HACHETTE WINE GUIDE 2002

THE FRENCH WINE BIBLE

HACHETTE WINE GUIDE

Editorial Director: Catherine Montalbetti

With the help of: Christian Asselin, INRA, *Vigne et Vin research unit*; Jean-François Bazin; Claude Bérenguer; Richard Bertin, *Oenologist*; Pierre Bidan, *Lecturer at ENSA, Montpellier*; Jean Bisson, *former Director of the INRA Viticultural Centre*; Jean-Pierre Callède, *Oenologist*; Pierre Casamayor, *Conference Director at the Science Faculty, Toulouse*; Béatrice de Chabert, *Oenologist*; Robert Cordonnier, *Director of Research at INRA*; Jean-Pierre Derouduille; Michel Dovaz; Michel Feuillat, *Lecturer at the Science Faculty, Dijon*; Pierre Huglin, *Research Director at INRA*; Robert Lala, *Oenologist*; Antoine Lebègue; Michel Le Seac'h; Jean-Pierre Martinez, *Chamber of Agriculture, Loir-et-Cher*; Mariska Pezzutto, *Oenologist*; Jacques Puisais, *honorary President of the Union Française des Oenologues*; Pascal Ribéreau-Gayon, *Former Dean of the Oenology Faculty, Bordeaux University II*; André Roth, *Agricultural Engineer*; Alex Schaeffer, *INRA, Director of the Vigne et Vin Research Centre*; Anne Seguin; Bernard Thévenet, *Agricultural Engineer*; Pierre Torrès, *Director of the Vine and Wine-growing Centre, Roussillon*.

Also: Patricia Abbou; Elisabeth Bonvarlet; Sylvie Chambadal; Isabelle Chotel; Nicole Crémer; Sylvie Hano; Micheline Martel; François Merveilleau; Diane Meur; Evelyne Werth; **Assistant editor:** Christine Cuperly; **Editorial secretary:** Anne Le Meur; **Computer processing:** Marie-Line Gros-Desormeaux; Sylvie Clochez; Martine Lavergne.

We should like to express our very grateful thanks to the 900 members of wine-tasting committees who met specially to help produce this guide, and who, as is customary, remain anonymous, and also to the organisations who kindly gave their support to the book or took part in general research: the Institut National des Appellations d'Origine, INAO; the Institut National de la Recherche Agronomique, INRA; the board of Consumption and Fraud Prevention; the Office National Interprofessionel des Vins and its regional delegations, ONIVINS; the CFCE; the DGDDI; the various professional committees, councils, federations and unions; the Institut des Produits de la Vigne of Montpellier and ENSAM; the Paul Sabatier University, Toulouse; the wine-growing unions and wine-growers' associations; the unions and federations for the Grands Crus; the wine-merchants' unions; the chamber of agriculture; the departmental analytical laboratories; the agricultural colleges of Amboise, Avize, Blanquefort, Bommes, Montagne-Saint-Emilion, Montreuil-Bellay and Nîmes-Rodilhan, the hotelier's colleges of Bastia and Tain l'Hermitage, the CFPPA at Hyères; the Institut Rhodanien; the Union Française des Oenologues and the Fédérations Régionale des Oenologues; the wine-brokers' unions; the Union de la Sommellerie Française and the Associations Régionales de Sommeliers; in Switzerland, the Office Fédéral de l'Agriculture, the Commission Fédérale du Contrôle du Commerce des Vins, the officers of the cantonal wine-growing services, the OVV, OPAV and OPAGE; in the Grand Duchy of Luxembourg, the Institut Viti-Vinicole Luxembourgeois; the Marque Nationale du Vin Luxembourgeois; the Fonds de Solidarité.

Layout: François Huertas; **Cartography:** Fabrice Le Goff; **Illustrations:** Véronique Chappée; **Photo credits:** pp. 13, 32: © Scope/M. Guillard; pp. 22, 28: © Scope/J. Guillard.

First published in the United Kingdom in 2002 by Hachette UK

Distributed in the United States of America by Sterling Publishing Co., Inc.
387 Park Avenue South, New York, NY 10016-8810

A CIP catalogue for this book is available from the British Library

ISBN 0-304-36248-4

English translation by Translate-A-Book, Oxford
Consultant Editor: Wink Lorch
Editors: S. Walton, L. Parry, M. Leitch, S. Hulme, H. Morgan, C. Whitehead, L. Eyre, J. Gilbert
Typeset by WestKey Ltd, Falmouth, Cornwall
Printed and bound in France by Aubin Imprimeur, Poitiers (E-mail: sales@aubin-imprimeur.fr)

Hachette UK
Cassell & Co
Wellington House
125 Strand
London
WC2R 0BB

HACHETTE WINE GUIDE 2002

THE FRENCH WINE BIBLE

HACHETTE

CONTENTS

CONTENTS

A selection of the best French wines

5

SYMBOLS

SYMBOLS USED IN THIS GUIDE

A photo of the label signifies that the wine is strongly recommended by the committee.

★★★ exceptional wine
★★ excellent wine
★ good wine

1999 vintage or year of wine tasted

□ still white wine ○ sparkling white wine
◖ still rosé wine ◕ sparkling rosé wine
■ still red wine ● sparkling red wine

50,000, 12,500 ... average number of bottles on offer

4 ha (10 acres): area of vineyard for this wine (in hectares and acres)

▬ aged in vat
● aged in cask
⊸ temperature regulation
☏ address
⊠ for sale on the premises
⍬ conditions of visit or tasting
☏ name of owner, if different from that mentioned in address

n.c. information not supplied

PRICES

Prices are shown in Euros and are for guidance only (average price of a bottle in France per case of 12). The equivalents in French francs (rounded to the nearest FF10) are given below. Conversion rate €1 = FF6.55957.

– €3	€3-€5	€5-€8	€8-€11	€11-€15
–FF20	FF20-30	FF30-50	FF50-70	FF70-100
€15-23	€23-30	€30-38	€38-46	€46-76
FF100-150	FF150-200	FF200-250	FF250-300	FF300-500
+€76				
+FF500				**€3-5**

Where the price is highlighted in red, this indicates good value for money

VINTAGES

㉒ **83** ㉟ |86| **89** ㊐ 91 |92| 93 **95 96** |97| **98**

83 91 — the vintages marked in red are ready to drink

93 95 — the vintages marked in black should be kept

|86| |92| — the vintages marked in black between two vertical lines are ready to drink but can be kept

83 95 — the best vintages are in bold

㊐ — exceptional vintages are circled

CONVERSIONS

Length		Weight		Volume	
1mm	0.0394 in	1g	0.035 oz	1 cu cm	0.061 cu in
1cm	0.394 in	1kg	2.2 lb	1 cu m	35.3 cu ft
1m	39.4 in	1kg	0.001 ton	1 cu m	1.31 cu yd
1m	1.09 yd	1 tonne	2,200 lb		
1km	0.621 miles	1 tonne	0.984 ton		

		Liquid Capacity			
Area		1ml	0.035 fl oz		
1sq cm	0.155 sq in	1l	0.53 pt (US pint = 16 fl oz)		
1sq m	10.76 sq ft	1hl (100 litre)	26.4 gal		
1sq m	1.2 sq yd				
1ha	2.47 acre				
1sq km	247 acres				
1sq km	0.386 sq miles				
1a (are)	0.25 acre				

Note: Conversions are into US measurements.

HOW THE GUIDE WORKS

The selection of the year

This guide contains details of the 9,000 best wines from France, Switzerland and Luxembourg, all tasted in the year 2001. This is an entirely new selection, focusing on the latest bottled vintage. These wines have been chosen for you by 900 experts during the course of blind tastings held by the *Hachette Wine Guide* of more than 30,000 wines from every appellation. In addition, while not given a separate entry, some thousand wines are featured in **bold type** in the entries that review producers' most highly rated wines.

An objective guide

The absence of any financial or promotional involvement by the producers, wine-merchants or co-operatives mentioned ensures the impartiality of the book, the sole aim of which is to be a wine-buying guide for consumers. The tasting notes should be used only to draw comparisons within the same appellation; it is, in fact, impossible to judge different appellations according to exactly the same criteria.

The tasting process and classification

Each unlabelled wine is examined by a jury. The colour, aroma and taste are described, and it is given a mark between 0 and 5.

0   faulty wine: eliminated
1   poor or mediocre wine: eliminated
2   wine typical of the area: worth a mention but not starred
3   good wine: **one star**
4   excellent wine: **two stars**
5   exceptional wine and a perfect example of the appellation: **three stars.**

Our choice

The wines whose labels are reproduced in the guide represent the 'coups de coeur'. These are wines that inspired our tasters to 'love at first sip', wines that are so good that they are particularly recommended to readers. References to wines being successful in previous years refer to previous editions of the French guide. References to a *Grappe d'or*, *Grappe d'argent* or *Grappe de bronze* refer to outstanding wines nominated as overall winners on publication of previous editions of the *Guide*.

Omissions

Some well-known and reputable wines are missing from this guide, either because the producers did not take part in, or were eliminated from, the tastings. Some wines were tasted and favourably assessed but additional information was not supplied; next to these wines you will see 'nc' (information not supplied).

Elsewhere, it is not surprising that there is no vintage or year for Vins d'Assemblage (mixed wines – for example, non-vintage champagnes), nor for liqueurs or sweet fortified wines, nor for those wines that are offered by different producers, supplied by wine-merchants or co-operatives.

Reader's guide

Because the object of this book is to advise the consumer on choosing wines, according to his or her individual taste, and to advise on the best value for money (where the price range is indicated in red), everything has been done to make this guide practical and easy to read.

It is important to read the general introduction as well as the ones to the regions and the appellations, because information common to all the wines is not repeated in each section.

Prices

The price range (average price per bottle for a case of 12) is subject to market trends and is given as a guide only. All prices are given in Euros. There is a guide to French franc equivalents on page 6.

Telephone numbers

In France telephone numbers have ten digits. If you want to phone or fax a French producer from abroad you need to dial the international code (00 from the UK and 011 from the USA) followed by the country code, which is 33 for France, and then the number, omitting the first zero. To telephone Switzerland and Luxembourg, the procedure is the same but the country code for Switzerland is 41 and for Luxembourg 352. E-mail addresses are also given where appropriate.

How to use this Guide

— The structure of the Guide is very simple.
- An introductory chapter discusses current issues and trends in French wine-making.
- The 'News from France's Vineyards' section gives up-to-date information on French wine-growing, an analysis of the 2000 vintage and regional economic information.
- A practical section, 'Wine – General', explains the techniques of cultivating the vine and wine-production.
- A 'Consumer's Guide' gives advice on buying, keeping and tasting wine and suggests the best food-wine combinations.

— The wines selected are listed:
- By region, in alphabetic order, followed by three sections devoted to Vins Doux Naturels, Vins de Liqueur and Vins de Pays. Further chapters cover a selection of wines from Luxembourg and Switzerland.
- By appellation, presented geographically within each region.
- Alphabetically within each appellation.
- Four indices at the back list appellations, communes, producers and wines featured.
- 49 original maps show the geographical distribution of the vineyards.
- Weights and measures are given in both metric and imperial for ease of use.

— How to interpret an entry:

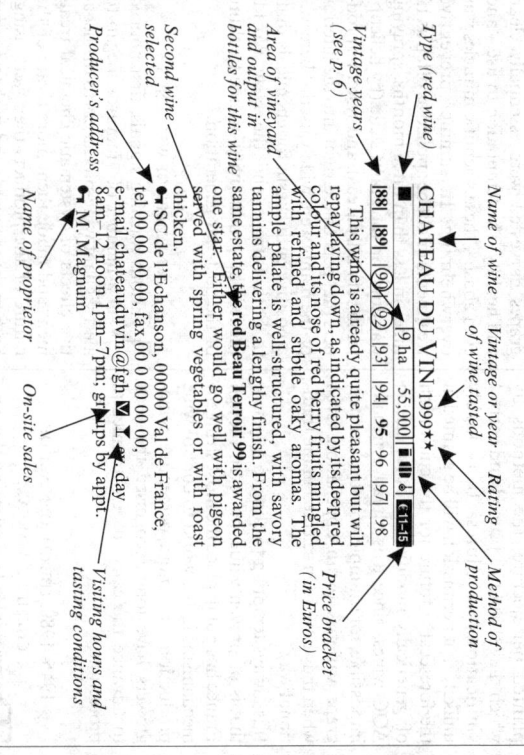

Name of wine   *Vintage or year of wine tasted*   *Rating*   *Method of production*

Type (red wine)

Vintage years (see p. 6)

CHATEAU DU VIN 1999★★

|88| |89| |90| |92| |93| |94| |95| 96 |97| 98

9 ha 55,000 €11-15

This wine is already quite pleasant but will repay laying down, as indicated by its deep red colour and its nose of red berry fruits mingled with refined and subtle oaky aromas. The ample palate is well-structured, with savory tannins delivering a lengthy finish. From the same estate, the red **Beau Terroir 99** is awarded one star. Either would go well with pigeon served with spring vegetables or with roast chicken.

● SC de l'Echanson, 00000 Val de France, tel 00 00 00, fax 00 0 00 00 00, e-mail chateauduvin@gh ● 1 ● day 8am-12 noon 1pm-7pm, groups by appt. ● M. Magnum

Area of vineyard and output in bottles for this wine

Second wine selected

Producer's address

Price bracket (in Euros)

Name of proprietor   *On-site sales*   *Visiting hours and tasting conditions*

RATIONALISED WINE CULTIVATION

In response to consumer demand, the *appellations d'origine contrôlée* (AOCs) of France are currently preparing to incorporate into their accepted production methods a practice that has now become widely known as 'rationalised cultivation' – an initiative entirely in keeping with the spirit of an institution that has supervised the production of quality wines for more than 65 years.

Consumers, influenced by a series of alarming news stories over the last decade, are becoming increasingly concerned with the wholesomeness and flavour of the food they buy. Wine-producers can justly take pride in the fact that they were pioneers in this field. Indeed, the whole AOC structure, which was created by statute in 1935, is aimed at offering the consumer a guarantee not only of the origin of the wine but also of its *terroir*, a term that encompasses a complex amalgam of natural factors, together with consistent production conditions, which are specifically laid down in the terms of each appellation. In addition to permitted grape varieties, the rules also specify the number of vines to be planted per hectare, the methods by which they should be pruned and correct vinification procedures. It is highly unlikely that permission will be granted in the foreseeable future for the cultivation of genetically modified vines for use in AOC wines, since it is already virtually impossible, for example, to introduce new grape varieties to an appellation, even when they have been selected in the traditional way.

It is always tempting to cling to a system that is of proven value, but even though France has put in place the most stringent mechanisms in the world to control wine production, the more perceptive wine-growers have long recognised the need to advance the cause of environmental protection.

1945–1980: THE GOLDEN AGE OF CHEMICAL WARFARE

The original rules governing the production of AOC wines did not, of course, take into account the use of herbicides and synthetic chemical treatments. These were, to all intents and purposes, non-existent in 1935, with the exceptions of sulphur dioxide, which was used against powdery mildew, copper sulphate, which was used against downy mildew, and arsenic compounds, which were used to treat the vine stocks. After the Second World War the tremendous progress made in organic chemistry supplied wine-growers the world over with unprecedented weapons with which to fight their enemies: insecticides and acaricides, rot-inhibitors of all kinds and even herbicides to reduce the need for soil maintenance. This struggle was made all the more relentless by the memory of the devastating effects of phylloxera, which came within an ace of wiping out the entire wine industry.

Enthusiasm was at its height in this era. There would be no more 'bad years', since even the worst weather had little effect on the volumes produced, and, above all, the grapes harvested were essentially clean and healthy. The temptation to use – and even abuse – these scientific miracles was overwhelming. In summer preventive treatments might be applied as often as 12 times in less than three months, spraying was done on the grand scale (by helicopter in very hilly areas), and systemic products that penetrated right into the interior of the plants were widely used. There was a positive enthusiasm for chemicals that, in both Europe and the New World, fuelled the productivity-oriented culture of the post-war generation.

A NUMBER OF WARNINGS

Various warning signals, first noticed in a number of vineyards, began to alert vigilant wine-producers to the negative effects of systematic chemical treatment and made them more aware of the nature of the products they were using, both in the vineyards and in the wineries. During the 1980s, for example, a ban was imposed on use of the fungicide procymidone, a 'miracle' product used to combat grey rot. An anti-cryptogamic agent of amazing penetrative power, it certainly protected the vines – but it was found that it penetrated them so profoundly that traces of it were found not only in the must but also in the finished wine. The United States government promptly outlawed both the use of this chemical and the importation of any wine containing so much as a trace of it.

THE RATIONALISED STRUGGLE: A PHASED RESPONSE

Today, ignoring environmental issues when considering the choice of production methods is regarded as indefensible. Public opinion is fully engaged with the issue and is demanding not just reflection but the action to back it up. Over the last decade many individual estates and groups of wine-growers have begun to practise rationalised cultivation. This involves reducing, and even eliminating, the use of fertilisers, studying plant diseases, using traps to monitor insect pests and destroying them only if absolutely necessary, and discontinuing the use of herbicides.

In the Gironde, Philippe Chéty, one of the pioneers of these methods, has been appointed president of the wine department of the regional Chamber of Agriculture. He is thus at the head of the most powerful engine for technical development in the department, an eloquent demonstration of the profession's support for a more considered approach to the issue of chemical protection. He himself has been practising these methods for 18 years and maintains that it is possible to avoid 25%–50% of treatments by limiting the growth of the vines and spraying only when strictly necessary. The Chamber of Agriculture's development agents, many of whom have been recruited in the last ten years, have all been trained in the new methods.

UNIFICATION OF METHODS?

The Beaujolais Development Committee of the Rhône Chamber of Agriculture undertook a similar project in 1990 when it launched its 'quality charter'. Over the years the number of wine-growers supporting the charter has steadily increased, topping 220 in 1999. An association with very rigorous terms of reference was set up in 1997 for those who wanted to develop the initiative still further, and this has followers in a number of other wine-producing areas. A certification bureau issues a guarantee stamp for use on labels to those who abide by its strict regulations.

These individual efforts could not fail to stir the leaders of the wine industry to action. If some producers clearly felt it necessary to go further and impose extra regulations on themselves, should not consideration for the environment be incorporated into the AOC rules? Until recently the only people to be concerned about this were organic producers on the fringes of the agricultural system, who were responding to the demands of a few consumers who were prepared to be militant for ecology's sake. Today it is a question of how to persuade everyone to adhere to the rules of rationalised agriculture.

VITICULTURE AND THE ENVIRONMENT

The Terroir and Environment Commission of the INAO is, therefore, faced with the task of offering extra guarantees to consumers. This was the principal point made in the report it submitted to the INAO National Council at its meeting on 26 April 2001. The main aim is to have written into the production conditions for each appellation those requirements that were not envisaged at the time of the creation of the AOC system in 1935: disinfecting the soil, correct use of fertilisers, herbicides and synthetic chemical treatments, weed-control, leaf-removal and the like. The idea of imposing general regulations on all the appellations was soon abandoned as being contrary to the AOC ethos. These are essentially decentralised organisations, the local *appellation d'origine* being the collective heritage and individual responsibility of every wine-producer. Moreover, the producers are professional people who are in the best position to know what is right for their own vineyards and to incorporate and apply these procedures accordingly. The Champagne region, which was seriously affected by problems arising from water pollution, already has its solutions in place, while in the Bordeaux region the wine-producers' trade associations are actively involved in advancing these environmental initiatives.

This venture has the potential to encourage the vast majority of wine-producers towards a greater respect for the environment. Any improvements in the care of vines must, of necessity, be reflected in the quality of the resulting wine.

Some consumers have opted to buy only organic products. Organic production does not totally prohibit the use of chemicals because the application of copper sulphate is still permitted, but the use of weedkillers and synthetic chemical treatments is banned. It particularly advocates soil tillage and the use of organic manure in place of chemical fertilisers. The AB (*agriculture biologique*, i.e. 'organically grown') labels issued by various approved organisations serve to guarantee the use of these methods, which are now recognised by the Ministry of Agriculture and registered in the relevant terms of reference.

Biodynamic viticulture goes much further but, so far, has few adherents other than a scattering of leading producers, such as Nicolas Joly at La Coulée de Serrant and Michel Chapoutier at Tain L'Hermitage. Initiated in 1924 by an Austrian, Rudolf Steiner, it is considered by its followers to be a genuine philosophy that seeks to put the grower in touch with the cosmos, since it takes account of the 'influence of the sun, the moon and the movements of the planets on all forms of life'.

Even though AOC viticulture as a whole may never follow these more extreme practices, it will nevertheless become 'rationalised' – which is what it should always have been, after all. It is a question of knowing how to get the best out of a *terroir* without abusing it. In that sense, great wines can never be anything other than rationally made.

JEAN-PIERRE DEROUDILLE

NEWS FROM FRANCE'S VINEYARDS

In 2000, France produced 59.9 million hl (1.5 billion gal) of wine (36% white and 64% red and rosé). While the internal market is still very significant, with an average consumption of 54 l (11.87 gal) per inhabitant per year, exports continue to constitute a major outlet. In 2000, 14.8 million hl (390 million gal) were sold abroad. Still appellation wines (VQPRD) accounted for 6.8 million hl (180 million gal) and earned FF18.9 billion (€2.88 billion). Export figures show a drop in volume (down 2.7%) compared with 1999, but the financial return on this category of wine has remained stable, whereas table wines, including regional wines, are undergoing a major crisis.

WHAT'S NEW IN ALSACE?

This region, where the wines have so long been identified only by their grape varieties, is beginning to lay greater stress on its Grands Crus. This is where the regionally specific *terroirs* should come into their own.

The winter of 2000 was kind to the whole of the Alsace region. The first leaves emerged around 20 April. Spring was changeable, damp in April and sunny in May, with periods of hot weather bringing on storms. Andlau, Brandhof, Moenchberg, Scherwiller and Ribeauvillé were struck by hail on 10, 11 and 13 May. Growth began a good two weeks early and extraordinarily early flowering occurred around 6 June. July saw the return of cooler, wetter weather, and then in August there were more storms, often accompanied by hail (on 25 July, they struck Orschwiller, Bergheim, Eguisheim and again, Ribeauvillé). Harvesting began on 11 September for the *crémants*, 21 September for still wines and 2 October for the late-harvested grapes and the *sélections de grains nobles*. The pickers found themselves getting very wet; it rained a great deal, particularly in mid-October, which created ideal conditions for noble rot. Botrytis developed quite early on and should result in some impressive wines, given that the picking was carried out quickly.

The 2000 yield reached around 1,214,624 hl (32 million gal), less than that of 1999 (which was around 1,240,000 hl, or 32.7 million gal), but above the annual average for the last five years. Average yield per hectare was almost 90 hl in 1999, whereas this time it was in the region of 85 hl. The volume of Alsace AOC was 1,008,744 hl (26.6 million gal), or 83% of the total production.

2000: THE YEAR OF RIESLING

Because of the frequent rain, the more delicate grape varieties, Muscat and Chasselas, were adversely affected and the wines may lack concentration. Some of the Pinots were attacked by rot. Many of the Auxerrois wines are fresh, rich and satisfying, while the Gewurztraminer is, for the most part, creditable, with a certain acidity that should allow it to keep reasonably well. The Pinot Gris yielded grapes that were splendidly ripe but often difficult to manage. Rigorously sorted and vinified, however, this variety did great credit to the vintage. The Sylvaner produced good wine, but it was the fairly late Riesling that was the year's winner, notably from Riquewihr and the surrounding areas.

ALSACE GRAND CRU: THE FIGUREHEAD WINE

The new statutory order of 24 January 2001 brought appreciable modifications to the regulations applicable to the Alsace Grand Cru AOC (accountable for 4% of the region's production: 1,600 ha/ 3,952 acres classed, 700 ha/1,729 acres planted). Any wine-grower intending to produce a Grand Cru must henceforth submit, before 1 March, a declaration specifying the name, grape varieties and the total area of the vineyard parcels intended for its production. New management regulations apply to all vines planted from 1 September 2000: a minimum of 4,500 plants per hectare will be enforced, as will a maximum distance of 2 m (2.2 yd) between the rows. Mechanical harvesting is banned.

The new authorised basic yield is 55 hl/ha (in place of the 70 hl/ha authorised by the previous statutory order), this being susceptible to an annual increase set by a variable PLC (the classification ceiling that fixes the maximum authorised yield for a wine still to be eligible for the AOC) of between 0% and 20%. It is hoped that an eventual figure of 66 hl/ha will be reached. The Alsace Grand Cru AOC may not yet represent a tremendous volume, but it is steadily increasing from year to year, having gone from 33,500 hl (884,000 gal) in 1995 to 48,500 hl (1.28 million gal) in 2000. Such an increase indicates something of a revolution: the Alsace wine-producers, who have historically given preference to their grape varieties, are turning more and more towards their *terroirs*, starting with the Grands Crus. A new regional identity is being forged, based on the best practice of matching grape variety to *terroir*. This is a trend that could lead, in the long term, to limiting the number of grape varieties permitted for each Grand Cru (at present these are Muscat, Pinot Gris, Riesling and Gewurztraminer), and also to the inclusion of Sylvaner – currently banned from use in Grand Cru wines – in some localities where conditions favour its production.

A MARKET IN SLIGHT DECLINE

After a period of euphoria (all-time record sales for 1999–2000 with 1,199,000 hl (31.65 million gal) or 160 million bottles, representing an increase of 4.3% in one year), the sales of still Alsace wines showed a slight decrease in 2000 (2% less volume with 155 million bottles). The best sales to foreign markets in recent years have been to Canada (+27%), Norway (+17%), Japan (+9%) and the USA (+8%), but the Netherlands are still (except for *crémant*) the best clients, taking 20% of the region's production. The German market has slipped to third place after having been the foremost outlet for 30 years, although if one includes *crémant* in the equation, Germany still maintains its leading position with 8.5 million bottles bought: more than Belgium and Luxembourg together (8.4 million bottles) and the Netherlands (8.1 million bottles).

Following its excellent performance in 1999, Crémant d'Alsace is also losing ground (down by 4% in 2000). With almost 20 million bottles produced, however, it remains the French market leader in sparkling wines outside Champagne. Its production in 2000 was 157,000 hl (4.14 million gal) – 13% of the overall volume of production for the region.

NEWS IN BRIEF FROM THE VINEYARDS

The INAO intends to modify the statutory order concerning the Crémant d'Alsace AOC to facilitate better transportation from the vineyards, with a resulting improvement in the quality of the grapes. Indeed, as with all wines made by traditional methods, the grapes should ideally be delivered to the press in an undamaged state. This requirement is stressed in the text that is in preparation. Facilities for reception and pressing will also be subject to regulation as and when the order is published.

WHAT'S NEW IN BEAUJOLAIS?

The great debate causing concern among the wine-growers of Beaujolais in 2000 was the subject of machine harvesting. Was this going to be accepted, flying in the face, as it would have done, of both custom and the regulations? In the end it hasn't been, but the controversy is still raging. That said, the wines of 2000 are Beaujolais through and through, whereas those of the previous year were somewhat atypical.

The 2000 vintage was a strange year. There were storms, but they did no damage. There was hot spring weather in April, with almost tropical humidity and a burning wind from the south. Mildew and black rot brought their share of problems to the heart of the luxuriant growth of the vines. Storms occurred, notably in early June, and then July was cold. August, however, made up for it. The grapes ripened early, and there was virtually no grey rot. The starting date for the harvest was 28 August, after the vineyards had enjoyed several weeks of sun. Harvesting continued until 20 September in conditions that were good from the point of view of both the weather and the state of the grapes. The 2000 harvest was the earliest of any in the last 30 years. A typical 'Beaujolais' year, unlike the previous one, which yielded meaty, structured wines, the 2000 vintage produced wines that were less acidic than normal and had plenty of fruit.

NO MECHANICAL HARVESTING

The harvest of 2000 yielded 1,396,835 hl (36.9 million gal). White Beaujolais continues to lose ground as a percentage of overall production, whereas Beaujolais and Beaujolais-Villages remain steady. With regard to the Crus (368,463 hl, or 9.7 million gal), the picture is one of relative stability except for Régnié (down 14.3%). The region's most recent AOC has not yet found its place as the tenth Cru. Also evident are slight reductions in the quantities of Chénas, Juliénas and Saint-Amour. Exports suffered a slight drop in volume (down by 1.9%), although their value continued to increase (by 3.2%). Germany is still the largest export market, taking 24.2% of the overall volume, but that nonetheless represents a 5.6% reduction on the previous year. On the other hand, figures for the UK show an increase of 5.1% in volume and 8.7% in value, despite strong competition there from New World wines. The Beaujolais Crus make up the largest part of the Japanese export market, which is the fifth largest market for the region's wines. Should machine harvesting be permitted in the south of the Beaujolais wine region? In a secret ballot of the regional committee, a large majority said no (36 against and five for, with two abstentions). This decision did not please all the wine-growers, several of whom had already ordered machines following the favourable opinion issued by the Union Viticole Beaujolaise.

60 MILLION BOTTLES OF *PRIMEUR*

The 2000 Beaujolais nouveau was launched for the first time in Seoul and St Petersburg. One third of the production of the region was sold as Beaujolais nouveau in 2000 (452,000 hl/11.9 million gal, or 60 million bottles). A new regulation for this category is being prepared. The wine-growers of Lantignié are considering producing a top-of-the-range *vin primeur* based on a notable estate in the village.

NEWS IN BRIEF FROM THE VINEYARDS

Burgundy's Saint-Vincent wine fair now has a rival. In 2001, the Fête des Crus du Beaujolais, hitherto based at Chiroubles, became a travelling event. It was held at Fleurie on 6 May 2000. In the spring of 2002, it will be held at Villié-Morgon. As a result of the ripeness of the Gamay grapes in 2000, as monitored by SICAREX (the local agricultural research station) and INRA (the National Institute of Agricultural Research), it was concluded that the late harvest had reduced the acidity in the wines and reinforced their colour.

One innovation for the year 2000: the Beaujolais wine-growers installed a vat-room in the very centre of Lyon, where they vinified 150 hl (3,960 gal).

In the south of the region, the Fête du Beaujolais Gourmand (the Beaujolais wine and food fair) at Tarare saw the birth of a new, exclusively feminine 'brotherhood' known as the Consoeurerie (Sisterhood) de la Tarandouille – the name referring to the *andouille*, or tripe sausage, made in Beaujolais.

The death of Louis Bréchard, known universally as 'Papa Bréchard', saddened everyone: one of the fathers of the AOC and a pillar of the wine-producing community for half a century, he died at the age of 96.

WHAT'S NEW IN BORDEAUX?

The last vintage of the century was an undoubted technical success, and a welcome boost to a mainly sluggish market for the great majority of wine-growers. Despite that, prices for the highest-rated crus internationally knew no ceiling.

The 2000 vintage in Bordeaux was one of superlatives – a word that applies both to the intemperance of the market and the quality of the harvest. It is true that such favourable weather conditions for the production of great wines had not been seen since 1989 and 1990. Proof of this is offered by the annual reference guide published by Professors Pascal Ribéreau-Gayon and Guy Guimberteau of the Oenology Faculty of Bordeaux University, which awards a grade to each vintage.

2000: A TUMULTUOUS YEAR

Meteorological and analytical records carried out under the same conditions for several decades now tend to confirm observations from other sources regarding global warming. It is not impossible that, in the long term, this could change the character of Bordeaux wines, having the same sort of impact as variations in methods of vine cultivation or oenological practices.

University academics have noticed a regular change in the average dates for the mid-point of flowering and colour-change during the 1970s, 1980s and 1990s. They have both come forward by two weeks over the course of the last 30 years. These figures, based on ten-year averages, also show an acceleration of this tendency over each previous period. Harvests are regularly seen to be earlier, and the grapes riper.

The 2000 vintage went even further than this long-term tendency, giving it an exceptional character. The mid-point of flowering, observed from 6 August, was extremely early. Although the weather had been particularly hot at the beginning of the year, there was seemingly no lack of moisture in the vines following the start of leaf-growth from April to June. The first onset of mildew, while quite virulent considering the conditions, was quickly stamped out.

The summer began badly with cold and rainy conditions at the beginning of July, but the weather turned hot and dry after the 15th of the month, conditions that were sustained remarkably throughout September. The maximum temperature exceeded 25° C for more than half the month, with three days on which it rose above 30° C.

RIPENESS AND QUALITY

On 18 September, at the last sampling before the harvest, the grapes had attained extraordinary ripeness, with a potential alcohol of 13.6% for the Merlot and 12.2% for the Cabernet Sauvignon. Even the super-ripe 1989 was far from achieving these readings. More remarkable still, quality went hand in hand with high yields, because the weight of 100 individual grapes was higher than any recorded for all the known great vintages.

Despite that, the ratio of polyphenols, or tannins, remained very high, a promise of good structure and complexity in the wines. While acidity levels were relatively low, they were nevertheless comparable to the great wines of 1989 and 1990. The final trump card held by the 2000 vintage was the excellent health of the grapes.

The last harvest of the century was therefore a memorable one, boosted by the clement weather that lasted until the end of September. Autumn only finally put in an appearance on 10 October, accompanied by heavy rain. After that the vineyards, in common with the rest of Europe, were not to see the sun again until January 2001.

The white grapes destined to make dry Bordeaux wines were picked in bright sunshine, fully ripe and in a perfectly clean state, all of which contributed to trouble-free vinification and successful wines. If there is one disappointment, it is in the aromas, which are somewhat lacking in fullness. It is well known that white grapes often prefer a cooler season in order to express their full potential. Undoubtedly, however, this vintage was more propitious for wines intended for keeping, particularly perhaps those matured in *barrique*, rather than for those with strong aromatic qualities. For the reds, on the other hand, it's a full house. Deep colour, tannins, fruit, suppleness – they were remarkable from the start, recalling the exceptionally supple wines of vintages like 1982 or 1989. The late-ripening Cabernet Sauvignon was, to be sure, picked in rainy conditions, but without coming to much harm. The 2000 vintage reds are destined to be up there with the greatest, wines that are already attractive in their early years, but that nonetheless have a potential life-span of several decades.

That just leaves the sweet wines, which suffered from the late-season rain that prevented noble rot from developing and doing its work. Many of the châteaux abandoned their final picking. The characteristic qualities of the Sauternes and Barsacs could therefore be affected, even though some well-made wines were produced.

The area planted with AOC vines having again increased by almost 2,000 ha (4,940 acres) since the last

Bordeaux harvest, it is not surprising that the yield was abundant. The declared yield in red AOC, including all appellations, has now reached 6,037,494 hl (159 million gal) against 5,965,896 hl (157 million gal) in 1999. Against that, the white wines – the poor relations of the Gironde vineyards – have seen their production further reduced from 912,797 hl (24 million gal) to 856,911 hl (22.6 million gal).

The increased quantities of red wine are a heavy burden on the market, especially for the regional AOCs. Thus rates that were already on a low trend at the beginning of the year 2000, with the wholesale price of a 900 l cask quoted at FF 8,500 (€1,296) by the producers, have fallen even further. During the whole of the 2000–2001 sales campaign, they remained stuck between FF 6,500 (€990) and FF 7,500 (€1,143), which effectively sets the wine-growers back by ten years. They have, however, managed to divide up the market, thanks to the Bordeaux Supérieur appellation, which was still quoted in June 2001 at FF8,000–8,500 (€1,220–1,296) the cask. The French consumer can buy a bottle of Bordeaux for an average price of FF18 (€2.74) and a bottle of Bordeaux Supérieur for FF24 (€3.66).

The fashion for rosé is certainly not faltering, since sales were up by 24% during the year 2000. Finally, however, the white wines are doing worse than ever. Between FF2,500 (€381) and FF4,000 (€610) the cask, they are in a critical state, despite the continuing decrease in area dedicated to their production. This is a great pity,

considering that white Bordeaux such as Entre-Deux-Mers and Graves can reach levels of quality worthy of other appellations making white wines that sell for two or three times the price.

PRIMEURS HAVE GONE MAD: THE TWO-SPEED WINE BUSINESS

Companies at the other end of the scale are most definitely not in crisis. These are the Grands Crus and their retinue of fashionable wines, buoyed up by the assessments of a few media critics tasting immature six-month-old wines that will only be bottled 14 or 16 months later. The sales campaign for wines sold *en primeur*, which ran from April to June 2001, was like a gauntlet thrown down in this depressed climate. Already the Crus Bourgeois and the Crus Classés were quoting increases of between 30% and 50%, using the excuse of the high value of the dollar coupled with the euro's weakness against sterling and the yen, and the acknowledged quality of the 2000 vintage, in which the *premiers* showed signs of the most extraordinary arrogance. Latour, Lafite, Mouton, Margaux and Haut-Brion carried unprecedented price tags of around FF1,400 (€213) a bottle. A few days before the opening of Vinexpo, the international wine exhibition held in Bordeaux from 17 to 21 June, that news had appeared in all the papers. And exports? According to the Centre Français de Commerce Extérieur (the French Office for Foreign Trade), they experienced a slight increase in volume – 2,173,395 hl (57.4 million gal) in 2000 as against 2,160,803 hl (57 million gal) in

1999 – but a small decrease in value of 1.19%, which nevertheless represents more than FF8 billion (€1.22 billion).

CHATEAUX SOLD

Whatever the direction of the market, estates are always changing hands. One example was the sale of Clos Fourtet, the Premier Grand Cru Classé of Saint-Emilion, by brothers André and Lucien Lurton to Philippe Cuvelier, a businessman from Paris who made his money in the wholesale paper industry. At FF280 million (€42.68 million) for the 20 ha (49 acres) of vines and the stock, it was undoubtedly the right time to buy. Similarly, the British Bass group, which has diversified from beer and spirits into the hotel trade, got rid of Château Lascombes, the Margaux Second Growth that they acquired in 1971. At FF500 million (€76.22 million) for 85 ha (210 acres), it was cheaper than Fourtet, but Saint-Emilion will always have the edge over the Médoc. The buyer is the American finance company, Colony Capital.

Another Saint-Emilion sale worth mentioning is that of Château Curé-Bon, a Grand Cru Classé of 4.5 ha (11 acres), which was bought by the Wertheimer brothers, owners of Chanel, Rauzan-Ségla in Margaux and Château Canon. Curé-Bon is due to disappear, with Canon being increased from 18 ha (44 acres) to 21.5 ha (53 acres), only the 3.5 ha (8.65 acres) that are actually situated on the Saint-Emilion plateau having been allowed to pass from the status of Grand Cru Classé to that of Premier Grand Cru Classé.

Another important sale concerned properties that still belonged to the Suez-Lyonnaise Group. Château Meyney (52 ha, or 128 acres, in Saint-Estèphe) and Château Plagnac (30 ha, or 74 acres, in Médoc) have been sold to Cordier-Mestrezat, which is part of the Languedoc co-operative, Val d'Orbieu-Listel. Finally, Clos des Jacobins and Château La Commanderie in Saint-Emilion were bought by the perfume manufacturer Marcel Frydmann of the Marionnaud Group.

WHAT'S NEW IN BURGUNDY?

The 2000 vintage is assured of a great future, for a bottle carrying that date on its neck-label will always excite interest. Its volume, while less than that of 1999, was the second largest in Burgundy's history, despite the uncertain weather that demanded constant vigilance.

While the all-time record production in 1999 was 1,608,214 hl (42.5 million gal), the 1,550,706 hl (40.9 million gal) produced in 2000 was higher than the average for the last five years (1,484,692 hl, or 39.2 million gal). White wines represented almost two-thirds of the harvest (943,180 hl, or 24.9 million gal), confirming previous trends, but there was also a slight increase in the reds (to a total of 607,526 hl, or 16 million gal). With reference to the previous vintage, the decrease arises mainly from less streamlined production methods and less generous allocations of ceiling limits (the permitted maximum yields). In white wines, the year produced some excellent Chablis. Among the reds, the Côte de Nuits has the advantage over the Côte de Beaune (the opposite of the case in 1999).

The decrease in the volume of white wine from 1999 to 2000 amounted to 9.4% in the villages of the Côte de Nuits, and a little less for Chablis (down by 5.7%) and for the Grands Crus of the Côte d'Or (down 5.8%), although the decrease in Chevalier-Montrachet and Le Montrachet was much greater. Elsewhere, everything remained stable. The only increases were in the Mâconnais communal appellations (up by 5.7%). The red wines of the Mâconnais (Mâcon and Mâcon Supérieur) also increased (by 1.6%), while Côtes de Nuits-Villages and Côtes de Beaune-Villages both suffered an appreciable drop (by 15.4% and 13.8% respectively). As regards the red Grands Crus of the Côte d'Or, the fall in volume was 7.7%, with big decreases in Griotte-Chambertin, Grands Echézeaux, Clos de Tart, Clos de Vougeot and Romanée Saint-Vivant.

18

VERY EARLY HARVESTS

Spared the storms at the end of December 1999, Burgundy experienced a very mild winter. The first leaves appeared quickly in early March. Everything went well right through May and June, with the hot weather favouring good growth. Flowering began in early June, with abundant setting of the buds. July was quite wet, cold and gloomy, but did nothing to check the advanced growing cycle, and the grapes ripened early. Hailstorms led to mildew and botrytis (2 and 4 July, and then 17 and 18 August in the Mâconnais). Despite the storms, July and August were, on the whole, quite cold. From the end of August, the ripening process was speeded up by an appreciable increase in temperatures, which simultaneously raised the quantities of natural sugars in the grapes and lowered their acidity. Botrytis was quite widespread, particularly in the Côte de Nuits. The storms held off until mid-September, but then returned in the Côte de Beaune. Overall, the grapes ripened beautifully, and this harvest was among the earliest of the decade from 1990 to 2000 in Burgundy (starting at the beginning of September in the Mâconnais).

PRICES: THE SLOWDOWN AFTER THE RISE

Lured by the historic vintage and the buoyant effect of demand from foreign buyers, Burgundy prices were on the increase (up by 11%) at the time of the Hospices de Beaune wine sales in November. The 1989 record was beaten, with FF47,577 (€7,252.6) for a 228 l (50 gal) cask (300 bottles). Red wines increased by 9% with an average rate per cask of FF44,872 (€6,840). The most prestigious wines, like Clos de la Roche and Mazis-Chambertin, were responsible for accentuating the price movement, with something like a 30% increase. Among the white wines, Bâtard-Montrachet increased by 30%, selling at FF158,086 (€24,098.5) the cask. However, the average overall increase for white Burgundy was 20%, and the average price of a cask FF61,123 (€9,317.5).

Later, the market slowed down a little. The following spring a cask of red was fetching FF24,912 (€3,797.6) at the Hospices de Nuits-Saint-Georges, a drop of 2.89%. The price of a cask of white wine (of which there were four only) really fell – by 28.57%.

Burgundy is holding up well on the external markets, with almost 90 million bottles sold during the 1999-2000 sales campaign, realising more than FF 3.5 billion (€0.53 billion). This represents stable volume with a 3% increase in value. The red wines were not favoured with a following wind in the markets, on account of their high prices and competition from abroad. With 62 million bottles, the whites took the lion's share, although purely on value, the reds were ahead. Two-thirds of the Burgundy exported goes to the UK (23 million bottles at a cost of FF752 million francs / €114.6 million), the USA (15 million bottles, but at FF811 million/€123.6 million), and to Germany (11 million bottles), and to Belgium (11 million bottles) and Japan (8 million bottles each).

NEWS IN BRIEF FROM THE VINEYARDS

Couchois, an area of 380 ha (939 acres) of vines belonging to individual estates in the north of the Saône-et-Loire region, near Maranges and the Côte Chalonnaise, is comprised of six villages: Couches, Dracy-lès-Couches, Saint-Jean-de-Trézy, Saint-Maurice-lès-Couches, Saint-Pierre-de-Varennes and Saint-Sernin-du-Plain. They could well benefit from the new addition of the geographical denomination Côtes du Couchois to that of AOC Bourgogne Rouge. It is not a matter of creating a new appellation, but of mentioning the place of origin within the regional AOC. Their first vintage was the 2000, with around 1,000 hl (26,400 gal) produced.

The lyre vine-training system has given rise to some discussion in certain wine-growing sectors. It is a system that uses V-shaped supports to grow the vines high and wide, and it first appeared in Burgundy 40 years ago. Several wine-growers make extensive use of this form of training, notably in the Auxey-Duresses and Hautes-Côtes-de-Beaune AOCs. It is also being used experimentally in the regional appellations of Côte Chalonnaise and Côtes du Couchois. This process does not form part of the regulations laid down for the AOC, and the relevant unions seem reluctant to introduce it, but if they do, the INAO will be obliged to ban these wine-growers from claiming AOC status for any parcels cultivated in this way. It is up to the profession to try to get the regulations changed, otherwise some 50 ha

(124 acres) using the lyre system will have to go back to conventional methods.

Yet again this year, OGM (the regulations relating to genetically modified wines) are exercising the wine-growers' attention. This time, it concerns the initiative led by Anne-Claude Leflaive of Puligny-Montrachet that was launched in 2000 by 24 wine-growers and *négociants-éleveurs* under the title l'Appel de Beaune (the Beaune Appeal). They are insisting on a moratorium on the introduction of OGM into the Burgundy appellations, because they fear this revolutionary development may harm the distinctive characteristics of their grape varieties.

In June 2001, the Caves des Hautes-Côtes merged with the Caves de la Vervelle (at Bligny-lès-Beaune), which vinifies 5,000 hl (132,000 gal). They are now the only co-operative in the Côte d'Or.

Antonin Rodet at Mercurey has acquired a part of the Aigle-à-Limoux estate. It constitutes 53 ha (131 acres), of which 27 ha (67 acres) are planted. Domaine Roux Père et Fils at Saint-Aubin is now installed at the Sainte-Croix estate at Aspiran in the Hérault after gaining a foothold at Lunel. Michel Picard of Chagny has taken control of Grandes Serres, a *négociant-éleveur* at Châteauneuf-du-Pape. The Alsace group Tresch has increased its Raoul Clerget site at Montagny-lès-Beaune, and concluded a partnership agreement with the Romuald Valot estate at Villers-la-Faye in the Hautes-Côtes-de-Nuits). Belvédère, an international group based in Beaune, is further increasing its Polish holdings, notably for the distribution of Bulgarian wines. The celebrated architect Frank Gehry will be constructing the Clos Jordan winery in Canada (not far from Niagara Falls) for the house of Jean-Claude Boisset.

Several companies (Denis Philibert, Goichot, L'Eglise and Chanson Père et Fils) are involved in judicial matters for a variety of reasons, none of which had been resolved at the time of going to press. No conclusions can be drawn at this time.

Highlights of the year 2002 include 26 and 27 January, with the Saint-Vincent travelling fair celebrated in the Côte Chalonnaise at Buxy, Montagny-lès-Buxy, Jully-lès-Buxy and Saint-Vallerin. In 2003, the intention is to organise the festival as a home-coming event at its original location of Château du Clos de Vougeot and environs. The Grands Jours de Bourgogne (Great Days of Burgundy) festival will take place between 17 and 24 March 2002.

WHAT'S NEW IN CHAMPAGNE?

A turbulent, trying year, plagued by hail, 2000 is not one that will easily be forgotten in Champagne. When the weather finally sorted itself out, however, quality turned out to be more than acceptable, and even though a great deal of champagne was drunk in celebration of the turn of the millennium, the year 2000 witnessed a marked decrease in yield over 1999, which was the greatest of all champagne vintages.

It was hardly an encouraging picture to begin with. Nature chose to display her powers across the entire gamut, by alternating cold, rainy weather with hot, stormy periods, which helped to upset the growing cycle of the vines. Winter was dry and very mild, with minimum temperatures more than 2° C (35.6° F) higher than normal. The first leaves appeared in mid-April in the course of a mild and very wet spring. Signs of mildew were noticed from the beginning of May onwards, as were early hailstorms and a first generation of larvae of the moth responsible for leaf curl.

AFTER THE PARASITES AND THE HAIL

May and June were particularly dry. Full flowering occurred on 11 June for Chardonnay, 12 June for Pinot Noir and 15 June for Pinot Meunier. Yellowing of the vines began soon after flowering had started, and became unusually widespread in the second half of June. This problem, which is seemingly linked to the use of weedkillers, was resistant to all those treatments – such as pollarding and trimming – that normally restore the healthy green growth. In the majority of cases, the situation only finally improved during July.

While the vines were slowly recovering their green colour, hailstorms battered the vineyards. On 2 July, a fall of hailstones the size of pigeons' eggs devastated 1,900 ha (4,700 acres) of vines. The year 2000, in company with 1971, was one of the century's worst years for hailstorms; by the eve of the harvest, 13,000 ha (32,000 acres), or 40% of the vineyards, had been damaged by them, and 2,900 ha (7,200 acres), or 9%, completely destroyed. During the month of August, the weather turned fine again. This dry, sunny period lasted throughout the harvest and allowed the pickers to gather bunches of grapes of well above-average weight – 150 g (5.25 oz) and more – and of perfectly clean quality. The fairly early harvest began on 11 September, and by a week later almost all the 100,000 pickers were hard at work.

The 2000 harvest totalled 1,188,910 casks (2,437,265 hl/64.3 million gal, one cask containing 205 l, or 44.8 gal). It was less than the two previous years, which both exceeded 1,220,000 casks (2,500,000 hl/ 66 million gal).

All the elements were thus in place for the production of some very fine wines. With a high potential alcohol reading in the region of 9.9% and an acidity level of 7.6 g/l, the 2000 vintage may not be as immediately appealing as the 1990, but the wines are clean and sound. After blending, each will be stamped with its classic identity.

THE VICISSITUDES OF A FLUCTUATING MARKET

Shipments of champagne for 2000 were 22% lower than in 1999 – a decrease caused by the classic phenomenon of 'precautionary buying', the great champagne occasion this time having been the night of 31 December 1999, rather than Saint Sylvester's Feast (New Year's Day) 2000.

According to the CFCE, the French commercial centre for external trade, there was a slight easing off in the volume of exports compared with 1999: 815,609 hl (21.5 million gal) as against 1,068,879 hl (28.2 million gal), a fall of 23.77%. This was accompanied by a drop in the overall value of exports, albeit to a lesser degree: sales were worth some FF 10 billion (€1.52 billion) compared with FF 12 billion (€1.83 billion) the previous year. Exactly the same trend can be seen for sparkling wines from other areas: a decline of around 25% in both volume and value. It was undoubtedly the year 2000 effect that made 1999 such an extraordinary year. The market trends for still appellation wines seem to be calmer, at least for those that have a high profile abroad.

The cost of property in the wine-production sector has increased by 17% in a year, with the price of vines having tripled within the last ten years. Wine-growers in the Aube region are waging a campaign to reclaim Champagne land that they consider was taken from them, most notably in the Côte des Bars, in the wake of the legislation of 1951. This mandated a reduction of the vine-growing area from a potential 16,000 ha (39,500 acres) accorded by the 1927 legislation to just 6,500 ha (16,000 acres) today.

NEWS IN BRIEF FROM THE VINEYARDS

Is there a conflict between Switzerland and the European Union? Agreements reached recently prohibit the village of Champagne (so-called since 895) in the Swiss canton of Vaud, from applying the name Champagne to the Bonvillars appellation wines it produces from its 28 ha (69 acres) of vines. Champagne's ruling body, the CIVC, has announced that the region began to adopt the practice of rationalised cultivation as of the beginning of 2001.

The champagne houses of Mumm and Perrier-Jouët have left the Hicks, Muse, Tate & First Group to return to the fold of Allied Domecq, at a price of FF 3,772 million (€575 million), having been bought for FF1,968 million (€300 million) in 1999. With the repurchase of SIMEXVI, Pommery has created a subsidiary company in Belgium named SA Pommery-Belgique.

Henkell & Söhnlein have bought the Gratien & Meyer Group (producers in both Champagne and Saumur). Meanwhile, the CIVC has obtained an order from the Paris courts banning the use of the name 'Champagne' by biscuit manufacturers Delos et Cantreau for their products. And yet the name has been in common use for the past 150 years to describe a particular type of biscuit.

WHAT'S NEW IN THE JURA?

Edgar Faure, noted politician and a great advocate for the wines of his *département*, used to say, 'Patience is the antechamber of happiness'. Indeed, it will require patience to wait until 2007 before enjoying the Vins Jaunes of the 2000 vintage. But the other Jura wines already herald a good year.

A mild winter gave way to a superb spring, lasting from April to June. Problem-free flowering started during the first week of June. The weather then deteriorated at the start of summer, with hail in the Arbois (30 June) and L'Etoile (1 July). The beginning of July was very wet. Temperatures dropped, slowing down growth to some extent. After a fairly stormy August, harvesting began half-way through September. At Château-Chalon, the first grapes were picked on 26 September, with the harvest ending in downpours. The Savagnin grapes suffered somewhat from late attacks of rot, while the Poulsard and Trousseau were affected by early mildew.

The 2000 Vins Jaunes, however, are on the right track and the other white wines, which are quite rich, are enjoying a fair wind too. Reds also have very good prospects, and will be ready to drink in 2002 or 2003.

The yield in 2000 was 97,826 hl (2.6 million gal), of which 31,380 hl (828,432 gal) were reds and rosés, 39,883 hl (1,052,911 gal) white wines and Vins Jaunes, and 13,875 hl (366,300 gal)

Crémant du Jura. The harvest showed a decline compared with the 110,750 hl (2.9 million gal) produced in 1999, but this region is particularly sensitive to bad weather conditions, and is accustomed to fluctuating production (it was only 16,354 hl/431,746 gal in 1991, for example). There is an appreciable improvement in the potential of the *crémant* wines, and the Château-Chalon maintains its market share. In this context, the Chardonnay and Pinot Noir varieties are somewhat akin to gatecrashers among the traditional grapes.

WHAT'S NEW IN SAVOY?

While yields remained stable, the quality of the wine in Savoy shows every sign of being excellent, with all records being broken in 2000 for richness and natural sugar levels. Even the 1997 vintage couldn't have improved on this performance. The wines have volume and class, making this a blessed vintage indeed.

W inter was mild, with the spring pleasant, quite sunny and dry. From April to June, the weather was positively heavenly. Flowering took place without a hitch at the beginning of June. July brought showers and August was changeable, but the harvest was very early, with most of the grapes being picked between 5 and 18 September. Volumes reached 140,000 hl (3.7 million gal), a slight increase over the previous year, which produced 138,300 hl (3.65 million gal).

The Savoy region has little scope for extending its area, but for a mere 1%

increase each year. All the new plantings are being made higher up the slopes. Wine-growers in the Jongieux sector have taken to producing a remarkable Roussette on a favourable part of the higher regions of Marestel. Savoy is bang up-to-date when it comes to combating erosion, the use of grassing between rows, control of yields and the rationalised war on pests and diseases.

Savoy is gradually shedding the widespread 'winter sports' image created by the very productive Jacquères grape variety (which, incidentally, performed brilliantly in 2000), and is determined to establish the personality of its wines by the use of other varieties, such as Roussanne (Bergeron), Altesse (Roussette) and the remarkable Mondeuse. At their best, they are wines of character, such as those produced, for example, by Chignin in Combe de Savoie, using the Bergeron and Mondeuse varieties. Some very fine wines are also being produced from Gamay, and the 2000 vintage was particularly favourable for this variety.

WHAT'S NEW IN LANGUEDOC AND ROUSSILLON?

While the final year of the 20th century gave a good account of itself, somewhat along the lines of the excellent 1998, and appears to be outstripping the more uneven 1999, it nevertheless saw, like a recurring nightmare, a return to the crisis of over-production. Table wines, including Vins de Pays, suffered a drop in sales, particularly in the export markets. This represents a new challenge for the region, which over the last 15 years has seen an unprecedented improvement in quality, as demonstrated in successive editions of the *Guide*: it accounted for 30 pages of the 1986 edition, with 63 in the present volume.

The year began badly, with serious flooding in Corbières in November 1999 arising from heavy rainstorms. Winter was dry, but the rainy periods that punctuated the fairly warm spring provided the water the vines needed. Flowering occurred early at the beginning of June, July was fairly cool and windy, and August was quite hot. Thanks to two rainy periods at the end of July and August, there was no shortage of water for the vines. Almost everywhere, the influence of the winds was beneficial to growth and the grapes ripened progressively during the first half of September, which was mostly dry and hot, accompanied by the occasional welcome shower. Harvesting, which varied between vineyards, took place between the end of August and the middle of October. Generally speaking, the bunches of grapes were clean and healthy. Their strong colour and the thickness of the skins augured well for rich, concentrated wines.

RICH AND RIPE WINES

In Languedoc, the 2000 vintage united concentration, alcohol content, complexity and finesse. Both the red and the white wines were seen to be very rich. Picpoul de Pinet offers all the vivacity and richness of aroma that characterise it in good years. The personality of the wines is gradually coming to the fore, and the *terroirs* are evident, resulting in some truly distinctive wines.

Roussillon's wines have the upfront fruitiness that will make them appeal to wine-lovers in a hurry, although they also have enough concentration to allow them to be laid down for several years. Wines from the Côtes du Roussillon, in particular, have a fine future.

Grenache, Carignan, Mourvèdre and Bourboulenc all did well this year, but the Syrah suffered somewhat from the dry conditions that plagued the area.

Because of its geographical position, Limoux is certainly a special case. Weather conditions were good, and the reflection of their *terroirs* is always markedly evident in these wines.

The total harvest in the Languedoc AOC reached 2,100,000 hl (55.4 million gal) of dry wines, added to which there were 45,887 hl (1.2 million gal) of naturally sweet wines (the Hérault Muscats). Production of dry wines in Roussillon was around 406,000 hl (10.7 million gal) and that of sweet wines 341,000 hl (9 million gal). The whole of the VQPRD production for Languedoc-Roussillon was in the region of 2,895,000 hl (76.4 million gal). This considerable quantity does not mean, however, that one can overlook the performance of table wines and Vins de Pays, which were affected by the overall fall in production rates: the Aude and Hérault *départements* alone produced 13.6 million hl (359 million gal) between them. Among the sweet wines, the Muscats are doing well. In 2000, they represented half of the Vin Doux Naturel production in Languedoc-Roussillon. In Roussillon, Muscat de Rivesaltes continued to make good progress, with the reassignment of vineyards previously producing AOC Rivesaltes resulting in an increase in volumes for the sweet

Muscat to 149,215 hl (3.94 million gal). Rivesaltes itself, with its 130,000 hl (3.43 million gal), remains in crisis. Maury, with a new team in place at the co-operative, is aiming at diversification by turning over part of its production to Côtes du Roussillon-Villages, while the market for Banyuls is still reasonably stable.

The export of appellation wines, while there has been a slight drop in volume to 1,036,000 hl (27.4 million gal), a decrease of 5.4%, is maintaining its value. The difficulties experienced by certain companies are the result both of the drop in these rates, especially for table wines, and of international competition. In recent years, however, this tendency has not prevented estates from leaving the co-operatives to start up on their own. In the Coteaux du Languedoc AOC, for example, the number of individually owned cellars registering harvests went from 446 in 1985 to 566 in 1999.

A NEW INTEREST IN WHITE WINES

The Collioure AOC is on a mission to add white wines to its repertoire of reds and rosés. A file is in preparation in reference to the production of 500 hl (13,200 gal) that is presently classified as Vin de Pays. Fitou, the senior member of the Languedoc–Roussillon AOCs and a specialist in red wines, is also seriously considering white wine production. The Tuchan co-operative has been producing whites experimentally for 20 years (around 400–500 hl, or 10,600–13,200 gal, in recent years), using Grenache Blanc, Macabeu and a maximum of 5% Muscat. As to the producers of Picpoul (a Coteaux du Languedoc AOC), they are campaigning for a specific Picpoul de Pinet AOC to be granted to their 40,000 hl (1.06 million gal).

NEWS IN BRIEF FROM THE VINEYARDS

After the floods of November 1999 (see the 2001 *Guide*) that devastated the Corbières vineyards, these have now been restored, thanks to widespread generosity, and so the Cascastel co-operative is now free of water. The thousands of hectares damaged in the Aude region have also been restored. Certain vineyards had to be relocated, such as those of Tuchan.

The epilogue to the controversy triggered last year by the investment project of California's Robert Mondavi at Aniane in the Hérault is that the new municipality, elected in March 2001, opposed the project and Mondavi withdrew. The company was to have invested FF55 million (€8.38 million) to clear 75 ha (185 acres) of land, of which 80% belonged to the village, plant them and establish a cellar. Since 1997, Mondavi has been marketing wines from the Pays d'Oc (under the Vichon Mediterranean brand) in the United States, occupying fourth place in that market, and selling to Japan, Latin America and the rest of Europe besides. A second brand, Arianna, is widely used as a house wine in American restaurants. In all, this represented a trading figure of FF84 million (€12.8 million) in 2000.

At the same time, investors came from all over France to show the colour of their money. Those from Burgundy were particularly active. Roux Père et Fils of Saint-Aubin acquired the Sainte-Croix estate at Aspiran in the Hérault, following the purchase of Château Saint-Séries at Lunel, which makes a red wine as well as a little AOC Clairette du Languedoc. A subsidiary of Worms et Cie, Antonin Rodet of Mercurey went into partnership with Jean-Louis Denois, creator of the Domaine de l'Aigle in the upper Aude valley, when it bought a part of his estate. Château des Mazes at Saint-Aunès in the Hérault was acquired by North American investors. Bordeaux group Castel, which acquired the Domaines de Virginie at Béziers and decided to transfer its bottling plant there from Sallèles in the Aude, has made substantial investments, encompassing 100,000 hl (2.64 million gal), 5,000 *barriques* and 100 million bottles a year.

24

WHAT'S NEW IN PROVENCE?

Amoureux à boire is Marie Mauron's charming description of the come-hither qualities of the 2000 vintage that marked a fitting finale to the 20th century. Though not exceptional, the year falls somewhere between good and very good. During the whole of the vines' growth cycle (April to September), Provence benefited from excellent, sunny and dry weather conditions, which enabled all the grape varieties to be brought in clean and healthy. The pre-growth season was mild, without any spring frosts, but with well-timed periods of rain making up for the dry earlier winter. Flowering began at the end of May or the beginning of June. July, and indeed June too, in some areas, were marked by a certain coolness, on account of the sharp winds. Summer remained dry, with only a few sporadic showers around 14 July. The vines held up relatively well in the dry periods, thanks to a satisfactory degree of night-time humidity. Some of the earlier varieties were picked from 15 August. In Bandol, harvesting began on 3 September.

RIPENESS AND CONCENTRATION

The high natural alcohol and satisfactory acidity of the vintage guaranteed good results for both red and white wines. If the vines suffered at all, it was from too much water, but the superb conditions in September ripened the grapes well, giving strong concentration to the wines. In the white wines, skin contact during vinification produced the desired results. The Carignan and Syrah both have plenty of body, the Grenache and Mourvèdre high degrees of alcohol. Among the reds, maturation conditions on the vine allowed for long fermentation periods, resulting in good, even excellent wines.

Volumes were greater than in the previous year: 1,334,000 hl (35.2 million gal) for all the AOCs, of which 56,832 hl (1.5 million gal) were whites (4.25%). Cassis produced some astonishing white wines. The micro-appellations, Palette and Bellet, maintained their rankings. Bandol results were somewhat diverse, but its reds continue to win points. Les Baux-de-Provence is an appellation gradually carving out a niche for itself. The Coteaux-d'Aix produced a good vintage in all three colours. As to the Coteaux Varois, their personality shone through clearly, particularly in the reds. Côtes de Provence offered elegant rosés. Some of its red wines could profit from being laid down, while some of the whites are of captivating quality.

Could the Côtes de Provence show off its specific *terroirs* to better advantage, though? The question has been asked now for several years, but little progress has been made. This seems disappointing, especially considering that the wine is selling well: 900,000 hl (23.8 million gal), a record, in the course of the 1999–2000 sales campaign (up 8.5% compared with the previous year), even though export sales were down (by 14.6% in volume, 7.6% in value).

In the Coteaux Varois, while the form of production for white wines is unchanged, the grape varieties used in the reds and rosés were reassessed for the 2000 harvest, with principal and secondary varieties being identified. Grenache, Cinsault, Mourvèdre and Syrah must now constitute 80% of the wines. Two of those varieties at least must be included, but neither may represent more than 90% of the total.

WHAT'S NEW IN CORSICA?

High temperatures and a dearth of rain characterised most of the vintage, other than in the north of the island. The southern part had no rain whatever throughout the long, burning summer months, so much so that the grapes ripened very early, the first being picked on 15 August. Because of the drought (it didn't rain until November), the grapes were in an excellent condition, clean and healthy, with just a few patches of rot being found in the north of the island.

The 2000 vintage unfolded beneath a blazing sun and a dry summer. Total volumes were greater than in the previous year, while quality was uneven but generally satisfactory.

Corsica produced 400,000 hl (10.6 million gal) of wine in 2000, around 200,000 hl (5.3 m gal) of that being in Vins de Pays and 80,000 hl (2.1 million gal) in table wines. The 2,510 ha (6,200 acres) in AOC areas (Vin de Corse 74%, Patrimonio 15%, Ajaccio 8%, Muscat du Cap Corse 3%) yielded 111,052 hl (2.9 million gal), a much greater quantity than in the previous year. That figure is made up of: 87,058 hl (2.3 million gal), 9% of it white, in Vin de Corse; 17,435 hl (460,000 gal) in

Patrimonio; 6,558 hl (173,000 gal) in Ajaccio; and 2,095 hl (55,000 gal) in Muscat du Cap Corse.

The main features of this harvest were its maturity and its acidity. In Ajaccio, however, the summer drought had stopped the Sciacarellu from ripening, causing the grapes to wither and making vinification difficult.

A very rare frost occurred during the night of 15 April 2001; temperatures down to −5 °C (23 °F) affected 1,000 ha (2,470 acres) situated between Bastia and Solenzara on the eastern coast. Patrimonio was not too badly hit. It is estimated that about 10% of the plots were totally destroyed.

WHAT'S NEW IN THE SOUTH-WEST?

The Grand Bassin Aquitain, which is comparable to the Aquitaine and Midi-Pyrénées regions, constitutes a geographical and climatic unit around the river Garonne and its tributaries. It is, therefore, hardly surprising that since Bordeaux produced a great vintage, the wines of the South-West also had a field day, with a few subtle differences owing to the fact that some grapes ripened a few days earlier than others, or to the nature of the grape varieties.

There was some bad weather during the first half of 2000 that had repercussions on the harvest. Heavy rains, notably from April to July, fell throughout the growing period of the vines from the first leaf-opening until after budding, with 250 mm (9.85 in) of rain falling in the Bergerac region alone. The vines were then attacked by mildew, and flowering took place in rather unfavourable conditions. Although the mildew was overcome in August, a little coulure and some millerandage were noted (both forms of failure of the vine to flower properly and to set fruit, leading to some tiny, unripe berries), all of which goes to explain why the quantities were slightly down throughout all the appellations. Fine weather then followed.

The wine-growers of Bergerac, given the superb, stable conditions of late summer, decided to wait until 20 September before starting their harvest, hoping that would produce better concentrations of phenolic compounds (tannins) and anthocyanins (colouring matter) in the grapes. This trend was repeated all over the South-West, where neither the weather during the second half of September, nor the state of health of the grapes, gave any cause for concern, unlike in previous years.

The reds were duly picked from the end of September, so as to obtain supple tannins. Some growers were even tempted to wait until mid-October, which turned out to be more of a gamble than they had barganied for, as the second half of October was very wet in the South-West. The whites, obviously, had been harvested earlier, in ideal conditions starting on 6 September in Bergerac. Grapes for the sweet wines were picked during the course of September. Scarcely any, apart from the botrytised sweet wines such as Monbazillac, suffered any harm, although the last ones to be picked had to be discarded because of the excessive humidity.

Despite some selection problems occurring from Gaillac to Madiran via Buzet and Cahors, the 2000 wines varied between excellent and exceptional, particularly the red wines, which are vividly coloured and rich in both aromas and tannins. The whites are flawless, though occasionally they lack the freshness and vivacity expected in the kinds of wines that are pleasant to drink young. Now that the vinification of white wines in barrel is becoming more commonplace, however, this is no longer regarded as a failing, since maturity and richness are what are increasingly sought after these days.

HIGH PRODUCTION, DESPITE
A SLIGHT FALL

Quantities harvested were slightly less than those registered in 1999, but the volumes remained significant nonetheless. The yield in Bergerac, taking into account all the appellations, went from 680,351 hl (18 million gal) in 1999 to 646,537 hl (17.1 million gal) in 2000, a small decrease of about 5%. It is noted, however, that the excellent quality of the wine allowed several lots to be reclassified. While white Bergerac, which is difficult to sell, saw its declared quantities drop by 12%, the white Côtes de Bergerac dropped by only 4%. Similarly, production of Pécharmant was reduced by only 2%.

GAILLAC'S PROGRESS

At Gaillac, the effect of this reclassification is clearly evident, and it is helped by the excellent market trends for this appellation. While the Tarn wine-growers have seen their overall production go down from 644,464 hl (17 million gal) in 1999 to 619,115 hl (16.3 million gal) in 2000, the total of AOC Gaillac wines increased from 15,679 hl (413,925 gal) to 184,564 hl (4.87 million gal) in 2000. The whites, up from 43,851 hl (1.16 million gal) to 45,858 hl (1.21 million gal) have benefited as much as the reds, up from 131,828 hl (3.48 million gal) to 138,706 hl (3.66 million gal). One significant fact is that, for the first time in 50 years, the Tarn wine-producing area has stopped shrinking and even grew by 72 ha (178 acres) in 2000, the AOC area having increased by 133 ha (329 acres). With a climate almost like that of the Languedoc, 2000 also turned out to be a vintage of great quality: ripe, easy, posing no vinification problems and resulting in well-structured wines. Gaillac is experiencing the same evolutionary process that Bordeaux underwent 20 or so years ago: the progressive eradication of table wine, the growing supremacy of the AOC and a concomitant improvement in quality. Cahors does not have the same characteristics, since its vineyards were almost entirely regenerated after the Second World War, basically as a VDQS that became an AOC in 1970. Vines are still being planted since the declared area was increased from 4,274 ha (10,558 acres) in 1999 to 4,427 ha (10,935 acres) in 2000, but production has nevertheless dropped slightly from 254,784 hl (6.73 million gal) to 243,911 hl (6.44 million gal). The Côtes du Frontonnais also underwent a small decline in production from 1999 to 2000, dropping from 128,196 hl (3.38 million gal) to 120,607 hl (3.18 million gal) declared. On the other hand, the Jurançon appellation (dry and sweet), which went from 46,768 hl (1.23 million gal) to 50,678 hl (1.34 million gal), was on the increase.

UNDER THE INFLUENCE OF BORDEAUX

The market for the wines of the South-West is variously oriented. Those vineyards that are closely related to the Bordeaux region, both in their grape varieties and their methods of cultivation, have suffered as if in sympathy with it.

At Buzet, the volume of exports fell appreciably. Significant stocks in Bergerac, resulting from the abundant harvest of 1999, have weighed against sales and prices: the quantities available (stocks plus harvest), which amounted to 1,098,383 hl (29 million gal) at the start of the sales campaign of 1999–2000, already 2.9% up on the sales campaign of 1999–2000, saw a further increase of 3.5%, reaching 1,136,382 hl (30 million gal) in September 2000. At Gaillac, on the other hand, wholesale prices of bulk red wines remained between FF660 (€100.61) and FF670 (€102.13) the hectolitre throughout the whole of the sales campaign, which is very close to the FF 6,500 (€ 990.85) charged for 900 l (equivalent to FF7.20, or €1.10, per litre) of regional AOC Bordeaux. Who would have believed this twenty years, or even a decade, ago?

The resurgence in the vineyards of the Midi of table wines also shows that the relentless competition between premium-priced AOC wines, a category that includes the Rhône as well as Bordeaux, could even have an influence on what used to be called 'wines for everyday drinking'.

Up against the twin difficulties of selling on the world markets and the rising cost of promotional sales drives, the wine-growers' unions of Bordeaux and the inter-professional bodies, have this year come out on the side of a political proposal that they had, for a long time, seen as superfluous, even dangerous. The Aquitaine regional council has created a Council for the Wines of Aquitaine (Conseil des vins d'Aquitaine, or CVA) – an association financed by the political institution that covers the whole administrative region, including Bordeaux. Pierre Cambar, formerly director of the regional wine-growers' union for the Bordeaux and Bordeaux Supérieur appellations, has been appointed Director and M. de Bosredon of Bergerac, as president. Prices for the South-West appellations are holding up rather better on account of the still reasonable property prices in the region (FF120,000–150,000, or €18.290–22.870, per hectare), which make it a welcome environment for investors. The planting taking place at Gaillac, and also Cahors and Lot-et-Garonne, are evidence of that.

Moreover, new vineyards are petitioning the venerable INAO to receive the supreme blessing of a promotion in status. A case in point is that of Saint-Sardos in Tarn-et-Garonne, which has been honourably mentioned many times in the *Guide*, and which is asking to be awarded the VDQS. The case in preparation should result in parcels of land being defined by next year, and the ministerial order could be signed in 2003.

WHAT'S NEW IN THE LOIRE VALLEY?

The year 2000 ended with the announcement, on 30 November, that UNESCO had declared the Loire Valley to be a World Heritage Site – a designation that will benefit the vineyards. The vines that have been coaxed forth from shale and limestone soils have, like the farms and châteaux, made their own contribution to the beauty of the Loire countryside.

IN THE NANTES REGION

The weather conditions in 2000 were less favourable than those of 1999. A mild winter and a wet spring encouraged the development of parasites, and July was short on sunshine. Fortunately, fine weather in August allowed the bulk of the harvest to be saved.

The result has been an even vintage of good average quality. The 2000 Muscadet is fruity and quite dry, with relatively high acid content.

The total production for the Nantes region (including the VDQS in the Vendée) reached 967,000 hl (25.5 million gal), or around 3% more than in 1999. Of that, 762,000 hl (30.1 million gal) was Muscadet. That corresponds, more or less, to the quantities sold. Stocks, which amount to no more than half of any harvest, therefore remain very low, with the result that from summer 2002 there is likely to be a shortage, since the 2001 harvest shows every sign of being a poor one. This is less on account of the frost that occurred on 20 April (the day the *Guide* tastings took place in that locality), which affected the northernmost vineyards, than because of the cool and very wet spring. The first leaf growth was so disappointing that it resulted in no more than half the normal quantities being produced. That could be a fatal blow to some of the more vulnerable estates, unless there is a significant rise in prices. That doesn't seem very likely. Despite maintaining good sales volume, especially of the *sur lie*, which increases by

about 6% year by year, prices remained depressed. As to exports, a strong improvement in the German, American and Japanese markets has failed to compensate for the serious downturn in the English market, which is the main outlet for Muscadet.

Price stagnation fuels tensions between the vine-growers and the *négociants*. Those among the latter who also make wines are gaining ground: in 2000–2001 they vinified 99,000 hl (2.61 million gal), which is more than 10% of the total production. While this was originally intended as a solution for small estates, however, the merchants have tended to go higher up the scale and handle the production from larger estates and châteaux. Co-operatives are still few and far between. Two or three small ones created in recent years have recently joined the Vignerons de La Noaille, which hopes to bring the volumes they produce up to the same level as their reputation.

The profession continues to ponder the creation of a future third level of Muscadet, intended to stand above the sub-regional appellations (Sèvre-et-Maine, Côtes de Grand-Lieu and Coteaux de la Loire).

IN ANJOU-SAUMUR

A great deal of rain, particularly in the spring and in September to October, meant that the 2000 vintage saw very little sunshine – 200 hours less than in an average year. However, temperatures stayed above average, and the months of May and June were very hot. The first leaves appeared ten days ahead of the average date, much as they had done the previous year. Mild, humid conditions encouraged proper growth but also brought mildew, which needed regular treatments. While flowering took place in optimal conditions, the vines lost their early advantage when the weather turned cool in July, and colour-change occurred at the normal time, between 20–23 August and 5–8 September.

Despite the rain, the grapes were hardly touched by rot, the fairly low daytime temperatures and the thick skins that they grew this year having slowed down the development of botrytis. The Cabernets were harvested at the end of October, and Chenin Blanc at the end of November, both in a good, healthy state. Gamay, Grolleau and Cabernet Franc were harvested under good conditions,

and the resulting wines are aromatically very rich. The reds have good colour and are perfectly balanced. The harvesting of the whites was put out of joint by the heavy rains in October and November. However, those parcels where the vigorous growth had been controlled did well. The grapes ripened successfully and the dry wines will be fruity and light; the sweet ones will be forthright in flavour, and extremely rich where the picking was late.

IN TOURAINE

While spring started at the end of February with three weeks of sun, the weather then became much cooler and the first leaves appeared around the normal date. The weather conditions – rainy in April, marked by a great deal of mist in May – also brought on the development of mildew. The summery period during the last three weeks in June favoured flowering, and then July brought more rain; August, though sunnier than July, was still wetter than normal. Fortunately, the weather turned fine as of 7 September, and held up until 8 October when the rain returned with a vengeance, persisting for over a month. All the grape varieties had larger berries than usual, with thicker skins that made them more resistant to botrytis.

Harvesting began on 12 September for the early varieties, like Gamay and Sauvignon Blanc, around the last week of September for Chenin and the Cabernets, and in the first week of October for the Chenin and Pineau d'Aunis of the Loir district.

The red wines are, in general, well structured, rounded and vividly coloured. This is a noble vintage particularly in Chinon, Bourgueil and Saint-Nicolas-de-Bourgueil. Reds from the Loir and Vendôme districts are quite supple. The dry white wines have good breeding. Chenin worked very well in the dry or demi-sec wines and in the Vouvrays and Montlouis, or as the basis for sparkling wines, but owing to the rain in October and November, 2000 is not a good year for sweet wines. The concentration of the grapes was no more than 14% potential alcohol: there were no *grains nobles* in this year. Hailstorms, moreover, affected the production of Montlouis.

A new Touraine AOC, Noble-Joué, has been recognised. It produces rosé or *gris* wines using a blend of Meunier, Pinot

Gris (20% minimum) and Pinot Noir (10% minimum) grapes, made at Chambray-lès-Tours, Esvres, Larçay, Saint-Avertin and Joué-lès-Tours. The new appellation makes its debut in the *Guide* with the 1999 vintage. Meanwhile, the Coteaux du Vendômois VDQS has been promoted to AOC.

THE CENTRAL AREA

The first leaves appeared around 15 April, a few days earlier than in an average year. Exceptional heat in May and June accelerated the growth of the vines, and flowering was practically over by the middle of June. A particularly cool and damp July, punctuated by storms, slowed down the development of the new bunches and obliged the vine-growers to keep a watch on the leaf-growth. Fortunately, August saw a return to fine weather, with moderate temperatures that permitted slow ripening of the grapes and refinement of their aromas. The last three weeks were excellent, ensuring that significant levels of sugar accumulated while good, balanced acidity was retained. The weather remained fine over the harvest period, allowing the growers to stagger the crop and pick the grapes from each parcel at the peak of ripeness. Harvesting of Pinot Gris began on 13 September, and on 18 September for Sauvignon Blanc. It lasted until 15 October for the latter grape variety, the Pinot Noir and Gamay having been picked in the meantime.

The white wines offer very complex aromas with a great deal of finesse, which reflect their *terroir* with fruity, mineral and sometimes herbaceous nuances. They show every sign of volume, firmness, length and character, auguring an attractive vintage. The best of them will keep several years.

The red wines are fruity and powerful. They will need fairly long maturation periods, depending on the origin of the grapes.

NEWS IN BRIEF FROM THE VINEYARDS

Following its Street Opera in 2000, the Comité Interprofessionnel des Vins de Nantes produced a comic opera, *Harlequin et Muscadine*, in honour of Muscadet *sur lie*, 'the wine that makes the whole town sing'. It also organised a roadshow presenting old vintages of Haute Expression (Muscadets officially designated as being of the highest quality) in several towns in Europe and North America. The Museum of Nantais Wine-making at Pallet has done its bit by installing new, more interactive displays.

In 2000, the Bonnezeaux appellation celebrated its 50th anniversary.

The scenic route through the vineyards in the heart of France (La Route des Vignobles du Coeur de France) was inaugurated on 26 February 2001 at Bourges. It was linked up with the Touraine vineyard route at Valençay on 4 May.

The 16th Loire Wine Salon will take place at Angers from Monday 4 to Wednesday 6 February 2002. The two principal invitees are the United States and Ireland.

WHAT'S NEW IN THE RHÔNE?

More haste, less speed! The old proverb was totally applicable to the year 2000, when vine-growth in the Rhône, long numbed by the effect of a winter that began very early, took off as soon as the first warm days arrived. The year finally turned out to be an early one, and a fortunate sequence of warmth, storms and mistral winds combined to produce wines of great richness.

One could not have guessed at the start of the year 2000 that it would prove to be one when everything came early. Even so, spectacular snowfalls – 23 cm (9 in) at Carpentras! – starting on 20 or 21 November 1999 made the news, and also happened to mark the day the *primeurs* were released in the Gard. Halfway through April, it seemed that the 2000 vintage would be a fairly late one compared with previous years, particularly with 1997 (25 days early), the year that certainly beat all the records for sunshine and heat. But the hot, sunny months of May and June allowed the vines to catch up. Flowering began on 20 May in the south and 23 May in the north, and by the end of June it was obvious that it was after all going to be an early vintage.

Following a particularly cold and wet July, the weather turned scorching hot on 14 August, with temperatures more than 1.8° C (3.24° F) above average, during which time conditions confirmed the likely precocity of the vintage. Harvesting began at the end of the month in the southern part of the Gard, and on 6 September in the northern Rhône. The healthy state of the grapes was remarkable; the yield in juice and the acidity were fairly low, while the alcoholic strength showed every sign of being high. The richness in polyphenolic compounds caused some people to compare 2000 with other great years.

However, the discrepancy between the ripeness of the skin (in terms of aroma, colour and tannin) and that of the pulp (sugars and acidity) has often been a factor in delaying harvesting. The storms of 20 September allowed further ripening of grapes that had been held back by the drought. The mistral, as always, played its part to perfection. Alternating changes of temperature between day and night facilitated generous levels of anthocyanin, which were above the average of the previous four years. The thickness of the skins and excellent health of the grapes allowed for long fermentation periods and very good extraction, promising wines that are vividly coloured, aromatic, rich in tannins and good for laying down: all the ingredients of a fine vintage.

The southern sector produced brightly coloured reds with purple highlights and splendidly soft tannins. The fruitiness of the Grenache is reminiscent of wild blackberries. Equally good fruit characterises the white wines, which have nuances of citrus fruits, apples and pears. The rosés are a lively colour, and offer aromas of red berries. The northern Rhône whites have good aromatic potential, already showing hints of white-fleshed fruits overlaid with floral touches. The red wines are remarkable for their colour, fruitiness and tannins that are quite evident but velvety in texture. Extraordinarily well served by the vintage conditions, they are highly distinguished wines that will be suitable for laying down.

The harvest of 2000 exceeded both of the two previous ones: 3,858,500 hl (101.9 million gal), as against 3,661,000 hl (96.6 million gal) in 1999. Côtes du

31   NEWS FROM FRANCE'S VINEYARDS

Rhône-Villages continues to grow: up from 317,700 hl (8.39 million gal) in 1999 to 336,150 hl (8.87 million gal) in 2000. Volumes are also on the increase in Châteauneuf-du-Pape.

FIFTEEN YEARS OF A

CHANGING MARKET

For a long time now, the restaurant trade has been the principal outlet for Rhône wines, usually as carafe wines to accompany an everyday meal. In 1987, this sector still represented 40% of the volume of sales, against 34% for home consumption and 27% for export. By 1999, consumption in the home (now 40%) had overtaken restaurants and café sales (which stood at 30%). In 2000, the sales of AOC wines for home consumption in the domestic market had increased by a further 3%.

Another positive trend over the last five years is the growing number of Rhône wines sent for export: it reached 30% of total sales, against 21% in 1994. Of all French regions, the Rhône is the one that shows the greatest increase in sales to other countries: it exported 798,301 hl (21.08 million gal), which represents more than FF1.7 billion (€259 million), with an increase in volume of 5.45% and in value of almost 15%.

NEWS IN BRIEF FROM THE VINEYARDS

A new co-operative, the Cave de Sauveterre, was created at Pujaut in the Gard. Situated right in the heart of the village, it is near to the N580, beside Cellier des Chartreux. The external vats, intended for the blending process, were air-lifted in by helicopter in an operation that delivered one 3,000-hl (79,000-gal) vat weighing 6 t, two 500-hl (13,200-gal) ones, each weighing 3 t, and four others holding 50 hl (1,320 gal) and weighing 1.5 t. In the Ventoux, a new group of producers has been established – the Vignobles du Ventoux, which consists of four co-operatives (Les Roches Blanches at Mormoiron, the Cave Saint-Marc at Caromb, Les Vignerons du Mont-Ventoux at Bedoin and La Courtoise at Saint-Didier). Altogether, they represent one-third of the total volume of the appellation.

Finally, the 'vin des papes', inaugurated in the vineyards of the Palais des Papes, has harvested its first crop. Les Compagnons du Ban des Vendanges (the organisation that issues harvesting certificates) held a memorable auction sale on 9 July 2001 in the superb Salle du Conclave. The proceeds of the sale went to the Mises en Scènes (Theatre Productions) Association, via the Reading in Hospitals project destined to help patients in the haematology department of Avignon Hospital.

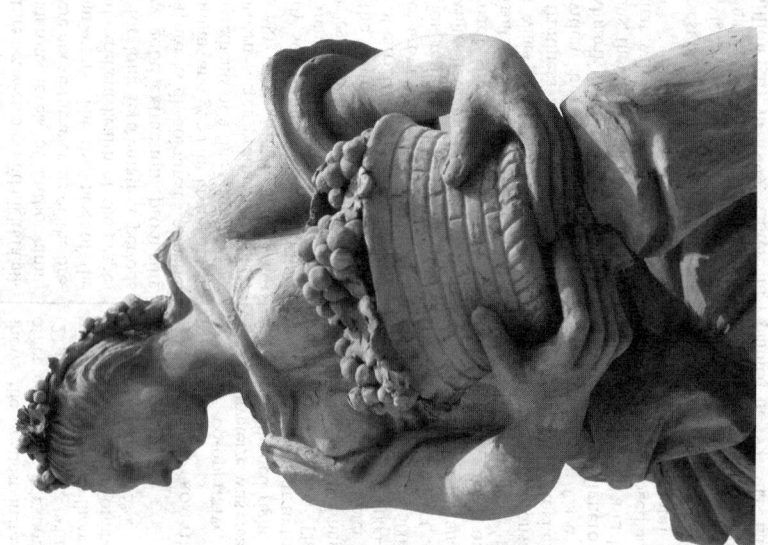

WINE

Wine is defined as 'the product obtained exclusively from partial or total alcoholic fermentation of grape must or fresh grapes, which can be pressed or whole'. All legal definitions require wine to have a minimum alcohol content of 8.5% vol or 9.5% vol, depending on the wine-growing area. The degree of alcohol is expressed in the percentage of the volume consisting of pure alcohol; 17 grams of sugar are needed for the must to produce 1% vol of alcohol by fermentation.

THE DIFFERENT TYPES OF WINE

European regulations, which incorporate French usage, distinguish between table wine and VQPRD. The Vins de Qualité Produits dans une Région Déterminée (VQPRD) are subject to certain controls. In France, they correspond to Appellations d'Origine Vins Délimités de Qualité Supérieure (AOVDQS) and to Vins d'Appellation d'Origine Contrôlée (AOC). It is worth noting that young vines (those under four years old) are excluded from appellations, because the wines they produce are too light to represent the appellation.

— Dry wines and sweet wines (*demi-secs*, *moelleux* and *doux*) are characterised by varying amounts of sugar. The production of sweet wine requires very ripe grapes, rich in sugar, of which only a part is transformed into alcohol by fermentation. Sauternes, for example, are particularly rich wines obtained from grapes whose sugar has been concentrated by *pourriture noble* (noble rot). They are often termed Grands Vins Liquoreux, not to be confused with Vins de Liqueurs, which are defined by European legislation (see below).

— Sparkling wines differ from still wines by the escape of carbon dioxide (the familiar 'pop') on opening – this comes from a second fermentation known as *prise de mousse*. In the traditional method, which used to be known as *méthode champenoise*, this is achieved in the bottle; if it is carried out in the vat, it is called the *cuve close* (tank) method.

— Vins Mousseux Gazéifiés also give off carbon dioxide on opening, but with these wines it has been added, either partially or totally. Vins Pétillants (lightly sparkling wines) have a carbon dioxide pressure of between 1 and 2.5 bars and need contain only 7% of alcohol. Pétillant de Raisin is obtained from the partial fermentation of grape must, and its alcohol content is low, the minimum being 1% vol.

— *Vins de Liqueur* (sweet fortified wines) are obtained by adding – before, during and after fermentation – pure alcohol, *eau-de-vie de vin* (wine brandy), concentrated grape must or a mixture of these products. The term 'mistelle' is not included in the European regulations, which refer to 'fresh grape must mixed with alcohol' (without fermentation). Pineau des Charentes, added to the grape must (without fermentation). Pineau des Charentes, Floc de Gascogne and Macvin du Jura belong in this category.

CULTIVATING THE VINE

The vine belongs to the genus *Vitis*, in which there are many species. Traditionally, wine is produced from different varieties of *Vitis vinifera*, which

Cultivating the vine

originated on the European continent. There are however, other species that originated on the American continent. Some of these are infertile, others produce wines with very particular organoleptic qualities (known as *foxé* or foxy), and these are not very popular. However, these 'American' varieties have a greater resistance to disease than *Vitis vinifera*. In the 1930s attempts were made to create hybrids that would be resistant to disease, like the American species, but would also produce wines of the same quality as *Vitis vinifera*. Unfortunately, these were a complete failure.

Vitis vinifera is susceptible to phylloxera, an insect that attacks the roots of the vine and that caused terrible devastation at the end of the 19th century. The development of a graft onto an American rootstock that was resistant to phylloxera led to a vinestock that had the properties of its own grape family but roots that could not be infected by the insect.

The species *Vitis vinifera* includes many varieties, known as *cépages*.

REGIONS	VARIETIES	CHARACTERISTICS
All the red Burgundy AOCs	Pinot	Fine wines to lay down
All the white Burgundy AOCs	Chardonnay	Fine wines to lay down
Beaujolais	Gamay	'Nouveau' or 'Primeur' wines or wines for rapid consumption
Northern Rhône (red)	Syrah	Fine wines to lay down
Northern Rhône (white)	Marsanne, Roussanne	Wines for medium to long-term maturing
Northern Rhône (white)	Viognier	Full-bodied wines to lay down
Southern Rhône, Languedoc, Côtes de Provence	Grenache, Cinsault Mourvèdre, Syrah	Full-bodied wines for medium to long-term maturing
Alsace (each variety, vinified separately, lends its name to the wine)	Riesling, Pinot Gris, Gewurztraminer, Sylvaner, Muscat . . .	Aromatic wines to be drunk quickly except for *Grands Crus*, *Vendanges Tardives* or *Sélections de Grains Nobles*
Champagne	Pinot, Chardonnay	Can be drunk on purchase
Loire (white)	Sauvignon	Aromatic wines to be drunk rapidly
Loire (white)	Muscadet	To be drunk quickly
Loire (white)	Chenin	Improve with age
Loire (red)	Cabernet Franc (Breton)	Short to long-term maturing
All the red Bordeaux, Bergerac and south-western AOCs	Cabernet Sauvignon, Cabernet Franc, Merlot	Fine wines to lay down
Madiran	Tannat, Cabernets	Fine wines to lay down
Bordeaux (white), Bergerac, Montravel, Monbazillac, Duras	Sémillon, Sauvignon, Muscadelle	Dry: for short to long-term maturing; Sweet dessert wines: for laying down;
Jurançon	Petit Manseng	Dry: short-term maturation;
	Gros Manseng	Sweet: long-term maturation

Each wine-growing region has chosen the most suitable variety for its area, but economic conditions and the tastes of consumers can also play a part in modifying what is planted. Some vineyards produce wine from a single variety (for example, Pinot Noir and Chardonnay in Burgundy and Riesling in Alsace). In other regions (for example, in Champagne and Bordeaux) the greatest wines are the result of blending several varieties with complementary characteristics. The varieties are themselves made up of 'individuals' (clones), which do not have identical characteristics (of productivity, rate of ripening, resistance to disease). The search is always on for the best stock. At the moment, research is being carried out into creating disease-resistant vines by genetic modification.

— Growing conditions have a decisive effect on the quality of wine. It is possible to increase yields considerably by changing fertilisation and pruning methods, choosing different stock and altering the density of the plants. It is not possible however to increase yields dramatically without affecting quality, except when nature intervenes; then quality is rarely compromised, and some of the greatest vintages have been produced from abundant harvests.

— In recent years the increase in yields has been linked to better growing conditions. The advisable limit depends on the style of the wine: for good red wines the maximum advisable yield is between 45 and 60 hl per ha and a little more for dry white wines. To produce very good wines, you also need vines that are ten years old or more, with a well-developed root system.

— The vine is susceptible to numerous diseases, various types of mildew and rot, which deplete the harvest and give the grapes a nasty taste, which is detectable in the wine. Wine-growers now have the means to treat these diseases effectively and this has certainly contributed to the general improvement in quality. In the past, a concern for security has probably led to an over-zealous use of chemical pesticides, but today they are used more prudently. In general, these chemical treatments are used only when absolutely necessary, and research within agricultural biology is now focusing on soil biodynamics, with the aim of creating natural conditions that will make the vine less susceptible to disease.

SOILS FOR WINE-GROWING: THE ADAPTATION OF VARIETIES TO SOIL AND CLIMATE

Taken in its broadest sense, the notion of 'soils for wine-growing', often referred to as *terroir*, brings together several different factors: biological (choice of variety), geographical, climatic, geological and pedological (types of soil). Added to these are the human, historical and commercial aspects: for example, the existence of the port at Bordeaux and its commerce with Scandinavian countries encouraged the wine-growers of the 18th century to improve the quality of their wines.

— In the northern hemisphere the vine is cultivated between the latitudes of 35° and 50°; it therefore has to adapt to very different climates. However, the most northerly vineyards usually cultivate only white varieties, which ripen slowly and whose grapes are resistant to early autumn frosts. In warmer climates, later fruiting varieties with high yields are grown. To make good wine you need well-ripened grapes, but the maturation process should not be too rapid nor too advanced because this leads to a loss in aroma; thus varieties are chosen with close attention paid to the maturation period. For the vineyards that are situated at the edges of climatic

Soils for wine-growing

zones, the big problem is inconsistency of climatic conditions during the maturation period.

Excessive dryness or humidity also play a part. The soil plays an essential role in the irrigation of the plant; in spring, during the growing period, it supplies the vines with water and allows any excess rain during maturation to drain away. Gravelly and chalky soils are particularly suited to this, but there are also highly reputable Crus that are grown on sandy and even clayey soils. Artificial drainage is sometimes used, and this accounts for the existence of high-quality Crus being grown on different types of soil, while neighbouring vineyards, with the same soil type, produce wine of varying quality.

The different types of soil and subsoil can affect the colour, aroma and taste of wines from the same variety and growing in the same climatic conditions. Wines can vary depending on whether the soil is chalky, clayey, sandy or gravelly or a combination of any of these. An increase in the proportion of clay in Graves makes the wine more acidic, more tannic and full bodied and less refined; a white Sauvignon takes on more flowery notes when grown on chalky, gravelly or marly soils. In any case, the vine is not particular about the quality of the soil on which it grows. In fact, poor soil is often a contributory factor in good wines, as the yield is limited and characteristics, such as colour, aroma and taste, are subsequently advanced.

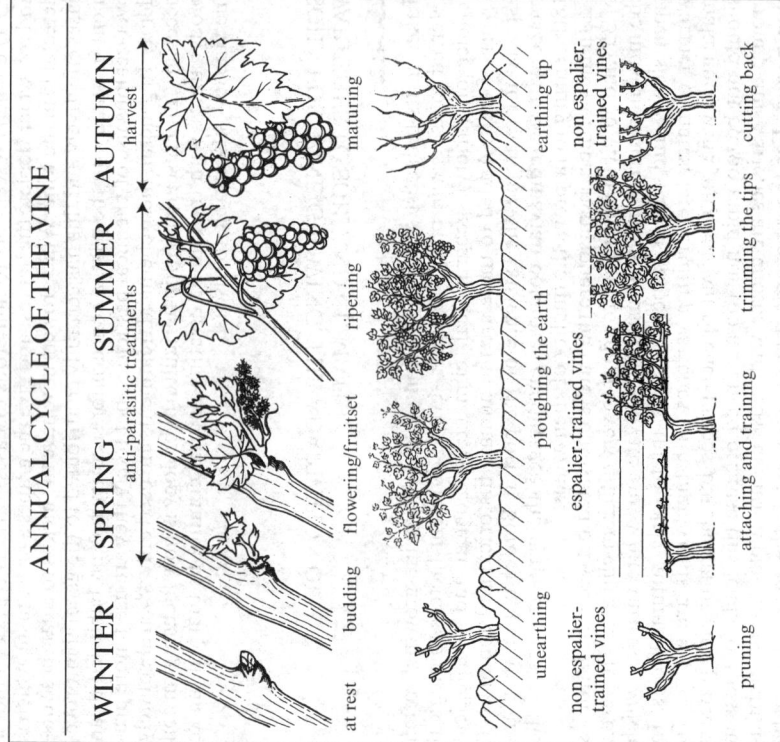

ANNUAL CYCLE OF THE VINE

WINTER | SPRING | SUMMER | AUTUMN

anti-parasitic treatments — harvest

at rest — budding — flowering/fruitset — ripening — maturing

unearthing — ploughing the earth — earthing up

non espalier-trained vines — espalier-trained vines — non espalier-trained vines

pruning — attaching and training — trimming the tips — cutting back

36

THE CYCLE OF WORK IN THE VINEYARD

Annual pruning, aimed at limiting excessive growth of the woody stem and giving a balanced yield, normally takes place between December and March. The potential number of buds is determined by the strength of the plant, and this has a direct effect on the size of the harvest. In spring the work consists of 'unearthing' the vines – the soil is raked into the middle of the row, creating a loose layer that should stay relatively dry.

— The ground is tended throughout the whole growing cycle, according to need: self-propagating plants are destroyed, the loose topsoil is maintained and loss of moisture through evaporation is prevented. Sometimes chemical herbicides are used for weeding; if they are applied to the whole vineyard, this is usually done at the end of winter and all ploughing is halted. This is known as 'non-cultivation' and represents a considerable saving. However, some environmentally aware producers prefer not to weed the rows, as the weeds act to limit the growth of the vines naturally.

— During the growing cycle, several different procedures are employed to limit excessive growth: *épamprage*, thinning out selected branches; *rognage*, trimming the tips; *effeuillage*, the removal of leaves, which allows the grapes to be more exposed to the sun; and *accolage*, training the shoots along wire espaliers. The wine-grower also has to protect the vines from disease, and to help him the Service for the Protection of Plants distributes information about various treatments, mainly sprays made from either natural or chemical products.

— Finally, in autumn, after the harvest, the earth is heaped up around the vines to protect them from the winter frosts; a furrow in the middle of the row allows rain water to run away, and fertiliser is sometimes dug in here as well.

GRAPES AND THE HARVEST

The degree of maturity of the grape is an essential factor in the quality of the wine. But even within the same region climatic conditions vary from one year to the next, leading to differences in the composition of the grapes, which in turn determines the characteristics of each vintage. Hot, dry weather is generally needed for the grapes to fully ripen, and the date to start picking must be fixed with great care, taking into account both the ripeness and the health of the grapes.

— Increasingly, manual harvesting is giving way to mechanical picking. The machines, fitted with 'beaters', knock the grapes on to a conveyor belt, and a fan is used to remove most of the leaves. The shock effect on the grapes detracts somewhat from their quality, especially where white grapes are concerned; the most reputable crus will be the last ones to use this form of grape-picking, despite the considerable progress that has been made in the design and construction of the machines. When the grapes are over-ripe at harvest-time, the level of acidity can be increased by adding tartaric acid, and if the grapes are under-ripe the acidity can be decreased by adding calcium carbonate. A wine that is not rich enough may not have a sufficiently high alcohol content and can be improved by adding concentrated must. Finally, in certain well-defined conditions, legislation allows for the adding of sugar to the must – this is known as 'chaptalisation'.

THE WINE-GROWER'S CALENDAR

JANUARY

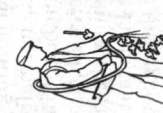

St Vincent's Day is the feast day of the patron saint of wine growers.

FEBRUARY

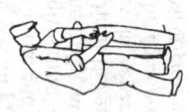

Wine contracts with the cold. Barrels need to be checked periodically and topped up if necessary. Malolactic fermentation should now be completed.

MARCH

Clear heaped-up earth away from the vines to let air circulate between them. Pruning should now be finished. Wines for early drinking should now be bottled.

APRIL

Before phylloxera, vines were trained on sticks. Nowadays, vines are trained along wire espaliers (except at l'Hermitage, Côte Rôtie and Condrieu).

MAY

This is the time to watch out for and protect against spring frosts. The spaces between the rows are ploughed.

JUNE

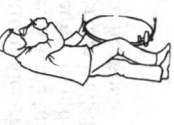

Vines are trained and the stems are pruned. The way the fruits set, known as the flowering, will determine the volume of the harvest.

JULY

Anti-parasitic treatments continue and the vines are studied carefully; this is a time when temperatures can vary enormously, and there is a risk of summer hail storms.

AUGUST

Disturbing the soil could be harmful to the vines, but a close look-out must be kept for parasites. In early-ripening regions, the vats and casks are prepared.

SEPTEMBER

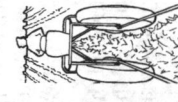

Grapes are picked and tested regularly for maturation in order to set a date for the harvest; harvest begins in Mediterranean areas.

OCTOBER

In most vineyards, it is harvest-time and wine-making begins. Wines for laying down are put in casks to mature.

NOVEMBER

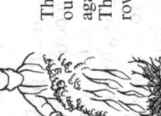

Young wines ready for drinking en primeur are bottled now. Progress of the nouveau wines is checked. The autumn cutback begins.

DECEMBER

The temperature in the wine-cellar is monitored to ensure alcoholic and malolactic fermentation.

THE MAKING OF WINE

The essential microbiological phenomenon that creates wine is alcoholic fermentation. The development of a type of yeast (*Saccharomyces cerevisiae*), which is not exposed to the air, breaks down the sugar into alcohol and carbon dioxide; numerous by-products appear (glycerol, succinic acid, ethyl esters etc), and these enhance the aroma and taste of the wine. The process of fermentation produces heat, and the vat may need to be cooled down by refrigeration.

In some cases, malolactic fermentation occurs after alcoholic fermentation; with the aid of certain bacteria, the malic acid is broken down into lactic acid and carbon dioxide. This results in a lowering of acidity, a smoothing out and refining of the aroma and a more stable wine. Red wines are always improved by this process, but it is not always so for white wines. Yeast and bacteria exist naturally on the grapes; they develop during the procedures carried out in the wineries, and often they are all that is needed to start fermentation. However, the use of dried commercial yeast is becoming more common because it allows more control of the fermentation process and avoids certain defects (odours caused by reduction or lack of aeration) associated with some naturally occurring yeast varieties. In some cases, a modified stock allows dormant aromas specific to a particular variety (Sauvignon) to be released from non-aromatic characteristics already existing in the grape. In any case, the quality and the character of the wine depend not wholly on the quality of the grape but also on natural factors, such as exposure and soil.

Yeast always develops before the bacteria, which begin to grow only when the yeast has stopped fermenting. If the yeast stops fermenting before all the sugar has been transformed into alcohol, the residual sugar can be broken down by the bacteria, producing acetic acid (volatile acid); this is a serious setback, known as *piqûre*. A recently discovered procedure allows toxic substances formed from the yeast itself to be eliminated. During the ageing process, bacteria are still present in the wine and could lead to serious problems, such as the decomposition of fruit elements of the wine, oxidation and the formation of acetic acid (a process in the making of vinegar). Today, however, the precautions used in vinification can help to avoid these risks.

THE DIFFERENT WINE-MAKING PROCESSES

Making red wine

In most cases, the grapes are first detached from their stalks and then crushed; the mixture of pulp, pips and skins is put into the fermenting vat along with a small dose of sulphur dioxide, which helps to protect against bacteria and oxidation. Once fermentation has started, the carbon dioxide lifts all the solid particles to the top of the vat where they form a solid mass called *chapeau* or *marc*.

Alcoholic fermentation takes place in the vat at the same time as the maceration of the skins and pips in the juice. It usually takes a minimum of five to eight days for the sugar to ferment completely; this is helped by allowing air in to increase the growth of the yeast and by controlling the temperature (at around 30°C/86°F) to avoid killing off the yeast. The maceration gives red wine its colour and much of its tannic structure. Wines that are to be aged should be rich in tannin and need a long period of

VINIFICATION OF RED WINE

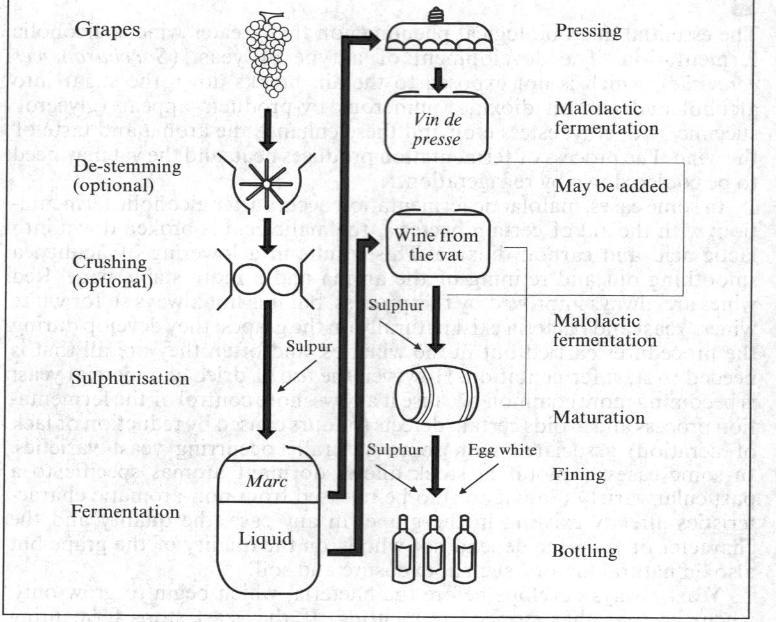

Grapes

De-stemming (optional)

Crushing (optional)

Sulphurisation

Fermentation

Pressing

Malolactic fermentation

May be added

Vin de presse

Wine from the vat

Malolactic fermentation

Maturation

Fining

Bottling

Marc

Liquid

Sulpur

Sulphur

Sulphur

Egg white

VINIFICATION OF WHITE WINE

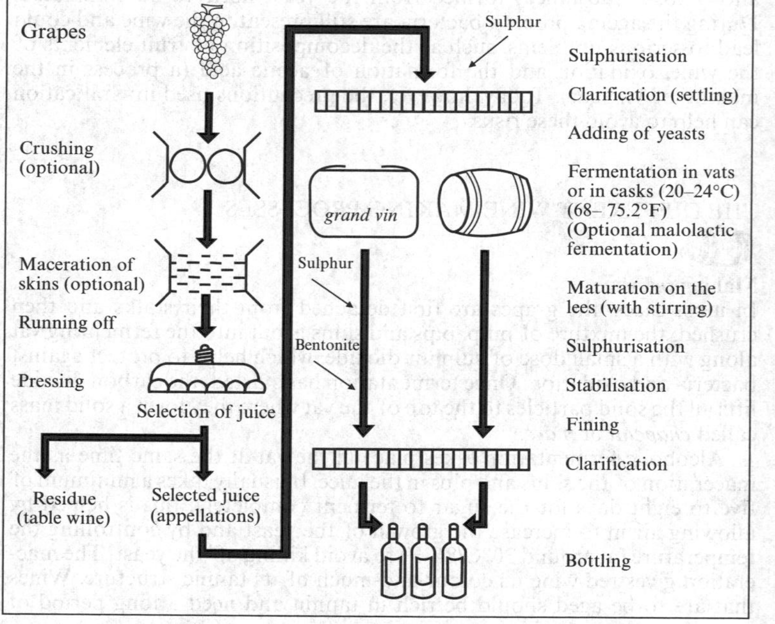

Grapes

Crushing (optional)

Maceration of skins (optional)

Running off

Pressing

Selection of juice

Selected juice (appellations)

Residue (table wine)

Sulphurisation

Clarification (settling)

Adding of yeasts

Fermentation in vats or in casks (20–24°C) (68–75.2°F) (Optional malolactic fermentation)

Maturation on the lees (with stirring)

Sulphurisation

Stabilisation

Fining

Clarification

Bottling

Sulphur

grand vin

Sulphur

Bentonite

maceration (two or three weeks) at 25–30°C (77–86°F). On the other hand, wines that are to be drunk young, such as Vins Nouveaux, should be fruity and not very tannic; these need to be macerated for only a few days.

— The liquid part of the mixture is then separated from the residue or *marc*. The liquid part is known as *vin de goutte* (free-run wine) or *grand vin*. The *marc* is then pressed and this gives what is known as *vin de presse*. *Vin de presse* is sometimes blended with *vin de goutte*, depending on defined criteria for taste and analysis. The wines are put into separate vats for the final settling and for malolactic fermentation to take place. With expensive, hand-made wines it is becoming more and more common for the liquid to be run off directly into small oak barrels in which malolactic fermentation takes place. Red wines thus acquire a more consistently complex character.

— This is the basic method, but other vinification procedures are of special interest, including thermovinification, continuous vinification and carbonic maceration.

Making rosé wine

Rosé, *clairet* (deep rosé) or *gris* (light rosé) wines are obtained by macerating, for varying lengths of time, grapes that are either strongly coloured or very lightly coloured. More often than not, they are vinified by pressing black grapes or by a short maceration process. For the latter, the vat is macerated for a short time before fermentation in order to extract their aroma. To achieve this you need perfectly healthy and ripe grapes in order to avoid defects in taste and aroma, such as bitterness and unpleasant odours. The juice is extracted by crushing the grapes, running off the juice and pressing. The *jus de presse* is fermented separately because it is inferior in quality. The white must, which is very susceptible to oxidation, is protected by the addition of sulphur dioxide. After the juice has been extracted, it will be clarified by a process known as *débourbage* (settling the sediment from the wine). During the whole fermentation process the vat has to be maintained at a temperature of between 20° and 24°C (68°F and 75.2°F) to protect the aroma.

Making white wine

There is a wide variety of types of white wine, each one with its own particular vinification technique and appropriate harvesting method. In most cases white wine results from the fermentation of grape juice, without the skins, which occurs after pressing. In some cases, however, the skins are macerated for a short time before fermentation in order to extract their aroma.

— The great Vins Blancs are vinified in barrels and consequently take on a succulent, woody character. This method also allows, among other things, an ageing on the yeast lees or sediments, which increases the richness and flavour of the wine. This development is accentuated by stirring the wine with a pole to keep the lees in suspension.

— In many cases malolactic fermentation is not required for white wines, which have a fresher more acid taste, and a second fermentation can often reduce the characteristic aromas of the variety. However, those white wines that have a fairly long ageing in casks (for example, white Burgundies) develop richness and volume during this second fermentation. They are also more stable biologically once bottled.

— Grapes very rich in sugar are needed for the vinification of sweet wines. Part of the sugar is transformed into alcohol, but the fermentation is stopped before it is completed by the addition of sulphur dioxide, and the yeast is eliminated by racking, by centrifuge or by pasteurisation.

The different stages of maturation

Sauternes and Barsacs, which are particularly rich in both alcohol (13 to 15% vol) and in sugar (50 to 100 g per litre), need very ripe grapes, which cannot be obtained by the normal ripening process. This requires the action on the grape of a fungus, *Botrytis cinerea*, to produce noble rot; the grapes are also harvested in successive stages according to the development of the noble rot.

THE DIFFERENT STAGES OF MATURATION

New wine is rough, cloudy and full of carbon dioxide. It needs *élevage* (clarification, stabilisation and refining) to prepare it for the next stage, that of bottling. The time this takes varies according to the type of wine: Vins Nouveaux are bottled a few weeks after vinification, whereas wines for laying down are aged for two or more years.

If the wine is kept in small containers, such as 225-litre oak barrels, clarification can be obtained by racking the wine (*soutirage*) and removing the sediments. If the wine is kept in large vats, however, centrifugation or other methods of filtration have to be used.

Because of its complexity, cloudiness and deposits can occur in the wine. These are totally natural phenomena of microbiological or chemical origin. When this happens in the bottle, it can be very serious, which is why stabilisation should take place beforehand.

Microbiological spoilage (acescency caused by bacteria or refermentation) can be avoided by preventing exposure to air and by keeping the container full. A topping-up process is carried out to prevent contact with air. Sulphur dioxide, which is both an antioxidant and an antiseptic, is often added, as is sorbic acid (an antiseptic) and ascorbic acid (an antioxidant).

The treatment of wines is born from necessity; the products added are relatively few, they do not affect the quality of the wine, and they have been proved to be harmless. Laboratory tests help to predict risks of instability and to limit treatments to what is absolutely essential. However, the modern approach to vinification is towards taking action immediately after vinification in order to limit the need for later treatments and the handling operations that these involve.

Refrigeration can help to prevent deposits of tartar before bottling. Metatartaric acid, which inhibits crystallisation, has an immediate but not a long-lasting effect. Fining consists of adding a protein, such as egg white or gelatine, to the wine. This has a coalescent action, taking out suspended particles that are liable to make the wine cloudy or to leave deposits at a later stage. The adding of substances (usually egg white) to red wine is an ancient practice, indispensable for getting rid of excess colouring matter that would otherwise line the inside of the bottle. Gum arabic has a similar effect and is used for table wines that are to be consumed soon after bottling. The coagulation of natural proteins in white wines is avoided by adding bentonite which is a protective colloid. An excess of certain metals such as iron or copper, can also lead to cloudiness; they can be eliminated by adding potassium ferrocyanide.

Elevage also contains a refining stage. First of all there is the elimination of any excess carbon dioxide that has been produced during fermentation. How this is done depends on the type of wine, for while it gives freshness to dry white wines and young wines, it has a coarsening effect on wines to be laid down, especially good red wines. The carefully controlled introduction of oxygen acts on the tannins of young red wines and is

42

indispensable for their later ageing in bottles. Controlled aeration happens naturally in oak casks, but it is possible to introduce precise amounts of oxygen; the technique is known as *microbullage*.

— When the wood is new, oak casks give wines tones of vanilla and toastiness, which harmonise perfectly with the aromas of the fruit. Allier oak (from the Tronçais forest) is more suitable than Limousin oak. The wood must be split and dried in the open air for three years before it is used. This is all part of the traditional method used for fine wines, but it is very expensive in terms of the cost of the casks, the manual labour involved and the loss of wine through evaporation. In addition, when the casks are old they can be a source of microbiological contamination and can sometimes do more harm than good. This type of ageing should be reserved for wines that are sufficiently rich for the oakiness not to dominate the fruity aromas of the wine and mask its typical characteristics. The contribution that oak can make depends on the structure of the wines (taking into account the length of ageing and the proportion of new casks), and care must be taken that the wine does not become too dry. Attempts have been made to simplify the process by, for example, macerating the wine with oak shavings or wood chips, but this is forbidden in the production of AOC wines.

AGEING

The word 'ageing' is specifically reserved for the slow transformation of wine in the bottle, with no exposure to the oxygen in the air. Bottling must be carried out with great care in very hygienic conditions. By this stage the wine has been thoroughly clarified and must not be contaminated. Care must also be taken to fill the bottles with the right quantity. Because of its elasticity and imperviousness to liquids, cork still remains the first choice for sealing bottles. However, it is advisable to re-cork bottles every 25 years or so, as cork is degradable. There are also two risks of contamination connected with corks: leaky bottles and a 'corky' taste.

— The changes that occur in the bottle are many and complex. There is, first of all, a change in colour, which is most evident in red wines. The bright red colour of young wines evolves into a more yellowy shade, resembling the colour of tiles or bricks. In very old wines the red is replaced by tones of brown and orange. This process of change is responsible for the deposits that are often present in very old wines. Bottle age also 'softens' the general structure of the wine by reducing the tannic element.

— It is during the ageing process in the bottle that aromas and the individual 'bouquets' of old wines develop. These developments are due to complex chemical changes that are still not fully understood but that do not involve esterification.

QUALITY CONTROL

Good wine is not necessarily great wine. A wine of quality can be anything from a table wine to a Grand Cru or any permutation in between. A distinction also has to be made between the human factors and natural factors that contribute to the quality of the wine. The first category is indispensable for a good wine, but a great wine requires very specific environmental conditions of soil and climate.

— Chemical analysis has helped to point out anomalies and defects, but it

Quality control

has its limitations when it comes to defining quality: in the final analysis, taste is the essential criterion. However, considerable progress has been made over the last 20 years in sensory analytical techniques, giving us a better understanding and knowledge of the physiology of odour and taste and of practical tasting conditions. Tasting expertise is playing an increasingly large part in gauging quality, in particular in the registration of AOC wines and in legal cases.

In fact, quality control has been subject to regulation for some time. The first official text was the French wine law of 1 August 1905 concerning commercial transactions. Regulations have progressed in step with developments in the understanding of the composition of wine and the changes that occur. With the help of chemical analysis, regulations define a minimum level of quality, thus eliminating major defects; they also encourage ways of improving this minimum level. The Consumers and Fraud Association is responsible for checking the analytical standards that have been established.

Added to this is the work carried out by the National Institute of Appellations d'Origine (INAO), which, in consultation with the *syndicats* concerned, lays down and controls production conditions, including production zones, varieties, planting and pruning methods, cultivation techniques, vinification, composition of musts and wines, and yields. This body is also responsible for representing AOC wines within France and abroad.

Finally, in every region, wine-growing *syndicats* defend the interests of their members, especially when it comes to matters concerning appellations. This work is often co-ordinated by councils, bodies or interprofessional committees that bring together representatives from various unions and from groups of producers and wine-merchants, as well as people from the professional and administrative worlds.

Pascal Ribéreau-Gayon

A CONSUMER'S GUIDE TO BUYING WINE

Buying wine is the easiest thing in the world: choosing wisely is the most difficult. If you were to consider everything that is on offer, you would find that there are several hundreds of thousands of different wines to choose from.

France alone produces tens of thousands of wines, each of which has its own individuality and characteristics. What distinguishes them in appearance, apart from their colour, is their label, hence the importance and care that the public and professional authorities attach to controlling the use and presentation of 'labelling'. It is also important for the buyer to understand a label's many 'mysteries'.

THE LABEL

The label fulfils several functions.

— The first is a legal one. It indicates who is responsible for the wine in case of any dispute. This could be a wine-merchant or the grower himself. In some cases this information is also indicated on the top of the cap or capsule.

— The second function of the label is very important, because it establishes the category to which the wine belongs: vin de table, Vin de Pays, AOVDQS or AOC; the last two of these have been assimilated into the European term Vin de Qualité Produit dans des Régions Déterminées (VQPRD).

AOC

This is the top class, the category for all the great wines. The label has to have 'XXXX Appellation Contrôlée' or 'Appellation XXXX Contrôlée' on it. This mentions the precise region, town or commune or even sometimes the cru (or *climat*, a part of a cru) where the vineyard is situated. To have the right to an AOC, a wine must have been produced according to 'local, loyal and consistent usage' – that is, it is from approved 'noble' varieties planted in specific vineyards and vinified according to regional traditions. The yield per hectare and alcoholic content (minimum and sometimes maximum) are also fixed by law. The wines are approved every year by a tasting committee.

— National regulations are supplemented by the institutionalised application of local customs. Thus, in Alsace the letters indicating the regional appellation are nearly always double the size of the name of the variety. In Burgundy on the other hand, only the Premiers Crus can be printed in letters that are the same size as those used for the appellation of the commune; the *climats* that are not in the highest classification can be mentioned only in small letters, half the size of the characters indicating the appellation. In addition, the communes of the Grands Crus do not appear on the labels, because these wines have their own individual appellations. These requirements are all given in detail in current French wine law.

45

How to read a label

HOW TO READ A LABEL

The label must identify the wine and indicate who is responsible for it. The last person in the production process is the bottler, and his name must also appear on the label. Each category of wine is subject to its own specific labelling regulations. The first duty of the label is to inform the consumer and to indicate which category the wine belongs to:

– Vin de table (origin, alcohol content, volume, name and address of bottler must all be mentioned; vintages, or years, are forbidden).
– Vins de Pays.
– Appellation d'Origine Vin Délimité de Qualité Supérieure (AOVDQS).
– Appellation d'Origine Contrôlée (AOC).

Alsace AOC

green fiscal stamp (on cap)

wine category (compulsory)

variety (only allowed if grapes are from one single variety)

volume (compulsory)

all other compulsory indications

necessary for export to certain countries

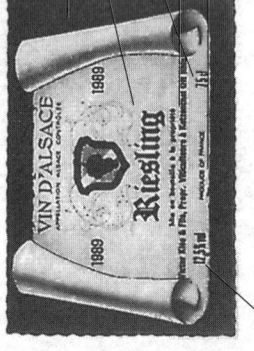

alcohol content in degrees (compulsory)

Bordeaux AOC

green fiscal stamp

brand (optional)

vintage (optional)

class of category (optional)

category (compulsory)

name and address of bottler (compulsory)

the word 'owner' (optional) fixes the status of the vineyard

optional

volume (compulsory)

necessary for export to certain countries

alcohol content in degrees (compulsory)

Burgundy AOC

green fiscal stamp

the vintage is often on a label around the neck of the bottle (optional)

name of the cru (optional); if the letters are the same size as those of the appellation, it is a Premier Cru

category (compulsory)

alcohol content (compulsory)

name and address of bottler (compulsory); also indicates that it is bottled at the property not by a wine-merchant

necessary for export to certain countries

volume (compulsory)

46

How to read a label

Champagne AOC

green fiscal stamp
of no great significance (optional)

compulsory

all Champagne is AOC, so this does not
figure on the rule that requires a reference to the
category of wine

brand and address (compulsory; it is taken
as read that it is bottled at the same
address)

volume (compulsory)

status of the vineyard and its professional
identification number (optional)

AOVDQS

green fiscal stamp

vintage (optional)

variety (optional, only allowed if grapes are
from one single variety)

name of the appellation (compulsory)

category (compulsory)

alcohol content (compulsory)

name and address of bottler (compulsory)

indicates whether bottled on premises
(optional)

stamp (compulsory)

volume (compulsory)

number (which indicates it has been
checked), compulsory in France

Vins de Pays

blue fiscal stamp

table wines are subject to the same
regulations. The words 'Vin de Pays' must
be followed by the name of the region
(compulsory)

'au domaine' optional

geographical area (compulsory)

name and address of bottler (compulsory)

alcohol content in degrees (compulsory)

volume (compulsory)

How to read a label

Appellation d'Origine Vin Délimité de Qualité Supérieure (AOVDQS)

The 'antechamber' of AOC, this category is sensibly subject to the same rules. AOVQDS wines are labelled after they have been tasted. The label must include the words 'Appellation d'Origine Vin Délimité de Qualité Supérieure' and its corresponding stamp. These are not wines for laying down, but some of them improve after being kept in cellars for a while.

Vins de Pays

The labels for Vins de Pays indicate which region the wine comes from, so you will see 'Vin de Pays de …' followed by the name of the region.

Wines in this category come from a legally defined list of more or less 'noble' grape varieties grown in large regional areas that are nevertheless 'limited'. Their alcoholic content, acidity and acidic volatility are all subject to controls. These are fresh, fruity and lively wines, to be drunk young. They are not suitable for laying down, and they can, in fact, deteriorate if kept.

Labels can contain other information that is not compulsory, unlike the above requirements, but is nevertheless subject to regulations. The terms 'Clos', 'Château' and 'Cru Classé', for example, can be used only in accordance with traditional usage and only if they refer to something that actually exists. What labels might lose in creativity they make up for in honesty, and the buyer should feel reassured that the information on labels is more credible nowadays than in times past.

Vintages and bottling

Two non-compulsory pieces of information on the bottle will interest the wine-lover: first, the vintage, which will either be on the label (which is the best option) or on another label attached to the neck of the bottle, and, second, the exact location of the bottling.

A keen wine-lover will be satisfied only with a label that indicates that bottling has taken place at the estate, property or château. Any other indication that does not establish a direct link between the place where the wine was vinified and where it was bottled is not of any great interest. No matter how accurate such phrases as 'bottled in the region of production', 'bottled by ourselves', 'bottled in our cellars', 'bottled by X (X being an intermediary)' may be, they do not have the same guarantee of origin as 'bottled at the property'.

The concern of the public authorities and of professional committees has always been twofold: first, to encourage producers to improve the quality of their wine and to check this by tasting before labelling and second to make sure that the wine described on the label is indeed the wine that is in the bottle, without any mixing, additions or substitutions. However, despite all sorts of precautions, including possible checks during transportation, the best guarantee of authenticity remains 'bottled at the property' (*mis en bouteille à la propriété*). This is because a wine-grower does not have the right to purchase other wine to store in his commercial cellar, which can contain only wine that he has produced himself.

Note that a co-operative that bottles its own wine can use the term 'bottled at the property'.

Caps

Most bottles are topped with a cap or capsule. Sometimes the cap bears a French government fiscal stamp, which is proof that all legal requirements have been fulfilled for its distribution. This clearance certificate is known colloquially as a *congé*, and that is why the caps are often referred to as *capsules congés*. When the bottles are not stamped, they have to be accompanied by a receipt or certificate issued by the nearest tax office (see the section on transporting wine).

The stamp shows the status of the producer (owner or wine-merchant) and the region of production. The caps do not officially have to be stamped or personalised, but in general one or the other is usually done.

Stamping corks

The producers of quality wine have felt the need to confirm the information on their labels by marking the corks as well. A label can become unstuck but a cork cannot; that is why the vintage and the origin of the wine are stamped on the cork. It is also a way of discouraging potential fraudsters who can no longer just replace the labels. Note that the appellation of AOC sparkling wines, must be mentioned on the cork.

HOW TO BUY WINE AND FROM WHOM

The ways in which wine is distributed are complex and vary from the very simple to the most convoluted, each method having its advantages and disadvantages. The ways in which wine is sold also take different forms according to the method of presentation (whether it is in bottles or in containers or personalised, and when it is bought, for example, if it is bought *en primeur* (before it is bottled).

Wines to drink and wines to keep

The procedures for buying wine to drink and buying wine for laying down are not the same: there are different methods for different purposes. Wines destined for immediate consumption are ready to drink as they are; these are 'nouveau' wines or Vins de Pays, of 'small' or 'medium' origin and modest vintages, which do not require much ageing. Or they may be great wines that have reached their peak (but these are practically impossible to find on the market).

In every case, but obviously more importantly for fine wines, it is essential that there is a rest period of two days to two weeks between purchasing (including transportation) and consumption. Old bottles should be transported with great care, in a vertical position and protected from knocks, to avoid any stirring up of sediments.

Wines for keeping or laying down should be bought young with the aim of ageing them. Always choose the best possible wines from the finest vintages; these are not only less likely to deteriorate over time but will improve over the years.

Buying in containers

Wine that is not bought in bottles is bought *en vrac* (in bulk, i.e., in containers). The term *en cercle* is reserved for wines in barrels, whereas *vrac* means plastic container of any kind, from a 220 hl steel tank on a truck to a 5-litre plastic container or glass demijohn.

Wine is sold in containers by co-operatives, by some wine-growers and wine-merchants, and even by some retailers. It is sometimes called wine sold *à la tireuse* or 'drawn by hand'. Usually, table wines or wines of medium quality are sold in this way; it is rare to find a good-quality wine sold in a container. In fact, in certain areas, it is forbidden — for example, Bordeaux Crus Classés cannot be sold in this way.

The wine-lover should be aware that even when a wine-grower says that the wine he is selling in containers is the same as the one that he is selling in

How to buy wine and from whom

bottles, this is not strictly true. He will always choose the best batches for the wine that he bottles himself.

— Buying wine in containers can represent a saving of about 25%, as it is common practice to pay, at most, the same price for a litre as you would pay for a 75cl bottle.

— The purchaser can also save on transport costs, but will have to buy corks and bottles if he or she does not have any to hand. If the transaction is made by the barrel, the costs (not very high in France) of returning the cask have also to be taken into account.

These are the most commonly used containers:

Bordeaux barrique	225 litres
Burgundy pièce	228 litres
Mâconnais pièce	216 litres
Chablis pièce	132 litres
Champagne pièce	205 litres

— Bottling, which can be fun when it is done with a group of friends, does not pose too many problems, whatever anyone might say, provided that certain elementary rules (see below) are adhered to.

Buying by the bottle

In France bottles can be bought from the wine-grower, from a co-operative, at a wine-merchant or at any of many other outlets.

— Where should a wine-lover in France go to get the best deal? For wines that are not widely distributed the best option is to go to the wine-grower, and there are many of these. To avoid paying the ever-increasing costs of transport for small quantities of wine, co-operatives are a good choice. In other cases, such a strategy is not as simple as it seems. It should be borne in mind that wine-growers and wine-merchants are not in competition with their distributors, and they are not going to sell their bottles more cheaply. In fact, a number of Bordeaux châteaux that do very little direct selling sell their bottles at an even higher price than retailers to discourage buyers who, through ignorance or for whatever other reason, persist in buying directly from the owners. For wines of repute prices are bound to be lower at the retailers, which can obtain much better deals by placing large orders, than an individual can obtain by buying a single case.

— A general rule can be drawn from this: it is not worth buying widely distributed wines direct from famous domains and châteaux, except when it is a rare vintage or a special reserve.

Buying en primeur

This method of buying wine, practised for several years in the Bordeaux region, was very successful during the 1980s. Today, it is probably better to talk about buying or selling by subscription. The principle is simple: you buy a wine before it has been aged or bottled, at a lower price than it would be sold at when it is ready to be delivered.

— Subscriptions are available for a limited time and for specified quantities, usually in the spring or the beginning of the summer that follows the harvest. The purchaser pays a deposit of half the total cost when he or she orders and the rest on delivery, i.e., 15 months later. In this way, the producer has ready cash and the buyer can make a profit if prices increase. This was the case from 1974–5 to the end of the 1980s. This type of transaction is similar to what, on the Stock Exchange, is known as a forward-exchange transaction.

— If, because of overproduction or an economic crisis, the price goes down between subscription and delivery, the subscribers pay more for their bottles than those who did not subscribe. This has happened in the past and could well happen again. In fact, some leading wine-merchants have been ruined in the past by trying to guarantee their supplies with this type of speculation. It is true that such speculators run more risks if their contract spans several years.

Under normal circumstances, buying wine *en primeur* is undoubtedly the only way to buy wine for less than its normal price (between 20% and 40% less). Opportunities to buy *en primeur* are organised by the wine-growers themselves, and also by wine-merchants and wine clubs.

Buying directly from the producer

Apart from the rather technical aspects described above, a visit to the producer, which is indispensable if the wine is not very widely distributed, gives the wine-lover a different kind of satisfaction from that of simply getting a bargain. Only by visiting the producers, the true 'fathers' of their wines, can oenophiles fully understand the meaning of *terroir* and its characteristics, appreciate the art of vinification, which brings out the very essence of the grape, and, finally, see the strong links that exist between a wine-grower and his wine — between a creator and his creation. It is a stage that needs to be experienced in order to 'drink well and drink better', as the French say. To truly appreciate a wine, nothing can replace a visit to the grower.

Buying from a co-operative

The quality of wines sold by co-operatives is improving all the time. They are well equipped for selling wines, either in containers or in bottles, at prices that are usually slightly lower than those of other sales outlets offering similar quality.

The principle underlying co-operatives is well known. The members bring in their harvested grapes, and those responsible for the technical side (usually oenologists) take care of the pressing, vinification and, in some appellations, the ageing and selling.

The fact that they usually produce several types of wine gives co-operatives an opportunity of either using the best grapes (by separating them out from the others) or of highlighting certain *terroirs* through separate vinifications. For the best co-operatives, the system of special payments for the ripest and noble grapes, coupled with the possibility of making and selling wines according to the quality of each individual delivery of grapes, opens up opportunities to produce quality wines or even wines for laying down. Other co-operatives remain suppliers of table wines and vins de pays that are not intended for ageing or laying down.

Buying from a wine-merchant

In France a wine-merchant, by definition, buys wines for resale. In addition, he or she may often be a vineyard owner. Such a merchant–owner may thus produce and sell his or her own wine, sell wine from independent producers without having to do anything other than arrange transportation (this is the case for Bordeaux wine-merchants who sell wines that have been château bottled) or may even have an exclusive contract with a single production unit. A merchant may be a *négociant-éleveur*, producing wines by assembling or mixing wines from the same appellation, but supplied by different growers; such a practice influences the final product twice: once by the choice of purchase and second by mixing the wines. Wine-merchants are usually located in the larger wine-growing areas, but there is, of course, nothing to stop a Burgundian wine-merchant from selling wine from Bordeaux or vice versa. The main purpose of a wine-merchant is to distribute and feed the retail network rather than to sell wines at much lower prices than retailers.

Buying from a cellarman (*caviste*) or a retailer

This is the easiest and quickest way of buying wine, and it is also the safest if the cellarman is sufficiently expert. Over the last few years, a number of shops specialising in the sale of quality wines have appeared. A good cellarman is someone who stores wines in good conditions but who also knows how to choose original wines from producers who love their work. In addition, a good retailer or cellarman should be able to advise clients, helping them to discover new wines and to choose appropriate wines to complement different types of food.

Supermarkets

In France buying quality wines in supermarkets has become a widespread practice, compared with the 1970s when it was rare. Whatever the location, the presentation in this type of shop is not always of the best, with problems such as too high a temperature, harsh neon lighting and the vertical storage of bottles. However, these oversights are becoming increasingly rare. Today in France, and elsewhere, many establishments possess specialised, well-equipped shelves where the bottles are stored horizontally and are classified by appellation. In France especially the wine-lover will find not only ordinary wines in supermarkets but also prestigious crus. The only wines not represented in supermarkets are appellations that are not widely distributed and wines from smaller vineyards. Contrary to common belief, it can be advantageous for the visitor to buy a prestigious bottle of French wine from a French supermarket.

Clubs

All over the world wine is delivered directly to wine-lovers, by the bottle or by the case, by so-called 'wine clubs', which offer their members a certain number of advantages, including serious and informed critiques. Often, the wines on offer are chosen by wine experts and well-known and competent personalities. There is a wide choice, which sometimes includes little-known wines. However, it is worth noting that many such 'clubs' are, in reality, wine-merchants.

Auction sales

In France, sales by auction, which are becoming increasingly fashionable and popular, are organised by auctioneers with the help of wine experts. Wherever the sale takes place, it is extremely important to know the origin of the bottles. If they have come from a good restaurant or from the cellar of a wine-lover who has had to relinquish some bottles for personal reasons, it is probable that they have been kept in very good condition. If they consist of smaller lots that have been brought together from various sources, there is nothing to guarantee that the wine has been kept properly.

— The appearance of the wine is the only indicator. The alert wine-lover will not bid for a bottle that is not filled to the correct level, nor for a white wine that is veering towards a darkish bronze colour, nor for red wine that looks 'tired'.

— It is rare to be able to buy great appellations that restaurateurs are interested in having on their lists at a bargain price; however, the lesser appellations, which are not so sought keenly after by professionals, are sometimes more affordable.

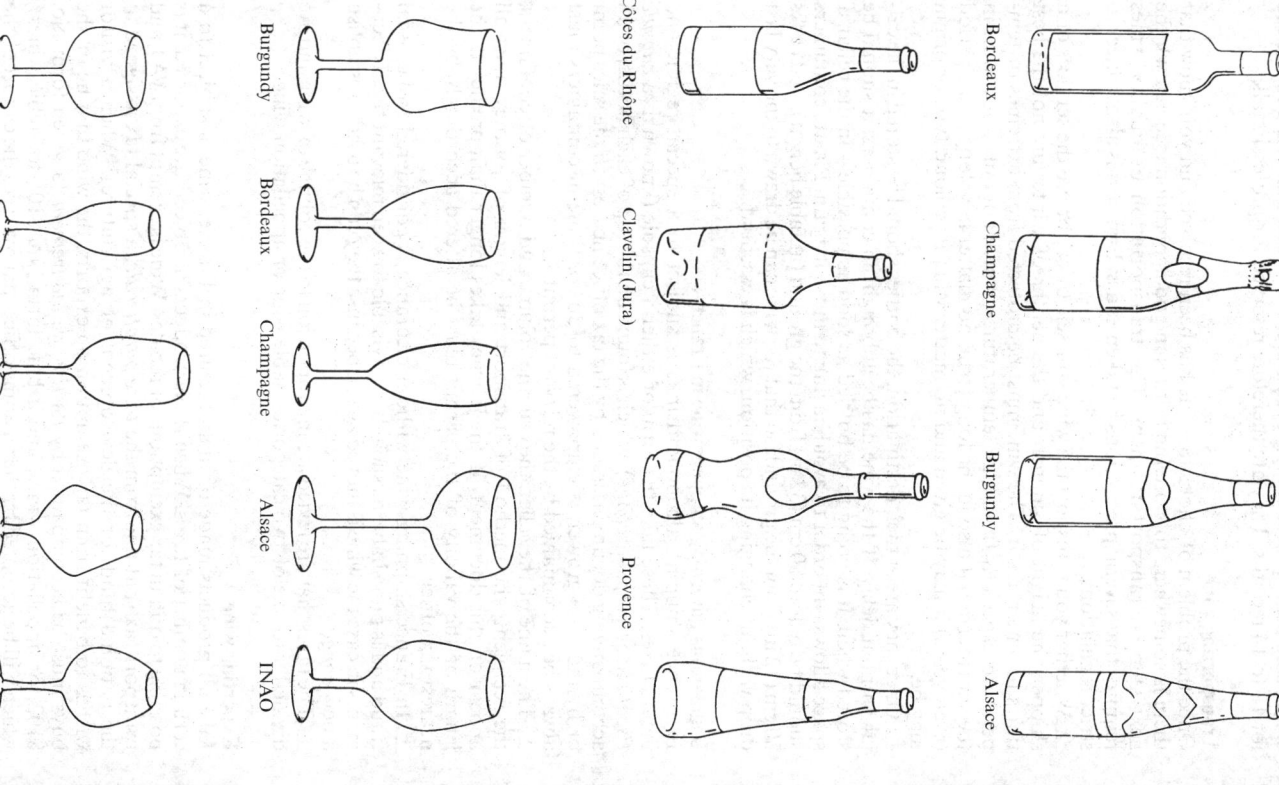

Bordeaux

Champagne

Burgundy

Alsace

Côtes du Rhône

Clavelin (Jura)

Provence

Burgundy

Bordeaux

Champagne

Alsace

INAO

Red wines

Sparkling wines

White wines

Young red and rosé wines

Old red wines

How to buy wine and from whom

The Hospices de Beaune wine auction and similar auctions

Wines sold during these charity events are sold in casks and have to be aged for 12 to 14 months. They are therefore reserved for professionals.

Transporting wine

Once the problem of choosing wine has been resolved and you know that there is somewhere to store the bottles in good condition (see below), the next step is transporting them. The transportation of quality wines requires that several precautions be taken and in France it is also subject to strict regulations.

Whether you transport the wine yourself by car or use the services of a shipper, the height of summer and the depths of winter are not the best times to undertake it. The wine must be protected from extremes of temperature, especially from high temperatures, which not only affect wine in the short term but also in the long term, no matter how long a rest period (even years) it may be given and no matter what its colour, type or origin may be.

Once they are at their destination, the bottles should be stored in the cellar without delay. If the wine has been bought in containers, it should be stored where it is going to be bottled as soon as possible – in the cellar if space allows – in order to avoid having to move it again. Plastic containers should be placed 80 cm (32 in) from the ground (at table height), and casks 30 cm (12 in) from the ground, so that the wine can be drawn to the very last drop without changing its position, which is essential.

Regulations governing shipping wine in France

In France shipping alcoholic drinks is subject to a special regime and incurs taxes. These take the form of either a capsule (known as a *capsule fiscalisée* or a *capsule congé*), which is found on the top of each bottle, or an accompanying document issued by the tax office nearest to the sales point or by the wine-grower, if empowered to do so. Wine in containers must always be accompanied by the relevant permit.

The name of the seller, the cru, the volume and number of containers, the recipient, the method of transport and length of journey must all appear on this document. If the journey takes longer than predicted, the length of the validity of the permit must be altered accordingly by the nearest tax office.

In France shipping wine without clearance is considered to be fiscal fraud and is punishable as such. It is advisable to keep relevant fiscal documents in case the wine is moved again, because they can be used to establish a new *congé*.

Exporting wine

Like all products made or manufactured in France, wine is subject to a certain number of taxes. When these products or objects are exported, it is possible to obtain tax exemptions or rebates. Wine is exempt from VAT and transport tax (but not from the *taxe parafiscale*, a special tax assigned to the national fund for the development of agriculture). When a visitor wishes to benefit from tax exemption on exports, the wine that he or she buys must be accompanied by its *titre de mouvement* (a green form No. 8102 for appellation wines, and a blue form No. 8101 for table wines), which will be accepted by the customs office that oversees the export of the merchandise. If the bottles have fiscal stamps the tax cannot be reclaimed. In order to benefit from a tax rebate, therefore, it is advisable to indicate to

The taxes that are levied are in proportion to the volume of wine and are divided into one of two categories: table wine or appellation wine.

the seller that the wine is intended for export at the time of purchase. It is also advisable to find out about importing wines and other alcoholic drinks into the countries concerned, as each country has its own regulations, which can range from import taxes to quotas to a blanket ban. Potential exporters of French wines should always contact their own customs authorities to clarify relevant regulations.

KEEPING WINE

Building up a good wine cellar involves a lot more than simply accumulating bottles. In addition to the principles already described, there are a number of important factors. One useful approach is to try to acquire wines of similar character and style, which need different lengths of time to age, so that they do not all reach their peak at the same time. It is also best to select wines that stay at their peak for the maximum possible period and so do not all need to be consumed within a short space of time. Choose a wide variety of wines so that you do not always have to drink the same sort, even if they are of the best, and so that you can be sure that there is always something appropriate to every occasion and to accompany all sorts of different food. Finally, there are two constraints that condition all other requirements – your budget and the size of the cellar space itself.

— A good cellar space should be enclosed, dark, free from vibration, noise and smells, and protected from draughts. At the same time it should be airy, not too dry nor too damp (a humidity level of about 75%). Most importantly, it should have a constant temperature of about 11°C (52°F).

— Cellars in towns rarely have all these characteristics. It is, therefore, important to try to improve the cellar before storing the wine by increasing or decreasing the ventilation as required. For example, it is possible to adjust the humidity of a too-dry cellar by introducing a basin of water and charcoal. If a cellar is too damp, dry it out by putting a layer of gravel on the floor and increasing the ventilation. If necessary the temperature can be regulated with the help of insulating panels, and, if vibration is a problem, by placing the racks on rubber blocks. If there is a central heating boiler nearby giving off oil fumes, the future will be less than bright for your wine.

— It is possible that a cellar may not be available or even if there is, that it may not be fit for use. In this case, there are two options: either buy a specially made unit that can store between 50 and 500 bottles, whose temperature and humidity are automatically regulated, or build a unit from scratch, somewhere at the back of your house or apartment. You will need a store-room in which the temperature is fairly constant and, if possible, does not rise above 16°C (60.8°F). Bear in mind that the higher the temperature the more quickly a wine ages and that it is not true, as was once commonly thought, that a wine that reaches its peak quickly in bad conditions is of the same quality as one that has matured slowly in a good cool cellar. Thus, fine wines that need to mature slowly should not be aged in a cellar, or any other type of store, that is too warm. Wine-lovers should plan their purchases and storage according to the premises that they have at their disposal.

Establishing a good cellar

Experience has shown that a cellar is always too small. The storage of the bottles has to be organised logically. A wine-rack with one or two rows has several advantages: it is not expensive, it can be installed straight away, and

Keeping wine

it gives easy access to the bottles. Unfortunately, it takes up a lot of room for the number of bottles stored. To gain extra space, the only way is to store the bottles in piles. In order to separate the stacks and have access to different wines you need to build, or have built, 'bins', which are made from breeze-blocks and which can contain 24, 36 or 48 bottles in stacks on two levels.

If there is enough room it is possible to raise the bins on planks. However, these will need to be checked regularly for rot as well as for the presence of insects that might attack the corks.

Two pieces of apparatus will complete the cellar: a maximum-and-minimum thermometer and a hygrometer to measure the humidity. Regular readings will help to correct any variations in temperature or humidity and to maintain the long-term requirements for ageing wines to best effect.

Bottling

If the wine has been transported in a container, it should be bottled as soon as possible; if it has been shipped by barrel, it is essential that it should rest for two weeks before bottling. This general advice needs to be tempered in light of the atmospheric conditions prevailing on the day chosen for bottling. Ideally, the weather should be mild, with high barometric pressure and no threat of rain or storms. In practice, the wine-lover will have to compromise between the ideal and the possible. However, no compromises should be made with the necessary equipment. First of all, the bottles should be used for all wines from the south-west and, possibly, from the Midi too, and Burgundy bottles for wines from the south-east, Beaujolais and Burgundy (always bearing in mind that there are other types of regional bottles for specific appellations).

If the bottles are to be stored in stacks, it should be noted that, whether they are Bordeaux or Burgundy in style, bottles are of varying thickness (some bottles have flat, or nearly flat, bases). As well as weight, the height and diameter also vary.

All bottles are suitable for keeping wine in, but the lighter bottles are less suitable for storing wine in stacks over a long period of time. In addition, if lighter gauge bottles are over-filled they can sometimes explode when the cork is forced into place.

Generally, it is better to use the heavier gauge bottles. It is almost as incongruous to bottle a great wine in light glass as it would be to use a clear glass bottle for a red wine. Custom dictates that these bottles should be used only for certain white wines, so that the colour can be clearly seen. However, white wines are particularly sensitive to the light, and this custom should be ignored. Their sensitivity to light is so great that champagne houses that sell wine in clear bottles always protect them with opaque paper or with a box.

Whichever type of bottle is chosen, it is essential that there are sufficient bottles and corks available before bottling is begun, because once under way this operation should be completed rapidly. If the cask or container is left open, the remaining wine may become oxidised and develop acescency, making the wine unfit to drink. Cleanliness is also essential, and the bottles should be scrupulously rinsed and dried before they are used.

Corks

Despite extensive research, cork remains the only material suitable for sealing bottles. Corks are not identical, differing in diameter, length and quality.

The diameter of the cork is always 6 mm (¼ in) larger than the bottleneck.

The better the wine, the longer the cork required. This is necessary for long-term ageing and is no more than due consideration for the wine and for those who will one day enjoy it.

The quality of a cork is more difficult to assess. It needs to be about ten years old to have the necessary suppleness. Good corks should not have those little cracks that are sometimes blocked up with cork powder – these are known as 'improved' corks. It is also possible to buy corks that have been stamped (or to have them stamped) with the vintage of the wine that is to be bottled.

Today, it is possible to buy ready-to-use corks, which are available in ozone-sterilised packaging. They are no longer moistened, but inserted dry, as this has proved to be the most successful method.

Filling the bottles

The ideal apparatus for filling bottles is a pump. There are two types: a piston pump and a vane pump, both of which are available in DIY stores for a modest price.

The bottle should be slightly tilted to let the wine run down the whole length of the side, to minimise the amount of oxidation and stirring up. This precaution is even more necessary for white wines. In no circumstances should a scum be allowed to appear on the surface of the liquid. The bottles should be filled as full as possible, so that the cork is in contact with the wine when the bottle is in an upright position. The cork should be inserted with the help of a special corking device that compresses the cork width-wise before insertion. There is a wide range of equipment available at varying prices for this purpose.

Labels

These can be attached with wallpaper paste or a mixture of flour and water. Simpler still, the labels can be moistened with milk and stuck on the bottles. The bottom edge of the label should be 3 cm (about 1 in) from the base of the bottle.

Perfectionists will add ready-made capsules to the top of the bottle with the aid of a little machine, or they will seal the tops with melted coloured wax, which can be bought from a cork merchant.

Storing wine in the cellar

As far as possible, the following rules should be observed: white wines should be stored close to the ground with the red wines on top; wines for long-term keeping should be stored on the less-accessible racks at the back, with bottles ready for drinking near the front.

Bottles bought or delivered in cardboard boxes should not be left in this type of packaging, unlike those delivered in wooden crates. Buyers who envisage reselling the wine should leave it in the crate, but others should not for two reasons: it takes up a lot of room, and it is a prime target for thieves. In any case, a cataloguing system (numerical, for example) will help to identify racks and bottles. This system can be logged in the most useful tool of the wine-cellar, the cellar book.

Three suggestions for your cellar

Everyone stocks his or her own cellar according to personal taste. The collections described on the following page are only suggestions and the main theme is diversity. Vins Nouveaux, and wines that gain nothing from being aged in the cellar do not feature in these lists. The fewer the bottles, the greater the need to maintain stocks. The prices in brackets are, of course, applicable only to France and are given as a guide only.

Keeping wine

A 50-bottle cellar (€600)

25 bottles of Bordeaux	17 red (Graves, Saint-Emilion, Médoc, Pomerol, Fronsac)
	8 white: 5 dry (Graves), 3 sweet (Sauternes-Barsac)
20 bottles of Burgundy	12 red (Côte de Nuits Crus, Côte de Beaune Crus)
	8 white (Chablis, Meursault, Puligny)
10 bottles of Vallée du Rhône	7 red (Côte-Rôtie, Hermitage, Châteauneuf-du-Pape)
	3 white (Hermitage, Condrieu)

A 150-bottle cellar (about €2,000)

Region		Red	White
40 Bordeaux	30 red	Fronsac	5 good, dry white wines
	10 white	Pomerol	
		Saint-Emilion	
		Graves	
		Médoc	5 Sainte-Croix-du-Mont
		(Crus Classés,	Sauternes-Barsac
		Crus Bourgeois)	
30 Burgundy	15 red	Côte de Nuits	Chablis
	15 white	Crus Côte de Beaune	Meursault
		Crus Côte Chalonnaise	Puligny-Montrachet
25 Vallée du Rhône	19 red	Côte-Rôtie	Condrieu
	6 white	Hermitage (red)	Hermitage (white)
		Cornas	Châteauneuf-du-Pape
		Saint-Joseph	(white)
		Châteauneuf-du-Pape	
		Gigondas Côtes-du-Rhône	
		Villages	
15 Vallée de la Loire	8 red	Bourgueil	Pouilly-Fumé
	7 white	Chinon	Vouvray
		Saumur-Champigny	Coteaux du Layon
10 South-west	7 red	Madiran	Jurançon (sweet and dry)
	3 white	Cahors	
8 South-east	6 red	Bandol	Cassis
	2 white	Palette (red)	Palette (white)
7 Alsace	(white)		Gewurztraminer
			Riesling
			Tokay
5 Jura	(white)		Vins Jaunes
			(yellow wines)
			Côtes du Jura-Arbois
10 Champagne and sparkling wines (readily accessible, as these wines do not improve with age)			Crémant de Loire Burgundy Alsace Various types of Champagne

A 300-bottle cellar

To create such a cellar is an investment of about €3,800 is needed. You double the numbers required for the 150-bottle cellar but should bear in mind that the more bottles you have, the longer the life of the wine has to be. This usually means, unfortunately, that despite discounts the wine is going to be more expensive.

The cellar book

This is the record, guide, judge and jury of the wine-lover. The following information should be recorded in the book: date acquired, number of bottles of each cru, precise identification details, price, presumed peak date, location in cellar and, possibly, tasting notes and details of ideal culinary accompaniments.

THE ART OF DRINKING

If drinking is a physiological necessity, drinking wine is a pleasure. This pleasure varies in intensity depending on the wine, the tasting conditions and the sensitivity of the taster.

Tasting

There are several types of wine-tasting, each suited to a particular end. The technical, analytical, comparative, triangular and so forth types of tasting are reserved for professionals. The wine-lover practises tasting purely for pleasure, to discover the quintessence of a wine, to learn how to put this into words and to improve the sensitivity of the nose and palate.

Tasting and, more generally, consumption of wine, should not take place anywhere and in any fashion. The location should be pleasant, well lit with natural light or 'daylight' lighting, which does not alter colours, preferably with light-coloured walls and free from any stray odours, such as perfume, smoke (tobacco and fire), cooking smells or flowers. The temperature should be between 18 and 20°C (64 to 68°F).

The choice of an appropriate glass is extremely important. It should be clear, so that the colour of the wine can be clearly seen, and if possible not too thick. It should have a tulip shape – that is it should not turn outwards at the top, which is often the case, but should in fact turn slightly inwards. The body of the glass should be separated from the foot by a stem. This prevents the glass from being warmed when it is held (by the stem) and makes it easier to swirl the wine; this is done in order to oxygenate the wine and to release its bouquet.

The shape of the glass is so important and has such an influence on the olfactory appreciation of wine (both taste and smell) that the Association Française de Normalisation (AFNOR) and the Instances Internationales de Normalisation (ISO) have, as a result of a study, adopted a glass that is eminently suitable for both taster and consumer. This type of glass, which is commonly referred to in France as 'the INAO glass', is not just for professionals but can be found in France in specialist shops. Over the last few years, French, German and Austrian glassmakers have considerably extended the choice of wine glasses available.

Tasting techniques

Tasting involves sight, smell, taste and touch – not touching with the fingers, of course, but with the mouth, which is sensitive to 'mechanical' effects of wine, such as temperature, consistency and fizz.

SIGHT

The first contact that a consumer has with wine is with the eye. Examining the visual appearance of the wine, which includes assessing its distinguishing colour, can reveal a lot of information. This is the first test. Whatever

Sight

the colour and tint of the wine, it should be clear, not cloudy. Any trace of streaks or cloudiness is a sign of disease and the wine should be rejected. Only small insoluble tartaric crystals (gravelle), which occur when there is a sudden cold spell, should be accepted; the quality of the wine is not affected by them.

The clarity of a wine can be tested by placing the glass between the eye and a source of light that should, if possible, be at the same height. The transparency of red wine can be determined by looking at it against a white background, such as a tablecloth or a piece of paper. The glass should be tilted and the surface, or 'disc', should form an ellipse; the shape can say a

Wine	Shade of colour	Interpretation
White	Almost colourless	Very young, well protected from oxidisation. Modern vinification in vat
	Very light yellow with hints of green	Young to very young. Vinified and aged in vat
	Straw yellow, golden yellow	Matured. Perhaps aged in wood
	Coppery gold, bronze gold	Already old
	Amber to black	Oxidised, too old
Rosé	Flecked white, partridge eye (soft corn colour) with hints of pink	Rosé obtained by pressing and light young rosés
	Very light, clear salmon-pink to red	Young, fruity rosé, ready to drink
	Pink with shades of yellow to onion skin	Beginning to be old for its type
Red	Purple	Very young. Good shade for nouveau Gamay and Beaujolais Nouveau (6 to 18 months)
	Pure red (cherry)	Neither young nor old. Peak period for wines which are neither nouveau nor for laying down (2–3 years)
	Red with bands of orange	Mature wine (short-term keeping). Beginning of ageing (3–7 years)
	Brownish red to brown	Only great wines have reached their peak when they are this colour. For others, it is too late.
Too light	Not pressed enough Rainy year Too large a yield Young vines Grapes not sufficiently ripe Rotten grapes Too short a time in vat Fermentation at low temperature	Light wines for short-term keeping Unexceptional vintages
Dark	Well pressed Low yield Old vines Successful vinification	Good or great wines Good future

60

lot about the age of the wine and how it has been kept. The next thing to examine is the actual shade of the colour. All young wines should be transparent, which is not the case with old, quality wines.

— The brilliance or luminosity of a wine is also important. If a wine is luminous it is lively; a dull wine will be lifeless. The intensity of colour, which is not to be confused with shade or tone, should also be taken into account.

— The intensity of the colour of red wines, which is the easiest to see, is the most telling.

— 'Legs' or 'tears', formed on the side of the glass when it is swirled around to breathe in the bouquet (see below) are also part of the visual aspect of wine. They are related to the alcoholic content: cognac always produces these, vins de pays rarely do so.

Examples of vocabulary used when talking about the appearance of wine:

Shades: purple, garnet, ruby, violet, cherry, peony
Intensity: light, strong, dark, deep, intense
Brilliance: matt, dull, sad, sparkling, brilliant
Clarity and transparency: opaque, hazy, veiled, crystalline, flawless

SMELL

Olfactory examination is the next test that wine has to undergo during tasting. Certain odours, such as volatile acidity (acescency, vinegar), and a corky smell discount wines straight away, but in most cases the bouquet – that is, the combination of odours released from the glass – is a new voyage of discovery each time.

— The aromatic components of the bouquet are expressed according to their volatility. What takes place is a kind of evaporation, and that is why the temperature at which wine is served is so important. If the wine is too cold, there will be no bouquet; too hot, and the result is too rapid evaporation, marked by aromas joining together, oxidation, the loss of highly volatile aromas and the release of abnormally heavy aromatic elements.

— The bouquet of a wine is like a kaleidoscope of scents that is forever changing; they emerge one after another depending on temperature and exposure to the air. This is why the way the glass is handled is important. First of all, the aromas released from a still glass are breathed in, then the glass is swirled around, and exposure to the air releases yet other scents.

— The quality of a wine is a function of the intensity and complexity of its bouquet. Mediocre wines have a small bouquet, if any; they usually have one note only and can be summed up very simply, in one word. On the other hand, great wines have full, deep bouquets, and their complexity is constantly changing.

— The vocabulary used to describe bouquets is almost infinite, because it uses analogy. Several classifications to describe them been put forward, but to simplify matters we will use the following characteristics: floral, fruity, vegetable (or herbaceous), spicy, balsamic, gamey, woody, smoky or burnt and chemical.

Examples of vocabulary used to describe the bouquet:

Flowers: violets, linden flowers, jasmine, elderflower, acacia, iris, peony
Fruits: raspberry, blackcurrant, cherry, Morello cherry, gooseberry, apricot, apple, banana, prune
Vegetable: grassy, fern, moss, undergrowth, damp ground, chalky, various mushrooms
Balsamic: resin, pine, terebinth (turpentine tree)
Gamey: meat, well-hung meat, game, civet, musk
Burnt: burnt, grilled, toasted, tobacco, dried hay, all roasted aromas (coffee etc).

Taste

TASTE

Having triumphantly passed through the two examinations of sight and smell, a wine's final test is that of taste.

A small amount of wine is taken into the mouth, where it is held, and a breath of air is also taken in and diffused throughout the oral cavity. If this is not possible, the wine is just swirled around the mouth. As the wine warms up in the mouth, it releases new aromas that are captured by the retronasal passage. The papillae (taste buds) on the tongue can detect only the four basic flavours – bitter, acidic, sweet and salty – which is why a person with a cold cannot taste wine (or food) because the retronasal passage is blocked.

In addition to the four flavours mentioned above, the mouth is also sensitive to the temperature of the wine, its viscosity, the presence or absence of carbon dioxide and astringency (the effect of astringency is the contraction of mucous membranes in response to tannin, which is felt as the absence of lubrication from the saliva glands).

It is by tasting that the balance and harmony of a wine is revealed or, conversely, that the characteristics of a badly constructed wine, which is not to be bought, are discovered.

White wines, light rosés and rosés are characterised by a good balance between acidity and sweetness.

Too much acidity: the wine is aggressive; not acidic enough, it is flat
Too sweet: the wine is heavy and thick; not sweet enough, it is thin and dull

In red wines there should be a balance between acidity, sweetness and tannin.

Excess acidity:	wine is too vigorous and often thin
Excess tannin:	wine is hard and astringent
Excess sweetness (rare):	heavy wine
Lack of acidity:	flabby wine
Lack of tannin:	unstructured, undefined wine
Lack of sweetness:	wine will dry out

A good wine balances the three components acidity, sweetness and tannin. These elements give it its richness of aroma. A great wine can be distinguished from a good wine by its rigorous, powerful but harmonious structure and the fullness of its aromatic complexity.

Examples of vocabulary used to describe the actual tasting of wine:

Minus points: unstructured, flabby, flat, thin, watery, limited, transparent, poor, heavy, massive, coarse, thick, unbalanced

Plus points: structured, well-built, well-constructed, balanced, fleshy (or full-bodied), elegant, fine, good texture, rich

After this analysis in the mouth, the wine is swallowed. The wine-lover then concentrates on measuring the persistence of its aromas, known familiarly as 'length on the palate'. This estimation is expressed in caudals, one unit being equal quite simply, to one second. The 'longer' a wine is, the better the quality. The 'length on the palate' alone is the only method of grading wines from the poorest to the greatest.

This measuring in seconds is very simple and at the same time very complicated. It concerns only the length of the aromas, not the structure of the wine (acidity, bitterness, sweetness or alcohol content), which cannot be measured in this way.

Identifying wine

Tasting, like consuming, is a way of appreciating wine. It involves tasting it

62

fully and deciding whether it is of average, good or excellent quality. Often, it is a matter of deciding whether it conforms to its type, so its origin also needs to be identified.

— Tasting to identify – that is recognition – is a sport, a kind of parlour game, but it is an impossible game to play without a minimum of information. It is easy enough to identify a variety such as a Cabernet Sauvignon, but to know whether it comes from Italy, Languedoc, California, Chile, Argentina, Australia or South Africa is another matter. If the range is limited to France, it is possible to identify the larger regions, but being more precise presents serious problems. If there were six glasses representing six Médoc appellations (Listrac, Moulis, Margaux, Saint-Julien, Pauillac, Saint-Estèphe), how many people would be able to guess which was which without making any mistakes?

— A classic experiment that anyone can try proves how difficult tasting can be: the taster, blindfolded, tastes in random order red wines with very little tannin and non-aromatic white wines, preferably oak-aged. The taster has simply to distinguish between red and white (and vice versa); it is very rare not to make a mistake! Paradoxically, it is much easier to recognise a very characteristic wine whose memory and taste lingers on in your memory – but what are the chances of being offered the same wine?

Tasting with a view to purchasing

When you visit a vineyard with a view to purchasing wine, the first step towards choosing the wine is to taste it. Tasting is an act both of appreciation and of comparison. It is easy to compare two or three wines, but the situation becomes more complicated when price has to be taken into account. With a fixed budget – and budgets are invariably fixed – purchases are automatically eliminated. The tasting is further complicated when the purpose of the wine (for example, as an accompaniment to different kinds of food) is considered. To guess what you might be eating in ten years' time, and consequently to buy an appropriate wine for the occasion, has something of the magician's art about it. Comparative tasting, easy and simple in principle, becomes a delicate matter when the buyer has to guess the necessary length of ageing and peak periods of various wines. Wine-growers themselves sometimes make mistakes when they try to envisage the future of their wines and it is not unknown for wine-growers to buy back their own wine, originally sold at cut-price, because they had thought wrongly, that it would age badly.

— Nevertheless, some general principles can help in the appreciation of wine. To age well, wines must have a solid structure. They must have a sufficient degree of alcohol, and chaptalisation (the adding of sugar, regulated by law) can be a contributory factor if necessary. It is also advisable to pay attention to the levels of acidity and tannin. A wine that is too supple because its acidity is low or very low (which can, nevertheless, taste very pleasant), will be fragile and its longevity uncertain. A wine that is low in tannin will also not have much of a future. In the first example, the grapes will have been over-exposed to the sun and heat; in the second, the grapes will not have ripened sufficiently, will have been attacked by rot or will have suffered an inappropriate vinification.

— These two components of wine, acidity and tannin, can be measured. Acidity can be calculated by its equivalence in sulphuric acid, in grams per litre or in pH, and tannin can be measured according to the Folain scale, but this needs to be carried out in a laboratory.

— A wine with less than three grams per litre of acidity does not have much of a future. It is more difficult to give an exact estimation of the level of tannin below which long-term keeping would be problematic, but it is

Peak (in years)

W = White; R = Red

Alsace (W): within the year	Vallée du Rhône, Southern (W): 2; (R): 4-8
Alsace Grand Cru (W): 1-4	Loire (W): 1-5; (R): 3-10 Loire, sweet, rich (W): 10-15
Alsace (late harvest) (W): 8-12	Périgord wines (W): 2-3; (R): 3-4
Jura (W): 4; 8	Périgord wines, sweet (W): 6-8
Jura, rosé: 6	Bordeaux (W): 2-3; (R): 6-8
Vin Jaune (W): 20	Bordeaux, fine (W): 4-10; (R): 10-15
Savoie (W): 1-2; (R): 2-4	Bordeaux, sweet (W): 10-15
Burgundy (W): 5 (R): 7	Jurançon, dry (W): 2-4
Burgundy, fine (W): 8-10; (R): 10-15	Jurançon, sweet, rich (W): 6-10
Mâcon (W): 2-3; (R): 1-2	Madiran (R): 5-12
Beaujolais (R): within the year	Cahors (R): 3-10
Beaujolais Crus (R): 1-4	Gaillac (W): 1-3; (R): 2-4
Vallée du Rhône, Northern (W):	Languedoc (W): 1-2; (R): 2-4
2-3; (R): 4-5	Côtes de Provence (W): 1-2; (R): 2-4
Côte-Rôtie, Hermitage etc. (W):	Corsican (W): 1-2; (R): 2-4
8; (R): 8-15	

NB:
Do not confuse peak period with maximum longevity.
A warm cellar or one with a variable temperature accelerates the ageing process.

useful to know what the scale is, as very ripe, smooth tannins are sometimes underestimated on tasting and are not always revealed.

In any case, wine should be tasted in good conditions, without the ambience of the wine-cellar taking over. Avoid tasting immediately after a meal or after consuming a liqueur, coffee, chocolate or mints, or after smoking. Beware if a wine-grower offers nuts, because they make any wine taste better! Beware also of cheese, as this changes the sensitivity of the palate; if absolutely necessary, eat a piece of plain bread.

Practising tasting

Like any other technique, tasting can be learned. It can be practised at home following the guidelines above or, if you are very keen, you can enrol on one of the ever-increasing number of courses offered by various private organisations. The best of such courses cover a whole range of topics in addition to just tasting, including food and wines, the discovery of the larger wine-producing areas (not only French regions) through tasting, an analysis of the influence of grape varieties, vintages and soils, the effect of vinification techniques and organised visits to wine estates in the company of the vineyard owner.

Serving wine

In a restaurant serving wine is the responsibility of the wine waiter. At home no wine waiter will be available, and it pays to learn some of the tricks of the trade. There are many of these, starting with choosing the bottles that are best suited to the dishes making up the meal and those that have reached their peak.

Individual taste does come into matching food and wine, but, centuries of experience have made it possible to establish some general principles, ideal combinations and major incompatibilities.

The rate at which wines age varies tremendously. The wine-lover who wants nothing but the best will be interested only in the wine's peak period. Depending on the appellation, variety, soil and vinification, this could be any time between one and twenty years. Depending on the year on the label, the same wine could age two or three times more rapidly. However, it is possible to establish average times that can be used as a basis and that can be adapted to the cellar and the information on the vintage cards.

Methods of serving

Care must be taken with the wine from its selection in the cellar to its arrival in the glass. The older the wine, the more care should be taken. The bottle should be taken from its stack and gently returned to an upright position, ready to be taken to table, unless it is going to be put straight into a special pouring basket.

— Wines of average quality should be served simply. A very old and consequently very delicate wine should be poured from the basket, where it has been carefully placed in the same position as it was in the stack. Younger wines and robust wines should be decanted, either to oxygenate them because they still contain gas left over from fermentation or to start oxidisation, which improves the taste of the wine, or simply to separate clear wine from sediment at the bottom of the bottle. In the last case, the wine must be decanted with care and should be done in front of a light source, traditionally a candle – a custom that predates the arrival of electric lighting and has no particular advantage – to allow the sediments and cloudy wine to stay in the bottle.

Opening the bottle and serving

Professor Peynaud, France's leading scientific authority on wine-tasting, maintains that it is not necessary to open a bottle a long time before drinking the wine, because the surface area of the wine that is exposed to the air (at the neck of the bottle) is too small to make a difference. However, the table on the following page summarises traditional usage that, if it does not always improve the wine, never spoils it.

Opening

The capsule should be cut below the ring or in the middle of it. The wine should never come into contact with the metal of the capsule. If the neck is sealed with wax, chip the wax away gently or, better still, remove the wax from the top part of the neck with a knife; this method is preferable because it does not disturb the wine or the bottle.

— To remove the cork, a traditional-style corkscrew (or one with arms, if handled gently) should be used. Theoretically, the cork should not be pierced all the way through. Once removed, it should be smelt to make sure that there are no bacterial odours present and that there is no corky smell. Afterwards, as a final test, the wine should be tasted before it is served.

White aromatic wines Red or white nouveau wines Red and white young wines Rosé wines	Open, drink straight away Bottle vertical
White Loire wines Sweet white wines	Open, wait an hour Bottle vertical
Young red wines Red wines at their peak	Decant half an hour to 2 hours before drinking
Old delicate red wines	Open in pouring basket and serve immediately; in some cases, decant and drink immediately

The right temperature

A wine can be completely spoiled by serving it at the wrong temperature; conversely a wine can be improved by being served at the right temperature. It is rare to achieve this without the help of a wine thermometer – a pocket version is handy for taking to restaurants and for dipping in the wine when at home. The temperature for serving wine depends on its appellation (its type), its age and, in a few cases, the temperature of the room. It should be remembered that wine warms up in the glass.

Bordeaux, fine wines, red	16–17°C	60.8–62.6°F
Burgundy, fine wines, red	15–16°C	59–60.8°F
Quality red wines	14–16°C	57.2–60.8°F
White, dry fine wines	14–16°C	57.2–60.8°F
Light, fruity, young red wines	11–12°C	51.8–53.6°F
Rosé wines, nouveau wines	10–12°C	50–53.6°F
Dry white wines, red Vins de Pays	10–12°C	50–53.6°F
Average white wines, white Vins de Pays	8–10°C	46.4–50°F
Champagne, sparkling	7–8°C	44.6–46.4°F
Sweet	6°C	42.8°F

These temperatures should be increased by one or two degrees if the wine is old.

— There is a tendency to serve wines slightly more chilled when they are offered as an apéritif and warmer when they are to accompany a meal. Similarly, the climate of the area and the temperature of the room should be taken into account; in very hot weather a wine drunk at 11°C (51.8°F) can seem icy and it is therefore advisable to serve it at 13° or even 14°C (55.4° or 57.2°F).

— Nevertheless, the 20°C (68°F) mark should not be passed because physico-chemical phenomena, independent of the environment, can cause irreversible changes, altering the qualities of the wine and the pleasure that we expect from it.

Glasses

Each region has its own particular glass. In practice, and to avoid being excessively purist, it is best to use either a universal-style glass (a tasting glass) or the two sorts most commonly used, the Bordeaux and the Burgundy. Whichever glass is used, it should be filled in moderation, nearer one-third full rather than half full.

In the restaurant

In the restaurant the wine waiter looks after the bottle and examines the cork but allows the person who ordered the wine to taste it. Before this, the wine waiter will have recommended wines to accompany the dishes.

— Reading the wine list is instructive, not only because it reveals the secrets of the cellar, which is its function, but because it is also indicative of the level of competence of the wine waiter, the cellar-master or the manager. A good wine list should definitely include the following information for each wine: appellation, vintage, place where it was bottled and the name of the wine-merchant or owner responsible for the wine. This last piece of information is often omitted – for no good reason.

— A good wine list should offer a wide range of appellations and a variety of vintages of different qualities (some restaurants have the annoying habit of offering only average quality vintages). An intelligent list should be adapted to the style or specialities of the cuisine and should offer a good selection of local wines.

— Sometimes, house wine is on offer. It is possible to buy a pleasant wine that does not benefit from an AOC, but these wines are never great wines.

Wine bistros and wine bars

In France there have always been wine bistros selling good-quality wine by the glass, often wines selected by the bistro owner on personal visits to vineyards. Selections of cold meat and cheese are usually on offer to customers in these establishments.

— In the 1970s a new generation of French wine bistros appeared, often referred to as 'wine bars'. The perfecting of an apparatus that protects wine in open bottles with a layer of nitrogen (*le cruover*) has allowed these establishments to offer customers very good wines with prestigious vintages. More sophisticated menus have been developed to accompany these wines.

VINTAGES

All quality wines have vintages. The only exceptions to this rule are a few particular wines and some Champagnes, whose own individual production involves the blending of several different years.

— Having said this, what should we make of a bottle that does not have a vintage? There are two possible reasons for the omission: either the year is inadmissible because its reputation is so tarnished within the appellation, or it cannot be given a year because it is a mixture of several years blended together (known among professionals as *vins de plusieurs années*). The quality of the product depends on the talent of the blender; generally, a blended wine is superior to each of its individual components, but it is not advisable to age this type of bottle. A wine from a great year is concentrated and balanced and is usually, but not always, the result of small yields, harvested early.

— In every case, great vintages come only from perfectly healthy grapes, untainted by rot. To obtain a great vintage, it does not matter what the weather is like at the beginning of the vegetative cycle. It can even be said that a few mishaps such as frost or *coulure* (the falling of young grapes before maturation) are a good thing, as they reduce the number of grapes per bunch, thus reducing the volume. On the other hand, the period between 15 August to harvest time (end of September) is crucial; a maximum of sun and heat are necessary. The year 1961, *the* year of the 20th century, was exemplary; everything happened as it should. On the other hand, 1963, 1965 and 1968 were disastrous years, because they suffered from a combination of cold and rain, which meant that the grapes did not mature properly. There was a glut and the grapes were swollen with water. The combination of rain and heat is not much better as warm water invites rot. This was the stumbling-block that tripped up the potentially great 1976 vintage in the south west. Progress in the development of treatments to protect grapes, in particular from the grape worm and from rot, have led to quality harvests that previously would have been spoiled. These treatments also make it possible to wait with equanimity for the grapes to ripen fully (which improves the quality) even if the immediate meteorological conditions are not encouraging. From 1978 onwards, there have been some excellent late-harvested vintages.

— It is customary to record and grade the quality of vintages in table form. These grades are averages only and do not take into account microclimates, or the heroic efforts of hand sorting the grapes at harvest time or the vagaries of the wine-making process. For example, a Graves, Domaine de

Vintages

Chevalier from 1965 – which elsewhere was a terrible year – proves that a great wine can be produced even during a year that is ranked at zero!

Vintage table (from 0 to 20)

	Bordeaux Red	Bordeaux White, Sweet	Bordeaux White, dry	Burgundy Red	Burgundy White	Champagne	Loire	Rhône	Alsace
1900	19	19	17	13		17			
1901	11	14							
1902									
1903	14	7	11					18	
1904	15	17		16		19			
1905	14	12							
1906	16	16		19	18				
1907	12	10		15					
1908	13	16							
1909	10	7							
1910									
1911	14	14		19	19	20	19	19	
1912	10	11							
1913	7	7							
1914	13	15				18			
1915	15	16		16	15	15	12	15	15
1916	15	15		13	11	12	11	10	10
1917	14	16		11	11	13	12	9	20
1918	16	12		13	12	12	11	14	4
1919	15	10		18	18	15	18	15	14
1920	17	16		13	14	14	11	13	11
1921	16	20		16	20	20	20	13	6
1922	9	11		9	16	4	7	6	14
1923	12	13		16	18	17	18	18	
1924	15	16		13	14	11	14	17	17
1925	6	11		6	5	3	4	8	18
1926	16	17		16	16	15	13	13	3
1927	7	14		7	5	5	3	4	3
1928	19	17		18	20	20	17	17	7
1929	20	20		20	19	19	18	19	15
1930							3	4	16
1931	2	2		2	3		3	5	
1932	2			2	3	3	3	3	
1933	11	9		16	18	16	17	17	
1934	17	17		17	18	17	16	17	

Vintages

	Bordeaux Red	Bordeaux White, Sweet	Bordeaux White, dry	Burgundy Red	Burgundy White	Champagne	Loire	Rhône	Alsace
1935	7	12		13	16	10	15	5	14
1936	7	11		9	10	9	12	13	9
1937	16	20		18	18	18	16	17	17
1938	8	12		14	10	10	15	8	9
1939	11	16		9	9	12	10	8	3
1940	13	12		12	8	9	11	5	10
1941	12	10		9	12	8	7	5	5
1942	12	16		14	16	10	11	14	14
1943	15	17		17	16	17	13	17	16
1944	13	11	12	10	10		6	8	
1945	20	20	18	20	18	20	19	18	20
1946	14	9	10	10	13	10	12	17	9
1947	18	20	18	18	18	18	20	18	17
1948	16	16	16	10	14	11	12		15
1949	19	20	18	20	18	17	16	17	19
1950	13	18	16	11	19	16	14	15	14
1951	8	6	6	7	6	7	7	8	8
1952	16	16	16	16	18	16	15	16	14
1953	19	17	16	18	17	17	18	14	18
1954	10			14	11	15	9	13	9
1955	16	19	18	15	18	19	16	15	17
1956	5				15		9	12	9
1957	10	15		14			13	16	13
1958	11	14		10	9		12	14	12
1959	19	20	18	19	17	17	19	15	20
1960	11	10	10	10	7	14	9	12	12
1961	20	15	16	18	17	16	16	18	19
1962	16	16	16	17	19	17	15	16	14
1963					10				
1964	16	9	13	16	17	18	16	14	18
1965			12				8		
1966	17	15	16	18	18	17	15	16	12
1967	14	18	16	15	16		13	15	14
1968									
1969	10	13	12	19	18	16	15	16	16
1970	17	17	18	15	15	17	15	15	14
1971	16	17	19	18	20	16	17	15	18
1972	10		9	11	13		9	14	9

Vintages

	Bordeaux Red	Bordeaux White, Sweet	Bordeaux White, dry	Burgundy Red	Burgundy White	Champagne	Loire	Rhône	Alsace
1973	13	12		12	16	16	16	13	16
1974	11	14		12	13	8	11	12	13
1975	18	17	18		11	18	15	10	15
1976	15	19	16	18	15	15	18	16	19
1977	12	7	14	11	12	9	11	11	12
1978	17	14	17	19	17	16	17	19	15
1979	16	18	18	15	16	15	14	16	16
1980	13	17	18	12	12	14	13	15	10
1981	16	16	17	14	15	15	15	14	17
1982	18	14	16	14	16	16	14	13	15
1983	17	17	16	15	16	15	12	16	20
1984	13	13	12	13	14	5	10	11	15
1985	18	15	14	17	17	17	16	16	19
1986	17	17	12	12	15	9	13	10	10
1987	13	11	16	12	11	10	13	8	13
1988	16	19	18	16	14	15	16	18	17
1989	18	19	18	16	18	16	20	16	16
1990	18	20	17	18	16	19	17	17	18
1991	13	14	13	14	15	11	12	13	13
1992	12	10	14	15	17	12	14	12	12
1993	13	8	15	14	13	12	13	13	13
1994	14	14	17	14	16	12	14	14	12
1995	16	18	17	14	16	16	17	16	12
1996	15	18	16	17	18	19	17	14	12
1997	14	18	14	14	17	15	16	14	13
1998	15	16	14	15	15	13	14	18	13
1999	14	17	13	13	12	15	12	16	10
2000	18	10	16	11	15	15	16	17	12

The areas encircled with a thick line indicate wines that should be cellared. Sweet wines from the Loire were given 20 for the year 1990.

Which vintages should be drunk now?

Wines evolve differently according to whether they are created during a gloomy year or a sunny year and also according to their appellation, their position in the hierarchy within the appellation, their vinification and their ageing, the latter stages of which depend also on the cellar in which they have been stored.

The vintage table includes only good wines from recent years, which are therefore available, provided they have been looked after correctly. It does not include exceptional wines or exceptional *cuvées*. Wines are graded at their peak, and the table does not include the current evolution of old vintages.

COOKING WITH WINE

Cooking with wine is not a recent phenomenon. The Roman gourmet Apicius gave us a recipe for suckling pig in wine sauce (it was a *Vin de Paille*, the grapes being ripened on a layer of straw). Wine is used in cooking for the flavour it brings to the dishes and for its digestive properties, which are due to the glycerine and tannin it contains. Even non-drinkers may approve, as alcohol all but disappears on cooking.

The history of cooking can be traced through wine. Wine marinades were invented to preserve pieces of meat – today we use them for their taste – and the reduction of marinades that took place during cooking was the origin of sauces. Sometimes, meat was actually cooked in wine marinades, a method that gave rise to the development of such dishes as stews, casseroles, court-bouillons and *oeufs en meurette* (eggs in red wine sauce).

Recommendations

Do not waste old vintages in cooking. It is expensive, ineffective and can be detrimental.

Never use vins ordinaires or very light wines in cooking; their reduction only brings out their lack of presence.

A corky taste disappears in cooking, so use bottles that have this defect.

Drink the same wine that has been used in the preparation of the dish or one that has the same origin as an accompaniment.

WINE VINEGAR

Wine is man's friend, but vinegar is wine's enemy. However, it would be wrong to conclude that vinegar is man's enemy too – wines and vinegars each have their roles to play in the range of flavours that people enjoy. To throw away quality wines that are a little musty, corky or oxidised would be a shame as they can easily be turned into vinegar. A domestic vinegar-maker is a 3- to 5-litre receptacle, made of wood or, even better, glazed earthenware, with a tap. The acidity of vinegar acts as a counterbalance to other flavours. To keep its fieriness in check, gourmet-style aromatic vinegars have been developed. Many strong flavours blend harmoniously together, including garlic, shallots, pickled onions, mustard grains, peppercorns, cloves, elderflower, chicory, rose petals, bay leaves, thyme, parsley and so on.

Recommendations

Never leave a vinegar-maker in a cellar.

Whenever the so-called *mère du vinaigre* or 'vinegar mother' (a viscous mass) develops in the vinegar, it should be quickly removed.

Place the vinegar-maker in a warm room at 20°C (68°F).

Never hermetically seal it because the acetic bacteria, which transform the alcohol in the wine into acetic acid, cannot live without air.

Never put herbs or spices in the vinegar-maker. The vinegar needs to be extracted from the vinegar-maker and placed with the seasoning in another receptacle, this time preferably hermetically sealed.

Never use wine that has no stated origin in the vinegar-maker.

The vinegar-maker must be in constant use. Each time vinegar is withdrawn from the vinegar-maker, an equivalent volume of wine should be added.

A vinegar that is left for more than two or three months will taste bitter. It will lose its wine flavour and will be of no use.

FOOD AND WINE

Nothing is more difficult than finding an ideal wine to accompany a dish. But should there be such a thing? The marrying of wine and food should not be a monogamous affair; the variety that French wines offer should be an opportunity to experiment, and a good cellar should allow us to experiment with different combinations in order to extend our range of eating and drinking pleasure.

HORS D'OEUVRE

ANCHOVY PUREE ON TOAST
- Côtes du Roussillon, rosé
- Coteaux d'Aix-en-Provence, rosé
- Alsace, Sylvaner

ASPARAGUS WITH CREAMY HOLLANDAISE SAUCE
- Alsace, Muscat

AVOCADO PEAR
- Champagne
- Bugey, white
- Bordeaux, dry

FOIE GRAS
- Barsac
- Corton-Charlemagne
- Listrac
- Banyuls Rimage

FOIE GRAS IN BRIOCHE
- Alsace Tokay, selection of quality wines
- Montrachet
- Pécharmant

FROGS' LEGS
- Corbières, white
- Entre-Deux-Mers
- Touraine Sauvignon

GRILLED FOIE GRAS
- Jurançon
- Graves, red
- Condrieu

GRILLED RED PEPPERS IN VINAIGRETTE
- Clairette de Bellegarde
- Muscadet
- Mâcon Lugny, white

PROVENÇALE ARTICHOKES
- Coteaux d'Aix-en-Provence, rosé
- Loire, rosé
- Bordeaux, rosé

SALADE NIÇOISE
- Alsace Sylvaner
- Côtes du Rhône, red
- Coteaux d'Aix-en-Provence, rosé

SNAILS À LA BOURGUIGNONNE
- Bourgogne Aligoté
- Alsace Riesling
- Touraine Sauvignon

SOYA BEAN SALAD
- Alsace Tokay
- Clairette du Languedoc
- Muscadet

COLD MEATS

BAYONNE HAM
- Côtes du Rhône-Villages
- Bordeaux, clairet
- Corbières, rosé

BRAISED HAM
- Alsace Tokay
- Côtes du Rhône, red
- Côtes du Roussillon, rosé

CHICKEN LIVER TERRINE
- Meursault-Charmes
- Saint-Nicolas de Bourgueil
- Morgon

COLD COOKED SAUSAGE
- Côtes du Rhône-Villages
- Beaujolais
- Côtes de Roussillon, rosé

HAM FLAVOURED WITH PARSLEY
- Chassagne Montrachet, white
- Coteaux de Tricastin, red
- Beaujolais, red

HARE PÂTE
- Côtes de Duras, red
- Saumur-Champigny
- Moulin à Vent

RILLETTES (POTTED PORK)
- Burgundy, red
- Alsace Pinot Noir
- Touraine Gamay

RILLONS (CUBES OF PORK)
- Touraine Cabernet
- Beaujolais-Villages
- Loire, rosé

SMOKED HAM (WILD BOAR)
- Côtes de Saint-Mont, red
- Bandol, red
- Sancerre, white

SHELLFISH

BROCHETTE OF SCALLOPS
- Graves, white
- Alsace Sylvaner
- Beaujolais-Villages, red

CHARENTAIS MUSSEL STEW
- Saint-Véran
- Bergerac, dry
- Haut-Poitou, Chardonnay

CLAMS WITH GRILLED CHEESE TOPPING
- Pacherenc du Vic-Bilh
- Rully, white
- Beaujolais, white

CRAB COCKTAIL
- Jurançon, dry
- Fiefs Vendéens, white
- Bordeaux Sauvignon, dry

CRAYFISH IN COURT-BOUILLON
- Sancerre, white
- Côtes du Rhône, white
- Gaillac, white

CRAYFISH WITH MAYONNAISE
- Patrimonio, white
- Alsace Riesling
- Savoie Apremont

SHELLFISH

BARQUETTES GIRONDINES (PASTRY SHELLS FILLED WITH A SELECTION OF SEA-FOOD)
- Bâtard-Montrachet
- Good-quality Graves, white
- Quincy

BOUILLABAISSE (FISH STEW)
- Côtes du Roussillon, white
- Coteaux d'Aix-en-Provence, white
- Muscadet des Coteaux de la Loire

BOURRIDE (CREAMY FISH SOUP WITH AIOLI)
- Coteaux d'Aix-en-Provence, white
- Loire, rosé
- Bordeaux, rosé

BRILL WITH WHITE WINE AND SHELLFISH SAUCE
- Graves, white
- Puligny-Montrachet
- Coteaux de Languedoc, white

COD IN GARLIC SAUCE (AÏOLI)
- Coteaux d'Aix-en-Provence, rosé
- Bordeaux, rosé
- Haut-Poitou, rosé

COLD HAKE WITH MAYONNAISE
- Pouilly-Fuissé
- Savoie
- Chignin
- Bergeron
- Bergerac
- Alsace Klevner

COQUILLES DE POISSON (SELECTION OF FISH SERVED IN SCALLOP SHELLS)
- Saint-Aubin, white
- Saumur, dry white
- Crozes-Hermitage, white

DUBLIN BAY PRAWNS IN COGNAC
- Chablis, Premier Cru
- Graves, white
- Muscadet de Sèvres-et-Maine

FRESH RAW MUSSELS
- Coteaux du Languedoc, white
- Muscadet de Sèvre-et-Maine
- Coteaux d'Aix-en-Provence, white

GRILLED LOBSTER
- Hermitage, white
- Pouilly-Fuissé
- Savennières

LOBSTER IN TOMATO AND WHITE WINE SAUCE
- Arbois, jaune
- Juliénas

MOULES MARINIÈRES
- Burgundy, white
- Alsace Pinot
- Bordeaux Sauvignon, dry

MUSSELS WITH SPINACH
- Muscadet
- Bouzeron Bourgogne
- Aligoté
- Coteaux Champenois, white

OYSTERS
- Muscadet
- Bourgogne Aligoté
- Chablis
- Beaujolais Nouveau, red

OYSTERS IN CHAMPAGNE
- Burgundy, Hautes-Côtes de Nuit, white
- Coteaux Champenois, white
- Roussette de Savoie

PRAWNS WITH MAYONNAISE
- Burgundy, white
- Alsace Riesling
- Haut-Poitou Sauvignon

SEAFOOD PLATTER
- Chablis
- Muscadet
- Alsace Sylvaner

SHELLFISH SALAD WITH CUCUMBER
- Graves, white
- Muscadet, white
- Alsace Klevner

STUFFED CLAMS
- Graves, white
- Montagny
- Anjou, white

STUFFED SQUID
- Mâcon-Villages
- Good-quality Côtes de Bordeaux
- Gaillac, rosé

FISH

DEEP-FRIED WHITING
- Alsace Gutedal
- Entre-Deux-Mers
- Seyssel

FILLET OF SOLE BONNE FEMME
- Graves, white
- Chablis, Grand Cru
- Sancerre, white

FILLET OF TURBOT IN FLAKY PASTRY
- Chevalier-Montrachet
- Crozes-Hermitage, white

FISH STEW
- Chablis, Premier Cru
- Arbois, white
- Alsace Riesling

FRESHWATER FISH STEW WITH WHITE WINE
- Meursault
- L'Étoile
- Mâcon-Villages

GRILLED COD
- Gros Plant du Pays Nantais
- Coteaux d'Aix-en-Provence, rosé
- Loire, rosé

GRILLED RED MULLET
- Chassagne-Montrachet, white
- Hermitage, white
- Bergerac

GRILLED SALMON STEAK
- Chassagne-Montrachet, white
- Cahors
- Côtes du Rhône, rosé

GRILLED SARDINES
- Clairette de Bellegarde
- Jurançon, dry
- Bourgogne Aligoté

GRILLED SEA-BASS
- Auxey-Duresses, white
- Bellet, white
- Bergerac, dry

LAMPREY IN RED WINE SAUCE
- Bergerac, red
- Bordeaux, rosé

MACKEREL IN WHITE WINE
- Alsace Sylvaner
- Haut-Poitou Sauvignon
- Quincy

MONKFISH
- Mâcon-Villages
- Châteauneuf-du-Pape, white
- Bandol, rosé

OYSTERS FROM ARCACHON IN WINE SAUCE
- Graves, white
- Bordeaux, dry
- Jurançon, dry

PAN-FRIED EEL WITH GARLIC AND PARSLEY
- Corbières, rosé
- Gros Plant du Pays Nantais
- Blaye, white

PIKE QUENELLES (DUMPLINGS) IN WINE SAUCE
- Montrachet
- Pouilly-Vinzelles
- Beaujolais-Villages, red

RED TUNA WITH ONIONS
- Coteaux d'Aix, white
- Coteaux du Languedoc, white
- Côtes de Duras Sauvignon

ROUILLE SÉTOISE (SELECTION OF SEA-FOOD IN SPICY GARLIC SAUCE)
- Clairette du Languedoc
- Côtes du Roussillon, rosé
- Loire, rosé

SALMON IN PASTRY
- Pouilly-Vinzelles
- Graves, white
- Loire, rosé

Red and white meat

SALMON ROE
- Haut-Poitou, rosé
- Graves, red
- Côtes du Rhône, red

SALT COD
- Haut-Poitou, rosé
- Bandol, rosé
- Corbières, rosé

SHAD WITH SORREL
- Anjou, white
- Loire, rosé
- Haut-Poitou, Chardonnay

SMALL FRIED FISH (WHITEBAIT)
- Beaujolais, white
- Béarn, white
- Fiefs Vendéens, white

SMOKED SALMON
- Puligny-Montrachet, Premier Cru

TROUT WITH ALMONDS
- Chassagne-Montrachet, white
- Alsace Klevner
- Côtes du Roussillon

TURBOT WITH HOLLANDAISE SAUCE
- Graves, white
- Saumur, white
- Hermitage, white

WHITE TUNA IN BASQUE SAUCE
- Graves, white
- Pacherenc de Vic-Bilh
- Gaillac, white

ZANDER (PIKE PERCH) IN BUTTERY SAUCE
- Muscadet
- Saumur, white
- Saint-Joseph, white

SOLE MEUNIÈRE
- Meursault, white
- Alsace Riesling
- Entre-Deux-Mers

SOUFFLÉ WITH CRAYFISH SAUCE
- Bâtard-Montrachet
- Crozes-Hermitage, white
- Bergerac, dry

STUFFED CARP
- Montagny
- Touraine, Azay-le-Rideau, white

STUFFED CRAB
- Alsace, Pinot
- Premières Côtes de Bordeaux, white
- Burgundy, white
- Muscadet

POUILLY-FUMÉ *(correction below)*
- Pouilly-Fumé
- Bordeaux Sauvignon, dry

RED AND WHITE MEAT

Lamb

COLD LAMB WITH MAYONNAISE
- Saint-Aubin, white
- Bordeaux, red
- Entre-Deux-Mers

FILLET OF LAMB EN CROÛTE
- Pomerol
- Mercurey
- Coteaux du Tricastin

LAMB CARBONADE
- Graves de Vayres, red
- Fitou
- Crozes-Hermitage, red

LAMB CURRY
- Montagne Saint-Emilion
- Alsace Tokay
- Côtes du Rhône

LAMB STEW (DAUBE)
- Patrimonio, red
- Côtes du Rhône-Villages, red
- Morgon

LAMB STEW (NAVARIN)
- Anjou, red
- Bordeaux Côtes-de-Francs, red
- Bourgogne Marsannay, red

LAMB STEW FLAVOURED WITH THYME
- Châteauneuf-du-Pape, red
- Saint-Chinian
- Fleurie

MARLY LAMB CHOPS (FROM BEST END OF NECK)
- Saint-Julien
- Ajaccio
- Coteaux du Lyonnais

ROAST BARON OF LAMB
- Haut-Médoc
- Savoie-Mondeuse
- Minervois

ROAST LAMB
- Morey-Saint-Denis

- Saint-Emilion
- Côte de Provence, red

SADDLE OF LAMB FLAVOURED WITH HERBS
- Vin de Corse, red
- Côtes du Rhône, red
- Coteaux de Giennois, red

SAUTÉED LAMB PROVENÇALE STYLE
- Gigondas
- Côtes de Provence, red
- Bourgogne Passetoutgrain, red

SHOULDER OF LAMB IN ONION SAUCE
- Hermitage, red
- Côtes de Bourg, red
- Moulin à Vent

STUFFED BREAST OF LAMB
- Côtes de Jura, red
- Graves, red
- Haut-Poitou Gamay

Beef

BEEF FONDUE BURGUNDY-STYLE
- Bordeaux, red
- Côtes du Ventoux, red
- Burgundy, rosé

BEEF STEW
- Buzet, red
- Côtes du Vivrais, red
- Arbois, red

BEEF STEW WITH RED WINE
- Lirac, red
- Côtes du Luberon, red
- Costières de Nîmes, red

BOEUF BOURGUIGNON
- Rully, red
- Saumur, red
- Côte du Marmandais, red

ENTRECÔTE STEAK WITH BORDELAISE SAUCE
- Saint-Julien
- Saint-Joseph, red
- Côtes du Roussillon-Villages

FILLET OF BEEF DUCHESSE
- Côte-Rôtie
- Gigondas
- Graves, red

FILLET STEAK WITH BÉARNAISE SAUCE
- Listrac
- Saint-Aubin, red
- Touraine Amboise, red

POT-AU-FEU
- Anjou, red
- Bordeaux, red
- Beaujolais, red

ROAST BEEF (COLD)
- Madiran
- Beaune, red
- Cahors

ROAST BEEF (HOT)
- Moulis
- Aloxe-Corton
- Côtes du Rhône, red

STEAK CHATEAUBRIAND
- Margaux
- Alsace Pinot
- Coteaux du Tricastin

STEAK MAITRE D'HOTEL (WITH PARSLEY AND LEMON SAUCE)
- Bergerac, red
- Arbois, rosé
- Chénas

Pork

ANDOUILLETTE (CHITTERLING SAUSAGE) WITH CREAM SAUCE
- Touraine, white
- Burgundy, white
- Saint-Joseph, white

CASSOULET (CASSEROLE OF WHITE BEANS AND PORK, GOOSE OR DUCK MEAT)
- Côtes du Frontonnais, red
- Minervois, red
- Bergerac, red

CHOUCROUTE
- Alsace Riesling
- Alsace Sylvaner

COLD ROAST PORK
- Burgundy, white
- Lirac, red
- Bordeaux, dry

CONFIT
- Tursan, red
- Corbières, red
- Cahors

COUNTRY-STYLE SOUP WITH CABBAGE
- Côtes du Luberon
- Côte de Brouilly
- Bourgogne Aligoté

GRILLED ANDOUILLETTE
- Coteaux Champenois, white
- Petit Chablis
- Beaujolais, red

GRILLED TOULOUSE SAUSAGE
- Saint-Joseph or Bergerac, red
- Côtes du Frontonnais, rosé

PORK CHOP WITH ONION AND WHITE WINE SAUCE
- Burgundy, white
- Côtes d'Auvergne, red
- Bordeaux, clairet

ROAST PORK FLAVOURED WITH SAGE
- Rully, white
- Côtes du Rhône, red
- Minervois, rosé

SHOULDER OF PORK WITH SAUVIGNON
- Bergerac, dry
- Menetou-Salon
- Bordeaux, rosé

STUFFED CABBAGE
- Côtes du Rhône, red
- Touraine Gamay
- Bordeaux Sauvignon, dry

SUCKLING PIG EN GELÉE
- Graves de Vayres, white
- Costières du Gard, rosé
- Beaujolais-Villages, red

Veal

BRAISED TOPSIDE OF VEAL
- Mâcon-Villages, white
- Côtes de Duras, red
- Brouilly

CALVES LIVER À L'ANGLAISE
- Médoc
- Coteaux d'Aix-en-Provence, red
- Haut-Poitou, rosé

GRILLED VEAL CHOP
- Côtes du Rhône, red
- Anjou, white
- Burgundy, rosé

KIDNEY BROCHETTES
- Cornas
- Beaujolais-Villages
- Coteaux du Languedoc, rosé

SAUTEED KIDNEYS IN VIN JAUNE
- Arbois, white
- Gaillac, Vin de Voile
- Bourgogne Aligoté

VEAL ESCALOPE IN BREADCRUMBS
- Côtes du Jura, white
- Corbières, white
- Côtes du Ventoux, red

VEAL KIDNEYS WITH MARROW-BONE
- Saint-Emilion
- Coteaux-Champigny
- Coteaux d'Aix-en-Provence, rosé

VEAL MARENGO (TOMATO AND WINE SAUCE)
- Côtes de Duras Merlot
- Alsace Klevner
- Coteaux du Tricastin, rosé
- Lirac, rosé

VEAL PARCELS
- Anjou Gamay
- Minervois, rosé
- Costières de Nîmes, white

VEAL STEW IN WHITE SAUCE À L'ANCIENNE
- Arbois, white
- Alsace Riesling, Grand Cru
- Côtes de Provence, rosé

VEAL SWEETBREADS WITH LANGOUSTINES
- Graves, white
- Alsace Tokay
- Bordeaux, rosé

POULTRY, RABBIT

BARBARY DUCK WITH OLIVES
- Savoie-Mondeuse, red
- Canon-Fronsac
- Anjou Cabernet, red

BREAST OF DUCK WITH GREEN PEPPER
- Saint-Joseph, red
- Bourgueil, red
- Bergerac, red

CHICKEN COOKED WITH SALT CRUST
- Listrac
- Mâcon-Villages, white
- Côtes du Rhône, red

CHICKEN CURRY
- Montagne Saint-Emilion
- Alsace Tokay
- Côtes du Rhône

CHICKEN WITH TRUFFLE SAUCE
- Chevalier-Montrachet
- Arbois, white
- Juliénas

COQ AU VIN
- Ladoix
- Côte de Beaune
- Touraine Cabernet

DUCK HEART BROCHETTES
- Saint-Georges-Saint-Emilion
- Chinon
- Côtes du Rhône-Villages

DUCK WITH ORANGE
- Côtes du Jura, jaune
- Cahors
- Graves, red

DUCK WITH TURNIPS
- Puisseguin Saint-Emilion
- Saumur-Champigny
- Coteaux d'Aix-en-Provence, red

DUCKLING WITH PEACHES
- Banyuls
- Chinon, red
- Graves, red

GUINEA-FOWL WITH ARMAGNAC
- Saint-Estèphe
- Chassagne-Montrachet, red
- Fleurie

PIGEON WITH DICED VEGETABLES
- Crozes-Hermitage, red
- Bordeaux, red
- Touraine Gamay

POULET BASQUAISE
- Côtes de Duras, Sauvignon
- Bordeaux, dry
- Coteaux du Languedoc, rosé

RABBIT FRICASEE
- Touraine, rosé
- Côtes de Blaye, white
- Beaujolais-Villages, red

ROAST CAPON
- Burgundy, white
- Touraine-Mesland
- Côtes du Rhône, rosé

ROAST RABBIT WITH MUSTARD
- Sancerre, red

- Tavel
- Côtes de Provence, white

SAUTEED CHICKEN WITH MOREL MUSHROOMS
- Savigny-lès-Beaune, red
- Arbois, white
- Sancerre, white

SPIT-ROASTED TURKEY
- Monthélie
- Graves, white

TURKEY WITH CHESTNUTS
- Saint-Joseph, red
- Sancerre, red
- Meursault, white

TURKEY ESCALOPES WITH ROQUEFORT
- Côtes du Jura, white
- Bourgogne Aligoté
- Coteaux d'Aix-en-Provence, rosé

GAME

- Châteaumeillant, rosé

STUFFED DUCK
- Saint-Emilion, Grand Cru
- Bandol, red
- Buzet, red

STUFFED GOOSE
- Anjou Cabernet, red
- Côtes du Marmandais, red
- Beaujolais-Villages

BRAISED WILD BOAR
- Fronsac
- Châteauneuf-du-Pape, red
- Moulin à Vent

FILLET OF WILD BOAR WITH BORDELAISE SAUCE
- Pomerol
- Bandol
- Gigondas

FLAMBEED WOODCOCK
- Pauillac
- Musigny
- Hermitage

HARE À LA ROYALE
- Saint-Joseph, red
- Volnay
- Pécharmant

HAUNCH OF WILD BOAR WITH VENISON SAUCE
- Chambertin
- Montagne Saint-Emilion
- Corbières, red

JUGGED HARE
- Canon-Fronsac
- Bonnes-Mares
- Minervois, red

PARTRIDGE À LA CATALANE
- Maury
- Côtes du Roussillon, red
- Beaujolais-Villages

PARTRIDGE WITH CABBAGE
- Burgundy, Irancy
- Arbois, rosé
- Cornas

PHEASANT IN CHARTREUSE
- Moulis
- Pommard
- Saint-Nicolas de Bourgueil

ROAST PARTRIDGE
- Haut-Médoc
- Vosne-Romanée
- Bourgueil

ROAST RABBIT
- Auxey-Duresses, red
- Puisseguin Saint-Emilion
- Crozes-Hermitage, red

ROAST WILD DUCK
- Saint-Emilion, Grand Cru
- Côte Rôtie
- Faugères

SADDLE OF HARE WITH JUNIPER
- Chambolle, Musigny
- Savoie-Mondeuse
- Saint-Chinian

VENISON CHOPS CONTI STYLE
- Lalande-de-Pomerol
- Côtes de Beaune, red
- Crozes-Hermitage, red

VENISON GRAND VENEUR
- Hermitage, red
- Corton, red
- Côtes de Roussillon, red

WILD DUCK IN RED WINE SAUCE
- Côte Rôtie
- Chinon, red
- Bordeaux, superior quality

WOODCOCK IN RED WINE SAUCE
- Saint-Julien
- Côte de Nuits-Villages
- Patrimonio

VEGETABLES

BRAISED CELERY
- Côtes de Ventoux, red
- Alsace Pinot Noir
- Touraine Sauvignon

DAUPHINOIS POTATOES
- Bordeaux Côtes de Castillon
- Châteauneuf-du-Pape, white
- Alsace Riesling

FRIED AUBERGINES
- Burgundy, red
- Beaujolais, red
- Bordeaux, dry

GREEN BEANS
- Côte de Beaune, white
- Sancerre, white
- Entre-Deux-Mers

MANGETOUT PEAS
- Graves, white
- Côtes du Rhône, red
- Alsace Riesling

MUSHROOMS
- Beaune, white
- Alsace Tokay
- Coteaux de Giennois, red

PASTA
- Côtes du Rhône, red
- Coteaux d'Aix, rosé

PETITS POIS
- Saint-Romain, white
- Côtes du Jura, white
- Touraine Sauvignon

SAUTEED MUSHROOMS MARBLED WITH PARSLEY
- Beaune, white
- Alsace Tokay
- Coteaux du Giennois, red

STUFFED PEPPERS
- Mâcon-Villages
- Côtes du Rhône, rosé
- Alsace Tokay

CHEESE

Made with cow's milk

BEAUFORT
- Arbois, jaune
- Meursault
- Vin de Savoie
- Chignin
- Bergeron

BLEU D'AUVERGNE
- Côtes de Bergerac, sweet
- Beaujolais
- Touraine Sauvignon

BLEU DE BRESSE
- Côtes du Jura, white
- Macon, red

BRIE
- Côtes de Bergerac, white
- Beaune, red
- Alsace Pinot Noir
- Coteaux du Languedoc, red

CAMEMBERT
- Bandol, red
- Côtes du Roussillon-Villages
- Beaujolais-Villages

CANTAL
- Coteaux du Vivarais, red
- Côtes de Provence, rosé
- Lirac, white

CARRE DE L'EST
- Saint-Joseph, red
- Coteaux d'Aix-en-Provence, red
- Brouilly

CARRE FRAIS
- Cahors
- Côtes du Roussillon, rosé
- Côtes du Rhône, white

CHAOURCE
- Montagne Saint-Emilion

- Cadillac
- Chénas

CÍTEAUX
- Aloxe-Corton
- Coteaux Champenois, red
- Fleurie

COMTE
- Graves, Château-Chalon, white
- Côtes du Luberon, white

EDAM DEMI-ETUVE
- Pauillac
- Fixin
- Costières de Nîmes, red

EPOISSES
- Savigny
- Côtes du Jura, red
- Côte de Brouilly

FOURME D'AMBERT
- L'Etoile, jaune
- Cérons
- Banyuls Rimage

GOUDA DEMI-ETUVE
- Saint-Estèphe
- Chinon
- Coteaux du Tricastin

LIVAROT
- Bonnezeaux

- Sainte-Croix-du-Mont
- Alsace Gewurztraminer

MAROILLES
- Jurançon
- Alsace, Gewurztraminer, late harvests

MIMOLETTE DEMI-ETUVE
- Graves, red
- Santenay
- Côtes du Rhône, red

MORBIER
- Gevrey-Chambertin
- Madiran
- Côtes du Ventoux, red

MUNSTER
- Coteaux du Layon-Villages
- Loupiac
- Alsace Gewurztraminer

CHEESE FONDUE
- Alsace Riesling
- Haut-Poitou Sauvignon

PONT L'EVEQUE
- Côtes du Rhône-Villages
- Côtes de Saint-Mont
- Bourgueil
- Nuit Saint-Georges

RACLETTE
- Vin de Savoie
- Apremont
- Côtes de Duras Sauvignon
- Juliénas

REBLOCHON
- Mercurey
- Lirac, red
- Touraine Gamay

RIGOTTE
- Bourgogne Hautes-Côtes de Nuits, red
- Côte du Forez

SAINT-AMOUR

SAINT MARCELLIN
- Faugères
- Tursan, red
- Chiroubles

SAINT-NECTAIRE
- Fronsac
- Burgundy, red
- Mâcon-Villages, white

VACHERIN
- Corton
- Bordeaux, Premières Côtes
- Barsac

Made with goat's milk:

CABECOU
- Burgundy, white
- Tavel
- Gaillac, white

CORSICAN GOAT'S CHEESE
- Patrimonio, white
- Cassis, white
- Costières de Nîmes, white

CROTTIN DE CHAVIGNOL
- Sancerre, white
- Bordeaux, dry

- Côte Roannaise

FRESH GOAT CHEESE
- Champagne
- Montlouis, medium dry
- Crémant d'Alsace

PELARDON
- Condrieu
- Roussette de Savoie
- Coteaux du Lyonnais, red

SAINTE-MAURE
- Rivesalles, white

- Alsace Tokay
- Cheverny Gamay

SELLES-SUR-CHER
- Coteaux de l'Aubance
- Cheverny
- Romorantin
- Sancerre, rosé

VALENÇAY
- Vouvray, sweet
- Haut-Poitou, rosé
- Valençay, Gamay

Made with ewe's milk:

CORSICAN EWE'S CHEESE
- Bourgogne, Irancy
- Ajaccio
- Côtes du Roussillon, red

EISBARECH
- Lalande-de-Pomerol

- Cornas

ROQUEFORT
- Marcillac
- Champagne
- Sauternes
- Muscat de Rivesalles

LARUNS
- Bordeaux, Côtes de Castillon
- Gaillac, red
- Côtes de Provence, red

DESSERTS

ALMOND CAKE
- Maury
- Bonnezeaux
- Muscat de Lunel

BRIOCHE
- Rivesalles, red
- Muscat de Beaumes-de-Venise
- Alsace, late harvest

CHOCOLATE CAKE
- Banyuls, Grand Cru
- Pineau des Charentes, rosé

CHRISTMAS LOG
- Champagne, medium dry
- Clairette de Die Tradition

CREME RENVERSEE
- Coteaux du Layon-Villages
- Sauternes

- Muscat de Saint-Jean de Minervois

ILE FLOTTANTE
- Loupiac
- Rivesalles, white
- Muscat de Rivesalles

KOUGLOF (CAKE FROM ALSACE)
- Quarts de Chaume
- Alsace, late harvests
- Muscat de Mireval

LEMON TART
- Alsace, various good quality wines
- Cérons
- Rivesalles, white

ORANGE FRUIT SALAD
- Sainte-Croix-du-Mont
- Rivesalles, white
- Muscat de Rivesalles

PRUNE FLAN
- Pineau des Charentes
- Anjou, Coteaux de la Loire
- Cadillac

STRAWBERRIES
- Muscat de Rivesalles
- Maury

TARTE TATIN
- Pineau des Charentes
- Arbois, Vin de Paille
- Jurançon

VANILLA ICE-CREAM WITH RASPBERRY SAUCE
- Loupiac
- Coteaux du Layon

Alsace

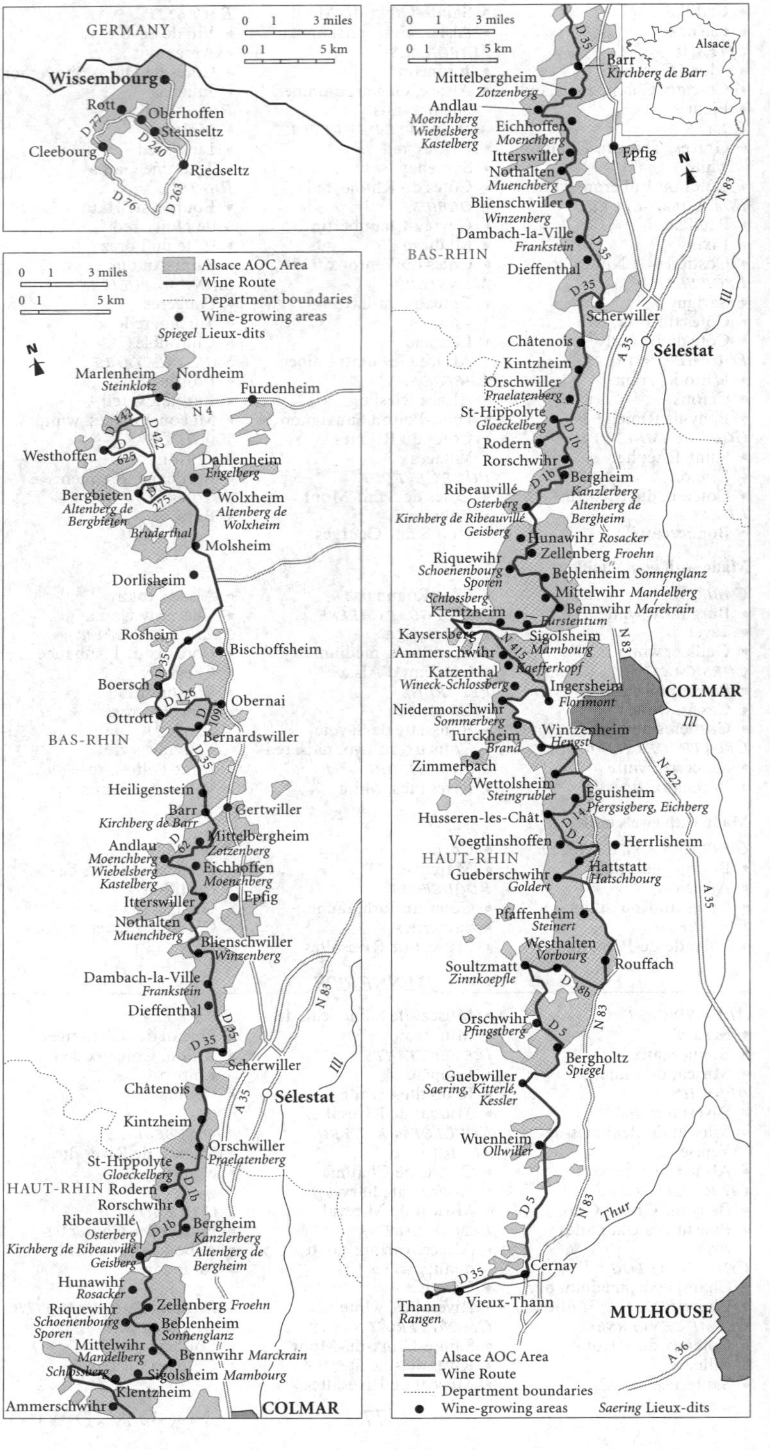
GERMANY
Wissembourg
Rott
Oberhoffen
Steinseltz
Cleebourg
Riedseltz
D 77
D 240
D 263
D 76
0 1 3 miles
0 1 5 km
Alsace AOC Area
Wine Route
Department boundaries
Wine-growing areas
Spiegel Lieux-dits
Marlenheim
Steinklotz
Nordheim
Furdenheim
N 4
D 142
D 422
D 625
Westhoffen
Dahlenheim
Engelberg
Wolxheim
Altenberg de Wolxheim
Bergbieten
Altenberg de Bergbieten
D 275
Bruderthal
Molsheim
Dorlisheim
Rosheim
Bischoffsheim
D 35
Boersch
D 126
Obernai
Ottrott
D 109
Bernardswiller
BAS-RHIN
Heiligenstein
Barr
Kirchberg de Barr
Gertwiller
Mittelbergheim
Zotzenberg
D 62
Andlau
Moenchberg
Wiebelsberg
Kastelberg
Eichhoffen
Moenchberg
Epfig
Itterswiller
Nothalten
Muenchberg
Blienschwiller
Winzenberg
Dambach-la-Ville
Frankstein
Dieffenthal
N 83
Scherwiller
A 35
Ill
Sélestat
Châtenois
Kintzheim
Orschwiller
Praelatenberg
St-Hippolyte
Gloeckelberg
HAUT-RHIN
Rodern
D 1b
Rorschwihr
Ribeauvillé
Osterberg
Kirchberg de Ribeauvillé
Geisberg
Bergheim
Kanzlerberg
Altenberg de Bergheim
Hunawihr
Rosacker
Zellenberg Froehn
Riquewihr
Schoenenbourg
Sporen
Beblenheim
Sonnenglanz
Mittelwihr
Mandelberg
Bennwihr Marckrain
Schlossberg
Sigolsheim Mambourg
Klentzheim
Ammerschwihr
COLMAR
Barr
Kirchberg de Barr
Alsace
Mittelbergheim
Zotzenberg
Andlau
Moenchberg
Wiebelsberg
Kastelberg
Eichhoffen
Moenchberg
Epfig
Itterswiller
Nothalten
Muenchberg
Blienschwiller
Winzenberg
Dambach-la-Ville
Frankstein
BAS-RHIN
Dieffenthal
Scherwiller
Châtenois
Sélestat
Kintzheim
Orschwiller
Praelatenberg
St-Hippolyte
Gloeckelberg
Rodern
Rorschwihr
Bergheim
Kanzlerberg
Altenberg de Bergheim
Ribeauvillé
Osterberg
Kirchberg de Ribeauvillé
Geisberg
Hunawihr Rosacker
Zellenberg Froehn
Riquewihr
Schoenenbourg
Sporen
Beblenheim Sonnenglanz
Mittelwihr Mandelberg
Schlossberg
Bennwihr Marckrain
Klentzheim
Furstentum
Kaysersberg
Sigolsheim
Mambourg
N 415
Ammerschwihr
Kaefferkopf
Katzenthal
Wineck-Schlossberg
Ingersheim
Florimont
COLMAR
Niedermorschwihr
Sommerberg
Turckheim
Brand
Wintzenheim
Hengst
N 422
Zimmerbach
Wettolsheim
Steingrubler
Eguisheim
Pfersigberg, Eichberg
Husseren-les-Chât.
D 14
D 1
Voegtlinshoffen
Herrlisheim
HAUT-RHIN
Hattstatt
Hatschbourg
Gueberschwihr
Goldert
A 35
Pfaffenheim
Steinert
Westhalten
Vorbourg
Rouffach
Soultzmatt
Zinnkoepfle
D 18b
Orschwihr
Pfingstberg
D 5
Bergholtz
Spiegel
Guebwiller
Saering, Kitterlé, Kessler
Wuenheim
Ollwiller
Thur
Cernay
Thann
Rangen
Vieux-Thann
MULHOUSE
A 36
Alsace AOC Area
Wine Route
Department boundaries
Wine-growing areas
Saering Lieux-dits

Alsace

Most of the Alsace wine region is on the hills that rise at the foot of the Vosges mountains and run eastward to the Rhine plain. The Vosges form a natural barrier between Alsace and the rest of France and help to create the region's individual climate. Because the moisture absorbed over the Atlantic falls as rain on the mountains, it leaves the eastern slopes only lightly watered. The average annual rainfall in the Colmar region is the lowest in France, less than 500 mm (19.7 in) a year. In summer the mountains also provide some protection from the cool Atlantic winds. Most importantly, however the undulating relief of the hills creates the minute variations in the micro-climates that ultimately contribute to the variety and quality of the vineyards.

The Alsace vineyards are also characterised by a great diversity in soil types. Some fifty million years ago, the recent past in geological terms, the Vosges and the Black Forest formed a single mass, created by a sequence of geological activity during the Tectonic era — floods, erosion and the folding of the earth's crust. From the Tertiary era, the central part of the mountains began to subside, creating, over time, a plain. As a result of this compression, nearly all the strata (layers of soil that had accumulated over different geological periods) were exposed along the line of schism. This is the area where the vineyards are located. In most of the wine-growing communes there are at least four or five different geological structures to the terrain.

The origins of the Alsatian vineyards are lost in the mists of time, but it is thought that the early inhabitants of the region probably harvested grapes, although organised cultivation did not take place until after the Roman conquest. In the wake of Germanic invasions in the 5th century, vine-growing fell into decline for a period, although manuscripts show the vineyards soon began to flourish again under powerful centres of Christianity such as bishoprics, abbeys and convents. Documents from before AD 900 cite more than 160 places where vines were cultivated.

The development of the vineyards continued uninterrupted until the 16th century, the period when wine-growing in Alsace was at its peak. The magnificent Renaissance-style houses that can be seen in the wine villages bear witness to the undoubted prosperity of the times, when great quantities of Alsatian wines were exported to every country in Europe. But the Thirty Years' War was devastating: pillage, famine, plague and destruction had catastrophic consequences for wine-growing and were ruinous for economic activity in the region.

When peace was restored cultivating vines and wineproduction were gradually put back on a stable footing and began again to flourish and expand. The areas of vineyards increased, but they were mainly planted with ordinary grape varieties, which meant wine was produced in quantity but was not necessarily of high quality. In 1731 a royal edict attempted to put a stop to this situation, but without much success. The expansion of the vineyards continued unabated after the Revolutions and by 1808 more than 23,000 ha (56,810 acres) were under vines, an area that increased to 30,000 ha (74,100 acres) by 1828. There was significant over-production of wine and the situation was made worse when the export market collapsed and the consumption of wine dropped as beer-drinking increased. At the same time, wines from southern France offered stiff competition, and they could now easily be shipped to the rest of France on the new railways. In Alsace the vines suffered from a variety of diseases, vine worm and phylloxera, which compounded the difficulties. From 1902 the once-extensive vineyards gradually diminished, and by 1948 the area of vine cultivation had fallen to 9,500 ha (23,456 acres), of which 7,500 ha (18,525 acres) was given the Alsace appellation.

The post-war economic boom and the increased professionalism of the wine-growers combined to drive the revival and redevelopment of the Alsace vineyards. They now cover an area of about 14,500 ha (35,815 acres) with an annual production which in 2000 amounted to 1,210,000 hl (31,944,000 gal) – 48,500 hl (1,280,400 gal) of Grands Crus and 157,000 hl (4,144,800 gal) of Crémant d'Alsace – and the wine is marketed throughout France and abroad. Exports represent about a quarter of total sales. The widespread improvements in the production and quality of Alsace wines were the collaborative work of the various professional groups which all agreed to limit the quantities of wine on the market. These groups included the wine-making wine-growers, co-operatives and négociants (local wine wholesalers), who were often also wine-growers themselves and who also bought large quantities of grapes from growers who did not vinify their own harvest.

The villages and towns along the Route du Vin hold wine festivals throughout the year. These are great tourist attractions and important cultural events for the region. The annual wine fair, held at Colmar in August, is undoubtedly the most important festival, and the ones held earlier in Guebwiller, Ammerschwihr, Ribeauvillé, Barr and Molsheim are also worth visiting. The most prestigious event is organised by the Confrérie Saint-Etienne, which was first established in the 14th century and revived in 1947.

The most distinctive attribute of Alsace wines is their aromatic perfume, which is at its best from grapes grown in cool, temperate areas where they ripen slowly and over a long time. The particular flavours naturally depend on the grape variety, and in Alsace wines are almost always labelled and sold under their grape variety, as distinct from most other French AOC wines which, as a rule, are named after the region or particular geographical location where the grapes are grown.

The grapes are harvested in October and transported as quickly as possible to the wine store for first pressing. Sometimes the grapes are stripped from the stalks, then they undergo a second pressing. The must that flows from the press is full of residual particles from pressing, such as fragments of grape flesh, pips, skins and stalks, which must be removed as quickly as possible by sedimentation or centrifugation. The clarified must then starts its fermentation. During this crucial phase enormous care has to be taken to avoid excessive temperatures. The young wine is often murky, and the wine-maker can use a variety of methods to clarify it, including racking, adding sulphur dioxide and fining. The developing wine is kept in vats or barrels until late spring when most of it is bottled. This method of production makes the dry white wines, which represent more than 90% of Alsace wine production.

The Alsace wines made from late-harvested grapes and the *sélection de grains nobles*, (wines made from late-harvested grapes that are individually selected from the bunch for their ripeness and sweetness) have had their own official appellation only since 1984. These wines are made under strictly regulated production guidelines, the most rigorous concerning the amount of sugar in the grapes. These wines are in a class of their own and, in addition to being very expensive, cannot be produced every year. Only certain grape varieties qualify for late harvesting, mainly Gewurztraminer, Pinot Gris and Riesling, but also Muscat, though more rarely.

Alsace wines are generally considered to be better when drunk young, and this is mostly true for the Sylvaner, Chasselas, Pinot Blanc varieties and Edelzwicker, a blend of varieties. But their youthfulness can mature and Riesling, Gewurztraminer and Pinot Gris often benefit from being kept for at least two years. There is no hard and fast rule, but some Grands Vins, made in years when the grapes are very ripe, can keep longer, sometimes for decades.

The Alsace appellation applies to all of the 110 areas of communal production and is restricted to the use of 11 grape varieties: Gewurztraminer, Riesling, Riesling Rhénan, Pinot Gris, Muscat Blanc à Petits Grains and Rosé à Petits Grains, Muscat Ottonel, Pinot Blanc, Auxerrois Blanc, Pinot Noir, Sylvaner and Chasselas Blanc and Rosé.

Alsace Klevener de Heiligenstein

Its rarity and elegance are what make it original. The wines are very well balanced and discreetly aromatic.

Klevener de Heiligenstein

Heiligenstein is no different from Vieux Traminer (or Savagnin Rose), which have been known in Alsace for centuries.

Mostly it has given way over time to the spicy 'Gewurztraminer' variant but has remained popular in Heiligenstein and five neighbouring communes.

ANDRE DOCK

Cuvée Tentation 1999★★		
☐		
0.2 ha	800	11-15

Although it belongs to the Savagnin family, Heiligenstein Klevener differs from Gewurztraminer in not being aromatic. All the same, it has a delicate, elegant fruitiness epitomised by this wine. The golden-yellow colour promises great maturity. The nose is great with aromas of crystallised fruits, which combine with those of pear and pineapple to give it a rare distinction. This perfectly integrated 99 wine is rich and satisfying. Delicious. (Residual sugar: 50 g/l, half-litre bottles.)

81

Alsace Sylvaner

It is not clear where the Sylvaner originated, but it has customarily been grown only in vineyards in Germany and the Lower Rhine in France, to which it is eminently suited. In Alsace this variety is particularly successful and regularly produces a large and reliable yield.

Sylvaner makes remarkably fresh, quite acid wines, which have a delicate fruitiness. There are two different types of Sylvaner on the market. The first, by far the better, comes from the well-exposed vineyards that do not produce over-large quantities of grapes. The second type is for those who like a particularly appealing, unpretentious, thirst-quenching wine. Sylvaner is an excellent accompaniment to sauerkraut, and is often drunk with shellfish and seafood. It goes particularly well with oysters.

CAVE VINICOLE D'ANDLAU-BARR
Mittelbergheim 1999

☐   n.c.   10,000 ■ ◾ **€3-5**

The Zotzenberg is a south-facing *terroir*, its soil a mixture of Jurassic limestone and marly limestone conglomerates. The Cave Vinicole has produced a Sylvaner with aromas of crystallised and exotic fruits (citrus and mango). After a lively attack, this wine has good balance and medium length.

☛ Cave vinicole d' Andlau et environs,
15, av. des Vosges, 67140 Barr,
tel. 03.88.08.90.53, fax 03.88.08.41.79 ☑
☨ by appt.

PATRICK BEYER 1999★★

☐   0.5 ha   3,000 ▥ **€3-5**

The commune of Epfig has been known for its wood production since the eighth century, and the Romanesque Church of

---

Alsace Sylvaner

balance and reveals its substantial body at the finish. Though ready to drink now, it could be left a while to reach its full potential. (Residual sugar: 11 g/l.)

☛ Dom. Daniel Ruff, 64, rue Principale,
67140 Heiligenstein, tel. 03.88.08.10.81,
fax 03.88.08.43.61 ☑ ☨ by appt.

☛ André et Christian Dock,
20, rue Principale, 67140 Heiligenstein,
tel. 03.88.08.02.69, fax 03.88.08.19.72 ☑
☨ ev. day 8am–12 noon 1pm–6pm

DOM. DOCK Cuvée Prestige 1999

☐   1.2 ha   8,000   **€5-8**

The Dock estate, with its 9 ha (22 acres) in the commune of Heiligenstein, exports a large part of its production to north-eastern Europe (Germany, The Netherlands and Belgium). Its 99 vintage is light yellow to pale gold in colour, very bright and clear. Though the nose as yet lacks great intensity and the finish is somewhat reserved, this wine is well made and spicy. (Residual sugar: 10 g/l.)

☛ André et Christian Dock,
20, rue Principale, 67140 Heiligenstein,
tel. 03.88.08.02.69, fax 03.88.08.19.72 ☑
☨ ev. day 8am–12 noon 1pm–6pm

PAUL DOCK Cuvée Prestige 1999★

☐   0.3 ha   2,000   **€8-11**

The production of Heiligenstein Klevener is confined to the village of that name and four surrounding communes: Bourgheim, Gertwiller, Goxwiller and Obernai. This vineyard lies several miles north of Barr, at the foot of Mont Sainte-Odile. Paul Dock's golden-yellow wine confirms the maturity of the grapes, grown at Heiligenstein. It is redolent of pear and quince. The palate echoes the bouquet perfectly: 'So much fruit!' observed one taster. This wine is made from overripe grapes, giving it a mellowness in keeping with its structure. (Residual sugar: 33 g/l.)

☛ Paul Dock, 55, rue Principale,
67140 Heiligenstein, tel. 03.88.08.02.49,
fax 03.88.08.02.49
☨ ev. day 9am–11.30 1.30pm–7pm

DANIEL RUFF L'Authentique 1999★

☐   0.6 ha   4 000 ▥ **€8-11**

It was in 1742 that Ehrhard Wantz, mayor of Heiligenstein, brought Klevener back from northern Italy. Though a valued variety, it witnessed a definite decline from the beginning of the 20th century, so much so that in 1970 only 3 ha (7 acres) were planted with it. Following its recognition as an Alsace appellation, it managed, fortunately, to recolonize the siliceous-clay, well-drained and dryish *terroir* that suits it. Daniel Ruff's Authentique Klevener lives up to its name. His strongyellow wine already expresses the characteristics of the variety. The palate has excellent

Sainte-Marguerite is full of interest. But if you come here, don't miss Patrick Bayer's estate; his Sylvaner, grown on limestone-clay, is remarkable. It releases aromas of fresh fruits and toasted bread which are both intense and persistent. After a good attack, this pleasant wine develops a delicate freshness before finishing on a note of hazelnut. 'I love it!' exclaimed one young member of the jury.

⚲ Patrick Bayer, 27, rue des Alliés, 67680 Epfig, tel. 03.88.85.50.21, fax 03.88.57.81.46 ☑ ♈ by appt.

E. BOECKEL

Mittelbergheim Vieilles vignes 1999★

1 ha   10,000   €5-8

The label designed by C. Spindler recalls the venerable tradition of the Boeckels and their Sylvaner, which comes from the great Zotzenberg and its surroundings. This wine has a range of aromas which begins with plant-like notes and hints of citrus, and opens out into crystallised fruits. The frank, fresh way in which it hits the palate is indicative of a well-mannered body, with peach and apricot aromas prominent. A lovely wine, true to type, pleasing and welcoming.

⚲ Emile Boeckel, 2, rue de la Montagne, 67140 Mittelbergheim, tel. 03.88.08.91.88, e-mail vins.boeckel@proveis.com ☑ ♈ by appt.

CAVE DE CLEEBOURG 1999

16.36 ha   24,000   €3-5

Created in 1946 in order to preserve wine-growing in the north of Alsace, the Cleebourg cellar draws on more than 180 ha (445 acres), thanks to its many members in the region. This vintage comes from a clayey-sandy terroir. True to type with its plant-like overtones (mown hay), it conveys a sense of balance and finishes on a hint of bitterness.

⚲ Cave vinicole de Cleebourg, rte du Vin, 67160 Cleebourg, tel. 03.88.94.50.33, fax 03.88.94.57.08, e-mail cave.cleebourg@wanadoo.fr ☑ ♈ ev. day 8am-12 noon 2pm-6pm; groups by appt.

GERARD DOLDER

Mittelbergheim 1999★★★

0.56 ha   5,300

Mittelbergheim is one of the loveliest villages in France. It dominates the plain, with its pretty 16th- and 17th-century houses; its streets abound with wine-growers' placards. It might be called the capital of Sylvaner.

Gérard Dolder's vintage certainly argues the case. Though restrained at first, the nose continues, exhaling floral, fruity and spicy notes. On the palate, you have the feeling of biting into a ripe, crunchy apple. Its fine balance persists through a long finish.

⚲ Gérard Dolder, 29, rue de la Montagne, 67140 Mittelbergheim, tel. 03.88.08.55.86 ☑ ♈ ev. day 9am-12 noon 2pm-6pm

PAUL FAHRER Réserve des Coteaux du Haut-Koenigsbourg 1999

0.2 ha   1,800   €3-5

The village of Orschwiller sits at the foot of the Haut-Koenigsbourg, the best-known and most-visited medieval château in Alsace. This family business, established more than 60 years ago, has 6 ha (15 acres) of vines. This wine, with its plant-like overtones, gradually opens out to disclose its fruitiness. After a clean attack, it shows its good balance and structure, leading to a slightly lemony finish.

⚲ Paul Fahrer, 3, pl. de La Mairie, 67600 Orschwiller, tel. 03.88.92.86.57, fax 03.88.92.20.41 ☑ ♈ by appt.

CHARLES FREY Frauenberg 1999★

0.5 ha   4,000   €5-8

The Freys have a biodynamic vineyard at Dambach, a town surrounded by medieval walls. Their Sylvaner, grown on granitic sands, exhales aromas that are delicate, one might almost say restrained. The well-balanced palate develops pleasingly, finishing on a persistent, lively note.

⚲ EARL Charles et Dominique Frey, 4, rue des Ours, 67650 Dambach-la-Ville, tel. 03.88.92.41.04, fax 03.88.92.62.23, e-mail frey.dom.bio@wanadoo.fr ☑ ♈ ev. day except Sun. 9am-12 noon 1.30pm-6pm

JEAN-MARIE HAAG

Vallée Noble Vieilles vignes 1999★

0.5 ha   5,200   €5-8

Soultzmatt is well known both for its mineral water and for its high-quality wines: the former to quench thirst, the latter to delight the senses. This young wine-grower, who started here in 1988, offers a Sylvaner from the Vallée Noble. Typical of the grape variety, it has a subtle bouquet and gradually opens to reveal good balance and suppleness due to its acidity being well absorbed.

⚲ Jean-Marie Haag, 17, rue des Chèvres, 68570 Soultzmatt, tel. 03.89.47.02.38, fax 03.89.47.64.79, e-mail jean-marie.haag@wanadoo.fr ☑ ♈ ev. day 9am-12 noon 2pm-6pm; Sun. and groups by appt.

JEAN HIRTZ ET FILS

Mittelbergheim 1999★

0.3 ha   1,200   €3-5

With its three centuries of history and experience, this family concern was taken over by Edy Hirtz in 1989, and today comprises 7.5 ha (19 acres) of vines. Its Mittelbergheim Sylvaner discloses subtle, yet restrained, aromas. The wine's fullness is

These two varieties are not too hard to cultivate and can produce excellent wines on mediocre soil. The wines are pleasantly fresh as well as having body and suppleness. In ten years the area given over to cultivating these two varieties has practically doubled, from 10% to 18% of the total vineyard.

In the range of Alsace wines, Pinot Blanc ranks just about in the middle, and it can outclass some Rieslings. When it comes to food, it goes well with a great range of dishes, although it is not especially good with cheese or desserts.

more marked on the palate. Its perfect balance continues through a finish of excellent length.
➤ GAEC Jean Hirtz et Fils, 13, rue Rotland, 67140 Mittelbergheim, tel. 03.88.08.47.90, fax 03.88.08.47.90 ☑
Y ev. day 9am–12 noon 1.30pm–7pm

LANDMANN Zellberg 1999★★★
☐ 1 ha 6,000 €5-8

The Landmann estate was established in 1995 by the merger of two family businesses. Since then its headquarters and 17th-century cellar have benefited from complete renovation. These efforts have been amply rewarded by the quality of this Zellberg Sylvaner. Aromas typical of the variety are complemented by notes of pepper and quince. A well-structured and supple wine with subtle, powerful length. Its persistence is the really distinguishing feature.
➤ Armand Landmann, 74, rte du Vin, 67680 Nothalten, tel. 03.88.92.41.12, fax 03.88.92.41.12 ☑ Y by appt.

DOM. DE LA VIEILLE FORGE 1999
☐ 0.15 ha 1,200 €5-8

Located where great-grandfather had his ancient forge, this cellar was created by a young oenologist in 1998. This Sylvaner is therefore one of his second-year wines. Clear-cut, with a slightly reticent nose, it has a fairly round-tasting palate. Though still somewhat closed, the wine should be fully open by the time the *Guide* is published.
➤ SCEA Wiehle, Dom. de la Vieille Forge, 5, rue de Hoen, 68980 Beblenheim, tel. 03.89.86.01.58, fax 03.89.47.86.37 ☑
Y by appt.

PIERRE ARNOLD Auxerrois 1999 €5-8
☐ 0.35 ha 2,500

Lots of Alsatian family estates have been in existence for two or three centuries. This one goes back to 1711. Pierre Arnold tends 6.5 ha (16 acres) of vines. He ages his wines for ten months in oak casks. His Auxerrois has an unambiguous nose with gorgeous fruity immediacy. The wine is balanced, authentic and persistent, with excellent body. A promising wine.
➤ Pierre Arnold, 16, rue de la Paix, 67650 Dambach-la-Ville, tel. 03.88.92.41.70, fax 03.88.92.62.95 ☑ Y ev. day 9am–7pm; Sun. by appt.

A. L. BAUR 1999 €5-8
☐ 0.56 ha 6,000

This Pinot Blanc was grown at Voegtlinshoffen, a belvedere 300 m (980 ft) up overlooking the Alsatian vines and plain. With its pale colour, and honest, fruity nose, plus a palate with medium yet well-balanced length, it is a fairly good representative of the variety. One of its predecessors was a *coup de coeur* in the 1999 edition of the *Guide*.
➤ A. L. Baur, 4, rue Roger-Frémeaux, 68420 Voegtlinshoffen, tel. 03.89.49.30.97, fax 03.89.49.21.37 ☑ by appt.

AIME CARL Roetel Auxerrois 1999 €3-5
☐ n.c. n.c.

This estate, which converted from general agriculture to specialise in vines 50 years or so ago, now enters the *Guide* as the son takes over (1999). His Auxerrois Pinot, with its relatively restrained nose, has a very fruity palate. A well-balanced wine that is very true to the variety.
➤ Alexandre Carl, 2, rue Saint-Sébastien, 67650 Dambach-la-Ville, tel. 03.88.92.60.51, fax 03.88.92.61.52 ☑ Y by appt.

Alsace Pinot or Klevner

Wine labelled with either of these names (the second is the old Alsace name) can be a blend of grape varieties, usually Pinot Blanc Vrai or Auxerrois Blanc.

MICHEL DIETRICH

Auxerrois Cuvée du Printemps 1999★

0.6 ha 4,000

Dambach-la-Ville still has its medieval town walls with ditches and three tower-gatehouses. Its narrow streets are lined with the ancient houses of wine-growers, like that of Michel Dietrich. His Printemps vintage, made from Auxerrois grapes, an earlier variety than Pinot, seems somewhat atypical owing to its aromas of burning. A quietly fruity, full, well-balanced, pleasing wine. Worth trying.

Michel Dietrich, 3, rue des Ours, 67650 Dambach-la-Ville, tel. 03.88.92.41.31, fax 03.88.92.62.88 ✓ ev. day except Sun. 9am–11.30am 1.30pm–7.30pm.

DREYER Eguisheim 1999★★

0.8 ha 6,000 €3-5

The Dreyer family live in the rue de Hautvillers. Eguisheim is reckoned to be the birthplace of Alsatian wine-growing and is twinned with that of Champagne. The producers here offer an excellent Pinot Blanc, as good as its immediate predecessor, which achieved the same rating. Though the nose is reserved at first, this 99 vintage goes on to reveal a gorgeous fruitiness that is honest and well-defined. True to the variety, it already has a full-tasting and agreeably round quality. A very attractive wine, that will go well with white meats served with a sauce.

GAEC Robert Dreyer et Fils, 17, rue de Hautvillers, 68420 Eguisheim, tel. 03.89.23.12.18, fax 03.89.41.61.45 ✓ by appt.

DOM. ANDRE EHRHART 1999

0.35 ha 2,500 €3-5

A family estate with a half-timbered house dating from 1737 in the centre of Wettolsheim, near Colmar. The Jury thought its Pinot Blanc was well made, with its initially reserved yet steadily strengthening aromas. The fruity, pleasingly well-balanced and persistent palate makes it a suitable accompaniment to any meal.

André Ehrhart et Fils, 68, rue Herzog, 68920 Wettolsheim, tel. 03.89.80.66.16, fax 03.89.79.44.20 ✓ ev. day except Sun. 8am–11.30am 2pm–6pm

FRITZ Auxerrois 1999★

0.3 ha 3,000

The vines of Ottrott, which stretch away from beneath the châteaux of Lutzelbourg and Rathsamhausen, constitute one of the preserves of Pinot Noir. Yet this Auxerrois proves that white varieties too can produce some fine wines grown on these *terroirs*. This 99 wine has intense aromas which mingle blackcurrant buds and plums with notes rather like brioche. With its winey palate, this is anything but a run-of-the-mill Pinot Blanc.

Fritz-Schmitt, 1, rue des Châteaux, 67530 Ottrott, tel. 03.88.95.98.06 ✓ by appt.
Schmitt

KIENTZLER Ribeauvillé 1999★

2.5 ha 9,200 €5-8

You will find this cellar out of town, an island in the middle of a sea of vines. Here André Kientzler serenely and meticulously produces wines from the 11 ha (27 acres) of vines that make up his estate. His Pinot Blanc yields intense aromas of ripe fruit. The powerful and unremittingly fruity palate has excellent balance. A pleasing, harmonious wine that will particularly suit white meats.

André Kientzler, 50, rte de Bergheim, 68150 Ribeauvillé, tel. 03.89.73.67.10, fax 03.89.73.35.81 ✓ by appt.

PIERRE KOCH ET FILS

Auxerrois 1999★

0.7 ha 6,000 €3-5

The one-street village of Nothalten has two Renaissance fountains. Pierre and François Koch tend 12 ha (30 acres) of vines nearby. Made from Auxerrois grapes, this 99 wine opens with fruity aromas subtly tinged with spice. The palate echoes this fruitiness, is well balanced and fresh. A well-blended, gulpable wine.

Pierre et François Koch, 2, rte du Vin, 67680 Nothalten, tel. 03.88.92.42.30, fax 03.88.92.62.91 ✓ ev. day 9am–12 noon 1.30pm–6pm

DOM. DE LA SINNE 1999

0.5 ha 4,000 €3-5

This 11-ha (27-acre) estate has converted to biodynamic methods, and now offers a Pinot Blanc with fresh, fruity aromas. The palate is quite well balanced, though slightly perturbed by residual sugar. It has excellent length and finishes with a hint of bitterness.

GAEC Jerome Geschickt et Fils, 1, pl. de la Sinne, 68770 Ammerschwihr, tel. 03.89.47.12.54, fax 03.89.47.44.76, e-mail geschickt@wanadoo.fr ✓ by appt.

FRANCOIS LICHTLE

Hohrain 1999★★★

0.18 ha 1,200 €5-8

Surrounded by vineyards, and dominated by the towers of the three châteaux of Haut Eguisheim, Husseren-les-Châteaux includes the highest point (390 m/1,280 ft) in the Alsatian wine region. No less a landmark is this Pinot Blanc, grown in the clay-sandstone of the Hohrain. Whether it's Pinot Noir or Pinot Blanc, François Lichtlé knows what he's doing with Pinots. Vinified in barrel, as tradition demands, this 99 vintage is

Alsace Pinot or Klevner

EMILE SCHILLINGER 1999 `€3-5`

0.2 ha 2,400

A 12th-century, three-storey belltower overlooks the village of Gueberschwihr and its vines. Here in this charming setting is the Schillinger estate of 5.5 ha (14 acres). Its Pinot Blanc did not elicit huge comment. Light and clear in appearance, somewhat restrained yet in some ways surprising, this wine is above all a pleasure to drink, which, after all, is the main thing.

➤ EARL, Emile Schillinger,
2, rue de la Chapelle, 68420 Gueberschwihr,
tel. 03.89.47.91.59, fax 03.89.47.91.75 ▼
Y by appt.

CAVE FRANCOIS SCHMITT 1999 `€3-5`

0.33 ha 3,000

François Schmitt took over the family smallholding of 3 ha (7 acres) in 1972. He increased the area to 11 ha (27 acres) and, together with his wife and now his son Frédéric, has a dynamic wine-growing estate. His is a model Pinot Blanc. Its golden colour is an invitation to inhale the aromas, which are extremely fruity with exotic, spicy overtones. The palate is both rich and fresh, full, aromatic, and remarkably long. A fine achievement.

➤ Cave François Schmitt, 19, rte de Soultzmatt, 68500 Orschwihr,
tel. 03.89.76.08.45, fax 03.89.76.44.02 ▼
Y by appt.

PIERRE SCHUELLER ET FILS 1999 `€3-5`

0.3 ha 3,300

Over its 150-year existence, this estate has been tended by four generations of wine-makers. Situated at an altitude of 300 m (984 ft), it dominates the Alsace plain. This Pinot Auxerrois is not, as yet, very fruity but is pleasing nonetheless. Although not particularly long-lasting on the palate, it is well-balanced and displays typical varietal nuances.

➤ Dom. Pierre Schueller, 4, rte du Vin, 68420 Husseren-les-Châteaux,
tel. 03.89.49.30.36, fax 03.89.49.30.36 ▼
Y by appt.

SPITZ ET FILS

Auxerrois Sélection 1999★★

0.35 ha 4,400

Dominique and Marie-Claude Spitz have been running an estate of 10 ha (25 acres) since 1983. Their expertise has frequently been praised. Take this Auxerrois. Its fruity citrus and peach bouquet is the result of beautifully ripe grapes. The palate is no less intense, true to type, well balanced, rich and quite winey, with a long-lasting, slightly overripe character that indicates good keeping potential.

➤ Spitz et Fils, 2–4, rte des Vins, 67650 Bienschwiller, tel. 03.88.92.61.20, fax 03.88.92.61.26 ▼ Y by appt.
➤ Dominique et Marie-Claude Spitz

---

a symphony of fruity, spicy notes. On the palate it is fresh, rich and powerful, a well-balanced, harmonious, elegant composition. A surprising wine, worth discovering.

➤ Dom. François Lichtlé, 17, rue des Vignerons, 68420 Husseren-les-Châteaux, tel. 03.89.49.31.34, fax 03.89.49.37.51, e-mail hlichtle@aol.com ▼ Y by appt.

CH. OLLWILLER

Clos de La Tourelle 1999★★

n.c. 10,000

Harvested at the château d'Ollwiller, in the south of the Alsatian wine region, the grapes are vinified and marketed by the Cave Vinicole du Vieil-Armand. This very pleasant 99 is characterised by overripe aromas enhanced by subtle spicy notes. This is the product of excellent fruit: intensely fruity, of course, and well balanced, finishing with a touch of freshness.

➤ Cave vinicole du Vieil-Armand, 3, rte de Cernay, 68360 Soultz-Wuenheim, tel. 03.89.76.73.75, fax 03.89.76.70.75 ▼ Y by appt.

JEAN RAPP Muhlweg Auxerrois 1999 `€5-8`

0.36 ha 1,500

Jean Rapp's family have been wine-growers since 1765. He cultivates 8 ha (20 acres) of vines in the north of the Alsatian wine region. His estate now enters the *Guide* with an Auxerrois imprinted by its 20 months in barrel. Its maturation is evident in the oaky, slightly hazelnut notes discernible when the wine arrives on the palate. The attack has life despite the wine's firm structure. A well-bred, atypical wine which will not leave you indifferent.

➤ Jean Rapp, 1, faubourg des Vosges, 67120 Dorlisheim, tel. 03.88.38.28.43, fax 03.88.38.28.43 ▼ Y by appt.

HUBERT REYSER 1999★★ `€5-8`

1 ha 6,000

This Klevner, from the northern section of the Route des Vins, west of Strasbourg, is full of freshness and ripe fruit. The aromas strengthen on the palate. Despite a hint of liveliness (a sign of youth), this well-made 99 is true to type and pleasant.

➤ EARL Hubert Reyser,
26, rue de la Chapelle, 67520 Nordheim, tel. 03.88.87.76.38, fax 03.88.87.59.67 ▼ Y by appt.

LUCAS ET ANDRE RIEFFEL

Klevner Vieilles vignes 1999 `€5-8`

0.4 ha 3,300

Although restrained, the aromas of this Pinot are pure and fresh, with a slight note of menthol. A pleasing, well-rounded, authentic and gulpable wine. 'The essence of Pinot,' concluded one Jury member.

➤ Lucas et André Rieffel,
11, rue Principale, 67140 Mittelbergheim, tel. 03.88.08.95.48, fax 03.88.08.28.94 ▼ Y by appt.

GERARD STINTZI 1999

1.6 ha 9,000 €5-8

In the last ten years, these growers have rebuilt two cellars, one with barrels, enlarged the property (now 8 ha/20 acres), and the new generation is getting ready to take over. The bouquet of this Pinot is full of fruit, with several developed notes, full, rich and well balanced. 'A typical product of a limestone-clay site,' wrote one taster.
● EARL Gérard Stintzi, 29, rue Principale, 68420 Husseren-les-Châteaux, tel. 03.89.49.30.10, fax 03.89.49.34.99 ▼ by appt.

ANTOINE STOFFEL Auxerrois 1999★★

0.72 ha 5,700 €5-8

This estate of slightly less than 8 ha (20 acres) lies in the heart of the vines of Eguisheim. Antoine Stoffel is loyal to the traditional techniques that he has wielded with expertise for nigh on forty years. What he has achieved with this Auxerrois is a wine with an intense nose of white flowers and a hint of pepper. Fresh and supple as it hits the palate, it opens on notes of (mainly crystal-lised) fruit. The body has vitality and remark-able length.
● Antoine Stoffel, 21, rue de Colmar, 68420 Eguisheim, tel. 03.89.41.32.03, fax 03.89.24.92.07 ▼ ev. day except Sun. 8am–12 noon 2pm–6pm

CAVE DE TURCKHEIM Rotenberg 1999★

2.5 ha 26,000 €5-8

Grown on a limestone-clay soil, this Pinot seems very restrained when first scented. It then steadily opens to evoke a basket of exotic fruits. The full, rich, well-balanced and persis-tent palate finishes on a hint of bitterness.
● Cave de Turckheim, 16, rue des Tuileries, 68230 Turckheim, tel. 03.89.30.23.60, fax 03.89.27.06.25 ▼ by appt.

CHARLES WANTZ Auxerrois 'R' 1999★

1 ha 6,000 €5-8

The wine-merchants Charles Wantz, headed by Erwin Moser and his wife, own a vineyard at Barr. The Auxerrois they offer makes a very pleasant first impression with its notes of fresh fruits. The same aromatic intensity similarly informs the palate, which is long-lasting and has a delightful hint of roundness.
● Charles Wantz, 36, rue Saint-Marc, 67140 Barr, tel. 03.88.08.90.44, fax 03.88.08.54.61, e-mail eliane.moser@fnac.net ▼ by appt.

ZEYSSOLFF Auxerrois 1999

2 ha 12,000 €5-8

Renowned for its Lebküchle (a type of spice loaf), the village of Gertwiller also produces some interesting wines, like this Auxerrois grown on limestone-clay and sandy soils.

Mixing aromas of white peach, honey and stewed fruit, the nose is rich and complex. After a pleasing attack, the wine goes on to display a round, gutsy character in the finish.
● G. Zeyssolff, 156, rte de Strasbourg, 67140 Gertwiller, tel. 03.88.08.91.60, fax 03.88.08.91.60, e-mail yuav.zeyssolff@wanadoo.fr ▼ by appt.

Alsace Riesling

Riesling is *the* grape variety of the Rhineland, and the Rhine valley is where it originated and flourished. It matures later than other varieties in the region and can be relied on to produce both quality and quantity. About 22% of the Alsace vineyard is planted with Riesling.

The Alsace Riesling is made in a dry style compared with the sweeter German Rieslings. Typically, there is a harmonious balance between its delicately fruity bouquet, good body and finely pronounced acidity. To fulfil its promise it must come from a sunny, sheltered *terroir*.

Riesling is planted in many other wine-growing countries, and there are at least ten other varieties that carry the Riesling name. Unless you specify Riesling Rhénan, the wines can be disappointing. On the gastronomic front, Riesling is particularly good when it is drunk with fish dishes, seafood and, naturally enough, a good Alsace sauerkraut or, alternatively, *coq au Riesling*. When the late-harvested grapes do not contain sufficient sugar, they are used as blending wines for *vins blancs liquoreux*.

ALLIMANT-LAUGNER 1999

2.6 ha 21,000 €5-8

Located on the edge of the Haut-Rhin *département*, Orschwiller is one of a string of villages below the Haut-Koenigsbourg. Hubert Laugner took over the family estate in 1984 and tends some 11 ha (27 acres) of vines. His Riesling has a restrained, subtle note, opening onto white

Alsace Riesling

peach and exotic fruits. Though the finish is slightly disappointing, the wine's good balance and fruit aromas provide interest. (Residual sugar: 5 g/l.)
- Allimant-Laugner, 10, Grand-Rue, 67600 Orschwiller, tel. 03.88.92.06.52, fax 03.88.82.76.38, e-mail alaugner@terre-net.fr  ev. day except Sun. 8am–7pm
- Hubert Laugner

DOM. YVES AMBERG
Damgraben Vieilles vignes 1999 · 1 ha · 5,000 · €5-8

Yves Amberg is unstinting both among his vines and in his cellar. His production is regularly applauded and sometimes takes away the prizes. His 1998 Damgraben Riesling was especially appreciated. The 99 version has a fine lemony nuance with a slightly mineral hint. The palate is a well-balanced continuation of the same characteristics, marrying the variety's typical freshness with an agreeable suppleness. (Residual sugar: 6 g/l.)
- Yves Amberg, 19, rue Frohholz, 67680 Epfig, tel. 03.88.85.51.28, fax 03.88.85.52.71 by appt.

COMTE D'ANDLAU-HOMBOURG 1999★
n.c. · 4,000 · €5-8

This wine estate, a property of the counts of Andlau-Hombourg, dates from the 12th century. The guiding principle of this Riesling is freshness. It is a well-balanced, exceedingly subtle wine, whose success lies in its fruity character. White peach and citrus notes give it class and elegance. (Residual sugar: 3.4 g/l.)
- Comtes d'Andlau-Hombourg, Château d'Ittenwiller, 67140 Saint-Pierre, tel. 03.88.08.13.30, fax 03.88.08.13.30 by appt.

MARC ANSTOTZ
Cuvée Catherine 1999★★ · 0.6 ha · 1,800

and accompany the lengthy finish. (Residual sugar: 12 g/l.)
- EARL Anstotz et Fils, 51, rue Balbach, 67310 Balbronn, tel. 03.88.50.30.55, fax 03.88.50.58.06 by appt.
- Marc Anstotz

LEON BAUR Elisabeth Stumpf 1999
1.2 ha · 10,000 · €5-8

The medieval township of Eguisheim, one of the places in which Alsatian wine-growing began, surrounds its château in three concentric circles. Rue du Rempart-Nord, in the northern part of the town, contains the headquarters of this family concern. Its Elisabeth Stumpf vintage, with its delicate, fruity aromas typified by grapefruit and pineapple, has a light body combining suppleness and freshness. (Residual sugar: 7 g/l.)
- Jean-Louis Baur, 22, rue du Rempart-Nord, 68420 Eguisheim, tel. 03.89.41.79.13, fax 03.89.41.93.72 by appt.

BESTHEIM Rebgarten 1999★
12 ha · 120,000 · €5-8

'Rebgarten' means 'vine garden'. The place-names containing the word are legion in Alsace. This particular one is located on a granitic soil, which finds its somewhat restrained floral and mineral expression in this Riesling. Though not hugely complex, this is a very authentic, well-balanced, spirited and subtle wine, both classic and full of promise. (Residual sugar: 10 g/l.)
- Cave de Bestheim-Bennwihr, 3, rue du Gal-de-Gaulle, 68630 Bennwihr, tel. 03.89.49.09.29, fax 03.89.49.09.20, e-mail bestheim@gofornet.com by appt.

JOSEPH CATTIN 1999★
6 ha · 48,000 · €5-8

The brothers Jacques and Jean-Marie Cattin have headed this estate since 1978. Their grandfather, Joseph, was a talented wine-grower. This Riesling, with its intense nose of white flowers and yellow fruits, has an excellent structure poised between roundness and freshness. It has a very long finish. A generous wine, typical of Alsace. (Residual sugar: 5 g/l.)
- Joseph Cattin, 18, rue Roger-Frémeaux, 68420 Voegtlinshoffen, tel. 03.89.49.30.21, fax 03.89.49.26.02, e-mail geattin@terre-net.fr ev. day 8am–12 noon 2pm–6pm; Sun. by appt.

DOM. VITICOLE DE LA VILLE DE COLMAR 1999
1.17 ha · 9,000 · €5-8

The city of Colmar's own wine estate took over from the Institut Oberlin, a research centre that opened in 1895. It covers 24 ha (59 acres) and is the pride of the capital of Alsatian wine-growing. This Riesling is extremely expressive, having a peach and cherry-plum fruitiness which increases when the wine is left to breathe. The body is

Balbronn, west of Strasbourg, deserves a visit as much for its fortified Romanesque church as for this estate, whose cellar contains both ancient carved tuns and this remarkable vintage, sadly a limited edition. Grown on limestone-clay soil with gypsum, this Riesling is highly redolent of slightly overripe citrus, a characteristic which also informs the palate. After a lively attack, the wine displays very good balance. The citrus nuances strengthen

excellent. Dense and rich, perhaps a little oversweet, but oozing with aromas, it moves to a finish of welcome freshness which contributes to its length. (Residual sugar: 4.8 g/l.)

🛒 Dom. viticole de la ville de Colmar, 2, rue Stauffen, 68000 Colmar, tel. 03.89.79.11.87, fax 03.89.80.38.66, e-mail cave@domaineviticoledecolmar.fr ☑ ev. day 8am–12 noon 2pm–6pm; groups by appt. cl. Aug.

MICHEL DIETRICH
Cuvée Lanzenberg

1.5 ha   8,000   €5-8

Cuvée Lanzenberg 1999★★

This Lanzenberg vintage remains closed at first, then releases a hint of pepper on opening onto a whole range of citrus fruits (mainly grapefruit and lemon) with, last of all, the merest mineral hint, which continues on the palate. The body is richly structured and overlain with a somewhat lively freshness. A lovely wine. (Residual sugar: 3.7 g/l.)

🛒 Michel Dietrich, 3, rue des Ours, 67650 Dambach-la-Ville, tel. 03.88.92.41.31, fax 03.88.92.62.88 ☑ ev. day except Sun. 9am–11.30am 1.30pm–7.30pm

HENRI EHRHART
Kaefferkopf d'Ammerschwihr

0.85 ha   4,200   €5-8

Kaefferkopf d'Ammerschwihr 1999★

The township of Ammerschwihr, which flourished in the 16th century, has kept its fortified elements: ramparts, high gate (13th-century), the Tour des Voleurs and Tour des Bourgeois. Today, its chief concern is the defence and promotion of its Kaefferkopf wines, such as this beautiful Riesling. Very fruity, a little overripe, set off by a mineral touch, this 99 wine reflects the granitic *terroir* from which it comes. Lively and fairly round, it impresses with its fullness and balance. (Residual sugar: 7 g/l.)

🛒 Henri Ehrhart, quartier des Fleurs, 68770 Ammerschwihr, tel. 03.89.78.23.74, fax 03.89.47.32.59 ☑ by appt.

DAVID ERMEL
Réserve particulière 1999

0.8 ha   7,500   €5-8

The famous fortified church at Hunawihr features on the label of this Riesling. The nose is subtle, expressive and essentially fruity, the palate has an average structure, supple at first, then turning quite lively and fresh. A down-to-earth Riesling, made by a family concern with 12 ha (30 acres). (Residual sugar: 4 g/l.)

🛒 David Ermel, 30, rte de Ribeauvillé, 68150 Hunawihr, tel. 03.89.73.61.71, fax 03.89.73.32.56 ☑ by appt.

ANDRE FALLER
Cuvée Julien 1999★★

0.15 ha   1,200   €8-11

A former Roman road crosses the charming village of Ittersviller, known equally for its wine and gastronomic prowess. This Riesling, grown on sandy-pebbly soil, strongly expresses the fruitiness of the variety and has characteristic mineral overtones. The palate is honest and fresh, fruity, authentic and well-balanced. (Residual sugar: 11 g/l.)

🛒 André Faller, 2, rte du Vin, 67140 Ittersviller, tel. 03.88.85.51.13, e-mail info@vins-faller.com ☑ ☑ by appt.

ROBERT FALLER ET FILS
Cuvée Bénédicte 1999★★

0.35 ha   3,000   €5-8

This wine, highly prized by the Jury, is named after Jean-Baptiste Faller's daughter, who took over the family estate in 1996 (12 ha/30 acres on the sunny *terroirs* of Ribeauvillé). The appeal of its complex aromatic range is immediate; aromas of white flowers mingle with fruity and mineral notes. The attack is full, almost explosive; the palate is both powerful and lively, having an intense fruitiness with balsamic nuances which prolong the pleasure of the bouquet. The balance and superb length of this remarkable wine is sustained by its freshness. (Residual sugar: 4 g/l.)

🛒 Robert Faller et Fils, 36, Grand-Rue, 68150 Ribeauvillé, tel. 03.89.73.60.47, fax 03.89.73.34.80, e-mail sarlfaller@aol.com ☑ ☑ by appt.

MARCEL FREYBURGER
Kaefferkopf 1999

n.c.   1,700   €5-8

This concern, established in 1951 by Sébastien Freyburger, today comprises 5 ha (12 acres) of vines; Christophe Freyburger has been in charge since 1994. This Riesling starts quietly, then opens onto a fresh fruitiness which has a slightly herbaceous quality. The palate is well balanced, but the wine needs time for the remaining sugar to blend in. (Residual sugar: 8 g/l.)

🛒 Marcel Freyburger, 13, Grand-Rue, 68770 Ammerschwihr, tel. 03.89.78.25.72, fax 03.89.78.15.50 ☑ ev. day 9am–12 noon 2pm–6pm; Sun. by appt.
🛒 Christophe Freyburger

FREY-SOHLER
Instant douceur Vendanges tardives 1998★★

0.9 ha   4,000   €15-23

Scherwiller is among the earliest centres of Riesling. Its alluvial gravelly soils are ideal for this grape variety, which is then able to achieve its full potential. The bright colour of this wine has golden glints; its aromas are of citrus and exotic fruits with nuances of lilac flowers and lily of the valley, the palate is smooth and rich, very supple and powerful. The elegant finish ends with a touch of crystallised citrus fruit.

➤ Frey-Sohler, 72, rue de l'Ortenbourg, 67750 Scherwiller, tel. 03.88.92.10.13, fax 03.88.82.57.11, e-mail freysohl@terre-net.fr ▼ ev. day 8am–12 noon 1.15pm–7pm; Sun. by appt.
● Sohler Frères

LUCIEN GANTZER 1999★

0.7 ha 5,000 €5-8

It is worth making a detour between Colmar and Rouffach to visit Gueberschwihr with its splendid Romanesque church tower. The Lucien Gantzer Estate cellar is in a picturesque street close to the lovely village square. The founder's eldest son took charge of this 5-ha (12-acre) estate in 1997. His golden Riesling exudes captivating aromas of crystallised fruits. Its richness and fullness combine with a subtle freshness to create a coherent, high-class product. (Residual sugar: 8 g/l.)

➤ SCEA Lucien Gantzer, 9, rue du Nord, 68420 Gueberschwihr, tel. 03.89.49.31.81, fax 03.89.49.23.34 ▼ by appt.

MICHEL GOETTELMANN 1999★

0.14 ha 1,600 €5-8

Michel Goettelmann took charge of this family concern in 1991. He makes wine from all the Alsatian varieties and has been selling direct since 1994. His Riesling is of the 'citrus' type, with the odd note of peach and a mineral nuance. A high-class, pleasing and well-balanced wine that finishes on a delightful note of lemony freshness.

➤ Michel Goettelmann,
27 A, rue des Goumiers, 67730 Châtenois, tel. 03.88.82.12.40, fax 03.88.82.12.40, e-mail mgoettelmann@wanadoo.fr ▼ ev. day 8am–12 noon 1pm–7pm

JOSEPH GSELL
Cuvée Modeste Gsell 1999

n.c. 2,000 €8-11

From its headquarters in a 300-year-old house, Joseph Gell has run the family estate since 1978. Grown on limestone-clay soil, this vintage is distinguished by its fullness, evident not simply by its fullness, evident not simply in the nose's excellent body. The wine is characterised however by warmth rather than freshness. The finish has a hint of bitterness. (Residual sugar: 8 g/l.)

➤ Joseph Gsell, 26, Grand-Rue, 68500 Orschwihr, tel. 03.89.76.95.11, fax 03.89.76.20.54 ▼ ev. day except Sun. 9am–7pm

DOM. GUNTZ
Ortenberg Cuvée Mathéus 1999★★

0.22 ha 1,600 €8-11

The label says it all: this estate, at Scherwiller, below the château de l'Ortenbourg, has seen 11 generations of winegrowers (the latest has been there since 1993). Experience and meticulous work have combined to produce this fine Riesling. Golden in colour, the wine opens with scents of lemon, nuances of overripe, almost crystallised fruits, and a hint of honey. The body is excellent, if aromatically still somewhat restrained. In a year or two the wine's fruitiness will come through more strongly. (Residual sugar: 23 g/l.)

➤ Christophe Guntz, 27, rue de Dambach, 67750 Scherwiller, tel. 03.88.58.30.30, fax 03.88.82.70.77 ▼ ev. day 8am–7pm; Sun. by appt.

ANDRE HARTMANN
Armoirie Hartmann 1999★

0.7 ha n.c. €8-11

Like a balcony overlooking the Alsace plain, the village of Voegtlinshoffen dominates a sea of vines. The Hartmann family has been established here since the 17th century. Its Armoirie Riesling is often praised. The 99 version has a subtle nose with restrained fruit aromas and an expressive palate with a fresh, pleasing balance. It will gain in assertiveness in the coming months. (Residual sugar: 10 g/l.)

➤ André Hartmann, 11, rue Roger-Frémeaux, 68420 Voegtlinshoffen, tel. 03.89.49.38.34, fax 03.89.49.26.18 ▼ ev. day except Sun. 9am–12 noon 2pm–6pm

HERTZOG Tradition 1999★

0.3 ha 3,500 €5-8

The earliest documents referring to winegrowing at Obermorschwihr are from the tenth century, when the vicus Morswilare (village of Morschwihr) was granted to the monastery of Saint Thomas by the bishop of Strasbourg. In the 15th century, the nearby abbey of Marbach had vast, prestigious vineyards. This very successful Riesling continues the tradition of bringing out the qualities of this terroir. Grown on limestone-clay, it exhales subtle fruit aromas with hints of peach and pear. A delicate, quite lemony freshness provides an elegant balance, and the well-balanced palate culminates in a long finish.

➤ EARL Sylvain Hertzog, 18, rte du Vin, 68420 Obermorschwihr, tel. 03.89.49.31.93, fax 03.89.49.28.85 ▼ ev. day 9am–7pm; Sun. by appt.

HUBER ET BLEGER
Schlossreben 1999

0.8 ha 8,000 €5-8

This estate of 16 ha (40 acres) has been run since 1977 by two brothers, Claude and Marc Huber. The local name, 'Schlosssreben', meaning 'castle vines', refers to the Haut-Koenigsbourg château, one of France's most-visited monuments, only several miles from Saint-Hippolyte. This terroir has produced a wine with a nose of average intensity, but containing interesting notes of pear and peach. Its freshness, length and a degree of fullness reflect the good quality of the grapes used. (Residual sugar: 8 g/l.)

➼ SCEA Huber et Bléger, 6, rte du Vin, 68590 Saint-Hippolyte, tel. 03.89.73.01.12, fax 03.89.73.00.81, e-mail huber.bleger@online.fr [V] [Y] ev. day 8am–12 noon 1.30pm–6.30pm

JACQUES ILTIS Schlossreben 1999★

0.35 ha 2,500 €5-8

Located at the foot of the Haut-Koenigsbourg, this 8.5-ha (21-acre) estate is tended by Christophe and Benoît, the sons of Jacques Iltis. The cellar contains oak casks bequeathed by their cooper ancestors. Oak is the medium in which this Riesling has developed; its charming aromas of white flowers and citrus (grapefruit) reflect the granitic soil in which the grapes were grown. These aromas reappear on the initially fresh palate. A well-balanced wine, with a hint of warmth, finishing on mineral notes. (Residual sugar: 5 g/l.)

➼ Jacques Iltis et Fils, 1, rue Schlossreben, 68590 Saint-Hippolyte, tel. 03.89.73.00.67, fax 03.89.73.01.82 [V] [Y] ev. day 8am–12 noon 2pm–6pm; Sun. by appt.

ROGER JUNG ET FILS Riquewihr 1999★

0.4 ha 3,500 €5-8

Rémy and Jacques Jung took over this 15-ha (37-acre) estate from their father Roger in 1989; it is located at Riquewihr, one of the most-visited wine-growing towns in Alsace. They aim for good quality, and have achieved it with this 99 wine. It is a fruity Riesling with spicy notes, reflected both in the nose and on the palate. First impressions on the palate are supple, leading to a pleasing fullness and freshness which guarantee a long finish. (Residual sugar: 4.5 g/l.)

➼ SARL Roger Jung et Fils, 23, rue de la 1ʳᵉ Armée, 68340 Riquewihr, tel. 03.89.47.92.17, fax 03.89.47.87.63, e-mail rjung@terre-net.fr [V] [Y] by appt.

HENRI KLEE Vieilles vignes 1999

1.3 ha 7,800 €5-8

Philippe Klee has been in charge of this concern since 1985, representing the ninth generation of a family which has made wine since 1624. His Riesling, produced from old vines, has an interesting nose of overripe notes (honey and wax). The wine strengthens on the palate with a good, intense, mouth-filling yet elegant body. The slightly supple finish is a sign to wait a year or two before drinking. ((Residual sugar: 6 g/l.)

➼ EARL Henri Klee et Fils, 11, Grand-Rue, 68230 Katzenthal, tel. 03.89.27.03.81, fax 03.89.27.28.17 [V] [Y] by appt.

KOEHLY Hahnenberg 1999

0.42 ha 2,000

Kintzheim is near Sélestat, on the road to the Haut-Koenigsbourg. Jean-Marie Koehly has headed this 15-ha (37-acre) vineyard since 1976. The Hahnenberg, a sandy-gravelly terroir, has left its mark on this Riesling. Its aromatic complexity mixes scents of flowers and fruit (apricot) with notes of overripeness and mineral nuances (gunflint). The wine's residual sugar is not yet sufficiently blended, indicating that some time needs to elapse for the wine to achieve better balance. (Residual sugar: 10 g/l.)

➼ Jean-Marie Koehly, 64, rue du Gal-de-Gaulle, 67600 Kientzheim, tel. 03.88.82.09.77, fax 03.88.82.09.77 [V] [Y] ev. day 8am–12 noon 1pm–7pm; cl. 20 Dec.–5 Jan.

JACQUES LINDENLAUB Stierkopf 1999

0.65 ha 4,600 €5-8

There is plenty for visitors to see in the village of Dorlisheim, near Molsheim: a Romanesque church, a well and Renaissance houses, not forgetting the ruins of the commandery of the Order of Saint John. A wine-growers' track takes the visitor through the vines to see the work of this vineyard. Grown on limestone-clay, its Riesling has restrained, subtle aromas which strengthen on the palate together with lemony nuances. The attack is supple, but is followed by a surge of liveliness and a fairly long finish. (Residual sugar: 8 g/l.)

➼ Jacques Lindenlaub, 6, ffg des Vosges, 67120 Dorlisheim, tel. 03.88.38.21.78, fax 03.88.38.55.38 [Y] by appt.

JEROME LORENTZ Réserve 1999★★

3 ha 20,000 €8-11

This well-respected wine-trading business also has its own estate (32 ha/79 acres of vines), its Réserve wine, grown on limestone-clay, exhales very intense fruit aromas. The same intensity is found on the palate, where the wine has power, dryness and depth, leading to an agreeable, persistent finish. (Residual sugar: 6 g/l.)

➼ Jérôme Lorentz, 1–3, rue des Vignerons, 68750 Bergheim, tel. 03.89.73.22.22, fax 03.89.73.30.49, e-mail lorentz@vins-lorentz.com [V] [Y] ev. day except Sun. 10am–12 noon 2pm–6.30pm
➼ Charles Lorentz

ANDRE MAULER Burgreben 1999★

0.34 ha 2,800 €5-8

Burgreben or 'castle-vines' is the name of this place, where the vineyard goes back to the early Middle Ages. The Mauler family have been here for four generations. They offer a Riesling whose nose is still restrained, opening on floral notes. The palate has good structure, with a mineral tendency. A promising, thoroughbred wine. (Residual sugar: 0.7 g/l.)

➼ André Mauler et successeurs, 3, rue Jean-Macé, 68980 Beblenheim, tel. 03.89.47.90.50, fax 03.89.47.80.08, e-mail c.mauler@caramail.com [V] [Y] by appt.

Alsace Riesling

METZ-GEIGER 1999★

☐   0.47 ha   2,900   ■   €3-5

This Riesling is from Epfig, the big wine-making village whose attractions include the Romanesque chapel of Sainte-Marguérite, situated away from the rest of the commune towards the plain. Grown on sandy clay, it has an intense nose of lemon and mint, with mineral nuances. It is lively, honest, and very fresh. Its acidity gives it great length and makes it a good accompaniment to fish. (Residual sugar: 5 g/l.)

☛ Metz-Geiger, 9, rue Fronholz, 67680 Epfig, tel. 03.88.85.55.21, fax 03.85.55.21 ☑ ⓨ by appt.

DENIS MEYER

Vendanges tardives 1998★★

☐   0.24 ha   1,100   ▥ €11-15

An ancient family of wine-growers established at Voegtlinshoffen since 1761 offers this intensely yellow wine, grown on a *terroir* of conchiferous limestone. The nose is full, subtle and rich, revealing above all aromas of crystallised fruit (apricot and citrus). The palate's balance and lingering finish are remarkable. The citrus aromas give this wine an unmatched subtlety. (Half-litre bottles.)

☛ Denis Meyer, 2, rte du Vin, 68420 Voegtlinshoffen, tel. 03.89.49.38.00, fax 03.89.49.26.52 ☑ ⓨ by appt.

MEYER-FONNE Kaefferkopf 1999★

☐   0.13 ha   900   ▥ €11-15

The 63-ha (156-acre) Kaefferkopf, a clayey-limestone-sandstone *terroir*, was officially recognised in 1932, though not as a grand cru. This Riesling makes its mark with its aromas of citrus and white flowers. The silky palate is full of fruits; its supple acidity and power make it a thoroughbred wine which will improve in quality in two to three years' time. (Residual sugar: 5 g/l.)

☛ Meyer-Fonné, 24, Grand-Rue, 68230 Katzenthal, tel. 03.89.27.16.50, fax 03.89.27.34.17 ☑ ⓨ by appt.

☛ François et Félix Meyer

JOS. MOELLINGER ET FILS

Sélection 1999

☐   0.75 ha   8,000   ■ €5-8

Joseph Moellinger marketed his first wines in 1945. Today, this 14-ha (35-acre) family estate near Colmar is run by his grandson Michel. His Sélection Riesling is immediately appealing. The nose is warm with smoky, brioche-style aromas; the attack is pleasing and on the soft side, leading to a straightforward acid freshness with notes of citrus and flowers. The finish is still a little unripe, but will improve in time. (Residual sugar: 6.3 g/l.)

☛ SCEA Jos. Moellinger et Fils, 6, rue de la 5ᵉ -D.-B., 68920 Wettolsheim, tel. 03.89.80.62.02, fax 03.89.80.04.94 ☑ ⓨ ev. day 8am–12 noon 1.30pm–7pm; cl. Oct.

FRANCIS MURE 1999★

☐   0.4 ha   2,500   ■ €5-8

The pulsatilla anemones, which herald spring on the heights of Westhalten, decorate the label of this light-golden Riesling. Though the nose still seems a little closed, it nonetheless has promise. Only on the palate does its full character come through in its fresh attack, good balance and great length. This 99 vintage will be ready in 2003. (Residual sugar: 2 g/l.)

☛ Francis Muré, 30, rue de Rouffach, 68250 Westhalten, tel. 03.89.47.64.20, fax 03.89.47.09.39 ☑ ⓨ by appt.

CAVE VINICOLE D'ORSCHWILLER-KINTZHEIM

Les Faîtières 1999

☐   n.c.   1,250,000   ■ €5-8

This co-operative, at the foot of the Haut-Koenigsbourg, offers a most honourable, impressively mouth-filling Riesling of medium length. With a little more freshness, it would have won a star. The palate's acidity blends with a fleshy quality and a certain roundness associated with notes of crystallised fruits. The intense nose of extremely ripe fruits is very attractive. (Residual sugar: 5 g/l.)

☛ Cave vinicole d'Orschwiller-Kintzheim, rte du Vin, BP 2, 67600 Orschwiller, tel. 03.88.92.09.87, fax 03.88.82.30.92 ☑ ⓨ by appt.

OTTER Sélection de grains nobles 1998★

☐   0.8 ha   2,000   ▥ ⓞ €30-38

This Riesling comes from a limestone *terroir*, which has influenced its flavour. Golden-yellow in colour, it has an extremely subtle nose dominated by aromas of overripe citrus. Light notes of grilling accompany the full, rich body. The fresh finish contains hints of crystallised citrus. A wine with a good future.

☛ Dom. François Otter et Fils, 4, rue du Muscat, 68420 Hattstatt, tel. 03.89.49.33.00, fax 03.89.49.38.69, e-mail ottjef@nucleus.fr ☑ ⓨ by appt.

VIGNOBLES REINHART

Sélection de grains nobles 1998★

☐   0.4 ha   2,500   ▥ €23-30

This Grains Nobles Sélection Riesling is made from juice containing more than 256 g/l of sugar. It has remarkably preserved the character of the grape variety, despite the use of noble rot. The colour of this 98 wine is an intense egg-yolk yellow, almost old gold. The bouquet has aromas of crystallised fruits, honey and peach, set off by complex mineral notes. The palate is both round and rich, with good freshness. A successful, well-balanced wine. (Half-litre bottles.)

☛ Pierre Reinhart, 7, rue du Printemps, 68500 Orschwihr, tel. 03.89.76.95.12, fax 03.89.74.84.08 ☑ ⓨ by appt.

PIERRE ET JEAN-PIERRE RIETSCH Stein 1999★

☐   0.46 ha   5,000   ▥ €5-8

Mittelbergheim is ranked among the hundred prettiest villages in France. The Rietsch family, who are wine-growers here, are regularly praised for the quality of their Rieslings and the originality of their labels. This 99 wine has complex and subtle aromas and a well-balanced palate. A most agreeable product which will be ready to drink in summer 2002. (Residual sugar: 9.2 g/l.)

☛ Pierre et Jean-Pierre Rietsch, 32, rue Principale, 67140 Mittelbergheim, tel. 03.88.08.00.64, fax 03.88.08.40.91, e-mail rietsch@wanadoo.fr ☑ ☖ by appt.

LA CAVE DU ROI DAGOBERT

Riesling de Wolxheim 1999

☐   2 ha   20,666   ▮▮ €5-8

The name of this cellar reminds us that the most famous of the Merovingian kings had vineyards in the northern part of the Alsatian wine region. Light yellow in the glass, this Riesling is still closed, but there are signs of rich, complex aromas emerging. There is good body and freshness through to the finish, but it will improve if left for a year or two. (Residual sugar: 6 g/l.)

☛ La cave du Roi Dagobert, 1, rue de Scharrachbergheim, 67310 Traenheim, tel. 03.88.50.69.00, fax 03.88.50.69.09, e-mail dagobert@cave-dagobert.com ☑ ☖ ev. day 8am–12 noon 2pm–6pm

RUHLMANN Cristal Granit 'S' 1999

☐   1 ha   6,600   ▮ €5-8

This estate, established in 1688, has greatly expanded over the last two decades, as much in area (now 17 ha/42 acres) as in exports. It offers a vintage from the Schlossberg, a granitic locality in Dambach (not to be confused with the grand cru of the same name in the Haut-Rhin *département*). A wine with notes of honeysuckle and rose, which reflect its *terroir*. The fresh, well-balanced and distinguished palate is characteristic of the variety. (Residual sugar: 2 g/l.)

☛ Ruhlmann, 34, rue du Mal-Foch, 67650 Dambach-la-Ville, tel. 03.88.92.41.86, fax 03.88.92.61.81 ☑ ☖ ev. day except Sun. 8am–12 noon 1.30pm–7pm

RUHLMANN-DIRRINGER

Cuvée réservée 1999★

☐   1.2 ha   10,000   ▮ €5-8

Hard by the fortified walls of Dambach, this property will interest lovers of good wines and of old buildings alike, for this 99 Riesling can be sampled beneath the ribbed vaults of its cellar dating from 1578. The bouquet's notes of citrus and crystallised fruits reappear on the palate along with a good freshness. A well-blended, authentic wine. (Residual sugar: 4 g/l.)

☛ Ruhlmann-Dirringer, 3, rue de Mullenheim, 67650 Dambach-la-Ville, tel. 03.88.92.40.28, fax 03.88.92.48.05 ☑

CLOS SAINTE-APOLLINE

Bollenberg Tradition 1999

☐   1.5 ha   5,000   ▥ €5-8

Established in 1887, the Bollenberg estate bears the name of a limestone-clay *terroir* typical of the wine-growing hills of southern Alsace. Its Tradition vintage has a nose of slight overripeness, with notes of ripe and crystallised fruit. A supple attack is followed by a balance which is already as it should be but will nevertheless improve still further if kept for a year or two. (Residual sugar: 2 g/l.)

☛ Clos Sainte-Apolline, Dom. du Bollenberg, 68250 Westhalten, tel. 03.89.49.67.10, fax 03.89.49.76.16, e-mail info@bollenberg.com ☑ ☖ ev. day 8am–8pm

SCHAEFFER-WOERLY

Clos du Bernstein 1999

☐   n.c.   1,700   ▮ €8-11

Vincent Woerly has run his family's 7-ha (17-acre) estate since 1987. The Clos du Bernstein Riesling produced by this granitic *terroir* is a subtle wine with a restrained bouquet which should open out over the coming months. After a fresh, not to say lively, attack, the excellent structure makes itself felt. The finish is pleasant and long. Wait a little while before opening. (Residual sugar: 12 g/l.)

☛ Schaeffer-Woerly, 3, pl. du Marché, 67650 Dambach-la-Ville, tel. 03.88.92.40.81, fax 03.88.92.49.87 ☑ ☖ ev. day 9am–12 noon 2pm–6pm by appt.

JEAN-PAUL SCHMITT

Rittersberg 1999

☐   1.5 ha   9,000   ▮ €8-11

The castle of Ortenbourg, stronghold of Rudolf of Habsburg in the 13th century, still impressively guards the entrance to the Val de Ville. In 1525 it provided the backdrop to the bloody epilogue to the Peasants' War a decisive episode in the Reformation. Today, on its slopes, Jean-Paul Schmitt grows 8 ha (20 acres) of vines acquired by his family in 1927. His Rittersberg vintage, which is aromatically still somewhat reserved, leaves an impression of freshness. The palate is subtle but strong, with notes of citrus, a tiny hint of bitterness and a long, interesting finish. (Residual sugar: 7 g/l.)

☛ Jean-Paul Schmitt, Hühnelmühle, 67750 Scherwiller, tel. 03.88.82.34.74, fax 03.88.82.33.95, e-mail vins.j.pschmitt@wanadoo.fr ☑ ☖ ev. day 10am–12 noon 1pm–6pm; Sun. 2pm–7pm; cl. 15 until 30 Jan.

SCHOENHEITZ Holder 1999

☐   0.3 ha   1,800   ▮ €5-8

Wihr-au-Val is located at the entrance to the vallée de Munster, which extends into the Vosges uplands. The Schoenheitz family have been here since the end of the 17th century.

☖ ev. day except Sun. 9am–11.45am 1.30pm–6.30pm

They have put new life into some interesting terrains, such as the Holder, the granitic *terroir* that produced this Riesling. A pleasing wine strongly redolent of flowers and spices, it has good balance and a fresh finish. (Residual sugar: 2 g/l.)

➤ Henri Schoenheitz, 1, rue de Walbach, 68230 Wihr-au-Val, tel. 03.89.71.03.96, fax 03.89.71.14.33 ◪ Ⴜ by appt.

JEAN-VICTOR SCHUTZ
Vieilles vignes 1999

□ 1.5 ha 7,000 ▪ ♦ €5-8

This wine-merchant, established in 1997, sells 95% of its wines outside France, particularly in The Netherlands, Belgium and Denmark. Pale yellow in appearance and slightly effervescent, this Riesling is averagely aromatic with some plant-like notes. Hints of citrus appear on the palate in a lively attack, along with a rounded, fresh flavour which will mature further in time. (Residual sugar: 13 g/l.)

➤ Jean-Victor Schutz, 34, rue du Mal.-Foch, 67650 Dambach-la-Ville, tel. 03.88.92.41.86, fax 03.88.92.61.81 Ⴜ by appt.

E. SPANNAGEL ET FILS
Côtes de Kientzheim Kirrenburg 1999

□ 0.08 ha 800 ▪ ♦ €5-8

Rémy Spannagel has been tending his family's estate near Colmar since 1995. All his vines are planted on slopes with granitic soils. The golden yellow of his Kirrenburg Riesling is a pointer to its excellent character. Here are aromas of overripe and dried fruits, a palate with good balance, slightly marked by alcohol, and a rich structure. It should mature fairly quickly. (Sucres résiduels: 5 g/l.)

➤ Eugène Spannagel et Fils, 11, rue de Cussac, 68240 Sigolsheim, tel. 03.89.78.25.90, fax 03.89.78.25.90, e-mail remy.spannagel@free.fr ◪ by appt.

ANDRE STENTZ Rosenberg 1999

□ 0.75 ha 4,000 ▪ ♦ €8-11

André Stentz's vineyard is in a commune near Colmar and dates from the 17th century. It went organic in the early 1980s. This Riesling has a fruity, subtle and elegant nose, but is more expressive on the palate. It is well balanced and finishes on a very slight note of roundness. (Residual sugar: 10 g/l.)

➤ André Stentz, 2, rue de la Batteuse, 68920 Wettolsheim, tel. 03.89.80.64.91, fax 03.89.79.59.75 ◪ Ⴜ by appt.

MICHELE ET JEAN-LUC STOECKLE Cuvée réservée 1999★

□ 1 ha 6,000 ▪ ♦ €5-8

For the last 20 years, Michèle and Jean-Luc Stoecklé have tended 6.5 ha (16 acres) of vines around Katzenthal, near Colmar. Their Cuvée Réservée, grown on granitic soil, betrays its origins. The aromas of flowers, liquorice and spices signal a high-quality product. A fresh, powerful wine, which shows its class in a beautiful finish.

➤ Michèle et Jean-Luc Stoecklé, 9, Grand-Rue, 68230 Katzenthal, tel. 03.89.27.05.08, fax 03.89.27.33.61 ◪ Ⴜ ev. day except Sun. afternoon 8am–12 noon 1pm–7pm

DOM. STOEFFLER
Kronenbourg 1999★

□ 0.5 ha 3,000 ▪ ♦ €5-8

In 1988, Martine and Vincent Stoeffler threw in their lot with each other, amalgamated their vineyards (around Barr and Ribeauvillé respectively) and wine-making expertise to form an estate of about 12 ha (30 acres). For more than ten years now, their commitment to quality has been bearing fruit, as this 99 vintage from the Kronenbourg shows. It immediately releases aromas of citrus and honey. The palate has lovely hints of well-ripened grapes in tune with a balanced structure which also has depth. A good wine to lay down for a while in the cellar. (Residual sugar: 5 g/l.)

➤ Dom. Martine et Vincent Stoeffler, 1, rue des Lièvres, 67140 Barr, tel. 03.88.08.52.50, fax 03.88.08.17.09, e-mail vins.stoeffler@wanadoo.fr ◪ Ⴜ by appt.

STRUSS Bildstoecklé 1999★

□ 0.19 ha 1,050 ▪ ♦ €5-8

The Struss family have some 5 ha (12 acres) at Obermorschwihr, a village whose wine-growing history is strongly linked to Marbach Abbey. A centre of Alsatian spirituality founded in the 11th century, the abbey held good vineyards on limestone-clay terrains. A limestone *terroir* has produced this full and expressive 99 with lemony aromas. Honest and supple as it hits the palate, it goes on to express citrus notes which blend with a certain overripe roundness. The fresh finish is very long. (Residual sugar: 10 g/l.)

➤ André Struss et Fils, 16, rue Principale, 68420 Obermorschwihr, tel. 03.89.49.36.71, fax 03.89.49.37.30 ◪ Ⴜ by appt.
● Philippe Struss

ANDRE THOMAS ET FILS
Sélection de grains nobles 1998★★

□ 0.5 ha 1,000 ▪ ♦ €23-30

Granitic *terroirs* suit Riesling marvellously well. The variety produces big grapes that are not very responsive to botrytis. But where noble rotting works, the results can be magical. This old-gold wine has a remarkably subtle nose, dominated by crystallised fruits with a note of mushroom and a nuance of fresh apricot. Very elegant. The palate is meltingly rich, coherent and exceedingly well structured.

EARL André Thomas et Fils, 3, rue des Seigneurs, 68770 Ammerschwihr, tel. 03.89.47.16.60, fax 03.89.47.37.22 ▼ by appt.

TRIMBACH
Cuvée Frédéric-Émile 1997★   5.5 ha   30,000   €15-23

This straw-yellow Riesling with its definite green lights comes from vines facing south and south-east, growing in limestone-clay or conchiferous limestone soils. Hence the nose contains not only delightful ripe-fruit aromas of white peach and fragrances of acacia but also strong mineral notes. The same features emerge on the palate, which is well balanced and powerfully aromatic. The rather lively and slightly lemony finish is well sustained by the fruit. Already an expressive wine, it has all it needs to age well.

F.E. Trimbach, 15, rte de Bergheim, 68150 Ribeauvillé, tel. 03.89.73.60.30, fax 03.89.73.89.04, e-mail contact@maison-trimbach.fr ▼ ▼ by appt.

VORBURGER 1999★   n.c.   n.c.   €5-8

This estate, established in the 1950s, is to be found at Voegtlinshoffen, a charming village perched above the vineyard. Its 99 wine has a nose of floral and spicy nuances. The body is substantial with richness, good balance and notes of overripeness. Its fresh acidity gives it dynamism and length. (Residual sugar: 3 g/l.)

Jean-Pierre Vorburger et Fils, 3, rue de la Source, 68420 Voegtlinshoffen, tel. 03.89.49.35.52, fax 03.89.86.40.56 ▼ ev. day except Sun. 8am-12 noon 1.30pm-6pm

CH. WAGENBOURG
Vallée Noble 1999   n.c.   7,000   €5-8

Soultzmatt is located at the entrance to the Vallée Noble, whose noble associations were embodied in the seven castles that guarded it. Château Wagenbourg is the only one that survives. The Klein family, whose ancestors were wine-growers in the village in the very early 17th century, settled here in 1905. Their Riesling, with its elegant citrus aromas, has a good attack, qualities of freshness and balance, and a delightfully round finish. (Residual sugar 3 g/l.)

Joseph et Jacky Klein, Ch. Wagenbourg, 25, rue de la Vallée, 68570 Soultzmatt, tel. 03.89.47.01.41, fax 03.89.47.65.61 ▼ ev. day except Sun. 8am-12 noon 1pm-7pm

WILLM 1999★   n.c.   n.c.

This wine-merchant belongs to the Eguisheim Wolfberger group. Its headquarters are at Barr, the wine-growing centre of the Bas-Rhin *département*, worth visiting especially for the Musée de la Folie Marco, a fine example of a sumptuous 18th-century residence. This 99 Riesling is an aromatic medley of crystallised fruit and white flowers with a touch of mineral. After a supple attack, the wine is delicate and well-structured, revealing a spicy character and fairly good length on the palate. (Residual sugar: 4 g/l.)

Alsace Willm, 32, rue du Dr-Sultzer, 67140 Barr, tel. 03.88.08.19.11, fax 03.88.08.56.21 ▼ by appt.

FERNAND ZIEGLER
Clos Saint-Ulrich 1999★   1.2 ha   3,130   €5-8

Fernand Ziegler is the latest scion of a family rooted in Alsatian wine-growing; the estate goes back to 1634, and he has been here nearly forty years. His experience comes through in this clean, fresh Riesling, whose aromas suggest citrus fruits. The palate is similarly fresh, with a fine complexity, a subtle structure and a finish with fruity notes. (Residual sugar: 2.5 g/l.)

EARL Fernand Ziegler et Fils, 7, rue des Vosges, 68150 Hunawihr, tel. 03.89.73.64.42, fax 03.89.73.71.38 ▼ by appt.

JEAN ZIEGLER   Seidenfaden 1999   0.6 ha   3,000   €5-8

This estate of less than 3 ha (7 acres) has already seen four generations of wine-growers. Riesling is part of Riquewihr's history and tradition. Grown on clay-gypsum soil, this version shows its breeding. Lively as it hits the palate, it has a supple structure and a finish that is still a little green. It needs more time. (Residual sugar: 12 g/l.)

Jean Ziegler, 3, chem. de la Daensch, 9, rue des Juifs, 68340 Riquewihr, tel. 03.89.47.96.47, fax 03.89.47.96.47, e-mail info@rotthus.com ▼ by appt.

ZIMMERMANN
Sélection première 1999★   0.7 ha   6,000   €5-8

Wine-growers from father to son since 1693, the Zimmermann family respect the traditions of wine-growing. Produced in the vicinity of the château du Haut-Koenigsbourg, this Riesling demonstrates a warm, mineral side recalling the flinty *terroir* from which it comes. There are subtle notes of peach and citrus, and a supple attack leading to good freshness. A well-balanced, delightful product. (Residual sugar: 7 g/l.)

EARL A. Zimmermann Fils, 3, Grand-Rue, 67600 Orschwiller, tel. 03.88.92.08.49, fax 03.88.92.94.55 ▼ by appt.

Alsace Muscat

Two varieties of Muscat are used to make this dry, aromatic white wine, which is reminiscent of the burst of flavour you get when biting into a fresh grape. One variety, traditionally called Muscat d'Alsace, is more accurately known as the Muscat de Frontignan. It is a late-maturing variety so it is planted on slopes with the best aspect. The second variety, which develops earlier and so is more widely grown, is the Muscat Ottonel. The two varieties are planted on 340 ha (840 acres), 2.4% of the Alsace vineyard. The Muscat d'Alsace is a pleasing and sometimes surprising speciality. It makes a good aperitif and is a good wine to serve at drinks parties. It goes well with cakes or salty nibbles like pretzels.

PIERRE-PAUL ZINK 1999 €5-8
0.8 ha 6,600

Here in Pfaffenheim, a village with a large number of wine-growers, Pierre-Paul Zink offers an expressive, engaging Riesling with a bouquet of citrus fruits and white flowers. As soon as it arrives on the palate its freshness is apparent, and it goes on to reveal good balance and length. It will blend in better if kept for a year or two. (Residual sugar: 2 g/l.)
➤ Pierre-Paul Zink, 27, rue de la Lauch, 68250 Pfaffenheim, tel. 03.89.49.60.87, fax 03.89.49.73.05 ☑ by appt.

CAMILLE BRAUN Bollenberg 1999★ €5-8
0.4 ha 2,500

The slopes of the Bollenberg are well known for their protected flora and the legend of the witches who come here on summer nights. Its limestone-clay terroir and this wine-grower's expertise have produced a Muscat with floral, slightly fruity notes. The palate does not have great length, but the attack is lovely, with a balance of freshness and roundness followed by an excellent presence of fruits. (Residual sugar: 9 g/l.)
➤ Camille Braun, 16, Grand-Rue, 68500 Orschwihr, tel. 03.89.76.95.20, fax 03.89.74.35.03 ☑ ev. day except Sun. 8am–12 noon 1.30–7pm

DOM. BERNARD ET DANIEL HAEGI Vendanges tardives 1998★ €15-23
0.25 ha 840

Muscat is undoubtedly one of the most fragile of the Alsatian grape varieties. Achieving a good dry wine is difficult in itself, but creating a Vendanges tardives is really an art form. Bernard and Daniel Haegi have done it, and deserve many congratulations. This brilliant yellow-gold wine has an extremely delicate aroma of fruits and a well-balanced palate of great finesse. Aromatically, the wine is still reserved; it just needs time. A very lovely product.
➤ Bernard et Daniel Haegi, 33, rue de la Montagne, 67140 Mittelbergheim, tel. 03.88.08.95.80, fax 03.88.08.91.20 ☑ ev. day except Sun. 8am–12 noon 1pm–6pm

HERTZOG 1999 €5-8
0.13 ha 1,500

Here at Obermorschwihr, the church is half-timbered, which is unique in Upper Alsace. This Muscat, with its rich, even somewhat robust palate is to be found at Sylvain Herzog's establishment. The bouquet has slightly grilled notes and hints of honey. The palate is round and well structured with a quite long finish. A wine to go with exotic dishes or an almond cake. (Residual sugar: 6 g/l.)
➤ EARL Sylvain Hertzog, 18, rte du Vin, 68420 Obermorschwihr, tel. 03.89.49.31.93, fax 03.89.49.28.85 ☑ ev. day 9am–7pm; Sun. by appt.

JEAN-LUC MEYER 1999 €5-8
0.24 ha 1,800

Jean-Luc Meyer has been running this estate since 1982. Today, it covers about 10 ha (25 acres). This pale-yellow Muscat with golden lights has a traditional dry character and is well made. The variety's aromatic influence and the wine's notes of crystallised fruits are intense. The palate starts with roundness, which then yields to a fruity freshness providing good length. (Residual sugar: 2 g/l.)
➤ Jean-Luc Meyer, 4, rue des Trois-Châteaux, 68420 Eguisheim, tel. 03.89.24.53.66, fax 03.89.41.66.46 ☑ by appt.

EDMOND RENTZ Réserve 1999★ €5-8
0.7 ha 5,000

This wine-grower has been tending 20 ha (49 acres) of vines at Zellenberg, a village perched on a hill, since 1954. The estate goes back to 1785, when the earliest plots were purchased. Grown on a limestone-clay terroir, this Muscat reveals a lovely fruitiness with nutty hints. There is a strong, slightly round grapey presence on the palate, which extends into quite a lengthy finish. (Residual sugar: 10 g/l.)
➤ EARL Dom. Edmond Rentz, 7, rte du Vin, 68340 Zellenberg, tel. 03.89.47.90.17, fax 03.89.47.97.27 ☑ ev. day except Sun. 9am–12 noon 2pm–6pm

LOUIS SCHERB ET FILS 1999★

☐ 0.48 ha 4,800 €5–8

A 12th-century belltower adorns the picturesque village of Gueberschwihr, equally known for its Feast of Friendship at the end of August. Though reserved at first, this Muscat opens out onto exotic, fairly complex notes. This honest and quite robust Muscat reveals elegance and character on the palate. A good aperitif. (Residual sugar: 4.9 g/l.)

EARL Joseph et André Scherb, 1, rte de Saint-Marc, 68420 Gueberschwihr, tel. 03.89.49.30.83, fax 03.89.49.30.65 V
ev. day 8am–12 noon 1pm–7pm; Sun. 9am–12 noon

JEAN-LOUIS SCHOEPFER 1999

☐ 0.35 ha 2,000 €5–8

The Schoepfer family have been winegrowers in Wettolsheim since 1656, with Gilles entering the family business in 1997. This is an authentic Alsatian Muscat, with a hint of acacia flowers, an honest attack, a palate with mouth-filling qualities and lots of life. A note of linden blossom gives it an air of spring. Try it with asparagus. (Residual sugar: 4 g/l.)

EARL Jean-Louis Schoepfer, 35, rue Herzog, 68920 Wettolsheim, tel. 03.89.80.71.29, fax 03.89.79.61.35, e-mail jlschoepfer@libertysurf.fr V
by appt.

DOM. STIRN Tradition 1999★

☐ 0.15 ha 1,200 €5–8

Fabien Stirn is a young oenologist who took over this property in 1999, realising his dream and exploring his passion for wine. This attractively bright Muscat, with its golden glints, exhales intense, complex aromas of violet, linden, blackberry, crystallised fruits and honey. The palate is balanced, round and full. An excellent aperitif or an enjoyable accompaniment to pan-fried crustaceans. (Residual sugar: 7 g/l.)

Fabien Stirn, Dom. Stirn, 3, rue du Château, 68240 Sigolsheim, tel. 03.89.47.30.58, fax 03.89.47.30.58 V
by appt.

Alsace Gewurztraminer

The grape variety used to make this wine is a particularly aromatic member of the Traminer family. In a treatise published in 1551 it was already being acknowledged as a variety that was typical of Alsace. Ideally suited to the Alsace *terroir*, it has been adapted over the centuries to create top-quality wines with a worldwide reputation.

It makes full-bodied, well-structured wines, which are basically dry but with some softness and have a marvellous, characteristic bouquet, which varies in power depending on the year and on where the grapes are grown. Gewurztraminer is an early-fruiting variety and has a limited and unreliable yield, but it produces very ripe grapes. About 2,500 ha (6,175 acres) are planted with Gewurztraminer, 17.6% of the Alsace wine region. It is often served as an aperitif or at drinks parties, and it is a good accompaniment to desserts, as well as being an excellent foil, particularly when full and rich in character, for strongly flavoured cheeses, such as Roquefort and Munster.

DOM. PIERRE ADAM Kaefferkopf 1999★

☐ 8 ha 6,000 €8–11

Pierre Adam founded this business in the 1950s. His son Rémy, who took over in the early 1990s, is today in charge of 11 ha (27 acres) of vines largely in the Kaefferkopf. That prestigious *terroir* with its limestone-clay soil is the source of this Gewurztraminer. It is already very expressive with its mixture of spice and crystallised-fruit aromas. The long, captivating palate makes it good for drinking with exotic specialities. (Residual sugar: 18 g/l.)

Dom. Pierre Adam, 8, rue du Lt-Louis-Mourier, 68770 Ammerschwihr, tel. 03.89.78.23.07, fax 03.89.47.39.68, e-mail info@domaine-adam.com V
ev. day 8am–12 noon 1pm–8pm

J.-B. ADAM Kaefferkopf Réserve particulière Cuvée Jean-Baptiste 1999★

☐ 1.5 ha 8,000 €11–15

At Ammerschwihr, the name Adam denotes a very traditional wine-growing and merchanting family who have been here since 1614. Ironically, this year's wine was judged extremely youthful. This Kaefferkopf has a bouquet combining roses and smokiness. The palate is fairly round, powerful, and very pleasant. Either drink as an aperitif or with Asian food. (Residual sugar:25 g/l.)

Jean-Baptiste Adam, 5, rue de l'Aigle, 68770 Ammerschwihr, tel. 03.89.78.23.21, fax 03.89.47.35.91, e-mail adam@jb-adam.com V ev. day except Sun. 8am–12 noon 2pm–6.30pm; groups by appt.

Alsace Gewurztraminer

LAURENT BANNWARTH
Bildstoecklé 1999★   ▯ €5-8   1.8 ha   12,142

☐   Laurent Bannwarth and his son tend more than 10 ha (25 acres) of vines, and have gained a reputation for the great maturity of their wines. Their Gewurztraminers are often singled out for praise. This one, grown on limestone-clay soil, demonstrates both richness and aromas typical of the variety. It is unusually full on the palate, with a richness and length that suits it for drinking as an aperitif and with desserts. (Residual sugar: 7.5 g/l.)

⚫➤ Laurent Bannwarth et Fils, 9, rte du Vin, 68420 Obermorschwihr, tel. 03.89.49.30.87, fax 03.89.49.29.02, e-mail bannwarth@calixo.net ☑ ⵌ by appt.

DOM. BARMES-BUECHER
Herrenweg 1999★   ▯ ⵌ €11-15   0.37 ha   2,000

☐   This reputable 15-ha (37-acre) estate derives from inter-family marriage. For three years now it has been subject to the exacting processes of biodynamics. Reflecting the gravelly *terroir* in which it was grown, this Gewurztraminer offers extremely intense aromas. The palate has a fine structure and very good length. An opulent wine. (Residual sugar: 10 g/l.)

⚫➤ Dom. Barmes-Buecher, 30, rue Sainte-Gertrude, 68920 Wettolsheim, tel. 03.89.80.62.92, fax 03.89.79.30.80, e-mail barmes-buecher@terre-net.fr ☑ ⵌ by appt.

BARON DE HOEN
Vendanges tardives 1998   ▯ ⵌ €15-23   20 ha   12,000

☐   The commune of Beblenheim, beneath the slopes of the Sonnenglanz, is one of the gems of the Alsatian wine region, offering visitors some splendid architectural sights, such as its wooden houses and a Gothic fountain. The Hoen company works a total of 250 ha (618 acres). The predominantly floral bouquet of this bright, light-yellow Gewurztraminer reflect its *terroir*. The delicate, well-structured palate is not yet fully integrated. A wine of excellent length that will be ready in three to five years' time.

⚫➤ SICA Baron de Hoen, 20, rue de Hoen, 68980 Beblenheim, tel. 03.89.47.89.93 ☑ ⵌ by appt.

EARL Baumann-Zirgel,
5, rue du Vignoble, 68630 Mittelwihr, tel. 03.89.47.90.40, fax 03.89.49.04.89 ☑ ⵌ ev. day 8.30am–12.30pm 2pm–7pm
⚫➤ J.-J. Zirgel

FRANCOIS BAUR 1999
▯▯ €11-15   0.78 ha   5,000

☐   This Gewurztraminer comes from an 11-ha (27-acre) estate in the heart of the little town of Turckheim, which includes a magnificent residence dating from the estate's foundation in 1741. Grown on a granitic *terroir*, this wine has an intense nose with notes of flowers and overripe fruits. The same aromatic complexity reappears on the airy, subtle palate. Suitable for exotic dishes. (Residual sugar: 20 g/l.)

⚫➤ François Baur Petit-Fils, 3, Grand-Rue, 68230 Turckheim, tel. 03.89.27.06.62, fax 03.89.27.47.21, e-mail vinsbaur@hotmail.com ☑ ⵌ by appt.

BECK – DOM. DU REMPART
Cuvée du Rempart 1999   ▯ €11-15   0.5 ha   2,000

☐   Gilbert Beck does not just tend his 9-ha (22-acre) estate, but puts his enthusiasm for the Alsatian *terroir* at his fellow wine-growers' service by offering their products in his own Maison des Grands Crus. His Cuvée du Rempart reflects its granitic *terroir*. After a supple attack, the palate is round but by no means unstructured. Lovely balance. (Residual sugar: 37 g/l.)

⚫➤ Beck, Dom. du Rempart, 5, rue des Remparts, 67650 Dambach-la-Ville, tel. 03.88.92.62.03, fax 03.88.92.49.40 ☑ ⵌ by appt.
⚫➤ Gilbert Beck

DOM. JEAN-MARC BERNHARD
Vieilles vignes 1999   ▯ €5-8   n.c.   n.c.

☐   After a year of travel and work placements that took him to new wine-growing countries, Frédéric Bernhard, an oenologist, has joined his father Jean-Marc on the ancestral estate, helping thus to perpetuate a tradition that goes back to the Empire. Now they have produced a seductively golden Gewurztraminer with aromas of flowers and crystallised fruits. The palate is very rich; though still dominated by a touch of unblended sugar, it should achieve balance and coherence with time. (Residual sugar: 19 g/l.)

BAUMANN ZIRGEL
Sélection de grains nobles 1998★★★   €23-30   1 ha   3,000

☐   Grown on limestone-clay soil, this Gewurztraminer is a fine example of a wine made from selected grapes which have been subject to noble rot. Slightly coppery in colour, it has a very complex bouquet comprising plum, quince, fruit (orange), almonds and wax. The same aromatic power appears on the palate right through to a lengthy finish. Every element combines to produce a masterpiece. (Half-litre bottles.)

- Domaine Jean-Marc Bernhard, 21, Grand-Rue, 68230 Katzenthal, tel. 03.89.27.05.34, fax 03.89.27.58.72, e-mail jeanmarcbernhard@online.fr [V]
- Y ev. day except Sun. 9am-12 noon 2pm-7pm

BESTHEIM Vendanges tardives 1998

□ 5.6l ha 17,000 | €15-23

During the Second World War, the village of Bennwihr and its vines were completely destroyed by artillery fire. To restore the vineyards and their production, a wine-growing operation was established in 1945, which later joined up with another at Westhalten and took the name of Bestheim. Here it offers a straw-yellow wine whose nose gently opens onto notes of flowers and mineral concentration. The palate displays fullness and concentration, but bears the imprint of a high sugar concentration. It should be kept for five years.

- Bestheim – Cave de Westhalten, 52, rte de Soultzmatt, 68250 Westhalten, tel. 03.89.49.09.29, fax 03.89.49.09.20, e-mail bestheim@goformet.com [V]
- Y by appt.

DOM. CLAUDE BLEGER Sélection de grains nobles 1998★★

□ 0.28 ha 2,200 | €23-30

Claude Bléger's genealogical tree goes back to the Thirty Years' War. His estate of 7 ha (17 acres) is at Orschwiller, a former fief of the château du Haut-Koenigsbourg, mentioned first in 823. This golden-yellow Gewurztraminer is very aromatic, redolent both of spices and liquorice. It is both thick and powerful, with a finely tuned balance and persistent traces of crystallised fruits (pear) perceptible on the palate. (Half-litre bottles)

- Dom. Claude Bléger, 23, Grand-Rue, 67600 Orschwiller, tel. 03.88.92.32.56, fax 03.88.82.59.95 [V] Y ev. day 9am-12.15pm 1.15pm-7.30pm

CAVE DE CLEEBOURG Oberberg Steinseltz 1999

□ 4.36 ha 7,000

Cleebourg, the 'Nordic' village: in the 17th and 18th centuries, Cleebourg and its neighbours were directly attached through marriage to the Swedish crown. Today, the wine-making co-operative (established in 1946) links together all the producers of Wissembourg in the northernmost part of the Alsatian wine region, where they cultivate some 180 ha (445 acres) of vines. Grown on a silty-clay terroir, this Gewurztraminer has an exuberant nose of lychees and exotic fruits. With its fairly supple attack and rather round palate, it is a wine for dessert. (Residual sugar: 8.5 g/l.)

- Cave vinicole de Cleebourg, rte du Vin, 67160 Cleebourg, tel. 03.88.94.50.33, fax 03.88.94.57.08, e-mail cave.cleebourg@wanadoo.fr [V] Y ev. day 8am-12 noon 2pm-6pm; groups by appt.

ROBERT FREUDENREICH ET FILS Sélection de grains nobles 1998★★

□ 1.12 ha 2,700 | €23-30

The marly limestone terroirs of Pfaffenheim, with their covering of calcareous shingle, are ideal for producing wines made from selected nobly-rotted grapes. This deep-yellow 98 with amber lights has a complex nose which emits aromas of crystallised fruits and spices with the characteristic

DOM. ANDRE EHRHART ET FILS Herrenweg 1999★

□ 0.8 ha 6,000 | €5-8

Wettolsheim, not far from Colmar, is a picturesque village entirely dedicated to viniculture. André Ehrhart's business is run from a residence dating from 1737. His wines regularly receive good notices. This Gewurztraminer, grown on a limestone-clay soil, is already very open, with a nose combining amylic and fruity notes. The palate, which is fairly full and rich, has an impressive finish. (Residual sugar: 8 g/l.)

- André Ehrhart et Fils, 8, rue Herzog, 68920 Wettolsheim, tel. 03.89.80.66.16, fax 03.89.79.44.20 [V] Y ev. day except Sun. 8am-11.30am 2pm-6pm

RENE FLEITH-ESCHARD Letzenberg 1999★

□ 0.7 ha 4,400 | €5-8

This estate is regularly singled out for praise. René Fleith has continually expanded his holding, and now has more than 9 ha (22 acres). His son Vincent joined him in 1995 with a view to further investment in the cellar. Reflecting its limestone-clay terroir, their Letzenberg Gewurztraminer still has a very young bouquet, with just the beginnings of fruity, overripe notes. With its round, well-integrated palate, this is a powerful wine made for keeping a long time. (Residual sugar: 25 g/l.)

- René Fleith-Eschard, lieu-dit Lange Matten, 68040 Ingersheim, tel. 03.89.27.24.19, fax 03.89.27.56.79 [V]
- Y by appt.
- René et Vincent Fleith

ANTOINE FONNE Kaefferkopf 1999★★

□ 1 ha 4,800 | €5-8

This small estate of 4 ha (10 acres) is at Ammerschwihr, one of the largest wine-growing communes in Alsace. It began specialising in wine-growing in the early 1970s, and, as this remarkable 99 vintage shows, has gained from being in the Kaefferkopf, a famous Alsatian terroir. The lightness of the granitic soil comes through in the elegant and intense aromas which are dominated by exotic fruits. The palate is well balanced and long. A thoroughbred, authentic Gewurztraminer that will be good as an aperitif and at the end of a meal. (Residual sugar: 17 g/l.)

- Antoine Fonné, 14, Grand-Rue, 68770 Ammerschwihr, tel. 03.89.47.37.90, fax 03.89.47.18.83 [V] Y by appt.

Alsace Gewurztraminer

undertone provided by noble rot. The voluptuous palate, without a trace of heaviness, remains in place all the way to a long finish. A wine with a brilliant future. (Half-litre bottles.) The estate has also produced a one-star wine, the dry **1999 Bergweingarten Gewurztraminer Sec**. Its winning features are a vibrant bouquet combining quince, melon and exotic fruits, and a fresh, well-balanced and long-lasting palate.

☛ Robert Freudenreich et Fils, 31, rue de l'Eglise, 68250 Pfaffenheim, tel. 03.89.49.60.88, fax 03.89.49.69.36 ☑ ☎ by appt.

FREY-SOHLER

Sélection de grains nobles 1998

☐ 0.9 ha n.c.   ▬ C 38-46

This wine, made from selected nobly-rotted grapes, comes from a *terroir* of alluvial gravels, which accounts for its open character and readiness for drinking straight away. Deep-yellow with golden lights, it is developing a powerful nose of spices and crystallised fruits. The same is apparent on the palate. A Gewurztraminer that is uncomplicated, but fresh, true to type and well balanced.

☛ Frey-Sohler, 72, rue de l'Ortenbourg, 67750 Scherwiller, tel. 03.88.92.10.13, fax 03.88.82.57.11, e-mail freysohl@terre-net.fr ☎ ev. day 8am–12 noon 1.15pm–7pm; Sun. by appt.
☛ Sohler Frères

PAUL GINGLINGER★

Vendanges tardives 1998★

☐ 0.7 ha 3,500   ▬ €15-23

Paul Ginglinger heads an estate of 12 ha (30 acres) that has been going since 1636. He is assisted by his son Michel, an oenologist with several years' experience. Together they have produced a golden wine with aromas of crystallised fruits. The body, full and flavoursome, gives an impression of power and richness. The wine's good balance bodes well for the future.

☛ Paul Ginglinger, 8, pl. Charles-de-Gaulle, 68420 Eguisheim, tel. 03.89.41.44.25, fax 03.89.24.94.88, e-mail ginglin@club-internet.fr ☑ ☎ by appt.

ANDRE HARTMANN

Terrasses du Hagelberg 1999

☐ 0.3 ha n.c.   €8-11

The terraces of the Hagelberg are the jewel in the crown of the André Hartmann estate. Painstakingly restored in 1991, they give the vineyard a romantic charm, besides favouring the early ripening of the grapes. The nose of this Gewurztraminer reflects the conchiferous limestone in which it was grown. It is, as one might expect, very floral. The spicy character of the wine emerges only at the finish. An elegant, well-structured wine that should have a long life. (Residual sugar: 30 g/l.)

☛ André Hartmann, 11, rue Roger-Frémeaux, 68420 Voegtlinshoffen, tel. 03.89.49.38.34, fax 03.89.49.26.18 ☑ ☎ ev. day except Sun. 9am–12 noon 2pm–6pm

HASSENFORDER 1999★

☐ 0.25 ha 1,000   ▬ €5-8

This Gewurztraminer comes from Nothalten, a village entirely given over to wine-growing. Gilbert Hassenforder has run this estate since 1977 and offers a Gewurztraminer grown on marly limestone. The wine still bears the aromatic traces of fermentation, hence the hint of banana. Lively as it hits the palate, the wine has good structure and will go well with cheeses and exotic specialities. (Residual sugar: 8.5 g/l.)

☛ Gilbert Hassenforder, 57, rte des Vins d'Alsace, 67680 Nothalten, tel. 03.88.92.41.81, fax 03.88.92.41.81 ☑ ☎ by appt.

BRUNO HERTZ Réserve 1999★

☐ 0.3 ha 2,000   ▬ €5-8

The headquarters of the wine-grower and oenologist Bruno Hertz lie in the centre of the medieval town of Eguisheim, which rates as one of the birthplaces of Alsatian wine. Here he has almost 6 ha (15 acres) of vines. Despite its limestone-clay origins, his Réserve Gewurztraminer already has a very intense and expressive bouquet with hints of citrus and apricot. With its fresh, strongly structured palate and good length, it will be equally suitable to drink as an aperitif or with an exotic dish. (Residual sugar: 5 g/l.)

☛ Bruno Hertz, 9, pl. de l'Eglise, 68420 Eguisheim, tel. 03.89.41.81.61, fax 03.89.41.68.32 ☑ ☎ by appt.

ALBERT HERTZ

Vendanges tardives 1998

☐ 0.35 ha 2,000   ▬ €15-23

Eguisheim is one of the prettiest large villages in Alsace. Pope Leo IX came from there, and in 2002 the town will celebrate the millennium of his birth. Albert Hertz has produced a straw-yellow wine with golden lights. The bouquet offers a complex range of exotic fruits, raisins and slight smokiness. The palate is silky and smooth, but somewhat conceals the character of the grape variety. It is already fairly mature.

☛ Albert Hertz, 3, rue du Riesling, 68420 Eguisheim, tel. 03.89.41.30.32, fax 03.89.23.99.23 ☑ ☎ by appt.

DOM. ROGER HEYBERGER

Bildstoeckle Sélection de grains nobles 1998★★

☐ 1 ha 4,000   ▬ €23-30

The colour is a lovely golden yellow with bright glints. The bouquet is fresh, mainly of rose-petals and spices. The palate is smooth and rich, slightly crystallised and with good length. This 98 vintage is not yet fully open. A little patience is required, but the wine has promise.

- Roger Heyberger et Fils,
5, rue Principale, 68420 Obermorschwihr,
tel. 03.89.49.30.01, fax 03.89.49.22.28 V
Y ev. day except Sun. 8am–12 noon
2pm–6pm

HORCHER
Sélection de grains nobles 1998★

0.25 ha 1,000 €23-30

In the commune of Mittelwihr, to the east of which is the Mandelberg Grand Cru known for its mild climate, both Riesling and Gewurztraminer varieties share the lime-light. Ernest Horcher offers a deep-amber wine with golden lights. Though still closed, the nose exhales the odd note of citrus. After a fine attack, the palate is velvety and makes an agreeable impression. Its aromatic content is intense and very long.

- Ernest Horcher et Fils,
6, rue du Vignoble, 68630 Mittelwihr,
tel. 03.89.47.93.26, fax 03.89.49.04.92 V
Y ev. day except Sun. 8am–12 noon
2pm–7pm

CLAUDE ET GEORGES HUMBRECHT 1999★

0.75 ha 7,000 €5-8

Gueberschwihr is famous not simply for its Romanesque belltower, but for its importance in the Alsatian wine region. Georges and Claude Humbrecht have worked here together since 1989. Though already quite open despite its limestone-clay origin, their Gewurztraminer releases aromas of banana and exotic fruits. Powerful and extremely long in the mouth, this is a dry wine that will go well with cheeses or Alsatian specialities. (Residual sugar: 6 g/l.)

- EARL Claude et Georges Humbrecht,
33, rue de Pfaffenheim,
68420 Gueberschwihr, tel. 03.89.49.31.51 V
Y by appt.

JEAN HUTTARD Prestige 1999★

0.5 ha 2,500 €5-8

Zellenberg is a splendid village perched on an outcropping spur to the east of Riquewihr. The Huttards have been established here, on the Route du Vin, for many generations. Despite its limestone-clay origins, their Gewurztraminer already has a very intense nose, with nuances of rose mingling with hints of exotic fruits and overripeness. The palate is well balanced, long and inviting, and reveals an excellent structure. (Residual sugar: 25 g/l.)

- Jean Huttard, 10, rte du Vin,
68340 Zellenberg, tel. 03.89.47.90.49,
fax 03.89.47.90.32 V Y ev. day except Mon.
9am–12 noon 2pm–6pm
- Jean-Claude Huttard

JEAN-CHARLES KIEFFER 1999★

0.3 ha 1,500 €5-8

Coming from a line of wine-growers going back to the 18th century, Jean-Charles Kieffer tends 9 ha (22 acres) of vines in the picturesque village of Itterswiller. The intense and very complex nose of his Gewurztraminer mixes traditional notes of citrus and crystallised fruits with other characteristics linked to overripeness. The full, well-structured palate has good length. The end-product of excellent raw material. (Residual sugar: 15 g/l.)

- Jean-Charles Kieffer, 7, rte des Vins,
67140 Itterswiller, tel. 03.88.85.59.80,
fax 03.88.57.81.44,
e-mail jean-charles-kieffer@wanadoo.fr V
Y ev. day 8am–12 noon 2pm–6pm

CAVE DE KIENTZHEIM-KAYSERSBERG
Altenberg 1999

9.83 ha 16,000 €8-11

This co-operative takes the production from 180 ha (445 acres) of vines from the neighbouring communes of Kayserberg and Kientzheim. Kientzheim contains the head-quarters of the Confrérie Saint-Étienne. The nose of this Gewurztraminer is of medium intensity, with developing aromas of tea and ripe fruits. The palate is well balanced and elegant ; though still young, it will open out well in time, like all wines grown on marly clay terroirs. (Residual sugar: 20 g/l.)

- Cave de Kientzheim-Kaysersberg,
10, rue des Vieux-Moulins, 68240 Kientzheim,
tel. 03.89.47.13.19, fax 03.89.47.34.38 V
Y by appt.

KLEIN AUX VIEUX REMPARTS
Schlossreben 1999★

0.75 ha 4,500 €8-11

The wines of this property are widely known and admired. The 8-ha (20-acre) estate is located at the foot of the Haut-Koenigsbourg and has been run since 1973 by Jean-Marie Klein. His 'castle wines' (Schlossreben) grow on a granitic soil that has given this Gewurztraminer its very elegant, fruity, toasty nose. After a fine attack on the palate, this 99 wine is lively and well struc-tured, and will suit any number of dishes. (Residual sugar: 7.5 g/l.)

- Françoise et Jean-Marie Klein – Aux Vieux Remparts, rte du Haut-Koenigsbourg, 68590 Saint-Hippolyte, tel. 03.89.73.00.41, fax 03.89.73.04.94 Y by appt.

PAUL KUBLER Weingarten 1999

0.22 ha 2,000 €8-11

Wine-growers for many generations since 1620, the Kubler family run an important estate at Soultzmatt, a charming village in the Vallée Noble. This Gewurztraminer, grown on sandstone, already has a very full, intense nose, with grape scents mingling with those produced by fermentation. The powerful, well-integrated palate also reflects the quality of the fruit used. (Residual sugar: 24 g/l.)

- EARL Paul Kubler, 103, rue de la Vallée, 68570 Soultzmatt, tel. 03.89.47.00.75, fax 03.89.47.65.45, e-mail kubler@

Alsace Gewurztraminer

KUEHN Kaefferkopf 1999★
□ n.c. 25,000 €8-11

Kuehn S.A. is a long-established wine-merchant at Ammerschwihr. Although it now belongs to the Cave Vinicole at Ingersheim, it has kept its autonomy and continues to look after its own superb 12-ha (30-acre) estate. Its Kaefferkopf Gewurztraminer has a very intense nose mingling floral and spicy notes, along with more unusual nuances of violet and crystallised fruits. With its thick, full palate, this is a well-balanced, thoroughbred wine which is full of promise. (Residual sugar: 20 g/l.)

➤ Kuehn SA, 3, Grand-Rue,
68770 Ammerschwihr, tel. 03.89.47.18.32 ☑ ❤ ev. day except Sun.
8am–12 noon 1pm–5pm

FRANCOIS LICHTLE
Sélection de grains nobles 1998★★
□ n.c. 600 €23-30

The village of Husseren-les-Châteaux, at 390 m (1,280 ft), is the highest in the Alsace wine region. It really came to life during the Revolution, when the villagers obtained the former lands of the abbey of Marbach. Grown on the local limestone-clay, this deep-yellow Gewurztraminer has glints of old gold. The intense and highly complex bouquet releases aromas of crystallised fruits and dried apricot. Generous and unctuous, this wine has richness and body, and remains well integrated through a very long finish. (Half-litre bottles.)

➤ Dom. François Lichtlé, 17, rue des Vignerons, 68420 Husseren-les-Châteaux, tel. 03.89.49.31.34, fax 03.89.49.37.51, e-mail hlichtle@aol.com ☑ ❤ by appt.

FRANCOIS LIPP
Sélection de grains nobles 1998★★
□ 0.46 ha 600 €30-38

The Lipp estate was established around 1825. It has 6.5 ha (16 acres) of vines and supplies the Brasserie Lipp in Paris and Zurich. The bright-yellow colour with old-gold glints gives this Gewurztraminer instant appeal. The nose is of the spicy variety. The palate is distinctive, perfectly balanced with hints of acacia. It has a crystallised character and 'smells of the sun,' as one taster recorded. A splendid wine.

➤ François Lipp et fils, 6, rte du Vin, 68420 Husseren-les-Châteaux, tel. 03.89.49.30.37, fax 03.89.49.32.23 ☑ ❤ by appt.

MARZOLF
Sélection de grains nobles 1998★
□ 0.25 ha 1,300 €30-38

Established at Gueberschwihr since 1844, this family has the good fortune to grow some of its vines on soils of the Goldert Grand Cru. Amber-yellow with old-gold glints, this 98 vintage is redolent of spices, toast and coffee. The palate is full and complex, perhaps still a little on the heavy side yet beautifully long. Wait a little for it to mature.

➤ GAEC Marzolf, 9, rte de Rouffach, 68420 Gueberschwihr, tel. 03.89.49.31.02, fax 03.89.49.20.84, e-mail vins@marzolf.fr ☑ ❤ by appt.

ALBERT MAURER 1999★
□ 1.05 ha 6,500 €5-8

Albert Maurer has been growing vines since 1965 and now runs a vineyard of 11 ha (27 acres) near the town of Barr. Being grown on limestone-clay, his Gewurztraminer has a restrained bouquet, which opens with spicy aromas. Fairly opulent as it hits the palate, this is a rich, well-structured and persistent wine. (Residual sugar: 14 g/l.)

➤ Albert Maurer, 11, rue du Vignoble, 67140 Eichhoffen, tel. 03.88.08.96.75, fax 03.88.08.59.98 ☑ ❤ ev. day except Sun. 8am–12 noon 1.30pm–6pm

GERARD METZ
Vieilles vignes Cuvée Prestige 1999★
□ 0.5 ha 3,000 €5-8

Wine-growers from father to son since around 1900 and today looking after 12 ha (30 acres) of vines, the Metz family owe their reputation not simply to their expertise but also to the diversity of the terroirs they cultivate. This Gewurztraminer reflects its clayey-sandy soil, which has endowed it with aromatic intensity, including notes of spices and liquorice. The fairly supple and well-balanced palate also demonstrates the excellence of the grapes used. (Residual sugar: 7 g/l.) It will go well with cheeses and desserts.

➤ Dom. Gérard Metz, 23, rte du Vin, 67140 Ittersviller, tel. 03.88.57.80.25, fax 03.88.57.81.42 ☑ ❤ by appt.
➤ Eric Casimir

DOM. RENE MEYER La Croix du
Ploeller Vieilles vignes Cuvée Martin 1999
□ 0.55 ha 5,400 €8-11

René Meyer has been making wine since 1959, and today works 8 ha (20 acres) of vines with his son. Made from 45-year-old vines grown on limestone-marl and magnificently exposed to the sun, this Cuvée Martin has a distinctively smoky nose. The palate is on the supple side, with all the structure required to provide good balance. It will be at its best in two to three years' time. (Residual sugar: 31 g/l.)

➤ EARL Dom. René Meyer et Fils, 14, Grand-Rue, 68230 Katzenthal, tel. 03.89.27.04.67, fax 03.89.27.50.59 ☑ ❤ by appt.

DOM. MOLTES Bergweingarten 1999★
□ 0.5 ha 2,500 €8-11

Descendants of a long line of wine-growers going back to the 18th century, Stéphane and Michaël Moltes took over the estate in 1997. The two brothers tend 11 ha (27 acres) of vines. The limestone-clay terroir of the Bergweingarten is ideal for making Gewurztraminer, and this one has a particularly authentic nose of spicy and fruity nuances. Fairly round and rich on the palate, it has an opulent feel with all the ingredients for a good aperitif or dessert wine. (Residual sugar: 20 g/l.)

♦ Dom. Antoine Moltès et Fils, 8–10, rue du Fossé, 68250 Pfaffenheim, tel. 03.89.49.60.85, fax 03.89.49.50.43, e-mail domaine@vins-moltes.com ☑
☂ ev. day 8am–12 noon 2pm–7pm

JULES MULLER Réserve 1999

3 ha | 20,000 | €8-11

Founded in 1886, the wine-merchant Jules Muller has retained its individuality despite belonging now to the Société Gustave Lorenz. It remains close to the soil inasmuch as it continues to tend its own vineyard of 12 ha (30 acres). Grown on limestone-clay soil, this Gewurztraminer has a developing nose of fruity and spicy aromas that are already very expressive. The powerful, fairly rich palate reflects the excellent grapes used. (Residual sugar: 6 g/l.)

♦ Jules Muller, 91, rue des Vignerons, 68750 Bergheim, tel. 03.89.73.22.21, fax 03.89.73.30.49 ☑ ☂ ev. day except Sun. 10am–12 noon 2pm–6.30pm
♦ Gustave Lorenz

CH. D'ORSCHWIHR Bollenberg 1999★★

1.3 ha | 10,000 | €5-9

A few years ago Hubert Hartmann took over this château with its 20-ha (49-acre) estate and gave it its present high reputation. His Bollenberg Gewurztraminer is developing a nose of very intense aromas of spices mingling with rose-petals. After a fine attack, the palate is powerful and dry, ideal for exotic dishes. (Residual sugar: 4 g/l.)

♦ Ch. d'Orschwihr, 1, rue du Centre, 68500 Orschwihr, tel. 03.89.74.25.00, fax 03.89.76.56.91, e-mail hh@chateau-or.com ☑ ☂ by appt.

OTTER Sélection de grains nobles 1998★★

0.34 ha | 1,600 | €30-38

The Otter estate has been at Hattstatt since 1890. This ancient town was fortified in the 12th century, and its surrounding walls are still visible. The estate offers a deep-yellow wine with amber lights. After a complex nose of exotic fruits and spices, the palate lengthens considerably to provide both richness and flavours of exotic fruits. Fruits and raisins remain evident in the long finish. A great wine.

♦ Dom. François Otter et Fils, 4, rue du Muscat, 68420 Hattstatt, tel. 03.89.49.33.00, fax 03.89.49.38.69, e-mail otjef@nucleus.fr ☑ ☂ by appt.
♦ Jean-François Otter

LES VIGNERONS DE PFAFFENHEIM ET GUEBERSCHWIHR Grande Réserve 1999★★

0.77 ha | 6,000

The cellar at Pfaffenheim merged with its opposite number at Gueberschwihr in 1968. Today its wines are made from 235 ha (580 acres) of vines, and some of them achieve top ratings. This Gewurztraminer combines both power and elegance. Redolent of fruit aromas, quince, and overripeness, it reveals its fullness and length on the palate. All the breeding in the terroir is present in this wine. (Residual sugar: 17 g/l.)

♦ Cave de Pfaffenheim, 5, rue du Chai, BP 33, 68250 Pfaffenheim, tel. 03.89.78.08.08, fax 03.89.49.71.65, e-mail cave@pfaffenheim.com ☑ ☂ ev. day 8am–12 noon 2pm–6pm

ERNEST PREISS Cuvée particulière 1999★

1.5 ha | 17,000 | €8-11

Having been spared by the world wars, Riquewihr has held on to its rich heritage, which makes it one of the most famous wine towns in Alsace. There are many winegrowers and merchants here to keep up the tradition. Ernest Preiss offers a Gewurztraminer whose nose is still young, with a hint of vanilla. The grape variety really comes through on the palate, which is both deep and spicy, and there is good length in the finish. This wine has everything it needs for long keeping. (Residual sugar: 9 g/l.)

♦ Ernest Preiss, rue Jacques-Preiss, BP 3, 68340 Riquewihr, tel. 03.89.47.91.21 ☑ ☂ by appt.

PREISS-ZIMMER Vieilles vignes 1999

3 ha | 26,000 | €8-11

This wine-merchant has its business in Riquewihr, a gem of the Alsatian wine region, both by virtue of its history and architecture, and the quality of its terroir. Preiss-Zimmer offer a Gewurztraminer that is still very young, as one would expect from its limestone-clay origins. The elegant note of exotic fruits is mainly evident on the palate. Both well structured and powerful, this is a good wine for keeping. (Residual sugar: 15 g/l.)

♦ SARL Preiss-Zimmer, 40, rue du Gal-de-Gaulle, 68340 Riquewihr, tel. 03.89.47.86.91, fax 03.89.27.35.33

VIGNOBLES REINHART Sélection de grains nobles 1998★

0.4 ha | 3,000 | €23-30

Orschwihr is one of Alsace's principal wine towns. Every year, at the foot of the Pfingstberg Grand Cru, it organises a *Nuit du Crémant*. Pierre Reinhart offers an intensely golden-yellow Gewurztraminer with amber lights and a bouquet with mild aromas of crystallised fruits. The palate is powerful, open and well developed with notes of crystallised pear prominent in a full range of aromas. (Half-litre bottles.)

♦ Pierre Reinhart, 7, rue du Printemps, 68500 Orschwihr, tel. 03.89.76.95.12, fax 03.89.74.84.08 ☂ by appt.

DOM. EDMOND RENTZ Sélection de grains nobles 1998★

1 ha | 1,800 | €30-38

Zellenberg is on a ridge, 285 m (935 ft) above sea-level; hence its nickname 'Little

Alsace Gewurztraminer

Toledo'. Here the ancestors of the Rentz family bought their first few rows of vines in 1785; now the estate runs to 20 ha (49 acres). Their yellow Gewurztraminer is subtle but restrained, with aromas of crystallised fruits and apricots. The palate is sweet, rich and powerful, finishing with an agreeable sensation of freshness. A wine that is virtually at its best. (Half-litre bottles.)

☛ EARL Dom. Edmond Rentz, 7, rte du Vin, 68340 Zellenberg, tel. 03.89.47.90.17, fax 03.89.47.97.27 ☑ ⟙ ev. day except Sun. 9am–12 noon 2pm–6pm

DOM. FRANCOIS RUNNER ET FILS
Bergweingarten 1999★

☐   0.83 ha 7,000   ⬛ €5-8

Francis-Claude took over this estate of 12 ha (30 acres) from his father. François Runner, in 1997. They make quality wines, which are regularly singled out for praise. Grown on limestone-clay soil, this Gewurztraminer has a developing nose of powerful floral aromas accompanied by toasty nuances. With its supple, perfectly balanced and very long palate, this is a wine of great elegance. Serve as an aperitif or with Asiatic specialities. (Residual sugar: 10 g/l.)

☛ Dom. François Runner et Fils, 1, rue de la Liberté, 68250 Pfaffenheim, tel. 03.89.49.62.89, fax 03.89.49.73.69 ☑ ⟙ ev. day 8am–12 noon 1pm–7pm; groups by appt.

SAULNIER
Vendanges tardives Vieilles vignes 1998★★

☐   0.29 ha 1,800   ⬛ €15-23

The riches of Gueberschwihr are to be found in its vines. Anyone can see this by simply strolling along its paved alleys where Renaissance houses open onto large courtyards, with spiral staircases and deep cellars. This is where Marco Saulnier established his business in 1992. He now offers a strawyellow Gewurztraminer with a bouquet of dried fruits and nuts, figs and apricots. The same notes are evident on the palate, which is concentrated, well blended, powerful, and classy. The very long finish has a hint of quince.

☛ Marco Saulnier, 43, rue Haute, 68420 Gueberschwihr, tel. 03.89.86.42.02, fax 03.89.49.34.82 ☑ ⟙ by appt.

SAULNIER 1999★★

☐   0.15 ha 1,200   ⬛ €5-8

Before establishing himself as a winegrower in 1992, Marco Saulnier gained his spurs with the Chambre d'Agriculture in the Haut-Rhin *département*. Despite its limestone-clay *terroir*, his Gewurztraminer is already highly scented with notes of spices and roses. This rich, powerful wine reflects the use of excellent fruit. (Residual sugar: 8 g/l.)

☛ Marco Saulnier, 43, rue Haute, 68420 Gueberschwihr, tel. 03.89.86.42.02, fax 03.89.49.34.82 ☑ ⟙ by appt.

MARTIN SCHAETZEL
Ammerschwihr Cuvée Isabelle 1999★

☐   0.6 ha 4,000   ⬛ €8-11

For 20 years Jean Schaetzel has managed to reconcile his activities as a professional instructor in viticulture with managing his own family estate of 8 ha (20 acres). Typical of its gravelly *terroir*, his Cuvée Isabelle already has a very intense bouquet, which is no less elegant for all that, combining roses, lychees and crystallised fruits. The palate is very rich. The roundness of the wine is perfectly counterbalanced by its solid structure. (Residual sugar: 19.6 g/l.)

☛ SARL Martin Schaetzel, 3, rue de la 5ᵉ -Division-Blindée, 68770 Ammerschwihr, tel. 03.89.47.11.39, fax 03.89.78.29.77 ☑ ⟙ by appt.

☛ Béa et Jean Schaetzel

DOM. JOSEPH SCHARSCH 1999★

☐   0.5 ha 4,000   ⬛ €5-8

When Joseph Scharsch took over this estate in 1970, it had only 2.5 ha (6 acres); now it extends to 10 ha (25 acres). This Gewurztraminer, grown on marly limestone soil, has an immature nose, but as soon as it hits the palate it reveals fullness, good structure and a certain roundness. A promising wine that will do well as an aperitif or with dessert. (Residual sugar: 9 g/l.) The same variety has produced a wine made from selected nobly-rotted grapes, the **Sélection de Grains Nobles 1998** for a half-litre bottle, which also gains one star. The palate is well balanced, the finish fresh, and the aromas (stewed fruits, oranges and mirabelles) powerful and elegant.

☛ Dom. Joseph Scharsch, 12, rue de l'Eglise, 67120 Wolxheim, tel. 03.88.38.30.61, fax 03.88.38.01.13, e-mail domaine.scharsch@wanadoo.fr ☑ ⟙ by appt.

SCHERB Sélection de grains nobles 1998★

☐   0.43 ha n.c.   ⬛ €23-30

The Gewurztraminer vines nestle between the green forest firs and the pink sandstone quarries of Gueberschwihr. This year's wine is deep yellow with lights of old gold. The nose of crystallised exotic fruits is enhanced by nuances of smoke and spices. The palate retains the same aromatic intensity, and is full and deep.

☛ Michel Scherb, 16, rue Haute, 68420 Gueberschwihr, tel. 03.89.49.26.82, fax 03.89.49.39.06 ☑ ⟙ by appt.

A. SCHERER Holzweg 1999★

☐   0.25 ha 1,500   ⬛ €8-11

This Gewurztraminer comes from Husseren-les-Châteaux, a picturesque village perched up high with an unbeatable view over the Alsace plain. The Scherer residence dates from 1750. The bouquet offers very pleasing aromas of ripe fruits and overripeness, reflecting all the nobility of the limestone-clay *terroir*. The solidly structured, balanced palate has a touch of sugar which reflects the quality of the harvest. (Residual sugar: 12 g/l.)

▲ Vignoble A. Scherer, 12, rte du Vin, BP 4, 68420 Husseren-les-Châteaux, tel. 03.89.49.30.33, fax 03.89.49.27.48, e-mail ascherer@wanadoo.fr ☑ ▼ ev. day except Sun. 8am–12 noon 1pm–6pm

DOM. PIERRE SCHILLÉ

Réserve 1999★

0.39 ha 3,700 €8-11

Pierre Schillé and his wife started bottling in the early 1960s. Their son Christophe took over the business in 1990 and now has a rich variety of *terroirs*. This Réserve Gewurztraminer is already open and blends spicy notes with floral scents. Given its very generous palate, this is a rich, well-structured wine with both length and excellent balance. (Residual sugar: 34 g/l.)

▲ Pierre Schillé et Fils, 14, rue du Stade, 68240 Sigolsheim, tel. 03.89.47.10.67, fax 03.89.47.39.12 ☑ ▼ by appt.

JEAN-LOUIS SCHOEPFER

Kirchacker 1999★

0.35 ha 2,500 €8-11

Jean-Louis Schoepfer, an enthusiastic wine-grower, was joined a few years ago by his two sons. They tend 10 ha (25 acres) of vines at Wettolsheim, near Colmar. Grown on siliceous clay, this Gewurztraminer offers a very intense bouquet of liquorice and orange peel. Rich and opulent, with a strong hint of over-ripeness, it has a very long palate. (Residual sugar: 7.5 g/l.)

▲ EARL Jean-Louis Schoepfer, 35, rue Herzog, 68920 Wettolsheim, tel. 03.89.80.71.29, fax 03.89.79.61.35, e-mail jlschoepfer@libertysurf.fr ☑ ▼ by appt.

J. SIEGLER 1999★

0.6 ha 3,300 €5-8

Jean Siegler is one of the many wine-growers established at Mittelwihr, a village known to connoisseurs for its Côte des Amandiers, also for its sunny aspect and grapes which ripen early. This wine has an intense bouquet despite its marly limestone origins, with aromas of roses, spices and ripe fruits. It has good balance and solid structure. This is a wine with both length and class. (Residual sugar: 10 g/l.)

▲ EARL Jean Siegler Père et Fils, Clos des Terres-Brunes, 26, rue des Merles, 68630 Mittelwihr, tel. 03.89.47.90.70, fax 03.89.49.01.78 ☑ ▼ ev. day 9am–7pm

LES VIGNERONS DE SIGOLSHEIM

Lieu-dit Vogelgarten 1999★

n.c. 38,000 €8-11

The co-operative at Sigolsheim was one of the first set up after the battles of the Colmar Pocket near the end of the Second World War. Although it now comes within the orbit of the co-operative at Turckheim, it continues to make wine at its original locations. This Gewurztraminer releases aromas of pineapple and banana. The attack is fresh and the spicy palate is notably long. (Residual sugar: 8 g/l.)

▲ La Cave de Sigolsheim, 11–15, rue Saint-Jacques, 68240 Sigolsheim, tel. 03.89.78.10.10, fax 03.89.78.21.93, e-mail la.cave.de.sigolsheim@gofornet.com ☑ ▼ ev. day 8am–12 noon 1.30pm–5.30pm

RENE SIMONIS Kaefferkopf 1999★

0.3 ha 1,800 €8-11

Descended from a line of wine-growers established at Ammerschwihr since the 17th century, Etienne Simonis has headed the estate since 1996. This year he offers a Kaefferkopf Gewurztraminer. Though grown in a granitic soil, this 99 wine still has a very young and restrained nose dominated by scents of flowers. Hints of exotic fruits appear on a palate that is both supple and well structured. An attractive wine with a fine future ahead of it. (Residual sugar: 40 g/l.)

▲ René et Etienne Simonis, 2, rue des Moulins, 68770 Ammerschwihr, tel. 03.89.47.30.79, fax 03.89.78.24.10 ☑ ▼ by appt.

SIPP-MACK Vieilles vignes 1999★★

1.48 ha 12,000 €8-11

The Sipp-Mack estate tends 17 ha (42 acres) of vines, making it larger than most family estates in Alsace. Its vines are divided between the communes of Hunawihr, Ribeauville and Bergheim. This Gewurztraminer, grown on marly-clay soil, has a superb bouquet which marries scents of fruit, flowers and honey. The palate is somewhat round yet very solidly structured to create a captivating wine made from remarkable fruit. (Residual sugar: 28 g/l.)

▲ Dom. Sipp-Mack, 1, rue des Vosges, 68150 Hunawihr, tel. 03.89.73.61.88, fax 03.89.73.36.70, e-mail sippmack@calixo.net ☑ ▼ by appt.

PAUL SPANNAGEL 1999★

0.35 ha 3,700 €5-8

The modern belltower, built after the destruction wrought by the Second World War, should not deceive the visitor. Katzenthal is a village full of history and viticultural traditions stretching back in time. Paul Spannagel has created a very floral Gewurztraminer, grown on limestone soil. A fresh attack is followed by good balance and length. This well-made 99 could be drunk as an aperitif, served with cheeses or drunk with dessert. (Residual sugar: 8 g/l.)

▲ Paul Spannagel et Fils, 1, Grand-Rue, 68230 Katzenthal, tel. 03.89.27.01.70, fax 03.89.27.45.93 ☑ ▼ ev. day except Sun. 8am–12 noon 2pm–7pm

VINCENT SPANNAGEL

Sélection de grains nobles 1998★★

0.36 ha 1,280 €25-30

Katzenthal is several miles west of Colmar. Nestling among its vines, the village is

dominated by the château de la Wineck. Here Vincent Spannagel has produced a very bright golden-yellow wine whose nose is subtly fruity with spicy overtones. The palate of this Gewurztraminer is powerful but well blended, with hints of crystallised fruits.
➤ Vincent Spannagel, 82, rue du Vignoble, 68230 Katzenthal, tel. 03.89.27.52.13, fax 03.89.27.56.48 ⟡ ⟡ by appt.

BERNARD STAEHLE
Cuvée Elise 1999★

☐ 0.6 ha 2,700 🔾 €5-8

Bernard Staehlé looks after more than 6 ha (15 acres) of vines in a commune near Colmar. His numerous stars in the *Guide* reflect the high level of his wine-making. His Cuvée Elise releases strong notes of quince and lychee. With its excellent balance, length and power, this wine will need two to three years' keeping to maximise its potential. (Residual sugar: 18 g/l.)
➤ EARL Bernard Staehlé, 15, rue Clemenceau, 68920 Wintzenheim, tel. 03.89.27.39.02, fax 03.89.27.59.37 ⟡ ⟡ by appt.

DOM. STOEFFLER
Vendanges tardives 1998★

☐ 0.6 ha 2,500 ⟡ ◆ €11-15

Martine and Vincent Stoeffler have an estate at Barr. In 1988, they merged their vineyard with that of Martine's parents at Ribeauvillé. Both are oenologists, and ply their craft with artistry. Their lovely light-yellow wine reveals an intense nose with the accent on stewed fruits and mirabelle jam. The palate is beautifully round (perhaps too much so, at present). The wine is both powerful and true to type: 'This Gewurztraminer is a great classic,' said one taster.
➤ Dom. Martine et Vincent Stoeffler, 1, rue des Lièvres, 67140 Barr, tel. 03.88.08.52.50, fax 03.88.08.17.09, e-mail vins.stoeffler@wanadoo.fr ⟡ ⟡ by appt.

THOMANN Clos du Letzenberg 1999

☐ 0.2 ha 2,152 ⟡ ◆ €8-11

The Thomann family cultivates a 7-ha (17-acre) estate of vines. In 1978 they began the gigantic project of restoring the coteau du Letzenberg, establishing terraces on its steep slopes. The result is a Gewurztraminer with golden lights and the variety's characteristic bouquet. With its well-structured palate, this is a long, generous wine, well suited for keeping. (Residual sugar: 12 g/l.)
➤ Vins Le Manoir, 56, rue de la Promenade, 68040 Ingersheim, tel. 03.89.27.23.69, fax 03.89.27.23.69, e-mail thomann@terre-net.fr ⟡ ⟡ by appt.
➤ Thomann

ANDRE THOMAS ET FILS
Vieilles vignes 1999

☐ 0.6 ha 3,000 €11-15

André and François Thomas are enthusiastic wine-growers who together tend 6 ha (15 acres) of vines and are currently turning to organic methods. Their Vieilles Vignes (old vines) wine, grown on limestone-clay soil, is still in an early phase. The nose is extremely subtle and the palate fairly rich, though it has a sufficiently acid structure to allow it to blossom fully after three or four years in the cellar. (Residual sugar: 30 g/l.)
➤ EARL André Thomas et Fils, 3, rue des Seigneurs, 68770 Ammerschwihr, tel. 03.89.47.16.60, fax 03.89.47.37.22 ⟡ by appt.

TRIMBACH Cuvée des Seigneurs de Ribeaupierre 1997★★

☐ 2.5 ha 12,000 ⟡ €15-23

This is a family estate wholly in the Alsatian tradition, meaning that it puts all its art into assembling vintages of great individuality, made to exacting standards. This intense straw-yellow Gewurztraminer with its slight golden glints has a concentrated, very authentic bouquet which runs through the grape variety's entire aromatic range: spices, roses, exotic fruits and notes of nutmeg. The palate is no less expressive, having a fairly rich, not to say opulent, balance. The lovely finish is smooth and long, deploying pure aromas without any heaviness. This is a very forthcoming wine.
➤ F.E. Trimbach, 15, rte de Bergheim, 68150 Ribeauvillé, tel. 03.89.73.60.30, fax 03.89.73.89.04. e-mail contact@maison-trimbach.fr ⟡ ⟡ by appt.

CHARLES WANTZ
Sélection de grains nobles 1998★

☐ 0.3 ha 1,000 €38-46

The Charles Wantz business was established several generations ago in Barr. Among the town's various economic activities, wine-growing has always been to the fore. Every year, around 14 July, there is a traditional wine festival for the wine-growers of the canton. This golden-yellow Gewurztraminer glistens with bright-amber lights before exhaling a subtle fruitiness with spicy nuances. It attacks the palate cleanly, then develops powerfully through to a spicy finish.
➤ Charles Wantz, 36, rue Saint-Marc, 67140 Barr, tel. 03.88.08.90.44, fax 03.88.08.54.61, e-mail eliane.moser@fnac.net ⟡ ⟡ by appt.

JEAN-PAUL WASSLER
Fronholz 1999★

☐ 0.37 ha 3,000 🔾 €8-11

Jean-Paul Wassler is a veteran wine-maker who took over this 12-ha (30-acre) estate in 1960, and led it into direct selling. Before that, it used to dispatch most of its production in bulk, mainly to Paris. This Gewurztraminer was grown on a limestone-clay *terroir* and has a nose which is both subtle and intense, evocative of lychees. The palate is equally expressive, with floral and exotic notes, and has both good balance and length. (Residual sugar: 17 g/l.)

WINTER Muhlforst 1999★

0.2 ha 2,000

This small estate of 4 ha (10 acres) at Hunwihr deals in high-quality vintages. This Gewurztraminer is still very young, and marked by its limestone-clay origins. The bouquet's smoky notes reveal a hint of over-ripeness. With its powerful, well-balanced palate, this wine is both generous and promising; it will reach its full potential after two years. (Residual sugar: 20 g/l.)

DOM. WEINBACH

Vendanges tardives Altenbourg 1998★

1 ha 4,000 €38-46

The Weinbach-Clos des Capucins estate is widely known; its wines are enjoyed at the best tables. More than half are bound for export. This bright golden-yellow wine has subtle citrus aromas. The palate is well structured, rich and powerful. There is good balance and a long fresh finish of citrus fruits. A wine with a future.

• Dom. Weinbach-Colette Faller et ses Filles, Clos des Capucins, 68240 Kaysersberg, tel. 03.89.47.13.21, fax 03.89.47.38.18 ▼ by appt.

• GAEC Jean-Paul Wassler, 1, rte d'Epfig, 67650 Blienschwiller, tel. 03.88.92.41.53, fax 03.88.92.63.11 ▼ by appt.
• Marc Wassler

JEAN-MICHEL WELTY

Bollenberg 1999★★

1.2 ha 10,000 €5-8

Jean-Michel Welty has been at the head of this business since 1984, and directs it from a historic former tithe-court, built in 1576. His Gewurztraminer is worthy of this setting, having a very intense nose with notes of spices, pear and citrus. The palate is rich and fleshy, with good structure and length. This wine will go with all sorts of food, including exotic specialities, cheeses and desserts. (Residual sugar: 13 g/l.)

• EARL dom. Jean-Michel Welty, 22-24, Grand-Rue, 68500 Orschwihr, tel. 03.89.76.09.03, fax 03.89.76.16.80, e-mail jean-michel-welty@terre-net.fr ▼ ev. day 8.30am–11.30am 2pm–7pm; Sun. by appt.

• Albert Winter, 17, rue Sainte-Hune, 68150 Hunawihr, tel. 03.89.73.62.95, fax 03.89.73.62.95 ▼ by appt.

WUNSCH & MANN

Sélection de grains nobles Collection Joseph Mann 1998

0.8 ha 2,400 €30-38

This business produces and deals in wines, and was established in Wettolsheim a long time ago. It has done much to promote the name of Alsatian wines. Its Gewurztraminer is golden yellow with amber lights, and releases notes of peach and mild spices. The palate is full and fruity but is still somewhat too sugary. It needs a little more time to blend in.

• Wunsch et Mann, 2, rue des Clefs, 68920 Wettolsheim, tel. 03.89.22.91.25, fax 03.89.80.05.21, e-mail wunsch-mann@wanadoo.fr ▼ by appt.
• Mann family

ZIEGLER-MAULER

Vendanges tardives Cuvée Inès 1998

0.4 ha 1,000 €23-30

In 1996, this estate of 5 ha (12 ha) was taken over by Philippe Ziegler, who had vinified its production since 1990. His Cuvée Inès is made from 50-year-old vines. The golden colour is very promising. The bouquet offers notes of marc brandy, which gives it a somewhat mature character. The powerful palate, with its crystallised aromas, is still strongly marked by the high percentage of residual sugar, which needs three years to blend in.

• Jean-Jacques Ziegler-Mauler Fils, 2, rue des Merles, 68630 Mittelwihr, tel. 03.89.47.90.37, fax 03.89.47.98.27 ▼ by appt.

Alsace Tokay-Pinot Gris

Pinot Gris has been known locally as Tokay d'Alsace for over four centuries. This is quite astonishing, because it is a variety that has never been grown in eastern Hungary (famous for Tokay). Legend has it, however, that Tokay was brought back to Alsace by General L. de Schwendi, who was the owner of a substantial vineyard in Alsace. The original area in which it was grown belonged to the historic Duchy of Burgundy, as did all the areas where Pinot is grown.

ALSACE

Alsace Tokay-Pinot Gris

Pinot Gris is planted on only 1,300 ha (3,211 acres) and produces a full-bodied, heavy, fine wine, which can easily be substituted for red wine to accompany meat dishes. At its most sumptuous, as it was in 1983, 1989 and 1990, which were exceptional vintages, it is one of the best possible accompaniments for foie gras.

DOM. PIERRE ADAM
Katzenstegel Cuvée Théo 1999★★   1 ha   7,000   €8-11

VIN D'ALSACE

DOMAINE PIERRE ADAM

TOKAY PINOT GRIS KATZENSTEGEL CUVÉE THÉO

This family business, founded in 1950 with just 1 ha (2.5 acres) of vines, has not stopped growing in both area and reputation. Today it has 11 ha (27 acres) and wins two stars for this Katzenstegel, grown on a sandy-gravel *terroir*. Last year's version was judged remarkable, while this Cuvée Théo is elegant, rich and long, its freshness well balanced by superb roundness. (Residual sugar: 22 g/l.)
- Dom. Pierre Adam, 8, rue du Lt-Louis-Mourier, 68770 Ammerschwihr, tel. 03.89.78.23.07, fax 03.89.47.39.68, e-mail info@domaine-adam.com
- ev. day 8am–12 noon 1pm–8pm

ANDRE ANCEL Quatre Saisons 1999   €5-8
0.23 ha   1,490

With its surrounding walls and castle-keep, Kayserberg still bears the stamp of the Middle Ages and Renaissance. The Ancel family have been tending vines around here for slightly more than a century. Their cellar contains rows of traditional tuns and small modern stainless-steel vats. This wine has a powerful nose combining the peach-like fruitiness and smoked apricot that typify the variety, aromas which reappear with intensity on the palate. After an honest, round attack, the wine is robust but remains very pleasant. (Residual sugar: 20 g/l.)
- EARL André Ancel, 3, rue du Collège, 68240 Kaysersberg, tel. 03.89.47.10.76, fax 03.89.78.13.78
- ev. day 8am–12 noon 1.30pm–7pm

VIGNOBLE FREDERIC ARBOGAST
Vieilles vignes 1999   €5-8
0.52 ha   3,600

The commune of Westhoffen lies in the northern part of the Alsatian wine region, west of Strasbourg. The Arbogast estate has been here for about thirty years. Grown on marly clay soil, this Tokay comes from old vines and has aromas of undergrowth and mushrooms. On the palate the fruit comes through subtly within a supple structure. A pleasing composition. (Residual sugar: 28 g/l.)
- EARL Frédéric Arbogast, 3, pl. de l'Eglise, 67310 Westhoffen, tel. 03.88.50.30.51, fax 03.88.50.30.51
- by appt.

DOM. BAUMANN Birgele 1999   €8-11
0.83 ha   9,000

This fairly new business has 14 ha (35 acres) of vines. It was formed in 1998 by Jean-Michel Baumann and Claude Wiss. Their 1999 Tokay has a restrained nose with the odd note of peach. This well-balanced, very lively wine is true to type and will achieve full maturity shortly. (Residual sugar: 30.6 g/l.)
- Dom. Baumann, 8, av. Méquillet, 68340 Riquewihr, tel. 03.89.47.92.14, fax 03.89.47.99.31, e-mail baumann@reperes.com by appt.

ANDRE BLANCK ET SES FILS
Cuvée Margaux 1999★   €8-11
1.5 ha   5,000

Acquired by André Blanck some fifty years ago, the Cour des Chevaliers de Malte once belonged to Lazare de Schwendi, who is credited with 'inventing' Tokay. So this is an appropriate site to grow Pinot Gris. This Cuvée Margaux has a complex bouquet full of flowers and ripe fruits. Its balance is a blend of rich grape matter and good freshness. It will be even better in two to three years. (Residual sugar: 25 g/l.)
- EARL André Blanck et Fils, Ancienne Cour des Chevaliers de Malte, 68240 Kientzheim, tel. 03.89.78.24.72, fax 03.89.47.17.07
- ev. day except Sun. 8am–7pm

HENRI BLEGER
Coteau du Haut-Koenigsbourg 1999★★   €8-11
0.38 ha   3,600

Saint-Hippolyte lies at the foot of the Haut-Koenigsbourg. Henri Bléger tends 8 ha (20 acres) of vines. His Renaissance (1562) cellar contains oak casks. This Tokay is not oak-matured, but for all that is a great wine. The very ripe, not to say overripe, fruit is evident to the nose, alongside smoky nuances. The palate has excellent structure and is rounded but balanced. The long, fresh finish gives the wine a frisky character which 'makes you want more'. A Tokay to go with foie gras. (Residual sugar: 11 g/l.)

108

● Henri Bléger, 2, rue Saint-Fulrade, 68590 Saint-Hippolyte, tel. 03.89.73.00.08, fax 03.89.73.05.93 ▼ by appt.

DOM. DU BOUXHOF
Vendanges tardives Cuvée Benjamin 1998★

17.78 ha | 1,400 | 23-30

Old parchments have been found tracing the history of the Bouxhof estate back eight centuries. This property of 7 ha (17 acres) is the only one in Alsace officially classified as an historic monument (1996). The wine is a deep golden yellow and releases a bouquet of concentrated aromas of crystallised fruits and aniseed. A thoroughbred Pinot Gris, balanced. A thoroughly balanced Pinot Gris, with recurring aniseed notes; its good supporting acidity will help it to age well.

● EARL François Edel et Fils, Dom. du Bouxhof, 68630 Mittelwihr, tel. 03.89.47.90.34, fax 03.89.47.84.82 ▼ ev. day 9am-7pm

CAMILLE BRAUN Lippelsberg 1999★

0.5 ha | 3,000 | €5-8

Camille Braun and his son belong to a wine-growing family with some two hundred years' experience. They tend 9.5 ha (23 acres) in the southern part of the Alsace wine region. They aim to get the best out of their *terroirs*, as this 99 Lippelsberg shows. Grown on sandstone-clay soil, it has a richly fruity nose with a touch of mineral, and an equally expressive palate. Full, rich and round, it has a good finish and a welcome freshness. (Residual sugar: 23 g/l.)

● Camille Braun, 16, Grand-Rue, 68500 Orschwihr, tel. 03.89.76.95.20, fax 03.89.74.35.03 ▼ ev. day except Sun. 8am-12 noon 1.30pm-7pm

DOM. BURGHART-SPETTEL
Réserve 1999★

0.35 ha | 2,900 | €5-8

This family estate, founded in 1948, has stayed loyal to tradition, especially in its commitment to oak-maturing. Its Réserve Pinot Gris has a lovely, already very ripe, fruitiness with a note of autumn undergrowth, aromas which reappear on the palate. Pleasantly balanced, having both freshness and a certain power, this 99 has a beautiful long finish.

● Dom. Burghart-Spettel, 9, rue du Vin, 68630 Mittelwihr, tel. 03.89.47.93.19, fax 03.89.49.07.62 ▼ by appt.

DOPFF ET IRION
Les Maquisards 1999★

3.5 ha | 21,000 | €8-11

Riquewihr and the lands of its château were the property of the Dukes of Wurtemberg from 1320 until the Revolution. Established in 1946, the Dopff and Irion business cultivates two estates, one of which is the château de Riquewihr (27 ha/67 acres). The name of Les Maquisards Pinot Gris was chosen by René Dopff, founder of the enterprise and a former member of the French Resistance. This bright golden-yellow 99 is a great classic. The extremely subtle nose releases notes of crystallised fruits and hay. The attack reveals the wine's freshness, power and solid structure. It needs time to reach its potential, but is worth waiting for. (Residual sugar: 14 g/l.)

● Dopff et Irion, Dom. du château de Riquewihr, 68340 Riquewihr, tel. 03.89.47.92.51, fax 03.89.47.98.90, e-mail post@dopff-irion.com ▼ by appt.

EINHART Westerberg 1999

1 ha | 3,000 | €5-8

The 99 version of this wine does not have the quality of some of its predecessors (the 94 and 96), but is a satisfying product. The nose is honest, subtle and true to type, with notes of honey and liquorice. The powerful, fresh palate has good balance. André Jost's watercolour on the label matches the impressions this wine creates in the nose and on the palate, with its nuances of warmth and freshness. (Residual sugar: 10 g/l.)

● Nicolas Einhart, 15, rue Principale, 67560 Rosenwiller, tel. 03.88.50.41.90, fax 03.88.50.29.27, e-mail info@einhart.com ▼ by appt.

FERNAND ENGEL ET FILS
Clos des Anges 1999★

n.c. | 7,300 | €8-11

This 99 Tokay marks the estate's 50th birthday. The nose gradually reveals its fruity aromas. The rich, powerful palate, still marked by sugar, has good length. A promising wine that should not be opened for a year or two. (Residual sugar: 35 g/l.)

● GAEC Fernand Engel et Fils, 1, rte du Vin, 68590 Rorschwihr, tel. 03.89.73.77.27, fax 03.89.73.63.70, e-mail fengel@terre-net.fr ▼ ev. day 8am-12 noon 1pm-6pm except Sun. 9am-12 noon

RENE FLECK 1999

n.c. | n.c. | €5-3

The label states 'René Fleck et fille' because in 1995 Nathalie Fleck joined her father on their estate in the Vallée Noble. Their 99 wine, grown on conchiferous limestone, opens slowly to reveal exotic notes, enhanced by hints of undergrowth. The balanced palate gives an impression of richness both when it hits the palate and through the long finish. There is a concluding touch of warmth. (Residual sugar: 10.5 g/l.)

● René Fleck et Fille, 27, rte d'Orschwihr, 68570 Soultzmatt, tel. 03.89.47.01.20, fax 03.89.47.09.24 ▼ by appt.

ROBERT FREUDENREICH
Côte de Rouffach 1999

0.34 ha | 3,500 | €8-11

The Freudenreichs, father and son, tend about 7 ha (17 acres) of vines using all the best traditional methods, such as harvesting by hand and the vinification and maturing of wines in oak. Their Tokay is very floral and spicy both in the nose and on the palate. This

is a pleasing wine with a smooth roundness and a spicy finish. (Residual sugar: 18 g/l.)
- Robert Freudenreich et Fils,
31, rue de l'Eglise, 68250 Pfaffenheim,
tel. 03.89.49.60.88, fax 03.89.49.69.36 ▼
Y by appt.

W. GISSELBRECHT
Réserve spéciale 1999

□   3 ha   28,000   €5-8

The fortified town of Dambach-la-Ville looks much the same as it must have done in the 18th century. It prides itself on having the largest area devoted to vines in Alsace. Gisselbrecht et Fils, besides its wine-merchant's activities, cultivates 17 ha (42 acres) of vines in Dambach and the neighbouring communes of Dieffenthal, Scherwiller and Châtenois. The bouquet of its Réserve Spéciale is still restrained, opening slightly onto one or two floral and smoky notes. The palate is already well balanced and is both powerful (an understatement) and persistent. (Residual sugar: 10 g/l.)
- Willy Gisselbrecht et Fils, 5, rte du Vin,
67650 Dambach-la-Ville, tel. 03.88.92.41.02,
fax 03.88.92.45.50 ▼ Y ev. day except Sun. 8am–12 noon 2pm–6pm

GOETZ 1999★★

□   0.6 ha   6,000   €5-8

They say that Napoleon liked Wolxheim wines; the village lies in the north of the region, on marly limestone soil. Mathieu Goetz has managed to obtain an extremely promising Pinot Gris from it. Though a little closed, the bouquet has a fine scent. The palate is well balanced, full and long. A wine for keeping, which could go with a large range of foods including poultry. (Residual sugar: 13 g/l.)
- Mathieu Goetz, 2, rue Jeanne-d'Arc,
67120 Wolxheim, tel. 03.88.38.10.47 ▼
Y by appt.

JOSEPH GSELL Cuvée César 1999★★

□   0.3 ha   1,500   ■   €8-11

This wine has both strength and power. The bouquet is subtle and intense, revealing its strength first in the nose and then on the palate, which is rich and well balanced with good structure. The fruity finish adds a note of elegance. (Residual sugar: 32 g/l.)
- Joseph Gsell, 26, Grand-Rue,
68500 Orschwihr, tel. 03.89.76.95.11,
fax 03.89.76.20.54 ▼
Y ev. day except Sun. 9am–7pm

JEAN-PAUL HAEFFELIN ET FILS
Cuvée Vieilles vignes 1999★

□   0.2 ha   2,000   ■   €5-8

This family has many generations of wine-making experience, founding their estate in 1770. In 1993, Daniel Haeffelin moved the business out of town, but they still welcome their visitors in the medieval town. This Tokay has a nose of crystallised fruits and white flowers and a well-balanced palate offering freshness and some power. This is a characteristic, easy-drinking wine with a good finish. (Residual sugar: 15 g/l.)
- Vignoble Daniel Haeffelin,
35, Grand-Rue, 68420 Eguisheim,
tel. 03.89.41.77.85, fax 03.89.23.32.43 ▼
Y by appt.

DOM. HENRI HAEFFELIN ET FILS Le Silex 1999★

□   0.5 ha   3,000   ■ €8-11

Guy Haeffelin has been in charge of this delightful property of 16 ha (40 acres) since 1988. His aim has been to 'capture the taste of the *terroir*'. Like last year, his Le Silex wine has caught the Jury's attention. Deep yellow in colour, its bouquet releases aromas of crystallised fruit and white flowers. Despite the current dominance of sugar, the attack is honest and fresh, introducing a palate whose richness creates a full, dense impression. (Residual sugar: 10 g/l.)
- Dom. Henri Haeffelin,
13, rue d'Eguisheim, 68920 Wettolsheim,
tel. 03.89.80.76.81, fax 03.89.79.67.05 ▼
Y ev. day 8am–12 noon 1pm–7pm; Sun. by appt.
- Guy Haeffelin

DOM. MATERNE HAEGELIN ET SES FILLES Cuvée Elise 1999

□   2 ha   17,900   €8-11

This wine bears the name of the youngest female representative of the estate. It too is young, with its still-restrained nose opening up, with its floral and fruity nuances that are a little overripe. The palate is supple and round, but has not yet achieved its correct balance, having too much acidity. It needs more time. (Residual sugar: 16 g/l.)
- Dom. Materne Haegelin et ses Filles,
45-47, Grand-Rue, 68500 Orschwihr,
tel. 03.89.76.95.17, fax 03.89.74.88.87,
e-mail filles@haegelin-materne.fr
Y ev. day 8am15–12 noon 1pm–6.30pm
- Régine Garnier

HAULLER
Cuvée Saint-Sébastien 1999★★

□   1 ha   11,000   €5-8

Since its foundation in 1830, this family estate has come a long way. It is involved in wine-trading and has its own 19 ha (47 acres) of vines, mainly on granitic soils. This Cuvée Saint-Sébastien is immediately attractive, with its expressive and complex nose combining notes of flowers, fruits and honey. On the palate it reveals a solid structure, good balance and length, despite its youth. A wine for drinking with good food: it would go well with a capon. (Residual sugar: 10 g/l.)
- J. Hauller et Fils, 3, rue de la Gare,
67650 Dambach-la-Ville, tel. 03.88.92.40.21,
fax 03.88.92.45.41, e-mail j.hauller@wanadoo.fr ▼ Y by appt.
- René Hauller

KLEIN-BRAND Cuvée Réserve 1999

0.55 ha 5,800 ▥ €5-8

The *terroirs* in the Vallée Noble usually produce rich, very characteristic wines, and this still-young 99 is a good example. It has a fine nose, combining white flowers (acacia) and pronounced notes of liquorice and mint. The same aromas reappear on the palate, which is fresh, well balanced and pleasant. (Residual sugar: 15 g/l.)

☛ Klein-Brand, 96, rue de la Vallée, 68570 Soultzmatt, tel. 03.89.47.00.08, fax 03.89.47.65.53 ▾ ev. day except Sun. 8am–12 noon 1.30pm–6pm

MARC KREYDENWEISS

Clos Rebberg 1999★★

0.4 ha 3,000 ▮♦ €11-15

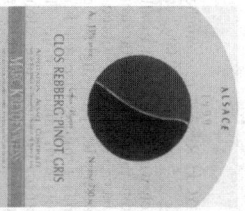

The unusually sober label of this Pinot Gris was designed by David Tremlet. The wine is produced organically on a 12-ha (30-acre) estate. Its bouquet is full of fruity aromas (ripe, dried and crystallized fruits) with a hint of honey. On the palate it has a very good, almost crisp body, and releases exotic flavours and notes of apricot. This wine is a real pleasure to drink. (Residual sugar: 8 g/l.)

☛ Dom. Marc Kreydenweiss, 12, rue Deharbe, 67140 Andlau, tel. 03.88.08.95.83, fax 03.88.08.41.16 ▾ by appt.

CELLIER DE LA WEISS

Ritzenthaler 1999★

3 ha 26,300 ▥♦

This Tokay was produced on an alluvial soil deposited by the Weiss and Fecht rivers, which flow down from the heights of the Vosges. It has a charming nose in which the scents of the grape variety are complemented by aromas of dried fruit. After a well-rounded attack, a fruity quince flavour lingers on to a long and pleasant finish. (Residual sugar: 16 g/l.)

☛ Cellier de La Weiss, BP 5, 68240 Kaysersberg, tel. 03.89.30.23.60, fax 03.89.27.35.33

MEISTERMANN Cuvée Prestige 1999

0.35 ha 4,000 ▥ €5-8

It is worth visiting Pfaffenheim to see the chapel of Notre-Dame-du-Schauenberg, a former place of pilgrimage from which there is a magnificent view over the Alsace plain. The village also boasts a large number of old wine-making firms. Michel Meistermann has

111

a modest, 4.5-ha (11-acre) estate and cellars equipped with traditional large wooden casks. The bouquet of his Cuvée Prestige is still restrained on the nose, but on the palate it is full and balanced and already has very good length. It will improve if kept for a year or two. (Residual sugar: 10 g/l.)

☛ Michel Meistermann, 37, rue de l'Eglise, 68250 Pfaffenheim, tel. 03.89.49.60.61, fax 03.89.49.79.30 ▾ by appt.

GILBERT MEYER Cuvée Prestige 1999

n.c. 2,400 ▥ €5-8

Coming from a marly limestone soil, this wine releases floral aromas against a slightly smoky background that is typical of the grape variety. This is a classic wine with a good structure, and although not particularly full-bodied, it is well balanced and pleasant. (Residual sugar: 18 g/l.)

☛ Gilbert Meyer, 5, rue du Schauenberg, 68420 Voegtlinshoffen, tel. 03.89.49.36.65, fax 03.89.86.42.45, e-mail vins.gilbert.meyer@wanadoo.fr ▾ by appt.

CHARLES NOLL 1999★

0.35 ha 2,500 ▥

Since 1983 Charles Noll has been running this family estate, which has 6 ha (15 acres) of vines planted mainly on limestone-clay soils. His Pinot Gris is pale yellow with green glints and has a bouquet typical of the grape variety. On the palate it is delightfully fine, fresh and very well balanced and makes an elegant overall impression. (Residual sugar: 14.6 g/l.)

☛ EARL Charles Noll, 2, rue de l'Ecole, 68630 Mittelwihr, tel. 03.89.47.93.21, fax 03.89.47.86.23 ▾ ev. day, 9am–9pm

PIERRE ET JEAN-PIERRE RIETSCH Rippelholz 1999★★

0.39 ha 2,500 ▮♦ €8-11

Once the property of the abbey at Andlau, Mittelbergheim has not only retained its picturesque charm but has also enhanced its reputation for wine-growing thanks to producers such as the Rietsch family. This Tokay, which comes from the marly limestone soils of the Rippelholz area, has an expressive, elegant nose of exotic fruits and is fine and pleasant on the palate, with plenty of body and excellent potential. A very promising wine, it

Alsace Tokay-Pinot Gris

should be kept for a few months. (Residual sugar: 36 g/l.)

➤ Pierre et Jean-Pierre Rietsch, 32, rue Principale, 67140 Mittelbergheim, tel. 03.88.08.00.64, fax 03.88.08.40.91, e-mail rietsch@wanadoo.fr ▼ ▼ by appt.

WILLY ROLLI-EDEL 1999★
☐ 0.34 ha 1,880 **€8-11**

Rorschwihr is one of a line of villages running to the south of the Haut-Koenigsbourg. Willy Rolli is a gifted wine-grower with an 11-ha (27-acre) family estate. His Pinot Gris opens with the smoky aromas of the grape variety, then releases notes of flowers and honey. On the palate its fullness, power and intense flavours make it a pleasant, well-balanced wine. (Residual sugar: 17 g/l.)

➤ Willy Rolli-Edel, 5, rue de l'Eglise, 68590 Rorschwihr, tel. 03.89.73.63.26, fax 03.89.73.83.50 ▼ ▼ by appt.

DANIEL RUFF Cuvée Julie 1999
☐ 0.6 ha 4,000 **€5-8**

This estate is located at Heiligstein, at the foot of Mont Sainte-Odile. It was founded in 1920, and although this is quite recent by Alsace standards, it already has 10 ha (25 acres) of vines. Its Cuvée Julie has aromas of overripe fruit, along with a few notes of amyl alcohol. Although not especially full-bodied on the palate, it is well balanced and quite round, with some hints of fruitiness. (Residual sugar: 9 g/l.)

➤ Dom. Daniel Ruff, 64, rue Principale, 67140 Heiligenstein, tel. 03.88.08.10.81, fax 03.88.08.43.61 ▼ ▼ by appt.

THOMANN Clos du Letzenberg
Sélection de grains nobles 1998★
☐ 0.26 ha 2,267 **€15-23**

Located between Ingersheim and Turckheim, the Letzenberg hillside faces south-east. It was abandoned after the First World War and restored to wine-growing by the present owner over the last 20 years or so. He was also responsible for the terraced layout. The wine has a deep straw-yellow colour and a rich, fine nose marked by crystallised fruits. It fills the palate very well, has good balance and is sure to keep well. (Half-litre bottles.)

➤ Vins Le Manoir, 56, rue de la Promenade, 68040 Ingersheim, tel. 03.89.27.23.69, fax 03.89.27.23.69, e-mail thomann@terre-net.fr ▼ ▼ by appt.

➤ Thomann

ANDRE THOMAS ET FILS
Cuvée particulière 1999
☐ 0.3 ha 1,500 **€11-15**

The Thomas family has produced many successful wines and this year offers a Tokay from a limestone-clay *terroir* with fine, fruity, elegant aromas. On the palate the wine reveals a rich, even somewhat fleshy structure. It is still slightly reserved and has a hint of bitterness at the finish. (Residual sugar: 40 g/l.)

➤ EARL André Thomas et Fils, 3, rue des Seigneurs, 68770 Ammerschwihr, tel. 03.89.47.16.60, fax 03.89.47.37.22 ▼ by appt.

TRIMBACH Réserve personnelle 1997★
☐ 4 ha 20,000 **€15-23**

Trimbach wines are served in all the best places, from prestigious restaurants to the Elysée Palace. This straw-coloured 97 has a very characteristic, spicy, slightly heavy nose and aromas ranging through honey and yellow fruits with mineral notes. The spicy quality returns on the palate, along with a fullness and a pleasant balance. The residual sugar makes its presence felt, giving a delightful overall impression with an aromatic finish.

➤ F.E. Trimbach, 15, rte de Bergheim, 68150 Ribeauvillé, tel. 03.89.73.60.30, fax 03.89.73.89.04, e-mail contact@maison-trimbach.fr ▼ ▼ by appt.

CLOS SAINTE-ODILE 1999
☐ n.c. 5,000 **€8-11**

The Clos Sainte-Odile is located on the heights of Obernai, where its wines are developed by a subsidiary of the Obernai Cave Vinicole. This one has typically strong smoky notes and hints of oak, along with a certain fruitiness. Sound and well balanced, it has a pleasantly acid quality, and was described by one taster as 'a likeable wine'. (Residual sugar: 7.5 g/l.)

➤ Sté vinicole Sainte-Odile, 30, rue du Gal-Leclerc, 67210 Obernai, tel. 03.88.47.60.29, fax 03.88.47.60.22 ▼ ▼ by appt.

VORBURGER
Sélection de grains nobles 1998★★
☐ n.c. n.c. **€15-23**

Founded in the 1950s, this family concern started to make its name in 1958 under Arsène Vorburger, and is now run by his grandson. It offers a golden-yellow Pinot Gris with a bouquet pleasantly marked by noble rot and undergrowth. Rich, opulent and spicy on the palate, it has a very fine acidic quality, which will ensure that it develops well. With its remarkably good length, it is not only a wine of great nobility but excellent value for money too. (Half-litre bottles.)

➤ Jean-Pierre Vorburger et Fils, 3, rue de la Source, 68420 Voegtlinshoffen, tel. 03.89.49.35.52, fax 03.89.86.40.56 ▼ ▼ ev. day except Sun. 8am-12 noon 1.30pm-6pm

LOUIS WALTER
Cuvée des Seigneurs 1999★
☐ 0.27 ha 2,800 **€8-11**

This family estate was founded in 1959 by Louis Walter and has been run since 1979 by his son Bernard on a 7-ha (17-acre) lime-stone-clay vineyard in the Pfaffenheim area. His Cuvée des Seigneurs has delightfully rich, complex and intense aromas with quince to the fore. On the palate its intense fruity flavours and well-balanced body make it a fine

Alsace Pinot Noir

Alsace is particularly renowned for its white wines, but it is not widely known that in the Middle Ages red grapes were widely grown. Pinot Noir then virtually disappeared from the area – it is the best red-wine grape variety in regions further south – but it has been reintroduced and is now cultivated in 1,294 ha (3,196 acres), some 8.5% of the Alsace area.

It is principally used to make a pleasant rosé that is dry and fruity, and, like other rosés, it can be drunk with a variety of different dishes. Increasing efforts are being made to produce red wines with Pinot Noir, and this is a welcome development.

BERNADETTE WELTY ET FILS 1999★★
0.55 ha   3,500   €8-11

Guy Welty took over the family estate in 1992. He has a vineyard of about 7 ha (17 acres), spread over four communes. This Tokay comes from a limestone-clay soil and opens with aromas of overripe fruit and notes of citrus fruits. The sweet attack is followed by a round and delightfully fruity quality on the palate. A very promising wine whose finish should become fully balanced in two to three years' time. (Residual sugar: 12 g/l.)
• Bernadette Welty et Fils,
15-17, Grand-Rue, 68500 Orschwihr,
tel. 03.89.76.95.21, fax 03.89.76.95.21 [V]
[Y] ev. day except Sun. 8am–12 noon 1.30pm–7pm

JEAN WEINGAND 1999
n.c.   45,000★

In addition to the family vineyard, the two Cattin brothers, Jacques and Jean-Marie, have developed a wine-merchants' business. Their Tokay opens with a strong old-gold colour and an intense nose of smoky notes followed by the scent of blood orange. On the palate the flavour is rich and well balanced. A wine that will mature well but that already has a great deal of charm. (Residual sugar: 12 g/l.)
• Jean Weingand, 19, rue Roger-Frémeaux, 68420 Voegtlinshoffen, tel. 03.89.49.30.21, fax 03.89.49.26.02 [Y] by appt.
• Jacques et Jean-Marie Cattin

impression. It will be at its best in a few months. (Residual sugar: 31 g/l.)
• Bernard Walter, 10, rue de la Tuilerie, 68250 Pfaffenheim, tel. 03.89.49.62.85, fax 03.89.49.62.85, e-mail stéphane-walter@wanadoo.fr [Y] by appt.

BARON KIRMANN 1999
Élevé en fût de chêne 1999★★
0.2 ha   1,500   €11-15

The vineyards of the Obernai region make outstanding Pinot Noir wines. This is demonstrated with great skill at the Kirmann estate, which was founded in 1630. Its 99 wine has an intense dark-red colour with purplish glints. The highly aromatic nose of soft fruits is dominated by morello cherries and blackberries. This full, rich wine has excellent balance on the palate and expressive tannins, which should be fully blended in two years' time. It delighted the tasters with its persistent notes of cherry at the finish. A Pinot Noir for longer maturing.
• Philippe Kirmann,
2, rue du Gal-de-Gaulle, 67560 Rosheim, tel. 03.88.50.43.01, fax 03.88.50.22.72 [V]
[Y] by appt.

PIERRE BECHT Cuvée Frédéric 1999★
0.5 ha   4,000   €5-8

Standing at the entrance to the Bruche valley, Dorlisheim can take pride in its vineyard on the foothills of the Lower Vosges. The aspect and soils are perfectly suited to bringing out the qualities of the most demanding grape varieties, as this Pinot Noir shows. It has a deep ruby colour with purplish glints and opens with a succession of soft-fruit aromas, mainly cherries and prunes. The oaky taste is well-dosed, adding just a touch of spiciness to the elegant overall impression. After a balanced attack, it is very supple on the palate and not particularly tannic. An excellent wine which will improve over the next three years.
• Pierre et Frédéric Becht,
26, fg des Vosges, 67120 Dorlisheim, tel. 03.88.38.18.22, fax 03.88.38.87.81 [V]
[Y] by appt.

FRANCOIS BLEGER Rouge de Saint-Hippolyte Vieilli en barrique 1999★
0.2 ha   1,500   €8-11

The red wines of Saint-Hippolyte are deeply rooted in the history of the Alsace region. Pinot Noir has always taken pride of place here, and rightly so. This ruby wine with purplish highlights has a fine, complex bouquet of undergrowth. Red-berry flavours appear on the palate, accompanied by rich tannins and an elegant oakiness. There is very good length at the finish.
• François Bléger, 63, rte du Vin, 68590 Saint-Hippolyte, tel. 03.89.73.06.07, fax 03.89.73.06.07, e-mail bleger.françois@liberty-surf.fr [V] [Y] by appt.

Alsace Pinot Noir

DOM. LEON BOESCH
Luss Vallée Noble 1999★★

■III €11–15   0.4 ha 2,500

The vines of the Vallée Noble are very well located, facing south to south-east. There Léon Boesch has produced a dark-ruby Pinot Noir, whose clarity is emphasised by its purplish highlights. On the nose oaky notes blend with red berries (blackberries and black-currants), the palate has a good tannic structure in which oak is clearly evident but never excessive. A full-bodied wine, its flavours include not only blackcurrant and blackberry but also a distinct hint of cherry. It will be at its best in a year or slightly longer.
- Dom. Léon Boesch, 6, rue Saint-Blaise, 68250 Westhalten, tel. 03.89.47.64.95 ☑ ▼ ev. day except Sun. 10am–12 noon 2pm–6pm
- Gérard Boesch

BOHN 1999
■   0.6 ha 3,400 €5–8

This vineyard was established in the 12th century by the monks of Baumgarten abbey on the steep slopes of the Ungersberg, which rise to 901 m (2,955 ft). The schist and sandstone *terroirs* leave their mark on the wines. This one has a warm, red colour with coppery glints and develops mild stewed-fruit aromas on the nose. On the palate the strong oaky tannins will need to mellow so that the wine's pleasant soft-fruit flavours can come through. Keep for a little while longer.
- Bernard Bohn, 1, chem. du Leh, 67140 Reichsfeld, tel. 03.88.85.58.78, fax 03.88.57.84.88 ☑ ▼ ev. day 8am–11.45am 1pm–6pm; Sun. by appt.

FRANCOIS BOHN Reserve 1999★
■III €5–8   0.2 ha 1,500

The Bohn family has been working this vineyard for many generations. Until 1998 they mainly sold grapes, but then they began to produce their own wines. It was a good decision, if this clearly characteristic, ruby Pinot Noir with darker glints is anything to go by. Although its fruity aromas and scents of undergrowth are still restrained, they bode well for a fine future. The supple, complex palate is still marked by tannins, but these will soften in time.
- François Bohn, 35, rue des Trois-Epis, 68040 Ingersheim, tel. 03.89.27.31.27, fax 03.89.27.31.27 ☑ ▼ by appt.

ANDRE DUSSOURT
Rouge de Blienschwiller Elevé en barrique
Réserve Prestige 1999★
■III €11–15   0.2 ha 1,450

These growers come from an old wine-making family that has been in the business since the 17th century. They were originally from Blienschwiller, but moved to Scherwiller after buying up the Bléger firm in 1961. Many of their vines are still at Blienschwiller, including those which produced this Pinot Noir. Its dark-red colour with mauve glints shows straightaway that it comes from good

stock. The fruity bouquet (morello cherries) is somewhat masked by vanilla from the oak, and the palate needs time to achieve the right balance. Nevertheless, all the signs are there to suggest that it will mature well.
- Dom. André Dussourt, 2, rue de Dambach, 67750 Scherwiller, tel. 03.88.92.10.27, fax 03.88.92.18.44, e-mail vins.dussourt@wordline.fr ☑ ▼ ev. day except Sun. 8am–12 noon 1.30pm–6pm
- Paul Dussourt

DOM. ENGEL 1999★
■   €5–8   1 ha 10,000

Located at the foot of the Haut-Koenigsbourg, Orschwiller was once a fiefdom of the castle. The Engel estate has 16 ha (40 acres) of vines, three-quarters of which are used for the Praelatenberg Grand Cru. The Pinot Noir has a fresh, brilliant colour, and pronounced aromas of black-currant and pronounced aromas of black-currant on the palate, which is fleshy, full and rich. This is a pleasant, characteristic wine with good length.
- Dom. Christian et Hubert Engel, 1, rue des Vignes, Haut-Koenigsbourg, 67600 Orschwiller, tel. 03.88.92.01.83, fax 03.88.82.25.09 ☑ ▼ ev. day 9am–11.30am 2pm–6pm

DOM. FLEISCHER 1999★
■   €5–8   0.55 ha 6,000

At Pfaffenheim, halfway between Colmar and Rouffach, the vineyards face south-south-east. The limestone-clay soils are composed of shingly conglomerates, and are perfectly suited to producing well-ripened Pinot Noir grapes. This 99 wine has a light-red colour, veering towards rosé, and releases fairly mild aromas of white flowers. On the palate it reveals a fresh, pleasant, smooth character. It will go well with light dishes such as white meats.
- Dom. Fleischer, 28, rue du Moulin, 68250 Pfaffenheim, tel. 03.89.49.62.70, fax 03.89.49.50.74 ☑ ▼ by appt.

J. FRITSCH 1999★
■   €5–8   0.37 ha 3,600

On the way into Kientzheim from the east, visitors can look around the château of the Confrérie de Saint-Etienne, then go next door to the Wine Museum which traces the history of local viticulture. The wine offered here by Joseph Fritsch has a deep, dark-red colour with subtle purplish glints. The nose is of medium intensity, with pronounced aromas of morello cherries, prunes and blackberries. The attack is clean, and the palate is full-flavoured. The balance is almost complete. In two or three years' time this Pinot Noir will achieve its full potential.
- EARL Joseph Fritsch, 31, Grand-Rue, 68240 Kientzheim, tel. 03.89.78.24.27, fax 03.89.78.24.27 ☑ ▼ by appt.

GEYER 1999★

0.35 ha   2,200   €5-8

Nothalten is surrounded by vineyards; to the west, they overlook the village from sunny hillsides facing east-south-east, while to the east they slope more gently beneath it. Roland Geyer owns 9 ha (22 acres) of vines here, and has produced a clear, deep-ruby Pinot Noir with purplish glints. The nose is marked by black cherries, blackberries and prunes. The attack is clear-cut, leading to a well-balanced palate; the tannins are clearly evident but not unduly so. The soft-fruit flavours re-emerge in the long, full finish.

☛ Dom. Roland Geyer, 148, rue du Vin, 67680 Nothalten, tel. 03.88.92.46.82, fax 03.88.92.63.19 Y by appt.

DOM. ROBERT HAAG ET FILS 1999

0.53 ha   4,188   €5-8

The commune of Schwerwiller, near Sélestat, has developed its vineyards on granitic and granitic-sandy terroirs. The wines in this area are full of lightness and good aromas. This Haag Pinot Noir is no exception; it has a brilliant-red colour and reveals a very floral, fruity nose. The finesse of the aromas is accentuated by a spicy note and a touch of toast. The palate is pleasant, and remains fresh right up to the finish.

☛ Dom. Robert Haag et Fils, 21, rue de la Mairie, 67750 Scherwiller, tel. 03.88.92.11.83, fax 03.88.82.15.85 V Y ev. day except Sun. 9am–12 noon
2pm–7pm
☛ François Haag

LEON HEITZMANN 1999★★★

0.4 ha   3,500   €8-11

The Léon Heitzmann firm is often praised, and in recent years has been awarded two coups de cœur. Yet again it confirms its high reputation by winning a further distinction for its 99 Pinot Noir. This is a rich, elegant wine with aromas of cherries accentuated by notes of blackcurrant. The palate is fine, full, rich and long, and supported by noble, very mature tannins. A wine which combines suppleness and a complex range of soft fruit flavours.

☛ Léon Heitzmann, 2, Grand-Rue, 68770 Ammerschwihr, tel. 03.89.47.10.64, fax 03.89.78.27.76 Y ev. day except Sun. 8am–12 noon 1.30pm–6pm

KIENTZ Coteaux de Blienschwiller 1999★

0.9 ha   6,500   €5-8

Granite soils heat up very quickly in the sun. This means that the grapes usually ripen early and produce wines which are expressive from the start. This intensely red Pinot Noir has a fresh bouquet with floral aromas and a fruity quality which is still restrained. The palate is full, characteristic and very powerful, and there is good length at the finish.

ARMAND HURST Vieilles vignes 1999★★

0.49 ha   4,000   €11-15

The Hurst estate has made its name with its Pinot Noir wines. This firm knows how to get the very best out of the granite terroirs of the Brand Grand Cru, where the old Pinot Noir vines for this wine are located. The wine has a ruby-red colour and an intensely fruity bouquet (blackcurrant) with a fine hint of oak. There is great fullness on the palate, and the tannins are already blended to perfection. A rich, forthcoming wine with red berry flavours and an exquisitely silky quality.

☛ Armand Hurst, 8, rue de la Chapelle, 68230 Turckheim, tel. 03.89.27.40.22, fax 03.89.27.47.67 Y by appt.

HORCHER 1999★

0.57 ha   4,800   €5-8

Mittelwihr stands on the Route du Vin, and is known for its almond trees, which means that its micro-climate is very well suited to growing vines. The terroirs in the area give the wines an unusual character. This Pinot Noir has an intense, very limpid ruby colour, a nose dominated by red berries (especially blackcurrants), and a palate further embellished by a fresh flavour of liquorice. A powerful, well-structured, full, rich wine with supple tannins which give it great presence.

☛ Ernest Horcher et Fils, 6, rue du Vignoble, 68630 Mittelwihr, tel. 03.89.47.93.26, fax 03.89.49.04.92 V Y ev. day except Sun. 8am–12 noon 2pm–7pm

EMILE HERZOG 1999★

0.21 ha   1,600   €8-11

Turckheim is a historic town which attracts many tourists and is known for having a traditional night watchman who does his rounds in the streets every evening in summer. The Herzog family is closely linked with the town, where it has been established since 1686. It offers a dark-red 99 with brown highlights. This pleasantly oaky Pinot Noir also has aromas of jam and plums in the nose, while the palate is dominated by stewed fruits enhanced by notes of cloves. A mouth-filling wine with a full, rich quality and a long, powerful finish.

☛ Emile Herzog, 28, rue du Florimont, 68230 Turckheim, tel. 03.89.27.08.79, e-mail e.herzog@laposte.net V Y by appt.

Alsace Pinot Noir

René Kientz Fils, 51, rte du Vin, 67650 Blienschwiller, tel. 03.88.92.49.06, fax 03.88.92.45.87 ☿ ⟁ by appt.

ANDRE KLEINKNECHT
Vieilli en barrique 1999★

■　0.2 ha　1,300　⬛ €8-11

Mittelbergheim is located to the south of Barr, and is well known not only for its picturesque architecture, but also for its vineyards and wines. With viticultural roots going back to 1621, André Kleinknecht produces wines on an estate of just over 9 ha (22 acres). Dark red in colour with brick-red highlights, his Pinot Noir has a bouquet based on oak with aromas of blackcurrant. The full, rich palate is agreeably forthcoming. The tannins are still very marked, but the wine has good prospects for the future (two to three years).

**André Kleinknecht, 45, rue Principale, 67140 Mittelbergheim, tel. 03.88.08.49.46, fax 03.88.08.49.46,
e-mail andre-kleinknecht@wanadoo.fr ☿
⟁ ev. day 10am–11.30am 1pm–7pm**

HUBERT KRICK Herrenweg 1999★

■　0.9 ha　6,000　⬛ €5-8

For many generations, Hubert Krick's vineyard has been established at Wintzenheim, a small town at the entrance to the Munster valley. This Pinot Noir comes from an alluvial *terroir* where the grapes ripen early because the soil has a high gravel content. It has a very strong red colour, an intense nose of soft fruits with shades of oak, and a pleasant, rich, opulent, fleshy palate with very good length. An excellent wine which is true to type and is both forthcoming and fluid on the palate.

**EARL Hubert Krick,
93–95, rue Clemenceau, 68920 Wintzenheim, tel. 03.89.27.00.01, fax 03.89.27.54.75 ☿
⟁ by appt.**

DOM. DE L'ANCIEN
MONASTÈRE Rouge de Saint-Léonard
Cuvée du Grand Chapitre 1999★★★

■　3 ha　3,066　⬛ €5-8

Saint-Léonard is located near Obernai and is very popular with tourists. This little town is one of the cradles of Alsace Pinot Noir, with renowned producers such as Bernard Hummel and his daughters. The dark-ruby colour of this complex 99 vintage augurs well for the future. Even though the nose is very much of the red berry type, it also has a prominent note of blackberries shaded with quince. The palate is silky and supported by very evident, mature tannins, and there is an exceptionally good balance between body, fruit and acidity.

**B. Hummel et ses Filles,
L'Ancien Monastère, 4, cour du Chapitre-Saint-Léonard, 67530 Boersch, tel. 03.88.95.81.21, fax 03.88.48.11.21, e-mail b.hummel@wanadoo.fr ☿ ⟁ ev. day 8.30am–12.30pm 1.30pm–7.30pm**

DOM. DE L'ECOLE
Côte de Rouffach 1999★

■　n.c.　4,000　⬛ €5-8

The Domaine de l'Ecole is part of the agricultural and viticultural training college at Rouffach. This experimental vineyard was founded in 1868 for teaching purposes, and since 1970 it has expanded and made a name for itself. Its Pinot Noir has a ruby-red colour with purplish highlights. The first impression on the nose is of a balance between the slightly oaky quality of the wine and its aromas of stewed fruit (prunes). Once it has been allowed to breathe for a while it develops scents of cherries and blackberries which show that it is true to type. The tannins on the palate are evident but not at all aggressive, indicating that this 99 wine is still young. There is good balance and length at the finish.

**Dom. de L'Ecole, Lycée viticole, 8, Aux Remparts, 68250 Rouffach, tel. 03.89.78.73.16, fax 03.89.78.73.01, e-mail expl.legta.rouffach@educagri.fr ☿
⟁ by appt.**

JEAN-LUC MADER
Cuvée Théophile 1999★★★

■　0.5 ha　2,500　⬛ €5-8

The commune of Hunawihr is best known for its fortified church, but visitors are attracted by other curiosities too, such as the stork park. The limestone-clay soils seem to be well suited to Pinot Noir, as can be seen from this Cuvée Théophile. Despite its beautiful ruby-red colour and powerfully fruity bouquet (soft fruits dominated by cherries) with delicate shades of oak, it is mainly on the palate that the wine really shows its qualities. It is rich, powerful and forthcoming, and was described by one of the tasters as 'marked by noble oak'. A fleshy wine with good length and a silkiness which further accentuates its elegance.

Jean-Luc Mader, 13, Grand-Rue, 68150 Hunawihr, tel. 03.89.73.80.32, fax 03.89.73.31.22 ☿ ⟁ by appt.

ALBERT MANN Vieilles vignes 1999

■　0.33 ha　2,500　⬛ €15-23

Wettolsheim is a few miles west of Colmar, and has a very large vineyard whose marly limestone soils are suited to every grape variety, and in particular to Pinot Noir. This

ROLLY GASSMANN Rodern 1999★

0.7 ha 3,000 €11-15

The highly-renowned firm of Rolly Gassmann regularly produces expressive wines which truly reflect its mastery of wine-making. This deep-red Pinot Noir already speaks volumes with an aromatic range that goes from fruit to slightly musky notes. It is expansive on the palate, leaving an impression of finesse, fullness and even richness. The finish has good length, but there is room for the flavours to open out more. A wine with great potential.

🍷 Rolly Gassmann, 2, rue de l'Eglise, 68590 Rorschwihr, tel. 03.89.73.63.28, fax 03.89.73.33.06 ☑ ☐ ev. day except Sun. 9am–11.45am 1.15pm–6pm

RINGENBACH-MOSER Réserve 1999

0.6 ha 5,500 €5-8

Sigolsheim is magnificently located at the point where the Kaysersberg valley, much visited by tourists, opens out into the plain. With its famous south-facing *terroirs*, it is a Mecca of Alsatian wine-growing. This 99 wine has a brilliant-red colour with cherry glints, and a fine bouquet with concentrated aromas. The attack is fruity, pleasant and delightfully fresh. 'A classic Pinot Noir,' as one taster described it.

🍷 Ringenbach-Moser, 12, rue du Vallon, 68240 Sigolsheim, tel. 03.89.47.11.23, fax 03.89.47.32.58 ☑ ☐ ev. day except Sat. Sun. 8.30am–11.30am 1.30pm–5.30pm

---

wine has a light-red colour with some brick-red glints, and a nose of fine oak with some hints of red berries. Although fairly rich, the palate is marked by tannins which are still too much in evidence. The finish is sinewy and needs time to mature.

🍷 Dom. Albert Mann, 13, rue du Château, 68920 Wettolsheim, tel. 03.89.80.62.00, fax 03.89.80.34.23, e-mail vins@mann-albert.com ☑ ☐ by appt.

🍷 Barthelmé

OTTER Barriques 1999★★★

0.39 ha 1,200 €8-11

The François Otter estate is located in the commune of Hattstatt, at the foot of the Hatschbourg *grand cru*. Their Pinot Noir is produced by traditional methods, without fining or filtration, and the 99 vintage is a supreme achievement and an example to all. It has a deep garnet colour with mauve high-lights which gives it great presence. The bouquet of morello cherries mingled with hints of leather and spicy oak is remarkable. It is highly expressive on the palate, with full, silky tannins. This is quite simply a perfect wine. 'Its potential for development is enormous,' say the tasters.

🍷 Dom. François Otter et Fils, 4, rue du Muscat, 68420 Hattstatt, tél. 03.89.49.33.00, fax 03.89.49.38.69, e-mail ottjef@nucleus.fr ☑ ☐ by appt.

PAUL SCHERER Réserve personnelle 1999★

0.4 ha 3,000 €5-8

Paul Scherer is one of the oldest wine-making firms in the commune of Husseren-les-Châteaux. The reputation it has earned for itself over five generations will be further enhanced by the quality of this remarkable, brilliant garnet-coloured Pinot Noir. The dense bouquet gives off a fresh blend of aromas of strawberries, raspberries and blackcurrants. The delightfully fine, balanced palate lingers into a long, fruity finish. A great wine.

🍷 EARL Paul Scherer et Fils, 40, rue Principale, 68420 Husseren-les-Châteaux, tel. 03.89.49.30.34, fax 03.89.86.41.67 ☑ ☐ by appt.

DOM. MAURICE SCHOECH 1999★

0.6 ha 4,500 €5-8

Sébastien and Jean-Léon Schoech have been running their father's vineyard since 1995. They have produced an excellent Pinot Noir which will reveal its full potential within two years. It has a red colour with orangey glints, an oaky bouquet with hints of stewed fruits, and notes of redcurrant jam and spices (pepper) on the palate. A robust, persistent wine which is developing plenty of body and has a finish of great finesse.

🍷 Dom. Maurice Schoech, 4, rte de Kientzheim, 68770 Ammerschwihr, tel. 03.89.78.25.78, fax 03.89.78.13.66 ☑ ☐ ev. day except Sun. 9am–12 noon 1.30pm–6pm

EMILE SCHWARTZ ET FILS Réserve personnelle 1999★

0.5 ha 4,500 €5-8

The village of Husseren-les-Châteaux stands to the west of Colmar, overlooking the local vineyards. Its very fine *terroirs* face south-south-east and include such prestigious names as the two grands crus, Pfersigberg and Eichberg. Emile Schwartz grows more than 6 ha (15 acres) of vines here. His Pinot Noir Réserve Personnelle has a very clear purple colour and a nose of cherry aromas mingled with scents of Mediterranean plants and notes of oak. After a rich attack, the palate is well balanced and complex, with a combination of fruit and pepper flavours.

EARL Emile Schwartz et Fils, 3, rue Principale, 68420 Husseren-les-Châteaux, tel. 03.89.49.30.61, fax 03.89.49.27.27 ev. day except Sun. 8am–12 noon 2pm–7pm; cl. 1–15 Sep.

JEAN-PAUL SIMONIS 1999
0.25 ha — 2,300 — €5-8

The first Pinot Noir on the Jean-Paul Simonis estate was produced in 1988. A decade later he offers this deep-purple wine with aromas of morello cherries and blackberries, along with hints of toast. The palate is rich, complex and powerful, with the same soft-fruit flavours as in the bouquet. The tannins are still very much in evidence, but will blend in better given time.

EARL Jean-Paul Simonis et Fils, 1, rue du Chasseur-M.-Besombes, 68770 Ammerschwihr, tel. 03.89.47.13.51, fax 03.89.47.13.51 by appt.
Jean-Marc Simonis

JEAN SIPP 1999★
2 ha — 10,000 — €11-15

Ribeauvillé is a busy town with several industries and a flourishing wine-making sector. With 20 ha (49 acres) of vines, the Sipp estate is one of the leading growers. Its excellent 99 Pinot Noir is a wine for longer maturing with a beautiful garnet colour. After a powerful, complex nose of fruit enhanced by oak from the barrel, it has great structure and a long finish on the palate. The tannins are not yet completely blended, but even so this wine has many qualities.

Dom. Jean Sipp, 60, rue de la Fraternité, 68150 Ribeauvillé, tel. 03.89.73.60.02, fax 03.89.73.82.38, e-mail domaine@jean-sipp.com by appt.
Jean-Jacques Sipp

DOM. J. SPERRY-KOBLOTH
Vieilles vignes 1999★
0.28 ha — 2,000 — €5-8

Blienschwiller is located just over a mile north of Dambach-la-Ville, in the midst of the granite hills of the lower Vosges. The two-mica granite soil is known for producing light, elegant wines, and this dark-red Pinot Noir with purplish glints is no exception. Ripe and dried fruits feature in a range of aromas mainly dominated by red berries (raspberries). On the palate the wine reveals great suppleness, flavours of dried fruit (figs) and a note of tobacco, finishing on a hint of blackcurrant which is not especially long but very fine.

Dom. J. Sperry-Kobloth, 50, rue du Winzenberg, 67650 Blienschwiller, tel. 03.88.92.40.66, fax 03.88.92.63.95 by appt.

JEAN-MARIE STRAUB 1999
0.35 ha — 3,000 — €5-8

Granite soils seem particularly well suited to Pinot Noir. Although the wines they produce are lighter, their aromas tend to be more intense and to develop earlier. This one has a very typical light-red colour with brick-red glints, and although the bouquet is still discreet, fine spicy scents are beginning to come through. The finish is a little short, but even so the palate is well constructed around fine tannins.

Jean-Marie Straub, 61, rte du Vin, 67600 Blienschwiller, tel. 03.88.92.40.42, fax 03.88.92.40.42 by appt.

HUGUES STROHM Rouge d'Obernai
Elevé en fût de chêne 1998★★
0.2 ha — 1,200 — €8-11

Hugues Strohm's vineyard is located in Obernai on a limestone-clay soil which is good for growing Pinot Noir. It has yielded this deep-ruby wine which is already very intense. It has a remarkably complex nose of red berries dominated by blackberries and accentuated by a hint of leather. With its full palate, very mature tannins and long finish, this 98 wine is very suitable for longer maturing; one taster predicted an ageing potential of 12 years.

Hugues Strohm, 33, rue de la Montagne, 67210 Obernai, tel. 03.88.49.93.51, fax 03.88.48.33.80 by appt.

WEHRLE 1999★
0.8 ha — 5,500 — €5-8

Husseren-les-Châteaux owes its name to the three castles that overlook the village. These are now in ruins, but visitors wishing to look around them can get there easily by going along the Route des Cinq Châteaux. The Wehrlé family has been in this commune since 1910, and now offers a light-red wine with a strikingly intense nose of oak mingled with cherries. The structure on the palate is light but well balanced. The tannins are not much in evidence, so the wine can be drunk immediately.

Maurice Wehrlé, 21, rue des Vignerons, 68420 Husseren-les-Châteaux, tel. 03.89.49.30.79, fax 03.89.49.29.60 by appt.

GERARD WEINZORN 1999★★
0.4 ha — 2,600 — €8-11

As you walk around Niedermorschwihr, guide book in hand, you will discover one treasure after another, including the Renaissance-style house of this wine-producer. Built in 1615, it is listed as a historic monument, and has a richly sculpted oriel window. You will also taste this deep-ruby wine with jam-like aromas of stewed fruits (strawberries and prunes) and hints of spice. The full, supple palate has high-quality tannins and a delightfully fine structure. With its perfect balance, this Pinot Noir is a great wine, ready to drink now.

Gérard Weinzorn et Fils, 133, rue des Trois-Epis, 68230 Niedermorschwihr, tel. 03.89.27.40.55, fax 03.89.27.04.23, e-mail contact@weinzorn.fr ev. day 8am–12pm 2pm–6pm

Alsace Grand Cru

As a way of promoting the best situated vineyards, a new appellation, Alsace Grand Cru, was established by decree in 1975. Strict limits were set on the quantity and quality of the designated vineyards qualifying for this appellation could produce, and the sugar content of the wine was also limited. They were to be vineyards growing only Gewurztraminer, Pinot Gris, Riesling and Muscat. Along with wines labelled with the seal of the Confrérie Saint-Etienne and some notable vintages, the vineyards that qualify produce the *nec plus ultra* of Alsace wines.

In 1983 a decree identified a group of 25 vineyards that qualified for the appellation, but the decree was rescinded and superseded by a new one on 17 December 1992. There are 50 official Grands Crus from 47 communes, although the decree mentions only 46, Rouffach having been omitted in error. Each vineyard covers an area of between 3.23 ha and 80.28 ha (8 and 198 acres), and each had to meet certain geological criteria appropriate to Grands Crus. The volume of wine produced by the Grands Crus is still modest: only 48,500 hl (1,280,400 gal in 2000.

New regulations were put in place after the 1987 harvest. They increased the minimum alcoholic content from 11 to 12 in Gewurztraminers and Tokay-Pinot Gris. At the same time, there were new requirements for labels to show the specific vineyard alongside the grape variety and the year, and this information also had to be shown on all administrative and commercial documentation.

Alsace Grand Cru Altenberg de Bergbieten

□ FREDERIC MOCHEL Muscat 1999★

0.32 ha   2,500   🍾 11–15

Of all the various Alsatian grape varieties, Muscat is the most demanding in terms of *terroir*. It needs a soil that is capable of keeping some water in reserve but also drains well, heats up rapidly and stores the heat, and faces south-south-east. The Altenberg de Bergbieten Grand Cru, from which this wine comes, suits these requirements perfectly. This green-yellow 99 with brilliant glints has a powerful Muscat aroma in the nose, with fine, elegant hints of spice. The palate sustains its good balance right up to a long, clean finish. (Residual sugar: 12 g/l.)

🍷 Frédéric Mochel, 56, rue Principale, 67310 Traenheim, tel. 03.88.50.38.67, fax 03.88.50.56.19 ✆ by appt.

□ CAVE D'OBERNAI Riesling 1999★

n.c.   16,000   🍷 5–8

The Cave Vinicole d'Obernai belongs to the Divinal group, one of the main operators in Alsace. Despite being a large organisation, it still makes every effort to bring out the qualities of the *terroir*. The marly clay soils of the Altenberg de Bergbieten Grand Cru come through in this Riesling, a very youthful wine but already beginning to reveal notes of citronella and toast on the nose. On the palate it is well balanced and aromatic, with a long finish. A wine which will be a good accompaniment to seafood. (Residual sugar: 2.5 g/l.)

🍷 Cave vinicole d' Obernai.
30, rue du Gal-Leclerc, 67210 Obernai, tel. 03.88.47.60.20, fax 03.88.47.60.22 ✆ by appt.

□ LA CAVE DU ROI DAGOBERT
Riesling 1999★★

1.5 ha   10,400   🍷 5–8

Another flagship of the Divinal group, located in the northern part of the Alsatian vineyard, is the Cave du Roi Dagobert, which for some years has been expanding its direct sales. Its wines, in particular the Rieslings, are regularly singled out. Their 99 wine has a very

119

Alsace Grand Cru Altenberg de Bergbieten

elegant nose combining lemon and bitter almonds. The palate is powerful and structured, and although there is a slight touch of residual sugar, it does not impair the overall balance. A long, very thoroughbred wine. (Residual sugar: 7 g/l.)

➤ La cave du Roi Dagobert, 1, rte de Scharrachbergheim, 67310 Traenheim, tel. 03.88.50.69.00, fax 03.88.50.69.09. e-mail dagobert@cave-dagobert.com ▼
Y ev. day 8am–12 noon 2pm–6pm

ANDRE REGIN Riesling 1999★
0.7 ha — 2,000 — €5-8

This 7.5-ha (19-acre) vineyard in the north of the Alsatian wine region has been run by André Regin since 1988. The commune of Wolxheim, with its Altenberg Grand Cru, is well known for its Rieslings. This one is still young, but already has all the potential you would expect from a wine grown on a limestone clay soil. It opens with a floral and mineral bouquet, followed by a clean, fresh attack. The palate has quite good length, finishing on citrus-fruit notes which suggest it would be a good wine to serve with seafood. (Residual sugar: 6.8 g/l.)

➤ André Regin, 2, rue Principale, 67120 Wolxheim, tel. 03.88.38.17.02, fax 03.88.38.17.02 ▼ Y by appt.

ZOELLER Riesling 1999★★★
0.95 ha — 6,600 — €5-8

This 10-ha (25-acre) vineyard was founded in 1900. The traditional methods of winemaking still used here have got the very best out of the Altenberg de Wolxheim Grand Cru. This Riesling's golden colour shows straightaway that it has exceptional body. The bouquet contains aromas of crystallised fruits and overripening. A full, rich, perfectly structured wine which will be a good acompaniment to the most refined fish dishes. (Residual sugar: 12 g/l.)

➤ EARL Maison Zoeller, 14, rue de l'Eglise, 67120 Wolxheim, tel. 03.88.38.15.90, fax 03.88.38.15.90, e-mail vins.Zoeller@wanadoo.fr ▼ Y ev. day except Sun. 9am–11.30am 2pm–7pm

Alsace Grand Cru Altenberg de Bergheim

GUSTAVE LORENTZ Riesling 1999
4 ha — 15,000 — €15-23

Although the Gustave Lorentz firm, founded in 1836, is well known as one of the main wine-merchants in Alsace, it also takes a keen interest in its 32 ha (79 acres) of vines, some of which are located in the heights of the Altenberg de Bergheim. This Riesling has a fine, floral nose, and a distinctively fresh, lemony palate. A characteristic wine with quite a long finish. (Residual sugar: 7 g/l.)

➤ Gustave Lorentz, 35, Grand-Rue, 68750 Bergheim, tel. 03.89.73.22.22, fax 03.89.73.30.49, e-mail lorentz@vins-lorentz.com ▼ Y ev. day except Sun. 10am–12 noon 2pm–6.30pm
➤ Charles Lorentz

Alsace Grand Cru Altenberg de Wolxheim

MUHLBERGER Riesling 1999
1.5 ha — 2,500 — €5-8

François Muhlberger runs a 13-ha (32-acre) estate with his son Robert. Although their Altenberg Riesling comes from a limestone-clay soil, it is already developing well, with mineral notes apparent in the bouquet. Well-structured and even rather rich, it is a long, balanced wine, which can be enjoyed straight away. (Residual sugar: 10 g/l.)

➤ Vignobles François Muhlberger, 1, rue de Strasbourg, 67120 Wolxheim, tel. 03.88.38.10.33, fax 03.88.38.47.65 ▼ Y ev. day 9am–12 noon 1pm–7pm

Alsace Grand Cru Brand

DOM. ALBERT BOXLER Tokay-pinot gris 1999★★
n.c. — n.c. — €11-15

Niedermorschwihr is surrounded by two granitic grands crus, the Sommerberg to the north and the Brand to the south. The Brand faces due south, and thus has maximum exposure to the sun. Its wines convey the warmth

of their *terroir*, this Tokay-Pinot Gris has a brilliant, straw-yellow colour and a fruity, smoky bouquet. Its power on the palate is combined with a rich, fleshy quality. The almost perfect balance is sustained right through its long finish. A very great wine. (Residual sugar: 36 g/l).
● Albert Boxler, 78, rue des Trois-Epis, 68230 Niedermorschwihr, tel. 03.89.27.11.32, fax 03.89.27.70.14, e-mail albert.boxler@online.fr ✓ by appt.

PAUL BUECHER

Tokay-pinot gris 1999★

0.35 ha 2,400 €11-15

Paul Buecher is one of the largest wine-growing concerns in the commune of Wettolsheim. It is currently run by Henri and Jean-Marc Buecher, who continually try to achieve greater complexity and the best possible match between grape variety and *terroir*. With its golden straw-yellow colour, intense aromas of fruit and overripening along with honey, and powerful, thoroughbred, balanced palate ending on a good note of supporting acidity, this is clearly a wine that has been made with great skill. It can be drunk for its own sake, without accompanying food. (Residual sugar: 24 g/l).
● Paul Buecher, 15, rue Sainte-Gertrude, 68920 Wettolsheim, tel. 03.89.80.64.73, fax 03.89.80.58.62 ✓ by appt.

DOPFF AU MOULIN

Gewurztraminer 1999★

3.3 ha 18,700 €11-15

Dopff au Moulin is a family firm which has been established at Riquewihr for a very long time. Its 70-ha (173-acre) vineyard in the commune of Turckheim is located on the Brand Grand Cru and is one of the best *terroirs* in Alsace. This wine delights from the start with its old-gold colour. It has an expressive bouquet of floral rose scents with slight hints of spice. There is a note of overripening on the palate. A balanced wine with a long, agreeable finish. (Residual sugar 12 g/l).
● SA Dopff au Moulin,
2. av. Jacques-Preiss, 68340 Riquewihr, tel. 03.89.49.09.69, fax 03.89.47.83.61 ✓ ev. day 9am-12 noon 2pm-6pm

ARMAND HURST

Riesling 1999★

0.88 ha 6,000 €8-11

Located to the west of Colmar at the entrance to the Munster valley, the little town of Turckheim gets the very best out of its exceptional vines, particularly those on the granite hillside of the Brand. Armand Hurst runs an 8-ha (20-acre) estate which has yielded a Riesling with a fine, floral bouquet. After this highly promising start, the full, well-structured palate confirms that the wine should develop well in time. Best served with fish or seafood. (Residual sugar: 9 g/l).
● Armand Hurst, 8, rue de la Chapelle, 68230 Turckheim, tel. 03.89.27.40.22, fax 03.89.27.47.67 ✓ by appt.

JOSMEYER

Riesling 1999★

0.3 ha 2,500 €15-23

Founded in 1854, this wine-merchant's business has a 25-ha (62-acre) vineyard which is being converted to organic methods. In keeping with the granite *terroir*, this Riesling has a very open bouquet, the intense fruity aromas mingling elegantly with a few notes of gunflint. With its good balance and structure on the palate, this is a thoroughbred wine to drink with the most delicate fish dishes. (Residual sugar: 4.9 g/l).
● SA Josmeyer et Fils, 76, rue Clemenceau, 68920 Winzenheim, tel. 03.89.27.91.90, fax 03.89.27.91.99, e-mail josmeyer@ wanadoo.fr ✓ by appt.

CAVE DE TURCKHEIM

Riesling 1999★★★

n.c. 35,000 €8-11

The Cave Vinicole at Turckheim is located just below the Brand Grand Cru, and plays a very important role here and throughout the valley. Its Grand Cru Riesling has a delightful bouquet with very expressive fruit aromas indicating great maturity. After an excellent attack on the palate, it reveals ripe fruit flavours and an unusually good structure. A well-balanced wine which will keep well and be a good accompaniment not only to fish but also to Asian specialities. (Residual sugar: 8.1 g/l).
● Cave de Turckheim, 16, rue des Tuileries, 68230 Turckheim, tel. 03.89.30.23.60, fax 03.89.27.06.25 ✓ by appt.

Alsace Grand Cru
Bruderthal

FREDERIC ARBOGAST

Gewurztraminer 1999★

0.27 ha 2,000 €8-11

This is a relatively recent estate which bottled its first wines in 1971. Some of its vines are on the Bruderthal *terroir* in the commune of Molsheim, and that is where this brilliant-gold wine comes from. Although the bouquet is still closed (as is normal for this *terroir*), it is now releasing some discreet aromas of quince and currants. The powerful palate is already expressive, and perhaps a little sweet because it is not sufficiently balanced. An excellent wine in the making. (Residual sugar: 32 g/l).
● EARL Frédéric Arbogast, 3, pl. de l'Eglise, 67310 Westhoffen, tel. 03.88.50.30.51, fax 03.88.50.30.51 ✓ by appt.

GERARD NEUMEYER

Gewurztraminer 1999★
☐ 0.79 ha 6,090 **Ⅲ €15-23**

The Gérard Neumeyer firm is established at Molsheim and owns a large number of the vines on the Bruderthal Grand Cru, a south-east-facing conchiferous limestone *terroir* which is suited to producing wines for longer maturing. It has yielded an excellent, 'typically limestone' **99 Tokay-Pinot Gris**, with a powerful bouquet of quince and smoke aromas. The mature, well-structured palate is balanced (residual sugar: 40 g/l.). Equally successful is this light-yellow Gewurztraminer with a complex range of fruit and flower aromas combined with mineral notes. Its palate is clear-cut, long, and underpinned by a fine structure. (Residual sugar: 41 g/l.)
➤ Dom. Gérard Neumeyer,
29, rue Ettore-Bugatti, 67120 Molsheim,
tel. 03.88.38.12.45, fax 03.88.38.11.27,
e-mail domaine.neumeyer@wanadoo.fr **N**
Y ev. day except Sun. 9am–12 noon
2pm–7pm

BERNARD WEBER Riesling 1999★★

☐ 1.5 ha 2,000 **▮ ♦ €11-15**

Bernard Weber took over this vineyard from his grandparents in 1974. He offers a 99 Grand Cru Riesling from a conchiferous limestone *terroir*. It already has a very intense nose of floral and mineral notes. The attack tends towards freshness, after which the wine reveals a very full structure and remarkably good length. (Residual sugar: 6 g/l.)
➤ Bernard Weber, 49, rue de Saverne,
67120 Molsheim, tel. 03.88.38.52.67,
fax 03.88.38.58.81, e-mail info@
bernard-weber.com **N Y** by appt.

Alsace Grand Cru Eichberg

CHARLES BAUR Riesling 1999★★

☐ 0.32 ha 2,800 **Ⅲ €11-15**

with a bouquet of floral aromas mingled with touches of citrus and exotic fruits, it shows extraordinary intensity on the palate. Powerful, structured and well-balanced, this is a wine with great potential which should have a remarkable future. (Residual sugar: 4 g/l.)
➤ Charles Baur, 29, Grand-Rue,
68420 Eguisheim, tel. 03.89.41.32.49,
fax 03.89.41.55.79, e-mail cave@
vinscharlesbaur.fr **N Y** ev. day except
Sun. 9am–12 noon 1.30pm–7pm
➤ Armand Baur

PAUL SCHNEIDER Riesling 1999★★

☐ 0.27 ha 1,800 **Ⅲ €8-11 N**

The Paul Schneider estate has its head office in a house built in 1663 which was once the tithe court of the Grand Provost of Strasbourg Cathedral. Its Grand Cru Riesling regularly appears in the *Guide*, varying in quality year by year from perfectly decent to quite dazzling. This 99 vintage is a great wine. In keeping with the siliceous limestone soils from which it comes, it has a bouquet combining lemon with exotic fruits. It is complex and fairly rich but very well structured on the palate, where the excellence of the raw material is clearly apparent. (Residual sugar: 6 g/l.)
➤ Paul Schneider et Fils,
1, rue de l'Hôpital, 68420 Eguisheim,
tel. 03.89.41.50.07, fax 03.89.41.30.57 **N**
Y ev. day 10am–12 noon 1.30pm–6.30pm;
Sun. by appt.

MAURICE WEHRLE

Tokay-pinot gris 1999★
☐ 0.3 ha 2,000 **▮ €8-11**

Overlooking the commune of Eguisheim, the Eichberg Grand Cru is a south-east-facing, marly limestone *terroir*. The main grape variety here is Gewurztraminer, but there is also a fair amount of Riesling and Tokay-Pinot Gris. The second of these has yielded a wine with a straw-yellow colour and a bouquet which is still closed, but even so suggests a complex range of elegant aromas. This thoroughbred, well-structured 99 will need to be kept for two years before it achieves its full balance. (Residual sugar: 17 g/l.)
➤ Maurice Wehrlé, 21, rue des Vignerons,
68420 Husseren-les-Châteaux,
tel. 03.89.49.30.79, fax 03.89.49.29.60 **N**
Y by appt.

PAUL ZINCK Gewurztraminer 1999★

☐ 0.5 ha 2,500 **▮ Ⅲ ♦ €8-11**

Famous for its stout fortifications, the town of Eguisheim keeps its reputation for wine-growing secure thanks to producers like Paul Zinck, who started bottling wines in 1970. Not only has this dynamic wine-maker been expanding his exports for some years now, he also opened a gourmet restaurant in 1990 and set up a new wine-making unit in 1995. Once again his Grand Cru Eichberg Gewurztraminer is featured in the *Guide*. The wine has an intense, floral bouquet, and is well structured and very long on the palate. Owing to a certain sweetness in the mouth it will be best

Armand Baur runs a 12-ha (30-acre) estate at Eguisheim, the famous wine-growing town where he was born. His Grand Cru Riesling is more than worthy of his birthplace. Starting

drunk as an aperitif or with dessert. (Residual sugar: 10 g/l.)

➤ SARL Paul Zinck, 18, rue des Trois-Châteaux, 68420 Eguisheim, tel. 03.89.41.19.11, fax 03.89.24.12.85, e-mail info@pzinck.fr ▣ ▼ by appt.

Alsace Grand Cru Florimont

RENE MEYER
Tokay-pinot gris 1999★★★

□   1,866   ▣ €11-15

The Florimont overlooks Ingersheim to the west. As its name suggests, this *terroir* has an interesting flora; vine tulips still bloom in spring on some of the plots. This 99 Tokay-Pinot Gris has a golden colour and a powerful, open nose of aromas ranging through notes of overripening and crystallised fruits. After a clean attack, the chief assets of the palate are its complexity, fullness and length. A wine bordering on the 'late-harvest' type, with excellent ageing potential. (Residual sugar: 35 g/l.)

➤ EARL Dom. René Meyer et Fils, 14, Grand-Rue, 68230 Katzenthal, tel. 03.89.27.04.67, fax 03.89.27.50.59 ▼ by appt.

BRUNO SORG
Riesling 1999★

n.c.   2,900

Bruno Sorg has been here since 1965, and all that time he has continually expanded his business. Today, he and his son run a 10-ha (25-acre) vineyard, divided between the communes of Eguisheim and Ingersheim. His Florimont Riesling comes from a limestone-clay soil. It is still young, but hints of white flowers and crystallised fruits are beginning to come through. After a fairly fresh attack, it is full, structured and long on the palate. A very well-balanced wine. (Residual sugar: 3 g/l.)

➤ Dom. Bruno Sorg, 8, rue Mgr-Stumpf, 68420 Eguisheim, tel. 03.89.41.80.85, fax 03.89.41.22.64 ▣ €8-11 ▼ by appt.

Alsace Grand Cru Frankstein

P. KIRSCHNER ET FILS
Riesling 1999★

□ 0.3 ha 2,120 ▣ €8-11

The previous vintage was awarded a *coup de cœur*, which indicates the skills of this business, which planted its first vines in 1800 and pioneered wine-bottling in the 19th century. This 99 Riesling comes from a granitic soil, and is both fruity and light. On the palate it is well structured and rich, with good length and plenty of potential for long ageing. (Residual sugar: 5 g/l.)

➤ Pierre Kirschner, 26, rue Théophile-Bader, 67650 Dambach-la-Ville, tel. 03.88.92.40.55, fax 03.88.92.62.54, e-mail kirschner@reperes.com ▣ ▼ ev. day except Sun. 8am–12 noon 1pm–7pm

RUHLMANN Gewurztraminer 1999★
□ 0.6 ha 5,400 ■ €11-15

Dambach-la-Ville is without doubt the major wine-producing commune in Alsace; the profession is very active here, with about 60 wine-makers marketing their produce. It also has its own grand cru, the Frankstein, which is located on a platform with a granitic, two-mica soil. This Gewurztraminer has a golden colour, and a nose which releases a little touch of overripening shaded with hints of crystallised fruits. On the palate the flavours of overripening are dominant. The attack is warm, and there is a long finish. (Residual sugar: 12 g/l.)

➤ Ruhlmann, 34, rue du Mal-Foch, 67650 Dambach-la-Ville, tel. 03.88.92.41.86, fax 03.88.92.61.81 ▣ ▼ ev. day except Sun. 8am–12 noon 1.30pm–7pm

Alsace Grand Cru Furstentum

JOSEPH FRITSCH
Gewurztraminer 1999★★

□ 0.3 ha 1,800 ■ €8-11

The Furstentum Grand Cru produces wonderfully expressive Gewurztraminers. This one, offered by Joseph Fritsch of Kientzheim, has a fairly light, very brilliant-yellow colour, and a nose dominated by exotic fruit and spicy aromas. It is still restrained on the palate, but one can already sense great subtlety of flavour, an almost perfect balance and a delightfully long, fruity finish. (Residual sugar: 39.4 g/l.)

➤ EARL Joseph Fritsch, 31, Grand-Rue, 68240 Kientzheim, tel. 03.89.78.24.27, fax 03.89.78.24.27 ▼ by appt.

ALBERT MANN
Riesling Vendanges tardives 1998★

□ 0.14 ha 600 ■ ♦ €23-30

The Mann family has diversified its *terroirs* and now has a stake on five grands crus. This Furstentum Riesling has a gold colour and aromas of crystallised fruits along with a note of coffee. The attack on the palate is clean and fresh. A balanced, full, rich wine, which should age very well over the next five years.

☛ Dom. Albert Mann, 13, rue du Château, 68920 Wettolsheim, tel. 03.89.80.62.00, fax 03.89.80.34.23, e-mail mann-albert.com ☒ ⴲ by appt.

ALBERT MANN

Gewurztraminer Vieilles vignes 1999★★ ◻ 0.6 ha 4,500 ▪ ◆ €11-15

With its exceptional location at the entrance to the Kaysersberg valley, the Furstentum has a south-south-easterly aspect which gives it maximum exposure to the sun all day long and also protects it from the north winds. The bouquet of this very brilliant, golden-yellow wine is still delicate, but is already showing promise with its complex aromas of mango and pineapple. It opens up quite quickly on the palate, displaying its power and good length with delightful finesse. The dominant flavour is of crystallised fruits. (Residual sugar: 34 g/l.)

☛ Dom. Albert Mann, 13, rue du Château, 68920 Wettolsheim, tel. 03.89.80.62.00, fax 03.89.80.34.23, e-mail vins@ mann-albert.com ☒ ⴲ by appt.
☛ Barthelmé

DOM. WEINBACH

Gewurztraminer Cuvée Laurence 1999★★ ◻ 1 ha 4,300 ⬛⬛ €30-38

One of the great names of the Alsace wine region is Colette Faller, who with her daughters runs the Weinbach estate in a masterly fashion, developing their wines with great subtlety. This Gewurztraminer has a golden colour and a spicy nose with a noble herbaceous quality. The very full, powerful palate is dominated by flavours of overripe fruit. The finish is vivid and long, although the sweetness still needs time to become better balanced. The tasters predict a great future for this wine. (Residual sugar: 65 g/l.)

☛ Dom. Weinbach-Colette Faller et ses Filles, Clos des Capucins, 68240 Kaysersberg, tel. 03.89.47.13.21, fax 03.89.47.38.18 ☒ ⴲ by appt.

KIENTZLER

Riesling 1999★ ◻ 1.3 ha 7,900 ⬛⬛ €15-23

Since 1975, André Kientzler has been running an 11-ha (27-acre) estate with a wealth of grand cru soils. The limestone-clay *terroir* of the Geisberg has yielded a Riesling with a very intense nose combining hints of smoke with notes of crystallised fruits and mineral touches. After an excellent attack, it is perfectly structured, complex and well

balanced. Clearly a wine with very good ageing potential. (Residual sugar: 3.5 g/l.)

☛ André Kientzler, 50, rte de Bergheim, 68150 Ribeauvillé, tel. 03.89.73.67.10, fax 03.89.73.35.81 ☒ ⴲ by appt.

KOEBERLE KREYER

Tokay-pinot gris 1999★★ ◻ 0.13 ha 800 ▪ ◆ €8-11

This sandy *terroir* is located on a granite platform. It catches a maximum of sun to the south, and is well suited to developing great wines, such as this Pinot Gris. It has an intensely yellow colour with green glints which shows its youth and great potential for development, then releases aromas of dried and even crystallised fruits (quince), along with a characteristic hint of smoke. On the palate it is quite simply superb: elegant, thoroughbred, excellently structured, smooth and rich. Judging by the perfect balance, this wine should keep for a long time. (Residual sugar: 60 g/l.)

☛ Koeberlé Kreyer, 28, rue du Pinot-Noir, 68590 Rodern, tel. 03.89.73.00.55, fax 03.89.73.00.55, e-mail fkoeberl@ fr.pakardbell.org ☒ ⴲ by appt.

CHARLES NOLL

Tokay-pinot gris 1999★ ◻ 0.1 ha 800 ⬛⬛ €8-11

This *terroir* has a light, sandy soil which heats up rapidly in spring and also encourages early ripening of the grapes. Pinot Gris does well in these conditions. This one delights the eye with a fairly pale, straw-yellow colour, lit up by a few green glints. The aromas of the bouquet suggest citrus fruits (mandarins), accentuated by a touch of smoke. The fresh, rich, powerful palate has the necessary degree of smooth fleshiness. Some tasters feel that this 99 wine is still a little young, but they are unanimous in predicting that it has an excellent future ahead. (Residual sugar: 21 g/l.)

Alsace Grand Cru Goldert

GROSS Riesling 1999★

0.16 ha 1,500 €6–11

Dominated by its superb, 36-m (118-ft) high Romanesque clock-tower, Gueberschwihr is one of the most famous communes in the Alsatian wine region. Of the many wine firms to be found here, Henri Gross produces many outstanding vintages. With its bouquet of citrus fruits and white flowers, this 99 wine is already displaying great aromatic intensity. Its full, long, structured palate shows good ageing potential. It will be enjoyable to drink with fish dishes in sauce. (Residual sugar: 6 g/l.)

● EARL Henri Gross et Fils, 11, rue du Nord, 68420 Gueberschwihr, tel. 03.89.49.24.49, fax 03.89.49.33.58 ☑ ♈ by appt.

LOUIS SCHERB ET FILS
Gewurztraminer 1999★

0.46 ha 3,900 €8–11

Gueberschwihr is one of the jewels of the Alsatian wine region. Located a few miles south of Colmar, it is well worth a visit, you will be captivated by the picturesque architecture of the wine-growers' houses. Coming from the town's Goldert Grand Cru, this light-yellow 99 has a nose of almond blossom, followed by a powerful, well-balanced palate. It has a very fresh quality which suggests that it will develop well over time. A delightfully fluid wine which will be a good accompaniment to various spicy dishes. (Residual sugar: 8.6 g/l.)

● EARL Joseph et André Scherb, 1, rte de Saint-Marc, 68420 Gueberschwihr, tel. 03.89.49.30.83, fax 03.89.49.30.65 ☑ ♈ ev. day 8am–12 noon 1pm–7pm; Sun. 9am–12 noon

MAURICE SCHUELLER
Gewurztraminer 1999

0.3 ha 2,500 ▮▮

This business started to market its wines in 1965. It has vines in the Goldert Grand Cru, which is certainly one of the best terroirs for bringing out the particular qualities of the Gewurztraminer grape. This pale-yellow wine has a bouquet of floral notes (roses). The palate is powerful, spicy, and supported by a good level of acidity which will ensure that it keeps very well. (Residual sugar: 19 g/l.)

● EARL Maurice Schueller, 17, rue Basse, 68420 Gueberschwihr, tel. 03.89.49.26.60 ☑ ♈ by appt.
● Marc Schueller

● EARL Charles Noll, 2, rue de l'Ecole, 68630 Mittelwihr, tel. 03.89.47.93.21, fax 03.89.47.86.23 ☑ ♈ ev. day 9am–9pm

Alsace Grand Cru Hatschbourg

BUECHER-FIX
Gewurztraminer 1999★★★

0.3 ha 2,500 €6–11

The Hatschbourg Grand Cru spans the communes of Hattstatt and Voegtlinshoffen and faces south. The main characteristics of this terroir are a marly limestone substratum covered mainly by gravel, with some deposits of loess and alluvium. It is a soil that yields wines for longer maturing, such as this exceptionally fine 99, which has a clear gold colour and produces tears on the glass. The bouquet has an intense scent of rose and aromas of overripening. This is an extraordinarily round, smooth wine, especially on the palate, where it sustains its great charm and appeal right up to an exotic finish enhanced by touches of spice. (Residual sugar: 30 g/l.)

● Buecher-Fix, 21, rue Sainte-Gertrude, 68920 Wettolsheim, tel. 03.89.30.12.30, fax 03.89.30.12.81, e-mail buecher@terre-net.fr ☑ ♈ by appt.

DOM. JOSEPH CATTIN
Tokay-pinot gris 1999

1.37 ha 10,000 €8–11

Joseph Cattin was one of the pioneering firms that created the Alsace wine region. The Cattin brothers still adhere to the policy of high quality that was initiated long ago by their ancestors. This clear, light-yellow wine with golden glints is pleasantly fruity with notes of green apples. Its slightly spicy, peppery attack is echoed by the flavours on the palate. The sense of balance which is beginning to develop is enlivened by a delightful freshness. (Residual sugar: 30 g/l.)

● Joseph Cattin, 18, rue Roger-Fremeaux, 68420 Voegtlinshoffen, tel. 03.89.49.30.21, fax 03.89.49.26.02, e-mail gcattin@terre-net.fr ☑ ♈ ev. day 8am–12 noon 2pm–6pm; Sun. by appt.
● Jacques et Jean-Marie Cattin

Alsace Grand Cru Hengst

Alsace Grand Cru Kastelberg

MOELLINGER Gewurztraminer 1999★

n.c.   4,000   € 5–8

The slopes of the Hengst Grand Cru are well-placed to catch the sun's rays. Its marly limestone soils are certainly some of the best for growing Gewurztraminer grapes. This brilliant, golden-yellow 99 is already very open in the nose, releasing a combination of faded rose, tobacco and spice aromas. After a clean attack, the palate are power, richness and smoothness. This high-quality wine will need six to eight years to achieve its full expression. (Residual sugar: 29.1 g/l.)

☛ SCEA Jos. Moellinger et Fils,
6, rue de la 5°-D.-B., 68920 Wettolsheim,
tel. 03.89.80.62.02, fax 03.89.80.04.94 ▼
Y ev. day 8am–12 noon 1.30pm–7pm; cl. Oct.

DOM. AIME STENTZ Clos du Vicus
Romain Tokay-pinot gris 1999★

n.c.   4,700   € 8–11

Located south of Wintzenheim and west of Wettolsheim are the towering slopes of the Hengst, a marly limestone *terroir* with a magnificent south-eastern aspect which is perfectly suited to a delicate grape variety like Pinot Gris. This wine has a light-yellow colour with golden glints, and releases subtle aromas of crystallised fruits. It is still closed, with a heavy, very fruity palate which is just beginning to develop some richness and smoothness. A wine for longer maturing which needs some time to reveal its full potential. (Residual sugar: 15 g/l.)

☛ Dom. Aimé Stentz et Fils,
37, rue Herzog, 68920 Wettolsheim,
tel. 03.89.80.63.77, fax 03.89.79.78.68,
e-mail stentz.c.@calcxo.net ▼ Y ev. day
except Sun. 8am–12 noon 2pm–6pm

DOM. AIME STENTZ ET FILS
Gewurztraminer Sélection de grains nobles 1998★★

0.19 ha   520   € 23–30

The Hengst yields great Gewurztraminer wines. This one has a brilliant, deep-yellow colour with amber highlights, and an assertive nose which not only releases the spicy aromas of the grape variety, but is lively and fresh as well. Its mouth-filling, smooth, rich palate reveals the same spicy freshness at the finish. This aromatic development is accompanied by crystallised fruits. A wine which has not yet opened up, but will do so once it has been kept for four or five years.

☛ Dom. Aimé Stentz et Fils,
37, rue Herzog, 68920 Wettolsheim,
tel. 03.89.80.63.77, fax 03.89.79.78.68,
e-mail stentz.c.@calcxo.net ▼ Y ev. day
except Sun. 8am–12 noon 2pm–6pm

ANDRE ET REMY GRESSER
Riesling 1999★

0.35 ha   2,500   € 11–15

In 1977 Rémy Gresser took over this 10-ha (25-acre) family estate with its vineyard founded at the time of Louis XIVth, the Sun King. He continually strives for quality, and for some years has been focusing on bringing out the qualities of his *terroirs*. He offers a Riesling from the shaly soils of the Kastelberg. It is a very young, but nonetheless elegant, wine with aromas of pears and quince, and a long, well-balanced palate. A wine with great promise. (Residual sugar: 6 g/l.)

☛ Dom. André et Rémy Gresser, 2, rue de l'Ecole, 67140 Andlau, tel. 03.88.08.95.88, fax 03.88.08.55.99, e-mail remy.gresser@wanadoo.fr ▼ Y ev. day except Sun. 8am–12 noon 2pm–7pm; Sun. by appt.

MARC KREYDENWEISS
Riesling 1999★

1 ha   4,000   € 23–30

Over the years the wines of Marc Kreydenweiss, who runs a 12-ha (30-acre) vineyard at Andlau, have become a benchmark in Alsace. Take for example this Kastelberg Riesling. Its intense nose of toast reflects the shaly soil it comes from, and the palate is very full, well structured and persistent, finishing on a nutty note. A very pleasant overall impression. (Residual sugar: 11 g/l.)

☛ Dom. Marc Kreydenweiss, 12, rue Deharbe, 67140 Andlau, tel. 03.88.08.95.83, fax 03.88.08.41.16 ▼ Y by appt.

GUY WACH Riesling 1999★★★

0.58 ha   4,400   € 11–15

Since 1979, Guy Wach has been running a 7-ha (17-acre) vineyard, and is frequently praised for his Grand Cru Rieslings. Given that his commune is over 1,000 years old, it is hardly surprising that he shows such respect for tradition. Or indeed that he continues to develop great wines for longer maturing, such as this Riesling with a very intense nose of passion-fruit. It has a fine attack, good

126

balance and excellent length, and is clearly produced from exceptional raw material. (Residual sugar: 12 g/l.)

● Guy Wach, Dom. des Marronniers, 5, rue la Commanderie, 67140 Andlau, tel. 03.88.08.93.20, fax 03.88.08.45.59 ▽ by appt.

Alsace Grand Cru Kirchberg de Barr

DOM. HERING Gewurztraminer 1999★

0.65 ha 4,200 €8-11

The wine-growing tradition has run in the Hering family since 1858. Jean-Daniel Hering's great-grandfather won further distinction by carrying out research into hybridisation in order to create a grafting stock especially suited to the conditions in the Alsace wine region. The bouquet of this light-yellow wine with brilliant glints is still restrained and, although very fine, still needs some time to open up. On the palate it has plenty of roundness and power, and a full body which will develop well. (Residual sugar: 25 g/l.)

● Dom. Hering, 6, rue Sulzer, 67140 Barr, tel. 03.88.08.90.07, fax 03.88.08.08.54, e-mail jdh@infonie.fr ▽ ▼ by appt.

PIERRE SPARR

Gewurztraminer Vendanges tardives 1998★

0.9 ha 10,000 €23-30

Pierre Sparr runs this estate with one of his cousins. He has made it his goal to produce high-quality wines, introducing innovative methods both in the vineyard and the barrel store. This Gewurztraminer has a golden-yellow colour. The bouquet has aromas of crystallised fruit and fresh figs, while the concentrated palate is enlivened by flavours of acacia honey. Figs and crystallised fruits reappear at the finish to round off this wine on a further note of sweetness. Excellent future prospects.

● SA Pierre Sparr et ses Fils, 2, rue de la 1ʳᵉ Armée, 68240 Sigolsheim, tel. 03.89.78.24.22, fax 03.89.47.32.62, e-mail vins-sparr@rmcnet.fr ▽ ▼ by appt.

Alsace Grand Cru Mambourg

CHARLES NOLL

Gewurztraminer 1999★★★

0.1 ha 900 €8-11

13% vol
ALSACE GRAND CRU
1999
Grand Cru Mandelberg
1999
GEWURZTRAMINER
75cl

The famous Mandelberg, or 'Almond-tree Mountain', seems to suit the Gewurztraminer grape exceedingly well. This 99 wine is a model of its type. Its colour is golden and its

Alsace Grand Cru Mandelberg

HARTWEG Riesling 1999★

0.26 ha 2,150 €8-11

Since 1972 Jean-Paul Hartweg has been running an 8-ha (20-acre) vineyard, and was joined by his son in 1996. The estate specialises in harvesting very ripe grapes. That is clearly apparent in this 99 Riesling, which comes from a marly limestone soil and certainly has a mature, if not overripe, quality. The bouquet is both floral and fruity (pears and apricots), while the palate is full and complex, with a good balance between exotic touches and a certain roundness. A wine with very good length, which can be drunk as an aperitif. (Residual sugar: 24 g/l.)

● Jean-Paul et Frank Hartweg, 39, rue Jean-Macé, 68980 Beblenheim, tel. 03.89.47.94.79, fax 03.89.49.00.83, e-mail frank.hartweg@free.fr ▽ ▼ ev. day except Sun. 8am–11.30am 1.30pm–6pm

JEAN-PAUL MAULER Gewurztraminer 1999★★

0.27 ha 2,300 €8-11

Coming from one of the oldest wine-producing families in Mittelwihr, Jean-Paul Mauler has made quite a name for himself. He has managed in a very short time to give his wines an original quality by creating a better match between soil and vines. This wine has a golden colour with brilliant glints, a nose of ripe fruits giving a sense of overripeness, and a very full palate coupled with a complex, spicy finish: all in all a remarkable Gewurztraminer. (Residual sugar: 17.5 g/l.)

● Jean-Paul Mauler, 3, pl. des Cigognes, 68630 Mittelwihr, tel. 03.89.47.93.23, fax 03.89.47.88.29 ▽ ▼ ev. day 8am–12.30pm 2pm–7pm

Alsace Grand Cru Moenchberg

Alsace Grand Cru Muenchberg

bouquet of roses and crystallised fruits makes a very intense impression. On the palate it explodes into a spectacular display of crystallised fruits and faded roses. With its perfect silkiness and wonderful richness, it is a real delight. A superb wine. (Residual sugar: 31.4 g/l.)

• EARL Charles Noll, 2, rue de l'Ecole, 68630 Mittelwihr, tel. 03.89.47.93.21, fax 03.89.47.86.23 ☑ ⟨ ev. day 9am–9pm

W. WURTZ Gewurztraminer 1999★
☐ 0.2 ha 2,000 ▮ €8-11

The Mandelberg is certainly one of the earliest-maturing *terroirs* in Alsace; the almond blossom there is the first sign of spring, and quite rightly it is classed as one of the grands crus. This wine has a brilliant, delicate pale-gold colour, and a nose which is already releasing very characteristic aromas of roses and ripe fruits. The balance on the palate is set off by a note of *pain d'épice* (spice cake). There is a delightfully fresh finish, which is a sign of good potential for development in the long term. (Residual sugar: 15 g/l.)

• Willy Wurtz et Fils, 6, rue du Bouxhof, 68630 Mittelwihr, tel. 03.89.47.93.16, fax 03.89.47.89.01 ☑ ⟨ ev. day 9am–7pm

ARMAND GILG Riesling 1999★
☐ 1 ha 6,800 ▮ ◆ €8-11

The Gilg estate, with its 22 ha (54 acres) of vines, is part of the wine-growing area around Mittelbergheim, one of the most beautiful villages in France, and is one of its leading vineyards both in terms of its size and reputation. This Riesling shows that it comes from a sandy soil with its bouquet of intense, elegant floral aromas. After a fairly fresh attack, there are hints of lemon on the palate which suggest that it will be a good accompaniment to any fish or seafood. (Residual sugar: 4 g/l.)

• Dom. Armand Gilg et Fils, 2, rue Rotland, 67140 Mittelbergheim, tel. 03.88.08.92.76, fax 03.88.08.25.91 ☑ ⟨ by appt.

RENE KOCH ET FILS Riesling 1999★
☐ 0.2 ha 1,200 ▮ €6-11

René Koch took over here in 1970. He has been joined by his son Michel, who represents the third generation. In recent years the 10-ha (25-acre) estate has produced a Riesling of very reliable quality from the volcanic, sandstone soils of the grand cru. This 99 version is still very young. The bouquet is dominated by notes of citrus fruits, while the palate is fresh, balanced and long. A wine with good potential, which will go well with fish or seafood. (Residual sugar: 5 g/l.)

• GAEC René et Michel Koch, 5, rue de la Fontaine, 67680 Nothalten, tel. 03.88.92.41.03, fax 03.88.92.63.99, e-mail vin-koch@oreka.com ☑ ⟨ by appt.

SAOULIAK Gewurztraminer Sélection de grains nobles 1998★★
☐ 0.12 ha 800 ▮ €38-46

This family business was founded in 1939 by the grandfather of Marie-Odile Saouliak, who has been running it since 1980 in association with her son. Its Gewurztraminer is golden-yellow in colour, with a bouquet revealing crystallised fruits and a strong element of oranges. A complex range of crystallised-fruit flavours reappears on the palate, this time in a rather Provençal register. The wine ends with a remarkable finish. (Half-litre bottles.)

• Saouliak, 102, rte des Vins, 67680 Nothalten, tel. 03.88.92.45.73 ☑ ⟨ ev. day 9am–12 noon 2pm–8pm

Alsace Grand Cru Marckrain

RENE BARTH Gewurztraminer 1999★
☐ 0.15 ha 1,100 ▮ €8-11

Michel Fonné took over this wine-producing estate from his uncle in 1989. An oenologist, he concentrates mainly on developing the production of *grand terroir* wines. This pale-gold 99 with green glints is very quickly beginning to release notes of exotic fruits and hints of spice. On the palate it is frank, very well balanced, and spicy. A wine with a long finish, which deserves to be kept for a while. (Residual sugar: 16 g/l.)

• Dom. Michel Fonné, 24, rue du Gal-de-Gaulle, 68630 Bennwihr, tel. 03.89.47.92.69, fax 03.89.49.04.86 ☑ ⟨ by appt.

VIEIL ARMAND Riesling 1999★

| | n.c. | n.c. | |

The Cave du Vieil Armand belongs to the Wolfberger group. It is located in the southern part of the Alsatian vineyards, as is the Ollwiller Grand Cru. Despite coming from limestone-clay soils, this Riesling is already very open in the nose, where there are mineral notes and hints of toast. After an excellent start, the wine is balanced and harmonious. (Residual sugar: 5 g/l.)
Cave vinicole du Vieil-Armand, 3, rte de Cernay, 68360 Soultz-Wuenheim, tel. 03.89.76.73.75, fax 03.89.76.70.75 ▼ by appt.

Alsace Grand Cru Osterberg

FERNAND FROEHLICH ET FILS

Riesling 1999 | 0.1 ha | 850 | €5-8

Along with his son, Fernand Froehlich grows more than 8 ha (20 acres) of vines at Ostheim, a village near Riquewihr and Colmar. He makes his début in the *Guide* with this '99 Riesling, grown on a limestone-clay *terroir*. It is still very young, but a fine mineral quality is already beginning to come through in the bouquet. After a fairly fresh opening, the palate is essentially lemony. A wine designed for longer maturing. (Residual sugar: 12 g/l.)
EARL Fernand Froehlich et Fils, 29, rue de Colmar, 68150 Ostheim, tel. 03.89.86.01.46, fax 03.89.86.01.54 ▼ ev. day 8am–12 noon 1.30pm–7.30pm; groups by appt.

Alsace Grand Cru Pfersigberg

CHARLES BAUR

Gewurztraminer 1999★ | 0.47 ha | 3,500 | €11-15

Armand Baur currently has a 12-ha (30-acre) vineyard which, being an oenologist, he runs very efficiently. His light-yellow, intensely brilliant Gewurztraminer is still closed, but even so it is already releasing some scents of spice and aniseed. There is excellent balance on the palate, despite the fact that the wine is still noticeably young. Two or three years of ageing will enable it to achieve its full potential. (Residual sugar: 13 g/l.)
Charles Baur, 29, Grand-Rue, 68420 Eguisheim, tel. 03.89.41.32.49, fax 03.89.41.55.79, e-mail cave@vincharlesbaur.fr ▼ ▼ ev. day except Sun. 9am–12 noon 1.30pm–7pm

LEON BAUR Gewurztraminer 1999★

| | 0.38 ha | 2,800 | €8-11

The Pfersigberg faces roughly east-south-east, and is composed of limestone shingle on a marly limestone soil. It yields wines of great finesse. This one has a light-yellow colour and an intensely aromatic nose dominated by spice. The well-balanced palate has a remarkable structure, lingering on to a finish of rose and violet flavours and fruity mango notes. (Residual sugar: 10 g/l.)
Jean-Louis Baur, 22, rue du Rempart-Nord, 68420 Eguisheim, tel. 03.89.41.79.13, fax 03.89.41.93.72 ▼ by appt.

EMILE BEYER

Riesling Vendanges tardives 1998★ | 0.51 ha | 2,304

The Beyer family has been established at Eguisheim since 1580. The current head office of the firm is in the old *Au Cheval Blanc* inn, whose cellar, dating from 1583, is still in use. This wine has a beautiful straw-yellow colour with orangey glints. The intense nose reveals aromas of orange along with hints of eucalyptus. The taster's first sensation on the palate is of great sweetness, which is then balanced by a vigorous finish. The impression of orange zest is very pronounced. A pleasant wine whose balance still needs to improve.
Emile Beyer, 7, pl. du Château Saint-Léon, 68420 Eguisheim, tel. 03.89.41.40.45, fax 03.89.41.64.21, e-mail info@emile-beyer.fr ▼ ev. day 9am–12 noon 2pm–6pm

ALBERT HERTZ Riesling 1999★

| | 0.3 ha | 2,500 | €8-11

Albert Hertz has been running this vineyard since 1976, and in 1993 was named Winemaker of the Year in the International Wine and Spirit Competition in London. From the marly limestone *terroir* of the Pfersigberg, he has produced a Riesling which is still young, with a nose dominated by citrus fruits. On the palate it is quite fresh, well-structured, long and very full-bodied. A wine to accompany good food. (Residual sugar: 4 g/l.)
Albert Hertz, 3, rue du Riesling, 68420 Eguisheim, tel. 03.89.41.30.32, fax 03.89.23.99.23 ▼ ▼ by appt.

Alsace Grand Cru Praelatenberg

DOM. ALLIMANT-LAUGNER
Riesling 1999★

□   0.34 ha   2,600   ■   €5-8

With more than 11 ha (27 acres) of vines, this is one of the top-ranking vineyards in Orschwiller. It draws its inspiration from the granite *terroir* of the Praelatenberg. Although still young, this Riesling already has an extremely elegant nose. Its intense, structured and very long palate shows that it comes from excellent raw material. A wine which is well-equipped for a long ageing period. (Residual sugar: 7 g/l.)

➤ Allimant-Laugner, 10, Grand-Rue, 67600 Orschwiller, tel. 03.88.92.06.52, fax 03.88.82.76.38, e-mail alaugner@terre-net.fr ☑

Ⓨ ev. day except Sun. 8am–7pm

➤ Hubert Laugner

DOM. ENGEL FRERES
Gewurztraminer 1999★

□   0.12 ha   1,000   ■   €8-11

The heights of the Haut-Koenigsbourg offer a view over the slopes of the Praelatenberg. This *terroir* is located on a granite platform covered by brown clay soils of varying thickness. The Engel estate has 7 ha (17 acres) of vines here. This golden-yellow wine has already opened out well, revealing floral notes and verbena aromas. The balanced palate is dominated by fruit flavours with an accent of roses. 'A delightful, finely peppery impression overall, leaning somewhat towards dried fruits,' wrote one of the tasters. (Residual sugar: 15 g/l.)

➤ Dom. Christian et Hubert Engel, 1, rue des Vignes, Haut-Koenigsbourg, 67600 Orschwiller, tel. 03.88.92.01.83, fax 03.88.82.25.09 ☑

Ⓨ ev. day 9am–11.30am 2pm–6pm

SIFFERT Gewurztraminer 1999★★

□   0.52 ha   6,600   ▥   €15-23

The Siffert estate is a very old Alsatian wine firm which celebrated its bicentenary in 1992. Some of its vines are located on the Praelatenberg *terroir*, which leaves the stamp of its complex subsoil on the wines it produces. This golden-yellow 99 reveals a very open nose of flowers and exotic fruits. On a palate dominated by crystallised fruits, there is plenty of fullness, some richness and a remarkable finish. A wine which will keep for three years. (Residual sugar: 49 g/l; half-litre bottles.)

➤ SCEA Dom. Siffert, 16, rte du Vin, 67600 Orschwiller, tel. 03.88.92.02.77, fax 03.88.82.70.02 ☑ Ⓨ ev. day 9am–12 noon 1.30pm–7pm; Sun. by appt.; cl. 15 Jan.–15 Feb.

➤ Maurice Siffert

130

FRANCOIS LICHTLE Riesling 1999★

□   0.17 ha   1,200   €11-15

The village of Hussern-les-Châteaux stands on a hill with a view over the whole Alsace plain, looking out first on the Pfersigberg Grand Cru, where the Lichtlé estate produces its very expressive wines. The intense nose of this Riesling has an aroma of peaches which seems to evoke the spirit of the area (its name means 'Peach-tree Mountain'), along with some notes of crystallised fruits. The very full, structured palate has plenty of body and slight notes of overripening. (Residual sugar: 6 g/l.)

➤ Dom. François Lichtlé, 17, rue des Vignerons, 68420 Husseren-les-Châteaux, tel. 03.89.49.31.34, fax 03.89.49.37.51, e-mail hlichtle@aol.com ☑ Ⓨ by appt.

JEAN-LOUIS ET FABIENNE MANN Riesling 1999★

□   0.4 ha   3,000   €8-11

Jean-Louis Mann took over the family business in 1982, but did not start bottling his own wines until 1998. He clearly has a talent for it: this superb 99 Riesling satisfies every requirement. Coming from a marly limestone soil, it develops an aromatic range of rare complexity, combining mineral notes with lemon and crystallised fruits. With a perfect structure and a certain amount of richness, this is a very promising wine. (Residual sugar: 8.5 g/l.)

➤ EARL Jean-Louis Mann, 11, rue du Traminer, 68420 Eguisheim, tel. 03.89.24.26.47, fax 03.89.24.09.41, e-mail mann.jean.louis@wanadoo.fr ☑ Ⓨ by appt.

Alsace Grand Cru Pfingstberg

ALBERT ZIEGLER
Gewurztraminer 1999★

□   0.3 ha   2,600   ■   €8-11

The Albert Ziegler estate is one of the major wine concerns in Orschwihr, a wine-producing commune par excellence. It grows some of its vines on the Pfingstberg, which faces south-south-east over the Orschwihr valley. This brilliant, golden-yellow Gewurztraminer has an intense bouquet of exotic fruits, accompanied by other dried fruits. The highly characteristic palate is powerful and long, with a finish dominated by faded roses and raisins. (Residual sugar: 12 g/l.)

➤ Albert Ziegler, 10, rue de l'Eglise, 68500 Orschwihr, tel. 03.89.76.01.12, fax 03.89.74.91.32 ☑

Ⓨ ev. day 8am–12 noon 1pm–7pm

CLOS SAINT-THEOBALD
Tokay-pinot gris Vendanges tardives 1998★★
□ 2 ha 3,000 €30-38

This 98 wine has a beautiful golden colour with amber glints, and aromas of crystallised fruits and beeswax. On the palate it is full, rich, mouth-filling and supported by an acidity which will enable it to keep for two or three years.

☎ Dom. Schoffit, 66-68 Nonnenholz-Weg, 68000 Colmar, tel. 03.89.24.41.14, fax 03.89.41.40.52 ▼ by appt.

CLOS SAINT-THEOBALD
Riesling Sélection de grains nobles 1998★
□ 1 ha 2,000 €38-46

This old-gold 98 has a bouquet of clean citrus-fruit notes. Crystallised-fruit flavours reappear on the palate, where, despite a high level of residual sugar, the balance is almost complete. This delightful wine will become even more refined once it has aged for a few years. (Half-litre bottles.) Another wine to mention is the **99 Gewurztraminer Sec**. It is a brilliant, golden wine much marked by over-ripening and sweetness, and is sure to develop well. (Residual sugar: 40 g/l.)

☎ Dom. Schoffit, 66-68 Nonnenholz-Weg, 68000 Colmar, tel. 03.89.24.41.14, fax 03.89.41.40.52 ▼ by appt.

WOLFBERGER
Tokay-pinot gris 1999★★★
□ n.c. 19,000 €23-30

Wolfberger is one of the leading wine estates in Alsace. It offers a wide range of wines grown on various *terroirs*. This Pinot Gris comes from the very steep slopes of the Rangen de Thann. It has a golden-yellow colour with many glittering highlights, and an astonishing bouquet of fine and exceptionally complex crystallised-fruit aromas. The palate is elegant, already well balanced, and quite simply superb. A wine with excellent future prospects, which will keep for three years. (Residual sugar: 60 g/l.)

☎ Cave Vinicole Wolfberger, 6, Grand-Rue, 68420 Eguisheim, tel. 03.89.22.20.20, fax 03.89.23.47.09 ▼ by appt.

CAVE VINICOLE DE HUNAWIHR
Tokay-pinot gris 1999★
□ 0.8 ha 5,300 €8-11

The wines produced in the commune of Hunawihr have been highly sought after for a very long time. In 1123 the bishops of Bâle and Saint-Dé were already quarrelling over tithes that were paid in wine. The area's reputation is just as high today, not least because it has added a grand cru to its array of assets. This golden-yellow wine with clear glints has a discreetly fruity nose with some notes of white flowers and mint. The palate is delightful, showing good balance reinforced by a certain degree of freshness. Despite its high residual sugar content, this is a pleasant wine with good length at the finish. (Residual sugar: 25 g/l.)

☎ Cave vinicole de Hunawihr, 48, rte de Ribeauvillé, 68150 Hunawihr, tel. 03.89.73.61.67, fax 03.89.73.33.95 ▼ ev. day 8am-12 noon 2pm-6pm

FRANCOIS SCHWACH ET FILS
Riesling 1999★
□ 0.2 ha 1,600 €8-11

This huge vineyard of 20 ha (49 acres) has developed a great deal over the last 20 years. It selects its *terroirs* with care, and uses modern equipment. The limestone-clay Rosacker Grand Cru has produced this Riesling, which has a very intense bouquet combining aromas of lemon, grapefruit and exotic fruits. After an excellent opening, the palate is powerful, quite supple and very long. A wine with good ageing potential. (Residual sugar: 8 g/l.)

☎ Dom. François Schwach et Fils, 28, rte de Ribeauvillé, 68150 Hunawihr, tel. 03.89.73.62.15, fax 03.89.73.37.84, e-mail schwach@mcnet.fr ▼ ev. day 9am-12 noon 1.30pm-6.30pm; groups by appt.; cl. Sun. from Jan. to Mar.

ALBERT WINTER
Riesling 1999
□ 0.2 ha 1,800 €8-11

This modest-sized vineyard of 4 ha (10 acres) has frequently been praised for its very fine wines. Grown on a limestone-clay soil, the 99 wine is still in its youthful phase. The bouquet combines hints of citrus fruits with notes of toast. With its well-balanced, harmonious palate, it has excellent ageing potential. (Residual sugar: 12 g/l.)

☎ Albert Winter, 17, rue Sainte-Hune, 68150 Hunawihr, tel. 03.89.73.62.95, fax 03.89.73.62.95 ▼ by appt.

Alsace Grand Cru Saering

DIRLER

Riesling Vendanges tardives 1998★★

☐ 0.31 ha ♦ 2,500 ■ ♦ €15-23

Jean Dirler, representing the new generation, took over here in 2000; he also got married, hence the business's new corporate name, Dirler-Cadé. The relationship between wine and *terroir* was closely observed for many years at this vineyard, long before the advent of the Alsace Grand Cru appellation. This Riesling comes from a sandy marl soil with an abundant gravel content. It has a pale-gold colour with brilliant-yellow glints, and releases a very high-quality nose of highly complex citrus and crystallised-fruit aromas. Although rich and full, the palate has enough freshness to make it remarkably elegant. Its notes of lime, grapefruit and exotic fruits give it a very long finish.

➤ EARL Dirler-Cadé, 13, rue d'Issenheim, 68500 Bergholtz, tel. 03.89.76.91.00, fax 03.89.76.85.97, e-mail jpdirler@terre-net.fr ✉ ✠ by appt.

JOSEPH LOBERGER

Tokay-pinot gris Cuvée Florian 1999★

☐ 0.4 ha ♦ 2,500 ■ ♦ €8-11

The Saering is one of the grands crus next to the point where the Guebwiller valley opens out into the plain. It has an interesting structure, with a sandy-clay soil which brings out the qualities of the most delicate grape varieties. Pinot Gris does well here, because water retention and heat are guaranteed. This one has a golden-yellow colour, a nose of peaches and quince with a hint of wax, and a balanced palate – a complex wine indeed. The fresh finish indicates good ageing potential. (Residual sugar: 23.2 g/l.)

➤ Joseph Loberger, 10, rue de Bergholtz-Zell, 68500 Bergholtz, tel. 03.89.76.88.03, fax 03.89.74.16.88 ✉ ✠ ev. day except Sun. 8am–12 noon 2pm–6pm

ERIC ROMINGER

Riesling 1999★ ■ ♦ €11-15

☐ 0.1 ha ♦ 500

Eric Rominger has been producing wine since 1986. He runs an 8-ha (20-acre) vineyard, and has just moved his cellar from Bergholtz to Westhalten. He has made a name for himself with his grand cru wines. Readers may be familiar with the ones from the Zinnkoepflé, which have won many awards. This Riesling comes from the Saering, a sandy-limestone *terroir* which has given the wine a very subtle nose combining lemon, mint and mineral aromas. With a very full palate which is rich but still has good balance and length, this 99 wine is characterised by its maturity. (Residual sugar: 8 g/l.)

Alsace Grand Cru Saering

➤ Eric Rominger, 16, rue Saint-Blaise, 68250 Westhalten, tel. 03.89.47.68.60, fax 03.89.47.68.61 ✉ ✠ by appt.

DOMAINES SCHLUMBERGER

Riesling 1999★

☐ 9 ha 20,000 ■ ♦ €11-15

The Schlumberger estates not only have the largest vine plantations in Alsace (145 ha/358 acres), they also rank among the greats in terms of reputation. They own most of the classified grand cru areas in the southerly Guebwiller region. This Saering Riesling has a particularly intense nose in which floral and mineral aromas mingle with a hint of liquorice. With its very well-balanced, long, harmonious palate, this is a wine to be drunk with fine food. (Residual sugar: 14 g/l.)

➤ Domaines Schlumberger, 100, rue Théodore-Deck, 68501 Guebwiller Cedex, tel. 03.89.74.27.00, fax 03.89.74.85.75, e-mail duschlum@aol.com ✉ ✠ by appt.

Alsace Grand Cru Schlossberg

ANDRÉ BLANCK

Riesling 1999★

☐ 2 ha 7,000 €8-11

The head office of the André Blanck estate is in the old Court of the Knights of Malta, a place laden with history which stands next to the no-less-famous Château de Schwendi where the Confrérie Saint-Étienne has its headquarters. The Schlossberg is a majestic hillside with a granitic sand soil. Riesling is the main grape variety here. This one is typical of the *terroir*, with a very floral nose which is already well open. The same intensity continues on the palate, which is balanced and long. Guaranteed ageing potential. The 97 vintage was awarded a *coup de coeur*. (Residual sugar: 6 g/l.) The estate also wins a star for its **98 Riesling de Vendanges Tardives**. The judges very much enjoyed its complex mineral and fruit aromas and rich, full palate. (Half-litre bottles.)

➤ EARL André Blanck et Fils, Ancienne Cour des Chevaliers de Malte, 68240 Kientzheim, tel. 03.89.78.24.72, fax 03.89.47.17.07 ✉ ✠ ev. day except Sun. 8am–7pm

JEAN DIETRICH

Riesling Vieilles vignes 1999★

☐ 0.45 ha 3,000 €8-11

The Dietrich estate has 11 ha (27 acres) of vines on the Kaysersberg, and is also associated with the highly reputable Schlossberg, one of the prime localities of the Alsace Granit *terroir*, it is still very young in the nose. After a fairly fresh attack, it is well structured and has good length. A wine of great

132

potential, which will go well with fish and seafood. (Residual sugar: 3 g/l.)
♦ Jean Dietrich, 4, rue de l'Oberhof, 68240 Kaysersberg, tel. 03.89.47.30.72 ▼
fax 03.89.47.30.72 ▼
▼ ev. day 10am–12 noon 2pm–6pm

Alsace Grand Cru Schoenenbourg

♦ Jean-Jacques Ziegler-Mauler Fils, 2, rue des Merles, 68630 Mittelwihr, tel. 03.89.47.90.37, fax 03.89.47.98.27 ▼
▼ by appt.

Alsace Grand Cru Schoenenbourg

DOPFF AU MOULIN Riesling 1999★
8 ha 47,000 €11-15

Dopff au Moulin was founded in 1634 and has remained a family concern. Not only are they a famous Riquewihr wine-merchant, they also run 70 ha (173 acres) of vines of their own, and know what *terroir* is all about. All the richness of the Schoenenbourg comes through in this Riesling, which already has a very intense nose of both floral and mineral aromas. It is on the palate, however, that this wine reveals its full power and complexity. With its very good length, it will be a worthy accompaniment to the most refined dishes. (Residual sugar: 6 g/l.)
♦ SA Dopff au Moulin, 2, av. Jacques-Preiss, 68340 Riquewihr, tel. 03.89.49.09.69, fax 03.89.47.83.61 ▼
▼ ev. day 9am–12 noon 2pm–6pm

ROGER JUNG ET FILS
Riesling Vendanges tardives 1998★★★
0.35 ha 2,200 €15-23

The little town of Riquewihr is known throughout the world for its history, of course, but also for its wine production. Roger Jung et Fils has its head office here, and its cellar is near the town's historic ramparts. With its gold colour and lemon glints, this wine shines in the glass. After a nose marked by citrus fruits (grapefruit), there is an exceptionally smooth, fleshy palate, on which the grapefruit flavour is complemented by very rich notes. The finish leaves a long impression of orange. An extraordinarily full wine.
♦ SARL Roger Jung et Fils, 23, rue de la 1re-Armée, 68340 Riquewihr, tel. 03.89.47.92.17, fax 03.89.47.87.63, e-mail rjung@terre-net.fr ▼ ▼ by appt.

JOSEPH FRITSCH Riesling 1999★★
0.3 ha 1,900 €5-8

Like all the wine-producers in Kientzheim, Joseph Fritsch offers his clientele the whole range of Alsatian wines, but this majestic Grand Cru Schlossberg takes pride of place. As one would expect from a Riesling grown on granite, it has excellent intensity in the nose. An extremely expressive, thoroughbred wine which combines elegance, structure and very good length. (Residual sugar: 6 g/l.)
♦ EARL Joseph Fritsch, 31, Grand-Rue, 68240 Kientzheim, tel. 03.89.78.24.27, fax 03.89.78.24.27 ▼ by appt.

SALZMANN Riesling 1999★
1.48 ha 4,300 €8-11

Descended from a line of wine-producers going back to 1526, the Salzmann-Thomann family offers an exceedingly good Riesling Grand Cru. Its elegant, very floral nose is characteristic of the granite *terroir* it comes from. It has a fine attack and is an expressive, well-balanced wine which will go well with fish dishes in sauce. (Residual sugar: 4 g/l.)
♦ Salzmann-Thomann, Dom. de l'Oberhof, 3, rue de l'Oberhof, 68240 Kaysersberg, tel. 03.89.47.10.26, fax 03.89.78.13.08 ▼ by appt.

FRANCOIS STOLL Riesling 1999★★
0.3 ha 2,007 €5-8

François Stoll comes from a line of wine-producers that dates back to 1767. His business is in the centre of Kaysersberg, a town renowned both for the beauty of its architecture and for the Schlossberg Grand Cru which has yielded this Riesling. Grown on granite, it has a very expressive nose of floral aromas mingled with hints of citrus fruits. With its well-balanced, opulent, very long palate, it will be a worthy accompaniment to the most refined fish dishes. (Residual sugar: 7.5 g/l.)
♦ GAEC François Stoll, 19, rue Basse-du-Rempart, 68240 Kaysersberg, tel. 03.89.78.23.10, fax 03.89.78.21.45 ▼ by appt.

ZIEGLER-MAULER
Les Murets Riesling 1999★
0.27 ha 1,200 €8-11

Philippe Ziegler took over this 5-ha (12-acre) vineyard in 1996. His Les Murets Schlossberg Grand Cru Riesling is frequently praised, and this vintage is particularly distinguished. The intense, highly complex nose shows from the start that it is very mature. The full, long palate has excellent balance. A wine to serve with cooked fish or lobster à l'américaine. (Residual sugar: 6 g/l.)

Alsace Grand Cru Sommerberg

JEAN KLACK Riesling 1999★

□ 0.35 ha 2,200 ▦ €8-11

Riquewihr is a world of old stone – as in this cellar which is as old as the estate, dating from 1628 – and great *terroirs*, such as the Schoenenbourg hillside. This Riesling has a highly elegant nose with aromas of white flowers and mandarin, followed by a lively, well-balanced palate. A very straightforward wine which expresses the typical qualities both of the grape variety and the marly limestone *terroir* that produced it. (Residual sugar: 9 g/l.)

➤ EARL Jean Klack et Fils,
18, rue de la 1ᵉ Armée, 68340 Riquewihr,
tel. 03.89.47.92.44, fax 03.89.47.84.72
✠ ev. day 9am–12 noon 2pm–8pm
➤ Daniel Klack

RAYMOND RENCK Riesling 1999★

□ 0.08 ha 600 ▦ €8-11

Colette and Gérard Schillinger-Renck took over this vineyard of somewhat more than 5 ha (12 acres) in 1996. They are great believers in traditional methods of wine-making, and lay great emphasis on bringing out the qualities of the *terroir*. The marly soil of the Schoenenbourg has left its mark on this Riesling, which still seems young, with a nose releasing hints of white flowers set off by a shade of liquorice. With its frank, fresh attack, good length and thoroughbred nature, this is a wine designed for a long ageing period. (Residual sugar: 3 g/l.)

➤ EARL Raymond Renck,
11, rue de Hoän, 68980 Beblenheim,
tel. 03.89.47.91.75, fax 03.89.47.91.75
✠ by appt.

FRANCOIS SCHWACH ET FILS

Riesling 1999

□ 0.13 ha 800 ▦ ♦ €11-15

Philippe Schwach, representing the third generation, joined his father on this estate in 1985. With 20 ha (49 acres) of vines, he is one of the largest wine producers in the region. The fact that his head office is in Hunawihr does not prevent him from developing his *terroirs*. His Schoenenbourg Riesling is already very open in the nose, which releases notes of white flowers. It is characterised by a fine attack and very good length. A wine which is well equipped for long ageing. (Residual sugar: 6.5 g/l.)

➤ Dom. François Schwach et Fils,
28, rte de Ribeauvillé, 68150 Hunawihr,
tel. 03.89.73.62.15, fax 03.89.73.37.84,
e-mail schwach@rmcnet.fr
✠ ev. day 9am–12 noon 1.30pm–6.30pm;
groups by appt.; cl. Sun. from Jan. to Mar.

Alsace Grand Cru Sommerberg

ALBERT BOXLER Riesling 1999★★

□ n.c. n.c. ▦ €8-11

The village of Niedermorschwihr stretches for a long way to the end of a valley overlooked by the Sommerberg hillside, and has a church which is architecturally very interesting. The Albert Boxler estate is a famous producer, and this 99 Riesling is just as remarkable as previous vintages. Coming from a granitic soil, it has an intense, very floral nose. Its fullness on the palate in no way prevents it from being an extremely well-balanced wine. (Residual sugar: 3 g/l.)

➤ Albert Boxler, 78, rue des Trois-Epis, 68230 Niedermorschwihr,
tel. 03.89.27.11.32, fax 03.89.27.70.14,
e-mail albert.boxler@online.fr
✠ by appt.

GERARD WEINZORN Riesling 1999★★

□ 0.5 ha 2,800 ▦ €11-15

The Renaissance-style house is listed as a historic monument. It dates back to 1619, as does the line of Claude Weinzorn's wine-producing ancestors. In 1992 he took over the estate, which regularly offers grand cru Rieslings (Sommerberg or Brand). This latest, in the 99 vintage, is truly remarkable. It was grown on a granitic soil, and is already very open in the nose, with floral aromas mingling with hints of citrus fruits. After a fairly supple attack, it quickly reveals a fine structure reinforced by a touch of overripening. (Residual sugar: 12.5 g/l.)

➤ Gérard Weinzorn et Fils, 133, rue des Trois-Epis, 68230 Niedermorschwihr,
tel. 03.89.27.40.55, fax 03.89.27.04.23,
e-mail contact@weinzorn.fr
✠ ev. day 8am–12 noon 2pm–6pm

Alsace Grand Cru Sonnenglanz

BARON DE HOEN

Tokay-pinot gris 1999★

□ n.c. 26,000 ▦ ♦ €8-11

The Hoen cellar, which belongs to the Cave Vinicole at Beblenheim, has a large vine plantation on the Sonnenglanz *terroir*. Its straw-yellow Pinot Gris opens with a nose of exotic fruits, quince and bergamot orange, mingled with hints of undergrowth. The well-structured palate is crisp, fruity (pineapple and peaches), balanced and long. Best left for a year or two until it achieves perfection. (Residual sugar: 25 g/l.)

🍷 SICA Baron de Hoen, 20, rue de Hoen, 68980 Beblenheim, tel. 03.89.47.89.93 ✓
Y by appt.

JEAN BECKER Gewurztraminer 1999★

0.6 ha 4,000 €11-15

The Becker firm in Zellenberg is renowned for its *terroir* wines. The Sonnenglanz in the neighbouring commune of Beblenheim has a rather heavy marly limestone soil which produces late-developing wines with very good ageing potential, like this Gewurztraminer. It has a pale-yellow colour, and a characteristic nose of fresh rose petals, followed by an agreeably full palate where, although still reserved, it is already revealing some overripe, spicy flavours. Needs to be kept for two years. (Residual sugar: 18 g/l.)

🍷 SA Jean Becker, 4, rte d'Ostheim, 68340 Zellenberg, tel. 03.89.47.99.57, fax 03.89.47.99.57 ✓
Y ev. day 8am-12 noon 2pm-6pm

JEAN-PAUL ET FRANK HARTWEG Tokay-pinot gris 1999★

0.2 ha 1,800 €8-11

Frank Hartweg took over the family estate in 1996, after studying viticulture and oenology in Burgundy. He has produced a very good Pinot Gris with a strong golden-yellow colour and fruity aromas mingled with some floral acacia notes. The same aromatic range reappears on a rich, full palate whose balance should improve with time. (Residual sugar: 44 g/l.)

🍷 Jean-Paul et Frank Hartweg, 39, rue Jean-Macé, 68980 Beblenheim, tel. 03.89.47.94.79, fax 03.89.49.00.83, e-mail frank.hartweg@free.fr ✓ Y ev. day except Sun. 8am-11.30am 1.30pm-6pm

HEIMBERGER Riesling 1999★

1.5 ha 8,000 €8-11

The Cave Vinicole at Beblenheim (near Riquewihr) has managed to retain its independence, thanks mainly to the talent of its wine-makers and the quality of its *terroirs*, which include more than one grand cru. Despite coming from a marly limestone soil, this Riesling is already very open in a remarkably fine nose dominated by floral scents. After an excellent attack, it has a well-blended structure and very good length. A balanced, thoroughbred wine. (Residual sugar: 5.3 g/l.)

🍷 Cave Vinicole de Beblenheim, 14, rue de Hoen, 68980 Beblenheim, tel. 03.89.47.90.02, fax 03.89.47.86.85 ✓
Y by appt.

BERNARD WURTZ Tokay-pinot gris 1999★

0.15 ha 600 €8-11

The Sonnenglanz has been a delimited area since the 1930s, and now belongs to the family of grands crus. The composition of its soil, which is fairly heavy but aerated by a chalky gravel structure, makes it an excellent *terroir* for Pinot Gris. This one has a strong yellow colour with green glints, and has a full bouquet combining quince and smoke aromas. A very fresh wine with a delightfully fine balance, plenty of richness and good length. (Residual sugar: 15 g/l.)

🍷 Bernard Wurtz, 12, rue du Château, 68630 Mittelwihr, tel. 03.89.47.93.24, fax 03.89.86.01.69 ✓ Y by appt.

Alsace Grand Cru Spiegel

LOBERGER Riesling 1999★★★

0.45 ha 3,200 €8-11

Descended from a line of wine producers going back to 1617, Joseph Loberger has been running a 6-ha (15-acre) estate since 1984. His Spiegel Riesling has an appealing nose of very intense exotic fruits aromas (mango and passion-fruit). After an excellent attack, the palate is lively, rich and long. A wine whose key features are its thoroughbred character and high quality. (Residual sugar: 7.2 g/l.)

🍷 Joseph Loberger, 10, rue de Bergholtz-Zell, 68500 Bergholtz, tel. 03.89.76.38.03, fax 03.89.74.16.88 ✓
Y ev. day except Sun. 8am-12 noon 2pm-6pm

DOM. SCHLUMBERGER Pinot gris 1999★

2.6 ha 21,000 €11-15

The Schlumberger estates are the largest vineyard-owners in Alsace, and also among the most highly regarded. They offer a wide range of *terroir* wines, such as this Pinot Gris grown on the terraced hillside of the Guebwiller valley. It has a brilliant-golden colour, and releases aromas of overripening and wax. There is a rich, full, forthcoming palate, which although still dominated by sweetness, is balanced by a delightful acidity. A very concentrated wine. (Residual sugar: 40 g/l.)

🍷 Domaines Schlumberger, 100, rue Théodore-Deck, 68501 Guebwiller Cedex, tel. 03.89.74.27.00, fax 03.89.74.85.75, e-mail duschlum@aol.com ✓ Y by appt.

Alsace Grand Cru Sporen

DOM. DE LA VIEILLE FORGE

Riesling 1999★

0.1 ha   450   €8-11

This business was taken over in 1998 by a young oenologist. The cellar is located on the site of his great-grandfather's forge, hence its name today. The jewel of the estate is the Sporen, which has now produced this Riesling with its very subtle bouquet of flowers and quince. There is a very good attack, and the structure on the palate copes perfectly with a slight touch of residual sugar. A very full-bodied wine. (Residual sugar: 3 g/l.)

☛ SCEA Wiehle, Dom. de la Vieille Forge, 5, rue de Hoen, 68980 Beblenheim, tel. 03.89.86.01.58, fax 03.89.47.86.37
Ⓨ by appt.

Alsace Grand Cru Steinert

KUENTZ Gewurztraminer 1999★

0.25 ha   2,000   €8-11

The mainly limestone soil of the Steinert is covered with a layer of gravel which gives it excellent aeration and ensures that the slightest ray of sun will heat it up very rapidly. It has produced this brilliant-golden Gewurztraminer, which has a moderately intense but very fine nose of floral aromas (faded roses). It is frank, characteristic, structured and impressively long on the palate, which finishes on renewed flavours of faded roses and violets. (Residual sugar: 22 g/l.)

☛ R. Kuentz et Fils, 22–24, rue du Fossé, 68250 Pfaffenheim, tel. 03.89.49.61.90, fax 03.89.49.77.17 Ⓥ Ⓨ ev. day 8am–12 noon 1.30pm–7pm; Sun. by appt.

Alsace Grand Cru Steingrübler

DOM. BARMES BUECHER

Riesling 1999★

0.31 ha   1,000   €15-23

François Barmès has been running this 15-ha (37-acre) vineyard since 1985. For the last three years he has moved into the demanding realm of organic growing in order to reflect the personality of the *terroir* as closely as possible. Although it comes from a limestone-clay soil, his Steingrübler Riesling already has an intense nose with a good balance between citrus-fruit notes and toast aromas resulting from slight overripening. With its very good attack and full, structured palate, this wine has all the power that excellent raw material can give. (Residual sugar: 6 g/l.)

☛ Dom. Barmès-Buecher, 30, rue Sainte-Gertrude, 68920 Wettolsheim, tel. 03.89.80.62.92, fax 03.89.79.30.80, e-mail barmes-buecher@terre-net.fr
Ⓨ by appt.

JOS. MOELLINGER ET FILS

Riesling 1999★

0.2 ha   1,600   €5-8

Joseph Moellinger started bottling wines here in 1945. Today the 14-ha (35-acre) estate is run by his grandson Michel. Not surprisingly for a wine grown on a marly limestone soil, his Steingrübler Riesling still needs time to open. The nose is beginning to release notes of gunflint, while the palate is characterised by a fairly frank attack, followed by a greater feeling of richness. A long, thoroughbred, wine, which will go well with many fine dishes. (Residual sugar: 5.9 g/l.)

☛ SCEA Jos. Moellinger et Fils, 6, rue de la 5ᵉ -D.-B., 68920 Wettolsheim, tel. 03.89.80.62.02, fax 03.89.80.04.94 Ⓥ Ⓨ ev. day 8am–12 noon 1.30pm–7pm; cl. Oct.

ANDRE STENTZ

Tokay-pinot gris 1999★

0.18 ha   1,250   €11-15

André Stentz comes from an old family of wine producers who went into viticulture as early as 1676. Since 1984 he has been interested in organic methods, and he now has a perfect mastery of the growing and winemaking techniques involved. This is an intensely yellow wine with a few paler glints. It is already very open in the nose, which has a touch of vanilla and brioche bread. On the palate it has a roundness which is not yet entirely blended. Even so, this suppleness is balanced by a delightful freshness, and enhanced by crystallised-fruit flavours. (Residual sugar: 30 g/l.)

☛ André Stentz, 2, rue de la Batteuse, 68920 Wettolsheim, tel. 03.89.80.64.91, fax 03.89.79.59.75 Ⓥ Ⓨ by appt.

Alsace Grand Cru Wiebelsberg

BOECKEL Riesling 1999★★ — 2.5 ha — 10,500 — €8-12

Located in the historic town centre of Mittelbergheim. The Boeckel firm owns 20 ha (49 acres) of vines. The sandy sandstone *terroir* of the Wiebelsberg has produced a Riesling with intense, surprising aromas of toast. Powerful, structured, long and thoroughbred: an unusual wine. (Residual sugar: 5 g/l.)

☎ Emile Boeckel, 2, rue de la Montagne, 67140 Mittelbergheim, tel. 03.88.08.91.91, fax 03.88.08.91.88, e-mail vins.boeckel@provins.com ▨ ▼ by appt.

Alsace Grand Cru Wineck-Schlossberg

JEAN-MARC BERNHARD Riesling 1999★ — 0.35 ha — n.c. — €8-11

Founded in 1802, this estate is run by Jean-Marc Bernhard, who for a year now has been assisted by his son. He owns plots on several grands crus, including the Wineck-Schlossberg. His Riesling is characterised not only by this granitic *terroir* but also by the overripeness of the grapes, which were harvested at the beginning of November. The nose is both floral and fruity, and there are lemony notes on the palate. The 1998 was awarded a *coup de cœur*. (Residual sugar: 7.2 g/l.)

☎ Domaine Jean-Marc Bernhard, 21, Grand-Rue, 68230 Katzenthal, tel. 03.89.27.05.34, fax 03.89.27.58.72, e-mail jeanmarcbernhard@online.fr ▨ ▼ ev. day except Sun. 9am–12 noon 2pm–7pm

JEAN-PAUL ECKLE Riesling 1999★ — 0.21 ha — 1,500 — €8-11

Jean-Paul Eckle, who has now been joined by his son, regularly offers very successful Rieslings (and indeed exceptional ones such as the 96 vintage) grown on the Wineck-Schlossberg. This one has an intense yellow colour, and reveals notes of honey and over-ripening in the nose. With its full, rich palate, it is well equipped for a long ageing period. A wine which will go well with fish dishes in sauce. (Residual sugar: 5 g/l.)

☎ Jean-Paul Eckle et Fils, 29, Grand-Rue, 68230 Katzenthal, tel. 03.89.27.09.41, fax 03.89.80.86.18 ▨ ▼ ev. day 8am–12 noon 1pm–7pm

Alsace Grand Cru Zinnkoepflé

HENRI KLEE Gewurztraminer Vendanges tardives 1998★★ — 0.35 ha — 1,800 — €15-23

The two-mica granite of the Wineck-Schlossberg Grand Cru has passed on all its nobility to this Henri Klee Gewurztraminer. It has a remarkable ochre-yellow colour, and a nose still marked by raisin aromas which has great potential for development. The palate was described by one taster as 'multi-dimensional': full and yet rangy, it is also well structured, and finishes sweetly on notes of exotic fruits. A delightfully fine, appealingly powerful wine. (Half-litre bottles.)

☎ EARL Henri Klée et Fils, 11, Grand-Rue, 68230 Katzenthal, tel. 03.89.27.03.81, fax 03.89.27.28.17 ▨ by appt.

Alsace Grand Cru Winzenberg

HUBERT METZ Gewurztraminer 1999★ — 0.63 ha — 3,000 — €8-11

Hubert Metz is established in Blienschwiller, in the old tithe cellar which dates from 1728. Until the French Revolution in 1789, tithes here were paid in grapes. This gold wine with amber glints reveals quince and crystallised-fruit aromas in the nose. These notes reappear on the palate—'with just a touch of alcohol which gives this wine a pleasant structure', said one of the tasters. The balance should be complete in three years' time. (Residual sugar: 21 g/l.) Another **1999 Riesling**. Its very intense nose closely reflects the granitic soil that produced it. It is quite fresh on the palate, ending on a note of lemon.

☎ Hubert Metz, 3, rue du Winzenberg, 67650 Blienschwiller, tel. 03.88.92.43.06, fax 03.88.92.62.08, e-mail hubertmetz@aol.com ▨ ▼ ev. day except Sun. 8am–7pm

Alsace Grand Cru Zinnkoepflé

DOM. LEON BOESCH Tokay-pinot gris Sélection de grains nobles 1998★ — 0.2 ha — n.c. — €46-76

The Zinnkoepflé is a marly limestone, conchiferous *terroir* which is very good for producing Sélection de Grains Nobles wines, as can be clearly seen from this straw-yellow Tokay-Pinot Gris. It has a complex aromatic range with hints of undergrowth, and makes an agreeable impression right from the attack. On the palate it develops a silky body, finishing with a real symphony of spicy aromas.

☛ Dom. Léon Boesch, 6, rue Saint-Blaise, 68250 Westhalten, tel. 03.89.47.01.83, fax 03.89.47.64.95 ☒ ☎ ev. day except Sun. 10am–12 noon 2pm–6pm

☛ Gérard Boesch

DIRINGER

Gewurztraminer Vendanges tardives 1998★   ▥ €15-23

☐   0.4 ha   1,800   ▤ ☎ €8-8

This family business was started as long ago as 1740. Since 1982 the two Diringers, Thomas and Sébastien, who is an oenologist, have been growing about 13 ha (32 acres) of vines, most of them on the Zinnkoepflé Grand Cru. Their pale-yellow Gewurztraminer has a fine, elegant nose, and also great richness and balance on the palate. Its very long finish remains unusually fresh.

☛ Dom. Diringer, 18, rue de Rouffach, 68250 Westhalten, tel. 03.89.47.01.06, fax 03.89.47.62.64, e-mail info@diringer.fr ☒ ☎ ev. day except Sun. 9am–12 noon 2pm–7pm

RENÉ FLECK Riesling 1999★   ▥ €5-8

☐   0.14 ha   1,200

René Fleck and his daughter, who joined him in running the estate in 1995, offer a Riesling with an interestingly complex aromatic range in a bouquet marked by lemony and mineral notes. A fine attack leads on to a long, well-balanced palate which has solid ageing potential. (Residual sugar: 14 g/l)

☛ René Fleck et Fille, 27, rte d'Orschwihr, 68570 Soultzmatt, tel. 03.89.47.01.20, fax 03.89.47.09.24 ☒ ☎ by appt.

JEAN-MARIE HAAG

Gewurztraminer Vendanges tardives 1998★   ▥ €15-23

☐   0.37 ha   1,200

Soultzmatt is a charming town nestling at the far end of the Vallée Noble. Although it owes its prestige to viticulture, there are other flourishing economic activities here, notably the Lisbeth mineral water spring and the metallurgical industry. Much of this late harvest comes from vines planted in 1920. It has produced a straw-yellow wine with golden glints, and a bouquet giving off powerful, fine aromas of flowers and exotic fruits. The palate is rich and already well balanced, with a moderately long finish on further floral notes.

☛ Jean-Marie Haag, 17, rue des Chèvres, 68570 Soultzmatt, tel. 03.89.47.02.38, fax 03.89.47.64.79, e-mail jean-marie.haag@wanadoo.fr ☒ ☎ ev. day 9am–12 noon 2pm–6pm; Sun. and groups sur by appt.

Gewurztraminer is a fine example. It opens with very complex aromas of crystallised fruits along with hints of figs. The very pleasant, silky palate already seems to be mature, revealing spicy flavours accompanied by the same fig notes as in the nose.

☛ EARL Paul Kubler, 103, rue de la Vallée, 68570 Soultzmatt, tel. 03.89.47.00.75, fax 03.89.47.65.45, e-mail kubler@lesvins.com ☒ ☎ by appt.

SEPPI LANDMANN Tokay-pinot gris

Sélection de grains nobles 1998★   +€76

☐   0.25 ha   1,000   ▤ ☎ +€76

Seppi Landmann came here in 1982, and has rapidly made a name for himself in Alsace. This Tokay-Pinot Gris comes from the early-maturing Zinnkoepflé terroir, and has an old-gold colour and a nose of cooked, caramel and mushroom aromas. With its intense, rich palate, this very silky wine has overripening. An excellent example of Sélection de Grains Nobles, with spicy notes. The 98 Riesling Sélection de Grains Nobles du Grand Cru Zinnkoepflé is singled out for its beautiful fruit flavours on the palate, and for its freshness.

☛ Seppi Landmann, 20, rue de la Vallée, 68570 Soultzmatt, tel. 03.89.47.09.33, fax 03.89.47.06.99, e-mail seppi.landmann@wanadoo.fr ☒ ☎ by appt.

FRANCIS MURE

Tokay-pinot gris 1999★★   €11-15

☐   0.3 ha   2,200

The Zinnkoepflé has an exceptionally good location; it is sheltered from the influence of the sea by the highest peaks of the Vosges to the west, and from the north winds by the top of the hillside where it lies on the south-facing slope. The limestone soil produces characteristic wines. This Pinot Gris has a deep golden-yellow colour, and a delightful, smoky nose with hints of quince. It has a rich, remarkably complex palate, and excellent ageing potential. As one of the tasters pointed out, this is 'a wine of very high quality which deserves to be kept in the cellar'. (Residual sugar: 35 g/l.)

☛ Francis Muré, 30, rue de Rouffach, 68250 Westhalten, tel. 03.89.47.64.20, fax 03.89.47.09.39 ☒ ☎ by appt.

BOECKEL Tokay-pinot gris 1999★   ▥ €8-11

☐   0.3 ha   2,050

Mention the Zotzenberg, and you immediately think of Mittelbergheim. This charming town is also the headquarters of the Boeckel firm, which is certainly one of the oldest in an

PAUL KUBLER Gewurztraminer

Sélection de grains nobles 1998★   ▤ ☎ €23-30

☐   0.3 ha   2,000

The Zinnkoepflé Grand Cru produces astonishing wines, of which this

area that has made a substantial contribution to the reputation of Alsatian wine. This Tokay-Pinot Gris has a golden-yellow colour, and a nose with a slight aroma of liquorice and developing scents of undergrowth. The attack is frank, and the palate is already very well balanced. A rich, almost dry, pleasantly full wine which will be a good accompaniment to subtle dishes. (Residual sugar: 12.5 g/l.)
- Emile Boeckel, 2, rue de la Montagne, 67140 Mittelbergheim, tel. 03.88.08.91.91, fax 03.88.08.91.88, e-mail vins.boeckel@proveis.com ☑ ▼ by appt.

BERNARD ET DANIEL HAEGI

Riesling 1999★

□ 0.3 ha 2,400 ▐ €5-8

This 8-ha (20-acre) vineyard is located in Mittelbergheim, one of the most beautiful villages in France, and benefits from the accumulated experience of three generations of producers. Their Riesling comes from the marly limestone Zotzenberg Grand Cru, and has the intense floral nose that is typical of the grape variety. It is lively, structured and long on the palate, as one would expect of a wine from this *terroir*. (Residual sugar: 2 g/l.)
- Bernard et Daniel Haegi, 33, rue de la Montagne, 67140 Mittelbergheim, tel. 03.88.08.95.80, fax 03.88.08.91.20 ☑
▼ ev. day except Sun. 8am-12 noon 1pm-6pm

FERNAND SELTZ ET FILS

Riesling 1999★★

□ 0.3 ha 2,500 ▐ €8-11

This vineyard of over 8 ha (20 acres) did not start bottling wines until 1988. It certainly hasn't wasted any time! Despite coming from a marly limestone soil, this Riesling is already very open in a nose of highly elegant lemony notes. It has a frank attack and is relatively supple on the palate, which is long and thoroughbred. A wine which will go well with the most delicate fish dishes. (Residual sugar: 4 g/l.)
- EARL Fernand Seltz et Fils, 42, rue Principale, 67140 Mittelbergheim, tel. 03.88.08.93.92, fax 03.88.08.93.92 ☑
▼ ev. day 8.30am-7pm; Sun. 8.30am-12 noon

A. WITTMANN FILS Riesling 1999★★

□ n.c. 2,660 €5-8

The Wittmann family has 8 ha (20 acres) of vines, and has been handing down the tradition of wine-growing from father to son since 1785. Their cellar actually dates back as far as 1558! This Riesling is developing a nose of very intense, well-balanced aromas of lemon, grapefruit and melon. With its lively attack and perfectly structured, long palate, this is a very high-quality wine with excellent ageing potential. (Residual sugar: 6 g/l.)
- EARL André Wittmann et Fils, 7-9, rue Principale, 67140 Mittelbergheim, tel. 03.88.08.95.79, fax 03.88.08.53.81 ☑
▼ by appt.

A. WITTMANN FILS

Gewurztraminer 1999★

□ 0.32 ha 2,000 ▌▐ €8-11

The Wittmann family grow some of their vines on the Zotzenberg hillside, whose marly clay soil produces wines for longer maturing. With its golden colour and delightful exotic-fruit aromas (especially mango), this Gewurztraminer is already a very self-assured wine. After a surprising attack, the palate has the same fruity notes as the nose, with added hints of menthol and aniseed at the finish. 'This wine will suit the enthusiast who wants to get off the beaten track,' wrote one taster. (Residual sugar: 20 g/l.)
- EARL André Wittmann et Fils, 7-9, rue Principale, 67140 Mittelbergheim, tel. 03.88.08.95.79, fax 03.88.08.53.81 ☑
▼ by appt.

Crémant d'Alsace

When this appellation was created in 1976, there was an immediate increase in production of sparkling wines made by the *méthode traditionnelle*, or Champagne method. They had always been produced, but on a smaller scale. Crémant d'Alsace is made from a blend of various grape varieties: Pinot Blanc, Auxerrois, Pinot Gris, Pinot Noir, Riesling and Chardonnay. The production of this sparkling wine, steadily gaining in reputation, increased to 157,000 hl (4,144,800 gal) in 2000.

ANDRE ANCEL

Riesling 1998★

○ 0.17 ha 1,100 ▐ €5-8

The Ancel family has been marketing bottled wines since 1928. The estate has 8.70 ha (21 acres) of vines, and has been run for 15 years now by André Ancel. His Crémant has a charming rosé colour, a fine sparkle, and a full, balanced, fruity palate with a delightfully harmonious finish.

Crémant d'Alsace

• EARL André Ancel, 3, rue du Collège, 68240 Kaysersberg, tel. 03.89.78.13.78 ▣ ▾ ev. day 8am–12 noon 1.30pm–7pm

RENE BARTH 1998★

○ 0.5 ha 3,500 ▪ €5-8

Michel Fonné comes from an old wine-producing family, and is a trained oenologist. He came here in 1989 to take over the business from his uncle. Made from a blend of Pinot and Riesling, his Crémant has a golden-yellow colour, a fresh, fruity palate, and an exotic note which will make it a good wine to drink as an aperitif.

• Dom. Michel Fonné, 24, rue du Gal-de-Gaulle, 68630 Bennwihr, tel. 03.89.47.92.69, fax 03.89.49.04.86, e-mail michel.fonne@wanadoo.fr ▾ by appt.

A. L. BAUR 1998★

○ 0.55 ha 5,600 ▪ €5-8

At the front of the Baur family's property, the visitor will find a row of vines representing the seven Alsatian grape varieties. This Crémant is made from Pinot-Auxerrois, which has given it a delightful nose of intense, fruity aromas. The palate is full and round, with very good length at the finish. A pleasantly mouth-filling, full-bodied wine, which will be good to drink with a meal.

• A. L. Baur, 4, rue Roger-Frémeaux, 68420 Voegtlinshoffen, tel. 03.89.49.30.97, fax 03.89.49.21.37 ▾ by appt.

BESTHEIM

○ n.c. n.c. ▪ €5-8

Bestheim is produced by the co-operative wine-producers' union in two villages, Bennwihr and Westhalten; they make their Crémants in Westhalten. This one has fruit and flower aromas. A slight roundness on the palate is balanced by freshness, which gives it some length at the finish. A smooth, gulpable Crémant.

• Cave de Bestheim-Bennwihr, 3, rue du Gal-de-Gaulle, 68630 Bennwihr, tel. 03.89.49.09.29, fax 03.89.49.09.20, e-mail bestheim@goformel.com ▾ by appt.

MAXIME BRAND

Rimmler Kapelle 1998★

○ 1.06 ha 6,700 ▣ €5-8

This property has a very old vaulted cellar which was probably once used for tithes. Here you will find this Crémant, which comes from a vineyard near the Saint-Michel Chapel. It has plenty of sparkle and an intense nose with a slightly exotic note. There is an excellent attack followed by more fruity notes on the palate, which has quite a supple, pleasant balance.

• Maxime Brand, 15, rue Principale, 67120 Ergersheim, tel. 03.88.38.18.87, fax 03.88.49.84.44 ▾ by appt.

JEAN-CLAUDE BUECHER 1999★

○ 0.33 ha 3,200 ▪ €5-8

Jean-Claude Buecher has been running the family business since 1980, and has chosen to specialise exclusively in Crémants d'Alsace. This wine is made from Pinot Noir, and has a pale pink colour, red berry aromas and a well-balanced palate.

• Jean-Claude Buecher, 31, rue des Vignes, 68920 Wettolsheim, tel. 03.89.80.14.01, fax 03.89.80.17.78 ▾ by appt.

DOM. DOCK 1999★

○ 0.5 ha 6,000 ▪ €5-8

Many monasteries, including Sainte-Odile, used to own wine-producing properties in the village of Heiligstein, which has Merovingian origins. The Dock family grows 9 ha (22 acres) of vines here. Their Crémant has a pale-yellow colour, a light mousse, and fine, discreet aromas of lemon and liquorice. The palate is pleasantly well balanced and fresh.

• André et Christian Dock, 20, rue Principale, 67140 Heiligenstein, tel. 03.88.08.02.69, fax 03.88.08.19.72 ▾ ev. day 8am–12 noon 1pm–6pm

DAVID ERMEL 1998★

○ 1.2 ha 12,000 ▪ ▮ €5-8

Visitors to Hunawihr should stroll around the tourist circuit or the wine trail, and of course pay a visit to a wine-producer's cellar such as this one. This Crémant has a pale-yellow colour and a fine, discreet nose of fruity aromas. The palate is fresh at first, then develops a body which is round and long.

• David Ermel, 30, rte de Ribeauvillé, 68150 Hunawihr, tel. 03.89.73.61.71, fax 03.89.73.32.56 ▾ by appt.

ANTOINE FONNE

Blanc de blancs 1998★

○ 0.32 ha 2,000 ▪ ▮ €5-8

This estate was founded in 1972. It has been run for about ten years now by René Fonné, who has 4 ha (10 acres) of vines. The wine has only a light mousse, but even so its aromas are fine and very floral. The combination of a full body, plenty of freshness and excellent length gives it all the elegance you would expect from a good aperitif.

• Antoine Fonné, 14, Grand-Rue, 68770 Ammerschwihr, tel. 03.89.47.37.90, fax 03.89.47.18.83 ▾ by appt.

LOUIS FREYBURGER ET FILS 1998★★

○ 0.33 ha 4,000 ▣ €5-8

André Freyburger has been running this 20-ha (49-acre) estate since 1972. In 1982 he started to produce Crémants Rosés. This one has a pink colour with slightly amber glints, good aromatic intensity and a round, long body on the palate.

• Dom. Louis Freyburger et Fils, 1, rue du Maire-Witzig, 68750 Bergheim, tél. 03.89.73.63.82, fax 03.89.73.37.72 ▾ by appt.

Crémant d'Alsace

JOSEPH GRUSS ET FILS 1999★★★

1.4 ha — 16,400 — €5-8

Built in 1559, this house in Eguisheim was once the headquarters of the Confrérie des Gourmets, a body of public officials who guaranteed the standard of the wine that was put on the market. Bernard Gruss and his son André still apply a policy of real quality here, and their wines are regularly singled out. This Crémant is based on Pinot-Auxerrois and Riesling, and deserves the highest of praise. With its hints of peach and citrus fruits in the nose, and delightful freshness combined with rich roundness on the palate, this wine is a splendid achievement.

☛ Dom. Gruss, 25, Grand-Rue, 68420 Eguisheim, tel. 03.89.41.28.78, fax 03.89.41.76.66, e-mail domainegruss@hotmail.com Ⓥ Ⓨ ev. day 8am–12 noon 1.30pm–6pm

ALBERT MAURER 1998★

1.5 ha — 12,000 — €5-8

The little wine-producing village of Eichhoffen is located near Andlau, well away from the main roads. Its history goes back as far as the Roman era. This Crémant has a slightly surprising brilliant-yellow colour and very long-lasting sparkle. It has intense fruity notes both in the nose and on the palate, which starts with a very good attack and lingers at the end into a long, pleasant finish.

☛ Albert Maurer, 11, rue du Vignoble, 67140 Eichhoffen, tel. 03.88.08.96.75, fax 03.88.08.59.98 Ⓥ Ⓨ ev. day except Sun. 8am–12 noon 1.30pm–6pm

PREISS-ZIMMER 1999★

15 ha — 150,000 — €5-8

Nestling behind its ramparts, the town of Riquewihr epitomises the traditions of Alsatian vineyard. No-one who walks up and down its narrow streets and visits its wine-cellars can fail to respond to its charm. This pale-yellow Crémant with green glints has a nose of citrus-fruit aromas which also shows a delightful personality. This develops further on the palate, right up to a frank, elegant finish.

☛ SARL Preiss-Zimmer, 40, rue du Gal-de-Gaulle, 68340 Riquewihr, tel. 03.89.47.86.91, fax 03.89.27.35.33

RUHLMANN 1998

0.9 ha — 8,000 — €5-8

The Château de l'Ortenbourg is located on the heights of Scherwiller. It has influenced the village's history, and its wine-growing and Riesling production still more so. This Crémant is a blend of Pinot Blanc and Riesling. It has elegant floral hints in the nose, and an expressive, very characteristic, slightly round palate with good balance and length.

☛ Gilbert Ruhlmann Fils, 31, rue de l'Ortenbourg, 67750 Scherwiller, tel. 03.88.92.03.21, fax 03.88.82.30.19, e-mail gruhlman@terre-net.fr Ⓥ Ⓨ by appt.

HUNOLD Cuvée du Paradis 1999

1.5 ha — 12,000 — €5-8

Le Paradis in Rouffach is a remarkable vine plantation at the top of the hill that overlooks the town. The Hunold family business has more than 12 ha (30 acres) of vines there. This Crémant is a blend of Chardonnay, Pinot and Riesling. It shows great finesse both in its nose of citrus fruit aromas and on the palate, where it has great presence. Best drunk at the start of a meal.

☛ EARL Bruno Hunold, 29, rue aux Quatre-Vents, 68250 Rouffach, tel. 03.89.49.60.57, fax 03.89.49.67.66 Ⓥ Ⓨ by appt.

HUBERT KRICK 1998

0.4 ha — 4,000 — €8-11

Wintzenheim is located very close to Colmar, below the Château de Hohlandsbourg and at the point where the town meets the vineyard. Hubert Krick has been running an 11.5-ha (28-acre) family vineyard here since 1982. His Crémant has a long-lasting sparkle and a nose of white-flower notes which reappear on the palate. A well-balanced, characteristic wine with good length.

☛ EARL Hubert Krick, 93–95, rue Clemenceau, 68920 Wintzenheim, tel. 03.89.27.00.01, fax 03.89.27.54.75 Ⓥ

PAUL SCHNEIDER 1999★

1.15 ha — 12,000 — €8-11

Every house in Eguisheim is full of history. The head office of the Schneider firm is in the old titthe court that once belonged to the Provost of Strasbourg Cathedral. The sparkle in this Crémant is very intense, as are the fruity notes in the nose and on the palate. A well-balanced, supple, fresh wine, which should be drunk as an aperitif.

☛ Paul Schneider et Fils, 1, rue de l'Hôpital, 68420 Eguisheim, tel. 03.89.41.50.07, fax 03.89.41.30.57 Ⓥ Ⓨ ev. day 10am–12 noon 1.30pm–6.30pm; Sun. by appt.

EMILE SCHWARTZ 1998

1.2 ha — 12,000 — €5-8

Emile Schwartz and his son Christian run a 6.5-ha (16-acre) estate, with vines stretching over the hillsides below the three castles at Eguisheim. This Crémant has fine, long-

141

ALSACE

lasting bubbles and pleasant, intense, characteristic Pinot aromas. It arrives very fresh on the palate, which gives it character without impairing its balance.

• EARL Émile Schwartz et Fils, 3, rue Principale, 68420 Husseren-les-Châteaux, tel. 03.89.49.30.61, fax 03.89.49.27.27 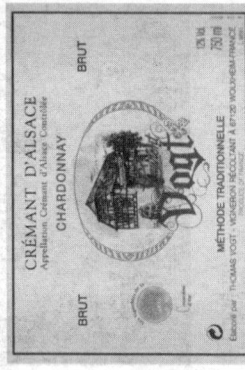, ev. day except Sun. 8am–12 noon 2pm–7pm; cl. 1 –15 Sept.

BRUNO SORG 1998★

| | n.c. | 9,000 | €5-8 |

Very close to the Church of Saint Léon, you can visit the Sorg estate's cellar, and perhaps try this Crémant. It has fine, fresh fruit aromas, with just a touch of freshness and a delightfully round quality. The fruit notes remain elegant on the palate.

• Dom. Bruno Sorg, 8, rue Mgr-Stumpf, 68420 Eguisheim, tel. 03.89.41.80.85, fax 03.89.41.22.64 ⊠ ☎ by appt.

SPITZ ET FILS
Blanc de noirs Fronholz 1998★

| | 0.54 ha | 6,200 | €5-8 |

Blienschwiller, which used to belong to the Bishop of Strasbourg, is a typical little wine-growing town with over 200 ha (500 acres) of vines and more than 50 wine-producers. For many years the Spitz estate has been pursuing a policy of high quality and making constant progress. This Crémant has a brilliant-golden colour and a fine mousse. Its elegant aromas both in the nose and on the palate contribute to an overall impression of harmony. A well-balanced, pleasant wine.

• Spitz et Fils, 2–4, rte des Vins, 67650 Blienschwiller, tel. 03.88.92.61.20, fax 03.88.92.61.26 ⊠ ☎ by appt.
• D. et M.-C. Spitz

STOFFEL 1998★

| | 0.69 ha | 6,000 | €5-8 |

Laden with history since Celtic and Roman times, the commune of Eguisheim has always taken great care over the reception it gives to tourists and wine-lovers. The Stoffel family contributes to this without fuss or ceremony. This Crémant has an intense, light sparkle, a pale gold colour, and very pronounced aromas of citrus fruits. After a fresh attack, the palate is well balanced and agreeably long.

• Antoine Stoffel, 21, rue de Colmar, 68420 Eguisheim, tel. 03.89.41.32.03, fax 03.89.24.92.07 ⊠ ☎ ev. day except Sun. 8am–12 noon 2pm–6pm

ULMER 1998★★

| | 40 ha | 4,600 | €5-8 |

The Ulmer estate was founded by the paternal grandfather, and now has some 12 ha (30 acres) of vines. This Crémant is based on just one grape variety, Pinot Blanc. It has a pale-yellow colour and intense aromas of white flowers and almonds. There is a fresh attack, after which the palate is long and remarkably well balanced.

• EARL Rémy Ulmer, 3, rue des Ciseaux, 67650 Rosheim, tel. 03.88.50.45.62, fax 03.88.50.45.62 ⊠ ☎ by appt.

LAURENT VOGT Chardonnay 1998★★

| | 0.4 ha | 4,800 | €8-11 |

In 1998, Thomas Vogt took over from his father Laurent. The estate has its head office in a beautiful, half-timbered house, and altogether grows 11 ha (27 acres) of vines. Only Chardonnay has been used to produce this moderately sparkling, light-yellow Crémant, which releases a delicate, well-developed nose of floral and fruity hints combined with toast and vanilla notes. The full, fresh palate is accentuated by some notes of roasting which continue into an exceptionally long finish. A superb, thoroughbred wine.

• EARL Laurent Vogt, 4, rue des Vignerons, 67120 Wolxheim, tel. 03.88.38.50.41, fax 03.88.38.50.41, e-mail thomas@domaine-vogt.com ⊠
• by appt.
• Thomas Vogt

CH. WAGENBOURG 1998★

| | 1.1 ha | 11,000 | €5-8 |

This estate, whose head office is in a castle built in 1506, has been run by Jacky and Mireille Klein since 1987. The Crémant here is made from Pinot Blanc grapes grown on a limestone clay *terroir*, and is as noble as the castle itself; it has a delightful range of intense fruity aromas which continue on the palate, and a lively freshness which will make it a very good accompaniment to a meal.

• Joseph et Jacky Klein, Ch. Wagenbourg, 25, rue de la Vallée, 68570 Soultzmatt, tel. 03.89.47.01.41, fax 03.89.47.65.61 ⊠
• ev. day. 8am–12 noon 1pm–7pm

ODILE ET DANIELLE WEBER 1998★

| | 0.4 ha | 2,500 | €5-11 |

The Weber sisters took over the family property in 1988, and since 1992 have been growing a little over 4 ha (10 acres) of vines by organic methods. They are developing a very interesting range of Alsatian wines. This Crémant has delicate, fruity aromas and some spicy notes. On the palate it is full-bodied, fine yet long, and pleasantly balanced.

• GAEC Odile et Danielle Weber, 14, rue de Colmar, 68420 Eguisheim, tel. 03.89.41.35.56, fax 03.89.41.35.56 ⊠ ☎ by appt.

The Côtes de Toul and the Moselle are the last remaining vineyards of the once flourishing wine-growing area of Lorraine. In their heyday, Lorraine wines were held in high esteem, and in 1890 the vineyards covered more than 30,000 ha (74,100 acres). The reputation of these two areas was at its height in the late 19th century. After that, various disasters contributed to its decline: the vines were destroyed by phylloxera, and the hybrid stock planted to replace them was of inferior quality; there was a slump in the wine industry in 1907; the battlefields of the First World War covered much of this part of eastern France; and the industrialisation of the region led to a massive exodus of workers from the country to the town to work in the factories. The local authorities ultimately acknowledged the originality of the wines produced in these vineyards, but it was not until 1951 that the Côtes de Toul and the Moselle wines were officially recognised, finally regaining their place among the old-established wines of France.

Côtes de Toul

Located just west of Toul and the elbow-bend of the Moselle, the Côtes de Toul vineyards cover eight communes along the hillside. Sedimentary layers from the eastern part of the Paris Basin have been eroded away to expose geological structures from the Jurassic period, mainly Oxford clay with significant deposits of calcareous scree, which gives good drainage. The slopes face south or south-east, and the semi-continental climate means high summer temperatures, which help to ripen the grapes. However, there are often frosts in spring.

The majority of the vineyards are planted with Gamay, although much is being replaced by Pinot Noir. The blending of these two varieties makes characteristic Vin Gris, which is obtained by direct pressing. To qualify as Vin Gris, the decree stipulates that at least 10% of Pinot Noir grapes must be blended with Gamay, which gives the wine greater roundness. Some Pinot Noir is made into single-variety red wines which are pleasant and full-bodied, while the locally grown Auxerrois makes light white wines.

The vineyards cover some 100 ha (247 acres), and produced 5,436 hl (145,141 gal) of wine in 2000.

As you leave Toul, there is a well signposted Route du Vin et de la Mirabelle, which takes you through the vineyard.

On 31 March 1998, the vineyard was officially recognised as an AOC.

■ VINCENT GORNY Pinot noir 2000★★

■ 1.2 ha 7,500 ■ €5-8

Vincent Gorny won the *coup de coeur* last year, and has succeeded perfectly in overcoming the difficulties of the 2000 vintage: witness the admirable, intense red colour of this wine, and its nose of very pronounced, exquisite soft-fruit aromas. The 12-year-old vines here have produced a wine of character, whose delightful palate is based on remarkably good balance.

Moselle AOVDQS

The vineyards are planted on the hillsides of the Moselle valley, which were originally layers of sedimentary rock at the eastern limit of the Paris Basin. The vineyards are clustered in three main centres: the first is south and west of Metz; the second in the region of Sierck-les-Bains, and the third along the Seille valley, around Vic-sur-Seille. Wine-making in this AOVDQS is influenced by that in neighbouring Luxembourg; the vines grow tall and wide producing dry, fruity white wines. In terms of quantity, the AOVDQS is still modest producing 1,633 hl (43,111 gal) in 2000, but the wine-growing area cannot expand because the land is broken up into very small plots.

DOM. DE LA LINOTTE Gris 2000★   €3-5

0.83 ha   8,000

After three years in the Champagne region, Marc Laroppe took over this estate in 1993. All his vines are planted in lyre formation. This wine has a beautiful, salmon-pink colour, and a pleasant, somewhat restrained, fruity nose. The palate is very well-balanced and delightfully long. Another wine from the same estate is a **2000 Auxerrois** which is fine, and balanced by a very pleasant acidity; it especially impressed the Jury.

➤ Marc Laroppe, 90, rue Victor-Hugo, 54200 Bruley, tel. 03.83.63.29.02, fax 03.83.63.00.39
Ⓨ ev. day 8.30am–7pm

MARCEL ET MICHEL LAROPPE Pinot noir 1999★   €5-8

4.5 ha   20,000

This family estate is one of the driving forces of the AOC. Respect for the environment, respect for the *terroir* and one year's maturation in barrel; all of these have produced a wine with a delightful red colour and a very beautiful nose of fine vanilla notes in which the grape variety comes through well despite the cover of oak. The palate is well balanced, with a long, harmonious finish. The **2000 Auxerrois**, which is not oak-matured, especially impressed the Jury with the subtlety of its fruit aromas.

➤ Marcel et Michel Laroppe, 253, rue de la République, 54200 Bruley, tel. 03.83.43.11.04, fax 03.83.43.36.92
Ⓨ ev. day except Sun. 8am–12 noon 1.30pm–7pm

LES VIGNERONS DU TOULOIS Gris 2000   €3-5

n.c.   7,000

Located on the Route de la Mirabelle, which is a famous Lorraine wine area, this co-operative is one of the most recently created cellars in France. It is also one of the smallest, comprising only about ten wine-growers. This *vin gris* has a beautiful salmon-pink colour with pink glints. Its fine nose is somewhat restrained but very agreeable. The palate is sweet and pleasant.

➤ Les Vignerons du Toulois, 43, pl. de la Mairie, 54113 Mont-le-Vignoble, tel. 03.83.62.59.93, fax 03.83.62.59.93
Ⓨ ev. day except Mon. 2pm–6pm

GAUTHIER Réserve de la porte des évêques Muller-Thurgau 2000★

0.2 ha   2,000

Claude Gauthier took over here in the year that marked the 200th anniversary of the French Revolution. He remains very attached to the history of his region, because his family was already growing vines under the Ancien Régime. This wine has a very pale colour and a very fine bouquet of floral notes. There are fruity notes on the palate, which is well balanced.

➤ Claude Gauthier, 4, pl. du Palais, 57630 Vic-sur-Seille, tel. 03.87.01.11.55, fax 03.87.01.11.55
Ⓨ by appt.

MICHEL MAURICE Auxerrois 2000★★   €3-5

0.67 ha   6,000

This vineyard in Ancy has a limestone-clay soil. Michel Maurice is offering a **2000 Rosé** which is a blend of Pinot Noir (70%) and Gamay, and has a ravishing salmon-pink colour and aromas of pear drops and flowers. It wins a star. The *coup de cœur* goes to this Auxerrois, however. Its colour is quite pale with green glints. The nose has a blackcurrant aroma and notes of lemon and exotic fruits. There is a full, well-balanced palate, tending towards citrus fruits.

● Michel Maurice, 1–3, pl. Foch, 57130 Ancy-sur-Moselle, tel. 03.87.30.90.07, fax 03.87.30.90.07, e-mail mauricem@ netcourrier.com ▼ Y by appt.

DOM. MUR DU CLOITRE
Muller Thurgau 2000

□ | 0.3 ha | 1,720 | €5-8

This estate is located 6 km (4 miles) from the Château de Sierck (11th century), and used to be run by the Carthusians at Rettel. In 1997 it was bought by Jean-Paul Paquet, so this 2000 vintage represents his fourth year of wine-growing. It has a very light, pale colour, and a nose which is still fairly discreet but does have some delightful mineral notes. The palate is lemony and very dry. A wine very much in keeping with the *terroir* from which it comes.

● Jean-Paul Paquet, chem. des Quatre-Vents, 57570 Berg-sur-Moselle, tel. 06.08.09.83.49, fax 06.87.67.44.29 ▼

OURY-SCHREIBER
Cuvée du Maréchal Fabert 2000

□ | 0.3 ha | 2,900 | €5-8

This little plot was once owned by Abraham de Fabert, who was a marshal under Louis XIV. It now belongs to Pascal Oury, whose estate has 6.18 ha (15 acres) of vines in all. This 2000 vintage is a blend of 60 % Pinot Gris, 30 % Gewurztraminer and 10 % Auxerrois. It has a beautiful, pale-green colour and a nose of floral scents and hints of hazelnut. The full, rich palate is marked by the 4.7 g of residual sugar. Two other wines are singled out here: the **2000 Auxerrois**, which has a pale colour with green glints, and is finely spicy, lemony, well balanced and long; and the oak-matured **2000 Pinot Noir**, which has an agreeable palate.

● Pascal Oury, 29, rue des Côtes, 57420 Marieulles-Vezon, tel. 03.87.52.09.02, fax 03.87.52.09.17 ▼ Y by appt.

J. SIMON-HOLLERICH
Pinot blanc 2000★

□ | n.c. | 4,500 | €3-5

Jeanne and Joseph have the same address, the same telephone number and the same label, and they are both offering a Pinot Blanc. Each wine has a ravishing colour with greenish glints, a very fine nose with lovely citrus-fruit aromas, and an agreeable, supple, delicately aromatic palate which is well-balanced and fresh.

● Jeanne Simon-Hollerich, 16, rue du Pressoir, 57480 Contz-les-Bains, tel. 03.82.83.74.81, fax 03.82.83.69.70 ▼ Y ev. day 8am–8pm

CH. DE VAUX
Les Hautes Bassières Pinot noir 2000★

■ | 1.3 ha | 10,200 | €5-8

Norbert and Marie-Geneviève Molozay are two young oenologists who in 1999 moved into the heart of the wine-making village of Vaux, taking over a château which was refurbished in 1870, and whose vaulted cellars date back to the 13th century. This light-red wine has been produced from hand-picked, 100 % de-stemmed grapes which were matured in oak barrels by traditional Burgundy methods. Its very classic nose has aromas of soft fruits and notes of oak. It is not quite rich enough on the palate to win two stars, but nonetheless has great potential. The finish is marked by notes of vanilla. Another delightful wine here (also winning one star) is the **2000 Blanc**. Produced from grapes macerated in their skins, it has subtle aromas of apricot, followed by white fruit notes on the palate, which are a sign that this will be a rich, long wine, to be drunk with the finest fish dishes.

● Marie-Geneviève et Norbert Molozay, Ch. de Vaux, 4, pl. Saint-Rémi, 57130 Vaux, tel. 03.87.60.20.64, fax 03.87.60.24.67 ▼ Y by appt.

Beaujolais

Officially, Beaujolais is part of the Burgundy wine-growing region, although it has become separately identified and through skilful promotion and marketing has become famous in its own right through the whole world. Who can be unaware of the much-trumpeted arrival of the Beaujolais Nouveau on the third Thursday of November? The soil and the topography of the Beaujolais differ significantly from the countryside of its celebrated neighbour, where the vineyard slopes form an almost straight north-south line. The steeper hills and deeper valleys of the Beaujolais mean many vineyards are frequently bathed in sunshine. The houses are different, too; rather than the roofs being covered by the flatter tiles of Burgundy, they are covered with bowed, Roman tiles which convey a Mediterranean flavour.

The Beaujolais region lies south of Burgundy, and is a gateway to southern France. There are 96 communes covering 23,000 ha (56,810 acres), stretching 50 km (31 miles) from north to south, through two departments, the Saône-et-Loire and the Rhône, and average 15 km (9 miles) wide, though narrower in the south. In the north, the Arlois is the border with the Mâconnais. In the east, on the other hand, the Saône plain, where the sparkling river meanders her slow majestic way south, makes a natural barrier. Julius Caesar remarked that the river moved so slowly that it was virtually impossible to judge in which direction it was flowing. To the west, the Beaujolais hills form the foothills of the Massif Central. The highest point, Mont Saint-Rigaux, 1,012 m (3,319 ft), is a gigantic mile-stone marking the junction of the lands of the Saône and Loire rivers. In the south, the Lyon wine country takes over as far as the city of Lyon itself, irrigated, as the saying goes, by three great 'rivers': the Rhône, the Saône and … the Beaujolais.

The great renown of Beaujolais wines owes a massive debt to Lyon. The wines are still sold in the city's famous small wine bars or *bouchons*, where they had a ready market after the highly successful expansion of the vineyards in the 18th century. Two hundred years previously, Villefranche-sur-Saône had become the region's capital, in place of Beaujeu, which had given the area its name. The lords of Beaujeu were skilful and wise; they carefully planned the expansion of their wealth and their domains, stimulated not least by their concern to protect themselves from their powerful neighbours, the Counts of Mâcon and Forez, the Abbots of Cluny and the Bishops of Lyon. The rapid development of the vineyard came about when Beaujolais was added to the ranks of the five Royal 'farms', areas which were exempted from certain taxes normally levied for transporting goods to Paris. For many years, Beaujolais produce was carried via the Briare canal.

146

Beaujolais

	Crus:
1	Saint-Amour
2	Juliénas
3	Chénas
4	Moulin-à-Vent
5	Fleurie
6	Chiroubles
7	Morgon
8	Régnié
9	Côte-de-Brouilly
10	Brouilly

Beaujolais Wine Routes
Beaujolais
Beaujolais-Villages
Department boundaries

BEAUJOLAIS

Today, Beaujolais produces an average of 1,400,000 hl (36,960,000 gal) of red wines of a distinctive character (there is virtually no white). With only the rare exception, Beaujolais reds are made from a single variety, the Gamay, a black-skinned grape with white flesh. This is one of the fundamental differences with Burgundy, where several varieties are grown. The wines produced fall into three appellations: Beaujolais, Beaujolais Supérieur and Beaujolais Villages, and there are also ten recognised Crus: Brouilly, Côte de Brouilly, Chénas, Chiroubles, Fleurie, Morgon, Juliénas, Moulin à Vent, Saint-Amour and Régnié. The first three appellations may apply to reds, whites or rosés, while the ten others are exclusively reds which qualify legally as AOC Bourgogne. Geologically speaking, the Beaujolais region was affected by the folding of the earth's crust in the Hercynian period of the Primary era and again in the Tertiary era when the Alps were formed. This was the era that created the relief of the present-day Beaujolais; the sedimentary deposits from the Secondary era were fractured when outcrops of rocks formed in the Primary period were pushed up. More recently, in the Quaternary era, glaciers and rivers flowing from west to east gouged out numerous valleys and fashioned the landscape from which outcrops of hard rock that are resistant to erosion stand out like islands. This is when the relief of the present-day Beaujolais was created with its eastern-facing slopes that descend like a gigantic staircase to the Saône.

Northern and southern Beaujolais have distinctive features and Villefranche-sur-Saône stands on an invisible dividing line between the two parts of the vineyard. The hills in the north are softly rounded and the bottoms of the valleys are filled with sand. It is a region of ancient rocks such as granite, porphyry, shale and diorite. As the granite has decomposed slowly over time, it has left siliceous sands, known locally as *gore*, which can vary in depth from a few tens of centimetres (inches) down to several metres (yards) and are areas of clay and sand. This poor, acid soil lacks organic matter and retains neither moisture nor nutrients, so it is prone to drying out though it is easy to work. This terrain, with other areas of shale, is where the local appellations and Beaujolais Villages wines are grown. The southern area has a larger proportion of sedimentary soil, with clay and limestone being found on the more steeply sloping hills. The soils are richer in limestone and sandstone than in the north. This area is known for its 'golden stones', which are coloured by ferrous oxide, giving a warm look to the buildings. The earth is richer and retains moisture better. This is where the AOC Beaujolais wines are grown. In both areas, vines prosper between altitudes of 190 and 550 m (623 and 1,804 ft). A background to these two distinct areas is Haut Beaujolais, an area of harder metamorphic rock which at over 600 m (1,968 ft) is covered by pine and chestnut forests and ferns. The best wine-growing land has a south-south-easterly aspect and lies between 190 and 350 m (623 and 1,148 ft).

The Beaujolais region is temperate though it has three competing prevailing climates: a continental influence, a maritime influence and another from the Mediterranean. Depending on the season, each of them can dominate and the change from one to another can be rapid and unexpected, making pressures and temperatures rise or plummet violently. Winters can be cold or wet; spring can be wet or dry; July and August are scorching when the desiccating wind blows up from the Midi, or drenched when there are rain and hail storms; autumn can be wet or hot. The average rainfall is 7.5 cm (2.95 in) and the temperature ranges from −20°C to +38°C (−4°F to +100°F). Throughout the region, however, there are tiny microclimates which do not follow the general rule and vines can flourish in situations which, on the face of it, should not be propitious. Generally speaking, the vineyards have good sunshine and enjoy good conditions for the grapes to ripen.

To describe the grape varieties planted in Beaujolais is particularly simple: 99% of the vineyards are planted with Gamay, often called 'Gamay Beaujolais' locally. In 1395, Philip the Brave banished Gamay from the Côte d'Or, considering it a 'disloyal plant', which it was, when compared with Pinot Noir. However, it is a very adaptable variety which can prosper in many different climates – some 33,000 ha (81,510 acres) are planted with Gamay in France and it is remarkably well suited to the soils of the Beaujolais. It has a trailing habit so has to be staked and supported for the first ten years of its life; in the north of the region you will see fields of vine props holding up the plants. It is susceptible to spring frosts and to the main parasites and vine diseases. The vines can bud early, at the end of March, but more usually in the second week of April. As the Beaujolais saying goes, 'When the vines shine in Saint George's tide, they are not late'. The flowering season is the first fortnight in June and the harvest starts in mid-September.

Varieties other than Gamay are also entitled to the appellation: Pinot Noir and Pinot Gris for red and rosé wines and Chardonnay and Aligoté for white wines. Until the year 2015, the expansion of Pinot Noir planting has been restricted to a total of 15% of the Beaujolais vineyard (currently very much less than that is planted); blends of red or rosé wines using up to a maximum of 15% of Pinot Noir or Pinot Gris, Chardonnay, Melon or Aligoté are also permitted. Vines are pruned in one of two ways: a hard prune, training the plant into the shape of a goblet or fan is used for all appellations, while for the Beaujolais appellation vines are pruned to one stem, known as a 'baguette' (the French word for the typical French loaf shape). Vines can also be pruned as cordons in the AOC Beaujolais vineyards.

All the red Beaujolais wines are made according to the same precepts: the bunches are kept whole and there is a short maceration period of three to seven days, depending on the type of wine. The technique used is classic fermentation for the 10–20% of juice produced when the grape skins are broken as the clusters are loaded into the vat; meanwhile intracellular fermentation ensures a quite considerable breaking down of malic acid which releases particular aromas. This is what gives Beaujolais wines their structure and their aromatic characteristics which are both enhanced and individually defined by the soil on which the vines are grown. Because so much of this technique depends on letting the grapes work by themselves, it is very difficult for the wine-maker to control the wine's development reliably in this early stage, given the unpredictability of the reactions between the volume of must released in relation to the entire content of the vat. On the whole, Beaujolais wines are dry but not tannic, supple, fruity and very aromatic; they are usually 12–13% volume, with a total acidity of 3.5 g/l in terms of H_2SO_4.

One of the common peculiarities in the Beaujolais vineyards is *métayage*, a system from the past but one that has persisted and still lives on. This means that the harvest and certain costs are shared between the grower and the owner, who provides the vineyard, lodgings, a vat room equipped with all that is required to make the grapes into wine, any products required during wine-making as well as the plantations of vines. The grower, or *métayer*, provides all the machinery required for cultivation, engages any workers, pays the pickers at harvest-time and ensures that the vines are kept in perfect condition. These management contracts start on St Martin's Day, 11 November, and many growers find it attractive to use them; 46% of Beaujolais vineyards are managed in this way compared with 45% which are managed by the owner. The remaining 9% of vineyards are run by tenant farmers. It is not unusual for growers to be owners of certain parcels of vineyards and *métayers* as well. A typical Beaujolais vineyard covers 7–10 ha (17–25 acres), and they tend to be smaller in the south, where mixed farming is more common, the vineyards are larger. Nineteen co-operatives vinify 30% of the grapes produced, while 85% of the wine is sold by growers and local shippers. AOC Beaujolais is sold by the 216-litre barrel, and AOC Beaujolais Villages and the Crus are sold by the 215-litre barrel. The wine is sold throughout the year but local incomes rise most appreciably when the Vins de Primeur, or new season's wines, are released onto the market. Some 50% of the wine is exported to Switzerland, Germany, Belgium, Luxembourg, Britain, the United States, the Netherlands, Denmark, Canada, Japan, Sweden and Italy.

Beaujolais Nouveau is red or rosé wine that comes only from the non-Cru appellations, usually from the Beaujolais or Beaujolais Villages appellations. The wines, grown on sandy granite soil in certain parts of Beaujolais Villages, are vinified after a short maceration which lasts only four days, creating soft, light wines with a mouthful of flavour. The colour is not particularly intense and the fruity perfumes sometimes have a hint of ripe banana. There are strict regulations which lay down the criteria the wine must meet and how it can be marketed. By mid-November, the Vins de Primeur are ready to be drunk around the world. In 1956 only 13,000 hl (343,200 gal) of this wine was sold; by 1970 the figure was 100,000 hl (2,640,000 gal), 200,000 hl (5,280,000 gal) in 1976, 400,000 hl (10,560,000 gal) in 1982, 500,000 hl (13,200,000 gal) in 1985, rising to 600,000 hl (15,840,000 gal) in 1990 and 630,576 hl (16,647,206 gal) in 2000. From 15 December, the Crus are tasted and judged, then marketed. The majority of sales of these are made after Easter. Beaujolais wines are not for keeping and most are consumed within two years. However, some particularly good bottles can be kept up to ten years and drink very well. The appeal of these wines lies in their freshness and the delicacy of their nose, reminiscent of flowers – peony, rose, violet, iris – and also certain fruits, including apricot, cherry, peach and summer fruits (berries).

Beaujolais and Beaujolais Supérieur

Nearly half of the wine produced is Appellation Beaujolais. Some 10,480 ha (27,470 acres), mainly south of Villefranche, provide an average of 672,790 hl (17,761,656 gal). Of this, 7,086 hl (187,070 gal) are white wines made from Chardonnay, 20% of the Chardonnay grapes being harvested in the small canton of La Chappelle-de-Guinchay, where the flinty soil of the Crus changes to the limestone terrain of the Mâconnais. In the area of the 'golden stones', east of Bois-d'Oingt and south of Villefranche, the red wines are aromatic with scents that are more fruity than flowery with even some traces of vegetation. These colourful wines are well-structured, if sometimes a little rustic, and keep quite well. In the upper part of the

Azergues valley, in the west of the region, the crystalline rocks give the wine a more flinty flavour which improves with age. The vineyards at the top of the slopes produce more sharply flavoured wines that are lighter in colour but also less heavy in hot years. The nine Caves Coopératives in this area have put a great deal of effort into developing their techniques and have significantly improved the economy of the area which produces about 75% of the 'Vins Primeurs'.

The Appellation

Beaujolais Supérieur does not come from a specifically defined area. To qualify for this appellation, the wines must be identified each year and are required to meet certain criteria: the must, at harvest, should have an alcoholic content 0.5° higher than the Appellation Beaujolais wines. Altogether, 4,000 hl (105,600 gal) are declared as Appellation Beaujolais Supérieur each year, principally from the area of AOC Beaujolais.

Villages are scattered and the architecture of the wine-growers' houses is attractive; traditionally they have the cellar at ground level and an exterior staircase leads to a canopied balcony and the living quarters. At the end of the 18th century, large vat rooms were built separately from the proprietor's house. The one at Lacenas, 6 km (4 miles) from Villefranche, which is on the domain of the Château de Montauzan, is the headquarters of the Confrérie des Compagnons du Beaujolais, established in 1947 to regulate and promote Beaujolais wines. Today, it is recognised internationally. The Confrérie des Grappilleurs des Pierres Dorées was set up in 1968 with the task of organising a whole range of festivals and fairs in the region. When it comes to downing a pot of Beaujolais, the heavy-bottomed bottle containing 46 cl of wine that is plonked on every bistro table, it goes perfectly with pork scratchings, tripe, black pudding, saucisson and charcuterie of all kinds and also with quenelles topped with cheese. The fresh young wines are a good accompaniment for dishes such as cardoons with bone marrow or gratiné potatoes and onions.

Beaujolais

ANTOINE BARRIER 2000

9 ha 73,000 €5-5

This purple-coloured wine is made in Saint-Georges-de-Reneins for the Leclerc supermarket chain. It has a well-developed nose of white flowers with hints of blackcurrant and red fruits. The full-bodied, rich palate is robust but well-balanced, and the wine should be drunk within the year, before it loses its primary fruit character.
☎ SCAMARK, 52, rue Camille-Desmoulins, 92135 Issy-les-Moulineaux, tel. 01.46.62.76.37, fax 01.46.44.38.32

CAVE DU BEAU VALLON
Au pays des pierres dorées 2000

12 ha 100,000 €5-8

The Beaujolais landscape is characterised by the local gold-coloured stone. Drystone walls criss-cross the vineyards, glinting like stacks of gold ingots, and the stone buildings of the villages shine in beautiful contrast to the vines that surround them. This wine co-operative from the heart of the region has produced a garnet-coloured wine with quite intense red-berry and apricot aromas. A light but rounded, supple and fruity character makes this an enjoyable wine that is ready to drink now.
☎ Cave du Beau Vallon, Le Beau Vallon, 69620 Theizé, tel. 04.74.71.48.00, fax 04.74.71.84.46, e-mail info@cave-beauvallon.com ☑ ☎ by appt.

CLAUDE BERGER 1999**

0.4 ha 2,000 €3-3

Claude Berger has been running the family estate for the past decade. Twenty-year-old vines are responsible for a glittering, green-gold wine, which has an elegant, fruity aroma with notes of lime-blossom and may-flower. On the palate the wine's fresh acidity is nicely balanced by a fruity, almond-scented flavour. The finish is lively and long. It should be drunk within the next two years and would be a fine accompaniment to pike.
☎ EARL Claude Berger, Le Chalier, 69480 Pommiers, tel. 04.74.65.07.09, fax 04.74.68.34.45 ☑ ☎ ev. day 10am–12 noon 2pm–6pm

CLAUDE BERNARDIN 2000

■ 2.5 ha 14,000 ■ ♦ €3-5

Bernardin's purple-red wine is matured in a vaulted cellar. It has a moderately aromatic nose of red berries and blackcurrants. Well-structured, with good fruit and a fairly long finish, this wine should be drunk within the next year.

➤ Claude Bernardin, Le Genetay, 69480 Lucenay, tel. 04.74.67.02.59, fax 04.74.62.00.19 ☑ ☒ by appt.

CH. DE BLACERET-ROY
Cuvée de l'Artiste 1999

☐ 1.5 ha 8,000 ■ €3-5

Wine-lovers visit this estate in great numbers. It has produced a distinctive wine with a dried-fruit nose with floral and mineral notes. A well-balanced palate and long finish make this a wine to enjoy over the next year.

➤ Thierry Canard, Ch. de Blaceret-Roy, 69460 Saint-Etienne-des-Oullières, tel. 04.74.03.45.42, fax 04.74.03.52.10 ☑ ☒ by appt.

DOM. DU BOIS DE LA BOSSE 2000★★

■ 3 ha 5,000 ■ €3-5

The Dumas family has cultivated this 12-ha (30-acre) estate since 1868. Their dark garnet-coloured Beaujolais has red-berry and spice aromas that continue and intensify on the palate. Very full-bodied and aromatic, this well-balanced, classy wine can be enjoyed over the next two or three years.

➤ EARL Georges Després, Le Vernay, 69460 Saint-Etienne-des-Oullières, tel. 04.74.03.48.98, fax 04.74.03.31.55 ☑ ☒ by appt.

DOM. DU BOIS DE LA GORGE 2000★

■ 1.5 ha 5,000 ■ €5-8

The estate, which dates back to 1620, houses a small gemstone museum that also contains an exhibition of old-fashioned tools. In one of its two cellars one can taste the **white Beaujolais 2000** that was singled out by the Jury, as well as this vivid ruby wine with its fine, fresh, red-berry nose. The formidable structure of this well-balanced wine does not get in the way of its refreshing style. An attractive wine, which could be served with charcuterie, it should be drunk within the next year or two.

➤ GFA du Bois de la Gorge, La Chanal, 69640 Jarnioux, tel. 04.74.03.82.89 ☑ ☒ by appt.
➤ M. Montessuy

DOM. DU BOIS DU JOUR
Bouquet de vieilles vignes 2000

■ 0.5 ha 3,500 ■ €3-5

Sandy, chalky-clay soils have created a dark garnet-red wine with a well-developed, spicy redcurrant and blackcurrant nose. On the palate the wine is still quite tannic, but nicely constructed and quite long. It is ready for drinking now and would go well with charcuterie as part of a picnic, according to the Jury.

The estate's **white Beaujolais 99** also impressed the Jury.

➤ Gilles Carreau, Lachanal, 69640 Cogny, tel. 04.74.67.41.40, fax 04.74.67.46.24 ☑ ☒ by appt.

LES VIGNERONS DE LA CAVE DE BULLY 2000

■ 520 ha 110,000 ■ ♦ €3-5

This co-operative wine cellar, formed in 1959, is one of the largest in Beaujolais, producing about 38,000 hl (over 1m gal) of wine. The Jury singled out its **white Beaujolais 2000** and **red Beaujolais Supérieur 2000**, as well as this simple Beaujolais. It has a youthful colour and a fresh grape and redcurrant nose. The fruity, supple, light but well-balanced palate makes this a wine that should be enjoyed within the year.

➤ Cave beaujolaise de Bully, 69210 Bully, tel. 04.74.01.27.77, fax 04.74.01.14.53 ☑ ☒ by appt.

CH. DE BUSSY 2000

■ 5 ha 35,000 ■ ♦ €3-5

A ruby-coloured wine with violet highlights, this Beaujolais was matured in the cellars of a château that was restored in 1892. While some red-berry aromas, with notes of blackberry and wild cherry, are discernible on both the nose and the palate, the wine is basically still closed up. The strong tannic attack suggests that this 2000 vintage needs at least a year to reach its full, fine potential.

➤ GFA Ch. de Bussy, Bussy, 69640 Saint-Julien, tel. 04.74.09.60.08
➤ Mme Ganem

MICHEL CARRON
Coteaux de Terre-Noire 2000

■ 1 ha 8,000 ■ ♦ €3-5

Michel Carron's **white Beaujolais 2000** was judged to be as good as his red. The garnet-coloured red has an appealing nose of red berries with a hint of pear drops. Fruity and rounded, it has a fairly light structure, making it suitable for immediate consumption.

➤ Michel Carron, Terre-Noire, 69620 Moiré, tel. 04.74.71.62.02, fax 04.74.71.62.02 ☑ ☒ by appt.

CH. DE CERCY 2000★

■ 10 ha 10,000 ■ ♦ €3-5

The estate, restored in 1972, has a function room that can hold up to 100 people. Its bright garnet Beaujolais has a powerfully aromatic nose of red berries with hints of fig and peach. as well as mineral notes. A fine and distinctive wine, it is extremely well-balanced and has good length. It should be enjoyed over the next year or two.

➤ Michel Picard, Cercy, 69640 Denicé, tel. 04.74.67.34.44, fax 04.74.67.32.35 ☑ ☒ by appt.

CH. DE CHANZE 1999

□   0.38 ha   3,500   €3-5

The estate, which vinifies 340 ha (840 acres), mostly planted with Gamay grapes, has developed a straw-yellow white Beaujolais with an aroma of grapefruit. As the wine is fairly acidic on the palate, it would benefit from being cellared for a few more months.

↳ Cave beaujolaise de Saint-Vérand, Le Bady, 69620 Saint-Vérand, tel. 04.74.71.73.19, fax 04.74.71.83.45, e-mail c.b.s.v.@wanadoo.fr ▣ ⊥ by appt.

PIERRE CHARMET
Cuvée la Ronze 2000★★

■   0.3 ha   2,500   €5-8

The output may be small, but the quality of this wine is very high. Deeply coloured, it has an expressive nose of red berries with floral notes. The enjoyably rounded and fruity first impression is followed by integrated tannins and a long finish. This well-balanced Beaujolais may be drunk over the next two years.

↳ Pierre Charmet, Le Martin, 69620 Le Breuil, tel. 04.74.71.80.67 ▣ ⊥ by appt.

JACQUES CHARMETANT 2000

■   6.5 ha   6,000   €3-5

Jacques Charmetant decided to become a wine-grower in 1996 and has been engaged ever since on a mission to improve the estate, some of whose vines are more than fifty years old. His ruby-coloured Beaujolais has a red-berry, violet and peony nose and a fine palate. Made in the classic regional style, this lively, mid-weight wine should be drunk within the year.

↳ Jacques Charmetant, pl. du 11-Novembre, 69480 Pommiers, tel. 04.74.65.12.34, fax 04.74.65.12.34, e-mail jacques.charmetant@wanadoo.fr ▣

DOM. CHATELUS DE LA ROCHE 2000

■   2 ha   n.c.   €5-8

Vines from south-west-facing slopes are the source of this bright ruby wine with strong blackcurrant aromas. Well-structured and with good body, this nicely crafted, balanced and aromatic wine is ready to drink now.

↳ Pascal Chatelus, La Roche, 69620 Saint-Laurent-d'Oingt, tel. 04.74.71.24.78, fax 04.74.71.28.36 ⊥ by appt.

DOMINIQUE CHERMETTE
Cuvée Vieilles vignes 2000

■   2 ha   15,000   €5-8

Dominique Chermette's parents bought this estate, which today covers more than 8 ha (20 acres), in 1958. Fifty-year-old vines growing on marl soils have produced a dark red wine with a bouquet of pear drops and morello cherries. It is full-bodied, powerful and lively on the palate, ending on a slightly tannic note. A few months in the cellar should be enough for the wine to attain its full potential.

↳ Dominique Chermette, Le Barnigat, 69620 Saint-Laurent-d'Oingt, tel. 04.74.71.20.05, fax 04.74.71.20.05 ▣ ⊥ by appt.

CLOS DES VIEUX MARRONNIERS 2000

■   4.5 ha   10,000   €3-5

This purple-red Beaujolais with its scent of blackcurrant is the product of vines planted on marl soils. Rich, well-balanced and long, it is full and rounded, and can only get better.

↳ Jean-Louis Large, 69380 Charnay, tel. 04.78.47.95.28, fax 04.78.47.95.28 ▣ ⊥ by appt.

ROLAND CORNU Tradition 2000★★

■   1 ha   5,000   €5-8

A clear ruby wine from the granite soil of southern Beaujolais, this has a rich bouquet of strawberries, raspberries and cinnamon, with further hints of liquorice and cloves. On the palate, it is as soft as silk. This wonderfully long, rich and fruity wine with dense, classy tannins may be drunk over the next two or three years. It would be a good complement to boeuf bourguignon.

↳ Roland Cornu, 275, allée du Mas, 69490 Sarcey, tel. 04.74.26.85.11, e-mail roland.cornu@wanadoo.fr ▣ ⊥ by appt.

DOM. DES COTEAUX DE LA ROCHE 2000★

□   0.25 ha   2,300   €5-8

This greenish-yellow wine has been made from vines growing on granite soil. It has a fresh, fine, mango-scented nose. An acidic opening combines with a fairly powerful, rounded and fruity structure to create a wine that should please even inexperienced palates. It is ready to drink now with fish or shellfish dishes. The estate's **red Beaujolais Vieilles vignes 2000** also impressed the Jury.

↳ EARL Joyet, La Roche, 69620 Létra, tel. 04.74.71.32.77, fax 04.74.71.32.77 ▣ ⊥ by appt.

DOM. DES CRETES
Cuvée des Varennes 2000★

▪ ■ 2.1 ha 17,000 ▪ ♦ €5-8

This bright red wine with purple highlights comes from vines planted on clay-silica soil along ridges that reach 350 m (1,144 ft). The well-structured, fruity and extremely rich palate immediately impresses. A wine with good length, it will be enjoyable for the next two years and would go well with grilled meats.

☛ GAEC Brondel Père et Fils, rte des Crêtes, 69480 Graves-sur-Anse, tel. 04.74.67.11.62, fax 04.74.60.24.30, e-mail domaine.descrete@wanadoo.fr ☑ ☲ by appt.

DOM. DE CRUIX 2000

■ n.c. 2.5 ha 15,000 ▪ €5-8

Ninety per cent of the wines sold by this estate have their labels printed directly on to the bottles. This bright red wine has a red-berry nose with spicy overtones. Lively, with good, well-balanced tannins, it develops well on the palate. A wine for laying down.

☛ Jean-Claude Brossette, Dom. de Cruix, 69620 Theizé, tel. 04.74.71.24.74, fax 04.74.71.29.16, e-mail jcbrossette@oreka.com ☑ ☲ by appt.

JEAN DESCROIX Cuvée du Clos 2000

■ n.c. 5,000 ▪ €3-5

This lively red has an appealing strawberry and redcurrant nose but is rather light on the palate. Very drinkable now, with no harsh notes, it would go well with hard cheeses.

☛ Jean et Michael Descroix, Bennevent, 69640 Denicé, tel. 04.74.67.30.74, fax 04.74.67.30.74 ☑ ☲ by appt.

JEAN-GABRIEL DEVAY
Cuvée des Jarlotiers 2000

■ 0.77 ha 4,500 ▪ €5-8

This wine comes from four plots of schist soil with good exposure. Medium-red, it has a nose of very ripe fruits and kirsch. These aromas are sustained on the palate. This full-bodied and well-structured wine has good length and is ready to drink now.

☛ Jean-Gabriel Devay, 10, chem. du Guéret, 69210 Bully, tel. 04.74.01.01.48, fax 04.74.01.09.04 ☑ ☲ by appt.

LES VIGNERONS DU DOURY
Cuvée Prestige 2000★★☆

■ 2 ha 3,000 ▪ ♦ €5-8

This cellar has just invested in a new type of wine-press. The Cuvée Prestige lives up to its name. Garnet-coloured, it has a complex nose of blackberries and bilberries. After a straightforward attack, soft, fruity tannins fill the mouth. This rich and well-balanced wine, consistently impressive throughout the tasting, will be enjoyable for the next two years. The estate's **Beaujolais Supérieur 2000** was awarded one star.

☛ Cave des Vignerons du Doury, Le Doury, 69620 Létra, tel. 04.74.71.30.52,

---

fax 04.74.71.35.28 ☑ ☲ ev. day except Mon. 9am–12 noon 2pm–6pm; Sun. 10am–12 noon 3pm–7pm

BERNARD DUMAS 2000★

■ ■ 1 ha 2,000 ▪ €3-5

This bright garnet wine was developed near the hillside village of Ternand. It has well-developed, spicy scents of red berries and peaches. Appealing kirsch and pear drop flavours are apparent on the fleshy palate. Supple tannins and a slightly acidic finish do not upset a well-balanced wine.

☛ Bernard Dumas, Les Ronzières, 69620 Ternand, tel. 04.74.71.38.57 ☑ ☲ by appt.

PIERRE ET PAUL DURDILLY
Les Grandes Coasses 2000★

■ 19 ha 50,000 ▪ ▮▮ ▪ €5-8

One hectare (2.5 acres) of the 20 which make up this estate is given over to the production of **white Beaujolais**; the **1999** was commended by the Jury. As for the red, it has a clear ruby colour, and a powerful pear drop and red-berry aroma with undertones of tobacco and cocoa. A rounded wine, it embraces the palate with fine tannins. Well-balanced, fruity and elegant, this wine is ready now as a perfect complement for white meat dishes.

☛ Pierre et Paul Durdilly, Dom. des Grandes Coasses, 69620 Le Bois-d'Oingt, tel. 04.74.71.65.11, fax 04.74.71.82.42 ☑ ☲ by appt.

HENRY FESSY 2000★

■ n.c. 30,000 ▪ ♦ €5-8

A rich red colour, this wine has a complex nose of very ripe fruits. Red fruit (cherry) flavours are apparent on the well-structured, reasonably long palate. An attractive wine to drink over the next two years.

☛ Henry Fessy, Bel-Air, 69220 Saint-Jean-d'Ardières, tel. 04.74.66.00.16, fax 04.74.69.61.67, e-mail vins.fessy@wanadoo.fr ☑ ☲ by appt.

JEAN-FRANCOIS GARLON
Cuvée Vieilles vignes 2000

■ 3 ha 20,000 ▪ €5-8

The Garlon family knows all there is to know about wine-making; it has been cultivating this estate since 1750. A pretty, clear purplish colour, the wine has a beguiling peach and apricot nose and a well-balanced palate. It is ready for drinking now.

☛ Jean-François Garlon, Le Bourg, 69620 Theizé, tel. 04.74.71.11.97, fax 04.74.71.23.30, e-mail jf.garlon@wanadoo.fr ☑ ☲ by appt.

DOM. JEAN-FELIX GERMAIN
1999★

☐ 0.75 ha 6,900 ▪ €5-8

This domaine is two hundred years old. Chardonnay grapes grown on marl soils have been transformed into a classic straw-yellow wine with a fresh, balanced, lemon and white-flower nose. After a lively opening, the wine has plenty of structure on the palate, and develops towards a fine, long finish. This well-balanced 99 may be drunk over the next two years, and would suit being served with fish.

Dom. Jean-Félix Germain, Les Crozettes, 69380 Charnay, tel. 04.78.43.94.52, fax 04.78.43.94.52 ❧ ev. day 8am–7pm

HENRI ET BERNARD GIRIN
Cuvée coteaux du Razet 2000★

1.5 ha 10,000 €5-8

A deep garnet wine with a nose of blackcurrant leaves and crushed strawberries is the result of high-extraction wine-making. Although it is quite rounded and full on the palate, young tannins emerge on the finish. The wine will remain enjoyable, and continue to improve, for the next two years. It could accompany cold meats or a poultry dish.

GAEC Henri et Bernard Girin, Aucherand, 69620 Saint-Vérand, tel. 04.74.71.63.49, fax 04.74.71.85.61, e-mail beaujolais.girin@free.fr ❧ ev. day except Sun. 8am–12 noon 2pm–7pm

CH. DU GRAND TALANCE

0.75 ha 7,000 €3-5

This pretty 42-ha (104-acre) estate has been in the same family since 1870. The straw-yellow white Beaujolais is made from grapes grown on alluvial clay soil. It has an appealing aroma of wisteria blossom and liquorice. Fruity and mineral flavours and a rich finish balance the fairly lively attack. The Jury also commended the **red Beaujolais 2000**.

Jean-Marc Truchot, GFA du Grand Talance, 69640 Denicé, tel. 04.74.67.55.04 ❧ by appt.

DOM. DU GUELET 2000

0.5 ha 2,000

This clear red wine has been matured in cellars that date from 1791. Fine fruity aromas combine with an easy-drinking, fresh palate. It is an attractive, delicate wine for immediate consumption.

Didier Puillat, Le Fournel, 69640 Rivolet, tel. 04.74.67.34.05, fax 04.74.67.34.05

VIGNOBLE GRANGE-NEUVE 2000

2.5 ha 8,000 €3-5

Denis Carron acquired a new 55-ha (136-acre) estate in 1994. Since 2000, he has also been renting out a *gîte* (*rural*) on the property. He has made a purple-garnet wine that has a powerful nose of blackcurrants with menthol notes. The structured palate has quite strong, young tannins, giving the wine a slightly rustic character. It needs time to develop. This Beaujolais, the result of modern wine-making technology, may be drunk over the next two years.

Denis Carron, chem. des Brosses, 69620 Frontenas, tel. 04.74.71.70.31, fax 04.74.71.86.30 ❧ by appt.

DOMAINE LAFOND
2000
BEAUJOLAIS

DOM. DE LA CHAMBARDE 2000★

3.44 ha 30,000 €5-8

Although the vineyards are 40 years old, the estate has only been making its own wines for the last 20 years. Granite soils have produced this ruby-coloured wine with violet highlights and a fruity, classic aroma. It is quite a substantial and well-structured wine with noble tannins and good length, and should keep well for one to two years.

Robert Peigneaux, Dom. de la Chambarde, 69620 Létra, tel. 04.74.71.32.43, fax 04.74.71.37.09, e-mail domaine.chambarde@wanadoo.fr ❧ by appt.

DOM. DE LA COMBE DES FEES

1999 0.3 ha 2,000 €5-8

The wine is named after the river that runs along the boundary of an estate that espouses environmentally sustainable agriculture. Chardonnay grapes, which flourish on the sandy granite soils here, have produced a golden wine that has a ripe grapey nose with hints of flowers and honey. The palate is well-balanced with a prominent acacia flavour. It should be drunk within the year with shellfish or shellfish dishes.

Jean-Charles Perrin, La Maison Jaune, 69460 Vaux-en-Beaujolais, tel. 04.74.03.24.55, fax 04.74.03.24.55 ❧ by appt.

DOM. DE LA FEUILLATA
Cuvée Elégance 2000★★

2 ha 5,000 €5-8

Fifty-year-old vines growing on granite soils have produced a wine that certainly lives up to its name. Its clear garnet colour and elegant, complex aromas of bilberries and blackberries, with hints of flowers and under-growth, impressed the Jury. The full-bodied palate with its superb structure of fine, rounded tannins and flavours of red berries lives up to the promise of the nose. This wine may be enjoyed over the next two years.

Dom. de La Feuillata, 69620 Saint-Vérand, tel. 04.74.71.74.53, fax 04.74.71.83.84 ❧ by appt.
Rollet

DOM. LAFOND 2000★★

12.5 ha 20,000 €3-5

The estate's **Brouilly 2000** was commended by the Jury, but this dark red wine with its potent red-berry nose was selected as a *coup de coeur*. Its intensely fruity aroma with overtones of vanilla, its good structure with supple tannins and its long finish all combine to create a seductive wine. This well-balanced, attractive Beaujolais is ready to drink now.

☛ EARL Dom. Lafond, Bel Air, 69220 Saint-Lager, tel. 04.74.66.04.46, fax 04.74.66.37.91 ▼ ▼ by appt.

DOM. DE LA GRANGE MENARD
Cuvée Vieilles vignes 2000★

■ 5 ha ■ ▲ 30,000 ■ €3-5

The vines on this 19-ha (47-acre) estate, which has been managed by Guy Pignard since 1980, have an average age of 45 years. They have produced an intense garnet wine with a powerful and complex nose of strawberries and blackcurrants, together with the banana/pear drop notes characteristic of Beaujolais. The pronounced, fruity attack is followed by a rich, full palate with well-structured tannins. This attractive wine is ready to drink now.

☛ Guy Pignard, Dom. de La Grange Ménard, 69400 Arnas, tel. 04.74.62.87.60, fax 04.74.62.87.60 ▼ by appt.

DOM. DE LA GRENOUILLERE
2000

■ 2.5 ha ■ ▲ 22,000 ■ ▲ €5-8

There has been a vineyard growing on these granite slopes since 1745. The 2000 vintage has a lively, strong red colour and a powerful pear drop aroma. Fine tannins and red-berry flavours fill the mouth to make a supple, medium-bodied wine that should be drunk within the year to accompany cold meats.

☛ Charles Bréchard, La Grenouillère, 69620 Chamelet, tel. 04.74.71.34.13, fax 04.74.71.36.22 ▼ ▼ by appt.

VIGNOBLE LA MANTELLIERE
2000

■ 1 ha ■ n.c. ■ €5-8

The wines of this 7.7-ha (19-acre) estate, near the medieval village of Oingt, are matured in wooden casks. A rich red Beaujolais, it has a pleasingly fruity and floral nose. The tannins, while now completely softened, nonetheless don't dominate the palate, and the wine has a good long finish. It should be drunk within the year.

☛ Christophe Braymand, Le Bourg, 69620 Le Breuil, tel. 04.74.71.85.72, fax 04.74.71.85.72 ▼ ▼ by appt.

DOM. DE LA NOISERAIE 1999
□

■ 0.5 ha ■ ▲ 2,500 ■ €8-11

The label is marked *Récolte tardive* (late harvest). Although the actual harvest date is not specified, it is quite clear that this strawyellow wine has been made from very ripe grapes. Its oaky character is immediately obvious both on the nose and on the palate, but the vanilla notes, which are still fairly dominant, are not overpowering. The relatively rich structure of the wine has allowed it to respond well to oak-ageing.

☛ Bernard Martin, Pizay, 69220 Saint-Jean-d'Ardières, tel. 04.74.66.36.58, fax 04.74.66.15.98 ▼ by appt.

DOM. DE LA REVOL 2000★

■ 3 ha ■ ▲ 5,000 ■ €3-5

The owners of this southern Beaujolais estate took back direct control of its management in 1982. They presented the jury with a **white Beaujolais 2000** that was duly singled out. The forthcoming red-berry nose and fleshy, powerful (but balanced) palate of this rich purplish-red wine were almost judged worthy of two stars. A harmonious wine that is ready to drink now, it will continue to be enjoyable throughout the coming year.

☛ Bruno Debourg, La Croix, 69490 Dareizé, tel. 04.74.05.78.01, fax 04.74.05.66.40 ▼ ▼ by appt.

DOM. LASSALLE 1999★
□

■ 0.16 ha ■ 1,500

Chardonnay grapes planted on marl slopes overlooking the Saône river valley have produced a light golden wine with a complex nose of honeysuckle, acacia and citrus fruits, with hints of dried fruits too. Its structured and rich palate has subtle acidity that is not immediately apparent. This attractive 99 is for drinking within the year with white meats or fish. The estate employs environmentally sustainable methods of cultivation.

☛ Jean-Pierre Lassalle, 1, chem. de Tredo, 69480 Morancé, tel. 04.78.43.63.97, fax 04.78.43.63.97, e-mail domaine.lassalle@wanadoo.fr ▼ ▼ Sat. 10am–6pm

CH. DE LAVERNETTE 1999
□

■ 2.5 ha ■ ▲ 6,000 ■ ▲ €5-8

Chardonnay grapes grown on clay-silica limestone soils have been made into a light yellow wine with green highlights. It has an appealingly fresh aroma redolent of citrus fruits. Light-bodied and well-balanced, this appealing 99 is for drinking now.

☛ Bertrand de Boissieu, Ch. de Lavernette, 71570 Leynes, tel. 03.85.35.63.21, fax 03.85.35.67.32, e-mail ba.de-boissieu@wanadoo.fr ▼ ▼ by appt.

CH. DE L'ECLAIR 2000★★

■ 2 ha ■ ▲ 11,000 ■ ▲ €5-8

This estate used to belong to Victor Vermorel, inventor of the *Eclair*, a shoulder-mounted vine-sprayer. Vines from the estate

were used to re-establish other vineyards after the catastrophic phylloxera epidemic. This is the second year running that the Beaujolais Grand Jury has awarded the estate a *coup de coeur*. A dark garnet wine, the 2000 has a subtle, complex aroma of strawberries, raspberries and blackberries. Fruity and fleshy, it is well-structured with fine tannins, and could be kept for one or two years. The **Château de l'Eclair 2000 Beaujolais-Villages** was also commended.

➤ SICAREX Beaujolais, Ch. de l'Eclair, 69400 Liergues, tel. 04.74.68.76.27, fax 04.74.68.76.27 ☑ ▼ by appt.

CH. DE LEYNES 1999★

2 ha | 10,000 | €5-8

Situated right on the border between the Mâcon and Beaujolais regions, this family estate is over 200 years old. It has yielded a pale yellow wine with golden highlights. A pleasing aroma of white flowers leads on to honey and spice flavours on the palate. This well-balanced 99 is both supple and long. An elegant Beaujolais, it may be drunk now with crab or lobster.

➤ Jean Bernard, Les Correaux, 71570 Leynes, tel. 03.85.35.11.59, fax 03.85.35.13.94, e-mail bernard-leynes@caramail.com ☑ ▼ by appt.

CAVE DES VIGNERONS DE LIERGUES 2000★

4 ha | 18,000 | €5-8

This co-operative cellar, the oldest in Beaujolais, today cultivates 500 ha (1,235 acres) of vines. It has made a fine, bright salmon-pink rosé. Clean and elegant grapey aromas lead on to an attractive fleshy and fruity palate that is nicely balanced. The wine is ready to drink now. Both the **white** and the **red Beaujolais 2000** made by this co-operative were also singled out by the Jury.

➤ Cave des Vignerons de Liergues, 69400 Liergues, tel. 04.74.65.86.00, fax 04.74.62.81.20 ☑ ▼ by appt.

LE PERE LA GROLLE 2000

30 ha | 260,000 | €3-5

This *négociant* has buying agreements with no fewer than 180 growers. The wine, which is the product of several vineyards, has a light red colour and a fine, pure, fruity nose. Well-structured with aromatic, dense tannins and a cherry-stone flavour on the finish, it is extremely attractive. Pere la Grolle would go well with charcuterie, and should be drunk within the next two years.

➤ Ets Pellerin, 435, rte du Beaujolais, 69830 Saint-Georges-de-Reneins, tel. 04.74.09.60.00, fax 04.74.09.60.17

DOM. LES PREVELIERES 2000★★

3.75 ha | 30,000 | €3-5

Marketed by Maison Thorin, a *négociant* that is part of the Boisset group, this purple-garnet wine has pleasing scents of strawberries and blackcurrants. It is fleshy with fairly rounded tannins, but manages to retain a certain freshness. A well-structured wine with a long finish, it has all the hallmarks of a Beaujolais that will cellar well. That said, it is ready to drink already, and would be at its best if served chilled, perhaps as an accompaniment to cold meats.

➤ Dom. Les Prévelières, Layet de Dessous, 69220 Oingt, tel. 04.74.69.09.10, fax 04.74.69.09.28

➤ Serge Morel

DOM. DU MARQUISON 2000★★

5 ha | 5,000 | €3-5

South-facing vineyards growing on marl soils have produced this purple-garnet wine with a complex, forthright aroma of strawberries and raspberries with further notes of blackcurrants and white flowers. An attractively rich aromatic attack of great finesse is followed by a balanced impression of fruity freshness and vinosity. This distinctive Beaujolais will be enjoyable for the next two years, and would best accompany red or white meat dishes and mild cheeses.

➤ Christian Vivier-Merle, EARL Dom. du Marquison, Les Verjouttes, 69620 Theizé, tel. 04.74.71.26.66, fax 04.74.71.10.32 ☑ ▼ by appt.

MEZIAT-BELOUZE 2000★

2.45 ha | 7,800

This light ruby-coloured wine has been made from grapes grown on clay-rich soils. It has a fresh, forthcoming nose of redcurrants and blackcurrants with a hint of pear drops. Fruity, supple and easy to drink, this very pleasing Beaujolais is a little on the light side, but nonetheless quite distinctive. It is for drinking within the year with grilled meats, kebabs or seafood.

RENE MARCHAND 2000

1.5 ha | 6,000 | €5-8

Marchand's Beaujolais is a dark red wine with a red-berry (raspberry) and floral nose. On the palate, its fairly powerful opening has ripe fruit aromas that linger through to the finish. Ready to drink now, it could be served with either a sirloin steak or a white meat. The Jury also singled out the **white Beaujolais 2000**.

➤ René Marchand, Les Meules, 69640 Cogny, tel. 04.74.67.33.25, fax 04.74.67.33.94 ☑ ▼ ev. day 8am–12 noon-2pm-7pm

DOM. MANOIR DU CARRA 2000

1.5 ha | 5,000 | €3-5

This estate is situated not far from the Château de Montmelas, which resembles Sleeping Beauty's castle. Its peony-red wine has aromas of pear drops and blackcurrants. After a fairly lively first impression, pear drop and red-berry flavours fill the mouth. This fine, well-balanced wine is ready to drink now.

➤ Jean-Noël Sambardier, Dom. Manoir du Carra, 69640 Denice, tel. 04.74.67.38.24, fax 04.74.67.40.61, e-mail jfsambardier@aol.com ☑ ▼ by appt.

➤ GAEC Méziat-Belouze, Rochefort, 69115 Chiroubles, tel. 04.74.69.11.81, fax 04.74.69.11.81 ⓥ Ⓨ by appt.

CH. DE MONTAUZAN

Elevé en fût de chêne 2000

■   1 ha   5,000   ▦ ▯ ⓑ   €3-5

In Lacenas, a village that was once part of the château's domain, there is a 400-year-old vat room. The vibrantly red Beaujolais it has produced has an attractive floral and spicy nose. A rounded, well-balanced and long wine, it is ready to drink now.

➤ SCI Dom. de Montauzan,
Ch. de Montauzan, 69640 Lacenas,
tel. 04.74.66.62.03, fax 04.74.69.61.38,
e-mail montauzan.com ⓥ Ⓨ by appt.

PIERRE MONTESSUY 2000★

■   1.2 ha   6,000   ▦   €5-8

This wine comes from an historic village that is overlooked by a fine 13th-century château. Grapes harvested from vines that are over 70 years old have been used to make an alluring purple-coloured wine that has a red-berry aroma with pear drop undertones. This refreshing, well-made wine should be drunk within the year.

➤ Pierre Montessuy, La Chanal 69640 Jarnioux, tel. 04.74.03.83.13 Ⓨ by appt.

DOM. PEROL

Cuvée Vieilles vignes 2000★

■   3.2 ha   10,000   ▦   €5-8

This 13-ha (32-acre) estate, established in 1806, was bought by the Pérol family in 1912. Seventy-year-old vines have yielded a purple-red wine that has a red-berry nose with floral overtones. The fresh and fruity palate is structured and well-balanced. A pleasant wine that should be drunk within the year, it would suit being served with a chicken dish or goats' cheese. The same estate's white **Clos du Château Lassalle 1999** was also commended.

➤ Frédéric Pérol, Colletière, 69380 Châtillon-d'Azergues, tel. 04.78.43.99.84, fax 04.78.43.99.84 Ⓨ ev. day except Sun. 2pm–8pm

DOM. DE PIERRE-FILANT 2000★

■   n.c.   ▥   €3-5

Surrounded by vineyards, woods and fields, the ancient fortified manor house now contains an aviary. The estate has produced an oak-aged, deep red wine with violet highlights and a scent of ripe red berries. The full-bodied palate is well-balanced, despite the presence of some youthful tannins. A finish of good length distinguishes a Beaujolais that is ready to drink now, but that should remain enjoyable until 2003.

➤ Emmanuel Fellot, Dom. de Pierre-Filant, 69640 Rivolet, tel. 04.74.67.37.75, fax 04.74.67.39.06 ⓥ Ⓨ ev. day 8am–7pm

RESERVE DU MAITRE DE CHAIS DE PIZAY 2000★

■   3.8 ha   18,000   ▦ ▯ ⓑ   €3-5

Gilles Perez holds a *métayage* (tenancy) in the vineyards of the Château de Pizay. His rich garnet Réserve has scents of wild strawberries and crystallised cherries. The chewy character of the wine is immediately apparent in its opening impression. Well-structured with good tannins and a long finish, this cuvée is just about ready for drinking now. It would complement grilled or richly sauced white meat dishes. It should keep for another one to two years.

➤ Gilles Perez, Pizay,
6920 Saint-Jean-d'Ardières,
tel. 04.74.66.26.10, fax 04.74.69.60.66
➤ Château de Pizay

DOM. DE POUILLY-LE-CHATEL

2000

□   0.8 ha   4,000   ▦   €5-8

A clear, bright wine made from vines growing on marl soils, this vintage has a complex, aromatic aroma of pears and mint, with a hint of lilies-of-the-valley. Full-bodied and fleshy, the well-balanced palate has now opened out attractively. The wine should be drunk within the year.

➤ Sylvaine et Bruno Chevalier,
Pouilly-le-Chatel, 69640 Denicé,
tel. 04.74.67.41.01, fax 04.74.67.37.86,
e-mail br.chevalier@free.fr ⓥ Ⓨ by appt.

DOM. DE ROTISSON Cuvée Prestige

Fleur de Lys Vieilles vignes 2000

■   1.8 ha   10,000   ▦ ▯ ⓑ   €5-8

Oenologist Didier Pouget has achieved a commendation in the *Guide* for the second year running. This time, it's a powerful garnet-coloured Cuvée Prestige with its powerful blackcurrant and vanilla aromas. The still youthful, austere tannins need to mature further in order for the wine to fulfil its excellent potential. It should be cellared for at least two to three years.

➤ Dom. de Rotisson, rte de Conzy,
69210 Saint-Germain-sur-L'Arbresle,
tel. 04.74.01.23.08, fax 04.74.01.55.41,
e-mail domaine-de-rotisson@wanadoo.fr ⓥ
Ⓨ ev. day except Sun. 9am–1pm 2.30pm–7pm
➤ Didier Pouget

Beaujolais Villages

The term 'Villages' was adopted to replace a multitude of commune names that used to be attached to the Beaujolais appellation to identify wines that were considered superior. Nearly all the producers opted for the name Beaujolais Villages.

munes, including eight in the canton of La Chapelle-de-Guinchay, qualify for the appellation Beaujolais Villages, but only 30 are entitled to add the name of the commune after it. Identifying wines as Beaujolais Villages has been helpful in marketing them since 1950. In 2000, the 6,022 ha (14,874 acres), located mostly between the Beaujolais and the Crus vineyards, produced 351,356 hl (9,275,798 gal) of red wine and 3,226 hl (85,166 gal) of whites.

The wines of the appellation grown nearest the Crus are cultivated under the same terms (pruned either in a goblet or fan shape; the alcoholic content of the must should be 0.5° higher than that required for Beaujolais). Grown on sandy granite soil, they are fruity, smooth wines with a beautiful, rich red colour, typical of the first pressings for the Vins Primeurs. The wines from granite soils on some upper slopes have enough character to develop, and drink well into the following year. Between these two extremes there is every shade of difference; some wines have finesse, a good nose and sufficient body to accompany dishes of all kinds, and gratify every taste; both pike with cream sauce and grilled Charolais steak will be well complemented by a good Beaujolais Villages.

DOM. DE BEL-AIR 2000

6 ha   n.c.   €5-8

An old-fashioned 'American' press was used in the making of this deep ruby-coloured wine. It has an open, fruity, redcurrant bouquet and a delightfully rich, soft palate with light tannins. This very appealing wine will be enjoyable for the next two years.

☛ EARL Lafont, Dom. de Bel-Air, 69430 Lantignié, tel. 04.74.04.82.08, fax 04.74.04.89.33 ▼ by appt.

DOM. FRANCOIS BEROUJON 2000★

6 ha   47,000   €5-8

There is a fine Norman priory in the village, which is located between Blacé and Vaux-en-Beaujolais. After sightseeing, you could visit the cellars of this estate, following the trail of the many actors and singers who have come here already. There, you may taste this dark-purple wine with its aromas of red berries. It is a full-bodied, structured and well-balanced wine with good length that is ready to drink now.

☛ François Beroujon, La Laveuse, 69460 Salles-Arbuissonnas, tel. 04.74.67.52.47, fax 04.74.67.52.47 ▼ by appt.

CH. DU BOST 2000

5 ha   40,000   €5-8

Here is an intense purple-coloured wine bottled by the négociant house of Thorin. It has an appealing, fairly powerful nose of red berries and wild cherries. Its very attractive, balanced, fruity and tannic palate makes this a wine for cellaring.

☛ Ch. du Bost, 69640 Blacé, tel. 04.74.69.09.10, fax 04.74.69.09.28
☛ de Geffier

CH. DU CARRE 2000

n.c.   n.c.   €5-8

A clear-red wine from a négociant house, this wine is fragrant with the aromas of strawberries, morello cherries and pear drops. It is an exceptionally soft wine but still well-balanced. Aromatic and attractively fresh, it is ready to drink now with pâté or with rosette, the dry pork sausage that is a special-ity of the Beaujolais region.

☛ Jacques Charlet, 71570 La Chapelle-de-Guinchay, tel. 03.85.36.82.41, fax 03.85.33.83.19

PIERRE CHANAU 2000★

20 ha   160,000   €3-5

This smooth, fruity wine is made by Thorin for the Auchan supermarket chain. Dark garnet-coloured, it has a fairly aromatic and complex nose of red and black fruits highlighted by a hint of pear drops. Fleshy and well-balanced, this very drinkable wine should not be kept too long before drinking.

☛ Auchan, 200, rue de la Recherche, 59650 Villeneuve-d'Ascq, tel. 04.74.69.09.10, fax 04.74.69.09.28 ▼ by appt.

DOM. DU CHAPITAL 2000

8 ha   9,000   €5-8

This estate, which dates back to 1850, is located off the D78, between Beaujeu and Lantignié. It has produced a ruby-coloured red wine with a fairly shy nose of flowers and overripe strawberries. On the palate, it is aromatic and long, and although still quite tannic, is just about ready to drink now.

☛ Bernard Desperrier, Le Chapital, 69430 Lantignié, tel. 04.74.04.82.79 ▼ by appt.

Beaujolais Villages

DOM. DES CHARMEUSES 2000 ■ ▥ 7,000 €3-5

1.2 ha 7,000

This estate, located 2 km (1.3 miles) from Beaujeu, the historic capital of Beaujolais, presented the Jury with a light ruby-coloured wine that has expressive aromas of flowers and red berries. The *nouveau*-style palate is light and supple. We suggest that this wine be served to accompany Roquefort cheese or a black cherry tart.

☛ Bruno Jambon, Le Charnay,
69430 Lantignié, tel. 04.74.69.53.93,
fax 04.74.69.53.95 � ▾ by appt.

CH. DU CHAYLARD Emeringes 2000 ■ €3-5

n.c. 7,000

Bernard Canard is the *métayer* (tenant grower) of the Château du Chaylard. He has made a wine with a delicate red-berry aroma. A fairly rich purple colour, it is reasonably well-constructed, if a little light, and would be a pleasing red for drinking within the year.

☛ Bernard et Josiane Canard,
Les Grandes Vignes, 69840 Emeringes,
tel. 04.74.04.44.49, fax 04.74.04.45.16,
e-mail bernard.canard@wanadoo.fr ▾
by appt.

RÉCOLTE CHERMIEUX 2000 ■ €5-8

2.7 ha 3,000

The village of Lantignié, to the north-west of Régnié, has a view of the 15th-century Château de la Roche-Thulon. Gérard Genty employs environmentally sustainable viticultural techniques to tend virtually 10 ha (25 acres) of vineyards. His light ruby-coloured wine has a very fragrant nose of overripe fruits (particularly strawberries). A charmingly forthright and aromatic opening is succeeded by assertive tannins, which linger through to the finish, but shouldn't need much longer to soften. This wine should be drunk within the year.

☛ Gérard Genty, Vaugervan,
69430 Lantignié, tel. 04.74.69.23.56,
fax 04.74.69.23.56 ▾ by appt.

DOM. DE CLAIRANDRE 2000 ■ ▥ 5,000 €5-8

1 ha 5,000

This 5-ha (12-acre) estate, located just off the D133 south of Saint-Etienne-la-Varenne, contains some vines that are 45 years old. Its bright garnet-coloured wine has an appealing red-berry nose with a hint of blackcurrant. On the palate, the light structure and aroma of pear drops give it a *nouveau* style. A fresh, pleasant wine for immediate consumption.

☛ André Chavanis, Champagne, 69460
Saint-Etienne-la-Varenne,
tel. 04.74.03.51.15, fax 04.74.03.53.97 ▾
by appt.

DOM. DE COLETTE 2000 ■ €5-8

5.5 ha 30,000

The grapes that go into Domaine de Colette's wines are hand-sorted at the winery. In 2000, they have yielded a purple-coloured wine with a powerful aroma of red berries, and a fleshy, aromatic palate with good

length. It is supple enough to be consumed within the year.

☛ Jacky Gauthier, Colette, 69430 Lantignié,
tel. 04.74.69.25.73, fax 04.74.69.25.14 ▾
by appt.

DOM. ANDRÉ COLONGE ET FILS 2000 ■ ▥ 60,000 €3-5

13 ha 60,000

The estate, listed eight times in the *Guide* and winner of the *Grappe d'argent* in 1996, was commended by the Jury for both of its **vintage 2000** wines: the **Fleurie** and the Beaujolais-Villages. The latter is a rich, ruby colour with pronounced tears in the glass, but with a somewhat closed nose. Slightly acidic blackcurrant flavours emerge on the palate. Reasonably long and well-made, this is an impressive wine that is ready to drink now.

☛ Dom. André Colonge et Fils,
Les Terres-Dessus, 69220 Lancié,
tel. 04.74.04.11.73, fax 04.74.04.12.68 ▾
by appt.

DOM. DES COMBIERS 2000 ■ €5-8

5 ha 3,000

A grape harvest scene from bygone days adorns the label of this rich ruby-coloured wine. Its fragrant bouquet of redcurrants and raspberries is followed by a fresh, fruity and elegant palate. This is a light wine for drinking within the year.

☛ Yves Savoye, Les Combiers,
69820 Vauxrenard, tel. 04.74.69.92.69,
fax 04.74.69.92.69 ▾ by appt.

PHILIPPE DESCHAMPS Cuvée Vieilles vignes 2000★ ■ €5-8

0.6 ha 4,000

This beautiful red wine with violet highlights has been made from stringently selected grapes after a harvest that suffered from *millerandage* (uneven grape development). Lingering aromas of red berries, cherries and blackcurrants are perceptible on this classically styled wine. It has a well-balanced palate that is both velvet-textured and full-flavoured. Although this wine is ready for immediate consumption, it will also keep for up to two years.

☛ Philippe Deschamps, Morne,
69430 Beaujeu, tel. 04.74.04.82.54,
fax 04.74.69.51.04 ▾ by appt.

GEORGES DUBOEUF 2000★★ ■ €3-5

n.c. 60,000

160

This famous *négociant* house established the Hameau en Beaujolais, a wine centre and museum. Its **Moulin-à-Vent 99** was singled out by the Jury. Both the **Régnié 2000** and this Beaujolais-Villages were awarded two stars. The Beaujolais-Villages was also selected as a *coup de cœur* by the Grand Jury. Rich, complex red and black fruit aromas precede a structured palate with lingering, attractive redcurrant and blackcurrant flavours. A distinctive wine, it may be drunk now, but could also be cellared for two to three years.

• SA Les Vins Georges Duboeuf, quartier de la Gare, B.P. 12, 71570 Romanèche-Thorins, tel. 03.85.35.34.20, fax 03.85.35.34.25, e-mail mcvgd@csi.com ▼ ev. day 9am–6pm at the Hameau en Beaujolais; cl. 1–15 Jan.

DOM. DES FORTIERES 2000
3.3 ha | 6,000 | €5-8

Aged for nine months in oak casks, this dark-red wine has a subtly spicy, fruity nose. An agreeably fresh first impression leads on to a well-rounded palate. It should be drunk within the year.

• Daniel Texier, Les Fortières, 69460 Blacé, tel. 04.74.67.58.57, fax 04.74.67.58.57, e-mail dtexier@vins-du-beaujolais.com ▼ by appt.

DOM. DES FOUDRES 2000
9.3 ha | 5,000 | €3-5

This clear ruby-coloured wine was produced near the village of Vaux-en-Beaujolais, famously satirised in Gabriel Chevallier's 1934 novel, *Clochemerle*. Fragrant with redberry and pear drop undertones, it is rounded, well-balanced and fresh. This light Beaujolais-Villages is ready to drink now.

• Roger Sanlaville, Le Plageret, 69460 Vaux-en-Beaujolais, tel. 04.74.03.24.03, fax 04.74.03.21.77 ▼ ev. day 7am–7pm

DOM. DE GIMELANDE 1999
0.42 ha | 1,800

The aroma of this typical Chardonnay is more developed than its bright, youthful colour would lead one to expect. On the palate, it displays a pleasing balance of clean flavours and restrained acidity. This light, quaffable wine is for drinking within the year.

• Armand Large, Dom. de Gimelande, Le Clerjon, 69640 Montmelas, tel. 04.74.67.30.95, fax 04.74.67.47.34 ▼

DAVID GOBET 2000
1 ha | 3,000 | €5-8

Fine blackcurrant aromas laced with hints of undergrowth bear witness to a high-temperature maceration of the grapes. The rounded, well-balanced and full-flavoured palate has a slightly tannic finish. A fine accompaniment for a grilled steak, this appealing wine should be drunk within the year.

• David Gobet, L'Ermitage, 69430 Régnié-Durette, tel. 04.74.69.22.10,

fax 04.74.69.22.10, e-mail dgobet@aol.fr ▼ by appt.

DOM. DU GRAND CHENE 2000★
6.5 ha | 13,330 | €5-8

Distributed by the Éventail des vignerons, this bright, deep ruby-coloured wine has fresh fruit aromas mixed with spices and a slight vegetal hint. A touch lively on entry, it is still quite attractive, a soft, light-bodied wine of character that is ready to drink now.

• André Jaffre, 69220 Charentay, tel. 04.74.06.10.10, fax 04.74.66.13.77 ▼ by appt.

DOM. DE GRY-SABLON 2000★★
3.8 ha | 18,000 | €5-8

Pre-fermentation maceration at carefully controlled temperatures has resulted in a purplish-red *coup de cœur* selection. A powerful, persistent aroma of red berries, particularly raspberries, combines with a full-bodied, well-structured palate on which some young tannins are still perceptible. The combination of an excellent opening, good length and a velvety finish indicates a wine that will respond well to two or three years in the cellar.

• Dominique Morel, Les Chavannes, 69840 Emeringes, tel. 04.74.04.45.35, fax 04.74.04.42.66, e-mail gry-sablon@wanadoo.fr ▼ ev. day except Sun. 8am–6pm

DOM. DES HAUTS BUYON 2000
1 ha | 5,000 | €5-8

The grapes used to make this wine come from an early-ripening vineyard that was harvested on 30 August 2000. They have produced a bright, clear, deep garnet wine with a fine, aromatic bouquet of red berries. Fruity, with firm, well-balanced structure, this appealing wine is ready to drink now.

• Christophe Paris, Buyon, 69460 Saint-Étienne-des-Oullières, tel. 04.74.03.52.25, fax 04.74.03.58.94 ▼ by appt.

DOM. DE LA BEAUCARNE Quintessence 2000★
0.6 ha | 4,000 | €5-8

A clear, dark garnet-coloured wine, Quintessence has a concentrated bouquet of irises and morello cherries with a further hint of hay. The Jury applauded the genuinely fruity character of its fleshy palate and noted faintly strong, spicy, wild cherry flavours on the finish. This attractive wine will be enjoyable for the next two years, and could be drunk with *boeuf bourguignon* or the Lyons speciality, *tablier de sapeur*: breaded, fried tripe.

➤ Michel Nesme, 69430 Beaujeu, tel. 04.74.04.86.23, fax 04.74.04.83.41 ⦿
Y by appt.

CH. DE LACARELLE 2000★★
■ 130 ha 100,000 ■ ⦿ €5-8

The vineyard has belonged to the same family since its establishment in 1775. Its 130 ha (321 acres) make it the largest estate in Beaujolais. This bright ruby-coloured wine with garnet highlights is redolent of raspberries and strawberries, with richer undertones of peach and vanilla. Rounded and full-bodied, the palate is nicely balanced by good acidity. This elegant wine should be drunk within the next two years, as an accompaniment to white meat dishes.

➤ Louis Durieu de Lacarelle, 69460 Saint-Etienne-des-Ouillières, tel. 04.74.03.40.80, fax 04.74.03.50.18, e-mail chateaudelacarelle@free.fr ⦿
Y by appt.

DOM. DE LA CHAPELLE DE VATRE Cuvée Allys 2000
■ 6.2 ha 7,000 ■ ⦿ €5-8

The vineyard dates from 1650, but the chapel it derives its name from is as old as the 12th century. The cherry-red wine has a slightly closed nose of redcurrants and raspberries intermixed with an aroma of very ripe blackcurrants. A pleasing opening impression is followed by a rather tannic palate to give a wine of some vinosity that should mature well, given time.

➤ Dom. de La Chapelle de Vâtre, Le Bourbon, 69840 Jullié, tel. 04.74.04.43.57, fax 04.74.04.04.27, e-mail dominique.capart@libertysurf.fr ⦿
Y by appt.
➤ Dominique Capart

VINCENT LACONDEMINE 2000★★
■ 3 ha 20,000 ■ ⦿ €5-8

This wine comes from a cellar that was renovated in 1999. Dark garnet-coloured, it has a complex, fragrant nose of cooked fruit and blackcurrants. Expert handling has ensured maximum extraction, resulting in a full-bodied and well-structured wine. Fresh, aromatic and balanced, this elegant red should be drunk within the next two or three years as an accompaniment to white meats or strong cheeses.

➤ Vincent Lacondemine, Le Moulin, 69430 Beaujeu, tel. 04.74.04.82.77, fax 04.74.69.27.61 Y by appt.

DOM. DE LA CROIX SAUNIER Sélection vieilles vignes 2000★
■ 3 ha 10,000

Sixty-year-old vines planted on south-facing, steep, sandy granite slopes have produced this very attractive, bright-purple wine. Aromas of red berries and spices lead on to a well-balanced and structured palate with good length. This is a generous wine for drinking within the year.

➤ GAEC dom. de La Croix Saunier, Jean Dulac et Fils, 69460 Vaux-en-Beaujolais, tel. 04.74.03.22.46, fax 04.74.03.28.97 ⦿
Y by appt.

DOM. DE LA MADONE Le Perréon 2000
■ 20 ha 80,000 ■ ⦿ €5-8

If you take a country walk in Beaujolais in the summer, you will be surrounded by the fragrance of ripe wild strawberries and raspberries, and it is always worth taking a break in the vineyards. At this domaine, 30-year-old vines have produced a ruby-coloured wine with violet highlights and a woody red-berry bouquet. This rounded and aromatic cuvée with fine length is ready for drinking now.

➤ Jean Bérerd et Fils, SCEA de La Madone, 69460 Le Perréon, tel. 04.74.03.21.85, fax 04.74.03.27.19 ⦿
Y by appt.

LA MERLATIERE 2000★
■ 16 ha 30,000 ■ ⦿ €5-8

The 20-ha (49-acre) family-run estate received a commendation for its **Moulin-à-Vent 2000**, but this rich garnet wine with attractive violet highlights, which makes up the bulk of its production, was awarded one star. Powerful from start to finish, its supple tannins and red-berry aromas linger well on the palate. Very well-made, it will continue to be forcefully impressive for the next two years, and would best accompany a sauced white meat dish or braised red meat.

➤ Gérard Gauthier, GAEC de La Merlatière, 69220 Lancié, tel. 04.74.04.13.29, fax 04.74.69.86.84 ⦿
Y by appt.

CUVEE DE LA MOUTONNIERE 2000★
■ 7 ha 30,000 ■ ⦿ €5-8

The Société des vins de Pizay markets the wines of several producers, including those on the land of the Château de Pizay. Now run as a winery and tourist complex, the Château has dungeons that date back to the 15th century. The Société presented the Jury with this rich garnet wine that has an appealing bouquet of red berries with an undertone of blackberries and a hint of blackcurrant. A well-balanced, warming wine, it has a pleasing taste of cherries on the finish. This wine is for drinking within the year with game terrines, charcuterie or cheeses.

➤ Sté des vins de Pizay, 69910 Villié-Morgon, tel. 04.74.66.26.10, fax 04.74.69.60.66

DOM. DE LA ROCHE THULON
2000★★ — 3.5 ha · 5,000 · €5-8

Domaine de la Roche Thulon — Beaujolais-Villages 2000

This garnet-red wine with its powerful, forthcoming, red-berry aroma has garnered Pascal Nigay, who has been managing the estate for ten years now, yet another *coup de coeur*. A rich, modulated attack is succeeded by well-balanced, beautifully complex flavours. Remarkably well-made and very typical, this wine will keep for many years.
♦ Pascal Nigay, Dom. de la Roche Thulon, 69430 Lantignié, tel. 04.74.69.23.14, fax 04.74.69.26.85 ▼ by appt.

DOM. DU MARRONNIER ROSE
2000 — 4 ha · 6,000 · €3-5

Wine-lovers in Japan, America and the Netherlands are already familiar with the Dory's wines, and their 2000 vintage won't disappoint anybody. With its dark cherry-red colour, it is bursting with fruit. Supple tannins are apparent on the palate after a lively, but subtle and balanced attack. Aromatic and well-made, it is a wine for drinking within the year.
♦ Sylvain et Nathalie Dory, Le Bourg, 69820 Vauxrenard, tel. 04.74.69.90.80, fax 04.74.69.90.80, e-mail natalie.dory@wanadoo.fr ▼ ▼ by appt.

DOM. DE LA TREILLE
Lancié 2000 — 2 ha · 2,500 · €5-8

This is a vivid, richly-coloured red wine that is echoed on the palate. Quite a fleshy wine, it still has some sinewy tannins that will need another two years to soften.
♦ EARL Jean-Paul et Hervé Gauthier, Les Frébouches, 69220 Lancié, tel. 04.74.04.11.03, fax 04.74.69.84.13, e-mail jean-paul.gauthier2@wanadoo.fr ▼ by appt.

DOM. DE LA TOUR DES BOURRONS
2000 — 3.5 ha · 3,000 · €3-5

Temperature-controlled carbonic maceration has resulted in a very aromatic, richly ruby-coloured wine. Fresh red berries with pear drop undertones are apparent on the nose. Soft, gentle and fruity, this easy-drinking Beaujolais-Villages is ready now.
♦ Bernard Guignier, Les Bourrons, 69820 Vauxrenard, tel. 04.74.69.92.05, fax 04.74.69.92.05 ▼ by appt.

DOM. CHRISTIAN MIOLANE
2000★ — 10.5 ha · 30,000 · €3-5

Grapes from 50-year-old vines, partially macerated at controlled temperatures, have created a deep ruby-coloured wine with a forthcoming bouquet of lemony blackberries and red berries. The rich and aromatic first impression is followed by a well-rounded, ample palate. A wine with character, it is best drunk young, within the next two years.
♦ Dom. Christian Miolane, La Folie, 69460 Salles-Arbuissonnas, tel. 04.74.67.52.67, fax 04.74.67.59.95 ▼

CEDRIC MARTIN
2000 — 3.5 ha · 4,500 · €3-5

The young wine-grower who has managed this estate since 1996 has made a dark red wine with an elegant fruity and floral nose. The wine's rich character is nicely balanced by seductive and persistent fruity aromas. It is a good, classic Beaujolais-Villages for drinking within the next 18 months.
♦ Cédric Martin, Les Verchères, 71570 Chânes, tel. 03.85.37.46.32, fax 03.85.37.46.32 ▼ by appt.

PATRICE MARTIN
2000★ — 2 ha · 4,000 · €3-5

This 23-year-old wine-grower has been in charge of the estate since 1998. His rich garnet wine has a slightly spicy, blackcurrant nose. Full-bodied with softened tannins, it has an ample yet elegant style. This long and heady wine is for drinking within the next two years. Patrice Martin's *Juliénas 2000* was also commended by the Jury.
♦ Patrice Martin, Les Verchères, 71570 Chânes, tel. 03.85.37.42.27, fax 03.85.37.47.43 ▼ ▼ by appt.

MOMMESSIN
Vieilles vignes 2000★ — 13.75 ha · 110,000 · €5-8

This purple-red wine is redolent of fresh grapes and red berries. It has an excellent fleshy, aromatic and long palate, adding up to a well-balanced wine that is for drinking within the year.
♦ Mommessin, Le Pont-des-Samsons, 69430 Quincié-en-Beaujolais, tel. 04.74.69.09.30, fax 04.74.69.09.28, e-mail information@mommessin.com ▼ by appt.

CH. DE MONVALLON
2000 — 2.04 ha · 4,000 · €5-8

The commune of Charentay spans seven hills and is home to several châteaux, including the Château d'Arginy, a 12th-century fortress that once belonged to the Knights Templar. The Château de Monvallon dates from the 19th century. Its 45-year-old vines have produced a very concentrated, dark garnet wine with a rather closed red-berry and liquorice nose. A fairly lively opening and chewy tannins make this a robust wine that should be cellared for several months before drinking.

🛒 Françoise et Benoît Chastel, La Grange-Bourbon, 69220 Charentay, tel. 04.74.66.86.60, fax 04.74.66.73.23 ☑ Ⴤ by appt.

DOM. DES NUGUES 2000★
■ 17.5 ha 70,000 ■ ♦ €5-8

The 2000 vintage marked the year that the wine-grower's son, Gilles, joined forces with his father on their 21.5-ha (53-acre) estate. They made a small quantity of **Morgon 2000**, commended by the Jury, as well as this garnet wine redolent of red berries. A fine, forthright attack is followed by a full-bodied, long palate whose flavours are still a little muted. In a few months, the aromas will have developed fully, and the wine will then be a fine companion for white meat dishes. It should be drunk within the next two years.

🛒 EARL Gelin, Les Pasquiers, 69220 Lancié, tel. 04.74.04.14.00, fax 04.74.04.16.73 ☑ Ⴤ by appt.

DOM. DU PENLOIS Lancié 2000★
■ 10 ha 35,000 ■ €5-8

After touring the 15th-century Château de Corcelles, drive 1 km (0.621 miles) down the road to visit this estate. The vineyard, at an altitude of 210 m (687 ft) in the commune of Lancié, has produced a dark-garnet wine with very attractive red-berry and blackcurrant aromas. The optimum level of extraction has resulted in a robust, full-bodied wine of great length. It will make a pleasant companion to game dishes over the next two years.

🛒 SCEA Besson Père et Fils, Dom. du Penlois, Cidex 558, 69220 Lancié, tel. 04.74.04.13.35, fax 04.74.69.82.07 ☑ Ⴤ by appt.

DOM. DU PERRIN 2000
■ 6 ha 10,000 ■ ♦ €5-8

The wine village of Le Perréon lies at the end of the ridge through the Beaujolais hills, on the D88. Roger Lacondemine has managed this estate since 1974. He has made a bright, pale-red wine with a complex and fairly intense bouquet of raspberries and strawberries, with hints of violet. After a fruity attack, it is light and very supple on the palate. This easy-drinking wine would be a good accompaniment to brawn.

🛒 Roger Lacondemine, Le Perrin, 69460 Le Perréon, tel. 04.74.03.24.69, fax 04.74.03.27.79 ☑ Ⴤ by appt.

ALAIN PEYTEL 2000
■ 0.13 ha 1,000 €3-5

Vines planted on sandy marl soil have produced a bright-red wine with vivid shades of raspberries, wild cherries and almonds. Supple at first, it quickly displays a powerful and slightly rustic character on the palate. Given time to develop, this well-made wine will be even more attractive.

🛒 Alain Peytel, Les Fouillouses, 69840 Juliénas, tel. 04.74.04.44.73, fax 04.74.04.48.39 ☑ Ⴤ by appt.
🛒 Peiller

CAVE COOPÉRATIVE DE SAINT-JULIEN 2000★★
■ 7 ha 5,800 €5-8

The most recently-formed (1988) of the 19 co-operative cellars in Beaujolais received a commendation for its **red Beaujolais 2000**, but truly impressed the Jury with this aromatic, garnet-coloured wine with purple highlights. Full bodied, rich, well-balanced and very long, with a beguiling, slightly spicy finish, this remarkable vintage should keep for at least two years. It would suit being served with a provençal-style daube.

🛒 Cave coopérative de Saint-Julien, Les Fournelles, 69640 Saint-Julien, tel. 04.74.67.57.46, fax 04.74.67.51.93, e-mail stjulien@vins-du-beaujolais.com ☑ Ⴤ by appt.

DOM. DE SOUZONS 2000
■ n.c. n.c. €5-8

Laurent Jambon is a young wine-grower who has only recently taken over the management of this estate. This is his first vintage. His lively red wine has attractive scents of red berries and blackcurrants. Despite some slight astringency, which should disappear very soon, the robust and fruity palate is very appealing. The Jury advises drinking this wine within the year with grilled fish.

🛒 Laurent Jambon, 69430 Lantignié, tel. 04.74.04.80.29, fax 04.74.69.29.50 ☑ Ⴤ by appt.

CH. DE VARENNES 1999
☐ 0.25 ha 1,100 ▥ €5-8

The 16th-century Château de Varennes is still proudly defended by its towers. This rich golden wine has been matured for ten months in barrel, and has the vanilla and toast aromas characteristic of oaked wine. Full-bodied and round, the wine has character, and would be enjoyable with fish in a creamy sauce.

🛒 SCI Ch. de Varennes, 69430 Quincié-en-Beaujolais, tel. 04.74.04.31.67, fax 04.74.69.00.69 ☑ Ⴤ by appt.
🛒 Charveriat

CH. DE VAUX 2000
■ 5 ha 20,000 ■ ♦ €3-5

Vaux-en-Beaujolais is not just notable for being the setting for Gabriel Chevallier's comic novel, *Clochemerle*. The Auguel ruins show that the village dates back to prehistoric times. This estate has been in the Vermont family since 1854, and this year Jacques Vermont's son, Yannick, has joined the enterprise. Their bright-red wine has floral and red-fruit aromas. Its fine vinosity, allied to a constitution that is still quite lively, suggest that it should be drunk within the year.

The **Château de Vaux white Beaujolais 2000** was also singled out.

Jacques et Yannick de Vermont, rue Louis de Vermont, 69460 Vaux-en-Beaujolais, tel. 04.74.03.20.03, fax 04.74.03.24.10 ▼ Ⲧ by appt.

Brouilly and Côte de Brouilly

On the last Saturday in August, the vineyards ring with song and music. Even though the harvest has not begun, crowds of walkers carrying baskets clamber 484 m (1,588 ft) up Mont Brouilly to the top where, near the chapel, bread, wine and salt are given away. From the summit there is a panoramic view over the Beaujolais, the Mâconnais, the Dombes and the Mont d'Or. There are two sister appellations next to each other, Brouilly and Côte de Brouilly, which have had many disputes about the precise limits of their territories.

Côte de Brouilly is an AOC, on the slopes of the mount which is hard granite and greenish-blue shale, nick-named 'green horn', or diorite. The mount is the remains of ancient volcanic activity or, according to legend, where the giant who dug out the Saône emptied his hod. Production, 18,800 hl (496,320 gal) from 325 ha (650 acres), covers four communes: Odenas, Saint-Lager, Cercié and Quincié. The Brouilly appellation runs around the foot of the mount, covering 1,315 ha (3,248 acres) and producing 75,800 hl (2,001,120 gal). Other neighbouring communes are Saint-Étienne-la-Varenne and Charentay while the famous 'Pisse Vieille' vineyard is in the Cercié commune.

CH. DE BAGNOLS 1999

9 ha 10,000 €5-8

An 18th-century château towers over this estate, which has been managed by Alain Ravier since 1983. The rich red 99 has an aroma of leather, liquorice and redcurrants, and its subtly fruity palate is full-bodied and silky. This attractive and well-balanced wine is for drinking over the next two years.

EARL Alain Ravier, Ch. de Bagnols, 69460 Saint-Étienne-la-Varenne, tel. 04.74.03.42.77, fax 04.74.03.42.77 ▼ Ⲧ ev. day 10am-12 noon 2pm-6pm

JEAN BARONNAT 2000★★

n.c. n.c. €5-8

This *négociant* house, based at Gleizé in Villefranche-sur-Saône, presented the Jury with three wines from the same vintage, all of which were highly rated. The **Morgon** received a commendation, while the **Beaujolais-Villages** was awarded one star. This intense garnet-coloured wine was awarded two stars. It has a pronounced raspberry and floral nose and a supple, rounded palate. An elegant and sustained combination of finesse and power, this wine is ready for drinking now, but could also be kept for another two years.

Maison Jean Baronnat, Les Bruyères, rte de Lacenas, 69400 Gleizé, tel. 04.74.68.59.20, fax 04.74.62.19.21, e-mail info@baronnat.com ▼ Ⲧ by appt.

CH. BEILLARD 2000

12 ha 40,000 €5-8

In Saint-Lager there is an extensively renovated medieval château, as well as several manor houses, making it an important stop on the route through Beaujolais. The estate has made a ruby-coloured Brouilly with purple highlights. It has a fragrant bouquet of strawberry and blackcurrant aromas, with hints of dried apricots. With a touch of liveliness on the full-bodied palate, this wine is for drinking within the year.

GFA Beillard, Brignais, 69220 Saint-Lager, tel. 04.74.09.60.08 ▼

CH. DE BRIANTE Réserve 2000

14.8 ha 15,000 €5-8

The Château de Briante, which dates from the 18th century, used to be owned by the man who founded the Union Beaujolaise in 1888, at the height of the phylloxera epidemic. These days, the gloriously coloured Réserve is bottled by the Monnessin company. It has a rich aroma of redcurrants and blackcurrants with a hint of pear drops. The fleshy palate is well-structured, but has youthful tannins that need to soften. We suggest cellaring this wine for one or two years.

Ch. de Briante, 69220 Saint-Lager, tel. 04.74.66.72.34, fax 04.74.66.73.94

PIERRE CHANAU 2000

■ n.c. 300,000 ■ ♦ €5-8

This is a wine made for large-scale distribution. Pale purple with an intense, spicy, raspberry and blackcurrant nose, it makes a vigorous first impression on the palate. The noticeable warmth that follows suggests that it will age well. This wine should be cellared for one or two years.

➤ J. Chanut, Les Chers, 69840 Juliénas, tel. 04.74.06.78.70, fax 04.74.06.78.71, e-mail avf@free.fr ▼ by appt.

DOM. DU CHATEAU DE LA VALETTE 2000

■ 2.74 ha 14,000 ■ ♦ €5-8

Jean-Pierre Crespin, from Charentay, also presented the same mark as this dark-red Brouilly that received the Jury with a **Côte de Brouilly** that received the same mark as this dark-red Brouilly. Its ripe-fruit aroma develops slowly on the palate, but it is still dominated by tannins for the time being. This structured, sinewy wine will respond well to being kept for two years.

➤ Jean-Pierre Crespin, Le Bourg, 69220 Charentay, tel. 04.74.66.81.96, fax 04.74.66.71.72 ▼ ▼ by appt.

PAUL CINQUIN Pisse-Vieille 2000

■ 3 ha 9,000 ■ ♦ €5-8

A wine from one of the most popular *climats* of Beaujolais, this clear-garnet Brouilly has a powerful aroma of peonies with overtones of strawberries and raspberries, and a velvety palate. A supple and fresh wine with a long finish, it would complement a white meat dish.

➤ Paul Cinquin, Les Nazins, 69220 Saint-Lager, tel. 04.74.66.80.00, fax 04.74.66.70.78 ▼ ▼ by appt.

DOM. CRET DES GARANCHES 2000★

■ 8 ha n.c. ■ ▥ ♦ €5-8

This dark-red wine with black tinges has been produced from 8 ha (20 acres) of the nine that make up this estate. Beautifully structured, fresh and fruity, this well-balanced Brouilly will keep for two to three years.

➤ Yvonne Dufaitre, Dom. Crêt des Garanches, 69460 Odenas, tel. 04.74.03.41.46, fax 04.74.03.51.65 ▼ ▼ by appt.

DOM. DIT BARRON 1999

■ 9 ha 10,000 ■ ♦ €5-8

When men were being conscripted into the army, an ancestor of the estate's owners received the title of Baron so that he could enlist in place of the real Baron's son for whom he worked, hence the name 'dit Barron', or 'so-called Barron'. The rich, red colour of the 1999 is showing slight hints of ageing. The aroma begins with black and red fruits and develops wild cherry and overripe blackcurrant tones. An attractive, well-balanced palate is still a bit tannic, but the wine should be ready for drinking during the course of 2002.

FABRICE DUCROUX

Vignobles des Côtes 2000

■ 0.64 ha 5,130 ■ ♦ €5-8

This estate, on the slopes of Mont Brouilly, has made a rich garnet wine redolent of blackcurrants and redcurrants, with a hint of pepper. The rounded palate is pleasing, despite being a little astringent. The wine could be drunk now with gammon, or kept for one or two years.

➤ Fabrice Ducroux, 69640 Saint-Julien, tel. 04.74.06.10.10, fax 04.74.66.13.77 ▼ ▼ by appt.

HENRY FESSY Cuvée Pur Sang 1999

■ n.c. 4,000 ■ ♦ €8-11

Dark ruby-coloured with a well-developed bouquet of ripe red berries and spices, this wine has an aromatic and somewhat tannic palate. A little rustic but true to type, it will respond well if allowed to breathe. It should be drunk within the year with roast meats or game.

➤ SCI Vignoble de Bel-Air, 69220 Saint-Jean-d'Ardières, tel. 04.74.66.00.16, fax 04.74.69.61.67, e-mail vins.fessy@ wanadoo.fr ▼ ▼ by appt.

➤ Henry Fessy

JEAN-FRANÇOIS GAGET 1999★

■ 6.2 ha 12,000 ■ ▥ €5-8

Jean-François Gaget, the grower at the Château de Pierreux, has made a dark-red wine with brick-red and pink highlights. The fine, elegant bouquet is reminiscent of peaches and flowers. Its fine structure, vinous and fresh, includes floral and cooked-fruit aromas on the palate. Full and vinous, it is a powerful wine with tannins that will have softened in a year or two.

➤ Jean-François Gaget, La Roche, 69460 Odenas, tel. 04.74.03.46.23, fax 04.74.03.51.40 ▼ ▼ by appt.

DANIEL GUILLET 2000

■ 1.25 ha 4,000 ▥ €5-8

Daniel Guillet has been managing this 7.5-ha (19-acre) estate since 1984. Of that total, 1.25 ha (3 acres) is dedicated to the production of this very clear, dark-red wine that is redolent of black fruits, strawberries and raspberries. Full and vinous, it is a powerful wine with tannins that will have softened in a year or two.

➤ Daniel Guillet, Les Lions, 69460 Odenas, tel. 04.74.03.48.06, fax 04.74.03.48.06 ▼ ▼ by appt.

DOM. DE JASSERON 2000

■ 1.26 ha 4,000 ■ ♦ €5-8

The product of 60-year-old vines, this dark ruby-coloured wine has fine, complex aromas of strawberries, raspberries and flowers. The rounded, slightly spicy, fruity palate is well-balanced, with supple tannins. This elegant

ANNE-MARIE JUILLARD
Cuvée Prestige 1999

1.35 ha   4,000   ⊞   €5-8

Anne-Marie Juillard acquired the La Sorbière estate in 2000. Subtle woody aromas are apparent on both the nose and the palate of this Brouilly. Mellow tannins and a fine texture dictate that this 99 is for drinking within the year. The Jury gave the **Régnié 2000** an equal mark.
➤ Anne-Marie Juillard, Bergeron, 69220 Saint-Lager, tel. 04.74.66.53.68 ☒ ☐ by appt.

CH. DE LA CHAIZE 2000

96.02 ha   450,000   ⊞   €5-8

Built in 1676 to the designs of Louis XIV's architect, François Mansart, and endowed with extensive vineyards, La Chaize is one of the most imposing châteaux in Beaujolais. The estate has an international reputation. Its 2000 vintage has a rich, red colour and a complex bouquet of red berries and violets. A forthright opening impression introduces a fruity, spicy palate. An elegant Brouilly, it is ready for drinking now.
➤ Marquise de Roussy de Sales, Ch. de La Chaize, 69460 Odenas, tel. 04.73.03.41.05, fax 04.74.03.52.73, e-mail chateaudelachaize@wanadoo.fr ☒ ☐ by appt.

JEAN-MARC LAFOREST 2000★

n.c.   34,000   ■   €5-8

The clear, dark garnet Brouilly can be tasted in the wine-maker's vaulted cellar. While the bouquet is full of red berries, pear drops and spices, the rounded palate is given volume by fine tannins wrapped in the flavours of red fruits. A well-balanced wine that retains some freshness, it should be drunk within the year.
➤ Jean-Marc Laforest, Chez le Bois, 69430 Régnié-Durette, tel. 04.74.04.35.03, fax 04.74.69.01.67 ☒ ☐ ev. day 8am-8pm

DOM. DE LA PISSEVIEILLE
Pissevieille 2000★

4 ha   15,000   ■   €5-8

Another wine from the Pissevieille *climat*, this red-violet Brouilly has a powerful aroma of strawberries, with mineral and toast undertones. It is a richly textured wine with a good balance of fruit and acidity. The slightly tannic finish suggests that it should be kept for two years.
➤ Mme Gaillard, La Pissevieille, 435, rte du Beaujolais, 69220 Cercié-en-Beaujolais, tel. 04.74.09.60.08

---

and extremely attractive wine is ready for drinking now.
➤ Georges Barjot, Grille-Midi, 69220 Saint-Jean-d'Ardières, tel. 04.74.66.47.34, fax 04.74.66.47.34 ☒ ☐ ev. day 8am-7pm

DOM. DE LA ROCHE SAINT MARTIN 2000★

7 ha   25,000   ■   €5-8

Jean-Jacques Béréziat has been managing this estate of just under 10 ha (25 acres) since 1989, and uses thermovinification techniques on half of the harvest. His **Côte de Brouilly 2000** was also commended by the Jury. This dark-red Brouilly with its bouquet of very ripe red berries was awarded a star. The fleshy and fruity palate is quite powerful, and needs to develop and soften further. A well-made wine that is true to its appellation, it should be drunk over the next two years.
➤ SCEA Jean-Jacques Béréziat, Briante, 69220 Saint-Lager, tel. 04.74.66.85.39, fax 04.74.66.70.54 ☒ ☐ by appt.

DOM. DE LA SAIGNE 2000

0.5 ha   3,500   ■

The grapes for this dark ruby-coloured Brouilly come from vines growing on steep granite slopes at a gradient of 25%. It has a discreet aroma of strawberries and pear drops, together with a hint of blackcurrant leaf. Lively, robust and tannic, this tightly-knit wine should be cellared for one or two years.
➤ EARL Lenoir Fils, Cimes de Cherves, 69430 Quincié-en-Beaujolais, tel. 04.74.69.02.03, fax 04.74.69.01.45 ☒ ☐ by appt.

DOM. DE LA VALETTE 2000★★

4 ha   20,000   ■   €5-8

This wine comes from the *négociant* house of J. Pellerin. It has a bright, clear-ruby colour and an intense bouquet of redcurrants and raspberries, with overtones of liquorice and cloves. Fine, rounded tannins are apparent in the velvety attack, and cherries dominate the palate's complex flavour. Charming, remarkably elegant and well-balanced, this wine is ready for drinking now, and will continue to be enjoyable for the next two years. It would complement a dish of chicken in a cream sauce with morels, or the Lyonnaise speciality *saucisson brioche* (sausage baked in brioche dough).
➤ Vins et Vignobles, 435, rte du Beaujolais, 69830 Saint-Georges-de-Reneins, tel. 04.74.09.60.00, fax 04.74.67.09.60, e-mail info@vinsetvignobles.com

LA VANDAME 2000

n.c.   n.c.   ■   €5-8

This red-purple wine has fine aromas of red berries and blackcurrants and a well-balanced, if slightly closed, palate. However, it should have developed fully before long, and may be drunk over the next two years. The same *négociant* wine was also commended for its **Domaine de Grand Croix 2000 Juliénas**.
➤ Dupond d'Halluin, B.P. 79, 69653 Villefranche-en-Beaujolais, tel. 04.74.60.34.74, fax 04.74.68.04.14

LE JARDIN DES RAVATYS 2000

■ 7 ha 10,000 ■ ◆ €5-8

The garden of Ravatys, depicted on the label, has Mont Brouilly as a backdrop and is particularly beautiful in spring. This ruby-coloured wine has a fine, attractive pear drop and blackcurrant nose, but is still a little lively on the palate. Its good structure, fruit and long finish suggest that it will keep for one or two years. It could be served with game.

☛ Institut Pasteur, Ch. des Ravatys, 69220 Saint-Lager, tel. 04.74.69.61.38 ⊻ ⅄ by appt.

LAURENT MARTRAY

Vieilles vignes 1999

■ 1.5 ha 8,000 ■ €5-8

This wine is made in the cellars of the Château de La Chaize. Dark ruby-coloured, it has a spicy (mostly clove-scented) aroma. The palate is robust, with astringent tannins that need several months to mature. The Jury felt that this wine would be ready to drink in late 2002, perhaps as an accompaniment to spicy charcuterie.

☛ Laurent Martray, Combiaty, 69460 Odenas, tel. 04.74.03.51.03, fax 04.74.03.50.92 ⊻ ⅄ by appt.
☛ de Roussy-Sales

DOM. DU MOULIN FAVRE

Cuvée vieilles vignes 2000★★

■ 8.5 ha 20,000 ■ ◆ €5-8

The wine is the product of a carefully-managed, semi-carbonic maceration, where the juice was allowed to remain in contact with the skins. The result is a distinctive, bright, rich garnet wine with an intense bouquet of cherries and bilberries mixed with coffee and chocolate. The well-balanced and long palate has a fruity, red-berry flavour and elegant structure that make it a pleasure to drink now, but also indicate that it should keep for another two or three years.

☛ Armand Vernus, Le Vieux-Bourg, 69460 Odenas, tel. 04.74.03.40.63, fax 04.74.03.40.76 ⊻ ⅄ by appt.

DOM. DES NAZINS 1999

■ 1.4 ha 8,200 ■ €8-11

Although this wine-growing family has lived in Saint-Lager for four centuries, the vineyard only dates back to 1900. It has produced a dark ruby-coloured wine with raspberry and cherry aromas. Supple, fresh and easy-drinking, it has a pleasing flavour of red berries and jam. It should be drunk with sausages cooked in wine or rolled pork brawn.

☛ Loïc Brac de La Perrière, Les Nazins, 69220 Saint-Lager, tel. 04.74.66.82.82, fax 04.74.66.72.05 ⊻ ⅄ by appt.

DOM. ROBERT PERROUD 1999

■ 5 ha 10,000 ▥ €5-8

Both the estate's **Côte de Brouilly 2000** and this 99 Brouilly support its slogan that the wines '... *sont le Pérou*' ('are worth the trouble'). A ruby colour with blueish highlights, the Brouilly has a forthcoming,

complex nose of very ripe fruits with toasty, spicy overtones. The balanced and structured palate reflect its thermovinification treatment. A well-made, balanced wine that is ready to drink now with game or red meat dishes, it could also be cellared for two to three years.

☛ Robert Perroud, Les Balloquets, 69460 Odenas, tel. 04.74.04.35.63, fax 04.74.04.32.46, e-mail robertperroud@wanadoo.fr ⊻ ⅄ by appt.

DOM. DE PIERREFAIT 1999

■ 2 ha 10,000 ■ €5-8

Thirty-year-old vines have produced a ruby-coloured wine that has a moderately intense nose of red berries, peonies and spices. The rounded, attractive first impression is followed by forthright tannins on the palate. This wine should be drunk within the year as an accompaniment to spiced duck breast.

☛ Claude Echallier, Creigne, 69460 Odenas, tel. 06.11.75.86.82 ⊻ ⅄ by appt.

DOM. DE PONCHON 2000

■ 3 ha 5,000 ■ €5-8

The same Régnié family has been making wine on this estate for four generations. Yves Durand has produced a garnet-coloured wine that has a complex bouquet of cherry jam and spices with a hint of vinosity. The elegant and classy palate is quite impressive. A distinctive and pleasing vintage, it should be drunk with the regional dish, *saucisson brioché* (sausages baked in brioche dough).

☛ Yves Durand, Ponchon, 69430 Régnié-Durette, tel. 04.74.04.34.78, fax 04.74.04.34.78 ⅄ ev. day 8am–8pm

CAVE BEAUJOLAISE DE QUINCIE 1999★

■ 4 ha 15,000 ■ ◆ €5-8

The co-operative's **Côte de Brouilly 99** and this clear-purple Brouilly were both awarded one star by the Jury. This wine has an elegant aroma of red berries and violets, and a fleshy and supple palate that is balanced by a nice touch of acidity. A balanced and well-structured wine, it should be drunk within the next two years.

☛ Cave beaujolaise de Quincié, Le Ribouillon, 69430 Quincié-en-Beaujolais, tel. 04.74.04.32.54, fax 04.74.69.01.30 ⊻ ⅄ by appt.

DOM. RUET 2000★

■ 4 ha 20,000 ■ ◆ €5-8

This 16-ha (40-acre) estate at the foot of Mont Brouilly has made a **Régnié 2000** that was commended by the Jury, as well as this dark-garnet Brouilly with its pronounced aromas of red berries, blackcurrants and flowers. The full-bodied, well-structured palate and long finish indicate a wine that will repay several months' keeping. Note that both the 1998 and 1999 vintages of Jean-Paul Ruet's Brouilly were selected as *coups de coeur*.

- Dom. Ruet, Voujon, 69220 Cercié-en-Beaujolais, tel. 04.74.66.85.00, fax 04.74.66.89.64, e-mail ruet.beaujolais@wanadoo.fr ☑ ☿ by appt.
- Jean-Paul Ruet.

DOM. DE SAINT-ENNEMOND
2000★

6 ha 30,000 €5-8

The 15-ha (37-acre) estate is named after a seventh-century Bishop of Lyons. *Chambres d'hôtes* (bed-and-breakfast rooms) are available. The dark-red 2000 vintage has a complex bouquet of peaches, strawberries and blackcurrants with a hint of pear drops. A well-made, fresh, lively and aromatic wine with a *nouveau* style, it is ready to drink now.
- Christian Béréziat, Saint-Ennemond, 69220 Cercié-en-Beaujolais, tel. 04.74.69.67.17, fax 04.74.69.67.29, e-mail christian.bereziat@wanadoo.fr ☑ ☿ ev. day 8am–7pm

DOM. DU SANCILLON 1999

3.9 ha 8,000 €5-8

Produced using a method that falls midway between classic Beaujolais wine-making and more modern thermovinification techniques, this dark, rich purple wine has a rapidly-opening and complex nose of white flowers and spices. Some judges enjoyed its gentle attack and floral aroma; the full texture and good structure of the palate impressed others. Drink this wine within the year, with game dishes.
- Charles Champier, Le Moulin Favre, 69460 Odenas, tel. 04.74.03.42.18, fax 04.74.03.30.62 ☑ ☿ by appt.
- Dom. Rolland.

DOM. JEANNE TATOUX
Garanche 2000

3 ha 9,730 €5-8

A wine from the vineyards of Charentay, marketed by the *Éventail des vignerons producteurs*. Garanche has a clear garnet colour and an aroma of humbugs developing towards strawberry and raspberry overtones. Drink this smooth, supple and appealing wine with a plate of cold meats.
- Jeanne Tatoux, 69220 Charentay, tel. 04.74.06.10.10, fax 04.74.66.13.77 ☑ ☿ by appt.

GEORGES VIORNERY 2000★

n.c. 14,000 €5-8

This dark-red wine was made in the village of Brouilly itself. It has an intensely aromatic nose of red and black fruits. The powerfully-structured palate has a subtle taste of raspberries. This is a wine with great potential that should be ready in two years' time.
- Georges Viornery, Brouilly, 69460 Odenas, tel. 04.74.03.41.44, fax 04.74.03.41.44 ☑ ☿ ev. day 8am–8pm

DOM. DE VURIL 1999

11.1 ha 35,000 €5-8

Granitic marl soils have produced a rich ruby-coloured Brouilly redolent of spicy, ripe red and black fruits. Its soft, full-bodied, fruity and long palate is very attractive, despite being a little thin. This wine is ready to drink now, with a Bresse chicken in truffle-flavoured juice.
- Gabriel Jambon, Chapoly, 69220 Charentay, tel. 04.74.66.84.98, fax 04.74.66.80.58 ☑ ☿ by appt.

Côte de Brouilly

DOM. BARON DE L'ECLUSE 1999★

5.11 ha 10,000 €5-8

This estate is run by Chantal Pégaz, founder and president of the *Étoiles en Beaujolais* group, a collective of a dozen women wine-makers, each of whom represents one of the 12 appellations of the region. Her 1999 vintage has a powerful bouquet of overripe fruits and blackcurrants, with toasty overtones. Ample, round and densely textured, this warm wine with its fine tannins and spicy finish is ready to drink now, but will also continue to improve over the next two years.
- SCI du Dom. Baron de l'Ecluse, L'Ecluse, 69460 Odenas, tel. 04.74.03.40.29, fax 04.74.03.53.50, e-mail vinbaron@aol.com ☑ ☿ by appt.

CAVE DES VIGNERONS DE BEL-AIR 2000★★

5 ha 42,000 €5-8

This co-operative cellar was established in 1929 when a group of wine-growers decided to join together and set up their own vat room. The dark-garnet Côte de Brouilly has a fine aroma of redcurrants and grapes, followed by a very attractive, fleshy palate with a persistent red-berry flavour. Even a slightly tannic finish cannot detract from this remarkable wine. It is ready to drink now, but could equally be kept for two years. The Jury also commended the **Beaujolais-Villages 2000** from the same cellar.
- Cave des Vignerons de Bel-Air, rte de Beaujeu, 69220 Saint-Jean-d'Ardières, tel. 04.74.06.16.05, fax 04.74.06.16.09, e-mail cvba@wanadoo.fr ☑ ☿ ev. day except Sun. 9am–12 noon 2pm–6pm

M. BONNETAIN 1999

3 ha 7,000 €8-11

The same family has run the vineyard tenancy of the Institut Pasteur since 1947. It has made a dark ruby-coloured wine with brick-red highlights. Fine mineral, undergrowth and spicy aromas are perceptible in the glass. A very attractive fleshy and fruity impression on the palate leads to a long, but

Côte de Brouilly

slightly edgy finish. The wine should be drunk within the year.
- Maurice Bonnetain, Le Bourg, 69220 Saint-Lager, tel. 04.74.66.81.49, fax 04.74.66.71.95 ▼ Υ by appt.

DOM. DU CHEMIN DE RONDE 2000★
■   3 ha   n.c.   ■ ♦ €5-8

Vines planted in north-eastern Beaujolais, on some of the hardest rocky terrain in Europe, have produced a garnet-coloured wine with a fine, ripe-fruit bouquet. Full, fleshy and well-balanced on the palate, it has soft tannins and plenty of complex fruit. A beguiling example of this appellation, it should be drunk within the next two years.
- Gérard Monteil, 70, Grande rue, 69220 Cercié-en-Beaujolais, tel. 04.74.66.80.50, fax 04.74.66.70.91 ▼ by appt.

DOM. CHEVALIER-METRAT 1999
■   2 ha   8,000   ■▥ €5-8

The harvest of 40-year-old vines planted in blue schist soils has been vinified using stainless steel vats containing oak staves. The resulting wine, with its lively red colour, has a fine aroma of blackberries and bilberries with mineral notes. Attractive and full-bodied on the palate, it is fruity with elegant oak tones. The 1999 is ready to drink now. The **red Beaujolais 2000**, the product of a half-hectare (1.2-acre) plot, was also commended by the Jury.
- Sylvain Métrat, Le Roux, 69460 Odenas, tel. 04.74.03.50.33, fax 04.74.03.37.24 ▼ Υ by appt.

DOM. DE CONROY 1999★
■   7.8 ha   25,000   ■▥ €5-8

This 12-ha (30-acre) estate dates back to the 17th century. It has produced a dark-red Côte de Brouilly with powerful aromas of blackberries and pears highlighted by mineral notes. Supple and clean-tasting with an attractive texture, it is still a little tannic on the finish. The wine will be ready for drinking during 2002, and should be allowed to breathe before serving.
- SCE des Dom. Saint-Charles, Le Blunzard, 69460 Saint-Etienne-la-Varenne, tel. 04.74.03.30.90, fax 04.74.03.30.80, e-mail saintcharles@sofradi.com ▼ Υ by appt.
- Jean de Saint-Charles

VALERIE DALAIS 1999
■   0.5 ha   2,000   ■▥ €5-8

This dark-garnet wine has been aged for 12 months in oak barrels. It has an attractive bouquet of pepper, saffron and leather. The robust and slightly rustic palate needs time to mature. We suggest waiting for a year before serving this wine with game.
- Valérie Dalais, La Grand-Raie, 69220 Saint-Lager, tel. 04.74.66.75.37, fax 04.74.66.75.77 ▼ Υ by appt.

DOM. DU FOUR A PAIN 2000★
■   2 ha   15,000   ■ ♦ €5-8

This purple-garnet wine is crystal-clear. The vinous bouquet has fine cherry scents, while the straightforward, rounded palate finishes with plenty of body. This well-made wine needs longer to develop, and should only be drunk in a year's time.
- SCI de L'Ecluse, 69220 Saint-Lager, tel. 04.74.09.60.08

CH. DU GRAND VERNAY 1999
■   n.c.   20,000   ■▥ €5-8

The estate, established in 1950, has been highly rated before by the *Guide*. This oak-aged, rich garnet-coloured wine with its concentrated aromas of morello cherries, ferns and hay, is made from grapes harvested from the south-facing slopes of Mont Brouilly. The appealing, if slightly nervy, opening impression is followed by a fine, fruity palate. This wine, which would happily accompany a terrine of wild boar, will continue to improve over the next two years.
- EARL Claude Geoffray, Ch. du Grand Vernay, 69220 Charentay, tel. 04.74.03.46.20, fax 04.74.03.47.46 ▼ Υ ev. day 9am–12.30pm 1.30pm–7.30pm

DOM. DE LA MADONE 2000
■   8 ha   10,000   ■▥ €5-8

This 12-ha (30-acre) estate is situated not far from the chapel on Mont Brouilly dedicated to Notre-Dame-du-Raisin, Our Lady of the Grape. It has made a darkly-coloured Côte de Brouilly with a well-developed bouquet of redcurrants, undergrowth and ferns. The solidly-structured and concentrated palate is already quite rounded and long, making this a wine for drinking over the next two years with grilled steak.
- EARL Dom. de La Madone, Les Maisons-Neuves, 69220 Saint-Lager, tel. 04.74.66.84.37, fax 04.74.66.70.65 ▼
- Daniel Trichard

DOM. DE LA PIERRE BLEUE 2000★★
■   4 ha   n.c.   ■ ♦ €5-8

The Jury awarded the **Beaujolais 2000 des Sables d'Or** one star. The estate's cellar, built in 1840, is geared up for receiving visitors. There, one can taste this bright, clear, deep-garnet Brouilly with purple highlights that was selected as a *coup*

de cœur. It has very attractive, intense aromas of red berries and violets. Supple tannins enveloped in fruity and floral flavours contribute to its perfect balance. This beautifully-made, extremely attractive wine is for drinking over the next two or three years.
➼ EARL Olivier Ravier, Dom. des Sables d'Or, Les Descours, 69220 Belleville-sur-Saône, tel. 04.74.66.12.66, fax 04.74.66.57.50, e-mail olivier.ravier@wanadoo.fr ⊠ Y ev. day 8am–6pm

DOM. J. LARGE 2000
3.2 ha   17,330   €5-8

This Côte de Brouilly, bottled by the *Éventail des producteurs à Corcelles*, has a subtle, toasty aroma of black fruits. The fruit on the palate is for the time being dominated by tannins, but the wine shows good potential. Its slightly rustic mineral finish suggests that it should be kept for at least a year.
➼ Michel Large, 69460 Odenas, tel. 04.74.06.10.10, fax 04.74.66.13.77 ⊠ Y by appt.

DOM. DE LA VOUTE DES CROZES 2000
3.5 ha   25,000   €5-8

Forty-year-old vines planted on granite and schist soils have produced a dark garnet wine with a concentrated aroma of peonies. The complex palate evolves quickly, revealing a rich texture and good tannins. This 2000 will reach its full potential if it is allowed to mature for another few months.
➼ Nicole Chanrion, Les Crozes, 80, Grande-Rue, 69220 Cercié-en-Beaujolais, tel. 04.74.66.80.37, fax 04.74.66.89.60 ⊠ Y by appt.

DOM. LES ROCHES BLEUES 1999★
2.65 ha   17,500   €5-8

The vaulted cellar of 15 m (16 yd) long where this deep-red 99 was matured had to be dynamited out of the rock. The wine has an appealing nose of fresh grapes and flowers. On the palate, it is very attractive and well-balanced, with overtones of cayenne pepper and gunflint. It is ready for drinking now.
➼ Dominique Lacondemine, Dom. Les Roches Bleues, 69460 Odenas, tel. 04.74.03.43.11, fax 04.74.03.50.06, e-mail lacondemine.dominique@wanadoo.fr ⊠ Y ev. day 8.30am–8pm. Sun. by appt.

DOM. MONBRIAND 2000
n.c.   13,000   €5-8

A wine from a Juliénas-based *négociant*, this Côte de Brouilly shows expressive aromas of cherries, with hints of pear drops and flowers. Well-balanced and lightly structured, this fine representative of its appellation is ready for drinking now.
➼ Jacques Dépagneux, Les Chers, 69840 Juliénas, tel. 04.74.06.78.70, fax 04.74.06.78.71, e-mail avf@free.fr ⊠ Y by appt.

DOM. ROLLAND 2000
6 ha   4,000   €8-11

This *négociant*, which was established in 1882, has made a very attractively-coloured, deep-garnet wine with a well-developed nose of wild cherries, blackcurrants and blackberries. After a supple first impression, the palate is quite firm. Ripe tannins and good acidity will help it to age well. A wine of great finesse, it will be very enjoyable in a year's time.
➼ Pierre Ferraud et Fils, 31, rue du Mal-Foch, 69220 Belleville, tel. 04.74.06.47.60, fax 04.74.66.05.50 ⊠ Y by appt.

CELLIER DES SAINT-ETIENNE 2000
12 ha   8,000   €5-8

The co-operative cellar, founded in 1957, is made up of 250 growers and vinifies 25,000 hl (660,000 gal) of wine a year. The garnet-coloured 2000 with purple highlights is redolent of red berries mixed with peonies, daffodils and the scent of undergrowth. Once the slightly tannic character of the wine has moderated, this well-made, fairly powerful cuvée with its subtle minerality will make a fine accompaniment to charcuterie. It is for drinking over the next two years.
➼ Cellier des Saint-Etienne, rue du Beaujolais, 69460 Saint-Etienne-des-Ouilleres, tel. 04.74.03.43.69, fax 04.74.03.48.29 ⊠ Y by appt.

DOM. DU SOULIER 2000
7 ha   6,000   €5-8

This dark-red wine with its complex bouquet of morello cherries, redcurrants and blackcurrants, mixed with iris, was made in one of the largest vaulted cellars in the Côte de Brouilly. The supple and quite powerful palate has a slightly tannic finish, but it should have softened within the year. It could then be served with jugged hare.
➼ Diane Juilliet, Dom. du Soulier, 69460 Odenas, tel. 04.74.03.49.01, fax 04.74.03.49.01 ⊠ Y by appt.

CH. THIVIN 2000★
8.3 ha   60,000   €5-8

Devastated by phylloxera in the 19th century, this estate was one of those that helped to mobilise the recovery of the Beaujolais vineyards. Its richly-coloured 2000 displays purple highlights at the rim. It has a generous aroma of red fruits (predominantly cherries). The soft and aromatic tannins on the palate are well-balanced and long. Powerful yet restrained, this wine is very true to type, and is ready to drink now. It would also keep for another two or three years.
➼ Claude Geoffray, Ch. Thivin, 69460 Odenas, tel. 04.74.03.47.53, fax 04.74.03.52.87 ⊠ Y by appt.

produced on the boggier and less hilly eastern part of the vineyard, is usually less full-bodied. This wine tends to be regarded as the poor relation of the Crus and, because of the size of the vineyard, is also limited to producing small quantities. The 17th-century cellar of the Coopérative du Château vinifies 45% of the appellation and is an impressive sight when it is full of large oak barrels, or *foudres*, filled with wine.

MICHEL ET REMI BENON 2000 ▪ €5-8
3 ha 13,000

Ten successive generations of the same family have run this estate. Its very youthful, bright ruby-coloured wine has all the characteristics to make it well suited for cellaring. Good, strong tannins make for a robust style that means it will need to be kept for two to three years, before being served as an accompaniment to game.
➤ GAEC Michel et Rémi Benon, Les Blémonts, 71570 La Chapelle-de-Guinchay, tel. 03.85.33.84.22, fax 03.85.33.89.54, e-mail benon@vins-du-beaujolais.com ☎ ev. day 8am–7pm

DOM. DU VADOT 1999★ ▪ €5-8
2 ha 8,000

Sixty-year-old vines planted on granite and schist soils have produced this dark-garnet wine with aromas of mineral, undergrowth and red fruits. Musky, warm flavours enrich the rounded and lengthy palate. This distinctive wine should be drunk over the next three years with charcuterie or red meats.
➤ Jean-Pierre Gouillon, Dom. du Vadot, Pont-de-Cherves, 69430 Quincié-en-Beaujolais, tel. 04.74.69.00.44 ☎ by appt.

ROBERT VERGER L'Ecluse 2000★ ▪ €5-8
9 ha 15,000

The 10.3-ha (25-acre) estate practises environmentally sustainable viticulture. Its cellar, renovated in 1996, has produced this clear-purple wine with well-developed, attractive aromas of red berries and violets. Subtle, slightly gamey aromas underpin the supple tannins on its well-structured palate. A very appealing wine, it should be drunk over the next two years.
➤ Robert Verger, L'Ecluse, 69220 Saint-Lager, tel. 04.74.66.82.09, fax 04.74.66.71.31 ☎ by appt.

Chénas

According to legend, a vast oak forest once covered this land. A woodcutter noticed that a wild vine had grown from a grape pip, apparently dropped by a bird. Convinced of divine intervention, the man set about making a clearing in the forest to cultivate the plant – which proved to be none other than the great Gamay, the black-skinned grape with white flesh.

Chénas is one of the smallest appellations in the Beaujolais, covering only 285 ha (704 acres) on the borders of the departments of Rhône and Saône-et-Loire. It produces 16,130 hl (425,832 gal) harvested from the communes of Chénas and La Chapelle-de-Guinchay. The wines produced on the steep granite slopes to the west are intensely coloured, strongly flavoured but not aggressively so, and release scents of rose and violet; they are not dissimilar to the perfumes of the wines from Moulin à Vent, which occupies most of the land in the commune. Chénas, which is

CH. BONNET Vieilles vignes 2000 ▪ €5-8
8 ha 30,000

Located 2 km (1.3 miles) from Moulin à Vent, this 13-ha (32-acre) estate uses cement vats and large oak barrels for its vinification. Sixty-year-old vines have produced a purple wine with aromas of ripe red berries. The strong, vanilla-scented tannins suggest that the wine needs more time to mature, and its flavours of strawberry and raspberry on a generally well-balanced palate will make the wait worthwhile.
➤ Pierre-Yves Perrachon, Ch. Bonnet, 71570 La Chapelle-de-Guinchay, tel. 03.85.36.70.41, fax 03.85.36.77.27, e-mail chbonnet@terre.net.fr ☎ by appt.

AMEDEE DEGRANGE 1999★ ▪ €5-8
0.12 ha 1,000

The Moulin à Vent and the Chénas, of the same vintage, were each awarded one star by the Jury. This garnet-coloured Chénas has an appealing, subtly oaky aroma. Its full-bodied palate is long and straightforward, and shows the influence of well-integrated oak. Keep it for two or three years, and then this lively, structured, powerful wine could accompany ham, or else roast veal with mushrooms.
➤ Amédée Degrange, Les Vérillats, 69840 Chénas, tel. 04.74.04.48.48, fax 04.74.04.46.35 ☎ ev. day 8am–12 noon 2pm–7pm

JEAN GEORGES ET FILS 1999 ▪ €5-8
2.7 ha 5,000

Twenty per cent of this family-run estate's production is exported to the United States,

Belgium and Germany. The 99 has an attractive, youthful and clear-garnet colour and a complex, ripe red-fruits nose, the slight oakiness of which reflects four months' ageing in barrel. This full-bodied, fleshy and well-structured wine is ready for drinking now, but could also be kept for a further one or two years. The estate's **Moulin à Vent 99** was also commended by the Jury.

➤ GAEC Jean Georges et Fils, Le Bourg, 69840 Chénas, tel. 04.74.04.42.77, fax 04.74.04.44.77,
e-mail jean-georges-et-fils@wanadoo.fr ☑
☒ by appt.

■
PASCAL GRANGER 2000
0.5 ha | 4,000 | €5-8

This Juliénas family has a 200-year history in the wine business. Its **Beaujolais-Villages Cuvée Spéciale 2000** was also singled out by the Jury. This clear ruby-coloured Chénas has discreet aromas of red fruits. The palate reveals stronger blackberry and blackcurrant flavours. A powerful wine with good, structured tannins, it is well-balanced and should be kept for a year or two.
➤ Germaine Granger, Les Poupets, 69840 Juliénas, tel. 04.74.04.44.79, fax 04.74.04.41.24 ☒ ☒ by appt.

■
DOM. DU GREFFEUR 1999
2 ha | 3,000

This estate was established in 1977 with cuttings from a parent vineyard. Its 99 is still very youthful. Its bouquet of ripe red fruits remains fairly closed at present. Slightly astringent tannins overwhelm the initial impression of roundness on the palate; they will need to age and soften.
➤ Jean-Claude Lespinasse, Les Marmets, 71570 La Chapelle-de-Guinchay, tel. 03.85.36.70.42, fax 03.85.33.85.49 ☒
☒ by appt.

■
HUBERT LAPIERRE
Cuvée spéciale Vieilli en fût de chêne 1999★
1 ha | 4,500 | €8-11

The purple-coloured Cuvée Spéciale, made from the harvest of 60-year-old vines, has been aged in oak for ten months. It has red-berry and oak aromas of great finesse. This fleshy and lively wine, with its rich, velvety tannins, will continue to improve. A very successful example of an oaked Beaujolais, it should remain enjoyable for a further two or three years, and would stand up well to richly sauced meat dishes.
➤ Hubert Lapierre, Les Gandelins, 71570 La Chapelle-de-Guinchay, tel. 03.85.36.74.89, fax 03.85.36.79.69 ☒
☒ by appt.

■
LE VIEUX DOMAINE 1999
1 ha | 3,000 | €5-8

Le Vieux Domaine was established in 1890 on the site of a presbytery that had been built the previous century. Its rich garnet-coloured 99 has a beguiling fruity aroma with oak and spice overtones. It shows all the positive characteristics of properly-managed barrel-ageing. The wine has a fairly light structure that suggests that it should be drunk over the next one to two years.
➤ EARL M.-C. et D. Joseph, Le Vieux Bourg, 69840 Chénas, tel. 04.74.04.48.08, fax 04.74.04.47.36,
e-mail le.vieux.domaine@wanadoo.fr ☑
☒ by appt.

■
DOM. DU MAUPAS 2000★
0.9 ha | 3,000 | €5-8

M. Lespinasse established this 7.5-ha (19-acre) estate in 1962. His **Juliénas 2000** received a commendation, but this clear ruby-coloured Chénas was awarded one star by the Jury. A generous bouquet of raspberries and morello cherries with overtones of pear drops precedes a well-structured palate. The fresh liveliness of the wine is sufficient to suggest that it will keep well. It should be cellared for several months, and then enjoyed over the next two to three years.
➤ H. et J. Lespinasse, Dom. du Maupas, 69840 Juliénas, tel. 03.85.36.75.86, fax 03.85.33.86.70 ☒ ☒ by appt.

■
DOM. DES PINS 1999
4.5 ha | 4,000 | €5-8

This light ruby-coloured 99 is a well-balanced wine with a delicate fruity aroma and a rounded, fine palate. For a cru, it is quite soft and straightforward, ready for drinking now, perhaps with sausages and lentils.
➤ Pascal Aufranc, En Rémont, 69840 Chénas, tel. 04.74.04.47.95, fax 04.74.04.47.95 ☒ ☒ by appt.

■
DOM. DU P'TIT PARADIS 2000
0.52 ha | 3,800 | €5-8

From the centre of the P'tit Paradis vineyard, one may savour a panoramic view of the Alps. The estate's bright-red Chénas has spicy fruit aromas. Full-bodied and agreeably lively on the palate, it is ready for drinking now.
➤ Denise et Francis Margerand, Les Pinchons, 69840 Chénas, tel. 04.74.04.48.71, fax 04.74.04.46.29 ☒ ☒ ev. day 8am–8pm

■
GEORGES ROSSI
Vignoble en Guinchay 2000★
2.5 ha | 9,330 | €5-8

The wine-grower purchased the estate in 1962 after decades of running it as a *métayage*, or tenancy. Its wines are marketed by the *Eventail des vignerons producteurs*. This bluish-red Chénas is both bright and clear with subtle aromas of blackcurrants and raspberries. The fruity, supple and silky first impression is offset by fairly prevalent ripe tannins. This well-balanced and elegant wine is ready for drinking now, and will remain enjoyable for another two or three years.
➤ Georges Rossi, 71570 La Chapelle-de-Guinchay, tel. 04.74.06.10.10, fax 04.74.66.13.77 ☒ ☒ by appt.

Chiroubles

Perched at 400 m (1,312 ft), Chiroubles is the highest of the Cru vineyards in Beaujolais. It covers 374 ha (924 acres) of light, impoverished granite sand, in a single commune, and produces 21,500 hl (567,600 gal) of red wine from the Gamay grape. Chiroubles is an elegant, delicate, charming and smooth wine, containing little tannin and with traces of violet perfumes. The Confrérie des Demoiselles de Chiroubles, supported by their Chevaliers, was created in 1996 to assist in the marketing of this wine which is sometimes referred to as 'the ladies' Beaujolais'. It is a wine for early drinking and is sometimes reminiscent of Fleurie or Morgon, which are neighbouring vineyards. Chiroubles is the perfect wine to drink with charcuterie. On the route to Fût d'Avenas, which leads out of the village towards the top of the mount, there is a *chalet de dégustation* where the wine can be tasted.

Every April, Chiroubles holds a festival to celebrate the memory of Victor Pulliat, born there in 1827. His considerable research into the pace of growth of different vine varieties and their comparative grafting qualities is world-famous. He made his observations in his domain at Tempéré and gathered a collection of over 2,000 vine varieties. Chiroubles has a cooperative cellar which vinifies 3,000 hl (79,200 gal) of the cru.

DOM. CHAPELLE SAINT-ROCH 2000★★

■   5 ha   3,330   ▬ ◈   €5-8

Forty-year-old vines planted on soil composed of granitic sand have produced a garnet-coloured Chiroubles redolent of redcurrants and pear drops, with spice and liquorice overtones. Its appealing, fresh and fruity attack persists on a cherry- and redcurrant-scented palate that is given body by powerful, rounded tannins. This is an elegant, easy-drinking wine that faithfully reflects its appellation. It should be enjoyed within the next two years with a roast haunch of venison.

➥ Gérard Chapuy, 69115 Chiroubles,
tel. 04.74.06.10.10, fax 04.74.66.13.77 ☑
▼ by appt.

DOM. DU CLOS VERDY 1999★★

■   5.5 ha   14,000   ▬ ◗◗◈   €5-8

This is the second year in a row that the estate has earned two stars. The clear garnet 99 has aromas of red fruits and kirsch, with spicy overtones of cinnamon, cloves, liquorice and saffron. A lively and aromatic opening impression is balanced by superbly integrated tannins, all wrapped up in the flavour of cherry preserve. Beguiling liquorice and mineral notes appear on the finish. A remarkable Chiroubles, it is ready for drinking now, alongside chicken cooked with cream and morels, but it will also keep for up to one year.

➥ Georges Boulon, pl. Victor-Pulliat,
69115 Chiroubles, tel. 04.74.04.27.27,
fax 04.74.69.13.16 ☑ ▼ ev. day 9am–
12 noon 2pm–6pm; Sat. Sun. by appt.

DOM. DU CRET DES BRUYERES 2000★

■   1.9 ha   6,000   ▬ ◈

The estate is located 800 m (870 yd) down the road from the 14th-century Château de la Pierre. It was commended for the **Régnié 2000** that makes up the bulk of its production,

---

DOM. DE TREMONT 2000★
Les Gandelins

■   2 ha   10,000   ▬   €5-8

The 19-ha (47-acre) estate, established in 1989, has produced a rich purple-red wine. Its powerful ripe fruit aroma with a hint of musk, and its rich, fleshy palate with very attractive tannins, combine to create a vintage that is worthy of the adjoining Moulin à Vent cru. It is supple enough to drink now, but could also be kept for two years.

➥ Daniel et Françoise Bouchacourt,
Les Jean-Loron, 71570 La Chapelle-de-
Guinchay, tel. 03.85.36.77.49,
fax 03.85.33.87.20 ☑ ▼ by appt.

while this purple-hued Chiroubles was awarded one star. An intense bouquet of blackcurrants and fresh red berries attests to thermovinification treatment. The fleshy, full and rounded palate is also fresh. Its finish is not exactly typical of Beaujolais, but doesn't spoil the balance of the wine. Those who appreciate this style may enjoy it over the next two years.

● GFA Desplace Frères, Aux Bruyères, 69430 Régnié-Durette, tel. 04.74.04.30.21, fax 04.74.04.30.55 ☒ by appt.

DOM. DUFOUX Cuvée Réservée 1999
1.65 ha 7,000 €5-8

This purple-red wine has an attractive nose of raspberries and redcurrants, with vanilla overtones and a hint of spice. After a fine first impression, fairly prominent tannins dominate the palate. Nevertheless, the crystallised fruit aromas perceptible on the finish help to balance this wine, which is ready for drinking now.

● Guy Morin, Le Bois, 69115 Chiroubles, tel. 04.74.69.13.29, fax 04.74.69.13.29 ☒
☒ ev. day 9am–8pm
● Marcel Dufoux

DOM. GOBET Vieilles vignes 1999★
0.85 ha 1,800 €5-8

Christophe Jeannet has run the 6-ha (15-acre) estate since 1998. His dark ruby-coloured 99 has a rich bouquet of red berries, vanilla and pepper. Very supple on the palate, this powerful, but not overwhelming, wine, with its fruity and peppery flavours, is well-balanced and attractive. It is for drinking within the year.

● Christophe Jeannet, Le Bourg, 69115 Chiroubles, tel. 04.74.04.21.04, fax 04.74.04.23.58, e-mail domaine.gobet@wanadoo.fr ☒ ☒ by appt.

DOM. DE LA CHAPELLE DES BOIS 1999★
0.24 ha 1,700 €5-8

Forty-year-old vines have produced a garnet-coloured wine with aromas of cherries and vanilla. It is lively and fresh, but not too light, and well-balanced despite the slightly chewy tannins apparent on the finish. We suggest keeping it until late 2002 to allow the wine to reach its full potential.

● EARL Coudert-Appert, Le Colombier, 69820 Fleurie, tel. 04.74.69.86.07, fax 04.74.04.12.66 ☒
☒ ev. day 8am–8pm; cl. in Jan.

DOM. DE LA COMBE AU LOUP 1999★
5 ha 38,000 €5-8

The 1998 vintage was selected as a *coup de coeur* in last year's edition of the *Guide*. This year, the estate has produced a **Régnié** that was commended by the Jury, and this garnet-coloured Chiroubles. It has forthcoming aromas of fresh red berries and morello cherries. The very well-balanced, fleshy palate has fine tannins and evolving flavours of

raspberries and redcurrants. This is a very attractive wine for drinking within the next three years.

● Méziat Père et Fils, Dom. de la Combe au Loup, Le Bourg, 69115 Chiroubles, tel. 04.74.04.02, fax 04.74.69.14.07 ☒ ☒ ev. day except Sun. 8.30am–12 noon 2pm–6.30pm

VIGNOBLE LA FONTENELLE 2000★★
5 ha 10,000 €5-8

A vineyard with south-east exposure has produced this very bright ruby-coloured wine with a rather shy nose of spicy red fruits and liquorice. The full, fleshy palate is sustained by tightly-knit, fine tannins. Ripe cherry flavours persist on a long, fresh-tasting finish. This attractive, vigorous Chiroubles is for drinking within the next two years with white meat dishes.

● Gobet-Jeannet, 69115 Chiroubles, tel. 04.74.06.10.10, fax 04.74.66.13.77 ☒ ☒ by appt.

ERIC MORIN Vieilles vignes 1999★★
1.5 ha 6,000 €8-11

Brueghel's *Dance of the Peasants* adorns the label, a picture that well suits the jovial style of this ruby-coloured wine. Well-developed aromas of red berries and peonies, with toasty coffee overtones, are sustained on the fleshy, full-bodied and well-structured palate. A distinctive and substantial Chiroubles, it will continue to be enjoyable for the next two to three years.

● Eric Morin, Javernand, 69115 Chiroubles, tel. 04.74.69.11.70, fax 04.74.04.22.28 ☒ ☒ by appt.

DOM. MORIN 2000★
4 ha 20,000 €5-8

The cellars of this estate are right in the centre of the village. They have produced a ruby-coloured wine with elegant aromas of raspberries, redcurrants and blackcurrants. Young tannins are immediately apparent on the palate, masking for the time being the concentrated blackcurrant fruit. A robust wine, it will certainly age well, and will be ready to drink in a year or two. It could then be served with dried Lyonnaise sausage.

● Guy Morin, Le Bois, 69115 Chiroubles, tel. 04.74.69.13.29, fax 04.74.69.13.29
☒ ev. day 9am–8pm

DOM. DU PETIT PUITS 2000
6 ha 20,000 €5-8

Vines growing on sandy granite soils have produced this ruby-coloured Chiroubles with its bouquet of faded roses, peonies, hay and red fruits. A bit light in texture, it is nevertheless well-made, straightforward and lively. This wine is for drinking within the year, perhaps as an accompaniment to sausages.

● Gilles Méziat, Le Verdy, 69115 Chiroubles, tel. 04.74.69.15.90, fax 04.74.04.27.71 ☒ ☒ ev. day 8am–7pm

Fleurie

A chapel surmounts the rounded hillock of the Fleurie and appears to keep a watchful eye over the vineyard that is planted entirely with Gamay. This is the Madonna of Fleurie and it marks the physical location of the third most important Cru after Brouilly and Morgon. The 875 ha (2,161 acres) of the vineyard are inside the commune boundaries and produce 50,028 hl (1,320,739 gal). The terrain is similar throughout the vineyard and made up of crystalline granite which contributes to the wine's finesse and charm. The wine can be drunk cool or at room temperature and, either way, it is the perfect accompaniment for *andouillette beaujolaise* made with Fleurie. It has the promise of the countryside in spring; light, bright and with a bouquet of iris and violets.

There are two wine-tasting cellars in the centre of the village, one near the town hall and the other in the Cave Coopérative which vinifies 30% of the cru. They offer a full range of local wines with evocative names: La Rochette, La Chapelle-des-Bois, Les Roches, Grille-Midi and la Joie-du-Palais.

CH. DU BOURG 2000★
5 ha   10,000   €5-8

A father and his sons manage the vineyards of this 18th-century château. They have made a bright ruby-coloured wine with an attractive nose of redcurrants and raspberries. After a lively, forthright initial impression, the palate is full-bodied, with supple tannins, fruity and long if a little sinewy on the finish. This wine needs to mature for another two years before it is drunk.
↦ Bruno Matray, La Treille, 69820 Fleurie, tel. 04.74.69.81.15, fax 04.74.69.86.80, e-mail matraybruno@free.fr Y by appt.

DOM. DU CALVAIRE DE ROCHE GRES 2000★
2.1 ha   15,000   €5-8

Not far from this estate, a procession of 13 rocks stands among the vines, erected in 1934 to represent the 13 Stations of the Cross (one short of the true number). The deep-garnet 2000 vintage has an intense aroma of red berries, particularly strawberries. On the palate, it is rich and clear-cut, with robust tannins. This long and structured Fleurie will continue to develop over the next three to four years.
↦ EARL Didier Desvignes, Saint-Joseph, 69910 Villié-Morgon, tel. 04.74.69.92.29, fax 04.74.69.97.54 Y by appt.

DOM. CHAINTREUIL
Cuvée Vieilles vignes 2000
3 ha   21,000   €5-8

A harvest of 97-year-old vines has been aged for seven months in oak barrels. The resulting purplish wine has pleasing aromas of red berries and blackcurrants, with a hint of plum. After a supple first impression, quite strong tannins are perceptible on the palate, but these will ripen given time. This well-balanced and long Fleurie should be kept for two years, before being served as an accompaniment to a red meat dish.
↦ SCEA Dom. Chaintreuil, La Chapelle-des-Bois, 69820 Fleurie, tel. 04.74.04.11.35, fax 04.74.04.10.40 Y by appt.

DOM. CHIGNARD Les Moriers 1999★
1 ha   7,000   €5-8

This dark-red wine, made from 50-year-old vines and matured in oak barrels, has a densely fruity bouquet that develops slowly. Its expressive, full-bodied, well-structured and balanced characteristics on the palate impressed the Jury. This is a wine for drinking within the next two years.
↦ Michel Chignard, Le Point du Jour, 69820 Fleurie, tel. 04.74.04.11.87, fax 04.74.69.81.97 Y ev. day except Sun. 8am–12 noon 1.30pm–7pm

CLOS DES GRANDS FERS 1999★★
0.75 ha   4,500   €5-8

Matured for ten months in oak, this clear garnet wine has a rich, complex bouquet of red fruits and wild cherries, mixed with vanilla and coffee. Right from the start, the intensely aromatic palate is impressively structured with a fine oaky character. This well-balanced, expansive wine will be enjoyable over the next two or three years. The Jury also commended the **Morgon Côte du Py 2000, Christian Bernard.**
↦ SARL Christian Bernard, Les Grands Fers, 69820 Fleurie, tel. 04.74.04.11.27, fax 04.74.69.86.64, e-mail chbernard@terre-net.fr Y ev. day except Sat. Sun. 9am–12 noon 2pm–5.30pm

DOM. COTEAU DE BEL-AIR
Cuvée Tradition 1999
n.c.   €5-8

Jean-Marie Appert owns 7 ha (17 acres) of vineyards. An area of one hectare (2.5 acres) is responsible for this pretty garnet-coloured wine, with its light fruity and floral aromas. The fruit-filled, rounded palate reflects the

elegant tannins. The wine will have reached its full potential in two years.
☎ Dom. Berrod, Le Vivier, 69820 Fleurie, tel. 04.74.69.83.83, fax 04.74.69.86.19 Ⓥ
Ⓨ by appt.

DOM. MÉTRAT ET FILS La Roilette 1999

2 ha | 12,000 | €8-11

"The estate's '98 vintage was selected as a *coup de cœur* last year. The '99 has a fine aroma of red fruits, with a hint of fresh butter. The supple and full-bodied palate is still a little tannic on the finish, but this is a well-made wine that will respond well to keeping. It will be ready for drinking in two years' time.
☎ Bernard Métrat, Le Brie, 69820 Fleurie, tel. 04.74.69.83.83, fax 04.74.69.86.19 Ⓥ
Ⓨ by appt.

DOM. MONROZIER Les Moriers 1999

2.15 ha | 4,500 | €8-11

"The estate has been within the same family ownership for the past two centuries. It has produced a garnet-coloured wine from the harvest of 50-year-old vines growing on pink granite soils. The complex bouquet of minerals and crystallised fruits shows good vinosity. A ripe texture and mature tannins on the palate attest to time spent in oak barrels. This distinctive wine is for drinking now.
☎ SCEA du dom. Monrozier, Les Moriers, 69820 Fleurie, tel. 04.74.69.83.78, fax 04.74.04.12.17 Ⓥ ev. day 10am–7pm

DOM. DE MONTGENAS 2000

5.75 ha | 26,660 | €5-8

Reasonably intense, pure aromas of red berries characterise this bright-red wine. The palate is quite full and supple with a nice touch of acidity, although it is lightly structured, making this a Fleurie for immediate consumption.
☎ Dom. de Montgenas, 69820 Fleurie, tel. 04.74.06.10.10, fax 04.74.66.13.77 Ⓥ
Ⓨ by appt.

DOM. PARDON 2000

n.c. | 19,000 | €5-8

"The ruby-coloured Fleurie from this Beaujolais *négociant* has a persistent ripe red-berry aroma with mineral overtones, followed by a well-balanced and fairly warm palate of considerable finesse. This is a wine for drinking over the next two years.
☎ Pardon et Fils, 39, rue du Gal-Leclerc, 69430 Beaujeu, tel. 04.74.04.86.97, fax 04.74.69.24.08, e-mail pardon-fils.vins@wanadoo.fr Ⓥ Ⓨ ev. day except Sat. Sun. 8am–12 noon 2pm–6pm

DOM. DU POINT DU JOUR 1999*

5.5 ha | 20,000 | €8-11

Jocelyne Depardon started working with her father in 1988, and took over the estate's management in 1995. Her clear-garnet wine has a cherry bouquet with hints of blackcurrant and liquorice. It is a chewy, full-bodied Fleurie that is structured and long

---

impact of six months' ageing in oak barrels. Complex and attractive with a good long finish, this Fleurie is for drinking within the next two years.
☎ Jean-Marie Appert, Bel-Air, 69115 Chiroubles, tel. 04.74.04.23.77, fax 04.74.69.17.19 Ⓨ by appt.

HENRY FESSY La Roilette 2000

n.c. | n.c. | €8-11

"The *négociant-éleveur* (merchant wine-maker), Henry Fessy, presented the Jury with this quite deeply-coloured Fleurie that has a subtle floral and fruity bouquet with spicy overtones. The attractive, fruity palate shows some vinosity, but is a little short on structure. A quaffable, well-made wine, it is intended for immediate consumption.
☎ Henry Fessy, Bel-Air, 69220 Saint-Jean-d'Ardières, tel. 04.74.66.00.16, fax 04.74.69.61.67, e-mail vins.fessy@wanadoo.fr Ⓥ Ⓨ by appt.

DOM. DE LA COUR PROFONDE 2000

4.7 ha | 14,000 | €5-8

"The estate derives its name from its location just below the commune of Chiroubles. Its Fleurie has been made from carefully sorted grapes grown on 50-year-old vines, and was vinified using a semi-carbonic maceration. It has a vermilion colour and a fine floral bouquet mixed with morello cherries and redcurrants. The attractive texture of its softened tannins blends with a slightly vegetal flavour on the palate to produce a fresh and well-balanced wine for drinking over the next three years.
☎ EARL Revollat, La Cour Profonde, 69115 Chiroubles, tel. 04.74.69.13.72, fax 04.74.04.22.84 Ⓥ ev. day 9am–7pm

DOM. DE LA MADONE La Madone 2000

8 ha | 30,000 | €5-8

From the Chapelle de la Madone, which is close to this estate, there is a beautiful view over the Saône valley. The ruby-coloured Fleurie made here has a fruity and floral bouquet. It is a light wine with a rounded and supple palate full of fresh fruit characteristics, and should be drunk within the next two years.
☎ Jean-Marc Després, La Madone, 69820 Fleurie, tel. 04.74.69.81.51, fax 04.74.69.81.93, e-mail jeanmardespres@aol.com Ⓥ
Ⓨ by appt.

DOM. LES ROCHES DU VIVIER 2000*

8 ha | 30,000 | €5-8

The harvest began on 30 August 2000. This vintage, made using semi-carbonic maceration, has a rich garnet colour and powerfully beguiling fruity and floral aromas. After a clean initial impression, the palate is full and fleshy with

Juliénas

A wine with an imperial heritage, Juliénas, with Moulin à Vent the leading wine of Beaujolais, does indeed owe its name to Julius Caesar, as does Jullié, another of the four communes which make up the vineyard (the others are Emeringes and Pruzilly, which is just over the border in Saône-et-Loire). The soil in the western part of the vineyard is granite while in the east the soil is sedimentary with ancient alluvial deposits. Its 606 ha (1,497 acres) are planted exclusively with Gamay, and produce 34,200 hl (902,880 gal) of well-structured wine. The richly-coloured wines drink well in the spring, after being kept only a few months. They are as vigorous and spirited as the characters on the frescoes in the Caveau de l'Eglise, the wine-tasting cellar in the centre of the town where, in November of each year, the Victor Peyrat prize ceremony is held. The prize is awarded to the artist, painter, writer or journalist who has celebrated the Crus with the most distinction. The actual prize consists of 104 bottles of wine, two for each weekend in the

year. The Cave Coopérative, situated in the old priory of the Château du Bois de la Salle, vinifies 30% of the appellation.

JEAN ET BENOIT AUJAS 1999 €5-8
9 ha   2,000

Father and son joined forces in 1993 to manage this 11-ha (27-acre), south-facing vineyard. The rich red 99 has complex aromas of blackcurrants and wild strawberries, with leather and tobacco. A light-bodied wine, it has a fresh, youthful character and is very true to type. Already easy to drink, perhaps with charcuterie or grilled meats, it will keep for another year.
↳ GAEC Jean et Benoît Aujas, La Ville, 69840 Juliénas, tel. 04.74.04.41.35 ☑
Y by appt.

DOM. DU BOIS DE LA SALLE €8-11
1.5 ha   8,000

Michel Jannin has run the 4.5-ha (11-acre) estate since 1974. His ruby-coloured 99 has garnet highlights at the rim. It also has a spicy floral aroma, and a fresh, well-balanced palate with fine tannins. This wine is ready for drinking now.
↳ Michel Janin, Bois de la Salle, 69840 Juliénas, tel. 04.74.04.44.74, fax 04.74.04.44.45 ☑ Y by appt.

BERNARD BROYER 2000★ €5-8
2 ha   8,000

This estate used to belong to the grandfather of Bernard Broyer's wife. The Jury commended its Chénas 2000, but awarded the Juliénas a star. A dark-red wine, it has a fresh grape and redcurrant aroma, with overtones of peonies and pepper. A clean attack leads on to a fruity and fleshy, well-structured palate, on which the youthful tannins show plenty of potential. This heady wine should reach its peak in a year's time, when it could be enjoyed with sauced meat dishes or with goats' cheese.
↳ Bernard Broyer, Les Bucherats, 69840 Juliénas, tel. 04.74.04.46.75, fax 04.74.04.45.18 ☑ Y ev. day 10am– 12 noon 2pm–7pm; cl. 15-31 Aug.

DOM. DU CLOS DU FIEF 2000 €5-8
7 ha   40,000

The fourth successive generation of the Tête family took over the helm of this 13-ha (32-acre) estate in 1980. Their ruby-violet wine, which is given a thermovinification treatment, has a powerful peony aroma with some musky overtones. The supple, well-balanced opening impression develops quickly to reveal rather restrained tannins. The Jury was split on how best to appreciate this wine: one group favoured drinking it now to enjoy its primary fruit, while the other suggested waiting for at least two years.
↳ Michel Tête, Les Gonnards, 69840 Juliénas, tel. 04.74.04.41.62, fax 04.74.04.47.09 ☑ Y by appt.

with big, promising tannins. A wine that will complement a haunch of venison or other red meat, it will be enjoyable for the next two to three years.
↳ Dom. du Point du Jour, Le Point du Jour, 69820 Fleurie, tel. 04.74.69.82.93, fax 04.74.69.82.87 ☑
Y ev. day except Sun. 8.30am–6.30pm
↳ GAEC Depardon-Copéret

ANDRE VAISSE Grille-Midi 2000 €5-8
4 ha   12,000

Environmentally sustainable methods are used to cultivate the vines that produce this garnet-coloured wine with its subtle aromas of red berries, pears and lilac. On the palate, it is fruity but still quite youthful. A well-balanced but somewhat thinly structured wine, it should be drunk within the year.
↳ André Vaisse, 69820 Fleurie, tel. 04.74.06.10.10, fax 04.74.66.13.77 ☑
Y by appt.

DOM. DU COTEAU DES FOUILLOUSES

Cuvée Vieilles vignes 2000
0.68 ha 5,000 €5-8

The 15-ha (37-acre) estate once belonged to the Beaujolais poet, Pierre Aguétant. Its oak-aged, clear-purplish wine has an attractive, vinous nose scented with raspberries and blackcurrants. The powerful and lively palate is still quite tannic, but this is a Juliénas that will age well over the next year or two.

● Roland Lattard, Le Bourg, 69840 Jullié, tel. 04.74.04.43.86, fax 04.74.04.43.86
Y by appt.

MAISON DESVIGNES 1999

n.c. 15,000 €5-8

The rich ruby-coloured Juliénas from this *négociant* has intense aromas of flowers and preserved fruits. Ripe fruit flavours are apparent on the soft but finely-structured palate, making this a well-balanced and attractive wine for immediate consumption.

● Maison Desvignes, rue Guillemet-Desvignes, 71570 La Chapelle-de-Guinchay, tel. 03.85.36.72.32, fax 03.85.36.74.02

CH. DE JULIÉNAS 1999

15 ha 20,000 €5-8

The *seigneur* of Beaujeu built a fortified manor house here in the 13th century. It was then rebuilt as a rather grand château in the 1700s. François Condemine and his son Thierry manage 35 ha (86 acres). Their elegantly structured, ruby-coloured Juliénas has a bouquet of red fruits with a hint of undergrowth. It is an attractive wine that is ready for drinking now.

● François et Thierry Condemine, Ch. de Juliénas, 69840 Juliénas, tel. 04.74.04.41.43, fax 04.74.04.42.38

CH. DE LA BOTTIÈRE 2000★

n.c. 30,000 €5-8

Records exist that place the Perrachon family in Juliénas as far back as 1601. Their deep-purplish wine, the product of thermovinification, has a well-developed, characteristic nose of blackcurrants, enlivened with a hint of black pepper. On the palate, it is extremely fruity and attractive. Maximum extraction and proper maturation have created a four-square wine that should be kept for one year before drinking.

● Jacques Perrachon, Dom. de La Bottière, 69840 Juliénas, tel. 03.85.36.75.42, fax 03.85.33.86.36

DOM. DE LA BOTTIÈRE-PAVILLON 2000

4 ha 28,000 €5-8

We're told that Peynet and Lino Ventura used to own this estate, whose wine was presented to the Jury by the *négociant*, Bouchacourt. It has a lively red colour, and an appealing bouquet of red fruits, peonies and spices. The aromatic first impression leads on to a palate that one might wish was a little more full-bodied. Although the tannins initially seem supple, they become much firmer on the finish. This pleasantly aromatic wine should be kept for a year or two to attain full maturity.

● Roland Bouchacourt, La Bottière-Pavillon, 69840 Juliénas, tel. 04.74.09.60.08

DOM. DE LA COMBE-DARROUX

Cuvée Prestige Vieilles vignes 1999
1.6 ha 10,000 €5-8

Pascal Guignet, who has run this estate since 1989, made this wine from old vines growing on the slopes of Bucherats. Matured in oak for eight months, the deeply-coloured 99 has a hint of vanilla on the nose and is quite lightly structured. Well-balanced and integrated oak, this appealing, easy-drinking wine is for immediate consumption.

● EARL Anne et Pascal Guignet, 71570 La Chapelle-de-Guinchay, tel. 04.74.06.70.90, fax 04.74.04.45.08, e-mail domaine.guignet@wanadoo.fr
Y by appt.

DOM. DE LA COTE DE BESSAY 1999

n.c. n.c. €5-8

This wine comes from a *négociant* house in Beaune. It has a clear, light-red colour and an attractive, subtle, bilberry and blackcurrant aroma with warm overtones. The powerful palate has structured tannins and a flavour of stone fruits. This well-made Juliénas is ready to drink now.

● HDV Distribution, rue du Dr-Barolet, Z.I. Beaune Vignolles, 21200 Beaune Cedex, tel. 03.80.24.70.07, fax 03.80.22.54.31, e-mail hdv@planeth.fr Y by appt.

DOM. DE LA COTE DE CHEVENAL 2000

1.25 ha 4,500 €5-8

The Bergeron brothers have jointly managed this 24-ha (59-acre) estate since 1996. Their rich red 2000 vintage is redolent of red fruits. The extremely aromatic, pepper-tinged palate is still dominated by only partially-ripened tannins. This is a very youthful wine that needs to be kept for at least a year. The Jury also commended the estate's **Fleurie 2000.**

● GAEC Jean-François et Pierre Bergeron, Les Rougelons, 69840 Emeringes, tel. 04.74.04.41.19, fax 04.74.04.40.72 Y ev. day 8am-12.30pm 1.30pm-7pm

DOM. LE CHAPON 2000★★

4.92 ha 12,000 €5-8

Jean Buiron's 1993 vintage was a memorably successful wine, and he has now been awarded two stars for this beautiful cherry-red 2000 with its fuschia-tinted highlights. Matured in oak for six months, it has a complex, powerful aroma of spicy red berries and stone fruits, impressions that are echoed

Morgon

Morgon is the second largest Cru after Brouilly, its vineyards located in a single commune. The 1,115 ha (2,754 acres) of AOC produce an average of 66,261 hl (1,749,290 gal) of

on the palate. A well-balanced wine with good vinosity and fine tannins, it is ready to drink now, but also shows the potential to age for a further two to three years.

☛ Jean Buiron, Le Chapon, 69840 Juliénas, tel. 04.74.04.40.39, fax 04.74.04.47.52 ☑ ⅋ by appt.

DOM. LE COTOYON 1999★

■ 1 ha 3,000 Ⅲ €5-8

This estate, located north of Juliénas itself, rents out two comfortable *gîtes* with a swimming pool attached. The elegant, dark-garnet 99 has been oak-aged for six months. Vanilla aromas are very apparent on the nose, while complex, persistent, oaky red fruit flavours emerge on the palate. This powerful, well-balanced and distinguished wine is enjoyable now, but could also be kept for two years.

☛ Frédéric Bénat, Les Ravinets, 71570 Pruzilly, tel. 03.85.35.12.90, fax 03.85.35.12.90 ☑ ⅋ by appt.

DOM. LES COTES DE LA ROCHE 1999★

■ 2 ha 6,000 ■ €5-8

The Descombes family have been wine-growers as far back as anyone can remember. Their garnet-coloured wine with purple highlights has strong, complex aromas of red berries and liquorice, with hints of anise and of undergrowth. The rich, fleshy and aromatic palate still bears the mark of youthful tannins. A fine Juliénas, this wine should be drunk over the next two or three years.

☛ EARL Joëlle et Gérard Descombes, Les Préaux, 69840 Jullié, tel. 04.74.04.42.05, fax 04.74.04.48.04 ☑ ⅋ by appt.

DOM. JEAN-PIERRE MARGERAND 2000

■ 6.15 ha 10,000 ■ €5-8

A dark-red wine made using semi-carbonic maceration, Margerand's 2000 vintage is red-olent of fresh fruits (grapes), lemon drops and mignonette flowers. Soft and pleasantly fruity, it is very slightly tannic on the finish. This wine is for drinking within the year, with cold meats or coq au vin.

☛ Jean-Pierre Margerand, Les Crots, 69840 Juliénas, tel. 04.74.04.40.86, fax 04.74.04.46.54 ☑ ⅋ by appt.

DOM. DES MARRANS 1999★

■ 0.8 ha 2,700 ■ €5-8

The estate, which extends over 16 ha (40 acres) and possesses some beautiful large oak barrels, offers two *chambres d'hôte*, bed-and-breakfast rooms. Its **Fleurie 99** was commended by the Jury, while this Juliénas was awarded one star. A pretty ruby-coloured wine with purple highlights, it has an intense and complex bouquet of blackberries and raspberries, with hints of gunflint and liquorice. An attractively fleshy and rounded first impression is followed by fairly firm structure. This stylish 99 should be cellared for another year before being served with *fondue bourguignonne*.

☛ Jean-Jacques et Liliane Melinand, Les Marrans, 69820 Fleurie, tel. 04.74.04.13.21, fax 04.74.69.82.45, e-mail melinand.m@wanadoo.fr ☑ ⅋ by appt.

DOM. MATRAY

Vieilles vignes Elevé en fût de chêne 1999

■ 1 ha 8,000 ⅢⅢ €5-8

The estate spans almost 10 ha (25 acres). This special cuvée, which has been aged in oak for ten months, is a rich ruby-coloured wine with a lightly oaked, spicy, floral aroma. Flavours of very ripe fruits follow a very firm opening impression, but this lively, full and rounded wine is ready for drinking now.

☛ GAEC Daniel et Lilian Matray, Les Paquelets, 69840 Juliénas, tel. 04.74.04.45.57, fax 04.74.04.47.63, e-mail domaine.matray@wanadoo.fr ☑ ⅋ ev. day 8am-8pm

JEAN-FRANCOIS PERRAUD 2000

■ 6.94 ha 6,000 ■ ⅃ €5-8

The Jury was particularly impressed by the consistently high quality of this estate's wines. Both the **red Beaujolais-Villages 2000** and this light-coloured Juliénas were commended. The latter has powerful aromas of red fruits and bilberries, underpinned by burnt notes. With its well-balanced, fresh and reasonably full-bodied palate, this wine is for drinking within the next two years.

☛ Jean-François Perraud, Les Chanoriers, 69840 Jullié, tel. 04.74.04.49.09, fax 04.74.04.49.09, e-mail jean.francois.perraud@wanadoo.fr ☑ ⅋ by appt.

BERNARD SANTE 1999★

■ 2.5 ha 18,000 ■ €5-8

Bernard Santé took over the family estate in 1980. He made this ruby-coloured Juliénas using semi-carbonic maceration from grapes produced by 68-year-old vines. It has a warm, rich, inviting nose of very ripe, almost jammy, fruit. On the palate, the acidity and tannins are beautifully balanced, all topped off by a highly attractive finish. This wine will continue to be enjoyable for another two years.

☛ Bernard Santé, rte de Juliénas, Les Blémonts, 71570 La Chapelle-de-Guinchay, tel. 03.85.33.82.81, fax 03.85.33.84.46 ☑ ⅋ by appt.

robust, generous, fruity wine with flavours of cherry, bitter cherry and apricot. It is often the most robust of the Crus and many of its characteristics come from the soil which is made from weathered, mainly alkaline shale with deposits of ferrous oxide and manganese, described by the local wine-makers as *terre pourrie* or rotten land. It is said of the Morgon wines that they *morgonne*, ie that they develop in their own unique way. The situation of the vineyard is particularly propitious for Gamay and makes a wine that is for keeping and which, with age, can take on some of the qualities of a red Burgundy. It is a robust enough wine to drink with *coq au vin*. The soil of the Py hill, which rises 300 m (984 ft) in a perfectly shaped rump near the old Roman road between Lyon and Autun, is typical of the area.

The commune of Villié-Morgon is justifiably proud to have been the first to promote their wines, encouraging wine-drinkers who appreciate Beaujolais to visit the wine-tasting cellars in the Château de Fonterenne which can cater for several hundred visitors. The cellar has a welcoming atmosphere which is very popular with the visitors and associations who visit.

DOM. AUCOEUR Cuvée Prestige 1999

1 ha　5,000　€5-8

The Aucoeur family offers tours of the estate's cellars and an introduction to wine-tasting, as well as this purple-red wine with its strong cherry aroma. Austere tannins are perceptible on the vinous palate, and we suggest waiting for a few months for the wine's oakiness to integrate.

Dom. Aucoeur, Le Rochaud, 69910 Villié-Morgon, tel. 04.74.04.22.10, fax 04.74.69.16.82　by appt.

RAYMOND BOULAND 1999

6 ha　10,000　€5-8　by appt.

The harvest of 60-year-old vines began on 10 September 1999 to make this clear ruby-coloured wine with its distinctive ripe cherry aroma. An initial rounded impression is succeeded by tannins that are still a little severe, but the wine does have promising length on the finish. The structure of this Morgon suggests that it will be ready for drinking in late 2002.

Raymond Bouland, Corcelette, 69910 Villié-Morgon, tel. 04.74.04.22.25, fax 04.74.04.22.25　by appt.

NOEL BULLIAT

Cuvée Vieilles vignes 1999**

0.7 ha　4,000　€5-8

A rich ruby-coloured wine made from 70-year-old vines, Bulliat's Morgon has aromas of black fruits and ripe cherries, together with a perfectly modulated oak. Fine tannins and a well-balanced structure will ensure that this wine may be drunk over the next two or three years. It should be served with poultry, either roasted or in a sauce.

Noël Bulliat, Le Colombier, 69910 Villié-Morgon, tel. 04.74.69.14.09　by appt.

JEAN-MARC BURGAUD

Côte du Py 1999*

6 ha　n.c.　€5-8

A cross at the summit of the Côte du Py marks the centre of this vineyard. It has produced a ruby-coloured wine with a spicy, toasty, wild cherry aroma. Fresh and full-bodied with fine, persistent tannins, this 1999, with its flavours of stone-fruits and wild peaches, is for drinking over the next two to three years.

Jean-Marc Burgaud, Morgon, 69910 Villié-Morgon, tel. 04.74.69.16.10, fax 04.74.69.16.10, e-mail jeanmarcburgaud@libertysurf.fr
ev. day 9am–12 noon 2pm–6pm

DOM. CALOT Tête de cuvée 1999

1.3 ha　9,000　€5-8

The estate was established in 1920, but the vines, which are planted on decomposed granite soils, are only about 40 years old. They have produced a very aromatic wine whose characteristic wild cherry nose is accented by elegant touches of iris and violet. A well-balanced wine of great finesse, it should be drunk within the year.

SCEA François et Jean Calot, Le Bourg, 69910 Villié-Morgon, tel. 04.74.04.20.55, fax 04.74.69.12.93
by appt.
GFA de Corcelette

DOM. DE CHANTEMERLE 2000*

3 ha　13,000　€5-9

This garnet wine has a fragrant, slightly spicy, strawberry and raspberry bouquet. It still has the vigorous attack and dominant tannins of a young wine, but it has the potential to age well, and should be allowed two years to reach its peak. It will then make a fine accompaniment to red meat dishes.

Claude Merle, 69910 Villié-Morgon, tel. 04.74.09.60.08

on the palate are both promising, and the wine may be enjoyed over the course of 2002.

☛ EARL Janine Chaffanjon, 210, rte de Pizay, 69220 Saint-Jean-d'Ardières, tel. 04.74.66.12.18, fax 04.74.66.09.37, e-mail st.paul@wanadoo.fr ☒ ⟙ ev. day except Sun. 8am–12 noon 2pm–6pm

DOM. GAGET Côte du Py 1999★

5.2 ha   30,000   ◼ €5-8

The wine-grower was joined by his son in 1999, and this clear, rich garnet wine made from 60-year-old vines is their first jointly-produced vintage. Although the cinnamon, clove and liquorice bouquet is a little muted, the rounded, well-structured and fleshy palate displays all the best characteristics of its well-known *terroir*. This beguiling wine, which was almost awarded two stars, will be enjoyable over the course of the next three years. It would be a fine accompaniment for a haunch of venison.

☛ Dom. Gaget, La Côte du Py, 69910 Villié-Morgon, tel. 04.74.04.20.75, fax 04.74.04.21.54 ☒ ⟙ by appt.

DOM. DES GAUDETS 2000★★

1 ha   10,000   ◼ €5-8

In 1993, father and son entered into a partnership to manage this vineyard of 50-year-old vines planted on schist soils. They have made a ruby-coloured wine with a scent of kirsch. The well-balanced palate has dense and persistent tannins, allied to flavours of wild peaches and overripe fruits. This Morgon will be enjoyable for the next two to three years.

☛ Noël et Christophe Sornay, Le Brye, 69910 Villié-Morgon, tel. 04.74.04.23.65, fax 04.74.69.10.70 ☒ ⟙ by appt.

ALAIN ET GEORGES GAUTHIER

1999   1.5 ha   11,300   ◼ ▥ €5-8

One half of this wine, which is made from 80-year-old vines planted on schist soils, has been matured in vat, while the other half has had five months in oak. The resulting garnet-coloured Morgon has a well-developed aroma of red berries with a hint of jasmine. Its rich texture reveals slightly chewy tannins that should be allowed to ripen for a few months. This will then be an attractive wine to serve at an informal dinner.

FRANCK CHAVY

Cuvée vieillie en fût de chêne 1999★

n.c.   9,000   ◼ ▥ ♦ €5-8

This Morgon has been vinified using modern technology and matured in a manner more commonly associated with Burgundy, yet it remains true to its appellation. It has a deep-red, youthful appearance, and an oaky bouquet with hints of red fruits. Displaying a good balance of oak and fine tannins on the palate, this distinctive wine is still full of youthful freshness, despite being quite rich. It will respond well to being kept for at least a year, and would complement game.

☛ Franck Chavy, Le Chazelay, 69430 Régnié-Durette, tel. 04.74.04.80.26, fax 04.74.69.20.00 ☒ ⟙ by appt.

LOUIS CHAVY 2000

n.c.   18,000   ◼ €8-11

A *négociant* based in the Côte d'Or made this wine. It has the floral and wild cherry aromas typical of a Morgon, but at present, young tannins dominate its rather light palate. The wine should be allowed to mature for a few months longer.

☛ Louis Chavy, Caveau la Vierge Romaine, pl. des Marronniers, 21190 Puligny-Montrachet, tel. 03.80.26.33.00, fax 03.80.24.14.84, e-mail mallet.b@eva-beaune.fr ☒ ⟙ ev. day 10am–6pm; cl. Nov.–Mar.

DOM. DU CHAZELAY 1999★

3 ha   10,000   ◼ €5-8

Made from the harvest of 60-year-old vines and aged in vats for seven months, this classically-styled purple-red wine has a pure, intense aroma of very ripe red berries. Firm tannic structure and full flavour characterise the distinctive palate. This is a well-balanced and powerful wine that should be drunk within the year with coq au vin.

☛ Henri Chavy, Le Chazelay, 69430 Régnié-Durette, tel. 04.74.69.24.34, fax 04.74.69.20.00 ☒ ⟙ by appt.

LA MAISON DES VIGNERONS DE CHIROUBLES

Cuvée de la Chenevière 1999★

2.72 ha   20,000   ◼ €5-8

The co-operative, formed in 1929, has made a rich purple Morgon with an attractive, fairly intense bouquet of red fruits. Soft tannins support the full-bodied and aromatic palate. This rounded and well-balanced classic Morgon is for drinking within the year with a roast leg of lamb.

☛ La Maison des Vignerons de Chiroubles, Le Bourg, 69115 Chiroubles, tel. 04.74.69.14.94, fax 04.74.69.10.59 ☒ ⟙ ev. day 10am–12.30pm 2.30pm–6pm

DOM. DE CLOS SAINT-PAUL 1999

1.3 ha   12,000   ◼ €5-8

This bright-garnet wine has a powerful bouquet of red berries with spicy overtones. The characteristic aromas and young tannins

🍷 Alain et Georges Gauthier, EARL des Rochauds, La Roche Pilée, 69910 Villié-Morgon, tel. 04.74.69.15.87, fax 04.74.69.15.87 ☎ by appt.

MADAME ARTHUR GEOFFROY

2000 | 0.58 ha | 4,000 | €5-8

Vines planted on schist soil have produced a garnet wine with scents of cherries and black fruits. The fleshy, rounded and wonderfully aromatic palate has a straightforward style and fine tannins. This wine is for drinking within the year with poultry or red meat dishes.

🍷 Louise Geoffroy, Le Pré Jourdan, BP 17, 69910 Villié-Morgon, tel. 04.74.04.23.57, fax 04.74.69.13.45 ☎ by appt.

DOM. DE GRY-SABLON 2000★★

2.3 ha | 17,000 | €5-8

This rich ruby-coloured wine can be sampled in the estate's newly-equipped tasting cellar. Bilberry and redcurrant jelly aromas develop slowly, gathering hints of saffron and cinnamon. Excellent tannins are enveloped by the wine's superbly rounded, rich textures. Its remarkable structure and long finish guarantee that this 2000 vintage will keep well for the next three to four years. It would perfectly complement a rib of beef.

🍷 Dominique Morel, Les Chavannes, 69840 Emeringes, tel. 04.74.04.45.35, fax 04.74.04.42.66, e-mail gry-sablon@wanadoo.fr ☎ ev. day except Sun. 8am-6pm

DOM. DE JAVERNIERE 2000★

1 ha | 6,600 | €5-8

Noël Lacoque, a fourth-generation wine-grower, has been managing this estate since 1974. He has made a wine with a gorgeous colour halfway between rubies and garnets. Powerful, pure aromas of violets, highlighted by hints of green peppers and spices, combine with a sturdy but balanced palate to create a robust and balanced wine that will age well. This distinctive Morgon will continue to seduce drinkers over the next three to four years.

🍷 Noël Lacoque, Javernière, 69910 Villié-Morgon, tel. 04.74.04.24.26 ☑

DOM. DE JAVERNIERE 2000★

1 ha | 5,000 | €5-8

Yet another Domaine de Javernière, this one is managed by the fifth generation of the Lacoque family. Their attractive ruby-coloured wine with purple highlights has well-developed oak overlaying an aroma of undergrowth, with hints of toast and leather. The wild-cherry and stone-fruit aromas characteristic of Morgon appear on the palate. A powerful wine with tightly-knit, persistent tannins, this 2000 vintage has the structure to stand up to three or four years' bottle-ageing, perhaps even longer.

🍷 Hervé Lacoque, Javernière, 69910 Villié-Morgon, tel. 04.74.04.26.64 ☑ ☎ by appt.

DOM. DE LA SERVE DES VIGNES

2000 | n.c. | n.c. | €8-11

The *négociant*, Pierre Dupond, presented the Jury with a well-made wine that has the rich mineral aromas typical of Morgon. Rather firm tannins follow a forthright attack, but this carefully-made, lengthy wine is beginning to round out and will soon be ready to drink.

🍷 Pierre Dupond, 235, rue de Thizy, 69653 Villefranche-sur-Saone, tel. 04.74.65.24.32, fax 04.74.68.04.14, e-mail p.dupond@seldon.fr

DOM. DE LA COTE DES CHARMES Les Charmes 2000

6 ha | 11,000 | €5-8

Jacques Trichard has been running this 9-ha (22-acre) estate since 1969. His garnet-coloured wine with purple highlights comes from the schist soils of the Les Charmes *climat*. It has a fine bouquet of wild cherries, and flavours of forest fruits, on its rich, structured palate. This well-made wine is suitable for keeping, and should be ready in two to three years' time.

🍷 Jacques Trichard, Les Charmes, 69910 Villié-Morgon, tel. 04.74.04.20.35, fax 04.74.69.13.49 ☑ ☎ by appt.

DOM. DE LA CHANAISE

Côte du Py 1999★

3.5 ha | 20,000 | €8-11

This family estate dates back to the 16th century. Its rich garnet-hued 99 has a complex and intense bouquet of stone fruits, dried fruits and peonies. A fleshy and fruity first impression is followed by supple and elegant tannins. Cask-ageing has imparted a subtle woody note to the fine ripe-fruit aromas perceptible on the palate. This attractive, classic Morgon has sufficient structure to last for up to three years.

🍷 Dominique Piron, Morgon, 69910 Villié-Morgon, tel. 04.74.69.10.20, fax 04.74.69.16.65, e-mail dominique-piron@domaines-piron.fr ☑ ☎ by appt.

DOM. DE LA BECHE

Cuvée Vieilles vignes 1999

2 ha | 12,000 | €5-8

Sixty-year-old vines planted on pebbly marl soil have produced a wine with a deliciously fruity bouquet. The tannins on its well-structured palate need to ripen for a few more months, however.

🍷 Olivier Depardon, Dom. de La Bèche, 69910 Villié-Morgon, tel. 04.74.04.21.88 ☑ ☎ by appt.

Moulin à Vent

The domain of the 'lord' of the Beaujolais Crus is 676 ha (1,670 acres) of vineyard stretching over the communes of Chénas in the Rhône and Romanèche-Thorins in Saône-et-Loire. The

CH. DE PIZAY 2000
■ 19 ha 150,000 €5-8

The château, with its square donjon, 15th-century turrets, 18th-century chapel, and various additions dating from both the Renaissance era and the 19th century, is run as a vast hotel complex and wine enterprise. As well as the white Beaujolais 2000 that was singled out by the jury, it has produced this ruby-coloured Morgon with a floral and fruity bouquet. The light but appealing palate makes this a wine for drinking within the year.
➤ SCEA Dom. Château de Pizay, 69220 Saint-Jean-d'Ardières, tel. 04.74.66.20.10, fax 04.74.69.60.66 ☑ by appt.

DOM. DE ROCHE SAINT JEAN
Côte de Py 1999★
■ 2.43 ha 5,500

The estate spans more than 13 ha (32 acres). A vineyard with south-east exposure has produced this rich ruby-coloured wine with a complex bouquet of very ripe red fruits. A rich opening impression is followed by a fleshy and attractive palate that is pure Morgon. This 99 should be drunk within the year, with either red or white meat dishes.
➤ SCEA Bernard Mathon, Bellevue, dom. de Roche-Saint-Jean, 69910 Villié-Morgon, tel. 04.74.04.23.92, fax 04.74.04.23.92 ☑ by appt.

MONIQUE ET MAURICE SORNAY
1999 n.c. 10,000 €5-8

The jurors unanimously praised this wine's vividly-perfumed bouquet (violet mixed with iris and fresh green pepper) and its seductive, aromatic tannins. Rounded and velvety, it is a distinctive and elegant wine for drinking within the year.
➤ EARL Sornay-Aucoeur, Fondlong, 69910 Villié-Morgon, tel. 04.74.04.22.97, fax 04.74.04.22.97 ☑ by appt.

DOM. DES SOUCHONS
Cuvée Tradition 1999★
■ 10 ha 60,000 €5-8

This domaine, which was established in 1752, has made a youthful-looking garnet wine from the harvest of 40-year-old vines growing on marl soil. It has an attractive, fine, fruity and floral aroma, and is soft on the palate. A charming, velvety wine, it could be drunk this year but will also keep well for another year or two.
➤ Serge Condemine-Pillet, Morgon-le-Bas, 69910 Villié-Morgon, tel. 04.74.69.14.45, fax 04.74.69.15.43, e-mail domainesouchons@free.fr ☑ ev. day 8am–12 noon 2pm–7pm; cl. 23 Dec.–2 Jan.

DOM. DE L'HERMINETTE 1999
■ 4 ha 20,000 €5-8

François Paquet is a négociant house with headquarters near the village of Vaux (immortalised in Clochemerle). Its rich garnet wine has subtle aromas of cherries and blackberries. The lively, tannic character of its full-bodied palate indicates that this 99, with its spicy (liquorice) finish, should be kept for several months. It will then make a fine companion for coq au vin.
➤ Maison François Paquet, B.P. 1, Le Trève, 69460 Le Perréon, tel. 04.74.02.10.10, fax 04.74.03.26.99 ☑

DOM. DU MARGUILLIER 2000
■ 6 ha 37,000 €5-8

This cherry-red wine exudes a spicy, clove-scented aroma. After a supple and rounded opening impression, the palate becomes more rustic and robust. This young Morgon has good potential, however, and should be given a year to mature.
➤ Noël et Christophe Sornay, 69830 Villié-Morgon, tel. 04.74.09.60.08

DOM. PASSOT-COLLONGE
Les Charmes 1999 n.c. 8,000 €5-8

This family-owned estate, located 800 m (870 yd) from the Château de Fontcrenne, was renovated in 1990. It has produced a luscious and powerful dark-garnet wine that is full-bodied and structured. This Morgon should be allowed to breathe and develop its full flavours, before being served with a game bird.
➤ Bernard et Monique Passot, Le Colombier, rte de Fleurie, 69910 Villié-Morgon, tel. 04.74.69.10.77, fax 04.74.69.13.59 ☑ by appt.

DOM. DES PILLETS
Vieilles vignes 1999★★
■ 8 ha 5,000 €5-8

The Roman road from Lyons to Autun crosses this vineyard that once belonged to the seigneurs of Fontcrenne de Villié. The dark-purple 1999 Morgon has intense, rich aromas of plum jam and quince jelly. Very ripe fruit flavours can be discerned on the well-balanced, soft, long palate. This remarkable wine will continue to be enjoyable for the next two to three years.
➤ GFA Les Pillets, Les Pillets, 69910 Villié-Morgon, tel. 04.74.04.21.60, fax 04.74.69.15.28 ☑ ev. day except Sun. 9am–12 noon 1.30pm–7pm; cl. 15 days in Aug, and 24 Dec.–2 Jan.
➤ Gérard Brisson

Moulin à Vent

emblem of the appellation is an ancient windmill at Les Thorins, standing proudly on the top of a gently rounded hillock, 240 m (787 ft) high, consisting of pure granite sand. The vineyard produces 38,600 hl (1,019,040 gal) of wine made from Gamay grapes. The thin topsoil is rich in manganese and other minerals which give the wines their strong, deep colour and scent of iris. These are full-bodied wines, sometimes reminiscent of their sturdier Burgundy cousins in the Côte-d'Or. Each year, in a traditional rite, the vintage is carried to the baptismal fonts in the local villages, starting at Romanèche-Thorins at the end of October and finishing at the 'capital' in early December.

Moulin à Vent can readily be drunk young, in its first few months, but also keeps well for a number of years. This 'prince' of wines was one of the first Crus recognised as an Appellation d'Origine Contrôlée in 1936, after its borders were legally defined by the Civil Tribunal in Mâcon. There are two wine-cellars where you can taste the wine: one at the foot of the windmill and the other at the edge of the main road. Moulin à Vent will accompany any dish and hold its own against many other reds.

DOM. BOURISSET
5 ha   35,000   2000

A vineyard near the famous windmill (*moulin à vent*) that gives its name to this appellation has produced this dark-garnet wine. It has a slightly shy, but attractive, bouquet of flowers and blackcurrants, with mineral overtones. The somewhat sinewy tannins evident on its youthful palate need more time to soften. A rich, concentrated and aromatic wine, it will be extremely enjoyable in two to three years.

• Collin-Bourisset Vins Fins, av. de la Gare, 71680 Crèches-sur-Saône, tel. 03.85.36.57.25, fax 03.85.37.15.38, e-mail cbourisset@gofornet.com by appt.

CH. BONNET Vieilles vignes 2000★
1.7 ha   12,000   €5-8   by appt.

Part of this pretty 7-ha (17-acre) estate, which dates back to 1630, is now being managed by the owner's son. His garnet-coloured wine has an evanescent, musky scent that develops towards spicy redcurrant and raspberry tones. The full aromatic character of this youthful 99 only becomes apparent on its lively and well-balanced palate. It should be drunk over the course of the next two years.

• Pierre-Yves Perrachon, Ch. Bonnet, 71570 La Chapelle-de-Guinchay, tel. 03.85.36.70.41, fax 03.85.36.77.27, e-mail chbonnet@terre.net.fr by appt.

PIERRE CHANAU 1999★
7.75 ha   60,000   €5-8

This light ruby-coloured 99 is made by Maison Thorin for the Auchan supermarket chain. It has intense, complex aromas of red and black fruits with floral and spicy overtones. There is a good balance of fruit and tannin on the palate, which lacks for nothing in vinosity. An attractive wine, it should be drunk within the next two years with red meats or a fish stew.

• Auchan, 200, rue de la Recherche, 59650 Villeneuve-d'Ascq, tel. 04.74.69.09.10, fax 04.74.69.09.28 by appt.

JACQUES CHARLET
Champ de Cour 2000

This is a light ruby-coloured wine with pretty purple highlights. It has very subtle but fine aromas of blackcurrants and cooked fruit. The well-balanced palate has a pronounced vegetal character at first, which is then superseded by long vanilla notes. This wine needs time to mature.

DOM. CHAMPAGNON 2000
2.99 ha   19,000   €5-8

This bright-red wine has been aged in barrel for six months. It has powerful aromas of cherries and blackcurrants that continue on to the palate. A supple and fruity first impression is followed by the more astringent impact of young tannins, but it will be a classy and easy-drinking wine if it is kept for another few months.

• EARL du Dom. Champagnon, Les Bruraux, 69840 Chénas, tel. 03.85.36.71.32, fax 03.85.36.72.00, e-mail champagnon.gaec@compuserve.com ev. day 8am-8pm

DOM. DE CHAMP DE COUR
Réserve 1999★
2 ha   15,000   €8-11

The Mommessin family owns this estate. Its 1999 Moulin à Vent has been aged for six months in used oak barrels from the family's Grand Cru Burgundy estate, *Clos de Tart*. This dark ruby-coloured wine has a fairly powerful vanilla aroma with floral hints, and its vinous, oaky palate has good balance. It should be drunk over the course of 2002.

• GFA Champ de Cour, 71570 Romanèche-Thorins, tel. 04.74.69.09.30, fax 04.74.69.09.28

Moulin à Vent

LA BRUYERE 1999
■ 1 ha 6,000 €15-23

This Moulin à Vent comes from a Beaune *négociant* house that generally specialises in Côte d'Or wines. The deep peony-red wine has an elegant aroma of vanilla-scented plums. A rounded and powerful wine, it is ready to drink now, but would improve further if kept for a year.
- Pierre André, Ch. de Corton-André, 21420 Aloxe-Corton, tel. 03.80.26.44.25, fax 03.80.26.43.57, e-mail pandre@axnet.fr

DOM. DE LA TEPPE 1999
■ 4.5 ha 9,000

Located 500 m (545 yd) from the Musée du Compagnonnage, which traces the history of the Carpenters' Guild, this fifth-generation family estate embraces more than 20 ha (49 acres) of vineyards. This rich ruby-coloured wine, with its complex bouquet of red fruits, dried flowers and undergrowth, displays attractive, spicy notes on the palate. The slightly tannic finish is beginning to soften, and the wine should be drunk within the year.
- EARL Robert et Pierre Bouzereau, Dom. de La Teppe, 71570 Romanèche-Thorins, tel. 03.85.35.52.47, fax 03.85.35.52.47 Y by appt.

J. GONARD ET FILS 2000★
■ 1 ha 7,000 €5-8

This *négociant* specialises in Mâconnais and Beaujolais wines. It presented the Jury with a dark-garnet wine redolent of spiced red berries and stone fruits. The powerful, rounded and fruity palate is nicely balanced. This well-made, attractive wine should be drunk within the next two years.
- J. Gonard et Fils, La Varenne, Jullie, 69840 Juliénas, tel. 04.74.04.45.20, fax 04.74.04.45.69 Y ev. day 9am–12 noon 2pm–7pm

- Jacques Charlet, 71570 La Chapelle-de-Guinchay, tel. 03.85.36.82.41, fax 03.85.33.83.19

DOM. GAY-COPERET 2000
■ 5 ha 8,000 €5-8

In an exemplary gesture of equality, this couple have named their estate with their combined surnames. Their dark, almost purple, red wine has a peony aroma with liquorice overtones and a robust, well-structured palate. Although it is still rather young and unsophisticated, it has great potential, and deserves to be kept for two to three years.
- Catherine et Maurice Gay, Les Vérillats, 69840 Chénas, tel. 04.74.04.48.86, fax 04.74.04.42.74
Y by appt.

DOM. DU HAUT-PONCIE 1999★
3.2 ha 6,800 €8-11

Vines growing on manganese-rich soils have produced this clear ruby-coloured wine with its pure, fine bouquet of vanilla and preserved red fruits. It is rich, well-balanced and long, with a rounded and well-structured palate that shows subtle oak influence with hints of liquorice. A classic Moulin à Vent, it is ready to drink now, but could also be kept for a further two years.
- Dom. du Haut-Poncié, 69820 Fleurie, tel. 04.74.04.16.06, fax 04.74.69.89.97 Y ev. day 8am–8pm; Sun. by appt.

CH. DES JACQUES 1999★
22 ha 20,000 €11-15

Traditional viticultural methods and a long pre-ferment maceration have resulted in a rich ruby-coloured wine with a bouquet of wild blackberries and mineral notes. This full and rich 99 is still lively, and has a more pronounced mineral character on the palate. It will continue to be enjoyable for the next two to three years, and would benefit from being treated like a burgundy and decanted before serving.
- Ch. des Jacques, 71570 Romanèche-Thorins, tel. 03.85.35.51.64, fax 03.85.35.59.15, e-mail chateau-des-jacques@wanadoo.fr Y by appt.
- Maison Louis Jadot

DOM. DE LA TOUR DU BIEF 1999
■ n.c. 9,800 €8-11

In Charnay, where this *négociant* has its headquarters, there is a church with a Norman apse and belfry. At first, this dark ruby-coloured wine has a rather restrained bouquet, but then liquorice and undergrowth aromas develop slowly. A well-balanced, fine and lengthy wine, it is mature now, and should be drunk within the next two years.
- Trénel Fils, 33, chem. du Buéry, 71850 Charnay-lès-Mâcon, tel. 03.85.34.48.20, fax 03.85.20.55.01, e-mail info@trenel.com
Y ev. day except Sun. 8am–12 noon 1.30pm–6pm; Mon. 1.30pm–6pm Sat. 8am–12 noon

DOM. JACQUES ET ANNIE LORON 2000★
La Rochelle 2000★
■ 2 ha 8,000 €5-8

A Chénas 2000, commended by the Jury, and then dark purple Moulin were both made from harvests of 50-year-old vines. An appealing rose and peony aroma is backed up by cinnamon and saffron overtones. This full-bodied, ample and well-structured wine will continue to develop for the next two or three years.
- EARL Jacques et Annie Loron, Les Blancs, 69840 Chénas, tel. 04.74.04.48.76, fax 04.74.04.42.14 Y by appt.

DOM. DU MATINAL 2000
■ 4 ha 8,000 €5-8

Both of the appellations encompassed by this 6.3-ha (16-acre) estate were commended by the Jury: a **Chénas 2000**, vat-aged for seven months, and this Moulin à Vent, which was matured in barrel for eight months. A delicate red in colour, it has a fine, persistent aroma of grapes and preserved fruits, with a hint of oak. The young and supple palate has just the right amount of body, wine is for drinking within the year.

➤ EARL Simone et Guy Braillon, Le Bourg, 69840 Chénas, tel. 04.74.04.47.64 fax 04.74.04.47.64 ▾ ev. day 9am–8pm; groups by appt.; cl. mid-Aug.

CH. DES MICHAUDS 2000

4 ha   6,400   €5-8

Matured in one of the most beautiful vaulted cellars in the region, this garnet-coloured wine, with its spicy aromas of flowers and fresh red fruits, is still youthful. Attractive tannins are perceptible on the long and fruity palate. This is a well-made wine which should be kept for a year so that it can continue developing and display its full potential.

➤ Ch. de Chénas, 69880 Chénas, tel. 04.74.06.10.10, fax 04.74.66.13.77 ▾

CH. DU MOULIN A VENT 1999★

29.4 ha   28,000   €8-11

This deep ruby-coloured wine has a complex bouquet of toast, spices and very ripe fruit. The fleshy, rich palate tastes of spicy preserved fruits. This wine is for drinking within the next two years with red meat or game. (The wine-maker has added the phrase *cuvée exceptionelle* to the label to distinguish it from the wine that was not cask-matured).

➤ Ch. du Moulin à Vent, 71570 Romanèche-Thorins, tel. 03.85.35.50.68, fax 03.85.35.20.06 ▾ ▾ ev. day 9am–12 noon 2pm–6pm; Sat. Sun. by appt.

➤ Flornoy-Bloud

DOM. DU MOULIN D'EOLE

Les Thorins Réserve 1999★

1.72 ha   13,000   €8-11

The 1998 vintage from this estate was selected as a *coup de cœur* last year. This time, the clear and bright ruby-coloured 99 was awarded one star. It has a fine red fruit aroma in which hints of liquorice, pepper, cinnamon and cloves are also perceptible. Ripe and persistent tannins coat the palate. This classy wine is ready to drink now, but will also keep, and continue to improve, for a further two years. It would be a fine complement to a haunch of venison.

➤ Philippe Guérin, Le Bourg, 69840 Chénas, tel. 04.74.04.46.88, fax 04.74.04.47.29 ▾ ▾ ev. day except Sun. 9am–12 noon 2pm–7pm

GEORGES ET MONIQUE PERRAUD 1999

1.26 ha   9,000   €5-8

Generations of the same family have been managing this estate since 1560. Their bright ruby-coloured 99 has a red-berry aroma with a strong vanilla accent. The appealingly fresh palate is still very oaky, but it should become more balanced as it matures. We suggest keeping it for one to two years.

➤ Georges et Monique Perraud, 69820 Vauxrenard, tel. 04.74.69.90.47 ▾ by appt.

LES VIGNERONS DU PRIEURE

Roche Gré 1999

n.c.   n.c.   €5-8

Eighty-three wine-growers joined together to establish this cellar in 1960. Now, there are 255 members working a total of 270 ha (670 acres). The clear, fortnight Moulin à Vent 99 has a fruity nose with slight vanilla overtones and is quite long on the palate. The overtly tannic structure of the wine should have softened in a few months' time.

➤ Les Vignerons du Prieuré, Ch., du Bois de la Salle, 69840 Juliénas, tel. 04.74.04.41.66, fax 04.74.04.47.05 ▾ by appt.

DOM. BENOIT TRICHARD

Mortperay 1999★

6.5 ha   30,000   €8-11

This wine-grower, who practises environmentally sustainable viticulture, is a regular in the *Guide*. This year, the Jury commended his **Brouilly 2000**, and awarded a star for this dark wine with brick-red highlights. Although a bit timid at first, the palate is rich, well-balanced and long. This beautifully-constituted wine has just the right degree of oak and plenty of personality. It should be drunk within the next two years.

➤ Dom. Benoît Trichard, Le Vieux-Bourg, 69460 Odenas, tel. 04.74.03.52.02, fax 04.74.03.52.02, e-mail dbtricha@ club-internet.fr ▾ by appt.

DOM. DU POURPRE 2000★

9.5 ha   20,000   €5-8

Both of the 2000 vintage wines made by this estate were selected for the *Guide*. The Jury commended the **Chénas**, and awarded this wine a star. The dark red Moulin à Vent has peony and rose aromas accented by a touch of cherry preserve. After a fresh initial impression, the wine is round, rich and soft on the palate. The dense, sinewy tannins that appear on the finish dictate that this wine should be kept for a further two or three years before drinking.

➤ EARL Dom. du Pourpre, Les Pinchons, 69840 Chénas, tel. 04.74.04.48.81, fax 04.74.04.49.22 ▾ ▾ ev. day 8am–8pm

➤ Méziat

Régnié

Régnié was officially recognised in 1988. This recent Cru closes the breach between Morgon to the north and Brouilly to the south, extending the limits of the ten Beaujolais appellations.

Apart from a tiny parcel of 5.93 ha (15 acres) on the neighbouring commune of Lantignié, the 746 ha (1,843 acres) of the appellation are all in the area of Régnié-Durette. As is the case with Morgon, its older sibling, the single village name Régnié designates the wine. Only 500 ha (1,235 acres) were declared as AOC Régnié in 2000 with an output of 28,900 hl (762,960 gal).

The aspect of the commune is north-west and south-east, so the vineyards get sun most of the day, and they may be planted on the hillsides from 300 m (984 ft) to as high as 500 m (1,640 ft) up.

The hillsides are part of the granite Fleurie range, and the mainly sandy and stony soil is exclusively planted to Gamay. There are, however, some areas which also contain some clay.

The vines are cultivated like all the other local appellations and the wines are made in the same way. However, an exception in the local regulations means that the wine-makers of Régnié are unable to request an AOC Bourgogne for their wines.

In the Caveau des Deux Clochers – the church it is next to has unusual architecture, symbolising wine – you can taste examples of the 33,880 hl (894,432 gal) of local wines. They are fruitily aromatic with scents of redcurrant, strawberries and flowers. Overall, they are fleshy and supple, well balanced and elegant, sometimes described as 'frivolous', 'fun' or 'feminine' wines.

DOM. DES BOIS 1999
■   1.32 ha   11,000   ■❙❶◗   €5-8

Visitors to the estate can take up room and board and, if they wish, receive an introduction to the arts of viticulture and wine-making. The very bright, ruby-coloured wine has a faintly spicy, cherry aroma. Light, balanced and fresh, this pleasing wine is for drinking now, with charcuterie.
- Roger and Marie-Hélène Labruyère, Les Bois, 69430 Régnié-Durette, tel. 04.74.04.24.09, fax 04.74.69.15.16, e-mail roger.labruyere@wanadoo.fr ☑
Y by appt.

DOM. DES BRAVES 2000
■   4 ha   10,000   ◗   €5-8

Franck Cinquin, who has managed this estate since 1989, has thermovinified his harvest to create a bright ruby-coloured wine with pretty purple highlights and great charm. It has complex and intense spicy ripe-fruit aromas. A rounded opening impression leads to a lively, vegetal palate that somewhat contradicts the expectations raised by the nose. This is a wine that should be kept for a while, although one taster felt that it was more or less ready now.
- Franck Cinquin, les Grandes Bruyères, 69430 Régnié-Durette, tel. 04.74.66.88.08, fax 04.74.66.88.08 ☑ by appt.
- Paul Cinquin

DOM. DES BRAVES 2000
■   9 ha   30,000   ◗   €5-8

Another wine to receive thermovinification treatment, this garnet-coloured Régnié has pronounced aromas of pear drops and black fruits. After a supple opening, the youthful palate displays a touch of acidity, but this is a fresh and fruity wine for drinking within the year.
- Paul Cinquin, Les Braves, 69430 Régnié-Durette, tel. 04.74.04.31.11, fax 04.74.04.32.17 ☑ Y by appt.

DOM. DES BUYATS 2000
■   1 ha   7,000   ◗   €5-8

The cellars of this domaine, which date back to 1822, have produced a purple-ruby wine with a lightly spicy and floral bouquet of red fruits. Rustic tannins dominate the firm, peppery palate for the time being, but in a year's time they will have ripened, and this well-balanced wine, with its appealing aroma, will be ready to drink.
- Pierre Coillard, Dom. des Buyats, Les Bulliats, 69430 Régnié-Durette, tel. 04.74.04.35.37, fax 04.74.69.02.93 ☑ Y by appt.

DOM. DE COLONAT
Cuvée Vieilles vignes 2000
■   0.76 ha   5,600   ■   €5-8

Bernard Collonge comes from a family of wine-makers that has cultivated this estate since the 17th century. Since taking over the estate in 1977, he has made several wines that have been selected as *coups de cœur* by the

Guide. This bright ruby-coloured 2000 vintage has a fine aroma of very ripe red berries. A well-balanced wine, it should be drunk within the year.

☎ Bernard Collonge, Dom. de Colonat, Saint-Joseph, 69910 Villié-Morgon, tel. 04.74.69.91.43, fax 04.74.69.92.47 [V]
[Y] by appt.

FRANCOIS ET MONIQUE DESIGAUD 1999*
4 ha | 4,000 | €5-8

The estate is equidistant from Villié-Morgon and Régnié-Durette, and overlooked by the nearby village of Saint-Joseph. The pretty, ruby-coloured 99 has powerful aromas of very ripe grapes and spices, which continue appealingly on to the palate. The fresh, clean attack announces a full-bodied wine with silky tannins. It should be kept for a few months before drinking.

☎ François et Monique Désigaud, Les Fûts, 69430 Régnié-Durette, tel. 04.74.69.92.68, fax 04.74.69.92.68 [V] [Y] by appt.

HOSPICES DE BEAUJEU
Cuvée La Plaigne 1999

This *négociant*, established in 1820, presented the Jury with a clear ruby-coloured wine that was bought at the famous candle-lit auction at the Hospices de Beaujeu. The vivid raspberry and redcurrant aromas with liquorice overtones blend with soft tannins on the palate. This soft, fresh and fruity wine can be enjoyed for the next two to three years, and would complement charcuterie.

☎ Pardon et Fils, 39, rue du Gai-Leclerc, 69430 Beaujeu, tel. 04.74.04.86.97, fax 04.74.69.24.08, e-mail pardon-fils.vins@wanadoo.fr [V] [Y] ev. day except Sat. Sun. 8am-12 noon 2pm-6pm; cl. Aug.

DOM. DOMINIQUE JAMBON
2000* | 3 ha | 4,000 | €5-8

Dominique Jambon acquired his own estate in 1995 after having been a *métayer* (a farmer) for many years. The Jury awarded a commendation to his **Morgon 2000**, and honoured this dark-purple Régnié with a star. It has a reasonably aromatic, complex nose of violets and black fruits (blackberries). A sound impression of fullness on the palate unfolds to reveal a well-structured, fruity wine that will age well. It should be kept for one year.

☎ Dominique Jambon, Arnas, 69430 Lantignié, tel. 04.74.04.80.59, fax 04.74.04.80.59 [Y] by appt.

DIDIER LAGNEAU 2000
1.8 ha | n.c. | €5-8

Didier Lagneau took over the running of the family estate in 1999. The spicy, red-berry aromas on the nose of his vivid red wine are echoed on the palate. Aromatic with nicely balanced, if slightly obtrusive, tannins, this is a wine for drinking within the year.

189

☎ Didier Lagneau, Huire, 69430 Quincié-en-Beaujolais, tel. 04.74.69.20.70, fax 04.74.04.89.44 [V] [Y] by appt.

GERARD ET JEANNINE LAGNEAU 2000
6.5 ha | 10,000 | €5-8

This family-owned estate has four *chambres d'hôte* (bed-and-breakfast rooms). Its **Beaujolais-Villages 2000** received a commendation from the Jury. This Régnié opens up quickly with subtle, spicy, raspberry aromas. The attractive palate is also fruity and spicy with a long finish, and has soft tannins that need a little more time. It should be drunk over the next two years.

☎ Gérard et Jeannine Lagneau, Huire, 69430 Quincié-en-Beaujolais, tel. 04.74.69.20.70, fax 04.74.04.89.44 [V] [Y] by appt.

DOM. DE LA GRANGE CHARTON 1999
3.44 ha | 25,000 | €5-8

The label on this wine depicts a traditional vineyard worker's home. The rich ruby-coloured 99 has a scent of redcurrants. After a straightforward opening impression, the palate is a little thinly-textured, with light tannins. This appealing wine is ready now, and should be drunk within the year with white meat dishes.

☎ Maison Thorin, Le Pont des Samsons, 69430 Quincié-en-Beaujolais, tel. 04.74.69.09.10, fax 04.74.69.09.28, e-mail information@maisonthorin.com

DOM. DE LA PLAIGNE 2000
9.5 ha | 40,000 | €5-8

This cuvée is a well-judged blend of traditionally vinified and thermovinified musts. It has a rich ruby colour and a bouquet of raspberries, dried fruits and flowers. The fruity, but rather lightly-structured palate suggests that this is a wine that should be consumed within the next two years.

☎ Gilles et Cécile Roux, La Plaigne, 69430 Régnié-Durette, tel. 04.74.04.80.86, fax 04.74.04.83.72 [V] [Y] by appt.

DENIS ET VALERIE MATRAY 1999
4.75 ha | 4,000 | €3-5

This family of wine-growers cultivates one of the vineyards of the Hospices de Beaujeu. Its wine has a youthful ruby colour and attractive spicy and fruity aromas. The fleshy, well-balanced and long palate is at just the right stage of development. Drink this wine within the year.

☎ Denis Matray, La Plaigne, 69430 Régnié-Durette, tel. 04.74.69.22.54, fax 04.74.69.22.54 [Y] ev. day except Sun. 9am-12 noon 2pm-7pm.

JEAN-LUC PROLANGE 2000**
6.3 ha | 10,000 | €3-5

This wine-grower began his career as the cellarman for the Hospices de Beaujeu estate. He has since taken over the family *métayage*.

Saint-Amour

The appellation has become a great favourite with wine-drinkers outside France and a large proportion of the wine is exported. Visitors to Plâtre-Durant can taste Saint-Amour in a cellar which was established in 1965, before continuing to the church and the town hall which, standing on a hill 309 m (1,014 ft) high, dominates the region. On the corner by the church there is a statue commemorating the conversion of the Roman soldier after whom the commune is named.

His very dark red wine with blue highlights has powerful and complex aromas of strawberries and violets, with mineral overtones and hints of very ripe blackcurrants and redcurrants. Seductively fleshy and rounded on the palate, it is an extremely full-flavoured and aromatic wine, with a slightly firmer tannic impression appearing right at the end. The wine's impressive grip and structure suggest that it will age well, and it should be kept for one to two years.

☞ Jean-Luc Prolange, Les Vergers, 69430 Régnié-Durette, tel. 04.74.69.00.22, fax 04.74.69.00.22, ☑ ⵂ by appt.
☞ Yemeniz

DOM. DE VERNUS 1999
■ 1.5 ha 3,500 ■ ♦ €5-8

The estate is named after the village in which it is located. It has made a carmine-hued wine with a well-developed bouquet of pepper, black fruits and lychees. Rounded and very aromatic on the palate, this is a slightly unusual, but attractive, wine that is ready to drink now.

☞ Alain Démule, La Roche, 69430 Quincié-en-Beaujolais, tel. 04.74.04.31.30, fax 04.74.04.31.37 ☑ ⵂ by appt.

CH. DE BELLEVERNE 2000
■ 4 ha 15,000 ■ ♦ €8-11

This wine has been made in the cellars of a château that dates from 1800. Purple-red in colour, it has rather shy toasty and spicy aromas. The palate is soft, with delicate bilberry and cherry flavours. A light but well-balanced wine, it is ready to drink now.

☞ Sylvie Bataillard, Ch. de Belleverne, rue Jules Chauvet, 71570 La Chapelle-de-Guinchay, tel. 03.85.36.71.06, fax 03.85.33.86.41 ☑ ⵂ ev. day except Sun. 8am–12 noon 1.30pm–6pm

Saint-Amour

All 317 ha (783 acres) of the Appellation Saint-Amour are in the department of Saône-et-Loire, producing some 18,244 hl (481,642 gal) of wine. The soil is decalcified sandstone and clay and granite pebbles, and forms the boundary between the primary rock of the south and the limestone soils of neighbouring Mâcon and Saint-Véran in the north. Two different approaches are taken to bringing out the qualities of the Gamay grape: the first, using grapes grown on the granite rocks, favours the traditional method of long fermentation in vats, creating wines with body and strong colour that are made to keep; the second is better adapted to Primeur wines which can be drunk early and so assuage the curiosity of wine-lovers. Saint-Amour goes well with snails, fried fish, frogs' legs, mushrooms and chicken with cream sauces.

DOM. DES BILLARDS 2000
■ n.c. n.c. ■ ♦ €5-8

The Jury awarded a commendation to the **Juliénas Domaine de la Vieille Église 2000**, which also belongs to the Loron family. This clear ruby-coloured wine has a red-berry and morello-cherry nose with complex mineral (flint) overtones. The aromatic character of the wine is confirmed on a supple and well-balanced palate. This softly textured, refreshing wine would be perfect served alongside a grilled steak on Valentine's Day, 2002.

☞ Ets Loron et Fils, Pontanevaux, 71570 La Chapelle-de-Guinchay, tel. 03.85.36.81.20, fax 03.85.33.83.19, e-mail vinloron@wanadoo.fr

DOM. DU CARJOT 2000
■ 3 ha 20,000 ■ ♦ €8-11

This *négociant* presented the Jury with a clear-purple, estate-bottled wine that has red-berry and toasted-almond aromas. Apricot flavours emerge on the supple, fruity and light palate. This is a wine for drinking within the year.

☞ La Réserve des Domaines, Les Chers, 69840 Juliénas, tel. 04.74.06.78.70, fax 04.74.06.78.71, e-mail avl@free.fr ⵂ by appt.
☞ Gilbert Giloux

CLOS DE LA BROSSE 2000
■ 1.08 ha 10,000 ■ ♦ €8-11

The Clos de la Brosse is an east-facing vineyard of 1.08 ha (3 acres). Its grapes have been made into a clear-garnet wine with a delicate red-berry aroma. Its beguiling palate is elegant and fruity, with ripe tannins. A finely-structured and well-made wine, the 2000 will be ready to drink in 2002. The Jury also commended the **Brouilly, Domaine de la Motte 2000** marketed by the same *négociant*.

↝ Paul Beaudet, rue Paul-Beaudet, 71570 Pontanevaux, tel. 03.85.36.72.76, fax 03.85.36.72.02, e-mail paulbeaudet@ compuserve.com ☑ ⟙ ev. day except Sat. Sun. 8am–12 noon 1.30pm–5.30pm; cl. Aug.

DOM. DES DUC 2000★

■ 9.5 ha 50,000 ■ ♦ €5-8

This domaine, which is made up of a group of vineyards, was established in 1985. It now encompasses 27.67 ha (68 acres). Its clear-purple 2000 vintage first attracts attention with its complex, spicy red-berry aroma. The concentrated palate is rich and vinous with good, ripe tannins. This is a full, rounded and well-balanced wine for drinking within the year.

↝ Dom. des Duc, La Plat, 71570 Saint-Amour-Bellevue, tel. 03.85.37.10.08, fax 03.85.36.55.75, e-mail duc@ vins-du-beaujolais.com ☑ ⟙ by appt.

DOM. DE L'ANCIEN RELAIS

Clos de la Brosse 1999

■ 1.1 ha 8,000 ■ €5-8

The *relais*, or post-house, was built in 1399. From its vaulted cellars have emerged a **Juliénas 99 Vieilles Vignes** that was commended by the Jury, as well as this bright ruby-coloured Saint-Amour, with its forthright aroma of spicy red berries. Wild-cherry and apricot flavours are discernible on the attractive palate, which is impressively structured. This wine is ready to drink now with red meat or offal dishes.

↝ EARL André Poitevin, Les Chamonards, 71570 Saint-Amour-Bellevue, tel. 03.85.37.16.05, fax 03.85.37.40.87 ☑ ⟙ by appt.

GÉRARD ET NATHALIE MARGERAND Champs grillés 1999

■ 0.38 ha 4,000 ■ €5-8

The estate's **Juliénas 99** was judged to be equally as good as this deep-red wine, which is redolent of red berries and blackcurrants. Fruity and spicy aromas appear on its powerful but well-balanced and very long palate. This Saint-Amour would complement game, and will be enjoyable for the next two to three years.

↝ Gérard et Nathalie Margerand, Les Capitans, 69840 Juliénas, tel. 04.74.04.46.53, fax 04.74.04.46.53 ☑ ⟙ by appt.

JEAN-JACQUES ET SYLVAINE MARTIN 2000★

■ 0.56 ha 3,500

The Martins have cultivated this estate since 1973. They presented the Jury with two

of the many wines that they produce, and both their **white Beaujolais 99** and this Saint-Amour were awarded one star. The dark ruby-coloured wine has peony and red-berry aromas. The fruity and fleshy first impression leads on to a powerful palate. Well-balanced and round, with a long finish of great finesse, this is an easy-going wine for drinking within the next two years alongside white meat or fish dishes.

↝ Jean-Jacques Martin, Les Verchères, 71570 Chânes, tel. 03.85.37.42.27, fax 03.85.37.47.43 ☑ ⟙ by appt.

DOM. DES PIERRES 2000

■ 6 ha 40,000 ■ €5-8

This estate is credited with introducing Beaujolais to a range of export markets, from Denmark to Japan. Its 2000 vintage was selected for its limpid-purple colour and spicy, floral and fruity nose. On the palate, this attractive, balanced and lengthy wine is quite rich and a little acidic, with appealing, light tannins. This Saint-Amour is for drinking within the year to accompany game.

↝ Georges Trichard, rte de Juliénas, 71570 La Chapelle-de-Guinchay, tel. 03.85.36.70.70, fax 03.85.33.82.31 ☑ ⟙ by appt.

JEAN-PIERRE TEISSÈDRE

Cuvée Prestige 1999

■ n.c. n.c. ■ €8-11

The garnet wine from this *négociant* based at Saint-Étienne-des-Ouillières has unusual aromas of leather and red berries that continue on to the palate. Full-bodied with a long finish, it is not a typical Saint-Amour, but will be a satisfying wine after it has aged for a year or two.

↝ Jean-Pierre Teissèdre, Les Grandes Bruyères, 69460 Saint-Étienne-des-Ouillières, tel. 04.74.03.48.02, fax 04.74.03.46.33, e-mail jp-teissedre.earl@ wanadoo.fr ☑ ⟙ by appt.

THOMAS LA CHEVALIÈRE

La Folie 2000★

■ 0.8 ha 5,000 ■ ♦ €8-11

A Watteau painting that depicts a scene of gay abandon is reproduced on the label, perhaps as an indication of the pleasures contained in the bottle. This clear-purple wine has well-developed and complex aromas of white flowers, peonies and red berries. A lively opening impression introduces a fleshy, rounded and fruity palate. This is a powerful and firmly-structured wine that would complement red meats in sauces, or a piece of Brie. It should be drunk within the next two years.

↝ Thomas La Chevalière, 69430 Beaujeu, tel. 04.74.04.84.97, fax 04.74.69.29.87 ☑ ⟙ ev. day except Sat. Sun. 8am–12 noon 2pm–6pm

Le Lyonnais

The vineyards that produce wines under the Coteaux du Lyonnais appellation are situated on the eastern slopes of the Massif Central. In the east they are bordered by the Rhône and the Saône, in the west by the Monts du Lyonnais. Their northern limit is the Beaujolais vineyards, and they go south as far as the Rhône valley. The historic vineyards of Lyon have been cultivated since Roman times and wine-growing reached its zenith at the end of the 16th century when religious institutions and wealthy merchants favoured and protected the cultivation of the vine. A land survey dating from 1836 identified 13,500 ha (33,345 acres) of vineyards. Phylloxera decimated them and the city of Lyon expanded significantly, thus reducing the area under vines. Nowadays it is down to only 346 ha (855 acres), divided among 49 communes which form a semi-circle to the west of the city, from Mont d'Or in the north to the Gier valley in the south.

The area is 40 km (25 miles) long and 30 km (19 miles) wide and is marked by a succession of valleys at about 250 m (820 ft) high, running south-west to north-east with hills reaching some 500 m (1,640 ft). The ground is varied, being made from granite, metamorphic and sedimentary rocks with alluvial or loess deposits. The soil is light with good drainage and is very shallow, as is common in wine-growing areas where the underlying geological structure is ancient rock.

Coteaux du Lyonnais

The three prevailing climates of Beaujolais are also found in this region, though there is a greater influence from Mediterranean weather. However, the topology of the area is particularly susceptible to the influences of the oceanic and continental climates which means the vines can be planted only up to 500 m (1,640 ft) and not on exposed, north-facing slopes. The best areas are on the plateau. The vine varieties planted are essentially Gamay, vinified according to the Beaujolais method to give appealing red wines which are the favourites of the local Lyonnais clientele. Chardonnay and Aligoté also qualify under the appellation and are used for making white wines. Vineyards must be planted at a density of 6,000 plants per hectare and are pruned either in the shape of a goblet, as in the Beaujolais, cordoned or reduced to a single stem. Production bases start at 60 hl/ha (648 gal per acre). Red wine has a minimum strength of 10° and a maximum strength of 13° while white wine goes from 9.5° to 12.5°. In 2000 20,276 hl (535,286 gal) of red and rosé and 2,050 hl (54,120 gal) of white were produced. The Cave Coopérative de Saint-Bel vinifies three-quarters of the harvest and is a significant force in the region where there is a good deal of mixed farming with large tracts of land being given over to cultivating fruit trees.

The Coteaux du Lyonnais became an AOC in 1984. They are fruity, fresh, well-scented wines which go perfectly with all sorts of Lyonnais pork dishes, including sausages, saveloys, pig's tails, salted pork, pigs' trotters, knuckles of ham, together with goats' cheeses of the region.

DOM. DU CLOS SAINT-MARC
2000

17 ha | 100,000 | €3-5

Grapes from 40-year-old vines growing on sandy granite soils have been harvested and vinified using a judicious combination of traditional and modern techniques, to create a deep ruby-coloured wine with an attractive red-berry aroma. Fairly light, but elegantly structured, with fresh and fruity tannins, this wine is for drinking within the next two years.

➤ GAEC du Clos Saint-Marc, 60, rue des Fontaines, 69440 Taluyers, tel. 04.78.48.26.78, fax 04.78.48.77.91 by appt.

PIERRE ET JEAN-MICHEL JOMARD 2000★

1 ha | 9,000 | €3-5

This family estate dates back to 1520. One of its three vats was used to vinify a **red Coteaux du Lyonnais 2000** that was commended by the Jury, as well as this pale-gold wine, with its aromas of honey and citrus fruits (lemon, orange, mandarin). Supple, rounded and mouth-filling, this well-balanced wine of great length is ready to drink now, but could also be kept for two to three years.

➤ Pierre et Jean-Michel Jomard, Le Morillon, 69210 Fleurieux-sur-l'Arbresle, tel. 04.74.01.02.27, fax 04.74.01.24.04

DOM. DE LA PETITE GALLEE
1999★★

2 ha | 12,000 | €5-8

This excellent 99, from an 11-ha (27-acre) estate located 15 km (10 miles) south of Lyons, just missed being selected as a *coup de coeur*. A rich green-gold colour, it has fresh and complex aromas of honey and lime blossom. This very well-crafted, fruity and well-balanced wine of fine length is enjoyable now, but will also keep for a further two years. Serve it with grilled chicken, roast veal or a salt-cod brandade. The Jury awarded the estate's **Vieilles Vignes du Rouge 2000** one star.

➤ Robert et Patrice Thollet, La Petite Gallée, 69390 Millery, tel. 04.78.46.24.30, fax 04.72.30.73.48 by appt.

ANNE MAZILLE 1999★★

0.3 ha | 2,500

DOM. DE BAPTISTE 2000★

3.5 ha | n.c. | €3-5

This grower also runs a vine nursery. His **red Beaujolais 2000, Domaine du Grand Lièvre**, was commended by the Jury, and this beautiful, ruby-coloured wine was awarded a star. It has powerful aromas of blackcurrants and pear drops, with complex overtones of musk and ferns. The silky, fresh palate has fine length. This very well-made, if atypical, Lyonnais red is powerful enough to last for another three years. It would complement *boeuf bourguignon*, pig cheek or stewed tripe.

➤ Bouteille Frères, Rotaval, 69380 Saint-Jean-des-Vignes, tel. 04.78.43.73.27, fax 04.78.43.08.94 by appt.

CAVE DE SAIN-BEL
L'Hommée 2000★★

30 ha | 40,000 | €5-8

The 1998 vintage of this wine was also selected as a *coup de coeur*. A deep garnet colour, it has fine, pure, blackcurrant and raspberry aromas. The full-bodied and well-structured palate displays a beguiling touch of sweetness, as well as classy, fruity tannins that persist on the long finish. This 2000 vintage will continue to be very enjoyable for the next three years, and would complement a Saint-Marcellin cheese. The **red Beaujolais 2000 Domaine du Soly** from the same cellar was awarded one star by the Jury. These are both excellent wines.

➤ Cave de Vignerons réunis, RN 89, 69210 Sain-Bel, tel. 04.74.01.11.33, fax 04.74.01.10.27 by appt.

Coteaux du Lyonnais

Thirty-year-old vines growing on granite soils have produced a richly-coloured green-gold wine that the Jury selected as a *coup de coeur*. It has very expressive honey and lemon aromas, and an impressively rich and full palate. This fruity, long and well-balanced wine could mature even longer; it will keep for at least two years, and could accompany fish or chicken in creamy sauces.

🛒 Anne Mazille, 10, rue du 8-Mai, 69390 Millery, tel. 04.72.30.14.91, fax 04.72.30.16.65  ⏰ by appt.

DOM. DE PETIT FROMENTIN

Vieilles vignes 2000

■   2 ha   13,200   ▪   ♦   €3-5

Vineyards on the historic Mont d'Or have produced a dark-red wine with purple highlights. The appealing, but subtle, red-berry aroma reveals an unusual hint of fennel. This fresh, well-balanced 2000 is for drinking within the year.

🛒 Decrenisse Père et Fils, Le Petit Fromentin, 69380 Chasselay, tel. 04.78.47.35.11, fax 04.78.47.35.11 ⏰ ev. day except Sun. 5pm–7.30pm

DOM. DE PRAPIN 2000

■   4 ha   30,000   ▪   €3-5

The estate is on the road that runs between Taluyers and Saint-Laurent-d'Agny, its vine-yards benefiting from a favourable *terroir*. The bright-garnet wine is full-bodied and aromatic, with a good, long finish. Youthful tannins ensure that it will keep for the next two to three years. It would complement pork. The **white wine**, made from Chardonnay grapes, also especially impressed the Jury.

🛒 Henri Jullian, Prapin, 69440 Taluyers, tel. 04.78.48.24.84, fax 04.78.48.24.84 ⏰ ev. day 9am–12 noon 2.30pm–7pm

Bordeaux is the ultimate symbol of wine, everywhere in the world, but visitors seeking an old wine town with beautiful rows of hogs-heads stretching along the port near the inviting wine stores of the shippers will be disappointed: the shippers have long since relocated to the indus-trial zones on the outskirts of the town, and the small cellar bars, where you could down a glass of sweet wine in the early morning, have practically disappeared. Echoes of another time, another way of life.

The history of wine in Bordeaux stretches back to ancient times. A wine trade was recorded in the area even before vines were culti-vated there. In the first half of the 1st century BC, some years before Roman legions invaded Aquitaine, merchants from Campania in Italy came to sell their wine to the Bordelais. Thus, in some ways, wine was the medium through which the people of Aquitaine first experienced Roman life. Vine-growing was under way during the 1st century AD, but it seems that more serious cultivation began in the 12th century. The marriage of Eleanor of Aquitaine to Henry Plantagenet, the future King Henry II of England, encouraged the export of 'clarets' (as the English called them) to Britain. The wines of the year were shipped to England before Christmas. In those days no one knew how to preserve wine, and it would deteriorate after a year as a result of natural chemical changes.

At the end of the 17th century claret encountered stiff competition from the introduction of new beverages – tea, coffee and choc-olate – and also from other, more robust wines from the Iberian peninsula. In addition, the foreign wars waged by Louis XIV led importing countries to levy punitive taxes on French wines. In spite of this, high society in England remained devoted to the flavour of claret. In the early 18th century some London shippers sought to create a new style of more refined wines, 'the new French clarets', which they bought young to lay down. In an inspired marketing initiative, shippers started to sell the wine in bottles that were corked and sealed to guarantee their origin, and could thus be sold at a premium. Almost imperceptibly, the connection between the *terroir*, the château and Grands Vins (fine wines) evolved, bringing about wines of a more reliable standard. Wines began to be judged, appreciated and priced according to their quality. As a consequence, wine-growers began to select land for cultivating the vines more carefully, limiting the amount of wine produced and improving the conditions for maturing the wines in casks. At the same time, they introduced new methods, protecting their wines during ageing through the use of sulphur dioxide and clarifying wine by fining or racking. The first ranking of the Bordeaux Crus was established at the end of the 18th century. In spite of the French Revolution and the Napoleonic Wars, which closed the English market for a period, the prestige of the Grands Vins of Bordeaux increased through the 19th century, as illustrated by the classification of the Crus du Médoc in 1855. This system, although not without its critics, is still in use today.

Following this period of growth, the Bordeaux vineyards were devastated by two major vine diseases, phylloxera and mildew, and suffered further from economic slumps and two world wars. Between 1960 and the end of the 1980s, however, Bordeaux recovered its prosperity by virtue of a remarkable improvement in the quality of its wines and a

BORDEAUX

significantly increased world-wide demand for fine wines in general. The hierarchy of Bordeaux's *terroirs* and crus regained some international respect, although the red wines benefited more than the whites. At the beginning of the 1990s the market suffered from a variety of economic factors affecting the structure of all the Bordeaux vineyards.

The Bordeaux vineyards are situated along three major waterways: the Garonne, the Dordogne and the estuary they both feed into, the Gironde. The environment they create – sunny, sheltered slopes and steady temperatures – is ideal for growing vines. These waterways have historically also played an important economic role as the means for transporting the wines to market. The climate in the Bordelais region is temperate, with average annual temperatures of 7.5°C (45.5°F) minimum and 17°C (62.6°F) maximum, and the vineyards are sheltered from ocean storms by pine forests. Winter frosts are rare (1956, 1985), but if the temperature drops to –2°C (28.4°F) or below in April and May the young shoots can be severely damaged or destroyed. The vines flower in June, and cool, rainy weather during this period can wash away the pollen: as a result the flowers do not pollinate and the grapes do not form. Spring frosts and summer rains alike can have a critical impact on the amount of grapes harvested and thus explain the great year-to-year variations in the quantity of wine produced. The final quality of the harvest depends on having hot, dry weather from July to October, particularly in the four weeks just before picking begins (in all, grapes need 2,008 hours of sun each year to ripen properly). The local climate is in fact fairly wet, 900 mm (35.5 in) of rain per year falling mainly in the spring, when the weather can be very poor. Autumns, on the other hand, are famously warm, and exceptional late-season weather has often saved many vintages. The reputation of the Grands Vins de Bordeaux depends entirely on this fortuitous combination of location and climate.

Along the Gironde the vine is cultivated on a variety of different soils; and no particular soil type determines the quality of the wine. Most of the Grands Crus red wines are from alluvial, sandy and gravelly soils, other reputable wines come from clay on limy subsoil, sandstone or even sedimentary clay. The vines for dry white wines grow equally well on soil with layers of sand or gravel, chalky soils, on alluvium or sandstone. Vines for sweet wines are usually grown on gravelly sand or clay. In every case, natural or mechanical methods of drainage and control over how much water the vines receive are essential factors in the production of good-quality wines, to the extent that fine wines with the same high reputation can be grown on soils of entirely different geological types. However, the distinctive aromatic flavours of the wines are influenced by the structure of the soils: the Médoc and Saint-Emilion wines are good examples. Here and elsewhere, the same soil type may well produce red wines, dry white wines and sweet white wines.

The Bordeaux vineyards covered 117,327 ha (289,798 acres) in 2000. At the end of the 19th century they extended over more than 150,000 ha (370,500 acres), but wine-growing was discontinued in some areas where the soil was inadequate. With the improvement of cultivating techniques, the total production has remained about the same, currently approaching 7 million hl (184,800,600 gal). While the average size of a vineyard is still about 7 ha (17 acres), changes in ownership have resulted in a progressive reduction in the number of producers (from 22,200 in 1983 to 16,000 in 1992, then from 13,358 in 1993 down to 12,852 in 1996).

ferent vine varieties with complementary qualities. Cabernet and Merlot are used to make red wines (about 90% of the vineyard area). Cabernet gives the wines their tannic structure, but the wines need to mature for a number of years if they are to reach optimum quality; Cabernet Sauvignon is a late-maturing grape, which, although resistant to rot, can have difficulty in ripening. Merlot makes for supple wines that develop more rapidly. The grapes fruit earlier and ripen well, but during the flowering season the pollen may be washed away by the spring rains and the young vines can be easily damaged by frost, while the grapes are susceptible to rot. Long practice has shown that best results are achieved by blending these two grape varieties in various proportions according to the soil in which they are grown and to the wine to be produced. The main variety used for white wine is Sémillon (52%), supplemented in some areas by Colombard (11%), above all by Sauvignon, which is ever more widely planted, and Muscadelle (15%), which has characteristic, very fine aromas. Ugni Blanc is now more rarely grown.

Vines are planted in rows and trained on espaliers. The density of vines varies considerably: as many as 10,000 plants per hectare in the vineyards of the Médoc and Graves Grand Crus, down to an average of 4,000 in the classified areas of Entre-Deux-Mers, and fewer than 2,500 when the plants are left to grow tall and are widely spaced out. At higher densities, each vine can be controlled to produce a limited number of bunches of grapes, allowing them to mature more easily. However, the costs of managing and cultivating such vineyards are greater and the grapes are more susceptible to rot. Cultivation of the vines requires meticulous care and attention all year round. In 1885, the science faculty of Bordeaux University discovered the *bouillie bordelaise*, or Bordeaux mixture, compounded of copper sulphate and lime, which proved particularly successful in combating mildew. Bordeaux mixture is still in use throughout the world, although modern wine-growers can now look to a large number of more ecologically friendly products to do the same job.

Bordeaux can boast many great vintages. The years for great reds were 1990, 1982, 1975, 1961 and 1959, but other years have also been excellent: 1989, 1988, 1985, 1983, 1981, 1979, 1978, 1976, 1970 and 1966. Unforgettable vintages from previous years were 1955, 1949, 1947, 1945, 1929 and 1928. It is worth stressing that recent years have seen a general improvement in the quality of vintages and a consequent reduction in mediocre ones. It may be that the vineyards have enjoyed better climatic conditions, but a greater contribution has come from improved working methods and the incorporation of research discoveries into cultivation and methods of vinification. The Bordeaux vineyards are situated on exceptional land for wine-growing, but sophisticated modern technologies now help to make the most of what nature was to offer; consequently, it is unlikely that the Gironde will produce any very poor vintages in the future.

Bordeaux's dry white wines may not feature prominently among the great vintages but sweet wines certainly do. To make a good sweet wine, the conditions for the development of noble rot are essential (see the introductory section, 'Wine' and the individual entries for the wines concerned).

The Bordeaux appellations

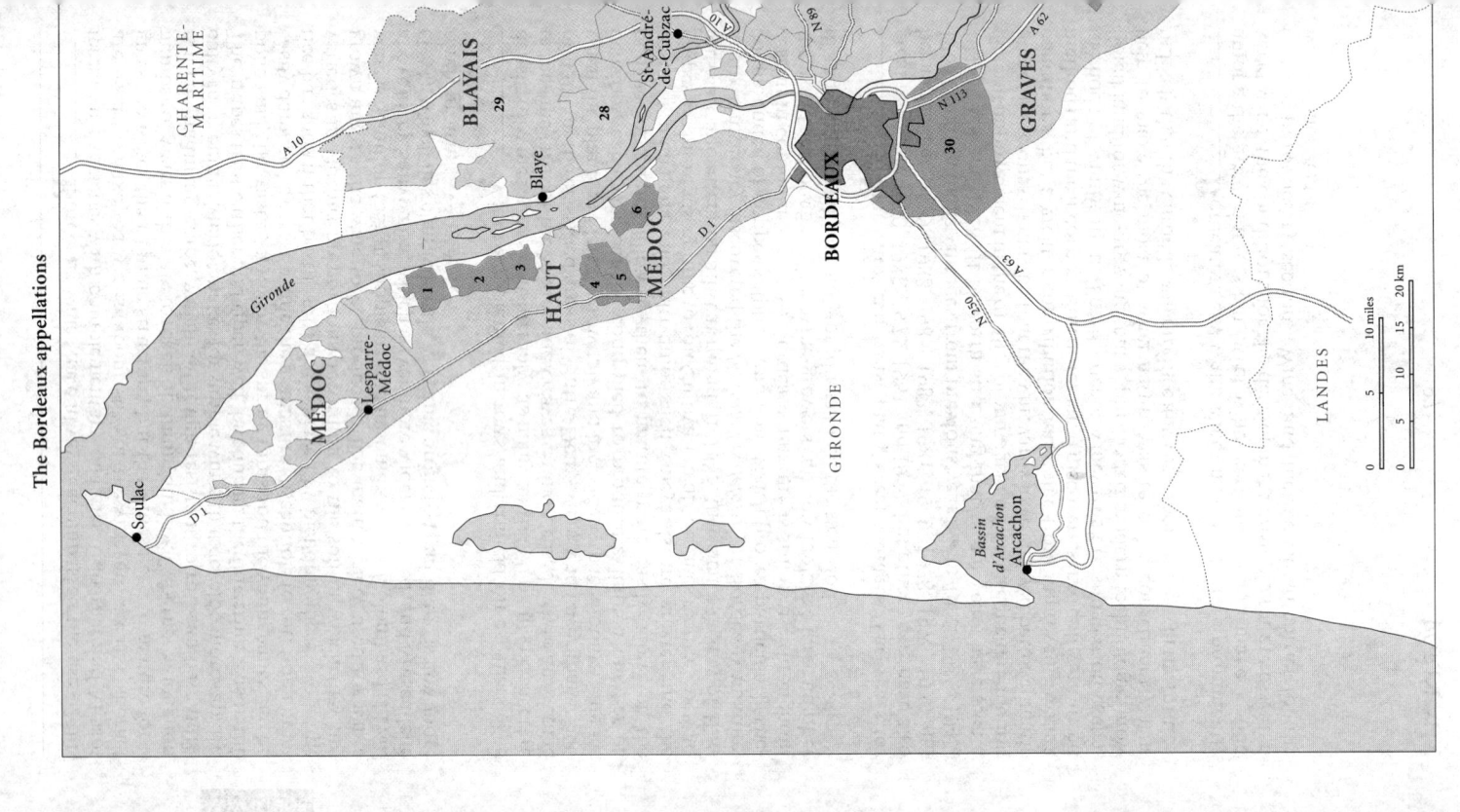

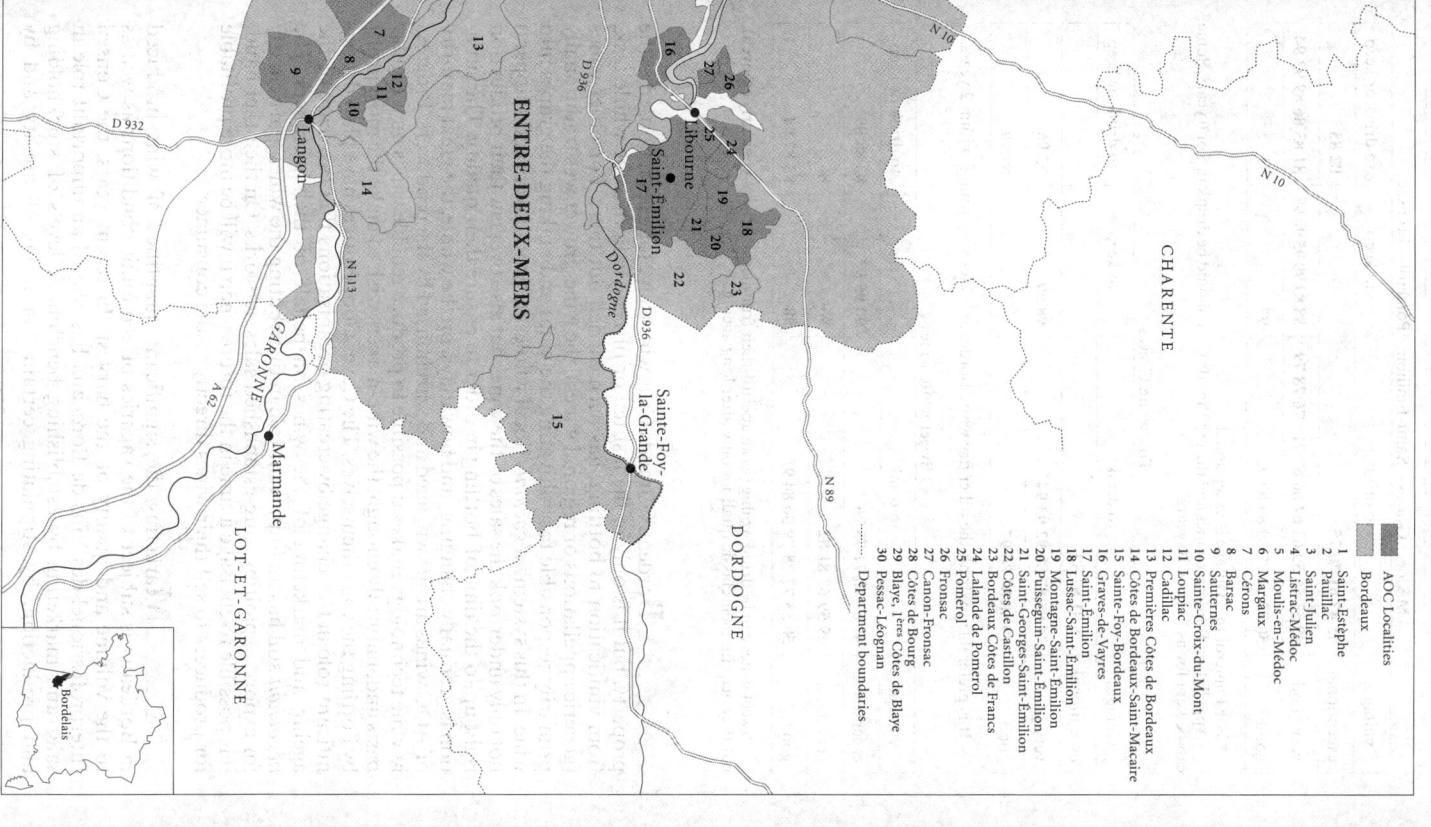

AOC Localities

Bordeaux

1 Saint-Estèphe
2 Pauillac
3 Saint-Julien
4 Listrac-Médoc
5 Moulis-en-Médoc
6 Margaux
7 Cérons
8 Barsac
9 Sauternes
10 Sainte-Croix-du-Mont
11 Loupiac
12 Cadillac
13 Premières Côtes de Bordeaux
14 Côtes de Bordeaux-Saint-Macaire
15 Sainte-Foy-Bordeaux
16 Graves-de-Vayres
17 Saint-Émilion
18 Lussac-Saint-Émilion
19 Montagne-Saint-Émilion
20 Puisseguin-Saint-Émilion
21 Saint-Georges-Saint-Émilion
22 Côtes de Castillon
23 Bordeaux Côtes de Francs
24 Lalande de Pomerol
25 Pomerol
26 Fronsac
27 Canon-Fronsac
28 Côtes de Bourg
29 Blaye, 1ers Côtes de Blaye
30 Pessac-Léognan

----- Department boundaries

ENTRE-DEUX-MERS

CHARENTE

DORDOGNE

LOT-ET-GARONNE

Langon

Saint-Émilion

Libourne

Sainte-Foy-la-Grande

Marmande

Bordelais

GARONNE

Dordogne

vintages	Médoc – Graves – Saint-Emilion – Pomerol – Fronsac		
	to drink	to keep	to drink or keep
exceptional	45 47 61 70 75		82 85
very good	49 53 55 59 62 64 66 67 71* 76 78 79	88 89 90 95 96 98	81 83 86 89 93 94
good	50 73 74 77 80 84 87 92	97	91

* For Pomerol this vintage is exceptional.

– Appellation Bordeaux wines and the red Vins de Côte should be drunk in 5 or 6 years. Some can be kept for as long as 10 years.

Dry white Graves

vintages	to drink	to keep	to drink or keep
exceptional	78 81 82 83		
very good	76 85 87 88 92 93 94	98 99	95 96
good	79 80 84 86 97		89 90

– It is preferable to drink the other dry white Bordeaux wines very young, within 2 years.

Sweet white wines

vintages	to drink	to keep	to drink or keep
exceptional	47 67 70 71 75 76	90 95 97	83 88 89
very good	49 59 62 81 82	96	86
good	50 55 77 78 79 80 84 91	98	85 87 94

– Sweet wines can be drunk young (as an aperitif their fruitiness can be particularly enjoyed), but they acquire their classic qualities only after long ageing.

Bordeaux Grands Crus wines have long been bottled at the property, but it is only in the last ten or fifteen years that the whole task, from vinification to bottling, has been carried out there. For other wines (generic appellations or regional wines), the wine-grower was traditionally primarily responsible for cultivating the vines and making the grapes into wine. In this system, *négociants* (local wholesale wine-buyers and shippers) not only undertook the sales of the wines but also oversaw their production right up to the time of bottling in order to ensure their quality. The situation is gradually changing, and nowadays, on the whole, the great majority of AOC wines are grown, aged and warehoused by the producers. Progress in wine technology makes it possible to produce reliable wines on a regular basis and, naturally enough, the wine-makers wish to make the most profit by bottling the wine themselves. The Caves Coopératives have played a significant role in this change by creating organisations that take care of the ageing and marketing of the wines on behalf of their members. The *négociant* still has an important role in distributing the wines, particularly for export, exploiting long-established sales networks. On the other hand, it is possible to envisage a time in the future when it will be more profitable for producers to sell their wines directly to the consumer.

Marketing the significant quantities of wine produced in Bordeaux is subject to the vagaries of economic conditions as well as to the volume and quality of the harvest. In recent years, the Conseil Interprofessionel des Vins de Bordeaux has played an important role in sales and marketing by establishing benchmark levels of stockholding and production, by stipulating certain conditions of quality and by implementing financial measures relating to the organisation of the market.

The regional *syndicats* or wine unions also protect the different Appellations d'Origine Contrôlées by defining criteria for quality. Under the management and control of INAO, they organise tastings at which all the wines produced each year are judged; they have the power to take away the appellation rights of a wine if its quality is deemed inadequate.

The various wine Confréries (Jurade in Saint-Emilion, Commanderie du Bontemps in Médoc and Graves, Connétablie in Guyenne and so on) organise regular festivals and popular events to promote Bordeaux wines. Their activities are co-ordinated by the Grand Conseil du Vin de Bordeaux.

All these promotional and marketing activities and production controls demonstrate that Bordeaux wines make up a major industry that is rigorously managed. The AOC wines produced in Bordeaux represent 26.54% of the all wines produced in France, with a volume of 6,897,946 hl (182,105,774 gal) in 2000, of which FF8,000 million (€1.2m) is earned through exports. The industry plays an important role in the life of the region, since it is estimated that one Girondin in six is directly or indirectly dependent on the activities of the wine industry. But for Gascony, the region of the Bordeaux wines, wine is more than simply a product of the economy. It is also, and above all, part of the culture. Behind the labels may lie châteaux with stunning architecture or simple peasant houses, but also the vineyards and the wine cellars where people work, applying their know-how and contributing their traditions and their memories to the production of great wine.

Bordeaux: the regional appellations

While it is relatively straightforward to identify the Appellation Communale wines, it is not so easy to understand what the Appellation Bordeaux means. In fact, the definition is quite simple: it applies to all good-quality wines produced within the boundaries of the department of the Gironde, excluding any that come from the sandy area to the west and south (namely La Lande, which has been set aside as a pine forest since the 19th century). Put more simply, the appellation applies to all wines from of the Gironde. All the wines produced there have the right to use it subject to meeting the fairly strict regulations concerning the selection of grape varieties, limits on quantities produced and so on. However, this simple provision conceals great variations. Indeed, rather than talking about a single Bordeaux appellation, it is more correct to talk about the Bordeaux appellations, which include red wine, rosé, clairets, both dry and white wines, and white or rosé sparkling wines. The variety of geographical origins for Bordeaux appellation wines gives rise to several types of wines that can claim the appellation. In some cases it means wines that are produced in parts of the Gironde that have the right to use only the Bordeaux appellation, such as the marshy districts (made up of alluvial soils) near the rivers or in parts of the Libournais (communes such as Saint-André-de-Cubzac, Guîtres, Coutras, for example). In other cases, the wines come from regions that also have

Bordeaux

the right to a specific appellation (Médoc, Saint-Emilion, Pomerol, and so on). Alternatively, a regional appellation can be used by a local appellation that may be less well known commercially (such as the Bordeaux Côtes-de-Francs, Bordeaux Haut-Benauge, Bordeaux Sainte-Foy or Bordeaux Saint-Macaire); the specific appellation is, in real terms, no more than an adjunct to the Appellation Régionale and, in fact, adds nothing to the intrinsic value of the product. In such cases, wine-makers are happier to rely on the image of the Bordeaux 'brand name'. Occasionally, Bordeaux wines may come from a property located in the production area of a particular, sometimes prestigious, appellation, an occurrence that can provoke a good deal of curiosity among inquisitive wine-lovers. But here, too, the explanation is not difficult to find: traditionally, many properties in the Gironde produced several types of wine (more usually both reds and whites); now, in numerous cases (Médoc, Saint-Emilion, Entre-Deux-Mers and Sauternes), the specific appellation applies to only one type. Consequently, the other wines produced are marketed as Bordeaux or Bordeaux Supérieur.

Appellations Régionales. Thus Bordeaux red wines are well-balanced, and delicate; generally they should be fruity but not too full-bodied, so they can be drunk young. The Bordeaux Supérieur reds tend to be more full-bodied; they are made from the best grapes and vinified by a method that will ensure they can keep for some time. They form a select group among Bordeaux wines.

Bordeaux clairets and rosés are made by allowing red-grape varieties to macerate for a short time; the clairets have a slightly more intense colour. They are fresh, fruity wines, but only a limited quantity is produced.

White Bordeaux wines are dry, lively, fruity wines. In recent years their quality has been improved by new techniques of vinification, but it should be said that this appellation does not yet enjoy the popularity it deserves. Some of these wines are 'demoted' to table wines, not least because the difference in profit is slight and it is sometimes easier to sell them as table wine than as Bordeaux Blanc. As a group, white Bordeaux Supérieur wines are luscious and rich; production, though, is small.

There is also an Appellation Crémant de Bordeaux. To qualify, all the grapes used must come from the designated Bordeaux appellation region. The second fermentation (the *prise de mousse*), must occur in bottle at wine cellars in the Bordeaux region.

Though these wines may be less celebrated than the Grands Crus, in a quantitative sense all these Bordeaux constitute the largest appellation of the Gironde with, in 2000 3,309,870 hl (87,380,568 gal) of red, 517,467 hl (13,661,129 gal) of white and 18,925 hl (499,620 gal) of sparkling Crémant de Bordeaux.

Taken at face value, the quantity of wine produced and the impressive area of the vineyards could lead one to suppose that there are few similarities among Bordeaux wines. The wines do indeed have distinctions in character, but they, also have qualities in common that give an overall identity to the

Bordeaux

■ ⅢⅢ €5-3

CLOS AMBRION
Vieilli en fût de chêne 1999

■   n.c.   7,000

With its intense, vigorous crimson colour and orange glints, it is clear from the start that this wine has real character. The same impression continues on the nose, which has a rich array of clove, cinnamon and incense notes. Oak appears slowly on the firm palate. This invigorating wine will open out when it has been left to age for a while.

- Bernard Faure, Ambrion, 33240 Lalande-de-Fronsac, tel. 06.68.48.82.25 ¶ by appt.

CH. BEAU-VAILLART 1999★
n.c. 100,000 €5-8

This wine is quite dark in colour, with some garnet glints, and there is a range of gamey aromas: fur, musk and old leather. The surprise comes on the palate, where the body is light, and dominated by fairly abundant and impetuous tannins. Keep it for one to two years to achieve a good balance. This is a wine that will appeal to traditionalists.

- Michel Boyer, Ch. Bellevue La Mongie, 33420 Génissac, tel. 05.57.24.48.43, fax 05.57.24.48.43
¶ ev. day 8am–12 noon 2–7pm; Sat. Sun. by appt.; cl. 15–30 Aug.

CH. BEL AIR PERPONCHER 1999★★
n.c. n.c. €5-8

This is the first mention in the *Guide* of a wine offered by the Despagne team, but you will find more of them featured prominently in the pages to come. The crimson colour is still very young, and the nose releases scents of tuberose and narcissus before the fruit aromas become apparent. Then comes the rich roundness of a fleshy palate, enhanced by soft tannins and opening out to a delightful long finish. This wine will go well with red meats and can be drunk now or over the next two or three years.

- GFA de Perponcher, 33420 Naujan-et-Postiac, tel. 05.57.84.55.08, fax 05.57.84.57.31, e-mail contact@vignobles-despagne.com
- J.-L. Despagne

CH. BELLE-GARDE
Cuvée élevée en fût de chêne 1999★★
9 ha 60,000 €3-5

It is clear how rich and full-bodied this wine is from its deep, dark colour. The nose releases a combination of fruit and oak aromas, with blackcurrants and prunes standing out against a well-integrated, oaky background and a chocolate note, which reveals a very strong Merlot influence. The same flavours come and go delightfully on the palate, which is supported by elegant tannins. There are excellent prospects for the future here.

- Eric Duffau, Ch. Belle-Garde, Monplaisir, 33420 Génissac, tel. 05.57.24.49.12, fax 05.57.24.41.28, e-mail eric.duffau@wanadoo.fr
¶ ev. day except Sun. 8am–12 noon 2–7pm; cl. 15–30 Aug.

CH. BONNEMET 1999★
23.77 ha 50,000 €3-5

This wine has a ruby colour with intense purplish glints, and a nose that is still very youthful and that is just beginning to develop a bouquet of undergrowth with a slight hint of meat. Fleshy and full-bodied from the attack, the palate gradually reveals the presence of underlying tannins, which will allow it to benefit from a good period of ageing (three to four years).

CH. ARNEAU-BOUCHER 1999★
22 ha 14,000 €5-8

This wine comes from a clay-limestone hilltop vineyard at Saint-Genès-de-Fronsac. Made entirely from Merlot grapes, it has a very promising deep red colour and a powerful, concentrated bouquet. The palate is supported by a tannic framework, which is gradually gaining in refinement. This will be a good wine to drink in about two years' time.

- EARL Jacques Sartron, 8, le Bourg, 33240 Saint-Genès-de-Fronsac, tel. 05.57.43.11.12, fax 05.57.43.56.34

DOM. DU BALLAT
L'Esprit du Ballat 1999★
3.5 ha 6,000 €8-11

It is no surprise to discover that this Esprit du Ballat comes from very near the homes where Mauriac and Toulouse-Lautrec found their inspiration. The wine, which has a crimson colour with peony highlights, offers a concentration of the fruit and body of extremely well-cultivated Merlot grapes. It is marked by truffles and liquorice, and the palate has a sense of muskiness along with a corresponding meaty richness. There is an accomplished range of flavours on the finish, where fruit (blackcurrant) competes with some hints of spice. Once it has aged for a while this wine will be even better. It will make a good accompaniment to stuffed quails.

- EARL Vignobles Trejaut, Dom. du Ballat 33490 Saint-André-du-Bois, tel. 05.56.76.42.83, fax 05.56.76.45.14

CH. DE BEAULIEU 1999
16.91 ha 65,000 €3-5

One legacy of Franco-British antagonism is the beautiful medieval walled town of Sauveterre-de-Guyenne, very close to Château de Beaulieu. It was also the British, of course, who were largely responsible for the early development of wine production in this region. This vintage comes from a grape blend consisting mainly of the Cabernets. The colour is rich and dark, but even so the nose is very fruity right from the start, with aromas of stewed fruits, prunes and black cherries. This full, structured wine is dominated by powerful tannins, which will become more subdued only after a good period of ageing. It has a long, vinous framework on the palate and will be a good buy for the enlightened wine-lover who is not in too much of a hurry.

- Cellier de La Bastide, Cave coop. vinicole, 33540 Sauveterre-de-Guyenne, tel. 05.56.61.55.21, fax 05.56.71.60.11
¶ ev. day except Sun. 9am–12.15pm 1.30–6.15pm; groups by appt.
- GFA de Beaulieu

Bordeaux

This wine is already pleasant to drink but can also be kept.

➤ Jean-Lou Debart, SCEA de Ch. Cablanc, 33350 Saint-Pey-de-Castets,
tel. 05.57.40.52.20, fax 05.57.40.72.65,
e-mail chcablanc@aol.com ⓂⓎ by appt.

CALVET RESERVE
Elevé en fût de chêne 1999★
167 ha   n.c.   ⒾⒷ €3-5

All the know-how of a highly reputed wine firm has gone into this Calvet Réserve: the selection of vineyards, a long vatting period, respect for the 'Calvet style', in the grape blend, oak maturation, and ageing in bottles. It's very well made, very Bordeaux, exclaimed the judges, who were clearly impressed by the wine's garnet colour and nose of charred, smoky aromas combined with raspberry notes. The elegant palate, with tannins enlivened by notes of undergrowth, completes the picture of a very fine wine.
➤ Calvet, 75, cours du Médoc, BP 11, 33028 Bordeaux Cedex, tel. 05.56.43.59.00, fax 05.56.43.17.78, e-mail calvet@calvet.com

CARREFOUR 1999★
n.c. 1,500,000   Ⓘ €3-5

The supermarket chain Carrefour has engaged Ginestet, the great Bordeaux wine firm, to develop its Bordeaux wines according to very strict specifications. The elegant label shows the name of the bottler, Bernard Taillan, which is the group to which Ginestet belongs, while Carrefour is mentioned on a neck collaret. This wine comes from a selection of plots over a 200-ha (494-acre) area, and you can buy it with your eyes closed and serve it to your best friends. It has a beautifully intense, crimson colour and rich, powerful aromas, which delight from the start. On the palate the tannins roll over the tongue in preparation for a fragrant, invigorating finish. It will be fully open in only a few months' time, but the wine-lover in a hurry will find it a pleasure to drink straight away.
➤ SA Maison Ginestet, 19, av. de Fontenille, 33360 Carignan-de-Bordeaux, tel. 05.56.68.81.82, fax 05.56.20.96.99, e-mail contact@ginestet.fr Ⓨ by appt.

CH. CAZALIS
Cuvée CL Fin de siècle 1998
6.5 ha   175,000   ⒾⒷ €5-8

The word Cazalis is derived from the name of a very ancient ancestor, Vital de Cazalé, who was a lord and soldier in the 13th century. This wine has a cherry colour and a nose that offers a whole basket of fruit aromas: not just blackberries, bilberries and prunes, but crystallised grapes as well. The palate is pleasant and well integrated, with an abundance of jam notes. Does that seem to evoke a flavour of 'fin-de-siècle' nostalgia? Never mind, the wine can be drunk quite happily in this new century.

CH. BONNET
Réserve Elevé en fût de chêne 1999★
57 ha   n.c.   ⒾⒷ €5-8

The wines at Château Bonnet have a noble heritage, coming as they do from an estate that existed long before the French Revolution. The beautiful 18th-century house is surrounded by outbuildings containing first-rate wine-growing and wine-making equipment, which is operated by highly reputed experts. The local clay-limestone and siliceous-clay soils have produced a high-quality wine, impregnated by oaky toast and vanilla on the nose, which releases fruity aromas of grape jelly and blackberries. This fleshy, full-bodied 99 is marked on the palate by a dominant Cabernet flavour and very mature tannins. There is a long, lingering finish on a note of spice.
➤ SCEA Vignobles André Lurton, Ch. Bonnet, 33420 Grézillac, tel. 05.57.25.58.58, fax 05.57.74.98.59, e-mail andrelurton@wanadoo.fr Ⓨ by appt.

CH. BRANDEAU 1999★
12 ha   92,000   Ⓘ €5-8

This 99 wine is crimson with brick-red glints, and a nose that subtly combines stewed fruits, tobacco and the aromas produced by 90% Merlot. The palate, which is both tannic and dense, has real complexity. This wine is already supple and will be a pleasure to drink until 2003.
➤ Philippe Hermouet, Clos du Roy, 33141 Saillans, tel. 05.57.55.07.41, fax 05.57.55.07.45, e-mail hermouetclosduroy@wanadoo.fr Ⓨ by appt.

CH. BUISSON-REDON 1999★
3 ha   40,000   Ⓘ €3-5

The garnet colour has slight brick-red glints, and the nose is muted and still reserved, with a developing aroma of fruit (raspberries). There is a surprising amount of body on the palate, where the tannin structure is unmasked and still substantial. This wine will benefit from being kept for a year or two.
➤ SCEA du Mayne-Vieil, 33133 Galgon, tel. 05.57.74.30.06, fax 05.57.84.39.33, e-mail mayne-vieil@aol.com ⓂⓎ by appt.
➤ Famille Seze

PRESTIGE DE CH. CABLANC 1999★
4.6 ha   40,000   ⒾⒷ €5-8

This wine has an intense red colour and a charming bouquet of vanilla and toast notes along with fairly delicate, but clearly evident, grape aromas, which bear witness to a harvest in a perfect state of health. The palate has a rich, silky body and pleasantly mouth-filling tannins, which give way to a creamy finish.

➤ Prodiffu, 17–19, rte des Vignerons, 33790 Landerrouat, tel. 05.56.61.33.73, fax 05.56.61.40.57, e-mail prodiffu@prodiffu.com
➤ Bernard Chavelard

204

Claude Billot, SCEA Dom. de Cazalis, 33350 Pujols-sur-Dordogne, tel. 05.57.40.72.72, fax 05.57.40.72.00, e-mail chateau.cazalis@wanadoo.fr
by appt.

CH. CAZEAU
Cuvée Prestige Vieilli en fût de chêne 1999

180 ha   100,000   €3-5

The orangey glints in this Cuvée Prestige's colour show that it is starting to develop. Very careful maturation in oak has been used to good advantage. The nose is marked with aromas of toast, while the elegant palate conveys a sense of the fullness and warmth of mature tannins. This wine would be good to drink with a leg of lamb, just before before going round the Vine and Wine Museum in Gornac.

SCI Domaines Cazeau et Percy, 33540 Sauveterre-de-Guyenne, tel. 05.56.71.50.76, fax 05.56.71.87.70, e-mail laguyennoise@wanadoo.fr
Anne-Marie et Michel Martin

CH. CHAPELLE SAINT-SAUVEUR
Elevé en fût de chêne 1999

50 ha   26,600   €3-5

Five different vineyards came together to form the Chapelle Saint-Sauveur château, next to which stands a little 18th-century chapel. This 99 wine has a deep crimson colour and a nose that initially releases hints of vegetation, especially undergrowth, then moves on to notes of jam (prunes and black cherries), all against a very pleasant, slightly vanilla background. The development on the palate is delightfully round and well balanced. Oaky flavours reappear at the finish, which is entirely unaggressive. This wine will go equally well with loin of lamb or fillet of beef with ceps.

SCEA des domaines Cazat-Beauchêne, 33570 Petit-Palais, tel. 05.57.69.86.92, fax 05.57.69.87.00, e-mail cazalio@aol.com
by appt.
S.F. Carere

CH. CLOS DU BOURG 1999★

4.75 ha   29,000   €8-11

This Château Clos du Bourg 99 is a fine example of good balance brought to the wine both by the quality of the grapes and also by the oak. The nose releases fruity aromas at first (blackberries and wild strawberries), then moves on to a vanilla and coconut register. It will be a matter of opinion and taste whether you serve it in the near future or keep it for a few more months.

Ch. Manieu, La Rivière, 33126 Fronsac, tel. 05.57.24.92.79, fax 05.57.24.92.78
ev. day except Sat. Sun. 10.30am–12 noon 2.30–6pm
Mme Léon

CH. COURTEY Cuvée Léon 1999★

4.89 ha   7,500   €3-5

The vines at Château Courtey are grown on hills imbued with the shadow of Toulouse-Lautrec, which hovers over the nearby Château Malromé. This Cuvée Léon has a very dense garnet colour and an enticingly vigorous palate, unfolding on a bed of tannins, which are already refined. The well-balanced finish makes this a pleasant wine, which is ready to serve with food now.

SCEA Courtey, 33490 Saint-Martial, tel. 05.56.76.42.56, fax 05.56.76.42.56
by appt.

CH. CRABITAN-BELLEVUE
Cuvée spéciale 1999

12 ha   15,000   €5-8

Bernard Solane's Cuvée Spéciale has a beautifully natural, clean colour and impressive, aromatic potential, which will become better balanced with time. There are blackcurrant, plum and cherry flavours on the palate, along with a tannin structure that is at present very dominant. Even so, this is a wine of character with fine prospects for the future.

GFA Bernard Solane et Fils, 33410 Sainte-Croix-du-Mont, tel. 05.56.62.01.53, fax 05.56.76.72.09
ev. day except Sun. 8am–12 noon 2–6pm

DOURTHE Numéro 1 1999

n.c.   600,000   €5-8

We had to wait five years after the creation of the famous Numéro 1 Bordeaux White for the launch of the Numéro 1 Bordeaux Red in 1993. With the benefit of rigorous cuvée pre-selection of the blends and a period of maturation in oak, both wines have been an indisputable success on the export market. This 99 version is a fine example of its appellation. It has a clear, brilliant garnet colour and a nose of very ripe fruits and cinnamon, which is not yet fully developed. There is a clean, slightly fresh attack on the palate, leading smoothly to sweet tannins with plenty of flavour. The wine has a long, lingering finish, with a few balsamic notes along the way. It is ready to drink now.

Dourthe, 35, rue de Bordeaux, 33290 Parempuyre, tel. 05.56.35.53.00, fax 05.56.35.53.29, e-mail contact@cvbg.com
by appt.

CH. DUCLA 1999★

30 ha   200,000   €5-8

This wine combines quality and quantity. It has a charming nose (plums and morello cherries), a body cloaked by silky tannins and a lingering finish on notes of plums and crystallised cherries. One star goes to the **Permanence V 99**, which has been matured in oak for a year and a half. This is already exceedingly pleasant, but it will also keep for three or four years.

GFA Dom. Mau, BP 1, 33190 Gironde-sur-Dropt, tel. 05.56.61.54.54, fax 05.56.71.10.45, e-mail info@chateau-ducla.com

CH. FAURET 1999★

■ 0.25 ha 1,600 🛢 €5–8

This wine's crimson colour fringed with violet is a sign of pleasures in store. These consist of fruity aromas and a palate which, despite a somewhat fresh attack, has elegant tannins and crystallised notes on the finish, indicating very ripe grapes. The wine will need to be kept in order to achieve its full potential (three to five years depending on conditions).

⚷ E. et N. Zecchi, GAEC Fauret, Les Arromans, 33420 Moulon, tel. 05.57.74.98.49 ☑ 🍷 by appt.

CH. FLEUR SAINT ESPERIT

Vieilli en fût de chêne 1999★

■ 0.88 ha 7,000 🛢 €3–5

Coming from a tiny plot on a sandy soil, planted with 100% Cabernet Franc vines and belonging to an owner from the Pomerol and Lalande AOCs, this 99 wine is in every respect unusual and captivating. It has a fresh, red colour with crimson glints. There is plenty of fruitiness along with slight hints of vanilla on the palate, which develops a succession of pepper and liquorice flavours interspersed with notes of the forest (humus and chanterelles). These complex aromas continue through to a finish which lends the wine a great deal of charm.

⚷ GFA V. et P. Fourreau, Chevrol, 33500 Néac, tel. 05.57.25.13.34, fax 05.57.51.91.79 ☑

DOM. FLORIMOND-LA-BREDE 1999★

■ 15 ha 60,000 ▮ 🌡 €3–5

This family property was reorganised by Louis Marinier, who 15 years ago was a tireless champion of Bordeaux wines. The estate stretches over clay-limestone hillsides close to the fortified citadel of Blaye. This delightful 99 wine is already quite far advanced in its development, and is therefore ready to be drunk. Its colour is a brilliant garnet, and its mainly Merlot content has given it grape-jelly aromas along with notes of peel and chocolate. The mature tannins are round and velvety. There is plenty of body here, and it has reached full maturity.

⚷ SCEA Vignobles Louis Marinier, Dom. Florimond-La Brède, 33390 Berson, tel. 05.57.64.39.07, fax 05.57.64.23.27, e-mail vignobleslouismarinier@wanadoo.fr ☑ 🍷 ev. day 8am–12 noon 2pm–6pm; Sat. Sun. by appt.; cl. Aug.

CH. FRAPPE PEYROT

Elevé en barrique 1999★

■ 15 ha 10,000 🛢 €5–8

The wine has a pleasant colour which gives off a dark purple gleam when it is swirled in the glass. After the powerful, spicy bouquet, the attack is frank and clean. This is still a young, lively wine, based on a structure with good tannins followed by an agreeable finish that will be even better when it has aged for a while. Wait until its youthfulness has passed.

⚷ Jean-Yves Arnaud, La Croix, 33410 Gabarnac, tel. 05.56.20.23.52, fax 05.56.20.23.52 ☑ 🍷 by appt.

CH. GEROME LAMBERTIE 1998★

■ 25 ha 50,000 ▮ 🌡 –€3

On his return from the seventh crusade, Alphonse de France (a brother of Saint-Louis) founded the beautiful walled town of Sainte-Foy-la-Grande (1255), which you must visit before tasting this mainly Merlot wine (70%). It has a garnet colour and a nose of fruit aromas and vegetable notes (green peppers). There is an elegant, fresh attack on the palate, followed by a delicate flavour of red berries which gives way to a full, elegant finish. The balance is such that you can drink a few bottles in the near future and keep the rest for a few more years.

⚷ EARL Jean-François Ossard, 3, La Lambertine, 33220 Pineuilh, tel. 05.57.46.12.04, fax 05.57.46.31.28

G. DE GINESTET 1999

■ 260 ha 2,000,000 ▮ 🌡 €3–5

Everyone knows what a vital contribution the *négociant-éleveur* makes to the international reputation of Bordeaux wines. The Ginestet firm offers some great brand names which enable it to play a decisive part in the region's success. This wine has a pleasant, translucent ruby colour, and appealing, subtle aromas of plums and blackcurrants, which so clearly express the fruit itself that they almost suggest 'early harvest'. A fragrant finish on the same aromatic register is accompanied by a few tannic echoes. This wine is ready to drink. Another Ginestet brand, the **Marquis de Chasse Bordeaux red 99**, receives the same rating.

⚷ SA Maison Ginestet, 19, av. de Fontenille, 33360 Carignan-de-Bordeaux, tel. 05.56.68.81.82, fax 05.56.20.96.99, e-mail contact@ginestet.fr 🍷 by appt.

CH. GIRUNDIA 1999★★

■ 3 ha 25,000 ▮ 🌡 €5–8

Based on a small selection of plots and an unusual grape blend (50% Merlot, 50% Malbec), this Blayais wine won over the Jury members with its beautiful, intense crimson colour fringed with ruby glints and its nose of crystallised fruits. It has great fullness on the palate, where the tannins are still powerful and full of flavour, giving way on the finish to a triumphant return of plums and crystallised cherries. This wine is for longer maturing, and will be a good accompaniment to woodcock.

⚷ SCEA Ch. Ségonzac, 39, Ségonzac, 33390 Saint-Genès-de-Blaye, tel. 05.57.42.18.16, fax 05.57.42.24.80, e-mail segonzac@chateau-segonzac.com ☑ 🍷 by appt.

CH. DES GRANDS BRIANDS

Elevé en fût de chêne 1998★

■ 7.5 ha 32,000 🛢 €3–5

The Merlot and Cabernet Sauvignon vines at this château have the advantage of a noble, rich gravel *terroir*. This has produced a wine whose great elegance and finesse show in its strong colour and very charming nose of peonies, faded roses, tea and honeysuckle. After a sweet attack it becomes slender and almost caressing on the palate. There is a simple, luscious finish on a very captivating note of oaky vanilla.

↬ Ch. du Grand Briand, ZAE de l'Arbalestrier, 33220 Pineuilh, tel. 05.57.41.91.50, fax 05.57.46.42.76 V
Y by appt.

CH. HAUT-CASTENET 1999★
■ 15 ha 120,000 €5-8 V

The Haut-Castenet estate is located at the heart of the Guyenne area, where 'the song of stone' still rises into the sky. You can see this not far away at the fortified abbey-church of Saint-Ferme (11th century) where the capitals recount the most beautiful scenes from the Old and New Testaments. This is where François Greffier, advised by oenologist J.-M. Jacob, makes and matures a wine with a brilliant ruby colour and a soft, round character. The fine, powerful bouquet continues on an ample, almost full-bodied palate where delightful young tannins are still clearly apparent. This handsome young star will be well suited to meat and game when it has lost its austerity.

↬ EARL François Greffier, Castenet, 33790 Auriolles, tel. 05.56.61.40.67, fax 05.56.61.38.82, e-mail ch.castenet@wanadoo.fr V Y by appt.

CH. GROSSOMBRE 1999★
■ 7 ha n.c. €5-8

A few miles from the flagship estate at Château Bonnet, Béatrice Lurton rules over the destiny of Château Grossombre, which is much more modest in size but whose wines enjoy a well-deserved reputation. This one has been matured in oak for a year, and comes from a grape blend dominated by Cabernet. It has a majestic colour and a delightfully fresh bouquet, and is a round, chocolatey wine with its rich flesh softens the abundant yet well-tempered tannins. With its fine toast notes, this is a wine of great elegance and fullness which is only just beginning to develop.

↬ Béatrice Lurton, BP 10, 33420 Grézillac, tel. 05.57.25.58.58, fax 05.57.74.98.59, e-mail andrelurton@andrelurton.com V

GRAND VOYAGEUR
Elevé en fût de chêne 1998
■ 2 ha 13,200

This Grand Voyageur wine still has a long journey ahead! It has a lovely, intense ruby colour, and a nose of ripe fruits and fruit stones, along with slight hints of spice and a note of oak which is still apparent. The palate has a powerful structure with clearly evident tannins. Mocha, cedar and a touch of pepper are the ingredients that go to make up this wine, but the recipe needs more time to balance out the different elements.

↬ Benoît et Valérie Calvet, 44, rue Barreyre, 33300 Bordeaux, tel. 05.57.87.01.87, fax 05.57.87.08.08, e-mail contact@bvcbordeaux.com

CH. HAUT-GAUSSENS 1999
■ 1 ha 5,000 €3-5

Of the 27 ha (67 acres) owned by this estate, only 1 ha (2.5 acres) was used for this oak-matured wine. It appeals straight away with its lovely light crimson colour. The nose is subtly divided between prunes and black-currants, which do not mask a delicate aroma of oak. The attack on the palate offers a well-integrated, elegant, lingering combination of aromas and flavours, followed by a long finish on notes of spice during which the tannins become more subdued. A few years of ageing will enable this wine to reach its full potential.

↬ Lhuillier, Guiard, 33620 Laruscade, tel. 05.57.68.50.99, fax 05.57.68.50.99 V
Y by appt.

CH. HAUT-MAZIERES 1999
■ 19.61 ha 164,000 €5-8 V

Although this 99 wine is still young, the brick-red glints in its colour and its flavours on the palate show that it is beginning to develop. The tannins are in the right place, and disappear of their own accord in a clean, supple finish which inspires complete confidence in the future of this wine.

↬ Union de producteurs de Rauzan, 33420 Rauzan, tel. 05.57.84.13.22, fax 05.57.84.12.67 Y by appt.

CH. HAUT PARABELLE 1999
■ 4 ha 20,000 €3-5

Every day the sun turns a complete circle around the east-west-facing hillsides of Haut Parabelle. Here even the Cabernet Sauvignon grape become fully ripe. It has produced this wine in equal shares with Merlot, and has given it a brilliant ruby colour. The body is supple and rich, and the tannins are already well integrated. The wine is ready to drink now.

↬ SCEA vignoble Yvan Brun, Coureau, 33330 Saint-Sulpice-de-Faleyrens, tel. 05.57.24.61.62 Y by appt.

CH. DE JABASTAS 1999★
■ 2 ha 15,000 €3-5

This wine comes from the smiling banks of the Dordogne, not far from where the Château de Vayres is reflected in the river. It shows all the qualities of its pleasant situation in an astonishingly brilliant, very strong garnet colour, an intense, delightfully fresh nose (raspberries and redcurrants), and a pleasant palate with a full body and a flavour of overripe morello cherries. It is ready to be served with good food now, but will also benefit from ageing for three years in a cool cellar.

↬ Jean-Marie Nadau, Ch. de Jabastas, 35, av. des Prades, 33450 Izon, tel. 05.57.84.97.13, fax 05.57.84.97.14 V

Bordeaux

CLOS JEAN 1999

■   5 ha   30,000   €5-8

In the middle of this hillside vineyard overlooking the Garonne, there is a beautiful 18th-century residence. The Bordeaux here is made from 80% Merlot, which has given it the grape's typical aromatic range based on an abundance of soft fruits and dark berries (blackcurrants, prunes and bilberries). The structure on the palate is very supple, round, and completely unaggressive. This is a traditional type of wine which is ready to drink now.

➤ SCEA vignobles Lionel Bord, Clos Jean, 33410 Loupiac, tel. 05.56.62.99.83, fax 05.56.62.93.55, e-mail closseau@ vignoblesbor.com ▼ Ⅰ ev. day 8.30am–12 noon 2pm–5.30pm; Sat. Sun. by appt.

CH. JOININ 1999★

■   15.48 ha   65,000   €3-5

This Entre-Deux-Mers estate belongs to the Mestreguilhems, who are owners of Château Pipeau at Saint-Emilion. This 99 has both the colour of black, overripe cherries and their aroma in the nose, where it is combined with bilberries and late-summer blackberries. The palate has an abundance of silky tannins, and follows a well-structured course. It will be the perfect wine to accompany an *entrecôte bordelaise*, and can be enjoyed in a year's time and for three or four years after that.

➤ Brigitte Mestreguilhem, 33420 Rauzan, tel. 05.57.24.72.95, fax 05.57.24.71.25, e-mail chateau.pipeau@wanadoo.fr ▼

CH. LA BARDONNE 1999★

■   6 ha   48,000   €3-5

This wine has been produced by traditional methods, and comes from a selection of plots spread over the high hillsides of the Blayais. It has a soft, dark colour and a slight aroma of oaky vanilla. The tannins are still prominent, but will soon become integrated on the palate with the flavour of very ripe grapes. This is a classic, well-structured wine which needs to be kept carefully for a while.

➤ Vignobles Alain Faure, Ch. Belair-Coubet, 33710 Saint-Ciers-de-Canesse, tel. 05.57.42.68.80, fax 05.57.42.68.81, e-mail belair-coubet@wanadoo.fr ▼ Ⅰ by appt.

CH. LA BASSANNE 1999★

■   3 ha   4,400   €3-5

This wine has been lovingly produced from meticulously selected plots. Catherine Perret has crafted its rosy colour, and watched over its powerful, vinous bouquet of soft fruit and spicy aromas. Velvety tannins add the final touch to this creation, which time (two or three years) will bring to perfection.

➤ Catherine Perret, La Grande-Côte, 33124 Aillas, tel. 05.56.65.33.17, fax 05.56.65.30.59 ▼ Ⅰ by appt.

DOM. DE LA COLOMBINE 1999★

■   n.c.   10,000   €3-5

This wine is made mainly from Merlot (80%), and has a rich, garnet-red colour and very intense, fruity aromas. The palate has a delightfully round body, velvety, well-balanced tannins and developing flavours of crystallised fruits, undergrowth and humus. It is a mouthwatering wine which is ready to be served straight away, and can be drunk throughout a meal.

➤ Les producteurs réunis de Puisseguin et Lussac-Saint-Emilion, Durand, 33500 Puisseguin, tel. 05.57.55.50.40, fax 05.57.74.57.43 ▼ Ⅰ by appt.
➤ Jean-Louis Rabiller

CH. LA COMMANDERIE DE QUEYRET 1999★

■   30 ha   180,000   €5-8

Judging by its high-tech equipment and working methods, the old and noble residence of the Knights Templar (13th century) has adapted exceedingly well to modern times. The proof is this vintage, which has an intense carmine colour and concentrated aromas of red berries and blackcurrants. The round, full-bodied palate reveals fruit flavours before moving on to a silky finish. This wine can be enjoyed immediately, or kept for three years.

➤ Claude Comin, Ch. La Commanderie, 33790 Saint-Antoine du Queyret, tel. 05.56.61.31.98, fax 05.56.61.34.22 ▼ Ⅰ by appt.

DOM. DE LA CROIX 1999

■   15 ha   20,000   €3-5

This wine has a beautiful ripe cherry colour, an intense nose, a round palate where you crunch right into the Merlot grape, and finally an invigorating, well-structured finish which will do justice to a weekend meal of *entrecôte* grilled on vine shoots. With this wine it's a matter of taste; you can either enjoy it now, or put it by until much later.

➤ Jean-Yves Arnaud, La Croix, 33910 Gabarnac, tel. 05.56.20.23.52, fax 05.56.20.23.52 ▼ Ⅰ by appt.

CH. LA CROIX DE NAUZE 1999★

■   2 ha   6,000   €3-5

As yet this wine's bouquet is hiding its light somewhat under a bushel, somewhere in the folds of its dark colour, no doubt; some floral notes (iris and tuberose) are coming to the palate, however, and lending fragrance to the palate. The body is balanced by tannins which, although still firm, are already mature. The balance is gradually taking shape, but it would be best to wait a year if not more until the wine reaches full maturity.

➤ Xavier Dangin, 39, Micouleau, 33330 Vignonet, tel. 05.57.84.53.01, fax 05.57.84.53.83 ▼ Ⅰ by appt.
➤ Elies-Brignet

CH. LAGARERE 1999

18.75 ha 150,000 €3-5

At the beginning of the 20th century, this property was equipped with a system of sluices that enabled it to be flooded in order to combat phylloxera. This 99 vintage owes everything to the bold way in which the new owners have reorganised the vineyard, brought in new barrel-store equipment, and introduced modern techniques. The result here is an intelligently extracted wine. The aromas are dominated by soft fruits (sloes and cherries), which seem to be more developed on the palate than in the nose. The youth of the tannins suggests that the wine should be drunk between 2002 and 2005.

Paul Gonfrier, Ch. de Marsan, 33550 Lestiac-sur-Garonne, tel. 05.56.72.14.38, fax 05.56.72.10.38, e-mail gonfier@terre-net.fr by appt.

CH. DE LAGORCE Réserve 1999★

1 ha 2,000 €8-11

This wine is a balanced blend of Cabernet Sauvignon and Cabernet Franc. Its appeal lies in the subtlety of its fragrances; the colour is very intense, and there is a range of concentrated, lingering aromas with any number of nuances (redcurrants, blackberries and cherries). The wine has a good, substantial structure which gives it real potential to age well.

Benjamin Mazeau, Ch. de Lagorce, 33760 Targon, tel. 05.56.23.60.73, fax 05.56.23.65.02 by appt.

CH. LA GRAVE 1999

6.2 ha n.c. €5-8

Virginie Tinon, the young woman who runs this château, has created her first vintage developed on the basis of lessons learned from her father to offer a wine with an abundance of phenolic body and whose rich colour is as dense as its delicate jam aromas of plums and blackberries. The sound tannic support on the palate will ensure that the wine has a life span of a few years, which it will need in order to open out fully.

EARL Vignoble Tinon, Ch. La Grave, 33410 Sainte-Croix-du-Mont, tel. 05.56.62.01.65, fax 05.56.62.00.04 by appt.

CH. LAGRAVE PARAN 1999★

9 ha 45,000 €3-5

This château's lovely clay and gravel hilltop vineyards are planted with Merlot (70%) and Cabernet Franc (30%), and are harvested every year strictly by hand-picking, which is very rare these days. This Bordeaux has a beautiful colour with brilliant glints, a charming nose, and a rich palate where it develops intense flavours of ripe fruits (grapes, prunes). These enhance a round, supple body whose velvety tannins are lingering and well balanced. This delightful wine will be a pleasure to drink tomorrow, but it will become even more appealing over the next two or three years.

EARL Pierre Lafon, Ch. Lagrave-Paran, 33490 Saint-André-du-Bois, tel. 05.56.76.42.74, fax 05.56.76.49.78 by appt.

CH. LALANDE-LABATUT Cuvée Prestige Elevé en fût de chêne 1999

15 ha 100,000 €5-8

The wine has a brilliant colour and a fruity, full, pleasant bouquet which opens on a bouquet of crystallised cherries and quince. The transparent structure barely reveals the presence of tannins, and softens a slender body with flavours of spices, cedar and cocoa. There is an impression of roundness at the finish, which is embellished by a delicately oaky note of smokiness.

SCEA Vignobles Falxa, 38, Labatut, 33370 Sallebouf, tel. 05.56.21.23.18, fax 05.56.21.20.98, e-mail chateau.lalande-labatut@wanadoo.fr by appt.

CH. LA MIRANDELLE 1999

8.66 ha 50,000 €3-5

Located in an old, traditional wine-growing commune, and in an area of fortified walled towns and ancient abbey-churches, this château runs a little sloping vineyard planted on clay-limestone soils. It has produced a delightful wine whose garnet colour, nose of ripe fruits and silky texture are most appealing. The tannins are very measured, and are only there to lend subtle support to a finish on primary flavours which suggest that this would be a good wine to drink as soon as the *Guide* comes out.

Cellier de La Bastide, Cave coop. vinicole, 33540 Sauveterre-de-Guyenne, tel. 05.56.61.55.21, fax 05.56.71.60.11 ev. day except Sun. 9am-12.15pm
Yves Moncontier

CH. LA MOTHE DU BARRY Cuvée Le Barry 1999★★

2 ha 14,000 €8-11

One hundred and fifty years of family tradition have not dissuaded Joël Duffau from launching resolutely into the age of modernism and innovation. This oak-matured Le Barry comes from a careful selection of plots. It has an impressive, deep colour as dark as night, and an exceptional bouquet of morello cherries in brandy, blackcurrants and bilberries. All of this blends together against a background of roasted coffee and balsamic fragrances. There is a feeling of full, warm maturity on the palate, where a hint of truffle points unmistakably to Merlot (75%) as the source of so much richness. A few years of ageing will add further polish to this excellent wine. The Cuvée Design 99 did not disgrace itself (one star) and totals 35,000 bottles.

Joël Duffau, Les Arromans n°2, 33420 Moulon, tel. 05.57.74.93.98, fax 05.57.84.66.10, e-mail lamothed@club-internet.fr ev. day except Sun. 8am-12 noon 2pm-7pm

Bordeaux

CH. LARROQUE

Vieilli en fût de chêne 1999★

■ 56 ha 224,000 ▥ €5-8

This wine has an intense garnet colour, a lovely dominant fruit aroma on the nose, a delicately toasty touch of oak, then a vigorous palate with a very round body. It comes from a good harvest, and the tannins are still fresh; the very concentrated grape flavour is still there, but it is combined with oak at the finish. You can drink this wine at your leisure.

☙ Boyer de La Giroday,
18, rte de Montignac, 33760 Ladaux,
tel. 05.57.34.54.00, fax 05.56.23.48.78,
e-mail vignobles-ducourt@wanadoo.fr ▥
☋ by appt.

LA VIEILLE EGLISE 1999★

■ 20 ha 133,000 ■ ♦ €4-3

The colour here is an engaging, brilliant, garnet with brick-red highlights. Equally encouraging and very expressive are the opening aromas in the nose, which are a happy combination of fruits (blackcurrants and blackberries) and nuances of undergrowth and humus. The palate is very round, and reveals flavours of musk. This 99 wine can be drunk immediately, 'on the fruit', or left to age for a year or two.

☙ Domainie de Sansac, Les Lèves,
33220 Sainte-Foy-la-Grande,
tel. 05.57.56.02.02, fax 05.57.56.02.22
☋ by appt.

CH. LE DROT 1998★

■ 12 ha 10,000 ■ ♦ €3-5

The Cabernets and Merlot combine here to produce a wine with a high, clear, carmine colour, and scents of soft kernel fruits (cherries) which leap out in the nose. Flavours of dark berries and iris take over on the palate to add colour to a tender, mouth-filling finish. This 98 wine is ready to drink, but for perfectionists it will keep as well.

☙ Jean-Guy Issard, 33190 Bagas,
tel. 05.56.71.46.25, fax 05.56.71.46.25 ▥
☋ by appt.

CH. LE FREGNE

Vieilli en fût de chêne 1999★

■ 3 ha 7,000 ▥ €3-5

For centuries Castelviel has been well-known for its depiction of the sin of lust, which is so delightfully portrayed on one of the capitals in its Romanesque church. A tasting at Château Le Frègne, however, will provide a modern version of the pleasures of the senses. This vintage has a crimson colour with shades of dark purple, and enchants the spirit with the subtlety of its well-integrated aromas of morello cherries mingled with a fine note of chocolate which shows the dominating influence of Merlot. On the palate there is also a slight hint of blackcurrant which draws attention away from a few undisciplined tannins. The wine develops plenty of flavour at the finish, and its medium-term future is not in any doubt.

☙ EARL Le Frègne, 33540 Castelviel,
tel. 05.56.61.97.56 ☋ by appt.
☙ Serge Rizzetto

CH. LE GRAND BESSAL 1999★

■ 2 ha 10,000 ■ ♦ €5-8

Saint-Germain-du-Puch is proud of the presence on its land of a venerable and very beautiful fortified house which was built in the 14th century, at the time when the Black Prince reigned over nearby Bordeaux. From the watchtowers of Grand Puch you can see Château Le Grand Bessac, which is very much part of the modern world; it has produced a wine with a bigaroon cherry colour, a nose of blackcurrants and hyacinths, and a palate that reveals gamey notes of leather and musk. You have to climb a bit high above the tannins to sense a return to the fruit, but two to four years of ageing should enable them to become better integrated and balanced.

☙ SCEA Echeverria, Ricard,
33750 Saint-Germain-du-Puch,
tel. 05.57.24.54.96, fax 05.57.24.02.05 ▥
☋ by appt.

CH. LE MAYNE 1999

■ 17 ha n.c. ■ ♦ €5-8

Purchased in 1987, this vast estate of 70 ha (173 acres) is equipped with a very modern barrel store. With its moderately intense colour, ruby glints and complex bouquet in which fruit competes with nuances of spice, this is a charming, elegant wine which will go well with white meats. The round, slightly spicy palate lingers on to a delightfully sweet finish which will make it a pleasure to drink in the near future.

☙ SCEA Ch. Le Mayne,
33220 Saint-Quentin-de-Caplong,
tel. 05.57.41.00.05 ☋ ev. day except Sat.
Sun. 8am–12 noon 2pm–6pm

CH. LE MOULIN DU ROULET 1999

■ 5 ha 20,000 ■■ ♦ €3-5

A young woman has created this lovely wine made from three Bordelais grape varieties (60% Merlot). The vines here are planted on a clay-limestone hilltop overlooked by a windmill. Fine and delicately marked by oak of good lineage, this well-structured, full-bodied palate where very mature flavours reappear at the finish. It will develop greater length with time, and will be a good accompaniment to game. This merchant also offers the

☙ Catherine et Patrick Bonnamy,
Moulin du Roulet, 33350 Sainte-Radegonde,
tel. 05.57.40.58.51, fax 05.57.40.58.51 ▥
☋ by appt.

CH. LE NOBLE 1999★

■ 23 ha 94,000 ■ ♦ €5-8

The wine has a light, translucent colour, but displays a liveliness and roundness which suggest bigaroon cherries and prunes. The tannins are well contained on a substantial, full-bodied palate where very mature flavours reappear at the finish. It will develop greater length with time, and will be a good accompaniment to game. This merchant also offers the

Château Tuilerie Rivière 99, which is recommended.

☛ Maison Sichel-Coste, 8, rue de la Poste, 33210 Langon, tel. 05.56.63.50.52, fax 05.56.63.42.28

LE VIEUX MOULIN Cuvée spéciale
Elevé en barrique de chêne 1999★

2 ha · 12,000 · €5-8

It is worth paying a visit to the barrel stores of the Mähler-Besse firm, whose very old vineyard is planted in the traditional Bordeaux wine merchants' district (Les Chartrons). Made from Merlot alone (which is very rare in Bordeaux), this wine has an intense black colour and releases a remarkable range of aromas in the nose: game, truffles and dried figs. In the same vein, the palate is full and well structured, revealing the supple character of very ripe Merlot. A delicate note of toasty oak reappears on the finish. The wine is already pleasant, but is also suitable for longer maturing.

☛ SA Mähler-Besse, 49, rue Camille-Godard, BP 23, 33026 Bordeaux, tel. 05.56.56.04.30, fax 05.56.56.04.59, e-mail france.mahler-besse@wanadoo.fr
Y by appt.

CH. LION BEAULIEU 1999★★

4 ha · n.c. · €5-8

As you would expect, the GFA de Lyon is already planning a regal future for this very youthful cru. An aromatic, powerful, fruity presence characterises this authentic, mouth-filling wine, which exhibits the simple qualities of a thoroughbred, fleshy Bordeaux with plenty of body and good balance.

☛ GFA de Lyon, 33420 Naujan-et-Postiac, tel. 05.57.84.55.08, fax 05.57.84.57.31, e-mail contact@vignobles-despagne.com
☛ J. Elissalde.

LES VINS DE LISENNES
Cuvée de l'Artiste 1999

n.c. · 15,000 · €3-5

The label, designed by the famous Romanian engraver Chirnoaga who stayed at the château, states that 'this wine is bottled at the property by B. Dumas for the wines of Lisennes'. The wine comes from a clay-limestone terroir divided equally between Merlot and Cabernet, and has a clean, frank colour that has already developed some brick-red glints. A fruity, mature, delightfully fine nose is the prelude to an attack where the body is in keeping with the light tannins. This is a well-integrated wine which can be drunk without fuss.

☛ Jean-Luc Soubie, Ch. de Lisennes, 33370 Tresses, tel. 05.57.34.13.03, fax 05.57.34.05.36, e-mail contact@lisennes.fr Y by appt.

CH. DE L'ORANGERIE 1999★

27.35 ha · 229,000 · €3-5

Since 1790 the Icard family has jealously held on to this beautiful wine-growing property, guarded by the old walled town of Sauveterre-de-Guyenne. On a homogeneous

---

LES CHARMILLES DES HAUTS DE PALETTE Elevé en fût de chêne 1999

12 ha · 50,000 · €3-5

This is the first wine in which the Cabernets have the same share as Merlot. The colour is light and scattered with beautiful vermilion glints. Impulsive aromas enliven a bouquet which is still somewhat restrained (blackcurrants and hyacinths). The finesse of this wine should be enjoyed without delay.

☛ SARL Les Hauts de Palette, 4bis, chem. de Palette, 33410 Béguey, tel. 05.56.62.94.85, fax 05.56.62.18.11, e-mail les-hauts-de-palette@wanadoo.fr

---

DOM. DE L'ESCOUACH
Elevé en fût de chêne 1999★★

1 ha · 6,000

A very small enclosure containing old Merlot vines planted on clay-limestone slopes has produced this wine, which has an intense, deep-red colour, and appeals from the start with its nose of vegetal aromas (green pepper and mushrooms). The rich, remarkably well-balanced palate has pleasant tannins, and is embellished by a mixture of spicy flavours along with liquorice notes. An ageing potential of a few years can be envisaged.

☛ Pierre Rabouy, 33350 Saint-Pey-de-Castets, tel. 05.57.40.51.16, fax 05.57.40.51.16

CH. LES VERGNES 1999★

n.c. · 133,000

This is a delightfully fine, light wine. It does not open up until it has been swirled in the glass, when some touches of fruit stone appear along with blackcurrants and a hint of raspberry. This carefully calculated delicacy quickly gives way to a charming, velvety attack on the palate. You should enjoy this subtle combination without delay before time begins to tell.

terroir of fortified land, they have built up a vineyard that is notable for the good balance between the three main Bordeaux grape varieties. This vintage has a fine, delicate crimson colour, and distinctive spicy notes which open on to a frank, supple palate with measured tannins. This is a very characteristic, sound Bordeaux, which can be opened immediately or kept for two or three years.
• Jean-Christophe Icard, Ch. de l'Orangerie, 33540 Saint-Félix-de-Fonc aude, tel. 05.56.71.53.67, fax 05.56.71.59.11, e-mail orangerie@quatermet.fr
Y by appt.

CH. MAISON NOBLE
Cuvée Prestige Vieill en fût de chêne 1999   1.7 ha   13,000   €5-8

This wine comes from a very small selection of plots of siliceous-clay soil planted with 90% Merlot. It has a brilliant crimson colour and a nose of cocoa, followed by a full palate which strongly reflects the dominant grape variety. A good balance between measured oak and wild flavours of undergrowth suggests that the wine should be drunk soon or kept for a short while.
• Bernard Sartron, Maison Noble, 33320 Maransin, tel. 05.57.69.19.36, fax 05.57.69.17.78 Y by appt.

CH. MAURINE 1999★★
16.7 ha   138,400   €5-8

This 99 wine captivates right from the start with a shimmering colour and a bouquet of soft fruits (bilberries and redcurrants) and shades of toast. It has a rich, vinous palate centring on a dense, well-extracted body with flavours of cinnamon and toast. This wine has a fine, long structure, and can be drunk straight away or kept for a while.
• Union de producteurs de Rauzan, 33420 Rauzan, tel. 05.57.84.13.22, fax 05.57.84.12.67 Y by appt.
• Jacques Chandes

CH. MERLIN FRONTENAC 1999
3 ha   10,000   €3-5

Frontenac is famous for the quality of the golden stone extracted from its age-old quarries. This vintage has a ruby colour with shades of violet, and a nose that opens on charming aromas of red berries and autumn undergrowth. The fragrances then move on to mushrooms, dried berries, and finally crystallised fruits. With its mouth-watering, supple, smooth palate, this 99 wine is ready to be served immediately.
• SA La Croix Merlin, 16, rte de Guibert, 33760 Frontenac, tel. 05.56.23.98.49, fax 05.56.23.97.22 Y by appt.

CH. DU MONT 1998★★
6 ha   30,000   €5-8

Sweet white wines do not have the monopoly of the hillsides of Sainte-Croix-du-Mont; beautiful black grapes are also grown here, and in some cases hand-picked, as at the Château du Mont. The colour of this 98 wine is very intense, dark, and fringed with dark purple. The complex nose has a caramel aroma along with hints of spice, a small amount of *rancio* and some balsamic notes. The tannins dominate the palate but do not mask the luscious flavour. Some will say that this powerful, concentrated Bordeaux is ready to drink now, others that it is suitable for longer ageing. But the two need not be mutually exclusive.
• Vignobles Hervé Chouvac, Ch. du Mont, 33410 Sainte-Croix-du-Mont, tel. 05.56.62.07.65, fax 05.56.62.07.58 Y by appt.

CH. MOTTE MAUCOURT
Vieill en fût de chêne 1999   5 ha   10,000   €5-8

The mural paintings in the medieval church at Saint-Genis-du-Bois attract tourists, as should this crimson wine, which is a real find. Its extreme concentration is apparent in its crystallised flavours, which follow on very precisely from a delightful nose marked by maturation in oak. A bilberry flavour emphasises the dominant fruity tonality of this wine. The palate is long, but will need to wait for two or three years until the tannins are more subdued.
• GAEC Villeneuve et Fils, Ch. Motte Maucourt, 33760 Saint-Genis-du-Bois, tel. 05.56.71.54.77, fax 05.56.71.64.23 Y ev. day except Sun. 9am–12 noon 2pm–7pm

CH. PEYRILLAC 1999
n.c.   20,000   €5-8

This 99 wine is still at the stage of primary aromas (blackcurrants and strawberries). There is a rolling tide of tannins on the palate, after which it gradually uncovers the skilful alchemy of flavours that are just beginning to open out, revealing a delightful developing bouquet of peonies and carnations. The wine needs time to achieve its full expression, and must be allowed to age for one or two years.
• Jean-Pierre Roussille, 97, rte de Terrefort, 33240 Saint-André-de-Cubzac, tel. 05.57.43.27.00, fax 05.57.43.69.95 Y by appt.

CH. PIERROUSSELLE 1999★★
25 ha   150,000   €3-5

This Château Pierrousselle was produced by Hélène Desplat, a distinguished oenologist at the Ginestet firm. It appealed to the judges because of its nose of soft fruits and ripe grapes. The main grape variety is Merlot, which gives a pleasant roundness to a palate with a good balance between richness and supple, lingering tannins. The label, otherwise written in French, states in English that this wine is specially selected for the Co-op.
• SA Maison Ginestet, 19, av. de Fontenille, 33360 Carignan-de-Bordeaux, tel. 05.56.68.81.82, fax 05.56.20.96.99, e-mail contact@ginestet.fr Y by appt.
• M. Lafon

CH. PONCHEMIN 1999★ — 12.98 ha — 50,000 — €3-5

This Bordeaux with intense garnet glints comes from a vineyard where Merlot (45%) is grown along with both of the Cabernets; its good vinosity is embellished with scents of stewed fruits and prunes. The round, full-bodied, well-structured palate is gamey and musky. The wine will benefit from a few years of ageing in a good cellar.

➤ SA Yvon Mau, BP 01, 33190 Gironde-sur-Dropt Cedex, tel. 05.56.61.54.54, fax 05.56.61.54.61

PREMIUS Elevé en fût de chêne 1999 — 12.09 ha — 100,000 — €5-8

This wine's carmine colour and fine aromas of oak and spice lead on to an appealing palate which is entirely impregnated with blackcurrants and crushed bilberries. The palate is structured around tannins that are unsubdued but full of flavour, and will need to settle down for a year or two. Under the same label, the **2000 Dry Bordeaux** is recommended. This is a tender, refreshing wine which can be drunk immediately with white meats.

➤ SA Yvon Mau, BP 01, 33190 Gironde-sur-Dropt Cedex, tel. 05.56.61.54.54, fax 05.56.61.54.61

CH. PREVOST 1999★ — 30 ha — 225,000 — €3-5

A few steps away from the imposing Benedictine abbey of La Sauve Majeure (1079), the Garzaro family has for several generations been growing vines on the clay-limestone slopes of the Baron. Their 99 wine is a traditional blend of Merlot, Cabernet Sauvignon and Cabernet Franc, and has a lovely, velvety ruby colour with crimson glints. It is still full of its first fruity aromas, and has now started to develop: its ample substance and powerful body bode well for the future.

➤ EARL Vignobles Elisabeth Garzaro, Ch. Le Prieur, 33750 Baron, tel. 05.56.30.16.16, fax 05.56.30.12.63, e-mail garzaro@vingarzaro.com ☟ by appt.

CH. RAUZAN DESPAGNE 1999★★ — n.c. — n.c. — €5-8

Thanks to their rigorous team, the Vignobles Despagne carry off numerous laurels in this *Guide* every year. The Grand Jury awarded a *coup de cœur* both to this Château Rauzan Despagne and to the Tour de Mirambeau, also in AOC Bordeaux. In accordance with the rules (no more than one label per producer in the same appellation), Rauzan Despagne is the winner. The bouquet is already assertive, with aromas of violets and irises that lend even more beauty to the ruby colour with dark purple glints. The palate caresses the tastebuds with flavours of cinnamon and cloves on a framework of tannins which are still in evidence but will gain in refinement after three to five years of ageing.

➤ GFA de Landeron, 33420 Naujan-et-Postiac, tel. 05.57.84.55.08, fax 05.57.84.57.31, e-mail contact@vignobles-despagne.com
➤ J.-L. Despagne

CH. RAUZAN DESPAGNE
Cuvée Passion 1999★★ — n.c. — n.c. — €11-15

The Cuvée Passion at Vignobles Despagne is a very great classic which features regularly in the *Guide*. This year is no exception. The colour is more than dark, it is black, and although very ripe fruit mingles in the nose with oak and spicy aromas of cinnamon and tobacco. This intense bouquet explodes in the warmth of the palate into an abundance of flavours that linger on to a fragrant, luscious finish. A long and virtuous period of ageing is essential.

➤ GFA de Landeron, 33420 Naujan-et-Postiac, tel. 05.57.84.55.08, fax 05.57.84.57.31, e-mail contact@vignobles-despagne.com
☟ by appt.

CH. DE RIBEBON 1999★ — 25 ha — 150,000 — €3-5

The wine has a high colour which is very attractive to the eye. The full palate reveals well-integrated tannins and good vinosity. Still in its adolescence, this 99 wine will not acquire an extended aromatic range, but it will gain in expression with time.

➤ Alain Aubert, 57 bis, av. de l'Europe, 33350 Saint-Magne-de-Castillon, tel. 05.57.40.04.30, fax 05.57.40.27.02
☟ by appt.

CH. SAINT-ANTOINE
Réserve du Château 1999★ — 80 ha — 400,000

This vast estate, planted around a very beautiful 19th-century house, devotes most of its vineyard to the production of this Bordeaux. It is a garnet colour with ruby glints, and an enchanting nose with a collection of intense floral aromas. It is very mouth-filling on the palate, where richness is accompanied by notes of spice and roasting. This is a very supple wine which has a rich body, is easy to drink, and will remain pleasant for a long time.

➤ Vignobles Aubert, Ch. La Couspaude, 33330 Saint-Emilion, tel. 05.57.40.15.76, fax 05.57.40.10.14 ☟ by appt.

CH. SAINT-FLORIN 1999

■ ♦ n.c. 450,000 ■ €3-5

Located on the clay-limestone slopes of Soussac, this vineyard has produced a well-balanced 99 wine which has an excellent, deep structure clearly dominated by Merlot, and releases both floral and fruity aromas. The wine has good staying power on the palate, where although it is mouth-filling it does not mask the young tannins. The Jury calls this a true 'country' wine, and suggests serving it with ham and cabbage.

➤ Jean-Marc Jolivet, Ch. Saint-Florin, 33790 Soussac, tel. 05.56.61.31.61, fax 05.56.61.34.87 ▼ ▼ by appt.

CH. DES SEIGNEURS DE POMMYERS 1999

■ 9 ha 25,700 ■ ♦ €5-8

This Seigneurs de Pommyers wine is proud of its history, which goes back to the 13th century, and although it has been produced by modern organic methods, it sings the virtues of tradition. Its colour has shades of dark purple, and it has a lovely nose of irises and violets which is full of the freshness of spring. Flavours in a neighbouring register (faded roses, peonies) emerge on the palate, where the structure is fine yet full. The tannins are not dominant, and leave the finish to languish on sweet scents of menthol.

➤ Jean-Luc Piva, Ch. des Seigneurs de Pommyers, 33540 Saint-Félix-de-Foncaude, tel. 05.56.71.65.16, fax 05.56.71.65.16 ▼ ▼ by appt.

SIRIUS Elevé en fût de chêne 1998★

■ n.c. 330,000 ■

Sirius means one thing in the firmament. Here on earth it means several hundred thousand bottles. The wine has a mysterious, very complex nose where musky scents mingle with spicy aromas of black tobacco and incense. This is followed by an integrated palate with liquorice forming a scented vault and fruit reappearing at the finish in a fragrant, fresh bouquet. This will be the perfect accompaniment to tender young roast rabbit.

➤ Maison Sichel-Coste, 8, rue de la Poste, 33210 Langon, tel. 05.56.63.50.52, fax 05.56.63.42.28

CH. TALMONT 1999★★

■ 77.53 ha 330,000 ■ ♦

This 99 wine won the unanimous support of the Jury from the start by the intensity of

its garnet colour fringed with carmine notes. The very ripe bouquet of blackcurrants and cherries in brandy is still developing. Violet and spice flavours give the palate great complexity. The structure is reinforced by a rich, round web of tannins which will ensure good ageing potential.

➤ Prodiffu, 17-19, rte des Vignerons, 33790 Landerrouat, tel. 05.56.61.33.73, fax 05.56.61.40.57, e-mail prodiffu@prodiffu.com

➤ Patrick Mourgues

CH. THIEULEY

Elevé en fût de chêne 1999★

■ n.c. 100,000 ■ €5-8

Founded at the dawn of the second millennium by Saint Gérard, the abbey at La Sauve Majeure was a powerful landed domain and a spiritual centre whose influence extended to England. Nowadays Château Thieuley is also known in England, but for very different reasons. This vintage has a beautiful crimson colour, and opens out straight away on to notes of stewed fruits and blackberries, while at the same time showing a leathery, musky character which may come as a surprise. The palate has a fine, concentrated body whose density softens the tannins in the background. Very mature Merlot grapes give it a full, silky finish on a note of truffles.

➤ Sté des Vignobles Francis Courselle, Ch. Thieuley, 33670 La Sauve, tel. 05.56.23.00.01, fax 05.56.23.34.37 ▼ ▼ by appt.

CH. TOUDENAC

Elevé en fût de chêne 1999★

■ 25 ha 120,000 ■ €5-8

Once you have admired the abbey at Blasimon, which is a fine example of Romanesque architecture, you must go and see the fortified watermill at Labarthe, built in the 14th century by Benedictine monks. After that a visit to Château Toudenac will bring you back to the pleasures of the senses. This wine is strongly marked by empyreumatic notes – coconut and delicate toast – and is vinous and powerful on the palate, where a highly elegant oaky flavour reappears on the finish.

➤ Vignobles Aubert, Ch. La Couspaude, 33330 Saint-Emilion, tel. 05.57.40.15.76, fax 05.57.40.10.14 ▼ by appt.

CH. TOUR DE BIOT

Cuvée Vieilles vignes 1999★

■ 3 ha 20,000 ■ ♦ €5-8

No-one can blame Gilles Gremen for growing these 3 ha (7 acres) of mainly Merlot (70%) vines separately in order to develop this wine. As its deep-crimson colour suggests, it is substantial and has rich, powerful, complex aromas that suggest fully ripe grapes. The high concentration on the palate, clearly evident, velvety tannins and a fine, fruity flavour give it good length and an ageing potential of two to three years.

214

lingers on into soft, vanilla flavours. Further fruit notes at the finish indicate that the ageing process has already begun.

Patrice Turtaut, Cousteau, 33540 Saint-Sulpice-de-Pommiers, tel. 05.56.71.59.54, fax 05.56.71.63.81 [V] [Y] by appt.

CH. VIEUX LIRON
Vieilli en fût de chêne 1998   5 ha   n.c.   €5-8

This 98 wine comes from an equal partnership between Merlot and Cabernet, grown on the gravel soils of Escoussans (north-east of Cadillac). It has a fresh, cherry colour and a simple but frank nose that suggests vine-blossom. The palate has a robust tannic structure and a substantial body with a long, balsamic finish. This splendid vigour will be mellowed by the aroma of a large jugged hare.

Danièle Mallard, Ch. Daniodnet-Plaisance, 33760 Escoussans, tel. 05.56.23.93.04, fax 05.57.34.40.78, e-mail mallard@net-courrier.com [V] [Y] by appt.

Bordeaux clairet

CH. BRAS D'ARGENT 2000★   1 ha   8,000   €5-8

From the top of its 100-m (328-ft) gravel hillside (a high peak in the Gironde!), this château looks out over the Beuve, a charming tributary of the Garonne. It has produced a very appealing clairet with a fine colour and garnet glints, and a velvety palate accentuated by a light tannic structure, which is just what it needs to avoid being confused with an ordinary rosé. It has floral aromas suggesting rose petals, and full flavours of vanilla and liquorice on the finish.

EARL Vignobles Belloc-Rochet, Ch. Brondelle, 33210 Langon, tel. 05.56.62.38.14, fax 05.56.62.23.14, e-mail chateau.brondelle@wanadoo.fr [V] [Y] by appt.

CH. DARZAC 2000★   10 ha   80,000   €5-8

Château Darzac has had tremendous success with its clairet, as can be seen from the fact that 10 ha (25 acres) of Merlot and Cabernet are allocated to it, thus enabling it to combine quality and quantity. This model clairet has a very fine and delicate bouquet with fresh, balanced, summery aromas, while the body is supple, smooth, liquoricy and slightly spicy, fading out slowly to leave behind a very soothing impression.

SCA Vignobles Claude Barthe, 22, rte de Bordeaux, 33420 Naujan-et-Postiac, tel. 05.57.84.55.04, fax 05.57.84.60.23, e-mail chateau.fondarzac@wanadoo.fr [V]

Gilles Gremen, EARL La Tour Rouge, 33220 La Roquille, tel. 05.57.41.26.49, fax 05.57.41.29.84 [V] [Y] by appt.

CH. TOUR DE MIRAMBEAU
1999★★   n.c.   n.c.

This year honours are showered not just on a very limited selection of a few acres, but on the entire cru, which is a tribute to the technical mastery of the Despagne team. This wine has a dense, deep crimson colour and a delicious nose. The attack shows good balance between silky tannins and fruit, and the palate has round, jam flavours of blackcurrants, plums and wild blackberries. The long, shimmering finish is unforgettable.

SCEA Vignobles Despagne, 33420 Naujan-et-Postiac, tel. 05.57.84.55.08, fax 05.57.84.57.31, e-mail contact@vignobles-despagne.com [V] [Y] by appt.
J.L. Despagne

CH. VALROSE 1998★   8 ha   5,000   €8-11

This is a wine with an intense Bordeaux colour and bluish glints, and an appealing nose of very ripe, concentrated grapes, along with notes of cocoa, caramel and vanilla which give it a sense of sweetness. After a very substantial attack, it is rich and full-bodied on the palate, where the tannins are of high quality. The wine is mouth-filling and elegant, and its very good balance will ensure that it has good ageing potential.

SCEA Michel Barthe, 18, Girolatte, 33420 Naujan-et-Postiac, tel. 05.57.84.55.23, fax 05.57.84.57.37 [V]

CH. VERMONT
Cuvée Prestige Elevé en fût 1998   30 ha   20,000   €5-8

The 19th-century house here contains a chapel and is surrounded by a vineyard which is run in a strictly traditional way and harvested by hand. The Cuvée Prestige has a beautiful, velvety, rich colour, and an evocative, fruity nose (cherries, prunes). This is a pleasant wine with silky tannins and a supple, fresh body opening on to a delightful finish on a note of oaky toast.

Vignobles Dufourg, Ch. Haut-Marchand, 33760 Targon, tel. 05.56.23.90.16, fax 05.56.23.45.30 [Y] by appt.

VIEUX CHATEAU RENAISSANCE
Vieilli en fût de chêne 1998★   5 ha   8,000   €3-5

Very long maceration of the grapes on their skins has helped this wine-maker to get the best out of the fruit. This Bordeaux has a purple colour which is as dark and intense as a ripe black grape, with aromas of crushed berries and grape jelly. After a luscious, tender start, the palate seems a little more severe when the tannins appear, but good balance becomes apparent as the palate

Bordeaux clairet

CH. DE FONTENILLE 2000★
6 ha · 50,000 · €3-5

Château de Fontenille stands very close to the Sauve-Majeure abbey, and is a beautiful 18th-century manor house which extends a very warm welcome to visitors. This rather light-pink, slightly orangey wine has a delightfully fruity nose of blackcurrants with just a hint of grapefruit. The palate is fresh, thoroughbred and elegant; the slight sparkle gives it a pleasant, lively quality, which combines extremely well with a finish on a pronounced note of pear drops.
➤ SC Ch. de Fontenille, 33670 La Sauve, tel. 05.56.23.03.26, fax 05.56.23.30.03, e-mail defraine@chateau-fontenille.com
Y by appt.
➤ Defraine

CH. LA BRETONNIERE 2000★
2 ha · 16,000 · €5-8

Château de la Bretonnière is offering a well-extracted clairet with quite an intense ruby colour and scents of ripe red berries which are as aromatic as a home-made raspberry coulis. On the palate it develops an excellent structure, a good, mouth-filling balance, and lingering flavours. This wine is already revealing all its finest assets, and should be drunk without further ado.
➤ Stéphane Heurlier,
EARL La Bretonnière, 33390 Mazion, tel. 05.57.64.59.23, fax 05.57.64.59.23
Y by appt.

CH. LANDEREAU 2000★
8 ha · 50,000 · €5-8

This clairet has a rather pale colour, but its aromas have the exuberance of fragrant elderberries in spring. Bergamot orange is there too to enliven a round, fresh palate. This is an ideal wine for a barbecue.
➤ SC Vignobles Michel Baylet,
Ch. Landereau, 33670 Sadirac,
tel. 05.56.30.64.28, fax 05.56.30.63.90
Y by appt.

CH. MALROME Aristide Bruant 2000★
0.7 ha · 6,600 · €5-8

This magnificent house with an inner courtyard dates back to the Middle Ages, and has had some famous 'lodgers': a minister of Napoleon III and the painter Toulouse-Lautrec, who gave the inspiration for this very good Aristide Bruant wine which has a lovely label showing a painting by the great master. The wine has a brilliant, pale-pink colour with salmon-pink glints and a delightfully fine, very elegant bouquet with an abundance of exotic fruit aromas and a slight touch of vanilla. The palate is round and balanced, and has pleasant flavours of oak and hazelnuts.
➤ Ch. Malromé, 33490 Saint-André-du-Bois,
tel. 05.56.76.44.92, fax 05.56.76.46.18,
e-mail v.lartigue@malrome.com
Y by appt.

CH. DE MARSAN 2000★
n.c. · 46,000 · €3-5

This clairet has a very appropriate, quite intense, lovely red colour, and distinguishes itself by the elegance of a body which is both round and dense, and by the infinite delicacy of its vine-blossom and blackcurrant flavours. The pleasure lingers on to a very spirited, smooth, balanced finish which leaves a sense of cleanness and fragrance on the palate.
➤ SCEA Gonfrier Frères, Ch. de Marsan, 33550 Lestiac-sur-Garonne,
tel. 05.56.72.14.38, fax 05.56.72.10.38,
e-mail gonfrier@terre-net.fr Y by appt.

CH. MOULIN DE PONCET 2000★
2.5 ha · 20,000 · €5-8

The clay-limestone slopes of Daignac (between La Sauve and Branne in Entre-Deux-Mers) are home to the Cabernet Sauvignon vineyard which produced this clairet. Its very fresh nose seems to belie the first signs of development apparent in its slightly brick-red colour. It is dominated throughout by wild strawberries and raspberries, and enlivened by a barely perceptible hint of sparkle. The clean, mouthwatering palate leads on to a lovely, fruity finish with very good length.
➤ Vignobles Ph. Barthe, Peyrefus, 33420 Daignac, tel. 05.57.84.55.90, fax 05.57.74.96.57, e-mail vbarthe@club-internet.fr Y by appt.

LES VIGNERONS DE SAINT-MARTIN 2000★
0.85 ha · 7,400 · €3-5

Just like their patron saint on his horse, the Vignerons de Saint-Martin have cut up their vineyard to devote a good-sized plot of pure Merlot to this smooth, pleasant clairet. Its very rich bouquet has a very strong personality, which fortunately is tempered by the finesse of the aromas on the palate. This in turn is embellished by a long, lingering finish on redcurrant and blackcurrant notes.
➤ Cave coop. vinicole de Génissac, 54, le Bourg, 33420 Génissac, tel. 05.57.55.55.65, fax 05.57.55.11.61 Y ev. day except Sun. 9am-12 noon 2pm-6pm; Sat. 9am-12 noon

Bordeaux sec

CH. DES ANTONINS 2000★★
2 ha · 8,000 · €3-5

In the 13th century, the monks of Saint Anthony lived here, and concocted a 'Saint-Vinage' potion with which they cured a convulsive disease known as Saint Anthony's Fire. Something of that miraculous balm must have been passed down to this wine, whose richness and balance appealed very much to our Jury. It is a cheerful alliance between Sauvignon (65%) and Sémillon

(35%), and has aromas of well-ripened grapes. No doubt about it, this wine is a real blessing!

♠ Geoffroy de Roquefeuil, Le Couvent, 33190 Pondaurat, tel. 05.56.61.00.08, fax 05.56.71.22.07 ▼ by appt.

BARTON ET GUESTIER
1725 Réserve du Fondateur 2000★

The founder of Barton et Guestier would no doubt be amazed by the excellence of this 2000 white which bears his name. It has a brilliant gold colour and summer-fruit aromas (pears and peaches). It then throws out a charming note of slight acidity on a palate with a velvety, almost padded texture, and finishes on a very pleasant Sauvignon note, acknowledging the main grape variety in the blend (20% Sémillon).

♠ Barton et Guestier, Ch. Magnol, 87, rue du Dehez, 33292 Blanquefort Cedex, tel. 05.56.95.48.00, fax 05.56.95.48.01, e-mail barton-e-guestier@seagram.com

CH. BAUDUC 2000★★

5.48 ha 4,000 €5-8

The beautiful old house here nestles in the midst of a wooded 70-ha (173-acre) park and a 30-ha (74-acre) vineyard, and has a winery where you can refresh yourself with this excellent Bordeaux. This vintage has a brilliant, pale yellow colour, and a concentrated bouquet of very ripe fruits and almonds. The palate is light and extremely fine, and its floral accents with shades of mint and passion-fruit are fully in keeping with the richness of over-ripe grapes. Balance, nose and body: this wine has everything it takes. It came very close to winning a *coup de cœur*.

♠ SCEA Vignobles Quinney, Ch. Bauduc, 33670 Créon, tel. 05.56.23.22.22, fax 05.56.23.06.05, e-mail team@bauduc.com ▼ by appt.

BEAU MAYNE 2000★

n.c. n.c. €3-5

The *négociant-éleveur* Dourthe offers this wine with a fairly light straw-yellow colour which is remarkably brilliant in the glass. A delicate, complex nose is full of notes of fennel and white roses that continue on the rich, fine palate. A few exotic fruit flavours (pineapple, grapefruit) embellish and prolong a delightfully fresh finish.

♠ Dourthe, 35, rue de Bordeaux, 33290 Parempuyre, tel. 05.56.35.53.00, fax 05.56.35.53.29, e-mail contact@cvbg.com ▼ by appt.

CAVE BEL-AIR 2000★

n.c. 30,000 €3-5

The Sichel firm prides itself on the fact that it produces the wines in its range itself. The firm's expertise is very well illustrated by this 100% Sauvignon with a nose of honey, apricots and melon. The same aromatic richness is intensified on the palate, within a register that is full of freshness. This is a lovely, balanced, subtle dry Bordeaux

♠ Maison Sichel-Coste, 8, rue de la Poste, 33210 Langon, tel. 05.56.63.50.52, fax 05.56.63.42.28

CH. BEL AIR PERPONCHER
2000★★

This Bordeaux has a sumptuous straw colour, and a combination of power and aromatic finesse. Its initial aromas of broom, elderberries and delicate boxwood are followed by notes of lemon and grapefruit peel which herald a fresh, slightly firm palate. A well-judged blend of 60% Sauvignon, 20% Sémillon and 20% Muscadelle gives the wine a supple, integrated, long, distinguished structure.

♠ GFA de Perponcher, 33420 Naujan-et-Postiac, tel. 05.57.84.55.08, fax 05.57.84.57.31, e-mail contact@vignobles-despagne.com ▼

▼ by appt.

♠ J.-L. Despagne

CH. BELLE-GARDE 2000★

3 ha n.c. €3-5

The wine has a brilliant, beautifully transparent golden colour, and a wonderfully soft nose of fresh butter with scents of vanilla. The round, very mature palate is full of velvety, well-integrated floral fragrances (broom and rose petals), combined with honey and hazelnuts which pleasantly caress the palate. This is a delightful, highly elegant wine with excellent future prospects.

♠ Eric Duffau, Ch. Belle-Garde, Monplaisir, 33420 Génissac, tel. 05.57.24.49.12, fax 05.57.24.41.28, e-mail eric.duffau@wanadoo.fr ▼

▼ ev. day except Sun. 8am-12 noon 2pm-7pm; cl. 15-30 Aug.

CH. BOIS-MALOT 2000★

0.6 ha 5,000 €5-8

The vineyard is planted on a gravelly clay soil with a gravel subsoil, and contains equal shares of Sémillon and Sauvignon vines. This wine has a good colour with green glints, and a nose of exotic fruits and broom. The palate is well balanced, quite full-bodied and pleasantly long. Chill this wine well before drinking it in small sips.

♠ SCEA Meynard et Fils, 133, rue des Valentons, 33450 Saint-Loubès, tel. 05.56.38.94.18, fax 05.56.38.92.47 ▼

▼ ev. day except Sun. 8.30am-12 noon 2pm-7pm; cl. Sat. pm.

CH. DE BONHOSTE 2000★★

6.87 ha 20,000 €5-8

The harmony of the surroundings and the affability of the hosts are by no means the least of the charms of this appropriately named Château Bonhoste. The pleasure of a visit is further enhanced by the products of the estate. The style of this Bordeaux asserts itself from the start; its fine, lemony aromas combined with a hint of orange zest and pineapple and merit close analysis. Peach and quince flavours glide over the tender, silky palate and linger on to a long, gentle, well-considered finish.

SCEA Vignobles Fournier, Ch. de Bonhoste, 33420 Saint-Jean-de-Blaignac, tel. 05.57.84.12.18, fax 05.57.84.15.36
by appt.

CHAI DE BORDES 2000★

n.c. 100,000 €3-5

This 2000 wine has a pale-yellow colour with green glints, and a somewhat timid nose which, when the wine is swirled in the glass, releases citrus-fruit aromas of lemon and orange peel. New flavours appear in the mouth: acacia blossom and beeswax fill the palate and add their charm to a slender body that finishes on a fresh, elegant, long note of Sauvignon.

Cheval-Quancard, La Mouline, 4, rue du Carbouney, 33560 Carbon-Blanc, tel. 05.57.77.88.88, fax 05.57.77.88.99, e-mail chevalquancard@chevalquancard.com by appt.

CH. BOURDICOTTE 2000★

3 ha 30,000 €3-5

This wine is a rather unusual blend of 90% Sauvignon and 10% Muscadelle. Both its colour and nose suggest the intoxicating charm of fresh-mown hay and the nostalgia of dried flowers. The same sense of autumn reappears on the palate, which is already quite developed, with well-balanced, pleasantly lingering flavours of figs, dried fruits and cherry stones.

SCEA Rolet Jarbin, Dom. de Bourdicotte, 33790 Cazaugitat, tel. 05.56.61.32.55, fax 05.56.61.38.26

CALVET RESERVE 2000

n.c. 33,000 €3-5

This pale-yellow Calvet Réserve owes its fruity elegance to its very high Sémillon content (80%), and its slight touch of mineral freshness to Sauvignon. The dense, vigorous body shows the advantages of a successful alliance between grape and oak. This well-balanced, long wine will go well with seafood and grilled fish.

Calvet, 75, cours du Médoc, BP 11, 33028 Bordeaux Cedex, tel. 05.56.43.59.00, fax 05.56.43.17.78, e-mail calvet@calvet.com

CHORUS Elevé en fût de chêne 1999

n.c. 12,000 €3-5

This Chorus has quite an intense, lemon-yellow colour, and reveals delicate floral aromas (eglantine and honeysuckle) when it is swirled in the glass. A very fine note of toast becomes more apparent on the palate, within a pleasantly acidic, subtly fruity structure. This fairly vigorous wine is developing an agreeably long finish which leaves the palate very clean. It will be a good accompaniment to seafood and shellfish.

J.J. Mortier et Cie, 62, bd Pierre-1er, 33000 Bordeaux, tel. 05.56.51.13.13, fax 05.57.85.92.77, e-mail mortier@mortier.com ev. day except Sat. Sun. 8am-6.30pm

CLOS DES CAPUCINS 2000★★

1.2 ha 9,000

This vintage has a slightly sparkling, grey-gold colour and a bouquet of well-ripened fruits and crystallised citrus fruits, combined with mineral notes (gunflint) and almonds. The mouthwatering, well-balanced palate has lingering fruity flavours sheathed in a substantial, almost creamy texture. The pleasure is prolonged by the overall sense of harmony.

SCEA Jean Médeville et Fils, Ch. Fayau, 33410 Cadillac, tel. 05.57.98.08.08, fax 05.56.62.18.22, e-mail medeville-jeanetfils@wanadoo.fr ev. day except Sat. Sun. 8.30am-12.30pm 2pm-6pm

CH. CRABITAN BELLEVUE 2000★

1 ha 8,000 €3-5

Along with his sweet wines, Bernard Solane practises his skill in the field of dry whites as well. This 2000 cuvée offers freshness without harshness, and is enlivened by springtime aromas of acacia, lily of the valley and citronella. It has a very straightforward, clean palate with well-integrated flavours, and will be a good accompaniment to any white meat in sauce.

GFA Bernard Solane et Fils, 33410 Sainte-Croix-du-Mont, tel. 05.56.62.01.53, fax 05.56.76.72.09 ev. day except Sun. 8am-12 noon 2pm-6pm

CH. DOISY-DAENE 2000★

6 ha 25,000 €11-15

This dry Bordeaux has been produced by two recognised masters of Bordeaux wine-making, Denis Dubourdieu and his father, who own this Sauternes-classified growth. It has a pale-gold colour and is a creation of great aromatic complexity, with a combination of lychee, pineapple and mango fragrances. It brings out the nobility of the oak in which it has been matured very well in a delightful note of toast, and leaves a very light, lively, satisfying impression on the palate.

EARL Vignobles P. et D. Dubourdieu, 10, quartier Gravas, 33720 Barsac, tel. 05.56.27.15.84, fax 05.56.27.18.99 by appt.

CH. FONREAUD Le Cygne 2000★

1.9 ha 14,000 €8-11

More than ten years ago Château Fonréaud revived an old tradition of Médoc white wines. At the beginning of the 20th century, a highly-reputed dry white wine known as 'Le Cygne' was produced here. This latest version at the end of the century comes from a blend in which Sauvignon (60%) is combined with equal shares of Muscadelle and Sémillon (20% each). It has a pale-yellow colour with green glints, and a bouquet which suggests the juicy flesh of nectarines and the 'roasted' aroma of overripe apricots. A flavour of ripe grapes fills a rich palate, on which notes of toast accompany this fruity melody like a voice in the background. There are more delights at the finish.

⚬ Ch. Fonréaud, 33480 Listrac-Médoc, tel. 05.56.58.02.43, fax 05.56.58.04.33 ▼
Y ev. day except Sat. Sun. 9am–11.30am 2pm–5.30pm
⚬ Héritiers Chanfreau

CH. FRANC-PERAT 2000★★   6 ha   30,000   €8-11

A fine siliceous-clay *terroir* planted with Sauvignon and Sémillon produced this luminous golden-yellow dry white. The nose is a sheer enchantment: vanilla, quince jam and white flowers. The same impression continues on the palate, which has a fresh, lively attack and remarkably good length. A pleasure like this calls for prompt gratification.

⚬ SCEA de Mont-Pérat, 33550 Capian, tel. 05.57.84.55.08, fax 05.57.84.57.31.
e-mail contact@vignobles-despagne.com
Y by appt.
⚬ J.-L. Despagne

CH. GAYON 2000★★   1.72 ha   8,000   €3-5

During the Revolution, a member of the family owning this beautiful and very old estate was the first victim of the Terror in the Bordeaux region. Nowadays the gentle slopes of Caudrot inspire serenity, as does the light-amber colour of this wine with its sweet fragrances of honey and acacia. Its delightful structure is rich enough to caress the taste-buds, and is sharpened at the finish by a refreshing note of menthol. With these excellent qualities it is not so much suitable for drinking as for sipping appreciatively, for instance as an aperitif. This elegant, thoroughbred wine is now at its peak.

⚬ Jean Crampes, Ch. Gayon, 33490 Caudrot, tel. 05.56.62.81.19, fax 05.56.62.71.24, e-mail jcrampes@chateau-gayon.com ▼ Y ev. day 8am–12 noon 2pm–6pm; Sat. Sun. by appt.

GINESTET

Vinifié et élevé en fût de chêne 2000   n.c.   100,000   €3-5

Tribute should be paid to the great Bordeaux wine-merchants who demonstrate that

the quantity of wine put on the market need not exclude quality. This wine delights from the start with its fresh-straw colour and aromas of dried figs and crystallised grapes. The rich, round palate reveals flavours of orange peel, and glides gently on to a vanilla and honey finish.

⚬ SA Maison Ginestet, 19, av. de Fontenille, 33360 Carignan-de-Bordeaux, tel. 05.56.68.81.82, fax 05.56.20.96.99, e-mail contact@ginestet.fr ▼ Y by appt.

CH. DU GRAND-MOUEYS 2000★   17 ha   n.c.   €3-5

There is an ancient, 6th-century Gallo-Roman villa here, and also a medieval chateau whose history should be gone into with caution, given that it reeks of sulphur and the acrid odour of the stake that was erected for the Knights Templar. Much more soothing is the elegant freshness of this 2000 wine, which is smooth both in the nose and on the palate, where there are flavours of crystallised fruits, peaches and apricots. There is a round finish on an abundance of soft honey notes.

⚬ SCA Les Trois Collines,
Ch. du Grand-Mouëys, 33550 Capian, tel. 05.57.97.04.44, fax 05.57.97.04.60, e-mail cavif.gm@ifrance.com ▼ Y by appt.

CH. DU GRAND PLANTIER 2000★★   1.5 ha   8,000   €5-8

Let's not beat around the bush, this wine is superb, bordering on first-class, and what is more well matured (on fine lees, needless to say). It owes its *coup de coeur* to its youthful, light-golden colour and the complexity of its powerful, captivating bouquet. The palate is full of bewitching, gossamer impressions of white flowers, lime-blossom and eglantine. Thoroughbred to the finish, this wine will be an inexhaustible source of happiness on every occasion.

⚬ GAEC des Vignobles Albucher, Ch. du Grand Plantier, 33410 Monprimblanc, tel. 05.56.62.99.03, fax 05.56.76.91.35 ▼
Y by appt.

CH. GUILLAUME BLANC

Elevé en fût 2000★   2.31 ha   n.c.   €3-5

The 98 wine won a *coup de coeur* in the 2000 *Guide*. The 2000 vintage is a captivating wine with an intense, golden-yellow colour whose brilliance recalls the gilded splendour of a

liquoreux. The aromas are marked by over-ripe, almost roasted fruit, and there is a very rich, powerful, fleshy palate with flavours of dried fruit (almonds) and crystallised apricots. A very sweet, vanilla finish marks this out as a vigorous wine, worthy to be drunk with langoustines cooked in Cognac.
➤ SCEA Ch. Guillaume, lieu-dit Guillaume-Blanc, 33220 Saint-Philippe-du-Seign al, tel. 05.57.41.91.50, fax 05.57.46.42.76 ☒ ☒ by appt.

CH. HAUT-GARRIGA 2000★   2 ha   10,000   €3-5

Château Haut-Garriga devotes 2 ha (5 acres) of Sémillon to this wine, which boasts a nose with an abundance of citrus-fruit peel aromas (oranges and mandarines), and very sweet, honeyed, slightly vanilla fragrances. Freshness is supplied by the flavours of verbena and bergamot orange on the palate. There is no acidity, however, and the roundness is delightful.
➤ EARL Vignobles C. Barreau et Fils, Garriga, 33420 Grézillac, tel. 05.57.74.90.06, fax 05.57.74.96.63 ☒ ☒ by appt.

CH. HAUT RIAN
Cuvée Excellence 1999★   2 ha   12,000   €5-8

When Michel Dietrich boldly named this wine 'Excellence' it really meant something to him, since he has put endless effort into developing it from Sémillon vines which are at least 35 years old. Sunny pineapple and grapefruit flavours flood the palate before giving way to a lovely note of slightly toasty oak on a long vanilla finish. The **2000 Dry Bordeaux** is not matured in oak and receives the same rating. It is delicate, tender wine whose attraction lies more in its balance than in its power.
➤ Michel Dietrich, La Bastide, 33410 Rions, tel. 05.56.76.95.01, fax 05.56.76.93.51 ☒ ☒ ev. day except Sun. 9am–12 noon 2pm–5.30pm; cl. 10-31 Aug.

CH. DU JUGE 2000★   8 ha   65,000   €5-8

This wine has a pale-gold colour in which one detects a slight sparkle. There is an intense nose of passion-fruit and mandarines, followed by a tender, rich palate that throws in some Muscat notes among the unusual flavours of quince and rhubarb. This is an adventurous wine which will appeal to curious spirits and is ultimately very captivating.
➤ Pierre Dupleich, Ch. du Juge, rte de Branne, 33410 Cadillac, tel. 05.56.62.17.77, fax 05.56.62.17.59, e-mail pierre.dupleich@wanadoo.fr ☒ by appt.
➤ David

LABOTTIERE 2000★   n.c.   n.c.   €3-5

This wine boasts a prestigious name, taken from a very beautiful private mansion in the old Saint-Seurin district of Bordeaux, which is a masterpiece of decorative delicacy in the best tradition of high French taste. Its lovely pale colour is clear and brilliant, and the bouquet has aromas of very ripe fruit, currants, dried apricots and bananas. This initial approach is confirmed by the flavours on the palate, where the very ripe, rich, warm Sauvignon is sufficient unto itself. The colourful, sweet finish on passion-fruit and lychee calls for a pikeperch or a roast capon.
➤ Cordier-Mestrezat et Domaines, 109, rue Achard, 33000 Bordeaux, tel. 05.56.11.29.00, fax 05.56.11.29.01

CH. LA CADERIE 2000★   2.09 ha 5,000   €5-8

The archives confirm that La Caderie was already producing wine during the Revolution. The tradition has been maintained and enhanced along the way by all the benefits of modern techniques. This wine comes from a harvest that was hand-picked on a plot where vines have been grown for over a century. It has a delightfully fine, elegant nose which opens on an aroma of toast before moving on to lemon and verbena. This bouquet is still apparent on the palate, which is round and fresh. Maturation on lees has made this a long, luscious, substantial wine.
➤ François Landais, Ch. La Caderie, 33910 Saint-Martin-du-Bois, tel. 05.57.49.41.32, fax 05.57.49.41.32 ☒ ☒ by appt.

LAITHWAITE 2000★★   n.c.   132,300   €3

This elegant, perfectly finished Sauvignon will appeal very much to the British market, both for its brilliant straw colour and for its delightfully fresh bouquet of citronella, verbena and orange blossom. After a firm, vigorous start, the wine reveals a supple body which is tender without being heavy, and has slight flavours of butter and toast. It remains alert to the finish, and will be a good accompaniment to grilled shad with fried aubergines or asparagus in white butter.
➤ SARL Direct Wines Ch. La Clarière Laithwaite, Les Confrères de La Clarière, 33350 Sainte-Colombe, tel. 05.57.47.95.14, fax 05.57.47.94.47 ☒ by appt.

CH. LAMOTHE DE HAUX 2000★   20 ha   200,000   €5-8

To produce 200,000 bottles of a wine like this is no mean feat. It has been achieved with this equal blend of Sauvignon and Sémillon, combined with 20% Muscadelle, and at least one can be sure of finding a bottle or two of this rich, opulent wine, which has a very contained note of acidity and autumn aromas of crab apples and quince. Given its one-star rating, the most modest of meals will become a banquet. It is ready to drink for pleasure without delay.

↦ Néel et Chombart, Ch. Lamothe de Haux, 33550 Haux, tel. 05.57.34.53.00, fax 05.56.23.24.49, e-mail neel-chombart@ chateau-lamothe.com ☑ ev. day except Sat. Sun. 9am–6pm

LEGENDE R 2000★

n.c. n.c.

Created by the Lafite team but distributed by Caves Nicolas, this Bordeaux comes from Sauvignon and Sémillon vines planted in Entre-Deux-Mers and Les Côtes, and is therefore a *vin de négoce*. It has been designed to be drunk while young, and with its lovely, fresh bouquet of lemon notes and fine, elegant palate, it achieves this objective to perfection.

↦ Domaines Barons de Rothschild Lafite Distribution, 33, rue de la Baume, 75008 Paris, tel. 01.53.89.78.00, fax 01.53.89.78.01

CH. DE L'ENCLOS 2000★★

1.2 ha 6,000 €8-11

This wine made from pure Sauvignon is a fine example of the grape variety's potential for high quality. Its great finesse in the nose (crystallised quince and white peaches) and clean, fruity palate give it a light, slender, and ultimately very appealing style. If drunk while still young, it will go best with seafood dishes or shad grilled over wood.

↦ Vignerons de Guyenne, Union des producteurs de Blasimon, 33540 Blasimon, tel. 05.56.71.55.28, fax 05.56.71.59.32 ☑
☙ by appt.
↦ Farges et Fils

CH. DE L'ESPERANCE 2000★

5 ha 40,000 €3-5

The Cazalis estate has allocated 5 ha (12 acres) of good clay-limestone soils to this wine made exclusively from Sauvignon. It has produced a white wine of a slightly surprising nature, with exotic fruit aromas (kiwi) and shades of blond tobacco and liquorice. The palate is extremely pleasant, soft and slightly biscuity, and has long, lingering notes of spice.

↦ SCEA Dom. de Cazalis, 33350 Pujols, tel. 05.57.40.72.72, fax 05.57.40.72.00, e-mail chateau-cazalis@wanadoo.fr ☑
☙ by appt.
↦ Claude Billot

CH. DE LOS 2000★

3 ha 30,000 €3-5

Although this 2000 vintage has the pale colour of acacia honey, it also has a very spirited bouquet of broom and boxwood, combined with complex notes of tar and incense. The tender, silky palate is well balanced to the finish and astonishingly fresh.

↦ SCEA Vignobles Siguié, 505, Petit-Moulin-Sud, 33760 Arbis, tel. 05.56.23.93.22, fax 05.56.23.45.75, e-mail signevignobles@wanadoo.fr ☑
☙ by appt.

BLANC DE LYNCH-BAGES 2000★

4.5 ha 36,000 €23-30

There is no doubt that these new white Médocs are formidable competitors, produced with an expertise which becomes more apparent every year. This Blanc de Lynch-Bages has a brilliant, pale colour and a becomingly modest nose enlivened by its bouquet of white flowers and boxwood. The palate is full of fresh notes (green peppers, agaric and citronella) which provide a fragrant, supple finish. This lively, thirst-quenching wine will greatly enhance a meal of cold hake.

MICHEL LYNCH 2000★

n.c. 200,000 €5-8

Nearly 200 years ago Michel Lynch was an illustrious figure in Médoc, known as an excellent wine-grower and the owner of Lynch-Bages. Today this is the brand name used by Jean-Michel Cazes in his merchant's business. The 2000 wine has an appealing, intense nose of floral nuances (jasmine and roses), and exotic fruit aromas (pineapple). A supple attack on the palate gives way to a full, rich body and a round, vigorous finish embellished by fruity flavours. The judges loved this delightful, mature wine.

↦ SNC Michel Lynch, BP 66, 33250 Pauillac, tel. 05.56.73.24.15, fax 05.56.59.26.42
↦ J.-M. Cazes

FLEUR DE LUZE 2000★

n.c. 27,000 €5-8

Since 1820 the Luze firm has been operating as a *negociant-éleveur*. This Fleur de Luze has a lovely, translucent gold colour, and a nose that offers a beautiful, skilfully balanced composition of springtime aromas of hawthorn blossom, lilacs and broom. The palate has a pleasantly mouth-filling, concentrated body with flavours of dried fruit (currants). The wine is a perfect combination of richness and freshness.

↦ A. de Luze et Fils, Dom. du Ribet, BP 59, 33451 Saint-Loubes Cedex, tel. 05.57.97.07.20, fax 05.57.97.07.27, e-mail deluze@grg.fr ☙ by appt.

JACQUES ET FRANCOIS LURTON 2000★

11 ha 109,000 €3-5

Jacques and François Lurton employ their dynamic commercial skills to produce this major Sauvignon wine, which is meticulously developed from well-selected grapes macerated on their skins. It has a brilliant, pale-gold colour and a fine yet powerful nose of privet blossom combined with mineral notes. The attack is fresh and suggests ripe, concentrated grapes. Hazelnuts add to the sense of balance at the finish, and the overall impression is of very good aromatic length.

↦ Jacques et François Lurton, Dom. de Poumeyrade, 33870 Vayres, tel. 05.57.74.72.74, fax 05.57.74.70.73, e-mail jflurton@jflurton.com

Bordeaux sec

➤ Jean-Michel Cazes, Ch. Lynch-Bages, 33250 Pauillac, tel. 05.56.73.24.00, fax 05.56.59.26.42, e-mail infochato@lynchbages.com
➤ Famille Cazes

MAYNE D'OLIVET 1999★★

☐   2 ha   12.000   €8-11

The Boidron family are real wine-growing and wine-making craftsmen, and have now opened up a new path by developing a high-class dry Bordeaux made from an innovative and very successful blend of Sauvignon Blanc, Muscadelle and Sémillon, and mainly Sauvignon Gris. Lychees, lemon and crystallised apricots are well balanced and integrated on a palate that is softly veiled with fine vanilla. This complex, mouth-filling array of flavours gives the wine excellent aromatic length.

➤ Jean-Noël Boidron, Ch. Corbin Michotte, 33330 Saint-Emilion, tel. 05.57.51.64.88, fax 05.57.51.56.30
Υ by appt.

MAYNE SANSAC 2000★

☐   5 ha   33.000   ■   ♦   €3-5

This wine has a beautiful, pale-gold colour with green glints and a bold, brilliant nose (citronella, mint and white flowers) against a fine, buttery background. The full, well-balanced body has a measured note of acidity, and starts on ripe fruits and honey before developing further on soft, satiny flavours. This is a delicate wine which can be drunk on its own as an aperitif, or with white meat.

➤ Domaine de Sansac, Les Lèves, 33220 Sainte-Foy-la-Grande, tel. 05.57.56.02.02, fax 05.57.56.02.22
Υ by appt.

CH. MOULIN DE PILLARDOT 2000

☐   3 ha   20.000   ■   €5-8

At Château de Pillardot, they take their time over making wines, maturing them for a long period on stirred lees. This one has a very floral bouquet, whose aromas of acacia, vine-blossom and broom form a sort of fragrant garland around a fresh palate of springtime flavours with a menthol finish and good length.

➤ Ch. Bourdicotte, Le Bourg, 33790 Cazaugitat, tel. 06.08.71.60.06, fax 05.56.61.38.26

PAVILLON BLANC DU CHATEAU MARGAUX 1999★★★

☐   n.c.   n.c.   ▥   €46-76

For some years now the Château Margaux Pavillon Blanc has been carving out a select place for itself among the greatest dry Bordeaux wines. This superb 99 is no exception. It has an appealing coppery colour and a remarkably complex bouquet combining fresh citrus fruit aromas with warmer notes of overripe fruit. The rich, dense, delicious palate also has a fine selection of flavours,

ranging from hazelnut butter to stewed pears. This powerful wine is as crunchy as a grape, and will be a worthy accompaniment to a fine fish dish in sauce.

➤ SC du Ch. Margaux, 33460 Margaux, tel. 05.57.88.83.83, fax 05.57.88.83.32

CH. PENIN 2000★

☐   2 ha   16.500   ▥   €5-8

Patrick Carteyron has added 15% of Sauvignon Gris to the traditional blend of his white Bordeaux. This is a powerful wine with a rich, complex combination of aromas from which grapefruit emerges particularly strongly. The fleshy, full-bodied palate allows its ripe fruit flavour to diversify into mandarines and dried apricots. 'At last some wine and ripe grapes!' exclaimed one delighted taster. Could there be a finer compliment?

➤ SCEA Patrick Carteyron, Ch. Penin, 33420 Genissac, tel. 05.57.24.46.98, fax 05.57.24.41.99 Υ by appt.

CH. PIERRAIL 2000★★

☐   10 ha   53.700   ■   ♦   €5-8

Once again Château Pierrail has brought out a top-of-the-range wine. It has a beautifully brilliant, straw-yellow colour, and a nose which successfully contrasts an aroma of toast with a floral explosion of honeysuckle and magnolia blossom. This is followed by an elegant, well-balanced palate, on which the same complex bouquet reappears and lingers on to a long finish. This is a really delightful wine, which should be served with a meal of the same class.

➤ EARL Ch. Pierrail, 33220 Margueron, tel. 05.57.41.21.75, fax 05.57.41.23.77, e-mail pierrail@chateau-pierrail.com Υ by appt.

CH. PIERRON 2000★

☐   8 ha   55.000   ■   ♦   €3-5

This large estate of about 100 ha (250 acres) is now run by the third generation. There are 8 ha (20 acres) of Sauvignon here, planted on a sandy, silty soil. The judges liked this wine's powerful aromas, which are both floral (broom) and fruity (white-fleshed fruits and green apples). Despite a somewhat sparkly attack, the palate becomes both rich and fresh. The springtime flavour of white flowers reappears on the finish, which is intense and long.

➤ GAEC Cardarelli, Laborne Nord, 33790 Massugas, tel. 05.56.61.48.13, fax 05.56.61.32.38

LE BLANC DU CHATEAU PRIEURÉ-LICHINE 2000★★
1.6 ha　7,000　€15-23

One envies the monks at the old priory, who had a communion wine reserved for them that was enough to bring the devil himself to his knees! This white Bordeaux made our judges swoon in profane adoration. It has an iris-yellow colour with touches of green apple, and a nose that sets off a real firework display of crystallised orange, grapefruit and orchard aromas: peaches, wild strawberries and apricots. The rich, fresh palate is embellished by toast and balsamic nuances.

• Ch. Prieuré-Lichine, 34, av. de la 5e-République, 33460 Cantenac, tel. 05.57.88.36.28, fax 05.57.88.78.93, e-mail prieure.lichine@wanadoo.fr ☑
Y by appt.
• M. Ballande

CH. REYNON Vieilles vignes 1999★
n.c.　72,000　€8-11

The old vines at Château Reynon have a well-established pedigree, and bear witness every year to the professionalism of the owner, who is an eminent promoter of new methods of white-wine vinification. Notable features here include hand-picking of grapes in a series of selections, and an obstinate search for the best possible aromatic extraction. This wine achieves its aim of bringing out the Sauvignon's full potential, with all its typical features and complexity. Its floral character (broom, rose petals) combines very well with a slight vegetal note, without masking the richness and velvet of a long, opulent palate.

• Denis et Florence Dubourdieu, Ch. Reynon, 33410 Béguey, tel. 05.56.62.96.51, fax 05.56.62.14.89, e-mail reynon@goformet.com ☑
Y by appt.

DOM. DE RICAUD 2000★
4.5 ha　36,000　€5-8

This estate is now run by a very sharp team, Régis Chaigne (a fount of new ideas) and his oenological adviser Jean-Louis. A high level of technical prowess has assured them of a place in the *Guide* for several years now. This 2000 wine combines the fruitiness of Sauvignon with the substantial roundness of Sémillon, while a slight touch of novelty (carnations and grape hyacinths) may well be the result of 5% of Muscadelle, which is not there by chance. Needless to say this wine is ready to drink now.

• Vignobles Chaigne et Fils, Ch. Ballan-Larquette, 33540 Saint-Laurent-du-Bois, tel. 05.56.76.46.02, fax 05.56.76.40.90, e-mail rchaigne@vins-bordeaux.fr ☑ Y by appt.

CH. DES ROCS 2000★
4.34 ha　20,000★

This is a delightfully polished creation. It has a colour as golden as acacia honey, then turns to the beehive again for its wax, before revealing its maturation on fine lees on

a very meaty palate with rich fragrances of vine-blossom. The full, rich finish will make this wine a good accompaniment to a plate of seafood.
• SCEA Vignobles Michel Bergey, Ch. Damis, 33490 Sainte-Foy-la-Longue, tel. 05.56.76.41.42, fax 05.56.76.46.42 ☑
Y by appt.
• F. Bellanger

CH. ROQUEFORT Tradition 2000★
32 ha　200,000　€5-8

Where white Bordeaux is concerned, Château de Roquefort is a model of quality. This Tradition is very floral (lily of the valley, hawthorn blossom and lilac), and has a frank, clean, powerful attack on the palate, whose richness and roundness combine well with a mineral flavour, carrying it through to a renewed floral note at the finish.
• SCE du Ch. Roquefort, 33760 Lugasson, tel. 05.23.97.48, fax 05.56.23.51.44, e-mail chateau-roquefort@wanadoo.fr ☑
Y by appt.

CH. TOUR DE MIRAMBEAU 2000★★

At J.-L. Despagne's, they know how to give you a really good grape flavour on the palate. That is certainly true of this 2000 Tour de Mirabeau, which has a sparkling green-gold colour, and melts you from the start with an aroma of vine-blossom, helped by a skilful combination of floral scents (acacia and elderberries). The supple, rich palate continues to delight with a succession of luscious flavours, scattered with cinnamon and grilled almonds.
• SCEA Vignobles Despagne, 33420 Naujan-et-Postiac, tel. 05.57.84.55.08, fax 05.57.84.57.31, e-mail contact@vignobles-despagne.com ☑
Y by appt.

CH. TURCAUD 1999★
2.4 ha　9,900　€5-8

Located at the heart of Entre-Deux-Mers, very close to the illustrious abbey at La Sauve Majeure, Château Turcaud produces Bordeaux white wines with a long-established reputation. This beautifully brilliant 99 wine has a pale-yellow colour with green glints, and an unmistakeable Sauvignon aroma enhanced by a fine note of oak. A frank, fresh attack is quickly followed by a developed, round palate with a combination of vanilla and crystallised fruit aromas. This is a wine to enjoy with friends.
• EARL Vignobles Robert, Ch. Turcaud, 33670 La Sauve, tel. 05.56.23.04.41, fax 05.56.23.35.85 ☑ Y by appt.

CH. VIEUX CARREFOUR 2000★
0.7 ha　4,000　€3-5

François Gabard, the owner of this château, can no longer count the generations between himself and the ancestor who first moved on to this property in 1745. His white

Bordeaux has an extremely elegant nose of peaches and lychees. Enlivened by a few sparkling bubbles, the round, utterly mouth-watering body combines honey and almond flavours with vanilla. The wine has a rich finish that will make it a good accompaniment to foie gras or game in a clear sauce.
🔑 EARL François Gabard, Le Carrefour, 33133 Galgon, tel. 05.57.74.30.77, fax 05.57.84.35.73 ☑ Ῑ by appt.

Bordeaux rosé

CH. BELLEVUE LA MONGIE 2000★

◪ 0.6 ha 5,000 ▮ ⫰ €3–5

This rosé makes a lovely raspberry disc in the glass. Its fresh, almost sharp bouquet of hawthorn and peonies also releases a few nuances of fresh almonds. The body is mouth-filling and fruity, and depends for its freshness on a slight touch of sparkle. This wine will make a delightful start to a meal, but it could also be served with dessert.
🔑 Michel Boyer, Ch. Bellevue La Mongie, 33420 Génissac, tel. 05.57.24.48.43, fax 05.57.24.48.43 ☑
Ῑ ev. day 8am–12 noon 2pm–7pm; Sat. Sun. by appt.; cl. 15–30 Aug.

CH. DE BONHOSTE 2000★

◪ 6 ha 13,000 ▮ ⫰ €5–8

This wine's colour is slight and pale, but as brilliant as a mountain stream. It has delicate rose-petal aromas, and a rather vigorous but very elegant attack on the palate. A slight touch of sparkle gives it a deliciously spritzy quality, which is well balanced by a soft menthol finish. This will be a good accompaniment to any white-fleshed fish.
🔑 SCEA Vignobles Fournier, Ch. de Bonhoste, 33420 Saint-Jean-de-Blaignac, tel. 05.57.84.12.18, fax 05.57.84.15.36 ☑
Ῑ by appt.

FEILLON FRERES ET FILS 2000★

◪ 0.33 ha 2,500 ▮ ⫰ €5–8

This rosé is the product of a perfect family collaboration in which everyone contributes their particular skills. It has a redcurrant colour and an intense nose (strawberries and raspberries), embellished by a slight hint of exotic fruits. The rather fresh, very clean attack tempts you on to the palate, which changes completely, becoming rich, almost warm, and filled by a certain softness which leaves an impression of general well-being.
🔑 Feillon Frères et Fils, Ch. Les Rocques, 33710 Saint-Seurin-de-Bourg, tel. 05.57.68.42.82, fax 05.57.68.36.25, e-mail feillon.vins.de.bordeaux@wanadoo.fr
☑ Ῑ ev. day 9am–12 noon 2pm–6pm; Sat. Sun. by appt.

GRANDES VERSANNES 2000★

◪ 4 ha 35,000 ▮ ⫰ €3–5

One star is the reward for the efforts of the Lugon producers, who have given this rosé the advantage of some well-exposed plots and the best possible choice of techniques. It has a brilliant, salmon-pink colour, and a bouquet marked by peaches and quince jelly. The palate achieves a perfect compromise between lemony freshness and the exotic charm of grapefruit and orange zest, before lingering on to a beautifully languid, fragrant finish.
🔑 Union de producteurs de Lugon, 6, rue Louis-Pasteur, 33240 Lugon, tel. 05.57.55.00.88, fax 05.57.84.83.16 ☑
Ῑ ev. day except Sun. 8.30am–12.30pm 2pm–6pm; groups by appt.

GRANGENEUVE 2000★

◪ 10 ha 13,000 ▮ ⫰ €3–5

The best wine-making techniques, in particular the introduction of low temperatures before fermentation begins, have gone into developing this rosé. It has a fresh, tender colour, and a nose of summer fragrances (nectarines and apricots). This is the prelude to the delights of a well-balanced palate supported by a long, slightly acid structure with a note of lightness contributed by a wild strawberry flavour.
🔑 Cave coop. de Grangeneuve, 33760 Romagne, tel. 05.57.97.09.40, fax 05.57.97.09.41 ☑ Ῑ ev. day except Sat. Sun. Mon. 8am–12 noon 2pm–5pm

CH. DE LABORDE 2000★

◪ 4.69 ha 14,000 ▮ ⫰ €3–5

This rosé is made from a blend strongly dominated by Cabernet Franc (80%). The character of the grape can be seen in the soft, purplish colour of the wine, and also in its nose of sweet strawberry and pear-drop aromas. There are delicate tannins on the palate that presents a well-balanced combination of a grilled almond flavour and a slight, lingering note of lemon.
🔑 Union de producteurs Baron d'Espiet, Lieu-dit La Fourcade, 33420 Espiet, tel. 05.57.24.24.08, fax 05.57.24.18.91, e-mail baron-espiet@dial.oleane.com ☑
Ῑ by appt.
🔑 Alain Duc

DOM. DE LA CROIX 2000★★

◪ 2 ha 7,000 ▮ €3–5

This rosé is a blend of the three Bordeaux grape varieties, grown on alluvial and clay-limestone soils. It has a lovely colour with glittering ruby glints, and a nose of great finesse with seemingly endless fragrances of hyacinths and roses. The long, caressing, voluptuous finish left the judges in a state of rapture.
🔑 Jean-Yves Arnaud, La Croix, 33410 Gabarnac, tel. 05.56.20.23.52, fax 05.56.20.23.52 ☑ Ῑ by appt.

CH. LA MICHELIERE 2000★
1.28 ha   11,200

This is a very pale rosé fringed with diaphanous tinges. It has delightfully subtle aromas which hover between peonies and redcurrants. The real delight comes on the palate, where the body is stripped of any reserve and has a pleasant, unexpected roundness. Its supple, fresh development makes it a wine to drink for pleasure, and a natural choice as an aperitif.

☛ SCEA Tobler et Fils, Ch. La Michelière, Lieu-dit Le Bourdieu, 33240 Saint-Romain-la-Virvée, tel. 05.57.58.16.39, fax 05.57.58.15.16 ☒ ⵌ by appt.

CH. LA RIVALERIE 2000★
0.75 ha   7,000

Just for fun, this château has set aside a very small *cuvée* to produce this rosé whose colour is a pastel shade of raspberry. It needs to be swirled around a bit before it releases its youthful nose of blackcurrants and grenadines. The run-off after maceration has produced a very extracted palate with a good balance between slightly acid and fruity flavours, and a spicy finish which gives it enough charm to be served throughout an autumn meal.

☛ SCEA La Rivalerie, 33390 Saint-Paul-de-Blaye, tel. 05.57.42.18.84, fax 05.57.42.14.27, e-mail info@la-rivalerie.fr ☒ ⵌ by appt.

LA ROSE CASTENET 2000★★
4 ha   34,000

You have to breathe in the buttery aromas of this Rose Castenet while standing in the welcome shade of the park here, which was planted in the Belle Epoque. With its scents of roasting (hazelnuts) and spices, and lovely sweetness on the palate, this rosé has a great deal of charm which completely won over the judges. A touch of strawberries lends colour to a beguiling finish.

☛ EARL François Greffier, Castenet, 33790 Auriolles, tel. 05.56.61.40.67, fax 05.56.61.38.82, e-mail ch.castenet@wanadoo.fr ☒ ⵌ by appt.

LA ROSE DE LOUDENNE 2000★
1 ha   6,000

At Loudenne there is no shortage of sources of inspiration for a high-quality rosé: for example the old pink walls of this 17th-century charterhouse, or the innumerable perfumes of a superb collection of old roses, not to mention the thousand and one possible combinations offered by 60 ha (148 acres) of various grape varieties. The colour of this Rose de Loudenne is a box of jewels containing complex, subtle shades of orange, pink and mauve. Equally complex is its nose of redcurrants with a slight vegetal hint that suggests tomato-plant leaves. There are peony and iris flavours on the palate, after which the aromas of the nose return for a fresh, fruity finish.

☛ SCS Ch. Loudenne, 33340 Saint-Yzans-de-Médoc, tel. 05.56.73.17.80, fax 05.56.09.02.87, e-mail chateau.loudenne@wanadoo.fr ☒ ⵌ ev. day except Sat. Sun. 9.30am–12 noon 2pm–5pm
● Dom. Lafragette

CH. PERAYNE 2000★
1.5 ha   10,000

Located very near Sauveterre, Château Perayne used to enjoy a great reputation.

CH. NAUDONNET PLAISANCE
Perle rose d'avril 2000★

1 ha   n.c.

Not many wines receive as much attentive care as these rosés do while they are being developed: hand-picking, maceration of the grapes before crushing and fermentation in barrel. At Naudonnet Plaisance nothing is too good for this Perle Rose d'Avril, which has a powerful, bewitching bouquet of mirabelle plums and cherries, against a background of honey finely marked by heather. This is a satiny, delicate wine which will go well with fine herb sauces or a *tarte Tatin*.

☛ Danièle Mallard, Ch. Naudonnet-Plaisance, 33760 Escoussans, tel. 05.56.23.93.04, fax 05.57.34.40.78, e-mail mallard@aol.com ⵌ by appt.

CH. MAISON NOBLE SAINT-MARTIN 2000★
3.5 ha   27,000

This Maison Noble, located very near Sauveterre-de-Guyenne, is built on the remains of a 14th-century feudal castle. Its 2000 rosé is very up to date and full of freshness, with an intense aroma of vine-blossom. A slight hint of sparkle reinforces its youth, without impairing a certain roundness on the palate, which has a soft, rich honey flavour and a beautiful, long finish on a note of liquorice.

☛ Michel Pelissie, Ch. Maison-Noble-Saint-Martin, 33340 Saint-Martin-du-Puy, tel. 05.56.71.86.53, fax 05.56.71.86.12, e-mail maison-noble@wanadoo.fr ☒ ⵌ by appt.

CH. MONTAUNOIR 2000★
1 ha   7,500

This *saignée* or run-off of Cabernet and Merlot has produced a juicy pink colour with raspberry glints, a real lifeblood as it were, which is brilliant, fresh, and sings as it flows into the glass. 'Very red berries,' said our tasters, with a touch of vanilla: the palate is fresh and bubbling with youth, and takes on a novel exotic note in a shade of pineapple. This is the perfect partner for a *déjeuner sur l'herbe* with friends.

☛ SCEA des Vignobles Ricard, Ch. de Vertheuil, 33410 Sainte-Croix-du-Mont, tel. 05.56.62.02.70, fax 05.56.76.73.23 ⵌ ev. day except Sun. 9am–12 noon 2pm–6pm

which its current owners who moved here in 1994 are endeavouring to restore. The proof is this lovely rosé, whose raspberry brilliance is very appealing to the eye. Aromas of green apples and blackcurrants dominate right through to the finish, where the structure picks up some wild strawberry fragrances along the way. You can drink this wine when you get back from visiting nearby Malagar, Malromé and Saint-Macaire.

• Henri Lüddecke, Ch. Perayne, 33490 Saint-André-du-Bois, tel. 05.57.98.16.20, fax 05.56.76.45.71, e-mail chateau.perayne@wanadoo.fr
Y by appt.

CH. SEGONZAC LA FORET 2000★

17 ha 15,000 €5-8

This wine has a lovely, frank, intense colour and aromas of midsummer fruits (white peaches) which linger on a pleasant, slightly fruity palate. The good, completely un-aggressive balance goes on delighting the tastebuds long after you have put down the glass. There is a silky, dense finish which seems to call for a partner that can match it, such as a very tender blanquette of veal.

• Grands Vins de Gironde, Dom du Ribet, 33450 Saint-Loubes, tel. 05.57.97.07.20, fax 05.57.97.07.27, e-mail jm.alige@gvg.fr
Y by appt.
• Jeanine Segonzac

Bordeaux supérieur

CH. BARREYRE 1999

6.5 ha 45,000 €5-8

The Petit Verdot grape variety plays a vital part in the extreme delicacy of this Cabernet Sauvignon by giving it a spicy freshness, along with a very special touch of violets. Fruit flavours of morello cherries and bilberries lend fragrance to a moderate structure, with the result that this wine will be ready to drink in the near future.

• SC Ch. Barreyre, 33460 Macau, tel. 05.57.88.07.64, fax 05.57.88.07.00
Y by appt.
• Giron

CH. BAULOS LA VERGNE 1999★

11 ha n.c. €5-8

The pretty little town of Saint-Germain-la-Rivière is reflected in the graceful meanders of the Dordogne, not far from Libourne. This crimson 99 will be glinting in our glasses for a long time to come. Its aromas are based on flowers (irises, hyacinths) and even more on the heady essences of midsummer fruits such as crushed raspberries and plums. This is a well-composed, full-bodied wine with a skilful tannic structure that confirms its ageing potential.

• Maison Yvan Dinand, Dom. de Baulos, 33240 Saint-Germain-la-Rivière, tel. 05.57.84.46.01, fax 05.57.84.81.36
Y by appt.

CH. BEL AIR PERPONCHER

Grande Cuvée 1999★★

n.c. n.c. 11-15

The Jury responded very enthusiastically to this Grande Cuvée. Its nose has an astonishing floral tonality. The palate is just as fragrant, with scents of irises, violets and elderberries embellishing a body which is somewhat austere in the attack. Flavours of stewed fruits and prunes appear at the finish, confirming that this is a wine with very good ageing potential.

• GFA de Perponcher, 33420 Naujan-et-Postiac, tel. 05.57.84.55.08, fax 05.57.84.57.31, e-mail contact@vignobles-despagne.com
Y by appt.
• J.-L. Despagne

CH. BELLEVUE LA MONGIE

Cuvée vieille en fût de chêne 1999★

2.5 ha 18,000 €5-8

Génissac is located to the south of Libourne, on the left bank of the Dordogne. The wines at this château never fail to make an impression. This vintage has a deep, crimson colour, and a substantial structure enhanced by a slight hint of pepper and shot through with gamey, musky notes. The palate is fleshy and rich, and the tannins have lost some of their vigour; they will help this delightful 99 to open out fully if it is given time to age. It will be a fine accompaniment to a well-ripened Brie.

• Michel Boyer, Ch. Bellevue La Mongie, 33420 Génissac, tel. 05.57.24.48.43, fax 05.57.24.48.43
Y ev. day 8am-12 noon 2pm-7pm; Sat. Sun. by appt.; cl. 15-30 Aug.

CH. DE BLASSAN

Cuvée spéciale Vieilli en fût de chêne 1999

5 ha 30,000 €5-8

This 31-ha (77-acre) estate is located in the Fronsadais. Its Bordeaux Supérieur has garnet and mauve glints, and a nose of musk and leather along with wild nuances of fur and civet. The whole appeal of this wine is that it does not try to be like anything other than itself. There is a fragrance a bit like the forest after rain on a palate which has powerful flavours, clean tannins and lingering notes of oak and chanterelles. This is a wine to serve with country dishes such as hare pâté, terrine of foie blond, and cold leg of lamb with mayonnaise.

• Guy Cenni, 33240 Lugon, tel. 05.57.84.40.91, fax 05.57.84.82.93
Y by appt.

CH. BOIS-MALOT
Tradition Elevé en fût de chêne neuf 1998★

7 ha · 33.500 · €8-11

At Château Bois-Malot they like to uphold tradition, as can be seen so well from this wine, which has involved hand-picking, a hand-sorting table, and a long vatting period. It has a crimson colour with slightly carmine glints, and a nose that releases a basket of fragrant fruit aromas 'with shades of Verlaine', as one taster put it. Its appeal lies more in its delicacy than in its power; the palate is silky and full of charm, ending on a long note of vanilla.

SCEA Meynard et Fils, 133, rte des Valentons, 33450 Saint-Loubes, tel. 05.56.38.94.18, fax 05.56.38.92.47

ev. day except Sun. 8.30am-12 noon 2pm-7pm; cl. Sat. pm

CH. DE BONHOSTE
Cuvée Prestige 1999★

n.c. · n.c.

This wine has a tender, brilliant colour through which you can see the light. Toast aromas and rich notes of vanilla are released in a nose which is still developing. Far from imposing itself, the palate appeals more by its charm and the delicacy of a body which is barely marked by disciplined tannins. The oak is still very much in evidence, which suggests that the wine should be kept for two or three years. The Cuvée Principale 99 from the same château is a classic, and is recommended.

SCEA Vignobles Fournier, Ch. de Bonhoste, 33420 Saint-Jean-de-Blaignac, tel. 05.57.84.12.18, fax 05.57.84.15.36

by appt.

Fournier Bern

CH. BOUTILLON 1998★

13 ha · 28,000 · €5-8

At this estate the wine-makers regard themselves as aesthetes, as artists, although there is no mention of the cinema – except when Claude Chabrol goes there to shoot a film (*Dr Popaul*). With its musk and venison aromas in the nose, and supple, firm body in which the tannins are still aggressive, this 98 wine has enough vigour to square up to a meal such as young guinea-fowl in Armagnac followed by a partly-steamed mimolette cheese.

SCEA Filippi-Gillet, Ch. Boutillon, 33540 Mesterieux, tel. 05.56.71.41.47, fax 05.56.71.32.21 by appt.

LES SENS DE BRANDA 1998★

n.c. · 150,000 · €5-8

Not only is Branda a medieval fort which was both a party and a witness to the tribulations of the Hundred Years' War, it has just been sumptuously restored and now offers a wonderful scented garden as well. Don't fail to visit it, or indeed to taste this 98 wine. It has a garnet colour fringed with orangey glints, and a nose of red berries in brandy and mouthwatering prunes, along with delicate notes of menthol. After that comes a rich, structured palate which will make this a good wine to serve with meat dishes in sauce or a sauté of chicken with chanterelles.

SA Leda, Ch. Branda, 33240 Cadillac-en-Fronsadais, tel. 05.57.94.09.20, fax 05.57.94.09.30

CH. DE CAMARSAC
Sélection Elevé en barrique 1999

9 ha · 68,000 · €5-8

Perched charmingly on its promontory, on the site of an ancient fortress where the Black Prince lived for a while, the present-day Château de Camarsac will soon be celebrating its 600th anniversary. Its Bordeaux Supérieur has a garnet colour with bronze glints, and a charming nose (red berries, liquorice and toast) which is the prelude to a clean, soft attack. There is a lovely texture that fills the palate pleasantly and embellishes it with floral notes of faded roses, violets and irises. The wine has a long, lingering finish on notes of toast, and can be served straight away with roast meat.

Bérénice Lurton, Ch. de Camarsac, 33750 Camarsac, tel. 05.56.30.11.02, fax 05.56.30.11.02 by appt.

CH. BRANDE-BERGERE 1999

4.5 ha · 26,000 · €5-8

This charterhouse was founded by an Irishman in 1780, but did not go in for wine-growing until 1850. The 99 wine is genuine and pleasant to the finish, starting with an intense red colour and complex berry aromas (sloes and bilberries). Its well-balanced presence on the palate will make it the perfect accompaniment to a good family meal.

EARL Ch. Brande-Bergère, 33230 Les Eglisottes, tel. 05.57.49.58.46, fax 05.57.49.51.52 by appt.

GFA Dalibot

CH. BROWN-LAMARTINE 1999★

11 ha · 80,000 · €8-11

This is another Jean-Michel Cazes vintage, although since then Christian Seely has taken over as director of the Axa-Millésimes estates which Jean-Michel Cazes brought up to a first-class standard by putting together a rigorous team. The 99 wine comes from the gravelly clay soils of Cantenac-en-Medoc, and from a blend of grapes largely dominated by Cabernet Sauvignon. It has a dark-garnet colour, and a notable and highly unusual nose of raspberry and oak notes. After an ample, full-bodied attack, the palate successfully combines a somewhat severe tannic structure with a dominant, cocoa-flavoured roundness. The wine has a crunchy fruitiness which means that it will be suitable to drink from now on.

Christian Seely, Ch. Brown-Lamartine, 33460 Cantenac, tel. 05.57.88.81.81, fax 05.57.88.81.90, e-mail info@chato@ cantenacbrown.com by appt.

Axa-Millésimes

Bordeaux supérieur

CH. CANEVAULT 1998★

■ 4.5 ha 24,000 ■ ♦ €5-8

The wine has a vermilion colour and a very sweet nose of morello cherries, followed by a rich, unctuous palate with smooth, delicious tannins and flavours of blackcurrants and raspberries. The overall impression is of delightful balance.

➦ SCEA Jean-Pierre Chaudet, Caneveau, 33240 Lugon, tel. 05.57.84.49.10, fax 05.57.84.42.07, e-mail scea-chaudet-j.p@wanadoo.fr ☑
☙ ev. day except Sun. 9am–12 noon 1.30pm–6pm
➦ Sylvie Chaudet

DOM. DE CANTEMERLE
Cuvée Prestige Vieilli en fût de chêne 1999

■ 10 ha 270,000 ■ ♦ €5-8

The youth of the two new owners does not prevent them from respecting tradition. They use the yeast from the *terroir*, but as a concession to technology they carry out a long maceration on the skins before fermentation. The result is a wine with plenty of colour and aroma: various spices and venison. It sits pleasantly on the palate, which is substantial and well structured. The oak is well warmed, and bodes well for the wine's future development.

➦ Vignobles Mabille, Dom. de Cantemerle, 33240 Saint-Gervais, tel. 05.57.43.11.39, fax 05.57.43.11.39, e-mail contact@domaine-cantemerle.com ☑ ☙ by appt.

CH. DE CAZENOVE 1999

■ 4 ha 25,000 ■ ♦ €5-8

'Sine labore nihil' is the motto of this Médoc estate. Its 99 wine has a lovely carmine-red colour, but only releases its bouquet slowly once the wine is swirled in the glass. It has a full, fairly firm structure of delightful tannins which rubs shoulders with the palate but is not yet integrated into it. This is a real wine for longer maturing, enlivened by very toasty oak and flavours of fruit and spices. The long, chewy finish suggests that it should be kept for several years.

➦ Louis de Cazenove, Ch. de Cazenove, 33460 Macau-en-Médoc, tel. 05.57.88.79.98, fax 05.57.88.79.98, e-mail cazessen@club-internet.fr ☑ ☙ by appt.

CHAPELLE DE BARBE 1999★

■ 8.3 ha 66,500 ■ ♦ €5-8

Much like the old Chapelle de Barbe built in 1636, which was a landmark for sailors navigating the estuary, this 99 wine is 'the model for red Bordeaux Supérieur', as one of the judges noted. Perhaps it is this long tradition that gives the wine such refinement in its delicate, complex bouquet of balsamic and sweet praliné aromas. The round palate has full, well-integrated tannins, and bears the stamp of old vines whose well-tempered vigour gives it power and concentration. With a few years of ageing, this wine will acquire an inimitable polish.

➦ SC villeneuvoise, Ch. de Barbe, 33710 Villeneuve, tel. 05.57.42.64.00, fax 05.57.64.94.10 ☑

CH. COURONNEAU Cuvée Pierre de Cartier Elevé en barrique 1999

■ 5 ha 20,000 ■ €8-11

Jacques Cartier's descendants lived in this superb 15th-century château, which is flanked by four watchtowers and surrounded by wide moats. This Cuvée Pierre de Cartier has a delightful crimson colour, and an intense nose of spicy and floral nuances (hyacinths and mint) along with a dominant oak note of fine toast. The palate is rich, long and concentrated, with a dense body into which the tannins are well integrated. This is a mature wine which already has a great deal of charm.

➦ Piat, Ch. de Couronneau, 33220 Ligueux, tel. 05.57.41.26.55, fax 05.57.41.27.58, e-mail chateau-couronneau@wanadoo.fr ☑ ☙ by appt.

DOM. DE COURTEILLAC 1999★★

■ 18.95 ha 96,000 ■ €8-11

Dominique Méneret bought this estate in 1998. This delightful wine has a dense, crimson colour fringed with dark purple, and an intense nose combining soft fruit aromas (redcurrants, cherries and blackcurrants) with a delicate, reserved note of oak. The palate is lusciously rich and fleshy, and as it develops reveals beautifully soft flavours of spices. There are still a few somewhat assertive tannins which make their presence felt, giving the wine a firm, long overall structure.

➦ Dom. de Courteillac, 33350 Ruch, tel. 05.57.40.79.48, fax 05.57.40.57.05
☙ by appt.
➦ D. Méneret

CH. COURTEY Cuvée Margo 1998★

■ 3 ha 9,000 ■ ■ ♦ €5-8

As its name suggests, this Cuvée Margo is a comely wine with crimson colour in its cheeks and wafting fragrances of vanilla and liquorice. Its supple, fresh, fairly lively body reveals some rather sharp tannins, which are accentuated by a slight touch of pepper, but in the end the structure seem to take charge again. This wine needs to be kept for two years.

➦ SCEA Courtey, 33490 Saint-Martial, tel. 05.56.76.42.56, fax 05.56.76.42.56 ☑ ☙ by appt.

CH. DE CUGAT
Cuvée Francis Meyer 1999★

■ 3 ha 10,000 ■ €8-11

This wine has a beautiful, velvety, garnet colour, and a complex nose in which notes of cedar and bergamot orange are up against a heavily dominant oak aroma. It is full of body, but needs time to achieve its full potential. The 99 Cuvée première from the same cru appealed to the judges with its fruity aromas and palate of spices and cinnamon. This very supple wine can be served without fuss in the next few months.

228

CH. DAMASE 1999★

🍷 Benoit Meyer, Ch. de Cugat, 33540 Blasimon, tel. 05.56.71.52.08, fax 05.56.71.60.29 ☑ ▼ by appt.

10 ha ◼ 80,000 ▦ €5-8

These gravelly-clay hillsides sloping down towards a meander in the Isle form a good partnership with their sole tenant, Merlot, which gets on very well here without any other grape variety. The deep-crimson colour of the wine is characteristic of this grape, as is the range of aromas: prunes, grape jelly, peel and truffles. Twelve months of maturation in high-quality oak have added scents of balsam wine and vanilla. This is a vigorous, thoroughbred wine whose civilized tannins give it good balance and ageing potential.

🍷 Xavier Milhade, Ch. Damase, 33910 Savignac-de-l'Isle, tel. 05.57.84.31.27, fax 05.57.84.31.27, e-mail milhadeg@aol.com

CH. DEGAS Elevé en fût de chêne 1999★

1.2 ha ◼ 8,000 ▦ €5-8

Marie-José Degas runs a most unusual vineyard: a real wine-growing botanical garden in fact, with one small vine which is over a hundred years old. This is the *nec plus ultra* of the Bordelais 'doctrine' that recommends a plurality of grape varieties. Needless to say, complexity is the key word where this wine is concerned. It has a bouquet with any number of resonances, and a supple, round, rich body which fills the palate with fruity notes (blackberries and cherries) and soft liquorice flavours. The tannins add substance to a well-balanced finish. This wine should be served with grilled meats.

🍷 Marie-José Degas, Ch. Degas, 33750 Saint-Germain-du-Puch, tel. 05.57.24.52.32, fax 05.57.24.03.72 ☑

CH. FAYAU 1998★★

25 ha ◼ 150,000 ▦ €5-8

The Medeville family has been growing wine at Château Fayau for seven generations on an exceptionally well-favoured *terroir* with soils consisting of gravel, clay and sand. This Bordeaux Supérieur is a fine example of what such a long tradition can produce. It has a carmine colour with bronze glints, and a bouquet of aromas with any number of spicy, floral and fruity nuances (violets and blackberries). The wine unfolds on a delightfully round palate against a background of red berry flavours. It is already excellent, but can also be kept.

🍷 SCEA Jean Médeville et Fils, Ch. Fayau, 33410 Cadillac, tel. 05.57.98.08.08, fax 05.56.62.18.22, e-mail medeville-jeanetfils@wanadoo.fr ☑ ▼ ev. day except Sat. Sun. 8.30am-12.30pm 2pm-6pm

CH. FONCHEREAU 1998★

20.05 ha ◼ 50,000 ▦ €3-5

This beautiful vineyard, located very near Bordeaux on the road to Libourne, is offering

a traditional blend of the three main Bordeaux grape varieties, in which Merlot is dominant (60%). It has a brilliant garnet colour and a very open nose with clean, fruity aromas of cherries, blackberries and blackcurrants. Mouthwatering flavours of spices and crystallised fruits fill the palate against a background of fine, elegant tannins. This wine has a precocious flair which can only get better as it ages.

🍷 SCA Ch. Fonchereau, BP 9, 33450 Montussan, tel. 05.56.72.96.12, fax 05.56.72.44.91, e-mail courrier@ fonchereau.com ☑ ▼ by appt.
🍷 Madar

CH. FREYNEAU 1998★

4.5 ha ◼ 30,000 ▦ €5-8

This 98 vintage attracts from the start with its dense, iridescent ruby colour with mauve glints, while its fine, thoroughbred, spicy nose is second to none. The palate has plenty of tannins and is delightfully firm. The wine will be soon be ready to drink with meat dishes in sauce.

🍷 GAEC Maulin et Fils, Ch. Freyneau, 33450 Montussan, tel. 05.56.72.95.46, fax 05.56.72.84.29, e-mail accueil@ chateau-freyneau.com ☑ ▼ by appt.

CH. DE FUSSIGNAC 1999

13 ha ◼ 75,000 ▦ €8-11

The beautiful Petit-Palais church was a frequent stopping-point on one of the roads to Santiago de Compostela. Château de Fussignac maintains the tradition of rearing animals as well as growing wine, and the grapes here are harvested by hand. The 99 wine has a fresh, powerful colour, and a complex bouquet of dried fruits and honey. The full, rich body opens out on a flavour of blackcurrant jelly, then continues to develop on to a long, rich, powerful finish. This wine is a real pleasure, to be enjoyed without delay.

🍷 Jean-François Carrille, pl. du Marcadieu, 33330 Saint-Emilion, tel. 05.57.24.74.46, fax 05.57.24.64.40, e-mail paul.carrille@ worldonline.fr ☑ ▼ by appt.

CH. GALAND Elevé en fût de chêne 1999★

3.58 ha ◼ 9,000 ▦ €8-11

Rigour is the order of the day here in every area: no weed-killers, just hard work; hand-picked harvesting in crates, sorting of the grapes, etc. This 99 wine comes from vines that are about 60 years old, and has a ruby colour with slight shades of carmine. There is a fine, highly expressive bouquet of fruit and toast notes, and an elegant palate where the flavours are very much in keeping with the nose. This delightful balance will suit rich dishes such as stuffed duck and ragout of woodpigeon.

🍷 Jean Galand, La Malatie, 33126 Fronsac, tel. 05.57.58.23.04, fax 05.57.58.20.81 ☑ ▼ by appt.

Bordeaux supérieur

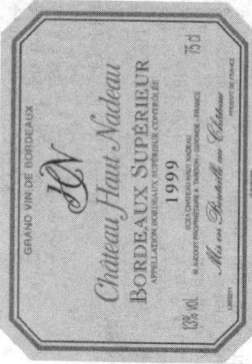

CH. GENLAIRE 1999

■   6.45 ha   114,000   ■ ♦

Château Genlaire is a pleasant little manor house set in the middle of its few acres of vines, which are unusual in that they comprise a clear majority (63%) of Cabernet Franc, and only 20% Merlot, with the remainder being made up by Cabernet Sauvignon. That no doubt explains the finesse of this wine's raspberry colour and the delicacy of its bouquet, which has tender fragrances of crystallised peaches and grapes dried on the vine. The dense, spicy palate lingers on to a finish which, although light, is not yet fully integrated. This wine will go well with delicate dishes, such as meats in white sauce, chanterelles and cream cheeses.

➤ Prodiffu, 17–19, rte des Vignerons, 33790 Landerrouat, tel. 05.56.61.40.57, fax 05.56.61.33.73,
e-mail prodiffu@prodiffu.com
➤ Jeanne Chauvel

CH. GRAND MONTEIL

Elevé en fût de chêne 1999

■   40 ha   320,700   ■ €5-8

This charming, unassuming château could well boast that it once belonged to Gustave Eiffel, and that around its admirable residence it has a park containing cedars and hundred-year-old magnolias, and a large wine-growing estate. This wine makes an enticing start with its lovely, brilliant red colour and powerful nose of spice notes and a slight hint of truffles. Undergrowth and agaric flavours take over on a delicate palate with a prominent structure of young tannins. It will be a worthy accompaniment to poultry and small game with mixed vegetables.

➤ Jean Téchenet, Ch. Grand Monteil, 33370 Salleboeuf, tel. 05.56.21.29.70, fax 05.56.78.39.91 ⅋ Ⴤ by appt.

CH. GREE-LAROQUE 1998★★

■   1.6 ha   7,000   ■ ⅷ ♦ €5-8

This young wine-grower came into the profession somewhat by chance, only to discover that he had a real vocation for it. There can be no doubt about this if his 98 wine is anything to go by; it is full of freshness and verve, has aromas of raspberries and blackcurrants and is supple and well balanced. Despite its impetuous tannins it is very easy to drink, and ends beautifully on a long note of oak.

➤ Benoît de Nyvenheim, Arnaud Laroque, 33910 Saint-Ciers-d'Abzac, tel. 05.57.49.45.42, fax 05.57.49.45.42 ⅋
Ⴤ by appt.

CH. HAUT NADEAU 1999★★

■   6 ha   45,000   ■ ⅷ ♦ €5-8

substantial tannins. This wine is a hymn to work well done; it is already superb, and can only grow in stature with time.

➤ SCEA Ch. Haut-Nadeau, 3, chem. d'Estévenadeau, 33760 Targon, tel. 05.56.20.44.07, fax 05.56.20.44.07 ⅋
➤ Audouit

CH. HAUT NIVELLE

Cuvée Prestige Vieilli en fût de chêne 1999★

■   18 ha   70,000   ⅷ €5-8

The wines at Haut Nivelle, in particular this Cuvée Prestige, add to the pleasure of discovering the marvels of Romanesque architecture that are scattered along the roads to Saint-Sauveur, Petit-Palais and Cornemps. This beautiful, cherry-red 99 wine has a delightful bouquet of spice and smoky aromas. The flavours on the palate are very soft, starting with some lovely vanilla notes, then moving on to tones of liquorice and leather. The tannins are young and fresh, but the round character of the wine will soften them with time. Watch it mature.

➤ SCEA Les Ducs d'Aquitaine, Favereau, 33660 Saint-Sauveur-de-Puyn ormand, tel. 05.57.69.69.69, fax 05.57.69.62.84,
e-mail vignobles@lepottier.com ⅋
➤ Le Pottier

CH. DES HUGUETS 1998★

■   5 ha   30,000   ■ ⅷ €5-8

The rich, gravelly, siliceous soils of Les Artigues-de-Lussac are very well-suited to this vineyard where three grape varieties (70% Merlot) are harvested by hand. The proof is this 98 wine, which shows its calibre throughout in its intense colour, notes of jam in the nose, and spicy flavours. The tender, round palate is well structured, and has a lingering, elegant finish.

➤ Vignobles Paul Bordes, Faize, 33570 Les Artigues-de-Lussac, tel. 05.57.24.33.66, fax 05.57.24.30.42,
e-mail vignoble.bordes.paul@wanadoo.fr
⅋ Ⴤ by appt.

CH. LA BASTIDE MONGIRON

Cuvée noire 1999★

■   1 ha   6,000   ⅷ ♦ €5-8

This Cuvée Noire lives up to its name; it does indeed have a very dark, almost opaque colour. It also has musky, very wild, leathery, slightly civet aromas which are the sign of a

Oenologist Patrick Audouit is real craftsman. He has put all his expertise into the development of this 99 wine, which comes from an estate belonging to his family. Its deep, velvety-black colour is the result of long maturation, as is the balance in the nose between blackberries and blackcurrants. The fullness on the palate is supported by good, strong structure on the palate. The wine has a delightful, robust, well-structured texture, with beautiful, grapey tannins and a very full, meaty body accompanied by oak flavours. This is a wine in the true Bordeaux tradition, with excellent prospects for the future.

♥ Jean-Michel Queyron,
Dom. de Mongiron, 33750 Nérigean,
tel. 05.57.24.53.16, fax 05.57.24.06.36 ☑
Y by appt.

CH. LA COMMANDERIE DE QUEYRET 1999★

| 20 ha | 120,000 | ■ | €5-8 |

Claude and Simone Comin run a *terroir* which was recognised 700 years ago by the Knights of Saint John of Jerusalem. They have produced a crimson wine with a complex bouquet containing a succession of aromas that are released when the wine is swirled in the glass. These are amplified on a palate with a smooth body which remains spicy right up to the long, voluptuous finish. A late boost in the tannins suggests that the wine should be kept for a while.

♥ Claude Comin, Ch. La Commanderie,
33790 Saint-Antoine du Queyret,
tel. 05.56.61.31.98, fax 05.56.61.34.22 ☑
Y by appt.

DOM. DE LA GRAVE
Cuvée Tradition 1999★

| 9 ha | 60,000 | ▦ | €3-5 |

The beautiful 18th-century charterhouse on this property is surrounded by gravelly-clay soils planted mainly with Merlot (80%). This rich, complex 99 releases floral notes of vanilla. It has a rich, unctuous presence on the palate, and the very mature tannins develop at a measured pace on a velvety structure: sure signs of high quality, which can only become even better with age.

♥ SCEA Roche, Perriche,
33750 Beychac-et-Caillau,
tel. 05.56.72.41.28, fax 05.56.72.41.28 ☑
Y ev. day 8am-7pm

DOM. DE LA GRAVE
R – Cuvée Prestige 1999★★

| 3 ha | 10,000 | ▦ | €5-8 |

Over 100 years ago the Roche family bought this estate from the local parish priest. They are still producing a wine here that is as dense and substantial as a monk's cowl, with a powerful, empyreumatic nose in which notes of roasting alternate with plum and peach jam aromas. The tannic structure is now becoming more refined, and the flavours of cedar and nutmeg add to the length of a finish which has great panache. This 99 wine should be kept for a fine, festive meal.

♥ SCEA Roche, Perriche,
33750 Beychac-et-Caillau,
tel. 05.56.72.41.28, fax 05.56.72.41.28
Y ev. day 8am-7pm

CH. LA MAZETTE
Cuvée fût de chêne 1999

| 25 ha | 120,000 | ▦ | €3-5 |

Merlot and Cabernet grown on clay and alluvial soils have produced a wine with a

Without exception the members of the Jury praised the fullness of this 98 wine. Its sumptuous crimson tints are as fresh and lively as its fragrances of carnations and hyacinths. This is a full-bodied, velvety, rich wine which comes from overripe grapes. It is elegant in every respect, and the civilised tannins on the finish are a sure sign of an excellent future.

♥ SCEA Pierre Dumeynieu, Roumagnac,
33126 La Rivière, tel. 05.57.24.98.48,
fax 05.57.24.90.44 ☑ Y by appt.

CH. LA MALATIE 1999★

| 1.49 ha | 11,500 | ▦ | €5-8 |

Two young wine-growers are now reaping the rewards of their efforts; their little vineyard, which they cultivate by traditional methods, has been selected for a wine with a Bordeaux colour and garnet glints. The nose has aromas of undergrowth and humus, along with very ripe fruit, while the palate is full of spicy flavours and a note of truffles. The tannins are still somewhat dense, but the wine has vigour as well as good length.

♥ Sautanier-Goumard, Lamarche,
33126 Fronsac, tel. 06.81.42.24.56,
fax 05.57.25.32.32,
e-mail chateau.la.malatie@wanadoo.fr ☑
Y by appt.

CH. LA MARECHALE 1998★★

| 1.75 ha | 10,000 | ▦ | €3-5 |

CH. LAGRAVE PARAN
Elevé en fût de chêne 1999★

| 2 ha | 12,000 | ▦ | €5-8 |

Cabernet Sauvignon reigns supreme here, and is ideal for the very gravelly soils on this estate. It shows all their characteristics in fine scents of resin, nutmeg and cedar, and finally vanilla notes which come from skilfully burnt oak. The attack is still somewhat muted, but balance is beginning to appear, showing a rich potential which will increase as the wine develops.

♥ EARL Pierre Lafon, Ch. Lagrave-Paran,
33490 Saint-André-du-Bois,
tel. 05.56.76.42.74, fax 05.56.76.49.78 ☑
Y by appt.

dark-red colour and powerful nose where the richness of the fruit flavours is highlighted by a slightly vegetal background. This full-bodied, fragrant 99 has an abundance of spice flavours and delightful tannins, along with notes of venison and leather. Its structure is full of flavours and it will make a good accompaniment to hot, spicy dishes.
Jean-Pierre Fourgadet, Ch. La Mazette,
33240 Saint-Romain-la-Virvée,
tel. 05.57.58.10.67, fax 05.57.58.18.54

CH. DE LA NAUZE 1999★

4 ha 10,000 €3–5

The Château de La Nause is offering a pleasant wine from the Saint-Emilion area, with a vermilion colour and a slightly mentholated nose. This supple, tender 99 has a liquoricy body and elegant, silky tannins. With its satiny quality and warm finish, it can be drunk in the near future.
Xavier Dangin, 39, Micouleau,
33330 Vignonet, tel. 05.57.84.53.01,
fax 05.57.84.53.83 by appt.
Elies-Brignet

CH. LANDEREAU

Cuvée Prestige 1999★

6 ha 30,000 €11–15

The Baylets at Château Landereau are wine-producers to the core. Their methods are well thought-out, in other words traditional: certain plots are hand-picked, some old vines are preserved and the grapes are sorted by hand. This Cuvée Prestige has a fresh, crimson colour and a developing bouquet of wild, almost meaty notes, which stand out against a subtle mixture of old rum and grilled almonds. The palate is alternately tender and round, and a slight hint of tannins appears on a smooth, long finish. From the same producer, the **white oak-matured Château Lhoste White 99** is recommended; it has notes of resin, undergrowth and chanterelles which suggest the forest, and balsamic flavours which come from the oak.
SC Vignobles Michel Baylet,
Ch. Landereau, 33670 Sadirac,
tel. 05.56.30.64.28, fax 05.56.30.63.90
by appt.

CH. LA SALARGUE 1999

10 ha 65,000 €3–5

This lovely, vigorous 99 has a red colour fringed with garnet, and a halo of crystallised fruit, almost caramelised aromas. It is substantial and well structured, with a variety of flavours in the musky register (leather and game), and tannins which are still very young and softened by the folds of its rich, fleshy body. It will reach full maturity in one to two years' time.
SCEA Vignoble Bruno Le Roy,
La Salargue, 33420 Moulon,
tel. 05.57.24.48.44, fax 05.57.24.49.93,
e-mail vignoble-bruno-le-roy@wanadoo.fr
by appt.

CH. LAUDUC

Cuvée Prestige Elevé en fût de chêne 1999

4 ha 26,500 €5–8

Château Lauduc's vineyards are spread out over the two rolling hills and valleys that have been reclaimed over the centuries from the medieval forest of Entre-Deux-Mers. The sense of serenity that the landscape here exudes despite its proximity to the regional capital can also be found in this 99 vintage. It has a garnet colour and a lovely nose of toast with a fine menthol note, followed by a pleasant, well-balanced palate which is fairly characteristic of expressive Merlot. The tannins are already quite developed, and are softened by flavours of honey and *pain d'épice* (spice loaf). You can drink this wine at your leisure.
GAEC Grandeau et Fils, Ch. Lauduc,
33370 Tresses, tel. 05.57.34.11.82,
fax 05.57.34.08.19,
e-mail maison.grandeau.lauduc@
wanadoo.fr by appt.

CH. LA VERRIERE 1999

4 ha 26,000 €5–8

This wine is a lovely blend of Merlot (60%) and the Cabernets, grown on the hillsides of Landerrouat. It has an intense, brilliant red colour, and a delightful bouquet of strongly concentrated fruit flavours (overripe grapes, bilberries and blackberries). The frank attack leads to a finish on notes of cedar. This wine is still developing, and will need two or three more years to open out fully.
EARL André Bessette, 8, La Verrière,
33790 Landerrouat, tel. 05.56.61.33.21,
fax 05.56.61.44.25 by appt.
André et Alain Bessette

CH. DE LA VIEILLE TOUR Réserve

Tradition Elevé en fût de chêne 1998★

7 ha 55,000 €8–11

This Réserve Tradition has a delightful crimson colour, and is very representative of the landscape and *terroir* it comes from; mushroom and even truffle notes reign supreme here, against a very evocative background of undergrowth. Oak finally becomes apparent on a vigorous, concentrated palate where the tannins will need to become softer. Keep this wine carefully for two or three years.
Vignobles Boissonneau,
33190 Saint-Michel-de-Lapujade,
tel. 05.56.61.72.14, fax 05.56.61.71.01,
e-mail vignobles.boissonneau@wanadoo.fr
by appt.

CH. LE GRAND CHEMIN

Elevé et vieilli en fût de chêne 1999★

9.52 ha 20,000 €5–8

The Merlot grape has given this wine its very intense, crimson colour and fresh, fragrant aromas of morello cherries and raspberries, set against notes of game and musk. The clean, vinous palate shows a good balance between its tannic content and a velvety body with nuances of chocolate. This is a well-balanced wine which can be drunk straight away.

↳ Christiane Bourseau, SCEA Le Grand-Chemin, Pradelle, 33240 Virsac, tel. 05.57.43.29.32, fax 05.57.43.39.57, e-mail christiane.bourseau@voila.fr ✉ ☎ ev. day 9am–1pm 2pm–7pm

CH. LE PIN BEAUSOLEIL 1999★

■ 4.7 ha 18,000 €11-15

This wine lives up to the regal reputation that it made for itself in the two previous *Guides*. It has a dark-garnet colour, and an extremely rich bouquet of overripe grapes along with eucalyptus and cinnamon. This delicate combination is strongly marked by a note of roasting that comes from high-quality oak. Given the exuberance of the tannins, the palate is not yet fully integrated, but it is only a matter of time.

↳ Arnaud Pauchet, Le Pin, 33420 Saint-Vincent-de-Perti gnas, tel. 05.57.84.02.56, fax 05.57.84.02.56, e-mail arno.pauchet@wanadoo.fr ✉ ☎ by appt.

CH. LE GRAND VERDUS

Grande Réserve

Elevé en barrique de chêne neuf 1999★

■ 7 ha 20,000 €11-15

Château Le Grand Verdus is a 16th-century fortified manor house. It is listed as a historic monument, and is one of the most prestigious residences in the Bordeaux wine-growing area. The present is just as important as the past here though, as is shown by the excellent ratings the château has already received in the *Guide*. This wine is the result of an uncompromising search for perfection (controlled grape yields, hand-picking), and has an intense crimson colour and a nose of plums in brandy and black cherries which opens up fully once the wine is swirled in the glass. Its good balance and softness create a great feeling of serenity. The **99 Cuvée Tradition** is also awarded a star. 'This wine has a long life ahead, and time will do great things for it', wrote one taster.

↳ Ph. et A. Legris de La Salle, Ch. Le Grand Verdus, 33670 Sadirac, tel. 05.56.30.50.90, fax 05.56.30.50.98, e-mail le.grand.verdus.legris.de.la.salle@wanad ✉ ☎ by appt.

CH. LE GRAND MOULIN

Fruit d'automne 2000★

□ 0.5 ha 4,000 €8-11

This luscious Fruit d'Automne comes from the north of the *département*, where it has been developed from Sauvignon Gris alone. It is well balanced and mouthwatering, and has pleasant, unusual ripe fruit notes along with well-integrated, oaky toast flavours. It is ready to drink now.

↳ GAEC du Grand Moulin, La Champagne, 33820 Saint-Aubin-de-Blaye, tel. 05.57.32.62.06, fax 05.57.32.73.73, e-mail jif@grandmoulin.com ✉ ☎ ev. day except Sun. 9am–12.30pm 2pm–7pm

↳ Reaud

CH. LESCALLE 1999

■ 20 ha 137,000 €5-8

This wine starts enticingly with a deep, black colour resulting from long maceration on the skins, and a nose of stewed fruit and jam aromas enriched by notes of roasting. The palate is concentrated, based on a substantial structure, and supported by tannins which are vigorous without being dominant. There is a long finish on renewed notes of vanilla and fruit. The wine will benefit from a few years of ageing.

↳ EURL Lescalle, 33460 Macau, tel. 05.57.88.07.64, fax 05.57.88.07.00 ✉ ☎ by appt.

CH. L'ESCART

Cuvée Omar Khayam 1999★★

■ 0.8 ha 5,600 €8-11

This limited-volume wine has been produced from a grape selection at the vineyard. Omar Khayam (the Persian poet and enologist of wine) would have extolled its very full body and dark-purple colour, and been intoxicated by its scents of cloves, resin and tobacco. The **Cuvée Prestige Julien 99** is recommended. This is a wine with very good ageing potential.

↳ SCEA Ch. L'Escart, 70, chem. Couvertaire, BP 8, 33450 Saint-Loubès, tel. 05.56.77.53.19, fax 05.56.77.68.59 ✉ ☎ by appt.

↳ Gerard Laurent

CH. LES GRAVIERES DE LA BRANDILLE 1998★

■ 26.37 ha 210,000 €5-8

This very sound 98 has a garnet colour on which time has already made its mark. When the wine is swirled in the glass it releases a bouquet of violets against a background of humus and dead leaves. After a tender attack, the palate is filled with roasted green pepper and truffle flavours. With its subdued tannins and well-balanced body, this is a very mature wine which is ready for the table and should be served without delay.

↳ EARL Jean-Pierre Borderie, 119, rue de la République, 33230 Saint-Médard-de-Guizières, tel. 05.57.69.72.84 ✉ ☎ ev. day except Sun. 8am–12 noon 2pm–7pm

CH. LES MAUBATS

Elevé en fût de chêne 1999

■ 3.4 ha 21,000 €5-8

Not only does this Château Les Maubats come from an area that was put to fire and the sword both during and after the Hundred Years' War, it was also matured near a hamlet which was destroyed during the Revolution. The name Les Maubats may evoke memories of those troubled times, but fortunately the

Bordeaux Supérieur here is in complete contrast, enabling us to sink into peaceful happiness as we enjoy its substantial body and reflect that this is the sign of a good terroir. Its full structure is full of fruity jam aromas. This is a wine with plenty of colour, whose virile personality will be particularly well suited to braised meats, game and soft cheeses.

➤ Robert Armellin,
Ch. Les Maubats, 33580 Roquebrune,
tel. 05.56.61.68.36, fax 05.56.61.69.10,
e-mail chateau.les.maubats@wanadoo.fr ☑
𝕀 by appt.

CH. LESTRILLE CAPMARTIN
Cuvée Tradition Elevé en fût de chêne 1999★★

▪   9 ha   70,000   ⬛ €5-8

Jean-Louis Roumage has developed this wine from a blend of Merlot (90%) and Cabernet Sauvignon. Twelve months of maturation in oak have given it a bouquet which is still young and releases notes of toast and cinnamon when the wine is swirled in the glass. The delight continues on a full, silky palate with a fragrant mixture of redcurrant and crushed blackberry flavours.

➤ EARL Jean-Louis Roumage, Lestrille,
33750 Saint-Germain-du-Puch,
tel. 05.57.24.51.02, fax 05.57.24.04.58,
e-mail jean-louis.roumage@wanadoo.fr ☑
𝕀 by appt.

CH. DE L'HERMITAGE
Vieilli en fût 1998★

▪   8.63 ha   30,000   ⬛ €5-8

It is said that Henri IV used to stop off at L'Hermitage when he went to visit his mother, Jeanne d'Albret. This extremely well-equipped estate has produced a 98 wine with a lovely crimson colour and an intense nose of toast and musky notes of leather and game. The supple, round attack is followed by a dense series of tannins which are a tiny bit aggressive, but are contained by a rich body, giving a real impression of balance. This wine has very good prospects for the future.

➤ EARL Gérard Lopez, L'Hermitage,
33540 Saint-Martin-du-Puy,
tel. 05.56.71.57.58, fax 05.56.71.65.00,
e-mail chateau-hermitage@wanadoo.fr ☑
𝕀 by appt.

CH. DE LUGAGNAC 1998★

▪   49 ha   140,000   ▪ ✦ €5-8

There has been a real renaissance at this château, where the very beautiful medieval residence has a vineyard which has been built up again over a quarter of a century. The Bon family has devoted all its energy to it, and their wines have been regularly singled out by the Guide. This deep, black 98 vintage has a nose of crystallised red berries, and a balanced, full-bodied palate which is delightfully round and has a long, aromatic finish. It will be ideal for meat dishes in sauce.

➤ Mylène et Maurice Bon,
SCEA du Ch. de Lugagnac, 33790 Pellegrue,
tel. 05.56.61.30.60, fax 05.56.61.38.48,
e-mail clugagnac@aol.com ☑
𝕀 ev. day 9am–12 noon 12pm–7pm

CH. MAJUREAU-SERCILLAN
Elevé en fût de chêne 1999

▪   10 ha   76,000   ⬛ €5-8

This wine stands out both for its elegant colour with brick-red glints and for a bouquet which is already rich and contains any number of aromas of undergrowth, dried leaves and very toasty oak. There is a warm, dense attack with gamey notes of venison and musk, after which the palate develops on flavours of fruit and crystallised grapes. The wine's prominent structure will make it a good match for rich, highly-seasoned dishes such as carbonade of lamb and rare entrecôte.

➤ Alain Vironneau, Le Majureau,
33240 Salignac, tel. 05.57.43.00.25,
fax 05.57.43.91.34 ☑ 𝕀 by appt.

L'ESPRIT DE MALROME
Elevé en barrique 1999★

▪   20 ha   60,000   ⬛ €5-8

This wine has a beautiful label showing the silhouette of Toulouse-Lautrec at the centre. It comes as no surprise to find that it has a rich, brilliant, old garnet colour. Also reminiscent of the painter's palette is the shimmering bouquet of violets and carnations, and the slight hint of pepper which enhances a lovely toast flavour on the palate. The slender body is packed with exuberant tannins and reveals a somewhat forthright structure. Time will do what is necessary to retouch this agreeable picture.

➤ Malromé, Ch. Malromé,
33490 Saint-André-du-Bois,
tel. 05.56.76.44.92, fax 05.56.76.46.18,
e-mail v.lartigue@malrome.com ☑
𝕀 by appt.
➤ Ph. Decroix

MARQUIS D'ABEYLIE
Elevé en fût de chêne 1998★

▪   4.5 ha   33,000   ⬛ €5-8

The Closerie d'Estiac presents its petit marquis; he has a ruddy complexion with slightly purplish blotches, but oh, such delicate perfumes of peonies and blackcurrant buds! He has plenty of flesh and is even quite well built. One senses a member of the old landed gentry who wears vine-blossom in his buttonhole and leaves behind a sort of fragrant web of truffle and tobacco. This wine will keep for two or three years.

➤ Closerie d'Estiac, Les Lèves,
33320 Sainte-Foy-la-Grande,
tel. 05.57.56.02.02, fax 05.57.56.02.22 ☑
𝕀 ev. day except Sun. Mon. 9.30am–
12.30pm 3.30pm–6pm

CH. MONIER LA FRAISSE 1998★★

▪   12 ha   22,000   ▪ ✦ €2-5

Located among walled towns and thousand-year-old abbeys, this vineyard on the hilltops of Sauveterre-de-Guyenne is unusual in that a clear majority of its area (70%) is devoted to the robust Cabernet Sauvignon grape, without which it is very difficult to make a *grand Bordeaux*. The wine has a dense, velvety, crimson colour and an impressive range of aromas. Crushed cherries, red-currants and blackberries are followed by a slight hint of menthol. An evident note of nutmeg on the palate gives way to a silky body. The main grape variety gives the wine flavour-ful but astringent tannins which call for a long ageing period of five or six years if not more.

→ Cellier de La Bastide, Cave coop. vinicole, 33540 Sauveterre-de-Guyenne, tel. 05.56.61.55.21, fax 05.56.71.60.11 [V], Y ev. day except Sun. 9am–12.15pm, 1.30pm–6.15pm; groups by appt.
→ Claude Laveix

DOM. DE MONREPOS 1999 — 10 ha — n.c. — €5-8

This 99 wine comes from a blend very heavily dominated by Merlot (85%) grown on a clay-limestone soil. It has a beautifully brilliant, intense red colour, a complex bouquet in which cocoa mingles with empyreumatic scents, and flavours of jam on the palate. There is a dense, rich finish which masks a barely perceptible tannic note and shows that the wine is now mature. It will age very well, for those who can wait to drink it.

→ EARL Vignobles D. et C. Devaud, Ch. de Faise, 33570 Les Artigues-de-Lussac, tel. 05.57.24.31.39, fax 05.57.24.34.17 [V]

CH. MOUTTE BLANC 1999★ — 2 ha — 12,000 — €5-8

The obsessive quest for high quality seems to be the austere rule that this young wine-maker has made for himself in life. His Bordeaux Supérieur has a very captivating bouquet of uncommon aromas of wild berries, crystallised apricots and overripe, dried grapes. There is a robust, substantial body and a rich, concentrated mid-palate, followed by a finish on cocoa and vanilla. This wine will attract a following.

→ Patrice de Bortoli, Ch. Moutte Blanc, 6, imp. de la Liberation, 33460 Macau, tel. 05.57.88.40.39, fax 05.57.88.40.39 [V], Y ev. day 9am–1pm 2pm–7pm

CH. MOULIN DE FERRAND 1999 — 7 ha — n.c. — €5-8

The Moulin de Ferrand confirms its place in the *Guide* with this 99 vintage. It has a lovely colour with many warm, bright notes, and a bouquet marked by fine, peppery spice aromas and soft-fruit fragrances. The round palate still has some harsh tannins, but time will heal this. If you are wise you will leave it to age for two years. This wine is widely distributed.

→ Vignobles Boissonneau, 33190 Saint-Michel-de-Lapujade, tel. 05.56.61.72.14, fax 05.56.61.71.01, e-mail vignobles.boissonneau@wanadoo.fr, Y by appt.

CH. PENIN Grande Selection 1999★★ — 7.5 ha — 53,000 — €8-11

Patrick Carteyron is one of the great stars of the appellation. After training as an oenologist he took over the family estate in 1982, and now every edition of the *Guide* features his wines among the 28–30% that are selected. This one was rated just below the Les Cailloux (see below), and also won a *coup de coeur*. It has a fresh, bluish glints and a developing yet deep bouquet with a complex base of bilberries and cloves. Maturation in oak has given it added nuances of roasting: a very promising

CH. NAUDONNET-PLAISANCE Vieilli en fût de chêne 1999★ — 20 ha — n.c. — €8-11

Escoussans is located between Cadillac and Targon, and belongs to Entre-Deux-Mers. This estate grows equal shares of Merlot and Cabernet. The wine starts delight-fully with a shimmering colour and a nose composed of undergrowth, truffle and humus notes which combine gracefully with a slight hint of oak as they continue on a round palate with soft tannins. This 99 wine is already pleasant to drink, but can also be kept in reserve for a few years.

→ Danièle Mallard,
→ Ch. Naudonnet-Plaisance, 33760 Escoussans, tel. 05.56.23.93.04, fax 05.57.34.40.78, e-mail mallard@net-courrier.com [V], Y by appt.

CH. PANCHILLE Cuvée Alix 1999★ — 3 ha — 17,000 — €5-8

This young wine-grower cultivates a clay and silt *terroir* wedged in a meander of the Dordogne, where he makes it a point of honour to hand-pick his harvests. His Cuvée Alix has a lovely, deep, cherry-red colour and is developing quite an expressive nose. The toast flavour appears on a round, supple body, and there is a long finish with a good sense of balance. The main wine here is the **Château Panchille 99**, which is recommended. Its civilized tannins are cloaked by black-currant and stewed-fruit flavours.

→ Pascal Sirat, 33500 Arveyres, tel. 05.57.51.57.39, fax 05.57.51.57.39 [V], Y by appt.

CH. PASCAUD Elevé en fût de chêne 1999★ — 3 ha — 20,000 — €8-11

The best thing about this 99 wine is that its grapes were selected from old vines. It has a classic Bordeaux colour and a range of vegetal aromas in a nose which opens on over-ripe, grapes dried on the vine and dried figs, then develops towards nuances of almonds and hazelnuts. Its balsamic fragrances are the sign of noble oak. This Château Pascaud has good prospects for a long career ahead.

→ SCEA Vignobles Avril, BP 12, 33133 Galgon, tel. 05.57.84.32.11, fax 05.57.74.38.62, e-mail ch.pascaud@aol.com [V], Y by appt.

Bordeaux supérieur

combination. The **Cuvée Tradition de Ch. Penin 99** has been aged in a vat and wins one star. Both the colour and the nose are a basket of fruits bursting with sunshine. The structure is made to last, but the wine is already a pure joy to drink.

☛ SCEA Patrick Carteyron, Ch. Penin, 33420 Génissac, tel. 05.57.24.46.98, fax 05.57.24.41.99 ▼ ⏱ by appt.

CH. PENIN Les Cailloux 1999★★
1.4 ha   6,700

This Les Cailloux comes, as its name suggests, from a gravel soil, and won its *coup de cœur* right from the start with its aromas of violets and irises. This springtime freshness gives way on the palate to notes of cinnamon and grilled almonds. The flavours of overripe grapes on sun-baked gravel slowly fade to a lingering, full-bodied finish. Still young and already full of flair, this wine will progress towards excellence as it ages.

☛ SCEA Patrick Carteyron, Ch. Penin, 33420 Génissac, tel. 05.57.24.41.99 ▼ ⏱ by appt.

CH. PETIT-FREYLON
Excellence Lyre 1999   €5-8
5 ha   10,000

Over the last few years the growing of vines in 'lyre formation' has become quite popular, especially among young wine-growers who are eager to try out new techniques. This is a fresh, young wine with a frank, lively colour and a nose of soft-fruit and prune aromas. Its body opens out on a rich, powerful, thoroughbred palate with notes of cherries and kirsch. There are still some rather vigorous tannins lurking in its very full body, but the battle is all but won; it won't be long now.

☛ EARL Vignobles Lagrange, Ch. Petit-Freylon, 33760 Saint-Genis-du-Bois, tel. 05.56.71.54.79, fax 05.56.71.59.90 ▼ ⏱ by appt.

CH. PEYRON SIMON
Vieilli en fût de chêne 1998★   €3-5
1.5 ha 10,000

There is a slight sense of nostalgia at the mention of this little vineyard, so close to Bordeaux, where time has stopped out of respect for the old way of working, without weedkillers. One can clearly sense the hand of the wine-maker behind this wine, which came close to winning a *coup de cœur*. It has a velvety, scarlet colour, and a bouquet combining dark berries and notes of coffee and leather. The long vanilla finish confirms the quality of a full-bodied palate with elegant tannins. It would not be surprising to learn in 2010 that this Bordeaux Supérieur is still around.

☛ J. Simon, 46, rte de Peyron, 33450 Montussan, tel. 05.56.72.94.73 ▼ ⏱ by appt.

CH. PIERRAIL 1998★   €8-11
19 ha   115,000

This beautiful, very old vineyard is overlooked by a superb 18th-century château which exudes a sense of history, since it was here that the Duchesse de Berry stopped for a while on her way to the Vendée while hatching her outlandish plot against Louis-Philippe (1832). The barrel store, on the other hand, is very much of our time, as can be seen from this deep-crimson 98 vintage. Its bouquet of fruit flavours (blackcurrants and bigaroon cherries) against a pleasant, vanilla background is followed by a palate with a substantial structure and tannins which are still rather lively but have plenty of flavour and will ensure that the wine has good ageing potential. It will be a worthy accompaniment to dishes with character (leg of lamb, fillet of duck breast, etc.).

☛ EARL Ch. Pierrail, 33220 Margueron, tel. 05.57.41.21.75, fax 05.57.41.23.77, e-mail pierrail@chateau-pierrail.com ▼ ⏱ by appt.

CH. PLAISANCE 1999★   €5-8
8 ha   57,000

This wine has a dense, deep colour and a range of aromas (prunes, morello cherries and dried apricots) which is tinged with a few touches of vanilla then with vegetal fragrances of mushrooms and truffles. The tannins are soft and well masked by the full, smooth body, which lingers on to a long, balanced finish on a fine note of oak.

☛ SCEA Ch. Plaisance, 33460 Macau, tel. 01.53.35.35.35 ▼ ⏱ by appt.
☛ Chollet

CH. PONCHARAC 1999   €3-5
15 ha   115,000

This is very much a wine from a clay-limestone *terroir*, with a beautiful, concentrated, very colourful appearance (crimson with shades of orange), and fruit aromas combined with notes of leather and fur which show all its youthful vigour. Its somewhat exuberant tannins still need a long time to develop, but the body is there, and is promisingly rich.

☛ SA Yvon Mau, BP 1, 33193 La Réole, tel. 05.56.61.54.54, fax 05.56.71.10.45, e-mail info@chateau-ducla.com
☛ Casasnovas

DOM. DU PONT ROUGE 1999   €3-5
11 ha   n.c.

The Cordier firm has exclusive rights over this estate at Soussans, but it belongs to

Château Tayac in the Margaux AOC. This lovely carmine-coloured 99 wine has an unusual nose which is both fruity and musky, and marked by emphatic notes of musk and leather. The tannins lend balance to a rich, vigorous body. The wine can be served immediately or kept for a while (two years).

● SC Ch. Tayac, Lieu-dit Tayac, BP 10, 33460 Soussans, tel. 05.57.88.33.06, fax 05.57.88.36.06
Υ ev. day 9am–12.30pm 2pm–6pm

PRINCE NOIR 1999

■ n.c. 130,000 ▯ € 3-5

Prince Noir is the brand name of a firm which has been exercising its passion for wine for almost three centuries! With every vintage their experience is challenged afresh by the whims of a changeable climate. The year 1999 was particularly difficult, when wine-producers such as those who worked over this Black Prince in its cradle were dedicated to producing an intense crimson colour and aromas of very ripe grapes, prunes and spices (cinnamon and liquorice). This is a wine with well-measured extraction, which will be a worthy accompaniment to any decent meal.

● Barton et Guestier, Ch. Magnol, 87, rue du Dehez, 33292 Blanquefort Cedex, tel. 05.56.95.48.00, fax 05.56.95.48.01, e-mail barton-e-guestier@seagram.com

CH. PUY-FAVEREAU 1999

■ n.c. 60,000 ▯ € 5-8

The rays of the midday and evening sun pour down on this hillside vineyard, which is very close to the Lussac-Saint-Emilion appellation. That explains this wine's soft-fruit bouquet, and its warm presence on the palate. It is now well on the way to being fully open.

● SCEA Les Ducs d'Aquitaine, Favereau, 33660 Saint-Sauveur-de-Puynormand, tel. 05.57.69.69.69, fax 05.57.69.62.84, e-mail vignobles@lepottier.com ▯
Υ by appt.
● Le Pottier

CH. DE RABOUCHET
Sélection première 1998★

■ 4 ha 20,000 ▯ € 5-8

This 4-ha (10-acre) hillside vineyard overlooking Sainte-Foy-la-Grande is remarkable for its limestone outcrops, which have produced a wine made from 70% Merlot and both Cabernets. Maceration at low temperature before fermentation has given it an intense ruby colour, and above all very pronounced fruit aromas which are the intentional result of this prolonged contact between the skins and juice of the crushed grapes. After a full-bodied, rich, fleshy attack, this 98 wine reveals some rather impetuous, almost astringent tannins on a characteristic palate with notes of leather, fur and game. The oak is evident, and is still dominant at the finish. Leave this wine to age for a few years.

● Fournier, GFA du Ch. de Rabouchet, 33220 Pineuilh, tel. 05.57.46.17.19, e-mail chfournier@infonie.fr ▯ Υ by appt.

CH. RAMBAUD 1999★

■ 7 ha 50,000 ▯ € 5-8

This limestone clay *terroir* where Merlot is the main grape variety (80%) is graced by the presence of a superb house which was built by a general of the Empire and looks down from the top of its hill over a meander in the Dordogne. The intensely crimson 99 wine has a delightful nose of toast, cocoa and spices. Its vanilla notes add elegance to a straightforward tannic structure. The balance is now developing, and although the wine is already pleasant it still needs to be kept for a while.

● SCEA Daniel Mouty, Ch. du Barry, 33350 Sainte-Terre, tel. 05.57.84.55.88, fax 05.57.74.92.99, e-mail daniel-mouty@wanadoo.fr ▯
Υ ev. day except Sat. Sun. 8am–5pm

CH. RECOUGNE 1999★★

■ 50 ha 300,000 ▯ € 5-8

The Milhade family runs this very beautiful estate on the hills of Fronsac. Their 99 wine has a highly elegant, iridescent garnet colour and an astonishingly rich nose of over-ripe berries mingled with a slight hint of violets and agaric. The judges were spellbound by the luscious, silky palate. The pleasant brioche finish suggests that the wine is ready to be enjoyed immediately. The new special *cuvée* here is the **Terra Recognita 99**, which wins one star. It comes from Merlot vines which are over 60 years old, and has very good tannins which will enable it to keep for a little while. Finally, one star goes to the **Château Tour d'Auron 99**, which is rich, full and round.

● SCEV Jean Milhade, Ch. Recougne, 33133 Galgon, tel. 05.57.55.48.90, fax 05.57.84.31.27

REIGNAC 1999★★

■ 27 ha 90,000 ▯ € 15-23

A beautiful 18th-century house and a greenhouse built by Eiffel are two good reasons for visiting this estate. Another is the wine here is the **Château de Reignac 99**, which is awarded one star in this appellation. This Reignac, a *cuvée spéciale* which is not restricted to a limited volume, was unanimously awarded a *coup de coeur* and took the very first place. What a lovely combination of grape, blackcurrant and redcurrant aromas along with beautifully finished oaky vanilla and accents of coconut! A roasted coffee note gives it complexity, and the palate is full of body and tender, fruity flavours. The tannins stay elegantly in the background, but will endure a long ageing period.

➤ SCI Ch. de Reignac, 33450 Saint-Loubès, tel. 05.56.20.41.05, fax 05.56.68.63.31 ☑
☉ by appt.
➤ Yves Vatelot

CH. ROC MEYNARD 1999
█   13 ha   55,000   ▥ ▯ ♦   €5-8

This vintage has a deep, clear, brilliant ruby colour, and is a delightfully powerful wine with good potential for development. The nose opens with an explosion of soft-fruit aromas which then mingle with fresh, slightly spicy notes. The velvety, substantial, full body fills the palate without masking the rich flavour of the tannins. There is a lingering finish on liquorice and slightly spicy notes which sink deep into the palate. This wine will reach its full potential in two or three years' time.

➤ Philippe Hermouet, Clos du Roy, 33141 Saillans, tel. 05.57.55.07.41, fax 05.57.55.07.45,
e-mail hermouetclosduroy@wanadoo.fr ☑
☉ by appt.

CH. SAINT-IGNAN 1999
█   15 ha   80,000   ▥ ▯ ♦   €5-8

This vineyard used to belong to the very beautiful Château du Bouilh in Côtes de Bourg. It offers a brilliant, crimson 99 with a developing bouquet which, although still reserved, is full of distinction, and releases fruity aromas along with truffles and spice. There is a vinous palate with a thoroughbred Madeira flavour and a dense body, which softens some rather lively tannins. This wine is still maturing, and should not be drunk in too much of a hurry.

➤ Feillon Frères et Fils, Ch. Les Rocques, 33710 Saint-Seurin-de-Bourg, tel. 05.57.68.42.82, fax 05.57.68.36.25,
☑ ☉ ev. day 9am–12 noon 2pm–6pm; Sat. Sun. by appt.

CH. DE SEGUIN Cuvée Prestige
Vieilli en barrique neuve 1998★
█   20.5 ha   150,000   ▥ ▯   €8-11

This very large estate is located on the outskirts of Bordeaux. Its aptly-named Cuvée Prestige has a glittering ruby colour and appealing aromas of spice. The palate develops a great sense of concentration within an elegant tannic structure. There are slight gamey aromas on a rich, silky finish which will make this wine especially well suited to spicy dishes. It will be pleasant to drink very soon, but will also benefit from being kept for quite a while.

➤ Michael et Gert Carl, Ch. de Seguin, 33360 Lignan-de-Bordeaux, tel. 05.57.97.19.75, fax 05.57.97.19.72,
e-mail info@chateau-seguin.fr ☑
☉ by appt.

SEIGNEUR DES ORMES
Cuvée réservée Elevé en fût de chêne 1998★★
█   1.7 ha   14,000   ▥ ▯   €5-8

This is the masterpiece of the Baron d'Espiet Union of Producers. Everything about it is great; it wins half the battle before it even hits the palate with a crimson colour and an intense nose of dark berries (blackcurrants and blackberries) accompanied by a very refined and well-integrated note of oak. This excellent impression is merely confirmed by what follows: a frank, clean, structured attack, smooth, flavourful tannins, and a lingering, alert, supple finish on an abundance of balsamic notes.

➤ Union de producteurs Baron d'Espiet, Lieu-dit La Fourcade, 33420 Espiet, tel. 05.57.24.24.08, fax 05.57.24.18.91,
e-mail baron-espiet@dial.oleane.com ☑
☉ by appt.

CH. TERTRE CABARON
Elevé en fût de chêne 1998★
█   1.75 ha   7,000   €5-8

This wine's beautiful, luminous red colour and nose of ripe fruits, spices and toast are the first signs of the high quality that lies in store on the palate, where subtle flavours of mocha and roasting are followed by a richly aromatic development. Soft, evanescent, spicy fragrances (nutmeg and cinnamon) linger on to a finish on soft notes of grilled almonds and oak.

➤ SCEA Dom. de Bastorre, 33540 Saint-Brice, tel. 05.56.71.54.19, fax 05.56.71.50.29 ☉ ☉ by appt.
➤ Mme Dugrand

CH. THIEULEY
Réserve Francis Courselle 1999★★
█   n.c.   50,000   ▥ ▯   €11-15

Château Thieuley
Réserve
Francis Courselle
1999
BORDEAUX SUPÉRIEUR
APPELLATION BORDEAUX SUPÉRIEUR CONTRÔLÉE
MIS EN BOUTEILLE AU CHÂTEAU
12% vol.   75cl

This vineyard has a high reputation, and not without reason. The wine (90% Merlot and 10% Cabernet Franc) comes from a gravelly clay soil and wins one of the highest ratings among the Bordeaux Supérieurs. It has a colour like 'a real cardinal's robe', as one taster put it, and an equally impressive nose of balsamic fragrances, sap, black olives, leather and humus. There is an astonishingly mouth-filling body on the palate, where tannins contribute to the flavour along with spices tempered by a delicate note of smoke. This is a nourishing wine, 'a meal in itself' as Alexis Lichine used to say, but it needs to be kept for a few years before it reaches its full potential.

- Sté des Vignobles Francis Courselle, Ch. Thieuley, 33670 La Sauve, tel. 05.56.23.00.01, fax 05.56.23.34.37 ☑ ☐ by appt.

CH. TOUR DE GILET 1999★
■ 3.9 ha 28,000 ■

This Bordeaux Supérieur comes from the Médoc, and is made from hand-picked Palus grapes. It has an inviting, spruce colour, an equally pleasant bouquet of black cherries with a slight hint of fresh redcurrants, and a very concentrated palate with flavours of red berries. It can be drunk without delay, but will improve with time. The Les Vieilles Vignes de Tour de Gilet 99 has been matured in oak for 16 months, and wins one star. It needs to be kept for two years.

- SC Ch. Tour de Gilet, Gilet, 33290 Ludon-Médoc, tel. 05.57.88.07.64, fax 05.57.88.07.00 ☑ ☐ by appt.
- Bachelot

CH. TOUR DE MIRAMBEAU
Cuvée Passion Elevé en fût de chêne 1999★★
■ n.c. n.c. ■ ■ €11–15

No doubt about it, the quality of a wine reflects the quality of the people who produce it. Château de Mirambeau is a figurehead of the appellation, and its wine-makers have put all their skills into this Cuvée Passion. It has a plum colour, and a bouquet of intense scents of blackcurrant liqueur and crushed redcurrants. The oak is evident and well proportioned. There is a round, full attack on the palate, which has flavours of ripe fruits and very soft, almost sweet oak. The velvety tannins make this a voluptuous, full-bodied wine which is already superb and will become even better with age.

- SCEA Vignobles Despagne, 33420 Naujan-et-Postiac, tel. 05.57.84.55.08, fax 05.57.84.57.31, e-mail contact@vignobles-despagne.com ☑
- by appt.
- J.-L. Despagne

CH. TROCARD Monrepos 1998★
■ 5 ha 25,000 ■ ■ €5–8

This Monrepos 98 comes from 5 ha (12 acres) of siliceous-clay soils devoted exclusively to good Merlot vines. It has a black colour and a very appealing, frisky nose of vanilla, fur and leather. The palate is vigorous, and has notes of undergrowth combined with oak flavours which are well balanced with fruit. The wine needs to be kept for two years.

- SCEA des Vignobles Trocard, 2, Les Petits-Jays-Ouest, 33570 Les Artigues-de-Lussac, tel. 05.57.55.57.90, fax 05.57.55.57.98, e-mail trocard@ wanadoo.fr ☑ ☐ ev. day except Sat. Sun. 8am–12 noon 2pm–5pm

CH. VERRIÈRE BELLEVUE 1999
■ 15 ha 30,000 ■ ■ €5–8

This wine's bouquet is as complex as the subsoil that produced it: white and red clay with an abundance of marine fossils and ferrous deposits. The full, vinous palate has a very long, flavoursome finish, and is quite delightful. It would not be a sacrilege to serve this wine quite soon.

- EARL Alice et Jean-Paul Bessette, 5, La Verrière, 33790 Landerrouat, tel. 05.56.61.36.91, fax 05.56.61.41.12 ☑ ☐ by appt.

CH. VIEUX BELLE-RIVE
Elevé en fût de chêne 1999
■ 2 ha 16,000 ■ ■ €5–8

This vintage comes from almost pure Merlot (90%), stylishly combined by a good wine-maker with 10% of Malbec, the main Cahors grape variety. It has an intense, garnet colour, scattered with slight brick-red glints, and a nose which is showing the first signs of development in its aromas of faded roses and peonies. The palate is quite full, and the tannins are becoming integrated into a body which will become more refined with time. This wine can be drunk over the next three years.

- Laurent Audigay, Ch. Vieux Belle-Rive, 33330 Saint-Sulpice-de-Faleyrens, tel. 05.57.21.66.77, fax 05.57.74.45.59 ☑

CH. VINCY 1998★
■ 12.9 ha 104,530 ■ ■ €5–8

Although the Union of Producers at Rauzan uses ultra-modern equipment, its vinification procedures are entirely in line with the Bordeaux orthodoxy. This château wine is typical of their methods; its red colour is quite moderate, as if not to overshadow blackcurrant, blackberry and cherry aromas which compete to dominate the nose. The round, powerful palate has a few slightly aggressive tannins which still need to mature, but the fruit is clearly evident, which means that the wine has all the flair that it needs to succeed.

- Union de producteurs de Rauzan, 33420 Rauzan, tel. 05.57.84.13.22, fax 05.57.84.12.67 ☐ by appt.
- G. Cresta

Crémant de Bordeaux

The sparkling Crémant de Bordeaux was created in 1990. It is made according to the same strict fermentation and ageing rules as all other Appellations Crémants, using traditional Bordelais grape varieties. Generally speaking, Crémants are white but they can also be rosé. Production figures for 2000 were 18,228 hl (481,219 gal) of which 696 hl (18,374 gal) were of rosé.

BROUETTE PETIT-FILS
Cuvée Réserve★

○ n.c. 17,200 €5-8

Where sparkling wines and in particular *crémants* are concerned, the Brouette firm (originally from Champagne) has been a model in the Bordeaux region for at least a hundred years now. The Cuvée Réserve here is made from pure Sémillon, and this has given it a lovely, clean yellow colour, aromas of brioche and honey, and a round, vanilla palate. This is a well-constructed wine with good length, and its softness does not prevent it from being lively and refreshing.

☛ SA Brouette Petit-Fils, Caves du Pain de Sucre, 33710 Bourg-sur-Gironde, tel. 05.57.68.42.09, fax 05.57.68.26.48 ☑ ⟙ ev. day except Sun. Mon. 9am–12 noon 2pm–6pm

A. CHAMVERMEIL 1999★

○ n.c. n.c. €5-8

This is a brand from Château d'Arsac in the Haut-Médoc. It is a well-constructed, very young wine with an abundance of fresh aromas: apples, quince and syringa. The fresh palate has flavours of beeswax and toasted brioche. Its good balance and length are very soothing, and suggest that it will be a good accompaniment to smoked salmon.

☛ Philippe Raoux, SA Marjolaine, Ch. d'Arsac, 33460 Arsac, tel. 05.56.58.83.90, fax 05.56.58.83.08 ☑

LE TREBUCHET 1999★★

○ 0.8 ha 6,000 €5-8

Château Trébuchet takes its name from a field catapult that was used during the Hundred Years' War, but its winery now contains equipment of a much more peaceable kind, which even so has produced a wine that conquered the hearts of our Jury. Everything about it is elegant: the very fine, twirling sparkle in its gleaming, golden colour, the bouquet of smoky, spicy, but also fruity aromas (William pears), and the well-developed, lingering palate, which ranks this wine among the élite of Bordeaux *crémants*. It wins a unanimous *coup de cœur*.

☛ Bernard Berger, Ch. Le Trébuchet, 33190 Les Esseintes, tel. 05.56.71.42.28, fax 05.56.71.30.16 ☑ ⟙ ev. day except Sun. 8am–12 noon 2pm–6pm

MILADY★

◑ n.c. 20,000 €5-8

This *crémant* caused a controversy among our Jury; some ranked it as excellent and others said that it was 'commercial' (although where's the harm in that?) It has a garnet-pink colour with very slight shades of brick-red, and a delightful nose of soft fruits (cherry stones and bilberries). There is more complexity on the palate, which reveals a hint of redcurrant and just a touch of blackcurrant. These very well-integrated impressions linger on in the same fruity register. This will be a good wine to drink on any occasion.

☛ Jean-Louis Ballarin, La Clotte, 33550 Haux, tel. 05.56.67.11.30, fax 05.56.67.54.60, e-mail ballarin@wanadoo.fr ☑ ⟙ by appt.

DU PRIEUR★

○ n.c. n.c. ▪ ♦ €8-11

The Garzaros were among the first producers to develop *crémant* wines, and this Crémant du Prieur shows the benefit of their experience. It has a brilliant, pale-gold colour with plenty of sparkle, an intense nose of toasty and buttery notes, and an alert, fresh palate embellished by citrus-fruit and vanilla flavours. It is already well balanced, and has an extremely pleasant, long finish.

☛ EARL Vignobles Garzaro, Ch. Le Prieur, 33750 Baron, tel. 05.56.30.16.16, fax 05.56.30.12.63, e-mail garzaro@vingarzaro.com ☑ ⟙ by appt.

Blayais and Bourgeais

Blayais and Bourgeais are two small regions on the border between the Charente department and the Gironde. They are delightful to come upon for the first time, since both contain historic sites: the prehistoric paintings in the Pair-Non-Pair caves are

Côtes de Blaye and Premières Côtes de Blaye

The fortress of Blaye was built by the great military engineer Vauban and is still completely intact. Today, the vineyards cover about 5,800 ha (14,524 acres) and are planted with both red and white grape varieties. The appellations Blaye and Blayais are used less and less frequently because the wine-growers prefer to produce wines using more noble vine varieties, which are entitled to the appellations Côtes de Blaye and Premières Côtes de Blaye. Nevertheless, 12,742 hl (336,389 gal) of Blaye was produced in 2000. The red wines of Premières Côtes de Blaye – 321,239 hl (8,480,710 gal) in 2000 – are intensely coloured and have an authentic simplicity, and are strong and fruity. The whites – 12,605 hl (332,772 gal) in 2000 – are aromatic. The Côtes de Blaye whites – 2,747 hl (72,521 gal) in 2000 – are mainly light-coloured dry wines that are best served at the beginning of a meal, while the red Premières Côtes go better with meat dishes and cheeses.

> **B**laye, Premières Côtes de Blaye, Côtes de Blaye, Bourg, Bourgeais, Côtes de Bourg, reds and whites ... there are so many that it is not always easy to be clear about the different appellations of the region. Nonetheless, it is possible to identify two main groups: the wines from Blaye, where the soil types are varied, and the ones from Bourg, which is geologically more uniform.

almost as splendid as the ones at Lascaux. Both Blaye and Bourg are fortified towns, and there are several small châteaux and old hunting lodges. The landscape of hills and valleys creates an intimate atmosphere, which is in sharp contrast to the almost maritime horizons of the banks of the estuary. This is the only place outside Russia and Iran where sturgeon have been caught; it has also been wine country since Gallo-Roman times, which gives this historic landscape a special charm. Up to the beginning of the 20th century there was a considerable production of white wines, used in the distillation of Cognac. Nowadays, white wine production has significantly declined against the much more economically viable reds.

Côtes de Blaye

☐ **DOM. DE LA NOUZILLETTE** 2000
4 ha 25,000 €3-5

This wine is a blend of Colombard (60%) and Sauvignon, harvested on 19 September 2000 and matured on fine lees. It is still somewhat restrained in the nose, but even so its floral and fruity notes make it very pleasant.
♣ GAEC du Moulin Borgne,
5, le Moulin Borgne, 33620 Marcenais,
tel. 05.57.68.70.25, fax 05.57.68.09.12 [V]
♥ ev. day 9am–8pm
♠ Cathernaud

☐ **CH. MAGDELEINE-BOUHOU** 2000
0.75 ha 5,700 €5-8

Located some 2 km (1 mile) from Blaye and its citadel, this vineyard is offering a supple, flavourful wine with some minor notes of fruit (citrus) and a slight acidity.
♣ Vignobles Rousseaud Père et Fils,
Ch. Magdeleine-Bouhou, 33390 Cars,
tel. 05.57.42.19.13, fax 05.57.42.85.27 [V]
♥ by appt.

Premières Côtes de Blaye

Premières Côtes de Blaye

CH. BERTHENON 1999★

■ 14 ha 83,000 ■ ♦ ▮ €5-8

Like many vineyards whose reputation goes far back in time, this château has a high-quality *terroir*. The full, elegant 99 is well constructed. The liquorice notes in the nose reappear on a long finish which leaves a delightful impression on the palate.

↪ GFA Henri Ponz, Ch. Berthenon, Le Barrail, 33390 Saint-Paul-de-Blaye, tel. 05.57.42.52.24, fax 05.57.42.52.24 ☑ ⋎ ev. day 8am–12 noon 2pm–7pm; Sat. Sun. by appt.

NECTAR DES BERTRANDS 1999★★

■ 2.5 ha 12,000 ▮ €11-15

The Dubois own 80 ha (200 acres) and develop a variety of wines. After winning a *coup de coeur* for the previous vintage, the

Cuvée Prestige 2000 wins two stars and can be taken completely on trust. This other wine was a runaway success with the Grand Jury. It is oak-matured, and displays real ambitions which it then fulfils as the tasting develops. The very beautiful colour is followed by a charming bouquet of well-integrated toasty aromas and soft fruit notes. The warm, velvety, delicious palate is equally expressive. This very promising 99 will be a worthy accompaniment to dishes of character in two to five years' time.

The Blayais and Bourgeais appellations

CHARENTE-MARITIME

Saint-Savin

Givrac-de-Blaye

→ BORDEAUX

Saint-André-de-Cubzac

Saint-Girons-d'Aiguerives

BLAYAIS

GIRONDE

Cartelegue

Saint-Aubin-de-Blaye

Mazion

Saint-Genes-de-Blaye

Ch. la Garde

Saint-Paul

Ch Launay

St-Trojean

BOURGEAIS

Ch. Berthou

Comps

Ch. Lamothe

Tauriac

Ch. du Bousquet

Ch. du Grand-Jour

Dordogne

Garonne

Saint-Ciers-sur-Gironde

Saint-Androny

Ch. le Menaudat

Fours

Ch. la Salle

Ch. Segonzac

St-Martin-la-Caussade

Cars

Ch. Barbé   Ch. Lescadre

Blaye

Plassac

Ch.1e Guiraud

Ch. de Barbe

Villeneuve

Ch. de la Croix-Millorit

Bayon

Ch. Tayac

Bourg

Gironde

The Blayais and Bourgeais appellations

☐ Blayais
☐ Bourgeais
······· Department boundaries

0   1   3 miles
0   1   5 km
N

A 10
01 N
N 137
D 659
D 937

242

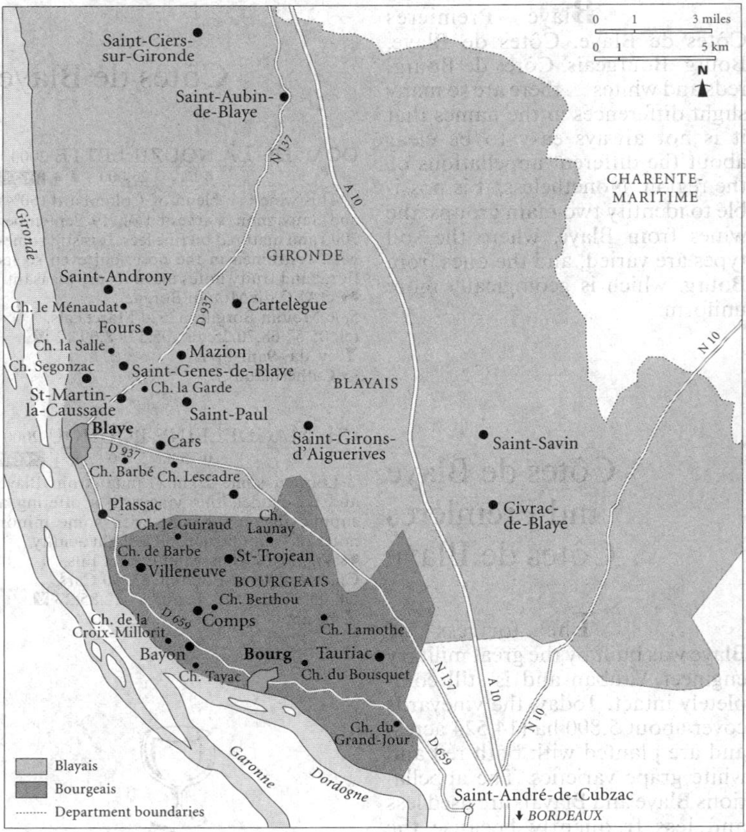

• EARL Vignobles Dubois et Fils, Les Bertrands, 33860 Reignac, tel. 05.57.32.40.27, fax 05.57.32.41.36, e-mail chateau.les.bertrands@wanadoo.fr ▼ by appt.

CH. BOIS-VERT 2000★
□

| 1 ha | 7,000 | | €5-8 |

The combination of both Sauvignons (*blanc* and *gris*) and Muscadelle has proved very successful in this supple, round wine which develops plenty of flavour on a palate of citrus fruit, white peach and exotic fruit notes. The **Prestige red 99** was also awarded one star.

• Patrick Penaud, 12, Boisvert, 33820 Saint-Caprais-de-Blaye, tel. 05.57.32.98.10, fax 05.57.32.98.10 ▼ by appt.

CH. CAILLETEAU BERGERON
Vieilli en fût de chêne 1999★

| 10 ha | 36,000 | | €5-8 |

This 99 wine has a crimson colour, a bouquet of elegant, mouthwatering aromas, and a palate combining oak and grape very successfully, all of which shows that it comes from a well-tended vineyard. The **white 2000** was also awarded one star for its very delightful nose of citrus fruits enhanced by an elegant note of vanilla which is a sign of well-closed maturation in oak.

• EARL Dartier et Fils, 33390 Mazion, tel. 05.57.42.11.10, fax 05.57.42.37.72 ▼ by appt.

CH. CANTELOUP 1999★★

| 4 ha | 20,000 | | €8-11 |

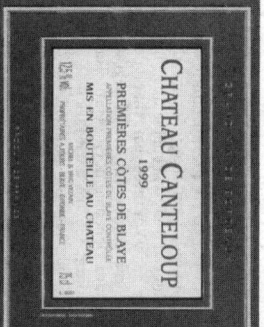

With this vintage Eric and Michel Vezain, who went into partnership in 1992, brilliantly confirm the success they achieved last year. The wine shows its strength from the start in a dark, almost black colour. The same power is apparent in the bouquet, which is both rich and complex and releases fruity and empyreumatic notes. The palate proves beyond further doubt that this very fine wine deserves pride of place in the cellar.

• Eric Vezain, Canteloup, 33390 Fours, tel. 05.57.42.13.16, fax 05.57.42.26.28 ▼ ev. day except Sun. 9am–12 noon 2pm–6.30pm

243

CH. CAP SAINT-MARTIN
Cuvée Prestige 1999★★

| 2 ha | 12,000 | | €8-11 |

This wine not only has the call of the ocean in its name, it also urges you most delightfully to sample the pleasure of drinking it, tempting you not only with its captivating colour, but also with a bouquet with any number of nuances: roast coffee, toast, prunes, etc. As for the palate, its substantial, full-bodied structure will ensure that the wine develops well over the next two to four years.

• SCEA des Vignobles Ardoin, 13, rte de Mazerolles, 33390 Saint-Martin-Lacaussade, tel. 05.57.42.91.73, fax 05.57.42.91.73, e-mail vignobles.ardoin@wanadoo.fr ▼ ev. day except Sun. 8am–12 noon 2pm–7pm; cl. 15–31 Aug.

CH. CORPS DE LOUP
Vieilli en fût de chêne 1999★

| 8 ha | 23,000 | | €5-8 |

This estate has produced a good-natured wine with a bouquet of toast and fruit notes supported by a hint of liquorice, and a long and well-made structure.

• Françoise Vidal-Leguenédal, Ch. Corps de Loup, 33390 Anglade, tel. 05.57.64.45.10, fax 05.57.64.45.10, e-mail chateau-corps-de-loup@wanadoo.fr ▼ ev. day 10am–12 noon 3pm–6.30pm; Sat. Sun. by appt.

GRAND VIN DE CH. DUBRAUD
1999

| 2 ha | 6,600 | | €11-15 |

This is a little *cuvée spéciale* which has been given its own name. It is very oaky and still somewhat rustic at the finish, and needs to develop, which its substantial structure will enable it to do if it is kept in the right conditions.

• Ch. Dubraud, 33920 Saint-Christoly-de-Blaye, tel. 05.57.42.45.30, fax 05.57.42.50.92, e-mail avida@terre-net.fr ▼ by appt.
• Alain et Céline Vidal

CH. FOUCHE 2000★
□

| 1.25 ha | 10,500 | | €3-5 |

The family has been here since the 17th century, but the buildings only date back to the early 1900s. This wine is made entirely from Sauvignon, and has interesting, very evident citrus notes both in the bouquet and on the palate. It is well balanced and fresh, and will go well with grilled shad.

• Vignobles Jean Bonnet, Ch. Fouché, 14, rue de la Gravette, 33620 Cubnezais, tel. 05.57.68.07.71, fax 05.57.68.06.08 ▼ by appt.

CH. FREDIGNAC Cuvée Prestige 1998

| 2 ha | 12,000 | | €5-8 |

Like many wines from the Blaye region, this 98 vintage comes mainly from Merlot, whose influence on its character can be felt in its bouquet of soft-fruit notes and relatively supple structure on the palate. It will need to be kept for a year or two until the oak becomes better integrated.

➧ Michel L'Amouller,
7, rue Emile-Frouard, 33390 Saint-Martin-Lacaussade, tel. 05.57.42.24.93, fax 05.57.42.00.64 ✅ Ⓨ by appt.

CH. GAUTHIER
Elevé en fût de chêne 1999★★

■ 10.35 ha 63,300 ▥ €5-8

Owned and made by the Pugnac co-operative, this wine displays all the expertise of its producers. It starts impressively with an intense colour and a particularly strong bouquet in which soft fruits are successfully combined with oak. The finishing touch is added by a palate which is powerful yet finely structured, and will ensure that it develops well.

➧ Union de producteurs de Pugnac, Bellevue, 33710 Pugnac, tel. 05.57.68.81.01, fax 05.57.68.83.17, e-mail udep.pugnac@wanadoo.fr Ⓨ by appt.
➧ Michel Massé

CH. DU GRAND BARRAIL
Révélation 1999★

■ 3 ha 19,500 ▥ €8-11

The firm of Vignobles Denis Lafon run several vineyards in the Blayais, and here offers a wine which has been matured for one year in new French barrels. The very expressive bouquet bears the stamp of oak, while the palate is supported by soft but evident tannins, and fills the mouth well before opening on to a peppery finish.

➧ Vignobles Denis Lafon, Bracaille 1, 33390 Cars, tel. 05.57.42.33.04, fax 05.57.42.08.92, e-mail denislafon@aol.com ✅ Ⓨ by appt.

DOM. DES GRAVES D'ARDONNEAU Cuvée Prestige
Vieilli en fût de chêne 1999★★

■ 4 ha 25,000 ▥ €5-8

This little Cuvée Prestige comes from a huge estate of 28 ha (69 acres), and has been developed with great care. It has a very elegant nose which is well supported by oak, and a palate based on round, expressive tannins and well-balanced flavours.

➧ Simon Rey et Fils, Dom. des Graves d'Ardonneau, 33620 Saint-Mariens, tel. 05.57.68.66.98, fax 05.57.68.19.30 ✅ Ⓨ ev. day except Sun. 8am–12.30pm 2.30pm–7pm

CH. HAUT CANTELOUP 2000★

□ 2.5 ha 10,000 ■ ♦ €3-5

This wine has been carefully developed using a diverse blend of grape varieties and maceration on the skins. It has an expressive character, with pleasant flavours of boxwood, citrus fruits and dried fruits on a well-balanced palate which is both rich and round.

➧ Sylvain Bordenave, 1, Salvert, 33390 Fours, tel. 05.57.42.36.69, fax 05.57.42.36.69 ✅ Ⓨ ev. day except Sun. 8am–12 noon 2pm–6pm

CH. HAUT GRELOT 2000★

□ 140 ha 100,000 ■ ♦

This vineyard was awarded a coup de coeur last year for its red Coteau de Methez, of which the 99 vintage is recommended. This 2000 white wine will surprise and delight many wine-lovers with its lovely aromas ranging from lychees to lemon.

➧ EARL Joël Bonneau, Au Grelot, 33820 Saint-Ciers-sur-Gironde, tel. 05.57.32.65.98, fax 05.57.32.71.81 ✅ Ⓨ ev. day except Sun. 9am–1pm 2pm–7pm

CH. DU HAUT GUERIN
Vieilli en fût de chêne 1998★

■ 3.6 ha 24,000 ▥ ♦ ♦

This wine, sold in numbered bottles, comes from gravelly clay hillside soils and has been matured in oak for 12 months. It still needs to become rounder, but is already more than delightful, not least because of its bitter chocolate note at the finish. There is a delicate bouquet of undergrowth, fruits and spices, and a round attack followed by a very good tannic structure on the palate.

➧ Alain Coureau, Ch. du Haut-Guérin, 33920 Saint-Savin, tel. 05.57.58.40.47, fax 05.57.58.93.09 ✅ Ⓨ ev. day 9am–9pm; cl. Aug.

CH. HAUT-TERRIER
Vieilli en barrique neuve 1999★

■ 40 ha 100,000 ▥ €6-11

This vineyard grows a large proportion of Merlot (95%), and has produced a wine which is clearly marked by that grape variety, with a very expressive bouquet of soft fruits and a pleasant roundness on the palate. That does not mean that there are no tannins in evidence, however; on the contrary, the full, well-balanced body will enable this wine to be kept for the two or three years that it needs for the oak to become completely integrated.

➧ Bernard Denéchaud, Ch. Haut-Terrier, 46, le Bourg, 33620 Saint-Mariens, tel. 05.57.68.53.54, fax 05.57.68.16.87, e-mail chateau-haut-terrier@wanadoo.fr Ⓨ by appt.

CH. LA BRAULTERIE 2000★

□ 1.5 ha 10,000 ■ ♦ €3-5

Sauvignon (80%) and Sémillon grown on siliceous-clay soils have produced this wine with a very lovely colour and an attractive bouquet of exotic fruits, lychees and yellow peach notes which are very much in keeping with the rich, full-bodied character of the palate.

➧ SCA La Braulterie-Morisset, Les Graves, 33390 Berson, tel. 05.57.64.39.51, fax 05.57.64.23.60, e-mail braulterie@wanadoo.fr ✅ Ⓨ ev. day except Sun. 9am–6pm

CH. LACAUSSADE SAINT-MARTIN 3 Moulins 2000

3 ha ▪ 20,000 ▥ €8-11

This wine comes from one of the oldest vineyards in the commune of Saint-Martin-Lacaussade, and is a blend of 90% Sémillon and 10% Sauvignon. It has a very complex bouquet (apricots, toast and crystallised berries) and a palate which is well balanced although still marked by oak. It needs to be kept until around St Valentine's Day 2002.

Jacques Chardat, Ch. Labrousse, 33390 Saint-Martin-Lacaussade, tel. 05.57.42.66.66, fax 05.57.64.36.20, e-mail bordeaux@vgus.com

CH. LA RAZ CAMAN

Elevé en fût de chêne 1998

n.c. ▪ 65,000 ▥ €8-11

This is an oak-matured wine from a vineyard which grows four grape varieties. It focuses resolutely on aromatic expression, offering pleasant notes of very ripe, almost overripe fruits. Although the tannins were still clearly in evidence on 24 April when the judges tasted the wine, they should be integrated by Christmas.

Jean-François Ponmeraud, Ch. La Raz Caman, 33390 Anglade, tel. 05.57.64.41.82, fax 05.57.64.41.77, e-mail info@la-raz-caman.com ▥ Υ by appt.

CH. LA ROSE BELLEVUE

Cuvée Prestige Elevé en fût de chêne 1999★

5 ha ▪ 25,000 ▥ €5-8

This Cuvée Prestige comes from a vast unit of over 40 ha (100 acres) in all, and has been marked by oak: this has been well dosed, however, and its touches of vanilla do not mask the fruit and the body. This is an elegant wine of great delicacy, with a rich, round, well-balanced palate and good length.

EARL vignobles Eymas et Fils, 5, Les Mouriers, 33820 Saint-Palais, tel. 05.57.32.66.54, fax 05.57.32.78.78, e-mail chateau.larosebellevue@freesbe.fr Υ ev. day 9am-7pm; cl. end Dec.

CH. DE LA SALLE 1999★

☐ 0.6 ha ▪ 4,500★★

This 18-ha (45-acre) estate has developed a little *cuvée* made from 100% Sauvignon grown on a clay-limestone soil. After 11 months of maturation in oak with stirring on lees, the wine has a splendid yellow colour with coppery glints, and an exceptionally

CH. LES HAUTS DE FONTARABIE 1999★

15 ha ▪ 110,000 ▪ €5-8

The vineyard here was bought in 1995 by the two daughters of Alain Faure. This wine has a lovely Bordeaux colour, an expressive bouquet of dark berries and game, and a well-structured palate. It needs to be kept, but

CH. LES GRAVES

Elevé en fût de chêne 1999★

5 ha ▪ 25,000 ▥ €5-8

This is a very young wine made from hand-picked Merlot (60%) and Cabernet Sauvignon grown on a gravelly-clay soil. It will need three or four years to develop its final personality, although this can already be sensed from its bouquet of subtle ripe-fruit aromas and full, well-balanced palate.

SCEA Jean-Pierre Pauvif, 15, rue Favereau, 33920 Saint-Vivien-de-Blaye, tel. 05.57.42.47.37, fax 05.57.42.55.89, e-mail info@chateau-les-graves.com ▥ Υ by appt.

CH. LE QUEYROUX

Le Joyau Elevé en barrique neuve 1998★

n.c. ▪ 600 ▥ €23-30

This tiny *cuvée* comes from a small, 1.5-ha (3.6-acre) vineyard where the work is done using a horse. It is an equal blend of Merlot and Cabernet Sauvignon, and has been matured in oak for 12 months. There is a bouquet of toasty and smoky notes, and a very well-structured palate with elegant tannins which will enable this wine to keep for four or five years.

Dominique Léandre-Chevalier, 6, lieu-dit Coulon, 33390 Anglade, tel. 05.57.64.46.54, fax 05.57.64.42.41 ▥ Υ by appt.

complex range of aromas mainly dominated by citrus fruits. With its lingering, fresh, well-balanced, expressive palate, it will keep for two or three years, although it is very pleasant already. This will be a worthy accompaniment to fish in white sauce.

SCEA Ch. de La Salle, 33390 Saint-Genès-de-Blaye, tel. 05.57.42.12.15, fax 05.57.42.87.11 ▥ Υ by appt.

Bonnin

CH. LE MENAUDAT

Cuvée réservée 1999★

5 ha ▪ 41,300 ▥ €5-8

This vineyard has a long-established reputation, and remains true to its tradition of high quality with this Cuvée Réservée. With its fresh almond, leather and ripe-fruit aromas, the bouquet is as complex as you could wish, while the palate is full, velvety and very well balanced.

SCEA FJDN Cruse, Le Menaudat, 33390 Saint-Androny, tel. 05.56.65.20.08, fax 05.57.64.40.29 ▥ Υ ev. day except Sun. 8am-12 noon 2pm-6pm; Sat. by appt.; cl. week of 15 Aug.

you should follow its progress regularly in order to catch it at its peak.

➣ Vignobles Alain Faure, Ch. Belair-Coubet, 33710 Saint-Ciers-de-Canesse, tel. 05.57.42.68.80, fax 05.57.42.68.81, e-mail belair-coubet@wanadoo.fr ☑ ☒ by appt.

CH. LE VIROU
Les Vieilles Vignes 1999★

■ 8 ha 48,000 ⬛ €5-8

This 99 wine comes from a vineyard belonging to a huge estate of over 100 ha (250 acres) in all, overlooked by an old 16th-century priory. It is a tannic, well-balanced wine of a truly classical type.

➣ SC Ch. Le Virou, Le Virou, 33920 Saint-Girons-d'Aiguevives, tel. 05.57.42.44.40, fax 05.57.42.44.40

CH. LOUMÈDE
Elevé en fût de chêne 1998★

■ 6 ha 44,000 ⬛ €5-8

This estate is located 800 m (half a mile) from the Gallo-Roman villa at Plassac. Although maturation in oak has marked this wine deeply with toast and caramelised aromas, its personality does not stop there. The round palate has plenty of tannic body and shows good balance and a great deal of concentration.

➣ SCE de Loumède, Ch. Loumède, 33390 Blaye, tel. 05.57.42.16.39, fax 05.57.42.25.30 ☑ ☒ by appt.

➣ Raynaud

CH. DE MANON 1999★★

□ 3.2 ha 20,000 ⬛ €8-11

The Bantégnies run a total of about 60 ha (148 acres) of vines, and here offer a wine from a plot registered as 'Manon', which belongs to the Bertinerie vineyard. It has a very bright gold colour which shines in the glass, and is both fresh and rich, maintaining a pleasant, thirst-quenching quality which is very much in keeping with its bouquet of mouthwatering toast, honey and *pain d'épice* (spice loaf) notes. It will go well with turbot, and will be ready to open this year.

➣ D. Bantégnies et Fils, Ch. Bertinerie, 33620 Cubnezais, tel. 05.57.68.70.74, fax 05.57.68.01.03 ☒ by appt.

CH. DES MATARDS
Cuvée Quentin Vinifié en fût de chêne 1999★

□ 1 ha 8,000 ⬛ €5-8

This oak-matured wine comes from a vineyard belonging to a large unit of over 40 ha (100 acres). It has real charm and a great deal of elegance, both in its bouquet of fine grapefruit and apricot notes and on the palate, where the balance is perfect.

➣ GAEC Terrigeol et Fils, 27, av. du Pont-de-la-Grâce, Le pas d'Ozelle, 33820 Saint-Ciers-sur-Gironde, tel. 05.57.32.61.96, fax 05.57.32.79.21, e-mail info@chateau-les-matards.com ☒ ☒ by appt.

CH. MAYNE-GUYON
Cuvée Héribert 1998★

■ 7.5 ha 33,500 ⬛ €8-11

Maturation in oak has marked the bouquet of this wine without spoiling the balance. The palate is well integrated and supported by supple, soft tannins. It has a round, rich structure which shows good ageing potential and gives the impression of a well-balanced wine.

➣ Ch. Mayne-Guyon, Mazerolles, 33390 Cars, tel. 05.57.42.09.59, fax 05.57.42.27.93 ☒ by appt.

➣ Fréteaud

CH. MONCONSEIL GAZIN
Grande Réserve Elevé en fût de chêne 1999★★

■ 2 ha 13,000 ⬛ €11-15

It is said that Charlemagne may once have held a council on the site where this beautiful manor house was built in about 1500. Fortunately we do not need to know for sure in order to appreciate this very delightful wine whose charming qualities will make it a good accompaniment to delicate meats. With that type of dish its fine flavours of ripe fruit and oak will open out to the full, as will its velvety tannins.

➣ Vignobles Michel Baudet, Ch. Monconseil Gazin, 33390 Plassac, tel. 05.57.42.16.63, fax 05.57.42.31.22, e-mail mbaudet@terre-net.fr ☑ ev, day except Sun. 9am–12.30pm 2pm–7pm

CH. MONTFOLLET
Vieilles vignes 1999★★

■ 3 ha 18,000 ⬛ €5-8

This wine has distinctively powerful aromas both in the nose and on the palate. The bouquet is dominated by a sense of roasting, but soft fruits come to the fore on the palate, where they are softened by notes of toast. This supple, rich, full, tannic wine is already pleasant, but it can also be kept.

➣ Cave coop. du Blayais, 9, Le Piquet, 33390 Cars, tel. 05.57.42.13.15, fax 05.57.42.84.92 ☒ by appt.

➣ SCEA Raimond

CH. PEYREDOULLE
Maine Criquau 1999★

■ 4 ha 30,000 ⬛ ■⬛ €8-11

This vineyard has a long-standing reputation, and remains true to its image with this wine, which promises much with its lovely carmine colour. Its bouquet, with its notes of black cherries, tobacco and roasting, and the powerful, well-balanced palate do not disappoint.

➣ Vignobles Germain et Associés, Ch. Peyredoulle, 33390 Berson, tel. 05.57.42.66.66, fax 05.57.64.36.20, e-mail bordeaux@vgas.com ☒ ☒ by appt.

CH. PRIEURE MALESAN
Elevé en fût de chêne 1999★

■ 53 ha 390,000 ⬛ €5-8

This wine not only has an exceptionally large volume of production, it also has an unusual bouquet with abundant notes of dried fruits, cocoa, vanilla and toast. Its complexity is confirmed on the palate, which offers fruit and toast flavours into a bargain. The wine is supported by a good structure with soft, silky tannins, and deserves to be kept for four to five years. It is distributed by the William Pitters company.

● SCEA Ch. Prieuré Malesan, 1, Perenne, 33390 Saint-Genès-de-Blaye, tel. 05.57.42.18.25, fax 05.57.42.15.86 ▼ by appt.

CH. SEGONZAC
Les Vieilles vignes 1998★

| 10 ha | 73,000 | €8-11 |

This vineyard is a fine production unit in terms of its buildings as well as its area. This 98 wine has much in its favour, both in its bouquet of stewed fruits, spice and oak aromas, and in its rich, fleshy structure on a palate with a substantial body which still needs to become rounder. The **Héritage 99** is recommended.

● SCEA Ch. Ségonzac, 39, Ségonzac, 33390 Saint-Genès-de-Blaye, tel. 05.57.42.18.16, fax 05.57.42.24.80, e-mail segonzac@chateau-segonzac.com ▼ by appt.

CH. TERRE-BLANQUE
Cuvée Noémie Elevé en fût de chêne 1999★★

| n.c. | 6,500 | €11-15 |

This wine is a numbered selection made from hand-picked grapes and matured in barrel. The quality is high throughout, starting with a bouquet of real complexity which is enriched by oak and moves from notes of toast to soft-fruit aromas. Equally good is the full, rich, powerful yet unaggressive palate, which indicates excellent ageing potential.

● Paul-Emmanuel Boulmé, Ch. Terre-Blanque, 33390 Saint-Genès-de-Blaye, tel. 05.57.42.18.48, fax 05.57.42.19.48, e-mail pe-boulme@chateau-terreblanque.com ▼ ▼ by appt.

EXCELLENCE DE TUTIAC
Vieilli en fût de chêne 1998★★

| 10 ha | 40,000 | €8-11 |

With 1,700 ha (4,200 acres) behind it, the Cave des Hauts de Gironde can make good use of its best vines to develop this *cuvée de prestige*. Its developed, complex bouquet starts with aromas of smoke, then opens out on to highly elegant notes of soft fruits. The palate continues in the same vein, leaving behind a lovely feeling of balance with its well-proportioned oak flavours and good body.

● Cave des Hauts de Gironde, La Cafourche, 33860 Marcillac, tel. 05.57.32.48.33, fax 05.57.32.49.63, e-mail contact@tutiac.com ▼ ▼ by appt.

Côtes de Bourg

The AOC covers about 3,876 ha (9,574 acres). The Merlot grape variety dominates and the reds – 226,648 hl (5,983,507 gal) in 2000 – often have a distinctively beautiful colour and a marked aroma of soft fruits. They are quite

CH. ROLAND LA GARDE
Prestige 1999★★

| 10 ha | 70,000 | €8-11 |

The name of this wine refers to the part played by Charlemagne and his nephew in the legendary history of the Blaye region. It is very much characterised by a rich, tannic structure which will ensure that it has the good ageing potential already suggested by the quality of the bouquet (blackcurrants, toast and flowers).

● Ch. Roland La Garde, 8, La Garde, 33390 Saint-Seurin-de-Cursac, tel. 05.57.42.32.29, fax 05.57.42.01.86, e-mail bruno.martin30@libertysurf.fr ▼ ev. day except Sun. 8am–12 noon 2pm–7pm

● Bruno Martin

DOM. DES ROSIERS
Elevé en fût de chêne 1999

| 2.5 ha | 18,600 | €5-8 |

This simple but well-made 99 should be drunk while young. It comes from a 15-ha (37-acre) estate with a characteristic range of Blaye grape varieties, and has been matured in oak for 12 months. There is a distinctive bouquet of roasted coffee combined with a mixture of gamey and dried fruit notes, and a palate that is well structured by fine tannins. This is already a good wine to serve with roast beef.

● Christian Blanchet, 10, La Borderie, 33820 Saint-Ciers-sur-Gironde, tel. 05.57.32.75.97, fax 05.57.32.78.37, e-mail cblanchet@wanadoo.fr ▼

CH. SAINT-AULAYE
Harmonie Elevé en fût de chêne 1999★

| 1 ha | 7,000 | €5-8 |

It is always exciting to discover old documents that tell the history of the family. That is what has just happened to the Berneauds, who have come upon a purchase deed for a plot bought in 1742. Such is life in the wine-growing business. This wine has been matured entirely in oak: it is supple and elegant, and has a good tannic structure, which will make it a delicious accompaniment to fine dishes such as quail with grapes or guinea-fowl with pineapples.

● SCEA vignoble J et H. Berneaud, 4, Saint-Aulaye, 33390 Mazion, tel. 05.57.42.11.14, fax 05.57.42.11.14, e-mail cberneaud@aol.com ▼ ▼ by appt.

Côtes de Bourg

tannic when young so in many cases may need to be kept. There are only a few whites – 2,752 hl (72,653 gal) in 2000 – which are generally dry and have a distinctive nose.

CH. BEL-AIR

Vieilli en fût de chêne 1998★

■ 0.5 ha 3,640 ▦ €5-8

This oak-matured wine comes from only a small part of a property totalling 20 ha (49 acres). It has a beautiful dark colour, an agreeable bouquet of soft-fruit aromas, and an equally pleasant palate with a supple, rich structure.

➤ GAEC Gayet Frères, Ch. Bel-Air,
33710 Samonac, tel. 05.57.68.26.67,
fax 05.57.68.26.67 ▨ ⓨ by appt.

CH. BELAIR-COUBET 1999★

■ n.c. 150,000 ■ ▦ ♦ €5-8

This wine was matured both in barrel and in tank, and is impressive not only in terms of volume of production, but also in the aromatic qualities of the bouquet and the tannic structure, although this still needs to become better integrated since the oak is still very evident. The **Château Tour Neuve 99** and the **Château Jansenant 99** also win one star.

➤ Vignobles Alain Faure,
Ch. Belair-Coubet, 33710 Saint-Ciers-de-Canesse, tel. 05.57.42.68.80,
fax 05.57.42.68.81, e-mail belair-coubet@wanadoo.fr ▨ ⓨ by appt.

CH. BRULESECAILLE 1999★★

■ 15 ha 80,000 ▦ €8-11

This vineyard is certainly one of the best known in the appellation, which is only fair when you consider how regularly it produces wines as good as this very delightful 99. It has a round, full-bodied, balanced and well-constructed palate which fully lives up to the promise of its lovely, dark colour. Everything suggests that it has excellent prospects for the future: the depth of its body, the balance between grape and oak, and a complex aromatic range (soft fruits, vanilla and toast) which will only increase if it is kept for three or four years. The **Blanc de Brulesécaille 2000** wins one star. This elegant and well-structured wine should be kept until the fruit flavours are stronger than the toast notes.

➤ GFA Rodet Recapet, Brulesécaille,
33710 Tauriac, tel. 05.57.68.40.31,
fax 05.57.68.21.27, e-mail cht.brulesecaille@freesbee.fr ▨ ⓨ by appt.

CH. CASTEL LA ROSE

Cuvée Sélection 1999★

■ 13 ha 40,000 ▦ €5-8

As at many vineyards in the Bourg region, Merlot features prominently among this château's range of grape varieties. It has a left its mark on this smooth, fruity wine, whose lovely flavours confirm the ageing potential of its body and long finish.

➤ GAEC Rémy Castel et Fils, 3, Laforêt,
33710 Villeneuve, tel. 05.57.64.86.61,
fax 05.57.64.90.07 ▨ ⓨ by appt.

CH. COLBERT

Cuvée Prestige Vieilli en fût de chêne 1999★

■ 2 ha 10,000 ▦ €5-8

This wine was matured in oak, and its beautiful colour, somewhere between ruby and garnet, inspires immediate confidence. Although still marked by oak, the bouquet has enough personality to release aromas of ripe fruits and chocolate along with musky notes. The full-bodied palate is supported by a good tannic structure, and has a real sense of balance. The **Cuvée Principale 99**, a real *vin de terroir*, is recommended.

➤ Duwer, Ch. Colbert, 33710 Comps,
tel. 05.57.64.95.04, fax 05.57.64.88.41 ▨
ⓨ ev. day 9am–6pm
➤ SCA Château Colbert

CH. DE COTS

Cuvée Prestige Elevé en fût de chêne 1998★★

■ n.c. 3,000 ▦ €8-11

This 15-ha (37-acre) vineyard is currently going over to organic methods. It offers a really delightful little *cuvée spéciale* which has been matured in new oak. With its pleasant colour, well-balanced bouquet of ripe fruits and oak, and substantial structure on the palate, it shows all the signs of needing to be kept for a while.

➤ Gilles Bergon, 3, Cots,
33710 Bayon-sur-Gironde,
tel. 05.57.64.82.79, fax 05.57.64.95.82 ▨
ⓨ ev. day 9am–12 noon 2pm–7pm

CH. COUBET 1998

■ n.c. 10,000 ■ ▦ ♦ €5-8

Michel Migné arrived on the family estate of 15 ha (37 acres) in 1996, and has produced a wine which, without being excessively powerful, does reveal a good tannic presence. The fruity bouquet and beautiful, very fresh colour give an overall impression of quality.

➤ Michel Migné, Ch. Coubet,
33710 Villeneuve, tel. 05.57.64.91.04 ▨
ⓨ by appt.

CH. CROUTE-CHARLUS

Vieilli en fût de chêne 1998★

■ 7.44 ha 11,000 ▦ €5-8

In 1995, Cédric Baudouin took over here from his grandfather Guy Sicard. He has maintained the tradition of using a diverse range of grapes, and now offers his oak-matured wine, which is a blend of 10% Malbec and three other Bordeaux varieties. The oak is still evident, especially on the palate, but does not mask the other flavours. This complex, full-bodied wine both needs and deserves to be kept for three to four years.

➤ Cédric Baudouin, Ch. Croûte-Charlus,
33710 Bourg-sur-Gironde,
tel. 05.57.68.25.67, fax 05.57.68.25.77
ⓨ by appt.

CH. FOUGAS

Cuvée Prestige Elevée en barrique 1999★★

| | 6 ha | 40,000 | 🍷 | €5-8 |

This vineyard has a lovely charterhouse on the road from Bourg to Pugnac, and enjoys a solid reputation which can only be reinforced by this Cuvée Prestige 99. It has a rich bouquet of beautiful, empyreumatic toast notes, and a substantial tannic structure which shows its power without losing its roundness. One star is awarded to the **Maldoror 99**, which has had a longer period of oak maturation and needs time to become more integrated. It won a *coup de coeur* for the 98 vintage.

↘ Jean-Yves Béchet, 33710 Lansac, tel. 05.57.68.42.15, fax 05.57.68.28.59 ☑
🍴 ev. day except Sat. Sun. 9am–6pm
↘ GFA Fougas

CH. GALAU 1999★★

| | 6.5 ha | 40,000 | 🍷 | €5-8 |

From the same producer as Château Nodoz (see below), this wine also came before the Grand Jury for a possible *coup de coeur*. Its aromas of roasting along with red berries and blackcurrants are highly elegant, as are its powerful tannins. This is a charming but also very powerful wine, which will keep for six to eight years.

↘ Magdeleine, Ch. Nodoz, 33710 Tauriac, tel. 05.57.68.41.03, fax 05.57.68.37.34 ☑
🍴 by appt.

CH. GARREAU 1999

| | 2.6 ha | 16,000 | 🍷 | €8-11 |

Despite a certain austerity at the finish, this wine makes a favourable impression with its well-balanced oak and fruit flavours. It will go well with a navarin of lamb.

↘ SCEA Ch. Garreau, La Fosse, 33710 Pugnac, tel. 05.57.68.90.75, fax 05.57.68.90.84 ☑ 🍴 ev. day except Sat. Sun. 8.15am–12 noon 1.30pm–5.30pm
🍴 Mme Guez

CH. GRAND LAUNAY

Réserve Lion noir 1999★

| | 6 ha | 30,000 | 🍷 | €8-11 |

This vineyard can be relied upon to produce high quality, and remains true to its tradition with this very well-composed wine. Maturation in oak has marked its bouquet with toast notes, but its personality goes on to reveal empyreumatic aromas and red-berry notes. It has a fresh, tannic palate which opens on to a beautiful finish.

↘ Michel Cosyns, Ch. Grand Launay, 33710 Teuillac, tel. 05.57.64.39.03, fax 05.57.64.22.32 ☑ 🍴 by appt.

CH. GRAVETTES-SAMONAC

Prestige Vieilli en fût de chêne 1999

| | 5 ha | 30,000 | 🍷 | €5-8 |

Made from a selection of the best oak-matured *cuvées* here, this dark-red wine is smooth and round, and has a pleasant range

of aromas with notes of fruit and roasting at the finish. The **Cuvée Tradition** is also recommended for its bouquet of floral and fruity fragrances.

↘ Gérard Griesse, Le Bourg, 33710 Samonac, tel. 05.57.68.21.16, fax 05.57.68.36.43 ☑ 🍴 by appt.

CH. GUERRY 1999

| | 22.95 ha | 140,000 | 🍷 | €8-11 |

Bordeaux wine-merchants may not have taken much interest in the vineyards of Bourg, but the same cannot be said of Bertrand de Rivoyre, who has been the owner here at Tauriac for three decades. His 99 wine has an elegant, carmine-red colour, and is already releasing fruity aromas in the nose. After a smooth attack, the palate is round and well balanced. This wine is pleasant to drink now, but can also be kept.

↘ SC du Ch. Guerry, 33710 Tauriac, tel. 05.57.68.20.78, fax 05.57.68.41.31 ☑
🍴 by appt.
↘ B. de Rivoyre

CH. GUIRAUD

Vieilli en fût de chêne 1998★

| | 4 ha | 21,600 | 🍷 | €8-11 |

Once again this vineyard has produced a highly successful wine. It has been oak-matured, and although the signs of this are still evident, especially at the finish, there is a good balance between oak and grape. This supple, pleasantly fragrant wine is already elegant, but will be at its best in two or three years' time.

↘ Jacky Bernard, 3, Guiraud, 33710 Saint-Ciers-de-Canesse, tel. 05.57.64.91.02, fax 05.57.64.91.46 ☑
🍴 by appt.

CH. HAUT-GUIRAUD

Péché du Roy Vieilli en fût de chêne 1999★★

| | 10 ha | 20,000 | 🍷◆ | €5-8 |

This oak-matured wine begins delicately with a restrained yet elegant bouquet of toast, mocha, spices, paprika and nutmeg. The full palate is supported by soft, fleshy tannins before opening on to an elegant, full-bodied finish. One star was awarded to the **Château Castaing**. It still has some rather harsh tannins, and needs to be kept for a while.

↘ EARL Bonnet et Fils, Ch. Haut-Guiraud, 33710 Saint-Ciers-de-Canesse, tel. 05.57.64.91.39, fax 05.57.64.88.05 ☑ 🍴 by appt.

CH. HAUT-MACO

Cuvée Jean-Bernard 1998★

| | 8 ha | 53,000 | 🍷◆ | €5-8 |

This estate made a major investment in 1991 with its semi-circular barrel-store. The wine comes from the vineyard's *cuvée prestige*. It is well constructed, but is particularly impressive for the quality of its bouquet of elegant, well-balanced aromas of ripe fruit combined with oak. The main wine here is the **98 Château Haut-Macó**, which is recommended; it is ready to drink now, whereas the

Cuvée Jean-Bernard will need to be kept for two or three years.

☛ Jean et Bernard Mallet, Ch. Haut-Macó, 33710 Tauriac, tel. 05.57.68.81.26, fax 05.57.68.91.97. ✉ ⴱ ev. day except Sun. 8am–12 noon 2pm–6pm.

CH. HAUT-MONDESIR 1999★

■   1.8 ha   12,000   ⫴ €11-15

This little vineyard belongs to an estate in the Blaye region (Mondésir-Gazin), and in this vintage offers a wine with plenty of aromatic intensity and substantial development on a palate embellished by good tannins and lovely notes of liquorice. This is a very good wine which should be kept until autumn 2002.

☛ Marc Pasquet, 10, Le Sablon, BP 7, 33390 Plassac, tel. 05.57.42.29.80, fax 05.57.42.84.46. ✉ ⴱ by appt.

CH. LABADIE

Vieilli en fût de chêne 1999★

■   9.2 ha   73,000   ⫴ ◆ €5-8

Although it does not equal some previous vintages, including the 98 which won a *coup de cœur* in last year's *Guide*, this wine has plenty to recommend it. The early promise of its strong colour is confirmed by its very intense bouquet of toast and vanilla notes, and its tannic yet round body on the palate. The **Château Laroche Joubert 99** is recommended, and will need to be kept for a while.

☛ Joël Dupuy, 1, Cagna, 33710 Mombrier, tel. 05.57.64.23.84, fax 05.57.64.23.85, e-mail vignoblesjdupuy@aol.com ✉ ⴱ by appt.

CH. DE LA BRUNETTE

Chêne de Brunette Elevé en fût 1999

■   0.5 ha   3,000   ⫴ €5-8

This oak-matured wine is somewhat arid at the finish. This youthful sin should disappear, however, leaving an expressive range of flavours (red berries, vanilla and cocoa). Its good structure is already quite well integrated.

☛ SCEA Lagarde Père et Fils, Dom. de La Brunette, 33710 Prignac-et-Marcamps, tel. 05.57.43.58.23, fax 05.57.43.01.21, e-mail chateau.de.la.brunette@wanadoo.fr ✉ ⴱ by appt.

CH. DE LA GRAVE Nectar 1999★

■   n.c.   15,000   ⫴ €11-15

Run from a feudal-looking château, this vineyard offers its *cuvée spéciale*. Maturation in oak has given it pleasant spice aromas which mingle with strawberry and crystallised fruit notes to form a lovely combination of flavours on a long, well-balanced palate.

☛ Philippe Bassereau, Ch. de La Grave, 33710 Bourg-sur-Gironde, tel. 05.57.68.41.49, fax 05.57.68.49.26, e-mail chateau.de.la-grave@wanadoo.fr ✉ ⴱ by appt.

CH. LA GROLET Tête de cuvée 1999★

■   1.5 ha   10,000   ⫴ €5-8

On this vast estate, only 1.5 ha (4 acres) are devoted to this numbered *cuvée spéciale*. It comes from 45-year-old Merlot vines, and is marked by maturation in oak and by the grape variety, which has given it a really delightful bouquet. The body already seems round, integrated and balanced.

☛ Jean-Luc Hubert, Ch. La Grolet, 33390 Cars, tel. 05.57.42.11.95, fax 05.57.42.38.15 ✉ ⴱ by appt.

LA PETITE CHARDONNE

Elevé en fût de chêne 1999★

■   4 ha   30,000   ⫴ €8-11

Vignobles Marinier mainly focus on their wineries, but they also have nearly 50 ha (124 acres) of vines in the Bourg region. They market selections from their best plots under the brand name La Petite Chardonne. Their Côtes de Bourg has a complex bouquet (vanilla, roast coffee, flowers and fleshy notes), and a pleasant structure which only needs a short ageing period (about two years) to become rounder.

☛ SCEA Vignobles Louis Marinier, Dom. Florimond-La Brède, 33390 Berson, tel. 05.57.64.39.07, fax 05.57.64.23.27, e-mail vignobleslouismarinier@wanadoo.fr ✉ ⴱ ev. day 8am–12 noon 2pm–6pm; Sat. Sun. by appt.; cl. Aug.

CH. LA TUILIERE

Les Armoiries 1998★

■   3 ha   15,000   ⫴ €11-15

The vineyard's star attraction is this wine made from 45-year-old vines and sold in numbered bottles. It needs to be kept for a while until the oak is better integrated, but it has a sufficiently substantial structure and powerful bouquet to ensure that this development goes ahead without any problem. The **Cuvée Principale** is recommended. This is also oak-matured, but comes from 25-year-old vines.

☛ Les Vignobles Philippe Estournet, Ch. La Tuilière, 33710 Saint-Ciers-de-Canesse, tel. 05.57.64.80.90, fax 05.57.64.89.97, e-mail chateaulatuiliere@minitel.net ✉ ⴱ by appt.

CH. LE BREUIL Cuvée du Dragon Elevé en fût de chêne 1998★

■   1.5 ha   11,000   ⫴ €5-8

Despite its name, this wine comes from a very attractive commune which has a beautiful church, located along the Gironde coast road. The same sense of peace and harmony can be found in the wine's bouquet, which offers a delightful combination of dark berry and truffle aromas with shades of vanilla and caramel. The long, tannic structure will ensure that it develops well as it ages.

☛ GAEC Doyen et Fils, Ch. Le Breuil, 33710 Bayon-sur-Gironde, tel. 05.57.64.80.10, fax 05.57.64.93.75, e-mail chateau.le.breuil@wanadoo.fr ✉ ⴱ ev. day except Sat. Sun. 9am–12 noon 3pm–7pm.

CH. LE SABLARD Cuvée Prestige
Elevée en fût de chêne neuf 1999

■ 6.3 ha 7,000 ■❙ €8-11

This oak-matured wine is still somewhat tannic at the finish. The oak is well combined with a balanced vinosity, however, and that will enable this youthful flaw to fade and allow the aromas of roast chestnuts, violets and soft fruits to become fully expressive.

➛ Jacques Buratti, 7, Le Rioucreux, 33920 Saint-Christoly-de-Blaye, tel. 05.57.42.57.67, fax 05.57.42.43.06
Ⓨ ev. day 9am–12 noon 2.30pm–6pm

CH. LES GRAVES DE VIAUD
Cuvée Tradition Vieilli en fût de chêne 1999

■ 10 ha 70,000 ■❙❙♦ €5-8

Château de Viaud was taken over in 1994 by new owners, and is now offering two wines. This one is not destined for lengthy keeping, but nevertheless it is well balanced and expressive, with good flavours developing on a combination of roasting and spice notes. The **Grande Cuvée** has been matured in oak for 12 months, and is recommended. It will need to be kept for two or three years until the oak has become fully integrated.

➛ Dom. de Viaud, 33710 Pugnac, tel. 05.57.68.94.37, fax 05.57.68.94.49
Ⓨ by appt.

CH. LE TERTRE DE LEYLE
Cuvée Réserve Elevé en fût de chêne 1998★

■ 1.1 ha 7,500 ❙❙ €5-8

This 16.6-ha (41-acre) estate is expanding over the years as it buys up neighbouring plots. This wine comes from a small *cuvée de prestige*, and is still strongly marked by its maturation in oak. The oak is of high quality, however, and has produced lovely notes of vanilla. The round, tannic structure is strong enough to guarantee that the wine will develop well.

➛ SC Vignobles Grandillon, Le Bourg, 33710 Teuillac, tel. 05.57.64.39.31, fax 05.57.64.24.18 Ⓨ by appt.

CH. MARTINAT
Vieilli en fût de chêne 1999★

■ n.c. 35,000 ■❙♦ €8-11

This wine still bears the stamp of maturation in oak clearly in a bouquet of coconut, vanilla and crystallised-fruit aromas. Nevertheless, as its dark, almost black colour suggests, it has a strong enough structure to keep until it is fully integrated.

➛ SCEV Marsaux-Donze, Ch. Martinat, 33710 Lansac, tel. 05.57.68.34.98, fax 05.57.68.35.39, e-mail donzels@aol.com
Ⓨ by appt.

➛ Eric et Bernard Latouche, Ch. Macay, 33710 Samonac, tel. 05.57.68.41.50, fax 05.57.68.35.23 Ⓨ by appt.

CH. MONTAIGUT
Vieilli et élevé en fût de chêne 2000

□ 1.8 ha 7,000 ■❙♦ €5-8

This is one of the few white wines still produced in the Côtes de Bourg appellation. Maturation in oak and a grape content of Sauvignon blended with Muscadelle (20%) and Sémillon (20%) have marked the bouquet with notes of boxwood and citrus fruits. The **Oak-matured red 99** is already delightful and is recommended.

➛ François de Pardieu, 2, Nodeau, 33710 Saint-Ciers-de-Canesse, tel. 05.57.64.92.49, fax 05.57.64.94.20 Ⓨ by appt.

CH. L'HOSPITAL Elevée en fût 1998★

■ 0.2 ha 10,000 ❙❙ €8-11

The current owners took over the property in July 1997, and this is the first vintage they can truly call their own. The results are more than encouraging: the wine has a deep, youthful colour, a fine, even elegant bouquet in which the oak is well integrated, and a supple, full-bodied palate with ripe fruit flavours.

➛ Christine et Bruno Duhamel, Ch. L'Hospital, 33710 Saint-Trojan, tel. 05.57.64.33.60, fax 05.57.64.33.60, e-mail alvitis@wanadoo.fr Ⓨ by appt.

CH. MACAY Original 1999

■ 3 ha 18,000 ■❙ €11-15

This wine comes from a plot where the grapes are hand-picked, and makes quite a captivating impression with its notes of lovely vanilla notes and good length on the palate.

CH. DU MOULIN-VIEUX 1998★

■ 15 ha 72,000 ❙❙ €5-8

The fact that this numbered, oak-matured wine has an unusually large volume of production merely makes one appreciate its qualities all the more. It has a bouquet of delicate soft-fruit fragrances against an oaky background, a full, rich palate and a well-balanced body which shows that it has been carefully developed.

➛ Jean-Pierre et Cédric Gorphe, 20 chem. du Moulin-Vieux, 33710 Tauriac, tel. 06.07.04.44.17, fax 05.57.68.29.75 Ⓨ by appt.

CH. NODOZ 1999★★

■ 10 ha 60,000 ❙❙ €8-11

This vineyard has a beautiful winery and a tasting-room which make it a favourite stopping-place on the 'wine-tourist' route. The main attraction here is the wine, however, which yet again is outstanding. With its very beautiful, dark-garnet colour, complex bouquet ranging from bitter chocolate to soft fruits, round attack and supple, elegant tannic structure, it has all it takes to make a great wine. It can be drunk in four to five years' time and from then until 2010 or 2012.

➤ Magdeleine, Ch. Nodoz, 33710 Tauriac, tel. 05.57.68.41.03, fax 05.57.68.37.34
Y by appt.

CH. PERTHUS 1998★
n.c.　■ €5-8

This wine comes from a vineyard located 300 m (330 yd) from the Pair-Non-Pair cave, which is one of the most important prehistoric sites in Aquitaine. There is more than a suggestion of the cave's famous frescoes in the wine's musky leather aromas, but although it has all the power of a neolithic hunter, it also has a well-integrated, soft quality which is more reminiscent of gentler times. The Cave de Tauriac also offered its **Etienne de Tauriac** brand, which is recommended.

➤ Cave de Bourg-Tauriac,
3, av. des Côtes-de-Bourg, 33710 Tauriac, tel. 05.57.94.07.07, fax 05.57.94.07.00,
e-mail cave.bourg-tauriac@wanadoo.fr
Y ev. day except Sun. 9am–12.30pm 1.30pm–6pm
➤ Claire Deffarge

CH. PEYCHAUD Maisomeuve 1999★
■ 6 ha 40,000 ■ €8-11

Vignobles Germain offers a lovely wine which combines good complexity in the nose (soft fruits, liquorice and overripe fruits) with a substantial, tannic, full-bodied structure. It can be drunk in two years' time and for four years after that.

➤ Vignobles Germain et Associés,
Ch. Peyredoulle, 33390 Berson,
tel. 05.57.42.66.66, fax 05.57.64.36.20,
e-mail bordeaux@ygas.com Y by appt.

CLOS DU PIAT Cuvée Louis 1999★★
3.5 ha 20,000 ■ €11-15

The Chétys are advocates if not apostles of environmentally sound growing methods, and have applied these principles to this little vineyard, which they bought in 1999. It has been a real success, as is shown by this delightful, oak-matured wine. It has a brilliant red colour, a bouquet of blackcurrants with nuances of liquorice, a fruity attack and a rich palate with well-integrated tannins, all of which give it excellent prospects for the future. Another wine, the **Château Mercier**, is recommended.

➤ Philippe et Christophe Chéty,
Ch. Mercier, 33710 Saint-Trojan,
tel. 05.57.42.66.99, fax 05.57.42.66.96,
e-mail info@chateau-mercier.fr Y ev. day except Sat. Sun. 8am–12 noon 2pm–5.30pm

RELAIS DE LA POSTE 1999 €5-8
n.c. 128,000 ■

This vineyard is named after an old post-house dating back to 1750, and offers a wine which is still somewhat austere at the finish but is well constructed and has good, complex

aromas (redcurrants, blackcurrants and faded roses).

➤ Vignobles Drode, Relais de la Poste, 33710 Teuillac, tel. 05.57.64.37.95, fax 05.57.64.37.95 Y by appt.

CH. REPIMPLET
Cuvée Amélie Julien 1999★★
■ 2.8 ha 18,000 ■ €8-11

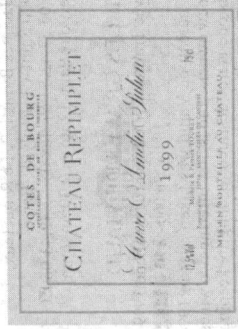

This vineyard made a great leap forward with its 96 vintage, but still needed to back it up with further proof. It has now done so with this lovely *cuvée de prestige*, which is not restricted to a limited volume of production. It starts with a dark-red colour, then develops a complex bouquet of ripe-fruit and spice aromas supported by vanilla. The rich, firm, long structure opens out on to beautiful notes of roasting, and can only lead to one conclusion: this wine deserves to be kept. The rich, expressive **Cuvée Principale 99** is recommended.

➤ Michèle et Patrick Touret, 4, Repimplet, 33710 Saint-Ciers-de-Canesse,
tel. 05.57.64.31.78, fax 05.57.64.31.78
Y by appt.

CH. DE ROUSSELET
Vieilli en fût de chêne 1998★
■ 2.5 ha 18,500 ■ €5-8

Although it is not particularly powerful, this wine attracts attention by its good balance and bouquet of fruit and chocolate aromas. The palate has a pleasant combination of oak and fruit flavours, and a beautiful, very long finish.

➤ EARL du Ch. de Rousselet,
33710 Saint-Trojan, tel. 05.57.64.32.18,
fax 05.57.64.32.18,
e-mail chateau.de.rousselet@wanadoo.fr
Y by appt.

CH. ROUSSELLE 1999★
n.c.　■ €8-11

An excellent *terroir* and a serious approach to growing, harvesting and vinification – all of which has produced this elegant, silky, well-balanced, expressive wine whose floral notes can be enjoyed before too long.

➤ Ch. Rousselle, 33710 Saint-Ciers-de-Canesse, tel. 05.57.42.16.62,
fax 05.57.42.19.51,
e-mail chateaurousselle@hotmail.com
Y ev. day 9am–12 noon 2pm–6pm; Sat. Sun. by appt.

CH. DE TASTE 1998

15 ha 80,000 ▥ €5-8

This wine comes from the undulating landscape of the commune of Lansac. It is supple and round, and its developing flavours are full of finesse and elegance.

♠ SCEA des Vignobles de Taste et Barrié, La Sablière, 33710 Lansac, tel. 05.57.68.40.34.

Le Libournais

Although there is no 'Appellation Libourne', the Libournais district exists in its own right. While Bordeaux is the major town and the Dordogne is the major waterway, Libourne has a distinct individuality in the Gironde and is not as dependent as other areas on the regional metropolis. It is not unusual for the Libournais to be distinguished from the Bordelais itself, with its less ostentatious architecture, its wine châteaux and wine-merchant quarter. But what sets the Libournais apart most of all is undoubtedly the concentration of the vineyards, which start right on the edge of the town and cover nearly the whole countryside in several communes, producing famous appellations, such as Fronsac, Pomerol and Saint-Emilion, on land that is parcelled up into small or medium-sized

CH. TOUR DES GRAVES

Vieilli en fût de chêne 2000★

□ 0.3 ha 1,500

Although white wines are not as common in Côtes de Bourg as they used to be, the tradition has not died out completely. This wine, has been developed and matured in oak with stirring on lees, and has a pleasant bouquet of citrus fruits and vanilla notes.

♠ GAEC Arnaud Frères, Le Poteau, 33710 Teuillac, tel. 05.57.64.32.02, fax 05.57.64.23.94 ✓ Ⓣ by appt.

CH. DE VIENS 1999★

23 ha 80,000 ▥ €5-8 €8-11

This concentrated, tannic wine still needs two or three years to become integrated and open, but its structure and body will enable it to do so without difficulty.

♠ Eric Merle, Château de Viens, 33710 Mombrier, tel. 05.57.68.24.80 ✓ Ⓣ by appt.

properties. Large properties, like those of the Médoc, or the wide expanses characteristic of Aquitaine, are practically unknown here.

The vineyard's individuality also comes from the varieties of grape grown: Merlot predominates, giving fruitiness and finesse to the wines, which are able to age well, even if they keep for less time than the appellations, made mainly from Cabernet-Sauvignon. On the other hand, they can be drunk a little sooner and accompany a variety of foods (red and white meat, cheeses and certain fish, such as lamprey).

Canon-Fronsac and Fronsac

The Fronsadais is bounded by the Dordogne and Isle rivers. The beautiful countryside is very divided up and has two hills, which offer magnificent views over the area. The region is a strategic point and under Charlemagne a sturdy fortress was built there; during the following centuries the area continued to play an important role in the history of France. Nowadays there is no trace of the original fortress, but the Fronsadais has some beautiful churches and numerous châteaux. Wine-growing is an ancient activity, and the vineyards, which cover six communes, produce individual wines that are balanced and full-bodied, while also being fine and distinguished. All the communes are entitled to use the Appellation Fronsac – 46,138 hl (1,218,043 gal) in 2000 – but of the wines produced on the limestone and clay slopes on a footing of opaline lime, only Fronsac and Saint-Michel-de-Fronsac are entitled to use the Appellation Canon-Fronsac – 16,462 hl (434,597 gal) in 2000.

Canon-Fronsac

CH. BARRABAQUE Prestige 1998★★

■   n.c.   n.c.   ⑨⑥   97   98

88 |89| 91 92 |94| ⑨⑤

When will this château ever stop? After three *coups de cœur* in a row, this magnificent 98 now wins a fourth, which is a rare feat in the *Guide*. The wine has a sumptuous, black colour and powerful, complex aromas which are marked by overripe fruits and perfectly balanced with oaky notes of vanilla and roasting. The real potential of this rich, dense 98 becomes apparent on the palate, which opens with a dazzling attack and develops with balance and finesse. The very long, aromatic finish shows just how well this wine will mature as it ages.

➥ SCEA Noël Père et Fils, Ch. Barrabaque, 33126 Fronsac, tel. 05.57.55.09.09,
fax 05.57.55.09.00,
e-mail chateaubarrabaque@yahoo.fr
Ⓨ by appt.

CH. BELLOY Cuvée Prestige 1998★

■   1 ha   6,619   Ⅲ €11-15

The château dates back to the Second Empire, and has upheld tradition while at the same time introducing modern techniques of planned growing and vinification. This limited *cuvée* is a great success; it has an emerging bouquet of ripe fruit, undergrowth and roasting aromas, and a velvety, balanced tannic structure which develops with finesse and good length. It needs to be kept for two to three years.

➥ SA Travers, BP 1, 33126 Fronsac,
tel. 05.57.24.98.05, fax 05.57.24.97.79 Ⓥ
Ⓨ by appt.
➥ GAF Bardibel

CH. CANON 1998★

■   1.35 ha   9,400   Ⅲ €11-15

There is barely more than 1 ha (2.5 acres) of Merlot on this vineyard belonging to the Moueix family, who always produce excellent wines on a par with this 98. It has a deep, intense colour and elegant aromas of ripe fruit, liquorice and vanilla, followed by a palate on which the velvety tannins develop with balance and finesse right up to a long, complex finish. The wine should have an ageing potential of at least four to six years.

➥ Ets Jean-Pierre Moueix,
54, quai du Priourat, 33500 Libourne,
tel. 05.57.51.78.96

CH. CANON DE BREM 1998

■   4.57 ha   31,000   Ⅲ €11-15

This 98 contains more than 60% Cabernet Franc, and has outstandingly elegant fragrances of menthol, leather and oak. After a tender, velvety attack, the wine develops with finesse. It will be ready to drink in two to three years' time.

➥ Ets Jean-Pierre Moueix,
54, quai du Priourat, 33500 Libourne,
tel. 05.57.51.78.96

CH. CANON SAINT-MICHEL 1998★

■   n.c.   12,500   Ⅲ €11-15

This is the first vintage produced by a young wine-grower who has just taken over his grandfather's property. The result is encouraging; the wine has a brilliant, intense colour, a bouquet of tobacco, toast and vanilla, and a very fruity (cherry) tannic structure which is elegant and well composed. The very long, concentrated finish on delicate notes of oak suggests an ageing potential of at least two to five years.

➥ Jean-Yves Millaire, Lamarche,
33126 Fronsac, tel. 06.08.33.81.11,
fax 06.57.25.07.38 Ⓥ Ⓨ by appt.

CH. CASSAGNE HAUT-CANON

La Truffière 1998★

■   13 ha   39,000   Ⅲ €11-15

86 88 **89** 90 91 |**93**| |94| 96 97 98

This wine's name refers to the truffle patch in the middle of the vineyard from which the owners harvest a few truffles every year. The 98 vintage has a dark colour with garnet glints, and fine, complex aromas of crystallised red berries and undergrowth along with a slightly gamey note. The palate plays on the balance between fruity tannins and elegant oak. This wine should be drunk within the next five years. The **Cuvée Classique** is recommended for its aromatic freshness and balanced floral flavours, and can be drunk straight away.

➥ Jean-Jacques Dubois,
Ch. Cassagne Haut-Canon,
33126 Saint-Michel-de-Fronsac,
tel. 05.57.51.63.98, fax 05.57.51.62.20,
e-mail jjdubois@club-internet.fr Ⓥ
Ⓨ by appt.

CLOS TOUMALIN 1998★

■   4 ha   10,000   ■ Ⅲ ◊ €11-15

This deep-crimson 98 is a blend of 50% Merlot, 25% Cabernet Sauvignon and 25% Cabernet Franc. It has a developing bouquet suggesting caramel, leather, menthol and crystallised fruits. On the palate it is a wine of character, with an attack of velvety tannins followed by a mouth-filling, concentrated body. The wine will be perfect in two to three years' time when the oak has become fully integrated.

♠ SC Vignobles Bouyge-Barthe, Ch. Gagnard, 33126 Fronsac, tel. 05.57.51.42.99, fax 05.57.51.10.83 ▼
Ϫ by appt.

CH. COMTE 1998★

3 ha   12,000   €11–15

The Merlot vines here (98%) are grown on the siliceous limestone soils of a hillside and have very good exposure to the sun. This wine has an intense, crimson colour, and aromas of bilberries, undergrowth, coffee and cocoa. The tannins are well structured, even lively in the attack, after which they develop pleasantly and with more softness and elegance up to a well-balanced finish. The wine will be ready to drink three to five years from now.
♠ Françoise Roux, Ch. Lagüe, 33126 Fronsac, tel. 05.57.51.24.68, fax 05.57.25.98.67 ▼ Ϫ by appt.

CH. COUSTOLLE 1998★

20 ha   n.c.   €8–11

90 93 94 |95| |96| |97| 98

This château regularly produces very good wines such as this 98, which has a clear, garnet colour with shimmering glints, and a delicate bouquet of ripe red berries with a slight hint of spice. The full, rich tannin structure asserts itself at the finish, but it should become more subdued after two or three years of ageing.
♠ GFA Vignobles Alain Roux, Ch. Coustolle, 33126 Fronsac, tel. 05.57.51.31.25, fax 05.57.74.00.32 ▼

CH. DU GABY 1998

9.35 ha   13,968   €11–15

The Khayat family bought this estate in 1999, which means that these two 98 wines were the last to be produced by owners who had been running the vineyard for 250 years. The first has a very frank bouquet of fresh red berries, and substantial tannins delicately cloaked by oaky vanilla. This wine is true to type, and can be drunk in two to five years' time. The second is **La Roche Gaby**, which is also recommended for its fruity character but has suppler tannins and is smooth and easy to drink. It has less ageing potential than the other wine, and should be drunk within the next three years.
♠ SCEA Vignoble famille Khayat, Ch. du Gaby, 33126 Fronsac, tel. 05.57.51.24.97, fax 05.57.25.18.99, e-mail chateau.du.gaby@wanadoo.fr ▼
Ϫ by appt.

CH. HAUT-MAZERIS 1998★

6.01 ha   39,000   €11–15

This very good 98 is a classic blend of Merlot (60%) and both Cabernets (40%). It has a fresh colour with delightful, ruby glints and a mainly fruity bouquet with delicate notes of cocoa. The tannins are powerful in the attack, then develop with finesse and no aggression until a fairly well-balanced finish. The wine will be ready to drink in two or three years' time.
♠ SCEA Ch. Haut-Mazeris, 33126 Saint-Michel-de-Fronsac, tel. 05.57.24.98.14, fax 05.57.24.91.07
Ϫ by appt.

CH. LA CROIX CANON 1998★

14 ha   74,000   €11–15

At this ideally located château, F. Veyssière, who runs the barrel-store, and oenologist Jean-Claude Berrouet have blended 81% Merlot with 19% Cabernet Franc to produce this very good 98 vintage. The garnet colour has crimson glints, and there is an expressive bouquet of spice, fruit and smoke aromas. The wine shows plenty of character on a full, well-structured palate with a particularly velvety finish. The balance will be perfect after two or five years of ageing.

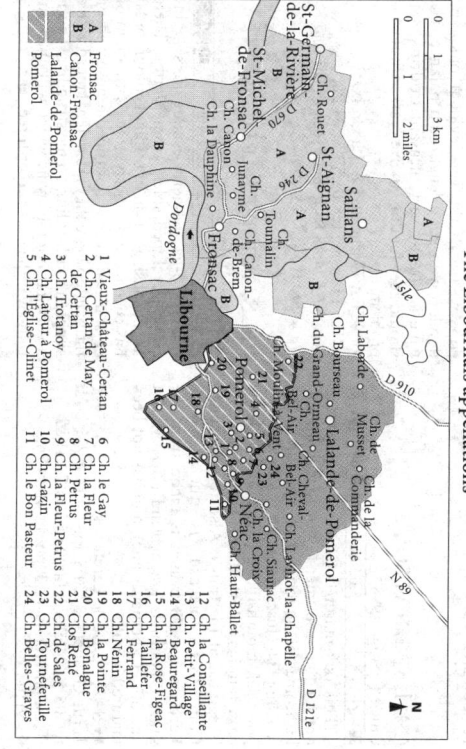

The Libournais appellations

Legend:
A Fronsac
B Canon-Fronsac
Lalande-de-Pomerol
Pomerol

1 Vieux-Château-Certan
2 Ch. Certan de May de Certan
3 Ch. Trotanoy
4 Ch. Latour à Pomerol
5 Ch. l'Église-Clinet
6 Ch. le Gay
7 Ch. la Fleur
8 Ch. Petrus
9 Ch. la Fleur-Petrus
10 Ch. Gazin
11 Ch. le Bon Pasteur
12 Ch. la Conseillante
13 Ch. Petit-Village
14 Ch. Beauregard
15 Ch. la Rose-Figeac
16 Ch. Taillefer
17 Ch. Ferrand
18 Ch. Nénin
19 Ch. la Pointe
20 Ch. Bonalgue
21 Clos René
22 Ch. de Sales
23 Ch. Tournefeuille
24 Ch. Belles-Graves

• SCEA Ch. Bodet, Ets Jean-Pierre Moueix 54, quai du Priourat, 33500 Libourne, tel. 05.57.55.05.80

LA FLEUR CAILLEAU 1998★★

◼ 3.6 ha 12,000 ◼◼◼ €11-15

85 86 88 92 |93| |94| **95 96 98**

Since 1990 this chateau has gone over to organic growing, and every year it produces excellent wines based essentially on Merlot (95%). This 98 wine has been matured in oak for 12 months. It has an intense, almost black colour, and a complex bouquet dominated by crystallised notes of prunes, peanuts and coffee. The tannins are rich and smooth in the attack, then become powerful, ripe and fleshy on a palate with a perfectly balanced finish. The fruitiness of the grape combines well with oak flavours which are not excessive. It was placed second by the Grand Jury, and only missed winning a *coup de coeur* by one vote. You can enjoy it in two to six years' time, but take care not to overdo it!

• Paul et Pascale Barre, La Grave, 33126 Fronsac, tel. 05.57.51.31.11, fax 05.57.25.08.61, e-mail p.p.barre@wanadoo.fr ✉ ☎ by appt.

CH. LAMARCHE CANON

Candelaire 1998 ◼ ◼◼◼ ♦ €8-11

|94| 95 |96| |97| 98

This wine is made from 90% Merlot grown on vines that are over 50 years old, and has been matured for 12 months in 400-litre oak barrels. It distinguished itself by its pleasant, fruity, tannic character and aromas of liquorice and oak at the finish. It is true to type, and should be left to age for two or three years.

• Eric Julien, Ch. Lamarche-Canon, 33126 Fronsac, tel. 05.57.51.28.13, fax 05.57.51.28.13, e-mail bordeaux@vgas.com ✉ ☎ ev. day except Sun. 8am-12 noon 2pm-6pm

CH. LARCHEVESQUE

Cuvée Prestige 1998★

◼ 3.62 ha 5,900 ◼◼◼ ♦ €11-15

This oak-matured Cuvée Prestige stands out for the deep intensity of its colour, and its aromas of liquorice, ripe fruits and oaky roasting. The luscious attack is followed by a powerful, mouth-filling palate, although the oaky tannins still need time to become more integrated at the finish. Also recommended from this vineyard is the **Château Larchevesque 98**, which is made from the same Libournais grape blend (70% Merlot and 30% Cabernet Franc), and has not been matured in oak.

• SARL Cave de Larchevesque, 1, rue Guadet, 33330 Saint-Emilion, tel. 05.57.24.67.78, fax 05.57.24.71.31 ✉ ☎ ev. day 10am-12.30pm 1.30pm-7pm

• Viaud

CH. MAZERIS

La Part des Anges 1998★★

◼ 1 ha 4,000 ◼◼◼ €8-11

Based on a selection from two plots of 50-year-old Merlot, this attractively named wine is remarkable for its year. It has an intense garnet colour, and complex aromas of ripe fruits, tobacco and menthol which combine well with a powerful note of oaky vanilla. The palate is predominantly fine and velvety, although the tannins are mouth-filling and very long. This is a wine which is not to be missed in four to ten years' time. A **Cuvée Classique** is recommended for its aromatic finesse and the silkiness of its tannic structure; it can be drunk one to three years from now.

• EARL de Courmuaud, Ch. Mazeris, 33126 Saint-Michel-de-Fronsac, tel. 05.57.24.96.93, fax 05.57.24.98.25, e-mail p.decournuaud@wanadoo.fr ✉ ☎ ev. day except Sun. 8am-1pm 2pm-7pm

CH. MAZERIS-BELLEVUE 1998

◼ 9.4 ha 65,000 ◼◼◼ €8-11

This château is located on the appellation's clay-limestone hillside, overlooking the beautiful church at Saint-Aignan. It has produced a good, interesting 98 with a dark-crimson colour, a floral and slightly fruity bouquet, and tender tannins which will become firmer as they develop. The wine appears to need two or three years of ageing.

• Jacques Bussier, Ch. Mazeris-Bellevue, 33126 Saint-Michel-de-Fronsac, tel. 05.57.24.98.19, fax 05.57.24.90.32, e-mail ch-mazeris-bellevue@wanadoo.fr ✉ ☎ ev. day 9am-6pm

CH. ROULLET 1998★

◼ 2.61 ha 10,000 ◼◼◼ ♦ €8-11

This little vineyard has been run by the same family from generation to generation, and produces excellent wines such as this fine, elegant 98, which is marked by intense notes of oak. On the palate the rich, velvety tannins cope well with the very evident oak, and develop with good length and balance. The wine is already very pleasant to drink, but should keep for three to five years without any problem.

• SCEA Dorneau, Ch. La Croix, 33126 Fronsac, tel. 05.57.51.31.28, fax 05.57.74.08.88, e-mail scea-dorneau@wanadoo.fr ✉ ☎ by appt.

CH. SAINT-BERNARD

Elevé en fût de chêne 1998★

◼ 0.26 ha 2,400 ◼◼◼ ♦ €5-8

This 26-ha (64-acre) estate offers a tiny *cuvée*, developed solely from Merlot. There are purplish glints in its brilliant colour, and it has cocoa and red-berry notes with a hint of crystallised prunes both in the nose and on the palate, where they are well balanced with a supple, mouth-filling tannic structure. This is a very harmonious wine which will open out fully over the next two or three years.

CH. BOURDIEU LA VALADE 1998★★

■ | n.c. | n.c. | 🍷 €8-11

With one foot in Canon and the other in Fronsac, Alain Roux knows what he is doing. This 98 has a brilliant crimson colour and an elegant bouquet of very ripe fruit, spice and toast aromas. After a smooth attack, the wine opens out as it develops on the palate, which is powerful, mature and well balanced. It is very characteristic of this appellation, and can be drunk in two to six years' time.
♠ GFA Vignobles Alain Roux, Ch. Coustolle, 33126 Fronsac,
tel. 05.57.51.31.25, fax 05.57.74.00.32 ☑
🍷 by appt.

CLOS DU ROY Cuvée Arthur 1998★

■ | 5 ha | 25,000 | 🍷 €8-11

The Cuvée Arthur is matured for one year in oak, and now represents 70% of the wine produced at Clos du Roy. The 98 wine has an intense colour, a developing bouquet of ripe fruits and vanilla, and a full, well-balanced tannic structure. There is a classic finish, which is somewhat severe but very long and holds out great promise for this wine's future in two to five years' time.
♠ Philippe Hermouet, Clos du Roy, 33141 Saillans, tel. 05.57.55.07.45,
e-mail hermouetclosduroy@wanadoo.fr ☑

CH. FONTENIL 1998

|88| |89| |90| 92 |93| |94| 95 96 |97| 98 | 9 ha | 55,000 | 🍷 €11-15

This château has belonged to Dany and Michel Rolland for 15 years, and now offers a 98 wine with a deep, almost black colour. Its intense aromas are dominated by coffee, smoke and vanilla. The powerful, full-bodied, very concentrated tannins are not yet allowing the fruit flavours to come through on the palate, where they are completely masked by oak. It will have to be kept for three to eight years.
♠ Michel et Dany Rolland, Catusseau, 33500 Pomerol, tel. 05.57.51.23.05,
fax 05.57.51.66.08 ☑

CH. GAGNARD 1998★

■ | 10 ha | 25,000 | 🍷 €8-11

This 98 wine is made from 50% Merlot and 50% Cabernet, a successful blend producing a bouquet of spice, ripe fruit and delicate oak notes, and good structure on the palate, where the strong, velvety tannins are particularly well softened and integrated thanks to well-controlled maturation. The wine has a very long finish, and will open out fully over the next five years.
♠ SC Vignobles Bouyge-Barthe, Ch. Gagnard, 33126 Fronsac,
tel. 05.57.51.42.99, fax 05.57.51.10.83 ☑

Fronsac

♠ Sébastien Gaucher, 1, Nardon, 33126 Saint-Michel-de-Fronsac, tel. 05.57.24.90.24, fax 05.57.24.90.24 ☑
🍷 by appt.

CH. TOUMALIN 1998★

94 95 96 98 | 7.5 ha | 48,000 | 🍷 €8-11

The d'Arfeuille family is established in Pomerol and Saint-Emilion, but does not neglect its Canon-Fronsac, which is a blend of 75% Merlot and Cabernet. This excellent wine has a ruby colour with slightly orangey glints. It has a restrained yet elegant bouquet, and supple, round tannins which develop with finesse and concentration and are perfectly balanced with a pleasant note of oaky vanilla. The wine should be drunk in two or three years' time.
♠ Françoise d'Arfeuille, Ch. Toumalin, 33126 Fronsac, tel. 05.57.51.02.11, fax 05.57.51.42.33 ☑ 🍷 by appt.

CH. VRAI CANON BOUCHE 1998★

|90| 91 |94| |95| 96 |97| 98 | 7 ha | 40,000 | 🍷 €11-15

In the 18th century the army used this plateau lying on stone quarries to test their cannons. Today wine is produced here in a calmer atmosphere and not without success, as can be seen from this 98 made from 90% Merlot. It has an intense, crimson colour, an elegant bouquet of red berries, blackberries and vanilla, and very evident tannins which are still concentrated and somewhat firm at the finish. It needs to be kept for four to five years until it opens out fully.
♠ Françoise Roux, Ch. Lagüe, 33126 Fronsac, tel. 05.57.51.24.68, fax 05.57.25.98.67 ☑ 🍷 by appt.

CH. BARRABAQUE 1998★

■ | n.c. | n.c. | 🍷 €8-11

This wine has been developed by one of the stars of the appellation, and is a blend of 70% Merlot and 30% Cabernet Franc. The colour is deep crimson, and the bouquet of soft fruits combined with oaky vanilla is still restrained. On the palate there is a supple, velvety structure which has spicy notes and develops on to a long, well-balanced finish. The wine is typical of this appellation, and will be ready to drink two or three years from now.
♠ SCEA Noël Père et Fils,
Ch. Barrabaque, 33126 Fronsac,
tel. 05.57.55.09.09, fax 05.57.55.09.00,
e-mail chateaubarrabaque@yahoo.fr ☑

Fronsac

CH. GRAND BARAIL 1998 ■ €5-8
1 ha   7,000

This Merlot has a distinctive bouquet of fruit (raspberry) and spice aromas. Its velvety, well-softened tannins are a little immature at the finish, but will enable the wine to be drunk now or kept for two or three years.

⌐ GFA Pierre Goujon,
Ch. Loiseau, 33240 Lalande-de-Fronsac,
tel. 05.57.58.14.02, fax 05.57.58.15.46 ⊠
⟉ by appt.

HAUT-CARLES 1998★★ ⊪ €15-23
7 ha   22,000

GRAND VIN DE BORDEAUX

FRONSAC

1998

HAUT - CARLES

Mis en bouteille à la propriété
APPELLATION FRONSAC CONTRÔLÉE
GEA Château de Carles, 33141 Saillans, France - A Château à Bordeaux, gironde

This property has a long history going back to the 15th century, and confirms its return to high quality by winning another *coup de coeur*. The wine comes from a selection of mainly Merlot plots with ideal exposure to the sun. It has a deep garnet colour and a complex bouquet of spices, toast, mocha and soft fruits. The round, velvety tannins are very mature and remarkably well balanced, and acquire great finesse and aromatic richness as they develop. This is an exceptional wine, and the other one here is the **98 Château de Carles**, which wins one star for its fruitiness and general good balance. It will be ready to drink two or three years from now.

⌐ SCEV Ch. de Carles, Ch. de Carles,
33141 Saillans, tel. 05.57.84.32.03,
fax 05.57.84.31.91 ⊠ **⟉** by appt.

CH. HAUT LARIVEAU 1998 ⊪ €11-15
6.5 ha   30,000

| 89 | [90] | 91 | 92 | [93] | [94] | 95 | 96 | [97] | [98] |

This property contains the remains of a 12th-century manor house, and produces a wine made exclusively from Merlot. The ruby colour has brick-red glints, and the light bouquet of coffee and smoke aromas is in the same register as the tannins, which are fresh in the attack then richer at the finish, where they are well balanced by oak. It should be drunk in the next three or four years.

⌐ B. et G. Hubau, Ch. Haut-Lariveau,
33126 Saint-Michel-de-Fronsac,
tel. 05.57.51.14.37, fax 05.57.51.53.45 ⊠
⟉ by appt.

CH. HAUT-MAZERIS 1998★ ⊪ €11-15
4.94 ha 37,000

The wine has a strong, garnet colour which gleams with brick-red glints, and a fresh bouquet of fruity and peppery aromas with a note of violets. On the palate the intense, silky tannins develop with a very fruity flavour (blackberries) combining finesse and power, and give this wine an ageing potential of three to five years.

⌐ SCEA Ch. Haut-Mazeris,
33126 Saint-Michel-de-Fronsac,
tel. 05.57.24.98.14, fax 05.57.24.91.07
⟉ by appt.

CH. JEANDEMAN La Chêneraie 1998★ €8-11
4 ha   16,000

Located at the highest point in the appellation, this château offers a wine which has been matured in oak for 12 months. It has an intense, ruby colour, and pleasant aromas of spices, herbs and blackcurrants along with a restrained note of oak. The highly expressive, very mature tannins are perfectly balanced with the oak flavour, which does stand out somewhat at the finish. This wine can be drunk now or kept for two to five years. Also recommended is the **Cuvée Classique**, which is not matured in oak. It can be enjoyed straight away for its maturity and good balance.

⌐ Roy-Trocard, Ch. Jeandeman,
33126 Fronsac, tel. 05.57.74.30.52,
fax 05.57.74.39.96, e-mail roy.trocard@
vnumail.com ⊠ **⟉** by appt.

CH. LA BRANDE 1998★ ⊪ €8-11
3 ha   23,000

La Brande is located on the border between the two communes of Galgon and Saillans. They say that this was the point where processions from the two villages ritually ended up in a fight between the Gascons and the Gabays (people from the North). Here you will find not only this wine, but also the **Château Moulin de Reynaud 98**, which is recommended. Both of them are fruity and spicy, with a delicate note of oak and a structure which, although rather simple at the finish, is clean and well balanced. These two good wines will be ready to enjoy in two or three years' time.

⌐ Vignoble Béraud, La Brande,
33141 Saillans, tel. 05.57.74.36.38,
fax 05.57.74.38.46 ⊠ **⟉** ev. day 9am–
12 noon 1.30pm–7pm; groups by appt.

CH. LA CROIX LAROQUE 1998 €8-11
12 ha   50,000

This small family property offers a pleasant 98 with delicate aromas of smoke, ganache (cream) and vanilla. After a fresh attack, it develops with plenty of body, but also with a certain austerity and firmness at the finish which call for an ageing period of two to four years.

⌐ Guy Morin, Ch. La Croix-Laroque,
33126 Fronsac, tel. 05.57.51.24.33,
fax 05.57.51.64.23 ⊠ **⟉** ev. day 9am–8pm

CH. DE LA DAUPHINE 1998★

9 ha 59,000 €11-15

This very beautiful charterhouse runs a vineyard in which Merlot reigns supreme (93%). This wine has a carmine-red colour and intense aromas of leather, red berries, vanilla and cocoa. The tannins on the palate are ample, mouth-filling, and well balanced by an elegant note of oak. This wine needs to age for two or three years until it opens out fully.

↝ Eis Jean-Pierre Moueix, 54, quai du Priourat, 33500 Libourne, tel. 05.57.51.78.96

CH. LA GARDE

Elevé en fût de chêne 1998

1.73 ha 6,000 €8-11

This small vineyard was purchased in 1997, and is worth visiting for its 98 wine, which has a brilliant red colour and an elegant bouquet of spices, flowers and soft fruits. The supple tannins are very evident at the finish. This wine should be kept for a year or two. The oak-matured **Cuvée Classique 98** is also recommended; it will delight wine-lovers looking for a supple, fruity wine which is ready to drink now.

↝ Ronald Wilmot, La Fontenelle, 33240 Lugon, tel. 05.57.84.82.13, fax 05.57.84.84.17 Y by appt.

CH. LA GRAVE 1998★

3.7 ha 15,000 €8-11

This wine comes from an organically grown vineyard, which is still quite rare in the Bordeaux wine area. The result is interesting: a deep-cherry colour, and fresh fragrances of raspberries, violets and pepper, embellished by a slight touch of oak. After a rich, intense attack, the wine develops with both power and finesse, but still needs at least three to five years to open out fully.

↝ Paul et Pascale Barre, La Grave, 33126 Fronsac, tel. 05.57.51.31.11, fax 05.57.25.08.61, e-mail p.p.barre@wanadoo.fr Y by appt.

CH. DE LA HUSTE 1998★

5 ha 29,000 €11-15

This property has been in the family since 1860, and habitually produces excellent wines such as this 98 vintage. It has an intense ruby colour shot through with black glints, and expressive aromas of red berries which are well combined with oaky toast notes. On the palate the wine is mouth-filling and powerful, while at the same time retaining a very elegant, fruity finesse at the finish. It can be drunk in two to five years' time. From the same producer, the **98 Château Dalem** wins one star. This is one of the leading establishments in the Fronsac region.

↝ Michel Rullier, Ch. de la Huste, 33141 Saillans, tel. 05.57.84.34.18, fax 05.57.74.39.85 Y by appt.

CH. LA VIEILLE CROIX

Cuvée DM 1998★★

5 ha 30,000 €8-11

The initials 'DM' are carved into the pediment of the château, and have given this wine its name. It comes from a south-facing *terroir* with a limestone and clay subsoil. It has an intense colour with ruby glints, and a nose still dominated by coffee, toast and vanilla aromas. The very young tannins are still rather fresh in the attack, after which they become rounder, richer and more mouth-filling as they develop. The wine opens out fully at the finish, where it shows great balance and fullness. This superb wine will be ready to drink three to six years from now.

↝ SCEA de La Vieille Croix, La Croix, 33141 Saillans, tel. 05.57.74.30.50, fax 05.57.84.30.96 Y by appt.

↝ Isabelle Dupuy

CH. LA ROUSSELLE 1998★★

4.2 ha 15,200 €11-15

|88| |89| |90| 91 92 |93| 94 |95| 96 |97| 98

Having had its glory days in the course of the last century, this property is now reaping the benefit of substantial restoration work over the last 30 years, both in the vineyard and in the barrel-stores. The result is magnificent, as can be seen from this 98 wine. It has an intense garnet colour with purplish lights, and powerful aromas of spices (pepper and ginger), red berries, vanilla and cocoa. The rich, mouth-filling impression on the palate is reinforced by an excellent balance in which the expressive tannins stand out at the finish. This wine should not be opened until three to eight years from now.

↝ Jacques et Viviane Davau, Ch. La Rousselle, 33126 La Rivière, tel. 05.57.24.96.73, fax 05.57.24.91.05 Y ev. day except Sun. 9am-12 noon 2pm-6pm

CH. DE LA RIVIERE 1998★

59 ha 200,000 €11-15

This magnificent château overlooking the Dordogne valley was founded in the 16th century and subsequently altered. It is well worth a visit, not just to admire the setting but also to appreciate the increasingly high quality of its wines, such as this violet-purple 98 with aromas of leather, ripe, slightly crystallised fruits (cherries) and toast. The supple attack on the palate gives way to a long, powerful structure which is still somewhat dominated by oak. The balance will be perfect two or three years from now.

↝ SA Ch. de La Rivière, BP 50, 33126 Fronsac, tel. 05.57.55.56.56, fax 05.57.24.94.39, e-mail info@chateau-de-la-riviere.com Y by appt.

↝ Jean Leprince

Canon-Fronsac

CH. LA VIEILLE CURE 1998★★

■ 20 ha 60,000 **IIID €15-23**

|88| |89| |90| |91| 92 93 |94| 95 |96| 97 98

This château has an excellent *terroir* on the hillsides at Saillans. It is regularly singled out by the *Guide*, and now wins a *coup de coeur* for this intense crimson 98 with brilliant ruby glints, and a powerful bouquet combining dark berries, vanilla and toast, along with a very agreeable mineral note. Just as powerful is the full-bodied, rich palate, which is still somewhat closed owing to oak maturation, but even so suggests a very long ageing period of at least four to eight years. A second wine here is the **Château Coutreau 98**, which is recommended for its fruitiness and roundness, and is ready to drink now.

➤ SNC Ch. La Vieille Cure,
1, Coutreau, 33141 Saillans,
tel. 05.57.84.32.05, fax 05.57.74.39.83,
e-mail vieillecur@aol.com ⅄ by appt.
➤ M. Ferenbach

CH. LES ROCHES DE FERRAND

Elevé en fût de chêne 1998

■ 5 ha 30,000 **IIID ♦ €8-11**

This château has been in the same family for many generations, and is often singled out in the *Guide* for the quality of its wines. This intense, garnet-coloured 98 has aromas of black cherries, musk and ginger. The tannins are rich and velvety, then somewhat bitter at the finish. This wine needs to be kept for three years.

➤ Rémy Rousselot, Ch. Les Roches de Ferrand, Huchat, 33126 Saint-Aignan, tel. 05.57.24.95.16, fax 05.57.24.91.44 ⅄ by appt.

CH. LES TROIS CROIX 1998★★

■ 13.71 ha 72,000 **IIID €15-23**

This château was awarded the *Grappe d'argent* in the 2001 *Guide*, after winning two consecutive *coups de coeur* for the 96 and 97 vintages. This year it came very close to pulling off a third, missing out by only one Grand Jury vote. Nevertheless, it is a sumptuous wine with an intense crimson colour with black glints and powerful, complex aromas of crystallised fruits, cocoa, roasting and cinnamon. Its dense, velvety tannic structure reflects the very ripe grapes used, while the exceptionally long, well-balanced finish is the mark of a very great wine at the top of its appellation.

➤ Famille Patrick Léon, Ch. Les Trois Croix, 33126 Fronsac, tel. 05.57.84.32.09, fax 05.57.84.34.03 ⅄ by appt.

CH. MANIEU 1998★

■ 4.24 ha 27,000 **IIID ♦ €11-15**

This château grows 95% Merlot on a clay-limestone molasse *terroir*. It offers an interesting 98 with a brilliant ruby colour, expressive aromas of blackcurrants, plums and oaky toast, and frank, well-structured tannins which develop with finesse and good length. This wine will be very pleasant in three to six years' time.

➤ Ch. Manieu, La Rivière, 33126 Fronsac, tel. 05.57.24.92.79, fax 05.57.24.92.78 ⅄ ⅄ ev. day except Sat. Sun. 10.30am–12 noon 2.30pm–6pm
➤ Mme Léon

CH. MAYNE-VIEIL

Cuvée Aliénor 1998★

■ 3 ha 20,000 **IIID €8-11**

The Cuvée Aliénor is a selection from 3 ha (7 acres) of Merlot, part of the 45 ha (111 acres) that make up this property. The 98 vintage stands out particularly for its brilliant deep-garnet colour and complex aromas of fruits, spices, undergrowth and vanilla. The tannins are rich in the attack, then powerful, balanced and also very long at the finish. The **Cuvée Principale** is recommended for its ripe fruit aromas and very classic structure. It is ready to drink now.

➤ SCEA du Mayne-Vieil, 33133 Galgon, tel. 05.57.74.30.06, fax 05.57.84.39.33, e-mail mayne-vieil@aol.com ⅄
⅄ by appt.
➤ Famille Sèze

CH. MOULIN HAUT-LAROQUE 1998★

■ 15 ha n.c. **IIID €15-23**

86 |88| ⑧⑨ |90| 91 |93| |94| 95 **96 97** 98

The fact that this château has been in the same family since the 16th century is sufficiently rare to be worthy of note by itself. It also regularly produces very good wines, thanks to its excellent *terroir* and the undisputed expertise of the owner. The complex bouquet of this 98 vintage suggests very ripe, crystallised fruits, vanilla and toast. The supple, rich, lingering tannins are well softened by an oaky note which is not excessive. The well-balanced structure indicates excellent ageing potential (at least three to eight years).

➤ Jean-Noël Hervé, Ch. Cardeneau, 33141 Saillans, tel. 05.57.84.32.07, fax 05.57.84.31.84, e-mail hervejnoel@aol.com ⅄ by appt.

CH. PÉTRARQUE 1998

■ 1.5 ha 7,800 **IIID ♦ €8-11**

This château bears the name of the 14th-century Italian poet Petrarch, who celebrated Laure de Noves in his sonnets. It

260

makes a high-quality wine with a dense, almost black colour and a delicate bouquet of violets, vanilla and liquorice. The full, fleshy tannins develop with finesse but without much length. This wine can be drunk in one to three years' time.
- GFA Chabiran, 1, av. de la Mairie, 33500 Néac, tel. 05.57.51.08.36, fax 05.57.25.93.44 ☑ by appt.

CH. PUY GUILHEM 1998★

7 ha   44,000   €11-15

This château was bought in 1995 by Annie and Jean-François Enixon, who since then have been putting their heart and their know-how into getting the best out of this very fine *terroir*. This deep-garnet coloured 98 wine has an expressive bouquet of red berries, pepper, vanilla and toast, and highly characteristic, soft tannins which are still somewhat marked by oak. The balance will be perfect in two to six years' time. The second wine is the **Château Puy Saint Vincent 98**. It is recommended for its aromatic freshness and a well-balanced structure which means that it is ready to drink now.
- SCEA Ch. Puy Guilhem, 33141 Saillans, tel. 05.57.84.32.08, fax 05.57.74.36.45 ☑
- ☑ by appt.
- M. et Mme J.-F. Enixon

CH. RENARD MONDESIR 1998★

|93| |94| |95| 96 |97| 98   7 ha   24,000   €11-15

This 98 wine is made from 95% Merlot, and is worth trying for its intense, clear colour, its open, pleasant bouquet of leather, spices and vanilla, and its powerful, well-balanced structure. The aromatic expression is even more intense at the finish; clearly this wine will benefit from two to five years of ageing.
- Xavier Chassagnoux, Ch. Renard, La Rivière, 33126 Fronsac, tel. 05.57.24.96.37, fax 05.57.24.90.18, e-mail chateau.renard.mondesir@wanadoo.fr ☑ ☑ by appt.

CH. RICHELIEU 1998★

12.5 ha   25,000   €8-11

As its name indicates, this château once belonged to the Richelieu family, and in particular to Marshal de Richelieu, nephew of the cardinal, who was known as 'Fronsac' at the court of Louis XIV. Here you will find a lovely 98 with concentrated aromas (mainly red berries and vanilla) and a powerful palate which is still marked by oak at the finish. It needs to be kept carefully for two to five years until it becomes more supple and integrated.
- EARL Ch. Richelieu, 1, chem. du Terre, 33126 Fronsac, tel. 05.57.51.13.94, fax 05.57.51.13.94 ☑
- ☑ ev. day 9.30am–12.30pm 2pm–6pm

CH. ROUET 1998

n.c.   n.c.   €11-15

This château has belonged to the same family since the end of the 18th century, and has now produced a fresh, very fruity 98 (redcurrants and raspberries). The intense, rather aggressive tannins need to age for a while until they are fully integrated.
- Patrick Danglade, Ch. Rouet, 33240 Saint-Germain-la-Rivière, tel. 05.57.84.40.24, fax 05.56.48.14.10
- ☑ by appt.

CH. ROUMAGNAC LA MARECHALE 1998★

93 |94| 95 96 97 98   4.93 ha   22,500   €5-8

This family property is ideally situated on south-south-east-facing hillsides overlooking the Dordogne valley, and is also worth visiting for its wines. The 98 vintage is marked by fragrances of undergrowth, oaky toast and pepper, and by a mouth-filling, highly characteristic and well-balanced tannic structure. It will open out completely in two to five years' time.
- SCEA Pierre Dumeynieu, Roumagnac, 33126 La Rivière, tel. 05.57.24.98.48, fax 05.57.24.90.44 ☑ ☑ by appt.

CH. STEVAL 1998

2.04 ha   1,000   €8-11

This is what is known as a 'garage wine'; unlike the Burgundy region, it is rare in Bordeaux to produce as few as 1,000 bottles. It is made from 100% Merlot, and is worth trying for its developing bouquet of spices and toast, and for its structure, which is well balanced although still dominated by oak. The balance should be complete after two to three years of ageing.
- Sébastien Gaucher, 1, Nardon, 33126 Saint-Michel-de-Fronsac, tel. 05.57.24.90.24, fax 05.57.24.90.24 ☑
- ☑ by appt.

CH. TOUR DU MOULIN
Cuvée particulière 1998★

7 ha   10,000   €11-15

This Cuvée Particulière has an intense, brilliant garnet colour and an expressive bouquet of caramel, figs, vanilla and prunes. On the palate the tannins develop with richness, good balance and very good length. The wine is almost ready to drink now, but will keep for two to five years. One star also goes to its **Cuvée Principale 98**, which is fruitier than the other wine at the moment, and is a very typical Fronsac. It can also be drunk now.
- SCEA Ch. Tour du Moulin, Le Moulin, 33141 Saillans, tel. 05.57.74.34.26, fax 05.57.74.34.26 ☑ by appt.
- J. et V. Dupuch

CH. VILLARS 1998★

20 ha   117,000   €11-15

This château is a founder member of 'Expression de Fronsac', a club which brings together some of the best properties in the appellation. It produces excellent wines such as this one, which has an intense ruby colour and powerful, concentrated aromas of spices, ripe fruit and vanilla. The elegant, velvety tannins are pleasantly embellished by an

Pomerol

appellation. As with all the great *terroirs*, Pomerol is the result of the action of a river, in this case the Isle, which began by breaking down the limestone substratum and strewing it with layers of stones that assisted further erosion. The result is a complicated muddle of gravel and smoothed stones which originated in the Massif Central. The soils are particularly complex and hard to identify separately. However, four general types can be identified: in the south, towards Libourne there is a sandy area; near Saint-Emilion gravel lies on sand or clay (the soil is similar to that found on the Plateau de Figeac); in the middle of the AOC the soil is gravel, sometimes on top of clay and sometimes underneath it (Pétrus); finally, in the north-east and north-west the gravel is finer and more sandy.

This variety of soils does not prevent Pomerol wines from having a basically common structure. They are very fragrant, round and supple with a real strength which allows them to keep for a long time although they can be drunk quite young. Their character means they go well with a range of different dishes and are just as good with sophisticated dishes as they are with simpler ones. In 2000, the appellation produced 36,992 hl (976,589 gal).

evident but well-proportioned note of oak. This is a wine for longer maturing, and will be ready to drink three to eight years from now. The **98 Château Moulin Haut Villars** is recommended for its intense fruitiness and sound, classic structure. It can be drunk in one or two years' time.

☛ Jean-Claude Gaudrie, Villars, 33141 Saillans, tel. 05.57.84.32.17, fax 05.57.84.31.25, e-mail chateau.villars@wanadoo.fr ◻ Ⴒ by appt.

Pomerol

Pomerol covers only about 800 ha (1,976 acres). It is one of the smallest appellations in the Gironde and one of the least interesting from an architectural point of view.

The 19th-century fashion for building wine châteaux in an eclectic architectural style appears not to have impressed the Pomerolais, who were happier with their rural or bourgeois houses. All the same, the appellation does boast the Château de Sales, built in the 17th century, which is undoubtedly the model for many of the charter-houses in the Gironde, and the Château Beauregard, which is one of the most beautiful houses built in the 18th century. A copy was built by the Guggenheims on their Long Island estate in New York.

The simplicity of the architecture is in harmony with this AOC, whose originality is staunchly defended by each individual, and where each inhabitant has his or her own vision, while seeking to maintain the harmony and cohesion of the community. This may explain why the wine-producers have been more than reticent in defining the guidelines for classifying the Crus.

The quality and specific nature of the *terroirs* alone should justify official recognition of the merit of the wines in this

CH. BEAUCHENE 1998★★

| ■ | 4.7 ha | 20,000 | 11 | €23-30 |

Ⓔ 96 **97 98**

Every year this vineyard offers a lovely old Merlot selection grown on a gravelly-clay *terroir* with iron slag, then remarkably well vinified and matured. This powerful, well-balanced 98 has a beautiful, black colour and crimson glints. The rich, very open bouquet combines aromas of ripe fruits with a superb note of toasty and burnt oak. The palate is thoroughbred, with a dense, full-bodied, well-structured body and good length. This is a great wine for longer maturing.

☛ Charles Leymarie et Fils, SCEA Clos Mazeyres, BP 132, 33502 Libourne Cedex, tel. 05.57.51.07.83, fax 05.57.51.99.94, e-mail leymarie@ch-leymarie.com

with a fine, spicy oak note. The full, powerful palate reveals rich, fleshy tannins which linger on to a long and beautifully flavourful finish.

🛒 Jean-Marie Bouldy, Lieu-dit René, 33500 Pomerol, tel. 05.57.51.20.47, fax 05.57.51.23.14 ☑ ⚘ by appt.

CH. BEAUREGARD 1998 ★★

■ 12 ha 60,000
75 78 81 (82) 83 84 85 86 [88] 89 [90] 92 ☐ €38-46 (98)

Beauregard is one of the most delightful of the 18th-century charterhouses in the Bordeaux area. Last year it won its first *coup de coeur* for a difficult vintage, and it repeats the same feat this year with a more classic wine. The 98 has all the qualities one looks for in a great Pomerol: a lovely, dark, almost black Bordeaux colour, a long succession of aromas in the nose (ripe dark berries, fine oak, cinnamon, vanilla, leather and truffles), and a palate with a smooth, rich, thoroughbred character and an excellent balance between grape and oak. This wine will keep for a long time (five to twenty years). The second wine here is the **98 Benjamin de Beauregard**, which will become velvety in three or four years' time. The 98 is elegant

🛒 SCEA Ch. Beauregard, 33500 Pomerol, tel. 05.57.51.13.36, fax 05.57.25.09.55, e-mail beauregard@dial.oleane.com ☑

CH. BEAU SOLEIL 1998 ★

■ 3.5 ha 19,500
☐ €30-38

This little vineyard grows mainly Merlot (with an additional 5% Sauvignon) on a sand and fine gravel soil. The dark garnet 98 wine has a developed fringe. The bouquet releases aromas of overripe fruit, jam and chocolate, along with a delightful note of oaky toast. The palate is powerful, round and well balanced, with evident but integrated tannins and a long, aromatic finish. This wine needs to be kept for two to three years until it becomes more open.

🛒 Anne-Marie Audy-Arcaute, Ch. Jonqueyres, 33750 Saint-Germain-du-Puch, tel. 05.56.68.55.88, fax 05.56.68.55.77, e-mail info@chateau-beausoleil.fr ☑

CH. BELLEGRAVE 1998 ★★

■ 7 ha 40,000
88 89 91 92 [93] [94] [95] [96] [97] 98 ☐ €15-23

This vineyard was bought in 1951 by Jean-Marie Bouldy's father. The 98 wine is a blend of three-quarters Merlot and one-quarter Cabernet Franc, and is a very well-constructed wine with an intense garnet colour. When it is swirled in the glass, the nose releases aromas of very ripe soft fruits, pleasantly combined

263

CH. BONALGUE 1998 ★

■ 5.5 ha 22,000
85 [86] [88] [89] [90] [93] [94] 95 96 97 98 ☐ €23-30

This 98 wine is made mainly from Merlot with an additional 15% Cabernet Franc, grown on soils containing a mixture of sand, clay and gravel. It has a high, garnet colour and an elegant, thoroughbred bouquet of truly noble oak and spice aromas. After a rich, smooth attack, the wine develops on a firm, powerful structure ending with a long, well-balanced finish. This very good wine is suitable for longer maturing.

🛒 SA Pierre Bourotte, 62, quai du Priourat, 33500 Libourne, tel. 05.57.51.62.17, fax 05.57.51.28.28, e-mail jeanbaptiste.audy@wanadoo.fr ⚘ by appt.

CH. BOURGNEUF-VAYRON 1998

■ 9 ha 41,000
[89] [90] 91 93 94 95 96 97 98 ☐ €30-38

This property has gravelly-clay *terroirs* where it grows mainly Merlot along with 10% Cabernet Franc. It offers a wine with a garnet colour and a nose which is still restrained, releasing musky and spicy notes combined with a slight hint of oak. The palate is very structured and concentrated, and has somewhat firm, austere tannins which will need a long ageing period to become softer.

🛒 Xavier Vayron, Ch. Bourgneuf-Vayron, 1, le Bourg-Neuf, 33500 Pomerol, tel. 05.57.51.42.03, fax 05.57.25.01.40 ☑ ⚘ by appt.

CH. CANTELAUZE 1998 ★

■ 1 ha 3,900
92 94 95 [96] 98

'Cantelauze' means 'the bird sings' in Provençal, and is the name that Jean-Noël Boidron, a well-known Bordeaux oenologist, has given to his little Pomerol vineyard, a tribute to the singing of the lark at harvest-time. His 98 wine is very good indeed, and has the colour of bigaroon cherries. The wine needs to be swirled in the glass slightly before the bouquet releases its oaky, empyreumatic aromas and notes of game. The structure is monumental, powerful, and well structured by plenty of oaky tannins, indicating that in a few years' time this will be an excellent Pomerol with a great deal of character.

🛒 Jean-Noël Boidron, 6, pl. Joffre, 33500 Libourne, tel. 05.57.51.64.88, fax 05.57.51.56.30 ☑ ⚘ by appt.

CH. CERTAN DE MAY DE CERTAN 1998*

5 ha 24,000 €46-76

85 86 88 |89| |90| 94 95 96 97 98

The de May family came from Scotland to serve the King of France in the Middle Ages. In the 16th century they were given the fief of Certan, and planted vines there. Their long history in the service of well-known and very elegant wine is confirmed by this vintage, which has a dark-garnet colour and a nose combining red-berry and oaky-toast aromas, along with spicy notes. On the palate the body is well balanced, supple in the attack, and still tannic on the finish, although not excessively so. This delightful wine should be ready to drink in two or three years' time.

Mme Barreau-Badar, Ch. Certan de May de Certan, 33500 Pomerol,
tel. 05.57.51.41.53, fax 05.57.51.88.51
by appt.

CLOS BEAUREGARD 1998

5 ha 30,000 €15-23

Jean-Michel Moueix took over this property in 1991. His sandy *terroir* on iron slag is planted with old vines made up of 60% Merlot, 25% Cabernet Franc and 15% Cabernet Sauvignon. This 98 wine has a lovely, intense garnet colour and a developing bouquet which is still very fresh and releases a note of menthol. The attack is supple and fresh, but the tannins are still harsh and need to mature a little. When the wine is ready, it will go well with red meats and game.

Jean-Michel Moueix, Ch. La Tour du Pin Figeac, 33330 Saint-Emilion,
tel. 05.57.74.18.44, fax 05.57.51.52.87
by appt.

CH. CLOS DE SALLES 1998

1.1 ha 6,600 €23-30

This small vineyard has been built up from a plot belonging to Château de Salles which was cut off by the railway when the line was first built. It grows 60% Merlot and 40% Cabernet on a gravel soil, and has produced a wine with a lovely dark-garnet colour and a bouquet which is already expressive (fruit, spice and menthol) but is still dominated by oak. A flavour of oak also reveals several years on the palate, which will need several years to become more subdued and develop finesse.

EARL du Ch. Clos de Salles, Ch. du Pintey, 33500 Libourne, tel. 05.57.51.03.04, fax 05.57.51.03.04, e-mail angeliquemerlet@hotmail.com by appt.

CLOS DU CLOCHER 1998**

4.3 ha 22,000 €30-38

82 83 |85| |86| |88| 89 |90| 92 |93| |94| 95 97 98

This vineyard sits in the shadow of the Pomerol church tower, very close to the town. Its gravelly-clay soils are planted with four-fifths Merlot and one-fifth Cabernet Franc, and this has produced a remarkable 98 with a magnificent, dark-garnet colour which is dense and very deep. There is a thoroughbred bouquet of crystallised red berry aromas which are well balanced with an elegant note of oaky vanilla. The palate is ample and fleshy, with a sumptuous, superbly concentrated body and velvety tannins. This is a very high-quality wine which should be kept for some years.

SC Clos du Clocher, BP 79, 33500 Libourne,
tel. 05.57.51.62.17, fax 05.57.51.28.28, e-mail jeanbaptiste.audy@wanadoo.fr
by appt.

CLOS DU PELERIN 1998

2.8 ha 12,000 €15-23

|93| |95| 96 |97| 98

This is a pleasant but still slightly rustic Pomerol which comes from sandy soils and is made from 80% Merlot and the two Cabernets. The nose is somewhat closed, and it releases its fruity blackcurrant notes. The powerful palate is constructed on tannins which will have to become a little more subdued.

Norbert Egreteau, Clos du Pèlerin, 3, chem. de Sales, 33500 Pomerol,
tel. 05.57.74.03.66, fax 05.57.25.06.17
by appt.

CLOS SAINT-ANDRE 1998**

0.6 ha 4,000 €23-30

In 1994 Daniel Mouty created this small vineyard, where he grows 35-year-old Merlot vines on a deep gravel soil. The wine has a dark, almost black Bordeaux colour, and a deep bouquet of dark berries and oaky toast. The palate is very concentrated and mouthfilling, combining the roundness of Merlot with the freshness of the tannins. These tactile sensations enhance the flavour of cocoa on the finish. This wine should appeal to lovers of both classic and modern wines.

SCEA Daniel Mouty, Ch. du Barry, 33350 Sainte-Terre, tel. 05.57.84.55.88, fax 05.57.74.92.99, e-mail daniel-mouty@wanadoo.fr
ev. day except Sat. Sun. 8am-5pm

CLOS TOULIFAUT 1998

2 ha 12,000 €15-23

In Pomerol Jean-Michel Moueix does not call his vineyards 'châteaux' but 'clos', both at Toulifaut and at Beauregard. Here as at Beauregard his old vines (60% Merlot, 30% Cabernet Franc and 10% Cabernet Sauvignon) are grown on sand and iron slag. The wine has a ruby colour fringed with brick-red glints, and a bouquet with an exotic character which releases notes of tobacco, oaky toast, liquorice, leather, and also a touch of dark berries. The supple, delicate palate finishes on silky tannins.

Jean-Michel Moueix, Ch. La Tour du Pin Figeac, 33330 Saint-Emilion,
tel. 05.57.74.18.44, fax 05.57.51.52.87
by appt.

CH. DELTOUR 1998

1.7 ha ☐ 10,000 ☐ 🍷 €8-11

This small vineyard is located in the René area to the west of the appellation, between the main roads to Paris and Périgueux. The vines are grown on a siliceous gravel soil, and consist of 70% Merlot along with both Cabernets and Pressac. This wine's developing bouquet is beginning to release aromas of red berries, mint and humus. The palate is still young, and has a ripe-fruit flavour and a slightly astringent tannic structure which will need a few years to become more refined.

➴ Jeanne Thouraud, lieu-dit René n°12, 33500 Pomerol, tel. 05.57.51.47.98, fax 05.57.25.99.23 ☑ 🍷 by appt.

CH. ELISEE Vieilli en fût de chêne 1998★

1.5 ha ☐ 10,600 ☐ 🍷 €15-23

This little Pomerol vineyard was purchased in 1987 by the Garzaro family, who gave it the first name of their ancestor. The *terroir* has a sandy gravel soil which is planted with 90% Merlot. The wine has a beautiful, deep-ruby colour, and a bouquet which is already expressive and releases aromas of soft-fruit, jam along with fine notes of oak. This Pomerol is full and fleshy on the palate, whose lovely round quality and tannic structure will enable it to keep well and be a good accompaniment to grilled meat.

➴ EARL Vignobles Garzaro, Ch. Le Prieur, 33750 Baron, tel. 05.56.30.16.16, fax 05.56.30.12.63, e-mail garzaro@vingarzaro.com 🍷 by appt.

CH. FRANC-MAILLET 1998★

5.1 ha ☐ 32,000 ☐ 🍷 €15-23

Since Jean-Baptiste Arpin bought the first vine plot here on his return from the First World War in 1919, three generations in succession have run this vineyard, which is located in the Maillet area and grows 80% Merlot and 20% Cabernet Franc on siliceous-gravel soils. The wine has a lovely, intense, garnet colour, and although still somewhat closed in the nose, releases concentrated, powerful fruity aromas when it is swirled in the glass. The same power is apparent on the palate, where the tannins are highly extracted and will need to age for six to seven years. The **Cuvée Jean-Baptiste 98** will also need to be kept until the oak becomes integrated. It wins one star.

➴ EARL Vignobles G. Arpin, Maillet, 33500 Pomerol, tel. 06.09.73.69.47, fax 05.57.51.96.75, e-mail gaelarpin@excite.com ☑ 🍷 by appt.

CH. GAZIN 1998

24.24 ha ☐ 46,908 ☐ 🍷 €46-76

| 70 | 75 | 76 | 78 | 79 | 80 | 81 | 82 | 83 | 84 | 85 | 86 | 87 |
| **88** | |89| | **90** | 91 | 92 | |93| | |94| | **95** | **96** | 97 |
| 98 |

The Gazin property has a great deal of charm, frequently wins honours and *coups de coeur* in the *Guide*, and is one of the oldest and most highly-reputed vineyards in Pomerol. This 98 wine is yet another reminder of the

great quality of the wine-maker here. It opens with a sumptuous, dark-garnet colour which is remarkably intense. The expressive, elegant bouquet gives off aromas of stewed prunes, caramel and vanilla, and shows a magnificent balance between fruit and oak. The palate is full-bodied, rich, ample and vinous, with a powerful, thoroughbred structure and a finish which seems to go on for ever and is delightfully well balanced. This is a very great classic: the sort of Pomerol that everyone loves. The second wine here is **L'Hospitalet de Gazin**, which is recommended for its aromas of stewed prunes, soft spices and tobacco, along with a slight hint of violets. It will be ready to drink in two or three years' time.

➴ SCEA Ch. Gazin, 33500 Pomerol, tel. 05.57.51.07.05, fax 05.57.51.69.96, e-mail chateau.gazin@wanadoo.fr ☑
➴ Famille Bailliencourt

CH. GOMBAUDE-GUILLOT 1998★

7.85 ha ☐ 24,000 ☐ 🍷 €30-38

| 86 | |89| |90| 91 |93| |94| **95** 96 98 |

This château is located in an old bistrot which was built at the same time as the church here in 1898. The 98 wine is made from 85% Merlot and 15% Cabernet Franc, and has a superb crimson colour with dark-purple glints. It combines very ripe soft-fruit aromas with an elegant oak note of toast and spices. The full, powerful structure reveals full-bodied, velvety tannins and an agreeably long finish. This excellent wine should be kept for three to five years and served with stewed duck.

➴ SCEA Famille Laval, 4, chem. des Grand-Vignes, 33500 Pomerol, tel. 05.57.51.17.40, fax 05.57.51.16.89 ☑
🍷 by appt.
➴ Claire Laval

CH. GOURPIE 1998

4.57 ha ☐ 13,000

This pleasant 98 has a very intense, garnet colour with a marked fringe. The expressive nose releases aromas of ripe fruits combined with notes of toast and cocoa and a floral touch of violets. There is a full-bodied, round palate with balanced, firm tannins. This is an agreeable wine which should be ready to drink two to three years from now.

SCEA Patrick et Sylvie Moze-Berthon, Bertin, 33570 Montagne, tel. 05.57.74.66.84, fax 05.57.74.58.70, e-mail chateau.rocher-gardat@wanadoo.fr
by appt.

CH. GRAND BEAUSEJOUR 1998★★ €38-46

0.65 ha 3,000

In 1998, Daniel Mouty bought a Merlot plot close to Château Figeac. Located near the main RN 89 road, the château is currently being renovated in its original Louis XV style, and should be ready to receive visitors very soon. This intense, dark-garnet 98 wine has a very limited volume of production; it is quite delightful and it has a bouquet of soft-fruit jam aromas along with a very pleasant note of oak. There is wonderful balance on the palate, which is full-bodied and mouth- filling and reveals rich, velvety tannins. This is great wine which is powerful and well balanced, and should be kept for three to five years.

SCEA Daniel Mouty.
Ch. du Barry, 33350 Sainte-Terre, tel. 05.57.84.55.88, fax 05.57.74.92.99, e-mail daniel-mouty@wanadoo.fr
ev. day except Sat. Sun. 8am–5pm

CH. GRAND MOULINET 1998★ €15-23

2 ha 12,000

|94| |96| 98

This small vineyard belongs to Château Haut-Surget in Lalande de Pomerol. It grows 90% Merlot on a sand and iron-oxide soil. The wine has a dark-crimson colour and a very expressive bouquet combining ripe-fruit aromas and a toasty oak note with a touch of menthol. There is a strong, complex palate with an oaky flavour which will appeal to some but may surprise others. This is a wine of character which needs to become a little more subdued.

Ollet-Fourreau, 33500 Néac, tel. 05.57.51.28.68, fax 05.57.51.91.79
by appt.

CH. GRANDS SILLONS GABACHOT 1998★ €15-23

4 ha 18,000

This vineyard belongs to a branch of the Janoueix family, which originally came from Corrèze and is now established in the Libourne region where they operate as wine-merchants and also own several vineyards. The old vines on this one are 70% Merlot, 20% Bouchet (Cabernet Franc) and 10% Pressac (Cot), and are grown on a varied soil with iron slag. The wine's colour has lovely, intense, garnet glints, and the bouquet is already expressive, with a dark-berry aroma (bilberry) and a spicy, well-integrated note of oak. There is a full-bodied attack, after which the oaky tannins quickly become apparent. You will need to wait three to eight years before serving this wine with dishes such as rare duck.

François Janoueix, 20, quai du Priourat, BP 135, 33502 Libourne Cedex, tel. 05.57.55.55.44, fax 05.57.51.83.70
by appt.

CH. GUILLOT 1998 €23-30

4.3 ha 24,000

82 83 85 86 88 |89| |93| |94| 95 96 97 98

This wine comes from siliceous-clay soils, and is a balanced blend of 70% Merlot and 30% Cabernet Franc. It has a lovely dark-garnet colour and a bouquet with a delightful note of oaky toast which does not mask the aromas of ripe red berries. The supple, delicate palate is fairly fine, and shows good balance between the body and the structure. This wine will be pleasant to drink within two to three years.

SCEA Vignobles Luquot, 152, av. de l'Epinette, 33500 Libourne, tel. 05.57.51.18.95, fax 05.57.25.10.59
by appt.

CH. HAUT-FERRAND 1998 €15-23

4 ha 25,000

82 83 85 86 88 91 92 93 |94| |95| 96 98

Coming from a selection from 4 ha (10 acres) of the 16 ha (40 acres) that Ferrand run in all, this wine has a dark-crimson colour and a nose which releases crystallised-fruit and leather aromas once the wine has been swirled in the glass. The palate needs two to three years of ageing to become more refined.

SCE du Ch. Ferrand, 33500 Pomerol, tel. 05.57.51.21.67, fax 05.57.25.01.41
by appt.
H. Gasparoux

CH. HAUT-TROPCHAUD 1998★★ €23-30

2 ha 15,000 98

88 |90| |93| |94| 95 96 |97| 98

This vineyard was bought in 1987 by Michel Coudroy. It is located on the very fine gravel soils of the high Pomerol terrace, and grows 80-year-old Merlot vines. The 98 wine has a lovely garnet colour, and gives off a complex, elegant bouquet of ripe-fruit, stewed-prune and cocoa aromas, combined with beautiful notes of vanilla, toast and roasting. After a round, full-bodied attack, the palate develops a rich, powerful body which has remarkable tannic concentration and is still firm on the finish. This is a very great wine which is worthy of a long ageing period.

Michel Coudroy, Maison-Neuve, 33570 Montagne, tel. 05.57.74.62.23, fax 05.57.74.64.18 by appt.

CH. LA BASSONNERIE 1998 €15-23

2.07 ha 12,000

96 97 98

The soil here is composed of gravel and old sands on a clay subsoil, and is planted with 60% Merlot and 40% Cabernet. This has produced a wine with a very clean, Bordeaux colour, and fresh red-berry aromas combined

266

Pomerol

with burnt-oak notes which veer slightly towards tar and continue on a full-bodied, balanced palate. The wine should be kept for two to three years until it becomes more expressive. From the same producer, the **Mayne René 98** is also recommended. This is a pleasant, 90% Merlot which will be ready in two years' time.

SCEA La Bassonnerie, 'René', 33300 Pomerol, tel. 06.09.73.12.78, fax 05.57.51.99.94, e-mail leymarie@ ch-leymarie.com **Y** by appt.

CH. LA CONSEILLANTE 1998★

								12 ha	n.c.		
82	**85**	**88**	**89**	**89**	91	**92**	**93**	95	96	97	98

This wine-growing estate is the archetypal Pomerol vineyard, and has been run by the Nicolas family for 300 years. Its gravelly-clay *terroir* is located between Petrus and Cheval Blanc, and is planted with 80% Merlot and 20% Cabernet Franc. This 98 Pomerol is a wine for longer maturing, with a beautiful colour and intense garnet glints. The complex bouquet combines floral (violets) and ripe-fruit aromas with spicy and empyreumatic notes of oak. The elegant yet full-bodied flavour on the palate is the sign of very ripe Merlot grapes and well-controlled oak. This wine will be ready to serve with a game bird from 2005 on.

SC Héritiers L. Nicolas, Ch. La Conseillante, 33500 Pomerol, tel. 05.57.51.15.32, fax 05.57.51.42.39 **Y** by appt.

CH. LA CROIX 1998

								10 ha	60,000		
86	**89**	**90**	92	94	**95**	**96**	97	98			

The La Croix vineyard stretches over the gravelly-sand soils of the high Pomerol terrace and its southern rim. A balanced blend of 60% Merlot, 20% Cabernet Franc and 20% Cabernet Sauvignon has produced a 98 wine with a fresh, intense ruby colour and a powerful, concentrated bouquet marked by notes of game and liquorice, with a flavour of violets at the finish. It should open out rapidly in the years to come. The palate has a dense tannic structure which as yet is somewhat austere, but will guarantee good ageing potential.

SC Ch. La Croix, 37, rue Pline-Parmentier, BP 192, 33506 Libourne Cedex, tel. 05.57.51.41.86, fax 05.57.51.53.16, e-mail info@ j-janoueix-bordeaux.com **V** by appt.

CH. LA CROIX DU CASSE 1998★

					9 ha	48,000		

This vineyard has a gravel, sand and iron-slag soil, and was reorganised after the frosts of 1956 on the basis of 70% Merlot and 30% Cabernet Franc. The 98 wine has a delightful, intense colour with garnet glints. The nose is

still somewhat lacking in fruit aromas, and develops on spicy but mainly very oaky notes. The palate has a powerful, full-bodied structure, and is supported by tannins which need to become more integrated. This wine will go well with saddle of hare in a cream sauce.

Jean-Michel Arcaute, Ch. Jonqueyres, Gam Audy, 33750 Saint-Germain-du-Puch, tel. 05.57.34.51.51, fax 05.56.30.11.45, e-mail info@gamaudy.com **Y** by appt.

CH. LA CROIX SAINT GEORGES 1998★

							3.5 ha	21,000		
82	83	85	86	**88**	**89**	**90**	92	**93**	**94**	**96**
97	98									

This château has undergone substantial restoration work, and a sculpture of Saint George on the façade of one of the barrel-stores is a reminder that the estate once belonged to the Order of the Hospitallers of Saint John of Jerusalem, who set up a hospice there to care for the sick and disabled. Today it is a wine-growing estate, and is offering a 95% Merlot 98. It has a dark, intense garnet colour and a complex, elegant bouquet of roasting and red-berry aromas. The full, round palate is supported by smooth, full-bodied tannins which are very well balanced. There is a very long, lingering finish.

SC Ch. La Croix, 37, rue Pline-Parmentier, BP 192, 33506 Libourne Cedex, tel. 05.57.51.41.86, fax 05.57.51.53.16, e-mail info@ j-janoueix-bordeaux.com **V** by appt.

CH. LAFLEUR 1998★★

						3.15 ha	12,000		
85	**86**	**88**	89	**90**	**92**	**93**	94	95	96	97	98

This is a very interesting vineyard, where Cabernet Franc is grown in equal proportion to Merlot, and the *terroir* has a varied soil combining gravel, clay and sand. This produces a Pomerol with character, which won a *coup de cœur* in 1993 and does so again this year. It has a magnificent, dark-garnet colour, is already powerful and complex in the nose, and shows a remarkably good balance between ripe fruit and fine oak. The palate is warm and extremely mouth-filling, with a finish on high-quality tannins. All in all, this is a delightfully well-balanced wine which is suitable for longer maturing. The second wine here is the **Pensées de Lafleur 98**, which is recommended.

267

BORDEAUX

CH. LA GANNE 1998★★

■   3 ha   13,300   €15-23

86   88 |90| |93| |94| 96 |97| **98**

This vineyard is located in the south-west of the appellation, and has been run for four generations by the Dubois-Lachaud family, who grow 80% Merlot and 20% Cabernet Franc on its sandy ferruginous soil. The 98 wine has a sumptuous colour and a fine yet complex bouquet which releases notes of cherries in brandy, vanilla, coffee and leather. The flavour is well balanced between power and elegance, and the oak does not mask the grape. This is a very well-made wine.

⚹ Michel Dubois, 224, av. Foch,
33500 Libourne, tel. 05.57.51.18.24,
fax 05.57.51.62.20, e-mail lagame@aol.com
✉ Y by appt.

CH. LA GRAVE TRIGANT DE BOISSET 1998

■   8.68 ha   50,000   €30-38

82   83   85   86 |88| |89| |(90)| |94| 95   96
98

With almost 9 ha (22 acres) of vines (89% Merlot and 11% Cabernet Franc) grown on gravelly-clay soils, this vineyard offers a pleasant, well-balanced 98 with a delightful, dark, intense cherry colour. The nose combines gamey aromas with balsamic fragrances and a fine, elegant note of oak, while the palate reveals round, full-bodied tannins which are rich and velvety, and linger on to a soft, smooth finish.

⚹ Ets Jean-Pierre Moueix, Ch. La Grave Trigant de Boisset, 33500 Pomerol

---

CH. LA POINTE 1998★★★

■   22 ha   110,000   €23-30

82   **83**   85   86 |89| |93| |94| 95   **96** |97|
98

Gilles Pauquet is the adviser on this property, which is run from a Directoire house and has astonished us once again by producing a 98 wine which is just as good as its 96 vintage. This one has all the attributes of a great Pomerol for longer maturing. It has a Bordeaux colour with black glints, and a powerful, complex bouquet in which aromas of violets, mocha, truffles, Merlot, oak and leather compete for attention. Thoroughbred flavours are structured by tannins with notes of liquorice and chocolate on a full-bodied, luscious palate which although powerful is

268

⚹ Sylvie et Jacques Guinaudeau, Grand Village, 33240 Mouillac, tel. 05.57.84.44.03, fax 05.57.84.83.31 **Y** by appt.
⚹ Marie Robin

CH. LA FLEUR DE PLINCE 1998★

■   0.28 ha n.c.   €23-30

This tiny vineyard was created in 1998 when Pierre Choukroun bought this 28-ha (69-acre) plot composed of 90% Merlot and 10% Cabernet. The wine has an intense garnet colour with glints which show that it is developing, and a powerful, vinous bouquet of stewed-fruit and crystallised-fruit aromas combined with notes of roasting. The palate is balanced and well structured, with rich, full-bodied tannins which develop on to a lingering finish.

⚹ Pierre Choukroun, Le Grand Moulinet, 33500 Pomerol, tel. 05.57.74.15.26, fax 05.57.74.15.27, e-mail gvbpc@wanadoo.fr **✉ Y** by appt.

CH. LAFLEUR-GAZIN 1998★

■   8.6 ha   51,000   €15-23

86   88 |89| |90| 92 |96| 97   98

This 98 wine is made mainly from Merlot (92%) grown on a sandy-clay soil, and has been developed by a team led by Jean-Claude Berrouet. It has an intense, deep colour and a pleasant bouquet of dried fruit and oaky toast notes along with a fresh touch of undergrowth. The structure is rich and well-balanced, with silky, integrated, well-constructed tannins and a very long finish. This wine has a long life ahead, and will go well with small game or an omelette with truffles.

⚹ Ets Jean-Pierre Moueix,
54, quai du Priourat, 33500 Libourne,
tel. 05.57.51.78.96
⚹ Mme Delfour-Borderie

CH. LA FLEUR-PETRUS 1998★★

■   10.41 ha   48,000   €46-76

82   83 |85| 86 |88| |(89)| 90   92 |94| 95   96
97   **98**

The same team develops and distributes both this wine and its big brother, Petrus. There are, however, certain slight differences between them in terms of *terroir* (in this case, a bit more gravel and a bit less clay) and grape blend (a little less Merlot and a little more Cabernet Franc). Petrus is certainly an exceptional wine, but La Fleur-Petrus is a remarkable, classic Pomerol; it has a very dark colour, very ripe aromas (prunes) with notes of oaky toast and leather, and a delightful roundness on the palate which is firmed up by dense grape and oak tannins. This wine will gain from opening up a little more, and should be drunk in five to seven years' time.

⚹ SC du Ch. La Fleur-Pétrus,
33500 Pomerol

also well balanced. This is an impressive wine, and is being sold at a very attractive price.
● SCE Ch. La Pointe-Pomerol, 33500 Pomerol, tel. 05.57.51.02.11, fax 05.57.51.42.33, e-mail chateau.lapointe@wanadoo.fr [V]
Y by appt.

CH. LA ROSE FIGEAC 1998*

■ 3 ha 18,000 [II] €:38-46

82 (85) 86 |88| |89| |90| 92 |93| |94| 95 96 97 98

This vineyard is located in the Figeac area, on a *terroir* containing a mixture of gravel and old sands. The 98 wine is a blend of 95% 50-year-old Merlot and 5% Cabernet Franc. It has an intense, young-ruby colour and releases an elegant, complex bouquet combining red-fruit aromas and floral scents of violets with a lovely note of oaky toast and hints of tar and liquorice. After a full-bodied, thoroughbred, vigorous attack, the palate develops on a firm, fleshy tannic structure which will guarantee good ageing potential. This wine will be a worthy accompaniment to game dishes.
● Vignobles Despagne-Rapin, Maison Blanche, 33570 Montagne, tel. 05.57.74.62.18, fax 05.57.74.58.98 [V]
Y by appt.

CH. LATOUR A POMEROL 1998*

■ 7.93 ha 42,000 [II] €:38-46

61 64 66 67 70 71 75 (76) 80 81 82 83
85 86 |87| 88 89 90 92 (93) 94 95 96

This vineyard belongs to Mme Lily Lacoste-Loubat, and is located close to the church in Pomerol. It grows 91% Merlot on a gravelly-sand soil, and under the direction of Jean-Claude Berrouet has produced a completely classic Pomerol with a very deep dark-garnet colour and a concentrated but as yet reserved bouquet of ripe-fruit aromas. The elegant palate develops a very good structure, with silky, high-quality tannins which linger on to a long finish. This wine deserves to be kept for five to eight years.
● Ets Jean-Pierre Moueix, 54, quai du Priourat, 33500 Libourne, tel. 05.57.51.78.96
● Lily Lacoste

CLOS DE LA VIEILLE EGLISE 1998***

■ 1998

■ 1.45 ha 9,500 [II] €:23-30

92 93 |94| 95 96 (98)

The vines here are 90% old Merlot and 10% Cabernet Franc, and the soil is gravelly clay. Our tasters were very keen on the density of this 98's deep, dark-garnet colour, and also the power and distinction of its bouquet, in which there is a good balance between stewed-fruit aromas and elegant notes of oak. The palate is concentrated, full and rich, with full-bodied, velvety tannins which linger on to a grandiose, very spicy finish.

● SCEA des Vignobles Trocard, 2, Les Petits-Jays-Ouest, 33570 Les Artigues-de-Lussac, tel. 05.57.55.57.90, fax 05.57.55.57.98, e-mail trocard@wanadoo.fr [V] Y ev. day except Sat. Sun. 8am–12 noon 2pm–5pm

CH. LE BON PASTEUR 1998***

■ 34,000 [II] €:46-76

78 79 81 (82) 83 |85| |86| |88| |89| |90| 92
93 94 (95) 96 97 (98)

Michel Rolland is a consultant to estates on every continent, and also exercises his talents brilliantly on his home territory, as can be seen from this superb 98 Pomerol, in which 75% Merlot is blended with Cabernet Franc. It has a dark, almost black colour, and a magnificent range of aromas combining very ripe fruits, powerful spices, and delightfully toasty oak. Its very rich flavours, full body and powerful yet well-controlled tannins make this a great wine for longer maturing which is both elegant and thoroughbred.
● SCEA Fermière des domaines Rolland, Maillet, 33500 Pomerol, tel. 05.57.51.23.05, fax 05.57.51.66.08 [V] Y by appt.

CH. LE CAILLOU 1998

■ 7 ha n.c. [II] ♦ €:15-23

|93| |94| |95| 98

This vineyard has been in the same family for over a century. The *terroir* here has a gravelly-sand soil mixed with iron slag. This 98 wine has a beautiful ruby colour with dark-purple glints, and is still a very young wine, with aromas of slightly acid red berries and leather, hints of oaky toast and vanilla, and a substantial structure with firm, powerful tannins which are still somewhat austere. All of this suggests that it has fine prospects for the future.
● André Giraud, Ch. Le Caillou, 41, rue de Catusseau, 33500 Pomerol, tel. 05.57.51.06.10, fax 05.57.51.74.95 [V]
Y by appt.
● GFA Giraud-Bélivier

CH. DU DOM. DE L'EGLISE 1998

■ 7 ha 35,000 [II] €:23-30

From three-quarters Merlot and one-quarter Cabernet Franc grown on gravel soils, this vineyard has produced a pleasant 98 wine with a lovely dark-garnet colour. The bouquet is still somewhat restrained, releasing only a few fruity aromas enhanced by fine touches of oak. The structure is firm and well balanced, and there is a charming attack, but the finish is rather austere, which means that the wine will need to be kept for several years until it becomes more supple.

➤ Indivision Castéja-Preben-Hansen, 33330 Saint-Emilion, tel. 05.56.00.00.70, fax 05.57.87.48.61

ESPRIT DE L'EGLISE 1998★★ 2 ha 10,000 €23-30

This second wine from Clos d'Eglise is developed from 75% Merlot and 25% Cabernet Franc. It has a lovely, black, bigaroon-cherry colour and a concentrated bouquet of very ripe Merlot, violets, vanilla and empyreumatic oak (mocha). The body is dense, full and structured by good, spicy oak tannins which are still somewhat dominant. This is a very well-made, modern Pomerol.

➤ Sylviane Garcin-Cathiard, SC Clos L'Eglise, 33500 Pomerol, tel. 05.56.64.05.22, fax 05.56.64.06.98, e-mail haut.bergey@wanadoo.fr

CH. L'ENCLOS 1998★

[85] [86] [88] [89] 91 [95] [96] 98

This classic wine-growing estate is located on the siliceous- clay soils in the west of the appellation. One landmark vintage here was a 47 which was served in 1959 at the royal court in Holland in honour of the British royalty. This very successful 98 will be ready to drink in a few years' time. For the moment it has an intense ruby colour and a bouquet which is already very fine, and releases fruits and aromas and notes of undergrowth. The structure is well balanced, round and full, with a lingering flavour of dark berries.

➤ SCEA du Ch. L'Enclos, 20, rue du Grand-Moulinet, 33500 Pomerol, tel. 05.57.51.04.62, fax 05.57.51.43.15, e-mail chateaulenclos@wanadoo.fr ▼ by appt.

CH. LES GRANDS SILLONS 1998 2 ha €15-23

This small family property was bought in 1952 by the great-grandfather of the current owner. The vineyard's sandy soil is planted with 45-year-old Merlot vines and an additional 15% Cabernet Sauvignon. This has produced a lovely 98 with a dark-garnet colour and aromas of red berries mingled with balsamic scents and nuances of undergrowth. The well-constructed palate has a firm, fresh body which will need a little time to become rounder.

➤ Philippe Dignac, Ch. Côtes de Bonde, 33570 Montagne, tel. 05.57.74.64.52, fax 05.57.74.55.88, e-mail dignac@enfrance.com ▼

CLOS DES LITANIES 1998 0.74 ha 4,500 €30-38

86 [90] 96 [97] 98

The rather quaint label here shows Brother Mathieu Bossuet, who became parish priest of Pomerol in 1514, reciting his litanies in this beautiful vineyard. This 98 wine is made exclusively from Merlot, and has a beautiful, deep, intense ruby colour and a nose of ripe-fruit aromas combined with lovely notes of oaky toast and vanilla. The palate is supple, silky, fine and elegant. This will be a pleasant wine to drink in two to three years' time.

➤ SC Ch. La Croix, 37, rue Pline-Parmentier, BP 192, 33506 Libourne Cedex, tel. 05.57.51.41.86, fax 05.57.51.53.16, e-mail info@j-janoueix-bordeaux.com ▼ ▼ by appt.

CH. MONTVIEL 1998★ 5 ha n.c.

88 89 [90] 91 [93] 94 [95] 96 97 98

This property grows 85% Merlot and 15% Cabernet Franc on a gravel soil. It has produced a very good 98 wine with an intense, garnet colour and an open bouquet of ripe-fruit aromas combined with notes of toast and roasting. The round, ample, full-bodied palate has a very good balance of grape and oak. It combines power and finesse, and should be kept for three to five years.

➤ SCA du Ch. Montviel, Grand-Moulinet, 33500 Pomerol, tel. 05.21.93.21.03 ▼ by appt.
➤ Yves et Catherine Péré-Vergé

CH. MOULINET 1998★ 13 ha 80,000

93 [94] [95] [96] 98

Nathalie Moueix-Guillot took over the running of this major and very old wine-growing estate after the death of her father Armand Moueix, who was a strong and very popular personality in Libourne wine-growing and sporting circles. The vines here are grown on a sandy-gravel soil, and consist of 60% Merlot, 30% Cabernet Sauvignon and 10% Cabernet Franc. The wine has a lovely dark-ruby colour, and a nose which is beginning to open on aromas of crystallised fruits and coffee along with an empyreumatic touch. The supple, round attack is closely followed by tannins which are still somewhat hard. In four to five years' time it will be ready to serve with meat and cheese.

➤ Nathalie et Marie-José Moueix, Ch. Fonplégade, BP 45, 33330 Saint-Emilion, tel. 05.57.74.43.11, fax 05.57.74.44.67, e-mail stephanyrosa@wanadoo.fr ▼ by appt.

CH. MOULINET-LASSERRE 1998★ 5 ha 25,000 €15-23

[89] [90] 91 92 93 94 95 96 97 98

Moulinet-Lasserre is no distance from Clos René. The vineyard consists of 70% Merlot, 20% Cabernet Franc and 10% Malbec, and has produced a wine with a very intense garnet colour and a bouquet which focuses on finesse, with a pure, liquoricy fruit aroma and a touch of leather. Despite its great density and obvious youth, this 98 wine still comfortably reflects the spirit of the appellation.

↬ SCEA Garde-Lasserre, Clos René, 33500 Pomerol, tel. 05.57.51.10.41, fax 05.57.51.16.28 ☑ by appt.
↬ J-M. Garde

CH. PETIT VILLAGE 1998 ★★

11 ha   42,000   €46-76

85 86 88 |89| 90 92 93 94 95 96 |97| 98

Christian Seely has taken over the management of Axa's Bordeaux estates, following the retirement of Michel Cazes. The gravelly *terroir* here is planted with 72% Merlot and 28% Cabernet, and has yielded a dark-garnet wine with an expressive bouquet of very ripe fruits, vanilla and oaky toast along with a touch of musk. The warm, dense palate is concentrated, and has an abundance of oak and fruit tannins. This delicious Pomerol should open out in five to ten years' time.

↬ Christian Seely, Ch. Petit Village, 33500 Pomerol, tel. 05.57.51.21.08, fax 05.57.51.87.31, e-mail infochato@petit-village.com ☑ by appt.
↬ AXA Millésimes

PETRUS 1998 ★★★

11.42 ha   30,000

61 67 71 74 75 76 78 |79| |81| |82| |83|
|85| |86| |87| |88| |89| 90 |92| 93 |94| |95|
|96| 97 |98|

In recent times this very consistent *terroir* has had a dazzling career and many hours of glory, starting at the time of the marriage of Princess Elizabeth, the future Queen of England. Today it is run by remarkable men, and Petrus is the standard bearer of the Pomerol appellation, all of whose features it displays with even more opulence in this vintage. Its magnificent Bordeaux colour is dark and almost black. The concentrated, exceedingly complex bouquet is a perfect combination of very ripe Merlot (95% of the blend) and very fine oak. There is a warm, powerful palate with full-bodied, truffle flavours and lingering tannins which are both dense and liquoricy, and indicate very good ageing potential.

↬ SC du Ch. Petrus, 33500 Pomerol

CH. PLINCE 1998 ★★

7.18 ha   45,000   €15-23

86 |89| |90| 91 92 |95| 96 98

This beautiful, 10-ha (25-acre) family property is located on sandy soils mixed with iron slag, where the vines are three-quarters Merlot and one-quarter Cabernet. The 98 wine appealed to our jury from the start with a sumptuous, deep, dark-crimson colour which has dark-purple glints on the surface. The bouquet is already very open and complex, combining very ripe soft-fruit aromas with notes of toast, vanilla and spice. The ample, full-bodied, powerful palate shows a good balance between grapey and oaky tannins. The finish is still rather firm, and will need a few years of ageing to become more refined.

↬ SCEV Moreau, Ch. Plince, 33500 Libourne, tel. 05.57.51.68.77, fax 05.57.51.43.39 ☑
☑ ev. day except Sat. Sun. 8am-12 noon 2.30pm-6.30pm; cl. Fri. 5pm

CLOS PLINCE 1998

1.15 ha   6,000   €15-23

This tiny vineyard was bought in 1996 by the Laval family, and is made up of 70% Merlot and 30% Cabernets which grow on a sandy soil. This pleasant and delightful 98 wine has a fresh ruby colour. At the moment the bouquet is somewhat dominated by oaky vanilla notes, but is opening on to aromas of red berries stewed in alcohol. The palate is robust and full-bodied, with firm, very evident tannins which should ensure that the wine develops well over an ageing period of three to five years.

↬ SCEA Famille Laval, 4, chem. des Grand-Vignes, 33500 Pomerol, tel. 05.57.51.17.40, fax 05.57.51.16.89 ☑
☑ by appt.

CH. POMEAUX 1998 ★★

3.78 ha   22,000   €46-76

This vineyard has made a sensational début with its first harvest! That may not seem difficult, given that the wine is made from pure Merlot grapes grown on a ferruginous gravel and clay soil. Even so, the result is impressive. The very dark colour has brown-black glints, and the nose releases a powerful yet subtle combination of red-berry, stewed-cherry and spice aromas, along with notes of mocha, leather and oaky toast (still somewhat dominant). The palate is warm, rich, dense and structured by finely-textured tannins which are still fresh and show that the wine has very good ageing potential. After a success like this we await further delights in the vintages to come.

↬ SCEA du Ch. Pomeaux, 6, Lieu-dit Touïfaut, 33500 Pomerol, tel. 05.57.51.98.88, fax 05.57.51.88.99, e-mail info@pomeaux.com ☑ by appt.
↬ M.A.T. Powers

Pomerol

CH. PONT-CLOQUET 1998

■ 0.53 ha 3,600 ▦ ♦ €30-38

Although its first vintage was as recent as 1996, this wine is developed from 50-year-old Merlot with an added 10% of Cabernet Sauvignon. It is a very fine, well-made Pomerol with a clear, intense garnet colour and a bouquet of ripe-fruit aromas and fine, elegant notes of oak. The supple, balanced palate is constructed on silky, fine, well-softened tannins, and has a very attractive finish.

⚲ Stéphanie Rousseau,
Petit Sorillon, 33230 Abzac,
tel. 05.57.49.06.10, fax 05.57.49.38.96,
e-mail vignoblerousseau@wanadoo.fr ▼
Ⓨ by appt.

CH. PRIEURS DE LA COMMANDERIE 1998★

86 88 |89| |90| 91 |⑨3| |94| 96 **97** 98
■ 3.5 ha 6,000 ▦ €23-30

This vineyard comprises a dozen or so plots scattered over the western part of Pomerol. It is run by the same technical team as Château La Dominique, which is a Saint-Emilion Grand Cru Classé belonging to the same owner. They offer a very good 98 wine with a slightly developed dark-garnet colour and aromas of stewed red berries along with scents of high-quality oak and very pleasant floral nuances. The palate is well balanced, and the round, full-bodied tannins linger delightfully on to a flavourful finish. This wine will go well with woodcock.

⚲ Clément Fayat, Ch. La Dominique,
33330 Saint-Emilion, tel. 05.57.51.31.36,
fax 05.57.51.63.04, e-mail info@
vignobles.fayat-group.com ▼ Ⓨ by appt.

CH. RATOUIN 1998★

■ 3.2 ha 15,000 ▦ €11-15

This small property has been in the same family for three generations. Château Ratouin is located on siliceous-gravel soils and planted with 70% Merlot and 30% Cabernet Franc. This 98 wine has an intense, deep colour and a concentrated, powerful bouquet with well-balanced aromas of stewed fruits, roasting, leather and high-quality oak. The palate has silky, full-bodied tannins and a rich, round structure, followed by a very pleasant, long, lingering finish.

⚲ SCEA Ch. Ratouin, Village de René,
33500 Pomerol, tel. 05.57.51.19.58,
fax 05.57.51.47.92 ▼ Ⓨ by appt.

CLOS RENE 1998★

|86| |88| |89| |90| 91 92 93 95 96 **97** 98
■ 12 ha 65,000 ▦ €15-23

This 98 wine comes from a sandy gravel *terroir*, and has been matured for 16 months in oak barrels, a quarter of which are new. It has a lovely garnet colour and a fine, fruity nose which releases spice and leather notes when the wine is swirled in the glass. The palate is still young, but the balanced tannins should make this a very appealing wine in three to five years' time.

⚲ SCEA Garde-Lasserre, Clos René,
33500 Pomerol, tel. 05.57.51.10.41,
fax 05.57.51.16.28 ▼ Ⓨ by appt.
⚲ J.-M. Garde

CH. ROUGET 1998★

|94| |95| |96| **97** 98
■ 18.5 ha 30,000 ▦ €23-30

This deep dark-garnet 98 wine comes from the gravelly-clay plateau. It has a nose of ripe and crystallised fruits (morello cherries), enhanced by an elegant note of oaky toast and roasting. The palate is round, full and powerful, with smooth, velvety, lingering tannins. This is a well-balanced wine which should reach maturity three to five years from now.

⚲ Ch. Rouget SGVP, 33500 Pomerol,
tel. 05.57.51.05.85, fax 05.57.55.22.45 ▼
Ⓨ by appt.
⚲ Labruyère

CH. SAINTE-MARIE 1998

■ 4.5 ha 26,000 ▦ €30-38

This family property is cultivated organically on sandy soils, and planted with two-thirds Merlot and one-third Cabernets. The wine has an intense, brilliant ruby colour and a warm, vinous bouquet of stewed fruit, coffee, chocolate and liquorice aromas. The balanced, expressive palate has a delightfully full body, integrated, velvety tannins, and very good length at the finish. The Jury made the unusual suggestion that it would go well with river fish.

⚲ J. Pélotier et Fille,
41, av. Georges-Pompidou, 33500 Libourne,
tel. 05.57.51.12.27, fax 05.57.51.12.27 ▼
Ⓨ by appt.

CH. DE SALES 1998

86 88 |89| |90| 92 94 |97| 98
■ 47.5 ha 160,000 ▦ ♦ €23-30

Sales has been in the same family for 400 years, and is architecturally one of the finest châteaux in the Bordeaux region. It has almost 50 ha (124 acres) of vines (70% Merlot, 15% Cabernet Franc and 15% Cabernet Sauvignon), grown on fine gravel and sand. Its very pleasant 98 wine has a lovely garnet colour with developed glints, and a nose which is still rather restrained but vinous, with aromas of stewed fruits. The palate is balanced, and its supple, round tannins compensate for a slight lack of power by a delightful elegance which will make the wine a worthy accompaniment to small game.

⚲ Bruno de Lambert, Ch. de Sales,
33500 Pomerol, tel. 05.57.51.04.92,
fax 05.57.25.23.91 ▼ Ⓨ by appt.

CH. DU TAILHAS 1998

97 98
■ 11 ha 60,000 ▦ ♦ €23-30

This 98 wine is made mainly from Merlot (70% of a blend of grapes grown on a mixture of sand and gravel on ferruginous *alios*), and has been matured for 20 months in new oak. It

272

has a light colour with brick-red glints, and a nose of fruit, liquorice and slightly truffly aromas which are still fresh. The elegant tannins lend a great deal of freshness to this pleasant wine, which will quite soon be ready to serve with red meats or lamprey.

🍴 Nébout et Fils, SC Ch. du Tailhas, 33500 Pomerol, tel. 05.57.51.26.02, fax 05.57.25.17.70 ▼ Y by appt.

CH. THIBEAUD-MAILLET 1998*

88 89 |90| 92 |93| 94 95 |96| 97 98
1 ha 6,167

This small vineyard is regularly selected by our tasters, and grows 85% Merlot and 15% Cabernet Franc on a gravelly-clay soil. The 98 wine focuses on finesse, with a lovely, dense ruby colour and crystallised-fruit and toast aromas in the nose. In two or three years' time it will be ready to serve with unhung game.

🍴 Roger et Andrée Duroux, Ch. Thibeaud-Maillet, 33500 Pomerol, tel. 05.57.51.82.68, fax 05.57.51.58.43 Y ev. day 9am–12 noon 2pm–8pm; cl. Mar.

CH. TROTANOY 1998**

79 80 82 85 86 87 |88| |89| |90| |92| |94|
95 96 97 98
7.16 ha 32,000 +76

The greatest gourmets in the world clamour after this wine, which comes from a very special, gravelly-clay soil which is hard in dry weather and becomes slippery in the moment there is a drop of rain. It's hard work for the wine-producer, but what a result! This 98 wine shows all the power and pedigree of the terroir in a very dense dark-garnet colour and an elegant bouquet in which oaky notes of grilling, toast and vanilla beautifully enhance the soft-fruit aromas. The structure is rich, and there is a full, fleshy body with an excellent tannic framework which will require wine-lovers to wait patiently while it ages for a little while.

🍴 SC du Ch. Trotanoy, 33500 Pomerol

CH. DE VALOIS 1998

7.66 ha 50,000 €15-23

This property was created in 1862, and was given the name Château de Valois in 1886. The soil here is aeolian sand sometimes mixed with gravel, and the grape range includes three-quarters Merlot. This 98 wine has a lovely garnet colour with glints which are still fresh, and releases a bouquet that is somewhat marked by oaky notes of toast and vanilla, with a slight underlying hint of fruit. The well-balanced palate has good concentration, but the firmness of the tannins at the finish means that it will need to be kept for a while.

🍴 SCEA des vignobles Leydet, Rouilledimat, 33500 Libourne, tel. 05.57.51.19.77, fax 05.57.51.00.62 ▼ Y by appt.

VIEUX CHATEAU CERTAN 1998***

81 82 83 85 86 |88| 89| |90| 92 93 |94|
95 96 97 98
14 ha 38,400 +76

Vieux Château Certan
Grand Vin
POMEROL
1998

This is the most European vineyard in Pomerol; the château was created at the beginning of the 16th century by a Scottish family, and since 1924 has been run with panache by a Belgian family. The 98 wine won unanimous praise for its splendid Bordeaux colour with black glints. It still has very fruity aromas (morello cherries, figs and prunes) against a background of fine oak, and the palate is full and round, with smooth tannins which give it the stamp of both grape and oak. In a word, this is a great, traditional, very well-balanced Pomerol.

🍴 SC du Vieux Château Certan, 33500 Pomerol, tel. 05.57.51.17.33, fax 05.57.25.35.08, e-mail vieuxchateaucertan@wanadoo.fr
🍴 by appt.
🍴 Thienpont

VIEUX CHATEAU FERRON 1998**

|89| |90| 93 |95| |96| 97 98
1.5 ha 10,000 €23-30

This is one of three vineyards in Pomerol run by the Entre-Deux-Mers wine-producers Garzaro, who grow 90% Merlot and 10% Cabernet Franc on its sand and gravel soil. The wine has a lovely garnet colour with slight brick-red glints. The nose has fine hints of oak and liquorice, and starts on a very 'Merlot' note of stewed prunes, along with a slight sense of musk (game). The silky, round, full-bodied palate is balanced by tannins which are now subdued, and will enable it to be drunk for two to eight years with beef with ceps or with game.

🍴 EARL Vignobles Elisabeth Garzaro, Ch. Le Prieur, 33750 Baron, tel. 05.56.30.16.16, fax 05.56.30.12.63, e-mail garzaro@vingarzaro.com ▼ Y by appt.

CH. VIEUX MAILLET 1998*

|95| 96 97 98
2.62 ha 12,500 €23-30

Vieux Mallet is a 4-ha (10-acre) property which was bought in 1994 by Isabelle Motte, and grows four-fifths Merlot and one-fifth Cabernet Franc on a clay and gravel soil. This

273

has produced a 98 wine with great presence, and a delightfully deep, intense ruby colour. The nose combines power and finesse; it has a perfect note of vanilla along with very ripe grape aromas and highly elegant scents of toast. This is an extremely well-structured wine, with lingering, rich, high-quality tannins and the characteristic good balance of a Pomerol.

Isabelle Motte, Ch. Vieux Maillet, 33500 Pomerol, tel. 05.57.51.04.67, fax 05.57.51.04.67, e-mail chateau.vieux.maillet@wanadoo.fr
by appt.

CH. VRAY CROIX DE GAY 1998★

3.66 ha　22,500　€15-23

85 86 88 |89| |90| |93| |94| 95 |97| 98

Olivier Guichard was a friend of General de Gaulle, and was one of the architects of his return to power in 1958. He ran a ministry, and continued to serve in the cabinet of Jacques Chaban-Delmas, who in 1969 appointed him Minister of Education. Now he runs this wine-growing estate, where the vines comprise 90% Merlot and 10% Cabernet Franc. This 98 wine has a ruby colour which is still young, and aromas of ripe fruits and soft spices along with notes of coffee and floral nuances. The palate is supple and delicate at first, then reveals velvety tannins which are followed by a delightfully mouth-filling, very vinous finish. This wine should be drunk in two to three years' time.

SCE Baronne Guichard, Ch. Siaurac, 33500 Néac, tel. 05.57.51.64.58, fax 05.57.51.41.56　by appt.
Olivier Guichard

CH. DES ANNEREAUX 1998★

20 ha　100,000　€8-11

This vineyard is ideally located at the heart of a clay and gravel terroir, and comprises 80% Merlot and 20% Cabernet vines. The wine has been oak-matured for 18 months. It has a brilliant, intense crimson colour, and a developed nose of spices, flowers, dark berries (blackcurrants and blackberries) and leather. On the palate the round, mature tannins develop very fully on flavours of liquorice and spices. The wine will be ready to drink in three to four years' time.

SCE du Ch. des Annereaux, 33500 Lalande-de-Pomerol, tel. 05.57.55.48.90, fax 05.57.84.31.27
by appt.
Mihade-Hessel

CH. BECHEREAU

Cuvée fût de chêne 1998

2.25 ha　14,000　€8-11

This supple, round wine has an intense colour and aromas of toast, leather and cinnamon. It should be drunk within the next three years.

SCE Jean-Michel Bertrand, Béchereau, 33570 Les Artigues-de-Lussac, tel. 05.57.24.31.22, fax 05.57.24.34.69
ev. day except Sun. 8am-12 noon 2pm-6pm

CH. DE BEL-AIR 1998★

16 ha　n.c.　€15-23

This old, 20-ha (50-acre) property has been owned by Jean-Pierre Musset since 1962. It is located on a gravel terroir with a classic grape range of Merlot (75%) and Cabernet, and now offers a wine with a deep, almost black colour, complex aromas of ripe and stewed fruits (blackcurrants and cherries), and full, velvety, highly characteristic tannins which develop with finesse. It has a certain freshness which will give good ageing potential. It will give great pleasure in two to five years' time.

Vignobles Jean-Pierre Musset, Ch. de Bel-Air, 33500 Lalande-de-Pomerol, tel. 05.57.51.40.07, fax 05.57.74.17.43, e-mail chateaudebelair@wanadoo.fr
by appt.

CH. BELLES-GRAVES 1998

16.2 ha　90,000　€11-15

For a long time this château was the 'official' supplier to Captain Cousteau's ship La Calypso. The 98 wine is very fruity (raspberries) and delicately oaky. The tannins are supple, delicious, very ripe and balanced, right up to a pleasant finish. This wine should be drunk within the next three years.

GFA Theallet-Piton, SC Ch. Belles-Graves, 33500 Néac, tel. 05.57.51.09.61, fax 05.57.51.01.41
by appt.

Lalande de Pomerol

The Hospitallers of the Knights of Saint John created this vineyard and its neighbour Pomerol; indeed, they also built the beautiful church in Lalande that dates from the 12th century. The vineyard covers about 1,120 ha (2,776 acres), growing classic Bordeaux grape varieties to make well-coloured red wines, which are powerful and have a good bouquet. They enjoy a good reputation and the best wines can rival Pomerols and Saint-Emilions. In 2000, 57,520 hl (1,518,528 gal) were declared.

274

CH. BOUQUET DE VIOLETTES

1998★ | 2.7 ha | 8,200 | €15-23

This small vineyard takes a great deal of care both in growing the vines and in developing its wines, beautiful, crimson colour with shades of ruby and its nose of delightful dark-berry, cherry, vanilla and cocoa aromas. The round, powerful tannins develop with smoothness and maturity. The somewhat severe finish needs two or three years of ageing to become rounder, which is not unusual in this AOC.

↝ Jean-Jacques Chollet, La Chapelle, 50210 Camprond, tel. 02.33.45.19.61, fax 02.33.45.35.54 ⅄ by appt.

CH. BOURSEAU 1998★

10 ha | 45,000 | €11-15

Located close to the magnificent 12th-century church in the village of Lalande, this property has an excellent clay and gravel *terroir* which has produced this blend of 10% Bouchet and the two traditional grape varieties. It has an intense colour, and its powerful aromas of ripe fruits and violets are accompanied by very fresh notes. The fairly firm tannins make for a palate which is substantial, full and long. This wine has good ageing potential and should be opened three to eight years from now.

↝ SARL Vignobles Véronique Gaboriaud-Bernard, Ch. Bourseau, 33500 Lalande-de-Pomerol, tel. 05.57.51.52.39, fax 05.57.51.70.19, e-mail matras@cavesparticulieres.com ▼ ⅄ ev. day 9am–12 noon 2pm–5.30pm

CH. CANON CHAIGNEAU 1998

24 ha | 24,000 | €11-15

This wine has notes of roasting (coffee and cocoa) and ripe fruits throughout, but although it is fairly full-bodied it is still very heavily dominated by oak. Everything should fall into place in two or three years' time.

↝ SCEA Marin Audra, 3 bis, rue Porte-Brunet, 33330 Saint-Emilion, tel. 05.57.24.69.13, fax 05.57.24.69.11, e-mail louis.marin@wanadoo.fr ⅄ by appt.

DOM. DU CHAPELAIN 1998

1.02 ha | 5,243

The label at this du Chapelain estate shows the Church of Saint-Jean de Lalande, whose superb façade recalls the Church of the Hospitallers of Saint John of Jerusalem. This little vineyard offers a pleasant 98 wine marked by elegant aromas of red berries, blackberries, vanilla and game. It will need to be kept for two or three years until the tannins become integrated.

↝ SCEA du Ch. L'Enclos, 20, rue du Grand-Moulinet, 33500 Pomerol, tel. 05.57.51.04.62, fax 05.57.51.43.15, e-mail chateaulenclos@wanadoo.fr ▼

CLOS DES TUILERIES 1998

2 ha | 2,500 | €8-11

This Clos offers a 98 wine with brick-red glints and a bouquet of menthol, liquorice and blackcurrant aromas supported by high-quality oak. On the palate the wine is supple and well balanced, and has evident, mature tannins which are highly characteristic of the appellation. It can be drunk now or kept for a few years.

↝ SCEA des Vignobles Francis Merlet, 46, rue de l'Europe, Goizet, 33910 Saint-Denis-de-Pile, tel. 05.57.84.25.19, fax 05.57.84.25.19 ⅄ by appt.

CLOS LES FOUGERAILLES 1998

2.25 ha | 5,000 | €8-11

This wine made from 100% Merlot has a distinctive fresh red colour; pleasant, delicately oaky red-berry aromas, and supple, round tannins which are well balanced at the finish. This is a very good wine which can be drunk in two or three years' time.

↝ SCEA du Ch. Coudreau, 1, rte de Robin, 33910 Saint-Denis-de-Pile, tel. 06.82.17.85.28, fax 06.57.74.26.77, e-mail chateau.coudreau@laposte.net ▼
↝ Vacher

CH. GRAND ORMEAU 1998★★

8 ha | 38,000 | €15-23

Jean-Claude Beton formed a passion for this vineyard in 1988, and embarked on a policy of high quality which has taken it to the very top. His excellent gravel *terroir* is used to best advantage with a yield of only 35 hl/ha, which is the first secret of great wines. This one gleams with dark-ruby lights, and its expressive bouquet suggests ripe fruits along with a very elegant note of empyreumatic oak. The finely-textured tannins create a dense structure with great concentration and richness. There is a very long, complex finish which indicates an excellent ageing potential of at least five to eight years.

↝ Ch. Grand Ormeau, 33500 Lalande-de-Pomerol, tel. 05.57.25.30.20, fax 05.57.25.22.80, e-mail grand.ormeau@wanadoo.fr ▼ ⅄ by appt.
↝ Jean-Claude Beton

CH. GRAND ORMEAU

Cuvée Madeleine 1998★★★ | 2.5 ha | 10,000 | €30-38

Jean-Claude Beton is the founder of the Orangina group, and has turned this property into a great vineyard. A unanimous *coup de coeur* is awarded to the Cuvée Madeleine, which comes from old vines grown on a gravel *terroir*. It has a very dark, intense colour and a complex mixture of spice (vanilla) and stewed soft-fruit aromas. The tannins are full and firm but also silky, and give an impression of power and good length. This is an exceptional wine which should be kept for five to ten years.

↝ Jean-Claude Beton

Lalande de Pomerol

CH. HAUT-SURGET 1998
■ 36 ha 100,000 ■ Ⅱ♦ €11-15

Haut-Surget is a very large property, and offers an agreeable wine. The Jury liked its garnet colour with purplish glints, and its floral and toast aromas accompanied by a note of red berries. On the palate the tannins are still heavily dominant, and it will take two to four years of ageing before the fruit flavours become fully expressive.

➤ Ollet-Fourreau, 33500 Néac,
tel. 05.57.51.28.68, fax 05.57.51.91.79 ☑
Ⴞ by appt.

CH. JEAN DE GUE
Cuvée Prestige 1998★★
■ 6.5 ha n.c. ■ ⅡⅠ♦ €11-15

After winning a *coup de coeur* and three stars for the 97 vintage, this château now offers a remarkable 98. It has a garnet colour with very brilliant ruby glints, and a complex bouquet of fruit aromas (blackcurrants), spices and truffles combined with more classic oak notes (vanilla and toast). The powerful, mature tannins are particularly rich and elegant, and give the palate a very fruity, spicy flavour. It will have to be kept carefully for five to six years.

➤ Vignobles Aubert, La Couspaude,
33330 Saint-Emilion, tel. 05.57.40.15.76,
fax 05.57.40.10.14 Ⴞ by appt.

CH. LA BORDERIE-MONDESIR
1998★
■ 2.2 ha 13,000 ■ ⅡⅠ♦ €11-15

Jean-Marie Rousseau grows a total of 44 ha (109 acres) of vines, and devotes 2 ha (5 acres) to this *cuvée*. In this vintage it is a blend of Cabernet Sauvignon and 90% Merlot, grown on a gravel soil with a subsoil containing clinker. The wine has a ruby colour with purplish glints, and gives off fragrances suggesting spices, red berries and leather. Its tannins are both round and powerful, and remain very elegant right up to the finish. This wine has good ageing potential, and will become completely expressive in two to five years' time.

➤ Jean-Marie Rousseau, Petit-Sorillon,
33230 Abzac, tel. 05.57.49.06.10,
fax 05.57.49.38.96,
e-mail vignoblesrousseau@wanadoo.fr ☑
Ⴞ by appt.

➤ Ch. Grand Ormeau,
33500 Lalande-de-Pomerol,
tel. 05.57.25.30.20, fax 05.57.25.22.80,
e-mail grand.ormeau@wanadoo.fr ☑
Ⴞ by appt.

CH. HAUT-CHAIGNEAU
Cuvée Prestige Elevé en fût de chêne 1998★
■ 11 ha 50,000 ■ ⅡⅠ €15-23

Pascal Chatonnet is a distinguished oenologist, and assists his father on the family properties. Together they produce excellent wines every year, such as this 98 with its deep, brilliant colour and expressive soft-fruit aromas (blackcurrants) combined with notes of oaky vanilla and toast. The tannins are very concentrated and powerful in the attack, then develop with finesse to a delightful finish. This wine should be kept for two to five years. The second wine here is the **Château Tour Saint-André 98**, which is recommended for its fruity, warm aromas and supple, balanced structure. It should be drunk sooner than the other wine.

➤ GFA J. et A. Chatonnet,
Ch. Haut-Chaigneau, 33500 Néac,
tel. 05.57.51.31.31, fax 05.57.25.08.93 ☑
Ⴞ by appt.

CH. HAUT-CHATAIN
Cuvée Prestige 1998★★
■ 1 ha 6,000 ■ ⅡⅠ €11-15

This Cuvée Prestige is a selection from 1 ha (2.5 acres) of 40-year-old vines on a property comprising 22 ha (54 acres) in all. The 98 wine is a delight from the start with its dark, deep colour and an intense bouquet of redberry jam, toast and tar. After a supple, dense attack, the palate reveals tannins which are mature, firm and very fruity (raspberries and wild strawberries). This wine is full of finesse, and should be drunk in two to eight years' time. The **Cuvée Classique** comes from 25-year-old vines with an added 10% Cabernet Franc, and wins one star for its good balance between ripe fruits and supple, elegant tannins. It can be drunk sooner than the first wine, in two to three years' time.

➤ Vignobles Rivière-Junquas,
Ch. Haut-Chatain, 33500 Néac,
tel. 05.57.25.98.48, fax 05.57.25.95.45 ☑
Ⴞ by appt.

CH. LA CROIX SAINT-JEAN 1998
■ 1.34 ha 8,000 ■ ⅡⅠ€11-15

This vineyard is passed down through the female side of the family, and is currently run by father and daughter. Their very pleasant wine has a brilliant, ruby colour and frank aromas of slightly toasty red berries. Its spicy tannins are well balanced, but also have a slight firmness which should fade after two to three years of ageing.

➤ Vignobles Raymond Tapon,
Lafleur Vachon, 33330 Saint-Emilion,
tel. 05.57.74.61.20, fax 05.57.74.61.19,
e-mail vinstapon@aol.com ☑ Ⴞ by appt.

Lalande de Pomerol

98 vintage has a brilliant colour, and fine, complex aromas suggesting liquorice, crystallised fruits and oaky vanilla. On the palate the mature, silky tannins are supported by a very full body, and the finish on a combination of oak and fruit flavours is very well balanced. This highly characteristic wine will keep for five to ten years.
↝ SA Pierre Bourotte, 62, quai du Priourat, 33500 Libourne, tel. 05.57.51.62.17, fax 05.57.51.23.28, e-mail jeanbaptiste.audy@wanadoo.fr ☑ ⟁ by appt.

CH. DE L'EVECHE 1998
10 ha 24,000 €8-11

This wine is recommended not only for its deep colour and elegant bouquet of ripe fruit and toast aromas, but also for its tannins which are full and velvety in the attack, then develop with charm but also a slight note of bitterness. 'A good, oaky toast Merlot,' noted the Jury, and indeed this grape variety does dominate the grape blend (60%). You are advised to keep this wine for two or three years.
↝ Vignobles Chaumet, Goujon, RN 89, 33500 Lalande-de-Pomerol, tel. 05.57.25.50.12, fax 05.57.25.51.48, e-mail vignobles.chaumet@wanadoo.fr ☑ ev. day except Sun. 8am-12 noon 2pm-6pm

CH. MONCETS 1998*
19 ha 30,000 €8-11

This beautiful 24-ha (59-acre) property boasts a very long history, and has produced an excellent 98 with concentrated aromas (dark berries and toast) and a structure which is still tannic. Its development on the palate is dominated by an elegant, smooth, lingering sense of balance and a very dense finish. This wine can be enjoyed in two to five years' time.
↝ de Jerphanion, Moncets, 33500 Néac, tel. 05.57.51.19.33, fax 05.57.51.56.24, e-mail bastidette@moncets.com ☑ ⟁ by appt.

CH. PERRON La Fleur 1998**
n.c. 10,000 €15-23

Dating back to 1647, Château Perron is one of the oldest in the Lalande commune, and has been owned by the same family for three generations. It offers a La Fleur cuvée which is in every respect remarkable, with a deep, dark colour, powerful, complex aromas of strawberries, raspberries, vanilla and cocoa, and very evident but very velvety tannins which are marked by great finesse and elegance at the finish. This will be a great wine once it has been kept for three to eight years.
↝ Michel-Pierre Massonie, Ch. Perron, BP 88, 33503 Libourne Cedex, tel. 05.57.51.40.29, fax 05.57.51.13.37 ☑ ⟁ by appt.

CH. LA FAURIE MAISON NEUVE
Elevé en fût de chêne 1998
3.8 ha 25,000 €8-11

This 98 wine comes from a good gravel terroir, and is worth trying for its intensely aromatic nose of spices, dark berries (blackcurrants), game, violets and vanilla. On the palate it is an agreeable wine with supple tannins. It can be drunk now for its fruit flavours or kept for two or three years.
↝ Michel Coudroy, Maison-Neuve, 33570 Montagne, tel. 05.57.74.62.23, fax 05.57.74.64.18 ☑ ⟁ by appt.

LA FLEUR DE BOUARD 1998*
n.c. 59,000 €15-23

The 98 vintage is the first made by the new owner, Hubert de Boüard, who is already the co-proprietor of Château Angelus and president of the Saint-Emilion syndicate. The wine has an intense garnet colour with black glints, and an expressive bouquet of ripe grapes and flowers which is also marked by rich vanilla and oak notes. On the palate the tannins are highly evident but very round and rich, giving a sense of great maturity. This wine will need two to three years of ageing until the oak is completely balanced, after which it will keep for a long time and will go well with small game.
↝ Hubert de Boüard de Laforest, SC Ch. La Fleur Saint-Georges, BP 7, 33500 Pomerol, tel. 05.57.25.25.13, fax 05.57.51.65.14, e-mail lafleurdebouard@libertysurf.fr ☑ ⟁ by appt.

CH. LA VALLIERE 1998*
1 ha 5,000 €8-11

This wine comes from a gravel terroir and a classic Libourne grape blend. It has a ruby colour with slightly brick-red glints, and a nose of complex ripe-fruit and crystallised-fruit aromas combined with musky notes (leather). The ample, mouth-filling tannins are quite full-bodied and long, and will enable this wine to be drunk in two years' time.
↝ SARL L. Dubost, Catusseau, 33500 Pomerol, tel. 05.57.51.74.57, fax 05.57.25.99.95 ☑ ⟁ by appt.

CH. LES CHAUMES 1998
3.5 ha 20,000 €8-11

This vineyard was purchased in 1977 by Alain Vigier, and now offers a pleasant wine with a bouquet of almonds and crystallised fruits, and complex, fairly firm tannins. From the same owner, the white Château La Croix 98 is also recommended.
↝ Alain Vigier, La Fleur des Prés, 33500 Pomerol, tel. 05.57.74.00.16, fax 05.57.51.87.70, e-mail vigier.alain@wanadoo.fr ☑ ⟁ by appt.

CH. LES HAUTS-CONSEILLANTS 1998*
9 ha 41,000 €11-15

This estate is located on a sandy silt terroir, and regularly produces excellent wines. This

Lalande de Pomerol

DOM. PONT DE GUESTRES 1998★

Elevé en fût de chêne 1998★

■ 2 ha 12,000 ■ ⑪ ⸙ €11-15

This family vineyard offers two different wines, each of which wins a star. The first is the Domaine Pont de Guestres (100% Merlot); it is characterised by intense oak notes which currently somewhat mask the fruit aromas and the quality of the very evident, lingering tannins. The second is the Château Au Pont de Guitres 98, which is a blend of 30% Cabernet Franc and Sauvignon but has had only six months of oak maturation as opposed to 12 months in the case of the previous wine. It is much more fruity, with very pleasant floral notes, and its tannins are supple, balanced and moderately full-bodied. It can be drunk very soon and certainly earlier than the first wine, which will need to age for two to five years.

➻ Rémy Rousselot, Ch. Les Roches de Ferrand, 05.57.24.95.16, fax 05.57.24.91.44 ⓥ
Ⓨ by appt.

CH. REAL-CAILLOU 1998★

■ 4.3 ha 25,000 ■ ⑪ €11-15

This wine is developed by the pupils at the Lycée de Montagne, which was founded in 1969 to train the wine-growers of the future. It is a very successful 98, with a lovely, intense, ruby colour and a developed bouquet of very ripe, stewed fruits and oaky roasting. On the palate the tannins are already delicious and charming, and should develop with finesse and balance in two to five years' time.

➻ Lycée viticole de Libourne-Montagne, Goujon, 33570 Montagne,
tel. 05.57.55.21.22, fax 05.57.51.66.13,
e-mail legta.libourne@educagri.fr ⓥ
Ⓨ ev. day except Sat. Sun. 8.30am–12 noon 1.30pm–5.30pm

CH. TOUR DE MARCHESSEAU 1998

■ 5 ha 35,000 ■ ⑪ ⸙ €8-11

This 98 wine comes from a lovely gravel terroir, and has an admirable, brilliant colour. It has restrained aromas of grilled fruit and leather, followed by a palate which is currently dominated by oak but is revealing flavours of very ripe fruit. It can be drunk now or kept for two or three years until the oak becomes more integrated. From the same owner, the Château La Croix des Moines 98 is recommended.
➻ SCEA des Vignobles Trocard,
2, Les Petits-Jays-Ouest, 33570 Les Artigues-de-Lussac, tel. 05.57.55.57.90,
fax 05.57.55.57.98, e-mail trocard@wanadoo.fr Ⓨ ev. day except Sat. Sun. 8am–12 noon 2pm–5pm

CH. DE VIAUD 1998★

■ 9 ha 54,300 ■ ⑪ €11-15

This château has a deep gravel soil and grows mainly Merlot (95%). Its 98 wine has an intense, brilliant garnet colour and a nose dominated by very ripe fruits (blackcurrants and blackberries) and delicate oak. On the palate the silky, velvety, lingering tannins confirm an impression of power, and hold out great promise for a very good ageing potential of four to eight years. From the same producer, the Château de Grand Chambellan 98 is recommended.
➻ SAS Ch. de Viaud,
33500 Lalande-de-Pomerol,
tel. 05.57.51.17.86, fax 05.57.51.79.77

ENCLOS DE VIAUD 1998★

■ 3.82 ha 21,300 ■ ⑪ €11-15

Coming from a sandy gravel terroir with a small clay content, this 98 wine is worth trying for its very beautiful crimson colour and its aromas of ripe red berries, blackcurrants and tobacco. The rich, full tannins fill a lingering palate which is not without freshness and has quite a spicy finish. The wine can be opened in three to five years' time.
➻ SARL de La Diligence, La Patache, 33500 Pomerol, tel. 05.57.55.38.03,
fax 05.57.55.38.01 ⓥ Ⓨ by appt.

CH. VIEUX CHEVROL 1998

■ 21 ha 100,000 ■ ⑪ €8-11

This 98 wine has an elegant, concentrated bouquet of red berries, and a pleasant, classic tannic structure which develops with a great deal of charm but without much complexity. It can be drunk now or kept for two to three years.
➻ Jean-Pierre Champseix, Vieux Chevrol, 33500 Néac, tel. 05.57.51.09.80,
fax 05.57.51.31.05 ⓥ Ⓨ by appt.

VIEUX CLOS CHAMBRUN 1998★

■ n.c. 2,400 ■ ⑪ €23-30

This limited cuvée has been matured in new oak, and is a blend of 50% Merlot and equal shares of the two Cabernets. It has a highly promising, intense garnet colour with mauve glints, and elegant fragrances of vanilla, dark berries, toast and violets followed by a balanced palate which develops powerfully. The fruit flavour is apparent, but is still dominated by oak. This will fade is two to three years' time.
➻ Jean-Jacques Chollet, La Chapelle, 50210 Camprond, tel. 02.33.45.19.61,
fax 02.33.45.35.54 ⓥ Ⓨ by appt.

Saint-Emilion and Saint-Emilion Grand Cru

Covering the slopes of a hill that looks down on the valley of the Dordogne, Saint-Emilion (3,300 inhabitants) is a peaceful and charming little wine village. But it is also a place full of history. It was once a stopping point on the pilgrims' route to Santiago de Compostela, a fortified town in the Hundred Years' War and the refuge of the Girondin deputies who were proscribed by the Convention during the Revolution, and there are a good number of historic ruins to see. Local legend has it that the vineyard was originally planted by Roman legionaries. It is more likely that its beginnings, at least part of them, were in the 13th century. However that may be, Saint-Emilion today is the centre of one of the most famous vineyards in the world. It extends over nine communes and is planted on a rich range of soils. A number of classic growths come from the lime plateau and clay on the limey subsoil around the village. They make wines of good colour, which are well-structured and full-bodied. The vineyards bordering Pomerol have a more gravelly soil and produce wines noted for their great finesse (this region also produces many Grands Crus). But the major ity of the Saint-Emilion appellation is on sandy alluvial soil, sloping down to the Dordogne, which produces very pleasant wines. With regard to the vine varieties, Merlot predominates but there is also Cabernet Franc, called 'Bouchet' in the region, and, in much lesser quantities, Cabernet Sauvignon.

One of the things that differentiates in the Saint-Emilion is the classification of the wines. It was only established recently, in 1955, and it is regularly and systematically reviewed (the first revision took place in 1958 and the most recent in 1996). The Saint-Emilion appellation can be used by all the wines produced in the commune itself and in the eight other communes surrounding it. The second appellation, Saint-Emilion Grand Cru, does not correspond to a defined *terroir*, but to particular wines that must satisfy the most rigorous criteria of quality and that are selected by expert tastings. The wines must be submitted to a second tasting before they are bottled. The châteaux are selected from the Saint-Emilion Grands Crus and the wines are then classified. In 1986 74 were classified, of which 11 were Premiers Grands Crus. In the 1996 classification 68 were classified and 13 were Premiers Grands Crus. They divide into two groups: A for two of them (Ausone and Cheval Blanc) and B for the other eleven. It is worth pointing out that the Union des Producteurs de Saint-Emilion is without question the largest Cave Cooperative in France to be located in a top AOC. In 2000 Saint-Emilion produced 100,141 hl (3,126,500 gal) and Saint-Emilion Grand Cru produced 175,180 hl (4,624,752).

The Hachette tastings were in two parts in the Appellation Saint-Emilion Grand Cru. One team tasted the Saint-Emilion Grands Crus Classés (without separating out the Premiers Crus), while a different team tasted the Saint-Emilion Grands Crus. The stars printed correspond to these two sets of criteria.

Saint-Emilion

CH. BARBEROUSSE
■ Cuvée Prestige 1998

| | 1 ha | 3,600 | ☐ €11-15 |

This tiny *cuvée* comes from old Merlot selected in the vineyard, vinified with care and matured in new oak for 15 months. The ruby

Saint-Emilion

colour has garnet glints, and the aromas of stewed red berries in the nose are dominated by toasty notes of new oak. The palate is delightfully mouth-filling, with round, rich, lingering and very mature tannins. This wine should be kept for two or three years until it achieves a better balance. The **Cuvée Principale 98** is recommended.

• GAEC Jean Puyol et Fils, Ch. Barberousse, 33330 Saint-Emilion, tel. 05.57.24.74.24, fax 05.57.24.62.77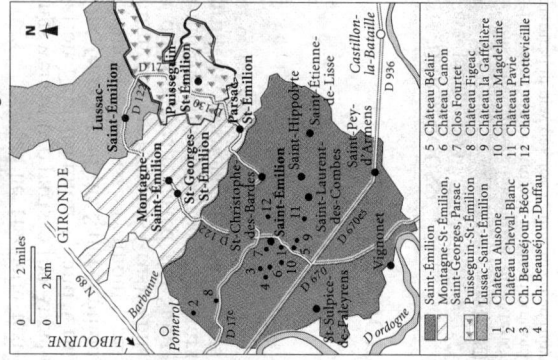
☎ by appt.

CH. BARRAIL-DESTIEU
Elevé en fût de chêne 1998

■ 1.17 ha 6,000 ▮▮▮ ♦ €8-11

This very small vineyard comprises equal shares of Merlot and Cabernet Franc, which are grown biodynamically on clay soils at the foot of a hillside. It was bought in 1995 by an owner from the neighbouring appellation of Côtes de Castillon, and now offers a very good 98 with a clear, brilliant garnet colour. The bouquet is dominated by toasty notes of high-quality oak and empyreumatic aromas. The supple, balanced palate is slightly marked by maturation in oak, but should become integrated in one to two years' time.

• GAEC Verger Fils, 4, chem. de Beauséjour, 33350 Saint-Magne-de-Castillon, tel. 05.57.40.13.14, fax 05.57.40.34.06
☎ by appt.

CH. BERTINAT LARTIGUE 1998

■ n.c. 15,000 ▮▮▮ ♦ €8-11

Danielle and Richard Dubois are wine-makers and oenologists, and produce this Saint-Emilion from 35-year-old vines grown on a ferruginous sand and gravel soil. The wine has a delightful ruby and carmine colour, and a nose which is still fresh, releasing aromas of fruit (cherries) and spices along with a touch of violets. The velvety palate is structured by peppery tannins, which give it an interesting character. This wine will be ready to drink in two to four years' time, and will go well with dishes such as roast veal in a cream sauce.

• Richard Dubois, Ch. Bertinat Lartigue, 33330 Saint-Sulpice-de-Faleyrens, tel. 05.57.24.72.75, fax 05.57.74.45.43, e-mail dubricru@aol.com
☎ ev. day 9am–11.30am 2.30pm–5.30pm; Sat. Sun. by appt.; cl. 14 Aug.–3 Sep.

CH. BEZINEAU 1998★★

■ 1.5 ha 7,000 ▮▮▮ ♦ €8-11

This Château Bézineau comes from a selection of 1.5 ha (4 acres) out of the 10 ha (25 acres) that the Faure family have been growing for more than six generations; the sandy *terroir* is planted with 80% Merlot and 20% Bouchet. Our experts liked this 98 wine's beautiful Bordeaux colour and its complex, intense bouquet of crystallised fruit, *pain d'épice* (spice loaf), fine oak and toast notes. The palate is very rich, with flavours of red berries, spices and cinnamon, and is structured by high-quality oaky tannins which do not mask the fruit. This will be an ideal accompaniment to magret of duck.

• SCEA vignobles Faure, Ch. Bézineau, 33330 Saint-Emilion, tel. 05.57.24.72.50, fax 05.57.24.72.50 ☎ by appt.

CH. BOIS CARDINAL 1998

■ 10 ha 10,000 ▮▮▮ €8-11

This cru was created in 1990, and is the second wine at Château La Fleur Cardinale. It is produced from Cabernet Sauvignon and 70% Merlot grown on clay-limestone soils with a rocky subsoil. This 98 wine has a lovely, ruby colour, which is fresh, lively and very intense. Its aromas of red berries and slight vegetal notes are embellished by a pleasant note of burnt liquoricy oak. The tannic structure is firm and as yet somewhat severe, but the tannins should rapidly become more refined. This wine should be kept for three to four years.

• Alain et Claude Asséo, Ch. Fleur Cardinale, 33330 Saint-Etienne-de-Lisse, tel. 05.57.40.14.05, fax 05.57.40.28.62, e-mail fleurcardinale@terre-net.fr
☎ by appt.

CH. BOIS GROULEY 1998

■ 6 ha 15,000 ▮▮▮ €8-11

This 98 wine is made from 60% Merlot, 30% Cabernet Franc and 10% Cabernet Sauvignon grown on a sand and gravel soil. It has a strong, intense, garnet colour and a very pleasant nose of crystallised red-berry aromas mingled with spicy nuances and notes of leather. The supple, round, full-bodied palate has velvety tannins and a very good structure. The wine can be kept for a year or two, or drunk straight away.

The Saint-Emilion region

Saint-Emilion
Montagne-Saint-Emilion
Saint-Georges, Parsac
Puisseguin-Saint-Emilion
Lussac-Saint-Emilion

1 Chateau Ausone
2 Chateau Cheval-Blanc
3 Ch. Beauséjour-Bécot
4 Ch. Beauséjour-Duffau
5 Chateau Bélair
6 Chateau Canon
7 Clos Fourtet
8 Chateau Figeac
9 Chateau la Gaffelière
10 Chateau Magdelaine
11 Chateau Pavie
12 Chateau Trottevieille

↝ Raymonde Lusseau, 276, Bois Grouley, 33330 Saint-Sulpice-de-Faleyrens, tel. 05.57.24.74.03, fax 05.57.24.67.19 ▼ by appt.

CH. CLOS JEAN VOISIN 1998

3.05 ha | 13,000 | €8-11

This wine is made half from Merlot and half from the Cabernets grown on old sands, and has a clear, light garnet colour with developed glints. The bouquet combines aromas of fresh and slightly acid red berries and musky leather notes with some fresh, vegetal nuances, and the structure is balanced, but the tannins and the finish are still firm. This wine should be allowed to age for two to three years before it is opened.

↝ Jacques Sautarel, Ch. Clos Jean Voisin, 33330 Saint-Emilion, tel. 05.57.24.67.10, fax 05.57.24.67.12 ▼ ▼ by appt.

CLOS LE BREGNET 1998

7 ha | 10,000 | €5-8

This fine, 13.5-ha (33.5-acre) property devotes 7 ha (17.3 acres) to making a Saint-Emilion wine and the remainder to making a Bordeaux. The well-balanced varietal blend (70% Merlot, 20% Cabernet Franc and 10% Cabernet Sauvignon, grown on sand and gravel) has yielded a pleasing 98, with a good, bright, garnet colour that is showing signs of development. The subtle, delicate nose combines fruity aromas with musky, leathery scents. The well-balanced palate is sustained by supple, silky tannins. Ready to drink now, this is a simple, honest wine.

↝ EARL Vignobles Coureau, Le Brégnet, 33330 Saint-Sulpice-de-Faleyrens, tel. 05.57.24.76.43, fax 05.57.24.76.43 ▼
▼ ev. day except Sun. 9am–12 noon 1.30–7pm

LE DE DASSAULT 1998*

10.33 ha | 48,000 | €11-15

Launched with the 97 vintage, this label replaces Château Mérissac as Château Dassault's second wine. A blend of two-thirds Merlot with one-third Cabernet from the youngest vines on the estate, this 98 is very pleasant. The ruby colour indicates good quality and has a vivid, deep purple glints. The bouquet is fresh and fruity, with spicy notes and a discreet oakiness. The tannins are obvious, but well rounded, giving excellent structure. Although ready to drink now, the wine will improve if it is aged for two to three years.

↝ SARL Ch. Dassault, 33330 Saint-Emilion, tel. 05.57.55.10.00, fax 05.57.55.10.01, e-mail lbv@chateaudassault.com ▼ ▼ by appt.

EPICURE Elevé en fût de chêne 1998*

n.c. | 20,000 | €8-11

Epicure is a brand belonging to the business owned by two Bordeaux personalities, the wine-merchants Bernard Pujol and Hubert de Boüard. They offer some interesting selections, including this very successful Saint-Emilion. Dark in colour, its nose, although still somewhat restrained, has a fruity, oaky richness. The palate has good body but finishes on tannins that are a little austere and will require several months' more ageing.

↝ Bordeaux Vins Sélection, 27, rue Roullet, 33800 Bordeaux, tel. 05.57.35.12.35, fax 05.57.35.12.36, e-mail bus.grands.crus@wanadoo.fr ▼

CH. FLEUR BADON 1998

4.38 ha | 21,066 | €8-11

This small vineyard, on siliceous soils at Saint-Laurent-des-Combes in the south-east of the appellation, is planted with 77% Merlot and 23% with Cabernets. A light, brick-red colour, the wine has an expressive nose that combines musky aromas and hints of undergrowth. The palate is mouth filling, with flavours of fruits and spices (green peppercorns) with minty nuances, in all, a surprising but interesting wine.

↝ Union de producteurs de Saint-Emilion, Haut-Gravet, BP 27, 33330 Saint-Emilion, tel. 05.57.24.70.71, fax 05.57.24.65.18, e-mail udp-vins.saint-emilion@gofornet.com
▼ ev. day except Sun. 8am–12 noon 2–6pm
↝ SCEA Vignobles Bost

CH. FRANCS BORIES 1998*

9.58 ha | 52,533 | €8-11

This vineyard at Vignonet, in the south of the appellation, is planted with 80% Merlot and 20% of the two Cabernets. The wine has an attractive, fresh colour and very ripe fruits on the nose, together with a gamey note. The rounded, well-balanced palate is pleasantly fruity, finishing on fine tannins.

↝ Union de producteurs de Saint-Emilion, Haut-Gravet, BP 27, 33330 Saint-Emilion, tel. 05.57.24.70.71, fax 05.57.24.65.18, e-mail udp-vins.saint-emilion@goiornet.com
▼ ev. day except Sun. 8am-12 noon 2–6pm
↝ J.-Cl. Arnaud and Gilles Roux

CH. GERBAUD 1998

n.c. | 5,000 | €8-11

The Chabrol family has owned this beautiful 15-hectare (37-acre) property since 1956. The wine is likeable both for its ruby colour with brick-red highlights and for its fruity, spicy aromas. The rounded palate reveals a persistent cherry flavour. The tannic structure is still a little firm, but that will allow this Saint-Emilion to be aged for a year or two.

↝ Patricia Chabrol, Ch. Gerbaud, 33330 Saint-Pey-d'Armens, tel. 06.03.27.00.32, fax 05.57.47.10.53, e-mail chateaugerbaud@wanadoo.fr ▼
▼ by appt.

CH. HAUTES VERSANNES 1998

13.61 ha | 80,000 | €8-11

Vinified by the co-operative at Saint-Emilion, this wine comes from a family-owned vineyard planted on the sandy gravel of Saint-Sulpice-de-Faleyrens. The supple, pleasant wine has an attractive ruby colour with orangey highlights, and it releases minty aromas when it is swirled in the glass. Its spicy palate would make it a fine accompaniment to grilled lamb chops.

Union de producteurs de Saint-Emilion, Haut-Gravet, BP 27, 33330 Saint-Emilion, tel. 05.57.24.70.71, fax 05.57.24.65.18, e-mail udp-vins.saint-emilion@gofornet.com

ev. day except Sun. 8am–12 noon 2–6pm

J.-Pierre et J.-Paul Lacoste

CH. HAUT GROS CAILLOU 1998   6 ha   43,000   €11-15

Making its first appearance in the *Guide* with its 93 vintage, this cru derives from sandy and limestone-clay soil planted with three-fifths Merlot to two-fifths Cabernet vines. This 98 shows signs of development in its garnet colour, orangey highlights and bouquet of stewed fruits, spices and good vanilla oak. Supple, rounded and well balanced, the wine has a pleasant length of flavour and is ready to drink now.

SCEA Haut Gros Caillou, 33330 Saint-Sulpice-de-Faleyrens, tel. 05.56.62.66.16, fax 05.56.76.93.30

by appt.

Alain Thiénot

CH. HAUT-RENAISSANCE 1998★   2.5 ha   16,000   €8-11

This château, which is no stranger to *coups de coeur*, this year offers a Saint-Emilion made from Merlot planted on limestone-clay and matured in a 17th-century barrel store. The tasters liked the wine's ruby colour and subtle yet powerful nose with overtones of black fruits and charred oak. The full, rounded structure demonstrates excellent balance between the fruit and the oak. With its long vanilla palate and liquorice finish, this rich wine will, in a few years' time, be good with coq au vin, beef stew or game.

SCEA des Vignobles Denis Barraud, Ch. Haut-Renaissance, 33330 Saint-Sulpice-de-Faleyrens, tel. 05.57.84.54.73, fax 05.57.84.52.07, e-mail denis.barraud@wanadoo.fr

by appt.

CH. HAUTS-MOUREAUX 1998   10.19 ha   74,666   €8-11

The vineyard at Saint-Etienne-de-Lisse consists of 86% Merlot and 14% Bouchet (Cabernet Franc) vines, grown on siliceous clay. The wine has a quite intense ruby colour. Supple and soft, it can be drunk fairly soon, perhaps with roast chicken.

Union de producteurs de Saint-Emilion, Haut-Gravet, BP 27, 33330 Saint-Emilion, tel. 05.57.24.70.71, fax 05.57.24.65.18, e-mail udp-vins.saint-emilion@gofornet.com

ev. day except Sun. 8am–12 noon 2–6pm

Vignobles Courrèche et Fils

CH. HAUT VEYRAC 1998★   7.5 ha   44,000   €8-11

This cru, located on the limestone-clay *terroirs* of Saint-Etienne-de-Lisse, is made up of three-quarters Merlot to one-quarter Cabernet Franc. It offers an intensely red 98 with very fresh, deep purple highlights. The powerful, complex nose contains notes of ripe red fruits. The palate reveals rounded, velvety tannins, which provide a long finish. Two to three years of ageing are required for this wine to reach its best.

SCA Ch. Haut Veyrac, 33330 Saint-Etienne-de-Lisse, tel. 05.57.40.02.26, fax 05.57.40.37.09

ev. day except Sun. Mon. 9.30am–6pm

G. Claverie, J. Castaing

CH. JUPILLE CARILLON
Elevé en fût de chêne 1998   n.c.   10,000

This charterhouse has been managed by Isabelle Visage since 1997, and the wine comes from her family's 9-ha (22.2-acre) vineyard. The dark soil, made up of sand and gravel, is planted with 85% Merlot. This ruby-coloured 98 has brick-red highlights and a pleasing nose of vanilla and menthol. The fresh palate reveals flavours of red fruits and spices, structured by tannins that are still a shade over-firm. Wait a while before drinking this wine with braised lamb or cheese.

SCEA des Vignobles Visage, Jupille, 33330 Saint-Sulpice-de-Faleyrens, tel. 05.57.24.62.92, fax 05.57.24.69.40

by appt.

CH. LA CAZE BELLEVUE 1998   9.3 ha   45,000   €5-8

This cru, which is from a 9.3-ha (23-acre) vineyard planted with 80% Merlot and 20% Cabernet Franc grown on a dark, sandy and gravelly soil, has made a very characteristic 98 wine. The nose combines red fruits (cherry and raspberry) with spicy nutmeg and violet notes. Initial impressions on the palate are of richness and fleshiness, leading to a tannic development that is unctuous but still a trifle over-firm. It is a wine to lay down for two or three years.

Philippe Faure, 7, rue de la Cité, 33330 Saint-Sulpice-de-Faleyrens, tel. 05.57.74.41.85, fax 05.57.74.41.85

by appt.

CH. DE LA COUR 1998★   n.c.   23,816   €8-11

Bought in 1995 by the young agriculturist Hugues Delacour, this cru has acquired a record for consistency. The château name honours a family ancestor and landowner, a Chevalier de la Cour who served under King Charles IX. This highly presentable 98, with its dark ruby colour, is redolent of the well-ripened red fruits that typify the Merlot variety, which accounts for 90% of the wine's blend. There is a good, rich structure, which fills the mouth well, although the finish is still a little austere. This is a wine that will be best appreciated in a few years' time.

EARL du Châtel Delacour, Ch. de La Cour, 33330 Vignonet, tel. 05.57.84.64.95, fax 05.57.84.65.00 by appt.

CH. LA CROIX BONNELLE 1998

3 ha   18,000   ■■ ♦   €8-11

Produced from the estate's youngest vines, which are grown on siliceous clay in the south-east of the appellation, this is Château La Bonnelle's second wine. It is a fresh, pleasing 98, with a vivid ruby hue and straightforward on the nose with fruity aromas. The rounded, supple palate is well structured. The slightly firm finish calls for a year's ageing.
- Vignobles Sulzer, La Bonnelle, 33330 Saint-Pey-d'Armens, tel. 05.57.47.15.12, fax 05.57.47.16.83 ☑
- ⟁ by appt.

CH. LA CROIX FOURCHE MALLARD Vieilli en fût de chêne 1998

2.5 ha   n.c.   €11-15

This cru of 2.5 ha (6 acres), which is mainly Merlot with a supplement of 10% of the two Cabernets and grown on sands and gravel, was acquired in the 1970s by the Mallard family, who came from the Entre-Deux-Mers and Sauternes districts. This 98 is a lovely vivid, intense red with deep purple highlights. The nose marries nuances of ripe fruits with aromas from the oak: vanilla, toast and spices. Appearing quite soft and fleshy to begin with, the tannins build on the palate and are a little firm on the finish. The wine needs another two or three years to achieve a proper balance.
- Danièle Mallard.
Ch. Naudonnet-Plaisance, 33760 Escoussans, tel. 05.56.23.93.04, fax 05.57.34.40.78, e-mail mallard@net-courrier.com ☑
- ⟁ by appt.

CH. LA FLEUR GARDEROSE 1998

1.56 ha   11,000   ■■ ♦   €8-11

Situated just outside Libourne, this cru is planted with two-thirds Merlot and one-third of the two Cabernets. It has produced an attractive 98 with a vivid ruby hue and a subtle, delicate bouquet, which is already charmingly expressive. The palate is soft and silky, warming and well structured, with dense tannins that are still somewhat over-firm. Keep for two to four years.
- GAEC Pueyo Frères, 15, av. de Gourinat, 33500 Libourne, tel. 05.57.51.71.12, fax 05.57.51.82.88, e-mail contact@belregard-figeac.com ☑ ⟁ by appt.

CH. LAGARDE BELLEVUE Vieilli en fût de chêne 1998★

1 ha   6,500   ■■   €8-11

From a tiny cru of 1 ha (2.5 acres) on deep sands mixed with gravel, this 98 is composed of four-fifths Merlot and one-fifth Cabernet Franc. The wine has excellent body, indicated by its attractive, deep ruby colour, and an emerging nose, which evokes red fruits with high-quality, oaky notes. The structure is sustained by rich, ripe tannins balanced by long-lasting flavours of fruits and liquorice. Very characteristic of the region, the wine should be left to age for two to three years or longer.
- SARL SOVIFA, 36 A, rue de la Dordogne, 33330 Saint-Sulpice-de-Faleyrens, tel. 05.57.24.68.83, fax 05.57.24.63.12 ☑ ⟁ by appt.
- Richard Bouvier

CH. LE MAINE 1998★★

4 ha   22,000   ■ ♦   €8-11

Located on sandy clay at Saint-Pey-d'Armens in the south-east of the appellation, this family property grows 80% Merlot and 20% Cabernet Franc. This remarkable 98 exhibits a sumptuous garnet colour and exhales powerful aromas of red fruits, which dominate fresher notes of liquorice and violet. The full, fleshy palate is well-structured with long-lasting, rich, velvety tannins. To get the best out of this delightful wine, lay it down for two to three years.
- Chantal Veyry, Ch. Maine-Reynaud, 33330 Saint-Pey-d'Armens, tel. 05.57.24.74.09, fax 05.57.24.64.81 ☑
- ⟁ by appt.

CH. LE SABLE Cuvée Prestige Elevé en fût de chêne 1998★

1.06 ha   6,000   ■   €11-15

This limited-production wine is made from 80% old Merlot and 20% Cabernet vines, vinified in the traditional way and matured in oak casks. A lovely ruby colour with deep purple highlights, this 98 has a subtle nose, with aromas of red fruits and toast. The palate is robust and well structured, and the powerful tannins, which are a trifle harsh for the moment, will gradually soften, given several years' ageing. The **Cuvée Principale**, which is not oak-matured but full of red fruitiness, also impressed the Jury.
- SARL Cave de Larchevesque, 1, rue Guadet, 33330 Saint-Emilion, tel. 05.57.24.67.78, fax 05.57.24.71.31 ☑
- ⟁ ev. day 10am-12.30pm 1.30-7pm
- Viaud

CH. LES MAURINS 1998★

2.5 ha   3,000   ■   €5-8

Chantal Pargade tends this small vineyard, which was planted by her father in 1981. A blend of Merlot (70%) and Cabernets (30%) has produced a wine with a youthful, intense colour and a bouquet redolent of fruit (blackcurrant) and spices. The fresh, rounded palate possesses promising tannins, which will need to soften further in the bottle before they reach their best. This wine will go well with red meats or cheeses.
- Chantal Pargade, 172, Les Maurins, 33330 Saint-Sulpice-de-Faleyrens, tel. 05.57.24.62.84, fax 05.57.24.62.84, e-mail ludovic.pargade@free.fr ☑
- ⟁ by appt.

CH. LES VIEUX MAURINS Cuvée
Prestige Vieilli en fût de chêne 1998★★

■ 1 ha 5,000 ⅢⅠ €11-15

This experiment was a masterstroke by the Goudal family, who devoted 1 ha (2.5 acres) of their 8-ha (20-acre) property to very old Merlot to produce this superbly oak-aged wine. The Jury was immediately attracted by the wine's remarkably intense, dense appearance, with depths of pure black and violet glints at the surface. The highly concentrated nose is still a little closed, but it already hints at aromas of jammy fruits, vanilla and violet that should soon evolve. No less concentrated, the fleshy palate possesses rich, substantial tannins that are long and flavoursome. This is definitely one to lay down.

→ Michel et Jocelyne Goudal,
Les Vieux-Maurins,
33330 Saint-Sulpice-de-Faleyrens,
tel. 05.57.24.62.96, fax 05.57.24.65.03,
e-mail les-vieux-maurins@wanadoo.fr ☑
Ⴤ by appt.

CH. LES VIEUX MAURINS 1998★

■ 7 ha 40,000 ◫ ♣ €8-11

Located on sandy soil with a limestone subsoil, this cru of 70% Merlot presents a successful, ruby-coloured 98. The nose, although still reticent, releases aromas of jammy, ripe, soft red fruit. The concentrated palate has rich, round tannins and a long finish, guaranteeing it a good future.

→ Michel et Jocelyne Goudal,
Les Vieux-Maurins,
33330 Saint-Sulpice-de-Faleyrens,
tel. 05.57.24.62.96, fax 05.57.24.65.03,
e-mail les-vieux-maurins@wanadoo.fr ☑
Ⴤ by appt.

CH. MONTREMBLANT 1998

■ 1 ha 5,000 ⅢⅠ €5-8

This unpretentious 98 has an attractive, characteristic, dark garnet colour. The nose is developing with aromas of jammy fruit and smoky notes. The well-balanced palate has agreeable, supple, silky tannins. Drink over the next three or four years.

→ GAEC Puyol, Ch. Montremblant,
33330 Saint-Emilion, tel. 05.57.24.74.24,
fax 05.57.24.62.77 ☑ Ⴤ by appt.

MOULIN DE SARPE 1998

■ 4 ha 25,000 ⅢⅠ €11-15

The Moulin de Sarpe was built on these limestone-clay soils in 1732 and belongs to the Association des Moulins de France. This pleasant 98 shows signs of development and on airing, undergrowth and red fruit aromas are released. The palate is supple, fresh and long-lasting with well-balanced tannins and a spicy flavour of nutmeg. Keep for two or three years.

→ Sté d'Exploitation du Ch. Haut-Sarpe,
BP 192, 33506 Libourne Cedex,
tel. 05.57.51.41.86, fax 05.57.51.53.16,
e-mail info@j-janoueix-bordeaux.com ☑
Ⴤ by appt.

CH. MOULIN DES GRAVES 1998

■ 9.05 ha 68,000 ◫ ♣ €8-11

This vineyard lies in the south of the AOC, near the small town of Vignonet, on iron-bearing sands and gravel. The blend of grape varieties is dominated by old Merlots with 10% of both Cabernet Franc and Cabernet Sauvignon. The result is a characteristic 98 with a deep, dark-ruby colour. It has agreeable, fresh aromas of soft red and dark berry fruit with pronounced cherry and black-currant. The well-balanced palate reveals good roundness and a well-made tannic structure. This pleasant and genuine Saint-Emilion may be drunk now or kept for up to three years.

→ EARL des Vignobles J.-F. Musset,
20, d'Arthus, 33330 Vignonet,
tel. 05.57.84.53.15, fax 05.57.84.53.15 ☑
Ⴤ by appt.

PAVILLON DU HAUT ROCHER
1998

■ 2 ha 14,900 ◫ ♣ €8-11

This label, created in 1874 by Jean de Monteil's great-grandfather, was revived in 1991 as the second wine of Château Haut-Rocher (a Saint-Emilion Grand Cru). This attractive 98's freshness is reflected in its vivid ruby colour with deep purple and mauve highlights. The flavourful nose has notes of soft red fruit, nut kernel and plums. It is well balanced by slightly firm and vigorous tannins that need several years in the cellar to soften.

→ Jean de Monteil, Ch. Haut Rocher,
33330 Saint-Etienne-de-Lisse,
tel. 05.57.40.18.09, fax 05.57.40.08.23,
e-mail ht.rocher@vins-jean-de-monteil.com
☑ Ⴤ by appt.

CH. PEREY-GROULEY 1998

■ 4.5 ha 30,000 ⅢⅠ ♣ €5-8

Florence and Alain Xan's vineyard covers 14.5 ha (35.8 acres). This cru consists of 90% Merlot planted on sandy-gravel soil in the south of the AOC. This brilliant, clear, garnet-coloured 98 already has characteristic aromas of soft red fruit on the nose but should open up fully in two to three years. On the palate it is supple, silky, delicate, fresh and fruity with a slight lack of concentration, compensated for by its remarkably vinosity.

♠ Vignobles Florence et Alain Xans, Percy, 33330 Saint-Sulpice-de-Faleyrens, tel. 06.80.72.84.87, fax 05.57.24.63.61 ☑
Y by appt.

PETIT CORBIN-DESPAGNE 1998

1 ha 4,000 €8-11

This is Château Grand Corbin-Despagne's second wine, from a hectare (2.47 acres) of young Merlot vines, produced in a limited edition of 4,000 bottles. It is an approachable, well-made wine with a fresh, youthful colour, a nose that is still slightly closed and a characteristic, well-balanced palate without any oakiness. Wait a while before drinking.

♠ SCEV Consorts Despagne, 33330 Saint-Emilion, Ch. Grand Corbin Despagne, 33330 Saint-Emilion, tel. 05.57.51.08.38, fax 05.57.51.29.18, e-mail grand-corbin-despagne.com
Y by appt.

CH. ROCHER-FIGEAC 1998

4 ha 24,000

Located at the gates of Libourne on gravel mixed with iron deposits, this family property was established around 1880. This pleasant 98 has a straightforward, lively ruby colour. Its restrained nose has an underlying complexity

CH. PEYROUQUET 1998

19.48 ha 91,708 €8-11

This vineyard, with 79% Merlot, is planted on a siliceous *terroir* at Saint-Pey d'Armens in the south-east of the appellation. This ruby-coloured wine has orange highlights and aromas of ripe fruit and spices with a hint of musk. Round and well-balanced with good tannins and a fruity flavour, this wine is pleasant but could mature another two to three years.

♠ Union de producteurs de Saint-Emilion, Haut-Gravet, BP 27, 33330 Saint-Emilion, tel. 05.57.24.70.71, fax 05.57.24.65.18, e-mail udp-vins.saint-emilion@goformet.com
Y ev. day except Sun. 8am-12 noon 2pm-6pm
♠ Maurice Cheminade

CH. QUEYRON PATARABET 1998★

9.43 ha 52,933 €8-11

This estate in the south of the commune of Saint-Emilion has almost 10 ha (24.7 acres) of siliceous soil exclusively planted with Merlot. This wine has an attractive ruby colour and jammy, liquorice aromas of well-ripened grapes with pronounced soft red fruit. The round, silky palate also has flavours of ripe fruit, developing on a structure of well-balanced and lasting tannins. In a year or two this excellent Saint-Emilion will be a good accompaniment to game.

♠ Union de producteurs de Saint-Emilion, Haut-Gravet, BP 27, 33330 Saint-Emilion, tel. 05.57.24.70.71, fax 05.57.24.65.18, e-mail udp-vins.saint-emilion@goformet.com
Y ev. day except Sun. 8am-12 noon 2pm-6pm
♠ EARL Vignobles Itey

CH. VIEUX LABARTHE 1998

9.06 ha 68,266 €8-11

This vineyard at Vignonet, in the south of the appellation, belongs to the Martins' heirs. It has an intense cherry colour and a still rather closed nose. On airing it releases notes of soft red fruit and undergrowth. The lively palate has a good vinosity with slightly rustic tannins. This interesting 98 will go well in several years time with red meat.

♠ Union de producteurs de Saint-Emilion, Haut-Gravet, BP 27, 33330 Saint-Emilion, tel. 05.57.24.70.71, fax 05.57.24.65.18, e-mail udp-vins.saint-emilion@goformet.com
Y ev. day except Sun. 8am-12 noon 2pm-6pm
♠ GAEC de Labarthe

CH. VIEUX LARTIGUE 1998★★

6.14 ha 25,000 €11-15

This cru, 80% Merlot and 20% Cabernet Franc, is located on sandy-gravel soils and together with skilled wine-growing, wine-making and traditional maturation, has produced a remarkable 98 with a deep, dense red

CH. TOINET-FOMBRAUGE 1998

6.25 ha 6,000 €8-11

This family property was bought from Château Fombrauge a century ago. Its limestone-clay *terroir* is today planted with 80% Merlot and 20% Bouchet. This pleasant 98 has an attractive colour and a subtle nose with fresh, fruity aromas. It is supple and soft on the palate with a raspberry flavour and pleasantly developing tannins.

♠ Bernard Sierra, Ch. Toinet-Fombrauge, 33330 Saint-Christophe-des-Bardes, tel. 05.57.24.77.70, fax 05.57.24.76.49 ☑
Y ev. day 10am-12 noon 3pm-7pm

of spices, smoke, plum and violet and the supple palate is round and well-balanced with good structure. This wine will be ready to drink within the next two years.

♠ Jean-Pierre Tournier, Tailhas, 194, rte de Saint-Emilion, 33500 Libourne, tel. 05.57.51.36.49, fax 05.57.51.98.70 ☑
Y by appt.

DOM. DU SEME 1998★

1.44 ha 5,000 €8-11

This small cru of 1.44 ha (3.55 acres) was purchased in 1995 by the Mérias family, who run a vineyard in the neighbouring AOCs of Lussac and Montagne-Saint-Emilion. A single-variety Merlot, this agreeable 98 has been well-matured in oak. Lively and intense in appearance, it has expressive aromas of jammy ripe fruit and an attractive oakiness of grilled and smoky notes. The well-integrated palate has supple and silky tannins. This wine is well-balanced with exceptional length and has a delightful fresh flavour.

♠ SCEA du Moulin Blanc, Le Moulin Blanc, 33570 Lussac-Saint-Emilion, tel. 05.57.74.50.27, fax 05.57.74.58.88, e-mail chateau-moulin-blanc@wanadoo.fr
☑ Y by appt.
♠ Brigitte Mérias

colour. This wine has aromas of soft red fruit, well integrated oak with grilled notes and hints of vanilla and spices. The palate is fleshy and full with firm, rich tannins that will ensure a good future.

➤ SC du ch. Vieux Lartigue,
33330 Saint-Sulpice-de-Faleyrens,
tel. 05.57.55.38.03, fax 05.57.55.38.01 ▼
🍷 by appt.

CH. YON SAINT-CHRISTOPHE
1998★

■   1.94 ha   13.300   ■ ▲ €8-11

A notable entry for this small vineyard, situated on the sandy clay *terroir* of Saint-Christophe-des-Bardes, which is tended by Côtes de Bourg growers wishing to diversify their output. This wine has an attractive intense ruby colour and on airing releases floral and fruity notes of violet and jammy blackberry. The smooth, fresh palate has flavours of ripe grapes. In a year or two, this lovely 98 will be an excellent accompaniment to roast lamb or fillet of duck.

➤ GFA Rodet Recapet, Brulesécaille,
33710 Tauriac, tel. 05.57.68.40.31,
fax 05.57.68.21.27, e-mail cht.brulesecaille@freesbee.fr ▼ 🍷 by appt.

already extremely complex and an extraordinarily rich palate. Put simply, this wine is a perfect balance of the classic and the original, of very good grapes and excellent oak, of power and elegance. It was this elegance that most impressed the Jury. This wine has a great future ahead of it.

➤ Famille Vauthier, Ch. Ausone,
33330 Saint-Emilion, tel. 05.57.24.70.26,
fax 05.57.74.47.39

CH. BARDE-HAUT 1998★

■   8.35 ha   38.000   ■ ■ ▲ €38-46

	95		96	97 98

Bought by Sylviane Garcin-Cathiard in September 2000, this estate lies on limestone-clay soil. This excellent 98, a blend of 85% Merlot and 15% Cabernet Franc, has a beautiful ruby colour. The powerful nose has aromas of charred oak with notes of stewed fruit. The well-structured palate has dense, fleshy, velvety tannins and a long finish.

➤ SC Ch. Barde-Haut,
33330 Saint-Christophe-des-Bardes,
tel. 05.56.64.05.22, fax 05.56.64.06.98 ▼
🍷 by appt.
➤ S. Garcin-Cathiard

CH. D' ARCIE 1998

■   6.9 ha   45.066   ■ ■ ▲ €8-11

This vineyard, located on sandy and siliceous clay soils at Saint-Pey-d'Armens, consists of three-quarters Merlot and one quarter Cabernets. This is an elegant and agreeable 98 with a complex and pleasing nose of well-ripened fruit, dried fruit and undergrowth with a touch of vanilla. It is well-balanced and has a medium structure, a fleshy body and an attractive finish.

➤ Union de producteurs de Saint-Emilion,
Haut-Gravet, BP 27, 33330 Saint-Emilion,
tel. 05.57.24.70.71, fax 05.57.24.65.18,
e-mail udp-vins.saint-emilion@gofornet.com
🍷 ev. day except Sun. 8am–12 noon 2pm–6pm
➤ SCEA Vignobles Soupre

CH. AUSONE 1998★★★

■ 1er gd cru A   7 ha   24.000   ■ ■ €76

61	64	75	76	78	79	80	81	82	83	85	86
88		89		90	92	93		94		96	97	98		

Great wines, like this magnificent Ausone, stand out even in blind tastings. Its secret may lie in the 50-year-old vines (half Merlot, half Bouchet) planted to the south of the town on a limestone-clay hillside where vines have grown for 2,000 years. The Jury were ecstatic about this wine and unanimous in awarding it a *coup de coeur*. It has a sumptuous, brilliant Bordeaux colour, a developing nose which is

CH. DU BARRY 1998★★

■   10 ha   58.000   ■ ■ €11-15

89		90	91 92	93	95 98

Located on a deep gravel soil in the south of the AOC and tended by Daniel Mouty and his daughter, this cru was established at the beginning of the 20th century by Daniel's grandfather, who came from the Auvergne. The 1995 vintage won a *coup de coeur* and this dark, intense ruby coloured 98 is also remarkable. The nose is a good blend of delicate, elegant oakiness and fruity aromas. The palate is rich and well-balanced, flavoursome and well-structured with fine quality tannins, long and lasting on the finish. This classy wine can be kept for up to five years.

☞ SCEA Daniel Mouy, Ch. du Barry, 33330 Sainte-Terre, tel. 05.57.84.55.88, fax 05.57.74.92.99, e-mail daniel-mouty@wanadoo.fr ☑
Y ev. day except Sat. Sun. 8am–5pm

CH. DU BASQUE 1998
■ 12.39 ha   79,989

Located on a sandy-clay soil in the south-east of the AOC, this cru consists mainly of Merlot with 15% Cabernet. Simple and agreeable with an attractive ruby colour, this pleasant 98 has a vinous nose of stewed soft red fruit. The round, supple palate has a firm, lively and tannic structure that needs to mature.

☞ Union de producteurs de Saint-Emilion, Haut-Gravet, BP 27, 33330 Saint-Emilion, tel. 05.57.24.70.71, fax 05.57.24.65.18, e-mail udp-vins.saint-emilion@gofornet.com
Y ev. day except Sun. 8am-12 noon 2pm–6pm
☞ SCEA Ch. du Basque

CH. BEAU-SÉJOUR BÉCOT 1998★
■ 1er gd cru B   16.52 ha   n.c.   ⊞ +76

75 78 79 81 82 83 (86) 87 (88) 89
90 91 92 93 94 95 96 97 98

This prestigious wine-growing estate lies on a fossil-bearing limestone-clay terroir on the Saint-Martin-de-Mazerat plateau, immediately west of the old town and is planted with 40-year-old vines (70% Merlot, 30% Cabernets). The Gallo-Roman furrows carved down to the rock prove the presence of vines here 2,000 years ago. This characterful 98 is still made by the Bécot family and has a dark cherry colour. The nose with fruity aromas of cherry brandy has touches of charred oak with a hint of spice and musk. The tannins on the robust, well-structured palate are a little austere, but guarantee a great wine in five to ten years.

☞ SCEA Beau-Séjour Bécot, 33330 Saint-Emilion, tel. 05.57.74.46.87, fax 05.57.24.66.88 Y by appt.

CH. BELLEFONT-BELCIER 1998
■ 8 ha   42,000   ⊞ €15-23

95 96 97 98

This vineyard, situated on the south-facing limestone hillside at Saint-Laurent-des-Combes to the east of the appellation, presents this selection from 8 ha (19.76 acres) of the vineyard's total surface area of 13 ha (32.11 acres). The blend of grape varieties is characteristic of Saint-Emilion. This is a vivid and intense garnet-coloured wine with complex aromas of dark berry fruit and spicy oak. The palate has a pronounced flavour of oak with notes of vanilla and coconut. At the moment the nose is more agreeable than the palate, which should settle down with three to four years' ageing.

☞ SCI Bellefont-Belcier, 33330 Saint-Laurent-des-Combes, tel. 05.57.24.72.16, fax 05.57.74.45.06, e-mail bellefontbelcier@aol.com ☑
Y by appt.

CH. BELLISLE MONDOTTE 1998
■ 4.5 ha   19,000   ⊞ €15-23

This lovely, dark-ruby 98 is still slightly restrained. On the nose there are fresh fruity aromas and subtle notes of undergrowth. This wine has a pleasant liveliness on the well-balanced palate and a good structure. Unpretentious yet pleasing, it will soon be ready to drink, in contrast with last year's 97, which pleasantly surprised everyone with its ageing qualities. Where wine is concerned, one year can be very different from another!

☞ SCEA Héritiers Escure, 33330 Saint-Laurent-des-Combes, tel. 05.57.74.41.17 ☑ Y by appt.

CH. BELREGARD-FIGEAC 1998
■ 2.83 ha   18,000   ⊞ €11-15

89 90 93 94 95 96 98

Thirty-year-old vines (68% Merlot, 32% Cabernets), grown on sandy-gravel soils in the Figeac area, have produced this lovely, deep purple 98. It has flowery, fruity aromas with a hint of musk. The fresh palate has a round, velvety texture and a slightly gamey character. This wine will be ready in three to five years' time.

☞ GAEC Pueyo Frères, 15, av. de Gourinat, 33500 Libourne, tel. 05.57.51.71.12, fax 05.57.51.82.88, e-mail contact@belregard-figeac.com ☑ Y by appt.

CH. BERGAT 1998
■ Gd cru clas.   n.c.   ⊞ €23-30

92 93 95 96 97 98

Although limestone-clay soils are common in the Saint-Emilion region, this cru's blend of grape varieties is less so, the 45% Cabernets give this wine its own character. It has an excellent ruby colour with garnet highlights and the nose has intense aromas of ripe fruit and finely toasted oak followed with buttery notes and touches of hazelnut. A well structured palate with long oaky tannins. Open within two to six years according to taste.

☞ Indivision Castéja-Preben-Hansen, 33330 Saint-Emilion, tel. 05.56.00.00.70, fax 05.57.87.48.61

CH. BERLIQUET 1998★★
■ Gd cru clas.   n.c.   23,000   ⊞ €30-38

88 89 91 92 93 94 95 96 97 98

Berliquet faces south-southwest on the limestone-clay plateau of La Magdelaine, next to the medieval town. This remarkable 98 is the result of the tremendous efforts put into both the vineyard and the wine cellars since 1996. It has a deep, dense colour and powerful, classy aromas of ripe fruit with an elegant, grilled and toasted oakiness. The concentrated palate has rich and fleshy tannins. This is a high-class wine with a promising future.

Saint-Emilion Grand Cru

1996 CLASSIFICATION OF SAINT-EMILION GRANDS CRUS

SAINT-EMILION, PREMIERS GRANDS CRUS CLASSÉS

A Château Ausone
Château Cheval Blanc

Château Belair
Château Canon
Clos Fourtet
Château Figeac
Château La Gaffelière
Château Magdelaine
Château Pavie
Château Trottevieille

B Château Angelus
Château Beau-Séjour (Bécot)
Château Beauséjour
(Duffau-Lagarrosse)

SAINT-EMILION, GRANDS CRUS CLASSÉS

Château Balestard La Tonnelle
Château Bellevue
Château Bergat
Château Berliquet
Château Cadet-Bon
Château Cadet-Piolat
Château Canon-La Gaffelière
Château Cap de Mourlin
Château Chauvin
Clos des Jacobins
Clos de L'Oratoire
Clos Saint-Martin
Château Corbin
Château Corbin-Michotte
Couvent des Jacobins
Château Curé Bon La Madeleine
Château Dassault
Château Faurie de Souchard
Château Fonplégade
Château Fonroque
Château Franc-Mayne
Château Grand Mayne
Château Grand-Pontet
Château Guadet Saint-Julien
Château Haut-Corbin
Château Haut-Sarpe
Château La Clotte
Château La Clusière
Château La Couspaude

Château La Dominique
Château La Marzelle
Château Laniote
Château Larcis-Ducasse
Château Larmande
Château Laroque
Château Laroze
Château L'Arrosée
Château La Serre
Château La Tour du Pin-Figeac
(Giraud-Belivier)
Château La Tour du Pin-Figeac
(Moueix)
Château La Tour-Figeac
Château Le Prieuré
Château Les Grandes Murailles
Château Matras
Château Moulin du Cadet
Château Pavie-Decesse
Château Pavie-Macquin
Château Petit-Faurie-de-Soutard
Château Ripeau
Château Saint-Georges Côte
Pavie
Château Soutard
Château Tertre Daugay
Château Troplong-Mondot
Château Villemaurine
Château Yon-Figeac

→ Patrick de Lesquen, SCEA Ch. Berliquet, 33330 Saint-Emilion, tel. 05.57.24.70.48, fax 05.57.24.70.24 Y by appt.

CH. BERNATEAU
Elevé en fût de chêne 1998★

12 ha 80,000 | €11-15

This Grand Cru is selected from 12 ha (29.64 acres) of the total 18 ha (44.46 acres) that make up this lovely hillside vineyard, cultivated for more than three generations by the Lavau family. The limestone-clay soil is planted with 82% Merlot and 18% Cabernets. This deep ruby-coloured 98 has purple highlights. Fine and elegant with a discreet charm, the nose has aromas of fresh fruit and toasted oak. The rich and iridescent palate has a powerful finish and although the tannins are fine, they need three to four years to soften. This wine will go well with roast pigeon.

→ Lavau, Ch. Bernateau,
33330 Saint-Etienne-de-Lisse,
tel. 05.57.40.18.19, fax 05.57.40.27.31

CH. BOUTISSE 1998★

23 ha 86,000 | €15-23

Xavier and Gérard Milhade have great hopes for this newly-acquired vineyard on limestone-clay soil. This ruby 98 has deep-purple highlights and an expressive, elegant nose with ripe fruit, toast and caramel. The charming, well-balanced structure has a good finish. Wait three to four years for the oak to blend in.

→ SCE Dom. Boutisse,
33330 Saint-Christophe-des-Bardes,
tel. 05.57.55.48.90, fax 05.57.84.31.27

Y by appt.
→ Milhade

CH. CADET-BON 1998★★

|90| 92 93 |94| 95 (96) |97| 98
Gd cru clas. 4.48 ha 20,800 | €25-30

This cru is situated to the north of the medieval town on the limestone-clay soils of the Butte du Cadet and consists of 70% Merlot and 30% Cabernet Franc. After ten years, it was finally classified in 1996 and won a coup de coeur in the 2000 Guide. This remarkable 98 has a dense, lively red colour and is developing powerful, vinous aromas of well-ripened jammy fruit with spicy, charred notes of good oak. The palate is full, fleshy tannins and a lasting finish.

→ Loriene SA, 1, Le Cadet,
33330 Saint-Emilion, tel. 05.57.74.43.20,
fax 05.57.24.66.41, e-mail loriene@
cadet-bon.com Y by appt.

CH. CADET-PEYCHEZ 1998

1.2 ha 6,000 | €8-11

This small cru has links with the classified growth of Faurie de Souchard. It is situated on the edge of the medieval town and comprises 80% Merlot grapes to 20% Cabernet Franc on limestone-clay soil. This intense ruby-coloured 98 has attractive aromas of ripe and jammy, soft red fruit with a hint of spice. The palate is round and supple with a well-balanced structure and good vinosity. This is an elegant wine and should be ready to drink in two to three years' time.

→ Françoise Sciard, Ch. Faurie de Souchard, 33330 Saint-Emilion, tel. 05.57.74.43.80, fax 05.57.74.43.96
Y by appt.

CH. CAILLOU D'ARTHUS
Vieilli en fût de chêne 1998

2.9 ha n.c. | €8-11

This pleasant 98 is made and marketed by local wine merchants Cordier-Mestrezat. On the nose this simple, pleasing aromas of soft red fruit in syrup. Supple, round and charming on the palate, its slight lack of richness is compensated for by an attractive fruitiness and elegance. Enjoy this easy-drinking wine now or keep for two to three years.

→ Jean-Denis Salvert, Ch. Caillou d'Arthus,
33330 Vignonet, tel. 05.57.80.93.30
Y by appt.

CH. CANON 1998★★

|89| |90| |94| 96 97 98
1er gd cru B 14 ha 30,000 | €38-46

This cru belongs to the Wertheimer family, who are also owners of the Chanel company, so naturally this lovely 98 belongs to the world of luxury products. Unlike many blends of perfume this wine has no secret ingredients; a classic blend of grape varieties, 80% Merlot to 20% Cabernet Franc planted on a limestone-clay soil. Perhaps the secret ingredient is the 14 ha (34.58 acres) of underground quarries? This wine has a superb colour and an elegant and complex nose with touches of bilberry, oak, chocolate, vanilla and peony. The charming palate has fresh tannins that indicate good laying down potential.

→ SC Ch. Canon, 33330 Saint-Emilion,
tel. 05.57.55.23.45, fax 05.57.24.68.00
Y by appt.

CLOS CANON 1998★★

14 ha 35,000 | €15-23

This excellent 98 grabbed the tasters' attention, with its superb, dense and deep, dark-ruby colour. The elegant, complex nose has jammy, dark fruit aromas with a hint of spice. The well-integrated full, fleshy palate has silky, velvety tannins which follow through to the long finish with flavours of stewed fruit.

→ SC Ch. Canon, 33330 Saint-Emilion,
tel. 05.57.55.23.45, fax 05.57.24.68.00
Y by appt.

CH. CAP DE MOURLIN 1998★

(82) 83 85 86 88 |89| |90| 92 93 |94| 96 98
Gd cru clas. 13.81 ha 65,000 | €15-23

These siliceous-clay and limestone-clay soils are planted with 65% Merlot and 35% Cabernets. This superb, dense, deep ruby-coloured 98 has not yet come out of its shell. It has notes of overripe soft red fruit and an elegant oakiness on the nose. The palate is robust, well-structured and generous, with rich tannins that are long and lasting on the finish. This wine should be ready in three to five years' time. This cru has been in the Capdemourlin family since the 17th century.

➤ SCEA Capdemourlin, Ch. Roudier, 33570 Montagne, tel. 05.57.74.62.06, fax 05.57.74.59.34 ⊠ ⟁ by appt.

CH. CAPET DUVERGER 1998

◼ n.c. 36,000 ⟁ €8–11

The sandy and siliceous soils of this domaine in Saint-Hippolyte grow a well-proportioned mix of grape varieties. A blend of two-thirds Merlot with one-third Cabernets has produced this agreeable 98 with a brilliant, dark ruby colour. It has aromas of ripe fruit and spices with well-softened oaky notes. A well-balanced, good quality structure with substantial body, this wine should develop well over the next two to three years.

➤ Union de producteurs de Saint-Emilion, Haut-Gravet, BP 27, 33330 Saint-Emilion, tel. 05.57.24.70.71, fax 05.57.24.65.18, e-mail udp-vins.saint-emilion@ gofornet.com ⟁ ev. day except Sun. 8am–12 noon 2pm–6pm
➤ EARL Héritiers Duverger

CH. CARDINAL-VILLEMAURINE 1998★

◼ 7 ha n.c. ⟁ €11–15

This château, located in the centre of the town, has matured one-third of this wine in vat and the other two-thirds in oak. This wine is a blend of 70% Merlot and 30% Cabernets grown on limestone-clay soil. A lovely Bigarreau cherry-red, this excellent 98 has intense aromas of soft red fruit, Griotte cherry and toasted vanilla and oak on the nose and a harmonious, round palate with well-balanced fruit and wood flavours. This wine is characteristic of both the appellation and the vintage and can be drunk in the next five to ten years.

➤ Jean-François Carrille, pl. du Marcadieu, 33330 Saint-Emilion, tel. 05.57.24.74.46, fax 05.57.24.64.40, e-mail paul.carrille@ worldonline.fr ⟁ ⟁ by appt.

CH. CARTEAU COTES DAUGAY 1998★

◼ 14.59 ha 80,000 ⟁ €11–15

82 83 86 88 [89] [90] 92 93 [94] [95] [96] [97] 98

This cru is situated on the limestone-clay and sandy hillsides of the first Saint Emilion slopes one comes to, when coming from Libourne. It is planted with three-quarters Merlot and one-quarter Cabernets. Every year this château is awarded one or two stars by the *Guide*. This attractive 98 has a superb, velvety purple colour with deep purple highlights. The nose is a rich and elegant blend of soft red fruit and spiced bread with a

pleasant, well-integrated oakiness. The full, rich and fleshy palate has the powerful structure of a wine that is good for laying down. The finish is long, tasty and flavourful. One taster suggested that it will go well with entrecôte steak in a wine-based sauce.

➤ SCEA Vignobles Jacques Bertrand, Ch. Carteau, 33330 Saint-Emilion, tel. 05.57.24.73.94, fax 05.57.24.69.07 ⊠ ⟁ by appt.

CH. DU CAUZE 1998★

◼ 20 ha 100,000 ⟁ €11–15

85 88 89 90 92 93 [94] 95 97 98

20 ha (49.4 acres) of this 24-ha (59.28-acre) estate are allocated to the production of this wine, made from vines that are 40–50 years old (90% Merlot) grown on limestone-clay in the north east of the AOC. It has a very dark garnet colour and strong prune aromas with a leathery, oaky touch. On the fleshy, well-structured palate, the slightly austere tannins show promise. This wine needs between three to nine years in the cellar.

➤ Bruno Laporte-Bayard, SC du Ch. du Cauze, 33330 Saint-Emilion, tel. 05.57.74.62.47, fax 05.57.74.59.12 ⊠ ⟁ by appt.

CH. CHAMPION 1998

◼ 7 ha 32,000 ⟁ €8–11

93 94 [95] [96] 98

The Bourrigaud family have for many generations worked these two Grands Crus, which are situated north of the town. This soft, agreeable 98 has an attractive, intense ruby colour and aromas of soft red fruit with a hint of oak on the nose. Its round structure is supple and fairly fruity but the tannins are a little firm and need one to two years to soften.

➤ SCEA Bourrigaud et Fils, Ch. Champion, 33330 Saint-Christophe-des-Bardes, tel. 05.57.74.43.98, fax 05.57.74.41.07, e-mail contact@ chateau-champion.com ⊠ ⟁ by appt.

CH. CHANTE ALOUETTE 1998

◼ 5 ha 28,000 ⟁ €11–15

[96] [97] 98

This 5-ha (12.35-acre) cru of Merlot (80%) and Cabernet (20%) is situated on sandy soil. It was taken over by his son Benoît. This elegant 98 has a lovely, brilliant ruby colour and floral aromas and a touch of menthol. The well-balanced structure has round, supple tannins and a long finish. This characteristic wine needs to be kept for two to three years.

➤ Guy d'Arfeuille, Ch. Chante Alouette, 33330 Saint-Emilion, tel. 05.57.24.71.81, fax 05.57.24.74.82 ⟁ ev. day except Sun. 9am–12 noon 2pm–7pm

DOM. CHANTE ALOUETTE CORMEIL 1998

■
③② 83 85 86 88 89 90 91 93 94 95 98   n.c.   32,000   ■ 🍷 €11-15

The vineyard situated on sand and iron deposits, consists of two-thirds Merlot and one-third Cabernets. This wine has a lovely dark ruby colour with purple highlights. On airing, the nose, although still a little closed, releases aromas of prune and undergrowth with a hint of musk. A rich and powerful palate opens out quickly with strong tannins that are still slightly rustic and need two or three years to soften.

• EARL Vignobles Yves Delol, Ch. Gueyrosse, 33500 Libourne, tel. 05.57.51.02.63, fax 05.57.51.93.39 ✓
Y by appt.

CH. CHAUVIN 1998

■ Gd cru clas.   12.49 ha   50,000
82 85 86 88 89 90 93 |94| |96| 98

This family property was acquired in 1891, and today consists of 15 ha (37.05 acres) that are run by two sisters. It is located on sandy-gravel soils planted with 80% Merlot to 20% Cabernet. This beautiful intense garnet-coloured 98 has aromas of ripe and jammy soft red fruit and an attractive oakiness with grilled and smoky notes. The lively, firm palate has a slightly austere tannic structure but guarantees a good future.

• SCEA Ch. Chauvin, Les Cabannes-Nord, 33330 Saint-Emilion, tel. 05.57.24.76.25, fax 05.57.74.41.34 ✓
Y by appt.
• Mmes Ondet-Février

CH. CHEVAL BLANC 1998★★

■ 1er gd cru A   35 ha   90,000
61 64 66 69 70 71 72 73 74 |75| 76 77
|78| |79| 80 |81| |82| 83 |85| 86 87 88 89
|92| |93| 94 95 96 97 98   ■ +76

Since 1764 this almost-mythical cru has been much written about. However, for Albert Frère, the Belgian financier, and Bernard Arnault, president of LVMH, who have also invested in Yquem, this 98 is their first harvest. For the last ten years, Pierre Lurton, who comes from one of the Bordeaux region's most important wine-growing families, has been running the estate. This excellent 98 bears something of their stamp, being both powerful and refined. It has a Bordeaux red colour with ruby highlights around the edges. The powerful palate is fleshy and rich in lively tannins that will, in time, develop finesse. This great wine is full of promise.

• SC du Cheval Blanc, 33330 Saint-Emilion, tel. 05.57.55.55.55, fax 05.57.55.55.50 Y by appt.

CLOS DE LA CURE 1998

■   6.87 ha   41,000   ■ 🍷 €11-15
|93| 95 96 97 98

It is here that the priests of Saint-Christophe-des-Bardes used to make their

wine, and although these days are gone the *clos* still exists. Its excellent limestone-clay *terroir* is planted with 78% Merlot and 22% Cabernets. This agreeable 98 has lively purple highlights and a lively nose with charred notes. Although still fresh on the palate, the wine is developing with fine, mellow tannins. It is youthful at the moment, but in two to three years' time will go well with game, red meat and cheese.

• Christian Bouyer, Ch. Milon, 33330 Saint-Christophe-des-Bardes, tel. 05.57.24.77.18, fax 05.57.24.64.20 ✓
Y by appt.

CH. CLOS DE SARPE 1998

■   3.68 ha   10,711   ■ 🍷 €30-38

This 4-ha (9.88-acre) cru, which once belonged to Baron Foussat de Bogeron, was bought by the current owner's grandfather in 1923. Located on a limestone-clay plateau and farmed organically, it has mainly Merlot with 15% Cabernet Franc vines. A lovely garnet colour with crimson highlights, this interesting 98 has spicy fruit, oak and chocolate aromas on the nose. After a firm, robust attack it reveals a rather harsh structure which needs several years to soften.

• SCA Beyney, Ch. Clos de Sarpe, 33330 Saint-Christophe-des-Bardes, tel. 05.57.24.72.39, fax 05.57.74.47.54 ✓
Y by appt.

CLOS DES MENUTS 1998★

■   36 ha   n.c.   ■ 🍷 €15-23
88 89 90 91 |95| |96| 98

This large 36-ha (88.92-acre) domaine markets its entire production under the same name. The cellars, situated in the heart of Saint-Emilion are dug out of the rocks. This promising and characteristic 98 has a bright ruby colour and attractive fruity aromas with spicy notes on the nose. The supple, round palate is well-balanced and well-structured by firm tannins that last through to the finish.

• SCEV Pierre Rivière, Clos des Menuts, 33330 Saint-Emilion, tel. 05.57.55.59.59, fax 05.57.55.59.51, e-mail mriviere@riviere-stemilion.com ✓
Y ev. day 9am–12 noon 2pm–6pm

CLOS FOURTET 1998★★

■ 1er gd cru B   n.c.   65,000   ■ 🍷 €46-76
71 73 74 75 76 78 79 81 82 83 |85| 86
87 |88| |89| |90| |91| 92 |93| |94| ㊟ 96 97
98

This 1998 vintage celebrates the 51st and, at the same time, one of the last vintages at Clos Fourtet for the Lourton family, who purchased the estate in 1948 and sold it in 2001 to Philippe Cuvelier. Clos Fourtet, situated near the church, is an archetypal Saint-Emilion Grand Cru. It consists of 85% Merlot on limestone-clay soil and has three levels of magnificent cellars housed in a former quarry. This excellent wine has a rich peony colour with peony highlights and a concentrated, complex nose with floral, fruity aromas of redcurrant and bilberry, with a note of toasty

oak. The explosive, energetic, fleshy and generous palate achieves an attractive balance between the Merlot and the oak. The lively, fine tannins guarantee a good future.
↪ SC Clos Fourtet, 33330 Saint-Emilion, tel. 05.57.24.70.90, fax 05.57.74.46.52
Ⓨ by appt.
↪ M. Cuvelier

CH. CLOS LA GRACE DIEU 1998★
■ 2 ha 6,000 III €15-23

This is the first harvest for Odile Audier who bought this small vineyard to the west of the town, next to the family property of La Grâce-Dieu-les-Menuts, in 1997. The 40-year-old vines, 80% Merlot and 20% Cabernets, are planted on various soils, namely brown sand, sandy-clay and iron deposits. This wine impressed our tasters with its dark, attractive appearance, dark berry fruit aromas and elegant oak. The rich palate is long and well-integrated. Wait several years and serve with red meat in a wine sauce.
↪ Odile Audier, La Grâce Dieu, 33330 Saint-Emilion, tel. 05.57.24.73.10, fax 05.57.74.45.92 Ⓨ Ⓨ by appt.

CLOS LA MADELEINE 1998
■ 2 ha 10,000 III €23-30

These 30-year-old vines, 60% Merlot and 40% Bouchet, grow on limestone-clay soil south of the town. This attractive 98 has a fine, youthful nose with both fruitiness and oakiness. The round palate has a lovely liquorice flavour. This wine will be good to drink very shortly.
↪ SA du Clos La Madeleine, La Gaffelière Ouest, BP 78, 33330 Saint-Emilion, tel. 05.57.55.38.03, fax 05.57.55.38.01 Ⓨ by appt.

CLOS SAINT-JULIEN 1998★
■ 1.5 ha 5,000 III €23-30

This small plot in the middle of town is still partly surrounded by walls built to protect a statue of Pomona, the Roman goddess of fruit and gardens (sadly stolen a few years ago). This pleasing 98 has an intense dark purple colour with bright ruby highlights. The powerful and elegant nose has jammy fruit, mocha, cinnamon and liquorice aromas with grilled notes. The rich, powerful palate is well-structured with lovely smooth tannins that lead to a long, flavoursome finish.
↪ SCEA Vignobles J.-J. Nouvel,
Ch. Gaillard, BP 84, 33330 Saint-Emilion, tel. 05.57.24.72.05, fax 05.57.74.40.03, e-mail chateau.gaillard@wanadoo.fr Ⓨ by appt.

CLOS SAINT-MARTIN 1998★
■ Gd cru clas. 1.33 ha 6,500 III €30-38
81 85 86 88 89 |90| 92 93 |95| |96| |97| 98

Once the vineyard of Saint Martin's Parish Church, this small domaine acquired by the Reiffers family in 1850 has limestone-clay soils planted with Merlot (70%) and Cabernet Franc (30%). This lovely 98 has a dark, dense garnet colour and a powerful and elegant nose with ripe, soft red fruit, toast and charred oak. The fresh, well-balanced and harmonious palate has a fine, mellow oakiness, silky, well-presented tannins and a long finish.
↪ GFA Les Grandes Murailles, Ch. Côte de Baleau, 33330 Saint-Emilion,
tel. 05.57.24.71.09, fax 05.57.24.69.72, e-mail lesgrandesmurailles@wanadoo.fr
Ⓨ by appt.

CLOS SAINT-VINCENT 1998
■ 4.68 ha 28,000 III €8-11

This cru, dedicated to the patron saint of the wine-makers, grows on sandy-gravel soil in the south of the appellation. This straightforward, characteristic 98 has a clear, lively, ruby colour. Strawberry aromas blend agreeably with a fine, slightly grilled oak quality. The well-balanced palate is supple, round and fresh, supported by delicate, silky tannins. This wine can be drunk soon.
↪ SC du Clos Saint-Vincent, Lansemen, 33330 Saint-Sulpice-de-Faleyrens, tel. 05.56.23.92.76, fax 05.56.23.61.65 Ⓨ
Ⓨ by appt.
↪ Latorse

CLOS TRIMOULET 1998
■ n.c. 52,000 III €11-15

This wine from 35-year-old vines (80% Merlot) has an attractive dense ruby colour with garnet highlights. The delicate nose has aromas of soft red fruit and a hint of musk. The palate is fruity, supple and slightly sharp, finishing on tannins that, although a little rustic, should mellow in two to five years' time.
↪ EARL Appollot, Clos Trimoulet, 33330 Saint-Emilion, tel. 05.57.24.71.96, fax 05.57.44.85.88 Ⓨ by appt.

CH. CORBIN 1998
■ Gd cru clas. 12.7 ha 80,000 III €23-30
64 75 79 81 (82) 83 85 86 |88| |89| |90|
93 94 |95| |96| 98

This estate, situated north-west of the town, is planted with 30-year-old vines, Merlot (80%), Bouchet (17%) and Malbec (Cot) (3%) on old sandy-clay soil. This wine's lovely ruby colour is complemented by a fruity nose of prune and redcurrant with spicy, oaky and toasty notes and, on airing, a touch of musk. The fresh, round palate has fine oak tannins and good fruitiness.
↪ SC Ch. Corbin, 33330 Saint-Emilion, tel. 05.57.25.20.30, fax 05.57.25.22.00, e-mail chateau.corbin@wanadoo.fr Ⓨ by appt.

CH. CORMEIL-FIGEAC 1998
■ 10 ha 50,000 III €15-23
82 83 86 88 89 90 91 92 94 95 96 98

This vineyard, situated on ancient sandy soil 2.5 km (1.55 miles) west of the town, is planted with Merlot (70%) and Cabernet Franc (30%). This promising 98 is characteristic of the Figeac district. It has a ruby colour and slightly oaky aromas with soft red fruit and a fresh, lively palate finishing on firm tannins. Robust and slightly rustic, in two to five years' time this wine will be a good accompaniment to game and red meat.

♠ SCEA Cormeil-Figeac, tel. 05.57.24.70.53, 33330 Saint-Emilion, fax 05.57.24.68.20, e-mail moreaud@ cormeil-figeac.com ☑ ☉ by appt.

♠ R. Moreaud

CH. COTE DE BALEAU 1998★

88 |95| 96 |98|

■ 8 ha 40,000 €11-15

This property has been in the Reiffer family since 1643. It is planted on limestone-clay with three-quarters Merlot to one-quarter Cabernets. This interesting 98 has a lovely intense ruby colour with garnet highlights. The youthful nose is still dominated by vanilla and oak aromas. The round attack on the palate is followed by a well-balanced structure, but the fruit here is also slightly overwhelmed by the oak. This wine can be drunk in two to three years due to its modern style.

♠ GFA Les Grandes Murailles, Ch. Côte de Baleau, 33330 Saint-Emilion, tel. 05.57.24.71.09, fax 05.57.24.69.72, e-mail lesgrandesmurailles@wanadoo.fr ☑ ☉ by appt.

COTES ROCHEUSES 1998

■ 35 ha 218,527 €6-11

This blend of 60% Merlot to 40% Cabernets is the most important wine produced in volume from L'Union des Producteurs de Saint-Emilion. It has a lovely ruby colour with crimson highlights with fruity, spicy aromas on the nose which also has delicate oakiness. The structure is not very intense, however it is well-balanced and due to its supple, silky tannins can be drunk soon.

♠ Union de producteurs de Saint-Emilion, Haut-Gravet, BP 27, 33330 Saint-Emilion, tel. 05.57.24.70.71, fax 05.57.24.65.18, e-mail udp-vins.saint-emilion@ gofornet.com ☑ ☉ ev. day except Sun. 8am-12 noon 2pm-6pm.

CH. COUDERT-PELLETAN

Vieilli en fût de chêne neuf 1998

■ 4 ha 24,000

86 88 92 |93| |94| 95 96 97 98

Planted on limestone-clay, this vineyard's Merlot (60%) and Cabernets (40%) have produced a fine, dark, ruby-coloured wine. It has fresh notes of undergrowth and blackcurrant on the nose and a fruity palate with tannins that need several more years to soften. In short, this is a characteristic 98 vintage.

♠ Pierre et Philippe Lavau, Ch. Coudert-Pelletan, BP 13, 33330 Saint-Christophe-des-Bardes, tel. 05.57.24.77.30, fax 05.57.24.66.24, e-mail coudert.pelletan@worldonline.fr ☑ ☉ ev. day 9am-12.30pm 2pm-6pm; Sat. Sun. by appt.

COUVENT DES JACOBINS 1998★★

■ Gd cru clas. 7 ha 30,000 €46-76

This 13th-century former monastery, situated in the heart of the medieval town, was abandoned in the French Revolution. Today it has become a listed building with wonderful walls and deep underground cellars. The vineyard is three-quarters Merlot and one-quarter Cabernet Franc. This superb 98 has a bright colour and opens out immediately on the nose with aromas of fresh soft red fruit, nut kernels, almonds and spicy notes. The powerful, rich palate has dense, smooth tannins and a long finish.

♠ SCEV Joinaud-Borde, 10, rue Guadet, 33330 Saint-Emilion, tel. 05.57.24.70.66, fax 05.57.24.62.51

CH. CROIX DE VIGNOT 1998★

■ 1.45 ha 9,500 €8-11

This tiny cru of 50-year-old Merlot is planted at the bottom of a hillside of limestone-clay near the ancient 'Seigneurie de Capet'. This agreeable 98 has an attractive ruby colour and a fine, complex nose of fruity, floral aromas with vanilla and spices. There is a lovely roundness on its full palate. This is a well-made wine with real potential.

♠ René Micheau-Maillou, 33330 Saint-Hippolyte, tel. 05.57.24.61.99, fax 05.57.24.61.99 ☑ ☉ by appt.

CH. CROQUE MICHOTTE 1998★★

91 |95| 96 98

■ 13.67 ha 59,000 €23-30

This beautiful 14-ha (34.58-acre) domaine near Pomerol was acquired in 1906 by Samuel Geoffrion, the present owner's great-grandfather. This pleasant 98, made from Merlot with 10% Cabernet Franc, is grown on ancient sandy gravel. It has a clear ruby colour and notes of cocoa and dark berry fruit on the nose with palate is full and fleshy with dense, powerful tannins that follow through to the long finish.

♠ GFA Geoffrion, Ch. Croque Michotte, 33330 Saint-Emilion, tel. 05.57.51.13.64, fax 05.57.51.07.81 ☑ ☉ by appt.

CH. CROS-FIGEAC 1998★★

■ 2.5 ha 7,000 €23-30

Acquired in 1998, this is the Querre family's latest property. They plan to improve the quality of this cru within five years, and are already well on their way with this remarkable 98. Dark purple in appearance, its nose is concentrated and classy with aromas of dark berry fruit, morello cherry, leather and vanilla against an oaky background. The palate is also long and complex; although a little overpowered by the good-quality oak, it finishes with ripe, classy tannins. This is a wine for laying down.

♠ SCEA Ch. Cros-Figeac, Hospices de La Madeleine, 33330 Saint-Emilion, tel. 05.57.55.51.60, fax 05.57.55.51.61 ☑

Saint-Emilion Grand Cru

CH. CRUZEAU 1998★
■ 4.4 ha   28.000   ■■ €11-15

This 16th-century château with pointed turrets was acquired by the Luquot family in 1897. Its vineyard consists of three-quarters Merlot to one-quarter Cabernet Franc grown on coarse, sandy soil. This lovely 98 has an attractive, intense ruby colour and aromas of jammy fruit, plum and liquorice with notes of spices and grilled coffee. The full, supple attack is followed by a firm tannic structure that should soften over the next three to four years.

↠ SCEA Vignobles Luquot,
152, av. de l'Epinette, 33500 Libourne,
tel. 05.57.51.18.95, fax 05.57.25.10.59 ☑
Ⴤ by appt.

CH. DASSAULT 1998★
■ Gd cru clas.   14.48 ha   77.000   ■■ €30-38
83 86 88 89 |90| 92 |94| |95| 96 98

Marcel Dassault, a well-known industrial leader, used to enjoy serving his own wine during aeronautic displays given by the group he had founded. Run today by his grandson Laurent, this vineyard on ancient sandy soil is made up of Merlot (65%), Cabernet Franc (30%) and Cabernet Sauvignon (5%). This excellent 98 vintage has a superb, bright, black cherry colour and a fine, elegant nose with lovely aromas of jammy fruits and toasty, spicy notes. After a supple, round attack, the palate opens to reveal length, dense and silky soft tannins.

↠ SARL Ch. Dassault,
33330 Saint-Emilion, tel. 05.57.55.10.00,
fax 05.57.55.10.01, e-mail lbv@
chateaudassault.com Ⴤ by appt.

CH. DESTIEUX 1998★
■   8.12 ha   32.000   ■■ €15-23
85 86 |88| |89| |90| 92 93 |94| |95| 96 97
98

This 8-ha (19.76-acre) domaine with its lovely views over the Dordogne valley regularly appears in the *Guide*. It presents here an intense ruby-coloured 98 with an elegant, harmonious nose of soft red and dark berry fruit with agreeable notes of toast and vanilla oak. The rich palate has a pleasant concentration of rounded, fleshy tannins, with good vinosity and length. This is a wine to keep.

↠ Dauriac, Ch. Destieux,
33330 Saint-Emilion, tel. 05.57.24.77.44,
fax 05.57.40.37.42 ☑ Ⴤ by appt.

CH. DESTIEUX BERGER 1998
■   8.63 ha   21.333   ■■ ◆ €8-11

Produced on the sands of Saint-Sulpice-de-Faleyrens, which are planted half with Merlot, half with Cabernet vines, this beautifully ruby wine has wonderful red fruit aromas blended with fine notes of slightly vanilla-tinged oak. On the palate it reveals a good tannic structure, nicely animated by a pleasing liveliness that provides a fresh finish.

↠ Union de producteurs de Saint-Emilion,
Haut-Gravet, BP 27, 33330 Saint-Emilion,
tel. 05.57.24.70.71, fax 05.57.24.65.18,
e-mail udp-vins.saint-emilion@
gofornet.com ☑ Ⴤ ev. day except Sun.
8am–12 noon 2pm–6pm
↠ Alain Cazenave

CH. FAUGERES 1998★★
■   20 ha   115.000   ■■ €23-30
|93| |94| 95 |96| |97| 98

At 500 m (545 yds) from Sainte-Colombe church, this estate has belonged to the Guisez family since 1823. This attractive 98, essentially a Merlot but with 10% Cabernet Franc and 5% Cabernet Sauvignon, spent 14 months in oak. The ruby colour is very intense and the complex, expressive nose has red fruit aromas with pleasant touches of burnt oak and nuances of tar and liquorice. The palate has superb body, is well-structured and substantial. The tannins are still firm and a little severe, but very promising.

↠ GFA C. et P. Guisez, Ch. Faugères,
33330 Saint-Etienne-de-Lisse,
tel. 05.57.40.34.99, fax 05.57.40.36.14,
e-mail faugeres@club-internet.fr ☑
Ⴤ by appt.

CH. DE FERRAND 1998★
■   28 ha   160.000   ■■ |90| |94| |95| 98
82 83 85 86 88

The remarkable 17th-century Château Ferrand, surrounded by woodland, reigns over a wine estate on limestone-clay that has produced this well-made, attractive 98 with a lively, intense ruby colour. The nose expresses jammy red fruits with very delicate notes of spices and vanilla. Well-structured with round, fleshy tannins, it is well balanced and long on the finish.

↠ Héritiers du Baron Bich, Ch. de Ferrand,
33330 Saint-Hippolyte, tel. 05.57.74.47.11,
fax 05.57.24.69.08 ☑ Ⴤ by appt.

CH. FERRAND-LARTIGUE 1998★
■   5.8 ha   24.000   ■■ €30-38
94 95 |96| 97 98

This cru has been regularly admired by our experts. Its wines are produced from 40-year-old vines planted on a variety of soils – sand, gravel and limestone-clay – and the varietal blend is 80% Merlot and 20% Cabernets. This attractive 98 has a lovely Bigarreau cherry colour. The nose opens with notes of flowers (violet), fruit (raspberry) and spices. The round, robust palate continues the fruity theme, and opens out to reveal rather austere tannins that need a further three to six years to tone down.

↠ Ferrand, Ch. Ferrand-Lartigue,
rte de Lartigue, 33330 Saint-Emilion,
tel. 05.57.74.46.19, fax 05.57.74.46.19,
e-mail vincent.rapin@libertysurf.fr

CH. FIGEAC 1998 ★★
■ 1 er gd cru B   37.5 ha   100,000

62 **64 66** (70) 71 **74 75 76 77 78 79 80**
|81| |82| |83| |85| |86| **87 88 89 90 92** |93|
|94| (95) **96** |97| **98**

Following the *coup de coeur* and *Grappe d'or* awarded for their classic 95, Figeac has done it again with this remarkable 98. This is a Grand Cru of character. Its history goes back to a Gallo-Roman villa, later replaced by a chateau that has been in the Manoncourt family since 1892. This wine is a mystery: the *terroir* and varietal blend are atypical and yet, when tasted blind, the Jury found it among the best of the Saint-Emilion classified Grand Crus. It's a real charmer, with its faultless presentation (classic Bordeaux red with purple lights) and refined nose of black berry fruit and toasted oak aromas. The elegant, harmonious palate has a long classy finish that cannot fail to appeal.

↝ SCEA Famille Manoncourt, Ch. Figeac, 33330 Saint-Emilion, tel. 05.57.24.72.26, fax 05.57.74.45.74, e-mail chateau-figeac@chateau-figeac.com ☎ by appt.

CH. FLEUR CARDINALE 1998 ★
■ 10 ha   50,000

82 83 85 86 88 89 (90) **93 94 95 96 97**

This limestone-clay *terroir* over rock is located to the east of the appellation. These 40-year-old vines (70% Merlot, 15% Cabernet Sauvignon and 15% Bouchet) have produced this garnet-coloured wine that is showing some signs of maturity. Well-made and well-matured, it has aromas of ripe fruit and vanilla, and is well-balanced, generous and fruity on the palate with a tannic structure that is still a little austere, as is normal in a young Grand Cru. The oak is not excessive and this wine should be ready to drink after two to three years.

↝ Alain et Claude Asséo, Ch. Fleur Cardinale, 33330 Saint-Etienne-de-Lisse, tel. 05.57.40.14.05, fax 05.57.40.28.62, e-mail fleurcardinale@terre-net.fr ✔

CH. FLEUR LARTIGUE 1998 ★
■ 5.46 ha   34,933   €8-11

This small vineyard of about 5.5 ha (12.35 acres) on sandy-gravel comprises 80% Merlot and 20% Cabernet Franc. This bright ruby 98 has aromas of ripe fruit and spices with hints of oak. The supple, round palate is well-balanced, with unctuous, velvety tannins that continue through to the finish.

↝ Union de producteurs de Saint-Emilion, Haut-Gravet, BP 27, 33330 Saint-Emilion, tel. 05.57.24.70.71, fax 05.57.24.65.18, e-mail udp-vins.saint-emilion@gofornet.com ☎ ev. day except Sun. 8am-12 noon 2pm-6pm

↝ SCEA Vignobles Chantureau

CH. FOMBRAUGE 1998 ★
■ 52 ha   165,000   €11-15

86 |88| |90| **91 92 93** (95) (96) |97| **98**

Recently acquired by the *négociant* Bernard Magrez, Fombrauge was built in 1679 and overlooks a vineyard of 75 ha (185.25 acres), planted on limestone-clay in the north-east of the appellation, have produced a wine that was much appreciated by the tasters. They liked the lovely Bigarreau cherry colour with its ruby lights. The wine needs to breathe before it yields its oaky, vanilla and mineral notes with stewed fruit. The full, velvety palate opens with ripe grapes and tannins that have a great future before them. A wine which will go well with an *entrecôte Bordelaise* in three to eight years' time.

↝ SA Ch. Fombrauge, 33330 Saint-Christophe-des-Bardes, tel. 05.57.24.77.12, fax 05.57.24.66.95, e-mail chateau@fombrauge.com ☎ by appt.

↝ B. Magrez

CH. FONPLEGADE 1998
■ Gd cru clas.   11.35 ha   n.c.

82 83 85 86 88 |90| **92** |93| |94| |95| **96** |97| **98**

The first vines were planted here by the Romans, as shown by the traces of furrows in the rock. The property is located on the south-ern slopes of Saint-Emilion in a sheltered part of the middle of the hillside. A lovely vivid ruby colour, this wine still has a slightly reticent nose. When the wine is aired, however, it reveals aromas of red fruit, vanilla and caramel. The structure is well-balanced, not terribly powerful, yet with good, ripe tannins which will soon mellow.

↝ Nathalie et Marie-José Moueix, Ch. Fonplégade, BP 45, 33330 Saint-Emilion, tel. 05.57.74.43.11, fax 05.57.74.44.67, e-mail stephanyrosa@vanadoo.fr ✔ ☎ by appt.

CH. FONRAZADE 1998 ★★
■ 8.5 ha   55,000   €11-15

86 |88| |90| |95| **96 98**

Only 8.5 ha (21 acres) have been selected for this great wine. With their knowledge of good wine-making, the owner and his daughter offer a remarkably successful 98 with a dark, extremely attractive Bordeaux red colour. When the wine is allowed to breathe, the nose reveals a fruity quality. The fine, elegant palate displays a lovely fruit-oak balance. This wine should be at its best

between the next three and twelve years. In the large complex over the barrel-store is a large reception room, where groups and seminars can be accommodated.
• Guy Balotte,
Ch. Fonrazade, 33330 Saint-Emilion, tel. 05.57.24.71.58, fax 05.57.74.40.87, e-mail chateau-fonrazade@wanadoo.fr ▼
Y ev. day 8am–12 noon 2pm–6pm

CH. FONROQUE 1998★

■ Gd cru clas.　19.26 ha　78,000　Ⅲ €15-23

81 82 83 85 86 88 89 [90] 92 93 95 [97] 98

This good-sized estate of about 20 ha (49.4 acres) on limestone-clay has produced this 90% Merlot with Cabernet Franc making up the rest. This is an attractive 98 with engaging, deep ruby colour and a nose that is still very fresh, opening with aromas of red fruit, prune and leather with notes of menthol, oak and liquorice. The round, fleshy palate is harmonious, with a lovely fruitiness supported by good grape tannins and oak, perfectly balanced and long. This is a good quality wine for laying down.
• Ets Jean-Pierre Moueix, 54, quai du Priourat, 33500 Libourne, tel. 05.57.51.78.96
• GFA Ch. Fonroque

CH. FRANC BIGAROUX 1998

■　6 ha　15,000　€11-15

Gilles Teyssier, the owner's nephew, tends an estate in the large village of Les Bigaroux on hot sands and deep gravel. The 98 presented is simple and pleasant, and will very soon be ready to drink. This is a garnet-coloured wine showing some maturity around the edge and ripe red fruit with agreeable grilled notes on the nose. The supple, round palate reveals very ripe, delicate tannins. Serve this wine with a partridge.
• EARL Gilles Teyssier, 50, av. de Saint-Emilion, 33330 Saint-Sulpice-de-Faleyrens, tel. 05.57.24.64.77, fax 05.57.24.64.77, e-mail gilles.teyssier@free.fr ▼ Y by appt.
• Francis Fretier

CH. FRANC GRACE-DIEU 1998★

■　8.49 ha　36,000　Ⅲ €11-15

The property takes its name from a former Cistercian priory, which enjoyed exemptions under the Ancien Régime. This vineyard is a classic combination of 70% Merlot and 30% Cabernets planted on brown sands and blue clay. The wine has an intense purple colour. The nose is still rather closed, but releases a few flowery notes (peony), fruit (lemon, blackcurrant) and fine oak (vanilla, toast). After a fresh and supple attack the palate opens out with tightly-knit, elegant tannins. In two to three years' time, this 98 will go well with game or an entrecôte steak.
• SEV Fournier, Ch. Franc Grace-Dieu, 33330 Saint-Emilion, tel. 05.57.24.66.18, fax 05.56.24.98.05 ▼ Y by appt.

CH. FRANC LA ROSE 1998★

■　3.8 ha　25,000　Ⅲ €11-15

In 1995 Jean-Louis Trocard acquired this small property in La Rose, north of the medieval town. The limestone-clay *terroir* is planted with 90% Merlot and 10% Cabernet Franc. In 1998, when the winery was being restored, he produced this wine with its dark purple appearance. It needs to breathe a little before yielding up its aromas of fruit, tobacco and leather and fine oakiness. The well-balanced, expressive and concentrated palate possesses silky tannins. This wine, with its rich character, will soon be ready to drink, and will be the ideal accompaniment to game.
• SCEA des Vignobles Trocard,
2, Les Petits-Jays-Ouest, 33570 Les Artigues-de-Lussac, tel. 05.57.55.57.90, fax 05.57.55.57.98, e-mail trocard@wanadoo.fr ▼ Y ev. day except Sat. Sun. 8am–12 noon 2pm–5pm

CH. FRANC-MAYNE 1998★

■ Gd cru clas.　5 ha　26,000　Ⅲ €23-30

85 86 [88] [89] [90] [92] 95 [96] [97] 98

In 1996, the Belgian *négociants* Georgy and Jean-Lou Fourcroy joined forces with Carlo and Hubert Clasen. Otto Lenselink, and Valérie and Benoît Calvet to buy this fine estate from the AXA group. They have done some excellent work since, notably with this 98, which has an intense ruby colour. Once the wine is aired, it releases aromas of dark berry fruit (blackcurrant), hazelnut and toasty oak. The very refined, elegant palate has both lovely ripe fruit and quality tannins. Drink this wine in three to four years with local dishes, pot-roasts and duck. Franc-Mayne is a member of the Châteaux et Hôtels de France and has five guest-rooms.
• Fourcroy, SCEA Ch. Franc-Mayne, La Gomerie, 33330 Saint-Emilion, tel. 05.57.24.62.61, fax 05.57.24.68.25 ▼ Y by appt.

CH. FRANC PATARABET 1998★

■　6 ha　26,000　Ⅲ €8-11

86 88 89 90 91 98

This cru in the heart of the Saint-Emilion appellation has a monolithic cellar. Merlot (60%) and Cabernets (40%) planted on siliceous clay soils have produced this lovely intense ruby wine. On the nose there is a pronounced, yet elegant, grilled oakiness with charred notes. Well-balanced, it has enough structure to cope with this current excess of oak influence, and should develop favourably over the coming three to five years.
• GFA Faure-Barraud, rue Guadet, BP 72, 33330 Saint-Emilion, tel. 05.57.24.65.93, fax 05.57.24.69.05, e-mail jn@franc-patarabet.com ▼ Y by appt.

CH. GAILLARD 1998★

■　11 ha　70,000　■ €11-15

This business has been in the family since 1792 and today comprises 19 ha (46.9 acres), of which 11 ha (27.2 acres) are devoted to

Château Gaillard. This vineyard, spread over three *communes*, possesses various soils, combining clay and sand. The varietal blend is 80% Merlot with the rest Cabernet Franc. Well-presented with an intense, lively purple colour, the nose, which reveals the odd note of red fruit and undergrowth tinged with vanilla, is not yet fully developed. The round, rich, unctuous and flavoursome palate has fruity and toasty flavours, a good lengthy structure and a firm finish.

➦ SCEA Vignobles J-J. Nouvel, Ch. Gaillard, BP 84, 33330 Saint-Emilion, tel. 05.57.24.72.05, fax 05.57.74.40.03, e-mail chateau.gaillard@wanadoo.fr Ⓥ Υ by appt.

CH. GALIUS 1998★

■ 10 ha 61,761 ■|■|♂ €11-15

This label is one of the flagships of the famous Saint-Emilion co-operative. It is made from a blend of 70% Merlot with 30% Cabernets. This well-made 98 has a lovely youthful, ruby colour, lively and intense. The nose releases well-ripened red and dark berry fruit aromas with an attractive vanilla and toasty oakiness. After a silky, round attack, the palate opens out to reveal its rich, fleshy structure with good tannins which are still firm on the finish, but will guarantee four to five years in the cellar. The **Royal 98** was commended out by the Jury.

➦ Union de producteurs de Saint-Emilion, Haut-Gravet, BP 27, 33330 Saint-Emilion, tel. 05.57.24.70.71, fax 05.57.24.65.18, e-mail udp-vins.saint-emilion@ gofornet.com Ⓥ Υ ev. day except Sun. 8am–12 noon 2pm–6pm

CH. GONTEY 1998★

■ 2.4 ha 12,000 ⓤ €15-23

This small vineyard has been tended by wine-growers from the Blayais-Bourgeais region since 1997. This wine has a fine, dense Bigarreau cherry colour. The nose reveals very ripe, dark berry fruit aromas with a charred note. The fresh, supple palate has a fruity, spicy flavour that finishes on quite prominent oak tannins. This 98 should reach its high point in four to six years.

➦ Laurence et Marc Pasquet, Grand Gontey, 33330 Saint-Emilion, tel. 05.57.42.29.80, fax 05.57.42.84.86 Ⓥ

CH. GRAND CORBIN-DESPAGNE 1998★

|89| |90| |93| |94| 95 96 97 98

■ 26.54 ha 101,000 ⓤ €15-23

The Despagne family, owners of this fine estate since 1812, have been in the Libournais since the beginning of the 17th century. They selectively pick grapes in the vineyard and sort them in the winery. This wine – from three parts Merlot to one of Cabernet Franc, both grown on sandy-clay in the north of the appellation – is a tribute to their methods. Dark and deep garnet in colour, it still has a slightly reticent nose with emerging aromas of ripe red fruits (raspberry) and spices, combined with elegant notes of toast and vanilla. The full, fleshy attack follows through on the palate with a dense, powerful tannic structure that should soften and integrate after several years in the cellar.

➦ SCEV Consorts Despagne, Ch. Grand Corbin Despagne, 33330 Saint-Emilion, tel. 05.57.51.08.38, fax 05.57.51.29.18, e-mail despagne@grand-corbin-despagne.com Ⓥ Υ by appt.

CH. GRAND-PONTET 1998★

■ Gd cru clas. 14 ha 70,000 ⓤ €15-23

85 86 88 |89| |90| 91 |93| |94| **95** 96 97 98

This property, formerly owned by Barton et Guestier, was purchased by the Bécot, Berjal and Pourquet families about twenty years ago. It sits on a limestone-clay plateau at the entrance of Saint-Emilion on the road to Libourne. This, their 98, three-quarters Merlot and one-quarter Cabernet Franc, has a sumptuous dark, dense purple colour and a powerful, expressive nose with jammy fruits, smoke, vanilla and roasted coffee. The palate has a lovely structure, firm and intense, with well-balanced tannins that will ensure good keeping.

➦ Ch. Grand-Pontet, 33330 Saint-Emilion, tel. 06.85.83.08.65 Υ by appt.

➦ Bécot-Pourquet

CH. GRANDS CHAMPS 1998★

■ 2 ha 13,000 ⓤ €11-15

This cru, essentially produced from old Merlot vines with one-fifth Cabernet (equal proportions of Franc and Sauvignon), comes from an estate of 18 ha (44.5 acres) which mainly makes Côtes de Castillon. It presents this splendidly deep garnet 98, which is lively at the edges. The nose is very expressive, with strong grilled notes and chocolate enlivened by an underlying fruitiness. The palate reveals a rich, firm, thoroughbred structure with good lengthy flavours. A good wine for laying down for three to five years before opening.

➦ Christophe Blanc, 2, av. de la Bourrée, 33330 Saint-Magne-de-Castillon, tel. 05.57.40.42.53, fax 05.53.40.42.53 Ⓥ

➦ Jean Blanc

CH. GUEYROSSE 1998★

86 90 92 93 94 96 |97| 98

■ 4.6 ha 20,000 ■|■|♂ €11-15

This is one of two crus nurtured by Yves Delol; this one located on sand and gravel at the entrance of Libourne. This dark purple 98 with garnet highlights presents an interesting nose which opens up with very ripe fruit, followed by vanilla oak and finishing on a strong gamey note. The robust, fleshy palate has an overripe flavour with dense, slightly coarse tannins. This is an old-fashioned Saint-Emilion, which in three to six years' time will go well with rich sauce dishes.

Saint-Emilion Grand Cru

CH. HAUT-BADETTE 1998   ■   €15-23

1.25 ha   7,500

This little 'Grand Cru' occupies slightly more than 1 ha (2.5 acres) out of the 21 ha (51.9 acres) cultivated by Jean Janoueix at Saint-Emilion. It consists of 90% Merlot complemented by 10% Cabernet Sauvignon planted on a siliceous and siliceous-clay *terroir*. This youthful-looking, ruby-coloured 98 has lively, fruity and delicately oaky aromas. On the palate the fresh, elegant redcurrant flavours and fresh tannins combine to produce a wine with a simple character that should be drunk fairly quickly with duck breast, white meats or mild cheeses.

➤ Sté d'Exploitation du Ch. Haut-Sarpe, BP 192, 33506 Libourne Cedex, tel. 05.57.51.41.86, fax 05.57.51.53.16, e-mail info@j-janoueix-bordeaux.com ▼
➤ J.-F. Janoueix

CH. HAUT-BRISSON 1998★★   ■   ⅠⅠⅠ   €15-23

9.38 ha   58,000

This is the new proprietors' second harvest. The cru, located on gravels and sand with iron deposits, is a splendid success composed of 60% Merlot, 30% Cabernet Sauvignon and 10% Cabernet Franc. It has a very dense, dark colour with black highlights. The powerful, concentrated nose comprises ripe grapes, charred and toasty oak combined with smoky and venison notes. The full, well-structured and lively palate has a fine chewiness and solid tannins which, though still a little austere, are very promising.

➤ SCEA Ch. Haut-Brisson, 33330 Vignonet, tel. 05.57.84.69.57, fax 05.57.74.93.11, e-mail haut.brisson@wanadoo.fr ▼ ▼ by appt.
➤ Kwok

CH. HAUT-CADET 1998   ■   ⅠⅠⅠ   ◊   €11-15

1.22 ha   8,266

Selectively-picked grapes from the numerous Bordelais vineyards owned by the Belgian *négociant* Roger Geens have gone to produce this wine. Half of the 80% Merlot component comes from vines grown on sandy-gravel soils rich in iron, the other half from limestone-clay. This 98 shows some maturity in its colour. It needs to be allowed to breathe before it opens to express its fruit and oak aromas. The palate reveals jammy fruit, and with evident yet mellow tannins the wine can be drunk in two to three years' time.

➤ SCEA Vignobles Rocher-Cap-de-Rive 1, 33350 Saint-Magne-de-Castillon, tel. 05.57.40.08.88, fax 05.57.40.19.93, e-mail vignoblesrochercaprive@wanadoo.fr

➤ EARL Vignobles Yves Delol, Ch. Gueyrosse, 33500 Libourne, tel. 05.57.51.02.63, fax 05.57.51.93.39 ▼ ▼ by appt.

CH. HAUT-CORBIN 1998★

■ Gd cru clas.   6.01 ha   36,000   ⅠⅠⅠ   €23-30

| 81 | 82 | 83 | 85 | 86 | 88 | 90 | 91 | 92 | 93 | 94 |
| 97 | 98 |

The 97 version of this cru near the Pomerol achieved a *coup de cœur*. This well-balanced 98 has spent 12 months in oak barrels (40% new). An attractive ruby colour with deep purple highlights, this wine is elegant and expressive. The nose has dark berry fruit derived from the fine oak and hints of smoke and tar. After a round, silky-smooth attack, the lengthy palate opens out to reveal a good structure with a firm finish. It needs to be laid down for several years.

➤ SC Ch. Haut-Corbin, 33330 Saint-Emilion, tel. 05.57.51.95.54, fax 05.57.51.90.93 ▼ ▼ by appt.

CH. HAUTE-NAUVE 1998★   8.51 ha   51,733   ■   ⅠⅠⅠ   ◊   €6-11

Grown on siliceous-clay, and comprised of 60% Merlot and 40% Cabernets, this wine has an attractive ruby appearance, and is bright. There are intense aromas of red and dark berry jammy fruits, with a fine, subtle oakiness and touches of vanilla and spice. The palate, with its obvious, chewy tannins, is well-balanced and long.

➤ Union de producteurs de Saint-Emilion, Haut-Gravet, BP 27, 33330 Saint-Emilion, tel. 05.57.24.70.71, fax 05.57.24.65.18, e-mail udp-vins.saint-emilion@gofornet.com ▼ ▼ ev. day except Sun. 8am-12 noon 2pm-6pm
➤ SCEA Ch. Haute-Nauve

CH. HAUT-GRAVET 1998★★

■   6.5 ha   44,000   ⅠⅠⅠ   €15-23

This is the first time this cru of 6.5 ha (16.15 acres) has appeared in the *Guide*, and it is stunning. This blend of 50% Merlot, 40% Cabernet Franc and 10% Cabernet Sauvignon is planted in the gravely zone of Saint-Sulpice-de-Faleyrens, in the south of the appellation. Our Jury was impressed by this 98's concentration and remarkable dark purple, extremely dense colour. The complex, highly expressive nose has ripe fruit aromas with a toasty, elegant oakiness. The rich, full and powerful palate reveals superb tannins that are flavoursome and long. This is a great wine that needs keeping for at least five years.

298

CH. HAUT-SEGOTTES 1998★★

8.7 ha | 40,000 | €11-15

88 89 90 92 93 94 96 98

No herbicides are used on this vineyard's Merlot (60%) and Cabernets (40%), grown on sandy-clay overlying iron deposits. The 98 has an intense nose of well-ripened red berry fruit and toasty oak. The finish is unaggressively robust but this beautiful wine should be laid down for at least four years, if not ten.

● Danielle André, Ch. Haut-Segottes,
33330 Saint-Emilion, tel. 05.57.24.60.98,
fax 05.57.24.74.29 [V] Y ev. day except Sun.
9am–12 noon 2pm–7pm

CH. HAUT VILLET 1998

5 ha | 31,000 | €15-23

This attractive 98, with its fine and crystal-clear ruby colour, already has intense aromas of flowers (violets), red fruits and spices (cinnamon). The robust and powerful palate has fruity, spicy flavours with notes of venison. Drink this wine in three to five years' time as an accompaniment to sauced dishes of game.

● Eric Lenormand, Ch. Haut-Villet,
33330 Saint-Etienne-de-Lisse,
tel. 05.57.47.97.60, fax 05.57.47.92.94,
e-mail haut.villet@free.fr [V] Y by appt.

CH. JACQUES-BLANC

Cuvée du Maître 1998★

7 ha | 40,000 | €11-15

89 90 93 95 98

Jacques Blanc, the founder of this cru, was an eminent Saint-Emilion personage in the 14th century. Today, the 21-ha (51.9-acre) vineyard practises biodynamic methods and 7 ha (17.3 acres) of old Merlot vines with a small amount (10%) of Cabernet Franc have resulted in this intense purple wine. The nose has ripe fruit aromas and a lovely grilled character with fine oak and fresh, slightly menthol nuances. Robust and energetic when it arrives on the palate, this wine opens out to become tasty and flavoursome. The tannins are round, fleshy and rich, and long on the finish.

● SCEA du Ch. Jacques-Blanc,
33330 Saint-Etienne-de-Lisse,
tel. 05.57.56.02.97, fax 05.57.40.18.01 [V]
Y by appt.

CH. JEAN VOISIN 1998★★

8 ha | 31,589 | €15-23

94 (95) 96 (97) 98

This Amédée vintage, selected from 8 ha (19.8 acres) of the 14-ha (34.6-acre) property, is an old friend to the *Guide*. Blending 70% Merlot and 30% Cabernets grown on siliceous-clay, it can always be relied upon. This lovely 98 has a remarkably fine dark purple colour. The nose is already very complex, with notes of jammy blackberry combining with flowers and oak. The well-balanced, harmonious palate has fleshiness and good length, sustained by dense yet smooth tannins. This fine 98 is a

---

● Alain Aubert, 57 bis, rte de Libourne,
33350 Saint-Magne-de-Castillon,
tel. 05.57.40.04.30, fax 05.57.40.27.02

CH. HAUT LA GRACE DIEU 1998★★

1.5 ha | 5,000 | €15-23

Bought in 1970 by Saby vineyards, this plot enjoys a favourable orientation on a limestone-clay hillside. The 50-year-old Merlot vines deserve careful handling: separate vinification, maturation and bottling. The result is this remarkable dark garnet 98 with a rich, complex nose of jammy red fruits and spices and charred aromas from its high-class, elegant oak. The palate is well-balanced with excellent body, and opens out with pleasant fullness. The tannic structure is closed and firm at present, but ought to soften after several years in the cellar.

● EARL Vignobles Jean-Bernard Saby
et Fils, Ch. Rozier,
33330 Saint-Laurent-des-Combes,
tel. 05.57.24.73.03, fax 05.57.24.67.77,
e-mail jean.saby@chateau-rozier.com [V]
Y by appt.

CH. HAUT-MONTIL 1998

7.22 ha | 44,800 | €8-11

This cru, mostly Merlot with 15% Cabernet Franc, comes from 7 ha (17.3 acres) of sandy gravel in the south of the appellation. This pretty, ruby-coloured 98 has a nose that opens with fresh aromas of red berry fruit. The supple, round and well-balanced palate has approachable tannins that allow this wine to be drunk straight away.

● Union de producteurs de Saint-Emilion,
Haut-Gravet, BP 27, 33330 Saint-Emilion,
tel. 05.57.24.70.71, fax 05.57.24.65.18,
e-mail udp-vins.saint-emilion@goformet.com
Y ev. day except Sun. 8am–12 noon 2pm–6pm
● SCEA Famille Vinceney

CH. HAUT-SARPE 1998★

Gd cru clas. | 13.25 ha | 79,000 | €23-30

85 86 88 89 90 92 93 94 95 96 98

Sited north-east of the town on the limestone-clay plateau linking Saint-Emilion with Saint-Christophe-des-Bardes, this elegant château presents a wine that blends 30% Cabernet Franc with Merlot. This fine 98 has deep, lively ruby colour. On the nose there are jammy fruit aromas blended with vanilla, cocoa and spices. The supple, round palate is well-balanced and harmonious with fine, elegant tannins that are long and flavoursome on the finish.

● Sté d'Exploitation du Ch. Haut-Sarpe,
BP 192, 33506 Libourne Cedex,
tel. 05.57.51.41.86, fax 05.57.51.53.16,
e-mail info@j-janoueix-bordeaux.com [V]
Y by appt.

good wine to lay down. The second wine, **Jean Voisin-Fagouet 98**, was also singled out by the Jury. It is supple, fresh, and already pleasant.
➤ SCEA du Ch. Jean Voisin, 33330 Saint-Emilion, tel. 05.57.24.70.40, fax 05.57.24.79.57, e-mail chassag@quaternet.fr ☑ ⵎ by appt.
➤ Chassagnoux

CH. LA BONNELLE 1998
■ 9.6 ha 60,000 ⵎ ♦ €11-15
93 |94| |95| 96 97 98

The Gironde-style residence dates from the beginning of the 19th century. The estate, a co-operative since 1990, has been making improvements and fitted out a new winery in 2000. An intense ruby colour, this 98 has a nose that combines aromas of red fruit and musk with grilled notes. The palate is robust and substantial. The somewhat severe tannins on the finish will need several years to mellow.
➤ Vignobles Sulzer, La Bonnelle, 33330 Saint-Pey-d'Armens, tel. 05.57.47.15.12, fax 05.57.47.16.83 ☑ ⵎ by appt.

CH. LA CHAPELLE-LESCOURS 1998★
■ 4.18 ha 27,000 ⵎ ♦ €11-15

This estate, taken over recently by the young oenologist François Quentin, has 50-year-old Merlot vines growing on a sandy-gravel hilltop. The youthful nose needs time to breathe in order to release its aromas of menthol, red fruit and mineral nuances. The palate has fullness and presence, flavours of fruit and undergrowth with solid tannins. The wine will be ready to drink in two years' time and reach its zenith in twelve years. It will be a good accompaniment to roast woodcock or a haunch of venison with *sauce grand veneur*.
➤ F. Quentin, Ch. La Chapelle-Lescours, 33330 Saint-Sulpice, tel. 05.57.74.41.22, fax 05.57.24.65.37, e-mail F.Quentin@free.fr ☑ ⵎ by appt.

CH. LA COMMANDERIE 1998
■ 5.35 ha n.c. ⵎ ♦ €11-15
82 85 88 |89| 91 92 |93| 94 |95| 96 98

On its mixed sand and gravel *terroir*, this cru is essentially Merlot with just 10% Cabernet Franc. It is managed by Cordier Estates and technically attached to Clos des Jacobins Cru Classé. The 98 has a fine garnet colour, dark and dense. The nose is powerful and winey with stewed fruit, leather and venison aromas. After robust, round and supple beginnings, the palate is well-presented but the firm finish will need several years' patience.
➤ Domaines Cordier, 160, cours du Médoc, 33300 Bordeaux, tel. 05.57.19.57.77, fax 05.57.19.57.87 ⵎ by appt.

CH. DE LA COUR 1998
■ n.c. 21,410 ⵎ ♦ €11-15
|95| |96| |97| 98

Created in 1995 by Hugues Delacour, a young wine-grower from Champagne, this 9-ha (22.2-acre) cru gets its name from an ancestor of the family, the Chevalier de La Cour, who served King Charles IX. This bright ruby 98 has a reticent but promising nose with notes of berry fruit and liquorice emerging. The well-balanced palate is very fruity with peppery notes and has an excellent tannic structure, which means that this wine can be laid down.
➤ EARL du Châtel Delacour, Ch. de La Cour, 33330 Vignonet, tel. 05.57.84.64.95, fax 05.57.84.65.00 ☑ ⵎ by appt.

CH. LA COUSPAUDE 1998★★
■ Gd cru clas. 7.01 ha 40,000 ⵎ €38-46
82 83 85 86 88 (89) |90| |91 92 |93| |94|
95 96 |97| 98

Classified since 1996, this cru is very active in the artistic world with its famous exhibitions. Not that it in any way neglects its viticultural role, as proved by this magnificent 98 matured in new oak. This is a typical Libourne-type blend, and has a superb dark and intense garnet colour. The nose is powerfully expressive with ripe fruit and elegant, toasty, charred oak. The structure is rich and full with the most lovely fleshy tannins, which are long on the finish.
➤ Vignobles Aubert, La Couspaude, 33330 Saint-Emilion, tel. 05.57.40.15.76, fax 05.57.40.10.14 ☑ ⵎ by appt.

CH. LA CROIZILLE 1998★★
■ 1.85 ha 4,425 ⵎ €38-46

Having bought this small vineyard, planted on limestone-clay, in 1996, Monsieur De Schepper is now in personal control. The 30-year-old vines, 70% Merlot with 30% Cabernet Sauvignon, have produced this magnificent dark purple, almost black, wine. The nose, already intense, is very promising; it has aromas of black berry fruit, vanilla and toasty oak. The palate is rich, complex and flavoursome with a beautifully dense tannic structure, making it a great wine for laying down. It could go on improving for six to ten years.
➤ SCEA Ch. Tour Baladoz, 33330 Saint-Laurent-des-Combes, tel. 05.57.88.94.17, fax 05.57.88.39.14, e-mail gdemour@aol.com ☑ ⵎ by appt.

CH. LA DOMINIQUE 1998
■ Gd cru clas. 18.5 ha 55,000 ⵎ €46-76
(82) 86 87 88 |89| |90| 91 92 |93| |94| 95
96 97 98

Located in the north-west of the appellation, this 22.5-ha (55.6-acre) estate dates from the 18th century and practises sustainable agriculture in selected plots. A bright and attractive, brilliant-ruby colour, this 98 has a discreet nose with just-emerging jammy fruit and vanilla aromas. The firm, powerful palate

300

reveals a strong concentration of tannins that need several years to integrate.

Clément Fayat, Ch. La Dominique, 33330 Saint-Emilion, tel. 05.57.51.31.36, fax 05.57.51.63.04, e-mail info@vignobles.fayat-group.com ☑ Y by appt.

CH. LA FAGNOUSE 1998★

■ 7 ha 40,000 €11-15

The Coutant family have 7 ha (17.3 acres) on limestone-clay in the east of the appellation. The classic Saint-Emilion blend of two-thirds Merlot and one-third Cabernet Franc has produced this ruby 98 that is true to type and well-balanced, with a delicately fruity (raspberry) bouquet. After a soft attack, the palate opens on tannins that have presence yet subtlety. This wine could be drunk fairly soon or laid down.

SCE Ch. La Fagnouse, 33330 Saint-Etienne-de-Lisse, tel. 05.57.40.11.49, fax 05.57.40.46.20 ☑ Y by appt.

Coutant

CH. LA FLEUR CRAVIGNAC 1998

■ 7.75 ha 51,400 €11-15

94 95 96 97 98

Regularly mentioned in the *Guide*, this cru is served in the restaurant of the French Parliament at the Lower House of the French Parliament. Intensely and attractively ruby in colour, it has very ripe red fruit aromas with buttery, musky notes. The full, round palate has a smooth tannic structure. Serve in two to three years with red meat, poultry and cheese.

SCEA Ch. Cravignac, 33330 Saint-Emilion, tel. 05.57.74.44.01, fax 05.57.84.56.70 ☑ Y by appt.

L. Beaupertuis

CH. LA FLEUR DE JAUGUE 1998

■ 3 ha 18,000 €11-15

|96| |97| 98

This cru has been in the Bigaud family since 1930. The wine is a La Croix de Jaugue selection (90% Merlot and 10% Cabernet Franc). Very dark ruby in colour, it has a nose that is still closed and needs to breathe a little before releasing its aromas of stewed fruit, spices (clove and pepper), incense and a slight oakiness. The structure is solid and sturdy. This old-fashioned wine will need several years before becoming an excellent accompaniment to roasted or sauced meats, or cheese.

Georges Bigaud, 150, av. du Gal-de-Gaulle, 33500 Libourne, tel. 05.57.51.51.29, fax 05.57.51.29.70 ☑ Y by appt.

CH. LA FLEUR DU CASSE 1998★

■ 1.2 ha 7,500 €11-15

This small cru, essentially old Merlot planted on limestone-clay with a 5% supplement of Cabernet Franc, was acquired in 1996 by the Garzaro family, who also cultivate a fine vineyard in Pomerol. Dark garnet in colour, this 98 is developing an intense and complex nose that is still somewhat dominated by notes of charred oak and liquorice, though there is an attractive underlying fruitiness. The palate displays good balance, with fleshy, substantial tannins, lots of elegance and a long finish, which all indicate that it will keep well.

EARL Vignobles Garzaro, Ch. Le Prieur, 33750 Baron, tel. 05.56.30.16.16, fax 05.56.30.12.63, e-mail garzaro@vingarzaro.com ☑ Y by appt.

CH. LA FLEUR PEREY

Cuvée Prestige Vieille en fût de chêne 1998

■ 3.5 ha 24,000 €11-15

93 |94| |95| |96| |97| |98|

Y by appt.

Fifty-year-old vines (80% Merlot and 20% Cabernets), planted on sandy gravel, are the source of this ruby *cuvée spéciale* with its bright carmine highlights. The pleasant nose has a blend of red fruit aromas with musky fur and leather and grilled, liquorice notes. The tannins are already silky and the palate has attractive length.

Vignobles Florence et Alain Xans, Perey, 33330 Saint-Sulpice-de-Faleyrens, tel. 06.80.72.84.87, fax 06.57.24.63.61 ☑ Y by appt.

CH. LA GAFFELIERE 1998

■ 1er gd cru B 18 ha 70,000 €38-46

75 |78| |79| 80 81 (82) 83 84 85 |86| 87 88 89 |90| 91 92 |93| |94| 95 96 |97| 98

There have been vines here for thousands of years, and this family has been here for centuries. We are at La Gaffelière, at the southern entrance to the medieval town, between Ausone and Pavie. The limestone-clay *terroir* is planted with 40-year-old vines (70% Merlot and 30% Cabernets). This attractive 98 fits the elegant and refined aristocratic image. The purple colour has carmine highlights. The nose is still a little austere but when left to breathe opens on notes of fruit (blackcurrant and cherry), spices (vanilla and cinnamon) and discreet oakiness. The palate is supple and delicate with tannins that display finesse and freshness. Individuality is the mark of this wine.

Léo de Malet Roquefort, Ch. La Gaffelière, 33330 Saint-Emilion, tel. 05.57.24.72.15, fax 05.57.24.69.06 ☑ Y by appt.

CH. LA GARELLE 1998

■ 8.35 ha 54,000 €11-15

In this 30-year-old vineyard on sandy soils at the foot of the Côte Pavie, the varietal mix is 80% Merlot, with the remaining 20% made up of the two Cabernets. This wine has a youthful, dark purple colour. The nose is very fruity. The attack on the palate is clean and well-structured, but the tannins quickly assert themselves, giving a rustic quality to the wine that will need four or five years to soften. Then this 98 will be a fitting accompaniment to white meat.

🗝 Jean-Luc Marette, Ch. La Garelle, 33330 Saint-Emilion, tel. 05.57.24.61.98, fax 05.57.24.75.22 ☑ Y by appt.

CH. LA GOMERIE 1998★★

■ 2.52 ha n.c. 🍷 +€76

95 **96** 97 **98**

In 1995, the owners of Beauséjour-Bécot took over this former vineyard of the Abbey of Fayze. The earliest record of vines here dates from 1276. During the French Revolution, the 200-ha (494-acre) estate was split up, and the remaining 2.5 ha (6.2 acres) represent the former priory's precinct. A single-variety Merlot, this remarkable 98 has a dark, deep purple colour. The very promising nose releases grilled aromas from good oak, which still overwhelms a pleasant fruitiness. The palate has good body and the rich, ripe tannins are long on the finish.

🗝 G. et D. Bécot, GFA La Gomerie, 33330 Saint-Emilion, tel. 05.57.74.46.87, fax 05.57.24.66.88, e-mail contact@beausejour-becot.com

CH. LA GRACE-DIEU-LES-MENUTS 1998

■ 13.35 ha 75,000 🍷 €15–23

86 88 89 91 93 94 95 |96| |97| 98

Taking its name from the nearby former priory, a pilgrims' halt on the road to Compostela, this domaine is made up of two-thirds Merlot and one-third Cabernets. The soils are siliceous and limestone-clay. This deeply-coloured wine has a fresh and fruity nose, influenced by the two Cabernets. The attack is elegant and lively. The tannins are still a bit rugged and will need some three to six years in order to become smooth. In due course, this 98 will go well with red meat or stews.

🗝 EARL Vignobles Pilotte-Audier, Ch. La Grâce-Dieu-les-Menuts, 33330 Saint-Emilion, tel. 05.57.24.73.10, fax 05.57.74.40.44 ☑ Y by appt.

CH. LAMARTRE 1998

■ 11.58 ha 53,457 🍷 €8–11

Grown on siliceous soils at Saint-Etienne-de-Lisse and made from 83% Merlot, this wine has a fine, pleasant nose with floral and spicy aromas and a hint of smoke. The palate is well-balanced with supple, silky tannins, which ought to result in a good easy-drinking wine in two years' time.

🗝 Union de producteurs de Saint-Emilion, Haut-Gravet, BP 27, 33330 Saint-Emilion, tel. 05.57.24.70.71, fax 05.57.24.65.18, e-mail udp-vins.saint-emilion@gofornet.com ☑ Y ev. day except Sun. 8am–12 noon 2pm–6pm

🗝 SCEA Ch. Lamartre

CH. DE LA NAUVE

Elevé en fût de chêne 1998

■ 3 ha 19,000 🍷 €11–15

This family property on the road from Libourne to Castillon in the south-east of the appellation has a sandy clay soil planted with 80% Merlot and 20% Cabernets. The wine has a pretty appearance. When allowed to breathe, it releases an individual mix of floral and fruity aromas with mineral notes (gunflint), oakiness and touches of leather and tobacco. The palate is expressive and well-balanced, with a harmonious finish. This agreeable 98 can be drunk quite soon.

🗝 SCEA Ch. de La Nauve, 9, Nauve-Sud, 33330 Saint-Laurent-des-Combes, tel. 05.57.24.71.89, fax 05.57.74.46.61, e-mail la-nauve@wanadoo.fr ☑

Y by appt.

🗝 Richard Veyry

CH. LANIOTE 1998

■ Gd cru clas. 5 ha 30,000 🍷 €15–23

89 93 |94| 95 96 98

The young owners of this cru have inherited not just the vines but also the grotto home of the 8th-century monk Emilion, the chapel of the Trinity (13th century) and some catacombs. Such responsibilities! Their 98 is a great success, with its intense, clear garnet colour and youthful nose of small red berries, floral perfumes (violet) and toasty notes from good quality oak. The firm, energetic structure reveals good power and very evident tannins, which are a trifle austere at present, but guarantee good ageing potential.

🗝 de La Filolie, Ch. Laniote, 33330 Saint-Emilion, tel. 05.57.24.70.80, fax 05.57.24.60.11, e-mail laniote@wanadoo.fr ☑

Y ev. day 8am–12 noon 2pm–6pm

CH. LAPLAGNOTTE-BELLEVUE 1998★

■ 5.54 ha 30,000 🍷 €15–23

|90| |93| |94| 96 |97| 98

This handsome property on siliceous-clay in the north-east of Saint-Emilion was bought by the Labarre family in 1990. This dark, intense ruby 98 reveals a mixture of fruit and well-ripened grapes, with grilled oaky notes on the nose. The well-balanced, harmonious palate has round, fleshy, lengthy tannins. A well-made, classic wine.

🗝 Claude de Labarre, Ch. Laplagnotte-Bellevue, 33330 Saint-Christophe-des-Bardes, tel. 05.57.24.78.67, fax 05.57.24.63.62, e-mail arnauddl@aol.com ☑ Y by appt.

CH. L'APOLLINE 1998

■ 2.8 ha 15,000 🍷 €11–15

Philippe and Perrine Genevey bought the vineyard in 1996. Their first two harvests have brought them recognition from the tasters. This cru they have named after their third daughter. Located in the south of the appellation, the 30-year-old vines consist of two-thirds Merlot, one-third Cabernet Sauvignon growing on a *terroir* of sand and clay over gravel. The wine has a pretty, youthful, dark appearance. The nose is fruity (fig) with buttery oaky notes. The palate is still unnervingly austere, revealing a strong extraction. It will need four to ten years to calm down.

• Genevey, EARL Ch. L'Apolline, 33330 Saint-Sulpice-de-Faleyrens, tel. 05.57.51.26.80, fax 05.57.51.26.80

CH. LARMANDE 1998★

■ Gd cru clas. 22.4 ha 95,000 €23-30

85 86 (88) |89| |90| 92 |93| 94 96 97 98

This lovely wine estate belonged to the Méneret-Capdemourlin family of Saint-Emilion for five centuries. In 1990 it came under the ownership of the La Mondiale insurance company. This is a good 98, a blend of two-thirds Merlot and one-third Cabernets. The vivid, intense ruby colour is firmed by the winey, very fruity nose with spicy, smoky notes. The powerful, firm structure seems a trifle austere at the moment, but bodes a good future in four to five years.

• SCE du Ch. Larmande, BP 26, 33330 Saint-Emilion, tel. 05.57.24.71.41, fax 05.57.74.42.80, e-mail chateau-larmande@wanadoo.fr

• La Mondiale

CH. LAROZE 1998★★

■ Gd cru clas. 27 ha 100,000 €15-23

85 86 88 89 |90| 91 92 |93| |94| 95 96 |97| 98

In 1610, the Gurchy family were already wine-producers at Saint-Emilion, in the lieu-dit of Mazerat. Between 1882 and 1885, they established Château Laroze, which today is cultivated by Guy Meslin, a direct descendant, who reminds us how important it is to attend to each vine-stock individually. His 27 ha (66.7 acres) of vines contain no fewer than 154,000 of them. Remarkably well-presented with its superb, deep, dense purple colour and lively deep violet highlights, this 98 is powerful and complex, with red berry fruit, spices and liquorice. The palate is rich and fleshy, revealing powerful, velvety tannins, which guarantee the keeping potential of this classic Saint-Emilion.

• Guy Meslin, Ch. Laroze, 33330 Saint-Emilion, tel. 05.57.24.79.79, fax 05.57.24.79.80, e-mail ch.laroze@wanadoo.fr Y by appt.

CH. LA SERRE 1998★

■ Gd cru clas. 6.5 ha 24,000 €15-23

|90| 92 |93| |95| |96| 98

Situated just 200 m (218 yds) from the walls of Saint-Emilion, this 7-ha (17.3-acre) cru lies east of the town on a limestone-clay plateau and comprises four-fifths Merlot, one-fifth Cabernet Franc. This attractive 98 has a lively, deep ruby appearance. The nose releases intense aromas of very ripe fruit accompanied by an extremely elegant oakiness. The palate is robust and well constructed with a good firm structure, the warranty of a great future.

• Luc d'Arfeuille, Ch. La Serre, 33330 Saint-Emilion, tel. 05.57.24.71.38, fax 05.57.24.63.01 Y by appt.

CH. DES LAUDES 1998★

■ 2.9 ha 18,000 €15-23

This is a new cru of around 3 ha (7.4 acres) out of the 5 ha (12.3 acres) cultivated by the associates of the GFA Haut-Saint-Georges. These new producers are very experienced in wine-making. Their 98 is deep and lively in appearance. On airing, it reveals a clean, elegant nose with a touch of Cabernet. The full palate has morello cherry flavours and finishes on tannins that are still firm. This is a good wine to lay down and will be ready four to ten years from now.

• GFA du Haut-Saint-Georges, Arvouet, BP 80, 33330 Vignonet, tel. 05.57.55.38.00, fax 05.57.55.38.01 Y ev. day except Sat. Sun. 9am–12.30pm 1.30pm–6pm

• B. Banton

CH. LA TOUR-FIGEAC 1998★

■ Gd cru clas. 12.5 ha 40,000 €30-38

82 83 85 86 89 |90| 93 |94| |95| 96 |97| 98

Though many crus have the famous name of Figeac in their titles, this one became independent in 1879. The vineyard, located on soils of mixed clays, ancient sand and gravel, is planted with 80% Merlot and 20% Cabernet Franc. Remarkably handsome, it is dark, with an almost black appearance deep down and nuances of purple near the surface. On the nose this 98 is still a little closed. The palate, however, displays superb concentration, dense and powerful tannins, richness, fleshiness and unctuousity. The oak is still very prominent, and the excellent body is promising.

• Otto Rettenmaier, BP 007, 33330 Saint-Emilion, tel. 05.57.51.77.62, fax 05.57.25.36.92 Y by appt.

CH. LA TOUR DU PIN FIGEAC 1998

■ Gd cru clas. 11 ha 69,000 €15-23

|88| |89| |90| 95 98

Separated from the prestigious Château Figeac in 1876, this 11-ha (27.2-acre) cru has belonged to the Giraud-Bélivier family since 1923. Sited on gravel and sandy-clay, the vineyard is three-quarters Merlot, one-quarter Cabernet Franc. The garnet colour of this elegant wine is beginning to show signs of maturity. The nose is still somewhat closed, but hints of fruity, spicy or oaky notes indicate the possibilities ahead. The well-structured, well-balanced palate is supported by firm, well-made tannins. Three to five years should see this wine open and offering its best.

• André Giraud, Ch. Le Caillou, 41, rue de Catusseau, 33500 Pomerol, tel. 05.57.51.06.10, fax 05.57.51.74.95

• Y by appt.

• GFA Giraud-Bélivier

CH. LAVALLADE 1998

■ 88 90 |95| 96 98 | 4 ha | 25,000 | ▦ €11-15

This cru is a family property. It is a selection from the best plots on the estate and represents one-third of the vineyard. It comprises 85% Merlot, 10% Cabernet Franc and 5% Cabernet Sauvignon. The colour is a fine dark garnet. The youthful nose is still reticent but will soon open on fresh, fruity notes. The palate is sturdy with tannins that are still a little hard, needing two to five years' ageing.
➤ SCEA Gaury et Fils, Ch. Lavallade, 33330 Saint-Christophe-des-Bardes, tel. 05.57.24.77.49, fax 05.57.24.64.83 ▣
⅄ by appt.

LE FER 1998★

■ | 2 ha | 6,000 | ▦ €23-30

Curiously, the label of this wine features a horseshoe. This 98, created by the Bordeaux *négoce* Mähler-Besse, is a single-variety Merlot made from 2 ha (4.9 acres) out of the 5 ha (12.3 acres) owned by the concern in the south of the appellation. Grown on siliceous-clay, this wine is a lovely deep purple with an already expressive and complex nose of flowers (hyacinth) and red fruit, with strong oaky, toasty notes. The attack is fresh and elegant, heralding a well-balanced development between the fruit and the oak. Round and mouthfilling, this wine is true to type and well-made.
➤ SA Mähler-Besse, 49, rue Camille-Godard, BP 23, 33026 Bordeaux, tel. 05.56.56.04.30, fax 05.56.56.04.59, e-mail france.mahler-besse@wanadoo.fr ▣
⅄ by appt.

CH. LE MERLE 1998

■ | 4 ha | 20,000 | ▦ ▤ ⚬ €11-15

Only Merlot is grown on this small property situated at Saint-Pey-d'Armens in the south-east of the appellation, recently joined to Vignobles Réunis. The wine has an attractive dense red colour, and on the nose blends fine, discreet notes of red fruit with nuances of toasty oak. Supple and well-balanced, this 98 will give pleasure in one to two years' time.

➤ SA Les Vignobles Réunis, 33330 Saint-Pey-d'Armens, tel. 05.56.81.57.86, fax 05.56.81.57.90, e-mail accueil@saint-lo-group.com ▣
⅄ by appt.

CH. LES CABANNES 1998

■ | 0.5 ha | 3,600 | ▦ €11-15

This property was bought in 1997 by a Canadian oenologist living in Bordeaux. A plot of old Merlot vines on deep gravel has produced this extremely small quantity. An agreeable, tasty 98 wine with an intense, lively ruby colour, its nose has aromas of blackcurrant and liquorice with floral perfumes (pinks) and toasty nuances of attractive oak. The supple, round, fleshy palate is well balanced with a very fruity finish. Drink now or keep two to three years.
➤ Peter Kjellberg, Les Cabannes, 33330 Saint-Sulpice-de-Faleyrens, tel. 05.57.24.62.86 ▣ ⅄ by appt.

CH. LES GRANDES MURAILLES 1998★

■ 88 | 1|89| 94 |95| |96| 97 98 | Gd cru clas. | 2 ha | 7,500 | ▦ €23-30

The large fortified walls alluded to in the name are vestiges of a 12th-century Jacobin friary and are emblematic of the appellation. The small vineyard they protect has belonged to the Reiffers family since 1643. Essentially a Merlot, grown on limestone-clay, this 98 has a superb vibrant and intense ruby colour with very bright violet-purple highlights. The expressive nose reveals aromas of dark berry fruit, prune and spices, combined with grilled and vanilla notes derived from excellent oak. After a supple and round attack, the palate opens out with a well-balanced structure equipped with firm tannins. This wine will suit laying down.
➤ GFA Les Grandes Murailles, Ch. Côte de Baleau, 33330 Saint-Emilion, tel. 05.57.24.71.09, fax 05.57.24.69.72, e-mail lesgrandesmurailles@wanadoo.fr
⅄ by appt.

LES PLANTES DU MAYNE 1998★

■ | n.c. | 13,000 | ▦ €15-23

This is a very interesting second wine, even if it is rather expensive. Produced and matured at Château Grand-Mayne, it has had the same care bestowed on it as the main wine. It has a Bigarreau colour with vermilion highlights. The nose is beginning to express aromas of red fruit with an oaky background. The palate is structured by tannins which are a little hard but elegant. Its denseness will contribute to its ageing potential.
➤ GFA Jean-Pierre Nony, Ch. Grand-Mayne, 33330 Saint-Emilion, tel. 05.57.74.42.50, fax 05.57.74.41.89, e-mail grand-mayne@grand-mayne.com ▣
⅄ by appt.

CH. LE LOUP 1998★

■ | 6.12 ha | 39,829 | ▤ ▦ ⚬ €8-11

From half Merlot, half Cabernet Franc grown on siliceous-clay to the north of Saint-Christophe-des-Bardes, this cru presents this attractive 98 which at first releases aromas of musky leather and venison, and then, when left to breathe, yields aromas of red fruit. The palate is well-structured, with powerful, firm tannins with a high quality vinosity. In two to three years' time this wine should be ready.
➤ Union de producteurs de Saint-Emilion, Haut-Gravet, BP 27, 33330 Saint-Emilion, tel. 05.57.24.70.71, fax 05.57.24.65.18, e-mail udp-vins.saint-emilion@gofornet.com ⅄ ev. day except Sun. 8am–12 noon 2pm–6pm
➤ Patrick Garrigue

■ **CH. L'ETAMPE 1998★**

1.82 ha 7,000 | £11–15

This is the first appearance in the *Guide* for this small cru (1.82 ha/4.5 acres), which was purchased and created in 1997. It is essentially consists of Merlot supplemented by 15% Cabernet Franc grown on sand and silt with subsoil of iron deposits. Dark ruby-red, youthful and intense, this 98 still displays violet highlights. Slightly dominated by an attractive oakiness with notes of vanilla and toast, it nevertheless yields pleasing aromas of ripe fruits. After a supple and round attack, it opens out on a lovely tannic structure, which is still rather firm on the finish and therefore calls for several years' patience.
➳ Ch. L'Etampe, RD 245, 33330 Saint-Emilion, tel. 05.56.44.27.71, fax 05.56.01.25.39 ☑ ☒ by appt.

■ **CH. LUCIE 1998**

4.3 ha 25,000 | £15–23

This is a small vineyard, which mainly consists of Merlot (95%) planted on various soils, namely sand, gravel and clay. The intense colour is youthful. On airing, the wine releases fruity, toasted aromas. The supple, fruity palate has fine, fresh tannins. Wait two to four years before drinking this wine with meat, including game.
➳ Michel Bertolussi, 316, Grands-Champs, 33330 Saint-Sulpice-de-Faleyrens, tel. 05.57.74.44.42, fax 05.57.24.73.00

■ **CH. LUSSEAU 1998★**

0.42 ha 2,700 | £15–23

Laurent Lusseau bought this really tiny cru of less than 0.5 ha (1.03 acres) from his uncle in 1993. The vines consist of 70% Merlot and 30% Bouchet planted on sandy-gravelly soil in the south of the appellation. This is a really nice 98 with an attractive dark-ruby colour and a predominantly oaky nose (roasted coffee and vanilla). The palate is full and rich, and opens to reveal tannins that are very evident yet agreeable. Still a little over-whelmed by the oak, it has good potential that ought to be appreciable in five to six years' time.
➳ Laurent Lusseau, 276, Percy-Nord, 33330 Saint-Sulpice-de-Faleyrens, tel. 05.57.74.46.54, fax 05.57.24.67.19

■ **CH. MAGDELAINE 1998**

1er gd cru B | 10.36 ha 33,000 | £38–46

70	75	78	79	80	83	85	86	87	88
89	90	92	93	94	95	96	97	98	

Magdelaine is a property belonging to the great Moueix family and is situated on both a limestone plateau and limestone-clay hillside. Thirty-year-old vines (90% Merlot and 10% Cabernet Franc) have yielded this lovely wine, which has spent 14 months in oak. The eye is immediately taken by the straightforward Bordeaux red colour. The oak influence is delicate both on the nose and on the palate. All is silky charm and softness, although the

---

still-tannic finish suggests that this wine could be kept for three to four years.
➳ Ets Jean-Pierre Moueix, 54, quai du Priourat, 33500 Libourne, tel. 05.57.51.78.96

■ **CH. MAGNAN 1998**

82 85 86 88 (89) 91 92 94 96 97 98

10 ha 50,000 | £11–15

This 10-ha (24.7-acre) cru forms part of a 25-ha (61.8-acre) estate bought by the Moreaud family in 1979. It is a classic Saint-Emilion blend grown on a *terroir* of ancient sand. This dark, good-looking 98 has an elegant nose with touches of oaky Cabernet, and a fruity, harmonious palate which softens to lengthy tannins on the finish. Wait a while before drinking it.
➳ SCEA Corneil-Figeac, BP 49, 33330 Saint-Emilion, tel. 05.57.24.70.53, fax 05.57.24.68.20, e-mail corneil-figeac.com ☑ ☒ by appt.
➳ R. Moreaud

■ **CH. MAGNAN LA GAFFELIERE 1998**

7.33 ha 48,000 | £11–15

This vineyard, planted on a sandy, rain-washed slope, comprises 65% Merlot, 25% Bouchet and 10% Cabernet Sauvignon. One-third matured in vat and two-thirds in oak, this wine has youthful character in all its aspects. The nose is still closed and releases its fruity, spicy aromas only when left to breathe and air. The palate has a clean, full attack, then displays fine but still-austere tannins which will require two to five years to become smooth.
➳ SA du Clos La Madeleine, La Gaffelière Ouest, BP 78, 33330 Saint-Emilion, tel. 05.57.55.38.03, fax 05.57.55.38.01 ☑ ☒ by appt.

■ **CH. MANGOT**
Cuvée Quintessence 1998★

2.75 ha 10,800 | £15–23

96 98

This wine is a selection from the 34 ha (84 acres) constituting this cru. The vines are all Merlot, 40 years old and planted on marine-based limestone in the east of the appellation. The colour is intense with some mature highlights. This vintage has a very oaky and toasty nose, hinting at prune, brandy, spices and a touch of musk. The generous palate has a very ripe Merlot flavour and on the finish the tannins show themselves to be fine and long. Serve in two to seven years' time.
➳ Vignobles Jean Petit, Ch. Mangot, 33330 Saint-Etienne-de-Lisse, tel. 05.57.40.18.23, fax 05.57.40.15.97, e-mail chmangot@terre-net.fr ☑ ☒ ev. day 8.30am–12 noon 2pm–6pm, Sat. Sun. by appt.

Saint-Emilion Grand Cru

CH. MATRAS 1998★
■ Gd cru clas.　8 ha　30,000　 ▮ ▯ ◷ €15-23
83 85 86 [90] [92] [93] [94] 97 98

The Matras barrels are stored in a former 17th-century chapel. This 98, the product of 50% Merlot, 50% Cabernet Franc, has a lovely garnet colour with deep violet lights. On the nose there is a blend of fresh aromas of red and dark berry fruit with grilled and charred notes from good oak. Full and smooth on the palate, this powerful, generous wine has good rich, dense tannins that have great length on the finish.

➤ Vignobles Véronique Gaboriaud,
Ch. Matras, 33330 Saint-Emilion,
tel. 05.57.51.52.39, fax 05.57.51.70.19 ▼
Ⓨ by appt.

CH. MAUVEZIN 1998
■　3.5 ha　15,000　 ▮ ▯ ◷ €23-30

This attractive and intense ruby-coloured wine reveals jammy red fruit and dried fruit aromas linked to pleasing grilled and toasty notes. Supple at first, the palate quickly unveils a strong tannic presence. Though a little firm at present, it should mellow after several years.

➤ GFA P. Cassat et Fils, BP 44,
33330 Saint-Emilion, tel. 05.57.24.72.36,
fax 05.57.74.48.54 ▼ Ⓨ by appt.

CH. MILON 1998
■　20 ha　43,000　 ▮ ▯ ◷ €8-11

The Bouyer-Arteau family cultivates nearly 27 ha (66.7 acres), including this fine wine-producing domaine. This cru, on siliceous clay and iron-bearing soils in the north of the appellation, comprises 80% Merlot and 20% Cabernets. The wine has a dark colour. Though still reserved, the nose opens on airing to reveal notes of flowers, cinnamon and vanilla. After a powerful, energetic attack, the palate displays tannins that are still firm but promising. This 98 should be ready for drinking in two to three years' time.

➤ Christian Bouyer, Ch. Milon,
33330 Saint-Christophe-des-Bardes,
tel. 05.57.24.77.18, fax 05.57.24.64.20 ▼
Ⓨ by appt.

CH. MOINE VIEUX 1998
■　3.5 ha　18,000　 ▮ ▯ €11-15

At this small property, sited on sand and gravel in the south of the appellation, there are 30-year-old vines typical of the Libourne region. This engaging 98 has a ruby colour with cherry highlights. The nose is already intense with red fruit, toasty oak and vanilla. The structure is very supple, pleasing and long with well-ripened Merlot flavours. The discreet tannins will allow this wine to be drunk quite soon, for example to accompany poultry in a wild mushroom sauce.

➤ SCE Moine Vieux, Lanseman,
33330 Saint-Sulpice-de-Faleyrens,
tel. 05.57.74.40.54, fax 05.57.74.40.54 ▼
Ⓨ by appt.
➤ P. Dentraygues

CH. MONBOUSQUET 1998★
■　33 ha　80,000　 ▮ ▯ ◷ €46-76
[93] [94] [95] 96 97 98

Acquired in 1992 by Gérard Perse, this cru is east of Saint-Sulpice-de-Faleyrens on gravelly clay. It comprises 60% Merlot, 30% Cabernet Franc and 10% Cabernet Sauvignon. The result is a dark garnet 98. The powerful nose is characterised by vanilla and toast, alongside ripe fruit aromas. The round, fleshy palate, rich and winey, is currently dominated by the oak of the barrels, but the wine will develop well in the coming years due to its excellent structure.

➤ SA Ch. Monbousquet,
33330 Saint-Sulpice-de-Faleyrens,
tel. 05.57.55.43.43, fax 05.57.24.63.99
➤ Gérard Perse

CH. MONLOT CAPET 1998★
■　7 ha　45,000　 ▮ ▯ €15-23
90 92 93 94 [95] [96] [97] 98

On limestone-clay at Saint-Hippolyte in the east of the appellation, this steady and reliable cru is regularly singled out by our experts. The purple colour of this 98 shows signs of development. The nose is already complex with aromas of medlar, blackcurrant and an attractively charred oakiness. The palate is fresh with fine, dense tannins. The wine should be enjoyable to drink in two to six years, when it will go very well with lamprey *Bordelaise*.

➤ Bernard Rivals, Ch. Monlot-Capet,
33330 Saint-Hippolyte, tel. 05.57.74.49.47,
fax 05.57.24.62.33, e-mail musset-rivals@
belair-monlot.com ▼ Ⓨ by appt.

CH. MOULIN GALHAUD 1998★★
■　2 ha　n.c.　 ▮ ▯ ◷ €15-23

The Galhaud family has been known in the world of Saint-Emilion wines for several generations, but this cru appeared in the *Guide* for the first time only last year – despite the difficulties of the 1997 harvest. The current manager only took over in 1996, so this year's 98 is a confirmation of her success. It represents the production of 2 ha (5 acres) of single-variety Merlot, grown on gravel and selected from the domaine's 5.6 ha (13.8 acres). The ruby colour is dark and dense. The nose is already a powerful mix of dark berry fruit, spices, vanilla, leather and liquorice. The palate is equally very rich, round, generous and fleshy, and finishes on velvety tannins. Authentically Saint-Emilion, this wine is a fine blend between well-ripened Merlot and vanilla oak.

➤ SCEA Martine Galhaud,
33330 Vignonet, tel. 05.57.97.39.73,
fax 05.57.97.39.74 ▼
Ⓨ ev. day 8am–12 noon 1pm–3pm

CH. MOULIN SAINT-GEORGES 1998★★

| 86 | 89 | 90 | 91 | 93 | 94 | 95 | 96 | 97 | 98 |

7 ha   35,000   € 30-38

This attractive property, located at the southern entrance to Saint-Emilion at the foot of Ausone (which is also cultivated by Alain Vauthier), is a classic Saint-Emilion vineyard, comprising 70% Merlot and 30% Cabernets on limestone-clay. The wine is also a classic and always of top quality. This fine, dark, ruby-coloured 98 has an intensely fruity but especially oaky nose with vanilla and very pleasant oaky palate has achieved a perfect balance between the red fruit flavours and the well-integrated tannins.

- Famille Vauthier, Ch. Ausone, 33330 Saint-Emilion, tel. 05.57.24.70.26, fax 05.57.24.47.39 ▼ ev. day except Sun. 8am–1pm 1.30pm–5.30pm; cl. Jan.

CH. ORISSE DU CASSE 1998

| 85 | 86 | 88 | 89 | 92 | 94 | 95 | 96 | 98 |

5.35 ha   12,500   € 11-15

Danielle and Richard Dubois are oenologists who aim to create traditional, crafted wines. Their terroir of gravelly sands and iron-bearing gravel has produced this deep-purple 98. The youthful nose is still very fruity (blackcurrant and redcurrant) and slightly oaky. The palate is very young and fresh, finishing with tannins that are firm and need several years' ageing to soften.

- Richard Dubois, Ch. Bertinat Lartigue, 33330 Saint-Sulpice-de-Faleyrens, tel. 05.57.24.72.75, fax 05.57.74.45.43, e-mail dubricru@aol.com ▼ ev. day 9am–11.30am 2.30pm–5.30pm; cl. 14 Aug–3 Sept.

CH. PARAN JUSTICE 1998

11.02 ha   48,666   € 8-11

This property, on siliceous-clay at Saint-Etienne-de-Lisse, is dominated by Merlot (68%). This agreeable 98 is ready to drink. A bright, clear garnet colour, it has a somewhat reticent nose with some floral aromas combined with musky, leathery notes. The supple, well-balanced palate reveals fine, generous tannins.

- Union de producteurs de Saint-Emilion, Haut-Gravet, BP 27, 33330 Saint-Emilion, tel. 05.57.24.70.71, fax 05.57.24.65.18, e-mail udp-vins.saint-emilion@goformet.com ▼ ev. day except Sun. 8am–12 noon 2pm–6pm
- Marie Boutros-Toni

CH. PATRIS 1998★★

| 88 | 90 | 92 | 93 | 95 | 96 | 97 | 98 |

7.59 ha   24,000   € 15-23

Michel Querre has been cultivating this cru, regularly commended by our tasters, since 1967. In 1996, he invested further in the property, a step that seems to have paid off, judging by his very good 97 (a difficult year) and this remarkable 98. The wine has a magnificent dark-purple colour and alluring aromas of jammy dark fruit and warm ginger-bread. Full, generous, and mouthfilling on the palate, it has mature, mellow tannins on the finish. This thoroughbred, sophisticated wine is the result of the use of fine grapes and expertly-handled vinification. Though already good, this wine should age well.

- Michel Querre, SCEA Ch. Patris, 33330 Saint-Emilion, tel. 05.57.55.51.60, fax 05.57.55.51.61 ▼ by appt.

CH. PAVIE 1998★

1er gd cru B   37 ha   80,000   € 76

| 87 | 88 | 89 | 90 | 91 | 92 | 93 | 94 | 95 | 96 | 98 |

This is Gérard Perse's first harvest and he presents a very successful 98. He acquired this important and prestigious domaine in 1998. It is located on the first line of cultivated hillsides and faces directly south. The terroir of limestone-clay and gravel is planted with 40-year-old vines; 60% Merlot and 40% Cabernets. A beautiful, dark, Bordeaux-red colour, almost black, this wine has a highly expressive nose of very ripe or stewed fruit, pastries, almonds, vanilla and coconut. The palate is generous, dense and flavoursome, revealing lots of tannins, grapes and oak. The oakiness is almost too much. This is a modern-style Pavie.

- Gérard Perse, SCA Ch. Pavie, 33330 Saint-Emilion, tel. 05.57.55.43.43, fax 05.57.24.63.99

CH. PAVIE DECESSE 1998★

Gd cru clas.   10 ha   33,000   € 76

| 83 | 85 | 86 | 88 | 89 | 90 | 91 | 92 | 93 | 94 | 96 | 97 | 98 |

The Perse family bought this 10-ha (24.7-acre) property in 1997. It is situated on the limestone-clay slopes of Côte Pavie and faces due south. Last year's version (the 97) was a coup de coeur, and this year's 98, essentially a Merlot with 10% Cabernet Franc, is also very good. The superb garnet colour, dark and intense, is complemented by a powerful nose of ripe red fruit and oaky elegance, all of which herald the concentration found on the palate. Although the tannins need several years' ageing, the structure is gorgeous.

- SCA Pavie-Decesse, 33330 Saint-Emilion, tel. 05.57.55.43.43, fax 05.57.24.63.99
- Gérard Perse

CH. PAVIE MACQUIN 1998★★

Gd cru clas.   11.89 ha   47,000   € 46-76

| 83 | 85 | 86 | 88 | 89 | 90 | 91 | 92 | 93 | 94 | 96 | 97 | 98 |

Close to the medieval town, this cru dominates Côte Pavie, being on top of the limestone-clay plateau. The method of cultivation is part sustainable, part biodynamic. Last year's 97 was a coup de coeur, and this year's 98 is remarkable, possessing a magnificent deep purple colour with deep mauve highlights. The nose is intense and very expressive with aromas of dark jammy fruit alongside charred notes of superb toasty oak. The powerful, rich palate reveals a dense, elegant, thoroughbred structure with a long finish. This is a fine wine for laying down.

➤ SCEA Ch. Pavie Macquin, 33330 Saint-Emilion, tel. 05.57.24.74.23, fax 05.57.24.63.78 ▼ Y by appt.
➤ Famille Corre-Macquin

CH. PETIT FOMBRAUGE 1998★★   2.5 ha   12,000   €15-23

CHATEAU
PETIT FOMBRAUGE
SAINT-EMILION GRAND CRU
1998
Pierre Lavau
Propriétaire, 33330 St-Christophe-des-Bardes

Pierre Lavau bought this small property at auction in 1996 and has invested a lot in it to bring it up to standard. His efforts began to be rewarded with his very first harvest, which was singled out by our experts. This 98 has conquered them completely, as they have awarded it a *coup de cœur*. They liked the deep ruby colour and slightly fruity nose, but what they appreciated most of all was the toasty oakiness. The very expressive palate has lots of red fruit and youthful but promising tannins. The good grapes and good workmanship in this wine can start to be enjoyed in two years' time, when it will go well with red meat and cheese.

➤ Pierre Lavau, Ch. Petit Fombrauge, 33330 Saint-Christophe-des-Bardes, tel. 05.57.24.77.30, fax 05.57.24.66.24, e-mail petitfombrauge@terre-net.fr ▼ Y by appt.

CH. PETIT-GRAVET 1998   3 ha   14,500   €11-15

This wine is the product of vines more than 40 years old (60% Merlot), planted on deep sand. The purple colour shows mature highlights. The pleasant nose has interesting finesse. The palate contains tannins that are enveloped in rich flesh, together with hints of leather and charred oak. The finish is already silky and will enable this wine to be drunk soon.

➤ SCE Ch. Petit-Gravet, 2, rue de la Madeleine, 33330 Saint-Emilion, tel. 06.82.10.64.75, fax 06.57.24.72.34, e-mail petit.gravet@wanadoo.fr ▼
Y by appt.
➤ Mme M.-L. Nouvel

CH. PETIT VAL 1998   9.25 ha 50,000

86 88 |89| |93| |95| 96 98

On a sandy, rainwashed slope to the north of Saint-Emilion, this cru offers a well-balanced varietal mix of 70% Merlot, 20% Cabernet Franc and 10% Cabernet Sauvignon. The light ruby of this 98 displays a few signs of development. The youthful nose reveals aromas of red fruit in brandy together with spicy, slightly oaky notes. The mouthfilling palate has good balance of fleshiness, good vinosity and tannins that are long on the finish.

➤ Michel Boutet, SC du Ch. Vieux Pourret, BP 70, 33330 Saint-Emilion, tel. 05.57.24.70.86, fax 05.57.24.68.30 ▼

CH. PIGANEAU 1998   n.c. 25,000   €8-11

This vineyard is situated near the Dordogne as you leave Libourne, where, in former days, one would have found the port of Saint-Emilion. The standing stone of Pierrefitte, the largest megalith in the Gironde, is also nearby. This lovely 98 has a bright, good-quality ruby colour and a very pleasant nose with fruity, spicy and oaky aromas. The supple, round palate does not have a very robust structure, but this is compensated for by the wine's finesse and charm. It is ideal for serving alongside rabbit with cranberries.

➤ SCEA J.-B. Brunot et Fils, 1, Jean-Melin, 33330 Saint-Emilion, tel. 05.57.55.09.99, fax 05.57.55.09.95, e-mail vignobles.brunot@wanadoo.fr ▼ Y by appt.

CH. PIPEAU 1998   35 ha 190,000

86 88 89 92 93 |94| |95| 96 97 98

Created around 1900 by the present owner's grandfather, this cru today comprises 35 ha (86.5 acres) of Merlot, along with 10% Cabernet Franc and 10% Cabernet Sauvignon. It is situated at the foot of the hillside to the south-east of Saint-Emilion on limestone-clay, sand and gravel *terroir*. This dark, intensely ruby-coloured 98 has a nose which, though still a little closed, reveals notes of red fruit and leather. The robust, solid structure has beautiful tannins which are somewhat closed and austere, but bid fair to a fine future.

➤ GAEC Mestreguilhem, Ch. Pipeau, 33330 Saint-Laurent-des-Combes, tel. 05.57.24.72.95, fax 05.57.24.71.25, e-mail chateau.pipeau@wanadoo.fr ▼ Y by appt.

CH. PLAISANCE 1998★   9 ha   54,000   €11-15

From a 9-ha (22.2-acre) selection out of the 16 ha (39.5 acres) cultivated by Xavier Mareschal since 1997 in the south of the appellation, this cru comprises 80% Merlot and 20% Cabernets. The soils are varied, being sand, gravel and clay. This highly successful 98 has a dark-ruby colour with garnet highlights. The aromas of red fruit are quickly overwhelmed by notes of roasted, vanilla oak. The elegant palate, also, is too oaky for the moment. This wine will be enjoyable between 2003 and 2013.

➤ SCEA ch. Plaisance, 33330 Saint-Sulpice-de-Faleyrens, tel. 05.57.24.78.85, fax 05.57.74.44.94 ✓
Y by appt.
● Xavier Mareschal

CH. DE PRESSAC 1998★   10 ha   49,000   €15-23

The claim of this château to history is twofold. It was here that the pact ending the Hundred Years' War was sealed in 1453, here too that the Noir de Pressac grape variety (Auxerrois) was first planted. The 40-ha (98.8-acre) estate was bought in 1997 by J.-F. and D. Quenin. This 98 has a magnificent appearance, almost black yet gleaming. The complex nose combines dark berry fruit and roasted vanilla-oak aromas. The elegant, classy palate finishes on superbly-textured tannins. In five to eight years this wine will be excellent with red meat and game.

➤ GFA Ch. de Pressac, 33330 Saint-Etienne-de-Lisse, tel. 05.57.40.18.02, fax 05.57.40.10.07, e-mail jfetdquenin@libertysurf.fr ✓
Y by appt.
● J.-F. et D. Quenin

CH. PUY MOUTON 1998   2 ha   n.c.   €11-15

Located on the siliceous-clay soils of Saint-Christophe-des-Bardes to the north of the appellation, this cru has produced a handsome ruby wine with purple highlights. The nose opens with touches of undergrowth, green peppercorns, toast and vanilla. The soft, round attack has a fruity flavour but the liquorice tannins have strong presence and need to age for two to five years.

➤ EARL Vignobles D. et C. Devand, Ch. de Faise, 33570 Les Artigues-de-Lussac, tel. 05.57.24.31.39, fax 05.57.24.34.17
Y by appt.

CH. QUERCY 1998★★   88 89 90 92 93 94 95 96 98   4.5 ha   20,000   €15-23

With its dark purple appearance and deep mauve highlights, this 98, grown on sandy-gravel soils, engaged our most exacting tasters. When left to breathe, it released intense aromas dominated by very high quality oak. The warm, generous palate combines concentration and richness with flavours of fruit, tobacco, and very refined tannins. A wine of character for real wine buffs, it will be at its best five to seven years from now.

➤ GFA du Ch. Quercy, 3, Grave, 33330 Vignonet, tel. 05.57.84.56.07, fax 05.57.84.54.82, e-mail chateauquercy@ wanadoo.fr ✓ Y by appt.

CH. QUERCY Marina Carine 1998★★   0.5 ha   1,000   €38-46

How does one best celebrate ten years in charge of a domaine? By issuing a rare wine. This vintage is limited to 1,000 bottles produced from 0.5 ha (1.24 acres) of gravel soil planted with 80% Merlot and 20% Bouchet vines that are 80 years old. The result could hardly fail to be remarkable, and our tasters confirmed it with two stars. The sumptuous, dark, Bordeaux-red colour, with its purple highlights, is matched by the powerful, complex nose, which reveals a succession of floral, fruity and gamey aromas against a background of charred oak. Rich and full, velvety and structured by mature tannins, the palate is a succession of powerful flavours. It is still a little overdominated by the oak, but the fruitiness returns on the fresh, flavourful finish. This is going to be an extraordinary wine in five to ten years' time.

➤ GFA du Ch. Quercy, 3, Grave, 33330 Vignonet, tel. 05.57.84.56.07, fax 05.57.84.54.82, e-mail chateauquercy@ wanadoo.fr ✓ Y by appt.

CH. RABY-JEAN VOISIN 1998   9.5 ha   60,000   €11-15

The Raby-Saugeon family acquired this cru on ancient sand and iron deposits in 1968. The varietal composition is 80% Merlot and 20% Cabernets. To the eye, this wine presents several changing shades of salmon-pink. The nose is very complex, more floral than fruity, mixing a hint of musk with a lot of toasty oak. The palate begins supple and round, then rapidly opens out with very oaky and vanilla flavours, which are dominant but should calm down in two to three years.

➤ Vignobles Raby-Saugeon, Ch. du Paradis, 33330 Saint-Emilion, tel. 05.57.55.07.20, fax 05.57.55.07.21, e-mail chateau.du.paradis@wanadoo.fr ✓
Y by appt.

CH. RIOU DE THAILLAS 1998★★   3 ha   10,000   €15-23

Recently acquired by Jean-Yves and Michèle Béchet, this small estate makes a fine entrance into the *Guide* with this remarkable 98. A single-variety Merlot, it has a dark, dense, garnet colour and is developing a concentrated nose with ripe fruit and elegant, high-class oakiness with charred, vanilla and cocoa notes. After a full, fleshy attack, the palate shows great length and finishes with a lovely, very rich and lengthy tannic texture. This is a great wine, which needs four to five years' ageing in the cellar.

➤ Michèle Béchet, Ch. Riou de Thaillas, 33330 Saint-Emilion, tel. 05.57.68.42.15, fax 05.57.68.28.59, e-mail jean-yves.bechet@wanadoo.fr ✓
Y by appt.

CH. ROC DE BOISSEAUX 1998★   92 93 94 97 98   5 ha   32,000   €8-11

This cru, located on the sandy-gravelly soils of Saint-Sulpice-de-Faleyrens, benefited from the advice of oenologist Gilles Pauquet and of Vitigestion. A deep-ruby 98, four-fifths Merlot, one-fifth Cabernet Franc, this wine reflects the excellent oak maturation period with its spicy, toasty notes that combine well with fresh red fruit aromas. The full, fleshy palate is mouthfilling with excellent balance and great length. This classic wine should be left to age three to five years in the cellar.

➤ SCEA du Ch. Roc de Boisseaux, Trapeau, 33330 Saint-Sulpice-de-Faleyrens, tel. 05.57.74.45.40, fax 05.57.88.07.00 Y by appt.
➤ GFA Mme Clowez

CH. ROCHEBELLE 1998★★

2.7 ha 15,000 €15-23

88 |89| |93| 96 97 **98**

Grown on an excellent limestone-clay *terroir*, 15% Cabernet Franc with Merlot have yielded this remarkable 98, handsomely presented with a dark, deep-ruby appearance. The powerful, harmonious nose has aromas of overripe fruit and prunes with spicy notes and a fresh hint of menthol. The full, round palate has a superb tannic texture and a long finish. A good wine for laying down.

➤ SCEA Philippe Faniest, Ch. Rochebelle, 33330 Saint-Laurent-des-Combes, tel. 06.07.32.37.94, fax 05.57.51.01.99, e-mail chateaurochebelle@grand-cru-st-emilion.c Y by appt.

CH. ROCHER BELLEVUE FIGEAC 1998★

7.5 ha n.c. €11-15

86 (88| |89| 91 92 94 95 96 97 **98**

Of the 10.5 ha (25.9 acres) that he cultivates, the owner of this domaine reserves 7.5 ha (18.5 acres) for this cru, located on ancient sand and gravel planted with 70% Merlot and 30% Cabernet Franc. This is thus a classic vineyard producing a classic, reliable wine. Deep Bordeaux-red in colour, the nose reveals an attractive oaky fruitiness. The palate displays an excellent concentration of dense, lengthy tannins. This wine is full of promise and should be left in the cellar for two to six years.

➤ SC Rocher Bellevue Figeac, 14, rue d'Aviau, 33000 Bordeaux, tel. 05.56.81.19.69, fax 05.56.81.19.69 Y by appt.
➤ Pierre Dutruilh

CH. ROLLAND-MAILLET 1998★★

3.35 ha 15,000 €11-15

82 85 86 |89| |90| |93| |94| 95 97 **98**

Michel Rolland, an oenologist with an international reputation, oversees this cru planted with three-quarters Merlot, one quarter Cabernet Franc. The dark and deep purple colour of this 98 still has lively, very youthful highlights. The nose is agreeable and intense, dominated by very ripe aromas of red and dark berry fruit spiced with a touch of well-balanced oak. The robust, fleshy palate is full and well-structured, superbly combining together the grape and oak tannins. This remarkable wine should be left, if possible, for three to four years before drinking.

➤ SCEA Fermière des domaines Rolland, Maillet, 33500 Pomerol, tel. 05.57.51.23.05, fax 05.57.51.66.08 Y by appt.

CH. ROL VALENTIN 1998★★

3.8 ha 12,000 €46-76

94 |95| 96 **98**

Eric Prissette is an enthusiast. He is as interested in top-level sport as he is in top-level wines. Wine-maker since 1994, he achieved his first *coup de cœur* with his 95, and has returned after a two-year absence to repeat the feat with this charming 98. It is a single-variety Merlot from 40-year-old vines grown on sand and gravel. The appeal of the sumptuous, dark Bordeaux-red, almost black, appearance is immediate. The nose is already a powerful, concentrated and elegant blend of very ripe Merlot and liquoricey, toasty oak. The palate is fleshy, dense and aristocratic, with lots of velvety tannins. Superb! Almost excessive, this wine will surprise certain wine connoisseurs, but it will repeatedly please and will hold its own with the richest food.

➤ Eric Prissette, Ch. Rol Valentin, 33330 Saint-Emilion, tel. 05.57.74.43.51, fax 05.57.74.45.13 Y by appt.

CH. ROYLLAND 1998★

4 ha 20,000 €11-15

90| 92 |93| |94| 95 96 **98**

Taken over by the current owners in 1989, this small vineyard is in the Mazerat loop on the south-west slope of Saint-Emilion. Its slightly limestone-tinged, sandy clay is mainly planted with Merlot, apart from 10% Cabernet Franc. A lively, intense ruby colour, this 98 has aromas of very ripe red and dark berry fruit with subtle and elegant, lightly toasty oak. The supple, harmonious palate has excellent structure, balanced by ripe and powerful tannins that guarantee a good future.

➤ GFA Roylland, 33330 Saint-Emilion, tel. 05.57.24.68.27, fax 05.57.24.65.25 Y by appt.
➤ Pascal Oddo et Chantal Vuitton

CH. ROZIER 1998

n.c. 90,000 €11-15

86 88 89 90 |93| |94| 96 |97| 98

Château Rozier, established in 1850, now has 22 ha (54.3 acres) of very varied *terroir* scattered over five *communes*. The varietal composition is Merlot with 15% Cabernet Franc and 5% Cabernet Sauvignon. This characteristic 98 has an intense ruby colour. The nose has an excellent blend of red fruit and toasty aromas from good oak. The palate is well balanced, with a round and fleshy attack followed by good structure and solid constitution. The finish is still a little severe, but should soften over the next two to three years.

🛒 EARL Vignobles Jean-Bernard Saby et Fils, Ch. Rozier, 33330 Saint-Laurent-des-Combes, tel. 05.57.24.73.03, fax 05.57.24.67.77, e-mail jean.saby@chateau-rozier.com ▼ by appt.

SAINT DOMINGUE 1998★★

■ 2.7 ha 6,000 €46-76

This new cru of 2.7 ha (6.7 acres) – all Merlot – is cultivated by the La Dominique technical team, and unites together plots adjoining this classified Grand Cru that were bought in 1998 by Clément Fayat. The richness and concentration of the wine delighted our tasters. The garnet colour is dark and dense, purple with violet highlights. The nose has aromas of red and dark jammy fruit that blend elegantly with oaky notes of cocoa, smoke and toasted almonds. The round palate has a silky, fleshy attack and opens out with a powerful tannic structure which will guarantee a good future.

🛒 Clément Fayat, Ch. La Dominique, 33330 Saint-Emilion, tel. 05.57.51.31.36, fax 05.57.51.63.04, e-mail info@vignobles.fayat-group.com ▼ by appt.

CH. SAINT-LO 1998

■ 9 ha 50,000 €11-15

The Consul of Thailand in Bordeaux entirely restored this 16th-century property in 1992. Made up of 85% Merlot and 15% Cabernet Franc planted on sandy-clay, this 98 has a clear garnet colour. The nose is quite intense with dark berry fruit, liquorice and musky, leathery notes, all accompanied by a fine, mellow oakiness. The palate is robust and supple, structured with tannins that are still a little firm on the finish and need three to four years' ageing.

🛒 SA Les Vignobles Réunis, 33330 Saint-Pey-d'Armens, tel. 05.56.81.57.86, fax 05.56.81.57.90, e-mail accueil@saint-lo-group.com ▼ by appt.

SANCTUS 1998

■ 3.7 ha 12,000 €46-76

This new cru's first vintage is made in collaboration with a Chilean wine-grower, Aurelio Montes, this 98 (two-thirds Merlot, one-third Cabernet Franc) has a vibrant ruby appearance. The delicate nose reveals stewed red fruit and good oak. The palate is well-balanced with roundness, fruit and elegant, fine tannins. It would be best to wait three to four years to appreciate this wine at its best.

🛒 SA Ch. La Bienfaisance, 39, le Bourg, 33330 Saint-Emilion, tel. 05.57.24.65.83, fax 05.57.24.78.26 ▼ by appt.

CH. SAINT-GEORGES COTE PAVIE 1998

■ Gd cru clas. 5 ha 28,000 €15-23

82 83 (85) 86 88 89 |90| 92 |95| 97 98

Located at the gates of the medieval town and facing south-southwest, this cru sits on a good slope of limestone-clay terroir. This 75% Merlot, 25% Cabernet Franc is very true to type. The garnet colour is well-presented but the nose is still closed. It yields, however, subtle aromas of fruit and flower with notes of chocolate. The well-balanced palate is fruity with evident but not aggressive tannins. Well-structured, it should mature in three to four years.

🛒 Marie-Gabrielle Masson, Ch. Saint-Georges Côte Pavie, 33330 Saint-Emilion, tel. 05.57.74.44.23 ▼ by appt.

CH. SANSONNET 1998

■ Gd cru clas. 7 ha 30,000 €11-15

The family of the Marquis d'Aulan, former owner of Piper-Heidsieck Champagne, acquired this property in 1999. Sansonnet belonged once to Louis XVIII's prime minister, Decazes. Here 35-year-old vines (70% Merlot, 30% Cabernets) grow on limestone-clay. This lovely 98 has aromas of very ripe fruit, spices and a pronounced oakiness on the nose. After a supple attack, the wine opens out with oaky ripe fruit flavours, which indicates that the wine will be ready to drink fairly soon.

🛒 Ch. Sansonnet, 33330 Saint-Emilion, tel. 03.26.88.75.81, fax 03.26.88.67.43
▼ by appt.
🛒 d'Aulan

CH. TERTRE DAUGAY 1998★

■ Gd cru clas. 13 ha 50,000 €23-30

82 83 86 88 |89| |90| |93| |94| 96 98

This cru is situated on the heights of Saint-Emilion's southern hillside. Planted on limestone-clay, it enjoys good exposure to the sun. This half-Merlot, half-Cabernet Franc 98 is an attractive and very youthful wine, with a lively and intense ruby colour. Aromas of red fruit dominate the powerful, generous nose along with fine oaky notes. The well-balanced, harmonious palate has an excellent mouthfilling character together with elegant, velvety tannins, which should be completely integrated in two to three years' time. This is a thoroughly traditional Saint-Emilion.

• Léo de Malet Roquefort, Ch. La Gaffelière, 33330 Saint-Emilion, tel. 05.57.24.72.15, fax 05.57.24.69.06 [V] [Y] by appt.

CH. TEYSSIER 1998
15.6 ha 65,208 €15-23

Purchased in 1994 by Jonathan Malthus, this fine residence is surrounded by a vineyard consisting mainly of Merlot with a small portion (15%) of Cabernet Franc. This attractive 98 has a shimmering garnet colour and aromas of stewed prune with jammy red fruit, liquorice oak and musky leather. The palate has a good mouthfilling character together with fleshy, potent tannins that become a little harsh on the finish. Clearly, this wine needs to age four or five years before it can be fully appreciated.

• Jonathan Maltus, Ch. Teyssier, 33330 Vignonet, tel. 05.57.84.63.54, fax 05.57.84.63.54, e-mail info@teyssier.fr [V] [Y] by appt.

CH. TOINET FOMBRAUGE 1998
1.05 ha 7,000 €11-15

93| |94| |95| |96| 97 98

The oldest vines of this estate are used in this appellation: Merlot (80%) and Cabernet Franc (20%) grown on limestone-clay. The wine has a lovely ruby colour and the nose evokes fresh red fruit and crushed nut kernels accompanied by fine oaky notes. The palate is robust and well-structured, opening with firm but promising tannins which should soften over the coming years.

• Bernard Sierra, Ch. Toinet-Fombrauge, 33330 Saint-Christophe-des-Bardes, tel. 05.57.24.77.70, fax 05.57.24.76.49 [V] [Y] ev. day 10am–12 noon 3pm–7pm

CH. TOURANS 1998
3.66 ha 24,888 €11-15

93| |94| 95| |96| 97| 98

This is one of the many Bordeaux crus of the firm of Roger Geens, the Belgian, négociant. This attractive bright ruby 98 is a blend of Merlot (80%) and Cabernet Sauvignon (20%) grown on limestone-clay. The nose is still closed, and the wine needs to be aired before releasing lactic and oaky notes. The palate is mouthfilling, but is rapidly overtaken by strong tannins. This characterful wine will either please or disconcert according to personal taste.

• SCEA Vignobles Rocher-Cap-de-Rive 1, 33350 Saint-Magne-de-Castillon, tel. 05.57.40.08.88, fax 05.57.40.19.93, e-mail vignoblesrochercaprive@wanadoo.fr

CH. TOUR BALADOZ 1998★
5 ha 30,000 €11-15

93| |94| 95| |96| 97| 98

Produced from 30-year-old vines (70% Merlot, 30% Cabernets) on limestone-clay in the east of the appellation, this 98 has an impressive near-black colour. The nose opens on jammy and charred notes. The palate starts supple and fleshy, then is swiftly structured by the oak tannins, which are good quality but a little firm. This wine needs to be laid down between three and twelve years, according to personal taste and storage conditions.

• SCEA Ch. Tour Baladoz, 33330 Saint-Laurent-des-Combes, tel. 05.57.88.94.17, fax 05.57.88.39.14, e-mail gdemour@aol.com [V] [Y] by appt.

CH. TOUR DES COMBES 1998
13 ha 51,000 €11-15

90| |94| |95| |96| 98

The vineyard (80% Merlot) sits on limestone-clay and sand at the foot of the hillside in Saint-Laurent-des-Combes. This attractive ruby-coloured 98 has a discreet nose with hints of freshness and fruit and several notes of spice. The palate is supple and round with agreeable fleshy tannins and red fruit flavours that return on the finish.

• SCE des Vignobles Darribéhaude, I. Au Sable, 33330 Saint-Laurent-des-Combes, tel. 05.57.24.70.04, fax 05.57.74.46.14 [V] [Y] by appt.

TOUR DU SÈME 1998★
3 ha 15,000 €15-23

This newcomer to the *Guide*, established in March 1998, has already impressed the Jury with this surprising wine, a vineyard selection from 3 ha (7.4 acres) of the property's 6 ha (14.8 acres) of 20-year-old vines planted on deep sand. The blend is typical, 60% Cabernets and 40% Merlot. The colour is a beautiful dark ruby. When the wine is aired, the nose, though still slightly closed, exhales scents of forest fruit, spices, tobacco and roasting coffee. The fresh, fruity palate has a mellow tannic structure which will permit this 98 to be drunk fairly soon.

• SARL Milens, Le Sème, 33330 Saint-Hippolyte, tel. 05.57.55.24.47, fax 05.57.55.24.44 [V] [Y] by appt.

CH. TOUR GRAND FAURIE 1998
13.8 ha 93,000 €11-15

88| |90| 94| |95| |96| 97| 98

This cru was bought at the beginning of the last century by Pierre Feytit, the great-grandfather of the current owner. The vines (86% Merlot, 12% Cabernet and a tiny proportion of Malbec, also known as Côt) are on average over 40 years old, planted on sandy soils overlying iron deposits and limestone-clay. The wine is bright with highlights showing some development. The nose is already fine and complex with notes of fruit and oak. The supple palate has a well-integrated tannic structure which indicates that this wine can be drunk fairly soon – ideal with a grilled sirloin steak served over vine shoots.

• Georgette Feytit, Ch. Tour Grand-Faurie, 33330 Saint-Emilion, tel. 05.57.24.73.75, fax 05.57.74.46.94, e-mail feytit@hotmail.com [V] [Y] by appt.

CH. TOUR RENAISSANCE 1998

89 |90| 91 92 93 94 |96| |97| 98 — 4 ha — 23,000 — €8-11

A regular sight in the *Guide*, this cru forms a part of the 48 ha (50.5 acres) cultivated by Daniel Mouty and owned by his wife Françoise who, like him, comes from an old wine-growing family. This superb, vibrant and intense ruby 98 presents a rich, expressive nose with aromas of ripe grapes and jammy fruit and a charming chocolatey oakiness. The palate is energetic and robust with a firm, long tannic structure which only needs a little time to soften.

☛ SCEA Daniel Mouty, Ch. du Barry, 33350 Sainte-Terre, tel. 05.57.84.55.88, fax 05.57.74.92.99, e-mail daniel-mouty@wanadoo.fr ☑

Ⓨ ev. day except Sat. Sun. 8am–5pm

CH. TRIMOULET 1998

94 |95| |96| |97| 98 — 8 ha — 48,000 — €11-15

This cru is 60% Merlot and 40% Cabernet Franc. This intensely-coloured 98 has aromas of fresh fruit combined with flowery notes. The palate is well structured with a dense tannic texture, which is a little closed at present but promising.

☛ Michel Jean, Ch. Trimoulet, 33330 Saint-Emilion, tel. 05.57.24.70.56, fax 05.57.74.41.69 Ⓨ by appt.

CH. TROPLONG-MONDOT 1998★

Gd cru clas.

82 83 85 86 88 |89| |90| 92 93 |95| |96| 97 98 — 25.32 ha — 83,800 — €38-46

This cru at Mondot, the highest point to the east of the town, was established in 1745 by the Sèze family. The domaine was constructed between 1850 and 1870 by Raymond Troplong, the president of the French Senate. Since 1936, this 30-ha (74.1-acre) cru has belonged to the Valette family. The vineyard comprises, classically, 80% Merlot and 20% Cabernets on a limestone-clay *terroir*. This lovely 98 wine is also a classic, and a high-quality one too, judging by its magnificent, dark – almost black – Bordeaux-red colour and rich, complex nose of very ripe grapes, prunes, chocolate, coffee, Bourbon vanilla and leather. The flavoursome palate is fruity and fleshy with quality tannins. This wine needs to be laid down and should be served in three to eight years, for example with game paté. The second wine, **Mondot 98** was also awarded a star. A harmonious wine with excellent balance between fruit and oak along with finely-grained tannins, it will be ready before the main wine.

☛ Christine Valette, Ch. Troplong-Mondot, 33330 Saint-Emilion, tel. 05.57.55.32.05, fax 05.57.55.32.07 ☑ Ⓨ by appt.

CH. TROTTEVIEILLE 1998★

1er grand cru B — n.c. — n.c.

82 85 86 88 90 93 94 |95| |96| |97| 98 — €38-46

This estate is crowned by an 18th-century charterhouse located several hundred metres north-east of Saint-Emilion. It enjoys magnificent views over the Dordogne Valley and the medieval part of the town, as well as Pomerol and Fronsac. The vineyard consists of half-Merlot and half-Cabernet vines, all about 40 years old, grown on limestone-clay. The wine has a dark, youthful-looking appearance. Once the wine has been left to breathe, the nose expresses a combination of roasted almonds and dark berry fruit. The lively, fresh palate includes plenty of vigorous tannins that will need five to ten years to mature. Saddle of venison or young wild boar will then accompany this wine very well.

☛ Indivision Castéja-Preben-Hansen, Ch. Trottevieille, 33330 Saint-Emilion, tel. 05.56.00.00.70, fax 05.57.87.48.61 ☑

Ⓨ by appt.

CH. DU VAL D'OR 1998

94 95 96 |97| 98 — 12.48 ha — n.c. — €11-15

This cru is named after the village of Orval in the Dordogne, where Philippe Bardet's grandfather originated. In the 19th century, one of his ancestors owned barges that used to take the barrels down-river to Bordeaux. Located in the south of the appellation, he has produced a dark-ruby wine with a fine, delicate nose evocative of berry fruit (raspberry) and toast. The palate is still very fruity and rich in firm tannins requiring only a short time to mature. Drink with red meat and game.

☛ SCEA des Vignobles Bardet, 17, la Cale, 33330 Vignonet, tel. 05.57.84.53.16, fax 05.57.74.93.47, e-mail vignobles@vignobles-bardet.fr Ⓨ by appt.

CH. VIEILLE TOUR LA ROSE 1998★

4.5 ha — 32,000 — €8-11

Of this attractive 10-ha (24.7-acre) estate, cultivated since 1946 by the Ybert family, some 4.5 ha (11.1 acres) are devoted to the Grand Cru. The soils form part of the La Rose sector of iron-bearing sand situated north of the town and are planted with 80% Merlot and 20% Cabernets. This alluring 98 has a dark, dense garnet colour and the nose, already intense, has very ripe, jammy grape and prune aromas, accompanied by a hint of leather. The palate is fleshy, dense and robust, structured with excellent grape tannins. This traditional-style Saint-Emilion will be a good accompaniment in two years' time to game, sauces, red meat and Pyrénéan cheeses.

☛ SCEA Vignobles Daniel Ybert, La Rose, 33330 Saint-Emilion, tel. 05.57.24.73.41, fax 05.57.74.44.83 ☑ Ⓨ by appt.

VIEUX CHATEAU L'ABBAYE 1998

■ 1.73 ha 10,000 ⅲ €11-15

|95| 96 97 98

Though restored, the 12th-century church of Saint-Christophe still has its *terroir* is lovely Romanesque porch. Here the *terroir* is limestone-clay over rock, planted with Merlot (85%) and Cabernet Franc (15%). This pretty ruby-coloured 98 has an expressive nose with flowery perfumes, notes of oak and a touch of pepper. The generous attack soon yields to the youthful tannins that will need two to three years to soften before the wine can be enjoyed.

➤ Françoise Lladères, Vieux château l'Abbaye, BP 69, 33330 Saint-Christophe-des-Bardes, tel. 05.57.47.98.76, fax 05.57.47.93.03  ☿ by appt.

VIEUX CHATEAU PELLETAN 1998

■ ⅲ ♦ 6.24 ha 23,300 ⅲ €8-11

This limestone-clay vineyard at the north of the AOC belongs to the Magnaudeix family, who also produce Vieux Larmande and Tertre de Sarpe. The varietal blend here is 80% Merlot and 20% Cabernet Franc. This dark-ruby wine has aromas of small red berries on the slightly oaky nose. The frank palate evolves on tannins that are still harsh and need several years' ageing to mellow. This is an old-fashioned Saint-Emilion, rustic and powerful.

➤ SCEA Vignobles Magnaudeix, Ch. Vieux Larmande, 33330 Saint-Emilion, tel. 05.57.24.60.49, fax 05.57.24.61.91 ☿ by appt.

CH. VIEUX GRAND FAURIE 1998

■ ⅲ ♦ 5 ha 26,000 ⅲ €8-11

Located north of the town, this cru consists of ancient sand planted with 30-year-old rootstock that are three-quarters Merlot. Attractively coloured with ruby highlights, this wine has a nose that needs a little airing before it releases warm aromas of jammy fruits. The supple, well-balanced palate has good concentration and tannins that are still a little harsh. It is a traditional-style Saint-Emilion that needs three to four years in the cellar.

➤ SCEA Bourrigaud et Fils, Ch. Vieux Grand Faurie, 33330 Saint-Emilion, tel. 05.57.74.43.98, fax 05.57.74.41.07, e-mail contact@chateau.champion.com ☿ ➤ Pascal

CH. VIEUX LARMANDE 1998

■ ⅲ ♦ 4.25 ha 23,400 ⅲ €11-15

|88| |90| 92 94 95 |96| |98|

This small family property, on siliceous-clay, comprises 30-year-old rootstock that are three-quarters Merlot and one-quarter Bouchet. The wine is a pretty, quite intense garnet colour. The nose is fruity (slightly acidic redcurrant) and subtle. The palate is

round and elegant with a similar fruitiness and excellent balance between the oak and grape tannins. This 98 is already harmonious and should mature quickly.

➤ SCEA Vignobles Magnaudeix, Ch. Vieux Larmande, 33330 Saint-Emilion, tel. 05.57.24.60.49, fax 05.57.24.61.91 ☿ by appt.

CH. VIEUX POURRET 1998★

■ 4.19 ha 24,000 ⅲ €11-15

86 88 |89| |90| |93| |94| 95 96 |97| 98

This cru, near the town, has belonged to Michel Boutet since 1980. This 98, a blend of 80% Merlot with 20% Cabernet Franc, was matured for 18 months in oak. A bright, clear garnet colour, nose of stewed red fruit, leather and spices, and a well-balanced palate all reflect the well-handled maturation. The tannins are supple and round with lovely fullness and strength, and then result in an agreeable, flavoursome finish.

➤ Michel Boutet, SC du Ch. Vieux Pourret, BP 70, 33330 Saint-Emilion, tel. 05.57.24.70.86, fax 05.57.24.68.30 ☿ ☿ by appt.

CH. VIEUX SARPE 1998★

■ 2.5 ha 15,000 ⅲ €15-23

At Haut-Sarpe, you can still see the furrows left in the rock from Roman times, and the vines are still here. This highly successful 98 has an intense ruby colour with carmine highlights. The youthful nose needs time to open out before it discloses red fruit (cherry) and spicy, meaty notes. This charming wine has a supple, round palate with relatively well-integrated tannins.

➤ Sté d'Exploitation du Ch. Haut-Sarpe, BP 192, 33506 Libourne Cedex, tel. 05.57.51.41.86, fax 05.57.51.53.16, e-mail info@j-janoueix-bordeaux.com ☿ ☿ by appt. ➤ J.F. Janoueix

CH. VILLEMAURINE 1998

■ Gd cru clas. 7 ha 48,000 ⅲ €23-30

85 86 88 |89| |90| 93 94 97 |98|

This attractive 98 has a lively, intense ruby colour with jammy aromas of small red berry fruit and touches of fig, vanilla and smoke. The supple, fine palate possesses silky tannins that are already agreeable.

➤ SCA Vignobles Robert Giraud, Dom. de Loiseau, BP 31, 33240 Saint-André-de-Cubzac, tel. 05.57.43.01.44, fax 05.57.43.08.75, e-mail direction@robertgiraud.com ☿ ☿ by appt.

Other appellations in the Saint-Emilion region

Several communes bordering Saint-Emilion and that used to be under its jurisdiction are permitted to put their name on their wine labels along with that of their famous neighbour. These are the Appellations Lussac Saint-Emilion, 1,437 ha (3,549 acres), producing 84,274 hl (2,224,834 gal), Montagne Saint-Emilion 1,575 ha (3,890 acres), producing 91,650 hl (2,419,560 gal), Puisseguin Saint-Emilion, 742 ha (1,835 acres) producing 43,037 hl (1,136,177 gal) and Saint-Georges Saint-Emilion, 183 ha (452 acres) producing 10,514 hl (277,570 gal). In fact, the last two correspond to two communes that have now joined Montagne. They are all located north-east of the small town, in a charming, topographically mixed region where a number of grand historic houses top the hills. The soils are very varied and the vine varieties are the same as Saint-Emilion; consequently, the quality of the wines is also much the same.

Lussac Saint-Emilion

CH. BEL-AIR 1998★★

| n.c. | 140,000 | ⅢⅢ♦ | €8–11 |

This fine 21-ha (51.9-acre) estate is situated on clay *terroir* with a subsoil of iron deposits. The wine is sumptuous, having an intense garnet colour with purple highlights and a rich, expressive nose still dominated by grilled, vanilla notes. The attack is smooth and generous then the palate opens out powerfully but also with lots of oak, which nevertheless quickly integrates. Extremely rich and complex, this wine has great keeping potential, at least four to six years.

↳ Jean-Noël Roi, EARL Ch. Bel-Air, 33570 Lussac, tel. 05.57.74.52.11, e-mail jean.roi@wanadoo.fr ☑ ⊤ by appt.

CH. BEL-AIR

Cuvée Jean Gabriel 1998★★

| 2 ha | 12,000 | ⅢⅢ | €11–15 |

This magnificent wine comes from selected vineyard plots of Merlot and Cabernets located on clay soil. Its 18 months in new oak will surely charm lovers of quality wines. The colour is purple verging on black, and the grilled, toasty aromas are enhanced by notes of ripe fruit on the complex nose. The silky, generous tannins are soft, rich, well-balanced and long. This is a remarkable wine, which should be aged at least four to ten years, if not longer.

↳ Jean-Noël Roi, EARL Ch. Bel-Air, 33570 Lussac, tel. 05.57.74.60.40, fax 05.57.74.52.11, e-mail jean.roi@wanadoo.fr ☑ ⊤ by appt.

CH. DE BELLEVUE 1998

| 12 ha | 84,000 | ⅢⅢ♦ | €8–11 |

A fine 18th-century charterhouse dominates the vineyard that has created this very elegant, supple and fruity (strawberry, peach) 98. The palate possesses a tannic complexity that needs a chance to mellow and integrate. Age for two to three years in a good cellar.

↳ Ch. Chatenoud et Fils, Ch. de Bellevue, 33570 Lussac, tel. 05.57.74.60.25, fax 05.57.74.53.69 ☑ ⊤ by appt.

CH. BONNIN 1998★★

| 2.5 ha | 15,000 | ⅢⅢ | €8–11 |

This château, only recently taken over by the present owner, obtained a star last year for its first vintage, the 97. This superb 98 is even better. The bright purple colour has black cherry glints. The expressive nose has grilled, vanilla and ripe fruit aromas. After a smooth and generous attack, the palate reveals powerful, flavoursome, well-integrated tannins; the year of oak maturation has been well-handled. The finish is particularly well-balanced and long, which indicates a good future, at least five to eight years.

↳ Philippe Bonnin, Pichon, 33570 Lussac-Saint-Emilion, tel. 05.57.74.53.12, fax 05.57.74.58.26 ☑ ⊤ by appt.

CH. DE BARBE-BLANCHE

Cuvée Henri IV 1998

| n.c. | 40,000 | ⅢⅢ | €11–15 |

In 2000, André Lurton acquired half-shares in André Magnon's estate. This Henri IV vintage, matured for a year in new oak, has a garnet colour with ruby highlights. The intense nose evokes ripe red fruit, vanilla and toast. Though not very concentrated, the tannins are evident and need two to three years.

↳ SCE Ch. de Barbe-Blanche, 33570 Lussac, tel. 05.57.25.58.58, fax 05.57.74.98.59 ☑ ⊤ by appt.
↳ André Lurton et André Magnon

315

Lussac Saint-Emilion

CH. DE BORDES B de B 1998 ■ ⅢⅢ♦ €8-11
0.25 ha 2,100

The production of this *cuvée* is very small. Matured for a year in oak, the wine has an intense garnet colour and a discreet yet elegant garnet colour and a discreet yet elegant fruitiness with blackcurrant, pepper and clove. The palate is rich with very evident tannins that need two to four years to soften and balance out.

⚲ Vignobles Paul Bordes, Faize, 33570 Les Artigues-de-Lussac,
tel. 05.57.24.33.66, fax 05.57.24.30.42,
e-mail vignobles.bordes.paul@wanadoo.fr
☑ ⴹ by appt.

CH. CAILLOU LES MARTINS 1998★ ■ ⅢⅢ♦ €5-8
8 ha 40,000

This small family concern regularly produces very good wines, like this bright purple-coloured 98. The youthful nose has charming fruity and smoky oak notes. The tannic structure has a supple attack and a powerful palate which has well-balanced grape tannins and oak. Drink within the next five years.

⚲ Jean-François Carrille, pl. du Marcadieu, 33330 Saint-Emilion, tel. 05.57.24.74.46, fax 05.57.24.64.40, e-mail paul.carrille@worldonline.fr ☑ ⴹ by appt.

CH. CHEREAU 1998 ■ ♦ €5-8
20 ha 60,000

This is a very Libourne-style varietal blend, with 70% Merlot and the remainder made up by Cabernets, planted on limestone-clay. The distinctive 98 has a very elegant floral (rose) aromas and a supple, well-integrated structure with a complex finish. Drink now or keep for two to three years.

⚲ SCEA Vignobles Silvestrini, 8, Chéreau, 33570 Lussac, tel. 05.57.74.50.76, fax 05.57.74.53.22 ☑ ⴹ by appt.

CH. DU COURLAT
Les raisins de la tradition Cuvée Jean-Baptiste
Fût de chêne 1998★ ⅢⅢ €11-15
4 ha 30,000

Produced from old vines, this wine was made in honour of the current owner's grandfather, who planted the vineyard. This brilliant garnet-coloured 98 has an expressive nose with lovely raspberry, violet, spicy and vanilla aromas. The palate is powerful and ripe but needs three to five years minimum to age and soften. **Château du Courlat 98** was singled out for its very fruity character, suppleness and harmony. It may be served now and for the coming two to three years.

⚲ SCA Pierre Bourotte, 62, quai du Priourat, 33500 Libourne, tel. 05.57.51.62.17, fax 05.57.51.28.28, e-mail jeanbaptiste.audy@wanadoo.fr
ⴹ by appt.

CH. CROIX DE RAMBEAU 1998 ■ ⅢⅢ♦ €8-11
6 ha 50,000

This has been a Trocard property since the middle of the 20th century. The château inaugurated a new winery in 2001. This pleasant 98 has a fresh and fruity nose with raspberry and violet. The tannic structure attacks with intensity, then opens out, but not without a certain austereness. When it has thrown off its youthfulness in one to three years' time, this will be a harmonious wine to go well with hare and similar game.

⚲ SCEA des Vignobles Trocard,
2, Les Petits-Jays-Ouest, 33570 Les Artigues-de-Lussac, tel. 05.57.55.57.90, fax 05.57.55.57.98, e-mail trocard@wanadoo.fr ☑ ⴹ ev. day except Sat. Sun. 8am–12 noon 2pm–5pm

CH. DE LA GRENIERE
Cuvée de la Chartreuse Elevé en barrique de chêne merrain 1998 ■ ⅢⅢ♦ €8-11
2.8 ha 15,000

The château of La Grenière presented two 1998 wines of equal quality. This oak-matured Cuvée de la Chartreuse has a fairly complex nose of dried fruit and intense, unctuous tannins that are still youthful on the finish. The **Cuvée Classique 98** is fresher, more fruity (redcurrant and blackcurrant) and slightly spicy. The tannins are already very pleasant. These two different styles of wine can be enjoyed in one to three years' time.

⚲ EARL Vignobles Dubreuil, Ch. de La Greniere, 33570 Lussac, tel. 05.57.74.64.96, fax 05.57.74.56.28, e-mail o.jp.dubreuil@m6net.fr ☑ ⴹ by appt.
⚲ Odette Dubreuil

CH. LA HAUTE CLAYMORE 1998★★ ■ ⅢⅢ €8-11
3 ha n.c.

This vineyard's English roots and history go back to the 14th century, when it belonged to the Cistercian monastery of Faise. It often appears in the *Guide* and has received an unanimous *coup de coeur* for this *cuvée spéciale*. It has a deep purple colour and an elegant nose that combines ripe fruit and grilled aromas with balsamic notes. The rich, clean attack with mellow tannins opens out powerfully with a very fruity body. Very characteristic, this high quality 98 will be even better after three to six years' ageing. **Cadet du Château Claymore 98**, the second wine, gains

316

one star. It is a very engaging and typical wine. Drink it within the next three or four years.
- EARL Vignobles D. et C. Devaud, Ch. de Faise, 33570 Les Artigues-de-Lussac, tel. 05.57.24.31.39, fax 05.57.24.34.17 ☑
- by appt.

CH. LA JORINE 1998*

3.55 ha | 25,000 | €5-8

This cru's label depicts the church at Cornemps. The château presented a very interesting 98 with an intense, deep garnet appearance and an already expressive nose with spices and coffee. The rich, well-structured tannins are accompanied by an excellent oakiness. The well-balanced, long finish indicates that the wine will benefit from two to five years in the cellar.
- EARL vignobles Fagard, Cornemps, 33570 Petit-Palais, tel. 05.57.69.73.19, fax 05.57.69.73.75 ☑ • by appt.

CH. DES LANDES 1998

24 ha | 25,000 | €5-8

The two Cabernets join the Merlot (80%) to constitute this 98 with its slightly tile-red colour and prominent, well-balanced tannic structure. The finish is still austere, but balance will be achieved in two to three years' time.
- EARL des vignobles des Landes, Ch. des Landes, 33570 Lussac-Saint-Emilion, tel. 05.57.74.68.05, fax 05.57.74.68.05, e-mail nicolaslassagne@aol.com ☑
- ev. day 8am-8pm
- Lassagne

CH. LE GRAND BOIS 1998*

0.89 ha | 70,000 | €8-11

We've already mentioned that the monolithic cellars in this château are well worth visiting. There you can also sample this superb single-variety Merlot, matured for 12 months in new oak. The very intense colour is quite arresting, and the nose has a combination of floral, red fruit and vanilla oak aromas. The palate is supple and spicy, then opens out with power, maturity and great balance. This is a very fine wine that can be drunk now or kept for three to six years.
- SARL Roc de Boissac, Pleniers de Boissac, 33570 Puisseguin, tel. 05.57.74.61.22, fax 05.57.74.59.54
- by appt.
- SCI de Boissac

CH. LES COUZINS Cuvée Prestige

Elevé en fût de chêne neuf 1998*

3 ha | 20,000 | €8-11

This Cuvée Prestige is the product of old Merlot (80%) and Cabernet Sauvignon (20%) vines. It has been in oak for a year. The purple colour has lovely ruby highlights. The intense nose evokes red berry fruit, coffee, cocoa and vanilla. The supple, rich tannins open out with power and balance, even though the oak is still prominent. Perfect harmony should be achieved in two to five years. The main wine, **Château Les Couzins 98**, gets a similar rating.

It is a 90% Merlot with great length and harmony; the maturation in oak is well-handled and respects the fruit.
- Robert Seize, Ch. Les Couzins, 33570 Lussac, tel. 05.57.74.60.67, fax 05.57.74.55.60 ☑
- ev. day 9am-12 noon 2pm-7pm, cl. Jan.

CH. LION PERRUCHON 1998

10.08 ha | n.c. | €8-11

This 65% Merlot has a distinctively intense garnet colour, a clean, fresh nose with redcurrant, blackcurrant and truffles, and a fairly powerful and characteristic tannic structure which needs time to soften. Drink in two to three years' time.
- Jean-Pierre Thézard, Ch. Lion Perruchon, 33570 Lussac, tel. 05.57.74.58.21, fax 05.57.74.58.39 ☑
- by appt.

CH. LUCAS Grand de Lucas Cuvée

Prestige Vieilli en fût de chêne 1998

5.25 ha | 35,000 | €8-11

It is said that Henri IV stayed in this château at the time of the Battle of Coutras. Today they produce good wines like this one with its elegant nose of blackcurrant and dried fruit. The palate has expressive, rich tannins that have finesse, but are not very long. Drink within two to three years.
- Frédéric Vauthier, Ch. Lucas, 33570 Lussac, tel. 05.57.74.62.46, e-mail info@ vins-lucas-vauthier.fr ☑ • by appt.

CH. DE LUSSAC 1998*

25 ha | 70,000 | €8-11

It is rather rare for a château to have the same name as its appellation, as is the case here. This wine has an intense colour with ruby highlights. The nose is just opening out with capsicum peppers, spices and violets. The palate is full and well-balanced. Already pleasant to drink, this wine will keep two to three years.
- Laviale, 15, rue de Lincent, 33570 Lussac-Saint-Emilion, tel. 05.57.74.65.55, fax 05.57.74.55.83 ☑
- by appt.

CH. LYONNAT 1998*

45 ha | 250,000 | €8-11

Lyonnat is a vast property with 80% Merlot, the remainder being devoted to the Cabernets. Matured for 14 months in oak, this superb 98 has a purple colour with bright highlights. The elegant aromas of roasted oak and red fruit are also appealing. The attack reveals smooth, ripe, well-balanced tannins. Drink in two to six years' time.
- SCEV Jean Milhade, Ch. Recougne, 33133 Galgon, tel. 05.57.55.48.90, fax 05.57.84.31.27 ☑

Lussac Saint-Emilion

CH. MAYNE BLANC
Cuvée Saint-Vincent 1998★

■ 6 ha 30,000 ■ **(I)** ◊ €11-15

This château, often honoured by the *Guide* and managed by Jean Boncheau and his son Charly, presents an excellent 98. The garnet colour is intense, while the youthful nose is reminiscent of roasts, vanilla, blackcurrant and cinnamon. The palate reveals intense, well-built tannins, richness and good balance. The finish is still tannic and needs two to five years to soften.

➤ EARL Jean Boncheau,
Ch. Mayne-Blanc, 33570 Lussac,
tel. 05.57.74.60.56, fax 05.57.74.51.77 ◪
☖ ev. day except Sun. 8am–12 noon 2pm–7pm; cl. Jan. Feb.

CH. DU MOULIN NOIR 1998

■ 6.8 ha 52,000 ■ **(I)** ◊ €8-11

If the address points to the Médoc, it is because this Libourne wine is overseen by the Vitigestion company. This well-presented 98 has a bright ruby colour and aromas of stewed fruit, smoke and a slight oakiness. The palate is supple and well-balanced with great finesse. Nonetheless, a hint of bitterness on the finish indicates a wait of one or two years.

➤ SC Ch. du Moulin Noir, Lescalle,
33460 Macau, tel. 05.57.88.07.64,
fax 05.57.88.07.00 ◪ ☖ by appt.

CH. PILOT LES MARTINS 1998★

■ 4 ha 24,000 ■ **(I)** ◊ €5-8

This is the first vintage of this new label which is a blend from selected plots of Merlot (70%) and Cabernet (30%) on gravelly clay. The wine has a bright and intense garnet colour with discreet and elegant aromas of stewed fruit and smoke. The tannins are very evident but well integrated, reflecting a well-judged maturation period. This will be a good wine to drink in two to four years' time.

➤ Jean-François Carrille, pl. du Marcadieu,
33330 Saint-Emilion, tel. 05.57.24.74.46,
fax 05.57.24.64.40, e-mail paul.carrille@worldonline.fr ◪ ☖ by appt.

CH. PONT DE PIERRE 1998

■ 12 ha 80,000 ■ ◊ €5-8

The *négociant* Yvon Mau owns and markets this estate's wine. It has a distinctive intense purple colour, a discreet nose of ripe and stewed fruits, a round, supple structure and a well-balanced finish. Such a straightforward wine will not keep for long – no longer than two to three years.

➤ SA Yvon Mau, BP 01,
33190 Gironde-sur-Dropt Cedex,
tel. 05.56.61.54.54, fax 05.56.71.10.45
➤ Vergniol

ROC DE LUSSAC
Cuvée des Druides 1998

■ n.c. 4,577 ■ ◊ €5-8

The co-operative cellar at Lussac has produced a very limited quantity of this wine. It has a bright and attractive purple colour and the nose has ripe fruit and floral aromas.

Initially supple and velvety, the tannins show excellent balance as they open out on the palate. This wine is ready to drink.

➤ Les producteurs réunis de Puisseguin et Lussac-Saint-Emilion, Durand,
33570 Puisseguin, tel. 05.57.55.50.40,
fax 05.57.74.57.43 ◪ ☖ by appt.

CH. DES ROCHERS 1998★

■ 2.78 ha 23,000 ■ **(I)** ◊ €8-11

This château estate, located on good-quality gravelly clay, is planted with 95% Merlot. The colour of the 98 is so dark it is almost black, and the aromas are intense, evocative of vanilla, violet, coconut and beeswax. The attack is very tannic, the palate opens out with good harmony and richness and unveils a strong oakiness. A perfect balance will be achieved in two to five years.

➤ SCE Vignobles Rousseau,
Petit Sorillon, 33230 Abzac,
tel. 05.57.49.06.10, fax 05.57.49.38.96,
e-mail rousseau.laurent2@wanadoo.fr ◪
☖ by appt.

CH. DE TABUTEAU 1998

■ 18.8 ha 140,000 ■

This significant château has produced an interesting 98 with a bright ruby colour and powerful aromas of jammy fruit and prunes. The tannins provide an agreeable attack and develop powerfully. It is imperative to wait two or three years, so that this wine can achieve the proper balance.

➤ Vignobles Bessou, Ch. Durand-Laplagne,
33570 Puisseguin, tel. 05.57.74.63.07,
fax 05.57.74.59.58 ◪ ☖ by appt.

CH. VERDU 1998★

■ 20 ha 13,500 ■ **(I)** ◊ €5-8

This bright, intensely-coloured 98 has red berry fruit aromas with smoky and stewed fruit notes. The tannic structure, supple at first, opens out with finesse and finely balanced flavours. This is a good wine to drink now or keep two to four years.

➤ SCEA Gaury-Dubos, 33230 Abzac,
tel. 05.57.74.51.16, fax 05.57.74.61.24 ◪
☖ by appt.

Montagne Saint-Emilion

CH. D' ARVOUET 1998★

■ 3.8 ha 18,000 ■ **(I)** ◊ €8-11

Located in the south-east of the appellation, this property employs modern techniques, which have resulted in this lovely 98, matured for 12 months in oak casks, one-third new. The garnet colour is still youthful but aromas with grilled notes. On the palate there are supple tannins which open out with

318

roundness and balance. The slightly austere finish is a sign that the wine needs two to five years in the cellar.

🍷 EARL Moreau, Ch. d'Arvouet, 33570 Montagne, tel. 05.57.74.56.60, fax 05.57.74.58.33, e-mail moreaulavoute@aol.com [V] [T] by appt.

CH. BECHEREAU 1998★

| 10 ha | 40,000 | €5-8 |

Ideally situated on limestone-clay, the estate comprises 75% Merlot and 25% Cabernet Franc. This purple wine with ruby highlights has a youthful nose with jammy fruit and game aromas, and a silky, well-balanced tannic structure that is very pleasant. The finish is already very harmonious and long, indicating that the wine could be drunk quite soon, though it will also keep several years.

🍷 SCE Jean-Michel Bertrand, Bechereau, 33570 Les Artigues-de-Lussac, tel. 05.57.24.31.22, fax 05.57.24.34.69 [T] ev. day except Sun. 8am–12 noon 2pm–6pm

CH. BONFORT 1998

| n.c. | n.c. | €8-11 |

This wine has a lively appearance and an elegant nose with delicately oaky, blackcurrant aromas. The round, characteristic tannins open out to reveal agreeable flavours right through to the finish. Drink now or keep for two to three years.

🍷 Cheval-Quancard, La Mouline, 4, rue du Carbonney, 33560 Carbon-Blanc, tel. 05.57.77.88.88, fax 05.57.77.88.99, e-mail chevalquancard@chevalquancard.com [T] by appt.

CH. CARDINAL 1998

| 9 ha | 50,000 | €11-15 |

This château, belonging to the same family since 1742, presents this well-made wine with an attractive suppleness and good balance between the fruit and smoky, lightly spicy oak. Its simplicity, however, means that it is not a wine for laying down.

🍷 SCEA Bertin et Fils, Dallau, 8, rte de Lamarche, 33910 Saint-Denis-de-Pile, tel. 05.57.84.21.17, fax 05.57.84.29.44

CH. CAZELON 1998

| 4 ha | 16,000 | €5-8 |

This pleasant 98 has an agreeable fruity character enlivened with a delicate touch of oak. Its fleshy, well-balanced structure develops towards a still-lively finish, which will require a further two or three years' ageing.

🍷 Denis Fourloubey, Cazelon, 33570 Montagne, tel. 05.57.74.58.78, fax 05.57.74.57.47 [V] [T] by appt.

CH. CHEVALIER SAINT-GEORGES 1998★

| 25,000 | €5-8 |

This château is situated on a good clay terroir planted with 80% Merlot and 20%

Cabernets. This ruby-coloured 98 with carmine highlights has leather, jam and floral aromas on the nose. Full and round on the attack, this is a rich wine that should develop well in the coming three years, though it may be opened now.

🍷 EARL Appollot, Clos Trimoulet, 33330 Saint-Emilion, tel. 05.57.24.71.96, fax 05.57.74.45.88 [V] [T] by appt.

CH. COUCY 1998★

| 20 ha | 80,000 | €8-11 |

This château, like Grande Barde, is run by Dominique Maurèze. A blend of 70% Merlot, 20% Cabernet Sauvignon and 10% Cabernet Franc grown on fine limestone-clay, this wine sports an intense colour complete with violet highlights. The youthful nose of red fruit aromas has elegance, while the palate is initially rich, before opening out with finesse and power, all perfectly-balanced with well-integrated oak. This is a classy wine that will be ready for drinking in two to three years' time.

🍷 Héritiers Maurèze, Ch. Coucy, 33570 Montagne, tel. 05.57.74.62.14, fax 05.57.74.56.07 [V] [T] by appt.

CH. CROIX BEAUSEJOUR
Elevé en fût 1998★★

| 6.5 ha | 19,000 | €5-8 |

This estate is located on a silt and limestone-clay terroir and has a large proportion of very old vines that have gone to produce this magnificently successful 98. The intense colour has ruby glints. The expressive nose evokes jammy fruit, prunes and vanilla. The tannins attack with fullness and vigour, then develop with richness and great delicacy without losing any of their strength. The very long, ripe finish bodes well for the future: give it between four and eight years.

🍷 Olivier Laporte, Ch. Croix-Beauséjour, Arraillh, 33570 Montagne, tel. 05.57.74.69.62, fax 05.57.74.59.21 [V] [T] by appt.

CH. FAIZEAU
Sélection Vieilles vignes 1998★★

| 10 ha | 39,000 | €11-15 |

This château, on the slopes of the Tertre de Calon, is often singled out in the *Guide*. The soils are sand, limestone, and molasse. This sumptuous 98 has a deep, black colour and

intense, complex aromas of fruits (blackberry, bilberries), toast and smoke designed to attract the wine-lover.

➤ SCE du Ch. Faizeau, 33570 Montagne, tel. 05.57.24.68.94, fax 05.57.24.60.37, e-mail chateau.faizeau@m6net.fr ▽

Ⴕ by appt.
➤ Chantal Lebreton

CH. GARDEROSE ★★

◼ 10 ha 20,000 ◼ ◆ €5-8

This wine, marketed by the *négociant* Yvon Mau, results from the vinification of grapes grown on various plots of gravelly clay. It is superb, with a colour that is simultaneously dark and sparkling, aromas of spices and ripe fruit that are still reticent but promising, and velvety tannins that are both concentrated and alluring. The finish is elegant, long and perfectly balanced. Drink this wine among friends in two or three years' time.

➤ SA Yvon Mau, BP 01, 33190 Gironde-sur-Dropt Cedex, tel. 05.56.61.54.54, fax 05.56.71.10.45
➤ Garde et Fils

CH. GAY MOULINS 1998 ★

◼ 2 ha 8,000 ◼ ◆ €11-15

This singular 98 has two particularities: it is the first wine for ten years to be bottled at the château; and the varietal blend is dominated by Cabernet Franc (75%), which is quite exceptional in the region. Yet it is unquestionably a success. The garnet colour is bright. The aromas of prune and ripe fruits are intense. The tannins are full and smooth when they attack the palate and then develop with finesse and length. Open this bottle in two to five years. The same producer's **Château des Moines 98**, an 80% Merlot, was singled out by the Jury.

➤ Vignobles Raymond Tapon, Ch. des Moines, 33570 Montagne, tel. 05.57.74.61.20, fax 05.57.74.61.19, e-mail vinstapon@aol.com ▽ Ⴕ by appt.

CH. GRAND BARAIL 1998 ★★

◼ 9 ha n.c. ◼ ◼ ◆ €5-8

This exceptional 98 blends 30% Cabernet Sauvignon with Merlot grapes from old vines. The results are impressive: a very concentrated black colour; complex, fine aromas of red fruit with grilled and vanilla notes; and a tannic structure which is initially supple and well-blended and then opens out with both power and elegance. The tannins are demonstrably from a very ripe harvest and are balanced by a well-integrated oakiness. Leave this wine in your cellar for three to ten years.

➤ EARL Vignobles D. et C. Devaud, Ch. de Faise, 33570 Les Artigues-de-Lussac, tel. 05.57.24.31.39, fax 05.57.24.34.17
Ⴕ by appt.

CH. GRAND BARIL Elevé en fût 1998

◼ 28 ha 21,210 ◼ ◆ €5-8

The viticultural college at Montagne teaches tomorrow's wine professionals. The students have made this attractive 98 as a part of their training in wine-growing. It has a

ruby colour with brick-red highlights. The discreet nose reveals some smoke and spice. The tannins are still a little severe, but will achieve a better balance after two or three years' ageing.

➤ Lycée viticole de Libourne-Montagne, Goujon, 33570 Montagne, tel. 05.57.55.21.22, fax 05.57.51.66.13, e-mail legta-libourne@educagri.fr ▽
Ⴕ ev. day except Sat. Sun. 8.30am–12 noon 1.30pm–5.30pm

CH. GUADET-PLAISANCE Cuvée Saint-Vincent Elevé en fût de chêne 1998 ★

◼ 2 ha 6,500 ◼ €8-11

This wine is a blend using 40-year-old vines (90%). The cherry-red colour shines with vibrant glints. The nose, still in the grip of forceful vanilla oak, has yet to awaken, while the tannins disclose a greater fruitiness and have good maturity. This is a well-made wine that needs three to five years' ageing for the oak to integrate.

➤ SCEA Vignobles Jean-Paul Deson, 2, av. Piney, 33330 Saint-Christophe-des-Bardes, tel. 05.57.24.77.40, fax 05.57.74.46.34 ▽
Ⴕ by appt.

CH. LA BASTIDETTE 1998

◼ 1.13 ha 6,000 ◼ ◼ ◆ €8-11

This interesting 98 is a blend of 70% Merlot and 30% Cabernet Franc. It has distinctive aromas of autumn leaves and peach, while the tannic structure is fresh and well-balanced, if not very powerful. This wine should be decanted and drunk in two or three years' time.

➤ de Jerphanion, Moncets, 33500 Néac, tel. 05.57.51.19.33, fax 05.57.51.56.24, e-mail bastidette@moncets.com ▽
Ⴕ by appt.

CH. LA CHAPELLE Elevé en fût de chêne 1998

◼ n.c. 18,000 ◼ ◼ ◆ €5-8

This attractive 98, from 90% Merlot, has a bright, intense colour with slight characteristic oakiness. The tannins are initially frank and somewhat lively, but then develop more roundness and balance. Drink within the next three years.

➤ SCEA du Ch. La Chapelle, Berlière, 33570 Montagne, tel. 05.57.24.78.33, fax 05.57.24.78.33 ▽ Ⴕ by appt.
➤ Thierry Demur

CH. LA COUROLLE Elevé en fût de chêne 1998

◼ 5 ha 30,000 ◼ ◼ ◆ €5-8

This attractive 98 is worth trying for its youthful aromas of prune and toasty oak as well as for its round yet solid structure, which is mature and displays a really classic character. The finish, however, shows that this is not a wine to keep – two to three years at most.

➤ Claude Guimberteau, Arriailh, 33570 Montagne, tel. 05.57.74.62.38, fax 05.57.74.50.78 ▽ Ⴕ by appt.

CH. LA COURONNE 1998*

11 ha · 42,000 · €8-11

This immediately appealing 98 is made exclusively from Merlot. The colour is bright purple and the aromas are very elegant and fruity. The tannins are full and round, then develop with charm, a certain vivacity and plenty of harmony. This is a very good wine that should be drunk within one to three years.

• EARL Thomas Thiou, Ch. La Couronne, 33570 Montagne, tel. 05.57.74.66.62, fax 05.57.74.51.65, e-mail Lacouronne@aol.com ⟐ by appt.

CLOS LA CROIX D'ARRIAILH 1998*

0.8 ha · 4,500 · €8-11

This Clos is a selection from vines over 50 years old, cultivated traditionally and using the most modern techniques for the vinification of the grapes. The nose is dominated by oak, yet on the palate the oakiness is very pleasant and perfectly integrated with the powerful, well-balanced tannins. This is a pleasant wine that should be left to age for two years.

• Olivier Laporte, Ch. Croix-Beauséjour, Arriailh, 33570 Montagne, tel. 05.57.74.69.62, fax 05.57.74.59.21 ⟐ by appt.

CH. LA FAUCONNERIE 1998*

0.88 ha · 6,000 · €5-8

This property is situated on the high limestone-clay plateaux of the appellation. The deep violet colour is complemented by complex aromas of fruit (blackcurrant) and well-integrated vanilla oak. The tannins are ripe, powerful and long. All is in place for this wine to reach its best in two to five years.

• Bernadette Paret, 33570 Montagne, tel. 05.57.74.65.47, fax 05.57.74.65.47 ⟐ Simone Paret

CH. LAFLEUR GRANDS-LANDES 1998

8 ha · 10,660 · €8-11

This property on a good gravel terroir was taken over in 1997 by a young oenologist. His second harvest has resulted in this wine, with its bright ruby colour and a nose dominated by very ripe, jammy fruit. The supple and elegant tannins have already developed somewhat, enabling this wine to be drunk now and over the next three years.

• EARL Vignobles Carrère, 9, rue de Lyon, Lamarche, 33910 Saint-Denis-de-Pile, tel. 05.57.24.31.75, fax 05.57.24.30.17 ⟐ by appt. ⟐ Isabelle Fort

CH. LA GRANDE BARDE 1998*

8.5 ha · 58,000 · €8-11

This attractive 98 is a blend of 80% Merlot, 18% Cabernets and 2% Malbec. The ruby colour has beautiful violet highlights. There are intense aromas of almond and red fruit accompanied by good oak. The palate has full, rich tannins and an agreeably flavourful middle palate and is beautifully balanced on the finish.

• SCE du Ch. La Grande-Barde, 33570 Montagne, tel. 05.57.74.64.98, fax 05.57.74.64.98 ⟐ by appt.

CH. MONTAIGUILLON 1998*

25 ha · 126,000 · €8-11

This estate has undergone constant renovation since 1949 and has regularly invested in its winery. This intensely-coloured 98 has deep purple highlights. The complex nose reveals spices, flowers, leather and well-handled oak maturation. The attack is supple and round; the tannins then display their rich and somewhat lively character, which indicates that this wine needs to be laid down for three to six years.

• Amart, Ch. Montaiguillon, 33570 Montagne, tel. 05.57.74.62.34, fax 05.57.74.59.07, e-mail chantalamart@montaiguillon.com ⟐ by appt.

L'ART DE MAISON NEUVE 1998

4 ha · 19,000 · €8-11

Michel Coudroy has been running this family estate since 1968. Two wines are presented this year. This one, L'Art, is a special single-variety Merlot created in 1998 with a very elegant label. It has distinctive aromas of caramel and cocoa, and a supple, pleasant structure enlivened with a pleasant oakiness. Cuvée Classique is more fruity: the tannins are supple and elegant but not very full. The two wines are ready to drink, but will also keep for two to four years.

• Michel Coudroy, Maison-Neuve, 33570 Montagne, tel. 05.57.74.62.23, fax 05.57.74.64.18 ⟐ by appt.

CH. LA TOUR CALON 1998

n.c. · 20,000 · €8-11

The large percentage (40%) of the two Cabernets in this 98 blend is most particularly evident on the nose with its aromas of cherry and spice. The palate is unctuous and quite powerful. The finish is still firm and oaky, needing two or three years to soften.

• Claude Lateyron, BP1, 33570 Montagne, tel. 05.57.74.50.00, fax 05.57.74.58.58 ⟐ ev. day except Sat. Sun. 8am-12 noon, 1.30pm-5.30pm

CH. LA PAPETERIE 1998

10 ha · 44,000 · €8-11

Located next to the Barbanne, a little river separating the Pays d'Oïl from the Pays d'Oc, this château presents an agreeable wine with a deep garnet colour. The nose has lovely smoky, liquorice aromas. The supple, harmonious tannins are not very powerful, which allows this wine to be drunk now and over the coming two or three years.

• Jean-Pierre Estager, 33-41, rue de Montaudon, 33500 Libourne, tel. 05.57.51.04.09, fax 05.57.25.13.38, e-mail estager@estager.com ⟐ by appt.

Montagne Saint-Emilion

CH. PLAISANCE 1998★

■ 17.44 ha 60,000 ■ €8-11

This château is on sandy soil and this intensely vibrant-coloured 98 is highly successful. It has a characteristic nose with delicately oaky red fruit, and supple, fine tannins, which open out with fullness and elegance. The finish is well-balanced, with noticeable aromas of walnut and prunes. This wine will be perfect in three or four years.

➤ Les Celliers de Bordeaux Benauge, 18, rte de Montignac, 33760 Ladaux, tel. 05.57.34.54.00, fax 05.56.23.48.78, e-mail celliers-bxbenauge@wanadoo.fr ✍
☻ by appt.

CH. ROC DE CALON
Cuvée Prestige 1998★★

■ 2.5 ha 14,000 ■ €8-11

This *cuvée* Prestige 98 comes from grapes selected from old Merlot (90%) and Cabernet Franc (10%) vines which have undergone vinification and maturation separately. It is a magnificent wine with a deep, shimmering appearance and a nose with morello cherry, prune and clove aromas with an elegant touch of oak. The palate is rich and ripe, giving a mouthfilling character with a very flavoursome finish. This is a thoroughbred wine with a long life ahead (at least five to eight years). The **Cuvée Classique 98** is singled out for the freshness of its small berry fruit flavours and supple, already pleasant structure.

➤ Bernard Laydis, Barreau, 33570 Montagne, tel. 05.57.74.63.99, fax 05.57.74.51.47, e-mail rocdecalon@wanadoo.fr ✍ ☻ by appt.

CH. ROCHER CALON 1998

■ 16 ha 40,000 ■ €5-8

This 98 is 95% Merlot, and the grape variety's character comes through in the aromatic hints of red fruit and truffles. The palate contains characteristic, well-balanced tannins. Drink within the next three years.

➤ SCEV Lagardère, Négrit, 33570 Montagne, tel. 05.57.74.61.63, fax 05.57.74.59.62 ✍ ☻ by appt.

CH. ROCHER CORBIN 1998★

■ 9.17 ha 62,000 ■ €8-11

This château is on the western flank of the Tertre de Calon, a limestone promontory overlooking the valley. It employs the most up-to-date techniques in both the vineyard and winery, and these are responsible for this lovely 98. The colour is very bright and the thoroughbred nose develops notes of tobacco, roasting coffee and red fruit. The tannic structure is powerful with great complexity of flavours. This wine will be at its best in two to five years' time.

➤ SCE du Ch. Rocher Corbin, 33570 Montagne, tel. 05.57.74.55.92, fax 05.57.74.53.15 ✍ ☻ by appt.
➤ Philippe Durand

CH. ROCHER-GARDAT 1998

■ 5.3 ha n.c. ■ €8-11

This is a quality wine, as is revealed by its pleasant aromas of jammy red fruit and well-balanced oakiness. The tannic structure is powerful and harmonious, true to the style of this vintage. Drink in two or three years' time.

➤ SCEA Patrick et Sylvie Moze-Berthon, Bertin, 33570 Montagne, tel. 05.57.74.66.84, fax 05.57.74.58.70, e-mail chateau.rocher-gardat@wanadoo.fr ☻ by appt.

CH. SAMION
Elevé en barrique de chêne 1998★★

■ 1.3 ha 12,000 ■ ■ ♦ €8-11

This property, which belongs to a Belgian group, consists of just 1.3 ha (3.2 acres) of marine-based limestone-clay. This remarkable 98 has a bright, intense purple colour and powerful aromas of red fruit and slightly tarry vanilla oak, which announce the presence of tannins that will develop with great maturity and richness. The very pleasant and well-balanced finish predicts a future for this wine of two to five years at least.

➤ SCEA Vignobles Rocher Cap de Rive 1, Ch. Cap d'Or, 33570 Montagne, tel. 05.57.40.08.88, fax 05.57.40.19.93, e-mail vignoblesrochercaprive@wanadoo.fr

CH. TEYSSIER 1998★

■ 19.2 ha 68,000 ■ €8-11

This large property of more than 50 ha (123.5 acres) is managed with a great deal of talent by the Bordeaux *négociant* Dourthe, as this very fine 98 shows. The colour is a dense purple. The aromas are intense and still dominated by a toasty oakiness. The supple, well-balanced tannic structure develops with increasing power and length. It is essential to wait two to five years before drinking this wine.

➤ Dourthe, 35, rue de Bordeaux, 33290 Parempuyre, tel. 05.56.35.53.00, fax 05.56.35.53.29, e-mail contact@cvbg.com ✍ ☻ by appt.
➤ GFA Durand-Teyssier

CH. VIEILLE TOUR MONTAGNE 1998★

■ 2.6 ha n.c. ■ ■ €8-11

Only Merlot is grown on this small estate of less than 3 ha (7.41 acres). The wine has excellent, intense aromas with elegant notes of fig, eucalyptus and game, with velvety, quite powerful and very well-balanced tannins. The freshness of the finish is very pleasant. Drink in the next two to five years.

➤ Pierre et André Durand, 33570 Montagne, tel. 05.57.74.62.02 ✍
☻ ev. day 9am–12 noon 2pm–6pm

VIEUX CHATEAU CALON
Sélection 1998★

■ n.c. n.c. ■ €5-8

Two or three years of ageing are required for this single-variety Merlot. The expressive nose reveals notes of musky leather and game, which will appeal to the connoisseurs. There is fruitiness here too, and the well-constructed palate has a dense, well-balanced structure. When the tannins are finally mellow, it will go well with hare.

- SCE Gros et Fils, Calon, 33570 Montagne, tel. 05.57.51.23.03, fax 05.57.25.36.14 Y by appt.

VIEUX CHATEAU DES ROCHERS 1998

4 ha	16,000	€5-8

Jean-Claude Rocher took over the family property in 1995. This 98 has a fine ruby colour and a youthful nose of ripe fruit (raspberry) and good-quality supple, round tannins. This is a wine to serve in two years' time with Sunday roasts.

- Jean-Claude Rocher, Mirande, 33570 Montagne, tel. 05.57.74.62.37, fax 05.57.25.18.14 Y by appt.
- Abel Rocher

VIEUX CHATEAU NEGRIT 1998★

7 ha	40,000	€5-8

This château, on a south-facing hillside, entrusts its wine to the *négociant* Yvon Mau, who handles its distribution. This purple-coloured 98 has garnet highlights. The nose is evocative of jammy fruit. The tannins are round and well-balanced; they develop powerfully but not aggressively. Drink now or keep for two or three years.

- SA Yvon Mau, BP 01, 33190 Gironde-sur-Dropt Cedex, tel. 05.56.61.54.54, fax 05.56.71.10.45
- Alexandre Blanc

VIEUX CHATEAU SAINT ANDRE 1998★★

10 ha	50,000	€8-11

This château belongs to Jean-Claude Berrouet who vinifies several Grands Crus, of which Petrus and several others are properties of the Moueix family. The soil is limestone and contains a number of Roman remains. This wine (80% Merlot, 20% Cabernet Franc) has a garnet red colour and reveals thoroughbred aromas of fruit, spices and fresh mint. The velvety and well-balanced structure is perfect. The flavoursome and long finish indicates good keeping potential, at least five to eight years.

- Jean-Claude Berrouet, 1, Samion, 33570 Montagne

CH. VIEUX MESSILE CASSAT
Elevé en fût de chêne 1998★

10 ha	48,000	€8-11

This château is planted with 70% Merlot and 30% Cabernet Franc. Bright and intense in appearance, this very lovely wine has characteristic aromas of fig, jammy fruit and elegant oak. The palate is round and generous, with a ripe, well-balanced finish. In two or three years' time, this wine will be a real delight.

- Vignobles Aubert, La Couspaude, 33330 Saint-Emilion, tel. 05.57.40.15.76, fax 05.57.40.10.14 Y by appt.

CH. VIEUX MOULINS DE CHEREAU 1998

5.5 ha	30,000	€5-8

This attractive 98 deserves the reader's attention for its supple, musky structure that develops with good balance and interesting maturity. Drink now or keep for two to three years.

- SCEA Vignobles Silvestrini, 8, Chéreau, 33570 Lussac, tel. 05.57.74.53.22 Y by appt.

Puisseguin Saint-Emilion

CH. BEL-AIR Cuvée de Bacchus
Vieilli en fût de chêne 1998★

5 ha	20,000	€8-11

These 17 ha (42 acres) of singly-owned vineyard date back to the 18th century. This *cuvée spéciale* is particularly successful. It has a partly-developed tile-red colour and elegant aromas of jammy fruit and toast. After the attack of round, supple tannins the palate opens with increasing power and class. The very rich, long finish indicates that the wine needs between three and five years in the cellar.

- SCEA Adoue Bel-Air, Bel-Air, 33570 Puisseguin, tel. 05.57.74.51.82, fax 05.57.74.59.94 Y ev. day 8am-1pm
- Adoue Frères

CH. BRANDA 1998★★★

5.5 ha	16,800	€15-23

Following its previous successful appearances in the *Guide*, this château obtains three stars this year; a rare accomplishment. The wine has a dark, almost black, colour that is at the same time bright with superb highlights. The complex aromas of ripe fruit, pepper and cinnamon blend well with the pleasing oaky notes of vanilla, cocoa and mocha. The dense, firm, rich tannins on the palate are magnificently mouthfilling. As it develops on the palate it becomes smooth, still retaining a strong oakiness, but the balance will be perfect after five to ten years' time. The master winery has done very well indeed!

- SC Ch. du Branda, Roques, 33570 Puisseguin, tel. 05.57.74.62.55, fax 05.57.74.57.33 Y by appt.

Puisseguin Saint-Emilion

CH. CHENE-VIEUX 1998
■   n.c.   27,100   ■   €5-8

This attractive 98 has a garnet colour with highlights that are already fading to a red-tile hue, a discreet nose with stewed jammy fruit and a palate with full, round, well-structured tannins. This pleasant wine should be drunk now.

☛ SCE Y. Foucard et Fils,
Ch. Chêne-Vieux, 33570 Puisseguin,
tel. 05.57.51.11.40, fax 05.57.25.36.45 ▼
▼ by appt.

CH. FAYAN Elevé en fût de chêne 1998★
■   10.77 ha   20,000   ■ ■ ♦   €5-8

Visiting this château, you can see exhibitions of paintings and sculptures as well as cars that are the stuff of legend. You can also sample this 98, with its delicate fruity aromas of blackcurrant and blackberry which blend well with its discreet and elegant oakiness. The evident, well-balanced tannins are in harmony with the oak influences. Drink within the next two to three years.

☛ SCEA Philippe Mounet, Ch. Fayan,
33570 Puisseguin, tel. 05.57.74.63.49,
fax 05.57.74.54.73 ▼ ev. day except Sun.
8am–12 noon 2pm–6pm

CH. FONGABAN 1998★★
■   7 ha   35,000   ■ ■ ♦   €8-11

Merlot (80%) and Cabernets (20%) on limestone-clay have yielded this magnificent wine with its deep colour and ruby highlights. There are complex aromas of fruit, nutmeg, vanilla and game. The firm, powerful attack persists on the balanced palate of velvety tannins and good long flavours (undergrowth). The oak still needs to integrate, which will necessitate keeping for three to eight years at least.

☛ SARL de Fongaban, 33570 Puisseguin,
tel. 05.57.74.54.07, fax 05.57.74.50.97 ▼
▼ by appt.

CH. GONTET 1998★★★
■   2 ha   10,000

Jean-Louis Robin has created a superb wine from a 2-ha (4.9-acre) selection, giving him top place this year in the appellation. The classic limestone-clay *terroir* is planted with 80% Merlot and 20% Cabernet. The dense garnet colour contains wonderful glints. The intense, complex nose is packed with black fruit, spices, jam and vanilla. The round,

elegant attack on the palate opens out with a sensation of powerful, well-balanced oaky tannins, which will soften after three to eight years' ageing in a good cellar.

☛ Jean-Loup Robin, Ch. Gontet,
33570 Puisseguin, tel. 05.57.84.28.16,
fax 05.57.84.29.13, e-mail chateau.gontet@
wanadoo.fr ▼ ▼ by appt.

CH. GRAND RIGAUD 1998
■   6 ha   15,000   ■ ■ ♦   €5-8

The Desplat family has owned this cru since 1935. This lovely 98 is distinguished above all for the finesse of its floral, slightly menthol nose, which develops with notes of prune, game and blackcurrant. The palate is silky and well-balanced. It is already pleasant to drink but would improve over several years.

☛ Guy Desplat, Grand Rigaud,
33570 Puisseguin, tel. 05.57.74.61.10,
fax 05.57.74.58.30 ▼ ▼ by appt.

CH. GUIBOT LA FOURVIEILLE
1998★★
■   10 ha   60,000   ■ ■ ♦   €8-11

This château belongs to one of the region's long-established families, one ancestor having gone with Maximilian on his conquest of Mexico in 1863. The excellent limestone-clay *terroir* gives its best in this lovely 98, a 90% Merlot with Cabernet Franc. Bright and dark in appearance, the nose is still somewhat closed, evocative of flowers, spices, blackcurrant, prune and vanilla. On the palate the tannins, which are firm, mouthfilling and very fruity, combine with an agreeable oakiness. Wait three to five years.

☛ Henri Bourlon, Ch. Guibeau,
33570 Puisseguin, tel. 05.57.55.22.75,
fax 05.57.74.58.52,
e-mail vignobles.henri.bourlon@wanadoo.fr
▼ ▼ by appt.

CH. HAUT-BERNAT
Vieilli en fût de chêne 1998★
■   5.65 ha   32,000   ■ ■   €8-11

Since its purchase in 1990, a great deal has been invested in this château, both in the vineyard and winery, allowing it to be counted among the best of the appellation. It gained a *coup de coeur* in last year's *Guide* for its 97, judged the best AOC wine. This bright, vibrantly-coloured 98 has fruity, roasting coffee and spice (clove) aromas. The round, fleshy tannins open on the finish with great complexity and a fairly intense oakiness. Drink in two to five years.

☛ SA Vignobles Bessineau, 8, Brousse,
BP 42, 33350 Belvès-de-Castillon,
tel. 05.57.56.05.55, fax 05.57.56.05.56,
e-mail bessineau@cote-montpezat.com ▼
▼ by appt.

CH. HAUT-FAYAN 1998★
■   7 ha   n.c.   ■ ■ ♦   €5-8

This intensely-coloured 98 has a garnet colour with lively highlights and elegant aromas of stewed fruit, liquorice and pine resin. The attack reveals round, mouthfilling tannins. The well-balanced palate opens with good fruitiness, indicating that this is a classy, honest wine that should give its best after two to three years in the cellar.

☛ SCEA Vignobles Guy Poitou,
Ch. Haut-Fayan, 33570 Puisseguin,
tel. 05.57.74.67.38, fax 05.57.74.54.82 ☑
Ⓨ ev. day 8am–12 noon 3pm–6pm

CH. LA CROIX GUILLOTIN 1998★

15 ha   90,000   €5-8

This wine, marketed by the *négociant* Yvon Mau, is deep ruby and has an elegant and complex nose with dark berry fruit and cinnamon. The structure, with its silky attack, subsequently reveals still-youthful tannins, which ought to be mellow by now. This wine is very characteristic of the appellation.

☛ Vignobles Paul Bordes,
Faize, 33570 Les Artigues-de-Lussac,
tel. 05.57.24.33.66, fax 05.57.24.30.42,
e-mail vignobles.bordes.paul@wanadoo.fr
☑ Ⓨ by appt.

CH. DES LAURETS 1998★★

20 ha   113,000   €8-11

This château, in the style of Napoleon III, commands a vast uninterrupted vineyard in the midst of 150 ha (370.5 acres) of land where you can also see the ruins of the Château Malengin, which date from the 12th century. This sumptuous, dark ruby wine offers complex aromas of red and dark berry fruit, toast, prunes and mint. The tannins are supple and powerful, perfectly ripe and very long. Open this high-class wine in three to six years' time.

☛ SA Ch. des Laurets, 33570 Puisseguin,
tel. 05.57.74.63.40, fax 05.57.74.65.34,
e-mail chateau-des-laurets@wanadoo.fr
Ⓨ by appt.

CH. DE MOLE 1998★

9.35 ha   60,000   €8-11

Having belonged to six generations of the same family, this château has latterly made progress, as this very successful intense garnet 98 proves. It has a complex nose with toasty fruit and vanilla and a palate with fleshy, powerful tannins, which open out with lots of complex flavours and length. This wine needs two to three years in the cellar.

☛ Ginette Lenier, Ch. de Môle,
33570 Puisseguin, tel. 05.57.74.60.86,
fax 05.57.74.60.86 ☑ Ⓨ by appt.

CH. MOUCHET

Vieilli en fût de chêne 1998

6.89 ha   8,000   €5-8

This wine, matured for 14 months in oak, is a blend of 70% Merlot with 15% of each of the two Cabernets. With its attractive garnet colour, still-lively highlights and youthful nose of spices and small red berries, it is instantly appealing. The palate has firm, slightly oaky tannins. Drink in two to three years' time.

☛ SCEA Ch. La Croix de Mouchet,
Mouchet, 33570 Montagne,
tel. 05.57.74.62.83, fax 05.57.74.59.61 ☑
☛ Grando

CH. DU MOULIN 1998★

8 ha   50,000   €5-8

A fine limestone-clay *terroir*, classic varietal blend and six months in oak have resulted in this very nice 98, with aromas of well-ripened red fruit. On the palate, the tannins are full and winey and a welcome acidity gives this wine undoubted ageing potential. It is a straightforward wine, which will delight drinkers in three to five years' time.

☛ SCEA Chanet et Fils, n° 1 Jacques,
33570 Puisseguin, tel. 05.57.74.60.85,
fax 05.57.74.59.90 Ⓨ by appt.

CH. DE PUISSEGUIN CURAT 1998★

3 ha   16,000   €5-8

Formerly a property of Jeanne d'Albret, this château was also managed for a while by Michel de Montaigne. Today's owners, undoubtedly less famous, have produced this high-quality wine. This intensely-coloured 98 has a very intense nose with leather, gunflint, blackcurrant and spices. The tannic structure, which has a rich and fruity attack, opens to reveal a powerful, mouthfilling quality. This is a delightful wine, which will be appreciated in three to five years' time.

☛ EARL du Ch. de Puisseguin-Curat,
33570 Puisseguin, tel. 05.57.74.51.06,
fax 05.57.74.54.29,
e-mail chateau-de-puisseguin-curat@wanadoo.fr Ⓨ by appt.
☛ Robin

CH. RIGAUD 1998★

3 ha   18,000   €8-11

This agreeable 98 has a bright colour with ruby highlights, a powerful and complex nose with gamey, leathery and spicy aromas, plus a pleasant structure that is all lace. It should be ready very soon.

☛ J. Taix, Rigaud, 33570 Puisseguin,
tel. 05.57.74.63.35, fax 05.57.74.50.34 ☑
Ⓨ by appt.

CH. ROC DE BERNON 1998

14.08 ha   64,000   €5-8

This château often receives honours in the *Guide* and last year was a *coup de cœur* winner. This lovely 98 has a delicately spicy, fruity, musky nose. The tannins on the palate

are initially supple and round, then gradually become firmer. This wine needs two to three years before it achieves a good balance.
➤ J.-M. Lenier, Ch. Roc de Bernon, 33570 Puisseguin, tel. 05.57.74.53.42, fax 05.57.74.53.42, e-mail roc.de.bernon@wanadoo.fr [V] [Y] by appt.

CH. ROC DE BOISSAC 1998★★

n.c.   n.c.   €8-11

In the late 19th century, this château belonged to Dr Poitou, the originator of the Bordeaux blend known to wine-growers the world over. If you come here, visit cellars that are unique in the *département* and taste this very fine 98 with its deep garnet colour and delicate aromas of fresh fruit and spices. The tannins begin supple and rich, then develop fullness, a sign of their potential. Enjoy this lengthy, classy wine in three to five years' time.
➤ SARL Roc de Boissac, Pleniers de Boissac, 33570 Puisseguin, tel. 05.57.74.61.22, fax 05.57.74.59.54 [V] [Y] by appt.

Saint-Georges Saint-Emilion

CH. BELAIR SAINT-GEORGES 1998★★

4 ha   20,000   €8-11

This small cru sits on a limestone-clay *terroir* and is planted with 80% Merlot and 20% Cabernets. The bright colour of this 98 is magnificent. On the nose there are complex aromas of coffee, toast and ripe, delicate fruit. After a smooth, dense attack, the palate develops power, good balance and a strong oakiness. The well-integrated finish is the sign of a great wine that ought to age well, three to six years at least.
➤ Nadine Pocci-Le Menn, Ch. Belair Saint-Georges, 33570 Montagne, tel. 05.57.74.65.40, fax 05.57.74.51.64 [V] [Y] by appt.

CH. CAP D'OR 1998

5.5 ha   44,000   €8-11

This château occupies a good-quality starfish-fossil and limestone-clay *terroir*. The result is this true-to-type 98 with smoky, ripe fruit and toasty oak. On the palate the rich yet evident tannins will doubtless soften over the next two to three years.
➤ SCEA Vignobles Rocher Cap de Rive 1, Ch. Cap d'Or, 33570 Montagne, tel. 05.57.40.08.83, fax 05.57.40.19.93, e-mail vignoblesrochercaprive@wanadoo.fr

CH. DIVON 1998

4.75 ha   n.c.   €8-11

This château has been in the same family since 1860. Tradition is therefore what counts here, as is the case with this 98. The youthful nose has pepper, flowers and red fruit aromas. The round, pleasant tannins are uncomplicated but sincere, if a little astringent on the finish. This wine will improve over the next three years.
➤ Christian Andrieu, Divon, 33570 Montagne, tel. 05.57.74.66.07 [V] [Y] by appt.

CH. HAUT-SAINT-GEORGES 1998★

3.5 ha   20,000   €11-15

Located on silty clay with iron deposits, this château has produced a quality 98 with 90% Merlot. The purple colour has lovely highlights and the nose is winey and fresh with hints of tobacco and truffles. After a rich, mellow attack the tannins open out with fullness and great youth. This wine is characteristic and should be drunk within two to five years.
➤ SCE du Ch. La Grande-Barde, 33570 Montagne, tel. 05.57.74.64.98, fax 05.57.74.64.98 [V] [Y] by appt.

CH. LA CROIX DE SAINT-GEORGES 1998★

6.58 ha   50,000

Once an integral part of the Château Saint-Georges, this is now an estate in its own right and grows equal proportions of Merlot and Cabernet. This still has a discreet nose showing touches of dark berry fruit, which are more evident on the palate, where the tannins are mellow, powerful, traditional and long. This wine will achieve its potential in three to six years' time.
➤ Jean de Coninck, Ch. du Pintey, 33500 Libourne, tel. 05.57.51.03.04, fax 05.57.51.03.04 [V] [Y] by appt.

CH. LE ROC DE TROQUARD 1998

3.05 ha   3,500   €5-8

Isabelle Visage's 98 'Roc' has a bright purple colour, a very delicate youthful nose which is honest and winey, and round, quite full tannins with no great complexity or length. All the same, this is a nice wine to drink now or keep two to three years.
➤ SCEA des Vignobles Visage, Jupille, 33330 Saint-Sulpice-de-Faleyrens, tel. 05.57.24.62.92, fax 05.57.24.69.40 [V] [Y] by appt.

CH. SAINT-GEORGES 1998★★★

45 ha   280,000   €15-23

92 93 94 **95** 96 **97** 98

The whole region is dominated by the towers of this magnificent 18th-century château. The same holds true of its wine. Every year it is honoured in the *Guide*. This year, though not a *coup de coeur*, it none the less gets a three-star rating, which is no less difficult to achieve! It has an intense colour with black highlights and powerful, elegant aromas of red fruit, cedar, and spices with a fine oaky note. The sophisticated tannins, smooth on the attack, are very ripe and well-structured which is proof of a well-handled

Côtes de Castillon

I In 1989 a new appellation was created: Côtes de Castillon. It applies to an area of 3,019 ha (79,702 acres), which was extracted from the Appellation Bordeaux Côtes de Castillon, that is, the nine communes of Belvès-de-Castillon, Castillon-la-Bataille, Saint-Magne-de-Castillon, Gardegan-et-Tourtirac, Sainte-Colombe, Saint-Genès-de-Castillon, Saint-Philippe-d'Aiguilhe, Les Salles-de-Castillon and Monbadon. Nonetheless, to leave the 'Bordeaux' group, the wine-growers are obliged to follow particularly strict rules of production, especially those that apply to density of plantation, which is limited to 5,000 plants per ha (2,000 per acre). Compliance has been set for the year 2010 to take account of the vines that are already planted. In 2000, 178,522 hl (4,712,981 gal) of wine were produced.

ARTHUS 1998★

n.c.　10,000　€8-11

Danielle, an oenologist, met Richard on one of the Bordeaux region's top estates, Château Petrus. Since then they have cultivated their vines together. These are 35 years old and are grown on a limestone plateau. This garnet-coloured 98 has aromas of cherry, blackberry and spices enhanced by pleasant grilled notes. On the palate, the powerful, well-balanced tannins add an agreeable vinosity, which continues on to the very long finish. Wait two to five years before opening.

➤ Richard Dubois, Ch. Bertinat Lartigue, 33330 Saint-Sulpice-de-Faleyrens, tel. 05.57.24.72.75, fax 05.57.74.45.43, e-mail dubricru@aol.com [V]
[Y] ev. day 9am-11.30am 2.30pm-5.30pm; Sat. Sun. by appt.; cl. 14 Aug-3 Sep.

maturation in wood. The generous, well-balanced finish offers every hope of a good future, at least five to ten years.

➤ Famille Desbois, Ch. Saint-Georges, 33570 Montagne, tel. 05.57.74.62.11, fax 05.57.74.58.62, e-mail g.desbois@chateau-saint-georges.com [V] [Y] by appt.

CH. BEAUSEJOUR

Elevé en fût de chêne 1998★★

5 ha　20,000　€5-8

This château practises biodynamic methods. In the winery the wine-making is well-mastered and the maturation handled as meticulously as possible, as this 98 shows. The colour is dense and deep. The aromas of very ripe fruit and notes of toasty oak are in perfect harmony. The supple and well-balanced, velvety tannins develop with great complexity and length through to a spicy finish that guarantees a fine future. This is a great wine.

➤ GAEC Verger Fils, 4, chem. de Beauséjour, 33350 Saint-Magne-de-Castillon, tel. 05.57.40.13.14, fax 05.57.40.34.06 [V]
[Y] by appt.
➤ Bernard et Gilles Verger

CH. BEL-AIR

Elevé en fût de chêne 1998★★

13 ha　50,000　€8-11

Legend has it that the druids once sacrificed animals here. Nowadays, things are more peaceful, and the production of high-quality wines is the main activity. This dark-garnet 98 is a fine example with its very delicate and winey, slightly liquorice nose with dark berry fruit and toast aromas. After a rather lively attack on the palate it opens out with richness, fullness and unctuousness. The long, very spicy finish is a sign of good ageing potential, at least four to eight years. The second wine, the **La Chapelle Monrepos 99** was singled out. It is an uncomplicated wine for drinking straight away.

➤ SCEA du Dom. de Bellair, 33350 Belvès-de-Castillon, tel. 06.80.13.02.12, fax 05.56.42.44.47 [V]
[Y] by appt.
➤ Patrick David

LE PIN DE BELCIER 1998★★

2 ha　4,000　€15-23

'Pin de Belcier' is a *cuvée spéciale* made from old vines (Merlot 80%, with Cabernet Franc). The Jury was impressed by its intense colour with ruby highlights and complex aromas of ripe fruit combined with vanilla-oak and powerful yet temperate grilled notes. The tannins are both robust and smooth, and there is an agreeable fruitiness on the middle palate. The superbly-balanced finish is very long and predicts a great future, at least five to ten years. The **Cuvée Principale du Château de Belcier 98**, a blend of four grape varieties, achieved one star.

➤ SCA Ch. de Belcier, 33350 Les Salles-de-Castillon, tel. 05.57.40.67.58, fax 05.57.40.67.58 [V]
[Y] by appt.
➤ MACIF

CH. BELLEVUE Cuvée Vieilles vignes

Vieilli en fût de chêne 1999★★

4 ha　12,000　€5-8

This skilfully-made *cuvée* comprises the produce of a selection of old Merlot vines

(90%) and Cabernet Franc 99 demonstrates with its intense purple colour and delightful aromas of jammy fruit, leather and grilled notes. The elegance of the attack is due to ripe, well-integrated tannins that are the result of good-quality maturation. The finish is particularly fruity and long. This is a very fine wine that came close to a *coup de cœur*. Drink in two to five years.

➤ Michel Lydoire,
Ch. Bellevue, 33350 Belvès-de-Castillon,
tel. 05.57.47.94.29, fax 05.57.47.94.29
Y by appt.

CH. BEYNAT Cuvée Léonard 1998★★

■ 2.5 ha 6,500 ⊞ €8-11

This *cuvée* is a selection of equal proportions of Merlot and Cabernet Sauvignon from 35-year-old vines. It has a deep garnet colour and aromas of cherry and leather with some grilled notes. The rich, powerful structure reveals richness, then fullness on the finish. This well-balanced wine is full of potential, which should show itself in two to six years' time. The Cuvée Classique 98 was singled out for its pleasantly menthol, spicy nose and for elegant, silky tannins.

➤ Xavier Borliachon, 27, rte de Beynat,
33350 Saint-Magne-de-Castillon,
tel. 05.57.40.01.14, fax 05.57.40.18.51
Y by appt.

CH. BREHAT 1998★

■ 8 ha 39,000 ⊞ €5-8

This château has belonged for some centuries to the family of Jean de Monteil. Here it presents this aromatic 98 which blends complex nuances of liquorice, red fruit, violets and Virginia tobacco. The palate has a full, attractive body with tannins that are still rather firm on the finish. Three to five years' ageing will result in a better balance.

➤ Jean de Monteil, Ch. Haut Rocher,
33330 Saint-Etienne-de-Lisse,
tel. 05.57.40.18.09, fax 05.57.40.08.23,
e-mail ht.rocher@vins-jean-de-monteil.com
Y by appt.

CH. CANTEGRIVE 1998★★

■ 16.73 ha 60,000 ⊞ €8-11

Acquired in 1990, this 23-ha (56.8-acre) property practises meticulous wine-making methods, as this remarkable 98 demonstrates. The garnet colour is dense, almost black. The aromas of well-ripened red fruit, leather and oak blend well with the winey, powerful, straightforward, long and spicy finish predicts a future of three to seven years for this lovely wine, which is characteristic of the appellation.

➤ SC Ch. Cantegrive, Terrasson,
33570 Monbadon, tel. 03.26.52.14.74,
fax 03.26.52.24.02 Y by appt.
➤ Doyard Frères

CH. CAP DE FAUGERES 1998★

■ 27 ha 108,000 ⊞ €8-11

No stranger to the *Guide* – remember last year's *coup de cœur* for the difficult harvest of 1997 – this château produces good wines every year. Such is the case with this lovely 98, which has a dense appearance and an intense and complex nose with well-ripened red fruit enlivened by an elegant oaky touch. The tannins are powerful but well-integrated and develop with notes of morello cherry and blackcurrant right through to a very well-balanced finish. Open this lovely wine in three to six years' time.

➤ GFA C. et P. Guisez, Ch. Cap de Faugères, 33350 Sainte-Colombe,
tel. 05.57.40.34.99, fax 05.57.40.36.14,
e-mail faugeres@club-internet.fr

CH. CASTEGENS Sélection première 1998★

■ 28 ha 25,000 ⊞ €5-8

This well-known château, which hosts the re-enactment of the Battle of Castillon, has belonged to the same family since the 15th century. The wine, too, is worth coming here for. This attractive 98 has a bright garnet colour and an intense nose with spices and jammy fruits. The supple attack on the palate opens out with silky yet powerful tannins that have great length. Wait two years or so before serving this wine.

➤ J.-L. de Fontenay, Ch. Castegens,
33350 Belvès-de-Castillon,
tel. 05.57.47.96.07, fax 05.57.47.91.61,
e-mail jldefontenay@wanadoo.fr
Y by appt.

CH. COTE MONTPEZAT 1999★★

■ 30 ha 150,000 ⊞ €8-11

Well-accustomed to receiving honours from the *Guide*, this cru almost gained a *coup de cœur* for this deep purple-coloured 99 with its pretty amber highlights. The intense and expressive nose has well-ripened red fruit, blueberry and vanilla aromas. The silky, fleshy tannins develop with finesse and good balance accompanied by elegant oaky notes. This lovely characterful wine should be drunk in two to six years' time.

➤ SA Vignobles Bessineau, 8, Brousse,
BP 42, 33350 Belvès-de-Castillon,
tel. 05.57.56.05.55, fax 05.57.56.05.56,
e-mail bessineau@cote-montpezat.com
Y by appt.

CH. DUBOIS-GRIMON 1998★★

■ 1 ha 6,000 ⊞ €15-23

Just 1 ha (2.47 acres) of Merlot (80%) and Cabernet Franc (20%) is reserved for this *cuvée spéciale*, representing one-tenth of the estate. The purple colour glints with bright ruby highlights. The powerful, complex nose has liquorice, prune and vanilla aromas. The supple, velvety tannins are perfectly ripe and blend well with the oakiness. The long, satin finish confers unquestionable charm upon this wine that will age extremely well (three to five years minimum).

➤ Gilbert Dubois, Ch. Grimon,
33350 Saint-Philippe-d'Aiguilhe,
tel. 05.57.40.67.58, fax 05.57.40.67.58

CH. FONTBAUDE

Vieilles vignes Elevé en fût de chêne 1999

3 ha | 15,000 | €8-11

This selection, taken from old vines, has produced a bright 99 with fruity aromas still dominated by a strong vanilla oakiness. The palate is smooth and supple, well-balanced with the wood influence, but the wine does not have great ageing potential. Drink straight away.

GAEC Sabaté-Zavan, 34, rue de l'Eglise, 33350 Saint-Magne-de-Castillon, tel. 05.57.40.06.58, fax 05.57.40.26.54, e-mail chateau.fontbaude@wanadoo.fr ☑ ⌾ by appt.

CH. GERBAY Elevé en fût de chêne 1998

12.23 ha | 15,000 | €5-8

This bright garnet-coloured 98 has an expressive nose with ripe fruit (raspberry). The supple, delicately oaky tannins open out with finesse but without great complexity. A nice wine to drink over the next two to three years.

Consorts Yerles, SCEA Ch. Gerbay, 33350 Gardegan, tel. 05.57.40.63.87, fax 05.57.40.66.39, e-mail gerbay@wanadoo.fr ☑ ⌾ by appt.

CH. GERMAN 1998★

30 ha | 50,000 | €5-8

This half-Merlot, half-Cabernets cru has produced a rich and complex 98. The youthful nose with ripe fruit and vanilla notes is very elegant, as are the silky, spicy, well-structured and well-integrated tannins that are the result of quality oak. This is a wine that will be at its best after two to three years in a good cellar. The same producer's **Château Hyot 98** was singled out by the Jury.

Alain Aubert, 57 bis, rte de Libourne, 33350 Saint-Magne-de-Castillon, tel. 05.57.40.04.30, fax 05.57.40.27.02

CH. GRAND TUILLAC 1999★

15 ha | 120,000 | €3-5

Located on the appellation's limestone plateau, this château has been in the same family for seven generations. Tradition is the hallmark of this violet-purple 99, with its agreeable youthful nose of ripe fruit and subtle oak aromas. After a powerful attack, the palate opens out with richness and length. This is a characterful wine which will be perfect in three to five years' time.

SCEA Lavigne, S. et L. Poitevin, Ch. Grand Tuillac, 33350 Saint-Philippe-d'Aiguilhe, tel. 05.57.40.60.09, fax 05.57.40.66.67, e-mail s.c.e.a.lavigne@wanadoo.fr ☑ ⌾ by appt.

CH. GRIMON 1998

4.5 ha | 36,000 | €5-8

This pleasant 98 has a blend of red fruit aromas, leather and subtle oak on the nose. On the palate the wine is supple and fresh, without great power, but well balanced and already drinking well.

Gilbert Dubois, Ch. Grimon, 33350 Saint-Philippe-d'Aiguilhe, tel. 05.57.40.67.58, fax 05.57.40.67.58 ☑

CH. HAUTE TERRASSE 1999

3.08 ha | 20,000 | €5-8

This agreeable 99 is the new owner's first harvest. It is a wine of character with aromas of leather and red berry fruit. The palate is supple and honest with an uncomplicated finish. Drink this characteristic wine over the next three years.

Pascal Bourrigaud, Champion, 33330 Saint-Emilion, tel. 05.57.74.43.98, fax 05.57.74.41.07, e-mail pascal.bourrigaud@producteurs.com ☑

CH. LA BRANDE 1999

n.c. | n.c. | €8-11

An estate with just one owner, this château presents an interesting 99 with an flavourful freshness (red fruit) and a lengthy, supple and well-integrated tannic structure. Drink now or leave to age several years.

Vignobles Jean Petit, Ch. Mangot, 33330 Saint-Etienne-de-Lisse, tel. 05.57.40.18.23, fax 05.57.40.15.97, e-mail chmangot@terre-net.fr ☑ ev. day 8.30am-12 noon 2pm-6pm; Sat, Sun. by appt.

DOM. DE LA CARESSE 1998★

n.c. | 60,000 | €8-11

The greatest care has gone into creating this lovely 98. It has a deep, bright garnet colour and aromas of well-ripened red fruit that blend well with the discreet oaky notes. The palate discloses full, round, spicy tannins and has a long, well-balanced and flavoursome finish. Open in two to five years' time.

Jean Blanc, 2, av. de la Bourrée, 33350 Saint-Magne-de-Castillon, tel. 05.57.40.07.59, fax 05.57.40.42.53 ☑

CH. LA CLARIERE LAITHWAITE 1998

4.6 ha | 24,500 | €8-11

This château, situated 1 km (0.62 miles) from Sainte-Colombe's flamboyant gothic church, produces very good wines that are sold mainly to an English wine club. Several other wines are available, like this attractive 98, which features an open, fruity, vanilla nose. The tannins, which have a fairly firm attack, open out with sincerity and length. Drink in about two years' time.

SARL Direct Wines Ch. La Clarière Laithwaite, Les Confrères de la Clarière, 33350 Sainte-Colombe, tel. 05.57.47.95.14, fax 05.57.47.94.47 ☑ ⌾ by appt.

CH. LA GRANDE MAYE

Elevé et vieilli en barrique de chêne 1998

12 ha | 60,000 | €8-11

This pleasant 98 has a toasty nose that is still somewhat reticent, but the fruitiness is evident on the palate which has supple well-integrated tannins and a vanilla oakiness. Drink over the next three years.

EARL P.L. Valade, 1, Le Plantey, 33350 Belvès-de-Castillon,
tel. 05.57.47.93.92, fax 05.57.47.93.92,
e-mail paul-valade@wanadoo.fr
by appt.

EXCELLENCE DE LAMARTINE
1999
2 ha 6,000 €11-15

Château Lamartine (17.5 ha/43.2 acres) produces this special single-variety Merlot. The 99 version has pronounced roasted-oak notes while red fruit makes a discreet appearance. The palate is concentrated and balanced. Drink now or keep for several years.

EARL Gourraud, 1, la Nauze, 33350 Saint-Philippe-d'Aiguilhe,
tel. 05.57.40.60.46, fax 05.57.40.66.01
ev. day except Sun. 9am–12 noon 2pm–7pm; cl. Sep.

CH. LAPEYRONIE 1998★★
4 ha 13,000 €11-15

Château Lapeyronie sits on an excellent limestone-clay *terroir* at Sainte-Colombe and benefits from modern wine-making and maturation methods. This attractive 98 is an illustration of these techniques. It has a deep garnet colour and grilled, toasted aromas with nuances of eucalyptus and cherries in kirsch. Direct and ripe on the attack, it has prominent tannins enhanced by the oakiness attributed to a well-handled maturation period. The finish is long and fruity. In two to five years' time, this will be a very fine wine indeed. The same owner's **Château La Font du Jeu 98** achieved one star.

SCEA Lapeyronie, 4, Castelmerle, 33350 Sainte-Colombe, tel. 05.57.40.19.27, fax 05.57.40.14.38 by appt.

CH. LA PIERRIERE
Cuvée Prestige 1998★
5 ha 32,420 €5-8

Built between the 13th and 16th centuries, this gorgeous château has belonged to the same family since 1607. Respect for tradition has not prevented modernity entering the winery, as the quality of this *cuvée Prestige* demonstrates. This delightful wine has a dense, dark colour and complex aromas of raspberry and cherry, with supple, well-blended tannins. Enjoy now or keep for two to three years. The **Cuvée Principale Château La Pierrière 99** (150,000 bottles, vat-matured) is marketed by Kressmanns. It is singled out for its sincerity.

R. et D. De Marcillac, Ch. la Pierrière, 33350 Gardegan, tel. 05.57.47.99.77, fax 05.57.47.92.58,
e-mail chateau.lapierriere@free.fr
by appt.

CH. LA RONCHERAIE
TERRASSON Cuvée Sereine 1998★
2 ha 6,000 €5-8

Having moved in here in 1997, these young wine-growers now present their first oak-matured wine. This Sereine is worth sampling, with its deep garnet colour, complex and intense aromas of grilled fruit and coffee and dense, well-knit tannic structure that opens out with richness, fullness and great freshness. The fruity, long finish gives a glimpse of a fine future, three to six years or longer.

EARL Roy-Vittaut, La Roncheraie-Terrasson, 33350 Belvès-de-Castillon,
tel. 05.57.47.94.12, fax 05.57.47.94.12,
e-mail la.roncheraie.terrasson@wanadoo.fr
by appt.
G. et A. Roy de Pianelli

CH. LA SENTINELLE
Elevé un an en fût de chêne 1999
4 ha 15,300 €5-8

This 25-ha (61.8-acre) vineyard, established in 1997 by a Parisian woman, presents a very fruity 99, enlivened by a light oaky note. Ripe yet powerful tannins indicate good potential.

Sté viticole du Dom. de Lézin, 11, Giraud-Arnaud, 33750 Saint-Germain-du-Puch, tel. 05.57.24.00.00,
fax 05.57.24.00.98 by appt.
Muriel Huillier

DOM. LA TUQUE BEL-AIR
Vieilli en fût de chêne neuf 1998
20 ha 45,000 €5-8

This domaine, established in 1854, has been owned since 1984 by a local man, originally from Saint-Emilion. It presents this pretty 98 with a ruby colour and a youthful nose of red berry fruit. The palate features supple, ripe tannins, though the finish is a little severe. The long full-flavoured finish indicates that the wine could be kept one to three years.

GAEC Jean Lavau et Fils, Ch. Coudert Pelletan, BP 13, 33330 Saint-Christophe-des-Bardes, tel. 05.57.24.77.30, fax 05.57.24.66.24,
e-mail coudert.pelletan@worldonline.fr
ev. day 9am–6pm; Sat. Sun. by appt.

CH. LAVERGNE 1999
5 ha 22,000 €3-5

Thierry Moro took over from his father in 1986. Though the parchment label of this wine seems a little outdated, the wine certainly isn't. Pleasant and fruity (raspberry, strawberry), it has a tannic palate that is supple, honest and relatively long. The good overall balance makes this wine agreeable to drink now, but it could be laid down for two to three years.

Thierry Moro, La Vergnasse, 33570 Saint-Cibard, tel. 05.57.40.65.75, fax 05.57.40.65.75 by appt.

LES MOULINS DE COUSSILLON
1998

2.12 ha 8,000 ■ €3-5

Pleasant, this wine has a youthful nose of spices, dead leaves and blackcurrant. The soft tannins have freshness and a harmonious balance. Drink in two or three years.
Arbo, Godard, 33570 Francs, tel. 05.57.40.65.77, fax 05.57.40.65.77. by appt.

CH. MOULIN DE CLOTTE Cuvée Dominique Vieilli en fût de chêne 1999★

0.5 ha 3,000 €5-8 by appt.

Grown on an estate of over 7 ha (around 17 acres), this Cuvée Dominique is produced in limited numbers. The colour is bright and intense, and the nose has red fruit and liquorice aromas with some roasted notes. The tannins, while prominent, are mouthfilling and in harmony on the finish and, being well-made, ought to soften out after two or three years.
SCEA Vignobles Dominique Chupin, Moulin de Clotte, 33350 Les Salles-de-Castillon, tel. 05.57.40.60.94, fax 05.57.40.66.68. by appt.

CH. PERVENCHE-PUY ARNAUD 1998★

8.5 ha 22,000 €5-8

Purchased by Thierry Valette in April 2000, this cru has undertaken large restoration work at its winery. Although this attractive 98 has not seen the benefits of this modernisation, it is nonetheless very successful. It has an intense garnet colour and a youthful nose with spices, liquorice and ripe fruit. An elegant attack with generous, powerful tannins that are in harmony with a pleasant oakiness. Drink in two to three years' time.
EARL Thierry Valette, 7, Puy Arnaud, 33350 Belvès-de-Castillon, tel. 05.57.47.90.33, fax 05.56.90.15.44. by appt.

CH. PEYROU 1998★★

5 ha 25,000 €8-11

Managed with meticulous care, talent and enthusiasm by a young oenologist, this château gained a unanimous *coup de coeur* for this splendid 98. The dark, very intense colour is instantly appealing. The aromas of red fruit and spices are well-balanced with the elegant vanilla oak. The tannins are at first velvety and then become rich and generous. It is powerful on the finish with an interesting youthfulness. This is an unusual wine, which needs to age for three to ten years. Let's have more like it!
Catherine Papon-Nouvel, Peyrou, 33350 Saint-Magne-de-Castillon, tel. 05.57.40.06.49, fax 05.57.74.40.03. by appt.

CH. PILLEBOIS
Vieilles vignes Vieilli en fût de chêne 1998

5 ha 14,000 €5-8

This estate belongs to Franc Lartigue of Saint-Émilion. The Côtes de Castillon produced here was singled out for its pleasant aromas of spices, vanilla and toast. The sincere, round tannins are well-balanced, though a little simple on the finish. Drink now or keep for two to three years.
Vignobles Marcel Petit, 6, chem. de Pillebois, 33350 Saint-Magne-de-Castillon, tel. 05.57.40.33.03, fax 05.57.40.06.05. by appt.

CH. DE PITRAY 1998★★

30 ha 210,000 €8-11

An estate of 100 ha (247 acres) surrounds the enormous Château de Pitray. Its premier wine, as the label says, is a selective harvest from less than one-third of the vineyard. The result is this impressive 98. The very dense colour and the intense, complex nose of red fruit, vanilla and coffee offer instant appeal. The powerful texture of the palate, characterised by fleshy, fruity (morello cherry) tannins is well balanced, with well-handled oakiness from the maturation in wood. A very fine wine that will be at its best after two to five years.
SC de La Frérie, Ch. de Pitray, 33350 Gardegan, tel. 05.57.40.63.38, fax 05.57.40.66.24, e-mail pitray@pitray.com by appt.
Comtesse de Boigne

CH. PUY GARANCE
Elevé en fût de chêne 1999

1 ha 3,000 €5-8

Frédéric Burriel took over part of the family estate in 1997. This *cuvée spéciale*, 98% Merlot, has an intense nose with toasty oak and slightly peppery aromas. On the attack the tannins are powerful then open out quickly. Drink during the next three years.
Frédéric Burriel, 33350 Belvès-de-Castillon, tel. 06.81.47.90.23, fax 05.57.40.11.15. by appt.

CH. ROBIN 1998★

12 ha 70,000 €8-11

Château Robin, established on south-east-facing slopes, is one of the jewels in the appellation's crown. The cherry-red 98 has complex aromas of blackcurrant, menthol and vanilla. The dense, well-integrated tannic structure is still firm on the finish. Perfect balance should be attained in two to three years and last for some time.

Côtes de Castillon

CH. ROQUEVIEILLE
Vieilli en fût de chêne 1998★

■ 11.41 ha 70,000 ⬛ €5-8

Located on a classic limestone-clay *terroir*, this cru presents this intensely-coloured 98 with a complex nose, which still has a pronounced toasty oakiness. The supple, ripe palate has morello cherry flavours structured with strong oak tannins. The general balance is good: open this wine in two to three years' time.

↦ SCEA Ch. Roquevieille,
33350 Saint-Philippe-d'Aiguilhe,
tel. 05.57.74.47.11, fax 05.57.24.69.08 ☑
☗ by appt.

CH. DE SAINT-PHILIPPE
Cuvée Helmina 1998★

■ n.c. 6,000 ⬛ ⬥ €8-11

Philippe Bécheau, the owner, belongs to the seventh generation of the family that purchased this property in 1750. The weight of tradition has not precluded the use of modern techniques in creating this Helmina. There are expressive ripe fruit aromas and strong oaky, roasted and vanilla notes. The tannins need to soften, but the very elegant finish is a sign of good ageing potential.

↦ EARL Vignobles Bécheau,
Ch. de Saint-Philippe, 33350 Saint-Philippe-d'Aiguilhe, tel. 05.57.40.60.21,
fax 05.57.40.62.28, e-mail pbécheau@terre-net.fr ☑ ☗ by appt.

CH. TERRASSON
Cuvée Prévenche 1998

■ 2 ha 12,000 ⬛ €5-8

Château Terrasson has two distinct 98 wines, both of which were singled out by the Jury. Cuvée Prévenche is oak-matured and characterised by aromas of dark berry fruit, vanilla and spices (cloves). The vat-matured **Vin Classique** is fruitier. In both cases, the tannins are supple and well balanced, but the oak-matured version has better ageing potential.

↦ EARL Christophe et Marie-Jo Lavau,
Ch. Terrasson, BP 9, 33570 Puisseguin,
tel. 05.57.56.06.65, fax 05.57.56.06.76,
e-mail clavau@terre-net.fr ☑ ☗ by appt.

VALMY DUBOURDIEU LANGE
1999★

■ 4.5 ha 20,000 ⬛ ⬛ ⬥ €15-23

Château de Chainchon is worth visiting as much for its architecture as for the quality of its wines. Its **Château de Chainchon Cuvée Prestige 99** receives the same rating as this 99. The bright purple colour is enticing, and the complex nose has nuances of blackcurrant, spice (vanilla) and cocoa. On the palate this wine is rich, full and very lengthy. It will be best appreciated after two to five years. It is worth remembering that the 98 version was a *coup de cœur*.

↦ Patrick Erésué, Ch. de Chainchon,
33350 Castillon-la-Bataille,
tel. 05.57.40.14.78, fax 05.57.40.25.45,
e-mail chateau.de.chainchon@wanadoo.fr
☑ ☗ by appt.

↦ Ch. Robin, 33350 Belvès-de-Castillon,
tel. 05.57.47.92.47, fax 05.57.47.94.45 ☑
☗ by appt.
↦ Sté Lurckroft

CH. ROC DE JOANIN 1998★

■ 1.5 ha 12,000 ⬛ ⬛ ⬥ €5-8

Yves Mirande purchased this estate in 1979. Since 1994, Pierre Mirande has officiated in the winery. This distinctive 98 has an intense ruby colour and complex aromas of well-ripened red fruit enlivened by a delicate oaky note. The concentrated tannic structure develops with finesse, and is in harmony with the qualities derived from the well-handled oak maturation. Drink in about two years' time.

↦ SCEA Vignobles Mirande, Ch. La Rose Côtes Rol, 33330 Saint-Emilion,
tel. 05.57.24.71.28, fax 05.57.74.40.42 ☑
☗ by appt.

CH. ROCHER LIDEYRE 1998

■ 37 ha 130,000 ⬛ ⬥ €5-8

This very large property presents this pleasant 98 with liquorice, tobacco and spice aromas. The tannins make a supple appearance on the palate, then the wine opens out with some liveliness. It needs one to three years for it to achieve harmony.

↦ SCEA Vignobles Bardet – Grands Vins de Gironde, Dom. du Ribet,
33450 Saint-Loubès, tel. 05.57.97.07.20,
fax 05.57.97.07.27, e-mail gvg@gvg.fr ☑

CH. ROQUE LE MAYNE
Elevé en fût de chêne 1999★★

■ 7 ha 43,000

After 12 months in new oak, this deep-purple blend of 70% Merlot, 25% Cabernet Sauvignon and 5% Côt reveals complex aromas of well-ripened red fruit, vanilla and chocolate. After a particularly mellow attack, the palate develops power and elegance. The fruitiness on the middle palate is well-balanced. Open this great wine in three to six years' time. The same owner's **Château la Bourrée 99** was singled out for its agreeable fruitiness and ripe tannins. It will be ready in a year or two from now.

↦ SCEA des vignobles Meynard,
10, rte de La Bourrée,
33350 Saint-Magne-de-Castillon,
tel. 05.57.40.17.32, fax 05.57.40.17.32,
e-mail vignobles-meynard@wanadoo.fr ☑
☗ by appt.

Bordeaux Côtes de Francs

The vineyard of Bordeaux Côtes de Francs is 12 km (7 miles) east of Saint-Emilion and encompasses the communes of Francs, Saint-Cibard and Tayac. The vines are planted on an excellent site, on the lime, clay and marly slopes of some of the highest hills in the Gironde. They almost all produce red wines, except for about 20 ha (50 acres), and are cultivated by some dynamic wine-growers and a Cave Coopérative. Between them, they produce some very attractive wines, which are rich, with a good bouquet. In 2000, 512 ha (1,265 acres) were under cultivation, producing 29,772 hl (785,981 gal) of wine.

VIGNOBLE D'ALFRED 1998

■   2 ha   n.c.   ▥ €8-11

Merlot (40%) and the two Cabernets in equal measure constitute this wine, which has matured for 16 months in oak. The shimmering colour has garnet highlights and the nose is complex with spices, red fruit and vanilla. The tannic structure is pleasant, though a little firm and light on the finish. It will need two to three years' time to gain some roundness.

✆ SCEA Lapeyronie, 4, Castelmerle, 33350 Sainte-Colombe, tel. 05.57.40.19.27, fax 05.57.40.14.38 ☑ ⊤ by appt.
✒ A. Charrier

CH. DE FRANCS
Les Cerisiers Vieilli en fût de chêne 1998★★

■   5 ha   18,000   ▥ €11-15

This *cuvée spéciale* from Château de Francs is produced from only 5 ha (12.4 acres) out of the property's total of 32 ha (79 acres). This wine is a blend of three-quarters Merlot and one-quarter Cabernet Franc, grown on an excellent limestone-clay *terroir*. Bright and intense in colour, its has fine, well-balanced aromas of red fruit and vanilla. The palate is full and generous with particularly ripe, well-integrated tannins that express themselves totally on the finish – a sign of excellent wine-making. Enjoy this wine in three to five years' time. The **white** 99 blends equal proportions of Sémillon and Sauvignon and has spent nine months in new oak. It is singled out for its lovely crystallised apricot, orange peel and caramelised vanilla flavours.

✆ SCEA Ch. de Francs, 33570 Francs, tel. 05.57.40.65.91, fax 05.57.40.63.04 ☑
✒ Hébrard et de Bouard

CH. GODARD BELLEVUE
Elevé en fût de chêne 1998

■   5.5 ha   13,500   ▥ €5-8

The vines here are 30 years old. Although at the tasting the nose emitted only a few roasted coffee notes, the wine had a fresh and oaky palate that was very pleasant. This is a wine that has good tannins and will be nice to drink over the next three years.

✆ Arbo, Godard, 33570 Francs, tel. 05.57.40.65.77, fax 05.57.40.65.77 ☑
✒ ⊤ by appt.

CH. LACLAVERIE 1998

■   9.5 ha   49,000   ▥ €5-8

This attractive 98 was singled out for its intense nose with well-ripened red fruit and toasted wood aromas and supple, well-balanced tannins. Nevertheless, it would be a good idea to wait two to three years for the oak to have an opportunity to soften.

✆ GFA Les Charmes-Godard, Lauriol, 33570 Saint-Cibard, tel. 05.57.56.07.47, fax 05.57.56.07.48, e-mail ch.puygueraud@
wanadoo.fr ☑ ⊤ by appt.
✒ Nicolas Thienpont

CH. LES CHARMES-GODARD
1999★★

□   1.65 ha   13,600   ▥ €8-11

This château has produced a superb white from Sémillon (65%), Sauvignon (20%) and Muscadelle (15%), matured for nine months on the lees in oak, with the yeasts being stirred. Bright pale-yellow in colour, this wine is instantly enticing. The palate is engaging with a lovely fullness and lots of richness. The blend of fruitiness (apricot) and vanilla-oak is perfect. This wine may be drunk straight away but will also age well over two to five years. The **red 98 Les Charmes Godard** was also singled out.

✆ GFA Les Charmes-Godard, Lauriol, 33570 Saint-Cibard, tel. 05.57.56.07.47, fax 05.57.56.07.48, e-mail ch.puygueraud@
wanadoo.fr ☑ ⊤ by appt.
✒ Nicolas Thienpont

CH. MARSAU 1998★★

■   5 ha   30,000   ▥ €11-15

Located on one of the highest sites in the appellation, Château Marsau enjoys a limestone-clay *terroir* entirely planted with Merlot. Already recommended in earlier editions, this cru has distinguished itself once more with this lovely 98. It has a garnet colour with black glints and a fresh nose with elegant aromas of redcurrant, cherry and liquorice. On the palate, the tannins are supple and frank, opening out with great richness, silkiness and balance. The fruity, long finish heralds a fine future, at least five to six years, maybe more. The wine is distributed by Dourthe company, presided over by Jean-Marie Chadronnier.

✆ Ch. Marsau, 'Bernaderie', 33570 Francs, tel. 05.57.40.67.23, fax 05.57.40.67.23, e-mail contact@cobg.com ⊤ by appt.
✒ S. et J.-M. Chadronnier

BORDEAUX

Between the Garonne and the Dordogne

The geographical region of Entre-Deux-Mers is the large triangular area bounded by the Garonne and Dordogne rivers and the south-east border of the department of the Gironde. Here, in one of the sunniest and most pleasant parts of Bordeaux, the vines occupy 23,000 ha (56,810 acres), about a quarter of the region's vineyard. The hilly terrain offers sweeping views as well as quiet corners adorned with fine examples of the traditional regional architecture (fortified manor-houses, small châteaux in green estates and larger numbers of fortified mills). Entre-Deux-Mers also lies at the heart of the Gironde's mythical past, with a rich heritage of beliefs and traditions dating from time immemorial.

Entre-Deux-Mers

The appellation Entre-Deux-Mers does not correspond exactly to the geographical area of Entre-Deux-Mers, excluding as it does some communes with their own appellations. It applies specifically to dry white wines produced under a set of regulations almost as rigorous as those for Appellation Bordeaux. As a matter of practice, the wine-growers try to keep their best white wines for this

CH. PUYANCHE
Elevé en fût de chêne 1998 — 1.5 ha | 4,000 | €4.5-8

This dry white wine, fermented and matured in oak, was admired for its aromas of flowers, citronella and wax. The palate has good length but already shows development. Drink it straight away.
Arbo, Godard, 33570 Francs, tel. 05.57.40.65.77, fax 05.57.40.65.77 by appt.

CH. PUYGUERAUD 1998★
35 ha | 59,500 | €11-15

This magnificent property, run by Nicolas Thienpont, is a stalwart of the appellation, as this interesting 98 demonstrates. It is made from 50% Merlot, 45% Cabernets and 5% Malbec and has spent 12 months in oak. The purple colour has pretty ruby lights. The elegant perfumes are evocative of pepper and blackberry. The fleshy, well-structured tannins combine well with a very agreeable winey character. It is a charming wine, which needs two to three years' time in a good cellar.
SC Ch. de Puygueraud, 33570 Saint-Cibard, tel. 05.57.56.07.47, fax 05.57.56.07.48, e-mail ch.puygueraud@wanadoo.fr by appt.

CH. NARDOU 1999★★
3 ha | 19,000 | €5-8

Acquired by the Dubart family in 1998, this estate is already beginning to be noticed – witness this superb 99. Deep-ruby in colour, it has complex, intense aromas of toasted oak and red fruit. The very fine tannins are robust and flavoursome; they combine well with the oak tannins on the finish. It will be a very fine wine when opened in three to five years' time. The second vintage, the red Château du Bois Meney 99, is not oak-matured, and was singled out for its fruity freshness and fleshy, elegant structure.
EARL Vignobles Florent Dubard, Nardou, 33570 Tayac, tel. 05.57.40.69.60, fax 05.57.40.69.20 by appt.

PELAN 1998★★
4 ha | 15,000 | €15-23

Once again this is a coup de coeur and it deserves the reader's attention. It is an 80% Cabernet Sauvignon grown on starfish-fossil limestone. The colour is dark purple and the nose a complex and intense combination of jam, vanilla, spices and roasted notes. The tannic structure is both powerful and elegant. This fleshy wine will need four to eight years to age. It will go well with grilled dishes or sauced meats.
Régis Moro, Champs-de-Mars, 33350 Saint-Philippe-d'Aiguilhe, tel. 05.57.40.63.49, fax 05.57.40.61.41 by appt.

appellation. As a result, production is voluntarily limited to 1,335 ha (3,298 acres) planted, producing 84,377 hl (2,227,553 gal) in 1999, and the annual tastings approving the wines are particularly demanding. The major grape variety is Sauvignon, giving the Entre-Deux-Mers whites their singular bouquet, to be appreciated particularly when the wine is young.

CH. DE BEAUREGARD-DUCOURT 2000★

☐   2 ha   n.c.   ■ ♦ ◗   €5-8

The Ducourt family is well known for its innovative spirit (reclaiming vineyards and new red wine vinifications during the 1970s and originality. This wine is a blend of Sémillon (63%), Sauvignon (34%) and 3% Ugni Blanc, a variety that is somewhat forgotten in this region. It is this last that probably accounts for the noticeable liveliness, typical of the sort of Entre-Deux-Mers that goes with oysters. Raisins, spring flowers and box with a lightly flavour a well-built body, which has a slightly bitter finish that will provide a good accompaniment to shellfish.

☎ SCEA Vignobles Ducourt, 18, rte de Montignac, 33760 Ladaux, tel. 05.57.34.54.00, fax 05.56.23.48.78, e-mail celliers-bxbenauge@wanadoo.fr ☑ Ⴤ by appt.

CH. BEL AIR 2000★★

☐   n.c.   n.c.   ■ ♦ ◗   €5-8

Stars and *coups de coeur* are, as previous editions have demonstrated, the stock-in-trade of J.-L. Despagne's inescapably talented team. This magisterial wine is a blend of Sauvignon, Sémillon and Muscadelle, in equal proportions. The powerful, full-flavoured nose reveals a stunning and complex combination that opens with springtime flowers and develops into exotic passion-fruit, lychee and pineapple aromas on a bed of acacia honey. The attack is explosive, the body round, concentrated and silky; the sensual finish has hints of liquorice. And yet the blend remains light and airy. It reveals the ripeness of the grapes during the harvest, their careful pressing and the impassioned and reflective forming of the wine through its vinification and maturation. Note (in the same AOC and year) **Rauzan d'Espagne** and **Tour de Mirambeau**, which are also rather good.

Between the Garonne and the Dordogne

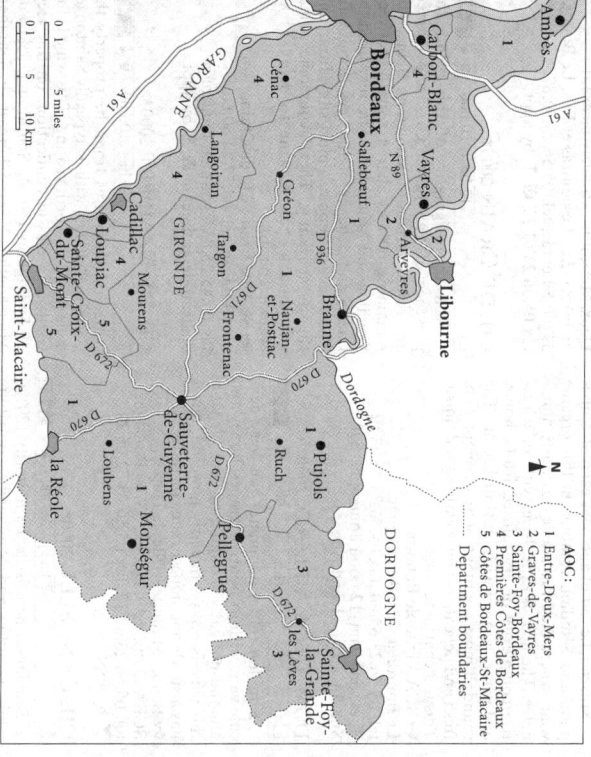

AOC:
1 Entre-Deux-Mers
2 Graves-de-Vayres
3 Sainte-Foy-Bordeaux
4 Premières Côtes de Bordeaux
5 Côtes de Bordeaux-St-Macaire

-------- Department boundaries

GFA de Perponcher, 33420 Naujan-et-Postiac, tel. 05.57.84.55.08, fax 05.57.84.57.31, e-mail contact@vignobles-despagne.com, Y by appt.

CH. BELLEVUE 2000
□ 7 ha 1,000 €3-5

A very classic wine, this 50% Sémillon and 50% Sauvignon blend is a cheerful basic wine for lovers of Entre-Deux-Mers. The floral complexity has touches of broom, and the fresh good humour of its body invites you to relax with friends after a fishing expedition.

SCEA Ch. Bellevue, 33540 Sauveterre-de-Guyenne, tel. 05.56.71.54.56, fax 05.56.71.83.95, e-mail postmaster@chateau-bellevue.com Y by appt.
D'Amécourt

CH. BONNET 2000★★
□ n.c. n.c. €5-8

Thanks to its owner, André Lurton, Château Bonnet is one of the producers that has influenced the history of Bordeaux wines over the last few decades. This wine is a splendid farewell to the 20th century with its finely presented nose of citrus (lime and grapefruit) and fitting light-yellow colour. Hiding its liveliness behind a rich attack, the palate has good presence that reflects the aromas on the nose. The successful Château Guibon 2000 was singled out by the Jury.

SCEA Vignobles André Lurton, Ch. Bonnet, 33420 Grézillac, tel. 05.57.25.58.58, fax 05.57.74.98.59, e-mail andrelurton@wanadoo.fr Y by appt.

DOM. DU BOURDIEU 2000★
□ 4.93 ha 37,000 €3-5

Muscadelle (50%) and 25% each of Sauvignon and Sémillon combine in this organic wine, where the Muscadelle obviously dominates. The nose is expressive, with an attractive complexity of crystallised fruits, honey and white caramel with hints of broom. The round, almost unctuous body develops rich, fresh and delicate flavours with a good finish. This is a charming wine.

SCA Vignoble Boudon, Le Bourdieu, 33760 Soulignac, tel. 05.56.23.65.60, fax 05.56.23.45.58 Y ev. day 9am–12 noon 2pm–6pm; Sat. Sun. by appt.; cl. end Aug.

DOM. DES CAILLOUX 2000
□ 6 ha 15,000 €3-5

Sémillon (60%) dominates this very delicate wine with its notes of grapes, honey and almond-nougat. Though fine and elegant, this wine is not particularly powerful, but it has a subtle and honest range of flavours.

Benoît Maulun et Nicole Dupuy, SCEA Dom. des Cailloux, 33760 Romagne, tel. 05.56.23.60.17, fax 05.56.23.32.05 Y by appt.

CH. CANDELEY 2000★
□ 7 ha 35,000 €3-5

Sauvignon here is in the minority (20%), while Sémillon and Muscadelle contribute

half-shares to the remainder of this flowery, fruity blend. The nose blends roses and lychees with a supple, mouthfilling citrus-fruit quality. The finish delivers a spark of liveliness to achieve a good overall balance. Drink with poultry, pork or goat's cheese.

Henri Devillaire, Toutifaut, 33790 Saint-Antoine du Queyret, tel. 05.56.61.31.46, fax 05.56.61.37.37 Y by appt.

CH. CASTENET-GREFFIER 2000★
□ 6 ha 44,000 €5-8

Established readers of the Guide will be familiar with the dignified, sedate abbey of Saint-Ferme, just 5 km (3 miles) from this château. This Sauvignon (75%), blended with Sémillon and Muscadelle, has wild and exotic aromas and a full body that attacks with suppleness, then becomes lively and finishes on lilac flowers. It is ideal for drinking with fish or cuts of pork, but there is no rush.

EARL François Greffier, Castenet, 33790 Auriolles, tel. 05.56.61.40.67, 05.56.61.38.82, e-mail ch.castenet@wanadoo.fr Y by appt.

CH. CHANTELOUVE 2000★★
□ 2.2 ha 19,000 €3-5

This is virtually the geographical heart of Entre-Deux-Mers. Sémillon (50%), Muscadelle (20%) and ripe Sauvignon (30%) have together produced this powerful yet delicate, harmonious nose, with its exotic fruit (lychee, pineapple, passion-fruit) and white-fleshed peach aromas with the merest hint of menthol. The palate is round with ripe, velvety nuances and notes of flavoursome pineapple. The freshness is discreet but effective. Though rather a characteristic Entre-Deux-Mers, it is extremely pleasant.

EARL J.C. Lescoutras et Fils, Le Bourg, 33760 Faleyras, tel. 05.56.23.90.87, fax 05.56.23.61.37 Y by appt.

CH. DE CRAIN 2000★
□ 12 ha 20,000 €3

Note the originality of this blend: the presence of Sauvignon Gris, a perfumed and round variant of Sauvignon Blanc. The remaining 60% is shared equally between Sémillon and Muscadelle. The Jury liked the finesse and delicacy of the very floral nose. The attack is supple, almost silky, fresh, and slightly sparkling. The flavoursome palate has good length. A wine to drink as an evening aperitif.

SCA de Crain, Ch. de Crain, 33750 Baron, tel. 05.57.24.50.66, fax 05.45.25.03.73, e-mail fougere@chateau-de-crain.com Y by appt.

CH. DE DAMBERT 2000★
□ 1.5 ha 10,000 €3

Several kilometres from the property the Castelvieil church, with its typically Saintonge-style porch, is worth visiting. This wine is the result of a classic vinification, on fine lees, of Sauvignon (50%), Sémillon (25%) and Muscadelle (25%). Château de Dambert releases, against a backdrop of broom, scents of white-flower honey and peaches. The palate has a citrus-fruit body that is a little heavy yet alluring. An alternative is the **La Grande Métairie 2000**. In this one, lemon, grapefruit and white-fleshed peach dominate the nose and palate enlivening the wine's round body. The development of these wines will be interesting to follow. Drink with fish, poultry or cheese.

🛒 SCEA Vignobles Bufféteau, LD Dambert, 33540 Gornac, tel. 05.56.61.97.59, fax 05.56.61.97.65 ▼ by appt.

CH. FONDARZAC 2000   n.c.   50,000   €5-8

The elegance of this Sauvignon (60%), Sémillon and Muscadelle blend is evident from its bright white colour with golden highlights. The nose reveals a fine mature complexity: white flowers, acacia and exotic fruit. The full, well-balanced palate is silky and finely sparkling and deserves to be noticed for its subtlety – one taster said it could be an ambassador for the appellation! The same owner is responsible for two other recommended wines: the **Château Darzac 2000**, which is a supple wine with touches of honey and acacia; and from the same château, the **Claude Barthe 99**, from selected plots (80% Sauvignon, 20% Sémillon) matured for six months in oak, which adds a smoky complexity to the crystallised fruit aromas and the honeyed roundness of the body. This one-star wine has a nice mineral note on the finish.

🛒 SCA Vignobles Claude Barthe, 22, rte de Bordeaux, 33420 Naujan-et-Postiac, tel. 05.57.84.55.04, fax 05.57.84.60.23, e-mail chateau.fondarzac@wanadoo.fr ▼ by appt.

CH. GRAND-JEAN 2000   14 ha   120,000   €3-5

About 3 km (7.41 acres) from La Sauve Majeure Abbey is this 83-ha (205-acre) estate, whose blend of Sémillon (60%), Sauvignon (30%) and Muscadelle, matured on the lees, offers a fresh, round, almost fleshy elegance. There are green fruit and slightly brioche-like flavours and the finish is a lively contrast to the rest. This wine would go well with seafood.

🛒 Michel Dulon, Ch. Grand-Jean, 33760 Soulignac, tel. 05.56.23.69.16, fax 05.57.34.41.29, e-mail dulon.vignobles@wanadoo.fr ▼ by appt.

CH. GROSSOMBRE 2000★   n.c.   n.c.   €5-8

This very typical Entre-Deux-Mers has a nose where floral notes combine with citrus fruit. The attack is lively, opening out with some richness on the palate which retains its freshness and then a certain fullness on the finish.

🛒 Béatrice Lurton, BP 10, 33420 Grézillac, tel. 05.57.25.58.58, fax 05.57.74.98.59, e-mail andrelurton@andrelurton.com ▼

CH. GUICHOT 2000★   2 ha   6,000   €3-5

The Jury liked the engaging complexity of this blend of Sauvignon (70%) and Muscadelle. It has finesse with aromas of white flowers, linden blossom, grapefruit, pear and apricot. The well-ripened grape quality found on the nose follows through onto the palate. This wine with its rich, fresh body and bitter citrus spark on the finish, will accompany fish (perhaps in a savoury crust) and shellfish.

🛒 André et Michèle Froissard, Guichot, 33790 Saint-Antoine du Queyret, tel. 05.56.61.36.99, fax 05.56.61.36.99 ▼ by appt.

CH. HAUT D'ARZAC 2000★   2 ha   12,000   €3-5

Somewhat characteristic, with an equal three-way split between Sauvignon, Sémillon and Muscadelle, this wine has a powerful Muscat-style nose with hints of white flowers (lilac and orange blossom) and fresh almonds. The full, rich palate is not yet fully open. The very long finish may surprise, but is interesting.

🛒 Gérard Boissonneau, 33420 Naujan-et-Postiac, tel. 05.57.74.91.12, fax 05.57.74.99.60 ▼ by appt.

CH. HAUT MAURIN 2000★   0.35 ha   2,660   €3

Several kilometres from Cadillac, this estate proposes several AOCs, one of them is this Entre-Deux-Mers, a blend of the three varieties (with 40% Sauvignon). The rich fullness of the palate is enhanced by hints of citrus fruit (orange zest) and broom honey, enlivened by fresh, lengthy notes of menthol. Time should improve the harmony.

🛒 EARL Vignobles Sanfourche, rue Grand-Village, 33410 Donzac, tel. 05.56.62.97.43, fax 05.56.62.16.87 ▼ by appt.

CH. HAUT POUGNAN 2000★   7 ha   55,000   €3-5

The pre- and post-fermentation macerations (regulated on fine lees) have given this wine a lovely Sauvignon (85%) character. There are complex aromas with fresh almonds and slightly lemony Muscat notes. The palate is round and long with hints of *kouglof* (a type of brioche that hails from Alsace). Though not a typical Entre-Deux-Mers, this wine is very good.

🛒 Ch. Haut Pougnan, 33670 Saint-Genès de Lombaud, tel. 05.56.23.06.00, fax 05.57.95.99.84 ▼ by appt.

🛒 Guéridon

CH. LA MIRANDELLE 2000★   4.3 ha   20,000   €3-5

Close to the ancient walls of one of the region's characteristic fortresses is this co-operative which, in contrast, has some impressive modern equipment. Château La Mirandelle has been selected by the co-operative for the quality of its limestone-clay *terroir* and very classic varietal composition. The 30% Muscadelle in this 2000 adds intense, exotic nuances to the lemony, floral aromas of the Sémillon (20%) and Sauvignon (50%). The lively, fresh body and fine menthol finish are signs of a good wine. The **Sauveterre**, perfumed with spring flowers and lychee, is produced from selected plots and includes 60% Sémillon and 10% Muscadelle. It was singled out for its 2000 version.

➤ Cellier de La Bastide, Cave coop. vinicole, 33540 Sauveterre-de-Guyenne, tel. 05.56.61.55.21, fax 05.56.71.60.11 ☑ ▮ ev. day except Sun. 9am–12.15pm 1.30pm–6.15pm; groups by appt.
➤ Moncontier

CH. LESTRILLE 2000★

□ 1.5 ha 13,000 ▮ ● €5-8

Reading the *Guide* over the last few years, one sees how Jean-Louis Roumage's solid reputation has come about for whites as well as reds. This lovely 2000 Entre-Deux-Mers (60% Sauvignon) is full of fruity harmony (grapefruit and pineapple) accompanied by orange blossom and acacia honey. Enjoy this attractive wine as an aperitif immediately.

➤ EARL Jean-Louis Roumage, Lestrille, 33750 Saint-Germain-du-Puch, tel. 05.57.24.51.02, fax 05.57.24.04.58, e-mail jean-louis.roumage@wanadoo.fr ☑ ▮ by appt.

LES VEYRIERS 2000★★

□ n.c. 6,000 ▮ ● €3

Only by a whisker did this superb classic miss being a *coup de cœur*. It has everything, from the beauty of its pale-yellow colour with emerald highlights to the strong, enticing and controlled fullness of aromas and flavours, combining ripe and crystallised fruits with spring or wild flowers. One member of the Jury described the finish as 'superb'. It is a blend of half Sémillon, half Sauvignon.

➤ C.C. Viticulteurs réunis de Sainte-Radegonde, 33350 Sainte-Radegonde, tel. 05.57.40.53.82, fax 05.57.40.55.99 ☑ ▮ ev. day except Sat. Sun. 8.30am–12.30pm 2pm–5pm

CH. LES VIEILLES TUILERIES 2000★

□ n.c. n.c. €3-5

Arbis, between the vast church at Targon and the huge château of Cadillac, heralds the Premières Côtes de Bordeaux. Muscadelle represents only 10%, and it is the Sauvignon (50%) and Sémillon (40%) that contribute mainly to the powerful aromas of broom tinged with menthol, grapefruit and orange peel. The fresh, supple palate is also perfumed with these fragrances, and it is attractively slightly sparkling which adds to the liveliness that continues right through to the finish. Try this refreshing wine with shellfish and grilled fish.

➤ SCEA des Vignobles Menguin, 194, Gouas, 33760 Arbis, tel. 05.56.23.61.70, fax 05.56.23.49.79 ☑ ▮ by appt.

MAINE-BRILLAND 2000

□ 10 ha 60,000 ▮ ● €3

Producta's Maine-Brilland is a very nice blend of equal proportions of Sémillon and Sauvignon enlivened by 10% Muscadelle. Hints of pineapple and ripe fruit soften the flavoursome freshness of the Sauvignon. The round palate has a lively finish. Drink it as an aperitif.

➤ Producta SA, 21, cours Xavier-Arnozan, 33082 Bordeaux Cedex, tel. 05.57.81.18.18, fax 05.56.81.22.12, e-mail producta@producta.com ▮ by appt.

CH. MARCEAU 2000★

□ 10.2 ha 61,200 ▮ ● €3-5

Sémillon (70%) is the variety which provides the foundation for this Château. The intense, citrus-fruit aromas with hints of brioche, box and fern, the supple, slightly sparkling attack, the fresh body and the more energetic finish are all marks of a very good Entre-Deux-Mers. **Château Canteloudette 2000** is a combination of Sémillon, Sauvignon and Muscadelle. Despite a reticent nose, it has a pleasing, lively and distinguished character with honey and box. It will improve with time but is already excellent with seafood. This wine earned one star, as did the **Fleur 2000**, a blend from the same source, tender and gulpable, with a contrasting nose of flowery and bold Muscat-like aromas. The discreet finish makes you want to refill the glass.

➤ Union de producteurs de Rauzan, 33420 Rauzan, tel. 05.57.84.13.22, fax 05.57.84.12.67 ☑ ▮ by appt.

CH. MARJOSSE 2000★

□ 6 ha 50,000 €3-5

The nearby ruins of the Château Curton modestly overlook an undulating landscape. Pierre Lurton is one of the grand masters of red wine-making at Cheval Blanc. Here, on his own territory, he shows that he can make a good white too. The slightly sparkling quality heightens the fresh aromas of Sauvignon (50% of the blend), and the well-balanced body opens out with notes of almond and fruit. This is a wine ideally served as an aperitif or with seafood. It is charming to look at with its pale colour and grey-gold glints.

➤ Pierre Lurton, Ch. Marjosse, 33420 Tizac-de-Curton, tel. 05.57.55.57.80, fax 05.57.55.57.84 ☑ ▮ by appt.

CH. MAYNE-CABANOT 2000★★

□ 5.6 ha 47,300 ▮ ● €3-5

The imposing medieval château (14th century) deserves a visit, like the important wine-cellar at Rauzan. This *coup de cœur* from Château Mayne-Cabanot celebrates the marriage of Sauvignon (76%) and Sémillon grapes harvested at full maturity, followed by perfect wine-making after maceration. The slightly sparkling character sets off the

...buoyant finesse on the attack of spring flowers, peaches and citronella, while the round, fleshy body opens with hints of grapefruit, menthol and pepper. Its complexity makes it a model of its appellation. Drink either as an aperitif or with meals. Its progress will be worth following.

☙ Union de producteurs de Rauzan, 33420 Rauzan, tel. 05.57.84.13.22, fax 05.57.84.12.67 ☑ ⊻ by appt.
☙ GFA Corbières

CH. MOULIN DE PONCET 2000★★
4 ha · 30,000 · €5-8

This is an attractive blend. Sauvignon (50%), Sémillon (30%) and Muscadelle (20%) grapes, harvested fully ripe and matured on fine lees, mingle springtime perfumes of hawthorn, orchards and vines in flower. The round, waxy, honeyed body finishes with an elegance and length that makes it ideal as an aperitif, and might suit certain cheeses, not least goat's cheese.

☙ Vignobles Ph. Barthe, Peyrefus, 33420 Daignac, tel. 05.57.84.55.90, fax 05.57.74.96.57, e-mail vbarthe@club-internet.fr ☑ ⊻ by appt.

CH. MYLORD 2000★
20 ha · 150,000 · €3-5

Like last year's version, this wine – made from equal parts of the three grape varieties – has a pleasing harmony. The maturation period on fine lees has enhanced the powerful aromas of citrus fruit and lychee, while the body is given extra edge by gentle bubbles. The finish is delightfully long and fresh.

☙ Michel et Alain Large, Ch. Mylord, 33420 Grézillac, tel. 05.57.84.52.19, fax 05.57.74.93.95, e-mail large@chateau-mylord.com ☑ ⊻ by appt.

CH. NARDIQUE LA GRAVIERE 2000★
13 ha · 65,000 · €5-8

A small proportion of Muscadelle (10%) adds interest to the blend of equal parts of Sauvignon and Sémillon. The nose is delicate and subtle. Though slightly bashful at first, it opens to reveal spring flowers, grapefruit and almonds. The fullness of flavour of the ripe fruit develops on the palate with insistent elegance. The tasty, fairly slender body is well-balanced with a lovely liveliness right through the finish. Keep this wine to serve with seafood or as an aperitif.

☙ Vignobles Thérèse, Ch. Nardique La Gravière, 33670 Saint-Genès-de-Lombaud, tel. 05.56.23.01.37, fax 05.56.23.25.89 ☑ ⊻ by appt.

CH. NINON 2000★
2.62 ha · 6,000 · €3-5

Painstaking, well-regulated vinification (with resting periods before and after fermentation) partly explains the success of this classic vintage (75% Sauvignon, 5% Muscadelle, 20% Sémillon). Fine notes of apple and pear combine well with those of citrus fruit and the aromas are further enhanced by smooth, crystallised nuances. The fine bubbles effectively enhance the harmony of the full body and add length to the finish of well-ripened fruit. Serve with seafood.

☙ Pierre Roubineau, 5, Tenot, 33420 Grézillac, tel. 05.57.84.62.41, fax 05.57.84.62.41 ☑ ⊻ by appt.

CH. SAINTE-MARIE
Vieilles vignes 2000★
60,000 · €5-8

This is an exemplary Entre-Deux-Mers. The Sauvignon (50%) displays elegant generosity, with moderate broom and box aromas. The body has flavours of peach, green apples and honey. This straightforward wine will be truly pleasurable either as an aperitif or purely for refreshment. **Cuvée Madlys 2000** comes from selected plots of Sauvignon (70%) and Sémillon (30%) grown on gravel, and matured in oak for six months. The complex nose reveals citrus fruit, pear drops and grape aromas, as well as toasty oak that shows itself in the charming spicy notes. The quality of the body is interesting with an oaky roundness and freshness of just-harvested grapes.

☙ Gilles et Stéphane Dupuch, 51, rte de Bordeaux, 33760 Targon, tel. 05.56.23.64.30, fax 05.56.23.66.80, e-mail ch.ste.marie@wanadoo.fr ☑ ⊻ by appt.

CH. VIGNOL 2000★
7 ha · 40,000 · €5-8

The château's main building is an original piece of Louisiana-style architecture, which reminds us that the creators were Bordeaux shippers. The influence of Sauvignon is very evident (60%, with 30% Sémillon) in the wine's round freshness and flavourful liveliness. Too much so? Some of the tasters would like readers' views about this.

☙ B. et D. Doublet, Ch. Vignol, 33750 Saint-Quentin-de-Baron, tel. 05.57.24.12.93, fax 05.57.24.12.83, e-mail bdoublet@club-internet.fr ⊻ by appt.

Graves de Vayres

Despite the similarity of the name, this wine-growing district on the left bank of the Dordogne, not far from Libourne, is not be confused with the Graves wine-growing area. Graves de Vayres is a relatively small, well-defined enclave of gravelly soil of a different type to that of Entre-Deux-Mers. The appellation has been used since the 19th century, though it was not officially recognised until 1931. Initially, it was used for dry or medium white wines, but currently there is an increase in the proportion of red wines which qualify for the appellation.

The total area of the vineyards is divided into 360 ha (889 acres) of red grape varieties and 165 ha (408 acres) of whites. A significant quantity of the reds is also sold as Appellation Régionale Bordeaux. In 2000 the production of AOC Graves de Vayres reached some 39,963 hl (1,055,023 gal), of which 7,871 hl (207,794 gal) were white wines.

CUVÉE DU BARON CHARLES
Elevé en fût de chêne 1998

■ 2 ha   15,000   ❚❚❙ €5-8

This wine is the product of 35-year-old Merlot (80%) and Cabernet Franc (20%) vines, matured 18 months in oak. This pleasant 98 is distinctive with its stewed fruit and roasted almond aromas, and supple, generous tannins that are already showing some maturity on the finish. Drink now or keep for a maximum of two to three years.

➼ Pierrette et Christian Labeille,
Ch. Le Tertre, 33870 Vayres,
tel. 05.57.74.76.91, fax 05.57.74.87.40 ◪
Ⴤ ev. day except Sun. 8am–7pm

CH. BARRE GENTILLOT 1999

■ 11.52 ha   40,000   ❚❙ ♦   €5-8

Founded in the 18th century, this estate is located 3 km (1.9 miles) from Château de Vayres. This attractive 99 is basically a Merlot (95%), with pronounced aromas of blackberries and dried fruit. The palate is supple and fruity but needs one to two years' to achieve a softer finish.

➼ SCEA Yvette Cazenave-Mahé,
Ch. de Barre, 33500 Arveyres,
tel. 05.57.24.80.26, fax 05.57.24.84.54,
e-mail chateau.de.barre@online.fr ◪
Ⴤ by appt.

CH. BUSSAC 1999

■ 20 ha   70,000   ❚❚❙ ♦   €5-8

Grown on gravelly soil and consisting of 80% Merlot, this wine has an intense ruby colour and a youthful nose in which aromas of vanilla and red fruit are just emerging. The supple, rich tannins develop with lots of finesse, thanks to the excellent integrated oakiness. A charming wine to be drunk in the next one to three years.

➼ SCEA Vignoble Cassignard,
33870 Vayres, tel. 05.57.24.52.14,
fax 05.57.24.06.00 ◪   Ⴤ by appt.

CH. CANTELAUDETTE
Elevé en fût de chêne 1999★

■ 2 ha   12,000   ❚❚❙   €5-8

This property, located on sandy-clay soil, presented this elegant, well-balanced wine with ripe fruit, flowers and vanilla oak aromas on the nose. After a fleshy attack the prominent tannins open out with some length. Two to three years in the cellar should enable this wine to mellow.

➼ Jean-Michel Chatelier,
Ch. Cantelaudette, 33500 Arveyres,
tel. 05.57.24.84.71, fax 05.57.24.83.41 ◪
Ⴤ by appt.

CH. DURAND-BAYLE 2000★

☐   n.c.   13,000   ❚❚❙   €5-8

Michel Gonet, the Champagne wine-grower, has invested a lot in Bordeaux, and it will not be long before his wines appear from the prestigious appellation in which he has just acquired a superb château. At the top of his 260 ha (642.2 acres), he is diversifying into Graves de Vayres. The most modern white wine vinification techniques have been used to produce this good quality 2000. Bright yellow-green in colour, it has an intense nose with aromas of acacia flowers and pineapple. The palate is supple and rich with finesse and harmony. It will be a real pleasure to drink either now or in two to three years. The red 99 is also awarded one star. It is mainly Merlot (80%) blended with Cabernet Franc, a silky and fruity wine with an oaky elegance. Drink over the next three years.

➼ SCEV Michel Gonet et Fils,
Ch. Lesparre, 33750 Beychac-et-Caillau,
tel. 05.57.24.51.23, fax 05.57.24.03.99,
e-mail vins.gonet@wanadoo.fr ◪
Ⴤ by appt.

CH. FAGE Elevé en fût de chêne 1999

■   n.c.   22,000   ❚❚❙   €5-8

This château, recently purchased by the négociant Joël Quancard, submits two different 99 wines, one oak-matured and the other not. They are of equal quality. Supple and full-flavoured, they are well-made, quite

340

fruity with well-balanced, ripe tannins. Drink in one to three years from now.
➤ SA Ch. Fage, 33500 Arveyres, tel. 04.67.39.10.51, fax 04.67.39.15.33 ☑

CH. GOUDICHAUD 1999★

■ 1 ha 5,000 | €5-8

This 18th-century manor house, built by a pupil of Gabriel, was once the summer residence of the archbishops of Bordeaux. It has produced this pleasing 99 with original aromas of cinnamon and exotic fruits. On the palate the tannins are still youthful and very evident with mineral notes on the finish. Typical of its region, this well-made wine should be drunk in two to three years from now.
➤ Paul Glotin, Ch. Goudichaud, 33750 Saint-Germain-du-Puch, tel. 05.57.22.27.60, fax 05.57.22.27.61 ☑

CH. HAUT-GAYAT 1999★

■ n.c. 105,000 | €5-8

This château, with its gravelly *terroir*, has been in the same family for eight generations. Its vines are half Merlot, half Cabernet Sauvignon. This dense ruby-red 99 has an expressive nose with spices and toasted oak. On the palate the tannins are supple, fresh, and already agreeable. Drink in two to three years from now.
➤ Marie-José Degas, Ch. Degas, 33750 Saint-Germain-du-Puch, tel. 05.57.24.52.32, fax 05.57.24.03.72 ☑

CH. LA CHAPELLE BELLEVUE

Prestige Elevé en barrique 1998★★

■ 2 ha 9,000 | €8-11

This superb 98 is somewhat untypical since the blend contains a large proportion of Cabernet Sauvignon (60%). The bright purple colour sparkles. The concentrated aromas of very ripe fruit blend well with toasty, vanilla notes. The meaty, robust, vigorous tannins develop with finesse and gorgeous balance. This extremely long and gorgeous wine should be put away in the cellar for three to six years.
➤ Lisette Labeille, Ch. La Chapelle Bellevue, chem. du Pin, 33870 Vayres, tel. 05.57.84.90.39, fax 05.57.74.82.40 ☑
Ƴ by appt.

GRAND VIN DU CH. LESPARRE

1999★★

■ 6 ha 30,000 | €15-23

This great wine, coming from the best plot of gravel, is the jewel in Château Lesparre's crown. It is produced and matured with every up-to-date modern technique and the result is impressive: a deep, dark colour, intense aromas of stewed fruit and toasty oak, and a robust, powerful tannic structure dominated by oak tannins that will need several years' ageing in order to soften. This is a very modern product that will appeal to those who like this style of wine. The red **Cuvée Classique 99 Château Lesparre** receives one star. It is certainly less oaky, but the oak is still very evident and will need two years' cellar time.
➤ SCEV Michel Gonet et Fils, Ch. Lesparre, 33750 Beychac-et-Caillau, tel. 05.57.24.51.23, fax 05.57.24.03.99, e-mail vins.gonet@wanadoo.fr ☑
Ƴ by appt.

CH. L'HOSANNE

Elevé en fût de chêne 1999★

□ 1 ha 5,000 | €5-8

This single-variety Sémillon, grown on clay-gravel, has undergone vinification in wood and has an alluring complexity of aromas (almonds, acacia flowers, pepper, vanilla) and an unctuous palate that is in perfect balance with the oak. It is a harmonious wine that can be drunk straight away.
➤ SCEA Chastel-Labat, 124, av. de Libourne, 33870 Vayres, tel. 05.57.74.70.55, fax 05.57.74.70.36 ☑ Ƴ by appt.

CH. PICHON-BELLEVUE

Cuvée Elisée 1999★

■ 2 ha 19,000 | €5-8

Pichon-Bellevue is a fine 40-ha (98.8-acre) property. This small-scale cru blends the three Aquitaine varieties with a large proportion of Merlot (75%). It is matured in oak for ten months. The colour is transparent cherry. The intense aromas are oaky and the palate's structure is fleshy and velvety, developing with good length with forest-fruit flavours. Drink it in the next three years. The **red Château Pichon-Bellevue 1999** is not oak-matured. It is singled out for its very agreeable palate, a smooth attack, fine balance and ripe fruit aromas.
➤ Ch. Pichon-Bellevue, 33870 Vayres, tel. 05.57.74.84.08, fax 05.57.84.95.04 ☑
Ƴ by appt.
➤ D. et L. Reclus

CH. TOUR DE GUEYRON 1999★

■ 1 ha n.c. | €5-8

Just 1 ha (2.47 acres) of gravel soil, split equally between Merlot and Cabernet Franc, has produced this ruby wine with aromas of well-ripened fruit and intense oakiness. The supple, round structure opens out with length, although the oak is still very overpowering. Wait two to four years to achieve a better blend.
➤ Pascal Sirat, 33500 Arveyres, tel. 05.57.51.57.39, fax 05.57.51.57.39 ☑
Ƴ by appt.

Sainte-Foy-Bordeaux

Saint-Foy, a medieval city of great tourist interest, is also a wine town, situated between Lot-en-Garonne and the Dordogne. Its 358 ha (884 acres) of vines produced 1,476 hl (38,966 gal) of white wine and 17,470 hl (461,208 gal) of red wine in 2000.

CH. DU CHAMP DES TREILLES

Sec Elevé en fût de chêne 2000★ ☐ **€5-8**

□ 2.25 ha 13,000

Jean Michel Comme, steward of Château Pontet, a classified Grand Cru at Pauillac, took over this family property in 1998. For the moment, he has distinguished himself with this 2000 dry white, which has a powerfully complex nose with pineapple, banana and vanilla aromas. The well-balanced, supple structure is still dominated by the oak influence but this should integrate in a year or two. A very limited edition old-vine Sémillon, **99 Sur des Vielles Vignes de Sémillon**, is also available. It is a rich wine, singled out for its agreeable fruity aromas of crystallised apricot and gingerbread. The palate is a little lively.

➤ Corinne Comme, Pibran, 33250 Pauillac, tel. 05.56.59.15.88, fax 05.56.59.15.88 ☑ ⟁ by appt.

CH. DES CHAPELAINS 1999★★

☐ **€5-8**

□ 1.2ha 9,500

This château has been in the same family since the 17th century but has only been making wine since 1991. Who could believe that a Saint-Foy-Bordeaux Sec could yield such riches? This *cuvée*, with its bright straw-yellow colour and golden highlights, has very fine, elegant aromas of acacia honey and crystallised orange. The oaky, vanilla and spicy notes appear subsequently on the palate, but are not excessive, and in perfect balance with the full, velvety structure. The finish has lots of richness and charm. It needs two to five years' cellar time, though it may be drunk straight away. Also singled out is the **red Château des Chapelains 99**, which has a lovely youthful nose and shows great potential.

➤ Pierre Charlot, Les Chapelains, 33220 Saint-André-et-Appelles, tel. 05.57.41.21.74, fax 05.57.41.27.42, e-mail chateaudeschapelains@wanadoo.fr ☑ ⟁ ev. day 8am–12 noon 2pm–6pm; Sat. Sun. by appt.

CH. CLAIRE ABBAYE

Elevé en fût de chêne 1999 ☐ **€5-8**

□ 4.5 ha 21,000

This domaine, comprising some 11 ha (27.2 acres) of vines planted on a limestone-

clay hillside, occupies a former Gallo-Roman site. After the remarkable success of its 98, this château offers a simpler 99, with a powerful nose dominated by Cabernet capsicum-type notes. On the palate, the tannins have yet to soften. But the general balance points to a good potential that will be realised over the next three years.

➤ Bruno Sellier de Brugière, Ch. Claire Abbaye, 33890 Gensac, tel. 05.57.47.42.04, fax 05.57.47.48.16, e-mail bruno.sellier@free.fr ☑ ⟁ by appt.

CH. HOSTENS-PICANT

Cuvée des Demoiselles 1999 ☐☐ **€11-15**

□ 10 ha 45,000

Sainte-Foy-la-Grande, a 13th-century fortress, did all it could in the 1990s to restore its quality wine-growing activity. This domaine has played a leading role in that project. Its white wine, produced and matured for 12 months in oak, deserves to be singled out for its expressive aromas of citrus fruit, peppery spices and flowers. After a supple and rich attack, the palate opens out to reveal floral character with some liveliness.

➤ Ch. Hostens-Picant, Grangeneuve Nord, 33220 Les Lèves-et-Thoumeyragues, tel. 05.57.46.38.11, fax 05.57.46.26.23, e-mail chateauhp@aol.com ☑ ⟁ by appt.

CH. LA CHAPELLE MAILLARD

Cuvée Prestige Elevé en fût de chêne 1999 ■ **€8-11**

■ n.c. 10,600

This 9-ha (22.2-acre) domaine practises biodynamic methods. The Cuvée Prestige is characterised by the elegance of the fruity, spicy aromas and powerful, well-balanced tannins. It will, however, be necessary to wait one to three years for the oak to soften.

➤ Ch. La Chapelle Maillard, 33220 Saint-Quentin-de-Caplong, tel. 05.57.41.26.13, fax 05.57.41.25.99, e-mail chateau@chapelle-maillard.com ☑ ⟁ by appt.

CH. L'ENCLOS Réserve de la Marquise

Elevé en fût de chêne 1999 ■ **€5-8**

■ 5.6 ha 41,000

Built in 1758, this château belongs to the president of the appellation's recently formed *syndicat*. Her knowledge of haute cuisine is reflected in her recommendation that this wine be served with vine leaves stuffed with *foie gras* and truffles accompanied by pan-fried cep mushrooms. That would be worth trying. This Réserve de la Marquise has a deep cherry colour. It has a discreet nose with hints of spices, flowers and oak. The tannins are full and velvety when they first arrive on the palate, then open out with simplicity but also harmony, which indicates that this wine will be very pleasant to drink in one to three years.

➤ SCEA Ch. L'Enclos, Dom. de L'Enclos, 33220 Pineuilh, tel. 05.57.46.55.97, fax 05.57.46.55.97, e-mail sceachateaulenclos@wanadoo.fr ⟁ by appt.

Premières Côtes de Bordeaux

The region of the Premières Côtes de Bordeaux stretches some sixty km (37 miles) along the right bank of the Garonne, from the gates of the city of Bordeaux to Cadillac. The vines are grown on slopes facing the river, which offer magnificent views. Soils here are very varied: along the Garonne it is a recent alluvial soil, producing some excellent red wines. On the slopes, gravelly and limey soils predominate, the amount of clay in the soil increasing further away from the river. The vines, the conditions of cultivation and methods of vinification are all in the classic Bordeaux mould. In all, this appellation consists of 2,868 ha (7,084 acres) planted for reds, with 470 ha (1,161 acres) planted for sweet whites; a significant proportion of the wines, mainly whites, are also sold under the Appellation Régionale Bordeaux. The red wines, of which 198,831 hl (5,249,138 gal) were produced in 2000, have a long-established reputation for their colour, body and strength, while those produced on the slopes above add a certain finesse to these qualities. The white wines, of which 17,933 hl (473,431 gal) were produced in 2000, are soft and increasingly tend towards the sweet.

The Appellation Côtes de Bordeaux Saint-Macaire is a south-easterly extension of the Premières Côtes de Bordeaux. The area makes supple, sweet white wines, producing 2,321 hl (61,274 gal) of wine in 2000.

CH. LES BAS-MONTS Sec 2000★★

☐   1 ha   7,800   ■ ♠   €3-5

Those who like authentic dry whites will love this single-variety Sauvignon grown on a classic *terroir* of limestone clay. The pale yellow colour is bright with coppery high-lights. The subtle nose has acacia, elderflower and honey aromas. On the palate, a full attack is followed by richness, fullness and remark-ably well-balanced flavours. Drink this very well-made wine now with fish or shellfish.

♠ GAEC Basso Frères, Au Raymond, 33220 Margueron, tel. 05.57.41.29.16, fax 05.57.41.29.16 ▼ by appt.

CH. MARTET Réserve de Famille 1999★

■   6.3 ha   30,000   ▥ €15-23

After the *coup de coeur* awarded for the 98, this château offers another really lovely single-variety Merlot, which this time only just missed two stars. The dense colour is almost black and the stunning perfumes evoke plums, vanilla and toast. The smooth, generous tannins give form to a very fine, long palate. Leave for three to six years in a good cellar. The second wine, **Les Hauts de Martet 99**, was singled out for its generous fruity character and powerful, pleasantly oaky tannic structure. It can be drunk whilst the other wine is ageing.

♠ SCEA Ch. Martet, 33220 Eynesse, tel. 05.57.41.00.49, fax 05.57.41.09.36, e-mail pdeconinck@deconinckwine.be ▼ by appt.
♠ Patrick de Coninck

CH. DES THIBEAUD 1999★★

■   1.5 ha   9,987   ▥ €5-8

Made from the fruits of a plot of old vines planted on limestone-clay, this three-quarters Cabernet 99 is a pleasant surprise. The bright garnet colour has purple highlights. The dark berry fruitiness, spiciness and vanilla-oak blend well with the full, powerful, mouth-filling tannins, and sloe and pepper flavours on the finish. This wine will be all the better for laying down for two to five years in a good cellar.

♠ Dom. Delaplace, Le Canton, 33220 Caplong, tel. 05.57.41.25.65, fax 05.57.41.27.84, e-mail chateau.des.thibeaud@free.fr ▼ by appt.

CH. VERRIERE BELLEVUE Moelleux 1999

☐   1 ha   4,000   ■ ♠   €8-11

Alice and Jean-Paul Bessette and their son Mathieu, who has a wine-growing qualifica-tion, own this vineyard on the slopes of Landerrouat. Made from successive selec-tions of late-harvested grapes, this sweet white wine has little bouquet yet but does have a rich, full palate with a fruity, honeyed finish. A little time is undoubtedly necessary.

♠ EARL Alice et Jean-Paul Bessette, 5, La Verrière, 33790 Landerrouat, tel. 05.56.61.36.91, fax 05.56.61.41.12 ▼ by appt.

343

Premières Côtes de Bordeaux

BARON DE GRAVELINES
Vieilli en fût de chêne 1999 ☐ €3-5
n.c.   n.c.   n.c.

Marketed by Yvon Mau, this wine follows current trends and has a strong oakiness. It is, however, quality oak, and the wine itself has an interesting bouquet somewhere between orange and lemon, good body and general balance.

➤ SA Yvon Mau, BP 01,
33190 Gironde-sur-Dropt Cedex,
tel. 05.56.61.54.54, fax 05.56.71.10.45

DOM. DU BARRAIL
La Charmille 1999★ 4 ha 24,000 €8-11

Yves Armand is best known for his sweet wines (Château La Rame). But his reds are no less indicative of his talents. The proof is in last year's lovely *coup de cœur*. The current 99 is also a very eloquent wine. It needs more time to blend, but the fruity, grilled notes on the nose and sturdy tannic structure show that it possesses real potential to develop into a really fine wine within four to five years.

➤ Yves Armand, Ch. La Rame,
33410 Sainte-Croix-du-Mont,
tel. 05.56.62.01.50, fax 05.56.62.01.94,
e-mail chateau.larame@wanadoo.fr ▼
☗ ev. day 8.30am–12 noon 1.30pm–7pm;
Sat. Sun. by appt.

CH. DU BIAC Elevé en barrique 1998
7 ha 26,000 €5-8

Both the nose and palate of this dark wine indicate that it is still youthful and austere and needs time to develop. The excellent structure indicates that it will be an interesting wine after three or four years.

➤ SCEA Ch. du Biac, 19, rte de Ruasse,
33550 Langoiran, tel. 05.56.67.19.98,
fax 05.56.67.32.63, e-mail palas@
quaternet.fr ▼ ☗ by appt.
➤ Patrick Rossini

CH. DE BIROT 1998★
17 ha 42,600 ☐ ♦ €5-8

There is a fine 18th-century residence on the slopes overlooking the Garonne, run by two great names of Bordeaux wine-growing: Fournier and Castéja. No wonder the cru nurses ambitions, and they are not vain ambitions either, as proved by this wine. Supple, round, structured with well-extracted tannins, it is already pleasant with its fine fruity and spicy aromas accompanied by a lovely note of musk. All the same, it will develop further and invites us to wait another two or three years.

➤ Fournier-Castéja, Ch. de Birot,
33410 Béguey, tel. 05.56.62.68.16,
fax 05.56.62.68.16, e-mail fournier.casteja@
wanadoo.fr ▼ ☗ by appt.

CH. BRETHOUS
Cuvée Prestige 1998★★ 12.5 ha 500,000 €8-11

The Verdiers' estate wisely avoids the traps of fashion. The making of trendy limited-edition wines is off the agenda. Oak is present, but knows its place; it is there to accompany the fruity body, not to supplant it. The result is a very lovely wine for laying down (wait five or six years) which shows youth in its Bordeaux-red colour and quality in its already complex nose, followed by a well-built, well-balanced structure.

➤ Denise et Cécile Verdier, Ch. Brethous,
33360 Camblanes, tel. 05.56.20.77.76,
fax 05.56.20.08.45 ▼ ☗ ev. day 8.30am–
12 noon 2pm–6pm; Sat. Sun. by appt.

CH. CARIGNAN 1999★
11 ha 40,000 €15-23

This is an enormous estate of some 145 ha (358.2 acres), of which 60 ha (148 acres) are planted with vines. It is dominated by a beautiful château that has known some Montesquieu owners, from Xaintrailles to the Montesquieu family. This well-balanced 99 has a complex nose. It will be a credit to its origins two to three years from now. The **Cuvée Prima 98** also gained one star for its elegant structure.

➤ GFA Philippe Pieraerts, Ch. Carignan,
33360 Carignan-de-Bordeaux,
tel. 05.56.21.21.30, fax 05.56.78.36.65,
e-mail tt@chateau-carignan.com ▼
☗ by appt.

CH. CARSIN Cuvée noire 1999★
21 ha 21,828 €11-15

This prestigious wine has been lovingly brought to fruition by its owner, the only Finnish wine-grower in the Bordeaux region. So much is clear from the lovely glossy dark-red colour and the aromas of leather, red fruit and toast. With its good structure of well-blended tannins on the palate the wine needs to be laid down for two to three years.

➤ Juha Berglund, Ch. Carsin, 33410 Rions,
tel. 05.56.76.93.06, fax 05.56.62.64.80,
e-mail chateau@carsin.com ▼ ☗ by appt.

CH. DES CEDRES
Elevé en fût de chêne 1999★
3 ha 18,600 €5-8

This wine has a pretty name, and its nose and palate are no less pleasing. If the nose expresses its personality with notes of red fruit, the palate stamps its identity with a sturdy body that should reach its optimum in the next two to three years.

♠ SCEA Vignobles Larroque, Ch. des Cèdres, 33550 Paillet, tel. 05.56.72.16.02, fax 05.56.72.34.44 ▼
Y by appt.

CH. CLOS DE MONS 1999
■ 1.47 ha 12,000 ▯▮ €5-8 ▼

This estate, purchased in 1996, acquired a winery in 1999. Merlot (65%), Cabernet Sauvignon (30%) and Cabernet Franc (5%) have contributed to the balance of this well-constructed deep purple wine. It will at its best within the next year or two.

♠ SC Ch. de Mons, 37, chem. de Peybotte, 33360 Lignan-de-Bordeaux, tel. 05.56.21.00.00, fax 05.56.21.00.01
Y by appt.
♠ Monfort-Davidsen

CLOS DU MOINE 1999★
□ 0.56 ha 3,000 ■ €3-5

This property has been in the same family since 1870, when the former owner of this vineyard chose to become a monk and sold the property. This wine, only made in very small quantities, is expressive both in terms of the floral and fruity notes on the nose and of the supple, round, full and fresh palate.

♠ Jean-Michel Barbot, Desclos, rte de Loupiac, 33410 Sainte-Croix-du-Mont, tel. 05.56.62.01.63, fax 05.56.62.06.09 ▼

CLOS SAINTE-ANNE 1999★
■ 3 ha 25,000 ▯▮ €8-11
Y by appt.

Although they mainly work in the Entre-Deux-Mers region, the Vignobles Courselle also produce wine here. The results are good, judging by this wine, whose elegance lies in the grilled notes on the nose and in the development of the flavours and ripe tannins on the palate. Wait two to three years for this delightful wine.

♠ Sté des Vignobles Francis Courselle, Ch. Thieuley, 33670 La Sauve, tel. 05.56.23.00.01, fax 05.56.23.34.37 ▼

CH. CRABITAN-BELLEVUE 1999★
■ 5 ha 9,000 ■ €5-8 Y

Although mainly present in the Sainte-Croix appellation, GFA Solane do not neglect their Premières Côtes. This pleasant wine is proof of that, with its suppleness, roundness, good balance and richness. It is a classic of the appellation.

♠ GFA Bernard Solane et Fils, 33410 Sainte-Croix-du-Mont, tel. 05.56.62.01.53, fax 05.56.76.72.09 ▼
Y ev. day except Sun. 8am–12 noon 2pm–6pm

CH. DUDON
Cuvée Jean-Baptiste Dudon 1998★
■ 2 ha 16,000 ▯▮ €5-8

Acquired by the Merlauts 40 years ago, this cru goes peacefully on its way with this characterful wine that has all the complexity of flavours and substance needed to become extremely elegant in two or three years' time.

♠ SARL Dudon, Ch. Dudon, 33880 Baurech, tel. 05.57.97.77.35, fax 05.57.97.77.39, e-mail jmdudon@alienor.fr ▼ Y by appt.
♠ Jean Merlaut

CH. FAUCHEY 1999
■ 5 ha 18,000 ▯▮ €5-8

The original castle here burned down when the Edict of Nantes was revoked, and it was rebuilt in neo-gothic style in 1855. This wine is extremely light and transparent in colour. It is above all supple and fresh, qualities that arrive on cue to enhance the appetising red berry fruit and vanilla aromas.

♠ SCEA Famille Salamanca, Ch. Fauchey, 33550 Villenave-de-Rions, tel. 05.56.72.30.60, fax 05.56.72.30.09, e-mail chateaufauchey@aol.com ▼
Y by appt.

CH. FRANC-PERAT 1999★★
■ n.c. n.c. ■ ▮▮ €8-11

You will find this producer often appears in this section of the Guide, because every year our Jury decides his wines are among the best. The superb Château Mont-Pérat appears later; in the meantime, consider this remarkable wine. It has intense well-balanced aromas of ripe fruit, vanilla and toast and a full, tannic palate, which guarantees a good future for this fine wine.

♠ SCEA de Mont-Pérat, 33550 Capian, tel. 05.57.84.55.08, fax 05.57.84.57.31, e-mail contact@vignobles-despagne.com
Y by appt.
♠ J.-L. Despagne

CH. GALLAND-DAST 1998★
■ 2.59 ha 20,000 ▯▮ €5-8

This discreet and pleasant property is responsible for this wine with personality. Supple, well-balanced, and long with a sturdy tannic structure, it shows every sign, given the right conditions, that the nose will open out with expressive red fruit aromas.

♠ SCEA du Ch. Galland-Dast, 33880 Cambes, tel. 05.56.20.87.54, fax 05.56.20.87.54 ▼

CH. DU GRAND PLANTIER 1999
■ 11 ha 22,000 ▯▮ €5-8

Producers in many appellations, the Vignobles Albucher here offer a Premières Côtes which, though uncomplicated, is well-made and has a pleasant roundness that is in harmony with its delightful floral and fruity aromas.

♠ GAEC des Vignobles Albucher, Ch. du Grand Plantier, 33410 Monprimblanc, tel. 05.56.62.99.03, fax 05.56.76.91.35 ▼
Y by appt.

Premières Côtes de Bordeaux

CH. GRIMONT Cuvée Prestige 1999★
■ 8 ha 55,000 ▦ €5-8

This wine is matured in oak. Its nose has retained a note of good-quality vanilla that is also perceived on the palate, where it combines with red fruit to create a well-balanced, supple, full and pleasant character. Given its good length, this wine may be laid down for three or four years.

➤ SCEA Pierre Yung et Fils, Ch. Grimont, 33360 Quinsac, tel. 05.56.20.86.18, fax 05.56.20.82.50 ▼ ☖ by appt.

CH. HAUT GAUDIN
Cuvée Prestige Elevé en fût de chêne 1998★ ■ €8-11
■ 5 ha 20,000

A 12-month maturation in oak has given this Cuvée Prestige spicy, vanilla notes that contribute to its elegance. Everything, from the glinting dark-ruby colour to the finish, confirms that this wine has good potential and will justify two to three years in the cellar. The **Cuvée Tradition 98**, matured in oak for only six months, was also awarded one star. It is already a pleasant wine and has good potential.

➤ Vignobles Dubourg, 33760 Escoussans, tel. 05.56.23.93.08, fax 05.56.23.65.77 ▼ ☖ ev. day except Sun. 8am–12 noon 2pm–6pm

CH. HAUT MAURIN 1999★
□ 2 ha n.c. ■ €3-5

This is the only sweet wine on offer from the Vignobles Sanfourche. It has elegant aromas and opens out to reveal a well-balanced structure which adds an overall suppleness and ripeness to the wine.

➤ EARL Vignobles Sanfourche, rue Grand-Village, 33410 Donzac, tel. 05.56.62.97.43, fax 05.56.62.16.87 ☖ by appt.

CH. JONCHET Cuvée Prestige 1998★
■ 6.5 ha 10,000 ▦ €5-8

This Cuvée Prestige is a good ambassador for its cru. The nose has a fine complexity of aromas (prune, oak and red fruit) and the palate is fresh, supple, silky, elegant and long, leaving the taster with a delightful memory.

➤ Philippe Rullaud, Ch.Jonchet, La Roberie, 33880 Cambes, tel. 05.56.21.34.16, fax 05.56.78.75.32 ▼ ☖ by appt.

CH. JOURDAN
Elevé en fût de chêne 1999★
■ 17.86 ha 93,000 ▦ €5-8

This property is a former Benedictine priory. The wine is currently marketed by the firm of Luze and has pleasant red berry fruit aromas. Although the palate is already supple, the wine has good potential due to its fine tannins and long finish.

➤ A. de Luze et Fils, Dom. du Ribet, BP 59, 33451 Saint-Loubes Cedex, tel. 05.57.97.07.20, fax 05.57.97.07.27, e-mail deluze@gvg.fr ▼ ☖ by appt.

CH. LA BERTRANDE
Elevé en fût de chêne 1999★★
■ 2.5 ha 12,000 ▦ €8-11

Although this wine has not benefited from the big improvements currently being undertaken at this cru, it is a limited edition matured in oak that is in excellent form. Supple, round and silky, as well as tannic, it opens out with ripe fruit on the nose and an interesting body that means it is already good to drink, though it has good ageing potential, too.

➤ Vignobles Anne-Marie Gillet, Ch. La Bertrande, 33410 Omet, tel. 05.56.62.19.64, fax 05.56.76.90.55, e-mail chateau.la.bertrande@wanadoo.fr ▼ ☖ by appt.

CH. LA CHEZE
Elevé en fût de chêne 1999★
■ 9 ha 40,000

Like many aristocratic residences in the neighbourhood, this château is reputed to have been used for hunting by the Duc d'Epernon. Today it is a cru taken over by two oenologists with an established reputation. They have every reason to be pleased with this 99, whose dark, glossy appearance predicts a good concentration. The nose has fine, complex aromas and there is a good combination of oak and fruit on the palate, which has a solid structure with fullness and length. All this shows that it is worth keeping this wine for three to five years.

➤ SCEA Ch. La Chèze, La Chaise, 33550 Capian, tel. 05.56.72.11.77, fax 05.56.23.01.51 ▼ ☖ by appt.

CH. LA CLYDE Cuvée Garde de la Clyde
Elevé en fût de chêne 1998★
■ 2 ha 12,000 ▦ €8-11

This wine, matured in oak, is ideal for laying down. The oak is still very pronounced. Yet the sturdy structure of this wine indicates that both oak and tannins will integrate well in time.

➤ EARL Philippe Cathala, Ch. La Clyde, 33550 Tabanac, tel. 05.56.67.56.84, fax 05.56.67.12.06 ▼ ☖ by appt.

CH. LA FORET
Elevé en fût de chêne 1999★
■ 2 ha 8,000 ▦ €5-8

Although the name of this cru honours the monks who cleared the forests in order to plant vines, this Premières Côtes has nothing in common with communion wine. The finesse of its aromas, with hints of red fruit, praline and oak, and its excellent tannic structure all testify to well-handled extraction and maturation.

➤ SCEA Ch. La Forêt, 33880 Cambes, tel. 05.56.21.31.25, fax 05.56.78.71.80 ▼ ☖ by appt.
➤ d'Herbigny

CH. LA PRIOULETTE 1998★

3 ha 10,000 €5-8

This estate, purchased by Pierre Bord in 1911, has stayed in the family. His grand-daughters Bénédicte and Valérie have been running it for the last five years. This wine is interesting with its expressive nose of red berry fruit and its solid tannic structure. It is an attractive wine that is already very good to drink, though it could be left in the cellar for a further two to three years.
➤ SC du Ch. La Prioulette, 33490 Saint-Maixant, tel. 05.56.62.01.97, fax 05.56.62.02.20 ⏐ by appt.

CH. LAROCHE 1999★★

13.5 ha 70,000 €5-8

This wine is as sturdily built as the château it comes from – a fine 18th-century residence constructed round a 16th-century tower. The intense aromas combine notes of under-growth and fruit. The concentrated, well-balanced palate has a supple attack, then reveals a tannic strength that calls for four to five years in the cellar.
➤ Martine Palau, Ch. Laroche, 33880 Baurech, tel. 05.56.21.31.03, fax 05.56.21.36.58, e-mail chateau.laroche@wanadoo.fr ⏐ by appt.

CH. LE DOYENNE 1999

8 ha 37,000 €8-11

Beautiful parkland gives this domaine added appeal. Though the wine is a little austere on the finish, it has an attractive balance and attractive fruity aromas of black-currant and morello cherry.
➤ SCEA du Doyenné, 27, chem. de Loupes, 33880 Saint-Caprais-de-Bordeaux, tel. 05.56.78.75.75, fax 05.56.21.30.09, e-mail doyenne@vieco.com ⏐ by appt.
➤ D. Watrin

CH. LESCURE 1998

□
2.3 ha 7,800 €3-5

Coming from Verdelais, whose church was attended by Mauriac and café patronised by Toulouse-Lautrec, this supple, rich wine is not for keeping, but will be extremely enjoy-able if drunk now.
➤ C.A.T. Ch. Lescure, 33490 Verdelais, tel. 05.57.98.04.68, fax 05.57.98.04.64, e-mail chateau.lescure@free.fr
➤ ⏐ by appt.
➤ S.P.E.G.

CH. LES HAUTS DE PALETTE

Elevé en fût de chêne 1998★
2.75 ha 20,000 €5-8

Made from half Merlot and half Cabernets, from a small vineyard, this wine is has a good, full, fleshy, long and well-balanced structure. Drink right away or keep for three to four years.
➤ SCEA Charles Yung et Fils, 8, chem. de Palette, 33410 Béguey, tel. 05.56.62.94.85, fax 05.56.62.18.11 ⏐ by appt.

CH. DE L'ESPINGLET 1999★

26 ha 120,000 €5-8

Grown on a fine estate renowned for years, this wine, which is marketed by Maison Ginestet, fulfills the promise of its beautiful purple colour. It has lovely aromas of red berry fruit and spices with prominent tobacco notes. This well-structured 99 has tannins that will be just right in one to two years' time.
➤ SA Maison Ginestet, 19, av. de Fontenille, 33360 Carignan-de-Bordeaux, tel. 05.56.68.81.82, fax 05.56.20.96.99, e-mail contact@ginestet.fr ⏐ by appt.
➤ EBG Raynaud

CH. DE LESTIAC

Cuvée Prestige Elevé en fût de chêne 1999★
55.7 ha 80,000 €5-8

Once again this cru, which can be relied on for its quality, has provided elegance in the form of this Cuvée Prestige. The nose is complex and appetising; ripe fruit and jam aromas of red berry fruit and grilled notes. The palate is full, long, fleshy and tannic. Another year or two, and it will be a very attractive wine. The red Château de Marsan 99 is not oak-matured and was singled out by the Jury.
➤ SCEA Gonfrier Frères, Ch. de Marsan, 33550 Lestiac-sur-Garonne, tel. 05.56.72.14.38, fax 05.56.72.10.38, e-mail gonfrier@terre-net.fr ⏐ by appt.

CH. LEZONGARS 1999★

10 ha 50,000 €5-8

This cru, overlooked by a lovely Palladian-inspired villa at the top of a hillside, has a fine quality terroir. Although the wine has a slightly austere finish, it has good quality aromas of red berry fruit and jam and an excellent structure. It needs three or four years.
➤ SC du Ch. Lezongars, 324, Roques-Nord, 33550 Villenave-de-Rions, tel. 05.56.72.18.06, fax 05.56.72.31.44, e-mail info@chateau-lezongars.com
➤ ⏐ by appt.

CH. MACALAN 1999★

2.65 ha 21,000 €5-8

Saint-Eulalie, where this wine hails from, is a commune in the north of the appellation with a rich heritage (a 13th-century church and an ancient abbey). The wine is resolutely elegant with ripe red berry fruit and roasted notes on the nose, and a supple, well-balanced and long palate.
➤ Jean-Jacques Hias, Ch. Macalan, 20, rue des Vignerons, 33560 Sainte-Eulalie, tel. 05.56.38.92.41, fax 05.56.38.92.41
➤ ⏐ by appt.

CH. MAINE-PASCAUD

Cuvée André Vieilli en fût de chêne 1998★
3 ha 20,000 €5-8

Though it does not rival certain earlier ver-sions, this wine has plenty of qualities. The colour is dense, the nose is expressive (fruits and spices) and the palate is supple, round

CH. MONT-PÉRAT 1999★★★ ▪ 10 ha ▦ 18,000 █ €15-23

Last year's version of this wine was a *coup de coeur*, as is this lovely 99. An impressive dark colour, and the nose emits aromas with a predilection for toasty notes. The oak is extremely well-handled and respects the wine's very fine quality.

☛ SCEA de Mont-Pérat, 33550 Capian, tel. 05.57.84.55.08, fax 05.57.84.57.31, e-mail contact@vignobles-despagne.com
Ⴘ by appt.

CH. OGIER DE GOURGUE 1999★ ▪ 4.5 ha ▦ 36,000 █ €8-11

Punching down by hand, and care over the percentage of new oak used, are both part of this oenologist-owner's aim to produce a wine that has keeping qualities, but avoids astringency. Despite a somewhat closed nose of discreet fruitiness, this objective has been achieved in the deep-coloured 99 with its purple highlights. The palate has richness right through to the silky finish.

☛ Josette Fourès, 41, av. de Gourgues, 33880 Saint-Caprais-de-Bordeaux, tel. 05.56.78.70.99, fax 05.56.76.46.18, e-mail v.lartigue@malrome.com [V]
Ⴘ by appt.

CH. DU PIRAS 1998★ ▪ 25 ha ▦ 175,000 █ €8-11

Grown on a large estate of 76 ha (187.7 acres), this wine needs to soften, which it will, thanks to its body, which has a good tannic structure. The intense, complex aromas of undergrowth, ripe fruit and spices are complemented by a musky note. The rich flavours are more forthcoming if the wine is decanted.

☛ SCA Les Trois Collines, Ch. du Grand-Mouÿs, 33550 Capian, tel. 05.57.97.04.44, fax 05.57.97.04.60, e-mail cavif.gm@ifrance.com [V] Ⴘ by appt.

CH. PRIEURE CANTELOUP
Cuvée Faustine Elevé en fût de chêne 1999★ ▪ 9.3 ha ▦ n.c. █ €5-8

This oak-matured wine manages to balance suppleness with concentration. The nose is still a little closed, but has an interesting fruitiness and a tannic structure that and well-balanced with good tannins. It will improve if left a year or two.

☛ Olivier Metzinger, SCEA du Ch. Pascaud, RD 10, 33410 Rions, tel. 05.56.62.60.58, fax 05.56.62.60.58 [V]
Ⴘ by appt.

CH. MALAGAR 1999★
☐ n.c. ▦ 4,000 █ €8-11

This estate once belonged to François Mauriac. This sweet, golden wine has beeswax and crystallised fruit aromas on the nose. The elegant palate has richness and fullness, and a pleasant oakiness that results in an interesting wine. It may be drunk and enjoyed right away.

☛ Domaines Cordier, 160, cours du Médoc, 33300 Bordeaux, tel. 05.57.19.57.77, fax 05.57.19.57.87 Ⴘ by appt.

CH. MARGOTON 1998★
☐ 3 ha ▦ 4,000 █ €5-8

There are equal proportions of Sémillon and Muscadelle in this *cuvée*, produced in limited quantity. Its richness is apparent both on the nose, with fine smoky notes, and in its supple, rich, full palate.

☛ Francine et Francis Courrèges, 31, chem. des Vignes, 33880 Saint-Caprais-de-Bordeaux, tel. 05.56.21.32.87, fax 05.56.21.37.18, e-mail f.courreges@gt-sa.com [V]
Ⴘ ev. day 8am–12 noon 2pm–6pm

CH. MEMOIRES
Vieilli en fût de chêne 1999★
n.c. ▦ 40,000 █ €5-8

Resisting the fashionable bias towards Merlot, this cru uses mainly Cabernet Sauvignon (60%). This vintage vindicates the practice. The colour is intense and the nose has personality with a pleasant combination of fruit and vanilla. The wine has concentration and very pronounced oak tannins, which point to a good future.

☛ SCEA Vignobles Ménard, Ch. Mémoires, 33490 Saint-Maixant, tel. 05.56.62.06.43, fax 05.56.62.04.32, e-mail memoires@aol.com [V] Ⴘ by appt.
☛ J.-François Ménard

CH. DE MONS
Elevé en fût de chêne 1998★
27 ha n.c. █ €3-5 ▦♦

This fine family estate sells through the Etablissements Cordier. It presents here an honest and robust wine, well-constructed ruby wine, which is fresh and robust with well-integrated oaky aromas. The wine is already drinking well, but calls for a little more time to soften.

☛ Ets D. Cordier, 53, rue du Dehez, 33290 Blanquefort, tel. 05.56.95.53.00, fax 05.56.95.53.01, e-mail florence.dobhels@cordier-wines.com
☛ GAEC Subra

needs time in order to open up (within four to five years).

• Xavier et Valerie Germe, 63, chem. du Loup, 33370 Yvrac, tel. 05.56.31.58.61, fax 05.56.56.00.00 ⊠ Y by appt.

CH. REYNON 1999* ■ 16 ha 75,000 €11-15

Though very 18th-century in style, chateau in fact dates from 1848. For those familiar with this cru, what is surprising about this year's 99 version is its suitability for drinking young – though it may indeed be kept. Those who begin drinking it in early 2002 will not be disappointed by the attractive fruity and powerful aromas, signalling excellent concentration, or by the well-balanced structure, which develops flavours of very ripe fruit and grilled notes. It has great elegance.

• Denis et Florence Dubourdieu, Ch. Reynon, 33410 Béguey, tel. 05.56.62.96.51, fax 05.56.62.14.89, e-mail reynon@goformet.com ⊠ Y by appt.

CH. ROQUEBERT ■ 1 ha 6,000 €8-11

Cuvée spéciale Oanna Elevé en fût neuf 1998

Produced from a small cuvée de prestige, this wine has an expressive nose. It is still has pronounced tannins and needs two or three years to mature.

• Christian et Philippe Neys, Ch. Roquebert, 33360 Quinsac, tel. 05.56.20.84.14, fax 05.56.20.84.14 ⊠ Y ev. day 9am–12 noon 2pm–6pm; Sat. Sun. by appt.

CH. DE TESTE 1999 □ 3 ha 14,000 €8-11

Laurent Réglat belongs to a well-established local family and presented this wine with a very well-handled palate. Beeswax, roasts, honey, acacia, lemon, jam all go to give the nose real charm. The red **Château Saint-Hubert 99** was also singled out by the Jury.

• EARL Vignobles Laurent Réglat, Ch. de Teste, 33410 Monprimblanc, tel. 05.56.62.92.76, fax 05.56.62.98.80, e-mail laurent.reglat@worldonline.fr ⊠ Y ev. day except Sat. Sun. 9am–12 noon 2.30pm–6pm, cl. 15–30 Aug.

CH. VIEILLE TOUR 1998* ■ 1.5 ha 9,000 €5-8

A fine vineyard of 33 ha (81.5 acres), this cru proposed a wine made entirely from Merlot. The variety has left its mark on the nose, which has fine fruity, spicy notes. The palate is agreeably supple. This well-constructed wine will be ready for drinking in a year or two.

• Arlette Gouin, 1, Lapradiasse, 33410 Laroque, tel. 05.56.62.61.21, fax 05.56.76.94.18, e-mail chateau.vieille.tour@wanadoo.fr ⊠ Y by appt.

Côtes de Bordeaux Saint-Macaire

CH. FAYARD 1999* □ 2.97 ha 10,000 €11-15

Saint-Macaire has retained its medieval ramparts, 16th-century houses and church of Saint-Sauveur with its 13th-century frescoes. Among the most beautiful towns in the Gironde, it is worth visiting, as is this 17th-century chateau. Made from old vines growing on a gravelly terroir, this attractive 1999 has a pretty colour with golden highlights and complex aromas of apricots, peaches and grapefruit with mineral and leather notes. The full, well-balanced palate is harmonious, rich and very long. Drink now or keep for two to three years.

• Jacques-Charles de Musset, Ch. Fayard, 33490 Le Pian-sur-Garonne, tel. 05.56.63.33.81, fax 05.56.63.60.20, e-mail chateau.fayard@wanadoo.fr
Y by appt.
• Saint-Michel SA

CH. PERAYNE 1999 □ 2.25 ha 1,350 €5-8

Philatelists will be delighted to find a postal services museum in Saint-Macaire at the Relais de poste d'Henri IV. This cuvée, produced in tiny amounts, is noteworthy for its attractive aromas of lime, flowers and pepper. Lively on the attack, this wine should benefit from two to three years' ageing, when it will be very pleasant to drink.

• Ch. Perayne, 33490 Saint-André-du-Bois, tel. 05.57.98.16.20, fax 05.56.76.45.71, e-mail chateau.perayne@wanadoo.fr ⊠ Y by appt.
• Henri Lüddecke.

The Graves Region

Bordeaux wines par excellence, those of the Graves have nothing to prove; from Roman times, the plantations, with their rows of vines, began to encircle the capital of Aquitaine and, according to Colomel, the agronomist, to produce 'a wine that keeps for a long time and which improves after several years'. The name 'Graves' was first recorded in the Middle Ages. At that time it designated all the countryside upstream from Bordeaux that lay between the left bank of the Garonne and the Landes plateau. Later, Sauternes was individually defined as a separate area within the Graves region that was devoted to producing sweet white wines.

Graves and Graves Supérieures

The Graves vineyards extend for some fifty km (31 miles) and owe their name to the structure of the soil, principally made up of terraces deposited by the Garonne or its predecessors, which left behind a great variety of stony débris (pebbles and gravels originating in the Pyrenees and the Massif Central).

Since 1987 not all the wines produced there are sold as Graves. Pessac-Léognan is now identified by a specific appellation, even though 'Vin de Graves', 'Grand Vin de Graves' or 'Cru Classé de Graves' may be printed on its labels. In precise terms, the description Appellation Graves applies to qualifying vineyards from the south of the region.

One of the peculiarities of Graves is the balance established between the areas devoted to red wines – nearly 2,376 ha (5,869 acres), excluding Pessac-Léognan – and those growing dry whites wines – more than 1,270 ha (3,137 acres). The red Graves, of which 137,957 hl (3,642,065 gal) were produced in 2000, have a fine, delicately smoky bouquet and an elegant, full-bodied structure which allows them to keep well. The dry white wines, 66,019 hl (1,742,902 gal) in 2000, and ranked amongst the best in the Gironde. The finest of them, many of which are now vinified and matured in barrels, develop in richness and complexity after several years. There are also some softer wines sold under the appellation Graves Supérieures which still claim their admirers.

CH. D'ARCHAMBEAU 2000★
10 ha n.c. €5-8
90 91 92 93 94 96 |98| |00|

Illats is well worth visiting for its pretty Romanesque church. At the same time, the visitor can discover several interesting crus, including this one. Fresh with an agreeable pale-yellow colour, this 2000 white is very alluring with its aromas of broom, passion fruit and a strong grapefruit note, which similarly returns on the palate.

➥ SARL Famille Dubourdieu, Archambeau, 33720 Illats, tel. 05.56.62.51.46, fax 05.56.62.47.98 ☑
Y by appt.

CH. D'ARDENNES 1999★★
25 ha 80,000 €8-11
88 (89) 90 92 93 94 96 |97| |98| 99

The reputation of the Château d'Ardennes is beyond dispute. All the same, no effort is spared where quality control is concerned. For proof, look no further than this lovely 99, which blends 45% Merlot, 40% Cabernet Sauvignon, 10% Cabernet Franc and 5% Petit Verdot. The dense colour predicts the fine body, amply supported by oak and fruity, grilled notes with a lengthy minerally character. The white 2000 was also commended.

➥ SCEA Ch. d'Ardennes, Ardennes, 33720 Illats, tel. 05.56.62.53.80, fax 05.56.62.43.67 ☑ Y by appt.
➥ François Dubrey

CH. D'ARRICAUD
Cuvée Prestige 1998★
2 ha 10,600 €11-15
(85) 88 89 |90| 91 93 |96| 98

Grown on a property with a fine panorama over the Sauternais and the Garonne, this wine (60% Merlot) still has a somewhat reticent nose. Nonetheless it has good substance and balance with good structure that is derived from well-handled oak maturation. Round and finely perfumed with acacia flowers and honey, the white 2000 was singled out by the jury.

➥ EARL Bouyx, Ch. d'Arricaud, 33720 Landiras, tel. 05.56.62.51.29, fax 05.56.62.41.47 ☑ Y by appt.

CH. BEAUREGARD-DUCASSE 1998★
23 ha 100,000 €8-11
|93| |94| 95 96 |97| |98|

The fine cru of nearly 40 ha (around 100 acres) is a family estate. This attractive wine is its principal product and needs time to develop, as the tannins are still very youthful. However, the wine has sufficient richness and energy for this to be achieved in two or three years. The nose has fine aromas of blackcurrant, forest fruit and light oak. It has a very pleasant finish. Equally powerful and elegant, the **Cuvée Bois Albert Duran** also obtained one star, as did the **Cuvée Albertine Peyri 2000**. The **2000 white** was also praised by the Jury.

☎ Jacques Perromat, Ducasse, 33210 Mazères, tel. 05.56.76.18,97, fax 05.56.76.17.73 ☑ ▼ by appt.

☛ GFA de Gaillote

CH. DE BEAU-SITE 1998
■   5 ha   14,000   €8–11

Made from grapes grown on a small vineyard plot and harvested by hand, this wine is very flavourful with balsamic notes and touches of stewed fruit. The pleasant tannins are fleshy. The **white 99** is equally recommended for its exotic aromas.

☎ SA Ch. de Beau-Site, Beau-Site, 33640 Portets, tel. 05.56.67.18.15, fax 05.56.67.38.12, e-mail chateaudebeausite@dial.deane.com

☑ ▼ by appt.

☛ Mme Dumergue

CH. BERGER 1998★★
■   1.64 ha   12,900   €8–11

Virtually a limited edition in volume terms, this wine performed really well throughout the tasting. The colour and nose are both

intense, while the latter's elegance and complexity follow through onto the palate with some length, leaving an impression of good harmony. A wine to keep for four to five years.

☎ SCA Ch. Berger, 6, chem. La Girafe, 33640 Portets, tel. 05.56.67.58.98, fax 05.56.67.04.88 ☑ ▼ by appt.

CH. BICHON CASSIGNOLS 1998★
■   3 ha   20,000   €8–11

Slightly over 12 ha (29.6 acres) in size, this cru was established in 1981 on sandy-gravelly soil. Although not yet fully mature, this wine already has much in its favour, such as the well-balanced, very dense structure and the pleasant aromas of red fruit and blackcurrant on the nose. The **white 99** is singled out for its very fine oakiness and exotic aromas.

☎ Jean-François Lespinasse, 50, av. Edouard-Capdeville, 33650 La Brède, tel. 05.56.20.28.20, fax 05.56.20.20.08, e-mail bichon.cassignols@wanadoo.fr ☑

▼ by appt.

CLOS BOURGELAT 1998
■   3.62 ha   28,000   €5–8

Grown at Cérons, like the sweet version, this half-Merlot, half-Cabernets wine does not express itself completely yet. But the excellent tannins and interesting aromas

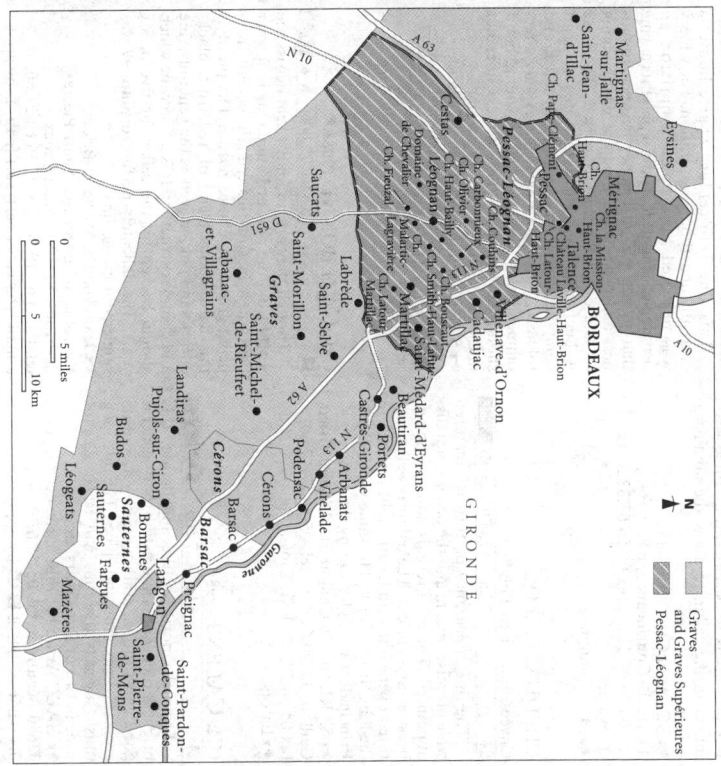

The Graves region

Graves and Graves Supérieures

Pessac-Léognan

351

BORDEAUX

(coconut, liquorice and smoke) are encouraging. The **white 2000** (100% Sémillon) is also recommended.

➤ Dominique Lafosse, Clos Bourgelat, 33720 Cérons, tel. 05.56.27.01.73, fax 05.56.27.13.72 ☑ ⦿ ev. day except Sun. 9am–12 noon 2pm–7pm; groups by appt.

CH. BRONDELLE 1999★★

15 ha — 80,000 — €8-11

For a long time, this cru produced only whites. Though the **white 2000** gains one star, the quality of the 99 red is wonderful. The complexity of the nose with iris, red fruit, raspberry and oak returns intact on the palate, creating a full-flavoured wine that is both traditional and modern. This fine wine should be tucked away in the cellar for five or six years.

➤ EARL Vignobles Belloc-Rochet, Ch. Brondelle, 33210 Langon, tel. 05.56.62.38.14, fax 05.56.62.23.14, e-mail chateau.brondelle@wanadoo.fr ☑ ⦿ by appt.

CH. CABANNIEUX

Elevé en barrique 1998★

13 ha — n.c. — €8-11

Situated as it is on slightly sloping gravel, this singly-owned vineyard has good drainage conditions. Expressive, well-structured and full, this pleasant 98 has spent ten months in oak and needs to be left two or three years longer in the cellar, to allow the tannins to soften.

➤ SCEA du Ch. Cabannieux, 44, rte du Courmeau, 33640 Portets, tel. 05.56.67.22.01, fax 05.56.67.32.54 ☑ ⦿ by appt.
➤ Mme Dudignac

CH. DU CAILLOU

Cuvée Saint-Cricq 1999★

2 ha — 7,000 — €5-8

The fine appearance of this oak-matured wine promises much, and the taster is not disappointed. The nose reveals notes of honey, beeswax and apricot. The palate is well-structured and opens out with length right through to the long, fruity finish. The same year's **Cuvée Principale** was singled out by the Jury.

➤ SARL Vignobles du Caillou, rte de Saint-Cricq, Caillou, 33720 Cérons, tel. 05.56.27.17.60, fax 05.56.27.00.31 ⦿ by appt.
➤ Latorse

CH. CALENS 1998★

6 ha — 7,500 — €5-8

From the north of the appellation, this bright garnet wine is interesting for its general good constitution, still severe as yet, and its aromas of ripe fruit and spices. The full, long finish suggests that this will be an elegant wine in two or three years' time.

➤ GAEC Artaud et Fils, 6, rue des Mages, 33640 Beautiran, tel. 05.56.67.05.48, fax 05.56.67.04.72 ☑ ⦿ by appt.

CH. DE CALLAC 1999★ — €11-15

20 ha — 120,000

This cru, recently taken over by Philippe Rivière, will be undergoing development over the coming years. Already this attractive 99 shows potential. Its nose, like its palate, blends ripe fruit and grilled, roasted notes. This well-constructed wine may be kept, though it is already ready for drinking. The **white 99** was singled out by the Jury. It will appeal to lovers of toasty oak.

➤ SCEA VM et Ph. Rivière, Ch. de Callac, 33720 Illats, tel. 05.57.55.59.59, fax 05.57.55.59.51, e-mail riviere@riviere-stemilion.com ☑ ⦿ by appt.

CH. CAMARSET 1999

1.2 ha — 6,000 — €5-8

This château, formerly attached to La Brède, has produced a wine that has undergone both vinification and maturation in oak. It bears the stamp of the oak, but despite its obvious presence, the wood has not overwhelmed the fruit or body, which is quite soft and pleasant.

➤ SCEA Camarset, Ch. Camarset, 33650 Saint-Morillon, tel. 05.56.20.31.94, fax 05.56.20.31.94 ☑

CH. DE CASTRES 1999★

14 ha — 41,000 — €11-15

This fine 18th-century charterhouse is currently undergoing restoration. The winery was designed by the new proprietor, an oenological engineer. The cru presents a wine that strikes a good balance between roundness and power, and it may be drunk young or laid down for a short period. The nose is beginning to open with notes of fruit compote (strawberry, raspberry), musk and tobacco. The **white 2000** achieves only a recommendation, because it is too young, but it should develop well; the oakiness does not mask its liveliness and exotic aromas.

➤ SARL Vignobles Rodrigues-Lalande, Ch. de Castres, 33640 Castres-sur-Gironde, tel. 05.56.67.51.51, fax 05.56.67.52.22 ☑ ⦿ by appt.

CH. CAZEBONNE 1998★★

12.6 ha — 72,000 — €5-8

Though they are no longer sent across the world from the port at Langon, as in former days, the wines of this cru still benefit from being grown on choice *terroir*. The proof is this harmonious blend of red fruit, blackcurrant and oak, as well as the generous, fine and complex structure. It is a fine wine which should be kept in the cellar for five or six years. The delicately perfumed **white 99** was singled out by the Jury.

➤ Jean-Marc et Marie-Jo Bridet, Vignobles de Bordeaux, Saint-Pierre-de-Mons, 33212 Langon Cedex, tel. 05.56.63.19.34, fax 05.56.63.21.60, e-mail lvb.sica@libertysurf.fr ☑ ⦿ by appt.

CH. DE CHANTEGRIVE 1999★★

■ | 30 ha | 100,000 | (III) | €8-11

This fine vineyard of 90 ha (222 acres) enjoys the benefit of sophisticated modern equipment. It regularly presents quality products, and this deep-red wine is part of that tradition. The prominent grilled notes denote oak, and the nose is robust, as indeed is the palate, where the tannins are spirited yet respectful of the fruit and oak, confirms the possibility of keeping this wine for longer than five years. The **white 99 Cuvée Caroline** was singled out by the Jury.

→ GFA Françoise et Henri Lévêque, Ch. de Chantegrive, 33720 Podensac, tel. 05.56.27.17.38, fax 05.56.27.29.42, e-mail courrier@chateau.chantegrive.com ☑ ¥ ev. day except Sun. 8am–12.30pm, 1.30pm–6pm

CH. CHERCHY-DESQUEYROUX 1999

□ | 0.75 ha | n.c. | €5-8

Fortunately for the Desqueyroux, their property extends to 18.65 ha (46.1 acres), so this vineyard and its round, full wine represent only a tiny proportion of their estate. The nose has initial fruity and mineral tones, then develops a Muscat-like touch.

→ SCEA Francis Desqueyroux et Fils, 1, rue Pourière, 33720 Budos, tel. 05.56.76.62.67, fax 05.56.76.66.92, e-mail vign.fdesqueyroux@wanadoo.fr ☑ ¥ by appt.

CH. CHERET-PITRES 1998

■ | 6.1 ha | 9,066 | | | €5-8

A little austere, notably on the finish, this wine needs a further two years to soften. Its structure and intense, complex nose with notes of musk and ripe fruit will permit it to mature well, given the right conditions.

→ Pascal et Caroline Dulugat, Ch. Cheret-Pitres, 33640 Portets, tel. 05.56.67.27.76, fax 05.56.67.27.76, e-mail chateau.cheret-pitres@wanadoo.fr ☑ ¥ by appt.

CLOS DU HEZ 1998★★

■ | 1 ha | 5,500 | (III) | €5-8

Like many other producers in the Sauternais, the Guignards also make Graves. No-one who tastes this harmonious 98 will be sorry about that! It is as expressive on its fruity, floral nose as on the palate. This quality wine has a good future ahead.

→ GAEC Philippe et Jacques Guignard, Ch. Lamothe Guignard, 33210 Sauternes, tel. 05.56.76.60.28, fax 05.56.76.69.05 ☑ ¥ ev. day 8am–12 noon 2pm–6pm; Sat. Sun. by appt.

CLOS FLORIDENE 1999★★

■ | 5 ha | 28,500 | (III) | €11-15
85 86 88 89 (90) 92 93 94 95 96 98 99

Denis Dubourdieu is a great specialist in white wine production. But he is also an all-round oenologist, who is no less a master of red wine-making. This wine follows many of predecessors; it balances tannins and body to create a round, elegant and generous wine. It is already pleasant with an elegant, charred and fruity nose, but could be laid down for four or five years.

→ Denis et Florence Dubourdieu, Ch. Reynon, 33410 Béguey, tel. 05.56.62.96.51, fax 05.56.62.14.89, e-mail reynon@gofornet.com ☑ ¥ by appt.

DOM. DE COUQUEREAU 1999

■ | 1.9 ha | 10,000 | (III) | €5-8

Merlot (80%) and Cabernet Sauvignon (20%) grown on gravelly soil have yielded this lovely ruby-coloured wine. The youthful nose does not hide the still-austere tannins that guarantee the future of this wine. The **white 99**, which one taster was able to detect as a single-variety Sémillon, also obtained a recommendation.

→ Amalia Gipoulou, 22, av. Adolphe-Demons, 33650 La Brède, tel. 05.56.20.32.27, fax 05.56.20.24.84 ☑ ¥ by appt.

CH. DOMS 1999

■ | 7 ha | 45,000 | (III) | €5-8

This domaine has a typical Bordeaux character, which can be seen in its architecture. The nose of this wine is just as fine and classic, with elegant hazelnut notes. Its very supple tannins produce a structure in harmony with the wine's flavours. The domaine's **red Cuvée Amélie 98** was also singled out by the Jury.

→ SCE Vignobles Parage, Ch. Doms, 33640 Portets, tel. 05.56.67.20.12, fax 05.56.67.31.89 ☑ ¥ by appt.

LA GRANDE CUVÉE DE DOURTHE 1998★★

■ | | | n.c. | 50,000 | (III) | €5-8

This Dourthe (part of the CVBG) label is one of the group's top wines. Lovely to look at, this is a blend of Cabernet and Merlot. The nose is astonishingly complex and original with notes of cherry, blackcurrant and oak along with very fresh eucalyptus notes. The classic palate, with its fine, well-balanced tannins, suggests a good future. The rich, round, long and elegant **white Grande Cuvée 99** gained one star.

→ Dourthe, 35, rue de Bordeaux, 33290 Parempuyre, tel. 05.56.35.53.00, fax 05.56.35.53.29, e-mail contact@cvbg.com ☑ ¥ by appt.

CH. DUVERGER Cuvée spéciale 1999★

□ | 1 ha | n.c. | (III) | €8-11

This prestigious wine, a single-variety Sémillon grown on limestone-clay, has received careful and attentive treatment. Behind the oaky notes which first take the taster's attention, an elegant nose opens out with lemon and beeswax. The palate is intense and flavourful, both rich and subtle. The **red Cuvée Spéciale 98** was singled out.

Graves

EPICURE Elevé en fût de chêne 1998★

▪ n.c. n.c. ▥ €11–15

'Epicure' is an attractive name that could be seen as a contradiction in terms, given the serious rather than hedonistic character of this wine. But perhaps the philosophical side of Epicureanism, as a love of virtue rather than of sensation, is what is meant here. Oak is very evident on both the nose and the palate but the structure is sufficiently well-built to support it, thanks to the sturdy grape-tannins that extend what is already a long finish.

➤ Bordeaux Vins Sélection,
27, rue Roullet, 33800 Bordeaux,
tel. 05.57.35.12.35, fax 05.57.35.12.36,
e-mail bus.grands.crus@wanadoo.fr ▥
➤ B. Pujol et H. de Bouard

CH. FERRANDE 2000★

☐ 5 ha 40,000 ▥ €5–8

This lovely cru, owned by the Castel family, ended the 20th century with an attractive wine with equal measures of Sauvignon and Sémillon. The tasters liked its golden yellow colour and flavourful character, which included notes of citrus fruit with a touch of mandarin orange on the finish. The **red 99** also received a recommendation. Wait one or two years for the oak to soften.

➤ Castel Frères, 21–24, rue Georges-Guynemer, 33290 Blanquefort,
tel. 05.56.95.54.00, fax 05.56.95.54.20

CH. DES FOUGERES

Clos Montesquieu 1999

☐ 9 ha 23,000 ▥ €11–15

The family of Montesquieu lends its prestigious signature to this simple yet very pleasant wine with its lemon, honey and citrus fruit nose. **Les Persanes de Montesquieu 98** is another label owned by the Montesquieu family, also *négociants*, and it, too, was singled out by the Jury.

➤ SCEA des Vignobles Montesquieu,
Aux Fougères, BP 53, 33650 La Brède,
tel. 05.56.78.45.45, fax 05.56.20.25.07,
e-mail montesquieu@
bordeaux-montesquieu.com ▥
➤ by appt.
➤ GFA Montesquieu

CH. DU GRAND BOS 1998★★

▪ 10.2 ha 54,000 ▥ €11–15

There has been wine-growing on this estate since the 17th century and it remains of the finest quality, as this 98 authoritatively shows. Its realises all the cru's ambitions. The classy dark colour and elegant nose with grilled notes of vanilla and cinnamon create a remarkable first impression. Then the palate divulges its rich, fleshy, well-constructed personality with a perfect balance of fruit and oak. The finish, in the same vein, confirms the potential of this very highly successful wine.

➤ SCEA du Ch. du Grand Bos,
33640 Castres, tel. 05.56.67.39.20,
fax 05.56.67.16.77 ▥ ➤ by appt.
➤ GFA de Gravesaltes

CH. GRAND MOUTA

Elevé en fût de chêne 1998★

▦ 2 ha 12,000 ▥ €5–8

Grown on a splendid vineyard in the south of the appellation, this wine opens out well during tasting. It has a deep colour and a very oaky nose, but also reveals prunes and jammy fruit. The palate is rich with excellent length.

➤ SCEA Dom. Latrille-Bonnin,
Petit-Mouta, 33210 Mazères,
tel. 05.56.63.41.70, fax 05.56.76.83.25 ▥
➤ by appt.
➤ GFA du Brion

CH. GRAVEYRON

Réserve du Château 1998★

▪ 6 ha 20,000 ▥ ♦ €5–8

This Cuvée Prestige has benefited from the care bestowed upon it. The garnet-colour, red berry-fruit aromas, roundness, mellow tannins and well-balanced finish make it good to drink now and also to keep. The **Cuvée Tradition** also gained one star. It is the same blend as the Réserve, but matured in oak for 12 months. Wait for the oak to blend.

➤ EARL Vignobles Pierre Cante,
67, rte des Graves, 33640 Portets,
tel. 05.56.67.23.69, fax 05.56.67.58.19 ▥ ➤ ev. day except Sun. 9am–12 noon 2pm–7pm

---

CH. DES GRAVIERES 1999★

▪ 15 ha 80,000 ▥ €5–8

The Labuzans are young oenologists who know all there is to know about modern techniques and how to use them to gain the best from their *terroir*. This wine proves how good their methods are, with its intense red colour and nose of musk and grilled notes. On the palate the tannins are prominent but not aggressive; there is a note of cherry on the finish.

➤ Vignobles Labuzan, Ch. des Gravières,
33640 Portets, tel. 05.56.67.15.70,
fax 05.56.67.07.50 ▥ ➤ by appt.

DOM. DU HAURET LALANDE

□ 2000 ★★

| | 1.65 ha | 12,800 | ▮▮👤 | €5-8 |

From the Barsac region and made at the Château Piada winery, this wine has some splendid origins. Full and flavoursome, it is worthy of its background, notably with its complexity of flavours and elegance: acacia flowers blended with grapefruit, and box with citrus fruit.

➥ EARL Lalande et Fils, Ch. Piada, 33720 Barsac, tel. 05.56.27.16.13, fax 05.56.27.26.30 ▼ ▼ ev. day 8am–12 noon 1.30pm–7pm: Sat. Sun. by appt.

CH. HAUT-GRAMONS

■ Elevé en fût de chêne 1998

| | 12 ha | 42,000 | ▮▮ | €6-11 |

Present on both sides of the Garonne, François and Frédéric Boudat here offer this clear wine with its spicy, red berry fruit nose. It is well balanced and fleshy with a tannic finish that needs to open out and soften.

➥ GAEC Cigana-Boudat, Ch. de Viaut, 33410 Mourens, tel. 05.56.61.98.13, fax 05.56.61.99.46 ▼ ▼ by appt.

CH. HAUT SELVE 1999 ★

□

| | 10 ha | 50,000 | ▮▮ | €11-15 |

Coming from the vast Saint-Selve estate, this wine, which has spent ten months in oak, is a blend of 60% Sauvignon with Sémillon. It has very fine aromas with elegant grilled notes and citrus fruit, plus a well-blended finish.

➥ SCA des Ch. de Branda et de Cadillac, 33240 Cadillac-en-Fronsadais, tel. 05.56.20.29.25, fax 05.56.78.47.63

LA CLOSIERE DE MAY 1999 ★

■

| | 1 ha | 6,000 | ▮▮ | €11-15 |

This wine comes from a small vineyard belonging to an owner from the north bank of the Garonne. The nose has original aromas of white oak and *rancio* with fresh menthol notes. The palate is supple and elegant with silky tannins, which are well suited to modern cuisine.

➥ Pierre Dupleich, Ch. du Juge, rte de Branne, 33410 Cadillac, tel. 05.56.62.17.77, fax 05.56.62.17.59, e-mail pierre.dupleich@wanadoo.fr ▼ ▼ by appt.

CH. LA FLEUR CLEMENCE

■ Elevé en fût de chêne 1999

| | 2 ha | 8,000 | ▮▮ | €11-15 |

The red Carbon d'Artigues 99 is quite oaky and was commended by the Jury. It is produced from grapes grown on 25-year-old vines and blends Merlot with Cabernets. The same maturation period (12 months in oak) characterises this Clemence 99, but the fruit is from 35-year-old vines and only Cabernet Sauvignon is blended with 60% Merlot. The wine has a fine Bordeaux-red colour. The nose is quite oaky but the palate is winey.

round, fleshy and flavoursome; the structure and aromas are perfect elegance.

➥ Ch. Carbon d'Artigues, 33720 Landiras, tel. 05.56.62.53.24, fax 05.56.62.53.24 ▼ ▼ by appt.

CH. LA FLEUR JONQUET 1999 ★

□

| | 1 ha | 7,500 | ▮▮ | €11-15 |

A blend of equal portions of Sémillon and Sauvignon, this attractive wine has a beautifully round, robust structure. It develops very interesting aromas, which combine spices and vanilla with exotic citrus fruit notes and overripeness.

➥ Laurence Lataste, 5, rue Amélie, 33200 Bordeaux, tel. 05.56.17.08.18, fax 05.57.22.12.54, e-mail l.lataste@enfrance.com ▼ ▼ by appt.

CH. DE LANDIRAS 1998 ★

■

| | n.c. | 8,400 | ▮▮ | €11-15 |

An aristocratic residence and place of pilgrimage, this estate is one of the most historic in the region. It is also a well-respected cru, as is confirmed by this attractive 98, which is both very well-structured and complex with alluring aromas of fruit, vanilla and toast. Wait three to five years before drinking. Equally harmonious is the white 99 (75% Sauvignon, 25% Sémillon), which achieved an equally-deserved star for its overall balance, in which the oak does not mask the fruit.

➥ SCA Dom. La Grave, Ch. de Landiras, 33720 Landiras, tel. 05.56.62.44.70, fax 05.56.62.43.78, e-mail mail@chateau-de-landiras ▼ ▼ by appt.

CH. LANGLET 1999 ★★

■

| | 2.09 ha | 15,000 | ▮▮ | €8-11 |

Though very active – and how! – in Pessac-Léognan with Château Latour-Martillac, the Kressmanns nevertheless do not neglect their interest in Graves. This well-structured and very promising wine is ample proof of that. The complexity of its nose is likely to charm the most exacting of tasters. Red and dark berry fruit, blackcurrant buds, vanilla, tobacco and smoke – what a flavourful excursion! The white 99 is recommended. 'Full of Sauvignon' wrote one taster, who of course did not actually know that the wine was made entirely from that variety.

➥ Domaines Kressmann, Ch. Latour-Martillac, 33650 Martillac, tel. 05.57.97.71.11, fax 05.57.97.71.17, e-mail latour-martillac@latour-martillac.com ▼ ▼ by appt.

CH. LA VIEILLE FRANCE 1998 ★

■

| | 3 ha | 20,000 | ▮▮ | €6-11 |

Grown in a vineyard divided equally between Merlot and Cabernet Sauvignon, this wine has a generous palate. It also has a fine, complex nose. Its body and length integrate excellent oak with a fine structure and call for four or five years' patience. The flavourful, rich and well-balanced white Cadet de la Vieille France 2000 also obtained a star. Bottled and distributed by Ginestet (with Carignan, the white Château Saint-Galier 99 is a selection from the vats of la Vieille France. It does not have enormous structure but has a pleasing floral character and was singled out by the Jury.

☛ Michel Dugoua, Ch. La Vieille France, 1, chem. du Malbec BP8, 33640 Portets, tel. 05.56.67.19.11, fax 05.56.67.17.54, e-mail courrier@chateau-la-vieille-france.fr ☑ ⟙ by appt.

CH. LE BOURDILLOT
Cuvée Prestige Elevé en fût de chêne 1999★ ▮▮▮ €8-11

0.81 ha n.c.

In the Graves appellation, the name of Haverlan has become a byword for quality. This 63% Cabernet Sauvignon blended with Merlot does no harm to that reputation. It is well balanced with interesting aromas of red fruit combining happily with spices. Though not a great wine for keeping, it could be drunk over the next two to three years. Equally deserving of a star are the **red Tentation 99** (fifty-fifty Cabernet Sauvignon and Merlot) and the **white 2000** (equal proportions of Sauvignon and Sémillon).

☛ Patrice Haverlan, 11, rue de l'Hospital, 33640 Portets, tel. 05.56.67.11.32, fax 05.56.67.11.32, e-mail patrice.haverlan@worldonline.fr ☑ ⟙ ev. day except Fri. Sat. Sun. 8am–12.30pm 1pm–5.30pm

CH. LE CHEC 1999★ ▮▮▮ €5-8

2.5 ha 8,000

Even if you don't give much credence to the legend explaining the origin of this cru's name, which is taken from the defeat of a Muslim in single combat by Montesquieu's ancestors, you cannot fail to appreciate this pale-golden wine with its elegant structure and pleasing oakiness. The **red 99** is singled out by the Jury. It needs to wait two or three years for the oakiness to soften.

☛ Christian Auney, La Girotte, 33650 La Brède, tel. 05.56.20.31.94, fax 05.56.20.31.94 ☑ ⟙ by appt.

CH. LEHOUL
Elevé en fût de chêne 1998★ ▮▮▮ €8-11

5 ha 25,000

Here they don't go in for the faddish and facile. Cabernet dominates (80%) and this superbly successful wine is all the better for it. Rich, round and with still very young tannins, the palate is a sure guarantor of its future, while the attraction of the nose lies in the combination of the warm notes of ripe fruit with the fresher nuances of heathland wild thyme. The **white 2000** is full-flavoured with rich linden flower and peach aromas. The **red Pavillon 98** opens with ripe tannins and notes of musk, spices and fruit (cherry). Both of these wines achieved a star.

☛ EARL Fonta et Fils, rte d'Auros, 33210 Langon, tel. 05.56.63.17.74, fax 05.56.63.06.06 ☑ ⟙ by appt.

CH. LE PAVILLON DE BOYREIN
1999 ▮ €5-8

13 ha 100,000

The finish is still quite austere, but this wine has an interesting nose with delicate notes of red fruit and leather, plus a supple, honest structure. Drink over the coming two years.

☛ SCEA Vignobles Pierre Bonnet, Le Pavillon de Boyrein, 33210 Roaillan, tel. 05.56.63.24.24, fax 05.56.62.31.59, e-mail vignobles-bonnet@wanadoo.fr ☑ ⟙ by appt.

CH. L'ETOILE 2000★ ▯ €5-8

n.c. 26,000

This pleasant, well-balanced 2000, produced by Pierre Coste, one of the great Bordeaux wine names, shows real generosity in its richness and full range of flavours; notes of box mingle with citrus fruits.

☛ Maison Sichel-Coste, 8, rue de la Poste, 33210 Langon, tel. 05.56.63.50.52, fax 05.56.63.42.28

CH. LE TUQUET 1998★ ▮▮ €8-11

35 ha 100,000

The monastery here dates back to 1730, the south façade is by Victor Louis, and the family of the missionary monk Father Charles de Foucauld was amongst its previous owners. On a more up-to-date note, the cellar was completely renovated in the 1990s. This well-constructed wine fulfils all the promise of its beautiful garnet colour, deriving a great deal of its charm from its aromas of lovely red berries, roasting coffee beans, smoke and prunes.

☛ GFA du Ch. Le Tuquet, Ch. Le Tuquet, 33640 Beautiran, tel. 05.56.20.21.23, fax 05.56.20.21.83 ☑ ⟙ by appt.
☛ Paul Ragon

CH. DE L'HOSPITAL 1998★★ ▮▮ €11-15

10 ha 60,000

At this cru, the development of the vines is monitored as carefully as the wine-making process. This results in remarkable wines such as this 98 with its impressively developed flavour. The combination of oak and red fruits is very successful. Concentrated, powerful and elegant, the structure leaves lingering memories of the extremely harmonious whole. This wine will benefit from laying down for three or four years. The **99 white**

confirms the care taken during harvesting and maturation. It was awarded one star for its subtle marriage of fruit and oak.

↝ SCS Vignobles Lafragette, Darrouban, 33640 Portets, tel. 05.56.73.17.80, fax 05.56.09.02.87 ☑ by appt.

M. DE MALLE 1999★★

n.c.　n.c.　■ ♦ €8-11

Produced from the gravel vineyards of Domaine de Malle, this wine has noble origins, which are evident in its appearance, bouquet (beautiful floral notes, mingled with apricot and tropical fruit) and fullness. Fresh and well balanced, it would go well with sauced fish dishes. The **Château de Cardaillon red 98** was commended by the Jury.

↝ Comtesse de Bournazel, Ch. de Malle, 33210 Preignac, tel. 05.56.62.36.86, fax 05.56.76.82.40, e-mail chateaudemalle@wanadoo.fr ☑ ☒ by appt.

CH. MAYNE D'IMBERT 1998★

20 ha　30,000　■ ♦ €5-8

In this age of micro-vinifications (making tiny quantities of particular *cuvées*), this wine remains faithful to the Bordeaux spirit in being produced in serious quantities. This makes its virtues, the elegant bouquet and balanced palate, all the more interesting.

↝ SCEA Vignobles Mauriac, 23, rue François-Mauriac, BP 58, 33720 Podensac, tel. 05.56.27.18.17, fax 05.56.27.21.16 ☒ by appt.

CH. MAYNE DU CROS 1999★

Elevé en fût de chêne

4 ha　8,000　■ ♦ €8-11

The product of a Cérons vineyard, this wine has been vinified with grapeskin maceration then matured in the cask. It has a strong yellow colour, and the complexity of its bouquet of mingled notes of tropical and citrus fruit, beeswax and mango immediately attracts attention. Its beautiful finish is slightly sharp and smoky. The Jury also commended the **Mayne du Cros red 98**, in which the Cabernets play the major role, with only 10% Merlot in the blend. It is well matured and balanced with a good body. It should be laid down for two years.

↝ SA Vignobles M. Boyer, Ch. du Cros, 33410 Loupiac, tel. 05.56.62.99.31, fax 05.56.62.12.59, e-mail contact@chateauducros.com ☒ ☒ ev. day 8am–12 noon 2pm–6pm; Sat. & Sun. by appt.

CLOS MOLEON

Vieilli en fût de chêne 1999

3 ha　16,000　■ ■ ♦ €8-11

The label is surprising and was no doubt intended as a visual pun: it is an image of Napoleon on horseback.... This simple, well-made wine is still a trifle austere but its tannic structure should round out. The very engaging bouquet develops good fruity notes.

CH. DE L'ORDONNANCE

Elevé en fût de chêne 1998★

1 ha　n.c.　■ ♦ €5-8

This barrel-matured wine, which is part of a small production, is currently oaky but given time and the right conditions, it promises to develop well as indicated by its garnet colour, youthful bouquet and beautiful structure.

↝ GAEC Bélis et Fils, Tourmilot, 33210 Langon, tel. 05.56.62.22.11, fax 05.56.62.22.11 ☑ ☒ by appt.

CH. LUDEMAN LA COTE 1999★★

9 ha　70,000　■ ♦ €5-8

This rapidly growing cru has doubled in area in less than 10 years, but this lovely 99 demonstrates that its expansion has not been at the expense of quality. Fleshy and well structured, without being aggressive, the wine is rich in flavour with perfectly integrated woody notes. It should be laid down for at least five years and will be suitable for serving with the more sophisticated dishes. The Jury also commended the **Clos des Majureaux red 99**. It is a simple, well-made, supple, fresh, unoaked wine, with violet aromas on the nose.

↝ SCEA Chaloupin-Lambrot, Ludeman, 33210 Langon, tel. 05.56.63.07.15, fax 05.56.63.48.17, e-mail m-bellocludeman@wanadoo.fr ☑ ☒ by appt.

CH. LUSSEAU 1998★

3.37 ha　6,000　■ ♦ €8-11

Built in 1805, this chateau is 4 km (2 miles) from La Brède. Twelve months' barrel maturation, a classic blend, which includes a little Malbec, and sandy, pebbled soil on a clay base, all contribute to this vintage. It has a lovely garnet colour, plenty of flesh and body, good tannins and a sustained bouquet, with fruity, toasty notes. A wine well equipped to hold its own in the future.

↝ Anne-Marie de Granvilliers-Quellien, Ch. Lusseau, 6, rte de Lusseau, 33640 Ayguemorte-les-Graves, tel. 05.56.67.01.67, fax 05.56.37.17.82 ☒ ev. day except Mon. Thu. Fri. 10am–12 noon, 2pm–6pm

CH. MAGNEAU Cuvée Julien 1999★★

4 ha　7,000　■ ♦ €8-11

Vinified in the barrel with grapeskin maceration and matured on the lees, this wine is the standard-bearer of the Ardurats. Fresh, with a delicate bouquet, vigorous and full-bodied, it holds its rank with aplomb. It benefits from oaky notes, which support the wine without overwhelming it. The Jury also praised the supple, pleasant **Château Magneau red 99**.

➤ EARL Vignobles Laurent Réglat,
Ch. de Teste, 33410 Monprimblanc,
tel. 05.56.62.92.76, fax 05.56.62.98.80,
e-mail laurent.reglat@worldonline.fr ☑
Ⓨ ev. day except Sat. & Sun. 9am–12 noon
2.30pm–6pm; cl. 15–30 Aug.

CH. DU MONT 1999★
☐   1 ha   3,000   ⅢⒹ   €5-8

This fresh, well-balanced, flavourful wine
is produced by a grower based mainly in Sainte-
Croix-du-Mont. It has been barrel-fermented
with stirring of the lees, giving it flavours of
tropical fruit and a citrus bouquet.
➤ Vignobles Hervé Chouvac, Ch. du Mont,
33410 Sainte-Croix-du-Mont,
tel. 05.56.62.07.65, fax 05.56.62.07.58 ☑
Ⓨ by appt.

CH. MOULIN DE CLAIRAC 2000★
☐   10 ha   70,000   ▤ ♦   €3-5

This well-constructed wine, produced by
Maison Ginestet, has a pleasant roundness,
which harmonises well with the delicacy of
its bouquet, in which jammy, toasted notes
mingle against a background of grapefruit.
➤ SA Maison Ginestet, 19, av. de
Fontenille, 33360 Carignan-de-Bordeaux,
tel. 05.56.68.81.82, fax 05.56.20.96.99,
e-mail contact@ginestet.fr Ⓨ by appt.
➤ Alain Pargade

CH. DU MOURET 2000★
☐   6 ha   53,000   ▤ ♦   €3-5

The Médevilles have been established in
Cadillac since 1826, and they have been producing wine from this vineyard in Roaillan for
a quarter of a century. This is long enough for
them to have developed a thorough knowledge of the *terroir* and to have learnt the best
way to express that understanding. This
knowledge is evident in the rounded, full-
bodied, lively, well-balanced wine.
➤ SCEA Jean Médeville et Fils,
Ch. Fayau, 33410 Cadillac,
tel. 05.57.98.08.08, fax 05.56.62.18.22,
e-mail medeville-jeanetfils@wanadoo.fr ☑
Ⓨ ev. day except Sat. & Sun. 8.30am–
12.30pm 2pm–6pm

CH. MOUTIN 2000★★
☐   1 ha   3,000   ⅢⒹ   €8-11

This 2000 white confirms the good impression given last year by the 97 red. Its richness,
body and bouquet of tropical fruit (passion-
fruit and mango) leave the taster with very
agreeable memories. The well-constructed **98
red**, still dominated by oak, was awarded a
star. It should be laid down for two or three
years.
➤ SC Jean Darriet,
Ch. Dauphiné-Rondillon, 33410 Loupiac,
tel. 05.56.62.61.75, fax 05.56.62.63.73,
e-mail vignoblesdarriet@wanadoo.fr ☑
Ⓨ ev. day 8am–12.30pm 2pm–6.30pm; Sat.
& Sun by appt. cl. 1–15 Aug.

CH. PERIN DE NAUDINE 1999
☐   3 ha   10,000   ⅢⒹ   €5-8

Olivier Colas started producing wine here
in 1996. Since then he has been expanding his
vineyard, which now covers 12 ha (30 acres).
This bright yellow wine is notable for the
harmony of its bouquet of citronella, white
peaches, spices and vanilla. The **Les Sphinx de
Naudine red 98** has well-rounded tannins,
backed by notes of red berries. It should be
laid down for one or two years.
➤ Ch. Périn de Naudine,
8, imp. des Domaines, 33640 Castres,
tel. 05.56.67.06.65, fax 05.56.67.59.68,
e-mail chateauperin@wanadoo.fr ☑
Ⓨ by appt.
➤ Olivier Colas

CH. PIRON 1998★★
▤   8 ha   30,000   ⅢⒹ   €5-8

This wine, the product of an ancient family
tradition and gravel *terroir*, is a blend of half
Merlot and half Cabernet Sauvignon. It was
matured for eighteen months and amply
amply fulfils the promise of its garnet colour
and dark highlights. The fullness and the concentration of its bouquet, woody with undertones of blackberry, are reproduced both on
the palate and in a sustained finish with lovely
mocha notes.
➤ Paul Boyreau, Ch. Piron,
33650 Saint-Morillon, tel. 05.56.20.25.61,
fax 05.56.78.48.36 ☑ Ⓨ by appt.

CH. PONT DE BRION 1999★★
▤   7 ha   35,000   ⅢⒹ   €8-11

This estate maintains its tradition for
reliable quality with this very good wine.
From its deep colour and delicate bouquet to
its tannins and balanced oaky body, everything indicates that it has a fine future. The
Pont de Brion white was awarded a star. It is
oaky but also exhibits exotic, tropical fruit
notes in its elegant development. The Jury
praised the very floral **99 Château Ludeman
Les Cèdres white**, from the very edge of the
AOC. It would make a pleasant aperitif.
➤ SCEA Molinari et Fils, Ludeman,
33210 Langon, tel. 05.56.63.09.52,
fax 05.56.63.13.47 ☑ Ⓨ by appt.

CH. DE PORTETS 1998
▤   14.12 ha   85,000   ▤ ▤ ♦   €8-11

The long history of this impressive château
goes back to the 13th century. The present
building dating back to the 18th century has
wrought-iron gates and a Renaissance pavil-
ion. Its well-structured 98, a blend of half
Merlot and half Cabernet, comes from vines
grown on a gravel soil. It has a pleasant colour
and a fruity, spicy bouquet, and should keep
well for two or three years.
➤ SCEA Théron-Portets,
Ch. de Portets, 33640 Portets,
tel. 05.56.67.12.30, fax 05.56.67.33.47,
e-mail vignobles.theron@wanadoo.fr ☑
Ⓨ by appt.
➤ Jean-Pierre Théron

CH. PROMS-BELLEVUE 1998
7 ha · 40,000 · €5-8

This wine, in which Cabernet Sauvignon dominates, comes from the south of the appellation. Its fruitiness is particularly marked. The first impression on the palate is supple and well rounded, but it also has an austere, firm finish, which should soften after the wine has been laid down for a year.

- SA Yvon Mau, BP 01, 33190 Gironde-sur-Dropt Cedex, tel. 05.56.61.54.54, fax 05.56.71.10.45
- J.-Cl. Labbe

CH. QUINCARNON 1998
5.5 ha · 26,000

This wine, which comes from the threshold of Sauternes, is a blend of equal parts Merlot and Cabernet Sauvignon. It has not yet completely come into its own, but the good, full, powerful structure, and the integrated tannins are already evident.

- Carlos Asseretto, Vignobles de Bordeaux, 33211 Saint-Pierre-de-Mons, tel. 05.56.63.19.34, fax 05.56.63.21.60, e-mail lvb.sica@libertysurf.fr by appt.

CH. RAHOUL 1998*
20 ha · 80,000 · €11-15

Rahoul and the team, headed by Alain Thienot, were awarded a *coup de coeur* last year for a 98 white Graves. In 2001, the Jury tasted the rich yet very delicate 98 and liked its bright, lively colour and its bouquet of red berries with smoky notes. The impression on the palate is full, robust and chewy, with ripe, well-rounded, long-lasting tannins. The finish has elegant, oaky notes. The **Château La Garance 99 white** was awarded a star. This elegant wine has a delicate bouquet of apples, pears and citrus fruit accompanied by a light oakiness.

- Alain Thienot, Ch. Rahoul, 4, rte du Courneau, 33640 Portets, tel. 05.56.67.01.12, fax 05.56.67.02.88, e-mail chateau-rahoul@alain-thienot.fr
- by appt.

CH. DE RESPIDE
Cuvée Callipyge Elevé en fût de chêne 1998*
5 ha · 18,000 · €8-11

The emphasis in this barrel-matured wine is on supple, velvety tannins which allow it to develop interesting flavours. The oak is, however, still rather dominant. A well-made wine, it should be laid down for about three years. The lingering, well-rounded, straight-forward **2000 Château de Respide white** was also awarded a star.

- SCEA Vignobles Franck Bonnet, Ch. de Respide, rte d'Auros, 33210 Langon, tel. 05.56.63.24.24, fax 05.56.62.31.59 by appt.

DAME DE RESPIDE 1998**
3.5 ha · 20,000 · €8-11

Château Respide Médeville, a cru as famous as its producer, the antique dealer of Sauternes', is represented here by its 'Dame'. It could not have chosen a better ambassador. The colour is rich; the strong bouquet has lovely leathery notes. Full and fleshy on the palate, with assertive tannins, it has, in short, everything required for a beautiful wine. It should be laid down for four or five years.

- Christian Médeville, Ch. Gilette, 33210 Preignac, tel. 05.56.76.28.44, fax 05.56.76.28.43, e-mail christian.medeville@wanadoo.fr
- by appt.

CH. ROQUETAILLADE LA GRANGE 1998**
23 ha · 150,000 · €8-11

This vineyard, which once belonged to the Château de Roquetaillade, one of the most beautiful historic buildings in the Gironde, is situated on excellent land. The Guignard brothers have set out to make the most of this in their wine. Their success can be measured in the complex, rich, flavourful wine, with its complex bouquet of spices and smoke, and its excellent balance: the result of a well-controlled ageing period. The **99 Château de Carolle red** was awarded one star. It should be laid down for three years.

- GAEC Guignard Frères, 33210 Mazères, tel. 05.56.76.14.23, fax 05.56.62.30.62, e-mail contact@roquetaillade.com
- by appt.

CH. SAINT-AGREVES 1998
11 ha · n.c. · €5-8

This wine has a slightly austere finish but softer attack. Its fresh, well-balanced blend successfully marries a fruity bouquet with more mature, spicy notes. It should be kept for two to three years.

- EARL Landry, Ch. Saint-Agrèves, 17, rue Joachim-de-Chalup, 33720 Landiras, tel. 05.56.62.50.85, fax 05.56.62.42.49, e-mail saint.agreves@free.fr ev. day except Sun. 9.30am–12.30pm 2.30pm–7pm.

CH. SAINT-HILAIRE
Cuvée fût neuf 1999*
2 ha · 4,500 · €5-8

This deliberately classical, well-rounded, fleshy, organic wine, 100% Sémillon, is nostalgically reminiscent of wines from a previous era, especially through its beeswax and acacia flowers bouquet.

- SARL H.-G. Guérin, Ch. Saint-Hilaire, 33640 Castres-Gironde, tel. 05.56.67.12.12, fax 05.56.67.53.23 by appt.

CH. SAINT-JEAN-DES-GRAVES 2000**
10 ha · n.c.

This cru, awarded a *coup de coeur* last year for its 98 red, is honoured again for this 2000 white, which brings the 20th century very happily to a close. The well-ripened Sauvignon, prominent in the blend, is also in the passion-fruit notes of the bouquet. The fruity, fleshy palate is very well balanced.

• J. David, Ch. Liot, 33720 Barsac, tel. 05.56.27.15.31, fax 05.56.27.14.42 [V]
Y by appt.

CH. SAINT-ROBERT ★★
Cuvée Poncet-Deville 1999★

■ 4 ha n.c. **[95]** €11-15

89 90 92 93 94 **[95]** 96 97 98 99

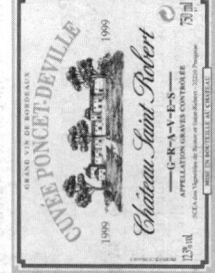

Grapes, hand-picked and selected, and careful treatment in the must and wine stages are usual practices at Saint-Robert. Both the colour and bouquet, with notes of spices and undergrowth, are elegant. The personality of this blend shows on the palate: flavourful, silky, full-bodied, well balanced. It promises to be a truly great wine in five years. The Cuvée Principale and the 99 white Cuvée Poncet-Deville were both awarded a star.
• SCEA Vignobles Bastor et Saint-Robert, Dom. de Lamontagne, 33210 Preignac, tel. 05.56.63.27.66, fax 05.56.76.87.03, e-mail bastor-lamontagne@dial.oleane.com
[V] Y by appt.
• Foncier-Vignobles

CH. DE SANSARIC
Cuvée Valentin 1998★

■ n.c. 1,000 €8-11

This wine, showing all the signs of careful production, is a blend of 50% Cabernet Sauvignon, 45% Merlot and 5% Malbec, which has been barrel-matured for 15 months. It has harmonious notes of warmed oak. Beautiful scents of morello cherry develop in the nose, whilst on the palate, integrated tannins make an elegant, well-constructed wine 'of the sort we like to find'. Discerning wine-lovers will like it already but it would benefit from being laid down for around three years. The fresh, fruity, delicately oaked 2000 white was awarded a star.

CH. DU SEUIL 1998★★

■ 7 ha 35,000 €8-11

This blend, 80% Merlot, 15% Cabernet Sauvignon, 5% Malbec, has been barrel-matured for 12 months. Although still somewhat closed, it does have an interesting bouquet backed by an oaky, generous, soft body. Given its well-integrated tannins, it will benefit from being laid down for a further two or three months.
• D. Abadie, 33640 Castres-Gironde, tel. 05.56.67.03.17, fax 05.56.67.59.53 [V]
Y by appt.
• Ch. du Seuil, 33720 Cérons, tel. 05.56.27.11.56, fax 05.56.27.28.79, e-mail chateau-du-seuil@wanadoo.fr [V]
Y by appt.
• T.-R. Watts

CH. SIMON 1998★★

■ 7 ha 12,000 €8-11

This blend, 70% Merlot and 30% Cabernet Sauvignon, is a good step forward for this cru. Very acceptable in its crimson colour and smoky bouquet, it is equally developed and well balanced on the palate, with its notes of undergrowth and balance between roundness and tannins.
• EARL Dufour, Ch. Simon, 33720 Barsac, tel. 05.56.27.15.35, fax 05.56.27.24.79, e-mail chateau.simon@worldonline.fr [V] Y by appt.

CH. TOUR DE CALENS 2000★

□ 1.1 ha 8,700 €5-8

Since 1987, the Doublets have been striving to maximise the use of their vineyard. This rich, lively, well-balanced wine has a particularly attractive bouquet of tropical fruit (bananas and mangoes). The Jury praised the very successful Tour De Calens Elevé en Fût de Chêne red 98.
• Bernard et Dominique Doublet, Ch. Tour de Calens, 33640 Beautiran, tel. 05.57.24.12.93, fax 05.57.24.12.83, e-mail b.doublet@club-internet.fr [V]
Y by appt.

CH. DU TOURTE 1999

■ 5 ha 26,000 €8-11

This cru, bought by the present owners in 1994, consists of 10 ha (25 acres) of deep gravel on a clay bed. Despite limited potential, this wine will benefit from laying down for two or three years, giving its bouquet time to reach the full complexity promised by its notes of red berries and spices. The Jury also mentioned the 99 Tourte white, which is still a little over-oaked.
• SCEA Ch. du Tourte, 33210 Toulenne, tel. 01.46.88.40.08, fax 01.46.88.01.45, e-mail hubert.arnaud@zza.fr Y by appt.

CH. TOURTEAU CHOLLET 1999★

■ 43.29 ha 249,600 €5-8

This 67-ha (165-acre) estate, run by Mestrezat since 1973, is situated in the heart of the southern Graves. This lovely stretch of vines, surrounded by pine trees, gives us a well-constructed wine, which promises, after being laid down to allow oak integration, to be very pleasant
• SC du Ch. Tourteau Chollet, La Croix-Bacalan, 109, rue Achard, BP 154, 33042 Bordeaux Cedex, tel. 05.56.11.29.00, fax 05.56.11.29.01 Y by appt.

CH. TRIGANT Cuvée Lartigue 1998

■ 0.7 ha 5,000 €8-11

This wine, benefiting from production on a cru in the Pessac appellation, is likely to be suitable for drinking young. This rounded, balanced and flavoursome 98 entirely fulfils its promise, but nevertheless could be kept for a short time.

• GFA du Ch. Trigant, chem. de Couhins, 33140 Villenave-d'Ornon, tel. 05.56.75.82.49, fax 05.56.75.82.49 Y by appt.
• Mme Seze

VIEUX CHATEAU GAUBERT
1999★★
■
83 85 86 87 |88| |89| |90| 91 |93| 94 95 97 98 99

25 ha | 60,000 | €11-15

It is frightening to think that this beautiful 18th-century house and its vineyard narrowly escaped being flattened by developers. Such a fate would have deprived us of this magnificent, dark red wine with its intense, complex bouquet of blackcurrant, ripe fruit, spices and leather. The expression on the palate of this superb, powerful, supple, soft wine guarantees its good future. The rich, elegant, complex and powerful **2000 Vieux Château Gaubert white**, the **99 Benjamin de Vieux Château Gaubert red** and the **2000 white** were all awarded stars. This is a very successful family of wines!

• Dominique Haverlan, Vieux Château Gaubert, 33640 Portets, tel. 05.56.67.52.76, fax 05.56.67.52.76 Y by appt.

CH. VILLA BEL-AIR 1999★★
■
24 ha | 144,000 | €8-11

If it is hard to get to the top, it is even harder to stay there, but this is just what Jean-Michel Cazes, Daniel Llose and Guy Delestrac have succeeded in doing. Once again, they have produced a wine in the true spirit of Bordeaux, which combines elegance and richness. It is sappy, supple and intense with a fine and complex bouquet of blackcurrant, spices and crystallised fruits. It deserves laying down for some considerable time. The well-oaked **2000 white** was also awarded two stars.

• Jean-Michel Cazes, Ch. Villa Bel-Air, 33650 Saint-Morillon, tel. 05.56.20.29.35, fax 05.56.78.44.80, e-mail infochato@villabelair.com Y by appt.

Graves Supérieures

CH. CHERCHY-DESQUEYROUX
1999★★
□
5.45 ha | 20,000 | €23-30

From the same producer as the Graves of the same name, this wine has an appealing bouquet, with notes of crystallised orange peel. A roastiness, characteristic of sweet wines, captures the attention on the rich and heady palate.

• SCEA Francis Desqueyroux et Fils, 1, rue Pourière, 33720 Budos, tél. 05.56.76.62.67, fax 05.56.76.66.92, e-mail vign.fdesqueyroux@wanadoo.fr Y by appt.

CH. LEHOUL 1999
□
1.2 ha | 2,800 | €8-11

This Sémillon wine, still bearing the mark of 16 months' barrel-maturation, needs time for oak integration. A darkish colour, its bouquet of elegant grilled notes is reflected in the well-rounded palate and the very ripe fruit flavours.

• EARL Fonta et Fils, rte d'Auros, 33210 Langon, tel. 05.56.63.06.06, fax 05.56.63.06.06 Y by appt.

DOM. DE MAREUIL 1999★
□
3 ha | 3,000 | €5-8

This traditional, extremely generously flavoured wine makes an agreeable play on nuances ranging from from crystallised mandarin to honey and beeswax.

• René Desert, 12, rte d'Illats, 33210 Pujols-sur-Ciron, tel. 05.56.76.69.70, fax 05.56.76.69.70 Y by appt.

CH. DE ROCHEFORT 1999★
□
1.92 ha | 2,000 | €5-8

This grower, who also produces wine in Sauternes, is well aware of just how demanding it is to make sweet and *moelleux* wines. Proof of this is this rounded, supple, powerful 99, with its truly fine bouquet, which is rich enough to be a true aperitif wine.

• Jean-Christophe Barbe, Ch. Laville, 33210 Preignac, tel. 05.56.63.59.45, fax 05.56.63.16.28 Y by appt.

Pessac-Léognan

Corresponding to the northern part of Graves (formerly called Hautes-Graves), the region of Pessac and Léognan is today an *Appellation Communale* similar to those of the Médoc. Its creation, historically justifiable, (medieval clarets were produced from the ancient vines that surrounded the towns) is supported by the originality of its soil. The terracing further south gives way to a much more irregular landscape. The area between Martillac and Mérignac consists of an archipelago of gravelly hilltops whose steep slopes guarantee good drainage and

Pessac-Léognan

whose soil, composed of a variety of different types of pebble, are excellent for wine-growing. Pessac-Léognan wines have great originality – a fact which specialists noticed long before the creation of the appellation, so much so that in 1855, at the time of the imperial classification, Haut-Brion became the only non-Médoc château to be classed (Premier Cru). Eventually in 1959, when the 16 Graves crus were classed, we find that all were in the present *Appellation Communale*.

The red wines (57,702 hl/1,523,330 gal in 2000), possess all the general characteristics of Graves wines, yet their bouquet, velvetiness and structure sets them apart. The white wines (13,561 hl/358,010 gal) are particularly suited to barrel-maturation and cellaring, allowing them to acquire great richness of flavour with fine notes of broom and lime blossom.

CH. BAHANS HAUT-BRION 1998★★
■　　　　n.c.　　n.c.　　🍷 £30-38

Like its illustrious older brother, this wine benefits from the meticulous care of the vineyard and winery teams. This dark 98, maroon with deep purple highlights, gets its expressive character from its aromas of waxed oak, leather and cherry brandy. The flavourful tannins contribute to the balance of this lovely whole, which finishes joyfully on an elegant peppery note.

➤ SA Dom. Clarence Dillon, BP 24, 33602 Pessac Cedex, tel. 05.56.00.29.30, fax 05.56.98.75.14, e-mail info@haut-brion.com

CH. BARET 1998★★
■　　　n.c.　　n.c.　　🍷 £8-11

This cru, located just outside Bordeaux, has been completely renovated over the last 20 years. This full, rich, well-structured wine with its substantial, well-extracted tannins shows that the last two decades of effort have not been in vain. Given that its garnet colour and red berry bouquet are of the same calibre, this lovely wine should be kept for four to five years and served with game and a good cut of red meat. The **99 white** was specially mentioned by the Jury.

➤ Héritiers André Ballande, Ch. Baret, 33140 Villenave-d'Ornon,
tel. 05.56.00.00.70, fax 05.56.52.29.54
🍷 by appt.

CH. BOUSCAUT 1998★
■Cru clas.　　n.c.　98,000　　📦 🍷 £15-23
76 79 **80 81** 82 83 84 **85** ⑧⑥ 87 |88| **89**
90 93 |94| 95 96 97

This cru, identified by its famous 18th-century name Haut Truchon, enjoys favourable topography, which contributes substantially to the quality of the wine produced, as this lovely 98 shows. Its present name is more poetic. The wine shows great balance and perfumes of vanilla, blackcurrant and leather. Given its substantial tannins, it should be laid down for about three years.

➤ Ch. Bouscaut, RN 113, 33140 Cadaujac, tel. 05.57.83.12.20, fax 05.57.83.12.21, e-mail cb@chateau-bouscaut.com ✉
🍷 by appt.
➤ Sophie Cogombles

CRUS CLASSÉS OF THE GRAVES REGION

NAME OF CRU CLASSÉ	TYPE OF WINE	NAME OF CRU CLASSÉ	TYPE OF WINE
Château Bouscaut	red and white	Château Laville-Haut-Brion	white
Château Carbonnieux	red and white	Château Malartic-Lagravière	red and white
Domaine de Chevalier	red and white	Château La Mission-Haut-Brion	red
Château Couhins	white	Château Olivier	red and white
Château Couhins-Lurton	white	Château Pape-Clément	red
Château de Fieuzal	red	Château Smith-Haut-Lafitte	red
Château Haut-Bailly	red	Château Latour-Haut-Brion	red
Château Haut-Brion	red	Château La Tour-Martillac	red and white

CH. BOUSCAUT 1999★★

□ Cru clas. 6 ha 22,000

| 82 | 83 | 85 | 86 | 88 | 89 | 90 | 93 | [95] | [96] | 97 |
| [98] | 99 | | | | | | | | | |

€15-23

Sophie Cogombles, who is as indifferent to media-inspired fashions as her father, Lucien Lurton, is aided by her husband, Laurent, in making wines she likes. This is all to the good, as it has resulted in this very lovely 98. The richness and complexity of its toasted almonds, acacia blossom, tropical fruit and coconut bouquet whets the appetite, and the fleshy, warm, perfectly balanced palate meets expectations. This is a truly great, well-balanced wine that will age well.

↝ Ch. Bouscaut, RN 113, 33140 Cadaujac, tel. 05.57.83.12.20, fax 05.57.83.12.21, e-mail cb@chateau-bouscaut.com V
Υ by appt.

CH. BROWN 1999

□ 3.81 ha 19,000 €15-15

Thanks to its consistent good quality, Château Brown has built up a solid following of those that like and appreciate its white wine. This wine, grown on sandy-gravelly soil, the fruit of responsible working methods, with its brilliant highlights, has a lovely bouquet of citrus and dried fruit and leaves a fresh, lively, fruity impression on the palate. It is already pleasant but will be at its peak in two to three years.

↝ Ch. Brown, allée John-Lewis-Brown, 33850 Léognan, tel. 05.56.87.08.10, fax 05.56.87.87.34, e-mail chateau.brown@wanadoo.fr V
↝ Bernard Barthe

CH. CANTELYS 1998

■ 25 ha 25,000

This wine, a blend of 70% Cabernet Sauvignon and 30% Merlot, is grown on fine gravel soil. Barrel-matured for 14 months, a lovely ruby colour, this wine develops a delicate, really fruity bouquet in which morello cherries and gooseberries mingle happily with spices and elegant oaky notes. Its coated tannins suggest it should be cellared for three to five years.

↝ SARL Daniel Cathiard, Ch. Cantelys, 33650 Martillac, tel. 05.57.83.11.22, fax 05.57.83.11.21 V Υ by appt.

CH. CARBONNIEUX 1998★

□ Cru clas. 45 ha 200,000

| 75 | 81 | 82 | 83 | 85 | 86 | 87 | [88] | [89] | [90] | [91] |
| [92] | [93] | [94] | [95] | 96 | [97] | 98 | | | | |

€11-15

The label bears witness to the often forgotten role played by monks in the wine-growing life of Bordeaux. This cru takes no half measures with this very lovely, powerful, complex wine with its toasty, morello-cherry bouquet, which opens on the palate to supple, powerful tannins. These rich tannins ensure that this wine will age well.

↝ SC des Grandes Graves, Ch. Carbonnieux, 33850 Léognan, tel. 05.57.96.56.20, fax 05.57.96.59.19, e-mail chateau.carbonnieux@wanadoo.fr V
Υ by appt.
↝ Perrin

CH. CARBONNIEUX 1999★

□ Cru clas. 45 ha 200,000

| 81 | 82 | 83 | 85 | 86 | 87 | 88 | [89] | [90] | [91] | 92 |
| [93] | [94] | [95] | [96] | 97 | [98] | 99 | | | | |

€15-23

The transparency of Carbonnieux white wine once resulted in it being exported to the Bosphorus as Carbonnieux mineral water. However, the colour of this wine is an unambiguous yellow. Discreet floral perfumes are unveiled, followed by a clear, honest, slightly oaky attack. On the palate the wine comes across as rich and elegant right up to its long, smoky finish. It should be cellared for two to three years.

↝ SC des Grandes Graves, Ch. Carbonnieux, 33850 Léognan, tel. 05.57.96.56.20, fax 05.57.96.59.19, e-mail chateau.carbonnieux@wanadoo.fr V
Υ by appt.

DOM. DE CHEVALIER 1998★★

■ Cru clas. 13 ha 80,000

| 64 | 66 | 70 | 73 | 75 | 78 | 79 | 83 | 84 | [85] | [86] | 87 |
| 88 | [89] | [90] | 91 | 92 | [93] | [94] | 96 | 97 | 98 | | |

€30-38

This pale-coloured-stone cru, which stands out against the dark green of the Landes forest, enjoys beautiful gravel soil on a clay-limestone base. This visually attractive wine has complex perfumes, enriched by a few toasty, truffled notes, which make it a veritable spice box. Flavourful tannins sustain the wine, which has plenty of length, and ensure it makes no secret of its ambition to be cellared for a long time. Judging by its promising powerful structure and bouquet, the wine-lover's patience will be repaid. The Jury specially mentioned its second label, **98 Esprit de Chevalier red**, which also requires cellaring, in this case for two to three years.

↝ SC Dom. de Chevalier, 33850 Léognan, tel. 05.56.64.16.16, fax 05.56.64.18.18, e-mail domainedechevalier@domainedechevalier.com Υ by appt.
↝ Famille Bernard

DOM. DE CHEVALIER 1998★★

□ Cru clas. 4 ha 15,000

| 82 | 83 | 85 | 86 | [89] | [90] | 91 | 92 | [93] | [94] | [96] |
| [97] | 98 | | | | | | | | | |

€38-46

The fame of Chevalier white wine bears no relation to the size of its source vineyard. Found on the world's most prestigious tables, we must surely envy the privileged few that will have the chance to savour the rich attack on the palate of this dense, vivacious 98, with its complex, oaky, citrus fruit bouquet. The Jury also specially mentioned the second wine **L'Esprit de Chevalier white**.

↝ SC Dom. de Chevalier, 33850 Léognan, tel. 05.56.64.16.16, fax 05.56.64.18.18, e-mail domainedechevalier@domainedechevalier.com Υ by appt.

CH. COUHINS-LURTON 1999★★ |||| €23-30
□ Cru clas. 5.5 ha n.c. |94|

82 83 85 86 87 88 89 |90| 91 |92| 93 |94| 95 |(96)| 97 98 |99|

André Lurton has thrown himself wholeheartedly into the rebirth of Couhins. This beautifully coloured 99 demonstrates, as have previous vintages, his successes. It develops a lovely bouquet in which notes of peach meet with tropical fruit and vanilla. On the palate it is supple, fruity, oaky and honeyed.

➜ SCEA Vignobles André Lurton, Ch. Bonnet, 33420 Grézillac, tel. 05.57.25.58.58, fax 05.57.74.98.59, e-mail andrelurton@wanadoo.fr ☑ ☒ by appt.

CH. DE CRUZEAU 1999★ |||| €8-11
□ 12 ha n.c. |99|

88 89 90 92 93 94 95 |96| |97| |98| |99|

This cru, situated in Saint-Médard-d'Eyrans, enjoys a southerly disposition. Although this wine is not the equal of the Couhins-Lurton from the same producer, it has a substantial, pleasant character confirmed by its up-front, toasted-almond, toasty, lychee and resin bouquet. The very pleasant fresh, powerful palate will no doubt improve after cellaring for two to three years. The Jury also specially mentioned the youthful 98 Cruzeau red with its notes of red berries, spices and coffee. This too will improve with time.

➜ SCEA Vignobles André Lurton, Ch. Bonnet, 33420 Grézillac, tel. 05.57.25.58.58, fax 05.57.74.98.59, e-mail andrelurton@wanadoo.fr ☑ ☒ by appt.

CH. FERRAN 1998★ |||| €8-11
■ 10 ha 60,000 |95|

83 85 88 89 |90| 94 |95| 97 98

This cru, like many properties in Martillac, was owned, long ago, by parliamentarians; its history is linked to that of the Montesquieu family. Despite its assertive tannins, a current fashion, this charming 98 is rich, full and unctuous on the palate with a bouquet enlivened by powerful perfumes of roasting coffee beans and crystallised fruits. It has all the signs of being a wine that will age well and should be cellared for at least three years. The 99 Ferran white was awarded a star for its delicious floral bouquet with laurel and box notes.

➜ Ch. Ferran, 33650 Martillac, tel. 06.07.41.86.00, fax 06.56.72.62.73 ☒ ☒ by appt.
➜ Hervé Béraud-Sudreau

CH. DE FIEUZAL 1998★★ |||| €38-46
■ Cru clas. 60 ha 150,000 |85|

70 75 76 77 78 79 80 81 82 83 84 |85| |86| |88| |89| |(90)| |91| 92 93 94 (95) (96) 97 98

This cru, in the control of the Banques Populaires in 1994, has a new owner this year. Admirably, it has kept up its regular standard of quality as illustrated by its two wines. The garnet 98, as eloquent as its bouquet of ripe fruit and toast, is gratifying and complex, on the palate due to substantial and straightforward tannins. It should be cellared for five to six years to allow the flavours to integrate and would then drink well with strongly flavoured duck dishes.

➜ SA Ch. de Fieuzal, 124, av. de Mont-de-Marsan, 33850 Léognan, tel. 05.56.64.77.86, fax 05.56.64.18.88 ☒ ☒ by appt.

CH. DE FIEUZAL 1999★★★ |||| €38-46
□ 18 ha 40,000 |(90)| 91 92 |93|

83 84 85 86 87 |88| |89| |89| |94| |95| |96| 97 98 (99)

This cru, closely involved in the renaissance of dry white Bordeaux wines, has once again distinguished itself through the quality of its wines. The gorgeous platinum-coloured 99 is impressive for its meatiness and length, which make it powerful without any trace of aggressiveness. Its intense, highly agreeable bouquet mingles fresh grapes and notes of ripe Sauvignon and spices. This superb wine should be cellared for at least three to four years. The Jury specially mentioned the lighter, highly perfumed second wine 99 L'Abeille de Fieuzal white, which has lovely box notes.

➜ SA Ch. de Fieuzal, 124, av. de Mont-de-Marsan, 33850 Léognan, tel. 05.56.64.77.86, fax 05.56.64.18.88 ☒ ☒ by appt.

CH. DE FRANCE 1998★ |||| €15-23
■ 29 ha 70,000 |(90)| 92 93 94 |95|

81 82 83 85 86 88 89 96 97 98

Bernard Thomassin, this year celebrating 30 years at the head of this cru, has succeeded in producing a wine with a lovely, spicy, powerful bouquet. On the palate the assertive but silky tannins are markedly oaky. This juicy wine has plenty of length. Everything points to this developing into a lovely wine after cellaring for five to seven years. The Jury commended the fine and elegant 99 Château de France white with its floral, toasty bouquet.

➜ SA Bernard Thomassin, Ch. de France, 98, av. de Mont-de-Marsan, 33850 Léognan, tel. 05.56.64.75.39, fax 05.56.64.72.13, e-mail chateau-de-france@chateau-de-france.com ☒ ☒ by appt.

CH. GAZIN ROCQUENCOURT 1998★
■ 5.1 ha 34,000 |||| €11-15

This cru, in the interests of quality improvement, presented this well-constructed 98, which strives towards finesse rather than power. On the palate it is supple and well balanced, and through its flavourful tannins supports the elegant perfumes of ripe grapes and spices.

➜ SCEA Ch. Gazin Rocquencourt, 74, av. de Cestas, 33850 Léognan, tel. 05.56.64.77.80, fax 05.56.64.77.89 ☒
➜ Michotte

CH. HAUT-BAILLY 1998★★

■ Cru clas.　26 ha　80,000

78 79 80 81 82 83 85 |86| 87 88 (89)
|92| 93 94 (95) 96 97 98 |90|　€30-38

This cru, awarded a *coup de coeur* last year for its 97, remains one of the most successful in the appellation. Right from the start, its lovely crimson colour with its deep purple highlights revealed its ability to age well. The bouquet, as complex and subtle as one could wish, with its perfumes of ripe fruit and vanilla fragrances, introduces a palate of an elegant, finish with hints of liquorice. The jury commended this cru's second label **98 La Parde de Haut Bailly red**, which will be good for drinking next year and would accompany veal or chicken.

Y by appt.
SCA du Ch. Haut-Bailly,
rte de Cadaujac, 33850 Léognan,
tel. 05.56.64.75.11, fax 05.56.64.53.60,
e-mail mail@chateau-haut-bailly.com

CH. HAUT-BERGEY 1998★★

■　13 ha　55,000

91 92 93 |94| 96 97 98　€23-30

This cru, called the 'maison noble de Pontey' in the 18th century, once covered more than 100 ha (247 acres). Today it is a more modest size at 32 ha (79 acres). This fact has not prevented it from ambitiously producing this superb deep-ruby wine with its equally intense bouquet. Its richness on the palate moves from blackcurrant and blackberry through to cocoa, toasty notes opening out along the way. The soft, well-structured palate with silky, powerful tannins bears witness to its noble heritage. This is a truly great wine that should be laid down for four to five years. Against background notes of toast, the Sauvignon, at *75%*, dominates in the 99 **Haut-Bergey white**.

Sylviane Garcin-Cathiard.
Ch. Haut-Bergey, BP 49, 33850 Léognan,
tel. 05.56.64.05.22, fax 05.56.64.06.98.
e-mail haut-bergey@wanadoo.fr [V]
Y by appt.

CH. HAUT-BRION 1998★★★

■ 1er cru clas.　43.2 ha　n.c.

73 74 |75| 76 77 78 |79| 81 |(82)| |83| 84
85 |86| 87 88 89 |(90)| |91| |92| |93| 94　€+476

This, the most ancient of the wine-growing châteaux in Bordeaux, is the only non-Médoc cru to have been classified in 1855. The 'Lord of Graves' justices once again the fame and the honours that have always been showered upon it. Its majestic, intense, deep colour affirms its youth. The bouquet, needless to say, is very beautiful and powerful, with notes of ripe fruit: morello cherries in brandy on a smoky, liquoricey background of great complexity. The voluptuously dense attack, however, makes the bouquet seem almost timid. Fine, perfectly balanced, elegantly fruity, dense tannins support the soft, full, monumental long impression on the palate. This wine states right to the finish, loud and clear, its exceptional ageing potential. It will take around ten years to reach its peak.

SA Dom. Clarence Dillon, BP 24,
33602 Pessac Cedex, tel. 05.56.00.29.30,
fax 05.56.98.75.14, e-mail info@
haut-brion.com

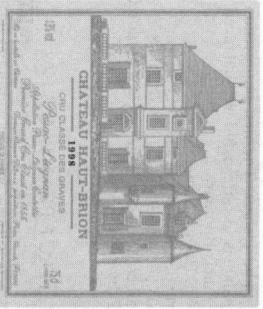

CH. HAUT-BRION 1999★★★

□　2.7 ha　n.c.

(82) 83 85 87 88 |89| |90| |93| |94| |95| |96|
|97| 98 (99)　€+476

Haut-Brion, an elegant manor dating back to the 16th and 17th centuries, was bought by Clarence Dillon in 1935. Today the Duchesse de Mouchy, joined this year by her son, Prince Robert de Luxembourg, presides over the vineyards. Although its white wines have never been classified, Haut-Brion has never proved itself unworthy. This stylish 99 was only one vote short of being chosen for a *coup de coeur*. The beautifully complex bouquet is reminiscent in turn of hazelnuts, fresh butter, citrus and exotic fruits and camomile. The palate is rich, powerful, flavourful and well balanced. This wine is obviously destined to age well.

SA Dom. Clarence Dillon,
BP 24, 33602 Pessac Cedex,
tel. 05.56.00.29.30, fax 05.56.98.75.14,
e-mail info@haut-brion.com

LES PLANTIERS DU HAUT-BRION 1999★

□　n.c.　n.c.

This wine, produced by the Haut-Brion team, is characteristic in its fruity bouquet (melon and citrus) of a Sémillon from Graves. The rounded, well-coated palate lives up to its noble origins, as does the flavourful finish with its fragrances of crystallised orange.

SA Dom. Clarence Dillon,
BP 24, 33602 Pessac Cedex,
tel. 05.56.00.29.30, fax 05.56.98.75.14,
e-mail info@haut-brion.com

CH. HAUT-LAGRANGE 1999★

□　1.7 ha　12,000

92 94 95 |96| 97 |98| |99|　€11-15

This blend, 5% Sauvignon gris, 45% Sauvignon and 50% Sémillon, results in a lovely pale yellow wine with a full bouquet of exotic fruits and lychees. The first impresssion on the palate is soft, fresh and well balanced.

⊶ Francis Boutemy,
SA Ch. Haut Lagrange,
31, rte de Loustalade, 33850 Léognan,
tel. 05.56.64.09.93, fax 05.56.64.10.08,
e-mail chateau-haut-lagrange@wanadoo.fr
☑ ⅄ by appt.

CH. HAUT-PLANTADE 1998

■ 5.67 ha 38,000 ⅲ €11-15

This is a lovely wine in a minor key. The bouquet reveals a fine oakiness mingled with red berries. The characterful flavour on the palate is, however, sufficiently substantial to indicate that the wine will age well.

⊶ GAEC Plantade Père et Fils,
Ch. Haut-Plantade, 33850 Léognan,
tel. 05.56.64.07.09, fax 05.56.64.02.24,
e-mail hautplantade@wanadoo.fr ☑
⅄ by appt.

CH. LAFONT MENAUT 1998★

■ 9 ha 50,000 ⅲ €8-11

This vineyard, which once belonged to Montesquieu, the author of *De l'esprit des lois* is fortunate in having beautiful Graves soil. Philibert Perrin refurbished it ten years ago. This wine, which illustrates the recent progress of the cru, combines a charming ruby colour with a powerful, complex, oak-dominated bouquet and a solid, round structure. In a final triumph, the finish is promisingly long and warm.

⊶ Philibert Perrin, Ch. Lafont Menaut,
33650 Martillac, tel. 05.57.96.56.20,
fax 05.57.96.59.19 ⅄ by appt.

CH. LA GARDE 1998★★

■ 48 ha 117,000 |90| 91 93 94 95 96 97 98

This château, dating back to 1739, built its cellars, which are well worth visiting, in 1882. These have been restored by the Dourthe concern, which bought the property in 1990. The carefully crafted wine, a blend of 60% Cabernet Sauvignon and 40% Merlot, grown on a beautiful Graves hilltop with a clay-lime-stone bed, should also be praised. Its brilliant, intense, crimson colour, immediately seduc-tive, is followed by the bouquet in which notes of roasting coffee beans, spices, cloves, ginger and red grapes mix. Its complexity is hard to resist. On the palate its development is pleas-ant and full, as fruit and oak mingle towards an equally seductive, long finish. This is a remarkable wine, which will be drinking well in three to four years, if not later, as an accom-paniment to game. The Jury commended the **99 La Garde white**, which is ready for drinking now.

⊶ SC du Ch. La Garde (Dourthe),
35, rue de Bordeaux, 33290 Parempuyre,
tel. 05.56.35.53.00, fax 05.56.35.53.29,
e-mail contact@cvbg.com ☑ ⅄ by appt.
⊶ Dourthe

CH. LAGRAVE-MARTILLAC 1998★

■ 30 ha 40,000 ⅲ €11-15

The power and elegance of a great wine is found in this second label from the Château Latour-Martillac, which is proud to offer a bouquet as rich as its tannic structure. This very lovely wine should be opened and drunk with red meat in four or five years' time. The Jury also commended the **99 Lagrave Martillac white** with its toasty notes, which, though still a little reserved, has great freshness.

⊶ Domaines Kressmann,
Ch. Latour-Martillac, 33650 Martillac,
tel. 05.57.97.71.11, fax 05.57.97.71.17,
e-mail latour-martillac@latour-martillac.com
⅄ by appt.
⊶ GFA Latour-Martillac

CH. LA LOUVIÈRE 1998

■ 35 ha n.c. ⅲ €23-30

75 80 81 82 83 86 |88| |89| |89| 91 92
93 94 95 96 97 98

La Louvière is a superb neoclassical château, displaying for all to see its monu-mental entrance staircase, crowned by Ionic capi-tals. Though it does not seek to rival earlier wines are surmounted by Ionic capi-tals. Though it does not seek to rival the 99 white, this intense garnet-red wine has a charming smoky, toasty perfumed bouquet. On the palate it reveals itself as being austere, even Jansenist. It will take three or four years for it to gain confidence.

⊶ SCEA Vignobles André Lurton, Ch.
Bonnet, 33420 Grézillac, tel. 05.57.25.58.58,
fax 05.57.74.98.59, e-mail andrelurton@
wanadoo.fr ☑ ⅄ by appt.

CH. LA LOUVIÈRE 1999★★

□ 15 ha n.c. ⅲ €23-30

86 88 89 |90| 91 92 93 |94| |95| |96| |97|
98 99

André Lurton, who celebrated 50 years of wine-growing this year, has many years of experience in the field of white-wine produc-tion. This well-balanced, complex, well-constructed 99 has an elegant perfume of box, mimosa and lemon in the bouquet to confirm this fact. Its honourable origins stand out, as does the fact that it will age well for two to three years. The second wine pre-sented, **99 L de La Louvière**, was also awarded a star.

⊶ SCEA Vignobles André Lurton, Ch.
Bonnet, 33420 Grézillac, tel. 05.57.25.58.58,
fax 05.57.74.98.59, e-mail andrelurton@
wanadoo.fr ☑ ⅄ by appt.

CH. LA MISSION HAUT-BRION 1998★★

Cru clas. 20.9 ha n.c. ⅲ +€76

78 80 81 |82| |83| 84 |85| |86| 87 |88| 89
|90| 92 |93| 94 95 |96| 97 98

This cru, once a rival of Haut-Brion, now part of it, owes the extraordinary quality of its wines to the soil and the ability of its suc-cessive managers. This very beautiful 98 with its garnet colour and crimson highlights has a dense, complex bouquet of cold smoke, spices and liquorice. Its powerful, generous attack and strong, substantial tannins on the palate carry through to a typical claret finish, with all its multiplicity of flavours. This impressive wine, the sort we have come to expect from Mission, should be laid down for ten to fifteen years. Equally well-structured is the second label from La Mission, **La Chapelle de la Mission Haut-Brion**, which was awarded a star. This could be opened sooner, in four to five years' time.

↠ SA Dom. Clarence Dillon,
BP 24, 33602 Pessac Cedex,
tel. 05.56.00.29.30, fax 05.56.98.75.14,
e-mail info@haut-brion.com

■ CH. LARRIVET-HAUT-BRION
□ 1999★   9 ha   25,000   [€]

88 89 90 |96| 97 |98| |99|

The grounds of this estate, with a little stream, the Larivet, running through them, are wonderful. The slightly amber-gold highlights in this wine are immediately seductive. Supple, well balanced, it develops gradually on the palate, releasing lovely flavours of citrus fruit. The happy alliance of oak and its body confirm careful production. The Jury commended the rather closed **98 red**.

↠ SCEA du Ch. Larrivet-Haut-Brion,
rue Haut-Brion, 33850 Léognan,
tel. 05.56.64.75.51, fax 05.56.64.53.47
Y by appt.
↠ Ph. Gervoson

■ DOM. DE LA SOLITUDE 1998
23 ha   70,000   [€11-15]

This cru, still owned by a community of nuns, reminds us of the role played by religious institutions in the historical development of Bordeaux. This rounded and well-balanced 98, produced by Olivier Bernard of the Domaine de Chevalier, has a pleasant bouquet with delicate notes of leather and cherries in brandy.

↠ SC Dom. de Chevalier,
Dom. de La Solitude, 33650 Martillac,
tel. 05.56.72.74.74, fax 05.56.72.52.00,
e-mail olivierbernard@
domainedelasolitude.com   Y by appt.

■ CH. LATOUR HAUT-BRION 1998★
■ Cru clas.   4.9 ha   n.c.   [€30-38]

78 79 80 81 (82)| |83| 84 |85| |86| 87 |88|
|89| |90| 92 |93| |94| 95 96 97 98

This cru, like its neighbour, La Mission, belongs to the Dillon group. It only produces red wines. Its densely textured 98 with its spicy finish, still a little severe on the midpalate, is, overall, round and full. The complex bouquet ranges from ripe, even overripe grapes, to leather. The palate shows its ability to age well.

↠ SA Dom. Clarence Dillon,
BP 24, 33602 Pessac Cedex,
tel. 05.56.00.29.30, fax 05.56.98.75.14,
e-mail info@haut-brion.com

Over a number of decades, the Kressmann family have carved out a solid reputation for their white wine and this superb 99 shows that their fame is not about to disappear. Limpid and shining, it has a powerful bouquet in which the toasty notes of the barrel mingle with perfumes of orange. The palate is equally complex, demonstrating a lovely sense of balance and freshness that make the

This cru near Carbonnieux is also owned by Antony Perrin, so the similarity between the two wines is not surprising. This harmonious 98 has balanced, well-integrated tannins and perfumes of morello cherries, roasting coffee beans and prunes. The **99 La Tour Léognan white** was also awarded a star. Its colour, bouquet and structure are in perfect harmony with its oakiness, which does not overwhelm its fruitiness.

↠ SC des Grandes Graves,
Ch. Carbonnieux, 33850 Léognan,
tel. 05.57.96.56.20, fax 05.57.96.59.19,
e-mail chateau.carbonnieux@wanadoo.fr
Y by appt.
↠ Perrin

■ CH. LA TOUR LEOGNAN 1998★
■   8 ha   40,000   [€8-11]

96 97 98

Visitors tasting this wine in the company of either Tristan or Loïc Kressmann will have no doubt as to their passion for wine. Any wine-lover tasting this very lovely 98 will be equally convinced. The powerful gamey bouquet carries through to the palate. The finish has a substantial tannic structure combined with great body and length, guaranteeing that this youthful, well-balanced wine will age well.

↠ Domaines Kressmann,
Ch. Latour-Martillac, 33650 Martillac,
tel. 05.57.97.71.11, fax 05.57.97.71.17,
e-mail latour-martillac@latour-martillac.com
Y by appt.
↠ GFA Latour-Martillac

■ CH. LATOUR-MARTILLAC 1998★★
■ Cru clas.   30 ha   126,000   [€23-30]

79 81 (82) 83 84 85 86 87 88 |89| 90 91
92 93 94 95 96 97 98

■ CH. LATOUR-MARTILLAC 1999★★★
□ Cru clas.   10 ha   42,000   [€23-30]

81 82 83 84 85 86 87 (88) 89 90 91 92
93 |94| |95| 96 97 |98| |99|

Pessac-Léognan

wine already very agreeable but also signal its ability to age well.

- Domaines Kressmann,
Ch. Latour-Martillac, 33650 Martillac,
tel. 05.57.97.71.11, fax 05.57.97.71.17,
e-mail latour-martillac@latour-martillac.com
- Y by appt.

CH. LAVILLE HAUT-BRION 1999★★ €38-45

Cru clas. 3.7 ha n.c.

81 82 83 |85| 87 88 (89) |90| 92 |93| |94| |95| |96| |97| (98) 99

This tiny vineyard is very much in the spirit of Graves and Haut-Brion in terms of its exceptional *terroir* and varieties, mainly Sémillon. This elegant, scintillating wine, pale with green highlights, has a fresh, floral bouquet typical of Sémillon. The palate is beautifully complex, with flavours of lime blossom, lemon and ripe pineapple, while the rich, fine structure indicates its ability to age well even though it is suitable for drinking now.

- SA Dom. Clarence Dillon,
BP 24, 33602 Pessac Cedex,
tel. 05.56.00.29.30, fax 05.56.98.75.14,
e-mail info@haut-brion.com

CH. LE PAPE 1998★ €15-23

5 ha 34,000

This cru, a small estate in Léognan, is run by a pretty monastery. Its wine, equally attractive, has a deep ruby colour, a bouquet with powerful notes of cinnamon, game, and red berries and a elegant, long tannic structure.

- Patrick Monjanel, 34, chem. le Pape,
33850 Léognan, tel. 05.56.64.10.90,
fax 05.56.64.17.78 V Y by appt.

CH. LE SARTRE 1999★ €11-15

7 ha 35,000

92 93 94 95 |96| 97 |98| 99

Situated on the edge of the Landes forest, Le Sartre sits on Günz Graves soil. It has belonged to the Perrins (Château Carbonnieux) since 1981. Today it has modern equipment which produces this rich, well-structured, interesting wine with its rich harmonious bouquet of vanilla, from barrel maturation, mingled with perfumes of citrus fruit and lime blossom.

- GFA des Ch. Le Sartre et Bois Martin,
33850 Léognan, tel. 05.57.96.56.20,
fax 05.57.96.59.19,
e-mail chateau.carbonnieux@wanadoo.fr V
- Y by appt.
- Perrin

CH. LES CARMES HAUT-BRION 1998★ €23-30

4.36 ha 22,000

80 82 83 85 88 |89| 90 91 92 93 94 |95| 96 97 |98|

This is a thoroughly charming cru, with its lake, 16th-century château and wooded grounds. Though still very young and rather closed, on aeration it develops a complex bouquet, in which toasty notes mingle with ripe fruit. Rich, fleshy and full, the palate structure indicates it should develop very well.

- Ch. Les Carmes Haut-Brion,
197, av. Jean-Cordier, 33600 Pessac,
tel. 05.56.51.49.43, fax 05.56.93.10.71,
e-mail chateau@les-carmes-haut-brion.com
- Y by appt.
- Didier Furt

CH. LESPAULT 1999 €11-15

1 ha 4,500

This attractive wine, 100% Sauvignon grown on deep gravel, harvested on 31st August, fermented in barrels and matured with stirring of the lees, although not tremendously full, is nonetheless agreeable. Flavours of citrus fruit, honeysuckle and ripe grapes lead into a fresh finish. It is a wine to be served with fish. The Jury also commended the **98 Château Lespault red** a supple, agreeable wine that will go well with an entrecôte steak in the spring of 2002.

- Domaines Kressmann,
Ch. Latour-Martillac, 33650 Martillac,
tel. 05.57.97.71.11, fax 05.57.97.71.17,
e-mail latour-martillac@latour-martillac.com
- Y by appt.
- SC Bolleau

CH. LE THIL COMTE CLARY 1999★ €11-15

n.c. 20,000

This cru should really be called the Countess Clary rather than the Count, given the extremely important role played in its history by Jeanne Clary, its owner in the second half of the 19th century. Descendants of her heirs have been discerning in their use of oak to respect the flavours of citrus fruit, peaches and yellow plums. It is full, lively and fresh and can be drunk now or laid down. The Jury also commended the **98 red**, on the light side for a Pessac-Léognan, but nonetheless agreeable.

- Ch. Le Thil Comte Clary,
Le Thil, 33850 Léognan, tel. 05.56.30.01.02,
fax 05.56.30.04.32, e-mail jean-de-laitre@chateau.le.thil.com V Y by appt.

CH. MALARTIC-LAGRAVIÈRE 1998★ €23-30

Cru clas. 23 ha 44,117

64 66 (70) 71 75 76 79 81 82 83 |85| |86| |88| |89| |90| |91| 92 |93| 95 96 97 98

This cru, as indicated on the label, belonged to a family of shipowners who were participants in the adventurous era when wines were shipped backwards and forwards across the Atlantic. However, any initiatory voyage is unnecessary for this lovely 98, with tones of stewed fruit and a full, concentrated palate, to reveal its qualities. The initially discreet bouquet reveals fruity perfumes backed by notes of roasting coffee beans. This impressive wine would go well with lamb casseroles. It is rare for the second wine presented by a cru to be as highly rated as the first but

CH. MALARTIC-LAGRAVIERE

1999
□ Cru clas. | 4 ha | 12,197
97 **98** |99|

This supple, well-balanced wine, 80% Sauvignon, 20% Sémillon, has a fine, delicate bouquet dominated by lovely citrus-fruit and orange-peel notes which complement toasty tones from the barrel. The Jury also commended the **99 Sillage de Malartic**, a similar type of wine. ... this is the case for the well-structured, seductive **Sillage de Malartic**.
♦ Ch. Malartic-Lagravière, 43, av. de Mont-de-Marsan, 33850 Léognan, tel. 05.56.64.75.08, fax 05.56.64.99.66, e-mail malartic-lagravière@ malartic-lagravière. Y by appt.
♦ A.-A. Bonnie

CLOS MARSALETTE 1999★

□ | 0.7 ha | 4,000 | ■■ | €11-15

The stage was set for success when the owners of Canon la Gaffelière, Haut-Lagrange and a land surveyor got together to create a cru. This extremely successful wine, half Sauvignon and half Sémillon, is concentrated and unctuous, with a lovely bouquet of lychees, coconut and grapefruit.
♦ SCEA Marsalette, 31, rte de Loustalade, 33850 Léognan, tel. 05.56.64.09.93, fax 05.56.64.10.08 Y by appt.

DOM. DE MERLET 1998

□ | 3 ha | 15,000 | ■ | €8-11

This wine with its initially closed bouquet was grown on a small 4-ha (10-acre) concern, replanted in 1989. It slowly opens into agreeable perfumes of fruit (plum), spices and liquorice. On the palate its elegance and balance indicate that it should be cellared for about three years.
♦ Indivision Tauzin, 35, cours du Mal-Leclerc, 33850 Léognan, tel. 05.56.64.77.74, fax 05.56.64.77.74 Y by appt.

CH. OLIVIER 1998★

■ Cru clas. | 35 ha | n.c.
82 83 |85| |86| 87 |88| |89| |90| 91 92 93
94 95 96 97 98

It was in this castle, with a moat still filled with water, that the Black Prince held Du Guesclin prisoner in the 14th century. This equally substantial, beautifully coloured 98, with its carmine nuances, exhibits a powerful bouquet in which red berries and blackberries mingle with spicy, vanilla, musky notes as if to reawaken the past and invite wine-lovers to enjoy a banquet of game.
♦ Jean-Jacques de Bethmann, Ch. Olivier, 33850 Léognan, tel. 05.56.64.75.16, fax 05.56.64.23, e-mail chateau-olivier@ wanadoo.fr Y by appt.

CH. PAPE CLEMENT 1998★★

■ Cru clas. | 20 ha | 80,000 | €38-46
75 78 79 80 (81) 82 83 **85** |86| 87 |88| 89
90 **91** 92 |93| |94| 95 96 97 98

This cru, owned by the well-known Bordeaux négotiant, Bernard Magrez, carries the name of a former owner, Bertrand de Got, who was elected pope in 1305. It is one of the most famous crus in Bordeaux. This beautifully presented 98 follows in the estates tradition. Its elegant colour with ruby, vermilian nuances is echoed in the intense, concentrated bouquet, which skilfully plays on spicy, fruity vanilla notes. It is equally rich on the palate, combining charm with a tannic structure that makes it a particularly classy wine.
♦ Bernard Magrez, Ch. Pape Clément, 33600 Pessac, tel. 05.57.26.38.38, fax 05.57.26.38.39, e-mail chateau@ pape-clement.com Y by appt.

CLEMENTIN DU PAPE CLEMENT 1999★

□ | 2.5 ha | n.c. | €15-23
92 (93) 94 |96| |97| **98** 99

It is not easy to succeed in marrying sweetness with liveliness, but this second wine which has a fine, elegant bouquet with toasty notes, succeeds whilst allowing its complexity to develop throughout the tasting. The agreeable, classically elegant **98 red** from Clement was also awarded a star.
♦ Bernard Magrez, Ch. Pape Clément, 33600 Pessac, tel. 05.57.26.38.38, fax 05.57.26.38.39, e-mail chateau@ pape-clement.com Y by appt.

CH. PICQUE CAILLOU 1998

■ | 14 ha | 51,066 | €15-23

Although ENITA is in the process of refurbishing a wine-growing estate in Mérignac, Picque Caillou is currently the only remaining vineyard in the commune. This fairly tannic, pepper-flavoured 98, a typical Cabernet, with a slightly severe finish, could be drunk young with a piperade but is also suitable for laying down.

Pessac-Léognan

GFA Ch. Picque Caillou, av. Pierre-Mendès-France, 33700 Mérignac, tel. 05.56.47.37.98, fax 05.56.97.99.37
by appt.
Calvet Paulin

CH. PONTAC MONPLAISIR 1998★
11 ha — 55,000 — €8-11
91 92 |94| 95 96 97 98

This cru, although just outside the city of Bordeaux, surrounded by its suburbs, manages to hold its own in the face of urban development. Its quality will attract supporters. This complex 98, with a bouquet ranging from leather to toast, is initially supple, almost sensual on the palate and then it develops as integrated oak and fruit harmonise. The successful **99 white** would go well with salmon, grilled with tarragon.

Jean et Alain Maufras, Ch. Pontac Monplaisir, 33140 Villenave-d'Ornon, tel. 05.56.87.08.21, fax 05.56.87.35.10
by appt.

CH. POUMEY 1998★
5 ha — 20,000 — €15-23

This cru, like Pape Clément, also owned by Bernard Magrez, is situated in Gradignan. It produces a wine that is characterful in its musky, charred bouquet and on the palate is unctuous, with a fullness that harmonises with its silky tannins.

Bernard Magrez, Ch. Pape Clément, 33600 Pessac, tel. 05.57.26.38.38, fax 05.57.26.38.39, e-mail chateau@pape-clement.com by appt.

CH. DE ROCHEMORIN 1998★
n.c. — n.c. — €8-11
85 86 88 89 90 91 92 |93| |94| 95 96 97 98

This wine, produced on an ancient fortified farm with its atmosphere of adventure, though still oaky, has a lovely, impressive bouquet of vanilla and toast. It is sufficiently structured to age for three or four years. It would drink well with quail served with spring vegetables. The **Rochemorin white 99**, floral and well balanced, receives one star.

SCEA Vignobles André Lurton, Ch. Bonnet, 33420 Grézillac, tel. 05.57.25.58.58, fax 05.57.74.98.59, e-mail andrelurton@wanadoo.fr by appt.

CH. DE ROUILLAC 1998★
7.5 ha — 18,000 — €15-23

Baron Haussmann entertained Napoléon III at Rouillac, serving him wines from this cru. It is not necessary to be a crowned head to be tempted by the integrated coffee, resin, ginger and clove bouquet of this wine or its fine-grained, oaky tannic structure.

SCS Vignobles Lafragette, Ch. de Rouillac, 33610 Canéjan, tel. 05.56.89.41.68, fax 05.56.89.41.68, e-mail vincent-painturaud@free.fr by appt.

CH. SEGUIN 1998
17 ha — 20,000 — €8-11

Considerable investment gave this vineyard a new lease of life in 1999. Of course this was of no benefit to this particular vintage. Red berries with notes of roasting coffee beans mingle in this rounded, well-structured wine with its good tannins.

SC Dom. de Seguin, chem. de la House, 33610 Canéjan, tel. 05.56.75.02.43, fax 05.56.89.35.41, e-mail chateau-seguin@wanadoo.fr by appt.

CH. SMITH HAUT LAFITTE 1999★★
11 ha — 45,000 — €30-38
88 89 90 91 92 93 94 |95| 96 |97| 98 99

Over the decades, Smith Haut Lafitte has carved out a solid reputation for the quality of its white wines. Think of the superb 98, last year's coup de cœur. This elegantly perfumed 99, mainly Sauvignon, supported by 5% Sauvignon gris and 5% Sémillon, has initial aromas of perfectly mature Sauvignon followed by more fruity notes as it opens. Only Gabriel Vialard, the excellent oenologist, knows how to make these perfumes constitute such a complex whole. The fleshy, very chewy wine is equally good on the palate, opening into a finish that indicates its ability to age well.

SARL D. Cathiard, 33650 Martillac, tel. 05.57.83.11.22, fax 05.57.83.11.21, e-mail smith-haut-lafitte@smith-haut-lafitte.co
by appt.

CH. SMITH HAUT LAFITTE 1998★★
Cru clas. — 44 ha — 110,000 — €30-38
61 62 70 71 72 73 75 80 82 83 85 86 87 |88| |89| |90| |91| 92 |93| 94 |95| 96 97 98

Though still characterised by the oak and slightly closed, it is already possible to predict that this wine will be extremely interesting in its maturity. Its youth, indicated by its colour, is confirmed in its lovely structure of long, rich, well-extracted tannins. The bouquet reveals leathery notes intermingled with ripe red berries.

SARL D. Cathiard, 33650 Martillac, tel. 05.57.83.11.22, fax 05.57.83.11.21, e-mail smith-haut-lafitte@smith-haut-lafitte.co by appt.

LES HAUTS DE SMITH 1998★
55 ha — 65,000 — €11-15

This second wine from Smith, with its red berries and blackcurrant notes, is supple and round with well-extracted tannins that guarantee its ageing potential without compromising its agreeable character. The Jury also commended the **99 Hauts de Smith white.**

SARL D. Cathiard, 33650 Martillac, tel. 05.57.83.11.22, fax 05.57.83.11.21, e-mail smith-haut-lafitte@smith-haut-lafitte.co by appt.

Médoc

Médoc occupies a place apart from the rest of the Gironde region, being virtually contained within the peninsula from which it gazes across the waters of the deep Gironde estuary. The Médoc and the Médocains may thus be seen as perfect illustrations of the Aquitaine temperament: they are both self-contained yet outward-looking. It is not unusual to find small family-run vineyards alongside grand, prestigious domains belonging to powerful French or foreign companies.

The Médoc vineyards (which represent only a part of the historically- and geographically-defined Médoc) occupy a strip more than 80 km (50 miles) long and 10 km (6 miles) wide. As a result, visitors can admire the great wine châteaux of the 19th century with their splendid, monumental wine stores and also make discoveries deep in the surrounding countryside. The terrain is very varied, offering flat, uniform landscapes around Margaux, hilly ridges towards Pauillac, and the entirely original world of the northern part of the Médoc, an unusual combination of terrestrial and maritime features. The area of the Médoc AOC covers about 15,408 ha (38,058 acres).

For those who enjoy investigating places off the beaten track, the Médoc is full of unexpected surprises. But its real riches lie in the gravelly terrain that slopes gently down towards the Gironde estuary. The soil is thin and poor in natural fertilisers, an excellent medium for the production of fine wines. In addition, the topography allows perfect drainage.

It has become usual to divide the Médoc into the Haut Médoc, from Blanquefort to Saint-Seurin-de-Cadourne, and the Bas Médoc, from Saint-Germain-d'Esteuil to Saint-Vivien. In the first area, six *Appellations Communales* produce the most famous wines. Virtually all of the 60 Crus Classés are from these appellations; however, five of them are labelled only as Appellation Haut-Médoc. The Crus Classés represent approximately 25% of the vineyard area, producing 20% of the wines and more than 40% of the income. In addition to the Crus Classés, the Médoc also produces a number of château-bottled Crus Bourgeois, which enjoy an excellent reputation. There are many Caves Coopératives in the Appellation Médoc and Appellation Haut-Médoc and also in three of the *Appellations Communales*.

The Médoc vineyard extends over 15,140 ha (37,396 acres) spread among eight AOCs, from north to south. There are two sub-regional appellations, Médoc and Haut-Médoc, comprising some 60% of the Médoc vineyards, and six *Appellations Communales*: Saint-Estèphe, Pauillac, Saint-Julien, Listrac-Médoc, Moulis en Médoc and Margaux (totalling 40% of the Médoc vineyards). The regional appellation is Bordeaux, as in the rest of the Bordeaux wine-growing area.

Cabernet Sauvignon was the traditional Médoc grape formerly; even so, it still accounts for 52% of the whole vineyard area. At 34%, Merlot is the second most important grape; its supple wines are of excellent quality and develop quickly so they can be drunk when still young. Cabernet Franc, which gives wine finesse, is planted on 10% of the area. The Petit Verdot and Malbec varieties are also planted, although they do not play a big role.

Médoc wines enjoy an exceptional reputation; they are among the most prestigious red wines produced either in France or in the rest of the world. They are noted for their beautiful ruby colour that takes on a tile-red hue

Médoc

Médoc

The whole of the Médoc vineyard, 15,408 ha (38,058 acres) has the right to the Appellation Médoc, although in practice it is used only in Bas Médoc (the northern sector of the peninsula, around Lesparre); the communes located between Blanquefort and

with age, and by their fruity aromas blending the spicy notes of Cabernet with hints of vanilla from the new oak barrels. Their tannic structure is dense and full, although the wines remain elegant and soft, and their perfect balance means they age remarkably well, softening without becoming thin and gaining in bouquet and flavour.

The Médoc and the Haut-Médoc appellations

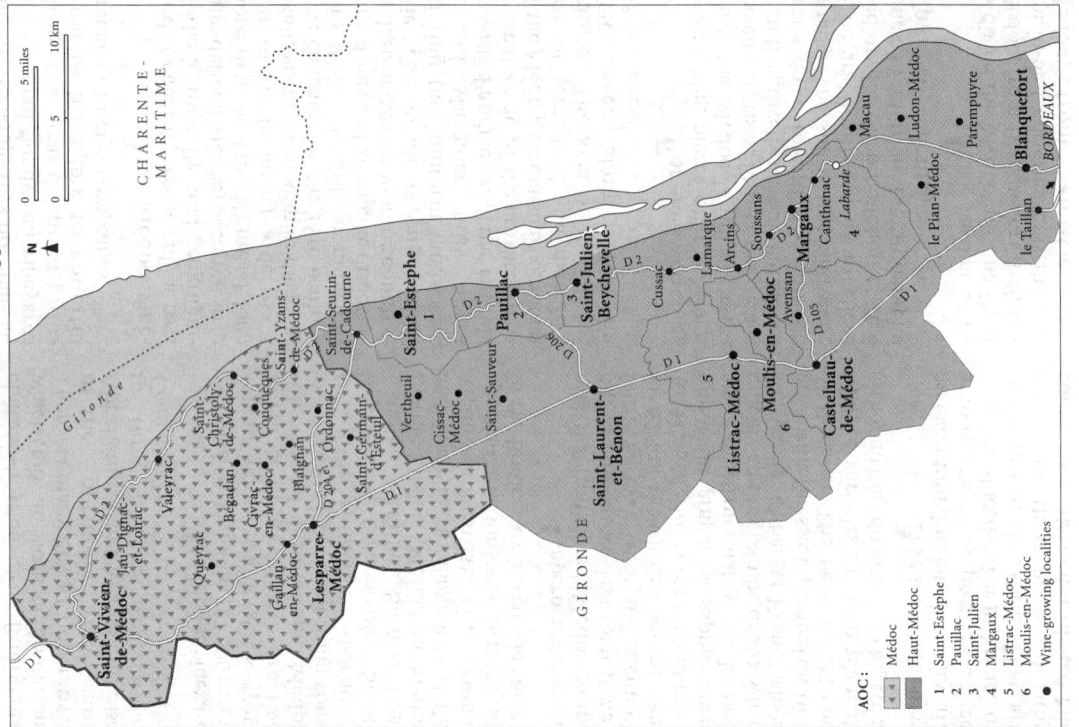

AOC:

- Médoc
- Haut-Médoc

1 Saint-Estèphe
2 Pauillac
3 Saint-Julien
4 Margaux
5 Listrac-Médoc
6 Moulis-en-Médoc
● Wine-growing localities

Saint-Seurin-de-Cadourne may apply for the Appellation Haut-Médoc or for a communal appellation within the area of their specific delimited territory. Nevertheless, Appellation Médoc remains the most significant, with an area of 5,039 ha (12,446 acres) and an output of 291,549 hl (7,696,894 gal) in 2000.

Noted for their intense colour, Médoc wines are made using a higher percentage of Merlot than those of Haut-Médoc and the *Appellations Communales*. The Merlot character makes itself felt in the fruity nose and round, mouth-filling flavour of these wines, some of which, grown on isolated, gravelly ridges, can develop great finesse and tannic depth.

CH. BELLEGRAVE Cuvée spéciale
Vieilli en fût de chêne neuf 1998★
■ Cru bourg.   2 ha   3,000   €11-15

This 20-ha (49-acre) estate has been in the same family for a century. Eighteen months maturation in new oak has had a very positive effect on this Cuvée Spéciale, a blend of half Cabernet and half Merlot. It has a delicate bouquet and powerful palate, with young but silky, flavourful tannins. It could be drunk now with game or cellared for three to five years. The Jury praised another 98 with 12 months oak ageing for its fresh, complex bouquet and sound structure. Predominantly Cabernet Sauvignon, grown on Garonne gravel, it too should be cellared.
↝ Christian Causseque, 8, rue de Janton, 33340 Valeyrac, tel. 05.56.41.53.82, fax 05.56.41.50.10 ☑ ⟙ by appt.

CH. BELLERIVE 1998
■ Cru bourg.   13 ha   20,000   €5-8

This surprisingly atypical 98, a blend of 50% Merlot, 35% Cabernet Sauvignon, 15% Cabernet Franc, cannot claim to rival previous vintages. The presentation is good, but the structure is still young; it could almost be mistaken for a New World wine, though perhaps it has more complexity. It should be decanted before serving.
↝ SCEA Ch. Bellerive-Perrin, 1, rte des Tourterelles, 33340 Valeyrac, tel. 05.56.41.52.13, fax 05.56.41.52.13 ☑
⟙ ev. day except Sun. 9am-6pm
↝ Melle Perrin

CH. BELLEVE 1998
■   2.5 ha   3,000

This cru, situated in Vertheuil, a village with a rich heritage, presented a blend of 70% Cabernet Sauvignon and 30% Merlot which does not need long cellaring. Its balance and truly elegant finish will make it pleasant to drink over the next five years.
↝ Luc Grimbert, 8, rue des Peupliers, Le Vignan, 33180 Vertheuil, tel. 06.08.92.45.91, fax 06.56.59.37.16 ☑ ⟙ by appt.

CH. BESSAN SEGUR
Elevé en fût de chêne 1998
■ Cru bourg.   38 ha   298,000   €8-11

This wine is a blend of 48% Merlot, 48% Cabernet Sauvignon with a touch of Cabernet Franc. The oak does not overwhelm the fruit despite six months barrel-maturation, which has given the bouquet noticeable toasty, grilled notes. This engaging, well-made complete 98 with coated tannins can be drunk young with grilled meat or kept for two or three years.
↝ Rémi Lacombe, Ch. Bessan Ségur, 33340 Civrac-en-Médoc, tel. 05.56.41.56.91, fax 05.56.41.59.06 ☑ ⟙ by appt.

CH. BOIS DE ROC 1998★
■ Cru artisan   10 ha   70,000   €5-8

85 86 89 90 92 93 96 97 98

Philippe Cazenave, an agricultural consultant in the 1960s, has been working this vineyard, planted on clay-limestone soil, for 30 years. Pleasingly, he includes Carménère (3%) and Petit Verdot (2%) among his varieties. This oaky 98 has the structure Médoc demands which will help it to develop nicely into a well-balanced wine in two to three years.
↝ GAF du Taillanet, Ch. Bois de Roc, 2, rue des Sarments, 33340 Saint-Yzans-de-Médoc, tel. 05.56.09.09.79, fax 05.56.09.06.29, e-mail boisderoc@aol.com ☑ ⟙ by appt.
↝ Ph. Cazenave

CH. BOURNAC
Elevé en fût de chêne 1998★★
■ Cru bourg.   13.5 ha   54,000   €8-11

This cru, which regularly appears in the *Guide*, is one of the safe bets in the appellation. Its very high quality *terroir* is in an area where limestone pebbles abound. An indication of its quality lies in its clear cellaring potential: it should be kept for five to six years. Deep coloured, it has a fruity bouquet with a thoroughly extracted tannic structure, and yet it remains elegant and fleshy.
↝ Bruno Secret, 11, rte des Petites-Granges, 33340 Civrac-en-Médoc, tel. 05.56.41.51.24, fax 05.56.41.51.24 ☑ ⟙ by appt.

CH. BREUILH 1998
■   4.2 ha   25,000   €8-11

Denis Bergey presented this wine, which though modest is agreeable in its perfume of red berries and vanilla and its fine, silky balance.
↝ Denis Bergey, 14, rte de Breuilh, 33340 Bégadan, tel. 05.56.41.53.62, fax 05.56.41.57.35 ☑

CH. DES BROUSTERAS
Vieilli en fût de chêne 1998★
■ Cru bourg.   25 ha   190,000   €8-11

The address of this cru, rue de l'Ancienne-Douane, is a reminder that Saint-Yzans is indeed a village of the Médoc *maritime*, situated on the edge of the estuary. This wine, light despite its good, deep-red colour, with complex aromas of blackcurrant, leather and vanilla, set off by very precise oak, should be at its best in about three years.

↘ SCF Ch. des Brousteras,
2, rue de l'Ancienne-Douane,
33340 Saint-Yzans-de-Médoc,
tel. 05.56.09.05.44, fax 05.56.09.04.21 ☑
☰ by appt.
↘ Renouil frères

CH. CANTEGRIC 1998★

Cru artisan 1 ha 6,000 €5-8

|95| |96| |97| 98

Although it modestly calls itself a Cru Artisan, this estate's ambition is evident in the quality of its production, a blend of 50% Cabernet Sauvignon, 10% Cabernet Franc and 40% Merlot, as this deep-coloured 98 with purplish highlights proves. Its complex, powerful, almost spell-binding bouquet of stewed red and black berries has substantial structure, supported by dense, velvety tannins.

↘ GFA du Ch. Cantegric,
10, av. Charles-de-Gaulle,
33340 Saint-Christoly-Médoc,
tel. 05.56.41.57.00, fax 05.56.41.89.36,
e-mail ch.cantegric@wanadoo.fr ☑
☰ by appt.
↘ Joany-Feugas

CH. CASTERA 1998★

Cru bourg. 63 ha 250,000 €11-15

|88| 89 |90| 95 96 97 98

The medieval origins of this château, surrounded by a beautiful park, overlooking Saint-Germain d'Esteuil, are obvious. This wine, from vines grown on clay-limestone, with its beautiful, slightly severe structure, is very far from being a light medieval *claret*. Its tannins and well-developed bouquet will enable it to age long enough for oak integration (three to four years).

↘ SNC Ch. Castéra,
33340 Saint-Germain-d'Esteuil,
tel. 05.56.73.20.60, fax 05.56.73.20.61,
e-mail chateaucastera@compuserve.com ☑
☰ by appt.

CH. CHANTELYS 1998★

Cru bourg. 8 ha 30,000 €11-15

Born a Courrian, Christine Braquessac bears two names synonymous with quality and authenticity in the Médoc, as this wine, with its youthful colour, testifies. Its bouquet of red berry, blackcurrant and black cherry notes is indicative of a wine that will develop into one with a substantial structure capable of cellaring for four or five years, perhaps longer if its development is carefully overseen. The generous, engaging second wine **Les Iris de Chantelys 98** should be drunk within three years.

↘ Ch. Chantelys, Lafon,
33340 Prignac-en-Médoc,
tel. 06.10.02.12.92, fax 06.56.09.09.07,
e-mail jfbraq@aol.com ☑ ☰ by appt.
↘ Christine Courrian

CLOS MALABUT 1998

4.15 ha 7,200 €5-8

This cru, situated on the headland on the western edge of Médoc, bears the full impact of the ocean. Its supple, full-bodied 98 is very agreeable on the palate. The characterful bouquet has plenty of fine, fruity, oaky notes. It should be drunk with poultry within two years.

↘ Nadine Wendling,
6, chem. des Séguelongue, Vensac,
33590 Saint-Vivien-de-Médoc,
tel. 05.56.09.49.16 ☑ ev. day
10.30am–12.30pm 5pm–7pm

COLLECTION PRIVEE D. CORDIER

Elevé en fût de chêne 1998 n.c. n.c. €5-8

This label from the house of Cordier may not be the very best, but it has plenty of character, both in its fruit-rich, berry bouquet and its well-integrated palate. It will be ready for drinking in one to two years.

↘ Ets D. Cordier,
53, rue du Dehez, 33290 Blanquefort,
tel. 05.56.95.53.00, fax 05.56.95.53.01,
e-mail florence.dobhels@cordier-wines.com

CH. DAVID 1998

Cru bourg. 10 ha 75,000 €8-11

This tannic wine, produced in Vensac, a village where beautiful windmill sails still turn and the soil has more sand than gravel, needs time to round out. A new generation runs the estate with this cru, and they have a new cellar. One to watch in the future.

↘ EARL Coutreau, Ch. David,
40, Grande-Rue, 33590 Vensac,
tel. 05.56.09.44.62, fax 05.56.09.59.09,
e-mail chateaudavid@online.fr ☑
☰ ev. day 9am–1pm 2pm–7pm; cl. during harvest.

CH. DES DEUX MOULINS 1998★

Cru bourg. 6 ha 30,000 €11-15

Situated on beautiful gravel overlooking the estuary, this cru benefits from quality *terroir* on which Merlot (60%), along with Cabernet Sauvignon, Cabernet Franc and Petit Verdot, grows. The wine-making takes advantage of this in producing a rich, full-bodied wine, with elegant, classy tannins. Not to be outdone, the complex bouquet, with its fruity, leathery notes, enlivened by a touch of oak, is equally good.

↘ SCEA Vignobles Moriau, 2, rte de Lesparre, 33340 Saint-Christoly-Médoc,
tel. 05.56.41.54.20, fax 05.56.41.37.63 ☑
☰ by appt.

LA GRANDE CUVEE DE DOURTHE 1998★★

n.c. n.c. €5-8

Grande Cuvée wines, produced by a partnership between a big *negociant-éleveur* and a number of vineyard owners, achieve their elegance through meticulous selection. The result of this, as far as this blend of 75% Cabernet Sauvignon and Cabernet Franc and

25% Merlot, matured in new barrels, is concerned, is exemplary. It has a lovely crimson colour with dark highlights, and a generous, full-bodied, concentrated palate, yielding a veritable explosion of flavours (vanilla, cocoa, liquorice, notes of burning, pepper and cloves ...). This a great Médoc classic that will go well with game.

☎ Dourthe, 35, rue de Bordeaux, 33290 Parempuyre, tel. 05.56.35.53.00, fax 05.56.35.53.29, e-mail contact@cvbg.com [V] [Y] by appt.

EPICURE 1998*

■ n.c.   20,000   [III] €11-15

This is a young label from Bernard Pujol, who for quite a long time managed Pape-Clément, and Hubert de Bouard, president of the Syndicat de Saint Emilion. It is a blend of 60% Merlot and 40% Cabernet Sauvignon. 'This is a fashionable wine', one taster wrote, meaning in effect that the bouquet is oaky. Nevertheless, it is well-balanced and the flavours should integrate given time.

☎ Bernard Pujol et Hubert de Bouard, 27, rue Rouillet, 33800 Bordeaux, tel. 05.57.35.12.35, fax 05.57.35.12.36, e-mail bus.grands.crus@wanadoo.fr [V]

CH. D'ESCOT 1998

■ Cru bourg.   18.8 ha   120,000   [III] €8-11

This cru is made up of two vineyards, one in Lesparre, the other in Saint-Christoly. Its austere 98, predominantly Cabernet Sauvignon (75%), has a lovely tannic structure which should ensure that it will develop well and become more rounded.

☎ SCEA du Ch. d'Escot, 33340 Lesparre-Médoc, tel. 05.56.41.06.92, fax 05.56.41.82.42 [V] [Y] ev. day except Sat. & Sun. 8.30am–12.30pm 1.30pm–5.30pm
☎ M. et Mme Rouy

CH. D'ESCURAC 1998

■ Cru bourg.   10 ha   60,000   [III] €11-15

Produced from vines grown on a beautiful gravel hilltop in the middle of the Queyrac marshes, this wine, a blend of 60% Merlot and 40% Cabernet Sauvignon, has a substantial structure to assist its development and allow its true character to appear over the next few years. In 2001, it had scents of flowers, sweet spices, red berries, toast and a warm finish. The second wine, **La Chapelle d'Escurac**, is a blend of the same varieties as the first, in equal parts. It will mature more quickly than

its elder brother. The Jury, captivated by its fineness and elegance, suggested serving it with pan-fried foie-gras accompanied by chanterelle mushrooms and buttered vegetables.

☎ Jean-Marc Landureau, Ch. d'Escurac, 33340 Civrac-en-Médoc, tel. 05.56.41.50.81, fax 05.56.41.36.48 [V] [Y] ev. day except Sat. & Sun. 9am–12 noon 2pm–5pm.

CH. FONTIS 1998

■ Cru bourg.   10 ha   40,000   [III] €11-15

This cru, well-sited at one of the highest points of the AOC (38 m/128 ft), benefits from quality *terroir*, gravel with some clay. This wine, a blend of Cabernet Sauvignon and Merlot in equal proportions, is still a little austere on the finish. It has spent 18 months in barrel and the lovely first impressions on the palate, following on from a beautiful bouquet with powerful notes of cocoa and red berries, are rather promising.

☎ Vincent Boivert, Ch. Fontis, 33340 Ordonnac, tel. 05.56.73.30.30, fax 05.56.73.30.31 [V] [Y] by appt.

CH. GARANCE HAUT GRENAT 1998*

■ 4.1 ha   30,000   [III] €8-11

Until 1997 this small family-run cru, situated on the clay-gravel *terroir* of Bégadan, had its wine produced at the co-operative. It now has a promising future as an autonomous concern. Its dark, intense-red 98 develops a lovely bouquet of crystallised red berries on a background of leather and spices. The oak is nicely controlled and integrated into a structure made up of solid constituents. Cellar until 2002 then drink for a further four or five years.

☎ Laurent Rebes, Ch. Garance Haut, 14, rue de la Reille, 33340 Bégadan, tel. 05.56.41.37.61, fax 05.56.41.37.61, e-mail l.rebes@free.fr [V] [Y] by appt.

GRAND SAINT-BRICE

Élevé en fût de chêne 1998*

■ 68.22 ha   111,900   [III] €5-8

The Saint-Yzans-Médoc co-operative, always consistent in quality, once more demonstrates its know-how with this wine. The oak (French and American) is present but discreet, providing good support for the bouquet and the structure. The very well-balanced, red berry aromas are nicely in harmony with the balance on the palate. This wine should be drunk in three to four years' time.

☎ Cave Saint-Brice, 33340 Saint-Yzans-de-Médoc, tel. 05.56.09.05.05, fax 05.56.09.01.92 [V] [Y] ev. day except Sat. & Sun. 8am–12 noon 2pm–6pm

CH. GREYSAC 1998*

■ Cru bourg.   60 ha   480,000   [III] €8-11

85 86 [88] [89] 91 93 94 [95] [96] [97] 98

This beautiful château, bought in 1973 by a group of friends, including Baron François de Gunzburg and Giovanni Agnelli, joined the

Union des Grands Crus nine years later, and is still worthy of its position, as confirmed by this characterful wine. The wine's structure harmonises with its upfront roundness, and the tobacco, liquorice and toast aromas make a dense, subtle whole.

• SA Domaines Codem, Ch. Greysac, 33340 Bégadan, tel. 05.56.73.26.56, fax 05.56.73.26.58 **•** by appt.

CH. GRIVIERE 1998★

| | Cru bourg. | 22 ha | n.c. | | | €11-15 |

| 93 | 94 | **95** | 96 | [97] | 98 |

This well-known cru, once owned by the Rozière family, prominent in the renaissance of the appellation in the 1970s, changed hands in 1991. This well-constructed blend, containing 58% Merlot, grown on clay-limestone soil, has no hesitation in showing off its charming aromas. The fine, natural perfumes mingling with notes of game, toast and spices accompany its pleasant palate development.

• Les Domaines CGR, rte de la Cardonne, 33340 Blaignan, tel. 05.56.73.31.51, fax 05.56.73.31.52, e-mail mguyon@domaines-cgr.com **•**

• ev. day except Sat. & Sun. 8.30am–12 noon 1.30pm–5pm; groups by appt.

CH. HAUT-BALIRAC
Vieilli en fût de chêne 1998★

| | | 2 ha | 7,000 | | | €5-8 |

Grapes from 2 ha (5 acres) of the 9-ha (22-acre) estate went into this special *cuvée*, a blend of 45% Merlot, 35% Cabernet Sauvignon, 15% Cabernet Franc, 3% Petit Verdot and a dash of Malbec grown on a soil of gravel mixed with sand. Barrel-matured for 12 months, this most attractive wine has an intense colour and a complex bouquet, showing both fruity and toasty notes. The palate is enjoyable from the start, but its richness promises a good development in the future.

• SCEA Haut-Balirac, 1, rte de Lousteauneuf, 33340 Valeyrac, tel. 05.56.41.55.93 **•** by appt.

• Cédric Chamaison

CH. HAUT BLAIGNAN
Elevage en barrique 1998

| | Cru artisan | 14.88 ha | 15,000 | | | €5-8 |

Bearing the title Cru Artisan, this wine, made from grapes grown on clay-limestone, reveals its Médoc origins in the quality of its tannic structure. Still a little severe, the tannin matches the power of the expressive bouquet, with its notes of overripe fruit, and suggests that this wine should be cellared for a short while.

• GAEC Brochard-Cahier, 19, rue de Verdun, 33340 Blaignan, tel. 05.56.09.04.70, fax 05.56.09.00.08 **•**

• ev. day 9am–12 noon 2pm–7pm

CH. HAUT BRISEY 1998★

| | Cru bourg. | n.c. | 90,000 | | | €5-8 |

| ⑧⑥ | 87 | **88** | **89** | 90 | 91 | 93 | 94 | **95** | 96 | 97 | 98 |

This estate was set up in 1983. Lovers of picturesque places will like the little harbour of Goulée, near the château. Anyone interested in archaeology should visit the Merovingian tombs, also nearby. This strongly expressive 98, a blend of 70% Cabernet Sauvignon and 20% Merlot, has powerful tannins that will integrate the skilfully handled oak. Its delicate perfume, with fine, spicy notes make for a pleasing wine to be cellared for three to four years. Apparently Christian and Corinne Denis also breed horses ....

• SCEA Ch. Haut Brisey, Sestignan, 33590 Jau-Dignac-et-Loirac, tel. 05.56.09.56.77, fax 05.56.73.98.36, e-mail hautbrisey@wanadoo.fr **•**

• by appt.

• Christian Denis

CH. HAUT-CANTELOUP
Collection 1998★★

| | Cru bourg. | 11 ha | 80,000 | | | €8-11 |

| 94 | 95 | [96| | [97] | 98 |

The harbour town of Saint-Christoly, with its sloping dock and custom house, clustered around its fairway, is one of the prettiest in the Gironde. This is the site of the cellars where this tremendously successful wine was produced. Its colour with violet highlights and expressive bouquet of ripe fruit, vanilla and coconut on a peppery background give great charm to its presentation. Structured and chewy, the palate holds its own right through to its long, well-balanced finish. This wine promises to age well and should be cellared for seven or eight years.

• SARL du Ch: Haut-Canteloup, 33340 Saint-Christoly-Médoc, tel. 05.56.41.58.98, fax 05.56.41.36.08 **•**

• by appt.

CH. HAUT-GARIN 1998

| | Cru bourg. | 6.5 ha | 11,000 | | | €5-8 |

| [93] | 94 | 96 | [97] | 98 |

Perhaps influenced by its somewhat nostalgic label, featuring a pair of oxen harnessed to a harvest cart, this wine joins the Médoc classics by virtue of the varieties in its blend, 60% of which is Cabernet Sauvignon, Cabernet Franc and Petit Verdot, its structure and its keeping potential. This does not prevent it from having a bouquet with plenty of person-ality, with fresh menthol notes complement-ing blackberry aromas.

↳ Gilles Huc, Lafon, 33340 Prignac-en-Médoc, tel. 05.56.09.00.02 ☑ Ⓨ ev. day 9am–12 noon 2pm–7pm; Sun. by appt.

CH. HAUT-GRAVAT 1998★

■ | 7.68 ha | 18,000 | €5-8

The cellar, a successful mix of wood and stainless steel, is so beautifully cared for that it is like going into a drawing-room, so it is not surprising that a well-made wine comes out of it. It is a blend of Cabernet Sauvignon, Caber-net Franc and Merlot in equal parts. The wood is, admittedly, still obvious but it is of a high quality; behind it can be detected a promising bouquet and silky tannic structure, giving excellent balance. In two to three years this will one of the most harmonious of wines.

↳ Sté Alain Lanneau, Ch. Haut-Gravat, 5, chem. du Clou, 33590 Jau-Dignac-et-Loirac, tel. 05.56.09.41.20, fax 05.56.73.98.06 ☑ Ⓨ by appt.

CH. HAUT-MYLES 1998

□ Cru bourg. | 12 ha | 80,000 | €8-11

This well-structured wine, produced on clay-limestone terroir, will improve on being cellared for three to four years, despite its already attractive personality and complex, intense bouquet. Its aromas of red berries, flowers and spices are a veritable gastronomic delight. One taster suggested serving it with coq au vin.

↳ Jean-Marc Landureau, Ch. d'Escurac, 33340 Civrac-en-Médoc, tel. 05.56.41.50.81, fax 05.56.41.36.48 Ⓨ ev. day except Sat. & Sun. 9am–12am 2pm–5pm

CH. HOURBANON 1998★

□ Cru bourg. | 5 ha | 30,000 | €5-8

This pretty estate is made up of a single parcel, on quality gravel terroir. Its deeply col-oured 98, a typical Médoc blend with only 24% Merlot, thanks to its structure has real ageing potential. The bouquet, currently dominated by oak following 18 months barrel-maturation, will open up in time.

↳ SC Delayat-Chemin. Ch. Hourbanon, 33340 Prignac-en-Médoc, tel. 05.56.41.02.88, fax 05.56.41.24.33, e-mail hugues.delayat@wanadoo.fr ☑ Ⓨ by appt.

CH. LABADIE 1998★★

|90| 92 93 94 |95| 96 97 98

□ Cru bourg. | 13.5 ha | 81,000 | €5-8

Y. Bibey, as well as being a prominent, like-able figure in the community, is also an excel-lent wine-grower. A particular achievement was the coup de cœur award last year for his 97, the product of a particularly difficult year. Yet again he proves his abilities with this well-constructed wine, made from grapes grown on clay-limestone, a blend of Merlot and Cabernet Sauvignon in equal propotions. A rich well-balanced structure supports this 98, which promises to develop very favourably, the more so given that its bouquet, with notes of roasting coffee beans, is every bit as attrac-tive as its palate flavours. When in Bégadan do not forget to admire the 11th-century apse in the church.

↳ GFA Bibey, 1, rte de Chassereau, Ch. Labadie, 33340 Bégadan, tel. 05.56.41.55.58, fax 05.56.41.39.47 ☑ Ⓨ by appt.

CH. LA CARDONNE 1998★

88 89 90 94 95 96 |97| 98

■ Cru bourg. | 86 ha | n.c. | €11-15

This cru, at more than 125 ha (309 acres), is one of the biggest estates in the area. Although it makes no claims to rival previous vintages, its singularly, well-rounded 98 with fruity, spicy flavours emphasises its agreeable character, right through to the finish.

↳ Les Domaines CGR, rte de la Cardonne, 33340 Blaignan, tel. 05.56.73.31.51, fax 05.56.73.31.52, e-mail mnguyon@domaines-cgr.com ☑ Ⓨ ev. day except Sat. & Sun. 8.30am– 12 noon 1.30pm–5pm; groups by appt.

CH. LA CHANDELLIÈRE Cuvée particulière Élevée en fût de chêne 1998★★

□ Cru bourg. | 21 ha | 35,000 | €8-11

This barrel-matured wine, 70% Cabernet Sauvignon and Cabernet Franc and 30% Merlot, grown on clay-limestone soil, lives up to the family's reputation. It has a beautiful, deep-purple colour and a seductive bouquet, whose lovely perfumes of ripe fruit (bilberry, redcurrant and morello cherry) are brought out by a light oakiness. Silky tannins develop around a rich structure on the palate, indicat-ing that the wine can either be drunk young with game or cellared for four or five years, even more, and then served with red meat.

↳ GAEC de Cazaillan, 16, rte des Petites-Granes, 33340 Civrac-en-Médoc, tel. 05.56.41.53.51, fax 05.56.41.53.51 ☑ Ⓨ by appt.
↳ Secret

CH. LA CLARE 1998★

□ Cru bourg. | 20 ha | 150,000 | €8-11

90 92 94 |95| 96 |97| 98

This lovely terroir is equal parts Garonnais gravel, Pyrenean gravel and clay-limestone. 'Is this a wine from the Boissenot school?', wondered one taster, and indeed this 98, has many assets. The first of these is a well-balanced structure which though a little tannic in the finish promises to develop well. The second is the charm of its bouquet. Although the full level of complexity is only just emerging, it can be glimpsed through its fruit and menthol notes, enriched by liquorice hints, which are of the highest standard.

↳ Paul de Rozières, Ch. La Clare, 33340 Bégadan, tel. 05.56.41.50.61, fax 05.56.41.50.69 ☑ Ⓨ ev. day 8am–6pm

Médoc

CH. LACOMBE NOAILLAC 1998★

■ Cru bourg.　15 ha　100,000　Ⅲ €8–11

The Lapalus, one of a small group of pioneers who relaunched viticulture both in Jau and at the tip of Médoc, are now amongst the main movers and shakers in the area. Their extremely successful 98, a happy marriage of fruit and oak, leaves a beautiful lingering in the memory. Its ruby colour, complex bouquet of cocoa and smoke lingering in the memory. Its ruby colour, complex bouquet and sound structure, suggest that this wine merits a period in the peace and calm of the cellar.

➽ SC Ch. Lacombe Noaillac,
Le Broustra, 33590 Jau-Dignac-et-Loirac,
tel. 05.56.41.50.18, fax 05.56.41.54.65,
e-mail info@les.trois.chateaux.com ▼

CH. LAFON 1998★★

■ Cru bourg.　8 ha　50,000

|93| ⑨⑤ 96 97 98

Nobody who knows Rémy Fauchey or his passion for the vine and its issue, will be surprised at the quality of this wine. This dark-red almost black 98, whose power and tannic richness burst out from the initial impression on the palate, is successful in every way from its colour to its long finish. The fresh, complex flavours, entirely in the same class, contribute in making this wine a classic Médoc for cellaring. It could be laid down for at least five years.

➽ Rémy Fauchey, Ch. Lafon,
33340 Prignac-en-Médoc,
tel. 05.56.09.02.17, fax 05.56.09.04.96 ▼
Ⲩ ev. day 9.30am–6pm

CH. LA HOURCADE

Vieilli en fût de chêne 1998★

■ Cru bourg.　15 ha　30,000　Ⅲ Ⅲ ♣ €5–8

96 97 98

If you are in Jau and want to find this cru, ask for Gino. Everyone in the village knows this former riding instructor who is mad about horses. This, however, does not stop him finding satisfaction in the art of viticulture. He even practises biodynamic cultivation. This wine, which introduces itself with a beautifully intense colour, with its promising bouquet with notes of spices and cloves and well-coated tannins on the palate, shows the integrity of the grower.

➽ Gino et Florent Cecchini,
Ch. La Hourcade, 7, rue de Noaillac,
33590 Jau-Dignac-et-Loirac,
tel. 05.56.09.53.61, fax 05.56.09.57.53 ▼
Ⲩ ev. day 9am–12 noon 2pm–8pm

CH. LALANDE DE GRAVELONGUE

La Croix Tête de cuvée 1998★

■　　3 ha　10,000　Ⅲ €15–23

This tiny prestige *cuvée* has been made traditionally; very deeply coloured it develops a forceful bouquet with notes of earthy roots. The full-bodied palate is backed by well-rounded tannins and well-integrated oak, resulting in a wine that can be either drunk young or cellared. The Jury also praised the **Cuvée Principale** (50,000 bottles), a well-constructed, rather more rustic wine.

➽ SCEA Lalande de Gravelongue,
19, rte de Troussas, 33340 Valeyrac,
tel. 05.56.41.59.68, fax 05.88.53.08.31,
e-mail gravelongue@libertysurf.fr ▼
Ⲩ by appt.

CH. LA PIROUETTE 1998

■ Cru bourg.　4 ha　25,000　Ⅲ €5–8

The reference to thoroughbreds on this label is not accidental: Yvan Roux is mad about horses, but this doesn't mean that he neglects his vines. The thoroughly reliable quality of his wine shows in its well-integrated tannins, which blend harmoniously with its fleshy silkiness.

➽ SCEA Yvan Roux, Semensan,
33590 Jau-Dignac-et-Loirac,
tel. 05.56.09.42.02, fax 05.56.09.42.02 ▼
Ⲩ by appt.

CH. L'ARGENTEYRE

Vieilles vignes Elevé en barrique 1998

■　　6 ha　38,000　Ⅲ €5–8

This wine is produced on an estate of 27 ha (67 acres) situated on gravel. Its youthful, blackcurrant and liquorice bouquet is rather austere, reminding us that Médocs benefit from being cellared for a time, to allow their true character to emerge.

➽ GAEC des vignobles Reich,
Ch. l'Argenteyre, Courbian, 33340 Bégadan,
tel. 05.56.41.52.34, fax 05.56.41.52.34 ▼
Ⲩ by appt.

CH. LA TILLE CAMELON

Elevé en fût de chêne 1998

■　　14.38 ha　29,460　Ⅲ €5–8

Although this simple, straightforward 98 is a cru wine, it was made by the Saint-Yzans co-operative. It is enhanced by a bouquet with pleasant notes of morello cherries.

➽ Cave Saint-Brice,
33340 Saint-Yzans-de-Médoc,
tel. 05.56.09.05.05, fax 05.56.09.01.92 ▼
Ⲩ ev. day except Sat. & Sun. 8am–12 noon 2pm–6pm

CH. LA TOUR DE BY 1998★

■ Cru bourg.　60 ha　500,000　▥ €11-15

82　83　85　86　|88|　|89|　|90|　91　|93|　|94|　95　96　|97|　98

This cru owes its name and emblem to its celebrated *tour à feu* (lighthouse), which dominates the Gironde, but it owes the reputation of its wines to the gravel hilltop on which it is situated. The *terroir* has consistently given good results, thanks largely to Marc Pagès, who today is preparing to hand over to his son-in-law. Here is a wine that confirms once again the quality of this estate, its elegant bouquet combines fruit with a note of undergrowth, whereas the structured and full-bodied palate shows serious ageing potential. It is not beyond the realms of possibility that this excellent 98 will earn a second star in two or three years time.

↬ Marc Pagès, Ch. La Tour de By, 33340 Bégadan, tel. 05.56.41.50.03, fax 05.56.41.36.10, e-mail la.tour.de.by@wanadoo.fr ☑ Ⴤ by appt.

CH. LAULAN DUCOS 1998★

20 ha　25,000　▥ €5-8

88　|89|　90　91　92　93　96　97　98

Here, Brigitte Ducos, who took over the running of the cru in 1997, has produced a delicately aromatic wine which marries tobacco and floral notes. This very typical, truly seductive 98 has a sound structure, which balances its oak with its body and fleshiness.

↬ SCEA Ch. Laulan Ducos, 4, rte de Vertamont, 33590 Jau-Dignac-et-Loirac, tel. 05.56.09.42.37, fax 05.56.09.48.40 ☑ Ⴤ by appt.
↬ Brigitte Ducos

CH. LE BERNARDOT 1998

■　12.27 ha　26,000　▥🕮

Maybe because they are not from a wine background, this Scottish/Japanese couple love talking passionately about wine – and they know what they are talking about, as this 98, a blend of 70% Cabernet Sauvignon and 30% Merlot, proves. The bouquet has blackcurrant and red berry perfumes and the palate has substantial tannins, which support the whole. It should be cellared for four to five years.

↬ Fujiko et John Robertson, Ch. Gaudin, 33590 Vensac, tel. 05.56.09.57.94, fax 05.56.73.98.87 Ⴤ by appt.

CH. LE BOURDIEU 1998★

■ Cru bourg.　23 ha　180,000　▥ €8-11

90　91　92　93　94　|95|　|96|　97　98

The engaging Baillys are wine-growers adept at bringing out the best in the appellation. Their seductive 98 was made with little fuss from grapes grown on the ridge surrounding the château. It has a simple, straightforward bouquet and a rich, well-constructed, well-balanced, finely oaked palate. Although currently a little closed, it should blossom in four to five years.

↬ Guy Bailly, Ch. Le Bourdieu, 1, rte de Troussas, 33340 Valeyrac, tel. 05.56.41.58.52, fax 05.56.41.36.09, e-mail lebourdieu@free.fr ☑ Ⴤ ev. day except Sat. & Sun. 9am–12 noon 2pm–6pm

CH. LE BREUIL RENAISSANCE

Excellence 1998★

■ n.c.　n.c.　▥ €8-11

This wine, which expanded rapidly in the 1990s, is situated less than 5 km (3 miles) from the picturesque little harbour of Goulée. This wine, currently pleasant, round, and fleshy with notes of roasting coffee beans, is still a little rustic. It needs to be cellared for two to three years to allow its character to emerge.

↬ Philippe Bérard, 6, rte du Bana, 33340 Bégadan, tel. 05.56.41.50.67, fax 05.56.41.36.77, e-mail phil.berard@wanadoo.fr ☑ Ⴤ by appt.

CH. LE PEY 1998★★

■ Cru bourg.　15 ha　105,000　▥ €8-11

This cru, extended by around 15 ha (37 acres) at the end of 2000, is carefully run by Claude Compagnet and his two sons. The reward for all their work is seen in this crimson wine, with ruby highlights. They have striven to highlight the oak in the notes of vanilla and toast in the bouquet but still there is sufficient structure to guarantee the ability to age well and to produce a well-balanced, well-made wine that will be ready in four to five years.

↬ SCEA Claude Compagnet, Ch. Le Pey, 33340 Bégadan, tel. 05.56.41.57.75, fax 05.56.41.53.23 ☑ Ⴤ ev. day except Sun. 9am–12 noon 2pm–6pm

CH. LES GRANDS CHENES

Cuvée Prestige 1998★★

■ Cru bourg.　7.16 ha　25,000　▥ €11-15

86　88　89　90　91　92　93　94　95　|96|　|97|　98

Bernard Magrez bought this cru, three years ago. It may be small but it has lovely gravel *terroir* and mature vines, consisting of 60% Cabernet Sauvignon, 5% Cabernet Franc and 35% Merlot. The quality of his production has been steadily improving. Here, he gives us an engaging wine with good oaky support. Its bouquet is particularly attractive, with toasty notes mingling with scents of undergrowth. The elegance on the palate makes it an agreeable wine already, yet suggests that it should be cellared for three or four years.

↬ SARL Ch. Les Grands Chênes, rte de Lesparre, 33340 Saint-Christoly-Médoc, tel. 05.56.41.35.69, fax 05.56.41.53.12 Ⴤ by appt.
↬ Bernard Magrez

CH. LES MOINES Prestige 1998★★

■ Cru bourg.　18 ha　140,000　▥ €8-11

86　88　89　90　91　92　|93|　94　95　96　|97|　98

One address to remember when visiting a Bordeaux vineyard is that of Claude

CH. LE TEMPLE 1998★
■ Cru bourg.   14 ha   100,000   **⫿⫿ ◆**   €8-11

Faithful to tradition, this cru seeks balance rather than simple power. The result is an agreeable wine with a bouquet of lovely violet, iris and liquorice notes. The well-coated, fleshy tannins lead naturally towards an elegant finish.

☛ Denis Bergey,
Ch. Le Temple, 33340 Valeyrac, tel. 05.56.41.53.62, fax 05.56.41.57.35, e-mail letemple@terre-net.fr ☑
Ⓨ ev. day except Sun. 8am–7.30pm

L'ÉTENDARD 1998
■   n.c.   15,000   **⫿⫿**   €5-8

Uni-Médoc have two cellars and replace a third of their 2,400 French oak barrels every year. A blend of 55% Cabernet Sauvignon and 45% Merlot, barrel-matured for ten months, this wine is simple and friendly, with agreeable aromas of cocoa and ripe fruit. The oak is nicely balanced.

☛ Uni-Médoc, 14, rte de Soulac, 33340 Gaillan, tel. 05.56.41.03.12, fax 05.56.41.00.66 ☑ Ⓨ by appt.

CH. LISTRAN 1998★
■ Cru bourg.   10 ha   50,000   **⫿⫿**   €5-8

This entirely replanted vineyard, set on a lovely gravel hilltop on the edge of Jau-et-Dignac, is very typical of the village of Jau-et-Dignac. Its beautiful, crimson 98, a blend of Merlot (39%), Cabernet Sauvignon, Cabernet Franc and Petit Verdot, lives up to its origins. Its youthfulness, indicated by its colour, is found again in its slightly burnt, red berry bouquet. With an immediate roundness, fragrance, full body and fleshiness, the palate will match dishes which feature duck, in two or three years.

☛ Arnaud Crété,
Ch. Listran, 33590 Jau-Dignac-et-Loirac, tel. 05.56.09.48.59, fax 05.56.09.58.70, e-mail crete@listran.com ☑
Ⓨ ev. day 9.30am–12.30pm 2pm–6pm; cl. 15 Sep.–15 Oct.

CH. LOIRAC Sélection 1998
■   6.54 ha   16,000   **⫿⫿**   €8-11

This wine, a blend of 70% Cabernet Sauvignon and 30% Merlot, has had 15 months barrel-maturation. A generous, unctuous palate supported by silky tannin follows its pleasant bouquet, with its fruity, spicy notes. It should be left for two or three years.

☛ SCA Ch. Loirac, 1, rte de Queyrac, 33590 Jau-Dignac-et-Loirac, tel. 06.08.46.68.21, fax 06.56.58.35.17, e-mail jllchtloirac@aol.com ☑ Ⓨ by appt.
☛ J.-L. Camelot

CH. LOUDENNE 1998★★
■ Cru bourg.   42 ha   280,000   **⫿⫿**   €11-15   (96)

⑧② 83 85 86 88 89 **90** 91 93 94 95 (96) 97 98

Loudenne enjoys an exceptional site on a mound of gravel on the edge of the Gironde. Its pink mansion, in British hands for over

Pourreau; equally likeable as he is passionate and meticulous, Claude is always very happy to show people around his estate. This could be an opportunity to taste this lovely Cuvée Prestige; a typical Medoc blend with 70% Cabernet Sauvignon. The bouquet, which develops fruity notes, and the palate are both well supported by its oak. Rich with a good body, this wine has the structure to be cellared for five to eight years which would facilitate complete integration.

☛ SCEA Vignobles Pourreau, 9, rue Château-Plumeau, 33340 Couquèques, tel. 05.56.41.38.06, fax 05.56.41.37.81 ☑ Ⓨ by appt.

CH. LES ORMES SORBET 1998★★
■ Cru bourg.   19 ha   100,000   **⫿⫿**   €11-15   (90)

78 81 83 85 86 88 89 (90) 91 92 93 94 95 96 97 98

Château Les Ormes Sorbet
MÉDOC
1998
CRU BOURGEOIS
APPELLATION MEDOC CONTROLEE
J. BOIVERT PROPRIETAIRE A COUQUEQUES, GIRONDE, FRANCE
MIS EN BOUTEILLE AU CHATEAU

The *terroir* of the village of Couquèques is so specific that it has given its name to a limestone bed. Guided by his oenologist, Jean Boissenot, Jean Boivert has again capitalised on this feature to reconfirm his fame. His majestic, crimson 98 is outstanding in its subtle, complex bouquet with fruity, smoky notes. The true spirit of Médoc wines is illustrated by the gentle and powerful structure. This is a bottle that should be forgotten in the cellar for about three or four years.

☛ Jean Boivert, Ch. Les Ormes-Sorbet, 33340 Couquèques, tel. 05.56.73.30.30, fax 05.56.73.30.31, e-mail ormes.sorbet@wanadoo.fr ☑ Ⓨ by appt.

CH. LES TUILERIES 1998★
■ Cru bourg.   11 ha   80,000   **⫿⫿**   €8-11

90 91 92 93 [94] **96** 98

Several of the old families of coopers have produced children with a vocation of wine-making, amongst these are the Dartiguenaves. This wine, a blend of Merlot, Cabernet Sauvignon and Cabernet Franc in equal parts, although still pronouncedly oaky, promises to develop well. Its bouquet, with its notes of menthol, its well-balanced initial impression on the palate and its unctuous, full-bodied personality are a good basis for this asssumption.

☛ Jean-Luc Dartiguenave, Ch. Les Tuileries, 33340 Saint-Yzans-de-Médoc, tel. 05.56.09.05.31, fax 05.56.09.02.43, e-mail chateau-les-tuileries@wanadoo.fr ☑
Ⓨ ev. day except Sat. & Sun. 9am–12 noon 2pm–6pm

120 years, has an extraordinary history, and it is hardly surprising that it produces distinguished wine. This 98, a blend of 60% Merlot and 40% Cabernet Sauvignon, is remarkable for its length and should be cellared for eight or ten years. It is a powerful wine, with velvety tannins and a rich first impression on the palate. The classy bouquet has notes of gingerbread, cinnamon and toast on a delicate background of jam. A real treat, it was only one vote short of a *coup de cœur*.

- SCS Ch. Loudenne, 33340 Saint-Yzans-de-Médoc, tel. 05.56.73.17.80, fax 05.56.09.02.87, e-mail chateau.loudenne@wanadoo.fr ☑ ⵑ ev. day except Sat. & Sun. 9.30am–12 noon 2pm–5pm
- Domaines Lafragette

CH. LOUSTEAUNEUF
Art et Tradition 1998★

■ Cru bourg.	10 ha	60,000	||| €8-11

93 94 |95| |96| 97 98

This wine, produced from selected grapes which have come from the estate's old vines, while well made, is currently slightly marred by its dominant oak but it will become elegant in three to five year's time.

- Bruno Segond.
2, rte de Lousteauneuf, 33340 Valeyrac, tel. 05.56.41.52.11, fax 05.56.41.38.52, e-mail chateau.lousteauneuf@wanadoo.fr ☑ ⵑ by appt.

MICHEL LYNCH 1998

■ n.c.		42,000	||| €8-11

As well as owning a number of famous crus, the Cazes are also *négociants*; currently they are in the process of expanding rapidly, with the construction of a new cellar in Macau. Michel Lynch is their label, Lynch Bages is their flagship. Well balanced, with an agreeable, ripe fruit, oaky bouquet, their Médoc could be drunk young or cellared for two to three years.

- SNC Michel Lynch, BP 66, 33250 Pauillac, tel. 05.56.73.24.15, fax 05.56.59.26.42

CH. MAREIL
Cuvée Prestige Elevé en fût de chêne 1998★

■	15 ha	25,700	||| €8-11

This cru, run by a firm woman with a lot of character, had its wine made by a co-operative for some time; this is the first vintage to have been made at the château. Though simple, it has promise. Well constructed around supple, silky tannins, it has savoury, black fruit flavours.

- EARL du Ch. Mareil, 4, chem. de Mareil, 33340 Ordonnac, tel. 05.56.09.00.32, fax 05.56.09.07.33, e-mail chateau.mareil@terre-net.fr ☑ ⵑ by appt.
- M. et Mme Brun

CH. DES MOULINS 1998

■ Cru artisan	9 ha	10,000	||| €5-8

Vertheuil was the site of a large abbey whose monks had several windmills, as its

splendid Romanesque church (a historic monument) continues to remind us. The name of this wine pays tribute to this. Despite the fact that its tannins would have benefited from being matured a little longer, this is still a classic Médoc. It will gain from being cellared for three or four years.

- Jean-Charles Prévosteau, Le Gouat, 33180 Vertheuil, tel. 05.56.41.95.20, fax 05.56.41.97.25 ☑ ⵑ by appt.

CH. NOAILLAC 1998

■ Cru bourg.	43 ha	203,000	||| €8-11

86 88 91 92 93 94 |95| **96** 97 98

This wine, produced by a vineyard with a high proportion of young vines, is situated on a gravel hilltop. First impressions are still austere, but by mid-palate the tannins are well-coated. It finishes with memories of delicate perfumes; red berries and an elegant touch of menthol.

- Ch. Noaillac, 33590 Jau-Dignac-et-Loirac, tel. 05.56.09.52.20, fax 05.56.09.58.75, e-mail noaillac@noaillac.com ☑ ⵑ by appt.

CH. NOURET
Elevé en fût de chêne 1998

■	5.37 ha	29,000	||| €5-8

Although this cru has its buildings in Civrac, its vines are in Bégadan. Still rather closed, this soundly structured wine, with aromas of liquorice, cocoa and blackcurrant is certainly interesting. Like any true Médoc, time is needed for the wine and wood to integrate.

- SCEA Ch. Nouret, 33340 Civrac-en-Médoc, tel. 05.56.41.50.40, fax 05.56.41.50.40 ☑ ⵑ ev. day 8am–6pm

CH. PATACHE D'AUX 1998★

■ Cru bourg.	43 ha	300,000	||| €11-15

82 83 **85** 86 88 **89** |90| 91 92 93 |94| 95 96 97 98

'Pataches d'aux' is a pretty name that takes us back to the days of stagecoaches. This wine, a blend of 20% Merlot, Cabernet Sauvignon, Cabernet Franc and 3% Petit Verdot, made from grapes grown on clay-limestone, has a lovely personality both in terms of its ripe red-berry bouquet and its palate with silky, well-integrated tannins. It should keep well.

- SA Patache d'Aux, 1, rue du 19-Mars, 33340 Bégadan, tel. 05.56.41.50.18, fax 05.56.41.54.65, e-mail info@les-trois-chateaux.com ☑ ⵑ by appt.

PAVILLON DE BELLEVUE 1998

■ n.c.		100,000	||| €8-11

Visitors interested in architecture will note that the renovated roofs of this co-operative have replaced the harsh reinforced concrete of the 1950s. Although the harsh tannins on the finish are still a little austere and need time to round out, this wine is, on the whole, fairly supple with agreeable, aromatic notes of red fruits and plums.

➤ SCAV Pavillon de Bellevue,
1, rte de Peyressan, 33340 Ordonnac,
tel. 05.56.09.04.13, fax 05.56.09.03.29 ▼
Y by appt.

CH. DU PERIER 1998★★

◼ Cru bourg.　7 ha　35,000
90 91 92 **93** 94 |95| 96 |97| **98**

This wine, 50% Merlot, has spent 12 months in barrels, 25% of which were new. Its ruby colour and powerful blackcurrant and red-berry perfumes signal youth. On the palate the initial impression of softness is replaced by a well-integrated tannic structure. This great classic, fleshy, long, substantial, rich Médoc must spend eight to ten years in the cellar.

➤ Bruno Saintout, Cartujac,
33112 Saint-Laurent-Médoc,
tel. 05.56.59.91.70, fax 05.56.59.46.13 ▼
Y by appt.

CH. PEY DE PONT

Vieilli en fût de chêne 1998★

◼ Cru bourg.　1.7 ha　14,000　€5-8

The ambitions of this cru, that withdrew from the co-operative system in 1998, are confirmed here, by this typical Médoc, a blend in which Cabernet Sauvignon (70%) dominates Merlot. The intense, brilliant colour delights the eye and the harmonious bouquet supports this, with its fine notes of prunes, blackcurrant and spices. On the palate, the tannins still need time (four to five years) to round out but guarantee the future of this wine, which bears witness to a work of great quality.

➤ EARL Henri Reich et Fils,
3, rte du Port-de-Goulée,
Trembleaux, 33340 Civrac-en-Médoc,
tel. 05.56.41.52.80, fax 05.56.41.52.80 ▼
Y ev. day 8am–12 noon 1.30pm–6pm

CH. PIGAUD 1998★

◼　4 ha　n.c.　€8-11

The bouquet of this wine, from the same producer as Château Bois de Roc, is also characterised by oak, with charred, almost burnt notes, but on the palate the oak integrates into a round structure, which supports pleasant little tannins. The whole is balanced and already a pleasant wine, although it could equally well wait a further two to three years.

➤ GAF Dom. du Taillanet, G. de Mour et Fils, 3, rue des Anciens-Combattants, 33460 Soussans, tel. 05.57.88.94.17, fax 05.57.88.39.14

CH. RAMAFORT 1998

◼ Cru bourg.　17 ha　n.c.　€11-15
96 97 |98|

Despite coming from the same producer as Château La Cardonne, this wine nevertheless, asserts its own personality in its blend of Cabernet Sauvignon and Cabernet Franc, in equal proportions. The result, a spicy, highly concentrated wine, will show itself at its best after light aeration and cellaring for two to three years.

➤ Les Domaines CGR,
rte de la Cardonne, 33340 Blaignan,
tel. 05.56.73.31.51, fax 05.56.73.31.52,
e-mail mguyon@domaines-cgr.com ▼
Y ev. day except Sat. & Sun. 8.30am–12 noon 1.30pm–5pm; groups by appt.

CH. RENE GEORGES

Cuvée Prestige Elevé en fût de chêne 1998★

◼　3 ha　5,500　€8-11

René Poitevin, a baker who came to viticulture when he took over the family business, remains a craftsman with a love for a job well done. How could anyone doubt this, looking at the brilliant colour of this Cuvée Prestige or savouring its lovely bouquet in which vanilla mingles harmoniously with black fruits? The dense, well-balanced, velvety palate is no less impressive. It should be cellared for five or six years. The **Château Poitevin**, again barrel-matured, was also specially mentioned.

➤ EARL Poitevin, 16, rue du 15-mars-62, 33590 Jau-Dignac-et-Loirac,
tel. 05.56.09.45.32, fax 05.56.04.45.32,
e-mail chateau.poitevin@voila.fr ▼
Y ev. day 8am–8pm

CH. ROLLAN DE BY 1998★★

◼ Cru bourg.　30 ha　150,000　€15-23
|89| 91 **93** |94| |95| **96** 97 **98**

True to form, this cru gives us a well-constructed wine that shows how well the combination of Merlot and gravel-clay has worked. This deep-coloured 98, still characterised by oak, has the necessary structure to assimilate it. Everything in this powerful, almost aggressive ensemble indicates that this wine will benefit from three to four years cellaring.

➤ Jean Guyon, Ch. Rollan de By,
33340 Bégadan, tel. 05.56.41.58.59,
fax 05.56.41.37.82, e-mail info@rollandeby.com ▼ Y by appt.

CH. SAINT-CHRISTOPHE 1998★

◼ Cru bourg.　30 ha　50,000　€11-15
94 |95| |96| 98

This wine, bearing the former name of the village, at that time the parish of Saint-Christoly, is a typical Médoc blend. Having been barrel-matured for 15 months it has plenty of character, with a bouquet in which gamey notes mingle with red berries. The tannins, still rather firm and vigorous, need time to round out, which will happen after several years.

➤ Patrick Gillet, Ch. Saint-Christophe,
33340 Saint-Christoly-Médoc,
tel. 05.56.41.57.22, fax 05.56.41.59.95 ▼
Y ev. day except Sun. 9am–6.30pm;
Sat. 9am–12 noon

CH. SAINT-HILAIRE
Vieilli en fût de chêne 1998

| | 8 ha | 60,000 | €5-8 |

Quercy, from its ancient windmills to its fortified church, has a discreet but not uninteresting heritage. Following its example, this wine is keeping its potential somewhat hidden at the moment but there are positive signs for the future; the fine, well-extracted tannins testify to a meticulous approach.

↬ EARL Adrien et Fabienne Uijtewaal, 13, chem. de la Rivière, 33340 Queyrac, tel. 05.56.59.80.88, fax 05.56.59.80.88
Y ev. day except Sat. & Sun. 9am–12 noon 2pm–6pm

CAVE SAINT-JEAN
Le Grand Art 1998★

| | n.c. | 50,000 | €5-8 |

The Saint-Jean cellar in Bégadan is one of the largest and most dynamic in Médoc, both in terms of quality control and supply traceability. This wine proves its seriousness with its beautiful, bright-red appearance and complex, expressive bouquet, in which oak mingles with red berries and violets. The supple, velvety, fleshy palate supported by rich, well-balanced tannins tells us clearly that it would be a pity to drink this wine until four or five years have passed.

↬ Cave Saint-Jean, 2, rte de Canissac, 33340 Bégadan, tel. 05.56.41.50.13, fax 05.56.41.50.78 Y ev. day except Sun. 8.30am–12.30pm 2pm–6pm (Fri. 5pm); Sat. 8.30am–12 noon

CH. SIPIAN 1998

| Cru bourg. | 25 ha | 90,000 | €8-11 |

This cru extending over 25 ha (62 acres) of Garonne gravel is planted with 60% Cabernet Sauvignon, 35% Merlot and 5% Petit Verdot. This vintage is a bright red wine with crimson highlights and a substantial structure. Although the finish is a little rough, it leaves memories of pleasant flavours in which pepper, smoke and touches of liquorice mingle. A wine to keep for three to four years.

↬ Vignobles Méhaye, SC Ch. Sipian, 28, rte du Port-de-Goulée, 33340 Valeyrac, tel. 05.56.41.56.05, fax 05.56.41.35.36, e-mail chateausipian@net-up.com
Y by appt.
B. et F. Méhaye

CH. TOUR BLANCHE 1998★

| Cru bourg. | 27 ha | 167,000 | €8-11 |

This wine, the work of Dominique Hessel, a striking Médoc personality, was produced from grapes grown on Garonne gravel and is entirely in keeping with the peninsula's spirit. Still somewhat closed, the bouquet gives hints of the increasing power to come. The fleshy, flavourful tannins on the palate confirm this impression.

↬ SVA Ch. Tour Blanche, 15, rte du Breuil, 33340 Saint-Christoly-Médoc, tel. 05.56.58.15.79, fax 05.56.58.39.89, e-mail hessel@moulin-a-vent.com
Y by appt.

CH. VERNOUS 1998

| Cru bourg. | 21.85 ha | 90,000 | €5-8 |

Owned by Roederer, the champagne house, this cru presented this well-constructed 98,

CH. TOUR CASTILLON 1998

| Cru bourg. | 10.47 ha | 6,500 | €5-8 |

'Everything comes to an end'. It takes a great deal of imagination when confronted by the paltry remains conserved on this estate, to recall that it is the site of one of the largest fortresses of medieval Aquitaine. Discreet oaky notes of vanilla and toast mingled with red berries agreeably support its wine, typical of the appellation, firm without being dense.

↬ EARL Vignobles Peyrusse, 3, rte du Fort-Castillon, 33340 Saint-Christoly-Médoc, tel. 05.56.41.54.98, fax 05.56.41.39.19
Y ev. day 9am–12 noon 1.30pm–6pm; Sat. & Sun. by appt.

CH. TOUR HAUT-CAUSSAN
1998★★

| 82 | 83 | 85 | 86 | [89] | [90] | 91 | 92 | 93 | 94 | 95 |
| 96 | 97 | 98 | | | | | | | | |

| Cru bourg. | 16 ha | 103,015 | €11-15 |

This cru, famous for the windmill, its emblem, benefits from quality *terroir*, a mix of gravel and clay-limestone and the passionate efforts of Philippe Courrian. Its elegant wine offers an open bouquet of grapes, redcurrants and prunes. Its chewiness and its tannins, both supple and firm, indicate that this wine should not be opened immediately; patience will be well rewarded. The second label **Château La Landotte 98**, a tasteful wine, commended by the Jury, is ready for opening now.

↬ Philippe Courrian, 33340 Blaignan, tel. 05.56.09.00.77, fax 05.56.09.06.26
Y by appt.

CH. TOUR PRIGNAC 1998

| Cru bourg. | 135.08 ha | 972,000 | €8-11 |

Produced by a vast estate, 250 ha (618 acres), owned by the Castel Frères group, this wine, barrel-matured for six months, has seductive aromas of warm oak, crushed strawberries and blackcurrant. Rounded and well balanced, it can be drunk immediately or else cellared for two to three years.

↬ Castel Frères, 21–24, rue Georges-Guynemer, 33290 Blanquefort, tel. 05.56.95.54.00, fax 05.56.95.54.20

TRADITION DES COLOMBIERS
1998

| | 132.1 ha | 100,000 | €8-11 |

This wine, both in its bouquet and on its palate, bears the mark of oak maturation. Its 'trendiness' will be appreciated by lovers of very oaky wines even when the fruit comes into its own.

↬ Cave Les Vieux Colombiers, 23, rue des Colombiers, 33340 Prignac-en-Médoc, tel. 05.56.09.01.02, fax 05.56.09.03.67
Y ev. day 8.30am–12.30pm 2pm–6pm

whose tannins, which developed throughout the tasting, will take another two or three years to round out.

☛ SCA du Ch. Vernous, Saint-Trélody, 33340 Lesparre, tel. 05.56.41.13.57, fax 05.56.41.21.12 ⵊ by appt.

CH. VIEUX PREZAT 1998

| ▉ | n.c. | 24,000 | ▥ €5–8 |

This wine, distributed by Cheval-Quancard, is simple but well made. Its pleasant bouquet has fine notes of soft red fruit in brandy. The wine will not need to be kept very long for it to be at its best.

☛ Cheval-Quancard, La Mouline, 4, rue du Carbouney, 33560 Carbon-Blanc, tel. 05.57.77.88.88, fax 05.57.77.88.99, e-mail chevalquancard@chevalquancard.com ⵊ by appt.

CH. VIEUX ROBIN

Bois de Lunier 1998★★

| ▉ Cru bourg. | 14.25 ha | 55,000 | ▥ ▥ ♦ €11–15 |

| 82| | 83 | **85**| | 86| | 87 | **98**| | **89**| | **90**| | **91** | |93| |
|94 | **95** | **96** | 97 | **98** |

Maryse and Didier Roba, heirs to a family tradition going back six generations, could have been happy simply maintaining the status of their cru. This is far from being the case, however, as they have proven, yet again, with their 'Bois de Lunier'. Their really enjoyable 98, which promises to age very well, will be at its best in eight to ten years. The astonishing richness of its bouquet, ranging from coffee and toast to quince, via apricot, strawberry and black fruits, is likely to yield some favourable comments in the cellar's visitors' book.

☛ SCE Ch. Vieux Robin, 33340 Bégadan, tel. 05.56.41.50.64, fax 05.56.41.37.85, e-mail contact@chateau-vieux-robin.com ⵊ
ⵊ by appt.
☛ Maryse et Didier Roba

Bordeaux wines was that of the Médoc in 1855 – that is, nearly a century before the other regions. This recognition arose directly from advances made in wine-growing in the Médoc area from the 18th century onwards. It was here in particular that the concept of quality came into being, along with new thinking about *terroirs* and crus, and an understanding that there was a relationship between the *terroir*, or specific vineyard, and the quality of a wine. Haut-Médoc wines are generous in character, with real finesse on the nose and, in general, good ageing qualities. They are best drunk at cool room temperature, and go as well with white meat and poultry as with the lighter sorts of game. Drunk young and served chilled, they can also accompany some fish dishes.

CH. D'AGASSAC 1998★★

| ▉ Cru bourg. | 23 ha | 120,000 | ▥ ▥ €11–15 |

| 95 | **96** | 97 | **98** |

Set between vines and marshes, an ancient fortified manor house whose towers reflect in the dark water of the pond-like moat, this cru found itself for a long period out of step with its prestigious past. When Groupama bought it in 1996 it regained its ranking. It is hard not to be seduced by the dark colour of this 98 and no easier to resist its delicate bouquet, with its notes of vanilla. The powerful, concentrated palate is equally pleasing; its tannins, as silky as one could wish, guarantee it will age well, although it is already pleasant.

☛ Château-d'Agassac, 15, rue du Château-d'Agassac, 33290 Ludon-Médoc, tel. 05.57.88.15.47, fax 05.57.88.17.61, e-mail contact@agassac.com ⵊ ⵊ by appt.
☛ Groupama

Haut-Médoc

Producing almost as much as the Appellation Médoc, with 250,453 hl (6,611,959 gal) in 2000 from 4,387 ha (10,836 acres), the Haut-Médoc wines have the edge on reputation, due in part to the presence of five Crus Classés grown within the AOC boundaries. Others are found in the six *Appellations Communales* contained within the Haut-Médoc area.

The first truly authoritative classification of

CH. D'ARCHE 1998★

| ▉ Cru bourg. | 9 ha | n.c. | ▥ ▥ €15–23 |

| 90| | 91 | 92 | 93 | |94| | |95| | **96** | |97| | |98| |

Distributed by Mähler-Besse, this wine may come as something of a surprise to loyal clients of the cru, in being able to be drunk fairly young. However, they won't be disappointed by its rounded personality and harmonious, aromatic, fruity qualities, which make it particularly pleasant.

☛ SA Mähler-Besse, 49, rue Camille-Godard, BP 23, 33026 Bordeaux, tel. 05.56.56.04.30, fax 05.56.56.04.59, e-mail france.mahler-besse@wanadoo.fr ⵊ
ⵊ by appt.

384

CH. ARNAULD 1998

■ Cru bourg.　25 ha　150,000　⦿ €11-15

82	83	85	⑧⑥				
97	98			91	92	93	95	96

Although the present church in the market town of Arcins only goes back to 1840, the parish is said to have had a priory on the route to Santiago de Compostela. Could this cru be a distant heir to this? This question should not hamper our enjoyment, in one or two years' time, of this delicate, well-balanced, well-structured wine with its fresh, menthol bouquet.

↪ SCEA Theil-Roggy, Ch. Arnauld, 33460 Arcins, tel. 05.57.88.89.10, fax 05.57.88.89.20 ☑ ᵞ ev. day except Sat. & Sun. 8.30am-12 noon 2pm-5.30pm

CH. D'AURILHAC 1998★★

■ Cru bourg.　11 ha　86,000　⦿ €8-11

96	97	98

This cru, consistent in quality and reasonable in price, two facts worth underlining, once more offers a pleasingly well-constructed wine. This powerful, aromatic 98 asserts its forceful personality through its lovely colour, extremely interesting bouquet, with notes of leather, strawberry and spices, and solid structure. Ample from the beginning, the palate promises to evolve favourably and age well. The **Château La Fagotte 98** from the same producer was praised.

↪ SCEA Ch. d'Aurilhac et La Fagotte, Senilhac, 33180 Saint-Seurin-de-Cadourne, tel. 05.56.59.35.32, fax 05.56.59.35.32 ☑

CH. BARATEAU 1998★

■ Cru bourg.　15 ha　90,000　⦿⦿ €6-11

85	86	[88]	[89]	[90]	[93]	[94]	95	96	[97]	98

In keeping with the spirit of the appellation, this cru does not neglect the so-called secondary varieties: Petit Verdot and Cabernet Franc (5% each), which complement the Cabernet Sauvignon and Merlot. Although its 98 is already agreeable thanks to its crystallised fruits bouquet, it could be kept for two to four years; its finish needs to become rounder even if the tannins are already supple.

↪ Sté Fermière Ch. Barateau, 33112 Saint-Laurent-Médoc, tel. 05.56.59.42.07, fax 05.56.59.49.91, e-mail cb@hroy.com ☑ ᵞ by appt.
↪ Famille Leroy

CH. BARREYRES 1998★

■ Cru bourg.　n.c.　546,300　⦿⦿ €11-15

95	[96]	97	98

An imposing château built around 1880 by Baron Dupérier de Larsan, presides over this cru, which extends over almost 100 ha (247 acres) and was acquired thirty years ago by the Castel family. Keeping the estate's image, the wine follows the best Médoc traditions, with its dense, deep colour announcing a well-constructed whole. Present but discreet oak supports the well-balanced, round structure.

CH. BEAUMONT 1998★

■ Cru bourg.　105 ha　500,000　⦿ €11-15

86	88	89	90	93	94		[95]	96	[97]	98

The architecture of this château is somewhat astonishing but equally so were some of its owners, amongst whom we find a Breton nobleman, a Honduran government minister, a Parisian industrialist, citizens of Milan, a lieutenant-colonel and a Venezuelan senator. This wine has just as much personality in its structure and toasty bouquet. Its ripe tannins with their oaky flavours indicate that it should be drunk between 2004 and 2008.

↪ SCE Ch. Beaumont, 33460 Cussac-Fort-Médoc, tel. 05.56.58.92.29, fax 05.56.58.90.94, e-mail chateau.beaumont@wanadoo.fr ☑
ᵞ by appt.

CH. BELGRAVE 1998★★

■ 5ème cru clas.　55 ha　245,000　⦿ €15-23

82	83	84	85	86	87	88	89	⑨⓪	91	92	93
[94]	95	96	97	98							

Shouldn't the name of this cru relate more to this region? Perhaps, but it does, in fact, refer to the London address of its former owners. However, it is really the quality of the gravel, nothing else, that allows the team, headed by Jacques Bégarie and Merete Larsen, once again to produce a wine such as this 98. Supported by full, powerful tannins, it proves to be a wine of real distinction in its fine, fruity and oaky bouquet. The whole is a beautiful piece of work that will drink excellently in four to five years. The second wine **Diane de Belgrave 98** does not rival the first, but was praised by the Jury for its fruitiness and integrated tannins.

↪ Dourthe, Ch. Belgrave, 35, rue de Bordeaux, 33290 Parempuyre, tel. 05.56.35.53.00, fax 05.56.35.53.29, e-mail contact@cvbg.com ☑ ᵞ by appt.

CH. BEL ORME

Tronquoy de Lalande 1998
■ Cru bourg.　26 ha　150,000　⦿ €11-15

95	[96]	97	98

The village of Saint-Seurin-de-Cadurne may not have any large, spectacular monuments but it is rich in small châteaux such as this one, whose architecture, so typical of the Gironde, was once attributed to Victor Louis. This distinctively aromatic 98, supported by a good tannic structure, still characterised by oak, will be ready to drink in two to three years from now.

↪ Jean-Michel Quié, Ch. Bel Orme, 33180 Saint-Seurin-de-Cadourne, tel. 05.56.59.38.29, fax 05.56.59.72.83 ☑
ᵞ by appt.

↪ Castel Frères, 21-24, rue Georges-Guynemer, 33290 Blanquefort, tel. 05.95.54.00, fax 05.06.95.54.20 ☑

Haut-Médoc

CH. BERNADOTTE 1998★

■ Cru bourg.　30 ha　n.c.　ⅢⅢ €15-23

Although this elegant château only dates back to 1860, the estate is named after the grandfather of the famous marshal of the First Empire. This wine benefits from lovely gravel *terroir*, and the Pichon Comtesse (Pauillac) team's know-how. It has fine, spicy flavours, supported by well-extracted tannins and a carefully balanced maturation that reveals its solid ageing potential.

➤ SC Ch. Le Fournas, Le Fournas-Nord, 33250 Saint-Sauveur, tel. 05.56.59.57.04, fax 05.56.59.57.04 ⴲ by appt.
➤ May-Eliane de Lencquesaing

CH. BERTRAND BRANEYRE 1998

■ Cru bourg.　13.9 ha　60,000　ⅢⅢ ♣ €11-15

Produced in Cissac, a viticultural village that is going through a real revival, this supple, agreeable wine has an interesting natural, friendly bouquet of cherries, blackcurrant and hazelnuts. Ludwig Cooreman bought the cru, which was in the family of its founder for two hundred years, in 1993.

➤ SARL Famille L. Cooreman, 13, rue de la Croix-des-Gunes, 33250 Cissac-Médoc, tel. 05.56.59.54.03, fax 05.56.59.59.46 ☑ ⴲ by appt.

LES BRULIERES DE BEYCHEVELLE 1998★

■　13 ha　84,000　ⅢⅢ €11-15

This wine, with its considerable presence, was produced by a Haut-Médoc vineyard belonging to Château Beychevelle, one of the most elegant and important of the Bordeaux mansions (AOC Saint-Julien). Dense crimson in colour it develops a lovely bouquet of ripe raisins. Still a little austere, the structure has good foundations, which call for the wine to be cellared for a further three to four years.

➤ SC Ch. Beychevelle, 33250 Saint-Julien-Beychevelle, tel. 05.56.73.20.70, fax 05.56.73.20.71, e-mail beychevelle@beychevelle.com ☑ ⴲ ev. day except Sat. & Sun. 10am–12 noon 2pm–5pm; groups by appt.
➤ Grands Millésimes de France

CH. DU BREUIL 1998★

■ Cru bourg.　16 ha　60,000　ⅢⅢ €8-11

The old, fortified château remains a repository of memories and, although now in ruins, it still generates a large number of mysterious stories. Its straightforward, powerful 98, by contrast, harbours no secrets; draped in a beautiful, dark colour it immediately announces its qualities, from the very expressive, musky bouquet to its structure, which signals its ability to age well. This is a great Haut-Médoc classic.

➤ Vialard, Ch. Cissac, 33250 Cissac-Médoc, tel. 05.56.59.58.13; fax 05.56.59.55.67, e-mail marie.vialard@ chateau-cissac.com ☑ ⴲ by appt.

CH. CAMBON LA PELOUSE 1998★★

■ Cru bourg.　32 ha　210,000　ⅢⅢ €8-11

The cellars of this ultra-modern, Californian-style winery bear witness to the effort that has gone into equipping it. That this has had a positive effect is amply demonstrated by this wine. The presentation is flawless, the intensity of the colour followed by a fine, complex bouquet with lovely notes of oak and little red and black berries. The full, powerful palate, supported by integrated tannins, finishes on memories of a successful whole, one that should be cellared for four or five years.

➤ Jean-Pierre Marie, SCEA Cambon La Pelouse, 5, chem. de Canteloup, 33460 Macau, tel. 05.57.88.40.32, fax 05.57.88.19.12 ☑ ⴲ by appt.

CH. CAMENSAC 1998★★

■ 5ème cru clas.　70 ha　285,000　ⅢⅢ €23-30

85　86 |88| 92　94 ⑨5 ⑨6 |97| 98

Camensac, wholeheartedly awarded a *coup de cœur* for its last three vintages, is situated on a hilltop of deep gravel. Its deep ruby colour, ripe fruits and prune bouquet and coated, slightly spicy tannic palate could well make a number of other crus jealous. This wine indisputably merits cellaring for a good five years.

➤ Ch. Camensac, rte de Saint-Julien, BP 9, 33112 Saint-Laurent-Médoc, tel. 05.56.59.41.69, fax 05.56.59.41.73 ☑ ⴲ by appt.

CH. CANTEMERLE 1998★★

■ 5ème cru clas.　67 ha　300,000　ⅢⅢ €23-30

81　82　83　⑧5 86　87 |88| |⑧9| |90| 91　92 |93| |94| 95　96　97　98

Although the grounds of this château, designed around 1850 by L.-B. Fischer, suffered a great deal of damage in the 1999 storm, it is still a beautiful estate. Its intensely coloured 98, still a little characterised by oak maturation, demonstrates it has sufficient resources to develop positively in the coming years. Its bouquet confirms its complexity on aeration and its long structure is supported by tannins that have no hard edges.

➤ SC Ch. Cantemerle, 1, chem. Guittot, 33460 Macau, tel. 05.57.97.02.82, fax 05.57.97.02.84, e-mail cantemerle@ cantemerle.com ⴲ by appt.
➤ groupe SMABTP

THE 1855 CLASSIFICATION REVIEWED IN 1973

PREMIERS CRUS (FIRST GROWTHS)
Château Lafite-Rothschild (Pauillac)
Château Latour (Pauillac)
Château Margaux (Margaux)
Château Mouton-Rothschild (Pauillac)
Château Haut-Brion (Pessac-Léognan)

SECONDS CRUS (SECOND GROWTHS)
Château Brane-Cantenac (Margaux)
Château Cos-d'Estournel (Saint-Estèphe)
Château Ducru-Beaucaillou (Saint-Julien)
Château Durfort-Vivens (Margaux)
Château Gruaud-Larose (Saint-Julien)
Château Lascombes (Margaux)
Château Léoville-Barton (Saint-Julien)
Château Léoville-Las-Cases (Saint-Julien)
Château Léoville-Poyferré (Saint-Julien)
Château Montrose (Saint-Estèphe)
Château Pichon-Longueville-Baron (Pauillac)
Château Pichon-Longueville-Comtesse-de-Lalande (Pauillac)
Château Rauzan-Ségla (Margaux)
Château Rauzan-Gassies (Margaux)

TROISIÈMES CRUS (THIRD GROWTHS)
Château Boyd-Cantenac (Margaux)
Château Cantenac-Brown (Margaux)
Château Calon-Ségur (Saint-Estèphe)
Château Desmirail (Margaux)
Château Ferrière (Margaux)
Château Giscours (Margaux)
Château d'Issan (Margaux)
Château Kirwan (Margaux)
Château Lagrange (Saint-Julien)
Château La Lagune (Haut-Médoc)
Château Langoa (Saint-Julien)
Château Malescot-Saint-Exupéry (Margaux)
Château Marquis d'Alesme-Becker (Margaux)
Château Palmer (Margaux)

QUATRIÈMES CRUS (FOURTH GROWTHS)
Château Beychevelle (Saint-Julien)
Château Branaire-Ducru (Saint-Julien)
Château Duhart-Milon-Rothschild (Pauillac)
Château Lafon-Rochet (Saint-Estèphe)
Château Marquis-de-Terme (Margaux)
Château Pouget (Margaux)
Château Prieuré-Lichine (Margaux)
Château Saint-Pierre (Saint-Julien)
Château Talbot (Saint-Julien)
Château La Tour-Carnet (Haut-Médoc)

CINQUIÈMES CRUS (FIFTH GROWTHS)
Château d'Armailhac (Pauillac)
Château Batailley (Pauillac)
Château Belgrave (Haut-Médoc)
Château Camensac (Haut-Médoc)
Château Cantemerle (Haut-Médoc)
Château Clerc-Milon (Pauillac)
Château Cos-Labory (Saint-Estèphe)
Château Croizet-Bages (Pauillac)
Château Dauzac (Margaux)
Château Grand-Puy-Ducasse (Pauillac)
Château Grand-Puy-Lacoste (Pauillac)
Château Haut-Bages-Libéral (Pauillac)
Château Haut-Batailley (Pauillac)
Château Lynch-Bages (Pauillac)
Château Lynch-Moussas (Pauillac)
Château Pédesclaux (Pauillac)
Château Pontet-Canet (Pauillac)
Château du Terre (Margaux)

THE SAUTERNES CRUS CLASSÉS OF 1855

PREMIER CRU SUPÉRIEUR (SUPERIOR FIRST GROWTH)
Château d'Yquem

PREMIERS CRUS (FIRST GROWTHS)
Château Climens
Château Coutet
Château Guiraud
Château Lafaurie-Peyraguey
Château La Tour-Blanche
Clos Haut-Peyraguey
Château Rabaud-Promis
Château Rayne-Vigneau
Château Rieussec
Château Sigalas-Rabaud
Château Suduiraut

SECONDS CRUS (SECOND GROWTHS)
Château d'Arche
Château Broustet
Château Caillou
Château Doisy-Daëne
Château Doisy-Dubroca
Château Doisy-Védrines
Château Filhot
Château Lamothe (Despujols)
Château Lamothe (Guignard)
Château de Malle
Château Myrat
Château Nairac
Château Romer
Château Romer-Du-Hayot
Château Suau

CH. DU CARTILLON 1998★

■Cru bourg. 45 ha 300,000 €8–11

This cru, on the boundaries of Moulis and Cussac, with its beautiful house, is situated on quality gravel. It puts this to good use with this wine, a typical Médoc blend. Seductively fresh in its red and black fruit, vanilla bouquet and well balanced on the palate this should be cellared for two to three years.

EARL Vignobles Robert Giraud, Ch. du Cartillon, 33460 Lamarque, tel. 05.57.43.01.44, fax 05.57.43.08.75, e-mail direction@robertgiraud.com V

DOM. DE CARTUJAC 1998

■Cru paysan 7 ha 25,000 €5–8

This wine, though still a little rustic, is, nevertheless, aromatically delicate in its black fruit and toast aromas. It would go well with rich poultry.

Bruno Saintout, SCEA de Cartujac, 20, Cartujac, 33112 Saint-Laurent-Médoc, tel. 05.56.59.91.70, fax 05.56.59.46.13 V
Y by appt.

CH. CHARMAIL 1998★★

■Cru bourg. 22 ha 107,000 €11–15

88 89 90 91 **92** 93 **|94|** |95| (96) **97** **98**

They say things come in threes and indeed Charmail has again been awarded a *coup de coeur.* Its brilliant, deep crimson colour is enough to understand why. The structure, with its ideal, ripe tannins, holds out promise and announces that this wine should be cellared for five to ten years. On the palate, a range of flavours pass from roasted roots to scorched notes, before revealing spices. The harmony, power and balance confirm excellent vinification and well-handled extraction.

Olivier Sèze, Ch. Charmail, 33180 Saint-Seurin-de-Cadourne, tel. 05.56.59.70.63, fax 05.56.59.39.20 V
Y by appt.

CHEVALIERS DU ROI SOLEIL 1998★

■ 5 ha 13,600 €5–8

Situated at the head of the access channel to the Port de la Lune, Cussac has a fort built by Vauban, whose lovely pediments honour Louis XIV and from which the co-operative wine-makers of the village took inspiration in naming their wine. This has not subdued the playful tone of this supple and pleasantly fruity wine, which owes more to the spirit of the Enlightenment than to the powerful strictness of the Classical age. The **Fort du Roy, Le Grand Art** was also praised by the Jury.

SCA les Viticulteurs du Fort-Médoc, 105, av. du Haut-Médoc, 33460 Cussac-Fort-Médoc, tel. 05.56.58.92.85, fax 05.56.58.92.86 V
Y by appt.

CH. CISSAC 1998★★

■Cru bourg. 36 ha 240,000 €15–23

Created in the 19th century by one of the present owner's ancestors, who brought several small crus together, this family-run estate has the advantage of being in an interesting cultural environment with Vertheuil Abbey and the 12th-century chancel of Cissac church nearby. This extremely subtle 98 is a perfect expression of a Médoc blend of 75% Cabernet Sauvignon, 20% Merlot and Petit Verdot. The powerful, elegant bouquet, playing on notes of fruit and vanilla, immediately reveals the nobility of this wine. Its rich, fleshy, well-structured palate calls for cellaring for three to four years.

Vialard, Ch. Cissac, 33250 Cissac-Médoc, tel. 05.56.59.58.13, fax 05.56.59.55.67, e-mail marie.vialard@chateau-cissac.com V Y by appt.

CH. CITRAN 1998★★

■Cru bourg. 90 ha 310,002 €15–23

88 **|89|** (90) **91** **92** **93** **|94|** (95) **96** **97** **98**

This 18th-century building inherited the moat that surrounds it from a small medieval castle, and its ancient origins are obvious. This very dense wine, discreetly perfumed with pleasant toasty, spicy notes, develops a substantial tannic structure. Fleshy, powerful and long, it asks for more time.

Antoine Merlaut, SA Ch. Citran, 33480 Avensan, tel. 05.56.58.21.01, fax 05.57.88.84.60, e-mail taillan@wanadoo.fr V Y by appt.

CH. CLEMENT-PICHON 1998★★

■Cru bourg. 25 ha 115,000 €11–15

85 **86** **88** **89** 90 94 |95| 97 **98**

The architecture of this château, inspired by the façade of Chenonceau, makes one think of the Loire but the wine is purely in the Médoc tradition. Dark red in colour, it is both tannic and soft. Well supported by oak, its bouquet of vanilla and toast, roundness, suppleness and velvetiness is seductive. It is richly structured and should be cellared for five or six years.

Clément Fayat, Château Clément-Pichon, 33290 Parempuyre, tel. 05.56.35.23.79, fax 05.56.35.85.23, e-mail info@vignobles.fayat-group.com V
Y ev. day except Sat. & Sun. 9am–1pm 2pm–6pm

CH. COLOMBE PEYLANDE

L'aïeul Léontin 1998

■   1 ha   5,000   (II) €11-15

This wine is produced from vines that are over 25 years old. Despite being slightly closed and still rustic, its balance and green-pepper and prune bouquet indicate that it should be lovely in three to four years' time.

☛ EARL Dedieu-Benoit, 6, chem. des Vignes, 33460 Cussac-Fort-Médoc, tel. 05.56.58.93.08, fax 05.57.88.50.81 ⊻

𝕐 by appt.

CH. DE COUDOT 1998

■ Cru artisan   5 ha   30,000   (II) €8-11

A newcomer to the *Guide*, this cru's wine is very typical of the appellation. The fine notes of red berries and vanilla in the bouquet and the evolving, powerful, ripe tannic palate make it a high-quality wine.

☛ SC du Ch. de Coudot, 9, imp. de Coudot, 33460 Cussac-Fort-Médoc, tel. 05.56.58.90.71, fax 05.57.88.50.47 ⊻

🍷 Blanchard

CH. COUFRAN 1998★

■ Cru bourg.   76 ha   500,000   (II) €11-15

| 82 | 83 | 85 | 86 | 88 | 89 | 90 | 93 | 94 | 95 | 96 | 97 |
| 98 | | | | | | | | | | | |

This wine, from the same producer as Château Verdignan, has very different *terroir* (dry, sandy gravel) and varieties (Merlot makes up 85%). The result is a wine with its own personality. Compared to the tight structure of the Verdignan, this wine has a rounded, charming side, which can be sensed both on the palate and in the bouquet, even if the fruitiness is, for the moment, still a little obscured by the oak.

☛ SCA Ch. Coufran, 33180 Saint-Seurin-de-Cadourne, tel. 05.56.59.31.02, fax 05.56.59.32.85

𝕐 by appt.

🍷 Miaihe

CH. DILLON 1998★

■ Cru bourg.   38 ha   160,000   (II) 𝟅 €8-11

| 82 | 83 | 85 | 86 | 88 | 89 | 90 | 91 | 93 | 94 | 95 |
| 96 | 97 | 98 | | | | | | | | |

Château Dillon is one of the last crus in the Blanquefort area to resist urban development, something it undoubtedly owes to its status as a *lycée agricole*. Its wine, highly typical in colour and bouquet, more than justifies this resistance. Supported by supple tannins, respectfully matured, it has very good ageing potential.

☛ Lycée agricole de Blanquefort, Ch. Dillon, BP 113, 33290 Blanquefort, tel. 05.56.95.39.94, fax 05.56.95.36.75, e-mail chateau-dillon@chateau-dillon.com

⊻ 𝕐 by appt.

🍷 Ministère de l'Agriculture

CH. DE GIRONVILLE 1998★

■ Cru bourg.   9 ha   63,000   (II) €8-11

Built on the site of an ancient fortified farmhouse, perhaps founded on a Gallo-Roman villa, this 18th-century château is associated with some disturbing legends. There is nothing frightening about its fresh, intensely coloured 98, however. The harmonious bouquet plays on notes of spices, toast and pepper. The palate is equally pleasant: supple and round with a good tannic structure. It should be cellared for two or three years. The **98 Château Belle-Vue**, a cru owned by the same producer, was commended by the Jury.

☛ SC de La Gironville, 69, rte de Louens, 33460 Macau, tel. 05.57.88.19.79, fax 05.57.88.41.79 𝕐 by appt.

CH. GRANDIS 1998★

■ Cru bourg.   9.6 ha   48,970   (II) €8-11

| 88 | 89 | 90 | 91 | 92 | 93 | 95 | 96 | 97 | 98 |

François Vergez, from a family that has been in Saint-Seurin since the 17th century, really knows the land in this area. He has succeeded in producing a happy marriage of oak with notes of vanilla and roasting coffee beans and fruit in his wine. Assertive tannins that should have rounded out in two to three years' time support the supple, well-constructed palate.

☛ François-Joseph Vergez, Ch. Grandis, 33180 Saint-Seurin-de-Cadourne, tel. 05.56.59.31.16, fax 05.56.59.39.85 ⊻

𝕐 by appt.

DOM. GRAND LAFONT 1998★

■ Cru artisan   n.c.   15,000   (II) €8-11

| 82 | 85 | 86 | 88 | 89 | 90 | 91 | 93 | 94 | 95 | 96 |
| 97 | 98 | | | | | | | | | |

This dark wine, made from grapes grown on beautiful gravel, comes from Ludon, a village in Haut-Médoc which has an interesting church with a fortified bell tower. It doesn't hide the fact that it has spent 24 months in barrels, 25% of which were new. The rich, oaky bouquet does not, however, obscure the fruit. The palate follows on in the same style: substantial, vinous, with an integrated, intense oakiness. Everything suggests it will keep well for three to four years.

☛ M. et Mme Lavanceau, Dom. Grand Lafont, 33290 Ludon-Médoc, tel. 05.57.88.44.31, fax 05.57.88.44.31 ⊻

𝕐 by appt.

CH. GUITTOT-FELLONNEAU 1998

■ Cru artisan   3.8 ha   21,000   (II) €8-11

From a country *auberge*, this wine is from 50% Merlot with the balance made up of two Cabernets. The deep ruby-red wine has a supple, well-structured palate which is in harmony with the fruity bouquet.

☛ Guy Constantin, Ch. Guittot-Fellonneau, 33460 Macau, tel. 05.57.88.47.81, fax 05.57.88.09.94 ⊻

𝕐 by appt.

CH. HANTEILLAN 1998

■ Cru bourg.   55 ha 408,000 🍴📖♦ €8-11

Compared with the deep colour of this wine, its bouquet may seem a little reserved. This delicacy, however, appears again in the soft character of the very expressive palate, aided by an almost silky structure. This agreeable wine should be drunk young.

➡ SA Ch. Hanteillan, 12, rte d'Hanteillan, 33250 Cissac, tel. 05.56.59.35.31, fax 05.56.59.31.51 ☑

🍷 ev. day except Sat. & Sun. 9am–12 noon 2pm–5.30pm; Fri. 9am–12 noon

CH. HAUT-BREGA 1998★

■   8 ha   48,000   📖 €8-11

This wine from Saint-Seurin, a blend of 65% Cabernet Sauvignon and Cabernet Franc and 35% Merlot, has good origins. Looking at its ruby colour, inhaling its fruity, spicy bouquet and appreciating its structure, this cannot be in doubt. Well made, its substantial character asserts its Haut-Médoc personality.

➡ Joseph Ambach, 16, rue des Frères-Razeau, 33180 Saint-Seurin-de-Cadourne, tel. 05.56.59.70.77, fax 05.56.59.62.50, e-mail cht.haut.brega@wanadoo.fr ☑

🍷 ev. day 10am–6pm; winter by appt.

CH. HAUT-LOGAT 1998

■ Cru bourg.   n.c.   n.c.   📖 €5-8

Marcel and Christian Quancard own this cru, which produced a substantially structured 98 supported by a broad palette of flavours (fruit, tobacco and liquorice). This will be at its best in two years' time. From the same domaine and same vintage, come **Château La Croix Margautot** and **Château Tour Saint-Joseph**, which have also received commendations.

➡ Cheval-Quancard, La Mouline, 4, rue du Carbouney, 33560 Carbon-Blanc, tel. 05.57.77.88.88, fax 05.57.77.88.99, e-mail chevalquancard@chevalquancard.com

🍷 by appt.

CH. HENNEBELLE 1998

■   10.5 ha 60,000   📖 €5-8

Coming from gravel and sandy gravel, this wine is a blend of 50% Merlot, 48% Cabernet Sauvignon and 2% Cabernet Franc. Robust and sappy, it has a number of assets, including a sound structure and a discreet but interesting bouquet of humus and undergrowth. This is an honest wine.

➡ Pierre Bonastre, 21, rte de Pauillac, 33460 Lamarque, tel. 05.56.58.94.07, fax 05.57.88.51.13

🍷 ev. day 8am–12 noon 3pm–7pm

CH. JULIEN 1998★

■ Cru bourg.   15 ha 70,000   📖 €8-11

The bouquet of this wine, from the same producer as Château Cap Léon Veyrin (Listrac) is characterised by its predominant variety (55% Merlot). Fleshiness, length and fullness on the palate all indicate that it will keep well.

➡ SCEA Vignobles Alain Meyre, Ch. Cap Léon Veyrin, 33480 Listrac-Médoc, tel. 05.56.58.07.28, fax 05.56.58.07.50 ☑ 🍷 ev. day except Sun. 9am–12 noon 2pm–6pm

KRESSMANN GRANDE RESERVE 1998★

■   n.c.   n.c.   🍴📖 €5-8

This barrel-matured wine, a blend of grapes from selected estates, has an agreeable bouquet with notes of vanilla, almond and jam. Its pleasant personality fits with its sound, full, fleshy structure and soft tannins. This is a well-made wine that should be laid down for three to five years.

➡ Kressmann, 35, rte de Bordeaux, 33290 Parempuyre, tel. 05.56.35.53.00, fax 05.56.35.53.29, e-mail contact@cvbg.com

🍷 by appt.

CH. LACOUR JACQUET 1998

■   5 ha 35,000   📖 €8-11

89 90 94 [95] [96] 97 98

This wine, a blend of 60% Cabernet Sauvignon, 35% Merlot, 3% Cabernet Franc and 2% Petit Verdot, comes from a cru which may, previously, have been on the route to Santiago de Compostela. It has an attractive, carmine colour and tannins, which though still rather severe, do not obscure the fruit. 'I very much like this wine, which should have rounded out in three to four years' time', wrote one taster.

➡ GAEC Lartigue, 70, av. du Haut-Médoc, 33460 Cussac-Fort-Médoc, tel. 05.56.58.91.55, fax 05.56.58.94.82 ☑

🍷 ev. day 10am–6pm

CH. LA FON DU BERGER 1998★

■   16 ha 60,000   📖 €8-11

Although, not particularly old, this estate, created in 1983, has done well with this tannic, full 98, whose complexity lasts throughout the tasting. It deserves to be cellared for two or three years.

➡ Gérard Bougès, Le Fournas, 33250 Saint-Sauveur, tel. 05.56.59.51.43, fax 05.56.73.90.61 ☑

🍷 ev. day 9am–12 noon 2pm–6pm

CH. LA HOURINGUE 1998

■ Cru bourg.   28 ha 150,000   📖 €11-15

This wine is from a vineyard behind the polo ground of Giscours, the estate that owns the cru. The blend, 55% Merlot, has an original bouquet of aniseed and menthol, mingled with red berries. Supple and agreeable, it should be at its best in two years' time.

➡ SAE Ch. Giscours, 10, rte de Giscours, 33460 Labarde, tel. 05.57.97.09.09, fax 05.57.97.09.00, e-mail giscours@chateau-giscours.fr

➡ by appt.

➡ Eric Albada Jelgersma

390

CH. LA LAGUNE 1998★★

■ 3ème cru clas.　n.c.　n.c.　€15-23

75　78　|81|　|82|　83　85　|86|　87　88　(89)　90
91　92　|93|　94　95　96　97　98

The mansion of this estate is recognised throughout the Médoc as a place not to be missed on any wine tour. It is also famous for its wine, a typical Médoc blend of 55% Cabernet Sauvignon, 15% Cabernet Franc and 10% Merlot. Barrel-matured, it has a strong, brilliant ruby colour. It asserts its personality in its chocolatey, toasty bouquet. Substantially built, supported by well-balanced tannins and with a beautiful body, it should be cellared for four to five years.

☛ Ch. La Lagune, 81, av. de l'Europe, 33290 Ludon-Médoc, tel. 05.57.88.82.77, fax 05.57.88.82.70 ☎ by appt.

☛ M. Ducellier.

CH. DE LAMARQUE 1998★

■ Cru bourg.　35.72 ha　180,000　€11-15

83　86　88　89　90　91　92　93　94　95　|96|　97　98

The little village of Lamarque, enlivened by the Bac de Blaye which flows through it, is right to be proud of its castle, whose towers have stood since the Hundred Years' War. The pretensions to longevity of its elegant, balanced 98 are much more modest. The fact that it has body and has been well matured should make it agreeable to drink in two years' time and be suitable for keeping for up to around ten years. Its younger brother, the **Château Cap de Haut 98**, praised by the Jury, is ready for drinking now.

☛ Gromand d'Evry, Ch de Lamarque, 33460 Lamarque, tel. 05.56.58.90.03, fax 05.56.58.93.43, e-mail chdelamarq@ aol.com ☎ by appt.

CH. LAMOTHE-CISSAC 1998

■ Cru bourg.　33 ha　200,000　€8-11

85　86　89　|90|　|94|　95　96　|98|

This cru, deep in the heart of the mysterious Médoc, is on the site of a Roman villa, as its topology and architecture confirm. Although still slightly dominated by the oak, this wine should be drunk young, in about a year, if its bouquet, with notes of undergrowth, brandied fruits, toast and cedar, is to be appreciated to the full. 'Well balanced from beginning to end', commented one taster.

☛ SC Ch. Lamothe, BP 3, 33250 Cissac-Médoc, tel. 05.56.59.58.16, fax 05.56.59.57.97, e-mail domaines.fabre@ enfrance.com ☎ by appt.

CH. LANESSAN 1998★

■ Cru bourg.　n.c.　280,000　€15-23

86　88　|90|　91　92　|93|　|94|　95　96　|97|　98

Château Lanesson, with its architecture, cellars, ancient family tradition dating back to 1793, coupled with its role in the development of wine tourism and *terroir*, is inseparable from the history of wine-growing in the Médoc, if not in France. Its 98, a blend of 75% Cabernet Sauvignon, 20% Merlot, 1.5% Cabernet Franc and 3.5% Petit Verdot, is faithful to its origins; classic in terms of its balance of finesse and power. It will be ready for drinking in three to four years' time. Produced on another estate, in the ownership of this family since 1962, the **Château de Sainte-Gemme 98**, was also commended by the Jury.

☛ SCEA Delbos-Bouteiller, Ch. Lanessan, 33460 Cussac-Fort-Médoc, tel. 05.56.58.94.80, fax 05.57.88.89.92, e-mail bouteiller@bouteiller.com ☎ ☎ ev. day 9am-12 noon 2pm-6pm

CH. LA PEYRE 1998★★

■ Cru artisan　n.c.　8,000　€5-8

|95|　96　|97|　98

The product of a vineyard where Merlot and Cabernet Sauvignon are grown in equal parts, this wine does nothing in half-measures. The colour is intense, the bouquet, powerful and full on the palate, though the fruit is still somewhat obscured by the oak. Behind this austerity it has ripe, long tannins confirming that it will benefit from cellaring for four to five years.

☛ EARL Vignobles Rabiller, Leyssac, 33180 Saint-Estèphe, tel. 05.56.59.32.51, fax 05.56.59.70.09 ☎ ☎ ev. day 10am-12 noon 2.30pm-7pm

CH. LAROSE-TRINTAUDON 1998★

■ Cru bourg.　53 ha　807,000　€8-11

81　82　83　85　86　87　88　89　|90|　91　92　93
|94|　95　96　97　98

The Bordeaux team that runs the vast estates belonging to AGF also run a Chilean cru, Las Casas del Toqui. Their Haut-Médoc, a blend of 60% Cabernet Sauvignon, 5% Cabernet Franc and 35% Merlot, is barrel-matured for 12 months. It has a sparkling bouquet of raspberry and blackcurrant on a firm oak background. The well-bred palate has refined tannins which give way to an elegant range of flavours. The **Château Larose Perganson 98**, a blend of 60% Cabernet Sauvignon and 40% Merlot, was awarded a star. This latter, also a very classic wine, will keep for longer than the first.

☛ SA Ch. Larose-Trintaudon, rte de Pauillac, 33112 Saint-Laurent-Médoc, tel. 05.56.59.41.72, fax 05.56.59.93.22, e-mail info@trintaudon.com ☎ ☎ by appt.

☛ AGF

CH. LA TOUR CARNET 1998★★

■ 4ème cru clas.　48 ha　240,000　€15-23

79　81　82　83　85　86　(88)　|89|　|90|　93　94
|96|　97　98

Readers will be familiar with La Tour Carnet and its almost one-thousand-year history; last March, Bernard Magrez invited some of the top celebrity chefs in France, Paul Bocuse, Francis Garcia, Pierre Troisgros along with the Gravellers, to its relaunch. Its 98 vintage is not a beneficiary but, nevertheless, has strong appeal in its dark livery with its deep-purple highlights. The bouquet is extremely fine with toasty, fruity notes and the palate seductively silky, thanks to its high-quality tannins.

➤ SCEA Ch. La Tour Carnet,
33112 Saint-Laurent-Médoc,
tel. 05.56.73.30.90, fax 05.56.59.48.54
Y by appt.
➤ Bernard Magrez

CH. DE LAUGA 1998★
■ Cru artisan   4.5 ha   30,000   ⅢⅠ €5-8

This is a true wine-growers' estate, where devotion to *terroir* can be felt. This well-structured wine has aromas of strawberries, red fruit and grapes accompanied by nicely developing oakiness. Sappy and robust, because it is still somewhat austere, it should be cellared for several years and then served with grilled meat.

➤ Christian Brun, 4, rue des Capérans,
33460 Cussac-Fort-Médoc,
tel. 05.56.58.92.83, fax 05.56.58.92.83 Ⅴ
Y ev. day 8am–7pm

CH. LE BOURDIEU VERTHEUIL 1998★
■ Cru bourg.   30 ha   200,000   ⅢⅠ €8-11

As this estate's name, which is probably of medieval origin, indicates, it has long been devoted to wine-growing. Its beautiful, deep 98 shows itself worthy of this rich heritage. It has a lovely, ripe-fruit bouquet, good structure, well-integrated tannins and a finish that completes the whole and confirms that it deserves cellaring for about five years.

➤ SC Ch. Le Bourdieu-Vertheuil,
33180 Vertheuil, tel. 05.56.41.98.01,
fax 05.56.41.99.32 Ⅴ Y by appt.

L'ERMITAGE DE CHASSE-SPLEEN 1998★
■   40 ha   250,000   ⅢⅠ €11-15

This wine, a blend of 35% Merlot, 65% Cabernet Sauvignon, was produced from vines in the Haut-Médoc appellation, specifically in the famous Moulis area. As well as an attractive deep-red colour, it has a lovely, red-and blackcurrant bouquet and a full, round palate, where the tannins harmonise with high-quality oak.

➤ Céline Villars-Foubet,
SA Ch. Chasse-Spleen, Grand-Poujeaux,
33480 Moulis-en-Médoc, tel. 05.56.58.02.37,
fax 05.57.88.84.40, e-mail jpfoubet@
chasse-spleen.com Y by appt.

CH. LIEUJEAN Cuvée prestige 1998
■ Cru bourg.   3 ha   15,000   ⅢⅠ €11-15

This wine, the product of selected plots of old vines – 3 ha (7 acres) out of 50 ha (124 acres) – is still characterised by its 12-months barrel-maturation but this has not spoilt the balance with the fruit.

➤ Ch. Lieujean,
33250 Saint-Sauveur-Médoc,
tel. 05.56.41.50.18, fax 05.56.41.54.65 Ⅴ

CH. LIVERSAN 1998★
■ Cru bourg.   25 ha   160,000

This cru, belonging to Prince Guy de Polignac, is currently worked by the GIE of Les Trois Châteaux. This is obviously a good arrangement, as testified by this wine whose dark-red colour gives a good indication of what is to follow. It develops a ripe raisins and toast bouquet and has a grip on the palate with its coated tannins.

➤ SCEA Ch. Liversan, 1, rte de Fonpiqueyre, 33250 Saint-Sauveur-Médoc, tel. 05.56.41.50.18, fax 05.56.41.54.65,
e-mail info@les-trois-chateaux.com Ⅴ
Y by appt.

CH. MALESCASSE 1998★
■ Cru bourg.   37 ha   160,000   ⅢⅠ €11-15

| 82 | 83 | 84 | 87 | **88** | **89** | **90** | 91 | 92 | 93 | **94** |
| 95 | 96 | 97 | 98 |

This château, built in 1830 in a typical Bordeaux style of architecture, clearly demonstrates just how much people used to care about displaying their wealth. Similarly, this 98 is showy with its intense, charred bouquet. Well-integrated tannins support the full, fleshy, generous palate. The Jury praised the second wine, **La Closerie de Malescasse 98**.

➤ Ch. Malescasse, 6, rte du Moulin-Rose, 33460 Lamarque, tel. 05.56.58.90.09,
fax 05.56.59.64.72, e-mail malescasse@
chateaumalescasse.com Ⅴ Y by appt.
➤ Alcatel Alstom

CH. DE MALLERET 1998
■ Cru bourg.   37 ha   120,000   ⅢⅠ €11-15

| 86 | 87 | **88** | **89** | **90** | 91 | 92 | 94 | **95** | **96** | |97| |
| |98| |

Its name, that of one of the big Longchamps races, reminds us that this château has owned a famous stud farm for a long time. This simple, well-constructed wine is not for keeping, as its ruby colour with its orangey fringe reveals, but it has youthful tannins and notes of peppers mingled with spices and fruit.

➤ SCEA du Ch. de Malleret,
Dom. du Ribet, 33450 Saint-Loubès,
tel. 05.57.97.07.20, fax 05.57.97.07.27
Y ev. day except Sat. & Sun. 9am–12 noon 2pm–5pm

CH. MAUCAMPS 1998★
■ Cru bourg.   18 ha   92,538   ⅢⅠ €11-15

| 82 | 83 | 85 | **86** | **88** | **89** | **90** | 93 | 94 | **95** | **96** |
| |97| | 98 |

Following in tradition, this cru presented a substantial, well-structured wine. The extraction has produced a blend that is still a little severe, despite soft initial impressions on the palate. This well-constructed 98, worthy of cellaring, has an interesting bouquet with warm notes of prunes, ripe grapes and morello cherries. It would go well with venison. The **98 Château Dasvin Bel Air** from the same producer was awarded a star, as was the **Château Laurac Les Vignes de Cabaleyran**. They both need time to open out.

• Ch. Maucamps, BP 11, 33460 Macau, tel. 05.57.88.07.64, fax 05.57.88.07.00 ☑
• by appt.
• Tessandier

CH. MEYRE Optima 1998★★

■ Cru bourg.　15.5 ha　15,000　■ ❙❙ ♦ €11-15 ☑

88 | 89 | 90 | 91 | 93 | 94 | [95] | 96 | [97] | 98

The Optima label, successor to the former owner's Cuvée Colette, is a characterful *cuvée de tête*. The assertiveness in the complex bouquet, with its notes of red berries, tobacco and leather, is carried onto the palate, where powerful tannins indicate that it should be cellared for five to six years.
• Ch. Meyre SA, 16, rte de Castelnau, 33480 Avensan, tel. 05.56.58.10.77, fax 05.56.58.13.20, e-mail chateau.meyre@wanadoo.fr ☑ ❙ Y ev. day except Sat. & Sun. 2pm-5pm; 1st Nov.-30th Mar. by appt.

CH. MICALET
Cuvée Réserve Elevé en fût de chêne 1998★★

■ Cru artisan　0.58 ha　3,600

Although not a star wine-tourist attraction, the cellar of this small cru has an air about it that plunges visitors into the estate's past. Its wine is, however, extremely up to date. It has a strong complex bouquet, created by the mix of aniseed with notes of roasting coffee beans, and develops a powerful, full structure. The tannins have the necessary strength to get the most out of the oak in three or four years.
• EARL Denis Fédieu, Ch. Micalet, 10, rue Jeanne-d'Arc, 33460 Cussac-Fort-Médoc, tel. 05.56.58.95.48, fax 05.56.58.96.85 ☑ ❙ Y ev. day except Sun. 9am-1pm 5pm-7pm; groups by appt.

CH. MILOUCA 1998★★

■ Cru artisan　1.5 ha　6,000　❙❙ €5-8

This cru, a small estate of 3 ha (7.5 acres) seeks to produce a wine in the pure Médoc tradition. It has succeeded brilliantly with this intense, maroon 98. It has an agreeable, complex bouquet and a well-balanced palate, with good ageing potential; long and elegant, it has all the characteristics of a true Haut-Médoc.
• Ind. Lartigue-Coulary, 33460 Cussac-Fort-Médoc, tel. 05.56.58.91.55, fax 05.56.58.94.82 ☑
• by appt.

CH. MOUTTE BLANC
Marguerite Déjean 1998★★

■ Cru artisan　0.36 ha　700

Micro-vineyard, micro-production but maxi-care; the marketing concept referred to as 'garage wine' that is comparable with the tiny plots found in Burgundy? It's a fair question, but should not detract from the merits of this full, long, well-constructed wine. Nearly black with as complex a bouquet as one could wish for – cherries, blackcurrant, resin and cedar – right through to its finish, all the signs point to this wine's excellent ageing potential.
• de Bortoli, 33, av. de la Coste, 33460 Macau, tel. 05.57.88.42.36, fax 05.57.88.42.36 ☑
• Y ev. day 10am-12 noon 2pm-7pm

CH. MURET 1998★

■ Cru bourg.　25 ha　80,000　■ ❙❙ ♦ €8-11 ☑

91 | 93 | 94 | [95] | 96 | 97 | 98

Here, this cru, close to the Brion archeological site, one of the natural curiosities of the Médoc, reconfirms its consistent quality. Its deep 98 develops a bouquet with generous notes of ripe, slightly crystallised fruits. Mouth-filling tannins agreeably coat the palate and the long finish confirms its ageing ability.
• SCA de Muret, Ch. Muret, 33180 Saint-Seurin-de-Cadourne, tel. 05.56.59.38.11, fax 05.56.59.37.03 ☑
• by appt.
• Boufflerd

CH. D'OSMOND 1998

■ Cru artisan　3.5 ha　20,000　❙❙ €5-8

This wine is produced by one of the small Crus Artisans that contribute to creating the personality of the viticulture in the Médoc. It is still a little rustic but sufficiently well constructed to be able to evolve well.
• Philippe Tressol, EARL des Gênes, 36, rte des Gênes, 33250 Cissac-Médoc, tel. 05.56.59.59.17, fax 05.56.59.59.17, e-mail chateaud'osmond@wanadoo.fr ☑
• by appt.

CH. PALOUMEY 1998★

■ Cru bourg.　13 ha　85,000　❙❙ €11-15

This wine, produced from young vines grown organically, certainly seems none the worse for this, neither in its very attractive colour nor in its pleasant vanilla bouquet nor in its supple, fine, long, well-balanced structure. The second wine, the **Château Haut-Carmaillet 98** was awarded the same rating.
• SA Ch. Paloumey, 50, rue Pouge-de-Beau, 33290 Ludon-Médoc, tel. 05.57.88.00.66, fax 05.57.88.00.67, e-mail chateaupaloumey@wanadoo.fr ☑
• by appt.

CH. PEYRABON 1998★

■ Cru bourg.　40.69 ha　125,185　■ ❙❙ €11-15

86 | 88 | [89] | [90] | 91 | 92 | 93 | [94] | 96 | [97] | 98

This cru, formerly owned by the Courcelles family, has belonged to the Millésima company since 1998. This typical 98 gets its character from emerging aromas of vanilla and caramel, a very agreeable palate and its tannic structure. It should be laid down for three or four years.
• SARL Ch. Peyrabon, 33250 Saint-Sauveur, tel. 05.56.59.57.10, fax 05.56.59.59.45, e-mail chateau.peyrabon@wanadoo.fr ☑
• by appt.

CH. PEYRE-LEBADE 1998★

■ Cru bourg.   n.c.   250,000   ⫿ €11-15

The mix of grape varieties, including 60% Merlot, in this vast vineyard may seem surprising but the generosity and palate structure, shown in the tasting, is definitely in the spirit of the Médoc. Since the bouquet, with its complex notes of ripe fruits is entirely up to the standard of the rest, this wine should age well. The other label, **Les Granges 98** is also very 'trendy', agreeable and flavourful. The Jury praised it.

➥ Cie vinicole Edmond de Rothschild,
Ch. Clarke, 33480 Listrac-Médoc,
tel. 05.56.58.38.00, fax 05.56.58.26.46,
e-mail chateau.clarke@wanadoo.fr ☑
➥ B. de Rothschild

CH. PONTOISE-CABARRUS 1998★

■ Cru bourg. ⫶   24 ha 180,000 ⫿ ♦ €8-11

85 86 88 89 90 92 93 94 95 96 |97| 98

François Tereygeol, a striking personality in Gironde viticulture, distinguished himself by introducing new formulae, such as VSI, *volume substituable individuel* (individual substitutable volume) to define quotas. However, he doesn't neglect his estate, as this highly coloured wine shows. Long and supported by well-judged oak, it exhibits seductive qualities in its ripe fruit bouquet.

➥ François Tereygeol,
Ch. Pontoise-Cabarrus, 33180 Saint-Seurin-de-Cadourne, tel. 05.56.59.34.92,
fax 05.56.59.72.42,
e-mail pontoise.cabarrus@wanadoo.fr ☑
⫯ ev. day except Sun. 9am–12 noon 2pm–5.30pm
➥ SCIA du Haut-Médoc

CH. RAMAGE LA BATISSE 1998★

■ Cru bourg.   33 ha 256,350 ⫿ ♦ €11-15

85 86 88 89 |90| 91 92 94 95 96 97 98

The serious approach to the running of this estate can be seen everywhere, from the level of financial investment to the involvement of the workforce in decision-making. It won a well-deserved *coup de coeur* for the intensely competitive 97 vintage and is honoured again for this rich and substantial 98 with its flawless tannic structure and truly agreeable, lovely, truffled, fruity bouquet. The Jury commended the second wine **Château du Terrey 98**.

➥ SCI Ch. Ramage La Batisse,
33250 Saint-Sauveur, tel. 05.56.59.57.24,
fax 05.56.59.54.14 ☑ ⫯ by appt.
➥ MACIF

CH. DU RAUX 1998★

■ Cru bourg.   16 ha 50,000 ⫿ ♦ €5-8

88 90 91 94 |95| |96| |98|

This cherry-red wine, which is produced from a vineyard with a high proportion of Merlot (60%), develops an agreeable, floral bouquet (violet and hyacinth). The palate is supple, round, elegant and extremely well constructed, with fine tannins.

➥ SCI du Raux, 33460 Cussac-Fort-Médoc,
tel. 05.56.58.91.07, fax 05.56.58.91.07 ☑
⫯ by appt.

CH. REYSSON

Réserve Vieilli en fût de chêne 1998

■ Cru bourg.   67 ha   66,600   ⫿ €11-15

This reserve *cuvée*, presented in numbered bottles, is still characterised by oak in the moment but should be very pleasant in one to two years. Remember the 96 was awarded a *coup de coeur* – it must be wonderful now. Mestrezat distributes this château's wine.

➥ SARL du Ch. Reysson, La Croix
Bacalan, 109, rue Achard, BP 154,
33042 Bordeaux Cedex, tel. 05.56.11.29.00,
fax 05.56.11.29.01 ⫯ by appt.

CH. SAINT-AHON 1998

■ Cru bourg.   30.5 ha 11,500 ⫿ ⫿♦ €11-15

This château, characterised by typical Napoléon III-style architecture, presented a well-made, agreeable, slender wine that aims at freshness and finesse. Good, well-integrated tannins make it ready to drink now and ensure it will age well for at least five years.

➥ Comte Bernard de Colbert,
Ch. Saint-Ahon, Caychac, 33290 Blanquefort,
tel. 05.56.35.06.45, fax 05.56.35.87.16 ☑
⫯ by appt.

CH. SAINT-PAUL 1998★★

■ Cru bourg.   20 ha 100,000 ⫿ €11-15

95 96 97 98

True to form, this cru presented a completely successful wine. Pure classicism predominates throughout the tasting. A complex toasty, red-berry, spicy, earthy bouquet, a soft first impression on the palate, silky, impressive tannins and plenty of fleshiness, all point to it being a great wine in four to five years, perhaps more.

➥ SC du Ch. Saint-Paul,
33180 Saint-Seurin-de-Cadourne,
tel. 05.56.59.34.72, fax 05.56.59.38.35 ☑
⫯ by appt.

CH. SÉNÉJAC 1998★★

■ Cru bourg.   n.c. 71,000   ⫿ ⫿♦ €11-15

89 90 91 |93| 94 95 96 97 98

This last vintage, produced under the auspices of Charles de Guigné, before Thierry Rustmann took over in 1999, has a garnet colour and complex bouquet, in which prunes and figs mingle with savoury notes. These and the balance on the palate, with a tannic structure that includes roundness, all augur well for its future development.

➥ M. et Mme Thierry Rustmann,
Ch. Sénéjac, 33290 Le Pian-Médoc,
tel. 05.56.70.20.11, fax 05.56.70.23.91
⫯ by appt.

LA BASTIDE DE SIRAN 1998★★

■   1 ha   7,200   ⫿ €8-11

Siran, like many crus in Margaux, has several plots of Haut-Médoc appellation. We owe this wine, with good ageing potential, to these, entirely planted with Cabernet Sauvignon. This is not for lovers of easy wines. High-quality tannins, a powerful bouquet of blackberry and blackcurrant and the excellent oak all point to a serious piece of work.

✒ SC du Ch. Siran,
Ch. Siran, 33460 Labarde,
tel. 05.57.88.34.04, fax 05.57.88.70.05,
e-mail chateau.siran@wanadoo.fr V
Ⓨ ev. day 10am–12.30pm 1.30pm–6pm
✒ William Alain Miailhe

CH. SOCIANDO-MALLET 1998 ★★★

■ 46 ha 230,000 ▦◗ €38–46

| [75] | 76 | 78 | 80 | 81 | [82] | 83 | 84 | 85 | 86 | 87 | [88] |
| [89] | [90] | 91 | [92] | [93] | 94 | [95] | [96] | 97 | [98] | | |

It may be hard to get to the top and even harder to stay there, but Jean Gautreau has done so for years. So there is no point concealing the pleasure this wine creates. It is exceptional, both in its bouquet and structure. Full, long, tannic and perfectly balanced, the palate flavour excellently rivals the explosion of aromas that mark the tasting. This wine will produce many positive comments in the cellar's visitors' book for five to six years and more. It is distributed by *négociants*. The second wine **La Demoiselle de Sociando-Mallet**, available on the estate, was also praised by the Jury. It could be drunk now, thanks to its silky, well-balanced tannins, but will become even better if cellared for two to four years.

✒ SCEA Jean Gautreau,
Ch. Sociando-Mallet,
33180 Saint-Seurin-de-Cadourne,
tel. 05.56.73.38.80, fax 05.56.73.38.88,
e-mail scea-jean-gautreau@wanadoo.fr
Ⓨ by appt.

CH. SOUDARS 1998 ★

■ Cru bourg. 22 ha 170,000 ▦ €11–15

| 82 | 83 | **85** | 86 | [89] | [90] | 91 | 92 | 93 | 94 | [95] |
| [96] | 97 | 98 | | | | | | | | |

This well-made wine is produced from a vineyard growing Merlot and Cabernet Sauvignon in equal quantities. Although its finish still needs to round out, the density of its bouquet of vanilla, cedar and fruits and the homogeneity of its structure indicate that it has everything it takes to make this happen.

✒ Vignobles E. F. Miailhe,
33180 Saint-Seurin-de-Cadourne,
tel. 05.56.59.31.02, fax 05.56.59.72.39
Ⓨ by appt.
✒ Eric Miailhe

CH. DU TAILLAN 1998 ★

■ Cru bourg. 24 ha 110,000 ▦◗▦ €8–11

The cellar and vat room of this cru, at the gates of the city of Bordeaux, is one of the oldest and most beautiful in the Bordeaux region. Its 98, from grapes grown on clay-limestone has an equally proud personality. A blend including 60% Merlot, its colour has as much depth as does its bouquet, with its notes of spices, roasting coffee beans, aniseed and menthol. It is both well rounded and tannic, with a substantial yet unaggressive structure, and would go well with game.

✒ SCEA Ch. du Taillan, 56, av. de La Croix, 33320 Le Taillan-Médoc,
tel. 05.57.47.00, fax 05.57.47.01,
e-mail chateau.taillan@wanadoo.fr V
Ⓨ by appt.

CH. TOUR DES GRAVES 1998

■ Cru bourg. 3 ha 20,000 €8–11

This straightforward blend, 65% Cabernet Sauvignon and 35% Merlot, is a supple wine with an agreeable flavour which creates an impression of freshness.

✒ Balleau, G. de Mour et Fils, 3, rue des Anciens-Combattants, 33460 Soussans, tel. 05.57.88.94.17, fax 05.57.88.39,14 V

CH. TOUR DU HAUT-MOULIN 1998 ★

■ Cru bourg. 32 ha 150,000 ▦ €11–15

| 78 | 79 | 81 | 82 | [83] | 84 | 85 | [86] | 87 | [88] | [89] |
| [90] | 91 | 92 | [93] | 94 | 95 | 96 | 97 | 98 | | |

A recognised safe bet in the appellation, this cru is traditional with this 50% Cabernet Sauvignon, 45% Merlot and 5% Petit Verdot blend. This dark ruby 98 will age well. Full, fleshy and substantial, with well-coated tannins, it highlights the bouquet's harmony, in which mingle toasty, oaky, spicy notes.

✒ SCEA Ch. Tour du Haut-Moulin, 7, rue des Aubarèdes, 33460 Cussac-Fort-Médoc, tel. 05.56.58.91.10, fax 05.56.58.99.30 V
Ⓨ by appt.
✒ Famille Poitou

CH. VERDIGNAN 1998 ★

■ Cru bourg. 50 ha 350,000 ▦ €11–15

| [86] | 88 | 89 | 90 | 93 | 94 | [95] | [96] | 98 |

This blend, 50% Cabernet Sauvignon, 5% Cabernet Franc and 45% Merlot, has been barrel-matured for 15 months. Its supporting tight structure will enable it to age well. Still closed and dominated by the oak, the bouquet, drawing on this structure, will open into fruity notes in three to five years.

✒ SC Ch. Verdignan,
33180 Saint-Seurin-de-Cadourne,
tel. 05.56.59.31.02, fax 05.56.81.32.35

Listrac-Médoc

This appellation corresponds exactly to the boundaries of the Listrac commune itself. The *appellation communale* is the furthest away from the Gironde estuary, and one of the few on the tourist routes to Soulac or from the Pointe-de-Grave. The *terroir* is most original, best described in geological terms as a hollowed-out dome in an anticlinal valley where erosion has created an inverse relief. To the west, along the edge of the forest, three ridges of Pyrenean gravel rise, their limestone slopes and subsoil giving good natural drainage. The centre of the AOC, the hollowed dome, is occupied by the Peyrelebade plain, which is composed of clay and lime soils. Finally, the ridges of the Graves by the Garonne rise to the east.

Listrac is a vigorous, robust wine, which has outgrown its former reputation for a somewhat crude quality. While some Listracs may be a little hard when young, the majority balance tannic strength with roundness. They all have a good capacity for keeping – 7 to 18 years, depending on the vintage. In 2000, the 663 ha (1,638 acres) produced 37,580 hl (992,112 gal).

CH. VIALLET-NOUHANT
Vieilli en fût de chêne 1998

■ Cru artisan   0.6 ha   4,800   ▦ €5-8

Alain Nouhant, a climatologist, was attracted to Bordeaux in 1993 when he chose to become a viticulturalist. This *micro-cuvée*, a blend of Cabernet Sauvignon and Merlot in equal proportions, is fairly trendy'. Its dark colour, rather closed bouquet and powerful, tannic palate signal a highly extracted wine. It should certainly be cellared.

➤ Alain Nouhant, 5, rue Jeanne-d'Arc, 33460 Cussac-Fort-Médoc,
tel. 05.57.88.51.43, fax 05.57.88.51.43,
e-mail alain.nouhant@libertysurf.fr ⟩
Ⴤ by appt.

CH. VICTORIA 1998★

■ Cru bourg.   80 ha   120,000   ▦ €11-15

The name is well chosen, as this château in some respects evokes the gentleness and elegance of English life in years gone by. Although characterised by oak, this wine shows a degree of softness in its tannic structure. It should be cellared for at least two or three years.

➤ SC Le Bourdieu, 33180 Vertheuil,
tel. 05.56.41.98.01, fax 05.56.41.99.32 ⟩
Ⴤ by appt.

CH. DE VILLAMBIS 1998

■ Cru bourg.   38 ha   n.c.   ▦ ⦿ €8-11

This wine, distributed by Dourthe and produced on a lovely estate, the Centre d'Aide par le Travail, is simple but well made. Its agreeable bouquet gives pride of place, on aeration, to ripe fruits, particularly black cherries.

➤ Ch. de Villambis, 33250 Cissac-Médoc,
tel. 05.56.35.53.00, fax 05.56.35.52.29,
e-mail contact@cvbg.com
➤ CAT Cissac-Médoc

CH. DE VILLEGEORGE 1998★

■ Cru bourg.   15 ha   67,800   ▦ €15-23

83 85 |86| 87 |89| |90| 93 94 95 **96** |97|
98

Although Merlot predominates in the mix of varieties grown on this estate, it is Cabernet Sauvignon that plays the major role in this blend. The result is a balanced, well-constructed wine that highlights fine notes of smoke and cherries. It is distributed by Bordeaux *négociants*. The Jury commended the cru's second wine, **Le Reflet de Villegeorge 98**, which is distributed by Lucien Lurton et Fils, Cadaujac.

➤ SC Les Grands Crus réunis, 2036 Chalet, 33480 Moulis-en-Médoc, tel. 05.56.58.22.01, fax 05.56.58.15.10, e-mail lgcr.wanadoo.fr
Ⴤ by appt.
➤ M.-L. Lurton-Roux

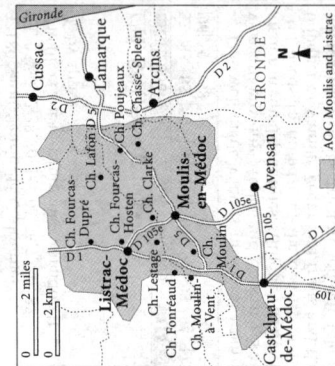

Moulis and Listrac

CH. CAP LÉON VEYRIN 1998★

■ Cru bourg.   15 ha   70,000   ⬛ €11-15
[90] 91 92 93 94 95 96 [97] 98

Although Merlot (60%) predominates in the mix of varieties, this elegant, classy 98 is less Merlot than in some previous years. It shows good ageing potential in its high-quality tannins and at the same time has a bouquet that is seductively complex, with scents of vanilla, truffles and raspberries. The structure will enable the oak, which still needs time, to integrate.
♠ SCEA Vignobles Alain Meyre, Ch. Cap Léon Veyrin, 33480 Listrac-Médoc, tel. 05.56.58.07.28, fax 05.56.58.07.50 ☑
Ⓨ ev. day except Sun. 9am-12 noon 2pm-6pm

CH. CLARKE 1998★★

■ Cru bourg.   54 ha   300,000   ⬛ €15-23
[94] 95 96 [97] 98
81 82 83 85 86 88 [89] [90] 91 92 93

Situated on limestone and clay-limestone terroir, this vineyard is original in its mix of varieties. It has a high proportion of Merlot (80%), with the rest Cabernet Sauvignon, which is evident this in its supple, flavourful 98, with its notes of red berries. Equally, its maturation, discernible in the touches of vanilla, is not hidden. Well balanced, well structured this wine needs to wait for one or two years before being enjoyed at its best.
♠ Cie vinicole Edmond de Rothschild, Ch. Clarke, 33480 Listrac-Médoc, tel. 05.56.38.38.00, fax 05.56.58.26.46, e-mail chateau.clarke@wanadoo.fr ☑
♠ Benjamin de Rothschild

CH. DONISSAN 1998

■ Cru bourg.   8.53 ha   43,000   ⬛ €8-11
81 82 83 85 86 [88] [89] [90] 91 92 [94] 96 [97] 98

This wine, from a modest estate, is pleasantly supple. Its bouquet with its delicate notes of red fruits is well supported by the oak. It will be pleasant if it is drunk when still young.
♠ Roger et Marie-Véronique Laporte, Ch. Donissan, 33480 Listrac-Médoc, tel. 05.56.58.04.77, fax 05.56.58.04.45 ☑
Ⓨ by appt.

CH. DUCLUZEAU 1998★

■ Cru bourg.   4.5 ha   36,000   ⬛ €8-11
81 (82) 83 85 86 [88] [89] [90] 91 92 [94] 96 [97] 98

This cru, listed in wine guides in the middle of the 19th century, still lives up to its past. Its remarkable gravel has given rise to this blend, 90% Cabernet Sauvignon, 10% Merlot, with its bouquet of incense and ripe fruits. Well rounded and fleshy, it nevertheless displays tannic notes and elegant oak. The flavour on the palate leads into a lovely caramelized, peppery finish.
♠ Mme J.-E. Borie, Ch. Ducluzeau, 33480 Listrac-Médoc, tel. 05.56.73.16.73, fax 05.56.59.27.37

GRAND L DU CHATEAU FONRÉAUD 1998

■ Cru bourg.   n.c.   50,000   ⬛ €11-15

This blend, 60% Cabernet Sauvignon, 30% Cabernet Franc and 10% Merlot, was presented by Château Fonréaud, one of the great houses of Bordeaux. Dark red in colour it has a fine, agreeable bouquet with woody notes and a round, pleasant palate.
♠ SA Mähler-Besse, 49, rue Camille-Godard, BP 23, 33026 Bordeaux, tel. 05.56.56.04.30, fax 05.56.56.04.59, e-mail france.mahler-besse@wanadoo.fr
Ⓨ by appt.

CH. FONRÉAUD 1998

■ Cru bourg.   33.55 ha   180,000   ⬛ €11-15
81 82 83 85 86 88 [89] [90] 91 92 [93]
95 96 97 98

This cru has remained typically Médocain in its mix of varieties: 60% Cabernet Sauvignon, 37% Merlot, 3% Petit Verdot. Its lovely estate, planted in gravel on a limestone base, has the same owner as Château Lestage. Its wine has a bouquet in which discreet fruit mingles with liquorice and musk. It needs to be cellared for two to three years to allow the tannins to round out.
♠ Ch. Fonréaud, 33480 Listrac-Médoc, tel. 05.56.58.02.43, fax 05.56.58.04.33 ☑
Ⓨ ev. day except Sat. & Sun. 9am-11.30am 2pm-5.30pm

CH. FOURCAS-DUMONT 1998★

■   30 ha   30,000   ⬛ €11-15

This château's wine was presented by Sichel. It is deep, brilliant colour attracts the taster. At the moment, the bouquet has oaky, vanilla tones, as does the palate, which displays a round, fairly fine structure and lengthy fruitiness. This is a wine that can be drunk young or cellared for three years to become more integrated.
♠ Maison Sichel-Coste, 8, rue de la Poste, 33210 Langon, tel. 05.56.63.50.52, fax 05.56.63.42.28

CH. FOURCAS DUPRÉ 1998

■ Cru bourg.   44 ha   250,000   ⬛ €11-15
(78) 79 81 82 83 [85] [86] [88] [89] [90] 91
92 93 [94] 95 96 [97] 98

This, one of the best-known crus in the appellation, grows Cabernet Sauvignon and Merlot in equal proportions, with 10% Cabernet Franc and 2% Petit Verdot, on gravel. It is a wine to be aged for some considerable time; at the time of the tasting, it was still closed, tannins dominating the whole, and so it should be left to 'sleep' in the cellar.
♠ Ch. Fourcas Dupré, 33480 Listrac-Médoc, tel. 05.56.58.01.07, fax 05.56.58.02.27 ☑ Ⓨ ev. day except Sat. & Sun. 8am-12 noon 2pm-5.30pm

Listrac-Médoc

CH. FOURCAS HOSTEN 1998★

■ Cru bourg. 46.67 ha 265,000 ▮▮▮ €11-15

75 78 81 |(82)| 83 85| 86| [88] [89] [90]
91 92 93 94| 95 96 97 98

This mansion, in the heart of the village at a stone's throw from the Romanesque church, still has vast grounds; this state of affairs is sufficiently rare to be worth mentioning. This deep-coloured wine, with an underlying note of vanilla thanks to its maturation, develops well, both in the bouquet and on the palate. It is an elegant wine that has enough power and length to suggest that it should be cellared for three or four years.

➤ SC du Ch. Fourcas-Hosten, rue de l'Eglise, 33480 Listrac-Médoc. tel. 05.56.58.01.15, fax 05.56.58.06.73, e-mail fourcas@club-internet.fr ▼
Y by appt.

GRAND LISTRAC
La Caravelle Elevé en fût de chêne 1998★

■ n.c. n.c. ▮▮▮ €11-15

This prestige *cuvée* from the co-operative, is faithful to the latter's traditions. Deep red in colour, it develops a bouquet with agreeable scents of liquorice and prunes before revealing a full and fleshy palate, which suggests that it will be ready to drink in about a year.

➤ Cave de vinification de Listrac-Médoc, 21, av. de Soulac, 33480 Listrac-Médoc, tel. 05.56.58.03.19, fax 05.56.58.07.22, e-mail grandlistrac@cave-listrac-médoc.com ▼ Y by appt.

CH. JANDER 1998

■ n.c. 50,000 ▮▮▮ €11-15

This is the first wine presented by this cru, which was created in 1998 from the merger of Château Listrac's vineyards with a part of those belonging to Sémillon-Mazeau. Dark with deep-purple highlights, its wine has a straightforward bouquet, which is still dominated by oak, and a sound structure. The relative austerity of its tannins confirms that patience will be required for it to reach maturity.

➤ SCE Les Vignobles Jander, 41, av. de Soulac, 33480 Listrac-Médoc, tel. 05.56.58.01.12, fax 05.56.58.01.57, e-mail vignobles.jander@wanadoo.fr ▼ Y ev. day 9am–12 noon 2pm–6pm

CH. LALANDE Cuvée spéciale 1998★

■ Cru bourg. 10.12 ha 25,000 ▮▮▮ €8-11

This estate, which has been in the same family for nine generations, includes Petit Verdot in its varieties. It distances itself from the frenzy of the media on this subject, knowing that authenticity is what matters. Its ruby 98 with its garnet highlights and expressive bouquet of blackcurrant, vanilla and roasting coffee beans is proof of this. The initial impression on the palate, its supple, round and substantial structure, needs time to round out. Another label from the same producer, marketed by Robert Giraud in Saint-André-de-Cubzac, the **Château Larosey 98**, is similar but entirely barrel-matured, and was also awarded a star.

➤ EARL Darriet-Lescoutra, Ch. Lalande, 33480 Listrac-Médoc, tel. 05.56.58.19.45, fax 05.56.58.15.62 ▼ Y ev. day 9am– 12 noon 2pm–7pm; Sun. by appt.

CH. LESTAGE 1998

■ Cru bourg. 39.73 ha 200,000 ▮▮▮ ♦ €11-15

81 82 83 85 [86] [89] [90] 91 92 |94| 95 96 97 98

This vast, ancient estate, presided over by its typical Napoléon III-style château, presented a wine with a delicate bouquet; though its tannins are still a little austere, it need not be cellared for more than three to four years.

➤ Ch. Lestage, 33480 Listrac-Médoc, tel. 05.56.58.02.43, fax 05.56.58.04.33 ▼ Y ev. day except Sat. & Sun. 9am–11.30am 2pm–5.30pm

CH. MAYNE LALANDE 1998★★

■ Cru bourg. 60,000 ▮▮▮ €11-15

85 86 88 [89] [90] 91 92 |94| |95| 96 97 98

Don't think that Bernard Lartigue set up home on the edge of the forest to get away from the world; he did it so that he could make agreeable wines such as this 98. The bouquet of spices, prunes, ripe fruit and oak fulfils all the promises of its ruby colour and palate. Fleshy, engaging and powerful all at the same time, it is a testament to careful work, which will keep very well.

➤ Bernard Lartigue, Le Mayne-de-Lalande, 33480 Listrac-Médoc, tel. 05.56.58.27.63, fax 05.56.58.22.41, e-mail b.lartigue@ terre-net.fr ▼ Y by appt.

CH. MOULIN DU BOURG 1998★

■ Cru bourg. 12 ha 80,000 ▮▮▮ €8-11

Once again this cru, part of Château Fourcas Doumont, has presented a wine that, though not particularly full, has a good structure and an agreeable bouquet with fruity notes.

➤ SCA Ch. Fourcas-Dumont, 12, rue Odilon-Redon, 33480 Listrac-Médoc, tel. 05.56.58.03.84, fax 05.56.58.01.20, e-mail info@chateau-fourcas-dumont.com ▼ Y ev. day 9am–12 noon 2pm–5pm; Sat. & Sun. by appt.
➤ MM. Lescoutra et Miquau

CH. PEYREDON LAGRAVETTE 1998★★

■ Cru bourg. 6.3 ha 35,000 ▮▮▮ ♦ €8-11

81 (82) 83 85 86 88 [89] [90] 91 92 93 |94|
|95| 96 97 98

This land has seemingly belonged to the same family since 6th November 1546, according to a title deed. Whatever the case, the quality of its dark-ruby 98 has a seductive bouquet of ripe fruits and oak and an equally seductive, fleshy and soft structure that is not overshadowed by its powerful and tannic side.

Margaux

Margaux is the only appellation name that is also a female first name. This is unlikely to have happened by chance. You have only to taste a glass of Margaux to savour the subtle relationship between wine and *terroir*.

Margaux wines are famous for keeping well, but they are equally distinguished for their suppleness and delicacy and for the elegance of their wonderfully fruity perfumes. They are the finest examples of generously tannic, soft wines to be proudly registered in the cellar book as wines for the long term.

The originality of Margaux comes from several different factors. Human input should not be underestimated. For example, Margaux growers have historically given less predominance to Cabernet Sauvignon than have the other great Médoc communes. Here, while still the minority variety, Merlot plays a more

---

● Paul Hostein, 2062 Médrac Est, Ch. Peyredon-Lagravette, 33480 Listrac-Médoc, tel. 05.56.58.05.55, fax 05.56.58.05.50 ▼
Ⓨ by appt.

■ CH. REVERDI Réserve personnelle 1998
□ Cru bourg. 15 ha n.c. £8-11

This wine, part of a numbered *cuvée*, doesn't hesitate to display its charms, a fact that makes it agreeable to drink right now. Black fruits and oaky notes permeate the bouquet whilst the no1 particularly strong palate develops into an elegant oakiness. The Jury also commended the **98 Château l'Ermitage**.

● SCEA Vignobles Christian Thomas, village Donissan, 33480 Listrac-Médoc, tel. 05.56.58.02.25, fax 05.56.58.06.56 ▼
Ⓨ ev. day except Sun. 9am–12 noon 2pm–6pm: cl. 20th Sep–20th Oct.

■ CH. SARANSOT-DUPRE 1998 ★★
□ Cru bourg. 15 ha 70,000 £11-15

70 71 75 78 81 **82** 83 85 **86** 88 |89| |90| 91 93 |94| **95** 96 97 **98**

Situated on predominantly clay-limestone *terroir*, this vineyard is 60% Merlot. This is noticeable in its wine, both in the red-berry bouquet and the supple, fleshy palate. Well balanced and well constructed, it deserves to be cellared for three or four years.

● Yves Raymond, Ch. Saransot-Dupré, 4, Grand-Rue, 33480 Listrac-Médoc, tel. 05.56.58.03.02, fax 05.56.58.07.64 ▼
Ⓨ ev. day except Sat. & Sun. 9am–12 noon 2pm–6pm

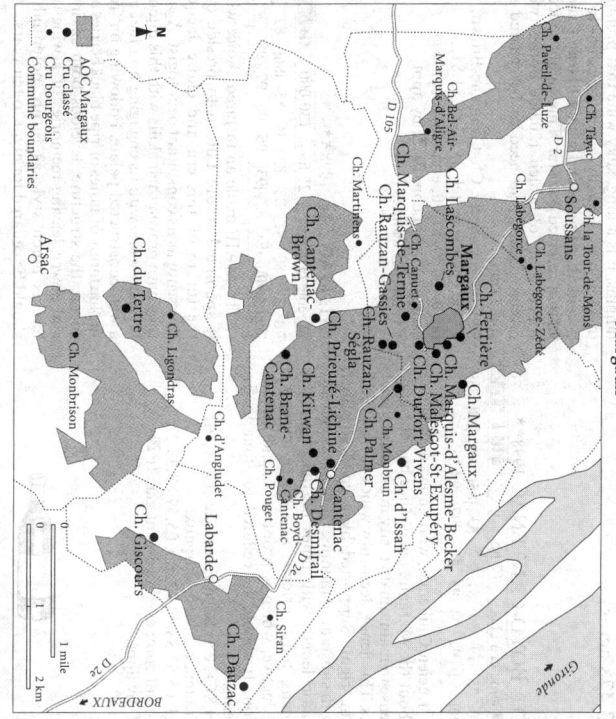

Map legend:
- AOC Margaux
- Cru classé
- Cru bourgeois
- Commune boundaries

Margaux

significant part. In addition, although the appellation stretches through five communes, namely Margaux and Cantenac, Soussans, Labarde and Arsac, only the soils that are best suited to growing vines for wine-making have been retained for the AOC. The result is a strikingly homogenous *terroir*, featuring a series of gravel ridges.

The ridges fall into two groups: on the periphery is a string of 'islands' separated by valleys, streams and boggy marsh; at the heart of the appellation, in the Margaux and Cantenac communes, what was formerly a plateau some 6 km (4 miles) by 2 km (1 mile) is now worn away into ridges by erosion. This is where the eighteen Grand Crus Classés of the appellation are grown.

The Margaux wines are remarkably elegant and should be drunk only with the finest-quality dishes such as Chateaubriand, duck, partridge or, in the local tradition, steak à la Bordelaise. In 2000 73,446 hl (1,938,974 gal) were produced from 1,408 ha (3,478 acres).

CH. BOYD-CANTENAC 1998 ★★

3ème cru clas.　17 ha　n.c.　€23–30
70 75 79 80 81 |82| 83 |85| 86 |88| |89|
|90| 91 92 94 95 |96| |97| 98

Lucien Guillemet, who knows a great deal about the Margaux *terroir*, has had the good sense to maintain diversity in his grape varieties. This dense, deep-ruby wine can only prove him right. Supported by a good structure, with substantial tannins, its richness and aromatic length with notes of roasting coffee beans, toast, brioche and spices (cloves) is seductive, which is proof of sound maturation. It should be cellared for four to five years.

↝ SCE Ch. Boyd-Cantenac et Pouget, Cantenac, 33460 Margaux, tel. 05.57.88.90.82, fax 05.57.88.33.27, e-mail contact@boyd-cantenac.fr ▶
Ⓣ by appt.

CH. BRANE-CANTENAC 1998 ★★

2ème cru clas.　90 ha　110,000　€38–46 |86|
70 71 75 76 78 79 81 82 83 84 85 |86| 97
87 |88| |89| |90| 91 92 93 94 95 |96| 97
98

This lovely estate has a modest house but a prestigious history; one of its owners, Baron de Brane, was one of the great viticultural figures at the beginning of the 19th century. He would have had no cause to be ashamed of this deep-coloured 98, made in the best Médoc tradition, whose ageing potential is as one could wish for, developing a bouquet that becomes increasingly full as it acquires oaky notes and tones of blackberry and blackcurrant. The Jury also favourably mentioned the **98 Baron de Brane**. It should be cellared for two or three years to allow its currently austere tannins time to integrate.

↝ SCEA du Ch. Brane-Cantenac, 33460 Cantenac, tel. 05.57.88.83.33, fax 05.57.88.72.51 Ⓣ by appt.
↝ Henri Lurton

CH. CANTENAC-BROWN 1998 ★★

3ème cru clas.　42 ha　144,000　€30–38
75 76 79 80 81 82 |83| 85 |86| |88| |89|
|90| 91 92 93 94 95 96 97 98

This château, a monumental brick-and-stone residence, houses a luxurious training centre for the executives of its owners, the Axa Group. It is a good bet that that they are not entirely indifferent to the contents of the cellar, of which this vintage is a good example, in its powerful, fine bouquet, and strong, elegant structure. Supported by high-quality tannins, it is a long, silky wine that promises to keep well. Equally tannic, needing to be decanted, is the second wine **Château Canuet 98** that received one star. This highly concentrated wine, of which 120,000 bottles were produced, will also need to be cellared for some time.

↝ Christian Seely, Ch. Cantenac-Brown, 33460 Cantenac, tel. 05.57.88.81.81, fax 05.57.88.81.90, e-mail infochato@cantenacbrown.com ▶ Ⓣ by appt.
↝ Axa Millésimes

CH. DAUZAC 1998 ★★

5ème cru clas.　25 ha　130,000　€30–38
78 79 80 81 82 83 84 85 |86| 87 |88|
|89| |90| 91 92 |93| 95 96 97 98

The MAIF made an inspired choice when it appointed André Lurton to preside over the future of this cru and chose Jacques Boissenot as its consultant oenologist. Again, they have proven their skills with this intense, brilliant wine, with its engaging bouquet and a well-constructed palate. Following on from the harmony of notes of ripe blackberries and cocoa, the structure develops both silkiness and power, leaving memories of a wine that has as much style as future potential. It should be cellared for eight to ten years.

400

CH. DEYREM VALENTIN 1998★

■ Cru bourg.　10 ha　65,000
75 76 81 82 **83** 85 |86| |88| |89| |90| 91
92 93 94 95 97 98　€15-23

Having crus such as Lascombes and Malescot as neighbours speaks volumes on the quality of the *terroir* of Deyrem. Its deep gravel has contributed an element of its elegance to the garnet colour and the bouquet of this well-structured 98, which is supported by dense but nicely ripe tannins that are elegantly integrated. It will be lovely in three or four years with roast duck.

● EARL des Vignobles Jean Sorge, Ch. Deyrem Valentin, 33460 Soussans, tel. 05.57.88.35.70, fax 05.57.88.36.84 ▼
Y by appt.

LA GRANDE CUVÉE DE DOURTHE 1998

■ n.c.　n.c.　€11-15

This well-balanced, well-integrated wine, produced by one of the best-known names on the Bordeaux wine market, develops a bouquet with original notes of crystallised fruits.

● Dourthe, 35, rue de Bordeaux, 33290 Parempuyre, tel. 05.56.35.53.00, fax 05.56.35.53.29, e-mail contact@cvbg.com ▼ Y by appt.

CH. DURFORT-VIVENS 1998★

■ 2ème cru clas.　39.82 ha　62,000
75 76 81 82 83 85 |86| |88| |89| |90| |93|
|94| **95** |96| |97| 98　€23-30

This cru has been playing a part in the history of the Médoc since the 13th century. Gonzague Lurton, who has been running it since 1992, has built a new vat and cellar as well as investing in the vines. His wine is a genuine Margaux, which exhibits good keeping potential alongside an engaging personality. The oak is sufficiently well administered to support the structure and the bouquet of red berries without being overwhelming. It should be cellared for five years.

● SCEA Ch. Durfort, Ch. Durfort-Vivens, 33460 Margaux, tel. 05.57.88.31.02, fax 05.57.88.60.60, e-mail infos@durfort-vivens.com Y by appt.
● Gonzague Lurton

CH. FERRIÈRE 1998★★

■ 3ème cru clas.　8 ha　33,000
70 75 78 81 83 84 **85** |86| 87 |88| 89
92 **93** **94** **95** **96** 97 **98**

Gabriel Ferrière, a royal courtier in Bordeaux, created this cru, one of the most ancient in Margaux, in the 16th century. Situated on choice *terroir*, today it is intelligently managed by Claire Villars-Lurton, who produces great wines. The garnet colour affords a glimpse of the promise of the bouquet and the palate. The former, moving from leather to brandied red berries, is as complex as it is classy, while the latter is silky, well constructed and very long. It is a wine that needs patience, as it should be cellared for four to eight years, but waiting will be rewarded. The Jury praised the second wine **Les Remparts de Ferrière 98**.

● Claire Villars, SA Ch. Ferrière, 33460 Margaux, tel. 05.57.88.76.65, fax 05.57.88.98.33, e-mail infos@ferriere.com Y by appt.

CH. GISCOURS 1998★

■ 3ème cru clas.　80 ha　300,000
75 78 81 82 83 85 |86| |88| |89| |90| 91
93 94 |97| 98　€23-30

This estates 80-ha (198-acre) vineyard represents only a small part of its 300-ha (741-acre) total, allowing for surrounding meadows, woods and marshes, all of which make a perfect environment for vines and wine. This wine confirms it all with its dark-red colour, bouquet with notes of toast and blackcurrant, and impressive palate, which opens into a full, long finish. The Jury commended its second wine, **La Sirène De Giscours 98**.

● SAE Ch. Giscours, 10, rte de Giscours, 33460 Labarde, tel. 05.57.97.09.09, fax 05.57.97.09.00, e-mail giscours@chateau-giscours.fr Y by appt.
● Albada Jelgersma

CH. HAUT BRETON LARIGAUDIÈRE 1998

■ Cru bourg.　12.46 ha　63,000
|90| 91 92 93　|94| 95 96 |97| 98　€15-23

Even though its structure is a little on the delicate side, this wine is well-constructed thanks to its fleshy but firm tannins, which reveal a balanced, classical structure that makes it agreeable.

● SCEA Ch. Haut Breton Larigaudière, 33460 Soussans, tel. 05.57.88.94.17, fax 05.57.88.39.14 Y by appt.
● de Schepper

CH. D'ISSAN 1998★

■ 3ème cru clas.　30 ha　110,000
82 83 85 86 87 |88| |89| |90| 92 93 **94**
95 96 97 98　€38-46

Château d'Issan wines, sufficiently famous in London at the beginning of the 18th century to be mentioned in a letter to the Prince of Wales, are still in the same class, two and a half centuries later! The wine's colour, with crimson highlights, is as intense as its complex bouquet, in which blackcurrant perfumes and toasty notes mingle. The silky, rich structure supported by elegant, well-integrated tannins, opens into a finish that picks up again on the notes of blackcurrant buds mingled with spices.

● Sté d'exploitation du Ch. Dauzac, 33460 Labarde-Margaux, tel. 05.57.88.32.10, fax 05.57.88.96.00 ▼
Y by appt.
● MAIF

Margaux

➤ SFV de Cantenac,
Ch. d'Issan, 33460 Cantenac,
tel. 05.57.88.35.91, fax 05.57.88.74.24,
e-mail issan@chateau-issan.com ✉
☎ by appt.
➤ Cruse

CH. KIRWAN 1998★

| 3ème cru clas. | 35 ha | 120,000 | €46-76 |

75 79 **81** 82 83 **85** ⑧⑥ |88| **89** 93 94 **95** 96 97 98

Built in 1780 by an Irishman, this was one of the first Médoc châteaux to be lived in permanently. In reflecting the mix of varieties, in which Cabernet Sauvignon and Cabernet Franc (together equalling 60%) and Petit Verdot (10%) play an important role, this wine follows in the Margaux tradition. Supported by well-integrated tannins, the structure is substantial but elegant. The result is a youthful, well-balanced wine, in which the complex, red-berry flavour, emerging from behind oaky notes, is highlighted. The Jury commended the second wine, the **Les Charmes de Kirwan 98**.

➤ Maison Schröder et Schÿler,
55, quai des Chartrons, 33000 Bordeaux,
tel. 05.57.87.64.55, fax 05.57.87.57.20,
e-mail mail@schroder-schyler.com ✉
☎ ev. day except Sat. & Sun. 9.30am–5.30pm
➤ J. H. Schÿler

CH. LABEGORCE-ZEDE 1998★

| | 27 ha | 100,000 | €15-23 |

82 ⑧③ |**85**| |**86**| |**88**| 89 90 91 **92** |**93**| |**94**| |**95**| 96 **97** 98

The château on the beautiful estate of this cru, owned by the same family as Vieux Château Pomerol, is surrounded by its vineyards. This bright 98, with cherry highlights, has an open, straightforward structure, not terribly powerful but pleasant, and is accompanied by an elegant bouquet of fresh fruits, wild berries and blackberries. It would go well with game birds or roast lamb.

➤ SCEA du Ch. Labégorce-Zédé,
33460 Soussans, tel. 05.57.88.71.31,
fax 05.57.88.72.54 ✉ ☎ by appt.
➤ L. Thienpont

LA BERLANDE 1998★★

| | 4 ha | 20,000 | €11-15 |

Henri Duboscq, the owner of Château Haut-Marbuzet, also a *négociant*, is past master in the art of wine selection. Here he has produced a complex, well-structured, concentrated wine, which gives full expression to the spirit of Margaux in its distinction and ageing potential. In order to derive the maximum pleasure from it, it should be cellared for around ten years.

➤ Brusina-Brandler, 3, quai de Bacalan,
33300 Bordeaux, tel. 05.56.39.26.77,
fax 05.56.69.16.84 ✉ ☎ by appt.

CH. LA GALIANE 1998

| | 5.67 ha | n.c. | €11-15 |

This wine, produced by one of the last surviving small properties in the appellation, though simple is, nevertheless, interesting in its suppleness, balance and bouquet of fine, spicy notes.

➤ SCEA René Renon, Ch. La Galiane,
33460 Soussans, tel. 05.57.88.35.27,
fax 05.57.88.70.59 ✉ ☎ by appt.

CH. LA GURGUE 1998★

| Cru bourg. | 10 ha | 36,500 | €15-23 |

82 83 **85** **86** 88 89 |**90**| |**95**| |**96**| |**97**| |98|

This wine, from the same producer as Château Ferrière, is more modest in its ambitions, but nevertheless perfectly typical. It has agreeable flavours, with notes of red berries and violets, a good body and silky tannins, all of which contribute to creating a rounded wine that will age well.

➤ Claire Villars, SA Ch. Ferrière,
33460 Margaux, tel. 05.57.88.76.65,
fax 05.57.88.98.33, e-mail infos@ferrière.com ✉ ☎ by appt.

CH. LARRUAU 1998

| Cru bourg. | n.c. | 700,000 | €11-15 |

86 |88| |89| **90** |93| |94| **95** 96 97 |98|

Although the most striking things about this wine are its suppleness and finesse, its agreeable bouquet of red berries expands onto the palate, which supports the bouquet without being overwhelmed by the oak.

➤ Bernard Château, 4, rue de La Trémoille,
33460 Margaux, tel. 05.57.88.35.50,
fax 05.57.88.76.69 ✉ ☎ by appt.

CH. LASCOMBES 1998★

| 2ème cru clas. | 50 ha | 200,000 | €30-38 |

70 76 79 **81** **82** 83 **85** ⑧⑥ |88| |89| |90|
93 **95** 96 |97| 98

This cru, which has just changed its owners, is found in the heart of the town and enjoys quality fine Guntz gravel *terroir*, so it is not surprising that this wine has plenty of character. Although clearly present, the oak doesn't obscure the personality of the bouquet or palate. From behind the musky notes emerge scents of roasting coffee beans, gingerbread and crystallised fruits. The powerful and tannic palate suggests that it should be aged.

➤ SV de Ch. Lascombes, 33460 Margaux,
tel. 05.57.88.70.66, fax 05.57.88.72.17,
e-mail chateaulascombes@wanadoo.fr ✉
☎ by appt.

CH. LA TOUR DE MONS 1998

| Cru bourg. | 22.4 ha | 159,000 | €11-15 |

Since changing hands in 1995, this cru has launched into a vast renovation programme. The first fruits of this wine, as seen in this wine, are very encouraging for the future. Its sappiness and elegance make it suitable for drinking now or else cellaring for two to three years.

➤ SCEA Ch. La Tour de Mons,
33460 Soussans, tel. 05.57.88.33.03,
fax 05.57.88.32.46 ✉ ☎ by appt.

CH. LE COTEAU 1998

10.5 ha 50,000 €8-11

This cru presents a well-structured wine with a substantial base of tannins. Although the finish could have been more elegant, the whole is seductive in its body, softness and intense bouquet of red berries. It should be cellared for three to five years.

Eric Léglise, 39, av. Jean-Luc-Vonderheyden, 33460 Arsac. tel. 05.56.58.82.30, fax 05.56.58.82.30
by appt.

CH. MALESCOT SAINT-EXUPERY 1998★★

3ème cru clas.	n.c.	105,500	€38-46 ✓

81 82 83 [85] [86] 88 89 90 [91] 92 93
94 95 96 98

This three-hundred-year-old cru is presided over by a château whose architecture is in the style of Napoléon III. Its wine has all the legendary elegance of Margaux. From the crimson colour right through to the finish, its taste is both powerful and delicate, thanks to the lovely scents and flavours of toasted bread and morello cherries. Full-bodied and extremely classy, this entirely successful 98 deserves a superb gourmet meal to complement it in five to ten years time, perhaps wood pigeon; an experience to remember as one of the great gastronomic events of the cellar diary.

SCEA Ch. Malescot Saint-Exupéry, 33460 Margaux, tel. 05.57.88.97.20, fax 05.57.88.97.21 by appt.
Roger Zuger

CH. MARGAUX 1998★★★

78 ha	n.c.	€76

59 [61] 66 70 71 [75] 77 78 [79] 80 [81]
[82] [83] 84 [85] [86] [87] 88 89 90 91
92 93 94 (95) (96) 97 (98)

There are not many crus that can claim to have achieved a perfect harmony between architecture and wine but Margaux certainly can. The nobility of this wine is a perfect reflection of the classical château and the cellars. This deep-garnet 98 introduces itself through its colour and goes on to display a complex, gourmet bouquet of mocha and brioche, followed by overripe fruit. The initial cocoa and vanilla flavours on the palate subsequently develop into notes of exotic oak and black fruit against an extremely classy, full, powerful and generous structure. Without doubt this wine should be laid down for several years.

SC du Ch. Margaux, 33460 Margaux, tel. 05.57.88.83.83, fax 05.57.88.83.32

CH. MARQUIS DE TERME 1998★★

4ème cru clas.	40 ha	165,000	€23-30

75 81 82 (83) 85 86 89 90 93 94 95 96
97 98

It may not appear very often under the spotlights of the catwalk, but this cru is nonetheless one of the safe bets of the appellation. The wine has proved this yet again. A beautiful, deep garnet colour, it unfolds a bouquet in which stewed fruits mingle with vanilla, before revealing a supple, rich, unctuous, tannic palate, which continues on to the harmonious finish. In short, this is a wine that should be cellared for at least five years.

SCA Ch. Marquis de Terme, 3, rte de Rauzan, BP 11, 33460 Margaux, tel. 05.57.88.30.01, fax 05.57.88.32.51, e-mail marquisterme@terre-net.fr
by appt.
Sèneclauze

CH. MARSAC SEGUINEAU 1998

Cru bourg.	10.23 ha	56,000	€15-23

95 [96] [97] 98

This cru, today owned by the group headed by Yves Barsalou, was created in the 18th century by the regrouping of some 115 plots. Despite a certain degree of austerity on the finish, its 98 has a fruity bouquet and a robust, fleshy structure. It should be cellared for three years.

SC du Ch. Marsac-Séguineau, La Croix Bacalan, 109, rue Achard, BP 154, 33042 Bordeaux Cedex, tel. 05.56.11.29.00, fax 05.56.11.29.01 by appt.

CH. MARTINENS 1998

25 ha	120,000	€11-15

Although originally built for two English women, this 18th-century château is a beautiful example of a Bordeaux landowner's house. Its finesse is reflected in this discreetly tannic wine, which is interesting in its suppleness and toasty ripe fruits bouquet.

Sté Fermière du Ch. Martinens, 33460 Cantenac, tel. 05.57.88.71.37, fax 05.57.88.38.35 by appt.
Mme Dulos et M. Seynat

CH. MONBRISON 1998★

Cru bourg.	13.2 ha	45,000	€15-23

82 83 [85] [86] 88 89| 90| 91 94 95 96
97 98

There is an underground passage beneath this charming house. The entrance to it is no doubt harder to find than the merits of this wine. From a beautiful, deep colour with violet highlights there emerges on an intense bouquet with notes of toast, roasting coffee beans, smoke and red berries. After initial suppleness, the palate develops simultaneously silky and powerful tannins. It should be cellared for five years to allow the oak to integrate.

➤ Laurent Vonderheyden, Ch. Monbrison, 33460 Arsac, tel. 05.56.58.80.04, fax 05.56.58.85.33 [V] [Y] by appt.
➤ E. M. Davis et Fils

CH. MONGRAVEY
Cuvée Prestige 1998★

■ 9 ha 12,000 [III] €15-23

Régis Bernaleau has been running this cru since 1981. This wine, a Cuvée Prestige, has real character. This is expressed in its dark red colour, its bouquet where menthol notes mingle with those of liquorice and blackcurrant, and in its rich, full, tannic structure. It should be cellared for four to five years.

➤ Régis Bernaleau, Ch. Mongravey, 33460 Arsac, tel. 05.56.58.84.51, fax 05.56.58.83.39,
e-mail chateau.mongravey@wanadoo.fr [V]
[Y] by appt.

CH. PALMER 1998★★

■ 3ème cru clas. 50 ha 120,000 [III] +€76
78 79 80 |81| |82| |83| 84 |85| [86] [88]
|89| 90 |91| |92| 93 94 95 96 97 98

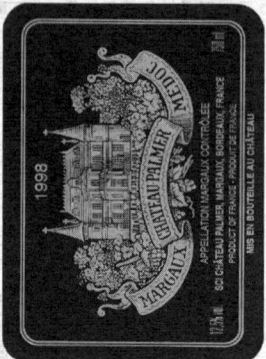

Although its building and its name only date back to the 19th century, this cru was already known in the 18th century under the name of the Château de Gasq. It is still one of the prime movers of the appellation, thanks to wines like this superb 98. Its richly promising dark-ruby colour fulfils its expectations. Its lovely, complex bouquet of vanilla, toast and liquorice is complemented by a full, powerful tannic structure in which the oak is perfectly mastered. The immensely long finish offers a lovely mix of ripe fruit and oak. This is a wine that will be at its best in eight or ten years.

➤ Ch. Palmer, Cantenac, 33460 Margaux, tel. 05.57.88.72.72, fax 05.57.88.37.16, e-mail chateau-palmer@chateau-palmer.com
[Y] by appt.

vanilla and cinnamon notes, and its palate, initially tremendously fresh, which develops a grand tannic structure that makes it more 'Jansenist' than its older brother. In short, this 98 deserves all the honours of the cellar.

➤ SC du Ch. Margaux, 33460 Margaux, tel. 05.57.88.83.83, fax 05.57.88.83.32

CH. POUGET 1998

■ 4ème cru clas. 10 ha n.c. [III] [♦] €15-23
75 85 86 88 |89| |90| 92 94 |95| |96| |97|
98

This wine, produced by the entirely independent cru, Boyd-Cantenac, gives priority to finesse. Well rounded, fleshy, tender and delicately perfumed, it has good balance, enabling it to integrate the flavours of the oak. In two or three years from now it should be at its best.

➤ SCE Ch. Boyd-Cantenac et Pouget, Cantenac, 33460 Margaux,
tel. 05.57.88.90.82, fax 05.57.88.33.27,
e-mail contact@boyd-cantenac.fr [V]
[Y] by appt.

CH. PRIEURE-LICHINE 1998★★★

■ 4ème cru clas. 40 ha 240,000 [III] [30-38]
82 83 86 |88| |89| |90| 91 |92| |93| 96 97
98

This is the last wine to have been produced by Sacha Lichine, as the estate changed hands in June 1999. The least one can say is that he 'went out' on a beautiful note. The bouquet, a model of elegance, is complex and original, with a gamey note. This is not an easy act to follow, but the palate succeeds in doing so in a very classy way. It manages to bring the wine and the oak together into a fleshy, full-bodied, rich whole. This 98 will be at its best in about ten years' time.

➤ Ch. Prieure-Lichine, 34, av. de la 5e-République, 33460 Cantenac,
tel. 05.57.88.36.28, fax 05.57.88.78.93,
e-mail prieure.lichine@wanadoo.fr [V]
[Y] by appt.
➤ GPE Ballande

CH. RAUZAN-GASSIES 1998★

■ 2ème cru clas. 30 ha 130,000 [III] €23-30
|93| |94| 96 97 98

This decent-sized cru, though by no means the largest in the appellation, has enough plots to take advantage of a large variety of soil types, so it is not surprising that it has produced a wine with a complex bouquet, in

PAVILLON ROUGE 1998★★

■ n.c. n.c. [III] €23-30
78 81 |82| |83| |84| |85| |86| |88| |89| |90|
92 |93| 94 95 96 97 98

Pavillon Rouge may only be a second wine, but it is from Château Margaux, hence its reputation. This is shown by its bouquet with its which notes of toasted coffee mingle with those of blackcurrant, redcurrant and bilberry. The powerful, silky tannins, well matched to the oak, will only take three to four years to integrate.

�¬ SCI Ch. Rauzan-Gassies, 33460 Margaux, tel. 05.57.88.71.88, fax 05.57.88.37.49 ☑ ⵌ by appt.
➬ J.-Michel Quié

CH. RAUZAN-SEGLA 1998 ★★★

■ 2ème cru clas. 51 ha 95,000 ⓘ €46-76
81 |83| |85| |88| |89| 90 91 92 93 94 95 |96| |97|

This cru, formerly owned by the Holt Group, has benefited from considerable financial investment. Thanks to this, its equipment is of high quality, as this superb 98 amply demonstrates. Right from its garnet colour to its finish, as flavourful as one could wish, elegance and power permeate the entire tasting. The fine, juicy bouquet plays on tasty, fruity, essentially red-berry notes, whilst on the palate generous, well-extracted tannins result in a well-structured, well-balanced whole, with superb length. This is a great wine; it would be a pity to open it for five years.

➬ Ch. Rauzan-Ségla, BP 56, 33460 Margaux, tel. 05.57.88.82.10, fax 05.57.88.34.54 ⵌ by appt.

SEGLA 1998 ★★

■ n.c. 95,000 ⓘ €11-15

Like a true lord of the manor, the first wine of Rauzan-Ségla is generous. It allowed little Ségla to play with the big boys, by taking the place of its elder brother and being presented to the *Grand Jury des coups de cœur*. Its perceptible elegance lies in the oaky notes of the bouquet, which also has notes of toasted hazelnuts. Without any loss of finesse, the palate has a full, classy character, which promises that the wine will age well. It should also be said that it is excellent value for money.

➬ Ch. Rauzan-Ségla, BP 56, 33460 Margaux, tel. 05.57.88.82.10, fax 05.57.88.34.54 ⵌ by appt.

CH. DES TROIS CHARDONS 1998

■ 2.88 ha 17,000 ⓘ €11-15
78 79 82 83 85 86 88 |89| |90| |94| |95| 96 97 |98|

Formerly cellar-masters and managers of Palmer, the Chardons work one of the last remaining Crus Artisans in the appellation. Their supple, elegant 98, with its delicate bouquet, is both rich and engaging, with a lovely finish.

➬ Claude et Yves Chardon, Issan, 33460 Cantenac, tel. 05.57.88.39.13, fax 05.57.88.33.94 ☑ ⵌ by appt.

CH. SIRAN 1998 ★

■ Cru bourg. 24 ha 90,000 ⓘ €23-30
66 78 79 80 81 82 83 85 86 87 88 |89| |90| 91 92 |93| 94 95 96 97 98

Before the waters of the Gironde and the Garonne were harnessed, the navigation channels came right up to this estate, where there was once a port for shipping wine. Let's hope wines in those days were all as good as this very successful 98. With deep-purple highlights its colour declares its youth, which is confirmed by the fleshy, tannic elegance and ensuing long finish. Already very elegant, it will be completely integrated in two to three years' time.

➬ SC du Ch. Siran, Ch. Siran, 33460 Labarde, tel. 05.57.88.34.04, fax 05.57.88.70.05, e-mail chateau.siran@wanadoo.fr ☑
ⵌ ev. day 10am–12.30pm 1.30pm–6pm
➬ William Alain Miailhe

CH. TAYAC 1998 ★

■ Cru bourg. 18 ha 134,000 ⓘ €11-15

Belonging to an estate of almost 40 ha (99 acres), this cru can be proud of its 98. As well as having an attractive, complex bouquet of roasting coffee beans, leather and stewed fruit, it has a round, full, well-structured palate. It should be laid down for three to five years.

➬ SC Ch. Tayac, Lieu-dit Tayac, BP 10, 33460 Soussans, tel. 05.57.88.33.06, fax 05.57.88.36.06 ☑
ⵌ ev. day 9am–12.30pm 2pm–6pm

CH. DU TERTRE 1998 ★★

■ 5ème cru clas. 50.4 ha 200,000 ⓘ €15-23
|90| 91 92 93 95 96 98

The ancient vaulted cellars that shelter the old vintages of this cru have, no doubt, room for a few bottles of this 98, which in every way promises to age well. It has a deep, dark colour and a bouquet whose powerful perfumes of blackberries, bilberries and crystallised cherries are supported by the delicate, toasty notes of the oak. The palate reveals a dense, tannic structure, whilst the finish lingers once more over the flavours of the bouquet.

➬ SEV Ch. du Tertre, chem. de Ligondras, 33460 Arsac, tel. 05.57.97.09.09, fax 05.57.97.09.00 ⵌ by appt.
➬ Albada Jelgersma

Moulis-en-Médoc

CH. VINCENT 1998★

■ Cru bourg. ■ 5 ha ■ 6,500 ■ €15-23

Although modest in size, this cru is much less so in terms of its wine and its *terroir*, situated amongst the Grand Crus Classés. This expressive and complex wine continues to develop throughout the tasting, with a round, full, long and well-balanced palate following on from a fruity bouquet with liquorice notes.

↝ Marthe Domec, Ch. Vincent, Issan, 33460 Cantenac, tel. 05.57.88.90.56, fax 05.44.18.02.70 ☑

Moulis-en-Médoc

An area consisting of a narrow ribbon 12 km (7 miles) long and only 300 or 400 m wide (328–438 yds), Moulis is the least extensive of the *appellations communales* in the Médoc. However, it offers a range of different *terroirs*.

As with Listrac, it falls into three main areas. The Bouqueyran area, to the west near the road from Bordeaux to Soulac, has a varied topography with limestone crests and a slope of ancient, Pyrenean gravel. In the centre, a plain of clay and limestone forms an extension of the Peyrelebade plain (see Listrac-Médoc). Finally, to the east and north-east, near the railway line, there rises a series of fine ridges of Garonne gravel forming a first-class *terroir* within which the famous hillocks of Grand-Poujeaux, Maucaillou and Médrac are clustered.

Moulis wines are soft and full, with a supple, delicate character. Even though they can be kept for some time (seven or eight years), they can develop more rapidly than wines from other communes in the area. The 2000 vintage produced 33,860 hl (893,904 gal) from 589 ha (1,455 acres).

CH. ANTHONIC 1998★

■ Cru bourg. ■ 20.54 ha 154,000 ■ III ♦ €11-15

82 83 **85** 86 88 **89** 90 91 92 93 94
95 96 97 98

Less than 800 m (2,627 feet) from the Romanesque church of Moulis, this cru has been run by Pierre Cordonnier since 1977. With its strong colour, this wine is true to its blend in which Merlot plays the leading role at 55%. Its bouquet has elegant notes of crystallised fruits and, thanks to its ripe tannins, it will be ready for drinking in two or three years.

↝ SCEA Pierre Cordonnier, Ch. Anthonic. 33480 Moulis-en-Médoc, tel. 05.56.58.34.60, fax 05.56.58.72.76, e-mail chateau.anthonic@terre-net.fr ☑
☑ ev. day 9am–12 noon 2pm–5.30pm; Sat. & Sun. by appt.

CH. BISTON-BRILLETTE 1998★

■ Cru bourg. ■ 21.5 ha 110,000 ■ €11-15

86 88 89 90 91 90 94 95 96 97 98

Once again, this cru confirms the quality of its production in a blend of half Cabernet Sauvignon and half Merlot. Supported by a substantial, well-coated tannic structure, it has a pleasing, very dark colour with red highlights. The bouquet is equally attractive with its notes of blackcurrant, cold tobacco, toast and cloves. Right through to the long finish, everything indicates that this is a wine that will age well for three or four years.

↝ EARL Ch. Biston-Brillette, Petit-Poujeaux, 33480 Moulis-en-Médoc, tel. 05.56.58.22.86, fax 05.56.58.13.16, e-mail contact@châteaubistonbrillette.com
☑ ☑ ev. day except Sun. 10am–12 noon 2pm–6pm; Sat. 10am–12 noon
↝ Michel Barbarin

CH. BOIS DE LA GRAVETTE 1998★

■ 3 ha ■ 20,000 ■ III €5-8

Although the cru only dates back to 1995, the Porcherons have been involved in wine-growing for a very long time. This wine, a blend of 52% Cabernet and 48% Merlot leaves one in no doubt about that. Although the fusion of oak and structure is not yet complete, the tannins and flavours of brandied red berries and cocoa are sufficiently present to ensure that it will develop favourably. It deserves to be cellared for four or five years.

↝ EARL Bois de la Gravette, 33480 Moulis-en-Médoc, tel. 05.56.58.22.11, fax 05.56.58.22.11 ☑ ev. day 8am–7pm
↝ Christian Porcheron

CH. BRILLETTE 1998★★

■ 40 ha 110,000 ■ III €15-23

94 95 96 98

On a lovely estate of more than 80 ha (197 acres) in total, this cru produces wine of outstanding quality, as evidenced by this well-balanced example. It is pleasing to gaze at its dark ruby colour, to smell and to discover its bouquet, a subtle marriage of fruit, spices, and toasty notes, and discover the

406

powerful palate structure, which calls for good ageing.
- SA Ch. Brillette,
33480 Moulis-en-Médoc, tel. 05.56.58.22.09,
fax 05.56.58.12.26 ☑ Y ev. day except Sat.
& Sun. 9am–12 noon 2pm–5.30pm

CH. CHASSE-SPLEEN 1998★★

■ Cru bourg.   40 ha   250,000   ⊕€23-30

75 76 **78** 79 80 **81 82** (**83**) |**85**| |**86**| |**88**|
|89| **90** 91 92 93 94 **95 96** 97 98

Everything is known about the history of this cru, from its creation in 1865 to the division of the estate in 1976 when it was bought by Jacques Merlaut, apart from the origin of its name. However, the estate's success is no secret in terms of its *terroir* quality and winemaking. The 98 offers ample evidence of this in its bouquet, which has delicate toasty, menthol, spicy and fruity notes (ripe fruits), and its well-rounded, supple, tannic structure. It is a lovely wine that doesn't need to be aged very long; it will be ready to drink in around three years.
- Céline Villars-Foubet,
SA Ch. Chasse-Spleen, Grand-Poujeaux,
33480 Moulis-en-Médoc, tel. 05.56.58.02.37,
fax 05.57.88.84.40, e-mail jpfoubet@
chasse-spleen.com Y by appt.

CH. CHEMIN ROYAL 1998

■ Cru bourg.   9.78 ha   60,000   ⊕€ 8-11

With a high proportion of Merlot (65%), some wine-lovers may be surprised by this wine's rapid integration However, they will not be disappointed by the bouquet with its charred notes and nuances of ripe fruits, or by its considerably long finish.
- Ch. Fonréaud, 33480 Listrac-Médoc,
tel. 05.56.58.02.43, fax 05.56.58.04.33 ☑
Y ev. day except Sat. & Sun. 9am–11.30am
2pm–5.30pm

CH. DUPLESSIS

■ Cru bourg.   18 ha   63,065   ⊕€ 8-11

From the same producer as Château Villegeorge (Haut-Médoc), this is a blend of 69% Merlot and three other Medoc varieties. Extremely clear in colour, with an attractive, discreet oakiness in the bouquet, and initial impressions of roundness, it is full bodied, with a later tannic evolution on the palate. It should improve over the next two to three years.
- SC Les Grands Crus Réunis,
2036, Chalet, 33480 Moulis-en-Médoc,
tel. 05.56.58.22.01, fax 05.56.58.15.10,
e-mail lgcr@wanadoo.fr Y by appt.
- Lurton-Roux

CH. DUPLESSIS FABRE 1998

■ Cru bourg.   2.5 ha   17,000   ⊕€11-15

90 91 92 93 94 |**95**| **96** 98

Once owned by the Duc de Richelieu, notorious for his intrigues and grand lifestyle during the reign of Louis XV, this cru differs from its sister cru, Maucaillou, in its mix of varieties: 55% Merlot and 45% Cabernet Sauvignon. The bouquet has fruity, spicy musky notes. On the palate, tannins mingle with toasty notes in a fairly linear structure. It should be cellared for one to two years.
- Ch. Maucaillou, quartier de la Gare,
33480 Moulis-en-Médoc,
tel. 05.56.58.01.23, fax 05.56.58.00.88
Y ev. day 10am–12 noon 2pm–6pm
- Philippe Dourthe

CH. DUTRUCH GRAND-POUJEAUX 1998

■ Cru bourg.   25 ha   170,000   ⊕€11-15

81 82 (**83**) **85** |**86**| |**88**| **89** |**90**| 93 |**94**| 95
96 |97| 98

Equipped with a new cellar and vats in 1999, this cru gives us a simple yet agreeable wine, particularly in the mocha notes of its bouquet. It should be cellared for two years.
- EARL François Cordonnier,
Ch. Dutruch Grand-Poujeaux,
33480 Moulis-en-Médoc,
tel. 05.56.58.02.55, fax 05.56.58.06.22,
e-mail chateau.dutruch@aquinet.net ☑
Y by appt.

CH. GUITIGNAN 1998

■ Cru bourg.   6 ha   40,000   ⊕€ 8-11

Vinified in the Listrac wine cellar, this is a simple wine as far as flavours on the palate are concerned but the bouquet, with its notes of red berries, and its more powerful tannic structure indicate that it will age well.
- Cave de vinification de Listrac,
21, av. de Soulac, 33480 Listrac-Médoc,
tel. 05.56.58.03.19, fax 05.56.58.07.22,
e-mail grandlistrac@cave-listrac-medoc.com
Y by appt.
- Annie Vidaller

CH. LA GARRICQ 1998★★

■   3 ha   20,000   ⊕€23-30

93 94 |95| 96 97 98

Although Martine Cazeneuve also produces wine in the Haut-Médoc appellation (Château Paloumey), it is this surprising Moulis wine that best demonstrates her know-how. In the elegant bouquet, oak leads into a dance of aromas, among which that of red berries is in step with the colour. Silky first impressions continue the celebration on the palate, where fruits and rounded tannins unite in harmony.
- SA Ch. Paloumey,
50, rue Pouge-de-Beau, 33290 Ludon-Médoc,
tel. 05.57.88.00.66, fax 05.57.88.00.67,
e-mail chateaupaloumey@wanadoo.fr ☑
Y by appt.

CH. LALAUDEY 1998★★

■   6.5 ha   24,000   ⊕€11-15

This Moulis, like the same producer's Margaux, Château Mongravey, has a substantial structure. Its bouquet, with emphatic notes of truffles, humus, leather and cold tobacco, is equally impressive. This is a wine that should be cellared for four or five years and checked regularly, as the tannins are already silky and ripe.

characterised by fruity, toasty and menthol notes, will open out. We should recall that the 96 vintage was one of the rare 'three stars' in the *Guide* to receive a *coup de cœur*.
➤ Ch. Maucaillou, quartier de la Gare, 33480 Moulis-en-Médoc, tel. 05.56.58.01.23, fax 05.56.58.00.88 ▼
▼ ev. day 10am–12 noon 2pm–6pm
➤ Philippe Dourthe

CH. MOULIN A VENT 1998 €11-15
■ Cru bourg. 25 ha n.c.

82 83 85 86 88 |89| |90| 91 95 |96| |97| 98

The cru, which has the same name as the *lieu-dit*, is situated on the highest hilltop to the west of the appellation. The structure it offers is unassertive, but the resiny notes in its bouquet and in the flavour on the palate remind us of the pine forest nearby. It should be cellared for one or two years.
➤ Dominique Hessel, Ch. Moulin a Vent, Bouqueyran, 33480 Moulis-en-Médoc, tel. 05.56.58.15.79, fax 05.56.58.39.89, e-mail hessel@moulin-a-vent.com ▼
▼ ev. day except Sat. & Sun. 9am–12 noon 2pm–6pm

CH. MYON DE L'ENCLOS 1998 €8-11
■ n.c. 20,000

95 |96| |97| 98

This wine, from the same producer as Château Mayne Lalande (Listrac), is more rustic but interesting in its potential for development over the next two to three years. Its dark colour, the bouquet mingling morello cherries with liquorice, the straightforward, massive attack and the austere follow-through are all pleasing.
➤ Bernard Lartigue, Le Mayne-de-Lalande, 33480 Listrac-Médoc, tel. 05.56.58.27.63, fax 05.56.58.22.41, e-mail b.lartigue@terre-net.fr ▼ by appt.

CH. PEY BERLAND 1998★
■ 0.85 ha 5,200 €15-23

The size of the vineyard explains why this wine, made entirely from Merlot, is atypical and simple, though well balanced, with a delicate bouquet. The fact that the vines are only eight years old is noteworthy.
➤ Jean Charpentier, Ch. Pey Berland, 33480 Moulis-en-Médoc, tel. 05.56.58.38.84, fax 05.56.58.38.84 ▼ by appt.

CH. POUJEAUX 1998★★ €23-30
■ Cru bourg. 53 ha 300,000

81 82 83 84 |85| |86| 87 |88| |89| 90 |91| |92| 93 94 95 96 97 98

With its lovely *terroir*, a Günz gravel hilltop in Poujaux and a family tradition going back 80 years, there is plenty to explain the well-deserved fame of the cru, which this wine is not about to ruin. It has a black velvet colour and a bouquet still characterised by oak, which gives it crusty, vanilla scents and glimpses of future development towards ripe fruits and spicy notes. The first impression is

➤ Régis Bernaleau, Ch. Mongravey, 33460 Arsac, tel. 05.56.58.84.51, fax 05.56.58.83.39, e-mail chateau.mongravey@wanadoo.fr ▼
▼ by appt.

CH. LA MOULINE 1998 €8-11
■ Cru bourg. n.c. n.c.

93 94 |95| 96 98

This wine, made before the cru was renovated in 1999, has tannins that are rather isolated on the palate but a bouquet with interesting notes of prunes and spices. It should be ready for drinking in one or two years.
➤ JLC Coubris, 90, rue Marcelin-Jourdan, 33200 Bordeaux, tel. 05.56.17.13.17, fax 05.56.17.13.18 ▼ ev. day except Sat. & Sun. 8am–12 noon 1pm–5pm; cl. Aug.

CH. LESTAGE-DARQUIER 1998 €8-11
■ Cru bourg. 8.29 ha 60,000

This light-coloured wine, produced on an estate which has been in the same family for six generations, has a simple, flavourful structure, pleasantly supported by notes of blackcurrant buds.
➤ EARL Bernard, Grand-Poujeaux, 33480 Moulis-en-Médoc, tel. 05.56.58.18.16, fax 05.56.58.38.42 ▼ by appt.

CH. MALMAISON 1998 €11-15
■ Cru bourg. 24 ha 45,000

88 89 90 91 92 93 94 95 96 97 98

The Clarke estate is so large it overflows into Listrac, making it possible for it to offer wines of different appellations, such as this Moulis, a blend of 61% Merlot and 39% Cabernet Sauvignon and Cabernet Franc. The colour follows the norm of the AOC and the bouquet mingles red berries with oaky notes, from 12 months' barrel-maturation. Right from the start the impression is substantial; later the palate puts the emphasis on the wood tannins. It should be laid down for three years.
➤ Cie vinicole Edmond de Rothschild, Ch. Clarke, 33480 Listrac-Médoc, tel. 05.56.58.38.00, fax 05.56.58.26.46, e-mail chateau.clarke@wanadoo.fr ▼
➤ Benjamin de Rothschild

CH. MAUCAILLOU 1998★
■ 69 ha 530,000 €23-30

81 82 83 85 86 87 |88| |89| |90| 91 92 93 94 |95| 96 97 98

This cru, owned by the Dourthe family, has a museum devoted to 'trades and professions of viticulture and vinification' – a must for any wine-lover. 'I have found the traditional spirit of the appellation,' noted one taster, delighted to find a wine made up of mainly Cabernet Sauvignon and Cabernet Franc, blended with 35% Merlot and 7% Petit Verdot. This substantially-structured 98 is not yet ready for drinking, but its present austerity is destined to disappear in three or four years, when its bouquet, currently

round and soft, the tannins are well coated and the finish is long. Everything indicates that this is going to be a lovely wine in a few years' time.

● Jean Theil SA, Ch. Poujeaux, 33480 Moulis-en-Médoc, tel. 05.56.58.02.96, fax 05.56.58.01.25, e-mail chateaupoujeaux@wanadoo.fr ☑
Ⴤ ev. day except Sat. & Sun. 9am–12 noon 2pm–5pm; by appt. 1st Oct–31st June

CH. RUAT PETIT POUJEAUX 1998

■ Cru bourg.   15 ha   45,000   ◨ £11-15   ☑

Pierre Goffre-Viaud, one of the big wine personalities of Bordeaux, completely renovated the estate 20 years ago. This wine, a beautiful cherry red with ruby highlights, has a lovely bouquet with notes of leather, grapes, crystallised fruits, raspberry and more. The soft initial impression is perfectly in tune with its structure, which, though lightly tannic, is pleasant right through into the finish.

● SCEA Vignobles Goffre-Viaud, Petit Poujeaux, 33480 Moulis-en-Médoc, tel. 05.56.58.25.15, fax 05.56.58.15.90 ☑
Ⴤ by appt.

Pauillac

With a population hardly greater than that of a large market town, Pauillac has a real urban feel, enhanced by a pleasure-boat harbour on the route of the Canal du Midi. The café terraces on the quay are the place to enjoy a plate of freshly caught shrimps from the estuary. But Pauillac is also, and above all, the capital of the Médoc wine-growing region, both by virtue of its geographical location in the middle of the vineyard and by the presence of three of the Premiers Crus Classés (Lafite, Latour and Mouton), which complete a really impressive tally of 18 Crus Classés. The co-operative produces a large quantity of wines. The appellation as a whole produced 64,357 hl (1,699,025 gal) from 1,178 ha (2,910 acres) in 2000.

The appellation is cut in two by the Chenal du Gahet, a small stream running through the middle of the two plateaus where the vines are grown. The area to the north, which takes its name from the hamlet of Pouyalet, is slightly higher, by about 30 m (98 ft) and has steeper slopes. It is the home of two of the Premiers Crus Classés (Lafite and Mouton) and enjoys an outstandingly fine balance between soil and subsoil, an attribute shared by the plateau of Saint-Lambert to the south. This second area stretches south from the Gahet to the Juillac Valley, where a small stream runs along the southern border of the commune and gives excellent drainage. The area's gravels, which are formed from large stones, are particularly distinctive on the terroir of its Premier Cru, Château Latour.

Pauillacs

Pauillacs from pure gravel ridges are very full-bodied wines, powerful and well-structured, but also fine and elegant, with a delicate bouquet. They develop very well as they age, and are worth waiting for. When mature, they can be served with confidence to accompany strongly flavoured dishes prepared with mushrooms, for instance, or to complement red meat, dark game meat or foie gras.

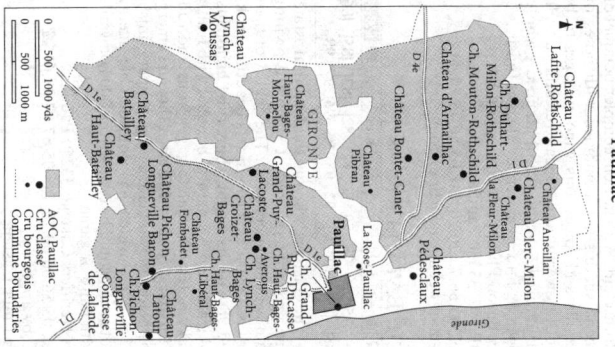

Pauillac

- Château Lafite-Rothschild
- Ch. Duhart-Milon-Rothschild
- Ch. Mouton-Rothschild
- Château Lynch-Moussas
- Château d'Armailhac
- Château Haut-Bages-Monpelou
- Château Pontet-Canet
- Château Clerc-Milon
- Château Pichran
- Château Haut-Batailley
- Château Batailley
- Château Grand-Puy-Lacoste
- Château Croizet-Bages
- Château Haut-Bages-Libéral
- Château Pichon-Longueville Baron
- Château Fonbadet
- Avensan
- Ch. Lynch-Bages
- Puy-Ducasse
- Ch. Haut-Bages
- La Rose-Pauillac
- Château Pédesclaux
- Ch. Pichon-Longueville Comtesse de Lalande
- Château Latour

GIRONDE

D 2   D 4e   D 1   D 206

AOC Pauillac
Cru classé
Cru bourgeois
Commune boundaries

0   500   1000 yds
0   500   1000 m

409

CH. D'ARMAILHAC 1998★★

■ 5ème cru clas.   50 ha   124,000   ▥ €23-30

72 |73| 74 75 78 79 **80 81 82** |83| **84** |85| |86| **87** |88| |89| **90** 92 93 |94| **95** 96 97 98

This cru has an emblem, borrowed from its neighbour Mouton Rothschild – a statue of Bacchus. Its genuine personality comes through in this lovely wine with its delicate bouquet of red berries, leather and charred notes. It is nicely rich, structured by silky tannins and full, guaranteeing that it will age well. The gentle, peppery finish is one of the most charming imaginable.

➤ Ch. d'Armailhac, 33250 Pauillac,
tel. 05.56.59.22.22, fax 05.56.73.20.44,
e-mail webmaster@bpdr.com
➤ Baronne Ph. de Rothschild GFA

CH. ARTIGUES ARNAUD 1998

■   39.18 ha   43,300   ■ ♦ €11-15

This estate presented a well-rounded, fleshy and richly textured wine, the work of the Grand-Puy Ducasse team, which represents the entire production of the cru. Though already agreeable with its fresh bouquet of red berries, it seems a little simple at the moment but promises to reveal some pleasant surprises in a few years' time.

➤ SC du Ch. Grand-Puy Ducasse,
La Croix Bacalan, 109, rue Achard, BP 154,
33042 Bordeaux Cedex, tel. 05.56.11.29.00,
fax 05.56.11.29.01 ▾ by appt.

BARON NATHANIEL 1998★★

■   n.c.   n.c.   €11-15

This label is a sign of the consistent quality of the *négociant*, Baron Philippe de Rothschild. With its rich, complex bouquet of cocoa successfully combined with notes of vanilla and spices, this wine manages to be both powerful and delicate, creating a well-structured, very well-balanced whole, opening into an extremely elegant finish.

➤ Baron Philippe de Rothschild SA,
BP 117, 33250 Pauillac,
tel. 05.56.73.20.20, fax 05.56.73.20.44,
e-mail webmaster@bpdr.com

CH. BATAILLEY 1998★★

■ 5ème cru clas.   55 ha   n.c.   ▥ €23-30

70 75 76 78 79 80 81 |82| **83** |85| |86| |88| |89| |90| 91 **92 93 95** |83| **96 97 98**

The Gastejas, who run this beautiful estate, are probably the oldest vineyard-owning family in the appellation. The quality of their cru is illustrated again in this beautiful dark-red 98 with its bright, shiny ruby highlights, which develops a natural bouquet with fruity, oaky notes. The palate is generous and full, with extraordinary Cabernet flavours emerging before moving into a long, peppery finish. This wine, which has considerable ageing potential, could be drunk from 2004 onwards with lamb or game.

➤ Héritiers Castéja, 33250 Pauillac,
tel. 05.56.00.00.70, fax 05.57.87.48.61 ▾
▾ by appt.
➤ Emile Castéja

CH. BELLEGRAVE 1998★

■ Cru bourg.   8 ha   50,000   ▥ €15-23

The Meffres, a family well known in the Rhône, bought 2.5 ha (6 acres) of this Pauillac cru from a San Francisco *négociant*, M. van der Voort, in 1997. Since then, they have increased the area of vines. This wine, barrel-matured for 12 months in 50% new oak, has seductive perfumes of ripe fruits and black-currants. Its fleshiness and body, with its rounded, supple tannins, ensure that it will improve in two or three years.

➤ Vignobles Meffre, rue Joseph-Vernet,
84810 Aubignan, tel. 05.56.59.06.47,
fax 05.90.65.03.73 ▾ ▾ by appt.

CH. CLERC MILON 1998★

■ 5ème cru clas.   30 ha   172,000   ▥ €30-38

|75| 76 78 79 |82| |83| |85| **86 87 88 89** 90 |92| |94| |95| **96 97** 98

This wine has a piece of 17th-century silverwork on its label, a pair of jesters housed in the Mouton museum. The charm of the wine lies in more than the label: its dark colour with its shades of vermilion is a pleasure to behold. Although the bouquet is initially a little closed, it opens into charred notes, whilst the palate reveals a substantially powerful, tannic structure, a generous texture and a seductive, liquoricey finish.

➤ Ch. Clerc Milon, 33250 Pauillac,
tel. 05.56.59.22.22, fax 05.56.73.20.44,
e-mail webmaster@bpdr.com
➤ Baronne Ph. de Rothschild GFA

CH. COLOMBIER-MONPELOU 1998

■ Cru bourg.   15 ha   110,000   ▥ €11-15

|94| **95 96 97** 98

Produced from vines grown on a plateau overlooking Pauillac, this wine with its velvety tannins has an agreeable personality, both in its engaging scents of ripe fruits and in its balsamic notes. Exotic flavours give it a likeable style.

➤ SC Vignobles Jugla,
Ch. Colombier-Monpelou, 33250 Pauillac,
tel. 05.56.59.01.48, fax 05.56.59.12.01 ▾
▾ by appt.

CH. CORDEILLAN-BAGES 1998★

■ Cru bourg.   2 ha   12,000   ▥ €30-38

|89| |91| 93 **94 95 96 97 98**

Cordeillan, a château-hotel, illustrates the revival in restoration work currently taking place in Médoc. It also produces high-quality wine, as can be seen from this example. The perfumes of black chocolate, spices and tropical fruits harmonise on the palate with the lovely structure and ripe, complex tannins. This is a well-balanced, powerful wine with plenty of character.

➤ Jean-Michel Cazes,
Ch. Cordeillan-Bages, 33250 Pauillac,
tel. 05.56.73.24.00, fax 05.56.59.26.42,
e-mail infochato@cordeillanbages.com
▾ by appt.

CH. CROIZET-BAGES 1998

■ 5ème cru clas. 28 ha 160,000 €15-23
93 94 [95] [96] [97] [98]

Its name is explained by the fact that the estate, created in the 16th century by the Bages family, became the property of the Croizets at the time of the Revolution. Its supple, fine 98 follows in the tradition of the cru. Delicacy and freshness rather than power are most noticeable in the bouquet, with its notes of slightly tart fruits, menthol, flowers and peppers, and in the flavour of simple tannins on the palate.

Jean-Michel Quié, Ch. Croizet-Bages, 33250 Pauillac, tel. 05.56.59.01.62, fax 05.56.59.23.39 [V] [Y] ev. day except Sun. & Mon. 9am–1pm 2pm–6pm

CH. DUHART-MILON 1998★★

■ 4ème cru clas. 67 ha 28,000 €46-76
61 70 75 76 79 80 81 [82] [83] [85] [86] 87 88 89 90 [91] [92] [93] [94] 95 96 97 98

As a port Pauillac had its pirates and one of them, Duhart, gave his name to this cru. That wine gives pride of place to grace, but that does not mean that it is not put together well. Its slender structure and elegant tannins go well with the blackcurrants, blackberries, liquorice, crystallised fruits and cocoa expressed in its bouquet, enlivened by charred, oaky notes. It forms a charming whole which should age very well. The Jury commended its second wine, the Moulin de Duhart 98. Shiny garnet in colour, with a discreet bouquet, it develops into a fine, pleasant structure and will be ready for drinking in two years.

Ch. Duhart-Milon, 33250 Pauillac

CH. FONBADET 1998

■ Cru bourg. n.c. 110,000 €15-23
75 76 78 79 81 [82] 83 85 [86] 87 [88] [89] [90] 91 93 95 96 97 98

Now being replanted, the grounds of this cru were severely affected by the gales that devastated Médoc, the rest of France and other parts of Europe in December 1999. As is often case with wines from this estate, the 98 will take two or three years to reveal its merits. However, a good future is promised by its tannins, very much in the Pauillac tradition, and its bouquet with its discreet notes of ripe fruits, spices and tobacco.

SCEA des Domaines Peyronie, Ch. Fonbadet, 33250 Pauillac, tel. 05.56.59.02.11, fax 05.56.59.22.61, e-mail pascale@chateaufonbadet.com [V] [Y] by appt.

CH. GAUDIN 1998

10 ha n.c. €11-15

Still rather severe, this wine is exclusively marketed by Cordier. Discreet scents of red berries mingle with the oak through to a spicy finish, giving an agreeable personality.

Linette Capdevielle, SCI du Ch. Gaudin, BP 12, 33250 Pauillac, tel. 05.56.59.24.39, fax 05.56.59.25.26

CH. GRAND-PUY DUCASSE 1998★

■ 5ème cru clas. 39 ha 174,000 €23-30
82 83 84 85 86 88 89 [90] 91 92 93 94 [95] 96 97 98

Like the château, a beautiful residence in the heart of Pauillac, this wine is a great classic in the best possible sense, both in its texture and in its tannins, indicating that it should be laid down for some considerable time. This will allow the bouquet, which is still only just emerging, to open out and strengthen the fruity, musky and spicy notes that are just starting to appear. The Jury commended the second wine, the Prélude à Grand-Puy Ducasse 98: its well-integrated tannins and oak should make it ready for drinking in 2002, accompanied by chicken and baby spring vegetables.

SC du Ch. Grand-Puy Ducasse, La Croix Bacalan, 109, rue Achard, BP 154, 33042 Bordeaux Cedex, tel. 05.56.11.29.00, fax 05.56.11.29.01 [Y] by appt.

CH. GRAND-PUY-LACOSTE 1998★★

■ 5ème cru clas. 50 ha 165,000 €30-38
61 66 70 71 75 76 78 81 82 [83] [85] [86] 87 88 89 90 [91] [92] [93] [94] 95 96 [97] 98

As the puy of its name suggests, this cru is situated on high ground. Thanks to the sensible management of François-Xavier Borie, this wine manages to derive the most from its terroir. Introduced by its dark garnet-red colour, it displays a wide palette of perfumes (red berries, spices, cherries, redcurrants and menthol, all sprinkled with vanilla). The generous, ripe tannins contribute to the balance of the palate and the long finish. They guarantee that this wine will age well. It should definitely be cellared for four years but, in the meantime, sampling the second wine would alleviate the agony of waiting – the pleasant Lacoste-Borie 98, also commended by the Jury.

Ch. Grand-Puy-Lacoste, 33250 Pauillac, tel. 05.56.73.16.73, fax 05.56.59.27.37 [Y] by appt.

CH. HAUT-BAGES LIBERAL 1998★★★

■ 5ème cru clas. 28 ha 117,000 €15-23
75 76 78 79 80 81 [82] [83] 84 [85] [86] 87 88 89 90 91 92 [93] [94] 95 96 97 [98]

In two separate parts, one overlooking the Gironde near Latour and the other on the Bages plateau, this cru has the benefit of quality terroir. You need look no further than the very beautiful dark 98 to be convinced of this. Should the slightest doubt remain, it will be quickly dispelled by the bouquet, an exceptionally distinguished palette of mainly crystallised fruits against a background of oak, with beautifully refined notes of chocolate

and coffee. It is impressive in its complexity. The dense, full, rich, fleshy and generous palate completes the picture marvellously and opens into a very lengthy finish. This is a great wine that should be laid down for several years. The second wine, more modest but nevertheless delicate and engaging,— **La Chapelle de Bages 98** — was awarded a star. Its bouquet of red berries and lovely, oaky notes lead into silky tannins.

☛ Claire Villars, Ch. Haut-Bages Libéral, 33250 Pauillac, tel. 05.57.88.76.65, fax 05.57.88.98.33, e-mail infos@haut-bages-liberal.com ☧ by appt.

CH. LA BECASSE 1998★

■ 4 ha   30,000   €23-30

91 92 93 |94| 95 96 |97| 98

This well-balanced wine, with its powerful but pleasantly-integrated tannins, mingles floral and toasty notes on the finish. This is a wine to be laid down for four or five years.

☛ Roland Fonteneau, 21, rue Edouard-de-Pontet, 33250 Pauillac, tel. 05.56.59.07.14, fax 05.56.59.18.44 ☑
☧ by appt.

CARRUADES DE LAFITE 1998★

■ n.c.   350,000   €30-38

85 |86| 87 88 89 90 91 92 |93| |94| 95
96 97 98

The second wine from Lafite proved more severe during tasting than the first (see below). Supported by firm but fleshy tannins, its substantial structure should ensure that it will age well.

☛ Ch. Lafite Rothschild, 33250 Pauillac, tel. 01.53.89.78.00, fax 01.53.89.78.01
☧ by appt.

CH. LAFITE ROTHSCHILD 1998★★★

■ 1er cru clas.   102 ha   260,000   +76

59 |6| 64 |66| 69 |70| 73 |75| 76 77 |78|
|79| |80| |81| |82| |83| |84| 85 86 |87| 88
89 90 92 93 94 95 96 97 98

The fashion for Lafite = this is one of the oldest vineyards in Médoc – started during the reign of Louis XV. The elegant residence presides over a majestically impressive circular cellar, designed by Ricardo Bofil. This wine is remarkable for its explosive bouquet, which develops scents of mocha and roasting coffee beans, with fruity notes lurking in the wings. The first impression and the flavour on the palate make that this is indeed a great Pauillac. Its power is accompanied by a great deal of elegance, resulting in a truly full, well-rounded wine. Supported by fine-grained tannins, the progression of flavours throughout the tasting is remarkable. The long, flavourful and well-balanced finish guarantees the future of this wine, which should be laid down for several years.

☛ Ch. Lafite Rothschild, 33250 Pauillac, tel. 01.53.89.78.00, fax 01.53.89.78.01
☧ by appt.

CH. HAUT-BATAILLEY 1998★

■ 5ème cru clas.   n.c.   105,000   €23-30

66 71 75 78 81 82 83 84 |85| |86| 87 88
89 90 91 |92| |93| 94 95 96 |97| 98

Although belonging to the owner of Château Grand-Puy-Lacoste, this cru has its own personality, with 10% Cabernet Franc contributing to the blend. There is a certain family resemblance in the garnet-red colour and in the sense of balance it demonstrates, but it asserts its identity in the toasty notes of the bouquet and in the roundness of its tannins. These, along with the lovely, toasty finish, indicate that it should be cellared for two or three years. The Jury singled out the second wine, the **Château La Tour L'Aspic 98**. 'There is a measure of tenderness in this wine,' noted one member of the Jury noted, when admiring its well-behaved tannins.

☛ SA Jean-Eugène Borie, 33250 Saint-Julien-Beychevelle, tel. 05.56.73.16.73, fax 05.56.59.27.37 ☧ by appt.
☛ Mme des Brest-Borie

DOM. IRIS DU GAYON 1998

■ Cru artisan   0.5 ha   1,500   €15-23

This discreet wine, produced from a cru so tiny that one might call it a 'micro-vineyard', has been barrel-matured for 16 months. It has a beautiful, purplish colour and a bouquet of black fruits and leather on an oaky background. The flavour on the palate, however, relies on the support of fairly simple tannins.

☛ Françoise Siri, Moulin du Gayon Pouyalet, 33250 Pauillac, tel. 05.56.59.03.82, fax 05.56.59.67.00 ☑ ☧ by appt.

CH. LA FLEUR MILON 1998★★

■ Cru bourg.   12.5 ha   85,000   ▯▯ €15-23

94 ⑤ 96 97 98

This cru, situated cheek by jowl with some of the great names of the wine aristocracy, is entitled to have grand ambitions and this 98 shows that they can be fulfilled. At the same time fresh, fleshy, rounded and dense, it has plenty of character. Its tannins can be relied upon to guarantee its future, whilst its bouquet, with its lovely floral and spicy notes, will give it a charming personality.

↬ SCE Ch. La Fleur Milon, Le Pouyalet, 33250 Pauillac, tel. 05.56.59.23.22 ☑ ☒ by appt.

↬ Héritiers Gimenez

CH. LA FLEUR PEYRABON 1998★

■ Cru bourg.   4.87 ha   30,841   ▯▯ €15-23

This cru, bought by the Millesima company in 1998 and now run by Patrick Bernard, dates back to the 18th century. This wine, whose still slightly austere tannins demand that it should be cellared for a while, is a lovely, shiny, ruby colour. Skilful maturation respects the fruit and the flavours, both of which result in satisfying complexity.

↬ SARL Ch. Peyrabon, 33250 Saint-Sauveur, tel. 05.56.59.57.10, fax 05.56.59.59.45, e-mail chateau.peyrabon@wanadoo.fr ☑ ☒ by appt.

↬ P. Bernard

LA ROSE PAUILLAC 1998

■ n.c.   70,000   ▯▯ €8-11

This label from the Pauillac co-operative has a fairly simple bouquet and a classical architecture, accompanied by clarity and power.

↬ La Rose Pauillac, 44, rue du Mal-Joffre, BP 14, 33250 Pauillac, tel. 05.56.59.26.00, fax 05.56.59.63.58 ☒ by appt.

CH. LATOUR 1998★★★

■ 1er cru clas.   43 ha   n.c.

⑥ 71 73 74 75 76 77 78 79 80
81 82 83 84 85 86 87 88 89 90 91
92 93 94 ⑤ 96 97 98

Wine may be a traditional product, but this does not mean that development of the crus should remain static. Despite, or possibly because of the burden of history, Latour is always at the forefront of change. It is forever modifying its cellar. Most importantly the wine remains as noble as this 98, which is endowed with all the social graces. Its lovely garnet colour and bouquet of roasting coffee beans, cocoa, spices and leather shows that it knows how to be assertive. The bouquet is confirmed in the flavours on the palate, where its ripe, opulent structure has silky, unctuous tannins making it essential to cellar the wine – for between ten to twenty years.

↬ SCV de Ch. Latour, Saint-Lambert, 33250 Pauillac, tel. 05.56.73.19.80, fax 05.56.73.19.81 ☒ by appt.

↬ François Pinault

GRAND VIN
CHATEAU
LYNCH BAGES
GRAND CRU CLASSÉ
PAUILLAC
1998

In the course of two generations, André and Jean-Michel Cazes have brought this ancient cru, situated on beautiful Garonne

CH. LYNCH-BAGES 1998★★★

■ 5ème cru clas.   90 ha   420,000   ▯▯ €46-76

70 71 75 78 79 80 81 82 83 84
85 86 87 88 89 90 91 92 93 94
95 96 97 98

LES FORTS DE LATOUR 1998★★

■ n.c.   n.c.   ▯▯ €46-76

80 81 82 83 85 86 87 88 89 90 92 94
95 96 97 98

It will be possible to enjoy this charming wine with its beautiful bouquet of fruit and leather and crystallised notes whilst waiting for the great wine from Château Latour to mature. However, do not be in too much of a hurry: this is a true Pauillac whose substantial structure, generous, concentrated tannins and long finish indicate that it should be cellared for three or four years.

↬ SCV de Ch. Latour, Saint-Lambert, 33250 Pauillac, tel. 05.56.73.19.80, fax 05.56.73.19.81 ☒ by appt.

↬ AGF

CH. LA TOURETTE 1998★

■ 3 ha   23,000   ▯▯ €15-23

A little austere in the finish, this wine, produced from a Pauillac plot belonging to the Château Larose-Trintaudon (Haut-Médoc) should be laid down for some time. The complexity of its bouquet and the quality of its structure, becoming increasingly powerful, guarantees that it will age well.

↬ SA Ch. Larose-Trintaudon, rte de Pauillac, 33112 Saint-Laurent-Médoc, tel. 05.56.59.41.72, fax 05.56.59.93.22, e-mail info@trintaudon.com ☑ ☒ by appt.

LES TOURELLES DE LONGUEVILLE 1998★

■ n.c.   180,000   ▯▯ €30-38

This second label from Pichon Baron reverses the proportions of the first, with 60% Merlot as against the 60% Cabernet Sauvignon in the great wine. Its slender body is seductively balanced and aromatic. The delicacy of its tannins will allow it to be fully enjoyed in two or three years.

↬ Christian Seely, Ch. Pichon-Longueville, 33250 Pauillac, tel. 05.56.73.17.28, fax 05.56.73.17.17, e-mail infochato@pichonlongueville.com ☑ ☒ by appt.

↬ Axa-Millésimes

gravel, up to the highest of standards. The extent of their success can be appreciated in this perfectly-balanced wine. Impressively black in colour, its generosity is demonstrated by the richness of its bouquet, in which the fruit is enlivened by the oak. The power of its tannins explodes on the palate without being the slightest bit aggressive; on the contrary, it proves to be extremely unctuous. Rich, silky, elegant and tightly structured, it should be cellared for five to ten years. The Jury commended the second wine, the **Château Haut Bages Averous 98**.

→ Jean-Michel Cazes, Ch. Lynch-Bages, 33250 Pauillac, tel. 05.56.73.24.00, fax 05.56.59.26.42, e-mail infochato@lynchbages.com [V]
→ Famille Cazes

CH. LYNCH-MOUSSAS 1998★

■ 5ème cru clas. n.c. n.c. [III] €30-38

81 82 **83** 85 86 88 [89] **90** [93] 95 96 [97] 98

Of Irish origin, the Lynch family gave the city of Bordeaux a mayor at the time of Napoleon as well as giving their name to the crus they owned. Like Batailly, this one is now owned by the Castéja family. Its soundly typical 98 has a full flavour on the palate, which has nicely integrated tannins, and its body and its long finish are promising. However, as a true Pauillac, it is also flavourful: its engaging bouquet has fruity and vanilla notes.

→ Emile Castéja, 33250 Pauillac, tel. 05.56.00.00.70, fax 05.57.87.48.61 [V] [Y] by appt.

CH. MOUTON ROTHSCHILD 1998★★★

■ 1er cru clas. 78 ha 275,000 [III] €76

71 72 73 74 [75] 76 77 [78] 79 80 81 82 83 [84] 85 86 [87] 88 89 90 [91] [92] 93 94 95 96 97 98

whilst on the palate it opens out still further into spicy tones of black pepper and flavours of crystallised fruits. The round, full and fleshy structure develops harmoniously, increasing in power and delicacy, leaving the memory of a noble wine brimming with charm that will age very well indeed. This is an archetypal Pauillac. The label is the work of the Mexican painter, Rufino Tamayo.

→ Ch. Mouton Rothschild, 33250 Pauillac, tel. 05.56.59.22.22, fax 05.56.73.20.44, e-mail webmaster@bpdr.com [V] [Y] by appt.
→ Baronne Ph. de Rothschild GFA

CH. PEDESCLAUX 1998

■ 5e cru clas. 12.5 ha 80,000 [III] €15-23

In 1821, Urbain Pédesclaux brought together several plots of land to create the cru to which he gave his name. This supple wine, with its well-coated tannins, will reach full maturity in two to three years when its bouquet of toasty notes, fruit kernels and liquorice will have opened out completely.

→ SCEA Ch. Pédesclaux, Padarnac, 33250 Pauillac, tel. 05.56.59.22.59, fax 05.56.59.63.19 [Y] by appt.

CH. PIBRAN 1998

■ Cru bourg. 10 ha 50,000 [III] €23-30

[88] [89] [90] 91 93 94 95 96 97 98

A neighbour of Pichon-Longueville Baron and belonging to the same group, this cru still has its own personality, which expresses itself here through the bouquet of this wine. Although still somewhat closed, it has a note of originality (*rancio*). The simple structure is sufficiently full-bodied to ensure that the wine will age well.

→ Christian Seely, Ch. Pibran, 33250 Pauillac, tel. 05.56.73.17.17, fax 05.56.73.17.28 [V]
→ Axa-Millésimes

CH. PICHON-LONGUEVILLE BARON 1998★★

■ 2ème cru clas. 70 ha 230,000 [III] €46-76 (90)

78 81 82 [83] 84 [85] [86] 87 [88] [89] 90 91 92 93 94 95 [96] 97 98

The Axa-Millésimes group has turned its château into a showcase; it has not simply invested in the fabric of the buildings and its cultural events. It has also spent money on equipment, as this wine effectively shows. Its bouquet is intense and complex in its development, moving from fruity components to the toasty note, without the latter overwhelming the former. The palate, which is classy and powerful, with well-integrated, very long tannins, is both engaging and promising. This is a wine that should reach maturity in five to seven years' time.

→ Christian Seely, Ch. Pichon-Longueville, 33250 Pauillac, tel. 05.56.73.17.17, fax 05.56.73.17.28, e-mail infochato@pichonlongueville.com [V] [Y] by appt.
→ Axa-Millésimes

With its vast cellar and museum of wine in art, exhibiting a collection of labels designed by famous artists, Mouton is of outstanding interest to tourists. However, this should not distract anyone's attention from what is really important: the quality of the *terroir* and the high standard of craftsmanship in both the vineyard and the cellar. The result is an exceptional wine, which fulfils all the promise of its deep cherry-red colour. The bouquet, as it moves from mocha to red berries, is a delight,

Saint-Estèphe

CH. PICHON-LONGUEVILLE COMTESSE DE LALANDE 1998★★

| 2ème cru clas. | 75 ha | n.c. | €46-76 |

66 70 71 75 76 78 79 80 81 82 83 84 **85| 86| 87 |88| 89| 90| 91| 92 |93| 94| 95 96 97 98**

Possibly because this is one of the few châteaux to have protected its archives and because it has been owned by only two families, May-Eliane de Lencquesaing has set herself the task of rediscovering the spirit of the Comtesse de Lalande. Thus, this wine, though it is far from having the definitive Pauillac personality, reveals assertiveness and an equally promising, remarkably fruity and finely oaky bouquet.

↳ SCI Ch. Pichon-Longueville Comtesse de Lalande, 33250 Pauillac, tel. 05.56.59.19.40, fax 05.56.59.26.56, e-mail pichon@pichon-lalande.com ◩ ▼ by appt.
↳ May-Eliane de Lencquesaing

CH. PONTET-CANET 1998★

| 5ème cru clas. | 40 ha | 200,000 | €30-38 |

6 70 75 76 77 78 79 81 82 **83 84 85| 86** 87 |88| **89| 90|** 91 92 93 |94| **95 96** 97 98

This estate, famous today as the location for the film *J'ai épousé une ombre*, has a cru, on the other hand that has been renowned since the 18th century. Faithful to tradition and to the appellation, it offers a substantially structured wine, which deserves to be cellared for some considerable time. Its assertive, extremely long-lasting tannins will ensure that it ages well, allowing the fruity, charred perfumes of its potent, intense bouquet to become increasingly fine.

↳ Alfred Tesseron, Ch. Pontet-Canet, 33250 Pauillac, tel. 05.56.59.04.04, fax 05.56.59.26.63, e-mail pontet@pontet-canet.com ◩ ▼ by appt.

RESERVE DE LA COMTESSE 1998★

| n.c. | n.c. | | €15-23 |

At Pichon-Comtesse, the marketing of the second wine is not new. The archives show that the 1874 vintage was sent to Moscow for the 1890 exhibition. After lapsing for a time, this custom of making a second wine, came back into use in 1973. This elegant 98 is entirely in the spirit of the cru, which is to be found in both the well-integrated, well-balanced tannins and the beautifully complex bouquet of red berries, mocha, toast and more. This is a very lovely wine that should be cellared for three or four years.

↳ SCI Ch. Pichon-Longueville Comtesse de Lalande, 33250 Pauillac, tel. 05.56.59.19.40, fax 05.56.59.26.56, e-mail pichon@pichon-lalande.com ◩ ▼ by appt.

CH. SAINTE-ANNE 1998★

| | 2.3 ha | 17,500 | €11-15 |

This wine, from a little vineyard belonging to an estate in Saint-Estèphe, seduced the Jury with the fruity, floral perfumes of its

bouquet, which are well supported by the oak. The rich, full and well-balanced palate is supported by a sound tannic base, which will ensure that the wine ages serenely and well.

↳ Dom. La Croix de Pez, Pez, 33180 Saint-Estèphe, tel. 05.56.59.37.23, fax 05.56.59.33.97 ◩ ▼ by appt.
↳ Guyonnaud

CH. TOUR PIBRAN 1998

| Cru bourg. | 10 ha | 65,000 | €11-15 |

Distributed by the *négociant*, this wine, whose emerging bouquet is very grapey, is still rather closed. Its substantial tannins are still dominated by the oak and need time to integrate.

↳ Compagnie Médocaine des Grands Crus, ZI, 7, rue Descartes, 33290 Blanquefort, tel. 05.56.95.54.95, fax 05.56.95.54.85, e-mail cmgc@medocaine.com
↳ J. Gounel

Saint-Estèphe

Not very far up the Garonne from Pauillac and its port lies Saint-Estèphe. Its charming rustic hamlets fittingly suggest a locale closely bound to the soil. Apart from a few acres that are part of the Appellation Pauillac, the Appellation Saint-Estèphe, which declared 1,231 ha (3,041 acres), producing 64,357 hl (1,699,025 gal) in 2000, encompasses the whole commune. As the most northerly of the six Médoc Appellations Communales, it has a fairly well-identified character, lying as it does at an average altitude of 40 m (130 ft) on gravelly soils that have a little more clay than the more southerly appellations. The Saint-Estèphe appellation includes five Crus Classés and the wines produced there have a noticeable tang of the *terroir*. Compared with other Médocs, the Saint-Estèphe wines have a higher degree of acidity in the grapes, a greater depth of colour and a more significant richness of tannin. They are very robust, and are excellent wines for laying down.

Saint-Estèphe

CH. ANDRON BLANQUET 1998★

■ Cru bourg.　16 ha　66,500　█ €11–15

75	76	79	81	82	83	85	86	87	88	[89]
[90]	91	92	[93]	[94]	[95]	96	97	98		

This cru, a sister of Cos Labory, is highly typical of the AOC in having 80% Cabernet Sauvignon and Cabernet Franc, planted in lovely Günz gravel. Its very bright, garnet-red wine is well balanced and harmonious, with fine, elegant tannins, which guarantee that it will age well. Its intense bouquet of spices with floral and fruity notes makes it a great classic.

•➤ SCE Dom. Audoy, Ch. Andron Blanquet, 33180 Saint-Estèphe, tel. 05.56.59.30.22, fax 05.56.59.73.52 ☑

CH. BEAU-SITE 1998★

■ Cru bourg.　n.c.　n.c.　█ €11–15

'The best vineyards can see the river', the saying goes. From the terrace of this house, one has a view over the vines and the estuary, which says a lot about the quality of the *terroir*. Powerful but well balanced, the wine is a fine ambassador for the estate. Although still a little dominated by the oak, it has the necessary richness and tannic strength for it to integrate as it ages. The finish is long and very elegant.

•➤ Héritiers Castéja, 33250 Pauillac, tel. 05.56.00.00.70, fax 05.57.87.48.61 ☑ by appt.

CH. BEL-AIR 1998★

■　4 ha　26,000　█ €11–15

This cru's reputation for consistent quality is maintained in this wine, which has a lovely presentation. Its garnet colour and its nicely complex bouquet, which offers notes of bilberry and spice, is followed by a well-balanced palate with long tannins, that have not yet entirely integrated.

•➤ SCEA du Ch. Bel Air, 4, chem. de Fontauge, 33180 Saint-Estèphe, tel. 05.56.58.21.03, fax 05.56.58.17.20, e-mail jfbraq@aol.com ☑ by appt.
•➤ J.-F. Braquessac

CH. CALON-SEGUR 1998★

■ 3ème cru clas.　90 ha　n.c.　█ €38–46

Calon, bishop of Poitiers, owned this cru in the Middle Ages and in the 18th century, the president of Ségur added his name to this château, which dates back to the 17th century. This wine, with its lovely ruby-red colour with purplish highlights, asserts its personality right from the start. Its bouquet of blackcurrants, blackberries and raspberries with musky overtones takes on plenty of character as the wine aerates. The, powerful, almost sappy palate has a lovely sense of balance and good ageing potential.

•➤ SCEA Ch. Calon-Ségur, 33180 Saint-Estèphe, tel. 05.56.59.30.08, fax 05.56.59.71.51 ☑ by appt.

CH. CHAMBERT-MARBUZET 1998★

■ Cru bourg.　8 ha　50,000　█ €15–23

66	76	79	81	82	83	[85]	[86]	[88]	[89]	[90]
91	92	[93]	[94]	[95]	96	97	98			

The talented man who produced this wine is none other than the owner of Haut-Marbuzet. Here he also gives us a lovely wine with a dense structure and a complex bouquet of cocoa, liquorice and red berries. Judging by the full, fruity finish, it will age very well.

•➤ Henri Duboscq et Fils,
Ch. Chambert-Marbuzet, 33180 Saint-Estèphe, tel. 05.56.59.30.54, fax 05.56.59.70.87 ☑
☒ ev. day except Sun. 10am–12 noon 2pm–6pm

CH. CLAUZET 1998

■ Cru bourg.　12 ha　73,000　█ €11–15

Maurice Velge is fond of reminding people that this vineyard is the realisation of a long dream and we happily believed it when we tasted this wine, whose structure promises to open out when it has been cellared for two or three years. Its present youthfulness bursts through in an attractive show; in the colour, with its violet highlights, as much as the emerging aromas of red berries on a background of toast and vanilla. The Jury also praised the **Château de Côme 98** from the same producer.

•➤ SA Maurice Velge, Leyssac, 33180 Saint-Estèphe, tel. 05.56.59.34.16, fax 05.56.59.37.11, e-mail chateauclauzet@wanadoo.fr ☑ ☒ ev. day except Sat. & Sun. 9am–12 noon 2pm–5pm

LES PAGODES DE COS 1998★

■　n.c.　110,000　█ €15–23

This second label from Cos (see below) is ruby in colour, with deep-purple highlights. Its rich, powerful structure remains well

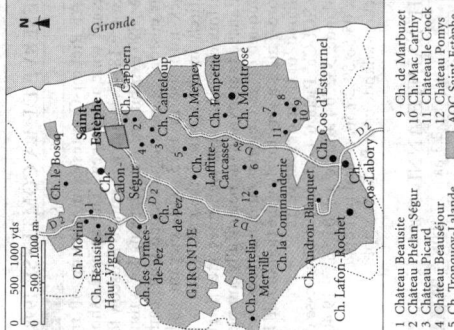

Saint-Estèphe

1　Château Beausite
2　Château Phélan-Ségur
3　Château Picard
4　Château Beauséjour
5　Ch. Tronquoy-Lalande
6　Château Houissant
7　Château Haut-Marbuzet
8　Ch. la Tour-de-Marbuzet
9　Ch. de Marbuzet
10　Ch. Mac Carthy
11　Château le Crock
12　Château Pomys
▨　Cru classé
▨　AOC Saint-Estèphe
▨　Cru bourgeois
⋯⋯　Commune boundaries

416

balanced and the bouquet is reminiscent of that of the first wine in its musky, spicy notes. It will go well with game in four or five years.

↪ Domaines Prats, 33180 Saint-Estèphe, tel. 05.56.73.15.50, fax 05.56.59.72.59, e-mail estournel@estournel.com
⑂ by appt.

COS D'ESTOURNEL 1998★★
■ 2ème cru clas.   65 ha   285,000   € 46-76

75 76 78 79 80 81 **82** 83 **85** **86** 87 88 89 **90** 91 **92** **93** **94** **95** **96** 97 98

A veritable oriental palace, Cos, as every-one in Médoc calls it, is quite simply a cellar completely dedicated to wine. It was sold once in 1998 and then changed hands again in 2000, but that did not change anything about the way the estate was run nor did it affect the quality of the wine, which has the benefit of exceptional *terroir*. This beautiful garnet 98 has an elegant bouquet with fine toasty, gamey notes mingled with ripe fruits, particularly blackcurrants. The palate comes up to the standard of the rest, with its silky tannins that have plenty of character. The whole concludes on a long, lingering finish that is full of promise.

↪ Domaines Prats, 33180 Saint-Estèphe, tel. 05.56.73.15.50, fax 05.56.59.72.59, e-mail estournel@estournel.com
⑂ by appt.

CH. COS LABORY 1998★★
■ 5ème cru clas.   18 ha   68,000   € 23-30

64 70 75 78 79 80 81 82 83 84 85 **86** 87 88 89 **90** 91 **92** 93 94 95 96 97 98

This cru succeeded in improving the quality of its production very significantly in the 1980s and today enjoys the reputation that its *terroir*, its classification, the people who run it and the quality of its wine, deserve. The lovely colour of this wine shows promise and what follows fulfils it. The bouquet plays on notes of ripe fruits, essentially blackcurrants and blackberries, spices (cinnamon) and toasted oak. The palate is full, powerful, elegant, well balanced and classy. The Jury also praised the second wine, **Le Charme Labory 98**. It is simpler but will also age well.

↪ SCE Domaines Audoy, Ch. Cos Labory, 33180 Saint-Estèphe, tel. 05.56.59.30.22, fax 05.56.59.73.52 ⑂ by appt.

417

CH. COUTELIN-MERVILLE 1998★
■ Cru bourg.   20.9 ha   154,000   € 11-15

A diverse mix of grapes and traditional vinification have resulted in this lovely, crimson wine, which has an intense bouquet. Although the oak still needs time to integrate, the full, tannic structure will ensure that this happens.

↪ G. Estager et Fils, Blanquet, 33180 Saint-Estèphe, tel. 05.56.59.32.10, fax 05.56.59.32.10 ⑂ by appt.

CH. HAUT-MARBUZET 1998★★★
■ Cru bourg.   55 ha   350,000   € 23-30

61 62 64 66 67 70 71 73 **75** **76** 77 **78** 79 **80** **81** **82** **83** **85** 86 88 89 90 |92| **93** **94** **95** **96** 97 **98**

In the almost 30 years that Henri Duboscq has been running this vineyard, he has both enlarged it and imprinted his personality upon it. He makes the wines he loves, which has resulted in one of the biggest successes of the year. The promise of the colour is more than fulfilled in the bouquet and the flavours on the palate. The former is as complex as one could wish, mingling overripe fruit with chocolate and toast. The latter is perfectly constructed, fresh and fruity, whilst remaining genuinely Saint-Estèphe. It leaves the taster with a sense of harmony, which almost tempts one to forget that this is a wine for cellaring.

↪ Henri Duboscq et Fils, Ch. Haut-Marbuzet, 33180 Saint-Estèphe, tel. 05.56.59.30.54, fax 05.56.59.70.87 ⑂ ev. day except Sun. 10am–12 noon 2pm–6pm

CH. LA COMMANDERIE 1998
■ Cru bourg.   9 ha   71,000   € 8-11

This engaging wine is produced from a vineyard where Merlot represents 50% of a mix of varieties. Its structure, though delicate, is sufficiently substantial to ensure that it will age well.

↪ EARL Ch. La Commanderie, Leyssac, 33180 Saint-Estèphe, tel. 05.56.59.32.30, fax 05.56.90.08.78 ⑂ by appt.

Saint-Estèphe

CH. LAFON-ROCHET 1998★★

4ème cru clas. 40 ha 144,000 ☐☐ ♦ €30-38

|64| 75 76 77 78 79 81 82 |83| 85 86
|88| |89| |90| |91| 92 93 |94| (95) 96 97 98

Improvements to the equipment are carried out on a regular basis on this cru and the year 2000 saw the construction of a new cellar. This wine is a blend of 39% Cabernet Sauvignon and 61% Merlot. Its highly nuanced bouquet is a perfect balance of liquorice, spices and black fruits. This sense of balance reappears on the palate, where well-executed extraction and real richness of flavour create a dense and complex whole, which is crowned by an extremely classy finish.

➤ SCF Ch. Lafon-Rochet,
33180 Saint-Estèphe, tel. 05.56.59.32.06,
fax 05.56.59.72.43, e-mail lafon@
lafon-rochet.com ☑ ☒ by appt.

➤ Tesseron

CH. LA PEYRE 1998

■ Cru artisan 6.5 ha 40,000 ☐☐ €11-15

This very young estate pulled off a great success with its 96. The 98, half Cabernet Sauvignon and half Merlot, has spent 15 months maturing in oak. There is no hiding this, as it is the oak that has the loudest voice at the moment. This is a powerful, long wine that should be cellared for four or five years.

➤ EARL Vignobles Rabiller, Leyssac,
33180 Saint-Estèphe, tel. 05.56.59.32.51,
fax 05.56.59.70.09 ☒ ev. day 10am–12 noon 2.30pm–7pm

CH. LE BOSCQ 1998★★

■ Cru bourg. 16.62 ha 48,000 ☐☐ €15-23

82 83 85 |86| (88| 89 90 |95| |96| |97| **98**

The Medoc house of Dourthe has always been good at choosing the crus that it distributes and those, like this one, that it cultivates, which keeps all the promises made by its beautiful, deep-ruby colour with its garnet highlights. The bouquet is impressively complex in its perfumes of black fruits and roasting coffee beans. The development on the palate has just as much character and reveals a remarkable structure. The superb finish signals a grand Saint-Estèphe that should be laid down for at least five years.

➤ Dourthe, 35, rue de Bordeaux,
33290 Parempuyre, tel. 05.56.35.53.00,
fax 05.56.35.53.29, e-mail contact@
cvbg.com ☑ ☒ by appt.

➤ GFA Le Boscq

CH. LE CROCK 1998★

■ Cru bourg. n.c. n.c. ☐☐ €11-15

90 |95| 96 97 98

Again, this cru has presented a well-constructed wine with a pleasant bouquet. It is nicely balanced, opting for finesse and unfolding fresh, delicate flavours in which the fruit and the oak are in harmony. The tasting ends on a long finish.

➤ Domaines Cuvelier, Ch. Le Crock,
33180 Saint-Estèphe, tel. 05.56.59.30.33,
e-mail cuvelier.bordeaux@wanadoo.fr ☑
☒ by appt.

CH. LES ORMES DE PEZ 1998★

■ Cru bourg. 33 ha 204,000 ☐☐ €23-30

81 |82| |83| 84 |85| |86| 87 |88| **89 90 91**
|92| 93 94 95 96 97 98

Like Château Lynch-Bages in Pauillac, this cru, owned by the Cazes, is one of the safe bets in the appellation. This deep-garnet 98 is a blend of 20% Merlot and 80% Cabernet Sauvignon and Cabernet Franc. It is thoroughly typical, dense but fine, with a bouquet that has agreeable perfumes of blackcurrants and redcurrants. Initially, the fruit is predominant on the palate, and it then gradually gives way to high-quality tannins, which linger lengthily through the finish. This is a wine that will age well.

➤ Jean-Michel Cazes, Ch. Les Ormes de Pez, 33180 Saint-Estèphe,
tel. 05.56.73.24.00, fax 05.56.59.26.42,
e-mail infochato@ormesdepez.com ☑

➤ Famille Cazes

CH. LILIAN LADOUYS 1998★

■ Cru bourg. 30 ha 200,000 ☐☐ €15-23

|89| |(90)| |91| 92 |93| |94| **95 96** 97 98

The quality of this cru has risen rapidly over the last few years. Its *terroir* is composed of 61% clay-limestone and 16% sandy gravel. This wine is a true Médoc in its blend and its suitably becoming colour. The bouquet, which is still a little closed, allows a glimpse of complex spicy, flowery notes. The well-extracted tannins are still firm. The Jury also praised the **La Devise de Liliane 98**.

➤ Ch. Lilian Ladouys, Blanquet,
33180 Saint-Estèphe, tel. 05.56.59.71.96,
fax 05.56.59.35.97 ☒ by appt.

➤ Natexis

CH. MARBUZET 1998★

■ Cru bourg. 7 ha 32,000 ☐☐ €15-23

75 76 78 **79** 81 **82** 83 84 |85| |86| 87
|88| |89| |(90)| 92 93 |94| **95 96** |98|

This Cru Bourgeois, owned by the Prat estates, is the younger sister of Cos d'Estournel. Its wine is well balanced and silky and knows how to express its own personality in its extremely subtle perfumes of flowers and fruits.

➤ Domaines Prats, 33180 Saint-Estèphe,
tel. 05.56.73.15.50, fax 05.56.59.72.59,
e-mail estournel@estournel.com ☒ by appt.

MARQUIS DE SAINT-ESTEPHE

Tradition Elevé en fût de chêne 1998

■ 34 ha 270,000 ☐☐ €11-15

The bouquet and flavours of this label from the Saint-Estèphe co-operative are still rather closed, but its sound body and still-young tannins will enable it to open out.

418

• Marquis de Saint-Estèphe, 2, rte du Médoc, 33180 Saint-Estèphe, tel. 05.56.73.35.30, fax 05.56.59.70.89, e-mail marquis.st.estephe@wanadoo.fr ▼
Ý ev. day except Sat. & Sun. 8.30am–12.15pm 2pm–6pm

CH. MONTROSE 1998★★

■ 2ème cru clas. 68 ha 196,500 ⅢⅢ £46-76

64 66 67 |70| |75| 76 78 |79| 81 |82| 83
|85| 86 87 88 89 90 |91| |92| |93| 94 95
96 97 98

This vast estate has a lovely *terroir* that can see the river, a view no doubt more interesting than the architecture of the château. Its 98, which is still oak-dominated, reveals a powerful, well-balanced, highly typical structure, which is accompanied by a bouquet in which cocoa, red berries and oak mingle agreeably. The tremendously long tannins will ensure that it ages well.
• Jean-Louis Charmolüe, SCEA du Ch. Montrose, 33180 Saint-Estèphe, tel. 05.56.59.30.12, fax 05.56.59.38.48 ▼
Ý by appt.

CH. PETIT BOCQ 1998

■ 7.74 ha 54,000 ⅢⅢ £15-23

94 95 96 97 98

This wine, which comes from a vineyard planted with *70%* Merlot, has an agreeable bouquet with a whole range of perfumes that moves from fruit to spices via brandied fruits. The initial impression on the palate is rounded and generous, and it then becomes more tannic with a structure that calls for cellaring for a short while.
• SCEA Lagneaux-Blaton, 3, rue de la Croix-de-Pez, B.P. 33, 33180 Saint-Estèphe, tel. 05.56.59.35.69, fax 05.56.59.32.11, e-mail petitbocq@hotmail.com ▼
Ý by appt.

CH. PHELAN SEGUR 1998★★

■ Cru bourg. 64 ha 180,000 ⅢⅢ £30-38

81 82 86 |88| |89| |90| |91| 92 93 |94| 95
96 97 98

This cru, on a beautiful estate overlooking the estuary, right next to the town, opts for elegance with this wine. The initial impression is fine, then tannins, whose gentleness testifies to high-quality extraction and good fruit, emerge on the palate. The finish, long without being overwhelming, has the same style. The Jury singled out the second wine, **Frank Phélan 98**.
• Ch. Phélan Ségur, 33180 Saint-Estèphe, tel. 05.56.59.74.00, fax 05.56.59.74.10, e-mail phelan.segur@wanadoo.fr
Ý by appt.
• X. Gardinier

CH. PICARD 1998★

■ Cru bourg. 8 ha 45,000 ⅢⅢ £11-15

This château, owned by the Mähler-Besse Group, who bought it in 1997 from Champagne Roederer, is less than 100 m (328 ft) from the Neoclassical parish church of Saint-Estèphe, which has a beautifully decorated interior. This 98 is a blend of 15% Merlot and 85% Cabernet Sauvignon, grown on a gravel hilltop. The tannins of the oak and wine still need to integrate but both are of high quality, as is the bouquet with its complex notes of fruit, roasting coffee beans and liquorice. The structure guarantees that this is a wine that will age well; the long toasty finish confirms it.
• SA Mähler-Besse, 49, rue Camille-Godard, BP 23, 33026 Bordeaux, tel. 05.56.56.04.30, fax 05.56.56.04.59, e-mail france.mahler-besse@wanadoo.fr ▼
Ý by appt.

CH. POMYS 1998

■ Cru bourg. 12 ha 65,000 ⅢⅢ ♦ £11-15

This estate, well known for its three-star château-hotel, along with its sister ship, the Château Saint-Estèphe constitutes a lovely 24-ha (59-acre) property. This 98 develops a well-balanced structure with fine tannins and a bouquet that moves from red berries through to floral notes. The Jury also praised the **Château Saint-Estèphe 98**.
• SARL Arnaud, Ch. Pomys, 33180 Saint-Estèphe, tel. 05.56.59.32.26, fax 05.56.59.35.24 ▼ Ý by appt.

CH. SEGUR DE CABANAC 1998★★

■ Cru bourg. 7.07 ha 45,000 ⅢⅢ £15-23

|86| 88 89 90 91 92 |93| |94| 95 96 |97|
98

Saint-Estèphe has links with the great Ségur family, the Bordeaux parliamentarians who wrote the history of Bordeaux wine, and are more generally associated with Pessac, Pauillac or Margaux. This wine pays well-deserved homage to the Ségur links, not just in its name but also in its extremely rich structure, which calls for the wine to be cellared for at least five years. The power of the bouquet, with its notes of toast, vanilla and red berries, allows us to view the future of this wine serenely.
• SCEA Guy Delon et Fils, Ch. Ségur de Cabanac, 33180 Saint-Estèphe, tel. 05.56.59.70.10, fax 05.56.59.73.94 ▼
Ý by appt.

CH. TOUR DE PEZ 1998★★

■ Cru bourg. 14 ha 80,000 ⅢⅢ £15-23

91 |93| |94| |95| 96 97 98

This cru is a beautiful unity, in size and in the quality of its *terroir* and in its wine, as this fully satisfactory 98 goes to show. Everything about this wine, throughout the tasting, is remarkable, from its garnet colour and its powerful bouquet, in which red berries mingle with toasty notes, to the palate, which is just as powerful and even more complex, with its almondy notes joining the fragrances of the bouquet. It is tannic and long and should be laid down for four or five years. The second wine, the **Château Les Hauts de Pez 98**, was awarded a star. It will also age well.

Saint-Julien

The vineyard of Saint-Julien is fairly small at 911 ha (2,250 acres) and producing 49,759 hl (1,313,638 gal) in 2000, and is located in the exact centre of the Haut-Médoc. Its wine can be thought of as a harmonious synthesis of Margaux and Pauillac, and so it is hardly surprising that Saint-Julien produces 11 Crus Classés (five of which are second growths). The wines reflect their *terroir*, offering a good balance between the qualities of Margaux (particularly their finesse) and the body of Pauillac wines. Generally speaking, Saint-Julien wines have a good colour, a fine, characteristic bouquet, good body, great richness and a beautifully aromatic flavour. It goes without saying that the wines in the 6.6 million bottles produced on average each year in Saint-Julien are far from all alike. Tasters with fine palates will distinguish between the Crus from the south (nearer to Margaux) and those from the north (which are closer to Pauillac), as well as between wines that come from nearer the estuary and those from further inland (near Saint-Laurent).

CH. TOUR DES TERMES 1998★★

■ Cru bourg.   15 ha   100,000   ▮▯ €11-15

| 81 | 82 | 83 | 84 | 85 | **86** | 88 | 89 | 92 | 93| 94| 95 |
| 96 | 97 | **98** | | | | | | | | | |

The mix of varieties on this cru, which has a high proportion of Merlot (50%), reflects a search for finesse and suppleness. This wine achieves the objective. Rich and complex in its flavours of ripe fruits, vanilla and toast, it is engaging whilst at the same time possessing a sound structure which gives support to the well-integrated oak. It will go well with game. The Jury also praised the attractively labelled **Fleur d'Ossian 98** from the same producer, which remains closed as the fruit is still completely dominated by the oak.

↬ Vignobles Jean Anney, Saint-Corbian, 33180 Saint-Estephe, tel. 05.56.59.32.89, fax 05.56.59.73.74 ▧ ▼ by appt.

↬ SA Ch. Tour de Pez, L'Hereteyre, 33180 Saint-Estephe, tel. 05.56.59.31.60, fax 05.56.59.71.12, e-mail chtpez@terre-net.fr ▧ ▼ ev. day except Sat. & Sun. 9.30am–12 noon 2pm–5pm; groups by appt.

CH. TRONQUOY LALANDE 1998★

■ Cru bourg.   17 ha   120,000   ▮▯ ♦ €11-15

| ⑧② | 83 | 85 | **86** | 87 | **88** | **89** | 90 | **91** | **93** | **94** |
| 95 | 96 | **98** | | | | | | | | |

The pretty 18th-century château of this cru presides over a vineyard growing 48% Merlot. This wine is a very attractive dark ruby in colour, with crimson highlights. The bouquet has real finesse, with perfumes of black fruits, enlivened by oaky notes. The well-balanced, elegant palate discloses a rich, velvety structure. This wine, still youthful, has a promising future ahead of it.

↬ Dourthe, 35, rue de Bordeaux, 33290 Parempuyre, tel. 05.56.35.53.00, fax 05.56.35.53.29, e-mail contact@cvbg.com ▧ ▼ by appt.
↬ Mme Casteja-Texier

Saint-Julien

The wine is Saint-Julien but the town is Saint-Julien-Beychevelle, making Saint-Julien the only Appellation Communale in the Haut-Médoc not to follow the standard practice of using the same name for both. The second name, it is true, has the drawback of being rather long. Both commune and appellation cover the same area, straddling two plateaux of pebbly and gravelly soil.

CH. BEYCHEVELLE 1998★★

■ 4ème cru clas.   55 ha   n.c.   ▮▮ €23-30

| 70 | 76 | 79 | 81 | 82 | 83 | 85 | **86** | **88** | **88**| |**89**| 90 |
| 91 | 92 | 93 | 94 | **95** | 96 | 97 | **98** | | | | |

Something halfway between a mansion and a palace, Beychevelle is one of the most beautiful wine châteaux in the Médoc. It is also a cru that has a remarkable *terroir*, as the excellence of its 98, which confirms the reputation of the 97, goes to prove. The perfumes of the pine forest rub shoulders with the spices that in earlier days perfumed the holds of the ships mooring up opposite the château to drop sail. These make up a bouquet whose complexity is enriched by gourmet notes of toasted bread, and strawberry jam. The palate is rich and balanced with a flavourful whole that displays its fleshiness and its potential, never ceasing to be elegant. This is a great Saint-Julien.

• SC Ch. Beychevelle,
33250 Saint-Julien-Beychevelle,
tel. 05.56.73.20.70, fax 05.56.73.20.71,
e-mail beychevelle@beychevelle.com
Y ev. day except Sat. & Sun. 10am–12 noon 2pm–5pm; groups by appt.

■ AMIRAL DE BEYCHEVELLE 1998★

19 ha   n.c.   €11–15

This second label from the Château Beychevelle has no claim to rival the first, but it creates no complexes and happily shows its worth. It has an expressive bouquet with notes of prunes, and a powerful, fleshy, well-rounded palate and will also age well.

• SC Ch. Beychevelle,
33250 Saint-Julien-Beychevelle,
tel. 05.56.73.20.70, fax 05.56.73.20.71,
e-mail beychevelle@beychevelle.com
Y ev. day except Sat. & Sun. 10am–12 noon 2pm–5pm; groups by appt.

■ CH. BRANAIRE Duluc-Ducru 1998★★

4ème cru clas.   n.c.   n.c.   €23–30

81 82 83 85 86 |88| 89 |90| 93 94 |95| 96 |97| 98

The renovation of the cru, undertaken ten years ago, has proven fruitful with this wine. It is entirely successful and testifies, in its finesse and ageing potential, to beautiful ingredients that have been intelligently worked. It should be laid down for five or six years while we dream about the captivating perfumes of liquorice, venison, menthol and prunes that the present bouquet allows us to glimpse.

• SAE du Ch. Branaire-Ducru,
33250 Saint-Julien-Beychevelle,
tel. 05.56.59.25.86, fax 05.56.59.16.26
Y by appt.

■ CH. DUCRU-BEAUCAILLOU 1998★★

2ème cru clas.   50 ha   210,000   €46–76

|61| 64 66 |70| 71 |75| 76 |78| 79 81 |82| 83 84 |85| |86| 87 88 89 90 91 92 |93| 94 |95| |96| |97| 98

Ducru, a superb mansion, surrounded by pavilions in a variety of styles, overlooks the estuary with its carefully aligned rows of vines. As one taster noted, in a blind tasting, 'don't forget, this wine is strongly marked by Cabernets'. It is indeed the case that the blend is made up of 65% Cabernet Sauvignon and 5% Cabernet Franc, with only 25% Merlot and 5% Petit Verdot. This is the excellent blend that makes Saint-Julien what it is. The power and elegance, that are typical of the cru, are realised to perfection in this wine. It has the additional bonus of possessing as rich and complex a bouquet as one could wish, with sunny notes of spices, cocoa and herbs, as well as a few touches of prunes and vanilla.

• SA Jean-Eugène Borie,
Ch. Ducru-Beaucaillou,
33250 Saint-Julien-Beychevelle,
tel. 05.56.73.16.73, fax 05.56.59.27.37
Y by appt.

■ CH. DULUC 1998★

n.c.   n.c.   €11–15

This wine, less ambitious than its older brother, Château Branaire, is nevertheless fine, with lacy tannins and flavours of roasting coffee beans and spices which make up a harmonious whole.

• SAE du Ch. Branaire-Ducru,
33250 Saint-Julien-Beychevelle,
tel. 05.56.59.25.86, fax 05.56.59.16.26
Y by appt.

■ CH. GLORIA 1998★

n.c.   n.c.   200,000   €23–30

64 66 70 71 |75| 76 |78| |79| 81 82 83 84 |85| |86| 87 |88| |89| |90| 93 94 |95| 96 97 98

Assisted by her husband, president of the Girondins de Bordeaux, Françoise Triaud is carrying on to great effect the work of her father, Henri Martin, who created this cru. Everything about the wine testifies to high-quality craftsmanship. It has a complex, elegant bouquet of green peppers and mocha, an subtle initial impression on the palate and fine, well-extracted tannins, supported by nicely judged oak.

• Domaines Martin, Ch. Gloria,
33250 Saint-Julien-Beychevelle,
tel. 05.56.59.08.18, fax 05.56.59.16.18
• Françoise Triaud

■ CH. GRUAUD-LAROSE 1998★

82 ha   254,000   €39–46

70 71 |75| 76 77 |78| 79 80 81 82 83 84 |85| |86| 87 |88| |89| 90 |91| 92 93 |94| |95| 96 |97| 98

This wine, the first to appear under the name of the present owners, the Taillan Group, will improve by being laid down. It testifies to their desire to keep up the standard

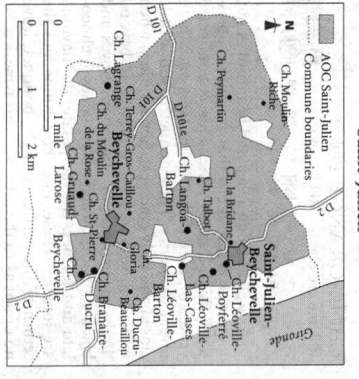

Saint-Julien

of quality and the renown of the cru. The promise of its beautiful, garnet-red colour is totally fulfilled in the bouquet with its lovely notes of red berries with a slight hint of musk, and the well-balanced, well-extracted structure on the palate. Its still oaky presence indicates that patience is in order.

➼ Ch. Gruaud-Larose, BP 6,
33250 Saint-Julien-Beychevelle,
tel. 05.56.73.15.20, fax 05.56.59.64.72,
e-mail contact@chateau-gruaud-larose.com
Y by appt.
➼ Bernard Taillan Vins

CH. LA BRIDANE 1998★ 〓 ⁂ ✸11-15

Cru bourg.	15 ha	n.c.
81	82	83	85	86	88	89	90		93		94		95	
96	97	98

Here three centuries of family tradition have forged a solid link with the *terroir*. This Cru Bourgeois gives evidence of this fact by its numerous merits; a lovely deep purple colour, a potent, classy bouquet, with beautiful notes of violet and roasting coffee beans, and a soft initial impression, followed by a structure with dense tannins and an opulent, liquoricey finish. It should be cellared for four or five years.

➼ Bruno Saintout, SCEA de Cartujac,
20, Cartujac, 33112 Saint-Laurent-Médoc,
tel. 05.56.59.91.70, fax 05.56.59.46.13 ✉
Y by appt.

LA CROIX DE BEAUCAILLOU 1998★ 〓 ✸23-30

	n.c.	77,000

This second label from Ducru-Beaucaillou declares its youthfulness and its ageing potential in its deep violet colour. Supported by ample, rich tannins, the structure accords perfectly with the jammy perfumes of the bouquet and the chocolatey flavours on the palate, resulting in a high-quality wine.

➼ SA Jean-Eugène Borie,
33250 Saint-Julien-Beychevelle,
tel. 05.56.73.16.73, fax 05.56.59.27.37
Y by appt.

CH. LAGRANGE 1998★★ 〓 ✸23-30

3ème cru clas.	109 ha	n.c.
79	81	82	83	85	86		87	88	89	90		91
92	93		94	95	96	97	98

As well as being a vast and beautiful estate, Lagrange is also a cru that produces consistently high-quality wine. This is confirmed yet again, even if this 98 hesitates initially to reveal its merits. The bouquet is still a little closed and only emerges after aeration; when it does, however, its complexity is beyond doubt, in its notes of cinnamon, cloves and black pepper, crowned with touches of chocolate and leather. On the palate, the tannins are intense. These, like the tannins and the return of the perfumes of the bouquet, leave no doubt as to the future of this wine.

➼ Ch. Lagrange,
33250 Saint-Julien-Beychevelle,
tel. 05.56.73.38.38, fax 05.56.59.26.09,
e-mail chateau-lagrange@
chateau-lagrange.com Y by appt.
➼ Suntory Ltd

LES FIEFS DE LAGRANGE 1998★ 〓 ✸15-23

	n.c.	n.c.

This second wine from Lagrange is undoubtedly rather more modest than the first. It is no less interesting, however, either in its bouquet that mingles musky notes and over-ripe fruit, or its tannins, which need to rest for a while, or its long, flavourful finish.

➼ Ch. Lagrange,
33250 Saint-Julien-Beychevelle,
tel. 05.56.73.38.38, fax 05.56.59.26.09,
e-mail chateau-lagrange@
chateau-lagrange.com Y by appt.

CH. LALANDE 1998 〓 ⁂ ✸11-15

	30 ha	200,000

There is nothing secret about this wine but this doesn't prevent it from looking agreeable with its deep-purple colour. After a supple initial impression, the flavour of the Cabernet comes out on the palate in true Médoc fashion against an oaky background. The somewhat rustic tannins still need to integrate for three or four years.

➼ Vignobles Meffre, rue Joseph-Vernet,
84810 Aubignan, tel. 05.56.59.06.47,
fax 04.90.65.03.73 ✉ Y by appt.

CH. LALANDE-BORIE 1998 〓 ⁂ ✸15-23

	18 ha	100,000

From the same producer as Ducru-Beaucaillou, this wine, though more monolithic, has charm in its delicate colour and sound flavours, both in the bouquet and on the palate.

➼ SA Jean-Eugène Borie,
33250 Saint-Julien-Beychevelle,
tel. 05.56.73.16.73, fax 05.56.59.27.37
Y by appt.

CH. LANGOA BARTON 1998★ 〓 ⁂ ♦ ✸23-30

3ème cru clas.	19 ha	90,000
70	75	76	78	80	81	82		83	85		86	88
89		91	92	93		94	95	96	97	98

In its elegance and comfort, Langoa is one of the best examples of a Bordeaux mansion. Apart from Mouton, it is the only classified cru that has had the same owners since 1855. Since 1821, it has been the family seat of the Bartons, who came from Ireland in 1722. Its intense and complex wine is also firmly in the spirit of Médoc. Well balanced thanks to its fine tannins, it will age well and should be cellared five or six years.

➼ Anthony Barton, Ch. Langoa Barton,
33250 Saint-Julien-Beychevelle,
tel. 05.56.59.06.05, fax 05.56.59.14.29
Y by appt.

CH. LÉOVILLE-BARTON 1998★★

■ 2ème cru clas.	46 ha	250,000	⬛ ♦	€ 30-38

64 67 70 71 75 76 78 79 80 81 |82| |83|
|85| 86 87 88 89 |90| |91| 92 |93| 94 95
96 97 98

as the château is Langoa; wine-lovers will, however, linger at length over this 98, a perfect blend of 80% Cabernet Sauvignon and Cabernet Franc and 20% Merlot that beautifully expresses the gravel *terroir*. It is a deep browny-red in colour and right from the start affords a glimpse of a bouquet that is as complex as one could wish. The first impression on the palate is full, fleshy and supple, moving through into a finish that is tannic but ripe and flavoursome. Everything indicates that this is a wine that should be cellared for eight or ten years.

♠ Anthony Barton, Ch. Léoville-Barton, 33250 Saint-Julien-Beychevelle, tel. 05.56.59.06.05, fax 05.56.59.14.29, e-mail chateau@leoville-barton.com
Y by appt.

CH. LÉOVILLE POYFERRÉ 1998★★

■ 2ème cru clas.	n.c.	n.c.	⬛	€ 30-38

76 78 79 80 81 |82| |83| 84 85 86 87
88 89 |90| |91| |92| |93| |94| 95 96 97 98

Poyferré, situated at the heart of the ancient Léoville estate, has the château and 80 ha (198 acres) of land. Its vines occupy one of the finest Graves hilltops in the AOC. The youthful 98, still characterised by oak, will need to be cellared for some considerable time. However, its dark colour with violet highlights, is already indicative of good future prospects. The bouquet's fine notes, of jam, spices and herbs (the fruit is not yet apparent) are followed by a highly structured, flavourful palate: rich and dense in body with a long liquoricey finish.

♠ Didier Cuvelier, Ch. Léoville Poyferré, 33250 Saint-Julien-Beychevelle, tel. 05.56.59.08.30, fax 05.56.59.60.09, e-mail lp.dc@leoville-poyferre.fr
Y by appt.

CH. MOULIN DE LA ROSE 1998★

■ Cru bourg.	4.65 ha	30,000	⬛	

|93| |94| 95 **96** |97| 98

This wine, although it comes from a small vineyard made up of a number of scattered plots, is anything but mediocre amongst the Saint-Julien crus. Its beautiful colour with deep-purple highlights, a lovely bouquet in which buttery, almost *rancio* notes, mingle with aromas of toast, cocoa, prunes and, of course, ripe fruit, a well-integrated structure, and a finish, somewhere between caramel and coffee, make it totally original.

♠ SCEA Guy Delon et Fils, Ch. Moulin de la Rose, 33250 Saint-Julien-Beychevelle, tel. 05.56.59.08.45, fax 05.56.59.73.94 V
Y by appt.

CH. TALBOT 1998★

■ 4ème cru clas.	102 ha	300,000	⬛	€ 30-38

78 79 80 81 |82| 83 84 |85| |86| 87 |88|
89 90 **93** 94 95 96 97 98

Talbot, standing proudly on a gravel hilltop overlooking the Gironde estuary, is a château that exudes comfort and enjoyment of life, in addition to having a superb wine-growing *terroir*. Who could doubt this after sampling the substantial character in this rounded 98 with its thoroughly engaging dark colour and caressing bouquet of coffee, vanilla and spices, with balsamic notes? Its fine well-coated tannins and its almost feminine harmony make it a lovely example of coffee. It must be laid down for four to five years.

CH. MOULIN RICHE 1998★

■	n.c.	n.c.	⬛	€ 15-23

|93| |94| 95 96 97 98

This second label from Léoville Poyferré is also well structured, and will be ready for drinking sooner than the first, thanks to its more integrated tannins.

♠ Didier Cuvelier, Ch. Léoville Poyferré, 33250 Saint-Julien-Beychevelle, tel. 05.56.59.08.30, fax 05.56.59.60.09, e-mail lp.dc@leoville-poyferre.fr Y by appt.

PORT CAILLAVET 1998★

■	4 ha	18,000	⬛	€ 11-15

This label from the *négociant* Henri Duboscq, created in memory of his mother, has a level of complexity in its toasty, fruity bouquet. Right from its serious first impressions, and carried by a beautiful, tasty, tannin structure, the full palate has all the signs that it will age well.

♠ Brusina-Brandler, 3, quai de Bacalan, 33300 Bordeaux, tel. 05.56.39.26.77, fax 05.56.69.16.84 V Y by appt.

CH. SAINT-PIERRE 1998★★

■ 4ème cru clas.	17 ha	58,000	⬛	€ 30-38

82 83 84 |85| |86| 87 |88| |89| |90| 91 92
|93| 94 **95** **96** 97 98

The architecture of this château may not be particularly aristocratic, but its history is typical of a number of Médoc crus. It was created in the 17th century, divided up in the second half of the 19th century, then put back together again in the 20th century by Henri Martin. This is a modern wine, despite its charmingly nostalgic label. The bouquet starts on delicate musky notes, which then mingle with vanilla, toast and ripe fruits. The delightfully full-bodied palate is supported by silky tannins, which lead to a long finish.

♠ Domaines Martin, Ch. Saint-Pierre, 33250 Saint-Julien-Beychevelle, tel. 05.56.59.08.18, fax 05.56.59.16.18 V
Y by appt.
♠ Françoise Triaud.

exactly like a sponge and, as the grapes shrivel, the juice evaporates and becomes concentrated. This makes for musts that are very rich in sugar.

Many problems have to be overcome to achieve this sweet must. The development of noble rot varies from grape to grape, so the vines must be picked several times, each time harvesting only individual grapes that are in their optimum state. The quantities produced per hectare are tiny, with a maximum amount permitted in Sauternes and Barsac of 25 hl per ha (270 gal per acre). The way the grapes reach over-ripeness is very unpredictable and depends entirely on climatic conditions, so it is an extremely risky time for the growers.

CH. TERREY GROS CAILLOUX

1998

■ Cru bourg.　n.c.　100,000　🔳 ▥ ◊ €11–15

This cru, made up of two small estates that have been brought together, remains faithful to its traditions with this well-constructed wine. It has an attractive, delicate, oaky, fruity bouquet and a good structure whose tannins still need time to round out.

🍷 SCEA du Ch. Terrey Gros Cailloux, 33250 Saint-Julien-Beychevelle, tel. 05.56.59.06.27, fax 05.56.59.29.32 ▥
☖ by appt.

CH. TEYNAC 1998★

■　　11.5 ha　50,000　🔳 €15–23

93	94	95	96	97	98

This cru, consistent in its quality, provides another good example of its know-how. Although the bouquet is somewhat closed, the emergence of elegant touches of vanilla and liquorice can be detected. Classical in the best possible taste, the palate flavour is supported by assertive but well-balanced, unaggressive tannins. This harmonious wine should be laid down for a time.

🍷 Ch. Teynac, Grand-rue, Beychevelle, 33250 Saint-Julien-Beychevelle, tel. 05.56.59.12.91, fax 05.56.59.46.12 ▥
☖ by appt.
🍷 F. et Ph. Pairault

Sweet White Wines

When you consult a wine map of the Gironde, you immediately notice that the appellations for the sweet wines (Vins Liquoreux) are clustered in a small region that straddles the Garonne, around its confluence with the River Ciron. Is this just a coincidence? Certainly not: the chill waters of this little river, whose entire course is shaded by leafy trees, contribute to a very particular micro-climate, encouraging *Botrytis cinerea*, the fungus that causes noble rot. In autumn, damp mornings and warm, sunny afternoons create ideal conditions for the fungus to develop on the perfectly ripe grapes, but without causing them to burst; the pips behave

This village with its fine 17th-century chateau, known as the Fontainebleau of the Gironde, is often thought of as the capital of the Premières Côtes. But, since 1980, it is also an appellation for sweet wines and produced 6,628 hl (174,979 gal) in 2000.

CH. DES CEDRES

Cuvée Prestige Elevée en fût de chêne 1999★

□　　1 ha　4,600　🔳 €5–8

This supple, powerful wine, from the same producer as the Premières Côtes of the same name has a distinctive flavour of honey, jam and orange marmalade and an elegant finish.

🍷 SCEA Vignobles Larroque, Ch. des Cèdres, 33550 Paillet, tel. 05.56.72.16.02, fax 05.56.72.34.44 ▥ ☖ by appt.

CLOS SAINTE-ANNE 1999★

□　　1 ha　6,000　🔳 €11–15

The fact that this wine was produced by Francis Courcelle is in itself a guarantee of quality. True to form, it performed brilliantly, throughout the tasting, with its golden colour, complex honey, pineapple, tropical crystallised fruits and hazelnut bouquet, and supple, concentrated, amply sweet, long structure.

set off by a captivating bouquet, in which hints of smoke, honey and crystallised fruits mingle with the main aroma, Virginia tobacco. The flavourful, complex palate it as powerful as it is subtle. This wine is already very pleasant indeed but will be at its best in two or three years.(50-cl bottles)

♠ SCEA Vignobles Ménard,
Ch. Mémoires, 33490 Saint-Maixant,
tel. 05.56.62.06.43, fax 05.56.62.04.32,
e-mail memoires@aol.com ▼ ✔ by appt.

CH. PEYBRUN 1999★★
□ 5.93 ha 10.000 ‖ €8-11

A family presence, on the same estate for almost four centuries, creates quality expectations. Mme de Loze lives up to these brilliantly with this superb 99, which is nicely affected by noble rot. It has a very pleasant appearance, a lovely, developing bouquet of crystallised fruits, which is well supported by oak and a full, well-balanced palate with sound sweetness. This is characterful wine that should be laid down for four or five years.
♠ Catherine de Loze, 41, rue Sainte-Cécile, 33000 Bordeaux, tel. 05.56.96.10.84, fax 05.56.96.10.84 ▼

♠ Sté Vignobles Francis Courselle,
Ch. Thieuley, 33670 La Sauve,
tel. 05.56.23.00.01, fax 05.56.23.34.37 ▼
✔ by appt.

CH. FAYAU 1998★★
□ 10 ha 32.000 ‖ €5-8

The Médevilles, *négociants* established in an 18th-century mansion in Cadillac are a great credit to the appellation with this very lovely 98. After a hesitant start the bouquet quickly reveals its finesse and complexity, characteristics which appear again on the palate. The power and intensity of this wine indicate that it will age well.
♠ SCEA Jean Médeville et Fils,
Ch. Fayau, 33410 Cadillac,
tel. 05.57.98.08.08, fax 05.56.62.18.22,
e-mail medeville-jeanetfils@wanadoo.fr ▼
✔ ev. day except Sat. & Sun. 8.30am–12.30pm 2pm–6pm

DOM. DU FILH Cuvée réservée 1998
□ 0.6 ha 2.000 ‖ €8-11

Christine Bouyre hopes to celebrate the 100th birthday of her grandmother (98 at the time of writing) in these cellars bought – by her grandmother – in 1945. This tiny special *cuvée* produced on the 20-ha (49-acre) domaine, a stylish, classical wine, has agreeable flavours of beeswax, broom and crystallised fruits, and leaves memories of a well-balanced, elegant whole.
♠ Christine Bouyre, Le Filh,
33410 Donzac, tel. 05.56.62.93.21,
fax 05.56.62.16.84 ▼ by appt.

CH. DU JUGE 1999★
□ n.c. n.c.

This wine lives up to its lovely straw-yellow colour, with pale-gold highlights, in its delicate bouquet with hints of honeysuckle, mandarin oranges, and fruit jelly and its well-balanced, extremely elegant, very agreeably flavoured palate. The Jury also praised the **Cru Quinette 98.**
♠ Pierre Dupleich, Ch. du Juge, rte de Branne, 33410 Cadillac, tel. 05.56.62.17.77, fax 05.56.62.17.59, e-mail pierre.dupleich@wanadoo.fr ▼ by appt.

CH. LA BERTRANDE 1999
□ 5 ha 20.000

This wine, from the producer of the Premières Côtes de Bordeaux of the same name despite having less character, does have agreeable, delicate flowery, fruity flavours, supported by a good long structure.
♠ Vignobles Anne-Marie Gillet,
Ch. La Bertrande, 33410 Omet,
tel. 05.56.62.19.64, fax 05.56.76.90.55,
e-mail chateau.la.bertrande@wanadoo.fr ▼ by appt.

CH. MEMOIRES Grains d'Or Elevé en fût de chêne 1999*
□ 5.75 ha 10.000 ‖ €8-11

This vineyard, consistent in its quality, has produced yet another beautiful-looking wine

425

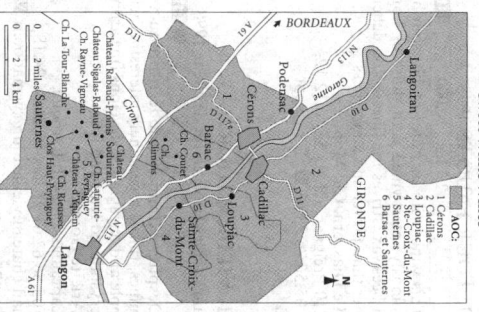

Sweet White Wines

AOC:
1 Cérons
2 Cadillac
3 Loupiac
4 Ste-Croix-du-Mont
5 Sauternes
6 Barsac et Sauternes

Loupiac

The Loupiac vineyard, which declared 14,549 hl (384,094 gal) from 401 ha (991 acres) in 2000, is very ancient, its existence first recorded in the 13th century. In aspect, *terroirs* and the vines grown there, this Appellation is very similar to the Appellation Sainte-Croix-du-Mont (see below). Yet, as one travels north, one can detect a subtle development in the flavour of the sweet wines, which become rounder, more in the style of the left bank.

CH. REYNON 1999★

□ 4.5 ha 16,000 ▥ €15-23

This wine, Denis Duburdieu's handiwork, achieves a good balance between power and suppleness. This basis enables the flavour to develop agreeable hints of crystallised fruits, fruit jelly, honey, apricots and white peaches. This wine, already pleasant and elegant, will achieve greatness in three to six years.

➥ Denis et Florence Dubourdieu,
Ch. Reynon, 33410 Béguey,
tel. 05.56.62.96.51, fax 05.56.62.14.89,
e-mail reynon@gofornet.com ▣ Ⴤ by appt.

DOM. DU ROC 1998

□ 4 ha 4,500 ▤ ♦ €8-11

Once again, this cru, with its consistent high standards of quality, has produced a beautiful looking, well-balanced wine with a delicate bouquet, which successfully creates a harmonious marriage between fruit-jelly flavours and hints of acacia flowers.

➥ Gérard Opérie, Dom. du Roc,
33410 Rions, tel. 05.56.62.61.69,
fax 05.56.62.17.78 ▣ Ⴤ by appt.

CH. DE TESTE 1999

□ 0.53 ha 2,800 ▤▥ ♦ €8-11

Here, Laurent Réglat, also a producer in the Premières Côtes, has produced a very small quantity of 100% Sémillon. Though still rather closed in it has an agreeable bouquet of crystallised fruits and spices.

➥ EARL Vignobles Laurent Réglat,
Ch. de Teste, 33410 Monprimblanc,
tel. 05.56.62.92.76, fax 05.56.62.98.80,
e-mail laurent.reglat@worldonline.fr ▣
Ⴤ ev. day except Sat. & Sun. 9am–12 noon
2.30pm–6pm; cl. 15–30 Aug.

CH. TOUR FAUGAS 1998

□ 2.7 ha 10,000 €11-15

This wine, with its notes of blossom harmoniously intertwined with those of honey and beeswax, strives for finesse and delicacy rather than power and jammyness

➥ Le Diascorn, Ch. Monteils,
33210 Preignac, tel. 05.56.76.12.12,
fax 05.56.76.28.63 ▣ Ⴤ by appt.

CH. VIEILLE TOUR

Grains nobles Elevé en fût de chêne 1998

□ n.c. 600 ▥ €11-15

Despite extremely modest production volumes, this is a genuinely interesting wine. Supple and engaging, it develops fine aromas of crystallised fruit and toast.

➥ Arlette Gouin,
1, Lapradiasse, 33410 Laroque,
tel. 05.56.62.61.21, fax 05.56.76.94.18,
e-mail chateau.vieille.tour@wanadoo.fr ▣
Ⴤ by appt.

CRU CHAMPON Crème de Tête 1998★

□ 1.8 ha 5,000 €8-11

This cru has been in the same family since 1793. Its attractive 98 was made from grapes harvested in mid-September. Supple, fresh, well balanced, its unctuous palate is complemented by the complexity of the bouquet, in which the perfumes of hazelnuts, mandarin oranges, jam and dried fruits mingle with those of noble rot.

➥ SCEA Yvan Réglat, Ch. Balot,
33410 Monprimblanc, tel. 05.56.62.98.96,
fax 05.56.62.19.48 ▣ Ⴤ by appt.

CH. DU CROS 1998★

□ 37 ha 35,000 ▥ €11-15

The 13th-century château is a place of cultural interest. The beautiful estate of le Cros belonged to the descendants of Montaigne, the author of the *Essais*, before Michel Boyer's grandfather bought it in 1921. The vineyards are well cared for. Though highly expressive with flavours of crystallised fruits and quince, the bouquet of this interesting yet straightforward 98 indicates that it is not in the same league as some earlier vintages.

➥ SA Vignobles M. Boyer, Ch. du Cros,
33410 Loupiac, tel. 05.56.62.99.31,
fax 05.56.62.12.59, e-mail contact@
chateauducros.com ▣ Ⴤ ev. day 8am–
12 noon 2pm–6pm; Sat. & Sun. by appt.

CH. DAUPHINE RONDILLON 1998

□ 18 ha 30,000 ▥ €8-11

This wine, from the same producer as Château Moutin (Graves), develops lovely, stewed, crystallised fruit and honeyed flavours that mingle with oaky, vanilla notes from 18 months barrel-maturation. It should be cellared for two years.

➥ SC Jean Darriet,
Ch. Dauphine-Rondillon, 33410 Loupiac,
tel. 05.56.62.61.75, fax 05.56.62.63.73,
e-mail vignoblesdarriet@wanadoo.fr ▣
Ⴤ ev. day 8am–12.30pm 2pm–6.30pm; Sat.
& Sun. by appt.; cl. 1–15 Aug.

CH. DU GRAND PLANTIER
Elevé en fût de chêne 1998
14 ha · 4,000 · €8-11
by appt.

This deep golden, barrel-matured Loupiac, distributed in numbered bottles, with its developing agreeable aromas of stewed fruit and honey and full-bodied palate, should be cellared for a few months to be appreciated at its best.

➥ GAEC des Vignobles Albucher, Ch. du Grand Plantier, 33410 Monprimblanc, tel. 05.56.62.99.03, fax 05.56.76.91.35
by appt.

CH. LA BERTRANDE 1998
3.59 ha · 15,000 · €8-11

At the time of writing, the cellars on this estate were undergoing renovation. The grape variety, Sémillon, is readily perceptible in the fruity bouquet of this fresh, rounded, well-constructed wine.

➥ Vignobles Anne-Marie Gillet, Ch. La Bertrande, 33410 Omet, tel. 05.56.62.19.64, fax 05.56.76.90.55, e-mail chateau.la.bertrande@wanadoo.fr
by appt.

CH. LA NERE 1998★
14 ha · 65,000 · €5-8

The Dulac-Séraphon estates consist of a fine group of vineyards made up of several crus in several different villages and appellations. This fresh, delicate, well-balanced Loupiac has great character, from its yellow colour and pleasant notes of crystallised, tropical fruits through to its supportive, round, full structure and long finish.

➥ SCEA Y. Dulac et J. Séraphon, 2, Pantoc, 33490 Verdelais, tel. 05.56.62.02.08, fax 05.56.76.71.49 by appt.

CH. LES ROQUES
Cuvée Frantz Elevé en fût de chêne 1999★★
3.5 ha · 2,500 · €15-23

Situated on a south-west facing hillside, bordering the Loupiac and Sainte-Croix-du-Mont AOCs, this cru has an exceptional view over Sauternes. The advantages of *terroir* are not just confined to the aspect, as this prestige *cuvée* proves in both its bouquet and palate. The former is fine, complex and full of surprises, with notes of dried fruits and orange peel. The latter is full, fleshy, rich and full of character. This is a wine to be cellared for four to five years.

➥ SCEA Ch. du Pavillon, 33410 Sainte-Croix-du-Mont, tel. 05.56.62.01.04, fax 05.56.62.00.92, e-mail a.v.fertal@wanadoo.fr by appt.
➥ Fertal

CH. DE LOUPIAC 1999★
2 ha · 6,600 · €15-23

Identified by its architecture, a mansion flanked by two pavilions, this château, situated near the 12th-century Romanesque church, really is in the spirit of Bordeaux. This barrel-matured wine acts as the standard-bearer for Sanfourche vineyards. The high quality oak, very much in evidence, contributes to the elegance of the whole palate as its vanilla mingles very satisfactorily with notes of acacia honey and menthol.

➥ Daniel Sanfourche, Ch. Loupiac-Gaudiet, 33410 Loupiac, tel. 05.56.62.98.88, fax 05.56.62.60.13, e-mail loupiac-gaudiet@atlantic-line.fr
by appt.
➥ Marc Ducau

CH. MEMOIRES 1999
5 ha · 9,900 · €5-8

Although Jean-François Ménard owns vineyards in other AOCs in the region, Loupiac is probably his favourite. This wine, in the complexity of its bouquet and full, fleshy body, shows all the evidence of careful craftsmanship. It should be cellared for three or four years.

➥ SCEA Vignobles Ménard, Ch. Mémoires, 33490 Saint-Maixant, tel. 05.56.62.06.43, fax 05.56.62.04.32, e-mail memoires@aol.com by appt.

CH. RONDILLON 1999
9.5 ha · 30,000 · €8-11

Following in the footsteps of a tradition dating back 200 years, the Bords have once more used *terroir* to advantage in this simple but well-balanced wine, which opts resolutely for finesse and elegance.

➥ SCEA Vignobles Bord, Ch. Rondillon, 33410 Loupiac, tel. 05.56.62.99.84, fax 05.56.62.93.55, e-mail lionelbord@vignoblesbord.com by appt.

Sainte-Croix-du-Mont

This area of steep hills overlooking the Garonne is comparatively little known, despite its considerable charm. The wines have long suffered from a reputation of being favourites at weddings and banquets, as have other Vins Liquoreux appellations from the right bank.

However, this appellation, which faces the Sauternes vineyards and which produced 16,155 hl (426,492 gal) from 429 ha (1,060 acres) in 2000, deserves better. The soil is good, mainly limestone with deposits of gravel, the micro-climate favouring the growth of noble rot. The grape varieties are similar to those grown in Sauternes, as are the methods of vinification. The wines are more rounded and soft rather than intensely sweet, with a pleasantly fruity taste. They can be served with the same dishes as their grander neighbours from the left bank, but their prices are more affordable, sufficiently so as to serve them as a sumptuous extra at drinks parties.

CH. DES ARROUCATS 1999   ■ ♦ €5-8

☐   23 ha   40,000

This deep golden wine engages us through both the scorched, toasty, jammy notes of its bouquet and its rich, slightly heady, well-rounded, fleshy structure.

↦ EARL des Vignobles Labat-Lapouge, Ch. des Arroucats,
33410 Sainte-Croix-du-Mont,
tel. 05.56.62.07.37, fax 05.57.98.06.29 ☒
☖ ev. day except Sun. 9am–12 noon 2pm–6pm
↦ Annie Lapouge

CH. CRABITAN-BELLEVUE

Cuvée spéciale 1998★   ▦ €8-11

☐   22 ha   13,000

This 46-ha (114-acre) estate presented a 24-months barrel-matured, 100% Sémillon Cuvée Spéciale. Though still being marked by high quality oak, this is a very lovely wine with good overall balance. It will, nevertheless, take five years for the fruit to assert its identity. This is another wine for devotees of the 'modern school'.

↦ GFA Bernard Solane et Fils,
33410 Sainte-Croix-du-Mont,
tel. 05.56.62.01.53, fax 05.56.76.72.09 ☒
☖ ev. day except Sun. 8am–12 noon 2pm–6pm

CH. LA GRAVE

Sentiers d'automne 1998★   ▦ €8-11

☐   11 ha   n.c.

Without beating around the bush, the barrel on the label tells us that this wine has been carefully cask-matured to ensure the contribution of the oak respects the wine's overall harmony. The bouquet and the palate flavour, which is round, rich, full and long, are evidence of well-managed noble rot followed by high-quality craftsmanship. The Jury also favourably mentioned the **Château Grand Peyrot 98**.

↦ Jean-Marie Tinon, Ch. La Grave,
33410 Sainte-Croix-du-Mont,
tel. 05.56.62.01.65, fax 05.56.62.00.04,
e-mail tinon@terre-net.fr ☒ ☖ by appt.

CH. LAMARQUE 1999★   ▦ €8-11

☐   15 ha   45,000

This cru, situated on a hillside overlooking the Garonne valley, enjoys its share of a good,

typical *terroir*, as shown by the presence of fossilized oyster beds. This asset, used to maximum advantage, produces lovely, very well-balanced wines. This wine, in which the personality of the structure and the bouquet has been respected in the maturation process, is no exception. Stewed fruit flavours with exotic notes give this wine real style, right through to its silky finish. It makes it just as enjoyable to drink now as it will be in three or four years' time.

↦ Bernard Darroman, Ch. Lamarque,
33410 Sainte-Croix-du-Mont,
tel. 05.56.62.01.21, fax 05.56.76.72.10 ☒

CH. LA RAME

Réserve du Château 1999★   ▦ €15-23

☐   20 ha   10,000

This agreeable 99 is the first wine to have benefited from Yves Armand's new 1,000-m² (10,760-sq ft) cellar. Although it doesn't claim to rival earlier vintages, many of whom have become legends, this wine shows harmony in its roundness, good balance and an elegant bouquet of flowers, honey and mangoes, set against a backdrop of beeswax.

↦ Yves Armand, Ch. La Rame,
33410 Sainte-Croix-du-Mont,
tel. 05.56.62.01.50, fax 05.56.62.01.94,
e-mail chateau.larame@wanadoo.fr ☒
☖ ev. day 8.30am–12 noon 1.30pm–7pm;
Sat. & Sun. by appt.

CH. LESCURE 1998   ▦ ■ ♦ €5-8

☐   4.34 ha   11,800

This cru, with its 1930s cellar, has been run by a co-operative association since 1993. It has produced a blend of 5% Muscadelle, 85% Sémillon and 10% Sauvignon. This likeable, well-rounded wine, which is very 'in character', has an agreeable bouquet of dried apricots and honey coupled with well-integrated oak and hints of noble rot.

↦ C.A.T. Ch. Lescure, 33490 Verdelais,
tel. 05.57.98.04.68, fax 05.57.98.04.64,
e-mail chateau.lescure@free.fr ☒
☖ by appt.
↦ S.P.E.G.

CH. LOUSTEAU-VIEIL

Cuvée Grande Réserve 1999   ▦ €11-15

☐   15 ha   44,000

Produced from a vineyard which sees – or rather glimpses – the Pyrenees from time to time, this prestige *cuvée* is a blend of 60% Sémillon, 25% Muscadelle and 15% Sauvignon. Although its oak is still very noticeable this is still a well-balanced wine with a seductively elegant bouquet, with notes of apricot and mirabelles. A wine to be cellared for a year or two and then served with lighter meats.

↦ Vignobles R. Sessacq, Ch. lousteau-Vieil,
33410 Sainte-Croix-du-Mont,
tel. 05.56.62.01.15, fax 05.56.62.01.68,
e-mail me.sessacq@infonie.fr ☒
☖ ev. day 9am–8pm
↦ Martine Sessacq

CH. DU MONT Cuvée Pierre 1999★★★

15 ha   10,000   €11-15

Although the Château du Mont is one of the *Guide's* regulars, it has now introduced a new wine under the label 'Pierre'. This wine, a true jewel, has everything going for it: a brilliant golden colour, a perfect bouquet with notes of crystallised fruit and a thoroughly genuine sweet, overripe, concentrated, unctuous, rich and exceptionally elegant palate. This is an exquisite wine, which testifies to excellent craftsmanship.

- Vignobles Hervé Chouvac.
- Ch. du Mont, 33410 Sainte-Croix-du-Mont, tel. 05.56.62.07.65, fax 05.56.62.07.58
- by appt.
- Paul Chouvac

CH. PEYROT-MARGES Réserve du château 1999

8 ha   10,000   €8-11

This *cuvée*, harvested mid-October, doesn't hide its barrel-maturation. Its really elegant development shows in its golden shining colour. Its honeyed, apricot bouquet links to supple, silky flavours on the palate, leaving memories of an agreeable ensemble.

- GAEC Vignobles Chassagnol.
- Bern, 33410 Gabarnac, tel. 05.56.62.98.00, fax 05.56.62.93.23 ev. day except Sun. 8am–12.30pm 2pm–7pm; Sat. by appt.

Cérons

Enclosed by the Graves region (an appellation that they can also claim, unlike the Sauternes and Barsac), the wines of Cérons offer a link between Barsac and the sweet Graves Supérieures. Production was 2,591 hl (68,402 gal) from 76 ha (188 acres) in 2000. These are, nonetheless, original wines, with a characteristic vigour and great finesse.

Barsac

All the wines carrying the Appellation Barsac can also be Appellation Sauternes. Barsac, which covers 616 ha (1,522 acres) and produced 13,504 hl (356,506 gal) in 2000, differs from the communes of the Sauternais proper by virtue of a less hilly terrain and by the stone walls that enclose many of the vineyards. The wines themselves differ from those of Sauternes, being slightly sweeter in character. However, like Sauternes, they may be served with desserts or, as is more and more popular, to accompany a starter of foie gras or strongly flavoured cheeses, such as Roquefort.

CH. DU CAILLOU 1998★

2 ha   6,000   €8-11

This wine, from the same producer as the Graves, though still characterised by oak, is interesting because of its full, long general structure and its lovely bouquet of hazelnuts and toast. It should be cellared for three to five years to allow the obvious, very powerful oak to fade.

- SARL Ch. du Caillou, rte de Saint-Cricq, Caillou, 33720 Cérons, tel. 05.56.27.17.60, fax 05.56.27.00.31 by appt.
- Latorse

CH. HURADIN 1998★★

1.28 ha   3,000   €8-11

This wine, produced from grapes grown on a plateau of gravel, still has a way to go before reaching its prime. Its agreeable personality is already visible in its bouquet of hazelnuts, acacia and crystallised orange and its well-rounded, full, long structure.

- SCEA Vignobles Y. Ricaud-Lafosse, Ch. Huradin, 33720 Cérons, tel. 05.56.27.09.97, fax 05.56.27.09.97 by appt.

CH. CLIMENS 1997★

1er cru clas.   29 ha   32,000   *€76

71 72 75 76 79 80 81 82 |83| |85| |86| **88 89** (90) |91| 94 95 97

This elegant, classical residence sits, in perfect harmony, amidst its vines. Following its example is this shining golden wine whose personality reveals seductive floral perfumes and expresses finesse and elegance. Honey and apricot still hold the stage on the palate, crystallised, dried fruit notes are not yet apparent.

Barsac

CH. ROUMIEU-LACOSTE 1999★★★

□ | n.c. | 15,600 | 🔲 €23-30

|90| |95| |96| |97| **98** **99**

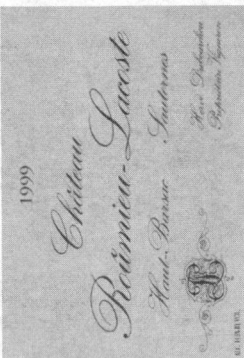

The Dubourdieu are a large family, not lacking in talent, as this superb 99 shows. Right from the start, the bouquet emerges majestically in an explosion of fragrances, ranging from crystallised fruits to hints of roast; these mingle harmoniously into a rich, complete, fine whole, simultaneously delicate and powerful. The palate, which gives free rein to a profusion of flavours, including apricots, raisins and toast is equally elegant, concentrated and complex. It is supported by a lovely structure and balanced oak, both indicating that this wine will age well.

☛ Hervé Dubourdieu,
Ch. Roûmieu-Lacoste, 33720 Barsac,
tel. 05.56.27.16.29, fax 05.56.27.02.65 ▼
▼ by appt.

☛ S. F. du Ch. Climens, 33720 Barsac,
tel. 05.56.27.15.33, fax 05.56.27.21.04,
e-mail contact@chateau-climens.fr ▼
▼ by appt.
☛ Bérénice Lurton

CH. FARLURET 1999★

□ | 9 ha | 10,000 | 🔲 €15-23

75 81 82 83 85 |88| |(89)| |90| |91| 94 95
|96| **97** 98 99

This wine, from the same producer as the Château Haut Bergeron (Sauternes), also opts for finesse in its lovely sweet bouquet, in which notes of raisins influenced by noble rot are warmed by a touch of vanilla, in a way that confirms a careful maturation.

☛ Hervé et Patrick Lamothe, 3, Piquey, 33210 Preignac, tel. 05.56.63.24.76,
fax 05.56.63.23.31, e-mail haut-bergeron@wanadoo.fr ▼ ▼ ev. day except Sun. 9am-12 noon 2pm-7pm

CH. NAIRAC 1997★★

□ 2ème cru clas. | 15 ha | 10,840 | 🔲 €38-46

73 74 75 76 79 80 **81** 82 |(83)| 85 |86| **88**
89 **90** |91| |92| |93| 94 **95** **96** **97**

Here, from the architecture of the château to the layout of the garden, the essence of perfection is everywhere, and this holds true for the production methods. How else could you explain the merits of this golden, straw-yellow wine. In the same class as its predecessors, it is as generous in its bouquet of over-ripe apricots and jam as it is on the palate, where its richness, complexity, a concentrated dimension and noble rot make it a very agreeable entity.

☛ Ch. Nairac, 33720 Barsac,
tel. 05.56.27.16.16, fax 05.56.27.26.50
▼ by appt.
☛ Nicole Tari

CH. ROUMIEU 1998

□ | 17 ha | 39,000 | €15-23

The supple, light, and unctuous quality of this wine is reflected in the subtlety of its bouquet, in which beeswax and orange mingle with iodized, fruity notes. It is bottled and distributed by the *negociant* Dourthe, CVBG in Parempuyre.

☛ Catherine Craveia-Goyaud,
Ch. Roumieu, 33720 Barsac,
tel. 05.56.27.21.01, fax 05.56.27.01.55
▼ by appt.

CH. SIMON 1998★

□ | 18 ha | 12,000 | 🔲 ◆ €11-15

Here, the Dufours, an old Barsac family, have produced a wine that is appealing in every way. From its fresh, elegant bouquet, mingling with notes of honey and mint, through to its development on the palate and then its lovely floral finish, enlivened by a touch of acacia, it is very agreeable.

☛ EARL Dufour, Ch. Simon,
33720 Barsac, tel. 05.56.27.15.35,
fax 05.56.27.24.79, e-mail chateau.simon@worldonline.fr ▼ ▼ by appt.

CH. SUAU 1999★

□ 2ème cru clas. | 8 ha | 19,000 | 🔲 ◆ €15-23

97 |98| |99|

This wine opts for suppleness, finesse and complexity, as confirmed by its bouquet of lychee, acacia honey and tropical fruits.

430

Sauternes

If you visit any of the châteaux in Sauternes, you will hear the story of the grower who one day had the brilliant, but perverse, idea of bringing in his harvest late, even though the grapes were over-ripe. However, if you go to five châteaux you will find that each grower has his own version of the story, which, naturally enough, took place on his property. The truth is, no one knows who 'invented' Sauternes, nor when it was invented, nor where.

While history in the

legend, there is no confusion about the geography of the area. The AOC covered an area of 1,624 ha (4,011 acres) in 2000. It produced 30,550 hl (806,520 gal) of wine. Every pebble in the five communes making up the appellation (including Barsac, which has its own appellation) is counted and every constituent recorded. The variety of soils and subsoils (limestone or chalk and clay under gravel) give a special character to each cru, with the most famous vineyards being planted on gravelly hillocks. The Sauternes wines are made from three grape varieties—Sémillon (70–80%), Sauvignon (20–30%) and Muscadelle; these are golden and luscious but also fine and delicate. Their 'toasted' bouquet develops very well with age, becoming rich and complex with notes of honey, hazelnut and crystallised orange. It is worth noting that Sauternes and Barsac were the only white wines to be classified in 1855.

CH. ANDOYSE DU HAYOT 1998

□   20 ha   36,000   ⊪▮◈

|90| |91| 93| 94| |95| |96| |97| 98

Sémillon (80%) and Muscadelle (20%) both love the clay-gravel soil of Sauternes. This fresh, sweet, golden 98, with its straw-coloured highlights, initially releasing perfumes of apples and pears, then hints of menthol, is ready for drinking now.

CH. D'ARMAJAN DES ORMES
1998★

□   7 ha   13,000   ⊪▮◈

|95| |96| 97 98

This ancient cru dating back to the 15th century has an 18th-century château. Its wine, which develops very beautifully throughout the tasting, showing that the estate is still in perfect order. It has a rich, dried-flowers, beeswax, quince bouquet and a full, supple, fleshy, flavoursome palate.

Ch. d'Armajan, 33210 Preignac, tel. 05.56.63.22.17, fax 05.56.63.21.55 ☑

CRU D'ARCHE-PUGNEAU 1998★

□   13 ha   10,000   ⊪▮◈   €15–23

The Daneys, a family with a tradition of wine-growing that goes back to the 18th century, have only been managing this cru since 1923. Their knowledge, passed down through the generations, can be seen in this lively, supple, full 98. It has plenty of character and a complex bouquet, in which beeswax mingles with flowers and notes of citrus fruits.

❧ Jean-Francis Daney, 24, le Biton, 33210 Preignac, tel. 05.56.63.50.55, fax 05.56.63.39.69, e-mail daney.francis.fr.free ☑ ☓ by appt.

❧ SCE Vignobles du Hayot, Ch. Andoyse, 33720 Barsac, tel. 05.56.27.15.37, fax 05.56.27.04.24, e-mail duhayot@usa.net ☑ ☓ by appt.

CH. BARONNE MATHILDE 1994

□   n.c.   n.c.   ⊪▮   €38–46

This wine, bearing *négociant* Baron Philippe de Rothschild's label, is pleasant in its buttery, cheesy bouquet with notes of raisins and apricots and interestingly in its full, concentrated palate.

❧ Baron Philippe de Rothschild SA, BP 117, 33250 Pauillac, tel. 05.56.73.20.20, fax 05.56.73.20.44, e-mail webmaster@bpdr.com

CRU BARREJATS 1997★★

□   2.6 ha   2,100   ⊪▮   €15–23

This cru consistently produces high-quality wine. Continuing in that tradition is this golden wine, whose colour is as agreeable as its oaky bouquet, with its hints of honey, crystallised apricots and currants. Rich and concentrated, it is becoming well balanced, but still has considerable development potential. The cru's second wine, the **Accabailles de Barréjats 98** was awarded a star.

❧ SCEA Barréjats, Clos de Gensac, Mareuil, 33210 Pujols-sur-Ciron, tel. 05.56.69.06, fax 05.56.76.69.06, e-mail mireille.daret@free.fr ☑ ☓ by appt.

❧ EARL Jacques et Guillaume Perromat, tel. 05.56.63.27.44.

❧ Mireille Daret et Ph. Andurand

Sauternes

CH. BASTOR-LAMONTAGNE 1998★

□   57 ha   64,000   ▦ ▥ ♦ €15-23   94 95

82 83 84 85 86 87 |88| |89| |90| 96 97 98

Here this valued, reliable, well-known Sauternes estate, almost a single parcel, presents a blend of 80% Sémillon and 20% Sauvignon from forty-year-old vines. A beautiful golden colour, it has an original bouquet, in which broom, crystallised fruits and beeswax mingle with lovely oak, and a well-balanced palate which leads into a truly elegant finish.
↬ SCEA Vignobles Bastor et Saint-Robert, Dom. de Lamontagne, 33210 Preignac, tel. 05.56.63.27.66, fax 05.56.76.87.03, e-mail bastor-lamontagne@dial.oleane.com
🅈 by appt.
↬ Foncier-Vignobles

CH. BECHEREAU 1998★

□   10.63 ha   33,000   ▦ ▥ €15-23

Vignobles Dumon produce wine in a number of appellations, but are biased towards Sauternes. Fresh, well balanced, well constructed and aromatic (acacia, fresh crystallised fruits, accompanied by lovely notes of liquoricey oak), their clear golden 98 shows that they know how to care for their wine.
↬ Les Vignobles Dumon,
Ch. Béchereau de Ruat, 33210 Bommes, tel. 05.56.76.61.73, fax 05.56.76.67.84 🅈
🅈 ev. day 9am–12 noon 2pm–5.30pm; Sat. & Sun. and groups by appt.

CH. CAILLOU Private Cuvée 1999★

□2ème cru clas.   n.c.   2,800   ▦ ▥ €38-46

The estate of this 13-hectare (32-acre) château, classified in 1855, produced this wine, which shows its pedigree, on a clay-limestone *terroir* in Haut Barsac. Right from the start, its colour, golden straw-yellow, makes its ambitions clear. Its agreeable bouquet with notes of honey, resin and citrus fruits is rather more distinctive. The pleasant, supple, rich, fruity, spicy palate leaves a lovely memory of a quality ensemble. It should be cellared for three years.
↬ Jean-Michel et Marie-Josée Pierre,
Ch. Caillou, 33720 Barsac,
tel. 05.56.27.16.38, fax 05.56.27.09.60 🅈
🅈 by appt.

CH. CAPLANE 1999★

□   3.5 ha   5,000   ▦ ▥ €11-15

This cru, a blend of 90% Sémillon and 10% Muscadelle, resolutely opts for elegance, especially in the bouquet with its successful marriage between honey and the extensive palette of fresh floral perfumes, blossom, roses and hawthorn. This pleasant wine has plenty of resources to ensure that it will age well.
↬ Guy David, 6, Moulin de Laubes, 33410 Laroque, tel. 05.56.62.93.76 🅈
🅈 by appt.
↬ Mme Garbay

CH. DE CARLES 1999

□   15.17 ha   40,000   ▦ ▥ ♦ €11-15

This Barsac cru has been in the same family since 1865. Here, this blend, 95% Sémillon and 5% Sauvignon, produces a supple, fresh wine with an engaging bouquet of tropical fruits (lychees and mangoes) mingled with honey and dried apricots.
↬ Michel Pascaud, Ch. de Carles, 33720 Barsac, tel. 05.56.27.07.19, fax 05.56.27.13.18, e-mail chateaudecarles@aol.com 🅈 by appt.

CLOS FONTAINE 1995

□   10 ha   5,000   ▥ €11-15

This simple but well-structured 95 has a nicely intense bouquet of very ripe fruit and freshness in its palate development.
↬ Claude Saint-Marc, Dom. du Petit de l'Eglise, 33210 Langon, tel. 05.56.62.24.78, fax 05.56.76.86.68 🅈 by appt.

CH. CLOSIOT 1998★★

□   4 ha   5,200

There is little chance of finding out if it is true that one of the routes to Santiago de Compostela went through this estate. The question need not prevent anyone from enjoying this lovely 98. Only the full palate equals the generosity of its bouquet with notes of toast, citrus fruits, honey, leather and dried fruits and the charming finish enlivened by little touches of orange peel. This wine deserves to be cellared for a bit, but it is already very enjoyable.
↬ Soizeau, Ch. Closiot, 33720 Barsac, tel. 05.56.27.05.92, fax 05.56.27.11.06, e-mail closiot@vins-sauternes.com 🅈
🅈 ev. day except Sat. & Sun. 9am–12 noon 2pm–6pm

CH. DU COY 1999★★

□   n.c.   18,000   ▦ ▥ €11-15

97 98 99

In 1999, Nicole Biarnès succeeded in making two radically different wines in Suau and Coy. The feminine personality of the Barsac contrasts with the invigorating qualities of the Sauternes. The latter, full and rich, has a bouquet that begins with fresh menthol perfumes, then moves to notes of raisins, crystallised oranges and honey. Still oaky, this is a wine that should be cellared for four or five years.
↬ Nicole Biarnès, Ch. de Navarro, 33720 Illats. tel. 05.56.27.20.27, fax 05.56.27.26.53 🅈 by appt.

CH. DOISY DAENE 1998★

□2ème cru clas.   15 ha   30,000   ▥ €23-30

50 71 |75| |76| |78| |79| |80| |81| |82| |83| 84 |85| |86| |88| |89| |90| |91| |94| 95 96 97 98

Pierre and Denis Dubourdieu, men of character, make the kind of white wines they like. Though full and well structured, this wine with its delightful straw-yellow colour and golden highlights strives for elegance

432

rather than power. The result is a well-balanced whole with elegant floral, toasty notes, which will open out fully in three to five years, although it is already fresh and extremely agreeable now.

CH. DUDON 1998

10.8 ha 18,565 ▥ €15-23

This fine, fresh, fruity modern wine with engaging perfumes of apricot, mingled with ripe fruit shows the progressive side of this very traditional producer, whose lovely 18th-century mansion, framed in towers and pavilions, has been in the owner's family since 1868.

• SCE du Ch. Dudon, 33720 Barsac, tel. 56.27.29.38, fax 56.27.29.38.
e-mail chateau.dudon.barsac@wanadoo.fr
✔ ☎ by appt.
• Allien

CH. DE FARGUES 1995★★

13 ha 15,000 ▥ €46-76

[47] [49] [53] [59] 62 (67) 71 [75] [76] [83]
84 85 [86] 87 [88] [89] [90] [91] [94] [95]

This country house, sitting at the foot of an ancient, majestic fortress, absorbs the peaceful atmosphere of the Langon countryside. However, the refined perfume of this wine: pear liqueur, broom, touches of quince and gingerbread on a background of menthol, evokes a more sophisticated world. Round, full, fine and fresh, the palate is of the same calibre: from a gentle beginning showing finesse and fullness in keeping with its mandarin, it suddenly emerges, enabling its strength and aromatic richness to break out.

• Comte Alexandre de Lur-Saluces, Ch. de Fargues, 33210 Fargues-de-Langon, tel. 05.57.98.04.20, fax 05.57.98.04.21.
e-mail fargues@chateau-de-fargues.com ✔
☎ by appt.

CH. FILHOT 1998★

□2ème cru clas. 60 ha 70,000 ▥ €23-30

81 82 83 85 86 88 89 91 92 95 97 98

Filhot, an impressive building completed just after the Revolution, was for some time called the Château de Sauternes, a title fully justified by this wine. An attractive straw-yellow in colour, with buttercup highlights, it develops a generous, complex toasty bouquet of crystallised and citrus fruit before revealing a full, powerful and expressive palate.

• SCEA du Ch. Filhot, 33210 Sauternes, tel. 05.56.76.61.09, fax 05.56.76.67.91.
e-mail filhot@filhot.com ✔ ☎ ev. day except Sun. 9am-12 noon 2pm-6pm
• Famille de Vaucelles

CH. GRAVAS 1998★

10.5 ha 30,000 ▥ €11-15

This medium-sized cru is typical of the vineyards of Barsac. This wine's bouquet is very nicely affected by noble rot. Full, rich and lively, the palate is also full of expression, playing with notes of blossom, acacia honey in the same aromatic combination as the bouquet. This is a well-balanced, seductive Sauternes with plenty of character.

• SCEA Domaines Bernard, Ch. Gravas, 33720 Barsac, tel. 05.56.27.06.91, fax 05.56.27.29.83 ✔
☎ ev. day 8am-12 noon 2pm-6pm

CH. GUIRAUD 1998★★

□1er cru clas. 85 ha n.c. ▥ €38-46

83 85 86 88 [89] (90) 92 [95] 96 (97) 98

This, the only Premier Cru apart from Yquem to be situated in the village of Sauternes, has a lovely terroir, so it will come as no surprise that it has produced a remarkable wine, which, in May 2001, had an expressive, complex bouquet with notes of peach, honey and apricot. It is a full, long wine, entirely in the spirit of the great sweet wines of Bordeaux, and although it will age well it is already pleasant and ready for drinking now. The Jury put forward the novel idea that it could be served with spiced Dublin Bay Prawns.

• SCA du Ch. Guiraud, 33210 Sauternes, tel. 05.56.76.61.01, fax 05.56.76.61.01.
e-mail xplanty@club-internet.fr ✔
☎ by appt.

CH. GUTERONDE DU HAYOT 1998★

35 ha 62,000 ▥ €11-15

The Hayot vineyards, a lovely estate situated in Barsac, have produced a promising wine. Still rather closed, the bouquet becomes more expressive on the palate, with notes of crystallised oranges on a backdrop of fruit jelly. The full robust and sappy structure is thoroughly well constructed. The old gold **Château Mayne du Hayot 99**, which has wonderful perfumes of apricot and crystallised orange marmalade, lingering on into the rich, powerful palate, was awarded a star.

• SCE Vignobles du Hayot, Ch. Andoyse, 33720 Barsac, tel. 05.56.27.15.37, fax 05.56.27.04.24, e-mail duhayot@usa.net
✔ ☎ by appt.

CH. HAUT-BERGERON 1999★

16 ha 40,000 ▥ €15-23

83 85 86 [88] [89] [90] 91 94 95 96 97 98 99

This serious, high-quality fresh, lively 99, is of the high standard that one would expect from a cru that has been in the same family for five generations. It is sustained by a perfect touch of acidity, whilst being full and well affected by noble rot. The bouquet still needs time, but is interesting diverse, with notes of gingerbread, stewed fruit and dried figs. The Jury commended the second wine from the same year **Château Fontebride.**

Sauternes

Hervé et Patrick Lamothe,
3, Piquey, 33210 Preignac,
tel. 05.56.63.24.76, fax 05.56.63.23.31,
e-mail haut-bergeron@wanadoo.fr,
ev. day except Sun. 9am–12 noon 2pm–7pm

CH. HAUT-GRILLON

Cuvée spéciale 1998★

Cru bourg. 8 ha 6,000 €15-23

This is an unreservedly ambitious wine, both in its enjoyably complex bouquet of apricots, crystallised oranges and honey and in its palate flavours. It is supple, rich and long – all indicators that this is a wine that will age well.

Odile Roumazeilles-Cameleyre, Ch. Grillon, 33720 Barsac, tel. 05.56.27.16.45, fax 05.56.27.12.18, ev. day 9am–12.30pm 2pm–7pm

CH. LAFAURIE-PEYRAGUEY 1998★

1er cru clas. 40 ha n.c. €30-38

| 75 | 76 | 79 | 80 | 81 | 82 | 83 | 84 | 85 | 86 | 87 |
| 88 | 89 | 90 | 91 | 92 | 93 | 94 | 95 | 96 | 97 | 98 |

This château, with its 13th-century entrance arch, surrounding wall and main building which date back to the 17th-century, has lovely vineyards, planted with 90% Sémillon, 8% Sauvignon and 2% Muscadelle, an efficient team and a very interesting cru. Clear evidence of this is provided by this truly typical wine, despite 1998 having been a very difficult year for sweet wines. It is well balanced and its personality, expressed in a delicate touch of noble rot, is discernible from the bouquet to its very agreeable finish. The Jury commended the second wine, **La Capelle de Lafaurie-Peyraguey 99.**

Domaines Cordier, 160, cours du Médoc, 33300 Bordeaux, tel. 05.57.19.57.77, fax 05.57.19.57.87, by appt.

CH. L'AGNET LA CARRIERE 1998★★

5 ha 14,000 €15-23

Set amidst a number of Bordeaux appellations, Mallard vineyards have once again produced a delightfully successful Sauternes. As it opens out in the course of the tasting, this increasingly complex 98 moves through a broad palette of flavours, including crystallised fruits, blossom and vanilla. The structure is equally impressive: rich and elegant, it would be at its most charming if it were served with rich, sauced chicken dishes accompanied by morel mushrooms.

Danièle Mallard, Ch. Naudonnet-Plaisance, 33760 Escoussans, tel. 05.56.23.93.04, fax 05.57.34.40.78, e-mail mallard@net-courrier.com, by appt.

CH. LAMOTHE GUIGNARD 1998★ €15-23

2ème cru clas. 18 ha 34,500

| 81 | 82 | (83) | 84 | 85 | 86 | 87 | 88 | 89 | 90 | 92 |
| 93 | 94 | 95 | 96 | 97 | 98 | | | | | |

This cru, set on a lovely clay-gravel hilltop, grows 90% Sémillon, 5% Sauvignon and 5% Muscadelle. Its well-rounded 98, the result of 12 months' barrel-maturation, combines the finesse of the bouquet (acacia, blossom and passion fruit) with the richness of the fleshy palate.

GAEC Philippe et Jacques Guignard, Ch. Lamothe Guignard, 33210 Sauternes, tel. 05.56.76.60.28, fax 05.56.76.69.05, ev. day 8am–12 noon 2pm–6pm; Sat. & Sun. by appt.

CH. LANGE 1998★ €11-15

n.c. 6,000

This wine, produced from grapes grown on an interesting *terroir*, gravel and clay-limestone, shows itself to be worthy of its origins. Although its bouquet is not yet definitive, already an interesting future can be expected from its notes of truffle and menthol. The full, generous palate opts for more fruity, toasty, spicy notes.

SCEA Daniel Picot, Ch. Lange, 33210 Bommes, tel. 05.56.76.61.69, fax 05.56.63.40.45, by appt.

CH. LANGE-REGLAT

Sélection royale 1998★ €30-38

2 ha 3,000

The merits of this prestige *cuvée* are just as interesting as its circular, rather original label design. Its merits are obvious in the strong oaky bouquet, which refrains from stifling the emerging perfumes of citrus fruits. The palate and the finish combine to create an elegant, engaging wine, with tropical flavours and considerable youth. The Jury praised the **Cuvée Spéciale 99.**

Bernard Réglat, Ch. de La Mazerolle, 33410 Monprimblanc, tel. 05.56.62.98.63, fax 05.56.62.17.98, e-mail reglat.bernard@wanadoo.fr, by appt.

CH. LARIBOTTE 1998★ €11-15

15.5 ha 10,000

A family-run estate like many others in Preignac, this cru keeps to tradition with this wine, which has a lovely bouquet of dried fruits and is silky, full and well-balanced on the palate.

Jean-Pierre Labiteau, quartier de Sanches, 33210 Preignac, tel. 05.56.23.27.88, fax 05.56.62.24.80, by appt.

CH. LA RIVIERE 1999★ €15-23

4 ha 9,000

This delicate 99, another wine from the Réglat family, this time produced by Guillaume, develops throughout the tasting. After a distinctive bouquet with lovely notes of honey and flowers on a waxy backdrop, its lively, elegant personality emerges on the palate.

● Guillaume Réglat, Ch. Cousteau, 33410 Monprimblanc, tel. 05.56.62.98.63, fax 05.56.62.17.98 ▼ by appt.

CH. LA TOUR BLANCHE 1996★★

☐ 1er cru clas. 34 ha n.c. ⫿ €30-38

[88] 62 75 79 80 [81] 82 [83] 84 [85] [86]
89 90 [91] [94] 95 96 97

This cru could have presented its 96 two years ago but chose to wait, and without doubt waiting was an inspiration. This beautiful yellow wine with golden highlights has an impressively deep, elegant bouquet, whose complexity emerges again on the palate, where crystallised and jellied fruit flavours mingle. It is perfectly balanced, and promises to be great in four to five years' time.
● Ch. La Tour Blanche, 33210 Bommes, tel. 05.57.98.02.73, fax 05.57.98.02.78, e-mail tour-blanche@tour-blanche.com ▼ ev. day except Sat. & Sun. 9am–11.30am
▼ Ministère de l'Agriculture

CH. LATREZOTTE 1999

⫿ 7.5 ha n.c. ⫿ €15-23

This golden-yellow wine, with a tropical fruit bouquet, on first impressions is simple and supple, but then, through its bouquet and well-structured finish, the wine takes on a more agreeable personality.
● Jan de Kok, Ch. Latrezotte, 33720 Barsac, tel. 05.56.27.16.50, fax 05.56.27.08.89 ▼ by appt.

CH. LAVILLE 1999★

☐ 13 ha 12,000 ⫿ €11-15

92 94 [95] 96 97 98 99

Although it does not rival the particularly successful 98 from the same cru, this distinctly engaging wine is as full of character in its bouquet as it is on the palate. The former declares its richness and complexity. The fleshy, full, well-balanced palate indicates good ageing potential. The unwooded Château Delmond was awarded a star, as was the Château Rochefort, from same producer, in the same year.
● EARL du Ch. Laville, 33210 Preignac, tel. 05.56.63.59.45, fax 05.56.63.16.28 ▼ ev. day except Sat. & Sun. 8am–12.30pm, 1.30pm–6.30pm
▼ Y. et C. Barbe

CH. LIOT 1999★

☐ 20 ha n.c. ⫿ €15-23

89 90 91 93 95 96 97 98 99

Yet again, diversity in the mix of varieties has produced a well-balanced wine with elegant aromas of fresh fruit mingling with touches of overripe fruit, creating a beautiful ensemble.
● J. David, Ch. Liot, 33720 Barsac, tel. 05.56.27.15.31, fax 05.56.27.14.42 ▼ by appt.

CH. DE MALLE 1999★★

☐ 2ème cru clas. 27 ha 30,000 ⫿ €30-38

71 [75] 76 81 83 [85] 86 87 [88] [89] [90]
91 [94] [95] 96 97 98 [99]

This cru, with its magnificent 17th-century residence, surrounded by lovely Italian gardens, is one of the prime tourist attractions in Sauternes. Its wine also has a strong personality. Tropical fruits, mainly guavas and passion-fruit, bring great power to the bouquet, which is enriched by notes of toast and liqueur. This full, lingering wine, has plenty of ageing potential, and though ready to drink now it deserves to be cellared for five to ten years. It was one vote short of a *coup de cœur*.
● Comtesse de Bournazel, Ch. de Malle, 33210 Preignac, tel. 05.56.62.36.86, fax 05.56.76.82.40, e-mail chateaudemalle@wanadoo.fr ▼ by appt.

CH. MONET 1999

☐ 2.1 ha 4,700 ⫿ €11-15

From the same producer as Château de Boudillot (Graves), this round, delicate agreeable wine, has a great deal of finesse in its flavours, which mingle ripe fruits, vanilla, honey and raisins.
● Patrice Haverlan, 11, rue de l'Hospital, 33640 Portets, tel. 05.56.67.11.32, fax 05.56.67.11.32, e-mail patrice.haverlan@worldonline.fr ▼ ▼ ev. day except Fri., Sat. & Sun. 8am–12.30pm 1pm–5.30pm

CH. DU MONT

Réserve du Château 1999★★

☐ 0.54 ha 1,200 ⫿ €11-15

This Réserve, from the same producer as the Sainte-Croix of the same name, is also a very interesting wine. A subtle pale-gold colour, it develops a beautifully intense bouquet, in which crystallised apricot, peaches, dried fruits and oak will soon integrate into a harmonious whole. The fleshy, well-constructed palate, with just enough acidity to give it depth, confirms the promise of the bouquet and indicates that this is a wine that should be cellared for five to ten years. It is only a pity that the quality is not matched by the quantity.
● Vignobles Hervé Chouvac, Ch. du Mont, 33410 Sainte-Croix-du-Mont, tel. 05.56.62.07.65, fax 05.56.62.07.58 ▼ by appt.

Sauternes

DOM. DE MONTEILS

Cuvée Sélection 1998★

□ 8 ha 4,800 ⅢⅡ▮ € 15-23

This top vintage has been thoroughly pampered, as one can tell from its complex, elegant bouquet that mingles honeyed, crystallised notes with dried apricots. Full, generous, balanced and long, the palate is also very appealing.

☛ SCEA Dom. de Monteils, 3, rte de Fargues, 33210 Preignac, tel. 05.56.62.24.05, fax 05.56.62.22.30, e-mail vins.sauternes@wanadoo.fr ☒ ⅄ by appt.

CH. DE MYRAT 1998

□ 2ème cru clas. 22 ha 34,000 ⅢⅡ € 23-30

Surrounded by vast grounds, this château brings to mind the long summer holidays of yesteryear. Unbelievably, it is still owned by the Pontac family, whose name is associated with the birth of the great Bordeaux crus. Myrat, replanted ten or so years ago, presents this lovely amber-coloured wine with notes of caramel, beeswax, dried fruits and spices, combined with its fleshiness and a state of evolution on the palate that provides real charm.

☛ Jacques de Pontac, Ch. de Myrat, 33720 Barsac, tel. 05.56.27.09.06, fax 05.56.27.11.75 ☒ ⅄ by appt.

CH. CRU PEYRAGUEY 1998★

□ 6.76 ha 19,000 ⅢⅡ € 15-23

| 75 | 76 | 79 | 82 | 83 | **85** | 86 | 88 | 89 | **90** | 91 |
| 94 | 95 | 96 | **97** | 98 |

This cru has a reputation for consistent quality. The round, full 98 rich in residual sugars, in which a whole variety of notes of blossom and beeswax mingle on the palate, opening into a warm finish.

☛ Vignobles Mussotte, 10, Miselle, 33210 Preignac, tel. 05.56.44.43.48, fax 05.56.44.43.48 ☒ ⅄ by appt.

CH. PIOT-DAVID 1998

□ 4 ha 11,000 ⅢⅡ € 11-15

Though well balanced, this wine, the product of a single parcel in a walled vineyard, should be cellared to allow the bouquet to completely open out and the oak to integrate.

☛ Jean-Luc David, Ch. Poncet, 33410 Omet, tel. 05.56.62.97.30, fax 05.56.62.66.76 ☒ ⅄ by appt.

PRIMO PALATUM 1998★★

□ 0.3 ha 600 ⅢⅡ € 46-76

Wine-growing on this 3-hectare (7-acre) estate is more like gardening. The result is a wine that is discreet but concentrated both in its bouquet and on the palate. Supported by high-quality oak, the bouquet moves from raisins to jellied fruit, from crystallised fruits to prunes. The full, fleshy, richness of the palate is classy. This label, a young *négociant* enterprise created in 1996, has chosen to go for small quantities sold at extremely high

prices. It would be nice to see it producing on a larger scale.

☛ Primo Palatum, 1, Cirette, 33190 Morizès, tel. 05.56.71.39.39, fax 05.56.71.39.40, e-mail primo-palatum@wanadoo.fr ☒ ☛ Xavier Copel

CH. DE RAYNE VIGNEAU 1998★★

□ 1er cru clas. 76.28 ha 128,000 ⅢⅡ € 30-38

| 85 | **86** | **88** | **89** | **90** | **91** | 92 | **94** | **95** | **96** | 97 |
| 98 |

Originally called the Domaine du Vigneau, this cru changed its name when owned by Catherine de Rayne, née Pontac, in the first half of the 19th century. Today, it is a vast estate with the know-how to make very beautiful wine, on a large scale, as this elegant 98 shows. Its bouquet, intense as it is complex, discloses perfumes that move from peach through grapes to acacia. Its structure is supple, well balanced and silky right through to its long finish, which is marked by notes of white peaches. The very well-balanced **Le Clos l'Abeilley 99**, a small enclave in the heart of Rayne-Vigneau, was awarded a star.

☛ SC du Ch. de Rayne Vigneau, La Croix Bacalan, 109, rue Achard BP 154, 33042 Bordeaux Cedex, tel. 05.56.11.29.00, fax 05.56.11.29.01 ⅄ by appt.

CH. RIEUSSEC 1998★★

□ 1er cru clas. 75 ha 90,000 ⅢⅡ € 46-76

62	67	70	71	**75**	**76**	**78**	[79]	[80]	[81]	82
83	84	85	**86**	87	88	**89**	[90]	92	**94**	95
96	**97**	98

This cru enjoys first-class *terroir*, whose full value has been realised thanks to considerable financial investment. Today it produces superb wines such as this very lovely 98, a magnificent example. Its bouquet, a successful marriage of honey, blossom and peaches does not belie the expressive promise of its golden colour. Simultaneously fresh, full, assertive and gently sweet, the flavours on its balanced palate leave room for a note of dried apricots to hold the stage. This wine will age remarkably well.

☛ Ch. Rieussec, 33210 Fargues-de-Langon, tel. 01.53.89.78.00, fax 01.53.89.78.01 ☒

CH. ROMER DU HAYOT 1998★

□ 2ème cru clas. 16 ha 23,600 ⅢⅡ € 15-23

| 75 | **76** | 79 | **81** | **82** | [83] | 85 | **86** | **88** | 89 | [90] |
| 91 | [93] | [95] | 96 | [97] | 98 |

This estate, classified in 1855, was divided up between a number of heirs in 1881. Decked out in its lovely golden colours, this wine reveals a powerful bouquet of blossom, dried fruits and honey. Flowery, well balanced and elegant on the palate, it could be cellared for some considerable time.

☛ SCE Vignobles du Hayot, Ch. Andoyse, 33720 Barsac, tel. 05.56.27.15.37, fax 05.56.27.04.24, e-mail duhayot@usa.net ☒ ⅄ by appt.

☛ André du Hayot

CH. ROUMIEU 1998
19.5 ha · 11,500 · ▥ 11-15

Is this a Barsac or a Sauternes? A claim could be made for both appellations, given that the vineyards are in the village of Barsac. This distinctly engaging, bright gold wine has a very agreeable bouquet of citrus fruit and vanilla, plenty of body and sweetness and lingers nicely on the palate.
→ Olivier Bernadet, Piguemate, 33720 Barsac, tel. 05.56.27.16.76, fax 05.56.27.05.97, e-mail olivier.bernadet@free.fr ▼ ⟁ by appt.

CH. SAINT-VINCENT 1998★★
7 ha · 12,000 · ▥ 15-23

This wine from the same producer as Château Chercy-Desqueyroux (Graves) develops harmoniously throughout the tasting. A beautiful gilded yellow in appearance, it reveals an intense, complex bouquet of crystallised fruit, vanilla, pears, acacia and broom and substantial, well-balanced flavours on the palate. This is a lovely, harmonious Sauternes that will age well.
→ SCEA Francis Desqueyroux et Fils, 1, rue Pourière, 33720 Budos, tel. 05.56.76.62.67, fax 05.56.76.66.92, e-mail vign.fdesqueyroux@wanadoo.fr ▼

CH. SIGALAS RABAUD 1999★★
1er cru clas. · 13.37 ha · n.c.
66 75 76 81 82 83 85 |86| 87 |88| |89|
|90| |91| |92| |94| (95) 96 97 98 |99|

Sigalas is not short on assets including its clay-gravel soil and a south-facing disposition. Yet again, Georges Pauli, Cordier's great oenologist, has put his talent to making the most of these elements. This wine, with its beautiful golden-yellow, slightly amber colour, is extremely elegantly aromatic, with notes of peaches mingling with ripe apricots, not forgetting the hints of acacia honey so characteristic of Sauternes. Equally typical is the well-structured, well-balanced, lingering palate. This 99 could be served with roast chicken and apricots. Sigalas' astonishing full, robust second wine **Le Cadet de Sigalas**

Rabaud 99, rich in enchanting perfumes, was also awarded two stars.
→ Ch. Sigalas-Rabaud, Bommes-Sauternes, 33210 Langon, tel. 05.56.11.29.00, fax 05.56.11.29.01
→ de Lambert des Granges

CH. D'YQUEM 1996★★★
1er cru sup. · n.c. · n.c.
21 29 37 42 |45| 53 55 59 (67) 70 71 |75|
|76| 80 |82| |83| |84| |85| |86| |87| |88| 89
90 91 93 94 (95) (96) · ▥ +76

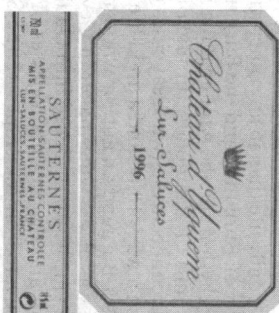

This château, a genuine fortified manor house, houses a number of treasures, including a chapel decorated with Italian frescoes. However, the main jewel in its crown is its wine, of which this rich 98 is a fine example. Although its richness can be seen in its brilliant colour, initially the bouquet seems a little timid, but it very quickly discloses a fresh, youthful, personality in its newly picked grape aromas, in addition to spicy notes from the oak. Full, rich and perfectly balanced, the palate is equally harmonious. Crystallised fruits, citrus peel, quince jelly, restrained power, are all part of this wine. The impressive length and finish predict its remarkable ageing possibilites. This is a huge classic.
→ Comte Alexandre de Lur-Saluces, Ch. d'Yquem, 33210 Sauternes, tel. 05.57.98.07.07, fax 05.57.98.07.08, e-mail info@yquem.fr ⟁ by appt.
→ LVMH

BURGUNDY

'Amiable and vinous Burgundy,' wrote the historian Michelet, and no wine-lover could fail to subscribe to his view. Around the world, Bordeaux, Champagne and Burgundy epitomise everything that's best in French fine wine, just as all are associated with the best in French gastronomy. The sheer variety of the wines from these three regions can satisfy every taste and complement the finest food.

In Burgundy the world of wine is more intricately involved with daily life than in any other wine-growing region: the culture and character of Burgundy and the Burgundians have been forged by the unchanging rhythms of the wine-making year. From the edge of the Auxerrois to the hills of Beaujolais, throughout the length and breadth of a province that connects the two great cities of Paris and Lyon, vines and wines have been a way of life, and a good life at that, since antiquity. Gaston Roupnel was a Burgundian author who wrote a history of the French countryside. He was also a wine-maker in Gevrey-Chambertin and, according to him, the vine was introduced into Gaul in the 6th century BC through Switzerland and the mountain passes of the Jura', ultimately being successfully cultivated on the slopes of the Saône and Rhône valleys. Other writers believe that Greek colonists in the Midi were responsible for introducing the cultivation of grapes to southern Gaul and thereafter bringing the knowledge north with trade. However, no-one can challenge the fact that vine cultivation quickly became very important in the Burgundy region, as some of the early reliefs exhibited in the archaeological museum in Dijon bear witness. And when, in the 4th century AD, the orator Eumenus addressed the Emperor Constantine at Autun, he eulogised the vines cultivated around Beaune as already 'admirable and ancient'.

In the Middle Ages the now long-established Burgundy wine trade was further re-shaped by a revolution in agricultural methods, in which the monks and the monastic movements of Cluny and Cîteaux played a vital role. Burgundy's vineyards gradually developed their mosaic of *climats*, or plots of ground, and their crus, while growers constantly aimed to improve the quality and individuality of their incomparable wines. During the reigns of the four dukes of Burgundy (1342–1477), rules were laid down to ensure that the high quality of the wines was maintained. Throughout the turbulent centuries that followed, Burgundian wines consistently remained at the forefront of reputation and quality, a position continued into modern times.

It is worth noting that not all wines produced today in the administrative region of Burgundy are, in fact, Burgundies. In the Nièvre department (administratively part of Burgundy, as are the departments of the Côte-d'Or, the Yonne and the Saône-et-Loire) the vineyards of Pouilly-sur-Loire belong to the vineyards of central France and the Loire valley. In addition, the Rhône department, which in terms of judicial and administrative authority belongs to Burgundy, is home to the Beaujolais area. The Beaujolais wine region is usually treated as an autonomous entity – except in commercial terms – because it grows a specific grape variety, the Gamay (see below). This is the approach followed by this guide (see the section on Beaujolais). So Burgundy is understood to mean the vineyards of the Yonne (lower Burgundy), the Côte-d'Or and the Saône-et-Loire, even though some wines produced in Beaujolais can also be sold under the Appellation Régionale Bourgogne.

Disregarding Beaujolais, which is planted with Gamay, a variety with black skin and white flesh, Burgundy's character as a wine-growing area is dominated by two grape varieties: Chardonnay, which produces white wines, and Pinot Noir, which produces red wines. In addition there are some other minor varieties, either throwbacks to earlier wine-making practices or specific varieties to suit particular *terrors*: Aligoté, for example, is a white grape producing the famous Bourgogne Aligoté, which is frequently used to make kir, a mixture of white wine and cassis (black-currant liqueur). The best quality Aligoté wines are produced in the small village of Bouzeron, very close to Chagny (Saône-et-Loire). The César, a red variety cultivated mainly in the region of Auxerre, is gradually falling from use. The Sacy produces Bourgogne Grand Ordinaire in the Yonne but is increasingly being replaced by Chardonnay. Gamay is used in Bourgogne Grand Ordinaire and is also mixed with Pinot Noir to make Bourgogne Passetoutgrain. Finally, Sauvignon, the famous aromatic grape variety planted in the vineyards of Sancerre and Pouilly-sur-Loire, is also grown in the region of Saint-Bris-le-Vineux in the Yonne. Currently bottled as AOVDQS Sauvignon de Saint-Bris, this wine is likely to become a recognised AOC in the near future.

Burgundy has a relatively uniform climate. It is mainly semi-continental (hot summers, cold winters) but is also affected by the Atlantic maritime climate, which reaches as far east as the edge of the Paris Basin. Thus it is the soil rather than climatic variations that gives the large number of wines grown in Burgundy their individual characteristics. As a rule, the vineyards are small plots of land mainly sited on a variety of out-crops of quite different geological origins, which can occur virtually side by side; these are the source of the rich palette of scents and flavours of the Burgundy crus. According to the specific chemical structure of the rock formation in each *climat*, or individual part of a vineyard, different wines with highly individual characteristics may be produced within a single appellation, thus complicating the overall classification and presentation of the Grands Vins de Bourgogne ... These *climats*, which often have particularly evocative names (La Renarde, Les Cailles, Genevrières, Clos de la Maréchale, Clos des Ormes, Montrecul), have existed since at least the 18th century. They are only a few hectares in size, and sometimes only several *ouvrées* (1 ouvrée = 428 m²/512 yds²) and correspond to a 'natural entity' which can be identified because of the specific character of the wine it produces' (A. Vedel). You can, in fact, see that there is sometimes less difference between two vines several hundred metres apart but in the *same climat* than there is between two neighbouring vines in two different *climats*.

There are four levels of appellation in the hierarchy of Burgundy wines: *Appellation Régionale* (56% of the production), *Villages* (or *Appellation Communale*) de Bourgogne, Premier Cru (12%) and Grand Cru (2%, consisting of 33 Grand Crus listed in the Côte-d'Or and Chablis). The number of legally defined *terroirs* or *climats* is very high; for example, 27 different denominations for the Premiers Crus are harvested in the commune of Nuits-Saint-Georges, all from barely a hundred hectares!

Recent scientific studies have confirmed earlier empirical observations about the relationship between the soils and the *lieux-dits* (names in common usage that identify a place) that gave rise to the appellations, the crus and the *climats*. Thus, for example, 59 different soil types can be identified by their external structure and physical chemistry (slope, stoniness, amount of clay and so on), all of which happen to match up with the boundaries between Grand Cru, Premier Cru, Villages and Régionale appellations.

Put more simply, and taking a more general geographical approach, it is usual to divide Burgundy's wine-growing area into four distinct zones: going from north to south these are the vineyards of the Yonne (or Basse Bourgogne), the Côte-d'Or (or Côte de Nuits and Côte de Beaune), the Côte Chalonnaise and the Mâconnais.

The Chablis vineyards are the best known vineyards of the Yonne. Chablis wines were held in high esteem by the Parisian court in medieval times, when river transport made it easy to sell the wines in the capital. Indeed, for a long time the wines of the Yonne were thought of as *the* wines of Burgundy. Nestling in the charming valley of the River Serein, the town of Noyers its medieval jewel, the Chablis vineyard is like a remote satellite 100 km (62 miles) north-west of the heart of the main Burgundy vineyard. The Chablis AOC area is quite spread out, covering more than 4,000 ha (9,880 acres) of hilly slopes of varied aspect, where a 'constellation of hamlets and a scattering of farms share the harvest of this dry, light, lively, delicately perfumed wine whose astonishing limpidity, lightly flecked with gold and green, delights the eye' (P. Poupon). Ten communes stretch south from Auxerre in the Auxerrois; in the vineyards of Irancy there are still a few hectares (some acres) planted with César, a variety that gives very tannic wines. Along with Coulanges-la-Vineuse, Irancy is undergoing rapid expansion. Saint-Bris-les-Vineux is Sauvignon country and shares the production of white wines with Chitry.

Three other vineyards in the Yonne were almost completely destroyed by phylloxera, although efforts are currently being made to revive them. Joigny, in the extreme north-west of Burgundy, covers an area of barely ten hectares (25 acres), but the vineyards are laid out on the hills surrounding the town and overlooking the River Yonne. A *vin gris*, which is an Appellation Bourgogne, is produced mainly for local consumption in addition to red and white wines. The vineyard of Tonnerre, on the approach to Épineuil, was once as famous as that of Auxerre; custom allows an Appellation Bourgogne-Épineuil. Finally, a small vineyard on the slopes of the celebrated hill at Vézelay, where the grand dukes of Burgundy themselves once owned a vineyard, has been back in production since 1979. These wines, sold as Appellation Bourgogne, should continue to benefit from the crowds of visitors to Vézelay's famous Romanesque basilica, which was once a place of pilgrimage.

The arid eroded limestone of the Langres plateau is the traditional invasion route from the north-east, both in the past and for today's tourists. It separates the Chablisien, the Auxerrois and the Tonnerrois from the Côte-d'Or, the so-called 'hillside of purple and gold', more simply referred to as 'La Côte', which is the product of complex geological events in the remote past. During the Tertiary era, following the formation of the Alps, the Bresse Sea covered the region, pounding the ancient Hercynian mountains of the Morvan. This ancient sea drained away over the millennia, depositing a variety of sedimentary limestone soils. There are also numerous parallel north-south faults dating from the birth of the Alps; the great Tertiary glaciations flowed from north to south, while combes were

Burgundy

Joigny
D 943
D 905
N 77
A 6
Auxerre
Chablis
D 965
Tonnerre
Montigny-sur-Aube
Châtillon-sur-Seine
YONNE
Coulanges-la-Vineuse
N 6
Vézelay
Avallon
0 20 miles
0 20 40 km
CÔTE-D'OR
Dijon
N 74
A 38
A 31
Marsannay-la-Côte
Fixin
Gevrey-Chambertin
Morey-Saint-Denis
Chambolle-Musigny
Vougeot
Vosne-Romanée
Nuits-Saint-Georges
CÔTE DE NUITS
HAUTES-CÔTES
Pernand-Vergelesses
Aloxe-Corton
A 36
Pommard
Chorey-lès-Beaune
Auxey-Duresses
Saint-Romain
Beaune
D 973
Meursault
Nolay
Puligny-Montrachet
Autun
Santenay
Chassagne-Montrachet
Dezize-lès-Maranges
Chagny
D 978
Bouzeron
Mercurey
Rully
N 73
CÔTE CHALONNAISE
Givry
Chalon-sur-Saône
N 80
Montagny-lès-Buxy
Buxy
D 978
Montceau-les-Mines
Tournus
SAÔNE-ET-LOIRE
D 980
Saône
MÂCONNAIS
Mâcon
Pouilly
Fuissé
Loché
Saint-Vérand
Vinzelles
A 40
Beaujeu
D 43
Local AOCs
Regional AOCs
Department boundaries
RHÔNE
RHÔNE
Villefranche-sur-Saône
BEAUJOLAIS
A 46
A 42
Burgundy
N 7
0 20 miles
0 20 40 km
LYON

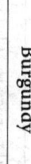

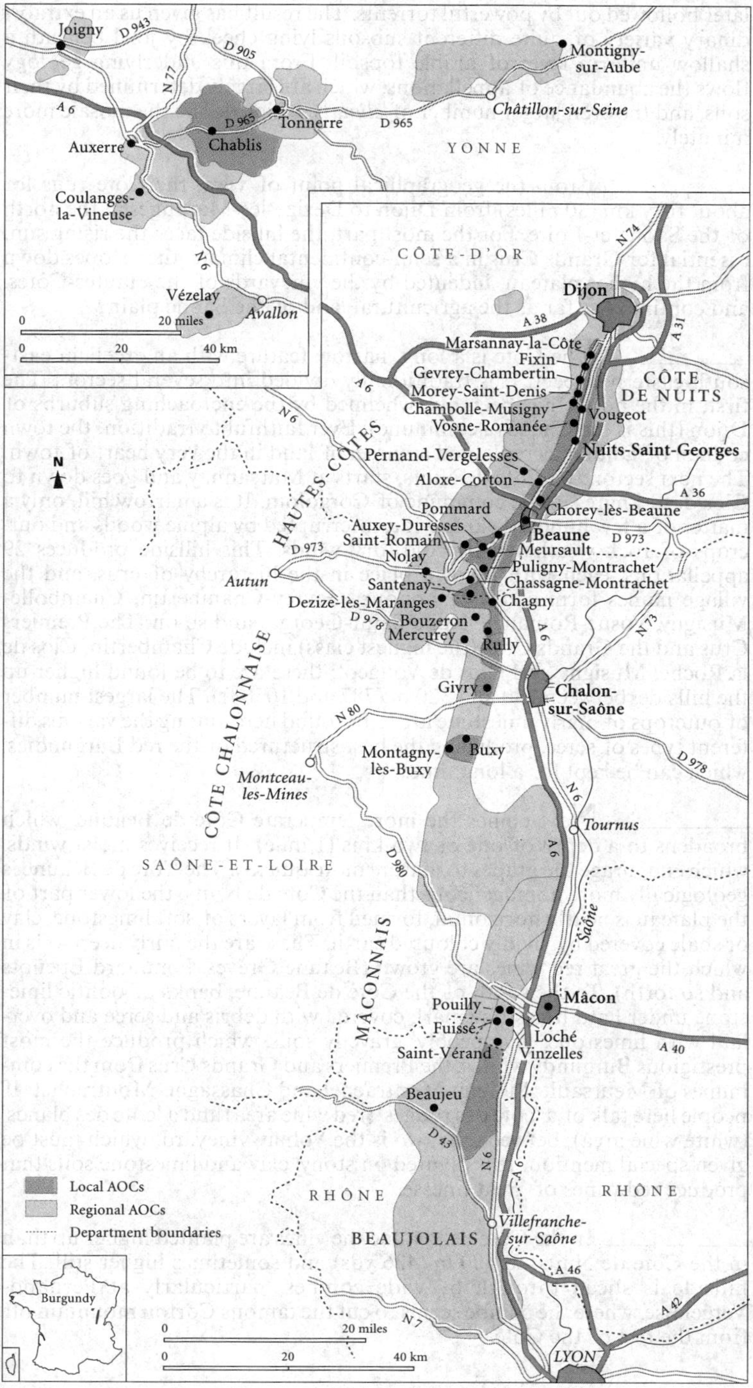

later hollowed out by powerful torrents. The result has given us an extraordinary variety of quite different subsoils lying cheek by jowl beneath a shallow uniform layer of arable topsoil. From this underlying geology flows the abundance of appellations, which are largely determined by their soils, and the even larger number of *climats*, which define the mosaic more minutely.

From the geographical point of view, the Côte runs for about fifty km (30 miles) from Dijon to Dezize-lès-Maranges in the north of the Saône-et-Loire. For the most part, the hillside faces the rising sun, essential for Grands Crus in a semi-continental climate, then slopes down from the higher plateau, indented by the vineyards of the Hautes-Côtes, and continues as far as the agricultural land of the Saône plain.

The Côte is a long, narrow feature with an excellent east-south-easterly aspect. It is traditionally divided into several sectors. The first, in the north, has been overwhelmed by the encroaching suburbs of Dijon (this is the Chenôve commune). Ever faithful to tradition, the town council of Dijon has replanted a parcel of land in the very heart of town. The next sector, the Côte de Nuits, starts at Marsannay and goes down to Clos des Langres in the commune of Corgoloin. It is a narrow hill, only a matter of a few hundred yards wide, interrupted by alpine woods and outcrops of rock weathered by cold, dry winds. This hillside produces 29 appellations, each with its own place in the hierarchy of crus, and the village names form a roll of honour: Gevrey-Chambertin, Chambolle-Musigny, Vosne-Romanée, Nuits-Saint-Georges and so on. The Premiers Crus and the Grands Crus (the highest class) include Chambertin, Clos de la Roche, Musigny and Clos de Vougeot; these are to be found higher up the hillside, between 240 and 320 m (787 and 1050 ft). The largest number of outcrops of marly limestone are to be found here among the various different types of scree, producing the best structured of the red Burgundies, which can be kept for a long time.

Next comes the more temperate Côte de Beaune, which broadens to a depth of one or two kms (1 mile). It receives moist winds, which encourage the grapes to mature more quickly. The Côte de Beaune is geologically more homogeneous than the Côte de Nuits; the lower part of the plateau is nearly horizontal, formed from layers of soft limestone, clay or shale covered by vividly coloured earth. These are the fairly deep soils in which the great red wines are grown (Beaune Grèves, Pommard Epenots and so forth). To the south of the Côte de Beaune, banks of oolitic limestone under hard limestone marl, covered with débris and scree and overlaid with limestone, give pebbly, gravelly soils, which produce the most prestigious Burgundy whites, the Premiers and Grands Crus from the communes of Meursault, Puligny-Montrachet and Chassagne-Montrachet. If people here talk of a 'côte des rouges' (red wine area) and a 'côte des blancs' (white wine area), between the two is the Volnay vineyard, which must be given special mention. It is planted on stony, clay and limestone soils that produce red wines of great finesse.

In the Côte de Beaune the vines are planted higher up than in the Côte de Nuits, to 400 m (436 yds) and sometimes higher still. The hillside is sliced through by wide combes, particularly at Pernand-Vergelesse, where the combe seems to cut the famous Corton mountain off from the rest of the Côte.

In the last thirty years sections of the Hautes-Côtes have been gradually replanted to produce Appellations Régionales Bourgognes Hautes-Côtes-de-Nuits and Bourgogne Hautes-Côtes de Beaune. The Aligoté grows at its best here, and the *terroir* shows off the wine's freshness to advantage. Other *terroirs* make excellent red wines from Pinot Noir, and these are characterised by scents of soft fruits such as raspberry and black-currant, which are also locally grown Burgundy specialities.

The countryside opens out somewhat in the Côte Chalonnaise, which covers 4,500 ha (11,115 acres). The linear structure of the basic relief softens into low-rising hills, which extend further to the west of the Saône valley. The geological structure differs again from the vineyards of the Côte d'Or; the soil rests on Jurassic limestone, on marl from the same period or even earlier or on sedimentary terrain made up of sandstone, limestone and marl. Red wines are produced from Pinot Noir in Mercurey, Givry and Rully, but the same communes also make white wines from Chardonnay, as does Montagny. Bouzeron, home of a highly reputable Aligoté, is also to be found here. There is a noteworthy vineyard on the way to Couches, which is dominated by its medieval château. The Roman-esque churches and ancient estates of the region are worth a visit and any tourist itinerary can easily be combined with a route through the vineyards.

The range of hills in the Mâconnais, with 5,700 ha (14,079 acres) of vineyards, opens up wide horizons where white Charolais cattle speckle the green meadows. The countryside was dear to the poet Lamartine – he came from Milly, a wine-producing village where he owned vineyards – and it is geologically simpler than the Chalonnais. The sedimentary soils from the Triassic and Jurassic periods are scored by east-west faults. Some twenty per cent of the wines are *Appellations Régionales* and 80% are *Appellations Communales* (Mâcon white and Mâcon red). The highest quality white wines are made from Chardonnay grapes, planted on dark lime-rich soil on the slopes at Pouilly, Solutré and Vergisson, which have a particularly good, sunny aspect; the wines are remarkable for their appearance and their capacity to keep a long time. Appellation Bourgogne reds and rosés are made from Pinot Noir, while the black-skinned Gamay with white juice produces the Mâcons that are harvested lower down the hills or on less well-exposed, flinty, alluvial soils with good drainage.

No matter how essential the local geology and climatic conditions may be, no picture of wine-growing in Burgundy would be complete without recognising the contribution that human effort makes to the vineyards and wines. The wine-makers have a deep attachment to their land, and in some villages the family names of many owners can be traced back for five hundred years. By the same token, some of the shipping companies were founded as long ago as the 18th century.

The Burgundy vineyard is divided into family-owned plots (domains), which cover very small areas. So a domain of four or five ha (12 acres) in, say, Nuits-Saint-Georges, can provide an adequate living for a worker and his family. It is rare to find producers who own and cultivate more than about ten ha (25 acres): for example, the illustrious Clos-Vougeot covers 50 ha (124 acres) and is divided among 70 owners. This par-celling up of the ownership of *climats* results in a greater diversity of wines and leads to a healthy rivalry among producers. In Burgundy a tasting will often consist of comparing two wines made from the same grape variety and from the same appellation but coming from different *climats*, or two wines made from the same grape and the same *climat* but from different years. Thus, in Burgundy, two basic elements must constantly be kept in mind when tasting the wines: the cru, or *climat*, and the year of the vintage; you must also allow for the personal touch of the wine-grower who makes them. From the technical point of view, Burgundian wine-makers are keen to maintain traditional methods, although this does not mean they are resistant to modernisation. As a result, the mechanisation of viticulture has developed, and many wine-makers have benefited greatly from new equipment and techniques. However, some traditions remain unchallenged by wine-growers and shippers alike, and one of the best examples is the maturing of wines in oak barrels.

In 1997, 3,500 domains were registered as dedicated solely to vines. They represent two-thirds of the 24,000 ha (59,280 acres) making Appellation d'Origine wines. Nineteen co-operatives are listed: the co-operative movement is very active in Chablis and the Côte Chalonnaise, and particularly so in the Mâconnais (13 cellars). They produce about 25% of the wines. Since the 18th century an important role has been played by the *négociants-éleveurs*, the merchants who buy wine from the grower and bring it on to bottling age in their own cellars. They sell more than 60% of the wine produced and own 35% of the total area of the Grands Crus of the Côte de Beaune. On their domains the merchants produce 8% of all the wine produced in Burgundy. This represents an average of 180 million bottles (105 million white and 75 million red) and generates a turnover of 5 thousand million francs (€762 m), of which more than half is earned from exports. Total exports approximate 3,000,000 hl (79,200,000 gal).

The importance of bringing on a wine (how it develops from its early youth to its optimum quality before it is bottled) demonstrates the significance of the *négociant-éleveur* to the system; in addition to being responsible for the sale of the wine, he also takes on a technical role. This technical and marketing knowledge lies at the heart of the harmonious professional relationship that has developed between wine-growers and merchants.

The Bureau Interprofessionnel des Vins de Bourgogne (BIVB), which initiates developments in the technical, economic and promotional fields, has three 'listening posts' at Mâcon, Beaune and Chablis. In 1934 the University of Burgundy was the first establishment in France, at least at university level, to set up and run courses in oenology and to offer a technical diploma. At the same time, the Confrérie des Chevaliers du Tastevin was founded to promote the reputation of Burgundy wines around the world. Its headquarters are at the Château du Clos-Vougeot and, with other local *confréries*, it makes a great contribution to keeping regional traditions alive. Without question, one of the most brilliant events is the auction sales in the Hospices de Beaune, first held in 1851. This is the meeting place of the international wine élite and the exchange for establishing the value of the Grands Crus. Together with the assembly of the Confrérie and the 'Paulée' in Meursault, the sale is one of the 'three glorious days of wine'. But the whole of Burgundy knows how to celebrate wine joyously, be it from a 228-litre hogshead or from a bottle. It does not take much to love Burgundy and its wines; it is simply a region that you can take away in your glass.

Appellations Régionales Bourgogne

The Appellation Bourgogne and the Appellation Bourgogne Grand Ordinaire, together with their related off-shoots or equivalents, account for the largest area of Burgundy's vineyards. They can be produced in the traditional wine communes of the department of the Yonne, the Côte-d'Or, the Saône-et-Loire and the canton of Villefranche-sur-Saône in the Rhône. In 2000, they produced a total of 361,917 hl (9,554,609 gal).

The registration of land use and, more specifically, the definition of the *terroirs* by establishing the borders of the parcels of land within the vineyards, created a hierarchy of *appellations régionales*. The Appellation Bourgogne Grand Ordinaire is the most common and the most productive in the areas defined. Using specified vines, Bourgogne Aligoté, Bourgogne Passetoutgrain and Crémant de Bourgogne are also produced in the same areas.

Bourgogne

The production area of this appellation is vast if you take into account the names of the different sub-regions (Hautes-Côtes, Côte Chalonnaise) or of the villages (Irancy, Chitry, and Epineuil) that can be added, each of which is a separate entity and is listed here as such. Given the extent of this appellation, it is not surprising that producers should have sought to personalise their wines and to persuade the regulator that the area of origin should be individually identified. In the Châtillon area, which is in the Côte-d'Or, the name of Massigny has been used in this way, even though the original vineyard has practically disappeared. More recently (and now as a matter of course) the wine-makers on the banks of the Yonne use the name of the village and add it after the words 'Appellation Bourgogne'. This is the case in Saint-Bris, the Côtes d'Auxerre on the right bank of the river and in Coulanges-la-Vineuse on the left bank.

The average volume of wine produced by the Appellation Bourgogne is about 155,000 hl (4,092,000 gal) a year. The white-wine producers make 78,726 hl (2,078,366 gal) of wine from Chardonnay vines, which are still known as Beaunois in the Yonne region. The Pinot Blanc, although referred to in the official texts and formerly grown more widely in the Hautes Côtes de Bourgogne, has now practically disappeared. In the past it was often confused with Chardonnay

Production of red and rosé wines from Pinot Noir is on average between 125,000 and 130,000 hl (3,300,000 and 3,432,000 gal) a year. Unfortunately, the Pinot Beurot grape has largely fallen from favour because it contained insufficient colour; it used to add remarkable finesse to red wines. In some years the volumes of wine declared can be augmented by wines that are downgraded from the Beaujolais Appellations Communales: Brouilly, Côte-de-Brouilly, Chénas, Chiroubles, Fleurie, Juliénas, Morgon, Moulin-à-Vent and Saint-Amour. These wines are made from the black Gamay grape only and have different characteristics. The production of rosé wines can increase in cool years when the grapes do not ripen well or when there is a great deal of grey rot, and they can be declared as Appellation Bourgogne Rosé or Bourgogne Clairet.

Bourgogne

To make things more difficult, some labels have the name of the *lieu-dit* (a name in common usage that identifies a place) where the wine was produced, in addition to the Appellation Bourgogne. Some old and reputable vineyards are examples justifying this practice: Chapitre à Chenôve and Des Montreculs keep alive names from the Dijon vineyards that are now smothered by the growth of the suburbs; another example is La Chapelle-Notre-Dame in Serrigny. As for the rest, some may be too easily confused with the Premiers Crus and may not always deserve the comparison.

CHRISTOPHE AUGUSTE
Coulanges-la-Vineuse 1999★

■ 11 ha 70,000 ■ ♦ *la Vineuse* €5-8

Coulanges is not known as *la Vineuse* (winey) for nothing. This warm, rich wine, with its morello cherry colour, opens with a certain contrasting freshness and is pleasant and light. A well-made wine, characteristic of the Auxerrois region, it will be drinking well until 2003.

☛ Christophe Auguste, 55, rue André-Vildieu, 89580 Coulanges-la-Vineuse, tel. 03.86.42.35.04, fax 03.86.42.51.81
Ⴤ by appt.

DOM. BERNAERT 1999★★
□ 5.92 ha 30,000 ■ €5-8

DOM. ALEXANDRE 1999
■ 1.8 ha 3,000 ■ ♦ €5-8

Aromas of coffee and raspberry combine together to create a lovely, intense nose. The fresh fruit flavours linger on the palate. This is a good, pleasant wine that will be ready to drink in a year at the most.

☛ Dom. Alexandre Père et Fils, pl. de la Mairie, 71150 Remigny, tel. 03.85.87.22.61, fax 03.85.87.22.61, e-mail domaine.alexandre@roonoo.net
Ⴤ by appt.

BERTRAND AMBROISE 1999★
□ n.c. n.c. ●● €5-8

Would you choose the **red 99 Vieilles vignes**? It has a delightful, lasting flavour of morello cherries. Or would you go for this white? Yellow with golden highlights, it is a vigorous, round wine, well made and with great promise but ready to enjoy now. Its nose is a real delight, flitting between iris and hazelnut. Either wine would be ideal for a Sunday lunch.

☛ Maison Bertrand Ambroise, rue de l'Eglise, 21700 Premeaux-Prissey, tel. 03.80.62.30.19, fax 03.80.62.38.69, e-mail bertrand.ambroise@wanadoo.fr
Ⴤ by appt.

MICHEL ARCELAIN 1999★
□ 0.16 ha 1,400 ●● €5-8

This white comes from Pommard, a region known for its red wines. Although it is superb right now, it could last another year or two. It is bright golden-yellow in colour, and its nose is already well developed, with notes of fruit and honey. The generous, intensely fruity palate has good length and elegance, and it would be a fine accompaniment for fish.

☛ Michel Arcelain, rue Mareau, 21630 Pommard, tel. 03.80.22.13.50, fax 03.80.22.13.50  Ⴤ by appt.

The potters of Accolay were well known, but unfortunately the arrival of the motorway has diverted the traffic from this spot on the old RN6. Here is an Accolay wine-producer whose Chardonnay receives the top *coup de cœur* of the Yonne. This vineyard has been fighting its way back to prominence since 1988. This warm 99 is pale yellow with silvery highlights and has a fresh lime and floral nose with a well-balanced, rich, long body that results in a beautiful harmony.

☛ Philippe Bernaert, 6, rte Nationale, 89460 Accolay, tel. 03.86.81.56.95, fax 03.86.81.69.33  Ⴤ by appt.

DOM. BORGNAT
Coulanges-la-Vineuse 1999★

□ 1 ha 2,000 ●● €5-8

If you are interested in visiting this region, there is a dovecote here that has been transformed into a gite and a wine-cellar that has been made into an inn. It is a lovely place, full of history. If you are not familiar with white Coulanges, you will have another pleasure in store. Appealing, but not very bright in colour, this has an attractive nose that hints at pineapple and vanilla. The palate is fresh on the attack, opening out immediately with an expressive and warm vinosity.

☛ EARL Dom. Benjamin Borgnat, 1, rue de l'Eglise, 89290 Escolives-Sainte-Camille, tel. 03.86.53.35.28, fax 03.86.53.65.00, e-mail domaineborgnat@wanadoo.fr
Ⴤ by appt.

446

PASCAL BOUCHARD

Côtes d'Auxerre Les Pierres blanches 1999★

n.c. 24,000 ■ ▯ ♦ €5-8

Act I is oaky, and Act II is fruity. Acts III and IV present the oak and the fruit with a mineral background, and finally Act V celebrates the successful combination of both. One couldn't ask for more. This wine has a distinct yellow colour and a nose with few aromas. It has a certain complexity and is more modern than classic, which makes it appealing to a wide audience. Isn't that what theatre is all about?

♠ Pascal Bouchard, 5 bis,
rue Porte-No1, 89800 Chablis,
tel. 03.86.42.18.64, fax 03.86.42.48.11,
e-mail pascal.bouchard@wanadoo.fr ▯
Ⴘ ev. day 10am–12.30pm 2pm–7pm; cl. Jan.

CELINE BOUDARD-COTE 1999★

0.65 ha 5,000 ■ €5-8

Céline Boudard-Coté studied in Bordeaux and then came back home in 1999 to take over the family estate. This is her first wine, and she deserves high praise for it. It has an intense colour, an expressive nose and a rich palate, which is still developing. You could serve this fine 99 to accompany a haunch of venison.

♠ Céline Boudard-Coté, Les Noirots,
Vaulinernes, 89700 Molosmes,
tel. 03.86.55.08.91, fax 03.86.55.13.47 ▯
Ⴘ ev. day 10am–8pm

DOM. DENIS BOUSSEY

Vieilles vignes 1999★

0.6 ha 3,600 ▯ €5-8

Monthélie boasts a 12th-century church that reflects the Cluny style. Perhaps it was in this very village that the first vines were planted before the Romans arrived. This wine is worth a look, at any rate. It is greeny-gold in colour and at the moment needs to breathe a little before presenting a fruity (lemon and grapefruit) nose with touches of vanilla from the oak. It opens on the palate with notes of almond, white peach and apricot, rounded off with a little hint of mint. A rich, elegant and mature wine, it has a long life ahead of it. We would recommend serving it with a fresh-water fish in cream sauce.

♠ Dom. Denis Boussey, 1, rue du
Pied-de-la-Vallée, 21190 Monthélie,
tel. 03.80.21.21.23, fax 03.80.21.62.46 ▯
Ⴘ ev. day except Sun. 8am–12 noon
1.30pm–6.30pm; cl. 5–25 Aug.

DOM. REGIS BOUVIER

Montre-Cul 1999★★

0.63 ha 2,500 ■ ▯ ♦ €5-8

Montre-Cul, a *climat* close to Dijon, is one of the few in this Burgundy appellation that has the right to give its name to the wine. This is a powerful 99, concentrated from start to finish with aromas of blueberries and mulberries. It has a great deal of potential for laying down, and you can happily put it in the cellar and forget it for a while.

MICHEL BOUZEREAU ET FILS

1999★

1 ha n.c. ♦ €8-11

This white Burgundy has a good colour, is pleasant to drink and comes from a great Chardonnay *terroir*, Meursault. Its pale, clear gold colour is shot through with green flecks, and its powerful nose is dominated by notes of honey. The palate is full, fleshy, well balanced and elegant.

♠ Michel Bouzereau et Fils, 3, rue de la
Planche-Meunière, 21190 Meursault,
tel. 03.80.21.20.74, fax 03.80.21.66.41 ▯

BROSSOLETTE 1999

2 ha 8,500 ■ ▯ ♦ €5-8

The renaissance of the Tonnerrois vineyard is a recent phenomenon, so the vines here have yet to age, but the men and women who are working for its future have shown real skill here. This wine, which is very characteristic of the vintage, has spent five months in barrel. The fruit flavours have been well handled, and although it isn't full (the vine stock is only nine years old) the palate is pleasant. It would make a fine accompaniment to an autumn picnic.

♠ J.J. et A.-C. Brossolette, 6, Grande-Rue,
89700 Molosmes, tel. 03.25.70.02.94,
fax 03.25.70.59.81 ▯ Ⴘ ev. day 8am–8pm

CHRISTOPHE BUISSON

Les Châtaigniers 1999★★★

n.c. n.c. ■ ▯ ♦ €5-8

Christophe Buisson started with precisely nothing in 1990, but he took an interest in his village, Saint-Romain in the Côte-d'Or, and rented, then bought some plots of vineyard, finally acquiring a winery. He has produced this deep red 99, which is garnet with touches of violet and mineral glints. It is very full, with a nose presenting ripe or overripe fruit. Delicacy and power vie for position, and it finishes on a spicy note. This wine will last a good three to four years.

♠ Christophe Buisson,
21190 Saint-Romain, tel. 03.80.21.63.92,
fax 03.80.21.67.03 ▯ Ⴘ by appt.

LES VIGNERONS DE BUXY 1999★★

1 ha 35,000 ■ ♦ €5-8

This wine, a pronounced yellow in colour, has a wonderfully rich, flavoursome palate and would go well with a fillet of pike-perch or even a rich, creamy sauce dish. A liquorice-like bitterness and cloves combine well together. The balance between acidity and alcohol is superb. It has great power and amazing length with an impressive finish. It is very characteristic of this style of wine.

♠ SICA Les Vignerons réunis à Buxy, rte de
Chalon-sur-Saône, 71390 Buxy,
tel. 03.85.92.03.80, fax 03.85.92.08.06

♠ Régis Bouvier, 52, rue de Mazy,
21160 Marsannay-la-Côte,
tel. 03.80.51.33.93, fax 03.80.58.75.07 ▯
Ⴘ by appt.

Bourgogne

DOM. CAILLOT Les Herbeux 1998★★ ▨ €5-8

☐ 1 ha 7,000

Les Herbeux is a *lieu-dit* situated on the wild, grassy side of Meursault. This lovely 98 is issue of the best wines of this prestigious appellation. From the start it is clear that it is a fleshy wine. Toasted almond comes through with a buttered croissant base and a little floral note. It is rich, with flavours of dried fruit on the palate. This perfection is more typical of Meursault than generic burgundy, and at such a price it will be snapped up!

☛ GAEC Dom. Caillot, 14, rue du Cromin, 21190 Meursault, tel. 03.80.21.21.70, fax 03.80.21.69.58 ▨ ☎ by appt.

MARIE-THERESE CANARD ET JEAN-MICHEL AUBINEL 1999★ €5-8

☐ 0.16 ha 1,500

Why should there be anything wrong with pleasure? Opening on a note of minerals and pineapple, this pale gold wine takes you in its arms and won't let you go. It has an amazing length, and its secondary aromas of pear and quince are appealing. Open it up and drink it straightaway.

☛ SCEV Canard-Aubinel, Mouhy, 71960 Prissé, tel. 03.85.20.21.43, fax 03.85.20.21.43 ▨ ☎ by appt.

DOM. CAPUANO-FERRERI ET FILS 1999★ €5-8

☐ n.c. n.c.

A *blanquette de veau* would bring out the best in this attractive 99, which should not be drunk too soon. Its deep peony note comes from a rather intense extraction process. The tannins mask its fullness, and it is quite rustic yet well balanced.

☛ John Capuano, 14, rue Chauchien, 21590 Santenay, tel. 03.80.20.64.12, fax 03.80.20.65.75 ▨ ☎ by appt.

MADAME EDMOND CHALMEAU Chitry 1999★ €5-8

☐ 1.8 ha 12,800

Chitry-le-Fort is known for its white wines and a fabulous Aligoté is sometimes produced here. This is a lovely, simple Chardonnay, which has won a *coup de coeur* in the past and demonstrates here that it hasn't lost its touch. The potential is only half-realised at present, with a good acidity and alcohol balance and an attractive aroma of white peaches.

☛ Mme Edmond Chalmeau, 20, rue du Ruisseau, 89530 Chitry-le-Fort, tel. 03.86.41.42.09, fax 03.86.41.46.84 ▨ ☎ by appt.

CHAMPY PERE ET CIE 1999★★ €8-11

■ n.c. 40,000

This Pinot Noir, the pride of the appellation, is a truly lovely wine. It has a good colour and the nose sets out wholeheartedly with a cocktail of soft fruit. Even the slightly aggressive tannins do not hinder the general harmony. Moreover, such complexity is rare in a regional AOC.

☛ Maison Champy, 5, rue du Grenier-à-Sel, 21200 Beaune, tel. 03.80.25.09.99, fax 03.80.25.09.95, e-mail champyprost@aol.com ▨ ☎ by appt.

☛ Pierre Meurgey

CHARLES DE FRANCE 1998★ €5-8

☐ n.c. 50,000

Charles is the name of one of Jean-Claude Boisset's sons. Perhaps this is where the name Charles de France comes from? Not that it matters: we are happy to pay homage to this golden, gentle Chardonnay with its ferny notes. It has a well-structured body, which is enlivened by a little hint of gingerbread. An agreeable wine to drink now, it can also be laid down.

☛ Jean-Claude Boisset, 5, quai Dumorey, 21700 Nuits-Saint-Georges, tel. 03.80.62.62.61, fax 03.80.62.37.38

DOM. PHILIPPE CHARLOPIN Cuvée Prestige 1998★★ €8-11

■ n.c. n.c.

This wine makes a grand entrance, and all eyes are immediately drawn to it. But then we are dealing with a rare creature, since it is extraordinary for a 98 vintage and exceptional for a regional appellation. Philippe Charlopin features frequently in our *Guide*, and let's just say that whatever he does is a success. Our advice? Get on your mobile now and call Gevrey.

☛ Philippe Charlopin, 18, rte de Dijon, 21220 Gevrey-Chambertin, tel. 03.80.51.81.18, fax 03.80.51.81.18 ▨ ☎ by appt.

JEAN-PIERRE CHARTON 1999★ €5-8

■ 3 ha 11,000

This Pinot Noir sings out with pride that it is from Burgundy. Indeed, this wine is very typical, pleasant, a little rustic, but spontaneous and lively. It presents itself well with a peony colour and a delicate and classy nose.

☛ Jean-Pierre Charton, 29, Grande-Rue, 71640 Mercurey, tel. 03.85.45.22.39, fax 03.85.45.22.39 ▨ ☎ by appt.

CLOS DU CHATEAU 1999★ €11-15

☐ 4.5 ha 30,000

This château, with its 19 ha (47 acres), belongs to Crédit Foncier and offers us a Burgundy that is full of character, although still distinctly oaky. Nevertheless, body and structure are of top quality and hold their own against the wood, the wine being full and powerful. This is a bottle for experienced wine-lovers.

☛ SCEA Dom. du Château de Puligny-Montrachet, 21190 Puligny-Montrachet, tel. 03.80.21.39.14, fax 03.80.21.39.07, e-mail chateaupul@aol.com ▨ ☎ by appt.

DOM. CHAUMONT PERE ET FILS 1999★

■ 1.5 ha 1,600 ■ €5-8

This estate has spent 30 years making organic wines, an unusual but perhaps significant fact. It now practises sustainable agriculture. This Burgundy takes us on a non-stop journey into the universe of Pinot Noir: it has a powerful intensity and fine clarity of colour, and aromas of black cherry combined with mocha. The black cherry then reappears on the palate with underlying undergrowth and humus flavours. It is very characteristic of the *terroir*.

♠ Dom. Chaumont Père et Fils, Le Clos Saint-Georges, 71640 Saint-Jean-de-Vaux, tel. 03.85.45.13.77, fax 03.85.45.27.77, e-mail didierchaumont@aol.com ⵝ
ⵏ by appt.

DOM. DES CHAZELLES 2000★

n.c. 6,000 €5-8

The Chaland family came here in 1967, leaving their co-operative wine-cellar in order to cultivate 6.20 ha (15.3 acres) of vineyard. 'This is a fine white Burgundy,' one of our tasters notes. This wine has a lovely Chardonnay character with its pale colour and green glints, pronounced hawthorn nose, and grapefruit flavour that wins out on the palate. A well-structured, attractive wine that is pleasant to drink now.

♠ Jean-Noël Chaland.
En Jean-Large, 71260 Viré,
tel. 03.85.33.11.18, fax 03.85.33.15.58 ⵝ
ⵏ ev. day except Sun. 8am–7pm

DOM. FRANCOIS COLLIN

Epineuil 1999★

4.9 ha n.c. €5-8

Philippe Collin took over this family estate in 2000, and has inherited a very successful 99 here with this attractive pleasant red. Deep violet ruby-red, with a nose which will mature further, showing stewed fruits and prune. A fruity palate with some oak showing and a round, fresh body that holds promise.

♠ Philippe Collin, Les Mulots, 89700 Tonnerre, tel. 03.86.75.93.84, fax 03.86.75.94.00, e-mail françois.collin@wanadoo.fr ⵏ by appt.

DOM. HENRI CLERC ET FILS

Les Riaux 1999★

2.33 ha 21,733 ■

This is an old Burgundy estate for which Chardonnay holds no secrets. This bright gold wine has a very pleasant nose of fresh fruit. Harmonious, well-balanced on the palate, with a fresh lemon finish to complete the picture. Over the next two or three years it will provide an excellent accompaniment to fish terrine.

♠ Dom. Henri Clerc et Fils, pl. des Marronniers, 21190 Puligny-Montrachet, tel. 03.80.21.32.74, fax 03.80.21.39.60 ⵝ
ⵏ ev. day 8.30am–11.45am 2pm–5.45pm
♠ Bernard Clerc

DOM. COLLOTTE 1999★

1 ha 4,000 ■ €5-8

This wine is made using the first rule of wine-making: you cannot make a good wine without good grapes. A wine of fine character, which is tannic without being astringent; full-bodied without being rich; supple and tasty. A brilliant deep red colour with a whole range of aromas in the nose, from leather to soft fruit. The rest, as we have said, is pure camaraderie. There is no point in laying down this wine.

♠ Dom. Collotte, 44, rue de Mazy, 21160 Marsannay-la-Côte, tel. 03.80.52.24.34, fax 03.80.58.74.40 ⵝ
ⵏ by appt.

COMTE DE MIGIEU 1999

n.c. n.c.

This wine is one produced by the Max group. The nose shows ripe fruit mixed with touches of honey and resin. A dash of alcohol on the palate accompanies the toastiness that comes from the wood, which ought to blend in after a few years in the cellar.

♠ Poulet Père et Fils, 6, rue de Chaux, BP 4, 21700 Nuits-Saint-Georges, tel. 03.80.62.43.02, fax 03.80.61.28.08

DOM. DE CORBETON 1999★★

n.c. 200,000 ■ €15-23

This is really top quality for this appellation. This pale straw wine shows its distinction and elegance from the very first moment with a powerful but restrained and elegant fruitiness. And then, light and subtle, it really shows its class. An A. Bichot wine that is produced under another name. It was nominated for a *coup de cœur*.

♠ Dom. de Corbeton, BP 47, 21202 Beaune Cedex, tel. 03.80.24.37.47, fax 03.80.24.37.38

DOM. DE COURCEL 1998★

0.7 ha 1,500 ■ €8-11

This 'simple' Burgundy 98 comes from a well-known estate in Pommard and is a very fine wine. Vanilla and blackcurrant dominate the powerful and intense aromas. A well-handled extraction leads to a similar phenomenon on the palate, whilst there are hints of Bigarreau cherry in the finish. Characteristic and rather chic.

♠ Dom. de Courcel, pl. de l'Eglise, 21630 Pommard, tel. 03.80.22.10.64, fax 03.80.24.98.73 ⵝ

DOM. DARNAT 1999★

1.2 ha 7,000 ■ €8-11

Henri Darnat took over the family estate in 1995. This white Burgundy, also from Meursault, is very true to its *terroir*. The nose defines the grape variety while the palate reveals a subtle and well-directed oakiness with underlying flavours of flowers and fruit. A well-presented wine.

Bourgogne

- Dom. Darnat, 20, rue des Forges, 21190 Meursault, tel. 03.80.21.23.30, fax 03.80.21.64.62, e-mail domaine.darnat@libertysurcl.fr [V] Y by appt.

RODOLPHE DEMOUGEOT 1999★ €5-8
0.49 ha 4,800

This vintage marks this estate's first production of white wine since it was founded in 1992. Ten months in barrel have not erased the typical characteristics of this wine with its pale straw colour and aromas of fresh fruit, almonds and undergrowth. Agreeable on the palate, the wine reveals a diversity of flavours, with richness and liveliness on the attack and liveliness on the citrus fruit finish. Already very pleasant.

- Dom. Rodolphe Demougeot, 2, rue du Clos-de-Mazeray, 21190 Meursault, tel. 03.80.21.28.99, fax 03.80.21.29.18 [V] Y by appt.

DESVIGNES 1998 €5-8
n.c. 12,000

This is a white Burgundy coming from a good Beaujolais estate. The colour is fine and delicate and the nose is floral with a note of cinnamon. Well-balanced, round, long and quite fruity on the palate, it can be enjoyed from now on.

- Maison Desvignes, rue Guillemet-Desvignes, Pontanevaux, 71570 La Chapelle-de-Guinchay, tel. 03.85.36.72.32, fax 03.85.36.74.02 Y by appt.

ANTOINE DONAT ET FILS
Côtes d'Auxerre Dessus-bon-boire 1999★★ €5-8
1.5 ha 7,000

This lovely 99 has been matured in oak, but no new oak is used since this would 'bludgeon' the wine to death. This is a connoisseur's wine, ruby-red tinged with deep purple, with fruity, spicy flavours typical of Pinot Noir.

- André Donat, 41, rue de Vallan, 89290 Vaux, tel. 03.86.53.89.99, fax 03.86.53.68.36 [V] Y ev. day 9am–12 noon 2pm–7pm; Sun. by appt.

DOM. DUBOIS D'ORGEVAL 1998 €5-8
n.c. n.c.

This deep ruby-red regional Burgundy has fairly typical gamey overtones. Its structure is particularly noteworthy, as is its distinctive Burgundy Pinot Noir character. A good wine.

- Dom. Dubois d'Orgeval, 3, rue Joseph-Bard, 21200 Chorey-les-Beaune, tel. 03.80.24.70.89, fax 03.80.22.45.02 [V] Y by appt.

GILLES DURAND 2000 €3-5
0.2 ha 1,650

This estate was founded in 1991 and has young vines (seven years old) which give us this interesting, though more rounded than fresh, rosé. The salmon-pink colour heralds a fruity nose with slight notes of acid drops. These flavours would go well with grilled dishes.

- Gilles Durand, Ferme de l'Hermitage, 89700 Tonnerre, tel. 03.86.54.46.70, fax 03.86.55.29.00 [V] Y by appt.

BERNARD DURY 1999★
0.61 ha 2,000

Bernard Dury has been cultivating his 7.45 ha (18.4 acres) since 1875. This bright gold wine has an expressive nose of linden and spring flowers. It is only on the palate that the wood flavours of vanilla show themselves, but the liveliness remains through to the finish and this wine is very well-balanced.

- Bernard Dury, rue du Château, hameau de Cissey, 21190 Meursault, tel. 03.80.21.48.44, fax 03.80.21.48.44 [V] Y by appt.

SYLVAIN DUSSORT
Cuvée des Ormes 1999★ €8-11
1.3 ha 9,000

This cuvée, which comes from a plot of 40-year-old vines, is very well-known to readers of the Guide. It is a bright gold colour with fragrances of flowers, honey and crystallised fruit on the nose. On the palate the attack is quite rich but then develops with oaky notes and a liveliness that will ensure a good future in two or three years. It will go well with fish in cream sauce.

- Sylvain Dussort, 12, rue Charles-Giraud, 21190 Meursault, tel. 03.80.21.27.50, fax 03.80.21.65.91, e-mail dussvins@aol.com [V] Y by appt.

DOM. FELIX
Côtes d'Auxerre Cuvée Saint-André 1998★★ €5-8
0.22 ha 2,000

This estate was founded in the 17th century and since 1987 has been run by Hervé Félix, who is particularly fond of his village, where the fine architecture is of great interest to anyone who likes ancient stone buildings. The St. Andrew's cross was once the rallying symbol for the Burgundians. This wine, which is dedicated to the same saint, certainly wins all the support it deserves. This deep yellow 98 still has a strong vanilla flavour but also possesses a richness and power, and an elegance, that are typical of this appellation. A wine worthy of sautéed scallops in a buttery sauce. The rosé 99 is good (one star), presenting delicate notes of citrus and soft fruit.

- Dom. Hervé Félix, 17, rue de Paris, 89530 Saint-Bris-le-Vineux, tel. 03.86.53.33.87, fax 03.86.53.61.64, e-mail felix@caves-particulieres.com [V] Y ev. day except Sun. 9am–11.30am 2pm–6.30pm

DOM. DE FISSEY 1999★ €5-8
1.5 ha 800

This agreeable 99, produced on the Chalonnais Côte, has more distant origins. Yves Léveillé actually lived in Paris until he moved here in 1993 and wasn't able to look after these vines from Montmartre. This is a satisfying result judging by this pleasant, vinous wine. The tannins are discreet, the

colour powerful and the classic aromas are awakening. A good example of its kind.

☛ Yves et Catherine Léveillé, Dom. de Fissey, 71390 Moroges, tel. 03.85.47.99.40 ✉ ⚟ by appt.

DOM. DES FROMANGES 1999★

n.c.	n.c.	€3-5

If this appellation ever had doubts about itself, this pale gold wine, which marries honey with flint, will soon convince you of the qualities and virtues of excellent white Burgundy. Lively and rich, this is pure delight.

☛ F. Protheau et Fils, Ch. d'Etroyes, 71640 Mercurey, tel. 03.85.98.99.10, fax 03.85.98.99.00, e-mail commercial@protheau.com ⚟ ev. day except Sun./Mon. 8am–12 noon 2pm–6pm

GILBERT ET PHILIPPE GERMAIN 1999★

0.2 ha	1,000	€3-5

This wine-producer took over his parents' estate in 1995. Here, he presents a subtle rosé with a natural liveliness that is enveloped in a pleasant roundness. Its shows some originality with a combination of light vanilla flavours and fruit. To drink at the start of a good meal.

☛ Philippe Germain, 21190 Nantoux, tel. 03.80.26.05.63, fax 03.80.26.05.12 ✓ ⚟ by appt.

DOM. FONTAINE DE LA VIERGE
Chitry 1999★★

2 ha	5,000	€5-8

This estate is situated 300 m (327 yds) from the fortified church of Chitry-le-Fort. Neither estate nor church should be missed on a visit to this region, and anyone who wants to recall the *pêche de vigne* aroma will be tempted by this wine. Fresh and extremely pleasant, it has real character. The palate, which has a light citrus flavour, appears more delicate than concentrated. This very attractive wine can be drunk immediately.

☛ Jean-Claude Biot, 5, chem. des Fossés, 89530 Chitry-le-Fort, tel. 03.86.41.42.79, fax 03.86.41.46.72 ⚟ by appt.

DOM. GRAND ROCHE
Côtes d'Auxerre 1999★★

4 ha	18,000	€5-8

Erick Lavallée used to be an accountant. In 1981, he became interested in cereal crops. In 1987, he became a wine-producer, and by the looks of this vintage, no one will be complaining about his decision. This cherry-red 99 possesses many characteristics of a Côtes d'Auxerre, managing to be wild without being

DOM. ANNE-MARIE GILLE
1999★★

0.24 ha	1,700	€5-8

Anne-Marie Gille belongs to an old family that has been at Comblanchien since the 16th century. She has headed the business since 1983 and inherited a cellar of spectacular old vintages. This wine, which is the kind of purple-red colour that an Impressionist might have used, has very classic aromas (undergrowth, mulberry) with a satisfying vinosity. On the palate it is equally impressive and the components are well-balanced. For example, the tannins are present but not aggressive, and the body is as rich as can be. This might well be a candidate for the *coup de coeur* in a couple of years' time. Meanwhile, nobody will complain if it is drunk with a dish of salt pork and lentils before December 2004.

☛ Dom. Anne-Marie Gille, 34, RN 74, 21700 Comblanchien, tel. 03.80.62.94.13, fax 03.80.62.99.88, e-mail gille@burgundywines.net ✓ ⚟ by appt.

GHISLAINE ET JEAN-HUGUES GOISOT
Côtes d'Auxerre 1999★★★

4 ha	20,000	€5-8

This estate, which is regularly singled out by our tasters, is based in an 11th-century former guardroom. The wine-making makes good use of the extraction process, and the fermentation period is long. This very sophisticated wine has a great deal of colour, lots of dark fruit, and is pretty impressive on the palate. The **Corps de Garde 99 red** is very similar to the first wine, and the **white 99** from the same *cuvée* gets a special mention: it is very woody and needs to wait two years before being ready to drink.

☛ Ghislaine et Jean-Hugues Goisot, 30, rue Bienvenu-Martin, 89530 Saint-Bris-le-Vineux, tel. 03.86.53.35.15, fax 03.86.53.62.03 ✓ ⚟ by appt.

aggressive. Such is the miracle of wine! Despite the freshness of its attack, the flavours stay under control on the palate. Its tannins are not overpowering and there is a pleasant aftertaste of fruit kernels.

➤ Erick Lavallée, Dom. Grand Roche, 6, rte de Chitry, 89530 Saint-Bris-le-Vineux, tel. 03.86.53.84.07, fax 03.86.53.88.36 ▼ by appt.

GRIFFE Côtes d'Auxerre 2000 ■ €5-8
1.07 ha 5,000

David Griffe has been in charge of the family estate since 1992. Chitry, where the estate is based, boasts a listed 14th-century church. What is there to say about this 2000 vintage? It has an interesting nose of sloes and soft fruit that continues through onto the palate. A light and engaging wine, it could be served this winter alongside a roast and a *gratin dauphinois*. The **bourgogne Chitry white 2000** receives the same mark, but one needs to wait a year or two before drinking.

➤ EARL Griffe, 15, rue du Beugnon, 89530 Chitry-le-Fort, tel. 03.86.41.41.06, fax 03.86.41.47.36 ▼ ♦ by appt.

DOM. PATRICK GUILLOT 1999★★ ■ ▥♦ €3-5
1.5 ha 5,000

The producers have managed to achieve the maximum colour in this wine. Mulberry is dominant on the nose, whilst on the palate there is a gentle flavour of soft fruit and subtle tannins. Although a little too direct at the moment, this wine is still a long way from being at its best and should be laid down for three to four years. It is certainly the best value for money of the series.

➤ Dom. Patrick Guillot, 9 A, rue de Vaugeailles, 71640 Mercurey, tel. 03.85.45.27.40, fax 03.85.45.28.57 ▼ by appt.

DOM. HARMAND-GEOFFROY 1999★ ▥ €8-11
0.63 ha 5,700

This wine hails from a pretty estate in Gevrey-Chambertin and is sold all over the world. It is a light garnet colour with two distinct levels to its nose: first there is raspberry, then more developed aromas such as undergrowth and pelt. The oak is well-handled, and the body full. A hint of acidity, on the other hand, gives the impression that it probably won't be suitable for keeping and the smooth, long finish needs to be taken advantage of in the next two to three years.

➤ Dom. Harmand-Geoffroy, 1, pl. des Lois, 21220 Gevrey-Chambertin, tel. 03.80.34.10.65, fax 03.80.34.13.72, e-mail harmand-geoffroy@wanadoo.fr ▼ by appt.

CUVEE HENRY DE VEZELAY Vézelay 1999★★ ▮▥♦ €5-8
32.93 ha 150,000

Vézelay is not only 'this ship that has anchored on the horizon' (in the words of the poet Paul Claudel), but also a fine wine cellar.

This co-operative was created in 1989 and here presents a full and fleshy Chardonnay that is very much in the spirit of the region. The colour is lovely and the nose indicates both subtleness and richness. The similarly named **red 99** receives one star and should be drunk soon with a fillet of duck breast. The **La Vézelienne 2000** also receives one star and needs to wait a year or two before drinking.

➤ Cave Henry de Vézelay, 89450 Saint-Père, tel. 03.86.33.29.62, fax 03.86.33.35.03 ▼ ev. day 10am–12 noon 2.30pm–6pm

HENRY FRERES 1999★★ ■ €5-8
5 ha 10,000

Pascal and Didier are brothers and have been working together for over ten years. This wonderful 99 made it as far as the Grand Jury for the *coup de coeur*. The colour is subtle, the nose reserved (although already with hints of honey, lemon and gunflint), then the palate reveals itself: delightful, delicate and well-structured.

➤ GAEC Henry Frères, 89800 Saint-Cyr-les-Colons, tel. 03.86.41.44.87, fax 03.86.41.41.48 ▼ by appt.

JOEL HUDELOT-BAILLET 1999★ ■ €5-8
0.93 ha 3,000

A generic Burgundy? More of a regional one, one might say. A deep intense colour with an interesting nose combining spices with ripe fruit. Rich, swaggering, almost untamed at the finish, this confident wine needs to wait a while.

➤ Joël Hudelot-Baillet, 21, rue Basse, 21220 Chambolle-Musigny, tel. 03.80.62.85.88, fax 03.80.62.49.83 ▼ by appt.

PATRICK HUGOT 1998★★ ■ ♦ €5-8
3.5 ha 5,000

The Tonnerrois is a vineyard to watch. Geologically very close to the Chablisien, and sometimes confused with it, it somehow managed – as is the case here – to create a little jewel of a Chardonnay. This white-gold 98, with peppery aromas of undergrowth, fresh and long in flavour, is now amongst the best around.

➤ Patrick Hugot, Le Grand Virey, 89700 Molosmes, tel. 03.86.55.16.11, fax 03.86.55.16.11 ▼ ev. day except Sun. 8am–12 noon 2pm–7pm

LES VIGNERONS D'IGE Elevé en fût de chêne 1999★ ▥ €5-8
3.5 ha 30,000

This wine, produced by a co-operative that produces wine from 280 ha (692 acres) of vines, has spent twelve months in barrel. It is a wickedly beautiful wine with its fiery purple colour. The nose is still wild with aromas of mulberries and blueberries and the oak is more apparent on the palate than the nose. A fairly typical wine that comes from the Mâconnais where Pinot Noir has a distinctive

quality. It is supple and well-balanced reveal-ing some extremely interesting qualities.
- Cave coop. des vignerons d'Igé, 71960 Igé, tel. 03.85.33.33.56, fax 03.85.33.41.85.
e-mail lesvigneronsdige@
lesvigneronsdige.com ☑ Ⓨ ev. day except Sun. 8am–12 noon 2pm–6pm

DOM. GUY-PIERRE JEAN ET FILS Les Champs Pourras 1999★

■   n.c.   n.c.   ▥ €5-8

This interesting 99 doesn't beat about the bush. Its deep violet colour looks more like that of a 2000 vintage, and on the nose the aromas of gooseberries and raspberries are expansive. On the palate it is still very closed. The strong wood influence, together with its structure and power, make it a suitable drink-ing partner for pungent local cheeses.
- Dom. Guy-Pierre Jean et Fils, rue des Cras, 21420 Aloxe-Corton, tel. 03.80.26.44.72, fax 03.80.26.45.36 ☑
Ⓨ by appt.

PHILIPPE ET FRANCOISE JOUBY
Côtes d'Auxerre 1998★

■   n.c.   n.c.   ▥ €5-8

This firmly-structured 98 doesn't skimp on chewiness. This is a true *vin de terroir*, sturdy underneath. This is a deep ruby-purple colour. It is reasonably char-acteristic of the appellation and can be kept for a moderate amount of time. The **white 99** is vibrant and receives a special mention from the Jury. Buy it, but don't open it straight away.
- Cave Françoise et Philippe Jouby, 8 bis, rte de Paris, 89530 Saint-Bris-le-Vineux, tel. 03.86.53.30.58, fax 03.86.53.30.58 ☑
Ⓨ by appt.

JULIUS CAESAR
Cuvée du Maître de poste 1998★

■   0.5 ha   3,000   ▥ €8-11

Julius Caesar is an unusual name for a wine, and one made in Burgundy too, where Julius was none too popular, Vercingetorix being the local hero. Leaving that aside, however, this deep ruby red 98 has lovely ripe flavours of soft fruit, darkening as a hint of blackcurrant appears, and combining a tannic structure with a fruity fullness. *Et tu ...*
Best drunk before the Ides of March.
- Marylène et Philippe Sorin, 12, rue de Paris, 89530 Saint-Bris-le-Vineux, tel. 03.86.53.60.76, fax 03.86.53.62.60, e-mail philippe.sorin@libertysurcl.fr ☑
Ⓨ by appt.

DOM. DE LA GALOPIERE 1999★

■   7 ha   3,000   ▥ ◉ €5-8

In 1982, Claire and Gabriel Fournier decided to dedicate themselves entirely to vineyards and wine. Today they work without weedkillers. This wine needs another year in the cellar before it is ready to drink. It is gutsy with aromas of ripe fruit and spices and has redcurrant flavours on the palate. A good chewy wine with strong yet mellow tannins, it will accompany a roasted red meat well.
- Claire et Gabriel Fournier, 6, rue de l'Eglise, 21200 Bligny-lès-Beaune, tel. 03.80.21.46.50, fax 03.80.21.49.93, e-mail c.g.fournier@wanadoo.fr ☑
Ⓨ by appt.

DOM. DE LA PERRIERE
Clos de La Perrière Monopole 1999★★

□   1 ha   6,000   ▥

If you are really looking for the best wine among the thousands belonging to this AOC, then try this clear-coloured 99, with its lightly toasted flavour, and appreciate its gently spicy aromas. On the palate there is a touch of freshness and finesse that combine delicately

DOM. DANIEL JUNOT
Elevé en fût de chêne 1999

□   0.4 ha   4,000   ▥

In the 17th century, at the village of Junay, situated 3 km (1.9 miles) from Tonnerre, there were vineyards belonging to the poet Boileau. This, however, is a very young vineyard that produces this *cuvée*. Well-made, yet without a

huge structure, with strong wood flavours that do not overpower the fruitiness.
- Daniel Junot, 7, Grande-Rue, 89700 Junay, tel. 03.86.54.40.93, fax 03.86.54.49.93. Ⓨ by appt.

DOM. DE L'ABBAYE DU PETIT QUINCY Epineuil 2000★

◩

This estate was taken over in 1990 by the Gruhier family: Madame Gruhier belongs to the Delaunays (a former *négoce-éleveur* based in Dijon, then in L'Etang-Vergy) and this *rosé de saignée* is a very successful vintage 2000. It is the colour of redcurrants, spicy and with fine complex aromas of pear drops, and a few citrus notes. To be drunk and enjoyed over the next few months.
- Dominique Gruhier, rue du Clos de Quincy, 89700 Epineuil, tel. 03.86.55.32.51, fax 03.86.55.32.50 ☑ Ⓨ ev. day except Sun. 9am–12 noon 2pm–6pm; Sat. by appt.

CH. DE LA BRUYERE
Elevé en fût de chêne 1999★

□   0.5 ha   3,000   ▥ ◉ €5-8

This château, owned by Borie since 1995, was first built in the Middle Ages and then completely redesigned in 1881. It has 8.6 ha (21.2 acres) of vineyards. Grown on lime-stone-clay, here the Chardonnay grape has produced a Burgundy wine that is balanced, well-structured and floral. Nine months of maturation in barrel have not spoilt its poten-tial. Best left unopened for the next year or two.
- Paul-Henry Borie, Ch. de La Bruyère, 71960 Igé, tel. 03.85.33.30.72, fax 03.85.33.40.65, e-mail mph.borie@wanadoo.fr ☑
Ⓨ ev. day 8am–12 noon 2pm–7pm

Bourgogne

with the lemony, menthol notes. A wine from the southern Côte d'Or.

☛ Dom. de La Perrière,
La Cave du Vincent Latour, 1, rte de Beaune, 21630 Pommard, tel. 03.80.24.62.25, fax 03.80.24.62.42, e-mail cecile.chenu@wanadoo.fr ▨ ♈ ev. day 10am–6pm

"L" DE MICHEL LAROCHE
Cuvée Prestige 1999★

☐ 13 ha 106,000 ▤ ♦ €5-8

Michel Laroche runs his own business and has agreed quality-control contracts with the wine-growers from whom he buys grapes. This wine, which is very typical, has a pale yellow colour and subtle flavours of honey and stewed fruit that give it character. A well-handled maturation period has produced a good quality wine, well-balanced and lasting.

☛ Michel Laroche, 22, rue Louis-Bro, BP 33, 89800 Chablis, tel. 03.86.42.89.28, fax 03.86.42.89.29, e-mail info@michellaroche.com ▨ ♈ by appt.

DOM. DE LA TOUR BAJOLE
Vieilles vignes 1998★

▤ 1.5 ha 9,000 ▥ €5-8

This estate, along with several wine-producers from Auxey-Duresses, played a pioneering role in growing the vines in the lyre formation, which is currently being tried out in the Hautes-Côtes. The black cherry colour is what one would expect for this grape variety. This wine has freshness, acidity and structure and will go well as an accompaniment to roasted or grilled white meat.

☛ M.-A. et J.-C. Dessendre,
Dom. de La Tour-Bajole, Les Ombrots, 71490 Saint-Maurice-lès-Couches, tel. 03.85.45.52.90, fax 03.85.45.52.90, e-mail domaine-de-la-tour-bajole@wanadoo.fr ▨ ♈ by appt.

CH. DE LA TOUR DE L'ANGE 1999
▤ 1.7 ha 10,000 ▥ ♦ €5-8

These vines are said to have once belonged to a hero of Mâconnais mythology, the famous Claude Brosse, who travelled to Versailles to ask Louis XIV to taste his wine. Here, we have a Mâconnais Pinot Noir produced in Gamay country. Bright, light ruby-red in colour, this delicate, clean 99 is suitable for everyday drinking.

☛ SCE Ch. de La Tour de l'Ange, chem. du bourg, 71850 Charnay-lès-Mâcon, tel. 03.85.34.96.67, fax 03.85.34.97.98, e-mail md.debryas@latourdelange.com ▨ ♈ by appt.

LATOUR-MABILLE 1999
☐ 0.8 ha 3,000 ▥ €5-8

Vincent Latour was 23 when he took over the family estate in 1998, and he is lucky enough to have inherited 45-year-old vines and a very fine Meursault terroir. This wine has a lovely floral freshness with a very upright character: the body is well-balanced and unpretentious. It needs just another year before being ready to drink.

☛ Jean Latour-Labille et Fils, 6, rue du 8-Mai, 21190 Meursault, tel. 03.80.21.22.49, fax 03.80.21.67.86 ▨ ♈ by appt.
☛ Vincent Latour

CH. DE LA VELLE 1999★
☐ 0.3 ha 3,000 ▥ €5-8

Sometimes you have to be bold enough to suggest wine and food combinations that will liven up the conversation when it flags a little, and you need the right wine to do this. Why not try this lovely 99 with a very sweet, banana-based dessert, or even flambéed Guide! This Chardonnay is lemon yellow in colour with a nose that tends towards citrus fruits (with a hint of fresh walnuts). It is very rich with a gentle citrus finish.

☛ Bertrand Darviot, Ch. de La Velle, 17, rue de La Velle, 21190 Meursault, tel. 03.80.21.22.83, fax 03.80.21.65.60, e-mail chateaudelavelle@infonie.fr ▨ ♈ by appt.

LES CAVES DE LA VERVELLE
Cuvée 1369 1999★★

▤ 2 ha 12,400 ▥ €8-11

The name of this wine is Cuvée 1369 which is the year the château of Bligny-lès-Beaune was built by Philibert Paillard, chancellor of Burgundy. A brilliant colour with vanilla aromas, this is a very fine wine. With a hint more richness it would have been perfect and would have achieved a coup de coeur.

☛ Ch. de Bligny-lès-Beaune,
Caves de la Vervelle, le Château, 21200 Bligny-lès-Beaune, tel. 03.80.21.47.38, fax 03.80.21.40.27 ▨
♈ ev. day 8am–12 noon 2pm–6pm

JACQUES LEMAIGRE 1999★★
▤ 0.2 ha 1,400 ▥ €5-8

This is a wine that knows when to put on a burst of speed – just at the moment of decision for the coup de coeur – and manages to arrive among the first at the finishing line. It is also one of the Guide's discoveries, as this is a little-known producer. This cherry-red wine with its delicate, complex nose, its pleasant acidity and perfect structure, belongs among the leaders. There are not many bottles to buy.

☛ Jacques Lemaigre, 2, rte de Paris-Genève, 89700 Dannemoine, tel. 03.86.55.54.84 ▨
♈ by appt.

SERGE LEPAGE
Côte Saint-Jacques 1999

▤ 0.48 ha 3,900 ▥ €5-8

Produced from just half a hectare (1.2 acres) of Pinot Noir, this wine holds aloft the torch for the wines from Joigny, the most northern area in the Burgundy region. This deep ruby-red 99 has a rather delicate nose (with a fine mineral note). The tannins are as they should be, enveloped in aromas of soft fruit and making the idea of two or three years' life in the cellar a feasible prospect. A vin gris 99, produced from a mixture of 70% Pinot Gris and 30% Pinot Noir that is pressed

454

straightaway as the grapes arrive from the harvest, is not without its own distinctive character, with flavours ranging from wild roses to hawthorn. It is recommended as a real thirst-quencher.

✦ Serge Lepage, 9, rue Principale, Grand Longueron, 89300 Champlay, tel. 03.86.62.05.58, fax 03.86.62.20.08 ☑
☕ by appt.

LES PIERRELEES Vieilles vignes 1999★

7.5 ha   6,000

Laurent Verot moved here in 1996 and puts on a fine performance for us with this deeply-coloured red with its powerful aromas of cherry and undergrowth. It has a big pair of lungs for a 'simple' Burgundy, mouthfilling and with great length.

✦ Laurent Verot, imp. des Petite-Chaumes, 71640 Germolles, tel. 03.85.45.15.07

MICHEL LORAIN 1999

5 ha   40,000

The pretty town of Joigny has been here since ancient Roman times. It is a place full of art and history, dominating the Yonne region. Although he has been producing wine for less than ten years, Michel Lorain shows his talents as a great wine-maker when we look at this wine. The subtle aromas of spring blossom and exotic overtones of almonds and mint are found both on the nose and the palate, which opens out powerfully and has good length. Delay a while before drinking it, as this promising 99 is worth waiting for.

✦ SCEV Michel Lorain, 12, fg de Paris, 89300 Joigny, tel. 03.86.62.06.70, fax 03.86.91.49.70 ☑ ☕ by appt.

DOM. NICOLAS MAILLET 2000★

0.4 ha   2,600

In 1999, Nicolas Maillet left the co-operative of which he was a member in order to produce wine himself, and judging by this elegant and well-designed wine, he has made a good job of it. It is mauve in colour, with an already very eloquent nose with very ripe cherries, while the palate is open and frank. A light but well-rounded wine.

✦ Dom. Nicolas Maillet, La Cure, 71960 Verzé, tel. 03.85.33.46.76, fax 03.85.33.46.76 ☑ ☕ by appt.

MALTOFF

Coulanges-la-Vineuse Cuvée Prestige 1999★★

0.5 ha   5,400

This Cuvée Prestige 99 has a lot of personality and character. It is peony-red in colour, while on the nose soft fruit leads the way, followed by vanilla. Supple and clean with a well-balanced palate, this excellent wine is very much in Coulanges style.

✦ Dom. Jean-Pierre Maltoff, 20, rue d'Aguesseau, 89580 Coulanges-la-Vineuse, tel. 03.86.42.32.48, fax 03.86.42.24.92, e-mail domaine/-p.maltoff@wanadoo.fr ☑
☕ by appt.

BOURGOGNE
COULANGES-LA-VINEUSE
DOMAINE MALTOFF
PRESTIGE

CAVE DES VIGNERONS DE MANCEY 1999★

n.c.   15,000

Mancey is the village near Tournus where phylloxera was first discovered in Burgundy. Since then, producers have worked hard to restore both vines and wines. This wine is clear and brilliant and the nose is a beguiling mix of undergrowth and fruit. The body is not massive, but its youthfulness and character indicate that it will be worth waiting for. The Cuvée Fût de Chêne 99 also went down well with the tasters.

✦ Cave des vignerons de Mancey, RN 6, En Velноux, 71700 Tournus, tel. 03.85.51.00.83, fax 03.85.51.71.20 ☑ ☕ by appt.

CATHERINE ET CLAUDE MARECHAL Cuvée Gravel 1999★

3.42 ha   15,300

Why is it called Cuvée Gravel? Because the subsoil in this area, east of Beaune, is mostly made up of gravel. This wine is an attractive colour with its pleasant cherry highlights with an aroma leaning towards small dark fruit such as blackcurrant or mulberries, while the palate, which is genuinely long, has the same flavours. This wine is good publicity for this grape variety.

✦ EARL Catherine et Claude Maréchal, 6, rte de Chalon, 21200 Bligny-lès-Beaune, tel. 03.80.21.44.37, fax 03.80.26.85.01 ☑ ☕ by appt.

DOM. DES MARRONNIERS 2000★★

1.08 ha   10,000

This most hospitable of wine-growers will go out of his way to show you around his vineyard, and this white Burgundy shares his affability. A bright straw-yellow in colour with floral, charred aromas on the nose, and both full and youthful on the palate. A well-made wine.

✦ Bernard Légland, Grande-Rue de Chablis, 89800 Préhy, tel. 03.86.41.42.70, fax 03.86.41.45.82 ☑ ☕ ev, day 9.30am–12 noon 1.30pm–7pm; cl 15 Aug–3 Sep.

DOM. DE MARSOIF 1999★★

2.45 ha   15,000

This estate was founded in 1991 and produced its first wine in 1994. It has connections with the Maison Rouge domaine in

Bourgogne

Tonnerois, while its tasting cellar is in Loir-et-Cher, all of which combine to achieve a *coup de cœur*. This is a superb white Burgundy, brilliant and intense, with a mineral flavour that is enough to make sparks fly from a flint. These 2.5 ha (6.2 acres) are a gift from the gods.

☛ SCEA de Marsoif, 1, rte de Verdes, 41160 Semerville, tel. 02.54.80.44.31, fax 02.54.80.43.26, e-mail rMar.oif@terre-net.fr ☑ ⦿ by appt.
☛ Martine Masson

DOM. MATHIAS Epineuil 1999★   ▣ 📖 €5-8
■ 7 ha 30,000

Alain Mathias was previously a vineyard worker, but then managed to establish his own business by taking on and renovating this Tonnerois vineyard. His wine is attractive-looking, with raspberry glints. Soft fruit on the nose, lively and fresh on the palate with notes of cherry. Altogether a fairly rounded wine.

☛ Alain Mathias, rte de Troyes, 89700 Epineuil, tel. 03.86.54.43.90, fax 03.86.54.47.75, e-mail domaine.alain.mathias@wanadoo.fr ☑ ⦿ by appt.

DOM. DE MAUPERTHUIS Les Truffières 1999   ▣ €5-8
☐ 1.35 ha 9,600

This estate of 4.55 ha (11.2 acres) was created in 1992. Their 'honest, straightforward' wine, which is produced from very young (five-year-old) vines, creates a good impression revealing fine citrus and mineral notes on both the nose and palate.

☛ Laurent Ternynck, EARL de Mauperthuis, Civry, 89440 Massangis, tel. 03.86.33.86.24, fax 03.86.33.86.24, e-mail ternynck@hotmail.com ☑ ⦿ by appt.

DOM. MOISSENET-BONNARD Les Maisons Dieu 1999★   📖 €5-8
☐ 0.29 ha 2,400

The strong aroma of blackcurrant bud, so much sought after by perfumeries, dominates the bouquet of this wine. This deep purple Pinot is still a little stiff but is in the process of softening. This *climat*, situated in Pommard, is not far from an *appellation communale*. Note also the **Cuvée de l'Oncle Paul 99**, which is commended by the Jury.

☛ Dom. Moissenet-Bonnard, rte d'Autun, 21630 Pommard, tel. 03.80.24.62.34, fax 03.80.22.30.04 ☑ ⦿ by appt.

MOMMESSIN La Clé Saint-Pierre 1999★   ▣ €8-11
■ 3.4 ha 20,000

This wine is packed with fruit: cherry in the colour, mulberries in the nose, blackcurrant and undergrowth on the palate. It is short on acidity but has a real kick to it and its prospects for the future are reasonably good. The keys of Saint Peter, which give this wine its name, have long been a feature of the family crest of this estate. The **white 99** deserves similar praise.

☛ Mommessin, Le Pont-des-Samsons, 69430 Quincié-en-Beaujolais, tel. 04.74.69.09.30, fax 04.74.69.09.28, e-mail information@mommessin.com

DOM. DE MONTPIERREUX 1998★   ▣ €5-8
☐ 3 ha 21,000

Montpierreux is renewing its links with its rich wine-producing past, and as evidence of this, they have produced this agreeable 98 which, though not particularly intense in colour, is very clear, and has a fresh, elegant nose. On the palate it is round and balanced, with mineral notes and good length. It would go well with a dish of fish in sauce.

☛ François Choné, Dom. de Montpierreux, rte de Chablis, 89290 Venoy, tel. 03.86.40.20.91, fax 03.86.40.28.00 ☑ ⦿ ev. day 9am-7pm

MICHEL MOREY-COFFINET 1999★★   ▣ €5-8
■ 1.2 ha 4,500

Thibault, one of the two sons of this family, has taken over the estate. This wine shows his talents with its deep red colour, its lovely brilliance, and wonderful combination of raspberry, cherry and mocha (soft fruit plus the oak influence). On the palate it is fresh and clean, quite supple in character, with solid and well-integrated tannins. A full wine with good length that will be at its best between 2003 and 2006.

☛ Dom. Michel Morey-Coffinet, 6, pl. du Grand-Four, 21190 Chassagne-Montrachet, tel. 03.80.21.31.71, fax 03.80.21.90.81, e-mail morey.coffinet@wanadoo.fr ☑ ⦿ by appt.

OLIVIER MORIN Chitry 1999★
☐ 3 ha 20,000 ▣ 📖 ♦

Chitry, a pretty village nestling in a valley surrounded by vineyards, is full of wine cellars which remind one just how old the tradition of wine-growing in this area is. It was here that one of the first Chardonnays was planted, in the Yonne valley. This particular wine is still a little closed on the nose but has length on the palate. The oak is still very evident and needs time to mellow. It would go well with a pike *au Chitry*.

456

● Olivier Morin, 2, chem. de Vaudu, 89530 Chitry-le-Fort, tel. 03.86.41.47.20, fax 03.86.41.47.20 ⓥ ⓣ by appt.

ANDRE ET JEAN-RENE NUDANT
La Chapelle Notre-Dame 1998★

■ 0.3 ha | 2,700 | €5-8

What is special about this wine? It is one of the few AOC *régionale* Burgundies to be officially allowed to be called after the *climat* where it is grown, in this case Notre-Dame-du-Chemin, which is just beside the main road at Ladoix. This is a light, fresh Pinot, ruby-red with brick-coloured glints, oaky with a sweet note of blackcurrant. It is characteristic of the style and will go well with roast meat.
● Dom. Nudant, 11, RN 74, 21550 Ladoix-Serrigny, tel. 03.80.26.40.48, fax 03.80.26.47.13, e-mail domaine.nudant@wanadoo.fr ⓥ
ⓣ by appt.

PINQUIER-BROVELLI 1999

■ 0.92 ha | 7,650 | €5-8

Thierry Pinquier has been running this estate since 1994. This wine is an attractive garnet colour with aromas hinting at vanilla and liquorice. The palate is very open, developing with true character, which makes this a wine that can be drunk now. It is very representative of the vintage.
● Thierry Pinquier,
5, rue Pierre-Mouchoux, 21190 Meursault, tel. 03.80.21.24.87, fax 03.80.21.61.09 ⓥ
ⓣ ex. day 8am–12.30pm 1pm–7pm

REBOURGEON-MURE 1999★★

■ 1.6 ha | 10,000 | €5-8

One day, Jean Bourgogne came to live in Pommard. The year was 1552, and that is how this ancient family line came into being. This 99 vintage, therefore, marks the 450th anniversary of the family's existence. It is garnet-red in colour, tinged with blue, with a charming, eager nose and good tannins revealing a touch of new oak on the nose. On the palate it is excellent: well-balanced, with a lovely range of flavours and silky tannins.
● Daniel Rebourgeon-Mure, Grande-Rue, 21630 Pommard, tel. 03.80.22.75.39, fax 03.80.22.71.00 ⓥ ⓣ by appt.

ARMELLE ET BERNARD RION 1999★★

■ 1 ha | 7,000 | €5-8

These wine-producers have more than one string to their bow: not only do they make wine, they also breed pedigree dogs (the bearded collie) and grow Burgundy truffles (*Tuber uncinatum*). This wine is violet-purple in colour, with complex, fruity aromas. It is still needs to open out but it has all the hallmarks of a great Burgundy to come. Top of the range for this appellation.
● Dom. Armelle et Bernard Rion, 8, rte Nationale, 21700 Vosne-Romanée, tel. 03.80.61.05.31, fax 03.80.61.24.60, e-mail rion@webwine.com ⓥ ⓣ by appt.

Domaine Saint Prix
BOURGOGNE
CÔTES D'AUXERRE

DOM. SAINTE-CLAIRE
Côtes d'Auxerre 1999★

■ n.c. | n.c. | €5-8

'I feel quite inclined to buy this', notes one member of the jury. This attractive 99 Pinot Noir is pale cherry-red in colour with a fruity but subtle nose. It is a little on the mineral side on the palate which is otherwise fruity. A well-made but quite simple wine which has developed a little and is ready to drink with the family evening meal. With its mineral notes and a lengthy finish, this estate's **Jean-Marc Brocard, Kimméridgien 99**, a white Burgundy receives one star.
● Jean-Marc Brocard, 3, rte de Chablis, 89800 Préhy, tel. 03.86.41.49.00, fax 03.86.41.49.09, e-mail brocard@brocard.fr ⓥ ⓣ by appt.

SAINT-HUBERT 1999

■ n.c. | n.c. | €11-15

This wine, made under the aegis of St. Hubert, the patron saint of hunters, is still developing its character. The nose has touches of strawberry jam and the palate is youthful yet elegant. This will appeal to people who like simple wines and don't want to wait. Open it now.
● Boisseaux-Estivant, 38, fg Saint-Nicolas, BP 107, 21200 Beaune, tel. 03.80.22.00.05, fax 03.80.24.19.73

DOM. SAINT-PANCRACE
Côtes d'Auxerre 2000★

□ 0.36 ha | 3,000 | €5-8

This wine is produced from a small estate in Auxerre (less than 1 ha/2.47 acres) and this is their second vintage, a wine whose exotic character makes it a good candidate to accompany a dish such as chicken with pineapple. It has a clear, pale colour, and some rather provocative aromas of banana and mango. Although young, over-lively and lacking in vanilla, it has a wonderful smoothness and an attractive fruity ripeness.
● Xavier Julien, Dom. Saint-Pancrace, 6, rue Lebeuf, 89000 Auxerre, tel. 03.86.51.69.71, fax 03.86.51.69.71 ⓥ ⓣ by appt.

DOM. SAINT-PRIX
Côtes d'Auxerre 1999★★

□ 2 ha | 12,000 | €5-8

This huge family estate has been making wine since way back in the 15th century, and always manages to win many of the top accolades in this *Guide*. This wine is no exception. 'Its aromas are so subtle one might think they'd been put together by a perfume blender rather than a wine-producer', wrote one of our tasters. This scintillating wine with its enticing aromas of jasmine and honeysuckle deserves a *coup de coeur*. The Bersan et Fils **Bourgogne Côtes d'Auxerre 99 red** deserves almost as much enthusiasm, and a *coup de coeur* at the very least.

• Dom. Bersan et Fils, 20, rue du Dr-Tardieux, 89530 Saint-Bris-le-Vineux, tel. 03.86.53.33.73, fax 03.86.53.38.45
Y by appt.

DOM. SAINT-PRIX
Côtes d'Auxerre 1999★★

| 5 ha | 30,000 | €5-8 |

The cherry-red colour of this wine recalls the fact that Auxerre was once pink with cherry blossom each spring. The nose is cherry-flavoured too. Marmotte cherries, perhaps? 'At last, a real wine!' writes one of our tasters. This devotion to the cherry theme makes one want to try it again. An absolute must.

• Dom. Bersan et Fils, 20, rue du Dr-Tardieux, 89530 Saint-Bris-le-Vineux, tel. 03.86.53.33.73, fax 03.86.53.38.45
Y by appt.

DOM. VINCENT SAUVESTRE
1999★

| 1.7 ha | 13,500 | €5-8 |

This wine possesses many varied qualities, from the black cherry colour to the lovely wild strawberry nose and the little peppery note on the finish of its fine, straightforward palate. The attack is gentle and its volume and body are perfect. Note also the delicious taste of fresh grapes which, oddly enough, has become a rare attribute in wine.

• Dom. Vincent Sauvestre, rte de Monthélie, 21190 Meursault, tel. 03.80.21.22.45, fax 03.80.21.28.05
Y by appt.

CLAUDE ET THOMAS SEGUIN
Côtes d'Auxerre 1999★

| 1.6 ha | 11,000 | €5-8 |

They take their time over things in Saint-Bris: the church, which was begun in the 13th century, was finished 300 years later, so is it any wonder that this 99 needs a little time (two or three years) to mature? It is deep ruby-red in colour with a hint of overripeness and a touch of the *terroir*. The tannins are well-integrated and it is moderately acidic with just the right amount of soft fruit.

• Claude et Thomas Seguin, 3 bis, rue Haute, 89530 Saint-Bris-le-Vineux, tel. 03.86.53.37.39, fax 03.86.53.61.12
Y by appt.

PAUL ET COLETTE SIMON 1999★

| 1 ha | 4,000 | €5-8 |

This is a Hautes-Côtes de Nuits and a half. It has such a powerful nose and great presence. A very pale colour and a nose with aromas of white nectarine, menthol and acacia; the palate is elegant and full of class, blending exotic fruit and grapefruit right up to the long finish. Very attractive and full of promise.

• Paul et Colette Simon, 21700 Marey-les-Fussey, tel. 03.80.62.93.35, fax 03.80.62.71.54, e-mail domaine@paul-simon.fr Y by appt.

CHRISTINE ET PASCAL SORIN
Côtes d'Auxerre 1999★★

| 1.5 ha | 4,600 | €5-8 |

In 1989, Pascal Sorin took over his grandparents' business and ever since then has been going from strength to strength. This Chardonnay opens with great gusto on the palate. It is pale yellow with green glints and has a very attractive texture. It has aromas of brioche and toast, typical of the grape variety, with a little mineral touch to give it a lift at the finish. Its finesse and well-balanced, fresh structure make it a wine to go with fish.

• Sorin-Coquard, 25, rue de Grisy, 89530 Saint-Bris-le-Vineux, tel. 03.86.53.37.76, fax 03.86.53.37.76
Y ev. day 8am–8.30pm; Sun. 8am–12.30pm
• Pascal Sorin

JEAN-PIERRE SORIN
Côtes d'Auxerre 1999★

| 0.65 ha | 4,000 | €5-8 |

Made using rigorous wine-making techniques and using the finest grapes, this wine has incomparable body and density. It appears very full and round with the potential to last several years. It has a powerful acidity (indicating its keeping potential) which at the moment dominates fine fruit and subtle tannins. Forget it for a year or two in your cellar.

• Madame Jean-Pierre Sorin, 6, rue de Grisy, 89530 Saint-Bris-le-Vineux, tel. 03.86.53.32.44, fax 03.86.53.37.76
Y ev. day 8am–8.30pm; Sun. 8am–12.30pm

MARYLENE ET PHILIPPE SORIN
Côtes d'Auxerre Réserve du Maître de Poste Fût de chêne 1998★

| 5.5 ha | 15,000 | €5-8 |

This former 18th-century coaching inn is at the centre of a 20-ha (49.4-acre) estate. This attractive 98 is bright ruby-red in colour with a few amber flecks. The aroma is double-edged, giving us leather and game on the one hand but also cherry and kirsch on the other. Its tannins and oakiness make it advisable to wait a while before drinking it.

• Marylène et Philippe Sorin, 12, rue de Paris, 89530 Saint-Bris-le-Vineux, tel. 03.86.53.60.76, fax 03.86.53.62.60, e-mail philippe.sorin@libertysurcl.fr
Y by appt.

JEAN-BAPTISTE THIBAUT

Chitry 1999★

| | 1.1 ha | 4,000 | | | €5-8 |

On this estate, you can visit a small ecological museum before, or after, buying this wine. It is an intensely-coloured wine (not bad for a 99), very much in the Chitry mould. The nose is gamey (leathery), while the young tannins are still a little prominent on the palate is already interesting. All in all, everything is heading in the right direction but it needs a year or two in the cellar.

➥ Jean-Baptiste Thibaut,
3, rue du Château, 89290 Quenne,
tel. 03.86.40.35.76, fax 03.86.40.27.70,
e-mail domaine-thibaut@wanadoo.fr ▼
Ⴤ by appt.

DOM. THOMAS 1999★

| | 0.88 ha | 7,500 | | | €8-11 |

This blood-red Pinot Noir from the Moillard family estate presents a basketful of fruity aromas lightly touched with vanilla. The wine is delicious on the palate and sets the standard for the appellation. Although the tannins are a little on the firm side, they are not unwelcome. A cheese buffet would make an ideal accompaniment.

➥ Dom. Thomas, chem. rural no. 29,
21700 Nuits-Saint-Georges,
tel. 03.80.62.42.00, fax 03.80.61.28.13,
e-mail nuicave@wanadoo.fr ▼
Ⴤ ev. day 10am–6pm; cl. Jan.

CH. DU VAL DE MERCY

Coulanges-la-Vineuse Réserve du Château 2000

| | 0.73 ha | 4,000 | | | €5-8 |

This estate was founded just ten years ago, and owns 18 ha (44.5 acres) in Chablis and 10 ha (24.7 acres) in Auxerrois. This 2000 vintage is the first of their wines to go before our Jury. It has a deep purple-red colour with a raspberry-ish nose, the result of good extraction. The warm palate is very characteristic.

➥ Dom. du Ch. du Val de Mercy,
8, promenade du Terre, 89530 Chitry,
tel. 03.86.41.48.00, fax 03.86.41.45.80,
e-mail chateauduval@aol.com ▼
Ⴤ by appt.
➥ Rudolf Mezoni

ALAIN VIGNOT

Côte Saint-Jacques 1999★

| | 4.16 ha | 22,000 | | | €5-8 |

This estate has been one of the key players in the renaissance of the Côte Saint-Jacques – a terroir which could otherwise easily have disappeared, which would have been a great pity – and this lovely 99 is proof of their labours. Red with blackcurrant glints and a rather untamed, gamey nose that has just a little provocative whiff of violet, this is an easy drinking wine, fresh, pleasant and very authentic, a far cry from so many 'manufactured' wines.

➥ Alain Vignot, 16, rue des Prés,
89300 Paroy-sur-Tholon, tel. 03.86.91.03.06,
fax 03.86.91.09.37 ▼ Ⴤ by appt.

DOM. ELISE VILLIERS 1999★

| | 0.5 ha | 3,000 | | | €5-8 |

To be a wine-producer in Vézelay means rubbing shoulders with the temporal and the spiritual, the mind and the heart, history and literature. It also means discovering the vines of the Dukes of Burgundy and participating in the renaissance of the former monastic estates. And this intense and forward 99 would be just the job to complement a strong local cheese. Although tannic, it is also direct; the attack goes right to the point and there is greater depth to explore. It may not be a very characteristic wine but it is interesting. The honeyed, buttery, rich and fresh Bourgogne Vézelay Le Clos 99 likewise is testament to the progress this estate has made in the last ten years, and receives a special mention from the Jury.

➥ Elise Villiers, Précy-le-Moult, 89450 Vézelay,
tel. 03.86.33.27.62, fax 03.86.33.27.62 ▼
Ⴤ by appt.

Bourgogne Grand Ordinaire

In real terms, the Appellations Bourgogne Bourgogne Ordinaire and Bourgogne Grand Ordinaire are used very rarely. When they are, the one that is less frequently used is Bourgogne Grand Ordinaire. This name may appear a little dull, but some terroirs on the margins of great vineyards can, nonetheless, produce some excellent wines that sold at very affordable prices. Almost all the Burgundy vine varieties can be used to produce white, red, rosé or clairet wines for this appellation.

The grapes used for white wine are Chardonnay or Melon. Although only a very few Melon vines remain, this variety reaches the heights of quality further west in France, where it is used to produce a reputable Muscadet in the Nantes region. The Aligoté is almost always declared as Appellation Bourgogne Aligoté.

The Sacy grape, now grown exclusively in the Yonne, was once grown in the whole Chablis area and in the Yonne river valley to produce sparkling wines for export; it is now used for Crémant de Bourgogne.

The principal varieties for red and rosé, are the traditional Burgundy grapes, Gamay Noir and Pinot Noir. In the Yonne the César variety, reserved exclusively for Burgundy wines, can still be used, particularly in Irancy, while the Tressot makes an appearance in the annals but never in the vineyards. The best wines made from Gamay are found in the Yonne, especially in Coulanges-la-Vineuse, where they are bottled under that appellation. The production of wines from this AOC was 10,300 hl (271,920 gal) in 2000.

CAVE DES VIGNERONS DE GENOUILLY 1999
4 ha 10,000 €5-8

The members of the Genouilly (Saône-et-Loire) co-operative make their Burgundy Grand Ordinaire from the Gamay grape. This full, meaty, well-structured wine is garnet in colour with slightly amber flecks and has an astringency that is not surprising. To drink during 2002.

Cave des vignerons de Genouilly, 71460 Genouilly, tel. 03.85.49.23.72, fax 03.85.49.23.58 ev. day except Sun. 8am–12 noon 2pm–6pm

OLIVIER MORIN 1999★
0.5 ha 2,000

This is a purely local grape variety that is too often forgotten, like the Melon de Bourgogne which they continue to use in Vézelay, or indeed the Sacy from Auxerre. Here, the Auxerre Gamay produces a wild, slightly foxy wine which will keep its *primeur* character for the next two or three years. A pleasant, crisp Burgundy Grand Ordinaire in the old style.

Olivier Morin, 2, chem. de Vaudu, 89530 Chitry-le-Fort, tel. 03.86.41.47.20, fax 03.86.41.47.20 by appt.

DOM. SYLVAIN PATAILLE 1999
0.4 ha 450 €3-5

This is the first crop of this Marsannay-la-Côte Gamay. There was a time when the light-hearted and generous Gamay grape made the fortune of local wine-makers, who used to sell it in Dijon to be drunk in bars. Pinot has taken over this role now, but the Gamay is still doing well. This cherry-red wine is rather gentle, with little in the way of aggressive tannins, but it needs a year or two to develop. The young wine-producer who made this delightful wine is a qualified oenologist.

Sylvain Pataille, 14, rue Neuve, 21160 Marsannay-la-Côte, tel. 03.80.52.49.49, fax 03.80.52.49.49 by appt.

DOM. ARMELLE ET BERNARD RION 1999
1 ha 7,000 €3-5

When a Vosne-Romanée estate adds Burgundy Grand Ordinaire to its list of wines, it is a little like the rabble entering Versailles in 1789. The price, however, makes this wine accessible to everyone. This is a youthful 99 with a fine colour and an upfront nose with jammy cherry aromas, followed by a palate that is classic for the appellation, though the fruit is a little astringent. It needs a year to mature.

Dom. Armelle et Bernard Rion, 8, rte Nationale, 21700 Vosne-Romanée, tel. 03.80.61.05.31, fax 03.80.61.24.60, e-mail rion@webiwine.com by appt.

Bourgogne Aligoté

This has been described as the 'Muscadet of Burgundy'. It is an excellent carafe wine to be drunk young, when it shows off the aromas of the variety at their best. Burgundians drink it for its freshness while they wait for the Chardonnay to mature. On the Côte Aligoté has been replaced by Chardonnay and has rather 'gone downhill', literally, in terms of the areas allotted to it; it was grown previously on the slopes. But the soils influence it just as much as any other variety and there are as many types of Aligoté as there are regions producing it. The Aligotés of Pernand were renowned for their suppleness and their fruity nose (before the vines were replaced with Chardonnay); the Aligotés of the Hautes-Côtes are sought after for their freshness and liveliness; those from Saint-Bris in the Yonne are light and pleasant to drink and seem to have borrowed traces of the elderflower scents found in Sauvignon.

BERTRAND AMBROISE 1999★

| n.c. | n.c. | 🍷 €5-8 |

This wine is an attractive gold colour, which, though lacking in intensity, is clear and bright. The nose is a more subtle affair offering, just a hint of minerals and ripe grapes. There is a certain fleshiness at first but then the palate opens out with a real liveliness. The overall harmony is guaranteed by its freshness.

♠ Maison Bertrand Ambroise, rue de l'Eglise, 21700 Premeaux-Prissey, tel. 03.80.62.30.19, fax 03.80.62.38.69, e-mail bertrand.ambroise@wanadoo.fr 🍷
Y by appt.

CH. BADER-MIMEUR 1998★

| 0.15 ha | 1,000 | 🍷 €5-8 |

One of our tasters – and let us remind you that this is a blind tasting, with only a number on the bottle, no name – writes in her notes: 'This wine has been produced in the manner of a Chardonnay'. Well done, sir! This Aligoté is from Chassagne-Montrachet, where it spent nine months in barrel and, consequently, has a strong character. One can hardly reproach it for that! A straw-gold colour and a remarkable nose with an interesting range of aromas: butter, menthol, almonds. It is rich rather than lively but has a little touch of acidity at the finish which adds freshness.

♠ Bader-Mimeur, 1, chem. du Château, 21190 Chassagne-Montrachet, tel. 03.80.21.30.22, fax 03.80.21.33.29 🍷
Y by appt.

CAVES DE BAILLY 2000★★

| 60 ha | 50,000 | 🍷 €5-8 |

Given that this wine was matured in the former quarries of Bailly at Saint-Bris-le-Vineux, it is hardly surprising that it has a mineral character to it. This 2000 vintage has all the essential qualities with its pretty glinting colour and hints of lime on the nose. It was in the running, after all, for a *coup de coeur*.

♠ SICA du Vignoble Auxerrois, Caves de Bailly, 89530 Saint-Bris-le-Vineux, tel. 03.86.53.77.77, fax 03.86.53.80.94 🍷
Y ev. day 8am–12 noon 2pm–6pm

DOM. BELIN-RAPET

Vieilles vignes 1998★

| 0.5 ha | 3,500 | 🍷 €5-8 |

This is a very pale wine with silvery glints. When swirled in the glass, it opens out with superb aromas of spring blossom and cut hay. Powerful and long with great concentration, it has floral and honeyed notes right through to the finish. This is a wine that can be drunk now.

♠ Dom. Belin-Rapet, imp. des Combottes, 21420 Pernand-Vergelesses, tel. 03.80.22.77.51, fax 03.80.22.76.59, e-mail domaine.belin.rapet@wanadoo.fr 🍷
Y ev. day 8am–8pm
♠ Ludovic Belin

461

JEAN-CLAUDE BOISSET 1999★

| n.c. | 40,000 | 🍷 €5-8 |

A wine as well-made as this would have no trouble coaxing a Burgundy snail from its shell. Attractive in colour, it offers light mineral aromas with hawthorn and honeysuckle followed by a charming attack that is immediately appealing. 'This is the kind of Aligoté I like,' notes one of our tasters. In the same group, the **Maison Morin Père et Fils 2000** also receives a star for its flowery elegance.

♠ Jean-Claude Boisset, 5, quai Dumorey, 21700 Nuits-Saint-Georges, tel. 03.80.62.62.61, fax 03.80.62.37.38

JEAN-CLAUDE BOUHEY ET FILS 1999★

| 12 ha | 16,000 | 🍷 €3-5 |

Villers-la-Faye is in the upper part of the Aligoté area in the Hautes-Côtes de Nuits. This wine is very characteristic of its type, with plenty of potential. The colour is pale, with green highlights; the bouquet is part floral, part mineral, and the palate is rather rich and full.

♠ GAEC Jean-Claude Bouhey et Fils, 7, rte de Magny, 21700 Villers-la-Faye, tel. 03.80.62.92.62, fax 03.80.62.74.07 🍷
Y by appt.

DOM. CAPUANO-FERRERI ET FILS 1999★

| n.c. | n.c. | 🍷 €5-8 |

This estate has already been singled out previously in the *Guide*. John has taken over from his father Gino and now produces his own *cuvées*, such as this one, which is really amazingly rich for an Aligoté. This lovely 99 is a deep golden yellow with a powerful nose (young oak, verbena, acacia) and a floral attack that is followed by the flavour of stewed fruit. It is full, warm, and lengthy and lacks only the stamp of the grape variety, although the wood influence is obvious.

♠ John Capuano, 14, rue Chauchien, 21590 Santenay, tel. 03.80.20.64.12, fax 03.80.20.65.75 🍷 Y by appt.

MADAME EDMOND CHALMEAU 1999★

| 3 ha | 18,000 | 🍷 €3-5 |

Madame Chalmeau, a wine-grower at Chitry-le-Fort, devotes 3 of her 8 ha (7.4 of the 19.8 acres) to Aligoté. This pale-coloured 99 lacks aroma but on the palate proves to be fairly winey, fruity and generous with a powerful opening that is supple and floral.

♠ Mme Edmond Chalmeau, 20, rue du Ruisseau, 89530 Chitry-le-Fort, tel. 03.86.41.42.09, fax 03.86.41.46.84 🍷
Y by appt.

Bourgogne Aligoté

DOM. CHARACHE-BERGERET
Vieilles vignes 1999★
☐ 4.3 ha 10,000 ■ €8-11

This wine-producer, who hails from Bouze (in the hills of Beaune), presents an interesting, elegant and likeable 99. Beneath a rather accentuated colour lies a pretty little Aligoté nose of cinnamon and acacia.

☞ Charache-Bergeret,
21200 Bouze-les-Beaune, tel. 03.80.26.00.86,
fax 03.80.26.00.86 ☒ Ⴤ by appt.

DOM. JEAN CHARTRON
Clos de la Combe 1999
☐ 0.5 ha 4,000 €5-8

Lime and green apple are obvious on the nose of this wine, though on closer inspection there is perhaps a hint of cooked pear and a hint of something floral. This agreeable 99 slips down nicely and will go well with an *andouillette*.

☞ Dom. Jean Chartron, 13, Grande-Rue,
21190 Puligny-Montrachet,
tel. 03.80.21.32.85, fax 03.80.21.36.35 ☒
Ⴤ ev. day 10h–12 noon 2pm–6pm; cl.
mid-Nov. until Mar.

PHILIPPE CHAVY 1998★
☐ 0.52 ha 2,000 €3-5

Combine maturation on lees in vat with a 98 vintage that has a tendency towards herbaceousness, and you get a wine that explodes on the palate. Ditto the aromas. There are a few floral and honeyed notes but this is Puligny, after all. One of the nicest wines in this tasting.

☞ Philippe Chavy, 22, Grande-Rue,
21190 Puligny-Montrachet,
tel. 03.80.21.92.41, fax 03.80.21.93.15,
e-mail chavyp@aol.com ☒ Ⴤ by appt.
☞ Pierre Thomas

LA CAVE DU CONNAISSEUR 1999★★
☐ 1 ha 6,000 €5-8

Competing in the final for the *coup de coeur* is not something every wine can achieve, but this one succeeded and it has gained its place on the podium with its attractive green-gold colour and superb lemony mineral note. It has a beautiful balance of richness and acidity.

☞ La Cave du Connaisseur,
rue des Moulins, BP 78, 89800 Chablis,
tel. 03.86.42.87.15, fax 03.86.42.49.84,
e-mail connaisseur@chablis.net ☒
Ⴤ ev. day 10am–6pm

DOM. DARNAT 1999★
☐ 0.18 ha 1,500 €5-8

This well-balanced 99 is fresh and fruity with just a hint of hazelnuts. The oak is present, of course: one has to understand that in Meursault they make wine – even Aligoté – in Meursault style.

☞ Dom. Darnat, 20, rue des Forges,
21190 Meursault, tel. 03.80.21.23.30,
fax 03.80.21.64.62, e-mail domaine.darnat@
libertysurcl.fr ☒ Ⴤ by appt.

JOCELYNE ET PHILIPPE DEFRANCE 1999★
☐ 5.39 ha 12,000 ■ ♦ €5-8

It is better to be an object of envy rather than pity, isn't it? This is a supple and fruity wine, white-gold in colour with a very intense nose. The hint of richness is welcomed. And its length? Very satisfactory. Best served as an aperitif with golden savoury cheese pastries.

☞ Philippe Defrance, 5, rue du Four,
89530 Saint-Bris-le-Vineux,
tel. 03.86.53.39.04, fax 03.86.53.66.46 ☒
Ⴤ by appt.

DOM. DENIS PERE ET FILS 1999★
☐ 0.8 ha 3,000 €5-8

A *jambon persillé* would go well with this wine that has well-balanced fruitiness and freshness which adds some interest to this characteristic Aligoté that is lacking in vigour. It has a golden colour, though not overly so; the nose is relatively closed but there are some floral aromas that could eventually open out.

☞ Dom. Denis Père et Fils,
chem. des Vignes-Blanches,
21420 Pernand-Vergelesses,
tel. 03.80.21.50.91, fax 03.80.26.10.32 ☒
Ⴤ by appt.

DOM. DENIZOT 1999★
☐ 5.3 ha 4,130 €5-8

At Bissey-sous-Cruchaud, a pleasant village north of Saône-et-Loire, they think of Aligoté as one of their children. It is that of Bouzeron but almost! This is a fresh wine, gentle and light with well-handled acidity.

☞ Dom. Christian et Bruno Denizot,
71390 Bissey-sous-Cruchaud,
tel. 03.85.92.13.34, fax 03.85.92.12.87,
e-mail denizot@caves-particulières.com ☒
Ⴤ ev. day except Sun. 8am–7pm

DOM. DESSUS BON BOIRE 1999
☐ 0.5 ha 4,500 €3-5

Not long ago Antoine Donat was responsible for reviving Pinot Noir and Chardonnay in the Auxerre vineyards. Here, André has replanted half a hectare (just over an acre) with Aligoté, and this wine justifies his action. Light in colour, though this grape variety is usually subtle in this respect, it has a pleasant nose based around citrus fruits and dried fruit aromas. Overall, a fresh and lively wine.

☞ André Donat, 41, rue de Vallan,
89290 Vaux, tel. 03.86.53.89.99,
fax 03.86.53.68.36 Ⴤ ev. day 9am–12 noon
2pm–7pm; Sun. by appt.

JEAN-FRANCOIS DICONNE 1999
☐ 2.3 ha 2,700 ■ ♦ €5-8

'If our ancestors are mentioned in the parish registers of 1626, then they must be there as hired hands, because the title 'owner' only came with the Revolution,' says Jean-François Diconne modestly. That's still more than two centuries ago! This wine is a deep lemon-yellow with a delicious nose

(fresh and full of fruity aromas such as apples and clementines), and slightly sparkling. It would go well with a starter – stuffed mussels, for example. A ripe wine with good length.
♦ Jean-François Dicomne, rue du Bourg, 71150 Remigny, tel. 03.85.87.20.01, fax 03.85.87.23.98 ☒ by appt.

GERARD DOREAU 1998
□ 0.39 ha · 3,000 · €5-8

This straw-coloured wine with green highlights has a nose that reveals oak influences. The aromas are heady: honey, toast and lightly spicy. This is one of those Aligotés produced in Chardonnay country which gives it a certain style of its own.
♦ Gérard Doreau, rue du Dessous, 21190 Monthélie, tel. 03.80.21.27.89, fax 03.80.21.62.19 ☒ by appt.

DOM. YVAN DUFOULEUR 1999★
□ 1 ha · 7,000 · €5-8

This attractive, pale-gold Aligoté comes from Nuits, which is red wine country. The nose is developed with citrus notes and a hint of honeysuckle. It is an excellent wine, not very characteristic of its type, but with good body and length.
♦ Dom. Yvan Dufouleur, 18, rue Thurot, 21700 Nuits-Saint-Georges, tel. 03.80.62.31.00, fax 03.80.62.31.00 ☒ by appt.

DOM. FONTAINE DE LA VIERGE 1999★
□ 7 ha · 30,000 · €3-5

There is no hiding the origins of this wine. It is clear and bright with good aromas of flint and wild flowers. Undeniably clean and straightforward.
♦ Jean-Claude Biot, 5, chem. des Fossés, 89530 Chitry-le-Fort, tel. 03.86.41.42.79, fax 03.86.41.46.72 ☒ by appt.

DIDIER FORNEROL 1999
□ 0.2 ha · 1,800 · €3-5

The colour of this wine with its pleasant highlights is what one would expect. The nose is explosive: all charcoal and flint. It is very rich on the palate with very mellow tannins, but makes up for it by finishing on a fresh, lively note. Good with snails.
♦ Didier Fornerol, 15, pl. de la Mairie, 21700 Corgoloin, tel. 03.80.62.93.09, fax 03.80.62.93.09 ☒ by appt.

GACHOT-MONOT 1999★
□ 0.52 ha · 4,700 · €3-5

There was a curate from Corgoloin who spent 15 years of his life as a missionary with the Eskimos. This Aligoté would have livened him up as he sat in his igloo in the freezing cold. It is a pleasant young wine with a pale straw-gold colour. The nose has a hint of citrus fruit but then it opens out showing the more typical aromas of its appellation, and the palate has a really refreshing attack.
♦ Dom. Gachot-Monot, 13, rue Humbert-de-Gillens, 21700 Gerland, tel. 03.80.62.50.95, fax 03.80.62.53.85 ☒ ev. day except Sat./Sun. 8am-12 noon 2pm-6pm

JEAN-HUGUES ET GHISLAINE GOISOT 1999★★
□ 7.68 ha · 56,000 · €5-8

This is the best Aligoté in the Yonne. From the very first glance, the first whiff, you can tell that this is a wine that is really true to type. Fruit followed by a little floral note on the nose, then a fresh and fruity palate that stays consistent right through to the classic mineral finish, and, as we've said, completely in the spirit of the grape variety and the Icaunais vineyard.
♦ Ghislaine et Jean-Hugues Goisot, 30, rue Bienvenu-Martin, 89530 Saint-Bris-le-Vineux, tel. 03.86.53.35.15, fax 03.86.53.62.03 ☒ by appt.

DOM. GOUFFIER Clos de Butte Soleil 1999★
□ 2.5 ha · 9,000 · €5-8

Fontaines is situated on the Côte Chalonnaise. It would be nice if the wine-producer could tell us more about this Clos de Butte Soleil. This clear straw 99 is a little closed, well-balanced and somewhat austere in character. It will undoubtedly be more eloquent in a couple of years' time. Meanwhile, it manages to be true to type in a way that has become very rare.
♦ Dom. Gouffier, 11, Grande-Rue, 71150 Fontaines, tel. 03.85.91.46.66, fax 03.85.91.46.98, e-mail jerome.gouffier@wanadoo.fr ☒ by appt.

DOM. GRAND ROCHE 2000★
□ 3 ha · 18,000 · €5-8

Erick Lavallée used to be an accountant until, in 1987, he decided to give it up and pursue a new way of life, and this wine certainly does him credit. It is pale with intense vegetal aromas, reminiscent of the Sauvignon grape. A pleasant wine with roundness, suppleness and well-balanced acidity that brings a lovely touch of citrus fruit to it.
♦ Dom. Grand Roche, rte de Chitry, 89530 Saint-Bris-le-Vineux, tel. 03.86.53.84.07, fax 03.86.53.88.36 ☒ by appt.
♦ Erick Lavallée

BLANCHE ET HENRI GROS 1999★
□ n.c. · 3,000 · €5-8

Drink this fine Aligoté with a little snack and it will perk you up. It is very pale and clear with a little hint of something exotic (mandarin), and flows on the palate like a mountain waterfall, beautifully fresh and full of life. It can be drunk now. Chamboeuf is the village in the Hautes-Côtes that can be reached by climbing the Lavaux valley from Gevrey.

Bourgogne Aligoté

DOM. JEAN GUITON 1999★
□   0.44 ha   3,000   ■ ◆   €5-8

Good attack, good acidity, good intensity. There may be more lively Aligotés around but this one holds its head up very well. It starts out with a vegetal character then opens out to become floral. A wine to keep for a year or two at least. Serve it with oysters.

➤ Dom. Jean Guiton,
4, rte de Pommard, 21200 Bligny-lès-Beaune,
tel. 03.80.26.82.88, fax 03.80.26.85.05,
e-mail guillaume-guiton@wanadoo.fr ☑
Ⴤ by appt.

JEAN-LUC HOUBLIN 1998★
□   0.59 ha   3,500   ■   €5-8

If you are passing Migé, it is well worth stopping off to visit their recently-restored windmill, and of course there is also this wine-cellar, which offers us a mineral-scented Aligoté with green highlights. This is a nicely concentrated, rich and fleshy wine with young fruit flavours.

➤ Dom. Jean-Luc Houblin, 1, passage des Vignes, 89580 Migé, tel. 03.86.41.69.87,
fax 03.86.41.71.95 ☑ Ⴤ ev. day 8am–8pm;
Sun. 8am–12.30pm; groups by appt.

FREDERIC JACOB 1999★
□   3 ha   6,000   €3-5

Frédéric Jacob took over the Jacob-Frerebeau estate in 1996. His Aligoté positively rampages down from the Hautes-Côtes with wild, warm, powerful notes. It is full and rich on the nose that opens with some ripe apricot aromas. A distinctive, pale straw-yellow wine with originality and just the right amount of vigour.

➤ Frédéric Jacob, 50, Grande-Rue,
21420 Changey-Echevronne,
tel. 03.80.21.55.58 ☑ Ⴤ by appt.

HUBERT JACOB-MAUCLAIR 1999
□   1.3 ha   4,000   ■   €5-8

This intense, brightly-coloured 99 hails from the Hautes-Côtes de Beaune. It has a slight sparkle to it that adds vigour. Its nose is elegant, floral and subtle with a pleasant hint of ferns. The attack is well-conducted, the balance assured.

➤ Hubert Jacob-Mauclair, 56, Grande-Rue, Changey, 21420 Echevronne,
tel. 03.80.21.57.07, fax 03.80.21.57.07 ☑
Ⴤ by appt.

DOM. REMI JOBARD 1999★★
□   1.5 ha   3,000   €5-8

This transparent, pale yellow Aligoté is well-structured and well-made with a promisingly fruity nose and a supple, gentle, well-rounded palate. Its attractive, delicately formed structure is the work of someone who really knows what he is doing. Its lemony character makes it a perfect accompaniment to seafood...

➤ Dom. Rémi Jobard, 12, rue Sudot,
21190 Meursault, tel. 03.80.21.20.23,
fax 03.80.21.67.69, e-mail rémi-jobard@
libertysurel.fr ☑ Ⴤ by appt.

JEAN-LUC JOILLOT 1999★
□   0.6 ha   6,000   €5-8

This wine has lime, lots of minerals, and a freshness and superb liveliness, with a firm, spicy structure flavoured with ripe fruit which gives it length and power.

➤ Jean-Luc Joillot, rue Marey-Monge,
21630 Pommard, tel. 03.80.24.20.26,
fax 03.80.24.67.54 ☑ Ⴤ by appt.

GILLES JOURDAN 1999★
□   0.3 ha   2,400   ■ ◆   €5-8

This Aligoté is very typical of the vintage and has a wonderful vigour about it. Its straightforward, typical mineral character is absolutely as it should be. It would go well with a plate of mussels.

➤ Gilles Jourdan, Grande-Rue,
21700 Corgoloin, tel. 03.80.62.76.31,
fax 03.80.62.98.55 ☑ Ⴤ by appt.

DOM. LAMY-PILLOT 1999★★
□   1.64 ha   9,400   ■ ◆   €5-8

This deep green-gold wine makes an impact from the start. The fresh almond nose doesn't give much away but hints at more to come. Its character is smooth and impulsive, with a powerful presence. A really superb wine and one which has no need of *crème de cassis* to make a perfect aperitif.

➤ Dom. Lamy-Pillot, 31, rte de Santenay,
21190 Chassagne-Montrachet,
tel. 03.80.21.30.52, fax 03.80.21.30.02,
e-mail lamy.pillot@wanadoo.fr ☑
Ⴤ by appt.

DANIEL LARGEOT 2000★
□   0.4 ha   3,600   €3-5

This wine has a crystalline appearance with a few glints. The nose is powerful with apples, spring blossom, and even butter. The acidity is well-incorporated, the attack nice and juicy, and there is a lovely aroma of gingerbread that appears later. It makes one want to visit Dijon.

➤ Daniel Largeot, 5, rue des Brenôts,
21200 Chorey-lès-Beaune,
tel. 03.80.22.15.10, fax 03.80.22.60.62 ☑
Ⴤ by appt.

DOM. LARUE 1999★
□   1.56 ha   5,200   ■ ◆   €5-8

This is a simple, straightforward wine, very true to type, pale gold in colour with green highlights. On the nose there are aromas of both unripe fruit and citrus fruits with a hint of almond. The palate is firm but fresh and long. It would go well with seafood.

➤ Dom. Larue, Gamay, 21190 Saint-Aubin,
tel. 03.80.21.30.74, fax 03.80.21.91.36 ☑
Ⴤ by appt.

DOM. MAILLARD PERE ET FILS
1999★
0.4 ha n.c. €5-8

Here is a mischievous little wine: young, enthusiastic, full of energy, not pompous, satisfying to both mind and body. It has a golden colour, and aromas of freshly-picked hawthorn, while on the palate there is gunflint and that little touch of elegance which only truly high-class wines possess. This wine needs a dish that is worthy of it.
➤ Dom. Maillard, 2, rue Joseph-Bard, 21200 Chorey-les-Beaune, tel. 03.80.22.10.67, fax 03.80.24.00.42 ☗

DOM. MAREY 1998
1 ha 5,000 €5-8

This estate has no connection with the Marey-Monge family who used to be so prominent in the Côte and the Hautes-Côtes. This Aligoté is so pale it looks almost white. Aromas of fern and mint nudge the nose in the right direction while the palate has good staying power. It is well-flavoured, attractive and full. Meuille, near Vergy, illustrates the success of the Hautes-Côtes since they were reclaimed for vineyards in the 1960s and 1970s.
➤ Dom. Marey, rue Bachot, 21700 Meuilley, tel. 03.80.61.12.44, fax 03.80.61.11.31, e-mail dommarey@aol.com ☑ ☗ by appt.

PASCAL MELLENOTTE 1999
1 ha 2,000 €3-5

Pale lemon-yellow, green apple on white bread, delicate lees, this refreshing wine is exceptionally agreeable. It may not have a long life expectancy but there is plenty of enjoyment to be had in the meantime, especially if served with seafood.
➤ Pascal Mellenotte, Le Martray, 71640 Mellecey, tel. 03.85.45.15.64, fax 03.85.45.15.64 ☗
☗ ev. day except Sun. 10am–7pm

ARMELLE ET JEAN-MICHEL MOLIN 1999★
0.3 ha 2,800 €3-5

This highly superior 99 will be ready to drink in 2002. Its colour has been carefully developed, the aromas are fine and it has a distinctly flinty flavour. The attack is both gentle and direct while on the palate it develops along the same mineral lines and is well-balanced at the finish. Don't use this wine for kir: it deserves something better, like a pike!
➤ EARL Armelle et Jean-Michel Molin, 54, rte des Grands-Crus, 21220 Fixin, tel. 03.80.52.21.28, fax 03.80.59.96.99 ☑

DOM. PAVELOT 1999★
0.9 ha 2,500 €5-8

The name of the Pavelot family is synonymous with the village of Pernand and has been so for centuries. This Aligoté is a good example for anyone who wants to get to know this appellation. Pale gold in colour with a delicate, floral character without a trace of aggression, but full of liveliness and vitality, it is well-structured and very characteristic.
➤ EARL Dom. Régis et Luc Pavelot, rue du Paulant, 21420 Pernand-Vergelesses, tel. 03.80.26.13.65, fax 03.80.26.13.65 ☗ by appt.

GEORGES ET THIERRY PINTE 1998
0.73 ha 2,600 €5-8

This pale yellow 98 has had time to develop intense spring blossom and mint aromas. There is a tiny hint of bitterness at the finish. A clean, direct wine, according to our tasters.
➤ GAEC Georges et Thierry Pinte, 11, rue du Jarron, 21420 Savigny-les-Beaune, tel. 03.80.21.51.59, fax 03.80.21.51.59 ☑

ERIC PANSIOT 1999★
3 ha 10,000 €5-8

This pale gold wine offers interesting aromas ranging from blackcurrant leaf to honeysuckle. Its fruity (lemony) acidity is just what people expect in this type of wine and it has a fullness that persists right through to the finish. Perhaps *jambon persillé* would go well with it?
➤ Eric Pansiot, Ch. de la Chaume, 21700 Corgoloin, tel. 03.80.62.94.32, fax 03.80.62.73.14 ☑ ☗ by appt.

NICOLAS PERE ET FILS 1999★
0.9 ha 5,000 €3-5

This wine has a pale gold colour with green highlights, gentle and lively at the same time, offering mineral aromas and a minty palate with a long fresh finish. The Jury liked its appearance and recommended that it would go well with a spicy or a sweet and sour dish.
➤ EARL du dom. Nicolas Père et Fils, 38, rte de Cirey, 21340 Nolay, tel. 03.80.21.82.92, fax 03.80.21.85.47 ☗ ev. day 9am–12 noon 1.30pm–7pm

DOM. HENRI NAUDIN-FERRAND 1999
1.81 ha 16,526 €3-5

The Hautes-Côtes de Nuits is the region where this grape variety seems to flourish best. It is like the 'promised land'. This wine is not very colourful but has a nose packed with aromas of spring flowers and remains interesting on the palate from the start through to the finish. Best drunk now.
➤ Dom. Henri Naudin-Ferrand, rue du Meix-Grenot, 21700 Magny-les-Villers, tel. 03.80.62.91.50, fax 03.80.62.91.77, e-mail dnaudin@ipac.fr ☑ ☗ by appt.

DOM. JACKY RENARD 1999 ■ ♦ €5-8

4.86 ha n.c.

This wine is a typical Yonne Aligoté with its bright, lively colour. The lovely nose is fresh and floral and the palate has a nice youthful spontaneity though not great length. Best drunk sooner rather than later.

↦ Jacky Renard, La Côte-de-Chaussan, 89530 Saint-Bris-le-Vineux,
tel. 03.86.53.38.58, fax 03.86.53.33.50 ▼
Ⴤ by appt.

CH. DE ROUGEON 1999★ ■ €5-8

8 ha n.c.

Bouchard Père et Fils is housed in cellars in the bastions of the 15th-century Beaune fortress. This is a good but not very characteristic Aligoté. It is attractive enough: greyish-gold in colour with an appealing scent of lime blossom followed by the aroma of fern, all of which is perfect. The palate, however, is round and lacks the liveliness normally attributed to this grape variety.

↦ Bouchard Père et Fils, Ch. de Beaune, 21200 Beaune, tel. 03.80.24.80.24,
fax 03.80.22.55.88, e-mail france@bouchard-pereetfils.com Ⴤ by appt.

PASCAL SORIN 1999★ ■ €3-5

2.2 ha 4,500

From the start things look good: the colour is lovely and bright; the partly vegetal, partly floral nose has a pretty hint of hazelnut, which does not come from the oak since it was matured in vat. A full wine, very round at first then suddenly bursting with flavour (grapefruit, notably) and with little acidity.

↦ Sorin-Coquard, 25, rue de Grisy, 89530 Saint-Bris-le-Vineux,
tel. 03.86.53.37.76, fax 03.86.53.37.76 ▼
Ⴤ ev. day 8am–8.30pm; Sun. 8am–12.30pm
↣ Pascal Sorin

PIERRE TAUPENOT 1998 ■ ⦆ €5-8

0.3 ha 2,780

There is nothing untoward in the colour of this wine. It moves nicely in the glass. The nose is average: citronella and hawthorn with a hint of herbaceousness. More rich than acidic but it manages to retain a certain freshness. Definitely a fine wine in true Côte de Beaune spirit.

↦ Pierre Taupenot, rue du Chevrotin, 21190 Saint-Romain, tel. 03.80.21.24.37,
fax 03.80.21.68.42 ▼ Ⴤ by appt.

VENOT 1999★ ■ €5-8

3 ha 3,000

This Côte Chalonnaise 99 brings to mind the old saying: 'young wine, rich Burgundy'. There is nothing Chardonnay-like about this wine. It has a lively character and a pleasant sharpness, and is complex and full, its lemon notes mingling with gentle spring flowers. It should reach perfection around the end of 2002 or the beginning of 2003.

↦ GAEC Venot, 'La Corvée', 71390 Moroges, tel. 03.85.47.90.20,
fax 03.85.47.90.20 ▼ Ⴤ by appt.

DOM. VERRET 2000★★ ■ ♦ €5-8

12.74 ha 110,000

This estate is a pioneer of direct sales in the Chablis region, and out of the 300,000 bottles which they have marketed this year, this one will not disappoint you. It has a clean look, a strong floral nose, and a pleasant spring-like palate with a little exotic touch that adds to its considerable charm. Best to take advantage of this without delay.

↦ Dom. Verret, 7, rte de Champs, BP 4, 89530 Saint-Bris-le-Vineux,
tel. 03.86.53.31.81, fax 03.86.53.89.61,
e-mail bruno.verret@wanadoo.fr ▼
Ⴤ by appt.

VEUVE HENRI MORONI 1999★ ■ €5-8

2 ha 6,500

Pale yellow with aromas of lemon, grapefruit, and touches of delicate flowers: this very fresh, fine wine is an Aligoté through and through and has all the qualities that one would expect. It may not be the liveliest but it certainly isn't dozy either.

↦ Veuve Henri Moroni, 1, rue de l'Abreuvoir, 21190 Puligny-Montrachet, tel. 03.80.21.30.48, fax 03.80.21.33.08,
e-mail veuve.moroni@wanadoo.fr ▼
Ⴤ by appt.

Bourgogne Passetoutgrain

This appellation applies exclusively to red and rosé wines produced in the inner part of the Bourgogne Grand Ordinaire area, and it requires the wines to be made from a blend of Pinot Noir and Gamay Noir grapes. The blend must contain a minimum of one-third of Pinot Noir. Current thinking holds that the best wines are made of roughly equal quantities of grapes from the two varieties, with a slight preponderance of Pinot Noir.

The rosé wines are obtained by the *saignée* method, a technical process distinct from the *vins gris*, which are obtained by the direct pressing of black grapes and vinifying them like white wines. In the *saignée* process the grapes are left to macerate, and the juice is extracted (or 'bled') only when the wine-maker has obtained the desired colour – which can very well occur in the middle of the night! Very little Passetoutgrain Rosé is made, and in general this appellation is regarded as a red wine. It is produced mainly in the Saône-et-Loire (about two-thirds), the remainder being made in the Côte d'Or or the Yonne valley. In 2000 production amounted to 61,090 hl (1,612,776 gal), while 71,708 hl (1,893,091 gal) were produced in 1999. The wines are light, deliciously flavoured and should be drunk young.

DOM. BOUZERAND-DUJARDIN
1999 ★★

| | 0.43 ha | 2,700 | |

On your marks ... get set ... Go! Hurry and don't stop until you reach this wonderful Passetoutgrain, which missed out on a *coup de coeur* by a hair's breadth. This is a delightful wine, sure to please. It has a deep garnet colour and aromas of blackcurrant and cherry with a hint of kirsch and is superbly refined on the palate; it is lively, fresh, a little on the warm side but firm. It certainly sets off on the right foot.

Dom. Bouzerand-Dujardin, pl. de l'Eglise, 21190 Monthélie, tel. 03.80.21.20.08, fax 03.80.21.28.16 V

JEAN BROCARD-GRIVOT 1999★

| | 0.26 ha | 1,370 | |

They have a good sense of balance in Reulle-Vergy: this wine is half Pinot, half Gamay. An honest, authentic 99, the colour of redcurrants and with a deep, well-structured nose (blackcurrant, white bread and spices). It is supple and would go well with barbecued kebabs.

Jean Brocard-Grivot, rue Basse, 21220 Reulle-Vergy, tel. 03.80.61.42.14 V

PIERRE CHANAU 1999

| n.c. | 156,977 | €3-5 |

This is a big company which commissions its wines from different *négociants*; in this case the wine comes from Philippe d'Argenval, as indicated on the label, which belongs to Antonin Rodet. A good, easy-drinking wine with a ruby red colour and distinctive flavour of undergrowth. The tannins are a little strong but the body has a lightness that is absolutely right for this wine. Drink it this winter with a pork hotpot.

Pierre Chanau, 71640 Mercurey, tel. 03.85.98.12.12, fax 03.85.45.25.49

GUY FONTAINE ET JACKY VION
1999★

| | 0.6 ha | 5,200 | €5-8 |

Situated halfway between Beaune and Chalon-sur-Saône, this family estate has been run since 1982 by two brothers-in-law who are regularly praised by our Juries. This blood-red Passetoutgrain 99 is a powerful wine with strong tannins and good length, best drunk now with a dish of roast pork and *pommes boulangères*.

GAEC des Vignerons, rue du Bourg, 7150 Remigny, tel. 03.85.87.03.35, fax 03.85.87.03.35 V by appt.

DOM. PIERRE GELIN 1999

| | 1.78 ha | 10,000 | €3-5 |

This Passetoutgrain is a deep, intense fiery red with a clean, straightforward nose. It is a blend of 70% Gamay, very characteristic with a well-structured, peppery palate. The tannins, on the other hand, would benefit from settling down a little.

Dom. Pierre Gelin, 2, rue du Chapitre, 21220 Fixin, tel. 03.80.52.45.24, fax 03.80.51.47.80 V Y ev. day except Sun. 9am–12 noon 2pm–5pm; Sat. by appt.
Stéphen Gelin

GILBERT ET PHILIPPE GERMAIN 1999

| | 1.5 ha | 5,000 | €3-5 |

If you ever find yourself wondering what would make the ideal accompaniment to a couple of eggs *en meurette* (eggs in a red wine sauce), then try this Hautes-Côtes de Beaune Passetoutgrain. It is made up of 70% Gamay to 30% Pinot, a combination which works well, creating a supple, gentle wine without great length but which hits the spot nicely.

Philippe Germain, 21190 Nantoux, tel. 03.80.26.05.63, fax 03.80.26.05.12 V Y by appt.

ROBERT GROFFIER ET FILS 1999

| n.c. | 5,000 | €5-8 |

This wine is easy to like. It is unbelievably deep red in colour and with wonderful exotic aromas of pomegranate and bitter orange. Lightly oaked, this is a youthful wine with character.

SARL Robert Groffier Père et Fils, 3–5, rue des Grands-Crus, 21220 Morey-Saint-Denis, tel. 03.80.34.31.53, fax 03.80.34.31.53 V

DOM. REMI JOBARD 1999★

| | 1 ha | 2,500 | €3-5 |

This is a red wine from a *village* of whites, and one which wears its deep, purplish-red colour with pride. The nose has a discreet aroma of fresh fruit, the attack is lively but soon develops a certain roundness; it is straightforward, clean and pleasant, with a slight touch of spicy warmth at the finish.

Bourgogne Passetoutgrain

•— Dom. Rémi Jobard, 12, rue Sudot,
21190 Meursault, tel. 03.80.21.67.69, e-mail rémi.jobard@
libertysurol.fr ☑ **Y** by appt.

DOM. DE LA CHAPELLE 1999
■ 3.5 ha 5,000 **€3-5**

This well-established 25-ha (61.7-acre)
estate has made this wine like a Beaujolais,
placing entire bunches of grapes into the vat.
This has created a nicely-coloured wine –
ruby-red with clear highlights – which opens
with soft red fruit. It is made up of 65%
Gamay which has a certain impact on the
flavour.

•— Bouthenet Père et Fils, Dom. de la
Chapelle, Eguilly, 71490 Couches,
tel. 03.85.45.54.76, fax 03.85.45.56.51 ☑
Y by appt.

DOM. DE LA FEUILLARDE 2000
■ 0.3 ha 2,600 **€5-8**

This Passetoutgrain 2000 comes from
southern Burgundy and it is an attractive
wine. Although very young, the Gamay, at
50%, is already performing, showing its gentle
and fresh side. Light in colour with an harmonious nose and palate, it is best drunk with
good friends now.

•— Lucien Thomas, Dom. de La Feuillarde,
71960 Prissé, tel. 03.85.34.31.50, e-mail contact@
domaine-feuillarde.com ☑
Y ev. day 8am–12 noon 1pm–7pm

LES CHAMPS DE L'ABBAYE 1999★
■ 1 ha 5,500 **€5-8**

This estate, which was only founded in
1996, has just converted to biodynamic
methods. This wine is 45% Pinot to 55%
Gamay. It has the characteristic fruity aromas
and a tasty, chewy palate that is well-
structured with reasonable depth and real
potential.

•— Alain Hasard, Les Champs de l'Abbaye,
3, pl. de l'Abbaye,
71510 Saint-Sernin-du-Plain,
tel. 03.85.45.59.32, fax 03.85.45.59.32 ☑
Y by appt.

GHISLAINE ET BERNARD
MARECHAL-CAILLOT 1999★
■ 3.13 ha 8,000 **€5-8**

This pleasant wine is a combination of 75%
Gamay and 25% Pinot Noir. The purple colour is
soft and easy to drink. The purple colour is a
little overdone but it is an excellent wine in its
category, with a supple fruitiness structured
with well-integrated tannins that makes it a
good bet for drinking from now. It would
make an excellent accompaniment to a joint
of veal with cream sauce and glazed carrots.

•— Bernard Maréchal-Caillot, 10, rte de
Chalon, 21200 Bligny-lès-Beaune,
tel. 03.80.21.44.55, fax 03.80.26.88.21 ☑
Y by appt.

DOM. DU MERLE 1999★
■ 1 ha 2,500 **€5-8**

This wine is made up of 65% Gamay, as is
normal for a Passetoutgrain. It is a brilliant,
clear cherry-red colour with jammy aromas,
very rich on the palate, and sturdy in character with surprisingly fine tannins. It is full-
bodied and already maturing. Best to open
and drink now.

•— Michel Morin, Sens,
71240 Sennecey-le-Grand,
tel. 03.85.44.75.38, fax 03.85.44.73.63,
e-mail domainemerle@yahoo.com ☑
Y ev. day 9.30am–7.30pm

PASCAL 1999★
■ 2 ha 15,000 **€5-8**

The presses of the Dukes of Burgundy,
which date from the 13th century, belong to
this estate in Chenôve which was founded in
1852. This Gevrey négociant has done a good
job with this wine. He has created a top-
quality Passetoutgrain which, with 60%
Gamay and 40% Pinot, deserves all our
respect. The colour is the deepest ruby red.
The nose is wild and blackcurrant. Structure,
body and harmony are all exactly as they
should be.

•— Pascal, Clos des Noirets,
21220 Gevrey-Chambertin,
tel. 03.80.34.37.82, fax 03.80.51.88.05 ☑
Y by appt.
•— Cheron

ROBERT SIRUGUE 1998★
■ 2.5 ha 15,000 ■Ⅱ❖ **€3-5**

Robert Sirugue and his children Marie-
France and Jean-Louis run this 11 ha
(27 acre) estate together. There are a thousand ways of making Passetoutgrain but
these people have got it right. There are also
several ways to blend it, in this case 30%
Gamay and 70% Pinot, but there is only one
way of really enjoying it: with a pot-au-feu.
This prettily-coloured 98 has just a hint of
blackcurrant on an otherwise fairly mature
leathery, smoky nose. The tannins remain
consistently strong in the background: this
wine is ready to drink now.

•— Robert Sirugue, 3, av. du Monument,
21700 Vosne-Romanée, tel. 03.80.61.00.64,
fax 03.80.61.27.57 **Y** by appt.

DOM. TAUPENOT-MERME 1998
■ n.c. 10,000 ■Ⅱ❖ **€5-8**

Jean Taupenot married Denise Merme, and
some 20 years later their children Virginie and
Romain are working on the estate. With a
blend of 30% Pinot and 70% Gamay, the
balance of this wine is obviously weighted
towards Gamay, but we're not complaining.
The colour is as expected. The nose with
aromas of blackberries, wild strawberries and
cooked prunes is simple and straightforward.
The palate is fresh on the attack, rustic as it
should be, with a certain vigour and a tannic
quality that add structure to its character.

468

the communes above the *appellations communales* and the crus of the Côte de Nuit. In 2000 these vineyards produced 29,717 hl (784,529 gal), of which 5,291 hl (139,682 gal) were white. The amount produced has increased significantly since 1970 when the vineyards used to produce more regional wines, essentially Bourgogne Aligoté. Extensive replanting has taken place since that time, and plants infected with phylloxera have been replanted.

In some years, the best exposed slopes produce wines that can rival some of the vineyards on the Côte; the best of them tend to be white, and it is a pity that more of the vineyards have not been planted with Chardonnay, which would undoubtedly give more reliable results more often. Along with the commitment to recreating the vineyard an equal effort has been put into encouraging tourism. In particular, a Maison des Hautes-Côtes gives visitors the chance to learn about the area and to taste the wines along with good local cuisine.

DOM. BARBIER ET FILS
Corvée de Villy 1998★

2.5 ha 12,000 €11-15

The Barbier et Fils estate was bought by fellow inhabitants of Nuits-Saint-Georges, Dufouleur Père et Fils, in 1995. The ruby colour of this wine is very typical of Burgundy, while a hint of cocoa and spice reveals a well-handled maturation in barrel. The palate, balanced by solid tannins, would benefit from one to two years in the cellar.

• Dom. Barbier et Fils, 15, rue Thurot, BP 27, 21700 Nuits-Saint-Georges, tel. 03.80.61.21.21, fax 03.80.61.10.65 ✓
Y by appt.
• Guy et Xavier Dufouleur

JEAN BOUCHARD 1999★

n.c. 34,500 €11-15

This is a very good wine. The colour is verging towards garnet, with a hint of pink at the edges. Blueberry, mulberry and dark fruit head up the list of aromas. The tannins do not overpower the full-bodied flavour of fruit.

• Jean Bouchard, BP 47, 21202 Beaune Cedex, tel. 03.80.24.37.27, fax 03.80.24.37.38

Bourgogne
Hautes-Côtes de
Nuit

The appellation Bourgogne Hautes-Côtes de Nuits is most often used for red, rosé and white wines produced in the 16 communes that lie in the hinterland of the Côte, together with parts of

DOM. VOARICK 1999★

8.25 ha 70,000 €5-8

This cherry-red wine with mauve glints would go well with a *forestière* pie. Its nose evokes all the melancholy of a Françoise Sagan character while its raspberry palate, with its backdrop of subtle tannins, is a more optimistic affair, opening and finishing on a supple note.

• Émile Voarick, 71640 Saint-Martin-sous-Montaigu, tel. 03.85.45.23.23, fax 03.85.45.16.37 ✓

DOM. VERRET 2000★★

2.5 ha 12,000 €5-8

This wine comes from a huge, 52 ha (128.4 acre) estate. It is two-thirds Gamay to one third Pinot, a successful blend. The colour is reddish-violet, the nose encouragingly blackcurranty. It is smooth and fruity, more lively than tannic, and makes one want to reach for the cured sausage and camembert.

• Dom. Verret, 7, rte de Champs, BP 4, 89530 Saint-Bris-le-Vineux, tel. 03.86.53.31.81, fax 03.86.53.89.61, e-mail bruno.verret@wanadoo.fr ✓
Y by appt.

JEAN-PIERRE TRUCHETET 1999★

0.63 ha 5,600 €3-5

This wine has a really deep, almost purple colour. The bouquet goes straight to the point: the fruit is well-placed with a little additional touch of spice and brambles (a rare but noticeable aroma). A full-bodied wine without being rustic; just as it should be.

• Jean-Pierre Truchetet, rue des Masers, 21700 Premeaux-Prissey, tel. 03.80.61.07.22, fax 03.80.61.34.35 ✓
Y ev. day except Sat. Sun. 9am–12 noon 2pm–7pm; cl. 15–31 Aug.

• Jean Taupenot-Merme, 33, rte des Grands-Crus, 21220 Morey-Saint-Denis, tel. 03.80.34.35.24, fax 03.80.51.83.41, e-mail domainetaupenot-merme@wanadoo.fr ✓ Y by appt.

DOM. CACHAT-OCQUIDANT ET FILS 1999★

■   61.91 ha   3,600   ⬛ €5-8

A garnet-coloured wine with bluish highlights and fruity but discreet aromas. It needs to be laid down for a while to develop its full potential. It is full rather than long, and round and well-structured with a very pleasant little hint of liquorice on the finish. The upper part of Ladoix marks the 'border' between Hautes Côtes de Nuits and Hautes Côtes de Beaune.

➤ Dom. Cachat-Ocquidant et Fils,
3, pl. du Souvenir, 21550 Ladoix-Serrigny,
tel. 03.80.26.45.30, fax 03.80.26.48.16 ☑

Ⓨ by appt.

F. CHAUVENET
Les Hauts de Charmont 1998★

■   n.c.   60,000   ⬛ €8-11

This wine has a lovely Burgundy ruby colour and a nose that is so floral, so flowery, so subtle and incredibly pretty that it puts one in mind of the author Colette who, in fact, once actually wrote an article about this estate, one of the oldest in Nuits (J.-Cl. Boisset is the present owner). A rich and generous wine, tannic but not excessively so. Refreshing, in a word.

➤ F. Chauvenet, 9, quai Fleury,
21700 Nuits-Saint-Georges,
tel. 03.80.62.61.43, fax 03.80.62.37.38.

RAOUL CLERGET 1999★

■   n.c.   30,000   ⬛ €5-8

The Clerget estate has been taken over by the Tresch family from Alsace. This Hautes-Côtes is still a little immature on the attack but develops pleasantly on the palate and shows some fullness. It is garnet red in colour with a scent of undergrowth and mushrooms. The palate follows the same lines, together with a classic fruity flavour. Best served with chicken at Sunday lunch.

➤ Raoul Clerget, chem. de la Pierre-qui-Vire,
21200 Montagny-lès-Beaune,
tel. 03.80.26.37.37, fax 03.80.24.14.81,
e-mail contacts@tresch.fr

➤ Tresch SA

DOM. YVAN DUFOULEUR
Les Dames Huguette 1998★

■   1.3 ha   6,000   ⬛ €8-11

The vines at Les Dames Huguettes are planted under television pylons, where they produce both red and white grapes. The estate receives a star for both colours: the red is deep garnet in colour, delicate and well-made, fitting all the criteria of the AOC despite having strong oak influences. Best to serve this with duck. From the same *climat*, the **white 98** has a delicate oakiness, while the **village red 99** is very harmonious.

➤ Dom. Yvan Dufouleur,
18, rue Thurot, 21700 Nuits-Saint-Georges,
tel. 03.80.62.31.00, fax 03.80.62.31.00 ☑

Ⓨ by appt.

GEISWEILER 1999

■   n.c.   10,000

The Geisweilers once played a pioneering role in the redevelopment of the Hautes-Côtes, most notably creating the huge vineyard at Bévy. Since then, they have become part of the Picard estate at Chagny. This 99 vintage has pretty ruby highlights, a nose that is still maturing (dark fruits, spices) and a palate that is straightforward on the attack. Its tannins are still rather austere but the wine is developing some length.

➤ Geisweiler, 4, rte de Dijon,
21700 Nuits-Saint-Georges,
tel. 03.85.87.51.21, fax 03.85.87.51.11

➤ M. Picard

DOM. GLANTENET 1999★★

☐   2.05 ha   8,000

The Glantenets, wine-makers since the 18th century, mature their wines in French oak. This particular example has spent a year in barrel. It has a fresh colour, and fine aromas of almond, citrus fruits and mint.

➤ Dom. Glantenet Père et Fils,
rue de l'Aye, 21700 Magny-lès-Villers,
tel. 03.80.62.91.61, fax 03.80.62.74.79,
e-mail domaine.glantenet@wanadoo.fr ☑

Ⓨ ev. day except Sun. 8am–12 noon 2pm–6pm

BLANCHE ET HENRI GROS
Cuvée de garde Vieilles vignes 1999★★

■   2.5 ha   4,500   ⬛ €8-11

Chambœuf is the northernmost *village* of the Hautes-Côtes de Nuits, and what a lovely surprise they have in store for us here. This elegant, powerful 99 has a lovely raspberry flavour. What more could one ask for? With its round palate and subtle tannins, this is certainly an attractive wine and should keep well.

➤ Henri Gros, 21220 Chambœuf,
tel. 03.80.51.81.20, fax 03.80.49.71.75 ☑

Ⓨ by appt.

DOM. GROS FRERE ET SOEUR 1999★★

■   6.5 ha   43,500   ⬛ €8-11

This lovely 99, produced by this prestigious estate in Vosne-Romanée, is one of the best and just missed receiving a *coup de cœur*. It has a wonderfully deep colour with attractive aromas of strawberry and mocha, and good tannins and length. A remarkably characteristic wine that should not be opened too soon. A **white 99** from the same estate receives one star. It is full with lasting flavours of flowers and fruit with that mineral note that only really great wines possess.

➤ SCE Gros Frère et Sœur, 6, rue des Grands-Crus, 21700 Vosne-Romanée,
tel. 03.80.61.12.43, fax 03.80.61.34.05 ☑

Ⓨ by appt.

➤ Bernard Gros

FREDERIC JACOB 1999

■   1 ha   3,000   ⬛ €5-8

Frédéric Jacob moved here in 1996. His wine is pleasant and well-made, without a huge amount of character, but interesting nevertheless. Lightly coloured with the nose showing both spice and fruit. Fresh and fruity, it would go perfectly with a plate of cold meats. A wine to be drunk for the pleasure of the moment without asking too many questions.

• Frédéric Jacob, 50, Grande-Rue, 21420 Changey-Echevronne, tel. 03.80.21.55.58 ✉ Y by appt.

JEAN-PHILIPPE MARCHAND
Cuvée Prestige Vieili en fût de chêne 1999★

This estate was founded in the 17th century and possesses an antique wine-press as well as guest rooms. Jean-Philippe Marchand has received high praise from our Jury in the past. This interesting 99 has the colour of very ripe cherries. The nose offers plenty of variety with aromas as diverse as fern and black-currant. It is a concentrated, well-structured, well-balanced, characteristic wine, pleasing with good length and agreeable tannins. It would make the prefect accompaniment to a rich sauce dish.

• Maison Jean-Philippe Marchand, 4, rue Souvert, 21220 Gevrey-Chambertin, tel. 03.80.34.33.60, fax 03.80.34.12.77, e-mail marchand@axnet.com ✉ Y by appt.

DOM. MOILLARD 1999
7.4 ha 40,000 €8-11

This clear wine, with its very expressive nose of vanilla and pear, has a peachy palate that finishes with a mineral note. It would go perfectly with a filet mignon of pork and prunes.

• Dom. Moillard, chem. rural 29, 2, rue François-Mignotte, 21700 Nuits-Saint-Georges, tel. 03.80.62.42.22, fax 03.80.61.28.13, e-mail nuicave@wanadoo.fr ✉ Y ev. day 10am–6pm; cl. Jan.

DOM. DE MONTMAIN
Les Genevrières 1998
6 ha 32,000 €15-23

Here we have an experienced wine-maker who has already been singled out by the Jury in the past. This particular red is closed on the attack but opens out revealing some spiciness. The finish is marked by sturdy tannins that need time to mellow. The prominent flavour of this wine is jammy red fruit. Best to wait two or three years before drinking.

• Dom. de Montmain, 21700 Villars-Fontaine, tel. 03.80.62.31.94, fax 03.80.61.02.31 ✉ Y ev. day except Sun. 8.30am–12 noon 1.30pm–6pm; Sat by appt.

DOM. HENRI NAUDIN-FERRAND Elevé en fût de chêne 1999
1.17 ha 9.310 €6-8

If you enjoy good cooking, choose a fillet of pikeperch in a crust of *pain d'épice* (Dijon is not far off) to go with this pale, straw-coloured 99. A little on the floral side but with enough acidity to balance things out, it doesn't have a great deal of body but has plenty of verve.

• Dom. Henri Naudin-Ferrand, rue du Meix-Grenot, 21700 Magny-lès-Villers, tel. 03.80.62.91.50, fax 03.80.62.91.77, e-mail dnaudin@ipac.fr ✉ Y by appt.

OLIVIER-GARD
Cuvée Tradition 1999★
1 ha 6,000 €5-8

This wine was produced at Corboin, a small hamlet that nestles on the plateau of Nuits-Saints-Georges. It has an elegant harmony: the colour sparkles, the aromas are fruity (though it needs to breathe). The quality of its palate and the charm of its finish promise plenty of pleasure to come.

• Dom. Olivier-Gard, Concour-et-Corbon, 21700 Nuits-Saint-Georges, tel. 03.80.61.00.43, fax 03.80.61.38.45 ✉ Y by appt.
• Manuel Olivier

ERIC PANSIOT Le Lieu Dieu 1999★★
0.6 ha 4,000 €5-8

The *climat* of Le Lieu Dieu is on the site of a former convent near Marey-lès-Fussey, high up in the Hautes-Côtes. This is a model example of Hautes-Côtes de Nuits wine. The Jury has, after all, judged it worthy of a *coup de coeur*. It has a gorgeous, honeyed touch and a brilliant, clear colour with sufficient structure to keep two to three years before opening.

• Eric Pansiot, Ch. de la Chaume, 21700 Corgoloin, tel. 03.80.62.94.32, fax 03.80.62.73.14 ✉ Y by appt.

CH. DE PREMEAUX 1999★
2.1 ha 8,000 €8-11

M. Pelletier, whose grandfather bought this château in 1933, has been running the 12.5-ha (31-acre) estate since 1982. This wine grips you firmly from the first glance: the colour is a very intense, bright garnet with violet high-lights. The nose is winey and blackcurranty. The palate doesn't disappoint: the body has a good richness and roundness but the fruit is little closed at the moment. This is a wine that is characteristic of its type. It can be opened and enjoyed now or kept for three to four years.

• Dom. du Ch. de Premeaux, 21700 Premeaux-Prissey, tel. 03.80.62.30.64, fax 03.80.62.39.28, e-mail chateau.de.premeaux@wanadoo.fr ✉ Y by appt.
• Pelletier

DOM. SAINT-SATURNIN 1999★
4 ha 26,000 €11-15

The 12th-century church of Saint-Saturnin at Vergy is situated in the heart of the Hautes-Côtes. This silky, garnet-red 99 with pink glints has an open, direct nose and real complexity. On the palate it is all silky smoothness, well-structured with just the right amount of acidity and satisfyingly long. It is a particularly attractive wine.

Bourgogne Hautes-Côtes de Nuit

➤ Vieilles Caves de Bourgogne &de; Bordeaux, 6 bis, bd Jacques-Copeau, 21200 Beaune, tel. 03.80.24.37.47, fax 03.80.24.37.38

PAUL ET COLETTE SIMON
Les Dames Huguette Vieilli en fût de chêne
1998★
■ □ 1 ha 6,000 ▥ €8-11

The vineyard of Les Dames Huguette in the hills of Nuits-Saint-Georges produces some of the best wines in the appellation. This wine shows good extraction with an authentic flavour of the *terroir* and that velvety-red colour of the *griotte* cherries. It has spent 18 months in barrels, 30% of them new, which gives it a liquorice flavour as it opens on the palate. Quite an unusual wine.
➤ Paul et Colette Simon,
21700 Marey-lès-Fussey, tel. 03.80.62.93.35, fax 03.80.62.71.54, e-mail domaine@ paul-simon.fr ▣ ▾ by appt.

GUY SIMON ET FILS
Vieilli en fût de chêne 1999★
■ □ 2 ha 6,000 ▥ €8-11

Guy Simon's son, who holds a BTS in oenology from the wine school in Beaune, now runs the estate. This Burlat cherry-coloured, spicy 99 has been matured in wood, using one-third new oak. It is impressive for its length on the nose and fullness on the palate. The oak is well-handled and the fruit well-established. The **Cuvée des Dames Huguette 99** also receives a special mention from the Jury. It comes from a well-known *climat* situated at the upper part of Nuits-Saint-Georges.
➤ Guy Simon et Fils,
21700 Marey-lès-Fussey, tel. 03.80.62.91.85, fax 03.80.62.71.82 ▣ ▾ by appt.

DOM. THEVENOT-LE BRUN ET FILS 1999★
□ 3.4 ha 14,400 ▤ ▥ ♦ €5-8

When he is not busy with wine, Thévenot-Le Brun the elder likes to perform in Shakespeare plays at the Avignon festival fringe. His wine, however, shows no signs of wondering whether 'to be or not to be'. This Chardonnay, which has a pale gold colour with silvery highlights and light toasty aromas, expresses *terroir* with a strong Hautes-Côtes accent. There is no point keeping this wine in the cellar: enjoy it now. The **Clos du Vignon white** also receives one star.
➤ Dom. Thévenot-Le Brun et Fils,
21700 Marey-lès-Fussey,
tel. 03.80.62.91.64, fax 03.80.62.99.81, e-mail thevenot-le-brun@wanadoo.fr ▣ ▾ by appt.

JEAN-PIERRE TRUCHETET
1998★★
□ 0.66 ha 5,700 ▥ €5-9

Situated at Premeaux-Prissey, a village which boasts two churches (one for Premeaux

and one for Prissey), both founded in the 13th century, this 8.5-ha (21-acre) estate has produced very attractive wine that has been matured for ten months in barrel. The Grand Jury unanimously awarded it a *coup de cœur* for its characteristic pale colour with green highlights and youthful mineral and floral aromas. Round and rich with plenty of body, it is only on the palate that it really expresses the mineral flavours that have already been presented on the nose. It is quite the most delightful wine in the appellation.
➤ Jean-Pierre Truchetet, rue des Masers, 21700 Premeaux-Prissey, tel. 03.80.61.07.22, fax 03.80.61.34.35 ▣ ▾ ev. day except Sat. Sun. 9am–12 noon 2pm–7pm; cl. 15-31 Aug.

DOM. ALAIN VERDET
Vieilles vignes 1998★★
□ 1.6 ha 5,000 ▥ €11-15

This estate has been using organic wine-growing methods since 1971, and this 98 was produced and matured for 18 months in new oak. It pleases in every way: the nose confirms what the eye sees and the palate follows through with the same flavours, all following a lovely floral path that is still a little lively but delicate. The finish is superb – real fireworks. In two to three years' time it will go perfectly with a dish of seafood.
➤ Alain Verdet, rue Combe A.-Naudon, 21700 Arcenant, tel. 03.80.61.08.10, fax 03.80.61.08.10 ▣ ▾ by appt.

CH. DE VILLERS-LA-FAYE 1999
■ 8 ha 13,000 ▥ €8-11

Serge Valot, wine-producer at the Hospices de Beaune – which is a stamp of nobility in Burgundy – has put his son Samuel in charge of the business. This crimson-purple 99 is as yet hesitant whether to go in the direction of oak or of dark red fruit. A delicate start on the palate which then lets the attractive tannins do all the talking at the finish. Sandrine Bonnaire shot a scene from Jacques Rivette's film about Joan of Arc here.
➤ Ch. de Villers-la-Faye, rue du Château, 21700 Villers-la-Faye, tel. 03.80.62.91.57, fax 03.80.62.71.32 ▣ ▾ by appt.
➤ Valot Père et Fils

Bourgogne Hautes-Côtes de Beaune

Bourgogne Hautes-Côtes de Beaune applies to about twenty communes, extending in the north into the Saône-et-Loire. In 2000 the quantity of wines produced under the appellation totalled 39,574 hl (1,044,754 gal), including 7,250 hl (191,400 gal) of white, rather more than the Hautes-Côtes de Nuits production. In situation, the two areas are quite similar, and a considerable area is given over to growing Aligoté and Gamay.

The Coopérative des Hautes-Côtes, which started life in Orches, a hamlet near Baubigny, is now based under the 'banner' of Pommard, at the intersection of the D973 and the main RN74, just south of Beaune. A significant amount of Bourgogne Hautes-Côtes de Beaune is vinified there. The vineyards have greatly developed since the years 1970–75, as in the north.

The countryside is more picturesque than that of the Hautes-Côtes de Nuits, and there are many places to visit, including Orches, La Rochepot and its château and Nolay, a little Burgundian village. It is worth adding that the Hautes-Côtes formerly grew a variety of crops and is still an area where soft fruits are grown to supply the liqueur-makers of Nuits-Saint-Georges and Dijon. The fruit liqueurs and brandies made from these blackcurrants and raspberries are of excellent quality. There is a single appellation for the pear brandy of Monts-de-Côte-d'Or, which is also made here.

DOM. BACHEY-LEGROS ET FILS
1999★ ■ 0.5 ha 600 €8-11

Taking the most ancient road from the village of Santenay-le-Haut, you will come across a country chapel dating from 1703 which sits opposite this estate, built in Burgundy style. This dark garnet-red 99 with bluish tones has a subtle nose where soft fruits combine with a balsamic touch. It is a rich, elegant wine balanced by tannins that are firm but not overpowering. It needs to wait a couple of years before being served, perhaps with a dish of eggs *en meurette*.

Christiane Bachey-Legros, 12, rue de la Charrière, 21590 Santenay, tel. 03.80.20.64.14 by appt.

DOM. BERGER-RIVE
Au Paradis 1999 ■ 3 ha 4,000 €5-8

It is important not to confuse the Château de Mercey, which is run by Antonin Rodet, with the Manoir de Mercey, which is the estate we are dealing with here. To avoid confusion, we will use Domaine Berger-Rive when talking about the Manoir. The vines here are high and wide, as authorised by the INAO in the Hautes-Côtes, and the *climat* has a lovely name: Au Paradis! As its violet-black colour suggests, this is a very concentrated wine with jammy fruit flavours, solid and tannic. It is worth waiting a while before serving it with a Charolais steak and/or strong cheese.

Dom. Gérard Berger-Rive et Fils, Manoir de Mercey, 71150 Cheilly-lès-Maranges, tel. 03.85.91.13.81, fax 03.85.91.17.06 by appt.

DANIEL BILLARD 1998★
0.44 ha 1,682 €5-8

Beneath a certain reserve, this has the makings of a great wine. One thinks of Van Gogh's words: 'Painting is reality plus temperament.' Here, maturity and concentration complement the delicate colour and the butter and hazelnut aromas. This wine could either be drunk now or laid down for a while. It is made by a Maranges wine-producer.

Daniel Billard, rue de Borgy, 71150 Dezize-lès-Maranges, tel. 03.85.91.15.60, fax 03.85.91.10.59

DOM. DU BOIS GUILLAUME
Les Champs Perdrix 1999★ □ 2.11 ha 12,000 €5-8

This young, pale yellow-gold wine really is faultless. It has an interesting texture with a very pleasant mineral note on the palate, which has an attractive length.

Jean-Yves Devevey, Dom. du Bois Guillaume, rue de Breuil, 71150 Demigny, tel. 03.85.49.91.11, fax 03.85.49.91.59, e-mail devevey-bois-guillaume@wanadoo.fr by appt.

PASCAL BOULEY 1998
■ 0.73 ha 2,400 ▥ €5-8

If you want to know what deep garnet-red looks like, then take a look at this wine. It is fruity (ripe, stewed fruit) with a hint of toastiness, and is well-structured, although it could do with a little more richness. It has a fine oakiness to it.

➤ Pascal Bouley, pl. de l'Eglise,
21190 Volnay, tel. 03.80.21.61.69,
fax 03.80.21.66.44 ▣ ▼ by appt.

G. BRZEZINSKI 1999
□ n.c. 3,000 €8-11

This estate used 'to belong to the Rivot family. On offer here is a ruby-red 99 with light brick-red highlights. It has an interesting fruity flavour as it opens on the palate, followed by something distinctly more gamey and wild. The texture is delicate, the tannins pleasant and docile. The way it is developing suggests that it should be drunk reasonably soon.

➤ G. Brzezinski, rte d'Autun,
21630 Pommard, tel. 03.80.22.23.99,
fax 03.80.22.28.33 ▣ ▼ ev. day except Sun.
8am–12 noon 2pm–6pm; cl. 23 Dec.–6 Jan.

CHRISTOPHE BUISSON
Les Pierres percées 1999★
■ n.c. n.c. ▤ ▥ €5-8

This estate was created in 1990 with nothing more than enthusiasm and guts. First the vines were rented, then little by little they were bought, and finally in 1999 a winery was bought in Beaune. Their wine is garnet-red in colour with bluish hues, and aromas of small-berried soft fruit. It is an honest, full wine with good tannins, a solid but not austere structure, rich and long: a good average.

➤ Christophe Buisson,
21190 Saint-Romain, tel. 03.80.21.63.92,
fax 03.80.21.67.03 ▣ ▼ by appt.

CAPITAIN-GAGNEROT
Les Gueulottes 1998★
□ 1.05 ha 7,000 ▤ ▥ €5-8

Since 1802, the Capitain family have had a proud family motto: 'Loyalty is my strength'. Their wine-cellar, which is cut out of the Corton mountain, is testimony to that determination. This wine, which still has a lively, young colour, at first encounter offers subtle aromas of soft white bread and toast. It is pleasant on the palate, rich, very dense and long, lingering well after the finish. There is no point in putting it in the cellar as it is ready to drink now.

➤ Maison Capitain-Gagnerot,
38, rte de Dijon, 21550 Ladoix-Serrigny,
tel. 03.80.26.41.36, fax 03.80.26.46.29 ▣
▼ by appt.

DENIS CARRE 1999★★
■ n.c. n.c. ▥ ▤ ▥ €5-8

This estate is highly acclaimed. It is characteristically-coloured, violet-tinged 99 is very, very young. The nose is showing hints of

strawberries and raspberries with a light oakiness in the background. It is well-structured, tannic and sturdy, even a little austere, but shows promise and is well-constructed. The **white 99** receives a special mention from the Jury: this is a light-hearted wine to be enjoyed at a festive occasion.

➤ Denis Carré, rue du Puits-Bouret,
21190 Meloisey, tel. 03.80.26.02.21,
fax 03.80.26.04.64 ▣ ▼ by appt.

DOM. FRANÇOIS CHARLES ET FILS 1999★
□ 1.5 ha 9,000 ▥ €5-8

Nantoux has rediscovered the taste for wine-making and this rather densely-coloured 99, perfumed with mirabelle, honey and toast, does its appellation credit. If it seems a little developed, that is only due to its maturity. This estate has been singled out by our Jury in the past for its red.

➤ EARL François Charles et Fils,
21190 Nantoux, tel. 03.80.26.01.20,
fax 03.80.26.04.84 ▣ ▼ by appt.

DOM. CHEVROT 1999★
■ 2 ha 13,000 €5-8

A loin of lamb would go down well with this supple, round though rigid Pinot Noir which has good length. It is deep garnet in colour with a scent of vanilla. A delicate wine, which one has to admit, makes a pleasant change from all those wines with overpowering tannins that have to be laid down for years before they can be drunk.

➤ Catherine et Fernand Chevrot,
Dom. Chevrot, 19, rte de Couches,
71150 Cheilly-lès-Maranges,
tel. 03.85.91.10.55, fax 03.85.91.13.24,
e-mail domaine.chevrot@wanadoo.fr ▣
▼ ev. day 9am–12 noon 2pm–6pm; Sun.
9am–12 noon

RAOUL CLERGET 1999★
■ n.c. 50,000 €5-8

At the very first glance this wine shows its intensity. On the nose there are aromas of tart red berries (Cornelian cherries, to be more precise). The attack is reasonably firm, the tannins precise, the acidity noticeable, the length average. It doesn't have great structure but is characteristic. The Raoul Clerget estate has recently been taken over and enlarged by the Tresch family from Alsace.

➤ Raoul Clerget,
chem. de la Pierre-qui-Vire,
21200 Montagny-lès-Beaune,
tel. 03.80.26.37.37, fax 03.80.24.14.81,
e-mail contacts@tresch.fr
➤ Tresch SA

Y. ET C. CONTAT-GRANGE 1999★
■ 2 ha 4,000 €5-8

There is a character called La Gazette who appears in the novels of Henri Vincenot and who was often to be found wandering through the streets of Hautes-Côtes de Beaune. This pleasant, black cherry-coloured wine with its aromas of undergrowth and ripe fruit would surely have tempted him to stop for a chat. This is a simple wine, not aggressive but on its guard, with the solid body expected from a sturdy Burgundy.

♠ EARL Yvon Contat-Grangé, Grande-Rue, 71150 Dezize-lès-Maranges, tel. 03.85.91.15.87, fax 03.85.91.12.54 ☑
Ⴤ by appt.

RODOLPHE DEMOUGEOT

Vieilles vignes 1999★

1 ha	6,000	€5-8

'This is not bad at all,' notes one Jury member in his notes. It has the colour of Griotte cherries and on the nose opens on black cherry, then heads off on a more musky, leathery note. On the attack it is subtle but soon opens to reveal a fine structure and an incredible chewiness. Keep it for two or three years in the cellar, then serve it with roast duck.

♠ Dom. Rodolphe Demougeot, 2, rue du Clos-de-Mazeray, 21190 Meursault, tel. 03.80.21.28.99, fax 03.80.21.29.18 ☑
Ⴤ by appt.

DOUDET-NAUDIN 1999★★

2.4 ha	18,000	€5-8

This is a really excellent wine, one of the best in the tasting. It has colour in abundance, a wonderfully true Pinot nose of pepper and blackcurrant, and such body, such fleshiness, such fruit! It wouldn't be unthinkable to drink it now but that would benefit from a year or two in the cellar.

♠ Doudet-Naudin, 3, rue Henri-Cyrot, BP 1, 21420 Savigny-lès-Beaune, tel. 03.80.21.51.74, fax 03.80.21.50.69 ☑

DOM. R. DUBOIS ET FILS

Les Monts Battois 1999★

0.9 ha	6,000	€5-8

Les Monts Battois is a justly famous *climat*. It was here, after all, that they created an experimental vineyard for Burgundy wine-makers, high up in Beaune-Savigny. This fresh and lively Chardonnay is yellow verging on green, with toasty, apricot aromas. An attractive grape makes for an attractive wine, and this wine is absolutely everything that this appellation ought to be.

♠ Dom. R. Dubois et Fils, rte de Nuits-Saint-Georges, 21700 Premeaux-Prissey, tel. 03.80.62.30.61, fax 03.80.61.24.07, e-mail rdubois@wanadoo.fr ☑ Ⴤ ev. day 8am-11.30am 2pm-6pm; Sat./Sun. by appt.

DOM. C. ET J.-M. DURAND 1999

2.5 ha	8,000	€5-8

Alexandre Dumas gave a very moving account of his visit to the Hautes-Côtes, and this ruby-red, spicy, rounded, fleshy wine provokes those same feelings. It has a full body and plenty of tannins, revealing wonderfully integrated flavours of blackcurrant and vanilla.

♠ Dom. Christine et Jean-Marc Durand, 1, rue de l'Eglise, 21200 Bouze-lès-Beaune, tel. 03.80.22.75.31, fax 03.80.26.02.57 ☑
Ⴤ by appt.

DOM. GLANTENET 1999★

3.17 ha	5,500	€5-8

Although this estate dates back to the 18th century, it has been producing its own wine only since 1997. This Chardonnay has a fresh, though not intense, colour. However, the nose is very attractive, with newly-baked bread and soft white dough aromas followed by citrus fruits and apples and pears. The attack remains on similarly lively, lemony notes with sufficient acidity to sanction a good three years in the cellar.

♠ Dom. Glantenet Père et Fils, rue de l'Aye, 21700 Magny-lès-Villers, tel. 03.80.62.91.61, fax 03.80.62.74.79, e-mail domaine.glantenet@wanadoo.fr ☑ Ⴤ ev. day except Sun. 8am-12 noon 2pm-6pm

LES CAVES DES HAUTES-CÔTES

La Dalignière Elevé en fût de chêne 1999

n.c.	21,000	€8-11

This co-operative has contributed a great deal to the redevelopment of the vineyards of the Hautes-Côtes. This oak-matured wine is strongly influenced by the wood. It is an open, friendly wine, sparkling purple in colour, fruity and peppery with well-blended tannins, but it is difficult to judge it properly at this stage.

♠ Les Caves des Hautes-Côtes, rte de Pommard, 21200 Beaune, tel. 03.80.25.01.00, fax 03.80.22.87.05, e-mail vincho@wanadoo.fr ☑ Ⴤ by appt.

HOSPICES DE DIJON

Chenovre Ermitage 1999★

10.12 ha	69,000	€8-11

In 1984, the regional and university hospital centre at Dijon decided, in an effort to get the best out of its land, to convert around ten hectares (24.75 acres) between Pernand and Savigny into vineyards, reviving the Chenovre-Ermitage estate. It is cultivated by workers from a community aid centre and produced by the château de Meursault (which belongs to the Boisseaux group). This agreeable 99 Hospices de Dijon is a subtle shade of greeny-gold, flowery and buttery, not very long but lively and fresh at the finish. The wine-making has been well-mastered.

♠ Hospices de Dijon, 5, rue du Collège, 21200 Beaune, tel. 03.80.24.53.01, fax 03.80.24.53.03 ☑ Ⴤ ev. day 9am-12 noon 2pm-6pm

DOM. A. ET B. LABRY 1999★

1.3 ha	2,500	€8-11

This is a 15.55-ha (38.45-acre) estate situated on the Côte and in the Hautes-Côtes de Beaune. *Carpe diem* says this wine: in other words, do not wait to enjoy the pleasure of drinking this delicately toasted, very well-

matured, supple, round wine, with its pale colour and its slight aroma of liquorice.
Dom. André et Bernard Labry, Melin, 21190 Auxey-Duresses, tel. 03.80.21.21.60, fax 03.80.21.64.15, e-mail domaine-labry@wanadoo.fr ☑ Y by appt.

LYCEE VITICOLE DE BEAUNE 1998★

☐ 1.03 ha 3,586 €5–8

The wine school of Beaune has often been acclaimed in this *Guide*. Its successful 98 receives the congratulations of the Jury, which is an achievement. It is yellowy-gold in colour with aromas of butter and hazelnut, minerally and fruity, and well-balanced. The oak is not overpowering although, apparently, the wine has spent some time in barrels that were made by the school of cooperage. The Minister of Agriculture ought to serve this wine from time to time at his own table.
Dom. du Lycée viticole de Beaune, 16, av. Charles-Jaffelin, 21200 Beaune, tel. 03.80.26.35.81, fax 03.80.22.76.69 ☑
Y ev. day except Sun. 8am–11.30am 2pm–5pm; Sat. 8am–11.30am

CH. MOROT-GAUDRY 1999★

☐ 0.2 ha 1,700 €5–8

Chateau Morot-Gaudry is based in an old windmill in the gorges of Cozanne, a small local river, between Maranges and the Hautes-Côtes. Their wine is clear and pale in colour with green glints, with touches of flint, even gunflint. It is round and fine, not very long, but pleasant nevertheless. Try serving it with a *pauchouse* – a stew made from fish from the Saône and Doubs rivers.
Morot-Gaudry, Moulin Pignot, 71150 Paris-l'Hôpital, tel. 03.85.91.11.09, fax 03.85.91.11.09 ☑ Y by appt.

DOM. HENRI NAUDIN-FERRAND 1999★

☐ 1.5 ha 13,532 €5–8

Magny-lès-Villers falls half in Hautes-Côtes de Nuits and half in Hautes-Côtes de Beaune. This wine hails from the latter part and has a classic colour. It has a vegetal touch on the nose and is typically Chardonnay; the palate starts with some fullness which is followed by ripe citrus fruits and a fine hint of lees. A wine with serious structure. Note also the **cuvée Orchis 98 red** if you like oakiness.
Dom. Henri Naudin-Ferrand, rue du Meix-Grenot, 21700 Magny-lès-Villers, tel. 03.80.62.91.50, fax 03.80.62.91.77, e-mail dnaudin@ipac.fr ☑ Y by appt.

DOM. PARIGOT PERE ET FILS 1999★

■ 2 ha 10,000 €8–11

This is an estate that truly knows its métier. This wine is a deep Bigarreau cherry-red in colour with a very long bouquet that begins on a roasted note and ends on a fruity one. It is well-constructed, robustly structured, already smooth, has a great deal of character and is very harmonious.
Dom. Parigot Père et Fils, rte de Pommard, 21190 Meloisey, tel. 03.80.26.01.70, fax 03.80.26.04.32 ☑
Y by appt.

CH. PHILIPPE-LE-HARDI

Clos de La Chaise Dieu 1999★

☐ 10.77 ha 100,000 €5–8

God's Chair? One could easily imagine God sitting on the Hautes-Côtes on the seventh day, settling down to relax and take a little time to enjoy his work. Perhaps He would also try this bright, golden wine with its subtle aromas of hazelnut and rather mineral character. It is pleasant on the palate, leaving a lovely freshness on the tastebuds.
Ch. de Santenay, BP 18, 21590 Santenay, tel. 03.80.20.61.87, fax 03.80.20.63.66 ☑
Y by appt.

DOM. PONSARD-CHEVALIER 1999

■ 1.79 ha 2,000 €5–8

Up hill and down dale, the Hautes-Côtes countryside goes from hills to valleys and back again. It is the same with this Pinot Noir: the attack is calm, reminiscent of fresh raspberries, then suddenly lively, aggressive tannins arrive. The colour is almost violet and its aromas are in keeping with the grape variety and the *terroir*.
Ponsard-Chevalier, 2, Les Tilles, 21590 Santenay, tel. 03.80.20.60.87, fax 03.80.20.61.10 ☑ Y by appt.

DOM. ROSSIGNOL-FEVRIER PERE ET FILS 1999★

■ 0.24 ha 1,800 €5–8

Roundness and fullness are the first impressions produced by this very sophisticated Pinot Noir. The colour is black cherry and the nose has a delicate aroma of liquorice and kirsch. This wine is obviously too young to show us everything on offer but the tannins are already softening and the finish is promising.
EARL Rossignol-Février, rue du Mont, 21190 Volnay, tel. 03.80.21.64.23, fax 03.80.21.67.74 ☑ Y by appt.
Frédéric Rossignol

DOM. SAINT-ANTOINE DES ECHARDS 1999★

☐ 0.41 ha 2,300 €5–8

This estate, which nestles in the heart of the lovely Cozanne valley, just at the edges of the Côte-d'Or and Saône-et-Loire, has produced a charmingly-coloured 99 with a subtle, lightly floral, then raspberry, aroma. It is so tantalising and alluring it makes one want to drink it right now. The palate has body and vigour, the aromas are interesting and original: all in all, a fully-formed character.
Franck Guérin, Dom. Saint-Antoine des Echards, rue Santenay, 21340 Change, tel. 03.85.91.10.40, fax 03.85.91.17.29 ☑
Y by appt.

CAVE DE SAINTE-MARIE-LA-BLANCHE 1999

1 ha   5,700   €8-11

This co-operative is certainly not short of dedication, working a total of 70 ha (173 acres) of vines, though there is only one hectare (2.47 acres) set aside for this wine. This is a smooth wine with mineral notes, which hits the spot nicely. The colour is yellowy-gold, the nose has hazelnut and buttered bread aromas. It is a little closed but still pleasant to drink as the palate is full, pleasant and authentic.

Cave de Sainte-Marie-la-Blanche, rte de Verdun, 21200 Sainte-Marie-la-Blanche, tel. 03.80.26.60.60, fax 03.80.26.54.47 ev. day except Sun. 8am–12 noon 2pm–7pm

MICHEL SERVEAU 1999★

3.19 ha   5,000   €5-8

At La Rochepot they know the meaning of colour. One has only to look up and admire the roofs of the château to get the idea. Thus this wine is garnet red and glossy in the style of the region. There is a little hint of redcurrant to it, another local trait. This is a full, good, and well-balanced wine that already tastes good, its structure makes three to four years in the cellar a reasonable plan.

Michel Serveau, rte de Beaune, 21340 La Rochepot, tel. 03.80.21.70.24, fax 03.80.21.71.87 by appt.

VAUCHER PERE ET FILS 1999★

n.c.   n.c.   €5-8

This estate formerly belonged to a Dijon négoce-éleveur and is now part of the Cottin group from Nuits (Labouré-Roi). Vaucher has created an intense rather than brightly-coloured 99 that is spicy and redolent of soft fruit berries, and keeps to this complexity of flavour on the palate. It doesn't have much body but does have a fleshy charm.

Vaucher Père et Fils, rue Lavoisier, 21700 Nuits-Saint-Georges, tel. 03.80.62.64.00, fax 03.80.62.64.10 by appt.

DOM. DES VIGNES BLANCHES 1998

0.64 ha   3,350   €5-8

The Léger family will greet you warmly if you visit their cellar at Paris-l'Hôpital, one of the villages in Saône-et-Loire which belong to this appellation. A deep, intense colour introduces this 98 wine with its aromas of strawberries and blackcurrant leaves. It is not yet 100% open but is attractive nevertheless.

Les Vignes Blanches, rue des Bayards, 71150 Paris-l'Hôpital, tel. 03.85.91.14.56 by appt.

DOM. DES VIGNES DES DEMOISELLES

Cuvée Amandine Poinsot 1999★

1.1 ha   6,400   €8-11

Everything is as it should be with this deep cherry-red Pinot Noir – the appellation, the vintage, the combination of flavours of soft fruit and vanilla. This somewhat tannic wine frolics along, just like the land which produced it: the Hautes-Côtes is full of steep paths and descents, and this wine is made along the same lines. It certainly isn't short of breath.

Gabriel Demangeot et Fils, rue de Berfey, 21340 Change, tel. 03.85.91.11.10, fax 03.85.91.16.83 by appt.

Crémant de Bourgogne

Like nearly all other French wine regions, Burgundy had its own appellation, the Bourgogne Mousseux, for the sparkling wines produced and made throughout the whole of the vineyard. Without being unnecessarily critical of the wine produced, it must be said that the quality was not consistent and nor, for the most part, did it compare with the reputation of the other wines of the region, undoubtedly because the base wines used were too heavy. A working group, established in 1974, laid down the rules for Crémant, setting out conditions for its production that were as strict as the ones in the Champagne region on which they were based.

A decree instituted in 1975 gave official approval to the enterprise, and eventually all the makers supported it, whether they really wanted to or not, because the Appellation Bourgogne Mousseux was terminated in 1984. After difficult beginnings, the Crémant de Bourgogne appellation is developing well and produced 74,130 hl (1,957,032, gal) in 2000.

477

Crémant de Bourgogne

BAILLY-LAPIERRE
Chardonnay 1998★

○　n.c.　50,000　■ ♦　€5-8

The **Blanc de Blancs Brut 98**, a blend of Chardonnay (70%) and Aligoté is well-structured, and lively enough to be kept up to two years. This *crémant* has fine, regular bubbles, hints of white blossom and green apple aromas. Rich and delicate without too much length, it is typical of Chardonnay. After thirty years of loyal service in the famous cellars at Bailly (Saint-Bris-le-Vineux) this new brand replaces the former name, 'Meurgis'.

↦ SICA du Vignoble Auxerrois, Caves de Bailly, 89530 Saint-Bris-le-Vineux,
tel. 03.86.53.77.77, fax 03.86.53.80.94 ☑
⅄ ev. day 8am–12 noon 2pm–6pm

DOM. BERGER-RIVE
Cuvée Saint-Hugues

○　0.98 ha 3,000　€5-8

This *cuvée* named after the owner's eldest son is a perfect example of a *crémant* wine. An attractive pale-straw colour with a very fine stream of bubbles, it is lively and spontaneous with a good mousse.

↦ Dom. Gérard Berger-Rive et Fils, Manoir de Mercey,
71150 Cheilly-lès-Maranges,
tel. 03.85.91.13.81, fax 03.85.91.17.06 ☑
⅄ by appt.

DOM. BILLARD ET FILS

○　n.c.　n.c.　€5-8

Supple and soft with a good finish, this *crémant* made from Pinot Noir is the work of Vitteaut-Alberti at Rully. Many wine-growers send their grapes away to a specialist to be made into sparkling wine. This wine, well-balanced on the palate, with a delicate nose and a fine, generous mousse, is a delight to the eye.

↦ Dom. Billard et Fils, 21340 La Rochepot,
tel. 03.80.21.87.94, fax 03.80.21.72.17 ☑
⅄ by appt.

CAVE DES VIGNERONS DE BISSEY Blanc de Blancs 1999★★

○　1.82 ha 19,000　■ ♦　€5-8

Chardonnay and Aligoté are in equal quantities in this blend. It is a superb wine, full of freshness and finesse with a floral nose and a well-defined, balanced body. This little co-operative in the north of the Saône-et-Loire could show quite a few how it's done. The **Rosé 99 Brut** is extremely attractive and retains a naive simplicity. Aligoté, Pinot and Gamay: a harmonious blend of these three grape varieties also received two stars.

↦ Cave de Vignerons de Bissey,
71390 Bissey-sous-Cruchaud,
tel. 03.85.92.05.00, fax 03.85.92.08.73 ☑
⅄ by appt.

DOM. ALBERT BOILLOT
Blanc de Noirs 1999★

○　0.22 ha 2,200　€5-8

The estate was established at Volnay at the end of the 17th century. Its Blanc de Noirs 99 has impact. A greenish-white in colour, it has bubbles that are fine and lasting. While not exceptional on the palate, it is acceptable, well-balanced and has quite a high *dosage*.

↦ SCE du Dom. Albert Boillot, ruelle Saint-Etienne, 21190 Volnay,
tel. 03.80.21.61.21, fax 03.80.21.61.21,
e-mail dom.albert.boillot@wanadoo.fr ☑
⅄ by appt.

SYLVAIN BOUHELIER 1998★

○　4 ha　9,000　■　€8-11

This young grower from the Châtillon area produced his first wine in 1993 and the results are highly commendable. This *crémant* has equal quantities of Pinot Blanc and Pinot Noir, a very good stream of roasted coffee and a lively mousse with aromas of roasted coffee and crystallised fruit. The initial fruitiness on the palate is followed by complex and mature flavours with unusual notes of ripe peaches and raisins.

↦ Sylvain Bouhelier, pl. Saint-Martin,
21400 Chaumont-le-Bois,
tel. 03.80.81.95.97, fax 03.80.81.95.97 ☑
⅄ by appt.

DOM. JEAN-MARIE BOUZEREAU
Blanc de blancs 1997★

○　0.25 ha 2,000　€5-8

Chardonnay from top to toe, this *crémant* is no mere bit-player; crystal-clear, it takes its place in the limelight. Sustained by its freshness and aromas of cream and biscuits, this wine's best quality is its vinosity. Were it not for the fine stream of bubbles, one might wonder whether it was a sparkling or still wine! An excellent example of the Traditional method that produces great sparkling wines.

↦ Dom. Jean-Marie Bouzereau, 7, rue Labbé, 21190 Meursault, tel. 03.80.21.62.41,
fax 03.80.21.24.39 ☑ ⅄ by appt.

DOM. JEAN CHARTRON
Blanc de blancs★

○　n.c.　1,500　€8-11

This is a typical Puligny Blanc de Blancs. A rich straw colour, this subtle wine with a lemon and grapefruit nose is simple and straightforward on the palate. Round and long, although a little light, it is still an enjoyable wine.

↦ Dom. Jean Chartron, 13, Grande-Rue, 21190 Puligny-Montrachet,
tel. 03.80.21.32.85, fax 03.80.21.36.35 ☑
⅄ ev. day 10am–12 noon 2pm–6pm;
cl. mid-Nov. to Mar.

CHEVALIER Prestige★★

○　n.c.　75,000　€5-8

This wine had many supporters when it took part in the final. It has a straw colour with a fine stream of crystal-clear bubbles and a buttery nose. A hint of green apples enhances its rich, unctuous flavour. Although it lacks a little in length to be really exceptional, this is more than an aperitif wine and would make a good accompaniment to a simple meal.

♠ Chevalier, 5, quai Dumorey, 21700 Nuits-Saint-Georges, tel. 03.80.62.61.47, fax 03.80.62.37.38

DOM. CHEVROT 1999★

0.6 ha · 4,000 · €5-8

Whether for a picnic or a traditional meal to celebrate the end of the grape harvest, the Chevrots are sure to open a bottle or two of this crémant. Made from 60% Pinot Noir and 40% Chardonnay, this wine has a fine, bright white mousse and a long-lasting stream of bubbles. Buttery and lemony, it is fresh and open with some expression on the palate.

♠ Catherine et Fernand Chevrot, Dom. Chevrot, 19, rte de Couches, 71150 Cheilly-lès-Maranges, tel. 03.85.91.10.55, fax 03.85.91.13.24, e-mail domaine.chevrot@wanadoo.fr ✓

Y ev. day 9am–12 noon 2pm–6pm; Sun. 9am–12 noon

DOM. DES COLOMBIERS 1999

0.8 ha · 2,000 · €5-8

This 100% Chardonnay comes from the south of Saône-et-Loire. It has a golden colour with a fine sparkle and lovely aromas of apple and hawthorn. There is perhaps a hint of oxidation. Its complex aromas are pleasant and it has character but should not be kept for long.

♠ EARL Dom. des Colombiers, Le Bourg, 71570 Saint-Vérand, tel. 03.85.37.45.65, fax 03.85.37.45.65 ✓ Y ev. day 2pm–6pm

♠ M. Berthelemy

DOM. CORNU 1997★

0.2 ha · n.c. · €5-8

Made by the excellent Delorme company at Rully, this classic crémant, citronella from its colour to its nose, with adequate sparkle, is ripe and distinctive as it opens. The body is traditional and calm. It can be served now.

♠ Dom. Cornu, rue du Meix-Grenot, 21700 Magny-lès-Villers, tel. 03.80.62.92.05, fax 03.80.62.72.22 ✓ Y by appt.

DELIANCE PERE ET FILS

Ruban vert★

5 ha · 22,000 · €5-8

A very lively sparkling wine made from Chardonnay (85%) blended with Pinot Noir. A golden colour with green highlights, floral and long, it is still young and has not yet reached its peak. Touches of bitterness and citrus fruit appear on the finish which together with its liveliness make an unusual wine.

♠ Dom. Deliance, 71640 Dracy-le-Fort, tel. 03.85.44.40.59, fax 03.85.44.36.13 ✓ Y ev. day except Sun. 9am–12 noon 2pm–7pm

CHARLES DURET

n.c. · 60,000 · €8-11

This estate in the Côtes de Nuits was managed for many years by a flamboyant figure among wine-growers, Bernard Barbier, and is today part of the German group G. Reh. Half Pinot blended with Chardonnay and Aligoté, this wine has an impressive sparkle with a light amber-yellow colour and strong exotic aromas of mango. Maturing and so needs to be drunk now.

♠ Moingeon, 4, rte de Dijon, 21700 Nuits-Saint-Georges, tel. 03.80.61.08.62, fax 03.80.62.36.38, e-mail cremantmoingeon@wanadoo.fr ✓ Y ev. day except Sun. 8am–12 noon 1.30pm–6pm

Crémant de Bourgogne

ANDRE DELORME Blanc de Noirs★★

n.c. · 67,000 · €5-8

The highly acclaimed and undisputed leader of Crémant de Bourgogne producers, Jean-François Delorme, is frequently awarded a coup de cœur. This Blanc de Noirs doesn't go for a dramatic effect but works at being characteristic with great success. It is slightly exotic and festive providing the perfect end to an evening. The Blanc de Blancs is in the same class, a perfect aperitif wine. The Rosé, with its fine, brilliant colour and attractive aromas, has been given a star. Perfect with chicken.

♠ André Delorme, Dom. de la Renarde, 2, rue de la République, 71150 Rully, tel. 03.85.87.10.12, fax 03.85.87.04.60, e-mail andre-delorme@wanadoo.fr ✓ Y ev. day except Sun. 9am–12 noon 2pm–7pm; Sat. –6pm, groups by appt.

DOM. DENIS PERE ET FILS★

0.2 ha · 1,200 · €5-8

Gold rather than green-gold, this crémant with its fine stream of bubbles opens on wild-flower notes. On the palate it is full and round indicating that it will keep well. The honey and lemon finish is delicious.

♠ Dom. Denis Père et Fils, chem. des Vignes-Blanches, 21420 Pernand-Vergelesses, tel. 03.80.21.50.91, fax 03.80.26.10.32 Y by appt.

DOM. DENIZOT★★

n.c. · 3,400 · €8-11

Denizot is a typical Burgundian name and one that appears frequently in the Guide; coup de cœur in the 2000 edition. The crémant from this domaine is always good and this one is superb. The tasters complimented its distinctiveness, personality and harmony, describing it simply as 'a pleasure to drink'. The 98 and 99 vintages are both a blend of 10% Gamay and 90% Pinot.

♠ Dom. Christian et Bruno Denizot, 71390 Bissey-sous-Cruchaud, tel. 03.85.92.13.34, fax 03.85.92.12.87, e-mail denizot@caves-particulieres.com ✓ Y ev. day except Sun. 8am–7pm

BERNARD DURY Blanc de Blancs

€5-8

n.c.   n.c.

90% Chardonnay with 10% Aligoté is a successful ratio. Yellow with a very lively sparkle, it has a nose of rye bread and dried apricots. The palate is full, vinous, and appears to have had only a light *dosage*.

⌂ Bernard Dury, rue du Château, hameau de Cissey, 21190 Meursault, tel. 03.80.21.48.44, fax 03.80.21.48.44 ☑
☖ by appt.

LES VIGNERONS DE HAUTE BOURGOGNE 1998★

€8-11

n.c.   18,000

This *crémant* might never have been produced had it not been for the courageous decision to revive the Châtillon vineyard (today a co-operative of 35 wine-growers cultivating 35 ha /86.5 acres). This *brut* with 60% Pinot Noir blended with Chardonnay gives a vivacious mousse with a lasting stream of bubbles. On the nose there are refreshing notes of hazelnut and apricot, lengthy and with all the freshness you could wish for. These two grape varieties (90% Pinot) also blend successfully together in the *cuvée* **Les Caves du Bois de Langres**. This wine, too, received a star.

⌂ SICA des Vignerons de Haute-Bourgogne, Les caves du Bois de Langres, 21400 Prusly-sur-Ource, tel. 03.80.91.07.60, fax 03.80.91.24.76
☖ ev. day except Mon. 9am–12 noon 2pm–7pm

LES CAVES DES HAUTES-COTES

n.c.   3 700   €5-8

The wine-makers of Orches have come a long way since the launch of their rosé and this co-operative is now well established in the area. Its *crémant* has a fine and pleasant, long-lasting stream of bubbles. Floral and above all toasty, its aroma is honest and modern in style. A good fruity attack but still developing ever so slightly. It should be drunk now.

⌂ Les Caves des Hautes-Côtes, rte de Pommard, 21200 Beaune, tel. 03.80.25.01.00, fax 03.80.22.87.05, e-mail vinchc@wanadoo.fr ☑ ☖ by appt.

LES VIGNERONS D'IGE★

€5-8

n.c.   150,000

The Igé co-operative, established in 1927, covers 280 ha (691.6 acres) and offers this *crémant* made with 20% Pinot Noir blended with Chardonnay. Its honeyed aspect with hints of beeswax and acacia is very attractive. Drink it at the next celebration, as it is not made for laying down.

⌂ Cave coop. des vignerons d'Igé, 71960 Igé, tel. 03.85.33.33.56, fax 03.85.33.41.85, e-mail lesvigneronsdige@ lesvigneronsdige.fr
☖ ev. day except Sun. 2pm–6pm

PIERRE JANNY La Maison bleue★★

€5-8

n.c.   n.c.

Made with chardonnay from Grande Bourgogne and blended by a *négociant* in the Saône-et-Loire, this wine has a distinguished green-gold colour. Young and fresh, the aroma opens with acacia blossom, which is characteristic of its grape variety, and unmistakable. A pronounced liveliness gives way to a pure fruitiness which stays on the palate. Perfect for drinking in the coming year, it would be excellent with a blackcurrant dessert.

⌂ Sté Pierre Janny, La Condemine, Cidex 1556, 71260 Péronne, tel. 03.85.23.96.20, fax 03.85.36.96.58, e-mail pierre-janny@wanadoo.fr

JEAN-HERVE JONNIER 1998★

€8-11

1 ha   8,000

Five thousand years ago there was a prehistoric civilization right here in Chassey-le-Camps whose roots are still deep in the earth. This 98 vintage has a delicate mousse and a light stream of bubbles. Lovely aromas of peach and hazelnut are followed by freshness and a good balance of richness and acidity. A fine example of the appellation.

⌂ Jean-Hervé Jonnier, Berculy, 71150 Chassey-le-Camp, tel. 03.85.87.21.90, fax 03.85.87.23.63 ☑
☖ ev. day 8am–12 noon 2pm–8pm

LES CAVES DE LA VERVELLE★

€5-8

1.15 ha 13,680

If you are looking for a fruity wine, this one is recommended. Classic in colour, it tends towards the exotic but retains its distinct flavour of green apples. It is well-structured and robust, made with 60% Pinot Noir, 30% Chardonnay and the remainder Aligoté.

⌂ Cave de Sainte-Marie-la-Blanche, rte de Verdun, 21200 Sainte-Marie-la-Blanche, tel. 03.80.26.60.60, fax 03.80.26.54.47 ☑
☖ ev. day except Sun. 8am–12 noon 2pm–7pm

CELLIER DE LA VIEILLE GRANGE 1999★

€5-8

0.71 ha 7,000

In 1969 Joachim Carlos began as a vineyard worker, then in 1980 started buying small plots of vines, and now he is a well-established producer at Beaune. Chardonnay with a small quantity of Aligoté, this pleasant 99 vintage presents a fleeting mousse. It has a pale colour, an aroma of sweet pastries, and is rounded on the palate, with a hint of flint. And it smells of grapes!

⌂ Cellier de La Vieille Grange, 27, bd Clemenceau, 21200 Beaune, tel. 03.80.22.40.06, fax 03.80.24.12.31
☖ ev. day 9am–12 noon 2pm–7pm
⌂ Joaquim Carlos

LOUIS LORON
Cuvée Prestige Blanc de Blancs★

n.c. 32,000 €5-8

Established in 1932, this Beaujolais company plans to hold open days in November when the *primeurs* are ready. This *crémant* is pure Chardonnay; the sparkle is vivacious and the nose is at first caramel, becoming very much 'Blanc de Blancs'. Full and long on the palate, it is truly characteristic of its type.

SA Louis Loron et Fils, Le Vivier, 69820 Fleurie, tel. 04.74.04.10.22, fax 04.74.69.84.19, e-mail infos@loron-et-fils.com ☑ ▼ ev. day except Sun. 8am–12 noon 1.30pm–6pm; Sat. 8.30am–12 noon

CAVE DE LUGNY★★

30 ha 300,000 €5-8

This co-operative is a former *coup de coeur* winner and produces wine from 1,470 ha (3,630 acres) of vines. It presented one of the best *crémants* of the tasting. The mousse and bubbles are not particularly noteworthy but then the powerful aroma of honeysuckle is unleashed and everything changes. So young, fruity, fresh and ultimately silky, this wine is singled out.

SCV Cave de Lugny, rue des Charmes, 71260 Lugny, tel. 03.85.33.22.85, fax 03.85.33.26.46, e-mail commercial@cave-lugny.com ☑ ▼ by appt.

DOM. DU MERLE Blanc de Blancs

0.3 ha 2,500 €5-8

'Le merle blanc!' The white blackbird! The Merle estate's *crémant* produced from 100% Chardonnay is gold in colour and bursting with fine, lively bubbles. It is fresh and dry with delicate, floral aromas reflecting all the typical Chardonnay characteristics in a pronounced Côte Châlonnaise style.

Michel Morin, Sens, 71240 Sennecey-le-Grand, tel. 03.85.44.75.38, fax 03.85.44.73.63, e-mail domainemerle@yahoo.com ☑ ▼ ev. day 9.30am–7.30pm

PICAMELOT 1999★★

n.c. 4,684 €8-11

This vineyard was established in 1926 by the wine-producer Louis Picamelot and his father Joseph, a cooper by trade. Theirs is an excellent rosé *crémant* aperitif wine which will delight all who drink it. Sparkling, with an imposing stream of bubbles in pale rose tones, this wine is well-balanced on the palate. Initial aromas are of raspberries, followed on the palate by lots of harmonious fruit. The sustained length carries on the theme of soft fruits, a pure Pinot Noir.

Louis Picamelot, 12, pl. de la Croix-Blanche, BP 2, 71150 Rully, tel. 03.85.87.13.60, fax 03.85.87.63.81 ☑ ▼ by appt.

CAVE DE PRISSE-SOLOGNY-VERZE

35.74 ha 120,000 €5-8

Lying in the heart of the valley immortalised by the 19th-century poet and politician Alphonse Lamartine, this co-operative produces wine from 900 ha (2,223 acres) of vineyards. Pure Chardonnay; filled with fine, delicate bubbles, the sparkle in this *crémant* is hinted at rather than overstated. It has lovely buttery aromas with tones of vanilla, cream and biscuit but stays warm, firm and solid on the palate.

Cave de Prisse-Sologny-Verzé, 71960 Prissé, tel. 03.85.37.88.06, fax 03.85.37.61.76, e-mail cave.prisse@wanadoo.fr ☑ ▼ by appt.

DOM. MICHEL PRUNIER 1998★

0.8 ha 5,000 €5-8

As a graduate of the wine-producers' college of Champagne at Aviz in the Marne, Michel Prunier knows the meaning of the word sparkling. Aligoté and Pinot Noir in equal quantities have produced this 98 vintage already at its peak so it needs to be drunk fairly soon. Presenting a good surge of bubbles in a light stream, and a buttery, brioche aroma, it is perfect on the palate and much too good merely to be served as an aperitif. Try it with oyster soup or poached eggs in a white wine and shallot sauce.

Michel Prunier, rte de Beaune, 21190 Auxey-Duresses, tel. 03.80.21.21.05, fax 03.80.21.64.73 ☑ ▼ by appt.

ALBERT SOUNIT Cuvée Prestige★★★

n.c. 34,000 €5-8

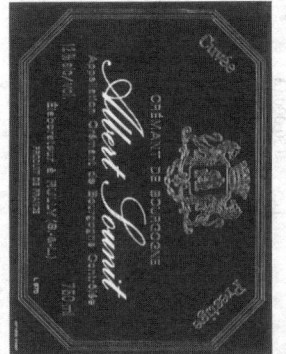

It is the toast of Copenhagen and even makes the Little Mermaid quiver with pleasure. Bought by its Danish importer almost 10 years ago, this company has been awarded its second *coup de coeur*. A blend of 60% Pinot Noir and 40% Chardonnay, this selection is classic perfection. Everything about it is fine, balanced, spontaneous and characteristic right up to the aroma of grapes. Its best quality is that you won't forget it easily.

Albert Sounit, 5, pl. du Champ-de-Foire, 71150 Rully, tel. 03.85.87.09.71, fax 03.85.87.09.71, e-mail albert-sounit@wanadoo.fr ☑ ▼ ev. day 8am–12 noon 2.30pm–6pm; Sat./Sun. by appt.

Crémant de Bourgogne

DOM. THEVENOT-LE BRUN ET FILS★★

€5-8

0.4 ha   4,000

This estate at Marey-le-Fussey in the Hautes Côtes de Nuits is very well-known. When they claim to blend 11% Pinot Gris (today something of a curiosity) with Pinot, Chardonnay and Aligoté, you can believe them. Apart from that, the blend smacks of alchemy and could well produce a gold-medal winner. A very clean wine with a young, light fruitiness, fresh and elegant ... in short, characteristic.

○☛ Dom. Thévenot-Le Brun et Fils,
21700 Marey-lès-Fussey, tel. 03.80.62.91.64,
fax 03.62.99.81,
e-mail thevenot-le-brun@wanadoo.fr ▼
▼ by appt.

CELINE AND LAURENT TRIPOZ 1999★

€8-11

1.2 ha   1,100

Its mousse is soft, its colour rich gold and it has grapefruit and (according to one taster) apricots on the nose which follows through onto the palate. This *crémant* is balanced and long and would be ideal with chicken in a cream sauce. If you are ever passing by, make time to visit this cellar, run by a couple with passionate dedication.

○☛ Céline and Laurent Tripoz,
pl. de la Mairie, 71000 Loché-Mâcon,
tel. 03.85.35.66.09, fax 03.85.35.64.23,
e-mail celine-laurent.tripoz@libertysurf.fr
▼ ▼ by appt.

VEUVE AMBAL Carte noire★

n.c.   150,000   €5-8

Marie Ambal, a sparkling Burgundian character, established this firm in 1898. Taken over a few years ago by a member of the Piffaut family, the estate presents a Carte Noir made from 60% Pinot and 40% Chardonnay. With bubbles that pack plenty of punch, a yellow-pink colour and an exuberant nose, this is a good wine with a pleasant palate.

○☛ SA Veuve Ambal, BP 1, 71150 Rully,
tel. 03.85.87.15.05, fax 03.85.87.30.15,
e-mail vveambal@aol.com ▼ ▼ by appt.

DOM. DES VIGNES DES DEMOISELLES 1999★

€8-11

0.35 ha   3,600

This one would make a truly regal *kir royal!* Made by Vitteaut-Alberti at Rully, this pleasant 99 vintage comes from a union of 70% Pinot Noir and 30% Aligoté. Its bubbles are well-dispersed within the pale-gold colour and it delights the nose with hazelnuts, toast and light floral notes. It is lively and fresh on the palate with lasting aromas of green fruit.

○☛ Gabriel Demangeot et Fils, rue de Berfey,
21340 Change, tel. 03.85.91.11.10,
fax 03.85.91.16.83 ▼ ▼ by appt.

L. VITTEAUT-ALBERTI 1999★★

8.5 ha   50,000   €5-8

Established 50 years ago, this family-run estate has lived up to all expectations. Its **Blanc de Blancs brut 98** was greatly admired by the Jury and awarded two stars. This wine made from 40% Pinot Noir, 40% Chardonnay and 20% Aligoté was also awarded two stars and came close to being selected for a *coup de cœur*. Its generous, creamy mousse invites you to enjoy the choice aromas of hawthorn, honeysuckle and exotic fruit. A roundness on the palate shows real personality, balance and length.

○☛ Gérard Vitteaut-Alberti,
20, rue du Pont-d'Arrot, 71150 Rully,
tel. 03.85.87.23.97, fax 03.85.87.16.24 ▼
▼ by appt.

Chablis

Despite having a reputation that has seen it imitated to a fantastic degree all around the world, the Chablis vineyard once nearly disappeared altogether. Catastrophic late frosts in 1957 and 1961 added to the difficulties of cultivating the vines on very steep hills with stony soils led to vine-growing being progressively abandoned; the value of land in the Grands Crus fell to laughably low prices and the people who bought then were very well advised. New systems of protection against frost and the development of mechanisation brought the vineyards back from the brink.

The appellation covers an area of 6,834 ha (16,880 acres), a proportion of which lies in the commune of Chablis itself while the rest is distributed among 19 of its neighbours; 4,274 ha (10,557 acres) are presently planted with vines. Production was 255,922 hl (6,756,341 gal) in 2000. The vines cover the steeply sloping hills on both sides of the Serein, a small tributary flowing into the Yonne. At this latitude, a south-south-easterly aspect is best for the grapes to ripen well, but in some of the more favoured locations vines may be planted on slopes facing away from the sun as well as towards it. The soil is made up of Jurassic marl or Kimmeridge clay (the other end of the rim of this geological basin is in Dorset, England, which is why it has this name) or Portland stone, which is limestone. These are the perfect soils for growing white wines, and in the 12th century the Cistercian monks of the Abbey of Pontigny realised this, most likely planting Chardonnay, known locally as Beaunois. Here, more than anywhere else, Chardonnay shows off the finesse and elegance which make it a superlative accompaniment to seafood, snails or charcuterie. The Premiers and Grands Crus will complement the choicest foods: chicken, fine charcuterie, fowl or white meat dishes, especially those prepared with wine.

Petit Chablis

This appellation is at the bottom of the hierarchy of wines in the Chablis area. In 2000 33,023 hl (871,807 gal) of wine were produced. The Petit Chablis is less aromatically complex than Chablis, with a greater degree of acidity, which gives its flavour a quality of greenness. It used to be served by the carafe, in the year of harvest, but it is now bottled. Held back by its name, it initially had great difficulty in getting established in its own right, but today the consumer seems to take less and less account of the diminutive adjective 'Petit'.

DOM. BILLAUD-SIMON 1999★

0.3 ha 2,400 €5-8

A charming label graces the bottles of this quality estate which has produced a good 99. Pale yellow in colour with a lemony aroma, it is lively and full-bodied. A simple and straightforward wine, perfect with seafood dishes.

➡ Dom. Billaud-Simon, 1, quai de Reugny, BP 46, 89800 Chablis, tel. 03.86.42.10.33, fax 03.86.42.48.77 ☑ ev. day except Sat./Sun. 9am–6pm; cl. 15 Aug–1 Sep.

PASCAL BOUCHARD 2000★

3 ha 24,000 €5-8

Yellow as a painter's water-colour, this wine expresses itself truly on the palate. Rose and sweet briar scents vie for attention as its nose opens out. It has youth, vigour, character and originality, qualities not found in all wines. Try it as an accompaniment to raw fish.

➡ Pascal Bouchard, 5 bis, rue Porte-Noël, 89800 Chablis, tel. 03.86.42.18.64, fax 03.86.42.48.11, e-mail pascal.bouchard@wanadoo.fr ☑ ev. day 10am–12.30pm 2pm–7pm; cl. Jan.

DOM. CHEVALLIER 1999★

0.75 ha 2,400 €5-8

With one or two exceptions it is unlikely that the 99 vintage will keep well but anyway, why deprive oneself of the pleasure of drinking it now? The Chardonnay from this estate, which practices sustainable agriculture, is a brilliant green-gold colour and has vegetal and mineral qualities in equal measure. It is supple on the palate with good acidity.

➡ Dom. Chevallier, 6, rue de l'École, 89290 Montallery-Venoy, tel. 03.86.40.27.04, fax 03.86.40.27.05 ☑ by appt.

DOM. JEAN COLLET ET FILS

1999★

0.9 ha 7,300 €5-8

Not an exceptional wine but well defined; yellow-gold in colour with a fresh and original aroma of gooseberries. The citrus fruit and flint attack is characteristic of the appellation. The pronounced liveliness is guaranteed to coax a dozen snails out of their shells.

➡ Dom. Jean Collet et Fils, 15, av. de la Liberté, 89800 Chablis, tel. 03.86.42.11.93, fax 03.86.42.47.43, e-mail collet.chablis@wanadoo.fr ☑ ev. day except Sun. 9am–12 noon 2pm–5.30pm; cl. Aug.

➡ Gilles Collet

DOM. JEAN-CLAUDE COURTAULT 1999★

5.6 ha 5,100 €5-8

This estate was created in 1984, part-purchased and part-rented, a very modest domaine at the time, that today covers 14.30 ha (35.3 acres). This is a charming little wine, supple, fresh and easy to drink. Full and natural, it will be at its best during the next two years, preferably with a seafood platter.

➡ Jean-Claude Courtault, 1, rte de Montfort, 89800 Lignorelles, tel. 03.86.47.50.59, fax 03.86.47.50.74 ☑ by appt.

DOM. ERIC DAMPT

Vieilles Vignes 1999

3 ha 21,000 €5-8

Old vines and Petit Chablis are well-matched here, and its inevitably the little one that reaps the benefit. This well structured, rich, long wine needs some aeration and

might benefit from being decanted. It would go well with fish cooked in a sauce.
☛ Eric Dampt, 16, rue de l'Ancien-Presbytère, 89700 Collan, tel. 03.86.55.36.28, fax 03.86.54.49.89, e-mail eric.dampt@libertysurf.fr ▸
Y by appt.

DOM. HERVE DAMPT
Cuvée Louis de Beaumont 1999★★
1 ha   7,000   €5-8

The white-golden colour, with hints of beeswax and acacia produce a great opening for this wine. It is very authentic, with a sensation of honey and flowers, and was one of the finalists for the *coup de cœur*.
☛ EARL Hervé Dampt, rue de Fleys, 89700 Collan, tel. 03.86.55.29.55, fax 03.86.54.49.89 ▸ Y by appt.

AGNES ET DIDIER DAUVISSAT 1999★
2.3 ha   2,000   €5-8

After visiting the remains of a Gallo-Roman estate 5 km (3 miles) north of Beine, it is worth carrying on and discovering this wine, which is excellent in every way. Whether oenology or mineralogy is responsible is an interesting question since it is distinctly flinty. Consistent and very pleasant on the palate, a genuine Petit Chablis.
☛ EARL Agnès et Didier Dauvissat, chem. de Beauroy, 89800 Beine, tel. 03.86.42.46.40, fax 03.86.42.80.82 ▸
Y ev. day 9am–12 noon 2pm–7pm

RENE ET VINCENT DAUVISSAT 1999★
0.4 ha   3,500   €5-8

'It's quite simply a question of continuity,' said the Dauvissats, when asked about themselves and their vineyard. Their wine reflects this answer. Clear, intense, floral and supple, and although not a wine that will move mountains, it is accessible and quite lively. All in all, very nicely balanced and a popular choice. It has the classic Kimeridgian identity that wine experts write about. One taster suggested that it would go well with leek tart and tarragon sauce, and for once everybody agreed.
☛ GAEC René et Vincent Dauvissat, 8, rue Emile-Zola, 89800 Chablis, tel. 03.86.42.11.58, fax 03.86.42.85.32

JEAN-PAUL DROIN 1999★
1.3 ha   10,000   €8-11

Benoît Droin's family goes back as far as 1547 and represents the 13th generation to be associated with wine in the Chablis area. He produced this first vintage in 1999 … welcome to the *Guide*, Benoît! The colour of this attractive wine is very characteristic, its complex aromas, including mineral and pear, are delicate and subtle, and it has a lively character.
☛ Dom. Jean-Paul Droin, 14 bis, rue Jean-Jaurès, 89800 Chablis, tel. 03.86.42.16.78, fax 03.86.42.42.09 ▸
Y by appt.

DOM. D'ELISE 1999★
7.02 ha 10,000   €5-8

This wine is a of good standard and ready to drink, as it shows no sign of developing. It is light in colour with a nice mineral quality on the nose, iodised but not very fruity, a characteristic wine and a marvellous complement to mature goat's cheese.
☛ Frédéric Prain, Côte de Léchet, 89800 Milly, tel. 03.86.42.40.82, fax 03.86.42.44.76 ▸ Y by appt.

DOM. FELIX 1999
1.31 ha 11,000   €5-8

Hervé de Félix, who took over the family estate in 1987, presented this good Petit Chablis 99. It has a strong gold colour and a bouquet that begins on a note of citrus fruit and ends with touches of honey and dried fruit. On the palate, on the other hand, it gives a fresh, rounded fruitiness. Overall a balanced and elegant wine.
☛ Dom. Hervé Félix, 17, rue de Paris, 89530 Saint-Bris-le-Vineux, tel. 03.86.53.33.87, fax 03.86.53.61.64, e-mail felix@caves-particulieres.▸
Y ev. day except Sun. 9am–1.30pm 2pm–6.30pm

DOM. FOURREY ET FILS 2000★
0.5 ha   3,400   €5-8

This wine fermented in vat, straw-gold in colour with a fresh fruit aroma, has all the characteristics of young wines made in this way. There is body and richness; in a word, wine. A good match for cooked ham, in a few months' time.
☛ Dom. Fourrey et Fils, 6, rue du Château, Milly, 89800 Chablis, tel. 03.86.42.14.80, fax 03.86.42.84.78 ▸ Y by appt.

MAISON JEAN-CLAUDE FROMONT 1999★
n.c.   25,000

The Château de Ligny, built some years ago by a wine merchant established at Bercy, has belonged to the Fromont family since 1994. This Petit Chablis, rich gold in colour, emits tempting, flattering, buttery aromas and is a credit to the vintage. One of the tasters suggested serving it with green asparagus on a bed of oyster mushrooms dressed with hazelnut oil.
☛ Maison Jean-Claude Fromont, Ch. de Ligny, 7, av. de Chablis, 89144 Ligny-le-Châtel, tel. 03.86.98.20.40, fax 03.86.47.40.72, e-mail accueil@chateau-de-ligny.com ▸ Y by appt.

DOM. HAMELIN 1999★
5.73 ha 44,000   €5-8

On a stroll through the vineyards at Lignorelles you may come across an old lime kiln; here you could pay a visit to Thierry Hamelin and taste this Petit Chablis. Its assertive personality will enable it to be kept for two to three years. It is honest, direct, as mineral as need be and full of character. Not a wine that can be ignored. A perfect accompaniment to ham in a Chablis sauce.

EARL Thierry Hamelin.

1, rue des Carillons, 89800 Lignorelles, tel. 03.86.47.54.60, fax 03.86.47.53.34 ev. day except Wed./Sun. 9.15am–12.15pm 2pm–6pm; cl. Aug.

DOM. DES ILES 1999★★   5.5 ha   45,000   €5-8

When selecting a wine to nominate for a *coup de cœur*, one wouldn't hesitate to choose this one. Really well-made, it expresses the personality of the vineyard with its pale-yellow colour and sparkling brilliance. The concentration of aromas is significant, revealing fruit and finesse with an opulent body. This Petit Chablis has all the hallmarks of a Chablis.

Gérard Tremblay, 12, rue de Poinchy, 89800 Chablis, tel. 03.86.42.40.98, fax 03.86.42.44.41 ev. day except Sun. 8am–12 noon 1.30pm–5.30pm; Sat. by appt.; cl. Aug.

DOM. DE LA CONCIERGERIE 1999   0.4 ha   3,000   €5-8

Christian Adine, a wine-grower with 25 years' experience, still lives in the old caretaker's lodge at the Château de Courgis where he was born. This pale greenish-yellow 99 seems well-balanced, natural, fruity and mineral, with potential to improve.

EARL Christian Adine, 2, allée du Château, 89800 Courgis, tel. 03.86.41.40.28, fax 03.86.41.45.75, e-mail nicole.adine@ free.fr by appt.

DOM. DE LA MOTTE 2000★   2 ha   10,000   €5-8

There is a 13th-century church at Beine, and not far from the village an artificial lake of 15 ha (37 acres), which supplies water for spraying the vines to protect them from frost. This wine is proof that the system works. White-gold in colour with a bouquet of honeysuckle and citrus fruit, which develop on aeration, it is characteristic of the appellation. The most pleasant surprise is reserved for the palate where the wine displays good length and a mineral quality. It will certainly keep for a couple of years.

SCEA Dom. de La Motte, 41, rue du Ruisseau, 89800 Beine, tel. 03.86.42.43.71, fax 03.86.42.49.63 ev. day except Wed. 8am–12 noon 2pm–6pm

Michaut – Robin

DOM. DE L'ORME 1999   1.3 ha   10,000

Pale yellow, brilliant and clear, this wine is very attractive. The aroma is faint at first but slowly reveals some vegetal qualities. It is generous, powerful and long on the palate with touches of the *terroir*, and maturity.

Dom. de L'Orme, 16, rue de Chablis, 89800 Lignorelles, tel. 03.86.47.41.60, fax 03.86.47.56.66 by appt.

DOM. DES MALANDES 1999★   1.2 ha   10,200   €5-8

Here is an estate that has been given more *coups de cœur* in previous years than all the other AOC wines in the whole Chablis area. This wine has a good initial colour and a lively nose with strong floral aromas. Rich and full on the palate, it is a wine with breeding. More Chablis than Petit Chablis, which one can't complain about! It would go well with a cooked fish dish.

Dom. des Malandes, 63, rue Auxerroise, 89800 Chablis, tel. 03.86.42.41.37, fax 03.86.42.41.97, e-mail contact@ domainedesmalandes.com by appt.

Marchive

DOM. DES MARRONNIERS 2000   2.5 ha   n.c.   €5-8

A former *coup de cœur* winner, this estate is a fine example of a Chablis vineyard. This wine is expressive on the nose, lively on the palate and develops aromas of exotic fruit, spring flowers and grapefruit. It deserves to be enjoyed while still young and fresh.

Bernard Légland, Grande-Rue de Chablis, 89800 Préhy, tel. 03.86.41.42.70, fax 03.86.41.45.82 ev. day 9.30am–12 noon 1.30pm–7pm; cl. 15 Aug.–3 Sep.

SYLVAIN MOSNIER 1999   0.75 ha   6,000   €5-8

Already well-developed, so ready to drink now, this wine is rich and fruity. Its ripeness is apparent in the colour and in its aromas of crystallised fruit. The opening is full and pleasant, finishing on a lively note.

Sylvain Mosnier, 4, rue Derrière-les-Murs, 89800 Beine, tel. 03.86.42.43.96, fax 03.86.42.42.88 by appt.

DE OLIVEIRA LECESTRE 2000   6.95 ha   30,000   €5-8

In 1978 Jacky Chatelain joined the Lucien De Oliveira estate which now extends over 40 ha (99 acres). 7 ha (17.3 acres) of which are dedicated to producing wine in this appellation. This 2000 vintage is very light in colour and full of aromas. It is delicate on the palate with citrus fruit flavours. It definitely won't disappoint the oysters.

GAEC De Oliveira Lecestre, 11, Grand-Rue, 89800 Fontenay-près-Chablis, tel. 03.86.42.40.78, fax 03.86.42.83.72 ev. day except Sun. 10am–12 noon 2pm–7pm; cl. 15–30 Aug.

Jacky Chatelain

DOM. DE PISSE-LOUP 1999★★   2.13 ha   10,000   €5-8

Comté cheese or a salmon tartare … This is a mouth-watering wine and the tasters dreamed up a thousand things to go with it. Purest Chardonnay, intense gold in colour, with elegant and floral aromas, this 99 vintage has a good, rich mineral base. A member of the Jury wrote: 'If it were up to me it would be

Petit Chablis

nominated for a *coup de coeur*, an opinion endorsed by the Grand Jury.

☛ SCEA Jacques Hugot et Jean Michaut, 1, rue de la Poterne, 89800 Beine, tel. 03.80.97.04.67, fax 03.80.97.04.67 ■ **Y** by appt.

☛ Jean-Marc Brocard, 3, rte de Chablis, 89800 Préhy, tel. 03.86.41.49.00, fax 03.86.41.49.09, e-mail brocard@ brocard.fr ■ **Y** by appt.

FRANCINE ET OLIVIER SAVARY 1999★

| □ | 2.5 ha | 20,000 | ■ | €8-11 |

With its beautiful green-gold colour, this wine reflects the characteristics of the Abbey at Pontigny … it has a firm, austere nose with a hint of the aromatic herbs found in all monastery gardens. Fresh and fruity on the palate, however, it has certainly not taken any vows of chastity or poverty.

☛ Francine et Olivier Savary, 4, chem. des Hâtes, 89800 Maligny, tel. 03.86.47.42.09, fax 03.86.45.55.80 ■ **Y** by appt.

SIMONNET-FEBVRE 1999★

| □ | 1.2 ha | 5,300 | ■ | €5-8 |

Established in 1840, the estate is currently run by Laurent Simonnet, who has achieved perfection from start to finish with this wine. Very pale, like the complexion of the youthful Colette, this Chardonnay starts off fruity and finishes on honeysuckle. Its bold opening achieves a honeyed balance, which is gratifying. An attractive 99 vintage which, like Bayard, is fearless and beyond reproach.

☛ Simonnet-Febvre, 9, av. d'Oberwesel, BP 12, 89800 Chablis, tel. 03.86.98.99.00, fax 03.86.98.99.01, e-mail simonnet@ chablis.net ■ **Y** ev. day 8am–11.30am 2pm–6pm; Sat./Sun. by appt.

☛ Simonnet

DENIS POMMIER 1999★

| □ | 3.5 ha | 16,000 | ■ | €5-8 |

Not as small as all that, this Petit Chablis is as good as what was formerly known as Chablis-Village or Côte de Chablis. Very soft and balanced, this really nice wine shows its youth in its pale-gold colour. Its flinty aromas, fullness, freshness and vinosity blend together on the palate with length and balance.

☛ Denis Pommier, 31, rue de Poinchy, 89800 Chablis, tel. 03.86.42.83.04, fax 03.86.42.17.80, e-mail denis.pommier@ liberty-surf.fr ■ **Y** ev. day 9am–12 noon 2pm–8pm; Sun. by appt.; cl. 24 Aug.–1 Sep.

DOM. JACKY RENARD 1999

| □ | 1.67 ha | n.c. | ■ | €5-8 |

A wine that is in no hurry, and well worth waiting for. Yellow-gold with straw highlights and hinting at dried figs and raisins, it is opulent rather than lively, suggesting a touch of overripeness in the grape. Not a wine to choose if you are looking for freshness, it is imposing and destined to accompany an innovative dish.

☛ Jacky Renard, La Côte-de-Chaussan, 89530 Saint-Bris-le-Vineux, tel. 03.86.53.38.58, fax 03.86.53.33.50 ■ **Y** by appt.

DOM. SAINTE-CLAIRE 1999★★

| □ | n.c. | n.c. | ■ | €5-8 |

No point in asking if the Petit Chablis will one day grow up, as it is already fully-grown, with a *coup de coeur* behind it! Jean-Marc Brocard has put on a very good show with this lively 99. Young and impulsive, this lightly-coloured, flowery wine with a touch of oak would go splendidly with a good helping of langoustines and artichokes in balsamic vinegar.

DOM. YVON VOCORET 1999★★

| □ | 3 ha | 7,900 | ■ | €5-8 |

After signing the visitors' book, if you are offered nothing more than this Petit Chablis to taste, your journey to this estate will have been well worthwhile. Rounded and very vinous, it is a match for some Chablis. A good gold-yellow colour, fruity and mineral, it is natural, full, and fine with good length.

☛ Dom. Yvon Vocoret, 9, chem. de Beaune, 89800 Maligny, tel. 03.86.47.51.60, fax 03.86.47.57.47 ■ **Y** ev. day 8am–7pm; Sun. by appt.

Chablis

In 2000 171,309 hl (4,522,558 gal) of Chablis were produced. This wine owes its inimitable qualities of freshness and lightness to the soils from which it springs. Ill-suited to cold and rainy years, when it acquires too much acidity, in warm years it gains a refreshing quality lacking in the Côte d'Or Chardonnays. It should be drunk young (in one to three years) but can be left to age for up to ten years or more, when it gains in complexity and in the richness of its bouquet.

DOM. DES AIRELLES 1999
11 ha | 5,000 | €5-8

There is an interesting 15th-century statue of the Virgin and Child in the church of Saint-Martin at Chichée. Here Thierry and Didier Robin have produced a classic wine which, although still young and lively in April 2001, was well-made enough to fulfil its potential with a well-balanced, dominant mineral tone against a floral background.
↠ Dom. des Airelles, 40, Grande-Rue, 89800 Chichée, tel. 03.86.42.80.49, fax 03.86.42.85.40 ☑ by appt.
↠ Jean Robin

DOM. BACHELIER
Vieilles vignes 1999★
1 ha | 6,283 | €6-11

The Bachelier family's history of wine-making goes back to 1833. Fifty-year-old vines have given this wine its brilliant, sunlit clarity and an open fruitiness with some mineral tones. A handsome, flawless 99 that has definite style, with crystallised fruit and a pepperiness resulting, perhaps, from the age of the vines. A wine to lay down.
↠ Dom. Bachelier, 13, rue Saint-Etienne, 89800 Villy, tel. 03.86.47.49.56, fax 03.86.47.57.96 ☑ by appt.

DOM. BESSON 2000
5.9 ha | 4,500 | €5-8

The colour is typical of the AOC: spring flowers and the freshness are in context. At first lively, then very dense, with a hint of bitterness, this poetic wine will age without the trace of a wrinkle over the next couple of years.
↠ EARL Dom. Alain Besson, rue de Valvan, 89800 Chablis, tel. 03.86.42.19.53, fax 03.86.42.49.46 ☑ by appt.

BLASONS DE BOURGOGNE 2000★
40 ha | 250,000 | €5-8

La Chablisienne makes wine from 1,100 ha (2,717 acres) of vineyards. In this lively and spirited wine, pleasant notes of mineral, honey and flowers are well balanced by good acidity and richness. Good to keep for three or four years. Another Chablis, **Laurent Dupaquis Le Millénium 98**, was also awarded a star.
↠ La Chablisienne, 8, bd Pasteur, BP 14, 89800 Chablis, tel. 03.86.42.89.89, fax 03.86.42.89.90, e-mail chab@chablisienne.com ☑
☑ ev. day 9am-12 noon 2pm-6pm

PASCAL BOUCHARD Grande Réserve du Domaine Vieilles vignes 1998★★
10 ha | 80,000 | €8-11

This estate often appears in the *Guide* and is no stranger to the *coup de cœur*. Made from their own *vieilles vignes*, matured for eight months in vat (30% of the harvest spends four months in oak), this 98 vintage is not just good, but a very high class wine. It has a strong yellow colour with green highlights, and a very clean bouquet that abounds in fruit. A fresh initial impact is followed by butteriness in a wine impressive both for its complexity and for its great potential.
↠ Pascal Bouchard, 5 bis, rue Porte-Noël, 89800 Chablis, tel. 03.86.42.18.64, fax 03.86.42.48.11, e-mail pascal.bouchard@wanadoo.fr ☑
☑ ev. day 10am-12.30pm 2pm-7pm; cl. Jan.

MADAME EDMOND CHALMEAU 1999★
2 ha | 12,000 | €5-8

The curtain goes up on honey and hawthorn blossom against a backdrop of pale yellow. Then the plot reveals a strong mineral theme sprinkled with spring flowers. Light and supple, it is very characteristic and stays true to its appellation. Marketed under the name of **Franck Chalmeau** (same telephone number and address, and in the same price bracket), a **Chablis 99** bears a strong resemblance to the first one.
↠ Mme Edmond Chalmeau, 20, rue du Ruisseau, 89530 Chitry-le-Fort, tel. 03.86.41.42.09, fax 03.86.41.46.84 ☑ by appt.

Chablis

DOM. DE CHANTEMERLE 1999★★ ☐ ■ €5-8

☐   11 ha   75,000

This estate could have lived out the rest of its days on the reputation of its famous Premier Cru, Homme Mort, but it has chosen to produce this remarkable Chablis as well. Light in colour with green highlights, fresh and mineral, it reflects its *terroir*. On the palate, it is everything one would expect. Don't lose any time as the price is very competitive. Parchment-style label.

➤ SCEA de Chantemerle, 27, rue du Serein, 89800 La Chapelle-Vaupelteigne,
tel. 03.86.42.18.95, fax 03.86.42.81.60 ▼
▼ by appt.
➤ Francis Boudin

DOM. DES CHENEVIÈRES 1999★★ ☐ ♦ €5-8

☐   7.5 ha   50,000

There are enough Tremblays in the Chablis area to fill the local telephone directory. Here we have one Bernard Tremblay assisted by Thierry Mothe, another local name. This lovely 99 vintage has a clear gold colour. The mineral aromas are as cool as antique marble and very pleasing to the palate; a wine that is serious, elegant and distinguished at the same time.

➤ Bernard Tremblay, Dom. des Chenevières, 1, rue des Vignes, 89800 La Chapelle-

Vaupelteigne, tel. 03.86.42.41.00, fax 03.86.42.48.08 ▼ ▼ by appt.

DOM. CHRISTOPHE ET FILS 1999★★ ☐ ■ €5-8

☐   0.33 ha   1,500

This name came up whilst selecting winners of the *coup de cœur*. The wine's delicate colour is flecked with pale tones and its nose is both floral and mineral. On the palate it is as serene and calm as the river Serein, rather imposing but always interesting. Not bad for a first wine! Their **Chablis Vieilles Vignes 99** was awarded a star, together with the incontestable and final comment: 'I like this wine!'

➤ Dom. Christophe et Fils, Ferme des Carrières, Fyé, 89800 Chablis,
tel. 03.86.55.23.10, fax 03.86.55.23.10 ▼
▼ by appt.

LA CAVE DU CONNAISSEUR 1999★ ☐ €5-8

☐   7 ha   40,000

Bis dat qui cito dedit: he who gives quickly gives twice. This very lively and direct wine does just that as it juggles aromas of herbs and green apples. Straw-yellow tinged with green, it is sure to develop well, having already acquired flavours rich in apricots, spring flowers and ferns. This relatively new

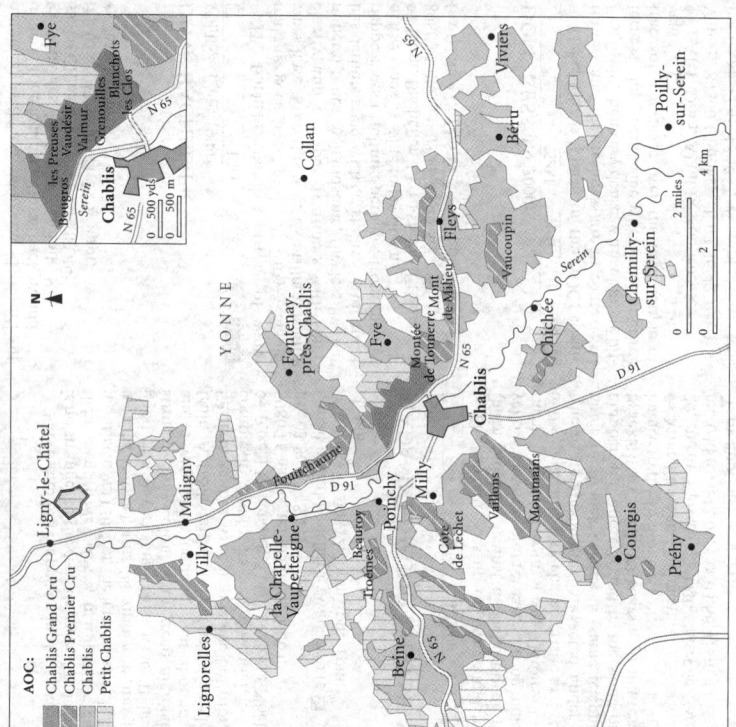

AOC:
- Chablis Grand Cru
- Chablis Premier Cru
- Chablis
- Petit Chablis

Chablis

company (1989) is installed in 12th- and 13th-century cellars.

♠ La Cave du Connaisseur,
rue des Moulins, BP 78, 89800 Chablis,
tel. 03.86.42.87.15, fax 03.86.42.49.84,
e-mail connaisseur@chablis.net ✓
Ⓣ ev. day 10am–6pm

DOM. BERNARD DEFAIX 1999★★

| 12 ha | 80,000 | ■ ♦ | €8–11 |

This attractive 99 offers us near-perfection for the vintage. A pale colour, but this is preferable to one obtained from a rapid and excessively forceful extraction. The nose, although not yet fully-developed, is nicely buttery and mineral when the wine is exposed to the air. The palate is fine and elegant; a clean wine that will remain superb for a long time.

♠ Dom. Bernard Defaix,
17, rue du Château, Milly, 89800 Chablis,
tel. 03.86.42.40.75, fax 03.86.42.40.28,
e-mail didier@bernard-defaix.com ✓
Ⓣ by appt.

DOM. JOSEPH ET XAVIER GARNIER 1999★★★

| 2.5 ha | 20,000 | ■ | €5–8 |

An aperitif wine, best appreciated on its own. Active and lively, its turbulent nature doesn't overpower the classic Chablis aromas of flint, spring flowers and toasted almonds. Very consistent, and already very pleasant to drink, it will keep until the middle of the decade.

♠ Dom. Garnier et Fils, chem. de Méré,
89144 Ligny-le-Châtel, tel. 03.86.47.47.12,
fax 03.86.98.09.95, e-mail domainegarnier@terre-net.fr ✓ Ⓣ by appt.

DOM. DES GENEVES

Vieilles vignes 1999★

| 0.6 ha | 4,800 | ■ | €5–8 |

This one is so appealing it almost merits an extra star. Pale yellow and light gold, green apples and lemons, just as it should be! This wine gives a flawless performance on the palate and has body and personality. Ham cooked with Chablis would seem the ideal partner for it.

♠ EARL Dom. des Genèves, 3, rte des Fourneaux, 89800 Fleys, tel. 03.86.42.10.15,
fax 03.86.42.47.34 Ⓣ by appt.
♠ Dominique Aufrère et Fils

DOM. GRAND ROCHE 2000★

| 6.5 ha | 40,000 | ■ | €5–8 |

The colour is pure Chablis ... and isn't honesty the best policy? It opens with ripe fruit and flowers followed by a slight over-ripeness. With a good combination of vivacity and richness of body, it will keep well.

♠ Erick Lavallée, Dom. Grand Roche,
6, rte de Chitry, 89530 Saint-Bris-le-Vineux,
tel. 03.86.53.84.07, fax 03.86.53.88.36 ✓
Ⓣ by appt.

THIERRY HAMELIN

Vieilles vignes 1999★★★

| 1.2 ha | 7,130 | ■ ♦ | €8–11 |

Primus inter pares, first among equals, this wine triumphed in the final for the *coup de cœur* while its companion, the *coup de cœur* 99, was classed as a normal *cuvée* on its own. What can be said about these two wines? The first is already quite strong in colour and offers a highly complex nose with playful aromas of spring flowers, dried fruits and minerals. All these flavours come through on the palate, rich and fresh at the same time. A wine with character to be reserved for a special meal. The green-gold colour of the second wine is dazzling and its typical flavours make it a great ambassador for Chablis wines.

♠ Dom. Thierry Hamelin,
1, imp. de la Grappe, 89800 Lignorelles,
tel. 03.86.47.52.79, fax 03.86.47.53.41 ✓
Ⓣ by appt.

DOM. DES HERITIERES 1999

| 4.5 ha | 36,000 | ■ ♦ | €8–11 |

This one is sufficiently full-bodied to be worth inviting to join you and your friends for roast veal with morel mushrooms. Although not particularly a good example of its kind, because it lacks that mineral note, it is subtle, balanced, fleshy and has enough length to be a good guest.

♠ Olivier Tricon, 15, rue de Chichée,
89800 Chablis, tel. 03.86.42.10.37,
fax 03.86.42.49.13

DOM. DES ILES 1999★

| 16 ha | 125,000 | ■ ♦ | €5–8 |

Good to look at, a good nose and starts out at a good pace. It is not a particularly exotic wine and more in tune with the authentic mineral tones of Chablis. A powerful wine, to be opened a year or two from now.

♠ Gérard Tremblay,
12, rue de Poinchy, 89800 Chablis,
tel. 03.86.42.40.98, fax 03.86.42.40.41 ✓
Ⓣ ev. day except Sun. 8am–12 noon 1.30pm–5.30pm; Sat. by appt., cl. Aug.

PIERRE JANNY 1999★

☐ n.c. 10,000 ▮ ♦ €8-11

Having transferred from Lyon to Chablis, this *négociant-éleveur* from the Mâconnais has a great affinity for the wines of Burgundy and Beaujolais. Although he is far from his home base, he is very intuitive, and presented a lively 99 vintage that asserts itself from start to gun-flint finish. Bright rather than coloured, the wine opens with citrus fruit and leaves the palate feeling satisfied. A wine worth keeping for two or three years.

☛ Sté Pierre Janny, La Condemine, Cidex 1556, 71260 Péronne, tel. 03.85.23.96.20, fax 03.85.36.96.58, e-mail pierre-janny@wanadoo.fr

DOM. DE LA MEULIERE 1999★★

☐ 8 ha 36,000 ▮ ♦ €5-8

When this well-balanced wine has softened a little it will be perfect. Green-gold in colour, it hits the spot with its direct fruitiness, mineral tones and well-balanced acidity. A good finish of ripe fruit.

☛ Chantal et Claude Laroche, Dom. de La Meulière, 18, rte de Mont-de-Milieu, 89800 Fleys, tel. 03.86.42.13.56, fax 03.86.42.19.32 ▼ by appt.

DOM. DE LA MOTTE
Vieilles vignes 1999★

☐ 1.3 ha 10,000 ▮ ♦ €8-11

An Epoisses (a Burgundian cheese) would be a good match for this wine, which displays all the usual Chardonnay hallmarks, without concealing the mark of its *terroir*: a mineral note on the nose which runs right through to the finish on the palate. Its freshness is positively inviting.

☛ SCEA Dom. de la Motte, 41, rue du Ruisseau, 89800 Beine, tel. 03.86.42.43.71, fax 03.86.42.49.63 ▼ ev. day except Wed. 8am–12 noon 2pm–6pm
☛ Michaut-Robin

DOM. LAROCHE Saint-Martin 1999★

☐ 61.57 ha 3,000 ▮ ♦ €11-15

Négociant and grower Michel Laroche is one of the prominent figures in the Chablis area. He presented three wines from his estates and all were awarded a star, the **Château de Chemilly 99** for its *cuvée normale* and its *cuvée* **Vieilles Vignes**, the first being very characteristic, the second mineral with overtones of dogrose, much richer and with less *terroir* character. Finally to this Saint-Martin, with its white-gold colour shot through with flecks of green, subtle with lasting aromas. It is well-made and a good example of its kind.

☛ Michel Laroche, 22, rue Louis-Bro, BP 33, 89800 Chablis, tel. 03.86.42.89.28, fax 03.86.42.89.29, e-mail info@ michellaroche.com ▼ ▼ by appt.

LES CAVES DE LA VERVELLE 1999★★

☐ 0.4 ha 2,700 ▮ ▮ ♦ €8-11

The members of this co-operative at Bligny-les-Beaune took second place on the podium. A real distinction for these prophets of Chablis! Harmonious and very open, this 99 vintage is beauty itself. A touch of oak brings out its silky purity. Richness goes hand in hand with finesse, combined with a strong floral personality of spring flowers. Ideal with grilled salmon in a dill sauce.

☛ Ch. de Bligny-les-Beaune, Caves de la Vervelle, le Château, 21200 Bligny-les-Beaune, tel. 03.80.21.47.38, fax 03.80.21.40.27 ▼ ▼ ev. day 8am–12 noon 2pm–6pm

DOM. DE L'EGLANTIERE 1999

☐ 50 ha 270,000 ▮ ♦ €8-11

Owner of 170 ha (419 acres) and a prominent figure in the Chablis vineyards, Jean Durup has played a major role in their development. He has produced a very characteristic wine, classic greenish-yellow in colour with a nose combining citrus fruits, spring flowers and flint. Not terribly lively on the palate but very pleasant.

☛ SA Jean Durup Père et Fils, 4, Grande-Rue, 89800 Maligny, tel. 03.86.47.44.49, fax 03.86.47.55.49, e-mail durup@club-internet.fr ▼

DOM. LONG-DEPAQUIT 1999★

☐ 22 ha 150,000 ▮ ♦ €6-11

Coming from a vineyard once belonging to the Cistercian abbey at Pontigny, this wine is typical of one from the Kimeridgean clay sub-soil. The clear, brilliant, pale-yellow colour is flecked with gold and judging by the nose, it will be a few months before the wine's strong mineral notes and liveliness unite successfully. The well-balanced palate promises three to four years of enjoyment.

☛ Ch. Long-Depaquit, 45, rue Auxerroise, 89800 Chablis, tel. 03.86.42.11.13, fax 03.86.42.81.89, e-mail longdepaquit@ wanadoo.fr ▼ ▼ ev. day except Sun. 9am–12.30pm 1pm–6pm
☛ Albert Bichot

DOM. DES MALANDES
Cuvée Tour du Roy Vieilles vignes 1999★

1.5 ha | 9,000 | €8-11

Winner of a *coup de cœur* several times in recent years, this estate is one of the corner-stones of the Chablis area. The colour of this 99 vintage is quite pale but bright, and the nose is fruity and mineral. Well-proportioned on the palate, it is a very well-made and characteristic *village* wine. The estate received a mention for its **Chablis 99** from an unnamed *cuvée*.

• Dom. des Malandes, 63, rue Auxerroise, 89800 Chablis, tel. 03.86.42.41.37, fax 03.86.42.41.97, e-mail contact@domainedesmalandes.com ⊻ ⊻ by appt.
• Marchive

DOM. LOUIS MOREAU 1999★★

24 ha | 60,000 | €8-11

This family-owned estate established in 1970, today covers 40 ha (99 acres) and exports 85% of its wine. Its flagship Chablis is superb, flamboyant and has a good future. First impressions are very pleasant and continue through to the finish; it displays a certain vigour but retains a characteristic harmony throughout.

• Louis Moreau,
10, Grande-Rue, 89800 Beine,
tel. 03.86.42.87.20, fax 03.86.42.45.59,
e-mail domaine.louismoreau@wanadoo.fr ⊻ ev. day 8am–12 noon 1.30pm–6pm; Sat. Sun. by appt.

DOM. ALAIN PAUTRE 1999★

10 ha | 40,000 | €5-8

A touch of originality is always welcome. This wine is certainly different with its flavours of underripe exotic fruit and grapefruit, developing into notes of orange and mint. Original, as we said and an ideal wine to fascinate connoisseurs.

• Alain Pautré, SCEA de Ronsien,
23, rue de Chablis, 89800 Lignorelles,
tel. 03.86.47.43.04, fax 03.86.47.46.54 ⊻

DOM. DE PERDRYCOURT
Cuvée Prestige 1999★

1 ha | 8,000 | €8-11

Established in 1987, this estate is jointly managed by Arlette Coury and her daughter Virginie. Appearance, nose, palate ... everything fine, as one writes on postcards. This wine's fruity freshness doesn't detract from its

DE OLIVEIRA LECESTRE 2000★

26.75 ha | 80,000 | €5-8

This distinguished 2000 has an ideal colour and its audacious aromas hold nothing back. Rich, lengthy enough and with reasonable body. To be enjoyed over the next two years.

• GAEC De Oliveira Lecestre,
11, Grand-Rue, 89800 Fontenay-près-Chablis,
tel. 03.86.42.40.78, fax 03.86.42.83.72 ⊻ ev. day except Sun. 10am–12 noon 2pm–7pm; cl. 15–30 Aug
• Jacky Chatelain

FRANCINE ET OLIVIER SAVARY
Sélection Vieilles vignes 1999★

1 ha | 8,000 | €8-11

If you haven't been here for a few years, you will discover some new stone cellars, vaulted in the old style. Everything about this 99 vintage is restrained: its pale colour, its nose of apricot and citrus fruit. When it comes to the palate, discretion is set aside; this is a responsive, full and well-balanced wine with good acidity. Six months in oak have not masked the fine mineral characteristics of Chablis.

• Francine et Olivier Savary, 4, chem. des Hâtes, 89800 Maligny, tel. 03.86.47.42.09, fax 03.86.45.55.80 ⊻ ⊻ by appt.

DOM. SEGUINOT-BORDET
Vieilles vignes 1999★★

10.5 ha | 3,000 | €8-11

The grandson took over this estate from his grandfather in 1998 and he certainly knows his job. His lovely 99 vintage was among the finalists in our tasting. Its gold colour is accompanied by a nose of linden flowers and flint. The mineral quality characteristic of this area of *Exogyra virgula* (sub-soil of fossilised shells) is what makes the wine supple, pleasant, concentrated and radiant on the palate. The wine-maker has achieved a good balance between the natural acidity and ripeness of the grapes. A worthy wine to serve with snails.

well-balanced body. It is a pale green-gold colour and respects the character of the appellation with its flowery apple, pear and mineral tones.

• EARL Arlette et Virginie Coury,
Dom. de Perdrycourt, 9, voie Romaine,
89230 Montigny-la-Resle,
tel. 03.86.41.82.07, fax 03.86.41.87.89,
e-mail domainecoury@wanadoo.fr ⊻ ev. day 8am–8pm

REGNARD 1998★

15 ha | 100,000 | €11-15

In 1984 Patrick de Ladoucette took over this firm in the Chablis area. Pale gold in colour with golden highlights, this wine has floral and mineral notes that last on the palate. Lively and balanced, it has all the Chablis characteristics.

• Régnard, 28, bd Tacussel, 89800 Chablis,
tel. 03.86.42.10.45, fax 03.86.42.48.67 ⊻ by appt.

DOM. DE PISSE-LOUP 1999★

2.1 ha | 2,000 | €5-8

Romuald Hugot has made a very attractive pale-gold wine. At first, the nose opens on ripe grapes and gunflint, then acacia and citrus fruit come to the fore in a fresh and balanced context. A wine to accompany any kind of grilled fish.

• Romuald Hugot, 30, rte Nationale, 89800 Beine, tel. 03.86.42.85.11, fax 03.86.42.85.11 ⊻ ⊻ by appt.

☛ Dom. Vocoret et Fils, 40, rte d'Auxerre, 89800 Chablis, tel. 03.86.42.12.53, fax 03.86.42.10.39, e-mail domainevocoret@wanadoo.fr ⊠ ⟡ by appt.

Chablis Premier Cru

Chablis Premier Cru comes from around thirty locations selected for their situation and the quality of their wines. They produced 45,968 hl (1,213,555 gal) in 2000. The comparison with Chablis lies chiefly in the Premier Cru's complex and lingering bouquet, the aromas offering a mixture of acacia honey, a touch of iodine and hints of vegetation. The amount produced per hectare is limited to 50 hl (1,320 gal per acre). All the winemakers agree that Chablis Premier Cru reaches a peak in its fifth year when it takes on a distinctive 'hazelnut' note. The most substantial examples are produced by the *climats* of La Montée de Tonnerre, Fourchaume, Mont de Milieu, Forêt, Butteaux and Côte de Léchet.

DOM. DES AIRELLES
Vaucoupin 1999   €8-11

1.2 ha   3,660   ⊞ ♦

Well-made but reserved, its colour is crystalline yellow-gold. The nose is fleeting, with buttery tones and tinges of acacia flowers. The attack is enough to make one believe in miracles: a mineral and fruity density, finishing with a touch of alcohol and bitterness. Thierry and Didier Robin took over their father's vineyard in 1996 and established the Domaine des Airelles the same year. It is situated on the right bank of Chichée.
☛ Dom. des Airelles, 40, Grande-Rue, 89800 Chichée, tel. 03.86.42.80.49, fax 03.86.42.85.40 ⊠ ⟡ by appt.
☛ Jean Robin

DOM. BARAT Vaillons 1999★★
€11-15

3 ha   15,000   ⊞ ♦

This estate unveiled a wide range of Premiers Crus: **Les Fourneaux**, **Mont de Milieu** and **Côte de Léchet 99** were all warmly praised. Heading the list is the Vaillons which was awarded another star ... and a *coup de cœur*. Very intense and full of finesse, mineral

☛ Roger Séguinot-Bordet, 4, rue de Méré, 89800 Maligny, tel. 03.86.47.44.42, fax 03.86.47.54.94, e-mail j.f.bordet@wanadoo.fr ⊠ ⟡ ev. day except Sun. 8am–6pm; Sat. 8am–12 noon; cl. 15 Aug.–1 Sep.

DOM. DE VAUDON★
6.9 ha   36,000   ⊞ €11-15

This company, from the Rue d'Enfer at Beaune needs no introduction. It owns 35 ha (86.5 acres) in the Chablis area and this wine comes from its own vineyards. Light gold in colour, it has a very pure nose, floral, mineral with a hint of honey. Well-balanced, rich and quite full-bodied, it is enhanced by delicate aromas and has good length. It is already very pleasant but will improve if kept for a while.
☛ Joseph Drouhin, 7, rue d'Enfer, 21200 Beaune, tel. 03.80.24.68.88, fax 03.80.22.43.14, e-mail maisondrouhin@drouhin.com ⟡ by appt.

DOM. DE VAUROUX
Vieilles vignes 1999★★   €8-11

3 ha   25,000   ⊞ ♦

If this wine were an ice-skater it would get full marks in the compulsory figures section. It has a bright golden colour and aromas of peach and hawthorn blossom with a mineral quality. It would also do pretty well in the free-skating section, with its programme including all the difficult movements impeccably performed from start to finish. Classy and extremely lively, it is a worthy representative of its flag. The *cuvée normale* of the **Village 99** was singled out by the Jury.
☛ SCEA Dom. de Vauroux, rte d'Avallon, BP 56, 89800 Chablis, tel. 03.86.42.10.37, fax 03.86.42.49.13 ⊠ ⟡ by appt.

DOM. VERRET 1999★★
2.4 ha   12,000   ⊞ €8-11

When the nose reaches the same heights as the palate this will be a very fine wine. Its complexity is already remarkable, suggesting pistachio nuts and lemon. Its structure and length will mature well, thanks to its good strong acidity. To quote Rabelais: '*lever matine n'est point bonheur, boire matin est le meilleur*' (there is no pleasure in early rising, drinking in the morning is the best), and for sheer pleasure this is just the wine to drink before lunch.
☛ Dom. Verret, 7, rte de Champs, BP 4, 89530 Saint-Bris-le-Vineux, tel. 03.86.53.31.81, fax 03.86.53.89.61, e-mail bruno.verret@wanadoo.fr ⊠ ⟡ by appt.

DOM. VOCORET ET FILS 1999★   €5-8
28 ha   140,000   ⊞⊞⊞ ♦

This wine's crystalline colour pleases from the start. The nose surprises with its aromas of very ripe exotic fruits and then the palate takes over, lively, clean and still developing. One of our tasters, who is an excellent wine merchant, thought that in a year or two this wine could well find a place on a restaurant's wine list.

Chablis Premier Cru

thought of that! The Mont de Milieu deserves its place among the great Premiers Crus. A hint of green in its soft yellow colour, a lemony, flinty nose, and a richness to round off the acidity. The *terroir* is clearly evident, and not overshadowed by the oak.
➤ Dom. du Chardonnay,
Moulin du Patis, 89800 Chablis,
tel. 03.86.42.48.03, fax 03.86.42.16.49,
e-mail domaine.chardonnay@free.fr ✓
Y by appt.

DOM. DU COLOMBIER
Fourchaume 1999★★ | 2.3 ha 15,000 €8-11

Fourchaume, extending towards the north of the Côte du Grand Cru, is perhaps the Prince of the Premiers Crus. Pale-yellow in colour with attractive green highlights, it opens with rocky minerals. Matured in vat, not oak, it is well made and characteristic, with a freshness and vigour that create an impressive harmony. Would go well with fillets of red mullet. The **Vaucoupin 99** was also awarded two stars.
➤ Dom. du Colombier,
Guy Mothe et ses Fils, 42, Grand-Rue,
89800 Fontenay-près-Chablis,
tel. 03.86.42.15.04, fax 03.86.42.49.67 ✓

LA CAVE DU CONNAISSEUR
Montmains 1999★ | 0.9 ha 3,500 €11-15

Why not do as Henry IV did and drink this Montmains with coq au vin? Or, as another taster suggested, with scallops cooked in cream ... Indeed, this full-flavoured 99 wine is suitable for drinking throughout a meal. It has a strong yellow colour and brims over with aromas of grapefruit and toast.
➤ La Cave du Connaisseur,
rue des Moulins, BP 78, 89800 Chablis,
tel. 03.86.42.87.15, fax 03.86.42.49.84,
e-mail connaisseur@chablis.net ✓
Y ev. day 10am–6pm

DOM. DANIEL DAMPT
Les Vaillons 1999★ | 5 ha 25,000 €11-15

Wines from Chablis and Beaune should not be too yellow, and indeed this 99 is not. It has fairly austere mineral notes but is nicely softened by the aroma of spring flowers, and should open out quickly. A perfect contrast to the flavour of sea-fish.
➤ Dom. Daniel Dampt,
1, rue des Violettes, 89800 Milly-Chablis,
tel. 03.86.42.47.23, fax 03.86.42.46.41,
e-mail domaine.dampt.defaix@wanadoo.fr ✓ Y by appt.

JEAN DAUVISSAT Montmains 1998★★
1.22 ha 10,000 €11-15

This agreeable Montmains 98 would go very well with freshwater fish. Light-yellow in colour and very mineral, it has strayed slightly off the beaten track with exotic

---

as tradition demands, we are definitely dealing with one of the best *climats* on the left bank (near Milly).
➤ EARL Dom. Barat, 6, rue de Léchet, Milly, 89800 Chablis, tel. 03.86.42.40.07, fax 03.86.42.47.88 ✓ Y by appt.

DOM. BILLAUD-SIMON
Fourchaume 1999★★★ | 0.25 ha 2,000

This one came top in the tasting with a unanimous *coup de coeur*; in fact the whole Jury put it in first place. What more is there to say? This classic Fourchaume has all the quality of a Premier Cru and is better than some Grand Cru wines. The **Montée de Tonnerre 99** was awarded two stars, the **Les Vaillons** and the **Mont de Milieu** one star each.
➤ Dom. Billaud-Simon, 1, quai de Reugny, BP 46, 89800 Chablis, tel. 03.86.42.10.33, fax 03.86.42.48.77 ✓ Y ev. day except Sat. Sun. 9am–6pm; cl. 15 Aug–1 Sep.

PASCAL BOUCHARD Beauroy 1999★
n.c. 75,000 €11-15

Formerly very sought-after but less well known nowadays, the name Beauroy is synonymous with a legendary Premier Cru. This pure gold 99 has a nose that opens with ripe fruit, making a good impression on the palate. Its length is well above average.
➤ Pascal Bouchard, 5 bis, rue Porte-Noël, 89800 Chablis, tel. 03.86.42.18.64, fax 03.86.42.48.11, e-mail pascal.bouchard@wanadoo.fr ✓ Y every day 10am–12.30pm 2pm–7pm; cl. Jan.

DOM. DU CHARDONNAY
Mont de Milieu 1999★ | 0.41 ha 2,400 €11-15

Calling itself Domaine du Chardonnay is indeed an inspired idea ... who would have

493

Chablis Premier Cru

touches such as passion-fruit. These aromas are followed through on the palate, with infinite freshness and charm.

☛ Caves Jean Dauvissat, 3, rue de Chichée, 89800 Chablis, tel. 03.86.42.14.62, fax 03.86.42.45.54, e-mail jean.dauvissat@terre-net.fr ⚑ Y by appt.

RENE ET VINCENT DAUVISSAT
Vaillons 1999★

☐   1.3 ha   11,000   🍾 €11-15

If you are in a hurry, choose the **Séchet 99**, which impressed the Jury and is ready for drinking now. If you have more time, take this fresh Vaillon 99 with its aromas of mousseron mushrooms and fruit. It is elegantly structured, quite lively and shows early signs of the appellation's characteristics which will become even more evident in a couple of years.

☛ GAEC René et Vincent Dauvissat, 8, rue Emile-Zola, 89800 Chablis, tel. 03.86.42.11.58, fax 03.86.42.85.32

DOM. DANIEL-ETIENNE DEFAIX-AU VIEUX CHATEAU
Vaillon 1997★★

☐   3 ha   9,000   🍾 €15-23

This estate was very proud to present the Vaillon 97 for tasting here as they are one of the few that market four- to eight-year-old wines. A good year showing a lot of maturity, this wine has subtle tones of honey and crystallised orange among the aromas of mousseron mushrooms. The mineral notes on the palate reflect a good, well-integrated *terroir* quality. It is developed and liable to improve further, given the chance.

☛ Daniel-Etienne Defaix, Au Vieux-Château, 14, rue Auxerroise, BP 50, 89800 Chablis, tel. 03.86.42.42.05, fax 03.86.42.48.56, e-mail chateau@chablisdefaix.com ⚑ Y ev. day 9am–12 noon 2pm–6pm; cl. 1 Jan.–15 Feb.

JEAN-PAUL DROIN Vaillons 1999★★

☐   4.8 ha   38,000   🍾 🍾 ◆ €11-15

and the vat work well together. The wine has superb presence, both on the nose which is fragrant, concentrated and elegant, and on the palate, where all these characteristics are recognized within a very promising structure.

☛ Dom. Jean-Paul Droin, 14 bis, rue Jean-Jaurès, 89800 Chablis, tel. 03.86.42.16.78, fax 03.86.42.42.09 ⚑ Y by appt.

JOSEPH DROUHIN Vaillons 1999★★

☐   2.2 ha   15,000   🍾 €15-23

This wine's colour is typical of the whiteness of Chablis, and the nose has aromas of peach, flower and honey. The first impression, which is clean and open, ends with a balance between richness and a good acidity. The mineral quality will probably take two or three years to develop, or perhaps even longer.

☛ Joseph Drouhin, 7, rue d'Enfer, 21200 Beaune, tel. 03.80.24.68.88, fax 03.80.22.43.14, e-mail maisondrouhin@drouhin.com ⚑ Y by appt.

GERARD DUPLESSIS
Montée de Tonnerre 1999★★

☐   1.2 ha   6,000   🍾 🍾 €8-11

The choice is between two wines: the round, untypical **Vaillon 98** (awarded two stars) with its crystallised fruit aromas, or this younger Montée de Tonnerre. It is bright gold with classic green highlights. The nose is strong and interesting with touches of broom and citrus fruit. On the palate the attack is supple, expanding and finishing splendidly on notes of oak.

☛ EARL Caves Duplessis, 5, quai de Reugny, 89800 Chablis, tel. 03.86.42.10.35, fax 03.86.42.11.11 ⚑ Y by appt.

DOM. D'ELISE Côte de Léchet 1999★

☐   0.1 ha   700   🍾 🍾 €11-15

This Côte de Léchet has an appropriate colour and a distinguished nose with a characteristic mineral expression. Well-structured and long, this 99 vintage should be kept three to four years.

☛ Frédéric Prain, Côte de Léchet, 89800 Milly, tel. 03.86.42.40.82, fax 03.86.42.44.76 ⚑ Y by appt.

WILLIAM FEVRE Beauroy 1999★★

n.c.   n.c.   🍾 🍾 ◆ €15-23

William Fèvre is an institution in Chablis and continues to be so thanks to J. Henriot. This wine is a credit to its label: gold with the requisite green glints, floral then mineral, it has all the richness one could want and finishes on a nice toasty note. The **Montée de Tonnerre 99** and the **Vignoble de Vaulorent, Fourchaume 99** were each awarded a star, products of the successful union of wine and oak.

☛ Dom. William Fèvre, 21, av. d'Oberwesel, 89800 Chablis, tel. 03.86.98.98.98, fax 03.86.98.99, e-mail france@williamfevre.com ⚑ Y ev. day except Sun. 9am–12 noon 2pm–6pm

Having won a *coup de coeur* not long ago for a Montée de Tonnerre, this estate never does things by halves. This year, the **Montmain, Montée de Tonnerre, Vaucoupin, Vosgros** were each awarded a star ... rest assured, this is very unusual. This wine was placed third by the *coup de coeur* Jury; it has so many characteristic qualities that it could serve as a model for the Chablis area. The oak

JEAN-CLAUDE FROMONT

☐ **Vaillons 1999** | n.c. | 7,000 | €8-11

To the eye its fairly light shade is faultless; the nose is overwhelmed by the aromas of acacia, and although it has a charming lightness, this is a serious wine with a great deal about it.

♠ Maison Jean-Claude Fromont, Ch. de Ligny, 7, av. de Chablis, 89144 Ligny-le-Châtel, tel. 03.86.98.20.40, fax 03.86.47.40.72, e-mail accueil@chateau-de-ligny.com ☑ ✟ by appt.

DOM. HAMELIN

☐ **Beauroy 1999★** | 3.89 ha | 32,800 | €11-15

This wine with its floral nose is supple on the attack, livening up a little as it goes on, but without losing its softness; then it manages a little touch of bitterness at the finish. While in the area, consider a visit to Lignorelles with its medieval lime-kiln.

♠ EARL Thierry Hamelin, 1, rue des Carillons, 89800 Lignorelles, tel. 03.86.47.54.60, fax 03.86.47.53.34 ☑ ✟ ev. day except Wed/Sun. 9.15am–12.15pm 2pm–6pm; cl. Aug.

JEAN-PIERRE GROSSOT

☐ **Mont de Milieu 1999★★** | 0.65 ha | 5,000 | €11-15

The **Vaucoupin 99** from this estate was awarded a star. The Mont de Milieu, which is perfectly balanced, underwent a double maturation in both oak and vat, that gives this wine an oaky finish. Characteristic in colour, nose and palate, this wine is elegance personified.

♠ Corinne et Jean-Pierre Grossot, 4, rte de Mont-de-Milieu, 89800 Fleys, tel. 03.86.42.44.64, fax 03.86.42.13.31 ☑ ✟ by appt.

DOM. ALAIN GAUTHERON

☐ **Les Fourneaux 1999★★** | 2.8 ha | 20,000 | €8-11

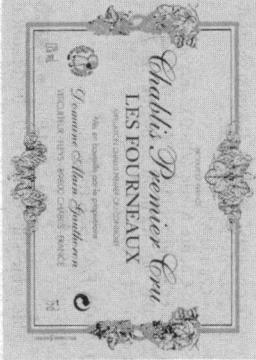

This is a small *climat* near to Fleys, and much sought after by enthusiasts for its exclusivity. Clear and mineral, then turning towards walnuts, this is a concentrated, structured wine building up to a very fresh and mentholated finish. The *terroir* appears in its full profundity, but this is a very restrained wine, nothing about it is excessive. Having all these qualities, this wine wins a *coup de cœur*. The **Vaucoupin 99** was awarded two stars, under a different label showing the winegrower's house surrounded by its vineyards.

♠ Alain Gautheron, 18, rue des Prégirots, 89800 Fleys, tel. 03.86.42.44.34, fax 03.86.42.44.50 ☑ ✟ by appt.

DOM. DES ILES

☐ **Côte de Léchet 1999★★** | 3 ha | 24,000 | €8-11

A bronze colour, this Côte de Léchet comes from an area between Poinchy et Milly. This remarkable Premier Cru often works wonders. Full-flavoured and fleshy, this well-made 99 is positively headstrong and will be at its best at the middle of this decade.

♠ Gérard Tremblay, 12, rue de Poinchy, 89800 Chablis, tel. 03.86.42.40.41 fax 03.86.42.40.98, ☑ ✟ ev. day except Sun. 8am–12 noon 1.30pm–5.30pm; Sat. by appt.; cl. Aug.

LES DOMAINES LA CHABLISIENNE

☐ **Mont de Milieu 1999★** | 6 ha | 40,000 | €15-23

The **Les Lys 99** is excellent for those who can wait, and so is the Mont de Milieu. What is special about this wine is its traditional colour and aromas of hawthorn, undergrowth and gunflint. It is a rich wine with hints of moss and lichen, characteristic of the *terroir*.

♠ La Chablisienne, 8, bd Pasteur, BP 14, 89800 Chablis, tel. 03.86.42.89.89, fax 03.86.42.89.90, e-mail chab@chablisienne.com ☑ ✟ ev. day 9am–12 noon 2pm–6pm

DOM. DE LA CONCIERGERIE

☐ **Butteaux 1999★** | 1.1 ha | 8,000 | €8-11

This *climat* is relatively unknown and rarely makes an appearance on wine labels; however, it is situated on the same slope as Forêt. This pale-coloured 99 is full of charm and class. Authentic with a good potential, it could be left to mature for a year.

♠ EARL Christian Adine, 2, allée du Château, 89800 Courgis, tel. 03.86.41.40.28, fax 03.86.41.45.75, e-mail nicole.adine@free.fr ☑ ✟ by appt.

LAMBLIN ET FILS

☐ **Fourchaumes 1999★★** | 3.5 ha | 24,000 | €11-15

The **Vaillon 99** from this estate, enthroned in the centre of a large slope to the south-west of Chablis, is one of the best Premiers Crus. Established here since 1690, the Lamblin family have produced a one-star wine that is full of energy. These Fourchaumes wines will give complete satisfaction. The crystalline colour is characteristic, as is the nose which is full of fruit and mineral notes mirroring the elegance and length of the palate. A wine to lay down.

- Lamblin et Fils, Maligny, 89800 Chablis, tel. 03.86.98.22.00, fax 03.86.47.50.12, e-mail infovin@lamblin.com ▼
- ev. day except Sun. 8am–12.30pm 2pm–5pm; Sat. 8am–12.30pm

DOM. DE LA TOUR★
Côte de Cuissy 1999
0.18 ha 1,500 €11–15

What a cast! Undergrowth, wild flowers, buttery overtones, toast ... all performing against a pale-gold backdrop. Very supple, this wine is pleasant and one might even say distinguished; not very lively, but quite straightforward. This family-owned estate was taken over in 1992 by M. Fabrici and has now moved from Chitry-le-Fort to Lignorelles.
- SCEA Dom. de La Tour, 3, rte de Montfort, 89800 Lignorelles, tel. 03.86.47.55.68, fax 03.86.47.55.86 ▼
- by appt.
- Fabrici

CH. DE MALIGNY
L'Homme mort 1999★★
5 ha 32,000 €11–15

Local legend has it that this climat, l'Homme Mort, was named after an English soldier killed in the Hundred Years War. This wine is much sought after by wine-lovers and regarded as an absolute must. The Durup family can go ahead and light the lamps at the Château de Maligny ... this well-balanced 99 is coup de coeur material. Slightly mineral, long, with almonds and honey on the palate, it has the classic Chablis colour.
- SA Jean Durup Père et Fils, 4, Grande-Rue, 89800 Maligny, tel. 03.86.47.44.49, fax 03.86.47.55.49, e-mail durup@club-internet.fr ▼
- by appt.

DOM. LONG-DEPAQUIT
Les Lys 1999
1.69 ha 12,000 €15–23

Once forming part of the royal domaine, Les Lys has an old-fashioned charm. Today, the Bichot du Chablisien vineyards are very well managed by Gérard Vullien from Savoie. This wine has noble connections but remains a democrat. Light gold in colour, it brims over with aromas ranging from orange peel to honey and has a lusciousness on the palate.
- Ch. Long-Depaquit, 45, rue Auxerroise, 89800 Chablis, tel. 03.86.42.11.13, wanado.fr ▼ ev. day except Sun. 9am–12.30pm 1pm–6pm
- Albert Bichot

DOM. DES MALANDES★★
Vau de Vey 1999
3.5 ha 29,800 €8–11

Last year this estate won a coup de coeur and this year they presented this Vau de Vey. Situated near Beine (or Beines, the name is still under discussion) this climat is one of those to have been recently nominated as Premier Cru. This wine has aromas of buds and fresh fruit. It is pale in colour with a well-controlled acidity on the palate, a very good length of flavour and an intriguing complexity.
- Dom. des Malandes, 63, rue Auxerroise, 89800 Chablis, tel. 03.86.42.41.37, fax 03.86.42.41.97, e-mail contact@domainedesmalandes.com ▼ by appt.
- Marchive

DOM. JEAN-CLAUDE MARTIN
Beauregards 1999★
n.c. 12,000 €8–11

This climat near Courgis is an extension of the Côte de Cuissy towards the south-west and the farthest away from the heart of the region's vineyards. This light-yellow wine presents a combination on the palate of richness, finesse and fresh fruit. It would be excellent with Gruyère-style cheese.
- Jean-Claude Martin, 5, rue de Chante-Merle, 89800 Courgis, tel. 03.86.41.40.33, fax 03.86.41.47.10 ▼ ev. day 9am–12 noon 2pm–7pm; Sat./Sun. by appt.; cl. 15–31 Aug.

J. MOREAU ET FILS
Vaucoupin 1998★★★
3 ha 24,000 €8–11

This wine stands out with its beautiful bright colour and aromas of quince and butter. The attack is supple, round with citrus fruits (grapefruit) and fresh hazelnuts. This is a Premier Cru with just the right amount of length and complexity.
- J. Moreau et Fils, La Croix Saint-Joseph, rte d'Auxerre, 89800 Chablis, tel. 03.86.42.88.00, fax 03.86.42.88.08, e-mail moreau@jmoreau-fils.com

MOREAU-NAUDET ET FILS
Vaillons 1999★★
1.7 ha 9,000 €11–15

This yellow-gold wine has a certain complexity. Dense and soft on the palate, it has pleasant flavours with well-blended vegetal tones embellished with mineral notes.
- GAEC Moreau-Naudet et Fils, 5, rue des Fossés, 89800 Chablis, tel. 03.86.42.14.83, fax 03.86.42.85.04 ▼ by appt.

DE OLIVEIRA LECESTRE
Côte de Fontenay Vieilles vignes 1999
0.5 ha 3,340 €8–11

Situated on the right bank with a good south-easterly exposure, this climat has begun rubbing shoulders with the great Premiers Crus. This successful 99 will be ready for drinking next year. There is a nice harmony between hawthorn blossom and vivacity. This wine will be a wonderful compliment to fillets of sole.
- GAEC De Oliveira Lecestre, 11, Grand-Rue, 89800 Fontenay-près-Chablis, tel. 03.86.42.40.78, fax 03.86.42.83.72 ▼ ev. day except Sun. 10am–12 noon 2pm–7pm; cl. 15–30 Aug.
- Jacky Chatelain

CHRISTIANE ET JEAN-CLAUDE OUDIN Vaucoupins 1999★

0.4 ha 3,200

This wine is crystalline with green highlights and knows its role by heart. Mineral with hints of iodine, it has something of the sea about it. This is an individual and self-confident wine, that will wake up the taste buds with its fullness and vegetal notes. Ready now to accompany a plate of oysters.
☎ Dom. Oudin, 5, rue du Pont, 89800 Chichée, tel. 03.86.42.44.29, fax 03.86.42.10.59 ✓ ⚑ by appt.

DOM. PINSON Vaugiraut 1999★

0.34 ha 2,900 €11-15

La Forêt 99 gets good marks and like the Montmain 99, this Vaugiraut 99 wine was awarded a star. Vaugiraut is situated on a very small, but high quality, area of the left bank near Chichée. This fine 99 has perfect clarity with delicious aromas of dried apricots and crystallised angelica. It plays scales on the palate with its varied notes of undergrowth and flint. Slightly chewy, it has spent six months in oak and six months in vat.
☎ SCEA Dom. Pinson, 5, quai Voltaire, 89800 Chablis, tel. 03.86.42.10.26, fax 03.86.42.49.94, e-mail contact@domaine-pinson.com ✓ ⚑ by appt.

DENIS RACE Montmains 1999★

5.22 ha 24,500 €8-11

This estate won a *coup de cœur* in the year 2000. The Jury placed **Vaillon** and **Mont de Milieu 99** on a similar level. Is this Montmains so popular because of its citrus fruit and mineral tones or is it due to its breeding? Whatever the reason, it makes the ideal accompaniment to goats' cheese.
☎ Denis Race, 5 A, rue de Chichée, 89800 Chablis, tel. 03.86.42.45.87, fax 03.86.42.81.23, e-mail domaine@chablisrace.com ✓ ⚑ by appt.

REGNARD Mont de Milieu 1998★

3 ha 25,000 €23-30

Established in 1860 by Zéphyr Regnard, this company was taken over in 1984 by Baron Patrick de Ladoucette. This is his Mont de Milieu, which as Raymond Dumay hoped, is dry, clear, perfumed, lively and light. Such richness on offer! A well-made wine which develops aromas of ripe grapes with mineral tones.
☎ Régnard, 28, bd Tacussel, 89800 Chablis, tel. 03.86.42.10.45, fax 03.86.42.48.67 ✓ ⚑ by appt.

DOM. GUY ROBIN ET FILS Montmains Vieilles vignes 1998★★

2 ha n.c. €8-11

A great success with excellent prospects … these simple words sum up the praise heaped on this Vieilles Vignes. It is a pleasant and full Chardonnay with a classic colour, complex nose and liveliness that is both spontaneous and honest. The **Mont de Milieu 98**, a wine to lay down, was also awarded a star.

☎ Guy Robin et Fils, 13, rue Berthelot, 89800 Chablis, tel. 03.86.42.12.63, fax 03.86.42.49.57 ✓ ⚑ ev. day 8am–7pm

FRANCINE ET OLIVIER SAVARY Fourchaume 1999★

0.7 ha 5,600 €8-11

The estate's fine, vaulted stone cellar has been open to visitors since 1999. Pale gold in colour with green glints, this Fourchaume is gentle on the palate. Citrus fruits, grapefruit and green apples blend together with a mineral touch.
☎ Francine et Olivier Savary, 4, chem. des Hâtes, 89800 Maligny, tel. 03.86.47.42.09, fax 03.86.45.55.80 ✓ ⚑ by appt.

DANIEL SEGUINOT Fourchaume 1999★★

3.8 ha 7,000 €11-15

Its brilliance makes one overlook its relative pallor, though Chablis wines really ought to be stronger in colour. The nose of apricots and *pêche de vignes* appears balanced: on the palate there is a riot of citrus fruits and an acidity that is noticeable but by no means excessive. Close your eyes and imagine it with ham cooked in Chablis.
☎ Daniel Seguinot, rte de Tonnerre, 89800 Maligny, tel. 03.86.47.51.40, fax 03.86.47.43.37 ✓ ⚑ ev. day 9am–12 noon 2pm–6pm

DOM. SERVIN Les Forêts 1999★

0.37 ha 2,800 €8-11

Light-yellow in colour with a fine nose; it is a pleasure to lose oneself in these aromas of a deep forest with mineral notes and pears. Fruitiness umpires a friendly contest between richness and acidity. An exciting finish.
☎ SCE Dom. Servin, 20, av. d'Oberwesel, 89800 Chablis, tel. 03.86.18.90.00, fax 03.86.18.90.01, e-mail servin@domaine-servin.fr ✓ ⚑ ev. day except Sun. 8am–12 noon 1.30pm–5.30pm

SIMONNET-FEBVRE Vaillons 1999★

2.1 ha 17,000 €11-15

If this one-time supplier to Tsar Nicholas II offered this particular wine to the present rulers in the Kremlin, it would light up all the gold in Red Square. Vegetal aromas develop towards more quince and hawthorn notes following aeration. It has good potential and displays all those characteristics looked for in Chablis but seldom found.
☎ Simonnet-Febvre, 9, av. d'Oberwesel, BP 12, 89800 Chablis, tel. 03.86.98.99.00, fax 03.86.98.99.01, e-mail simonnet@chablis.net ✓ ⚑ ev. day 8am–11.30am 2pm–6pm; Sat/Sun. by appt.

DOM. DE VAUROUX Montée de Tonnerre 1999★

1.11 ha 9,000 €11-15

This estate's label depicts a *cabotte*, which is the Côte d'Or name for a hut where farming tools are stored. This Montée de Tonnerre is going places! Gold-green with a young, supple nose of eucalyptus, citrus fruits and acacia, it is a wine to enjoy straight away. From the same producer comes the **Domaine des Héritières, Montmains 98**, which was also awarded a star.

➤ SCEA Dom. de Vauroux, rte d'Avallon, BP 56, 89800 Chablis, tel. 03.86.42.10.37, fax 03.86.42.49.13 ▶ by appt.
➤ Olivier Tricon

DOM. VOCORET ET FILS ★★ €8-11
La Forêt 1999

4.7 ha 35,000

We also commended the **Vaillon 99**, which is as delicious and promising as that which comes from one of the best *climats* on the left bank of the river Serein. This La Forêt is white-gold in colour and conjures up aromas ranging from toasted almonds to buttered bread. Its elegance and length would not be out of place in the grandest of culinary environments.

➤ Dom. Vocoret et Fils, 40, rte d'Auxerre, 89800 Chablis, tel. 03.86.42.12.53, fax 03.86.42.10.39, e-mail domainevocoret@wanadoo.fr ▶ by appt.

DOM. VRIGNAUD Fourchaume 1999★ €8-11

5.4 ha 5,000

This estate used to sell the grapes it grew, but since Guillaume Vrignaud arrived in the early part of the 1990s, he has been making and marketing the wine himself. His Fourchaume is well-structured with smoky, overripe aromas. Very pleasant on the palate, it has flavours of undergrowth and mushrooms enhanced by notes of crystallised fruits and toasted almonds.

➤ Dom. Vrignaud, 10, rue de Beauvoir, 89800 Fontenay-près-Chablis, tel. 03.86.42.15.69, fax 03.86.42.40.06, e-mail guillaume.vrignaud@wanadoo.fr ▶ by appt.

Chablis Grand Cru

Grown on the best exposed hills on the right bank of the Yonne and divided into seven *lieux-dits* (Blanchot, Bougros, les Clos, Grenouille, Preuses, Valmur and Vaudésir), Chablis Grand Cru is a clear cut above its juniors. Chablis Grand Cru is, at its peak, a most complete wine with a lingering aroma and a certain bite from the *terroir* (a sedimentary layer of stones and clay) that distinguishes it from its rivals further to the south. It has an astonishing capacity for ageing, requiring between eight and 15 years to develop harmoniously and to acquire its unforgettable gunflint bouquet (in the best Clos, it even has traces of gunpowder!).

JEAN-CLAUDE BESSIN Valmur 1999 €15-23
1.28 ha 5,000

This clean-looking 99 has unusually intense aromas of ripe fruit; the palate, which doesn't have great length, has the same flavours. Valmur is considered one of the most romantic Grand Cru wines, no doubt owing to its great variation in moods created by the considerable differences in altitude and exposure.

➤ Jean-Claude Bessin, 3, rue de la Planchotte, 89800 Chablis, tel. 03.86.42.46.77, fax 03.86.42.85.30 ▶ by appt.

DOM. BESSON Vaudésir 1999★★ €15-23
1.43 ha 1,200

This wine has great potential and is already very open for such a young Grand Cru. Pale-yellow in colour with green apples and hazelnut notes indicating a well-handled use of oak, it has a strong mineral finish. This generous opening is characteristic of both the vintage and the appellation.

➤ EARL Dom. Alain Besson, rue de Valvan, 89800 Chablis, tel. 03.86.42.19.53, fax 03.86.42.49.46 ▶ by appt.

DOM. BILLAUD-SIMON €23-30
Les Preuses 1999★

n.c. 2,500

One is always spoiled for choice in this cellar: last year the Vaudésir 98 won a *coup de coeur*, this year the **Vaudésir 99** was commended by the Jury and **Les Clos 99** was awarded a star. Take note of Les Preuses with its long-lasting fruitiness and mineral presence. It is an elegant, promising wine that lives up to its Grand Cru ranking.

➤ Dom. Billaud-Simon, 1, quai de Reugny, BP 46, 89800 Chablis, tel. 03.86.42.10.33, fax 03.86.42.48.77 ▶ ev. day except Sat./Sun. 9am–6pm; cl.15 Aug–1 Sep.

JEAN-MARC BROCARD €15-23
Vaudésir 1999

n.c. n.c.

This wine has a yellow colour and an intense open nose hinting at spring flowers and nuts. A wine worth waiting for as it will improve with age, it would make a marvellous accompaniment to baked fish.

➤ Jean-Marc Brocard, 3, rte de Chablis, 89800 Préhy, tel. 03.86.41.49.00, fax 03.86.41.49.09, e-mail brocard@brocard.fr ▶ by appt.

DOM. JEAN COLLET ET FILS
Valmur 1999★
0.51 ha 3,500 €15-23

"This wine has a good classic colour, the nose is slow to open but finally reveals a touch of fruit and almonds. It is delicate and very fine, thanks to good oak integration. The attack is intense and lively with a lightly honeyed richness. Well-made and interesting, it is finely balanced between a touch of freshness and a touch of alcohol.

↝ Dom. Jean Collet et Fils, 15, av. de la Liberté, 89800 Chablis, tel. 03.86.42.11.93, fax 03.86.42.47.43, e-mail collet.chablis@wanadoo.fr [V] [Y] ev. day except Sun. 9am–12 noon 2pm–5.30pm; cl. Aug.

DOM. DU COLOMBIER
Bougros 1999★★
1.2 ha n.c. €11-15

"This climat is situated at the end of the slope of the Grand Cru near Maligny. Enterprising, unctuous and sometimes robust, this 99 vintage is not easily forgotten ... it is a model of its kind and comes close to perfection! Subtle initially with a pale-gold colour, it quickly reveals its upfront aromas and flavours, finishing with exotic and ripe fruit. A really great wine.

↝ Dom. du Colombier,
Guy Mothe et ses Fils, 42, Grand-Rue, 89800 Fontenay-près-Chablis,
tel. 03.86.42.15.04, fax 03.86.42.49.67 [V]
↝ Mothe frères

RENE ET VINCENT DAUVISSAT
Les Preuses 1999★
0.96 ha 6,000 €15-23

"This estate has won a coup de coeur many times in the past. This well-made 99, with its aromas of undergrowth and truffles, has a delicate touch of oak with richness and fullness beneath. It will keep well. Take note, too, of the Les Clos 99, a lively wine which has lots of mineral qualities and is still young with a good future; it also won a star.

↝ GAEC René et Vincent Dauvissat,
8, rue Emile-Zola, 89800 Chablis,
tel. 03.86.42.11.58, fax 03.86.42.85.32

JEAN-PAUL DROIN Les Clos 1999★★★
1 ha 7,000 €15-23

"All these wines are good, and some even better than good. Grenouille et Vaudésir 99 is recognisable as a true Grand Cru by its well-balanced nose and palate. This brilliant estate is in a class of its own and the Les Clos gave us great pleasure. It is a superb wine from start to finish, subtle, elegant and perfectly characteristic. The sheer delight of a Grand Cru as big as Mount Everest – perfect.

↝ Dom. Jean-Paul Droin,
14 bis, rue Jean-Jaurès, 89800 Chablis,
tel. 03.86.42.16.78, fax 03.86.42.42.09 [V]
[Y] by appt.

JOSEPH DROUHIN Vaudésir 1999★
1.4 ha n.c. €30-38

"Joseph Drouin, like many local companies, has had a long interest in this vineyard and now has a foothold. This nicely-balanced wine is white-gold in colour with notes of vanilla and pear. Admirable for its freshness, its length of flavour and its well-controlled oak, it should be laid down for three years before drinking.

↝ Joseph Drouhin, 7, rue d'Enfer,
21200 Beaune, tel. 03.80.24.68.88,
fax 03.80.22.43.14, e-mail maisondrouhin@drouhin.com [Y] by appt.

DOM. WILLIAM FEVRE
Les Preuses 1999★★★
2.55 ha n.c. €30-38

CHABLIS GRAND CRU
LES PREUSES
Domaine WILLIAM FEVRE
1999

"The William Fèvre estate (taken over by the Henriot Champagne family, owners of Bouchard Père et Fils) invited the Jury to taste the 99 vintage of all seven climats of the Grand Cru. All of them were selected and this one was awarded a coup de coeur by the Grand Jury of seven (the 98 Preuses was already coup de coeur last year). A restrained gold colour with green flecks, it has aromas of the fresh fruit, revealing mousseron mushrooms and flint in the purest tradition. Nothing goes better with a shellfish platter. This estate holds 15.5% of the total area of this Grand Cru. The Bianchot 99 was awarded two stars and is also absolutely characteristic.

↝ Dom. William Fèvre, 21, av. d'Oberwessel, 89800 Chablis, tel. 03.86.98.98.98,
fax 03.86.98.98.99, e-mail france@williamfevre.com [V] [Y] ev. day except Sun. 9am–12 noon 2pm–6pm

DOM. WILLIAM FEVRE
Grenouilles 1999★★
0.57 ha n.c. €30-38

"Here we have Fèvre-Henriot's other Grands Crus, all 99s and all in the same price bracket. Commended but not given a star, the Bougros côte Bougerots is still dominated by oak. Stars were awarded to the Les Clos, where the taste of oak does not mask the mineral tones of the terroir, and to the Valmur, another Grand Cru fermented in oak, which is floral, fresh and classy. Two stars went to the Vaudésir, which is a beautiful, lacy wine with citrus fruits reinforced to great effect by a note of oak. Lastly,

Grenouilles 99, floral, mineral, well-made and of course ready to lay down.
• Dom. William Fèvre, 21, av. d'Oberwesel, 89800 Chablis, tel. 03.86.98.98.98, fax 03.86.98.98.99, e-mail france@williamfevre.com ▣ ☖ ev. day except Sun. 9am–12 noon 2pm–6pm

DOM. DES ILES Vaudésir 1999

0.63 ha 3,500 ▣ □ ◊ €23–30

This agreeable 99 should be tasted again in a short while as its youth gives it a somewhat lively side, which will no doubt calm down with maturity. Its virtues, apart from its brilliant clarity, include a bouquet with hints of violets, hawthorn and liquorice, a well-made body and undoubted presence.
• Gérard Tremblay, 12, rue de Poinchy, 89800 Chablis, tel. 03.86.42.40.98, fax 03.86.42.40.41 ▣ ☖ ev. day except Sun. 8am–12 noon 1.30pm–5.30pm; Sat. by appt.; cl. Aug.

LA CHABLISIENNE Les Preuses 1999★

3.9 ha 23,000 ▣ □ ◊ €23–30

Jean-Luc Balacey (of Viviers), who recently succeeded Jaques Fèvre as president of the co-operative, presents a Les Preuses which is fresh, lively and elegant. The colour is perfect and the nose has all the Chablis characteristics, such as mineral and lemons, while flavours of almonds and acacia flowers blend well together.
• La Chablisienne, 8, bd Pasteur, BP 14, 89800 Chablis, tel. 03.86.42.89.89, fax 03.86.42.89.90, e-mail chab@chablisienne.com ▣ ☖ ev. day except Sun. 2pm–6pm

DOM. LONG-DEPAQUIT Moutonne Monopole 1998★

2.35 ha 15,000 ▣ □ ◊ €23–30

One no longer hears about La Moutonne in the Chablis area, which once straddled Les Preuses and Vaudésir. But did you know that the Long-Depaquit estate (which belongs to the Bichot company), has held this jewel in its possession for more than 200 years? This charming 98 is a queen among wines and worth noting. It has a luminous white-gold colour, as Chablis was in the last century, and has a rich nose with touches of broom, hazelnut and menthol. Its charmingly peachy palate is more supple than concentrated, but promises well for the future.

• Dom. de La Moutonne, 45, rue Auxerroise, 89800 Chablis, tel. 03.86.42.11.13, fax 03.86.42.81.89, e-mail longdepaquit@wanadoo.fr ▣ ☖ ev. day except Sun. 9am–12.30pm 1pm–6pm
• Albert Bichot

DOM. DES MALANDES Vaudésir 1999★

0.9 ha 6,300 ▣ □ ◊ €15–23

This wine is very clear, blending flint with pine resin, and then a very exotic palate of lychees and mangoes. It is lively and well-made, although still too young to express itself fully.
• Dom. des Malandes, 63, rue Auxerroise, 89800 Chablis, tel. 03.86.42.41.37, fax 03.86.42.41.97, e-mail contact@domainedesmalandes.com ☖ by appt.

MOREAU-NAUDET ET FILS Valmur 1999

0.6 ha 3,500 ▣ □ ◊ €15–23

Alfred Naudet was a strong character who between the wars played an important part in the INAO (National Institute for Appellations of Origin of wines) and was one of the people responsible for marking out the Chablis AOC. Stéphan is his grandson; in 1950 a marriage between members of the Naudet and Moreau families gave rise to the hyphenated name and a total holding of 15 ha (37 acres). The estate has 60 a (1.5 acres) in Valmur. This uncharacteristic 99 vintage has good oak and golden, floral tones that open out towards honey and beeswax. It needs to mature for two to three years.
• GAEC Moreau-Naudet et Fils, 5, rue des Fossés, 89800 Chablis, tel. 03.86.42.14.83, fax 03.86.42.85.04 ☖ by appt.

L DE LAROCHE Les Bouguerots 1999★

n.c. n.c. ▣ □ ◊ €30–38

Les Bougros is a wine with wonderful aromas of sage and honeysuckle that grab your attention. It is very supple on the palate with a stylish attack, but is probably not destined to keep for any great length of time (three to four years).
• Michel Laroche, 22, rue Louis-Bro, BP 33, 89800 Chablis, tel. 03.86.42.89.28, fax 03.86.42.89.29, e-mail info@michellaroche.com ☖ by appt.

DOM. PINSON Les Clos 1999★★

2.57 ha 12,000 ▣ □ ◊ €15–23

Les Clos must be the oldest *climat* in the Chablis area and its wines are of legendary firmness, so worth waiting a few years for. This beautiful 99 confirms this, with emerald flecks contrasting marvellously with its golden colour. The aromas of citrus fruits and vanilla are subtle and restrained, the palate reaches a climax with a note of quince. This fine wine has sufficient acidity to keep well, magnificent concentration, and already the beginnings of maturity.
• SCEA Dom. Pinson, 5, quai Voltaire, 89800 Chablis, tel. 03.86.42.10.26, fax 03.86.42.49.94, e-mail contact@domaine-pinson.com ☖ by appt.

DENIS RACE Blanchot 1999★

0.3 ha 1,873 ▣ □ ◊ €8–11

A clear gold colour, this is an expressive and complex wine with aromas of ripe fruit. It is round, pleasant and quite mineral on the palate but could do with being slightly more lively. It would make a wonderful partner to fish cooked in cream.

Denis Race, 5 A, rue de Chichée, 89800 Chablis, tel 03.86.42.45.87, fax 03.86.42.81.23, e-mail domaine@chablisrace.com ☑ ▼ by appt.

REGNARD Les Preuses 1998
☐ 0.4 ha 2,000 ■ ♦ €38-46

Gold with green glints, this wine has a characteristic Chablis colour. An intense nose blends fruit with minerals and tar. After the generous attack the body shows itself to be more straightforward but already mature, finishing with a hint of citrus fruit peel.

Régnard, 28, bd Tacussel, 89800 Chablis, tel. 03.86.42.10.45, fax 03.86.42.48.67 ☑ by appt.

DOM. SERVIN Blanchot 1999★
☐ 0.91 ha 4,000 ■ €15-23

Looking at both the estate and this year's Grand Cru is a pleasure. The **Les Clos** (one star) and the **Bougros** (singled out by the jury) are among the wines rated by our tasters and can be bought with confidence. The best is the Blanchot which is golden and floral, in the exotic style now generally accepted. It does not have enormous length but its unexpected fruitiness gives it originality. Supple and pleasant, a wine that will go far.

SCE Dom. Servin, 20, av. d'Oberwesel, 89800 Chablis, tel. 03.86.18.90.01, fax 03.86.18.90.01, e-mail servin@domaine-servin.fr ☑ ▼ ev. day except Sun. 8am–12 noon 1.30pm–5.30pm

DOM. SIMONNET Les Preuses 1999★
☐ 0.33 ha 700 ■ €23-30

This well-structured 99 is gold with green flecks and has a nose which subtly opens out with butteriness and well-ripened fruit. It is rich and full on the palate with toast flavours and would go well with lobster. A wine ready to drink now. **Valmur 99**, another oak-matured Grand Cru, was singled out, but the oak still dominates, making it difficult to assess.

Simonnet-Febvre, 9, av. d'Oberwesel, BP 12, 89800 Chablis, tel. 03.86.98.99.00, fax 03.86.98.99.01, e-mail simonnet@chablis.net ☑ ▼ ev. day 8am–11.30am 2pm–6pm; Sat/Sun. by appt.

DOM. VOCORET ET FILS Les Clos 1999★
☐ 1.62 ha 10,000 ■ ■ ♦ €15-23

Here we are in Les Clos and in the presence of a wine with a future. It has hints of honeysuckle and touches of mineral on the nose and conceals a potential strength which will eventually explode. It does however need keeping for two to three years.

Dom. Vocoret et Fils, 40, rte d'Auxerre, 89800 Chablis, tel. 03.86.42.12.53, fax 03.86.42.10.39, e-mail domainevocoret@wanadoo.fr ☑ ▼ by appt.

501

Irancy

The fame of this small vineyard, located about 15 km (9 miles) south of Auxerre, was acknowledged when it became an AOC commune.

The red wines of Irancy have acquired something of a reputation thanks to the César or Romain, a local grape variety which may go back as far as Gallic times. It is a rather temperamental variety, capable of giving the best and the worst of results. When production is low to average, it stamps a particularly tannic character on the wine that makes for very long-term keeping. On the other hand, when the volume of production is high, the César does not easily lend itself to good wine-making, and this is why it is not a compulsory ingredient for the appellation.

The Pinot Noir variety is the main one used, and on the slopes of Irancy it makes a high-quality, very fruity and ruddy-coloured wine. The terroir takes its character mainly from the topographical situation of the vineyard, essentially laid out on slopes forming a bowl with the village standing in the hollow. This terroir also borders on the two neighbouring communes of Vincelotte and Cravant, whose Côte de Palotte wines were once very highly thought of. Production was 6,935 hl (183,084 gal) in 2000.

CAVES BIENVENU 1999★
■ 12 ha 72,000 ■ ■ ♦ €8-11

The Bienvenu cellars would have felt at home two thousand years ago, like many of the AOC wine-makers. They presented an Irancy with no César in it, even though they are one of the last strongholds of this seriously endangered grape variety. It was a pleasure to taste this dark red 99, rich and fine with its expressive nose of red berries and velvety tannins.

EARL Caves Bienvenu, rue Soufflot, 89290 Irancy, tel. 03.86.42.22.51, fax 03.86.42.37.12 ☑ ▼ by appt.

BERNARD CANTIN

Elevé en fût de chêne 1998

■ 7.8 ha 25,000 ▦ € 5–8

Bernard Cantin has been here for the last 40 years. One hundred per cent Pinot Noir, this wine is round on the palate with a pleasant oak flavour. It plays its cards with a certain pleasure. Fresh cherry-red in colour, it continues with aromas of morello cherries. This wine needs keeping for a while as oak and tannins still dominate the palate.

☛ Bernard Cantin,
35, chem. des Fosses, 89290 Irancy,
tel. 03.86.42.21.96, fax 03.86.42.21.96 ▼
Ⓧ ev. day 8am–12 noon 1.30pm–8pm

ANITA ET JEAN-PIERRE COLINOT 1999★

■ n.c. n.c.

This Irancy that comes from the best *climats*, such as Palotte, Mazelots and Les Cailles, is a garnet-red, traditional wine with strong tannins. Made from 100% Pinot Noir, it has good acidity, which guarantees that it will keep. Don't expect anything of it for at least two years.

☛ Anita et Jean-Pierre Colinot, 1, rue des Chariats, 89290 Irancy, tel. 03.86.42.33.25, fax 03.86.42.33.40 ▼ Ⓧ by appt.

ROGER DELALOGE 1999★

■ 3 ha 20,000 ▦ € 5–8

This garnet-coloured wine is 99.9% Pinot Noir with a tiny 0.1% César, and has a toasty nose with touches of oak and soft fruit. Fresh with a normal intensity of aromas, the fruitiness of the nose is reflected on the palate. This wine is interesting and full-bodied but needs to mature a little.

☛ Roger Delaloge, 1, ruelle du Milieu, 89290 Irancy, tel. 03.86.42.20.94, fax 03.86.42.33.40 ▼ Ⓧ by appt.

FRANCK GIVAUDIN 1999★★

■ 5 ha 15,000 ▦ € 8–11

Franck Givaudin, a great admirer of the beautiful countryside around the Morvan and Puisaye, took over the family estate in 1998. This fine, well-made 99 with a drop of César in an ocean of Pinot Noir, is the product of a controlled yield and reflects the Irancy *terroir* well. A medium ruby-coloured wine with a marvellous balance of fruit and tannins, it is a recommended accompaniment to roast duck.

☛ Franck Givaudin, sentier de la Bergère, 89290 Irancy, tel. 03.86.42.20.67, fax 03.86.42.54.33 ▼ Ⓧ by appt.

DOM. GRAND ROCHE 1998★

■ 0.5 ha 2,600 ▦ € 5–8

This relatively new estate was established in 1987 and is situated at the heart of the Auxerre wine-growing area. It presented a colourful, dark ruby wine, made with 100% Pinot Noir. The nose opens with blackberries and bilberries, and in contrast to this dark side, the palate becomes rosier with a fiery touches of ripe, almost jammy, fruits. The

initial impression is solid and concentrated. One of the tasters suggested that it would go well with a prime cut of beef and roasted shallots, whilst another preferred string cheeses.

☛ Dom. Grand Roche, rte de Chitry, 89530 Saint-Bris-le-Vineux, tel. 03.86.53.84.07, fax 03.86.53.88.36 ▼
Ⓧ by appt.
☛ Erick Lavallée

DOM. HEIMBOURGER 1999

■ 2 ha 10,000 ▦ ▦ € 5–8

This estate has passed from father to son, as is traditional in this area; Olivier took over from Pierre in 1994. This violet-red Irancy opens with blackcurrants and stays on this intense note, covering the whole range from bud to berry. The tannins in this 100% Pinot Noir are already well-integrated and it is ready to drink.

☛ Heimbourger Père et Fils, 5, rue de la Porte-de-Cravant, 89800 Saint-Cyr-les-Colons, tel. 03.86.41.40.88, fax 03.86.41.48.33 ▼
Ⓧ by appt.

ROBERT MESLIN 1999★

■ 15,000

This peony-red 99 is 100% Pinot Noir with a raspberry bouquet which could still open up a little more … its tannins are well-integrated and it has wonderful acidity. A well-balanced wine to drink young but it could mature a little more.

☛ Robert Meslin, 35, rue Soufflot, 89290 Irancy, tel. 03.86.42.31.43, fax 03.86.42.51.28 ▼ Ⓧ by appt.

DOM. DES REMPARTS 1999

■ 3 ha 20,000

In this garnet-red 99, it is pleasing to find 8% César. This tannic, slightly austere but well-made and structured wine will be improved by two or three more years in the bottle.

☛ Dom. des Remparts, 6, rte de Champs, 89530 Saint-Bris-le-Vineux, tel. 03.86.53.33.59, fax 03.86.53.62.12 ▼
Ⓧ by appt.
☛ Sorin

THIERRY RICHOUX

Elevage en fût 1999★

■ 4 ha 20,000 ▦ ◈ € 8–11

Red in colour with dark fruit completing the picture, this wine bears witness to good wine-making, fine oak, powerful fruit and great potential. Our tasters thought it would keep well for five years.

☛ Thierry Richoux, 73, rue Soufflot, 89290 Irancy, tel. 03.86.42.21.60, fax 03.86.42.34.95Ⓧ by appt.

DOM. SAINT-GERMAIN 1999★

■ 6.5 ha 30,000 ▦ ◈ € 8–11

A passion for wine is something relatively new for Christophe Ferrari; however, it has culminated in this fine wine made with 100% Pinot Noir. With aromas of liquorice and

502

cinnamon, this light red 99 doesn't show great length on the palate but is superbly fragrant. The finish is tannic and slightly astringent, spontaneous and authentic. It would marry well with a rabbit cooked in a mustard sauce.

Christophe Ferrari, 7, chem. des Fosses, 89290 Irancy, tel. 03.86.42.33.43, fax 03.86.42.39.30 ▼ by appt.

HUBERT ET JEAN-PAUL TABIT
Haut Champreux 1999
■ 1 ha 6,000 ■Ⅲ♦ €6-11

This Irancy made with 100% Pinot Noir has a clear ruby colour and redcurrant aromas which give it a lyrical and very drinkable quality. If you are visiting the area, stop at the estate's museum of wine-production to view its large collection of vine-growing and wine-making tools.

Hubert et Jean-Paul Tabit, 2, rue Dorée, 89530 Saint-Bris-le-Vineux, tel. 03.86.53.33.83, fax 03.86.53.67.97, e-mail tabit@wanadoo.fr ☑ ▼ ev. day 8am–12 noon 2pm–8pm; Sun. by appt.

Sauvignon de Saint-Bris AOVDQS

This wine used to be a more modest affair, but it is now of superior quality and, as the appellation suggests, is made from the Sauvignon grape in the communes of Saint-Bris-le-Vineux, Chitry, Irancy and parts of the communes of Quenne, Saint-Cyr-les-Colons and Cravant. It is grown mainly on areas of limestone plateaux from which it draws a certain aromatic intensity. In contrast to wines made from the same grape variety in the Loire Valley and the Sancerre, the Sauvignon de Saint-Bris generally goes through a malolactic fermentation, though this does not affect its perfumed, supple character. These qualities are shown to best advantage when its alcoholic content reaches around 12°. Saint-Bris is due to become an AOC very soon.

PHILIPPE DEFRANCE 1999★
■ 3.6 ha 8,000 ■♦ €5-8

The English adore Sauvignon wines and this one should have no difficulty making the Channel crossing. Its green highlights are accompanied by vegetal aromas of violets and blackcurrant leaves. Restrained and nicely-balanced rather than vigorous, it finishes with a perfumed freshness.

Philippe Defrance, 5, rue du Four, 89530 Saint-Bris-le-Vineux, tel. 03.86.53.39.04, fax 03.86.53.66.46 ☑ by appt.

DOM. FELIX 1999
□ 2.17 ha 20,000 ■♦ €5-8

The Félix family have been wine-growers since 1690 and their present vine stock is more than 30 years old. It is reassuring to know that Sauvignon vines have been extensively replanted in the Saint-Bris-le-Vineux area during recent years and are no longer an endangered species. This wine has a fairly intense colour and a bouquet leaning towards ripe fruits. Not very lengthy but an agreeable wine and suitable for drinking on any occasion.

Dom. Hervé Félix, 17, rue de Paris, 89530 Saint-Bris-le-Vineux, tel. 03.86.53.33.87, fax 03.86.53.61.64, e-mail felix@caves-particulieres.com ☑ ▼ ev. day except Sun. 9am–11.30am 2pm–6.30pm.

GHISLAINE ET JEAN-HUGUES GOISOT 1999★★★
□ 5.43 ha 39,000 ■♦ €5-8

This superb and praiseworthy 99 vintage was produced by cellars that go back to the 15th century, making them among the oldest in Burgundy. It has all the Sauvignon characteristics: aromas of mixed herbs, cumin, a hint of curry, fresh fruit and an attractive colour. On the palate, freshness and maturity carry on a lively exchange. A remarkable wine for this appellation and ready to drink in now. The Cuvée du Corps de Garde Gourmand 99 was awarded a star. Its tones of lightly crystallised exotic fruits are astonishing.

Ghislaine et Jean-Hugues Goisot, 30, rue Bienvenu-Martin, 89530 Saint-Bris-le-Vineux, tel. 03.86.53.35.15, fax 03.86.53.62.03 ☑

It is gold in colour with aromas of tropical fruits, such as mangoes, which blend with the classical tones of apricots forming a very powerful combination. This softens on the palate and becomes simple and light.

➤ Dom. Sorin-Defrance, 11*bis*, rue de Paris, 89530 Saint-Bris-le-Vineux, tel. 03.86.53.32.99, fax 03.86.53.34.44 ☑
🍷 ev. day 8am–12 noon 2pm–7pm

DOM. GRAND ROCHE 2000

5 ha | 35,000 | €5-8

Erick Lavallée was an accountant who, towards the end of the 1980s, decided to become a wine-producer. His 2000 vintage is straw-gold... or rosey-gold?... with a nose of blackcurrant leaf. The palate is soft and livened up by a citrus fruit acidity giving it a certain balance. It will keep for one to two years and is great served with shellfish.

➤ Erick Lavallée, Dom. Grand Roche, 6, rte de Chitry, 89530 Saint-Bris-le-Vineux, tel. 03.86.53.84.07, fax 03.86.53.88.36 ☑
🍷 by appt.

J. MOREAU ET FILS 2000★★

12 ha | 115,200 | €3-5

Imported from the Loire, the Sauvignon vines have formed a permanent relationship with the Auxerre area and this wine is a result of their union. Grey-gold in colour, this wine has aromas which tend towards the exotic, but also touches of lilac and roses. Pleasant, rich, full and embellished with notes of lemon, which are probably due to its youth, it was described by one of our tasters as a wine to drink for pure self-indulgence. This company from the Chablis area has still retained its personality even though it is now part of Vins J-Cl. Boisset.

➤ J. Moreau et Fils, La Croix Saint-Joseph, rte d'Auxerre, 89800 Chablis, tel. 03.86.42.88.00, fax 03.86.42.88.08, e-mail moreau@jmoreau-fils.com

DOM. JACKY RENARD 1999★★

5.5 ha | n.c. | €5-8

This wine, intense gold in colour, has the characteristic aromas of its grape variety. The first impression is fresh and perfumed, the body quickly following suit with great concentration. Remarkable for this particular year and ready to drink now, this festive wine would be a good accompaniment to white meat or fish, or as an aperitif.

➤ Jacky Renard, La Côte-de-Chaussan, 89530 Saint-Bris-le-Vineux, tel. 03.86.53.38.58, fax 03.86.53.33.50 ☑
🍷 by appt.

DOM. SAINTE CLAIRE 2000★

n.c. | n.c. | €3-5

Jean-Marie Brocard built this estate in 1975. He presented this lovely 2000, an extremely young wine with a nose that opens slowly on floral and fruity notes and continues towards the exotic. The attack is soft and the palate remains delicate, elegant and well-balanced. It is ready to drink now.

➤ Jean-Marc Brocard, 3, rte de Chablis, 89800 Préhy, tel. 03.86.41.49.00, fax 03.86.41.49.09, e-mail brocard@brocard.fr ☑ 🍷 by appt.

DOM. SORIN DE FRANCE

La Cuvée 2000

13 ha | 105,000 | €3-5

This is a large estate of 39 ha (96.3 acres), of which 13 ha (32 acres) produce this VDQS,

---

La Côte de Nuits

Marsannay

Geographers are still discussing where the northern limits of the Côte de Nuits should be drawn. During the 19th century, flourishing vineyards in communes around Dijon made up the Côte Dijonnaise. Today, apart from a few remaining vines like Marcs d'Or and Montrecreuls, Dijon's urban sprawl has forced the vineyards to the south of the city, and even Chenôve has difficulty in keeping its pretty hillside planted with vines.

At one time, Marsannay, then Couchey, supplied the town with Grands Ordinaires, but failed to obtain recognition as AOC Communales in 1935. Little by little, the wine-growers replanted the terroirs with Pinot, starting the tradition of making rosé which is identified as a local appellation: 'Bourgogne Rosé de Marsannay'. Then red and white wines of the pre-phylloxera era were rediscovered and, after more than twenty-five years of effort and research, the AOC Marsannay was registered in 1987 for all three colours. There is also a local Burgundy peculiarity, the 'Marsannay Rosé', which is produced on the lower slopes on gravelly soil. This vineyard occupies a larger area than those given to the red and white wines, which can be grown only on the slopes of the three communes of Chenôve, Marsannay-la-Côte and Couchey.

These sturdy, red wines are a little harsh in their youth and must wait a few years to mature. It is most unusual to find white wines in the Côte de Nuits, but the Chardonnay and the Pinot Blanc find the marly soils particularly well adapted to their needs and these whites are particularly sought after for their finesse and solid body.

The vineyards produced 6,002 hl (158,453 gal) of red and rosé wine and 1,603 hl (42,319 gal) of white in 2000. The hillsides are currently being replanted.

DOM. CHARLES AUDOIN 1999★
2.5 ha 20,000 €5-8 ✔

This rosé has long been in competition with Tavel wine for top position. As H.W. Yoxall once wrote, it shows 'a sweet frivolity'. This pale 99 has just the right amount of mineral notes. The body is generous and the length average. A red **Les Favières 99** is all soft fruit, has a true Pinot-style elegance and is singled out by the Jury.
• Dom. Charles Audoin, 7, rue de la Boulotte, 21160 Marsannay-la-Côte, tel. 03.80.52.34.24, fax 03.80.58.74.34
Y by appt.

DOM. BART
Les Champs-Salomon 1998★
1.4 ha 6,500 €8-11

This wine has a distinct red colour with mulberries, leather and pepper on the nose, a theme which continues on the palate combining with jammy red berry fruit. All in all, this is a good wine that would benefit from laying down.
• Dom. Bart, 23, rue Moreau, 21160 Marsannay-la-Côte, tel. 03.80.51.49.76, fax 03.80.51.23.43
Y by appt.

REGIS BOUVIER Clos du Roy 1999
2.07 ha 12,000 €8-11 ✔
Clos du Roy 1999

Le Clos du Roy is situated near Chenove and has thankfully managed to escape the encroaching urbanisation of the town: it has been famous for centuries and is one of the best crus of the appellation. This mauve 99 has a subtle aroma of mulberries, mouthfilling with well-integrated tannins. The **Longeroies Vieilles Vignes 99**, which is also singled out by the Jury, is still a very young wine but will develop with fruit and elegance in two or three years' time.
• Régis Bouvier, 52, rue de Mazy, 21160 Marsannay-la-Côte, tel. 03.80.51.33.93, fax 03.80.58.75.07
Y by appt.

RENE BOUVIER Le Clos 1999★★
2.03 ha 10,000 €11-15 ✔

Marsannay is the only 'tricolour' wine in Burgundy, since it comes in red, rosé and white. This charming, golden 99 is all vanilla and mint. It has good vitality and a lingering note of apricot which contributes to the remarkable balance between the acidity and sweetness of its structure. The **Vieilles Vignes 99**, which receives one star, is also worth considering.
• EARL René Bouvier, 2, rue Neuve, 21160 Marsannay-la-Côte, tel. 03.80.52.21.37, fax 03.80.59.95.96
Y by appt.

MARC BROCOT Les Echézeaux 1999
0.75 ha 5,100 €8-11

This brilliant ruby-red Marsannay has a lovely fruity, floral nose while the palate is all soft fruit from start to finish. 'At last, a real Pinot!' exclaims one taster, who suggests waiting a year before serving this wine with Sunday lunch.
• Marc Brocot, 34, rue du Carré, 21160 Marsannay-la-Côte, tel. 03.80.52.19.99, fax 03.80.59.84.39
Y by appt.

DOM. PHILIPPE CHARLOPIN-PARIZOT
En Montchenevoy 1998★★
n.c. n.c. €11-15 ✔

1998
MARSANNAY
Appellation d'origine Contrôlée
"EN MONTCHENEVOY"

Philippe Charlopin has already been singled out in this *Guide* for his red 95, and this year he has achieved a *coup de coeur* with this beautiful, fine wine. This is a wine that has been expertly matured in the barrel. It is a brilliant violet-red colour and there are lovely soft fruit flavours with an underlying spiciness. The maturation in oak has been expertly handled; harmonious and long, it will benefit from laying down. A lot of praise for one wine, perhaps, but well-deserved.
• Philippe Charlopin, 18, rte de Dijon, 21220 Gevrey-Chambertin, tel. 03.80.51.81.18, fax 03.80.51.81.18
Y by appt.

CH. DE MARSANNAY 1999★

6.27 ha   30,000   €5-8

In the 18th century, a large house was built on the foundations of the old château, which was destroyed in 1513. This kept the same name and became known as Château Marsannay. This pale rosé wine has a delicate, floral nose with a little sharpness on the palate and would go well with a *mâchon campagnard*. It is a good, well-made wine produced by the André Boisseaux's estates. The Echezeaux 98 red is a supple, round wine that seems a good bet for laying down. It is singled out by the Jury. The white Les Champs Perdrix 98 receives one star. This climat is situated in Couchey, on the top of the hillside. The wine is ready to drink now.

Ch. de Marsannay, rte des Grands-Crus, BP 78, 21160 Marsannay-la-Côte, tel. 03.80.51.71.11, fax 03.80.51.71.12
ev. day 10am–12 noon 2pm–6.30pm

DOM. TRAPET PERE ET FILS 1999★

0.3 ha   n.c.   €11-15

Unable to expand his estate in Gevrey, Jean Trapet bought up 1.6 ha (4 acres) of vines in Marsannay, mostly red but with a little white as well. This wine is already very attractive: the colour is youthful, the perfumes, in the words of the writer Roupnel, are those of freshly-opened roses at dawn. It is a very good example of its type: smooth, classy and good for keeping.

Dom. Trapet Père et Fils, 53, rte de Beaune, 21220 Gevrey-Chambertin, tel. 03.80.34.30.40, fax 03.80.51.86.34, e-mail message@domaine-trapet.com
by appt.

BERNARD COILLOT PERE ET FILS

Les Grasses Têtes 1999★

0.5 ha   5,000   €11-15

André Coillot, one-time owner of this climat that is situated right at the top of this hillside, was considered the father of rosé. Here, however, he presents his red and white. The Pinot Noir has a strong, deep-red colour. It is fresh and lively, quite supple with subtle vanilla flavours and little in the way of tannins. It should be drunk without pondering over it too much. Note that the red Les Boivins 99 also receives one star. These wines will benefit from age. In white 99, the Marsannay is singled out by the Jury.

Bernard Coillot Père et Fils, 31, rue du Château, 21160 Marsannay-la-Côte, tel. 03.80.52.17.59, fax 03.80.52.12.75, e-mail domcoil@aol.com   by appt.

DOM. JEAN FOURNIER

Les Echezeaux 1999★

0.9 ha   6,000   €8-11

Situated 200 m (218 yds) from a 13th-century dovecote is an estate that already existed in Louis XIII's time, and is known as far afield as Japan and the USA. Their Marsannay is very characteristic (there is also Echezeaux in this AOC). Its bright ruby-red colour is attractive and cherry aromas appealing. On the palate it is moderately full and well-balanced and has a lovely elegant finish with fine, gentle tannins. The white 99 seems to have potential and is singled out by the Jury.

Dom. Jean Fournier, 29–34, rue du Château, 21160 Marsannay-la-Côte, tel. 03.80.52.24.38, fax 03.80.52.77.40
by appt.

ALAIN GUYARD Les Etales 1998

1 ha   4,000   €5-8

This wine has been matured 18 months in oak. It has a golden colour and is developing an intensity of aromas with undergrowth and mushroom. The fresh attack balances well with a nice richness that is accompanied by a few oaky, hot buttered-croissant notes. 'It could do with ageing, but it's good: go on, drink it!' is the advice of one taster.

Alain Guyard, 10, rue du Puits-de-Têt, 21160 Marsannay-la-Côte, tel. 03.80.52.14.46, fax 03.80.52.67.36
by appt.

DOM. HUGUENOT PERE ET FILS 1999★

2.5 ha   20,000   €5-8

This estate's rosé was once the pride of Marsannay, and happily the reputation is upheld. This bright salmon-pink 99 has a fresh, slightly redcurrant nose and a very pleasant and full on the palate. The red Les Echezeaux 98 en Marsannay is a decent wine and is singled out by the Jury.

Huguenot Père et Fils, 7, ruelle du Carron, 21160 Marsannay-la-Côte, tel. 03.80.52.11.56, fax 03.80.52.60.47, e-mail domaine.huguenot@wanadoo.fr
by appt.

Fixin

After visiting the wine presses of the Dukes of Burgundy in Chenôve and tasting some Marsannay, the wine tourist arrives at Fixin, the first in a series of communes that give their names to various Appellations d'Origine Contrôlée. Here growers produce mainly red wines – 3,722 hl (98,261 gal) of red wine and 100 hl (2,640 gal) of white – which are sturdy, well-structured, often tannic, and keep well. They can also request the Appellation Côte-de-Nuits-Villages at the time of the harvest.

The climats Hervelets, Arvelets, Clos du Chapitre and Clos Napoléon, all classed as Premiers Crus, are among the best known, though the best of all is Clos de la Perrière, which has been described by eminent Burgundian writers as a 'Cuvée Hors Classe' (a wine beyond class) and has been compared to Chambertin; the vineyard extends a little into the commune of Brochon and neighbouring Miex-Bas.

DOM. BART Hervelets 1998
■ 1er cru 1.42 ha 5,000 €11–15

This wine has a moderately intense colour. The nose has a balsamic and toasty notes. After a gentle, supple attack, it is quite oaky on the palate. A very simple wine, best drunk without asking too many questions.
↪ Dom. Bart, 23, rue Moreau, 21160 Marsannay-la-Côte, tel. 03.80.51.49.76, fax 03.80.51.23.43 ☑
Ⴅ by appt.

VINCENT ET DENIS BERTHAUT
Les Arvelets 1999★
■ 1er cru 1 ha 5,000 ☖☖☖& €15–23

A red **Les Crais 99**? Why not? However, we preferred this pure and clear wine with its lively aromas of crystallised fruit. A supple, fresh attack with average length but good flavours on the palate. This estate has been awarded several *coups de coeur* in the past.
↪ Vincent et Denis Berthaut, 9, rue Noisot, 21220 Fixin, tel. 03.80.52.45.48, fax 03.80.51.31.05, e-mail denis.berthaut@wanadoo.fr ☑
Ⴅ ev. day 10am–12 noon 2pm–6pm

RENE BOUVIER Crais de chêne 1999
■ 1.09 ha 4,000 ☖☖ €11–15

This *climat* is situated right on the edge of Couchey, at the north of the appellation. The tannins and acidity of this 99 are a portent of good things to come. Indeed, the structure is so perfect it can contemplate the future

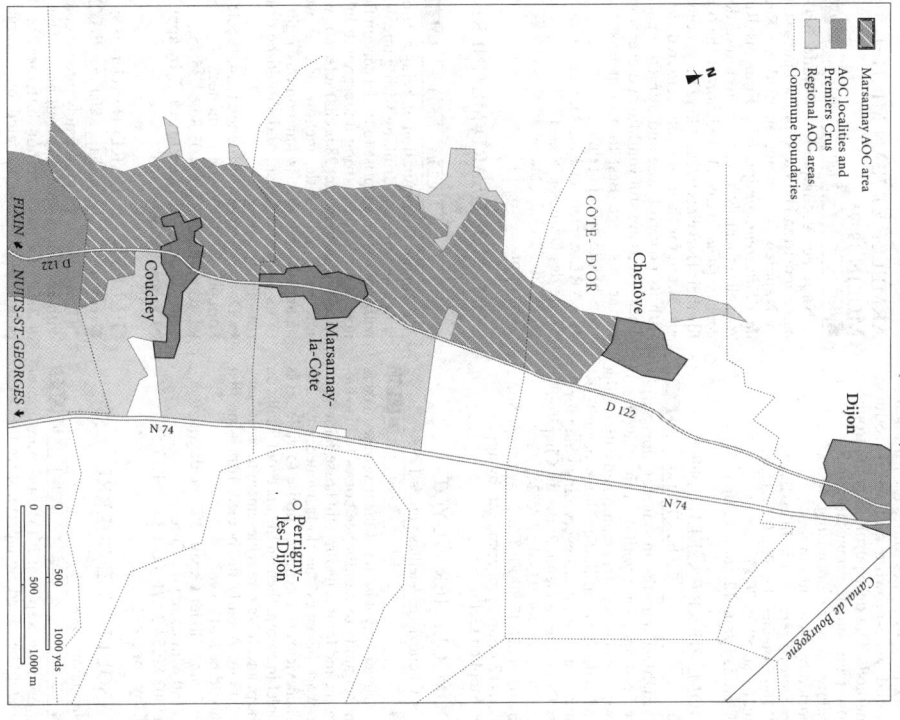

FIXIN ◂ D 122
NUITS-ST-GEORGES ◂

Couchey

Marsannay-
la-Côte

Chenôve

CÔTE D'OR

D 122

N 74

Dj_i_n

N 74

o Perrigny-
les-Dijon

Canal de Bourgogne

Côte de Nuits (North 1)

◼ Marsannay AOC area
▨ AOC localities and Premiers Crus
▨ Regional AOC areas
Commune boundaries

0   500   1000 yds
0   500   1000 m

BURGUNDY

without any worries. Already, one can detect a touch of leather in the aroma, and the colour is a deep shade of purple.

➤ EARL René Bouvier, 2, rue Neuve, 21160 Marsannay-la-Côte, tel. 03.80.52.21.37, fax 03.80.59.95.96 ▼
⟶ by appt.

C. CHARTON FILS 1998★

| | n.c. | n.c. | |

Opinions differ on one point: is this wine better drunk young or should it be left to age? Forget politics. This is the kind of thing that livens up dinner-table conversation! This fleshy, tannic wine is deep cherry-red in colour with raspberry fruit on the nose, agreeable and reasonably long on the palate.

➤ C. Charton Fils, 38, fg Saint-Nicolas, BP 107, 21200 Beaune, tel. 03.80.22.00.05, fax 03.80.24.19.73 ▼

DOM. DEREY FRERES

Hervelets 1999★

| 1er cru | 0.9 ha | 2,000 | €15-23 |

Tenant farmers from Dijon, Derey Frères work the clos of Les Marcs d'Or using traditional wine-growing and wine-producing methods. This deep purple 99 emits aromas of soft fruit and is remarkably subtle on the palate. A very promising wine, well-supported by pleasant tannins.

➤ Derey Frères, 1, rue Jules-Ferry, 21160 Couchey, tel. 03.80.52.15.04, fax 03.80.58.76.70 ▼
⟶ ev. day 9am–12 noon 1.30pm–7pm

DOM. PIERRE GELIN 1998★

| | 2.2 ha | 11,000 | €8-11 |

Eighteen months in oak for this purple, amber-tinged wine with its fruity flavours of grapes and stewed fruit combined with vanilla and oak. It is full-bodied, long, beautifully made: in short, it has everything going for it.

➤ Dom. Pierre Gelin, 2, rue du Chapitre, 21220 Fixin, tel. 03.80.52.45.24, fax 03.80.51.47.80 ▼ ⟶ ev. day except Sun. 9am–12 noon 2pm–5pm; Sat. by appt.
➤ Stéphen Gelin

DOM. OLIVIER GUYOT

Les Chenevières Vieilles vignes 1999

| | 1 ha | 2,700 | €11-15 |

Olivier Guyot is one of the first wine-makers in Burgundy to reintroduce horses to his vineyards, and Indigo, his draught horse, allows him to work his vines 'the old-fashioned way'. His Chenevières is a hymn of praise to violet: it is violet in colour, then on the nose and finally on the palate. It is a rare achievement to create such harmony. A fairly full-bodied, firm wine that should be laid down.

➤ Dom. Olivier Guyot, 39, rue de Mazy, 21160 Marsannay-la-Côte, tel. 03.80.52.39.71, fax 03.80.51.17.58
⟶ by appt.

JABOULET-VERCHERRE

Napoléon 1998

| | n.c. | 12,000 | €15-23 |

A Cuvée Napoléon? It should more appropriately be called Bonaparte, since this well-made but very young wine is still in the early stages of its career – it hasn't reached Austerlitz yet. It has a dark garnet colour with a delicate raspberry aroma on the nose. The tannins are strong at first but integrate gradually with the soft fruit flavours. It ought to go down well with red meat.

➤ Maison Jaboulet-Vercherre, 5, rue Colbert, 21200 Beaune, tel. 03.80.22.25.22, fax 03.80.22.03.94 ▼
➤ P. Jaboulet-Vercherre

JOLIET PERE ET FILS

Clos de La Perrière 1998

| 1er cru | 4.5 ha | 15,000 | €11-15 |

This clos has been in the family for over 200 years, and counts among the most historical on the Côte. This clear ruby 98 is all musk and ripe soft fruit. It has enough body and richness to merit a wait of at least two years to develop fully.

➤ EARL Joliet père et fils, La Perrière, 21220 Fixin, tel. 03.80.52.47.85, fax 03.80.51.99.90, e-mail joliet@webiwine.com ▼ ⟶ ev. day 8am–6pm

ARMELLE ET JEAN-MICHEL MOLIN 1999★

| | 3 ha | 7,000 | €8-11 |

Napoleon's companion Claude Noisot came here twice in his days, and he built a statue in Napoleon's honour, entitled Le Réveil de l'Empereur, sculpted by François Rude. Armelle et Jean-Michel Molin were awarded a coup de cœur in the 2000 edition of the Guide for their Hervelets 97, and here they receive a just award for their superbly-coloured village with its powerful nose and attractive palate. The tannins are still youthful and overpowering at this stage. Best to wait at least three years before drinking this.

➤ EARL Armelle et Jean-Michel Molin, 54, rte des Grands-Crus, 21220 Fixin, tel. 03.80.52.21.28, fax 03.80.59.96.99 ▼
⟶ by appt.

DOM. MONGEARD-MUGNERET 1998★

| | 1.2 ha | 5,500 | €11-15 |

Fixin has the reputation of being a 'winter wine', suitable for drinking with game, so it will come as no surprise to find a certain fiery note here. With a strong undergrowth influence, this deep garnet 98 is characteristic with soft fruit and subtle, mellow oak. A well-balanced wine that is harmonious right up to its attractive finish, and should be drunk reasonably young.

➤ Dom. Mongeard-Mugneret, 14, rue de la Fontaine, 21700 Vosne-Romanée, tel. 03.80.61.11.95, fax 03.80.62.35.75, e-mail mongeard@axnet.fr ▼ ⟶ by appt.
➤ Vincent Mongeard

GILLES VAILLARD Hervelets 1999

| 1er cru | 0.7 ha | 1,200 | €11-15 |

This wine has a moderately intense colour with both floral and soft fruit notes. This fin de siècle 99 has a certain bitterness on the palate that is compensated by a surge of

Gevrey-Chambertin

The wines of this appellation are robust and powerful when grown on the hillside, elegant and subtle when grown at the foot of the hill. With regard to the lower vineyard, some have taken the inaccurate view that the part running down to the Dijon-Beaune railway line should not qualify as Appellation Gevrey-Chambertin. This view makes a mockery of what Gevrey's wine-makers know as fact, but it gives us the opportunity to explain the background. At various times in the past, the hill has been the site of a great deal of different geological activity, some of which was the result of glacial action in the Quaternary era; a base of Bajocian limestone is overlaid by different layers of chalky soil with clay particles and pebbles. The combe of Lavaux was a sort of channel down which deposits ran, causing a huge plug of waste to be deposited at its foot, made of identical or similar minerals to those found at the top of the hillside. In some places, the soils are simply deeper, so further away from the substratum. But they form essentially the same base, with its layers of limestone pebbles, giving rise to the elegant, subtle wines mentioned above.

North of Gevrey, three *appellations communales* are produced in the commune of Brochon: Fixin on a small part of the Clos de la Perrière, Côtes de Nuits-Villages on the northern part (at Préau and Queue-de-Hareng) and Gevrey-Chambertin in the south.

Of these, the Appellation Communale Gevrey-Chambertin is not only the biggest producer by volume – 19,034 hl (502,367 gal) in 2000 but also the home of a number of world-famous Grands Crus producing in total less than 3,890 hl (102,696 gal) in 2000. The combe of Lavaux divides the commune in two. To the north we find, among other *climats*, Les Evocelles (which borders on Brochon), Les Champeaux, La Combe Aux Moines (once the walk of Cluny Abbey, where the monks were the first important growers of Gevrey), Les Cazetiers, Le Clos Saint-Jacques, Les Varoilles, etc. South of the village, the crus are less numerous because nearly the whole of the slope produces Grand Cru wines, for example the *climats* of Fonteny, Petite-Chapelle, Clos-Prieur, etc.

---

sincerity, elegance and softness. It is best to wait two or three years before drinking it as these elements are still developing.

♠ Gilles Vaillard, 42, rte de Beaune, 21220 Gevrey-Chambertin, tel. 03.80.51.80.30 ✓ by appt.

DOM. DU VIEUX COLLEGE 1998 ■ 1.6 ha 4,000 ⊞ €8-11 ✓ by appt.

Coq au vin would go wonderfully with this wine. Its amber-tinged purple colour shows some age, but this minerally 98 with undergrowth notes is well-structured and sturdy, though still austere. It is one for laying down, that's for sure: this isn't a wine that should be taken from its cradle too soon.

♠ Jean-Pierre et Eric Guyard, 4, rue du Vieux-Collège, 21160 Marsannay-la-Côte, tel. 03.80.52.12.43, fax 03.80.52.95.85 ✓

Gevrey-Chambertin

PIERRE ANDRE
Les Vignes d'l'Isabelle 1999★
■ 0.8 ha 3,500 ⊞ €38-46

Les Vignes d'Isabelle, a *climat* next to the RN 74, has produced this lovely, deep-coloured wine with intense aromas of cherry, kirsch and chocolate. On the palate it develops gradually without aggression, despite the sturdy tannins, with nuances of fresh cherry again.

♠ Pierre André, Ch. de Corton-André, 21420 Aloxe-Corton, tel. 03.80.26.44.25, fax 03.80.26.43.57, e-mail pandre@axnet.fr ✓ ev. day 10am–6pm

DOM. ARLAUD PERE ET FILS 1999★
■ 0.8 ha n.c. ⊞ €15-23

This wine is tannic and powerful but not overly so. It has a deep ruby colour and a bouquet that opens with blackcurrant, then brings us vanilla, moss and undergrowth. Soft, fine tannins make this a harmonious wine that could be kept for the next ten years or so.

♠ SCEA Dom. Arlaud Père et Fils, 43, rte des Grands-Crus, 21220 Morey-Saint-Denis,

Gevrey-Chambertin

tel. 03.80.34.32.65, fax 03.80.58.52.09,
e-mail cyprien.arlaud@wanadoo.fr ✇
⚑ by appt.

DOM. DES BEAUMONT

Les Cherbaudes 1999★★
■ 1er cru   0.4 ha   2,400   €23–30

Alongside the real **Vieilles Vignes en Gevrey
Village 99** ('real' because the vines are over 50
years old, and because this wine was awarded
a star and will go fantastically well, in three or
four years' time, with a Charolais steak), the
Jury also showed its appreciation for this
Premier Cru, a 'real' wine to open amongst
friends. The colour is deep and intense,
the nose fruity (red and black berry fruits)
and delicately-spiced. The palate is well-
constructed and elegant right up to the finish.
If you like young wines, this one will go well
with a joint of meat flavoured with truffles. If
you'd rather it matured, keep it in a good
cellar for eight to ten years.

➡ Dom. des Beaumont,
9, rue Ribordot, 21220 Morey-Saint-Denis,
tel. 03.80.51.87.89, fax 03.80.51.87.89 ✇
⚑ by appt.

JEAN-CLAUDE BOISSET 1998★
■   n.c.   45,000   €15–23

It was in Gevrey-Chambertin that Jean-
Claude Boisset planted his first vines, in the
Bel-Air *climat*. He knows the area well, therefore, and this *village* is the best proof one
could have of that fact. It is brilliant purple
in colour, lively and delicate, with a cherry
flavour that confirms it as a classic wine that
will keep well. Coq au vin would make the
perfect accompaniment.

➡ Jean-Claude Boisset, 5, quai Dumorey,
21700 Nuits-Saint-Georges,
tel. 03.80.62.62.61, fax 03.80.62.37.38

RENE BOUVIER 1999
■   1.02 ha   4,000   €15–23

This is a well-balanced *village* with both
colour and texture in harmony, its bouquet
combining well a muskiness and fruitiness
with well-integrated oak. Although a little
on the austere side at first, its warmth and
chewiness soon win out. It would go well with
marinated meat if you have the patience to
wait two to five years.

Côte de Nuits (North 2)

Grands Crus
AOC localities and Premiers Crus
Regional AOC areas
Commune boundaries

CÔTE-D'OR

DIJON

N 74

Fixey

Fixin

Brochon

**Gevrey-
Chambertin**

Mazis-
Chambertin

Ruchottes-
Chambertin

D 122

510

● EARL René Bouvier, 2, rue Neuve, 21160 Marsannay-la-Côte, tel. 03.80.52.21.37, fax 03.80.59.95.96 Y by appt.

DOM. PHILIPPE CHARLOPIN-PARIZOT

■ Vieilles vignes 1998★★★ | n.c. | n.c. | €23-30 ▼

Philippe Charlopin has kept two lovely surprises in store for the Gevrey-Chambertin tasters: this particular example won the Jury's unanimous approval – they judged it to have reached 'perfection'. This is a gorgeous-looking wine, dark garnet-red with attractive violet highlights. The oaky influence is perfectly balanced by the Pinot Noir characteristics. Texture, concentration, everything about it is superb. Charlopin (who is the former president of the association of Roi Chambertin) has managed to create wine that is worthy of a Grand Cru. The *climat* **La Justice 98** also wins two stars.

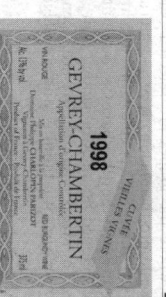

● Philippe Charlopin, 18, rte de Dijon, 21220 Gevrey-Chambertin, tel. 03.80.51.81.18, fax 03.80.51.81.18

DOM. PIERRE DAMOY

■ Clos Tamisot 1999★ | 1.45 ha | 5,400 | €23-30

The *clos* of Le Tamisot is more or less the Damoy family's back garden: people in Gevrey won't grow grass where they can grow vines. This particular wine is already quite mature. It has a dark cherry-red colour with a blend of toasted pepper, blueberry and kirsch aromas. The tannins could be more prominent but overall this is a rich, supple, mellow wine. It has an appealing soft fruit touch on the finish.

● Dom. Pierre Damoy, 11, rue du Mal-de-Lattre-de-Tassigny, 21220 Gevrey-Chambertin, tel. 03.80.34.30.47, fax 03.80.58.54.79

DOM. DROUHIN-LAROZE

■ 1999★★ | 0.67 ha | 3,000 | €15-23

Jean-Baptiste Laroze founded this estate in 1850. On the day after the end of the First World War, Antoinette Laroze married Alexandre Drouhin: the rest is history. This is a wine that is worthy of your attention: its colour is a remarkably bright blackcurrant; along the aroma, though slightly reserved, follows the same blackcurranty lines; then a light spicy note completes the picture. The palate is young but cannot be faulted, from start to finish. Proof indeed that this very famous estate will be living up to its reputation for years to come.

● Dom. Drouhin-Laroze, 2, rue du Chambertin, 21220 Gevrey-Chambertin, tel. 03.80.34.31.49, fax 03.80.51.83.70 ▼ Y by appt.
● Bernard-Philippe Drouhin

DOM. DUPONT-TISSERANDOT

■ Lavaux Saint-Jacques 1999★ | 0.98 ha | n.c. | €15-23

A good forecast is announced for this lovely 99. It has undergone lots of extraction which shows in the intense colour and nose of wild berries, undergrowth and curry spices, and with top-class tannins. It is already full despite its youth, and with time will become simply sumptuous. The **village 99** will make an equally good addition to your cellar: it is commended by the Jury.

● GAEC Dupont-Tisserandot, 2, pl. des Marronniers, 21220 Gevrey-Chambertin, tel. 03.80.34.10.50, fax 03.80.58.50.71 ▼

FAIVELEY

■ Les Marchais 1998★ | 1.08 ha | 3,700 | €23-30

I can still recall Gabriel Tortochot saying 'Marchais! Where am I going to sell a wine with a name like that?' This fine, cherry-red wine is a generous-spirited affair, with toasty aromas tending equally towards mulberry and liquorice. Clean, well-structured with sturdy tannins, it is a good example of its type. Obviously this wine should be laid down. The **Premier Cru Combe aux Moines 98** also receives one star, and has an equally fine profile. Keep it for four or five years in the cellar.

● Dom. Faiveley, 8, rue du Tribourg, 21701 Nuits-Saint-Georges Cedex, tel. 03.80.61.04.55, fax 03.80.62.33.37, e-mail bourgognes-faiveley@wanadoo.fr Y by appt.

DOM. JEAN FOURNIER

■ 1999★ | 0.55 ha | 3,000 | €11-15

This gorgeous-looking wine seduces on first encounter with its crushed berry fruit and raspberry coulis aromas. Only the tannins hold things up a little, though there is nothing surprising in that at this age. The overall structure is impressively clean but wait at least a year after this *Guide* is published before opening the first bottle to check how many more years it needs in the cellar.

● Dom. Jean Fournier, 29–34, rue du Château, 21160 Marsannay-la-Côte, tel. 03.80.52.24.38, fax 03.80.52.77.40 ▼

ALEX GAMBAL

■ Vieilles vignes 1998 | n.c. | 1,200 | €15-23

Alex Gambal is an American who came to Burgundy in 1997 to work as a *négociant*. The wine he presents here is one that he has not actually matured himself. It is a very good example of this AOC as much in its colour as in the fruity aromas, although a slight burnt note testifies to the 18 months it has spent in wood. There is plenty of fruit on the palate, well-rounded tannins and a long finish.

EURL maison Alex Gambal,
4, rue Jacques-Vincent, 21200 Beaune,
tel. 03.80.22.75.81, fax 03.80.22.21.66,
e-mail agbeaune@aol.com ▶ by appt.

DOM. ROBERT GROFFIER PERE ET FILS 1999★

	0.85 ha 4,800	€15-23

One can never forget the image of the founder of this well-known estate, Jules Groffier, taking part in a cycling competition in Gevrey, pedalling like a madman. This year the estate presents a very characteristic Pinot *village* that is already quite drinkable, though not without promise of things to come. Our advice is to drink it while it is gentle and still youthful.

SARL Robert Groffier Père et Fils,
3–5, rte des Grands-Crus, 21220 Morey-Saint-Denis, tel. 03.80.34.31.53,
fax 03.80.34.31.53 ▶ by appt.

GUILLARD Les Corbeaux 1998★

1er cru	0.48 ha 2,800	€15-23

These vines were bought in 1993 from Suzanne Thomas, sister of Madeleine Thomas-Collignon (*cuvée* des Mazis-Chambertin des Hospices de Beaune). If you want to discover the real character of the cru, open this distinguished ruby-red with its winey, toasty nose and sensuous, fine palate. This is an example of the true style of Pinot when its character is respected rather than forced. Equally interesting is the Aux Corvées Vieilles Vignes 98 en Village, which is a very companionable wine.

SC Guillard, 3, rue des Halles,
21220 Gevrey-Chambertin,
tel. 03.80.34.32.44 ▶ by appt.

JEAN-MICHEL GUILLON Les Champonnets 1999★

1er cru	1.1 ha 5,700	€15-23

This estate is only 20 years old but it is no greenhorn in producing wine. Although its Village Vieilles Vignes 99 is well worth recommending, this wine is even better. It has a wild colour with the tiniest tinge of violet. Redcurrant and vanilla are in perfect harmony on the nose and from the first moment on the palate it is fleshy, sensual and sturdy with some structure and excellent body.

Jean-Michel Guillon, 33, rte de Beaune,
21220 Gevrey-Chambertin,
tel. 03.80.51.83.98, fax 03.80.51.85.59,
e-mail eurlguillon@aol.com ▶ by appt.

DOM. GUYON 1999★★

	0.4 ha 2,900	€15-23

This is one of those small estates that are little known elsewhere but which have always been and continue to be one of the great pleasures of this *Guide*. You will find that their name features amongst the prizewinners throughout the appellations. This blue-black Gevrey has an incredible range of aromas from blueberry, raspberry and fruit coulis to vine cuttings and spices. There is a little hint of oak, but it is not excessive, with ripe fruit and silky tannins. This is a vintage that should be left in peace to mature.

EARL Dom. Guyon, 11-16, RN 74,
21700 Vosne-Romanée, tel. 03.80.61.02.46,
fax 03.80.62.36.56 ▶ by appt.

DOM. ANTONIN GUYON 1998★★

	2.4 ha 15,000	€15-23

This estate makes it into our *Guide* every year. They have a sorting table in their winecellar where the grapes are selected before being put into the pneumatic press for crushing. This wine is dark purple with bluish hues; it is quite oaky but this balances out quite a well-developed bouquet of jammy fruit and spices. The attack is straightforward, opening out with smooth tannins and an elegant finish.

Dom. Antonin Guyon,
21420 Savigny-les-Beaune,
tel. 03.80.67.13.24, fax 03.80.66.85.87,
e-mail vins@guyon-bourgogne.com ▶
by appt.

DOM. HARMAND-GEOFFROY La Bossière 1999★

1er cru	0.29 ha 2,000	€23-30

This well-made, crystalline, ruby-red cru is the monopoly of the Harmand-Geoffroy family. From the very moment it opens on the palate the tannins are evident: it will go perfectly with a dish of wild boar but will be a long while before the fruit is ready to meet. However, there is every reason to feel confident about the future of this wine, with its deep cherry-red colour, its soft fruit on the nose, its oaky and spicy notes. Both the Clos Prieur 99 en Village and the Premier Cru La Perrière 99 receive a star. Nor should you neglect the 30,000 bottles of the recommended village 99, which will have to wait for the tannins to blend in before being served up with coq au vin.

Dom. Harmand-Geoffroy, 1, pl. des Lois,
21220 Gevrey-Chambertin,
tel. 03.80.34.10.65, fax 03.80.34.13.72,
e-mail harmand-geoffroy@wanadoo.fr ▶
by appt.

DOM. HERESZTYN Les Corbeaux 1999★★

1er cru	0.19 ha 1,100	€23-30

On offer here is a Les Corbeaux. This vineyard once belonged to the author of these lines (who will remain entirely faithful to the tasters' notes, Ed.) This is a wine that makes one want to share it with one's best friends: it has a very pure colour and delicate aromas of blackcurrant and spice. Wonderfully fruity with well-measured tannins and solid potential for the future. All this reveals the quality of its origins (the vine stock is 60 years old). Also noteworthy is the Premier Cru Les Champonnets 99, which is very well-structured, quite sturdy with pronounced tannins. The Jury gave it one star.

Dom. Heresztyn, 27, rue Richebourg,
21220 Gevrey-Chambertin,
tel. 03.80.34.13.99, fax 03.80.34.13.99,
e-mail domaine.heresztyn@wanadoo.fr ▶
by appt.

DOM. HUMBERT FRERES
Craipillot 1999★★

1er cru | 0.21 ha 1,100 | €23-30

Saint Aignan is patron saint of this village, and from his Romanesque bell-tower he watches over a Premier Cru that is one of the best in its appellation. This is what Gevrey ought to be like: highly-coloured with slight blackcurrant notes and arriving on the palate with power, grace and a lovely richness that is balanced by well-manipulated tannins. All in all, a lovely wine.

→ Dom. Humbert Freres, rue de Planteligone, 21220 Gevrey-Chambertin, tel. 03.80.51.80.14, fax 03.80.51.80.14
Y by appt.

DOM. LOUIS JADOT
Clos Saint-Jacques 1998★★

1er cru | 1 ha 4,300 | €46-76

Encircled by walls, with a little oratory in the centre, this is one of the oldest *clos* in Burgundy. Only the vicissitudes of history can explain its absence from among the Grands Crus whose rank it equals. This deep garnet-red 98, overflowing with the ripe cherry aromas, is a fine example of what they can produce. It is rich and complex, fleshy and full. The oak is well-integrated and it has good length. What more enticing invitation to visit Saint-Jacques could there be?

→ Maison Louis Jadot, 21, rue Eugène-Spuller, 21200 Beaune, tel. 03.80.22.10.57, fax 03.80.22.56.03, e-mail contact@louisjadot.com
Y by appt.

JANE ET SYLVAIN

n.c. | 2,500 | €11-15

This is one of the few wines, if not the only one in Burgundy, to put only the producers' first names on the label. Like Romeo and Juliet, Jane and Sylvain are happy just to exist. This 99 is a little too much on the toasty side but it looks good, and is deep and rich on the palate. Best to wait a few years before drinking it. Jane belongs to the Bernollin family.

→ EARL Jane et Sylvain, 9, rue du Chêne, 21220 Gevrey-Chambertin, tel. 03.90.34.16.83, fax 03.80.34.16.83
Y by appt.

LIGNIER-MICHELOT 1999★

0.5 ha 2,500 | €11-15

If Nono, the character from Gaston Roupnel's novel, were to return to Gevrey, he would open this wine to drink with friends. This is neither a very intense nor very concentrated wine but it has a delicious nose of cherry jam and a harmonious, round and attractive palate with ripe grape flavours. In a year's time it will be perfect. The wine has spent 13 months in oak, 30% new, and this has been well-handled, since all the component parts are in the right place.

→ Dom. Lignier-Michelot, 11, rue Haute, 21220 Morey-Saint-Denis, tel. 03.80.34.31.13, fax 03.80.58.52.16
Y by appt.

DOM. MICHEL MAGNIEN ET FILS
Les Seuvrées Vieilles vignes 1999★★

1.26 ha 9,200 | €15-23

This estate produces Grands Crus but also makes this remarkable, deeply-coloured, youthful *village*. The nose is slightly smoky, showing well-handled oak, with delicate nuances of mulberry and blackcurrant. The palate follows along the same lines: the body is rich, the tannins very long, and the elegant woody flavours combine well with the fruit. In two or three year's time this wine will reveal all its charm but it could just as easily spend ten years in the cellar.

→ EARL Michel Magnien et Fils, 4, rue Ribordot, 21220 Morey-Saint-Denis, tel. 03.80.51.82.98, fax 03.80.58.51.76
Y by appt.

DOM. MICHEL MAGNIEN ET FILS
Les Cazetiers 1999★★

1er cru | 0.25 ha 1,800 | €23-30

This deep, dark Cazetiers is stunning. It is subtle at first but then its aromas of Griotte cherries, mulberry and spice are joined by wild, aggressive notes. Then, on the palate, it fairly explodes, delivering all that has been hinted at; powerful, velvety, structured with fine tannins. The characteristic flavours of this Premier Cru leave us quite simply amazed.

→ EARL Michel Magnien et Fils, 4, rue Ribordot, 21220 Morey-Saint-Denis, tel. 03.80.51.82.98, fax 03.80.58.51.76
Y by appt.

DOM. MARCHAND FRERES
En Songe 1999★

0.2 ha 1,200 | €15-23

En Songe ... 'in a dream'—what a name for a Burgundy *climat!* It owes little to dreams, however, and more to the harsh reality of the past: it was once a piece of seigneurial land, situated near the château of the Cluny abbots and was worked on their behalf. Having said that, we now live in a republic and this brightly-coloured 99 embodies all the democratic values that new oak and *crème de cassis* can bring! This is a sturdy, solid Gevrey that has its feet on the ground.

→ Dom. Marchand Freres, 1, pl. du Monument, 21220 Gevrey-Chambertin, tel. 03.80.62.10.97, fax 03.80.62.11.01, e-mail dmarc2000@aol.com Y ev. day except Sun./Mon. 9am-12 noon 2pm-7pm

Gevrey-Chambertin

DOM. THIERRY MORTET 1999★★
■ 3 ha 14,000 ■■ €15-23

Gevrey didn't take the name Chambertin for nothing. A *village* of such high quality can look the most illustrious crus straight in the eye. It has the colour of 1950s Hollywood – a Technicolor sunset. The nose is very fresh with strawberry notes while the palate is mouthfilling with plenty of body. Best served in two to three years' time.

❦ Dom. Thierry Mortet, 16, pl. des Marronniers, 21220 Gevrey-Chambertin, tel. 03.80.51.85.07, fax 03.80.34.16.80 ☑ ☎ by appt.

PIERRE NAIGEON
Les Fontenys 1999★
■ 1er cru 0.09 ha 300 ■■ €30-38

With the help of Pascal Roblet, a wine-producer from Bligny-les-Beaune, Pierre Naigeon has taken over the estate from Jean-Pierre, his late father. This Fontenys 99 is a passionate affair. It is very dark in colour and manages to celebrate youth while at the same time showing a most promising maturity. Vinosity and well-balanced tannins are to the fore.

❦ Pierre Naigeon, BP 59, 21220 Gevrey-Chambertin, tel. 03.80.34.14.87, fax 03.80.58.51.18, e-mail naigeon@aol.com ☎ by appt.

GERARD QUIVY Les Corbeaux 1999
■ 1er cru 0.16 ha 1,000 ■■ €23-30

This estate is based in a lovely old house situated between the town hall and the post office on Gevrey-Chambertin. This Corbeaux is on top form this year, with its light, spring-like colour, its fine bouquet of cherry and raspberry and its feather-light touch on the palate. It has a delicate, light texture allowing the tannins full and free expression. Best to wait a while before drinking it.

❦ Gérard Quivy, 7, rue Gaston-Roupnel, 21220 Gevrey-Chambertin, tel. 03.80.34.31.02, fax 03.80.34.31.02 ☑ ☎ ev. day except Fri. 9am–12 noon 2pm–6.30pm; cl. Jan.

DOM. HENRI REBOURSEAU 1998★
■ 7.02 ha 14,511 ■■ ♦ €15-23

Twenty years ago, Régis de Surrel succeeded his grandfather, who was a leading wine figure in Clos de Vougeot and in Chambertin. His deep red 98 is a clean, direct wine with a real Gevrey character. The flavour of fresh cherry blends well with the vanilla and oak; the body is in the process of softening and has length. A wine that would taste delicious served with a Nuits ham.

❦ NSE Dom. Henri Rebourseau, 10, pl. du Monument, 21220 Gevrey-Chambertin, tel. 03.80.51.88.94, fax 03.80.34.12.82, e-mail rebourseal@aol.com ☑ ☎ by appt.

DOM. HENRI RICHARD 1998
■ 2.07 ha n.c. ■■ €11-15

This rather dark cherry-red wine is chocolatey, opening on blackcurrant or mulberry. Mature and musky, it is a well-proportioned wine, quite structured and promising. It needs to wait a while before drinking because of the powerful tannins.

❦ SCE Henri Richard, 75, rte de Beaune, 21220 Gevrey-Chambertin, tel. 03.80.34.35.81, fax 03.80.34.35.81 ☑ ☎ ev. day 9am–12 noon 2pm–6pm; Sun. by appt.; cl. 15–31 Aug.

CAVE PRIVEE D'ANTONIN RODET
Les Estournelles Saint-Jacques 1998★
■ 1er cru n.c. 866 ■■ €38-46

Jacky Rigaud, a wine-writer from Gevrey-Chambertin, begins his book on the region's wines with the words: 'It is the *terroirs* that do the talking here …'. This wine shows exactly that. This Estournelles is a classic ruby colour tinged with brick red; the nose is very much of the *terroir* with a little hint of cherries in *eau-de-vie*. This velvety, well-structured 98 has plenty of body on the palate and should be enjoyed now.

❦ Antonin Rodet, 71640 Mercurey, tel. 03.85.98.12.12, fax 03.85.45.25.49, e-mail rodet@rodet.com ☑ ☎ ev. day except Sat./Sun. 9am–12 noon 2pm–6pm

GERARD SEGUIN
Vieilles vignes 1998★
■ 1.25 ha 6,000 ■■ €11-15

This is a valiant little estate, belonging to a deeply-rooted family that counts a former local mayor among its members. This wine has a medium intense colour with aromas of vanilla and crystallised fruits, and the palate is as it should be: it has sufficient acidity, approachable tannins, an acceptable structure and a satisfying length. The wine is characteristic of the AOC for this vintage.

❦ Gérard Seguin, 11–15, rue de l'Aumônerie, 21220 Gevrey-Chambertin, tel. 03.80.34.38.72, fax 03.80.34.17.41 ☑ ☎ by appt.

DOM. TAUPENOT-MERME
Bel Air 1998★
■ 1er cru n.c. 2,700 ■■ €23-30

Bel Air is a *climat* situated high up just above the Grands Crus, overlooking the vines below; sometimes you can even see Mont Blanc from here. This year the estate presents an imposing wine, almost bewitchingly haughty, with marvellous Pinot aromas. It is very characteristic and true to its *terroir*. Best tackled in five to ten years' time with a rabbit *en papillote* and young vegetables.

❦ Jean Taupenot-Merme, 33, rte des Grands-Crus, 21220 Morey-Saint-Denis, tel. 03.80.34.35.24, fax 03.80.51.83.41, e-mail domainetaupenot-merme@wanadoo.fr ☑ ☎ by appt.

DOM. TORTOCHOT Les Corvées 1998
■ 0.86 ha 6,000 ■■ €11-15

Be warned that the *rue de l'Eglise* does not lead to the 12th-century church of Saint-Aignan. You will have to save your visit there until you have been to the estate. Sadly, Gaby departed this life recently, leaving us with this Les Corvées, which was produced by his

514

daughter, Chantal. This is a very delicate wine, ruby-red in colour with notes of Griotte cherries and strawberries. It is a subtle but direct village with soft fruit flavours from start to finish.

- Dom. Tortochot, 12, rue de l'Eglise, 21220 Gevrey-Chambertin, tel. 03.80.34.30.68, fax 03.80.34.18.80
- Y by appt.
- Chantal et Michel Tortochot

DOM. DES VAROILLES
La Romanée 1998

1er cru	n.c.	n.c.	€23-30

Burgundy is a complex wine region and one often needs a good guide to find one's way around. There is a Romanée in Gevrey but there are several others elsewhere as well. This one is situated on the right-hand side as you enter the Lavaux valley and has a pretty *maison de quatres heures* (where they used to keep the tools and roast chestnuts) set right in the middle. This light brick-red 98 has an excellent nose of dark fruits and fine spices. The tannins are very silky but are they sufficient to allow this wine to keep? The Jury is still out.

- SCI Dom. des Varoilles, rue de l'Ancien-Hôpital, 21220 Gevrey-Chambertin, tel. 03.80.34.30.30. fax 03.80.51.88.99

DOM. DU VIEUX COLLÈGE
Les Champeaux 1999

1er cru	0.3 ha	1,300	€15-23

This ruby-red Pinot Noir tinged with garnet has subtle aromas of Bigarreau cherries and blackcurrants on the nose. Its personality is only just beginning to emerge: there is a light touch of blackcurrant leaf but the palate is closed and the character musky. This wine needs another four to five years.

- Jean-Pierre et Eric Guyard, 4, rue du Vieux-Collège, 21160 Marsannay-la-Côte, tel. 03.80.52.12.43, fax 03.80.52.55.85
- Y by appt.

Chambertin

Bertin, who was a wine-maker in Gevrey, owned a parcel of vineyard neighbouring the Clos de Bèze and, noting the quality of the wines the monks made there, planted the same vines and produced a similar wine. This was the 'Champ de Bertin', or Bertin's field, from which evolved the name Chamberin. In 1999 the AOC produced 506 hl (13,358 gal).

DOM. HUBERT CAMUS 1998*

Gd cru	1.69 ha	n.c.	€30-38

Hubert Camus has taken on many professional responsibilities in the Burgundy wine-making world, but his Chambertin 98 shows that he remains faithful to the Camus tradition of creating elegant, light, smooth, silky wines. That, at least, is the opinion of our tasters. Even the colour of this wine remains cherry red through and through. The aroma touches on blackcurrant with a hint of liquorice-flavoured vanilla in the background.

- SCEA Dom. Camus Père et Fils, 21, rue du Mal-de-Lattre-de-Tassigny, 21220 Gevrey-Chambertin, tel. 03.80.34.30.64, fax 03.80.51.87.93
- Y by appt.
- Hubert Camus

PHILIPPE CHARLOPIN POUR MADAME BARON 1999*

Gd cru	n.c.	n.c.	€46-76

We like the fact that the label gives both the name of the owner, Jocelyne Baron, and that of the producer who is in charge of these vines and this wine, Philippe Charlopin. This is useful information and we wish it were given more often. Philippe Charlopin uses a wine-making method that draws the maximum from the grapes in terms of both colour and aroma (which in this case is a well-balanced blend of flowers and toast). The palate is round, the tannins subtle and delicate, and on the finish there is a welcome note of freshness. All in all, this is a very harmonious wine.

- Philippe Charlopin-Baron, 18, rte de Dijon, 21220 Gevrey-Chambertin, tel. 03.80.51.81.18, fax 03.80.51.81.27
- Y by appt.

DOM. PIERRE DAMOY 1999**

Gd cru	0.47 ha	2,100	€46-76

Julien Damoy started out as a small grocer in Yvetot, then went to Paris, and opened many grocery stores there. Having made his fortune, he fell in love with Burgundy wine and founded the Tamisot estate in Gevrey. His Chambertin 99 is a superb puzzle, the pieces of which will probably all fit together in around ten years' time. The very dark colour testifies to a vigorous pressing, which is also perceptible on the palate. There are hints of blueberries and good-quality oak. It will be best to wait at least five years before drinking.

- Dom. Pierre Damoy, 11, rue du Mal-de-Lattre-de-Tassigny, 21220 Gevrey-Chambertin, tel. 03.80.34.30.47, fax 03.80.58.54.79

CH. DE MARSANNAY 1998

Gd cru	0.09 ha	448	€46-76

This bright ruby-red wine has a youthful nose that opens with aromas of kirsch and cocoa. It is fresh and acidic, the attack shows flair, and the firm tannins add decent structure. This wine comes from the Boisseaux group (notably the Château de Meursault) and needs to spend three or four years in the cellar.

• Ch. de Marsannay, rte des Grands-Crus, BP 78, 21160 Marsannay-la-Côte, tel. 03.80.51.71.11. fax 03.80.51.71.12 ▼ Y ev. day 10am–12 noon 2pm–6.30pm

DOM. HENRI REBOURSEAU 1998★ ▮▮▮ €76
■ Gd cru 0.79 ha 2,049

The flesh may at times be weak but this is not the case here. This is a rich wine that seems to be built on good, firm tannins. It is consistent on all counts – colour, nose and palate – and has both well-balanced elegance and finesse, with enough structure to assure its future. The grandfather of Jean de Surrel, who now runs this 14-ha (34.6-acre) estate, was once president of the Chambertin and Clos de Vougeot Syndical.

• NSE Dom. Henri Rebourseau, 10, pl. du Monument, 21220 Gevrey-Chambertin, tel. 03.80.51.88.94, fax 03.80.34.12.82, e-mail rebourseau@aol.com ▼ Y by appt.

DOM. LOUIS REMY 1999
■ Gd cru 0.35 ha 800
[93] 96 97 98 99

This estate has been in the family since 1820 and boasts vaulted wine-cellars on two floors that date from the 17th and 18th centuries. This wine has an intense garnet-red colour but the nose is closed. The must extraction has been well-handled and the tannins are firm. It is still developing but has enough good qualities now to have been commended by the Jury, which is not the case with so many other wines.

• Dom. Louis Remy, 1, pl. du Monument, 21220 Morey-Saint-Denis, tel. 03.80.34.32.59, fax 03.80.34.32.59 ▼ Y by appt.

DOM. ROSSIGNOL-TRAPET 1998★ ▮▮▮ €38-46
■ Gd cru 1.6 ha 4,200

This dark ruby-red 98 is a complex wine. Its aromas are already quite mature – blackcurrant and leather, prunes and game – but on the palate its strength, acidity and very prominent tannins point more towards a wine that should be laid down, and whose richness and softness will only develop later. How much later? About four or five years.

• Dom. Rossignol-Trapet, 3, rue de la Petite-Issue, 21220 Gevrey-Chambertin, tel. 03.80.51.87.26, fax 03.80.34.31.63, e-mail info@rossignol-trapet.com ▼ Y by appt.

DOM. ARMAND ROUSSEAU PERE ET FILS 1999★★
■ Gd cru 2.15 ha 10,600 ▮▮▮ €46-76

Serena Sutcliffe sees Charles Rousseau as 'the most colourful and generous personality in Burgundy'. He has much to live up to: his father Armand was a great figure in Gevrey in the first half of the 20th century. This Chambertin shows his character: the colour is bright and attractive; the nose is all leather, black cherry and liquoricey spices, and the body is graceful as an angel! The terroir is fully respected, as are traditional wine-making methods. This is a wine with a clear

conscience: 'There is no reason to make it any differently', writes one taster. Note that out of six judges, four gave it a coup de coeur. If only they had all agreed …

• Dom. Armand Rousseau, 1, rue de l'Aumônerie, 21220 Gevrey-Chambertin, tel. 03.80.34.30.55, fax 03.80.58.50.25, e-mail contact@domaine-rousseau.com

DOM. TRAPET PERE ET FILS 1999★
■ Gd cru n.c. n.c. ▮▮▮ €46-76
96 98 99

Gaston Roupnel saw Chambertin as a 'miracle of nature', though fortunately it is one that is in the hands of wine-producers who know exactly what they are doing! This extremely concentrated 99 is clearly preparing itself for a glorious future. All the tasters agreed on that. It is almost black in colour with an already markedly fruity nose. Its ripe and lengthy tannins made one taster comment: 'At last, here is a great Chambertin in the making.' This is the way they make them on this estate.

• Dom. Trapet Père et Fils, 53, rte de Beaune, 21220 Gevrey-Chambertin, tel. 03.80.34.30.40. fax 03.80.51.86.34, e-mail message@domaine-trapet.com ▼ Y by appt.

Chambertin-Clos de Bèze

In 630 the monks from the Abbey at Bèze planted a vineyard on a small parcel of land which produced a particularly highly rated wine; today the appellation bearing the abbey's name covers about 15 ha (37 acres); the wines can also be called Chambertin. In 2000, 462 hl (12,197 gal) of wine were produced.

DOM. PIERRE DAMOY 1999★
■ Gd cru 5.36 ha 13,000 ▮▮▮ €46-76

This Bèze clos has been praised by the Guide in the past. Here it presents a deep purple wine, intense and dark, with aromas of blackcurrant leaf and prunes, which continue on the palate with well-blended and lightly oaky tannins. The 5.35 ha 96 ca (13.5 acres) of this estate (which was formerly the Serre estate of Meursault) were bought by Julien Damoy in around 1920.

• Dom. Pierre Damoy, 11, rue du Mal-de-Lattre-de-Tassigny, 21220 Gevrey-Chambertin, tel. 03.80.34.30.47, fax 03.80.58.54.79

DOM. DROUHIN-LAROZE 1999

■ Gd cru   1.5 ha   4,000   € 46–76

This very old estate, which was founded in the same year that Alexander Dumas published *The Black Tulip*, has produced a wine which will be very pleasant to drink in a few years' time. Right now it is all oak, but its straightforwardness and structure are promising, with a few hints of soft fruit just beginning to break through the casing of tannins.

• Dom. Drouhin-Laroze, 21220 Gevrey-Chambertin, tel. 03.80.34.31.49, fax 03.80.51.83.70 ▼
Y by appt.
• Bernard et Philippe Drouhin

DOM. GROFFIER PERE ET FILS

1999★

■ Gd cru   n.c.   1,500   € 46–76

93 95 96 97 **98** 99

Last year this estate was awarded a *coup de coeur* for its 98, and this year, too, its efforts do not go unrewarded. This wine certainly has an incredible intensity: the aroma, with some raspberry notes, remains very timid but has potential. The acidity is as it should be and is well-balanced by the tannins. The oak is well-handled and there is an aftertaste of Burlat cherry. Everything will be well-integrated in two, three, or even four years' time.

• Dom. Robert et Serge Groffier, 3–5, rte des Grands-Crus, 21220 Morey-Saint-Denis, tel. 03.80.34.31.53, fax 03.80.34.31.53 ▼

Other Grands Crus from Gevrey-Chambertin

Surrounding the two previous vineyards is a huddle of others which, while not quite their equal, nonetheless bear a family resemblance. The regulations for producing these wines are slightly less demanding, but the wines share the sturdiness, strength and fullness, with a hint of liquorice, that generally distinguish Gevrey wines. These are Les Latricières (about 7 ha/17 acres); Les Charmes (31 ha/77 acres); Les Mazoyères, which can also be called Charmes (the reverse is not allowed); Les Mazis, including Les Mazis-Haut (about 8 ha/20 acres) and Les Mazis-Bas (4 ha/10 acres); and Les Ruchottes, which comes from the word *roichot* meaning a rocky

DOM. ROSSIGNOL-TRAPET 1998

■ Gd cru   0.75 ha   2,600   € 30–38

Gevrey is the first village to have obtained, in 1847, the right to add to its name that of its *terroir*, Chambertin. It is well-worth visiting the old village of Gevrey before going to see the best estates, such as this one. There is a simple calculation that sums up this 98 vintage: ruby-red plus cherry plus silk. At the moment it is closed on all three counts but there is faith in its future. Although the palate is closed at the moment, the tannins are good, and in five or six years' time they will be as smooth as can be.

• Dom. Rossignol-Trapet, 3, rue de la Petite-Issue, 21220 Gevrey-Chambertin, tel. 03.80.51.87.26, fax 03.80.34.31.63, e-mail info@rossignol-trapet.com ▼
Y by appt.

DOM. TRAPET 1999★

■ Gd cru   n.c.   n.c.   € 46–76

Henry Miller kept a label from a bottle of Latricières on his desk at Big Sur and wrote about the wine in his book *Memories, memories*. He would doubtless have liked this deep-coloured wine. As the wine breathes and opens, the aromas of dark fruits explode from

place, and which covers a tiny area comprising Les Ruchottes-du-Dessus (1.92 ha/4.7 acres) and Les Ruchottes-du-Bas (1.27 ha/3.1 acres); Les Griottes, where wild cherries are supposed to have grown (5.48 ha/13.5 acres); and finally, Les Chapelles (5.39 ha/13.3 acres), its name deriving from the chapel built in 1155 by monks from the Abbey at Bèze, but destroyed during the French Revolution.

Latricières-Chambertin

DOM. LOUIS REMY 1999★

■ Gd cru   0.6 ha   2,000   € 46–76

Lamartine published his *Méditations poétiques* in 1820, the year in which the Morey-Saint-Denis estate was founded. This is their Grand Cru, from the northern part of the estate, just above the *clos de la Roche*. It has an attractive deep violet colour and is developing with a blackcurrant leaf note: a classic journey that starts off on the right foot. It is attractive for a 99 with roundness, fullness and a well-balanced oakiness that continues to show through to the finish. A bottle to open in around four or five years' time.

• Dom. Louis Remy, 1, pl. du Monument, 21220 Morey-Saint-Denis, tel. 03.80.34.32.59, fax 03.80.34.32.59 ▼
Y by appt.

the glass. It is powerful and fresh with good, mature tannins without any aggression. In three or four years' time it will be the perfect accompaniment to a wild boar dish, though it will have to be decanted. Jean and Jean-Louis Trapet have more than seven generations of wine-producing history behind them and they export over 60% of the 60,000 bottles they produce every year.

🔑 Dom. Trapet Père et Fils, 53, rte de Beaune, 21220 Gevrey-Chambertin, tel. 03.80.34.30.40. fax 03.80.51.86.34, e-mail message@domaine-trapet.com V
Y by appt.

Chapelle-Chambertin

DOM. PIERRE DAMOY 1999★★

■Gd cru 2.22 ha 7,200 € 46–76

The original chapel that was built in 1155 and rebuilt in 1547 by the Bishop of Bethelehem (who was repatriated to Clamecy) was, sadly, completely destroyed in 1830. It has, however, left us with this charming, clear wine. It sings only one song: black cherry in colour and also on the nose. It is the result of well-ripened grapes and well-handled wine-making. It is, in short, more on the rich side than anything else, but in five to eight years' time who knows what heights it might be capable of reaching?

🔑 Dom. Pierre Damoy, 11, rue du Mal-de-Lattre-de-Tassigny, 21220 Gevrey-Chambertin, tel. 03.80.34.30.47, fax 03.80.58.54.79

DOM. ROSSIGNOL-TRAPET 1998

■Gd cru 0.54 ha 2,200 € 30–38

|92| |(93)| 97 98

As expected from a Grand Cru, this is a wine with a musky note but it is not overly so. It has plenty of body and a lovely full fruitiness, with a tough tannic structure that will mellow after two or three years spent in the cellar. Slightly cavalier for a Grand Cru but, these days, that counts for something!

🔑 Dom. Rossignol-Trapet, 3, rue de la Petite-Issue, 21220 Gevrey-Chambertin, tel. 03.80.51.87.26, fax 03.80.34.31.63, e-mail info@rossignol-trapet.com V
Y by appt.

DOM. TRAPET PERE ET FILS 1999

■Gd cru n.c. n.c. € 46–76

91 |94| 95 96 **98** 99

This wine is a very deep garnet-red in colour. Its toasty, smoky aromas grab your attention from the start and then open out with a musky note, with just the merest hint of fruit penetrating through. Overall, it is a well-structured wine with an oaky depth.

🔑 Dom. Trapet Père et Fils, 53, rte de Beaune, 21220 Gevrey-Chambertin, tel. 03.80.34.30.40. fax 03.80.51.86.34, e-mail message@domaine-trapet.com V
Y by appt.

Charmes-Chambertin

DOM. ARLAUD 1999★

■Gd cru n.c. n.c. € 23–30

This estate has the experience of both owner and tenant farmer on this Grand Cru. It presents an attractive 99 that has a fine nose with elegant oak and a lovely range of ripe fruit aromas. Although the acidity is pronounced on the finish, this liveliness, coupled with a solid tannic structure, gives the wine promise for the future.

🔑 SCEA Dom. Arlaud Père et Fils, 43, rte des Grands-Crus, 21220 Morey-Saint-Denis, tel. 03.80.34.32.65, fax 03.80.58.52.09, e-mail cyprien.arlaud@wanadoo.fr V
Y by appt.

DOM. PHILIPPE CHARLOPIN 1999★

■Gd cru n.c. n.c. € 38–46

(85) **88** |89| **91** 92 **94** 95 |97| 99

This wine has all the qualities one might expect from a promising Grand Cru. The colour is a brilliant, deep cherry-red; the bouquet is open with soft fruit and liquorice, and an attractive oaky note; then an elegant attack reveals fine substance. It opens out on the palate with interesting length and prominent but well-blended tannins. In five years' time it will have attained a glorious maturity.

🔑 Philippe Charlopin, 18, rte de Dijon, 21220 Gevrey-Chambertin, tel. 03.80.51.81.18, fax 03.80.51.81.18
Y by appt.

F. CHAUVENET 1998

■Gd cru n.c. 3,000 € 46–76

This Charmes certainly isn't lacking in charm! The colour is purple or garnet depending on the light. It opens with a delicate note of Griotte cherry before moving onto more serious aromas of almond kernels and prunes. It is fine, with light soft fruit flavours, but still tannic, which means it would be best drunk around 2005, perhaps with a truffle omelette. This estate belongs to the Jean-Claude Boisset group.

🔑 F. Chauvenet, 9, quai Fleury, 21700 Nuits-Saint-Georges, tel. 03.80.62.61.43, fax 03.80.62.37.38

DOM. DUJAC 1999★

■Gd cru 0.78 ha 4,000 € 38–46

Representative of the appellation (the vine stock was originally bought from Alfred Jacqot in 1977 and is situated near Morey), this flavoursome 99 has an expressive, fruity, slightly balsamic nose. It is not particularly concentrated but its rather prominent tannins are quite well-rounded. Jacques Seysses discovered that he preferred making wine to running the Belin biscuit business, and he and his American wife, Rosalind, have recently bought something else to keep them busy: the

Triennes estate at Nans-les-Pins (*vin de pays du Var*):

- Dom. Dujac, 7, rue de la Bussière, 21220 Morey-Saint-Denis, tel. 03.80.34.01.00, fax 03.80.34.01.09, e-mail dujac@dujac.com ▼
- Seysses

DOM. DOMINIQUE GALLOIS

1999★★

Gd cru	0.3 ha	1,800

96 97 98 **99**

Dominique Gallois ran a restaurant in Dijon before taking over the family estate in 1989. He found some incredible papers in his attic, which he has recently offered to a Californian researcher as archive material for a wonderful thesis on Gaston Roupnel. From his cellar, this Charmes is truly splendid, among the finest of the Chambertins tasted this year. It is dark and clear with aromas of jammy Griotte cherries and on the palate it combines richness, power and fineness. 'Easily on the same level as a Chambertin,' notes one of the best Burgundian oenologists.

- Dominique Gallois, 9, rue Mal-de-Lattre-de-Tassigny, 21220 Gevrey-Chambertin, tel. 03.80.34.11.99, fax 03.80.34.38.62 ▼
- Y by appt.

DOM. HUMBERT FRÈRES 1999★

Gd cru	0.21 ha	1,100	€38-46

96 98 99

This wine has a fine black-cherry colour. Aromas of coffee, leather, toast and wild cherries mingle on the nose and its oakiness is evident. Full-bodied, powerful and rich, it can be opened in three to four years.

- Dom. Humbert Frères, rue de Planteligone, 21220 Gevrey-Chambertin, tel. 03.80.51.80.14, fax 03.80.51.80.14
- Y r.-v.

DOM. HENRI PERROT-MINOT

1998★

Gd cru	0.7 ha	4,000	€30-38

It is difficult to imagine a better version of this wine. It has a purplish, almost garnet colour. The oak is evident in the direct bouquet, which has the hint of almond kernels typifying this vintage. There is absolutely no doubt that this full, warm, liquorice-flavoured and very long 98 will eventually settle down and come into its own in four or five years' time. It definitely has potential.

- Henri Perrot-Minot, 54, rte des Grands-Crus, 21220 Morey-Saint-Denis, tel. 03.80.34.32.51, fax 03.80.34.13.57 ▼
- Y r.-v.

CAVE PRIVÉE D'ANTONIN RODET 1998★

Gd cru	n.c.	608	€46-76

This *cave privée* will be good to drink in a few years' time. Hurry to buy a bottle because the production is very small. Indeed, let's hope that there will be enough left by the time the *Guide* is published. This well-made Charmes is all friendliness and harmony. The soft fruit (cherry) nose is nicely open. The palate has good power and is mouthfilling, structured with straightforward tannins that are still a little austere. A ruby-red colour with some bluish highlights around the edges shows its youthfulness. It will be best to wait three or four years before drinking.

- Antonin Rodet, 71640 Mercurey, tel. 03.85.98.12.12, fax 03.85.45.25.49, e-mail rodet@rodet.com ▼
- Y ev. day except Sat. Sun. 9am-12 noon 2pm-6pm

DOM. TAUPENOT-MERME 1998★

Gd cru	n.c.	6,900	€38-46

96 97 98

This alluring wine has powerful aromas of cinnamon, spice and game that emerge with the enthusiasm of a wine passing from youth to maturity. The colour is magnificent and theatrical. The palate is somewhat reserved with grilled, liquorice flavours lacking passion.

- Jean Taupenot-Merme, 33, rte des Grands-Crus, 21220 Morey-Saint-Denis, tel. 03.80.34.35.24, fax 03.80.51.83.41, e-mail domainetaupenot-merme@ wanadoo.fr ▼ Y by appt.

DOM. TORTOCHOT 1998

Gd cru	0.57 ha	2,000	€30-38

91 92 **93** 94 95 96 98

Spare a thought for Gaby Tortochot, who recently left this life to join his old friends. He had managed to assure his succession before going and he also had the time to taste this 98 red wine as it was still very young. This dark ruby-red wine is attractive, with aromas of undergrowth and very ripe fruit: a classic combination. Slightly austere tannins hold it back a little but the attack is supple and the body smooth. Open it in two to three years' time.

- Dom. Tortochot, 12, rue de l'Église, 21220 Gevrey-Chambertin, tel. 03.80.34.30.68, fax 03.80.34.18.80 ▼
- Chantal et Michel Tortochot

Griotte-Chambertin

DOM. MARCHAND FRERES 1999

■ Gd cru 0.12 ha 900 ▥ €30-38

Griotte isn't easy to find. The total production of this Grand Cru amounts to no more than 10,000 bottles, which are exported all over the world. This estate produces 900 bottles that come from three of the small plots known as *ouvrées*. The wine, with its clear garnet colour, already has mature aromas of leather and prunes, along with notes of cinnamon and toast contributed by the oak. Fans of this AOC will know that it's the tannins that count, not the acidity. This is a wine to be put aside for a minimum of five years.

➤ Dom. Marchand Freres, 1, pl. du Monument, 21220 Gevrey-Chambertin, tel. 03.80.62.10.97, fax 03.80.62.11.01, e-mail dmarc2000@aol.com ▥ ev. day except Sun. Mon. 9am–12 noon 2pm–7pm

DOM. PONSOT 1998★★

■ Gd cru 1 ha 1,653 ▥ €76

When the weather is good, Ponsot father and son hold delightful tasting evenings on the vine-covered verandah of the Clos de Vougeot. We should raise a big Burgundy cheer, therefore, in honour of this superb, intensely garnet-coloured wine. The nose is direct but reserved, with aromas of dark fruit developing with hints of undergrowth. Blackcurrant and cherry blend with liquorice on the palate. 'Young wine, rich Burgundy', as the saying goes: this is a tough wine with a great future, yet it is already very full-bodied. Its length seduced the Jury. Put this bottle in your cellar; you can open it in three years' time but it will keep another eight to fifteen years.

➤ Dom. Ponsot, 21, rue de la Montagne, BP 11, 21220 Morey-Saint-Denis, tel. 03.80.34.32.46, fax 03.80.58.51.70, e-mail info@domaine-ponsot.com

still austere on the palate but has enough substance and promise to ensure a sound future.

➤ Philippe Charlopin, 18, rte de Dijon, 21220 Gevrey-Chambertin, tel. 03.80.51.81.18, fax 03.80.51.81.18 ▼ by appt.

FAIVELEY 1998

■ 1.2 ha 4,300 ▥ €46-76

The Faiveley domaine is well established in Gevrey (formerly the Grésigny property). It presents here a purple 98 with cherry glints that has good aromas (mainly kirsch) but is still awakening. The palate has similar flavours accompanied by notes of blueberry and blackcurrant. The tannins are closed and a little austere at the moment. Wait two or three years for this wine to open up.

➤ Bourgognes Faiveley, 8, rue du Tribourg, 21701 Nuits-Saint-Georges, tel. 03.80.61.04.55, fax 03.80.62.33.37, e-mail bourgognes.faiveley@wanadoo.fr ▼

JEAN-MICHEL GUILLON 1999

■ Gd cru 0.16 ha 1,090 ▥ €30-38

When you travel through Gevrey by car, 'past Guillon's place' as they say here, you see dozens of covers of our *Guide* on the wall: this estate has won plenty of awards! After a 98 that won two stars, the Jury has singled out its Mazis 99. With its clean, bright violet colour and aromas of stewed prunes, this is a decent wine with dominant oak. Of course, it is not yet ready to drink and the fruit has yet to come through. Having said that, it certainly passes muster, which many don't.

➤ Jean-Michel Guillon, 33, rte de Beaune, 21220 Gevrey-Chambertin, tel. 03.80.51.83.98, fax 03.80.51.85.59, e-mail eurlguillon@aol.com ▥ ▼ by appt.

DOM. HARMAND-GEOFFROY 1999★

■ Gd cru 0.7 ha 4,200 ▥ €30-38

This 9-ha (22.2-acre) estate is one of the leading lights of Burgundy. This is a well-made Mazis 99 even if the attack is a little reserved and lacking in expression. The colour is lively and the nose is dominated by grilled aromas, but the fruit will soon have the upper hand. On the palate it is straightforward and consistent. You'll need to wait four or five years for the richness to develop but this is already well above average.

➤ Dom. Harmand-Geoffroy, 1, pl. des Lois, 21220 Gevrey-Chambertin, tel. 03.80.34.10.65, fax 03.80.34.13.72, e-mail harmand-geoffroy@wanadoo.fr ▼ by appt.

DOM. HENRI REBOURSEAU 1998

■ Gd cru 0.96 ha 3,042 ▥ €38-46

If you come in on the D122 from Gevrey, Mazis-Chambertin is the first Grand Cru you'll encounter. It has produced this wine which has been matured in oak for 18 months, as its closed tannins testify. It has an intense colour and a nose that combines mineral notes and stewed fruits with a touch of

Mazis-Chambertin

DOM. PHILIPPE CHARLOPIN 1999★

■ Gd cru n.c. n.c. ▥ €46-76

The name of Charlopin first appears in the records in 1420. If you don't have 500 years of wine-making behind you, nobody will take you seriously, in Burgundy anyway. This wine, still strongly oaky, needs to spend some time in the cellar before appearing on the table in around 2010. This is not, after all, the chapter on young wines! An intense, concentrated colour and a generous and open aroma, with notes of freshly picked blackcurrants. It is

oakiness that all hold promise for the future. It needs two or three years for the richness to develop and flavours to integrate.

♠ NSE Dom. Henri Rebourseau, 10, pl. du Monument, 21220 Gevrey-Chambertin, tel. 03.80.51.88.94, fax 03.80.34.12.82, e-mail rebourseal@aol.com ✉ Υ by appt.

DOM. HENRI PERROT-MINOT

1998 ★★

Gd cru	0.8 ha	4,000

Mazoyères has tended to be rather neglected recently but is making a welcome comeback. Passionate and impetuous with a persistent violet colour, this has the primary aromas of a very young, oaky wine with raspberry or even mulberry fruit. The palate is full, which makes all the difference. A very high quality wine.

♠ Henri Perrot-Minot, 54, rte des Grands-Crus, 21220 Morey-Saint-Denis, tel. 03.80.34.32.51, fax 03.80.34.13.57 ✉ Υ by appt.

Mazoyères-Chambertin

DOM. HENRI RICHARD 1999 ★★

Gd cru	1.11 ha	5,500	€ 30-38

Gaston Roupnel would be happy. The great Burgundian writer lived in Gevrey and sold these vines in 1938 to the Richard family. He would have loved to read the comment: 'A wine that does its appellation credit'. There are very few Mazoyères on the market. This one is very typical of its vintage: a wine of character, full of life but without great length, hovering between the flavour of strawberries and something rather wilder. The oak influence is not overpowering, and what there is supports the fruit effectively.

♠ SCE Henri Richard, 75, rte de Beaune, 21220 Gevrey-Chambertin, tel. 03.80.34.35.81, fax 03.80.34.35.81 ✉ Υ ev. day 9am-12 noon 2pm-6pm; Sun. by appt.; cl. 15-31 Aug.

Ruchottes-Chambertin

CH. DE MARSANNAY 1998

Gd cru	0.1 ha	448	€ 46-76

The label refers to the 'tournament of the Charlemagne Tree', which took place at Marsannay in medieval times, when all the

leading knights had to fight each other. This traditional Ruchottes is still closed, austere and uncompromising, with a firm, sharp attack. It has great length, which is an advantage, since it will be a long battle. Attractive nevertheless.

♠ Ch. de Marsannay, rte des Grands-Crus, BP 78, 21160 Marsannay-la-Côte, tel. 03.80.51.71.11, fax 03.80.51.71.12 ✉ Υ ev. day 10am-12 noon 2pm-6.30pm

DOM. ARMAND ROUSSEAU

Clos des Ruchottes 1999 ★★

Gd cru	1.06 ha	6,400	€ 38-46

The *Clos des Ruchottes* is a monopoly of this domaine and represents one-third of the Grand Cru. The Thomas-Bassot family who owned it in the 19th century built the gate and walls. This admirable 99 has produced a fine must. The ruby-red colour is as it should be; it has notes of undergrowth, vegetation and plums with firmness, power and length. This is a great wine that has plenty of body and fills the mouth nicely. Best drunk in four or five years' time.

♠ Dom. Armand Rousseau, 1, rue de l'Aumônerie, 21220 Gevrey-Chambertin, tel. 03.80.34.30.55, fax 03.80.58.50.25, e-mail contact@domaine-rousseau.com

♠ Ch. Rousseau

Morey-Saint-Denis

Covering a little more than 100 ha (247 acres), Morey-Saint-Denis is one of the smallest *appellations communales* in the Côte de Nuits. You can find some excellent Premier Crus and five Grands Crus which qualify for the Appellation d'Origine Contrôlée: Clos de Tart, Clos Saint-Denis, Bonnes-Mares (only a part), Clos de la Roche and Clos des Lambrays.

The appellation, which produced 4,324 hl (114,154 gal) in 2000, of which 188 hl (4,963 gal) were white, is squeezed between Gevrey and Chambolle and could be said to be halfway between the strength of the first and the finesse of the second. On the Friday before the sale at the Hospices de Nuits (which takes place in the third week in March) the wine-makers put Morey-Saint-Denis, and only this wine, on sale to the

Morey-Saint-Denis

public at the festival of the 'Carrefour de Dionysos', held in the village hall.

DOM. PIERRE AMIOT ET FILS 1999★

▥ 2 ha 4,500 🍷 €11–15

Jean-Louis succeeded Pierre, then Didier succeeded Jean-Louis in 1993. This is how it goes in the Amiot family, as in many of the wine-producing families that end up becoming dynasties. This Pinot-red 99 is already developing notes of kirsch and cherries in *eau-de-vie*, with an underlying touch of oak. The natural tannins are interesting, with a presence that is a gauge of the wine's longevity. There is a little touch of warmth with some spice in the background: best to wait two or three years before drinking. Ditto the **Premier Cru aux Charmes 99**, which is singled out by the Jury.

• Dom. Pierre Amiot et Fils,
27, Grande-Rue, 21220 Morey-Saint-Denis,
tel. 03.80.34.34.28, fax 03.80.58.51.17
Ⴑ by appt.

DOM. ARLAUD PERE ET FILS

Les Ruchots 1999★

▥ 1er cru 0.7 ha n.c. 🍷 €15–23

This *climat* is situated on the edge of Chambolle. Although the tannins and oak still need time to integrate, the wine is already pleasant to drink. The deep ruby-red colour has been achieved by a significant period of time in vat. Very good legs and abundant tears show in the glass and on the nose there are attractive blackcurrant fruit aromas. It has a delightful harmony. Other good wines include the intense, concentrated **village 99** as well as the **Premier Cru aux Chezeaux 99**. They all get one star.

• SCEA Dom. Arlaud Père et Fils, 43, rte des Grands-Crus, 21220 Morey-Saint-Denis,
tel. 03.80.34.32.65, fax 03.80.58.52.09,
e-mail cyprien.arlaud@wanadoo.fr ▣
Ⴑ by appt.

DOM. DES BEAUMONT 1999

▥ 1 ha 6,000 🍷 €11–15

This 5-ha (12.4-acre) estate was only founded in 1991 and already exports 60% of its production. This wine remains a *village* in character, opening with rather vegetal aromas evolving towards spice and tobacco. It has a strong oak character that should soften with time. The Jury also singles out the **Premier Cru red 99**. This wine should become more powerful but is already rich in aromas (blackcurrant, strawberry, raspberry, quince) with a dense oaky structure.

• Dom. des Beaumont, 9, rue Ribordot,
21220 Morey-Saint-Denis,
tel. 03.80.51.87.89, fax 03.80.51.87.89 ▣
Ⴑ by appt.

REGIS BOUVIER

En la Rue de Vergy 1999

▥ 0.53 ha 3,000 🍷 €11–15

As its name suggests, this *climat* is on the road to the Hautes-Côtes, heading towards the old château at Vergy. This dark cherry-red 99 is a real product of the vintage. It is clean and straightforward on the nose and just on the verge of opening out. The length is average but there is lots of fruit.

• Régis Bouvier, 52, rue de Mazy,
21160 Marsannay-la-Côte,
tel. 03.80.51.33.93, fax 03.80.58.75.07 ▣
Ⴑ by appt.

DOM. PHILIPPE CHARLOPIN 1998★★

▥ n.c. n.c. 🍷 €15–23

Philippe Charlopin seems to be everywhere in the Côte de Nuits which is welcome news, since his wines are so good! This deep red 98 has a fine nose of toast and *pain d'épice* with just a hint of fresh grapes. At the first impression it is full and round, then the tannins make their presence felt, without destroying the balance or length, combining an elegant oakiness with a flavour of cherries in *eau-de-vie*. This is a superb wine made in the traditional style.

• Philippe Charlopin, 18, rte de Dijon,
21220 Gevrey-Chambertin,
tel. 03.80.51.81.18, fax 03.80.51.81.18 ▣
Ⴑ by appt.

DOM. DROUHIN-LAROZE 1999★

▥ 0.2 ha 1,000 🍷 €15–23

Of the 12 ha (29.6 acres) owned by this family, this wine represents only 20 ares (2,392 sq yds). That's Burgundy for you. This wine has a brilliant ruby colour with a touch of mauve. On the nose there are light oak and soft fruit aromas. Though lively on the attack, it's almost unctuous. 'Fine wine-making', notes one taster who comes from one of the best estates in the Côte.

• Dom. Drouhin-Laroze, 2, rue du Chambertin, 21220 Gevrey-Chambertin,
tel. 03.80.34.31.49, fax 03.80.51.83.70
Ⴑ by appt.
• Bernard et Philippe Drouhin

DUFOULEUR PERE ET FILS

Monts-Luisants 1998★

▥ 1er cru n.c. 3,100 🍷 €23–30

The *climat* of Les Monts-Luisants is on the top of the hillside where the vine leaves shine even at night, so they say. It produces both white and red wine. This Pinot Noir has a characteristic colour for a 98 vintage, with an expressive musk aromas. Its full-bodied palate could have been painted by Rubens. There is a tiny touch of alcohol that is scarcely noticeable.

• Dufouleur Père et Fils, 15, rue Thurot,
BP 27, 21700 Nuits-Saint-Georges,
tel. 03.80.61.21.21, fax 03.80.61.10.65 ▣
Ⴑ by appt.

DOM. JEAN FERY ET FILS 1998

■ 0.5 ha 3,000 €11-15

This wine is an averagely deep ruby-red colour but with a fine lustre. Its body presents a mixture of cherry, undergrowth and cocoa. A fresh, light 98, very representative of the *village* of the appellation, it is less robust than we traditionally expect from this wine but that makes it more accessible.

☛ Dom. Jean Fery et Fils, 21420 Echevronne, tel. 03.80.21.59.60, fax 03.80.21.59.59 ⍐ by appt.

FORGEOT 1999★★

■ n.c. n.c. €15-23

Here, Bouchard Père et Fils present one of the finest wines of the tasting. This classically-made wine is well-structured, liquoricy with well-balanced tannins and oak. It is deep garnet in colour with an attractive bouquet (Griotte cherry at first followed by ripe fruit) and a strong character. Best to put it to one side and keep it to open with a special roast.

☛ Grands Vins Forgeot, 15, rue du Château, 21200 Beaune, tel. 03.80.24.80.50

DOM. HERESZTYN

■ Les Millandes 1999★

■ 0.37 ha 1,800 €38-46

This *climat* has already a fine reputation, and this estate certainly pulls out all the stops. Both the nose and colour are wonderfully intense. Against a backdrop of a violet-red sunset, there are aromas of mulberry, blackcurrant and fruits in *eau-de-vie*. This complex and distinguished wine, powerful and well-made, is sufficiently well-structured to guarantee a long life.

☛ Dom. Heresztyn, 27, rue Richebourg, 21200 Gevrey-Chambertin, tel. 03.80.34.13.99, fax 03.80.34.13.99, e-mail domaine.heresztyn@wanadoo.fr ⍐

LIGNIER-MICHELOT

■ Aux Charmes 1999★

■ 0.24 ha 1,300 €15-23

'These wines lack nothing,' wrote Dr Jules Lavalle (1855) in his chapter on Morey wines. And to judge by this wine, he was right. It is pure Pinot-red in colour with a very winey, rather wild, open nose. The structure is beautiful, combining both elegance and liveliness. This wine would go well with a *griotte à la Vincenot*, if someone happens to bring a wild boar back from the hunt. A **En la Rue de Vergy 99** is also worth noting. It receives one star.

☛ Dom. Lignier-Michelot, 11, rue Haute, 21220 Morey-Saint-Denis, tel. 03.80.34.31.13, fax 03.80.58.52.16 ⍐

DOM. MICHEL MAGNIEN ET FILS

■ Le Très Girard 1999★

■ 0.49 ha 3,400 €15-23

This *climat* has become reasonably well known thanks to a restaurant that took the same name. This delicately-coloured 99 has aromas of liquorice, fur and mulberries on the nose. The fruity theme is continued on the palate where the oak is well-blended. This is a wine that will soon be perfectly drinkable, since the tannins are not too overpowering and the palate has plenty of flesh. The honest and classically-made **village 99 red** is also appealing but it would be best to wait two or three years before opening it.

☛ EARL Michel Magnien et Fils, 4, rue Ribordot, 21220 Morey-Saint-Denis, tel. 03.80.51.82.98, fax 03.80.58.51.76 ⍐ ⍏ by appt.

DOM. MICHEL NOËLLAT ET FILS 1999★

■ 1.3 ha 3,600 €15-23

There are some classic rules of wine-making that are hard to beat. The combination of roundness, richness and fullness, for a start, or the balance between alcohol and acidity. This wine is not particularly well-structured but it does follow these rules. Add to this an attractive ruby-red colour plus aromas of humus and fresh fruit (raspberries) and a lovely toastiness from the oak, and you have a very decent wine.

☛ SCEA Dom. Michel Noëllat et Fils, 5, rue de la Fontaine, 21700 Vosne-Romanée, tel. 03.80.61.36.87, fax 03.80.61.18.10 ⍐ ⍏ by appt.

DOM. HERVE SIGAUT

■ Les Charrières 1999★

■ n.c. 4,000 €15-23

Les Charrières is separated from the Clos de la Roche by the *Route des Grands Crus*. It has produced this attractive 99 packed with aromas of liquorice, raspberry, Griotte cherry, cocoa and fur. The wine is still a long way from achieving its full potential, but it will in due course. At the moment it has body and ripe fruit and would go well with a leg of lamb.

☛ Hervé Sigaut, 12, rue des Champs, 21220 Chambolle-Musigny, tel. 03.80.62.80.28, fax 03.80.62.84.40 ⍐ ⍏ by appt.

Clos de la Roche, de Tart, de Saint-Denis, des Lambrays

The Clos de la Roche – which despite its name is not a walled vineyard – covers the biggest surface area (about 16 ha/

40 acres), and includes various *lieux-dits* or named locations; it produced 486 hl (12,830 gal) in 1998, 700 hl (18,480 gal) in 1999 and 652 hl (17,213 gal) in 2000. Clos Saint-Denis, about 6.5 ha (16 acres), is also unwalled, and it too incorporates a group of *lieux-dits* 270 hl (7,128 gal). These two Crus are parcelled into small plots and cultivated by numerous growers. The Clos de Tart is entirely enclosed by one grower. It is about 7 ha (17 acres) and the wines are vinified and matured on the property – 220 hl (5,808 gal) in 2000; the cellar on two levels is well worth a visit. The Clos de Lambrays has one main grower, but it is a group of several plots and *lieux-dits*: Les Bouchots, Les Larrêts or Clos de Lambrays and Le Meix-Rentier. It covers just under 9 ha (22 acres), 8.5 (21 acres) of which are cultivated by the same grower. It produced 383 hl (10,111 gal) in 1999 and 331 hl (8,738 gal) in 2000.

Clos de la Roche

DOM. ARLAUD 1999★

■ Gd cru   n.c.   n.c.   ■■ €23-30

A young soldier from the Ardèche, Joseph Arlaud, was passing through Morey during the war. There, he fell in love with Renée Amiot and thanks to the vagaries of history, both this estate and their son Hervé were born. This is a very well-presented 99. Its blueberry jam nose offers a few toasted notes before opening on more leathery lines. It has body, acidity and the true structure of a Grand Cru in the making.
↘ SCEA Dom. Arlaud Père et Fils, 43, rte des Grands-Crus, 21220 Morey-Saint-Denis, tel. 03.80.34.32.65, fax 03.80.58.52.09, e-mail cyprien.arlaud@wanadoo.fr ☑
Y by appt.

DOM. DUJAC 1999★

■ Gd cru   1.95 ha   10,200   ■■ €46-76

Jacques Seysses has owned this magnificent estate since 1968. He has always been extremely careful about the quality of his grapes, and in growing vines as in making wine, he always aims to achieve the best result. People often say that Clos de La Roche is the most structured of the Morey *Grands Crus*, and this wine goes along with that. It has a faultless dark purple colour. The nose with aromas of raspberry, mulberry, blackcurrant and mild tobacco has also a wild and musky character. Although it is still rather tannic, the palate has the right degree of acidity and well-handled, long tannins. In five to eight years' time this wine will be truly great.
↘ Dom. Dujac, 7, rue de la Bussière, 21220 Morey-Saint-Denis, tel. 03.80.34.01.00, fax 03.80.34.01.09, e-mail dujac@dujac.com ☑
↘ Jacques Seysses

DOM. PONSOT

Cuvée vieilles vignes 1998

■ Gd cru   3.2 ha   6,779   ■■ +★76

This tiny estate is famous for producing wine using the most natural methods: maturation on the lees, bottling without fining or filtration 'on a clear night during the moon's last quarter, as the label says. Father and son, both absolute pillars of the association of the *Chevaliers du Tastevin*, have created a 98 that is red as a magistrate's gown. The nose of stewed fruit and spices has wild animal notes too. The palate is still reserved, so we will have to hope that the wait is worthwhile.
↘ Dom. Ponsot, 21, rue de la Montagne, BP 11, 21220 Morey-Saint-Denis, tel. 03.80.34.32.46, fax 03.80.58.51.70. e-mail info@domaine-ponsot.com

POULET PERE ET FILS 1999

■ Gd cru   n.c.   n.c.   ■■ €46-76

This cherry-red wine, more intense than brilliant in colour, has a rather 'New World'-style nose, with brandied fruit aromas adding a firm, assertive character. The attack is straightforward and clean, though without great structure. However, its fresh acidity, subtle softness and touch of high-class elegance are sufficient for it to feature here. You might say it has a rather seductive, delicate style, but these clichés shouldn't be taken as gospel.
↘ Poulet Père et Fils, 6, rue de Chaux, BP 4, 21700 Nuits-Saint-Georges, tel. 03.80.62.43.02, fax 03.80.61.28.08

Clos Saint-Denis

DOM. ARLAUD 1999

■ Gd cru   n.c.   n.c.   ■■ €23-30

This estate won a *coup de cœur* in the 1996 *Guide* for its subtle 92 vintage. In contrast, this one is demonstrative right from its violet colour up to the fiery finish. Musky smells and tastes soften powerful tannins, and if this were not a Grand Cru, one might describe it as sturdy: it is a noble peasant with its feet firmly on the ground.
↘ SCEA Dom. Arlaud Père et Fils, 43, rte des Grands-Crus, 21220 Morey-Saint-Denis, tel. 03.80.34.32.65, fax 03.80.58.52.09, e-mail cyprien.arlaud@wanadoo.fr ☑
Y by appt.

COTE - D'OR

Conceur

la Romanée
Romanée Conti
la Grande-Rue

Richebourg
Romanée-
St-Vivant

la Tâche

Vosne-
Romanée

Grands-
Echézeaux

Echézeaux

Clos
de Vougeot

Musigny

Vougeot

Chambolle-
Musigny

D 122

D 122

Bonnes
Mares

Clos des
Lambrays

Clos
de
Tart

Clos
St-Denis

Clos de
la Roche

Morey-
Saint-Denis

Latricières-
Chambertin

Mazoyères-
Chambertin

Chambertin

Charmes-
Chambertin
ou

Griotte-
Chambertin

Chapelle-
Chambertin
Clos-de-Bèze

Ruchottes-
Chambertin

Mazis
Chambertin

Gevrey-
Chambertin

Chambertin
Clos-de-Bèze

N 74

N 74

N 74

Flagey-
Echézeaux

Gilly

Grands Crus

AOC localities and Premiers Crus

Regional AOC areas

Commune boundaries

N

0   500   1000 yds

0   500   1000 m

palate follows along the same lines: straightforward and structured with well-measured tannins. Its finish – though austere, of course, at this age – is long and promising: give it five to eight years.

➽ Mommessin, Dom. du Clos de Tart, 7, rte des Grands-Crus, 21220 Morey-Saint-Denis, tel. 03.80.34.30.91, fax 03.80.24.60.01 ▶

DOM. PHILIPPE CHARLOPIN 1999★

| Gd cru | n.c. | n.c. | €38-46 |

People call this *clos* the 'Mozart of the Côte de Nuits,' and this wine certainly lives up to the name. This is a supple and tender wine, dark red in colour, delicate on the nose with floral and vanilla aromas. It is full flavoured, all silk and lace – exactly how one imagines it should be.

➽ Philippe Charlopin, 18, rte de Dijon, 21220 Gevrey-Chambertin, tel. 03.80.51.81.18, fax 03.80.51.81.18
Ⲧ by appt.

DOM. HERESZTYN 1999★

| Gd cru | 0.23 ha | 1,400 | €46-76 |

The deep, full palate of this wine complements the violet-purple colour and aromas of cherry preserved in alcohol. The well-balanced, pleasant palate is well-structured with fine oak, while the fruit and tannins are as expected in a still-developing 99.

➽ Dom. Heresztyn, 27, rue Richebourg, 21220 Gevrey-Chambertin, tel. 03.80.34.13.99, fax 03.80.34.13.99, e-mail domaine.heresztyn@wanadoo.fr ▶
Ⲧ by appt.

REINE PEDAUQUE 1999

| Gd cru | n.c. | n.c. |

In contrast to the saint after which it was named (who was decapitated), this Saint-Denis is in no danger of losing its head. It comes from the collegiate church of Vergy in the Hautes-Côtes. The colour is a bright garnet-red, the nose musky and wild, beginning on a spicy note and then becoming rather biting. The attack is straightforward and solid, expanding on the palate to reveal a full-bodied structure.

➽ Reine Pédauque, Le Village, 21420 Aloxe-Corton, tel. 03.80.25.00.00. fax 03.80.26.42.00. e-mail rpedauque@axnet.fr Ⲧ by appt.

Clos des Lambrays

DOM. DES LAMBRAYS 1998★★

| Gd cru | 8.66 ha | 30,000 | €46-76 |

79 81 **82** 83 **85** 88 **89** [90] 92 [93] 94 **95** 96 97 **98**

Nestled between the Clos de Tart and the Clos Saint-Denis, this Grand Cru has only recently been established. It has been achieved by joining several separate plots of vineyard that were worked in the 19th century. The *clos*, which sits high on the hillside and is surrounded by walls, owes its renaissance to Thierry Brouin, an oenologist who has been running it since 1980. Here he presents a garnet-red 98 with dark purple highlights – just as one might expect. There are the beginnings of a rich, complex, bouquet of cherry, mulberry and plum with an appropriate hint of vanilla. A velvety wine with an elegant hint of mocha, it can safely look forward to a minimum of five to eight years in the cellar. 'Worthy of its rank,' writes one enthusiastic taster.

➽ Dom. des Lambrays, 31, rue Basse, 21220 Morey-Saint-Denis, tel. 03.80.51.84.33, fax 03.80.51.81.97 ▶
Ⲧ by appt.
➽ Freund

Chambolle Musigny

The Musigny name alone sets the pitch in the orchestral sweep of wines in this region. This is a commune of enormous reputation despite its tiny area, founded on the quality of its wines and the fame of its Premiers Crus, the most celebrated of which is the *climat* of Les Amoureuses. But Chambolle also has Charmes, Chabiots, Cras,

526

Clos de Tart

MOMMESSIN 1999★★

| Gd cru | 7.53 ha | 20,000 | €46-76 |

64 **69** 76 78 **82** 83 84 [85] **86** [88] [89] [90] [93] 95 96 97 98 99

The Knights Hospitallers of Brochon gave this vineyard as a gift, in 1141, to the Abbey of Notre-Dame de Tart. It was not yet called the Clos de Tart, and probably wasn't until the 15th century. It was bought in 1932 by the Mommessin family, and today is run by Sylvain Pitiot, the author of several important books on Burgundy wine. This lovely dark-red 99 has a very oaky, charred nose with a few hints of Griotte cherry and raspberry just beginning to show through. The

Fousselottes, Groseilles and Lavrottes as well. The small village, with its narrow streets shaded by trees, has magnificent cellars (Domaine des Musigny). In 2000, the vineyard produced 6,793 hl (179,335 gal).

The Chambolle wines are elegant, subtle and soft, combining the strength of Bonnes-Mares and the finesse of Musigny; within the Côte de Nuits this area represents a transition from one type of *terroir* to another.

DOM. ARLAUD PERE ET FILS
1999★★

0.7 ha | n.c. | €11-15

This Pinot Noir is as black as ink. It is a little slow to show itself, but then, once it does, what a range of flavours! Spices, vanilla, blackcurrant ... The tannins are very prominent but there is an exceptional richness which indicates great potential. Superb: a great wine for laying down.

SCEA Dom. Arlaud Père et Fils, 43, rte des Grands-Crus, 21220 Morey-Saint-Denis, tel. 03.80.34.32.65, fax 03.80.58.52.09, e-mail cyprien.arlaud@wanadoo.fr
by appt.

ALBERT BICHOT 1998★

n.c. | 10,000 | €23-30

'The eye must be seduced and delighted,' reads an old tasting manual. Here the wine has a bright blood-red colour and a classic nose with vanilla and blackcurrant. The structure is as solid as the walls of Château Clos de Vougeot. What is needed now is time for the character to develop. Keep it for at least two to three years in the cellar.

Maison Albert Bichot, 6 *bis*, bd Jacques-Copeau, 21200 Beaune, tel. 03.80.24.37.37, fax 03.80.24.37.38

SYLVAIN CATHIARD
Les Clos de l'Orme 1999★

0.43 ha | 2,500 | €15-23

Everyone was in agreement about this wine, which won a *coup de cœur* two years ago for the 97 vintage. The colour is brilliant with violet glints, but at present the wine remains rather closed with pronounced wood flavours. There are no doubts, however, that it has real potential: the fruit is beginning to peek through and it has all the right qualities at heart. We are betting on it.

Sylvain Cathiard, 20, rue de la Goillotte, 21700 Vosne-Romanée, tel. 03.80.62.36.01, fax 03.80.61.18.21 by appt.

527

DOM. PHILIPPE CHARLOPIN-PARIZOT 1998★★

n.c. | n.c. | €15-23

This simple *village* is a deserving winner of a *coup de cœur*. It is almost up to the level of a Premier Cru. The colour is a very dark garnet with bluish hues. The mulberry and blackcurrant nose is fantastic, the attack well-measured and well-constructed. It has perfect harmony and, quite simply, is truly great. One taster – while awarding it the *coup de cœur* – notes that the finish is still dominated by oak, but this will mellow over four years.

Philippe Charlopin, 18, rte de Dijon, 21220 Gevrey-Chambertin, tel. 03.80.51.81.18, fax 03.80.51.81.18
by appt.

F. CHAUVENET 1998★

n.c. | 9,000 | €23-30

Françoise Chauvenet was famous in Nuits-Saint-Georges where she was highly respected for being one of the few female wine-tasters. Things have moved on since the 19th century. She would have liked this perfectly-coloured Pinot Noir with its lovely direct nose of blackcurrant leaf, freshness of ripe fruit and delightful tannins. It is on the level of a Premier Cru, and can be laid down for a long time. This label forms part of J.-Cl. Boisset's group.

F. Chauvenet, 9, quai Fleury, 21700 Nuits-Saint-Georges, tel. 03.80.62.61.43, fax 03.80.62.37.38

GUY COQUARD 1999

1er cru | 0.49 ha | 3,200 | €15-23

This is a good wine for getting to know this appellation, since its fruit, roundness and fullness are very characteristic. The concentrated palate shows a slight hardness on the finish but this will soften with time. It is dark, almost dull red in colour, with a most impressive bouquet where one encounters, among other things, orange peel and *pêche de vigne* in syrup. A promising vintage that will go perfectly with a roast pigeon.

Guy Coquard, 55, rte des Grands-Crus, 21220 Morey-Saint-Denis, tel. 03.80.34.38.88, fax 03.80.51.58.66
by appt.

HENRI FELETTIG 1999★

2.6 ha | 9,000 | €11-15

This rather glamorous wine has a pale, 'back to nature' colour. Its aromas of raspberry and blackcurrant leaf are very smart

Chambolle Musigny

and upmarket. The palate is attractive and supple with an underpinning of liquorice which rings bells. Do not wait too long for this wine: youth is not eternal.

☛ GAEC Henri Felettig, rue du Tilleul, 21220 Chambolle-Musigny, tel. 03.80.62.85.09, fax 03.80.62.86.41 ☑
Ⲭ by appt.

DOM. FOUGERAY DE BEAUCLAIR Les Veroilles 1999★★
■ 0.08 ha 500 ‖‖ €23-30

This lovely, reserved, discreet 99 illustrates its appellation and vintage beautifully. Its wonderful primary aromas give the impression of a wine that has just come from the barrel. Its attack is glorious, changing tone abruptly from spicy, peppery flavours and pine to blackcurrant or blueberry on the palate. A great deal of skill has gone into making this wine, and its future is secure. Not far of a *coup de coeur*.

☛ Dom. Fougeray de Beauclair, 44, rue de Mazy, 21160 Marsannay-la-Côte, tel. 03.80.52.21.12, fax 03.80.58.73.83, e-mail fougeraydebeauclair@wanadoo.fr ☑
Ⲭ ev. day 8am–12 noon 2pm–6pm

ROBERT GROFFIER PERE ET FILS
Les Hauts-Doix 1999★★
■ 1er cru 1 ha 4.500 ‖‖ €30-38

This estate is always close to success. Les Hauts-Doix is a *climat* next to Les Amoureuses and the wine it produced this year is close to a *coup de coeur*. The colour is dense and dark, and the nose opens with a blend of cinnamon and charred notes which are followed by blackcurrant. It is full of fruit, faultlessly well-balanced, and looks as if it will last forever. The **Premier Cru Les Sentiers 99** is a very characteristic Chambolle and has been matured in fine oak, which is present but not prominent on the palate. We like it as much as the other one.

☛ SARL Robert Groffier Père et Fils, 3-5, rte des Grands-Crus, 21220 Morey-Saint-Denis, tel. 03.80.34.31.53, fax 03.80.34.31.53 ☑
Ⲭ by appt.

DOM. A.-F. GROS 1999★
■ 0.39 ha 2.600 ‖‖ €15-23

This Chambolle has character: it is forceful, tough and sturdy. It comes from several vineyard plots that are scattered here and there: Fremières, Derrière le Four, Le Pas de Chat, Les Athets. The colour is an attractively intense red, the raspberry nose lively and the palate full of character, as we have said. There is not much in the way of oak. It will go well with game or a Maroilles cheese.

☛ Dom. A.-F. Gros, La Garelle, 21630 Pommard, tel. 03.80.22.61.85, fax 03.80.24.03.16, e-mail gros.anne-françoise@wanadoo.fr ☑
Ⲭ by appt.

DOM. HERESZTYN 1999★★
■ 0.37 ha 2.500 ‖‖ €15-23

This is the wine of the future. It would be hard to find a wine redder than this! It is so dark it is almost black. The nose is complex, combining raspberry and ferns. It is superb on the palate, a little on the heavy side but glorious nevertheless. A wine like this could manage the unlikely feat of bringing together a cheese from the abbey of La Pierre-qui-Vire and a chocolate cake. Yes, indeed. It has mulberry and an amazing concentration of blackcurrant flavours and, of course, a *coup de coeur*.

☛ Dom. Heresztyn, 27, rue Richebourg, 21220 Gevrey-Chambertin, tel. 03.80.34.13.99, fax 03.80.34.13.99, e-mail domaine.heresztyn@wanadoo.fr ☑
Ⲭ by appt.

LIGNIER-MICHELOT 1999★
■ 1.4 ha 3.500 ‖‖ ◆ €11-15

There are a few violet highlights in this otherwise deep-red wine. The aromas are honest and straightforward with fine notes of tobacco, spices and mulberry. This rich, warming, well-constructed 99 does its village proud.

☛ Dom. Lignier-Michelot, 11, rue Haute, 21220 Morey-Saint-Denis, tel. 03.80.34.31.13, fax 03.80.58.52.16 ☑
Ⲭ by appt.

DOM. MACHARD DE GRAMONT
Les Nazoires 1998★★
■ 0.25 ha 1.300 ‖‖ €15-23

The colour of this wine is a fine, youthful cherry-red. The nose is elegant, beginning on a smoky note before opening with floral fragrances accompanied by a touch of toastiness. The palate is not particularly powerful but does reflect the delicacy of the wines from this village. A lovely, subtle, fine wine that should be drunk soon (within two to five years).

☛ SCE Dom. Machard de Gramont, Le Clos, rue Pique, BP 105, 21703 Prémeaux-Prissey, tel. 03.80.61.15.25, fax 03.80.61.06.39 ☑ Ⲭ by appt.

JEAN-PAUL MAGNIEN

■ Les Sentiers 1999

■ 1er cru | 0.41 ha 2,000 | €15-23

In the opening pages of *Les Aristocrates*, a novel by Michel de Saint-Pierre, the twins who feature in the story secretly empty the family wine-cellar and drink a Chambolle Musigny straight from the bottle. We think this wine deserves a little more respect. It is clear and limpid, with strawberries and stewed fruits on the nose, well-balanced with a certain finesse: a good wine, in short.

• Jean-Paul Magnien, 5, ruelle de l'Eglise, 21220 Morey-Saint-Denis, tel. 03.80.51.83.10, fax 03.80.58.53.27 ▼
Y by appt.

DOM. THIERRY MORTET

■ Les Beaux Bruns 1999

■ 1er cru | 0.25 ha 1,500 | €23-30

Les Beaux Bruns is a *climat* situated in the middle of the appellation. As clear a wine as you could hope to find, with well-defined aromas that are fairly typical of Chambolle. On the palate there is soft fruit and fullness with a touch of bitterness that in two to five years will disappear. With his **Village 99**, Thierry Mortet manages to produce a high-class wine that combines balance with freshness. Its aromas of mulberries, blueberries, spices and delicately oaky notes confirm a well-measured extraction process.

• Dom. Thierry Mortet, 16, pl. des Marronniers, 21220 Gevrey-Chambertin, tel. 03.80.51.85.07, fax 03.80.34.16.80 ▼
Y by appt.

JACQUES-FREDERIC MUGNIER

■ Les Fuées 1998★

■ 1er cru | 0.71 ha 2,000 | €30-38

Les Fuées runs alongside the Bonnes Mares slope. This deep purple wine sings in the glass. The aroma of blackcurrant leaf does not come as a surprise since the Mugnier family was for many years a prominent producer of liqueurs in Dijon. With some aeration, the wine releases a more complex fruit aroma. The palate is pleasant but not entirely open, promising better things to come. The Château Chambolle-Musigny dates from the 18th century.

• Jacques-Frédéric Mugnier, Ch. de Chambolle-Musigny, 21220 Chambolle-Musigny, tel. 03.80.62.85.39, fax 03.80.62.87.36

DOM. MICHEL NOELLAT ET FILS

■ Les Feuillottes 1999★

■ 1er cru | 0.45 ha 1,200 | €23-30

This is the kind of wine that people always grab hold of if ever they get the chance. This wine has a Bigarreau cherry colour with aromas of fern and cocoa (a light touch of the lees). Its character is full and floral, and it has good length on the palate but needs a year or two for the oak to mellow.

DOM. HERVE SIGNAUT

■ Les Sentiers Vieilles vignes 1999★★

■ 1er cru | n.c. 4,500 | €15-23

One of our tasters was very keen to give this wine a *coup de cœur*. Presenting a very pleasant and companionable palate, it looks good, is well-made, and has plenty of fruit. The colour is dark red with tinges of violet round the edges and the nose has complex aromas of fruit in *eau-de-vie* or even fruit liqueur with a dash of well-measured oak thrown in. Les Sentiers is near Morey, just below the Bonnes Mares.

• Hervé Sigaut, 12, rue des Champs, 21220 Chambolle-Musigny, tel. 03.80.62.80.28, fax 03.80.62.84.40 ▼
Y by appt.

DOM. ROBERT SIRUGUE

■ Les Mombies 1999★

■ 0.3 ha 1,650 | €15-23

Twenty-five per cent new oak was used in maturing this youthful 99, which means that the wood is still very pronounced, though the body seems well-structured. Its bouquet is powerful and spicy with aromas of wild strawberry and blueberry creeping through. One of our tasters would like to drink it 'in three or four years' time with something spicy, like a tagine'.

• SCEA Dom. Michel Noëllat et Fils, 5, rue de la Fontaine, 21700 Vosne-Romanée, tel. 03.80.61.36.87, fax 03.80.61.18.10 ▼
Y by appt.

LAURENT ROUMIER 1998★

■ 1.4 ha 5,000 | €15-23

'He who drinks good wine sees God': the Cistercian monks lived near Chambolle and their maxim is perfectly apt here. This glinting bright ruby-red 98 has a lovely nose with Griotte cherries and cloves. From the first moment it opens on the palate, you know that this is a good wine. It has depth and length – all the right qualities are there, and with elegance.

• Dom. Laurent Roumier, rue de Vergy, 21220 Chambolle-Musigny, tel. 03.80.62.83.60, fax 03.80.62.84.10 ▼
Y by appt.

REMI SEGUIN 1998★

■ 0.51 ha n.c. | €11-15

Harvested on 20 September 1998, these 55-year-old vines have produced a wine that is very characteristic of the AOC. There are a lot of blue hues in the garnet-red colour of this wine, revealing its youth. The nose is fruity and fresh and the palate full with a hint of new oak, which was noted by the Jury. The tannins are rounded and well-integrated, silky-smooth and long. Good for the first ten years of this century.

• Rémi Seguin, 19, rue de Citeaux, 21640 Gilly-lès-Citeaux, tel. 03.80.62.89.61, fax 03.80.62.80.92 ▼ Y by appt.

DOM. TAUPENOT-MERME 1998★

🍇 Robert Sirugue, 3, av. du Monument, 21700 Vosne-Romanée, tel. 03.80.61.00.64, fax 03.80.61.27.57 ▼ Y by appt.

n.c.	5,000	€15-23

This intense ruby-red 98 has a fiery nose with aromas of undergrowth and dark fruit. The tannins are soft and the finish reasonably long. Its charms will last a good ten years. Best served with a duck and truffles or a simple *filet mignon*. The **Premier Cru La Combe d'Orveau 98**, which is commended by the Jury, needs to wait for the oak to integrate and mellow.

🍇 Jean Taupenot-Merme, 33, rte des Grands-Crus, 21220 Morey-Saint-Denis, tel. 03.80.34.35.24, fax 03.80.51.83.41, e-mail domainetaupenot-merme@wanadoo.fr ▼ Y by appt.

HENRI DE VILLAMONT
Les Groseilles 1998★★

1er cru	0.67 ha	2,500	€23-30

This estate was taken over some while ago by the Swiss group Schenk and has been producing good wines. Its 85 received a *coup de coeur* in the 1989 *Guide*. This wine, *coupe de coeur* purple edged with vermilion, has real texture and deep, full aromas of blackcurrant and leather. It is rich, solid and generous – what more could one ask? A fine future awaits it.

🍇 SA Henri de Villamont, rue du Dr-Guyot, 21420 Savigny-les-Beaune, tel. 03.80.24.70.07, fax 03.80.22.54.31, e-mail hdv@planetb.fr ▼ Y ev. day except Tue. 10.30am–6pm; cl. 15 Nov.–15 Mar.

JEAN-LUC AEGERTER 1999

Gd cru	0.12 ha	600	€46-76

A *négociant-éleveur* can not always get a good Bonnes Mares. Jean-Luc Aegerter, however, manages it frequently, and has done it again this year. His wine is deep purple with pink highlights round the edge. The nose is still youthful and although the wine has a good solid structure, it is still too young to demonstrate its true worth.

🍇 Jean-Luc Aegerter; 49, rue Henri-Challand, 21700 Nuits-Saint-Georges, tel. 03.80.61.02.88, fax 03.80.62.37.99 ▼

Bonnes-Mares

This appellation, which produced 613 hl (16,183 gal) in 1999 and 559 hl (14,758 gal) in 2000, spreads into the commune of Morey along the wall of the Clos de Tart, but most of it is located in Chambolle. This is a Grand Cru par excellence. The wines of Bonnes-Mares are full, vinous and rich and have the capacity to keep for a long time. After a few years of ageing, they make excellent accompaniments to rich stews or game birds.

DOM. ARLAUD 1999★

Gd cru	0.2 ha	n.c.	€30-38

91 92 ⑨③ 95 96 ⑨⑦ 99

This brilliant scarlet 99 has a delicate nose and a long palate, and although the wood is pronounced, it doesn't overwhelm the soft fruit flavours. There is a certain chewiness, a decent amount of acidity and a little touch of bitterness on the finish: it is tannic and austere, as it should be at this age. The 93 vintage gained a *coup de coeur* in the 1997 *Guide*. This plot of 20 ares (0.5 acres) was bought in the early 1940s by the Valby family from Morey.

🍇 SCEA Dom. Arlaud Père et Fils, 43, rte des Grands-Crus, 21220 Morey-Saint-Denis, tel. 03.80.34.32.65, fax 03.80.58.52.09, e-mail cyprien.arlaud@wanadoo.fr ▼ Y by appt.

DOM. BART 1999★★

Gd cru	1.01 ha	2,500	€38-46

This wine almost gets three stars. It really is wonderful. This is the 'charming Grand Cru' which Terry Robards mentions in his dictionary of wine. Its colour is a velvety dark red and yet brilliant at the same time; it offers delicate mulberry and macerated fruit aromas, and then explodes on the palate with elegance and refinement. The body is dense but not tightly-knit, the richness sensual, the finish tender. This is a really classy wine that truly knows its stuff and will be very good for a very long time to come.

🍇 Dom. Bart, 23, rue Moreau, 21160 Marsannay-la-Côte, tel. 03.80.51.49.76, fax 03.80.51.23.43 ▼ Y by appt.

DOM. DROUHIN-LAROZE 1999★★

Gd cru	1.5 ha	4,000	€38-46

95 96 98 99

In 1921 Alexandre Drouhin inherited this estate, originally founded in 1850, and afterwards set about buying up plots of land in this Grand Cru. These vineyards are in the middle part of the appellation and some vine stock here dates as far back as 1928. This is a high-quality wine with a very youthful colour (ruby verging on purple) and on the nose there is still a prominent woodiness, though aromas of violet and black cherry are beginning to show through. On the palate, the tannins are also pronounced but, having all the qualities of a Grand Cru, it should keep well for a long time. To quote one of our tasters: 'The fruit is all there, tantalising our curiosity and our greed.'

🍇 Dom. Drouhin-Laroze, 2, rue du Chambertin, 21220 Gevrey-Chambertin, tel. 03.80.34.31.49, fax 03.80.51.83.70 ▼ Y by appt.
🍇 Bernard Philippe Drouhin

This is the smallest commune of the Côte, only 80 ha (198 acres) in area. Of these, the famous Clos occupies 50 ha (124 acres). Here you can find several Premiers Crus, the best-known being the Clos Blanc (white wines) and the Clos de la Perrière. Production rose to 710 hl (18,744 gal) in 2000, of which 163 hl (4,303 gal) were white.

DOM. FOUGERAY DE BEAUCLAIR 1999*

■ Gd cru	1.6 ha	3,000	⊞ €46-76

88 89 90 **92** [**93**] [**94**] [**95**] 96 **97** 98 99

This Bonnes Mares produced by the Clair family from Morey-Saint-Denis is for real connoisseurs. It has an intense black cherry colour and, although not very forthcoming, it has a few musky notes that are just about detectable. It is full and tannic, very concentrated and very much a Morey wine. There is an intense fruitiness here which is just waiting for the opportunity to express itself in five or six years' time.

➽ Dom. Fougeray de Beauclair, 44, rue de Mazy, 21160 Marsannay-la-Côte, tel. 03.80.52.21.12, fax 03.80.58.73.83, e-mail fougeraydebeauclair@wanadoo.fr 🗑
Ⴤ ev. day 8am-12 noon 2pm-6pm

ROBERT GROFFIER PERE ET FILS 1999★★

■ Gd cru	0.98 ha	n.c.	⊞ €46-76

93 94 96 **97** **98** 99

This almost 1-ha (2.47-acre) plot was bought in 1933 from the Peloux estate and has been in the family ever since. The garnet-purple of this wine is dappled with ruby flecks that resemble stained glass. Its aromas combine Griotte cherries and rose aromas before opening out with fresh grapes. The attack is smooth, the body extremely well-balanced. It has both power and smoothness — not bad!

➽ SARL Robert Groffier Père et Fils, 3-5, rte des Grands-Crus, 21220 Morey-Saint-Denis, tel. 03.80.34.31.53, fax 03.80.34.31.53 🗑
Ⴤ by appt.

LAURENT ROUMIER 1999★

■ Gd cru	0.15 ha	600	⊞ €46-76

This small estate, which in California would be called a 'boutique winery', was painstakingly built up ten years ago from rented vineyards. They make top-quality wine here. Four *cuvées* of Bonnes Mares have resulted in this crimson-red wine. The rather oaky nose has touches of mango and spicy herbs. Full-bodied and generous, it has appealing delicacy and length, with a structure that allows the fruit full freedom of expression.

➽ Dom. Laurent Roumier, rue de Vergy, 21220 Chambolle-Musigny, tel. 03.80.62.83.60, fax 03.80.73.84.10 🗑
Ⴤ by appt.

DOM. BERTAGNA

Clos de la Perrière Monopole 1998★★

■ 1er cru	2.25 ha	8,500	⊞ €15-23

This *clos* is situated in the former quarry that provided the Cîteaux monks with the stone to build their château and its walls. This very fine wine can either be drunk now or spend years in the cellar. The colour is deep, with a real Burgundy character; the nose is complex with a slight hint of truffles and a few notes of raspberry jam. The palate is well-structured, revealing a beautifully harmonious balance. The director of the Domaine des Hospices de Beaune comes from the Bertagna estate which gives some indication of the level we are at here.

➽ Dom. Bertagna, 16, rue du Vieux-Château, 21640 Vougeot, tel. 03.80.62.86.04, fax 03.80.62.82.58 🗑
Ⴤ by appt.

CHRISTIAN CLERGET

Les Petits Vougeot 1998

■ 1er cru	0.47 ha	2,500	⊞ €15-23

If you go up the path that leads to the château, this *climat* is on the right-hand side. The 97 vintage of this wine was remarkable, and here is the estate's deep ruby-red 98 version of the same. This rather severe wine is extremely well-made but is still firmly closed on all counts. Its well-balanced, elegant tannins and long finish give great hope for the future.

➽ Christian Clerget, 10, ancienne RN 74, 21640 Vougeot, tel. 03.80.62.87.37, fax 03.80.62.84.37 🗑 Ⴤ by appt.

DOM. ROUX PERE ET FILS

Les Petits Vougeot 1998

■ 1er cru	1.2 ha	6,000	⊞ €23-30

This estate cultivates a large plot of the Vougeot AOC and they mature their wine for 18 months in oak, 30% new. The colour of this attractive 98 is superb: garnet-red, deep, brilliant and clear. It's promising, in short. Then, from the first impression on the nose, the oak dominates right up to the finish. It will be three to five years before this wine softens sufficiently to be judged in its maturity. It is sure to go well with game or meat in sauce.

☛ Dom. Roux Père et Fils, 21190 Saint-Aubin, tel. 03.80.21.32.92, fax 03.80.21.35.00 ▼ Ⴤ by appt.

Clos de Vougeot

Much has already been written about the Clos de Vougeot and the seventy plus growers who share its 50 ha (124 acres) and production of 2,100 hl (55,440 gal) as registered in 1999 with 1,896 hl (50,054 gal) declared in 2000. Its great appeal is not just a matter of chance, but because it is good and consequently everyone in the world wants some. Of course, distinctions must be made between the wines at the top of the vineyard, those in the middle and those in the lower part, but nevertheless, when the monks of the medieval Abbey of Cîteaux built their high enclosing wall, they had chosen their site very well.

Founded at the beginning of the 12th century, the Clos rapidly grew to its present size; the surrounding wall predates the 15th century. The real appeal of the Clos itself can be tasted in the quality of the wines a few years after they have been bottled. In addition, the château itself, built in the 12th century and extended in the 16th century, is worth taking time to visit. The oldest parts are the cellar, nowadays used for meetings of the Confrérie des Chevaliers du Tastevin, its present owners, and the vat room, with its four magnificent 12th-century wine presses, one in each corner.

BERTRAND AMBROISE 1999★
Gd cru   n.c.   n.c.   ▮ €46-76

The colour of this wine has a perfect brilliance. The nose still has strong wood notes but the attack is full and powerful, the body concentrated yet friendly and inviting, with unassuming tannins that will make this a pleasant wine to drink amongst friends in four to five years' time.

☛ Maison Bertrand Ambroise, rue de l'Eglise, 21700 Premeaux-Prissey, tel. 03.80.62.30.19, fax 03.80.62.38.69, e-mail bertrand.ambroise@wanadoo.fr ▼ Ⴤ by appt.

PIERRE ANDRE 1998
Gd cru   1.09 ha   3,300   ▮ +€76

This 1.09-ha (2.7-acres) plot is part of the Ouvrard inheritance. It is situated at the top of the *clos* near the Grands-Echézeaux and was acquired by the Liger-Belair family in 1889, and then by Pierre André in 1933. This is a dark ruby-red 98 with copper highlights and aromas of animal pelts and jammy fruit. It has a lot of charm with a smooth fruitiness on the palate, a direct and flavoursome character and decent structure. The **Reine Pédauque 99** has greater potential for laying down, with its solid tannic foundation hinting at the great delicacy held in reserve for the future.

☛ Pierre André, Ch. de Corton-André, 21420 Aloxe-Corton, tel. 03.80.26.44.25, fax 03.80.26.43.57, e-mail pandre@axnet.fr Ⴤ ev. day 10am–6pm

CAPITAIN-GAGNEROT 1998
Gd cru   0.17 ha   900   ▮ €38-46

This plot of 17 ares 12 centiares (0.42 acre) in the high part of the *clos* has been in the Capitain family since the Léonce Bocquet sale in 1920. Their fresh coloured, rather pale 98 is not an imposing wine: its nose of Griotte cherries and raspberries is on the delicate side. The same rather pleasant character is found on the palate. Forget serving this with venison and go for a chicken instead.

☛ Maison Capitain-Gagnerot, 38, rte de Dijon, 21550 Ladoix-Serrigny, tel. 03.80.26.41.36, fax 03.80.26.46.29 ▼ Ⴤ by appt.

DOM. PHILIPPE CHARLOPIN 1999★
Gd cru   n.c.   n.c.   ▮ €38-46

Colonel Bisson ordered his soldiers to present arms in front of the Clos de Vougeot. So we too can pay civil homage to this rather powerful, high-class, rich 99. Its colour has luminous tones. At first there is vegetation in the aroma, and then it develops along fruitier lines. There is no denying there is alcohol here, with its hint of Griotte cherries in *eau-de-vie*, but its sound structure and length guarantee a good eight to ten years' life ahead of it.

☛ Philippe Charlopin, 18, rte de Dijon, 21220 Gevrey-Chambertin, tel. 03.80.51.81.18, fax 03.80.51.81.18
Ⴤ by appt.

DOM. HENRI CLERC ET FILS 1998★
Gd cru   0.3 ha   1,582   ▮ €38-46

This plot, situated near the RN 74, used to belong to the British group IDV and is now part of the Piat company. This brilliant and very dark garnet-red 98 with golden-brown highlights has characteristic aromas of leather, brandied fruits and blackcurrant. A very slight warmth does not upset the harmony of a genuine Grand Cru which one could – if really keen – drink now. Otherwise, it is best to wait five or six years.

Dom. Henri Clerc et Fils, pl. des Marronniers, 21190 Puligny-Montrachet, tel. 03.80.21.32.74, fax 03.80.21.39.60
ev. day 8.30am–11.45am 2pm–17.45pm

CH. GENOT-BOULANGER 1998

| ■ Gd cru | n.c. | n.c. |

A few brick-coloured highlights show through the garnet tone of this wine, followed on the nose by fairly characteristic aromas of musk, leather, and ripe, even jammy fruit. On the palate the wine is austere and introverted

533

DOM. DROUHIN-LAROZE 1999★★

| ■ Gd cru | 1 ha | 3,000 | €36-46 |

83 86 [88] 89 91 93 94 95 96 97 98 99

This estate manages to be among the front-runners for a *coup de coeur*. Philippe Drouhin make their Clos de Vougeot from a vineyard plot situated at the top part of the *clos*, near the château. This wine has a garnet colour with deep purple glints; the nose is gamey, scented with undergrowth, while the attack is spirited and rich in blackcurrant. The middle palate is slightly overwhelmed by the oak but the tannins are good quality. This is a wine with real potential.

Dom. Drouhin-Laroze, 2, rue du Chambertin, 21220 Gevrey-Chambertin, tel. 03.80.34.31.49, fax 03.80.51.83.70
by appt.

FAIVELEY 1998★★

| ■ Gd cru | 1.28 ha | 5,700 | €46-76 |

This superb wine is the product of three plots of land, each in a different corner of the *clos*. This brilliantly-coloured 98 runs the whole gamut of classic aromas: from truffles to leather, blueberries to mushrooms. It is full-bodied and rich, its character respected by a well-closed barrel, and it is still tannic, so it needs patience. In five years' time it will be perfect, and will taste delicious with a game bird.

Bourgognes Faiveley, 8, rue du Tribourg, 21701 Nuits-Saint-Georges, tel. 03.80.61.04.55, fax 03.80.62.33.37, e-mail bourgognes.faiveley@wanadoo.fr

---

DOM. FOREY PERE ET FILS 1999★

| ■ Gd cru | 0.4 ha | 1,570 | €30-38 |

This dark-violet wine is young and still very much dominated by the flavour of new oak. Although a few notes of soft fruit are beginning to break through, this is a wine that should not on any account be touched for at least four to five years. The attack is straightforward and clean, while the pronounced tannins add a little note of bitterness at the finish, which is quite normal.

Dom. Forey Pere et Fils, 2, rue Derrière-le-Four, 21700 Vosne-Romanée, tel. 03.80.61.12.63
by appt.

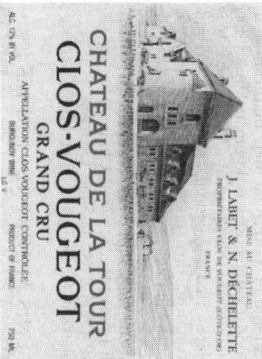

J. LABET & N. DÉCHELETTE
AL. 12% BY VOL.
CHATEAU DE LA TOUR
CLOS-VOUGEOT
GRAND CRU
APPELLATION CLOS VOUGEOT CONTROLEE
BURGUNDY WINE LC V
PRODUCT OF FRANCE
750 ML.

---

as a young Grand Cru should be. This is a slow-developing 98 with prominent woody flavours, which needs to spend five to eight years in a decent cellar.

SCEV Ch. Génot-Boulanger, 25, rue de Citeaux, 21190 Meursault, tel. 03.80.21.49.20, fax 03.80.21.49.21.
by appt.
Mme Delaby

ALAIN HUDELOT-NOELLAT 1999★

| ■ Gd cru | 0.69 ha | 3,800 | €30-38 |

This wine has a youthful colour, a dark ruby-red tinged with violet. The nose, also very youthful, is not very forthcoming, just hinting at a few blackcurrant, cocoa and fine tobacco notes. The fresh palate is not lacking in vigour but the body is somewhat rich; its vinosity, fullness and well-blended oak make this a promising wine which can be drunk from 2005 onwards. It would go very well with venison steak.

Alain Hudelot-Noëllat, Ancienne rte Nationale, 21640 Chambolle-Musigny, tel. 03.80.62.85.17, fax 03.80.62.83.13
by appt.

LOUIS JADOT 1999

| ■ Gd cru | 2.2 ha | 12,000 | €46-76 |

The owners of the Louis Jadot company are American, though the Gagey family actually run the business, and they do a very good job. This very youthful 99 is not particularly communicative. The colour is pleasant, the nose fresh and subtle with a light hint of musk and a touch of blackcurrant leaf. The attack is round, the palate full but the tannins are still in need of some discipline. Best laid down for four to six years.

Maison Louis Jadot, 21, rue Eugène-Spuller, 21200 Beaune, tel. 03.80.22.10.57, fax 03.80.22.56.03, e-mail contact@louisjadot.com by appt.

CH. DE LA TOUR 1998★★

| ■ Gd cru | 5.4 ha | n.c. | €46-76 |

85 86 87 [88] [89] 90 91 93 94 95 96 97 98

The biggest property right in the heart of the *clos* returns in force with a *coup de coeur* voted unanimously by the Grand Jury. This purple wine with its deep, dark glints is appealing from the start. Its balsamic and fruity nose shows a certain originality of character. It is exceptionally full on the palate, which is built on tannins that are both prominent and well integrated, and above all it has an absolutely breathtaking length. This is a very fine wine that possesses all the depth that one expects from a Grand Cru.

• Ch. de La Tour, Clos de Vougeot, 21640 Vougeot, tel. 03.80.62.86.13, fax 03.80.62.82.72, e-mail contact@ chateaudelatour.com ☑ ⛬ ev. day except Mon.10.30am–6.30pm; cl. 30 Nov.–1 Apr.
• François Labet

LUPÉ-CHOLET 1998★
■ Gd cru   0.75 ha   3,800   ⟐ €46-76

These days the Lupé-Cholet business belongs to the A. Bichot company. On offer here is a fairly standard dark red, almost black, 98. Its aromas take us on walks in the forest, drawing in the smell of the forest-floor after rain. On the palate the tannins are still young but the structure is good. All round, this is a good-quality wine that would be best kept in the cellar for the next four to five years.

• Lupé-Cholet, 17, av. du Gal-De-Gaulle, 21700 Nuits-Saint-Georges, tel. 03.80.61.25.02, fax 03.80.24.37.38

CH. DE MARSANNAY 1998★★
■ Gd cru   0.21 ha   1,040   ⟐ €46-76

This wine just missed a *coup de coeur* by a few votes. It has a dark garnet-red colour with amber highlights and very characteristic truffle aromas. Its acidity and tannins harmonise beautifully with the flavours of raspberry and undergrowth that are the mark of a truly great wine, a real Grand Cru. This wine is remarkably characteristic of the appellation. The Château de Marsannay has connections with Château de Meursault (owned by the Boisseaux family).

• Ch. de Marsannay, rte des Grands-Crus, BP 78, 21160 Marsannay-la-Côte, tel. 03.80.51.71.11, fax 03.80.51.71.12 ☑ ⛬ ev. day 10am–12 noon 2pm–6pm

LOUIS MAX 1999
■ Gd Cru   n.c.   1,300   ⟐ +€76

This garnet-coloured, very oaky 99 has undergone a well-handled maturation in wood. On the nose it is dominated by aromas of liquorice, black tea and red berries. It is quite a rich and complex wine with a tannic structure; the spicy (liquorice-flavoured) finish combines with blackcurrant and mulberries. In four to five years' time it will go wonderfully well with roast venison.

• Louis Max, 6, rue de Chaux, BP 4, 21700 Nuits-Saint-Georges, tel. 03.80.62.43.01, fax 03.80.62.43.16

DENIS MUGNERET ET FILS 1999★
■ Gd cru   0.72 ha   1,800   ⟐ €30-38

90 93 [94] 95 97 98 99

This vineyard plot belongs to the Liger-Belair family of Nuits-Saint-Georges and has been run by this estate on tenant farming lines since 1969. It borders the wall of the Rue de Morland, near Flagey, in the middle of the *clos*. Their garnet-coloured 99 with vermilion highlights is all blackcurrant, aromatic herbs, and kirsch. It is fairly youthful on the palate and needs to blend and soften because, although winey, long and well-structured, it remains rather closed. In five to eight years' time it will go well with a dish of beef in red wine.

• Denis et Dominique Mugneret, 9, rue de la Fontaine, 21700 Vosne-Romanée, tel. 03.80.61.00.97, fax 03.80.61.24.54 ☑ ⛬ by appt.
• Liger-Belair

DOM. MICHEL NOËLLAT ET FILS 1999★
■ Gd cru   n.c.   2,000   ⟐ €30-46

One certainly wouldn't drink this with jugged hare but it would go well with red meat. However, don't hurry this elegant 99. For the moment it remains very closed, just hinting at brandied and stewed fruit. The finesse and aromas will probably not come into their own for the next eight to ten years. A good level of acidity makes this the perfect wine for laying down and there are even some notes of violet.

• SCEA Dom. Michel Noëllat et Fils, 5, rue de la Fontaine, 21700 Vosne-Romanée, tel. 03.80.61.36.87, fax 03.80.61.18.10 ⛬ by appt.

DOM. HENRI REBOURSEAU 1998★
■ Gd cru   2.21 ha   9,460   ⟐ €46-76

89 90 92 [93] 94 95 96 97 98

This wine-producer, the grandson of a former president of the Syndicat du Clos de Vougeot, is lucky enough to have 2.21 ha (5.46 acres) of vines, right in the heart of the Grand Cru. These vineyards have been in the family since 1915 and have only changed hands four times since 1110! This brilliant black-cherry 98 presents perfectly classic aromas of truffle and undergrowth. It is still tannic and warm but has a solid structure and should become well balanced in around three years' time.

• NSE Dom. Henri Rebourseau, 10, pl. du Monument, 21220 Gevrey-Chambertin, tel. 03.80.51.88.94, fax 03.80.34.12.82, e-mail rebourseau1@aol.com ☑ ⛬ by appt.

LAURENT ROUMIER 1999★
■ Gd cru   0.6 ha   900   ⟐ €30-38

Alexis Lichine used to say that Clos de Vougeot is a wine 'which lasts long after it has been drunk.' That's how it is with this ruby-vermilion wine. On the nose there is something resembling mulberry juice. The structure is not the greatest but it is fruity, well balanced, and probably grown on a very good soil. It will doubtless be a very pleasant wine in around three or four years' time.

• Dom. Laurent Roumier, rue de Vergy, 21220 Chambolle-Musigny, tel. 03.80.62.83.60, fax 03.80.62.84.10 ⛬ by appt.

DOM. TORTOCHOT 1998

■ Gd cru   0.21 ha   900   III €38–46

This vineyard plot of 20.33 ha (50.2 acres) was bought from the Grivelotte-Cusset family in 1955 and, as is often the case in the *clos*, runs in a slender line from east to west. This deep, dark red 98 presents very well, with strong aromas of game and leather. The tannins are currently very powerful but the structure does not suggest that this wine can be laid down for very long. Best to wait two years and see how it develops.

● Dom. Tortochot, 12, rue de l'Eglise, 21220 Gevrey-Chambertin, tel. 03.80.34.30.68, fax 03.80.34.18.80
Y by appt.
● Chantal et Michel Tortochot

Echézeaux and Grands-Echézeaux

To the south of the commune of Flagey-Echézeaux, with its village to the east on the flatter land, like Gilly-lès-Cîteaux (see map). Its border runs along the wall of the Clos de Vougeot, to the top of the upper slopes, taking in some of the lower slopes. The vineyard on the lower slopes falls under the Appellation Vosne-Romanée. On the hills there are two Grands Crus next to each other: Le Grands-Echézeaux and L'Echézeaux. The first covers about 9 ha (22 acres) on several *lieux-dits* and produced only 314 hl (8,290 gal) in 2000, while the second covers more than 30 ha (74 acres), producing 1,363 hl (35,983 gal) in 2000.

The wines of these two Crus, the most prestigious of which is the Grands-Echézeaux, are very 'Burgundian': sturdy, well-structured, intensely aromatic and very expensive. They are mostly cultivated by wine-growers from Vosne and Flagey.

Echézeaux

JACQUES CACHEUX ET FILS 1999★★

■ Gd cru   1.07 ha   4,500   III €38–46

This estate does not use insecticides and has chosen to practise sustainable agricultural methods. This is a remarkable Grand Cru and one that is very characteristic of its AOC. The colour is black cherry, the nose mulberry and blackcurrant with vanilla, the attack pleasant. There are no surprises as it opens out. The tannins are harmonious and very well-integrated in a balanced, lengthy palate where the oak influence is still present but well-handled. It needs to spend five to eight years in the cellar. It comes from *climats* of En Orveaux and Cruots.

● Jacques Cacheux et Fils, 58, Route Nationale, 21700 Vosne-Romanée, tel. 03.80.61.01.84, fax 03.80.61.01.84,
e-mail cacheux.j.et.fils@wanadoo.fr
Y by appt.

DOM. FRANCOIS CAPITAIN ET FILS 1999★★

■ Gd cru   0.32 ha   1,500   III €38–46

Jacques Puisais recommends a leg of lamb braised with onions as the dish to really get the best out of Echézeaux. It is worth taking his word for it, and this wine would be ideal to put his theory to the test. Strongly coloured with a classic nose of blackcurrant, strawberry and prunes, it has a subtle oakiness which enhances its two main characteristics of elegance and power. It is a very good example of its type and has an excellent palate: a great wine for laying down.

● Maison Capitain-Gagnerot, 38, rte de Dijon, 21550 Ladoix-Serrigny, tel. 03.80.26.41.36, fax 03.80.26.46.29 V
Y by appt.

DOM. PHILIPPE CHARLOPIN 1999

■ Gd cru   n.c.   n.c.   III €46–76

Philippe Charlopin has often come to Vosne to ask: Jvice from the legendary Henri Jayer. This wine lacks a little depth but possesses charm and tenderness with mellow vanilla notes. The colour is robust and attractive nose presents firstly sloes and then mulberries. Best tasted with a *citeaux* rather than an *epoisses* (local Burgundy cheeses).

● Philippe Charlopin, 18, rte de Dijon, 21220 Gevrey-Chambertin, tel. 03.80.51.81.18, fax 03.80.51.81.18
Y by appt.

CHRISTIAN CLERGET 1998★★

■ Gd cru   1.1 ha   4,600   III €23–30

87 |89| |90| 91 92 93 |94| 95 97 **98**

In 1870, the Clerget family moved to an estate 1 km (0.6 miles) from Château Clos de Vougeot. This deep ruby 98 is just beginning to reveal some tantalising redcurrant aromas. It is starting to develop but has yet to reach maturity, and is well-balanced with just the right amount of acidity and already silky smooth tannins. The aromas return just at the right moment.

➤ Christian Clerget, 10, ancienne RN 74, 21640 Vougeot, tel. 03.80.62.87.37, fax 03.80.62.84.37 ◪ ⓨ by appt.

DOM. DUJAC 1999★

■ Gd cru 0.7 ha 3,600 ⬛ €46-76

This vineyard of 68 ares 72 centiares (1.7 acres) in the Champs Traversins is 100% cloned, since Jacques Seysses adopted this technique just as soon as it had been mastered. The end result is a wine with a pleasantly subtle colour, avoiding excessive extraction, and a slightly smoky, liquorice nose with a hint of flowers. The palate is more harmonious than powerful. It is a sensual wine with a two- to three-year life ahead of it.

➤ Dom. Dujac, 7, rue de la Bussière, 21220 Morey-Saint-Denis, tel. 03.80.34.01.00, fax 03.80.34.01.09, e-mail dujac@dujac.com ◪
➤ Jacques Seysses

FAIVELEY 1998

■ Gd cru 0.86 ha 3,800 ⬛ €46-76

This violet-red 98 from the En Orveaux climat has a full aroma with notes of wild rose and raspberries. It is still a little coarse; the attack is straightforward and ample. However, the oak is prominent, so it needs a few years to mature.

➤ Bourgognes Faiveley, 8, rue du Tribourg, 21701 Nuits-Saint-Georges, tel. 03.80.61.04.55, fax 03.80.62.33.37, e-mail bourgognes.faiveley@wanadoo.fr ◪

DOM. FOREY PERE ET FILS 1999★

■ Gd cru 0.3 ha 1,580 ⬛ €30-38

This estate produced Romanée for the estate of Liger-Bélair for a long time. Here is a nicely coloured, very young-looking 99. Its nose, which at first is oaky, really opens out with aromas of blackcurrant and preserved cherries. The strong extraction shows on the palate, so it needs to spend a good few years in the cellar, where it will become a great wine.

➤ Dom. Forey Père et Fils, 2, rue Derrière-le-Four, 21700 Vosne-Romanée, tel. 03.80.61.09.68, fax 03.80.61.12.63 ◪
ⓨ by appt.

DOM. A.-F. GROS 1999★★

■ Gd cru 0.26 ha 1,400 99 ⬛ €38-46

89 90 94 96 97 98 **99**

This is the first harvest from the estate of François Parent, who has consolidated vines that he inherited from his family with those of A.-F. Gros. This authentic, deep garnet Grand Cru has charming aromas of mulberries and blueberries. The firm tannins and notes of liquorice and mocha reveal its youth. It has a well-defined palate and is perfect for laying down.

➤ Dom. A.-F. Gros, La Garelle, 21630 Pommard, tel. 03.80.22.61.85, fax 03.80.24.03.16, e-mail gros.anne-françoise@wanadoo.fr ◪

DOM. GUYON 1999★

■ Gd cru n.c. 1,200 ⬛ €38-46

85 86 [88] [89] [90] 92 94 95 99

This cherry-black 99 from the En Orveaux climat owes its deep colour to an intensive extraction. Its nose at first is very floral (violets), then as the wine is opens out, it explodes with a more intense aroma of leather. Likewise, the first impression on the palate is pleasant and round, then the very firm tannins arrive in force. It is hardly necessary to point out that this wine needs plenty of time to mature.

➤ EARL Dom. Guyon, 11-16, RN 74, 21700 Vosne-Romanée, tel. 03.80.61.02.46, fax 03.80.62.36.56 ◪ ⓨ by appt.

DOM. FRANCOIS LAMARCHE 1999★

■ Gd cru 1.31 ha 6,700 ⬛ €39-46

Should this wine be drunk young for pleasure in two or three years, or put aside for the next six or seven years? This is a lovely garnet-red 99 with aromas of black cherry and touches of mocha. It is round and rich and comes from Les Cruots, on the Champs Traversins. The tannins are still fairly prominent but its fullness gives hope for better things to come. It has all the right qualities. A game bird would be the perfect accompaniment.

➤ Dom. François Lamarche, 9, rue des Communes, 21700 Vosne-Romanée, tel. 03.80.61.07.94, fax 03.80.61.24.31 ◪
ⓨ by appt.

DOM. DE LA ROMANEE CONTI 1999★★★

■ Gd cru 4.67 ha 14,651 ⬛ +★76

The similarity of this wine to the 1990 vintage is immediately apparent on the nose and then on the palate, but it has more richness, more flesh, more force, though also more delicacy. Its very dark colour resembles that of black tulips. The extremely mature nose is demonstrative and the palate opens with rare concentration: this is Pinot Noir in all its glory. This wine is the product of the first of two harvests that take place in the estate's vineyards; this is dependent upon the ripeness of the grapes. The second, which is a little less concentrated, has produced a **Premier Cru Vosne-Romanée 99**. In using this method, the estate is bringing back a practice that was common in the 1930s; the second harvest then produced a wine called 'Duvault-Blochet' (the name of the owner of Romanée Conti in the 19th century).

➤ SC du Dom. de La Romanée-Conti, 1, rue Derrière-le-Four, 21700 Vosne-Romanée, tel. 03.80.62.48.80, fax 03.80.61.05.72

MONGEARD-MUGNERET 1999★

Gd cru 2.16 ha 10,500 €30-38

This is a fine 25-ha (61.8-acre) estate which our readers know well. It is worth noting that the Jury tastes the Grands Crus without knowing any more than that there are several Grands Crus in the village. In this case, one of the tasters immediately recognised that he was tasting an Echézeaux. This lovely 99 has an authentic Pinot colour without too much extraction. There are very ripe aromas of dark fruit which move onto floral notes when the wine is aerated. The elegant palate blends flavours of fruit and oak: the oak is still dominant – inevitably at this age – but the result remains well-balanced. It will need to spend five to eight years in the cellar.

☛ Dom. Mongeard-Mugneret, 14, rue de la Fontaine, 21700 Vosne-Romanée, tel. 03.80.61.11.95, fax 03.80.62.35.75, e-mail mongeard@aanet.fr ⳾ by appt.

97 98 99

DENIS MUGNERET ET FILS 1999★

Gd cru 0.43 ha 1,800 €30-38

This garnet Echézeaux with violet highlights is beautifully balanced: it has a very complex nose combining a light floral touch with classic notes of soft fruit and spicy, toasted oak. It has a lovely length and well-blended tannins, though the oak is still the most prominent note on the finish. The Jury notes that it will go best with white meat.

☛ Denis et Dominique Mugneret, 9, rue de la Fontaine, 21700 Vosne-Romanée, tel. 03.80.61.00.97, fax 03.80.61.24.54 ⳾ by appt.

DOM. DES PERDRIX 1998★

Gd cru 1.15 ha 4,553 €46-76

Bertrand Devillard and his wife (Antonin Rodet) bought this estate in 1996. This dark ruby-red 98 is very much at home here, though it obviously needs a little time to develop and refine. Aromas of blackcurrant, redcurrant and oak are just beginning to show through, and the attack is clean although the palate is a little austere. The length of its firm, liquorice-flavoured tannins is promising.

☛ B. et C. Devillard, Dom. des Perdrix, Ch. de Champ Renard, 71640 Mercurey, tel. 03.85.98.12.12, fax 03.85.45.25.49

DOM. JACQUES PRIEUR 1998★

Gd cru 0.35 ha 1,150 €46-76

This vast estate, which is a frequent winner of coups de coeur in the Burgundy appellations, has done extremely well with this difficult vintage. Their wine is dark violet, almost the colour of a moonless night, with a youthful nose of grape must, cherries, mulberries and blueberries, and an attractive subtle oakiness. It is fruity with dense, ripe, fleshy, almost Rubenesque tannins, and has good roundness. Well-constructed with a lovely texture, this wine should be left to mature for the next two to five years.

☛ Dom. Jacques Prieur, 6, rue des Santenots, 21190 Meursault, tel. 03.80.21.23.85, fax 03.80.21.29.19 ⳾ by appt.

DOM. FABRICE VIGOT 1999★

Gd cru 0.59 ha 1,200 €46-76

90 91 92 93 **94** 96 97 99

This is an interesting, even a complex wine. The attack is both round and well-structured, leading to a full, rather distinguished palate with an attractive density. The acidity, tannins and alcohol all have something to say, but on the finish there is good length. There are pronounced aromas of *pain d'épice* and cinnamon with a discreet note of jammy red fruit. The colour is quite usual in these days of strongly-coloured wines.

☛ Dom. Fabrice Vigot, 20, rue de la Fontaine, 21700 Vosne-Romanée, tel. 03.80.61.13.01, fax 03.80.61.13.01

Grands-Echézeaux

JOSEPH DROUHIN 1998★★

Gd cru 0.47 ha 2,100 €76

This was Henri Vincenot's favourite wine, and he was a true Burgundy connoisseur! Lovely soft fruit and new oak are apparent in this dark, brilliantly-coloured 98. It is generous and straightforward on the attack and the palate is well-balanced with ripe fruit flavours and fine, well-integrated tannins, and good length. Best to wait two to three years and then serve it over the following five.

☛ Joseph Drouhin, 7, rue d'Enfer, 21200 Beaune, tel. 03.80.24.68.88, fax 03.80.22.43.14, e-mail maisondrouhin@drouhin.com ⳾ by appt.

DOM. F. MARTENOT 1998★★

Gd cru n.c. 946 €30-38

HDV Distribution is one of the subsidiaries of the Swiss group Schenk (Martenot, from Villamont). This is certainly a fine Grands Echézeaux, just going to show that it is possible for a *négoce-éleveur* to work miracles. The colour is clear, and the nose explicit (cherry, liquorice, vanilla) and the palate overflowing with complexity. This is a great wine with plenty of potential. The 99 is also a good bet.

☛ HDV Distribution, rue du Dr-Barolet, ZI Beaune-Vignolles, 21209 Beaune Cedex, tel. 03.80.24.70.07, fax 03.80.22.54.31, e-mail hdv@planetb.fr ⳾ by appt.

DOM. MONGEARD-MUGNERET 1999★

Gd cru   0.9 ha   5,000   €46-76

This domaine was very successful with the 91 vintage. It has been worth waiting four years to taste this wine with its attractive, deep colour. For the moment the oak is prominent but soft fruit notes are beginning to work their way through. It is well-structured and round, powerful but harmonious, and has depth. 'Drink it young with a creamy sauce dish, or more mature with braised meat and carrots'. This gastronomic taster is one of the great stalwarts of Burgundy winemaking.

➽ Dom. Mongeard-Mugneret, 14, rue de la Fontaine, 21700 Vosne-Romanée, tel. 03.80.61.11.95, fax 03.80.62.35.75, e-mail mongeard@axnet.fr ▼ ▼ by appt.

Vosne-Romanée

H ere again, the Burgundian customs are well respected; the name of the vineyard is better known than that of the village. Like Gevrey-Chambertin, this commune is the site of many Grands Crus and next to them are a number of famous *climats* such as Les Suchots, Les Beaux-Monts, Les Malconsorts and many others. The Appellation Vosne-Romanée produced 5,030 hl (132,792 gal) in 1999 and 6,860 hl (181,104 gal) in 2000.

DOM. CHARLES ALLEXANT ET FILS 1999★

0.25 ha   1,500   €11-15

The distiller Charles Allexant bought his first vines here in 1957. Today, the estate stretches over 14 ha (34.6 acres). His Vosne is a bright, powerfully-coloured wine. The palate is straightforward, structured and full, with flavours ranging from leather right through to cherries in *eau-de-vie*. Its elegance and liquorice finish leave a good impression and promise a great future.

➽ SCE Dom. Charles Allexant et Fils, rue du Château, Cissey, 21190 Merceuil, tel. 03.80.26.83.27, fax 03.80.26.84.04 ▼ ▼ ev. day 8am-12 noon 1.30pm-6pm; Sat./Sun. by appt.

JACQUES CACHEUX ET FILS

Les Suchots 1999★★

1er cru   0.43 ha   2,500   €30-38

This Vosne, with its velvety garnet-black colour, has a bouquet which is still closed and a little musky, showing Griotte cherries on aeration, and then blackcurrant leaf. A strong extraction has produced this powerful, concentrated wine with good volume, richness and a mellow tannin structure. It has a particular style but will mature well over the next five to ten years or longer.

➽ Jacques Cacheux et Fils, 58, Route Nationale, 21700 Vosne-Romanée, tel. 03.80.61.01.84, fax 03.80.61.01.84, e-mail cacheux.j.et.fils@wanadoo.fr ▼ ▼ by appt.

SYLVAIN CATHIARD

Aux Malconsorts 1999★

1er cru   0.74 ha   4,800

From reading just one of the tasting notes we have the general opinion of this wine: 'A very fine wine, attractive with well-blended tannins, good length on the palate and skilfully-handled new oak. Rather moreish.' The aromas of blackcurrant and vanilla are expected after such a very deep red colour. We also recommend the elegant, smoky and consistent **En Orveaux 99**.

➽ Sylvain Cathiard, 20, rue de la Goillotte, 21700 Vosne-Romanée, tel. 03.80.62.36.01, fax 03.80.61.18.21 ▼ by appt.

CHRISTIAN CLERGET

Les Violettes 1998

0.38 ha   2,000   €11-15

'This is a distinguished wine with all the fineness and qualities of its class,' notes one taster. It is full and solid with good tannins and has a very youthful colour which another Jury member describes as 'Burgundy red'. It needs to remain in the cellar for two to three years, and then be tasted again to gauge its development.

➽ Christian Clerget, 10, ancienne RN 74, 21640 Vougeot, tel. 03.80.62.87.37, fax 03.80.62.84.37 ▼ by appt.

FRANCOIS CONFURON-GINDRE

Les Chaumes Vieilles vignes 1999

1er cru   0.37 ha   1,350   €15-23

Both the Chaumes and the **Les Beaumonts 99** are of similar quality. The Chaumes is a pretty ruby-red with a mineral notes in the aroma, which is developing slowly towards soft fruit. The palate concentrates on stewed fruit and tannins, which still need time to soften.

➽ François Confuron-Gindre, 21700 Vosne-Romanée, tel. 03.80.61.20.84, fax 03.80.62.31.29 ▼ ▼ by appt.

DOM. FOUGERAY DE BEAUCLAIR Les Damodes 1999★★★

0.2 ha   1,000   €23-30

Vosne-Romanée really is 'the pearl of the Côte de Nuits'. The proof is this wine from

Les Damodes, a *climat* that is situated right on the edge of Nuits-Saint-Georges. Its colour is very dark with deep purple highlights. The nose, delicate and attractive, is all fruit. The palate is well-structured with rasberry flavours just showing through. This is a lovely 'natural' wine punctuated by a little note of bitterness from the tannins, which ought to soften in two years.

☎ Dom. Fougeray de Beauclair, 44, rue de Mazy, 21160 Marsannay-la-Côte, tel. 03.80.52.21.12, fax 03.80.58.73.83, e-mail fougeuraydebeauclair@wanadoo.fr ☑
Ⓨ ev. day 8am-12 noon 2pm-6pm

ALEX GAMBAL Les Suchots 1998★

■ 1er cru   n.c.   900   €30-38

Alex Gambal, originally from the USA, came to work in Beaune as a *négociant-éleveur* in 1997. He has been producing wine himself since 1999. Here is an attractive 98 which still has pronounced wood characteristics but with lots of *pain d'épice* and a little mulberry beginning to show through. Its rather austere and powerful style indicates that it will need laying down for a good while, since it is still developing and has not yet said all it has to say.

☎ EURL maison Alex Gambal, 4, rue Jacques-Vincent, 21200 Beaune, tel. 03.80.22.75.81, fax 03.80.22.21.66, e-mail agbeaune@aol.com ☑ Ⓨ by appt.

BLANCHE ET HENRI GROS

■   0.49 ha   1,200   €15-23

The colour of this wine is very characteristic of its vintage. Its nose is youthful and not very expressive, with the oak masking the few notes of ripe fruit and violets. The palate is very modern with fine tannins but still dominated by the oak. Five to ten years in the cellar will bring out more of the Pinot flavours.

☎ Henri Gros, 21220 Chamboeuf, tel. 03.80.51.81.20, fax 03.80.49.71.75 ☑

DOM. A.-F. GROS Aux Réas 1999★★

■   1.65 ha   9,300   €15-23

Anne-Françoise Parent-Gros, who won a *coup de coeur* last year for her Richebourg, runs Les Réas, a *climat* which has been in the Gros family for over a century. This wine is deep red with purple round the edges and reveals a few hints of woodland and floral scents before exploding on the palate with powerful raspberry flavours. It is concentrated, very full and has both glamour and presence. One need have no worries about laying it down for a long time. The **Clos de la Fontaine 99** obtains one star.

☎ Dom. A.-F. Gros, La Garelle, 21630 Pommard, tel. 03.80.22.61.85, fax 03.80.24.03.16, e-mail gros.anne-françoise@wanadoo.fr ☑
Ⓨ by appt.

MICHEL GROS

■ 1er cru   2.12 ha   13,000   €30-38

Michel Gros has been running this vineyard since 1978. He presents an attractive **village 99** and this dark garnet Clos des Réas with violet highlights. The nose is all ripe dark fruits, mild tobacco and *pain d'épice*, with an oaky structure. The body is the result of an strong pressing, which is confirmed in the attack, and then in the way the wine opens with a structure of firm, silky tannins. Best to wait four or five years before serving this wine with a duck roasted with Griotte cherries.

☎ Dom. Michel Gros, 7, rue des Communes, 21700 Vosne-Romanée, tel. 03.80.61.04.69, fax 03.80.61.22.29 ☑
Ⓨ by appt.

DOM. GROS FRERE ET SOEUR

■   1999★

    3.72 ha   27,200   €15-23

This attractive, well-made wine comes from one of the many Gros estates in Vosne-Romanée. Its colour is intense and brilliant with deep purple hues. When the wine is swirled in the glass, woodland aromas of undergrowth and ripe mulberries surge up, with a gamey note following not far behind. The tannins are already very pleasant while an overall harmony is achieved by its richness and length. Ready to drink, but also has a long life ahead of it.

Ⓨ by appt.
☎ Bernard Gros
Grands-Crus, 21700 Vosne-Romanée, tel. 03.80.61.12.43, fax 03.80.61.34.05 ☑

DOM. GUYON

Les Charmes de Mazières 1999★

■   0.2 ha   1,200   €23-30

This estate, which won *coups de coeur* for its 97 and 98 Les Orveaux, is a big-league player in Burgundy wine. This *cuvée spéciale* comes from a group of different vineyard plots. It represents its vintage well with its reddish-violet colour and aromas of toast and then fruit. The oak influence has not been entirely eliminated and at the moment it overwhelms the fullness and richness of the flavours, but this wine has a secure future ahead of it.

☎ EARL Dom. Guyon, 11-16, RN 74, 21700 Vosne-Romanée, tel. 03.80.61.02.46, fax 03.80.62.36.56 Ⓨ by appt.

HUDELOT-NOELLAT

Les Malconsorts 1999★★

■ 1er cru   0.14 ha   900   €23-30

Just try turning down the pleasures that this wine has to offer! Beneath a very intense ruby-black colour, the aromas centre in turns around violet and blackcurrant. It has a perfect, full, round body with a fine balance that enhances its more spontaneous charms. Les Malconsorts is the *climat* nearest to La Tâche. Note also the very fine **Les Suchots 99**,

Vosne-Romanée

which receives one star for its exquisite range of flavours.

☞ Alain Hudelot-Noëllat, Ancienne rte Nationale, 21640 Chambolle-Musigny, tel. 03.80.62.85.17, fax 03.80.62.83.13 ▽
Ⴡ by appt.

DOM. CHANTAL LESCURE
Les Suchots 1999★

■ 1er cru   0.4 ha   2,400   ⫼ €23–30

This Les Suchots has a wonderful colour (dark cherry with violet highlights), due to an excellent extraction, and lovely aromas (mulberry and blueberry). Dark fruits open on the palate combined with notes of tobacco. The wine still has a pronounced oakiness but has plenty of potential and should definitely be laid down. If drunk young it will go well with wild boar, or with woodcock when more mature.

☞ Dom. Chantal Lescure, 34 A, rue Thurot, 21700 Nuits-Saint-Georges,
tel. 03.80.61.16.79, fax 03.80.61.36.64,
e-mail contact@domaine-lescure.com ▽
Ⴡ by appt.

BERTRAND MACHARD DE
GRAMONT Aux Réas 1998

■   0.53 ha   1,800   ⫼ €15–23

This wine cellar is moving this year. Here is a wine that needs to mature further. It has an excellent appearance and the nose is full of warm aromas of spice and chocolate. Then on the palate the richness of the structure reveals itself. Although the tannins are already very soft, the wine remains very youthful in character.

☞ Bertrand Machard de Gramont,
13, rue de Vergy, 21700 Nuits-Saint-Georges,
tel. 03.80.61.16.96, fax 03.80.61.16.96 ▽
Ⴡ by appt.

DOM. MONGEARD-MUGNERET
Les Orveaux 1999★★

■ 1er cru   1.08 ha   7,000   ⫼ €23–30

This *climat* is situated in Flagey-Echézeaux and part of it is Grand Cru (Echézeaux). On offer here is a wine that is very much a product of its vintage and that will be delicious in a few years' time. The colour is beautifully clear with ruby reflections. There is a pronounced flavour of vanilla at present but the attack is good, the body rich, and it has an innate elegance about it. It is a little lively in the finish, so leave it to soften and open up fully in a good cellar.

☞ Dom. Mongeard-Mugneret, 14, rue de la Fontaine, 21700 Vosne-Romanée,
tel. 03.80.61.11.95, fax 03.80.61.24.22 ▽
e-mail mongeard@axnet.fr ▽ Ⴡ by appt.

DENIS MUGNERET ET FILS 1999★

■   1.5 ha   9,000   ⫼ €15–23

This deep ruby-coloured wine has superb brightness. The nose is more reserved, with aromas of blackcurrant, undergrowth and soft fruit preceding a delicate palate that is well-structured and youthful. It will go well with a small game bird, but not for a good while yet.

☞ Denis et Dominique Mugneret, 9, rue de la Fontaine, 21700 Vosne-Romanée,
tel. 03.80.61.00.97, fax 03.80.61.24.54 ▽
Ⴡ by appt.

DOM. MICHEL NOËLLAT ET FILS
Les Suchots 1999★

■ 1er cru   1.37 ha   3,900   ⫼ €23–30

We liked the **Les Beaux Monts 99** just as much as this Les Suchots. What is more, the 92 and 93 vintages were recently awarded the *coup de coeur*. There is a tradition of fine wine-making here. This cherry-black 99 is flavoured with truffle and coffee. Its tannins are tightly-packed but nevertheless already well-integrated and long: the coffee returns in the aftertaste, just preceding a flavour of Griotte cherries in *eau-de-vie*. This is an old-fashioned wine which should not be opened for the next five years at least and which will go well with venison.

☞ SCEA Dom. Michel Noëllat et Fils,
5, rue de la Fontaine, 21700 Vosne-Romanée,
tel. 03.80.61.36.87, fax 03.80.61.18.10 ▽
Ⴡ by appt.

DOM. DES PERDRIX 1998★

■   1.05 ha   5,168   ⫼ €30–38

The Les Perdrix estate was taken over by Antonin Rodet in 1996. This densely-coloured 98 shows not the slightest sign of development. The nose remains closed with just a few floral notes creeping through. The round, lengthy body has a slight tannic astringency. It will open up, however, given four or five years to mature, and in the long run will be a wholly satisfying wine, worthy of a capon.

☞ B. et C. Devillard, Dom. des Perdrix,
Ch. de Champ Renard, 71640 Mercurey,
tel. 03.85.98.12.12, fax 03.85.45.25.49 ▽
Ⴡ by appt.

DOM. ROBERT SIRUGUE
Les Petits Monts 1999★

■   0.6 ha   3,300   ⫼ €23–30

This is a fine and well-made wine with an intense, brilliant, ruby-red colour. Its aromas are undeniably dominated by oak, making it a little monolithic in character, but there is also a very discernible and effective note of blackcurrant and a hint of spring blossom. The palate is full and generous and already very smooth even though the wood is still prominent. It will soften after four or five years, as will the *village* 99, which is singled out by the Jury for its fine maturity;

🕭 Robert Sirugue, 3, av. du Monument, 21700 Vosne-Romanée, tel. 03.80.61.00.64, fax 03.80.61.27.57 Y by appt.

Richebourg, Romanée, Romanée-Conti, Romanée-Saint-Vivant, Grande Rue, La Tâche

These Crus are all equally prestigious and it would be difficult to pick out the greatest. Romanée-Conti undoubtedly enjoys the greatest fame, and through history there have been numerous references to the 'exquisite quality' of the wine. The famous vineyard of Romanée was eyed covetously by the great and the good of the ancien régime, though Madame de Pompadour failed to win it when she was pitted against the Prince of Conti who acquired it in 1760. Until the Second World War, the vines were not grafted and were treated with sulphur carbonate to protect them against phylloxera. These had later to be grubbed up and the first harvest of the new vines took place in 1952. Romanée-Conti, cultivated by a single grower on 1.8 ha (4.5 acres), is one of the most famous and expensive wines in the world.

The Romanée vineyards cover 0.83 ha (2 acres), Richebourg 8 ha (20 acres), Romanée-Saint-Vivant 9.5 ha (23.5 acres) and the Tâche covers a little more than 6 ha (15 acres). As with all the Grands Crus, the volumes produced are in the region of 20 to 30 hl per ha (216 to 324 gal per acre), depending on the year. Together, these Grands Crus produced no more than 920 hl (24,288 gal) in 2000, of which 292 hl (7,709 gal) were Richebourg and 284.48 hl (7,510.27 gal) Romanée-Saint-Vivant. Grande Rue became an accredited Grand Cru on 2 July 1992.

Richebourg

DOM. A.-F. GROS 1999★★

| Gd cru | 0.6 ha | 3,100 | ⊞ | +€76 |

89 90 **91** 92 [93] [94] **95** 97 **98** 99

Y by appt.

As this estate has already been awarded the *coup de cœur* for its Richebourg four times, it belongs among the true greats. This is an epic wine that has received an impressive pressing: it is intense and winey right from the colour through to the lovely coffee bean aromas. Note that the Grands Crus are never sold alone, but accompanied. It used to be the same with Tokay two hundred years ago.

🕭 Dom. A.-F. Gros, La Garelle, 21630 Pommard, tel. 03.80.24.03.16, fax 03.80.24.03.17, e-mail gros.anne-françoise@wanadoo.fr Ⓥ
Y by appt.

ALAIN HUDELOT-NOËLLAT

1999★★★

| Gd cru | 0.28 ha | 1,500 | ⊞ | +€76 |

The name of Richebourg is enough to fill a glass by itself. These seven *ouvrées* (small plots) of land have produced a sumptuous 99 which receives a unanimous *coup de cœur* from the Grand Jury. The colour is ruby with garnet highlights, and the aroma is deep, complex and smooth, revealing ripe, spicy fruit. It is a fiery wine, as oaky as it should be (that is to say, reasonably so) and needs to be laid down for a long time. It has a good, solid structure and an irresistible charm: in short, this is a great wine.

🕭 Alain Hudelot-Noëllat, Ancienne rte Nationale, 21640 Chambolle-Musigny, tel. 03.80.62.85.17, fax 03.80.62.83.13 Ⓥ

DENIS MUGNERET ET FILS 1999

| [93] Gd cru | 0.52 ha | 1,200 | ⊞ | +€76 |

[93] 94 95 96 97 98 99

This wine is closed on all counts, and amazingly austere. It really is under lock and key. Youthful, introvert and still trying to come to terms with its own power. Don't even think about drinking it for five years at least. The 93 vintage was awarded a *coup de cœur*.

🕭 Denis et Dominique Mugneret, 9, rue de la Fontaine, 21700 Vosne-Romanée, tel. 03.80.61.00.97, fax 03.80.61.24.54 Ⓥ

Romanée-Saint-Vivant

DOM. FOLLIN-ARBELET 1998

| ■ Gd cru | 0.4 ha | 900 | ▥ | +€ 76 |

This estate was part of the Poisot inheritance that came from the Latour family in 1898. The vineyards are now part of Aloxe-Corton's domaine. This is a dense, deep garnet wine with a slightly jammy, tannic character and a life expectancy of around five years. It is robust enough to go well with jugged hare.

➤ Dom. Follin-Arbelet, Les Vercots, 21420 Aloxe-Corton, tel. 03.80.26.46.73, fax 03.80.26.43.32 ▣ ⅄ by appt.

CH. DES GUETTES 1999★

| ■ Gd cru | n.c. | 600 | ▥ | +€ 76 |

This peony-coloured 99 with dark hues has a slightly secretive nose that suggests undergrowth and spice. The attack is confident, the body interesting, but for the moment the very young tannins are wholly dominated by the flavour of new oak. Let's not exaggerate: a good after five to ten years. This one promises much pleasure in the future.

➤ François Parent, Ch. des Guettes, 14 bis, rue Pierre-Joigneaux, 21200 Beaune, tel. 03.80.22.61.85, fax 03.80.24.03.16, e-mail gros.anne.francoise@wanadoo.fr ▣ ⅄ by appt.

ALAIN HUDELOT-NOELLAT 1999★★

| ■ Gd cru | 0.48 ha | 2,500 | ▥ | +€ 76 |

It is rare that the same estate is awarded a *coup de cœur* for two Vosne-Romanée Grands Crus. This Saint-Vivant (the product of a mere half-hectare/1.24 acres) is cardinal red, very intense but characteristic of the vintage. The aromas are deep and concentrated, with blueberries, blackcurrants and spices. The wine is tannic but also smooth and voluptuous. Still very young, this wine is one you should have in your cellar. It will be best enjoyed after 2010.

➤ Alain Hudelot-Noëllat, Ancienne rte Nationale, 21640 Chambolle-Musigny, tel. 03.80.62.85.17, fax 03.80.62.83.13 ▣ ⅄ by appt.

DOM. DE LA ROMANÉE-CONTI 1999★★★

| ■ Gd cru | 5.28 ha | 12,855 | ▥ | +€ 76 |

67 72 73 75 76 78 ⑦ ⑨ 80 81 82 87 89 91 92 95 97 98 99

Thanks to this estate, the ancient Abbey of Saint-Vivant de Vergy in the Hautes-Côtes de Nuits is being restored. What a superb 99! Although still a little tannic, it is good and chewy, full-bodied and already completely captivating. From the first, the nose reveals that this wine was harvested at absolutely the right moment. The wine's youth is accompanied by the austerity that is usual in this Grand Cru, but it also acknowledges the exceptional power of the vintage.

➤ SC du Dom. de La Romanée-Conti, 1, rue Derrière-le-Four, 21700 Vosne-Romanée, tel. 03.80.62.48.80. fax 03.80.61.05.72

LOUIS LATOUR
Les Quatre Journaux 1998

| ■ Gd cru | 0.76 ha | 2,000 | ▥ | +€ 76 |

What a story! The relics of this Vendée saint were widely scattered when the Vikings invaded, and then ended up being buried a few feet from here. For 650 years, the monastery of Saint-Vivant devoted all its attentions to this vineyard. This *clos* has carried the Latour name since 1898. That makes just three owners in over a thousand years. This delightful 98 is more delicate than robust, despite its prominent tannins. It has a sparkling ruby colour and a musky nose with a few fruity notes. It will go very well with a woodcock in three to five years.

➤ Dom. Louis Latour, 18, rue des Tonneliers, 21204 Beaune, tel. 03.80.24.81.00. fax 03.80.22.36.21, e-mail louislatour@louislatour.com ⅄ by appt.

La Grande Rue

DOM. FRANCOIS LAMARCHE 1999★

| ■ Gd cru | 1.65 ha | 7,000 | ▥ | €46-76 |

89 ⑨⓪ 91 92 93 94 95 98 99

Nestled between Romanée-Conti and La Tâche, this vineyard has all the qualities of its illustrious neighbours. It is a monopoly of the François Lamarche domaine and, since it was only recognised in 1992, is the most recent of the Grands Crus. As usual with this vintage, the wine has a very deep and intense ruby-red colour. Its nose holds no surprises: it is high-class, spicy and liquorice-flavoured. A wine with a wild side to it, as fans of the Grand Cru will know. Likewise, the rich chewiness, powerful and concentrated, is very characteristic. The Jury was overawed by its

The best-known Premier Cru vineyards are: Nuits-Saint-Georges, which is reputed to have been a vineyard as early as the year 1000; Les Vaucrains which produces robust wines; Les Cailles; Les Champs-Perdrix (the 'partridge fields'); Les Porets, in the commune of Nuits, the name of which comes from *poirets* or little pears, and indeed produces a pronounced flavour of wild pears; the various clos named la Maréchale: des Argillières, des Forêts-Saint-Georges, des Corvées, de l'Arlot and sur Prémeaux. The vineyards produced 13,900 hl (366,960 gal) in 2000, of which 251 hl (6,626 gal) were white wines.

Nuits-Saint-Georges

Nuits-Saint-Georges is the little wine capital of Burgundy. It also has a Hospices vineyard, which holds the annual wine auction on the Sunday before Palm Sunday. Many of the wine-shippers have their head offices in the town as do the liqueur-makers who produce Cassis de Bourgogne, and the makers of sparkling wines which have evolved today as Crémant de Bourgogne. The administrative headquarters of the Confrérie des Chevaliers du Tastevin is also to be found here.

JEAN-CLAUDE BOISSET 1998

n.c. | 25,000 | €15-23

'Wine-making is not in my blood,' says Jean-Claude Boisset, who started from scratch in 1961 and today heads a huge wine-making empire. On offer here is a classic 98, which ought to keep well. The musky, black-currant-leaf aroma runs along traditional lines. Likewise, its youthfulness and strong tannins are entirely in character. Don't start roasting the chicken with morel mushrooms quite yet.

Jean-Claude Boisset, 5, quai Dumorey, 21700 Nuits-Saint-Georges, tel. 03.80.62.62.61, fax 03.80.62.37.38

JACQUES CACHEUX ET FILS

Au bas de Combe 1999

0.52 ha 3,800 | €15-23

This Bas de Combe *climat* is close to Vosne-Romanée. This wine is dense and dark with deep-purple hues. Initially, the aromas speak of blueberries but then the conversation turns to spices, which is how it opens on the palate. The tannic structure is still firm, the pressing more obvious than the

Nuits-Saint-Georges

Nuits-Saint-Georges, a little town of 5,000 inhabitants, does not produce the Grands Crus of its northerly neighbour; the appellation spreads into the commune of Premeaux which borders it to the south. However, the many Premiers Crus to be found here have a deserved reputation and in this, the most northerly Appellation Communale of the Côte de Nuits, we find a very different type of wine being made in the *climats*. The wines here generally have a higher tannin content, which means they can keep a long time.

DOM. DE LA ROMANÉE-CONTI

1999 ★★★

Gd cru | 6.06 ha 16,640 | +76

97 98 99 | 72 73 75 78 79 80 81 82 87 89 91 92

La Tâche

Although the 98 vintage will not be at its best for a long time to come, this 99 (12.5% to 13% natural potential alcohol) will be ready to drink much sooner, and is clearly one of the top wines of this year. What finesse! What length! What perfection! This is a fantastically harmonious wine with great breeding and richness.

SC du Dom. de La Romanée-Conti, 1, rue Derrière-le-Four, 21700 Vosne-Romanée, tel. 03.80.62.48.80, fax 03.80.61.05.72

---

length, and they assure us that this wine has a long future.

Dom. François Lamarche, 9, rue des Communes, 21700 Vosne-Romanée, tel. 03.80.61.07.94, fax 03.80.61.24.31

by appt.

complexity, but after three or four years in the cellar all will be well.

SYLVAIN CATHIARD

Aux Murgers 1999

1er cru   0.48 ha   2,800   €23-30

This wine is tannic and full of wicked passion. Bright ruby-red in colour, fruity and very Pinot-like, this is a fairly light-bodied wine whose palate, much more sensible than its nose, has a pronounced oakiness that ought to soften after three to four years in the cellar. There is a little hint of kirsch on the finish.

Sylvain Cathiard, 20, rue de la Goillotte, 21700 Vosne-Romanée, tel. 03.80.62.36.01, fax 03.80.61.18.21 by appt.

CHARTRON ET TREBUCHET

1998

n.c.   2,300   €30-38

Produced by one of the leading lights of Burgundy wine-making, this wine has an unexceptional, rather light colour. A discreet oakiness provides good support for the notes of blackcurrant and mulberry, which appear again on the palate. Whether this *village* will improve further and soften with a little time in the cellar remains to be seen.

Chartron et Trébuchet, 13, Grande-Rue, 21190 Puligny-Montrachet, tel. 03.80.21.32.85, fax 03.80.21.36.35, e-mail jmchartron@chartron-trebuchet.com ev. day 10am–12 noon 2pm–6pm; cl. mid-Nov.-Mar.

DOM. JEAN CHAUVENET

Les Vaucrains 1999

1er cru   0.41 ha   2,700   €30-38

Jules Verne mentions a bottle of Nuits in his book *Round the Moon*. This particular wine, which has a certain panache, could well have inspired him. It has a light purplish colour that reveals its youthfulness, and a very typical Nuits nose of game, undergrowth and soft fruit. It is not very full at the moment but the potential is bursting with fresh, spring-like flavours. Note also the much fresher and rounder **Rue de Chaux 99**, which is commended by the Jury, and the **Premier Cru Les Perrières 99**, which is a really ambitious, top-flight wine that receives two stars. Finally, the full-bodied and well-structured **village 99** receives one star.

SCE Dom. Jean Chauvenet, 3, rue de Gilly, 21700 Nuits-Saint-Georges, tel. 03.80.61.00.72, fax 03.80.61.12.87 by appt.

CHAUVENET-CHOPIN

Aux Thorey 1999

1er cru   0.52 ha   3,000   €15-23

This inspirational wine-maker won the *coup de coeur* last year for a 98 vintage. This wine-grower offers a very pleasant **village 99** (one star) as well as this Aux Thorey. Les Thorey is a *climat* situated on the right as you go up the Combe de la Serrée. It is dark red edged with violet and the bouquet, a little reserved at the outset, soon relaxes and opens up. Its tannins are ripe but not quite fully developed, though they seem to be heading in the right direction.

Chauvenet-Chopin, 97, rue Félix-Tisserand, 21700 Nuits-Saint-Georges, tel. 03.80.61.28.11, fax 03.80.61.20.02 by appt.

A. CHOPIN ET FILS

Les Murgers 1999★★

1er cru   0.39 ha   2,300   €15-23

People should take note of this estate. It has been awarded the *coup de coeur* for a 95 vintage of the same wine, and this time only just missed out on another one. This deep ruby-mauve 99 has bright, clean highlights and a dazzling, engaging, raspberry freshness. It is already drinking well but in a couple of years' time will be even better. Its length, with a little spicy note, is quite astonishing. There simply is no point explaining: it just has to be tried. In the *village* category, note the **Bas de Combes 99** obtains one star.

Dom. A. Chopin et Fils, RN 74, 21700 Comblanchien, tel. 03.80.62.92.60, fax 03.80.62.70.78 by appt.

DOM. DU CLOS SAINT MARC

Clos des Argillières 1998★

1er cru   1 ha   n.c.   €30-38

Les Argillières is in Premeaux-Prissey where the Clos Saint-Marc, with its attractive little house set right in the middle of the vineyard, is situated. Their wine is a pretty shade of red with aromas of aniseed and liquorice and a rather tannic character. Overall, a well-balanced, round wine with some complexity and decent length. Alternatively, you can always choose its twin, the **Premier Cru Clos Saint-Marc 98** that looks as if it has the potential for a long life in the cellar.

Bouchard Père et Fils, Ch. de Beaune, 21200 Beaune, tel. 03.80.24.80.24, fax 03.80.22.55.88, e-mail france@bouchard-pereetfils.com by appt.

R. DUBOIS ET FILS 1998★

3.3 ha   12,000   €11-15

Régis Dubois has handed over to the younger generation, Raphaël et Béatrice, but his position as president of the Viti and his numerous responsibilities mean that he remains a solid, well-respected Burgundian. This tannic and dense *village* has been made in the traditional way, with a pleasant additional hint of Griotte cherries that makes it more accessible. With its cherry-red colour and fine oakiness, it would partner a wild boar terrine, but not for the next two to three years.

Dom. R. Dubois et Fils, rte de Nuits-Saint-Georges, 21700 Premeaux-Prissey, tel. 03.80.61.24.07, e-mail rdubois@wanadoo.fr ev. day 8am–11.30am 2pm–6pm; Sat./Sun. by appt.

DOM. GUY DUFOULEUR

Clos des Perrières 1998★

■ 1er cru | 0.93 ha | 6,000 | €22-30

If his wine is anything to go by, the mayor of Nuits has nothing to fear when it comes to his re-election. The **Premier Cru Les Poulettes 98** gets one star in the very first ballot. Skilful wine-making has produced this very intense Les Perrières. A little mineral note adds originality, while blackcurrant dominates on the middle palate. The combination of finesse and robustness guarantees this wine a long life ahead.

☛ Dom. Guy Dufouleur, 18, rue Thurot, 21700 Nuits-Saint-Georges, tel. 03.80.62.31.00, fax 03.80.62.31.00 ☑
Y by appt.
Y Guy et Xavier Dufouleur

DOM. DUPONT-TISSERANDOT

1999

■ | 0.29 ha | 1,800 | €11-15

This wine has a frank, deep colour but the nose is still closed. It is hard to tell if the aromas are blackcurrant bud or blackcurrant leaf. There is no disputing its cleanness, or the finesse on the palate, with its expressive finish. It has two to three years of expansion ahead of it.

☛ GAEC Dupont-Tisserandot, 22, pl. des Marronniers, 21220 Gevrey-Chambertin, tel. 03.80.34.10.50, fax 03.80.58.50.71 ☑
Y by appt.

FAIVELEY

Les Porêts Saint-Georges 1998★

■ 1er cru | 1.69 ha | 7,000 | €30-38

The name Faiveley is synonymous with Nuits-Saint-Georges, Tastevin and Co. The Jury commended the **Premier Cru Aux Chaignots 98**, which is very characteristic but needs time to develop, since it has an overpowering body at the moment. This wine will bring more immediate pleasure. It has a limpid colour and is clear at the edges. The nose is all jammy fruit, but with freshness, and on the palate it opens tenderly, then becomes supple and powerful. We predict three to eight years in the cellar.

☛ Dom. Faiveley, 8, rue du Tribourg, 21701 Nuits-Saint-Georges Cedex, tel. 03.80.61.04.55, fax 03.80.62.33.37, e-mail bourgognes-faiveley@wanadoo.fr
Y by appt.

CAVEAU DES FLEURIERES

Vieilles vignes 1998

■ | n.c. | 900 | €15-23

This wine has a very pronounced red colour, with a nose and palate presenting little red berry fruits and gentle tannins. As is so often the case in Burgundy – even, or especially, for a 98 – this is a wine you'll need to wait three to five years for.

☛ Caveau des Fleurières, 50, rue du Gal-de-Gaulle, BP 63, 21702 Nuits-Saint-Georges, tel. 03.80.61.10.30, fax 03.80.61.35.76, e-mail info@javouhey.net ☑
Y ev. day 9am–7pm

PHILIPPE GAVIGNET

Les Chaboeufs 1999★

■ 1er cru | 1 ha | 6,000 | €15-23

This is a wine that needs to be allowed to develop in peace and quiet. Deep garnet in colour with aromas that hover between Burlat cherry and pepper, it is not the fleshiest wine, but that is no great fault. It has good structure on the palate, which is smooth, harmonious and typical of this vintage. The **Les Pruliers Premier Cru 99** has similar qualities and is also singled out along with, in the *village* category, **Les Argillats 99**, which is simpler in style but successful nevertheless.

☛ Dom. Philippe Gavignet, 36, rue Dr-Louis-Legrand, 21700 Nuits-Saint-Georges, tel. 03.80.61.09.41, fax 03.80.61.03.56 ☑ Y ev. day 8am–12 noon 2pm–6pm; Sat./Sun. by appt.

DOM. ANNE-MARIE GILLE

Les Brulées 1999

■ 1er cru | 1.21 ha | 6,500 | €11-15

This bottle has one of those old-fashioned parchment labels with curling edges: it looks like a throwback to something from a much earlier time. Garnet-red in colour, it presents a lovely combination of blueberries and pepper blended with vanilla from the oak. The palate is lively and the prominent tannins should calm down in three to four years' time.

☛ Dom. Anne-Marie Gille, 34, RN 74, 21700 Comblanchien, tel. 03.80.62.94.13, fax 03.80.62.99.88, e-mail gille@burgundywines.net ☑ Y by appt.

DOM. HENRI GOUGES

Clos des Porrets-Saint-Georges 1998★★

■ 1er cru | 3.5 ha | 10,000 | €15-23

The much-lamented Henri Gouges was one of the founders of the AOC. People used to call him the 'gendarme of Burgundy' because of the inflexibility of his opinions about wine. This wine, which is dedicated to his memory, has a warm crimson colour. It has been made with consummate skill, and just goes to show how a great *terroir* can make superb wine without conforming to the fashion of high extraction. It should be opened in three years' time, and then can be drunk over the following ten years.

☛ Dom. Henri Gouges, 7, rue du Moulin, 21700 Nuits-Saint-Georges, tel. 03.80.61.04.40, fax 03.80.61.32.84

DOM. GUYON

Les Herbues 1999★★

■ 1er cru | 0.22 ha | 1,600 | €15-23

It was a memorable moment when the crew of the Apollo XV baptised a lunar crater on 25 July 1971 with a bottle of Nuits. This wine would have been perfect for the occasion: the Les Herbues *climat*, next to Vosne-Romanée, wins a *coup de cœur* for this intense ruby-red wine with delicate violet hues. The nose is a little severe but then on aeration it opens with fine aromas of fresh fruit and spice. It is a supple wine and although the texture is developing a silkiness, the attack has a reassuring solidity. A lively, vigorous wine with solidity.

Nuits-Saint-Georges

DENIS MUGNERET ET FILS

Les Boudots 1999★

■ 1er cru　0.6 ha　2,400　Ⅲ €15-23

This attractive 99 would liven up an evening. It has depth of colour, and musky, leathery aromas with a hint of liquorice that comes from well-blended oak. On the palate it is slightly tannic but nevertheless has round-ness and medium length. This estate has pre-viously been acclaimed for its **Saint-Georges 94**. Their **Saint-Georges 99** also obtains one star.

➤ Denis et Dominique Mugneret, 9, rue de la Fontaine, 21700 Vosne-Romanée, tel. 03.80.61.00.97, fax 03.80.61.24.54 ⊠

DOM. MICHEL NOELLAT ET FILS

1999★

■　1.3 ha　3,000　Ⅲ €15-23

This pitch-black *village* has an intense and complex nose that needs to open up a little. A straightforward and vinous attack, good quality with an interesting, liquorice-flavoured body. You will need to lay it down for at least two years.

➤ SCEA Dom. Michel Noëllat et Fils, 5, rue de la Fontaine, 21700 Vosne-Romanée, tel. 03.80.61.36.87, fax 03.80.61.18.10 ⊠
Ⓨ by appt.

DOM. DES PERDRIX 1998★

■　1.16 ha　4,256　Ⅲ €30-38

This estate has been taken over by Antonin Rodet and is an endless source of goodies. This wine is dark cherry-red with lively, sprightly aromas. A rich, lively and well-balanced palate, though of course not a wine you should drink too soon. The **Premier Cru aux Perdrix 98** is also commended. It is much more complex, a real Premier Cru.

➤ B. et C. Devillard, Dom. des Perdrix, Ch. de Champ Renard, 71640 Mercurey, tel. 03.85.98.12.12, fax 03.85.45.25.49 ⊠
Ⓨ by appt.

CH. DE PREMEAUX

Clos des Argillières 1999★

■ 1er cru　0.5 ha　2,500　Ⅲ €15-23

This estate was bought in 1933 by the current owner's grandfather. This gorgeous black cherry-coloured wine has spent 18 months maturing in oak. It has sprinted aromas of leather, crusty bread, and jammy fruit. The acidic attack is followed by a good structure of youthful tannins with pleasant, fruity flavours on the middle palate, opening out to reveal a lovely fullness later.

➤ Dom. du Ch. de Premeaux, 21700 Premeaux-Prissey, tel. 03.80.62.30.64, fax 03.80.62.39.28, e-mail chateau.de.premeaux@wanadoo.fr ⊠
Ⓨ by appt.

HENRI ET GILLES REMORIQUET

Rue de Chaux 1999★

■ 1er cru　0.4 ha　2,000　Ⅲ €15-23

This well-presented wine is garnet-red, almost black in colour and very

remarkable length and well-integrated oak. A high-class *village*.

➤ EARL Dom. Guyon, 11-16, RN 74, 21700 Vosne-Romanée, tel. 03.80.61.02.46, fax 03.80.62.36.56 ⊠ Ⓨ by appt.

ALAIN HUDELOT-NOELLAT

Les Murgers 1999

■ 1er cru　0.68 ha　4,500　Ⅲ €23-30

This wine is very characteristic of the AOC. It has a lively colour, with notes of leather and undergrowth, followed by very character-istic woodland flavours of the *terroir* and pro-nounced oakiness: it has great potential for laying down but needs to be kept an eye on.

➤ Alain Hudelot-Noëllat, Ancienne rte Nationale, 21640 Chambolle-Musigny, tel. 03.80.62.85.17, fax 03.80.62.83.13 ⊠
Ⓨ by appt.

DOM. DE L'ARLOT

Clos de l'Arlot 1998★★

□ 1er cru　1 ha　3,500　Ⅲ €30-38

This monopoly, visible from the main road, is situated in Premeaux beside the historic house and garden of Viénot. The wine has an intense gold colour with deep yellow-green highlights, and well-blended toasty and floral aromas. It is as solid as the pillars in the store-room of the Clos de Vougeot. Full, rich, and heavy, it needs a year or two before its full complexity develops. The **Clos des Forêts Saint-Georges Premier Cru 98** receives one star. Serve it with chicken in white sauce.

➤ Dom. de L'Arlot, Premeaux, 21700 Nuits-Saint-Georges, tel. 03.80.61.01.92, fax 03.80.61.04.22 ⊠
Ⓨ by appt.
➤ Axa Millésimes

BERTRAND MACHARD DE GRAMONT

Les Hauts Pruliers 1998★

■　0.58 ha　2,800　Ⅲ €15-23

This wine-cellar is moving premises soon but as yet we don't know where, although this wine is worth seeking out. 'A glass of Nuits will set you up for the night', as they say at Tastevin, and this wine will give you the opportunity to find out if this is true. It is a very delicate wine with finesse, balance, subtle tannins, nicely blended oak and pleasant, consistent aromas including Griotte cherries. Sweet dreams!

➤ Bertrand Machard de Gramont, 13, rue de Vergy, 21700 Nuits-Saint-Georges, tel. 03.80.61.16.96, fax 03.80.61.16.96 ⊠
Ⓨ by appt.

characteristic. Its aromas are complex and concentrated. Blackcurrant and blackberries follow a hint of liquorice in this powerful, tannic, structured and balanced wine. Also on offer here is a *village*, **Les Allots 99**, which was commended by the Jury.

• SCE Henri et Gilles Remoriquet, 25, rue de Charmois, 21700 Nuits-Saint-Georges, tel. 03.80.61.24.84, fax 03.80.61.36.63, e-mail domaine.remoriquet@wanadoo.fr V
Y by appt.

DOM. ARMELLE ET BERNARD RION Les Murgers 1998

■ 1er cru   0.4 ha   2,000   ID £15-23

This attractive 98 has a very characteristic Pinot colour, and diverse aromas of spices, coffee and blackcurrant. A good-looking wine that lacks a little concentration, although powerfully structured.

• Dom. Armelle et Bernard Rion, 8, rte Nationale, 21700 Vosne-Romanée, tel. 03.80.61.05.31, fax 03.80.61.24.60, e-mail rion@webwine.com V Y by appt.

DOM. DANIEL RION ET FILS Vieilles vignes 1998★

■   0.8 ha   5,000   ID £15-23

This wine is still closed but will open up eventually; it needs time to develop. It has a lovely, deep-red colour with bluish highlights and scents of violets and spices. The powerful oak and fruit have been successfully handled, and with its good structure it stands out from the crowd.

• Dom. Daniel Rion et Fils, RN 74, 21700 Premeaux, tel. 03.80.62.31.28, fax 03.80.61.13.41, e-mail contact@ domaine-daniel-rion.com V

CAVE PRIVEE D'ANTONIN RODET Les Porêts 1998★

■ 1er cru   n.c.   912

There is only a small quantity of Les Porêts, so we hope that there will still be some left when this *Guide* is published! It has a fresh nose with hints of mocha coffee. Harmonious and pleasant colour and an elegant, reserved but concentrated and, although closed at the moment, this wine should develop beautifully over the next four to five years.

• Antonin Rodet, 71640 Mercurey, tel. 03.85.98.12.12, fax 03.85.45.25.49, e-mail rodet@rodet.com V Y ev. day except Sat. Sun. 9am-12 noon-6pm

RENE TARDY Aux Argillats 1998★

■ 1er cru   0.39 ha   2,400

This estate is situated 50 m (55 yards) from the church of Saint-Symphorien, which was built in 1280. Les Argillats is on the Vosne-Romanée side of Nuits; the clay soil here produces a wine with a reputation for being austere, coming into its own later in life. This wine with its youthful colour and soft red fruitiness has a forward, pleasant character. However, its acidity means that a three-year wait would be worthwhile. Joël Tardy's brother is a wine-maker in Oregon.

• Dom. René Tardy et Fils, 32, rue Caumont-Bréon, 21700 Nuits-Saint-Georges, tel. 03.80.61.20.5y0, fax 03.80.61.36.96, e-mail tardyrene@aol.com V Y by appt.
• Joël Tardy

PIERRE THIBERT Rue de Chaux Vieille vigne 1999★

■ 1er cru   0.28 ha   1,650   ID £15-23

This appellation is in good form, and these family vineyards, farmed on a tenant basis have produced a really top quality Premier Cru. It is deep ruby-red in colour, as expected, and has delicate aromas with soft flavours of vanilla and liquorice on the palate. It has a good body and gripping tannins that cause no concern as they will mellow with time.

• Pierre Thibert, 76, Grande-Rue, 21700 Corgoloin, tel. 03.80.62.73.40, fax 03.80.62.73.40. V Y by appt.

DOM. JEAN-PIERRE TRUCHETET 1998

■   1.63 ha   2,600   ID £15-22

The light-brown highlights in this wine indicate that it is beginning to mature – these things happen, it is not the end of the world. The intense nose opens on Griotte cherries, preserved grapes and chocolate. The palate with aromas of cherry and oak is pleasant from start to finish. It needs to spend two to three years in the cellar.

• Jean-Pierre Truchetet, rue des Masers, 21700 Premeaux-Prissey, tel. 03.80.61.07.22, fax 03.80.61.34.35 V
Y ev. day except Sat./Sun. 9am-12 noon 2pm-7pm; cl. 15-31 Aug.

Côte de Nuits-Villages

After the village of Prémeaux, the vineyard dwindles to only about 200 m (218 yd) at Corgoloin, the narrowest point on the Côte. Here, the 'mountain' is not so high and the administrative jurisdiction of the Appellation Côte de Nuits-Villages, once known as Vins Fins de la Côte de Nuits, stops at the level of the Clos des Langres above Corgoloin. Between them are two communes: Prissey, associated with Prémeaux, and Comblanchien, famous for a particular kind of limestone (incorrectly called marble) which is extracted from the quarries in the hills. They both have *terroirs* that are entitled to be called *Appellation Communale*. But the

Côte de Nuits-Villages

areas of these three communes are too limited to have their own appellation, so Brochon and Fixin became associated with them to share the unique Appellation Côte de Nuits-Villages, which in 2000 produced 7,200 hl (190,080 gal) of wine, of which 224 hl (5,914 gal) were whites. You can find excellent wines at affordable prices here.

DOM. CHARLES ALLEXANT ET FILS Aux Montagnes Cuvée Prestige 1999★★

■ 1.85 ha 10,000 ● €8-11

Aux Montagnes is a Comblanchien *climat*, not far from an area of marble quarrying. However, there is not the slightest trace of mineral in this wine with its deep, floral aromas. It is a sensuous wine with an attractive, rich and fleshy palate. You can drink it now but it has not yet had its last word.

●→ SCE Dom. Charles Allexant et Fils, rue du Château, Cissey, 21190 Merceuil, tel. 03.80.26.83.27, fax 03.80.26.84.04 ☑ ▼ ev. day 8am–12 noon 1.30pm–6pm; Sat./Sun. by appt.

BERTRAND AMBROISE 1999★

■ n.c. n.c. ● €11-15

Do not expect to be able to drink this wine in the near future: it needs several years in the cellar before it will realise its potential. However, its length and the suppleness of its tannins seem to indicate that it is on the right track.

●→ Maison Bertrand Ambroise, rue de l'Eglise, 21700 Premeaux-Prissey, tel. 03.80.62.30.19, fax 03.80.62.38.69, e-mail bertrand.ambroise@wanadoo.fr ☑ ▼ by appt.

RENE BOUVIER 1999★

■ 0.49 ha 2.500 ● €11-15

This has all the qualities of a great wine: a fine colour with dense, deep highlights and an attractive nose with floral aromas followed by a tannic backdrop (inevitable at this age but no cause for concern). An undeniable success for the appellation.

●→ EARL René Bouvier, 2, rue Neuve, 21160 Marsannay-la-Côte, tel. 03.80.52.21.37, fax 03.80.59.95.96 ☑ ▼ by appt.

CHAUVENET-CHOPIN 1999★

■ 1.5 ha 8,000 ● €8-11

This clear, brilliant and attractive, deep ruby-red wine is worth waiting for. A well-made structure in harmony with its intense nose suggests two to three years are needed before drinking.

●→ Chauvenet-Chopin, 97, rue Félix-Tisserand, 21700 Nuits-Saint-Georges, tel. 03.80.61.28.11, fax 03.80.61.20.02 ☑ ▼ by appt.

DOM. A. CHOPIN ET FILS Vieilles vignes 1999★★

■ 1 ha 4,500 ● €8-11

Comblanchien marble is often compared to that of Carrare, and by the same token this incredibly promising wine could easily be compared with the greats. It has a bright black-cherry colour and on the nose there are intense aromas of stewed fruit, which are very much in the spirit of the appellation. After a supple opening, the palate is full and solid right up to its superb finish. It would be best to wait for at least two years to get the most from its charms.

●→ Dom. A. Chopin et Fils, RN 74, 21700 Comblanchien, tel. 03.80.62.92.60, fax 03.80.62.70.78 ☑ ▼ by appt.

BERNARD COILLOT PERE ET FILS 1999

■ 0.5 ha 3,000 ● €11-15

To really get to know this appellation you need to look at both sides of it. This wine is from the northern side (Fixin, Brochon). Purple with a light crimson tinge round the edge, the bouquet is not yet forthcoming giving out subtle aromas of cocoa and jammy fruit. The wine is powerful and tannic as it opens on the palate and certainly not lacking in potential. Open in two years' time and serve with beef.

●→ Bernard Coillot Père et Fils, 31, rue du Château, 21160 Marsannay-la-Côte, tel. 03.80.52.17.59, fax 03.80.52.12.75, e-mail domcoil@aol.com ☑ ▼ by appt.

DESERTAUX-FERRAND 1999

□ 1.12 ha 9,000 ■ ● €8-11

This appellation of mainly red wines is slowly starting to produce white. This whitish-gold wine with aromas of pear and quince has a light touch of acidity, a mineral palate and a smooth finish. The powerful and well-balanced **red Les Perrières 99** needs a year or two in the cellar before drinking.

●→ Dom. Desertaux-Ferrand, Grande-Rue, 21700 Corgoloin, tel. 03.80.62.98.40, fax 03.80.62.70.32, e-mail desertaux@erb.com ☑ ▼ by appt.

R. DUBOIS ET FILS Les Monts de Boncourt 1999★

□ 0.8 ha 5,000 ● €8-11

Situated in the village of Corgoloin, this *climat* is one of the most southern in the Côte de Nuits. Its Chardonnay with aromas of yellow fruit, honey and a touch of vanilla would go well with apple pie. A well-balanced palate with a touch of pear and a pleasant suppleness. Drink it in two years' time.

↪ Dom. R. Dubois et Fils, rte de Nuits-Saint-Georges, 21700 Premeaux-Prissey, tel. 03.80.62.30.61, fax 03.80.61.24.07, e-mail rdubois@wanadoo.fr ☑ ▼ ev. day 8am-11.30am 2pm-6pm; Sat/Sun. by appt.

DOM. JEAN FERY ET FILS
Le Clos de Magny 1998★

n.c.   8,000 ||| €8-11

This clear, peony-coloured wine is characteristic. The nose is all musk and fur, the palate all soft fruit and well-balanced tannins. It is already very pleasant to drink.

↪ Dom. Jean Fery et Fils, 21420 Echevronne, tel. 03.80.21.59.60, fax 03.80.21.59.59 ▼ by appt.

PHILIPPE GAVIGNET 1999★★

0.5 ha   3,000 ||| €8-11

A leg of lamb would make the perfect accompaniment to this garnet 99, with its brightness around the edge of the glass, and its pleasant, oaky flavour. Everything about it is delightful: the roundness, the alcohol, and the fruity flavour. With wines like this, the appellation can rest assured. Excellent value for money.

↪ Dom. Philippe Gavignet, 36, rue Dr-Louis-Legrand, 21700 Nuits-Saint-Georges, tel. 03.80.61.09.41, fax 03.80.61.03.56 ☑ ▼ ev. day 8am–12 noon 2pm–6pm; Sat./Sun. by appt.

CHRISTIAN GROS
Les Vignottes 1999★

0.6 ha   n.c. ||| €8-11

The name of the *climat* was rarely given in this AOC. However, it is now becoming quite frequent, in order to distinguish the wines and make them more personal. Les Vignottes is in Premeaux, just below the Clos de la Maréchale. This clear ruby-red, fruity wine has a nice, open nose and a well-composed palate. It needs to wait a year or two before being served with chicken.

↪ Christian Gros, rue de la Chaume, 21700 Premeaux-Prissey, tel. 03.80.61.39.77 ▼ by appt.

GILLES JOURDAN 1999★

1.02 ha   4,000 ||| €8-11

This wine-producer took over the family estate in 1997. His wine has plenty of life and an attractive, intense purple colour with floral aromas. The palate has a note of liveliness and a fresh, round attack. It would be perfect with eggs in a red wine sauce.

↪ Gilles Jourdan, Grande-Rue, 21700 Corgoloin, tel. 03.80.62.76.31, fax 03.80.62.98.55 ▼ by appt.

Some domaines are very successful every year and this is one of them. It already boasts a large collection of *coups de coeur* congratulations. Claire Naudin! This impressively-coloured wine has toasted notes on the nose and huge potential on the palate. Everything is there; well-defined and well-balanced; it is good enough to accompany game. Worth noting also is a **Clos de Magny 98 red**, which receives one star.

↪ Dom. Henri Naudin-Ferrand, rue du Meix-Grenot, 21700 Magny-les-Villers, tel. 03.80.62.91.50, fax 03.80.62.91.77, e-mail dnaudin@pac.fr ☑ ▼ by appt.

DOM. LALEURE-PIOT
Les Bellevues 1999★

0.84 ha   5,700 ||| €8-11

This wine comes from a *climat* on top of the hillside next to the Comblanchien quarries. A dark colour without the slightest trace of development, it is very much in the spirit of the appellation. It has a rich, clean, straightforward, intense nose and fine tannins blended with fresh, ripe soft, red fruit. It is not far off being awarded a second star.

↪ Dom. Laleure-Piot, rue de Pralot, 21420 Pernand-Vergelesses, tel. 03.80.21.52.37, fax 03.80.21.59.48, e-mail laleure.piot@wanadoo.fr ▼ ev. day 8am–12 noon 2pm–6pm; Sat/Sun. by appt.

DOM. DE LA POULETTE 1999★

0.75 ha   n.c. ||| €11-15

This domaine has been handed down through the female side of the family for six generations. Today, it is Françoise Michaut-Audidier who is in charge. Her well-structured 99 is guaranteed a long life in the cellar – if you feel inclined to lay it down. It has a deep-gold colour with a lovely rich palate. Full and complex, it has a well-balanced oakiness and a very pleasant liquorice finish. Among the many illustrious visitors to this wine-cellar is Pope Jean XXIII who, when he was still a papal nuncio, came to bless France's vineyards from the top of the Montagne de Beaune.

↪ Dom. de La Poulette, 103, Grande-Rue, 21700 Corgoloin, tel. 03.80.62.98.02, fax 03.45.25.43.23 ▼ by appt.
↪ Mme F. Michaut-Audidier

DOM. HENRI NAUDIN-FERRAND
Vieilles vignes 1998★★★

1.55 ha   9,028 ||| €11-15

(20,486 gal) of white in 2000, the Appellation Ladoix is little known, but deserves better.

Another oddity: even though Ladoix was given a favourable classification by the Comité de Viticulture de Beaune in 1860, it was not awarded any Premiers Crus. This was put right by the INAO in 1978. The main Premiers Crus are La Macaude, La Corvée and Le Clou d'Orge, which produce wines with the same characteristics as those from the Côte de Nuits; Les Mourottes (Basses and Hautes) which have a wild appeal, and the Bois-Roussot, planted on 'lava'.

DOM. D'ARDHUY 1999★
■ 1er cru   1.5 ha   8,000   🔲 €11-15

Treat this interesting 99 vintage with caution as it needs to soften and will be infinitely superior in two to three years' time. Ladoix comes from *doué* which in Burgundian is an underground stream from the Vaucluse. Similarly, this wine likes to disappear and then come back in full force. A radiant dark-red with touches of red berried fruit and toast. Rich and generous, its fortunes are definitely rising.
● Dom. d'Ardhuy, Clos des Langres, 21700 Corgoloin, tel. 03.80.62.98.73, fax 03.80.62.95.15,
e-mail domaine.ardhuy@wanadoo.fr ☑
Ⓨ ev. day except Sun. 10am–12 noon 2pm–6pm

BOISSEAUX-ESTIVANT 1998★
■   n.c.   n.c.   🔲 €15-23

This garnet cherry-coloured wine's aromas and tannins work very well together. While the aromas are smooth, its flavours are beginning to develop in strength. It is a full-bodied wine with superb concentration but will need at least two years to really fulfil its potential.
● Boisseaux-Estivant, 38, fg Saint-Nicolas, BP 107, 21200 Beaune, tel. 03.80.22.00.05, fax 03.80.24.19.73

DOM. CACHAT-OCQUIDANT ET FILS Les Madonnes Vieilles vignes 1999★
■   1.2 ha   5,200   🔲 €11-15

This excellent estate is situated at the foot of the Corton hill. In this AOC, two *villages* are both equally successful: a 99 *red*, and this Griotte cherry-coloured Madonnes. The nose has wild notes of animal pelts and toast, and the rich, powerful body is very expressive of the *terroir*. The tannins are well-structured and there is certainly some fruit. In two to three years' time it will be interesting.
● Dom. Cachat-Ocquidant et Fils, 3, pl. du Souvenir, 21550 Ladoix-Serrigny, tel. 03.80.26.45.30, fax 03.80.26.48.16 ☑
Ⓨ by appt.

CHARLES VIÉNOT
Cuvée Roi de Saxe 1998
■   n.c.   45,000   🔲 €11-15

This wine is dedicated to the king of Saxony who once honoured the Viénot family by ordering wine from them. It has a garnet-red colour with aromas of dark berries mixed with sweet spices. The opening is fresh, the middle palate full-bodied, even luscious, as it should be for this appellation. Its fine tannic body would go very well with game.
● Charles Viénot, 5, quai Dumorey, BP 102, 21703 Nuits-Saint-Georges, tel. 03.80.62.61.41, fax 03.80.62.37.38

La Côte de Beaune

Ladoix

Three small villages – Serrigny near the railway line, Ladoix on the RN74, and Buisson at the end of the Côte de Nuits – make up the commune of Ladoix-Serrigny. The *Appellation Communale* is Ladoix. The hamlet of Buisson is located exactly at the geographical conjunction of the Côtes de Nuits and the Côtes de Beaune. The administrative border stops at the commune of Corgoloin, but the hill itself continues further on as do the vineyards and the wine. The Corton 'mountain' rises beyond the combe of Magny which marks the physical separation. The steep inclines made up of layers of marl have many south- and west-facing slopes, making this one of the best wine-growing areas on the Côte.

The various aspects give the Appellation Ladoix a variety of different types of wine, added to which its white wines are exceptionally well adapted to growing on the Argovian marlstone soils. This is the case with Les Gréchons, for example, which is grown on the same geological soils as Corton-Charlemagne further south, though it has a less favourable aspect. The wines from this location have distinctive characteristics. Having produced 3,861 hl (101,930 gal) of red wine and 776 hl

CAPITAIN-GAGNEROT

La Micaude 1998★

■ 1er cru | 1.64 ha 9,000 | ⬥ €11-15

This domaine has won a *coup de coeur* twice for past vintages and often pulls out its Micaude as a trump card. As it is now, Garnet-red in colour, this bottle does not allow the oak to overwhelm the note of raspberry. The body needs to soften but it has depth and does its best to live up to the family motto: 'Loyalty is my strength'. It definitely needs a few years in the cellar.

☛ Maison Capitain-Gagnerot, 38, rte de Dijon, 21550 Ladoix-Serrigny, tel. 03.80.26.41.36, fax 03.80.26.46.29 ⬥

⬥ by appt.

DOM. CHAUDAT

Côte de Beaune 1998★

■ 0.15 ha 700 | ⬥ €8-11

This really good wine has an old-fashioned parchment label (a Burgundian tradition). Medium intense in colour with attractive hints of blackberry, and a fullness and complexity as it hits the palate, it is very characteristic of the *terroir* and vintage, and should be put to one side ... or drunk straight away if you like young wines. The choice is yours.

☛ Dom. Odile Chaudat, 41, voie Romaine, 21700 Corgoloin, tel. 03.80.62.92.31, fax 03.80.62.92.31 ⬥ ⬥ by appt.

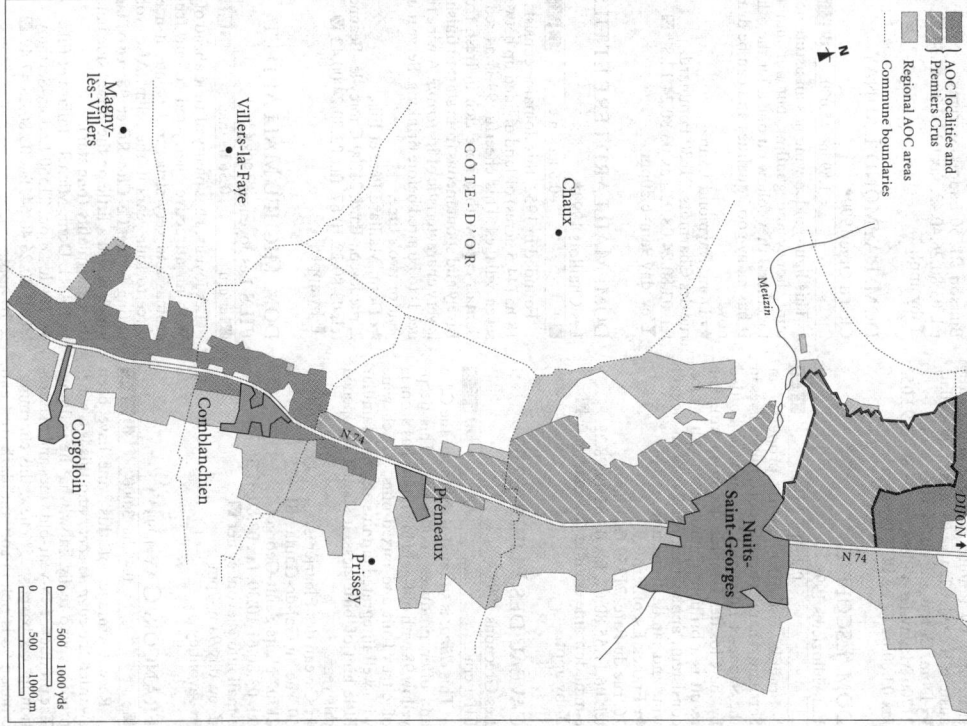

Côte de Nuits (South)

N

CÔTE-D'OR

Magny-lès-Villers

Villers-la-Faye

Chaux

Corgoloin

Comblanchien

N 74

Prissey

Premeaux

Meuzin

Nuits-Saint-Georges

DIJON →

N 74

AOC localities and Premiers Crus

Regional AOC areas

Commune boundaries

0   500   1000 yds

0   500   1000 m

CHEVALIER PERE ET FILS
Les Gréchons ★
□ 1er cru   0.47 ha   2,500

This wine is the beautiful sunbeam-yellow of Cinderella's ball gown. Like the Prince, its aromas are generous: honey, beeswax and bitter almond. Lively, round and successful, it will surely have a happy ending.

•ϼ SCE Chevalier Père et Fils, Buisson, 21550 Ladoix-Serrigny, tel. 03.80.26.46.30, fax 03.80.26.41.47 **ⓥ ❦** by appt.

DOM. CORNU 1998
■   0.96 ha   6,000   **Ⅲ €11-15**

This wine-producer previously won a *coup de cœur* for a 90 vintage. This wine is not yet fully open but has a fine body and a good ruby colour with glints of brick-red. The nose has interesting aromas of undergrowth, damp earth and humus, while the palate is well-structured by tannins that are still a little austere. It needs a few years in the wine-cellar.

•ϼ Dom. Cornu, rue du Meix-Grenot, 21700 Magny-lès-Villers, tel. 03.80.62.92.05, fax 03.80.62.72.22 **ⓥ ❦** by appt.

DOM. ESCOFFIER
Les Vallozières 1998
□   0.26 ha   2,100   **€8-11**

Franck Escoffier owns property at Serrigny, a hamlet near Ladoix, but he lives in the Saône-et-Loire and has his wine bottled by the Clos des Langres (La Juvinière). The result is a brilliant Chardonnay with a nice, consistent, appley fruitiness. It is an elegant wine and can be drunk now.

•ϼ Franck Escoffier, 16, rue du Parc, 71350 Géanges, tel. 06.11.55.80.67, fax 03.85.49.98.22, e-mail domaine.escoffier@wanadoo.fr **ⓥ ❦** by appt.

CAVEAU DES FLEURIERES
Les Gréchons 1998
□ 1er cru   n.c.   900   **Ⅲ €15-23**

This *climat* is situated at the top of the Côte and often produces good wines. This deep-yellow 98 with old-gold highlights has aromas of citrus fruit and mixed nuts. A rich wine with well-integrated tannins and that familiar little hint of bitterness, it should be opened this year.

•ϼ Caveau des Fleurières, 50, rue du Gal-de-Gaulle, BP 63, 21702 Nuits-Saint-Georges, tel. 03.80.61.10.30, fax 03.80.61.35.76, e-mail info@javouhey.net **ⓥ** **❦** ev. day 9am–7pm
•ϼ Javouhey

FRANCOIS GAY 1998 ★★
■   0.49 ha   3,000   **Ⅲ €8-11**

Recent vintages of this wine have been awarded the *coup de cœur* and this is a wine-producer who really know what he is doing. The product of 45-year-old vines and maturation in oak barrels. 25% new, this charming, crimson 98 is rich in soft and dark fruit and

---

slips effortlessly onto the palate. An adequate body with pleasant tannins and a fruity finish. Best kept for three to four years but, if you like young wines, already quite drinkable.

•ϼ EARL François Gay, 9, rue des Fiètres, 21200 Chorey-lès-Beaune, tel. 03.80.22.69.58, fax 03.80.24.71.42 **ⓥ**

DOM. ROBERT ET RAYMOND JACOB 1999 ★
□   0.7 ha   5,000   **Ⅲ €8-11**

Cervantes only had one arm and yet he was a great writer: this Ladoix does not have much of a body and yet it is a good wine. It has a light colour and a supple palate. The only exception to its lightness are the rather aggressive aromas of honey, acacia, flint and toast. A subtle oakiness does not overwhelm the floral flavours on the finish.

•ϼ Dom. Robert et Raymond Jacob, Buisson, 21550 Ladoix-Serrigny, tel. 03.80.26.40.42, fax 03.80.26.49.34 **ⓥ** **❦** by appt.

DOM. RAYMOND LAUNAY
Clou d'Orge 1999 ★
□   1.89 ha   15,000   **Ⅲ €11-15**

This light-golden wine has an astute nose: mint, honey and gunflint, but not jumbled together – they follow on one after the other. It has many good qualities and can be drunk now.

•ϼ Dom. Raymond Launay, rue des Charmots, 21630 Pommard, tel. 03.80.24.08.03, fax 03.80.24.12.87 **ⓥ** **❦** ev. day 9am–6.30pm

DOM. MAILLARD PERE ET FILS
Les Chaillots 1999 ★
■   0.5 ha   n.c.   **Ⅲ €11-15**

Founded in 1952, this domaine consists of 18 ha (44.5 acres) of land divided up between seven villages. This cheerful 99 is as red as Santa's cape with a nose rich in fresh fruit. Lively and spontaneous from start to finish, it is very characteristic of its *terroir*. A wine that needs to be aired before drinking. Serve it in a year or two's time.

•ϼ Dom. Maillard Père et Fils, 2, rue Joseph-Bard, 21200 Chorey-lès-Beaune, tel. 03.80.22.10.67, fax 03.80.24.00.42 **ⓥ** **❦** by appt.

DOM. MICHEL MALLARD ET FILS Les Joyeuses 1998 ★
■ 1er cru   0.36 ha   n.c.   **Ⅲ €11-15**

Les Joyeuses has plenty of time ahead of it. With an attractive cherry-red colour, fruity aromas and very structured palate, it needs three to four years in the cellar. Also worth noting is the **Le Clos Royer 98 red village**, which is still a little on the closed side but of the same quality (one star).

•ϼ EARL Dom. Michel Mallard et Fils, 43, rte de Dijon, 21550 Ladoix-Serrigny, tel. 03.80.26.40.64, fax 03.80.26.47.49 **ⓥ** **❦** by appt.

CATHERINE ET CLAUDE MARÉCHAL, Les Chaillots 1999★

■ n.c. ⊞ 3,900 €11-15

This purple-garnet wine is still youthful in character and would benefit from being decanted. The aromas spring no surprises and are as burnt and blackcurranty as one would expect. After a clean, straightforward opening, the structure is very consistent with tannins that need to soften. It has potential for laying down (three to four years).

☎ EARL Catherine et Claude Maréchal, 6, rte de Chalon, 21200 Bligny-lès-Beaune, tel. 03.80.21.44.37, fax 03.80.26.85.01 [V]
Y by appt.

GHISLAINE ET BERNARD MARÉCHAL-CAILLOT
Côte de Beaune 1999★

■ 1.81 ha ⊞ 4,800 €8-11

This wine is very straightforward with an attractive, soft red colour and a pleasant nose of dark fruit and soft oak. Supple and fruity with silky tannins, it can be drunk now and for the next four or five years.

☎ Bernard Maréchal-Caillot, 10, rte de Chalon, 21200 Bligny-lès-Beaune, tel. 03.80.21.44.55, fax 03.80.26.88.21 [V]
Y by appt.

DOM. MARTIN-DUFOUR 1999

■ 0.45 ha ⊞ 3,200 €8-11

This wine is too young, and needs to be left for a while to calm down, although it does have an interesting complexity. The colour is faultless and the nose has a nice combination of soft red fruits and vanilla. It has a crisp palate, a pleasant finish, and won't disappoint.

☎ Dom. Martin-Dufour, 4a, rue des Moutots, 21200 Chorey-lès-Beaune, tel. 03.80.22.18.39, fax 03.80.22.18.39

DOM. NUDANT Les Gréchons 1999★

□ 1er cru 0.6 ha ⊞ 3,000 €15-23

The Premier Cru Les Buis 98 red will be a very nice wine in three or four years' time. However, if one had to choose, it would be this lively young Chardonnay. A straw-yellow colour with silvery glints, it has generous aromas of acacia and toast. The palate is lively, the tannins supple and it has a pleasant richness on the finish. One unusual idea suggested by a taster is to try serving it with a Mont d'Or cheese.

☎ Dom. Nudant, 11, RN 74, 21550 Ladoix-Serrigny, tel. 03.80.26.40.48, fax 03.80.26.47.13,
e-mail domaine.nudant@wanadoo.fr [V]
Y by appt.

DOM. PARENT La Corvée 1998★

■ 1er cru n.c. ⊞ 3,600

The 35-year-old vines on this estate are divided into plots and the wines matured for 16 months in oak. This bright red, forthright 98 has a delicately peppery nose with a hint of strawberry. The palate stays within the traditional limits, but it is a fresh and lively wine that is gradually opening up. Drink it between Easter 2002 and Christmas 2007.

☎ Dom. Parent, pl. de l'Eglise, 21630 Pommard, tel. 03.80.22.15.08, fax 03.80.24.19.33,
e-mail parent-pommard@axnet.fr [V]
Y by appt.

DOM. PRIN 1998★★

■ 0.97 ha ⊞ 3,000 €11-15
■
Y by appt.

This pure, simple *village* 98 is a rare find. A *coup de cœur* goes to a wine with a splendid colour and a subtle nose of soft, slightly jammy fruit. Well made and well matured, this is the kind of wine people want to have in their cellar. It is concentrated and powerful but not overly so, tannic but well balanced, and will keep for the next four to five years. The Premier Cru Les Joyeuses 98 red will make another welcome addition to your cellar. It gets one star and also has good potential for laying down. Two excellent value-for-money wines.

☎ Dom. Prin, 12, rue de Serrigny, Cidex 10, 21550 Ladoix-Serrigny, tel. 03.80.26.40.63, fax 03.80.26.46.16 [V] Y by appt.

Aloxe-Corton

O of the total classified as Corton and Corton-Charlemagne, the Appellation Aloxe-Corton applies only to a very small part of the smallest commune of the Côte de Beaune; it produced 5,826 hl (153,806 gal) of red wine and 28.8 hl (760 gal) of white wine in 2000. The Premiers Crus from here have a fine reputation: Les Maréchaudes, Les Valozières and Les Lolières (Grandes and Petites) are the best-known.

Aloxe-Corton

The commune is an important shipping centre and there are several châteaux, resplendent with magnificent glazed tiles, that are worth a visit. The Latour family owns a magnificent domain where the 19th-century vat room is a model of its type for making Burgundy wines.

DOM. CACHAT-OCQUIDANT ET FILS Les Maréchaudes 1999★

■ 1er cru 0.15 ha 1,148   〓 €15-23

Les Maréchaudes is a very old *climat*, mentioned as far back as 1253 (*vinea en Mareschaul*) and was at one time marshland. Vines grow well here and produce good fruit. This wine is fruity on the nose with the typical colour of this vintage and a full, well-structured palate. In two or three years' time this wine will slip down very nicely.

☛ Dom. Cachat-Ocquidant et Fils, 3, pl. du Souvenir, 21550 Ladoix-Serrigny, tel. 03.80.26.45.30, fax 03.80.26.48.16 ▼ ☖ by appt.

CAPITAIN-GAGNEROT 1998★

■ 0.61 ha 3,000   〓 €15-23

This family domaine, created in 1802, has been run since 1987 by Michael Capitain, a very experienced taster. This wine has a pleasant body of ripe fruit with noticeable but well-rounded tannins, delicate and very long. It has good acidity, guaranteeing it at least five years in the cellar.

☛ Maison Capitain-Gagnerot, 38, rte de Dijon, 21550 Ladoix-Serrigny, tel. 03.80.26.41.36, fax 03.80.26.46.29 ▼ ☖ by appt.

DOM. DUBOIS-CACHAT 1999

■ 0.32 ha 1,500   〓 €11-15

This bright, deep-garnet 99 is already open with aromas of crushed fruit and fresh flowers. Although the tannins are still very youthful, it is rich and well-balanced with a

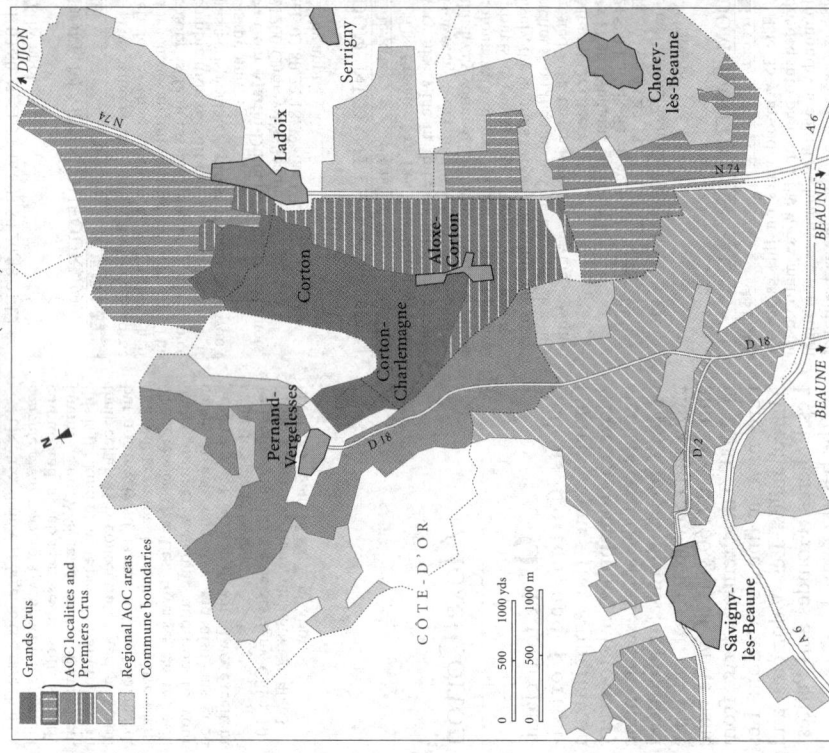

Côte de Beaune (North)

Grands Crus

AOC localities and Premiers Crus

Regional AOC areas
Commune boundaries

dense body which will express itself better in three years' time.

↠ Jean-Pierre Dubois, 2, Grande-Rue, 21200 Chorey-lès-Beaune, tel. 03.80.22.27.83, fax 03.80.22.27.83 ☑
Y by appt.

P. DUBREUIL-FONTAINE PERE ET FILS 1999

	n.c.	n.c.	€11-15

This softly-coloured wine has a toasty nose with red fruit aromas and a supple, well-blended palate. Although not very lengthy, this wine has turned out quite successfully and would go nicely with a steak.

↠ Dom. Dubreuil-Fontaine Père et Fils, 21420 Pernand-Vergelesses, tel. 03.80.21.55.43, fax 03.80.21.51.69, e-mail dubreuil.fontaine@wanadoo.fr ☑
Y by appt.

DUFOULEUR PERE ET FILS 1998★★

	n.c.	2,000	€30-38

This bright, deep ruby-red wine is complex, with ripe aromas of fruit and spice. It has a delightful opening, well-structured body, soft and subtle tannins, and a long finish. This wine is already quite drinkable but has potential for a longer life.

↠ Dufouleur Père et Fils, 15, rue Thurot, BP 27, 21700 Nuits-Saint-Georges, tel. 03.80.61.21.21, fax 03.80.61.10.65 ☑

DOM. LIONEL DUFOUR Les Valozières 1999★

1er cru	0.34 ha 2,800	€46-76

The flavours of fruit and oak go well together in this attractive wine. The colour has hues of ruby and there are delicate aromas of fresh fruit and vanilla. It is stylish, a little fiery, round, fruity and yet biting with quite a distinctive oaky flavour.

↠ SCI Lionel Dufour, 7, rte de Monthélie, 21190 Meursault, tel. 03.80.21.67.02, fax 03.87.69.71.13

DOM. FOLLIN-ARBELET Clos du Chapitre 1999★

1er cru	1 ha 5,000	€15-23

We apologise, but we cannot find this Clos du Chapitre on the map. Having said that, it must exist somewhere. This deep garnet-coloured wine has aromas of vanilla blended with stewed fruit and blackberries. This tannic and vinous wine will need time to express itself more fully. Also worth noting is the **Premier Cru Les Vercots 99**, a modern wine, which was awarded one star and is going to prove a popular choice.

↠ Dom. Follin-Arbelet, Les Vercots, 21420 Aloxe-Corton, tel. 03.80.26.46.73, fax 03.80.26.43.32 ☑ Y by appt.

FRANCOIS GAY 1998★

	0.73 ha 4,500	€15-23

This brilliant garnet-red 98 is well balanced. Everything is in its proper place, from start to finish: a peppery character with stoned fruits and prunes; a gentle attack where the flavour of the wine gradually appears from behind prominent tannins; and a pronounced finish of Griotte cherries. This combination should produce a very pleasant wine in two to three years' time.

↠ EARL François Gay, 9, rue des Fiètes, 21200 Chorey-lès-Beaune, tel. 03.80.22.69.58, fax 03.80.24.71.42 ☑
Y by appt.

CHRISTIAN GROS Les Petites Lolières 1998

1er cru	0.16 ha n.c.	€11-15

A ruby Burgundy? Yes it does exist, and here it is, with a subtle nose and a full, well-structured palate which needs the edges rounding off a little. This wine is consistent with well-handled oak. It should be left in the cellar until it acquires that calm fullness associated with great wines.

↠ Christian Gros, rue de la Chaume, 21700 Premeaux-Prissey, tel. 03.80.61.29.74, fax 03.80.61.39.77 ☑ Y by appt.

DOM. GUYON Les Guerets 1999★★

1er cru	0.09 ha 690	€23-30

This domaine next to Pernand previously won a *coup de cœur* for its 96 vintage. This year it presents a highly-coloured, very open wine with powerful aromas of leather, spices and prunes. The pronounced, rich palate has a hint of ground pepper. A touch of acidity on the finish indicates a wine that, if given the chance, will last.

↠ EARL Dom. Guyon, 11-16, RN 74, 21700 Vosne-Romanée, tel. 03.80.61.02.46, fax 03.80.62.36.56 ☑ Y by appt.

DOM. ROBERT ET RAYMOND JACOB 1999

1er cru	1 ha 6,000	€11-15

This tender redcurrant-coloured wine has a complex nose with notes of fresh berries, almonds, hazelnuts, and leather. The palate is soft, silky and almost buttery, finishing on a note of cherry. This wine doesn't have a fantastic structure but is pleasant and elegant.

↠ Dom. Robert et Raymond Jacob, Buisson, 21550 Ladoix-Serrigny, tel. 03.80.26.40.42, fax 03.80.26.49.34 ☑
Y by appt.

DOM. DE LA GALOPIERE Les Valozières 1999★★

1er cru	0.29 ha 1,500	€15-23

This wine has a superb colour with wonderful aromas of cherry and spices along with a velvety, silky palate. Soft with a lasting finish, the Pinot grape's character comes out beautifully in this top quality wine.

Claire et Gabriel Fournier,
6, rue de l'Eglise, 21200 Bligny-lès-Beaune,
tel. 03.80.21.46.50. fax 03.80.21.49.93,
e-mail c.g.fournier@wanadoo.fr ☑
☖ by appt.

DOM. LALEURE-PIOT 1999★

█ 0.2 ha 1,300 ◉ €11–15

The future looks sunny for this Griotte cherry-red 99. It has an attractive, deep colour and the bouquet, although closed at first, finally opens up with toast and fruit. It is robust, rich and powerful at the finish, without being overly so. This wine has not added the name of Corton to Aloxe for nothing.

☛ Dom. Laleure-Piot, rue de Pralot,
21420 Pernand-Vergelesses,
tel. 03.80.21.52.37, fax 03.80.21.59.48,
e-mail laleure.piot@wanadoo.fr ☑ ☖ ev. day 8am–12 noon 2pm–6pm; Sat./Sun. by appt.

DANIEL LARGEOT 1999★

█ 0.6 ha 4,000 ◉ €15–23

This wine's colour has very attractive bluish shades to it – a much-valued characteristic of the Pinot grape. With its strong, Griotte cherry flavour, delicate oakiness with plenty of depth, and a hint of cherry brandy, it is just as a pleasant drinking wine should be. If you wait, it is bound to reveal even greater and more ambitious things to come.

☛ Daniel Largeot, 5, rue des Brenôts,
21200 Chorey-lès-Beaune,
tel. 03.80.22.15.10. fax 03.80.22.60.62 ☑
☖ by appt.

DOM. LOUIS LATOUR 1998★

█ 3.15 ha 15,000 ◉ €11–15

Louis Latour is to Aloxe-Corton what Louis XIV is to Versailles. Today, his domaine covers 50 ha (123.5 acres), 28 ha (69 acres) of which are devoted to the AOC Grand Cru. This pale-ruby 98 with vermilion highlights opens up when exposed to the air, with aromas of truffles and undergrowth. The Griotte cherry flavour bravely resists the powerful tannins on the palate, waiting for that precious resource – time – which brings order to everything and every wine.

☛ Maison Latour, 18, rue des Tonneliers,
21200 Beaune, tel. 03.80.24.81.00.
fax 03.80.22.36.21, e-mail louislatour@
louislatour.com ☖ by appt.

DOM. MAILLARD PERE ET FILS 1999★

█ 1 ha n.c. ◉ €11–15

This wine's colour is somewhere between crimson and purple. The nose has aromas of leather and blackcurrant with a hint of violet. It has grilled notes from the barrel and elegant tannins followed by soft, red fruit. On the whole, a well-structured wine and a good example of its type. It can be opened now.

☛ Dom. Maillard Père et Fils, 2, rue Joseph-Bard, 21200 Chorey-lès-Beaune,
tel. 03.80.22.10.67, fax 03.80.24.00.42 ☑
☖ by appt.

DOM. MICHEL MALLARD ET FILS Les Valozières 1998★

█ 1er cru 1.2 ha 7,500 ◉ €15–23

Should one choose the Valozières 98 or the **village 98**, which was commended by the Jury? Both are well thought of by our tasters. This serene ruby-red Premier Cru has a pleasant, pure and subtle aroma that opens gradually with freshly-picked cherries. The *terroir* is reflected on the palate. Chewy and sturdy … it really needs to be laid down for a while.

☛ EARL Dom. Michel Mallard et Fils,
43, rte de Dijon, 21550 Ladoix-Serrigny,
tel. 03.80.26.40.64, fax 03.80.26.47.49 ☑
☖ by appt.

MORIN PERE ET FILS 1998★

█ n.c. 12,000 ◉ €15–23

This is a well-made wine, both bright and deep-red in colour with a still-subtle nose of nicely ripe soft, red fruit and oak. The round attack is followed by a concentrated, solid palate. When it comes to life it will be splendid. Jean-Claude Boisset wines have taken over Morin. The wine-cellars, which date from 1747, are worth a visit.

☛ Morin Père et Fils, 9, quai Fleury,
21700 Nuits-Saint-Georges,
tel. 03.80.61.19.51, fax 03.80.61.05.10 ☑
☖ ev. day 9am–12 noon 2pm–6pm; summer 9am–7pm

DOM. NUDANT La Coutière 1998★

█ 1er cru 0.79 ha 4,500 ◉ €15–23

Under review … as one says of a good wine that is too immature to be properly judged. This dark-red wine has a lovely range of aromas: leather, liquorice, bilberry and gunflint. The structure needs to open out and develop and its power needs to be tempered a little, all of which seem quite possible. Another fine wine, the **Valozières 98**, can be chosen without hesitation, or else the **Clos de la Boulotte 98**, which was commended by the Jury. All three need to spend two to five years in the cellar.

☛ Dom. Nudant, 11,
RN 74, 21550 Ladoix-Serrigny,
tel. 03.80.26.40.48, fax 03.80.26.47.13,
e-mail domaine.nudant@wanadoo.fr ☑
☖ by appt.

DOM. DU PAVILLON Clos des Maréchaudes 1998★★

█ 1er cru 1.41 ha 8,800 ◉ €23–30

This is a very attractive, purple-coloured wine. The nose of roasted aromas and ripe fruit is very pure. A straightforward opening is followed by a well-balanced palate with very firm, soft tannins. It is solid, classy, long and haughty, and will keep well.

☛ Dom. du Pavillon,
6 *bis*, bd Jacques-Copeau, 21200 Beaune,
tel. 03.80.24.37.37, fax 03.80.24.37.38

Pernand-Vergelesses

The village of Pernand is situated where two valleys meet, facing due south, and it is, beyond the slightest doubt, the most typical wine village on the Côte. Narrow streets, deep cellars, vine-clothed hillsides, enthusiastic growers and subtle wines have built the village a solid reputation, and of course the old Burgundian families have made a significant contribution, too. In 2000, 4,015 hl (105,996 gal) of red wines were produced; the most famous Premier Cru here is L'Ile des Vergelesses which has great finesse and fully deserves its reputation. Some excellent white wines are also made – 2,074 hl (54,754) in 2000.

DOM. CHRISTIAN PERRIN
Les Boutières 1999
0.94 ha 5,776 | €11-15

This lovely deep ruby-red coloured wine with blue-black highlights has a subtle nose of stoned fruits. The palate keeps you waiting at first, then finally expresses small soft, red fruit and prominent tannins; this wine is worth waiting a long time for.

Christian Perrin, 14, rue de Corton, 21550 Ladoix-Serrigny, tel. 03.80.26.40.93, fax 03.80.26.48.40 Y ev. day except Sun. 8am–12 noon 2pm–6pm

CH. PHILIPPE-LE-HARDI
Les Brunettes et Planchots 1999
2.14 ha 16,000 | €11-15

This climat is right in the heart of the region. This slightly brick-red wine has aromas which build up gradually: first a touch of lace, then a light fruitiness, followed by an oaky note, and finally there is raspberry or strawberry. It is superb on the palate. This unusual 99 goes from strength to strength, but its delicacy of character is not for everyone.

Ch. de Santenay, BP 18, 21590 Santenay, tel. 03.80.20.61.87, fax 03.80.20.63.66 V Y by appt.

ROGER ET JOËL REMY 1999★
n.c. n.c. | €11-15

This dark-ruby wine with purple highlights is adventurous. The nose already gives away its character. It has a long palate with good acidity, soft tannins and a slight sharpness on the finish. It needs five to ten years in the cellar.

SCEA Roger et Joël Rémy, 4, rue du Paradis, 21200 Sainte-Marie-la-Blanche, tel. 03.80.26.60.80. fax 03.80.26.53.03 V Y ev. day except Sun. 8am–12 noon 2pm–6pm

CAVE DE SAINTE-MARIE-LA-BLANCHE 1998
0.25 ha 1,900 | €11-15

Sainte-Marie-la-Blanche, a village to the east of Beaune, created this cooperative in 1957. This interesting 98 has plenty of colour and aromas; there is coffee, fruit and undergrowth in the bouquet, while the palate is pleasant but austerly constructed. It should open up sometime between now and 2003.

Cave de Sainte-Marie-la-Blanche, rte de Verdun, 21200 Sainte-Marie-la-Blanche, tel. 03.80.26.60.60. fax 03.80.26.54.47 V Y ev. day except Sun. 8am–12 noon 2pm–7pm

DOM. CACHAT-OCQUIDANT ET FILS 1999★
□ 0.22 ha 1,300 | €11-15

This straw-gold coloured wine has green flecks and a very elegant nose of spring blossom and brioche. The palate, which develops along similar lines, is balanced and pleasant, well-balanced wine. The red 99 en village also receives one star; it has aromas of ripe Griotte cherries, and the firmness and vigour needed to survive three or four years in the cellar.

Dom. Cachat-Ocquidant et Fils, 3, pl. du Souvenir, 21550 Ladoix-Serrigny, tel. 03.80.26.45.30. fax 03.80.26.48.16 V Y by appt.

CHAMPY PERE ET CIE 1999★
□ n.c. 3,600 | €15-23

This golden Chardonnay has a brilliant intensity that suits its age, and an elegant floral bouquet. It is still on the oaky side but this will soften with time. It is fresh and full on the palate with attractive fruity aromas; a pleasant, well-balanced wine.

Maison Champy, 5, rue du Grenier-à-Sel, 21200 Beaune, tel. 03.80.25.09.99, fax 03.80.25.09.95, e-mail champyprost@aol.com V Y by appt.

DOM. CHANDON DE BRIAILLES
Ile des Vergelesses 1998★
1er cru
4 ha 12,000 | €15-23

This domaine has a long and noble history in Burgundy, and boasts an 18th-century château with traditional French-style gardens. This wine is not yet open, but has brilliance, delicacy and a hint of astringency, which will guarantee it two to three years' life in the cellar.

Dom. Chandon de Briailles,
1, rue Soeur-Goby, 21420 Savigny-les-Beaune,
tel. 03.80.21.52.31, fax 03.80.21.59.15
By appt.
de Nicolay

CHARTRON ET TREBUCHET 1999★ €15-23
n.c. 9,000

This pale 99 is faintly tinged with gold. Aromas of hazelnut and honey emerge gradually from beneath an oaky flavour. The richness and fullness of the palate are perfectly balanced and it lives up to the promises of the nose, creating a fine *village* which should be drunk between 2002 and 2003.

Chartron et Trébuchet,
13, Grande-Rue, 21190 Puligny-Montrachet,
tel. 03.80.21.32.85, fax 03.80.21.36.35,
e-mail jmchartron@chartron-trebuchet.com
ev. day 10am–12 noon 2pm–6pm; cl. mid-Nov.-Mar.

DOM. DENIS PERE ET FILS 1999★ €8-11
2 ha 6,000

This dark garnet-red *village* with bluish glints looks very youthful. However, there are already aromas of blackcurrant and blackberries on the nose. The palate is robust but also very pleasurable, with nicely balanced fruit and tannins, guaranteeing it four to five years' life in the cellar. The agreeable L'Ile des Vergelesses 99 red was singled out for its raspberry aromas and its oak-influenced freshness on the palate, and will doubtless improve with age.

Dom. Denis Père et Fils,
chem. des Vignes-Blanches,
21420 Pernand-Vergelesses,
tel. 03.80.21.50.91, fax 03.80.26.10.32
By appt.

DOM. P. DUBREUIL-FONTAINE PERE ET FILS Clos Berthet 1999★★ €15-23
1 ha 5,000

This beautifully golden Clos Berthet (a family monopoly) is a pleasant wine. It is straightforward, open, rich, fresh and fruity. Also worthy of note is a **village 99 white**, which was singled out and would go very well with a grilled *andouillette*.

Dom. Dubreuil-Fontaine Père et Fils,
21420 Pernand-Vergelesses,
tel. 03.80.21.55.43, fax 03.80.21.51.69,
e-mail dubreuil.fontaine@wanadoo.fr
By appt.

DUFOULEUR PERE ET FILS 1998★ €15-23
n.c. 900

This very clear-coloured wine with shades of amber takes us straight to the bakery with its delicious aromas of brioche and hot croissant. With a fresh attack and well-balanced palate, its luscious flavour confirms the aromas. This is a very elegant wine.

Dufouleur Père et Fils, 15, rue Thurot, BP 27, 21700 Nuits-Saint-Georges, tel. 03.80.61.21.21, fax 03.80.61.10.65
By appt.

DOM. JEAN-JACQUES GIRARD €11-15
Les Belles Filles 1999★
0.35 ha 2,700

Simply by calling itself Les Belles Filles, 'The Lovely Girls', (the genuine name of the *climat*), this Pernand makes itself immediately more attractive. However, with its bright-gold colour and its hazelnut notes, it certainly has no need of a pretty name to make it one of the best whites on offer. It is powerful with good acidity and fruity aromas that are still a little closed but ready to soften. It can be laid down for a year or two before drinking.

Dom. Jean-Jacques Girard,
16, rue de Citeaux, 21420 Savigny-les-Beaune,
tel. 03.80.21.56.15, fax 03.80.26.10.08
By appt.

DOM. DOMINIQUE GUYON 1998★ €15-23
Les Vergelesses 1er cru
0.58 ha 3,600

The structure of this wine is light and fruity. Full-bodied and red-garnet in colour with still-developing aromas, and a palate that is heading in the right direction, this is a wine that will go down well in Finland, as the Guyon family supplies that consulate in Dijon. The **white Antonin Guyon village 99**, named after the owner, was commended by the Jury.

Dom. Dominique Guyon,
21420 Savigny-lès-Beaune,
tel. 03.80.67.13.24, fax 03.80.66.85.87,
e-mail vins@guyon-bourgogne.com
By appt.

JACOB-FREREBEAU 1999★ €5-8
0.3 ha 2,000

You could almost lose yourself looking into this wine's crimson highlights. The nose has aromas of dark fruit with a touch of raspberry. The youthful palate has sufficient structure and well-proportioned tannins to make this a serious bet for the future. It has a nice fullness but needs to wait at least two years before being opened.

Frédéric Jacob, 50, Grande-Rue,
21420 Changey-Echevronne,
tel. 03.80.21.55.58 By appt.

LES VILLAGES DE JAFFELIN 1998★ €11-15
n.c. 12,000

The deep, dark red of this wine has come straight from the canvas of a Dutch Master. The nose opens with undergrowth, followed by a complex blend of cherry and peony. The effect on the palate is at first subtle, becoming increasingly musky. An old-fashioned roast would seem the most appropriate dish to accompany it.

- Jaffelin, 2, rue Paradis, 21200 Beaune, tel. 03.80.22.12.49, fax 03.80.24.91.87

DOM. LALEURE-PIOT

Les Vergelesses 1999★

1er cru | 1.7 ha | 12,000 | €11-15

A previous *coup de cœur* winner, this year the domaine presented this brilliant cherry-red Les Vergelesses. It has a delightful nose of almonds, mushrooms, and fruits in *eau-de-vie*; the palate is a little lacking in fruitiness but has good potential. **L'Ile des Vergelesses 99 red** receives one star, as does a very fine **white Premier Cru 99**, which is ready to drink, preferably with fish.

- Dom. Laleure-Piot, rue de Pralot, 21420 Pernand-Vergelesses, tel. 03.80.21.52.37, fax 03.80.21.59.48, e-mail laleure.piot@wanadoo.fr ☑ Y ev. day 8am–12 noon 2pm–6pm; Sat/Sun. by appt.

PIERRE MAREY ET FILS 1999★

□ | 2.45 ha | 13,000 | €11-15

This wine is pale and light-gold in colour with green highlights. The nose is still on the closed side but has hints of floral aromas with touches of butter and vanilla. After a fine opening on the palate, the wine is lively with well-balanced citrus fruit flavours. It develops with elegance, has good length, and should be drunk over the next three years, preferably with white meat.

- EARL Pierre Marey et Fils, rue Jacques-Copeau, 21420 Pernand-Vergelesses, tel. 03.80.21.51.71, fax 03.80.26.10.48 ☑

DOM. PAVELOT En Caradeux 1999★

1er cru | 1.3 ha | 7,000 | €6-11

They say in Burgundy, 'If you can see Pernand, you're not in it'; the village, nestled on a hill, can be seen from afar. This garnet-red wine has aromas of blackcurrant and blackberry with a luscious jammy red fruit flavour on the palate. This wine should not be drunk straight away. Worth noting also is the **red Les Vergelesses 98**, a good old-fashioned Burgundy.

- EARL Dom. Régis et Luc Pavelot, rue du Paulant, 21420 Pernand-Vergelesses, tel. 03.80.26.13.65, fax 03.80.26.13.65 ☑

JEAN-MARC PAVELOT

Les Vergelesses 1998★

1er cru | 0.6 ha | 3,000 | €11-15

Although this Les Vergelesses 98 is ready to be served, two to three years in the cellar will do it no harm. The colour of ripe cherries, with lengthy secondary aromas, it is rich and round on the palate and fairly oaky with soft, gentle tannins.

- Jean-Marc Pavelot, 1, chem. des Guettottes, 21420 Savigny-lès-Beaune, tel. 03.80.21.55.21, fax 03.80.21.59.73 ☑ Y by appt.

CH. ROSSIGNOL-JEANNIARD

Les Fichots 1999★★

1er cru | 1.05 ha | 5,000 | €11-15

This is a lovely, dark-garnet wine with blackcurrant and cherry giving an impression of maturity. It has a refined, full and generous palate with very subtle tannins. This wine will become more powerful with time.

- Ch. Rossignol-Jeanniard, rue de Mont, 21190 Volnay, tel. 03.80.21.62.43, fax 03.80.21.27.61 ☑ Y by appt.

DOM. NICOLAS ROSSIGNOL 1999

□ | 0.4 ha | 2,200 | €8-11

This wine's intense purple colour is a good sign. The aromas are still subtle and the concentrated and complex palate is developing well. The tannins are a little narrow but should blend in with time and there is a charming flavour of fruit preserved in alcohol.

- Nicolas Rossignol, rue de Mont, 21190 Volnay, tel. 03.80.21.62.43, fax 03.80.21.27.61 ☑ Y by appt.

DOM. ROLLIN PERE ET FILS 1999

□ | 1.5 ha | 9,000 | €11-15

This wine is a brilliant gold colour. The nose opens on typical Chardonnay tones of acacia and hawthorn. After a subtle attack the palate gradually opens, eventually revealing pronounced lemony flavours. It is fine, balanced, and elegant: a lovely ensemble.

- Rollin Père et Fils, rte des Vergelesses, 21420 Pernand-Vergelesses, tel. 03.80.21.57.31, fax 03.80.26.10.38 ☑ Y by appt.

DOM. RAPET PERE ET FILS

Ile des Vergelesses 1999★

1er cru | 0.65 ha | 3,000 | €15-23

The Rapet domaine was very much involved with a well-known local theatre. This bottle of red Ile has a delicate floral aroma with a fruity, full-bodied and promising palate. **The white village 98, the white Premier Cru 99, and the red Les Vergelesses Premier Cru 98** all receive one star. Not a bad show, really.

- Dom. Rapet Père et Fils, 21420 Pernand-Vergelesses, tel. 03.80.21.59.94, fax 03.80.21.54.01, ☑ Y by appt.

ALBERT PONNELLE

Les Vergelesses 1998★

1er cru | n.c. | n.c. | €15-23

The opening is graceful and supple, but as expected at this age, the palate is slightly severe with tannins that still need to soften. The wine has a pleasant pale colour, with aromas of figs and prunes.

- Albert Ponnelle, Clos Saint-Nicolas, BP 107, 21200 Beaune, tel. 03.80.22.00.05, fax 03.80.24.19.73, e-mail info@albert-ponnelle.com ☑ Y by appt.

of red. The prominent oak flavour does not obscure the notes of liquorice and fruit. Its concentration and strength are qualities of a Grand Cru. Its fresh, velvety chewiness, flavour of blackcurrant, and soft, smooth palate all add to the pleasure.

↘ Maison Bertrand Ambroise, rue de l'Eglise, 21700 Premeaux-Prissey, tel. 03.80.62.30.19, fax 03.80.62.38.69, e-mail bertrand.ambroise@wanadoo.fr ☑
Ŧ by appt.

DOM. THIÉLY 1999

□   0.6 ha   2,700 ||| €11-15

The label on this bottle is in the old parchment-style with curling edges that used to be the style in Burgundy. This wine has aromas of caramel, vanilla and apple with a gentle richness, good quality structure and a fruity finish.

↘ Dom. Thiély, rue de Vergy, 21420 Pernand-Vergelesses, tel. 03.80.21.54.86, fax 03.80.26.11.92 ☑
Ŧ by appt.

Corton

The 'Corton Mountain' is made up of different types of soil and produces different wines at different levels of the slope. Topped with woods that grow on hard limestone from the Rauracian period (Superior Oxfordian), the Argovian marlstone emerges as white soil for several score metres, and is particularly good for white wines. These soils also cover shelves of pearly limestone incorporating numerous large oyster shells, overlaid by brown soil favourable for producing red wines.

The name of the *lieu-dit* appears under the Appellation Corton, and can be used for white wines but is mainly known for reds. Les Bressandes is produced on the red soils, which give the wine power and finesse. On the other hand, on the higher slopes of Les Renardes, Les Languettes and the Clos du Roy, the white soils produce well-structured red wines which, as they age, take on the gamey, 'sauvage' scents that can be found in the Mourottes de Ladoix. Corton is the biggest producer of the Grand Crus – 3,776 hl (99,686 gal) of red and 138 hl (3,643 gal) of white wine in 2000.

BERTRAND AMBROISE

Le Rognet 1999★★

■ Gd cru   n.c.   n.c. ||| €46-76

This is a flavourful wine and very Corton in style. It would be hard to find a darker shade

ARNOUX PERE ET FILS

Rognet 1999★

■ Gd cru   0.33 ha   1,500 ||| €23-30

82 83 |89| |90| |91| 92 **97** 98 99

This plot of land was bought in 1984 from the Charles Viénot estate. The result is this highly-coloured 99 with excellent aromas of toast blended with subtle soft red fruit. It has a smooth, velvety palate but its structure, concentration, and fruit reveal a determined character. It has a good future ahead of it.

↘ Arnoux Père et Fils, rue des Brenôts, 21200 Chorey-lès-Beaune, tel. 03.80.22.57.98, fax 03.80.22.16.85 ☑
Ŧ by appt.

JEAN-CLAUDE BELLAND

Grèves 1999

■ Gd cru   0.55 ha   3,200 ||| €23-30

This wine marks the tenth anniversary of wine-production for the domaine's owner. It is more black than scarlet and … dare one say it? Stendhalian? Its aromas of grape-brandy continue with Griotte cherry and raspberry. The full palate lives up to its colour. This relatively unknown *climat* is situated between Bressandes and Perrières. The **Perrières 99** has strong but decent tannins. One taster who likes complex and fine aromas detected a hint of violet, and recommends opening this bottle between 2003 and 2006.

↘ Jean-Claude Belland, 21590 Santenay, tel. 03.80.20.61.90. fax 03.80.20.65.60 ☑
Ŧ by appt.

BONNEAU DU MARTRAY 1998★

■ Gd cru   1.5 ha   5,000 ||| €38-46

|80| 86 87 88 |89| |90| 91 92 |93| **94** 95 **96** 97 98

This is one of the rare estates that produces only Grand Crus, from a single plot of land: 9.5 ha (23.5 acres) in Corton-Charlemagne and 1.5 ha (3.7 acres) for this Corton. This agreeable 98 is bright red with violet highlights, firm and well structured. It has aromas of cherry and vanilla and is straightforward and full, rather in the style of a Renardes, a very nice wine.

↘ Dom. Bonneau du Martray, 21420 Pernand-Vergelesses, tel. 03.80.21.50.64, fax 03.80.21.57.19 ☑
↘ de la Morinière

DOM. HENRI ET GILLES BUISSON
Le Rognet-et-Corton 1998

| Gd cru | 0.32 ha | 1,800 | €23-30 |

This bottle has a perfect label that states the exact name of this Grand Cru. The wine itself is a typical 98 vintage, lacking complexity. On both the nose and palate there is a lot of oak with notes of blackcurrant, suggesting a strong pressing. In five to eight years' time, this wine should have softened.

- Dom. Henri et Gilles Buisson, imp. du Clou, 21190 Saint-Romain, tel. 03.80.21.27.91, fax 03.80.21.64.87
- by appt.
- Gilles Buisson

DOM. CACHAT-OCQUIDANT ET FILS
Clos des Vergennes 1999

| Gd cru | 1.42 ha | 5,600 | €23-30 |

86 87 88 [90] 91 95 96 97 98 99

Les Vergennes is very aristocratic, situated as it is between le Rognet-et-Corton and les Maréchaudes. This example is well structured, and has delicate tannins with pepper and liquorice touches and aromas of soft fruit. It needs a long time in the cellar.

- Dom. Cachat-Ocquidant et Fils, 3, pl. du Souvenir, 21550 Ladoix-Serrigny, tel. 03.80.26.45.30, fax 03.80.26.48.16
- by appt.

CAPITAIN-GAGNEROT
Les Renardes 1998

| Gd cru | 0.33 ha | 1,500 | €30-38 |

82 83 85 86 88 (89) 90 91 92 96 97 98

In a difficult vintage, this wine is one of the stars of this estate. It is a lovely Burgundy-red in colour; the nose is spicy and fresh but not very intense and still difficult to judge. The oaky palate obscures the flavour of the *terroir*, which should be more in evidence in three or four years' time.

- Maison Capitain-Gagnerot, 38, rte de Dijon, 21550 Ladoix-Serrigny, tel. 03.80.26.41.36, fax 03.80.26.46.29
- by appt.

DOM. CHANDON DE BRIAILLES
Les Maréchaudes 1998★

| Gd cru | 0.32 ha | 1,500 | €30-38 |

This beautiful estate was founded in the 18th century and its inhabitants have always been involved in wine-making and the arts. Situated in Ladoix, this *climat* has produced a subtle red wine, the sign of a measured and elegant pressing. The nose is like a French garden, well-organised with aromas of flowers and soft red fruit. On the palate, the tannins are noticeable without being bitter and the oak is discreet and non-intrusive. Best to wait at least three years.

- Dom. Chandon de Briailles, 1, rue Soeur-Goby, 21420 Savigny-lès-Beaune, tel. 03.80.21.52.31, fax 03.80.21.59.15
- by appt.
- de Nicolay

CH. CORTON GRANCEY 1998★

| Gd cru | 17 ha | 36,000 | €30-38 |

Louis Latour, one of the great *négociants-éleveurs* of the Côte d'Or, bought this château in 1890 and became one of the largest Grands Crus owners. The deep colour of this shy 98 shows signs of developing. The bouquet is closed, revealing a subtle oakiness that very slowly begins to soften and the delicate palate has tannins that although beginning to soften are still quite austere. Open it in two years to try it, but it may need longer. The **Le Clos de la Vigne au Saint 98** was sufficiently inspiring for the Jury to single it out.

- Dom. Louis Latour, 18, rue des Tonneliers, 21200 Beaune, tel. 03.80.24.81.00, fax 03.80.22.36.21, e-mail louislatour@louislatour.com
- by appt.

JOSEPH DROUHIN Bressandes 1998★

| Gd cru | 0.25 ha | 1,200 | €38-46 |

This Bressandes is made in the style of a Renardes. For a 98, the ruby-red colour has kept all its intensity. On the nose, strawberry aromas combine with undergrowth, musk and pepper. The palate is open and has the same complex aromas as the nose with a little more freshness and fine tannins. 'A really nice Corton, just as we like them,' notes one Jury member, which is a real compliment.

- Joseph Drouhin, 7, rue d'Enfer, 21200 Beaune, tel. 03.80.24.68.88, fax 03.80.22.43.14, e-mail maisondrouhin@drouhin.com
- by appt.

DUFOULEUR PÈRE ET FILS 1998

| Gd cru | n.c. | 900 | €38-46 |

Wild aromas with touches of cooked fruit, already well-matured, do not detract from this wine's youthful palate. The attack is strong and the tannins are well-tamed. This 98 has violet notes and notable potential (in two to five years).

- Dufouleur Père et Fils, 15, rue Thurot, BP 27, 21700 Nuits-Saint-Georges, tel. 03.80.61.21.21, fax 03.80.61.10.65
- by appt.

DOM. DUPONT-TISSERANDOT
Le Rognet 1999★

| Gd cru | 0.32 ha | 1,800 | €23-30 |

This wine has a lot going for it: a black cherry colour with aromas of blackcurrant, coffee and oak. It has depth and charm, and is a good option for laying down.

- GAEC Dupont-Tisserandot, 2, pl. des Marronniers, 21220 Gevrey-Chambertin, tel. 03.80.34.10.50, fax 03.80.58.50.71
- by appt.

CLOS DES CORTONS FAIVELEY 1998★★

| Gd cru | 2.97 ha | 12,800 | €46-76 |

85 86 88 89 [90] 91 92 [94] (95) 96 97 98

Long before the creation of the AOCs, a court hearing in Dijon decided that in order to avoid any confusion, this vineyard ought to use the owner's name. This good-quality 98, with its deep, dark-red colour and authentic structure, is a credit to the Faiveley family. The palate is still tannic and confirms the high-quality oak nose. It needs a good five to ten years in the cellar.

• Bourgognes Faiveley, 8, rue du Tribourg, 21701 Nuits-Saint-Georges, tel. 03.80.61.04.55, fax 03.80.62.33.37, e-mail bourgognes.faiveley@wanadoo.fr ▼

DOM. FOLLIN-ARBELET 1999

■ Gd cru 0.4 ha 2,000 ⬛ €23-30

This light, fresh 99 has aromas of cherry jam, toast and cinnamon with well-blended tannins and raspberry on the middle palate. This soft, calm wine should be drunk in a year or two's time.

• Dom. Follin-Arbelet, Les Vercots, 21420 Aloxe-Corton, tel. 03.80.26.46.73, fax 03.80.26.43.32 ▼ ▼ by appt.

DOM. ANNE-MARIE GILLE

Les Renardes 1999

■ Gd cru 0.16 ha 600 ⬛ €23-30

This wine has a deep, youthful colour with violet highlights. On the nose there is a vanilla-flavoured oakiness with subtle strawberry and raspberry touches. On the palate the oak blends well with the fruit in an adequate structure. It needs two to four years in the cellar.

• Dom. Anne-Marie Gille, 34, RN 74, 21700 Comblanchien, tel. 03.80.62.94.13, fax 03.80.62.99.88, e-mail gille@burgundywines.net ▼ ▼ by appt.

CHRISTIAN GROS ★

Les Renardes 1998 ★

■ Gd cru 0.65 ha n.c. ⬛ €23-30

Christian Gros's mother comes from a long line of wine-producers who go back as far as 1750; she has been running this domaine since 1973. This wine is representative of its climat. Red with violet highlights, it is strongly perfumed with jammy fruits, stewed prunes, woodland scents and spices. Although it needs time to come together, it has the means to do so. It has a nice chewiness and well-concentrated tannins, both holding back in order to guarantee our pleasure in five to seven years' time, preferably with roast duck.

• Christian Gros, rue de la Chaume, 21700 Premeaux-Prissey, tel. 03.80.61.29.74, fax 03.80.61.39.77 ▼ ▼ by appt.

DOM. ANTONIN GUYON

Bressandes 1998

■ Gd cru 0.86 ha 4,000 ⬛ €30-38

This wine has an intense colour and a nose already open on soft red fruit despite a still very strong oakiness. It has a well-balanced palate, fine tannins, decent toasted aromas and oaky length. It should be a good bet in two years' time.

• Dom. Antonin Guyon, 21420 Savigny-lès-Beaune, tel. 03.80.67.13.24, fax 03.80.66.85.87, e-mail vins@guyon-bourgogne.com ▼ ▼ by appt.

DOM. MICHEL ET LAURENT JUILLOT Perrières 1999

■ Gd cru n.c. 5,000 ⬛ €30-38

This Corton Perrières is produced in a climat 240 m (785 ft) above sea level. It is matured in oak, 30 % of which is new and very noticeable, leaving very little room for the cherry—just a note of kirsch. The toasted, grilled flavour brings a great deal of austerity to a wine which should come into its own in three to four years' time.

• Dom. Michel et Laurent Juillot, 59, Grande-Rue, BP 10. 71640 Mercurey, tel. 03.85.98.99.89, fax 03.85.98.99.88, e-mail infos@domaine.michel.juillot.fr ▼ ▼ by appt.

DOM. LALEURE-PIOT

Le Rognet 1999 ★

■ Gd cru 0.33 ha 1,600 ⬛ €23-30

Here we have two 99s right next to each other: a Bressandes 99, and this classic, highly concentrated Corton, good for laying down. Reddish-black in colour with pronounced kirsch and raspberry aromas and subtle touches of oak, it has fullness and good acidity which promise a fine future. Last year the 98 vintage was awarded one of our coups de coeur.

• Dom. Laleure-Piot, rue de Pralot, 21420 Pernand-Vergelesses, tel. 03.80.21.52.37, fax 03.80.21.59.48, e-mail laleure.piot@wanadoo.fr ▼ ▼ ev. day 8am–12 noon 2pm–6pm; Sat./ Sun. by appt.

• Frédéric Laleure

DOM. MAILLARD PÈRE ET FILS 1999 ★

□ Gd cru 0.34 ha n.c. ⬛ €23-30

97 98 99

This estate was awarded a coup de coeur last year for its 1998 vintage, and this promising white Corton 99 is also capable of success. It has a lovely clarity which is characteristic of the appellation and rank of Grand Cru. Hazelnut, acacia and flint aromas suggest its future complexity. It has a lively temperament and a well-established structure.

• Dom. Maillard Père et Fils, 2, rue Joseph-Bard, 21200 Chorey-les-Beaune, tel. 03.80.22.10.67, fax 03.80.24.00.42 ▼ ▼ by appt.

FRANÇOISE MALDANT

Renardes 1999 ★

■ Gd cru 0.33 ha 800 ⬛ €23-30

'Will make a good wine when the flavour of the oak has softened.' It has an intense cherry-red colour and roasted aromas with a few gamey notes. Its round tannins still need to soften, which, according to the experts, should take between three and five years.

Françoise Maldant, 27, Grande-Rue, 21200 Chorey-les-Beaune, tel. 03.80.22.11.94, fax 03.80.24.10.40 V

DOM. MICHEL MALLARD ET FILS

Les Maréchaudes 1998*

|93| |94| 96 98

Gd cru | 0.31 ha | 1,600 | €30-38

This wine has a soft red fruit attack and a strong tannic structure. It needs a long period of five to ten years in the cellar, after which it will go nicely with grilled steak. It is a dark-sunset colour and has a Griotte cherry aroma with oaky touches. An attractive wine, worthy of its rank.

EARL Dom. Michel Mallard et Fils, 43, rte de Dijon, 21550 Ladoix-Serrigny, tel. 03.80.26.40.64, fax 03.80.26.47.49 V

D. MEUNEVEAUX Chaumes 1999**

Gd cru | 0.3 ha | 1,300 | €15-23

It is possible to know everything about Corton and not know where Chaumes is: when you leave Aloxe, go towards Pernand and you will see Chaumes on the left after La Vigne au Saint. It is not a very well-known *climat* but this fine and elegant wine is impressive. Its lightness is misleading; the structure is superb and very characteristic of Pinot. It has an intense garnet-red colour with a hint of roses. Wait four years before serving this wine. A very competitive price.

Didier Meuneveaux, 9, pl. des Brunettes, 21420 Aloxe-Corton, tel. 03.80.26.42.33, fax 03.80.26.48.60 V Y by appt.

DOM. NUDANT Bressandes 1999

Gd cru | 0.6 ha | 2,500 | €30-38

The Nudant family has been here since 1747 and owns nearly 13 ha (32 acres) of land. This Bressandes has a perfect, intense garnet colour. The nose opens on ripe, soft red fruit followed by an aroma of mocha indicating a very powerful oakiness. The full palate follows the same lines; the oak will need to soften over the next three to four years before one can judge the true value of this wine.

Dom. Nudant, 11, RN 74, 21550 Ladoix-Serrigny, tel. 03.80.26.40.48, fax 03.80.26.47.13, e-mail domaine.nudant@wanadoo.fr V Y by appt.

DOM. DU PAVILLON

Clos des Maréchaudes 1998**

Gd cru | 0.54 ha | 3,000 | €46-76

This estate, which since 1994 has belonged to the Albert Bichot company, consists of 4 ha (9.9 acres) surrounded by a dry-stone wall, which together with the main house and wine cellars make a charming picture. This flaming ruby-red wine is slightly aggressive on the nose but long and well structured. It can be served young with a venison steak, but could equally well be kept for up to ten years.

Dom. du Pavillon, 6bis, bd Jacques-Copeau, 21200 Beaune, tel. 03.80.24.37.37, fax 03.80.24.37.38

DOM. PRIN Bressandes 1998*

Gd cru | 0.68 ha 3,300 | €30-38

They say that Les Bressandes flows from a spring and flows on the palate; this is a wine with a reputation for being supple and easy to drink. This powerful 98 is developing slightly in colour but its nose of spices and dark fruit is still closed. On the palate there are the beginnings of an impressive body and a useful touch of astringency from the tannins, providing structure. This Corton is made with the future (the next decade) in mind. A precious investment!

Dom. Prin, 12, rue de Serrigny, Cidex 10, 21550 Ladoix-Serrigny, tel. 03.80.26.40.63, fax 03.80.26.46.16 V Y by appt.

DOM. RAPET PERE ET FILS

Pougets 1999*

|93| 96 |97| 98 99

Gd cru | n.c. | 2,400 | €30-38

The **red Corton 99** is developing well and, like the Pougets, was awarded one star. This mainly white-wine area generally produces affable reds. Almost black in colour with a flavour of dark fruit, this is a consistent wine with unique personality, and good for laying down. Although a little tannic today, it is worth waiting for. It will be drinkable in four to five years' time, but can be kept for up to twelve years.

Dom. Rapet Père et Fils, 21420 Pernand-Vergelesses, tel. 03.80.21.59.94, fax 03.80.21.54.01 V Y by appt.

COMTE SENARD

Clos des Meix Monopole 1999**

88 89 90 93 96 |97| 99

Gd cru | 1.6 ha | 7,000 | €23-30

This estate, one of the first to be founded in Burgundy, opened a *table d'hôte* in 1999 and between March and November offers wine-tasting lunches. This *climat*, next to La Vigne au Saint, has created a very delicate wine from this monopoly *clos*. A powerful ruby-red in colour with subtle and straightforward aromas of Griotte cherry; it has a well-blended body with a ripe, almost jammy flavour and good tannins. It will be at its best in four to six years' time.

SCE du Dom. Comte Senard, 7, rempart Saint-Jean, 21200 Beaune, tel. 03.80.24.21.65, fax 03.80.24.21.44 V Y by appt.

DOM. MICHEL VOARICK

Renardes 1999**

Gd cru | 0.5 ha | 1,500 | €23-30

Pierre Voarick was a wine-producer for the Hospices de Beaune for many years (*cuvée Docteur Peste*) until together with his son Michel he founded this estate. The excellent **Languettes 99** was awarded one star and is worth considering if the Renardes is no longer available. Better still is this deep-garnet 99, which opens very softly with fresh strawberries and crème de cassis, then shows its true colours in a long, characterful body. This wine will probably become more concentrated but needs to be laid down for at least four years.

↳ SCEA Michel Voarick, 2, pl. du Chapitre, 21420 Aloxe-Corton, tel. 03.80.26.40.44, fax 03.80.26.41.22, e-mail voarick.michel@aol.com [V]
↳ by appt.

Corton-Charlemagne

The Appellation Charlemagne, which until 1948 could have Aligoté grapes added to it, is no longer used. In 2000, Appellation Corton-Charlemagne produced 2,432 hl (64,205 gal), most of it grown in the communes of Pernand-Vergelesses and Aloxe-Corton. The wines of this appellation – which owe their name to the Emperor Charles the Great who apparently ordered white grapes to be planted so the wines would not stain his beard – are a lovely greenish-gold and reach their peak after five or ten years.

JEAN-LUC AEGERTER 1999
□Gd cru n.c. 2,400 €38-46

This well-made 99 is a good average for the appellation. It needs to be kept for about four years, although it is already fairly open with its character starting to show. It has a white-gold colour and balanced floral and vanilla aromas, and would go well with a fish paté.

↳ Jean-Luc Aegerter, 49, rue Henri-Challand, 21700 Nuits-Saint-Georges, tel. 03.80.61.02.88, fax 03.80.62.37.99 [V]
↳ by appt.

DOM. BONNEAU DU MARTRAY 1998★
□Gd cru 9.5 ha 54,000 €46-76
79 83 |90| |91| |92| 93 95 96 97 98

This estate owns 9.5 hectatres (23.5 acres) of Corton-Charlemagne and is a real part of the history of Burgundy wine. This pale-gold 98 has a complex nose of hazelnut, chamomile and lime, and a subtle palate that is not yet very rich. This wine will be ready in five to ten years' time. The domaine has been awarded two coups de cœur in the past.

↳ Dom. Bonneau du Martray, 21420 Pernand-Vergelesses, tel. 03.80.21.50.64, fax 03.80.21.57.19 [V]
↳ de La Morinière

PHILIPPE BOUCHARD 1999★
□Gd cru n.c. n.c. €46-76

This white-gold 99 seems to have an endless future ahead of it. Well-balanced and generous with vanilla aromas, it is livened up by a touch of acidity on both the attack and the finish. It has a wonderfully straightforward flavour but needs a long time to develop its richness.

↳ Philippe Bouchard, 21420 Aloxe-Corton, tel. 03.80.25.00.00, fax 03.80.26.42.00. e-mail vinibeaune@bourgogne.net
↳ by appt.

DOM. BOUCHARD PÈRE ET FILS 1998★
□Gd cru 3.25 ha n.c. €46-76

Bouchard Père et Fils present this golden-yellow 98 which is still developing and has great laying down potential. Toasted aromas combine with hawthorn and truffle, followed by a lasting mineral tone bringing variation to the powerful flavours. It would go perfectly with a barbecued lobster.

↳ Bouchard Père et Fils, Ch. de Beaune, 21200 Beaune, tel. 03.80.24.80.24, fax 03.80.22.55.88, e-mail france@bouchard-pereetfils.com ↳ by appt.

CHAMPY 1999★
□Gd cru n.c. 2 700 €46-76

'The only way to overcome a problem is to survive it,' said Talleyrand. There is no doubt that this complex 99 will do just that and in two or three years' time develop into a lovely wine. A golden colour with highlights of emerald green and carefully defined mineral and citrus fruit aromas, it has a smooth and lively palate and flavours of apples and pears.

↳ Maison Champy, 5, rue du Grenier-à-Sel, 21200 Beaune, tel. 03.80.25.09.99, fax 03.80.25.09.95, e-mail champyprost@aol.com [V] ↳ by appt.

MAURICE ET ANNE-MARIE CHAPUIS 1999
□Gd cru 1 ha 4,000 €23-30

This pale-yellow 99 with grey highlights has an open nose of acacia and pineapple with an attractive, full, well-made palate. There is a touch of soft white bread with just enough acidity. It will progress over the next five years.

↳ Maurice Chapuis, 21420 Aloxe-Corton, tel. 03.80.26.40.99, fax 03.80.26.40.89 [V] ↳ by appt.

CHEVALIER PÈRE ET FILS 1998★
□Gd cru 0.22 ha 1,200 €38-46

This estate founded in 1985 now covers 11 ha (27.2 acres) This brilliant-yellow 98 has a flint and acacia nose accompanied by a

vanilla flavour that comes from well-mastered oak. The palate opens on a straightforward, fresh note, followed by touches of lime.
- SCE Chevalier Père et Fils, Buisson, 21550 Ladoix-Serrigny, tel. 03.80.26.46.30, fax 03.80.26.41.47 ▼ by appt.

DOM. DUBREUIL-FONTAINE PÈRE ET FILS 1999★

□ Gd cru   0.76 ha 3,800   [€ 30–38]

Pierre Dubreuil was a leading Burgundy wine-producer who would have been proud of this successful 99. This is a rich wine with well-tempered oak, 35% new barrels, and a yeast stirring on the lees. An attractive colour, the nose a mixture of cinnamon and pear and a straightforward attack with well-balanced acidity and alcohol; it is made for laying down, although it can be appreciated from 2003.
- Dom. Dubreuil-Fontaine Père et Fils, 21420 Pernand-Vergelesses, tel. 03.80.21.55.43, fax 03.80.21.51.69, e-mail dubreuil.fontaine@wanadoo.fr ▼
- by appt.
- Bernard Dubreuil

CH. GENOT-BOULANGER 1998★

□ Gd cru   0.29 ha 870   [€ 46–76]

We need to be patient with this wine. Its colour is already a lovely shade of gold but its citrus-fruit bouquet needs to open up more to do justice to the aromas of spring blossom. It is light on the palate with a spicy and mineral base and should realise its full potential in two years' time. It will go well with a crayfish.
- SCEV Ch. Génot-Boulanger, 25, rue de Cîteaux, 21190 Meursault, tel. 03.80.21.49.20, fax 03.80.21.49.21, e-mail genot.boulanger@wanadoo.fr ▼
- by appt.
- M. Delaby

DOM. ANTONIN GUYON 1999

□ Gd cru   0.55 ha 3,500   [€ 46–76]

[92] [93] [94] 95 **96** 97 98 99

This clear, brilliant gold-coloured wine has oaky aromas of hazelnut and vanilla blended with a few floral notes. It is lively and round but also powerful and concentrated. An informal, friendly wine which will be at its best in three to four years' time.
- Dom. Antonin Guyon, 21420 Savigny-lès-Beaune, tel. 03.80.67.13.24, fax 03.80.66.85.87, e-mail vins@guyon-bourgogne.com ▼
- by appt.

DOM. MICHEL JUILLOT 1999

□ Gd cru   n.c. 3,000   [€ 46–76]

Charlemagne gave this estate, as a gift, to the Canons of Saulieu in 775 and they kept it for a thousand years. This interesting 99 is a green-gold colour and has floral aromas ('ylang-ylang' was suggested by one taster), followed by a flavour of apples. It has sufficient length and a good acidity, and is a wine that will keep for up to five years.
- Dom. Michel et Laurent Juillot, 59, Grande-Rue, BP 10, 71640 Mercurey, tel. 03.85.98.99.89, fax 03.85.98.99.88, e-mail info@domaine.michel.juillot.fr ▼
- by appt.

DOM. LALEURE-PIOT 1999★

□ Gd cru   0.31 ha 1,500   [€ 38–46]

This magnificent 99 reached the 'final' for a coup de cœur. The structure of this wine is a true reflection of both the terroir and the quality of its wine-making. A perfect colour with aromas of fern, lemon verbena and hazelnut, it has a powerful attack with a mineral tone and an interesting complexity. It can be laid down for a long time and is rich enough to accompany foie gras.
- Dom. Laleure-Piot, rue de Pralot, 21420 Pernand-Vergelesses, tel. 03.80.21.52.37, fax 03.80.21.59.48, e-mail laleure_piot@wanadoo.fr ▼
- ev. day 8am–12 noon 2pm–6pm; Sat./ Sun. by appt.

LOUIS LATOUR 1998

□ Gd cru   9.65 ha 45,000   [€ 46–76]

This wine-cellar at Corton-Grancey is one of the most prestigious places in the region. This pleasant 98, although light in style, has a fine body. It is yellow-green in colour and has a lemon and mineral nose with a subtle oakiness on the palate. A touch of vanilla softens the lively finish. A wine which will gain in stature as it matures.
- Dom. Louis Latour, 18, rue des Tonneliers, 21204 Beaune, tel. 03.80.24.81.00, fax 03.80.22.36.21, e-mail louislatour@louislatour.com
- by appt.

LOUIS LEQUIN 1999★★

□ Gd cru   0.8 ha 604   [€ 38–46]

This very concentrated, firm and powerful 99 is not yet fully open. It has an intense colour, aromas of ripe grapes, and well-proportioned oakiness. It needs to become more supple and to soften. Even though the quantity is so small it is certainly worth the effort. In a few years' time this wine will go well with a seafood gratin.
- Dom. Louis Lequin, 1, rue du Pasquier-du-Pont, 21590 Santenay, tel. 03.80.20.63.82, fax 03.80.20.67.14, e-mail louis.lequin@wanadoo.fr ▼
- by appt.

DOM. MARATRAY-DUBREUIL 1999

□ Gd cru   0.4 ha 2,000   [€ 23–30]

Of the total 14 ha (34.6 acres) that make up this estate, under half (a hectare (just under one acre) is dedicated to this light-gold wine. This pleasant 99 has characteristic aromas of pear, white bread and gunflint. It has an adequate but agreeable structure with a sharp freshness indicating that it should be laid down for three to five years.

➤ Dom. Maratray-Dubreuil, 5, pl. du Souvenir, 21550 Ladoix-Serrigny, tel 03.80.26.41.09, fax 03.80.26.49.07 ▣ Y by appt.

PIERRE MAREY ET FILS 1999★★
☐ Gd cru   0.9 ha   3,000   ▮▮ €30-38

This estate has almost a hectare (over two acres) of vines of Grand Cru. In the past a *coup de coeur* was awarded for their 91 vintage. This light straw-coloured 99 has a very classic, lengthy and complex nose with aromas of dried fruit, exotic crystallised fruit and ripe grapes. The fieryness on the palate, which is not surprising at this age, is well balanced with the acidity. This is a wine that can be laid down for a long time.

➤ EARL Pierre Marey et Fils, rue Jacques-Copeau, 21420 Pernand-Vergelesses, tel 03.80.21.51.71, fax 03.80.26.10.48 ▣ Y by appt.

DOM. DU PAVILLON 1999★★★
☐ Gd cru   1.09 ha   6,000   ▮▮ €46-76

Long before it became famous for chefs Dumaine and Loiseau, Charlemagne gave Saulieu the white vines of Corton. This majestic 99 is awarded a *coup de coeur* by a unanimous vote. Pure, shining gold in colour, it has aromas of almonds, butter, subtle mineral and floral notes, and a charming oakiness. On the palate, intensity and freshness are well balanced right through to the classy finish. This is a demanding, successful wine, and characteristic of its *terroir*. The Pavillon estate is part of the A. Bichon company.

➤ Dom. du Pavillon, 6bis, bd Jacques-Copeau, 21200 Beaune, tel 03.80.24.37.37, fax 03.80.24.37.38

DOM. RAPET PERE ET FILS 1999★★
☐ Gd cru   2.5 ha   9,000   ▮▮ €30-38

This wine is not called Charlemagne for nothing! It has an attractive colour but its bouquet with aromas of peach and grapefruit is its crowning glory. Cinnamon joins the flavours on the palate which has a full, well-balanced structure. This wine should not be kept waiting more than three to four years.

➤ Dom. Rapet Père et Fils, 21420 Pernand-Vergelesses, tel 03.80.21.59.94, fax 03.80.21.54.01 ▣ Y by appt.

REINE PEDAUQUE 1999★
☐ Gd cru   n.c.   n.c.   ▮▮ €46-76

The name La Reine Pédauque is inspired by an ancient mythical figure sculpted on cathedrals. This wine's intense fruitiness, attractive liveliness and overall harmony explain its success. It has pronounced golden highlights and peachy, apricot aromas with mineral notes. Open in two to eight years' time.

➤ Reine Pedauque, Le Village, 21420 Aloxe-Corton, tel 03.80.25.00.00. fax 03.80.26.42.00. e-mail rpedauque@axnet.fr Y by appt.

DOM. ROLLIN PERE ET FILS 1999
☐ Gd cru   0.4 ha   2,300   ▮▮ €30-38

This wine has the colour of a Corton, but a toasted oaky flavour overpowers the citrus fruit. It has a straightforward structure with good acidity and can be laid down for four to five years.

➤ Rollin Père et Fils, rte des Vergelesses, 21420 Pernand-Vergelesses, tel 03.80.21.57.31, fax 03.80.26.10.38 ▣ Y by appt.

DOM. DES TERREGELESSES 1999★
☐ Gd cru   0.4 ha   1,500   ▮▮ €38-46

This is the Comte Sénard estate under another name but run by the same family. Philippe Senard is following in the footsteps of his father, notably at the Grand Conseil du Tastevin. This delicately golden Corton-Charlemagne with charred aromas reveals itself as a wine for laying down. It is rich with aromas of brioche and dried apricot flavours. There is a hint of bitterness due to young tannins, which three to five years will soften, if you can wait that long.

➤ Dom. des Terregelesses, 7, rempart Saint-Jean, 21200 Beaune, tel 03.80.24.21.65, fax 03.80.24.21.44 ▣ Y by appt.

Savigny-lès-Beaune

Savigny is another typical wine village. The spirit of the *terroir* is well in evidence here, and the Confrérie de la Cousinerie de Bourgogne is the symbol of Burgundian hospitality. The 'Cousins' swear to welcome their guests 'with bottles on the table and their hearts in their hands'.

Savigny wines are reputedly 'nourishing, prove the existence of God and stave off death'; they are fruity, supple and elegant, and are pleasant to drink young though they also age well. In 2000, the AOC produced 14,614 hl (385,810 gal) of red wine and 1,848 hl (48,787 gal) of white.

ARNOUX PERE ET FILS
Les Vergelesses 1999★
■ 0.28 ha 1,400 €11-15

A vibrant red colour, this wine's tannins are still on the closed side. It has a lively palate with blackcurrant and raspberry flavours, a fruity fullness and good length. On the point of being ready to drink, this pleasant wine will still be enjoyable in the second half of the decade.

☛ Arnoux Père et Fils, rue des Brenôts,
21200 Chorey-lès-Beaune,
tel 03.80.22.57.98, fax 03.80.22.16.85 ☑
☛ by appt.

DOM. BARBIER ET FILS
Les Fourches 1998★
■ 0.39 ha 2,400 €15-23

Bought by Dufouleur Père et Fils in 1995, this estate has family connections with the Grand Maître of the Confrérie des Chevaliers du Tastevin. Les Fourches, a *climat* on the Pernand side, has produced this velvety, dark garnet-red 98. On the nose there are aromas of blackberry and mulberry, and on the palate flavours of fruit are emerging from beneath the strong tannins. This is a wine of character that will be good for laying down.

☛ Dom. Barbier et Fils, 15, rue Thurot,
21700 Nuits-Saint-Georges,
tel 03.80.61.21.21, fax 03.80.61.10.65 ☑
☛ Guy et Xavier Dufouleur

BOISSEAUX-ESTIVANT
Les Dentellières 1999★
□ n.c. n.c. €23-30

This wine is good even though it doesn't appear among the *climats* featured in the most serious wine map of the region. This is an intricate Chardonnay, pale lemon in colour with grey tones and well-integrated aromas of toast and fruit. It has an elegant attack with striking complexity and good acidity. Another three or four years and it will be perfect. The **red Charton Fils 98** is awarded one star.

☛ Boisseaux-Estivant, 38, fg Saint-Nicolas,
BP 107, 21200 Beaune, tel 03.80.22.00.05,
fax 03.80.24.19.73

CHRISTOPHE BUISSON
Le Mouttier Amet 1999★
■ n.c. n.c. €11-15

Christophe Buisson has two strings to his bow. He is a wine-producer but he also races motorcycles and in April 2000 won the 17th 'Vineyard Endurance Race' in Chablis. This Savigny, however, has nothing in common with a Yamaha 250. It is characteristically Pinot in style, with black cherry, and possesses all the grace and elegance of the appellation.

☛ Christophe Buisson,
21190 Saint-Romain,
fax 03.80.21.67.03 ☑ ☛ by appt.

DOM. CAMUS-BRUCHON
Aux Grands Liards Vieilles vignes 1999★★
■ 0.52 ha 2,700 €11-15

The clock can't be turned back but one can prepare the future, a good idea for this attractive 99 with its ripe cherry colour and pronounced aromas of blackberry. A good opening is followed by a pleasant suppleness and soft finish. It is already very agreeable on the palate but can also be laid down.

☛ Lucien Camus-Bruchon,
Les Cruottes, 16, rue de Chorey,
21420 Savigny-lès-Beaune,
tel 03.80.21.51.08, fax 03.80.26.10.21 ☑

DENIS CARRE 1999★
■ n.c. n.c. €8-11

The oak needs time to integrate in this interesting 99, which has an intense ruby-garnet colour with a hint of toast followed by a fullness, good quality tannins and a satisfying length. This wine needs to be kept for at least three years.

☛ Denis Carré, rue du Puits-Bouret,
21190 Meloisey, tel 03.80.26.02.21,
fax 03.80.26.04.64 ☑ ☛ by appt.

DOM. CHANDON DE BRIAILLES
Les Lavières 1998★
■ 1er cru 2.5 ha 11,000 €15-23

This light-coloured wine has a lovely iris fragrance and the attack is supple. When visiting the Chandon de Briailles Domaine, you discover not only the delights of the wine-cellar but an interesting and elegant building with a theatrical atmosphere. This domaine has been practising organic methods for the last ten years.

☛ Dom. Chandon de Briailles,
1, rue Soeur-Goby, 21420 Savigny-lès-Beaune,
tel 03.80.21.52.31, fax 03.80.21.59.15 ☑ ☛ by appt.
☛ de Nicolay

RODOLPHE DEMOUGEOT
Les Bourgeots 1999★
■ 0.75 ha 3,500 €11-15

Rodolphe Demougeot won a *coup de coeur* for the 98 vintage from the same *climat*. Les Bourgeots is situated opposite Les Feuillets at Les Narbatons. This colourful 99 is a rich wine with a full, round, consistent and finely-textured palate. The bouquet has strong violet aromas and then opens out to reveal the quality oak influence.

• Dom. Rodolphe Demougeot, 2, rue du Clos-de-Mazeray, 21190 Meursault, tel 03.80.21.28.99, fax 03.80.21.29.18
Y by appt.

DOUDET-NAUDIN 1999★★

■ 1er cru   3 ha   15,000   €11-15

A soft red Premier Cru Les Peuillets 99 is awarded one star, while this village, though a little less velvety, gets our preferred vote. It has a powerful, complex nose and a strong, lively attack. It has a good structure with a well-blended oak that needs to integrate. It will develop well with time.

• Doudet-Naudin, 3, rue Henri-Cyrot, BP 1, 21420 Savigny-lès-Beaune, tel 03.80.21.51.74, fax 03.80.21.50.69
Y by appt.
• Yves Doudet

BERNARD DUBOIS ET FILS

Clos des Guettes 1998★

■ 1er cru   0.81 ha   5,000   €15-23

There is the choice here between three bottles of the same quality: the village, Les Ratausses 98 red and 99 white and this Clos des Guettes with its light brick-red hues, its aromas of peony, undergrowth and, if you search hard enough, apricot jam. It is characterised by its freshness and fine tannins. Well balanced with well-integrated oak, this wine will stay beautifully harmonious for the next two to three years.

• Dom. Bernard Dubois et Fils, 8, rue des Chobins, 21200 Chorey-lès-Beaune, tel 03.80.22.13.56, fax 03.80.24.61.43
Y by appt.

PHILIPPE DUBREUIL-CORDIER

□ 1999   0.72 ha 2,400   €8-11

Opinions differed about this wine. Everyone agreed that the colour was excellent as well as the richness of toasted hazelnut and flint aromas. However, the palate was described by one taster as lively and another as characteristic of the appellation and vintage. Everyone found a hint of spiced bread and agreed that in three to four years' time it will be a fine wine. The 95 white previously won a coup de coeur.

• Philippe Dubreuil, 4, rue Péjot, 21420 Savigny-lès-Beaune, tel 03.80.21.53.73, fax 03.80.26.11.46
Y by appt.

DOM. LOIS DUFOULEUR

Les Planchots 1998★

■ 0.33 ha 2,097   €11-15

We have not been able to locate this vineyard on the map. It was acquired in 1997 from SAFER (an organization that controls France's agricultural land) and this is its second year of production. This wine has a garnet colour with crimson highlights and the

nose opens on woody spices and soft dark berry fruit. It is tannic, robust and lengthy but has not yet been opened up to the world.

• Dom. Loïs Dufouleur, 8, bd Bretonnière, 21200 Beaune, tel 03.80.22.70.34, fax 03.80.24.04.28
Y by appt.

MAURICE ECARD ET FILS

Les Serpentières 1998★

■ 1er cru   2.5 ha   12,000   €15-23

This wine is deep, dark red with a subtle oakiness. The palate is full with noticeable but controlled tannins, which make it good for laying down. Its aromas lie between damp earth and wood smoke, followed by strawberry and soft red fruit. The red Premier Cru Les Narbantons 98 is also a great wine. The vines on this estate are tended by hand and no weedkillers are used.

• Maurice Ecard et Fils, 11, rue Chanson-Maldant, 21420 Savigny-lès-Beaune, tel 03.80.21.50.61, fax 03.80.26.11.05
Y by appt.

DOM. FOUGERAY DE BEAUCLAIR Les Golardes 1998★

□ 0.26 ha 1,500   €11-15

Les Golardes is situated on the right as you go up towards Bouilland. This wine is a strong yellow colour and has a nose that is developing. The palate is rich, spicy, fleshy and a little fiery. Fougeray de Beauclair is the amalgam of three names: Jean-Louis Fougeray, Evelyne Beauvais and Bernard Clair. One has to create nobility!

• Dom. Fougeray de Beauclair, 44, rue de Mazy, 21160 Marsannay-la-Côte, tel 03.80.52.21.12, fax 03.80.58.73.83, e-mail fougeraydebeauclair@wanadoo.fr
Y ev. day 8am–12 noon 2pm–6pm

FRANCOIS GAY 1998★

■ 1er cru   0.69 ha 4,200   €11-15

This brilliant 98 with its lovely intense garnet colour has spent 18 months in oak (25% new). Although still a little reserved, it has subtle touches of dark berry fruit and spice on the nose. The palate is full with pleasant, lengthy tannins. You will need to wait three to four years for this wine.

• EARL François Gay, 9, rue des Fiètres, 21200 Chorey-lès-Beaune, tel 03.80.22.69.58, fax 03.80.24.71.42
Y by appt.

MICHEL GAY Vergelesses 1999★

■ 1er cru   0.4 ha   2,200   €11-15

This wine is too young to express its full potential. However, it has a brilliant, dark ruby colour and there are signs of development on the nose. The tannic and fruity palate shows potential, with a hint of maturity. This wine needs to be kept for at least two years.

• Michel Gay, 1b, rue des Brenôts, 21200 Chorey-lès-Beaune, tel 03.80.22.22.73, fax 03.80.22.95.78
Y by appt.

DOM. A.-F. GROS

Clos des Guettes 1999★

1er cru   0.66 ha   5,000

Anne-Françoise Parent-Gros bought the *clos* des Guettes in 1995 from the Pinoteau de Rodinger family. Serious and dedicated, she makes the wines in the same way as her predecessors. This wine is garnet-red with violet highlights; it has subtle vegetal and vanilla notes and a clean palate with well-integrated and expressive tannins.

👃 Dom. A.-F. Gros,
La Garelle, 21630 Pommard,
tel 03.80.22.61.85, fax 03.80.24.03.16,
e-mail gros.anne-françoise@wanadoo.fr
👍 by appt.
👃 Anne-Françoise Parent-Gros

DOM. PHILIPPE GIRARD

Les Lavières Vieilles vignes 1999★

1er cru   0.34 ha   1,000   €11-15

Make a note of the **red Premiers Crus Les Narbantons** and **Les Rouvrettes 99**, which are worth going all the way to Beaune for. Les Lavières takes up a large part of the hillside overlooking Pernand. This wine has undergone a strong pressing but in contrast the aromas are delicate and lightly floral, suggestive of hawthorn, which is uncommon in a Pinot Noir. On the palate there is a strong fruity flavour. This is a full, structured and classy wine with a pleasant finish.

👃 Dom. Philippe Girard,
37, rue Gal-Leclerc, 21420 Savigny-lès-Beaune,
tel 03.80.21.57.97, fax 03.80.26.14.84
👍 by appt.

JEAN-MICHEL GIBOULOT

1.3 ha   5,000   €11-15

There is no need for long introductions: this wine is so friendly, attractive and pleasant on the palate, it is bound to please. This clear gold-coloured wine is very accessible. At first it has little in the way of aromas, but it opens to reveal floral notes.

👃 Jean-Michel Giboulot,
27, rue Gal-Leclerc, 21420 Savigny-lès-Beaune,
tel 03.80.21.52.30, fax 03.80.21.52.30
👍 by appt.

CH. GENOT-BOULANGER

Aux Vergelesses 1998★

1er cru   0.2 ha   980   €15-23

This is a well-balanced wine, substantial and successful for its year. Its fruity and ripe aromas combine with just the right amount of oak. Pale straw in colour with a buttery nose, this attractive 98 shows the first signs of maturation. This estate, which has belonged to the Génot-Delaby family since 1974, boasts 17 white and 16 red AOCs.

👃 SCEV Ch. Génot-Boulanger,
25, rue de Cîteaux, 21190 Meursault,
tel 03.80.21.49.20, fax 03.80.21.49.21,
e-mail genot.boulanger@wanadoo.fr
👍 by appt.

DOM. PIERRE GUILLEMOT

Aux Serpentières 1999★

1er cru   1.7 ha   6,000   €11-15

People who have never heard Pierre Guillemot give his opinion at a tasting have missed out. The 97, 91 and 89 vintages are among the wines from this estate that in the past were awarded a *coup de coeur*. This brilliant cherry-red 99 was commended. Admittedly, its oak flavour helps it a little but in a few years it will be able to stand on its own two feet. In four to five years, when fully matured, it will be the perfect accompaniment to duck salmi. The **red Premier Cru Les Jarrons 99** stays in the Savigny spirit and is awarded one star.

👃 SCE du Dom. Pierre Guillemot,
1, rue Boulanger-et-Vallée,
21420 Savigny-lès-Beaune,
tel 03.80.21.50.40, fax 03.80.21.59.98
👍 by appt.

DOM. JEAN GUITON 1998★

2.48 ha   4,500   €8-11

Jean Guiton has a typical Burgundian philosophy. He does not look for complexity but contents himself with creating this wine. Pale in colour, fine and light with aromas of undergrowth and fresh almonds, this wine has a supple and attractive palate and is easy to drink without being simplistic.

👃 Dom. Jean Guiton, 4, rte de Pommard,
21200 Bligny-lès-Beaune,
tel 03.80.26.82.88, fax 03.80.26.85.05,
e-mail guillaume-guiton@wanadoo.fr
👍 by appt.

DOM. GUYON Les Peuillets 1999★★

1er cru   0.25 ha   1,800   €11-15

This wine was a candidate for a *coup de coeur*. The red, almost black colour is followed through in the bouquet, with blackberry, blackcurrant and charred aromas. Both the oak and the tannins will take time to blend in but the wine has undergone a strong pressing and is substantial with a clean and open attack. It will go very nicely with game.

👃 EARL Dom. Guyon, 11-16, RN 74,
21700 Vosne-Romanée, tel 03.80.61.02.46,
fax 03.80.62.36.56   👍 by appt.

DOM. LUCIEN JACOB

Vergelesses 1999★

1er cru   0.8 ha   4,000

This estate has been run since 1989 by Jean-Michel, Christine and Chantal Jacob, and with 19 ha (47 acres) there is plenty to keep them busy. Lucien Jacob, however, has not retired: he is a member of the local council and recently a member of parliament for the Côte d'Or. This Les Vergelesses is clear red in colour and has aromas of blackcurrant and blackberries. The wine's freshness makes up for a rather firm approach. It is definitely good for laying down but shouldn't be kept for more than five years.

👃 Dom. Lucien Jacob, 21420 Echevronne,
tel 03.80.21.52.15, fax 03.80.21.55.65,
e-mail lucien-jacob@wanadoo.fr
👍 by appt.

Savigny-lès-Beaune

The *climat* of Les Clous is situated near Savigny-lès-Beaune, and means 'les Clos' in old Burgundian. This is an oaky but well-blended wine. It is supple and approachable on the palate with a floral, smoky finesse and, like most of its peers, has that touch of bitterness on the finish. We recommend drinking it within the next three years.

☞ Pierre Lebreuil, 17, rue Chanson-Maldant, Les Guettottes, 21420 Savigny-lès-Beaune, tel 03.80.21.52.95, fax 03.80.26.10.82, e-mail jean-baptiste.lebreuil@wanadoo.fr ▼
Ⓣ ev. day 10am–11.30am 2pm–6pm

DOM. MACHARD DE GRAMONT
Les Vergelesses 1999★
☐ 1er cru   0.2 ha   1,400   ‖‖ €11-15

This is an excellent example of a Savigny wine, exactly what one expects from the appellation. This white gold Chardonnay has fine oak flavours followed by ripe fruit. The well-matured palate is pleasant with attractive floral flavours. These vineyards once belonged to Léonce Bocquet who restored the Château Clos de Vougeot. The 96 vintage was awarded a *coup de coeur* in the 2000 edition of the *Guide*.

☞ SCE Dom. Machard de Gramont, Le Clos, rue Pique, BP 105, 21703 Prémeaux-Prissey, tel 03.80.61.15.25, fax 03.80.61.06.39 ▼ Ⓣ by appt.

DOM. MAILLARD PERE ET FILS
1999★
‖   1.8 ha   n.c.   ‖‖ €11-15

'The soil of Savigny is not lacking in depth,' so Camille Rodier tells us. The same could be said of this pleasant 99 with its deep colour and intense aromas of soft red fruit and toast on the palate. This is a well-structured wine with tannins that do not overwhelm the fruit.

☞ Dom. Maillard Père et Fils, 2, rue Joseph-Bard, 21200 Chorey-lès-Beaune, tel 03.80.22.10.67, fax 03.80.24.00.42 ▼ Ⓣ by appt.

DOM. MICHEL MALLARD ET FILS Les Serpentières 1998★
‖ 1er cru   1.1 ha   6,000   ‖‖ €11-15

Serpentières is not easy to find, hidden on the slopes of Pernand. Its wines are generally considered among the most delicate. This fine, light wine with its Griotte cherry aromas confirms this reputation. Vanilla, coffee and mocha flavours are dominated by the oakiness, this is no cause for concern: it will all blend together with time.

☞ EARL Dom. Michel Mallard et Fils, 43, rte de Dijon, 21550 Ladoix-Serrigny, tel 03.80.26.40.64, fax 03.80.26.47.49 ▼ Ⓣ by appt.

GHISLAINE ET BERNARD MARECHAL-CAILLOT 1999★
‖   2.22 ha   6,000   ‖‖ €11-15

This wine is rich even in colour but its body is also characteristic of the grape variety and *terroir*. The nose has aromas of soft red fruit

DOM. PATRICK JACOB-GIRARD
Aux Gravains 1998★★
‖ 1er cru   1.36 ha   6,000   ‖‖ €11-15

In the space of four generations this wine-producing family has expanded its estate from 4 ha (9.88 acres) to just over 8 ha (19.76 8 acres). This superb wine has a deep ruby-red colour and complex aromas of strawberry, cherry and spice. It has a gentle attack followed by strawberry flavours. The tannins are a little austere at first but soften out and a flavour of truffles appears. What a lovely surprise!

☞ Dom. Jacob-Girard, 2, rue de Cîteaux, 21420 Savigny-lès-Beaune, tel 03.80.21.52.29, fax 03.80.26.19.07 ▼ Ⓣ by appt.

DOM. DE LA GALOPIERE 1999★
‖   0.8 ha   3,500   ‖‖ €8-11

Claire and Gabriel Fournier gave up mixed farming 20 years ago in order to devote themselves entirely to wine-making. There is very little to say except that this wine is lovely, has a rich colour, fruity nose with well-blended aromas of kirsch. It is well-balanced, not too oaky, and clearly a good example of its type.

☞ Claire et Gabriel Fournier, 6, rue de l'Eglise, 21200 Bligny-lès-Beaune, tel 03.80.21.46.50, fax 03.80.21.49.93, e-mail c.g.fournier@wanadoo.fr ▼ Ⓣ by appt.

DANIEL LARGEOT 1999★★
‖   0.6 ha   3,500   ‖‖ €8-11

This *village* was unanimously voted a *coup de coeur*, a remarkable feat to pull off. Cherry red in colour with garnet highlights and a subtle nose of floral and light vanillary notes. This simple wine has a lasting fruitiness, is round and full on the palate, well-balanced and strong. Good value for money.

☞ Daniel Largeot, 5, rue des Brenôts, 21200 Chorey-lès-Beaune, tel 03.80.22.15.10, fax 03.80.22.60.62 ▼ Ⓣ by appt.

DOM. LES GUETTOTTES
Aux Clous 1999★
☐   0.2 ha   1,500   ‖‖ €11-15

Pierre Lebreuil took over his mother's vineyard in 1964 and since 1998 his son has joined him in running this 7.5-ha (18.52-acre) estate.

with a hint of oak and the well-balanced palate has subtle tannins. It finishes with notes of alcohol and although reserved today, will open up shortly.

➜ Bernard Maréchal-Caillot, 10, rue de Chalon, 21200 Bligny-lès-Beaune, tel 03.80.21.44.55, fax 03.80.26.88.21 ☑
Y by appt.

OLIVIER PERE ET FILS
Les Peuillets 1999★
1er cru   1 ha   4,000   €11-15

One has confidence in the future of this wine just by looking at it. It has a deep, rich and intense colour, confirmed by the nose with notes of nutmeg and brandied prunes. The palate is pleasant, generous and rich. This wine fully reflects its terroir and needs to be laid down. It would go beautifully with a roast turkey, but next Christmas would be too soon.

➜ Olivier Père et Fils, 5, rue Gaudin, 21590 Santenay, tel 03.80.20.61.35, fax 03.80.20.64.82, e-mail antoine.olivier2@wanadoo.fr ☑ Y by appt.

DOM. PARIGOT PERE ET FILS
Les Peuillets 1999★
1er cru   0.21 ha   1,500   €11-15

This climat situated near Beaune has produced an agreeable 99, still a little reserved cherry in colour, it has a delicate nose with a hint of redcurrant and a touch of violet. After a straightforward attack the palate is well-structured with good, rich tannins. It needs to be laid down for two to three years.

➜ Dom. Parigot Père et Fils, rte de Pommard, 21190 Meloisey, tel 03.80.26.01.70, fax 03.80.26.04.32 ☑

PATRIARCHE PERE ET FILS 1998
n.c.   5,800   €5-8

How can one taste this wine without thinking of André Boisseaux's amazing 'Wine-cellar for the year 2000' where he had put away many wonderful wines which were finally opened up and tasted with great seriousness. This classic purple 98 with aromas of blackcurrant is a pure, straightforward and simple wine, which is what makes it interesting. To hell with complexity, let's just enjoy the wine.

➜ Patriarche Père et Fils, 5, rue du College, 21200 Beaune, tel 03.80.24.53.01, fax 03.80.24.53.03 ☑
Y ev. day 9am–12 noon 2pm–6pm

JEAN-MARC PAVELOT 1999★★
0.75 ha   6,000   €8-11

This wine-producer was awarded a coup de coeur for his 85 and 93 vintages. Like an architect, he manages to use the eye of an artist and the skill of a builder in his wine-making. This excellent 99 has a pleasing and graceful colour with many tones. The nose is mineral, which is found again on the palate with an acidity that still needs to soften. This is a well-made, invigorating and decisive wine. Also worth noting is the red Premier Cru 98 La Dominode awarded two stars and very characteristic of the appellation. The red Aux Guettes obtains one star.

➜ Jean-Marc Pavelot, 1, chem. des Guettottes, 21420 Savigny-lès-Beaune, tel 03.80.21.55.21, fax 03.80.21.59.73 ☑
Y by appt.

GEORGES ET THIERRY PINTE
1998★
1.13 ha   1,800   €8-11

Choose a grilled steak rather than a marinade or strong sauce to accompany this village. This is a supple and elegant wine, cherry from the first glance right through to its fruity finish. After a lively attack, it is calm, vinous and long.

➜ GAEC Georges et Thierry Pinte, 11, rue du Jarron, 21420 Savigny-lès-Beaune, tel 03.80.21.51.59, fax 03.80.21.51.59 ☑
Y by appt.

DOM. DU PRIEURE
Les Lavières 1999★
1er cru   0.77 ha   4,000   €11-15

The 86 vintage won a coup de coeur in the 1990 edition of the Guide, and this years entry is also very pleasing. This wine is a lovely ruby red with aromas of fruit and vanillary raspberry on the rich and agreeable nose. The fresh palate is slightly fleshy with a pleasant roundness. It is a wonderful wine and would go well with a fillet of beef. The red village Les Grands Picotins 98 is another fine wine.

➜ Jean-Michel Maurice, Dom. du Prieuré, 23, rte de Beaune, 21420 Savigny-lès-Beaune, tel 03.80.21.54.27, fax 03.80.21.59.77, e-mail maurice.jean-michel@wanadoo.fr ☑
Y by appt.

DOM. RAPET PERE ET FILS 1999★
n.c.   n.c.   3,000   €11-15

Which wine would you take to a desert island? Why not this one? You can open it in three to four years' time when the first boat is spotted on the horizon ... This wine has an attractive colour and a fruity, menthol nose. It is full, rich, distinctive and powerful and comes from one of the most beautiful villages on the Côte.

➜ Dom. Rapet Père et Fils, 21420 Pernand-Vergelesses, tel 03.80.21.59.94, fax 03.80.21.54.01 ☑
Y by appt.

REINE PEDAUQUE 1999★
n.c.   n.c.   3,000   €11-15

This wine is brilliant, attractive, round and smooth but needs time to develop. It has plenty to offer but is in no hurry. A rich body follows this friendly appearance.

➜ Reine Pédauque, Le Village, 21420 Aloxe-Corton, tel 03.80.25.00.00, fax 03.80.26.42.00, e-mail rpedauque@axnet.fr Y by appt.

the village's *lieux-dits* are neighbours to Savigny. In 2000, the *Appellation Communale* produced 6,188 hl (163,363 gal) of red wine and 227 hl (5,993 gal) of white.

SEGUIN-MANUEL
Goudelettes 1999★★
□ 0.5 ha 2,000 III €11-15

Les Lavières received a *coup de coeur* for its 95 vintage. It represents a Les Goudelettes (a *climat* situated on the hillside in the direction of Bouilland). It has a straightforward red colour with golden highlights and the nose opens on blossom and citrus fruit. It will need a watchful eye as it matures. It is rich and fleshy with elegant oaky notes. The 13th-century Cistercian cellars, where these wines are matured, are worth a visit.

Dom. Seguin-Manuel, 15, rue Paul-Maldant, 21420 Savigny-lès-Beaune, tel 03.80.21.50.42, fax 03.80.21.59.38, e-mail seguin-manuel@worldonline.fr
ev. day 8am–12 noon 2pm–5pm
Pierre Seguin

DOM. THIELY Côte de Beaune 1999★
■ n.c. 1,800 III €15-15

Founded in 1870 by the present wine-producer's ancestors, this is the only estate in this series that bears the name of the Côte de Beaune. This bright red Savigny combines the toasty, vanillary aromas of oak with the wine's fruity aromas of blackcurrant and cherry. The palate is tannic but at the same time pleasantly integrated. The finish is a little vigorous as usual in a young wine which needs to mature. It needs to be laid down for two years.

Dom. Thiély, rue de Vergy, 21420 Pernand-Vergelesses, tel 03.80.21.54.86, fax 03.80.26.11.92
by appt.

HENRI DE VILLAMONT
Clos des Guettes 1998★★
■ 1er cru 1.91 ha 9,000 III €15-23

This Burgundy branch of the Swiss group Schenk has its base in the magnificent property of Léonce Bocquet (a legendary figure in Burgundy wine-making) in Savigny. Henri de Villamont, however is an imaginary name but the wine is very real. It is out of the ordinary in fact. Red with copper hues and aromas of blackcurrant and undergrowth. It is a well-made wine, powerful and full of vigour.

SA Henri de Villamont, rue du Dr-Guyot, 21420 Savigny-lès-Beaune, tel 03.80.21.54.31, e-mail hdv@planetb.fr ev. day except Tue. 10.30am–6pm; cl. 15 Nov–15 Mar.

DOM. CHARLES ALLEXANT ET FILS Les Beaumonts 1999★
■ 1.04 ha 4,500 III €8-11

One had to be on form in 1999 to produce this excellent and supple Pinot Noir, which can be drunk young without fuss. It confirms the saying: 'Chorey does not speak, it sings.' Deeply coloured with an intense nose of stewed-fruit and a touch of brandied cherry on the middle palate.

SCE Dom. Charles Allexant et Fils, rue du Château, Cissey, 21190 Merceuil, tel 03.80.26.83.27, fax 03.80.26.84.04
ev. day 8am–12 noon 1.30pm–6pm; Sat. Sun. by appt.

ARNOUX PERE ET FILS
Les Confrelins 1999★
■ 1.8 ha 9,600 III €11-15

Chorey used to be referred to as a 'medicinal wine' and was frequently used to add substance to the rather pale *cuvées* of the neighbouring crus. These qualities are in evidence here. This is a soft wine but its structure is tannic and robust with a body of pronounced fruity aromas. It is attractive in appearance with a light raspberry nose. The *climat* is situated right at the edge of the Beaune AOC.

Arnoux Père et Fils, rue des Brenôts, 21200 Chorey-lès-Beaune, tel 03.80.22.57.98, fax 03.80.22.16.85
by appt.

DOM. BELIN-RAPET
Les Bons Ores 1999
■ 0.25 ha 1,250

This is a classic wine: the colour reflects the redcurrants and raspberries aromas on the nose. It is well-balanced, fresh and reasonably tannic with subtle oak. This is a good wine which needs to wait a year or two before being ready to drink. This estate was created in 1983.

Dom. Belin-Rapet, imp. des Combottes, 21420 Pernand-Vergelesses, tel 03.80.22.77.51, fax 03.80.22.76.59, e-mail domaine.belin.rapet@wanadoo.fr
ev. day 8am–8pm
Ludovic Belin

MAURICE CHAPUIS 1998★★
□ 1 ha 4,500 III €8-11

This wine was nearly awarded a *coup de coeur*. It has a gold colour with green highlights and a pleasant, open nose with floral aromas and notes of dried fruit. It is fresh, round and fruity and will go beautifully with a fillet of pikeperch served with citrus fruit.

572

Chorey-lès-Beaune

Chorey-lès-Beaune is situated on flat land, opposite the pile of scree at the foot of the Combe de Bouilland, and some of

- Maurice Chapuis, 21420 Aloxe-Corton, tel 03.80.26.40.99, fax 03.80.26.40.89 ☑
Y by appt.

JOSEPH DROUHIN 1998

■ n.c. n.c. | €11-15 ☑

This wine is ruby red with copper hues and opens with almonds and dried fruit. The body is straightforward and honest with a note of cherry on the middle palate. Its tannins guarantee a good structure; best to wait two years for the finish to soften.

- Joseph Drouhin, 7, rue d'Enfer, 21200 Beaune, tel 03.80.24.68.88, fax 03.80.22.43.14, e-mail maisondrouhin@drouhin.com Y by appt.

DOM. DUBOIS-CACHAT 1999★

0.5 ha 2,000 | €8-11 ☑
Y by appt.

This is a poetic wine but unfortunately there are only 2,000 bottles of it. It has a light colour and a strong oakiness with crystallised cherry. It is well integrated and would go well with a Brie de Meaux, Reblochon or a Cîteaux cheese.

- Dom. Dubois-Cachat, 2. Grande-Rue, 21200 Chorey-lès-Beaune, tel 03.80.22.27.83, fax 03.80.22.27.83 ☑

XAVIER DUCLERT
Les Beaumonts 1998

■ n.c. n.c. | €11-15 ☑

This clean, brilliant Chorey has an original label setting off this pale coloured wine with aromas of undergrowth and leather, which has strong tannins that need to soften. This *climat* is situated right on the edge of Savigny.

- Xavier Duclert, 2bis, pl. Carnot, 21200 Beaune, tel 03.80.22.74.77, fax 03.80.22.74.77, e-mail xavier.duclert@fnac.net ☑ Y ev. day except Sun. Mon. 10am–12.30pm 2.30pm–7pm

FRANCOIS GAY 1998★

2.75 ha 15,000 | €8-11 ☑

This wine has a magnificent colour: deep, dark ruby red with violet highlights, and has real brilliance. The nose combines bilberries, blackberries, vanilla and liquorice with great delicacy. The palate continues along the same theme with youthfulness and confidence. In three or four years this will be a great wine.

- EARL François Gay, 9, rue des Fiètres, 21200 Chorey-lès-Beaune, tel 03.80.22.69.58, fax 03.80.24.71.42 ☑

MICHEL GAY 1998

3.6 ha 14,000 | €8-11 ☑

This is a wine that Lady Chatterley's lover might have taken on a country picnic. It has an intense red colour and rich aromas of eucalyptus, warm bread-crust and vanilla. It has fresh cherry on the palate with a light peppery flavour, smooth tannins and a rustic-ity similar to D.H. Lawrence's celebrated character.

DOM. GUYON Les Bons Ores 1999★★

0.87 ha 6,400 | €11-15 ☑

The only thing that separates this *climat* from Aloxe-Corton is the Route National 74. The Guyon family gave up making barley and beer in order to devote themselves to vines and wine. This successful 99 is softer and less powerful than the previous vintage, described in the 2001 *Guide*. It has a spontaneous character with a light richness, good acidity and aromas of kirsch and prunes on the palate. It is ready to drink.

- EARL Dom. Guyon, 11–16, RN 74, 21700 Vosne-Romanée, tel 03.80.61.02.46, fax 03.80.62.36.56 ☑ Y by appt.

DOM. LALEURE-PIOT
Les Champs longs 1999★

1.92 ha 13,000 | €8-11 ☑

This generous 99 is fiery, full-bodied, rich, robust, fleshy and round all at the same time. A wine with so many virtues! Its brilliant colour just adds to the list. The nose however has a hint of undergrowth and nothing more, a year or two in the cellar will improve this.

- Dom. Laleure-Piot, rue de Pralot, 21420 Pernand-Vergelesses, tel 03.80.21.52.37, fax 03.80.21.59.48, e-mail laleure.piot@wanadoo.fr ☑ Y ev. day 8am–12 noon 2pm–6pm; Sat. Sun. by appt.

DANIEL LARGEOT
Les Beaumonts 1999★

1.5 ha 8,000 | €8-11 ☑

This wine has the violet colour of vine-leaves in the autumn. Its aromas range from musk to soft fruit and roasted coffee. It has a well integrated structure that still needs to soften. A touch of acidity means that it can be kept for two to three years.

- Daniel Largeot, 5, rue des Brenôts, 21200 Chorey-lès-Beaune, tel 03.80.22.15.10, fax 03.80.22.60.62 ☑ Y by appt.

DOM. MAILLARD PERE ET FILS
1999

This estate of seven villages is one of the largest in Chorey-lès-Beaune. This garnet-coloured 99 opens gradually with ripe, mature aromas. It is characteristic of Pinot Noir from this part of the Côte. It has supple tannins, moderate acidity, with fruit that has been well pressed and kirsch on the finish: in short, a harmonious wine.

- Dom. Maillard Père et Fils, 2, rue Joseph-Bard, 21200 Chorey-lès-Beaune, tel 03.80.22.10.67, fax 03.80.24.00.42 ☑ Y by appt.

Grèves, Les Teurons and Les Champimonts. In 2000, the AOC produced 16,276 hl (429,686 gal) of red wine and 2,020 hl (53,328 gal) of white.

BERTRAND AMBROISE
Saint-Désiré 1999★

■   n.c.   n.c.   ◫ **€ 11-15**

This is an attractive wine with violet highlights and a hint of fruit on the nose. This Saint-Désiré (a *climat* which is situated at the top of the hillside, on the Pommard side) is tannic, firm, and reserved. Its weak level of acidity suggests that it should be drunk over the next two to three years.

• Maison Bertrand Ambroise, rue de l'Eglise, 21700 Premeaux-Prissey, tel 03.80.62.30.19, fax 03.80.62.38.69, e-mail bertrand.ambroise@wanadoo.fr ⊠
Y by appt.

ARNOUX PERE ET FILS
Les Cent Vignes 1999★

■ 1er cru   0.49 ha   2,500   ◫ **€ 15-23**

Les Cent Vignes, produced using traditional wine-making methods and 14 months' oak maturation, is on top form this year. This is a superb-looking wine with an affable, smoky fragrance. Not extraordinary in length but the soft red fruit is just right. It is a strong, well-balanced, well-made and complex wine.

• Arnoux Père et Fils, rue des Brenôts, 21200 Chorey-lès-Beaune,
tel 03.80.22.57.98, fax 03.80.22.16.85 ⊠

Beaune

The Appellation Beaune is one of the biggest on the Côte in terms of area. But Beaune, a town of some 20,000 inhabitants, is also and above all the wine capital of Burgundy, the headquarters of many wine shippers, and one of the most attractive tourist towns in France. The Hospices de Beaune wine sales have become an event with a world-wide reputation and are certainly one of the most celebrated of all the Burgundy charity sales. Situated at the hub of a motorway network, Beaune will undoubtedly continue to develop its appeal as a tourist destination.

Beaune is best known for its powerful and distinctive red wines. Its geographical advantages mean that a large part of the vineyard has been classified as Premiers Crus; amongst the most prestigious we should list Les Bressandes, Le Clos du Roi, Les

ROGER ET JOEL REMY
Les Beaumonts 1999

■   2 ha   12,000   ◫ **€ 5-8**

An English taster was very impressed by this full, well-balanced wine with its aromas of undergrowth and soft red fruit. The rest of the Jury liked its honesty and distinctiveness, but also recommended waiting two to three years for the tannins, which are still slightly rustic, to soften.

• SCEA Roger et Joël Rémy, 4, rue du Paradis, 21200 Sainte-Marie-la-Blanche, tel 03.80.26.60.80, fax 03.80.26.53.03 ⊠
Y ev. day except Sun. 8am–12 noon 2pm–6pm

DOM. GEORGES ROY ET FILS
1999★

☐   0.38 ha   1,800   ◫ **€ 8-11**

Everyone agreed that this pleasant and precisely-made wine is very expressive. It has a lively colour with hints of lemon, which appear again in the bouquet with honeysuckle and a note of vanilla. This is a rich, lengthy and easy-to-drink wine with well-defined fruit.

• Dom. Georges Roy et Fils, 20, rue des Moutots, 21200 Chorey-lès-Beaune, tel 03.80.22.16.28, fax 03.80.24.76.38 ⊠
Y by appt.

BALLOT-MILLOT ET FILS
Epenottes 1999★

■ 1er cru   0.43 ha   2,500   ◫ **€ 15-23**

This wine has lovely aromas of fresh cherry with a hint of pepper. It is firm, well-balanced and lengthy, with no bitterness and little acidity. If in any doubt, keep it no longer than two years.

• Ballot-Millot et Fils, 9, rue de la Goutte-d'Or, BP 33, 21190 Meursault, tel 03.80.21.21.39, fax 03.80.21.65.92 ⊠
Y by appt.

GUILLEMETTE ET XAVIER BESSON Les Champs Pimont 1999

■ 1er cru   0.72 ha   1,500   ◫ **€ 11-15**

This Premier Cru Beaune is made in a 17th-century wine-cellar. It has a dark colour with shades of garnet and a slightly overripe nose. It would appeal to lovers of rich, round wines, although it is not without a certain liveliness. There is a pronounced flavour of ripe fruit on the palate.

• Dom. Guillemette et Xavier Besson, 9, rue des Bois-Chevaux, 71640 Givry, tel 03.85.44.42.44, fax 03.85.44.42.44 ⊠
Y by appt.

DOM. GABRIEL BILLARD

Les Epenottes 1999★

1er cru 0.2 ha 900 [€11-15]

This Premier Cru is situated on the Pommard side of the hillside. It has a satiny appearance, spicy nose and a touch of peony on the finish. The palate is elegant rather than powerful, but straightforward and substantial. It should not be opened for at least two years.

SCEA Dom. Gabriel Billard, imp. de la Commaraine, 21630 Pommard, tel 03.80.22.27.82, fax 03.85.49.49.02 ✉ by appt.

DOM. GABRIEL BOUCHARD

Clos du Roi 1999★

1er cru 0.65 ha 2,300 [€15-23]

This estate was awarded a *coup de coeur* for their 88 and 91 vintages and presents here a **red Premier Cru Cent Vignes 98** which is on the same level as this rather regal Clos du Roi. This wine has a cardinal-red colour with aromas of freshly picked raspberries and hints of undergrowth. It is full, classy and although still a little closed, is characteristic of a Beaune wine.

Dom. Gabriel Bouchard, 4, rue du Tribunal, 21200 Beaune, tel 03.80.22.68.63

Alain Bouchard

DOM. BOUCHARD PERE ET FILS

Grèves Vigne de l'Enfant Jésus 1998★

1er cru 4 ha n.c. [€38-46]

This Beaune company, which used to be run by J. Henriot, presents here two fine wines. The **white Clos Saint-Landry Premier Cru 98** is superb and well-balanced with heavenly aromas of almond and honey. Then the miraculous Enfant Jésus of Beaune (the most famous one in Europe, along with the one from Prague) gives its name to a very impressive wine. This ancient vineyard situated in Les Grèves once belonged to the Carmelites, This wine has a clear ruby-red colour with aromas of vanilla and mocha on the nose and a youthful, jammy, fruity palate.

Bouchard Père et Fils, Ch. de Beaune, 21200 Beaune, tel 03.80.24.80.24, fax 03.80.22.55.88, e-mail france@bouchard-pereetfils.com ✉ by appt.

REYANE ET PASCAL BOULEY

1999★★

0.64 ha 3,600 [€8-11]

This is an intensely coloured 99 and although its nose is still closed, it has a characteristic Beaune character from start to finish. Full and distinctive, it has an impressive roundness. This is a wine to drink in two to three years' time.

Pascal Bouley, pl. de l'Eglise, 21190 Volnay, tel 03.80.21.61.69, fax 03.80.21.66.44 ✉ by appt.

DOM. CAUVARD

Clos de la Maladière 1998

□ 0.85 ha 4,000 [€11-15]

You can drink this clear, brilliant wine soon or lay it down for a while. It is pleasant, well-balanced, rich and full with that note of honey characteristic of a Chardonnay that has spent 14 months in oak.

Dom. Cauvard, 34 bis, rue de Savigny, 21200 Beaune, tel 03.80.22.29.77, fax 03.80.24.06.03, e-mail domaine.cauvard@wanadoo.fr ✉ by appt.

CHAMPY PERE ET CIE

Champs-Pimont 1999

1er cru 0.65 ha 3,600 [€23-30]

Marcel Proust mentions in one of his books the pleasure to be had in walking in Beaune, a walk that surely involves passing through the crus. Champs-Pimont is situated next to Montée Rouge in the middle of the appellation. This classy 99 has a magnificent colour and leathery, fruity aromas on the nose. It is long on the palate with a vigorous attack and tannins that need to soften and blend.

Maison Champy, 5, rue du Grenier-à-Sel, 21200 Beaune, tel 03.80.25.09.99, fax 03.80.25.09.95, e-mail champyprost@aol.com ✉ by appt.

Pierre Meurgey, Pierre Beuchet

DOM. CHANGARNIER

Les Bélissands 1999

1er cru 0.45 ha 1,400 [€15-23]

Bélissands is situated at the bottom of the hillside where the the vineyard starts to face towards Pommard. This pleasant 99 has a lovely colour with aromas of undergrowth. There are pronounced tannins on the palate although the Griotte cherry is working to create a certain roundness. Accept it as it is and drink it now.

Dom. Changarnier, pl. du Puits, 21190 Monthélie, tel 03.80.21.22.18, fax 03.80.21.68.21, e-mail changarnier@aol.com ✉ by appt. ev. day except Sun. 9am–12 noon 2pm–7pm

DOM. CHARACHE-BERGERET

Les Pirolles 1999★

0.24 ha 1,500 [€11-15]

René and Jacqueline Charache founded this estate in 1976. Today, their two sons have joined them in running the 19 ha (47 acres) covering 12 appellations. This wine is from a *climat* situated along the Route National 74 on the right hand side of the road going towards Chagny and Pommard. It has a brilliant colour and a complex range of subtle aromas, such as kirsch with a touch of mineral. On the palate it is Pinot Noir through and through. It is best to wait a while before drinking this wine.

Charache-Bergeret, 21200 Bouze-lès-Beaune, tel 03.80.26.00.86, fax 03.80.26.00.86 ✉ by appt.

DOM. DU CHATEAU DE MEURSAULT Cent-vignes 1998

1er cru   1.9 ha   9,000   **€23-30**

The old name for Cent-Vignes is Sanvignes, (*Sinevineis* is quoted as far back as 1295) and there used to be a Gallo-Roman hamlet here near the fountain of Les Marconnets. This wine is pale red with light brick-red hues. It has a stewed fruit flavour with a freshness that manages to soften the tannins.

⚲ Dom. du Château de Meursault, 21190 Meursault, tel 03.80.26.22.75, fax 03.80.26.22.76 ▼ ▼ by appt.

CH. DE CITEAUX Teurons 1999

1er cru   0.4 ha   2,800   **€11-15**

Perhaps the name of this *climat* comes from the word *terre* meaning hillock or mound. The wine is an example of old-fashioned wine-making. It is developing in the right direction but the attack is held back by stubborn tannins. It has a superb brilliance in colour with well-blended oak and notes of black-currant leaf on the nose. It needs to be laid down for three to five years.

⚲ Dom. Philippe Bouzereau,
Ch. de Citeaux, 18–20, rue de Citeaux, BP 25, 21190 Meursault, tel 03.80.21.20.32, fax 03.80.21.64.34, e-mail info@ domaine.bouzereau.fr ▼ ▼ by appt.

DOM. HENRI CLERC ET FILS Chaume Gaufriot 1998★

1er cru   0.3 ha   1,882   **€11-15**

Bernard Clerc has been running this 22-ha (54.3-acre) estate, created in the 17th century, since 1965. This *climat* is situated on top of a hillside above La Montée Rouge. This *village* has an invigorating deep garnet colour with dark tobacco, nutmeg and a subtle aroma of oak on the nose. It has a soft attack and abrupt finish with firm tannins and should develop well.

⚲ Dom. Henri Clerc et Fils, pl. des Marronniers, 21190 Puligny-Montrachet, tel 03.80.21.32.74, fax 03.80.21.39.60 ▼ ▼ ev. day 8.30am–11.45am 2pm–5.45pm
⚲ Bernard Clerc

COUVENT DES CORDELIERS 1998

1er cru   n.c.   7,800   **€23-30**

This characteristic 98 has highlights that are a little developed, and a nose with aromas of figs and grapes. It has a fine palate with a touch of cherry that softens lively tannins and oak that needs to blend in and soften. This enterprise is the sister company of Patriarche, both of which were owned by André Boisseaux, who went to his secret cellar in the year 2000. This wine is dedicated to his memory.

⚲ Caves du Couvent des Cordeliers, rue de l'Hôtel-Dieu, 21200 Beaune, tel 03.80.25.08.85, fax 03.80.25.08.21 ▼ ▼ ev. day 9.30am–12 noon 2pm–6pm

YVES DARVIOT Clos des Mouches 1998

1er cru   0.7 ha   3,800   **€15-23**

This estate is situated in the heart of Beaune and covers 3 ha (7.4 acres). This Clos des Mouches is a classic ruby-red in colour, a charming wine with a pleasant flavour of wild strawberries although the strong tannins are still obscuring the fruit. It has a temporary austerity which three to four years in the cellar will render more amenable. In the *village* category the **red Chaume-Gaufriot 98** gets the same mark and needs to be laid down for two years.

⚲ Yves Darviot, 2, pl. Morimont, 21200 Beaune, tel 03.80.24.74.87, fax 03.80.22.02.89, e-mail ydarviot@ club-internet.fr ▼ ▼ by appt.

RODOLPHE DEMOUGEOT Les Epenotes 1999★

  n.c.   2,000   **€11-15**

This intense purple *village* with crimson highlights opens with a fanfare. It has aromas of soft red fruit and a touch of tobacco which continues through to the palate. It has a strong structure and needs to wait four to five years.

⚲ Dom. Rodolphe Demougeot,
2, rue du Clos-de-Mazeray, 21190 Meursault, tel 03.80.21.28.99, fax 03.80.21.29.18 ▼ ▼ by appt.

DOUDET-NAUDIN Les Grèves 1999

1er cru   0.35 ha   2,431   **€15-23**

This wine was not far off a *coup de coeur!* One taster had doubts but all the others thought it perfect. It is dark blackcurrant in colour with an oaky nose and real fullness on the palate. There are flavours of new oak but Griotte cherry and liquorice are also present. This estate celebrated its 150th anniversary in 1999.

⚲ Doudet-Naudin, 3, rue Henri-Cyrot, BP 1, 21420 Savigny-les-Beaune, tel 03.80.21.51.74, fax 03.80.21.50.69 ▼ ▼ by appt.

JOSEPH DROUHIN Clos des Mouches 1998★★

  15 ha   n.c.   **€30-38**

Le Clos des Mouches under the name of Drouhin is never a disappointment. Having won a *coup de coeur* for the 92, 91, 86 and 85 vintages, to some extent it is out of the competition. This wine has a flamboyant ruby colour and a concentrated nose of cherry jam. A gentle opening leads to a firm, tender and smooth fullness.

⚲ Joseph Drouhin, 7, rue d'Enfer, 21200 Beaune, tel 03.80.24.68.88, fax 03.80.22.43.14, e-mail maisondrouhin@ drouhin.com ▼ by appt.

DOM. DUBOIS D'ORGEVAL 1998★★

  n.c.   1,200   **€11-15**

This youthful wine will keep well and is one of the best in this series. It has a deep ruby-red

576

colour, with violet glints, and aromas of cherry and bilberry. It has both presence and a perfect structure, with tannins that evoke nutmegs and cloves. It needs at least three to five years in the cellar.

🕴 Dom. Dubois d'Orgeval,
3, rue Joseph-Bard, 21200 Chorey-lès-Beaune, tel 03.80.24.70.89, fax 03.80.22.45.02 ☑

DOM. LOIS DUFOULEUR

■ 1er cru   Le Clos du Roi 1999★

| 0.31 ha | 2,086 | €15-23 |

Presented here are three red wines from different *climats*, each receiving one star. There is the **Clos du Dessus des Marconnets 99**, the **Les Cent Vignes Premier Cru 99**, and this beautifully brilliant wine which several tasters placed high on their lists. There are subtle blackcurrant and wild strawberry aromas on the nose; the palate continues in the same spirit with well-blended oak. This wine can be drunk within the year as it has started to mature, but could also be laid down for three to four years.

🕴 Dom. Loïs Dufouleur, 8, bd Bretonnière, 21200 Beaune, tel 03.80.22.70.34, fax 03.80.24.04.28 ☑ ☂ by appt.

DUFOULEUR PERE ET FILS

■ 1er cru   Les Grèves 1998★

| n.c. | 2,500 | €30-38 |

This is a wine to keep for a long time. It has an attractive Pinot colour but the nose is not very open, but that will come. Structure and body are there, but not yet fully formed.

🕴 Dufouleur Père et Fils, 15, rue Thurot, BP 27, 21700 Nuits-Saint-Georges, tel 03.80.61.21.21, fax 03.80.61.10.65 ☑ ☂ by appt.

CH. DES GUETTES

■ 1er cru   Les Boucherottes 1999★

| 0.3 ha | 2,300 | €15-23 |

This is the first harvest for François Parent, who combined the vineyards inherited from his family with those of Anne-Françoise Gros. The result is not bad at all! This pleasant 99 has a dark, almost black colour with an intense and fruity nose. It has a normal astringency and well-balanced strength and richness. The unusual label features Burgundy truffles.

🕴 François Parent, Ch. des Guettes, 14bis, rue Pierre-Joigneaux, 21200 Beaune, tel 03.80.22.61.85, fax 03.80.24.03.16, e-mail gros.anne.francoise@wanadoo.fr ☑ ☂ by appt.

DOMAINES JABOULET-VERCHERRE

□ 1er cru   Les Bressandes 1999

| 0.9 ha | 6,415 | €15-23 |

This wine has a white-gold colour with green highlights; the nose has yet to develop but the palate is well-balanced. Richness and liveliness are combined well with flavours of toast and fruit. This wine will go well, in two years' time, with fish cooked in a sauce.

🕴 Maison Jaboulet-Vercherre, 5, rue Colbert, 21200 Beaune, tel 03.80.22.25.22, fax 03.80.22.03.94 ☑

JEAN GAGNEROT   Clos du Roi 1999

■ 1er cru   n.c.   3,000   €11-15

This wine has a similar character to that of La Reine Pédauque: it is deep purple in colour, courtly and refined. Complex and toasty, it evokes both redcurrant and peony. Well-made and well-structured, with a rustic side to it that doesn't detract from its charms, it is worthy of its appellation.

🕴 Jean Gagnerot, 21420 Aloxe-Corton, tel 03.80.25.00.00, fax 03.80.26.42.00, e-mail vinibeaune@bourgogne.net

DOM. JESSIAUME PERE ET FILS

■ 1er cru   Cent-Vignes 1999

| 1.16 ha | 7,200 | €15-23 |

This wine has a violet-red colour and raspberry aromas. The palate is supple, fresh, fruit and lengthy with a fiery finish. A wine one can have confidence in, that will be at its best in three to four years' time.

🕴 Dom. Jessiaume Père et Fils, 10, rue de la Gare, 21590 Santenay, tel 03.80.20.60.03, fax 03.80.20.62.87 ☑ ☂ by appt.

DOM. PIERRE LABET

□   Clos des Monsnières 1999

| 1 ha | 5,000 | €15-23 |

This deep, golden-yellow *village* with green highlights has a gorgeous nose with aromas of toast, ripe fruit and hints of menthol. The palate is less complex but would go well with a sole meunière. The **red Premier Cru Coucherias 99** is very young. It has a powerful nose and a vigorous palate with a pronounced grilled quality that will need at least two years to soften. Its austerity will, with time, give way to the fruit.

🕴 Dom. Pierre Labet, Clos de Vougeot, 21640 Vougeot, tel 03.80.62.86.13, fax 03.80.62.82.72, e-mail contact@chateaudelatour.com ☑ ☂ ev. day except Tue. 10.30am-7pm; cl. 15 Nov.-Easter
🕴 François Labet

DOM. DE LA CONFRERIE 1999

■   0.7 ha   2,000   €11-15

This estate has been built up over generations and only took the name Confrérie in 1991. This violet-ruby *village* is lightly fruity with a youthfulness that pleads in its favour. Time will soften its tannins.

🕴 EARL Jean Pauchard et Fils, Dom. de la Confrérie, rue Perraudin, 21340 Cirey-lès-Nolay, tel 03.80.21.70.27, e-mail domj.pauchard@wanadoo.fr ☑ ☂ by appt.

DOM. DE LA CRÉA

Les Cent Vignes 1999★

■ 1er cru   0.5 ha   2,600   ⦿ €11-15

Cécile Chenu has been running this estate since 1992. Presented here is an interesting wine with a nose showing both a delicate Pinot character and the *terroir*. It has a classic coloured wine with a bold, forceful attack. This wine is structured with well-controlled tannins. It will be at its best in two years' time.

• Cécile Chenu-Repolt,
La cave de Pommard, 1, rte de Beaune,
21630 Pommard, tel 03.80.24.62.25,
fax 03.80.24.62.42, e-mail cecile.chenu@
wanadoo.fr 🗹 ➤ ev. day 10am–6pm

MICHEL LAHAYE

Les Bons Feuvres 1998★

■   0.44 ha   1,200   ⦿ €11-15

This excellent *village* is a deep garnet red in colour with aromas of nuts and mild spices on the nose. This is a well-made wine with a solid and youthful attack, well-proportioned, full and expansive. It is still very young and needs to spend a few years in the cellar.

• Michel Lahaye, pl. de l'Église,
21630 Pommard, tel 03.80.22.52.22 🗹
➤ by appt.

DANIEL LARGEOT Les Grèves 1999★

■ 1er cru   0.6 ha   3,500   ⦿ €15-23

This estate received a *coup de cœur* for its 95 and 96 vintages. This lovely 99 gives a clear picture of the character of this Les Grèves, even though it is not fully developed. The violet glints are of the right hue, and the smoothness of the tannins, the flavour of the fruit is not overwhelmed by the delicate oakiness. There is black cherry on the middle palate with jammy notes. This is a wine you should have in your cellar.

• Daniel Largeot, 5, rue des Brenôts,
21200 Chorey-les-Beaune,
tel 03.80.22.15.10, fax 03.80.22.60.62 🗹
➤ by appt.

CH. DE LA VELLE Cent vignes 1998★

■ 1er cru   0.24 ha   750   ⦿ €11-15

This pale garnet-coloured wine is lengthy on the palate with a Pinot-style nose. From the opening to the finish it is light and pleasurable with a lovely vinosity. Also not to be missed is the rich and promising red **Premier Cru Les Marconnets 98**, which has an interesting musky and toasty nose, and the **white Les Marconnets 99**, which will be very good in two years' time, as will the **Clos des Monsnières 99**. They all receive one star.

• Bertrand Darviot, Ch. de La Velle,
17, rue de La Velle, 21190 Meursault,
tel 03.80.21.22.83, fax 03.80.21.65.60.
e-mail chateaudelavelle@infonie.fr 🗹
➤ by appt.

LYCÉE VITICOLE DE BEAUNE

La Montée Rouge 1998★

■ 1er cru   0.8 ha   4,104   ⦿ €11-15

Respiciamus atque prospiciamus: 'We look behind us and we look before us' is the college of viticulture's motto. This clear garnet-coloured 98 reveals its complexity from the beginning. There are aromas of raspberry, juniper, moss and leather. It is silky-smooth with a straightforward, delicious roundness. The **red Perrières 99 Premier Cru** is direct and was commended by the Jury.

• Dom. du Lycée viticole de Beaune,
16, av. Charles-Jaffelin, 21200 Beaune,
tel 03.80.26.35.81, fax 03.80.22.76.69 🗹
➤ ev. day except Sun. 8am–11.30am 2pm–
5pm; Sat. 8am–11.30am

DOM. MAILLARD PÈRE ET FILS

1999★

■   1.4 ha   n.c.   ⦿ €11-15

This promising 99 has a deep, clear ruby-red colour and a youthful, subtle nose of grapes and mild spices. It has a fresh attack, which opens with a certain oakiness and dark berry fruit. This is a straightforward, promising, rich and powerful wine that can be drunk from now on.

• Dom. Maillard Père et Fils,
2, rue Joseph-Bard, 21200 Chorey-lès-Beaune,
tel 03.80.22.10.67, fax 03.80.24.00.42 🗹

DOM. RENÉ MONNIER

Cent-Vignes 1999★★

■ 1er cru   1.7 ha   7,000   ⦿ €11-15

The first thing you notice about this agreeable 99 is its subtle, discreet aromas, such as blackcurrant liqueur. It has a dark flame-red colour with violet highlights and a full and lively palate with fine tannins. The **red Premier Cru Toussaints 99** was singled out and awarded one star.

• Dom. René Monnier,
6, rue du Dr-Rolland, 21190 Meursault,
tel 03.80.21.29.32, fax 03.80.21.61.79 🗹
➤ ev. day 8am–12 noon 2pm–6pm
• M. et Mme Bouillot

DOM. PARIGOT PÈRE ET FILS

Les Aigrots 1999★★

■ 1er cru   1.23 ha   8,000   ⦿ €11-15

This excellent 99 comes from a *climat* on the Pommard side of the hillside near Le Clos des Mouches and its real potential. It has a wonderful deep red colour and aromas of ripe fruit on the nose. This wine has an elegant, supple, delicate and liquorice-flavoured body with smooth tannins and an excellent structure. 1 will go well with a guinea fowl dish. Also recommended is the rich and powerful, **red Premier Cru Grèves 99**, the 87 version of which won a *coup de cœur*.

• Dom. Parigot Père et Fils,
rte de Pommard, 21190 Meloisey,
tel 03.80.26.01.70. fax 03.80.26.04.32 🗹
➤ by appt.

CH. PHILIPPE-LE-HARDI
Clos du Roi 1999
■ 1er cru 0.83 ha 6,200 €11-15

This wine has the clean, straightforward colour of its vintage (dark red with violet highlights). The nose is rich in dark berry fruit with aromas of vanilla and toast. It is a well-made, potentially elegant wine with good tannins and notes of Griotte cherries and blackcurrant on the palate. It will improve with three years in the cellar.

Ch. de Santenay, BP 18, 21590 Santenay, tel 03.80.20.61.87, fax 03.80.20.63.66
by appt.

THIERRY PINQUIER-BROVELLI
Les Chaumes Gauffriot 1999★
■ 0.3 ha 1,600 €8-11

Thierry Pinquier's father is 73 years old and still continues to work in his vineyards. Pinquier has been running the estate since 1994. Presented here is a brilliant ruby-coloured 99 with a nose that opens on strong roasted notes, due to the oak maturation. Well-structured, it needs to be laid down for three years.

Thierry Pinquier, 5, rue Pierre-Mouchoux, 21190 Meursault, tel 03.80.21.24.87, fax 03.80.21.61.09
ev. day 8am-12.30pm 1pm-7pm

ALBERT PONNELLE
Clos du Roi 1998★
■ 1er cru n.c. n.c. €23-30

This Clos du Roi is a little rustic around its regal edges. It has a medium-intense garnet colour and an open nose with stewed fruit aromas. It has a pronounced richness with a firm finish. The structure and texture are good quality with a strong blackcurrant flavour.

Albert Ponnelle, Clos Saint-Nicolas, BP 107, 21200 Beaune, tel 03.80.22.00.05, fax 03.80.24.19.73, e-mail info@albert-ponnelle.com
by appt.
Louis Ponnelle

DOM. JACQUES PRIEUR
Grèves 1998★
■ 1er cru 1.7 ha 6,000 €15-23

'Beaune makes one want to fall ill', said Viollet-le-Duc on visiting the Hôtel-Dieu. This wine is full of comfort: well-balanced with pleasant fruitiness, a rich velvety-red colour and a light vanilla fragrance. 'I wish I had made this,' confesses one of our tasters, a hard compliment to beat. He recommends drinking it with game. The **white les Champs Pimont 98** was praised by the Jury, but needs to be laid down for a while as the oak is too prominent.

Dom. Jacques Prieur, 6, rue des Santenots, 21190 Meursault, tel 03.80.21.23.85, fax 03.80.21.29.19
by appt.

DOM. RAPET PÈRE ET FILS
Grèves 1999
■ 1er cru 0.36 ha 2,000 €15-23

Vincent Rapet has recently taken over the running of this very old family estate, which dates back as far as the 18th century. This pleasant 99 predates his arrival. It has a charming colour with a nose of fresh moss. The tannins are still a little solid but a red-currant flavour on the middle palate, decent length, and the overall character give this wine great hope for the future.

Dom. Rapet Père et Fils, 21420 Pernand-Vergelesses, tel 03.80.21.59.94, fax 03.80.21.54.01
by appt.

DOM. REBOURGEON-MURE
Les Vignes Franches 1999★
■ 1er cru 0.62 ha 3,000 €11-15

The vines here in Beaune are venerable (70 years old) but this estate based in Pommard supposedly goes back to the 16th century. The wine has an intense garnet colour with purple highlights and a charming nose with aromas of stewed fruit, followed by a supple attack and well-balanced palate with tannins that enhance the flavours of black-currant, blackberry and raspberry. This is an attractive wine with a pleasant finish, which will need to be laid down for two to four years.

Daniel Rebourgeon-Mure, Grande-Rue, 21630 Pommard, tel 03.80.22.75.39, fax 03.80.22.71.00
by appt.

ROGER ET JOËL REMY
Les Cent Vignes 1999
■ 1er cru n.c. n.c. €8-11

This wine is quite open and has a complex character. There is a flavour of oak, but thanks to its fullness and length it will probably develop well. A strong, characterful wine, with tannins that still need to soften.

SCEA Roger et Joël Rémy, 4, rue du Paradis, 21200 Sainte-Marie-la-Blanche, tel 03.80.26.60.80, fax 03.80.26.53.03
ev. day except Sun. 8am-12 noon 2pm-6pm

DOM. NICOLAS ROSSIGNOL
1999★★
■ 1er cru 0.45 ha 2,500 €8-11

Nicolas Rossignol only took over this estate in 1997 and already he has achieved a

BEAUNE
Appellation Beaune contrôlée
1999
NICOLAS ROSSIGNOL
Volnay (Côte d'Or) France

Côte de Beaune

The Appellation Côte de Beaune is not to be confused with Côte de Beaune-Villages, and can be produced only on a few specified places on the Beaune slopes. The appellation declared 890 hl (23,496 gal) of red wine and 583 hl (15,391 gal) of white in 2000.

JOSEPH DROUHIN 1998★   €15-23

n.c.   n.c.

This wine should open up soon: one's eye is immediately attracted by the brilliance of its cherry-red colour. The nose is not forthcoming, waiting for the next 12 months to pass before it speaks out. The palate, in contrast, is all jammy soft fruit, well-balanced with fine tannins that need to soften a little. This is a wine worthy of its rank.

➤ Joseph Drouhin, 7, rue d'Enfer, 21200 Beaune, tel 03.80.24.68.88, fax 03.80.22.43.14, e-mail maisondrouhin@drouhin.com ☎ by appt.

DOM. LOIS DUFOULEUR

Les Longes 1999★   €11-15

■   0.75 ha   5,000

This deep red 99 is an attractive wine. Youthful and fresh on the nose, it has finesse and roundness on the palate: this is a Pinot that knows its stuff. A rather supple style with a touch of jammy vigour that opens out on the middle palate.

➤ Dom. Lois Dufouleur, 8, bd Bretonnière, 21200 Beaune, tel 03.80.22.70.34, fax 03.80.24.04.28 ☑ ☎ by appt.

EMMANUEL GIBOULOT

La Grande Châtelaine 1999★   €8-11

□   2.34 ha   3,000

This rich, lemony wine has a lively gold colour and is not one to be missed. A well-measured roundness and good acid structure add charm to the fruitiness. There is a little hint of hazelnut on the finish. It is not particularly full but is good for this type of wine. The **white Les Pierres Blanches 99** likewise gets one star.

➤ Emmanuel Giboulot, Combertault, 21200 Beaune, tel 03.80.26.52.85, fax 03.80.26.53.67 ☑ ☎ by appt.

DOM. CHANTAL LESCURE

Le Clos des Topes Bizot 1999★   €8-11

■   4.28 ha   3,000

With its very ripe cherry colour and elegant cherry nose, this wine keeps to the same theme. This Beaune (from the top of the hillside, on the Savigny side) has all the right qualities to develop well: body, concentration and structure. There is a pleasant little touch of liquorice on the finish.

580

---

coup de cœur! This wine has a flaming red colour and an appealing nose with beautiful fruity notes. On the palate, it is pleasing in every way, with finesse, elegance, structure and, more than that, it is a perfect example of its type. This is just the kind of wine people want.

➤ Nicolas Rossignol, rue de Mont, 21190 Volnay, tel 03.80.21.62.43, fax 03.80.21.27.61 ☑ ☎ by appt.

DOM. ROSSIGNOL-FEVRIER PERE ET FILS

Les Chardonnereux 1998★★   €8-11

■   0.46 ha   2,800

This is one of those *climats* which, fortunately, prevents the further urbanisation of Beaune on the vineyard side, here at the exit leading to Pommard. As to the wine, it has all the qualities of a marvellous *village*. It is appealing but not selfish. An intense colour with an interesting nose (peony, violet, black pepper); winey, full and with a very sensual aftertaste. This is not an exaggeration: it is all there in our tasters' notes.

➤ EARL Rossignol-Février, rue du Mont, 21190 Volnay, tel 03.80.21.64.23, fax 03.80.21.67.74 ☑ ☎ by appt.

➤ Frédéric Rossignol

DOM. ROSSIGNOL-TRAPET

Teurons 1998★   €15-23

■ 1er cru   1.2 ha   7,600

Rossignol has one foot in the Côte de Beaune, while Trapet has a foot in the Côte de Nuits. Together, these two wine-making lineages have produced this dark purple Teurons. There are a few grilled notes on the nose that opens to reveal some musky aromas, then very ripe fruit. The tannins are powerful but attractive. This is a charming wine with lovely length. It ought to be left to age for a few years (four to six) when it will be even better.

➤ Dom. Rossignol-Trapet, 3, rue de la Petite-Issue, 21220 Gevrey-Chambertin, tel 03.80.51.87.26, fax 03.80.34.31.63, e-mail info@rossignol-trapet.com ☑ ☎ by appt.

DOM. VOARICK Montée Rouge 1998   €15-23

■   0.92 ha   5,800

This estate has been bought by Michel Picard. Here is a clear, pale cherry-red wine with a complex nose that opens on floral aromas of roses and peonies, then shows more developed, fruity notes. The fineness of the fruit and the floral character fill the palate with soft, velvety flavours. This wine is like a ballerina: light, high-flying, and with a very long stride.

➤ Emile Voarick, 71640 Saint-Martin-sous-Montaigu, tel 03.85.45.23.23, fax 03.85.45.16.37 ☑ ☎ ev. day 8am–12 noon 2pm–6pm

➤ Dom. Chantal Lesure, 34 A, rue Thurot, 21700 Nuits-Saint-Georges, tel 03.80.61.16.79, fax 03.80.61.36.64, e-mail contact@domaine-lesure.com Ⓥ by appt.

DOM. POULLEAU PERE ET FILS
Les Mondes Rondes 1999★

■ 3.2 ha 9,000 €5-8

In the whites, we recommend the 99 *climat* Grande Châtelaine, which gets one star, in the red, the Mondes Rondes from the same year. This wine comes from the very summit of the Montagne de Beaune. It needs time to develop but has a fine concentration of colour and aromas (undergrowth and ripe fruit), and a rich and powerful character with slightly rustic tannins that will become more supple with time.
➤ Dom. Poulleau Père et Fils, rue du Pied-de-la-Vallée, 21190 Volnay, tel 03.80.21.26.52, fax 03.80.21.64.03 Ⓥ by appt.

Pommard

This appellation is the best-known Burgundy outside France. The vineyard produced 16,472 hl (434,861 gal) in 1999 and 14,753 hl (389,479 gal) in 2000. Argovian marlstone is here replaced by soft limestone, and the vines it produces are sturdy, tannic and good for keeping. The best *climats* are classified as Premier Crus, of which the most celebrated are Les Rugiens and Les Épenots.

BALLOT-MILLOT ET FILS
Pézerolles 1999★

■ 1er cru 0.7 ha 2,700 €15-23

The 2001 festival of Saint-Vincent owes a lot to this very dedicated wine-producer, although his duties do not prevent him from looking after his wines. This Pézerolles, which is somewhere between purple and garnet in colour, is very tempting. On the nose there are delicious aromas of ripe fruit. On the palate, it is satisfyingly full and solidly structured. Even the light note of bitterness on the finish is in no way surprising or even unpleasant. It needs to be laid down for at least three years.
➤ Ballot-Millot et Fils, 9, rue de la Goutte-d'Or, BP 33, 21190 Meursault, tel 03.80.21.21.39, fax 03.80.21.65.92 Ⓥ by appt.

DOM. GABRIEL BILLARD
Charmots 1998★

■ 1er cru 0.4 ha 1,800 €15-23

Laurence Jobard and Mireille Desmonet's involvement with wine-production is a successful one. They have already gained two *coups de cœur* (for their 90 and 97 vintages) in previous editions of the *Guide* and thoroughly know their craft. This light ruby-red wine is very fruity. The palate is still rather fiery but promising, with jammy soft fruit and blackcurrant leaf combined with good oak. There is an elegant finesse about this wine, which will come into its own in three to five years' time.
➤ SCEA Dom. Gabriel Billard, imp. de la Commaraine, 21630 Pommard, tel 03.80.22.27.82, fax 03.85.49.49.02 Ⓥ by appt.

DOM. BILLARD-GONNET
Rugiens-Bas 1998★

■ 1er cru 0.25 ha 1,500 €23-30

This is a truly fine wine. It has a bright colour, and aromas of leather and raspberry. Its tannins are still determinedly firm, but, as Saint Bernard said, 'One should leave time for time.' This estate owns vineyard plots in eight Premiers Crus in this appellation. Other wines that we recommend include the **Premier Cru Clos de Verger 98**, which receives one star for the lovely fruitiness that is the result of a good pressing, and the well-made **Premier Cru Chaponnières 98**, which especially impressed the Jury.
➤ Dom. Billard-Gonnet, tel 03.80.22.17.33, fax 03.80.22.68.92 Ⓨ by appt.

ERIC BOIGELOT 1998★

■ 0.35 ha 2,200 €15-23

This is a lovely brilliant red wine with purple highlights. The nose is hovering between cherry and dark fruit (bilberries), with some additional musky notes. A well-structured wine that needs to spend two or three years in the cellar.
➤ Eric Boigelot, 21, rue des Forges, 21190 Meursault, tel 03.80.21.65.85, fax 03.80.21.66.01 Ⓨ by appt.

ROGER BELLAND Les Cras 1999★★

■ 0.98 ha 5,000 €15-23

This Les Cras has the colour of very ripe cherries on the tree. The *climat* is situated just below the Premiers Crus, on the Volnay side. Good maceration has produced dark berry fruit and prune aromas, and the palate is extremely full-bodied and vinous. The tannins will blend in: they already show signs of doing so. This is a really good wine with plenty of potential for laying down (five to ten years).
➤ Dom. Roger Belland, 3, rue de la Chapelle, BP 13, 21590 Santenay, tel 03.80.20.60.95, fax 03.80.20.63.93, e-mail belland.roger@wanadoo.fr Ⓥ by appt.

Pommard

DOM. ALBERT BOILLOT
Les Chanlins-Bas 1999
1er cru 0.25 ha 1,700 €11-15

You might find the austere **Premier Cru En Argillière 99**, which needs laying down, interesting, or you might prefer this very characteristic vermilion wine: it has real personality, and is fruity and very agreeable on the palate. Harmonious with mild spices and fine tannins, this attractive wine, like the other example, needs to be laid down.

☛ SCE du Dom. Albert Boillot, ruelle Saint-Etienne, 21190 Volnay, tel 03.80.21.61.21, fax 03.80.21.61.21, e-mail dom.albert.boillot@wanadoo.fr
Y by appt.

MICHEL BOUZEREAU ET FILS
Les Cras 1998★
0.35 ha n.c. €15-23

'At last, a real Pommard!' exclaimed one of our Jury members. This dark garnet 98 is already very open with notes of fresh fruit. The palate strongly reflects the *terroir*; everything else is in harmony, with strength and elegance, power and length. Just the wine for a coq au Pommard, that old rival to coq au Chambertin.

☛ Michel Bouzereau et Fils, 3, rue de la Planche-Meunière, 21190 Meursault, tel 03.80.21.20.74, fax 03.80.21.66.41
Y by appt.

DOM. CAILLOT 1998★★
2 ha 5,000 €15-23

This wine has a dark purple colour and on the nose there are aromas of leather and toasted almonds, followed by a vinous palate with a well-structured finish. It is a traditional wine that is made to last and is not afraid to show its teeth. The Jury vouches for it.

☛ GAEC Dom. Caillot, 14, rue du Cromin, 21190 Meursault, tel 03.80.21.21.70, fax 03.80.21.69.58
Y by appt.

DENIS CARRE Les Charmots 1999★★
1er cru n.c. n.c. €15-23

DOM. DU CHATEAU DE MEURSAULT Les Petits Noizons 1998★
1.5 ha 7,000 €23-30

One simply cannot remain indifferent to this dark ruby-red 98. It comes from a very stony terrain high on the hillside, where it stares the sun straight in the eyes when the church clock strikes midday. The nose is lovely, with mulberry and flint aromas; the palate follows along the same lines while the tannins get stronger and stronger. It is a real Pommard, winey and delicate, and definitely good for laying down for a long time.

☛ Dom. du Château de Meursault, 21190 Meursault, tel 03.80.26.22.75, fax 03.80.26.22.76
Y by appt.

DOM. Y. CLERGET Les Rugiens 1998★
1er cru 0.85 ha 4,000 €23-30

This Les Rugiens is very intense in colour. At first the nose is closed but on aeration reveals a fruity aroma that gradually becomes more identifiable as Griotte cherries. A mouthfilling palate with reasonable tannins and a subtle oakiness. Don't wait too long before drinking it.

☛ Dom. Y. Clerget, rue de la Combe, 21190 Volnay, tel 03.80.21.61.56, fax 03.80.21.64.57
Y by appt.

ALAIN COCHE-BIZOUARD
La Platière 1999★
0.36 ha 2,200 €15-23

This Pommard *climat* of La Platière faces the *médito* (south) all along the valley. The wine is red with brick-red highlights, very fruity with good liquorice notes. This is a moderate wine in all respects, with distinction and personality.

☛ EARL Alain Coche-Bizouard, 5, rue de Mazeray, 21190 Meursault, tel 03.80.21.28.41, fax 03.80.21.22.38
Y by appt.

DOM. COSTE-CAUMARTIN
Le Clos des Boucherottes 1998★
1er cru 1.81 ha 10,000 €15-23

For around 200 years the Coste-Caumartin family made ovens and stoves before turning their hands to wines and wine-making. This Clos des Boucherottes is a monopoly situated right at the edge of Beaune. This dark vermilion 98 is all soft red fruit and spices. It may not be a wine you can keep for long, but with such fruitiness that is both soft and velvety, it will be pleasant to drink over the next three to four years.

☛ SCE du dom. Coste-Caumartin, rue du Parc, 21630 Pommard, tel 03.80.22.45.04, fax 03.80.22.65.22, e-mail coste.caumartin@wanadoo.fr
Y ev. day 9am–12 noon 2pm–7pm; Sun. by appt.
☛ Jérôme Sordet

☛ Denis Carré, rue du Puits-Bouret, 21190 Meloisey, tel 03.80.26.02.21, fax 03.80.26.04.64
Y by appt.

This wine-producer often appears in the *Guide* and is much praised for his wine. Here he receives a *coup de cœur* for this wine by a unanimous vote from the Jury. The colour is almost as black as ink. The oak has the good taste not to overwhelm the fruit, which is all grapes and Griotte cherries with well-integrated tannins. It is superbly chewy.

582

DOM. DE COURCEL

■ 1er cru   Les Frémiers 1998★

n.c.   2,000   ▥ 23–30

This 16th-century estate has already been praised in the past by our Jury. This **Bigarreau** and **Marmot** (the famous Auxerrois cherry) red 98 achieves a certain complexity with its vanilla and soft fruit. It is still rather solid but has a nice liveliness on the palate, where the tannins are approachable and promising. However, it needs to spend at least another two years in the cellar. The **Premeir Cru Grand Clos des Epenots 98** was commended by the Jury. It is a wine with prominent but elegant tannins that will keep well.

⌕ Dom. de Courcel, pl. de l'Eglise, 21630 Pommard, tel 03.80.22.10.64, fax 03.80.24.98.73 ☑

DOM. CYROT-BUTHIAU

■ 1er cru   Les Arvelets 1999★

0.22 ha   1,100   ▥ 15–23

Wait for the right occasion, or even a special occasion, before opening this lovely garnet wine with purple highlights. A wonderful nose with aromas of moss, undergrowth, blackberry liqueur, mocha. On the palate, strawberry, raspberry and Griotte cherry jam all integrate well with the oak: the tannins are still firm and need to soften and blend in. This wine has a life of at least eight to ten years ahead of it.

⌕ Dom. Cyrot-Buthiau, rie d'Autun, 21630 Pommard, tel 03.80.22.06.56, fax 03.80.24.00.86, e-mail cyrot.buthiau@wanadoo.fr ☑ ⏱ by appt.

Côte de Beaune (North Central region)

Monthélie

Volnay

Pommard

CÔTE-D'OR

BEAUNE

| | AOC localities and Premiers Crus |
| | Regional AOC areas |

Commune boundaries

0   500   1000 m
0   500   1000 yds

VINCENT DANCER
Les Pézerolles 1999★★
■ 1er cru   31 ha   1,500   ▮▮▮ €15-23

This wine has a lovely bouquet that journeys at a pleasantly leisurely pace from blackcurrant leaf to mulberry aromas with an underlying muskiness. This fresh and lively, charming wine positively overwhelms the palate with all its qualities, which is doubtless why it has won a *coup de coeur*, honouring the fourth vintage for this young wine-producer.
☛ Vincent Dancer, 23, rte de Santenay, 21190 Chassagne-Montrachet, tel 03.80.21.94.48, fax 03.80.21.94.48, e-mail vincentdancer@aol.com ▼
Ⴤ by appt.

MARCEL DECHAUME 1999★★
■ 0.6 ha   1,500   ▮▮▮ €11-15

This wine has a perfect colour with aromas of blackcurrant enhanced by undergrowth, followed by a lovely floral freshness. On the palate it is faultless: slender and long. It has our vote.
☛ Marcel Dechaume, 9, rue du Château, 21200 Sainte-Marie-la-Blanche, tel 03.80.26.60.23, fax 03.80.26.60.23 ▼
Ⴤ by appt.

HENRI DELAGRANGE ET FILS
Les Vaumuriens Hauts 1999★
■ 0.62 ha   3,900   ▮▮▮ €11-15

This *climat* is situated above Les Rugiens on the same slope, opposite Volnay. This wine is particularly inspired. The colour may well be average for a 99, but it has a lovely nose that opens with musk and follows through to pepper via cherry. The palate is supple and pleasant, and has good continuity about it. You don't need a set of keys to open it up: it is thoroughly accessible and easy to drink.
☛ Dom. Henri Delagrange et Fils, rue de la Cure, 21190 Volnay, tel 03.80.21.61.88, fax 03.80.21.67.09 ▼ Ⴤ by appt.

GERARD DOREAU 1999
■ 0.44 ha   3,000   ▮▮▮ €11-15

At the moment, this crystal-clear wine shows little development. Aromas of redcurrant emerge with a few spicy notes. It doesn't have a massive body but has good acidity and is well-structured. Its richness argues in its favour and urges you to lay it down for a few years.

☛ Gérard Doreau, rue du Dessous, 21190 Monthélie, tel 03.80.21.27.89, fax 03.80.21.62.19 ▼ Ⴤ by appt.

CH. DE DRACY 1998
■ 0.4 ha   2,000   ▮▮▮ €30-38

The Château de Dracy was originally a military fortress built in 1298. It has been restored many times over the years but nothing can detract from its proud beauty. The wine tasted is bottled by the Bichot company. It looked lovely but at first the nose was very closed. After it was allowed to breathe, a blackcurrant fragrance emerged, accompanied by mocha notes from the wood. The tannic palate reveals body, structure, and liquorice flavours. The verdict is clear: it needs to age for two to three years.
☛ SCA Ch. de Dracy, 71490 Dracy-les-Couches, tel 03.85.49.62.13 Ⴤ by appt.
☛ Benoît de Charette

DOM. CHRISTINE ET JEAN-MARC DURAND 1999★
■ 1.1 ha   3,000   ▮▮▮ €11-15

This is a wine with a taste for freedom. It takes off on the palate with well-balanced power and finesse. The tannins are present but not aggressive. The colour is half-ruby, half-garnet, the nose has roasted coffee aromas with mulberry and violet notes. Enjoy it while you can!
☛ Dom. Christine et Jean-Marc Durand, 1, rue de l'Eglise, 21200 Bouze-les-Beaune, tel 03.80.22.75.31, fax 03.80.26.02.57 ▼

CH. GENOT-BOULANGER
Clos Blanc 1998★
■ 1er cru   0.32 ha   1,500   ▮▮▮ €23-30

Don't be misled: Le Clos Blanc (which is situated next to Les Epenots) is a red wine. The colour is a pronounced shade of purple with black cherry highlights, the bouquet subtle but clean, revealing elderberries, mulberries and black cherry again. On the palate it is rich and tannic with good *terroir* flavours. It could easily stand up to a ten-year stay in the cellar.
☛ SCEV Ch. Génot-Boulanger, 25, rue de Citeaux, 21190 Meursault, tel 03.80.21.49.20. fax 03.80.21.49.21, e-mail genot.boulanger@wanadoo.fr ▼
Ⴤ by appt.
☛ M. Delaby

CH. DES GUETTES
Les Pézerolles 1999★
■ 1er cru   0.3 ha   1,300   ▮▮▮ €23-30

This is a small plot on a *climat* which is situated just above Les Epenots and which covers almost 6 ha (14.6 acres). A youthful wine, well made with delicacy and elegance at the outset, developing along more forceful lines. Although it has a classic dark garnet colour, its slightly balsamic, spicy nose with gamey aromas ('hare's stomach', as specialists call it) is certainly unusual. The body, although well-constructed, needs to develop.

• François Parent, Ch. des Guettes,14bis, rue Pierre-Joigneaux, 21200 Beaune, tel 03.80.22.61.85, fax 03.80.24.03.16, e-mail gros.anne.francoise@wanadoo.fr ▼ by appt.

HOSPICES DE BEAUNE
Cuvée Dames de la Charité 1999★★

■ 1er cru n.c. 600 €15-23

Is it worthy of its label? Yes, it certainly is, since our tasters, who are not aware of its identity, are not backward in their praise of this exemplary wine. It is dark and deep, elegant with a pronounced yet well-handled oakiness, and the dark berry fruit flavours are expressive with a little hint of *eau-de-vie*. It is very structured, very long and very young: this wine will keep well.

• Les Caves des Hautes-Côtes de Pommard, 21200 Beaune, tel 03.80.25.01.00. fax 03.80.22.87.05, e-mail vinche@ wanadoo.fr ▼ ▼ by appt.

DOM. HUBER-VERDEREAU 1999★

■ 0.4 ha 1,600 €11-15

This very young 99,with its bright garnet colour, has both class and panache! The aromas are all raspberry. Firmly structured, it is a rich, fleshy, harmonious wine. The wisest decision is not to drink it too soon.

• Dom. Huber-Verdereau, rue de la Cave, 21190 Volnay, tel 03.80.22.51.50. fax 03.80.22.48.32, e-mail huber-verdereau@ huber-verdereau.com ▼ ▼ by appt.

JEAN-LUC JOILLOT
Les Rugiens 1999★★

■ 0.5 ha 1,800 €23-30

Les Rugiens is the very embodiment of the appellation, and is honoured here by a *coup de cœur* which particularly recalls its origins: this is a top-class *climat* that goes back a long way, and ought to encourage you to tour the area. The wine is intensely purple, all pepper and blackcurrant aromas, structured and fleshy on the palate; it is well constructed and in four to five years' time will be perfect. This estate's *Les Noizons* gained a *coup de cœur* in 1994; the **99** obtains a star, as does the **Premier Cru Les Petits Epenots**.

• Jean-Luc Joillot, rue Marey-Monge, 21630 Pommard, tel 03.80.24.20.26, fax 03.80.24.67.54 ▼ ▼ by appt.

DOM. DE LA CREA 1999★

■ 0.5 ha 2,500 €15-23

This wine has a crystal-clear vermilion colour. Its aromas are all blackcurrant, undergrowth and violet. It develops well on the palate, where the pressing of the fruit has been very effective, while the oak remains subtle. It is a fresh, lively and charming 99 which can be drunk now or be laid down in a decent cellar for the next five years.

• Cécile Chenu-Repolt, La cave de Pommard, 1, rte de Beaune, 21630 Pommard, tel 03.80.24.62.25, fax 03.80.24.62.42, e-mail cecile.chenu@ wanadoo.fr ▼ ▼ by appt.

DOM. DE LA GALOPIERE 1999★

■ 0.9 ha 5,000 €15-23

A ruby red with purple highlights, this wine has an abundant nose with violet (a classic aroma in the Côte de Nuits, less frequent in the Côte de Beaune) and wild strawberries. Soft fruit invades a well-constructed and straightforward palate that has a decent level of acidity. Drink it in ten years' time and it will still be on top form.

• Claire et Gabriel Fournier, 6, rue de l'Eglise, 21200 Bligny-lès-Beaune, tel 03.80.21.46.50, fax 03.80.21.49.93, e-mail c.g.fournier@wanadoo.fr ▼ by appt.

DOM. LAHAYE PERE ET FILS
Les Arvelets 1998★

■ 0.52 ha 2,400 €15-23

This *climat* runs the length of the valley leading to the Hautes-Côtes. It produces an uncomplicated wine that would go well with a beef bourguignon. A straightforward, clear ruby colour with a frank nose full of hunting smells, and a very firm structure. It is very characteristic of the grape variety.

• Lahaye Père et Fils, pl. de l'Eglise, 21630 Pommard, tel 03.80.24.10.47, fax 03.80.24.07.65 ▼ ▼ ev. day except Sun. 9am–12 noon 2pm–6pm

LOUIS LATOUR Epenots 1998★

■ 1er cru 0.41 ha 5,000 €23-30

In *Madame Bovary*, Flaubert's characters drink Pommard. It is a wine, he writes, 'which excites the faculties.' This ruby-coloured wine certainly runs along these lines, with a nose that opens gradually with musk and under-growth. This elegant 98 is a fine wine for laying down, with lovely richness and ele-gance. It is very representative of its appellation.

• Maison Latour, 18, rue des Tonneliers, 21200 Beaune, tel 03.80.24.81.00. fax 03.80.22.36.21, e-mail louislatour@ louislatour.com ▼ by appt.

LA TOUR BLONDEAU 1998★

■ n.c. n.c. €23-30

This wine, which comes from Bouchard Père et Fils, has light brick-red colour. The nose has wonderful aromas, all musk and mushrooms, while on the palate a flavour of walnuts takes over. The tannins are firm, the length decent. It is, when all is said and done, a very typical 98 that is developing well.

➤ Grands Vins Forgeot, 15, rue du Château, 21200 Beaune, tel 03.80.24.80.50

DOM. RAYMOND LAUNAY
Chaponnières 1998★
■ 1er cru   60 ha   2,500   €23-30

Raymond Launay, who gave his name to this estate, is sadly no longer with us. This dark-garnet Premier Cru garners many compliments. On the nose it shows a strong personality (very concentrated blackcurrant and prunes). A full, round, winey, subtle and soft wine with good origins and a good future ahead of it, yet developing along rather strong, powerful lines. Think about serving it with game.

➤ Dom. Raymond Launay, rue des Charmots, 21630 Pommard, tel 03.80.24.08.03, fax 03.80.24.12.87
Ⓨ ev. day 9am-6.30pm

LES CAVES DE LA VERVELLE 1999★
■   0.85 ha   5,900   €15-23

This deep vermilion wine with blackcurrant leaf notes needs time for its tannins to soften. The attack is straightforward and it has well-balanced acidity. This former domaine of Château de Bligny-lès-Beaune, which Suntory and the GMF used to own, has been taken over by local producers of the Cru.

➤ Ch. de Bligny-lès-Beaune, Caves de la Vervelle, le Château, 21200 Bligny-lès-Beaune, tel 03.80.21.47.38, fax 03.80.21.40.27
Ⓨ ev. day 8am-12 noon 2pm-6pm

DOM. LEJEUNE 1998
■   0.85 ha   1,800

When you have been a professor of wine-growing, you are not afraid of producing wine in your own way, a fact that explains the originality of this fermentation period (20-25 days, using whole bunches of grapes, gradual crushing of the grapes followed by daily punching down of the cap). The result is this 98 whose colour is gradually beginning to develop, and which has aromas that centre around wild strawberries and blackcurrant leaf. It is quite a heady wine and should be opened in two years' time.

➤ Dom. Lejeune, pl. de l'Eglise, 21630 Pommard, tel 03.80.22.90.88, fax 03.80.22.90.88, e-mail domaine-lejeune@wanadoo.fr
Ⓨ by appt.
➤ Famille Jullien de Pommerol

DOM. CHANTAL LESCURE
Les Bertins 1999
■ 1er cru   2 ha   3,000   €23-30

This little-known *climat* nestles between Poutures and Fremiers. The wine is red with garnet round the edges. It has a pleasant but noticeable oakiness and the tannins are still rather lively. Characteristic with a good future ahead of it.

➤ Dom. Chantal Lescure, 34 A, rue Thurot, 21700 Nuits-Saint-Georges, tel 03.80.61.16.79, fax 03.80.61.36.64, e-mail contact@domaine-lescure.com
Ⓨ by appt.

DOM. MAILLARD PERE ET FILS
La Chanière 1999★
■   n.c.   n.c.   €15-23

This domaine celebrates its 50th anniversary this year; it was created by Daniel Maillard in 1952. This wine belies the image of Pommards as austere and robust. On the contrary, it is deeply sensual and full of charm. Intensely garnet, on the nose it is very attractive, all soft fruits. Best to put it aside for two to three years.

➤ Dom. Maillard, 2, rue Joseph-Bard, 21200 Chorey-lès-Beaune, tel 03.80.22.10.67, fax 03.80.24.00.42
Ⓨ by appt.

CATHERINE ET CLAUDE MARECHAL La Chanière 1999★★
■   0.87 ha   3,000   €15-23

This sumptuous, fleshy and full-bodied Chanière comes from an area between La Petite Combe and La Grande Combe. It is an elegant black-cherry colour with intense, defined aromas of almond kernels and kirsch, a perfect combination that continues the entire length of the palate. It is already ready to drink but is also capable of waiting a year or two.

➤ EARL Catherine et Claude Maréchal, 6, rte de Chalon, 21200 Bligny-lès-Beaune, tel 03.80.21.44.37, fax 03.80.26.85.01
Ⓨ by appt.

DOM. MOISSENET-BONNARD
Les Pézerolles 1999
■ 1er cru   0.26 ha   1,600   €15-23

The puzzle does not quite fit together yet, but gradually the pieces are falling into place for this intense, bright purple wine with its aromas of soft fruit. The palate at the moment is as light as a feather. The strong acidity seems to be a plus here, along with its good tannic structure and agreeable length. **Les Charmots Premier Cru 99** is well-balanced with a good blend of fresh fruit and soft tannins. It gets the same mark. Both wines can be laid down.

➤ Dom. Moissenet-Bonnard, rte d'Autun, 21630 Pommard, tel 03.80.24.62.34, fax 03.80.22.30.04
Ⓨ by appt.

BERTRAND DE MONCENY
Vieille Racheuse 1999
■   n.c.   12,000   €15-23

Does this *climat* exist on some old land register? Jean-Pierre Nié knows his subject well and has plenty of imagination. This purple, fragrant raspberry-flavoured wine is still tannic but has plenty of character. It needs time to mature.

Cie des Vins d'Autrefois, abbaye Saint-Martin, 53, av. de l'Aigue, 21200 Beaune, tel 03.80.26.33.00, fax 03.80.24.14.84, e-mail mallet.b@cva-beaune.fr
➤ Jean-Pierre Nié

DOM. RENE MONNIER
Les Vignots 1999★

| 0.77 ha | 4,000 | €11-15 |

This powerful 99 will go wonderfully with a good Epoisses cheese. The pressing has been extensive, resulting in a wine with a strong, self-willed character. The colour is red tinged with violet, the nose is modest with a note of blackcurrant. The wine needs to mellow: leave the tannins to soften and the richness to develop for three to four years in the cellar.
➤ Dom. René Monnier, 6, rue du Dr-Rolland, 21190 Meursault, tel 03.80.21.29.32, fax 03.80.21.61.79
⏰ ev. day 8am-12 noon 2pm-6pm
➤ M. et Mme Bouillot

DOM. DE MONTILLE
Rugiens 1999

| 1.1 ha | 5,000 | €46-76 |

This estate, which has been in the same family since the 17th century, presented a cherry-red Rugiens with brilliant violet highlights. The nose is expressive, with intense aromas of crushed and overripe soft fruit. The attack is straightforward, then the tannins turn up in force. This wine needs time to develop some fruit on the palate: we recommend five to six years in the cellar.
➤ Hubert de Montille, rue du Pied-de-la-Vallée, 21190 Volnay, tel 03.80.21.62.67, fax 03.80.21.67.14

DOM. DES OBIERS
Rugiens 1999★

| 0.45 ha | 1,500 | €23-30 |

This Rugiens has a very prominent Pommard character that sticks closely to the rule book: a deep, dark garnet colour edged with cherry hues; a complex nose with musky aromas combined with soft fruit, mocha and undergrowth; richness with rather fine tannins. It seems to have a very real potential for the future.
➤ Dom. des Obiers, chem. rural 29, 21700 Nuits-Saint-Georges, tel 03.80.62.42.00, fax 03.80.61.28.13, e-mail nuicave@wanadoo.fr
⏰ ev. day 10am-6pm; cl. Jan.

DOM. PARENT
Les Rugiens 1998★

| n.c. | 1,500 | €30-38 |

This deep ruby wine blazes with a still-youthful brightness. It follows all the requisite rules: its aromas are untamed, all cherry and leather. It is quite austere at first encounter, then grows silky-smooth, exploding with red fruit that makes its tannins disappear almost entirely. It is easy to drink and can be enjoyed from now on. Another Premier Cru worth noting is the **Les Arvelets 99**, which gets one star and should only be opened in three, five or ten years.

➤ Dom. Parent, pl. de l'Eglise, 21630 Pommard, tel 03.80.22.15.08, fax 03.80.24.19.33, e-mail parent-pommard@axnet.fr
⏰ by appt.

DOM. PARIGOT PERE ET FILS
Les Vignots 1999★★

| 0.5 ha | 3,300 | €15-23 |

This domaine is celebrating its tenth anniversary in style with this remarkable 99. It is a crystal-clear purple tinted with violet, and is the very incarnation of a majestic, powerful, domineering Pommard that can also show a delicate side. The wine-making is of the highest quality, and this is a top-quality wine that should be served with a jugged hare or, failing that, a rabbit. Besides this, we recommend the **Premier Cru Charmots 99**, which gets one star and is an extremely honest, rich wine.
➤ Dom. Parigot Père et Fils, rte de Pommard, 21190 Meloisey, tel 03.80.26.01.70, fax 03.80.26.04.32
⏰ by appt.

VINCENT ET MARIE-CHRISTINE PERRIN 1999★

| 0.5 ha | 3,000 | €15-23 |

This is a veritable colossus of Rhodes with a formidable structure, satisfying acidity and prominent tannins. Put it under lock and key for at least five years in your cellar. It is a deep ruby red with a nose that, when it opens, suggests moss.
➤ Vincent Perrin, 21190 Volnay, tel 03.80.21.62.18, fax 03.80.21.68.09
⏰ by appt.

ALBERT PONNELLE 1999★
1er cru

| n.c. | n.c. | €23-30 |

This black cherry, dense, very dark *village* has a rather unspectacular nose that is still very closed. On the palate it is more animated, rich and powerful, with all the right elements present and correct. Wait two years.
➤ Albert Ponnelle, Clos Saint-Nicolas, BP 107, 21200 Beaune, tel 03.80.22.00.05, fax 03.80.24.19.73, e-mail info@albert-ponnelle.com
⏰ by appt.
➤ Louis Ponnelle

MICHEL REBOURGEON
Rugiens 1998★
1er cru

| 0.17 ha | 964 | €15-23 |

This Rugiens does not do things by halves. The colour is still very youthful, the clean and straightforward nose favours aromas of cherry and undergrowth, and there is a decent balance on the palate between acidity and tannins. Everything, in short, points to a good-quality wine with real potential for laying down, for this round and robust wine is far from having had its say.
➤ Michel Rebourgeon, pl. de l'Europe, 21630 Pommard, tel 03.80.22.22.83, fax 03.80.22.90.64 ⏰ by appt.

DOM. REBOURGEON-MURE★

1998

▪ 1.52 ha 3,900 🍷 €11-15

The Rebourgeon-Mure family has been in Pommard since the 16th century. They presented four different wines, each one receiving one star. The three **Premiers Crus, Clos des Arvelets, Clos Micault** and **Grands Épenots**, all belong to the excellent **99** vintage. This particular wine is a garnet-coloured *village* with mauve highlights. Blackcurrant jam mixes with mild spices, while the oak is already well-integrated. In short, it offers remarkable finesse and freshness from beginning to end. Both the Pinot and the appellation work together nicely. It would go down very well with game.

☛ Daniel Rebourgeon-Mure, Grande-Rue, 21630 Pommard, tel 03.80.22.75.39, fax 03.80.22.71.00 ✉ ☒ by appt.

DOM. NICOLAS ROSSIGNOL

1999★

▪ 0.35 ha 2,000 🍷 €11-15

Why does Alfred Hitchcock, in one of his films, hide state secrets in a bottle of Pommard? There is less suspense involved here in this complex and spicy 99 that will mature well. The wine follows a seamless path: there is a touch of austerity at this stage due to rather lively tannins, but two to three years in the cellar will soften it and ensure a happy ending for all concerned.

☛ Nicolas Rossignol, rue de Mont, 21190 Volnay, tel 03.80.21.62.43, fax 03.80.21.27.61 ✉ ☒ by appt.

DOM. VINCENT SAUVESTRE★

Clos De La Platière 1999★

▪ n.c. n.c. 🍷 €23-30

This clean and bright 99 possesses the kind of svelte, smooth, rich tannins that they simply don't make any more. It sits well on the palate right from the start, with its nose is fine and satisfying with a fruity elegance. This is not a wine that can be laid down for long.

☛ Dom. Vincent Sauvestre, rte de Monthélie, 21190 Meursault, tel 03.80.21.22.45, fax 03.80.21.28.05 ✉ ☒ by appt.

VAUCHER PÈRE ET FILS 1999★

▪ n.c. n.c. 🍷 €15-23

There is a school of drawing that stresses the importance of purity of line: precision and simplicity are paramount. This Pinot Noir belongs to that school. It is clear, perfumed with blackcurrant, has a good level of liveliness and acidity, excellent length, and is full of liveliness and richness. In short, it is a very classic and fine wine. Vaucher Père et Fils is an old Dijon business that has been taken over by the Cottin brothers at Nuits (Labouré-Roi).

☛ Vaucher Père et Fils, rue Lavoisier, 21700 Nuits-Saint-Georges, tel 03.80.62.64.00. fax 03.80.62.64.10 ☒ by appt.

VAUDOISEY-CREUSEFOND

Charmots 1998

▪ 1er cru 0.25 ha 1,500 🍷 €15-23

This wine has a smooth Burgundy colour and a pleasing nose where soft fruit, undergrowth and oak all sit together side by side. On the palate, the tannins are still youthful but they are not aggressive: one can detect mulberry and blackcurrant flavours. It will most probably be at its best in 2004 or 2005.

☛ Vaudoisey-Creusefond, rte d'Autun, 21630 Pommard, tel 03.80.22.48.63, fax 03.80.24.16.81 ✉ ☒ by appt.

JOSEPH VOILLOT 1999★

▪ 2 ha 10,000 🍷 €11-15

Guillaume Paradin wrote 500 years ago that Pommard is 'the flower of all the wines of Beaune' (that is, of the Beaune region). This wine confirms it. It has an intense red colour with smooth, satiny highlights; the nose has some charred notes and blackcurrant, and the palate is as smooth as silk. There is a good crispy fruitiness with just the right amount of roundness that enables it to be enjoyed young in two years' time.

☛ Dom. Joseph Voillot, pl. de l'Eglise, 21190 Volnay, tel 03.80.21.62.27, fax 03.80.21.66.63, e-mail joseph.voillot@mageos.com ✉ ☒ by appt.

Volnay

Snuggling in the hollow of the hill, the village of Volnay is as pretty as a postcard. Though less well known than Pommard to the north, the appellation yields nothing to its neighbour and the wines have all the finesse you could hope for. They vary from the lightness of Les Santenots, situated on the neighbouring commune of Meursault, to the robustness and vigour of the Clos des Chênes or the Clos des Champans. We shall not list all of them here for fear of omitting some. Le Clos des Soixante Ouvrées is another very well-known wine, and provides the opportunity to explain the origin of the word: an *ouvrée* dates from the Middle Ages and measures four ares and twenty-eight centiares, representing a basic unit of vineyard soil that a worker could break up in a day, using a pick. This area corresponds to 428 m² (512 yds²).

Many 19th-century writers have referred to Volnay wines. When the Viscount de Vergnette addressed the Congrès des Vignerons Français in 1845, he finished his erudite report with the following words: 'The wines of Volnay will continue for a long time into the future to be the best wines in the world, as they were in the 16th century under our Dukes who owned the de Caille-du-Roy vineyards there.', 'Cailleray' then 'Caillerets'. In 1999, 11,362 hl (299,957 gal) of Volnay were produced and 9,855 hl (260,172 gal) in 2000.

DOM. CHARLES ALLEXANT ET FILS Le Village 1999★

■ 1er cru   0.51 ha 3,000   ⊞ €11-15

'There is a certain subtle rusticity to this wine,' notes one of our tasters. As its name implies, this *climat* is close to the village. The wine has a pale garnet colour with aromas of blackcurrant leaf and oak. Violet holds sway on a calm, gentle palate, while the blackcurrant body is enlivened by a little fieriness.

🍴 SCE Dom. Charles Allexant et Fils, rue du Château, Cissey, 21190 Merceuil, tel 03.80.26.83.27, fax 03.80.26.84.04 V
Y ev. day 8am–12 noon 1.30pm–6pm; Sat/Sun. by appt.

ROGER BELLAND Santenots 1999★

■ 1er cru   0.25 ha 1,000   ⊞ €15-23

Les Santenots is like a little corner that has been carved out for Volnay in the commune of Meursault because the land is so obviously good for red wine. This is a traditional wine, and it ought to please. The colour is black cherry, there is kirsch on the nose, and cherry on the palate; the common denominator is not difficult to find. It has a nice texture, but its strong oaky flavour means it needs to be left to age.

🍴 Dom. Roger Belland, 3, rue de la Chapelle, BP 13, 21590 Santenay, tel 03.80.20.60.95, fax 03.80.20.63.93, e-mail belland.roger@wanadoo.fr V
Y by appt.

CHRISTIAN BELLANG Clos des Chênes 1999★

■ 1er cru   0.7 ha   900   ⊞ €15-23

Christian Bellang took over his father's vineyards in 1964. In 1999, his son joined him in running the estate. This Volnay is medium-intense in colour, which is fine – better than a highly-extracted colour. Redcurrant aromas are accompanied by toast in celebration of

the union between the Pinot Noir and the wood. The wine is fresh on the attack and warm on the finish, playing in both fields a little. It has been produced in a very classic manner, and the result is very decent. An equally classic partner for this wine would be a chicken with cream sauce.

🍴 Dom. Christian Bellang et Fils, 2, rue de Mazeray, 21190 Meursault, tel 03.80.21.22.61, fax 03.80.21.68.50 V
Y by appt.

ERIC BOIGELOT Les Santenots 1998★

■ 1er cru   0.16 ha 900   ⊞ €15-23

During the time of the Dukes of Burgundy, Volnay played an important part in diplomatic negotiations. It is a particularly conciliating wine and this one is no exception. There is peace and harmony in the garnet-red colour. The nose undertakes to continue the discussion. A hint of jam confirms the maturity of the whole affair. Finally, the acidity and the tannins sign a pact of friendship.

🍴 Eric Boigelot, 21, rue des Forges, 21190 Meursault, tel 03.80.21.65.85, fax 03.80.21.66.01 V Y by appt.

DOM. BOUCHARD PERE ET FILS Clos des Chênes 1998★

■ 1er cru   0.85 ha n.c.   ⊞ ♦ €23-30

This wine fits in with the picture that we have of modern Volnay wines. The Clos des Chênes borders with Monthélie and is also next to Cailleret, the *nec plus ultra* of *climats*. This deep-red 98 has only a delicate bouquet (a hint of cherry-stone, a touch of vanilla) but it develops powerfully on the palate. It is a firm, structured, tannic Pinot Noir. Age will temper the severity of its youth.

🍴 Bouchard Père et Fils, Ch. de Beaune, 21200 Beaune, tel 03.80.24.80.24, fax 03.80.22.55.88, e-mail france@bouchard-perefils.com Y by appt.

DOM. DENIS BOUSSEY Taillepieds 1999★

■ 1er cru   0.21 ha 1,200   ⊞ €15-23

This estate has frequently pleased our Jury. Here, it presents a Premier Cru that comes from Aargau limestone, which is very light and quite chalky. Taillepieds is said to produce delicate wines and that is certainly the case here. This is a clear, bright wine with aromas of fresh soft fruit and vanilla (which comes from the oak). It receives a star for its freshness and roundness.

🍴 Dom. Denis Boussey, 1, rue du Pied-de-la-Vallée, 21190 Monthélie, tel 03.80.21.21.23, fax 03.80.21.62.46 V
Y ev. day except Sun. 8am–12 noon 1.30pm–6.30pm; cl. 5-25 Aug.

DOM. FRANCOIS BUFFET Champans 1998★★

■ 1er cru   112 ha 2,200   ⊞ €15-23

Although this wine didn't quite make a *coup de cœur*, it was selected for the final. This medium-intense garnet Champans is the stuff of legends. It has an amazing complex nose (dark berry fruit, leather, musk), and attacks with gusto. Richness and structure only add to the merits of this top-of-the-range 98. The Clos des Chênes 98 receives one star. Both these wines need to spend two to three years in the cellar.

•– Dom. François Buffet, petite place de l'Eglise, 21190 Volnay, tel 03.80.21.62.74, fax 03.80.21.65.82, e-mail dfbuffet@aol.com ▼ ▼ by appt.

DOM. FRANCOIS CHARLES ET FILS Clos de la Cave 1999★   III €11-15

■ 0.4 ha 1,800

This is the complete opposite of the kind of wine that is easy to drink and gives everything up to the first comer. It has a deep, dark purple colour and a firm, complex character. Mineral notes mingle with ripe soft fruit. It is full on the attack with plenty of body; direct, with a long raspberry finish. The wine-cellar here is a natural cavity, a little crater formed by water erosion.

•– EARL François Charles et Fils, 21190 Nantoux, tel 03.80.26.01.20, fax 03.80.26.04.84 ▼ ▼ by appt.

HENRI DELAGRANGE ET FILS Vieilles vignes 1999★   III €11-15

■ 1.9 ha 10,000

These wines spend 16 months in oak, 25% new. Young guinea fowl would seem to be the perfect accompaniment to this almost perfectly characteristic wine. Its colour hovers between ruby and garnet, on the nose it ranges from vanilla to mulberries, and the body is Volnay from top to toe. A straightforward attack, supple tannins, no bitterness and a really fruity finish. An affordable wine that is ready to drink now.

•– Dom. Henri Delagrange et Fils, rue de la Cure, 21190 Volnay, tel 03.80.21.61.88, fax 03.80.21.67.09 ▼ ▼ by appt.

JEAN GAGNEROT 1999★   III €15-23

■ n.c. 2,500

This dark-purple Volnay has good origins. Its nose hovers between mineral notes and ripe soft fruit. This theme turns up again on the palate where the wine seems to have good presence. The finish has vigorous tannins but also a very pleasant hint of Griotte cherries. We will be in for some nice surprises when it is fully mature.

•– Jean Gagnerot, 21420 Aloxe-Corton, tel 03.80.25.00.00, fax 03.80.26.42.00, e-mail vinibeaune@bourgogne.net

CH. GENOT-BOULANGER Les Aussy 1998★★   III €15-23

■ 0.4 ha 1,650

Let us taste this wine again in ten years' time! It comes from a climat near Cailleret. A beautiful wine that has the red colour of a stained-glass window caught in the sunlight. The nose is still closed but has a certain richness hiding in the background. It is powerful and well structured, fine and elegant, and capable of making the journey from the year 2000 to 2010 without a hitch. It will go wonderfully with a game terrine or a roast duck.

•– SCEV Ch. Génot-Boulanger, 25, rue de Cîteaux, 21190 Meursault, tel 03.80.21.49.20, fax 03.80.21.49.21, e-mail genot.boulanger@wanadoo.fr ▼ ▼ by appt.
•– Mme Delaby

BERNARD ET LOUIS GLANTENAY Les Santenots 1998★   III €15-23

■ 1er cru 0.67 ha 2,072

The 14th-century church of Saint-Cyr in Volnay boasts a fine 16th-century altarpiece, the Adoration of the Magi. This estate has been in Volnay for generations. The wine is a brilliant ruby red with aromas of leather and game. It is not particularly open but for a 98 is developing well. There is a little hint of pine bark, something resiny about it, and plenty of acidity and chewiness. In two or three years' time everyone will want to open it.

•– SCE Bernard et Louis Glantenay, rue de Vaut, 21190 Volnay, tel 03.80.21.62.20, fax 03.80.21.67.78, e-mail glantenay@waliea9.com ▼ ▼ by appt.

DOUDET-NAUDIN 1999   III €15-23

■ 1.05 ha 1,798

Yves Doudet heads this family-run business which was founded in 1849. This Volnay village has an unusually pale colour. The nose is typically Pinot. There is not a great deal of tannic structure but there is an interesting intensity of flavours. A good characteristic wine with an easy, accessible style.

•– Doudet-Naudin, 3, rue Henri-Cyrot, BP 1, 21420 Savigny-lès-Beaune, tel 03.80.21.51.74, fax 03.80.21.50.69 ▼ ▼ by appt.
•– Yves Doudet

JEAN GUITON Les Petits Poisots 1998★★   III €11-15

■ 0.35 ha 2,000

Bossuet secretly adored Volnay wine and would happily dip his pen in ink to sing its praises. The Petits Poisots (a climat situated along the RN 74 between Pommard and Meursault) would have provided him with ample inspiration. What a wine, indeed! What finesse and style! You feel as if you are breathing cherries and biting into the flesh of the fruit. The colour is an elegant, perfect pure ruby red.

•– Dom. Jean Guiton, 4, rte de Pommard, 21200 Bligny-lès-Beaune, tel 03.80.26.82.88, fax 03.80.26.85.05, e-mail guillaume-guiton@wanadoo.fr ▼ ▼ by appt.

DOM. ANTONIN GUYON Clos des Chênes 1998★   III €23-30

■ 1er cru 0.87 ha 4,800

This dark purple wine is a fine example of good wine-making combined with high-quality grapes. On the nose there are floral notes which turn peppery towards the end.

The palate is round with enough body to develop well. Everything works together to create an impression of richness.

↳ Dom. Antonin Guyon, 21420 Savigny-lès-Beaune, tel 03.80.67.13.24, fax 03.80.66.85.87, e-mail vin@guyon-bourgogne.com [V] [Y] by appt.

JAFFELIN Santenots 1998★

| ■ 1er cru | n.c. | 1,200 | €23-30 |

'This is a wine one should have in one's cellar,' notes one of the tasters. The peony colour with dark shades is charming. On the nose are aromas of rose, blackberry and precious woods. Although there is a slight touch of dryness on the finish, its elegance and distinction make it worthy of praise. The Jaffelin company belongs to J.-Cl. Boisset, but is run independently from Beaune.

↳ Jaffelin, 2, rue Paradis, 21200 Beaune, tel 03.80.22.12.49, fax 03.80.24.91.87

DOM. LA POUSSE D'OR

En Caillerets Clos des 60 Ouvrées Monopole 1998

| ■ 1er cru | 2.39 ha n.c. | €23-30 |

Patrick Landanger took over the Pousse d'Or estate in 1998. It was created by Gérard Potel who had most notably developed the Clos des Caillerets. This attractive 98 has a fairly ordinary colour with a few light brick-red highlights. The nose shows some good oak and opens on a complex note. Although not very long, this wine livens up the whole palate in a really harmonious way.

↳ Dom. de La Pousse d'Or, rue de la Chapelle, 21190 Volnay, tel 03.80.21.61.33, fax 03.80.21.29.97, e-mail patrick@la-pousse-d'or.fr [V] [Y] by appt.

↳ Patrick Landanger

LES CAVES DE LA VERVELLE 1999

| ■ | 1.65 ha 11,400 | €15-23 |

'Between Pommard and Meursault,' they say here, 'Volnay always comes out on top!' Indeed. A typically-coloured 99, ruby red with youthful highlights. The nose is charming, all fruit and nut kernel, ink and smoke. On the palate everything is silky and soft. The acidity is not too strong, or the oakiness too overpowering, since this wine has a good five years ahead of it.

↳ Ch. de Bligny-lès-Beaune, Caves de la Vervelle, le Château, 21200 Bligny-lès-Beaune, tel 03.80.21.47.38, fax 03.80.21.40.27 [Y] ev. day 8am-12 noon 2pm-6pm

HUBERT DE MONTILLE

Mitans 1999★

| ■ 1er cru | 0.7 ha 4,500 | €38-46 |

This is an historic estate. Its Mitans is a dusky violet with dark, shadowy highlights. Its nose is lacy, seductive and redolent of bilberry coulis. It has a warm chewiness. It has everything it needs, in short, to spend a while in the cellar until you are ready to drink it.

↳ Hubert de Montille, rue du Pied-de-la-Vallée, 21190 Volnay, tel 03.80.21.62.67, fax 03.80.21.67.14 [V]

DOM. ANNICK PARENT

Fremiets 1998★

| ■ 1er cru | n.c. | €15-23 |

This is a Premier Cru from the Pommard side of the hill. It is such a characteristic Volnay that it cannot help but make a good impression. The colour is perfect, the nose has dominant kirsch aromas. The noticeable oakiness will soften in two to three years' time and allow the black cherry flavour to liven up the concentrated, mouth-filling palate.

↳ Dom. Annick Parent, rue du Château-Gaillard, 21190 Monthélie, tel 03.80.21.21.98, fax 03.80.21.21.98, e-mail annick.parent@wanadoo.fr [V] [Y] by appt.

DOM. PARIGOT PERE ET FILS

Les Echards 1999★

| ■ | 0.72 ha 4,800 | €11-15 |

This Echards (a *climat* situated just below les Champans and Ronceret) is a dark ruby red. Although the aromas are rather strong (prunes and cherry jam), the structure is perfectly satisfactory: the flesh is fruity, the body full of vigour. An affordable wine, a little on the commercial side, but then what is wrong with simply tasting nice?

↳ Dom. Parigot Pere et Fils, rte de Pommard, 21190 Meloisey, tel 03.80.26.01.70, fax 03.80.26.04.32 [Y] by appt.

DOM. PONSARD-CHEVALIER

Cros Martin 1999

| ■ | 0.39 ha 1,000 | €11-15 |

An attractively-coloured 99 with youthful highlights. The nose opens on ripe fruit, then becomes more floral, and although there is less complexity on the palate, overall it is well-made. The finish is very clean with well-handled tannins.

↳ Ponsard-Chevalier, 2, Les Tilles, 21590 Santenay, tel 03.80.20.60.87, fax 03.80.20.61.10 [Y] by appt.

DOM. POUILLEAU PERE ET FILS 1999★

| ■ 1er cru | 0.2 ha 900 | €15-23 |

This wine is like the rocket Ariane on her launch pad. Once it has successfully taken off, this bottle will send some very fine flavours into orbit. It is more clear than bright, with a good balance of vanilla and cherry. It has a pronounced *terroir* flavour but at the same time reveals a remarkable openness and approachability (the tannins are particularly soft). Best to wait three to six years. The village La Cuvée Vieilles Vignes 99 will be just right in a year or two's time.

↳ Dom. Pouilleau Pere et Fils, rue du Pied-de-la-Vallée, 21190 Volnay, tel 03.80.21.26.52, fax 03.80.21.64.03 [V]

DOM. JACQUES PRIEUR★

Clos des Santenots 1998★

■ 1er cru   1.19 ha   2,000   ⏲ €30-38

This estate won a *coup de cœur* last year. This year's offering is not quite of the same calibre, although it is a very good average. There is a hint of raspberry just detectable on the mainly mocha nose. Acidity and tannins are in harmony. On the palate it is developing some supple and tender notes. This wine is close to being at its best. The domaine has been taken over by the Antonin Rodet company.

● Dom. Jacques Prieur, 6, rue des Santenots, 21190 Meursault,
tel 03.80.21.23.85, fax 03.80.21.29.19 ▼ ▼ by appt.

DOM. PRIEUR-BRUNET

Santenots 1998★

■ 1er cru   n.c.   n.c.   ⏲ €23-30

A deep ruby colour with a lovely clear brightness and a sophisticated and intense bouquet. The structure is what one might expect from a Santenots: full, fleshy, supple and deep. It is not yet fully open and needs to wait two to three years.

● Dom. Prieur-Brunet, rue de Narosse, 21590 Santenay, tel 03.80.20.60.56, fax 03.80.20.64.31, e-mail uny-prieur@prieursantenay.com ▼ ▼ by appt.

DOM. REBOURGEON-MURE★★★

Caillerets 1999★★★

■ 1er cru   0.32 ha   1,800   ⏲ €15-23

Heaven knows if there was even any competition! This Caillerets carries off the first prize. It presents a purple colour, a musky nose and then a marvellous alchemy takes place, with well-blended oakiness, a perfect balance between tannins and fruit, a fine complexity, superb length and an extraordinary elegance. What is the greatest compliment a taster can give to a wine? 'I wish I'd made this myself.' Note also the **Santenots 98**: it is beautifully harmonious and obtains two stars.

● Daniel Rebourgeon-Mure, Grande-Rue, 21630 Pommard, tel 03.80.22.75.39, fax 03.80.22.71.00 ▼ ▼ by appt.

REINE PEDAUQUE Santenots 1999

■ 1er cru   n.c.   4,200   ⏲ €15-23

This wine has undergone a strong pressing. The colour is black cherry, the nose all liquorice and spices. Its character appears more winey than fruity, and the tannins, which are a little tough at present, suggest that one should forget this wine for a while in the cellar.

● Reine Pédauque, Le Village, 21420 Aloxe-Corton, tel 03.80.25.00.00. fax 03.80.26.42.00. e-mail rpedauque@axnet.fr ▼ by appt.

NICOLAS ROSSIGNOL Fremiets 1999

■ 1er cru   0.17 ha   800   ⏲ €15-23

Nicolas Rossignol has been here since 1997, and has successfully produced a micro *cuvée*, which has a characteristic elegance. The colour is black with garnet highlights – or it might be the opposite. The crushed fruit, the black cherry, the toasty wood flavour, the cocoa finish, the balanced structure – everything conspires to encourage this young man in his efforts.

● Nicolas Rossignol, rue de Mont, 21190 Volnay, tel 03.80.21.62.43, fax 03.80.21.27.61 ▼ by appt.

DOM. REGIS ROSSIGNOL-CHANGARNIER 1998★

■ 1er cru   0.8 ha   3,600   ⏲ €15-23

This is an attractive, well-made wine, light in tone, with a slightly amber-tinged colour that sets the scene for a fresh and floral nose and a full flavour on the palate. A lovely wine, despite a tannic note that will disappear after a year or two in the cellar. It is lengthy, persistent and convincing. The **village 98** obtains the same mark and will be more immediately drinkable.

● Régis Rossignol, rue d'Amour, 21190 Volnay, tel 03.80.21.61.59, fax 03.80.21.61.59 ▼ by appt.

DOM. ROSSIGNOL-FEVRIER PERE ET FILS 1999★

■ 1er cru   1.37 ha   5,000   ⏲ €11-15

This domaine reminds us on its label that its wine has been grown, matured and aged at the foot of Notre-Dame des Vignes. This attractive 99 has a cardinal purple colour and plenty of fruit. Although it is still austere before too long as it has well-structured tannins.

● EARL Rossignol-Février, rue du Mont, 21190 Volnay, tel 03.80.21.64.23, fax 03.80.21.67.74 ▼ by appt.

● Frédéric Rossignol

CH. ROSSIGNOL-JEANNIARD

Santenots 1999★

■ 1er cru   1.5 ha   7,000   ⏲ €15-23

This rich, round, fleshy wine has an impressive intense colour. The nose, with some cajoling, has some good things to offer (bilberry jam). Finally, there is a huge concentration on

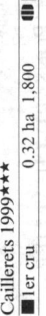

the palate, which is unctuous. There is not much acidity; don't keep it too long.

● Ch. Rossignol-Jeanniard, rue de Mont, 21190 Volnay, tel 03.80.21.62.43, fax 03.80.21.27.61 ☑ ☏ by appt.

CHRISTOPHE VAUDOISEY

■ 1er cru

Clos des Chênes 1999★

| | n.c. | n.c. | €15-23 |

The garnet-red colour of this wine sets the scene nicely, with the curtain opening at the moment when the rather wild and spicy aromas match the strength of those of cocoa and stewed prunes. The following acts see good structure, concentration, richness and fieriness with an oaky theme. This wine definitely belongs among the 'modern' wines rather than the 'old-fashioned' ones.

● Christophe Vaudoisey, pl. de l'Eglise, 21190 Volnay, tel 03.80.21.20.14, fax 03.80.21.27.80 ☑ ☏ by appt.

JOSEPH VOILLOT 1999★★

■ | 2 ha | 12,000 | €15-23 |

This dark, intensely-coloured wine with its complex nose, has a fine Pinot character. The tannins have good texture, which makes them relatively supple. As a whole, it is well-structured, the product of a very sure-handed technological wine-making approach. Its open charm indicates that it should be drunk over the next year.

● Dom. Joseph Voillot, pl. de l'Eglise, 21190 Volnay, tel 03.80.21.62.27, fax 03.80.21.66.63, e-mail joseph.voillot@mageos.com ☑ ☏ by appt.

Monthélie

The combe of Saint-Romain separates the *terroirs* producing red wines from those producing whites. Monthélie is on the south-facing slope of the combe. This little village is somewhat overshadowed by its more famous neighbours but produces wines of excellent quality. In 2000 production totalled 4,982 hl (131,525 gal) of red wine and 575 hl (15,180 gal) of white.

DOM. DENIS BOUSSEY

■ **Les Hauts Brins 1999**

□ | 1.16 ha | 6,000 | €11-15 |

This *climat* on the Volnay side of the hill has produced a deep-red wine with an interesting intensity on the nose which has powerful, red fruit aromas. Its texture is supple and soft with elegant tannins, and generally it seems very harmonious. Two to three years in the cellar will not go amiss. The **red, Premier Cru Les Champs Fulliot 99** should likewise develop well. Give it at least three years.

● Dom. Denis Boussey 1, rue du Pied-de-la-Vallée, 21190 Monthélie, tel 03.80.21.21.23, fax 03.80.21.62.46 ☑ ☏ ev. day except Sun. 8am–12 noon 1.30pm–6.30pm; cl. 5–25 Aug.

ERIC BOIGELOT Sur la Velle 1998★

■ 1er cru

□ | 0.25 ha | 1,500 | €11-15 |

Do you remember *Le Petit Prince?* 'It is the time you have given up for your rose that makes your rose so important.' It is the same for this wine, which is far from being at its best and needs to be laid down, but it will be time well spent! The colour is lovely and bright with dark cherry hues, the nose is still closed, oaky and toasty, but this 98 will be very harmonious one day: its richness and length guarantee it.

● Eric Boigelot, 21, rue des Forges, 21190 Meursault, tel 03.80.21.65.85, fax 03.80.21.66.01 ☑ ☏ by appt.

---

supple with an attractive middle palate. Subtle tannins without astringency are testimony to a maturation in wood that respects the wine.

● Guy Bocard, 4, rue de Mazeray, 21190 Meursault, tel 03.80.21.64.92 ☑ ☏ by appt.

JACQUES BOIGELOT

■ 1er cru

Les Champs-Fulliot 1998★★

□ | 0.39 ha | 2,800 | €11-15 |

If the spelling of this *climat* on the label is questionable (Fulliot instead of Fuilliot), the wine, on the other hand, gets 10 out of 10. It is a bright red, with the Pinot grape spelling out each aroma in turn: blackcurrant, blackberry, strawberry jam, then toast. Then on the palate there is something like brandied fruit. It is a very tasty, pleasant wine, and one there is little point leaving to age longer, although it could easily survive the next two years without coming to any harm.

● Jacques Boigelot, 21190 Monthélie, tel 03.80.21.22.81, fax 03.80.21.66.01 ☑ ☏ by appt.

DOM. GUY BOCARD Toisières 1999★

□ | 0.12 ha | 900 | €11-15 |

If you know the area well, you will know that this *climat* is situated just before Meursault, not far from Les Champs Fulliot. It produces this wine with a clear, bright garnet colour with bluish highlights. The nose is long and complex with bluish highlights. The nose is long and complex with bluish highlights (leather, pear-drops, vanilla-flavoured fruits). The attack is very

DOM. BOUZERAND-DUJARDIN 1999

□ | 0.8 ha | 3,300 | €8-11 |

This pale gold 99 has aromas of citrus fruit and honey accompanied by a little hint of butter. The oakiness is pleasant on the palate, which has a round body with just the right degree of acidity.

Monthélie

» Dom. Bouzerand-Dujardin, pl. de l'Eglise, 21190 Monthélie, tel 03.80.21.20.08, fax 03.80.21.28.16 ▼ ☧ by appt.

DOM. CHANGARNIER 1999★
□ 0.25 ha 1,800 🍷 €11-15

The church of Monthélie was designed in the Romanesque Cluny style (12th century). It overlooks this AOC, which is more of a red wine appellation than a white. Therefore, here we have in the **red** category a **Premier Cru Champs-Fulliot 99** and the **village 99**, each of which is especially commended by the Jury. In white there is a *village* that is all yellowy gold, full of pear and mineral notes. A powerful and full-bodied wine with nice liveliness and good fruitiness on the palate, it is sufficiently well-built and concentrated to last for two to three years, and would go well with brill in cream sauce.

» Dom. Changarnier, pl. du Puits, 21190 Monthélie, tel 03.80.21.22.18, fax 03.80.21.68.21, e-mail changarnier@aol.com ▼ ☧ ev. day except Sun. 9am–12 noon 2pm–7pm

RODOLPHE DEMOUGEOT
La Combe Danay 1999★★
■ 0.3 ha 2,000 🍷 €11-15

This estate, founded in 1992, today covers 7 ha (17.3 acres). Following the advice of wine-expert Kyriakos Kynigopoulos, they mature their wines for 12 months in wood, one quarter of which is new. The wine has undergone a strong pressing to extract this intense colour. The nose is packed with fruit and has light oaky notes. The first impression is good, and is confirmed on the palate, which is full and complex. It opens up revealing prominent but round tannins that guarantee a good potential for laying down.

» Dom. Rodolphe Demougeot, 2, rue du Clos-de-Mazeray, 21190 Meursault, tel 03.80.21.28.99, fax 03.80.21.29.18 ☧ by appt.

PAUL GARAUDET
Le Clos Gauthey 1999★
■ 1er cru 1.1 ha 5,000 🍷 €11-15

This garnet-red wine has a light toasty quality, thanks to well-handled oak, with jammy Griotte cherries. It has some way to go, which is normal at this age. The solid, well-balanced structure has a rather severe character but this will soften with time. Its secondary aromas (blackcurrant leaf and jammy fruit) inspire confidence for the future.

» Paul Garaudet, imp. de l'Eglise, 21190 Monthélie, tel 03.80.21.28.78, fax 03.80.21.66.04 ☧ by appt.

---

needs to be savoured. It has well-balanced toast and soft fruit, and a structured, expressive, lengthy palate. It needs to spend two to three years in the cellar before being served with game.

» Philippe Germain, 21190 Nantoux, tel 03.80.26.05.63, fax 03.80.26.05.12 ▼ ☧ by appt.

LOUIS LATOUR 1998
□ n.c. 1,000 🍷 €11-15

Founded in 1797, the Maison Latour has been based in Beaune since 1867. This wine, matured 12 months in wood, has very clear colour with an intense nose where flowers and orange peel combine with a touch of oak. The palate is simpler but clean, round and ready to drink.

» Maison Louis Latour, 18, rue les Tonneliers, 21204 Beaune Cedex, tel 03.80.24.81.10. fax 03.80.22.36.21, e-mail louislatour@louislatour.com ☧ by appt.

DOM. RENE MONNIER 1999★★
■ 0.47 ha 2,000 🍷 €8-11

There is nothing fake about this wonderful 99, which is the winner of our *coup de coeur*! The colour is a dense, violet-tinted garnet; the aromas are all ripe, crushed strawberries with a hint of elegant oakiness. After a supple and full attack, the well-structured palate opens out with soft fruit and mellow tannins. For a *village*, the quality is unbeatable. And then the tasters make our mouths water by suggesting that the best dish to accompany this wine would be rabbit with cabbage.

» Dom. René Monnier, 6, rue du Dr-Rolland, 21190 Meursault, tel 03.80.21.29.32, fax 03.80.21.61.79 ▼ ☧ ev. day 8am–12 noon 2pm–6pm
» M. et Mme Bouillot

CH. DE MONTHELIE 1998★★
■ 2 ha 7,750 🍷 €11-15

This wine is bottled at the château, and at a real 18th-century one at that. The colour is attractive, the nose delicate, mainly raspberry supported by a hint of vanilla and cinnamon. The tannins are smooth. It is a real treat and has admirable density. Very fine indeed for a 98.

GILBERT ET PHILIPPE GERMAIN 1999★
■ 2.5 ha 5,000 🍷 €8-11

Philippe Germain took over his parents' 11-ha (27-acre) estate in 1995. It is based in Nantoux, a pretty wine-making village whose 15th-century church has a two-sided bell-tower. This deep and brilliant ruby Pinot Noir

594

☛ EARL, Eric de Suremain, rue du Pied-de-la-Vallée, 21190 Monthélie, tel 03.80.21.23.32, fax 03.80.21.66.37 ☒

DOM. J. PARENT Clos Gauthey 1999★
■ 1er cru 1.13 ha 2,700 ▮▮ €11-15

This domaine can pride itself on the fact that it once had Thomas Jefferson as a customer. The Clos Gauthey offers the delights of an 18th-century house with a park dating from 1900. It is surrounded by the vines that have produced this lovely wine with its black highlights and touches of sloes and blackcurrant leaf. It is mouthfilling and rich with plenty of body. Also worth noting is the **red Premier Cru Champs Fulliot 99**, which would be best complemented by wild boar.

☛ Chantal Parent, rue du Château-Gaillard, 21190 Monthélie, tel 03.80.21.21.98, fax 03.80.21.21.98, e-mail annick.parent@wanadoo.fr ☒
☒ by appt.

DOM. PINQUIER-BROVELLI 1999★
■ 1.2 ha 7,000 ▮▮ €8-11

Thierry Pinquier's father was a local wine labourer, and he created this estate through sheer hard work, managing to pull together 5 ha (12.35 acres) over 45 years. This magnificent-looking 99 has some lovely vanilla aromas that are in the process of integrating. It is an elegant and fine wine, almost soft, very appealing on the middle palate and with an attractive fiery note. Its tannins are firm but delicate.

☛ Thierry Pinquier, 5, rue Pierre-Mouchoux, 21190 Meursault, tel 03.80.21.24.87, fax 03.80.21.61.09 ☒
☒ ev. day 8am–12.30pm 1pm–7pm

VINCENT PONT Les Duresses 1999★
■ 1er cru 0.18 ha 1,000 ▮▮ €11-15

Vincent Pont bought his first vines in 1979. Today he is in charge of 6 ha (14.8 acres). He matures his wines in oak. Les Duresses is a *climat* with one part in Monthélie and the largest part in Auxey. This is a deep ruby-red 99. The nose is a blend of aromas of brandied fruit with toasty oak. One taster detected a note of aniseed. The palate is perfectly satisfactory, boasting both body and fullness, and tannins are already quite approachable.

☛ Vincent Pont, rue des Etoiles, 21190 Auxey-Duresses, tel 03.80.21.27.00, fax 03.80.21.24.49 ☒ ☒ by appt.

DOM. JEAN-PIERRE ET LAURENT PRUNIER 1999
■ 0.41 ha 3,000 ▮▮ €8-11

This estate covers 9 ha (22.2 acres) and this Monthélie, which comes from a 41-are plot (0.9 acre), has been matured a year in wood. It has a garnet colour with bluish highlights and an attractive floral richness on the nose. The suppleness and lack of astringency are also pleasing. A hint of alcohol warms it up a little.

595

Auxey-Duresses

Two wine slopes are to be found at Auxey-Duresses. The red Premier Crus of Duresses and Le Val are highly regarded. The 'Meursault' slope produces excellent white wines which, although they lack the reputation of the great appellations, are very affordable. This appellation produced 1,921 hl (50,714 gal) of white wine in 2000, and 4,572 hl (120,701 gal) of red.

Auxey-Duresses

CAVE PRIVEE D'ANTONIN RODET 1998★
■ n.c. 1,170 ▮▮ ♦ €15-23

Nadine Gublin, who is the cellarmaster and oenologist of the great Mercurey company, is the guiding hand behind this deep, dark 98. The Jury was attracted by its fine, complex nose where the cherry does a solo dance. On the palate the wine opens out and reveals prominent tannins that do not in any way trouble its richness, balance, or length. Drink it in two years' time, then serve it over the following three or four together with a side of beef.

☛ Antonin Rodet, 71640 Mercurey, tel 03.85.98.12.12, fax 03.85.45.25.49, e-mail rodet@rodet.com ☒ ☒ ev. day except Sat./Sun. 9am–12 noon 2pm–6pm

PRUNIER-DAMY Les Duresses 1999★
■ 1er cru 0.42 ha 2,500 ▮▮ €11-15

This year's offering from Philippe Prunier is a straightforward wine that is becoming more powerful as it develops. Its colour is very typical of the year, its nose is subtle and intense, all fruit and oak. The robust, soft structure with its elegant tannins does not destroy the flavour of the Pinot and allows one to envisage a fine future for this wine. Its *village* appellation, the **Clos de Ressi 99 red** receives special praise from the Jury. Its well-blended tannins suggest it can be drunk over the next two years.

☛ Philippe Prunier-Damy, rue du Pont-Boillot, 21190 Auxey-Duresses, tel 03.80.21.60.38, fax 03.80.21.26.64 ☒
☒ by appt.

☛ Dom. Jean-Pierre et Laurent Prunier, rue Traversière, 21190 Auxey-Duresses, tel 03.80.21.27.51, fax 03.80.21.27.51 ☒
☒ by appt.

CORINNE ET PASCAL ARNAUD-PONT Le Reugne 1999★

▢ 1er cru　0.43 ha　1,100　▥ €11-15

Peaches or pears? This wine with its delicate fruitiness. The *climat* is the next one down the slopes from Les Duresses and is therefore very similar. This successful 99 vintage has a good, clear, gold colour and the nose at first offers subtle fruity aromas. Dense and opulent, it comes effortlessly to life, backed up by plenty of vitality.

☛ Pascal et Corinne Arnaud-Pont,
36, av. Théophile-Gautier, 75016 Paris,
tel. 01.42.24.74.80 ☑

JEAN-NOEL BAZIN 1998★

■ 1er cru　0.5 ha　3,000　　€8-11

The colour is youthful, bright, limpid; the nose a touch wild toned down by the aroma of blackcurrant leaf. It has softness with cherry notes and is superbly well-balanced, making it very characteristic of the appellation. This 98 vintage is a really genuine wine.

☛ Jean-Noël Bazin, Les Petits Vergers,
21340 La Rochepot, tel. 03.80.21.75.49,
fax 03.80.21.83.71 ☑ ☒ by appt.

DOM. GUY BOCARD 1999★

■ 1er cru　0.19 ha　1,180　▥ €11-15

The villages of Meursault and Auxey-Duresses are only 3 km (1.9 miles) apart, and both have churches dating in part back to the 15th century which are worth a visit. Guy Bocard has vineyards in both AOCs. Fermented for 12 months in oak, this blackish-purple, very vinous 99 vintage with its aromas of blackcurrants and elderberries and very concentrated body holds lots of promise. A wine likely to interest collectors.

☛ Guy Bocard, 4, rue de Mazeray,
21190 Meursault, tel. 03.80.21.26.06,
fax 03.80.21.64.92 ☒ ☒ by appt.

DENIS CARRE Bas des Duresses 1999★

■ 1er cru　n.c.　n.c.　▥ €11-15

A model of its kind. This wine with its intense black cherry colour has barely begun to open, but already shows a rich, solid structure. It has a great deal of character and, while still in hiding, it is not a shrinking violet. It is already very rich and fleshy. Make a note, too, of the one-star **red Village 99**, which is very pleasant and accessible.

☛ Denis Carré, rue du Puits-Bouret,
21190 Meloisey, tel. 03.80.26.02.21,
fax 03.80.26.04.64 ☒ ☒ by appt.

LOUIS CHAVY 1998★

■　n.c.　4,200

The colour sparkles. Very typical of the vintage, this wine is lively with youthful, open aromas. The touches of vegetation and liquorice carry through onto the palate acting together to give the wine great density and concentration.

☛ Louis Chavy, Caveau la Vierge Romaine,
pl. des Marronniers, 21190 Puligny-Montrachet, tel. 03.80.26.33.00,
fax 03.80.24.14.84,
e-mail mallet.b@cva-beaune.fr ☑
☒ ev. day 10am–6pm; cl. Nov. to Mar.

CHRISTIAN CHOLET-PELLETIER 1999★

▢　0.25 ha　800　　€8-11

Full of energy and determination, this wine knows where it is going and how to get there. It has a luminous brilliant colour and the nose reveals buttery notes with vanilla and citrus fruits. The initial impact is quite fleshy, the body pleasant and full. Uncork it now, if you like. This estate gained a *coup de cœur* in 2000 for its 97 vintage.

☛ Christian Cholet,
21190 Corcelles-les-Arts,
tel. 03.80.21.47.76, fax 03.80.21.47.76 ☑
☒ ev. day 8am–12 noon 2pm–6pm

CH. DE CITEAUX Les Duresses 1999★

■ 1er cru　0.45 ha　3,000　▥ €11-15

The Burgundians soften everything. That's why they say Auxey, rather than Auxey, to avoid pronouncing the harsh 'x' sound. And indeed, this wine is full and complete, round and generous on the palate. The tannins are a little harsh but very good, and the finish a positive fanfare. This deep garnet-red Duresses 99 with its light floral notes would make a **sound** addition to your cellar. The **Domaine Boulard 99** is grown, produced, matured and bottled by Philippe Bouzereau and also gains one star.

☛ Dom. Philippe Bouzereau,
Ch. de Citeaux, 18–20, rue de Citeaux,
BP 25, 21190 Meursault, tel. 03.80.21.20.32,
fax 03.80.21.64.34, e-mail info@
domaine.bouzereau.fr ☑ ☒ by appt.

CLOS DU MOULIN AUX MOINES 1999

■　2.5 ha　12,500　▥ €8-11

Established in a magnificently-restored ancient mill, part of the Cluny Abbey, this estate also has accommodation for guests. This garnet-red wine opens on red fruit combined with pronounced oaky, toasty notes. The same aromas are found on the mouth-filling palate. A wine of this structure and length may be left to mature for another two to three years.

☛ Emile Hanique, Dom. du Moulin aux Moines, 21190 Auxey-Duresses,
tel. 03.80.21.60.79, fax 03.80.21.60.79 ☑
☒ ev. day 9am–12.30pm 2pm–7pm

DOM. JEAN-PIERRE DICONNE Les Grands Champs 1999★

■ 1er cru　0.65 ha　3,500　▥ €11-15

Jean-Pierre Diconne is proud of his village with its 15th-century church, and the surrounding region. He recommends a visit to the Hôtel-Dieu at Beaune (8 km/5 miles) to see its multi-panelled painting of Van der Weyden's *Last Judgement*. His wines are worthy of interest too. The one-star red **Premier Cru Les Duresses 99** could well find a place in your cellar, as could this one, with its fine, dark-red colour and with garnet highlights. While concentrated and powerful, it nevertheless has attractive fruit (blackcurrant), and although very pleasant now it will benefit from laying down.

↘ Jean-Pierre Diconne, rue de la Velle, 21190 Auxey-Duresses, tel. 03.80.21.25.60, fax 03.80.21.26.80 ▼ by appt.

JEAN GAGNEROT 1998★★
n.c.　4,000　€11-15

Auxey in its purest state, very true to type, with solid potential. Everything about it is intense, from the first glimpse down to the *foudron* (a Burgundian word meaning the dregs in the bottom of the bottle). A brilliant purple colour – the colour of passion; aromas of violets and peonies on the nose; flavours of raspberry jam with very fine tannins and an impeccable structure.

↘ Jean Gagnerot, 21420 Aloxe-Corton, tel. 03.80.25.00.00, fax 03.80.26.42.00, e-mail vinibeaune@bourgogne.net
▼ by appt.

LES VILLAGES DE JAFFELIN 1998★
n.c.　7,000　€11-15

Light cherry-red in colour, this is a gamey, untamed wine that has real impact. After opening out a little, however, it ends up on a note of sweet spices. It is straightforward with a good, consistent, lengthy finish – very characteristic. Jaffelin forms part of the Jean-Claude Boisset company but its wine-growing and wine-making is managed autonomously.

↘ Jaffelin, 2, rue Paradis, 21200 Beaune, tel. 03.80.22.12.49, fax 03.80.24.91.87

DOM. JESSIAUME PERE ET FILS
1er cru Les Ecusseaux 1999★
0.32 ha　2,100　€15-23

An estate that has remained faithful to this *climat*, near to Bas des Duresses, at the foot of the hillside. This white wine has an interesting pale-gold colour and aromas of hawthorn. The oak from the barrel is not overpowering, the fruitiness balances well with the toasty notes. This well-formed 99 will be ready for drinking in two or three years' time.

↘ Dom. Jessiaume Père et Fils, 10, rue de la Gare, 21590 Santenay, tel. 03.80.20.60.03, fax 03.80.20.62.87 ▼ by appt.

HENRI LATOUR ET FILS 1999★
3.17 ha　11,000　€8-11

A good, intense garnet-red colour, opening with scents of undergrowth and cooked red fruits, this *village* has good, firm, yet soft and mellow tannins. Fruity, elegant, with a touch of vanilla from the oak, it will develop well over the next three to four years.

↘ Henri Latour et Fils, rte de Beaune, 21190 Auxey-Duresses, tel. 03.80.21.65.49, fax 03.80.21.63.08 ▼ by appt.

CATHERINE ET CLAUDE MARECHAL 1999★
n.c.　5,400　€11-15

This intense ruby-red, purple-rimmed 99, which came close to being awarded two stars, is packed with aromas of morello cherries and a light, coffee note derived from the oak. The extensive extraction process shows, particularly on the palate, with the power and concentration of tannins that need a little longer to mellow. It may safely be left to mature for three to four years.

↘ EARL Catherine et Claude Maréchal, 6, rte de Chalon, 21200 Bligny-lès-Beaune, tel. 03.80.21.44.37, fax 03.80.26.85.01 ▼ by appt.

DOM. JEAN PASCAL ET FILS 1999★
1.37 ha　5,400　€11-15

A pale gold colour, the bouquet is very open with appealing aromas of citrus fruits and white flowers. There is a great deal of freshness and character in this wine, which has plenty of length. It would make a pleasant aperitif.

↘ SARL Dom. Jean Pascal et Fils, 20, Grande-Rue, 21190 Puligny-Montrachet, tel. 03.80.21.34.57, fax 03.80.21.90.25 ▼ by appt.

DOM. PIGUET-CHOUET
Les Boutonniers 1999
0.38 ha　1,200　€8-11

Max and Anne-Marye Piguet-Chouet have three sons, so the future of their vineyards is assured. Are you familiar with this *climat* – the last one near Auxey going towards Meursault? Chardonnay does well here. Lemon-yellow in colour, this 99 vintage has a nose that is far from banal. Pineapple, perhaps? Fleshy and fine, though without any great length, it is ready to drink now. It will please those who like a slightly over-mature wine, with secondary aromas of cherry-plums.

↘ Max et Anne-Marye Piguet-Chouet, rte de Meursault, 21190 Auxey-Duresses, tel. 03.80.21.25.78, fax 03.80.21.68.31 ▼ by appt.

PIGUET-GIRARDIN
1er cru Les Grands Champs 1998
5 ha　1,200　€8-11

Les Grands Champs is situated below the Val. With a lively colour, delicate and light fruity aromas, this supple wine is representative of its type and category.

↘ SCE Piguet-Girardin, rue du Meix, 21190 Auxey-Duresses, tel. 03.80.21.60.26, fax 03.80.21.66.61 ▼ by appt.

VINCENT PONT 1999★
1er cru Les Grands Champs 1998
0.7 ha　1,800　€11-15

The **red Village 99** is fresh and fruity with a structure of well-ripened grapes. A notch above – and this is normal – the Premier Cru. Purple in colour with a youthful spirit, it has

Saint-Romain

This vineyard is situated midway between the Côte and the Hautes Côtes. The wines of Saint-Romain – 4,113 hl (108,583 gal) – are mainly whites – 2,098 hl (55,387 gal) in 2000, fruity, fresh-flavoured and, according to the wine-makers, always ready to give more than they promise when young. The location itself is magnificent and very much worth a special trip to see.

aromas of blackcurrants and morello cherries. On the palate it has all the acidity and tannins needed to make a good, solid wine to lay down.

➤ Vincent Pont, rue des Etoiles, 21190 Auxey-Duresses, tel. 03.80.21.27.00, fax 03.80.21.24.49 ⁓ by appt.

DOM. JEAN-PIERRE ET LAURENT PRUNIER 1999

◻ 1.7 ha 5,000 ▥ €8-11

Clothes don't always make the man, but this wine's luminous colour certainly indicates a fine product. Freshly-baked croissants, vanilla, exotic fruits … all these are present in the undeniably complex nose. Its oakiness is delicate and well-integrated. It has a slight aggressiveness, even a little greenness, due to its youth.

➤ Dom. Jean-Pierre et Laurent Prunier, rue Traversière, 21190 Auxey-Duresses, tel. 03.80.21.27.51, fax 03.80.21.27.51 ▣ ⁓ by appt.

PASCAL PRUNIER 1999★

■ 0.38 ha 2,400

Everyone in Auxey is called Prunier… well, nearly everyone. And everybody makes good wine! Pascal Prunier has frequently been praised in the past by our Jury. On the palate, this *village* wine is concentrated and fine at the same time. A wine to please wine-lovers who like chewy fruit. It has a purple colour with garnet highlights and a wide-open nose of kirsch and cherries in eau de vie.

➤ Dom. Pascal Prunier-Bonheur, 23, rue des Plantes, 21190 Meursault, tel. 03.80.21.66.56, fax 03.80.21.67.33, e-mail pascal.prunier-bonheur@wanadoo.fr ▣ ⁓ by appt.

PRUNIER-DAMY Clos du Val 1999★

■ 1er cru 0.16 ha 1,000 ▥ €11-15

At Auxey, wine presses have replaced the many mills that used to be found along the river, but that's nothing to complain about. This cherry-red 99, strong in vinosity, doesn't skimp on aromas: musk, leather, right through to jammy fruits. An imposing attack but with suppleness. Tannic but pleasurable. To drink, perhaps, with Boeuf Bourguignon?

➤ Philippe Prunier-Damy, rue du Pont-Boillot, 21190 Auxey-Duresses, tel. 03.80.21.60.38, fax 03.80.21.26.64 ▣ ⁓ by appt.

PIERRE TAUPENOT

Les Duresses 1998★

■ 1er cru 1.03 ha 1,389 ▥ ▥ €11-15

Saint-Romain is the birthplace of the Taupenot family, some of whom are also at Morey. This brilliant, ruby-red 98 is Duresses to its very soul. The nose opens well, but has not yet reached its full potential. On the palate, the *terroir* is expressed in the classic manner, with a little touch of bitterness.

➤ Pierre Taupenot, rue du Chevrotin, 21190 Saint-Romain, tel. 03.80.21.24.37, fax 03.80.21.68.42 ▣ ⁓ by appt.

FRANCOIS D'ALLAINES 1998★

◻ n.c. 6,000 ▥ €11-15

If Roland Thevenin (who always spoke with praise of the village of Saint-Romain) came back to earth, he would see that his beloved appellation has made great progress! This golden Chardonnay with green glints has tremendous style. Eleven months on lees in barrels (10% of them new). Flint and acacia, the spirit of the *terroir*. Lively, it has stamina and can be left to mature a while. Lime and cinnamon give uplift to the finish.

➤ François d'Allaines, La Corvée du Paquier, 71150 Demigny, tel. 03.85.49.90.16, fax 03.85.49.90.19, e-mail francois@dallaines.com ⁓ by appt.

BERTRAND AMBROISE 1999★★

◻ n.c. n.c. ▥ ▥ ♦ €11-15

Clinging to its fleshy richness, as the village of Saint-Romain clings to its cliff, this Chardonnay is a dense canary-yellow. The oak is elegant, within a context of honey touched with hawthorn. Well-balanced, harmonious, it need have no worries: it will be enjoyed over the next two years.

➤ Maison Bertrand Ambroise, rue de l'Eglise, 21700 Premeaux-Prissey, tel. 03.80.62.30.19, fax 03.80.62.38.69, e-mail bertrand.ambroise@wanadoo.fr ▣

CHRISTOPHE BUISSON

Sous le Château 1999★

◻ n.c. n.c. ▥ ▥ ♦ €11-15

If the **red Sous le Château 99**, which was singled out by the Jury, is to your taste, this same appellation and same *climat* has produced a white with good complex aromas showing citrus fruits. Warm and full at the finish, it also shows elegance and finesse. A brilliant colour highlighted with gold, and lingering lemon and hazelnut notes.

➤ Christophe Buisson, 21190 Saint-Romain, tel. 03.80.21.63.92, fax 03.80.21.67.03 ▣ ⁓ by appt.

DOM. HENRI ET GILLES BUISSON Sous la Velle 1998★
1.27 ha 9,000 · €8-11

A pale colour but full of promise. It doesn't push itself forward, and is all the better for that. Characteristic with a lemony and mineral nose so typical of Chardonnay grown beside rock, it is long on the palate, which retains both these aromas. A very lively wine that should go perfectly with seafood.
➤ Dom. Henri et Gilles Buisson, imp. du Clou, 21190 Saint-Romain, tel. 03.80.21.27.91, fax 03.80.21.64.87 ✓
Ⓣ by appt.
➤ Gilles Buisson

DENIS CARRE Le Jarron 1999★★★
€8-11

Denis Carré is awarded the *palme d'or* for his red Jarron 99. Its colour is mid-way between purple and black, on the nose it is violets and blackberries. On the palate, its concentration and generosity make it a superb and unusual Saint-Romain. The supreme honour of the *coup de coeur* was unanimously awarded by the Grand Jury.
➤ Denis Carré, rue du Puits-Bouret, 21190 Meloisey, tel. 03.80.26.02.21, fax 03.80.26.04.64 Ⓣ by appt.

CHAMPY PERE ET CIE 1999★★★
n.c. 2,400 · €15-23

This remarkable wine is the 'baseline man' of the vintage: the one that everyone lines up on. A clear gold colour with toast (well-handled oak) and white flowers on the nose, supple and lively and sufficiently acidic, this remarkable 99 even manages to come up with a touch of bitter almonds when one least expects it. This long-standing Beaune company (founded in 1720), taken over by the Meurgey family, has produced a great wine.
➤ Maison Champy, 5, rue du Grenier-à-Sel, 21200 Beaune, tel. 03.80.25.09.95, fax 03.80.25.09.99, e-mail champyprost@aol.com ✓ Ⓣ by appt.
➤ Pierre Meurgey, Pierre Beuchet

DOM. DU CHATEAU DE PULIGNY-MONTRACHET 1999★
0.46 ha 3,000 · €11-15

A yellow-gold wine with an open nose with notes of vanilla but also vegetation, with fresh grass and white flowers. On the attack the acidity and sweetness are clearly trying to work together while richness predominates. The palate is overwhelmed with butter and liquorice. 'Finally, a real wine,' wrote one member of the Jury.
➤ SCEA Dom. du Château de Puligny-Montrachet, 21190 Puligny-Montrachet, tel. 03.80.21.39.14, fax 03.80.21.39.07, e-mail chateaupul@aol.com ✓ Ⓣ by appt.

GERMAIN PERE ET FILS Sous le Château 1999★
1.46 ha 5,000 · €8-11

A good range of colours, right through to deep shades of purple. In the discreet bouquet one can distinguish only a light cherry aroma and an agreeable oakiness. The attack is vinous with a certain rustic quality that has the merit of simplicity. The wine has interesting depth, cherry reappearing to add continuity. Full-bodied and round, a very good wine.
➤ EARL Dom. Germain Pere et Fils, rue de la Pierre-Ronde, 21190 Saint-Romain, tel. 03.80.21.60.15, fax 03.80.21.67.87 ✓
Ⓣ by appt.

DOM. DE LA CREA Sous Roche 1999★
1 ha 6,000 · €8-11

It is still too soon to evaluate this wine, but it is going in the right direction and the Jury had every confidence in it. A dark cherry-red colour, vinous, with spicy aromas, and tannins that dominate initially but are well-integrated at the finish, it has all the characteristics of the AOC.
➤ Cécile Chenu-Repolt, La cave de Pommard, 1, rte de Beaune, 21630 Pommard, tel. 03.80.24.62.42, fax 03.80.24.62.44, e-mail cecile.chenu@wanadoo.fr ✓ ev. day 10am–6pm

DOM. DES MARGOTIERES 1999
n.c. 3,000 · €8-11

Monica and Gilles Buisson have both signed the label, which is adorned with cherubs and the legend, '*Le vin, la plus aimable des boissons, date de l'enfance du monde*'. (Wine, the most likeable of drinks, dates back to the time when the world was in its infancy). History may well dispute this claim but wine-lovers will take it to their hearts. This cherry-red 99 is bursting with raspberries and blackberries. It is a light, agreeable wine, of medium length, with well-integrated oak but still fairly tannic, and just the right degree of acidity.
➤ Dom. des Margotières, 21190 Saint-Romain, tel. 03.80.21.27.91, fax 03.80.21.64.87

POULET PÈRE ET FILS 1998★★

□   n.c.   1,800   €23-30

Numbered amongst the finalists for the *coup de coeur*, this wine begins with the word 'very'. In all the tasting notes one reads, 'very elegant', 'very long', 'very fine on the palate', 'a very fine wine', 'very well-made', etc. Slightly milky yellow in colour, with a floral and mineral freshness, this 98 is remarkable for its sincere and straightforward richness and has great class. A branded wine from the Louis Max company.

☛ Poulet Père et Fils, 6, rue de Chaux, BP 4, 21700 Nuits-Saint-Georges, tel. 03.80.62.43.02, fax 03.80.61.28.08

DOM. VINCENT PRUNIER 1999★

■   0.82 ha   6,000   €8-11

'*Goûtons voir, oui, oui, oui, goûtons voir si le vin est bon …*' (Let us taste, yes, yes, yes, let us taste the wine to see if it is good) … goes the Burgundian song. Yes, this wine is good. A clear, if not very pronounced, colour with a nose of redcurrants and fresh cream: a lovely combination. With its distinctive aromas, this is a pleasant wine and ready to drink now. Vincent Prunier does not come from an established wine-making family and he took a BTS in wine-making at Beaune college before coming here in 1988. He started with just 3.5 ha (8.6 acres) of vineyard but, today he reigns over 11 ha (27 acres).

☛ Vincent Prunier, rte de Beaune, 21190 Auxey-Duresses, tel. 03.80.21.27.77, fax 03.80.21.68.87 ▼ by appt.

PASCAL PRUNIER 1999

□   0.92 ha   6,000   €8-11

Brother to Saint Lupicin, Saint Romain spent his life as a hermit in a cave in the Jura, but this wine would surely have tempted him out of his lair. Its pale-yellow appearance would have astonished him. There is nothing diabolical about the almond and acacia nose with its hint of mushrooms. Everything – its unaggressive liveliness, its little hint of hazelnuts – is positively angelic. He would be well-advised to take his time over it, though, since it needs keeping for another one to two years.

☛ Dom. Pascal Prunier-Bonheur, 23, rue des Plantes, 21190 Meursault, tel. 03.80.21.66.56, fax 03.80.21.67.33, e-mail pascal.prunier-bonheur@wanadoo.fr ▼ ▼ by appt.

PRUNIER-DAMY Sous le château 1999

■   0.19 ha   1,200   €8-11

This wine is simple and honest, which is better than having fake characteristics. The colour, somewhere between cherry-red and purple, the nose still developing, this wine has a good balance of tannins and acidity with a light, soft oaky fruitiness. A wine that is still closed and needs time, although more of its qualities were revealed after airing.

☛ Philippe Prunier-Damy, rue du Pont-Boillot, 21190 Auxey-Duresses, tel. 03.80.21.60.38, fax 03.80.21.26.64 ▼ ▼ by appt.

PIERRE TAUPENOT

Côte de Beaune 1998

■   2.36 ha   8,887   €8-11

Its colour has brick-red highlights, a sign that it should be drunk soon. The bouquet covers the whole range from vanilla, to spices, on blackcurrants, and moving onto spices. Vinous and pleasant, this is a straightforward, well-balanced wine.

☛ Pierre Taupenot, rue du Chevrotin, 21190 Saint-Romain, tel. 03.80.21.24.37, fax 03.80.21.68.42 ▼ by appt.

CHARLES VIÉNOT 1998★★

■   n.c.   5,000   €11-15

One of the historic figures of the Côte, Charles Viénot used to be a leading light at all the festivals. The estate now forms part of Les Vins J.-Cl. Boisset and carries on the tradition. It is a pleasure to linger over this wine with its liquid-gold colour and flowery, citrus fruit aromas. On the palate there is as rich suppleness which would compliment ripe perch cooked in cream. This attractive 98 vintage will improve still further.

☛ Charles Viénot, 5, quai Dumorey, BP 102, 21703 Nuits-Saint-Georges, tel. 03.80.62.61.41, fax 03.80.62.37.38

Meursault

The area producing great white Burgundies really begins at Meursault. In 2000, 19,716 hl (520,502 gal) were produced, and the Premiers Crus are famous world-wide: Les Perrières, Les Charmes, Les Poruzots, Les Genevrières, Les Gouttes d'Or, etc. They combine subtlety and strength, flavours of bracken and grilled almond, and the appeal to be drunk young and the quality to keep. Meursault is undoubtedly the 'capital of white Burgundy wines'. A small amount of red wine – 500 hl (13,200 gal) – is also produced.

The 'little châteaux' which still exist in Meursault are relics of a former opulence, and bear witness to a long tradition of famous wines from the area. The festival known as La Paulée began here as a communal banquet that everyone enjoyed at the end of the harvest. It became a traditional event marking the third of the 'Trois Glorieuses', the annual three-day Burgundy wine festival.

FRANCOIS D'ALLAINES 1998★

n.c. 1,650 €23-30

This is a new brand, created in 1990, which, according to the tradition of a *négoce-éleveur*, buys grapes and produces its own *cuvées*. This one is a musketeer in action! It attacks with vivacity and, while it does not have a long reach, it knows how to use its weapon. It wears the golden uniform of the guards of Monseigneur de Chardonnay and its nose opens on mature aromas, particularly of pears. Not surprisingly it has warmth too, but with well-balanced acidity. It should be laid down for several seasons.
➜ François d'Allaines, La Corvée du Paquier, 71150 Demigny, tel. 03.85.49.90.16, fax 03.85.49.90.19, e-mail francois@dallaines.com Y by appt.

BALLOT-MILLOT ET FILS
Les Narvaux 1999★

0.46 ha 2,100 €15-23

By next Saint Vincent's day this wine could make one want to return to Meursault every year. It shows no sign of ostentation but expresses above all the delicacy, freshness and balance typical of a Les Narvaux which, as everyone knows, is a neighbour of Les Genevrières. It is pale gold and, already very good now, it will become more complex later. The **Premier Cru Charmes 99** was also awarded a star.
➜ Ballot-Millot et Fils, 9, rue de la Goutte-d'Or, BP 33, 21190 Meursault, tel. 03.80.21.21.39, fax 03.80.21.65.92 V by appt.

DOM. GUY BOCARD
Les Narvaux 1998★

0.3 ha 1,800 €15-23

Let's tour the whole cellar and hand out the stars; for example, **Village Vieilles Vignes 98**, one star, and **Premier Cru Charmes 99**, commended by the Jury. This wine tops the honours list: straw-yellow with gold highlights and a light attack of blackcurrant leaf, fresh and fruity on the palate. It asks nothing more than to show its best qualities.
➜ Guy Bocard, 4, rue de Mazeray, 21190 Meursault, tel. 03.80.21.26.06, fax 03.80.21.64.92 Y by appt.

BOUCHARD PERE ET FILS
Les Clous 1998

8.66 ha n.c. €23-30

This *climat* is the highest one on the hillside. The wine presented here is a straw-yellow colour highlighted with green. The interesting, floral nose is only just beginning to open out and on the palate it is long rather than full, but overall is well-balanced. Most noticeably it presents a distinctive little touch of personality which holds the attention.
➜ Bouchard Père et Fils, Ch. de Beaune, 21200 Beaune, tel. 03.80.24.80.24, fax 03.80.22.55.88, e-mail france@bouchard-pereetfils.com Y by appt.

This estate is not unknown to our readers and its **Premier Cru Genevrières 97** won a *coup de cœur* in 2000. The 99 vintage gets two stars. But it is this Les Grands Charrons which takes second place on the podium. The finesse of aromas (predominantly honeysuckle), the brilliant gold colour, the instantly noticeable balance of good fruitness with just the right amount of the oak and elegant length – all these combine to make this a great wine. Also worthy of note is the **Les Tessons 99**, which will have more to offer, and which was awarded a star.
➜ Michel Bouzereau et Fils, 3, rue de la Planche-Meunière, 21190 Meursault, tel. 03.80.21.20.74, fax 03.80.21.66.41 V by appt.

DOM. HUBERT BOUZEREAU-GRUERE
Charmes 1999★

1er cru 0.65 ha 2,000 €23-30

Open this Charmes for tasting in four or five years; it is all silk, lace, honeysuckle and dried fruits, and worth leaving to integrate further and continue maturing. Daughters Marie-Laure and Marie-Anne assure the future alongside their father, Hubert Bouzereau.
➜ Hubert Bouzereau-Gruère, 22 a, rue de la Velle, 21190 Meursault, tel. 03.80.21.20.05, fax 03.80.21.68.16 Y by appt.

JOSEPH DE BUCY Bouchères 1999★★

1er cru n.c. 1,160 €23-30

This estate was taken over from the Jean Germain de Meursault company in 1996

GILLES BOUTON
Blagny La Jeunelotte 1999★★

1er cru 0.44 ha 3,700 €15-23

La Jeunelotte is unmistakably a Meursault-Blagny, bordering on a Puligny. This one was much admired. The oak does not obscure the grape variety and while unremarkable on the palate, it is absolutely honest with notes of sweet almonds and lemon. An excellent wine for keeping a little while, already rounded and drinking well now.
➜ Gilles Bouton, Gamay, 21190 Saint-Aubin, tel. 03.80.21.32.63, fax 03.80.21.90.74 V by appt.

MICHEL BOUZEREAU ET FILS
Les Grands Charrons 1999★★

n.c. 8,000 €15-23

MICHEL BOUZEREAU ET FILS
MEURSAULT
"LES GRANDS CHARRONS"
1999

and installed at Beaune, beneath the town ramparts. This wine from the 99 vintage is ranked among the best: limpid gold in colour, it makes an impression right from the first impact of the nose; butter and acacia, citrus fruits and honey are happily present right through to the finish. The oak is well-handled. Well worth keeping for a special occasion.

Maison Joseph de Bucy,
34, rue Eugène-Spuller, 21200 Beaune,
tel. 03.80.24.91.60, fax 03.80.24.91.54,
e-mail jodebucy@aol.com Ⓥ Ⓨ by appt.

DOM. CAILLOT Le Limozin 1998★
0.4 ha 2,500 €15-23

The estate was awarded the *coup de coeur* for a 97 vintage in last year's *Guide*. While it may not win first prize, this wine is a worthy representative of Meursault. Brilliant light gold, it opens out with elegance and richness on an impressive structure. This 98 has all the qualities of the 95 vintage, with an already pronounced character. Have the oak on standby with the cream and morel mushrooms! Also of note was the **Clos du Cromin 98**: brioche, peaches, butter and toast. As rounded and rich as one could wish, and ready to drink.

GAEC Dom. Caillot, 14, rue du Cromin, 21190 Meursault, tel. 03.80.21.21.70, fax 03.80.21.69.58 Ⓥ Ⓨ by appt.

mellowed, will be very representative of its kind. Its richness, well-rounded structure and length hold promise. It was here in 1098, the year the Cistercian order was founded, that the monks of Citeaux first planted vines. Also commended by the Jury was the **Premier Cru Perrières 99**.

Dom. Philippe Bouzereau,
Ch. de Citeaux, 18-20, rue de Citeaux,
BP 25, 21190 Meursault, tel. 03.80.21.20.32,
fax 03.80.21.64.34, e-mail info@
domaine.bouzereau.fr Ⓥ Ⓨ by appt.

ALAIN COCHE-BIZOUARD 1999★
0.4 ha 2,400 €8-11

This is a red Meursault, something of a rarity, with just the right oak balance. It is charming with massive fruitiness. The nose starts with blackcurrant, leading on to gamey, smoky notes. These are confirmed on a palate that has a good structure with excellent tannins. One enthusiastic taster suggested serving it with quail stuffed with foie gras. Consider also the white **Meursault Goutte d'Or 98**, Thomas Jefferson's favourite Premier Cru, which was awarded a star for its slightly liquorice-tinged honeysuckle aromas and the fruitiness on the palate, which is both lively and fresh.

EARL Alain Coche-Bizouard,
5, rue de Mazeray, 21190 Meursault,
tel. 03.80.21.28.41, fax 03.80.21.22.38 Ⓥ
Ⓨ by appt.

VINCENT DANCER Perrières 1999★★
1er cru 0.29 ha 1,800 €15-23

Vincent Dancer, established since 1996, has appeared in the *Guide* before. Here he presents a wine awarded two stars: this lovely 99 vintage is definitely worthy of a place in your cellar, but not for longer than one to two years. Bursting with white flowers and limes, it has a clear, white-gold colour and shows an oakiness that is contained by the lively, subtle, almost airy, richness that dominates the scene. Would it go well with a Poularde de Bresse? On reflection, yes!

Vincent Dancer, 23, rte de Santenay,
21190 Chassagne-Montrachet,
tel. 03.80.21.94.48, fax 03.80.21.94.48,
e-mail vincentdancer@aol.com Ⓥ
Ⓨ by appt.

JOSEPH DROUHIN
En Luraule 1999★★
0.45 ha n.c.

DOM. CHANGARNIER 1999
0.26 ha 2,000 €11-15

The estate has been going for ten, perhaps fifteen, generations: they have lost count. What does count is this brilliant gold 99 with its hint of mushrooms on a fruity background of apples and pears. Fairly characteristic but undeniably rich with well-controlled power, it will be ready for drinking in a year or two.

Dom. Changarnier, pl. du Puits,
21190 Monthélie, tel. 03.80.21.22.18,
fax 03.80.21.68.21, e-mail changarnier@
aol.com Ⓥ Ⓨ ev. day except Sun. 9am–
12 noon 2pm–7pm

DOM. DU CHATEAU DE PULIGNY-MONTRACHET 1999★
0.73 ha 5,000 €15-23

'*Vérité contre tout*' (Truth above all), is the proud motto of this estate, taken over recently by the Crédit Foncier de France. Very oaky, this wine has an attractive appearance and a complex and seductive nose. Clean and rich, it offers fruity flavours of apples and pears with a good toastiness, a sign that the oak is well-integrated.

SCEA Dom. du Château de Puligny-Montrachet, 21190 Puligny-Montrachet,
tel. 03.80.21.39.14, fax 03.80.21.39.07,
e-mail chateaupul@aol.com Ⓥ Ⓨ by appt.

CH. DE CITEAUX Les Narvaux 1999★
0.65 ha 4,000 €15-23

A warm gold colour with green flecks and an open bouquet with toasty notes complemented by citrus fruits, this 99, when it has

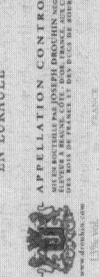

The En Luraule *climat* lies between Les Gouttes d'Or and Les Grands Charrons. This wine has a clear, radiant colour. It is mocha, nougat, pastries; at Meursault they are fond of brioche. It is charmingly fleshy, well-balanced, finely-oaked, seductive. One taster described it as 'a wine that stays in the mouth'.

☎ Joseph Drouhin, 7, rue d'Enfer, 21200 Beaune, tel. 03.80.24.68.88, fax 03.80.22.43.14, e-mail maisondrouhin@drouhin.com Ⓨ by appt.

DOM. EMILE JOBARD

Les Tillets 1999★

☐ 0.36 ha 1,900 €11-15

This pale-gold colour, this aroma of budding acacia, this roundness, all carry a conviction which arouses optimism, despite this wine's present slight tendency to withdraw into itself. A few years in the cellar will see an improvement.

☎ Dom. Emile Jobard, 1, rue de la Barre, 21190 Meursault, tel. 03.80.21.26.43, fax 03.80.21.60.91 Ⓥ Ⓨ by appt.
☎ Jobard-Morey

DOM. DE LA GALOPIÈRE

Les Chevalières 1999★

☐ 0.23 ha 1,500 €15-23

Les Luchets was made famous by a play, written and performed by the actor/wine-grower Jean-Marc Roulot. His Les Chevalières is a fine, heraldic-gold colour. The grape variety, the *terroir*, the oak, are all participants in a chivalrous tournament, but the wine is sufficiently fleshy to stand the pace for some time, without losing its spurs.

☎ Claire et Gabriel Fournier, 6, rue de l'Eglise, 21200 Bligny-lès-Beaune, tel. 03.80.21.46.50, fax 03.80.21.49.93, e-mail c.g.fournier@wanadoo.fr Ⓥ
Ⓨ by appt.

Côte de Beaune (South Central region)

Legend:
- Grands Crus
- AOC localités and Premiers Crus
- Regional AOC areas
- Commune boundaries

SYLVAIN LANGOUREAU
Blagny La Pièce sous le bois 1999★

□ 1er cru   0.45 ha   3,600   €15-23

The Langoureau family arrived in Burgundy at the end of the 19th century. The head of the estate has been in charge since 1988. This is his Meursault-Blagny, a relative of Puligny. A floral, white-gold 99, with appealing, well-tempered yet impressive oak on the palate. While it lacks just a touch of 'bite' it is a high-quality wine.

Sylvain Langoureau, Hameau de Gamay, 21190 Saint-Aubin, tel. 03.80.21.39.99, fax 03.80.21.39.99 by appt.

LA P'TIOTE CAVE Bouchères 1998★★★

□ 1er cru   n.c.   n.c.   €23-30

Les Bouchères is situated in the best area in the heart of the AOC village, alongside its neighbours, Goutte d'Or and Poruzot. This delightful 98 has a very fresh, white gold colour with aromas of honey, tinged with toasted almonds. Still a little reserved and austere, this wine is worth waiting for, as it is very promising.

EARL La P'tiote Cave, 71150 Chassey-le-Camp, tel. 03.85.87.15.21, fax 03.85.87.28.08 ev. day 9am–12 noon 2pm–6pm Mugnier Père et Fils

JEAN LATOUR-LABILLE ET FILS 1999★

■   0.56 ha   3,000   €8-11

Vincent Latour took over this estate in 1998 at the age of 23. Therefore, these are his first wines. Somewhat lost amongst so many whites, this deep purple wine gallantly defends the honour of the reds. Soft and rich at the start, it is well-structured and full, offering aromas of prunes in eau-de-vie on the middle palate. Also worth noting is the red Premier Cru Les Cras 99, full of volume and well-structured with strong oak influence, as is the white Perrières Premier Cru that will take a long time to give up its secrets.

Jean Latour-Labille et Fils, 6, rue du 8-Mai, 21190 Meursault, tel. 03.80.21.22.49, fax 03.80.21.67.86 by appt. Vincent Latour

OLIVIER LEFLAIVE Charmes 1998★

□ 1er cru   1.2 ha   7,400   €38-46

Rich, full, powerful ... this is hardly a wine that inspires pity, or begs for charity. It has all the gold it needs in its colour. Its fruity aromas show just a hint of development. The result is emphatically a Chardonnay, characteristically opulent, which imposes itself forcefully on the palate. One member of the Jury, who is also a great chef, wrote simply, 'Perfect for the restaurant: send in the Poulet de Bresse cooked with cream and morel mushrooms'.

Olivier Leflaive, pl. du Monument, 21190 Puligny-Montrachet, tel. 03.80.21.37.65, fax 03.80.21.33.94, e-mail leflaive-olivier@dial.oleane.com by appt.

DOM. MAILLARD PÈRE ET FILS 1999★

□   0.23 ha   n.c.   €15-23

This is the wine to drink with a fish terrine. It isn't very full but has a fine, light elegant body. Its beauty is complex ... Acidity and sweetness go hand in hand. The colour is impeccable, the nose has fresh hazelnuts, lightly toasted. It is a true *village*.

Dom. Maillard Père et Fils, 2, rue Joseph-Bard, 21200 Chorey-lès-Beaune, tel. 03.80.22.10.67, fax 03.80.24.00.42 by appt.

DOM. MAROSLAVAC-LEGER
Les Murgers 1999★

□   0.25 ha   1,700   €15-23

The full name of Les Murgers is 'Murger de Monthélie', which is close to this village. The 'murger' is a pile of stones dug out of the earth centuries ago. This clear, intense 99, slightly oaky with underdeveloped floral aroma, shows a fruitiness on the palate that, remarkably, continues through to the finish.

Dom. Maroslavac-Leger, 43, Grande-Rue, 21190 Puligny-Montrachet, tel. 03.80.21.31.23, fax 03.80.21.91.39, e-mail maroslavac.leger@wanadoo.fr by appt.

CH. DE MEURSAULT 1998

□ 1er cru   5 ha   30,000   €30-38

A cherub, sweet and tender! Its qualities are not instantly apparent: light gold in colour, oaky, tentatively hawthorn with an underlying toastiness. It is very smooth but with good consistency that has weight and suggests it would be suitable with white meat cooked in a sauce.

Dom. du Château de Meursault, 21190 Meursault, tel. 03.80.26.22.75, fax 03.80.26.22.76 by appt.

DOM. MICHELOT MÈRE ET FILLE Clos du Cromin 1999★

□   0.98 ha   1,500   €15-23

Domaine Michelot Mère et Fille. This new Burgundy will never cease to surprise us. Geneviève took over her father's estate in 1998, in partnership with her daughter Veronique. On the label there is a picture of her grandmother, along with a note stating that the wine is not filtered. With a strong fruit presence on its length, fine colour and, for the moment, strong oaky notes, this is a good example of the 99 vintage that should be ready in another 18 months.

Dom. Michelot Mère et Fille, 24, rue de la Velle, 21190 Meursault, tel. 03.80.21.68.99, fax 03.80.21.27.65 by appt.

MOILLARD Clos du Cromin 1999★

□   1.6 ha   7,500   €23-30

Always very forward in their development, these vines close to Volnay-Santenot are generally harvested quite early. They have produced this light gold 99 with hawthorn and toasted almonds, appealing on the palate and of very acceptable length. Not many high points but it is in keeping with expectations; a true *village*.

↗ Dom. Moillard, chem. rural 29, 2, rue François-Mignotte, 21700 Nuits-Saint-Georges, tel. 03.80.62.42.22, fax 03.80.61.28.13, e-mail nuicave@wanadoo.fr ☑ ☒ ev. day 10am–6pm; cl. Jan.

BERTRAND DE MONCENY
Bellevue 1999★

□ ■   n.c.   12,000   €23-30

This is a good Meursault of characteristic structure. Very classic, with lemony and floral notes, touches of ripe grapes, and a charming attack. It is rich, but not overly so, has a pure fruitiness and is agreeably soft. Bellevue does not seem to be a *climat*, and Bertrand de Monceny is one of the J.-P Nié brands.

↗ Cie des Vins d'Autrefois, abbaye Saint-Martin, 53, av. de l'Aigue, 21200 Beaune, tel. 03.80.26.33.00, fax 03.80.24.14.84, e-mail mallet.b@cva-beaune.fr
↗ Jean-Pierre Nié

PIGUET-GIRARDIN
Vieilles vignes 1999

□   2 ha   n.c.   €11-15

This is an example of a restrained 99 vintage. Limpid pale-gold without being conspicuous; a nose of hazelnuts, butter and the flesh of oranges. Its suppleness is quite pronounced; it has not great structure but has a pleasant character with almond notes.

↗ SCE Piguet-Girardin, rue du Meix, 21190 Auxey-Duresses, tel. 03.80.21.60.26, fax 03.80.21.66.61 ☒ ☒ by appt.

CAVE PRIVEE D'ANTONIN RODET
Perrières 1998★★

□ 1er cru   n.c.   608   €38-46

Awarded a *coup de coeur*, this one is phenomenal! A massive wine, almost completely developed, putting the Perrières in tune with the *terroir*. Menthol, flint and lemon all herald a pronounced opulence that would not disgrace a Meursault. The Grand Jury put it in first place.

↗ Antonin Rodet, 71640 Mercurey, tel. 03.85.98.12.12, fax 03.85.45.25.49, e-mail rodet@rodet.com ☑ ☒ ev. day except Sat. Sun. 9am–12 noon 2pm–6pm.

ROPITEAU 1999★

■   n.c.   6,000   €11-15

Red Meursault is a rare beast, but when it has Ropiteau on the label it needs no further proof of its identity. The Boisset family shows great wisdom in retaining the tradition and know-how of the companies it takes over. This vermilion-red 99 has appealing gamey and spicy notes. Immediately evident is its well-blended structure where the tannins support the fruitiness without restricting it. A wine with good potential richness. The **white Premier Cru Perrières 98**, full, rich and warming with a toasty, apricot nose, was also awarded a star.

↗ Ropiteau Frères, 13, rue du 11-Novembre, 21190 Meursault, tel. 03.80.21.69.20, fax 03.80.21.69.29 ☑ ☒ ev. day 9am–7pm; cl. mid-Nov. to Easter

DE SOUSA-BOULEY
Les Millerans 1999★

□   0.51 ha   1,800   €11-15

Down in the village, this *climat* has produced a wine that will go well with pike quenelles or fresh-water crayfish. It has light-green highlights with toasty aromas including a hint of mushrooms. Long and quite lively, with a romantic hazelnut note.

↗ Albert de Sousa-Bouley, 25, RN 74, 21190 Meursault, tel. 03.80.21.22.79, fax 03.80.21.66.76 ☑ ☒ ev. day 8am–8pm

HENRI DE VILLAMONT 1999

□   n.c.   12,000   €23-30

This very green wine, presented by a Burgundy subsidiary of the Swiss group Schenk, has a grapefruit and lime nose that is very lively. Rich and round, but with good acidity, it is without doubt a wine to lay down. It tends towards citrus fruits on the palate.

↗ SA Henri de Villamont, rue du Dr-Guyot, 21420 Savigny-lès-Beaune, tel. 03.80.24.70.07, fax 03.80.22.54.31, e-mail hdv@planetb.fr ☒ ☒ ev. day except Tue. 10.30am–6pm; cl. 15 Nov.–15 Mar.

Blagny

The Blagny vineyard, straddling the communes of Meursault and Puligny-Montrachet, is a self-contained vineyard that grew up around the village. Remarkable red wines are produced under the Appellation Blagny – 256 hl (6,758 gal) in 2000 – but the majority of the area is planted with Chardonnay, producing Meursault Premier Cru or Puligny-Montrachet Premier Cru, depending on the commune.

DOM. HENRI CLERC ET FILS

Sous le Dos d'Ane 1998★   🌐 €23–30

94 95 **96** 97 98

Established in the 16th century, this estate traditionally sent its harvest to a *négoce*, until 1965 when Bernard Clerc started making his own wine. An intense garnet-red with a slightly mauve tinge, his wine fulfils its duties on the nose with finesse: wild cherries, prunes, boxwood, dead leaves. Its tannins form a good structure that needs to mature for several years. The Dos d'Ane is still astringent and needs to mellow but it is promising (should be laid down for five to six years).

➤ Dom. Henri Clerc et Fils, pl. des Marronniers, 21190 Puligny-Montrachet, tel. 03.80.21.32.74, fax 03.80.21.39.60 ☑

➤ Bernard Clerc

DOM. CHARLES ALLEXANT ET FILS Les Meix 1999

▢   0.41 ha   2,500   🌐 €15–23

Limpid with golden highlights, this wine has hazelnuts and lilacs on the nose. It starts with an agreeable finesse that bathes in freshness. Acidity? No problem. The finish? A hint of liquorice. This *climat* is found just below Les Pucelles. It has Puligny characteristics and should receive an honourable mention.

➤ SCE Dom. Charles Allexant et Fils, rue du Château, Cissey, 21190 Merceuil, tel. 03.80.26.83.27, fax 03.80.26.84.04 ☑

Ⓨ ev. day 8am–12 noon 1.30pm–6pm; Sat./Sun. by appt.

MICHEL BOUZEREAU

Les Champs Gains 1999★

▢ 1er cru   0.3 ha   n.c.   🌐 €23–30

At an altitude of more than 300 m (981 ft), and on the Blagny hillside, Les Champs Gains is the highest Premier Cru in the whole of the area surrounding Montrachet. This wine conforms exactly to the standard model for the appellation and *climat*. Delicate and floral, it seeks to seduce rather than to convince and the acidity offers some relief. It is undeniably light but has class.

➤ Michel Bouzereau et Fils, 3, rue de la Planche-Meunière, 21190 Meursault, tel. 03.80.21.20.74, fax 03.80.21.66.41 ☑

Ⓨ by appt.

Puligny-Montrachet

Puligny-Montrachet is the fulcrum of the Côte d'Or white wines, situated between its two neighbours, Meursault to the north and Chassagne to the south. The vineyards of this small, peaceful commune occupy half the area of those in Meursault and are two-thirds the size of those in Chassagne, but despite their apparently modest extent they produce the greatest Grand Cru white wines in Burgundy, sharing the Montrachet name with Chassagne.

The geologists of the University of Dijon have discovered that the Grands Crus are located on an outcrop of Bathonian limestone, giving them greater finesse, harmony and aromatic subtlety than the neighbouring marlstone. The AOC produced 11,120 hl (293,568 gal) of white wines and 258 hl (6,811 gal) of red in 2000.

The other *climats* and Premier Crus of the commune have a notably expressive bouquet smelling of vegetation with hints of essential oils and vegetal resins.

DOM. CAILLOT Les Pucelles 1998★★

▢ 1er cru   0.22 ha   350   🌐 €39–46

In his book, published in 1831, Doctor Morelot mentioned the touch of vanilla found in Burgundy wines, which proves that this is nothing new. Marvellous in every way, pert rather than modest, this Les Pucelles is still too toasty to be evaluated at the moment, but in two or three years it will satisfy the most demanding wine-drinker. There is a magnificent wine waiting to be discovered.

➤ GAEC Dom. Caillot, 14, rue du Cromin, 21190 Meursault, tel. 03.80.21.21.70, fax 03.80.21.69.58 ☑ by appt.

DOM. JEAN CHARTRON

Les Folatières 1999★

▢ 1er cru   0.5 ha   3,500   🌐 €46–76

Delicacy or lightness? That was the question our tasters asked themselves. That said, they are not amateurs; one of them, without knowing what the wine was, wrote on his slip: 'Comes from below Puligny'. Precisely, this is a Les Folatières. Light in colour and well-presented with traces of hazelnut on the nose, this 99 vintage is freshness personified, with spring blossom and an apple and pear fruitiness. A fine Premier Cru, gentle rather than pungent. Also of interest is the **Clos de la Pucelle 99**, which gets the same mark.

➤ Dom. Jean Chartron, 13, Grande-Rue, 21190 Puligny-Montrachet, tel. 03.80.21.32.85, fax 03.80.21.36.35 ☑

Ⓨ ev. day 10am–12 noon 2pm–6pm; cl. mid-Nov. to Mar.

DOM. DU CHATEAU DE PULIGNY-MONTRACHET 1999★

1.5 ha 10,000 €23-30

Sempé, the cartoonist, used to come to tastings here. The freshness in this wine would have pleased him. The colour is an intense yellow, the oak is concentrated and the complex aromas (beeswax, cloves) clearly definable. The almost unanimous verdict was that this will be a great wine in two to four years.

☎ SCEA Dom. du Château de Puligny-Montrachet, 21190 Puligny-Montrachet, tel. 03.80.21.39.14, fax 03.80.21.39.07, e-mail chateaupul@aol.com ▾ ▾ by appt.

DOM. DUPONT-FAHN

Les Grands Champs 1999★

n.c. 1,200 €11-15

You see Le Clavaillon? Les Grands Champs is its neighbour. The gold of a thousand flames shines here. The first thing to reach the nose is freshness, followed by full-bodied notes of citrus fruits and finally the vanilla takes over. What richness and fleshiness on the palate! A wine to drink with fish? Undoubtedly, and it had better be a big one!

☎ Michel Dupont-Fahn, 21190 Monthélie, tel. 03.80.21.26.78, fax 03.80.21.21.22 ▾ by appt.

RAYMOND DUREUIL-JANTHIAL

1er cru Les Champs Gains 1999

0.19 ha 1,200 €23-30

Having married the only daughter of a wine-producer from Rully, this wine-grower now has one foot in the Côte de Beaune and the other in the Côte Chalonnaise. This Premier Cru, unctuous at first, then lively with well-integrated oak, is well-structured but needs to mature. Its notes of toastiness, with nuances of citrus fruits, and its light-gold colour make a very good impression.

☎ Raymond Dureuil-Janthial, rue de la Buisserolle, 71150 Rully, tel. 03.85.87.02.37, fax 03.85.87.00.24 ▾ ev. day 9am–12 noon-3pm-7pm; Sun. by appt.

CH. GENOT-BOULANGER

Les Nosroyes 1998

1.1 ha 4,900 €15-23

This *climat* is near Les Perrières, but anywhere in Puligny one is never far from Paradise. Green-gold? More lime-green. The wine-lover will find the nose has lilac blossom, pine resin and even gunflint. The oak has not yet entirely disappeared and it gives the impression of being very young. If you want to drink it reasonably soon it will need decanting.

☎ SCEV Ch. Génot-Boulanger, 25, rue de Cîteaux, 21190 Meursault, tel. 03.80.21.49.20, fax 03.80.21.49.21, e-mail genot.boulanger@wanadoo.fr ▾ by appt.

DOM. HUBERT LAMY

Les Tremblots 1999★

0.9 ha 7,900 €15-23

Les Tremblots is bright in colour with a nose of hazelnut butter and good length on the palate. Its great variety of aromas make this an interesting wine but its reserved manner and low acidity indicate that it's not likely keep more than two or three years.

☎ Dom. Hubert Lamy, Paradis, 21190 Saint-Aubin, tel. 03.80.21.32.55, fax 03.80.21.38.32 ▾ ▾ by appt.

SYLVAIN LANGOUREAU

La Garenne 1999★★

0.55 ha 4,400 €15-23

Two very good wines: the **Premier Cru Les Chalumeaux 99** (one star) and, even better, this one. La Garenne is on the road up to Blagny. Under its golden exterior this is a wine that touches of honey and fresh butter, fit for Red Riding Hood's basket. Rich and round, it is still showing slightly too much alcohol, but of the ripeness of the grape and the complexity of the nose will have plenty to work on during the two to five years it needs to spend in the cellar. It could even be served with salmon in a tartare sauce.

☎ Sylvain Langoureau, Hameau de Gamay, 21190 Saint-Aubin, tel. 03.80.21.39.99, fax 03.80.21.39.99 ▾ ▾ by appt.

DOM. LARUE Les Garennes 1999★

1er cru

0.59 ha 4,500 €23-30

Crystalline and shot through with the famous green glints, this wine appears mature though still very young. Honeysuckle, a charred note and a touch of mineral are all combined here. Subtle and powerful at the same time on the palate, it is almost ready to drink.

☎ Dom. Larue, Gamay, 21190 Saint-Aubin, tel. 03.80.21.30.74, fax 03.80.21.91.36 ▾ by appt.

ROLAND MAROSLAVAC-LEGER

Les Combettes 1999

1er cru

0.16 ha 1,000 €23-30

This Les Combettes has the pronounced aroma and flavour of hazelnuts. A good colour, it is a wine that seduces the palate with a touch of Meursault (which is right next door). The structure tends to be sustained by alcohol. It will have developed its 'sting' in two years' time.

☎ Dom. Maroslavac-Léger, 43, Grande-Rue, 21190 Puligny-Montrachet, tel. 03.80.21.31.23, fax 03.80.21.91.39, e-mail maroslavac.leger@wanadoo.fr ▾ by appt.

PROSPER MAUFOUX 1998★

n.c. n.c. €23-30

A strong gold colour with green highlights, this vigorous 98 is still full of strength. A wine that goes to the head, as we used to say. Light floral honey with notes of toasted almonds, the nose is very pleasing. The first impression on the palate is slightly harsh but leads to a solid, well-founded structure while still keeping its strict, dense aspect. In two to three years it will be well-balanced and probably more round.

↘ Prosper Maufoux, pl. du Jet-d'Eau, 21590 Santenay, tel. 03.80.20.60.40, fax 03.80.20.63.26,
e-mail prosper.maufoux@wanadoo.fr ▼
Ⓨ by appt.

DOM. BERNARD MILLOT 1999★ □ Ⓜ €11–15
0.45 ha 1,500

A pale straw colour with classic green highlights that invite you to look deeper. Agreeably, though delicately, fruity (cherry plums), the nose reveals a background of floral notes. Initially fresh on the palate, the same aromas develop with good length and with an underlying richness. It is an attractive wine and very true to type.

↘ EARL Bernard Millot,
27, rue de Mazeray, 21190 Meursault, tel. 03.80.21.20.91, fax 03.80.21.62.50 ▼
Ⓨ by appt.

DOM. JEAN PASCAL ET FILS 1999★ □ Ⓜ €15–23
3.3 ha 6,000

Pale gold with grey flecks in colour with a freshness touched with lemon and ferns, this wine has an elegant profile, slender on the palate, though not at all thin. The fruitiness is very much in evidence. Soft with a very long finish, it shows good promise for the future. An excellent *village* wine.

↘ SARL Dom. Jean Pascal et Fils,
20, Grande-Rue, 21190 Puligny-Montrachet, tel. 03.80.21.34.57, fax 03.80.21.90.25 ▼
Ⓨ by appt.

FERNAND ET LAURENT PILLOT
Noyers Brets 1999★ □ Ⓜ €15–23

The Noyet Brets *climat* is south of the village, between Enseignères and Tremblots. Deep yellow-gold, this lovely 99 vintage presents a good quality bouquet that is very promising and has an impressive palate. It has all it needs to mature well. Supple with touches of almonds, vinous and rich, it tempts you to drink it now but you would be well-advised to lay it down for a further two to five years.

↘ Fernand and Laurent Pillot, 13, rue des Champgains, 21190 Chassagne-Montrachet, tel. 03.80.21.33.64, fax 03.80.21.92.60,
e-mail lfpillot@club-internet.fr ▼
Ⓨ by appt.

REINE PEDAUQUE 1999 □ Ⓜ €15–23
n.c. 9,000

This wine will come into its own once it has matured but this will take time. It is a typical Chardonnay with light, toasty aromas but, as we have said, it needs to be kept for two – perhaps five – years.

↘ Reine Pédauque,
Le Village, 21420 Aloxe-Corton,
tel. 03.80.25.00.00, fax 03.80.26.42.00,
e-mail rpedauque@axnet.fr Ⓨ by appt.

CAVE PRIVEE D'ANTONIN RODET Hameau de Blagny 1998 Ⓜ €46–76
□ 1er cru n.c. 718

Here one is at Blagny, physically. Unctuous, velvety and supple, this is a wine to leave for one to two years before enjoying its slightly unusual, but compelling charm.

↘ Antonin Rodet, 71640 Mercurey,
tel. 03.85.98.12.12, fax 03.85.45.25.49,
e-mail rodet@rodet.com ▼ Ⓨ ev. day except Sat. Sun. 9am–12 noon 2pm–6pm

ROPITEAU 1999★ □ Ⓜ €15–23
n.c. 10,000

Direct, clean, this is a very dry wine. Yellow and green in colour, in keeping with tradition, very perfumed (fruit, vanilla), and still improving. On the palate it is round and agreeable, with notes of almonds and hazelnuts and noticeably good length. The Ropiteau estate is, undoubtedly, one of the flagship companies of the Jean-Claude Boisset family of wine-producers.

↘ Ropiteau Frères,
13, rue du 11-Novembre, 21190 Meursault, tel. 03.80.21.69.20, fax 03.80.21.69.29 ▼
Ⓨ ev. day 9am–7pm; cl. mid-Nov. to Easter

DOM. ROUX PERE ET FILS
Les Enseignères 1999★ □ Ⓜ €23–30
0.33 ha 2,300

Euripides taught us that character is what counts, and here is the proof. This attractive 99 has a well-balanced structure and harmony. Fairly light gold in colour, it has aromas of almonds and ripe apple and pear. It should develop well. The 97 vintage won a *coup de coeur* in 2000. This enterprising family has recently established itself in the Languedoc region, as have many other Burgundy companies.

↘ Dom. Roux Père et Fils,
21190 Saint-Aubin, tel. 03.80.21.32.92,
fax 03.80.21.35.00 ▼ Ⓨ by appt.

RENE TARDY ET FILS 1999★ □ Ⓜ €15–23
0.39 ha 2,900

Joël Tardy has managed this estate since 1985. He bought this plot of vineyards together with 35 shareholders, all lovers of fine wines. This one will have to wait for several years to deliver all that it promises. At the moment it is all youthful freshness and seduced the entire Jury, except for one taster who would have preferred it to have more personality. We will have to wait two or three years to see.

↘ Dom. René Tardy et Fils, 32, rue Caumont-Bréon, 21700 Nuits-Saint-Georges,
tel. 03.80.61.20.50, fax 03.80.61.36.96,
e-mail tardyrene@aol.com ▼ Ⓨ by appt.

VAUCHER PERE ET FILS 1999★ □ Ⓜ €23–30
n.c. n.c.

This warmly-coloured, bright gold 99 has complex aromas of toast and oak hinting at butter and acacia. Its structure, well-balanced in the French way, gives a full, round but firm wine, slightly developed perhaps, but with

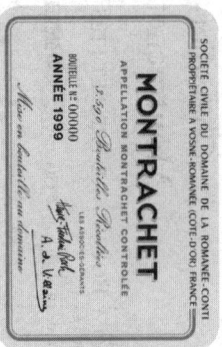

enough acidity to give hope of an interesting future. Vaucher was bought by the Cottin family (Labouré-Roi at Nuits).

♠ Vaucher Père et Fils, rue Lavoisier, 21700 Nuits-Saint-Georges, tel. 03.80.62.64.00, fax 03.80.62.64.10

Y by appt.

Montrachet, Chevalier, Bâtard, Bienvenus Bâtard, Criots Bâtard

In the recent past, the most astonishing characteristic of the Grands Crus was that they took quite some time before fully revealing the exceptional quality expected of them. It could mean waiting ten years for a 'great' Montrachet to reach maturity or five years for the Bâtard and its cohorts; the Chevalier-Montrachet alone seemed to be more expressive much earlier.

However, in the last few years some of the Montrachet pressings show a bouquet of exceptional power and complex flavours whose quality can be appreciated immediately, without having to guess how they may develop in the future. The amount of wine is very small: all the Montrachet Grands Crus accounted for only 1,512.23 hl (39,922.87 gal) in 2000.

Montrachet

DOM. DE LA ROMANEE-CONTI

1999★★★
□ Gd cru   0.67 ha   3,590   ▦ +€76
|83| |86| ⑨⓪ |91| 93 97 98 ⑨⑨

Jasmine can be satisfied with her work (Jasmine being the work horse, a *Comtois* from the Franche-Comté, belonging to Sébastien Denis which, since 1999, has been used for ploughing on the estate in Romanée-

Conti, Montrachet and a part of Richebourg), for this 99 vintage has developed very well. Harvested very late and extremely mature, it has nonetheless retained its freshness. A point to remember about Montrachet wines: 1998, a year which produced botrytis, produced an opulent, honeyed wine; in this following year, with no botrytis, the wine is less honeyed, more subtle, rigorous, almost austere, but fascinatingly seductive. It may not reflect the roundness of the beauties in a baroque painting, but it offers purity of line and is in perfect taste. An impression of lightness goes along with a dazzling density.

♠ SC du Dom. de La Romanée-Conti, 1, rue Derrière-le-Four, 21700 Vosne-Romanée, tel. 03.80.62.48.80, fax 03.80.61.05.72

OLIVIER LEFLAIVE 1999★★

□ Gd cru   n.c.   n.c.   ▦ +€76

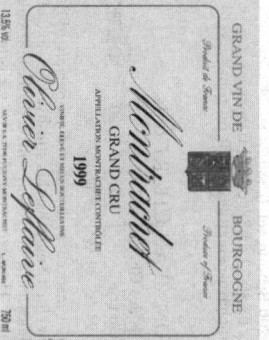

'This is not a wine, it's an event' said Frank M. Schoonmaker about a Montrachet. This is a warm golden-coloured 99 that is rich and dry, unctuous and sophisticated, its already very open nose boasts peaches, wild roses and mandarin peel. On the palate it is very clean and pure with an added mineral note and a long finish. It will be a great wine in a few years, and for many years to come.

♠ Olivier Leflaive, pl. du Monument, 21190 Puligny-Montrachet, tel. 03.80.21.37.65, fax 03.80.21.33.94, e-mail leflaive-olivier@dial.oleane.com ✉

Y by appt.

Chevalier-Montrachet

Chevalier-Montrachet

DOM. BOUCHARD PERE ET FILS
1998★★★

| □ Gd cru | 2.54 ha | n.c. | 🍷 | +€76 |

Domaine Bouchard Père & Fils
1998
CHEVALIER-MONTRACHET
APPELLATION CHEVALIER-MONTRACHET CONTRÔLÉE
GRAND CRU
CE VIN A ÉTÉ RÉCOLTÉ, ÉLEVÉ ET MIS EN BOUTEILLE PAR
BOUCHARD PÈRE & FILS
CHÂTEAU DE BEAUNE, CÔTE D'OR, FRANCE
PRODUCE OF FRANCE - PRODUIT DE FRANCE

When in Beaune make sure to visit this domaine, owned by Henriot Champagne since 1995: its superb cellars are housed in the bastions of the 15th-century fortress. Bouchard is the most important estate of this Grand Cru. This lovely 98, very classic in colour, offers bold aromas of pineapple, walnuts and even rose-water. On the palate it follows through with a classy complexity and a strong attack, lively and very elegant but with a certain opulence.

☛ Bouchard Père et Fils, Ch. de Beaune, 21200 Beaune, tel. 03.80.24.80.24, fax 03.80.22.55.88, e-mail france@bouchard-pereetfils.com ☎ by appt.

DOM. JEAN CHARTRON
Clos des Chevaliers 1999★

| □ Gd cru | 0.55 ha | 2,000 | 🍷 | +€76 |

91 92 93 94 **|95|** 96 **|97|** **98** 99

Fermented and matured in barrels (40% new) for 12 months, this still-lively 99, like all adolescents, is passing through the difficult stage. However, its already well-defined colour inspires confidence. The bouquet opens gradually with a variety of aromas: verbena, lemon, ginger. With a well-balanced acidity this wine is pleasant to drink already, so enjoy it without waiting too long (three to five years).

☛ Dom. Jean Chartron, 13, Grande-Rue, 21190 Puligny-Montrachet, tel. 03.80.21.32.85, fax 03.80.21.36.35 ☑ ☎ ev. day 10am–12 noon 2pm–6pm; cl. mid-nov. to Mar.

LOUIS LATOUR Les Demoiselles 1998

| □ Gd cru | 0.59 ha | 2,400 | 🍷 | +€76 |

These vineyards have quite a history. The demoiselles referred to are Adèle and Julie Voillot and their story began in the middle of the 19th century. For a time the estate belonged to Léonce Bocquet, then Louis Jadot, and finally Louis Latour acquired it in 1913. As to the wine, Les Demoiselles is a beautiful colour with pronounced highlights. The aroma? Beeswax, austere and reserved, evocative of the Carmelite convent at Beaune. It is not to today's taste but it still exists. Will these Demoiselles blossom out within the next ten years?

☛ Dom. Louis Latour, 18, rue des Tonneliers, 21204 Beaune, tel. 03.80.24.81.00, fax 03.80.22.36.21, e-mail louislatour@louislatour.com ☎ by appt.

Bâtard-Montrachet

DOM. BACHELET-RAMONET PERE ET FILS
1999★★★

| □ Gd cru | 0.5 ha | 1,500 | 🍷 | €46-76 |

Complex, well-balanced and very luminous, this wine seduces right from the start. Spring flowers, warm brioche, toast, honey: it could be the echo of Jean Lenoir, a native of the area, describing the aromas of Chassagne wines. The attack is perfectly straightforward, the oak delicate, the middle palate full of ripe fruit with an unexpected touch of bitterness. Don't be impatient, it needs to be laid down for a long time.

☛ Dom. Bachelet-Ramonet Père et Fils, 11, rue du Parterre, 21190 Chassagne-Montrachet, tel. 03.80.21.32.49, fax 03.80.21.91.41 ☑ ☎ by appt.

LOUIS LEQUIN 1999★★

| □ Gd cru | 0.12 ha | 810 | 🍷 | €46-76 |

94 95 98 99

Finalist, and a close runner-up for a *coup de coeur*, this is – as they used to say during the age of the *Toison d'or* (order of the Golden Fleece, founded in the 15th century by Philip the Good, Duke of Burgundy) – the *Grand Bâtard de Bourgogne* (the great Bastard of Burgundy), magnificent in gold with crystal-line highlights. Extraordinarily full-bodied and immensely distinctive with flavours of almonds, honey and honeysuckle, rich, dense and fleshy, the structure is significant. The alcohol is strong but this need not give concern, it is normal in a Montrachet. This wine has enormous potential. The plot, situated close to Chassagne, was bought by Jean Lequin in 1938 (part of the former Lequin-Roussot estate, which was divided up for reasons of succession).

☛ Louis Lequin, 1, rue du Pasquier-du-Pont, 21590 Santenay, tel. 03.80.20.63.82, fax 03.80.20.67.14, e-mail louis.lequin@wanadoo.fr ☑ ☎ by appt.

Bienvenues-Bâtard-Montrachet

RENE LEQUIN-COLIN 1999★★
□ Gd cru   0.12 ha   750   €46-76

This plot of land, situated on the Chassagne slope, was created when a family estate was split in half by the succession laws and has been known as Lequin since 1938. It has yielded this superb 99. Its colour is direct and clean. Acacia flowers and hazelnuts balance the toastiness on the nose. On the palate it is seduction personified, silky and generous, bountiful. Full of character, this wine, however, is not straightforward and needs time to reveal all its qualities. We mustn't forget that a *coup de coeur* was awarded last year to the three-star 98 vintage.

♠ EARL René Lequin-Colin, 10, rue de Lavau, 21590 Santenay, tel. 03.80.20.66.71, fax 03.80.20.66.70, e-mail renelequin@aol.com ✓ Y by appt.

VEUVE HENRI MORONI 1999★
□ Gd cru   0.32 ha   1,800   €46-76

Established in 1922 by Henri Moroni, this *négoce* company was taken over by Marc Domain and his wife Jacqueline, to complement their wine-producing business. It presents here a bronze-coloured and very intense wine which, a while after opening, reveals aromas of honey and toast. The character is already evident and will assert itself from year to year. For the moment the wine is fairly reserved and has prominent mineral characteristics.

♠ Veuve Henri Moroni, 1, rue de l'Abreuvoir, 21190 Puligny-Montrachet, tel. 03.80.21.30.48, fax 03.80.21.33.08, e-mail veuve.moroni@wanadoo.fr ✓ Y by appt.

JEAN-CLAUDE BACHELET 1998★★
□ Gd cru   0.09 ha   n.c.   €38-46

A plot of 9 a 42 ca (1,196 sq yds), acquired by the Dupaquier family in 1960, has produced this wine with a fine, strong green-gold colour and aromas of spring flowers with some orange marmalade peeking through. Its acidity obviously indicates that this is a wine that will keep a long time. Finesse? In its delicate lacy finish, the tasters were delighted to identify truffles and amber alongside the classic characteristics of this Grand Cru. Indisputably a great wine which in ten years' time – or even longer – will be much talked about.

♠ Jean-Claude Bachelet, rue de la Fontaine, 21190 Saint-Aubin, tel. 03.80.21.31.01, fax 03.80.21.97.71, e-mail j.c-bachelet@aol.com ✓ Y by appt.

DOM. BACHELET-RAMONET PERE ET FILS 1999★
□ Gd cru   0.28 ha   500   €46-76

This pale-gold wine has brilliance. The oak is still very pronounced but it is surrounded by an lively combination of wild roses, verbena, lemons, apples and pears. All this carries through to the palate where there is also noticeable acidity. It finishes on buttery notes with toasty nuances. To lay down for five to ten years, when it will go well with a Poularde de Bresse.

♠ Dom. Bachelet-Ramonet Père et Fils, 11, rue du Parterre, 21190 Chassagne-Montrachet, tel. 03.80.21.32.49, fax 03.80.21.91.41 ✓ Y by appt.

CHARTRON ET TREBUCHET 1999★★
□ Gd cru   n.c.   600   +76

Here the president of the *Bureau Interprofessionel des Vins de Bourgogne* (Interprofessional Bureau for Burgundy Wines) is carrying on his own business. The wine is pale gold with green highlights. The aroma doesn't hide the 12 months spent in good oak but opens progressively on wild roses, linden flower and honey. Its balance and finesse, the delicacy of the tannins from the oak, and the aromas of ripe fruits (citrus fruits) left the Jurors lost in admiration for so much elegance. It will give pleasure for eight to fifteen years.

♠ Chartron and Trébuchet, 13, Grande-Rue, 21190 Puligny-Montrachet, tel. 03.80.21.32.85, fax 03.80.21.36.35, e-mail jmchartron@chartron-trebuchet.com ✓ Y ev. day 10am-12 noon 2pm-6pm; cl. mid-Nov. to Mar.

DOM. HENRI CLERC ET FILS 1999★★
□ Gd cru   0.46 ha   1,646   €46-76

This Grand Cru is a small plot out of the 22 ha (54.3 acres) which make up this large estate. The wine has a very intense gold colour with green glints; the bouquet is particularly active and captivating, with crystallised citrus fruits, orange flowers, but also a certain toastiness and smokiness. Tightly textured, this wine is full and round, complete, touched with vanilla from the oak that should integrate well. Set it aside to drink with a turbot in cream sauce.

the Chassagnes. In 2000, the whites produced 8,803 hl (232,399 gal) and the reds 6,282 hl (165,845 gal).

DOM. GUY AMIOT ET FILS

Les Vergers 1998

□ 1er cru   0.6 ha   3,000   [€] 23–30

In 1985, Guy Amiot took over the family estate, established in 1920. The 50-year-old Chardonnay stock is the result of rigorous mass selection. With powerful mineral characteristics, the wine has a delicate but very clean appearance. The bouquet declares itself: the brilliance of marble, flint, with a sprinkling of fine hazelnuts. The initial impact is upfront with an apple and pear fruitiness and there is sufficient acidity to add balance to the wine right up to the touch of liquorice on the finish. Ready to drink now.

- GAEC Guy Amiot et Fils, 13, rue du Grand-Puits, 21190 Chassagne-Montrachet, tel. 03.80.21.38.62, fax 03.80.21.90.80, e-mail domaine.amiotguyetfils@wanadoo.fr
- [Y] by appt.

- Dom. Henri Clerc et Fils, pl. des Marronniers, 21190 Puligny-Montrachet, tel. 03.80.21.32.74, fax 03.80.21.39.60 [V]
- ev. day 8.30am–11.45am 2pm–5.45pm
- Bernard Clerc

DOM. GUILLEMARD-CLERC 1999★

□ Gd cru   n.c.   n.c.   [€] 38–46

A well-made wine, very long and robust; the first impression on the palate is fresh, the middle palate fleshy, and the finish quite plausible. Honey and acacia are found on the bouquet, together with gunflint. The colour is very intense. This is a wine to drink in another three to five years.

- Dom. Guillemard-Clerc, 19, rue Drouhin, 21190 Puligny-Montrachet, tel. 03.80.21.34.22, fax 03.80.21.94.84, e-mail guillemard-clerc.domaine.wanadoo.fr [V]
- [Y] by appt.
- Franck Guillemard

Criots-Bâtard-Montrachet

ROGER BELLAND 1999★★

□ Gd cru   0.64 ha   3,200

89 |94| |95| 96 98

The Grand Jury considered this wine for a coup de cœur. Yellow-gold, brilliant, it is the product of a plot of land bought in 1982 from the Marcilly group. On the nose one detects that the grapes were very ripe when harvested. It takes us from orange flowers to gingerbread, passing through some mineral notes, and on to vanilla derived from the oak. Young and rich, this wine has a good future. Right now, it is suave and unctuous.

- Dom. Roger Belland, 3, rue de la Chapelle, BP 13, 21590 Santenay, tel. 03.80.20.60.95, fax 03.80.20.63.93, e-mail belland.roger@wanadoo.fr [V]
- [Y] by appt.

Chassagne-Montrachet

A new combe rises at Saint-Aubin, running alongside the RN6, and more or less marks the southern limit of white wine production before red wines begin; Les Ruchottes vineyard is at the dividing line. Clos Saint-Jean and Clos Morgeot, both sturdy, vigorous wines, are the most famous of

DOM. BACHELET-RAMONET PERE ET FILS Caillerets 1999★

□ 1er cru   0.45 ha   2,000   [€] 15–23

Bachelet and Ramonet, two well-known families in the village, got together to produce this well-rounded, rich wine. After its bright yellow colour one takes pleasure in inhaling honey, white peaches, grapefruit: a nose with grace and finesse. Grapefruit is also present on the palate, titillating the taste buds. A wine that should not be opened for another two years. The same goes for the white **Premier Cru La Romanée 99**, a wonderful wine, and note also the white **Premier Cru La Grande Montagne 99**.

- Dom. Bachelet-Ramonet Père et Fils, 11, rue du Parterre, 21190 Chassagne-Montrachet, tel. 03.80.21.32.49, fax 03.80.21.91.41 [V] [Y] by appt.

DOM. BACHEY-LEGROS ET FILS

Morgeot 1999★

□ 1er cru   1.92 ha   3,000   [€] 15–23

Situated at Santenay-le-Haut, this estate is established in a beautiful old house, as pictured on the label. The **Village 99**, garnet-purple with pink highlights, was singled out for its morello cherry nose and solid structure that still masks the agreeable traits of this wine. Give it time. This Premier Cru should also be allowed to mature for at least another two years. It is oaky but has a fruity freshness.

- Christiane Bachey-Legros, 12, rue de la Charrière, 21590 Santenay, tel. 03.80.20.64.14 [Y] by appt.

JEAN-CLAUDE BELLAND

Morgeot Clos Charreau 1999★

□ 1er cru   0.48 ha   2,500   [€] 15–23

The Clos Charreau is one of the *climats* united under the name of Morgeot. This *climat* is situated along the road leading to Santenay. This very dark, garnet-red 99 is already quite rich with a good structure of aromas. Very characteristic of a Chassagne, concentrated and slightly aggressive with touches of sloe and blackberry, it hasn't yet come to terms with its tannins. Be patient.

☎ Jean-Claude Belland, 21590 Santenay, tel. 03.80.20.61.90, fax 03.80.20.65.60 Ⓥ
Ⓨ by appt.

ROGER BELLAND
■ 1er cru

Morgeot Clos Pitois 1999★ | 1.71 ha | 9,000 | ⊞ €11–15

Coup de cœur last year, this estate returns this year with a very dark garnet-red, morello cherry Pinot with bluish glints. A superb nose with plums and jammy fruit, and a good background oakiness that is very pleasing. It is not excessively long on the palate but it has good structure together with suppleness and great aromatic flavour. A red Chassagne as they should be. The white **Premier Cru Clos Pitois 99** will also be a good wine in time.

☎ Dom. Roger Belland, 3, rue de la Chapelle, BP 13, 21590 Santenay, tel. 03.80.20.60.95, fax 03.80.20.63.93, e-mail belland.roger@wanadoo.fr Ⓥ
Ⓨ by appt.

JEAN BOUCHARD 1999★
■ | n.c. | 16,000 | ⊞ €15–23

Splendidly attired for the ball, this Pinot Noir swings between vanilla and dark berry fruits before finally imposing itself. Astringent, undoubtedly, but packed with complementary qualities and showing considerable potential. The future will smile on it, there is no doubt about that.

☎ Jean Bouchard, BP 47, 21202 Beaune Cedex, tel. 03.80.24.37.27, fax 03.80.24.37.38

BOUCHARD AINE ET FILS
□ 1er cru

Morgeot 1999★ | n.c. | 2,000 | ⊞ €30–38

A chicken breast in cream would go well with this Chardonnay, which is not a Morgeot for nothing. Light, almost transparent, it comes to life with notes of hot croissants and fresh butter. A mineral note and a certain roundness combine well with the oakiness on the palate. A good wine that needs to age a little but already gives pleasure to body and soul.

☎ Bouchard Aîné et Fils, Hôtel du Conseiller-du-Roy, 4, bd Mal-Foch, 21200 Beaune, tel. 03.80.24.24.00, fax 03.80.24.64.12 Ⓥ
Ⓨ ev. day 9.30am–12.30pm 2pm–6.30pm

GILLES BOUTON
■

Les Voillenots Dessous 1999 | 0.86 ha | 6,000 | ⊞ €8–11

Don't expect this wine to have the complexity of a Bergman film. It is simple, sincere, direct and transparent. A good colour without excessive brilliance; a good nose, concentrating on dried fruits. The tannins from the oak have not completely disappeared from the picture but the wine is quite mellow. About average for the appellation.

☎ Gilles Bouton, Gamay, 21190 Saint-Aubin, tel. 03.80.21.32.63, fax 03.80.21.90.74 Ⓥ Ⓨ by appt.

DOM. HUBERT BOUZEREAU-GRUERE Les Blanchots Dessous 1999
■ 1er cru | 0.23 ha | 1,500 | ⊞ €15–23

This estate is a neighbour of the Criots, Bâtard and Montrachet. Its Blanchot Dessous is nicely limpid, intense to look at and distinctly aromatic (ferns, hyacinths). It's a tender-hearted wine; drink it and feel at peace with the world.

☎ Hubert Bouzereau-Gruère, 22a, rue de la Velle, 21190 Meursault, tel. 03.80.21.20.05, fax 03.80.21.68.16 Ⓥ Ⓨ by appt.

CH. DE CITEAUX Les Pasquelles 1999
□ 1er cru | 0.15 ha | 1,000 | ⊞ €23–30

Golden straw-yellow, this wine might have come straight out of the bakery. Aromas of warm bread, croissants, brioche, with touches of vanilla. On the palate, a little bite shows a satisfactory acidity that balances its richness and fullness. This wine comes from a *climat* near Puligny and Montrachet, the most southerly part of the appellation.

☎ Dom. Philippe Bouzereau, Ch. de Citeaux, 18–20, rue de Citeaux, BP 25, 21190 Meursault, tel. 03.80.21.20.32, fax 03.80.21.64.34, e-mail info@domaine.bouzereau.fr Ⓥ Ⓨ by appt.

BERNARD COLIN ET FILS
□ 1er cru

Les Caillerets 1998★★ | n.c. | n.c. | ⊞ €15–23

Eight generations have worked this 8-ha (19.8-acre) estate, the last one having been there since the Fifth Republic was founded. This wine-maker has already proved his skill. This year two of his wines achieved a *coup de cœur*, which is a rare achievement. The white **Premier Cru Les Chenevottes 98** was awarded this *ad honorem* distinction (placed third by the Grand Jury) as was this rich golden Les Caillerets. Fresh with notes of brioche, already complex (pears, dried fruits) and with perfectly-controlled opulence on the palate, this wine is without ostentation – Chardonnay in its purest state. Take note, too, of the white **Premier Cru Clos Saint-Jean 98**, awarded one star, as was the very characteristic white **Village 98**, a wine with great character and ready to drink, though it will keep a while.

☎ Bernard Colin et Fils, 22, rue Charles-Paquelin, 21190 Chassagne-Montrachet, tel. 03.80.21.32.78, fax 03.80.21.93.23 Ⓥ
Ⓨ ev. day 8.30am–12.30pm 2pm–7pm; Sun. by appt.

DOM. MARC COLIN ET FILS

Les Caillerets 1999★

☐ 1er cru   1 ha   6,500   ⦿ €23-30

There are only a very few bottles left on the estate so you may have to get this from a wine-merchant, or settle for the **red Village 99**, which was commended by the Jury. The Les Caillerets is superior. Its colour is lively, warm, radiant, worthy of a Premier Cru, well up to standard. The oak, certainly, is no mere onlooker, but the mineral notes are beginning to surface. There is freshness at the start on the palate, leading on to a delicate fruitiness which lasts through to the finish where we find a pleasant citrus fruit note. Already drinkable, yet with a good future ahead of it.

☛ Marc Colin et Fils, hameau de Gamay, 21190 Saint-Aubin, tel. 03.80.21.30.43, fax 03.80.21.90.04 ▼

DEMESSEY Morgeot 1999

☐ 1er cru   n.c.   2,400   ⦿ €30-38

The colour is typical of the AOC and the nose is still overpowered by the oak. On the other hand there is good acidity and plenty of richness on the palate, with tentative hints of lemon and spring flowers. Definitely one to lay down.

☛ SARL Demessey, Ch. de Messey, 71700 Ozenay, tel. 03.85.51.33.83, fax 03.85.51.33.82, e-mail vin@demessey.com ▼ ☒ by appt.
☛ Marc Dumont

DUPERRIER-ADAM

Les Caillerets 1998★

■   0.2 ha   n.c.   ⦿ €15-23

A flamboyant garnet-red, this wine is not very forthcoming on the nose which has very young Pinot aromas that have been enhanced by 15 months in oak. It is on the palate that it expresses itself. With an excellent body balanced with good acidity and a generous fleshiness, it should be a fine wine in five to eight years' time.

☛ SCA Duperrier-Adam, 3, pl. des Noyers, 21190 Chassagne-Montrachet, tel. 03.80.21.31.10, fax 03.80.21.31.10 ▼ ☒ ev. day 9am–12 noon 6pm–5pm; Sat./Sun. by appt.; cl. Aug.

ALEX GAMBAL La Maltroie 1998

☐ 1er cru   0.16 ha   1,300   ⦿ €23-30

When an American falls in love with Burgundy and sets up as a *négociant-éleveur* in Beaune, the result is a Maltroie full of freshness from top to toe, lively in colour and and youthful on the palate. It is not surprising to find aromas of toast, green apples and a certain mineral note. Not a very powerful wine but fine, delicate and ideal to drink with trout.

☛ EURL Maison Alex Gambal, 4, rue Jacques-Vincent, 21200 Beaune, tel. 03.80.22.75.81, fax 03.80.22.21.66, e-mail agbeaune@aol.com ▼ ☒ by appt.

VINCENT GIRARDIN

La Boudriotte 1999★★

■ 1er cru   0.5 ha   3,000   ⦿ €15-23

This wine-grower came within a whisker of a *coup de coeur*. His Boudriotte is a great success with its velvety colour edged with purple, and a nose that opens generously with blackcurrant, enhanced by a few floral notes. It is tightly-knit but without harshness. Its tannins are present but subtle, with an obvious oakiness: a wine to lay down for three to five years.

☛ Caveau des Grands Crus, pl. de la Bascule, 21190 Chassagne-Montrachet, tel. 03.80.21.96.06, fax 03.80.21.96.23 ☒ ev. day 10am–1pm 2pm–6pm
☛ Vincent Girardin

DOM. VINCENT ET FRANCOIS JOUARD La Maltroie 1998★

☐ 1er cru   0.48 ha   3,000

A delightful Chardonnay, gold with green glints. Its bouquet of apples and pears, spring blossom, is harmonious and expressive. An elegant yet complex wine with richness, finesse, and lasting aromas, but lacking a little in strength. It needs to be kept two to three years. A good future also awaits the **white Premier Cru Morgeot 99** (one star), and the **Premier Cru Les Chaumées 99** (the highest *climat* of the hillside, facing Saint-Aubin); the latter is singled out by the Jury for its aromas of honeysuckle and its good balance.

☛ Dom. Vincent et François Jouard, 2, pl. de l'Eglise, 21190 Chassagne-Montrachet, tel. 03.80.21.30.25, fax 03.80.21.96.27 ▼ ☒ by appt.

GABRIEL JOUARD Les Baudines 1998

☐ 1er cru   1.3 ha   3,000   ⦿ €11-15

For six generations this family has been *propriétaire-récoltante* at Chassagne, and one can understand them never wanting to leave these vineyards. High up on the Santenay hillside, this *climat* produces a deep gold, slightly amber Chardonnay with a nose that is a little developed and opens with wax, citrus fruits, smokiness. Quite well-balanced on the palate, it is ready to drink now.

☛ EARL Dom. Gabriel Jouard Pere et Fils, 3, rue du Petit-Puits, 21190 Chassagne-Montrachet, tel. 03.80.21.30.30, fax 03.80.21.30.30 ▼ ☒ by appt.

LABOURE-ROI 1998

■   n.c.   n.c.   ⦿ €11-15

The estate was taken over by the Cottin family of Nuits-Saint-Georges. It presents a *village* of a pleasing, intense colour. Initially the nose is slightly gamey, opening out towards raspberry jam. Its initial impact is fruity (ripe cherries) with pronounced tannins that make it somewhat austere. It should, however, mature well if laid down for three to five years.

☛ Labouré-Roi, rue Lavoisier, 21700 Nuits-Saint-Georges, tel. 03.80.62.64.00, fax 03.80.62.64.10 ☒ by appt.

CH. DE LA CHARRIERE

Clos Saint-Jean 1999
☐ 1er cru　0.45 ha　2,400　€15-23

This one needs to be left a while as the oak has not yet integrated, but it seems to have all the qualities needed to age well: there are good, it does not lack power and there are already interesting mineral and liquorice notes. It should be kept for at least two years. Also commended was the **red Village Les Champs de Morjot 99**, full of dark fruit on the nose, rich and balanced on the palate; one to lay down for two or three years.
● Dom. Yves Girardin,
1, rte des Maranges, 21590 Santenay,
tel. 03.80.20.64.36, fax 03.80.20.66.32 ▼
Ⴤ by appt.
● Cournut

CH. DE LA MALTROYE Clos du
Château de la Maltroye Monopole 1999★
☐ 1er cru　1.18 ha　9,200　€23-30

This wine's very light colour, although not remarkable, remains within the classic parameters. On the nose there are aromas of russet apples with an underlying floral touch. The fruit becomes softer on the palate, making way for vanilla and brioche flavours. The acidity is still evident but will integrate in time. The fish destined to be cooked in a cream sauce to accompany it can be left to swim for another two to three years. Among the **red Premiers Crus** the **Monopole** from the same *climat*, and **La Boudriotte** were each awarded one star. Both are wines to lay down.
● Ch. de La Maltroye, 16, rue de la Murée, 21190 Chassagne-Montrachet,
tel. 03.80.21.32.45, fax 03.80.21.34.54 ▼
Ⴤ by appt.

DOM. HUBERT LAMY 1999★★
☐　0.16 ha　1,350　€23-30

Well worth looking at is the **red Goujonne Vieilles Vignes 99 Village**, a full and well-structured, one-star wine, and this white *village*. A brilliant light colour with an expressive nose of exotic fruit opening out with touches of almonds and toast. Rich, forthright, not too powerful but quite concentrated, it will be ready to drink in two to three years.
● Dom. Hubert Lamy, Paradis,
21190 Saint-Aubin, tel. 03.80.21.32.55, fax 03.80.21.38.32 ▼ Ⴤ by appt.

DOM. LARUE 1999★
☐　0.3 ha　1,500　€11-15

A lyrical and very lively Chardonnay with a pale-yellow colour and an acacia and exotic fruit nose with delicate oakiness. Powerful and round, it eventually resolves any conflict on the palate. Open in character, with volume and fruitiness, this is a very successful *village*.
● Dom. Larue, Gamay, 21190 Saint-Aubin, tel. 03.80.21.30.74, fax 03.80.21.91.36 ▼
Ⴤ by appt.

OLIVIER LEFLAIVE

Les Blanchots 1998★
☐ 1er cru　0.35 ha　n.c.　€38-46

Only the width of a road separates the Blanchots from Montrachet. This Premier Cru only just missed becoming a Grand Cru like Les Criots. Wine-lovers know these little secrets. This dense golden-yellow 98 has an expressive nose of hazelnuts and honey and, though initially lively, it follows through pleasantly on the palate with silkiness and length, finishing with a light touch of bitterness and liquorice which will allow it to keep for two or three years. Suitable to drink with a fish terrine.
● Olivier Leflaive, pl. du Monument, 21190 Puligny-Montrachet,
tel. 03.80.21.37.65, fax 03.80.21.33.94,
e-mail leflaive-olivier@dial.oleane.com ▼
Ⴤ by appt.

LOUIS LEQUIN Morgeot 1999
☐ 1er cru　0.13 ha　2,100　€11-15

Louis Lequin was wine-maker at the Hospices de Beaune and in 1872 he founded this private estate. The barrels here are made of oak from the forests of Tronçais and Bertrange. This wine is very full with a blue-tinged garnet-red colour, a sign of its youth, and a violet-scented bouquet that gives one the impression of breathing in a whole garden. Additional raspberry nuances and ripe fruit appear on the palate after a full-flavoured attack. Its tannins become evident at the finish and will need time to integrate (to be laid down for three to five years).
● Louis Lequin,
1, rue du Pasquier-du-Pont, 21590 Santenay,
tel. 03.80.20.63.82, fax 03.80.20.67.14,
e-mail louis.lequin@wanadoo.fr ▼

RENE LEQUIN-COLIN

Les Vergers 1999★★
☐ 1er cru　0.45 ha　3,700　€15-23

There are wines that make one feel at peace with life – this one is one of them. Les Vergers is not far from Montrachet and the relationship is clear to see. Yellow with gold highlights, beautifully fresh to the eye, this is a slightly toasty Chardonnay with very ripe aromas, superb on the palate. A great treat. Nothing about it is exaggerated or exuberant, everything is as it should be: full, round and classy. The same applies to the **red Premier Cru Morgeot 99**, smooth with raspberry notes.
● EARL René Lequin-Colin, 10, rue de Lavau, 21590 Santenay, tel. 03.80.20.66.71, fax 03.80.20.66.70, e-mail renelequin@aol.com ▼ Ⴤ by appt.

DOM. DU DUC DE MAGENTA
Morgeot Clos de La Chapelle 1998★★
☐ 1er cru　2.8 ha　12,000　€46-76

'Here I am and here I'll stay,' this wine seems to be saying: offspring of the Duc de Magenta and descendant of the Maréchal de Mac-Mahon of the Château de Sully, it is

DOMAINE DU DUC DE MAGENTA

PREMIER CRU

CHASSAGNE-MONTRACHET

"MORGEOT"

MONOPOLE CLOS DE LA CHAPELLE

APPELLATION CONTRÔLÉE

LOUIS JADOT

NÉGOCIANT ÉLEVEUR À BEAUNE, CÔTE-D'OR, FRANCE

PRODUIT DE FRANCE

---

undisputed winner of a *coup de coeur*, brilliant green-gold in colour. Its elegant nose combines a delicate oakiness with notes of pears and grapefruit. Expressive on the palate, reflecting good *terroir*, with well-integrated oak, this wine is destined to be at its peak in five to six years.

• Maison Louis Jadot,
21, rue Eugène-Spuller, 21200 Beaune, tel. 03.80.22.10.57, fax 03.80.22.56.03, e-mail contact@louisjadot.com ▼ by appt.

MICHEL MOREY-COFFINET★

Les Caillerets 1999★ □1er cru 0.7 ha 4,500 €23-30

A brilliant yellow colour, typically limpid. The aromas are subtle, with a few floral touches and a hint of toasted almonds. It is slightly acidic but this blends well with the freshness and well-balanced, elegant fruity flavours. This very pleasant wine heralds the arrival on the estate of one of the two sons, Thibault Morey. Make a note, too, of the **red Village 99**, one star, which should be enjoyed at this youthful, fruity stage.

• Dom. Michel Morey-Coffinet, 6, pl. du Grand-Four, 21190 Chassagne-Montrachet, tel. 03.80.21.31.71, fax 03.80.21.90.81, e-mail morey.coffinet@wanadoo.fr ▼ by appt.

PIGUET-GIRARDIN Morgeot 1999★★

■1er cru 0.5 ha 2,000 €11-15

The result of the merging of two estates, D. Pinguet and A.-M. Girardin, the domaine presents here a wine that would go well with spring lamb. Garnet-red, lightly tinged with blue, it is intense and rich, both to the eye and on the nose (plums, cherries), and very accessible. The little touch of alcohol will soften, given time. Its fantastic length is particularly notable. It is a top-level Premier Cru.

• SCE Piguet-Girardin, rue du Meix, 21190 Auxey-Duresses, tel. 03.80.21.60.26, fax 03.80.21.66.61 ▼ by appt.

FERNAND ET LAURENT PILLOT★★

Les Vergers 1999★★ □1er cru 0.91 ha 6,300 €15-23

This estate is only a few metres from the famous quarries where the Chassagne stone (used in the construction of the Trocadéro, Bercy and the Pyramid at the Louvre) is extracted. However, this superb Chardonnay, a perfect example of its appellation and vintage, is more fruity than mineral. Its youthful colour, very fresh scents of toast and pineapple, and balance between fullness and acidity make it the ideal wine to drink with a grilled bass and *beurre blanc* (a shallot butter sauce) in two years' time. Take a look also at the **white Village 99**, lightly sparkling and quite flowery.

• Fernand and Laurent Pillot, 13, rue des Champgains, 21190 Chassagne-Montrachet, tel. 03.80.21.33.64, fax 03.80.21.92.60, e-mail lfpillot@club-internet.fr ▼ by appt.

DOM. VINCENT PRUNIER 1999★★

■ 0.24 ha 1,765 €11-15

Vincent Prunier was born into winegrowing and obtained the *Brevet de Technicien Agricole, viti-oenologie* (diploma in viticulture/oenology) in 1988. Since then he has come a long way. His wine reflects modern extraction methods with its colour of dark purple ink, very intense for this grape variety. An attractive, long-legged 99 with an open bouquet of blackcurrants and blackberries. Rich and fleshy with a touch of liquorice, it has everything one could wish for. Even its tannins are very civilized.

• Vincent Prunier, rte de Beaune, 21190 Auxey-Duresses, tel. 03.80.21.27.77, fax 03.80.21.68.87 ▼ by appt.

ANTONIN RODET 1998★★

□ n.c. 4,473 €38-46

A round of applause for this very representative 98. Straw-yellow in colour, it favours the more exotic aromas, yet allows the toastiness of the oak to come through. Full and warming, it should be laid down for several years.

• Antonin Rodet, 71640 Mercurey, tel. 03.85.98.12.12, fax 03.85.45.25.49, e-mail rodet@rodet.com ▼ ▼ ev. day except Sat/Sun. 9am–12 noon 2pm–6pm

ROPITEAU Morgeot 1998

□1er cru n.c. 3,000 €23-30

'*Coûte que coûte, il faut que j'en goûte*' (At all costs, I must taste it), is the legend on an old pottery dish from Burgundy. The saying comes to mind at the sight of this pale-gold Morgeot with its greyish highlights. Look closer and find that hazelnuts and honey have joined forces and signed a pact of friendship. The wine lacks fullness but the velvety palate compensates for this. It has all the distinction of this grape variety in its most hallowed cradle. The estate has been taken over by J.-Cl. Boisset Wines.

• Ropiteau Frères,
13, rue du 11-Novembre, 21190 Meursault, tel. 03.80.21.69.20, fax 03.80.21.69.29 ▼ ▼ ev. day 9am–7pm; cl. mid-Nov. to Easter

DOM. ROUX PÈRE ET FILS

Les Macherelles 1999 □1er cru 0.45 ha 3,200 €23-30

This Premier Cru forms part of the vineyards to the north of the village. Very light gold with green flecks, the wine has a clean,

Saint-Aubin

S aint-Aubin is topographically the neighbour of the Hautes-Côtes, but some of the commune borders Chassagne to the south and Puligny and Blagny to the east. The Murgers des Dents de Chien, Saint-Aubin's Premier Cru, is grown only a very short distance from Chevalier-Montrachet and Les Caillerets and it must be said that the Saint-Aubin Premier Cru is fully their equal in quality. The vineyards have begun to produce a little more red wine — 2,916 hl (76,982 gal) in 2000 — but the whites — 4,822 hl (127,301 gal) — reveal St Aubin at its best.

attractive nose with aromas of hawthorn and fresh butter. On the palate it is more severe, less expressive but with a certain liveliness. The wine has potential and, at this stage, shows no sign of tiredness. Have confidence.
☛ Dom. Roux Père et Fils, 21190 Saint-Aubin, tel. 03.80.21.32.92, fax 03.80.21.35.00 [V] [Y] by appt.

BERTRAND AMBROISE
Murgers des Dents de Chien 1999★

□ ler cru   n.c.   n.c.   [€15-23]

Murgers des Dents de Chien: 'murgers' are piles of stones collected over the centuries from among the vines; les Dents de Chien (dog's teeth) are long, narrow parcels of vineyard. This 99 vintage is perfectly-balanced. A straightforward wine, with well-judged acidity and richness, that makes the most of its charm. With its fine yellow colour and delightful nose, with minerally and flowery aromas, it has all the qualities of a good Saint-Aubin. Superlatively 'terroir'.
☛ Maison Bertrand Ambroise, rue de l'Eglise, 21700 Premeaux-Prissey, tel. 03.80.62.30.19, fax 03.80.62.38.69, e-mail bertrand.ambroise@wanadoo.fr [V] [Y] by appt.

☛ Jean-Noël Bazin, Les Petits Vergers, 21340 La Rochepot, tel. 03.80.21.75.49, fax 03.80.21.83.71 [V] by appt.

GILLES BOUTON

□ ler cru   Les Champlots 1999★   0.13 ha 1,000   [€8-11]

Those who have been awarded a coup de coeur (in this case for a 95 vintage) are already counted among the 'happy few', a small, esteemed band. Four of these wines have been commended by the Jury: the Premier Cru Les Champlots 99 red; the Premiers Crus Murgers des Dents de Chiens and En Remilly 99 white; and this one, which stands out from the rest. One often finds a Les Champlots in the place of honour: this wine, with its freshness of honeysuckle is a touch austere but ready to explode.
☛ Gilles Bouton, 21190 Saint-Aubin, tel. 03.80.21.90.74 [V] [Y] by appt.

DOM. DE BRULLY Les Cortons 1999★

□ ler cru   0.67 ha 4,500   [€15-23]

Here it is again, our coup de coeur of last year for a 98 vintage; this time presenting a climat Les Cortons 99 white, which will make a perfect talking point when wine-lovers get together round a table. A great wine, still in hiding but with discernible aromas of peaches. It has a good structure and is already taking shape. Also the Jury commended the Premier Cru Les Frionnes 99 red. All elegance and roundness — a wine for the future.
☛ Dom. de Brully, 21190 Saint-Aubin, tel. 03.80.21.32.92, fax 03.80.21.35.00 [V]
[Y] by appt.
☛ Roux

G. BRZEZINSKI
Murgers des Dents de Chien 1999★★

□ ler cru   n.c.   1,000   [€15-23]

This wine was proposed for a coup de coeur and sits at the right hand of the winner. Readers of the Guide are aware that this climat is near to the prodigious Montrachet family. This gold-coloured 99, exactly the shade it should be, has a pleasant nose: apples, dried fruit. Very well-balanced with the fruit staying sensibly in the background, it is a Premier Cru worthy of the name, fine, classy, not for drinking right away.
☛ G. Brzezinski, rte d'Autun, 21630 Pommard, tel. 03.80.22.28.33 [Y] ev. day except Sun. 8am–12 noon 2pm–6pm; cl. 23 Dec–6 Jan.

DOM. JEAN CHARTRON
Les Murgers des Dents de Chien 1999

□ ler cru   0.55 ha 4,000   [€23-30]

Twelve months in oak (40% new) has not prevented the this wine from turning out rich and ripe, clear and brilliant at the rim, with citrus fruit and peachy fruit clearly evident. Its well-balanced palate has a richness that, the Jury felt, is due to the ripeness of the grapes. It still has something in reserve.

JEAN-NOEL BAZIN 1999

□ ler cru   0.5 ha 3,000   [€11-15]

Like Saint Romain, Saint Aubin wanted to give himself a little respite. To 'voir à voir', as they say in the Côte, meaning: to take time to relax and view things with a clear head. With that in mind, here is a village full of good intentions with a direct approach (straw, apple purée) and an assertive body. It is more rich than concentrated: these are still very young vines.

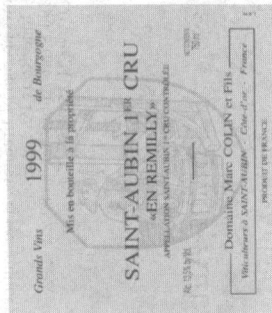

•– Dom. Jean Chartron, 13, Grande-Rue, 21190 Puligny-Montrachet, tel. 03.80.21.32.85, fax 03.80.21.36.35 ⬚
Ⲧ ev. day 10am–12 noon 2pm–6pm; cl. mid-Nov. to Mar.

CH. DE CHASSAGNE-MONTRACHET Le Charmois 1999★

| ☐1er cru | 5.68 ha | 31,000 | ⬚ €15-23 |

Intense green-gold, this is the kind of colour one dreams about. Apart from the toasted almond aroma – well-balanced, incidentally – there are touches of spring blossom and mineral notes. The attack is frank, decisive, the acidity controlled, very rich, and the palate is in keeping with the nose.
•– Ch. de Chassagne-Montrachet, 21190 Chassagne-Montrachet, tel. 03.85.87.51.00, fax 03.85.87.51.11
•– Michel Picard

DOM. DU CHATEAU DE PULIGNY-MONTRACHET

En Remilly 1999★

| ☐1er cru | 1.34 ha | 9,000 | ⬚ €15-23 |

This oaky wine lacks neither charm nor authenticity. Beneath its classic appearance, dried fruit and flint compete for attention. Delicately honeyed and wholly convincing.
•– SCEA Dom. du Château de Puligny-Montrachet, 21190 Puligny-Montrachet, tel. 03.80.21.39.14, fax 03.80.21.39.07, e-mail chateaupul@aol.com ⬚ Ⲧ by appt.

FRANCOISE ET DENIS CLAIR

Les Murgers des Dents de Chien 1999★

| ☐1er cru | 0.88 ha | n.c. | ⬚ €11-15 |

Vinification has taken place in oak barrels, 30% new oak, the yeast stirred until spring; this brilliant gold 99 is has delightful aromas (subtle oak, toast, hazelnuts, acacia flowers). The initial freshness remains on the palate: a well-bred wine to lay down for five to six years.
•– Françoise et Denis Clair, 14, rue de la Chapelle, 21590 Santenay, tel. 03.80.20.61.96, fax 03.80.20.65.19
Ⲧ by appt.

BERNARD COLIN ET FILS

En Remilly 1998★

| ☐1er cru | 0.4 ha | n.c. | ⬚ €8-11 |

With its light but attractive colour, this Remilly has beautiful floral aromas with touches of ripe citrus fruit. Fresh, fruity and soft, it is still youthful on the palate. Although enjoyable to drink at this stage it would be better to let it mature and develop all its complexity.
•– Bernard Colin et Fils, 22, rue Charles-Paquelin, 21190 Chassagne-Montrachet, tel. 03.80.21.32.78, fax 03.80.21.93.23 ⬚
Ⲧ ev. day 8.30am–12.30pm 2pm–7pm; Sun. by appt.

DOM. MARC COLIN ET FILS

En Remilly 1999★★

| ☐1er cru | 2 ha | 10,000 | ⬚ €11-15 |

Being a proprietor in Montrachet is the equivalent of having a noble title in Burgundy. 'A wine-grower of exemplary modesty and integrity,' someone wrote about this one. Michèle, his wife, came from Saint-Aubin when they married. His Remilly (neighbour of Chevalier-Montrachet) is so splendid that it won him a *coup de cœur*. It is easily the equal of a Premier Cru Puligny or Meursault with its intense, complex nose that combines fruit and flowers, almonds, and toastiness from the oak. It has a well-balanced palate with an elegant finish. Also singled out is the **Premier Cru La Châtenière 99 white** which was awarded one star, as was the **white La Fontenotte 99.**
•– Marc Colin et Fils, hameau de Gamay, 21190 Saint-Aubin, tel. 03.80.21.30.43, fax 03.80.21.90.04 ⬚

COUVENT DES CORDELIERS 1998

| ☐ | n.c. | 4,900 | ⬚ €11-15 |

This wine has a wonderful lively, shimmering colour. The nose, however, is strictly orthodox; flint and acacia. An echo of these same aromas appear on the palate, which gives an impression of unity despite a certain vivacity in the attack, and you feel, as you set down your glass, that you have not wasted your time.
•– Caves du Couvent des Cordeliers, rue de l'Hôtel-Dieu, 21200 Beaune, tel. 03.80.25.08.85, fax 03.80.25.08.21 ⬚
Ⲧ ev. day 9.30am–12 noon 2pm–6pm

DUPERRIER-ADAM

Sur le Sentier du Clou 1999★

| ☐1er cru | 0.23 ha | n.c. | ⬚ €8-11 |

Le Sentier du Clou? In the old Burgundy language the word 'clou' meant a vineyard enclosure. This deep garnet-red Pinot presents a slightly jammy nose. Demonstrative, amiable but powerful, it is well-structured. Its youthfulness indicates that it needs laying down in a good cellar for three to four years.
•– SCA Duperrier-Adam, 3, pl. des Noyers, 21190 Chassagne-Montrachet, tel. 03.80.21.31.10, fax 03.80.21.31.10 ⬚
Ⲧ ev. day 9am–12 noon 2pm–5pm; Sat./Sun. by appt.; cl. Aug.

ECHANSONNERIE DU GOÛT VINAGE

□1er cru   1 ha   6,000   €30-38

This wine, bearing one of the most surprising labels in the wine-producing region, was presented by l'Echansonnerie de l'Ordre du Goût Vinage de France. The label reads: 'dedicated to excellence in wines favoured by those men considered worthy of esteem'. How very bizarre! That said, the wine is very acceptable. Its gold colour, aromas of apricots and white-fleshed peaches, and potentially pleasing structure all speak in its favour. The **Premier Cru Murgers des Dents de Chien 99 red** is also worth mentioning.

☎ Echansonnerie du Goût Vinage, rte de Moince, 57420 Louvigny, tel. 03.87.69.79.69, fax 03.87.69.71.13

CHRISTOPHE GUILLO

□1er cru   0.95 ha   6,000   €8-11

Les Murgers des Dents de Chien 1999★

The **Les Murgers des Dents de Chien 99 white** and its red twin were both placed in the same category. We opted finally for the latter one because of its delicacy (wild strawberries, bilberries) and the astonishing balance between the firm tannins and the overall finesse. Coming from a white wine *terroir*, it would be ideal with oeufs en meurette (eggs poached in red wine).

☎ Christophe Guillo, Dom. des Meix, 21200 Combertault, tel. 03.80.26.67.05, fax 03.80.26.67.05 [V] [Y] by appt.

MICHEL LAMANTHE 1999★

□1er cru   0.7 ha   4,000

The Romanesque church at Saint-Aubin is a fine building dating back to the 10th century. Church and wine have come through one thousand years of history together. This pale-yellow 99 with gold highlights shows evidence of a good maturation: the fine oakiness on the nose opens with a few floral notes, then a powerful, round palate with dried fruit and a mineral touch, and superb length. A worthy wine to accompany a fine fish dish.

☎ Michel Lamanthe, 21190 Saint-Aubin, tel. 03.80.21.33.23, fax 03.80.21.93.96 [V] [Y] by appt.

LES VILLAGES DE JAFFELIN

1999★

□   n.c.   5,000   €15-23

Abbot of Tincillac and bishop of Angers, the good Saint Aubin frequently performed miracles and was very popular. This Chardonnay obviously received his blessings. Toast and fresh butter; you could almost drink it at breakfast. It has a mineral structure, in keeping with the *terroir*. The Jaffelin company was taken over by Jean-Claude Boisset but has retained autonomy in managing the estate.

☎ Jaffelin, 2, rue Paradis, 21200 Beaune, tel. 03.80.22.12.49, fax 03.80.24.91.87

DOM. LARUE

□1er cru   Murgers des Dents de Chien 1999★★

0.93 ha   6,900   €11-15

The quality of this 99 vintage is what we expected. The gold colour is a little frugal but the nose has finesse and the palate is passionately divided between mineral notes and richness.

☎ Dom. Larue, Gamay, 21190 Saint-Aubin, tel. 03.80.21.30.74, fax 03.80.21.91.36 [V] [Y] by appt.

SYLVAIN LANGOUREAU

En Remilly 1999★

□1er cru   1.4 ha   9,800   €11-15

A *coup de coeur* was awarded to this estate for a 96 vintage. Sylvain Langoureau, with a builder friend, has since constructed the vaulted cellar where this 99 En Remilly was stored. Pale yellow with good legs, it is a pure Premier Cru, and plays the grapefruit card with finesse. This follows through on the palate, accompanied by bitter almonds. Still very young, this wine is like a block of marble waiting for a sculptor. The result will be a beautiful work of art in two or three years. A **Les Frionnes Premier Cru white** also received the same rating.

☎ Sylvain Langoureau, Hameau de Gamay, 21190 Saint-Aubin, tel. 03.80.21.39.99, fax 03.80.21.39.99 [V] [Y] by appt.

DOM. HUBERT LAMY

En Remilly 1999★

□1er cru   1.1 ha   10,000   €15-23

A star was awarded to the **Premier Cru La Chatenière 99 white**, a wine from very good stock, and to a **village La Princée 99**, also white. The En Remilly was slightly better – very fruity, supple and appealing, classic green-gold in colour with an attractive floral nose. Dry and mineral, it comes from very good stock. Ready to drink now if you are impatient but, equally, may be laid down.

☎ Dom. Hubert Lamy, Paradis, 21190 Saint-Aubin, tel. 03.80.21.38.32 [V] [Y] by appt.

☎ Olivier et Hubert Lamy

DOM. LAMY-PILLOT

Les Argilliers 1999

■   0.54 ha   3,400   €8-11

Strong and brilliant in colour, this Les Argilliers is very fruity, with grapey aromas and flavours. It has all the qualities of a young wine in the process of developing. If you prefer a Chardonnay, the **Les Pucelles 99** has real personality and should please you.

☎ Dom. Lamy-Pillot, 31, rte de Santenay, 21190 Chassagne-Montrachet, tel. 03.80.21.30.52, fax 03.80.21.30.02, e-mail lamy.pillot@wanadoo.fr [V] [Y] by appt.

Saint-Aubin

OLIVIER LEFLAIVE

Le Charmois 1998★

☐ 1er cru   1.8 ha   10,000   🍷 €15-23

This floral, toasty 98 has great clarity and luminosity. Its balsamic tendencies are followed by a full, well-structured palate. However, this is a wine that will not benefit from keeping for very long, and should be drunk now. Formerly co-manager of the Leflaive estate, Olivier Leflaive has now branched out on his own as a wine-grower, merchant and proprietor of a traditional restaurant.

☛ Olivier Leflaive, pl. du Monument, 21190 Puligny-Montrachet, tel. 03.80.21.37.65, fax 03.80.21.33.94, e-mail leflaive-olivier@dial.oleane.com ☑

🍷 by appt.

DOM. MAROSLAVAC-LEGER

Les Murgers des Dents de Chien 1999★

☐ 1er cru   0.34 ha   2,100   🍶 🍷 €15-23

Roland Maroslavac's grandfather was an immigrant from Yugoslavia who arrived in France in 1930 looking for work. By his own efforts he built up this estate that presents this wonderfully intense wine (good colour, floral and smoky nose), full and long on the palate. This very attractive Saint-Aubin needs a few more years in the cellar.

☛ Dom. Maroslavac-Leger, 43, Grande-Rue, 21190 Puligny-Montrachet, tel. 03.80.21.31.23, fax 03.80.21.91.39, e-mail maroslavac.leger@wanadoo.fr ☑

🍷 by appt.

CH. PHILIPPE-LE-HARDI

En Vesvau 1999

☐   0.94 ha   8,000   🍷 €11-15

Very pale straw with green glints, this wine wears the white Burgundy colours. The nose speaks of spring blossom with a good oaky structure. Frank, balanced and lively, on the palate it bears all the hallmarks of a charming, elegant and still very young wine.

☛ Ch. de Santenay, BP 18, 21590 Santenay, tel. 03.80.20.61.87, fax 03.80.20.63.66 ☑

🍷 by appt.

BERNARD PRUDHON

Les Castets 1999★

◼ 1er cru   0.64 ha   1,500   🍷 €8-11

Les Castets is very close to the village and next to a *climat* with the amusing – though seemingly unjustified – name of Derrière chez Edouard (behind Edward's place). This garnet-red 99 with pink highlights hints gently at soft red fruit and vanilla. A well-made wine that is completely in character, with pronounced tannins, at the moment it is a touch brusque and appropriate for laying down.

☛ Bernard Prudhon, 21190 Saint-Aubin, tel. 03.80.21.35.66 ☑

HENRI PRUDHON

Les Frionnes 1999★

◼ 1er cru   2 ha   12,000   🍶 🍷 €8-11

The **Premier Cru Sur Gamay 99 white** is an interesting wine and was singled out by the Jury. It is always amusing to surprise one's guests with such a wine. But in our opinion this Frionnes is better: velvety with a fine nose (cherries) and characterised by rare finesse.

☛ Henri Prudhon et Fils, 21190 Saint-Aubin, tel. 03.80.21.36.70, fax 03.80.21.91.55 ☑

🍷 by appt.

☛ Gérard Prudhon

DOM. ROUX PERE ET FILS

La Pucelle 1999★

☐   2.5 ha   15,000   🍷 €11-15

This is an important family and one that makes good wines. *Coup de coeur* for a 97 vintage, this La Pucelle 99 has very strong emerald highlights. The nose reveals peaches and apples together with a lovely oakiness. This dense and effective wine, slightly balsamic on the palate, is destined to be consumed in the near future. The **Premier Cru Les Frionnes 99 red** will make a good consolation prize if the previous one is already sold out. It was awarded one star and could stay in your cellar for three to five years.

☛ Dom. Roux Père et Fils, 21190 Saint-Aubin, tel. 03.80.21.32.92, fax 03.80.21.35.00 ☑

🍷 by appt.

MICHEL SERVEAU

En l'Ebaupin 1999★

☐   0.15 ha   1,000   🍷 €8-11

This *climat* near to Les Pucelles is at the far end of the slope going towards La Rochepot. It has produced a strong garnet-red 99 with a nose that is fruity at first (cherries) then very intense. On the palate it is full-flavoured, heady and fleshy, though still youthful. While its quality is not in doubt, more time in the cellar is essential (two to three years).

☛ Michel Serveau, rte de Beaune, 21340 La Rochepot, tel. 03.80.21.70.24, fax 03.80.21.71.87 ☑

🍷 by appt.

GERARD THOMAS

Murgers des Dents de Chien 1998★

☐ 1er cru   1.7 ha   10,800   🍷 €8-11

Sparkle, brilliance – this lively wine has everything going for it: flint encircled with fresh almonds and hawthorn, pleasant on the palate. It has excellent prospects. You could also try the **Premier Cru La Chatenière 98 white** (one star) or go for a change of colour with the **Premier Cru Les Frionnes 99 red**, which was commended by the Jury and needs to be kept for another two years.

☛ Gérard Thomas, 21190 Saint-Aubin, tel. 03.80.21.32.57, fax 03.80.21.36.51 ☑

🍷 by appt.

Santenay

The village of Santenay is dominated by the Trois-Croix mountain and, thanks to its salt-water spa which has the most lithium-rich waters in the whole of Europe, it has become a famous spa resort. The village has many attractions, among which are some excellent red wines. Les Gravières, La Comme and Beauregard are the best-known Crus. As at Chassagne, the vines of Santenay are often trained in the *Cordon de Royat* method. The two appellations of Chassagne and Santenay edge over into the Commune de Remigny, in Saône-et-Loire, where we find the appellations of Cheilly, Sampigny and Dezize-lès-Maranges, now included under the Appellation Maranges. In 2000 the AOC Santenay produced 1,937 hl (51,137 gal) of white wine and 13,982 hl (369,125 gal) of red wine.

DOM. ALEXANDRE
■ Les Champs Claude 1999★★

2.25 ha 2,000 ▥ €8-11

This *climat* belongs to a plot of vines within the appellation situated near Remigny. This attractive wine has a ruby-red colour tinged with purple, and notes of blackcurrant and liquorice. Its fine structure, good length and remarkable complexity all go to make up a wine that is among the best. The **Premier Cru Gravières 99 red** (one star) is harsh, but once it has opened out you must tell us what you think of it.

☛ Dom. Alexandre Père et Fils, pl. de la Mairie, 71150 Remigny, tel. 03.85.87.22.61, fax 03.85.87.22.61,
e-mail domaine.alexandre@roonoo.net ✓

DOM. BACHEY-LEGROS ET FILS
■ Clos des Hâtes 1999

0.88 ha 3,500 ▥ ▥ €8-11

The typically Burgundian architecture of this estate, full of charm, is pictured on the wine label. This is how Santenay wines used to be, with very dark garnet-red colour and aromas of ripe fruits that tiptoe softly on the nose. Its well-structured body is still firm and closed. The Jury suggests it should be laid down for four to five years.

☛ Christiane Bachey-Legros,
12, rue de la Charrière, 21590 Santenay,
tel. 03.80.20.64.14 ✓ ▼ by appt.

DOM. BART En Bièvau 1998★
■ 0.6 ha 3,200 ▥ €11-15

Red to dark-red in colour, very clear and intense, this wine has a nose that is still youthful but shows some raspberries and flowers in a setting of vanilla. This is a Bièvau, that excellent *village* which is often the equal of a Premier Cru. It is pleasant on the palate with an adequate structure and well-developed fruitiness. The slight hint of bitterness didn't seem to worry those tasters who were aware of it.

☛ Dom. Bart, 23, rue Moreau,
21160 Marsannay-la-Côte,
tel. 03.80.51.49.76, fax 03.80.51.23.43 ✓
▼ by appt.

JEAN-CLAUDE BELLAND
■ 1er cru Clos des Gravières 1999

1.21 ha 7,400 ▥ €11-15

'The vineyards at Santenay are among those which are cultivated with the greatest possible care'; this was the opinion of Dr. Jules Lavalle in the middle of the 19th century. This is a wine that needs a little coaxing but which does not hesitate on the well-rounded attack. Enhanced by a touch of liquorice, it is lighter than most of its fellow wines, but charming.

☛ Jean-Claude Belland, 21590 Santenay,
tel. 03.80.20.61.90, fax 03.80.20.65.60 ✓

ROGER BELLAND
■ 1er cru Beauregard 1999★★

3.22 ha 15,000 ▥ €11-15

This *climat*, like La Comme, flourishes on the side of the hill. Almost inky, but nonetheless limpid, this wine has the most attractive nose imaginable: raspberries, toast, liquorice. Round and powerful, direct and concentrated, it is clearly a wine to lay down. Also recommended are the **Premier Crus Les Commes red** and the **Les Gravières 99 red**, also the **Charmes Village 99 red**. All were awarded two stars and will be ready to serve at fine meals in two, three or four years' time.

☛ Dom. Roger Belland,
3, rue de la Chapelle, BP 13, 21590 Santenay,
tel. 03.80.20.60.95, fax 03.80.20.63.93,
e-mail belland.roger@wanadoo.fr ✓
▼ by appt.

ALBERT BICHOT 1998★

■   n.c.   14,000   ▭◨◧ ♦ €15-23

It is like a fairytale castle: the tannins form the keep; the outer walls surrounding it are slender rather than rounded. You will have gathered that this characteristic 98 has something of a fortified structure about it. It can withstand several years of siege. The colour and the nose are typical Pinot.

↳ Maison Albert Bichot, 6 bis, bd
Jacques-Copeau, 21200 Beaune,
tel. 03.80.24.37.37, fax 03.80.24.37.38

BOUCHARD PÈRE ET FILS

Passe-temps 1998★

■1er cru   n.c.   n.c.   ▭◨◧ ♦ €15-23

Where does the name Passe-temps (pastime) come from? Perhaps because one needed to pass time in this vineyard to cultivate it properly, suggests M.-H. Landrieu-Lussigny, the author of a work on the origins of names and places on the Côte. This medium ruby-red 98 overwhelms the nose with strawberry and raspberry aromas. On the palate it is very full, tannic, approachable, but nevertheless a candidate for the waiting room.

↳ Bouchard Père et Fils, Ch. de Beaune,
21200 Beaune, tel. 03.80.24.80.24,
fax 03.80.22.55.88, e-mail France@
bouchard-pereetfils.com ♈ by appt.

DOM. DE BRULLY

Grand Clos Rousseau 1999

■1er cru   0.6 ha   3,200   ▭◧ €15-23

There are wines that appear to be simple but which turn out to be more complex. This one has a strong colour with very little bouquet at the moment. On the palate it is full and supple, despite a tannic quality that, all things being equal, should mellow.

↳ Dom. de Brully, 21190 Saint-Aubin,
tel. 03.80.21.32.92, fax 03.80.21.35.00 ▼
♈ by appt.
↳ Roux

DOM. CAPUANO-FERRERI ET FILS Les Gravières 1999★

■1er cru   n.c.   n.c.   ▭◧ €11-15

This Premier Cru wants to please. Deep purple, it doesn't give a great deal away at first, but then ... the aromas of chestnuts combined with young blackcurrant buds appear. Very good on the palate, showing character.

↳ Capuano-Ferreri et Fils,
1, rue de la Croix-Sorine, 21590 Santenay,
tel. 03.80.20.64.12, fax 03.80.20.65.75 ▼
♈ by appt.

DOM. DU CHATEAU DE MERCEY

■1998   1.13 ha   5,000   ▭◧ €11-15

Taken over by Antonin Rodet several years ago, this estate, founded in 1603, produces a deep cherry-red village with aromas of spices (nutmeg) and ripe soft fruit which need a little aeration. Tannic, but not excessively so, and

well-structured, it should be laid down for two years.
↳ Ch. de Mercey,
71150 Cheilly-lès-Maranges,
tel. 03.85.91.13.19, fax 03.85.91.16.28 ▼
♈ by appt.

FRANÇOISE ET DENIS CLAIR

Clos Genet 1999★★★

■   1.3 ha   6,000   ▭◨◧ €8-11

This wine came out on top among our coups de coeur. But then, the Clos Genet is at the very centre of the village, isn't it? And doesn't it frequently make the final list? Anyway, as villages go, it's first-rate and remarkably good value for money. A deep, intense garnet-red, with an expressive nose (ripe fruit, toast), on the palate it has exceptional complexity and marvellous roundness, and finishes with cherries in eau-de-vie. A wine for serious wine-lovers. The Village 99 red was awarded a star. It is a wine with character and shows itself to be very well-balanced.

↳ Françoise et Denis Clair,
14, rue de la Chapelle, 21590 Santenay,
tel. 03.80.20.61.96, fax 03.80.20.65.19 ▼
♈ by appt.

MICHEL CLAIR

Clos de Tavannes 1999★

■1er cru   0.21 ha   1,200   ▭◧ €8-11

Already a very attractive wine, the one-star Clos Genet 99 Village red was amongst our recommendations. As to this very well-made Premier Cru, it is not terribly fruity but is on the point of becoming complex, and the aromas are beginning to emerge. This heady wine has the kind of richness that benefits from a few years in the cellar. It will bear them well and be all the better for them.

↳ Dom. Michel Clair, 2, rue de Lavau,
21590 Santenay, tel. 03.80.20.62.55,
fax 03.80.20.65.37 ▼ ♈ by appt.

Y. ET C. CONTAT-GRANGE

Saint Jean de Narosse 1999★

■   1 ha   3,700   ▭◧ €8-11

The AOC hamlet of Saint-Jean-de-Narosse is surrounded by steep slopes; this gives a garnet-coloured wine with ruby highlights and morello-cherry aromas. It shows strong extraction of colour and aromas, but the body seems rich, tannic and structured, capable of waiting until the middle of this decade. The 93 vintage received a *coup de coeur* in our 1996 edition.

➤ EARL Yvon Contal-Grangé, Grande-Rue, 71150 Dezize-lès-Maranges, tel. 03.85.91.15.87, fax 03.85.91.12.54 ☑ by appt.

JEAN-FRANCOIS DICONNE

En Charron 1998

■ | 2.7 ha | 4,000 | €8-11

This wine has a brilliant, purple-garnet colour and on the nose it is oaky with an occasional untamed note of blackberries. This is a full-bodied *village* and very frank: rich, mouthfilling, *structured*. The fruitiness is definitely there but held in check by the biting tannins. Leave it to mature for one or two years.

➤ Jean-François Diconne, rue du Bourg, 71150 Remigny, tel. 03.85.87.20.01, fax 03.85.87.23.98 ☑ by appt.

DOM. GUY DUFOULEUR

Clos Genêts 1998

■ | 1.68 ha | 10,000 | €11-15

The purple colour of morello cherries, with aromas tending slightly towards leather, this is a wine of guaranteed quality. One can tell it is still reserved, with a certain harshness, but that will no doubt disappear in two or three years' time.

➤ Dom. Guy Dufouleur, 18, rue Thurot, 21700 Nuits-Saint-Georges, tel. 03.80.62.31.00, fax 03.80.62.31.00 ☑ by appt.

DOM. VINCENT GIRARDIN

Les Gravières 1999★★★

■ 1er cru | 1 ha | 5,500 | €11-15

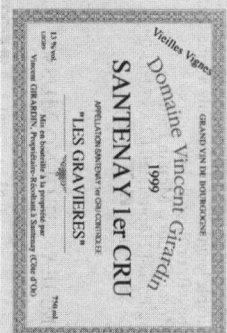

The plot is well carried out. It suggests a significant extraction, with its incredible garnet-black colour, powerful aromas of peonies and pears, and great concentration. Then along comes a note of elegance, a touch of distinction. If you are interested in a Chardonnay, try the fresh, minerally and toasty **Premier Cru Clos du Beauregard 99 white**.

➤ Caveau des Grands Crus, pl. de la Bascule, 21190 Chassagne-Montrachet, tel. 03.80.21.96.06, fax 03.80.21.96.23 ☑ ev. day 10am–1pm 2pm–6pm
➤ Vincent Girardin

DOM. DES HAUTES CORNIERES

1998★★

■ | 6 ha | 36,000 | €8-11

Our tasters considered awarding it a *coup de coeur*, which means you can have complete confidence in this wine from the 98 vintage that shows real personality. Brilliant purple, it is predominantly gamey, musky but doesn't neglect its fresh fruity side. The tannins are silky and well-blended, and a more than adequate acidity will allow this elegant wine to keep for quite a long time.

➤ Ph. Chapelle et Fils.
Dom. des Hautes-Cornières, 21590 Santenay, tel. 03.80.20.60.09, fax 03.80.20.61.01 ☑ ev. day except Sun. 9am–12 noon 2pm–6pm

DOM. LOUIS JADOT

Clos de Malte 1998★

□ | 1.5 ha | 5,400 | €15-23

Already very appealing to the eye with its brilliant, yellow-gold colour, this wine is clearly still very young with a dominant oakiness. However, as the nose penetrates the nose and there is a taste of hazelnuts on the tip of the tongue. The palate is balanced and totally taken up by oaky nuances. Wait at least a year before drinking it, with smoked salmon.

➤ Maison Louis Jadot, 21, rue Eugène-Spuller, 21200 Beaune, tel. 03.80.22.10.57, fax 03.80.22.56.03, e-mail contact@louisjadot.com ☑ by appt.

DOM. JESSIAUME PERE ET FILS

Gravières 1999★

□ 1er cru | 0.54 ha | 4,200 | €23-30

A golden colour and an admirable nose combining mineral notes and hints of citrus fruit, crushed grapes and honey. Full and rich, fleshy, generous, it will age well. The **Premier Cru Gravières 99 red** is also worthy of interest. It is a strongly concentrated wine with a promising future. One star.

➤ Dom. Jessiaume Pere et Fils, 10, rue de la Gare, 21590 Santenay, tel. 03.80.20.60.03, fax 03.80.20.62.87 ☑ by appt.

GABRIEL JOUARD

1998★

■ | 1.3 ha | 2,500 | €8-11

To appreciate the many aspects of this wine one must not be put off by its oakiness. Very open, accessible, it has style. On the palate it opens out to become full and fruity (blackcurrant, blackberries) while the tannins are still very noticeable. However, it has real quality that tips the balance in its favour, as long as one doesn't drink it too soon.

➤ EARL Dom. Gabriel Jouard Pere et Fils, 3, rue du Petit-Puits, 21190 Chassagne-Montrachet, tel. 03.80.21.30.30, fax 03.80.21.30.30 ☑ by appt.

Santenay

DOM. HUBERT LAMY
Clos des Hâtes Vieilles vignes 1999★★

◼ 0.7 ha 2,300 ⫿⫿ €11-15

The 98 vintage of this wine was awarded a *coup de coeur* last year. Passing on to this one, the result is almost as good. Nocturnal in colour (blackness melting into blueness), fairly oaky (it will need time to mellow), it has the temperament of a teacher. It likes to explain, demonstrate, and is very good at it – but make it wait a while in the cellar.

➤ Dom. Hubert Lamy, Paradis,
21190 Saint-Aubin, tel. 03.80.21.32.55,
fax 03.80.21.38.32 ⊠ ⛾ by appt.

DOM. RAYMOND LAUNAY
Clos de Gatsulard 1998

◼ 2.95 ha 7,000 ⫿⫿ €11-15

Spare a thought for Raymond Launay, the great Burgundian figure of the Mutualité Agricole (an agricultural organisation), now deceased. This Santenay *climat* was one of his classics, in the same way as the Le Clos is a monopoly. The colour is slightly slatey and the nose hints at raspberries. Closed on the palate, this robust 98 still shows a certain complexity enhanced by the flavour of cherry-stones.

➤ Dom. Raymond Launay,
rue des Charmots, 21630 Pommard,
tel. 03.80.24.08.03, fax 03.80.24.12.87 ⊠
⛾ ev. day 9am–6.30pm

RENE LEQUIN-COLIN
Les Charmes 1999★

◼ 0.46 ha 3,300 ⫿⫿ €8-11

Awarded one star, the **Les Hâtes 99 Village white** may have ethereal charms. And speaking of Les Charmes, this red one collected all the votes. Deep garnet-red with a nose full liquorice and floral aromas, it is mouthfilling on the palate, with flavours that last through to the finish. The statue of Saint Vincent, entrusted to the care of the family in 2001, watches over the cellars!

➤ EARL René Lequin-Colin, 10, rue de Lavau, 21590 Santenay, tel. 03.80.20.66.71, fax 03.80.20.66.70, e-mail renelequin@aol.com ⊠ ⛾ by appt.

JEROME MASSON
Beaurepaire 1999★

◼ 1er cru 0.78 ha 600 ⫿⫿ €11-15

Jérôme Masson took over from his parents (first Maurice, then Nadine) in 1998. He follows in their footsteps with this fine example of the appellation. Very intense – almost black – in appearance, the Premier Cru wavers between spices and red berries before revealing all that is expected of it on the palate. The liquorice finish still has a tannic touch that will mellow after two or three years in the cellar.

➤ Jérôme Masson, rue Haute,
21340 La Rochepot, tel. 03.80.21.72.42,
fax 03.80.21.72.42 ⊠ ⛾ by appt.

MESTRE PERE ET FILS
Passe-Temps 1998

◼ 1er cru 1.25 ha 3,500 ⫿⫿ €11-15

What a joy to have such an agreeable Passe-Temps (literally 'pastime')! A lively colour with a generous, slightly jammy aroma (blackcurrants); it is very long – as long as a day without wine. On the palate it still leans towards blackcurrant. A trifle monolithic, but then, so are the supporting pillars of the château's cellars at Clos de Vougeot …

➤ Mestre Père et Fils, 12, pl. du Jet-d'Eau, 21590 Santenay, tel. 03.80.20.60.11, fax 03.80.20.60.97, e-mail gilbert-mestre@wanadoo.fr ⊠ ⛾ by appt.

MOMMESSIN
Clos Rousseau 1998★

◼ 1er cru 1.2 ha 6,000 ⫿⫿ €11-15

A true Janus. Its ruby colour is undoubtedly Burgundian (Burgundy-red), and while its bouquet is characteristic, musky and fruity, it is doubly so on the palate. On the one hand, it is structured, tannic, a perfect example of the appellation; on the other, delicate in the extreme, wild roses, cherry-stones. A wine destined to become pure silk! Mommessin belongs to Vins J.-Cl. Boisset.

➤ Mommessin, Le Pont-des-Samsons,
69430 Quincié-en-Beaujolais,
tel. 04.74.69.09.30, fax 04.74.69.09.28,
e-mail information@mommessin.com
⛾ by appt.

CH. MOROT-GAUDRY 1998★★

◼ 0.67 ha 1,000 ⫿⫿ €8-11

An old mill, worked by this family from 1852 to 1965, has been converted into wine-making premises. This lovely 98 vintage holds some real trumps in its hand: a beautiful, limpid colour and an open bouquet packed with damp undergrowth and fern aromas; a substantial palate, rich and complex, with creditable length. This is certainly a wine that can be left for three to four years.

➤ Morot-Gaudry, Moulin Pignot,
71150 Paris-l'Hôpital, tel. 03.85.91.11.09,
fax 03.85.91.11.09 ⊠ ⛾ by appt.

DOM. JEAN ET GENO MUSSO
1999

◼ 0.63 ha 4,000 ⫿⫿ €8-11

Winner of the *Grappe d'argent* in our 1991 edition, this domaine extends all over the Côte Chalonaise: Château de Sassangy, Clos de Prieuré at Rosey. It has been practising organic methods since 1984. Its attractive 99 vintage has a light but well-balanced structure. Clear red with raspberry shades, it holds onto this theme through to the finish. An admirable restraint marks it out from its neighbours.

➤ Jean et Geno Musso, Le château,
71390 Sassangy, tel. 03.85.96.18.61,
fax 03.85.96.18.62 ⊠ ⛾ by appt.

LUCIEN MUZARD ET FILS

Clos de Tavannes 1999★★

0.99 ha · 3,000 · €11-15 · 1er cru

M. de Saulx-Tavannes, that great figure from Burgundian history, would have enjoyed this wine with a rib of beef before the start of a battle. Truly a wine that puts its heart into its work. A strong ruby in colour, it has aromas touching on liquorice and blackcurrant. A trifle austere, no doubt because of its age, but with an acidity that will keep it in top form, it was considered for a *coup de cœur*. Also commended by the Jury was the **Premier Cru Maladière 99 red**.

Lucien Muzard et Fils, 11 *bis*, rue de la Cour-Verreuil, 21590 Santenay, tel. 03.80.20.61.85, fax 03.80.20.66.02, e-mail lucien-muzard-et-fils@wanadoo.fr by appt.

NICOLAS PERE ET FILS 1999★

0.35 ha · 2,000 · €8-11

The Côte d'Or begins here, approaching from the south anyway, as this Pinot Noir, with its flag flying high, shows. With slight amber highlights, it initially delivers an aroma of ink that tends to disappear on aeration, opening out with cinnamon and fresh almonds. Balanced, and both firmly structured and soft at the same time, it presents an example of a Pinot Noir which has remained true to its origins, without being subjected to excessive extraction.

EARL du dom. Nicolas Père et Fils, 38, rue de Cirey, 21340 Nolay, tel. 03.80.21.82.92, fax 03.80.21.85.47 ev. day 9am–12 noon 1.30pm–7pm

Côte de Beaune (South)

Map labels: Mercey · Sampigny-les-Maranges · Dezize-les-Maranges · Cheilly-les-Maranges · Santenay-Haut · Santenay-Bas · Chassagne-Montrachet · CÔTE-D'OR · SAÔNE-ET-LOIRE · CHALON-SUR-SAÔNE · N 6 · D 113

AOC localities and Premiers Crus
Regional AOC areas
Department boundaries
Commune boundaries

0 500 1000 yds
0 500 1000 m

DOM. CLAUDE NOUVEAU ★
Les Charmes Dessus 1998 ★
■ 0.9 ha 5,500 | €8-11

The **Premier Cru Grand Clos Rousseau 98 red** was commended by the Jury. The Les Charmes Dessus *climat* is near to the Clos Rousseau, on the Maranges side. It produces this satiny, crimson-purple Pinot Noir. Its nose, with aromas of musky leather and light red berries, is not yet fully open but already has sound framework, with good tannic structure and keeping qualities.
☛ EARL Dom. Claude Nouveau, Marchezeuil, 21340 Change, tel. 03.85.91.13.34, fax 03.85.91.10.39 ☒ ☒ by appt.

OLIVIER PÈRE ET FILS
Le Bièvaux 1999
□ 3.5 ha 10,000 | €11-15

Golden-yellow like the bulk of the 99 vintage, this Chardonnay's nose contains aromas of flint with touches of incense which add interest. Characteristic, it behaves well on the palate.
☛ Olivier Père et Fils, 5, rue Gaudin, 21590 Santenay, tel. 03.80.20.61.35, fax 03.80.20.64.82, e-mail antoine.olivier2@wanadoo.fr ☒ ☒ by appt.

PIGUET-GIRARDIN Comme 1999 ★
■ 1er cru 1.4 ha 5,500 | ★ €11-15

In the casino at Santenay, this wine's bouquet would bring it so much luck it could double its stake. It carries a touch of vinosity in a cocktail where one can detect strawberries, vanilla and pebbles from the vineyard. But don't mistake it for an inveterate gambler. On the contrary it shows prudence, almost austerity in its concentration. It has plenty of time before it (two years).
☛ SCE Piguet-Girardin, rue du Meix, 21190 Auxey-Duresses, tel. 03.80.21.60.26, fax 03.80.21.66.61 ☒ ☒ by appt.

DOM. PONSARD-CHEVALIER
Les Daumelles 1999 ★
□ 0.22 ha 1,600 | €8-11

Les Daumelles? We admit we didn't know it, and it is not on the map. That said, there thousands of such *lieux-dits* (localities). Light-yellow in colour with butter and hazelnuts, this is a wine which is fresh and stylish, with a touch of vivacity to liven up the scene.
☛ Ponsard-Chevalier, 2, Les Tilles, 21590 Santenay, tel. 03.80.20.61.10 ☒ ☒ by appt.

DOM. PRIEUR-BRUNET
Clos Rousseau 1999
□ 1er cru 0.25 ha 1,500 | €15-23

From water-nymph to the god of wine ... the spa town of Santenay houses both these marvels. Bacchus is expressed here in white. While it does not have great structure, its lively, lemony freshness, and its supple and pleasant attack on the palate with pronounced citrus fruit flavours, do capture one's attention.
☛ Dom. Prieur-Brunet, rue de Narosse, 21590 Santenay, tel. 03.80.20.60.56, fax 03.80.20.64.31, e-mail uny-prieur@prieursantenay.com ☒ ☒ by appt.

JEAN-CLAUDE REGNAUDOT ★
Grand Clos Rousseau 1999 ★
■ 0.32 ha 2,100 | €8-11

When its passion has calmed down, this should be a remarkable wine. Attired with distinction, reserving the few attributes of its bouquet for blackberries, its tannins are still powerful. Hold fast for two or three years before drinking it with a coq au vin.
☛ Jean-Claude Regnaudot, Grande-Rue, 71150 Dezize-les-Maranges, tel. 03.85.91.15.95, fax 03.85.91.16.45 ☒ ☒ by appt.

BERNARD REGNAUDOT 1999 ★
■ 1 ha 3,000 | €8-11

Les Maranges is not far from here. This dark-red 99 has a light nose of fruit preserved in alcohol. Balanced and generous, the palate suggests it should be laid down for two years.
☛ Bernard Regnaudot, rte de Nolay, 71150 Dezize-les-Maranges, tel. 03.85.91.14.90, fax 03.85.91.14.90 ☒ ☒ by appt.

SORINE ET FILS Clos Rousseau 1998 ★
■ 1er cru 0.4 ha 2,500 | €8-11

A cellar you could find your way around with your eyes closed. Our Jury chose three wines: the **Premier Cru Beaurepaire 99 red**, the **Village 98 white**, and this attractive, half-flowery, half-fruity Clos Rousseau. From the start, this wine shows an agreeable suppleness that develops solidly with vigorous, chewy tannins. There is no doubt that it will age well. This family, who migrated to Paris for a while, has been in the area a long time (look at places like Croix Sorine and Derrière chez Sorine).
☛ Dom. Sorine et Fils, 4, rue Petit, Le Haut-Village, 21590 Santenay, tel. 03.80.20.61.65, fax 03.80.20.61.65 ☒ ☒ by appt.

DOM. DES VIGNES DES DEMOISELLES 1999 ★
■ 1.07 ha 7,700 | €11-15

The 98 vintage won a *coup de cœur* last year. Here's the subtle and well-made 99 which has a purple colour and a very fine, even delicate nose. Its tannins have this same characteristic. A certain vivacity enlivens the whole, perfectly-balanced picture. Last but not least, the wine is not overwhelmed by oakiness. Well done.
☛ Gabriel Demangeot et Fils, rue de Berfey, 21340 Change, tel. 03.85.91.11.10, fax 03.85.91.16.83 ☒ ☒ by appt.

JEAN-MARC VINCENT

Les Gravières 1998★

1er cru	1.15 ha	1,000	£11-15

This is an unusual label showing a picture of the bottle, bearing a label picturing the bottle ... and so on to infinity. Having succeeded his 91-year-old grandfather in 1997, Jean-Marc Vincent has produced this Premier Cru which has a pronounced colour, an interesting nose (vanilla, nutmeg, liquorice) and good structure. It needs to be left in peace for a couple of years.

→ Jean-Marc Vincent, 3, rue Sainte-Agathe, 21590 Santenay, tel. 03.80.20.67.37, fax 03.80.20.67.37, e-mail vincent.j@wanadoo.fr Y by appt.

Marañges

The Marañges vineyard is in Saône-et-Loire (Chailly, Dezize and Sampigny). Since 1989, following a reorganisation, it has had its own AOC, which includes six Premiers Crus. Wine production here is predominantly of red, with some white; the reds may also be labelled AOC Côte de Beaune-Villages, which was how they were previously sold. The wines are fruity, full-bodied and well-structured; they can age for between five and ten years. In 2000 9,122 hl (240,821 gal) of AOC Marañges were produced, of which 232 hl (6,125 gal) were white.

DOM. ALEXANDRE PERE ET FILS

Les Clos Roussots 1999★

1er cru	n.c.	n.c.	€8-11

The colour of this wine fully reflects its youthfulness but it is making great strides towards maturity. The nose, too, is still adolescent with red berry aromas. It has great keeping potential thanks to its powerful structure.

→ Dom. Alexandre Père et Fils, pl. de la Mairie, 71150 Remigny, tel. 03.85.87.22.61, fax 03.85.87.22.61, e-mail domaine.alexandre@roonoo.net [V] Y by appt.

DOM. BACHELET

Vieilles vignes 1998★

	3.5 ha	18,000	€5-8

This wine-grower has previously won a coup de cœur for his 94 red, but this time he presented his Fussière Premier Cru white 99. It has a clear colour, round and perfumed, and obtained the same mark as this Cuvée Vielles Vignes, made from Pinot Noir. Between dark ruby and garnet, the latter offers a toasty nose marked by the terroir, and becomes nicely supple on the palate. This wine is in great form and needs to go back into the cellar to acquire a little sheen.

→ Dom. Bernard Bachelet et Fils, rue des Marañges, 71150 Dezize-lès-Marañges, tel. 03.85.91.16.11, fax 03.85.91.16.48 [V] Y by appt.

DANIEL BILLARD La Fussière 1999

1er cru	1.17 ha	n.c.	€8-11

Henri Vincenot wrote charmingly about Les Marañges, home of his wife and her family. He understood the secret soul of the area and praised it, as does this spontaneous and very unaffected wine, with its rural aromas of blackberries and bilberries, and its gripping tannins. A wine to lay down for a year or two.

→ Daniel Billard, rue de Borgy, 71150 Dezize-lès-Marañges, tel. 03.85.91.15.60, fax 03.85.91.10.59 [V] Y by appt.

DOM. JEAN-FRANCOIS BOUTHENET Sur le chêne 1999

	0.37 ha	3,000	€8-11

Remarkable for its very pronounced terroir flavours, this 99 vintage is typically 'Les Marañges.' An appealing palate with flowers and brioche, supple almost bordering on sweet, it has a strong gold-yellow colour. The nose is closed at the moment but that will change.

→ Jean-François Bouthenet, Mercey, 71150 Cheilly-lès-Marañges, tel. 03.85.91.14.29, fax 03.85.91.18.24 [V] Y by appt.

ROGER BELLAND La Fussière 1999★

1er cru	1 ha	5,500	€8-11

As Catullus said, 'Effort is rewarded by victory.' It is not difficult to measure the effort, from vine to cellar, that went into producing this serene and joyous wine with its relatively soft oakiness (which needs to integrate further to bring out the spirit of the Pinot grape) and refined elegance. Spicy morello cherry flows in its wake on the palate.

→ Dom. Roger Belland, 3, rue de la Chapelle, BP 13, 21590 Santenay, tel. 03.80.20.60.95, fax 03.80.20.63.93, e-mail belland.roger@wanadoo.fr [V]

DOM. MARC BOUTHENET

La Fussière 1999★

1er cru	0.75 ha	4,500	€8-11

'I am young, it is true, but of well-bred spirit ...,' 'This lovely 99, positively bursting with colour, has a well-controlled oakiness that allows the fruit to show through, and shows well on the palate right through to the attractive finish. Also worth mentioning.

while we are about it, is the lasting note of raspberries.

Dom. Marc Bouthenet, Mercey, 10–11, rue Saint-Louis, 71150 Cheilly-lès-Maranges, tel. 03.85.91.16.51, fax 03.85.91.13.52 ☑ Y by appt.

PIERRE BRESSON Les Meurées 1999 · €8-11

0.2 ha · 1,000

This *climat*, situated near to Cheilly, is represented here by a white with notes of fresh citrus fruits. It has supple, light tones; simple, in a word. A wine for drinking in the coming year.

Dom. Pierre Bresson, Le Pont, 71150 Cheilly-lès-Maranges, tel. 03.85.91.15.58, fax 03.85.91.17.37 ☑ Y by appt.

DOM. MAURICE CHARLEUX ET FILS Le Clos des Rois 1999★ · €8-11

1er cru · 0.3 ha · 1,800

Two red wines, both equally praiseworthy: a **Fussière 99** that is well-balanced and has great potential, and this Clos des Rois (a *climat* next to Sampigny, which is near Loyères and Clos Roussots). Dark ruby in colour, it has well-blended oak and a nose with good depth. Its fine structure reveals some cherry-stone flavours; a Premier Cru that is very typical. In 1999, Maurice Charleux passed the baton to his son Vincent, and these are his first wines.

EARL Maurice Charleux et Fils, Petite-Rue, 71150 Dezize-lès-Maranges, tel. 03.85.91.15.15, fax 03.85.91.11.81 ☑ Y by appt.

DOM. CHEVROT 1999 · €8-11

0.7 ha · 4,000

The **99 Domaine red** allows a few notes of blackcurrant to show through; the palate is still closed and will take its time. As to this white, it has a spring-like colour and scarcely any aroma but becomes supple, mineral and fruity on the palate. Not particularly powerful but overflowing with charm.

Catherine et Fernand Chevrot, Dom. Chevrot, 19, rte de Couches, 71150 Cheilly-lès-Maranges, tel. 03.85.91.10.55, fax 03.85.91.13.24, e-mail domaine.chevrot@wanadoo.fr ☑ Y ev. day 9am–12 noon 2pm–6pm; Sun. 9am–12 noon

Y. ET C. CONTAT-GRANGE 1999 · €5-8

1.2 ha · 4,000

Diamond-shaped and without illustration, this is one of the most unusual labels of the region. Definitely an *haute couture* appearance. The nose, however, has little to say for itself. A very powerful 99 and certainly not to be pitied. Let us have faith in its promises.

EARL Yvon Contat-Grangé, Grande-Rue, 71150 Dezize-lès-Maranges, tel. 03.85.91.15.87, fax 03.85.91.12.54 ☑ Y by appt.

MARINOT-VERDUN 1998 · €8-11

n.c. · 4,500

No need to go in for target-shooting: the match is won before it starts. This interesting 98 has already developed somewhat, its aromas show some maturity. The jammy style is in keeping with the slightly rustic character but there is nothing disagreeable about it, nor should there be. From this autumn onwards, it would go well with a wild-boar stew.

Marinot-Verdun, Cave de Mazenay, 71510 Saint-Sernin-du-Plain, tel. 03.85.49.67.19, fax 03.85.45.57.21 ☑ Y ev. day except Sun. 8am–12 noon 1.30pm–6pm

DOM. RENE MONNIER Clos de la Fussière 1999

1er cru · 1.2 ha · 5,000

A war-horse among the Premier Crus of this AOC, this *clos*, a monopoly, produces this wine that has not yet had its say. It has a garnet-red colour with purple, almost black, highlights. The aromas of damp undergrowth combine with vanilla. The body is lively, and tannins are undergoing a transformation that will ensure a long life.

Dom. René Monnier, 6, rue du Dr-Rolland, 21190 Meursault, tel. 03.80.21.29.32, fax 03.80.21.61.79 ☑ Y ev. day 8am–12 noon 2pm–6pm
M. et Mme Bouillot

DOM. CLAUDE NOUVEAU 1998★ · €8-11

1.1 ha · 6,000

This red *village* immediately caught our interest. The nose has complex, diverse aromas of damp undergrowth, moss and strawberries. This still-young wine has a structure with very fine, firm tannins. Ready to drink in four to six years. Let us also recommend a **Fussière Premier Cru 98 red**, in case the former is no longer available; it had a similar rating but only obtained a mention as it is a Premier Cru.

EARL Dom. Claude Nouveau, Marchezeuil, 21340 Change, tel. 03.85.91.13.34, fax 03.85.91.10.39 ☑ Y by appt.

DOM. PONSARD-CHEVALIER Clos des Rois 1998★ · €8-11

1er cru · 0.34 ha · 2,000

This wine from the 98 vintage has a persistent colour. On the nose it is astonishingly complex and fruity and caresses the palate with its well-balanced, long, silky body. Very typical, despite the presence of well-structured tannins. A wine that will keep for four to five years.

Ponsard-Chevalier, 2, Les Tilles, 21590 Santenay, tel. 03.80.20.60.87, fax 03.80.20.61.10 ☑ Y by appt.

Côte de Beaune-Villages

Not to be confused with the Côte de Nuits-Villages appellation, which has its own special production area, the Côte de Beaune-Villages appellation is not confined to a specific place but may be used by all the red-wine *Appellations Communales* in the Côte de Beaune, with the exception of the *Appellations Communales* in the Côte de Beaune, Aloxe-Corton, Pommard and Volnay. In 2000, 210 hl (5,544 gal) were produced.

DOM. GUY DIDIER 1999★

0.91 ha 6,500 €11-15

The strong extraction shows in the colour of this wine. The nose, initially tempted by liquorice, opts for bilberries. The attack is solid, spirited, quite firm, the length satisfactory, coming back to dark berry fruit. A very characteristic 99, this wine needs to age two or three years before being served with marinated meats.

• Dom. Guy Didier, chem. rural n° 29, 21700 Nuits-Saint-Georges, tel. 03.80.62.42.00, fax 03.80.61.28.13, e-mail nuicave@wanadoo.fr
Y ev. day 10am–6pm; cl. Jan.

La Côte Chalonnaise

Bourgogne Côte Chalonnaise

The AOC Bourgogne Côte Chalonnaise was created on 27 February 1990. It comprises 44 communes, which produced 27,335 hl (721,644 gal) of red wine and 8,990 hl (237,336 gal) of white in 2000. According to the system also applied in the Hautes-Côtes, agreements about quality are reached following a second tasting to supplement the compulsory tasting that takes place everywhere.

Located between Chagny and Saint-Gengoux-le-National (Saône et Loire), the Côte Chalonnaise has an individual identity that deserves the recognition it has received.

BERNARD REGNAUDOT

Clos des Rois 1999★

1er cru 1 ha 6,500 €8-11

This wine should not be woken up too soon as it needs to open out before its proper values can be appreciated. Product of Sampigny, it couldn't be more strongly-coloured. Its tannins confer a vegetal side that will tone down, as will the touch of astringency that is not a permanent feature. Strawberry jam is already discernible on the horizon.

• Bernard Regnaudot, rte de Nolay, 71150 Dezize-lès-Maranges, tel. 03.85.91.14.90, fax 03.85.91.14.90
Y by appt.

JEAN-CLAUDE REGNAUDOT ET FILS Les Clos Roussots 1999★

1er cru 0.52 ha 3,600 €8-11

The Saint-Vincent travelling wine fair has contributed a great deal to the awareness of the Maranges AOC. This excellent Premier Cru, which has undergone significant extraction during vinification, has produced this lovely 99 with an imposing structure that will slim down as it matures. It has a vinous and youthful nose and a brilliant garnet colour. Wait for three to five years before partnering it with a *civet de lièvre* (a rich hare and red-wine stew).

• Jean-Claude Regnaudot, Grande-Rue, 71150 Dezize-lès-Maranges, tel. 03.85.91.15.95, fax 03.85.91.16.45
Y by appt.

DOM. DES ROUGES-QUEUES 1999

0.8 ha 2,800 €8-11

Installed in 1997, the Vanteys (he from Burgundy and she from the Valais) have vines growing here that are 65 years old. This wine's nose does not say anything immediately but opens finally with fine spices. After a fairly lively attack the tannins become apparent: the structure is strong and should hold up well, since it is developing on the palate with a good fruity foundation.

• Jean-Yves Vantey, 10, rue Saint-Antoine, 71150 Sampigny-lès-Maranges, tel. 03.85.91.18.69, fax 03.85.91.18.69
Y by appt.

MICHEL SARRAZIN ET FILS

Côte de Beaune 1999★

1.5 ha 8,000 €8-11

They hardly ever write 'Maranges Côte de Beaune' on labels nowadays, though they are entitled to do so. The name of the capital of Burgundy is obviously a selling point. This year this wine-producer presented a wine with the kind of vegetal attack on the nose that is very common in this appellation; small dark berry fruit and vanilla are also present. This tannic 99 tinged with liquorice needs to be laid down in the cellar for two or three years.

• Michel Sarrazin et Fils, Charnailles, 71640 Jambles, tel. 03.85.44.30.57, fax 03.85.44.31.22
Y by appt.

Bourgogne Côte Chalonnaise

CH. DE CARY POTET

Vieilles vignes 1999★

■   2 ha   4,500   ◫ €8-11

Belonging to the same family since 1750, this estate survived the Revolution and has known all the subsequent regimes. This is a well-balanced 99 with a purple-red colour and a full aroma retaining a blackcurrant-leaf aspect on the palate. Its potential guarantees it a happy future; its tannic and oaky temperament will soften over time.

↪ Charles et Pierre du Besset, Ch. de Cary Potet, 71390 Buxy, tel. 03.85.92.14.48, fax 03.85.92.11.88 ☑ Y by appt.

DOM. CHAUMONT PÈRE ET FILS

1999★

■   0.6 ha   3,100   ◫ €5-8

For almost 30 years now this 9-ha (22.2-acre) estate has been using organic methods. Now it practises sustainable agriculture, and here is its latest offspring: rich in colour, not very responsive on the nose, with musky, animal and soft fruit aromas. Very full, round and pleasantly fruity, it has well-balanced acidity and a good tannin quality. All this points to a fine future. It would go well with boeuf Bourguignon.

↪ Dom. Chaumont Père et Fils, Le Clos Saint-Georges, 71640 Saint-Jean-de-Vaux, tel. 03.85.45.13.77, fax 03.85.45.27.77, e-mail didierchaumont@aol.com ☑ Y by appt.

DANIEL DAVANTURE ET FILS

1998★

■   9.6 ha   6,000   ■ €5-8

It is only two kilometres (1.2 miles) from this estate to the 12th-century village church – the distance needed to locate this good Burgundy which is very characteristic of its appellation, smelling sweetly of the *terroir* for. Daniel Davanture, who succeeded his father, Louis, took sons Damien and Eric into partnership in 1996. Saint-Désert, the name of the village, is not as deserted as all that!

↪ Daniel Davanture et Fils,
GAEC des Murgers, rue de La Montée, 71390 Saint-Désert, tel. 03.85.47.90.42, fax 03.85.47.99.88 ☑ Y by appt.

CAVE DES VIGNERONS DE GENOUILLY 1999★

□   10 ha   20,000   ■ ◆ €3-5

Of the 65 ha (160.5 acres) owned in common by this co-operative, ten (24.7 acres) are dedicated to this slightly gold-tinted Chardonnay. On the nose there is a blend of mineral and toasted nuts. A tiny exotic touch is followed by a fine richness enlivened by a certain acidity; overall it has good length. As to the **99 red**, it is a chewy wine with character,

and was awarded a star. Keep it for two to three years if possible.

↪ Cave des vignerons de Genouilly, 71460 Genouilly, tel. 03.85.49.23.72, fax 03.85.49.23.58 ☑ Y ev. day except Sun. 8am–12 noon 2pm–6pm

DOM. MICHEL GOUBARD ET FILS Mont-Avril 1999

■   7 ha   50,000   ■ ◫ ◆ €5-8

Mont-Avril is one of the rare *climats* to have made a name for itself in the Côte Chalonnaise, thanks to the Goubard family who have done a great deal for vines and wine. Its purple highlights, aromas of smokiness and red berries, its supple attack and vivacity, make this fruity 99 a wine to drink now with a rustic dish like *andouille* (a type of sausage) with beans, or a veal and carrot stew.

↪ Dom. Michel Goubard et Fils, Basseville, 71390 Saint-Désert, tel. 03.85.47.91.06, fax 03.85.47.98.12 ☑ Y ev. day 8am–7pm; Sat./Sun. by appt.

DOM. GOUFFIER

Clos de Petite Combe 1999

■   0.55 ha   3,000   ◫ €8-11

Its fairly intense, garnet-ruby colour showing no sign of excessive extraction, this wine is moderate at heart. The purity of the fruit (as much scarlet as black – this wine knows its Stendhal) is accompanied by a delicate note of vanilla. Severe on the palate, clean-cut and robust, it still has a trace of tender fruitiness. While it is not a marathon runner, it does well at middle-distance and will be very good in one to two years' time.

↪ Dom. Gouffier, 11, Grande-Rue, 71150 Fontaines, tel. 03.85.91.46.98, fax 03.85.91.46.98, e-mail jerome.gouffier@wanadoo.fr ☑ Y by appt.

PIERRE D'HEILLY ET MARTINE HUBERDEAU 1999

■   2 ha   15,300   ■ ◫ ◆ €5-8

The estate is established at the foot of Mont-Avril sur Moroges. In the 18th century, the Abbot of Courtépée mentioned finding in this area 'a good little wine-growing district called Butte-Sèche, with vines from Dijon'; could this be for it? At any rate this is a very well-made cherry-red wine with a raspberry aroma, robust on the palate with the right amount of vinosity. A well-constructed wine which will easily last three to four years. The estate has been practising organic methods since 1978.

↪ EARL d'Heilly-Huberdeau, Cercot, 71390 Moroges, tel. 03.85.47.95.27, fax 03.85.47.98.97 ☑ Y by appt.

DOM. FRANCE LECHENAULT 1999★★

□   0.68 ha   2,000   ◫ €5-8

The late France Léchenault was the senator-mayor of Bouzeron, and her daughter Claudette has followed her into politics. This Chardonnay with its fresh and fruity notes of verbena and fresh almonds is wonderfully approachable. Radical in spirit, its opulent richness is tempered by a welcome acidity. The **red 99** has a very good basic structure and will be tremendous in one to two years. It was also awarded two stars.

☛ Dom. France Léchenault, 11, rue des Dames, 71150 Bouzeron, tel. 03.85.87.17.56, fax 03.85.91.27.17 ▼

DOM. LES DAVIGNOLLES 1999★★

3.5 ha 3,000 €5-8

This estate, acquired in 1997 by Denis Vessot, started out with 4.5 ha (11 acres), mostly of Pinot. This still-firm 99 will age attractively. A good intense colour; blackcurrants and blackberries are complemented by a reasonable oakiness. A wine which is shaping up nicely, it is elegant right through to the finish.

☛ Denis Vessot, Le Bourg, 71640 Barizey, tel. 03.85.44.59.79, fax 03.85.44.59.79 ▼ ev. day 8am–7pm

DOM. MASSE PÈRE ET FILS
Les Vignes Devant 1999★

0.2 ha 1,500 €5-8

This wine has a touch of charm which works very well and earns it a place among the best. Very pale gold with copper highlights, it is particularly full in its aromas: citronella and hazelnuts. There is also a hint of mushrooms on the supple, unctuous, appealing palate.

☛ Dom. Masse Père et Fils, 71640 Barizey, tel. 03.85.44.36.73 ▼ ev. day 8am–8pm

DOM. MASSE PÈRE ET FILS 1999

5 ha 8,000 €5-8

Cherry-red to the eye, kirsch on the nose, this wine is constant in its allegiances. Powerful and vinous, it has plenty to say on the palate and is loyal to the cherry (the two really are inseparable) while at the same time the tannins are integrating in the style of a Pinot Noir from the Côte Chalonnaise. Don't open it yet!

☛ Dom. Masse Père et Fils, 71640 Barizey, tel. 03.85.44.36.73 ▼ ev. day 8am–8pm

DOM. MAZOYER
Sous Saint-Germain 1999

5 ha 12,000 €5-8

'Definitely destined for a *cassolette d'escargots à la vigneronne*' (snails cooked in an earthenware dish), the Jury decided, inspired by this frank, round, fleshy wine with its very dark colour and brilliant purple highlights. Spicy, it is very appealing, though not particularly long.

☛ Dom. Mazoyer, imp. du Ruisseau, 71390 Saint-Désert, tel. 03.85.47.95.28, fax 03.85.47.98.91 ▼ by appt.

DOM. DES MOIROTS 1999

2.3 ha 7,000 €5-8

The product of vines cultivated for 35 years, this wine has a dark-purple, inky colour which leaves the nose in peace, not asking too much of it: just a few musky aromas and gamey notes. In contrast, it is very open on the palate, tannic and tending towards game. The *oeufs en meurette* (eggs poached in red wine) will have to wait one to two years.

☛ Dom. des Moirots, 14, rue des Moirots, 71390 Bissey-sous-Cruchaud, tel. 03.85.92.16.93, fax 03.85.92.16.93 ▼

☛ Lucien et Christophe Denizot

DOM. ROBERT SIZE ET FILS 1999

1.2 ha 7,000 €5-8

Bright ruby in colour, it needs a quarter-turn before opening with redcurrants and cherries. It doesn't lose sight of its objectives and smooths its tannins without seeking to complicate things. Simple, light, rustic, it rests happily within its category.

☛ Dom. Robert Size et Fils, Le Bourg, 71640 Saint-Martin-sous-Montaigu, tel. 03.85.45.11.72, fax 03.85.45.27.66, e-mail alainc@size.fr ▼

FLORENCE ET MARTIAL THÉVENOT 1999

2.4 ha 2,000 €5-8

A Pinot Noir of good intensity which is developing aromas of macerated fruit with roasted notes. A style that is a follower of the Côte Chalonnaise scene.

☛ Florence et Martial Thévenot, 4, rue du Champ-de-l'Orme, 71510 Aluze, tel. 03.85.45.18.43, fax 03.85.45.09.98 ▼ by appt.

VENOT La Corvée 1999★

0.7 ha 3,000 €5-8

It would be difficult to be more brilliant! The nose starts with damp undergrowth and balsamic aromas and then opens out and turns religious (notes of incense). The attack is all strength and vigour and on the palate is rich and unctuous with a certain fleshiness. On the finish it returns to the theme with honeyed, toasty flavours.

☛ GAEC Venot, 'La Corvée', 71390 Moroges, tel. 03.85.47.90.20, fax 03.85.47.90.20 ▼ by appt.

A. ET P. DE VILLAINE
Les Clous 1999★★

3 ha n.c. +76

The new Mayor of Bouzeron, Aubert de Villaine, together with his wife Pamela, here present a 99 vintage with a charming colour. With sweet spices and orange colour, the nose is careful not to forget a touch of hawthorn blossom. This is a wine to drink in two years time when we can still appreciate its youthfulness. Among the red wines, the **La Digoine 99** received the same rating for its dark colour, concentrated nose of soft fruit and liquorice, and very fine, long tannins.

☛ A. et P. de Villaine, 2, rue de la Fontaine, 71150 Bouzeron, tel. 03.85.91.20.50, fax 03.85.87.04.10, e-mail dom.devillaine@wanadoo.fr ▼ by appt.

Bouzeron

Bouzeron is a little village between Chagny and Rully, well-known for its wines made from the Aligoté grape, the variety most evident in the commune's vineyard of around 62 ha (153 acres). Planted on slopes slanting east-south-east, on mainly chalky soil, Aligoté makes lively white wine with lots of character, developing into complex wines of a 'sharp roundness'. The Appellation Bourgogne Aligoté Bouzeron was created in 1979, being replaced in 1998 by the *Appellation Communale* Bouzeron. In 2000, 4,040 hl (106,656 gal) were declared.

BOUCHARD PERE ET FILS 1999
☐   n.c.   n.c.   €8–11

A little severe and lively but one shouldn't reproach it for not having a typical Chardonnay style. The colour is faultless; the nose very intense, opening with young blackcurrant leaves. Not the least bit disagreeable. On the palate it is charming, supple and as easy as ABC.

☛ Bouchard Père et Fils, Ch. de Beaune, 21200 Beaune, tel. 03.80.24.80.24, fax 03.80.22.55.88, e-mail france@bouchard-pereetfils.com ☒ by appt.

PIERRE COGNY ET DAVID DEPRES 1999★★
☐   5.87 ha 10,000   €5–8

A salmon tartare with cucumber? Why not? One really should do justice to this very pale-straw coloured wine with its appealing nose of fruits and spring blossom, lacking neither fullness nor length and very characteristic of the vintage.

☛ Pierre Cogny et David Déprés, GAEC de La Vieille Fontaine, 71150 Bouzeron, tel. 03.85.87.19.96, fax 03.85.87.19.96 ☒ by appt.

DOM. PATRICK GUILLOT
☐   1.52 ha 2,800   €5–8

The winner's spot on the podium for this brilliant Aligoté. To the eye it has fine green highlights; on the nose it plays skilfully on various levels ranging from lemony freshness to a flowery quality. The Grand Jury awarded it a *coup de cœur* for its depth, richness and complexity, upheld by the liveliness of the AOC.

☛ Dom. Patrick Guillot, 9 A, rue de Vaugeailles, 71640 Mercurey, tel. 03.85.45.27.40, fax 03.85.45.28.57 ☒ ☒ by appt.

DOM. DE LA RENARDE
Les Cordères 1999★
☐   1.7 ha 14,000 ■■ ☒ €5–8

'I am proud to be a Burgundian'! One may certainly sing that while drinking a wine such as this one. This very pale, barely-golden 99 reveals green apples and flint, then a round attack followed by a surge of freshness on the palate.

☛ André Delorme, Dom. de la Renarde, 2, rue de la République, 71150 Rully, tel. 03.85.87.10.12, fax 03.85.87.04.60, e-mail andre-delorme@wanadoo.fr ☒ ev. day except Sun. 9am–12 noon 2pm–7pm, Sat. 6pm, groups by appt.
☛ J.-F. Delorme

LOUIS LATOUR 1999★
☐   n.c.   25,000   ■ ☒ €5–8

One is truly looking at a rare bird. This highly drinkable wine has the finest green-gold colour with green apples, at first, on the nose and then a lemony finish.

☛ Maison Latour, 18, rue des Tonneliers, 21200 Beaune, tel. 03.80.24.81.00, fax 03.80.22.36.21, e-mail louislatour@louislatour.com ☒ by appt.

PAUL REITZ 1999
☐   n.c.   30,000   €8–11

The fairly low-key colour has green glints; the nose remains timid for the moment, but the wine is irreproachable on the palate. Its vitality is no great surprise, coming as it does from a grape variety that has nothing sleepy about it.

☛ Maison Paul Reitz, 124, Grande-Rue, 21700 Corgoloin, tel. 03.80.62.93.07, fax 03.80.62.96.83, e-mail paul.reitz@telepost.fr ☒

A. ET P. DE VILLAINE 1999★★
☐   10 ha   50,000   ■ ☒ €5–8

Aubert de Villaine, proprietor of this estate since 1973, divides his time between Vosne-Romanée, Bouzeron and the rest of the world. He has contributed greatly to the recognition of this appellation and presents here a wine with a very classic colour, and aromas of apples, pears and citrus fruit. More complex than concentrated, its future is guaranteed with charm and sincerity. A taster recommended serving it with a Roquefort and walnut tart.

☛ A. et P. de Villaine, 2, rue de la Fontaine, 71150 Bouzeron, tel. 03.85.91.20.50, fax 03.85.87.04.10, e-mail dom.devillaine@wanadoo.fr ☒ ☒ by appt.

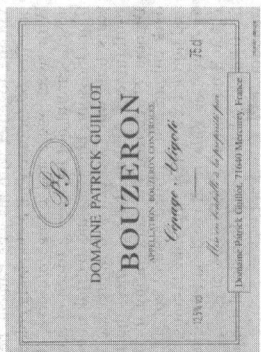

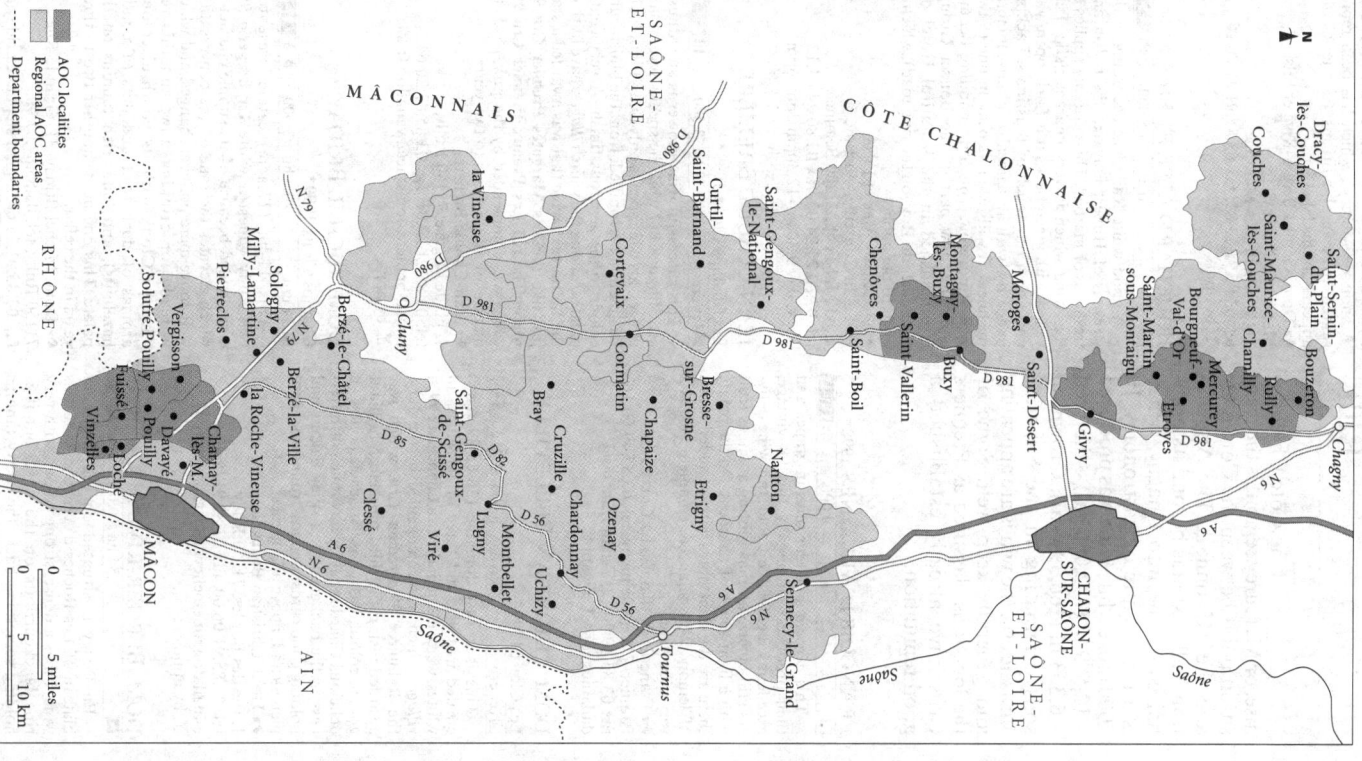

Côte Chalonnaise and the Mâconnais

Rully

The Côte Chalonnaise, or Mercurey region, is the transition point between the Côte-d'Or and the Mâconnais. The Appellation Rully extends beyond its original commune into Chagny, which is a local centre of gastronomy. In 2000 more white wine was produced – 12,579 hl (332,086 gal) – than red – 6,303 hl (166,399 gal). Grown on soils originating in the Superior Jurassic era, the wines are appealing and generally keep well. Some of the locations classified as Premiers Crus have already established a good reputation.

FRANCOIS D'ALLAINES 1998★
☐　　n.c.　9,000　Ⅲ €11-15

This négociant-éleveur buys in grapes and then produces, judging by this 98 vintage, excellent wine. Brilliant gold, this wine delivers still-elusive aromas hinting at citrus fruit with a light touch of oakiness. On the palate there are the same notes with an added touch of lemon. Well-balanced, complete, this is a very nice wine.

☛ François d'Allaines, La Corvée du Paquier, 71150 Demigny, tel. 03.85.49.90.16, fax 03.85.49.90.19, e-mail francois@dallaines.com ☖ by appt.

DOM. CHRISTIAN BELLEVILLE
Les Cloux 1999★
☐ 1er cru　3.6 ha　6,000　Ⅲ ☖ ♦ €8-11

This is a vast domaine (36 ha/89 acres) created in 1982, and three of its wines, all whites, were selected: the **Les Chauchoux 99**, a *village*, which was commended by the Jury, the **Rabourcé 99 Premier Cru**, which was awarded a star, the third musketeer, brilliant gold in colour, has a nose of acacia honey – a delicious Chardonnay. A tiny touch of bitterness in the background, a spicy flavour and holding good cards: richness, roundness, suppleness and, above all, openess.

☛ Dom. Christian Belleville, 1, rue des Bordes, 71150 Rully, tel. 03.85.91.06.00, fax 03.85.91.06.01, e-mail domaine-belleville@wanadoo.fr ☖ by appt.

DOM. BERGER-RIVE En Rosey 1999★
■　　3.54 ha 10,000　Ⅲ €5-8

En Rosey is situated on the dominant plateau of Les Roches d'Agneux. As to this wine, it has a grave, strong colour, with very ripe blackcurrants on the nose, but it is holding something back: the chewy tannins have a strong character. Recommended with a

civet de lièvre (a rich hare stew). Note that 'Manoir de Mercey', which has been represented in several editions of the *Guide*, appears on this label.

☛ Dom. Gérard Berger-Rive et Fils, Manoir de Mercey, 71150 Cheilly-lès-Maranges, tel. 03.85.91.13.81, fax 03.85.91.17.06 ☒

BOUCHARD AINE ET FILS 1999★
☐　　n.c.　65,000　Ⅲ €5-8

A good white Rully has, according to the writings of Hubert Duyker, 'the polish and freshness of marble'. This certainly applies to this wine which is very characteristic. Pale yellow with green flecks it is fairly open with nuts and a tiny touch of toastiness. Lacking in acidity, with an agreeable, almost mineral freshness, it will reach its peak in one to two years from now. This long-standing Beaune company, now part of the Boisset Group, is established in the beautiful Hôtel du Conseiller du Roy (on the ring road), which is open to the public.

☛ Bouchard Ainé et Fils, Hôtel du Conseiller-du-Roy, 4, bd Mal-Foch, 21200 Beaune, tel. 03.80.24.24.00, fax 03.80.24.64.12 ☖ ev. day 9.30am–12.30pm 2pm–6pm

JEAN-CLAUDE BRELIERE
Les Champs Cloux 1999★★
■ 1er cru　0.78 ha　3,500　Ⅲ €11-15

This successful wine-grower is an enthusiastic linguist but while he speaks several languages, his wine speaks only one – Pinot Noir. Distinction personified, from the bluish-ruby colour to the generous finish. A very gentle palate. Among the white *villages*, each have faith in the **La Barre**, a wine that was awarded a star, just like the **Les Margotés Premier Cru 99 white**. The **red Les Préaux Premier Cru 99**, which was commended by the Jury, needs to mature for another one to two years.

☛ Jean-Claude Brelière, 1, pl. de l'Eglise, 71150 Rully, tel. 03.85.91.22.01, fax 03.85.87.20.64, e-mail breliere.domaine@wanadoo.fr ☖ by appt.

DOM. MICHEL BRIDAY
Champs Cloux 1999★
■ 1er cru　0.6 ha　3,000　Ⅲ ☖ ♦ €11-15

This 11-ha (27-acre) estate presented two Rully wines: a white **La Bergerie 99**, commended because of its supple character, which elevates the tone of the conversation well above mere polite exchanges, and which is ready for drinking now; and this red Champs Cloux with its youthful colour, aromas of dark fruit and nuts (almonds, hazelnuts), and long, rich tannins on the palate. This one needs another two to three years in the cellar.

☛ Dom. Michel Briday, 31, Grande-Rue, 71150 Rully, tel. 03.85.87.07.90, fax 03.85.91.25.68, e-mail stephane.briday@wanadoo.fr ☒ ☖ by appt.

LOUIS CHAVY 1999*

n.c. 24,000 €11-15

One of our tasters suggested serving this wine with frogs' legs. It doesn't go un-noticed, this bright 99! Pale with green highlights and with its aromas of grapefruit and limes, it has a holiday feel about it. Its lively freshness, a trifle vigorous, combines with toasty notes. A certain personality will be revealed in one to two years.

↘ Louis Chavy, Caveau la Vierge Romaine, pl. des Marronniers, 21190 Puligny-Montrachet, tel. 03.80.26.33.00, fax 03.80.24.14.84,
e-mail mallet.b@eva-beaune.fr ☑
📞 ev. day 10am–6pm; cl. Nov. to Mar.

JOSEPH DROUHIN 1999**

n.c. n.c. €11-15

Established in 1880, this great Beaune wine-producer also has a foot in the Côte Chalonnaise. The new oak influence is attractive in this straw-coloured wine with green glints. It has toasty, grilled notes that don't overwhelm the fruitiness. On the palate, its warm buttery flavours are enhanced by a strong acidity which should guarantee it long life. Ready to drink in two to three years. If you are a regular follower of the *Guide* you will remember that the 96 vintage was *coup de coeur*.

↘ Joseph Drouhin, 7, rue d'Enfer, 21200 Beaune, tel. 03.80.24.68.88, fax 03.80.22.43.14, e-mail maisondrouhin@ drouhin.com 📞 by appt.

DUFOULEUR PÈRE ET FILS

Margotey Elevé en fût de chêne 1999**

1er cru n.c. 1,800 €15-23

Product of the hillside known as 'du château' the Premier Cru **Meix Cadot 99 white** was commended by the Jury. Its rich, round body is likely to become complex, but only at the end of its maturation, two or three springs hence. As to this Margotey, finely-oaked, a lively gold colour with gold highlights, it is rich and tender, long and full-flavoured.

↘ Dufouleur Père et Fils, 15, rue Thurot, BP 27, 21700 Nuits-Saint-Georges, tel. 03.80.61.21.21, fax 03.80.61.10.65 ☑
📞 by appt.

RAYMOND DUREUIL-JANTHIAL 1998*

1.47 ha 8,000 €11-15

The underground 18th-century cellars house the barrels that have produced a white **Rully 99** with a palate which combines menthol, pineapple and toast. The oakiness has length, giving it its style with a certain mineral note. As for this red Rully, matured in oak for two years, it has a magnificent youthful colour. Well-balanced, fruity and fresh, it will perform admirably at dinner.

↘ Raymond Dureuil-Janthial, rue de la Buisserolle, 71150 Rully, tel. 03.85.87.02.37, fax 03.85.87.00.24 ☑ 📞 ev. day 9am–12 noon 3pm–7pm; Sun. by appt.

VINCENT DUREUIL-JANTHIAL

Le Meix Cadot 1999*

1er cru 0.44 ha 2,500 €11-15

Coup de coeur last year for a 98 vintage, this graduate of the Lycée Viticole at Beaune became established here in 1994, which shows that he has quickly made his way in life. We enjoyed the **Premier Cru Les Margotés 99 white**, commended by the Jury, also the **white village 99**, which was awarded a star. However, the Jury preferred this golden Meix Cadot which has some peach notes when it opens out. Good balance and directness of flavour; the fruitiness leaves its mark on the palate.

↘ Vincent Dureuil-Janthial, rue de la Buisserolle, 71150 Rully, tel. 03.85.87.26.32, fax 03.85.87.15.01, e-mail vincent.dureuil@ wanadoo.fr ☑ 📞 by appt.

DUVERNAY PÈRE ET FILS

Les Champs Cloux 1999**

1er cru 3 ha 13,000 €8-11

Established in 1973, this family estate was taken over by the three sons in 1999. What is there to say about this first vintage? One can spend quite a time over the **Premier Cru Les Raclots 99 white** that was commended, but all things considered, this Pinot is more impressive. A fine ruby-coloured wine but the nose has to be coaxed to open, which it does with peonies and spices. The attack is vibrant, the terroir mineral, the structure full, rich and elegant. A true Premier Cru.

↘ Dom. Duvernay, 4, rue de l'Hôpital, 71150 Rully, tel. 03.85.87.04.69, fax 03.85.87.09.17 ☑
📞 ev. day 8am–12 noon 1.30pm–7pm

GUY FONTAINE ET JACKY VION

La Chaponnière 1998*

0.5 ha 2,900 €8-11

'*Fontaine, je ne boirai pas de ton eau mais de ton vin!*' (Fountain, I will not drink your water ... but your wine). This is something one would happily say to Guy Fontaine, one of the co-proprietors of the estate. Just look at this wine: a gilded-white colour, it reveals a fragrant, honeyed richness that is tinged with citrus fruit on the palate. With some richness, good liveliness, clean and genuine at the finish, it plays an intelligent game. In a **red village 99**, a welcoming **Bergerie** should win your approval with a dish of *oeufs en meurette* (eggs poached in red wine). It was given the same mark.

↘ GAEC des Vignerons, rue du Bourg, 71150 Remigny, tel. 03.85.87.03.35, fax 03.85.87.03.35 ☑ 📞 by appt.

DOM. DE LA CROIX JACQUELET 1998*

2.49 ha 16,276 €11-15

This wine was produced by the Faiveley family in the Côte Chalonnaise. A golden-yellow colour, combining mushrooms and exotic fruits with toastiness on the nose. Fairly acidic but, on the whole, pleasant and well-balanced, it should go well with pike quenelles.

▶ Dom. de La Croix Jacquelet, SBEV, 71640 Mercurey, tel. 03.85.45.12.23, fax 03.85.45.26.42 ⚑ Y ev. day 8am–12 noon 1.30pm–5.30pm; Sat./Sun. by appt.

DOM. DE LA FOLIE
Clos de Bellecroix 1999★

■ 4.52 ha 11,300 €8-11

This estate is the birthplace of the 'seventh art': it once belonged to E.J. Marey, inventor of a forerunner of the cine-camera. This wine, on the other hand, is not likely to display any artistic temperament. Garnet-red with bluish highlights, expressive and open (violets, blackcurrants), it is fresh and light. A wine for immediate enjoyment. Worth noting: several *coups de coeur* awarded in the past.

▶ Dom. de La Folie, 71150 Chagny, tel. 03.85.87.18.59, fax 03.85.87.03.53, e-mail domaine.de.la.folie@wanadoo.fr ⚑
Y ev. day 9am–7pm
▶ Noël-Bouton

DOM. DE LA RENARDE Varot 1999

□ 17.64 ha 55,000 €8-11

A notable figure in Rully, Jean-François Delorme has of course been awarded *coup de coeur* in this AOC. This attractive 99 has a good appearance with a clear colour. It reveals some floral and mineral qualities. Simple and light, almost casual, it will be perfectly at home at the table.

▶ André Delorme, Dom. de la Renarde, 2, rue de la République, 71150 Rully, tel. 03.85.87.10.12, fax 03.85.87.04.60, e-mail andre-delorme@wanadoo.fr ⚑
Y ev. day except Sun. 9am–12 noon 2pm–7pm, Sat. 6pm, groups by appt.
▶ J.-F. Delorme

LES CAVES DE LA VERVELLE 1999★★

□ 1.2 ha 7,700 €11-15

The new team at Château de Bligny-lès-Beaune may congratulate itself on a quality product. This Rully is exemplary. Nuts, flint and hawthorn form an amicable trio on the nose. It is full and fresh on the palate with an appreciable richness that is brought into focus by a good degree of concentration. This 99 vintage has great depth and is so typical it could serve as the standard model.

▶ Les caves de La Vervelle, Le Château, 21200 Bligny-les-Beaune, tel. 03.80.21.47.38, fax 03.80.21.40.27 ⚑
Y ev. day 8am–12 noon 2pm–6pm

LA VIEILLE FONTAINE
Grésigny 1998

□ 1er cru 0.55 ha 2,500 €5-8

Brilliant gold-yellow, this wine from the Mont-Palais–Margotée sector has aromas of citrus fruit and flowers. Light at first, then lively with a vegetal note, it finishes with an exotic touch.

▶ Pierre Cogny et David Déprés, GAEC de La Vieille Fontaine, 71150 Bouzeron, tel. 03.85.87.19.96, fax 03.85.87.19.96 ⚑
Y by appt.

DOM. DE L'ECETTE 1998★

■ 2 ha 5,000 €8-11

This purplish-red 98 has a bouquet that is both wide and deep, with a fruity complexity that is only beginning to make its presence felt. The fruitiness reappears on the palate. The structure is very good, the vigour and length particularly dynamic. To lay down for one to two years.

▶ GAEC Jean et Vincent Daux, Dom. de L'Ecette, 21, rue de Geley, 71150 Rully, tel. 03.85.91.21.52, fax 03.85.91.24.33 ⚑
Y by appt.

LE MANOIR MURISALTIEN 1998★★

■ n.c. 15,000 €11-15

The Château de Messy domaine, between Tournus and Cluny, has 17 ha (42 acres) of AOC vineyards. Marc Dumont also owns the Manoir Murisaltien at Meursault and is building vast cellars beside the Clos de Mazeray. While this Rully is the colour of peonies, the nose and palate are more evocative of cherry-stones. Very characteristic, this fine wine is not yet at its peak. It needs another two to three years to achieve its full potential.

▶ Le Manoir Murisaltien, 4, rue du Clos Mazeray, 21190 Meursault, tel. 03.80.21.21.83, fax 03.80.21.66.48 ⚑
Y by appt.
▶ Marc Dumont

DOM. ANDRE LHERITIER 1998★
Clos Roch

■ 0.4 ha n.c. €8-11

This wine has class, with its light gold colour of admirable intensity and aromas and flavours of a basketful of freshly-picked mushrooms. Citrus fruit also plays a part. The acidity is right, the balance assured. Already harmonious, this 98 will improve further with time (two to three years).

▶ André Lhéritier, 4, bd de la Liberté, 71150 Chagny, tel. 03.85.87.00.09 ⚑
Y ev. day 8.30am–11.30am 2pm–7pm

MUGNIER PERE ET FILS
La Pucelle 1998★

□ 1er cru n.c. n.c. €8-11

This La Pucelle is very reserved. Its summery gold-yellow colour is transparent. Its aromas hint at hazelnuts, vanilla and minerals. On the palate it has a little floral side, some length, and a calm, rather than lively, temperament. Very characteristic of the 98 vintage.

▶ EARL La P'tiote Cave, 71150 Chassey-le-Camp, tel. 03.85.87.15.21, fax 03.85.87.28.08 ⚑
Y ev. day 9am–12 noon 2pm–6pm

ALBERT PONNELLE 1998★

□ n.c. n.c. €11–15

Ponnelle is a fairly common name in the Côte. There are several *négoce-éléveurs* called Ponnelle and one has to check the first name: Albert in this case. This Rully is a pleasant colour; the nose is well-integrated (citrus fruit) and the attack full of energy. Will this 98 acquire a little richness as it ages? One hopes so, and the way it is developing seems promising.

Albert Ponnelle, Clos Saint-Nicolas, BP 107, 21200 Beaune, tel. 03.80.22.00.05, fax 03.80.24.19.73, e-mail info@albert-ponnelle.com by appt.

Louis Ponnelle

CH. DE RULLY 1998

□ 24.64 ha 113,112 €11–15

The Counts of Ternay lived here for 800 years, and an ancestral wineglass which holds 3 l (5 pt) is kept here. The management of this estate is in the hands of Antonin Rodet. Pale gold colour, toasty, and quite lively, this Rully, though not of noble stock, is an honest representative of the middle-class.

Dom. du Ch. de Rully, 71640 Mercurey, tel. 03.85.98.12.12, fax 03.85.45.25.49

by appt. with Antonin Rodet

Comte R. de Ternay

DOM. DE RULLY SAINT-MICHEL

Les Cloux 1999★

□ 1er cru 1.5 ha 3,820 €8–11

Once belonging to the Minister of Finance to Napoléon III (the Château Saint-Michel at Rully is now a hotel management training centre), this wine-producing estate is still cultivated by his descendants. The Rully has a pale straw-white colour with a freshness touching on menthol and a richness enhanced by apricot. The **Premeir Cru Les Champs Cloux 99 red** is tender and velvety and of similar quality.

Dom. de Rully Saint-Michel, rue du Château, 71150 Rully, tel. 03.85.91.28.63, fax 03.85.87.12.12 ev. day 9am–6pm

Mme de Bodard

DOM. SAINT-JACQUES

La Fosse 1999★

■ 1er cru 0.98 ha 3,800 €8–11

One of the stopping-places on the pilgrim route to Santiago de Compostella, this domaine has 13th-century cellars and some 18th-century wine presses displayed in the vat room. This wine is a product of one of the *climats* belonging to the group comprising Marissou, Chapitre, etc., which is situated at the foot of the great hillside. Already a garnet shade, it hints at toasted almonds. On both the nose and the palate there is a pronounced oakiness with morello cherry flavours and a good structure that should develop well. Still tannic, it is a sword still in its sheath. When it emerges (in five years?) it will provide a fine encounter. The same *climat* was awarded a *coup de coeur* in the year 2000, for a 96 vintage.

Christophe-Jean Grandmougin, 11, rue Saint-Jacques, 71150 Rully, tel. 03.85.87.23.79, fax 03.85.87.17.34

by appt.

ALBERT SOUNIT

Cloux l'Ouvrier 1999★

□ 1.1 ha 1,800 €8–11

Gilt-edged, as buttery as a buttered crumpet, this wine stands out because of its great length on the palate. It is without doubt rich and round, with the good nature of an approachable wine. However, it is the length that has the edge on all its other qualities. Established in 1851, this company has for several years been owned by K. Kjellerup, a Danish importer of Burgundy wines.

Albert Sounit, 5, pl. du Champ-de-Foire, 71150 Rully, tel. 03.85.87.20.71, fax 03.85.87.09.71, e-mail albert-sounit@wanadoo.fr ev. day 8am–12 noon 2.30pm–6pm; Sat./Sun. by appt.

K. Kjellerup

DOM. ROLAND SOUNIT

Les Cailloux 1999★

□ 0.5 ha 3,500 €8–11

This Meursault wine-grower owns 17 ha (42 acres). From his Rully wines he submitted an exotic **Village Les Crays 99 white**, which was commended by the Jury, and this Les Cailloux which has all the expected intensity of a young wine. The nose is full of ripe, bordering on exotic, fruit aromas that make a pleasant impression. Slightly over-ripe grapes, perhaps? Indeed, this very ripe aspect is also found on the palate. Rich, powerful – a wine that excites the tastebuds.

SCEA Dom. Roland Sounit, rte de Monthélie, 21190 Meursault, tel. 03.80.21.22.45, fax 03.80.21.28.05

ERIC DE SUREMAIN Préaux 1998★

■ 1 ha 5,300 €8–11

An estate that uses biodynamic methods and whose products are sold on every continent. Deep purple in colour, this Rully presents a nose that is not yet open but heading in the right direction: the oak is already well-integrated. Well-structured and tannic with a touch of astringency, this wine shows good extraction, and is forthright on the palate with a powerful attack. It will need time to soften and reveal its hidden depths.

EARL Eric de Suremain, rue du Pied-de-la-Vallée, 21190 Monthélie, tel. 03.80.21.23.32, fax 03.80.21.66.37

by appt.

Mercurey

Mercurey is 12 km (7 miles) north-west of Chalon-sur-Saône, on the edge of the Chagny-Cluny road, and borders the Rully vineyard to the south. This appellation communale produces the largest volume of wine on the Côte Chalonnaise: in 2000 31,000 hl (818,400 gal), 4,134 hl (109,138 gal) of which were white wines. It extends into three communes: Mercurey, Saint-Martin-sous-Montaigu and Borgneuf-Val-d'Or.

Some locations are also classified as Premier Cru. The wines are generally light and pleasant, with some keeping qualities.

JEAN-LUC AEGERTER
Réserve personnelle 1998 ■ n.c. 6,000 ❙❙❙ €11–15

This *négociant-éleveur*, from the Nuits area, managed Labouré-Roi, as well as Louis Roederer in Champagne before he took over the firm of Pierre Gruber and set up on his own. This wine's garnet-red colour and aroma of small red berries are very enticing. Fresh and concentrated, with good acidity, it should be kept for two to three years.

➛ Jean-Luc Aegerter,
49, rue Henri-Challand, 21700 Nuits-Saint-Georges, tel. 03.80.61.02.88,
fax 03.80.62.37.99 ☑ ❦ by appt.

DOM. BRINTET La Perrière 1999
■ 0.5 ha 3,000 ❙❙❙ €8–11

This beautiful 13-ha (32-acre) estate has been run by Luc Brintet since 1984. This wine has an intense red colour and has opted firmly for kirsch on the nose. As round as the globe, it notches up a number of points in its favour on the palate. Fruity with a touch of oakiness, it is well-balanced.

➛ Dom. Luc Brintet, Grande-Rue,
71640 Mercurey, tel. 03.85.45.14.50,
fax 03.85.45.28.23 ☑ ❦ by appt.

DOM. CHANZY Les Carabys 1998
□ n.c. n.c. ❙❙❙ €8–11

Slightly smoky for a Chardonnay with notes of walnuts and almonds and an unyielding structure – that is its character, because it has been matured in barrel (40% new oak). The fruit does not fade at the finish and the oakiness stays in place. It is ready to drink from now on.

➛ Daniel Chanzy, 1, rue de la Fontaine,
71150 Bouzeron, tel. 03.85.87.23.69,
fax 03.85.91.24.92, e-mail daniel.chanzy@
wanadoo.fr ☑ ❦ by appt.

JEAN-PIERRE CHARTON
Vieilles vignes 1999★
■ 2.5 ha 11,000 ❙❙❙ €8–11

This 7-ha (17.3-acre) estate must admire the *Compagnons du Devoir* (an organisation dealing with traditional crafts), if one is to judge by the label which shows the fine work of the master carpenter. It also loves its own work: look at this full-bodied wine. Slightly purplish in colour, on the nose it reveals a perfect harmony of blackcurrant, *pain d'épice*, and hazelnut aromas. Fleshy on the palate, not excessively tannic and without any harshness. The oak is well handled.

➛ Jean-Pierre Charton, 29, Grande-Rue,
71640 Mercurey, tel. 03.85.45.22.39,
fax 03.85.45.22.39 ☑ ❦ by appt.

DOM. DU CHATEAU DE MERCEY 1998★★
■ 11 ha 15,000 ❙❙❙ €11–15

This domaine is managed by Antonin Rodet; brilliantly, it must be said. This wine is very distinguished with its black cherry colour and aromas of raspberry coulis, almost peonies. This fruity quality on the nose opens further to reveal spicy, peppery notes. The tannins have sheathed their claws. The concentration is excellent. A worthy example of its appellation that is ready to drink now.

➛ Ch. de Mercey,
71150 Cheilly-lès-Maranges,
tel. 03.85.91.13.19, fax 03.85.91.16.28 ☑ ❦ by appt.

DEMESSEY 1999
□ n.c. 4,500 ❙❙❙ €11–15

Owner of the Château de Messey, between Tournus and Cluny, Marc Dumont is also a *négociant*. This is his Mercurey. A radiant, clear pale gold in colour, it has an exotic nose with notes of pineapple, guava and vanilla. Well-rounded, very rich, well-structured and, although it needs time to mature, it is already a very pleasant wine. Without great depth but ideal to drink with hors d'oeuvres.

➛ SARL Demessey, Ch. de Messey,
71700 Ozenay, tel. 03.85.51.33.83,
fax 03.85.51.33.82, e-mail vin@
demessey.com ☑ ❦ by appt.

DOUDET-NAUDIN 1999★★★
■ 0.8 ha 4,998 ❙❙❙ €11–15

The domain was established by this Savigny-lès-Beaune family in 1849. This pretty village is famous as the birthplace of the Comte de La Loyère who, around the same time, instituted the practice of planting vines in rows. This is a superb wine. Velvety: no other word comes to mind to define this vibrant *coup de coeur*. A very concentrated red colour with very ripe fruit and a light oakiness, its attack is direct. On the palate it is

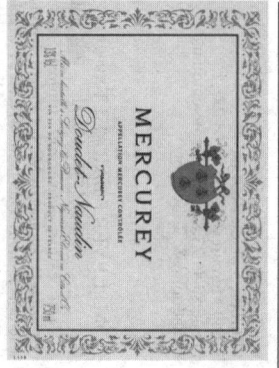

DOM. PATRICK GUILLOT

Clos des Montaigu 1999★★

■ 1er cru   0.81 ha   4,800   [€ 8-11]

Mercurey has been described as 'the iron hand in the velvet glove' and this one fits that description well: plenty of body, power and prominent tannins in this pleasant wine. There is good continuity between the nose and palate, both revealing notes of vanilla and morello cherry. This wine is among the best.

↣ Dom. Patrick Guillot,
9 A, rue de Vaugeailles, 71640 Mercurey,
tel. 03.85.45.27.40, fax 03.85.45.28.57 ☑
Y by appt.

DOM. EMILE JUILLOT

Les Croichots 1999★★

■ 1er cru   0.64 ha   3,500   [€ 8-11]

Established at the beginning of the 20th century, this estate covers 12 ha (29.6 acres). Les Croichots is the near-perfect result of all the different factors. Fruit, oak, tannins, richness, freshness: all these combine superbly within the wine. The colour is beautiful, the very open nose has aromas of blackberries and bilberries. It will perhaps not keep very long but is, for the moment, charming and lovely.

↣ EARL N. et J.-C. Theulot,
Dom. Emile Juillot, clos Laurent,
71640 Mercurey, tel. 03.85.45.13.87,
fax 03.85.45.28.07, e-mail e.juillot.theulot@wanadoo.fr ☑
Y by appt.

DOM. MICHEL ET LAURENT JUILLOT Champs Martin 1998

□   n.c.   3,500   [€ 15-23]

This flinty *climat*, made up of rocks that have broken down to fine particles, is renowned for the suppleness and finesse of its wines. This light-coloured Chardonnay, vegetal on the nose (fresh grass in springtime), is long on the palate which has a touch of acidity and flavours of marmalade combining with the vegetal tones. If you go to the Hostellerie du Val d'Or at Mercurey, order their Coquilles St. Jacques with whipped butter.

↣ Dom. Michel et Laurent Juillot,
59, Grande-Rue, BP 10, 71640 Mercurey,
tel. 03.85.98.99.89, fax 03.85.98.99.88,
e-mail infos@domaine.michel.juillot.fr ☑
Y by appt.

DOM. DE LA CHARMEE 1998

■   n.c.   3,000   [€ 8-11]

Leaving Cluny tourists can take the 'circuit des Brigands' ('the brigands' way) which dates from the insurrections of 1789, and pass through Péronne, where the home of the *négoce* who presented this Mercurey is situated. A touch austere? Undoubtedly, but

---

soft and long and opens out wonderfully to reveal all its qualities. Such potential indicates a great future. It is the product of significant, but well-judged extraction.

↣ Doudet-Naudin, 3, rue Henri-Cyrot,
BP 1, 21420 Savigny-lès-Beaune,
tel. 03.80.21.51.74, fax 03.80.21.50.69 ☑
Y by appt.
↣ Yves Doudet

CH. D'ETROYES

Champmartins 1999★★

□ 1er cru   0.25 ha   1,800

This wine from the 99 vintage achieved a *coup de coeur* apparently without even trying. An intense gold colour, it has a good nose (mocha-vanilla, and the tiniest hint of Viennese pastries). On the palate it excels with a superb richness and hazelnuts and almonds. Truly remarkable and far above average. Note that no *coup de coeur* was awarded to this estate last year but it is back with a vengeance! The **Premier Cru Les Combins 99 red** received one star. It needs to be laid down for two to three years.

↣ F. Protheau et Fils, Ch. d'Etroyes,
71640 Mercurey, tel. 03.85.98.99.10,
fax 03.85.98.99.00, e-mail commercial@protheau.com ☑ Y ev. day except Sun.
Mon. 8am–12 noon 2pm–6pm
↣ Famille Maurice Protheau

DOM. GOUFFIER

Clos de la Charmée 1999

■   0.88 ha   5,000   [€ 8-11]

A 13-ha (32.1-acre) domaine which was established in 1850. This purplish-garnet wine, opening on blackcurrants, is well-structured with fine tannins. Its suppleness means it is ready to drink. Note a hint of tobacco on the finish.

↣ Dom. Gouffier, 11, Grande-Rue,
71150 Fontaines, tel. 03.85.91.49.66,
fax 03.85.91.46.98, e-mail jerome.gouffier@wanadoo.fr ☑ Y by appt.

Mercury

this wine is fresh on the attack, lively and fruity on the palate. On the nose there are crushed berries, especially strawberries, followed by a spiciness derived from the maturation in oak. The colour is a straightforward red.

- Sté Pierre Janny, La Condemine, Cidex 1556, 71260 Péronne, tel. 03.85.23.96.20, fax 03.85.36.96.58, e-mail pierre-janny@wanadoo.fr

DOM. DE LA CROIX JACQUELET
La Perrière 1998★
■ 1.26 ha 3,873 |||| €11-15

Part of the Faiveley vineyards, this vast Mercurey domaine has more than one *coup de coeur* to its credit (95, 92 and 91 vintages). Light ruby in colour, this wine is delightful, with aromas of raspberry and vanilla. On the palate there are dominant flavours of fruit coulis and it has a sophisticated body that is already mellow and complex. The **white Village 98**, without a *climat* name, was given the same rating.

- Dom. de La Croix Jacquelet, SBEV, 71640 Mercurey, tel. 03.85.45.12.23, fax 03.85.45.26.42 ☑ ☎ ev. day 8am–12 noon 1.30pm–5.30pm; Sat./Sun. by appt.

DOM. LA MARCHE
Les Caudroyes 1999★★
☐ n.c. 4,500 |||| €46-76

What is hidden behind this label, designed in the form of theatre-stage curtains? The first act is clear and brilliant, the second floral and a touch toasty. The third, lively and round; the fourth honeyed on the middle palate. The fifth, fine and complex. This company – native to the area – has found its place in the spotlight.

- Louis Max, 6, rue de Chaux, BP 4, 21700 Nuits-Saint-Georges, tel. 03.80.62.43.01, fax 03.80.62.43.16

DOM. DE LA RENARDE 1999
■ 3.01 ha 18,000 |||| €8-11

The impression of the *terroir* is evident here, as a result of a vinification that favours finesse. A well-extracted colour is followed by a jammy fruitiness with fullness and length: this Pinot Noir is perfectly at home on the palate. In brief, a very nice Mercurey.

- André Delorme, Dom. de la Renarde, 2, rue de la République, 71150 Rully, tel. 03.85.87.10.12, fax 03.85.87.04.60, e-mail andre-delorme@wanadoo.fr ☑ ☎ ev. day except Sun. 9am–12 noon 2pm–7pm, Sat. 6pm, groups by appt.

DOM. DE L'EUROPE
Le Nectar d'Icare 1999★
■ 1 ha 4,000 |||| €5-8

When Chantal Côte, the Belgian painter, met Paul Cinquin, wine-grower at Mercurey, they created this estate, and an extraordinary label which takes you up in a hot air balloon, a zeppelin. This is a brilliant cherry-red Mercurey and on the nose has burnt aromas. Fresh, very young and well made.

- Chantal Côte et Guy Cinquin, Dom. de l'Europe, 5 pl. du Bourgneuf, 71640 Mercurey, tel. 06.08.04.28.12, fax 06.85.45.23,82, e-mail cote-cinquin@wanadoo.fr ☑ ☎ by appt.

DOM. LEVERT-BARAULT 1999★
■ 6.56 ha 44,000 |||| €8-11

This estate covering almost 8 ha (19.8 acres) belongs to Michel Picard, who is also a *negociant*. This is his Mercurey which has an intense ruby colour enlivened by mauve hues. Blackberries and bilberries adorn the bouquet, and while initially restrained on the palate, it opens out to become fleshy, velvety and delicate.

- Dom. Levert-Barault, rue de Mercurey, 71640 Mercurey, tel. 03.85.87.51.00, fax 03.85.87.51.11
- Michel Picard

DOM. LORENZON
Les Champs Martin Cuvée Carline 1999★★★
■ 1er cru 0.5 ha 1,200 |||| €15-23

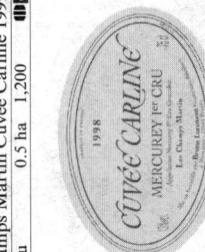

This producer is one of this year's best. This *cuvée* made from old vines, without fining or filtration, was matured for 12 months in oak, half of which was new. It is a very rich wine with an intense, almost black, purple colour and a clean and expressive nose with touches of jammy fruit. Superbly-made, firm with good keeping qualities. This same **Premier Cru** made from younger vines and without a *cuvée* name, obtained two stars, as did the **Mercurey Village 99**.

- Dom. Bruno Lorenzon, 14, rue du Reu, 71640 Mercurey, tel. 03.85.45.13.51, fax 03.85.45.15.52 ☑ ☎ by appt.

MAISON FRANCOIS MARTENOT
Chapomne 1999★
■ n.c. 26,000 ■|||| ♦ €8-11

A very classic wine, even though extraction is a modern wine-making practice. You can see it in the deep, sombre colour. You can smell it in the aromas of little dark berries. You can taste it in the fruitiness and the tannins that combine to add complexity. A wine to lay down.

- HDV Distribution, rue du Dr-Barolet, ZI Beaune-Vignolles, 21209 Beaune Cedex, tel. 03.80.24.70.07, fax 03.80.22.54.31, e-mail hdv@planetb.fr ☎ by appt.

DOM. DU MEIX-FOULOT

Clos du château de Montaigu 1998★

■ 1er cru 1.92 ha 9,000 €11-15

Henry IV demolished the mediaeval fortress of Montaigu. Fortunately the vineyards in the surrounding area have preserved the memory of the château (the Clos is a monopoly). This lively, homogeneous purple 98 is full-flavoured but firm and closed at the moment. Its structure, however, has richness and body. Still a little severe and not yet sufficiently integrated, this wine has enough potential to develop well.

● Dom. du Meix-Foulot, 71640 Mercurey, tel. 03.85.45.13.92, fax 03.85.45.28.10 ✓
● by appt.
● Paul de Launay

DOM. L. MENAND PÈRE ET FILS

Clos des Combins 1999★

■ 1er cru 3 ha 15,000 €8-11

The white Premier Cru Clos des Combins 99 was commended by the Jury: it seems well-structured. The red version has a dark purple, inky colour and aromas of over-ripe fruit, vanilla and toastiness from the oak. After a good attack it develops on the palate with fine tannins which play a useful part in harmonising the character. Needs to wait but not for too long.

● Dom. L. Menand Père et Fils, Chamerose, 71640 Mercurey, tel. 03.85.45.19.19, fax 03.85.45.10.23 ✓
● by appt.

DOM. VINCENT MEUNIER

Les Fourneaux 1999★

■ 1.3 ha 3,200 €8-11

Les Fourneaux is one of the best *climats* of the appellation. This figurehead wine has a beautiful garnet-red colour and a restrained nose that promises to open with finesse and elegance. Its suppleness, softness of the fruit, and smooth tannins complement a refined, well-proportioned silhouette. It will become more assertive in time.

● Vincent Meunier, EARL du Gai Logis, rue des Milandes, 71640 Mellecey, tel. 03.85.45.15.73 ✓ ● by appt.

MUGNIER PÈRE ET FILS

Clos des Hayes 1998

■ 1er cru n.c. n.c.

Without hesitation: blackcurrant. From head to toe, this wine is blackcurrant. Blackcurrant the whole way through. Canon Kir, who gave us the famous aperitif, would have chosen this light, structured, slightly astringent and rather elegant wine.

● EARL La P'tiote Cave, 71150 Chassey-le-Camp, tel. 03.85.87.15.21, fax 03.85.87.28.08 ✓
● ev. day 9am–12 noon 2pm–6pm

LOUIS PICAMELOT 1998

■ 1er cru 1 ha 1,800 €11-15

This Mercurey is submitted by a Rully company. Its dark cherry-red colour is dramatic. The very intense nose is full of leather and gamey, musky aromas with a few burnt notes also appearing. The roundness on the palate is balanced by a touch of acidity. True to type and full of promise.

● Louis Picamelot, 12, pl. de la Croix-Blanche, BP 2, 71150 Rully, tel. 03.85.87.13.60, fax 03.85.87.63.81 ✓
● by appt.

PICARD PÈRE ET FILS

Les Croichots 1999★

■ 1er cru 0.51 ha 2,500 €11-15

Could Aluze, which is built on a promontory, be the Gallo-Roman Alesia, as those who excavated the site claim? The archaeologists are still divided over this matter. Gallo-Roman or not, it is the site of this wine-producing estate. Its Mercurey? The product of a good but moderate extraction. Garnet-red in colour with a nice fruity nose (cherries) that opens delicately, this Premier Cru is instantly attractive; lively, fresh and fruity, agreeable and ready for the table. It is full and its tannins already mellow.

● GAEC du dom. des Vignes sous Les Ouches, Au bourg, 71510 Aluze, tel. 03.85.45.16.34, fax 03.85.45.15.91 ✓
● by appt.

OLIVIER RAQUILLET

Les Vellées 1999★★

■ 1er cru 0.85 ha 6,500 €8-11

Olivier Raquillet has managed the family estate since 1998. Here, he has two winners. The oak influence in the wine is expressive and indicates the quality of the maturation. This lovely 99 with its colour of morello cherries with blue highlights opens pleasantly with blackcurrants. It is long on the palate with subtle finesse and needs to be laid down for one to two years, after which its success is guaranteed. If you can, take the red Village 99 too, a totally persuasive wine (one star).

● Olivier Raquillet, Chamirey, 71640 Mercurey, tel. 03.85.45.18.38 ✓
● by appt.

CAVE DE SAINTE-MARIE-LA-BLANCHE 1999★

■ 1 ha 5,900 €8-11

Often it comes out of nowhere – that little something that strikes a chord. It is here in this ripe cherry-coloured wine with red-currant and wild strawberry aromas, structured, long, integrated. Youthful and not yet softened, but with superb reserve and spirit. Established in 1957, this little co-operative makes wine with grapes from 70 ha (173 acre) of vines.

● Cave de Sainte-Marie-la-Blanche, rte de Verdun, 21200 Sainte-Marie-la-Blanche, tel. 03.80.26.60.60, fax 03.80.26.54.47 ✓
● ev. day except Sun. 8am–12 noon 2pm–7pm

DOM. PATRICK SIZE
Vignes de Château-Beau 1999 ■ €8-11
■ 0.57 ha 3,500

'The Burgundy that bears the name of a god': Mercurey, of course. Saint Vincent would not be pleased, but he is broad-minded. This Château-Beau 99 (the most southerly *climat* of the AOC, near Saint-Martin-sous-Montaigu) is purple in colour. The fresh, youthful nose has notes of wild flowers. On the palate it is unusual, paradoxical and very interesting: crystallised violets, strawberry jam.

↘ Dom. Patrick Size, imp. de l'Eglise, 71640 Saint-Martin-sous-Montaigu, tel. 03.85.45.23.05, fax 03.85.45.23.05, e-mail patrick.size@libertysurf.fr ☑
Y by appt.

DOM. ROBERT SIZE ET FILS
Les Velley 1999 ■ €11-15
■ 1er cru 1.16 ha 7,000

An effort has been made to produce a decorative label. What to say about the colour of this Premier Cru? It is bright black-cherry. The nose is toasty at first but soon opens out with blackcurrants. Good and mouthfilling, with enough acidity and a touch of tannin. Rustic, but not in any pejorative sense. A wine to lay down for two years.

↘ Dom. Robert Size et Fils, Le Bourg, 71640 Saint-Martin-sous-Montaigu, tel. 03.85.45.11.72, fax 03.85.45.27.66, e-mail alain@size.fr ☑ Y by appt.

DOM. TREMEAUX PERE ET FILS
Les Croichots 1998 ■ €8-11
■ 1er cru 1.69 ha 3,000

Somewhere between purple and ruby in colour, this is a generous wine. A supple attack, smooth, it develops aromas of kirsch and starts to open out with soft red fruit. Well-structured and already satisfying to drink.

↘ Dom. Trémeaux Père et Fils, 10, rue Jamproyes, 71640 Mercurey, tel. 03.85.45.23.03, fax 03.85.45.23.03 ☑
Y by appt.

DOM. TUPINIER-BAUTISTA
En Sazenay 1999★ ■ €8-11
■ 1er cru 1.14 ha 7,000

This wine is perfectly in tune with its identity. The colour is not particularly remarkable but after that it is all fresh fruitiness. A tender temperament with a touch of bitterness, completely classic. Jaques Tupinier retired quite a while ago; Manuel (Manu to his friends) is rugby mad, but his Pinot Noir is not one to kick the ball into touch.

↘ Manuel Bautista, Touches, 71640 Mercurey, tel. 03.85.45.26.38, fax 03.85.45.27.99, e-mail mcbautista@caramail.com ☑ Y by appt.

DOM. LAURENT VEROT
Vieilles vignes 1999★★
■ 0.6 ha 4,000

'Every man is master of his own fate' says the Latin proverb. This *village* doesn't rely on anybody to fight its cause. A fine, rich colour, with aromas hinting at fruit and the *terroir*. Very silky on the palate, reflecting the care and attention that went into making it. And indeed, it came close to being selected for a *coup de coeur*.

↘ Laurent Verot, imp. des Petite-Chaumes, 71640 Germolles, tel. 03.85.45.15.07 ☑
Y by appt.

Givry is 6 km (4 miles) south of Mercurey, and is a typical Burgundian village with a wealth of historic monuments. Givry is claimed to have been the favourite wine of Henri IV of France, and mainly red wines are produced – 10,314 hl (272,290 gal) in 2000). However, the whites – 2,154 hl (56,866 gal) in 2000 – are also of interest. Prices are very affordable. The appellation lies principally in the commune of Givry but spills over slightly into Jambles and Dracy-le-Fort.

GUILLEMETTE ET XAVIER BESSON
Le Petit Pretán 1999
□ 0.4 ha 3,000

The *Festival des Musicaves* (held here at the end of June and beginning of July) combines concerts and wine tastings. This is an amazing 99 Givry. Its richness is visible to the naked eye. The nose is very attractive with half-floral, half-roasted aromas. On the palate it has a pleasant, citronella freshness; a wine that is really getting into its stride and showing signs of excellent keeping qualities. Undoubtedly good value. Another one to mark in your little book is the **Petit Prétan 99 red.**

↘ Dom. Guillemette et Xavier Besson, 9, rue des Bois-Chevaux, 71640 Givry, tel. 03.85.44.42.44, fax 03.85.44.42.44 ☑
Y by appt.

CHANUT FRERES 1999
■ n.c. 4,900 ■ €8-11

The colour of this wine is well within the ruby-red range. The nose is quite complex: black cherries, perfectly in keeping with a

Pinot. Tannins, richness, roundness, freshness and vitality combine in this well-balanced wine. On the finish there is a slight aftertaste of *marc* (spirit distilled from grape residues).

☛ Alliance des vins fins, Les Chers, 69840 Juliénas, tel. 04.74.06.78.70, fax 04.74.06.78.71

DOM. CHOFFLET-VALDENAIRE
Les Galafres 1999

□ 1er cru | 1 ha | 6,000 | €8-11

There is a little touch of nutmeg on the nose that suggests overripeness in the grapes. Quite a pale colour, while on the palate it is far from being reserved. This is a wine for the future, with good mineral qualities: one to lay down in the cellar and forget, as it is still at the adolescent stage.

☛ Dom. Chofflet-Valdenaire, Russilly, 71640 Givry, tel. 03.85.44.34.78, fax 03.85.44.45.25 ☒ ☗ by appt.

DOM. DU CLOS SALOMON 1999★★

□ 1er cru | 6.8 ha | 40,000 | €5-9

This *clos* is the monopoly of a family that has been here for three centuries. One need have no qualms about waiting for this Clos Salomon, one of the appellation's top names. Purplish and subtle, the bouquet has notes of undergrowth and soft red fruit blended with toasty touches from the oak. On the palate it is well-constructed. What more can one say? A high quality wine with good promise; one to drink in three or four years' time.

☛ Dom. du Clos Salomon, 16, rue du Clos-Salomon, 71640 Givry, tel. 03.85.44.32.24, fax 03.85.44.49.79 ☒ ☗ du Gardin-Perrotto

DANIEL DAVANTURE ET FILS
1999★

□ | 0.18 ha | 1,500 | €5-8

Eight generations of wine-producers preceded Daniel Davanture's three sons, who took over from him in 1996. Light gold, this wine has lovely brioche aromas. On the palate it has body and richness and shows good length after aeration, while the oak is well-integrated. Good luck to this 99 vintage, which has undoubted reserves and is an honest representative of its *terroir*.

☛ Davanture, GAEC des Murgers, rue de la Montée, 71390 Saint-Désert, tel. 03.85.47.90.42, fax 03.85.47.95.57 ☒

PROPRIÉTÉ DESVIGNES
Clos Charlé 1999

□ 1er cru | 0.5 ha | 3,500 | €8-11

During the last decade of the 20th century there were some good wines. Witness this Clos Charlé, one of the finest of the appellation. Although lacking in aroma, it has a summery colour and a palate that is totally beyond reproach. A noble wine, complete and very characteristic of a Givry, it has great potential.

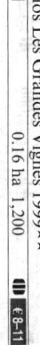

Congratulations are due to Gérard and Laurent Parize: they have run this estate since 1980 and have already been highly acclaimed for their red; and this year they receive a *coup de cœur* for their white. What a wonderful wine! Its nose positively explodes: buttery, toasty. On the palate you will find everything you could wish for. The Jury were unstinting in their praise of its richness, acidity, appearance, complexity, and fruitiness (apples and pears). A fine example of good wine-making. Also consider the **Champ Nalot 99**, in both red and white. The red (two stars) is appealing with its dark colour and interesting nose that combines fine oak with dark fruit, and its rich, velvety, powerful palate. The one-star

☛ Propriété Desvignes, 36, rue de Jambles, Poncey, 71640 Givry, tel. 03.85.44.37.81, fax 03.85.44.43.53 ☒ ☗ by appt.

DIDIER ERKER
Les Bois Chevaux 1999★

■ | 1.2 ha | 5,000 | €5-8

In the old days Burgundy wines were vermilion in colour and this one is a throwback. It carries with it a basket of fruity and vanilla aromas, and tannins that are fine but still quite evident, resulting in an agreeable roundness and length on the palate. Among the reds, the **Grands Prétans 99** was awarded a star. Elegant, tender and velvety, this is a well-made, successful wine.

☛ Didier Erker, 7 bis, bd Saint-Martin, 71640 Givry, tel. 03.85.44.39.62, fax 03.85.44.39.62, e-mail Erker@givry.net ☒ ☗ ev. day 8am-7pm

DOM. DE LA FERTE
La Servoisine 1998★

■ | 0.67 ha | 5,168 | €11-15

La Ferté is an old Cistercian Abbey near Givry. This dark, almost black 98 has staying power. Solid, powerful, very chewy, still youthful and rustic at the moment, it promises well for the future. This estate's **red Village 98**, full and fleshy with good structure, was commended by the Jury. Drink it with a boeuf bourguignon.

☛ Antonin Rodet, 71640 Mercurey, tel. 03.85.98.12.12, fax 03.85.45.25.49, e-mail rodet@rodet.com ☒ ☗ ev. day except Sat./Sun. 9am-12 noon 2pm-6pm

LA SAULERAIE
Clos Les Grandes Vignes 1999★★

□ | 0.16 ha | 1,200 | €8-11

JEAN TATRAUX ET FILS 1999★

■ 3.5 ha 10,000 €5-8

'I want everyone to be sincere,' insisted Alceste, in Molière's *La Misanthrope*. He would not have needed to say it twice to this deep garnet-coloured wine with blackcurrants and blackberries, a supple attack and well-structured body. Not much fullness but with an authenticity that argues its case far better than any words could.

➤ EARL Jean Tatraux et Fils, 20, rue de Lorène, 71640 Givry, tel. 03.85.44.36.89, fax 03.85.44.59.43 ☑ ☒ by appt.

DOM. THÉNARD 1999★

□ 2.22 ha 14,000 €5-8

At the heart of the fabulous Montrachet area, this estate played its part in the history of French wines. It was here that Baron Thénard discovered a way of combating phylloxera using carbon bisulphide. This very pale Givry, with its perfect limpidity and green highlights, has a delightful nose with aromas of hawthorn and acacia. It is beautiful on the palate, bursting with minerals and delicate honey notes, its richness tempered by good acidity. The **red Clos Saint-Pierre 99** was commended by the Jury.

➤ Dom. Thénard, 7, rue de l'Hôtel-de-Ville, 71640 Givry, tel. 03.85.44.31.36, fax 03.85.44.47.83 ☑ ☒ by appt.

DOM. VOARICK 1999

■ 1.88 ha 13,600 €8-11

Blood-red, this wine identifies itself right from the start. The nose is attractive and full of freshness with notes of raspberry and vanilla, the body fleshy with a touch of liquorice. A well-made wine that needs to mature a little more.

➤ Emile Voarick, 71640 Saint-Martin-sous-Montaigu, tel. 03.85.45.23.23, fax 03.85.45.16.37 ☑ ☒ ev. day 8am–12 noon 2pm–6pm
➤ Dom. Michel Picard

Montagny

Producing only white wines, Montagny, which is the southernmost village of the region, heralds the neighbouring Mâconnais. The appellation can be produced in four communes: Montagny, Buxy, Saint-Vallerin and Jully-lès-Buxy. A *climat* can only be claimed in the commune of Montagny. Production in 2000 reached 16,338 hl (431,323 gal).

white is already very good but will improve still further over one or two years.

➤ Gérard et Laurent Parize, 18, rue des Faussillons, 71640 Givry, tel. 03.85.44.38.60, fax 03.85.44.43.54, e-mail laurentparize@wanadoo.fr ☑ ☒ ev. day 9am–7pm; groups by appt.

DOM. MASSE PÈRE ET FILS

Champ Lalot 1999

■ 0.5 ha 3,500

The colour shows some development and this is confirmed by its aromas of cooked fruit. The attack, however, is fresh and fruity, and the wine has agreeable vinosity with good tannins. It will be ready to drink soon.

➤ Dom. Masse Père et Fils, 71640 Barizey, tel. 03.85.44.36.73 ☒ ev. day 8am–8pm

GÉRARD MOUTON Clos Jus 1998

□ 1er cru €8-11 2 ha 11,000

This classic, ruby-coloured Clos Jus is all finesse with its notes of blackcurrant. It is perhaps not a legendary Premier Cru but its balance and length are very pleasant. Opinions about it differed, and the Jury discussed it at great length: had it been a *village*, they would have given it a higher rating.

➤ SCEA Gérard Mouton, 6, rue de l'Orcène, Poncey, 71640 Givry, tel. 03.85.44.37.99, fax 03.85.44.48.19 ☑ ☒ by appt.

MICHEL SARRAZIN Champ Lalot 1999★★★

■ 4 ha 25,000 €8-11

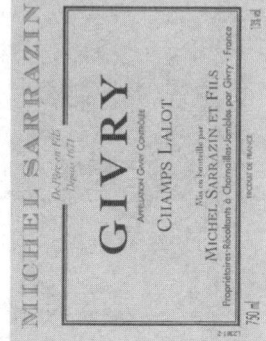

Already well-known to readers of the *Guide*, Michel Sarrazin has once more taken the highest place on the podium. This wine, matured for 12 months in barrel, has pronounced oakiness; it is instantly appealing. Its deep, dark colour is a direct result of the wine-making methods used. A full-bodied wine with a complex nose (peonies, prunes) and a fine palate which is full and fleshy. The oak is not overwhelming. A modern wine for well-informed wine-lovers.

➤ Michel Sarrazin et Fils, Charnailles, 71640 Jambles, tel. 03.85.44.30.57, fax 03.85.44.31.22 ☑ ☒ by appt.

DOM. ARNOUX PERE ET FILS 1999★

0.2 ha · 1,200 · €5-8

This wine has style and good presence with a colour that is absolutely right. Its aromas? Grapefruit and limes with touches of spice and mineral notes. It seems to have been made using very ripe grapes. Powerful and concentrated, it would go well with a hot main dish.

☛ Dom. Arnoux Père et Fils, 7, rue du Lavoir, 71390 Buxy, tel. 03.85.92.11.06, fax 03.85.92.19.28 ⊻ ⊺ by appt.

BOUCHARD PERE ET FILS 1999★

n.c. · n.c. · €8-11

One can understand why the great poet, André Frénaud, so often sang the praises of Montagny. Here, Chardonnay is more than willing to show a lyrical and passionate side, as this already very open, full-bodied and floral 99 vintage shows. Very slightly honeyed, full of finesse, it is developing exotic (grapefruit) notes without losing any of its openness and elegance.

☛ Bouchard Père et Fils, Ch. de Beaune, 21200 Beaune, tel. 03.80.24.80.24, fax 03.80.22.55.88, e-mail france@bouchard-pereetfils.com ⊺ by appt.

LES VIGNERONS REUNIS A BUXY

Les Chagnots 1999★

5.3 ha · 26,000 · €8-11

This co-operative makes wine using the grapes from 860 ha (2,124 acres) of vineyards in the Côte Chalonnaise and Maconnais. It presented this medium-intense 99 which is already open with fruit and citrus fruits. Mouthfilling, powerfully structured and vivacious with a certain mineral character, this dry wine has plenty of bite and will keep well for one or two years before partnering a seafood platter. The **Cuvée Spéciale Premier Cru La Buxynoise 99** has undergone a short period of skin-contact before vinification, followed by ten months in wood. The oak influence, however, is not overwhelming. The richness on the palate and the peach, quince and exotic fruit flavours make it suitable to serve with foie gras. The Jury awarded it one star.

☛ SICA Les Vignerons réunis à Buxy, rte de Chalon-sur-Saône, 71390 Buxy, tel. 03.85.92.03.80, fax 03.85.92.08.06 ⊻

CH. DE CARY POTET

Les Burnins 1999★

1.5 ha · 9,000 · €8-11

This estate, which surrounds a most charming château, has belonged to the same family since 1750. Hervé, author of Tintin and Snowy, has paid a visit here. Doesn't a bottle of Burgundy appear in the early editions of his book *Black Gold*? The gold of this wine is tinged with green. The nose is in hiding but is enchanting on the palate, clearly reflecting its *terroir* and breeding. A suitable wine to accompany any kind of fish.

☛ Charles et Pierre du Besset, Ch. de Cary Potet, 71390 Buxy, tel. 03.85.92.11.88 ⊻ ⊺ by appt.

CHARTRON ET TREBUCHET 1999

n.c. · 9,000 · €11-15

Matured for nine months in oak, 20% of it new, this Montagny from an important wine-producer is pleasing in every way: its limpid gold colour with silver highlights; its nose with aromas of citrus fruits, dried fruits, a hint of butter and a light touch of oak; its powerful palate. All this makes it a very tempting prospect. It should stay in the cellar for two years.

☛ Chartron et Trébuchet, 13, Grande-Rue, 21190 Puligny-Montrachet, tel. 03.80.21.32.85, fax 03.80.21.36.35, e-mail jmchartron@chartron-trebuchet.com

⊻ ⊺ ev. day 10am–12 noon 2pm–6pm; cl. mid-Nov.–Mar.

CH. DE DAVENAY

Clos Chaudron 1999

4.42 ha · 36,000 · €8-11

The colour of this wine is restrained but brilliant; the nose is floral, indicating its youth. On the palate there is freshness with liquorice hints and good acidity all sharpened by a touch of flint. Very characteristic, it is a wine to lay down for three years. The estate is managed by the Picard company of Chagny.

☛ Dom. du Château de Davenay, 71390 Buxy, tel. 03.85.45.16.37, fax 03.85.45.16.37

☛ Michel Picard

DOM. DE LA GUICHE 1999★

4 ha · 30,000 · €8-11

A brilliant, intense gold colour highlighted with green, this wine has a straightforward, open nose, mainly floral with a touch of crystallised fruits. On the palate it is slightly buttery with blossom and limes: well-balanced, it has good potential. One can imagine it going well with a chicken with a creamy sauce during the coming three years.

☛ SICA Les Vignerons réunis à Buxy, rte de Chalon-sur-Saône, 71390 Buxy, tel. 03.85.92.03.80, fax 03.85.92.08.06 ⊻

CH. DE LA SAULE

Elevé en fût de chêne 1999★

3 ha · 20,000 · €11-15

Alain Roy, who manages this 17-ha (42-acre) estate, says of himself: 'Born on 14 July, Bastille Day, I am a typical *feu d'artifice* (firework).' There is nothing artificial about his straw-coloured Montagny: lemony and mineral, this is an honest wine. Very honest. On the palate it is round and buttery, lemony and floral (hawthorn), effective and expressive. This is definitely an address to remember within this appellation.

☛ Alain Roy, La Saule, 71390 Montagny, tel. 03.85.92.11.83, fax 03.85.92.08.12 ⊻

⊺ by appt.

rosé wines. The white wines can also be called Pinot-Chardonnay-Mâcon and Mâcon-Villages. The vineyard is huge and, from the region of Tournus to the suburbs of Mâcon, the great variety of situations and aspects produces an equally wide range of different wines.

The area of Virée, Clessé, Lugny and Chardonnay is well-suited to producing the light, pleasant white wines for which it is known. A large number of wine-growers have grouped together in co-operatives to vinify their harvest and market their wines, and production has developed significantly as a result. In 2000 250,037 hl (6,600,977 gal) of white wine and 50,202 hl (1,325,333 gal) of red wine were produced.

OLIVIER LEFLAIVE 1999★

□ 1er cru   3 ha   18,000   €11-15

Pineapple and dried fruits, light pear and a hint of oak, this is a wine that has both ancient and modern aspects. A flawless green-gold colour, it has a strong, vivacious attack with a little mineral note on the finish. A fine piece of work, there's no doubt.

➤ Olivier Leflaive, pl. du Monument, 21190 Puligny-Montrachet, tel. 03.80.21.37.65, fax 03.80.21.33.94, e-mail leflaive-olivier@dial.oleane.com
Y by appt.

DOM. DES MOIROTS

Le Vieux Château 1999

□ 1er cru   3.59 ha 13,500   €8-11

Denizot ... this truly Burgundian name often appears in Henri Vincenot's novels. Pale gold, with aromas of dried pears and apples, this fruity 99 is notable for its pleasant fullness, freshness and general balance. Only 20% was matured in barrel for 11 months. A wine for drinking with any fish.

➤ Dom. des Moirots, 14, rue des Moirots, 71390 Bissey-sous-Cruchaud, tel. 03.85.92.16.93, fax 03.85.92.16.93
Y by appt.
➤ Lucien et Christophe Denizot

JEAN-CLAUDE PIGNERET 1999★

□ 1er cru   1.44 ha 1,100   €5-8

These vineyards, with their south-south-eastern exposure, have been in the Pigneret family since 1700. Golden yellow, disconcerting at first but definitely on the way to being exotic, this is a charming wine which no doubt owes its style to an aromatic Chardonnay that has been matured for six months in barrel. It is very unusual. To sum up, it was much enjoyed but one would need to know what one is dealing with.

➤ Jean-Claude Pigneret, rue de la Pompe, 71390 Saint-Désert, tel. 03.85.47.94.40
Y by appt.

Le Mâconnais

Mâcon, Mâcon Supérieur and Mâcon-Villages

The appellations Mâcon, Mâcon Supérieur and Mâcon followed by the commune of origin are used for red, white and

DOM. DU BICHERON 1999★

   1 ha   1,500   €5-8

Situated to the north of Mâcon in the commune of Péronne, this family-run estate with 18 ha (44.5 acres) of vineyards is mainly planted with Chardonnay. Just one hectare (2.5 acres) is reserved for the Gamay that produces a deep ruby-red wine with purple highlights. The nose is restrained, spicy, fruity (redcurrants), while the palate has a supple attack and a good balance of richness and tannins. The finish is acidic but this should have softened by now. Drink it over the next couple of years.

➤ Daniel Rousset, Saint-Pierre-de-Lanques, 71260 Péronne, tel. 03.85.36.94.53, fax 03.85.36.99.80 Y by appt.

CAVE DE CHARNAY-LES-MACON

Charnay 2000★★

   5.68 ha 40,000   €5-8

Almost 6 ha (14.8 acres) of vines were picked by hand and underwent carbonic maceration to produce clear deep-ruby wine. The wine-makers at the Cave de Charnay can be justly proud of the fine red fruit flavours, particularly raspberries, that complement the richness on the palate with its well-integrated and restrained tannins. The openness of this supple, fruity wine makes it particularly good with a picnic.

♠ Cave de Charnay, En Condemine, 71850 Charnay-lès-Mâcon, tel. 03.85.34.54.24, fax 03.85.34.86.84 ▣
Y by appt.

JEAN-MICHEL COMBIER
Serrières Sélection vieilles vignes 2000★

◻ 0.8 ha | 2,500 | ▣ €5-8

Coming from the steep slopes of Serrières, with their sandy soil and granite base, this Gamay is typical, though it does need time to mature. It has a beautiful, intense garnet-red colour, the not-yet-open nose shows some soft red fruit. On the palate, in contrast, it is already expressive with good structure, tannins that are evident but not the least aggressive, and a heady finish. To drink in a year or two with grilled meats.
♠ Jean-Michel Combier, Les Provenchères, 71960 Serrières, tel. 03.85.35.75.80, fax 03.85.35.79.67 ▣ Y by appt.

DOM. CORDIER PÈRE ET FILS
1999★

◻ 2.22 ha | 14,000 | ▣ €8-11

This white Mâcon confirms everything that is said every year about this estate. It has a clean, bright, golden colour and interesting aromas of fresh fruit, of confectionery, even a touch of overripeness. The 12 months spent in barrel are still noticeable, but the richness and general balance of this wine promise some pleasant moments in two or three years' time.
♠ Dom. Cordier Père et Fils, 71960 Fuissé, tel. 03.85.35.62.89, fax 03.85.35.64.01 ▣ Y by appt.

DOM. DES DEUX ROCHES
Pierreclos 1999★★

◻ 2 ha | 12,000 | ▣ €5-8

This domaine is one of the great signatures of the appellation. It distinguishes itself this year with two remarkable wines from the 99 vintage. The first is a white Mâcon, brilliant with gold highlights and an imposing, complex range of aromas from honey, yellow peaches, orange peel and bergamot to toast; it has good balance and impressive length on the palate. The second is this red Mâcon Pierreclos, which has been the source of much debate between those who support and those who oppose maturation in oak. The Jury was nevertheless impressed by this intense, deep cherry-red wine. The fine, expressive nose reveals spices, blackcurrants, blackberries and a hint of vanilla. On the palate it is balanced, quite rich with a pronounced oaky finish. It will need a year to reach its full potential, after which it will be ready to be served with an entrecôte steak.
♠ Dom. des Deux Roches, 71960 Davayé, tel. 03.85.35.86.51, fax 03.85.35.86.12 ▣ Y by appt.

MARIE-ODILE FREROT ET DANIEL DYON
2000★

◻ 0.95 ha | 1,700 | ■ €3-5

Rosé wines are still only produced in limited quantities in the Mâconnais. This one, made with Gamay, is obtained partly by the saignée method and partly by direct pressing. The combination gives a wine of a light, salmon colour with a subtle nose of fresh fruit (strawberries, mangoes). Agreeable on the palate, it finishes on lemony notes. 'A thirst-quenching wine, fresh and easy to drink,' said one taster.
♠ Marie-Odile Frérot et Daniel Dyon, Venuzre, 71240 Etrigny, tel. 03.85.92.24.31, fax 03.85.92.24.31 ▣ Y by appt.

LES VIGNERONS D'IGE
La Berthelotte 2000★

■ 3 ha | 25,000 | ■ €5-8

Established in 1927 and now incorporating 280 ha (692 acres) of vineyards, this co-operative is renowned for the quality of its red wines. The Mâcon Igé 2000 was commended for its acid–fruit balance and tenacious finish, which make it a good wine to drink with pork. This La Berthelotte with its intense, brilliant purple colour, has an open nose with ripe red fruit (strawberries, raspberries) with some mineral notes. It is balanced and classy on the palate with fruity and floral (peony) flavours. A good result in what was a difficult year.
♠ Cave coop. des vignerons d'Igé, 71960 Igé, tel. 03.85.33.33.56, fax 03.85.33.41.85, e-mail lesvigneronsdige@wanadoo.fr ▣ Y ev. day except Sun. 8am–12 noon 2pm–6pm

CH. DE LA BRUYÈRE
Igé Vieilles vignes 1999★

■ 1.5 ha | 5,042 | ▣ €5-8

This magnificent 12th-century château is surrounded by 9 ha (22 acres) of vineyards nesting behind the Igé hills. This Mâcon with its lovely, intense garnet colour has a particularly fine nose with aromas of crystallised fruits, vanilla and toasted bread. On the palate, which remains rather reserved, it is well-structured but the tannins are still a little firm and the oak is prominent due the maturation in wood. A wine with character that would be best left for a year or two.
♠ Paul-Henry Borie, Ch. de La Bruyère, 71960 Igé, tel. 03.85.33.40.65, fax 03.85.33.40.65, e-mail mph.borie@wanadoo.fr ▣ Y ev. day 8am–12 noon 2pm–7pm

DOM. DE LA COMBE DE BRAY
Bray 1997★★

■ 4.5 ha | 10,000 | ■ €5-8

When you leave Cluny, with its abbey, allow yourself be guided to these fabulous Bray hill-sides where the clay-limestone soil invests the Gamay with extraordinary keeping potential. The proof shows in this red Mâcon 97, which was exuberantly praised by the Jury. Dark ruby in colour, it is already showing brilliant orange highlights. The nose, displaying some maturity, has underlying aromas of wood-land, game and spices, accentuated by hints of fresh red fruit. On the palate it is balanced, well-structured and peppery with notes of young blackcurrant shoots. The well-integrated tannins give it a very velvety finish. A great wine at its best; serve it with grilled meat.

• Henri Lafarge, Dom. de La Combe, 71250 Bray, tel. 03.85.50.02.18, fax 03.85.05.37 ☑ ▼ by appt.

DOM. DE LA CROIX SENAILLET 2000★

☐ 1.87 ha 15,000 ◼ ▮ €8-11

This estate, as always, is in the forefront of the Mâconnais scene. Produced from young vines planted on clay soil, this fine, pale green-gold wine has elegant aromas of spring flowers and a fruity, full palate with a certain liveliness. It would go well with a seafood platter.

• Richard and Stéphane Martin, Dom. de La Croix Senaillet, En Coland, 71960 Davayé, tel. 03.85.35.82.83, fax 03.85.35.87.22 ☑ ▼ by appt.

DOM. NICOLAS MAILLET Verzé 2000★

◼ 0.25 ha 2,100 ◼ ▮ €3-5

Nicholas Maillet left the co-operative in 1999 to pursue his own destiny, and here obtains a star for this wine from his second harvest. Grown on 70-year-old vines, the grapes are handpicked and the wine made using carbonic maceration, which gives it a brilliant red colour with intense aromas (banana, melon, strawberries). Following a supple attack, the fruity aromas re-emerge together with well-blended tannins. A wine to serve with cold meats.

• Dom. Nicolas Maillet, La Cure, 71960 Verzé, tel. 03.85.33.46.76, fax 03.85.33.46.76 ☑ ▼ by appt.

DOM. MATHIAS Chaintré 2000★★★

◼ 0.3 ha 2,500 ◼ ▮ €5-8

Domaine Mathias
PRODUIT DE FRANCE
Mâcon Chaintré
Appellation Mâcon Chaintré Contrôlée
MIS EN BOUTEILLE À LA PROPRIÉTÉ
Domaine Mathias • Propriétaires • Viticulteurs • 71570 Chaintré

Béatrice and Gilles Mathias are young wine-growers with 10 ha (24.7 acres) of vineyards, largely producing Chardonnay. Here they presented this red wine, made from Gamay, which, according to the Grand Jury, is so remarkably characteristic that it is a standard-bearer for the appellation. Its colour is cherry-red with ruby highlights. The aromas of blackcurrants, fresh cherries and raspberries are enchanting. On the palate it is full and fresh with good structure and balance, finishing on a note of morello cherries in brandy. A wine to serve with rabbit and spring vegetables.

• Béatrice et Gilles Mathias, Dom. Mathias, rue Saint-Vincent, 71570 Chaintré, tel. 03.85.27.00.50, fax 03.85.27.00.52 ☑ ▼ by appt.

DOM. DE MONTERRAIN Serrières 2000

◼ n.c. n.c. ◼ €5-8

The vineyards of this domaine are situated on the Serrières hills with their granite soil. The resultant Gamay has produced this clear, dark-red wine. There are intense aromas of cooked fruit, blackcurrants and blackcurrant jam. With its good structure on the palate and full-flavoured length, this is far from being a classic Mâcon, but it is an ideal wine to serve with mature cheeses.

• Patrick et Martine Ferret, Dom. de Monterrain, 71960 Serrières, tel. 03.85.35.73.47, fax 03.85.35.75.36 ☑ ▼ by appt.

PASCAL PAUGET 2000★★

◼ 0.75 ha 3,000 ◫ ▮ €5-8

Close to the magnificent town of Tournus, Préty is the only Burgundy vineyard on the left bank of the river Saône, a circumstance that has conferred a particular character to this beautiful, intense purple-coloured wine with its lovely aromas of red fruit (raspberry coulis), spices and vanilla. While the attack is still quite oaky, the structure is rich and well-balanced; it shows every sign of giving great pleasure in two or three years' time. Also worth noting is the red Mâcon Tournus 99 which was awarded a star for its richness and fullness of flavour; it is ready for drinking now.

• Pascal Pauget, La Croisette, 71700 Tournus, tel. 03.85.32.53.15, fax 03.85.51.72.67 ☑ ▼ by appt.

DOM. SAUMAIZE-MICHELIN Les Bruyères 1999★★★

◼ 0.2 ha 1,500 ◫ ▮ €5-8

Specialising in white wines, Christine and Roger Saumaize show us here that they can also make reds. With 20 ares (half an acre) of Gamay planted on siliceous soil, this wine was produced using carbonic maceration and matured for ten months in oak, giving exceptional results. Garnet-red with purplish highlights, it has a nose that clearly reflects the time spent in oak. The secondary aromas reveal cooked fruit, spices (nutmeg) and violets. On the palate it is colossal with tremendous structure, concentrated but integrated tannins, and a very long finish of cherries and jam. A work of art!

• Dom. Roger et Christine Saumaize-Michelin, Le Martelet, 71960 Vergisson, tel. 03.85.35.84.05, fax 03.85.35.86.77 ☑ ▼ by appt.

DOM. SIMONIN Bussières 1999★

◼ 0.28 ha 2,400 ◼ ▮ €8-11

Bussières, a charming wine-growing village, is part of the famous Golden Triangle of red Mâcon, renowned for its terroir wines.

appealed to the Jury with its intense aromas of redcurrants, stewed fruits and eucalyptus. Very lacey on the palate, it is a light and very smooth wine and would be delightful with cold meats.

☛ Céline et Laurent Tripoz, pl. de la Mairie, 71000 Loché-Mâcon, tel. 03.85.35.66.09, fax 03.85.35.64.23, e-mail celine-laurent.tripoz@libertysurf.fr

Intensely plum-coloured, this one is packed with aromas of red stoned fruits, spices (cinnamon and aniseed) and gunflint. This supple 99 holds up well on the palate with good tannins and a long, spicy finish. 'A very genuine wine,' one taster called it.

☛ Dom. Simonin, Le Bourg, 71960 Vergisson, tel. 03.85.35.84.72, fax 03.85.35.85.34

DOM. DU TERROIR DE JOCELYN
Bussières 2000 ■ n.c. ■ 3,000 €3-5

Lamartine, who in 1836 wrote *Jocelyn*, a chronicle of the private thoughts of the parish priest of Bussières, was born just one km (0.62 miles) from this estate, which is worth a visit. Ask to taste this Mâcon Bussières, which attracted the attention of our Jury, with its garnet colour and purple glints, its restrained nose of slightly acidic red berries (redcurrants, wild cherries) and its powerful, strong palate.

☛ EARL Daniel et Annie Martinot, Les Fuchats, 71960 Bussières, tel. 03.85.36.65.05, fax 03.85.36.65.05

THORIN Commanderie des Sarments du Mâconnais 2000★★ ■ 12 ha ■ 60,000 €5-5

We pay tribute to the well-mastered vinification and maturation shown here by this Quincié-en-Beaune wine-producer, who presented this exceptional and modestly-priced wine. It has a dazzling deep-garnet colour and intense and fine aromas – on the primary level for the moment: boiled sweets, raspberries and violets. On the palate it is powerful and full-bodied with silky tannins and a liquorice finish that is never-ending. A fine wine that should be drunk from now on to enjoy its very pleasant aromas to the full.

☛ Maison Thorin, Le Pont des Samsons, 69430 Quincié-en-Beaujolais, tel. 04.74.69.09.30, fax 04.74.69.09.29, e-mail information@maisonthorin.com

CELINE ET LAURENT TRIPOZ
1999★ ■ 0.4 ha ■ 3,000 €5-8

Laurent Tripoz established himself here on 10 ha (24.7 acres) in 1986. Harvesting by hand has produced this bright red wine, which

DIDIER TRIPOZ
Clos des Tournons 2000★ ■ 2 ha ■ 10,000 €3-5

The Clos des Tournons was bought in 1938 by *négociant* Eugène Chevalier. The grapes grown here were used only for making sparkling wines until 1988, when Didier Tripoz took it over and started making still wines. This deep ruby-coloured 2000 has a very agreeable bouquet of macerated fruits (cherries in *eau-de-vie*) and spices. Soft red fruit dominates on the palate where the tannins are evident but not excessive; the balance is pleasant despite a slightly acidic finish. 'A wine with colour: fresh, fruity and thirst-quenching,' said one taster. Suitable to drink with a family meal.

☛ Didier Tripoz, 450, chem. des Tournons, 71850 Charnay-lès-Mâcon, tel. 03.85.34.14.52, fax 03.85.20.24.99, e-mail didiertripoz@wanadoo.fr

Mâcon Supérieur

LES TEPPES MARIUS 2000 ■ 3 ha ■ 25,000 €5-8

This wine is a clear, intense cherry-red colour. The nose opens with agreeable aromas of soft red fruit and grapes with a touch of banana. After a very fresh, slightly sparkling attack, a whole assortment of small fruits (blackcurrants, raspberries, redcurrants) is released on the palate, together with supple tannins. This lush wine would be a pleasure to drink with fresh goats' cheeses.

☛ Collin-Bourisset Vins Fins, av. de la Gare, 71680 Crêches-sur-Saône, tel. 03.85.36.57.25, fax 03.85.37.15.38, e-mail cbourisset@goformet.com

LORON ET FILS 2000 ■ n.c. ■ n.c. €5-8

This light-coloured red wine with ruby highlights has a fresh nose of morello cherries and redcurrants. Very well-balanced, its structure is a little light but fruity; to drink in the coming year with cold meats.

☛ Ets Loron et Fils, Pontanevaux, 71570 La Chapelle-de-Guinchay, tel. 03.85.36.81.20, fax 03.85.33.83.19, e-mail vinloron@wanadoo.fr

Mâcon-Villages

DOM. DES PIERRES ROUGES 1999★

□ | 3 ha | 2,000 | ■ | €5-8

This domaine, better known for its Saint-Véran and its Beaujolais, presented this AOC, produced from vines planted forty or so years ago in clay-limestone soil. It has a beautiful, intense ruby colour with a nose revealing boiled sweet aromas and fruity notes of red cherries which carry through to the palate and stay for some time. A good example of the Gamay grape; serve with grilled red meat.
➽ Dom. des Pierres Rouges, La Place, 71570 Chasselas, tel. 03.85.35.12.25, fax 03.85.35.10.96 ✓ ▾ by appt.
➽ Jullin

DOM. RONGIER 1999★

□ | 1 ha | 5,000 | ■ | €5-8

This characteristic 99 comes from the granite ground of the village of Clessé, better known for its white wines. Made by using carbonic maceration, it has an intense garnet colour and a complex nose that opens on notes of red fruit, spices and violets. On the palate it is flavoursome, fleshy, structured and well-balanced. True to type and agreeable, this wine is ready to drink now but could well wait another year.
➽ EARL Claudius Rongier et Fils, rue du Mur, 71260 Clessé, tel. 03.85.36.94.05, fax 03.85.36.94.05 ✓ ▾ by appt.

Mâcon-Villages

JEAN BARONNAT 2000

□ | n.c. | n.c. | ■ | ● | €5-8

A traditional family company, established at the start of the 20th century, the firm of Baronnat submitted a fine Mâcon 2000 with a bright, lively yellow colour. The Jury liked the delicate fragrances of white-fleshed peaches and honey, which were also found on the palate. Balanced and agreeable, this is a wine that will become more expressive after a few extra months in bottle.
➽ Maison Jean Baronnat, Les Bruyères, 491, rte de Lacenas, 69400 Gleizé, tel. 04.74.68.59.20, fax 04.74.62.19.21, e-mail info@baronnat.com ✓ ▾ by appt.

FRANCOIS BOURDON 1999

□ | 0.64 ha | 5,300 | €5-8

Awarded a coup de cœur for the 97 vintage, François Bourdon owns some magnificent terroirs. This clear, pale-gold 99 has an agreeably fruity bouquet. Soft, supple and tender, it is full-flavoured wine that would be a happy match for flavoursome white meats.
➽ François Bourdon, Pouilly, 71960 Solutré-Pouilly, tel. 03.85.35.81.44, fax 03.85.35.81.44 ✓ ▾ by appt.

DOM. DES BURDINES 2000★

□ | 2.8 ha | 20,000 | ■ | ● | €5-8

This négoce business was founded in 1821. What is there to say about its 2000 vintage? The colour is brilliant, touched with green-gold. The fine nose features floral and mineral notes. The round attack has notes of apples and pears, becoming more lively and fine on the palate. 'A good, characteristic Mâcon,' was one taster's verdict.
➽ Collin-Bourisset Vins Fins, av. de la Gare, 71680 Crêches-sur-Saône, tel. 03.85.36.57.25, fax 03.85.37.15.38, e-mail cbourisset@goformet.com ✓ by appt.

CHAMPY ET CIE

Uchizy Les Ravières 1999★

□ | n.c. | 4,000 | ■ | ▥ | ● | €8-11

Négociant at Beaune, the Champy company, of which Pierre Muergey is the chairman, presented a beautifully-made wine. Clean and brilliant, the colour shows its youth. The expressive nose tends more towards oakiness with notes of toast, smoke and vanilla, followed by touches of golden peaches, butter and honey. On the palate the union of oak and wine is well balanced, and the elegant toasty flavours include hints of sweet pastries. A wine to drink in one to two years' time with fish in a cream sauce.
➽ Maison Champy, 5, rue du Grenier-à-Sel, 21200 Beaune, tel. 03.80.25.09.99, fax 03.80.25.09.95, e-mail champyprost@aol.com ✓ ▾ by appt.

CAVE DE CHARNAY-LES-MACON

Charnay 2000

□ | 24.32 ha | 30,000 | ■ | ● | €5-8

This medium-sized co-operative produced this excellent, bright, straw-coloured Charnay. The aromas are typical of Chardonnay, enhanced with an agreeable hint of fennel. On the palate, after a slightly sparkling attack, it opens equally fresh with lemon and toast flavours. It has richness and roundness too. A good wine to drink with well-matured goats' cheese.
➽ Cave de Charnay-lès-Mâcon, 71850 Charnay-lès-Mâcon, tel. 03.85.34.54.24, fax 03.85.34.86.84 ▾ by appt.

DOM. CHENE La Roche Vineuse 1999★

□ | 7 ha | 13,000 | €8-11

Newcomers to the Guide, these winegrowers left the co-operative in 1999 to launch themselves into wine-making and marketing. Their first vintage has been very successful. This intense green-gold wine has a nose with ferns and gunflint; round and well-balanced on the palate, it is very attractive. Very characteristic, it will benefit from being left for a few months.
➽ Dom. Chêne, Ch. Chardon, 71960 Berzé-la-Ville, tel. 03.85.37.65.30, fax 03.85.37.75.39 ▾ ▾ by appt.

DOM. CLOS GAILLARD

Soluté 2000★

■ 3.3 ha ▬ 4,000 €5-8

Product of the clay-limestone soil of Soluté, this wine has delicate aromas of dried fruit and spring flowers which follow through with some length on the palate; the finish has lasting fruity notes (peaches, apricots, citrus fruits). Well-made, green-gold in colour with lovely clarity, it needs to be kept for one to two years to achieve its full potential.

⚘ EARL Gérald Favre, 71960 Soluté-Pouilly, tel. 03.85.35.87.50, e-mail gérald.favre@ free.fr ▾ by appt.

DOM. FICHET Igé Vieilles vignes 1999

■ 0.7 ha ▬ 7,000 €5-8

Igé is a typical Mâconnais village, where this 19-ha (47-acre) family estate is situated. Over the years it has acquired a solid reputation. This elegant 99, the product of old Chardonnay vines growing halfway up the slope in clay-limestone soil, is pale yellow with green highlights. It shows a great deal of finesse and light citrus fruit aromas. Very upfront, fresh with fruity flavours, it will be ready to drink in the spring with goats' cheeses.

⚘ Dom. Fichet, Le Martoret, 71960 Igé, tel. 03.85.33.30.46, fax 03.85.33.44.45, e-mail olivier.fichet@wanadoo.fr ▾ by appt.

ANDRE DEPARDON

Les Condemines 2000★

■ 0.75 ha ▬ 7,330 €5-8

André Depardon's Mâcon-Villages is grown on the limestone soil of a *terroir* situated on a steep slope. The south-west exposure gives the ideal amount of sun needed to ripen the grapes. It has a clear, greenish-yellow colour and aromas of honey and spring flowers on the nose, supported by a good mineral quality. The same mineral characteristic – typical of the *terroir* – is repeated on the palate. Upright and honest, this wine would go well with grilled fish.

⚘ André Depardon, 71570 Leynes, tel. 04.74.06.10.10, fax 04.74.66.13.77 ▾ by appt.

DOM. ELOY 2000★

■ 4 ha ▬ 5,000

Jean-Yves Eloy, with more than ten years' experience, offers a brilliant light-yellow *village* with good intense aromas dominated by mineral and fruity notes. The flavours on the palate confirm its spring-like charm. This approachable, well-balanced wine has a fresh finish. Destined to be drunk as an aperitif.

⚘ Jean-Yves Eloy, Le Plan, 71960 Fuissé, tel. 03.85.35.67.03, fax 03.85.35.67.07 ▾ by appt.

CAVE DES GRANDS CRUS BLANCS Loché 2000★

■ 16.4 ha ▬ 50,000 €5-8

This co-operative makes wine from the harvest of 130 ha (321 acres) of vineyards at Vinzelles and the surrounding villages. A clear yellow in the glass, its Mâcon-Loché 2000 has a fine and complex nose of marshmallow and crystallised fruit with a little floral note. The palate is generous and structured, with medium length and a fresh finish. The **Mâcon-Vinzelles 2000** was commended by the Jury for its characteristic fruitiness.

⚘ Cave des Grands Crus blancs, 71680 Vinzelles, tel. 03.85.35.61.88, fax 03.85.35.60.43 ▾ by appt.

DOM. DE FUSSIACUS Fuissé 2000★★

■ 3 ha ▬ 23,000 €5-8

Jean-Paul Paquet, despite his many union duties, is an excellent wine-grower, very attached to his *terroir* and well able to bring out its qualities, as demonstrated by this remarkable wine. It received nothing but praise for its intense, straw-yellow colour and its complex aromas of ripe fruits, currants, citrus fruits and hazelnuts. Its finesse and generous richness are appealing on the palate, and the concentrated, powerful finish confirms that this wine should age well.

⚘ Jean-Paul Paquet, 71960 Fuissé, tel. 03.85.27.01.06, fax 03.85.27.01.07, e-mail fussiacus@wanadoo.fr ▾ by appt.

DOM. DES GERBEAUX

Soluté 2000★

■ 0.4 ha ▬ 3,600 €5-8

Using a traditional wine-making method respecting the raw materials, Jean-Michel Drouin has produced a wine of great character, with developing toasty, fruity aromas. With good presence on the palate, this Soluté is well-balanced and retains an attractive liveliness that promises well for the future. A wine to buy in any frame of mind.

⚘ Jean-Michel Drouin, Les Gerbeaux, 71960 Soluté-Pouilly, tel. 03.85.35.80.17, fax 03.85.35.87.12 ▾ by appt.

DOM. GONON 1999★★

■ 40 ha ▬ 3,700 €5-8

Vergisson is a charming wine-making town nestling between two famous rocks (Soluté and Vergisson). This wine has an astonishing sparkling green-gold colour that is still fresh, and the bouquet opens with an explosion of aromas: honey, mild tobacco and citrus fruit. On the palate it is full and minerally with a touch of acidity which serves to liven up the wine. Typical of its appellation and vintage, this is a wine to drink from now on with goats' cheese.

⚘ Dom. Gonon, 71960 Vergisson, tel. 03.85.37.78.42, fax 03.85.37.77.14, e-mail jigonon@domaine-gonon.com ▾ by appt.

Mâcon-Villages

DOM. MARC GREFFET
Solutré-Pouilly 1999★

☐ 0.8 ha 5,000 ▥ €5-8

This wine comes from the rare clay soil of Solutré, and was made in large wooden casks. It has a clear, light-gold colour and aromas of white peaches and delicately-flavoured pears. Expressive, well-balanced with a good, full-flavoured structur, it has a touch of acidity that augurs well for the future.

• Marc Greffet, 71960 Solutré-Pouilly, tel. 03.85.35.83.82, fax 03.85.35.84.24 ▤
Ⅰ by appt.

DOM. GUEUGNON-REMOND
1999

☐ 0.8 ha 4,000 ▥ ◆ €5-8

This little family estate, taken over in 1997 by the daughter and son-in-law of the previous owners, has 9 ha (22.2 acres) of vineyards. Although slightly austere in appearance, this pale yellow Mâcon-village opens with a nose of spring flowers, honey and hazelnuts. With its direct attack and good balance, it is very characteristic of the appellation. Ready to drink now as an aperitif!

• Dom. Gueugnon-Remond, chem. de la Cave, 71850 Charnay-lès-Mâcon, tel. 03.85.29.23.88, fax 03.85.20.20.72 ▤
Ⅰ by appt.

DOM. LACHARME ET FILS
La Roche-Vineuse Vieilles vignes
Elevé en fût de chêne 1999★★

☐ 1.7 ha 8,000 ▥ ◆ €5-8

At this family estate in La Roche-Vineuse, this wine was matured for 12 months in barrels made of oak from the forest of Tronçay. The result is remarkable. Lemon-yellow with green highlights, it is a delightful wine with a complex range of aromas: crystallised fruit, honey, roasted coffee. On the palate the attack is supple, opening with a great deal of richness and some lasting charred notes. This lovely wine will improve still further if laid down for two to three years.

• Dom. Lacharme et Fils, Le Pied du Mont, 71960 La Roche-Vineuse, tel. 03.85.36.61.80, fax 03.85.37.77.02 ▤
Ⅰ by appt.

DOM. DE LA GARENNE
Azé 1999★★

☐ 3 ha 30,000 ▥ €5-8

This estate is situated near the prehistoric caves at Azé. Since 1986, when it invested in

and established this cellar and vineyard that until then did not exist, the domaine has been producing this remarkable wine with a clear, green colour with sparkling highlights. The nose is charming, made up of floral and fruity (grapes, pears) notes with a few touches of agreeable damp undergrowth. On the palate it is fine, well-balanced and has good length. A wine with character, to lay down for two years before serving with fairly mature goats cheese.

• Périnet et Renoud-Grappin, Dom. de La Garenne, rte de Péronne, 71260 Azé, tel. 04.74.55.06.08, fax 04.74.55.10.08 ▤

DOM. DE LALANDE
Chânes Les Serreudières 1999★★

☐ 1.5 ha 5,000 ▥

Dominique Cornin fired the Jury with enthusiasm for this intense, topaz-coloured wine. The appealing nose offers a complex range of aromas: grapefruit, orange marmalade, acid-drops, nuances of honeysuckle and cinnamon. Quite supple on the palate, it shows power and richness, with flavours like jellied fruit and peaches in syrup, all ending on a mentholated finish. A very expressive wine, ready to drink now, but which will bear laying down for a few years.

• Dominique Cornin, chem. du Roy-de-Croix, 71570 Chaintré, tel. 03.85.37.43.58, fax 03.85.37.43.58, e-mail dominique.cornin@fnac.net ▤
Ⅰ by appt.

DOM. MICHEL LAPIERRE
Solutré-Pouilly 1999★

☐ 0.6 ha 3,000 ▥ ◆ €5-8

Grown on clay-limestone soil, at the foot of the majestic Solutré rock, this wine is a beautiful, pale-gold colour. The open bouquet combines peaches, lemons and acacia. Round and lively, the palate has a number of trump cards, notably its slightly acidic and fruity finish. A well-made wine that is ready to drink now.

• Dom. Michel Lapierre, 71960 Solutré-Pouilly, tel. 03.85.35.80.45, fax 03.85.35.87.61 ▤ Ⅰ by appt.

DOM. LAROCHETTE-MANCIAT
Charnay Chuffailles 2000

☐ 0.55 ha 4,800 ▥ ◆ €5-8

A few green highlights are reflected in the pale, crystalline colour of this wine. Delicate,

DOM. DE LA DENANTE 2000★★

☐ 1.5 ha 8,000 ▥ €5-8

The Jury was won over by this pale-yellow wine with its complex and elegant aromas of fresh fruit and green grass. It has great finesse with a well-balanced palate that finishes on notes of crystallised orange peel and honey. Ready to drink now.

• Robert Martin, Les Peiguins, 71960 Davayé, tel. 03.85.35.82.88, fax 03.85.35.86.71 ▤ Ⅰ by appt.

it needs to be aired for a few minutes to release its floral notes. On the other hand, the body is full and pleasant, well-balanced and with good length. To drink in this coming year, with *andouillette* (a sausage made with pigs' intestines).

↟ Dom. Larochette-Manciat, rue du Lavoir, 71570 Chaintré, tel. 03.85.35.61.50, fax 03.85.35.67.06, e-mail o.larochette@club-internet.fr ☑ ⦿ by appt.

DOM. DE LA SARAZINIERE

Bussières Cuvée Claude Seigneuret
Vieilles vignes 1999★ | 1 ha | 6,000 | €5-8

Normally it is Philippe Trébignaud's red wines that get him noticed, but this year it was a white *cuvée* which brought him a recommendation. Made according to the traditional Burgundy method (vinification and maturation in used oak casks) this wine has a brilliant gold colour. Aggressive at first, the nose is tamed by high-class notes of butter and vanilla. Finely oaky, the palate is balanced with a great richness of flavours (toast, citrus fruit). A very well-made wine in which grape and oak cohabit in perfect harmony. To drink from this autumn with a bass baked in a salt crust.

↟ Philippe Trébignaud, Dom. de La Sarazinière, 71960 Bussières, tel. 03.85.37.76.04, fax 03.85.37.76.23, e-mail philippe.trebignaud@wanadoo.fr ☑ by appt.

CH. DE LA TOUR PENET 2000 | n.c. | n.c. | €5-8

A pale and bright wine with subtle mineral (gunflint) and vegetal (freshly-mown grass) notes on the nose. It explodes on the palate with grapey flavours that give it roundness and balance. Serve it with cold meats.

↟ Jacques Charlet, 71570 La Chapelle-de-Guinchay, tel. 03.85.36.82.41, fax 03.85.33.83.19

DOM. DE LA TOUR VAYON

Pierreclos 1999★ | 0.6 ha | 5,429 | €5-8

Creating a vineyard in the Mâconnais is not an easy project but, nevertheless, Jean-Marie Pidault has done just that. Starting from nothing in 1995, he now farms more than 6 ha (14.8 acres) but has only been making wine with his own grapes since 1999. His first vintage was very successful; this agreeable, green-gold wine has floral and fruity aromas of good intensity. On the palate, it has a well-rounded and a good, emphatic finish. One to watch.

↟ Jean-Marie Pidault, La Condemine, 71960 Pierreclos, tel. 03.85.35.71.78, fax 03.85.34.78.03 ☑ by appt.

CAVE DE LUGNY

Chardonnay Réserve du Millénaire 2000 | 5 ha | 60,000 |

Established in the heart of the Mâconnais, this co-operative makes wine from more than

653

1,400 ha (3,458 acres). Thanks to modern equipment and remarkable public relations, it has made a great contribution to the renown of the wines of the region, such as this copper-yellow wine with green highlights. Its nose opens on notes of cooked fruit (pears in syrup), dried fruit and a mineral touch. Lively on the palate, supple and generous, it is the very model of a successful Mâcon-Village.

↟ SCV Cave de Lugny, rue des Charmes, 71260 Lugny, tel. 03.85.33.22.85, fax 03.85.33.26.46, e-mail commercial@cave-lugny.com ☑ ⦿ by appt.

DOM. NICOLAS MAILLET

Verzé 2000 | 0.5 ha | 5,000 | €5-8

Recently installed here, Nicholas Maillet matures his wines in a magnificent vaulted cellar. This wine, from his second vintage, has a very light, pale-gold colour, and reveals a youthfulness on the nose that is very fresh and promising (notes of fruit and spring flowers). This youthful character is confirmed on the palate. A wine well worth waiting a year for.

↟ Dom. Nicolas Maillet, 71960 Verzé, tel. 03.85.33.46.76, fax 03.85.33.46.76 ☑ by appt.

DOM. DES MAILLETTES

Davayé 2000★ | 1.4 ha | 12,000 | €5-8

A product of silty-clay soil, this light and fresh Mâcon-Davayé has a nose that opens out with floral notes (roses and acacia) with a balancing hint of spice (cinnamon). Stimulating and round on the palate, it has an appealing, slightly acid attack. Still very young, it needs to be laid down for one or two years to give it time to become more balanced.

↟ Guy Saumaize, Les Maillettes, 71960 Davayé, tel. 03.85.35.82.65, fax 03.85.35.86.69 ☑ by appt.

DOM. MANCIAT-PONCET

Charnay Les Chênes 1999★ | 5.9 ha | 45,000 | €5-8

This attractive, bright wine was presented by Claude Manciat, head of the family estate since 1952, which makes him an experienced wine-maker by any standards. This white wine, almost crystalline 99 opens on touches of nuts (hazelnuts) and oaky notes. Following an almost sparkling attack, it balances out on the palate and has a citrus fruit finish that adds freshness.

↟ Dom. Manciat-Poncet, 65, chem. des Gérards, Levigny, 71850 Charnay-lès-Mâcon, tel. 03.85.34.18.77, fax 03.85.29.17.59 ☑ by appt.

DOM. MICHEL

Clessé Vieilles vignes 1999★★ | 1 ha | 7,000 | €8-11

This estate produces wines that are typical of the clay-limestone sector of Clessé. The Jury was particularly impressed by the complex nose of this *village* with its associated notes of apples and pears, acacia flowers and damp woodland scents. On the palate it is powerful and pleasant with ripe fruit flavours right through to the finish. This characteristic wine would be ideal with foie gras.

• Dom. René Michel et ses Fils, Cray, 71260 Clessé, tel. 03.85.36.94.27, fax 03.85.36.99.63 [V] Y by appt.

DOM. RENE PERRATON

Loché 1999★   €5-8   1.85 ha   17,000

Produced from vines planted in silty-clay soil more than fifty years ago, this wine is an example of this estate's outstanding work. Fine and delicate aromas, accompanied by touches of spice, emanate from this brilliant gold-coloured wine. It has body, length and excellent balance on the palate. Its slightly peppery finish is agreeable and amusing.

• Dom. René Perraton, rue du Paradis, 71570 Chaintré, tel. 03.85.35.63.36, fax 03.85.35.67.45 [V] Y by appt.

CAVE DE PRISSE-SOLOGNY-VERZE 2000★

€5-8   227.36 ha   100,000

When you have duly admired the magnificent countryside in the valley, birthplace of the poet Lamartine, you could visit the cellars belonging to this group of wine-makers and taste this wine, produced in many different varieties. Its colour is light yellow and clear, its elegant nose has honey and well-ripened fruit aromas; powerful on the palate, it has long, agreeable flavours. It is a pleasing wine with great finesse, and would go very well with goats' cheeses.

• Cave de Prissé-Sologny-Verzé, 71960 Prissé, tel. 03.85.37.88.06, fax 03.85.37.61.76, e-mail cave.prisse@wanadoo.fr [V] Y by appt.

RIJCKAERT

Montbellet En Pottes Vieilles vignes 1999★   €11-15   0.59 ha   4,200

Jean Rijckaert, a Belgian, set up in business in the Mâconnais and in the Jura in 1998, and his company is already offering some excellent wines, such as this Montbellet, from ten-year-old vines (not a great age for these vines). The wine has a brilliant green-gold colour and a fine and complex nose based on notes of vanilla and toast, well-supported by the typical mineral qualities of Montbellet wines. After a supple and vigorous attack, the impressive oaky structure re-emerges quite strongly but in three or four years' time it will have given the wine a wonderful density.

• SARL Rijckaert, En Correaux, 71570 Leynes, tel. 03.85.35.15.09, fax 03.85.35.15.09, e-mail jeanrijckaert@aol.com [V] Y by appt.

DOM. DU ROURE DE PAULIN

Fuissé 2000★★   €5-8   0.6 ha   5,000

Coming from a 60 are (less than half an acre) plot with clay-limestone soil, this wine from the long-awaited 2000 vintage is far from disappointing. Its fine and upright nose with spring flowers and spices, its frank and full attack, long finish and positive character make it a worthy representative of the appellation.

• Dom. du Roure de Paulin, 71960 Fuissé, tel. 03.85.35.65.48, fax 03.85.35.68.50 [V] Y by appt.

DOM. SAINT-DENIS

Chardonnay 1999★★   €8-11   1.8 ha   14,000

Hubert Laferrère, the only independent wine-maker at Lugny, says: 'My job involves keeping a constant eye on the natural environment, both from a pedological and a biological point of view. Respect for it, linked to an understanding of the balance involved, is the only way to obtain terroir wines.' And to demonstrate the truth of his statement he has produced two fine wines from the 99 vintage: the Jury seems to have preferred this one for its finesse and delicacy. Its aromas are those of a bride's bouquet: acacia flowers, honeysuckle, lilies. Extremely subtle, it is balanced and soft on the palate. The two-star **Mâcon-Villages Lugny**, with its intense yellow colour, opens with explosive aromas of ripe fruit and muscat grapes, and is round and full on the palate.

• Hubert Laferrère, rte de Péronne, 71260 Lugny, tel. 03.85.33.24.33, fax 03.85.33.25.02, e-mail saintdenis@free.fr [V] Y by appt.

RAPHAEL ET GERARD SALLET

Chardonnay 1999★   €5-8   0.54 ha   4,800

These 21 ha (52 acres) of vineyards near Tournus make up one of the leading estates of this appellation. Raphaël Sallet and his father Gérard aim at producing fine wines that specifically express the characteristic qualities of their terroir. This pale-gold 99 with greenish highlights has a nice, very fresh nose made up of mineral notes, citrus fruit and acid-drops. It is round and fine on the palate where it shows excellent structure and has an uplifting finish. One star also goes to the **Mâcon Uchizy 2000**, which has a very characteristic nose but still needs to open up on the palate, and to the **Clos des Ravières 99**, matured in wood.

• EARL Raphaël et Gérard Sallet, rte de Chardonnay, 71700 Uchizy, tel. 03.85.40.50.45, fax 03.85.40.58.05 [V] Y by appt.

DOM. SAUMAIZE-MICHELIN

Les Sertaux 1999★   €5-8   1 ha   4,500

Christine and Roger Saumaize have handled the wood maturation with great care, which is not easy with a Mâcon. The oak shows itself in the toasty, vanilla aromas on the nose but on the palate the wine is round and well-balanced, finishing with a very fresh lemony touch. Mouthfilling, it is already very

DOM. DES GERBEAUX

Cuvée Prestige Très vieilles vignes 1999★

□   0.4 ha   2,800   [€11-15]

Béatrice and Jean-Michel Drouin, who preside brilliantly over the fortunes of this estate, are ardent supporters of the appellation. Faithful readers of the Guide will not be surprised to find three of their wines chosen again this year. This one is appealing with its light, pale-yellow colour and subtle aromas (spring flowers, hawthorn, dried fruits and toast) and its balance of wine and oak. It is a fresh, fruity wine that could be laid down for four to five years. Just as elegant is the **Terroir de Pouilly et Fuissé 2000**, still rather reserved at the moment but with fine potential, notably because of the richness on the palate. As to the **Terroir de Solutré 2000**, it is already manifesting, loud and clear, exotic notes of

CH. FUISSE Les Brûlés 1999★★

□   1.8 ha   4,000   [€15-23]

Les Brûlés, a monopoly of Château Fuissé, owes its name to its full southern exposure that produces exceptionally mature grapes from which an eminent wine-maker, Jean-Jacques Vincent, knows exactly how to bring out the best. A brilliant green-gold colour, this elegant 99 has a fine, complex nose with oak and vanilla touches sustained by notes of ripe grapes and mild spices. On the palate it shows perfect balance and the oak is well-handled. It has good length. One taster felt it would go well with a sea-perch *en croûte*. A star was awarded to the famous *cuvée* **Vieilles Vignes 99**, which is still a touch reserved for the moment but has everything it needs to become a lovely wine in one to two years' time.

• SC Ch. de Fuissé, 71960 Fuissé, tel. 03.85.35.61.44, fax 03.85.35.67.34, e-mail jean-jacques.vincent@wanadoo.fr ☑
🍷 by appt.
• Jean-Jacques Vincent

DOM. DE FUSSIACUS

Vieilles vignes 1999★

□   2.5 ha   10,000   [€11-15]

This domaine reputedly takes its name from a Roman nobleman, popularly believed to be the founder of the village of Fuissé. This light yellow Vieilles Vignes 99 with bright glints has a touch of oakiness on the nose, opening out with floral and fruity aromas. It is very lacey on the palate, finishing with a lingering touch of welcome acidity. Good served with sautéed scallops.

• Jean-Paul Paquet, 71960 Fuissé, tel. 03.85.27.01.06, fax 03.85.27.01.07, e-mail fussiacus@wanadoo.fr ☑ 🍷 by appt.

DOM. DE LALANDE

Clos Reyssié 1999★

□   n.c.   3,500   [€11-15]

Situated on the magnificent east-facing hillside in the village of Chaintré, the Clos its green highlights lies in its toasty, buttery aromas and its remarkable balance on the palate. A wine that will benefit from a year or two in the cellar.

• Pierre Dupont, 235, rue de Thizy, 69653 Villefranche-sur-Saô ne, tel. 04.74.65.24.32, fax 04.74.68.04.14, e-mail p.dupont@seldon.fr

YVES GIROUX Cuvée Chêne 1999★

□   1 ha   3,500   [€11-15]

Very delicate with notes of linden blossom, honey and undergrowth, this intense gold-coloured wine is powerful, round and long on the palate; it needs to be laid down for several years. 'It could be drunk in a year's time or laid down for 15 years,' one taster concluded.

• Dom. Yves Giroux, Les Molards, 71960 Solutré-Pouilly, tel. 03.85.35.63.64, fax 03.85.32.90.08 ☑ 🍷 by appt.

DOM. JEAN GOYON 1999★

□   2 ha   5,000   ■ ◖ [€8-11]

At the foot of the Solutré rock, Jean Goyon has created this delicate wine, product of 40-year-old vines, with the pronounced aroma of spring flowers that is characteristic of the Chardonnay grape grown in clay-limestone soil. It should be drunk now to appreciate its freshness.

• Jean Goyon, Au Bourg, 71960 Solutré-Pouilly, tel. 03.85.35.81.15, fax 03.85.35.87.03 ☑ 🍷 by appt.

MME RENE GUERIN La Roche 2000

□   0.18 ha   1,200   [€11-15]

Intense gold-yellow in colour, this Pouilly-Fuissé, though dry, shows all the traits of overripe grapes. The powerful, fruity nose has crystallised fruit aromas. The attack is straightforward; on the palate it is round and full, enhanced by an attractive freshness resulting from its well-adjusted acidity. The flavours on the middle palate are exotic and honeyed. A wine to serve from now onwards, with foie gras.

• Mme René Guérin, Le Martelet, 71960 Vergisson, tel. 03.85.35.84.39 ☑ 🍷 by appt.

LA CROIX-PARDON 1999★★

□   6 ha   40,000   ■ ◖ [€11-15]

Erected in the 19th century to watch over the Pouilly-Fuissé appellation, La Croix-Pardon does indeed seem to have protected this wine. Draped in amber-gold, it is packed with powerful aromas where crystallised fruits, wax polish and honey all combine together. Round and full on the palate, it has buttery, honeyed flavours. 'A rich, full and satisfying wine, was one taster's opinion.

• Joseph Burrier, Ch. de Beauregard, 71960 Fuissé, tel. 03.85.35.60.76, fax 03.85.35.66.04, e-mail joseph.burrier@mageos.com ☑
• F.-M. Burrier

PIERRE DUPOND 2000

n.c.   n.c.

A *négoce* specialising in Beaujolais wines, Pierre Dupond here presented this Pouilly-Fuissé which caught the Jury's attention. The appealing quality of this 2000 vintage with

tel. 03.85.3...
by appt.

FRANCOIS BOURDON

Le Clos Cuvée réservée 1999

0.53 ha 1,000 €6-11

At the head of this 13-ha (32-acre) estate since 1995, François Bourdon uses traditional methods of vinification, with a fairly

...AUVIGUE Vieilles vignes 1999★

1.25 ha 10,000 €11-15

...Auvigue company, a traditional family ...ess, produces wines that are classy and ...istic, thanks to careful selection of ...ried out by Jean-Pierre and Michel ...minated *coup de cœur* in the last ...he 98 vintage, this Vielles Vignes ...wing year has an attractive ...r and a delicate nose, with ...able charred notes. There is ...la on the well-rounded palate ...well-balanced with a fine acidic ...Also commended by the Jury was the ...s Chailloux 99, which is ready to drink now.

DOM. DE FUSSIACUS

Vieilles vignes 1999★

2.5 ha 10,000

This domaine reputedly takes its na... to be the founder nobleman, popularly ... from a Roman nobleman...

LAURENT HUET 1999

0.8 ha 2,500 €5-8

In the centre of the picturesque market town of Clessé, Laurent Huet produces and matures his wines in the traditional manner, without adding yeast. Head of this tiny, 1.2-ha (3-acre) estate, he takes care of the *terroirs* and produces wines of considerable richness, such as this one. It has an intense yellow-gold colour; the nose is rich in ripe fruits and honey. The palate is full with powerful flavours, the structure dense. A wine to drink now, as an aperitif.

Jean-Noël Chaland, En Jean-Large, 71260 Viré, tel. 03.85.33.11.18, fax 03.85.33.15.58
ev. day except Sun. 8am–7pm

Laurent Huet, La Croix de Fer, 71260 Clessé, tel. 03.85.36.96.99, by appt.

DOM. RENE MICHEL ET FILS

Vieilles vignes 1999★

10 ha 70,000 €6-11

this wine-producing estate was founded in the date engraved on the keystone of the the doorway that is pictured on the the three Michel brothers inherited for all aspects of wine-making for this *terroir* from their father by hand, no yeast is added, no fermentation on fine lees Vignes (the average age years) aroused considerab... drunk now...

Reyssié produces wines of great elegance. The result of vinification and maturation in oak for a year, with the yeasts stirred repeatedly, this wine is a particularly brilliant, delicate pale-gold colour. The exotic fruit aromas combine perfectly with the intense, toasty, oak notes. A round palate with a lemony attack and good length, and notes of hazelnuts and toasted almonds on the finish. A wine to serve as an aperitif.

↦ Dominique Cornin,
chem. du Roy-de-Croix, 71570 Chaintré,
tel. 03.85.37.43.58, fax 03.85.37.43.58,
e-mail dominique.cornin@fnac.net ☑
Ⴈ by appt.

DOM. LAROCHETTE-MANCIAT
Grande Réserve 1999★★

| | 0.5 ha | 2,000 | | €15-23 |

Established in the centre of the village of Chaintré, in 1999 Marie-Pierre and Olivier Larochette built their cellar where you may try this wine that so enthused our tasters. An attractive, intense yellow-gold colour, it releases a thousand aromas: ripe fruits, honey, butter, gingerbread. What a delight! Nor is the palate to be outdone, with its straightforward attack, crystallised citrus fruit flavours, and liquorice finish giving it an attractive freshness. As to the Les Petites Bruyères 99, it was awarded a star for its appealing floral nose, clean attack, roundness and suppleness on the palate. The Vieilles Vignes 99 was singled out by the Jury.

↦ Dom. Larochette-Manciat, rue du Lavoir, 71570 Chaintré, tel. 03.85.35.61.50, fax 03.85.35.67.06, e-mail o.larochette@club-internet.fr ☑ Ⴈ by appt.
↦ O. et M.-P. Larochette

DOM. LA SOUFRANDISE
Levrouté Vieilles vignes 1999★

| | 1 ha | 6,000 | | €15-23 |

This luminous, saffron-yellow wine presents a whole festival of aromas: ripe pears, confectionery (caramels, crystallised orange peel), white flowers (honeysuckle). A full, well-balanced and structured palate there are fruity flavours (pineapple, dried apricots). A most successful wine from Françoise and Nicolas Melin, who on this occasion held back harvesting the grapes until 5 October 1999. Apart from that, the Vieilles Vignes 99 was singled out particularly for the finesse of its aromas (honey and spices); it will be ready for drinking now.

↦ Françoise et Nicolas Melin,
EARL Dom. La Soufrandise, 71960 Fuissé, tel. 03.85.35.64.04, fax 03.85.35.65.57 ☑

DOM. MANCIAT-PONCET
Les Crays 1999★

| | 4.5 ha | 15,000 | | €11-15 |

This estate, which now covers 11 ha (27.2 acres), has been handed down from father to son since 1870. The attention of the Jury was caught by this Pouilly-Fuissé which is well-balanced and promising. An attractive pale-yellow colour with green flecks, it has intense aromas of white flowers on the nose. On the palate it is full and complex, with a good aromatic length. A wine that will achieve its full potential in time.

↦ Dom. Manciat-Poncet,
65, chem. des Gérards, Levigny,
71850 Charnay-lès-Mâcon,
tel. 03.85.34.18.77, fax 03.85.29.17.59 ☑
Ⴈ by appt.
↦ Claude Manciat

PROSPER MAUFOUX 1999

| | n.c. | n.c. | | €15-23 |

The négoce Prosper Maufoux, established at Santenay, has magnificent 18th-century cellars. This Pouilly-Fuissé with its agreeable nose of apples, pears and honey is pale-gold in colour. After a good initial impact on the palate, it opens with power and richness, finishing on lemony notes that provide an attractive freshness.

↦ Prosper Maufoux, pl. du Jet-d'Eau, 21590 Santenay, tel. 03.80.20.60.40, fax 03.80.20.63.26,
e-mail prosper.maufoux@wanadoo.fr ☑
Ⴈ by appt.

PATRIARCHE PERE ET FILS 1999★

| | n.c. | 35,000 | | €15-23 |

The Patriarche company, the biggest négoce in the Place Beaunoise, near the famous Hospices de Beaune, selected this attractive pale yellow wine for our tasting. The nose remains subtle but the fine, elegant palate exhibits all the fruity flavours characteristic of Chardonnay. A real classic!

↦ Patriarche Père et Fils, 5, rue du Collège, 21200 Beaune, tel. 03.80.24.53.03, fax 03.80.24.53.01,
Ⴈ ev. day 9am-12 noon 2pm-6pm

MARCEL PERRET
Cuvée Vieilles vignes 2000★

| | 4 ha | 2,500 | | €8-11 |

Installed here since 1977, Marcel Perret has produced a 2000 vintage in the tradition of the terroir, which expresses the Chardonnay grape-variety to perfection. The intense nose has white flower aromas (acacia); it is slightly mineral, enhanced with notes of liquorice. After a frank attack, one discovers a palate that is full and long with flavours of tarte au citron (lemon tart). Typical of the vintage, this wine could be drunk now, but will improve still further if laid down for four to six years.

↦ Marcel Perret, Le Haut de Pouilly,
71960 Solutré-Pouilly, tel. 03.85.35.81.64,
fax 03.85.35.81.64 ☑ Ⴈ by appt.

CH. DES RONTETS Pierrefolle 1999

| | 0.69 ha | 5,099 | | €11-15 |

Established in 1995, this young Franco-Italian couple demonstrate their expertise with this brilliant, intense gold wine. The nose, still restrained on the day of the tasting, was, however, not lacking in complexity, toasted with aromas of peaches and apricots,

Pouilly-Fuissé

hazelnuts and ripe fruits. On the palate the attack was rich and dense and revealed a good balance of fleshiness and acidity. The pleasure was prolonged with notes of peaches and apricots.

Claire et Fabio Gazeau-Montrasi, Ch. des Rontets, 71960 Fuissé, tel. 03.85.32.90.18, fax 03.85.35.66.80, e-mail chateaurontets@compuserve.com ▼ by appt.

DOM. SAUMAIZE-MICHELIN
Vigne blanche 1999★★ — 2 ha — 12,000 — €8-11

'Respect for the *terroir* and the vine,' is the creed of Christine and Roger Saumaize who own this 8.5-ha (21-acre) estate in the magnificent village of Vergisson. They are obviously right because, once again, they submitted outstanding wines for the tasting. An intense green-gold colour, this wine charms from the start with an expressive and subtle nose, made up of a thousand floral and fruity aromas backed up by toasty notes. The attack is supple and richly flavoured (pears, citrus fruits, vanilla), the palate elegant and lengthy. A work of art!

Dom. Roger et Christine Saumaize-Michelin, Le Martelet, 71960 Vergisson, tel. 03.85.35.84.05, fax 03.85.35.86.77 ▼ by appt.

DOM. SIMONIN Vieilles vignes 1999★★
2 ha — n.c. — €11-15

This wine with great potential is the product of old vines grown in vineyards with superb exposure. Still very young, it nevertheless unveils a nose of great complexity with toasty notes mingled with mocha, delicately enhanced by a touch of aniseed. Elegant and well-balanced on the palate, it has attractive honey and butter flavours. The already excellent balance of oak in the wine is an auspicious sign for its future. A wine to lay down for four to five years.

Dom. Simonin, Le Bourg, 71960 Vergisson, tel. 03.85.35.84.72, fax 03.85.35.85.34 ▼ by appt.

DOM. THIBERT PERE ET FILS
Vignes de la Côte 1999★ — 0.15 ha — 1,400 — €11-15

The Thibert estate satisfied the Jury's requirements with the first vintage of this *terroir* wine. The product of vines averaging 55 years in age, picked by hand on 9 October 1999 and matured in oak for 17 months, this wine is characterised by its fullness and complexity. A luminous green-gold colour, with a nose where fruity (pear) notes combine with spring flowers, vanilla and flint. The palate, after the soft attack, is well-balanced and finishes on slightly acid notes that add a great deal of freshness. To drink in two or three years' time, with a good lobster.

GAEC Dom. Thibert Père et Fils, Le Bourg, 71960 Fuissé, tel. 03.85.35.61.79, fax 03.85.35.66.21, e-mail domthibe@club-internet.fr ▼ by appt.

DOM. TRANCHAND 1999★
1.2 ha — 8,000 — €11-15

The Collin-Bourisset company was established in 1821 at Crèches-sur-Saône, a town on the border between the Mâcon and Beaujolais regions. It is managed with passionate enthusiasm by Edward Steeves, an American who fell in love with France, its culture and particularly its wines. This one, with its attractive yellow-gold colour, will attract you from the word go with its intense floral nose with a touch of oakiness. The attack is fine and agreeable; oak provides the vital link on the palate and furthers the good length. Best forgotten in the cellar for a few years before serving with a salmon *en croûte*.

Collin-Bourisset Vins Fins, av. de la Gare, 71680 Crèches-sur-Saône, tel. 03.85.36.57.25, fax 03.85.37.15.38, e-mail cbourisset@goformet.com ▼ by appt.

DOM. DES TROIS TILLEULS 2000★★
5 ha — 30,000 — €11-15

Ninety per cent of the production of this very reputable *négociant* is exported, so those who get the chance to taste this wine from the mythical 2000 vintage can consider themselves fortunate. Its green-gold colour is particularly brilliant; the white flowers of the nose blend perfectly with the vanilla and mocha nuances derived from the wood. The attack is straightforward, clean, still dominated by the oak, but the wine is so well-structured that it will easily excel. A wine to lay down for four to six years and then to drink with poultry dishes.

Paul Beaudet, rue Paul-Beaudet, 71570 Pontanevaux, tel. 03.85.36.72.76, fax 03.85.36.72.02, e-mail paulbeaudet@compuserve.com ▼ ev. day except Sat./Sun. 8am–12 noon 1.30pm–5.30pm; cl. Aug.

VESSIGAUD Vieilles vignes 1999★★
3 ha — 20,000 — €11-15

Made from grapes picked by hand, this Pouilly-Fuissé has an attractive straw-yellow colour, clear and brilliant. On the nose, spring flowers blend with vegetal notes. The powerful attack, the fullness and richness on the palate, the slightly fiery finish, all make a wine that reflects its *terroir*, right in the heart of the appellation where the Vessigaud estate, so well-known to our readers, is situated. A wine to recommend with the finest of fish dishes.

◆ Dom. Vessigaud Pere et Fils, hameau de Pouilly, 71960 Solutré-Pouilly, tel. 03.85.35.81.18, fax 03.85.35.84.29 [V]
[Y] ev. day except Sun. 8.30–12 noon 1.30pm–7pm

DOM. DES VIEILLES PIERRES
Vieilles vignes Les Crays 1999★★

0.67 ha 2,630 [€11–15]

Awarded a *coup de cœur* last year, Jean-Jacques Litaud knows how to astonish taste-buds with superb wines produced from very old vines (on average 90 years of age). This wine has a radiant colour, pale-gold with green highlights. Then the nose casts a spell of dried fruits, vanilla, spring flowers. On the palate the balance is disturbed at the moment by an oaky presence that is not yet integrated, but this wine already has a structure showing a good balance of acidity to richness. One to lay down for four or five years.

◆ Jean-Jacques Litaud, Les Nembrets, 71960 Vergisson, tel. 03.85.35.85.69, fax 03.85.35.86.26,
e-mail jean-jacques.litaud@wanadoo.fr [V]
[Y] by appt.

CH. VITALLIS Vieilles vignes 2000★

2 ha 12,000 [€11–15]

This château, situated at the centre of the pretty village of Fuissé in the Mâcon region, has belonged to the Dutron family since 1835. The 2000 vintage with its characteristic gold colour and green glints reveals very fresh aromas of lemon together with notes of verbena. On the palate it is rich and well-balanced, though a touch biting on the finish. 'A rich and satisfying wine,' one taster decided. Excellent in a year or so, and until 2006 at least, with crayfish, giant prawns or a fish terrine.

◆ EARL Denis Dutron, 71960 Fuissé, tel. 03.85.35.64.42, fax 03.85.35.66.47 [V]
[Y] by appt.

Pouilly-Loché and Pouilly Vinzelles

These small appellations in the communes of Loché and Vinzelles are much less well-known than their neighbour. They produce wines of the same style as Pouilly-Fuissé, though perhaps with a little less body. Only white wines are produced, in 2000, Loché made 1,880 hl (49,632 gal) and Vinzelles 2,959 hl (78,118 gal).

Pouilly-Loché

DOM. CORDIER PERE ET FILS
1999★★

0.5 ha 2,500 [€11–15]

Unquestionably, the Cordier estate has performed an amazing feat with this yellow-gold 99. A wine with a remarkably complex nose: coffee, hazelnuts and hints of vanilla. On the palate the oak is evident but well-handled, and provides good balance and great length. A wine to reserve for very special occasions.

◆ Dom. Cordier Pere et Fils, 71960 Fuissé, tel. 03.85.35.62.89, fax 03.85.35.64.01 [V]
[Y] by appt.

ALAIN DELAYE 1999

0.99 ha 7,800

High above the octagonal clock tower on the Roman church of Loché, this domaine clings to the hillside surrounded by vineyards where this Pouilly-Loché comes from. Hand-picked, this *cuvée* was matured partly in stainless steel vats and partly in oak, then blended to give this wine with an attractive, pale, green-highlighted colour. Its nose is still closed but the palate reveals lively lemony flavours and has good length. Perfect to accompany one of the local Mâcon goats' cheeses.

◆ Alain Delaye, Les Mûres, 71000 Loché-Mâcon, tel. 03.85.35.61.63, fax 03.85.35.61.63 [Y] by appt.

DOM. GIROUX Au Bûcher 1999★

1.2 ha 6,000 [€8–11]

Situated on the hillsides of Fuissé and Loché, facing the rocks of Solutré and Vergisson, is this estate which covers over 7 ha (17.3 acres). At the head of the organisation since 1973, Monique and Yves Giroux make *terroir* wines, such as this very promising, pale green-gold 99. The nose is still restrained but opens with considerable elegant notes of mineral and gunflint. Rich with toasty flavours on the palate, it finishes on a slightly acid, very fresh note.

◆ Dom. Yves Giroux, Les Molards, 71960 Fuissé, tel. 03.85.35.63.64, fax 03.85.32.90.08 [Y] by appt.

CAVE DES GRANDS CRUS BLANCS 1999★★

14.35 ha 50,000 [€8–11]

Situated at the point where tourist routes converge, the Cave des Grands Crus Blancs makes wine from 130 ha (321 acres) of vines. Yet again, this year it has produced a top-class wine. Yellow-gold in colour with a floral nose, balanced and powerful on the palate, very stylish, this wine is completely characteristic of the AOC. It should be perfect by the time the *Guide* is published. The **Les Mûres 99** received a star.

◆ Cave des Grands Crus blancs, 71680 Vinzelles, tel. 03.85.35.61.88, fax 03.85.35.60.43 [V] [Y] by appt.

Pouilly Vinzelles

DOM. SAINT-PHILBERT

Clos des Rocs 1998★

□   2.4 ha   2,500   ▥   €8–11

This magnificent, family-owned estate, nestled in the centre of the village of Loché, was enlarged in 1999, thanks to the ingenuity and perseverance of Philippe Bérard from Vigneroscope, a museum which traces the history of vines and wine, which is well worth making a detour to visit. At the end of the tour you may perhaps have the opportunity to taste this Clos des Rocs, a very fresh, lemony, appealing wine, or you could ask for the **Pouilly-Loché 99**, which was singled out for its great finesse and elegance.

➤ Philippe Bérard, Dom. Saint-Philibert, 71000 Loché-Mâcon, tel. 04.78.43.24.96, fax 04.78.35.90.87, e-mail berard-loche@wanadoo.fr ▥ ϒ by appt.

CELINE ET LAURENT TRIPOZ 1999★★

□   0.2 ha   1,500   ▥   €8–11

After visiting the picturesque little town of Loché and its pretty little Roman church, you could go and see Céline and Laurent Tripoz, who would certainly make you very welcome. This enthusiastic young couple now have a 10-ha (24.7-acre) estate, and put tremendous care and effort into the production of high-quality wines. This appealing 99 charms both the eye and the nose, where fruit and toast blend together. The palate, very round and full, is structured with an elegant oakiness, demonstrating a very well-handled maturation.

➤ Céline et Laurent Tripoz, pl. de la Mairie, 71000 Loché-Mâcon, tel. 03.85.35.66.09, fax 03.85.35.64.23, e-mail celine-laurent.tripoz@libertysurf.fr ▥ ϒ by appt.

2000. Produced from 30-year-old vines, this wine has been both made and matured for six months in oak. The Jury was unstinting in its praises of the intensely concentrated bouquet with notes of currants and crystallised citrus fruits, enlivened by a touch of vanilla. Supple, full and rich at the same time, the palate displays a good balance with an perfect lemony finish that will result in a truly dazzling wine in a few (three to five years' time.

➤ Jean-Paul Paquet, 71960 Fuissé, tel. 03.85.27.01.06, fax 03.85.27.01.07, e-mail fussiacus@wanadoo.fr ▥ ϒ by appt.

CAVE DES GRANDS CRUS BLANCS 1999★

□   16.46 ha   100,000   ▥ ■   €8–11

A bright gold colour, this wine has a rich and complex nose. It is altogether fruity: apricot, William pears and notes of aniseed. Mouthfilling, round and very agreeable on the palate, it finishes on an exotic flavour. No doubt about it, this wine would be the perfect partner for the famous *choucroute maison* served by the chef in charge of the wine-cellar at the Cave des Grands Crus Blancs.

➤ Cave des Grands Crus blancs, 71680 Vinzelles, tel. 03.85.35.61.88, fax 03.85.35.60.43 ▥ ϒ by appt.

DOM. MATHIAS 1999★

□   1 ha   8,000   ▥   €8–11

This wine is the product of grapes from 40-year-old vines grown on clay-limestone soil with a tremendous amount of care. Its captivating aroma combines peaches, apricots and grapefruit; very pure on the palate, it has a lemony finish. A wine to drink as soon as the *Guide* comes out – just for the pleasure of it.

➤ Béatrice et Gilles Mathias, Dom. Mathias, rue Saint-Vincent, 71570 Chaintré, tel. 03.85.27.00.50, fax 03.85.27.00.52 ▥ ϒ by appt.

DOM. DES PERELLES 1999★

□   0.6 ha   2,000   ▥   €8–11

Jean-Marc Thibert's wines, which bear the imprint of the clay-limestone *terroir*, are well made and always need a little time to soften out. This one has a lovely pale-gold colour, almost crystalline. Moderately intense, the nose is floral with light toasty notes associated with the eight months maturation in oak. On the palate the attack is delicate, opening out with flavours of russet apples and acacia. One taster described it as 'thirst-quenching'.

➤ Jean-Marc Thibert, Les Pérelles, 71680 Crèches-sur-Saône, tel. 03.85.37.14.56, fax 03.85.37.46.02 ▥ ϒ by appt.

DOM. RENE PERRATON

Les Buchardières 2000

□   0.26 ha   2,000   ▥ ■   €5–8

The view from this estate over the Saône valley and the first hills of the Beaujolais is breathtaking, but this wine comes from a plot opposite the village of Chaintré, just on the

Pouilly Vinzelles

DOM. DE FUSSIACUS 2000★★

□   0.35 ha   2,600   ▥   €8–11

Chosen by an overwhelming majority last year, for a Saint-Véran 99, Jean-Paul Paquet has done it again with a Pouilly Vinzelles

edge of the little town of Vinzelles. Made from handpicked grapes, it has a lively gold colour and notes of toast, honey and fresh almonds. Agreeable on the palate with good balance and elegant, flavourful length: grapefruit and exotic fruits. One to serve with a pike in *beurre blanc*.

↬ Dom. René Perraton, rue du Paradis, 71570 Chaintré, tel. 03.85.35.63.36, fax 03.85.35.67.45 ▣ ▼ by appt.

DOM. THIBERT PERE ET FILS

1999★   ▣ €8-11

Not satisfied with winning a *coup de coeur* for its Mâcon-Villages, the Thibert estate has also earned itself an honourable place for its Pouilly Vinzelles. Made from the grapes from 45-year-old vines grown on a marly slope and harvested on 22 September, this wine was produced and matured in large oak casks for nine months. The result is a wine 'with character', as one taster put it. Notes of toast and meadow hay compete with aromas of vanilla and brioche. Supple, full and well-balanced on the palate, the finish is lemon-flavoured and has great freshness. Wait three to five years before serving it with frogs' legs.

↬ GAEC Dom. Thibert Père et Fils, Le Bourg, 71960 Fuissé, tel. 03.85.35.61.79, fax 03.85.35.66.21, e-mail domthibe@club-internet.fr ▣ ▼ by appt.

CH. DE VINZELLES 1998★   n.c.   n.c.   ▣ €5-8

This is one of the last family-owned *négociants* in the Mâconnais region. We salute here its longevity, which is without doubt not unconnected with its expertise in both buying and producing wine. This clear yellow '98 has an intense nose revealing notes of dried apricots and linden blossom. Full, supple and round, the palate has toasty flavours together with hawthorn and fresh almonds, and its lemony finish leaves one looking forward to the pleasure of drinking it in two or three years' time.

↬ Ets Loron et Fils, Pontanevaux, 71570 La Chapelle-de-Guinchay, tel. 03.85.36.81.20, fax 03.85.33.83.19, e-mail vinloron@wanadoo.fr

Saint-Véran

P roducing only white wines in eight communes in the Saône-et-Loire, Saint-Véran is the last of the Mâcon appellations to be created (1971). In 2000, 40,247 hl (1,062,521 gal) were produced, and in quality the wines are somewhere between Pouilly and the Mâcons that are followed by the village name. The wines are light, elegant, fruity and accompany the first courses of meals wonderfully well.

G rown mainly on limestone soil, this appellation marks the southern limit of the Mâconnais.

DOM. ACERBIS 1999★   n.c.   n.c.   ▣ €5-8

Submitted by Pierre Janny, a small wine-merchant in the Mâconnais, this is a very characteristic Saint-Véran with an agreeable, almond-paste fragrance. It has a well-balanced, velvety palate with a lemony, honeyed finish. An expressive and modestly-priced wine.

↬ Sté Pierre Janny, La Condemine, Cidex 1556, 71260 Péronne, tel. 03.85.23.96.20, fax 03.85.36.96.58, e-mail pierre-janny@wanadoo.fr

AUVIGUE Les Chênes 1999   0.6 ha   5,000   ▣ €5-8

For this Les Chênes, the Auvigne company selected musts from good sources which were then matured for four months in lots of two to four wines. Intense aromas of crystallised fruits, pears in syrup and *pain d'épice* emanate from this brilliant yellow-gold wine. Only on the palate did the tasters detect the oak, but it was accompanied by a good structure prolonged by a vanilla finish. To drink with poultry in a cream sauce.

↬ Vins Auvigue, Le Moulin du pont, 71850 Charnay-lès-Mâcon, tel. 03.85.34.17.36, fax 03.85.34.75.88, e-mail vins.auvigue@wanadoo.fr ▣ ▼ by appt.

CAVE DE CHAINTRE 2000★★   17.88 ha   60,000   ▣ €5-8

Built on the remains of a Gallo-Roman villa, this co-operative presented a remarkable wine. Intense and complex, the nose has notes of crystallised fruits, honeysuckle and almonds. The rich, full, structured and very classy palate has a touch of overripeness on the finish. Wait one to two years before drinking it with a fish terrine.

↬ Cave de Chaintré, 71570 Chaintré, tel. 03.85.35.61.61, fax 03.85.35.61.48 ▣ ▼ by appt.

DOM. DU CHALET POUILLY 1999   3 ha   6,000   ▣ €5-8

A wine with an attractive, brilliant pale-gold colour and a complex, intense nose with mangoes and crystallised fruit enlivened by oaky and floral notes. The straightforward attack opens with notes of fresh butter. Mouthfilling and round-bodied with a lengthy oaky finish, this well-structured wine will need another year to assimilate its oak.

Saint-Véran

B. Léger-Plumet,
Dom. du Chalet Pouilly, Les Gerbeaux,
71960 Solutré-Pouilly, tel. 03.85.35.80.07,
fax 03.85.35.85.95 ✔ ⟁ by appt.

DOM. CORDIER PERE ET FILS
Les Crais 1999★★★

☐   0.25 ha   1,200   ⬤ €15-23

GRAND VIN DE BOURGOGNE
SAINT-VÉRAN
APPELLATION SAINT-VÉRAN CONTROLÉE
"LES CRAIS"
MIS EN BOUTEILLE AU
Domaine CORDIER Père & Fils

Three wines with *coup de coeur* in the same edition of the *Guide* – two of them Saint-Véran – this is the Cordier estate's record, which is fast becoming unbeatable in Mâconnais wines. Make your way through the slopes of the Fuissé heights to the wine-cellar where you will be welcomed by Roger Cordier and his son Christophe, and perhaps have the good fortune to taste this wine, produced in limited quantity, which enchanted the Jury. This very intense gold-coloured 99 has a powerful nose with aromas of ripe fruit (peaches, apricots), wax and honey uplifted by notes of vanilla and toast from the wood. On the palate everything rises to a crescendo, the attack, supple at first, becomes rich and powerful; the imprint of the oak is deeply-rooted. A 'monster' of a wine. The **Le clos à la Côte 99**, also nominated by an overwhelming majority, was awarded second place by the Grand Jury. Younger sibling of the previous wine, it is notable for its light, greenish-gold colour and fresh, lemony nose. On the palate it is well-balanced, fine, and the finish is accented by fresh citrus fruits. Lacey to perfection!

Dom. Cordier Pere et Fils, 71960 Fuissé,
tel. 03.85.35.62.89, fax 03.85.35.64.01
⟁ by appt.

DOM. CORSIN Tirage précoce 2000★

☐   2.5 ha   20,000   ▮ ♦ €5-8

This is one of the leading estates of the appellation. With grapes handpicked on 11 September, produced, matured, then bottled six months later, this wine is already very outgoing. A fine, pale-yellow colour, it presents aromas of confectionery, spring flowers and citrus fruits. After a slightly sparkling initial impact, roundness and good balance are revealed on the palate. 'A heavenly wine which will make a good aperitif,' said one Juror.

Dom. Corsin, Les Plantés, 71960 Davayé,
tel. 03.85.35.83.69, fax 03.85.35.86.64 ✔
⟁ by appt.

DOM. DES DEUX ROCHES
Les Terres noires 1999★★

☐   3 ha   20,000   ▮ ⬤ ♦ €8-11

This family-owned wine-producing business covers 35 ha (86.5 acres) of vineyards in Mâconnais, and also owns an estate in the Languedoc, near to Limoux. Well-used to being honoured by the *Guide*, it has distinguished itself again this year with this radiant amber-coloured wine. The subtle, slightly oaky nose is followed by a round, full palate which has good length while still retaining freshness. The oak is still very prominent; it needs laying down for a year or two to reach maturity. To drink with a fine fish dish.

Dom. des Deux Roches, 71960 Davayé,
tel. 03.85.35.86.51, fax 03.85.35.86.12 ✔
⟁ by appt.

JOSEPH DROUHIN 1999★

☐   n.c.   21,000   ▮ €8-11

Bright gold in colour, this wine has aromas of pears and white flowers (acacia, honeysuckle) that are rediscovered on the very well-balanced palate, which has great finesse: all these things go to make up a wine that is one of the very best. The Jury was particularly appreciative of its general balance. Of course, this Saint-Véran was submitted by that prestigious *négoce* from the Côte-d'Or, Joseph Drouhin.

Joseph Drouhin, 7, rue d'Enfer,
21200 Beaune, tel. 03.80.24.68.88,
fax 03.80.22.43.14, e-mail maisondrouhin@
drouhin.com ⟁ by appt.

PIERRE DUPOND 2000★

☐   n.c.   ▮ €8-11

Presented by a good *négociant* from Beaujolais, this crystalline Saint-Véran has great presence, thanks to its fresh aromas of apples and pears and wild flowers. Following a lively attack, the palate develops with harmony and finishes on notes of citrus fruits. A wine to serve chilled with a snack.

Pierre Dupond, 235, rue de Thizy,
69653 Villefranche-sur-Saône,
tel. 04.74.65.24.32, fax 04.74.68.04.14,
e-mail p.dupond@seldon.fr

DOM. MARC GREFFET 1999★

☐   0.6 ha   5,000   ⬤ €5-8

At the foot of the Solutré rock there is a museum housing prehistoric exhibits, which is not to be missed. This glittering lemon-yellow wine is also not one to be passed over. The nose combines very agreeable notes of fresh almonds and vanilla. On the palate it is refreshing and well-balanced. The limestone *terroir* has left a good imprint on this 99 vintage, matured for a year in oak. Already very pleasant, it may be left to age for one to two years.

Marc Greffet, 71960 Solutré-Pouilly,
tel. 03.85.35.83.82, fax 03.85.35.84.24 ✔
⟁ by appt.

DOM. GUEUGNON-REMOND
Vieilles vignes 1999

0.92 ha 7,990 €5-8

In 1997, Veronique, the daughter, and her husband, Jean-Christophe, took over the family business and since that time have worked unceasingly to bring out the very 'core' of the terroir. This wine, product of 20-year-old vines, has a range of aromas but shows mainly spring flowers. Very sincere and well-balanced on the palate, it finishes on a pleasant grapey note. 'A very promising terroir wine,' stressed one taster. It would go well with a dish of deep-fried small fish from the river Saône.

↬ Dom. Gueugnon-Remond, chem. de la Cave, 71850 Charnay-les-Macon, tel. 03.85.29.23.88, fax 03.85.20.20.72 V
Y by appt.
↬ Remond

DOM. DE LA DENANTE 2000*

5.5 ha 30,000 €5-8

Robert Martin, who uses very traditional methods of vinification and maturation, will welcome you warmly to his wine-cellar. Established at Davayé about 20 years ago, he always presents sound wines with plenty of character. This one, with its intense green-gold colour, has a complex nose of ripe fruit (quince) and citronella refreshed by a note of menthol. Fresh and agreeable, almost acidic, well-structured and full-bodied on the palate, this is a wine to keep for two to three years.
↬ Robert Martin, Les Peiguins, 71960 Davayé, tel. 03.85.35.82.88, fax 03.85.35.86.71 V Y by appt.

DOM. DE LA CROIX SENAILLET
Les Rochats 1999**

2.5 ha 6,000 €8-11

This estate, which now covers 22 ha (54.3 acres), was taken over by the two sons, Richard and Stéphane Martin, in 1991. In 1999, following renovation and building work to extend the winery, they decided to produce a wine using only the grapes from their old vines growing on the best hillsides of Davayé, and to mature it separately from the rest. The result is very persuasive, judging by this glittering yellow-gold wine. While it has a subtle nose of spring flowers and dried fruits, it is powerful and round on the palate. La cuvée La Grande Bruyère 99 also obtained two stars: its delicate aromas combine spring flowers with an agreeable vegetal note of fern. On the palate it is direct and full, finishing with lemony flavours. Commended by the Jury was the Saint-Véran 99, a cuvée blend of different terroirs and more classically made. A suitable wine to drink as an apéritif.
↬ Richard et Stéphane Martin, Dom. de La Croix Senaillet, En Coland, 71960 Davayé, tel. 03.85.35.82.83, fax 03.85.35.87.22 V

DOM. L'ERMITE DE SAINT-VERAN Jully Vieilles vignes 1999*

0.71 ha 4,200 €5-8

At the top of a hill in the southern-most part of the appellation, you will find the magnificent village of Saint-Vérand (with a d). It is near to this village that Gérard Martin owns 71 ares (about two-thirds of an acre) of very old vines (70 years on average) which he maintains in perfect condition in order to produce this wine, which has a beautiful, lively, brilliant green-gold colour. The subtle, floral (honeysuckle and acacia) nose paves the way to a palate that is lively and round at the same

DOM. DE LA FEUILLARDE
Vieilles vignes 1999

1.5 ha 8,000 €8-11

The roots of 60-year-old vines have searched deep into the clay-limestone soil to produce this authentic Saint-Véran which, for the moment, is still a little reserved. In two to four years' time it will be an interesting wine to serve with grilled fish.
↬ Lucien Thomas, Dom. de La Feuillarde, 71960 Prissé, tel. 03.85.34.54.45, fax 03.85.34.31.50, e-mail contact@domaine-feuillarde.com
Y ev. day 8am–12 noon 1pm–7pm

DOM. DE LALANDE 1999*

0.5 ha 4,000 €5-8

Established at the foot of the Chaintré hillsides, Dominique Cornin strives to get the best out of his terroir, using ploughing to control weeds and grassing down. This very well-made Saint-Véran is testimony to good vinification and maturation techniques. It has a brilliant pale-yellow colour with green flecks. The complex nose reveals notes of fresh fruits (William pears, cherry-plums), raisins and hazelnuts, enhanced by a pleasant touch of cinnamon. Supple and full on the palate, round, well-balanced and fruity throughout (citrus fruits), this will be a pleasant wine to drink in a year or two.
↬ Dominique Cornin, chem. du Roy-de-Croix, 71570 Chaintré, tel. 03.85.37.43.58, fax 03.85.37.43.58, e-mail dominique.cornin@fnac.net V
Y by appt.

DOM. LA MAISON
Les Condemines Vieilles vignes 1999**

6 ha 9,000 €5-8

Perhaps as a tribute to his father, Georges, co-founder of the Saint-Véran cru just thirty years ago, Jean Chagny has distinguished himself by producing this remarkable wine. Gold-coloured with green highlights, it has an attractive nose with crystallised fruits and touches of cinnamon and raisins. The same theme is carried over onto the full, structured palate. The lemon finish adds a fine freshness. The ideal wine to accompany snails.
↬ Jean Chagny, Au bourg, 71570 Leynes, tel. 03.85.35.10.16, fax 03.85.35.12.09, e-mail domaine.la.maison@free.fr V
Y by appt.

Saint-Véran

time. A fresh and characteristic wine that needs to be laid down for two or three years before being served with *andouillette* (a sausage made with pigs'intestines).

➤ Gérard Martin, Les Truges,
71570 Saint-Vérand, tel. 03.85.36.51.09,
fax 03.85.37.47.89 ☑ ☎ by appt.

CH. DE LEYNES Vieilles vignes 1999★★

1.5 ha   10,000   €8-11

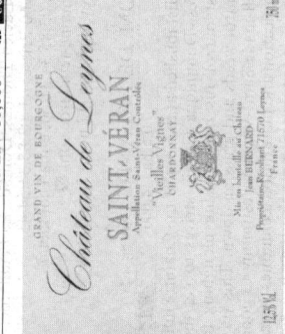

A centenary park, a real Mâconnais house with a great gallery, a family who have been wine-growers since the start of the 18th century: Jean Bernard, as becomes the worthy heir to this estate, makes high-quality wines like this one, which thrilled the tasters' palates. The colour is intense, luminous gold. The nose has aromas suggestive of breakfast: butter, toast, coffee, vanilla. Liveliness and roundness are the two main characteristics found on the palate, which finishes on some refreshing mineral notes. An undeniable success.

➤ Jean Bernard, Ch. de Leynes,
71570 Leynes, tel. 03.85.35.11.59,
fax 03.85.35.13.94, e-mail bernard-leynes@
caramail.com ☑ ☎ by appt.

DOM. DES MAILLETTES
En Pommard 2000★

0.8 ha   6,500   €5-8

Guy Saumaize, heir of a family of wine-growers established more than a century ago in the region, is also a nurseryman specialising in vines and, as you have probably realised, Chardonnay is his speciality. The light colour of this Saint-Véran En Pommard augurs an agreeable wine. The nose confirms this first impression with attractive aromas of spring flowers, gunflint and lemon. Round and supple on the palate, this personable 2000 is a rich and satisfying wine.

➤ Guy Saumaize, Les Maillettes,
71960 Davayé, tel. 03.85.35.82.65,
fax 03.85.35.86.69 ☑ ☎ by appt.

DOM. DES PERELLES 2000★

0.5 ha   4,200   €5-8

Head of this estate since 1976, Jean-Marc Thibert presents this brilliant green-gold wine with its characteristic nose of spring flowers and lemon enhanced by notes of oak and vanilla. After a fresh and smooth attack, the balance is redressed by a significant liveliness on the palate, finishing with long toasty notes.

This soundly-made 2000 should develop well over the next two to four years.

➤ Jean-Marc Thibert, Les Perelles,
71860 Crèches-sur-Saône,
tel. 03.85.37.14.56, fax 03.85.37.46.02 ☑
☎ by appt.

DOM. DES PONCETYS
Tradition 1999★

1.4 ha   11,100   €5-8

The Guigue de Maind family gave this estate to the bishopric of Autun in 1872. From 1905 to 1963 it belonged to the department of Saône-et-Loire, which then donated it to the State for use as a school of wine-growing, from where a good number of the wine-producers in the area have graduated. This Tradition has an attractive pale green-gold colour. The fairly intense nose opens with notes of spring flowers and the round, fresh palate finishes on a delicate, mineral note. From the same vintage, the **Cuvée Prestige** also obtained a star, but it will need laying down for several years as, for the moment, the oak is still too pronounced.

➤ Lycée viticole de Mâcon-Davayé,
Dom. des Poncetys, 71960 Davayé,
tel. 03.85.33.56.20, fax 03.85.35.86.34,
e-mail legta.macon@wanadoo.fr ☑ ☎ ev.
day except Sun. 9am–12 noon 2pm–5.30pm

CAVE DE PRISSE-SOLOGNY-VERZE

Dernière cuvée du millénaire 1999★

176.09 ha   25,000   €5-8

Wine-producers from the three Mâconnais wine co-operatives – Prissé, Sologny and Verze – have amalgamated, resulting in a combined holding of 900 ha (2,223 acres) of vines. They presented this intense gold wine which has a pure, very expressive nose of vanilla, butter, apricots and pineapple. After a lively attack, a good balance is obtained between the richness and acidity, finishing with a sumptuous fruitiness.

➤ Cave de Prissé-Sologny-Verzé,
71960 Prissé, tel. 03.85.37.88.06,
fax 03.85.37.61.76, e-mail cave.prisse@
wanadoo.fr ☑ ☎ by appt.

PASCAL RENOUD-GRAPPIN 1999

1.6 ha   1,164   €5-8

Pascal Renoud-Grappin is a young wine-producer who set up on his own in 1996, after undergoing on-the-job training with established wine-growers in the region. He presented a clear white-gold wine with aromas composed of citrus fruits and dried fruit, and a fresh, slightly acidic palate. 'A fruity wine that would go well with seafood,' was one taster's suggestion.

➤ Pascal Renoud-Grappin, Les Plantes,
71960 Davayé, tel. 03.85.35.81.35 ☑
☎ ev. day except Sun. 8am–8pm

DOM. SAUMAIZE-MICHELIN

☐ Les vieilles vignes 1999★

| 0.7 ha | 5,000 | 🔲 €8-11 |

Sixty per cent of this estate's production is exported to a number of countries around the world – as far away as New Zealand. An attractive, intense yellow-gold colour, this wine releases notes of smoke and hazelnuts combined with intense aromas of vanilla, toast and butter that come from ten months in wood. The attack is soft and round, and the palate has an oaky foundation that is more than ready to blend in. A great wine, which needs one to two years more to mature.

- Dom. Roger et Christine Saumaize-Michelin, Le Martelet, 71960 Vergisson, tel. 03.85.35.84.05, fax 03.85.35.86.77 ☑
- Ⴤ by appt.

JEAN-LUC TISSIER Les Crais 2000

| 2.2 ha | 8,000 | €5-3 |

Jean-Luc Tissier, a passionate wine-grower and in charge of 9 ha (22.2 acres) of vineyards, has not failed with this symbolic 2000 vintage. His Les Crais, product of clay-lime-stone soil, is a beautiful golden-yellow. Its nose with ripe fruits (pears) heralds a round and vinous palate where crystallised fruit give the cue for the citrus fruits to emerge. This wine is at its peak of perfection.

- Jean-Luc Tissier, Les Pasquiers, 71570 Leynes, tel. 03.85.35.10.31, fax 03.85.35.13.04 ☑ Ⴤ by appt.
- Roger Tissier

DOM. DES VALANGES

☐ Cuvée hors Classe 1999★★

| n.c. | 12,000 | 🔲 €11-15 |

This domaine is a collector of coups de coeur; Michel Paquet, the dedicated wine-grower at its head is also president of the Union of Wine-producers of Saint-Véran. The Cuvée hors Classe, made with grapes from the oldest vines on the estate, is worthy of its name. It was matured for nine months, partly in wood and partly in vat. Its intense and brilliant green-gold colour proclaims a great wine; the quite intense nose of flowers and apricots confirms this. As to the rest, it is perfection itself on the palate, its structure is very well-balanced, and the finish is dazzling.

- Michel Paquet, Dom. des Valanges, 71960 Davayé, tel. 03.85.35.85.03, fax 03.85.35.86.67, e-mail domaine-des-valanges@wanadoo.fr ☑ Ⴤ by appt.

DOM. DES VIEILLES PIERRES

Les Pommards 1999

| 1.3 ha | 5,600 | 🔲 €8-11 |

This renowned terroir, situated on a steep slope with a north-west exposure near to Davayé, has produced, as expected, a wine of great purity that is still subtle. The nose opens on mineral and floral (honeysuckle) notes; it is followed by a freshness on the palate that also expresses a significant mineral quality. This still somewhat reserved wine will benefit from a peaceful spell in the cellar before being served with lobster.

- Jean-Jacques Litaud, Les Nembrets, 71960 Vergisson, tel. 03.85.35.85.69, fax 03.85.35.86.26, e-mail jean-jacques.litaud@wanadoo.fr ☑ Ⴤ by appt.

CHAMPAGNE

The wine of kings and princes and now the wine for every celebration, champagne is cloaked in glory and prestige and conveys to the world all that is French elegance and seductiveness. Its reputation has as much to do with its history as with its particular characteristics, which means, for many, that only wine from Champagne is *the* champagne; however, it is not as simple as that …

The Champagne region, which is situated less than 200 km (125 miles) north-east of Paris, contains three Appellations d'Origine Contrôlée, Champagne, Coteaux Champenois and Rosé des Riceys, but the last two of these produce only around 100,000 bottles. This northernmost wine-growing region in France extends chiefly over the Marne and the Aube regions, with small areas in the Aisne, Seine-et-Marne and Haute-Marne. The total vineyard area covers 31,458 ha (77,701 acres), of which 30,407 ha (75,105 acres) was in production in 2000.

Between them, Reims and Épernay in the Marne share the role of capital of Champagne. The former has the additional appeal of its monuments and museums, which draw crowds of visitors who, at the same time, can discover the cellars belonging to the 'great houses', many of which are very ancient.

The whole of the wine-growing area has a similar, undulating countryside, where four main regions are traditionally identified. In La Montagne de Reims some of the vineyards face north and are on sandy soil. The Côte des Blancs, just outside Épernay, benefits from a relatively predictable climate, the valley of the Marne (21,652 ha/53,480 acres), extending into the vineyards in the Aisne, where 2,804 ha (6,926 acres) are planted, and where the river flows between chalky hills, the slopes of both banks are covered in vines. Here, despite what one might expect, the quality of the grapes produced rarely varies, whether the vineyards face north or south. Finally, there is the vineyard of the Aube, 6,649 ha (16,423 acres) in the extreme south-east of the appellation, and separated from the other three areas by a 75-km (47-mile) zone where no vines are grown. The Aube is higher and more susceptible to spring frosts than the other areas, yet it produces wines of no lesser quality. This is where you find the only *appellation communale*: Rosé des Riceys. The Haute-Marne encompasses 68 ha (168 acres) and the Seine-et-Marne 47 ha (116 acres).

As the sea retreated some 70 million years ago upheavals caused by tellurian quakes ensued, forming a chalk base that is permeable and rich in essential minerals and brings finesse to the wines of Champagne. A shallow layer of clay and limestone covers the subsoil on nearly 60% of the land devoted to vines. In the Aube, the soil composition is marl, which is closer to that found in neighbouring Burgundy.

If frost – and at this latitude, spring frosts are frequent – makes reliable production difficult, the climatic extremes are nevertheless tempered by extensive mountain forests, which balance out the mild Atlantic maritime climate and the harsher continental one, maintaining a certain level of humidity. The lack of extreme heat is also a determining factor in the fine quality of the wines. Naturally enough, the choice of grape variety

668

is made in the context of the wine-growing and climatic conditions. Of the 31,458 ha (77,701 acres) devoted to vine-growing, Pinot Noir takes up 11,934 ha (29,477 acres), Pinot Meunier 10,781 ha (26,629 acres) and Chardonnay 8,650 ha (21,366 acres). Other varieties – Pinot Blanc, Pinot Gris, Petit Meslier and Arbanne – share the remaining area under cultivation. The wine-making industry provides 31,000 jobs for the region, including 14,695 wine-growers and producers.

The particular demands of the champagne method, which takes a number of years (three on average and many more for vintage years), requires that nearly 900,000 bottles are kept in storage at any one time. Annual production, which was 2,349,993 hl (62,039,815 gal) in 1999, represents 11% of the volume of wine produced in France. It also represents 30.6% in value and 33.1% in volume of all French wines exported in 1999, with Britain, Germany and the United States topping the list of importing countries, followed by Switzerland, Belgium, Italy, Holland and Japan.

Wine has been made in Champagne since at least the time of the Roman invasion. The first wines to be produced were white, later production was of red and then 'gris' (grey), which is white or nearly white wine that comes from pressing black grapes. At an early stage the wine had the irritating habit of fizzing up in the barrels. Systematic bottling of these unstable wines was invented in England, to where, until around 1700, the wine had been delivered in barrels. This had the result of allowing the carbon dioxide to dissolve in the wine, and sparkling wine was born. Dom Pérignon, the procurator of the abbey in Hautvillers and a forward-looking blending technician, produced the best wines at his abbey; he was also able to sell them for the highest prices.

In 1728 the king's council authorised the transportation of wine in bottles; a year later, the first champagne house was founded: Ruinart. Others were to follow, including Moët in 1743, but the majority of the great houses were started or established in the 19th century. In 1804 Madame Clicquot launched the first rosé champagne, and from 1830 the first labels to be stuck on bottles appeared. From 1860 Madame Pommery was famous for her *brut* wines, while around 1870 the first vintage champagnes began to appear. In 1884 Raymond Abelé invented the first disgorging rack cooled with ice, before phylloxera and two world wars ravaged the vineyards. A great deal of modernisation has taken place in the half century since: wooden barrels have for the most part yielded to stainless-steel vats, fining and finishing have been automated and, nowadays, *remuage* or riddling – shifting the angle of the bottle to make the deposit gravitate towards the cork – is being mechanised as well.

A large number of wine-growers in Champagne belong to a category known as grape producers, who 'sell by the kilo (2.2lb)'. They sell all or a proportion of their harvest to the great houses, which vinify, make and sell the wines. This practice has led the champagne makers' trade association to set recommended prices for the grapes and to give each commune a classification depending on the quality of the grapes produced: this is known as the *échelle des crus* (scale of the crus). The wines made in wine-making communes are classified on this descending scale, which first appeared at the end of the 19th century. Wines classified as 100% have the right to be called Grand Cru, those from 99% to 90% may be called Premier Cru; the normal appellation is classified between 89% and 80%. The price of grapes is set according to the percentage allocated to the commune. The maximum amount of grapes produced on each hectare (2.5 acres) is altered

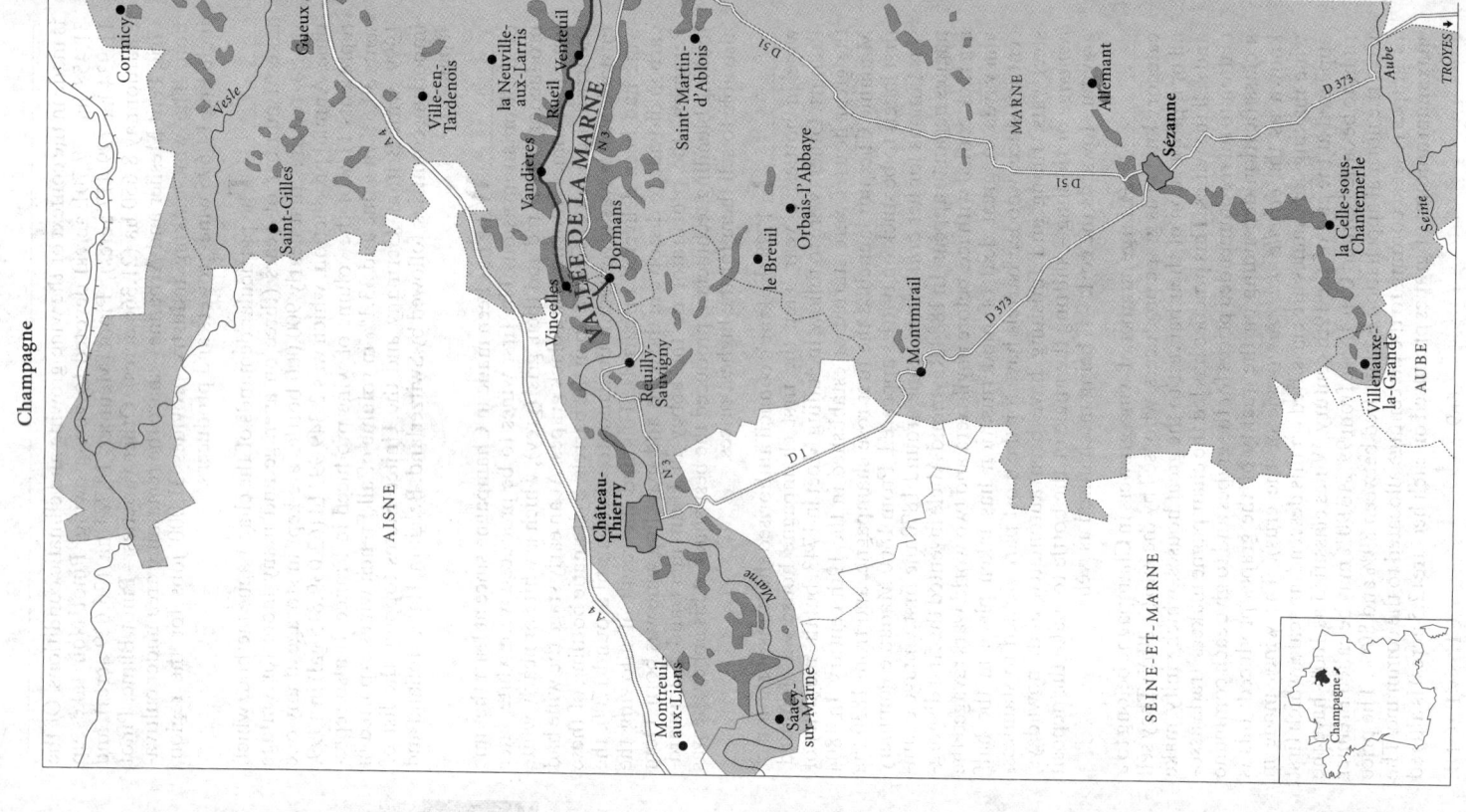

Champagne

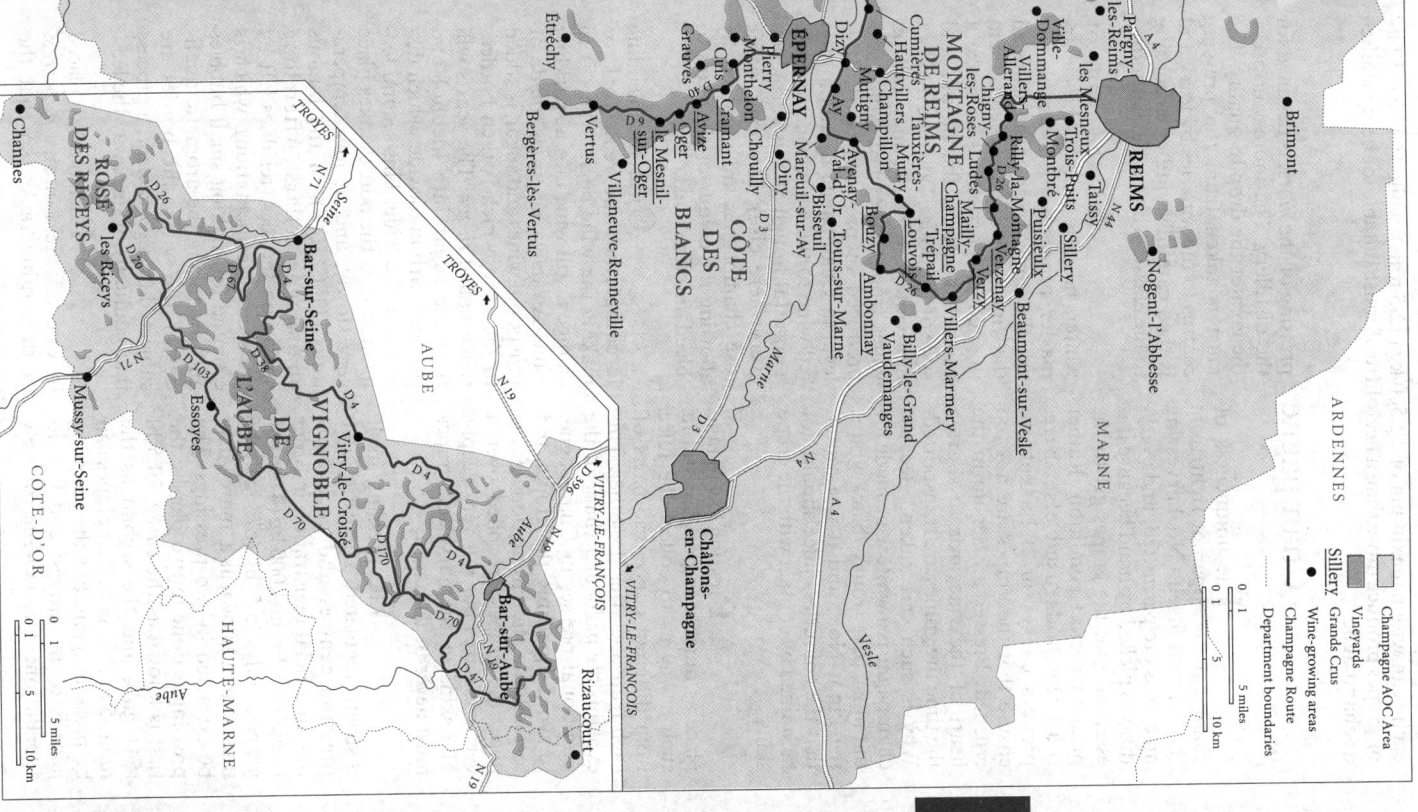

CHAMPAGNE

Champagne

The uniqueness of champagne is apparent right from the harvest itself. No harvesting machines are permitted, and everything is picked by hand because it is essential that the grapes get to the press in perfect condition. Rather than the hods used elsewhere, pickers carry small baskets to ensure that the grapes are not too crushed. Presses are set up in the heart of the vineyards to shorten the time the grapes are transported. Why is such care taken? Because champagne is a white wine made for the most part from a black grape, the Pinot Noir, and it is essential that the colourless juice should not be stained by contact with the grape skins.

Pressing has to take place as quickly as possible and in such a way as to collect the juice from different concentric parts of each fruit one after the other. This explains the particular shape of the traditional presses in Champagne: to avoid squashing the grapes and to facilitate the circulation of juice, the grapes are piled over a very wide area but not very deeply. The skins of the harvested grapes must never be damaged.

The pressing itself is strictly regulated. There are 2,000 pressing centres and each must obtain official registration in order to operate. From 4,000 kg (4 ton) of grapes, only 25.5 hl (673 gal) of must, a unit known as a 'marc', may be extracted in two pressings. The pressing is done in two phases: the first is known as the *cuvée*, 20.5 hl (541 gal), and the second as the *taille*, 5 hl (132 gal). The grapes can be pressed again, but the resulting juice is of no interest and has no appellation. The *rebêche*, or new

pressing of the *marc*, is destined for the distillery. The more you press, the greater the drop in quality. The must is taken from the pressing centres to the wineries by lorry and is then carefully vinified according to the classic white wine method.

At the end of winter, in early spring, the cellarmaster proceeds to 'assemble' or mix the *cuvée*. To do so, he tastes all the wines available and blends them in such proportions as to make a wine that reflects the flavour and style of the house. When he makes a non-vintage wine, he may call on wines from the reserve, which was produced in previous years. It is legal in Champagne to add a little red wine to the white wine to make a rosé (although this is forbidden everywhere else). However, some rosé champagnes are obtained by allowing the colour of the skins to 'bleed' into the must.

Once the blending is completed, the real work of making the wine begins. This is to change a still wine into a sparkling wine. A *liqueur de tirage*, made of yeasts, old wines and sugar, is added to the wine, which is then bottled: this is called *tirage*. The yeasts will turn the sugar into alcohol and produce carbon dioxide, which dissolves in the wine. This second fermentation in the bottles takes place very slowly, and at low temperatures (11°C/51°F), in the famous champagne cellars. After long ageing on the lees (residues left by the second fermentation), which is essential for making small bubbles and producing the aromatic qualities of the wines, the bottles are subjected to *dégorgement*, a process that gradually drains away the lees.

Each bottle is placed in one of the famous *pupitres*, or disgorging racks, so that the

each year, with a maximum of 12,500 kg (12.5 tons), while 160 kg (352 lb) of grapes produce more than a hectolitre of must suitable for being vinified as champagne.

deposits will settle in the neck of the bottle, beneath the cork. For two or three months the bottles will be periodically shaken and tilted, neck down, until the wine is perfectly clear (automated riddling in a gyropallet is on the increase). To evacuate the deposit, the neck is frozen in a refrigerating bath and the cork is removed; once the deposit is expelled, the bottle is topped up with a wine that may or may not be sweetened: this is the *dosage*. If pure wine is added, a 100% brut wine is obtained (Brut Sauvage from Piper-Heidsieck, Ultra-Brut from Laurent-Perrier, and champagnes known as *non-dosés*, or not sweetened, and now called Brut Nature). If only a very small amount (1%) of sweetened wine is added, the champagne is Brut; a content of 2% to 5% produces dry champagne; 5% to 8% produces demi-sec; and 8% to 15% sweet. The bottles are then shaken to blend the wines together and set to rest again to allow the taste of the yeast to disappear. They are then labelled and released onto the market. From then on the champagne is ready to be appreciated at the top of its form. Allowing it to age for too long can only harm it: serious houses flatter themselves that they put their wines on sale only when they have reached their peak.

Some excellent wines made from the first pressing, together with numerous 'reserve' wines (for the non-vintages), the talent of the cellar-master, with his finely judged, minimal, undetectable dosing, and the long maturing of the champagne on the lees will combine to produce wines of the highest quality. But it is rare for a buyer to be fully informed about all these issues, and certainly there is no guarantee that the information will be accurate.

What can be read on a champagne label? The brand and the name of the maker; the

dosage (brut, sec and so on); the year or lack of a year; the phrase *blanc de blancs* when only white grapes have been used in the wine; when possible (though this is rare), the commune of origin of the grapes, and finally, sometimes, but less and less often, the qualitative classification of the grapes: Grand Cru for the 17 communes that have the right to the description or Premier Cru for 41 others. The professional standing of the producer must appear, printed in small letters: NM (*négociant-manipulant*), meaning a merchant-winemaker; RM (*récoltant-manipulant*), a grower making champagne from his or her own grapes, with 5% bought in from other sources; CM (*Co-opérative de manipulation*), a co-operative that makes and sells its own champagne using grapes from its member growers; MA (*marque d'acheteur*), the brand of the buyer; RC (*récoltant-coopérateur*), a small grower who sends his grapes to one or several co-operatives to be made into champagne because he does not have the equipment to do so himself, and who receives the finished champagne to sell; SR (*société de récoltants*) a registered firm set up by champagne growers of the same family who pool their production resources; or ND (*négociant-distributeur*), meaning a merchant who distributes wine bought from others.

What can be gleaned from all this? Simply that the Champenois have deliberately adopted a sales policy that is focused on the brand. A customer will, therefore, order Moët et Chandon, Bollinger or Taittinger because he or she prefers the flavour and style adopted by this or that brand. It is the same for the champagnes produced by the *négociants-manipulants*, the co-operatives and related brands, but not for the *récoltants-manipulants*, who, to qualify as such, make champagne only from their own grapes, generally grouped in a single commune.

Champagne

These champagnes are the so-called Monocrus, and the name of the Cru will generally appear on the label.

Although there is only the one appellation, 'champagne', a great many different champagnes exist, and the range of characteristics of flavour, smell and appearance can readily satisfy the different needs and varying tastes of every drinker. So, champagne can be blanc de blancs, blanc de noirs (from Pinot Meunier, Pinot Noir or from both) or blends of blanc de blancs and blanc de noirs in any imaginable proportion. It can be from one cru alone or from several, originating from a Grand Cru, a Premier Cru or communes of lesser prestige. It can be vintage or non-vintage (the non-vintage champagnes can be made from young wines or be made up from wines from the reserve, and they are sometimes produced from an assemblage of vintage years). It can be non-dosed or very variably dosed and it can undergo short or long maturation on the lees. It may be disgorged for a longer or shorter time, or be white or rosé (which is obtained either by blending or by bleeding). Then again, most of these options can be combined together in different ways, so there is in fact an infinite number of champagnes. Whatever the type, the general consensus is that the best champagne has matured for a long time on the lees (five to ten years), and is consumed, in France at least, in the six months following disgorgement.

Given all this, it is easy to understand why the price of bottles can vary so widely and why there are wines at the top of the range or special wines, *cuvées spéciales*. It is unfortunately true that, among the better known brands, the cheapest champagnes are the least appealing. On the other hand, the big price differences between the upper range (vintage champagnes) and the top-price wines do not always guarantee an equivalent step in quality.

Champagne should be drunk when it is between 7° and 9°C (44.6–48.2°F), chilled for the blancs de blancs and young champagnes, not so cold for the vintage and sweeter champagnes. In addition to the classic 75cl bottle, champagne is also sold in a quarter bottle, a half, a magnum (twice a single bottle), Jeroboam (4 bottles), Methuselah (8 bottles) and Salmanazar (12 bottles). The bottle should be cooled gradually by immersing it in a champagne bucket containing water and ice. To remove the cork, take off the wire cage and foil. If the cork is likely to be pushed out by the pressure, allow it to come out with the cage and foil. If the cork resists, hold it in one hand and turn the bottle with the other. The cork should be removed slowly and noiselessly, avoiding rapid decompression.

Champagne should not be served in goblets but in tall, slender glasses that are completely dry and free from any traces of detergent, which will kill the bubbles and the foam. It can be drunk equally well as an apéritif as with starters and non-oily fish. The richer wines, mostly blanc de noirs, and the great vintages are frequently served with meat dishes with sauce. Drink a demi-sec wine rather than a brut with dessert or sweet dishes, because the sugar in the dish will over-emphasise the palate's sensitivity to the acidity of the brut.

The most recent vintages are 1982, a great vintage everywhere; 1983, straightforward; 1984 was not a vintage, so we can ignore it; 1985, good bottles; 1986, average quality, few wines declared a vintage; 1987, a bad year; 1988, 1989 and 1990, three wonderful years to enjoy; 1991, poor, generally not declared a vintage; 1992, 1993 and 1994, average years; a few important houses declared 1992 and 1993 a vintage; 1995, the best year since 1990; 1996, a great year, declared a vintage in January 2000.

674

AGRAPART ET FILS Blanc de Blancs

6 ha · 20,000 · €11-15

This vineyard features regularly in the *Guide* for its blancs de blancs. There is nothing surprising about that, for the Agraparts have been producing wine in the Côtes des Blancs for over a century. They currently cultivate 9.6 ha (24 acres) and pride themselves on the fact that 'there's life in the old dog yet'. The characteristic oakiness of the 96 and 97 wines is found in this blanc de blancs. It is very young, still retaining the bread-like aroma of fermentation. Flavours of spiciness and liquorice mingle on the palate. The estate was also commended for two other blancs de blancs: the **Reserve**, produced from the harvests of 1995 and 1996 and commended for its freshness and balance, and the imposing, brioche-flavoured **93**. (RM)

☛ EARL Agrapart et Fils, 57, av. Jean-Jaurès, 51190 Avize, tel. 03.26.57.51.38, fax 03.26.57.05.06, e-mail champagne.agrapart@wanadoo.fr
☖ by appt.

GILLES ALLAIT 1996★

0.2 ha · 1,500 · €11-15

Gilles Allait cultivates a 3.5-ha vineyard at Passy-Grigny, near Dormans. His Chardonnays are matured for six months in barrel. His 96 vintage, a blend of equal parts Chardonnay and Pinot Meunier, has swiftly reached its peak. Its finesse, structure and full-bodied richness make it an ideal accompaniment for white meats. The **Cuvée Tradition**, produced from Pinot Meunier, complemented by 5% Chardonnay, was also commended for its well-balanced richness. (RC)

☛ Gilles Allait, 2, rue du Château, 51700 Passy-Grigny, tel. 03.26.52.92.19, fax 03.26.52.97.22 ☖ by appt.

JEAN-ANTOINE ARISTON Carte Blanche

1.5 ha · 15,000 · €11-15

The village of Brouillet is situated to the west of Reims. Jean-Antoine Ariston, who has 6.5 ha (16 acres) of vines at his disposal, took over from a long line of wine-producers in 1962, and he launched his champagne in 1975. The Carte Blanche is made up of 60% Chardonnay and 40% Pinot Noir, from the 1998 harvest. It has a fine, delicate bouquet. Flavours of citrus fruits lend freshness to the palate. (RM)

☛ Jean-Antoine Ariston, 4, rue Haute, 51170 Brouillet, tel. 03.26.97.47.02, fax 03.26.97.49.75, e-mail champagne.ariston@wanadoo.fr
☖ ev. day 8am-12 noon; 2-6pm

ARISTON FILS 1995

2 ha · 7,000 · €15-23

The Aristons have been producing wine since the vineyard was first established in 1794. Rémi took over in 1964, and has been joined by his son, Paul-Vincent. The estate, which covers 9 ha (22 acres), also offers guest rooms. The colour of its deep-yellow 95 suggests advanced development, a character that is less pronounced on the palate, where its roundness and balance can be more fully appreciated. (RM)

☛ Rémi Ariston, 4 et 8, Grande-Rue, 51170 Brouillet, tel. 03.26.97.43.46, fax 03.26.97.49.34, e-mail champagne.ariston.fils@wanadoo.fr
☖ ev. day 9am-12 noon, 1.30-6pm; Sun. 10am-12 noon; 3-5pm; cl. 3rd wk. Aug.

MICHEL ARNOULD ET FILS Tradition★

Gd Cru · 6 ha · 40,000 · €11-15

Michel Arnould has been in business for 40 years. He was fortunate to acquire some vineyards at Verzenay, a village in the Montagne de Reims classified as Grand Cru, where the wines are noted for their fine character. Nowadays, he cultivates 12 ha (30 acres). The Tradition, a blanc de noirs (100% Pinot Noir) derived from the harvests of 1996 and 1997, is full, sophisticated and well balanced – a fine example of a mature wine. (RM)

☛ Michel Arnould et Fils, 28, rue de Mailly, 51360 Verzenay, tel. 03.26.49.40.06, fax 03.26.49.44.61, e-mail michelarnould@wanadoo.fr ☖ by appt.

NICOLAS FRANCOIS AUBRY Sablé rosé 1996

1er Cru · 10 ha · 2,500 · €15-23

The Aubrys have been making wine since the time of the French Revolution. They operate a vineyard of 16 ha (40 acres) and produce champagnes of great originality. This rosé, made from direct pressing of the grapes, is lightly sparkling. The two Pinots dominate, supplemented by 20% Chardonnay (1996 harvest). The orange-pink colour and complex bouquet of fruit, butter and vanilla anticipate a wine that is supple and fresh on the palate. It could be served with salmon or with cheese. (RM)

☛ SCEV Champagne L. Aubry Fils, 4-6, Grande-Rue, 51390 Jouy-lès-Reims, tel. 03.26.49.20.07, fax 03.26.49.75.27 ☖ by appt.

AUTREAU DE CHAMPILLON Les Perles de La Dhuy 1996★

9.7 ha · 10,000 · €15-23

The Autreau family has dedicated itself to the vine since 1670. Their champagne was created in 1955, and they now manage 27 ha (67 acres) on the slopes of the Montagne de Reims, between Ay and Hautvillers. This particularly white *cuvée* contains only 10% Pinot Noir. Its floral and liquorice bouquet and highly structured palate contribute to a wine of impressive length. (NM)

☛ SARL Vignobles Champenois, 15, rue René-Baudet, 51160 Champillon, tel. 03.26.59.46.00, fax 03.26.59.44.85 ☖ ev. day 9am-12 noon; 2-6pm; Sat. Sun. by appt.; cl. 16-20 Aug.
☛ Eric Autréau

AUTREAU-LASNOT★★
1 ha 4,500 €11-15

This estate, established in 1932, covers 10 ha (25 acres) of vines at Venteuil and Châtillon, districts on the right bank of the river Marne. The darkish-coloured rosé is made from the three champagne grape varieties. Its flavours of wild fruits are captivatingly complex, embracing blackberries and soft red fruits, and the pronounced acidity underscores its freshness. The **Cuvée Prestige 97**, half from black grapes and half from white, received a star for its youthfulness, freshness and balance, while the commended **Carte d'or** again owes its brioche and charred notes to all three grapes, harvested between 1995 and 1997. (RM)

➤ Champagne Autréau-Lasnot, 6, rue du Château, 51480 Venteuil, tel. 03.26.58.49.35, fax 03.26.58.65.44 ☑ ⌧ by appt.
➤ Gérard Autréau

AYALA Blanc de Blancs 1996
n.c. n.c. €23-30

The Ayala estate, which has 85 ha (210 acres) of vines at its disposal, was established under the Second Empire. It submitted a very fine (and commended) **Brut 96**, which was made predominantly from black grapes. From the same vintage comes this greenish-gold, crystal-clear blanc de blancs, with its exceedingly young, citrussy, fruity bouquet and great potential. (NM)

➤ Champagne Ayala, 2, bd du Nord, BP 6, 51160 Ay, tel. 03.26.55.15.44, fax 03.26.51.09.04 ☑ ⌧ by appt.
➤ Ducellier

BAGNOST PERE ET FILS
Cuvée de Reserve
1.25 ha 10,000 €11-15

This modest, family-run vineyard of 8 ha (20 acres) was founded in 1889, and is situated in the area of Pierry, to the south of Epernay. It distinguished itself with a *coup de coeur* in the previous edition of the *Guide*, and this year three of its wines were singled out by the Jury. This **Cuvée de Reserve**, made from three champagne harvests in 1998, is very youthful, with an intense bouquet and sharp, vigorous palate. Also commended were the **rosé**, for its fruity vinosity, and the **93 Blanc de Blancs**, which was chosen for its mineral character. (RM)

➤ Champagne Bagnost Pere et Fils, 30, rue du Gal-de-Gaulle, 51530 Pierry, tel. 03.26.54.04.22, fax 03.26.55.27.17 ⌧ ev. day except Sun. 9am–12 noon; 2–6pm

CHRISTIAN BANNIERE★
Gd Cru 0.5 ha 2,000 €11-15

Christian Bannière launched his champagne in 1948. Although he has only a few hectares under vine, location is all important. Bouzy is a village on the southern slope of the Montagne de Reims, classified as Grand Cru and renowned for its Pinot Noir. That grape variety dominates the blend of this *brut rosé* (80%, the balance is Chardonnay). Both its bouquet and palate evoke complex, rich, warm flavours of cherries, raspberries, flowers, honey and quince. The **Tradition Grand Cru**, as with the previous blend, is lively, robust and spicy. (RM)

➤ Christian Bannière, 5, rue Yvonnet, 51150 Bouzy, tel. 03.26.57.08.15, fax 03.26.59.35.02 ☑ ⌧ by appt.

PAUL BARA Grand Rosé de Bouzy★
Gd Cru 11.05 ha 10,000 €15-23

The vineyard was established around 1833 and began to be developed after 1860. Today it accounts for 11 ha (27 acres) at Bouzy, a Grand Cru village. Not surprisingly, Pinot Noir, king of the grape varieties in this district, dominates the Bara blends. The Grand Rosé is, therefore, very deeply coloured, containing 88% Pinot to just 12% Chardonnay. A range of flavours mingle on the palate: almonds, honey, citrus and red fruits. It is the sort of wine that used to be described as 'feminine'. It is suitable as an aperitif or with food. The **Special Club 97 Grand Cru** also received a commendation. This light, fresh, floral wine is made up of 70% Pinot Noir and 30% Chardonnay. (RM)

➤ Champagne Paul Bara, 4, rue Yvonnet, 51150 Bouzy, tel. 03.26.57.00.50, fax 03.26.57.81.24 ☑ ⌧ by appt.

BARDOUX PERE ET FILS Réserve
3 ha 3,060 €15-23

The birth of Pierre Bardoux at Villedommange in the Montagne de Reims in 1684 established a dynasty of wine-growers, and Jules and Prudent Bardoux launched their champagne in 1929. In 1973 Pascal Bardoux resumed production on the family estate, which in those days consisted of just 4 ha (10 acres) of vines. Its Réserve, drawn from the harvests of 1993, 1994 and 1995, is made up of two-thirds black grapes to one-third white. This complex, lingering, honeyed wine shows evident *dosage* and is appropriate for the dinner-table. The **rosé** and the **93 Cuvée Prudent Bardoux 1er** Cru were also commended by the Jury. Both are champagnes in which Chardonnay plays almost as significant a role as Pinot Meunier. The first was commended for its balance and length; the second for its very ripe fruit and its maturity. (RM)

➤ Pascal Bardoux, 5–7, rue Saint-Vincent, 51390 Villedommange, tel. 03.26.49.25.35, fax 03.26.49.23.15, e-mail contact@champagne-bardoux.com ☑ by appt.

E. BARNAUT Blanc de Noirs
Gd Cru 2.5 ha 20,000 €11-15

Philippe Secondé took over the family-run vineyard in 1987, and his champagne bears the name of his ancestor, who founded the estate in 1874. Today he cultivates 14.5 ha (36 acres) at Bouzy, and it isn't in the least surprising to find him commended for a Pinot Noir blanc de noirs, produced from the 1997 harvest, topped up with reserve wines. Its fresh, opening impression is followed by length and balance on the palate. The flavours

676

are intense and appealing, with overtones of white fruits, quince and stone fruits. (RM)

Y by appt.

♦ Philippe Secondé

BARON ALBERT Tradition

n.c. — 150,000 — €11-15

The Albert family has been working the vineyard at Charly-sur-Marne since 1677, but it was not until 1946, under the direction of Albert Baron, that the vineyard started producing champagne. Today, the estate has 30 ha (74 acres) under vine. Claude Baron's wines do not undergo malolactic fermentation. His Tradition wine consists of 90% Pinot Meunier and 10% Chardonnay from the 1996 and 1997 vintages. This simple, floral champagne offers good balance. (NM)

♦ Champagne Baron Albert,
1, rue des Chaillots, Grand-Porteron,
02310 Charly-sur-Marne,
tel. 03.23.82.02.65, fax 03.23.82.02.44,
e-mail champagnebaronalbert@wanadoo.fr
Y by appt.

BARON-FUENTE 1995★

n.c. — 50,000 —

Baron-Fuenté champagne originated in the late 1960s as a result of the marriage between Dolores Fuenté and Gabriel Baron, heir to a long tradition of wine-producers dating back to the 17th century. The company has recently modernised its production methods, and from its current selection of champagnes the 95 vintage, a half white and half black *cuvée* (with 20% Pinot Meunier), emerged as the Jury's favourite. It has a fine bouquet of citrus fruits and a well-rounded palate with charred undertones. Two other *cuvées* deserve mention: the *Esprit de Baron-Fuenté* (the new name for the Prestige Cuvée), which was made from all three champagne grapes and commended for its originality and length, and the **Tradition**, which is a blend of 75% Pinot Meunier and 25% Chardonnay. (NM)

♦ Champagne Baron-Fuente, 21, av. Fernand-Drouet, 02310 Charly-sur-Marne, tel. 03.23.82.01.97, fax 03.23.82.12.00, e-mail champagne.baron-fuente@wanadoo.fr

BAUCHET PERE ET FILS Sélection

1er Cru — n.c. — 65,000 — €11-15

Established at Bisseuil in the Marne valley and founded by the Bauchet brothers, this company owns a major vineyard of 36 ha (89 acres) in the regions of the Côte des Blancs and the Aube. Its Sélection, made from half black grapes and half white, is particularly noteworthy for its fine, expressive and complex bouquet, which mingles flavours of fruit and confectionery. In comparison, the palate is a little lacking, but its first impressions are lively and fresh enough. The **95 1ᵉʳ Cru** also won a commendation from the Jury. With its flavours of brioche and honey,

Chardonnay makes its mark as the dominant grape variety (70% of the blend). (RM)

♦ Sté Bauchet Frères, rue de la Crayère, 51150 Bisseuil, tel. 03.26.58.92.12, fax 03.26.58.94.74,
e-mail bauchet.champagne@wanadoo.fr
Y by appt.

BAUGET-JOUETTE Blanc de Blancs 1994★

n.c. — n.c. — €30-38

Vine-growers since 1822, the Baugets launched their champagne brand in 1973. Today, they manage a vineyard of 14.5 ha (36 acres), and in 2001 they submitted a rare (and expensive) 94. Champagnes from this vintage are relatively rare, because conditions that year were not exactly favourable. This is a fine exception and an unqualified success. Fruity, toasty and floral in the bouquet, it develops powerfully on the palate and could quite easily be served with foie gras. The **rosé**, made up of 60% Chardonnay and 40% Pinot Meunier, including 14% red wine, also received a commendation. Its bouquet may be understated, but its fine palate is certainly well balanced. (NM)

♦ Champagne Bauget-Jouette,
1, rue Chanfleury, 51200 Epernay,
tel. 03.26.54.44.05, fax 03.26.55.37.99,
e-mail champagne.bauget@wanadoo.fr
Y by appt.

BAUSER Blanc de Noirs

n.c. — 44,000 — €11-15

The vineyard, which today covers 12 ha (30 acres), was established in 1963, launching its champagne brand in 1975. The estate is established at Les Riceys, a Pinot Noir stronghold, and the house makes two blancs de noirs from that grape variety. The first, produced from grapes harvested in 1997, is suitable as an aperitif. Flavours of red fruits and lemon add liveliness and freshness to the wine. The **95**, very close in character to the previous champagne, achieved the same rating. (RM)

♦ EARL René Bauser, rte de Tonnerre, 10340 Les Riceys, tel. 03.25.29.32.92, fax 03.25.29.96.29,
e-mail champagne-bauser@worldonline.fr
Y by appt.

ANDRE BEAUFORT Demi-sec★★

Gd Cru — 1.6 ha — 1,000 — €38-46

Jacques Beaufort is an organic producer, who shows the date of disgorgement of his wines on the labels. The demi-sec he submitted is likely to be seen as something of a milestone, since this is the first time in the history of the *Guide* that a champagne of this type has generated sufficient enthusiasm to be proposed for a *coup de coeur* – missing it by only one vote. Composed of a blend of 80% Pinot Noir and 20% Chardonnay, it exhibits all the characteristics of a complex and well-balanced *brut*. Its maker has succeeded in avoiding both heaviness and the common failing of excessive sweetening, which is usually an attempt to combat the acidity that is essential to all champagnes. This demi-sec is

Champagne

a brilliant exercise in style and a wine worthy of foie gras. (RM)

➻ Jacques Beaufort, 1, rue de Vaudemanges, 51150 Ambonnay, tel. 03.26.57.01.50, fax 03.26.52.83.50 ☑
Υ by appt.

HERBERT BEAUFORT

Blanc de Blancs Cuvée du Mélomane★

◯ Gd cru   3 ha   14,000   ∎ €15-23

The Beauforts were vine-growers in the 18th century, and Marcellin began the champagne operation at the beginning of the 20th century. Production, however, really took off in the 1930s, under the direction of Herbert, whose name has been passed down to the current owners, Henry and Hugues Beaufort. Together, they work approximately 17 ha (42 acres) of vines, of which 13 ha (32 acres) are Grands Crus. Despite coming from Bouzy, a village famous for its Pinot Noir, Cuvée du Mélomane comes entirely from Chardonnay grapes, harvested in 1997 and 1998. The Jury described this blanc de blancs as 'a serious wine'. Its principal assets are its aromatic range, with floral notes, dried fruits and hazelnuts all registering, and its fine balance. (RM)

➻ Champagne Herbert Beaufort, 32, rue de Tours-sur-Marne, 51150 Bouzy, tel. 03.26.57.01.34, fax 03.26.57.09.08 ☑
Υ by appt.

➻ Henry et Hugues Beaufort

BEAUMET

◯   n.c.   ∎ ♦ €15-23

Maison Beaumet, which was founded in 1879 and taken over by Jacques Trouillard in 1977, is an estate of 121 ha (298 acres). Its rosé, made exclusively from black varieties contains 30% Pinot Meunier, and is a fine, minerally wine, with good fruit (cherries) and balance. (NM)

➻ Champagne Beaumet, Ch. Malakoff, 3, rue Malakoff, 51207 Epernay Cedex, tel. 03.26.59.50.10, fax 03.26.54.78.52, e-mail chateau.malakoff@wanadoo.fr
➻ J. Trouillard

BEAUMONT DES CRAYERES

Grand Prestige★

◯   10 ha   33,000   ‖‖ €11-15

This co-operative, established in 1955, consists of more than 200 growers who oversee the production of an estate that is subdivided into many scattered vineyard plots. The Grand Prestige is a blend of the three champagne grapes (40% Chardonnay, 40% Pinot Noir and 20% Pinot Meunier). Flavours of green apples and citrus fruits indicate a lively palate that is fresh, lemony and well balanced. (CM)

➻ Champagne Beaumont des Crayères, BP 1030, 51318 Epernay Cedex, tel. 03.26.55.29.40, fax 03.26.54.26.30, e-mail champagne-beaumont@wanadoo.fr
☑ **Υ** ev. day 10am–12 noon; 2–6pm; cl. Sat. Sun. from Christmas to Easter.

FRANCOISE BEDEL Blanc de noirs

◯   3.4 ha   20, 275   ‖‖ ⚫ €11-15

This wine-grower took over the family estate in 1976. The estate is situated on both banks of the river Marne in the region of Château-Thierry. Since 1998, production has been biodynamic. Pinot Meunier, the estate's dominant grape variety, forms the base of this particular blanc de noirs, a blend produced largely from the 1996 harvest, topped up with 1995 reserve wines. It was commended for its expressive and complex bouquet, with aromas of undergrowth and dried fruits, and for its rich and well-developed palate. (RM)

➻ Champagne Françoise Bédel, 71, Grande-Rue, 02310 Crouttes-sur-Marne, tel. 03.23.82.15.80, fax 03.23.82.11.49, e-mail chFbedel@quid-info.fr ☑ **Υ** by appt.

L. BENARD-PITOIS

◯ 1er cru   n.c.   ∎ ‖‖ €15-23

In 1991 Raoul Bénard took over the estate, which had been founded in 1938 by his grandfather. It covers 10 ha (25 acres), made up of two Grands Crus and four Premiers Crus. Its rosé 1ᵉʳ Cru is made up of 56% Pinot Noir and 34% Chardonnay, harvested in 1996, with 10% of red wine in the blend. The bouquet exhibits aromas of strawberries and redcurrants with smoky undertones, while the palate is supple and fresh. It could be served as an aperitif or to accompany an entrée. (RM)

➻ Champagne L. Bénard-Pitois, 23, rue Duval, 51160 Mareuil-sur-Ay, tel. 03.26.52.60.28, fax 03.26.52.60.12 ☑

BERECHE ET FILS Reflet d'Antan

◯ 1er cru   0.3 ha   1,000   ∎ €15-23

This family-run estate possesses 8 ha (20 acres) of vines and is situated in the Montagne de Reims. The champagnes are made in oak barrels and matured under traditional cork stoppers. This particular cuvée divided the Jury, with the tasters agreeing on one point only: its originality. Its bouquet offers aromas of pine bark and crystallised fruits, followed by intense, vigorous fruit flavours on the palate. Reactions to it ranged from perplexity on the part of some tasters to enthusiasm from others. (RM)

➻ Champagne Bérèche et Fils, Le Craon-de-Ludes, BP 18, 51500 Ludes, tel. 03.26.61.13.28, fax 03.26.61.14.14 ☑
Υ by appt.

CH. BERTHELOT Carte noire★

◯ Gd cru   2.05 ha   n.c.   ∎ €11-15

Managed by Christian Berthelot since 1982, this small estate is located at Avize, a village classified as Grand Cru. Both of these Côte des Blancs champagnes are produced from Chardonnay alone. The first, made exclusively from grapes harvested in 1998, combines richness, finesse and elegance, while the other wine, the **Grand Cru Blanc de Blancs**, which was produced from the 1996 and 1997 harvests, is supple and lingering, albeit a little weighed down by its high *dosage*. (RM)

Christian Berthelot, 32, rue Ernest-Valle, 51190 Avize, tel. 03.26.57.58.99, fax 03.26.51.87.26 V Y by appt.

PAUL BERTHELOT Blason d'or

n.c. €11-15

This *négociant* house, founded in 1884, is located at Dizy, near Epernay and it has 22 ha (54 acres) under vine. The Blason d'or, made from half black grapes and half white, has a bouquet of crystallised fruits and fresh butter, with hints of toastiness. Its fresh, vigorous palate has noticeable overtones of hazelnut. The **Cuvée Prestige 2000**, sourced from the 1995 harvest, is a blend of 70% Chardonnay with 30% Pinot Noir and conjures up aromas of fresh citrus fruits. It achieved the same rating. (NM)

SARL Paul Berthelot, 889, av. du Gal-Leclerc, 51530 Dizy, tel. 03.26.55.23.83, fax 03.26.54.36.31 V Y by appt.

BILLECART-SALMON Blanc de Blancs 1995★

n.c. 15,000 €46-76

This enterprise, founded in 1818 at Mareuil-sur-Ay, has been making its presence felt since the 19th century, both in the USA and among the Russian aristocracy. The estate, which remains a family concern, is always orientated towards the top of the range. This 95 champagne has been cold-settled and fermented at a temperature of 13°C (55°F), and it has managed to retain not only the subtlety of the Chardonnay grape, but also its richness, complexity and elegance. It is a great blanc de blancs, well balanced and long. The **Grande Cuvée 89**, a fine wine that has matured rapidly, also received a star. It is a blend of 60% Pinot Noir and 40% Chardonnay and has a golden-yellow colour, perfect opening, toastiness, elegance and complexity. This is a champagne at its peak and would work well as an accompaniment for zander served en croûte. Finally, a commendation goes to the **Cuvée Nicolas François Billecart 95**, which contains a blend of grape identical to the previous wine, and full of power, finesse and elegance. (NM)

Champagne Billecart-Salmon, 40, rue Carnot, 51160 Mareuil-sur-Ay, tel. 03.26.52.60.22, fax 03.26.52.64.88, e-mail billecart@champagne-billecart.fr V Y by appt.

BINET 1992★★

n.c. n.c. €23-30

Founded in 1849 by Léon Binet, this establishment changed hands several times after the Second World War, before merging with the Prin Group in the year 2000. The 92 vintage (three-quarters black grapes to one-quarter white) charmed the tasters with its simultaneous aromas of crystallised fruits, pepper and honey and the floral finesse of its flavours. The Jury also commended the **Brut Elite**, which is a blend of 60% Pinots with 40%

Chardonnay. A light, very fresh champagne. (NM)

Champagne Binet, 31, rue de Reims, 51500 Rilly-la-Montagne, tel. 03.26.88.05.00, fax 03.26.88.05.05, e-mail info@champagne-binet.com V Y by appt.

CH. DE BLIGNY Chardonnay

5.1 ha 51,000 €11-15

It is unusual to see such a reference on a Chardonnay label, but here we have an example of one of the champagne 'châteaux'. Situated in the Aube region, it has connections with the house of G.-H. Martel & Co. After an absence, it reappears in the *Guide* with a blanc de blancs, produced from the harvests of 1995 and 1996. The wine excels itself with its sheer fullness and lusciousness, characteristics that are reinforced by skilful *dosage*. The **95 Blanc de Blancs** also received a commendation for its roundness and generosity. (RM)

Ch. de Bligny, 10200 Bligny, tel. 03.25.27.40.11, fax 03.25.27.04.52 V
ev. day except Sat. Sun. 9am–12 noon; 2–5.30pm
Rapeneau

H. BLIN ET CIE 1995★

5 ha 40,000 €15-23

This group of producers was founded by Henri Blin in 1947. Nowadays, there are approximately 100 members, who produce wine from the estate's 120 ha (296 acres). This 95 is made from both white and black grape varieties, in equal proportions (of which 30% is Pinot Meunier.) It is a biscuity-flavoured, soft and pleasant wine. The **Tradition**, short of being a blanc de noirs, has Pinot Meunier very much in evidence (77% of the blend). It has a spicy bouquet, ample roundness and the capacity to age well. (CM)

SC Champagne H. Blin et Cie, 5, rue de Verdun, 51700 Vincelles, tel. 03.26.58.20.04, fax 03.26.58.29.67, e-mail contact@champagne-blin.com V Y by appt.

R. BLIN ET FILS Sélection★★

n.c. n.c. €11-15

Gilles and Madeleine Blin cultivate 11 ha (27 acres) of vines in the Saint-Thierry Massif, to the north-west of Reims, a location immersed in champagne history. An abbey located in the area had a reputation for producing highly acclaimed wines. Made from 90% Pinot Noir and 10% Chardonnay, this

Champagne

particular champagne won the hearts of the Jury. Its intense golden colour glitters with rosy highlights. Powerful aromas are followed by ample, full-bodied and well-balanced fruity flavours. A champagne to be served at mealtimes, it could accompany the heaviest of dishes. Two other *cuvées* received a star. The **Grande Tradition**, of which the composition is in inverse proportions to the previous champagne (90% Chardonnay to 10% Pinot Noir) has a complex, charred bouquet and lingers well on the palate, with flavours of crystallised fruits and raspberries. **Carte Blanche**, a blanc de noirs with a strong emphasis on Pinot Meunier (80%), is well-rounded, structured and complete. (RM)

➤ R. Blin et Fils, 11, rue du Point-du-Jour, 51140 Trigny, tel. 03.26.03.19.63, fax 03.26.03.10.97, e-mail champagne-blin-et-fils.fr ☒ ☐ by appt.

TH. BLONDEL Blanc de Blancs 1996★

○ 1er cru   4 ha   n.c.   ☐ ♦ €11-15

Established in 1904 by great-grandfather Blondel, a lawyer from Rilly-la-Montagne, this estate has been converted into a family-run, commercial enterprise, and since 1985 has been making its own proprietary champagne. It cultivates 9.5 ha (23 acres) of vines in the Montagne de Reims. With three *cuvées*, each earning a star, this establishment has certainly earned its stripes! This 96 blanc de blancs offers fresh, peachy fruitiness, and is structured and long. The **Blanc de Blancs 1er Cru Vieux Millésime 95** starts softly with finesse and elegance. As for the **Carte d'or**, produced from a blend of 70% Pinot Noir and 30% Chardonnay, from the harvests of 1996 and 1997, it creates a lively first impression and is a well-structured wine. (NM)

➤ Th. Blondel, Dom. des Monts-Fournois, BP 12, 51500 Ludes, tel. 03.26.03.43.92, fax 03.26.03.44.10 ☒ ☐ by appt.

BOIZEL Réserve

○   n.c.   400,000 ☐ ♦ €15-23

This vineyard was founded in 1834 by Auguste Boizel. Although allied to the BCI Group, which became BCC in 1994, this establishment has remained firmly in the hands of its founders' descendant, Evelyne Roques-Boizel. In 2001, three of the estate's champagnes impressed the Jury. The Brut **Réserve** *cuvée* contains more black grapes than white (55% Pinot Noir and 15% Meunier). Its bouquet mingles floral notes with aromas of hazelnuts, while the palate is firm but short. The **rosé**, 10% short of being a blanc de noirs (50% Pinot Noir, of which 8% is vinified as red, and 40% Meunier), is pale rose-coloured in appearance and light on the palate. The **blanc de blancs** (always good value from Boizel) is a fine, minerally young wine. (NM)

Champagne Boizel,
46, av. de Champagne, 51200 Epernay,
tel. 03.26.55.21.51, fax 03.26.54.31.83,
e-mail evboizel@boisel.fr
➤ Groupe Boizel-Chanoine

BOLLINGER Grande Année 1992★★

○   n.c.   n.c.   ☐ ♦ €46-76

This famous establishment dates back to 1829 and remains family-run, because Ghislain de Montgolfier, a director since 1994, is descended from its original founders. With the back-up of a vast vineyard of approximately 150 ha (370 acres), the estate produces nearly twice the company's required output. Bollinger makes champagnes of great character. Grande Année is the vintage wine. As with all other wines produced at Bollinger, Pinot Noir is the dominant grape variety, complemented by Chardonnay: together, they represent the two constituents of the blend. The base wines are aged in oak. This 92 offers a complex, smooth and full-flavoured assembly, where hints of undergrowth mingle with notes of vanilla and butter. The palate is fresh and extremely well-balanced. A very vivid and powerful champagne, it made the tasters' thoughts turn to chicken with *girolles*. The *coup de coeur* awards itself. (NM)

➤ Bollinger, 16, rue Jules-Lobet, 51160 Ay, tel. 03.26.53.33.66, fax 03.26.54.85.59

BOLLINGER R.D. Extra brut 1988★★

○   n.c.   n.c.   ☐ ♦ €46-76

This champagne is produced from 72% Pinot Noir and 28% Chardonnay, fermented and matured in oak barrels, aged leisurely on the lees, and recently disgorged in order to preserve its freshness. Awarded a *coup de coeur*, last year, it does not disappoint. With its lightly oaky taste from the barrel maturation, this powerful, full-bodied and complete champagne is at its peak. The **Special Cuvée** also exhibits characteristics of strength and maturity, and was awarded a star. It is made from the three champagne grapes – 60% Pinot Noir, 15% Pinot Meunier and 25% Chardonnay. (NM)

➤ Bollinger, 16, rue Jules-Lobet, 51160 Ay, tel. 03.26.53.33.66, fax 03.26.54.85.59

BONNAIRE Blanc de Blancs★★

○ Gd cru   9 ha   n.c.   ☐ ♦ €11-15

This vineyard is located at Cramant, a village famous for its Chardonnay. Established in 1932 by Fernand Bouquemont, it has remained in the hands of its descendants, who today cultivate 13.5 ha (33 acres) in the Côte des Blancs and 8.5 ha (21 acres) in the Marne Valley. Buttery and toasty with undertones of caramel, powerful and fruity on the palate, this blanc de blancs is highly rated as a classic of its style. The **Blanc de Blancs 96 Grand Cru Cuvée Prestige** was commended. It is produced from Cramant Chardonnay, which lends it structure, power and richness. (RM)

- Jean-Louis Bonnaire, 120, rue d'Epernay, 51530 Cramant, tel. 03.26.57.07.31, fax 03.26.57.59.17. ev. day 9am-12 noon, 2pm-5pm; Sat. Sun. by appt.; f. Aug.

BONNET-PONSON★

| | n.c. | n.c. | ■ ▮▮ ▴ | €11-15 |

This family of wine-producers, established since 1835 at Chamery in the Montagne de Reims, currently manages around 10 ha (25 acres) of vines. The three champagne grapes (60% Pinot Noir, 10% Pinot Meunier and 30% Chardonnay), drawn from the vintages between 1996 and 1999, and topped up with a small quantity of red wine come together to make up this rosé. It has a slight coppery-coloured appearance, and is light but well-balanced on the palate. The **Cuvée Jules Bonnet 96** is a blanc de noirs derived entirely from the Pinot Noir grape, and vinified in oak barrels (the juice stirred with wooden batons). It also receives a star for its balance, its rounded opening impression and its finesse. (RM)

- Thierry Bonnet, 20, rue du Sourd, 51500 Chamery, tel. 03.26.97.65.40, fax 03.26.97.67.11, e-mail champagne.bonnet.ponson@wanadoo.fr by appt.

FRANCK BONVILLE
Blanc de Blancs Sélection

| Gd cru | 15 ha | 100,000 | ■ ▴ | €11-15 |

Frank Bonville, a wine-grower from Avize in the Côte des Blancs, produced his first champagnes in 1945. The vineyard is actually managed by Gilles Bonville, who tends 15 ha (37 acres) of vines. The Blanc de Blancs Sélection, a non-vintage wine, brings together the harvests of 1996, 1997 and 1998. Full of youth, well rounded, fruity and buttery, it would go well with white fish. The **Blanc de Blancs 93 Grand Cru**, which also won a commendation, exhibits flavours of honey and dried fruits, and is well balanced and consistently fresh. (RM)

- Champagne Franck Bonville, 9, rue Pasteur, 51190 Avize, tel. 03.26.57.52.30, fax 03.26.57.59.90, e-mail franck-bonville@wanadoo.fr by appt.

BOUCHE PÈRE ET FILS
Cuvée Réservée

| | n.c. | 300,000 | ■ ▴ | €15-23 |

This family-run vineyard, established in 1945, comprises 35 ha (86 acres) spread over a number of crus. The Reserve Cuvée, made from half white grapes and half black (including 20% Pinot Meunier), contains 20% reserve wines. Its flavours of spicy, cooked fruits linger on a full-bodied palate. (NM)

- Champagne Bouché Père et Fils, 10, rue Charles-de-Gaulle, 51530 Pierry, tel. 03.26.54.12.44, fax 03.26.55.07.02. by appt.

RAYMOND BOULARD Réserve★

| | n.c. | 35,000 | ■ ▮▮ ▴ | €15-23 |

Wine-producers since 1792, the Boulards established their champagne house in 1952. Nowadays, they cultivate around 10 ha (25 acres) of vines, located on the slopes of the Montagne de Reims and in the Marne Valley. Some of their wines are matured in oak. All the champagnes nominated obtained a star. The Reserve Cuvée, produced from all three champagne grapes (45% Pinot Meunier, 35% Pinot Noir and 20% Chardonnay), is drawn from four vintages: 1998, 1997, 1996 and 1995. This champagne is full, fresh and well balanced, with overtones of acacia, mirabelle plums and white fruits. The **96**, made from half-and-half black and white grapes, mingles lemony flavours with hints of mineral and caramel. It is exceedingly lively, in common with the majority of champagnes from this vintage. The **rosé**, a rosé de noirs, is a blend of the two Pinots, harvested in 1997 and vinified on the skins of the grapes. This gives an impression of richness, with notes of strawberry preserve. Flavourful, with good vinosity, it is nonetheless an elegant wine. (NM)

- Champagne Raymond Boulard, 1, rue du Tambour, 51480 La Neuville-aux-Larris, tel. 03.26.58.12.08, fax 03.26.61.54.92, e-mail info@champagne-boulard.fr by appt.

JEAN-PAUL BOULONNAIS
Tradition★

| 1er Cru | 5 ha | 15,000 | ■ | €11-15 |

The Boulonnais family have been wine-producers for five generations, and have built up a vineyard of 5 ha (12 acres). They are based at Vertus, in the south of the Côte des Blancs. Their Tradition is a very pale wine (80% Chardonnay to 20% Pinot Noir). It has a floral and spicy bouquet, and a supple first impression that reveals its freshness. Although the **rosé** (100% Pinot Noir) has no great length, it does have a powerful bouquet and well-rounded palate. (NM)

- Jean-Paul Boulonnais, 14, rue de l'Abbaye, 51130 Vertus, tel. 03.26.52.22.23.41, fax 03.26.52.27.55 by appt.

R. BOURDELOIS 1995★

| | n.c. | 12,000 | ■ | €15-23 |

This grower-wine-maker is based at the village of Dizy, opposite Epernay in the Marne Valley. Its 95 is a blend of equal parts white grapes and black (of which 15% are Pinot Meunier). The bouquet mingles aromas of citrus fruits with hints of toasted bread. After a clean start, the palate displays full-flavoured roundness with notes of brioche. (RM)

- Raymond Bourdelois, 737, av. du Gal-Leclerc, 51530 Dizy, tel. 03.26.55.29.81, fax 03.26.55.23.34, by appt.

Champagne

BOURGEOIS-BOULONNAIS

Blanc de blancs

○ 1er cru   5 ha   n.c.   ■ €11-15

Vertus, a Premier Cru village in the south of the Côte des Blancs, is where Alain Bourgeois works his 5.5-ha (14-acre) vineyard. He submitted a classic blanc de blancs, with a discreet bouquet and honeyed, vinous, well-structured palate. (RM)

➤ Champagne Bourgeois-Boulonnais,
8, rue de l'Abbaye, 51130 Vertus,
tel. 03.26.52.26.73, fax 03.26.52.06.55 ☑
Y by appt.

BOUTILLEZ-GUER Tradition★★

○   2 ha   12,000   ■ €11-15

The village of Villers-Marmery, situated in the Montagne de Reims, is these days renowned for its Chardonnays. Here, Boutillez's predecessors have cultivated the vine for almost five centuries. The Tradition cuvée is noticeably pale-coloured (80% Chardonnay to 20% Pinot Noir), and fell just short of a coup de coeur. It won over the Jury with its floral and honeyed aromas and its remarkably well-balanced, lingering palate. 'A perfect wine', wrote one taster. (RM)

➤ Champagne Boutillez-Guer,
38, rue Pasteur, 51380 Villers-Marmery,
tel. 03.26.97.91.38, fax 03.26.97.94.95 ☑
Y by appt.
➤ Marc Boutillez

G. BOUTILLEZ-VIGNON

Blanc de blancs★

○ 1er cru   1 ha   2,500   ■ €11-15

This is a different branch of the Boutillez family, also from Villers-Marmery, established here since 1524. They cultivate a vineyard of 5 ha (12 acres), and launched their champagne in 1976. Their blanc de blancs non-vintage is produced from the harvests of 1997 and 1998. It is lively, floral and has good length, winning approval for its elegance. (RM)

➤ G. Boutillez-Vignon,
26, rue Pasteur, 51380 Villers-Marmery,
tel. 03.26.97.95.87, fax 03.26.97.97.23 ☑
Y ev. day 8am–12 noon; 2pm–6pm; Sat.
Sun. by appt.; f. 15 Aug.–5 Sept.

BRATEAU-MOREAUX★

○   4.75 ha   25,742   ■ €3-11

It took four generations of wine-producers before this label saw the light of day in 1990. The vineyard extends over 5.5 ha (14 acres) at Leuvrigny, a village in the Marne Valley that produces, so it has been suggested, the very best Pinot Meunier. It is this grape variety, from the 1998 vintage, that makes up 100% of this blanc de noirs. It certainly made a favourable impression upon the Jury. This is a floral, well-rounded, soft and very fruity champagne. (RM)

➤ Dominique Brateau, 12, rue Douchy,
51700 Leuvrigny, tel. 03.26.58.00.99,
fax 03.26.52.83.61 ☑ Y by appt.

BRETON FILS Prestige★

○   17 ha   10,000   ♦ €15-23

In the early 1950s, Ange Breton launched the vineyard's first cuvée of 500 bottles. During the winter of that year, he dug out a cellar from the chalk soil beneath his property. Today, the estate accounts for 17 ha (42 acres) located, not only in the Sézannais, to the south of Congy, but also in the Marne Valley. The estate is managed by the sons of the family: with Yann in charge of the vines and Johann overseeing the cellar. Three of their champagnes have been nominated. Although all three reveal generous dosage, they are nevertheless well balanced. The Jury preferred their Prestige Cuvée (60% Chardonnay, with citrus fruit flavours. (RM)

➤ SCEV Breton Fils,
12, rue Courte-Pilate, 51270 Congy,
tel. 03.26.59.31.03, fax 03.26.59.30.60 ☑
Y ev. day 8am–12 noon; 1.30pm–6pm
➤ Ange Breton

BRICE Verzenay★

○ Gd Cru   n.c.   ♦ €15-23

Although this commercial enterprise, managed by Jean-Paul Brice, was only set up as recently as 1994, the Brices have actually been established at Bouzy since the 17th century. They specialise in producing cru champagnes. This one, from Verzenay, is a blend of 90% Pinot Noir and 10% Chardonnay, made up of the 1998 harvest, backed up by some reserve wine. The bouquet gives off aromas of flowers and bread-dough. A lively start on the palate is followed by lingering toasty flavours. (NM)

➤ Jean-Paul Brice,
3, rue Yvonnet, 51150 Bouzy,
tel. 03.26.52.06.60, fax 03.26.57.05.07,
e-mail champagnebrice@wanadoo.fr ☑
Y by appt.

LAURENT BOUY★

○ Gd cru   1.2 ha   9,600   ■ €11-15

Laurent Bouy, who comes from a long line of wine-makers, has been working a 4.5-ha (11-acre) vineyard at the Grand Cru village of Verzy in the Montagne de Reims since 1977. He submitted a cuvée made of half black and half white grapes, a blend of wines from the years 1993 to 1996. Its aromas are powerful and mature, while its assertive palate has balance and length. A champagne of great character. (RM)

➤ Laurent Bouy,
7, rue de l'Ancienne-Eglise, 51380 Verzy,
tel. 03.26.97.93.23 ☑ Y by appt.

BRICOUT Cuvée Arthur Bricout
○Gd Cru　n.c.　n.c.　■ £23-30 ▼

Founded in 1820, the house of Koch became Bricout towards the end of the 19th century. It finally assumed the name Bricout in 1990, and has formed part of the Delbeck Group since 1998. Cuvée Arthur Bricout comprises 70% Chardonnay and 30% Pinot Noir. Buttery layers and scents of crystallised fruits announce a full-bodied and complex palate. A champagne to accompany sauced fish dishes. (NM)

♠ SA Champagne Bricout et Koch, 59, rte de Cramant, 51190 Avize, tel. 03.26.53.30.00, fax 03.26.57.59.26 ▼
▼ by appt.

BROCHET-HERVIEUX★
○1er Cru　n.c.　n.c.　£11-15

Based in Ecueil, a village near Reims, this estate encompasses 16 ha (40 acres) of vines. It has been producing champagne commercially since the end of the Second World War. This estate submitted a highly rated 1er Cru rosé. The wine in question is almost a blanc de noirs (with just 5% Chardonnay). Light salmon in colour, it mingles aromas of crystallised fruits with notes of toasted bread – flavours that are extended to the well-balanced and satisfying palate. The 95 1er Cru is a blend of 85% black grapes and 15% Chardonnay. It has good vinosity, intensity and overtones of crystallised fruits, but is beginning to show its age. It received a commendation. (RM)

♠ Brochet-Hervieux, 12, rue de Villers-aux-Nouds, 51500 Ecueil, tel. 03.26.49.77.44, fax 03.26.49.77.17 ▼
▼ by appt.

ANDRE BROCHOT Cuvée★
○　1 ha　n.c.　£11-15

This estate, situated to the south of Epernay, has been producing champagne since 1949. It nominated a blanc de noirs produced from Pinot Meunier. Its appearance catches the eye with its delightful rosy highlights. The bouquet offers a profusion of fruity aromas, while the palate is lively, full and long. (RM)

♠ Francis Brochot, 21, rue de Champagne, 51530 Vinay, tel. 03.26.59.91.39, fax 03.26.59.91.39 ▼ by appt.

BRUGNON★
○　5 ha　20,000　£11-15

Alain Brugnon represents the third generation to work this estate. It was his grandfather, Maurice, who first started champagne production. The property cultivates vineyards in the area of Ecueil (to the south-west of Reims) and in Rilly-la-Montagne in the Marne Valley. Its Brut Non-Vintage is dominated by black grapes (50% Pinot Noir and 30% Meunier) harvested in 1997, 1998 and 1999. It is an intensely rich champagne, with both bouquet and palate exhibiting appley overtones. The same rating applies to the 96, a blend of two-thirds white grapes to one-third black. A fine, floral wine, it is a true

representative of its vintage, with its lemony emphasis and fresh, lively characteristics. This youthful champagne would be suitable as an aperitif. The Sélection, an identical blend to the previous wine and very similar in style, was also commended by the Jury. (RM)

♠ EARL Champagne Brugnon, 1, rue Brûlée, 51500 Ecueil, tel. 03.26.49.25.95, fax 03.26.49.76.56, e-mail brugnon@cder.fr ▼ ▼ by appt.

EDOUARD BRUN ET CIE 1996★★
○　n.c.　27,000　■ £15-23

This establishment was founded by Edouard Brun in 1898, associated with Edmond Lefèvre in 1939, and is today run by the latter's daughter. Alcoholic fermentation takes place in barrel and the malolactic in tank. This mineral, iodine-scented, lemony wine is noticeably fresh and lively, with flavours of citrus fruits dominating the palate. Another star was awarded to the Réserve 1er Cru. It comprises twice the quantity of black grapes as white, and is blended from the 1996, 1997 and 1998 vintages. It is at once a rounded and vigorous wine. (NM)

♠ Edouard Brun et Cie, 14, rue Marcel-Mailly, BP 11, 51160 Ay, tel. 03.26.55.20.11, fax 03.26.51.94.29 ▼
▼ ev. day 8.30am–12 noon; 2pm–6pm; Sat., Sun. by appt.

CHRISTIAN BUSIN Réserve
○Gd Cru　0.5 ha　5,000　£11-15

Christian Busin cultivates 6 ha (15 acres) of vines in the adjacent villages of Verzenay and Verzy, two Grands Crus on the Montagne de Reims. His champagne, which combines 80% Pinot Noir with 20% Chardonnay, has a discreet floral bouquet and a soft, well-rounded palate, with flavours of small, fleshy fruits. (RM)

♠ Christian Busin, 4, rue d'Uzès, 51360 Verzenay, tel. 03.26.49.40.94, fax 03.26.49.44.19, e-mail lucbusin@aol.com ▼ by appt.

JACQUES BUSIN Réserve 1995★★
○Gd Cru　2 ha　10,000　■ £11-15

Based in the region of the Montagne de Reims, Jacques Busin enjoys the rare privilege of owning vines in four Grands Crus (Verzy, Verzenay, Ambonnay and Sillery), an advantage that enables him to produce some highly original champagne blends. This half-black, half-white cuvée certainly succeeded in swaying the Jury. A fine, complex champagne, it combines hints of dried fruits, toast and brioche with light musky flavours. Structured, rich, balanced and elegant, it would go well with fish and white meats. Some bottles of the **Cuvée 2000 Grand Cru** remain. This wine is a blend of 75% Pinot Noir and 25% Chardonnay, and in 2001 had clearly improved, as it then gained two stars. Complex and long, with a fine opening impression, this champagne has reached its peak. Finally, the estate was commended for its **Carte d'or Grand Cru**, a blend of 60% Pinot Noir and 40% Chardonnay, harvested in 1997 and 1998. Its bouquet evokes dried fruits, and its apricot flavour is emphasised by the vigorous character of the wine. (RM)

Jacques Busin, 17, rue Thiers, 51360 Verzenay, tel. 03.26.49.40.36, fax 03.26.49.81.11, e-mail jacques-busin@wanadoo.fr ▼ ▼ by appt.

GUY CADEL
6 ha 5,000 €11-15

Already established in viticulture in the 19th century, the Cadel family became grower-producers in 1960. Today, they cultivate 10 ha (25 acres) of vines. Their rosé is a blend of Pinot Meunier (60%) and Chardonnay from the 1997 and 1998 harvests. This easy-drinking, attractive champagne has good balance, underlined by flawless *dosage*. (RM)

Champagne Guy Cadel, 13, rue Jean-Jaurès, 51530 Mardeuil, tel. 03.26.55.24.59, fax 03.26.55.25.83, e-mail guycadel@terre-net.fr ▼ ▼ by appt.
M.Thiébault

CANARD-DUCHENE
Charles VII Grande Cuvée★★★
n.c. n.c. €23-30

Founded in 1868, this estate came about as a result of the marriage of Victor Canard (carpenter and cooper) to Léonie Duchêne, daughter of a wine-grower. The vineyard was taken over by Veuve Clicquot in 1978 and, eight years on, joined the LVMH group. Composed of 44% Pinot Noir, 42% Chardonnay and 14% Pinot Meunier, the Charles VII Grande Cuvée represents the top of Canard-Duchêne's range. The Jury was unanimous. The tasters emphasised its finesse, freshness, balance and length, as well as the complexity of its full-flavoured palate, which mingles toasty, smoky notes with hints of honey and brioche. Furthermore, this excellent Grande Cuvée is reasonably priced. The **Cuvée Charles VII Blanc de Noirs** is worthy of commendation, as is the **Brut Non-Vintage**, which combines 80% of the two Pinots with 20% Chardonnay. (NM)

Canard-Duchêne, 1, rue Edmond-Canard, 51500 Ludes, tel. 03.26.61.11.60, fax 03.26.49.60.17, e-mail info@canard-duchene.fr ▼
ev. day except Sun. Mon. 11am-1pm; 2.30pm-5pm f. 15 Oct.-1 Apr.

JEAN-YVES DE CARLINI 1997★
Gd cru 2 ha 3,500 €15-23

The estate was founded by R. de Carlini in 1955, taking on the name of Jean-Yves de Carlini in 1984. It comprises 6.7 ha (17 acres) of Grands Crus in the Montagne de Reims. Its 97 vintage, an unusual year, is made up of equal parts Chardonnay and Pinot Noir. Both bouquet and palate exhibit characteristics of honeyed, rich, crystallised fruits. The **Reserve** from this producer was also commended. It too is made half from black grapes and half from white but, unlike the previous wine, it is derived from several years' harvests (1999, plus 1998, 1997 and 1996). This is a champagne for drinking in the afternoon. (RM)

Jean-Yves de Carlini, 13, rue de Mailly, 51360 Verzenay, tel. 03.26.49.43.91, fax 03.26.49.46.46 ▼ ▼ by appt.

CASTELLANE Croix rouge 1991
12 ha 100,000 €15-23

Founded in 1895 in Epernay, this house has made its mark on the local landscape, thanks to the belfry that towers above its head office. (Built in 1904, it was designed by Auguste Marius Toudoire, architect of the Gare de Lyon in Paris.) The estate's founder, Vicomte Florens de Castellane, renowned for his entertaining during the Belle Epoque era, chose as his trademark the St Andrew's Cross, which still adorns the labels to this day. The 91 vintage, dominated by Chardonnay (80%), offers no great length, but makes up for it with its attractive, toasty, floral and lemony flavours. **Commodore 90** equally impressed the Jury and deserves a mention for its flavourful palate, which mingles toasted notes with very ripe fruits: apples, peaches and pears. (NM)

Champagne de Castellane, 57, rue de Verdun, BP 136, 51204 Epernay Cedex, tel. 03.26.51.19.19, fax 03.26.54.24.81, e-mail info@castellane.com ▼
ev. day 10am–12 noon; 2pm–6pm; cl. 23 Dec.–3 March

CATTIER 1995★
1er Cru 18 ha 40,000 €15-23

The Cattiers have owned vineyards for nearly two and a half centuries, and have been producing champagne since 1920. Their estate remains independent to this day, comprising 18 ha (44 acres) of Premiers Crus in the Marne Valley. The three champagne grapes (40% Pinot Noir, 30% Pinot Noir and 30% Chardonnay) make up this *cuvée*, which particularly impressed the Jury with its rich, citrus-fruit flavours and the finesse of its finish. Also commended were the **Brut 1er Cru**, predominantly black grapes (with 20%

Chardonnay), and the famous **Clos du Moulin 1er Cru**, made up of half black grapes and half white; the former for its sensitive *dosage*, the latter for its delightful vivacity. (NM)
- Cattier, 6–11, rue Dom-Pérignon, 51500 Chigny-les-Roses, tel. 03.26.03.42.11, fax 03.26.03.43.13, e-mail jeancatt@cattier.com ☑ Y ev. day except Sat. Sun. 9am–11am; 2pm–5pm; groups by appt.

CHANOINE

Tsarine 1995★ n.c. n.c. €15-23

The Chanoine brothers' company was founded in 1730, a year after that doyenne of champagne houses – Ruinart – was established. It has re-emerged today as an ultra-modern complex of cellars in Reims. During the 19th century, Russia provided Chanoine's main market, from whence this *cuvée* acquired its name. The wine certainly does justice to the great 95 vintage. Its lightly honeyed bouquet is discreet, while the palate has impact, clearly demonstrating its complexity and elegance in a successful

CLAUDE CAZALS

Carte Blanche 3 ha 20,000 €11-15

Ernest Cazals founded his estate in 1897. A century later, Claude Cazals works a vineyard of 9 ha (22 acres) in the Côte des Blancs. Carte Blanche is simply a blanc de blancs from the harvests of 1997, reinforced by wines from 1995 and 1996. It combines liveliness, freshness and suppleness. His **Vive Grand Cru Extra Brut** is also a non-dosed blanc de blancs – a difficult feat to pull off. This fine, lingering champagne deserved its commendation by the Jury. (RC)
- Champagne Claude Cazals, 28, rue du Grand-Mont, 51190 Le Mesnil-sur-Oger, tel. 03.26.57.52.26, fax 03.26.57.78.43 ☑
Y by appt.

CHARLES DE CAZANOVE

Demi-Sec Tradition Père et Fils★ n.c. n.c. €11-15

This unimposing yet important family-run enterprise was founded in 1811 at Avize, and has remained independent to the present day, although it is now located at Epernay. It has been particularly successful with its demi-sec, a category of champagne in which good results are notoriously difficult to achieve. Made from 50% Pinot Noir, 20% Meunier and 30% Chardonnay, the wine uses only the first (and best) free-run juice of the grapes. It possesses a fine, discreet bouquet of floral broom, and an attractive and well-balanced palate – the sort of champagne that would make an ideal accompaniment for desserts. Those looking for an aperitif could plump for the **Tradition Père et Fils Rosé**, made up of 95% Chardonnay and 5% Pinot Noir red wine. It combines freshness and fullness, and offers attractive flavours of red fruits and wild berries. (NM)
- Charles de Cazanove, 1, rue des Cotelles, 51200 Epernay, tel. 03.26.59.57.40, fax 03.26.54.16.38
- Lombard

CHARDONNET ET FILS

Blanc de Blancs★★ 1 ha 4,000 €11-15

The Chardonnets, who established their champagne in 1970, work 4 ha (10 acres) of vines in the Côte des Blancs and the Marne Valley. They submitted a classic blanc de blancs, with flavours of almonds and toasted bread. Rich and rounded, this champagne has already reached its peak. Another *cuvée*, **Tradition** (70% Chardonnay to 30% Pinot Noir, from the years 1995 to 1997), deserves commendation for its lemony vitality and its length. (RM)
- Michel et Lionel Chardonnet, 7, rue de l'Abattoir, 51190 Avize, tel. 03.26.57.91.73, fax 03.26.57.84.46 ☑ Y by appt.

ROLAND CHARDIN

Cuvée Prestige 1996 1 ha 5,000 €11-15

The Avirey-Lingey vineyard in the Aube region was established in 1980, and today encompasses 6.5 ha (16 acres) of vines. Its Prestige Brut is made up of 85% Chardonnay and 15% Pinot Noir. It exhibits flavours of white fruits, green apples and lemon. The palate is supple, but fleeting. (RM)
- Roland Chardin, 25, rue de l'Eglise, 10340 Avirey-Lingey, tel. 03.25.29.33.90, fax 03.25.29.14.01 ☑ Y by appt.

combination of crystallised fruits and freshness – no mean feat! Another champagne to make a strong impression on the Jury was the **Grande Réserve**, which received a commendation. (NM)
- Champagne Chanoine Frères, allée du Vignoble, 51100 Reims, tel. 03.26.36.61.60, fax 03.26.36.66.62, e-mail chanoine-freres@wanadoo.fr

JACQUES CHAPUT 1999

9 ha 90,000 €8-11

This vineyard of 12 ha (30 acres) is situated in Arrentières, in the Aube region. The black label indicates a champagne that is almost a blanc de noirs (with only 10% Chardonnay). The wine exhibits floral notes and flavours of crystallised fruits. Its yellow-labelled cousin, a **95 Blanc de Blancs**, is equally noteworthy. This lively champagne would make an ideal aperitif. (NM)
- Champagne Jacques Chaput, La Haie-Vignée, 10200 Arrentières, tel. 03.25.27.00.14, fax 03.25.27.01.75 ☑
Y by appt.

GUY CHARLEMAGNE

Brut Extra★★ 6 ha 50,000 €11-15

This straw-coloured wine, a blend of Chardonnay (60%) and Pinot Noir, is a powerful and well-balanced champagne with fine bubbles. One of the tasters commented that 'the middle palate offers a whole gamut of interesting and aromatic flavours: fully ripe white peach, quince, pear' adding 'I like this one very much'. The **96 Mesnillésime Blanc de**

Champagne

Blancs was commended for its light, floral texture. (SR)

🍇 Guy Charlemagne, 4, rue de La Brèche-d'Oger, 51190 Le Mesnil-sur-Oger, tel. 03.26.57.52.98, fax 03.26.57.97.81 ▣
☎ by appt.

CHARLIER ET FILS Carte noire★

○ 14 ha · 50,000 · €11-15

This 14-ha (35-acre) vineyard is situated in the Marne Valley. Oak is very much in evidence *chez* Charlier: the wines certainly reflect their vinification in large wooden vats. Carte Noire is dominated by 75% Pinot Meunier (a speciality of the district), with Pinot Noir and Chardonnay completing the blend. This is a rounded, well-balanced and appealing champagne. The **Prestige Rosé** was also awarded a star. It is a rosé de noirs made up of 80% Pinot Noir and 20% Pinot Meunier. Flavours of cooked fruits (morello cherries and quince) contribute to its roundness. (RM)

🍇 Champagne Charlier et Fils, 4, rue des Pervenches, Aux Foudres de Chêne, 51700 Montigny-sous-Châtillon, tel. 03.26.58.35.18, fax 03.26.58.02.31, e-mail champagne.charlier@wanadoo.fr ▣
☎ by appt.

J. CHARPENTIER Réserve★

○ 3.5 ha · 35,000 · €11-15

The Charpentiers, champagne-makers since 1954, manage a vineyard of 12 ha (30 acres) on the right bank of the Marne Valley. Their Réserve is a blanc de noirs (80% Pinot Meunier). Its bouquet may be somewhat reserved, but the palate is certainly full, spicy and assertive. (RM)

🍇 Jacky Charpentier, 88, rue de Reuil, 51700 Villers-sous-Châtillon, tel. 03.26.58.05.78, fax 03.26.58.36.59 ▣
☎ by appt.

CHARTOGNE-TAILLET Cuvée Fiacre Taillet★

○ n.c. · 2,500 · €15-23

Philippe Chartogne is based at Merfy, a village near Saint-Thierry, one of the original champagne vineyards. The Chartogne-Taillet family is descended from vine-growers who have left behind an extremely interesting set of records spanning a century of viticultural activity (1750–1850). The estate today covers 11 ha (27 acres) of vines. This *cuvée* is made up of Chardonnay (60%) and Pinot Noir (40%) harvested in 1996, only part of which has undergone malolactic fermentation. Aromas of dried fruits and toast dominate the bouquet, while slightly acidic notes of red berries enhance the sense of balance on the palate. A pleasant aperitif champagne. (RM)

🍇 Philippe Chartogne-Taillet, 37–39, Grande-Rue, 51220 Merfy, tel. 03.26.03.10.17, fax 03.26.03.19.15, e-mail chartogne.taillet@wanadoo.fr ▣
☎ by appt.

CHASSENAY D'ARCE Cuvée Privilège★

○ n.c. · 110,000 · €11-15

Chassenay d'Arce is the name of an important Aube co-operative established in 1956, which today cultivates 310 ha (766 acres) of vines. Privilège is made up of 40% Chardonnay to 60% Pinot Noir. Floral scents are very much in evidence, together with a hint of honey. The **rosé** also deserves a commendation. Its high proportion of Pinot Noir (85%) lends suppleness and roundness to the wine. (CM)

🍇 Champagne Chassenay d'Arce, 10110 Ville-sur-Arce, tel. 03.25.38.30.70, fax 03.25.38.79.17, e-mail champagne-chassenay-darce@wanadoo.fr ▣
☎ by appt.

GUY DE CHASSEY 1993★

○ Gd Cru · 0.5 ha · 3,000 · €15-23

This family-run vineyard is based at Louvois, a village classified as Grand Cru. The wine is a classic blend of Pinot Noir and Chardonnay, in a 60:40 ratio. It offers aromas of citrus fruits, and is lively, powerful and long on the palate. Also commended was the Grand Cru **Nicolas d'Olivet, Cuvée Reservée**, an identical blend to the previous wine, but from the 1995 harvest. It is a champagne of high standard, remarkable for its liveliness. (RM)

🍇 Champagne Guy de Chassey, 1, pl. de la Demi-Lune, 51150 Louvois, tel. 03.26.57.04.45, fax 03.26.57.82.08, e-mail mo.de.chassey@wanadoo.fr ▣
☎ ev. day 9am–12 noon; 2pm–6.30pm

CHAUDRON ET FILS

○ n.c. · €11-15

The Chaudron family, based in the Grand Cru village of Verzenay, has had an unbroken record of champagne production since 1820. They submitted a non-vintage *brut* that is a blend of 70% Pinot Noir to 30% Chardonnay. Aromas of citrus and exotic fruits and hazelnuts precede a complex palate of good vinosity. (RM)

🍇 Champagne Chaudron, 2, rue de Beaumont, 51360 Verzenay, tel. 03.26.50.68.68, fax 03.26.50.08.71, e-mail champagnechaudron@wanadoo.fr ▣
☎ by appt.

A. CHAUVET Cachet Rouge 1990★

○ n.c. · €15-23

The house of Chauvet has been producing wine at Tours-sur-Marne since 1848. Out of the vast range of champagnes on offer, this Cachet Rouge 90 highlights the role of the Pinot Noir grape. Despite being cellared for ten years, it surprised the Jury with its striking youthfulness. A star was also awarded to the **Grand Rosé**, essentially a Chardonnay coloured with Bouzy red wine and made in the *demi-mousse* style. It is a happy marriage of power and finesse. (NM)

♠ Champagne Chauvet, 41, av. de Champagne, 51150 Tours-sur-Marne, tel. 03.26.58.92.37, fax 03.26.58.96.31 V
Y by appt.
♠ Famille Paillard-Chauvet

MARC CHAUVET

○ 7 ha · 60,000 · €11-15 · V

This estate launched its champagne in 1964 (although the two previous generations have also cultivated the vine). Its vineyard extends over 12 ha (30 acres). The non-vintage *brut* is produced from the three champagne grapes, in equal proportions, having undergone a partial malolactic fermentation. Delicate flavours of acacia make quite an impact on the palate. (RM)

♠ Champagne Marc Chauvet, 3, rue de la Liberté, 51500 Rilly-la-Montagne, tel. 03.26.03.42.71, fax 03.26.03.42.38, e-mail chauvet@eder.fr V Y by appt.

HENRI CHAUVET ET FILS

Blanc de Noirs ★ ○ 5 ha · 30,000 · €11-15

Henri Chauvet was a nurseryman and viticulturist at the beginning of the 20th century, which is when he produced his first wines. His successors, René, Henri and now Damien, manage a vineyard of 8 ha (20 acres) near Rilly-la-Montagne on the Montagne de Reims. Although this blanc de noirs has a delicate bouquet, its first impressions are firm and straightforward, and the balance is enticing. Two other champagnes received commendations: the **96 Blanc de Blancs**, which has a direct, lemony style, and the **Réserve**, which achieves its good balance by means of a skilful blend of Pinot Noir (60%) with Chardonnay. (RM)

♠ Damien Chauvet, 6, rue de la Liberté, 51500 Rilly-la-Montagne, tel. 03.26.03.42.69, fax 03.26.03.45.14, e-mail contact@champagne-chauvet.com V
Y by appt.

ANDRE CHEMIN ★★

○ 1er Cru · 0.5 ha · n.c.

André Chemin established his champagne in 1948, and was succeeded by his son in 1971. Today his grandson, Sébastien, is in charge of the 6.5-ha (16-acre) vineyard, which is situated in the Montagne de Reims. The rosé is a rosé de noirs made entirely from Pinot Noir. Tasters singled it out for the rarity of its qualities: roundness without heaviness, and freshness without excessive acidity. 15% Chardonnay, was commended for its roundness of palate and well-balanced finish. (RM)

♠ Champagne André Chemin, 3, rue de Châtillon, 51500 Sacy, tel. 03.26.49.22.42, fax 03.26.49.74.89, e-mail sebastian.chemin@wanadoo.fr V
♠ Jean-Luc Chemin

ARNAUD DE CHEURLIN ★

○ 0.5 ha · n.c. · €11-15 · V

This label has been in existence since 1981. The estate of 6 ha (15 acres) is located at Celles-sur-Ource, near Bar-sur-Aube. Its rosé is composed solely of Pinot Noir that has undergone a short maceration. Subtlety is not its strong point – it is more about richness and fullness – but its jammy fruit, with hints of brioche, make it suitable for the dinner table. The well-made **Réserve**, dominated by Pinot Noir (75%, with the rest Chardonnay), also received a star from the Jury. (RM)

♠ Arnaud de Cheurlin, 58, Grande-Rue, 10110 Celles-sur-Ource, tel. 03.25.38.53.90, fax 03.25.38.58.07 Y by appt.
♠ Eisentrager

RICHARD CHEURLIN Brut H 1996★

○ 0.7 ha · 4,000 · €11-15

Here is another Cheurlin from Celles-sur-Ource in the Aube. Since its establishment in 1978, this estate has expanded to 8.3 ha (20.5 acres). Its Brut H, a blend of 70% Pinot Noir and 30% Chardonnay, reaffirms the fine reputation of the 96 vintage. Its freshness, length and finesse are combined with flavours of dried fruits and floral notes to make a well-balanced wine that is clearly still very young. The **97 Cuvée Jeanne** was also commended. This vigorous wine mingles elements of lemon and grapefruit on its flavourful palate. (RM)

♠ Richard Cheurlin, 16, rue des Huguenots, 10110 Celles-sur-Ource, tel. 03.25.38.55.04, fax 03.25.38.58.33 Y by appt.

CHEURLIN DANGIN Cuvée Spéciale

○ 3 ha · 8,000 · €11-15

Although the Cheurlins have had a presence in Celles-sur-Ource, in the Côte des Bars district of the Aube, for generations, the Cheurlin-Dangin champagne was launched as recently as 1960. Their Cuvée Spéciale, produced from 1996 and 1997 wines, is based on equal parts Pinot Noir and Chardonnay, but is dominated by the power of the black grapes, which impose their roundness and fruitiness on the palate. (RM)

♠ Champagne Cheurlin-Dangin, 17, Grande-Rue, BP 2, 10110 Celles-sur-Ource, tel. 03.25.38.50.26, fax 03.25.38.58.51 V
Y by appt.

CHEURLIN ET FILS Prestige

○ n.c. · 55,000 · €11-15

This estate, established in 1960, maintains a sizeable vineyard of 25 ha (62 acres) on the slopes of the Côte des Bars. Its Prestige wine is made up of 70% Pinot Noir and 30% Chardonnay, harvested in 1998. The intense bouquet conjures up hints of crystallised fruits and honey, with notes of citrus fruits and cinnamon emerging on the palate. (NM)

♠ Champagne Cheurlin et Fils, 13, rue de la Gare, 10250 Gyé-sur-Seine, tel. 03.25.38.20.27, fax 03.25.38.24.01, e-mail champcheurlin@aol.fr Y ev. day except Sun. 9am-12 noon 2pm-6pm

Champagne

GASTON CHIQUET Tradition

○ 1er Cru   13 ha   115,000 ▪ ♦ €11-15

Nicolas Chiquet cultivated the vine during the reign of Louis XV. Fernand and Gaston Chiquet began making champagne in 1919, with Gaston launching his own label in 1935. Nowadays, his son, Claude, and his grandchildren run the 22.5-ha (56-acre) vineyard at Dizy, near Epernay. The three champagne grapes (45% Meunier, 20% Pinot Noir and 35% Chardonnay) from the 1996 and particularly the 1997 harvests, contribute to the straightforward, extremely lively Tradition. It has only one drawback – its youth. The **Grand Cru Ay Blanc de Blancs** was also commended by the Jury. This one is a bit of a curiosity, as the village of Ay, a neighbour of Dizy, is famous for its Pinot Noir. Produced from the 1997 harvest, this well-balanced *cuvée* has an aromatic palate that mingles notes of pears, crystallised fruits and praline. (RM)

↣ Gaston Chiquet, 912, av. du Gal-Leclerc, 51530 Dizy, tel. 03.26.55.22.02, fax 03.26.51.83.81, e-mail info@gaston-chiquet.com ▢ ▼ by appt.

CHARLES CLEMENT
Gustave Belon★★★

○   175 ha   n.c.   €11-15

Charles Clément was one of the original founders of the co-operative at Colombé-le-Sec, an Aube village near the other Colombey, where General de Gaulle is buried. Established in 1956 with 18 members, the operation today numbers 202, cultivating among them 175 ha (432 acres) of vines. The company has been skilfully producing its own wines since 1980 – a fact to which this year's excellent results bear testimony. For instance, the present wine, which is 2% short of being a blanc de blancs, has a complex bouquet that combines intensity with finesse, while the well-structured, lively and brioche-flavoured palate, with its touch of exotic fruits, leaves a lasting impression of balance – a perfect ensemble. The 91 vintage, made from half black grapes and half white, offers an expressive bouquet that mingles citrus with crystallised fruits, and has great freshness on the palate. If it were not for the hint of bitterness on the finish, this champagne would have received two stars. As for the non-vintage **brut** with the dark-blue label, a blend of all three champagne grapes, it certainly won the hearts of the Jury with its toasty, crystallised aromas and fine balance. It also received a star. (CM)

SCV Champagne Charles Clément, rue Saint-Antoine, 10200 Colombé-le-Sec, tel. 03.25.92.50.71, fax 03.25.92.50.79, e-mail champagne-charles-clement@wanadoo.fr ▢ ▼ ev. day except Sun. 8am–12 noon; 1.30pm–5.30pm

CLEMENT ET FILS

○   6 ha   3,500   ▪ €11-15

This property, set up by grandfather Clément in 1950, today accounts for 6 ha (15 acres) on the bank of the Congy, between the Côte des Blancs and the slopes of the Sézannais. It submitted a rosé, based on Pinot Meunier (75%), blended with Chardonnay. This champagne has a complex bouquet and leaves a lingering impression of freshness. (NM)

↣ GAEC Champagne Clément et Fils, 15, rue des Prés, 51270 Congy, tel. 03.26.59.31.19, fax 03.26.59.22.63 ▢ ▼ by appt.

CLERAMBAULT Cuvée Tradition★

○   140 ha   120,000   ▪ ♦ €11-5

Founded in 1951, this group of Aube producers cultivates a vineyard of 140 ha (346 acres). Its Tradition Cuvée, a blanc ce noirs derived from the two Pinots, offers pleasant floral scents. It is well balanced, but has rather noticeable *dosage*. Although the **92 Blanc de Blancs** has a somewhat fleeting finish, it nonetheless received a commendation for its flavourful palate, full of flora, honeyed notes. (CM)

↣ Champagne Clérambault, 122, Grande-Rue, 10250 Neuville-sur-Seine, tel. 03.25.38.38.60, fax 03.25.38.24.36, e-mail champagne-clerambault@wanadoo.fr ▢ ▼ ev. day except Sun. 8am–12 noon; 2pm–6pm

JOEL CLOSSON★

○   0.5 ha   4,000   ▪ €11-15

Although the Closson family has been based at Saulchery in the Marne Valley for around four centuries, it did not commence champagne production until 1984, under the direction of Joël Closson, who today runs a 5-ha (12-acre) vineyard. A blend of 1997 and 1998 wines, the estate's rosé is largely composed of black grapes (90% of the blend, of which 60% is Meunier). Its colour is attributable to the 20% proportion of red wine. The fresh fruitiness is commendable, as are the supple opening impression and fine length. In the blanc sector, the **Cuvée Prestige**, identical in both composition and age, received a commendation for its straightforward lemony finesse. (RM)

↣ Joël Closson, 155, rte Nationale, 02310 Saulchery, tel. 03.23.70.17.34, fax 03.23.70.15.24 ▢ ▼ ev. day except Sun. 8am–12 noon; 2pm–6pm

PAUL CLOUET★

○ Gd Cru   3 ha   n.c.   ▪ ♦ €11-15

The Clouets manage a vineyard in the village of Bouzy, famous for red wines made from Pinot Noir – a grape variety very much in evidence in this Grand Cru, which only uses 30% Chardonnay. The champagne is perfectly true to type, with its fine structure and length. The **rosé** and the **Cuvée Prestige Grand Cru** were both commended: the former for its fruitiness and good balance, the latter for its firm, full-bodied character. (RM)

● Paul Clouet, 10, rue Jeanne-d'Arc, 51150 Bouzy, tel. 03.26.57.07.31, fax 03.26.52.64.65, e-mail champagne-paul-clouet@wanadoo.fr ev. day 10am–12 noon; 2pm–5pm

MICHEL COCTEAUX Réserve★

○   2 ha   12,000   €11–15

This vineyard of 9.5 ha (23 acres), situated in the south of the Marne region, was established in 1965. Its Réserve is a blanc de blancs and exhibits all the typical characteristics of that style – citrus-fruit aromas, honeyed overtones and well-balanced freshness. (RM)

● Michel Cocteaux, 12, rue du Château, 51260 Montgenost, tel. 03.26.80.49.09, fax 03.26.80.44.60 by appt.

COLLARD-CHARDELLE 1986★★

○   n.c.   6,000   €15–23

Situated in the Marne Valley, this estate has been in production for over a century, although each generation has managed to leave its individual stamp upon the champagne. Today, the vineyard covers approximately 8 ha (20 acres). It entered a well-developed 86 that came before the *coup de coeur* Grand Jury, and just fell short of gaining that distinction. Pinot Meunier is the major player in the blend (70%), accompanied by a little Pinot Noir (10%) and Chardonnay (20%). The elegance and complexity of its aromatic palate emphasise toasty, charred flavours, along with hints of honey and fruit. Two other *cuvées* were each awarded a star. The **96 Cuvée Prestige** and the **Non-Vintage** version of the same wine, both blends of the 1996 and 1997 harvests. The former is vanilla scented, lemony, lively and powerful; the latter vinous and more mature. (RM)

● EARL Collard-Chardelle, 68, rue de Reuil, 51700 Villers-sous-Châtillon, tel. 03.26.58.00.50, fax 03.26.58.34.76 by appt.

COLLARD-PICARD Cuvée Prestige

○   2 ha   6,000   €15–23

A well-established vine-grower, Olivier Collard, took over part of the family estate in 1996 and cultivates some 6 ha (15 acres) of vines. His **Cuvée Prestige**, from half black and half white grapes, is derived mainly from the 1998 harvest, but topped up by 1997 and a small amount of 1996 wine. It exhibits plenty of finesse, with aromas of citrus fruits and toast; there is also evidence of generous *dosage*. The same observations apply to the **96 Cuvée Prestige**, a similarly constituted blend, which was commended for its richness and length. (RM)

● Champagne Collard-Picard, 61, rue du Château, 51700 Villers-sous-Châtillon, tel. 03.26.52.36.93, fax 03.26.58.34.76, e-mail champcp51@aol.com by appt.

RAOUL COLLET★

○   15 ha   n.c.   €11–15

This group of producers, whose members' vineyards now extend to 600 ha (1,482 acres), made its first champagne in 1921. Their **rosé** is composed exclusively of Pinot Noir. It creates an immediate impression with its salmon-coloured, slightly orangey appearance and its combination of blackcurrant and may-blossom aromas. Preserved red fruits, and notes of brioche, emerge on the palate. The **93 Carte d'Or** also received a star. This champagne is freshly scented, with a palate that combines fullness, balance and length. (CM)

● Champagne Raoul Collet, 14, bd Pasteur, 51160 Aÿ, tel. 03.26.55.15.88, fax 03.26.54.02.40 by appt.

CHARLES COLLIN★★

○   n.c.   100,000   €11–15

Established in 1952, this group of wine-producers collectively manages an area of 250 ha (618 acres). Their output is around 900,000 bottles per annum. Drawn mainly from the 1998 harvest, with a little wine added from 1997, the group's non-vintage *brut* is predominantly Pinot Noir (85%), topped up with Chardonnay. It impressed the Jury with its aromatic palate, mingling flavours of apricots, peaches, cherries and other stone-fruits, and for its finesse, balance and length. The **90** consists of slightly more Chardonnay (30%). It is well developed, showing no loss of freshness, and receives a commendation. (CM)

● Champagne Charles Collin, 27, rue des Pressoirs, BP 1, 10360 Fontette, tel. 03.25.38.31.00, fax 03.25.29.68.64, e-mail champagne-charles-collin@wanadoo.fr by appt.

DANIEL COLLIN Tradition★

○   2 ha   22,000   €11–15

This estate is situated in the south-western part of the Marne Valley, near the Saint-Gond marshes. Founded in 1959 by Daniel Collin, it has since been taken over by his son Hervé, who cultivates a vineyard of 4 ha (10 acres). This **Tradition** is a blend of 1997 and 1998 harvests, and is a blanc de noirs (60% Meunier and 40% Pinot Noir, with attractive pink highlights. An aromatic range of flavours, combining apple, pear and quince is just as evident in the bouquet as on the palate. Another champagne from this estate, made from the 1996 and 1997 harvests, warranted a commendation, namely the **rosé**. It is a similar blend to the previous wine, soft and generous, and would be an appropriate wine for the dinner table. (RM)

● Daniel Collin, 3, rue Caye, 51270 Baye, tel. 03.26.52.80.50, fax 03.26.52.33.62 by appt.

Champagne

COMTE DE NOIRON Coeur de Cuvée★
n.c.   50,000   ■ ◫   €15–23

This predominantly black-grape wine goes under one of the many Rapeneau-G.H. Martel family brand names. Made up of 80% Pinot (of which 30% is Pinot Meunier) from the harvests of 1997 and 1998, it has a floral, fresh character, with evident *dosage* and good length. (NM)

➡ Champagne Maxim's, 17, rue des Créneaux, 51100 Reims, tel. 03.26.82.70.67, fax 03.26.82.19.12 ⦿ ▼ by appt.

JACQUES COPINET
Blanc de Blancs Sélection★★
6 ha   5,000   ■ ◫   €11–15

Jacques Copinet set up this vineyard in late 1975. Situated in the Sézanne region, it covers an area of 7 ha (17 acres). The Chardonnays that go into this *cuvée* were harvested in 1995, 1996 and 1997. This fine, young, minerally champagne has great length. The **Cuvée Marie Étienne**, blended from the same years, is another blanc de blancs. Its delicate bouquet, combining flavours of lime-blossom and vanilla, and its fine balance, earned it a star. (RM)

➡ Jacques Copinet, 11, rue de l'Ormeau, 51260 Montgenost, tel. 03.26.80.49.14, fax 03.26.80.44.61, e-mail champagne.copinet@wanadoo.fr ⦿ ▼ by appt.

CORDEUIL PERE ET FILS 1995★
n.c.   5,000   ■ ◫   €11–15

Although this 7.5-ha (19-acre) vineyard goes back many years, its champagne was only created in 1974. This 95 vintage (a good year) comprises 75% Pinot Noir and 25% Chardonnay, and has undergone only partial malolactic fermentation. It is a very young-looking wine, with a bouquet of crystallised fruits, and a level of acidity on the palate that enhances the impression of firmness – a very well-balanced wine. (RM)

➡ Champagne Cordeuil, 2, rue de Fontette, 10360 Noé-les-Mallets, tel. 03.25.29.65.37, fax 03.25.29.65.37 ⦿ ▼ ev. day 8.30am–12 noon; 2pm–7pm

COUCHE PERE ET FILS★
5 ha   39,800   €8–11

This Auboise estate began production in 1972, and comprises 8 ha (20 acres) of vines. The current generation has been at the helm since 1996. Their non-vintage *brut* is a blend of 30% Chardonnay with 70% Pinot Noir, harvested in 1997 and 1998. A mixture of honey and exotic fruits mingles on the bouquet, while the palate proves superbly fresh. (RM)

➡ EARL Champagne Couche, 29, Grande-Rue, 10110 Buxeuil, tel. 03.25.38.53.96, fax 03.25.38.41.69 ⦿ ▼ by appt.

ROGER COULON
Prestige Ch. de Vallier★
0.5 ha   5,000   ■ ◫ ◕   €15–23

The vineyard near Reims, where eight generations of the Coulon family have cultivated the vine, was founded in 1806. Today, it covers 9 ha (22 acres). This *cuvée prestige* is a blend of 20% Pinot Noir, matured for two years in barrel, and 80% Chardonnay, from the 1991 and 1992 harvests. It has a vinous, complex and powerful bouquet, and its well-structured palate is reminiscent of small red berries. An autumn champagne, was the conclusion of one member of the Jury. (RM)

➡ Éric Coulon, 12, rue de la Vigne-du-Roi, 51390 Vrigny, tel. 03.26.03.61.65, fax 03.26.03.43.68, e-mail champagne.coulon.roger@wanadoo.fr ⦿ ▼ by appt.

ALAIN COUVREUR
Blanc de Blancs Cuvée de Réserve★
n.c.   n.c.   ■ ◫   €11–15

This 5.5-ha (14-acre) vineyard is situated at Prouilly, to the west of Reims. Its blanc de blancs Reserve Cuvée is produced from 1990 Chardonnay. Fleshy, rich and unctuous, the wine appears to be fully developed. It could be served as an accompaniment to a sauced meat dish. (RM)

➡ Alain Couvreur, 18, Grande-Rue, 51140 Prouilly, tel. 03.26.48.58.95, fax 03.26.48.26.29 ⦿ ▼ by appt.

DOMINIQUE CRETE ET FILS
Réserve
4 ha   30,000   ■ ◫   €11–15

The current generation, represented by Dominique Crété, took over management of this estate in 1984, with the present label succeeding that of Roland Crété et Fils. The vineyard, at Moussy, extends to 7 ha (17 acres). This Réserve is produced from 80% Pinot Meunier and 20% Chardonnay. It reveals floral scents, with overtones of apple and lemon, in a simple, forthright style. (RM)

➡ Dominique Crété, 63, rte Nationale, 51530 Moussy, tel. 03.26.54.52.10, fax 03.26.52.79.93 ⦿ ▼ by appt.

LYCEE AGRICOLE DE CREZANCY
Cuvée Euphrasie-Guynemer 1995
0.8 ha   2,000   ■   €11–15

The pupils of the agricultural school at Crézancy in the Aisne region have a vineyard of almost 3 ha (7 acres) at their disposal for their practical studies. Their Euphrasie-Guynemer wine is made from a blend of 40% Pinot Meunier and 60% Chardonnay. Its initial bouquet of flowers and undergrowth is followed by light, smoky flavours of crystallised fruits, backed up by good vinosity. It would make a suitable accompaniment for food. (RM)

- Lycée agricole et viticole de Crézancy, rue de Paris, 02650 Crézancy, tel. 03.23.71.50.70, fax 03.23.71.50.71 ▼ by appt.

COMTE AUDOIN DE DAMPIERRE Cuvée des Ambassadeurs

n.c.   100,000   €15-23 ▼

Cuvée des Ambassadeurs, a champagne made from half black grapes and half white, is derived from 1er Cru sites. Diplomats will drink it as an aperitif for its lightness and expressive bouquet, which mingles floral notes with a hint of menthol. Equally commended was the **95 Grand Vintage**, a generous wine made up of 60% Pinot Noir and 40% Chardonnay. (MA)

- Comte Audoin de Dampierre, 3, pl. Boisseau, 51140 Chenay, tel. 03.26.03.11.13, fax 03.26.03.18.05, e-mail champagne.dampierre@wanadoo.fr ▼ by appt.

PAUL DANGIN ET FILS Cuvée du Cinquantenaire 1996★★

2 ha   10,000   €11-15

At the beginning of the 20th century, Joseph Dangin was cultivating his ancestors' vineyard, which used to belong to the abbey at Mores founded by Saint Bernard of Clairvaux in the 12th century. This *cuvée* was created to celebrate the 50th anniversary of the brand that Paul Dangin founded in 1947. Today, his sons and grandsons manage a vineyard of 30 ha (74 acres). They submitted a predominantly white-grape 96 Vintage (90% Chardonnay) that carries all before it, combining citrus-fruit aromas with balance and length. (RM)

- SCEV Paul Dangin et Fils, 11, rue du Pont, 10110 Celles-sur-Ource, tel. 03.25.38.50.27, fax 03.25.38.58.08, e-mail c.dangin@champagne-dangin.com ▼

DAUTEL-CADOT Cuvée Prestige

n.c.   n.c.   €11-15

René Dautel, successor to several generations of vine-growers, launched his champagne in 1971. He is based in the Aube region, cultivating a vineyard of more than 8 ha (20 acres). His Prestige Cuvée draws on equal proportions of Pinot Noir and Chardonnay, harvested in 1994. It has a complex bouquet and a well-balanced palate, with overtones of citrus fruits. **Carte Blanche**, a blanc de blancs produced from the 1995 harvest, was similarly commended as a champagne that charms with its vivacity and hazelnut flavour. (RM)

- Dautel-Cadot, 10, rue Saint-Vincent, 10110 Loches-sur-Ource, tel. 03.25.29.61.12, fax 03.25.29.72.16 ▼ by appt.
- René Dautel

PH. DAVIAUX-QUINET Blanc de Blancs 1996★

Gd Cru   0.35 ha   2,700   €11-15

This young brand was created in 1988 by Philippe Daviaux-Quinet, the descendant of a vine-growing family. His vineyard covers almost 4 ha (10 acres) near the Grand Cru village of Chouilly, in the vicinity of Epernay. It is fast becoming apparent that the 1996 vintage has produced wines of impressive potential longevity, as is perfectly illustrated by this blanc de blancs. It exhibits a lively start, good balance and fine length – a promising combination. (RM)

- Philippe Daviaux-Quinet, 4, rue de la Noue-Coutard, 51530 Chouilly, tel. 03.26.54.44.03, fax 03.26.54.74.81 ▼

JACQUES DEFRANCE★★

10 ha   50,000   €11-15 ▼

This Auboise estate, first established in 1900, cultivates 10 ha (25 acres) of vines, producing both champagne and Rosé des Riceys. Its brand was launched in 1973. The non-vintage *brut* is almost a blanc de noirs, made from Pinot Noir with just a little Chardonnay (10%) thrown in for good measure. The tasters praised its intense bouquet, its fullness, roundness and length. The **rosé** receives a star for its concentrated flavours of red fruits and grapefruit. (RM)

- Jacques Defrance, 28, rue de la Plante, 10340 Les Riceys, tel. 03.25.29.32.20, fax 03.25.29.77.83 ▼ by appt.

DEHOURS Confidentielle

n.c.   2,000   €11-15

This *négociant* house was set up in 1930 by Ludovic Dehours and is today run by his descendants. Confidentielle comprises 60% Pinot Noir and 30% Chardonnay, with 10% reserve wines. It is a fresh, simple, well-structured champagne with pleasant *dosage*. (NM)

- Champagne Dehours et Fils, 2, rue de la Chapelle, Cerseuil, 51700 Mareuil-le-Port, tel. 03.26.52.71.75, fax 03.26.52.73.83, e-mail champagne-dehours@wanadoo.fr ▼

DELAHAIE★

n.c.   20,000   €11-15

This non-vintage *brut* is produced from the harvests of 1996 and 1997, and is a blend of 60% Pinot Meunier, with 20% each of Pinot Noir and Chardonnay. It is a floral, brioche-scented and perfectly balanced wine. The same company's **Cuvée Sublime** also received a star. With the emphasis on Chardonnay (85%), it owes its flavours of quince and honey to that grape variety, and its feeling of roundness to its age. (NM)

- Brochet, 22, rue des Rocherets, 51200 Epernay, tel. 03.26.54.08.74, fax 03.26.54.34.45, e-mail champagne.delahaie@wanadoo.fr ▼ by appt.

DELAMOTTE Blanc de Blancs★★

n.c.   n.c.   €25-30

Delamotte, founded in 1760, is one of the longest-established champagne houses. Today, it belongs to Laurent-Perrier, as does Salon, its next-door neighbour at Mesnil-sur-Oger in the Côte des Blancs. The

Chardonnays that have been used to produce this champagne were harvested in 1996 and 1997. They introduce finesse, richness, complexity and length to this model wine. (NM)

➤ Champagne Delamotte, 5, rue de la Brèche-d'Oger, 51190 Le Mesnil-sur-Oger, tel. 03.26.57.51.65, fax 03.26.57.79.29

ANDRE DELAUNOIS Carte d'or €11-15
7.6 ha 18,000

Vine-grower Edmond Delaunois has been in business since the 1920s. Nowadays, the third and fourth generations of Delaunois carry on the family tradition. Their vineyard covers 7.6 ha (19 acres) in the Montagne de Reims. Their Carte d'Or is composed of the three champagne grape varieties in proportions of 25% each (harvested in 1997 and 1998), supplemented by 25% reserve wine. Its flavours of crystallised fruits are already well developed, yet it also retains its freshness, making it an ideal aperitif. (RM)

➤ SCE André Delaunois,
17, rue Roger-Salengro, BP 42,
51500 Rilly-la-Montagne,
tel. 03.26.03.42.87, fax 03.26.03.45.40,
e-mail champagne.a.delaunois@wanadoo.fr
⅋ by appt.

DELAVENNE PERE ET FILS €15-23
Cuvée 3e Millénaire 1995★
Gd cru 0.96 ha 10,000

Descendants of the founder of this family-run estate, which was established in 1920, now run the 8-ha (20-acre) vineyard. Their 95 vintage Cuvée 3e Millénaire combines 60% Pinot Noir with 40% Chardonnay. Its complex bouquet augurs well for its development, while the palate attracts attention for its balance. The rosé, a blend of 50% Pinot Noir and 35% Chardonnay, owes its hue to the addition of 15% Bouzy red wine. It deserved a commendation for its freshness, attributed to the harvests of 1997 and 1998. (RM)

➤ Delavenne Père et Fils, 6, rue de Tours,
51150 Bouzy, tel. 03.26.57.02.04,
fax 03.26.58.82.93 ⅋ ev. day except Sun. Mon. 10am–12 noon; 2pm–5pm

DELBECK Bouzy★
Gd Cru n.c. n.c. €23-30

Delbeck prides itself on having been the chosen supplier of the French Court, during the July Monarchy. The estate has changed hands several times, however, in the period since the Second World War. Three champagnes, each from a different Grand Cru village, were honoured by the Jury. The Bouzy has a ripe bouquet and a complex and balanced palate, and is made up of 70% Pinot Noir and 30% Chardonnay. A Cramant Grand Cru Blanc de Blancs, floral, fine and fresh, also received a star. The Ay Grand Cru (80% Pinot Noir and 20% Chardonnay), just a notch below and narrowly missing out on a star, showed evidence of unsubtle dosage. It was commended, though, for its milky caramel and fresh almond flavours. (NM)

➤ Champagne Delbeck, 39, rue du Gal-Sarrail, BP 77, 51053 Reims Cedex, tel. 03.26.77.58.00, fax 03.26.77.58.01, e-mail info@delbeck.com
➤ Martin de La Giraudière

DELOUVIN NOWACK Carte d'or €11-15
5 ha 30,000

Although the Delouvins have been growing vines at Vandières in the Marne Valley since the 16th century, they only started bottling their own wine around 1930. Their Carte d'Or is a blanc de noirs, made from the 1997 and 1998 harvests of Pinot Meunier. This rich champagne has flavours of red fruits and dried apricots, and would appear already to have reached its optimum stage of development. The 95 Extra Sélection is a blend of equal parts Chardonnay and Pinot Meunier. It is similar to the previous wine, apart from its more discernible dosage and it receives the same rating. (RM)

➤ Champagne Delouvin-Nowack,
29, rue Principale, 51700 Vandières,
tel. 03.26.58.02.70, fax 03.26.57.10.11
⅋ by appt.
➤ Bertrand Delouvin

YVES DELOZANNE Tradition €11-15
7.5 ha 15,000

The Delozannes have been wine-growers for five generations, selling their grapes on to the trade. About 30 years ago, they became producers themselves, today cultivating an 8.5-ha (21-acre) vineyard. Their Tradition is almost a blanc de noirs, being made from 90% Pinot Meunier. This is a mature champagne, showing generous dosage. (RM)

➤ Yves Delozanne, 67, rue de Savigny,
51170 Serzy-et-Prin, tel. 03.26.97.40.18,
fax 03.26.97.49.14 ⅋ by appt.

SERGE DEMIERE Réserve★★ €11-15
Gd cru 1.5 ha 15,000

Serge Demière cultivates a 6-ha (15-acre) vineyard at Ambonnay, a Grand Cru village in the Montagne de Reims. His Réserve cuvée, a blend of 60% Pinot Noir and 40% Chardonnay, harvested in 1997, has been aged in oak. It made a strong impression on the Jury, with some members almost ready to award it a coup de coeur. Its powerful toasty aromas were much admired, as was the discernible note of maturity. The attractive, balanced palate shows evidence of generous dosage. The Tradition 1er Cru, which derives from the 1998 harvest, earned a star for its balance, freshness and length. (RM)

➤ Serge Demière,
7, rue de la Commanderie, 51150 Ambonnay,
tel. 03.26.57.07.79, fax 03.26.57.82.15
⅋ by appt.

DEMILLY DE BAERE €11-15
Brut 0 Cuvée Carte d'or
4 ha 2,000

Gérard Demilly is a descendant of the Bligny family, who have been cultivating vines since 1624. Having founded his own brand in

1975, he manages a vineyard of 4 ha (10 acres) in the Côte des Bars district of the Aube, which includes a small quantity of Pinot Blanc – an unusual grape variety of Champagne. It accounts for 10% of this complex non-dosed *brut*, which is otherwise made up of the more classic Chardonnay (20%), Pinot Meunier (5%) and Pinot Noir (65%). That last variety indeed is very much in evidence in this vinous champagne, with its fruit compôte flavours, making it a suitable accompaniment to food. (NM)

● Gérard Demilly, rue du Château, 10200 Bligny, tel. 03.25.27.45.02, fax 03.25.27.45.02.
✉ ❖ e-mail champagne-demilly@barsuraube.net

MICHEL DERVIN Cuvée MD★

○   3 ha   24,133   ■ | ● £11-15

This commercial wine enterprise was established in 1983. Its Cuvée MD is a blanc de noirs (80% Pinot Meunier) that hasn't undergone malolactic fermentation. It has an expressive bouquet and a fresh first impression, leading on to a well-balanced palate. (NM)

● Michel Dervin, rue de Belval,
51480 Cuchery, tel. 03.26.58.15.22,
fax 03.26.58.11.12, e-mail dervin.michel@wanadoo.fr ❖ ❖ by appt.

DESBORDES-AMIAUD Tradition★

○ 1er Cru   n.c.   20,000   ■ £11-15

This estate, close to the Ville des Sacres in the Marne Valley, comprises 9 ha (22 acres) of vines. Since 1935, its management has been all-female. This champagne, made from the three champagne grape varieties, has not undergone malolactic fermentation – a fact that explains its striking freshness. The finesse of its toasty flavours impressed the Jury. (RM)

● Marie-Christine Desbordes, 2, rue de Villers-aux-Nouds, 51500 Ecueil,
tel. 03.26.49.77.58, fax 03.26.49.27.34 ❖
❖ by appt.

A. DESMOULINS ET CIE★

○   n.c.   n.c.   £15-23

This *négociant* house has been a family business since it was first established in 1908 by Albert Desmoulins. It submitted a copper-coloured rosé, with flavours of red fruits and blackcurrant leaves. Although its supple, fleshy palate is not that long, it is nonetheless an attractive wine. The **Cuvée Prestige**, which is made predominantly from white grapes, shows some less-than-subtle *dosage*, but still obtained a commendation for its finesse and length. (NM)

● Champagne A. Desmoulins et Cie,
44, av. Foch, B.P. 10, 51201 Epernay Cedex,
tel. 03.26.54.24.24, fax 03.26.54.26.15 ❖

PAUL DETHUNE★

○ Gd Cru   6 ha   27,000   ■ | ■ £11-15

The Dethune family has been established at Ambonnay since 1620, and is fortunate

---

enough to have at its disposal a vineyard of 7 ha (17 acres) in that Grand Cru. It is justly proud of its viticultural roots, its 'tailor-made' cellars and its ranks of large wooden fermentation casks. Indeed, this particular *cuvée* is composed of wines that have been aged in oak. A complex blend of 70% Pinot Noir and 30% Chardonnay (including 30% reserve wines), it has biscuity, toasty flavours commended for its red-fruit intensity. (RM)

● Paul Déthune, 2, rue du Moulin,
51150 Ambonnay, tel. 03.26.57.01.88,
fax 03.26.57.09.31 ❖ ❖ ev. day except Sun. 9am–12 noon; 2pm–5pm, cl. 2 – 15 Jan.

DEUTZ William Deutz 1995★

○   n.c.   850,000   ■ | ● £46-76

This house was founded in 1838, and has been managed by Roederer since 1973. Three of its champagnes received commendations. The **Classic**, a blend of the three champagne grapes in equal proportions, harvested between 1995 and 1997, has a subtle bouquet, but is balanced and elegant. The **95 Blanc de Blancs** remains very youthful for the time being, while the **95 Amour de Deutz**, a blanc de blancs with a forthright start and a perceptible *dosage*, has flavours of beeswax and toasted bread. The star goes to the 95 William Deutz (35% Chardonnay and 65% Pinots), a champagne representative of its year – long on the palate and, as one member of the Jury put it, 'just what one would expect from a special *cuvée*'. (NM)

● Champagne Deutz, 16, rue Jeanson,
51160 Ay, tel. 03.26.56.94.00,
fax 03.26.56.94.10 ❖ ❖ by appt.

DIDIER-DESTREZ 3e Millénaire★

○   1.5 ha   3,000   ■ £11-15

Jean Didier cultivates his 5 ha (12 acres) of vines at Saint-Martin d'Ablois, a few kilometres to the south-west of Epernay. He took over from his father, the creator of the brand, in 1971. The 3° Millénaire is a blend of equal parts Pinot Noir and Chardonnay. It is a floral, brioche-scented and well-balanced champagne. The **Cuvée Prestige**, a Chardonnay-dominated blend (60%), was also commended for its very fine bouquet, with aromas of dried flowers and overtones of toasted bread on the palate. (RM)

● Jean Didier, 48, rue de Vinay,
51530 Saint-Martin-d'Ablois,
tel. 03.26.59.90.25, fax 03.26.59.91.63 ❖
❖ by appt.

DOM BASLE
Réserve Cuvée Raisins et Passions

○ Gd cru   0.25 ha   2,000   ■ £11-15

Damien Lallement is in a fortunate position: he owns vines in the Grand Cru villages of Verzenay and Verzy in the Montagne de Reims. This *cuvée* comes from the single Verzy vintage of 1995, and is comprised of 80% Pinot Noir and 20% Chardonnay. This is a full-bodied, vigorous champagne of great character, with greengage fruit flavours. The

693

CHAMPAGNE

brut is a blend of identical proportions of the same grape varieties, but grown in Verzenay and Verzy and drawn from the 1996 and 1998 harvests. It is fruity, with notes of brioche and pronounced nutty flavours. This champagne received a commendation for its lightness and length. (RM)

Champagne Lallement-Deville, 28, rue Irénée-Gass, BP 29, 51380 Verzy, tel. 03.26.97.95.90, fax 03.26.97.98.25

Y by appt.

Damien Lallement

DOQUET-JEANMAIRE★

1er Cru   7 ha   3,000   €11-15

A blend of Vertus red wines and Chardonnay from the Côte des Blancs, this rosé is definitely an aperitif wine. The *dosage* is perfect, and its flavours of red fruits and wild berries certainly enamoured the Jury. Its good structure suggests that it could be laid down for a year or two. (SR)

Doquet-Jeanmaire, 44, chem. du Moulin de la Cense-Bizet, 51130 Vertus, tel. 03.26.52.16.50, fax 03.26.59.36.71, e-mail doquet.jeanmaire@wanadoo.fr

Y by appt.

DIDIER DOUÉ Prestige★

0.5 ha   n.c.   €11-15

Didier Doué established his vineyard in 1973, and then turned his attention to fitting out his cellar and finally, in 1980, launched his champagne. The estate is based at Montgueux, a Chardonnay enclave in an Auboise vineyard that tends to favour red grapes. The fine Prestige, which comprises 70% Chardonnay and 30% Pinot Noir, has aromas of honey and dried fruits, and is well balanced and long on the palate. (RM)

Didier Doué, chem. des Vignes, 10300 Montgueux, tel. 03.25.79.44.33, fax 03.25.79.40.04

Y by appt.

ETIENNE DOUÉ Cuvée Prestige 1995

0.5 ha   n.c.   €15-23

This 4.5-ha (11-acre) estate is situated at Montgueux, not far from Troyes. It launched its champagne in 1977. Although there is no indication on the label, the Prestige Cuvée is a blanc de blancs. A lively 95 with a forthright opening impression, it has perceptible *dosage*. (RM)

Etienne Doué, 11, rte de Troyes, 10300 Montgueux, tel. 03.25.74.84.41, fax 03.25.79.00.47

Y by appt.

DOURDON-VIEILLARD

Grande Réserve★★

1.5 ha   8,000   €11-15

This grower-wine-maker cultivates a vineyard of 9.5 ha (23 acres) in the Marne Valley. Its Grande Réserve is mainly Chardonnay (60%), supplemented by the two Pinots in equal proportions. It offers flavours of buttered toast and has a perfectly balanced palate. The **Vieilles Vignes Brut** is a blanc de noirs made from Pinot Meunier (70%) and Pinot Noir (30%), harvested in 1997. It was

commended for its clean characteristics and length. (RM)

Dourdon-Vieillard, 7, rue du Château, 51480 Reuil, tel. 03.26.58.06.38, fax 03.26.58.35.13, e-mail dourdonvieillard@aol.com

Y by appt.

R. DOYARD ET FILS

Oeil-de-perdrix, Collection de l'An I 1996

1er Cru   7 ha   3,500   €15-23

The Doyards are based in the south of the Côte des Blancs and oversee 7 ha (17 acres) of vines. They became grower-wine-makers in 1927. Maurice Doyard, the first of the line, also co-founded the CIVC (Comité Interprofessional des Vins de Champagne). Oeil-de-Perdrix is white with rose-coloured highlights It comprises one-third Chardonnay (vinified *en barrique*) and two-thirds Pinot Noir. Structured and lightly oaky, with a panoply of rich flavours (cooked fruits, honey, notes of buttered brioche), this champagne is destined for the dinner table. The **95 Blanc de Blancs 1er Cru** is composed of 25% oaked wines. Its flavours of dried fruits, as well as its praiseworthy richness and power, helped it gain a commendation. (RM)

Champagne Robert Doyard et Fils, 61, av. de Bammental, 51130 Vertus, tel. 03.26.52.14.74, fax 03.26.52.24.02, e-mail champagne.doyard@wanadoo.fr

Y ev. day except Sat. Sun. 8am–12 noon; 1.30pm–6pm, cl. Aug.

DOYARD-MAHÉ

Cuvée Blanc de Blancs Carte d'or

1er Cru   n.c.   €11-15

Maurice Doyard's grandson Philippe runs a 6-ha (15-acre) vineyard at Vertus on the Côte des Blancs. Two of his 1er Cru wines were commended by the Jury: the Carte d'Or, produced from Chardonnays harvested between 1995 and 1998, a superb-looking wine, with a citrus-fruit bouquet and lively palate; and the round and supple rosé, composed of 88% Chardonnay and 12% red wine that has been aged in oak for six months. (RM)

Philippe Doyard-Mahé, Moulin d'Argensole, 51130 Vertus, tel. 03.26.52.23.85, fax 03.26.59.36.69

Y ev. day sf dim. 10am–12 noon; 2pm–6pm

DRAPPIER Grande Sendrée 1995★

n.c.   69,800   €23-30

Louis Drappier founded the estate in 1808 at Urville in the Côte des Bars. Today, this 30-ha (74-acre) vineyard is cultivated by his descendants, who take a certain pride in the fact that their cellars were originally established by the Cistercian monks of Clairvaux. The Drappiers were also once flattered by a visit from their famous neighbour, General de Gaulle. Their special *cuvée*, Grande Sendrée, is a blend of 55% Pinot Noir and 45% Chardonnay. Its flavours of citrus fruits and *pain d'épice* are reinforced by exemplary *dosage*. This well-balanced champagne has now reached its peak. The **95 Signature Blanc de Blancs** was also commended by the Jury for its good balance. Finally, lovers of vintage champagne will take to the predominantly black-grape **79 Carte d'Or** (90% Pinots). This beautifully integrated wine should be drunk now. (NM)

● Champagne Drappier, Grande-Rue, 10200 Urville, tel. 03.25.27.40.15, fax 03.25.27.41.19, e-mail info@champagne-drappier.com ☑ ▼ by appt.

DRIANT-VALENTIN
Grande Réserve Extra Brut★★

○ 1er Cru	1 ha	6,000	■ ♦	€11-15

Having taken over in 1972, Jacques Driant represents the fourth generation to work this village near Avize. Its Grande Réserve, a 1er Cru blend of 80% Chardonnay and 20% Pinot Noir, harvested in 1993 and 1995. An absence of dosage contributes to the success of this wine, because the tasters highlighted its excellent construction, its finesse and its fine present construction, its finesse and its fine previous wine and in identical proportions, was commended for its balance and freshness. (RM)

● Jacques Driant, 4, imp. de la Ferme, 51190 Grauves, tel. 03.26.59.72.26, fax 03.26.59.76.55 ▼ by appt.

GERARD DUBOIS Tradition★

○	6 ha	6,000	■ ♦	€11-15

Gérard Dubois started producing wine in 1970 on the family estate established by his grandfather in 1920. The vineyard extends over 6 ha (15 acres) of vines. Its Tradition is made up of the three grape varieties (of which 30% is Chardonnay), harvested in 1996 and 1997. It is a good non-vintage brut, with floral flavours and a touch of confectionery. The well-balanced palate is fresh and lightly acidic. The non-vintage **Réserve Blanc de Blancs**, made from the 1995 harvest, received a commendation from the Jury. It mingles floral flavours with notes of vanilla and honey, and exhibits an assertive freshness. (RM)

● Gérard Dubois, 67, rue Ernest-Vallé, 51190 Avize, tel. 03.26.57.58.60, fax 03.26.57.41.94, e-mail gerardhdubois@wanadoo.fr ☑ ▼ by appt.

HERVE DUBOIS
Blanc de Blancs Réserve★

○ Gd Cru	2 ha	5,000	■	€11-15

Hervé Dubois started producing wine in 1980 in Avize, a Grand Cru village in the Côte des Blancs. His estate comprises 4.4 ha (11 acres) of vines. Its Grand Cru wines, the **95 Blanc de Blancs** and this Réserve, are both produced from 100% Chardonnay, and were both awarded a star. They are two very similar champagnes, young, fruity and elegant. (RM)

● Hervé Dubois, 67, rue Ernest-Vallé, 51190 Avize, tel. 03.26.57.52.45, fax 03.26.57.99.26 ▼ by appt.

ROBERT DUFOUR ET FILS
Tradition

○	n.c.	n.c.	■	€11-15

This Tradition, a blanc de noirs made from Pinot Noir, is the product of a 14-ha (35-acre) vineyard in the Aube. Its aromatic palate, with its flavours of white-fleshed fruits and honeyed notes, is well balanced and long. (RM)

● EARL Robert Dufour, 4, rue de la Croix-Malot, 10110 Landreville, tel. 03.25.29.66.19, fax 03.25.38.56.50 ☑ by appt.

J. DUMANGIN FILS

○ 1er Cru	5.2 ha	2,700	■	€11-15

This estate of 5.5 ha (14 acres) is based at Chigny-les-Roses, a Premier Cru village in the Montagne de Reims. Made from half black grapes and half white, this rosé is fruity, robust and long. It has certainly reached its peak. (RM)

● Jacky Dumangin Fils, 3, rue de Rilly, 51500 Chigny-les-Roses, tel. 03.26.03.46.34, fax 03.26.03.45.61, e-mail info@champagne-dumangin.fr ☑ ▼ by appt.

DUMENIL★

○ 1er Cru	6.5 ha	41,000	■	€11-15

The vineyard was established in 1905, and its champagne launched in 1925, by the Rebeyrolle family, which still remains at the helm of the Duménil enterprise. The vineyard covers 10.6 ha (26 acres) in the area around Chigny-les-Roses on the Montagne de Reims. The three champagne grapes play equal parts in this non-vintage brut, harvested in 1996 and 1997. This is a well-structured champagne, with a flavour of grapefruit and a fresh finish. The **Cuvée Prestige**, made from half black grapes and half white, mingles flavours of fresh fruits and hazelnuts. It is supple, delicate and long. (RM)

● Duménil, rue des Vignes, 51500 Chigny-les-Roses, tel. 03.26.03.44.48, fax 03.26.03.45.25, e-mail info@champagne-dumenil.com ☑ ▼ by appt.

● Rebeyrolle

DANIEL DUMONT
Cuvée d'Excellence 1995

○	0.6 ha	5,000	■	€15-23

Daniel Dumont started in the wine trade in 1962. He expanded his parents' business by taking on a vineyard, and is today in charge of a 10-ha (25-acre) estate in the Marne Valley. He is also a nurseryman. His lemony and toasty-scented 95 Cuvée d'Excellence is a blend of 70% Chardonnay and 30% Pinot Noir. Its lively first impression is followed by a softer note of freshness on the palate. (RM)

● Daniel Dumont, 11, rue Gambetta, 51500 Rilly-la-Montagne, tel. 03.26.03.40.67, fax 03.26.03.44.82 ☑ by appt.

R. DUMONT ET FILS 1996★

○	2 ha	9,700	■ ♦	€15-23

The Dumonts have been in wine production at Champignol-Lez-Mondeville in the

Aube for around two centuries, cultivating 22 ha (54 acres) of vines today. They submitted a 96 vintage – made from 60% Pinot Noir and 40% Chardonnay – a champagne from a prestigious year, and one that is worth cellaring. It certainly lives up to its promise, delivering great freshness and balance. The lingering finish offers vivacious flavours of crystallised fruits. (RM)

☛ R. Dumont et Fils,
10200 Champignol-lez-Mondeville,
tel. 03.25.27.45.95, fax 03.25.27.45.97 🔽
🍷 by appt.

DUVAL-LEROY
Fleur de Champagne Rosé de saignée★★

| ○ | n.c. | ■ | 75,000 | €15-23 |

The Duval–Leroy enterprise, founded in 1859, is the most important operation in the Côte des Blancs. Carol Duval has successfully managed this 150-ha (370-acre) vineyard since 1991. Three of the estate's champagnes have been honoured. Although the blancs de blancs (as well as the white-dominated *cuvées* that consist of at least 75% Chardonnay) represent the house speciality, this *rosé de saignée*, 100% Pinot Noir, has to be its crowning glory. Its fine reputation is clearly justified. This year, several members of the Jury were keen to award it a *coup de coeur*. Its fine pale appearance (the aim of most champagne producers) and its fruity finish add up to a winning formula. It also exhibits roundness, complexity, freshness and perfect *dosage*. Duval-Leroy also received a commendation for its **blanc de noirs** (60% Pinot Noir), a well-structured, balanced, fresh and supple wine, and for its **95 Extra-Brut**. The latter is more representative of the estate's output, with 80% Chardonnay and 20% Pinot Noir making up the blend. This champagne was highly rated for its straightforward character, its fine structure and its length. One taster suggested that it would be suitable as an accompaniment for a small game-bird. (NM)

☛ Champagne Duval-Leroy, 69, av. de Bammental, B.P. 37, 51130 Vertus,
tel. 03.26.52.10.75, fax 03.26.52.37.10,
e-mail champagne@duval-leroy.com 🔽
🍷 by appt.
☛ Carol Duval

CHARLES ELLNER Réserve

| ○ | n.c. | | 250,000 | ■ €11-15 |

Charles-Emile Ellner was a grower-winemaker before the First World War. His son Pierre has expanded the vineyard and increased sales. The house, which remains family-run, added another string to its bow in 1972: it diversified into the *négociant* sector of the champagne trade. The estate comprises 54 ha (133 acres) of vines, dotted throughout the various regions of Champagne, but mainly located in the area around Epernay. The Réserve, produced from the 1995 and 1996 harvests, has a slight preponderance of Chardonnay (60%, to 40% Pinot Noir). It is a floral-scented, lively and well-balanced wine. (NM)

☛ Champagne Charles Ellner,
6, rue Côte-Legris, 51200 Epernay,
tel. 03.26.55.60.25, fax 03.26.51.54.00,
e-mail info@champagne-ellner.com 🔽
🍷 by appt.

ESTERLIN Cuvée Elzévia

| ○ | n.c. | | 25,000 | ■ €15-23 |

Founded in 1948, this group of Epernay producers collectively manages an area of 120 ha (296 acres) of vines. Its Elzévia Cuvée is a blanc de blancs, harvested in 1996. This champagne has not undergone malolactic fermentation – an unusual strategy for a naturally acidic wine. That, however, goes some way to explain the lemony-flavoured vitality observed by the tasters in this very youthful wine. (CM)

☛ Champagne Esterlin, 25, av. de Champagne, BP 342, 51334 Epernay Cedex,
tel. 03.26.59.71.52, fax 03.26.59.77.72,
e-mail contact@champagne-esterlin.fr 🔽
🍷 by appt.

CHRISTIAN ETIENNE Tradition

| ○ | 6 ha | ■ | 10,000 | ■ €11-15 |

This family estate was established in 1978, and today cultivates a 9-ha (22-acre) vineyard in the Aube. The mainly black-grape Tradition (90% Pinot Noir), derived from the 1995, 1996 and 1997 harvests, is fresh, appears vigorous and displays aromas of green apples and citrus fruits. It would make a suitable accompaniment for shellfish. **Prestige**, a blend of 70% Chardonnay to 30% Pinot Noir, made from grapes harvested in 1996, deserved a commendation for its freshness, elegance and finesse. (RM)

☛ Christian Etienne, rue de la Fontaine, 10200 Meurville, tel. 03.25.27.46.66, fax 03.25.27.45.84 🔽 by appt.

JEAN-MARIE ETIENNE★

| ○ 1er cru | 3.6 ha | ■ | 26,000 | ■ €11-15 |

The Etiennes, who have been vine-growers for four generations, are based at Cumières, a Premier Cru village near Epernay. Jean-Marie Etienne launched his brand name in 1958, and was later succeeded in the business by his sons, Daniel and Pascal. They have been very successful with this well-balanced, young, predominantly black-grape *brut*, produced from the 1993, 1995 and 1996 harvests. It is made up of 50% Meunier, 30% Pinot Noir and the rest Chardonnay. A star, too, goes to the **Cuvée Spéciale** (comprising 55% Chardonnay, with the remaining 45% being made up of the two Pinots). This champagne combines flavours of fig and quince, and offers good length. (RM)

☛ Etienne, 33, rue Louis-Dupont, 51480 Cumières, tel. 03.26.51.66.62, fax 03.26.55.04.65 🔽 by appt.

FRANCOIS FAGOT★★

| ○ | 0.7 ha | ■ | 7,500 | ■ €11-15 |

François Fagot cultivates a 7-ha (17-acre) vineyard in the Montagne de Reims. His rosé, from the 1996 and 1997 harvests, has been vinified by the *saignée* method – a short

maceration period on the red grape-skins – and is therefore a rosé de noirs (80% Pinot Noir). It impressed the Jury with its full, rounded, structured, warm, powerful and balanced qualities. With so many adjectives, it had to receive a *coup de coeur!* The mainly black-grape **95** (just 10% Chardonnay) was also commended for its lively first impression and its firm finish. (NM)

☎ SARL François Fagot, 26, rue Gambetta, 51500 Rilly-la-Montagne, tel. 03.26.03.42.56, fax 03.26.03.41.19, e-mail fagot@wanadoo.fr 🍷 by appt.

FALLET-DART Grande Sélection

○ | 10 ha | 50,922 | €11-15

Fifteen generations of the Fallet-Darts have tended the vine since the family first began production in 1610. Today, they cultivate a vineyard of 16.5 ha (41 acres) at Aisne. This *cuvée* is a blanc de noirs made from a blend of the two Pinots, from the 1996 and 1997 harvests. It has overtones of strawberries and raspberries. These fruity flavours are equally apparent in the **rosé**, which also received a commendation. (RM)

☎ Fallet-Dart, Drachy, 2, rue des Clos-du-Mont, 02310 Charly-sur-Marne, tel. 03.23.82.01.73, fax 03.23.82.19.15 🍷 by appt.

FANIEL-FILAINE

n.c. | 30,000 | €11-15

The Faniels have been vine-growers since 1696. Tr...y, together with the Filaines, they cultiv... 5.5 ha (14 acres) in the Marne Val...y. Their non-vintage *brut* is a blanc de noirs, with a strong emphasis on Pinot Meunier (80%) – a grape variety that gives this wine its light balance and floral flavours. The **Réserve** (30% Chardonnay and 70% of the two Pinots) and the **Cuvée Eugénie Blanc de Blancs** were both commended for their freshness and suppleness. (NM)

☎ Faniel-Filaine, 77, rue Paul-Douce, 51480 Damery, tel. 03.26.58.03.26, fax 03.26.58.03.26 🍷 by appt.

SERGE FAYE Tradition★

○ 1er Cru | 3 ha | n.c. | €11-15

Situated at Louvois (facing south from the Montagne de Reims), this 4-ha (10-acre) estate was established by Robert Faÿe in 1952 and has, since 1984, been managed by his son, Serge. Produced from the 1997 and 1998 harvests, the **Tradition** is a blend of 80% Pinot Noir and 20% Chardonnay. With its scent of pink grapefruit, this is a soft and attractive

champagne, with appropriate levels of *dosage*. The **Réserve 1er Cru**, from the harvests of 1996 and 1997, contains more Chardonnay (40%). It was specially commended for its liveliness and youth. (RM)

☎ Serge Faÿe, 2 bis, rue André-Le-Nôtre, 51150 Louvois, tel. 03.26.57.81.66, fax 03.26.59.45.12 🍷 by appt.

M FÉRAT ET FILS Cuvée Prestige 1995

○ 1er Cru | n.c. | €15-23

Pascal Férat has been managing this 2-ha (5-acre) vineyard at Vertus in the south of the Côte des Blancs since 1976. The almost blanc de blancs **95** (only 6% Pinot Noir) was commended for its rather discreet bouquet. It offers a rounded first impression and a balanced palate. (RM)

☎ Pascal Férat, rte de la Cense-Bizet, 51130 Vertus, tel. 03.26.52.25.22, fax 03.26.52.23.82 🍷 by appt.

NICOLAS FEUILLATTE Cuvée Spéciale 1996★★

○ 1er Cru | n.c. | n.c. | €15-23

These two quality champagnes bear the brand name of the prestigious wine-production centre at Chouilly, which handles grapes from 2,130 ha (5,260 acres) of vineyard. The **Cuvée Spéciale**, a blend of 40% Pinot Noir, 40% Chardonnay and 20% Meunier, particularly impressed the Jury. The tasters were enamoured of its complexity, its power and the length of its flavours, which include grapefruit, floral hints and ripe fruits. The predominantly black-grape **96 Rosé** (90% of both Pinots) was commended for its menthol-scented, lightly tannic fruitiness. (CM)

☎ Champagne Nicolas Feuillatte, BP 210, Chouilly, 51210 Montmirail, tel. 03.26.59.55.50, fax 03.26.59.55.82 🍷 by appt.

JEAN-MARIE FÉVRIER Cuvée Sélection★★

○ | 2.3 ha | n.c. | €11-15

Jean-Marie Février is based in the Aube and, with his two sons, cultivates 12 ha (30 acres) of vines. The **Sélection Cuvée**, a blanc de noirs, is floral and remarkably well balanced on the palate. It would be best served with a meal. (NM)

☎ SA Champagne Jean-Marie Février, 5, rue des Vignes, 10250 Gyé-sur-Seine, tel. 03.25.38.23.93, fax 03.25.29.94.58 🍷 by appt.

BERNARD FIGUET Cuvée de Réserve★★

○ | 4 ha | 30,000 | €11-15

Having inherited an estate established in 1930, Bernard Figuet became a grower-wine-maker after the war. Now, joined by Eric, he manages a 10.5-ha (26-acre) vineyard in the Marne Valley, at Saulchery near Charly-sur-Marne. This **Réserve Cuvée** is the product of a classic blend of half black grapes and half white, and contains 30% Meunier. The tasters were impressed by its elegance and

vitality, its floral flavours and its well-balanced, fresh palate. Indeed, it came close to receiving a coup de coeur. It awaits discovery by the readers of this Guide! (RM)
- EARL Bernard et Eric Figuet, 14, rte Nationale, 02310 Saulchery, tel. 03.23.70.16.32, fax 03.23.70.17.22
- by appt.

ALEXANDRE FILAINE

Cuvée Spéciale   0.5 ha   n.c.   €11-15

The Filaines, based at Damery in the Marne Valley, have dedicated themselves to vine-growing for five centuries. They have submitted their Special Cuvée, a blend of two-thirds black grapes and one-third white, in which the very young 1998 base wines have been aged in oak. That natural impression makes for an interestingly spicy champagne. 'A well-thought-out and carefully made wine', concluded one member of the Jury. It awaits discovery by the readers of this Guide. (RM)
- Fabrice Gass, 17, rue Poincaré, 51480 Damery, tel. 03.26.58.88.39
- by appt.

FLEURY PERE ET FILS 1995

3 ha   n.c.   €23-30

Although this Auboise brand was launched in 1929, the estate dates back to the end of the previous century. Today, Jean-Pierre Fleury manages the 13-ha (32-acre) biodynamically-run vineyard. Who knows, perhaps astrological influences favoured the 93 vintage. Anyway, this difficult vintage gained a coup de coeur last year. Produced from an identical blend of 80% Pinot Noir and 20% Chardonnay, the rounded and structured 95 had to settle for a commendation. (NM)
- Champagne Fleury, 43, Grande-Rue, 10250 Courteron, tel. 03.25.38.20.28, fax 03.25.38.24.65   by appt.

G. FLUTEAU Carte Blanche★

2 ha   18,000   €11-15

This small Auboise négociant was founded in 1935 and today manages 8 ha (20 acres) of vines. Its Carte Blanche is a blanc de noirs made from Pinot Noir. Two-thirds of the grape content is from the 1998 harvest, with the balance drawn from 1997. This champagne has an intense bouquet and palate, with red-berried fruitiness, and appears unusually well developed for its age. The rich and fresh 97 Cuvée Prestige, a blanc de blancs, received a commendation. (NM)
- SARL Hérard et Fluteau, 5, rue de la Nation, 10250 Gyé-sur-Seine, tel. 03.25.38.20.02, fax 03.25.38.24.84, e-mail champagne.fluteau@wanadoo.fr   ev. day except Sun. 9am–12 noon; 2pm–6pm

FORGET-BRIMONT

1er Cru   n.c.   €11-15

Louis Forget was a wine-grower at the beginning of the 20th century, while Eugène was the first to develop the estate's champagne. Today, Michel manages 10 ha (25 acres) of vines. The house is situated on the Montagne de Reims. Pinot Noir (60%), Meunier (25%) and Chardonnay (15%) make up this lively and fruity wine, which has both freshness and good structure. (NM)
- Forget-Brimont, rte de Louvois, 51500 Ludes, tel. 03.26.61.10.45, fax 03.26.61.11.58   ev. day except Sun. 8am–12 noon; 1.30pm–6pm; Sat. by appt.
- cl. Aug.
- Michel Forget

FORGET-CHEMIN★

1er Cru   6 ha   5,000   €11-15

Thierry Forget has followed in the footsteps of three generations of wine-producers and today cultivates a vineyard of 12 ha (30 acres) in the Marne Valley. Dominated by black grapes (75% Pinots, of which 50% is Pinot Noir), his non-vintage rosé is coloured with 17% red wine. The 1996, 1997 and 1998 harvests were drawn upon to make up this fruity, cherry-flavoured champagne. It offers a fine start and a powerful, lingering finish. Similar observations were made about the 96 Special Club, a champagne made up of half black grapes and half white, with hints of brioche and a lively, rounded character. It would be a good accompaniment to grilled lobster. (RM)
- Champagne Forget-Chemin, 15, rue Victor-Hugo, 51500 Ludes, tel. 03.26.61.12.17, fax 03.26.61.14.51, e-mail champagne.forget-chemin@voila.fr
- by appt.

FOURNAISE-THIBAUT 1995★

1 ha   5,000   €11-15

Daniel Fournaise manages a 3-ha (7-acre) vineyard at Châtillon-sur-Marne. Half-black, half-white 95 has a honeyed, well-balanced palate, and is already at its peak. The rosé also won a star. Produced from the 1997 and 1998 harvests, it owes everything to its Pinot Meunier content. With its impressive structure, discernible dosage and powerful richness, it is a champagne destined for the dinner table. (RM)
- Daniel Fournaise, 2, rue des Boucheries, 51700 Châtillon-sur-Marne, tel. 03.26.58.06.44, fax 03.26.51.60.91
- by appt.

TH. FOURNIER Cuvée de réserve

6 ha   50,000   €11-15

Thierry Fournier took over the family estate at Festigny on the left bank of the Marne in 1983. His Cuvée de Réserve is made up of three-quarters black grapes (of which a quarter are Pinot Noir), harvested in 1997 and 1998. Its flavourful palate mingles overtones of apricots and nuts. Despite its youth, this is a well-balanced champagne. (RM)
- Thierry Fournier, 8, rue du Moulin, Meuville, 51700 Festigny, tel. 03.25.58.04.23, fax 03.26.58.09.91, e-mail thierry.fournier7@wanadoo.fr
- by appt.

PHILIPPE FOURRIER Réserve★★ ■ £11-15

This champagne, a blend of 60% Pinot Noir and 40% Chardonnay, hails from the Aube. It is unquestionably the — densely structured and gently evolved. It is a glittering, pale-coloured champagne with a forthright, fruity, honeyed flavours and a fresh, citrus-fruit finish. (SR)

♠ Champagne Philippe Fourrier, rte de Bar-sur-Aube, 10200 Baroville, tel. 03.25.27.13.44, fax 03.25.27.12.49, e-mail champagne.fourrier@wanadoo.fr ▼ by appt.

FRANCOIS-BROSSOLETTE
Tradition ○ 8 ha 28,900 ■ ♦ £11-15

The Brossolettes cultivate a 12-ha (30-acre) vineyard at Polisy in the Aube. Tradition is made up of 75% Pinots to 25% Chardonnay, harvested in 1997 and 1998. This highly intense champagne starts on a lively note, but evidence of its *dosage* soon becomes apparent. The *blanc de blancs*, from the harvests of 1996, 1997 and 1998, was also commended for its supple start and fresh, lingering finish. (RM)

♠ François-Brossolette, 42, Grande-Rue, 10110 Polisy, tel. 03.25.38.57.17, fax 03.25.38.51.56 ▼ by appt.

RENE FRESNE Cuvée d'Argent
○ 2 ha 16,000 ■ ♦ £11-15

This estate, in the Montagne de Reims, was established in 1921, and taken over by Bruno Fresne in 1969. The vineyard extends over 8 ha (20 acres) of vines. The Cuvée d'Argent is made from half black grapes and half white, from the harvests of 1996 and 1997. It is floral and lemony-tasting, and its good balance makes it a suitable aperitif wine. (RM)

♠ Champagne René Fresne, 20, rue du Franc-Mousset, 51500 Sermiers, tel. 03.26.97.60.38 ▼ by appt.

FRESNET-BAUDOT ♀ Gd Cru
○ 0.5 ha 1,000 ■ Ⅲ ♦ £11-15

The Fresnets cultivate vineyards at Verzy, Mailly-Champagne and Sillery, three Grand Cru villages. Chardonnay plays the major role (60%) in their non-vintage rosé. It is pale in colour, with a pearly sheen and a slight reddish tint that can be attributed to the presence of red wine from Sillery (a vineyard with a good reputation). It exhibits distinct flavours of morello cherries and red fruits. (RM)

♠ Fresnet-Baudot, 9, rte de Puisieulx, 51500 Sillery, tel. 03.26.49.11.74, fax 03.26.49.10.72, e-mail courrier@champagne-fresnet-baudot.fr ▼ by appt.

FRESNET-JUILLET Sélection
○ 1 ha 10,000 ■ ♦ £11-15

Gérard Fresnet, who is based at Verzy in the Montagne de Reims, carved out something of a name for himself when he launched his champagne in 1954. His son Vincent, who joined the business in 1999, currently manages a vineyard of 9 ha (22 acres). The Selection is a blanc de noirs made of Pinot Noirs, harvested in 1996, 1997 and 1998. Its fine but discreet bouquet is followed by a light palate. (NM)

♠ Champagne Fresnet-Juillet, 10, rue de Beaumont, 51380 Verzy, tel. 03.26.97.93.40, fax 03.26.97.92.55, e-mail fresnet.juillet@wanadoo.fr ▼ ev. day except Sun. 9am–12 noon 2pm–5pm

MICHEL FURDYNA Prestige 1996★
○ 1 ha 5,900 ■ £11-15

Michel Furdyna started wine production in 1974 and today cultivates an 8-ha (20-acre) vineyard in the Aube. He submitted a fine 96, made of equal parts black and white grapes; a well-balanced, young, fruity champagne with overtones of white-fleshed and citrus fruits. The commended **Carte Blanche** comprises an abundance of Pinot Noir (80%), plus two white grape varieties—Chardonnay and Pinot Blanc (perfectly legal in champagne!). This wine has a complex bouquet and a well-balanced palate, despite its perceptible *dosage*. (RM)

♠ Champagne Michel Furdyna, 13, rue du Trot, 10110 Celles-sur-Ource, tel. 03.25.38.54.20, fax 03.25.38.25.63, e-mail champagne.furdyna@wanadoo.fr ▼ by appt.

GABRIEL-PAGIN ET FILS Carte d'or
○ 7.69 ha n.c. ■ £11-15

This family-run estate, founded in 1946, is located near Mareuil-sur-Ay and comprises 9.6 ha (24 acres) of vines. Their Carte d'Or is a blanc de noirs made from Pinot Noir. This champagne's dominant characteristic is strength rather than subtlety. Its fruity intensity is reminiscent of peaches, apricots and quince. The **Prestige Roger Gabriel**, made from half black grapes and half white, has a pleasant bouquet that combines notes of hawthorn, lemon and brioche – flavours that linger lightly on the palate. It too was commended. (RM)

G. DE BARFONTARC Extra Quality
○ 90 ha 150,000 ■ £11-15

This co-operative is located in the Côte des Bars district of the Aube, a short distance from the Royal Glassmakers at Bayel and the abbey at Clairvaux. The cellar, established in 1964, markets its champagne under the G. de Barfontarc brand. Extra Quality is a blend of Pinot Meunier (45%), Pinot Noir (40%) and Chardonnay, harvested in 1997 and 1998. It is a straightforward, well-balanced and reasonably lively champagne. Also commended was the **96. Exception**, a half-black and half-white, lightly evolved wine, with hints of farmyard, leather, coffee and acacia. (CM)

♠ Champagne G. de Barfontarc, rte de Bar-sur-Aube, 10200 Baroville, tel. 03.25.27.07.09, fax 03.25.27.23.00, e-mail g.de.barfontarc@wanadoo.fr ▼ ev. day except Sun. 8.30am–12 noon; 2pm–4.30pm

Pascal Gabriel, 4, rue des Remparts, 51160 Avenay-Val-d'Or, tel. 03.26.52.31.03, fax 03.26.58.87.20 ▼ ⌶ by appt.

LUC GAIDOZ Grande Réserve★ €15-23

n.c. 1,000

Luc Gaidoz set up production in 1983 at Ludes in the Montagne de Reims. His Grande Réserve is made up of three-quarters black grapes (50% Meunier), harvested in 1992 and 1993. Scented with citrus fruits, its rounded, powerful and lengthy palate make it a good wine to go with food. His **Tradition**, which exhibits pronounced Pinot Meunier characteristics (80%, supplemented by Pinot Noir and Chardonnay in equal proportions) was also commended. Produced from the harvests of 1997 and 1998, it has developed rapidly and already seems soothingly rich. It is now (2001) ready to drink. (RM)

Luc Gaidoz, 4, rue Gambetta, 51500 Ludes, tel. 03.26.61.13.73, e-mail lgaidoz@wanadoo.fr ▼ ⌶ by appt.

GAIDOZ-FORGET Réserve★ €15-23

n.c. 3,000

This Réserve has all the hallmarks of a Montagne de Reims wine-grower. Made from the harvests of 1992 and 1993, it comprises 75% black grapes (50% of which are Pinot Meunier). Its mingled flavours of acacia honey and brioche impressed the Jury. (RM)

Gaidoz-Forget, 1, rue Carnot, 51500 Ludes, tel. 03.26.61.13.03, fax 03.26.61.11.65 ⌶ by appt.

GAILLARD-GIROT €11-15

3.5 ha 25,000

This 3.5-ha (9-acre) estate based at Mardeuil near Epernay entered a non-vintage *brut* made from the 1997 harvest. This mainly black-grape champagne (85% Pinots, of which 78% is Pinot Meunier) has a fruity bouquet and palate, with aromas of pears and apples. (RM)

Gaillard-Girot, 43, rue Victor-Hugo, 51530 Mardeuil, tel. 03.26.51.64.59, fax 03.26.51.70.59, e-mail champagne-gaillard-girot@wanadoo.fr ⌶ by appt.

GARDET Charles Gardet 1995 €23-30

n.c. 32,000

This vintage *cuvée* is a tribute to Charles Gardet, who in 1895 established the company that is today based at Chigny-les-Roses in the Montagne de Reims. It is a blend of two-thirds white grapes to one-third black (both Pinots, in equal proportions). Its bouquet combines flavours of toasted bread with cocoa beans – an indication that the wine is well developed – while its balanced palate remains young and fresh. (NM)

Gardet, 13, rue Georges-Legros, 51500 Chigny-les-Roses, tel. 03.26.03.42.03, fax 03.26.03.43.95, e-mail info@champagne-gardet.com ▼ ⌶ by appt.

BERNARD GAUCHER Carte d'or €11-15

8 ha 65,000 ▪ ⌂

Established in 1972, this estate comprises a 12-ha (30-acre) vineyard at Arconville in the Aube. Its Carte d'Or is dominated by black grapes (80%), derived from the 1997 harvest, supplemented by 1996 reserve wines. It exhibits fresh, lemony and well-balanced flavours. (RM)

Bernard Gaucher, Grande-Rue, 10200 Arconville, tel. 03.25.27.87.31, fax 03.25.27.85.84 ▼ ⌶ by appt.

GAUDINAT-BOIVIN 1996★ €11-15

0.2 ha 1,600

This 96 vintage, a blend of Chardonnay and Pinot Meunier in equal proportions, was produced in the Marne Valley. It has an expressive bouquet, with flavours of toast and crystallised fruits. It is fresh on the palate, with good length and balance. (RM)

Gaudinat-Boivin, 6, rue des Vignes, Mesnil-le-Huttier, 51700 Festigny, tel. 03.26.58.01.52, fax 03.26.58.97.47 ▼ ⌶ by appt.

SERGE GAUDRILLER★ €11-5

Gd Cru 6 ha n.c.

This non-vintage *brut* hails from the Grand Cru village of Louvois, on the south slope of the Montagne de Reims. It is a blend of 70% Pinot Noir with 30% Chardonnay from the 1996 harvest. The bouquet is expressive and appealing, and the lively start on the palate is followed by impressions of roundness and balance. (RM)

Serge Gaudriller, 2, pl. de la Demi-Lune, 51150 Louvois, tel. 03.26.57.03.59, fax 03.26.57.03.59 ▼ ⌶ by appt.

GAUTHEROT★ €11-15

n.c. 4,000 ▪ ⌂

François Gautherot's two grandfathers established themselves in champagne production in 1935. This 12-ha (30-acre) Auboise estate is proud to number the French Navy amongst its customers. Produced from Pinot Noir harvested in 1988, its rosé has a profusion of red fruit flavours – cherries in particular. This is a powerful champagne of good vinosity. (RM)

François Gautherot, 29, Grande-Rue, 10110 Celles-sur-Ource, tel. 03.25.38.50.03, fax 03.25.38.58.14, e-mail gautherot@champagne-gautherot.com ▼ ⌶ by appt.

GAUTHIER 1993★ €15-23

n.c. 81,000

Founded by Charles-Alexandre Gauthier in 1858, the house was bought out a century later by Gaston Burtin (Marne et Champagne). Its half-black, half-white 93 vintage is floral, fresh and subtly well balanced. (NM)

Marre et Champagne, 22, rue Maurice-Cerveaux, 51200 Epernay, tel. 03.26.78.50.50, fax 03.26.78.50.99, e-mail ir.fo@m-c-d.fr ▼

MICHEL GENET
Brut-Esprit★

○Gd Cru 2.5 ha 26,000 €11-15

The label bears the name of the estate's founder. Today, however, the enterprise is managed by his sons, Vincent and Antoine. The 7-ha (17-acre) vineyard is planted predominantly with Chardonnay, the base grape variety of Brut-Esprit, which is to be found once again in the *Guide* this year. Its golden-green appearance, its floral and citrus-fruit bouquet and fine, elegant palate, with hazelnut overtones, all add up to an exemplary blanc de blancs. The **96 Grande Réserve Blanc de Blancs Grand Cru** is very much in the same style as the previous wine. It would perhaps be better kept for a year or so. (RM)

➤ Michel Genet,
22, rue des Partelaines, 51530 Chouilly,
tel. 03.26.55.40.51, fax 03.26.59.16.92.
e-mail champagne.genet.michel@
wanadoo.fr ○ ▼ by appt.

PIERRE GERBAIS L'Originale

○ 0.5 ha 3,000 €23-30

This house, which comprises a vineyard of almost 14 ha (35 acres) in the Aube, has submitted an appropriately named blanc de blancs. Although the information does not appear on the label, it is made not from Chardonnay but from Pinot Blanc – the only champagne of this type to appear in the *Guide*. It has an intense, golden-yellow appearance and a minerally, well-developed bouquet with leathery and gamey overtones. All is in balance on the palate. 'Atypical', was the tasters' verdict. 'A likeable curiosity'. (NM)

➤ Pierre Gerbais, 13, rue du Pont,
BP 17, 10110 Celles-sur-Ource,
tel. 03.25.38.51.29, fax 03.25.38.55.17 ▼
○ ▼ ev. day 9am–12 noon; 2pm–6pm

PIERRE GIMONNET ET FILS
Chardonnay Spécial Club 1996★

○1er Cru n.c. 19,600

The Gimonnets have been cultivating the vine since 1750, and producing wines from their grapes since 1935. Their vineyard is planted entirely with Chardonnay. Located exclusively on the Côte des Blancs, it is divided between 12 ha (30 acres) of Grand Cru land around Chouilly and Cramant, supported by some in the Premier Cru village of Cuis. The base wine of the 96 Spécial Club has not been chaptalised. It possesses floral and mineral aromas, and an eloquent mixture of white peach and vine blossom flavours on the palate. The **95 Millésime de Collection** was commended for its elegance and finesse. (RM)

➤ Pierre Gimonnet et Fils,
1, rue de la République, 51530 Cuis,
tel. 03.26.59.78.70, fax 03.26.59.79.84 ▼
○ ▼ ev. day except Sun. 8.30am–12 noon;
2pm–6pm; Sat. by appt.; cl. 15–31 Aug.

GIMONNET-GONET
Blanc de Blancs Cuvée Prestige★

○ 1 ha 5,000 €11-15

The Gimonnets and Gonets are two well-known Côte des Blancs families. Their estate comprises a 9.2-ha (23-acre) vineyard, planted mainly with Chardonnay. Two non-vintage *brut* champagnes produced from the 1997 harvest have earned places in the *Guide*. The more successful of the two is the Cuvée Prestige Blanc de Blancs. Both its bouquet and palate are seductively light, fresh and well balanced. The half-black, half-white **Tradition** was also commended by the Jury for its commanding presence on the palate. (RM)

➤ Gimonnet-Gonet,
166, rue du Gal-de-Gaulle, 51530 Cramant,
tel. 03.26.57.51.44, fax 03.26.58.00.03 ▼
○ ▼ ev. day 8am–12 noon; 1.30–7pm, Sat.
Sun. by appt.; cl. 7–25 Aug.

GIMONNET-OGER Grande Réserve

○ 10,000 €11-15

Gimonnet-Oger's Grande Réserve has a golden-green appearance and a vigorous, expressive bouquet. An impression of freshness lingers on the palate, which is redolent of fresh herbs and ferns, making for a lively, attractive champagne. (RM)

➤ Jean-Luc Gimonnet,
7, rue Jean-Mermoz, 51530 Cuis,
tel. 03.26.59.86.50, fax 03.26.59.86.51,
e-mail champagne.gimonnet-oger@
wanadoo.fr ○ ▼ by appt.

BERNARD GIRARDIN
Cuvée de Réserve★

○ 1 ha 5,000 €11-15

Ten years ago, Sandrine Brités took over from her father, who founded this estate in 1970 at Mancy behind the Côte des Blancs. Her Cuvée de Réserve, produced from 60% Chardonnay, 30% Pinot Meunier and 10% Pinot Noir, from the 1995 harvest, offers a bouquet of toasted brioche, backed up by a rounded, full, fresh and balanced palate. The **Cuvée BG** received a commendation. A blend of the three champagne grapes in identical proportions, but drawn from different years (1997, plus some 1996 and 1995 reserve wines), it too displays a brioche-scented bouquet, as well as fine presence and roundness on the palate – all the characteristics of a mature wine. (RM)

➤ Sandrine Brités-Girardin, Champagne
Bernard-Girardin, 14, Grande-Rue,
51530 Mancy, tel. 03.26.59.70.78,
fax 03.26.51.55.45, e-mail sandrine.brites@
wanadoo.fr ○ ▼ by appt.

PAUL GOBILLARD Blanc de Blancs

○Gd Cru n.c. 8,000 €15-23

Paul Gobillard, a wine-grower at Pierry during the Second Empire, has bequeathed his name to this brand. The house took on the additional role of *négociant* in 1941. It submitted a blanc de blancs of impeccable pedigree, produced from Chouilly and Cramant

Chardonnay, with a little from Mesnil-sur-Oger, harvested in 1995, 1996 and 1997. This champagne is supple, rich, vinous, complex and elegant. (NM)

☛ Paul Gobillard, Ch. de Pierry,
BP 1, 51530 Pierry, tel. 03.26.54.05.11,
fax 03.26.54.46.03 ☙ ⚕ by appt.

J.-M. GOBILLARD ET FILS
Blanc de Blancs★★

○ 1er Cru   2.5 ha 20,000 ▪ ♨ €11–15

This company's tasting cellar was set up in 1955, and is located opposite the abbey of Hautvillers, made famous by Dom Pérignon. Its vineyard extends over 25 ha (62 acres). After bestowing a *coup de cœur* last year, the Jury has this time awarded two stars to the fresh, fruity, rounded and balanced blanc de blancs, a blend of the 1997 and 1998 harvests. **Privilège des Moines** received one star. It is a blend of 70% Chardonnay and 30% Pinot Noir, from the 1995 and (mainly) 1996 harvests. The base wine was fermented in barrel with baton-stirring of the must; a vinification method that has produced a champagne of character. Flavours of white cocoa-blossom, oaky vanilla and blackcurrants, combined with a hint of menthol, mingle on the palate. (NM)

☛ Champagne J.-M. Gobillard et Fils,
38, rue de l'Eglise, BP 8, 51160 Hautvillers,
tel. 03.26.51.00.24, fax 03.26.51.00.18,
e-mail champagne-gobillard@wanadoo.fr ☙
⚕ by appt.

GODME PERE ET FILS Réserve★

○ 1er Cru   6 ha 50,000 €15–23

This 11.5-ha (28-acre) property enjoys an enviable location amidst the Grand Cru villages of Verzenay, Verzy and Beaumont-sur-Vesle and the Premiers Crus of Villers-Marmery and Villedommange. Its half-black, half-white Réserve creates quite an impression with its intensely toasty bouquet, which leads on to a complex, well-balanced palate that is showing slight signs of evolution. The **Carte Noire** Grand Cru was also commended. A blend of Pinot Noir (70%) and Chardonnay, its structure, balance and length caught the attention of the Jury. (RM)

☛ Champagne Godmé Père et Fils,
10, rue de Verzy, 51360 Verzenay,
tel. 03.26.49.48.70, fax 03.26.49.45.30 ☙
⚕ by appt.

PAUL GOERG Chardonnay 1996

○ 1er Cru   n.c. 102,000 ▪ €15–23

Founded in 1950, this group of wine-producers at Vertus on the Côte des Blancs comprises around 100 members collectively cultivating 120 ha (296 acres) of vines. Their brand was established in 1985. Balanced, fine, floral and lingering, the 96 blanc de blancs narrowly missed out on a star. The **95 Cuvée du Centenaire** was also commended by the Jury. Although it shows some evidence of development, it was praised for its buttery, toasty flavours and its elegance. (CM)

☛ Champagne Paul Goerg,
4, pl. du Mont-Chenil, 51130 Vertus,
tel. 03.26.52.15.31, fax 03.26.52.23.96,
e-mail champagne-goerg@wanadoo.fr ☙
⚕ by appt.

FRANCOIS GONET
Blanc de Blancs Réserve 1995

○   2 ha 10,000 ▪ €11–15

In the Côte des Blancs there are many Gonets, so forenames are significant. François Gonet has been a champagne-producer for about 30 years, and has gradually expanded his vineyards in the Marne Valley. His Réserve Blanc de Blancs is produced from Chardonnay harvested in 1995. Powerful, ripe flavours of apples and pears emerge on both the bouquet and the palate of this fresh, young champagne. (RM)

☛ François Gonet, 5, rue du Stade,
51190 Le Mesnil-sur-Oger,
tel. 03.26.57.53.71, fax 03.26.57.93.66 ☙
⚕ by appt.

MICHEL GONET Blanc de Blancs★

○ Gd Cru   30 ha 100,000 ▪ €11–15

Six generations of vine-growers have preceded Michel Gonet, who today cultivates 40 ha (99 acres) of vines, not only on the Côte des Blancs, but also at Vinchy in the Sézannais and at Montgueux and Fravaux (Pinot Noir) in the Aube. (This is to say nothing of his Bordeaux vineyards!) This Grand Cru blanc de blancs is made from a blend of Chardonnays from Oger and Mesnil-sur-Oger, harvested in 1997, 1998 and 1999. A bouquet of nuts and white peach is followed by a fine palate that combines delicacy, freshness and intensity. (RM)

☛ SCEV Michel Gonet et Fils, 196, av. Jean-Jaurès, 51190 Avize, tel. 03.26.57.50.56, fax 03.26.57.91.98, e-mail vinsgonet@wanadoo.fr ☙ ⚕ by appt.

PHILIPPE GONET Blanc de Blancs★★

○   3 ha 10,000 ▪ €15–23

Here is yet another Gonet from the Côte des Blancs, this one with a vineyard of around 20 ha (49 acres). His blanc de blancs is a blend of the 1996 and 1997 harvests. Firm, round and full-flavoured, it would go well with a sauced fish dish. The **96 Spécial Club Blanc de Blancs** receives a star for its elegance, which is enhanced by the characteristic liveliness of this vintage. (RM)

☛ Champagne Philippe Gonet, 1, rue de la Brèche-d'Oger, 51190 Le Mesnil-sur-Oger, tel. 03.26.57.53.47, fax 03.26.57.51.03, email philippe.gonet@wanadoo.fr ☙
⚕ by appt.

GONET-MEDEVILLE An 2000

○   0.5 ha 1,000

Bordeaux and Champagne have joined forces in this enterprise, with the marriage in 2000 of Xavier Gonet (of the Côte des Blancs Gonets) to Julie Médeville (of the Sauternes family that owns Châteaux Gilette and Les Justices). Their recently established estate comprises 8 ha (20 acres) of vines at Bisseuil, not far from Mareuil-sur-Ay. The non-vintage *brut* is a white-dominated blend (90% Chardonnay) drawn from the 1995 and 1996 harvests. A bouquet of considerable youth and freshness. (RM)

Xavier Gonet, 1, chem. de la Cavotte, 51150 Bisseuil, tel. 03.26.57.75.60, fax 03.56.76.28.43 by appt.

GONET SULCOVA★   1 ha   n.c.   €15-23

This brand, like that above, was also born of a marriage, having 15 ha (37 acres) of vines at its disposal. The rosé is a rosé de noirs, produced from Pinot Noirs harvested in 1996 and 1997. It has a slightly aged, evolved appearance, with aromas of musk and ripe wild strawberries preceding a powerful and structured palate. The **Vincent Gonet** (a blend of 60% Pinot Noir with 40% Chardonnay, from the years 1996 to 1998) received a commendation from the Jury. This rich, powerful and lingering champagne would make a suitable accompaniment to food. (RM)

SCEV Beauregard, 13, rue Henri-Martin, 51200 Epernay, tel. 03.26.54.37.63, fax 03.26.54.87.73, e-mail gonet-sulcova@wanadoo.fr by appt.

Vincent Gonet

GOSSET   Grand Millésime 1996★★   n.c.   200,000   €46-76

An old-established family from Ay handed on its famous name to Béatrice Cointreau in 1993. This *cuvée*, which has not undergone malolactic fermentation, is made up of 62% Chardonnay and 38% Pinot Noir. Elegant aromas of spices, vanilla and oak are reinforced on the palate by a flavour of crystallised lemon zest. The **Grand Rosé**, a blend of 56% Chardonnay with 35% Pinot Noir, is coloured with 9% Grand Cru red wine. This champagne was commended for its roundness and length. (NM)

Champagne Gosset, 69, rue Jules-Blondeau, BP 7, 51160 Ay, tel. 03.26.56.99.53, fax 03.26.51.55.88, e-mail info@champagne-gosset.com by appt.

GOSSET-BRABANT   1er Cru   0.5 ha   3,000   €11-15

This 7.5-ha (19-acre) estate was established in 1930. It is situated in the Grand Cru village of Ay, which has a fine reputation for Pinot Noir. The rosé blend is dominated by Pinot Noir (with only 20% Chardonnay), drawn from the years 1997 and 1998. It is coloured with 12% Ay red wine. Its bouquet releases red fruit aromas (wild strawberries in particular), which continue through to the supple, fresh palate. The **Cuvée de Réserve Grand Cru d'Ay** was also commended by the Jury. Flavours of red fruits are just as apparent within the bouquet as on the palate. (RM)

Gosset-Brabant, 23, bd du Mal-de-Lattre-de-Tassigny, 51160 Ay, tel. 03.26.55.17.42, fax 03.26.54.31.33, e-mail gosset-brabant@wanadoo.fr by appt.

GOUSSARD ET DAUPHIN Prestige★   2 ha   5,800   €11-15

In 1989 the oenologist Didier Goussard joined forces with his brother-in-law in order to make champagne. Their vineyard comprises 7 ha (17 acres). Chardonnay dominates this Prestige, despite the fact that the estate is near Les Riceys, more famous for its Pinot Noir. This year, the champagne is a blend of wines from the years 1995, 1996 and 1997. Scents of flowers and white-fleshed fruits mingle on the bouquet, while the palate is both vigorous and well balanced. (RM)

Goussard et Dauphin, GAEC du Val de Sarce, 2, chem. Saint-Vincent, 10340 Avirey-Lingey, tel. 03.25.29.30.03, fax 03.25.29.85.96, e-mail goussard.dauphin@wanadoo.fr by appt.

GOUTORBE Traditional Cuvée★   n.c.   4,000   €11-15

René Goutorbe runs an 18-ha (44-acre) vineyard in the famous Grand Cru village of Ay. His Traditional Cuvée this year owes everything to Pinot Noir. A structured, balanced, honeyed champagne, it would go well with grilled fish. The commended **95 Grand Cru** (with its emphasis on black grapes) has floral, brioche flavours and would make a good aperitif. Notably, both *cuvées* have a discernible *dosage*. (RM)

René Goutorbe, 11, rue Jeanson, 51160 Ay, tel. 03.26.55.19.47, fax 03.26.54.85.11 by appt.

ALFRED GRATIEN 1991★   n.c.   30,000   €38-46

The house, founded in 1864 by Alfred Gratien, still remains in the hands of his descendants, Alain and Gérard Seydoux. Members of the Jaeger family, who manage the cellar, have also handed responsibility down the line for three generations – a clear indication of the family's dedication to tradition. The company adheres to certain traditional techniques, such as vinification in small 205-litre (54-gal) oak barrels and secondary fermentation under cork. This 91 vintage, produced from all three champagne grapes, has reached its peak. It exudes scents of honey and beeswax, and seems sweet and well rounded on the palate. Its slightly acidic character makes it a good choice for desserts. The **96 Cuvée Paradis**, also made from the three grape varieties, owes a great deal to its Chardonnay content (61%). First impressions are soft and lingering, and it received a commendation. (NM)

Champagne Alfred Gratien, 30, rue Maurice-Cerveaux, BP 3, 51201 Epernay Cedex, tel. 03.26.54.53.44, fax 03.26.54.38.20, e-mail contact@alfredgratien.com by appt.

Champagne

GRUET 1996

○ n.c. 33,438 ■ ♦ €11-15

Claude Gruet's predecessors were already cultivating vines in the Côte des Bars during the era of the Sun King. Today, the family estate comprises 10 ha (25 acres). This fresh, aromatic and well-balanced 96 is composed of Pinot Noir (75%), supplemented by Chardonnay. The **95** vintage, which is made from the same grape varieties in the same proportions, exhibits a bouquet and palate of buttered brioche and honey. It too received a commendation. (NM)

➤ SARL Champagne Gruet,
48, Grande-Rue, 10110 Buxeuil,
tel. 03.25.38.54.94, fax 03.25.38.51.84,
e-mail champagne-gruet@wanadoo.fr ☑
☑ ev. day 8.30am–12 noon; 2pm–6pm; Sat. Sun. by appt.; cl. w/c. 15 Aug.

MAURICE GRUMIER Tradition

○ 6 ha n.c. ■ €11-15

Situated in the Marne valley at Venteuil, this family-run estate encompasses 7.5 ha (19 acres) of vines. Although the Maurice Grumier label has been around since 1945, this enterprise also produces champagnes under a different brand name. The estate, managed by Guy Grumier since 1968, is now run jointly with Fabien. Their Tradition *cuvée* is a blanc de noirs, produced from the two Pinots (with 80% Meunier), harvested in 1997 and 1998. This is a simple and well-balanced champagne, with flavours of pears and apples. The **Réserve**, a blend of the three champagne grapes in equal proportions, from the years 1996 and 1997, was commended for its fruity freshness. (RM)

➤ Guy Grumier, 13, rte d'Arty,
51480 Venteuil, tel. 03.26.58.48.10,
fax 03.26.58.66.08 ☑ ☑ by appt.

RENE GUE Blanc de Blancs Carte d'or★

○ 0.6 ha 5,000 €11-15

This estate, close to Epernay, was established in 1954, and today consists of a 6.5-ha (16-acre) vineyard. Its non-vintage blanc de blancs is drawn from the 1996 harvest. It attracted the attention of the Jury with its complex bouquet of fading honey and caramel notes. Firmness and length distinguish the biscuity palate. (RM)

➤ Philippe Gué, 2, rue de Monthelon,
51530 Chouilly, tel. 03.26.54.50.32,
fax 03.26.54.01.45 ☑ ☑ by appt.

P. GUERRE ET FILS Tradition

○ 8.5 ha n.c. ⑩ €11-15

The Guerres, vine-growers on the right bank of the Marne valley for several generations, became grower-wine-makers in the 1950s. Today, they cultivate vineyards split between eight different *terroirs*. Their Tradition is a classic blend of the two Pinots (60%) with Chardonnay (40%), from the harvests of 1996, 1997 and 1998. It is a fresh, young and fairly elegant champagne. (RM)

➤ Michel Guerre, 3, rue de Champagne,
51480 Venteuil, tel. 03.26.58.62.72,
fax 03.26.58.64.06 ☑
☑ ev. day 9am–11.30am; 2pm–5pm

ROMAIN GUISTEL Réserve

○ 1 ha 10,000 ■ €11-15

This 5-ha (12.4-acre) estate in the Marne Valley submitted a non-vintage *brut* blanc de noirs dominated by Pinot Meunier (70%), harvested in 1997 and 1998. A lightly developed bouquet of brioche is followed by a well-balanced palate with flavours of preserved fruits. (NM)

➤ Champagne Romain Guistel, 1, rue des Remparts-de-l'Ouest, 51480 Damery,
tel. 03.26.58.40.40 ☑ ☑ by appt.

HAMM Sélection★

○ n.c. 40,000 ■ €11-15

Henri Hamm, who became a wine-producer in 1910, established his own *négociant* business in 1930. His descendants continue to make a success of this Ay-based company. The Selection *cuvée*, for which the base wines have not undergone malolactic fermentation, is a blend of mainly black grapes (80% of the two Pinots, in equal proportions). A bouquet of pears and citrus fruits continues on to the silky, well-rounded palate. (NM)

➤ Champagne Hamm,
16, rue N.-Philipponnat, 51160 Ay,
tel. 03.26.55.44.19, fax 03.26.51.98.68 ☑
☑ ev. day 9am–12 noon; 2pm–6pm; Sat. Sun. by appt.

HARLIN Grand Rosé

○ 1.8 ha 15,000 €15-23

'Maison C. Harlin et Cie was founded in 1848,' according to the label of this grower-wine-maker from Tours-sur-Marne. The bouquet and palate of this onion-skin-coloured rosé are reminiscent of small red berries, and are distinguished by roundness and finesse. Also commended was the **Grand Chardonnay**, a noticeably more evolved blanc de blancs with honeyed and pronounced spicy flavours. (NM)

➤ Harlin, 41, av. de Champagne,
51150 Tours-sur-Marne, tel. 03.26.51.88.95,
fax 03.26.58.96.31 ☑ ☑ by appt.

HARLIN PERE ET FILS

Prestige 1995★★

○ 2 ha 1,500 ■ €11-15

This estate in the Marne Valley encompasses 8 ha (20 acres) of vines. Its Prestige, a blend of 40% Chardonnay and 60% Pinot Noir, reflects all the excellent characteristics of this particular year. It possesses a fine bouquet of crystallised fruits and vanilla, and a palate that is as powerful as it is well balanced. The **Grand Cru**, made from 1997 wines, is a blend of Pinot Noir and Chardonnay in the same proportions as the previous wine. It offers a lively start, which then softens on the palate. For this it earned a recommendation. (RM)

♠ Harlin Père et Fils, 8, rue de la Fontaine, 51700 Port-à-Binson, tel. 03.26.58.34.38, fax 03.26.58.63.78 ▼ ev. day except Sun. 9am-12 noon, 2pm-6pm

JEAN-NOEL HATON
Cuvée Prestige★★
n.c.　n.c.　€ 15-23

This estate, founded in 1928 at Damery in the Marne Valley, comprises 23 ha (57 acres) of vines. The half-black, half-white Cuvée Prestige exudes aromas of crystallised quince, toasted bread and brioche on the bouquet, and fruity notes on the palate backed by hints of pepper and menthol. The rosé, which is produced from three-quarters black grapes (including 50% Meunier), also impressed the Jury. This champagne, with its red and black fruit flavours, has an invigoratingly lively character. (NM)

♠ Jean-Noël Haton, tel. 03.26.58.40.45, 51480 Damery, tel. 03.26.58.63.55 ▼ by appt. fax 03.26.58.63.55

LUDOVIC HATTE
Réserve
7 ha　10,000　€ 11-15

This is a 7-ha (17-acre) estate located in four Grand Cru villages on the Montagne de Reims. Its Réserve contains 80% black grapes, and is derived from the 1995 and 1996 harvests. It creates a lively first impression, with brioche notes on both the bouquet and palate – a very direct style of champagne. (RM)

♠ Ludovic Hatté, 3, rue Thiers, 51360 Verzenay, tel. 03.26.49.43.94, fax 03.26.49.81.96 ▼ by appt.

MARC HEBRART
1er Cru　Prestige 1995★★
5,000　€ 15-23

Marc Hébrart, who established this estate in 1963, was joined by his son Jean-Paul in 1983. A highly fragmented vineyard, it comprises no fewer than 65 plots of vines, scattered among six different villages. The 95 Prestige is a classic blend of 60% Pinot Noir and 40% Chardonnay, with both grape varieties leaving their mark on the complex, richly fruity, buttery, brioche-scented bouquet. One taster, impressed by its intensity, elegance and length, suggested awarding it a coup de coeur. 'I shall be buying this', he wrote in his notes. The vigorous quality of the wine only adds to its overall attraction. (RM)

♠ Marc Hébrart, 18-20, rue du Pont, 51160 Mareuil-sur-Aÿ, tel. 03.26.52.60.75, fax 03.26.52.92.64 ▼ by appt.

HEIDSIECK & CO MONOPOLE
Diamant bleu 1995★
n.c.　30,000　€ 30-38

Founded by Florens Louis Heidsieck in 1785, this house has been highly esteemed since before the First World War, as a supplier to several European courts, including that of Tsar Nicholas II. The enterprise changed hands several times during the course of the 20th century. In 1923, it was taken over by Edouard Mignot, who added the 'Monopole' to the brand name. The estate passed to Munm, then part of the Seagram group, in 1972, before being finally bought out by Vranken in 1996. The present Diamant Bleu is made from half black grapes and half white, of a particularly prestigious year. This powerful, lingering, buttery, brioche-flavoured 95 is at its peak. Two other champagnes received commendations. The **Blue Top** is a classic non-vintage *brut*, made from a blend of the three champagne varieties (including 80% Pinots), while the **96 Gold Top** is a blend of 60% Pinot Noir and 40% Chardonnay. The latter is a champagne of great vitality, albeit with a closing note of slight bitterness. (NM)

♠ Heidsieck & Co Monopole, 17, av. de Champagne, 51200 Epernay, tel. 03.26.59.50.50, fax 03.26.52.19.65 ▼
♠ P-F Vranken

D. HENRIET-BAZIN 1993★
Gd Cru　3 ha　10,000　€ 11-15

This estate has been around for more than a century. It enjoys the benefits of both a black-grape Grand Cru vineyard at Verzenay, and an excellent white-grape 1er Cru at Villers-Marmery. Its vineyards cover a total area of 7.5 ha (19 acres). The estate submitted an unusual vintage – a rare 93, blended from 70% Pinot Noir and 30% Chardonnay. This champagne offers fruity notes of apple and lemon on both bouquet and palate, a fortnight-opening impression announces, a palate of great intensity and length. (RM)

♠ D. Henriet-Bazin, 9 bis, rue Dom-Pérignon, 51380 Villers-Marmery, tel. 03.26.97.96.81, fax 03.26.97.97.30 ▼ by appt.

HENRIOT
Cuvée des Enchanteleurs 1988★
103 ha　50,000　€ 46-76

This champagne owes its origin to a widow: Appoline Henriot lost her husband in the year that she founded the estate, in 1808. Today, the vineyard is managed by Joseph Henriot, who gives it his undivided attention, despite having other commitments in Burgundy. The particularly light Cuvée des Enchanteleurs is dominated by white grapes (56% Chardonnay to 44% Pinot Noir). The 88 vintage has distinctive, well-developed aromas of undergrowth and game backed up by toasty notes but, as an ensemble, shows a restrained quality that made a favourable impression on the Jury. The palate is remarkably fresh for a 13-year-old champagne. Another star was awarded to the 95 (47% Chardonnay to 53% Pinot Noir), which delighted the tasters with its balance and freshness. (NM)

♠ Champagne Henriot, 3, pl. des Droits-de-l'Homme, B.P. 457, 51066 Reims, tel. 03.26.89.53.00, fax 03.26.89.53.10 ▼ by appt.

PAUL HERARD
Cuvée Paul
1.5 ha　12,000　€ 11-15

This champagne pays tribute to its founder, Paul Hérard. Nowadays, this Auboise house, established in 1925, is run by his descendants, who cultivate 11 ha (27 acres) in the Côte des Bars. It is a classic blend of 60% Chardonnay and 40% Pinot Noir, harvested in 1997, a wine of character, fresh and long, with a certain smoky note to it. Also commended was the **Blanc de Noirs**, produced from the 1998 and 1999 harvests. Its straightforward start, and its overall balance and vivacity, despite a hint of bitterness, are what caught the attention of the Jury. (NM)

☛ Champagne Paul Hérard,
33, Grande-Rue, 10250 Neuville-sur-Seine,
tel. 03.25.38.20.14, fax 03.25.38.25.05 Ⓥ
Ⓨ by appt.

DIDIER HERBERT

○1er Cru   4 ha   40.000   ▪ ♠   €11-15

Didier Herbert elected to become a *négociant*, managing a vineyard of 7 ha (17 acres) at Rilly-la-Montagne. His *brut* is produced from the three champagne grapes in equal proportions, harvested in 1997 and 1998. This complex champagne particularly impressed the Jury, with its combination of floral and mineral flavours. It is suitable for serving with chicken. Also commended was the **96 Platinum I**" Cru, which is a blend of 60% Chardonnay and 40% Pinot Noir. It combines flavours of citrus fruits with toasty, peppery notes. Its only drawback is its youth. (NM)

☛ Didier Herbert, 32, rue de Reims,
51500 Rilly-la-Montagne,
tel. 03.26.03.41.53, fax 03.26.03.44.64,
e-mail champagne-herbert@terre-net.fr Ⓥ
Ⓨ by appt.

STEPHANE HERBERT

○   n.c.   n.c.   €15-23

Stéphane Herbert is based in the Montagne de Reims area. The non-vintage *brut* he submitted has a fruity bouquet and a honeyed, balanced palate of fine length. The overall impression is enhanced by a hint of maturity. (RM)

☛ Stéphane Herbert, 11, rue Roger
Salengro, 51500 Rilly-la-Montagne,
tel. 03.26.03.49.93, fax 03.26.02.01.39
Ⓨ by appt.

M. HOSTOMME Blanc de Blancs

○Gd Cru   6 ha   50.000   ▪ ♠   €11-15

This *négociant* manages 10 ha (25 acres) of vines in a prime location in the Chardonnay-dedicated Grand Cru village of Chouilly. The estate was commended twice for its aperitif-style champagnes. The first is a non-vintage blend of wines from the years 1997 and 1998. Its honeyed bouquet and palate exude charming finesse. The second, an expressive **95 Blanc de Blancs Grand Cru**, was singled out for its balance, and particularly for its length. (NM)

☛ M. Hostomme et Fils,
5, rue de l'Allée, 51530 Chouilly,
tel. 03.26.55.40.79, fax 03.26.55.08.55,
e-mail champagne.hostomme@wanadoo.fr
Ⓥ Ⓨ by appt.

HUGUENOT-TASSIN Cuvée Tradition

○   n.c.   25.000   ▪   €11-15

This grower-wine-maker cultivates a mixture of grape varieties that deserves to be commended for its originality: Chardonnay, Pinot Blanc and Pinot Noir (with 50% old vine stocks). Pinot Blanc and Pinot Noir contribute in equal proportions to the Cuvée Tradition (45% of each, with 10% Chardonnay). Its subtle, floral bouquet is complemented by lychee and citrus-fruit flavours. Not a hint of *dosage* can be detected on the well-balanced palate. (RM)

☛ Benoît Huguenot, 4, rue du Val-Lune,
10110 Celles-sur-Ource, tel. 03.25.38.54.49,
fax 03.25.38.50.40 Ⓥ Ⓨ by appt.

IVERNEL Prestige★

○   n.c.   50.000   ▪ ♠   €15-23

Philipponnat, Gosset and Ivernel are three well-established Aÿ families, dating back to the 15th century. The ancestors of Gustave Ivernel, founder of the brand in 1890, were already well known throughout France for their wines in Renaissance times. Ivernel was taken over by Gosset in 1989. The mainly black-grape Prestige is made up of 30% Chardonnay with 55% Pinot Noir and 15% Meunier. It is fresh, rounded and well structured. (NM)

☛ Champagne Ivernel, B.P. 15, 51160 Aÿ,
tel. 03.26.55.21.10, fax 03.26.51.55.88 Ⓥ
Ⓨ by appt.

ROBERT JACOB 1996★

○   4 ha   7,000   ▪ ♠   €11-15

The brand was created by Robert Jacob in 1950, and taken over by his son Daniel ten years later. The 6-ha (15-acre) vineyard is located among four villages in the Bar and Aube districts. Two of the estate's champagnes received a star each. The lightly charred, subtly scented 96 is made up of two-thirds Chardonnay to one-third Pinot Noir. It is a lively and extremely youthful wine. The same description applies to the **Prestige**, a blanc de blancs from the harvest of 1996. This champagne reveals exotic fruit flavours with biscuity undertones. Notwithstanding these characteristics, it too remains a very young wine. (RM)

☛ Champagne R. Jacob, 14, rue de Morres,
10110 Merrey-sur-Arce, tel. 03.25.29.83.74,
fax 03.25.29.34.86 Ⓥ Ⓨ by appt.
☛ Daniel Jacob

JACQUART

Blanc de Blancs Mosaïque 1996★★

○   n.c.   n.c.   ▪ ♠   €23-30

Established in 1962, this important co-operative brings together 850 members and cultivates 1,000 ha (2,470 acres) of vines. The estate submitted a 96 blanc de blancs, a champagne representative of both its grape variety and its vintage, in that it has a lively start, fresh finish, fine balance and good length. The half-black, half-white **92 Tradition**, a fruity wine with a well-developed bouquet, was awarded one star. The non-vintage **Brut**

de Nominée was also commended for its lightly acidic, lemony characteristics. (CM)
- SA Jacquart, 6, rue de Mars, 51100 Reims, tel. 03.26.07.88.40, fax 03.26.07.12.07, e-mail jacquart@ebc.net

ANDRE JACQUART ET FILS
Blanc de Blancs 1996★★

Gd Cru   1.5 ha   10,000   €15-23

Michel Jacquart originally established a 1.8-ha (4.5-acre) vineyard. His son André and his grandchildren, Chantal and Pierre, have been so successful at vine-growing that the third generation now finds itself in charge of an area of 20 ha (49 acres) of vines in the Côte des Blancs. They submitted a fine 96 vintage. Unlike certain other wines of this year, this champagne seems not to be marked by the characteristic 96 acidity. Its freshness, moreover, remains impressive. It has a floral, hawthorn-scented bouquet and a fine lingering palate. (RM)
- André Jacquart et Fils, 23, rue des Zalieux, 51190 Le Mesnil-sur-Oger, tel. 03.26.57.52.29, fax 03.26.57.78.14, e-mail info@champagne.a-jacquart-et-fils.com
- by appt.

YVES JACQUES Tradition Réserve

10 ha   5,000   €11-15

The Jacques family estate was founded in 1932 at Baye in the Sézannais. Its 10-ha (25-acre) vineyard is located not only at Baye, but also at Sézanne, Troissy and Argançon in the Aube. Their Tradition Réserve is a blend of 75% Pinots (of which 50% is Meunier) and 25% Chardonnay, drawn from the years 1993-1995. With its flavours of grapefruit and other ripe fruits, it exhibits a distinct complexity. This year (2001), it is ready to drink. The Sélection Réserve also impressed the jury. Drawn from the harvests of 1994, 1995 and 1996, this vanilla-scented and fruity blanc de blancs contains a slight hint of bitterness, but nonetheless received a commendation. (RM)
- Champagne Yves Jacques, 1, rue de Montpertuis, 51270 Baye, tel. 03.26.52.80.77, fax 03.26.52.80.77

JACQUESSON ET FILS Perfection★

n.c.   n.c.   €23-30

Founded at Châlons in 1798, Jacquesson et Fils is one of Champagne's oldest houses. In the past, it has enjoyed great prosperity, producing around one million bottles in 1867, but with output declining thereafter and, at one point, almost ceasing altogether. Since 1974, production has been boosted by the Chiquet family of Dizy. A third of the base wine for the Perfection has been aged in oak. It is made up of 62% Pinots (40% Meunier and 22% Pinot Noir) and 38% Chardonnay, and consists of a blend of premiers crus and grands crus, harvested between 1995 and 1997. Its overall impression is one of balance and lightness. (NM)
- Champagne Jacquesson et Fils, 68, rue du Colonel-Fabien, 51530 Dizy, tel. 03.26.55.68.11, fax 03.26.51.06.25, e-mail champagne.jacquesson@wanadoo.fr
- by appt.

JACQUINET-DUMEZ★

1er Cru   1 ha   n.c.   €11-15

Following in the footsteps of Henri Dumez and Jean-Guy Jacquinet, Olivier Dumez represents the third generation of grower-wine-makers to work this estate near Reims. He cultivates 7 ha (17 acres) of vines, exclusively classified as Premier Cru. His rosé is composed entirely of Pinots (65% Pinot Noir and 25% Meunier, with 10% Coteaux Champenois red wine). This exceedingly pale rosé has mingled aromas of raspberries and blackcurrants in the bouquet, followed by a supple, mature palate with honeyed overtones. A star also goes to the half-white, half-black (Pinot Noir) 96 Cuvée l'Excellence. This is a fairly mature champagne, with toasty flavours and good structure. It would make an excellent aperitif. (RM)
- Jacquinet-Dumez, 26, rue de Reims, 51370 Les Mesneux, tel. 03.26.36.25.25, fax 03.26.36.58.92, e-mail jacquinet-dumez@aol.com
- by appt.

JAEGER-LIGNEUL Sélection

n.c.   n.c.   €11-15

This family-run enterprise is based at Reuil in the Marne Valley. Its predominantly lemon-flavoured Sélection is a blanc de noirs made from Pinot Meunier. It is a supple and well-rounded champagne. (RM)
- Jaeger-Ligneul, 2 bis, Grande-Rue, 51480 Reuil, tel. 03.26.58.02.68, fax 03.26.58.02.68
- by appt.

PIERRE JAMAIN Cuvée Caroline★

1 ha   7,700   €11-15

The estate was established by Pierre Jamain in 1962, and taken over by his daughter Elisabeth in 1985. The vineyard is located in the extreme south of the Marne, on the Aube border. Although it does not state as much on the label, the Cuvée Caroline is a blanc de blancs, produced from the 1997 harvest. This extremely youthful, well-balanced champagne, with its flavours of white-fleshed fruits and nuts, should be served as an aperitif. (RM)
- EARL Pierre Jamain, 1, rue des Tuileries, 51260 La Celle-sur-Chantemerle, tel. 03.26.80.21.64, fax 03.26.80.29.32
- by appt.

E. JAMART ET CIE

n.c.   5,000   €11-15

Founded by Emilien Jamart in 1934, this house, with its head office at Saint-Martin-d'Ablois, south of Epernay, remains a family-run operation. Its intensely dark-coloured rosé, made exclusively from Pinot Meunier harvested in 1997 and 1998, was commended for its flavours of raspberries and redcurrants. Also commended was the

Réserve, a blend of 80% Meunier and 20% Chardonnay that exhibits a lively, floral character. Both champagnes would make good aperitifs. (NM)

- E. Jamart et Cie, 13, rue Marcel-Soyeux, 51530 Saint-Martin-d'Ablois, tel. 03.26.59.92.78, fax 03.26.59.95.23, e-mail champagne.jamart@wanadoo.fr
- ev. day 9am-12 noon; 2pm-6pm; Sun. by appt., cl. 15-31 Aug.
- J.-Michel Oudart

JANISSON-BARADON ET FILS
Collection du Millénaire 1996★

1 ha   5,148   €15-23

Georges Baradon and his son-in-law established this champagne in 1922. The company tradition was carried on by Michel Janisson, and then by his son Richard and grandson Cyril. The 70% vintage is a blend of 30% Pinot Noir to 70% Chardonnay. It has mingled flavours of caramel and cooked fruits, and is powerful on the palate. (RM)

- SCEV Janisson-Baradon, 65, rue Chaude-Ruelle et 2, rue des Vignerons, 51200 Epernay, tel. 03.26.54.45.85, fax 03.26.54.25.54, e-mail info@champagne-janisson.com by appt.
- M. et C. Janisson

RENE JARDIN Blanc de Blancs Vieilles vignes Cuvée Louis René★★
Gd Cru   2 ha   16,000   €15-23

René Jardin started producing champagne in 1889. His successors expanded the enterprise, and today cultivate 22 ha (54 acres) of the three champagne grape varieties, located in several *terroirs*: Bouzy and Les Riceys, the Côte des Blancs and the Marne Valley. The Cuvée Louis René narrowly missed out on a *coup de coeur*. This champagne is produced from 40-year-old Chardonnay vines, harvested in 1993 and 1995. Its complex, intense bouquet, with its attractive brioche aromas, made a big impression on the Jury. The **rosé**, which is a rosé de noirs from Pinot Noir harvested in 1997 and 1998, takes its colour from a red wine that is also derived from old vines. This champagne received a commendation for its pleasantly soft bouquet, which includes hints of undergrowth. (RM)

- SCEV Champagne René Jardin, 3, rue Charpentier-Laurain, 51190 Le Mesnil-sur-Oger, tel. 03.26.57.50.26, fax 03.26.57.98.22, e-mail contact@champagne-jardin.fr by appt.

JEANMAIRE Cuvée Blanc de Blancs
n.c.   80,000   €15-23

Founded by André Jeanmaire in 1933, this enterprise was taken over by the Trouillards in 1981, with Oudinot and Beaumet having an equal holding. The 121-ha (299-acre) Trouillard vineyard produces three very similar branded champagnes, with the blanc de blancs being Jeanmaire's brainchild. It is firm and fresh, distinguished by the finesse of its citrus fruit and honey flavours, and by its striking youthfulness. (NM)

- Champagne Jeanmaire, 3, rue Malakoff, 51207 Epernay, tel. 03.26.59.50.10, fax 03.26.54.78.52, e-mail champagne.jeanmaire@wanadoo.fr
- J. Trouillard

RENE JOLLY Blanc de noirs
n.c.   n.c.   €11-15

The Jollys manage this 10-ha (25-acre) Aube vineyard, originally founded in 1737. René Jolly, creator of the brand, still insists, at the age of 87, on manual *remuage* for his champagnes. The estate submitted this blanc de noirs, produced entirely from Pinot Noir. It offers a fresh opening impression and a pleasing, rounded, honeyed palate. The **rosé**, a blend of Pinot Noir and Chardonnay, was singled out for its raspberry and blackcurrant flavours and its lively character. (RM)

- Hervé Jolly, 10, rue de la Gare, 10110 Landreville, tel. 03.25.38.50.91, fax 03.25.38.30.51 by appt.

BERTRAND JOREZ Prestige★
1er Cru   n.c.   n.c.   €11-15

Jorez Prestige contains 40% Chardonnay and 43% Pinot Meunier, with a balance of Pinot Noir, harvested in 1996. Its fresh, floral bouquet heralds an expressive and well-balanced palate. It would go well with white fish or as an aperitif (RC)

- EARL Bertrand Jorez, 13, rue de Reims, 51500 Ludes, tel. 03.26.61.14.05, fax 03.26.61.14.96 by appt.

JEAN JOSSELIN Blanc de Blancs 1996
0.84 ha   1,876   €15-23

Jean-Pierre Josselin took over in 1980 from a long line of vine-growers who have been established in the Aube since the Second Empire. The estate covers 10 ha (25 acres) of vines, not far from Les Riceys. Its 96 blanc de blancs was commended for its minerally, charred bouquet and for its clean start. Similar observations were made about the **Tradition**, a blend of 60% Pinot Noir and 40% Chardonnay, harvested in 1998. This champagne exhibits a supple palate of fruity, smoky flavours. (RM)

- Jean-Pierre Josselin, 14, rue des Vannes, 10250 Gyé-sur-Seine, tel. 03.25.38.25.00, fax 03.25.38.25.00 by appt.

KRUG★★
1988★★

n.c.   n.c.   -€76

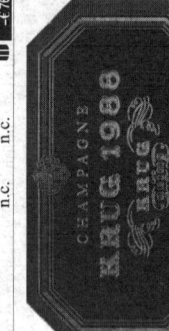

Founded in 1843, the house of Krug focuses on the upper end of the champagne market. Although the house came under the umbrella of LVMH in 1991, the Krug master-blenders refused to go with the flow of a larger corporation, preferring instead to stick to the tried and tested formula on which their fine reputation was built. Their record reflects these standards: five champagnes listed with two stars (see also the next entry) and numerous *coups de coeur* all over the place... These are precious and expensive *cuvées*, all figuring in the highest price bracket. This 88 vintage, a blend of 50% Pinot Noir, 18% Meunier and 32% Chardonnay, delighted the Jury with its power, balance and length. It has an extremely youthful appearance for its age, and has been oaked to perfection. It was awarded a *coup de coeur* for its superb longevity. (NM)

- Krug Vins fins de Champagne, 5, rue Coquebert, B.P. 22, 51100 Reims, tel. 03.26.84.44.20, fax 03.26.84.44.49, e-mail krug@krug.fr [V] [Y] by appt.

KRUG ★★

n.c.   n.c.   [III] ★€76

The Krug rosé received a *coup de coeur*, as it did in 2001, but the rules of the *Guide* forbid the reproduction of more than one label per producer from the same appellation. Although the rosé does not seem to belong within the Krug tradition, it may nonetheless be considered to have its place within the range of this great Reims house. Basically, it is a Grande Cuvée, tinted with the red wine from the Krug vineyard at Ay, which gives it much colour. The complex bouquet merges oak and fruity notes. A palate of crystallised citrus fruit flavours, and its vinosity, fullness and perfect balance encourage one to drink it throughout a meal. The following three wines also received two stars each. The **Grande Cuvée**, a blend of old reserve wines dominated by black grapes (45–55% Pinot Noir and 15–20% Pinot Meunier, with 25–30% Chardonnay) has a well-developed floral and offers floral, honeyed flavours and a palate of long, smooth complexity. The **88 Clos du Mesnil** is the archetypal oaked blanc de blancs; it came within a hair's breadth of three stars. The half-white, half-black (19% Meunier) **81 Collection** is the most beautiful and best-preserved champagne from this difficult vintage. Its expressive, toasty aromas and supple balance led one of the tasters to compare it to a Meursault. (NM)

- Krug Vins fins de Champagne, 5, rue Coquebert, B.P. 22, 51100 Reims, tel. 03.26.84.44.20, fax 03.26.84.44.49, e-mail krug@krug.fr [V] [Y] by appt.

MICHEL LABBE ET FILS Prestige

1 ha   5,000   €15-23

The Labbé family has been established in the Montagne de Reims since the end of the 19th century. Nowadays, they cultivate approximately 10 ha (25 acres) of vines. The Jury was impressed by the half-black, half-white Brut Prestige – in particular, its attractively toasty, toasty bouquet with its overtones of mocha, and its lively, lemony palate. (RM)

- Champagne Michel Labbé et Fils, 5, chem. du Hasat, 51500 Chamery, tel. 03.26.97.65.45, fax 03.26.97.67.42 [V] [Y] by appt.
- Didier Labbé

LACROIX Grande Réserve ★

n.c.   15,000   [III] €11-15

Based in the Marne Valley, this enterprise has been producing champagne since 1974. The Lacroix family manages an 11-ha (27-acre) vineyard. Meticulous vinification procedures include manual *remuage* and a cellar equipped with wooden casks. Grande Réserve is made up of three-quarters black grapes (of which 25% is Meunier) to one-quarter white. Both bouquet and palate exhibit floral flavours (white flowers and violets, notably). **Tradition**, which has a stronger quotient of black grapes (70% Pinot Meunier and 20% Pinot Noir to 10% Chardonnay, harvested in 1996 and 1997), was commended by the Jury for its aromas of nuts and red fruits, and its fine balance. (RM)

- Champagne Jean Lacroix, 14, rue des Genêts, 51700 Montigny-sous-Châtillon, tel. 03.26.58.35.17, fax 03.26.58.36.39 [V] [Y] ev. day 9am–12 noon; 2pm–5pm; Sun by appt.; cl. 10–31 Aug.

LACROIX-TRIAULAIRE ET FILS

Prestige 1996 ★

n.c.   3,700   [III] €11-15

François Lacroix set up production in 1972, and today cultivates a 7.3-ha (18-acre) Aube vineyard. Black and white grapes blend harmoniously in the make-up of this fine and elegant champagne. The Prestige is certainly representative of its year, with its smoky, toasty aromas and firmness of palate. (RM)

- Lacroix-Triaulaire, 4, rue de La Motte, 10110 Merrey-sur-Arce, tel. 03.25.29.83.59
[V] [Y] by appt.

CHARLES LAFITTE Grande Cuvée ★

n.c.   1,600,000   €11-15

When Vranken took over Charles Lafitte in 1983, the champagne enterprise also adopted the brand name of the cognac. This full-blooded Grande Cuvée is an equally creditable product. It draws on approximately equal proportions of the three champagne grapes (40% Chardonnay, with equal quantities of both Pinots). A subtle bouquet is followed by an assertively long palate with evident *dosage*. The half-black, half-white **96 Orgueil de France** received the same rating. It is a good example of the liveliness, elegance and richness of the 1996 vintage. The straight **96** was also awarded a star. Produced from the three champagne grapes, it is made in a similar style to the previous wine. (NM)

- Charles Lafitte, Champ Rouen, 51150 Tours-sur-Marne, tel. 03.26.52.50.50, fax 03.26.52.19.65 [V]
- P.-F. Vranken

Champagne

BENOÎT LAHAYE★

◯Gd Cru   0.6 ha   2,000   ▮▮▮   €11–15

Benoît Lahaye took over the family vineyard of 4.5 ha (11 acres) in the early 1990s. The estate enjoys a prime *terroir* at the Grand Cru village of Bouzy. It has produced a rosé from brief maceration of 1998 and 1999 Pinot Noir grapes. The wines in question do not undergo malolactic fermentation, but half have been aged in oak for six months. The result is a cheery, young, purplish-hued champagne, with raspberry and violet flavours enhancing its delicate balance. (RM)

☛ Benoît Lahaye, 33, rue Jeanne-d'Arc, 51150 Bouzy, tel. 03.26.52.79.94, fax 03.26.52.79.94, e-mail lahaye.benoit@wanadoo.fr ☒ ▾ by appt.

LAHAYE-WAROQUIER Prestige★

◯Gd cru   0.5 ha   2,000   €15–23

Here is another Benoît Lahaye brand (see above) that took over a champagne house created by Lucien Waroquier in 1950. Its blanc de noirs, from the harvests of 1996 and 1997, offers a bouquet of toasted almonds, hazelnuts and undergrowth. Fresh, balanced and long on the palate, it would make a suitable accompaniment for any rich food. (RM)

☛ Benoît Lahaye, 33, rue Jeanne-d'Arc, 51150 Bouzy, tel. 03.26.57.03.05, fax 03.26.52.79.94, e-mail lahaye.benoit@wanadoo.fr ☒ ▾ by appt.

JEAN-JACQUES LAMOUREUX

◯   5 ha   25,000   ▮   €11–15

The Jean-Jacques Lamoureux operation made its first champagne in 1985. This 7.5-ha (18.5-acre) estate is located in the environs of Les Riceys, a village well known for its Pinot Noir. Indeed, this grape variety makes up the bulk (80%) of the Brut Réserve, with a balance of Chardonnay: both varieties coming from the 1999 harvest. This lively, light champagne has a discreetly musky bouquet. (RM)

☛ Jean-Jacques Lamoureux, 27 *bis*, rue du Gal-de-Gaulle, 10340 Les Riceys, tel. 03.25.29.11.55, fax 03.25.29.69.22 ☒ ▾ by appt.

VINCENT LAMOUREUX★

◯   0.5 ha   1,500   ▮   €11–15

This other Lamoureux family, from Les Riceys, has been producing champagne since 1988. It submitted a rosé from the 1996 harvest – a vivid, brick-coloured wine that owes its success to the Pinot Noir grape. Its fruity bouquet and palate, with hints of crystallised grapefruit, were highly rated by the Jury. (RM)

☛ Vincent Lamoureux, 2, rue du Sénateur-Lesaché, 10340 Les Riceys, tel. 03.25.29.39.32, fax 03.25.29.80.30 ☒ ▾ by appt.

LANCELOT-GOUSSARD

Cuvée Brio 1995★

◯   0.7 ha   4,400   €15–23

Claude Lancelot continues a tradition of three generations of wine-growers. Today, the estate produces champagne under two different labels, Lancelot-Goussard and Lancelot Fils, from a vineyard covering around 5 ha (12 acres). Although the estate is based in the Côte des Blancs, Pinot Noir plays a significant role in the composition of its *cuvées*. That grape variety, with Chardonnay, represents 40% of this most classic of blends, Cuvée Brio. It possesses a vinous and supple palate, with strong flavours of ripe fruits and hints of crystallised fruits. The **Tradition Saint-Jean Lancelot Fils rosé**, made from 100% Pinot Noir, received a commendation for its glowing red appearance – an attribute that could also be applied to both its bouquet and palate. It is just made for devotees of this type of rosé. (RM)

☛ Lancelot-Goussard, 30, rue Ernest-Vallé, 51190 Avize, tel. 03.26.57.94.68, fax 03.26.57.79.02 ☒ ▾ by appt.

☛ Claude Lancelot

P. LANCELOT-ROYER

Blanc de Blancs Cuvée de Réserve R.R. ★

◯   2 ha   12,000   €11–15

Cramant is located at the heart of the Côte des Blancs. The Lancelot family have a long history in this village, having been here for eleven generations. Originally vine-growers, they became grower-wine-makers in 1930, and nowadays operate a 4.5-ha (11-acre) estate. This blanc de blancs is produced from a blend of one-third 1997 wines to two-thirds 1998. Its characteristics – an aromatic palate, with contrasting notes of quince, honey, butter, lychees, undergrowth and toast – all contribute to the typical blanc de blancs style. One taster called it 'a great champagne for an aperitif'. The balanced and skilfully dosed **96 Blanc de Blancs**, which is unusually supple for this vintage, also received one star. (RM)

☛ EARL P. Lancelot-Royer, 540, rue du Gal-de-Gaulle, 51530 Cramant, tel. 03.26.57.51.41, fax 03.26.57.12.25, e-mail champagne.lancelot.royer@cder.fr ☒ ▾ by appt.

LANSON Noble Cuvée 1989★

◯   n.c.   n.c.   €46–76

In 1760, Lanson – one of the longest-established champagne houses – bore the name of its founder, François Delamotte, a senior magistrate of Reims. It was not until 1856 that it took the name of one Lanson, an associate of Delamotte. Although the company was bought out in 1991, its cellar-master Jean-Paul Gandon is still re-inning the fort. He is very much against malolactic fermentation. The Noble Cuvée from the prestigious vintage of 1989 is a top-of-the-range champagne, made from a cla-sic blend of 60% Chardonnay to 40% Pinot Noir. It has now reached its peak, and should be d ink straight away for its complexity, fullness and fusion of crystallised apricot and honey

grapes, in almost equal proportions (53% Pinot Noir, 47% Chardonnay). This champagne, with its buttery, toasty flavours, exhibits all the generous characteristics of the vintage. Also commended was the lively and well-balanced **Rosé Label**, produced from all three champagne grapes (53% Pinot Noir, 32% Chardonnay and 15% Meunier). (NM)
☎ Lanson, 12, bd Lundy, 51100 Reims, tel. 03.26.78.50.50, fax 03.26.78.53.88 ▼
Ⓨ by appt.

P. LARDENNOIS Sélection★

Extra brut★

◯ Gd Cru   0.3 ha   1,000   €15-23

Lardennois is based at Verzy in the Montagne de Reims. Its Sélection is a blend of two-thirds Pinot Noir to one-third Chardonnay, from the years 1992 to 1994. This rich champagne is now at its peak. Its powerful character, with smoky flavours, and its fullness and complexity, all make it a suitable wine to serve at dinner. (RM)
☎ Carnot, 51380 Verzy, tel. 03.26.97.91.23, fax 03.26.97.97.69 Ⓨ by appt.

DE L'ARGENTAINE Tradition

◯   40 ha   360,000   €11-15

The Union wine co-operative, based at Vandières in the Marne Valley, markets its product under the L'Argentaine brand name. Their Tradition, derived from the harvests of 1995, 1996 and 1997, is a blend of the three champagne grapes, with a preponderance of the two Pinots (70% Meunier, 20% Pinot Noir). Lemony and floral, it was commended for its elegance. (CM)
☎ Coopérative vinicole L'Union, Cidex 318, 51700 Vandières, tel. 03.26.58.68.68, fax 03.26.58.68.69, e-mail delargentaine@wanadoo.fr ▼ Ⓨ by appt.

GUY LARMANDIER

Cramant Blanc de Blancs★★

◯ Gd Cru   4 ha   30,000   €11-15

An equally talented grower and producer, Jules Larmandier was among the top grower-wine-makers in the Côte des Blancs. His descendants, among them Guy, expanded the vineyard, and the 9-ha (22-acre) estate is currently managed by Colette Larmandier and her son François. This non-vintage Cramant won the admiration of the Jury with its characteristic bouquet of great floral finesse. Its perfectly balanced palate and optimum freshness also made it a favourable impression. This is a collector's Chardonnay. The **96 Cramant Cuvée Prestige Grand Cru** received a commendation. Its powerful, floral bouquet has that hint of green apples so often found in the 96 vintage wines. Its clean palate, by contrast, is both delicate and intricate. (RM)
☎ EARL Champagne Guy Larmandier, 30, rue du Gal-Koenig, 51130 Vertus, tel. 03.26.52.12.41, fax 03.26.52.19.38 ▼
Ⓨ by appt.

LARMANDIER-BERNIER

Blanc de Blancs Vieilles vignes de cramant

Extra brut★★

◯ Gd Cru   n.c.   n.c.   €15-23

This label resulted from the marriage of Philippe Larmandier and Elisabeth Bernier. Following the premature death of her husband, Elisabeth has managed the estate with authority, and her son Pierre has successfully maintained the brand's reputation for excellent quality. A company that prides itself on subtle *dosages*, it submitted a non-dosed champagne that is every bit as remarkable as the previous year's. To succeed with a 96 Extra Brut is something of a *tour de force*. Indeed, it would be well-nigh impossible, were it not for some venerable 50-year-old vine stocks. This cheery, floral-scented champagne of great finesse, length, purity and, above all, perfect balance. The **95 Special Club Premier Cru Blanc de Blancs** received a commendation for its minerally palate of dried and crystallised fruits and its good length. (RM)
☎ Champagne Larmandier-Bernier, 43, rue du 28-Août, 51130 Vertus, tel. 03.26.52.13.24, fax 03.26.52.21.00, e-mail larmandier@terre-net.fr ▼
Ⓨ by appt.

LARMANDIER PERE ET FILS

Blanc de Blancs Perlé de Larmandier 1997★

◯ 1er Cru   n.c.   n.c.   €15-23

The famous Jules Larmandier brand has been taken over by Françoise Gimonnet (née Larmandier) and her sons, Olivier and Didier. Perlé, a lightly sparkling blanc de blancs, was the signature wine of Jules Larmandier. This fine Perlé is composed of 70% Cramant and Chouilly wines (two Grand Crus) with 30% Cuis wine, from the 1997 vintage. It possesses fresh, fruity flavours and is extremely young. Two other champagnes, both blancs de blancs, also received a star each: the toasty, floral, lively **96 Special Club**, and the well-balanced, long but light **Premier Cru**, a blend from the harvests of 1993, 1997 and 1998, and an excellent aperitif champagne. (RM)
☎ Larmandier Père et Fils, 1, rue de la République, 51530 Cuis, tel. 03.26.57.52.19, fax 03.26.59.79.84 ▼
Ⓨ ev. day except Sun. 8.30am-12 noon 2pm-6pm; Sat. by appt.; cl. Aug.
☎ Famille Gimonnet-Larmandier

P. LASSALLE-HANIN

Cuvée de réserve

◯   9 ha   30,000   €11-15

Established in the early 1950s, this estate comprises 9 ha (22 acres) of vines at Chigny-les-Roses in the Montagne de Reims. Its Cuvée de Réserve is made up of the three champagne grapes, harvested in 1998, supplemented by 20% of reserve wines. This wine was commended by the Jury for its delicate bouquet of pear compote and peaches, and its appealing, restrained palate. (RM)

CH. DE L'AUCHE Tradition★★

○   n.c.   200,000 ■ ⬩ €11–15

The Janvry co-operative vinifies the produce of 122 ha (301 acres) of vines, marketing its products under two brand names of Prestige des Sacres and Château de l'Auche. Their Tradition, a blanc de noirs produced from the two Pinots (with 90% Pinot Meunier), from the years 1996 to 1999, created quite a frisson amongst the tasters, with its elegant, ethereal, integrated bouquet, and is well-balanced and fruity palate. It came within a hair's breadth of a *coup de coeur*. The **Cuvée Sélection**, made up of an identical blend but from earlier years (1995 to 1998), received one star. Similar in style to the previous champagne, it delivers floral scents and good length. (CM)

❧ Coop. vinicole de Germigny-Janvry-Rosnay, rue de Germigny, 51390 Janvry, tel. 03.26.03.63.40, fax 03.26.03.66.93 ☑
Ⓨ by appt.

PAUL LAURENT

Cuvée du Fondateur Réserve

○   10 ha   100,000 ■ ⬩ €11–15

This champagne typifies the output of the Paul Laurent enterprise. The house is based at Bethon, a village in the south of the Marne *département*, on the border of the Seine-et-Marne. The Cuvée du Fondateur contains 70% Pinot Noir with 30% Chardonnay, harvested in 1999. Well balanced and firm, with suggestions of apples and pears on both bouquet and palate, it made one taster think of drinking with grilled sea-bream with courgettes au gratin. (NM)

❧ Paul Laurent, 4, rue des Pressoirs, 51260 Bethon, tel. 03.26.81.91.11, fax 03.26.81.91.22,
e-mail champagnepaullaurent@wanadoo.fr
Ⓨ ev. day 9am–12 noon; 2pm–6pm;
cl. 31 Jul.–30 Aug.

LAURENT-PERRIER

Grand Siècle Lumière du Millénaire 1990★★

○   n.c.   ■ ⬩ +€76

This house, originally named Pierlot and subsequently renamed Leroy-Pierlot, was founded during the First Empire in 1812. It adopted the title Laurent-Perrier in 1881, following the marriage of Eugène Laurent and Mathilde-Emilie Perrier. At the time of the outbreak of the First World War, it was a very prosperous enterprise. It was badly affected, however, by the hostilities and, at one point, almost folded. In 1938, it was taken over by Marie-Louise de Nonancourt. Her son, Bernard, transformed the business into one of today's greatest champagne houses. Last year, this Prestige *cuvée*, made up of half black grapes and half white, was awarded a *coup de coeur*. It exhibits all the characteristics of its vintage: strength, opulence and suppleness, as well as balance and complexity. (NM)

❧ Champagne Laurent-Perrier, Dom. de Tours-sur-Marne, 51150 Tours-sur-Marne, tel. 03.26.58.91.22, fax 03.26.58.77.29 ☑

ALBERT LE BRUN Vieille France★

○   n.c.   30,000 ■ ▦ ⬩ €15–23

Founded in 1860 at Avize and transferred in 1963 to Châlons-sur-Marne (known today as Châlons-en-Champagne), this house has changed hands several times over the years. A bottle inspired by the 18th century encloses this rosé which combines a coppery-red appearance with a bouquet of cherries, raspberries and wild strawberries. It has a full and fruity palate. (NM)

❧ SCV Albert Le Brun, 93, av. de Paris, 51000 Châlons-en-Champagne, tel. 03.26.68.18.68, fax 03.26.21.53.31 ☑
Ⓨ by appt.
❧ Patrick Raulet

PAUL LEBRUN

Blanc de Blancs Grande Réserve 1996★

○   5 ha   50,000 ■ ⬩ €11–15

This house at Cramant in the Côte des Blancs was founded by Henri Lebrun, and celebrates its centenary in the year 2002. Throughout its history, this 16.5-ha (41-acre), Chardonnay-dedicated vineyard has remained family-owned. Chardonnay forms the basis of the three nominated *cuvées*. Highly characteristic of this grape variety and typical of its history, the 96 vintage offers a floral, biscuity bouquet of great finesse. It is a fresh, vigorous champagne. The equally well-structured, minerally and lengthy **93 Blanc de Blancs** also received a star, while the **96 Cuvée Prestige Blanc de Blancs** was commended for the liveliness of its vanilla and acacia honey style. (NM)

❧ SA Champagne Vignier-Lebrun, 35, rue Nestor-Gaunel, 51530 Cramant, tel. 03.26.57.54.88, fax 03.26.57.90.02 ☑
Ⓨ by appt.
❧ M. P. Vignier

LE BRUN DE NEUVILLE

Cuvée Sélection

○   n.c.   70,000 ■ ⬩ €11–15

This group of producers was established in 1963, and today manages a 145-ha (358-acre) vineyard. The group's output is dominated by the Chardonnay grape. In fact, it accounts for 80% of this *cuvée*, which is produced from the 1997 harvest (the balance being made up of Pinot Noir). It is a minerally, lively and long champagne. The Jury was also impressed by the honeyed and strongly dosed **92**, which is only 5% off being a blanc de blancs. The **Cuvée Chardonnay**, produced from the 1997 harvest, with its charred and powerful palate, was also noticeably dosed. (CM)

❧ Champagne Le Brun de Neuville, rte de Chantemerle, 51260 Bethon, tel. 03.26.80.48.43, fax 03.26.80.43.28, e-mail lebrundeneuville@wanadoo.fr ☑
Ⓨ by appt.

❧ Champagne P. Lassalle-Hanin, 2, rue des Vignes, 51500 Chigny-les-Roses, tel. 03.26.03.40.96, fax 03.26.03.42.10 ☑
Ⓨ by appt.

LE BRUN-SERVENAY
1994 Cuvée Club Trésor★★

◯ Gd Cru ■ 0.8 ha ▮ 4,000 ■ ▮ ⓔ 15-23

Based at Avize in the Côte des Blancs, this enterprise has been producing champagne since 1945. Its 8-ha (20-acre) vineyard is lucky enough to be planted with old vines, which goes to explain how a 1994 wine can be described as being 80 years of age! This non-chaptalised champagne is produced from a blend of 80% Chardonnay, 10% Pinot Noir and 10% Pinot Meunier, and has not undergone malolactic fermentation. The 94 vintage, although coming from a notoriously difficult year, is unsurpassable, with its acacia and hazelnut bouquet, and flavours of honey and citrus fruits on the palate. The **Brut Réserve**, produced from the three principal grapes (50% Chardonnay with both Pinots in equal proportions, from the harvests of 1994 to 1997), is commended by the Jury for its light, floral character. (RM)

☏ EARL Le Brun-Servenay,
14, pl. Léon-Bourgeois, 51190 Avize,
tel. 03.26.57.52.75, fax 03.26.57.02.71 Ⓥ
Ⓨ by appt.

LECLAIRE-THIEFAINE
Blanc de Blancs Cuvée Sainte-Apolline★

◯ Gd Cru ■ 1 ha ▮ 5,000 ■ ⓔ 11-15

This grower-wine-maker from Avize in the Côte des Blancs cultivates 4 ha (10 acres) of vines, presides over a floral, balanced and long blanc de blancs of great finesse. The same house, under the Leclaire-Gaspard label, also submitted its **90 Carte d'Or Grand Cru**, a balanced and powerful champagne of striking freshness, despite its being 11 years old. (RM)

☏ Dom. des Champagnes Leclaire, 22–24, rue Pasteur, 51190 Avize, tel. 03.26.57.55.66, fax 03.26.55.34.98,
e-mail champagne.leclaire.thiefaine@wanadoo.fr Ⓥ Ⓨ by appt.

LECLERC BRIANT
Divine 1990★★

◯ 1.5 ha ▮ 10,000 ■ ▮ ⓔ 30-38

There are records of a Leclerc cultivating the vine at Ay in 1664. Louis Leclerc sold his first bottle of wine in 1872. Today, Pascal Leclerc Briant manages an organic vineyard of 30 ha (74 acres), located between the Montagne de Reims and the Marne Valley, which he has also converted to biodynamic principles. This enterprise has become something of a tourist attraction where, amongst other activities, visitors can try their hand at mountaineering, abseiling down to the wine cellars, which are 30 metres deep. They can also try the champagne, perhaps the 90 Divine, which is made up of half black grapes and half white. This wine is typical of its vintage: powerful and full bodied with flavours of quince – all characteristics that reflect its age. Two other *cuvées* received a star each: the **96 Rubis Rosé de Noirs Extra-Brut**, a highly coloured, cherry-fruited, full and powerful champagne that would go well with a rare leg of lamb, and **Les Crayères Collection**

713

LECLERC-MONDET 1995★★

◯ 1 ha ▮ 9,000 ■ ▮ ⓔ 11-15

Situated in the Marne Valley, this vineyard was established by Henri Leclerc in the early 1950s. Nowadays, the estate is managed by his grandsons, who submitted a half-white, half-black 95 vintage (of which 20% is Pinot Meunier). The tasters were just as impressed by its finesse, elegance and flavours of honey and citrus fruits as by its fine length. (RM)

☏ Champagne Leclerc-Mondet,
5, rue Beethoven, 02850 Trélou-sur-Marne,
tel. 03.23.70.26.40, fax 03.23.70.10.59 Ⓥ
Ⓨ by appt.

LEGOUGE-COPIN★★
Cuvée Bulle de Folie★★

◯ 0.8 ha ▮ 2,000 ■ ▮ ⓔ 11-15

This estate was established in the 1930s in the Marne Valley. In 1962, Serge Copin launched its champagne brand. The enterprise was later taken over by his eldest daughter, Jocelyne, who, in 1992, introduced this new label, incorporating her married name, Legouge. Pinot Noir, supplemented by Chardonnay, accounts for 75% of this rosé blend from the harvests of 1995 and 1997. Compliments flowed: 'a rounded, spicy and very powerful champagne'. The *brut* **Tradition**, a blanc de noirs (70% Meunier) from the harvests of 1996 and 1998, was commended for its smoky qualities and its generosity of flavour. (RM)

☏ Champagne Legouge-Copin,
6, rue de l'Abbé-Bernard, 51700 Verneuil,
tel. 03.26.52.96.89, fax 03.26.51.85.62 Ⓥ
Ⓨ by appt.

ERIC LEGRAND
Cuvée Bulle de Folie★★

◯ 0.4 ha ▮ 4,200 ■ ▮ ⓔ 15-23

Founded in 1982, this Auboise estate consists of 7 ha (17 acres) of vines. Their Bulle de Folie has a fine, pale golden appearance with greenish highlights, and is actually a blanc de blancs, although it does not say so on the label. This fine champagne, based on wines from the 1997 harvest, certainly impressed the tasters, who commented favourably on its balance, vivacity and fruity, honeyed, buttery flavours on the palate. The **Réserve**, made from exceedingly ripe grapes, is rounded and vinous on the palate, with flavours of honey and liquorice, and was awarded a star. It is a champagne to accompany white meats. The **Prestige**, produced from the harvests of 1997 and 1998, and dominated by Chardonnay (70%), received a

Les Authentiques Blanc de Noirs, a fine, long and well-balanced champagne, from a Premier Cru vineyard, harvested in 1995 and 1996. (NM)

☏ Champagne Leclerc-Briant, 67, rue Chaude-Ruelle, B.P. 108, 51204 Epernay Cedex, tel. 03.26.54.45.33, fax 03.26.54.49.59,
e-mail pascal.leclercbriant@wanadoo.fr Ⓥ
Ⓨ ev. day 9am–11.30am; 1.30pm–5.30pm; Sat, Sun, by appt.; cl. 5-25 Aug.
☏ Pascal Leclerc-Briant

commendation. It has enough finesse to make a good aperitif champagne. (RM)

☛ Eric Legrand,
39, Grande-Rue, 10110 Celles-sur-Ource,
tel. 03.25.38.55.07, fax 03.25.38.56.84,
e-mail champagne.legrand.fr ✉
🍷 ev. day except Wed. Sun. 9am–12.30pm;
2pm–6pm; cl. 15 Aug.–5 Sep.

R. ET L. LEGRAS Blanc de Blancs
Cuvée Saint-Vincent 1990★★

○ Gd Cru   10 ha   60,000   ▦ ♦ €23-30

The Legras family has been established at Chouilly in the Côte des Blancs for around two centuries. Their estate encompasses 14 ha (35 acres) of vines in the area surrounding the village, planted almost exclusively with Chardonnay. Their Cuvée Saint-Vincent, produced from the estate's oldest vines, received nothing but compliments from the Jury: 'Excellent, a noble wine, a connoisseur's wine, a wine of character …'. Its strengths are good balance, finesse and length. It would go well with sauced fish dishes, as indeed would the **92 Cuvée Présidence Blanc de Blancs Grand Cru**, which was awarded a star. This elegant champagne exhibits flavours of citrus fruits and vanilla. The **Blanc de Blancs Non-Vintage**, drawn from the harvests of 1995 and 1996, received a commendation. Although it doesn't have quite the length on the palate as the previous champagnes, it is nonetheless well balanced and rich. (NM)

☛ Champagne R. et L. Legras,
10, rue des Partelaines, 51530 Chouilly,
tel. 03.26.54.50.79, fax 03.26.54.88.74,
e-mail champagne-r.l.legras@wanadoo.fr ✉
🍷 by appt.

LELARGE-PUGEOT Cuvée Prestige★★

○   0.5 ha   4,000   ▦ €11-15

Heir to a vine-growing lineage that dates back to 1850, Dominique Lelarge took over this estate in 1990. The vineyard is located at Vrigny, west of Reims. The three champagne grapes (60% Chardonnay and the two Pinots in equal proportions), harvested in 1996, combine to make up this cuvée, which has an expressive, fruity bouquet with notes of brioche. It offers a lively start, followed by great length – qualities that assure it a great future. (RM)

☛ Dominique Lelarge,
30, rue Saint-Vincent, 51390 Vrigny,
tel. 03.26.03.69.43, fax 03.26.03.68.93,
e-mail champagnelelarge-pugeot@
wanadoo.fr ✉ 🍷 ev. day except Sun. 9am–
12 noon; 2pm–6pm

PATRICE LEMAIRE 1996★

○   n.c.   2,000   ▦ €11-15

In 1988, Patrice Lemaire took over this family-run estate that was founded in 1920 on the left bank of the Marne. Although it is not stated on the label, this 96 vintage is in fact a blanc de blancs champagne, its bouquet mingles flavours of fruit compote with mineral undertones to make an exceptionally lively wine. (RM)

PHILIPPE LEMAIRE Dame de Louis★

○   3 ha   n.c.   ▦ ▦ €8-11

Philippe Lemaire has been producing champagne since 1992, cultivating a vineyard on the left bank of the Marne. His champagnes, two of which received a star, are vinified in both stainless steel and oak. The Dame de Louis, a predominantly black-grape cuvée (50% Meunier, 30% Pinot Noir), was singled out for its suppleness, roundness and flavour of pears. The **95** is a blanc de blancs (although not stated as such on the label). Its bouquet mixes hints of may-blossom with buttery notes. The opening impression is of a supple and well-balanced wine. (RM)

☛ Philippe Lemaire, 4, rue de La Liberté,
51480 Oeuilly, tel. 03.26.58.30.82,
fax 03.26.52.92.44 ✉ 🍷 by appt.

R.C. LEMAIRE Chardonnay 1996★★

○ 1er Cru   0.5 ha   3,000   ▦ €30-38

The R.C. Lemaire champagne label was launched in 1945. Gilles Tournant, who has been at the head of the enterprise since 1975, manages 11 ha (27 acres) of vines in the Marne Valley. The winery's vinification methods reflect his personal input. He refuses, for example, to carry out malolactic fermentation, and prefers to vinify and age the wines in barrel for eight months. It is not surprising, therefore, that this very young 96 Chardonnay, which needs further time to mature, has a classic non-malolactic character. With its fine structure and spring-like flavours of green apples and lemons, it is a champagne worth waiting for! The **Select Réserve**, a blanc de noirs produced from Pinot Meunier (aged in tank), received a commendation. This floral champagne remains remarkably fresh, considering that it is made from Pinot Meunier grapes harvested in 1996 and 1997. (RM)

☛ Gilles Tournant, rue de la Glacière,
51700 Villers-sous-Châtillon,
tel. 03.26.58.36.79, fax 03.26.58.39.28,
e-mail tournant@clubinternet.fr ✉
🍷 by appt.

LEMAIRE-RASSELET
Cuvée Tradition★★

○   9.2 ha   15,000   ▦ ♦ €11-15

The Lemaire-Rasselet champagne was launched in 1946. Its vineyard extends over an area of more than 9 ha (22 acres) on the left bank of the Marne. Françoise Lemaire has produced a very fine non-vintage **brut**, composed almost entirely of black grapes, harvested in 1996 and 1997. The tasters were impressed by its expressive bouquet of apple and caramel aromas and its integrated, well-balanced character. The very attractive **95** also received a star. Produced from the three champagne grapes in equal proportions, it offers an appealing bouquet of nougat and crystallised fruits, as well as a sufficiently vigorous palate. (RM)

- SCEV Lemaire-Rasselet, 5, rue de la Croix-Saint-Jean, 51480 Boursault, tel. 03.26.58.44.85, fax 03.26.58.09.47 ▼ by appt.

A. R. LENOBLE ★
○ Gd Cru 7 ha 220,000 ■ €15-23 ▼

This house was founded in 1941 by a courtier, A.R. Grasser, and has been managed by his descendants ever since. The vineyard comprises 18 ha (44 acres). The Reserve is a blend of the three champagne grapes in almost equal proportions (but with 40% Chardonnay), harvested in 1998. It has a fruity bouquet and its first impression on the palate is fresh, with just a touch of greenness. The 95 Blanc de Blancs Grand Cru also earned a star. This champagne is all freshness and softness on the palate, and its brioche-scented bouquet is very appealing. (NM)

- Champagne Lenoble, 35, rue Paul-Douce, 51480 Damery, tel. 03.26.58.42.60, fax 03.26.58.65.57, e-mail champagne.lenoble@wanadoo.fr ▼ by appt.
- Malassagne

LIEBART-REGNIER ★★ 8 ha 46,000 €11-15

Situated in the Marne Valley in the area around Baslieux-sous-Châtillon and Vauciennes, this estate comprises an 8-ha (20-acre) vineyard. Its predominantly black-grape non-vintage *brut* (50% Pinot Meunier and 40% Pinot Noir, from the years 1997 and 1998) greatly enthused certain of the tasters, who would happily have awarded it a *coup de coeur*. Its bouquet of red fruits, apples and pears, and flavours of peaches and apricots on the palate, all add up to an excellent, generous wine. The 96 Excelia is a classic blend of Pinot Noir (70%) and Chardonnay. Its vigorous opening impression, and its balance and freshness, all won the approval of the Jury, who awarded it a star. (RM)

- Liébart-Régnier, 6, rue Saint-Vincent, 51700 Baslieux-sous-Châtillon, tel. 03.26.58.11.60, fax 03.26.52.34.60, e-mail liebart-regnier@wanadoo.fr ▼ by appt.
- Laurent Liébart

LILBERT-FILS Blanc de Blancs Perle ★
○ Gd Cru n.c. 2,000 €11-15

This grower-wine-maker is a blanc de blancs specialist. He works a vineyard in the Grand Cru village of Cramant. His Cuvée Perle is composed of a blend of half 1995 wines, with the rest from the harvests of 1991 to 1994. It is a champagne with a bouquet of exotic fruits, and well-integrated, vanilla flavours. The Blanc de Blancs Grand Cru Non-Vintage, harvested in 1996 and 1997, was commended for its aperitif qualities – freshness and good balance. (RM)

- Georges Lilbert, 223, rue du Moutier BP 14, 51530 Cramant, tel. 03.26.57.50.16, fax 03.26.58.93.86 ▼ by appt.

JOSEPH LORIOT-PAGEL
Blanc de Blancs 1996
○ 1 ha 5,000 ■

This label was born of the union of two viticultural families: the Loriots, owners of four crus in the Marne Valley, and the Pagels, proprietors at Avize and Cramant on the Côte des Blancs. The combined estate comprises approximately 8 ha (20 acres) of vines. Two of its champagnes were commended by the Jury. First was this rounded, light 96 Blanc de Blancs, with its noticeable *dosage*, and the other was the predominantly black-grape Carte d'Or (65% Pinot Meunier, 22% Pinot Noir), drawn from the harvests of 1996 to 1998. The latter conjures up white flowers in

BERNARD LONCLAS
Blanc de Blancs ★
○ 3 ha 2,500 €11-15

Bernard Lonclas is proud of the fact that he planted his own vineyard and launched his proprietary champagne in 1979. His 5.7-ha (14-acre) estate is based on the south-eastern outskirts of the appellation (Bassuet is near Vitry-le-François). This blanc de blancs is nonetheless a successful wine, despite its peripheral location. Produced from the years 1997 and 1998, it has now reached its peak. Rounded, vinous and true to type, it has plenty of character. (RM)

- Bernard Lonclas, chemin de Travent, 51300 Bassuet, tel. 03.26.73.98.20 ▼ by appt.

GERARD LORIOT Selection
○ 8,000 €11-15

Gérard Loriot took over the estate in 1981, following in the footsteps of a long line of vine-growers dating back to the Second Empire. He cultivates 5 ha (12 acres) of vines on the left bank of the Marne. This half-black, half-white *cuvée* is powerful, long and well developed. (RM)

- Gérard Loriot, rue Saint-Vincent, Le Mesnil-le-Huttier, 51700 Festigny, tel. 03.26.58.35.32, fax 03.26.51.93.71 ▼ by appt.

MICHEL LORIOT Carte d'or
○ 4 ha 35,000 €11-15

The Loriots have been producing champagne in the Marne Valley since 1931. Michel Loriot, who took over in 1977, also launched his own *marque*. Nowadays, he cultivates a little over 6 ha (15 acres) of vines. His Carte d'Or is a blanc de noirs produced from Pinot Meunier, harvested in 1997 and 1998. Floral and lemony, it is full on the palate, with perceptible *dosage*. Also commended was the *rosé*, which is a rosé de noirs (85% Pinot Meunier), made from the same vintages as the preceding champagne. Balanced and long, it would go well with white meats. (RM)

- Michel Loriot, 13, rue de Bel-Air, 51700 Festigny, tel. 03.26.58.03.98, fax 03.26.58.03.98, e-mail info@champagne-michelloriot.com ▼ by appt.

the bouquet, while the palate shows signs of maturity. (RM)

➤ Joseph Loriot, 33, rue de la République, 51700 Festigny, tel. 03.26.58.33.53, fax 03.26.58.05.37 ▼ Ⅰ by appt.

YVES LOUVET Cuvée de Sélection★★
4.5 ha · 20,000 · €11-15

Yves Louvet cultivates a 6.5-ha (16-acres) vineyard at Tauxières, on the south slope of the Montagne de Reims. Pinot Noir dominates all three of the champagnes that he submitted, accounting for 75% of the blend in each case, supplemented by Chardonnay. The Cuvée de Sélection is made up of grapes harvested in 1997. Its subtle bouquet of fresh butter and honey is followed by a straightforward, attractive palate, with balsamic overtones. One star was awarded to the **93** vintage. This honeyed champagne with its notes of preserved fruits and its fine length gives neither its age nor its *dosage* away. (RM)

➤ Yves Louvet, 21, rue du Poncet, 51150 Tauxières, tel. 03.26.57.03.27, fax 03.26.57.67.77 ▼ Ⅰ by appt.

LOYAUX-GORET★
Cuvée du Millénaire★
6.43 ha · 2,000 · €11-15

Situated near Passy-sur-Marne on the Aisne, this 6.5-ha (16-acre) vineyard was established in 1958. This largely black-grape wine (80% Pinots, of which 50% is Meunier) is produced from the harvests of 1990 and 1996. Its lightness, to which it owes its elegance, only slightly masks the maturity of the wine. (RM)

➤ Loyaux-Goret, 4, rue des Sites, 51480 Vauciennes, tel. 03.26.58.62.87, fax 03.26.58.67.34 ▼ Ⅰ by appt.

PHILIPPE DE LOZEY 1996★★
n.c. · 6,200 · €23-30

This Auboise house, managed by Daniel and Philippe Cheurlin, has excelled itself this year with a splendid wine – a 96 vintage made from half Pinot Noir and half Chardonnay. Its delicately lemony bouquet leads, almost stealthily, to a superb, clean, forthright, lively, full, balanced and elegant palate. A true 96! (NM)

➤ Champagne Philippe de Lozey. 72, Grande-Rue, B.P. 3, 10110 Celles-sur-Ource, tel. 03.25.38.51.34, fax 03.25.38.54.80, e-mail de.lozey@wanadoo.fr ▼
Ⅰ by appt.
➤ Ph. Cheurlin

LUCAS CARTON★
n.c. · 100,000 · €15-23

This label, launched by Vranken in 1998, bears the name of a grand Parisian restaurant that opened its doors in 1839. The blend of 70% Chardonnay and 30% Pinot Noir lends a certain elegance to this fresh, light champagne with its reserved bouquet. (NM)

➤ Lucas Carton, Ch. des Castaignes, 51270 Montmort-Lucy, tel. 03.26.59.80.00, fax 03.26.59.80.08
➤ P.-F. Vranken

M. MAILLART Blanc de Blancs 1993★
0.5 ha · 3,300 · €15-23

A village very close to Reims, a line of vine-producers dating back to 1720, that first inscribed its name on a label in 1965, and a 8.4-ha (21-acre) vineyard, are the factors at work in the creation of this floral-scented blanc de blancs. It is a fresh, balanced and well-structured champagne. (RM)

➤ Michel Maillart, 13, rue de Villers, 51500 Ecueil, tel. 03.26.49.77.89, fax 03.26.49.24.79, e-mail m.maillart@free.fr ▼ Ⅰ by appt.

MAILLY GRAND CRU La Terre 1996
Gd Cru · n.c. · 25,000 · €23-30

This 70-ha (173-acre) co-operative, established in 1929, is in a unique position in Champagne for two reasons: first, membership is reserved exclusively for those growers who own plots of vines in Mailly, and secondly, its wines bear the name of that Grand Cru village on the Montagne de Reims. Both blends commended by the Jury are made up of 75% Pinot Noir, with a balance of Chardonnay: the supple, rounded, smoky, lemony **96** La Terre, and the distinctly mature, yet straightforward, top-of-the-range **88 Les Echansons**, which also shows suppleness and roundness. (CM)

➤ Champagne Mailly Grand Cru, 28, rue de la Libération, 51500 Mailly-Champagne, tel. 03.26.49.41.10, fax 03.26.49.42.27, e-mail contact@champagne-mailly.com ▼ Ⅰ by appt.

HENRI MANDOIS
Victor Mandois 1996★★
4 ha · 30,000 · €15-23

This *cuvée* pays tribute to Victor Mandois, who produced the first Mandois champagnes in 1930. The house remains family-run, and today cultivates 30 ha (74 acres) of vines dotted around several villages. This very pale 96 (70% Chardonnay), with its light floral bouquet, starts on a lively note. The palate, by contrast, has honey and citrus fruit flavours that emphasise the robustness of a champagne that should grace the dinner table. The non-vintage **Cuvée de Réserve** received one star. A fine, well-constructed *brut* wine, it is made up of the three champagne grapes. Another star went to the **Rosé Premier Cru**. Produced by the *saignée* method from the two Pinots, this is a rich, vividly coloured champagne that would also go well with food. (NM)

♠ **Champagne Henri Mandois**, 66, rue du Gal-de-Gaulle, 51530 Pierry, tel. 03.26.54.03.18, fax 03.26.51.53.66 ⓥ ⓨ by appt.

MANSARD

○ 1er Cru   n.c.   60,000   ▮■ ❚ €11-15

The Rapeneau family has a high profile in the Champagne region. Mansard is one of their brand names. This *cuvée* is a classic blend of 40% Pinot Noir to 60% Chardonnay, from the 1997 harvest, and exhibits a classic honeyed, fresh character on the palate, albeit with evident *dosage*. (NM)

♠ Champagne Mansard-Baillet, 14, rue Chaude-Ruelle, 51200 Epernay, tel. 03.26.54.18.55, fax 03.26.51.99.50 ⓥ ⓨ ev. day except Sat. Sun. 8am–11.30am; 1.30pm–5pm
♠ Rapeneau

DIDIER MARC★

○   3.5 ha   2,000   ■ €11-15

Didier Marc is a recently established champagne label, but with strong viticultural roots that date back to the 18th century. The present wine is a pale-coloured rosé de noirs (85% Pinot Meunier), from the years 1998 and 1997. Its bouquet resembles apples more closely than red fruits, and it has a vinous palate that mingles flavours of apples and pears with notes of blackcurrant. The overall effect is very appealing. (RM)

♠ Didier Marc, 11, rue Dom-Pérignon, 51480 Fleury-la-Rivière, tel. 03.26.58.60.69, fax 03.26.52.84.20, e-mail champagnedidiermarc@orenka.com ⓥ ⓨ ev. day 8am–12 noon; 2pm–7pm; cl. 15–31 Aug.

PATRICE MARC Ultima Forsan★

○   0.15 ha   1,500   €11-15

Established in 1975, Patrice Marc cultivates a 3-ha (7-acre) vineyard at Fleury-la-Rivière. On display in the cellar is a wine-press that saw service from 1889 until 1991! Ultima Forsan ('maybe the last'), a name with a certain epicurean charm, is used to describe this mature *cuvée*, which is composed of more black grapes than white (40% Pinot Noir and 20% Meunier, to 40% Chardonnay). One-third of the grapes were harvested in 1996 and two-thirds in 1997. This wine will delight lovers of mature champagne: several tasters envisaged it as the perfect accompaniment for an intimate *dîner à deux*. The Jury was impressed by its gilded appearance and its bouquet of dried fruits, mirabelle plums and floral overtones. They approved of its intricate yet well-constructed palate. This wine would be delightful throughout a meal. It is ready to drink now. (RM)

♠ Patrice Marc, 1, rue du Creux-Chemin, 51480 Fleury-la-Rivière, tel. 03.26.58.46.88, fax 03.26.59.48.21, e-mail contact@champagne-marc.com ⓥ ⓨ by appt.

A. MARGAINE

Blanc de Blancs Spécial Club 1996★

○   0.7 ha   5,000   ■ €15-23

Gaston Margaine founded the estate in 1910, and succeeding generations — André, Bernard and Arnaud — expanded the enterprise. The 6.5-ha (16-acre) vineyard at Villers-Marmery on the Montagne de Reims enjoys a fine reputation for its Chardonnays. Indeed, they make a significant contribution to the elegance of this floral, balanced and fresh champagne. The predominantly white-grape **Cuvée Traditionnelle Premier Cru** (87% Chardonnay), produced from the 1998 harvest, received a commendation. It is similar in style to the previous champagne, but is shorter on the finish. (RM)

♠ Champagne A. Margaine, 3, av. de Champagne, 51380 Villers-Marmery, tel. 03.26.97.92.13, fax 03.26.97.97.45 ⓥ ⓨ by appt.

MARGUET-BONNERAVE

○ Gd Cru   2 ha   16,000   €11-15

Christian Marguet cultivates a 13-ha (32-acre) vineyard situated in a prime *terroir* in three Grands Crus of the Montagne de Reims: Ambonnay, Bouzy and Mailly. The base wine for this non-vintage rosé, a blend of 80% Pinot Noir to 20% Chardonnay, is drawn from the harvests of 1996 to 1998. Ambonnay red wine adds the colour. This is a powerful and long champagne with plenty of character, well suited to the dinner table. (RM)

♠ Marguet-Bonnerave, 14, rue de Bouzy, 51150 Ambonnay, tel. 03.26.57.01.08, fax 03.26.57.09.98, e-mail info@champagne-bonnerave.com ⓥ ⓨ by appt.

MARIE STUART Cuvée de la Reine

○   n.c.   n.c.   ▮■ ❚ €15-23

Originally created in 1867, the Marie-Stuart brand name changed hands several times before being acquired by Alain Thiénot. This special *cuvée* is a credit to the Chardonnay grape, the variety that accounts for 90% of the blend (with the balance being Pinot Noir). This powerful, rounded, supple and harmonious champagne, with its aromas of *pain d'épice* and biscuity notes, won the unanimous approval of the Jury. (NM)

♠ Champagne Marie-Stuart, 8, pl. de la République, 51100 Reims, tel. 03.26.77.50.50, fax 03.26.77.50.59, e-mail marie.stuart@wanadoo.fr
♠ Thiénot

MARTEAUX-GUYARD Réserve

○   13 ha   30,000   ▮■ ❚ €11-15

Joël Marteaux oversees the family vineyard of 13 ha (32 acres) in the Marne Valley, near Château-Thierry. The estate's champagne was launched in 1978. Its Reserve is composed mainly of Pinots (80%, of which 45% is Meunier), from the harvest of 1997, and is a floral-scented, young and vigorous wine. (RM)

• Joël Marteaux,
63, Grande-Rue, 02400 Bonneil,
tel. 03.23.82.90.04, fax 03.23.82.05.69,
e-mail champagnemarteauxguyard@
hotmail.fr ▶
Ƴ ev. day 8am–12 noon; 1pm–7pm

G. H. MARTEL & CO Prestige★

30 ha 300,000 ■ ♦ €15-23

The house of G.H. Martel was founded in 1869, and came under the control of the Rapeneau family in the late 1970s. The 80-ha (198-acre) estate spearheads a group that includes several brands. The Prestige is a blend of 70% Pinot Noir and 30% Chardonnay, from the harvests of 1996 and 1997. It is a pleasant and fresh champagne that would go well with salmon *en croûte*. The *brut rosé*, from the harvests of 1997 and 1998, is blended from 30% Chardonnay, 55% Pinot Noir and 15% Bouzy red wine, the last of which gives it its colour. This champagne was commended for its bouquet of spices, hazelnuts and vanilla, and is rounded and fresh palate. (NM)

• Champagne G.H. Martel,
69, av. de Champagne, BP 1011,
51318 Epernay Cedex, tel. 03.26.51.06.33,
fax 03.26.54.41.52 ▶
• Rapeneau

P. LOUIS MARTIN Bouzy 1996★

Gd Cru 1.5 ha 7,000 ■ ♦ €11-15

Although this champagne is produced by a grower-wine-maker, its brand name is controlled by the Rapeneau family. Paul-Louis Martin is based at Bouzy, a Grand Cru village in the Montagne de Reims. The estate is commended for two champagnes. Black grapes dominate each of its classic blends in a ratio of 70% Pinot Noir to 30% Chardonnay. The fresh, young and powerful 96 creates a lively first impression. Another star went to the **Non-Vintage Brut**, from the years 1996 and 1997, which offers elegance, freshness and fine balance. (RM)

• Champagne Paul-Louis Martin,
3, rue d'Ambonnay, BP 4, 51150 Bouzy,
tel. 03.26.57.01.27, fax 03.26.57.83.25 ▶
• Rapeneau

MARX-BARBIER ET FILS

6 ha n.c. ■ €11-15

A good, classic, non-vintage *brut*, this champagne is a blend of 25% Chardonnay, 40% Pinot Meunier and 35% Pinot Noir from the harvest of 1998. An elegant citrus fruit bouquet is followed by a full, honeyed yet fresh palate. (RM)

• Champagne Marx-Barbier et Fils,
1, rue du Château, 51480 Venteuil,
tel. 03.26.58.48.39, fax 03.26.58.67.06,
e-mail marx-barbieretfils@wanadoo.fr ▶
Ƴ by appt.

D. MASSIN Cuvée de Réserve

0.3 ha 3,000 ■ ♦

Dominique Massin, who oversees this 11-ha (27-acre) vineyard, launched his champagne in 1975. He submitted a rosé de noirs (100% Pinot Noir from the 1998 harvest). This fruity champagne, on which the bouquet is more intense than the palate, has reached its peak. The 96, a blend of Pinot Noir (60%) and Chardonnay, was equally commended. It offers a lively bouquet of citrus fruits, and a youthful, persistent palate that appears well rounded for its vintage. (RM)

• Dominique Massin, rue Coulon,
10110 Ville-sur-Arce, tel. 03.25.38.74.97,
fax 03.25.38.77.51 ▶ Ƴ by appt.

THIERRY MASSIN Sélection★

n.c. 49,000 ■ €11-15

This 10-ha (25-acre) vineyard in the Aube launched its champagne in 1977. The estate is managed by Thierry Massin and his sister Dominique. The Sélection is made from the 1998 harvest, topped up with reserve wines from 1996 and 1997. This floral blanc de noirs (Pinot Noir) has aromas of butter and liquorice, and is rounded and well balanced on the palate. The predominantly black-grape **Réserve** (85% Pinot Noir), from the same years, was also awarded a star, for its flavours of apples and pears, its vivacity and its length. The fairly light, pear- and honey-scented **Prestige**, a blend of 70% Pinot Noir and 30% Chardonnay from the harvests of 1996 and 1997, received a commendation. (RM)

• Thierry Massin,
6, rue des Deux-Bar, 10110 Ville-sur-Arce,
tel. 03.25.38.74.01, fax 03.25.38.79.10,
e-mail champagne.thierry.massin@
wanadoo.fr ▶ Ƴ ev. day 9am–12 noon;
1.30pm–6.30pm; Sat. Sun. by appt.

REMY MASSIN ET FILS

Cuvée Tradition

9.5 ha 79,000 ■ ♦ €11-15

Sylvère, the son of Rémy Massin, took over this vineyard of 20 ha (49 acres) in the Aube in 1981. His Cuvée Tradition, produced from the harvests of 1997 and 1998, owes much to the Pinot Noir grape. Its bouquet is more highly developed than its palate, and although this champagne possesses no great length, its elegance certainly attracted the Jury's attention. The firm, fresh **Prestige**, made from half black grapes and half white, harvested in 1996 and 1998, also received a commendation. It is a champagne that offers youth and vivacity in abundance. (RM)

• Champagne Rémy Massin et Fils,
34, Grande-Rue, 10110 Ville-sur-Arce,
tel. 03.25.38.74.09, fax 03.25.38.77.67,
e-mail remy.massin.fils@wanadoo.fr ▶
Ƴ ev. day 10am–12 noon 2pm–6pm; Sat.
Sun. by appt.

SERGE MATHIEU Cuvée Prestige★★

4 ha 25,000 ■ ♦ €11-15

Following in the footsteps of several generations of vine-growers, Serge Mathieu took over this estate in 1970, and decided to develop his own champagne. Today, he cultivates a vineyard of 11 ha (27 acres) near Les Riceys, in the Aube. His Prestige Cuvée is a classic blend of 70% Pinot Noir and 30% Chardonnay, produced from grapes harvested in 1996 and 1997. This floral champagne, with its spicy bouquet and palate, is well balanced. The **Select Tête de Cuvée** is derived from half black grapes and half white in two particularly good years – 1995 and 1996 – and received a commendation. With its aromas of honey and citrus fruits and mineral undertones, it is a youthful champagne. (RM)

� Champagne Serge Mathieu,
6, rue des Vignes, 10340 Avirey-Lingey,
tel. 03.25.29.32.58, fax 03.25.29.11.57,
e-mail champagne.mathieu@wanadoo.fr ▼
Y by appt.

MATHIEU-PRINCET
Blanc de Blancs★

| ○ | 1 ha | 8,000 | €15-23 | ▼ |

This 8-ha (20-acre) estate near Avize on the Côte des Blancs was established in 1960. Readers of last year's *Guide* will be familiar with the name Mathieu-Princet, thanks to two listed champagnes: a superb 95 and an extremely successful 93. Here we have a a champagne from the 1994 harvest, albeit a non-vintage. A powerful blanc de blancs, full-bodied and long; it is a wine of character. (RM)

➍ SARL champagne Mathieu-Princet,
16, rue Bruyère, 51190 Grauves,
tel. 03.26.59.73.72, fax 03.26.59.77.75 ▼

PASCAL MAZET

| ○ | 2 ha | n.c. | €11-15 |

Pascal Mazet is based in the Montagne de Reims. His meticulous vinification methods involve the use of large wooden casks and small oak barrels, particularly for storing the estate's reserve wines. His non-vintage *brut* is made from a traditional local blend: 30% white and 70% black grapes. Pinot Meunier, however, plays a major role (50%). With its scents of white flowers, this wine offers everything one would expect of this style of champagne. (RM)

➍ Pascal Mazet,
8, rue des Carrières, 51500 Chigny-les-Roses,
tel. 03.26.03.41.13, fax 03.26.03.41.74,
e-mail champagne.mazet@free.fr ▼
Y by appt.

GUY MEA

| ○ 1er Cru | 4 ha | n.c. | €11-15 |

The estate is located on the south slope of the Montagne de Reims. Its non-vintage *brut* is a product of the 1998 harvest. It comprises two-thirds Pinot Noir to one-third Chardonnay, and is a well-balanced, young and fresh champagne. (RM)

➍ SCE La Voie des Loups, Chez Guy Méa,
1, rue de l'Eglise, 51150 Louvois,
tel. 03.26.57.03.42, fax 03.26.57.66.44 ▼

MERCIER 1995

| ○ | n.c. | n.c. |

Eugène Mercier, who founded this house in 1858, has played a positive and significant role in the democratisation of champagne.

His knowledge and understanding of advertising have equipped him with the means to promote and expand his own business. Consider, for example, the immense cellars at Epernay, a fine tourist attraction. The company has been owned by Moët et Chandon since 1970. This 95 vintage, a blend of 15% Pinot Meunier with Pinot Noir and Chardonnay in equal proportions, bears all the Mercier hallmarks. It is vinous, fleshy, full and well-integrated – a champagne suitable for serving with even the richest dishes. (NM)

➍ Champagne Mercier,
75, av. de Champagne, 51200 Epernay,
tel. 03.26.51.22.00, fax 03.26.54.84.23
Y by appt.

DE MERIC 1993★★

| ○ | n.c. | n.c. | ♨ €15-23 |

Founded in 1960 by Christian Besserat, this house has retained some 60 or so old oak barrels. A highly classic blend of 70% Pinot Noir and 30% Chardonnay, this 93 vintage has been aged in oak. Its aromas of honey and crystallised apricots, its vinosity and, above all, its length were unanimously praised by the Jury. (NM)

➍ SA Christian Besserat Père et Fils,
Champagne de Meric, 17, rue Gambetta,
51160 Ay, tel. 03.26.55.20.72,
fax 03.26.55.69.23 ▼ by appt.

J.B. MICHEL
Blanc de Blancs Vieilli en tonneau de chêne★

| ○ | 1 ha | 7,000 | €11-15 |

Bruno Michel is based at Pierry, to the south of Epernay. The vines on his 13-ha (32-acre) estate have an average age of more than 30 years. Wine-making procedures are streamlined, and the barrel-store houses approximately 100 oak casks of 225-litre (59-gal) capacity. Although this champagne has been 'produced in oak barrels', it is not, however, an oaky wine. On the contrary, vinification in barrel has served only to enhance its softness and complexity. It has a supple and well-balanced palate, and would make a suitable aperitif or accompaniment for an entrée. (RM)

➍ Bruno Michel, 4, allée de la
Vieille-Ferme, 51530 Pierry,
tel. 03.26.55.10.54, fax 03.26.54.75.77,
e-mail champagne.j.b.michel@cder.fr ▼
Y by appt.

PAUL MICHEL
Chardonnay Carte Blanche

| ○ 1er Cru | 10 ha | n.c. | €11-15 |

This Côte des Blancs estate comprises 18 ha (44 acres) of vines. It submitted a blanc de blancs demi-sec, produced from the 1997 harvest. This smoky, lemony champagne is fresh and, above all, extremely young. (RM)

➍ SARL champagne Paul Michel, 20,
Grande-Rue, 51530 Cuis, tel. 03.23.59.79.77,
fax 03.26.59.72.12 ▼ ev. day except Sat.
Sun. 9am–12 noon; 2pm–5pm; cl. Aug.
➍ Philippe et Denis Michel

GUY MICHEL ET FILS★

○   n.c.   93,716   ■ €11-15

The present label may well be a recent addition, but the Michels have been producing champagne at Pierry for 150 years. Their vineyard extends over an area of 20 ha (49 acres). This is yet another *cuvée* that comprises 70% black grapes and 30% white. The blend here, however, is dominated by Pinot Meunier (50%), and is produced from the 1998 harvest. Its complex bouquet, and its fresh, structured and long palate, earned it a star. The same rating was awarded to the **blanc de blancs**, with its beautifully intense aroma of brioche, its forthright start and its length on the palate. It would make a very refined aperitif. (RM)

☛ SCEV champagne Guy Michel et Fils, 54, av Léon-Bourgeois, BP 25, 51530 Pierry, tel. 03.26.54.67.12 ☑ ☎ by appt.

CHARLES MIGNON

Grande Réserve★

○ 1er Cru   n.c.   n.c.   ■ €11-15

This recently established Epernay house (1995) received a star for its Brut Grande Réserve, a young, elegant, fresh, vigorous, and yet extremely well-balanced champagne. The **Blanc de Blancs Premier Cru Non-Vintage** received a commendation for its suppleness and its charred, floral, spicy flavours. (NM)

☛ Charles Mignon, 1, av. de Champagne, 51200 Epernay, tel. 03.26.58.33.33, fax 03.26.51.54.10, e-mail bruno.mignon@champagne-mignon.fr ☑ ☎ by appt.

PIERRE MIGNON Brut Prestige★

○   4 ha   n.c.   ■ €11-15

Founded in 1970 at Breuil, this family-run business today cultivates 12 ha (30 acres) of vines. Their Brut Prestige is a blend of 65% Pinot Meunier, 20% Chardonnay and 15% Pinot Noir. Its pale-golden appearance has straw-coloured highlights. Ripe quince and apple flavours intermingle in a wine that combines richness and freshness. Another star was awarded to the equally appealing **90 Cuvée Madame**. (NM)

☛ Pierre Mignon, 5, rue des Grappes-d'Or, 51210 Le Breuil, tel. 03.26.59.22.03, fax 03.26.59.26.74, e-mail p.mignon@lemel.fr ☑ ☎ by appt.

MIGNON ET PIERREL

Cuvée Florale★★

○ 1er Cru   n.c.   n.c.   ■ €15-23

This recently established house (1990) puts its champagnes in the most unconventional bottles: the glass is entirely enveloped in a plastic film of green, blue or pink. The contents, on the other hand, are distinctly more conventional – a classic blend of 60% Chardonnay to 40% Pinot Noir. A brioche-like bouquet, a forthright opening impression and exotic fruit flavours that linger on the palate are its hallmarks. The **95 Cuvée Florale Premier Cru**, a blanc de blancs (albeit not labelled as such), received one star. This wine

opens with floral, honeyed scents and ends on a note of citrus fruits. Finally, a commendation was given to the non-vintage *brut*, **Marquis de La Fayette Cuvée Prestige**. This overwhelmingly black-grape champagne (90% Pinot Noir) is light bodied, with flavours of apple and menthol. (NM)

☛ SA Pierrel et Associés, 26, rue Henri-Dunant, 51200 Epernay, tel. 03.26.51.00.90, fax 03.26.51.69.40, e-mail champagne@pierrel.fr ☑ ☎ by appt.

JEAN MILAN

Blanc de Blancs Cuvée Spécial★

○ Gd Cru   n.c.   n.c.   ■ €11-15

Established in 1864, this house is managed nowadays by a descendant of the founder. It comprises 6 ha (15 acres) of vines in the Côte des Blancs, which are dedicated to Chardonnay. Among its blancs de blancs this Brut Cuvée Spécial, from the harvests of 1996 and 1997, with its discreet bouquet, lively start, balance, youth and freshness, gained the admiration of the Jury. (NM)

☛ Champagne Milan, 6, rue d'Avize, 51190 Oger, tel. 03.26.57.50.09, fax 03.26.57.78.47, e-mail info@champagne-milan.com ☑ ☎ ev. day 10am–12.30pm; 2pm–6pm; Sun. by appt.

☛ Henry-Pol Milan

MOET ET CHANDON

Brut Imperial 1995★

○   n.c.   n.c.   ■ €30-33

Moët et Chandon, one of the oldest and most prestigious champagne houses, was founded in 1743 by Claude Moët. It has been famous from the start, thanks to its royal patronage. Since the early 1960s, it has witnessed major expansion, and today is the main champagne producer of the LVMH group. The 95 Brut Impérial is a blend of equal parts Pinot Noir and Chardonnay, with a dash of Pinot Meunier. Its bouquet offers light, crystallised fruit scents, and the palate is rich and powerful. (NM)

☛ Champagne Moët et Chandon, 20, av. de Champagne, 51200 Epernay, tel. 03.26.51.20.00, fax 03.26.54.84.23 ☑ ☎ ev. day 9.30am–11.30am; 2pm–4.30pm; groups by appt.

MOET ET CHANDON

Dom Pérignon 1993★

○   n.c.   n.c.   ■ +€76

It may not be common knowledge, but the prestigious Dom Pérignon brand name, synonymous with fine champagne, originally belonged to Mercier (in turn owned by Moët since 1970). It was offered to Francine Durand-Mercier, Eugène's grand-daughter, when she married Paul Chandon. Its launch under the Moët et Chandon label, during the inaugural voyage of the steamship *Normandie* to New York in 1936, was an immediate success. The first vintage was the 21, beyond a shadow of a doubt the finest of the century. Dom Pérignon blends its black and white grapes in more or less equal proportions, but this may vary according to the vintage. Both black and white can boast a fine pedigree. The former hail from Chouilly, Avize, Mesnil and Oger, the latter from Bouzy, Verzenay, Mailly, Ay and Ambonnay, with a small quantity, as a symbolic gesture, from Dom Pérignon's old base of Hautvillers. The 93 harvest, a modest year on the whole, is very successful in this instance. With its almondy bouquet, initial impressions are of a straightforward and well-balanced wine, with flavours of citrus fruits lingering on the finish. (NM)

☎ Champagne Moët et Chandon, 20, av. de Champagne, 51200 Epernay, tel. 03.26.51.20.00, fax 03.26.54.84.23 ✉
⊤ ev. day 9.30am–11.30am; 2pm–4.30pm; groups by appt.

ERNEST MONMARTHE

70e Anniversaire 1995★

○ 1er Cru	n.c.	10,000	€11-23

Certain key dates define the history of this estate: 1737, when the Monmarthes set up this enterprise in the Montagne de Reims; 1930, when Ernest Monmarthe started marketing his first champagnes; and 1990, when Jean-Guy took over the estate. It consists of 17 ha (42 acres) of vines around the Premier Cru village where his ancestors were originally based. The Ernest Monmarthe *cuvée* celebrates the 70th anniversary of the launch of the original Monmarthe label. Made from half white grapes and half black (with 25% of Meunier), this champagne releases an intense bouquet of honey and crystallised fruits, and excels itself with its power and balance. A commendation was awarded to another Premier Cru, the **Grande Réserve**, also half white and half black and produced from the harvests of 1994 to 1996, a very soft rosé. (RM)

☎ Jean-Guy Monmarthe, 38, rue Victor-Hugo, 51500 Ludes, tel. 03.26.61.10.99, fax 03.26.61.12.67, e-mail champagne-monmarthe@wanadoo.fr
⊤ by appt.

PIERRE MONCUIT

Blanc de Blancs 1995★★

○ Gd Cru	12 ha	25,000	€15-23

Located at Mesnil-sur-Oger in the heart of the Côte des Blancs, this enterprise specialises in Grand Cru blancs de blancs. The vineyard was established in 1889, and its first wine was produced in 1928. The 95 vintage was highly rated by the Jury. Its crystallised fruity bouquet (with the emphasis on quince) and its balanced and liquoricey palate, point to a wine that has reached its peak. The **95 Nicole Moncuit Vieilles Vignes**, produced from 80-year-old vines, was commended for its elegance and finesse. The same rating was accorded to the **Cuvée de Réserve**, with its soft first impression and forthright, well-balanced palate. (RM)

☎ Champagne Pierre Moncuit, 11, rue Persault-Maheu, 51190 Le Mesnil-sur-Oger, tel. 03.26.57.52.65, fax 03.26.57.97.89 ✉

MONDET Tradition★

○	4 ha	12,000	€11-15

This 10.5-ha (26-acre) estate, founded in 1928, is situated not far from the abbey at Hautvillers. The Tradition is made up of 80% Pinot Noir to 20% Chardonnay. Two-thirds of the grapes derive from the 1996 harvest, with the rest from 1995. The wines have been aged in oak. This champagne, with its aromas of toasted brioche, has a particularly full and supple palate. (NM)

☎ Champagne Mondet, 2, rue Dom-Pérignon, 51480 Cormoyeux, tel. 03.26.58.64.15, fax 03.26.58.44.00 ✉
⊤ by appt.
☚ Francis Mondet

MONTAUDON★

○	100 ha	800,000	€11-15

The Montaudon brand was created in 1891. Today, the estate comprises 35 ha (86 acres). Its non-vintage *brut* is made from three-quarters black grapes (of which 25% is Pinot Meunier) and one-quarter white, harvested between 1996 and 1998. This is a classic blend for a classic champagne, offering roundness, balance and very good length. (NM)

☎ Champagne Montaudon, 6, rue Ponsardin, 51100 Reims, tel. 03.26.86.70.80, fax 03.26.86.70.87 ✉

DANIEL MOREAU

Carte Noire Blanc de Noirs★★

○	2.5 ha	20,000	€11-15

This family-run estate was established in 1875, and has been producing champagne since 1978. Its 4.5-ha (11-acre) vineyard is situated in the Marne Valley, where Daniel Moreau is quite a Pinot Meunier champion (see his entry under Coteaux Champenois). His balanced, full and expressive blanc de noirs, from the harvests of 1996 and 1997, is clearly derived from the Pinot Meunier grape. His **Carte d'Or** is a blanc de blancs, whose complexity, roundness, vinosity, balance and length earned it a star. It is a champagne destined for the dinner table. (RM)

☎ Daniel Moreau, 5, rue du Moulin, 51700 Vandières, tel. 03.26.58.01.64, fax 03.26.58.15.64 ⊤ by appt.

MOREL PERE ET FILS

○	3 ha	4,000	€11-15

For many years, the Morels have produced nothing but Rosé des Riceys. Since 1997, however, Pascal Morel has been making champagnes too, as typified by this rosé. Naturally produced from Pinot (in this instance Pinot Noir), it has undergone a brief maceration on the skins. Red fruit flavours harmonise appetisingly on a fresh, well-rounded and balanced palate. (RM)

☎ Pascal Morel Père et Fils, 93, rue du Gal-de-Gaulle, 10340 Les Riceys, tel. 03.25.29.10.88, fax 03.25.29.66.72 ✉
⊤ by appt.

MORIZE PERE ET FILS Réserve★

○ 11 ha 45,545 ▮ ◆ €11-15

Based at Les Riceys in the Aube, this 11-ha (27-acre) estate submitted a predominantly black-grape (85% Pinot Noir) Réserve, sourced from the harvest of 1996, with proportions of 1994 and 1995. The strengths of this well-balanced wine are its freshness and its length. By contrast, the 96 contains more Chardonnay than anything else (85%). It won a commendation from the Jury for its complex bouquet of citrus fruits, pepper, tobacco and leather – impressions that continue on to the palate. (RM)

☛ Morize Père et Fils, 122, rue du Gal-de-Gaulle, 10340 Les Riceys, tel. 03.25.29.30.02, fax 03.25.38.20.22 ▼
Ⴗ by appt.

PIERRE MORLET 1996

○ 1er Cru 1.5 ha 13,000 ▮ ▮▯ ◆ €11-15

Pierre Morlet is a grower and *négociant*, based at Avenay-Val-d'Or. His 96 vintage is made from a blend of 62% Pinot Noir and 38% Chardonnay, grown on the Grand Cru vineyard of Ay and the Premiers Crus of Avenay-Val-d'Or and Mutigny. The must is fermented in oak barrels, and the result is a fine, elegant champagne with citrus fruit flavours, and a hint of bitterness on the finish that reveals its extreme youth. (NM)

☛ Champagne Pierre Morlet, 7, rue Paulin-Paris, 51160 Avenay-Val-d'Or, tel. 03.26.52.32.32, fax 03.26.59.77.13 ▼
Ⴗ by appt.

CORINNE MOUTARD Tradition★

○ n.c. 20,000 ▮ ◆ €11-15

This family-run estate comprises 6 ha (15 acres) of vines in the Aube. Corinne Moutard has been marketing a champagne under her own name since 1998. The Tradition is, indeed, a traditional blend of 70% Pinots (of which 10% is Meunier) and 30% Chardonnay. This *cuvée* offers a subtle, yet exquisite bouquet, a forthright opening impression and a well-balanced palate. The **rosé**, which is a rosé de noirs, also received a star for its bouquet of nuts and fruit compote, and for its smoky, fruity palate. (NM)

☛ Corinne Moutard, 51, Grande-Rue, 10110 Polisy, tel. 03.25.38.52.47, fax 03.25.29.37.46 ▼ Ⴗ by appt.

JEAN MOUTARDIER Carte d'or★

○ 23 ha 210,000 ▮ ◆ €11-15

Despite its somewhat remote location on the western outskirts of the Champagne growing area, in the Surmelin Valley (nearer to Montmirail than to Epernay), this 23-ha (57-acre) estate, founded in 1920, has featured regularly in the *Guide*. Its grape blend favours Pinot Meunier (a variety that this house has made something of a speciality). The Carte d'Or therefore draws heavily upon Meunier, which makes up 90% of the blend, backed up by 10% Chardonnay. Some of the base wines in the blend are reserve wines that have been aged in oak. The resulting champagne has an

intense, well-developed palate of great length. (NM)

☛ Champagne Jean Moutardier, 51210 Le Breuil, tel. 03.26.59.21.09, fax 03.26.59.21.25, e-mail moutard.j@ebc.net ▼ Ⴗ by appt.

MOUTARD PERE ET FILS

Extra-brut

○ 3.5 ha 20,000 ▮ ◆ €15-23

The Moutards have been making champagne since 1927. François Moutard has a particular interest in the region's rare grape varieties, and even makes one champagne from unblended Arbanne! This Extra Brut, though, is made in a more classic idiom, from half white grapes and half black (Pinot Noir). Non-dosed, and with a subtle, floral bouquet, its lively first impressions are followed by a clean and clearly defined palate. (NM)

☛ Champagne Moutard-Diligent, 6, rue des Ponts, 10110 Buxeuil, tel. 03.25.38.50.73, fax 03.25.38.57.72, e-mail champagne.moutard@wanadoo.fr ▼
Ⴗ by appt.

Y. MOUZON LECLERE Carte d'or

○ 1er Cru 1,800 ▮ ◆ €11-15

Although the brand only dates back as far as 1959, the Mouzon Leclère estate has been producing champagne since pre-war days. Based in the Montagne de Reims, it encompasses 10 ha (25 acres) of vines. The Carte d'Or, which does not undergo malolactic fermentation, comprises 80% Chardonnay and 20% Pinot Noir (from the harvests of 1994 and 1995). It has a fruity bouquet and a generously firm palate. (RM)

☛ Yvon Mouzon, 1, rue Haute-des-Carrières, 51380 Verzy, tel. 03.26.97.91.19, fax 03.26.97.97.89 ▼
Ⴗ by appt.

PH. MOUZON-LEROUX

Grande Réserve

○ Gd Cru n.c. 80,000 ▮ ◆ €11-15

Philippe Mouzon cultivates 10 ha (25 acres) of vines near Verzy, a Grand Cru village in the Montagne de Reims. Two of the estate's champagnes bottled under the Mouzon-Leroux label received commendations. Both *cuvées* are blends of Pinot Noir and Chardonnay, but in inverse proportions to each other. The Grande Réserve is dominated by black grapes (80%), with 58% of the wine derived from the 1997 harvest, topped up with reserve wines from 1993 to 1996. It is a vinous and well-balanced champagne, with evident *dosage*. The **95 Grand Cru**, on the other hand, contains 80% Chardonnay. Its delicate, floral bouquet contrasts appealingly with its rounded, if vigorous palate. Another Grand Cru *cuvée*, in this instance a non-vintage, bottled under the **R. Mouzon–Juillet** label, was also commended by the Jury. This intense, honeyed and highly evolved champagne, is made up of two-thirds Chardonnay to one-third Pinot Noir, from the harvests of 90 (30%) and 91 (70%). It would go well with red meats (RM)

♠ EARL Mouzon-Leroux, 16, rue Basse-des-Carrières, 51380 Verzy, tel. 03.26.97.96.68, fax 03.26.97.97.67 V
Y by appt.

G.H. MUMM ET CIE Cordon Rouge★

| ○ | 750 ha | 5,000,000 | ■ ■ | €15-23 |

Founded in 1827 by two Germans, even before the First World War this famous Reims house was already exporting around three million bottles a year. Despite its success, Mumm has encountered turbulent times over the years. Since 1969, the company has operated as a division of various major American conglomerates (Allied Domecq is its present owner). Cordon Rouge, a tribute to the Légion d'honneur, has been in existence since 1875. The current release consists of 70% black grapes (45% Pinot Noir and 25% Meunier), and contains 10% reserve wines. Unlike the honorific Cordon Rouge, it isn't just restricted to a small number of customers. At once fresh and well rounded, it will win itself countless admirers. The 96 also received a star. This blend, too, is dominated by black grapes (62%), but from Grand Cru vineyards. It is powerful, lingering and most definitely a youthful wine. Yet another star went to Mumm de Cramant, a Grand Cru blanc de blancs made in the lightly sparkling style. It was praised for its elegance and its fine, complex bouquet of flowers and brioche. (NM)

♠ G.-H. Mumm et Cie, 29, rue du Champ-de-Mars, 51100 Reims, tel. 03.26.49.59.69, fax 03.26.40.46.13, e-mail mumm@mumm.fr V Y by appt.
♠ Allied Domecq

NAPOLEON 1991

| ○ | | n.c. | | €23-30 |

Maison Prieur, founded in 1825 at Vertus, has exclusive rights to the Napoléon brand name. Curiously, in view of the name's implications, it was originally targeted at the Russian market. The Napoléon operation likes to age its wines, and therefore submitted a well-developed 91 made from half black grapes and half white. It has both length and noticeable dosage. (NM)

♠ Champagne Napoléon, 2, rue de Villers-aux-Bois, 51130 Vertus, tel. 03.26.52.11.74, fax 03.26.52.29.10 V
♠ Ch. et A. Prieur

CHARLES ORBAN

Cuvée Spéciale 2000★★

| ○ | 1 ha | 6,000 | ■ ■ | €15-23 |

Charles Orban champagne is one of Maison Rapeneau's brands. This cuvée is produced exclusively from a 9-ha (22-acre) vineyard owned by a grower-wine-maker based at Troissy in the Marne Valley. Largely dominated by Chardonnay (80%), supplemented by Pinot Noir, the grapes in this blend were harvested in 1996 and 1997. The result is an extremely attractive champagne whose success can be attributed not only to its fine, lively, buttery, toasty bouquet, with hints of

honeyed apples and pears, but also to its well-balanced, fresh and lingering palate. (RM)

♠ Champagne Charles Orban, 44, rue de Paris, 51700 Troissy, tel. 03.26.52.70.05, fax 03.26.52.74.66 V Y ev. day except Sat. Sun. 10am-12 noon; 2pm-6pm.
♠ Rapeneau

CUVÉE ORPALE Blanc de Blancs 1990

| ○ Gd Cru | | n.c. | 25,000 | ■ ■ | €30-38 |

Based at Avize in the Côte des Blancs, Union Champagne co-ordinates around ten co-operatives that together manage approximately 1,000 ha (2,470 acres) of vines. Its marque brand names are marketed under either grande marque brand names or under its own labels. Saint-Gall (a name worth looking out for) and Orpale. The latter is a top-of-the-range cuvée. Tasters identified two outstanding characteristics: it is 'very 90', in other words, opulent, supple and lightly evolved, and it is also 'very blanc de blancs', i.e. full of finesse, and exhibiting the classic aromatic range of a Chardonnay wine: toast, butter and hazelnuts. (CM)

♠ Union Champagne, 7, rue Pasteur, 51190 Avize, tel. 03.26.57.94.22, fax 03.26.57.57.98, e-mail info@de-saint-gall.com V Y by appt.

OUDINOT Brut Cuvée★

| ○ | | n.c. | 700,000 | ■ ■ | €15-23 |

Founded in 1889 at Avize, this house was taken over in 1981 by Jacques Trouillard, proprietor not only of 121 ha (299 acres) of vines, but also of the Jeanmaire and Beaumet brand names. This fine, lively non-vintage brut is made from the three champagne grapes in virtually equal proportions. It would make a good aperitif. (NM)

♠ Champagne Oudinot, ch. Malakoff, 3, rue Malakoff, 51207 Epernay, tel. 03.26.59.50.10, fax 03.26.54.78.52, e-mail chateau.malakoff@wanadoo.fr
♠ M. et J. Trouillard

BRUNO PAILLARD 1995★

| ○ | | n.c. | | ■ ■ ■ | €23-30 |

Founded in 1981 by Bruno Paillard, this is one of the more recently established champagne houses. Its cuvées fall into the higher price-bracket, and three-quarters of its output is destined for the export market. Restaurateurs and owners of private cellars also account for a large number of Paillard's clients. Composed of two-thirds black grapes (45% Pinot Noir and 19% Meunier, to 36% Chardonnay), this 95 brut is brioche scented, rich and long. The Première Cuvée was equally highly rated. Produced from similar proportions to the 95 (45% Pinot Noir, 22% Meunier, 33% Chardonnay), it is a fruity, rounded, expressive and perfectly balanced wine. The Première Cuvée rosé, dominated by Pinot Noir (85% to 15% Chardonnay), received yet another star. It has a gentle pink appearance in the glass, and is lively and powerful on the palate. Apart from the rose, Bruno

Paillard's champagnes are partially – or indeed, in the case of the commended **90 NPU (Nec plus ultra)** – entirely oaked. (NM)

➤ Champagne Bruno Paillard,
av. de Champagne, 51100 Reims,
tel. 03.26.36.20.22, fax 03.26.36.57.72,
e-mail brunopaillard@aol.com
Y by appt.

AMAZONE DE PALMER

○ n.c. n.c. ■ ♦ €23–30

Originally a group of Grand Cru producers, the Palmer organisation went on to expand into more humble *terroirs*. Amazone is a classic blend of half black grapes and half white, and is the only champagne to be marketed in an oval-shaped bottle. This powerful, vinous, honeyed wine will delight aficionados of more mature champagnes. It will doubtless find its way on to dinner tables, served with meats. Equally commended was the **Non-Vintage Brut**, produced from two-thirds Chardonnay (62%) to one-third of both Pinots. Well balanced, with citrus fruit flavours, it would make a pleasing aperitif (CM)

➤ Champagne Palmer et C°, 67, rue Jacquart, 51100 Reims, tel. 03.26.07.35.07, fax 03.26.07.45.24 **Y** by appt.

PANNIER 1996★

○ n.c. 18.386 ■ ♦ €15–23

This enterprise bears the name of Eugène Pannier, founder of a champagne house that he later transferred to the control of his son. In 1971, the brand was relaunched by COVAMA, a co-operative group of grape-suppliers. The enterprise is based at Château-Thierry in the Aisne district of the Marne Valley, famed for being the birthplace of Jean de la Fontaine. It has 600 ha (1,480 acres) of vines at its disposal. The 96 vintage, produced from the three champagne grapes, was particularly well received by the Jury. Its balance, freshness and length all came in for high praise. A commendation was awarded to the **rosé** – again, a blend of all three varieties, but with a preponderance of Pinot Meunier. Deep pink, almost red, in appearance, it is a well-structured, vinous and supple champagne (CM)

➤ SCVM COVAMA, 25, rue Roger-Catillon, B.P. 55, 02403 Château-Thierry Cedex, tel. 03.23.69.51.30, fax 03.23.69.51.31, e-mail chppannier@aol.com  **Y** by appt.

PAQUES ET FILS

Chardonnay Cuvée Aurore★★

○ 1er Cru 0.25 ha 2,000 ■ ♦ €15–23

Founded in 1905, by the great-grandfather of the current incumbents, this estate of approximately 10 ha (25 acres) is situated in the Montagne de Reims, in the vicinity of the Premier Cru village of Rilly. It created quite a stir with two highly rated wines. Aurore is a blanc de blancs, born of two exceptional years, 1995 and 1996. The tasters were greatly impressed by its freshness and finesse, and forecast a promising future for it. It would make a fine aperitif, or an accompaniment for

fish and shellfish. The **95 Carte Rouge** received one star. Fruity, honeyed and smoky, this champagne distinguishes itself by its power and great character. (RM)

➤ Paques et Fils, 1, rue Valmy, 51500 Rilly-la-Montagne,
tel. 03.26.03.42.53, fax 03.26.03.40.29,
e-mail phil.paques@wanadoo.fr
Y by appt.

DENIS PATOUX Carte d'or★★

○ n.c. n.c. ■ ♦ €11–15

Denis Patoux's family has been committed to the vine since 1900. However, it was grandfather Patoux who first entered the champagne market in 1945. Today, this enterprise, based at Vandières in the Marne Valley, comprises 8 ha (20 acres) of vines, planted along the right bank of the river. The Carte d'Or makes its mark in an utterly forthright fashion: the clean, fruity, lively bouquet; the fresh, impeccably fruity palate, with its suggestion of white peach; the fine balance and length of the wine. This excellent champagne would be equally good as an aperitif or with fish. Spicy, vigorous and long, the **Non-Vintage Brut** earned itself one star. (RM)

➤ Denis Patoux, 1, rue Bailly, 51700 Vandières, tel. 03.26.58.36.34, fax 03.26.59.16.10 **Y** by appt.

PEHU–SIMONET Sélection★★

○ Gd Cru 2 ha 17,000 ■ ♦ €11–15

The Péhu-Simonet label came about as a result of the union of two families in 1978. Nowadays, the estate comprises 5 ha (12 acres) of vines at Verzenay, a village in the Montagne de Reims classified as 100% on the *échelle des crus*. The three garlanded champagnes are, moreover, all Grands Crus. 'This is it!', 'I like this wine!,' commented two of the tasters about the Sélection *cuvée*, made from three-quarters Pinot Noir backed up by Chardonnay. It is a blend of grapes from the 1998 harvest, with contributions from 1994 to 1997 – a fleshy, full, long and structured wine that should be served with red meat. The **Cuvée Spéciale rosé** is made up of 80% Pinot Noir (some of which is red wine) and 20% Chardonnay, harvested between the years 1994 and 1997. Its fine presence, balance and length earned it a star. Finally, the **93 Cuvée Junior** also deserves a mention. Blended from half black grapes and half white, this ripe and full champagne mingles flavours of stewed fruits with hints of brioche. (RM)

♠ Péhu-Simonet, 7, rue de la Gare, BP 22, 51360 Verzenay, tel. 03.26.49.43.20, fax 03.26.49.45.06 ☒ ♈ by appt.

JEAN-MICHEL PELLETIER

Tradition ★★

○   2.5 ha   22,000   €11-15

This non-vintage *brut* is a blend of grapes from the years 1996, 1997 and 1998, containing 90% Pinot Meunier. Oenologist Jean-Michel Pelletier has succeeded in producing a complex, rounded, floral and fruity champagne with light *dosage* – a pleasing and well-balanced wine. (RC)
♠ Jean-Michel Pelletier, 22, rue Bruslard, 51700 Passy-Grigny, tel. 03.26.52.65.86, fax 03.26.52.65.86 ☒ ♈ by appt.

JEAN PERNET Tradition

○   6 ha   30,000   €11-15

This house manages 15.5 ha (38 acres) of vines, and has been marketing its champagne since 1947. Their Tradition is a blend of 60% Pinots (of which 10% is Meunier) and 40% Chardonnay, from the harvest of 1997 and 1998. It offers an intense, honeyed bouquet and a light, fresh palate. The **Reserve Chardonnay Grand Cru**, a blend of 1996 and 1997 wines, was also commended by the Jury. Although somewhat fleeting on the finish, this is a rounded and well-balanced champagne. (NM)
♠ Champagne Jean Pernet, 6, rue de la Brèche-d'Oger, 51190 Le Mesnil-sur-Oger, tel. 03.26.57.54.24, fax 03.26.57.96.98 ☒ ♈ by appt.

PERNET-LEBRUN ★

○   n.c.   2,000   €11-15

This vineyard near Mancy has been cultivated by five generations of growers. Pinot Meunier (58%) is the dominant grape in this rosé blend, supplemented by 12% Pinot Noir and 30% Chardonnay, harvested in 1998. A salmon-coloured wine, with orangey tints, it exhibits aromas of honey and raspberries, and is well balanced on the palate. The **95 Authentick** received a further star from the Jury. A blend of the three champagne grapes in equal proportions, it is toasty, vigorous and light in texture. **Cuvée d'Argent-Sol** is a half-and-half blend of white and black (Meunier) grapes, from the harvest of 1997. As with the previous champagne, it was praised for its balance and length. (RM)
♠ Pernet-Lebrun, Ancien-Moulin, 51530 Mancy, tel. 03.26.59.71.63, fax 03.26.57.10.42 ☒ ♈ by appt.

JOSEPH PERRIER Cuvée Royale ★

○   n.c.   500,000   €15-23

One of the two Châlons-en-Champagne houses, founded in 1825 by Joseph Perrier and sold in 1888 to one Paul Pithois, this enterprise was owned for a short while by Laurent-Perrier, before being taken over by Alain Thiénot. The non-vintage Cuvée Royale is made up of the three champagne grapes in equal proportions. It has good balance and finesse, showing lemony notes both in the bouquet and on the palate. Two other champagnes, both in the upper price bracket, received commendations. The **Cuvée Royale rosé**, dominated by black grapes (75% Pinot Noir to 25% Chardonnay), is extremely well balanced and marked by noticeable pear-drop flavours, while the **95 Cuvée Royale**, which is a virtually half-and-half blend of black and white grapes (with 55% Pinot Noir), was also described as well balanced. (NM)
♠ SA Champagne Joseph Perrier, 69, av. de Paris, B.P. 31, 51000 Châlons-en-Champagne, tel. 03.26.68.29.51, fax 03.26.70.57.16 ☒ ♈ by appt.

DANIEL PERRIN Cuvée Prestige

○   1.5 ha   10,000   €11-15

This 12-ha (30-acre) vineyard in the Aube is managed by two brothers who have been producing their own champagnes since 1957. Their Prestige Cuvée is made up of two-thirds black grapes (Pinot Noir) to one-third white, from the harvest of 1998. The Jury was impressed by its bouquet of fleshy fruits and its lemony palate, which has perceptible *dosage*. (RM)
♠ EARL Champagne Daniel Perrin, 10200 Urville, tel. 03.25.27.40.36, fax 03.25.27.74.57 ☒ ♈ by appt.

PERSEVAL-FARGE

Cuvée Jean-Baptiste

○ 1er Cru   2 ha   2,000   €15-23

Isabelle and Benoist Perseval cultivate 4 ha (10 acres) of vines on five different plots around Chamery in the Montagne de Reims. Jean-Baptiste is a classic blend of 60% Chardonnay and 40% Meunier, from the harvests of 1993 to 1995. Brioche and almonds mingle in the bouquet, while the light-bodied palate conjures up citrus fruits. (RM)
♠ Isabelle et Benoist Perseval, 12, rue du Voisin, 51500 Chamery, tel. 03.26.97.64.70, fax 03.26.97.67.67, e-mail champagne.perseval-farge@wanadoo.fr ☒ ♈ by appt.

PERTOIS-MORISET

Blanc de Blancs 1995

○ Gd cru   12 ha   30,000   €15-23

Dominique Pertois cultivates 18 ha (44 acres) of vines at Mesnil-sur-Oger, a Grand Cru village in the heart of the Côte des Blancs. He submitted a blanc de blancs with a honeyed, mocha-scented bouquet – a characteristic indicative of a well-developed wine. Its sharply angled palate is typical of the vivacity of the 95 vintage. (RM)
♠ Dominique Pertois, 13, av. de la République, 51190 Le Mesnil-sur-Oger, tel. 03.26.57.52.14, fax 03.26.57.78.98 ☒ ♈ ev. day except Sun. 8am–12 noon, 2pm–6pm; cl. Aug.

PIERRE PETERS

Blanc de Blancs Cuvée de Réserve   €11-15

○Gd Cru   10 ha   100,000

This producer, from a well-known Mesnil-sur-Oger family, manages a 17.5-ha (43-acre) vineyard planted entirely with Chardonnay. Two of his blanc de blancs (both very different *cuvées*), were commended by the Jury. The Réserve has mingled aromas of butter, caramel and honey on the bouquet, and a supple palate with evident *dosage*. The **Extra Brut**, on the other hand, is strikingly fresh, with hazelnuts on the bouquet and a fine, lingering palate that finishes on a note of citrus fruits. (RM)

☛ Champagne Pierre Peters, 26, rue des Lombards, 51190 Le Mesnil-sur-Oger, tel. 03.26.57.50.32, fax 03.26.57.97.71 ✉
✠ by appt.
☛ F. Peters

PETITJEAN-PIENNE

Blanc de Blancs★   €11-15

○Gd Cru   1.75 ha   8,800

This family has been established at Cramant in the Côte des Blancs for four generations. It manages a vineyard in the vicinity of Avize, itself a Grand Cru village. It is represented by a floral-scented blanc de blancs with a full-bodied, mature palate. (RM)

☛ Petitjean-Pienne, 4, allée des Bouleaux, 51530 Cramant, tel. 03.26.57.58.26, fax 03.26.59.34.09, e-mail petitjean-pienne@wanadoo.fr ✉ ✠ by appt.

MAURICE PHILIPPART

Prestige 1990★   €15-23

○Gd Cru   6 ha   11,236

Nicaise – a typical champagne name – was already cultivating a vineyard in 1827. Maurice, who was a grower in the period between the wars, bequeathed his name to the champagne that was marketed by Paul from 1956. Franck took over in 1993, and today cultivates 6 ha (15 acres) of vines. The estate is based at Chigny in the Montagne de Reims. The 90 Prestige, a blend of 40% Pinot Noir and 60% Chardonnay, is very representative of its year. In other words, it is rich, soft, full and long, with well-developed, emphatic flavours of very ripe fruits. One could imagine this champagne accompanying a dish of chicken with truffles. (RM)

☛ Maurice Philippart,
16, rue de Rilly, 51500 Chigny-les-Roses, tel. 03.26.03.42.44, fax 03.26.03.46.05, e-mail franck.philippart1@libertysurf.fr ✉
✠ ev. day except Sun. 9am–11.30am; 2pm–6pm; Sat. by appt.
☛ Franck Philippart

PHILIPPONNAT

Clos des Goisses 1990★★   €46-76

○   5.5 ha   n.c.

This house's emblem, a red and gold chequered coat of arms, dates back to 1697. Although the Philipponnat family has owned vines since that era, it was not involved in champagne production until the time of the

Second Empire. The house was founded in 1910 by Auguste and Pierre Philipponnat. Boizel Chanoine Champagne has owned and managed the 17-ha (42-acre) estate since 1997. The renowned Clos des Goisses, a 5.5-ha (14-acre) south-facing, sloping vineyard enclosed within walls, was acquired in 1935. It is reserved exclusively for vintage champagnes. The 90 Clos des Goisses, composed of 70% Pinot Noir and 30% Chardonnay, has not undergone malolactic fermentation. Several tasters were extremely enthusiastic: 'Superb!' concluded one who recommended it for a *coup de coeur*. This magnificent, full, structured and extremely long champagne exudes flavours of hazelnuts and almonds. The **91 Sublime Réserve Blanc de Blancs** received a commendation. Given weight by its *dosage*, it is a champagne that has reached its peak. (NM)

☛ SA Champagne Philipponnat,
13, rue du Pont, 51160 Mareuil-sur-Ay, tel. 03.26.56.93.00, fax 03.26.56.93.18, e-mail info@champagnephilipponnat.com
✠ by appt.

PIERREL   Cuvée Arabesque★   €15-23

○   n.c.   n.c.

Pierrel is the brand name of an Epernay house that also produces champagnes under the Mignon et Pierrel label (look out for this name) as well as that of Marquis de la Fayette. The Arabesque is produced entirely from Chardonnay, although the designation 'blanc de blancs' does not appear on the simple, diamond-shaped label. 'Complex, rounded, balanced and long, it would make a good champagne for serving at a special reception', suggested one taster. Two other Premier Cru champagnes were commended: the **Non-Vintage Brut**, a fleeting but well-balanced blend of 60% Chardonnay and 40% Pinot Noir, and the **95 Grande Cuvée**, which is 5% off being a blanc de blancs. This latter is lively and long, with flavours of citrus fruits. (NM)

☛ SA Pierrel et Associés, 26, rue Henri-Dunant, 51200 Epernay, tel. 03.26.51.00.90, fax 03.26.51.69.40, e-mail champagne@pierrel.fr ✉ ✠ by appt.

PIERSON-CUVELIER

Prestige Carte d'or★   €11-15

○Gd Cru   2.5 ha   5,000

The vineyard is 100 years old. Its first champagnes were produced in 1928, and the brand was launched 50 years later. The estate is based at Louvois, a village in the Montagne de Reims that is classified 100% on the *échelle des crus*. The two champagnes submitted are all Grands Crus. The Jury preferred the Carte d'Or, a prestige blanc de noirs produced from the harvests of 1994 to 1996. A powerful, rich, well-structured champagne with preserved fruit flavours and a long finish, it would go well with white meats. The **rosé**, drawn from the harvests of 1995 to 1997, received a commendation. This champagne is a blend of *saignée* rosé, some Bouzy red wine from the same *cuvée* and a quantity of blanc de noirs.

Its intense colour, power and length make it a suitable champagne to serve at dinner. (RM)

François Pierson-Cuvelier, 4, rue de Verzy, 51150 Louvois, tel. 03.26.57.03.72, fax 03.26.51.83.84 ▼ by appt.

PIPER-HEIDSIECK 1995★
n.c.　n.c.　€23-30

This house is one of the three branches that resulted from the 1835 breakup of the company founded in 1785 by Florens Louis Heidsieck. Since 1990, the house has, like Charles Heidsieck, been owned by Rémy Cointreau. The 95 vintage is produced from the two 'noble' grape varieties, Pinot Noir and Chardonnay. It is a champagne of great character and, as one taster concluded, should be 'reserved for true devotees of champagne' - so underlining its elegance, intensity and finesse. (NM)

Piper-Heidsieck, 51, bd Henry-Vasnier, 51100 Reims, tel. 03.26.84.43.00, fax 03.26.84.43.49 ▼ by appt.

PLOYEZ-JACQUEMART 1995★
1.4 ha　14,000　€38-46

The négociant arm of this viticultural enterprise, which dates back to 1860, was set up in 1930, and has remained family-run ever since. The estate is based in the Montagne de Reims. The floral, balanced and fresh 95 is composed of a classic blend of 40% Pinot Noir and 60% Chardonnay. (NM)

Champagne Ployez-Jacquemart, 8, rue Astoin, 51500 Ludes, tel. 03.26.61.11.87, fax 03.26.61.12.20 ▼ by appt.

POL ROGER Blanc de blancs 1995★
n.c.　n.c.　€38-46

Pol Roger founded this house in 1849. The forename 'Pol' was incorporated in the surname at the beginning of the 20th century, and since then the enterprise has been under the management of Maurice Pol-Roger, Georges Pol-Roger, Jacques Pol-Roger and, finally, Christian Pol-Roger (who today jointly manages the business with his cousin Christian de Billy). The 95 vintage, a blend of 60% Pinot Noir and 40% Chardonnay, is a generous, rounded, full and perfectly balanced champagne. (NM)

SA Pol Roger, 1, rue Henri-Lelarge, 51200 Epernay, tel. 03.26.59.58.00, fax 03.26.55.25.70, e-mail polroger@abc.net ▼ by appt.

POMMERY Louise 1989★
45 ha　n.c.　€46-76

The LVMH group has owned the Pommery estate and its 300 ha (741 acres) of vines since 1990. Its brand name originated with the house of Dubois-Gosset, which was taken over by Narcisse Greno, who, in 1836, formed an association with Louis-Alexandre Pommery. However, it was Louise, the wife of the latter, who was instrumental in developing the business after her husband's death in 1858. She created the brut champagne, and also acquired a top-quality vineyard. The Cuvée Louise that is named after her is a prestige wine. It is made up of a blend of 60% Chardonnay and 40% Pinot Noir. Tasters were enthralled by this 89 vintage, a fitting tribute to one of the great widows of Champagne. Their notes read: 'delicious, unctuous, voluptuous, warming, succulent, brioche, almonds, dried fruits, a brilliant finish'. The Grand Jury was unanimous in awarding a coup de cœur. (NM)

Pommery, 5, pl. du Gal-Gouraud, B.P. 87, 51100 Reims, tel. 03.26.61.63.98, fax 03.26.61.63.98 ▼ by appt.
LVMH

VIRGILE PORTIER
Blanc de Blancs Cuvée Madeleine
1 ha　2,000　€15-23

This estate, founded by Virgile Portier in 1924, today comprises 8 ha (20 acres) of vines. The vinification takes place in oak, avoiding the use of malolactic fermentation. This non-vintage blanc de blancs, produced from the 1995 harvest, has a lightly oaked bouquet of great presence, revealing buttery notes with citrus fruit undertones, and a rich palate. It has now reached its peak. (RM)

SARL Virgile Portier, 21, rte Nationale, 51360 Beaumont-sur-Vesle, tel. 03.26.03.90.15, fax 03.26.03.99.31 ▼ ev. day 8am-12 noon; 2pm-7pm; Sun. by appt.

ROGER POUILLON ET FILS
5ème Anniversaire Fleur de Mareuil★
1er Cru　0.5 ha　3,000　€19-23

Founded by Roger Pouillon in 1947, this estate comprises 6.5 ha (16 acres) at Mareuil-sur-Aÿ, as well as at several other locations dotted throughout the Champagne region. It has a long-standing reputation for the production of oaked wines, and indeed Fabrice, grandson of the founder, worked in Sauternes and Burgundy before joining his father in the business in 1998. Needless to say, Fleur de Mareuil, which is made from half black grapes and half white drawn from the 1996 and 1997 harvests, has been vinified in barrel with stirring of the lees. Its complex aromatic range combines notes of light oak, vanilla and nuts. These flavours appear a touch over-evolved on the palate. (RM)

Roger Pouillon et Fils, 3, rue de la Couple, 51160 Mareuil-sur-Aÿ, tel. 03.26.52.60.08, fax 03.26.59.49.83, e-mail contact@champagne-pouillon.com

PRESTIGE DES SACRES

Reserve Spéciale★

○ n.c. 🍷 150,000 ■ 🍴 €11-15

The Germigny-Janvry-Rosnay co-operative was founded in 1961, and has been marketing champagne since 1970. Its two brand names are Château de l'Auche and Prestige des Sacres. This *cuvée* is a blend of the three champagne grapes, from the harvests of 1995 to 1998. A bouquet of fruits, spices and honey is followed by a clean opening impression and a full, brioche-flavoured palate. Under the same label, the **Nectar de Saint-Rémi Blanc de Blancs**, produced from the harvests of 1993 and 1994, received a commendation for its bouquet of nuts and soft spices, and for its palate of lingering, wild fruit flavours. (CM)

☛ Coop. vinicole de Germigny-Janvry-Rosnay, rue de Germigny, 51390 Janvry, tel. 03.26.03.63.40, fax 03.26.03.66.93 Ⓥ

🍷 by appt.

YANNICK PREVOTEAU

La Perle des Treilles

○ 🍷 0.6 ha 4,000 🍴 €15-23

Five generations of the same family have cultivated this 9.5-ha (23-acre) vineyard, its champagne label being launched in 1970. Yannick Prévoteau's wines do not undergo malolactic fermentation. La Perle des Treilles is made up of a blend of 60% Pinot Noir and 40% Chardonnay. It has a fruity bouquet of apples and pears, and a well-balanced, honeyed palate of good length. (RM)

☛ Yannick Prévoteau,
4 bis, av. de Champagne, 51480 Damery, tel. 03.26.58.41.65, fax 03.26.58.61.05 Ⓥ

🍷 ev. day 8am–12 noon; 1pm–7pm

ACHILLE PRINCIER

Grand Art 1995★

○ n.c. 🍷 10,000 ■■ €30-38

This Epernay house, which includes various commercial operations, was set up in 1955. The Grand Art bottle is made in an old-fashioned design, with its cork secured in the old-fashioned way with twine, in accordance with the royal ordinance of 1735 (replacing the more familiar wire cage). Made from half black grapes and half white, this *cuvée* is a blend of wines from two white and three black Grands Crus. Its elegant and intense acacia-honey bouquet is followed by a rounded, rich palate that seems relatively evolved for a 95 vintage. (NM)

☛ Achille Princier,
9, rue Jean-Chandon-Moët, 51207 Epernay, tel. 03.26.54.04.06, fax 03.26.59.16.90 Ⓥ

🍷 ev. day 10am–7pm

☛ J.-Cl. Hébert

PRIN PERE ET FILS

Blanc de Blancs 1995★

○ n.c. 🍷 🍴 €23-30

The Prin family dedicates itself to this *négociant* house at Avize on the Côte des Blancs. Its outstanding 95 blanc de blancs has a smoky bouquet and a firm start on the

palate. It is a balanced, structured wine with good length. (NM)

☛ Champagne Prin Père et Fils,
28, rue Ernest-Valle, 51190 Avize, tel. 03.26.53.54.55, fax 03.26.53.54.56 Ⓥ

🍷 by appt.

DIDIER RAIMOND Tradition★★

○ 🍷 1.5 ha 10,500 ■ €11-15

This family enterprise has been expanding since 1980, and settled at Epernay in 1994. It comprises a vineyard of 5.4 ha (13 acres), and stores its reserve wines in cask. The three champagnes selected are drawn from the years 1997 and 1998. The Tradition, which received a *coup de coeur* in the previous edition of the *Guide*, remains just as impressive this year. Produced from two-thirds white grapes to one-third black (of which 10% is Meunier); it is an elegant, lively, rounded and well-balanced champagne. The coppery, almost brick-coloured **rosé**, a blend of 90% Charcconnay and 10% both Pinots, is a distinguished, but slightly overdosed wine that reveals light, fresh, red-fruit flavours. It earned one star. A commendation went to the elegant, oaky, complex, vigorous **Cuvée Sublime Blanc de Blancs**. (RM)

☛ Dicier Raimond, 39, rue des Petits-Prés, 51200 Epernay, tel. 03.26.54.39.05, fax 03.26.54.51.70,
e-mail champagnedidier.raimond@wanadoo.fr Ⓥ 🍷 by appt.

CUVEE DU REDEMPTEUR

Blanc de Blancs

○ 🍷 0.5 ha n.c. ■■ €11-15

This wine is a tribute, from his successors, to Edmond Dubois, nicknamed 'The Redeemer following his role in the 1911 champagne-growers' revolt. Today, the Dubois family cultivates a 7-ha (17-acre) vineyard in the vicinity of Venteuil in the Marne Valley. This blanc de blancs has been vinified in oak. It is full and balanced, albeit noticeably dosed. (RM)

☛ EARL du Rédempteur Dubois Père et Fils, rue d'Arty, 51480 Venteuil, tel. 03.26.58.48.37, fax 03.26.58.63.46 Ⓥ

🍷 ev. day 8am–12 noon; 2pm–5.30pm; Sat. Sun. by appt.

☛ Claude Dubois

PASCAL REDON Cuvée du Hordon★★

○ 1er Cru 🍷 0.3 ha 3,000 ■ 🍴 €15-23

This recently established estate of 4.3 ha (11 acres) has achieved marvellous results with its three commended champagnes. Hordon, made from half black grapes and half white, has an attractive bouquet of brioche and *pain d'épice*. Its palate is lively and young, with good length. The **95**, which is 5% away from being a blanc de blancs, was equally remarkable, not only for its bouquet of mingled crystallised fruits and toast, but also for its power and fine balance. In a lower price-bracket, the **Tradition** was awarded one star. This fine, floral, vigorous and well-balanced champagne is a blend of 80%

Chardonnay and 20% Pinot Noir. It would make a perfect accompaniment for fish dishes. (RM)

● Pascal Redon, 2, rue de la Mairie, 51380 Trépail, tel. 03.26.57.06.02, fax 03.26.58.66.54 ■ Y by appt.

BERNARD REMY Prestige★

◯   2 ha   7,000   ■ ♨ ▮ €11-15

This 7-ha (17-acre) estate has been very successful with its Prestige, which is produced from 60% white grapes and 40% black (of which 10% is Meunier). The base wines are drawn from the harvests of 1996 and 1997. A floral, brioche-scented champagne, it offers a lively start, intriguing length and perceptible *dosage*. The **rosé**, produced from black grapes harvested in 1996 and 1997, was also awarded a star. It has a scent of raspberries on the bouquet, and fresh red-fruit flavours on the finish. (RM)

● Bernard Rémy, 19, rue des Auges, 51120 Allemant, tel. 03.26.80.60.34, fax 03.26.80.37.18 ■ Y by appt.

● Françoise Rémy

MARC RIGOLOT Blanc de Blancs 1992★★

◯   2 ha   9,233   ♨ ▮ €15-23

This wine-grower cultivates a 4-ha (10-acre) vineyard not far from Epernay. His 92 blanc de blancs, from a fairly rare vintage, made quite an impression on the Jury with its well-developed, honeyed and buttery bouquet, and its brioche-flavoured and lingering palate. (RM)

● Champagne Marc Rigolot, 54, rue Julien-Ducos, 51530 Saint-Martin-d'Ablois, tel. 03.26.59.95.52, fax 03.26.59.94.95, e-mail champagne.rm@wanadoo.fr ☑ Y by appt.

BERTRAND ROBERT Cuvée Séduction 1995★

◯   n.c.   3,000   ▯ ♨ ▮ €15-23

André Robert is a grower in Mesnil-sur-Oger, a Grand Cru village in the heart of the Côte des Blancs. His Séduction certainly lives up to its fine name. It is a blend of 75% Mesnil-sur-Oger Chardonnay and 25% Vertus Pinot Noir, both fermented in oak. Its lively bouquet offers notes of honey, toast and violets, while its fine, firm palate is lightly oaked, but turns out to have impressive length. (RM)

● Champagne André Robert, 15, rue de l'Orme, B.P. 5, 51190 Le Mesnil-sur-Oger, tel. 03.26.57.59.41, fax 03.26.57.54.90 ☑
Y ev. day 9am-12 noon, 2pm-7pm; Sat. Sun. by appt.

● Bertrand Robert

ERIC RODEZ Blanc de Blancs

◯   6.12 ha   n.c.   ▯ ♨ ▮ €11-15

Eric Rodez cultivates a little over 6 ha (15 acres) in the *terroir* of Ambonnay, a Grand Cru village in the Montagne de Reims. His skilful vinification procedures strike a fine balance between partial malolactic fermentation and alcoholic fermentation in oak. This approach enables him to produce wines of great complexity. His fresh, floral and lingering blanc de blancs stands out for its youthfulness. The **Cuvée des Crayères**, which received a commendation, was equally expressive and complex, although the *dosage* makes itself felt. (RM)

● Eric Rodez, 4, rue d'Isse, 51150 Ambonnay, tel. 03.26.57.04.93, fax 03.26.57.02.15, e-mail e.rodez@champagne-rodez.fr ☑ Y by appt.

LOUIS ROEDERER Brut Premier★★

◯   n.c.   n.c.   ■ ♨ ▮ €23-30

This prestigious house owes its name to a company founded in 1760 by Dubois Père et Fils. When Louis Roederer inherited the estate in 1833, he renamed the business after himself, and then proceeded to make his fortune, expanding sales in the American and Russian export markets. His son built on these achievements by creating the famous Cristal *cuvée* for Tsar Alexander II in 1876. Today, the house remains in family hands, and manages 200 ha (494 acres), split between three Champagne regions. The Brut Premier is produced from two-thirds black grapes (56% Pinot Noir and 10% Meunier) and one-third Chardonnay. The Réserve wines that have been aged in oak constitute 10% of the blend. This is a fresh champagne that mingles flavours of spices, butter, lemon and hazelnuts. (NM)

● Champagne Louis Roederer, 21, bd Lundy, 51100 Reims, tel. 03.26.40.42.11, fax 03.26.47.66.51, e-mail com@champagne-roederer.com

ROGGE CERESER Reserve Cuvée★

◯   n.c.   1,919   ■ ♨ ▮ €11-15

Based at Passy-Grigny, not far from the Marne Valley, this 6.5-ha (16-acre) estate has been producing champagne since 1997. Once again, it submitted its almost blanc de noirs Réserve Cuvée. This year, however, it contains 7% Chardonnay in addition to its 93% of Pinots (of which 78% is Meunier), and the grapes have been drawn from the 1999 harvest. Its rose-like, floral bouquet and its smoky palate make for a classic non-vintage *brut*. (RM)

● SCEV Rogge Cereser, 1, imp. des Bergeries, 51700 Passy-Grigny, tel. 03.26.52.96.05, fax 03.26.52.07.73 ☑ Y by appt.

JACQUES ROUSSEAUX Réserve Cuvée★

◯ Gd Cru   1 ha   10,400   ■ ♨ ▮ €11-15

This 8-ha (20-acre) family enterprise is based at Verzenay, a Grand Cru village on the Montagne de Reims. Its Réserve Cuvée is made up of two-thirds black grapes, to one-third white, and is a blend of wines from the 1998 harvest, plus reserve wines from 1995 to 1997. It possesses a honeyed, velvety bouquet and a rounded, soft palate. Another star was awarded to the **Cuvée Montgolfière**, a blend of half black grapes and half white from the harvest of 1998. It offers crystallised fruit flavours, richness and length. (RM)

♠ Jacques Rousseaux,
5, rue de Puisieulx, 51360 Verzenay,
tel. 03.26.49.42.73, fax 03.26.49.40.72,
e-mail champagne.jacques.rousseaux@cder.fr ☑ ▼ by appt.

ROUSSEAUX-BATTEUX

○   0.25 ha 2,000   ■ £11-15

This Grand Cru Verzenay estate comprises a vineyard of just over 3 ha (7 acres). It submitted a rosé de noirs, derived from the harvests of 1997 and 1998. With cherries and kirsch on the bouquet, this champagne has a supple, honeyed palate with evident dosage. (RM)

♠ Rousseaux-Batteux, 17, rue de Mailly, 51360 Verzenay, tel. 03.26.49.81.81, fax 03.26.49.48.49 ☑ ▼ by appt.

ROUSSEAUX-FRESNET Prestige

○Gd Cru   0.15 ha 1,500   ■ £15-23

Jean-Brice Rousseaux-Fresnet is based at Verzenay on the Montagne de Reims, following in the footsteps of several generations of wine-growers. Today, the estate encompasses 3.5 ha (9 acres) of vines. The predominantly black-grape Prestige (90% Pinot Noir) has a delicate bouquet, but is a lively and fresh on the palate, despite its rather noticeable dosage. (RM)

♠ Jean-Brice Rousseaux-Fresnet, 21, rue Chanzy, BP 12, 51360 Verzenay, tel. 03.26.49.45.66, fax 03.26.49.40.09 ☑ ▼ by appt.

ROYER PERE ET FILS

○   1 ha   6,000   ■ £11-15

Founded in 1960, this estate consists of a 21-ha (52-acre) vineyard in the Côte des Bars district of the Aube. Its brut rosé, from the harvest of 1998, owes everything to the Pinot Noir grape. It displays aromas of kirsch and cherries, and is assertively powerful on the palate – a champagne for the dinner table. (RM)

♠ Champagne Royer Père et Fils, 120, Grande-Rue, 10110 Landreville, tel. 03.25.38.52.16, fax 03.25.38.37.17, e-mail champagne.royer@wanadoo.fr ☑ ▼ by appt.

RUELLE-PERTOIS

Blanc de Blancs Cuvée de Réserve

○1er Cru   2.5 ha 10,000   ■ £11-15

This family-run estate, based at Moussy to the south-west of Epernay, comprises a 6-ha (15-acre) vineyard. Its blanc de blancs, drawn from the harvests of 1997 and 1998, mingles aromas of apples and almonds on the bouquet, and gives an impression of softness, despite its obvious youth, on the palate. Some tasters were aware of its dosage. (RM)

♠ Michel Ruelle-Pertois,
11, rue de Champagne, 51530 Moussy,
tel. C3.26.54.05.12, fax 03.26.52.87.58 ☑
▼ ev. day 8.30am–12 noon; 1.30pm–7pm. Sat. Sun. by appt.; cl. 7–31 Aug.
♠ Michel Ruelle

DOM. RUINART 1988★★★

○   n.c.   n.c.   ■   ■ +76

The oldest champagne house of them all was founded in 1729 by Nicolas Ruinart, nephew of Dom Ruinart, a contemporary of Dom Pérignon. In 1963, the enterprise was taken over by Moët et Chandon, which later became one of the divisions of the LVMH group. The tasters did not waver in their decision: they awarded the 86 Dom Ruinart rosé a coup de cœur, and have bestowed the same distinction upon the 88 vintage. An 'old' rosé is something of a contradiction in terms, yet this 13-year-old wine succeeded in charming the Jury: 'velvet', harmony, complexity, balance, length, vivacity, an accomplished wine, a fine first impression, wonderfully developed' – in short, a coup de cœur. Whereas the 86 Dom Ruinart rosé is composed of approximately 80% Chardonnay and 20% Pinot Noir, the white wine is produced entirely from Chardonnay. The 93 Dom Ruinart white was awarded one star for its floral intensity and its extreme finesse. Bear in mind, however, that the 93 vintage will develop at a faster rate than the 88 has done. (NM)

♠ Champagne Ruinart, 4, rue des Crayères, BP 85, 51053 Reims Cedex, tel. 03.26.77.51.51, fax 03.26.82.88.43 ☑ ▼ by appt.

RENE RUTAT Grande Réserve

○1er Cru   10,000   n.c.   ■ £11-15

René Rutat, who inherited the family estate, embarked on champagne production in 1960, and his son Michel took over the enterprise in 1985. The vineyard is made up of 6 ha (15 acres) of vines, distributed in 27 separate plots around Vertus on the Côte des Blancs. René Rutat champagnes, however, remain steadfastly blanc de blancs, even though they are not designated as such on the label. This particular cuvée is a blend of grapes from the 1996 harvest (70%) and from 1997 (30%). A fresh, young and powerful champagne, it exhibits impressive length. (RM)

♠ Champagne René Rutat, av. du Gal-de-Gaulle, 51130 Vertus, tel. 03.26.52.14.79, fax 03.26.52.97.36, e-mail champagne.rutat@terre-net.fr ☑ ▼ by appt.

LOUIS DE SACY

Cuvée Tentation 1985★

Gd Cru   3 ha   10,000   €15-23

The Sacy family has had a presence in Verzy since 1633. Alain Sacy, the descendant of a line of 12 generations of growers, manages a 25-ha (62-acre) estate. Its plots are located not only in the Marne Valley and Reims, but also in the Montagne de Reims. The 85 vintage is a blanc de noirs (20% Meunier). It is a full, rounded and straightforward wine of good length. Despite some evidence of dosage, the wine shows no signs of its age. The Non-Vintage Brut Grand Cru, Verzenay, is produced from the 1997 harvest, is a classic blend of 40% white grapes and 60% black (of which 20% is Meunier). This champagne is fruity, intense and still developing. (NM)

🍇 Champagne Louis de Sacy, 6, rue de Verzenay, B.P. 2, 51380 Verzy, tel. 03.26.97.91.13, fax 03.26.97.94.25, e-mail contact@champagne-louis-de-sacy.fr ▼ ev. day except Sat. Sun. 8am–12 noon; 2pm–6pm

SAINT-CHAMANT

Blanc de Blancs 1993★

n.c.   16,007   €15-23

Christian Coquillette cultivates 11.5 ha (28 acres) of vines on the Côte des Blancs. His champagnes owe everything to the Chardonnay grape. Despite its toasty and crystallised fruit aromas, and its short, but rounded and sophisticated palate, this 93 vintage certainly succeeds in hiding its age! The **92 Brut Intégral**, on the other hand, is simple, straightforward and firm. This commended wine will delight lovers of non-dosed champagnes. (RM)

🍇 Christian Coquillette, Champagne Saint-Chamant, 50, av. Paul-Chandon, 51200 Épernay, tel. 03.26.54.38.00, fax 03.26.54.96.55 ▼ by appt.

DE SAINT-GALL Blanc de Blancs

1er Cru   n.c.   100,000   €15-23

This is a brand name of the Union Champagne at Avize, an important vinification centre that acts on behalf of both big-name and lesser-known brands. Its Chardonnay wines have a good reputation. This non-vintage brut, with its aromas of ripe berry fruits, is firm and fresh on the palate. The **95 Blanc de Blancs Premier Cru** is lively, elegant and light bodied, and also received a commendation. (CM)

🍇 Union Champagne, 7, rue Pasteur, 51190 Avize, tel. 03.26.57.94.22, fax 03.26.57.57.98 e-mail info@ de-saint-gall.com ▼ by appt.

SALMON 1996★

6.5 ha   6,900

This family-run estate in the Ardres Valley has been producing champagne since 1958. It submitted a 96 vintage – an excellent year – produced from 70% Pinot Meunier and 30% Chardonnay. Its delicate bouquet mingles minerally, buttery notes of crystallised fruits. After a soft initial impression, a certain vivacity makes itself felt on the palate, leading to a lingering finish. (RM)

🍇 EARL Champagne Salmon, 21-23, rue du Capitaine-Chesnais, 51170 Chaumuzy, tel. 03.26.61.82.36, fax 03.26.61.80.24 ▼ by appt.

SANGER Blanc de Blancs★

Gd Cru   n.c.   n.c.

The production of the Champagne School of Viticulture based at Avize, a Grand Cru village on the Côte des Blancs, has been marketed under the Sanger label since 1952. This year, the Jury again preferred its non-vintage blanc de blancs, a champagne with a floral bouquet and supple palate. Still in the Grand Cru category, the powerful, rounded, rich and generously dosed **95 Blanc de Blancs** received a commendation, as indeed did the **96**. The latter, a blend of two-thirds black grapes to one-third white, mixes citrus fruits with brioche on the bouquet, and is full and well balanced on the palate. Both champagnes fall into the upper price-bracket. (CM)

SALON Blanc de Blancs 1990★

n.c.   45,000   +€76

The 90 succeeds the 88, the 33rd vintage produced by this meticulous house that makes only vintage champagnes. It insists upon white grapes, exclusively drawn from the Grand Cru village of Mesnil-sur-Oger. The golden-yellow 90 surprised some of the tasters with its well-developed richness (a characteristic of this particular vintage). All the tasters, however, hailed it as a great blanc de blancs, generous, powerful and destined to be served with haute cuisine. (NM)

🍇 Champagne Salon, 5190 Le Mesnil-sur-Oger, tel. 03.26.57.51.65, fax 03.26.57.79.29 ▼ by appt.

DENIS SALOMON Réserve★★

1.2 ha   9,326   €11-15

Established in 1974, Salomon owns a vineyard on the right bank of the Marne. It performed strongly this year, with three of its champagnes winning accolades. The best of these is the Réserve, a blend of 70% Pinot Meunier and 30% Chardonnay, drawn from the harvests of 1997 and 1998. Its intense aromas of crystallised fruits and its long and well-structured palate add up to a remarkable ensemble. The **Cuvée Prestige**, a blanc de noirs (with 30% Pinot Meunier) from the harvest of 1998, was awarded one star for its liveliness. The **Cuvée Elégance**, a blanc de blancs from the 1994 and 1995 harvests, offers a distinctive style composed of complexity and roundness. It received a commendation. (RM)

🍇 Denis Salomon, 5, rue Principale, 51700 Vandières, tel. 03.26.58.05.77, fax 03.26.58.00.25, e-mail denis.salomon@ wanadoo.fr ▼ by appt.

Coopérative des Anciens Elèves du lycée viticole d'Avize, 51190 Avize, tel. 03.26.57.79.79, fax 03.26.57.78.58 ▼ ▼ ev. day except Sat. Sun. 8am–12 noon; 2pm–6pm

CAMILLE SAVÈS 1996★★
○ Gd Cru   4.3 ha   15,030   €15-23

Hervé Savès took over the estate from Camille in 1982. He manages a 9-ha (22-acre) vineyard, of which 7.5 ha (18.5 acres) are Grand Cru and the remainder Premier Cru. It was established in 1894, the outcome of the marriage of Eugène Savès, an agricultural engineer, to Anaïs Jolicoeur, daughter of a Bouzy grower. Savès submitted a remarkable 96 vintage, a blend of 75% Pinot Noir with Chardonnay. As with all champagnes produced by this grower, the 96 has not undergone malolactic fermentation. Its eye-catching appearance (it has pink highlights), its honeyed and fruity bouquet, and its red fruit flavours on the palate, are clear indications of the wine's wonderful freshness. The **Cuvée de Réserve Grand Cru**, a blend of 60% Chardonnay with Pinot Noir, drawn from the 1996 harvest with the addition of 1995 reserve wine, has been aged in cask. It was commended by the Jury. This fruity, smoky wine is well balanced and round. (RM)
Camille Savès, 4, rue de Condé, 51150 Bouzy, tel. 03.26.57.00.33, fax 03.26.57.03.83 ▼ ▼ ev. day except Sun. 8am–12.30pm; 1.30pm–7pm
Hervé Savès

FRANCOIS SECONDE
Blanc de Blancs 1996★★
○ Gd Cru   0.7 ha   2,500   €15-23

François Secondé, who is in charge of this 5-ha (12-acre) vineyard, is one of the very few grower-wine-makers in the Grand Cru commune of Sillery. His fresh and well-balanced 96 blanc de blancs has a complex, elegant bouquet and a lingering finish. His rosé, also a Grand Cru, owes everything to the Pinot Noir grape. Produced from the 1999 harvest, this salmon-coloured champagne offers intense, red-fruit flavours. It is a well-balanced, rounded, fresh and lively wine: delightful characteristics that earned it a star. **Clavier** is a fine-tuned, harmonious blend of 70% Chardonnay and 30% Pinot Noir. This commended champagne would make a good apéritif. (RM)
François Secondé, 6, rue des Galipes, 51500 Sillery, tel. 03.26.49.16.67, fax 03.26.49.11.55, e-mail francoisseconde@wanadoo.fr ▼ by appt.

CRISTIAN SENEZ Carte Verte★   €11-15
15ha   120,000

Established in 1973, Cristian Senez currently manages a 30-ha (74-acre) vineyard in the Aube. In 1985, he made the decision to become a négociant. He submitted a champagne, made half from black grapes and half from white, that has not undergone malolactic fermentation. This cuvée is drawn from the 1998 harvest, supplemented by 1997 reserve wine. Its bouquet may be somewhat restrained, but the palate certainly comes up with a few pleasant surprises, with its flavours of almonds and nougat. (NM)
Champagne Cristian Senez, 6, Grande-Rue, 10360 Fontette, tel. 03.25.29.60.62, fax 03.25.29.64.63, e-mail champagne.senez@wanadoo.fr ▼ by appt.

SERVEAUX FILS 1996★   €15-23
○ 1 ha   3,500

In 1993, Pascal Serveaux took over an estate that was founded by his father in 1956. Based in the Marne Valley, the vineyard has expanded steadily over the years, and today extends to 11.6 ha (29 acres) of vines. The 96 vintage is made up of 40% Pinot Noir and 60% Chardonnay. Flavours of quince, strawberry and lemon contribute to a **fresh and well-balanced champagne**. The **blanc de blancs**, produced from the harvests of 1996 and 1997, was commended by the Jury. Fresh, elegant and fine, with lemony, exotic overtones, this is a very young champagne that would benefit from cellaring. (RM)
Pascal Serveaux, 2, rue de Champagne, 02850 Passy-sur-Marne, tel. 03.23.70.35.65, fax 03.23.70.15.99, e-mail serveauxp@aol.com ▼ by appt.

SIMART-MOREAU
Cuvée des Crayères 1996
○ Gd Cru   0.4 ha   3,000   €11-15

Situated at Chouilly, this estate was established in the mid-1970s and today comprises 4 ha (10 acres) of vines. The Crayères blanc de blancs is the house's flagship wine. It offers a subtle bouquet, and proves to be extremely fresh on the palate. This is a well-balanced champagne with good length. A few tasters thought that its noticeable *dosage* would compensate for its extreme youth. (RM)
Pascal Simart, 9, rue du Moulin, 51530 Chouilly, tel. 03.26.55.42.06, fax 03.26.57.53.66, e-mail simart.moreau@wanadoo.fr ▼ by appt.

A. SOUTIRAN-PELLETIER
Blanc de Noirs   €23-30
○ n.c.   n.c.

Established in 1970, this estate is based at Ambonnay, a Grand Cru village in the Montagne de Reims. As well as cultivating a 7.3-ha (18-acre) vineyard, this enterprise supplements its requirements by purchasing grapes from a further 12.5 ha (31 acres). The blanc de noirs is produced from Pinot Noir, harvested in 1995, 1996 and 1998. Its golden-yellow appearance suggests maturity, as do the the tertiary aromas of crystallised fruits. (NM)
Soutiran-Pelletier, 12, rue Saint-Vincent, 51150 Ambonnay, tel. 03.26.57.07.87, fax 03.26.57.81.74, e-mail alain.soutiran@wanadoo.fr ▼ ▼ ev. day except Sun. 9am–12 noon; 2pm–6pm

STEPHANE ET FILS Carte Blanche★

6.5 ha   15,000   ◯ 11-15

Based at Boursault on the left bank of the Marne, Xavier Foin cultivates a 6.5-ha (16-acre) vineyard that was originally planted by his great-grandfather, Auguste, a vineyard worker in the early years of the 20th century. The Carte Blanche is virtually a blanc de noirs (with just 5% Chardonnay). The two Pinots, present in equal proportions, were harvested in 1997 and 1998. The wine's bouquet conjures up scents of orchard fruits, while the palate is marked by great vivacity, despite the noticeable *dosage*. (RM)

✆ EARL Stéphane et Fils, 1, pl. Berry, 51480 Boursault, tel. 03.26.58.40.81, fax 03.26.51.03.79, e-mail champ.stephane@wanadoo.fr ☑ ⟙ by appt.

✆ Xavier Foin

SUGOT-FENEUIL

Cuvée 2000 Bulles 1995

◯ Gd Cru   1 ha   5,000   15-23

Four generations of wine-producers have cultivated this 10-ha (25-acre) estate at Cramant, a Grand Cru village on the Côte des Blancs. The 95 blanc de blancs impressed the Jury with its rich aromas of toasted brioche, and its vigorous, lemony palate and good length. (RM)

✆ Champagne Sugot-Feneuil, 40, imp. de la Mairie, 51530 Cramant, tel. 03.26.57.53.54, fax 03.26.57.17.01 ⟙ by appt.

TAITTINGER Prestige★

n.c.   n.c.   ◯ 23-30

Taittinger can be traced back to the house founded in 1734 by Jacques Fourneaux, a champagne *négociant*. Some two centuries later, the house was taken over by the Taittinger family, who to this day remain proprietors of the vast 260-ha (642-acre) vineyard. Pinot Noir dominates the Prestige rosé, backed up by Chardonnay: it contains 72% of that variety (of which 13% is vinified on the skins, for colour). It has a salmon-tinged appearance, and exhibits fruitiness, balance, liveliness and length. The **96 Brut** received a commendation for its appealing bouquet, with strong overtones of white flowers, and its powerful vinosity. This year (2001) the champagne, however, is still very young, and would benefit from being cellared for a year or two before it enters the realms of star ratings. (NM)

✆ Taittinger, 9, pl. Saint-Nicaise, 51100 Reims, tel. 03.26.85.45.35, fax 03.26.85.17.46 ⟙ by appt.

TAITTINGER Blanc de Blancs Comtes de Champagne 1995★

n.c.   502,300   ◯ +76

Launched in 1957, Taittinger's famous prestige *cuvée*, sold in bulbous, 18th-century-style bottles, is a blanc de blancs, and quite accustomed to receiving *coups de cœurs*. Its name makes reference to the earls who reigned supreme over the region during the Middle Ages, right up to its reunification with France in 1284. It also bears the seal of Thibaud IV who, according to the ballad writers, was one of the most famous minstrels of his day. The produce of some of the finest crus of the Côte des Blancs goes into it. A mere 6% of the blend is vinified in new oak. Its clear, pale yellow appearance, with its delicate bubbles, reflects the grape variety. It possesses a pleasing, subtly buttery bouquet, which is also evocative of bread dough and wax. Lively first impressions are followed by a light and delicate palate, with lemon and vanilla notes and, according to some tasters, rather noticeable *dosage*. (NM)

✆ Taittinger, 9, pl. Saint-Nicaise, 51100 Reims, tel. 03.26.85.17.46 ⟙ by appt.

TARLANT Brut Zéro

◯ n.c.   15,000   11-15

Pierre Tarlant was a grower in the Aisne district during the reign of Louis XIV. A century later, shortly before the French Revolution, the Tarlants took up residence at Oeuilly in the Marne Valley, where the family has remained to this day. In the 19th century, they supplied the Paris cabarets with red and white wines. However, it was not until the late 1920s that they started producing champagne. Today, Jean-Mary, the eleventh generation of the family – assisted by his son Benoît – cultivates the 13 ha (32 acres) of vines. Their Brut Zéro is a blend of the three champagne grapes in equal proportions, and is produced from the 1994 and 1995 harvests, supplemented by grapes from the 1996 harvest. It is a well developed, but also balanced, champagne. Also commended was the half-black and half-white **Cuvée Louis**, produced from the harvests of 1994 and 1995 and vinified in oak. A highly intricate, spicy and oaky wine, it would make a good partner for grilled seabass with fennel. (RM)

✆ Champagne Tarlant, 51480 Oeuilly, tel. 03.26.58.30.60, fax 03.26.58.37.31, e-mail champagne@tarlant.com ☑ ⟙ by appt.

J. DE TELMONT Blanc de Blancs 1996

◯ 5 ha   n.c.   11-15

Based at Damery in the Marne Valley, the L'hopital family has been dedicated to vine-growing for many years, and is responsible for building up this important 32-ha (79-acre) vineyard. The 96 blanc de blancs contains grapes from the Côte des Blancs, the Sézannais and the Marne Valley. This aperitif-style champagne is floral, lemony and light. Also commended was the **93 Grand Couronnement Blanc de Blancs**, a blend of superior grapes from Mesnil, Avize and Chouilly. This champagne exhibits a fresh bouquet and a structured, well-balanced palate. (NM)

✆ Champagne J. de Telmont, 1, av. de Champagne, 51480 Damery, tel. 03.26.58.40.33, fax 03.26.58.63.93, e-mail telmont@wanadoo.fr ⟙ by appt.

12 ha (30 acres) on the banks of the Marne. Tribaut has been producing its own champagne since 1976. The blanc de blancs, produced from grapes harvested in 1997, topped up with reserve wines, is a classic of its kind, an immensely seductive wine full of fresh, buttery, hazelnut aromas, and with elegance and balance on the palate. (RM)

➤ Champagne G. Tribaut, 88, rue d'Eguisheim, B.P. 5, 51160 Hautvillers, tel. 03.26.59.40.57, fax 03.26.59.43.74, e-mail champagne.tribaut@wanadoo.fr ▼
Ⓨ ev day 9am–12 noon; 2pm–6.30pm

TRIBAUT-SCHLOESSER

Grande Reserve★

Ⓞ   10.01 ha 40,000 ▦ ⑪▯ € 11–15

Founded in 1929, this house manages a 30-ha (74-acre) vineyard. Its rosé de noirs is produced from the harvests of 1997 and 1998. The Jury concluded, unanimously, that this is a 'very intricate' wine – soft, fresh, elegant and of great delicacy. (NM)

➤ Tribaut-Schloesser, 21, rue Saint-Vincent, 51480 Romery, tel. 03.26.58.64.21, fax 03.26.58.44.08 ▼ Ⓨ by appt.

TRICHET-DIDIER Reserve

Ⓞ 1er Cru   2 ha   18,000   ▦ ♦ € 11–15

This small estate of 2.8 ha (7 acres) is situated in the village of Trois-Puits, very close to Reims. Its vines were planted in the early 1950s by the grandparents of Pierre Trichet, who became a négociant in 1998. This wine is composed mainly of Pinots (79%, of which is 60% is Meunier), from grapes harvested in 1997. Light on the palate, it captivates with its fine, flcral, elegant bouquet. (NM)

➤ SARL Pierre Trichet, 11, rue du Petit-Trois-Puits, 51500 Trois-Puits, tel. 03.26.82.64.10, fax 03.26.97.80.99 ▼ Ⓨ ev. day 8am–12 noon; 1.30pm–8pm

ALFRED TRITANT★

Ⓞ Gd Cru   3.37 ha 3,000   ▦ € 11–15

'We cultivate a vineyard of 3.37 ha [8.32 acres],' was the producer's precise comment, and certainly in the Grand Cru village of Bouzy on the Montagne de Reims, where he is based, every square inch of land is like gold dust. Tritant's holding has indeed been put to good use. Three of its champagnes have achieved a star, all being Grands Crus, and all containing a majority of Pinot Noir, which reigns supreme at Bouzy. The rosé is a blend of 70% Pinot Noir to 30% Chardonnay, from the harvests of 1995 to 1998. This pale-coloured champagne is attractively supple and light, but lacks for nothing in length. Among the whites, the Cuvée Prestige is made from an almost identical blend of grapes (with 65% Pinot), but from the 1996 to 1998 harvests. This champagne is full, vinous and well balanced. Finally, the 95, produced from the same grape varieties in exactly the same proportions as the previous ones, offers a floral bouquet with buttery riotes, and a powerful, lingering palate. (RM)

JACKY THERREY★

Cuvée François 1996★

Ⓞ   1 ha   5,000   € 11–15

Jacky Therrey produced his first wines in 1965. Based in the Aube, he cultivates a vineyard of 6 ha (15 acres), located in the excellent Montgueux terroir (renowned for its Chardonnays) and also at Celles-sur-Ource. The Cuvée François shows up well in the 1996 vintage. With its bouquet of almonds and toast, this highly successful, vigorous, elegant blanc de blancs has great potential. As last year, the rosé also received a star. Produced from 1998 Pinot Noir, it is a deliciously fresh champagne. Both bouquet and palate offer a veritable basket of raspberries, strawberries and blackcurrants. (RM)

➤ Jacky Therrey, 8, rte de Montgueux, La Grange-au-Rez, 10300 Montgueux, tel. 03.25.70.30.87, fax 03.25.70.30.84 ▼ Ⓨ by appt.

ALAIN THIENOT

Grande Cuvée 1995★

Ⓞ   n.c.   ▦ ♦ € 38–46

Alain Thiénot has many commitments, what with his own champagne brand, the Marie Stuart and Joseph Perrier champagnes, and three châteaux in Bordeaux. The Grande Cuvée is a blend of 60% Chardonnay and 40% Pinot Noir. Very ripe fruits impose themselves on both bouquet and palate in a wine that has now reached its peak. The 96 rosé, a blend of the three champagne grapes, received a commendation. The liveliness so typical of this vintage is clearly reflected in its intensely fruity character. (NM)

➤ Alain Thiénot,
4, rue Joseph-Cugnot, 51500 Taissy, tel. 03.26.77.50.10, fax 03.26.77.50.19, e-mail vignobles.alain-thienot@ alain-thienot.fr ▼ Ⓨ by appt.

MICHEL TIXIER

Réserve Grande Année★

Ⓞ   0.6 ha   4,000   ▦ € 11–15

Michel Tixier has been established in the Montagne de Reims since 1962, cultivating 4.4 ha (11 acres) of vines. His rosé impressed the Jury with its assertively fruity character, and the aromatic complexity of both its bouquet and palate. It is a supple, fresh, long and extremely well-balanced champagne. (RM)

➤ Champagne Michel Tixier,
8, rue des Vignes, 51500 Chigny-les-Roses, tel. 03.26.03.42.61, fax 03.26.03.41.80 ▼ Ⓨ by appt.

G. TRIBAUT Blanc de Blancs★

Ⓞ   n.c.   5,084   € 11–15

This vineyard is situated 300 m (325 yd) from the abbey of Hautvillers, where Dom Pérignon was once based. The Tribaut estate is on the rue d'Eguisheim (named after an Alsace wine town that prides itself on being the cradle of Alsatian wine, and which also boasts a rue d'Hautvillers!). The vineyard was established in 1935, and today comprises

- Alfred Tritant, 23, rue de Tours, 51150 Bouzy, tel. 03.26.57.01.16, fax 03.26.58.49.56, e-mail champagne-tritant@wanadoo.fr  ev. day 9am–12 noon; 2pm–6pm; Sat. Sun. by appt.

JEAN-CLAUDE VALLOIS
Blanc de Blancs 1995★★

○ | 4 ha | 23,185 | €11-15

Jean-Claude Vallois cultivates a 6-ha (15-acre) vineyard at Cuis, not far from Epernay. His 95 blanc de blancs displays all the fine characteristics of that excellent vintage. Its buttery, honeyed bouquet is everything one could hope for and its well-balanced palate mingles flavours of crystal-lised fruits, wax and toast. His **Assemblage Noble Blanc de Blancs**, sourced from the harvests of 1996 and 1997, was awarded one star. It has an intense, floral, lemony bouquet, a fresh opening impression, and a sense of live-liness that is reinforced by a lingering finish of citrus fruits. (RM)
- Jean-Claude Vallois, 4, rte des Caves, 51530 Cuis, tel. 03.26.59.78.46, fax 03.26.58.16.73 by appt.

VARNIER-FANNIERE
Cuvée Saint-Denis★

○ Gd cru | 0.6 ha | 5,000 | €15-23

A member of the Fannière family was culti-vating the vine at Avize in 1860, but it was Jean Fannière, in the 1950s, who decided to produce his own champagne. The enterprise was then taken over, first by his son-in-law Guy Varnier, and later by his grandson, Denis. The 4-ha (10-acre) vineyard is situated on the Côte des Blancs, looking towards the Grands Crus of Oger and Cramant. Although not particularly long on the palate, its blanc de blancs, produced from the harvests of 1996, 1998 and 1999, is enticingly fresh, rounded and elegant. (RM)
- Champagne Varnier-Fannière, 23, rempart du Midi, 51190 Avize, tel. 03.26.57.53.36, fax 03.26.57.17.07. e-mail contact@varnier-fanniere.com
- by appt.
- Denis Varnier

F. VAUVERSIN Blanc de Blancs★

○ Gd Cru | n.c. | 7,000 | €11-15

The Vauversins were growers as long ago as 1640, but have only been marketing their own wines since 1930. Their 3-ha (7-acre) estate is situated in the heart of the Côte des Blancs, and this champagne owes everything to the Chardonnay grape. Its biscuity, buttery bouquet, its structured, supple and rounded palate, and its full-bodied richness all contrib-ute to a highly beguiling wine. (RM)
- Champagne Vauversin, 9 bis, rue de Flavigny, 51190 Oger, tel. 03.26.57.51.01, fax 03.26.51.64.44, e-mail bruno.vauversin@wanadoo.fr by appt.

VAZART-COQUART ET FILS
Blanc de Blancs Grand Bouquet 1995★★

○ Gd Cru | 11 ha | 10,000 | €15-23

This vineyard of 11 ha (27 acres) was established by Louis and Jacques Vazart in the 1950s. The business is based at Chouilly, near Epernay. This is another 95 vintage – a great year – that lives up to expectations. Its flavours are simultaneously powerful and refined, complex and elegant, and its fine, lively and lingering palate suggests a seem-ingly eternal youth! (RM)
- Champagne Vazart-Coquart, 6, rue des Partelaines, 51530 Chouilly, tel. 03.26.55.40.04, fax 03.26.55.15.94, e-mail vazart@cder.fr by appt.

DE VENOGE
Brut Sélect Cordon Bleu★★

○ | n.c. | n.c. | €15-23

This famous house, founded in 1837 and bought out by BCC in 1988, was originally set up by a Swiss, Henri-Marc de Venoge. The house has been something of a pioneer in the area of wine labels. Its Cordon Bleu brand name, which became its registered trade mark in 1864, bears the insignia of the Order of the Holy Spirit, an emblem that also graces many an aristocratic coat of arms. De Venoge has excelled itself with three remarkable cham-pagnes, one of which, the Sélect Cordon Bleu, was awarded a *coup de cœur*. A blend of 75% Pinots (of which 25% is Meunier), this wine delighted the tasters with its freshness and floral, fruity flavours of ripe apples and pears, mingled with notes of baked brioche. Its pedi-gree, harmonious balance, power and finesse all combine to create a charming whole. With an even higher black-grape content, the **95** (85% Pinots, of which 15% is Meunier) amazed the jury with its balance, power and length. The **93 Grand Vin des Princes**, a blanc de blancs, charmed with its flavour of toasted almonds, its freshness and complexity. (NM)
- Champagne de Venoge, 46, av. de Champagne, 51200 Epernay, tel. 03.26.53.34.34, fax 03.26.53.34.35

J.-L. VERGNON
Blanc de Blancs Extra Brut★★

○ Gd Cru | n.c. | 45,000 | €11-15

The Vergnon estate, based in the Grand Cru village of Mesnil-sur-Oger, was founded in 1950, comprising just over 5 ha (12 acres) of vines. From its location, therefore, it is not surprising that blanc de blancs has become the vineyard's speciality. Often highly rated in the *Guide*, its extra-brut, non-dosed *cuvées* allow the Chardonnay grape to speak for itself. This particular champagne, produced from the harvests of 1996 and 1997, offers wonderful floral freshness and finesse. It is powerful and well balanced on the palate. (RM)

☛ SCEV J.-L. Vergnon, 1, Grande-Rue, 51190 Le Mesnil-sur-Oger,
tel. 03.26.57.53.86, fax 03.26.52.07.06 ▨ ☙ ev. day 8am–12 noon; 2pm–6pm; Sat. Sun. by appt.

GEORGES VESSELLE★

| ○Gd Cru | 10 ha | 90,000 | ■ | €15-23 |

The Vesselles have put down roots at Bouzy, a Montagne de Reims village where Georges has been Mayor for 25 years. He inherited a small vineyard that had been handed down from father to son since the 16th century, which increased his holdings to 17.5 ha (43 acres) from which a wide range of champagnes is produced. Pinot Noir, the supreme grape variety of this Grand Cru, tends to dominate his wines (usually to the extent of 90%). Two of his *cuvées* have been equally successful this year, earning a star each. This Brut Grand Cru was produced from the recent harvests of 1997 and 1998, and is particularly fruity and long. The **Juline**, which is always drawn from older wines, is a blend of the 1988, 1989 and 1990 vintages. This more highly evolved champagne conjures up flavours of jellied fruits, and is full, ripe and generous on the palate. (NM)

☛ Georges Vesselle, 16, rue des Postes, 51150 Bouzy, tel. 03.26.57.00.15,
fax 03.26.57.09.20, e-mail contact@champagne-vesselle.fr ▨ ☙ ev. day except Sat. Sun. 9am–12 noon; 2pm–5pm

MAURICE VESSELLE★

| ○Gd Cru | n.c. | n.c. | ■ | €15-23 |

Maurice Vesselle is another of the Vesselle dynasty of Bouzy. He cultivates 8.5 ha (21 acres) of vines, at Bouzy and at Tours-sur-Marne, both Grands Crus. His wines do not undergo malolactic fermentation, which explains why his rosé, produced from the 1991 harvest, has not aged but has nonetheless developed a certain complexity. The product of a short maceration of Pinot Noir, this champagne captivated the Jury with its crystallised red-fruit flavours, its balance and its length. The **85 Grand Cru** favours Pinot Noir (85% of the blend) and, as with the previous wine, is also hiding its age. It has a subtle yet concentrated bouquet, and deserves a commendation. (RM)

☛ Maurice Vesselle, 2, rue Yvonnet, 51150 Bouzy, tel. 03.26.57.00.81,
fax 03.26.57.83.08 ▨ ☙ by appt.

VEUVE A. DEVAUX Cuvée D★

| ○ | 200 ha | 30,000 | ■ | €23-30 |

This house was founded in 1846 and was taken over by the Union Auboise in 1986. It comprises 800 growers, cultivating 1,400 ha

(3,460 acres), Cuvée D is made up of two-thirds Pinot Noir, with a balance of Chardonnay, from the 1995 harvest, plus some wines from 1992 to 1994 that have been aged in barrel. Although its floral bouquet is lightly evolved, its citrus-fruit palate remains quite lively. The same grape varieties, in the same proportions, make up the **Grande Réserve**, but here they come from the 1993, 1995 and 1996 harvests. This champagne deserved a commendation for its fruity, minerally bouquet and its fine balance. (CM)

☛ Union Auboise des prod. de vin de Champagne, Dom. de Villeneuve, 10110 Bar-sur-Seine, tel. 03.25.38.30.65, e-mail info@champagne-devaux.fr ☙ by appt.

VEUVE CLICQUOT PONSARDIN

La Grande Dame 1990★

| ○ | n.c. | n.c. | ■ | +76 |

This famous house, founded in 1772, was taken over by a 27-year-old widow in 1805 (a positively revolutionary development in those days). She employed some exceptional colleagues, including Edouard Werlé, who became her business partner in 1821. The latter's descendants continued to expand the business up until 1987, when the LVMH group acquired it. It was the first house to market a rosé wine, a style that remains a Veuve Clicquot speciality to this day. The rosé version of Grande Dame, the house's prestige wine, comprises 39% Chardonnay and 61% Pinot Noir (15% of which is red wine from Bouzy). Its orangey-pink colour and honeyed aromas are indications of the maturity to be expected of a 90 vintage, but it also remains lively and fresh. The **95 Réserve rosé** has a greater Pinot content – 64% Pinot Noir (of which 15% is Bouzy red), 8% Meunier and 28% Chardonnay – and exhibits floral, honeyed and brioche-like flavours, while the **95 Vintage Réserve** is a blend of two-thirds black to one-third white grapes, and is a ripe, intense wine that will need to be kept. (NM)

☛ Veuve Clicquot-Ponsardin, 12, rue du Temple, 51100 Reims, tel. 03.26.89.54.40, fax 03.26.40.60.17 ▨ ☙ by appt.

VEUVE DOUSSOT 1996★★

| ○ | 18.3 ha | 6,800 | ■ | ♦ | €11-15 |

The Joly family cultivates an 18-ha (44-acre) vineyard in the Aube, and has been marketing a champagne since 1973. The 96 vintage made quite an impression on the tasters, showing all the promise of this fine year. It has an intricate bouquet of white flowers, and a full, rich and perfectly balanced palate of citrus fruits, apricots and honey. The **rosé**, 100% Pinot Noir, received one star. It has mingled flavours of quince pear and red fruits. Because of its *dosage*, it would be best served with desserts. (RM)

☛ Joly, 1, rue de Chatet, 10360 Noé-les-Mallets, tel. 03.25.29.60.61, fax 03.25.29.11.78 ▨ ☙ by appt.

VEUVE FOURNY ET FILS
Cuvée du Clos Faubourg Notre Dame 1996★
○ 1er Cru   0.12 ha   1,200   €30-38

The Fourny family has been involved in viticulture since the time of the Second Empire, and has been producing wines since the 1930s. Monique Fourny has managed the enterprise, which is based in the Côte des Blancs, since the death of her husband in 1979. Nowadays, she is assisted by her two sons. Clos Faubourg Notre Dame is an authentic walled vineyard, planted exclusively with old Chardonnay vines of 50 years of age. The wine is a blend of three wines that have been vinified in barrel for nine months, with stirring of the lees, and then fined but not filtered. Powerful, structured and musky, it is at once fresh and evolved in character, an assertive wine that could distract the novice champagne-lover! It is the type of champagne that could accompany a meal - specifically, substantial white meat dishes. (NM)

● Champagne Veuve Fourny et Fils, 2-5, rue du Mesnil, 51130 Vertus, tel. 03.26.52.16.30, fax 03.26.52.20.13, e-mail info@champagne-veuve-fourny.com
Y ev. day 9am-12 noon, 2.30pm-6pm

VEUVE MAITRE-GEOFFROY
Carte d'or Selection 1996★
○ 1er Cru   2 ha   8,000   €11-15

Thierry Maitre cultivates 9.5 ha (23 acres) of vines at Cumières, a Premier Cru village in the Marne Valley. He took over a label that his great-grandmother created in 1878. This floral, buttery, brioche-scented 96 is a blend of 60% Chardonnay and 40% Pinot Noir. It is a well-balanced, attractively light champagne that would make a good aperitif. (RM)

● Veuve Maitre-Geoffroy, 116, rue Gaston-Poittevin, 51480 Cumières, tel. 03.26.55.29.87, fax 03.26.51.85.77, e-mail thierry.maitre@worldonline.fr
Y by appt.

MARCEL VEZIEN★
   10 ha   80,000   €11-15

Four generations of the Vézien family have dedicated themselves to vine-growing. Armand battled with phylloxera, Henri expanded the vineyard, Marcel launched the brand in 1978, and today Jean-Pierre directs this 14-ha (35-acre) estate in the Aube. Three champagnes were honoured. The Jury's favourite was the non-vintage brut, drawn from the harvests of 1998 and 1999. This champagne is almost a blanc de noirs (with just 5% of Chardonnay). Its two outstanding qualities are its fruitiness and its freshness, sustained by the dosage. The balanced, floral and light-bodied Selection is dominated by Pinot Noir (80%), and is a blend of the 1997 and 1998 harvests. This cuvée received a commendation, as indeed did the 94 Armand Vézien, a champagne full of floral finesse. (NM)

● SCEV Champagne Marcel Vézien et Fils, 68, Grande-Rue, 10110 Celles-sur-Ource, tel. 03.25.38.50.22, fax 03.25.38.56.09
Y ev. day 8.30am-6pm; Sat. Sun. by appt.

FLORENT VIARD Blanc de Blancs★
○ 1er Cru   0.75 ha   6,000   €11-15

This family-run enterprise was established in 1994 at Vertus on the Côte des Blancs. It comprises a 2-ha (5-acre) vineyard, of which 1.7 ha (4.2 acres) is devoted to Chardonnay. The blanc de blancs is a product of the harvests of 1994 to 1997. An expressive, floral, almondy bouquet, a lively, spicy start, and a note of menthol on the finish all add up to a champagne of great finesse. The 96 Premier Cru received a commendation. It is a blanc de blancs of pleasing freshness and roundness. (RM)

● Champagne Florent Viard, 3, rue du Donjon, 51130 Vertus, tel. 03.26.52.16.76, fax 03.26.51.60.82
Y by appt.

VIARD ROGUE Prestige Cuvée 1995
○   1 ha   2,000   €11-15

This family-run enterprise was established in 1973, and manages a vineyard of 6 ha (15 acres) in the Côte des Blancs. At 5% off a blanc de blancs, this 95 vintage has a well-developed bouquet. On the palate, however, it has retained its freshness, and turns out to be a well-balanced champagne. (RM)

● Champagne Viard Rogué, 33, rue du 28-août-1944, 51130 Vertus, tel. 03.26.52.16.76, fax 03.26.59.36.66
Y by appt.

VILMART Coeur de Cuvée 1993★★
○   0.4 ha   4,000   €30-38

Founded in 1890 by Désiré Vilmart, this Montagne de Reims estate is currently managed by Laurent Champs, his great-grandson. The vineyard comprises 11 ha (27 acres) of Premier Cru land. Very strict vinification procedures are followed. The vintage wines are fermented in oak casks of 225 l (59 gal), and the non-vintages in large wooden vats. The 93 Coeur de Cuvée is dominated by white grapes (80%), and comes from 50-year-old vines. Its complex bouquet mingles aromas of tobacco, liquorice, spices and apricots, and its honeyed palate is at once rounded and lively. This is a champagne to serve with sauced fish dishes. The Grand Cellier, a blend of 75% Chardonnay with Pinot Noir, produced from the harvests of 1997 and 1998, received a commendation. Its complex bouquet reveals oaky, toasty notes that recur (along with hints of green apples) on its generous palate. (RM)

● Champagne Vilmart et Cie, 5, rue des Gravières, 51500 Rilly-la-Montagne, tel. 03.26.03.40.01, fax 03.26.03.46.57, e-mail laurent.champs@champagnevilmart.fr
Y by appt.

● Laurent Champs

VOIRIN-DESMOULINS
Cuvée Prestige 1994★★
○ Gd Cru   3 ha   5,000   €15-22

This estate, based at Chouilly, near Epernay, comprises 9 ha (22 acres) of vines. Its 94 Cuvée Prestige, a blend of 70% Chardonnay with Pinot Noir, is a remarkably

Coteaux Champenois

Called Vins Nature de Champagne, or still wines, they became AOC in 1974 and took the name of Coteaux Champenois. They are white, red or, more rarely, rosé still wines. Drink the whites with respect and a degree of historical curiosity, remembering that they are a survival from ancient times, before champagne was created. Like champagne itself, Coteaux Champenois can be made from black grapes vinified to make white wine (blanc de noirs), from white grapes (blanc de blancs) or from mixed wines.

The best known Coteaux Champenois Rouge carries the name of the celebrated commune of Bouzy (a Grand Cru of the Pinot Noir). In this commune you can admire one of the two strangest vineyards in the world (the other is at Ay). A huge notice proclaims 'old, pre-phylloxera French vines'; these would be virtually indistinguishable from the others were they not free-growing, following an ancient technique that has been abandoned everywhere else. All the work is done by hand using old tools. The House of Bollinger maintains this jewel, which is intended for making the rarest and most expensive champagne of all.

The Coteaux Champenois wines are drunk young, at a temperature of 7–8°C (44.6–46.4°F) for the whites and sold in silkscreen-printed bottles). Both wines are young and lively, with flavours of lemon and vanilla, and both have great elegance. They would make fine aperitif champagnes. (RM)

Waris-Larmandier, 608, rempart du Nord, 51190 Avize, tel. 03.26.57.79.05, fax 03.26.52.79.52 ▼ by appt.

successful champagne for a much-decried year. When it was judged in 1999, it was deemed to be 'youthful, lively and fresh'. It has since developed considerably. Its aromas have gained in complexity, with buttery, honeyed and smoky notes, and that smoky element, joined by flavours of quince and crystallised fruits, returns on the supple, rounded and markedly lengthy palate. This is a champagne of real character, destined to be drunk by connoisseurs as an aperitif, or as a fine accompaniment for entrées. (RM)

SCEV Voirin-Desmoulins, 24, rue des Partelaines, 51530 Chouilly, tel. 03.26.54.50.30, fax 03.26.52.87.87 ▼ by appt.

VRANKEN Demoiselle Cuvée 21 1995★★

n.c.　20,000　£46–76

Over the years, Paul Vranken has carved out for himself a highly enviable position in the viticultural world. Champagne Vranken was founded in 1976, and its special *cuvée*, Demoiselle, sold in elegantly shaped, Art Nouveau bottles, was launched in 1985. The Demoiselle wines have since been sprinkled with stars, particularly so in the case of Cuvée 21, the Demoiselle prestige champagne, which always attracts eulogies. Although not described as such on the label, it is a blanc de blancs. The tasters praised its complex bouquet of exotic fruits, and a palate that is not just well balanced, but elegant, youthful, charming and long. It was described as the very 'essence' of champagne. Two other, less expensive *cuvées* each received a star. The **Grande Cuvée** is a blend of 60% Chardonnay and 40% Pinots (of which 10% is Meunier). Marked by the character of the white grape, this fresh, long and complex champagne exhibits floral and citrus fruit flavours. Finally, another blanc de blancs, the **96 Tête de Cuvée Premier Cru**, is a light and honeyed champagne that would make a fine aperitif. (NM)

Vranken, 42, av. de Champagne, 51200 Epernay, tel. 03.26.59.50.50, fax 03.26.52.19.65 ▼
▼ ev. day 9.30am–4.30pm; Sat. 10am–4pm; Sun. and groups by appt.
P.-F. Vranken

WARIS-LARMANDIER
Blanc de Blancs Cuvée Empreinte★

○Gd Cru　0.22 ha 2,500　€15–23

Waris-Larmandier is an estate of recent provenance, given that its vineyard was only planted in 1984, and its first champagne launched in 1991. It submitted two similar blancs de blancs, both highly successful and both produced from the harvest of 1998: Cuvée Empreinte and **Collection** (the latter

accompanying dishes that go with very dry wines, and at 9–10°C (48.2–50°F) for the reds, to accompany light dishes (white meats and oysters). In exceptional years, they may be left to age.

☐ GATINOIS Aÿ 1997★★

| ■ | 0.2 ha | 2,000 | ⦀ | €15-23 |

🐌 Philippe Doyard-Mahé, Moulin d'Argensole, 51130 Vertus, tel. 03.26.52.23.85, fax 03.26.59.36.69 ☑
🍷 ev. day except Sun. 10am–12 noon; 2pm–6pm

A coup de coeur in Coteaux Champenois is a rarity, but here is a heart-warming exception. This Pinot Noir hails from the Chauffour vineyard at Aÿ. Grapes from 45-year-old Pinot vines are de-stemmed before undergoing a slow fermentation. The wine is then matured in barrel for three years. It has a deep purple appearance and an ample, well-structured palate, with a remarkable array of peppery, toasty and fruity flavours – a wine that would go particularly well with duck.

🍷 by appt.
🐌 P. Cheval-Gatinois

☐ HERBERT BEAUFORT Bouzy 1996

| ■ | 3 ha | 8,500 | ⦀ | €15-23 |

Beaufort ferments and macerates his Pinot Noir for approximately two weeks. The wine then lies in tank for a year, before spending another two years in oak. This gives the wine its deep colour and its fruity, lightly oaky character, as well as lending it great suppleness.

🐌 Champagne Beaufort, 32, rue de Tours-sur-Marne, 51150 Bouzy, tel. 03.26.57.01.34, fax 03.26.57.09.08 ☑
🍷 by appt.
🐌 Henry et Hugues Beaufort

☐ CHARLES DE CAZANOVE 1993

| ■ | n.c. | n.c. | ■ ⦀ ♦ | €11-15 |

This family-run house, established in 1811, bears the name of its founder. This interesting wine is made entirely from Pinot Meunier and oak-matured, as it should be, in champagne casks. The bright ruby colour looks slightly evolved, and the wine is beginning to show its age on the palate too. Its tannins are well integrated, and perfect balance has been attained. As such, the wine is at its peak.

🐌 Charles de Cazanove, 1, rue des Cotelles, 51200 Epernay, tel. 03.26.59.57.40, fax 03.26.54.16.38 ☑
🐌 Lombard

☐ PAUL CLOUET Bouzy

| ■ | n.c. | n.c. | ⦀ | €11-15 |

A ruby-red wine, with a developed Pinot bouquet, this Bouzy makes a gentle impression on the palate, with velvety red fruit flavours and integrated tannins. It would make a good accompaniment to red meats and soft cheeses.

🐌 Paul Clouet, 10, rue Jeanne-d'Arc, 51150 Bouzy, tel. 03.26.57.07.31, fax 03.26.52.64.65,
e-mail champagne-paul-clouet@wanadoo.fr
🍷 ev. day 10am–12 noon; 2pm–5pm

☐ DOYARD-MAHE Vertus

| ■ | 0.6 ha | n.c. |

At the beginning of the 20th century, the Argensole mill used to generate the electricity that powered the sewing machines used in making straw muffs to protect the wine bottles. A century later, the estate located here has submitted a wine produced from Pinot Noir, harvested in 1995 and 1996, and given an extended barrel-ageing. Its deep garnet colour anticipates aromas of red and black fruits, but the tannins on its powerful palate need time to soften.

☐ J.-M. GOBILLARD ET FILS Hautvillers★

| ■ | 0.6 ha | 2,000 | ⦀ | €11-15 |

This red wine comes from the village where Dom Pérignon worked between 1668 and 1715. The Pinot Noir has been de-stemmed, the wine baton-stirred and then matured in oak. Although a non-vintage wine, it is the produce of the 1999 harvest. Fruity, lightly oaked, rounded and vanilla flavoured, it would go well with grilled meats.

🐌 Champagne J.-M. Gobillard et Fils, 38, rue de l'Eglise, BP 8, 51160 Hautvillers, tel. 03.26.51.00.24, fax 03.26.51.00.18,
e-mail champagne-gobillard@wanadoo.fr ☑
🍷 by appt.

☐ VINCENT LAMOUREUX 1998★

| ■ | 0.5 ha | 1,500 | ■ ⦀ | €8-11 |

Here is a red Coteaux Champenois from Les Riceys, the village famed for its Pinot Noirs and its eponymous rosé. It is a rather faintly coloured Pinot Noir, almost a 'red-rosé', as one of the tasters put it. The bouquet is lively, floral and lightly oaky, as befits a wine that has only spent three months in barrel. Descriptions such as 'supple, very supple, smooth, easy-drinking' recur in the tasters' notes.

➤ Vincent Lamoureux, 2, rue du Sénateur-Lesaché, 10340 Les Riceys, tel. 03.25.29.39.32, fax 03.25.29.80.30 Ⓥ Y by appt.

DANIEL MOREAU 1999★★★　0.2 ha　500　€8-11

This wine is an impeccable ruby red, and has a complex bouquet of cherries, blackcurrants and liquorice. Its rounded, well-integrated, balanced palate exhibits great finesse, making it the best Coteaux Champenois to be made entirely from Pinot Meunier in this year's *Guide*. Even more remarkable is the fact that the grapes were harvested in 1999, a year of somewhat dubious reputation. Daniel Moreau has been producing wine since 1978, and hereby confirms his viticultural *savoir-faire*.

➤ Daniel Moreau, 5, rue du Moulin, 51700 Vandières, tel. 03.26.58.01.64, fax 03.26.58.15.64 Ⓥ Y by appt.

PIERRE PAILLARD Bouzy 1997　1 ha　5 733　€11-15

It goes without saying that this red Bouzy is produced from 100% Pinot Noir. A light-bodied wine with a scent of kirsch, its appearance reflects its age. It would make a fine accompaniment for *Brie de Meaux*.

➤ Pierre Paillard, 2, rue du XXᵉ Siècle, 51150 Bouzy, tel. 03.26.57.08.04, fax 03.26.57.83.03, e-mail benoit.paillard@wanadoo.fr Ⓥ Y ev. day except Sun. 9.30am–11.30am; 2.30–5pm; cl. 10–31 Aug.

ROGER POUILLON ET FILS
Vieilles vignes　0.3 ha　n.c.　€11-15

This Pinot Noir has undergone eight days' cold maceration and eighteen months' maturation in barrel. It has an intense, brick-red colour and a fruity, oaky bouquet, but its fleshy, powerful structure on the palate can't mask either its astringency or its advanced stage of development.

➤ Roger Pouillon et Fils, 3, rue de la Couple, 51160 Mareuil-sur-Ay, tel. 03.26.52.60.08, fax 03.26.59.49.83, e-mail contact@champagne-pouillon.com Ⓥ Y by appt.

PATRICK SOUTIRAN
Ambonnay 1996　0.5 ha　1,000　€11-15

The medieval market square of Ambonnay has a church, Saint-Réole, that dates back to the 12th century. This is very much a wine-producing village, where the Soutiran family has plied its trade for five generations. The attractive-looking 96 has a moderately intense bouquet of red fruits, but is more powerful on the palate. It is still very youthful, however, and will need about a year or two to soften, whereupon it would go well with coq au vin – cooked in Ambonnay red, of course.

➤ Patrick Soutiran, 3, rue des Crayères, 51150 Ambonnay, tel. 03.26.57.08.18, fax 03.26.57.81.87, e-mail patrick.soutiran@wanadoo.fr Ⓥ Y by appt.

EMMANUEL TASSIN
Les Froles 1998★　0.25 ha　700　€8-11

The 1996 vintage of Emmanuel Tassin's Coteaux Champenois was awarded a *coup de cœur*. 1998 proved to be a more difficult year, but he has made a success of it nonetheless. Having undergone fermentation and maceration for a good week, the wine is fined but not filtered, and then aged for 15 months in oak barrels (of which 25% are new). It has an intense colour, and a powerful bouquet of red fruits and oak. The freshness and fine length on the palate are enhanced by well-integrated tannins.

➤ Emmanuel Tassin, 104, Grande-Rue, 10110 Celles-sur-Ource, tel. 03.25.38.59.44, fax 03.25.29.94.59 Ⓥ Y by appt.

B. VESSELLE Bouzy　1.5 ha　15, 000　€11-15

Bruno Vesselle, son of Georges, has been producing wine under his own name since 1994. His Bouzy undergoes a careful vinification, with 70% of the grapes passing through a crusher-destemmer, before the wine is matured in cask for two years. Its bright red appearance and its classic Pinot bouquet of cherries are reinforced by a balanced palate, with well-integrated tannins supporting the fruit.

➤ Georges Vesselle, 16, rue des Postes, 51150 Bouzy, tel. 03.26.57.00.15, fax 03.26.57.09.20, e-mail contact@champagne-vesselle.fr Y ev. day except Sat. Sun. 9am–12 noon; 2pm–5pm

MAURICE VESSELLE Bouzy 1992　n.c.　n.c.　€11-15

The Pinot Noir grapes used in Maurice Vesselle's Bouzy are not de-stemmed. He punches down the cap of grapeskins manually during the fermentation, and then gives the wine two years' maturation in oak. This 1992, tasted on 19 April 2001, can't help but show its age. It is nonetheless an interesting wine, with a bouquet reminiscent of prunes and preserved fruits, and a palate that is supple and still enjoyable. For all that, its decline can't be too far off.

➤ Maurice Vesselle, 2, rue Yvonnet, 51150 Bouzy, tel. 03.26.57.00.81, fax 03.26.57.83.08 Y by appt.

Rosé des Riceys

The three villages of Les Riceys (Haut, Haute-Rive and Bas) are located in the extreme south of the Aube, not far from Bar-sur-Seine. The commune of Les Riceys consists of three appellations: Champagne, Coteaux Champenois and Rosé des Riceys. The last is a still wine of great rarity – only 819 hl (21,622 gal) were harvested in 1999 and 640 hl (16,896 gal) in 2000 – and of great quality: it is one of the best rosés in France. The wine was already being drunk in the reign of Louis XIV and is said to have been taken to Versailles by the builders who were digging the foundations of the château and who came from Les Riceys.

This rosé is the result of vinification that includes a short maceration of Pinot Noir with a natural alcohol level that cannot be less than 10%. The maceration must be stopped – *saigner la cuve* or bleeding the vat – at the precise moment that the unique Riceys flavour appears, otherwise it vanishes. Only the rosés with this special flavour are labelled. The Rosé des Riceys is matured in vat and drunk young, at 8–9°C (46.4–48.2°F), as an aperitif or with a first course. Matured in barrels, it can develop over three to ten years and should then be served at 10–12°C (50–53.6°F) throughout the meal.

BAUSER 1999*

1 ha 5,500 [11-15]

Both René Bauser's sons have joined him on this vineyard, which was established in 1963. Their Rosé des Riceys is a very fine, intensely coloured wine. Its scents of raspberries, cherry-stones and spices announce a complex palate that, although still tannic, is nonetheless well balanced.

EARL René Bauser,
rte de Tonnerre, 10340 Les Riceys,
tel. 03.25.29.32.92, fax 03.25.29.96.29,
e-mail champagne-bauser@worldonline.fr
by appt.

ALEXANDRE BONNET 1997*

6 ha 14,675 [15-23]

This famous Riceys house became part of the BCC group, managed by Philippe Baijot, in 1998. The '97 was produced before the merger, and is therefore a product of the Bonnet family. It is showing its age with its brick-coloured highlights and its well-developed bouquet, in which gamey hints accompany the scents of strawberries and blackcurrants. The palate is fruity, peppery, balanced and long.

SA vignobles Alexandre Bonnet,
138, rue du Gal-de-Gaulle, 10340 Les Riceys,
tel. 03.25.29.30.93, fax 03.25.29.38.65,
e-mail info@alexandrebonnet.com
by appt.

GUY DE FOREZ 1998*

1 ha 9,300 [11-15]

This estate comprises 8.5 ha (21 acres) of vines. Each year, it allocates 1 ha (approximately 2.5 acres) of Pinot Noir to the production of Rosé des Riceys. This particular wine has been fermented for 72 hours, and has then been left to age in oak for three months. Its deep cherry colour with brick-red highlights did not go unnoticed, but neither did its bouquet of dried rose-petals and preserved red fruits. Its lively, spicy quality contributes to a wine of good balance.

SCEA du Val du Lei, rte de Tonnerre,
10340 Les Riceys, tel. 03.25.29.98.73,
fax 03.25.38.23.01 ev. day except Sun.
9am–12 noon, 2pm–7pm; cl. 15–31 Aug.
• Sylvie Wenner

JEAN-JACQUES LAMOUREUX

1998

0.5 ha 2,500 [11-15]

The ancient village of Les Riceys boasts three long-established houses that enhance its charm. The one that produced this champagne dates back to the 18th century. It is a clear, bright, brick-coloured wine with the typical Riceys bouquet (elegantly fruity and vanilla-tinged), and a light palate with silky tannins. It would go well with all grilled meats.

Jean-Jacques Lamoureux, 27 bis, rue du
Gal-de-Gaulle, 10340 Les Riceys,
tel. 03.25.29.11.55, fax 03.25.29.69.22
by appt.

VINCENT LAMOUREUX 1999

0.5 ha 2,000 [11-15]

The intensity of its colour is such that this wine could be seen either as a very dark rosé or as a very light red. Its bouquet exhibits extreme youth – not surprisingly, as it was made in 1999. A slight oakiness is apparent on the palate, along with some fruity notes, making for a wine of great freshness.

Vincent Lamoureux, 2, rue du
Sénateur-Lesaché, 10340 Les Riceys,
tel. 03.25.29.39.32, fax 03.25.29.80.30
by appt.

Rosé des Riceys

MOREL PERE ET FILS 1998 🍷 ⬛ ⬛ €11–15

n.c.   10,000

The carefully selected grapes are accommodated in ancient, vaulted cellars, and the wines aged in oak casks. Clear and bright, this almost cherry-coloured wine is developing aromas of red fruits and spices. Its integrated tannins, good balance and respectable length make it a suitable accompaniment to a terrine of poultry.

☞ Pascal Morel Père et Fils,
93, rue du Gal-de-Gaulle, 10340 Les Riceys,
tel. 03.25.29.10.88, fax 03.25.29.66.72 ⬛
🍷 by appt.

PASCAL WALCZAK 1999★★ ⬛ ⬛ 🍷 €11–15

0.25 ha 1,500

A *coup de cœur* couldn't have been closer! One member of the Jury described this wine as 'the best Rosé des Riceys tasted', while another called it 'a real charmer, superb'. In a word, this 1999 is a classic of its type. Its colour is intense and the fine, complex bouquet mingles notes of vanilla and toast with scents of wild berries. The fruity, fresh, expressive palate is integrated and well balanced. A truly delightful wine.

☞ Pascal Walczak, Parc Saint-Vincent,
10340 Les Riceys, tel. 03.25.29.39.85,
fax 03.25.29.62.05 ⬛ 🍷 ev. day except Sun
8am–12 noon; 1.30pm–7pm

Jura

A mirror-image of the vineyards of the Haute Bourgogne, the Jura vineyards occupy the slopes that descend from the first plateau of the Jura mountains to the plain below. The wine-growing region runs from north to south across the whole department, from the area of Salins-les-Bains in the north to Saint-Amour in the south. Compared with the Côte-d'Or, across the valley, the Jura slopes are scattered and irregular, with many different aspects and exposures. Vines are cultivated only on the most favourably sited slopes, at an altitude of between 250 and 400 m (820–1,312 ft). The vineyard covers about 1,828 ha (4,515 acres) from which about 110,758 hl (2,924,011 gal) were produced in the abundant year of 1999.

The classic continental climate is unusually exaggerated, because of both the general westward orientation of the region and the particular characteristics of its Jurassic contours, especially the boxed-off features known as 'blind alleys'. Winters are harsh, and the summer weather is unreliable, but there are often many hot days. The harvest takes place over a fairly long period, even extending into November because of the difficulties the grapes have in ripening fully. The soils are in the main sedimentary Triassic deposits, or liassic deposits of Jurassic marl, particularly in the north, and there is also a chalk overlay, mostly found in the south of the department. The local grape varieties are perfectly adapted to the clay soils and produce wines of a remarkably specific regional character. The vines need to be trained quite high to raise the grapes above damaging autumn humidity. They are pruned en courgées – that is, in long, arching stems such as can be found on the similar soils of the Mâconnais. If one can believe the writings of Pliny, vine cultivation in the region dates back to at least the beginning of the Christian era; and there is no doubt that the Jura vineyards, particularly appreciated by Henri IV of France, were very much in fashion from the Middle Ages.

The old, peaceful city of Arbois, the wine capital of the region, is full of charm. There are many reminders that the great 19th-century scientist Louis Pasteur, who spent his youth in Arbois, frequently returned to it. It was here, using the vines that grew at his family home, that he began his researches into fermentation that were to prove so important to the nascent science of oenology (from the Greek *oinos*, meaning wine) and that led, among other things, to the discovery that harmful micro-organisms could be killed by heat, a technique still known as pasteurisation.

JURA

Local grape varieties grow alongside later arrivals from Burgundy. One of the native varieties, the Poulsard (or Ploussard), from the lower foothills of the Jura mountains, was apparently only ever cultivated in the Revermont, a geographical area that also includes the Bugey vineyard, where it is known as the Mècle. This very pretty grape, with its large, oblong berries, is deliciously perfumed and has a thin, lightly coloured skin containing little tannin. A typical grape variety for rosé wines, it is more often used here to make red wines. The Trousseau, another local grape variety is, on the other hand, rich in both colour and tannin, and it, too, produces classic red wines that are characteristic of the Appellations d'Origine du Jura. The Pinot Noir, imported from Burgundy, is most frequently added in small quantities in the making of red wines. It also has an important future in the vinification of white wines made from black grapes intended for assembly with blanc de blancs to make high-quality sparkling wines. As in Burgundy, the Chardonnay grows perfectly successfully on the clay soils and gives the white wines their unmatched bouquet. The Savagnin, a local white grape variety, is cultivated on the poorest marly soils and, after six careful years of development on ullage in barrel, produces the magnificent Vin Jaune, or 'yellow wine', a Jura classic. Vin de Paille (straw wine) is also produced in small quantities in the Jura.

The region appears to be particularly favourable for obtaining excellent sparkling wine made, as previously mentioned, from blending blanc de noirs (Pinot Noir), white juice from black grapes, with blanc de blancs (Chardonnay), or white juice from white grapes. To achieve their high standards of quality and in order to ensure the necessary freshness, these sparkling wines have to be made from grapes selected at a particular stage of ripeness.

The white and red wines are classic in style, but, apparently because of the appeal of Vin Jaune, growers try to give them a highly developed character that is almost oxidised. Half a century ago, even some red wines were aged for more than a hundred years, but now makers have returned to more normal time frames for the wine's development.

As for the rosé, it is a lightly coloured red wine with low tannin, more frequently resembling red wine than rosés from other vineyards. Because of this, it can be kept for a time. It goes very well with fairly light dishes, the real reds – particularly those made from Trousseau grapes – being kept for more strongly flavoured dishes. The whites accompany the usual dishes, white meats and fish; the older whites partner Comté cheese very well. Vin Jaune excels with Comté and also with Roquefort and some other dishes for which it can be difficult to find an appropriate wine, such as duck with orange or dishes with sauce américaine.

Arbois

This is the best known of the Appellations d'Origine du Jura, and the name applies to all types of wines produced in the 12 communes in the Arbois region, which cover about 849 ha (2,097 acres). In 2000 production reached about 42,236 hl (1,115,030 gal), of which 23,340 hl (616,176 gal) were reds and rosé, 18,354 hl (484,546 gal) were whites and yellows, 352 hl (9,293 gal) were Vin de Paille and about 190 hl (5,016 gal) were sparkling. The Triassic marls of the *terroir* influence the quite particular character of the rosés made from Poulsard grapes.

744

FRUITIÈRE VINICOLE D'ARBOIS
Poulsard 1998

55 ha | 200,000 | €5-8

The co-operative was formed in 1906 and now has 28 members. It owns three tasting rooms in Arbois and one in Arc-et-Senans (where you should visit the Royal salt-works, which were constructed in 1775 by Claude Nicolas Ledoux, who dreamed of building an ideal city). The staff of the Fruitière Vinicole d'Arbois go to great lengths to make you feel welcome. On offer is an Arbois rosé made from Poulsard grapes. The wine is a lovely pale shade of pink with a perfumed and fruity nose. It is still closed and needs a little time to soften. The underlying notes of woodland fruit that are already showing through are interesting.

➤ Fruitière vinicole d'Arbois, 2, rue des Fossés, 39600 Arbois, tel. 03.84.66.11.67, fax 03.84.37.48.80 ▼ by appt.

LUCIEN AVIET
Cuvée des Géologues 1999★

0.6 ha | n.c.

The famous Cuvée des Géologues is made by a real wine-making character, known to all Jura fans as Bacchus: he now collaborates with his son, Vincent. This wine is dedicated to geologists, but it has been meticulously examined by our tasting-experts, who found common ground with the former. This is an interesting wine from all perspectives, with red fruit and vegetal aromas on the nose, a rush of liveliness on the palate, where a good deal of freshness emerges. There is also alcohol and tannin that add to the balance alongside the fruitiness. A fine, technically well-made wine that does not betray the basic attributes of the terroir.

➤ Lucien Aviet et Fils, Caveau de Bacchus, 39600 Montigny-lès-Arsures, tel. 03.84.66.11.02 ▼ by appt.

PAUL BENOIT
Pupillin Chardonnay 1999★

3 ha | 20,000 | €8-11

The nose is intense and subtle. Flowery with a freshness (of menthol and aniseed), it opens with a certain fruitiness. It is well balanced on the palate, where it is full and aromatic. The finish is light and could be better, but there is a truly lovely roundness. A dish of veal and shallots will really show it off, but it would not be out of place as an aperitif.

➤ Paul Benoit, rue du Chardonnay, La Chenevière, 39600 Pupillin, tel. 03.84.37.43.72, fax 03.84.66.24.61 ▼ ev. day 9am–7pm

COLETTE ET CLAUDE BULABOIS
1997★★

2.2 ha | 3,000 | €8-11

A remarkable 97: Colette and Claude Bulabois have used great skill here. Thirty-five per cent of the vineyard is planted with Savagnin. The nose is powerful and very typical, with complex oaky, buttery, toasty and dried fruit notes. The wine is round yet not heavy on the palate, and lightly oaked, showing some concentration and richness of flavour. The evolution of the wine *sous voile* (under a film of yeast), shows it off to perfection. It has good keeping qualities but can already be enjoyed with a mushroom pastry, for example. The red **Cuvée Vieilles Vignes 99** is a blend of Ploussard, Pinot Noir and Trousseau grapes and is matured in oak for 12 months. It has a Pinot nose and is an easy-drinking wine that merited the Jury's praise.

➤ Claude et Colette Bulabois, 1, Petite-Rue, 39600 Villette-lès-Arbois, tel. 03.84.66.01.93 ▼ ev. day 5–7.30pm

JOSEPH DORBON Ploussard 1999★★

0.35 ha | 1,600 | €5-8

Joseph Dorbon has been running his own 3 ha (7.4 acres) vineyard since 1996. This Poulsard, bottled at the end of August, 2000, has a very pleasant nose, with aromas of strawberry and morello cherry. The wine is still lively, although it is well made with good structure, with rich tannins. Given its structure, it could almost be mistaken for a Trousseau. The aromas of red fruit, undergrowth, spices and menthol are elegant. A fine, good wine that is just waiting to accompany a venison stew or roast partridge. The **Cuvée Vieilles Vignes 98** is made from Chardonnay only and matured for 22 months in oak without undergoing racking or topping-up. It was praised for its aromas of cooked fruit, nuttiness and freshly baked biscuits. A fine pairing with a dish of morel mushrooms in cream.

➤ Joseph Dorbon, pl. de la Liberté, 39600 Vadans, tel. 03.84.37.47.93, fax 03.84.37.47.93 ▼ ev. day 10am–7pm

Jura

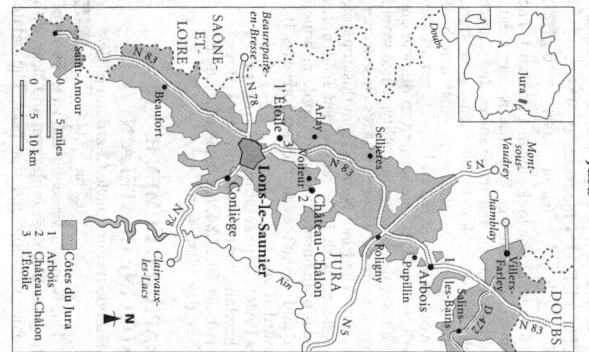

1 Côtes du Jura
2 Arbois
3 Château-Chalon
3 l'Étoile

DANIEL DUGOIS Chardonnay 1998★

☐   1 ha   4,000   ▥ €5–8

Daniel Dugois, who has a portrait of Henri IV emblazoned on his wine labels, has been managing his 780 ha (1,927 acres) of vineyard since 1973. This white wine, made exclusively from Chardonnay grapes, is pale gold. It has fruity aromas with alluring vanilla undertones. It is full bodied with a hint of acidity, which suggests a long future ahead. A well-made wine that will reveal its subtlety in time. The red **Trousseau 99**, also awarded a star, is musky on the nose and balanced on the palate, with attractive tannins. It is ready to drink now or can be left to age for several years.

☛ Daniel Dugois, 4, rue de la Mirode, 39600 Les Arsures, tel. 03.84.66.03.41, fax 03.84.37.44.59 ▼ by appt.

DOM. FORET

Instant Flora Trousseau 1999★

■   1 ha   3,000   ▥ €11–15

Life is a succession of moments. The Forêt domaine presents a 'Floral Moment' with the Trousseau grape. The nose has a lovely intensity, although it is likely to open and give more. Pine sap is much in evidence. The palate opens with roundness and suppleness and finishes with a strong vinous note. To drink with grilled meat or game. The blend of two-thirds Chardonnay and one-third Savagnin, matured for 10 months in wood, produced a lovely **Arbois sec 98**. The nose is complex, with hazelnut, walnut and almond, and has a promising freshness. It impressed the Jury.

☛ Dom. Foret, 13, rue de la Faïencerie, 39600 Arbois, tel. 03.84.66.23.01, fax 03.84.66.10.98 ▼ by appt.

RAPHAEL FUMEY ET ADELINE CHATELAIN Ploussard 1999★★

■   0.6 ha   3,000   ▥ €5–8

Just what one looks for in a Poulsard. The ruby is enchanting! The nose is very clean, with aromas of red fruit, spices and quince jelly. It is difficult to follow such a great start. This elegant 99 is full with great length of flavour of stewed red fruit and is remarkably well balanced. If one wanted to quibble one could say it is lacking in acidity, which would give it more suppleness, but it's close to perfection. The **Pinot Noir 98** from this domaine is packed with little red-berried fruit notes and is both harmonious and supple, although it could stay in the cellar for several years. It is awarded one star.

☛ EARL Raphaël Fumey et Adeline Chatelain, 39600 Montigny-lès-Arsures, tel. 03.84.66.27.84, fax 03.84.66.27.84 ▼ ▼ ev. day 10am–6pm

RAPHAEL FUMEY ET ADELINE CHATELAIN

Méthode traditionnelle Chardonnay 1998

○   0.5 ha   3,000   ▥ €5–8

This is so effervescent it almost leaps out of the glass. The nose is pleasant and clean with aromas of apple and ripe pear. The palate,

which is far from disappointing, is frank and lively. An easy-drinking wine to suit a whole range of occasions.

☛ EARL Raphaël Fumey et Adeline Chatelain, 39600 Montigny-lès-Arsures, tel. 03.84.66.27.84, fax 03.84.66.27.84 ▼ ▼ ev. day 10am–6pm

MICHEL GAHIER

Trousseau Grands Vergers 1999★

■   1 ha   4,000   ▥ €8–11

A young wine-maker, Michel Gahier, has run this domaine since 1990. He makes two wines using Trousseau grapes, including this Grands Vergers, with its distinguished, intense nose with spicy and fruity notes. The full-bodied 99 is dominated by the tannins and oak flavours are present, but it is a lovely wine in which the technical skill of the winemaker is evident. It will be more eloquent in three to five years. The **Chardonnay 98** is also awarded a star. Over its 24 months in cask it has matured to a very attractive golden-yellow. Hazelnut and honeyed tones fill the mouth, and it has substantial length. Good value for money.

☛ Michel Gahier, pl. de l'Eglise, 39600 Montigny-lès-Arsures, tel. 03.84.66.17.63, fax 03.84.66.17.63 ▼ by appt.

DOM. AMELIE GUILLOT

Poulsard Vieilles vignes Rouge

Tradition 1999★★★

■   1.5 ha   2,500   ▥ €8–11

A young woman tends these old vines: a partnership that bodes well for the future. It is a typical Poulsard, light in colour with orangey flecks. The nose is also true to the grape variety. There is a tannic richness on the palate but with suppleness and balance. The wine is a fine example of the Poulsard variety produced using flawless wine-making techniques. The oenology studies paid off.

☛ Amelie Guillot, 1, rue du Coin-des-Côtes, 39600 Molamboz, tel. 03.84.66.04.00, fax 03.84.66.04.00, e-mail amelie.guillot@wanadoo.fr ▼ ▼ ev. day 2–8pm

LA CAVE DE LA REINE JEANNE

Poulsard 1999★

■   5 ha   30,000   ▥ €5–8

Bénédicte and Stéphane Tissot set up their *négoriant* business in 1977 in superb cellars or the Place d'Arbois. Here, it is not wine that is for sale but grapes, which means that Stéphane is cited as a wine-maker on the bottles. This pure Poulsard is clear ruby. Redcurrant jelly and strawberries jump out of the glass. A slight acidity on the palate adds freshness. It would be a pity not to take advantage of this fruity 99 and to drink it, perhaps with a terrine. The pure Chardonnay **white Arbois 99** received the same marks; 60% of the wine is fermented in barrels, 40% is matured in metal vats. It is flowery, lemony and vanillary following through with buttery tones and hints of ripe apples.

• Le Cellier des Tiercelines, 54, Grande-Rue, 39600 Arbois, tel. 03.84.66.25.79, fax 03.84.66.25.08 ⊠
• Bénédicte et Stéphane Tissot

DOM. DE LA PINTE

Trousseau 1998★★

■ 1 ha   3,500   ⊞ €8-11

If you go to the domaine you should visit the cellars that Roger Martin built in 1955. There are three, all 70 m (76 yds) long; one is used for this red Arbois made exclusively from Trousseau grapes. There is a good depth of colour, and even though the nose is not very powerful it has elegant aromas of cherry in *eau-de-vie* with a background of vanilla. A well-balanced palate with a dominant fruiti-ness accompanied by mellow, well-integrated oak. Nonetheless, it is an unusual wine due to premature ageing, which almost gives it a Burgundian aspect. The tasting panel agreed it would go with with beef tournedos and mushrooms but could equally well accom-pany guinea fowl with blackcurrants.
• Dom. de La Pinte, rte de Lyon, 39600 Arbois, tel. 03.84.66.06.47, fax 03.84.66.24.58 ⊠ ▼ ev. day 9am–12 noon 1.30–6pm; Sun. by by appt.

DOM. DE LA RENARDIERE

Pupillin Ploussard 1999★★

■ 2.2 ha   14,000   ⊞ €5-8

When a crisis occurs some wine-makers offer extraordinary solidarity and support. This was Jean-Michel Petit's experience when he had a serious accident a few years ago. His wine is as convivial as you might imagine, which may be an expression of this support. This Poulsard is pleasant, just as it should be. It has an elegant, even a thoroughbred, nose and is well structured with body and mature, supple tannins. Full flavoured with red fruit and spices, all in perfect harmony, this Poulsard is closer in colour to a rosé but is typical and serves as a good reference point.
• Jean-Michel Petit, rue du Chardonnay, 39600 Pupillin, tel. 03.84.66.25.10, fax 03.84.66.25.70, e-mail renardiere@libertysurf.fr ▼ ev. day except Sun. 10am–12 noon 2–7pm

DOM. DE LA TOURNELLE

Chardonnay 1999★★

□ 2 ha   9,000   ⊞ €8-11

Pascal Clairet has made his living from his wines for ten years, and that deserves to be cel-ebrated. The nose of this Arbois is developed and powerful and already complex and elegant. Honey, caramel and buttery tones are very noticeable. On the palate it has a very fine structure with perfect balance between acidity, roundness and alcohol. It is very expressive with flowery perfumes that open to reveal buttery and honey tones. A characteris-tic, concentrated wine which retains its fresh-ness and finesse. It will go well with fish in cream sauce. The **Poulsard Vieilles Vignes 99** would be good with a terrine eaten among

friends; it was especially singled out by the Jury.
• Pascal Clairet, 5, Petite-Place, 39600 Arbois, tel. 03.84.66.25.76, fax 03.84.66.27.15 ⊠ ▼ ev. day except Sun. 10am–12.30pm 2.30–7pm

DOM. LIGIER PERE ET FILS

Trousseau 1999★★

■ 0.7 ha   4,000   ⊞ €5-8

The Ligiers take part in many wine trade shows and exhibitions, so you are sure to come across them. This hand-harvested Trousseau Arbois red is the one to try. The nose is intense, spicy and lightly oaked. Red fruit flavours are at the core of the palate, which has both body and balance. For imme-diate drinking with duck breast *confit* with honey and morel mushrooms, this 99 wine can also wait for three to five years.
• Dom. Ligier Pere et Fils, 7, rue de Poligny, 39380 Mont-sous-Vaudrey, tel. 03.84.71.74.75, fax 03.84.81.59.82, e-mail ligier@netcourrier.com ⊠ ▼ by appt.

DOM. LIGIER PERE ET FILS

Poulsard 1999★★★

■ 1 ha   6,000   ⊞ €5-8

Here, wine-loving friends, is an investment you will not regret. This Poulsard is marvel-lous. Everything about it is beautiful, starting with its ruby colour flickering orange. The bouquet is unruly, 'masculine', even spicy, and well structured with an unusual aromatic register. The mouth is silkier and attractively fleshy and a pleasure to taste. The balance is superb: strawberry, cherries in brandy, game. It is a genuine Poulsard but shows kinship with the Trousseau, almost as if the neigh-bouring vines had communicated their viril-ity. Roast deer with bilberries and this wine would make an unforgettable feast.
• Dom. Ligier Pere et Fils, 7, rue de Poligny, 39380 Mont-sous-Vaudrey, tel. 03.84.71.74.75, fax 03.84.81.59.82, e-mail ligier@netcourrier.com ⊠ by appt.

FREDERIC LORNET

Chardonnay 1999★

□ 1.2 ha   7,000   ⊞ €5-8

Frédéric Lornet lives in an ancient abbey and has run this domaine since 1981. Last year he was awarded a *coup de coeur* for **Trousseau des Dames 98**. The well-made **99** of the same vintage has good body and structure though at the tasting the oak was dominant; it was recommended. As for this Arbois Chardonnay, it has an intense nose with complexity: mineral notes, bitter almond and a touch of roasted coffee beans. The acidity is slightly high, but it adds a pleasant freshness to this fruity 99 with an attractive aftertaste. The wine was a little young when tasted, but it holds promise for the future. To be drunk from 2002 with a *galette des rois* (a seasonal almond cake baked for the Feast of the Kings on 6 January), and then good for the next five years.

☞ Frédéric Lornet, L'Abbaye, 39600 Montigny-lès-Arsures, tel. 03.84.37.44.95, fax 03.84.37.40.17 ⊠ ▼ by appt.

DOM. MARTIN FAUDOT Pinot 1999★ €5-8
0.8 ha 3,000

Michel Faudot and Jean-Pierre Martin vinify Pinot Noir separately to make a varietal *cuvée*. This rather pale 99 has a definitive red fruit nose enhanced by a touch of oak. The tannin flavours are supported by a light but balanced structure. A wine to wait for. The **Arbois pur Chardonnay 99** is matured in vat for six months and was awarded the same marks. A brilliant pale gold colour with rich dried fruit and flowers on the nose, it develops on the palate with hints of citrus fruit and peach.

☞ Dom. Martin-Faudot, 1, rue Bardenet, 39600 Mesnay, tel. 03.84.66.29.97, fax 03.84.66.29.84, e-mail info@domaine-martin.fr ⊠ ▼ by appt.

JEAN-FRANCOIS NEVERS 1996★ €8-11
1 ha 3,000

Jean-François Nevers is the head of a traditionally run family property that is based in a little street in Arbois near the Musée de la Vigne et du Vin (the Vine and Wine Museum). The old-gold 96 already has a mature nose with hints of spicy and vanilla aromas with a mineral aspect. The palate is rich but already mature. A very fine wine that should be drunk straight away.

☞ Jean-François Nevers, 4, rue du Collège, 39600 Arbois, tel. 03.84.66.01.73, fax 03.84.37.49.68 ⊠ ▼ by appt.

PIERRE OVERNOY Pupillin poulsard 1998★ €8-11
1.5 ha n.c.

Pierre Overnoy is known well beyond the Jura region. He set up in 1968 and was an early convert to organic cultivation, long before it became fashionable. He is a passionate purist who, for example, has a horror of the use of SO^2 (sulphur dioxide). His Poulsard red is not very limpid but this is not the wine-maker's fault. The nose is powerful, long and elegant, mingling very ripe strawberry, quince jelly and redcurrant jelly. The palate follows through with the same notes, not forgetting to mention the well-integrated tannins and good balance. It is ready to drink now, for both organic purists and the rest of us. The **white Arbois Pupillin See 99** was awarded the same marks. It is golden, heady, mouthfilling and will hold its own with any spicy food.

☞ Pierre Overnoy, rue du Ploussard, 39600 Pupillin, tel. 03.84.66.14.60, fax 03.84.66.14.60 ⊠ ▼ by appt.

DESIRE PETIT ET FILS Vin de paille 1997★★★ €15-23
0.84 ha 3,700

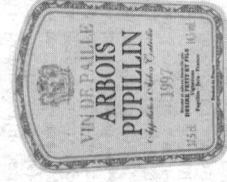

Produced by two brothers, Gérard and Marcel Petit, this 97 is made up of one third Poulsard, one third Chardonnay and one third Savagnin grapes, in a perfectly balanced equation. The talent of the wine-makers has drawn the best out of each of the grape varieties in this Vin de Paille. The nose is powerful and elegant, releasing giddy-making aromas of honey, dates and quince jelly. This is very rich and intensely full-flavoured with a sublime balance of lively acidity and fullness; its harmony makes it a text-book wine. All the tasters agreed that it can wait for no less than 50 years!

☞ Dom. Désiré Petit, rue du Ploussard, 39600 Pupillin, tel. 03.84.66.01.20, fax 03.84.66.26.59 ⊠ ▼ by appt.
☞ Gérard et Marcel Petit

MARCEL POUX Vin jaune 1987 €15-23
n.c. 5,000

Marcel Poux is the brand name for the wines that the Henri Maire company produces for the restaurant trade. This Vin Jaune is amber toned. The nose is still somewhat closed but this wine is supple in the mouth. It has a straightforward palate yet is fine and elegant and can be drunk from now.

☞ Marcel Poux, SARL Gevin, 39600 Arbois, tel. 03.84.66.12.34, fax 03.84.37.42.42

PRE-LEVERON Chardonnay Vieilles vignes 1999 €8-11
1 ha 6,000

The SARL Rijckaert is a wine-maker in the Mâconnais and a shipper. This white Arbois has an intense nose with notes of very ripe, white-fleshed fruit. This full-flavoured 99 is alcoholic but also has good acidity. It should be drunk fairly soon and would accompany *quenelles* very well.

☞ SARL Rijckaert, Correaux, 71570 Leynes, tel. 03.85.35.15.09, fax 03.85.35.15.09, e-mail jeanrijckaert@aol.com ⊠ ▼ by appt.
☞ Dominique Horbach

JACQUES PUFFENEY

Les Bérangères Trousseau 1999★

0.8 ha — 4,500 — €11-15
[V] [Y] by appt.

Trousseau vines account for only 5% of the grape varieties grown in Jura's vineyards, but at Montigny-les-Arsures we are at the capital, and naturally enough, Jacques Puffeney grows some. This Bérangères is truly red with noticeable violet hues. It is full, with a concentrated nose of blackberry jam, blackcurrant leaf and bilberry jam aromas. The palate is rich and full bodied. It is Burgundian in style and was judged to be attractive but without any strong characteristics of the terroir.

→ Jacques Puffeney, quartier Saint-Laurent, 39600 Montigny-lès-Arsures, tel. 03.84.66.10.89, fax 03.84.66.10.89 [V]
[Y] by appt.

ROLET PERE ET FILS

Trousseau 1999★★

6 ha — 30,000 — €8-11

The Rolet family's wines go to Belgium, Switzerland and Japan, where they are greatly enjoyed. This Trousseau is not a cool colour but a superb, vivid garnet. It has a well-bred nose with choice, seductive blackcurrant aromas. It is supple but still fills the mouth well. It has substance and a certain fleshiness. Red fruit and ripe cherry emerge. Its authenticity and desired richness will enchant. It would be wise to wait for two years.

FRUITIERE VINICOLE DE PUPILLIN Pupillin Pinot noir 1999

3 ha — 10,000 — €5-8

In Pupillin the name of the commune may be attached to the Arbois AOC. This is in recognition of its reputation, and since its establishment in 1906 the Fruitière Vinicole has participated in that fame. This red has an intense, slightly herbaceous nose and this same vegetal aspect is reproduced on the palate, with added spicy notes. This wine should wait a few years.

→ Fruitière vinicole de Pupillin, 39600 Pupillin, tel. 03.84.66.12.88, fax 03.84.37.47.16 [Y] by appt.

DOM. ROLET PERE ET FILS

Vin jaune 1994

6 ha — 10,000 — €23-30

When Désiré Rolet established this domaine in 1946 he probably did not imagine that he, and subsequently his children, would turn it into the second biggest vineyard in the Jura, covering 61 ha (15 acres) in the AOCs of Arbois, Côtes-du-Jura and l'Etoile. This is a powerful Vin Jaune, which is lively and typical. As a whole, it is characteristic, but in no circumstances should it be opened for five years.

→ Dom. Rolet Père et Fils, rte de Dole, 39600 Arbois, tel. 03.84.66.00.05, fax 03.84.37.41.41, e-mail rolet@wanadoo.fr
[V] [Y] by appt.

DOM. DU SORBIEF 1998★★★

n.c. — 35,000 — €11-15

The Henri Maire company has owned this domaine since 1963. There are 66 ha (163 acres) on red marl growing Poulsard and Trousseau, with a few hectares producing a rosé-style wine that is fermented for around 10 days. The attractive 98 is the colour of hen pheasant's plumage and has a very fruity nose, with redcurrant, quince jelly and strawberry. The palate has an impressive complexity and richness. Both alcoholic and full, this wine has a remarkable finish. It is packed with flavour: morello cherry, wild strawberry and cinnamon aromas that go on forever. Time to serve it with roast woodcock.

→ SCV des domaines Henri Maire, 39600 Arbois, tel. 03.84.66.42.42, e-mail info@henri-maire.fr [V] [Y] by appt.

ANDRE ET MIREILLE TISSOT

Vin jaune 1993★

2 ha — 7,000 — €23-30

The vineyard has a firm commitment to environmentally-friendly techniques and a complete conversion to organic cultivation in the domaine has begun. This Vin Jaune was matured in cask for seven years, we are told (the minimum time stipulated is six years and three months). This shows on the nose, which is intense and marked with an attractive oakiness. It is elegant, well balanced and full bodied on the palate. The finish is still a little lively but this is a very young wine. This wine has turned out to be a success for a vintage that was considered trickly.

→ André et Mireille Tissot, 39600 Montigny-lès-Arsures, tel. 03.84.66.25.08 [V] [Y] by appt.
fax 03.84.66.08.27,
→ André et Stéphane Tissot

DOM. DE SAINT-PIERRE

Cuvée Renaud 1997

3.65 ha — 10,000 — €5-8

This vineyard produces white wines only, and this is quite rare in the Jura. It makes a pure Chardonnay but also vinifies a wine blended from Chardonnay and Savagnin, like this golden-yellow 97. It has an intense bouquet and releases pleasant honeyed notes. The mouth is lively and spiced. Try a glass after a visit to the Romanesque church or the feudal tower that adjoin the domain. Match it up with a lamb curry.

→ EARL Hubert et Renaud Moyne, Dom. de Saint-Pierre, 39600 Mathenay, tel. 03.84.37.56.80, fax 03.84.37.56.80 [V]
[Y] by appt.

→ Dom. Rolet Père et Fils, rte de Dole, 39600 Arbois, tel. 03.84.66.00.056, fax 03.84.37.41.41, e-mail rolet@wanadoo.fr
[V] [Y] by appt.

ANDRE ET MIREILLE TISSOT
Trousseau 1999★ 4 ha 20,000 €8-11

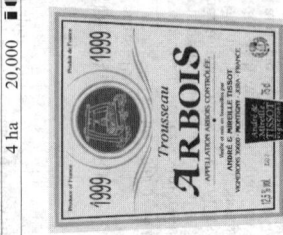

A brief history of this Trousseau: the harvest is hand-picked at the end of September, very rigorous selection, a month of fermentation, three months in vat and a year in cask. Take a look at the result: dark garnet delicately tinged with tile-red, a classy nose, which opens with musk and finishes with lightly toasty aromas and a few underlying blackcurrant tones. It is full and fleshy yet there is a pleasant suppleness. Its balance and harmony make it both lush and complex. A very fine wine that will improve over a number of years. To be enjoyed with dishes of red meat or game.
➤ André et Mireille Tissot, 39600 Montigny-lès-Arsures, tel. 03.84.66.25.08 ☑ ☏ by appt.
➤ André et Stephane Tissot

JEAN-LOUIS TISSOT
Vin jaune 1993★★ 2 ha 2,000 €15-23

Jean-Louis Tissot left the Fruitière Vinicole d'Arbois in 1976 to set up a business, producing and selling his own wine. This Vin Jaune has an intense nose with a beautiful harmony of dried fruit aromas. The powerful, rich and complex palate is full of flavour and has a very long finish. It is a well-balanced wine, made with the care of a perfectionist. Worthy of a fine foie gras. One taster suggested it would go well with frogs' legs.
➤ Jean-Louis Tissot, Vauxelles, 39600 Montigny-lès-Arsures, tel. 03.84.66.13.08, fax 03.84.66.08.09 ☑ ☏ by appt.

JEAN-LOUIS TISSOT
Trousseau 1999★ 2 ha 8,000 €8-11

A beautiful cherry-red colour. An attractive fruity nose, flitting between jam and spice. The structure is balanced and the fruit on good form. It is well made and very attractive. This is a good, approachable example of a Trousseau, the wine to share with friends.
➤ Jean-Louis Tissot, Vauxelles, 39600 Montigny-lès-Arsures, tel. 03.84.66.13.08, fax 03.84.66.08.09 ☑ ☏ by appt.

DOM. TREUVEY
Pinot noir Chantemerle 1999★ 0.5 ha 2,000 €5-8

Jean-Louis Treuvey took over from his father in the autumn of 1998. This wine is from his first Pinot Noir harvest. It has an intense, spicy and vanilla nose with a firm, rich attack. The oak flavours are well integrated within a well-balanced structure. It is pleasant to drink right away but still has a lot to offer and will age for a few years.
➤ Jean-Louis Treuvey, 20, Petite rue, 39600 Villette-lès-Arbois, tel. 03.84.66.14.51, fax 03.84.66.14.51 ☑ ☏ by appt.
➤ Gérard Treuvey

Château-Chalon

The most prestigious of the Jura wines is exclusively the famous Vin de Voile, produced on 45 ha (111 acres). This is a Vin Jaune, made according to strict regulations. The grape is harvested in a remarkable landscape of black liassic marl, overlooked by towering cliffs on top of which the old village is perched. Production is limited but in 2000 it reached 1,717 hl (43,329 gal). The wine is put on sale precisely six years and three months after the harvest. It is worth noting that the producers themselves, who are constantly concerned to maintain a high level of quality, refused the AOC classification for the harvests of 1974, 1980 and 1984.

DOM. BERTHET-BONDET 1994 4 ha 8,000 23-30

Nea-ly half the surface area of this domaine is used to make Château-Chalon. Take the opportunity of tasting this vintage in Jean Berthet-Bondet's lovely property in the village. It is a distinct golden colour. The nose is straightforward, open and powerful. A few walnuty notes emerge from the well-balanced palate. This very young wine needs at least three years to mature.
➤ Dom. Berthet-Bondet, 39210 Château-Chalon, tel. 03.84.44.60.48, fax 03.84.44.61.13, e-mail domaine.berthet.bondet@wanadoo.fr ☑ ☏ by appt.

BLONDEAU ET FILS 1986★

3 ha | 3,000 | €23-30

A Château-Chalon 1986 is becoming a rarity! This one is a pale, slightly coppery colour. The nose is complex and shows over-ripe fruit, slightly crystalised. The palate is open out in the glass. The palate divided tasters' opinions; one expected more personality, others judged it had already matured. All agreed the wine can be enjoyed now but also has good keeping properties.

• Dom. Blondeau et Fils, 39210 Menétru-le-Vignoble, tel. 03.84.44.90.56, fax 03.84.44.90.56, e-mail blondeau@blondeau-vignerons.com ✓ ⚡ by appt.

MARCEL CABELIER 1993★

3 ha | 3,000 | €23-30

This merchant joined the Grands Chais de France company in 1986. He submitted a beautiful golden-yellow 93 enhanced by pretty green glints, an open nose, with dried fruit, walnut and toasty aromas. On the palate the flavours are simple but direct with good balance. Keep in the cellar for at least two years.

• Cie des Grands Vins du Jura, rte de Champagnole, 39570 Crançot, tel. 03.84.87.61.30, fax 03.84.48.21.36, e-mail jura@grandschais.fr ✓ ⚡ ev. day

RESERVE CATHERINE DE RYE 1985★

n.c. | 10,000 | €30-38

You will not find such a huge stock of Château-Chalon anywhere else. This famous merchant, the most important in the appellation, also owns a vineyard in Château-Chalon. This means it can submit a vintage that is no longer very young. Its beautiful coppery colour is very intense. The nose evokes a Vin de Paille because its dried fruit, toasted walnuts and spiced bread aromas are so dominant. The same range of flavours shows on the palate with that touch of acidity that is totally typical of Vins Jaunes. This 85 is mature and could be drunk now, but its structure means it has a number of years ahead of it.

• SCV des domaines Henri Maire, 39600 Arbois, tel. 03.84.66.12.34, fax 03.84.66.42.42, e-mail info@henri-maire.fr ✓ ⚡ by appt.

JEAN-MARIE COURBET 1994

2 ha | 2,000 | €23-30

Jean-Marie Courbet is located in Nevy-sur-Seille, a small village in a valley on the road to the Abbey of Baume-les-Messieurs. His Château-Chalon is pale gold with a few green glints. The nose is delicate with pretty walnut notes and a background of roasted coffee that also follows through on the fine, lengthy palate. It has an obvious Vin Jaune personality.

• Jean-Marie Courbet, rue du Moulin, 39210 Nevy-sur-Seille, tel. 03.84.85.28.70, fax 03.84.44.68.88 ✓ ⚡ by appt.

DESIRE PETIT ET FILS 1994★

0.26 ha | 1,400 | €23-30

The owners originate from Arbois. Gérard and Marcel Petit have only 26 ares (0.6 acre) but hold onto them with real determination. This Château-Chalon has a fabulous nose. Walnut and hazelnut are there in strength on a toasty background that the tasters really enjoyed. A well-balanced palate with good length. This wine, characteristic of the appellation, should open out in two to five years.

• Gérard and Marcel Petit, rue du Ploussard, 39600 Pupillin, tel. 03.84.66.01.20, fax 03.84.66.26.59 ✓ by appt.

FRUITIERE VINICOLE DE VOITEUR 1990★

15 ha | 40,000 | €23-30

From the village of Château-Chalon there is a perfect view of the Fruitière Vinicole de Voiteur, on the Nevy-sur-Seille road. This lovely 90 has been allowed to mature in these cellars. The nose is forward and lengthy, with walnut and toastiness, and the palate is well balanced and powerful with wonderful flavours of walnut, hazelnut and toastiness, particularly on the middle palate. Waiting a little would certainly improve it, but drinking it now certainly gives great pleasure.

• Fruitière vinicole de Voiteur, 39210 Voiteur, Nevy-sur-Seille, tel. 03.84.85.21.29, fax 03.84.85.27.67, e-mail voiteur@fruitiere-vinicole-voiteur.fr ✓ ⚡ by appt.

J. ET B. DURAND-PERRON 1993

n.c. | 1,500 | €23-30

Jacques Durand will undoubtedly remind you that Château-Chalon, like all Vins Jaunes, should be drunk at room temperature, around 15° C/59° F. The 93 is a lovely golden colour. The nose is very attractive with walnut, hazelnut, curry and a hint of toastiness. The wine is harmonious and balanced but without a robust structure although appealingly full flavoured.

• Jacques et Barbara Durand-Perron, 9, rue des Roches, 39210 Voiteur, tel. 03.84.44.66.80, fax 03.84.44.62.75 ✓ by appt.

PHILIPPE PELTIER 1994

2 ha | 1,400 | €23-30

This domaine of 8 ha (20 acres) was created by Pierre Peltier in 1938 and, since 1990, has been run by Philippe Peltier. A quarter of the property is dedicated to this appellation. The colour of the 94 is already well pronounced. The nose starts off with fresh walnut and toasty notes. The wine is not very complex but can be enjoyed for its fruitiness. Needs to mature so it can be savoured fully.

• Philippe Peltier, Caveau du Terroir, 39210 Menétru-le-Vignoble, tel. 03.84.44.90.79 ✓ by appt.

Côtes du Jura

The appellation incorporates the whole area of the vineyard producing fine wines. In 2000 the area of plantation was 619 ha (1,529 acres) which produced 30,687 hl (810,137 gal) of all types of wine: 20,621 hl (544,394 gal) of white wine or Vin Jaune, 8,040 hl (212,256 gal) of red wine), 720 hl (19,008 gal) of Vin de Paille and 1,306 hl (34,478 gal) of sparkling wine.

CH. D'ARLAY Corail 1996
■ 7 ha 25,000 ▥ ▥ ▣ ◆ €8-11

The lineage of this domaine, which has been owned by princes from Spain, England and France since AD560, is one of the most prestigious in France. Today, it is run by Alain de Laguiche. This Corail is produced from the maceration of five grape varieties: Pinot, Trousseau, Poulsard, Chardonnay and Savagnin. This results in a rosé with cherried hues. The nose is reminiscent of undergrowth with hints of morello cherry with cocoa and cinnamon as well. After a fresh attack, the palate develops some roundness supported by soft yet evident tannins. This 96 is ready to accompany oriental cuisine or grilled fish.
➦ Alain de Laguiche, Ch. d'Arlay, rte de Saint-Germain, 39140 Arlay,
tel. 03.84.85.04.22, fax 03.84.48.17.96,
e-mail chateau@arlay.com ▣
🍷 ev. day except Sun. 8–12 noon 2–6pm

BERNARD BADOZ Vin jaune 1993★
□ 1.5 ha 3,000 ▥ ▣ €23-30

Bernard Badoz got this rare pearl of a Vin Jaune ready for La Percée, the wine festival that was inaugurated at Poligny in 1997. For this 93 discretion is the watchword for both the nose and the palate. It is, however, very balanced and elegant. Pike with *beurre blanc* would make an ideal companion.
➦ Bernard Badoz, 15, rue du Collège, 39800 Poligny, tel. 03.84.37.11.85,
fax 03.84.37.11.18 ▣ 🍷 ev. day 8–7pm

BERNARD BADOZ Trousseau 1999★
■ 1 ha 6,000 ▣ €8-11

Bernard Badoz produces several red wines, including single variety Poulsards or Trousseau-Poulsard blends. This single variety Trousseau, with its eye-catching, vermilion colour, is no shrinking violet. It has a lovely nose packed with red fruit with light musky aromas. A good, well-structured wine. It would be a good accompaniment for wild boar.

➦ Bernard Badoz, 15, rue du Collège, 39800 Poligny, tel. 03.84.37.11.85,
fax 03.84.37.11.18 ▣ 🍷 ev. day 8–7pm

BAUD PERE ET FILS
Chardonnay 1999★
□ 5 ha 15,000 ▥ ▥ €5-8

Alain and Jean-Michel Baud inform us that a founding ancestor established the domaine in 1642. They produce this Côtes du Jura on Triassic Jurassian marls. It is made totally of Chardonnay and has a perfumed nose with flowery, citrus and hazelnut notes. The palate is well balanced with a slight acidity that uplifts the attractive fruitiness. Delicious as an aperitif.
➦ Dom. Baud Père et Fils, rte de Voiteur, 39210 Le Vernois, tel. 03.84.25.31.41,
fax 03.84.25.30.09 ▣ 🍷 by appt.

BERNARD FRERES
Chardonnay Aux grandes Vignes 1997★★★
■ 1 ha 2,880 ▥ €5-8

Gevingey hosted the Vin Jaune festival during the famous La Percée wine festival. This Chardonnay 97, made using both tanks and barrels, was much appreciated. The powerful, classy nose releases complex nuances of toasty and smoky aromas. This Côtes du Jura is rich on the palate and well balanced with the right amount of acidity, which gives the freshness to support the delicate fruitiness. It is a superb wine, which comes from south of Revermont, an area that is little known for vineyards though it harbours great talents.
➦ Bernard Frères, 15, rue Principale, 39570 Gevingey, tel. 03.84.47.33.99 ▣ 🍷 by appt.

DOM. BERTHET-BONDET
Tradition 1998★
□ 4 ha 10,000 ▥ €8-11

Jean Berthet-Bondet makes Château-Chalon, but he also uses Savagnin blended with Chardonnay for his Côtes du Jura. The nose of this 98 is fresh and very upfront. It opens with cherry and endive tones then reveals honey, butter and apple. A typical wine, yet with character, it should be left for a while to develop fully and reveal its true personality. To be drunk with scallops in a creamy sauce or with Morbier cheese.
➦ Dom. Berthet-Bondet, 39210 Château-Chalon, tel. 03.84.44.60.48,
fax 03.84.44.61.13,
e-mail domaine.berthet.bondet@wanadoo.fr
▣ 🍷 by appt.

DOM. BERTHET-BONDET
Tradition 1999★
■ 0.5 ha 3,500 ▣ ◆ €5-8

All three red grape varieties permitted in the Côtes du Jura AOC are used to make this wine. It has an attractive cherry-red colour and an intense nose with redcurrant, blackcurrant leaf and a certain spiciness. A full fruity palate with good, soft tannins. One taster described it as 'a wine to quench your thirst'. Its fruitiness makes it an ideal accompaniment for grilled meats.

752

• Dom. Berthet-Bondet, 39210 Château-Chalon, tel. 03.84.44.61.13, fax 03.84.44.60.48, e-mail domaine.berthet.bondet@wanadoo.fr
Y by appt.

DOM. LUC ET SYLVIE BOILLEY
Vin jaune 1992   n.c.   n.c.   €15-23

This yellow Côtes du Jura is grown on clay-limestone soils and initially the nose is discreet but opens to reveal mentholated and toasted aromas. It is light, supple and very harmonious on the palate. Well made and not too overpowering: ideal for people who want to try Vin Jaune for the first time. Worth trying with *blanquette de veau*.
• Dom. Luc et Sylvie Boilley, rte de Domblans, 39210 Saint-Germain-le-Arlay, tel. 03.84.44.97.33, fax 03.84.37.71.21
Y by appt.

PHILIPPE BUTIN **Vin jaune 1994★★★**
0.7 ha   1,600   €23-30

Philippe Butin has been the head of this family enterprise since 1981. As well as his Château-Chalon, he also produces another Vin Jaune in the Côtes du Jura appellation. At first the nose is delicate, but as this 94 opens out it shows characteristic walnut and spice aromas. A powerful palate with an excellent liveliness, with touches of walnut and lemon, which suggests good keeping qualities. The wine is not ready yet but holds promise for the future; its *jaune à l'ancienne* style impressed the Jury. To accompany it, choose *coq aux morilles* (cockerel with morel mushrooms) or Comté cheese.
• Philippe Butin, 21, rue de la Combe, 39210 Lavigny, tel. 03.84.25.36.26, fax 03.84.25.39.18 ev. day 8-7pm

CAVEAU DES BYARDS
Chardonnay 1998★★★   n.c.   12,000   €5-8

'I'll buy it,' declared one of our tasters after this very fine wine was highly rated by the Jury. The nose is delicate at first and has great finesse and elegance with attractive blackcurrant leaf and toasty aromas. A good attack follows with acidity that adds freshness and supports the fruit. This wine does not have great length but the touch of acidity is so pleasant that it creates almost perfect harmony. Ideal to serve with pan-fried scallops.
• Caveau des Byards, 39210 Le Vernois, tel. 03.84.25.33.52, fax 03.84.25.38.02
Y by appt.

MARCEL CABELIER
Grande tradition 1996★★   1 ha   8,500   €5-8

The Compagnie des Grands Vins du Jura is part of the Grands Chais de France group and has two retail outlets, one at Crançot and the other at the Maison des Vignerons in Lons-le-Saunier, in the Jura prefecture. A golden-coloured wine is made from 70% Chardonnay and 30% Savagnin and matured in Burgundy-style barrels. The characteristic, intense nose reveals great freshness. The excellent flowery attack is supported by a firm structure. Mouth filling and full flavoured with hazelnut and spice, this harmonious blend is a good example of the Jura *terroir*. Drink now with a veal escalope. The **Trousseau 99** from the same company, is mouth filling, which is astonishing for this variety, and it received high praise from the tasters.
• Cie des Grands Vins du Jura, rte de Champagnole, 39570 Crançot, tel. 03.84.87.61.30, fax 03.84.48.21.36, e-mail jura@grandschais.fr
Y ev. day 8-12 noon 1-6pm

DANIEL ET PASCAL CHALANDARD **1999★**
0.5 ha   2,000   ■

Before launching into wine-growing, Daniel Chalandard worked as a chemical technician, but that was more than 30 years ago. He favours sustainable agriculture and presented a red wine made from Trousseau which divided the Jury: some found it had a remarkable nose while others felt the explosive aromas were less than characteristic and that it lacked depth. On the other hand, they all agreed that this 99 with its strong temperament, would go well with venison.
• GAEC du Vieux Pressoir, rte de Voiteur, BP 30, 39210 Le Vernois, tel. 03.84.25.31.15, fax 03.84.25.37.62 Y by appt.

DANIEL ET PASCAL CHALANDARD **Cuvée Axel 1998★★★**
4 ha   15,000   €5-8

This wine, 70% Chardonnay and 30% Savagnin, is left to mature for 24 months in barrels, and it bowled over the whole jury. This 98 is a clear, brilliant straw-yellow and leaves tear-shaped drops on the side of the glass. But none of the tasters wept over this wine: the nose opens with heavenly aromas of hazelnut, almond, minerals and dried morel. The wine is characterised by a robust yet well-balanced structure, which has surprising length. On the middle palate the flavours develop a mineral quality, reminiscent of a Château-Chalon. It is well structured and typical, a first-class wine, which just calls for dishes with cream sauce. Besides which it is ready to drink!

• GAEC du Vieux Pressoir, rte de Voiteur, BP 30, 39210 Le Vernois, tel. 03.84.25.31.15, fax 03.84.25.37.62 ⚐ by appt.

DENIS ET MARIE CHEVASSU
Pinot noir 1999★
▪ 0.5 ha 2,500 €5-8

Wine and cheese always make a good partnership as is evident on this farm, where the milk from the dairy herd is used to make the famous Comté cheese. It would go well with this deep red wine. It is made entirely from Pinot Noir, and the nose of pronounced, ripe morello cherry and blackberry gives it away. Fresh and fruity on the palate.

• Denis Chevassu, Granges Bernard, 39210 Menétru-le-Vignoble, tel. 03.84.85.23.67, fax 03.84.85.23.67 ⚐ by appt.

ELISABETH ET BERNARD CLERC Cuvée du pré Cottin 1999★
□ 1,5 ha 3 000 €5-8

This wine is matured for two years in cask and is a blend, with Chardonnay being in larger proportion than the Savagnin. The nose opens with delicate aromas of honey and white blossom. The palate is typically delicate and well structured. This 99 will be ready soon to drink with celeriac purée (often a problematic dish for a wine) or a leek tart.

• Elisabeth Clerc, rue de Recanoz, 39230 Mantry, tel. 03.84.85.58.37 ⚐ by appt.

JEAN-MARIE COURBET
Trousseau 1999★★★
▪ n.c. 3,500 €5-8

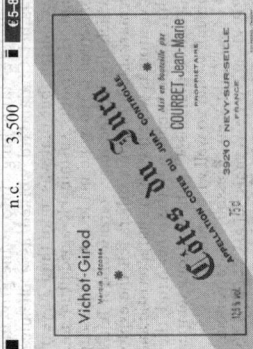

The President of the Société de Viticulture du Jura can be proud of this wine, a product of his property in Nevy-sur-Seille. Freshness and elegance are the primary qualities of this single-variety Trousseau, which has not been near an oak cask in its life. It spent 15 months in stainless steel vats. A powerful nose with red fruit, and very round on the palate. Morello cherry, spices, blackberry and even elderflower are prominent. It is an exceptional wine and will accompany many dishes, particularly game birds.

• Jean-Marie Courbet, rue du Moulin, 39210 Nevy-sur-Seille, tel. 03.84.85.28.70, fax 03.84.44.68.88 ⚐ by appt.

DOM. VICTOR CREDOZ
Pinot 1999★
▪ 0.6 ha 2,500 €5-8

Daniel and Jean-Claude Credoz run this domaine of 10.5 ha (26 acres), which was established in 1859 and is just 3 km (1.9 miles) outside Château-Chalon. This Pinot Noir is matured in 228-l, Burgundy-type casks and, to the eye, it already exhibits a detectable maturity with orange highlights. Strawberry jam on the nose and powerful but ready to drink with a tournedos steak with mushrooms.

• Dom. Victor Credoz, 39210 Menétru-le-Vignoble, tel. 06.80.43.17.44, fax 06.84.44.62.41 ⚐ ev. day 8-12 noon 1-7pm

DOM. GRAND FRERES
Vin de paille 1997★
□ 1 ha 5,000 €15-23

Emmanuel, the son of one of the Grand brothers, has just come back from the GAEC and replaced Dominique, who has left the domaine. This well-organised team submitted a Vin de Paille that has pretty amber lights yet is not intense in colour. The nose is very rich and has great finesse. Orange peel, menthol and cinnamon all vie with each other. Though it may not be very full flavoured on the palate at the moment, this 97 has enough character to keep for between 10 and 15 years.

• Dom. Grand Frères, rue du Savagnin, 39230 Passenans, tel. 03.84.85.28.88, fax 03.84.44.67.47 ⚐ ev. day 9am–12 noon 2–6pm; cl. Sat. Sun. in Jan and Feb.

DOM. GRAND FRERES 1999★★
▪ 2.5 ha 13,000 €5-8

It has taken the best of each of the Jura grape varieties to produce a wine that is somewhat solid in style. The colour is deep and the nose of red fruit, spices, undergrowth and mushroom is already showing a little maturity. The attack is direct, the tannins are distinguishable, and the flavours are mature. Its structure suggests this Côtes du Jura is capable of ageing well; it should reach its peak in five years.

• Dom. Grand Frères, rue du Savagnin, 39230 Passenans, tel. 03.84.85.28.88, fax 03.84.44.67.47 ⚐ ev. day 9am–12 noon 2–6pm; cl. Sat. Sun. in Jan and Feb.

CH. GREA Vin de paille 1997★
□ 0.5 ha 800 €15-23

A Vin de Paille, made mainly from white grape varieties, which is not backward in coming forward. Its beautiful amber colour

754

is instantly seductive. The nose has a hint of oak, but interesting notes of caramel and quince jelly also emerge. The palate is well balanced and shows volume and length with a background of flavours of crystallised fruit and pear. To be drunk in the next decade. The powerful and long **white 97**, made of 80% Chardonnay to 20% Savagnin, is recommended. It is appealing. This friendly wine-maker has *chambres d'hôtes* in the Château Gréa, which dates back to the 17th century.

● Nicolas Caire, Ch. Gréa, 39190 Rotalier, tel. 06.81.83.67.80, fax 06.84.25.05.47 ☑
Y by appt.

CAVEAU DES JACOBINS
Savagnin 1996★

1.9 ha 13,300 €11-15

This co-operative, which was established in 1907, is based in the old Jacobin church that dates back to the 13th-century. Its '96 has great class and is maturing in an interesting way; apple-scented on the nose, very characteristic on the palate with aromas of dried fruit and walnuts, which show well on the middle palate. Powerful with just the right amount of acidity. A Jura wine to the core. People who enjoy a nice, light little wine should not try this.

● Caveau des Jacobins, rue Nicolas-Appert, 39800 Poligny, tel. 03.84.37.01.37, fax 03.84.37.30.47.
e-mail caveaudesjacobins@free.fr ☑
Y ev. day 9.30am–12 noon 2–6.30pm

CLAUDE JOLY Le Monceau 1998

1 ha 4,000 €6-11

At the dawn of the new millennium Cédric joined up with Claude Joly again in an EARL. This Monceau wine is very reluctant to show off its nose; it needs time to open. Even though Savagnin is one of the grape varieties in the blend, it is not enormously evident on the palate. Nonetheless, it has class and should be left to mature.

● EARL Claude et Cédric Joly, chem. des Patarattes, 39190 Rotalier, tel. 03.84.25.04.14, fax 03.84.25.14.48 ☑
Y by appt.

ALAIN LABET
Fleur de Marne La Bardette 1997★★

0.6 ha 1,200 €11-15

It is possible to find a truer Jurassian type but this wine leaves a strong impression nonetheless. It is pale and clear, brilliant yellow in colour. The powerful, elegant nose wavers between liquorice and roasted coffee and has notes of citrus fruit and fresh apricot. The supple and rich palate is balanced by a lively finish. It has good length and well-integrated oak.

● Alain Labet, pl. du Village, 39190 Rotalier, tel. 03.84.25.11.13, fax 03.84.25.06.75 ☑ Y by appt.

DOM. LABET
Chardonnay Les Varrons 1998★★★

0.4 ha 2,400 €6-11

Only a Chardonnay, matured in cask for eighteen months, no doubt with passion and professionalism, could offer such a pleasing end result. The toasty, buttery aromas are exceptional in a Côtes du Jura. These wood aromas are also found on the full, well-balanced palate. Whether drunk now or left a while, this wine will provide a pleasing accompaniment to many different dishes.

● Alain Labet, pl. du Village, 39190 Rotalier, tel. 03.84.25.06.75 ☑ Y by appt.

FREDERIC LAMBERT
Chardonnay 1998★

0.75 ha 2,000 €5-8

Frédéric Lambert acquired his first plot of vines in 1993. He did everything necessary to achieve his goal: to sell all his wine production. Judging by this wine, he looks set to achieve this. It is old-gold in colour. The nose is complex with some oxidation which is typical of the style. This powerful, attractive 98 is elegant and characteristic of the AOC. It is good now but could easily wait another five years. A red **Côtes du Jura 99**, made solely from Trousseau grapes, was singled out by the Jury because of its musky nose, its fruity palate and its good structure.

● Frédéric Lambert, Pont du bourg, 39230 Le Chateley, tel. 03.84.85.53.98, fax 03.84.25.97.83 ☑ Y by appt.

LA VIGNIERE Vin de paille 1997★

n.c. 10,000 €15-23

This large Arbois enterprise and the most significant owner of Jura vineyards, presents one of its works of art. The nose is open with spices and quince. At first round, the palate is mouthfilling, well-balanced and long with a silky finish. It will provide a good accompaniment to *foie gras* or could be served as an aperitif.

● Henri Maire SA, Dom. de Boichailles, 39600 Arbois, tel. 03.84.66.12.34, fax 03.84.66.42.42, e-mail info@henri-maire.fr ☑ Y by appt.

DOM. MOREL THIBAUT
Tradition 1998

2 ha 6,000 €5-8

The winery of this domaine is near the L'école de Laiterie (the dairy farming school), in the town centre of Poligny, capital of the region. This Côtes du Jura is the fruit of more or less equal proportions of Chardonnay and Savagnin. The nose is fresh and intense. It is still lively so needs time to develop and mature. This is 'an athlete of the future', according to one taster.

● Dom. Morel-Thibaut, 8, rue Coittier, 39800 Poligny, tel. 03.84.37.07.61, fax 03.84.37.07.61 ☑
Y ev. day 3–7pm; Sun. 10am–12 noon

DOM. PIGNIER Trousseau 1999★

■ 0.65 ha 3,000 ▯ €5-8

This ancient, monastic vineyard has been owned by the same family since the 18th century. On another historical note, Rouget de Lisle, who composed *La Marseillaise* in 1792, was a wine-maker in Montaigu. The same wine from the previous vintage was considered to be remarkable. This 99 needs a little more time to develop but the nose is just beginning to awaken and show its fruity side. There is good structure on the palate, achieved by its maturation in wood. This is a well-made wine, ideal for serving with red meat.

➤ Dom. Pignier, Cellier des Chartreux, 39570 Montaigu, tel. 03.84.24.24.30, fax 03.84.47.46.00. ☑ ▾ ev. day 8-12 noon 1.30-7pm; Sun. 8-12 noon

AUGUSTE PIROU Vin de paille 1997★

▯ n.c. 11,000 ▯ €11-15

Henri-Michel Maire, son of the famous Henri Maire, is the manager of this company. The intense nose indicates some of the complexity of this Vin de Paille. It has tobacco, cinnamon and leather aromas, with a certain fleshiness showing on the finish. It is fullbodied on the palate where the same nuances come through. A balanced wine that could well wait fifteen years.

➤ Auguste Pirou, Les Caves Royales, 39600 Arbois, tel. 03.84.66.42.71, fax 03.84.66.42.70, e-mail info@auguste-pirou.fr

XAVIER REVERCHON

Saint Savin 1998

▯ 0.7 ha 5,000 ▯ €5-8

In the centre of Poligny, near the 11th-century Mouthier-le-Vieillard church, Xavier Reverchon continues in the family wine-making tradition. This white Côtes du Jura has a very pleasant, enticing nose of hazelnut and sweet honey. It is still a little lively on the palate but overall an attractive wine that would provide an admirable accompaniment to a dish in a rich sauce.

➤ Xavier Reverchon, EARL de Chantemerle, 2, rue de Clos, 39800 Poligny, tel. 03.84.37.02.58, fax 03.84.37.00.58 ☑ ▾ by appt.

PIERRE RICHARD Poulsard 1999

■ 0.5 ha 2,000 ▯ €5-8

Pierre Richard's grandfather bought the property in 1919. His 96 Vin de Paille was awarded a *coup de cœur* last year. This Côtes du Jura, made exclusively from Poulsard grapes, is one of the wide range of Jura wines produced by the vineyard. It is a pretty, salmony colour. At first the nose has toasty tones which open out, becoming musky. Though not rich, the palate is supple and it finishes on a very appealing cherry note. It should be drunk chilled with grilled meats.

➤ Dom. Pierre Richard, 39210 Le Vernois, tel. 03.84.25.33.27, fax 03.84.25.36.13 ☑ ▾ by appt.

JEAN RIJCKAERT

Chardonnay Les Sarres 1999

▯ 1.5 ha 14,000 ▯ €5-8

This Côtes du Jura is produced at Les Planches near Arbois and is the handiwork o` a wine-maker who also has a base in the Saône-et-Loire. It has a flowery, fruity but lightly-oaked nose, and has more characteristics of the grape variety (Chardonnay) than of the *terroir*. It has a clean, lively and fruity palate without a strong character of the Jura.

➤ SARL Rijckaert, Correaux, 71570 Leynes, tel. 03.85.35.15.09, fax 03.85.35.15.09, e-mail jeanrijckaert@aol.ccm ☑ ▾ by appt.

DOM. DE SAVAGNY

Chardonnay 1998★

▯ 2 ha 6,000 ▯ €5-8

The old-gold colour of this wine holds a promise of riches to come, and the taster only has to plunge his nose into the glass to smell the aroma of success. This Côtes du Jura is powerful, spicy and complex. It is round and elegant with a good acidity underpinning the structure. The long finish has a pleasant freshness with hints of ripe fruit.

➤ Claude Rousselot-Pailley, 140, rue Neuve, 39210 Lavigny, tel. 03.84.25.38.38, fax 03.84.25.31.25 ☑ ▾ by appt.

JEAN TRESY ET FILS

Poulsard 1999★★

■ 0.6 ha 3,000

A local rhyme suggests that, when looking for historic monuments and fine art, there is not much in Passenans to make a visitor stop, but when it comes to food and drink, it's another story. Passenans is a charming village, nonetheless, but with this Poulsard wine it's the wine-maker who is the star attraction! This 99 has a spicy, vegetal nose that leans towards cherry aromas. On the palate it is both mouthfilling and full-flavoured. It is a good example of a red Jura wine and it will be at its best in two to three years from now.

➤ Jean Trésy et Fils, rte des Longevernes, 39230 Passenans, tel. 03.84.85.22.40, fax 03.84.44.99.73, e-mail tresy.vin@wanadoo.fr ☑ ▾ by appt.

FRUITIERE VINICOLE DE VOITEUR Cuvée Prestige 1997★★

▯ 12,000 ■ ▯ €8-11

'Fruitière' is the name used for co-operatives in Franche-Comté. This one produces wines from 75 ha (185 acres). The Cuvée Prestige is made up of 80% Chardonnay and 20% Savagnin grapes. Fruity aromas emerge from the glass, quickly enhanced by notes of walnut and spices. The palate is firm and well-structured with a dash of acidity. It is powerful and has a range of flavours which will open up. This is a characterful wine, made from successful blend of two grape varieties.

➤ Fruitière vinicole de Voiteur, 60, rue de Nevy-sur-Seille, 39210 Voiteur, tel. 03.84.85.21.29, fax 03.84.85.27.67, e-mail voiteur@fruitiere-vinicole-voiteur.fr ☑ ▾ by appt.

Crémant du Jura

The AOC Crémant du Jura was recognised by a decree of 9 October 1995, and it applies to sweet *mousseux* wines made from grapes harvested within the production area of the AOC Côtes du Jura and vinified according to the strict rules applying to Vins Crémants. The approved red-grape varieties are the Poulsard (or Ploussard), Pinot Noir (known locally as Gros Noirien), Pinot Gris and Le Trousseau. The white varieties are the Savagnin (known locally as Naturé), Chardonnay (known as Melon d'Arbois or Gamay Blanc). In 2000, a total of 14,985 hl (395,604 gal) was declared.

FRUITIÈRE VINICOLE D'ARBOIS
1998★   30 ha   150,000   €5-8

Managing a co-operative with 128 members is a difficult task. The *crémant* of this well-known Fruitière has been produced with great attention to balance. The nose is light and delicate with nuances of white blossoms, citrus fruit and quince. On the palate, it is fruity and flavourful with good length.
• Fruitière vinicole d'Arbois, 2, rue des Fossés, 39600 Arbois, tel. 03.84.66.11.67, fax 03.84.37.48.80 ▼ by appt.

CAVEAU DES BYARDS 1998
n.c.   16,000   €5-8

This wine has a lovely appearance: a fine, constant stream of bubbles. The nose is still discreet but hints at lemons and green apples. Abundantly full on the palate without being too round or over-vigorous, this is a well-made *crémant*.
• Caveau des Byards, 39210 Le Vernois, tel. 03.84.25.33.52, fax 03.84.25.38.02 ▼ by appt.

MARCEL CABELIER 1998★
60 ha   300,000   €5-8

This Crémant du Jura is made from Chardonnay grapes. The bubbles are not very fine but they rise swiftly to the surface of the wine. The nose is attractive with aromas of fresh grape, apple, lemon and a floral touch. The flavours on the palate follow on from those on the nose. A very good aperitif wine.
• Cie des Grands Vins du Jura, rte de Champagnole, 39570 Crançot, tel. 03.84.87.61.30, fax 03.84.48.21.36, e-mail jura@grandschais.fr ▼
▼ ev. day 8-12 noon 1-6pm

DANIEL ET PASCAL CHALANDARD 1999★
1.5 ha   4,000   €5-8

This *crémant* is a blend of Chardonnay and Pinot Noir. Pretty bubbles rise rhythmically to the surface of this very pale yellow wine. It is not very forthcoming on the nose but reveals more on the palate, which is attractively fresh with flavours of fruit and brioche.
• GAEC du Vieux Pressoir, rue de Voiteur, BP 30, 39210 Le Vernois, tel. 03.84.25.37.62 ▼ by appt.

DENIS CHEVASSU 1999★★
n.c.   2,000   €5-8

The Chevassu family love making wine even though they also raise cattle on their land. The quality of the bubbles in this wine shows their success. The mousse is well-formed, and the pale yellow colour with its bronzed highlights is the precursor to a lively, rich and complex nose. It is flowery to begin with, and opens out with citrus, mainly lemony tones. It is attractive on the palate and has a long, green apple finish. This wine has an excellent harmony.
• Denis Chevassu, Granges Bernard, 39210 Menétru-le-Vignoble, tel. 03.84.85.23.67, fax 03.84.85.23.67 ▼ by appt.

DOM. VICTOR CREDOZ 1999★
2 ha   7,000   €5-8

Founded by Victor Credoz in 1859, this 10-ha (25-acre) domaine is now run by Daniel and Jean-Claude Credoz. This *crémant* has a fine mousse with a continuous stream of bubbles. It is fairly floral on the nose and also on the palate, which is very round.
• Dom. Victor Credoz, 39210 Menétru-le-Vignoble, tel. 06.80.43.17.44, fax 06.84.44.62.41 ▼ ev. day 8-12 noon 1-7pm

DOM. GRAND FRERES Prestige
3 ha   25,000   €8-11

This *crémant* Blanc de Blancs is produced in the last property before leaving the village of Passenans for Frontenay. Its very fine bubbles rise energetically in the glass. The nose is delicate with hints of yeast and apple, which add freshness. A well-balanced wine.
• Dom. Grand Frères, rue du Savagnin, 39230 Passenans, tel. 03.84.85.28.88, fax 03.84.44.67.47 ▼ ev. day 9am-12 noon 2-6pm; cl. Sat. Sun. in Jan. and Feb.

CAVEAU DES JACOBINS
2.3 ha   21,148   €5-8

In 1271 Alix de Méranie gave this Jacobin convent to the preacher-friars of Poligny. Its church transformed into a winery, it has been making wine for more than 80 years. Maybe convents aren't in everyone's gift, but this sparkling young *crémant* is certainly worth offering your friends. The nose is flowery and develops nicely upon opening.

☛ Caveau des Jacobins, rue Nicolas-Appert, 39600 Poligny, tel. 03.84.37.01.37, fax 03.84.37.30.47, e-mail caveaudesjacobins@free.fr
Ⓨ ev. day 9.30am–12 noon 2–6.30pm

DOM. DE LA TOURNELLE 1999★ ■ €8-11

○   0.5 ha   3,000

Pascal Clairet has a gift for hospitality and entertainment. He organises a music festival at his property and serves up cold meats, cheese, wine and music. This *crémant* has the same expressive exuberance: the bubbles race to the surface. Green apple aromas dominate on the nose and the fruit is also evident on the palate with a good acid balance. With its lovely freshness this wine is easy to drink.

☛ Pascal Clairet, 5, Petite-Place, 39600 Arbois, tel. 03.84.66.25.76, fax 03.84.66.27.15 Ⓥ Ⓨ ev. day except Sun. 10am–12.30pm 2.30–7pm

DOM. LIGIER PERE ET FILS 1998 ■ €5-8

○   0.6 ha   4,000

This is a *crémant* in a hurry with a frothy mousse and bubbles that explode on the surface of this pale-gold wine, highlighted with rosy pink. It is clean on the nose and lively, but not aggressive on the palate, exactly the way it should be. It has an attractive fruitiness that makes it a pleasant aperitif.

☛ Dom. Ligier Père et Fils, 7, rte de Poligny, 39380 Mont-sous-Vaudrey, tel. 03.84.71.74.75, fax 03.84.81.59.82, e-mail ligier@netcourrier.com Ⓥ Ⓨ by appt.

FREDERIC LORNET★ ■ €5-8

○   1 ha   6,600

The mousse is fine and even. The nose is intense and very pleasant: after a first citrus note, more expressive aromas of pear and ripe fruit emerge. The very fine bubbles escape from a fresh fruity palate with good length.

☛ Frédéric Lornet, L'Abbaye, 39600 Montigny-les-Arsures, tel. 03.84.37.44.95, fax 03.84.37.40.17 Ⓥ Ⓨ by appt.

DESIRE PETIT 1999 ■ €5-8

○   0.63 ha   5,600

Made from Pinot Noir, this rosé *crémant* has a long-lived mousse. A lovely raspberry colour with a fruity palate and with a relatively sweet finish due to a high *dosage*.

FRUITIERE VINICOLE DE PUPILLIN 1999 ■ 2 ha 18,000

○

The harvest from relatively young vines goes to make this *crémant*. This is a good choice, since sparkling wines do not require grapes from mature vines as still wines do. The mousse is long lasting in this pale yellow wine. Lemon and exotic fruit are detectable on the nose. A more limited *dosage* would probably have made a fresher wine but it is still very complex.

☛ Fruitière vinicole de Pupillin, 39600 Pupillin, tel. 03.84.66.12.88, fax 03.84.37.47.16 Ⓥ Ⓨ by appt.

XAVIER REVERCHON 1998★ ■ €5-8

○   1 ha   9,600

Chardonnay with a dash of Pinot Noir and watch out for the fizz! This yellow, lightly pink-coloured wine has lively bubbles. It has a slightly sharp nose with tones of lemon, apple and grape. It is direct, fine and clean. On the palate it has finesse and good structure with just the right acidity. A high-class *crémant*, ideal for celebrating the New Year.

☛ Xavier Reverchon, EARL de Chantemerle, 2, rue de Clos, 39800 Poligny, tel. 03.84.37.02.58, fax 03.84.37.00.58 Ⓥ Ⓨ by appt.

JACQUES TISSOT 1998★ ■ €5-8

○   2.5 ha   12,000

The bubbles die away quickly but the nose is attractive, somewhere between bread crusts and russet apples. Good body on the palate although not particularly fresh and youthful, but it has good balance and genuine maturity. This *crémant* should be drunk now with a meal, rather than as an aperitif.

☛ Jacques Tissot, 39, rue de Courcelles, 39600 Arbois, tel. 03.84.66.14.27, fax 03.84.66.24.88 Ⓥ Ⓨ by appt.

JEAN-YVES VAPILLON 1998 ■ €5-8

○   0.5 ha   3,500

Jean-Yves Vapillon will welcome you in the village of Lons-le-Saunier, on the road to Macornay. He makes his *crémant* from Chardonnay. A golden-yellow colour with bubbles rushing to the surface. Starting with a fruity, slightly menthol nose, the flavours on the palate contain citrus notes while the finish is reminiscent of orange blossom.

☛ Jean-Yves Vapillon, 120, rte de Macornay, 39000 Lons-le-Saunier, tel. 03.84.47.45.65, fax 03.84.43.21.88 Ⓥ Ⓨ ev. day except Mon. Sun. 2–6.30pm

---

The village owes its name, 'The Star', to a certain type

758

of fossilised plant found in the rocks of the area, cross-sections of the plant (a sea lily) form a five-pointed star. In 2000 the vineyards, which cover 76 ha (188 acres), produced 3,800 hl (100,320 gal) of white, yellow, straw and sparkling wine.

DOM. GENELETTI
Vin de paille 1997★★

□   0.4 ha   1,900   €15-23

Lots of Chardonnay, a dose of Savagnin and a dash of Poulsard make up the blend that Michel Geneletti and his son put together to make this wine. It is the colour of ginger bread and the nose has the same fragrances. From the attack it is evident that this is a great Vin de Paille with a robust structure and a full-flavoured richness of dried dates, all in perfect harmony. Excellent with apple tart flavoured with cinnamon.
➤ Dom. Michel Geneletti et Fils, 373, rue de l'Eglise, 39570 L'Etoile, tel. 03.84.47.46.25, fax 03.84.47.38.18 ☑ Y by appt.

CH. DE L'ETOILE Vin jaune 1993★★

□   5 ha   10,500   €23-30

This gleaming, golden wine is approachable. The vinous nose has aromas of brioche and honey. The palate is well-balanced with a good structure. A wine of considerable length with flavours of green walnuts and citronella. This remarkable example of the 93 vintage is ready to drink now but can be left to mature further. This domaine has been awarded numerous coups de coeur.
➤ Vandelle et Fils, Ch. de L'Etoile, 994, rue Bouillod, 39570 L'Etoile, tel. 03.84.47.33.07, fax 03.84.24.93.52 ☑ Y by appt.

DOM. DE MONTBOURGEAU
1997★★

□   n.c.   2,000   €11-15

The Montbourgeau property has been making this Savagnin wine since 1993: this very particular grape variety expresses itself in a different way here than in Vin Jaune. It has taken four years maturation in vat then in oak cask to create this golden, rich wine with its clean nose. It has mineral tones but also cut hay and green walnut, but this complexity is no drawback. On the palate, it is full-flavoured and the acidity and alcohol are very elegant. It will be quite at home with chicken in a sauce or a blanquette.
➤ Jean Gros, Dom. de Montbourgeau, 39570 L'Etoile, tel. 03.84.47.32.96, fax 03.84.24.41.44 ☑ Y by appt.

DOM. DE MONTBOURGEAU
Vin jaune 1994★★

□   1 ha   2,000   €23-30

Jean Gros has produced Vin Jaune on blue and grey marls since 1985. The vinification of this wine takes place in oak casks over several years. On the nose, its typical characteristics are still quite hard to detect but it opens with notes of fresh walnut. The palate is still very fresh with a strong lemon note. This is obviously a wine that should be put away for ten years or more and will develop into a very high quality wine.
➤ Jean Gros, Dom. de Montbourgeau, 39570 L'Etoile, tel. 03.84.47.32.96, fax 03.84.24.41.44 ☑ Y by appt.

DOM. DE MONTBOURGEAU
Vin de paille 1997★★

□   n.c.   2,000   €15-23

Jean Gros handed on all his wisdom and skill on the making of Vin Jaune to his daughter, Nicole Deriaux. This was a coup de coeur last year and this year the Jury was equally impressed by this wine that is strongly scented with orange peel. There is a good dose of raisin on the palate with a spice and honey-toned finish. Well-balanced and with good length. Without a doubt, this is an attractive wine that is a very typical Vin de Paille. Serve it with orange fruit tart and happiness will abound.
➤ Jean Gros, Dom. de Montbourgeau, 39570 L'Etoile, tel. 03.84.24.41.44 ☑ Y by appt.

CH. DE PERSANGES
Vin de paille 1997★★★

□   0.5 ha   2,000   €11-15

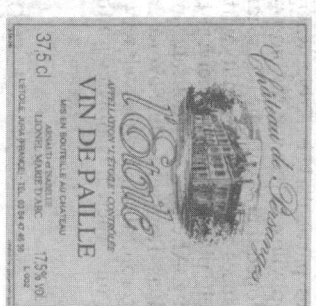

37.5 cl · APPELLATION L'ETOILE CONTRÔLÉE · Château de Persanges · VIN DE PAILLE · MIS EN BOUTEILLE AU CHÂTEAU · LIONEL MARIE D'ARC, PROPRIÉTAIRE-RÉCOLTANT À L'ETOILE, JURA FRANCE · 75% VOL

Arnaud Lionel-Marie d'Arc and his wife Isabelle give some of the work in the vineyard to young people with special educational needs. This Vin de Paille serves as a showpiece in wine-making. The 97 is a pale wheat colour with a very pretty honey, crystallised-orange, apricot and raisin nose. The transition from nose to mouth is perfectly harmonious and flavours are magnificent. Apricot is dominant but crystallised orange peel is always somewhere in the background. There are no traces of cloying flavours at the finish where the balance is superb. Drink now or at some time in the future, this is a very fine vin liquoreux.
➤ Ch. de Persanges, rte de Saint-Didier, 39570 L'Etoile, tel. 03.84.47.46.56, fax 03.84.47.46.56 ☑ Y ev. day 9.30am–12 noon 2.30-7pm; cl. Sun. Mon.
➤ Lionel-Marie d'Arc

SAVOY

From the French shore of Lake Geneva to the Isère valley, in the departments of Savoie and Haute-Savoie, the vineyards occupy favourable lower slopes of the Alps. The vineyard is constantly expanding, currently nearly 1,800 ha (4,446 acres); and year on year, produces about 130,000 hl (3,432,000 gal). The individual wine-growing areas together form a complex mosaic dictated by the shapes of the various valleys, which are planted in bigger or smaller islets of cultivation. This geographical diversity is echoed in local climatic variations, which are either exaggerated by the relief or tempered by the proximity of Lake Geneva and the Lac du Bourget.

Vin de Savoie and Roussette de Savoie are regional appellations, used nearly everywhere; they may be followed by the name of a cru, but apply exclusively to still wines which, for the Roussettes, mean whites only. Wines from Crépy and Sayssel each have a right to their own appellation.

Because of the widely dispersed vineyards, numerous grape varieties are in use but, in fact, many are planted in only limited amounts: this is particularly true of Pinot Noir and Chardonnay. The main varieties are two reds and four whites, alongside others that produce specifically local wines. Gamay, imported from neighbouring Beaujolais post-phylloxera, produces fresh, light red wines to be drunk in the year of production. Mondeuse, a local, quality variety, produces full-bodied red wines, particularly in Arbin, where it is the only variety under cultivation. Pre-phylloxera this was the most widely grown variety in Savoy, and it is to be hoped that it will one day regain its rightful place, because the wines it produces are of good quality with terrific character. Jacquère is the most widely planted white variety; it produces fresh, light white to be drunk young. Altesse, a very delicate variety, typically Savoyard, produces wines sold as Roussette de Savoie. Finally, Roussanne, locally known as Bergeron, also produces white wines of very high quality, especially in Chignin, where it is grown with the cross variety Chignin-Bergeron.

Crépy   DOM. LE CHALET 2000★

☐   2 ha   13,000   ▥ €5-8

This wine demands great concentration when tasting. It is a beautiful yellow colour and has a complex nose, with peach and dried fruit and touches of spice. The palate is rich and powerful. This is a wine with interesting potential and it will be ideal with cheese-based Savoy specialities.

●▬ Jacques Métral, Dom. Le Chalet, 74140 Loisin, tel. 04.50.94.10.60, fax 04.50.94.18.39 ☑ ⍉ ev. day except Sun. 9am–12 noon 2–7pm

Chasselas is the only variety planted in the 80-ha (198-acre) Crépy vineyard, as it is on the shores of Lake Geneva. It produces about 4,800 hl (126,720 gal) of light white wine. This little region obtained its AOC in 1948.

760

Vin de Savoie

The vineyard classed as Appellation Vin de Savoie is generally to be found on the ancient glacial moraines (continuous linear deposits of rocks and gravel left by glaciers), or on scree, which because of its geographical dispersal contributes to great diversity in the wines; these are frequently identified by adding a local denomination to the regional appellation. On the French shore of Lake Geneva, in Marin, Ripaille and Marignan, Chasselas produces light, white, often slightly fizzy wines, which are best drunk young. Other areas grow different varieties and, depending on the soil types, produce white or red wines. From north to south, from Ayze to the banks of the Arve

river, sparkling and fizzy whites give way (south of the Appellation Seyssel) to the red wines of the Lac du Bourget and La Chautagne, where the reds in particular have a marked character. South of Chambéry, the flanks of Mont Granier produce fresh white wines such as the Apremont and the Cru des Abymes, a vineyard established on a site where the mountain collapsed in 1248, killing thousands of people. Facing it, Monterminod has been smothered by housing developments, but has retained a vineyard which produces remarkable wines; next to it lie the vineyards of Saint-Jeoire-Prieuré, on the far side of Challes-les-Eaux, then Chignin, where the fame of the Bergeron grape is absolutely justified. Going up the Isère on the right bank, the south-east-facing slopes are occupied by the crus of Montmélian,

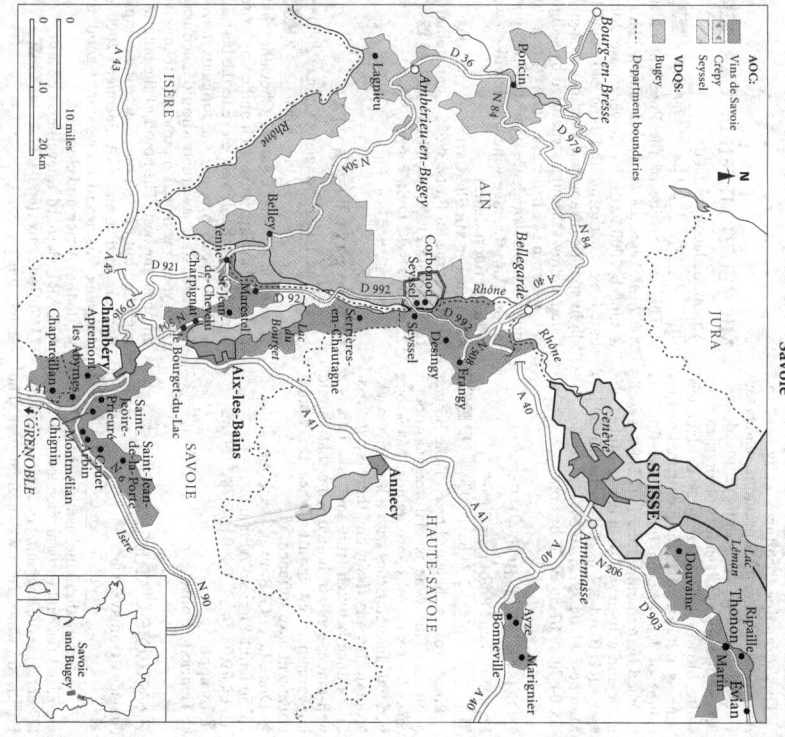

AOC:
- Vins de Savoie
- Crépy
- Seyssel

VDQS:

Bugey

Department boundaries

N

0   10   20 km
0   10 miles

Savoie and Bugey

Arbin, Cruet and Saint-Jean-de-la-Porte.

Produced only in limited quantities, around 130,000 hl (3,432,000 gal), in a region very popular with tourists, the Savoie wines are mainly drunk young, mostly locally, and sold into a market where demand sometimes outstrips supply. The white Savoy wines go well with freshwater and sea fish, while the reds (made from Gamay) are very versatile. It is a shame to drink the Mondeuse reds too young as they need several years to develop and soften: these high-quality wines accompany strongly flavoured dishes such as game, the excellent Tomme de Savoie and the famous Reblochon cheeses.

BLARD ET FILS Apremont Cuvée

Thomas Vieilles vignes 2000★ □ ■ ♦ €5-8 0.6 ha 5,000

This domaine produces Abymes and Apremont. This year's Apremont, made from vines that are forty-something years old, has a very subtle nose with shades of characteristic white blossom. The lightness of Jacquère wines is to be found on the palate that betrays a hint of lemon even though the finish is touched by mineral notes. This 2000 is well-made and will go well with fish in sauce.
➤ EARL Blard et Fils, Le Darbé, 73800 Les Marches, tel. 04.79.28.16.64, fax 04.79.28.01.35 ⍌ ⅂ by appt.

DOM. G. ET G. BOUVET

Le Beau Chêne Pinot noir 2000★ ■ ❚❚ €5-8 2.94 ha 90,000

Pinot Noir is the war horse of the Bouvet domaine. This wine is matured in wooden casks for six months and the nose has strong varietal characteristics with a liquorice background. It is very fleshy and there is a successful balance between fruit and oak. This is a well-made, well-structured wine that should improve in a few months when the vanilla finish will have softened.
➤ Dom. G. et G. Bouvet, Fréterive, 73250 Saint-Pierre-d'Albigny, tel. 04.79.28.54.11, fax 04.79.28.51.97 ⅂ by appt.
➤ Henriette Bouvet

FRANCOIS CARREL ET FILS

Jongieux Gamay 2000★ ■ ♦ €-5 2.5 ha n.c.

This family domaine, established in 1949, increased the vineyard surface area to 11 ha (27 acres) at the beginning of the 21st century. For Savoy wines 2000 was a great year. The

reds are spectacular as shown by their deep, dark colour with ruby dominating. The first impression instantly shows a hint of morello cherry that has good length. Round and already soft tannins make an approachable wine. This is an easy drinking wine which, from the autumn of 2001, will go well with grilled meat. The extremely elegant **white 2000**, made from Jacquère was picked out for praise by the Jury with one taster noting, 'this is an intellectual wine'. Fruity, citrus fruit, roses, mineral touches all add to its subtlety.
➤ François et Eric Carrel, 73170 Jongieux, tel. 04.79.44.02.20, fax 04.79.44.03.73 ⍌ ⅂ by appt.

CATHERINE ET BRUNO CARTIER Apremont Jacquère 2000★

□ €2-5 6.5 ha 56,000

The vines that produce the grapes for this wine are planted on soil from the Upper Cretaceous era which forms part of the *terroir* of the AOC. It fairly explodes with mineral flavours at the first impression. Round, even powerful, with typical fruit aromas of a mature wine. This wine will last a number of years.
➤ Bruno Cartier, Saint-Vit, 73190 Apremont, tel. 04.79.28.20.05, fax 04.79.71.64.75 ⅂ by appt.

MICHEL ET MIREILLE CARTIER Apremont Jacquère 2000★

□ €5-8 2.2 ha 150,000

This is the wine of the President of the *Syndicat Régional des Vins de Savoie*. This is a superb 2000, with its flowery nose dominated by hawthorne and lime blossom. Its slight sparkle disappears quickly and a good balance shows through structured by a slight, yet welcome, bitterness. The finish has mineral tones, which are typical in this appellation. An attractive wine which will go well with the finest dishes.
➤ Michel et Mireille Cartier, EARL du Château, rue du Puits, 38530 Chaparellan, tel. 04.76.45.21.26, fax 04.76.45.21.67 ⍌ ⅂ ev. day 8-12 noon 2-6pm

BERNARD ET CHANTAL CHEVALLIER Jongieux Gamay 2000★★

■ €2-5 2.73 ha 8,000

Jean-Pierre and Chantal Chevallier have produced an impessive, rich and complex red wine. It is probably very close to the best that a Gamay can produce on Jongieux *terroir*. The two stars awarded should encourage these young winemakers to count themselves amongst the best. The power of the tannins is beguiling but doesn't overpower the complex flavours and aromas. A **Jacquère 2000 en Jongieux** was awarded one star: a good, dry white that is rich and eloquent.
➤ EARL Bernard Chevallier, Le Haut, 73170 Jongieux, tel. 04.79.44.00.33 ⍌ ⅂ by appt.

DOM. DU COLOMBIER
Apremont 2000★★★
□   1.2 ha   13,000   ■   €5-8

An exceptional wine that only just missed getting a *coup de cœur*. A classic, beautiful, pale gold with a precise, almost brutal character without any flounces. It is very fine and long, revealing real class at the finish. The best marks for a wine in this appellation.
● Michel Tardy, EARL du Colombier, Saint-André, 73800 Les Marches, tel. 04.79.28.13.93, fax 04.79.71.57.64 ▼ by appt.

MADAME ALEXIS GENOUX
Arbin Mondeuse 2000★★
□   0.9 ha   7,000   ■   €5-8

Mme Genoux shares the vineyard with her sons. This is her own wine. While the nose is already very open, and gives off aromas of dark, small-berried fruit, the palate is virtually inexpressive. However, hiding behind this young harshness is a remarkably well-structured wine that has lots of character. It would be advisable to cellar this Arbin right away and leave it to mature for a good few years.
● Mme Alexis Genoux, 335, chem. des Moulins, 73800 Arbin, tel. 04.79.84.24.30 ▼ ev. day 8-12 noon 2-6pm

ANDRE GENOUX Arbin Mondeuse
Cuvée Comte Rouge 1999★★
□   0.5 ha   4,000   Ⅲ   €5-8

The production from a small plot of forty-year-old vines has resulted in this delicious 99 wine with its vanilla nose enlivened with notes of red fruits. On the palate it is soft, delicate, yet evident tannins. In all, this is a civilised, velvety wine which will be a happy companion to red meat.
● André Genoux, 450, chem. des Moulins, 73800 Arbin, tel. 04.79.65.24.32 ▼ by appt.

CHARLES GONNET Chignin 2000
□   6 ha   60,000   ■   €5-8

The pale colour, only faintly enhanced by a few silvery-green highlights, is misleading because this wine immediately releases a joyous panoply of aromas where yellow-fleshed fruit, white blossoms and hazelnut tones all blend together. A lovely wine with a slightly bitter, acid tone on the finish which will have softened by now.
● Charles Gonnet, Chef-lieu, 73800 Chignin, tel. 04.79.28.09.89, fax 04.79.71.55.91, e-mail charles.gonnet@wanadoo.fr ▼ by appt.

JEAN-PIERRE ET PHILIPPE GRISARD
Saint-Jean-de-la-Porte Mondeuse 1999
□   1.2 ha   8,000   Ⅲ ■   €5-8

It is quite an achievement to have come through the selection process with a 99 vintage. Our Jury commented favourably on this wine, which is endowed with a full-flavoured palate dominated by red fruit. The structure explodes on the palate with its vigorous tannins that need more time to mellow.
● Jean-Pierre et Philippe Grisard, Chef-lieu, 73250 Fréterive, tel. 04.79.28.54.09, fax 04.79.71.41.36 ▼ ev. day except Sun. 8-12 noon 1.30-6.30pm

EDMOND JACQUIN ET FILS
Mondeuse 2000
■   2 ha   15,000   ■   €5-8

Here is a lovely red wine with tones of purple and ruby. The nose has typical black-currant aromas and the palate is full-bodied and long. The silky nature of the tannins and their length show how well the extraction has been carried out. A classic, well-balanced Mondeuse that is made to share with friends.
● Edmond Jacquin et Fils, Le Haut, 73170 Jongieux, tel. 04.79.44.02.35, fax 04.79.44.03.05 ▼ by appt.

DOM. LA COMBE DES GRAND'VIGNES Chignin 2000
□   5 ha   20,000   ■   €5-8

No surprises with this lovely green-gold, white wine. It has an intense and open nose where flowery aromas dominate and, on the palate, it does not hold back: after a clean, fresh attack, lemony aromas emerge.
● Denis et Didier Berthollier, Dom. La Combe des Grand'Vignes, Le Viviers, 73800 Chignin, tel. 04.79.28.11.75, fax 04.79.28.16.22, e-mail berthollier@chignin.com ▼ by appt.

LES ROCAILLES
Apremont Jacquère 2000★★
□   7 ha   120,000   ■   €5-8

Our Jury particularly enjoyed this very complex wine which has noticeable residual sugars though they are well-integrated. It is a lovely green-gold and releases fragrances of violet and white blossoms. On the palate there is ripe fruit which expresses the richness of the grape, at the finish there are various mineral tones. There is also the stamp of the *terroir* that is discreet but subtle.
● Pierre Boniface, Les Rocailles, Saint-André, 73800 Les Marches, tel. 04.79.28.14.50, fax 04.79.28.16.82, e-mail pierre.boniface@wanadoo.fr ▼ ev. day except Sat. Sun. 8.30-12 noon 2-6pm

DOM. DE L'IDYLLE
Cruet Jacquère 2000
□   8 ha   40,000   ■   €3-5

The Tiollier brothers are located at the foot of the Cruet hills. Their red and white wines are produced with care and attention. Their knowledge and technical skill shine through in this spontaneous white with spring fragrances. Vinification at low temperature has left its mark; it is frank and characteristic, very representative of the appellation.

SAVOY

Vin de Savoie

☛ Ph. et F. Tiollier, Dom. de l'Idylle, Saint-Laurent, 73800 Cruet, tel. 04.79.84.30.58, fax 04.79.65.26.26 ▼ ☨ by appt.

DOM. MICHEL MAGNE
Apremont Tête de cuvée 2000★★
☐ 1.2 ha 7,000 ■ ♦ €5-8

This Apremont comes from vineyards on rock and rubble soil created when Mont Granier collapsed in 1248. The exceptional harvest of 2000 has led to this fullness and complexity. Our Jury enjoyed the exotic fruit flavours of mango. This wine is well-structured and round yet also has a remarkable balance resulting from a touch of freshness and its lightly lemony finish.
☛ Michel Magne, Saint-André, 38530 Chapareillan, tel. 04.79.28.07.91, fax 04.79.28.17.96 ▼ ☨ ev. day except Sun. 2–6pm

M. ET X. MILLION-ROUSSEAU
Jongieux Jacquère 2000★★
☐ 1.5 ha 11,000 ■ €3-5

Michel Million grows vines on the little hillside of the Coteau de Monthoux, which is classified in the Cru Jongieux. Above all, he makes excellent white wines. The excellent harvest of 2000 has allowed him to produce this remarkable dry white Jacquère. Here again, the flavours are infinitely varied. Liquorice and more volatile aromas such as box bush and white blossoms vie with each other. The palate is an enchanted forest of fruit with a lasting finish. A rare and precious Jacquère.
☛ M. et X. Million-Rousseau, Monthoux, 73170 Saint-Jean-de-Chevelu, tel. 04.79.36.83.93, fax 04.79.36.83.93 ▼ ☨ ev. day except Sun. 8–12 noon 2–7pm

DOM. MARC PORTAZ Abymes 2000★
☐ 1 ha 8,000 ■ €5-8

The Jury remarked on the intense yellow of this wine. Rich and full with remarkable length, full-flavoured with lots of citrus notes. The Portaz (father and son) are nurturing a very good vintage that is shown at its best here.
☛ EARL Dom. Marc Portaz, allée du Colombier, 38530 Chapareillan, tel. 04.76.45.23.51, fax 04.76.45.57.60 ☨ by appt.

ANDRE ET MICHEL QUENARD
Chignin Mondeuse Vieilles vignes Coteau de Torméry 2000★★★
■ 1.38 ha 10,000 ■ ☷ €5-8

The Jury was unanimous in awarding a *coup de cœur* to this lovely Mondeuse with its nose of liquoricey, red-berried fruit. On the palate the flavours are extraordinary showing a mix of blackcurrant and bilberries with a cocoa finish. The tannins are silky and soft giving the wine extraordinary length. The wine has already lost a great deal of its wild

aggressiveness but it will calm down a great deal more after a few year's ageing.
☛ André et Michel Quenard, Tormery, 73800 Chignin, tel. 04.79.28.12.75, fax 04.79.28.09.60 ▼ ☨ by appt.

ANDRE ET MICHEL QUENARD
Chignin Bergeron Les Terrasses Coteau de Torméry 2000★★
☐ 3 ha 13,000 ■ ♦ €8-11

The Savoyard chef, Marc Veyrat, who is one of the most inventive restaurant owners in France, has a passion for this vineyard, which is not surprising. The Jury awarded a *coup de cœur* to their Mondeuse and congratulated them on this remarkable Chignin Bergeron made from grapes harvested by successive, selective pickings. Slow fermentation produces a very complex and open wine. In spite of its alcoholic strength, it retains a good balance which is clear proof of the quality of the extraction process. This should be bought now and left to develop for a few years.
☛ André et Michel Quenard, Torméry, 73800 Chignin, tel. 04.79.28.12.75, fax 04.79.28.09.60 ▼ ☨ by appt.

DOM. J.-PIERRE ET J.-FRANCOIS QUENARD
Chignin Bergeron Vieilles vignes 2000★
☐ 1 ha 7,000 ■ ♦ €5-8

The domaine is at the foot of the towers of the ancient Château de Chignin and is run by Jean-François Quénard, who has a diploma in Oenology from Dijon University. Three wines were presented, three selected for tasting. This Bergeron, with a very fruity bouquet, is a real success. It is very fresh but quickly moves on to present a roundness which is derived from the quality of the grapes which are harvested by successive pickings. The wine still has an attractive freshness which gives it elegance. A classy wine to lay down in the cellar without a moment's thought. The other white wine, made from Jacquère grapes, **Anne de la Biguerne 2000**, is full and complex with good length and is awarded a star.
☛ Dom. J.-Pierre et J.-François Quénard, Caveau de la Tour Villard, Le Villard, 73800 Chignin, tel. 04.79.28.08.29, fax 04.79.28.18.92 ▼ ☨ by appt.

DOM. J.-PIERRE ET J.-FRANCOIS QUENARD

Mondeuse 2000★★

■   0.3 ha   2,500   ■   €5-8

The wine-makers have poured heart and soul into this wine. This year, the *vendanges en vert* preceded the main harvest. Having optimal maturity, the wine is magnificent both on the nose and on the palate. The full-ness, length and complexity of the nose make it a wine of rare quality. As soon as possible, buy some to lay down in the cellar.

● Dom. J.-Pierre et J.-François Quenard, Caveau de la Tour Villard, Le Villard, 73800 Chignin, tel. 04.79.28.08.29, fax 04.79.28.18.92 ✆ by appt.

LES FILS DE RENE QUENARD

Chignin 2000★★

■   1 ha   8,000   ■   €5-8

The Quénard brothers are particularly attentive to the cultivation of their plot of Pinot. They have again produced an excellent wine this year. It has an untamed nose with strong, musky notes and a full-bodied palate. There is a coupling of strength and finesse to the boldly-drawn finish. Some little time will be necessary for this wine to reach its peak of eloquence.

● Les Fils de René Quénard, Les Tours, cidex 4707, 73800 Chignin, tel. 04.79.28.01.15, fax 04.79.28.18.98 ✆ by appt.

PHILIPPE RAVIER

Chignin Bergeron 2000★

■   3.6 ha   n.c.   ■

Philippe Ravier's vines are planted on the Coteaux de Francin, in one of the best situations in the appellation. This wine expresses its origins: it is both powerful on the nose and on the palate. It can be left to mature nicely in the cellar for a few years.

● Philippe Ravier, Léché, 73800 Myans, tel. 04.79.28.17.75, fax 04.79.28.17.75 ✆ by appt.

GILBERT TARDY Apremont 2000★

■   1 ha   9,000   ■   €3-5

One of the most classic Apremont wines. It was still very youthful on the day of the tasting. Using traditional vinification methods results in a wine that expresses the characteristics of the *terroir* with vigour. The nose is floral and the palate should soften for it to be ready to drink from now on.

● Gilbert Tardy, La Plantée, 73190 Apremont, tel. 04.79.28.23.78, fax 04.79.28.23.78 ✆ by appt.

LES FILS DE CHARLES TROSSET

Arbin Mondeuse 2000★

■   4 ha   n.c.   ■   €5-8

The Trosset brothers make regular appearances in the *Guide* and, again this year, presented an Arbin with a very open nose and deep-red colour. The wine is a festival of hot-and-spicy, red-fruit and menthol tones, veering towards undergrowth, which are present through to the finish. On the palate the structure is defined with liquorice tannins that give it excellent balance.

● SCEA Les Fils de Charles Trosset, chem. des Moulins, 73800 Arbin, tel. 04.79.84.30.99, fax 04.79.84.30.99 ✆ by appt.

CLAUDE TARDY Abymes 2000★

■   3.1 ha   10,000   ■   €3-5

This vineyard is on the highest parts of the only commune in Isère which belongs to the area producing Vin de Savoie (Chapareillan). Claude Tardy has produced a very attractive little wine. He pays meticulous attention to his raw material which comes from sixty-year-old vines. This lovely wine has both liveliness and length on the palate. Flowery tones with an emphasis on lime flower precede the smooth palate that is full of freshness with citrus notes that are typical of a good Abymes.

● Claude Tardy, Saint-Marcel, 38530 Chapareillan, tel. 04.76.45.24.97 ✆ by appt.

JEAN VULLIEN ET FILS

Chignin Bergeron 2000★

■   1.8 ha   14,000   ■   €5-8

The Vullien family have invested in the Coteaux de Montmélian over a number of years. It has been well worth it and the result has fulfilled their greatest hopes, to judge by this Chignin Bergeron with its delicate peach and apricot aromas. The palate is fresh and clean, and with agreeable length, supported by a well-contained liveliness. A pleasant wine where finesse and elegance predominate. It should go well with grilled fish or white meats. A **Mondeuse Saint-Jean-de-la-Porte 2000** is also awarded one star. This cru is undergoing a full rebirth and promises great things.

DOM. VIALLET

Apremont Jacquère Vieilles vignes 2000

■   8 ha   40,000   ■   €3-5

This 18-ha (45-acre) domaine was established in 1966 and Pierre Viallet has been running it since 1983. Our Jury was keen to make special mention of this discreetly charming Apremont which is a lovely pale gold. The nose suggests some maturity on apple and pear fruit. It is very attractive on the palate releasing a succession of flavours which have roundness. The wine was vinified on the lees at low temperature, but is almost too well-behaved for the vintage.

● GAEC Dom. Viallet, rte de Myans, 73190 Apremont, tel. 04.79.28.33.29, fax 04.79.28.20.68, e-mail viallet@aol.com ✆ ✆ ev. day except Sun. 8-12 noon 2-6pm

Roussette de Savoie

M ade exclusively from the Altesse grape (following a new decree dated 18 March 1998), the Roussette de Savoie is mainly found in Frangy, along the River Usses, in Monthoux and in Marestel, on the shore of the Lac du Bourget. The habit of serving the Roussettes too young is a shame since, as they open with age, they are splendid with fish and white meat dishes, and form a perfect accompaniment to the local Beaufort cheese.

☞ EARL Jean Vullien et Fils,
La Grande Roue, 73250 Fréterive,
tel. 04.79.28.61.58, fax 04.79.28.69.37,
e-mail domaine.jean.vullien.et.fils@
wanadoo.fr 🅥 🍷 ev. day except Sun.
8.30–12 noon 2–6.30pm

JEAN-PIERRE ET PHILIPPE GRISARD 1999★

☐   1.24 ha   10,000   🍷 🔲   €5-8

The Grisards run a nursery and vineyards in Fréterive, the neighbouring commune to Saint-Pierre d'Albigny and the Château of Miolans where the Marquis de Sade was incarcerated in 1772. This wine emits aromas of ripe fruit and spices. The palate has a very attractive, frank and lively attack. At the finish there are perceptible notes of apricot and pear. A pleasant wine that could be served with fish in sauce.

☞ Jean-Pierre et Philippe Grisard,
Chef-lieu, 73250 Fréterive,
tel. 04.79.28.54.09, fax 04.79.71.41.36 🅥
🍷 ev. day except Sun. 8–12 noon 1.30–
6.30pm

EDMOND JACQUIN ET FILS 1999★

Marestel   1.5 ha   12,000   🍷 🔲   €5-8

The Jacquins are one of the wine-growing families who have decided to develop good local products for sale. This hauntingly charming wine is one of them. It is undoubtedly built for keeping. It is very powerful but retains an almost indefinable, genuine softness.

☞ Edmond Jacquin et Fils, Le Haut,
73170 Jongieux, tel. 04.79.44.02.35,
fax 04.79.44.03.05 🅥 🍷 by appt.

LA CAVE DU PRIEURE

Marestel 2000★

☐   2 ha   14,000   🍷 🔲   €5-8

The Barlets are another renowned winemaking family and their cellar is in the ancient 14th-century priory. This wine comes from an area of the *terroir* that is being reclaimed by local winegrowers. The slightly closed nose has honey scents and fine finesse, followed by a balanced palate with great finesse, with an acid structure that is its guarantor of a long life. To be put in the cellar now and drunk in not too much of a hurry: pleasure guaranteed.

☞ Raymond Barlet et Fils, La Cave du
Prieuré, 73170 Jongieux, tel. 04.79.44.02.22,
fax 04.79.44.03.07 🅥 🍷 by appt.

DOM. LA COMBE DES GRAND VIGNES Baron Decouz 2000★

☐   0.36 ha   2,500

Didier Berthollier joined his brother Denis on the domaine in 2000. This pair of young producers have set themselves the task of reclaiming the quality soils on the hills of La Combe de Savoie. This wine was judged by the Jury as being an almost perfect example of the Roussette de Savoie with its open nose with both flower and fruit aromas, enlivened with a hint of spice. On the palate it is fresh, clean and well balanced. Very successful, given that the wine is made from still very young, (six-year-old) vines. By the time you read this it will have already developed

DOM. G. BLANC ET FILS 2000

☐   0.6 ha   5,800   🍷 🔲   €5-8

The Blancs, a father and son team, know how to get the best from this rubble-filled *terroir* in Les Abymes. Year after year, the Jury remarks on the quality of their Roussette de Savoie. This wine is retiring but subtle, though it ultimately reveals itself without too much reluctance: it is lively at first, then reveals its aromas of fruit and almonds and a full and harmonious palate. It is ready to drink now.

☞ Dom. Gilbert Blanc et Fils, 73, chem. de
Revaison, 73190 Saint-Baldoph,
tel. 04.79.28.36.90, fax 04.79.28.36.90 🅥
🍷 ev. day except Tue. Sun. 9am–12 noon
3–7pm

GILBERT BOUCHEZ 2000★★

☐   1 ha   8,000   🍷 🔲   €5-8

Gilbert Bouchez has not always been a full-time wine-maker but his love of wine has never wavered. He has already won a star for his 99 vintage and has achieved another this year. The nose has a depth marked by truffle and vanilla tones: the palate is full and round, leading to a characterful finish of ripe fruit. A quality wine that needs to be laid down in the cellar now. It should provide an elegant accompaniment for Savoy soufflés or similar dishes.

☞ Gilbert Bouchez, Saint-Laurent,
73800 Cruet, tel. 04.79.84.30.91,
fax 04.79.84.30.50 🅥 🍷 by appt.

JEAN VULLIEN ET FILS 2000★★★

1.8 ha · 15,000 · €5–8

Jean, David and Olivier Vullien presented a high-class Roussette de Savoie. The nose has depth with notes of fresh butter, hazelnut, even almond, and a very rich palate with substantial length. A great ambassador for this AOC. It should be a pleasure to drink as an aperitif or with a starter at a gourmet meal.

ETIENNE SAINT-GERMAIN 2000★★

0.7 ha · 4,000 · €5–8

Etienne Saint-Germain came to La Combe de Savoie in 1997 and, with this 2000 vintage, makes his first appearance in this edition of the Guide. The Jury was bewitched by the richness of its nose where nuances of dried fruit dominate. On the palate, it is both full and powerful. A well-structured wine with appealing length and good firm acidity that will ensure a good future.

• Etienne Saint-Germain, rte du col du Frêne, 73250 Saint-Pierre-d'Albigny, tel. 04.79.28.61.68, fax 04.79.28.61.68 ☑ ⚥ ev. day except Sun. 5–7pm in summer only.

maturity and the traces of residual sugars will have integrated.

• Denis et Didier Berthollier, Dom. La Combe des Grand'Vignes, Le Viviers, 73800 Chignin, tel. 04.79.28.11.75, fax 04.79.28.16.22, e-mail berthollier@ chignin.com ☑ ⚥ by appt.

JEAN PERRIER ET FILS
Haute Sélection 1998★

n.c. · 4,200 · €5–8

In the year 2000, the Perrier firm built a 2,000 m² (2,400 yd²) air-conditioned store room as part of their on-going development programme. From the wide range of Vins de Savoie proposed by this shipper, it is quite usual for one to be selected for the Guide. This year, the Jury particularly enjoyed the Roussette which has a definitive beeswax aroma. Silky on the palate but with good, well-balanced acidity, it shows a very characteristic style of development in this type of wine, and the Savoyard wine-makers are far from exhausting all its possibilities.

• Jean Perrier et Fils, Saint-André, 73800 Les Marches, tel. 04.79.28.11.45, fax 04.79.28.09.91, e-mail vperrier@ vins-perrier.com ☑ ⚥ ev. day except Sat. Sun. 8–12 noon 2–6pm

• Gilbert Perrier

Seyssel

The still wines from this appellation are made solely with the Altesse grape variety. The few Molette vines grown in Seyssel are blended with Altesse for the appellation's sparkling wines which are released for sale three years after bottling for the second fermentation. These local grape varieties contribute finesse and a particular bouquet to the wines of Seyssel, notably the scent of violets. The appellation covers around 75 ha (185 acres).

LA TACCONNIERE 2000★

12 ha · 80,000 · €3–5

The Mollex company has been in the winegrowing business for five generations and is the owner of the biggest vineyard in the AOC, which covers 25 ha (62 acres). The complex nose of this wine, made from Altesse grapes, is seductive and has strong grilled almond and iris aromas. On the palate it is soft and alluring. Well-balanced, round, and powerful showing great finesse with a back-up of residual sugars on the finish.

• Dom. Maison Mollex, Corbonod, 01420 Seyssel, tel. 04.50.56.12.20, fax 04.50.56.17.29 ☑ ⚥ by appt.

MAISON MOLLEX
Méthode traditionnelle 1997★

○ 3 ha · 30,000 · €5–8

Our jury was enchanted by this Seyssel that is matured for a long time on the lees. The floral aromas have great delicacy and it will please anyone who loves bubbles. On the palate there are pleasant, fresh and mellow flavours. An attractive wine to serve as an aperitif.

• Dom. Maison Mollex, Corbonod, 01420 Seyssel, tel. 04.50.56.12.20, fax 04.50.56.17.29 ☑ ⚥ by appt.

• EARL Jean Vullien et Fils, La Grande Roue, 73250 Fréterive, tel. 04.79.28.61.58, fax 04.79.28.69.37, e-mail domaine.jean.vullien.et.fils@ wanadoo.fr ☑ ⚥ ev. day except Sun. 8.30– 12 noon 2–6.30pm

Bugey

Bugey AOVDQS

Located in the Ain department, the Bugey vineyard occupies the lower slopes of the Jura from Bourg-en-Bresse to Ambérieu-en-Bugey (to the extreme south of Revermont), as well as those which run down to the right bank of the Rhône, from Seyssel to Lagnieu. A large vineyard at one time, it is now smaller and more dispersed.

For the most part, it stands on fairly steep slopes of limestone scree. The grape varieties reflect the area's famous neighbours: for reds, the Jura Poulsard – restricted to blending with sparkling wines from Cerdon – is grown alongside Mondeuse from Savoie and Pinot Noir and Gamay from Burgundy. For the whites, Jacquère and Altesse compete with Chardonnay (the most widely grown variety) and Aligoté, as well as Molette, the only truly local variety.

BANCET L'unique 1999★

⬛ ▢ 1.5 ha 12,000 🍾 ▥ ◆ €5-8

The Duport brothers presented this original blend of Pinot and Mondeuse. It is made by traditional vinification methods *avec pigeage*. A very expressive nose with leather and cooked fruit aromas. This wine is already remarkably well-developed and the tannins will be tame by now.

↳ Maison Duport, Le Lavoir,
01680 Groslée, tel. 04.74.39.74.33,
fax 04.74.39.74.33 ▨ Ⴤ by appt.

CELLIER DE BEL AIR
Milvendre Chardonnay 1999★★

▢ 1 ha 9,000 ▥ €5-8

This vineyard occupies the sunny slopes of the Grand Colombier mountain in the Ain and has been owned by the Riboud family for 25 years. This lovely 99 wine was both fermented and matured in oak casks and on the palate it shows great harmony which is an indication of a successful partnership. The wine is already attractive but it would be a pity not to allow it to mature because it seems to have the capacity to develop further. The **Chardonnay 2000** was awarded one star. One to drink with a platter of seafood.

↳ Michelle Férier, Dom. du Cellier de Bel-Air, 01350 Culoz, tel. 04.79.87.04.20, fax 04.79.87.18.23, e-mail domainebelair@free.fr ▨ Ⴤ ev. day 9am–12 noon 3–7pm

CHRISTIAN BOLLIET Cerdon
Méthode ancestrale Cuvée spéciale 2000★

◖ 0.44 ha 4,400 €5-8

Every year, Christian Bolliet soldiers on and submits a single varietal wine made from Poulsard grapes. Its pinkish colour is discreet but on the palate, by contrast, it is full, almost sweet. The hazelnut aromas need time to develop and open out to their best and then the wine will be wonderfully harmonious.

↳ Christian Bolliet, Hameau de Bôches, 01450 Saint-Alban, tel. 04.74.37.37.21, fax 04.74.37.37.69 ▨ Ⴤ by appt.

BONNARD FILS
Montagnieu Mondeuse 1999★★

⬛ 0.65 ha 4,000 €5-8

The Bonnard brothers, established since 1987, submitted two of their Vins du Bugey: the elegant, unctuous **Roussette 99** that gently caresses the palate is awarded one star and will go will with fish with *beurre blanc*; the Mondeuse was matured in wood. Even though the grapes are undoubtedly of top quality, the jury found the wood influence was noticeable. Nonetheless, this is a well-structured wine with obvious capacities for keeping. It is produced using wine-making practices that pay great attention to the quality of the grapes harvested and, after partial stemming, the maceration is lengthy. This wine should be left in the cellar for several years and then served with a *civet*.

↳ GAEC Bonnard Fils, Crept, 01470 Seillonnaz, tel. 04.74.36.14.50, fax 04.74.36.14.50 ▨ Ⴤ ev. day except Sun. 8–12 noon 2–7pm

768

LE CAVEAU BUGISTE
Chardonnay 2000★
6 ha 35,000 €5-8

This domaine is in Vongnes, a beautiful village in Bugey renowned for its copious flowers, and on the property there is a museum with a substantial exhibition of implements used for cultivating vines. There is also a collection of stone masons' tools and a slide show. In addition, they sell high-quality local products. This vintage 2000 has an attention-grabbing personality with elegance. It is an easy-drinking, fresh and fruity wine that is ready from now on.

Le Caveau Bugiste, 01350 Vongnes, tel. 04.79.87.92.32, fax 04.79.87.91.11
ev. day 9am–12 noon 2–7pm

P. CHARLIN Montagnieu 1999★★★
2.5 ha 23,000 €5-8

A double success for Patrick Charlin. There are few locations in Savoy or Le Bugey where Pinot Noir can be grown successfully but Patrick Charlin has produced a winning red Bugey 99 which wins one star. He went one better when he was unanimously awarded a *coup de cœur* for this fine sparkling wine with its delicate, persistent stream of bubbles. The palate is very delicate and leaves an impressive length. A real pleasure to drink among friends and highly recommended as an aperitif.

Patrick Charlin, Le Richenard, 01680 Groslée, tel. 04.74.39.73.54, fax 04.74.39.75.16
by appt.

CLOS DE LA BIERLE
Méthode traditionnelle 1999
0.5 ha 5,000 €8-11

This is a new entry in the *Guide*: Thierry Troccon set up in 1985 and has specialised in sparkling wine. This is very typical of his Bugey wines. There is a lightness throughout this wine which has a symphony of floral aromas, and a general harmony and delicacy that give this wine undoubted charm.

Thierry Troccon, Leymiat, 01450 Poncin, tel. 04.74.37.25.55, fax 04.74.37.28.82, e-mail labierle@aol.com
ev. day 9am–7pm

DUCOLOMB Mondeuse 2000★★
0.85 ha 8,000 €3-5

This is Pierre Ducolomb's first appearance in the *Guide*. Part of Lhuis, his commune, is made up of excellent soil where red grapes flourish and produce successful red wines. At the tasting, members of the Jury considered this to be an authentic *vin de terroir*. It has a very rich full-flavoured nose ranging from well-ripened red fruit to spicy notes that are typical of the grape variety. On the palate, it is a turmoil of tannins, acidity and wonderful richness that have yet to find perfect balance. Without a doubt, this wine will be ready to drink from now on, but do not rush to uncork the bottle.

Pierre Ducolomb, 01680 Lhuis, tel. 04.74.39.82.58, fax 04.74.39.82.58
by appt.

MARJORIE GUINET ET BERNARD RONDEAU
Cerdon Méthode ancestrale 2000★★
2 ha 15,000 €5-8

Marjorie and Bernard Rondeau set up in 1998 and specialise in producing Cerdon. Last year they won their first *coup de cœur* and this year they have pulled off another with this wine that enchanted the Jury. They must be congratulated for their success. This aromatic sparkling wine, very rare in France, is a must for a fashionable aperitif. It is beyond reproach at the technical level. This attractive wine combines together small-berried, red-fruit flavours and has obtained a subtle balance between sugar and acidity. A wonderfully attractive wine. It is worth remembering that Cerdon only contains 8% volume of alcohol.

Marjorie Guinet et Bernard Rondeau, Cornelle, 01640 Boyeux-Saint-Jérôme, tel. 04.74.37.12.34, fax 04.74.37.12.34
by appt.

FRANCK PEILLOT
Roussette de Montagnieu 2000★
1.25 ha 10,000 €8-11

Franck Peillot comes from a family that has been devoted to wine since 1900 and he took up the torch in 1995. Like his father Jean, before him, Franck is deeply attached to the Altesse grape variety, the beacon of the

Bugey AOVDQS

appellation, and is committed to developing its potential. Mission accomplished with this wine which has been produced from 50-year-old vines. Its nose is dominated by exotic and citrus fruits and the first impression on the palate is clean and fresh. The wine then moves on and becomes very complex with well-balanced alcohol and acidity. It is unfussy, lively and very elegant and will go well with pan-fried *foie gras*. Equally very successful is the **red Bugey 2000** made from Mondeuse but it should be given time for the tannins to mellow, then served with coq au vin *rouge* using Mondeuse in the recipe.

● Franck Peillot, Au village,
01470 Montagnieu, tel. 04.74.36.71.56,
fax 04.74.36.14.12  ☎ Y by appt.

JEAN-PIERRE TISSOT 2000★

■   1.14 ha 10,900   ■   ●   €3-5

■

A warm hand to the first appearance of Jean-Pierre Tissot and his son Thierry, who has a solid training as an engineer. They only started up in 2001 and have set themselves the ambitious task of reclaiming some of the hills of the Coteaux de Vaux-en-Bugey. The wine is made from a harvest where the grapes are picked in bunches and put whole into the vat. The wine has a very intense colour. The nose has strong red-fruit aromas and it is followed by a fresh, slightly alcoholic and well-balanced palate. The structure is formed with well-softened tannins which guarantee it will be impeccable by now.

● Jean-Pierre Tissot, quai du Buizin,
01150 Vaux-en-Bugey, tel. 04.74.35.80.55,
e-mail thierrytissot@hotmail.com ✉
Y by appt.

LANGUEDOC AND ROUSSILLON

From the southern edge of the Massif Central to the eastern regions of the Pyrenees, the Languedoc-Roussillon vineyards stretch over four coastal departments: the Gard, the Hérault, the Aude and the Pyrénées-Orientales. This substantial area can be visualized as a ring of hills and mountains running down to the coastal plain. Descending from the heights to sea level there are four successive types of terrain. The highest is a mountainous region, formed mostly from the ancient rocks of the Massif Central: below is a region of rocky outcrops and arid moors (the garrigue), which is the oldest wine-growing areas in the region; further down still is the rolling alluvial plain, quite sheltered, with a number of low-lying slopes (200 m/656 ft); the fourth, the coastal area itself, is a continuous strip of low-lying beaches and lagoons, recently developed into one of Europe's liveliest holiday spots. Greek traders and colonists may have planted vines near their settlements in the region as early as the eighth century BC. Under the Romans, the Languedoc vineyard developed rapidly, competing with Roman vineyards in Italy to such an extent that in 92 AD Emperor Domitian ordered half the area of the vineyards to be grubbed up! For two centuries vine cultivation was limited to the Narbonne area, but in 270 Probus annulled the decrees of 92, giving the vineyards of Languedoc-Roussillon a new start. Production was maintained under the Visigoths, but perished during the Saracen invasions of the ninth century. The beginning of the 11th century marked the rebirth of the vineyard, with monasteries and abbeys playing a significant role. At that time the vines were largely confined to the hillsides, the plains being reserved for food crops.

The wine trade grew considerably during the 14th and 15th centuries as new techniques emerged and the number of vineyards increased. Brandy-making became established in the 16th and 17th centuries.

In the 17th and 18th centuries the economic life of the region began to take off: a new port was built at Sète, the Canal des Deux Mers was opened, and the old Roman road was reconstructed. Along with the development of local weaving and silk industries, this economic revival gave a new impetus to vine-growing. A growing export trade of wines and brandies was significantly assisted by the new transport infrastructure.

New vineyards were planted in the plain, utilising the latest ideas about vine-growing *terroirs*. At that time sweet wines occupied a substantial area. The construction of the railways, between 1850 and 1880, shortened distances and guaranteed the opening of new markets whose needs were to be met by the plentiful production of vineyards that were replanted after the phylloxera crisis.

Taking advantage of propitious soils on the slopes in the Gard, the Hérault, Minervois, Corbières and Roussillon, a new vineyard, planted with traditional vine varieties, was developed in the 1950s, adjacent to vineyards that had been the glory of Languedoc-Roussillon a century before. A large number of wines were subsequently recategorised as AOVDQS and AOC, part of a general move to produce higher quality wines in the region.

771

Wine-growing in the Languedoc-Roussillon takes place in a range of very different conditions as regards altitude, proximity to the sea, growth on terraces or on slopes, soils and *terroirs*.

The soils and the *terroirs* include schist from the primary mountains, as at Banyuls and Maury, in Corbières, Minervois and at Saint-Chinian; sandstone from the Liassic or the Triassic periods, which often alternate with marl, as in Corbières and at Saint-Jean-de-Blanquière; gravel terraces and smoothed pebbles from the Quaternary era, an excellent *terroir* for the vine, to be found at Rivesaltes, Val-d'Orbieu, Caunes-Minervois in the Méjanelle or les Costières de Nîmes. Limestone and stony

Languedoc

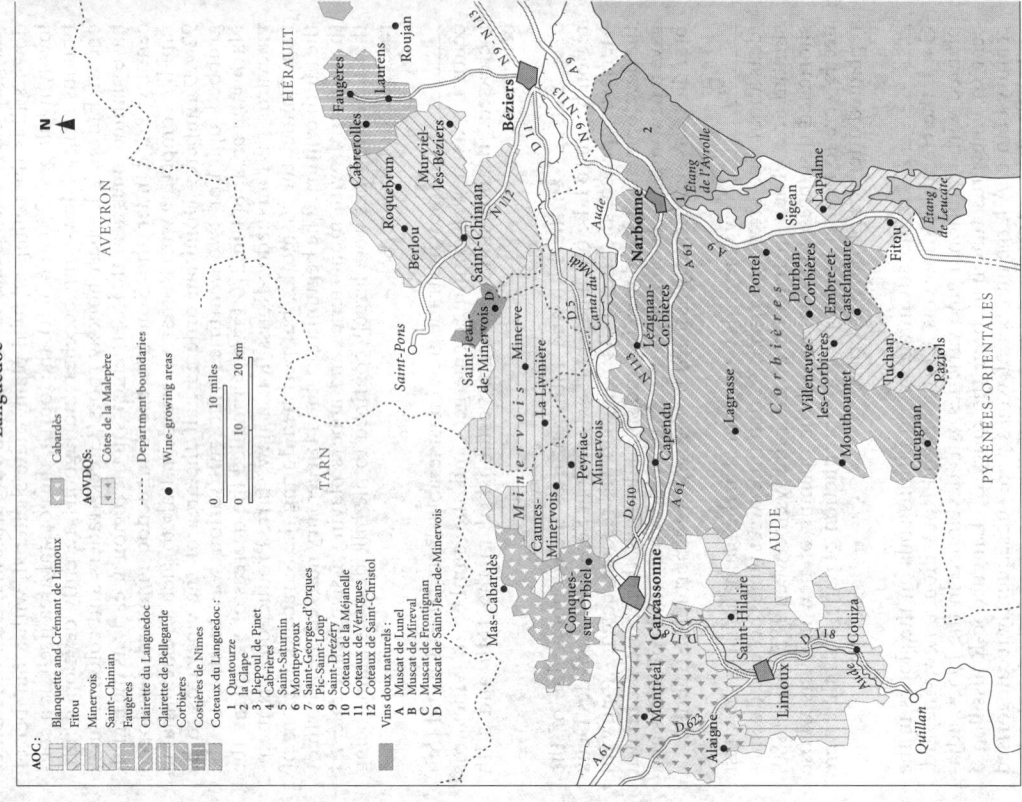

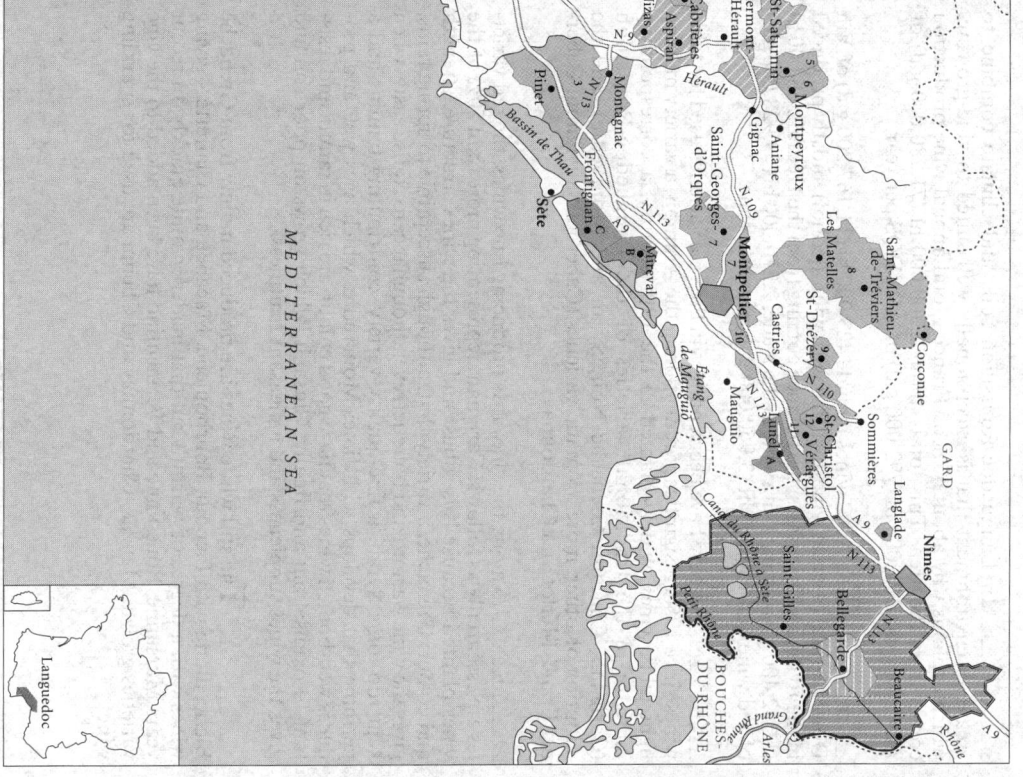

terrain, occurring as slopes or as plateaux, as in Roussillon, Corbières and Minervois contrasts with the recent alluvial soils of the Languedoc slopes, as well as with the arenas of granite and gneiss found at Les Fenouillèdes.

The Mediterranean climate, prone as it is to extremes of weather, is a unifying feature throughout Languedoc-Roussillon. It is the hottest region in France (the average annual temperature is close to 14°C/57°F, with temperatures that often exceed 30°C/86°F in July and August); rainfall is infrequent, unreliable and falls unevenly across the area. The warm season, from 15 May to 15 August, is always significantly dry. In many areas in Languedoc-Roussillon vines or olives are the only crops it is possible to grow. Only 350 mm (14 in) of rain falls on Barcarès, the driest area in France. However, the quantity of rain can vary by three depending on the place – 400 mm (16 in) on the coast, 1,200 mm (47 in) in the mountains. The winds make the climate even drier when they blow from the land (the Mistral, Cers or Tramontane); on the other hand, winds blowing from the sea temper the effects of the heat and bring a welcome humidity for the vines.

The network of watercourses is particularly dense. There are at least 20 rivers, which may swiftly become torrents after storms or dry up altogether during periods of drought. These rivers have contributed substantially to the formation of the landscape and to the *terroir* of the Rhône valley as far as Têt in the Pyrénés-Orientales.

In Languedoc-Roussillon soils and climate combine to create an environment that is exceptionally well suited to vine-growing, which explains why about 40% of France's total annual wine production comes from the area. This totals about 2,700,000 hl (71,280,000 gal) of AOC wines and 30,000 hl (792,000 gal) of AOVDQS per year.

The AOC wines include 423,000 hl (11,167,200 gal) of Vin Doux Naturel (a sweet wine, fortified with wine alcohol), mostly produced in the Pyrénées-Orientales, the balance coming from the Hérault; 66,000 hl (1,742,400 gal) of sparkling wine in the Aude; 2,270,000 hl (59,928,000 gal) of red wine and 150,000 hl (3,960,000 gal) of white wine.

There have been changes in the vine varieties used for table wines since 1950: a significant reduction in the Aramon, a variety making light table wines, widely planted in the 19th century, a corresponding increase in the traditional varieties of the Languedoc-Roussillon (Carignan, Cinsault, Grenache Noir, Syrah and Mourvèdre), and the adoption of other, more aromatic varieties (Cabernet Sauvignon, Cabernet Franc, Merlot and Chardonnay).

Among the vineyards producing fine wines, the red varieties are essentially as follows: Carignan, representing more than 50% of the vines planted because it is robust and gives the wines structure, strength and colour; Grenache, a variety that, although susceptible to spring rains, gives the wine warmth and bouquet, even though it can oxidise easily when kept too long; Syrah, a fine-quality variety, contributing tannins and a perfume that develops with time; Mourvèdre, which ages well and produces well-bodied wines that have good colour, are rich in tannin and resistant to oxidisation; and finally, Cinsault, which grows on poor soil and gives the wines suppleness and a pleasant fruitiness.

The still white wines are produced mainly from Grenache Blanc, along with Picpoul, Bourboulenc, Macabeu and Clairette – giving wines with a degree of warmth but that maderise quite quickly. In recent years Marsanne, Roussanne and Vermentino have been added to the vine varieties grown. Mauzac, Chardonnay and Chenin are used for sparkling wines.

Blanquette de Limoux and Blanquette Méthode Ancestrale

The monks of Saint-Hilaire Abbey, which is near Limoux, noticed that their wines went into a second fermentation and were the first people to make Blanquette de Limoux. Three varieties are used to make the wine: Mauzac (90% minimum), Chenin and Chardonnay. The last two of these were introduced in place of Clairette, and they give Blanquette its characteristic acidity and aromatic finesse.

Blanquette de Limoux

Limoux is made according to the Méthode Traditionelle (Champagne method) in three different styles as brut (dry), demi-sec (medium dry) or doux (sweet).

Blanquette Méthode Ancestrale

Ancestrale is a separate AOC, and the method used is kept secret. The characteristic difference of its production lies in a final fermentation in the bottle. Today, modern techniques allow a low-alcohol sweet wine to be produced from 100% Mauzac.

AIMERY Méthode ancestrale

○ Suave et Fruitée Demi-sec

500 ha	150,000	€5-8

The co-operative cellar regularly makes a distinctive Blanquette *méthode ancestrale* wine, which is the result of constantly evolving technology that nonetheless remains true to the wine's origins. The bouquet has notes of stewed apples and honey with a hint of roses. On the palate it is very sweet. Indeed, some thought it reminiscent of a cider, which

suggests that it would go well with apples and crêpes.
🍴 Aimery-Sieur d'Arques, av. de Carcassonne, BP 30, 11303 Limoux Cedex, tel. 04.68.74.63.00, fax 04.68.74.63.12, e-mail service@sieurdarques.com
🍷 by appt.

AIMERY Brut Tête de cuvée ★★

500 ha	150,000	€5-8

Long gone is the time when members of the co-operative would bring their harvest to the press-pump in the middle of the courtyard. Today, the technical equipment here is state-of-the-art, and the result is an attractive pale yellow wine with green highlights and fine, vigorous streams of bubbles. The nose is dominated by acacia flowers, and the delicate palate, which has hints of brioche, finishes on an attractive, fresh, mineral note.
🍴 Aimery-Sieur d'Arques, av. de Carcassonne, BP 30, 11303 Limoux Cedex, tel. 04.68.74.63.00, fax 04.68.74.63.12, e-mail service@sieurdarques.com

---

CLUB DES SOMMELIERS Brut ★

500 ha	150,000	€5-8

The clubbable *sommeliers* who make this wine have produced a highly authentic Blanquette de Limoux, made from 90% Mauzac grapes. Aromatically intense, with the classic predominant note of green apples, it has a full, generous palate with smoky overtones. It all adds up to a Blanquette that is true to type, attractive, well balanced and ready to drink.
🍴 Aimery-Sieur d'Arques, av. de Carcassonne, BP 30, 11303 Limoux Cedex, tel. 04.68.74.63.00, fax 04.68.74.63.12, e-mail service@sieurdarques.com
🍷 by appt.

DOM. COLLIN

○ Brut Cuvée Jean-Philippe 1999 ★★

20 ha	60,000	€3-5

Cuvée Jean-Philippe is well known to readers of the *Guide*. It is a wine that honours the technical expertise, skills and single-mindedness of its cellar-master, M. Rosier. A bright yellow wine with green highlights and a delicate mousse, it has toasted aromas allied to scents of fresh citrus fruits. The full palate fulfils the promise of the nose and is remarkable for its superb balance.

Crémant de Limoux

Even though the Crémant de Limoux was officially categorised only as recently as 21 August 1990, it is a tried and tested product. The strict regulations originally laid down for the production of Limoux are very close to those used for Crémant, so there is no difficulty in including the Limouxins in this elite group.

The mature wines have been appearing in wine stores for some time now, and customers are learning to appreciate the subtle blend of the personality and character of Mauzac, the elegance and roundness of Chardonnay and the youth and freshness of Chenin.

GUINOT Brut Cuvée réservée★ €5-8

○ 9 ha 40,000

The family own three estates, one of which is situated on the site of a Gallo-Roman town. And while the Guinots may now have an Internet site, they nonetheless retain the time-honoured methods of manual *remuage* and disgorgement to create their wines. This attractive, lively wine releases scents of peach and apricot, evolving towards honey, while the well-balanced, aromatic and complex palate leads up to a fresh and lively finish.

• Maison Guinot, 3, av. Chemin-de-Ronde, 11304 Limoux, tel. 04.68.31.01.33, fax 04.68.31.60.05, e-mail guinot@blanquette.fr ▼ ev. day except Sat. Sun. 9am–12 noon 2pm–6pm

ROBERT Brut Cinquantenaire 1998★ €8-11

○ 6 ha 22,100

The Roberts are a family concern. Although the estate, with its magnificent scenery, encourages relaxation, work has to come first, with everyone playing their part. The youthful character of this *cinquantenaire* (50th anniversary) wine belies its name. Fine bubbles in a steady stream, an attractive pale yellow colour with golden highlights, intense, complex notes of peach and green apple and a well-balanced palate with a hint of grapefruit add up to a wine of remarkable freshness: an excellent choice for a celebration meal.

• GFA Robert, Dom. de Fourn, 11300 Pieusse, tel. 04.68.31.15.03, fax 04.68.31.77.65 ▼ by appt.

TAILHAN-CAVAILLES 1999★★ €5-8

○ 4 ha 20,000

When he settled here in 1999 Alain Cavaillés took over the vineyard from M. Tailhan and began vinifying his wines on the latter's property, forming an association of the two names. Since 2001 he has been supervising the production in his own brand-new cellar. Already singled out for praise last year, he is again commended for this intense, complex 99, the aromas of which develop from roasted notes towards peach and honey. The palate has appreciable liveliness, accompanied by good balance and a finish hinting at citrus fruits.

• Alain Cavaillès, 11300 Magrie, tel. 04.68.31.66.14, fax 04.68.31.11.01, e-mail cavailles.alain@wanadoo.fr ▼ by appt.

AIMERY Cuvée brut★ €5-8

○ 500 ha 150,000

Here is yet another side to the talents of the young team at Sieur d'Arques. Every year they organise an auction presided over by some of France's greatest chefs, the proceeds going towards the restoration of old belltowers. The operation is called 'Toques et Clochers' (remember the name). This light golden wine charmed the Jury with its mingled aromas of peach and pear. After an attractive, straightforward opening, the wine emerges further as full-bodied, well balanced and lively: a pleasure to drink.

• Aimery-Sieur d'Arques, av. de Carcassonne, BP 30, 11303 Limoux Cedex, tel. 04.68.74.63.00, fax 04.68.74.63.12, e-mail servico@sieurdarques.com

▼ by appt.

• Vignerons du Sieur d'Arques

GUINOT Impérial du Millénaire★ €11-15

○ 1.3 ha 5,000

Established in the Limoux region since the 16th century, the house of Guinot is part of the history of Blanquette and *crémant* wines. This special *cuvée*, a blend of the 1997 and 1998 vintages, has spent some time in oak. Its pale gold appearance is further enhanced by fine, energetic bubbles. The nose is subtle and attractive, offering delicate fruity and floral impressions. On the palate the wine is pleasingly fresh, with an attractive finish that is evocative of passion-fruit.

• Maison Guinot, 3, av. Chemin-de-Ronde, 11304 Limoux, tel. 04.68.31.01.33, fax 04.68.31.60.05, e-mail guinot@blanquette.fr ▼ ev. day except Sat. Sun. 9am–12 noon 2pm–6pm

J. LAURENS

Cuvée Domaine Tête de cuvée 1999★★★

○   10 ha   23,501   ■ ▲ €8–11

Michel Dervin, from the Champagne region, settled in the Limouxin in 1983. Thanks to great technical mastery and strict attention to the grapes, he has created a remarkable wine. The attractive appearance is most inviting. The rich, complex palate has great appeal, being both well integrated and possessed of a fresh, powerful finish.

↣ SARL Dervin, rte de La Digne-d'Amont, 11300 La Digne d'Aval, tel. 04.68.31.61.61, fax 04.68.31.61.61, e-mail dervin.michel@ wanadoo.fr ✔ ⊺ by appt.

MICHEL OLIVIER

Tête de cuvée 1999★

○   6 ha   28,000   €5–8

Frequently mentioned in the Guide, this erstwhile champagne house has stayed true to form with its delicate Limoux sparkler. The Jury admired the continuous stream of bubbles in the wine, its pale yellow colour with green highlights and the appealing bouquet of yellow flowers and citrus fruits. It strikes the palate with vigour, power and elegance. A well-balanced wine to appreciate among friends as an apéritif and throughout a meal.

↣ Dom. Collin-Rosier, rue Farman, 11300 Limoux, tel. 04.68.31.48.38, fax 04.68.31.34.16 ⊺ by appt.

SIEUR D'ARQUES 1998★

○   500 ha   150,000   €8–11

Alain Gayda is an oenologist working for the market leaders in Limoux and is president of the Oenologues de France: clearly a man who knows how to pick a team and impart his expertise. No wonder the Sieur d'Arques cellar keeps cropping up in different sections of this chapter. Hints of toastiness, borne aloft on a beguiling mousse, are followed on the full, well-balanced palate by an impression of richness that blends well with the toastiness. A good apéritif wine.

↣ Aimery-Sieur d'Arques, av. de Carcassonne, BP 30, 11303 Limoux Cedex, tel. 04.68.74.63.00, fax 04.68.74.63.12, e-mail service@sieurdarques.com ⊺ by appt.

Limoux

T he Appellation Limoux Nature, recognised in 1938, was in reality a wine used as the base in the making of Appellation Blanquette de Limoux, and all the shippers used to handle a little of it.

I n 1981 this AOC regrettably saw the use of the term 'Nature' being prohibited, and it became simply Limoux. The wine is still made from 100% Mauzac but has slowly declined, while the wines de Limoux are a blend of Chenin, Chardonnay and Mauzac.

T his appellation has started up again and was included for the first time at the harvest of 1992. It may now be made from a mixture of Chenin and Chardonnay grapes, but Mauzac must still be present. Unusually, fermentation and development until 1 May must be carried out in oak barrels. The energetic Limouxin team is now starting to reap the benefits of all their hard work.

DOM. BEGUDE 1999

□   8 ha   24,000   ‖‖ €11–15

Not long established in the region, the Domaine des Comtes Méditerranéens, based at La Livinière in the Minervois, offers this Bégude estate wine. Its second vintage is a purely organic product. It seems a safe bet that this wine will crop up in future editions of the Guide. The light, even shy bouquet features white flowers, together with notes of quince and peach. A firm, oaky Limoux with a mildly tannic finish, it needs a little more time to develop.

↣ Dom. Bégude, 11300 Cepie, tel. 04.68.91.42.63, fax 04.68.91.62.15, e-mail framboissier@compuserve.com

DOM. DE L'AIGLE Les Aigles 1999★★

□   4 ha   35,000   ‖‖ €11–15

Jean-Louis Denois, a travelling oenologist, has decided to make the Limoux appellation his priority. A product of the Haute-Vallée, this clear, pale-yellow 99 is a great success. It offers a fine, appealing bouquet with hints of chestnut and a well-balanced palate with notes of hazelnut and the minty freshness of early morning.

↣ Dom. de L'Aigle, 11300 Roquetaillade, tel. 04.68.31.39.12, fax 04.68.31.39.14 ✔ ⊺ by appt. ↣ Jean-Louis Denois

TOQUES ET CLOCHERS Terroir

Haute Vallée Elevé en fût de chêne 1999★★★

□   50 ha   35,000   ‖‖ €11–15

The house of Sieur d'Arques has made a speciality of vinification by terroir, resulting in four distinct cuvées: Terroir d'Autan, Océanique, Méditerranéen and Terroir Haute-Vallée. This last features most often in the Guide. A semi-mountainous district

Clairette de Bellegarde

Nîmes. Production of this wine, with its characteristic bouquet, totalled 1,695 hl (44,748 gal) in 2000.

with a robust climate, this is the preferred terrain of the Chardonnay grape. The colour is vibrant straw yellow, the bouquet is powerfully spicy with a touch of acacia, and the palate is full and well balanced: a combination that really enthused the Jury. Recommended as an accompaniment to sauced fish dishes or grilled prawns, this wine is already great and will remain so until 2003.
- Aimery-Sieur d'Arques, av. de Carcassonne, BP 30, 11303 Limoux Cedex, tel. 04.68.74.63.00, fax 04.68.74.63.12, e-mail servico@sieurdarques.com
Y by appt.
- Vignerons du sieur d'Arques

MAS CARLOT Cuvée Tradition 2000★   7 ha   35,000   €3-5

In 1998 the oenologist Nathalie Blanc-Mares took over the estate bought in 1986 by her father, Paul-Antoine Blanc. She has not neglected this little-known appellation on the fringes of Costières de Nîmes. The wine is very true to the single variety from which it is made. Light straw yellow, it has a complex nose of ripe peaches, orange-blossom and pâtisserie. The full, rounded palate of this heady Clairette finishes classically with a hint of bitterness.
- Nathalie Blanc-Mares, Mas Carlot, rte de Redessan, Ch. Paul Blanc, 30127 Bellegarde, tel. 04.66.01.11.83, fax 04.66.01.62.74
Y ev. day 8am–12 noon 2pm–5pm; Sat. Sun. by appt.

TOQUES ET CLOCHERS
Autan Elevé en fût de chêne 1999   50 ha   35,000   €11-15

The Terroir d'Autan, which comes from the very heart of the appellation, is the most characteristically *limouxin* of the four *terroir cuvées* (see above), marrying the subtlety and freshness of the **Océanique** with the fuller character of the **Terroir Méditerranéen**. A pale yellow wine with aromas of white flowers mixed with toasty notes, it has a pleasing, full, well-balanced palate of great length. A successful marriage of wine and oak-ageing.
- Aimery-Sieur d'Arques, av. de Carcassonne, BP 30, 11303 Limoux Cedex, tel. 04.68.74.63.00, fax 04.68.74.63.12, e-mail servico@sieurdarques.com
Y by appt.

Clairette de Languedoc

The vines are cultivated over 112 ha (277 acres) in eight communes in the Hérault valley and produced 4,344 hl (114,682 gal) in 2000. After vinification at low temperature, with a minimum of oxidation, a generous white wine is produced with an intense yellow robe. It can be dry, medium or sweet. As it ages, it acquires a *rancio*, toasted flavour, that finds its fans. It goes well with Bourride Sétoise, a local fish stew.

LA CLAIRETTE D'ADISSAN 2000   12.5 ha   50,000   €5-8

Adissan is the birthplace of Clairette du Languedoc. Let yourself be charmed by this pale-golden wine, with its bouquet of ripe fruit (pear, quince) and crystallised lemon aromas, backed up by hints of toast. Full and fleshy, this successful wine is at once sprightly and velvet textured.
- Cave coop. La Clairette d'Adissan, 34230 Adissan, tel. 04.67.25.01.07, fax 04.67.25.37.76, e-mail clairette.adissan@wanadoo.fr
Y ev. day except Sun. 9am–12 noon 3pm–6pm

Clairette de Bellegarde

This AOC was recognised in 1949. Clairette de Bellegarde is produced on red, stony soil in the south-eastern part of the Costières de Nîmes, in a small region that is squeezed between Beaucaire and Saint-Gilles, and between Arles and

Corbières wines, categorised VDQS from 1951, became AOC in 1985. The extent of the appellation covers 87 communes, producing 656,000 hl (17,318,400 gal) in 2000, (7% of white and rosé and 93% of red). They are powerful wines, ranging between 11% and 13% alcohol, produced from vineyards planted with a maximum of 60% of Carignan vines.

Les Corbières is a typical wine-growing area in that it is hardly suitable for any other type of crop. Yet it is a difficult region to classify because, although the Mediterranean influence dominates, there is also a certain degree of maritime Atlantic influence to the west. The great diversity of soil types, the preponderance of Carignan and the partitioning of plots due to the very broken relief contribute to a sense of uniqueness.

CH. AIGUILLOUX
Cuvée des Trois Seigneurs 1999

5.65 ha 30,000 €8-11

Trois Seigneurs is so-called because the *terroir* lies on the borders of the ancient counties of Narbonne, Durban and Lézignan. The wine is made from the three principal Corbières varieties, Carignan (55%), Grenache (25%) and Syrah (20%), which are harvested manually, vinified with maceration of the whole grapes and oak-matured for 12 months. Delightful aromatic intensity distinguishes a bouquet of fruits in brandy, overripe strawberries and fresh grass. On the palate this well-balanced Corbières makes a good opening impression, following it up with fine structure, freshness and well-integrated tannins.

• Marthe et François Lemarié, Ch. Aiguilloux, 11200 Thézan-des-Corbières, tel. 04.68.43.32.71, fax 04.68.43.30.66, e-mail aiguilloux@wanadoo.fr ev. day 10am–12 noon 2pm–6pm

CH. DES AUZINES
Cuvée des Hautes Terres 1999

2 ha 6,000 €8-11

Les Auzines, a vineyard site near Lagrasse, overlooked by Mt Alaric and overlooking the gorges of the Alsou valley, is situated at the relatively low altitude of 270 m (883 ft). In spite of that, the Carignan grape is not equipped to appear at its best here, which is why Cuvée des Hautes Terres doesn't contain any of it. The wine has an honest, direct and intense bouquet, followed by an attractive, full, young palate, which needs more time.

• Yves Jalliet, Ch. des Auzines, 11220 Lagrasse, tel. 04.68.43.12.05, fax 04.68.43.16.67 ev. day 9am–7pm

CH. BEAUREGARD MIROUZE
Cuvée Prestige 1999

1.28 ha 6,000 €11-15

Nicolas Mirouze represents the seventh generation of his family to work this estate, and he knows how to respond to his *terroir*. It is not easy to produce great wines on these sandstone soils. He has had to replace the Carignan with Syrah but has kept some of the garrigue and of pepper, enhanced by a little oak. Full and rich, with well-integrated tannins, it is an elegant wine that can be drunk straightaway.

• Nicolas Mirouze, Ch. Beauregard, 11200 Bizanet, tel. 04.68.45.19.35, fax 04.68.45.10.07, e-mail nmirouze@beauregard-mirouze.com by appt.

CH. BEL-EVEQUE 1998

11 ha 30,300 €5-8

Being an actor involves portraying a certain character, and Pierre Richard is not lacking in this respect. Nor is his wine. Château Bel-Evêque is intensely dark in colour with almost black, glossy highlights. The bouquet is appealing, being clean and ripe with fascinating aromas of preserved fruits. With its long-lasting palate, this warming, concentrated wine has an attractive finish that, though perhaps a trifle overstated, contributes texture and personality.

• SCEA Pierre Richard, Ch. Bel-Evêque, 11430 Gruissan, tel. 04.68.75.00.48, fax 04.68.49.09.23 ev. day except Sun. & Mon. 10am–1pm 3pm–6pm

CH. BERTRAND 2000★

1 ha 6,500 €3-5

'From grape to bottle' is a formula that encapsulates the wine-grower's craft. Roger Bertrand became one in order to realise a long-held dream of his father. He has succeeded on two counts: with this rosé, which is quite powerful but also lively, well structured and possessed of a pleasingly fruity, aromatic intensity, and with a 98 red, **Cuvée Réservée du Domaine de Longueroche.**

• Dom. de Longueroche, 11200 Saint-André-de-Roquelongue, tel. 04.68.41.48.26, fax 04.68.32.22.43, e-mail domaine.de.longueroche@wanadoo.fr by appt.
• Roger Bertrand.

CASTELMAURE Cuvée no 3 1999★

■   10 ha   25,000   ▥ €15-23

This wine has a number rather than a name, which seems somewhat anachronistic in this environment of rocks and stones, burning garrigue, brilliant sunshine, steep-sloping vineyards and the distinctive local twang in the wine-makers accents. On tasting the wine, however, the words come pouring out: bright, ruby-coloured, oaky, vanilla, ripe fruits, toasty and then spicy aromas, good presence on the palate, harmony, balance, dense tannins, fullness and length. Already an interesting wine, this one has great potential.

↪ SCV Castelmaure, 4, rte des Cannelles,
11360 Embres-et-Castelmaure,
tel. 04.68.45.91.83, fax 04.68.45.83.56,
e-mail castelmaure@wanadoo.fr ▼
🍷 ev. day except Sat. & Sun. 9am–12 noon
2pm–6pm

DOM. DES CHANDELLES 1998★

■   4 ha   10,000   ▥ €11-15

We can all agree on the logic of this British wine-maker's career. Once an accountant, he became sufficiently smitten by wine to train as an oenologist and to study French viticulture. He bought vineyard land in the Aude, making the wise decision to avoid Carignan in this western part of the Corbières appellation, and has invested in modern, rationalised wine-making technology, while not neglecting the tradition of oak-maturation. He has now given wine-lovers a peppery, well-balanced 98 that is very fine on the palate and has great length.

↪ Dom. des Chandelles, 4, chem. des Pins,
11800 Floure, tel. 04.68.79.00.10,
fax 04.68.79.21.92 ▼ 🍷 by appt.
↪ P. et S. Munday

BLANC DE BLANCS DES DEMOISELLES 2000★★

☐   n.c.   30,000   ■ ◈

The Demoiselle is ageless: every year, she is renewed. She is pleasing on the eye, a discreet perfume of white flowers, and underneath it all, genuine personality. With its full and exquisitely soft-textured palate, this wine has balance, roundness, freshness and languorous length. Allow yourself to be seduced!

↪ SCV Cellier des Demoiselles, 5, rue de la Cave, 11220 Saint-Laurent-de-l a-Cabrerisse, tel. 04.68.44.02.73, fax 04.68.44.07.05 ▼
🍷 ev. day except Sun. 8am–12 noon
2pm–6pm

imprint, was the only wine to distinguish itself. Although of average intensity, it nevertheless has personality. Spicy and overripe on the palate, supple, full and rounded, it has very gentle tannins accompanied by a hint of liquorice – in short, a nice marriage of wine and oak.

↪ SCEA des Aireles, 21, av. des Plages,
11540 Roquefort-des-Corbières,
tel. 04.68.48.23.88, fax 04.68.48.23.88 ▥
🍷 by appt.

CH. ETANG DES COLOMBES
Bicentenaire Vieilles vignes 1999★★

■   17 ha   90,000

Henri Gualco is a wine-maker at ease with himself. Everything he does is directed towards making the best Corbières and delighting the taster. This *cuvée* is dominated by Grenache, and supplemented by Syrah with a dash of Mourvèdre. The grape-harvest was carried out by hand. Eight months in oak have proved sufficient to perfect the wine. Its aromatic profile is certainly distinguished, being distantly redolent of the garrigue. The palate, after a smooth yet textured opening, has plenty of character. Balanced, well integrated and lifted by a hint of freshness, it concludes on a spicy finish.

↪ Henri Gualco,
Ch. Etang des Colombes, 11200 Cruscades,
tel. 04.68.27.00.03, fax 04.68.27.24.63,
e-mail christophe.gualco@wanadoo.fr ▥
🍷 ev. day 8am–12 noon 2pm–7pm

DOM. DE FONTSAINTE
Réserve la Demoiselle 1999★

■   8 ha   41,000   €5-8

Bruno Laboucarié is a model wine-grower. His eye is alert to any fine touches needed by his vines, and his expert taster's palate helps him in his vinification and cellar management. Hence, although 1999 was a tricky year, his Réserve la Demoiselle has a variety of distinctive aromatic characteristics, such as vanilla, red-fruit preserve, and notes of roasting coffee beans. The palate is honest and supple, with well-judged oakiness, and is not without a hint of freshness, well-integrated tannins, and above all great length.

↪ SEP Laboucarié, Dom. de Fontsainte,
11200 Boutenac, tel. 04.68.27.07.63,
fax 04.68.27.62.01 ▥ 🍷 ev. day except Sun.
10am–12 noon 2pm–6pm

CH. GAUBERT
Cuvée Philharmonie 1998

■   3 ha   10,000   ▥ ◈ €8-11

Blended from Syrah and Grenache grapes grown in the extreme west of Corbières, and slowly matured in temperature-controlled conditions in a brand-new cellar, this wine spent three months in the vat and nine in oak. It is redolent of the garrigue (thyme especially) and is pleasingly smooth, somewhat

DOM. DOHIN LE ROY
Cuvée la Bruyère 1999

■   6.25 ha   30,000   ■ ▥ €8-11

While it may not be obvious from the name, Roquefort-des-Corbières overlooks the Mediterranean. In 1999, this maritime *terroir* did not enjoy the usual benefits of its location. Cuvée la Bruyère, with its strong Mourvèdre

780

spicy, with a strong finish. Would suit saddle of venison with cherries.
→ Gilles Cavayé, EARL dom. Gaubert,
11220 Arquettes-en-Val, tel. 04.68.24.04.49

DOM. DU GRAND CRES
Cuvée majeure 1998★★

■   12 ha   3,000   €11-15

Pascaline and Hervé Leferrer's wine takes its time, needing to mature before it may be tasted. After decanting, it releases slightly vegetal aromas, an impression that is also perceptible on the palate. On the nose the wine is enhanced by clean and forthright oakiness, with an excellent balance between alcohol and tannin.
→ Hervé and Pascaline Leferrer,
Dom. du Grand Crès, 40, av. de la Mer,
11200 Ferrals-les-Corbières,
tel. 04.68.43.69.08, fax 04.68.43.58.99
Y by appt.

CH. HAUTERIVE LE HAUT 2000★

□   1 ha   6,500   €3-5

The Reulet family has its winery amidst the Miocene-era gravel soils characteristic of the Boutenac terroir, where their 17th-century family property is to be found. Old Grenache Blanc vines and a smattering of Macabéo make up this very attractive white wine, with discreet herbaceous notes, a well-balanced palate and very long finish.
→ SCEA Reulet, Ch. Hauterive-le-Haut,
11200 Boutenac, tel. 04.68.27.62.00,
fax 04.68.27.62.00 Y by appt.

CH. HAUTERIVE LE VIEUX 1999★

■   3 ha   1,338

A former tenant-holding of Fontfroide, this estate probably became a vineyard as early as the 11th century. Its Corbières is the fruit of tradition: half Carignan and a quarter each of Grenache and Syrah, it is given a lengthy maceration of the whole grapes, is matured entirely in the vat and is bottled at the end of the second winter. The result is a wine of hugely intense colour, with aromas of preserved fruits and cocoa. Its pleasant, full, rounded palate is marked by tannins that are still quite pronounced, but that should calm down after a few months in the bottle.
→ André Cambriel, Ch. Hauterive-le-Vieux,
65, av. Saint-Marc, 11200 Ornaisons,
tel. 04.68.27.43.08, fax 04.68.27.43.08
Y ev. day except Sun. 9am–12.15pm
4.30pm–7.30pm; winter by appt.

CH. HAUT-GLEON 1999★

■   20 ha   35,000

Coming from Narbonne, you will find that Château Haut-Gléon stands at the gateway of the Hautes Corbières district in the terroir of Durban. Carignan grapes are in the majority (60%), accompanied by Grenache and Syrah. Restrained yields, hand-picking, a state-of-the-art winery and eight months in oak have yielded a Corbières of very fine concentra-tion, with an intense, complex nose of vanilla and toast: a wine with power. The fleshy, rather warm palate is supported by a generous tannic structure.
→ Ch. Haut-Gléon,
Villesèque-des-Corbières, 11360 Durban,
tel. 04.68.48.85.95, fax 04.68.48.46.20,
e-mail chateauhautgleon@wanadoo.fr
Y ev. day 9am–12 noon 1.30pm–5pm
→ Duhamel

CH. LA BASTIDE 1999★ Optimée

■   10 ha   20,000   €8-11

This is a south-facing Corbières estate, although to the north may be glimpsed the terraces of Minervois. The wine is true to its appellation, despite its high proportion of Syrah, set off by Grenache. With the authentic Corbières garnet colour and violet highlights, it displays aromas of spices, toast, some discreet oakiness and a slight touch of musk. The richly constituted palate is pleasing and full, built on subtle, silky tannins and generally well balanced – a wine for drinking within the year.
→ Ch. La Bastide, 11200 Escales,
tel. 04.68.27.08.47, fax 04.68.27.26.81
Y by appt.
→ Guilhem Durand

CH. LA DOMEQUE 1998★

■   8.25 ha   55,000   €5-8

A chapel was founded here in the Carolingian era, although the estate has only borne its name since the 16th century. This dark, vibrant wine with black glints has a subtle, discreet yet elegant nose of ripe black fruits. A hint of evolution adds to its lustre. The almost fragile palate, still slightly marked by oak, turns out to be otherwise very well integrated, smooth, velvety and long-lasting, with just a final spark of tannin.
→ Frédéric Roger, 19, av. E.-Babou,
BP 90, 11200 Lézignan-Corbières,
tel. 04.68.27.84.50, fax 04.68.27.84.51
Y ev. day 9am–12 noon 2pm–6pm; Sat. Sun. by appt.

CH. LA PUJADE
Cuvée Charlemagne 1999★

■   4 ha   20,000   €5-8

This Corbières is a distinctive blend of Mourvèdre (60%), old-vine Carignan (20%), Syrah and Grenache, matured in oak for 15 months. Intensely deep garnet in colour with purple highlights, this unusual wine has a very potent nose, which begins with notes of oak, leads on through vanilla and finishes with a touch of toastiness. The forthright, full, rich and rounded palate delivers flavours of dried fruits and has a very long finish. An already interesting wine that promises more.
→ Ch. La Pujade,
11200 Ferrals-les-Corbières,
tel. 04.68.43.55.65, fax 04.68.43.56.16,
e-mail chateaupujade@aol.com
Y by appt.
→ Mennesson

CH. DE LASTOURS
Apparences 2000★★
n.c.   5,000   €8-11

The château has many noteworthy features. Historically, it goes back to Roman times, being sited close to the Via Domitiana. Nowadays, it is on the Paris-Dakar motor-racing route and contains some test-tracks. It also provides for disabled people to participate directly in the tending of the vineyard. The wine itself has aromas of peony, pear and kirsch, with the same flavours coming through on the palate, fittingly enhanced by slight spritziness. The secret of its success is the dash of Muscat that underpins a blend of Bourboulenc and Grenache Blanc.
➤ Centre d'Aide par le Travail, Ch. de Lastours, 11490 Portel-des-Corbières, tel. 04.68.48.29.17, fax 04.68.48.29.14, e-mail portel.chateaudelastours@wanadoo.fr ▾ by appt.

DOM. LAS VALS 1999
5 ha   5,000   €23-30

Alongside the white vines of the Château de la Baronne, there is an estate planted exclusively with red varieties on the eastern slopes of the Alaric. This is Las Vals. Paul and Jean Lignères, in their first harvest, have produced a wine predominantly from Mourvèdre grapes. The somewhat closed nose is already spicy, and the palate is warm and generous, sustained by tannins that make their presence felt, but not aggressively so. Wait a few months.
➤ Suzette Lignères, Ch. La Baronne, 11700 Fontcouverte, tel. 04.68.43.90.20, fax 04.68.43.96.73, e-mail chateaulabaronne@net-up.com ▾ by appt.

CH. LA VOULTE-GASPARETS
Cuvée réservée 1999★
22 ha   120,000   €6-11

Patrick Reverdy and Château La Voulte-Gasparets – its vines, its cellar and its wine – need no further introduction. See last year's edition of the Guide. There is space here only to describe the pleasure that is renewed with this slightly faded, but attractive, purple-hued 99. It has subtle but powerful aromas with the authentic accents of its terroir, which deserves to be considered a cru. The same impression returns on the palate, which is well-structured, concentrated, full and generous, perfect in fact. Tannins contribute to the wine's length, and are sure to help it age well.
➤ Patrick Reverdy, Ch. La Voulte-Gasparets, 11200 Boutenac, tel. 04.68.27.07.86, fax 04.68.27.41.33, e-mail chateau-la-voulte-gasparets@wanadoo.fr ▾ ev. day 9am-12 noon 2pm-6pm

CH. LES OLLIEUX 2000★
3.24 ha   11,000   €5-8

Made from Grenache, Cinsault, Syrah and a few Carignan grapes grown on the southern slopes of the Pinada, in the heart of the Boutenac terroir, this vat-matured rosé is now in its early prime. It is attractively fruity, with a hint of pear drops. The slight prickle of gas gives it both interest and youthful vitality.
➤ François-Xavier Surbezy, Ch. Les Ollieux, 11200 Montséret, tel. 04.68.43.32.61, fax 04.68.43.30.78, e-mail ollieux@free.fr ▾ ev. day 8.30am-8pm; Sat. Sun. 10am-8pm

CH. LES PALAIS
Cuvée Randolin 1999★
10 ha   45,000   €8-11

Xavier de Volontat by no means rests on his laurels. The terroir may remain the same, but the plantings of Syrah and Grenache are growing older, with a consequent improvement in quality. Cellar techniques are developing in the direction of what has been dubbed 'traditional modernity'. This 1999 Randolin has a powerful bouquet, with smooth, vanilla aromas. Its concentrated palate offers the usual good tannins and a tell-tale note of cocoa.
➤ Ch. Les Palais, 11220 Saint-Laurent-de-la-Cabrerisse, tel. 04.68.44.01.63, fax 04.68.44.07.42 ▾ ev. day 9am–12 noon 2pm–7pm; Sun. by appt.
➤ X. de Volontat

CH. DE L'HORTE
Grande Réserve 1999★★★
3 ha   9,500   €11-15

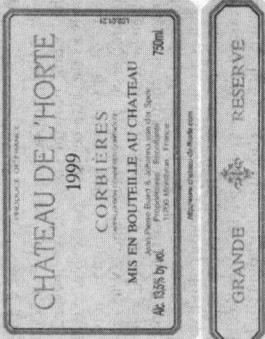

The estate is on the northern fringe of Corbières, where the sandstone terrain, covered in pines, bears the vines on its slopes. Here are to be found proud local boy Jean-Pierre Biard, and Johanna, whose accent wavers between the tones of the North and those of the Midi. Their wine is a perfectly authentic Corbières. A deep and dense ruby, it has powerful aromas of mocha and coffee, a gorgeously rounded attack, integration and balance, ripe fruit and fullness. This is a wine with body, texture and, crowning it all, a soft-toned finish that seems to go on for ever.
➤ Jean-Pierre Biard et Johanna Van der Spek, Ch. de L'Horte, 11700 Montbrun-des-Corbières, tel. 04.68.43.91.70, fax 04.68.43.95.36, e-mail horte@wanadoo.fr ▾ by appt.

CH. DE LUC
Cuvée des Murets Elevé en fût de chêne 1999
■ 10 ha 50,000 ▮▮ €5-8

The château is the former residence of the lord of Saint-Geniès, governor of Narbonne under Louis XIII. Here are the oak barrels that once contained Cuvée des Murets, harvested in 1999 by Louis Fabre. Deep red wine are spiciness contributed by the oak, a touch of musk and a hint of evolution, all elegantly blending together. After an uncomplicated opening impression, the palate displays good structure, and a return of the same aromatic complexity. The tannins on the finish still need time to soften.
♠ Louis Fabre, rue du Château, 11200 Luc-sur-Orbieu, tel. 04.68.27.10.80, fax 04.68.27.38.19, e-mail chateau.luc@aol.com ☑ Ⴘ by appt.

CH. MAYLANDIE Cuvée Prestige 1998
■ 2.5 ha 13,000 ▮▮ €5-8

This estate, which lies in the vicinity of various old abbeys and Cathar castles, offers *gîte* accommodation to devotees of both ancient buildings and the wines of Corbières. This 1998 is in its prime. Dark but lively, it has an intense nose that is still full of primary fruit, and yet also has notes of preserved prunes and mineral nuances. Its strong concentration, its still youthful tannins and the as yet somewhat jolting finish do not impair the impression of fullness on the palate. Leave this wine in the cellar and forget about it for a year, for it shows great promise.
♠ Maymil, Ch. Maylandie, 11200 Ferrals-les-Corbières, tel. 04.68.43.66.50, fax 04.68.43.69.42, e-mail maymil@infonie.fr ☑ Ⴘ ev. day 9am-8pm

CH. MERVILLE 1999★
■ 6 ha 35,000 ▮▮▮ €8-11

François and Jacques Lurton are Bordeaux-based, but with an interest in Corbières. Although they are not producers here, they have taken on the year-round responsibility of vinifying, maturing and bottling some of the estate's harvest. Limiting the proportion of Carignan used, they have nevertheless preserved the authenticity of the *terroir*. Aromas of liquorice, tobacco, spices and vanilla are followed by multiple, oak-enhanced flavours which make for a supple, fleshy and rather fresh-tasting wine. This easy-drinking 99 should give good pleasure. It would be very good with stuffed quail or flambéed woodcock.
♠ Jacques et François Lurton, Dom. de Poumeyrade, 33870 Vayres, tel. 05.57.74.72.74, fax 05.57.74.70.73, e-mail jflurton@jflurton.com

CH. MEUNIER SAINT-LOUIS
A Capella 1999★★★
■ 5 ha 34,000 ▮▮ €8-11

In 1999, a watchful eye on the part of the grower here counted for more than agricultural warnings against swarms of the vine moth *Lobesia botrana*. Philippe Pasquier-Meunier mounted a successful guard, and was able to deliver to Martine, the cellar-mistress, some splendid grapes for her A Capella *cuvée* – a wine that has been highly rated in past editions. It reappears now with a similar profile: an intense, deep but subtle colour somewhere between purple and black, and a powerful, extremely elegant bouquet, mingling flowers, red fruits, vanilla and pepper. The palate is straightforward and attractive, upholstered with silky tannins that blend in with the same aromatic complexity as informed the nose. This is all but perfection.
♠ Ph. Pasquier-Meunier, Ch. Meunier Saint-Louis, 11200 Boutenac, tel. 04.68.27.09.69, fax 04.68.27.53.34 ☑ by appt.

CH. PECH-LATT Alix 1998★
■ 3 ha 12,000 ▮▮ €23-30

This property is a former dependency of the Benedictine abbey of Lagrasse, founded in the eighth century. Its vineyard is planted on limestone deposits from Mount Alaric. The wine itself, with its strong accents of morello cherry and its elegant tannins, comes from a rigorous selection of Grenache (25%), Syrah (30%), Mourvèdre (5%) and Carignan (40%), and is given a long vatting and 12 months' oak maturation.
♠ SC Ch. Pech-Latt, 11220 Lagrasse, tel. 04.68.43.11.40, fax 04.68.58.11.41 ☑ Ⴘ ev. day 8am-12 noon 1.30pm-5.30pm; Sat. & Sun. by appt.

CH. PRIEURE BORDE-ROUGE
Cuvée Signature 1999★
■ 4.3 ha 25,000 ▮▮ €5-8

Natacha and Alain Quenchen are as enamoured of their estate as ever, as passionate about the craft of wine-growing, and the vines respond to their enthusiasm. This is among the best of the 99s, with a satisfyingly expressive, complex nose that comprises tea, cherries and raspberries, a rounded, full palate, the warmth of which is perfectly balanced by fine tannins, and a flawless finish. It could accompany a spiced *aiguillette* of duck.
♠ SCEA Devillers-Quenchen, Ch. Prieuré Borde-Rouge, 11220 Lagrasse, tel. 04.68.43.12.55, fax 04.68.43.12.51, e-mail quenchen@aol.com ☑ Ⴘ ev. day 9am-6pm

SEIGNEUR DE QUERIBUS 1999★
■ 25 ha 6,000 ▮▮ €5-8

At the foot of the Cathar citadels, there are still some pious souls. Today's purists, however, are not Cathars, but those who show their devotion to the *terroir* by selecting the right vines and varieties, respecting the grapes by hand-picking, and doing justice to the harvest by macerating the whole grapes and not trying to 'improve' the wine with oak-ageing. This co-operative offers a very aromatic 99 (violets, crushed strawberries and notes of thyme) that is easy-drinking and fruity, with a hint of menthol and forthright but supple tannins.

Vignerons du château de Quéribus, 11350 Cucugnan, tel. 04.68.45.41.61, fax 04.68.45.02.25
ev. day 10am–12 noon 2pm–7pm.

ROQUE SESTIERE
Carte blanche 1999★★

3 ha 6,200 €5-8

Commended in the 2000 *Guide* for its old-vine white Corbières, Roque Sestière is equally reputed for its red. Roland Lagarde, the master wine-grower, has made a notably good 99. He has managed to combine the authenticity of Carignan with the elegance of Syrah, and their ageing in oak has given the wine extra character. The palate is reminiscent of a superior cru wine. A great Corbières.

EARL Roland Lagarde, rue des Étangs, 11200 Luc-sur-Orbieu, tel. 04.68.27.18.00, fax 04.68.27.18.00 by appt.

ROSEE D'OCTOBRE 2000★

4 ha 5,000 €3-5

The Haute Corbières, around Quéribus and Cucugnan, is a unique *terroir* that produces a one-off rosé. Congratulations on the 2000 vintage go to the wine-growers of Padern and Montgaillard, in honour of this fresh, welcoming, elegant, well-balanced, silky wine and its red-fruit flavours.

Les Terroirs du Vertige, 11350 Padern, tel. 04.68.45.41.76, fax 04.68.45.02.55 by appt.

DOM. ROUIRE-SEGUR 2000★★

5 ha 7,000 €3-5

Geneviève Bourdel is a heart-and-soul wine-grower, who every year cossets her grape harvest to get the best from her rosé. Her 2000 vintage is a wonderful success. The recipe is still the same: a predominance of Syrah on a Grenache base, with a touch of Cinsault. The result is a wine of crystalline appearance and a range of intense aromas that develops from delicate flowers to berry fruits. The palate opens with an attack that, although quite fresh, is also rounded and soft. A well-integrated wine of great subtlety.

Geneviève Bourdel, Dom. Rouire-Ségur, 11220 Ribaute, tel. 04.68.27.19.76, fax 04.68.27.62.51 by appt.

CH. SAINT-JAMES Prieuré 1999★★

2.9 ha 20,000 €5-8

Henri Gualco entirely rejuvenated Château Saint-James before handing it over to his son Christophe. This excellent *terroir* of scree and fine deposits, between the garrigue and Orbieu, has been replanted, on account of its rather pebbly character and elevated position, primarily with Grenache, alongside Syrah and some Mourvèdre. Christophe's task has been to allow these new vines to express themselves. His supple, down-to-earth 99 has ripe fruit and a discreet note of vanilla. A pleasing wine.

Christophe Gualco, Ch. Saint-James, 11200 Nevian, tel. 04.68.27.00.03
by appt.

SEXTANT SEDUCTION 1998★

n.c. 11,000 €11-15

Occasionally, one comes across a wine that resembles its grower, but it is more unusual to find a wine that is like the cellar-master, especially that of a co-operative. Yet Sextant *is* Alain Cros, which, with its strong personality and solid, direct, generous character. Though a little austere, this wine has no 'side': its generosity is evident in its interestingly complex aromas, and the developing flavours of ripe fruits and black olives.

Vignerons du Mont Tenarel d'Octaviana, 53, rue de la Coopérative, 11200 Ornaisons, tel. 04.68.27.09.76, fax 04.68.27.58.15
ev. day except Sun. 8am–12 noon 2pm–6pm; Sat. 8am–12 noon

TERRA VINEA 1999★

5 ha 20,000 €8-11

This cuvée has profited from the care bestowed on it by oenologist Luc Mazot: faultless selection of source material, harvesting as late as possible, whole-grape vinification, early transfer to cask. Cosseted 80 m (260 ft) underground, in a former gypsum works, the wine has attractively spicy, warm, almost charred aromas. With notes of vanilla on the palate, this is a rounded, full, robust wine of excellent length, with a touch of violet on the finish.

Caves Rocbère, 11490 Portel-des-Corbières, tel. 04.68.48.28.05, fax 04.68.48.45.92
ev. day 9am–12 noon 2pm–7pm

CH. DU VIEUX PARC
La Sélection 1999★

10 ha 50,000 €8-11

A man who loves both nature and sport, Louis Panis is no less passionate about the art of wine-growing. This perfect 99 has a blackberry bouquet, a tiny touch of musk and, as ever, a suggestion of undergrowth. Its fine structure of well-integrated tannins is perfumed with a fresh hint of the garrigue heathland, which lends it elegance and fluidity. To be recommended with roast lamb.

Louis Panis, Ch. du Vieux Parc, av. des Vignerons, 11200 Conilhac-Corbières, tel. 04.68.27.47.44, fax 04.68.27.38.29
by appt.

LE BLANC DU DOMAINE DE VILLEMAJOU
Vinifié en barrique 2000★

7 ha 40,000 €5-8

A good *terroir* cannot lie. Previous editions of the *Guide* have commended Gérard Bertrand for his red and rosé wines. This time, it's a white, but one still bearing his trademark style of oak maturation. This light strawyellow wine with its lively, clear appearance, has a powerful, unusual bouquet of wellbred, toasty oak. The palate is fresh and complex, with well-sustained aromas. The wine is ready for drinking now, but will certainly be just as interesting in two or three years' time.

↝ Dom. Gérard Bertrand, 11200 Saint-André-de-Roquelongue, tel. 04.68.42.68.68, fax 04.68.45.11.73 ▼

Y by appt.

CH. DE VILLENOUVETTE
Cuvée Marcel Barsalou 1998 ★★★

■   4 ha   14,000   €8-11 ▼

PRODUCT OF FRANCE

CHATEAU DE VILLENOUVETTE
Cuvée Marcel Barsalou
CORBIÈRES
1998

In the last century, this former abbey became the site of the Château de Villenouvette, built by Garnier (of Paris Opera House fame). The surrounding vineyard sits on a pebbly, quick-draining terrain in which the roots have to seek out the least traces of moisture to quench their thirst. Hence the strong concentration of fine Syrah and perfect Carignan grapes that Eric Barsalou has brought together here. A remarkably well-handled maturation in oak has contributed much to this exceptional and complex 98. Aromas of black fruits, cooked fruits and undergrowth give of their all when the wine is decanted. The palate exhibits integrated tannins, richness and roundness. This long-lasting, well-balanced Corbières exudes class.

↝ Vignerons de La Méditerranée, ZI Plaisance,12, rue du Rec-de-Veyret, BP 414, 11104 Narbonne Cedex, tel. 04.68.42.75.00, fax 04.68.42.75.01, e-mail rhirtz@listel.fr

Y by appt.

↝ SCEA vignobles Villenouvette

Costières de Nîmes

Maynes, Vauvert, Saint-Gilles and Beaucaire, south-east of Nîmes and north of the Camargue. In 2000, 237,218 hl (6,262,555 gal) of wine were sold under the classification of Appellation Costières de Nîmes (67% of red, 30% of rosé and 3% of white), which is produced in an area covered by 24 communes. The rosés go well with the typical charcuterie of the Cévennes, the whites are a natural complement to seafood and Mediterranean fish, and the reds, which are warm and full-bodied, are especially good with grilled meats. An energetic wine society, the Ordre de la Boisson de la Stricte Observance des Costières de Nîmes, has recently revived local wine-related traditions originally established in 1703. A wine route runs through the region, starting from Nîmes.

Costières de Nîmes

Some 25,000 ha (61,750 acres) of land have been classified as AOC of which 12,000 ha (29,640 acres) are currently planted. Red, rosé or white wines are produced from sunny slopes of smoothed pebbles within a rectangular area bounded by the towns of

CH. AMPHOUX 2000 ★

■   n.c.   17,000   €5-8

Tended by Alain Giran since 1997, this 30-ha (74-acre) estate is devoted to the production of AOC wines. The dark, glossy red has a diversity of aromas that impressed the tasters: undergrowth, violets, spices (pepper). The palate has richness and volume, with tannins that are very evident but silky. The long finish has a flavour of liquorice. An attractive wine with body.

↝ EARL Alain Giran, Ch. Amphoux, rue de La Chicanette, 30640 Beauvoisin, tel. 04.66.01.92.57, fax 04.66.01.97.73

DOM. DES ARMASSONS 2000

■   n.c.   200,000   €3-5

This very deep blue-black co-operative wine has a bouquet that is still closed, and yet hints at red fruits, blackcurrants and spices. The austere tannins will need some time to soften for the wine to express itself properly, but its potential is not in doubt.

↝ SCA Les Vignerons de Jonquières, 20, rue de Nîmes, 30300 Jonquières-Saint-Vincent, tel. 04.66.74.50.07, fax 04.66.74.49.40, e-mail cave.jonquieres@wanadoo.fr ▼ Y by appt.

CH. DES AVEYLANS 2000 ★

■   3.2 ha   22,000   €3-5

A proportion of 70% Syrah has been blended with Grenache to make the 2000 vintage of this wine. Planted on gravel soils, the vines have yielded an attractive, deeply coloured wine with purple highlights. Its youth is full of promise. Though the nose is still closed (aromas of grapeskins), it is sustained by a well-balanced structure in which

Costières de Nîmes

the powerful tannins are still austere. Wait a year. The 97 version gained a *coup de coeur* in the 1999 *Guide*.
➤ EARL Hubert Sendra, Dom. des Aveylans, 30127 Bellegarde, tel. 04.66.70.10.28, fax 04.66.01.02.26 Ⓨ
Ⓨ by appt.

DOM. BARBE-CAILLETTE

Délice de Jovis 2000★

10.5 ha 8,000 €3-5

Two women, one a literature teacher, the other a midwife, decided to establish a wine estate under the aegis of Jupiter. This is their first vintage, and very encouraging it is, too. An attractive bright pink colour, it has an intense and elegant nose of roses, and then fruit (strawberries). The palate has a flavour of pear drops, and a slight spritziness enhances the balance, which is both subtle and supple.
➤ SCEA Barbe-Caillette, Mas Jovis, chem. de Barbe-Caillette, 30600 Vauvert, tel. 04.66.51.34.97, fax 04.66.51.39.21, e-mail pascal.peloce@wanadoo.fr
Ⓨ ev. day 11am–5pm

CH. BEAUBOIS Cuvée Elégance 2000★

5 ha 15,000 €5-8

The parents tend a very fine property of 53 ha (131 acres) to the north of the lake of Scamandre; their son François works in the vineyard, while the daughter Fanny is in charge of the wine-making. As is often the case with the 2000 wines, the colour is very deep purple with violet highlights. The structure is as elegant as the name suggests, and the tannins, rather obvious at present, will soften with time.
➤ SCEA Ch. Beaubois, 30640 Franquevaux, tel. 04.66.73.30.59, fax 04.66.73.33.02, e-mail fannyboyer@chateau-beaubois.com
Ⓨ Ⓨ ev. day 8am–12 noon 2pm–6pm
➤ Boyer

LOUIS BERNARD 2000★

n.c. 200,000 €3-5

Based at Orange, this *négociant* has a strong presence in the appellation. This branded wine has a pleasing purple colour. Its bouquet of grapeskins evokes the harvest. The rounded, full palate, sustained by supple tannins, makes for an easy-drinking wine.
➤ Les Domaines Bernard, rte de Sérignan, 84100 Orange, tel. 04.90.11.86.86, fax 04.90.34.87.30, e-mail sagon@domaines-bernard.fr

CH. PAUL BLANC 2000★

1 ha 3,000 €5-8

Paul Blanc established this estate in 1989. His daughter is an oenologist and has been managing it since 1998. This beautiful golden-yellow wine with green highlights is a single-variety Roussanne grown on red pebbly soils. Behind the very evident oak is discovered the hugely complex aromatic mix of vanilla, pineapple, well-ripened peach and crystallised lemon. The palate is full and unctuous, but a final hint of acidity lends lightness, and is a guarantee of long life. Wait at least one to two years.
➤ Nathalie Blanc-Mares, Mas Carlot, rte de Redessan, ch. Paul Blanc, 30127 Bellegarde, tel. 04.66.01.11.83, fax 04.66.01.62.74 Ⓨ
Ⓨ ev. day 8am–12 noon 2pm–5pm; Sat. Sun. by appt.
➤ Paul Blanc

CH. BOLCHET Tradition 2000★★★

3.8 ha 26,000 €5-8

This estate has made a glittering entry into the *Guide*! Its two red wines vied for the *coup de coeur*. The **Cuvée Prestige red 2000** receives two stars; it is a wine in which Syrah (75%) plays an important role, dominating the bouquet as well as its imposing structure on the palate. Yet in the end, the Cuvée Tradition (50% Syrah) took the top prize for its intense colour and black sheen, and the complex, forthcoming bouquet of fruits of the forest and rich blackcurrant, in which the back of the nose catches a medley of spices and red fruits. After a full-blooded attack on the palate, the wine's balance is faultless. The tannins are superb: powerful and young, yet noble and promising. The finish is very long and well balanced. A particular success, given that 2000 was not that easy a vintage.
➤ Béatrice Becamel, Ch. Bolchet, 30132 Caissargues, tel. 04.66.38.05.65, fax 04.66.29.14.79 Ⓨ Ⓨ ev. day except Sat. & Sun. 8.30am–12 noon 2pm–7pm

MAS DES BRESSADES

Cuvée Tradition 2000★

5 ha 30,000 €3-5

From the pebbly Rhône *terroir*, Cyril Marès has obtained a *rosé de saignée* with pleasingly intense aromas that are predominantly of small berry fruits (redcurrants and raspberries). The palate is attractively round and has good structure.
➤ Cyril Marès, Mas des Bressades, Le Grand-Plagnol, 30129 Manduel, tel. 04.66.01.66.00, fax 04.66.01.80.20 Ⓨ
Ⓨ by appt.

CH. CADENETTE 2000★

24 ha 25,000 €3-5

The Dideron family has been running this estate on the edge of the Camargue since 1962. This wine, with its bright cherry-red highlights, has an intense and delicate fruiti-ness that mingles raspberries, blackcurrants and strawberry fruit-drops. The slightly acid palate is replete with fruit flavours that persist through to a warming finish. The same producer's **rosé 2000 du Domaine de La Guillaumette** similarly gains a one-star rating. It is fruity, full and supple.

☛ Pierre Dideron, La Cadenette, 30600 Vestric-et-Candiac, tel. 04.66.88.21.76, fax 04.66.88.20.59, e-mail chbommel@club-internet.fr ☑
Ⓨ by appt.

■ DOM. DE CAMPAGNOL 2000★

| 6 ha | 41,000 | €5-8 |

The attractive purple colour is pleasing to the eye. A hint of musk, typical of young Syrah, quickly yields to complex aromas of red fruits and violets. The palate is well balanced and silky, with a first impression of suppleness. Offering uncomplicated pleasure, this is a wine that can be drunk straightaway.

☛ Marc Jacquet, Dom. de Campagnol, quartier Grès, 30540 Milhaud, tel. 04.66.74.20.44, fax 04.66.74.18.29, e-mail domaine.campagnol@wanadoo.fr ☑
Ⓨ by appt.

■ MAS CARLOT Cuvée Tradition 2000★

| 7.5 ha | 50,000 | €3-5 |

Two wines impressed the tasters equally: **Les Jeunes Vignes de Carlot white 2000**, with its peach-skin aromas and a note of lemon; black, and a nose that, though still restrained, hints at violets and spices (cinnamon). The full, long-lasting palate has dense tannins and lots of promise.

☛ Nathalie Blanc-Mares, Mas Carlot, rte de Redessan, ch. Paul Blanc, 30127 Bellegarde, tel. 04.66.01.11.83, fax 04.66.01.62.74 ☑
Ⓨ ev. day 8am–12 noon 2pm–5pm: Sat. & Sun. by appt.
☛ Paul Blanc

■ CH. GRANDE CASSAGNE 2000★

| 10 ha | 80,000 | €3-5 |

Hippolyte Dardé, a Parisian wine-merchant, bought this estate in 1887. His descendants have survived all the crises in the Languedoc, but have also enjoyed the successes. Two of their wines are particularly noteworthy. This red wine has a bright purple colour and a powerful bouquet of garrigue aromas and a notes of cooked fruits. The tannins are still very prominent, but support the well-balanced structure of the wine all the way to its warming finish. The other wine, a **rosé 2000** that is redolent of white flowers and fruits, is sustained by good acidity, balanced by roundness and fullness.

☛ Dardé Fils, La Grande Cassagne, 30800 Saint-Gilles, tel. 04.66.87.32.90, fax 04.66.87.32.90 ☑
Ⓨ by appt.

■ CH. GUIOT 2000★

| 35 ha | 230,000 | €3-5 |

This estate lies on one of the routes to Santiago de Compostela, and was acquired

by the Cornut family in 1977. In addition to a very successful **rosé 2000**, this wine has the characteristic deep colouring of the reds of the vintage. The nose is still closed, but there are burgeoning aromas of red fruits and a hint of smokiness. After a rounded opening impression, the palate displays good structure, with dominant tannins guaranteeing that it will age well.

☛ GFA Ch. Guiot, Dom. de Guiot, 30800 Saint-Gilles, tel. 04.66.73.30.86, fax 04.66.73.32.09 ☑ Ⓨ by appt.
☛ Cornut

■ HAUT MOULIN D'EOLE 2000★

| 6 ha | 40,000 | €5-8 |

The co-operative, established in 1928, is located by a windmill that has watched over the vineyard for two centuries. This blend of 80% Syrah with Grenache is an attractive deep red colour. The nose immediately displays fresh, attractive aromas in which herbaceous, red-fruit and grape-skin scents predominate. After a straightforward opening impression, the palate is well balanced by softening tannins that will allow the wine to be enjoyed in a year's time.

☛ SCA Les Vignerons de Beauvoisin, av. de la Gare, 30640 Beauvoisin, tel. 04.66.01.37.14, fax 04.66.01.85.73, e-mail vignerons.beauvoisin@costieres.com ☑ Ⓨ ev. day except Sun. 9am–12 noon 2.30pm–7pm

---

■ DOM. DU HAUT PLATEAU 2000★

| 3 ha | 20,000 | €3-5 |

This wine is made in the image of the surrounding Camargue. Its bluish-black appearance is deep like the sea. Impetuous, full of life and verve, like the horses depicted on the label, its length on the palate leaves an impression of great fullness.

☛ Denis Fournier, Dom. du Haut-Plateau, 30129 Manduel, tel. 04.66.20.31.78, fax 04.66.20.20.53, e-mail FDenis2501@aol.com ☑ Ⓨ by appt.

■ CH. LA COURBADE 2000★

| n.c. | 170,000 | €3-5 |

The colour is deep, with dark purple nuances. Red fruits and violets are uppermost in the bouquet, with pepper and liquorice bringing up the rear. The tannins are still too young and robust, but help to give this warm, full-bodied wine its solid structure. **Domaine de La Figueirasse red 2000** from the same *negociant* is similarly rated.

☛ Les Domaines Bernard, rte de Sérignan, 84100 Orange, tel. 04.90.11.86.86, fax 04.90.34.37.30, e-mail sagon@domaines-bernard.fr ☑
☛ Boucoiran

☐ CH. LAMARGUE 2000★

| 15 ha | 90,000 | €5-8 |

Grenache Blanc (65%), Roussanne (25%) and Rolle, planted on a soil of pebbles and clay, have produced this very clear yellow wine with bright highlights. The nose is floral in type, peach-skin with an attractive hint of lemon, offering great freshness. Its excellent balance on the palate makes it a wine that is good for drinking now, with fish and shellfish.

SCI du Dom. de Lamargue, rte de Vauvert, 30800 Saint-Gilles, tel. 04.66.87.31.89, fax 04.66.87.41.87, e-mail domaine.de.lamargue@wanadoo.fr
by appt.
C. Bonomi

CH. DE L'AMARINE
Cuvée des Bernis 2000★

4 ha　25,000　€5-8

Grenache Blanc (90%) and Roussanne planted on gravel soils have produced this very appealing bright-yellow wine with a scent of dried apricots and more dried fruits on the palate. Round and full, with a slight bite on the finish, this is a well-balanced wine.

SCA Ch. de L'Amarine, Ch. de Campuget, 30129 Manduel, tel. 04.66.20.20.15, fax 04.66.20.60.57, e-mail campuget@wanadoo.fr day except Sun. 10am–12 noon 2pm–6pm
Famille Dalle

DOM. DE LA PATIENCE 2000★

2 ha　4,000　€3-5

An estate whose name appears to encourage a wise approach makes its debut in the *Guide*. Its rosé is a lively colour and has fine, intense floral aromas (roses), with fruity (strawberry) and slight pear-drop notes. The palate is fleshy, full and supple, without any biting acidity. A pleasant, well-balanced wine that will go well with white meats.

EARL dom. de La Patience, chem. des Marguerites, 30320 Bezouce, tel. 04.66.37.40.99, fax 04.66.37.40.99 from Thu. to Sat. 9am–12 noon 2pm–6pm
Christophe Aguilar

DOM. DE L'ARBRE SACRE 2000★

21.6 ha　170,000　€3

This wine has an inviting violet-purple colour, and clearly discernible red fruits on the bouquet. The palate opens roundly enough, and then displays enveloping, high-quality tannins, leading to a warm finish.

La Compagnie rhodanienne, chemin Neuf, 30210 Castillon-du-Gard, tel. 04.66.37.49.50, fax 04.66.37.49.51
by appt.

CH. LA TOUR DE BERAUD 2000★

12 ha　66,660　€3

An ancient fire-tower stands over the estate, and gives its name to this inky-black wine. The complex, powerful bouquet displays perfumes of undergrowth, violets and blackcurrants, then develops towards musky notes. Its structure is sustained by firm tannins through to a warming finish. A successful blend.

François Collard, Ch. des Mourgues du Grès, 30300 Beaucaire, tel. 04.66.59.46.10, fax 04.66.59.34.21 ev. day except Sun. 9am–12 noon 2pm–6pm; Sat. by appt.

CH. DE LA TUILERIE
Vieilles vignes 2000★

3.7 ha　26,000　€8-11

This wine is a blend of one-fifth Grenache from 40-year-old vines with four-fifths Syrah from vines of 25 years old. Thirty per cent of the *cuvée* was matured in oak casks – the new cellar contains 600 barrels – and the resulting wine is a garnet colour with brownish highlights. The elegance of its complex aromas (slight oakiness, toastiness, sweet spices) is a treat for the nose. Long-lasting peppery spice flavours emerge on the palate; this is a warming wine supported by supple tannins. It may be drunk now with red meats.

Chantal et Pierre-Yves Comte, Ch. de La Tuilerie, rte de Saint-Gilles, 30900 Nîmes, tel. 04.66.70.07.52, fax 04.66.70.04.36, e-mail vins@chateautuilerie.com
by appt.

MAS CORINNE 2000★

2.5 ha　20,000　€3

Syrah grapes, grown on pebbly clay soils, have yielded a garnet-coloured wine with delightful violet highlights. The nose is pleasantly complex (violets, soft fruitiness, toasty vanilla notes). On the palate, elegant structure with very evident tannins is revealed – the result of successful vinification and maturation.

La Compagnie rhodanienne, chemin Neuf, 30210 Castillon-du-Gard, tel. 04.66.37.49.50, fax 04.66.37.49.51
by appt.
A. Dalmas

CH. MOURGUES DU GRES
Terre d'Argence 2000★★

5 ha　30,000　€5-8

One of the star-turns in the appellation, Mourgues du Grès offers some superb wines. The leading wine, with its deep colour, has the edge over another red, the **Les Galets Roulés 2000**, which nonetheless receives one star. The musky bouquet has touches of red fruits and beautifully complex notes of undergrowth. Firm tannins do not militate against the impression of a well-balanced wine that is elegant, generous and long-lasting. As to whites, both the white **Terre d'Argence** and **Galets Dorés 2000** receive two stars, like the **2000 rosés: Les Galets Roses**, which is very classic, ideal for exotic or spicy food, and the oak-matured **Capitelles des Mourgues**, which is very fruity, with enough richness to accompany sauced dishes.

François Collard, Ch. des Mourgues du Grès, 30300 Beaucaire, tel. 04.66.59.46.10, fax 04.66.59.34.21 ev. day except Sun. 9am–12 noon 2pm–6pm; Sat. by appt.

CH. DE NAGES
Cuvée Joseph Torrès 2000★

5.5 ha　28,000　€11-15

After ten years' viticultural experience in the United States, Michel Gassier took over from his father in 1999. This beautiful golden-yellow wine is 95% Roussanne, with the remainder Grenache Blanc. The bouquet is composed of heady perfumes of honey and beeswax, while its full, ample-bodied palate offers up burnt notes at the back of the nose. The finish is long and attractive. A superbly judged, oak-aged wine that will further surprise in a year or two.

↝ Vignobles Michel Gassier, Ch. de Nages, 30132 Caissargues, tel. 04.66.38.44.30, fax 04.66.38.44.21, e-mail m_gassier@chateaudenages.com ☑
Υ by appt.

DOM. DU PERE GUILLOT 2000★★

| 1.5 ha | 13,300 | €3 |

Le Père Guillot is a Beaujolais estate in Morgon. The business has also had a presence in the Gard *département* since 1995, and now makes its entry into the *Guide*. The colour of this rosé is a pretty, tender pink. Its subtle, attractive nose has an immediate intensity of fruit aromas, which strengthen on the palate. Well balanced with a touch of acidity that adds freshness, this elegant wine is ready now.

↝ Dom. du Père Guillot, rte du Pont-des-Tourradons, 30740 Le Cailar, tel. 04.66.88.69.60, fax 04.66.88.69.61, e-mail laurent.guillot3@wanadoo.fr
Υ by appt.
↝ GFA du Grand Bourry

PREFERENCE 2000★

| n.c. | 20,000 | €3 |

This is a very deeply coloured blend of half-Grenache, half-Syrah. The bouquet is a mix of red berry fruits, preserved fruits and new leather. Some ageing is needed in order to tame the currently dominant tannins.

↝ SCA Costières et Soleil, rue Emile-Bilhau, 30510 Générac, tel. 04.66.01.31.31, fax 04.66.01.38.85 ☑
Υ ev. day except Sun. 10am–12.30pm 3.30pm–7pm

CH. DE RATY 2000★

| 10.8 ha | 80,000 | €3-5 |

This is one of the oldest châteaux in Costières, its wines produced by the Générac co-operative. This very dark 2000 vintage has a still-discreet nose of violets and fruits that should develop over time. The palate, after a round, straightforward first impression, goes on to reveal quality tannins that are very evident but not too astringent, leading to an attractive finish.

↝ SCA Costières et Soleil, rue Emile-Bilhau, 30510 Générac, tel. 04.66.01.31.31, fax 04.66.01.38.85
Υ ev. day except Sun. 10am–12.30pm 3.30pm–7pm

DOM. SAINT-ANTOINE

Cuvée réservée 2000★

| 11 ha | 5,000 | €3-5 |

The colour is so dark, it is almost black. For the time being, the bouquet is still quite discreet, and the aromas are more perceptible on the palate. Several more years are needed for this wine to mature, and for its very severe

tannic structure to calm down. On the other hand, the rosé 2000, also a one-star wine, is already good to drink. Fresh, lively, long and full of flavour, it will go well with fish.

↝ Jean-Louis Emmanuel, Dom. Saint-Antoine, 30800 Saint-Gilles, tel. 04.66.01.87.29, fax 04.66.01.87.29 ☑
Υ by appt.

CH. SAINT-CYRGUES 2000★★

| n.c. | 7,000 | €5-8 |

The colour is a uniform pale gold, the aromas are of peach skins, and the well-balanced palate has interesting levels of acidity for this particular year. The château gains one star for its 2000 red. Red fruits and berries (blackcurrants and bilberries) share a bouquet enhanced by a hint of spice. Full and rounded, despite its powerful tannins, this is a wine dominated by the presence of Syrah, very true to its *terroir*.

↝ SCEA de Mercurio, Ch. Saint-Cyrgues, 30800 Saint-Gilles, tel. 04.66.87.31.72, fax 04.66.87.70.76, e-mail g.demercurio@ free.fr ☑ Υ by appt.

DOM. SAINT-ETIENNE 2000★

| 12 ha | 5,000 | €3-5 |

Located on the Costières de Nîmes and Côtes du Rhône border, this estate, well known to readers of the *Guide*, offers wines from both appellations. This attractive, sun-filled Costières has a bouquet that marries aromas of fresh fruits, adding up to a supple and well-balanced whole. It may be drunk now.

↝ Michel Coullomb, Dom. Saint-Etienne, fg du Pont, 30490 Montfrin, tel. 04.66.57.50.20, fax 04.66.57.22.78 ☑
Υ by appt.

CH. SILEX 2000★★

| 16 ha | 53,000 | €5-8 |

This estate, acquired in 1999 by Domaine Saint-Bénézet, enjoys the benefit of a talented manager. This highly attractive deep-purple wine releases complex aromas of red fruits and pepper, with slight vegetal hints too. The attack is rounded and full, and the palate continues pleasantly, sustained by velvety, quality tannins. Its good balance should guarantee it a life of two to three years.

↝ SCEA Saint-Bénézet, Dom. Saint-Bénézet, 30800 Saint-Gilles, tel. 06.16.57.32.02, fax 06.66.70.05.11 ☑
Υ ev. day except Sun. 8am–7pm
↝ Bosse-Platière

CH. VESSIERE 2000★

| 20 ha | 180,000 | €5-8 |

Twenty-five-year-old Syrah (80%) and 18-year-old Grenache (20%) vines, grown on the gravelly soils of the Costières, have yielded this intense red wine. The bouquet is still timid, with very discreet aromas of cooked fruits, followed by more complex, vegetally tinged notes of red fruits. After a rounded first impression, the structure of the wine

Coteaux du Languedoc

is sturdy, sustained by tannins that are still immature, and leading up to a warming finish.

⚑ Philippe Teulon, Ch. Vessière, 30800 Saint-Gilles, tel. 04.66.73.30.66, fax 04.66.73.33.04, e-mail chateau.vessiere@pol.fr ☑
Ⴑ by appt.

Coteaux du Languedoc

These wines are grown in an area of moors and hills stretching from Narbonne to Nîmes. A total of 168 communes, five of which are in the Aude and 19 in the Gard, the remainder in the Hérault, contribute to the appellation, specialising in red and rosé wines. AOC Coteaux du Languedoc has been an Appellation Générale since 1985, added to which are 11 specific denominations of red and rosé wines: La Clape and Quatourze in the Aude, Cabrières, Montpeyroux, Saint-Saturnin, Pic-Saint-Loup, Saint-Georges-d'Orques, Les Coteaux de la Méjanelle, Saint-Drézéry, Saint-Christol and the Coteaux de Vérargues in the Hérault; there are also two white denominations: La Clape and Picpoul de Pinet.

All are descended from wines that have been renowned for centuries. In 2000, the Coteaux du Languedoc produced, from 9,900 ha (24,453 acres), 62,552 hl (1,651,373 gal) of white wine and 449,182 hl (11,858,404 gal) of red and rosé wine.

ABBAYE DES MONGES
La Clape 2000★
■ 2 ha 13,000 ■ ♦ €3-5

A Cistercian convent was founded in this area at the start of the 12th century. The wine-growing tradition has continued right down to the 2000 vintage, and the estate receives a star for its **white**, and also for this red, which has a fine purple colour with violet highlights. It is redolent of toast, red fruits and a hint of musk. The tannins are evident but not excessive, and its warming palate suggests that it would go well with lamb roasted in herbs.

⚑ Paul de Chefdebien, 45, rue Parerie, 11100 Narbonne, tel. 04.68.42.36.27, fax 04.68.41.53.07, e-mail dechefdebien-marco@wanadoo.fr ☑
Ⴑ by appt.

ABBAYE DE VALMAGNE
Cuvée de Turenne 1999★
■ 15 ha 24,000 ■ ♦ €8-11

Tradition continues in this oratory dedicated to the vine and wine, one of the last Cistercian abbeys to honour its viticultural vocation, but now in lay hands. The 1999 is a deep, dense red, redolent of the garrigue heathlands, fruity and spicy, with discreet oakiness that heralds a rich, full palate of fine, concentrated body and length. Try also the **white 2000 de l'Abbaye**, which is all flowers and fruits, and comes highly commended by a panel of experienced tasters.

⚑ Philippe d'Allaines, Abbaye de Valmagne, 34560 Villeveyrac, tel. 04.67.78.06.09, fax 04.67.78.02.50 ☑
Ⴑ by appt.

ARNAUD DE NEFFIEZ
Élevé en fût de chêne 1999★
■ 5 ha 10,000 ■■■ €8-11

The marriage of Arnaud de Neffiez and **Catherine de Saint-Juéry**, the latter receiving a commendation, is made to last. Their constancy is heartening. Both are a deep garnet colour and have bouquets of ripe fruits, which on the Neffiez is a trifle shy, subtly oaky, charred, chocolatey, but more open (with toasty and floral notes) in the case of the Saint-Juéry. The Neffiez's powerful tannins contrast with the velvety elegance of the Saint-Juéry, but their well-balanced and long-lasting palates unite them once more.

⚑ Cave coop. de Neffies, av. de la Gare, 34320 Neffies, tel. 04.67.24.61.98, fax 04.67.24.62.12 ☑

DOM. HONORE AUDRAN
Cuvée Terroir 1999★★★
■ 1 ha 4,000 ■■■ ♦ €8-11

In a wild, spellbinding landscape of hot red shades that has so captivated his heart, Luc Biscarlet continues his father's passion for viticulture. Wines like this put one in a state of grace. Biscarlet's Terroir *cuvée* contains nothing to criticise. Its dark purple, almost black, colour is an invitation to mystery and dreams, which deepen as you scent the aromas: liquorice and hints of the garrigue, truffles and jam being cooked. The immediately powerful, rich palate has great length and character, and is the fruit of extremely skilful handling.

GAEC Luc Biscarlet Père et Fils, 8, chem. du Moulin, 34700 Le Bosc, tel. 04.67.44.73.44, fax 04.67.44.73.44 ▼
Y by appt.

CH. BELLES EAUX

Elevé en fût de chêne 1998

| 5.6 ha | 30,000 | €5-8 |

A wine-growing château since 1824, Belles Eaux offers a purple 98 with a complex, attractive bouquet of red fruits, bursting with sunshine, toast and spice. The reticent palate exhibits tannins that are still austere, and that necessitate three to four years' keeping.
Ch. Belles Eaux, 34720 Caux, tel. 04.67.09.30.95, fax 04.67.09.30.95 ▼
Y ev. day except Sat. 10am–12 noon 4pm–6pm

DOM. BELLES PIERRES

Les Clauzes de Jo 1998★

| 3 ha | 8,000 | €8-11 |

In this village founded in Roman times, Damien Coste has a vineyard that receives his every attention. This 1998 wine honours his father. Still strong in colour, it regales the nose with charred and fruity notes. The well-balanced palate marries strength and lightness to make a wine of character that is by no means dominated by its twelve months in oak.
Damien Coste, 24, rue des Clauzes, 34570 Murviel-les-Montpellier, tel. 04.67.47.30.43, fax 04.67.47.30.43 ▼

CH. BERANGER

Picpoul de Pinet 2000★

| 40 ha | 300,000 | €3-5 |

You won't regret stopping at this cellar and being served, on an oyster-shaped counter, with these three Picpoul de Pinet wines, all of which impressed the Jury. The **Cuvée Hugues de Beauvignac 2000** and the **Cuvée Prestige 99**, which spent ten months in oak, were both commended. The starred 2000 vintage that ended the millennium is pale with green nuances, and mixes aromas of citrus fruits (lemon, grapefruit) with aniseed. The palate's roundness is appropriately cut by its acidity.
A great classic.
Cave Les Costières de Pomérols, 34810 Pomérols, tel. 04.67.77.01.59, fax 04.67.77.21, e-mail pomerols@mnet.fr ▼ Y by appt.

MAS BRUGUIERE

Pic Saint-Loup La Grenadière 1999★

| 3.5 ha | 18,000 | €11-15 |

For more than 25 years, Mas Bruguière has been one of the estates at the forefront of developments in the beautiful Languedoc region. Its wines are utterly reliable. The **L'Arbouse red 2000**, which gained a commendation, is already very attractive, despite its youth. But La Grenadière, with its irresistible deep purple colour, has both a complex bouquet (smoke, the garrigue, ripe fruits and undergrowth) and a generous, yet well-structured palate. This is a well-integrated wine that finishes on subtle notes of tobacco.
Guilhem Bruguière, 34270 Valflaunès, tel. 04.67.55.20.97, fax 04.67.55.20.97 ▼
Y by appt.

MAS BRUNET

Elevé en fût de chêne 1999

| 0.9 ha | 7,300 | €5-8 |

This lovely golden-yellow 99 has an intense, subtly oaky bouquet with strong notes of citrus fruits and toast. Lively, round and soft, with admirable length, it will be at its best in a year or even two.
GAEC du Dom. de Brunet, Mas Brunet, rte de Saint-Jean-de-Buèges, 34380 Causse-de-la-Selle, tel. 04.67.73.10.57, fax 04.67.73.12.89 ▼
Y by appt.
M. Coulet

LES VIGNERONS DE CABRIERES

Cabrières Fulcran Cabanon 2000★★

| 15 ha | 40,000 | €5-8 |

Three wines are presented by the Vignerons de Cabrières, who are increasingly getting the best out of their terroirs. Take, for example, this Fulcran Cabanon, a leading wine of its type, with its resplendent youth. Deep red in colour with violet highlights and already aromatically expressive, it is highly perfumed with red fruits, nutmeg, cocoa and menthol. The palate does not disappoint, with its round, mouth-filling character and length; the tannins promise great things in a couple of years' time. Note also these two one-star wines: the subtly oaky **Château Cabrières Terres des Guilhem**, and the **Prieuré Saint-Martin des Crozes, Elevé en Fût de Chêne**, which is still somewhat closed up. These would both be best left for three to five years before opening.
Cave des Vignerons de Cabrières, 34800 Cabrières, tel. 04.67.88.91.60, fax 04.67.88.00.15, e-mail sea.cabrieres@wanadoo.fr ▼ Y ev. day except Sun. 9am–12 noon 2pm–6pm

MAS CAL DEMOURA

Pierre d'Alipe 1999★

| 4.4 ha | 19,000 | €11-15 |

Cal Demoura in the local dialect means 'you must stay'. On the soil, it goes without saying, Jean-Pierre Jullien offers some further exquisite wines. **L'Infidèle 99, Elevé en Fût**, commended by the Jury, promises to be superb in years to come. Pierre d'Alipe is a currently more approachable wine with a deep blackberry colour. The bouquet offers attractive aromatic complexity, with hints of dried flowers, spices and red fruits. Finesse, roundness and dense tannins characterise the balance on the palate. Though already opened up, the wine does not lack concentration, and could wait a further five years or so. Give a thought, too, to the elegant and classic **rosé 2000**, also a one-star wine.
Jean-Pierre Jullien, Mas Cal Demoura, 34725 Jonquières, tel. 04.67.88.61.51, fax 04.67.88.61.51 ▼ Y by appt.

Coteaux du Languedoc

CH. DE CAPITOUL
La Clape Les Rocailles 2000★

■ 3 ha 10,000 ■ €5-8

A former property of the canons of Saint-Just Cathedral in Narbonne, Capitoul offers its Rocailles *cuvées*, the white version of which last year so impressed the Grand Jury. This version is salmon-pink, and displays gorgeously caramelised aromas of exotic fruits. It is also developing a roundly balanced palate full of flavour and length. The **white 2000** also impressed, and is duly commended this year.

➤ Ch. de Capitoul,
rte de Gruissan, 11100 Narbonne,
tel. 04.68.49.23.30, fax 04.68.49.55.71,
e-mail chateau.capitoul@wanadoo.fr ☑
Ⓨ ev. day 8am–8pm
➤ Charles Mock

DOM. DE CASSAGNOLE 2000★

■ 1 ha 2,500 ■ €3-5

The Cassagnole vineyard is at Assas, 2 km (1.3 miles) from the château and its ruined medieval fortifications. The **red 99** gains a commendation, but the rosé was even more attractive, with its soft and tender character. Light in colour, it has a fresh, fruity bouquet (strawberries and citrus fruits) and a supple, well-balanced, roundly inviting palate. Delicious.

➤ Jean-Marie Sabatier, Dom. de Cassagnole, chem. de Bellevue, 34820 Assas, tel. 04.67.55.30.02, fax 04.67.55.30.02 ☑
Ⓨ by appt.

CH. DE CAZENEUVE
Pic Saint-Loup Le Roc des Mates 2000★★★

■ 3 ha 15,000 ■ €11-15

The president of the Pic Saint-Loup syndicate really knows how to get the best out of this stony vineyard surrounded by garrigue heathland. His **Cuvée Le Sang du Calvaire 2000** gains two stars, but the Pic Saint-Loup *terroir* comes into its own in this Roc des Mates. Top-quality grapes, ripened to perfection, have resulted in a purple, almost mysterious colour. The bouquet is rich and powerful, mixing notes of small black jammy fruits, black olives and almonds, with liquorice and a medley of other spices. The fullness and integration of the flavours and tannins, allied to its great length on the palate, entice one to taste the wine over and over simply for the pleasure of it. But those who have the patience to wait a further two to five years will be handsomely rewarded.

➤ André Leenhardt, Ch. de Cazeneuve, 34270 Lauret, tel. 04.67.59.07.49, fax 04.67.59.06.91 ☑ Ⓨ by appt.

DOM. CHARTREUSE DE MOUGERES Clos de l'Abbaye
Elevé en fût de chêne 1999★

■ 2 ha 10,000 ■ €5-8

Convents, as is well known, favour meditation. Prepare to attain divine grace with the Clos 99 from the *chartreuses* at Mougères! The deep ruby colour with dark purple nuances is a delight, as is the bouquet, which is floral and mineral, toasty and spicy. Let yourself be drawn in by the joyful, long-lasting palate, which is all fullness, roundness and elegance.

➤ Sareh Bonne Terre,
rte de Béziers, 34120 Tourbes,
tel. 04.67.98.40.01, fax 04.67.98.46.39,
e-mail nicolas.lebecq@libertysurf.fr ☑
Ⓨ Tues.-Sat. 9am–12 noon 2pm–5pm

MAS DES CHIMERES 1999★

■ 3 ha 19,000 ■ €8-11

If life, love and their illusions are tending to lose you in the labyrinth of lost hearts, stop at Dardé's and try his wine. It is dark as ebony, with a bouquet that is at once mineral, roasted and floral, like the garrigue heathland, and a palate that is magnificently sculpted, elegant, delicate and extremely long-lasting. The oak, however, is still somewhat over-dominant. Give it two to three years to settle down.

➤ Guilhem Dardé, Mas des Chimères, 34800 Octon, tel. 04.67.96.22.70, fax 04.67.88.07.00 ☑ Ⓨ by appt.

CLOS MARIE
Pic Saint-Loup Simon 1998★

■ 3 ha 14,000 ■ €5-8

The 1998 vintage was characterised by wines of very high concentration, all the more so if severe pruning was undertaken and harvesting was done 'green' to produce restricted yields. This Pic Saint-Loup is a direct result of such good practices. It is a dark wine with a rich, complex bouquet expressive of the garrigue, of roasting, of blackcurrants, fruits in brandy and spices (a hint of liquorice). On the palate, the dense body and still-compacted tannins suggest that the wine should be left for four to five years before drinking.

➤ Christophe Peyrus, Clos Marie, 34270 Lauret, tel. 04.67.59.06.96, fax 04.67.59.08.56 ☑ Ⓨ by appt.

DOM. PHILIPPE COMBES 1998★

■ 1.75 ha 5,000 ■ €11-15

Here is a wine-grower returning to the *Guide* in splendid form after a few years' absence. This wine is remarkable, with its deep and intense ruby colour, and rich and complex aromas of red fruits and spices, enhanced by a touch of leather and undergrowth. A four-square first impression introduces a concentrated palate with powerful tannic structure which, though very obtrusive for the time being, shows good breeding.

➤ Philippe Combes, 32, av. de Lodève, 34725 Saint-André-de-Sang onis, tel. 04.67.25.24.21, fax 04.67.57.28.20 ☑ Ⓨ ev. day 9.30am–7pm

CH. CONDAMINE BERTRAND

Elixir 2000★★   2 ha   n.c.   €15-23

Condamine Bertrand has been a family estate since 1792, and runs to 52 ha (128 acres). Its Elixir 2000 is a darkly coloured wine with black highlights. The bouquet is striking: intense and complex, it discharges wine with preserved fruits, spices and undergrowth, with brioche-like toasted and charred notes. The palate begins straightforward and full, and goes on to disclose a powerful structure of silky, long-lasting tannins.

Bertrand Jany.
Ch. Condamine Bertrand, 34230 Paulhan, tel. 04.67.25.27.96, fax 04.67.25.07.55, e-mail chateau.condamineber@free.fr
ev. day except Sun. 10am–12 noon 2pm–6pm

DOM. COSTE ROUGE 2000★

18.46 ha   35,000

Selection of grapes by plot has made it possible at Gabian to create this intensely red wine with violet highlights and an opulent bouquet of red and black fruits, the garrigue and spices. After a down-to-earth first impression, the palate is beautifully structured, well-wrought and impressively long. At barely more than one year old, this is already a grown-up wine.

Cave coopérative La Carignano,
13, rte de Pouzolles, 34320 Gabian,
tel. 04.67.24.65.64, fax 04.67.24.80.98,
e-mail stéphane.pouyet@libertysurf.fr

COURSAC Elevé en fût de chêne 1999★   0.35 ha   1,600

This wine's attractive bright purple colour is a sure sign of oak maturation. The oaky notes evident in the bouquet blend with aromas of toast and spices. The palate is dominated by tannins, but they are sufficiently balanced by its richness. An elegant wine that impressed the Jury. Drink from spring 2002 to accompany duck breast.

SCA Les Vignerons de Carnas,
30260 Carnas, tel. 04.66.77.30.76,
fax 04.66.77.14.20   ev. day except Sun.
8am–12 noon 2pm–6pm

CH. CREYSSELS Picpoul de Pinet 2000

2.5 ha   7,500

This 16th-century house and estate are located 500 m (550 yards) from the Via Domitiana, close to the lake of Thau. The white wine indubitably belongs to the Picpoul de Pinet family, given its pale-gold colour and aromas of citrus fruits (lemon and grapefruit). Though predominantly fresh-tasting, the palate has an appealing warmth that gives it balance. Excellent, of course, with oysters. The white 2000 Elevé en Fût will be better with grilled fish or white meats in a year or two.

J. et M. Benau, Dom. de Creyssels,
34140 Mèze, tel. 04.67.43.80.82,
fax 04.67.18.82.06   ev. day except Mon.
10am–12 noon 4pm–6.30pm

DOM. DEVOIS DU CLAUS

Pic Saint-Loup 1999★   1.9 ha   8,300   €8-11

These are early days for Devois du Claus as an individual cellar, and this wine marks its honourable entry into the Guide. Dark in colour, it has an authentic bouquet of very ripe, jammy fruits. The palate is both round and concentrated, with excellent length and balance.

Dom. Devois du Claus, 38, imp. du Porche, 34270 Saint-Mathieu-de-Tréviers, tel. 06.75.37.19.58, fax 06.67.55.06.86
by appt.
André Gely

DOM. DURAND-CAMILLO 1999★★

3 ha   9,000   €5-8

This wine is a precious commodity, which every year rewards the care that is bestowed upon it. The 1999 vintage is a mottled red with violet highlights. Within its aromatic range may be detected hints of toastiness, tempting aromas of cherries in brandy, jammy fruits and spices. The palate is rounded, fleshy and balanced, with well-balanced length and supportive, if still quite compacted, tannins. Patience is required.

Armand Durand, 26, av. de Fontès, 34720 Caux, tel. 04.67.09.32.46, fax 04.67.09.32.46, e-mail durand.armand@wanadoo.fr   by appt.

ERMITAGE DU PIC SAINT-LOUP

Pic Saint-Loup Cuvée Sainte-Agnès 1999   6 ha   30,000   €8-11

The highly distinctive label on the bottle depicts a fine escutcheon decorated with three fishes. Equally worthy of note is the wine inside it, with its deep purple highlights and its subtle bouquet of Indian spices and red fruits. On the palate, it is soft-textured and appealing: a down-to-earth, food-friendly wine.

Ravaille, GAEC Ermitage du Pic Saint-Loup, Cazevieille,
34270 Saint-Mathieu-de-Tréviers,
tel. 04.67.55.20.15, fax 04.67.55.23.49
by appt.

DOM. FELINES JOURDAN

Picpoul de Pinet 2000★   30 ha   100,000   €3-5

This is an attractive Picpoul de Pinet that is very true to type. Its colour is light with golden highlights, while the bouquet is marked by fruity notes jostling with aromas of white flowers and honey. The palatal balance marries fullness with that acidic edge that is so characteristic of the terroir. A certain fleshiness on the finish suggests that the grapes were picked at optimum ripeness.

GAEC du Relais Jourdan,
Dom. Félines Jourdan, 34140 Mèze,
tel. 04.67.43.69.29, fax 04.67.43.69.29,
e-mail felines-jourdan@free.fr
by appt.

DOM. FERRI ARNAUD La Clape

Cuvée Romain Elevé en fût de chêne 1999★★

■ 1.5 ha 6,500 🍷 €11-15

Between the rocks and the sea, at Fleury-d'Aude, the stony, sun-drenched *terroir* of La Clape speaks fully and eloquently through purple, the bouquet intense, with aromas of toasty oak, truffles and violets. The palate is rich and solidly structured, its strong presence sustained by well-managed oak maturation. No wonder this fine 99 came close to being a *coup de coeur*. You will not be disappointed either by **La Clape 99**, another classic wine that merited a commendation by the Jury.

🍷 EARL Ferri Arnaud, av. de l'Hérault, 11560 Fleury-d'Aude, tel. 04.68.33.62.43, fax 04.68.33.74.38 ☑

🍴 ev. day 9.30am–1pm 3pm–8pm

🍷 Richard Ferri

CH. DE FLAUGERGUES La

Méjanelle Cuvée fût de chêne 1998★

■ 6.5 ha 28,000 🍷 €11-15

Flaugergues is the oldest of Montpellier's follies, being a historic monument whose château and gardens are open to visitors. Its wines and the typical *terroir* of round pebbles also merit a detour. The **white Sommelière 2000** receives a commendation. The 98 red has been carefully matured in oak. With its lovely garnet colour, aromas of stewed fruits and spices, not forgetting the rounded palate and tannic presence, it is a wine with a future.

🍷 Henri de Colbert, Ch. de Flaugergues,1744, av. Albert-Einstein, 34000 Montpellier, tel. 04.99.52.66.34, fax 04.99.52.66.44, e-mail colbert@flaugergues.com ☑ 🍴 by appt.

FOULAQUIER

Pic Saint-Loup L'Orphée 2000★★

■ 2 ha 10,000 🍷 €5-8

A grand entrance into the *Guide* is made by this 8-ha (20-acre) estate in the heart of this Pic Saint-Loup *terroir*. The Foulaquier property has been recently re-equipped to get the

best results from its top-quality hand-harvested grapes. Its purple colour indicates the wine's depth. The bouquet is intense and complex, marrying aromas of pink peppercorns and eucalyptus that are extremely inviting and that reappear on the palate. Lovers of good food and wine, assured of its fleshy and mouth-filling character, with its aromatic richness and silky yet sturdy tannic structure, will not mind keeping this wine for a year or two to develop.

🍷 SCEA du dom. Foulaquier, Mas Foulaquier, 34270 Claret, tel. 04.67.59.96.94, fax 04.67.59.96.94, e-mail mas.foulaquier@free.fr ☑ 🍴 by appt.

🍷 Pierre et Maïté Jequier

MAS DE FOURNEL

Pic Saint-Loup Cuvée classique 1999★

■ 3 ha 5,000

The star awarded is evidence of the constant quality of Mas de Fournel, which achieved a *coup de coeur* last year with its Cuvée Pierre. This lovely deep red, with its intense bouquet and provocative aromatic range of blackcurrants, black olives, liquorice and cocoa, has a palate of enveloping softness that is underlined by its charming balance and estimable length.

🍷 Gérard Jeanjean, SCEA Mas de Fournel, 34270 Valflaunès, tel. 04.67.55.22.12, fax 04.67.55.22.12 ☑ 🍴 ev. day 9am–6pm

DOM. GALTIER Kermès 1998★

■ 2 ha 7,000 🍷 €5-8

Lise Carbonne took over the estate in 1995, and her success is evident in this intensely purple 98 with its matching highlights. The rich and elegant bouquet reveals scents of well-ripened red fruits against a background of grilled, spicy, chocolate and mocha notes, which testify to the subtleness of the oak. The palate is round and unctuous, subtly balanced and laudably long.

🍷 Lise Carbonne, Dom. Galtier, lieu-dit Mas-Maury, 34490 Murviel-lès-Béziers, tel. 04.67.37.85.14, fax 04.67.37.97.43 ☑ 🍴 ev. day 10am–12 noon 3pm–6.30pm

MAS GRANIER Les Grès 1999★★

■ 2 ha 5,000 🍷 €8-11

After the white that gained two stars in the *Guide* last year, it's now the turn of the red. The Aspères *terroir* never ceases to surprise, but the Granier brothers are working on upgrading it. The Jury had a real weakness for this wine, firstly because of its superb dark purple colour, and then for its rich aromatic range, which features notes of coffee, red-fruit preserves, pepper and wax. Last but not least, the palate fulfils all expectations, with its generosity, concentrated, elegant body and excellent length. One taster confessed that he wanted to drink it there and then ...

🍷 EARL Granier, Mas Montel, 30250 Aspères, tel. 04.66.80.01.21, fax 04.66.80.01.87, e-mail montel@wanadoo.fr ☑ 🍴 ev. day except Sun. 9am–12 noon 2pm–7pm

CH. FONDOUCE Réserve 2000★

■ 7.5 ha 11,000 🍷 €3-5

There is nothing strange about an ancient estate like Fondouce being associated with the Languedoc's viticultural renaissance. This red Réserve 2000, with its pleasing violet overtones, is the proof. The bouquet releases aromas of jammy fruits (morello cherries and prunes), deliciously underlined by spices, and while the palate has the tenderness of youth, it is also full, long-lasting and sturdy, owing to its surprisingly well-structured tannins. Worth trying too is the commended **Fondouce 2000**.

🍷 Jean-Claude Magnien, Ch. Fondouce, rte de Roujan, 34120 Pezenas, tel. 04.67.76.06.03, fax 04 67.76.46.39, e-mail sicla@wanadoo.fr ☑ 🍴 ev. day except Sat. & Sun. 10am–12 noon 3pm–7pm

DOM. DE GRANOUPIAC 1999*

3.65 ha   19,500   €5-8

Going from Montpellier towards Le Larzac, you come across the wide limestone terraces of Granoupiac. More laurels are awarded this year to this estate: one star for its oak-matured Cuvée Les Cresses 99, and another for this wine with its dark appearance and attractive aromas of smoke, cooked fruits and spices. Its roundness and silky tannins enable it to give an impression of simultaneous strength and subtlety. A totally reliable wine.

↳ Claude Flavard, Dom. de Granoupiac, 34725 Saint-André-de-Sangonis, tel. 04.67.57.58.28, fax 04.67.57.95.83, e-mail cflavard@infonie.fr Y by appt.

CH. GRÈS SAINT-PAUL

Antonin 1999**

11.25 ha   48,000   €11-15

After last year's *coup de cœur*, Grès Saint-Paul show again that their wines are among the best. This was not an easy vintage, but here the pebbly *terroir* and the wine-grower's talent got the upper hand. This dense, bilberry-coloured wine has complex perfumes of spices, well-ripened red fruits and chocolate. The palate is high quality, with a generous character and dense, elegant tannins. The wine's concentration and powerful flavours are guarantees of great promise.

↳ Ch. Grès Saint-Paul, rte de Restinclières, 34400 Lunel, tel. 04.67.71.27.90, fax 04.67.71.73.76, e-mail contact@gres-saint-paul.com Y ev. day except Sun. 10am-12 noon 3pm-7pm

↳ Servière

DOM. GUINAND

Saint-Christol Cuvée fût de chêne 1998*

2 ha   10,000   €8-11

This estate, which has been in the same family since the end of the 19th century, offers a high-quality *cuvée* that can be enjoyed from now on. Its oak maturation blends perfectly with the aromas of fruits and the garrigue. The palate is round and supple, with hints of sweet spices, and the finish harmonious.

↳ Dom. Guinand, 36, rue de l'Espargne, 34400 Saint-Christol, tel. 04.67.86.85.55, fax 04.67.86.07.59 Y ev. day except Sun. 10am-12 noon 3pm-6pm

MAS HAUT-BUIS Coste Cavre 1999

n.c.   7,000   €15-23

The Cirque de Navacelles, visible from the edge of the Larzac plateau, well deserves its two stars in the *Guide Bleu*, as it is a listed site. But don't forget to call in on Olivier Jeantet if you visit the area. His cellars are on the Larzac *causse* (the limestone plateau). Jeantet does nothing by halves, creating wines that are superbly concentrated, like this one, which deserves to be tasted again in about five years' time. Deep red with black highlights, this promising 99 has a bouquet that needs to lose some of its dominant woody notes. The palate has an air of distinction, but the wine's potential is at present masked by the reticence of youth. Still, it has a great future ahead of it. The same goes for Les Carlines 99, also commended.

↳ Olivier Jeantet, 34520 La Vacquerie, tel. 04.67.44.12.13, fax 04.67.44.12.13 Y by appt.

CH. HAUT-CHRISTIN 1999*

4 ha   25,000   €5-8

This is the easternmost district in the Coteaux du Languedoc, in the heart of the Sommières, and has stamped its character on this intensely garnet-coloured 99. The bouquet displays aromas of leather and roasting, as well as cherries in brandy, which make a strong return on the finish. The structure of the wine is already ripe, and fills the mouth well. The **rosé 2000**, though not star-rated, has attractive floral notes.

↳ André et Marie-France Mahuziès, rte d'Aubais, 30250 Junas, tel. 04.66.80.95.90, fax 04.66.80.95.90, e-mail mahuzies@aol.com Y ev. day 9am-12 noon 2pm-6pm; groups and Sun. by appt.

LES COTEAUX DES HAUTES GARRIGUES Pic Saint-Loup

Hameau des Biranques 1999*

7 ha   10,000   €3-5

Grown on a stony *terroir* that gives the Syrah and Grenache varieties scope for boundless expression, this wine ravishes the eye with its garnet colour and youthful highlights. Red fruits mingle with spices to provide a bouquet of considerable intensity. Charred and mineral notes, together with soft tannins, offer the illusion of a return to the wine's source, a journey to the heart of the vineyard.

↳ Cave coop. des coteaux des Hautes Garrigues, 198, rte du Pic-Saint-Loup, 34380 Saint-Martin-de-Londres, tel. 04.67.55.00.12, fax 04.67.55.78.54 Y by appt.

DOM. HORTALA

La Clape Tradition 1999*

4.5 ha   26,000   €5-8

In 1999, Jean-Marie Hortala took over this family vineyard set in a stony landscape of garrigue, sun and wind. The results are his one-star Les Hauts de Bouisset red 99, and this similarly rated wine with its elegant purple appearance. Garrigue, liquorice and menthol all establish the bouquet's character. The palate has real personality, with tannins that make their presence felt after a silky opening impression. There is still a future in store for this wine.

↳ Jean-Marie Hortala, 20, rue Diderot, 11560 Fleury-d'Aude, tel. 04.68.33.37.74, fax 04.68.33.37.75, e-mail vins-hortala@wanadoo.fr Y by appt.

CH. DES HOSPITALIERS 2000★

□ 1.2 ha 5,000 ▪ ♦ €3-5

In the 12th century, the Knights of Malta made a clearing in the forest to plant vines. Maybe this wine represents the soul of that ancient vineyard? Its gleaming, light-yellow colour is a delight, as is the subtle and intense bouquet of small white fruits and citrus. The well-integrated palate has a good balance of richness and liveliness, and the finish is soft and long. Try also the one-star **Cuvée Prestige rosé 2000**, with its bouquet of broom and mandarin orange, and its palate of red fruits, figs and blackcurrants.

•→ Martin-Pierrat, rond-point du Gal-Chaffard, 34400 Saint-Christol, tel. 04.67.86.01.15, fax 04.67.86.00.19, e-mail serge.martin-pierrat@wanadoo.fr ▼
Ⅰ ev. day 8am–8pm

CH. ICARD
Saint-Georges d'Orgues 2000★★

▪ n.c. 7,000 ■ €5-8

In 1999, Laurent Icard threw off his co-operative moorings and launched himself as an independent wine-grower. His reward: two stars. This beautiful dark red wine with its many violet highlights unveils aromas of leather, violet and the garrigue. After a forth-right opening impression, the palate reveals a powerful structure with obvious, yet velvety tannins, and good overall length.

•→ Laurent Icard, rte de Saint-Georges-d'Orgues, 34570 Pignan, tel. 06.82.43.54.66, fax 04.67.75.31.63, e-mail laurent.icard@wanadoo.fr ▼
Ⅰ Wed. Fri. Sat. 9am–12 noon 3pm–7pm

DOM. JORDY
Elevé en fût de chêne 1999★

▪ 3 ha 4,500 ■ €5-8

The red earth in the countryside around Loiras, a few kilometres south of Lodève, is a source of fascination to walkers. But there are also schist soils in this region, and these are responsible for this garnet-coloured 99 with its violet highlights. The bouquet exudes subtle notes of musk, black fruits and sweet spices. The opening impression is round and warming, but the palate reveals tannins that, though still a trifle young, give it strength. Open the wine an hour before serving.

•→ Frédéric Jordy, Loiras, 9, rte de Salelles, 34700 Le Bosc, tel. 04.67.44.70.30, fax 04.67.44.76.54, e-mail frederic.jordy@wanadoo.fr ▼
Ⅰ ev. day except Sun. 8am–8pm

MAS DE LA BARBEN
Cuvée Les Lauzières 1999★

▪ 3 ha 12,000 ■ ♦ €8-11

The Hermanns acquired this 60-ha (148-acre) estate on the edge of Nîmes in 1999. The terrain is a very stony limestone-clay. This intense ruby-coloured cuvée is redolent of a basket of red fruits with liquorice. The palate, warm and full, with its well-integrated structure and excellent length, has a very Mediterranean profile.

•→ Mas de La Barben, rte de Sauve, 30900 Nîmes, tel. 04.66.81.15.88, fax 04.66.63.80.43, e-mail marcel.hermann@wanadoo.fr ▼
Ⅰ ev. day except Sun. 10am–12 noon 2pm–7pm
•→ Marcel Hermann

CUVEE JACQUES ARNAL
Elevé en fût de chêne 1999★★

▪ 3.5 ha 20,000 ■ €8-11

With this wine, we are once more on the pilgrims' route to Santiago de Compostela. Hence the name **Cuvée Saint-Jacques, white 2000**, a wine already familiar to our readers and which this year gains a star. Side by side with it is this Jacques Arnal *cuvée*, whose lovely violet-purple highlights and bouquet of cooked red fruits and spices yield to a well-developed palate of great fullness, sustained by well-integrated tannins. The wine's subtle notes of oak, far from invading the palate, are evidence of well-managed maturation in the barrel. Visitors to the winery may see the new cellars where it all takes place, which were built in 2000.

•→ SCA vignerons de Saint-Félix, 21, av. Marcelin-Albert, 34725 Saint-Félix-de-Lodez, tel. 04.67.96.60.61, fax 04.67.88.61.77 ▼
Ⅰ by appt.

DOM. DE LA COSTE Saint-Christol
Cuvée sélectionnée Elevé en fût 1999★

▪ 10 ha 7,110 ■■ €5-8

The vineyard is located in the Villafranchine hills in the *terroir* of Saint-Christol, a place where working as a family still makes sense. Now, and for some years to come – for this is a wine that will last – you will be able to admire the intense purple colour and fruity, vanilla and mineral aromas that give this oak-matured wine its charm. The estate's success is apparent also in its **Domaine de La Coste red 99**, which earns a commendation, as well as in the **rosé 2000**, which earns a star for its tempting, tender fuschia tones, its subtle, delectable fruitiness and its ethereal balance.

•→ Luc et Elisabeth Moynier, Dom. de La Coste, 34400 Saint-Christol, tel. 04.67.86.02.10, fax 04.67.86.07.71 ▼
Ⅰ ev. day except Sun. 9am–12 noon 2pm–7pm

DOM. LA CROIX CHAPTAL
Cuvée Charles Elevé en fût de chêne 1999★★

▪ 3.5 ha 16,000 ■■ €8-11

Charles Pacaud's estate, which he has managed since 1999, makes a majestic entrance into the *Guide*. His wine's authenticity derives from the pebbles and gravel terraces between the Larzac and the Mediterranean on which it is grown. Intense in appearance, it is redolent of spices, ripe fruits and undergrowth. The palate is silky, rich and full, velvety yet powerful. Hachette is laying bets on this grower.

Pacaud-Chaptal, Cambous, chem. de Bages, 34725 Saint-André-de-Sangonis, tel. 06.82.16.77.82, fax 04.67.16.09.36, e-mail lacroixchaptal@wanadoo.fr
- by appt.
- Charles Pacaud

CH. DE LA DEVEZE MONNIER 2000 □

La Devèze Monnier has its vines in the foothills of the Cévennes, where sun and breezes help to perfect the grapes that have yielded this pale-yellow wine with its attractive halo of yellow and green highlights. The elegant bouquet is characterised by flowers and peaches, while the palate is round and delicate, full and soft, long and harmonious. A 2000 vintage that would well suit *dorade royale* (gilthead bream).

- Damais, GAEC du Dom. de la Devèze, 34190 Montoulieu, tel. 04.67.73.70.21, fax 04.67.73.32.40, e-mail domaine@deveze.com ☑ ▼ by appt.
- Cadène Frères

CH. DE LANCYRE
Pic Saint-Loup Grande Cuvée 1999★

1.5 ha	4,000	€11-15

Lancyre makes a mark every year with its bright-amber white, a wine whose intense and refined bouquet mingles aromas of toast, caramel, flowers and spices with crystallised citrus fruits, exotic fruits and honey. The palate is full and silky, rich and concentrated, with bewitching softness and length. The **red Grande Cuvée 99** was also applauded. Dark in appearance, it has intense aromas of black fruits and smoke. The powerfully structured palate, however, will need two or three years' more keeping to reach its best.

- GAEC de Lancyre, Lancyre, 34270 Valflaunès, tel. 04.67.55.22.28, fax 04.67.55.23.84 ▼ by appt.
- Valentine Durand

CH. DE LA NEGLY La Côte 2000★

18.37 ha	95,000	€5-8

Château de La Négly has produced some fine 2000 wines: a **white Cuvée Marine**, which was commended; a **rosé Cuvée Les Embruns** (the word means sea-spray; the estate being right by the sea), one star; and this La Côte 2000, which echoes the 1998 *coup de cœur*. This deeply coloured red releases charred aromas of cooked red fruits, with a subtle hint of menthol. The well-structured and generous palate is equipped with sturdy tannins, to the extent that there need be no rush to drink it yet.

- SCEA Ch. de La Négly, 11560 Fleury-d'Aude, tel. 04.68.32.36.28, fax 04.68.32.10.69, e-mail lanegly@wanadoo.fr ☑ ▼ by appt.
- Jean Paux-Rosset

CH. LANGLADE Prestige 1999

2.5 ha	6,000	€5-8

The 1999 vintage produced generally supple wines, but the rule was broken at Château Langlade. Its wine is an intense red colour, with a notably strong bouquet of blackcurrants, coffee, leather and toast. The palate has very evident tannins and unabashed oakiness. Patience is required.

- Ch. Langlade, chem. des Aires, 30980 Langlade, tel. 04.66.81.30.22, fax 04.67.59.14.50, e-mail chateau.langlade@freesbee.fr ☑
- by appt.

DOM. DE LA PROSE Saint-Georges d'Orques Grande Cuvée 1999★★

2 ha	4,200	€15-23

The La Prose estate is building upon its splendid launch. Despite the capricious nature of the 1999 vintage, the Saint-Georges d'Orques *terroir* has combined with Mortillet expertise to produce a blackberry-hued wine with complex aromas of spices, fruit compote and smoke. The wine's richness on the palate is supported by tannins that are both sturdy and subtle. Members of the Jury felt that they had tasted this wine a little too soon, and believe it has a great future ahead of it.

- de Mortillet, Dom. de La Prose, 34570 Pignan, tel. 04.67.03.08.30, fax 04.67.03.48.70 ▼ by appt.

CH. LA ROQUE □
Pic Saint-Loup Cupa Numismae 1999★★

15 ha	55,000	€8-11

Almost twenty years of stubborn effort have enabled Château La Roque to guarantee us some excellent products – like this intensely coloured 99 red with violet hints, its powerful scents of blackcurrants, vanilla and roasting, and its matching hint of the garrigue. This round, full, mouth-filling and superbly well-balanced wine, with its subtle, unctuously soft tannins, is quite remarkable.

- Jack Boutin, Ch. La Roque, 34270 Fontanès, tel. 04.67.55.34.47, fax 04.67.55.10.18 ▼ ev. day except Sun. 10am-12 noon 2pm-6pm

CH. LA SAUVAGEONNE □
Cuvée Prestige 2000★

5.5 ha	20,000	€5-8

You could say that La Sauvageonne is a sort of Carmen amidst the busty foothills of the Larzac. With its usual dark appearance, perfumed with scents of the garrigue and undergrowth, it is gorgeously fleshy on the palate, sensuously shaped and desirably long: a real forbidden fruit.

- EARL Gaëtan Ponce et Fils, 34700 Saint-Jean-de-la-Blaquière, tel. 04.67.44.71.74, fax 04.67.44.71.02 ▼ ev. day 8am-12 noon 2pm-7pm

CH. DE LASCAUX □
Blanc classique 2000★

n.c.	27,000	€6-8

This 2000 wine has a very pale-yellow appearance with green highlights around the edges and an intense, elegant bouquet of *pain d'épice* and flowers. The palate opens with a forthright, lively first impression, followed by fullness and length. An exquisitely harmonious wine.

- ☛ Jean-Benoît Cavalier, Ch. de Lascaux, 34270 Vacquières, tel. 04.67.59.00.08, fax 04.67.59.06.06, e-mail j.bcavalier@wanadoo.fr ☑ Ⴤ by appt.

MAS DE LA SERANNE

Le Clos des Immortelles 1999★

| ■ | 0.8 ha | 6,375 | | ■ €8-11 |

With its light-red colour and scattered brown highlights, this is a wine that exudes subtly oaky, fruity notes, and is round, smooth, soft but persistent on the palate. The **rosé 2000**, with its jammy, spicy strawberry and raspberry aromas, is round and rich on the palate and drew much favourable comment from the Jury.

- ☛ Venture, Mas de La Seranne, 34150 Aniane, tel. 04.67.57.37.99, fax 04.67.57.37.99, e-mail mas.seranne@wanadoo.fr ☑ Ⴤ by appt.

DOM. DES LAURIERS

Picpoul de Pinet 2000★

| □ | 10 ha | 15,000 | | ■ €5-8 |

This white wine with green highlights was grown on gravelly red soils at Castelnau-de-Guers. The Jury particularly remarked on the aromas of overripe fruits and the warm, full palate. The slightly bitter touch on the finish is not unusual in a Picpoul de Pinet, and will contrast well with the iodine in Bouzigues oysters if drunk as an accompaniment to them.

- ☛ Dom. des Lauriers, 15, rte de Pézenas, 34120 Castelnau-de-Guers, tel. 04.67.98.18.20, fax 04.67.98.96.49, e-mail cabral.marc@wanadoo.fr ☑ Ⴤ by appt.

CH. LA VERNEDE

Elevé en fût de chêne 1999★

| ■ | 2.5 ha | 14,500 | | ■ €6-11 |

The slopes of Château La Vernède, which turn their indolent faces into the furnace of the Mediterranean climate, show their distinction with this oak-matured, dark red wine, redolent of very ripe, caramelised and spicy red fruits. Its tannins are well honed and supple, yet have presence, supporting a palate that is exceptionally long-lasting. Don't forget the **Tradition** from the same vintage, which obtained a commendation.

- ☛ Jean-Marc Ribet, Ch. La Vernède, 34440 Nissan-lez-Enserune, tel. 04.67.37.00.30, fax 04.67.37.60.11 ☑ Ⴤ ev. day except Sun. 10am–1pm 3pm–7pm

L'AYAL Montpeyroux 1999

| ■ | 3.8 ha | 13,000 | ■ ◆ | €5-8 |

The local winds lend their name to this *cuvée*. The *Ayal* is, in Occitan, the wind that blows up from the south-east. A gorgeous ruby colour, the wine has a discreet, subtle, soft bouquet of sweet preserved fruits, which

lends a certain bramble-like balance to the palate. It may be drunk now.

- ☛ Cave de Montpeyroux, 5, pl. François-Villon, 34150 Montpeyroux, tel. 04.67.96.61.08, fax 04.67.88.50.91, e-mail cave.montpeyroux@wordonline.fr ☑ Ⴤ by appt.

CH. DE L'ENGARRAN

Saint-Georges d'Orques Cuvée Quetton

Saint-Georges 1999★

| ■ | 3.5 ha | 16,000 | ■ €11-15 |

Scarcely out of the barrel and already in our glasses, the youthful-looking Quetton also has very forward, equally youthful tannins. Their presence is also confirmed in the bouquet, which has aromas of spices, bay-leaves and cocoa. The Jury is sure that this wine will provide great interest in the future, but it does need time. In the meantime, you can savour the **rosé 2000**, which was commended for its subtlety and fruitiness. If you get the chance, call in at this magnificent 18th-century château when there is a heritage open-day. You are bound to succumb to its charm.

- ☛ SCEA du Ch. de L'Engarran, 34880 Laverune, tel. 04.67.47.00.02, fax 04.67.27.87.89, e-mail lengarran@wanadoo.fr ☑ Ⴤ ev. day 10am–7pm
- ☛ Grill

LES BARONS Picpoul de Pinet

Guillaume de Guerse 2000★★

| □ | 12 ha | 60,000 | | ■ €5-8 |

Is it the variation of exposure among the various vineyard plots that explains the complexity of this very fine white wine? Or is it the soils, all of them limey and formed from marine or river sediments? Wherever the explanation lies, this Picpoul is brilliantly expressive of its *terroir*, with its lively golden-yellow colour and the bouquet that is dominated by orchard fruits, citrus fruits and sweet spices. The palate is concentrated, round and energetic, typifying the appellation, and the finish reveals a tiny, tender touch of bitterness. Drink with seafood or goats' cheese, and you will not be disappointed. Another Picpoul, **Les Sautarochs 2000**, was given a commendation. It would go well with oysters.

- ☛ Cave coop. de Castelnau-de-Guers, 26, rte de Florensac, 34120 Castelnau-de-Guers, tel. 04.67.98.13.55, fax 04.67.98.86.55 ☑ Ⴤ by appt.

LES COTEAUX DU PIC

Pic Saint-Loup Sélection 2000★

| ■ | 40 ha | 60,000 | | ■ €5-8 |

The wine-growers of Le Pic represent a *terroir* of several communes tucked away on the outskirts of Le Pic Saint-Loup, a little mountain of 638 m (2,090 ft) that can be climbed in two hours. Grapes from selected plots express this richness and diversity in a dark wine with deep purple highlights. An aromatic medley of spices, olives and the garrigue is harmoniously supported by a powerful tannic texture that will need two or three years to soften.

Michel et Marcelle Causse, ancien chem. d'Anduze, 34270 Fontanès, tel. 04.67.55.21.41, fax 04.67.55.21.41
by appt.

CH. L'EUZIERE
Cuvée Les Escarboucles 1999★

12 ha · 16,000 · €8-11

This *cuvée* is a fine blend of *terroir* and expert wine-making. It is a true-to-type garnet-coloured Pic Saint-Loup with aromas of the garrigue and of almonds, while the rounded and spicy palate shows excellent balance that would enable it to be drunk now. 'Would go well with a lamb stew with ceps and black olives, remarked one taster.

SCA Les Coteaux du Pic, 34270 Saint-Mathieu-de-Tréviers, tel. 04.67.55.81.19, fax 04.67.55.81.20, e-mail cave@coteaux-du-pic.com
by appt.

DOM. LES FERRAGERES
Pic Saint-Loup 1999★

30 ha · 25,750 · €5-8

Grown in the heart of the Pic Saint-Loup district, this wine from the Ferragères estate featured in last year's *Guide*. Already at its best, it owes its attractive purple colour and violet highlights to traditional vinification, which is also responsible for the successful marriage of heady fruit aromas and wild scents of the garrigue. The same charming mix persists onto the palate, where a cherry fruitiness mingles with sweet spices, supported by elegant tannins.

SA Bessière, 40, rue du Port, 34140 Mèze, tel. 04.67.18.40.40, fax 04.67.43.77.03

LES HAUTS DE LUNES
Elevé en fût de chêne 1998★★

5 ha · n.c. · €11-15

The Jeanjeans extract the quintessence of the *terroir* from a limestone plateau known as the *désert d'Aumelas*. Dark and intense in appearance, the wine has a bouquet that reveals notes of roasting, vanilla, and a discreet, elegant oakiness. The palate shows concentrated body, powerful tannins and great aromatic persistence that will allow it to age with no trouble at all.

Philippe et Frédéric Jeanjean, Mas de Lunes, 34230 Cabrials, tel. 04.67.88.41.34, fax 04.67.88.41.33

CH. LE THOU
2000★

2.9 ha · 15,000 · €11-15

Beneath an ancient stone keep, in the calm of the cellar, slumbers this violet-tinged, purple-red wine. Its complex bouquet exudes notes of menthol, liquorice, and smokily roasted fruits and spices. The palate is delicious – full, smooth, supple and yet concentrated – with tannins that are already mature, yet will ensure continued development.

SCEA de Ferrier de Montal, Ch. Le Thou, 34410 Sauvian, tel. 04.67.32.16.42, fax 04.67.32.16.42

CH. DE MARMORIERES
La Clape 2000★

2 ha · 6,000 · €5-8

Marmorières is now in its seventh generation of wine-growers, a sound tradition that has seen many harvests, and affirms itself once again this year with this delicately salmon-pink, pale rosé. The bouquet comprises aromas of citrus fruits, white flowers, honey and eucalyptus, with a lively, subtly balanced and lengthy palate. The Jury also commended the oak-matured **red 99**, which

CH. DE L'HOSPITALET
La Clape Summum 2000

8 ha · 26,000 · €8-11

Here, in the heart of La Clape, you can stay the night, enjoy some Mediterranean cooking, saunter round the various museums, and visit the vast cellar where this golden-hued white wine comes from. The Jury liked the character of its aromas, which range from toastiness to oak, and from ripe fruits to dried ones. Perhaps the palate does not have quite the intensity of the bouquet, but would still do justice to *bourride de baudroie* (a garlicky Mediterranean fish dish).

Dom. de L'Hospitalet, 11100 Narbonne, tel. 04.68.45.27.10, fax 04.68.45.27.17, e-mail info@domaine.hospitalet.com
by appt.

L'ORMARINE Picpoul de Pinet Cuvée
Prestige Cuvée des Oenologues 2000★

30 ha · 20,000 · €3-5

Visiting the Pinet cellar is a must when you are in the vicinity of this small village 10 km (6.5 miles) from the Etang de Thau lake. With its pale-yellow appearance and bouquet of citrus fruits hinting at menthol, this wine is true-to-type to the appellation. Its good balance, liveliness and aromatic freshness on the palate make it a good partner for shellfish.

Cave de L'Ormarine, 1, av. du Picpoul, 34850 Pinet, tel. 04.67.77.03.10, fax 04.67.77.76.23, e-mail ormarine@mnet.fr
by appt.

DOM. DE L'HORTUS
Pic Saint-Loup 1998★

17.8 ha · 80,000 · €15-23

Nestling at the foot of the Pic Saint-Loup, the Hortus vineyard is like a jewel set in the garrigue. And sure enough, bay, thyme and black olives are precisely what come through in the bouquet of this elegant wine with its sweet fruitiness, silky tannins, classy balance and excellent length. Like its equivalents from previous years, this fine 98 will easily keep for two to three years.

Jean Orliac, Dom. de L'Hortus, 34270 Valflaunes, tel. 04.67.55.31.20, fax 04.67.55.38.03
by appt.

Coteaux du Languedoc

would suit winter meals as well as great gastronomic occasions.

➤ De Woillemont, SCEA de Marmorières, 11110 Vinassan, tel. 04.68.45.23.64, fax 04.68.45.59.39 ☑ ☒ by appt.

CH. MAZERS 1999★

■　　　10 ha　12,000　　⭐ €5–8

The Fontès cellar can always be relied upon to produce some excellent **rosés**, and not surprisingly, **Prieuré Saint-Hippolyte** again receives a star. Château Mazers 99 completes the range. An intense purple with subtle hints of blue, this new arrival is redolent of fruits in brandy, dried figs and spices. The palate is smooth, straightforward and subtly oaky.

➤ Cave coop. La Fontesole, bd Jules-Ferry, 34320 Fontès, tel. 04.67.25.14.25, fax 04.67.25.30.66, e-mail la.fontesole@libertysurf.fr ☑ ☒ ev. day except Sun. 8am–12 noon 2pm–6pm

CH. MIRE L'ÉTANG

La Clape Cuvée des ducs de Fleury Elevé en fût de chêne 1999★

■　　　9 ha　7,000　　■ €11–15

The Mire l'Etang vineyard extends in terraces on the *massif* of La Clape. It overlooks the lakes and the Mediterranean. The windy maritime climate gives this *terroir* its special character, discernible in both the **Cuvée Corail 2000**, which receives a commendation, and this 99 red. Its dark appearance has fleeting brown highlights. The bouquet is immediately sharp and intense, with notes of spices, roasting, blackcurrants and undergrowth. On the palate, it is generous and well structured, its length sustained by soft tannins. The oak maturation is discreet and well judged. Also commended was the **white 2000**.

➤ Ch. Mire L'Étang, 11560 Fleury-d'Aude, tel. 04.68.33.62.84, fax 04.68.33.99.30 ☑ ☒ by appt.
➤ Chamayrac

CH. DE MONTPEZAT

La Pharaonne 1999

■　　　1 ha　n.c.　　■ €11–15

Montpezat dates back to the 16th century. The château was embellished in the 19th century, during a period of high splendour. Currently, the vineyard makes successful wines like this dark 99 red with its abundant violet overtones and attractive oaky bouquet, characterised by charred, spicy notes and aromas of overripe red fruits. The roundness, body and structure of the palate make for a particularly well-balanced wine.

➤ Christophe Blanc, Ch. de Montpezat, rte de Roujan, 34120 Pezenas, tel. 04.67.98.10.84, fax 04.67.98.98.78, e-mail contact@chateau-montpezat.com ☑ ☒ ev. day 10am–12 noon 2pm–7pm; winter by appt.

DOM. DE MORIN-LANGARAN

Picpoul de Pinet 2000★

▢　　　6.58 ha 21,000　　■ €3–5

This is a lovely place to halt on the road from Mèze to Pinet. Moran-Langaran's authentic Picpoul de Pinet (with the white label) is a bright, clear wine with green highlights, and has a bouquet that is at once fresh and ripe, with scents of citrus and exotic fruits. The palate has both warmth and the sort of vivacity that sets the tastebuds tingling. Alongside it in the cellar is **Saint-Jean des Sources 2000**, which was also commended by the Jury.

➤ Albert Morin, Dom. Morin-Langaran, 34140 Mèze, tel. 04.67.43.71.76, fax 04.67.43.33.60 ☒ ☒ by appt.

MORTIÈS

Pic Saint-Loup Jamais content 1999★★★

■　　　3 ha　6,000　　■ €11–15

The year 1999 saw the sixth vintage at Mortiès, the crowning achievement of which was this intensely coloured '*Jamais content*' with its halo of violet highlights and concentrated, rich bouquet. The aromas are of toast, liquorice, spicy, fruity, and menthol notes, plus hints of violets and the garrigue. Similarly powerful on the palate, it opens straightforwardly, and then reveals very concentrated, full body in which the tannins, though still noticeable, are quite silky. The finish seems to go on for ever. The estate's main vintage, **Le Mortiès 99**, is still a little closed but gains a commendation.

➤ GAEC du mas de Mortiès, 34270 Saint-Jean-de-Cuculles, tel. 04.67.55.11.12, fax 04.67.55.11.12 ☑ ☒ by appt.
➤ Jorcin-Duchemin

MAS MOURIES Amarante 2000★

■　　　2 ha　9,000　　■ €8–11

Located in the region of the Terres de Sommières, Mas Mouriès offers a wine of impetuous youth. It has a purple colour with violet highlights, red-fruit and chocolate aromas, and a somewhat rustic palate whose tannins will lose their rough edges in time. The long-lasting flavours indicate that the wine has a good future.

➤ Eric Bouet, Mas Mouriès, 30260 Vic-le-Fesq, tel. 04.66.77.87.13, fax 04.66.77.87.13 ☑ ☒ by appt.

DOM. DU NOUVEAU MONDE
1998★

10 ha   30,000   €6-11

This estate confirms the commitment to quality set in stone here some years ago. Its magnificently well-made deep-garnet 98 has a spicy and fruity bouquet that is still a little closed up. The palate, however, certainly seems to be ready, being full, soft, structured and balanced, as well as appreciably long. The Jury also commended the **Cuvée Le Nouveau Monde Fût de Chêne 98**, which is still in its first flush of youth.

Dom. Any et Jacques Gauch, Dom. Le Nouveau Monde, 34350 Vendres, tel. 04.67.37.33.68, fax 04.67.37.58.15
by appt.

NOVI 1998★★

12.45 ha   5,000   €15-23

Mas de Novi (in the 11th century, the wine-store of the abbey at Valmagne) recently opened a superb winery that this *cuvée* no doubt spent time. It still looks very youthful, being a deep purple in colour. The bouquet is a warm mixture of vanilla and ripe, spicy fruits. The palate is fleshy and richly structured, qualities that will in time take this wine to remarkable heights. A successful marriage of expression of the *terroir* with well-judged oak maturation.

SA Saint-Jean du Noviciat, Mas de Novi, 34350 Montagnac, tel. 04.67.24.07.32, fax 04.67.24.07.32
ev. day 8am–12 noon 1pm–7pm

CH. DU PARC
Elevé en fût de chêne 2000★

n.c.   6,000   €11-15

Having acquired invaluable knowledge and experience at Château des Ollieux, Arnaud l'Epine returned to the family estate, which he runs on organic principles. He has made a wise decision, as this intensely coloured wine demonstrates, with its aromas of ripe fruits, prunes and bay-leaves mingling with subtle oaky and spicy notes. On the palate, the tannins make their presence felt, but are soft and very long, sustained by excellent structure. Drink now, or over the next three or four years.

Arnaud L'Epine, Ch. du Parc, rte de Caux, 34120 Pezenas, tel. 04.67.98.01.59, fax 04.67.98.01.59, e-mail lep1959@aol.com
by appt.

CH. PECH-CELEYRAN
La Clape Tradition 1999

40 ha   200,000   €5-8

If you went back in time in search of a celebrity connection, you would come across a relative of the château's former owners. For the last four generations, Pech-Celeyran has belonged to the Saint-Exupérys. As for this 99 red, it has an elegant appearance with brown highlights, but what impressed the Jury was the original-ity of its bouquet: the note of garrigue and hint of menthol. The palate is restrained and well balanced, with a liquorice finish. Understandably, given the vintage, it is a less concentrated wine than its immediate predecessor.

Jacques de Saint-Exupéry, Ch. Pech-Celeyran, 11110 Salles-d'Aude, tel. 04.68.33.50.04, fax 04.68.33.36.12, e-mail saint-exupery@pech-celeyran.com
ev. day 9am–7.30pm

CH. PECH REDON La Clape
L'Epervier Elevé en fût de chêne 1999★

n.c.   40,000   €8-11

The superb location in which this estate is situated may be found along the winding and picturesque road that climbs to the top of the Pech-Redon. The climatic conditions in 1999 were less favourable than those of the previous year. Nonetheless, this is an extremely good wine. Garnet-red in colour, it has spicy aromas of red fruits and leather. The palate is round and silky, making for a very appealing wine.

Christophe Bousquet, Ch. Pech Redon, rte de Gruissan, 11100 Narbonne, tel. 04.68.90.41.22, fax 04.68.65.11.48, e-mail bousquet@terre-net.fr ev. day except Sun. 9am–12 noon 2pm–7pm

CH. DE PINET Picpoul de Pinet 2000★

n.c.   20,000   €5-8

This wine, which is the product of feminine expertise, is a very traditional Picpoul de Pinet, as is evidenced by its pale colour and golden highlights, and its aromas of citrus fruits, in which mandarin mingles with lemon. The palate is subtle, well balanced and elegant. A wine made to go with shellfish, needless to say, but which would also suit grilled sea-bass.

Ch. de Pinet, 34850 Pinet, tel. 04.68.32.16.67, fax 04.68.32.16.39
ev. day 10am–1pm 3pm–7pm; cl. Jan.

DOM. PUECH Cuvée spéciale 1999★

2 ha   5,700   €8-11

The Puech estate's vineyard lies several kilometres to the north of Montpellier. In addition to the **Cuvée des Grands-Devois 99** that was commended by the Jury, this wine, with its dark, glossy appearance, was remarked upon for the intensity of its aromas, in which red fruits mingle with spices. The rich, warm, velvety palate is not lacking in subtlety. One to keep.

GAEC Dom. Puech, 25, rue du Four, 34980 Saint-Clément-de-Rivière, tel. 04.67.84.12.31, fax 04.67.66.63.16, e-mail domaine.puech@hotmail.com
by appt.

CH. PUECH-HAUT
Saint-Drézéry Tête de cuvée 1999★★

30 ha   72,000   €15-23

Puech-Haut needs no introduction. It already has a very distinguished record, and this year's *Guide* confirms the château's exper-tise once again. The colour of this *coup de*

Coteaux du Languedoc

coeur Tête de Cuvée red is very intense, almost black, with violet nuances. The bouquet is very expressive, with charred aromas of black fruits, dried fruits and spices, together with an oakiness that needs more time to soften. The classy palate is powerful, well balanced and long, with a structure of commanding presence that suggests it will keep for up to ten years. Also worth mentioning are the **Prestige red 99** and **rosé 2000**, which both gain commendations, and the **Tête de cuvée white 99** (one star) and **Clos du Pic, red 99** (two stars) the last two made by the talented Matthieu Bru.

♦ SCEA Ch. Puech-Haut, 2250, rte de Teyran, 34160 Saint-Drézéry, tel. 04.67.86.93.70, fax 04.67.86.94.07, e-mail chateau.puech-haut@wanadoo.fr ⊻
⛏ by appt.
♦ Gérard Bru

DOM. DU ROC BLANC
Picpoul de Pinet 2000★★
□ 10 ha 37,000 €3-5

This pretty white comes from a *terroir* of red clay. As soon as it is poured, it reveals itself. Pale, green-tinged in appearance, it exudes aromas of exotic fruits and grapefruit. The palate opens with a fresh, lively attack, leading to impressions of roundness and richness that somehow manage not to mask that acidic edge that is so quintessentially Picpoul de Pinet. It would be an excellent accompaniment to Bouzigues oysters, as would the **Terres Rouges 2000** that received a commendation from the Jury.

♦ Cave coopérative de Montagnac, 15, rte d'Aumes, 34530 Montagnac, tel. 04.67.24.03.74, fax 04.67.24.14.78
⛏ by appt.

ROUCAILLAT 1999
□ 3.5 ha 14,000 €8-11

Anybody who gets the chance to taste them at three or four years old will notice that the white wines of Comberousse still show signs of a seemingly eternal youth. That is why this pale golden-yellow 99, with its hints of menthol, caramelised citrus fruits, white fruits and small flowers, together with its rich, balanced and lengthy palate, will need two or three years of keeping before it is ready to give of its all.

♦ Alain Reder, Comberousse, rte de Gignac, 34660 Cournonterral, tel. 04.67.85.05.18, fax 04.67.85.05.18 ⊻
⛏ by appt.

CH. ROUMANIERES
Cuvée Tradition 1999★
▪ 3.5 ha 20,000 €8-11

In former days, pilgrims en route for Santiago de Compostela would stop at Roumanières, where one imagines they would down many flagons. Today, the pilgrims have been replaced by rambling holiday-makers who might come to sample, for instance, this delicate, devilishly fruity and well-balanced wine. It has warmth, gentleness and excellent length. Otherwise, they could try the commended **Cuvée Les Garrics red 99**, for all that it is still very young and wrapped up in its oak, or the **rosé, Cuvée Tradition**, a one-star wine for those who appreciate freshness.

♦ Robert et Catherine Gravegeal, EARL Ch. Roumanières, 34160 Garrigues, tel. 04.67.86.91.71, fax 04.67.86.82.00, e-mail roumanières@net-up.com ⊻
⛏ ev. day except Sun. & Mon. 9am–12 noon 3pm–7pm

CH. RICARDELLE La Clape 2000★
▪ 16.5 ha 90,000 €5-8

The vines of Château Ricardelle have their roots at the very gates of Narbonne, on the side closest to the charming little port of Gruissan. Youth is no bar to this wine, with its light purple colour, unreserved bouquet of blackcurrants, leather and the garrigue, and its easy-drinking, well-balanced palate. It can be enjoyed straightaway.

♦ Ch. Ricardelle, rte de Gruissan, 11100 Narbonne, tel. 04.68.65.21.00, fax 04.68.32.58.36, e-mail ricardelle@wanadoo.fr ⊻ ⛏ ev. day 9am–6pm
♦ Pellegrini

CH. RIVIERE LE HAUT
La Clape Clos des Myrtes 2000★
□ 1 ha 5,300 €8-11

Situated opposite the lakes, Château Rivière le Haut enjoys ideal conditions for producing expressive white wines. The delicate appearance and subtle bouquet of this one, which sends out aromas of small white flowers and aniseed and scents of the garrigue, are supported to advantage by the classy palate. True to the La Clape designation, it has roundness, liveliness and a mouthfilling, spicy finish, all of which suggest that it would go well with either grilled sea-bream or shellfish.

♦ Josiane Segondy, Ch. Rivière Le Haut, 11560 Fleury-d'Aude, tel. 04.68.33.61.33, fax 04.68.33.90.32, e-mail rivierelehaut@wanadoo.fr ⊻ ⛏ ev. day except Sat. & Sun. 9am–12 noon 2pm–5pm

DOM. SAINT-ANDRIEU

Montpeyroux Exception 1998★ ■ 1.5 ha 1,800 €15-23

At Saint-Andrieu, a family estate planted on the typical *terroirs* of Montpeyroux, everything, from the viticultural regime to the use of manual harvesting, aims to respect the grapes and extract their essence. The bright garnet Exception *cuvée* is subtle and elegant, mixing small red fruits and blackcurrant-leaf aromas both in the bouquet and on the palate. An alliance of suppleness and sweet spice puts the finishing touch to this delicious wine, which is ready to drink now.

☞ Renée-Marie et Charles Giner, 1, chem. des Faysses, 34150 Montpeyroux, tel. 04.67.96.61.37, fax 04.67.96.63.20
Y by appt.

CLOS SAINTE-CAMELLE 1998★

■ 3.5 ha 10,000 €5-8

Catherine Do's first vintage in the appellation is testimony to her talent as a grower in unlocking the potential of her *terroir*. The wine is full of surprises. Its dense colour is still bright and young-looking, while the mineral notes and aromas of well-ripened fruits integrate well with the palate's roundness and fullness, even if the close-packed tannins need to wait a little longer. The **rosé 2000** has distinctive subtlety and personality, which is why the Jury has rewarded it with a star.

☞ EARL dom. de Campaucels, rte de Saint-Pons-de-Mauchiens, 34530 Montagnac, tel. 04.67.24.19.16, fax 04.67.24.12.64, e-mail campaucels.domaine@mageos.com
Y by appt.
☞ Catherine Do

CLOS SAINTE-PAULINE

La Vertu 1999★★ ■ 4 ha 10,000 €8-11

The Rolle, Grenache Blanc and Clairette varieties contribute distinct aromas of citrus fruits, smokiness and box-hedge, which come together on the palate to form a well-balanced wine that is full and gentle, lively and smooth, long and warming. Eel stew was one taster's suggested accompaniment, duck with olives that of another.

☞ Alexandre Pagès, rte d'Usclas, 34230 Paulhan, tel. 04.67.25.29.42, fax 04.67.25.29.42 Y by appt.

CH. SAINT-JEAN 1998

■ 4 ha 32,000 €8-11

At La Blaquière, scattered among the gorges of purple earth, are a number of dark schist soils that have yielded some attractively distinguished wines, like this Château Saint-Jean. A red of moderate intensity, full of fruits and spices, it has a supple, rounded palate with good balance and excellent length.

☞ SCAV Les vignerons de Saint-Jean-de-la-Blaquière, 1, rte de Lodève, 34700 Saint-Jean-de-la-Bl aquière, tel. 04.67.44.90.40, fax 04.67.44.90.42
Y by appt.

CH. SAINT-JEAN DE BUEGES 1999

■ 5 ha 15,000 €8-11

Arriving at Saint-Jean-de-Buèges, a tiny village with an ambience of the Middle Ages, was one of the most unforgettable experiences of our meander through the Languedoc. The quintessence of the wines of this *terroir* lies in their finesse. Brilliant garnet in appearance, with a bouquet that is full of red fruits and spices, this delightful *cuvée* has a palate of great discretion and subtlety.

☞ Cave des Coteaux de Buèges, rte des Graves, 34380 Saint-Jean-de-Buèges, tel. 04.67.73.13.73, fax 04.67.73.12.38
Y by appt.

DOM. SAINT-JEAN DE L'ARBOUSIER 2000

■ 5.5 ha 40,000 €5-8

This was an ancient Templar property in 1235. Its vineyard nestles in the garrigue, scarcely 5 km (3.5 miles) from Castries, famous for its magnificent château. The Jury selected two wines: the **white 2000**, and this 2000 red. With its purple colour, discreetly subtle bouquet of spices and red fruits, and its supple, soft-textured palate, it already makes good drinking. Christmas visitors to the cellar will see a large crib decorated with no fewer than 80 ornamental figurines.

☞ EARL Saint-Jean-de-l'Arbousier, Dom. Saint-Jean-de-l'Arbousier, 34160 Castries, tel. 04.67.87.04.13, fax 04.67.70.15.18, e-mail dom-stjean.de.larbousier@club-internet.f Y by appt.
☞ Viguier

CH. SAINT-MARTIN-DE-LA-GARRIGUE 2000

□ 5.35 ha 40,000 €5-8

This year, Saint-Martin-de-la-Garrigue offers us a fine pale-yellow 2000 with golden highlights indicating great ripeness. The bouquet gives off scents of citrus fruits and small white flowers, sustained by buttery, toasty notes. The forthright, supple, mouth-filling palate is gracefully balanced, with a warming feel on the finish.

☞ SCEA Saint-Martin de la Garrigue, Dom. Saint-Martin de la Garrigue, 34530 Montagnac, tel. 04.67.24.00.40, fax 04.67.24.16.15, e-mail jezabalia(@stmartingarrigue.com Y ev. day 8am-12 noon 1pm-5pm; Sat. & Sun. by appt.
☞ Umberto Guida

DOM. DES SAUVAIRE 2000★

■ 1.7 ha 11,000 €3-5

Hervé Sauvaire was discovered by the *Guide* last year with his very first vintage. He has fulfilled that early promise with this garnet-red 2000, which, like its attractive predecessor, is redolent of red fruits and spices.

The palate is rounded, well balanced and already delicious to drink.

→ Hervé Sauvaire, Mas de Reilhe, 30260 Crespian, tel. 04.66.77.89.71, fax 04.66.77.89.71, e-mail hervé.sauvaire@terre-net.fr ✓ ⦿ by appt.

SEIGNEUR DES DEUX VIERGES
Elevé en fût de chêne 1999★★★

13.8 ha 38,000 ▮ IID €8-11

The wine-growers of Saint-Saturnin have attained the summit of their art with this *cuvée*, in which the *terroir* reigns supreme, and the cellar-master proves himself a fine exponent of it. A feast of spices and liquorice wafts up from the purple, near-black depths. This *soi-disant* 'Lord of the Two Virgins' has a full-blooded, powerful palate, endowed with an unctuousness and (some would say) a virile constitution – a classy wine, certainly. Whether to drink it now or wait is purely a matter of taste. Note also the **Seigneur des Deux Vierges white 2000**, which merits a star for its balance and finesse.

→ Les Vins de Saint-Saturnin, rte d'Arboras, 34725 Saint-Saturnin-de-Lucian, tel. 04.67.96.61.52, fax 04.67.88.60.13 ✓ ⦿ by appt.

DOM. SOUYRIS 2000★

4 ha 15,000 ▮ €8-11

The Souyris estate, planted between the Larzac and the Mediterranean, makes a fine debut in the *Guide* with this dark purple 2000 vintage. It has delightful aromas of red fruits and the garrigue, but it is above all the silky palate, with its subtlety and balance that impressed the Jury.

→ Guilhem Souyris, 301, chem. de la Roque, 34725 Saint-Félix-de-Lodez, tel. 04.67.96.68.70, fax 04.67.96.68.70 ✓ ⦿ ev. day 8am–8pm

CH. DE TARAILHAN La Clape 1999

2 ha 5,000 ▮ ▮ €5-8

The bottle bears an enchanting label, complete with a tiny musical score, that is fully justified by the contents. A bright garnet-red wine, it has aromas of morello cherries and the garrigue in the bouquet. After a full-blooded opening impression, the palate discloses its still somewhat lively tannins. It will need a few more months ageing in the bottle.

→ Jean-Yves Duret, SCEA dom. du château de Tarailhan, 11560 Fleury-d'Aude, tel. 04.68.33.91.88, fax 04.68.33.91.81, e-mail tarailhan@wanadoo.fr ✓ ⦿ by appt.

→ François Duret

DOM. DE TERRE MEGERE
Les Dolomies 1999★

3 ha 15,000 ▮ ▮ €5-8

Michel Moreau is very familiar with his parcel of red garrigue *terroir* nestling in the folds of the Grès de Montpellier. The **white Galopine 2000**, commended by the Jury, bears eloquent witness of his talents, as does this Dolomies 99 with its dense colour and aromas of leather, bay-leaves and very ripe fruits. The full, velvety palate will be even more expressive if the wine is decanted. It is a feast of liquorice, silky tannins and … dreams.

→ Michel Moreau, Dom. de Terre Mégère, Cour de Village, 34660 Cournonsec, tel. 04.67.85.42.85, fax 04.67.85.25.12, e-mail terremegere@wanadoo.fr ⦿ ev. day except Sun. 3pm–7pm; Sat. 9am–12.30pm

DOM. LES THERONS
Saint-Saturnin Cuvée Sélection 1999★★

4 ha 20,000 ▮ €5-8

This grower's estate is located on two *terroirs* within the appellation. His **Château Mandagot Grande Réserve 99, Montpeyroux** gains a star. But this patiently matured wine is full of complex flavours of blackberries, blackcurrants and smoke. Its very fine mouth-filling quality, balance and tannic structure add up to an elegant wine that may be drunk now.

→ Jean-François Vallat, Dom. Les Thérons, 34150 Montpeyroux, tel. 04.67.96.64.06, fax 04.67.96.67.63 ✓ ⦿ by appt.

RESERVE VERMEIL
Vermeil du Crès 2000★

4 ha 12,500 ▮ ▮ €3-5

Youthful Syrah and Grenache vines are planted on gravelly slopes only two minutes from the shore. The best grapes, with the former variety in the majority, are selected to make enticing wines, notably this dark purple Reserve 2000, with its shades of violet and aromas of blackcurrants, cherries, liquorice and spices. The palate is rounded, supple, well balanced and classy. Worth noting too is the **Vermeil du Crès boisé**, a commended wine that is still maturing, and the one-star rosé **Marine**, which is ready to drink right now.

→ SCAV les Vignerons de Sérignan, av. Roger-Audoux, 34410 Sérignan, tel. 04.67.32.23.26, fax 04.67.32.59.66 ✓ ⦿ ev. day except Sun. 9am–12 noon 3pm–6pm

DOM. DES VIGNES HAUTES
Pic Saint-Loup 1999★

3 ha 10,000 ▮ ▮ IID €8-11

Corconne's Pic Saint-Loup is a regular in the *Guide*. It received a star last year, and is this year similarly distinguished for its **rosé 2000, Domaine du Tourtourel**, which earns a commendation, as well as this *cuvée*, which is still quite young. It bodes well for keeping, with its dark, rather violet colour, aromas of red fruits, toast and menthol that develop in the glass, and its powerful palate that is firmly structured by oaky tannins.

● SCA La Gravette, 30260 Corconne, tel. 04.66.77.32.75, fax 04.66.77.13.56, e-mail lagravette@wanadoo.fr [V] [Y] ev. day 8am–12 noon 2pm–6pm; groups by appt.

CH. DE VIRES La Clape Cuvée Prestige
Elevé en fût de chêne 1999

■ 2 ha 4,500

Two de Vires wines have been judged successful this year: the very fruity **blanc 2000**, **Carte Or**, and this 99 red, with its deep, sombre colour. The first impression on the nose is of oak, followed by morello cherries and spices. The palate is still young and marked by that oak, with dense, obvious tannins that will need a little time to soften.

● GFA du Dom. de Vires, rte de Narbonne-Plage, 11100 Narbonne, tel. 04.68.45.30.80, fax 04.68.45.25.22 [V] [Y] ev. day 9am–12 noon 2pm–7pm

DOM. ZUMBAUM-TOMASI
Pic Saint-Loup Clos Maginial 1999★★

■ 4.35 ha 13,300 €11-15 [V]

This estate, on the road to Verriers, recently went organic, and stunned us last year with its fine 98. This dark, almost secretive 99 with violet highlights is a confirmation of that talent. The bouquet is a medley of spices, smokiness and vanilla, while the palate is rich and powerful but well balanced.

● Zumbaum-Tomasi, rue Cagarel, 34270 Claret, tel. 04.67.02.82.84, fax 04.67.02.82.84 [V] [Y] by appt.

Faugères

The wines from Faugères have been AOC since 1982, as have those of its neighbour, Saint-Chinian. The region of production covers seven communes north of Pézenas and Béziers and south of Bédarieux, and produced 83,490 hl (2,204,136 gal) of wine from 1,866 ha (4,609 acres) in 2000. The vineyards are planted quite high – 250 m (820 ft) – on steeply sloping hillsides situated on the lower, poorly fertile, schist outcrops of the Cévennes. Faugères is a heady wine with a good purple colour and characteristic perfumes of the garrigue and summer fruits.

CH. CAUSSINIOJOULS 1999★★★

■ 20 ha 30,000 €8-11

The wine-growers of the Faugères co-operative have married state-of-the-art technology with rigorous grape selection to produce a wine that went all the way to the Grand Jury, as well as their **Mas Olivier**, which also obtains two stars. This beautifully deep red wine has an aromatic ambience of great finesse, comprising red fruits and spices. Caussiniojouls is an extremely pleasurable wine: the palate is soft, with the kinds of toasty notes and integrated tannins that make it an authentic product of the schistose soils of Faugères. It would go very well with duck breast.

● Cave Coop. Faugères, Mas Olivier, 34600 Faugères, tel. 04.67.95.08.80, fax 04.67.95.14.67, e-mail lescrus.faugeres@free.fr [V] [Y] ev. day 9am–12 noon 2pm–7pm

CH. ANGLADE Comète 1998★

■ 5 ha 10,000 €11-15

This deep and intense wine is a classic blend of Grenache (60%), Syrah (35%) and Mourvèdre (5%). Its bouquet is captivating and generous, offering aromas of red fruits mixed with coffee overtones. The palate, supported by evident tannins, has a vanilla-tinged finish. This beautifully made wine needs time.

● Marie Rigaud, Ch. Anglade, 34600 Caussiniojouls, tel. 05.59.84.16.23, fax 05.59.84.16.23, e-mail chateau.anglade@wanadoo.fr [V] [Y] by appt.

ABBAYE SILVA PLANA
Songe de l'abbé 1999★

■ 7 ha 26,000 €8-11

A judicious blend of 42% Syrah, 36% Grenache, 15% Carignan and 7% Mourvèdre, a marvellous *terroir*, rigorous grape selection, and perfectly *regulated* vinification and maturation have combined to produce this very fine wine. Dark red in colour, it has a mineral bouquet that moves into spices, while the palate has overripe fruity aromas and a vanilla finish that confers elegance and good balance on it. This harmonious Faugères is ready to drink.

● SCEA Bouchard-Guy, 3, rue de Fraisse, 34290 Alignan-du-Vent, tel. 04.67.24.91.67, fax 04.67.24.94.21 [Y] by appt.

CH. DES ADOUZES
Elevé et vieilli en fût de chêne 1999★

■ 5 ha 12,000 €5-8

This estate, near an 11th-century chapel, was established several generations ago. Its wine is purple in colour, with discreet perfumes of violets and sweet spices. The rounded, subtle tannins are in excellent balance with the fruit. The **rosé 2000** also received a star.

● Jean-Claude Estève, Tras du Castel, 34320 Roquessels, tel. 04.67.90.24.11, fax 04.67.90.12.74 [Y] by appt.

Faugères

CH. CHENAIE Les Douves 1999★

■ 4 ha | 16,000 | €8–11

The Chabbert family acquired the dungeon and the second part of this 11th-century castle in order to restore them. Les Douves is very dark with violet nuances, and an intense bouquet that mixes notes of roasting and vanilla. The palate has excellent body and vigorous tannins, but this is still a young wine.

➴ EARL André Chabbert et Fils, Ch. Chenaie, 34600 Caussiniojouls, tel. 04.67.95.48.10, fax 04.67.95.44.98 **V** **Y** by appt.

CH. DES ESTANILLES 1999★★

■ 5 ha | 30,000 | €15–23

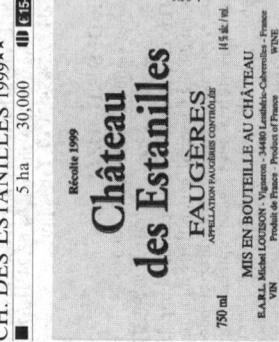

Yet again this estate, whose two-hundred-barrel cellar is open to view, gains a *coup de coeur*. This sumptuous 99, with its deep, brooding colour, has a very fine bouquet of cocoa marked by spicy and toasty notes. After a supple, fruity opening impression, the concentrated palate is full and sturdily built, with silky tannins adorning the long finish. This is a wine of majestic harmony.

➴ Michel Louison, Ch. des Estanilles, 34480 Cabrerolles, tel. 04.67.90.29.25, fax 04.67.90.10.99 **V Y** by appt.

DOM. DE FENOUILLET 1999★

■ 3 ha | 8,000 | €5–8

The firm of Jeanjean has its headquarters at Saint-Félix-de-Lodez, but manages a vineyard at Faugères and matures its wines at the Laurens cellar. This carefully selected *cuvée* is strongly marked by its *terroir*, the grapes are picked by hand when they are slightly over-ripe. Purple in colour, the wine is intensely aromatic, with notes of red fruits and vanilla. Firm tannins make their presence felt on the palate and sustain the wine's long, soft finish.

➴ Jeanjean, BP 1, 34725 Saint-Félix-de-Lodez, tel. 04.67.88.80.00, fax 04.67.96.65.67

DOM. DU FRAISSE 1999★★

■ 13 ha | 65,000 | €5–8

Twenty-year-old vines and 12 months of oak maturation are the secrets behind this *cuvée* with its characteristic schist bouquet that combines notes of charring and gun flint. The overall balance makes for a fascinating wine. Already attractive and full of character, it possesses excellent structure that should help it to mature well as the years pass.

➴ Jacques Pons, 1 bis, rue du Chemin-de-Ronde, 34480 Autignac, tel. 04.67.90.23.40, fax 04.67.90.10.20, e-mail jacques.pons@wanadoo.fr **V Y** by appt.

CH. GREZAN

Cuvée Arnaud Lubac 1999★★

■ 11 ha | 40,000

This estate belongs to a château that was once a command-post of the Knights Templar, and the foundations of which date back to the 12th century. Its 19th-century architecture is also interesting, with its *trompe l'oeil* enclosure. The wine is the genuine article and full of potential. This is evident from its intense colour, its aromas of cooked fruits with notes of menthol, and the silky tannins. A mouth-filling, richly elegant, extremely attractive Faugères that needs keeping in order to develop its full potential. Enjoy it with some Mediterranean cooking in the château's own restaurant. The Jury also awarded one star to **Les Schistes dorés 98**, which will also need another two years of keeping.

➴ Ch. Grézan, RD 909, 34480 Laurens, tel. 04.67.90.27.46, fax 04.67.90.29.01, e-mail chateau-grezan@wanadoo.fr **V** **Y** ev. day except Sun. 9.30am–12 noon 2pm–6.30pm

CH. HAUT LIGNIERES 2000★

■ 2 ha | 7,000 | €5–8

Those in search of enjoyment need look no further than this wine. It has a perfect mauve colour, and a complex, powerful bouquet of jasmine and fresh raspberries, and a rounded, superbly balanced palate. Drink as an aperitif or with grilled fish. Then again, you could do worse than drink this rosé on its home ground, simultaneously looking out upon the superb Cévennes landscape in which it was grown.

➴ Elke Kreutzfeld, lieu-dit Bel-Air, 34600 Faugères, tel. 04.67.95.38.27, fax 04.67.95.78.51 **V Y** by appt.

CH. DE LA LIQUIERE Cistus 1999★

■ 6 ha | 21,000 | €11–15

Here is a family property that has existed for many generations, and where respect for the *terroir* and the environment go hand in hand. Made from 40% Syrah and equal proportions of Carignan, Grenache and Mourvèdre grapes, this is a true-to-type, intensely coloured Faugères. Though the bouquet is still a little closed up, there is plenty of indication on the palate that the wine will age well. Try it with a Languedoc dish, such as duck with tiny *picholine* olives.

➴ Ch. de La Liquière, 34480 Cabrerolles, tel. 04.67.90.29.20, fax 04.67.90.10.00, e-mail bvidal@terre-net.fr **V Y** by appt.

➴ Vidal-Dumoulin

Wine label (Château des Estanilles):

Récolte 1999

Château des Estanilles

FAUGÈRES
APPELLATION FAUGÈRES CONTRÔLÉE

750 ml

MIS EN BOUTEILLE AU CHÂTEAU
EARL Michel LOUISON - Vigneron - 34480 Lenthéric-Cabrerolles - France
VIN   Produit de France - Product of France   WINE

14% alc./vol.

L.S 916

806

DOM. DE LA REYNARDIERE
1999★

6 ha | 6,000 | €5-8

A black label identifies a *cuvée* that the tasters greatly admired. Ripe red in appearance, its aromas of very deep red fruits are accompanied by notes of leather and toast. The wine's power on the palate is underscored by its dense tannins. Drink it now, or keep it for two to three years.

● SCEA Dom. de la Reynardière, 7, cours Jean-Moulin, 34480 Saint-Geniès-de-Fontedit, tel. 04.67.36.25.75, fax 04.67.36.15.80 ▼ ev. day except Sun. 10am-12 noon 2pm-7pm
● Mège-Pons

MOULIN DE CIFFRE 1999★

6 ha | 25,000 | €8-11

The talented Lésineau family may not hail from Faugères, but they have a fine understanding of the *terroir* and its people. Their rich, sun-soaked wine is intensely red, and has a bouquet that, though still slightly closed up, reveals predominant smoky and spicy notes. After an excellent initial impression, the palate displays tannins that still need time to soften, but the wine's overall balance is full of promise that should be fulfilled in a few months' time.

● Lésineau, SARL Ch. Moulin de Ciffre, 34480 Autignac, tel. 04.67.90.11.45, fax 04.67.90.12.05, e-mail info@moulindeciffre.com ▼ by appt.

DOM. OLLIER-TAILLEFER
Grande Réserve 1999★★

6 ha | 30,000 | €5-8

Thanks to its schist *terroir* and excellent exposure, this estate enjoys the most favourable conditions for producing a highly authentic expression of its appellation. The Jury's attention was caught by this wine, **Castel Fossibus 99**, but even more by this wine, which takes time to disclose its character. The bouquet evokes roasting game, while the full, concentrated attack and subsequent development of forthright tannins are equally indicative of remarkable potential.

● Dom. Ollier-Taillefer, rte de Gabian, 34320 Fos, tel. 04.67.90.24.59, fax 04.67.90.12.15 ▼ by appt.
● Alain Ollier

DOM. DES PRES-LASSES 1999★

3 ha | 5,000 | €8-11

This is the first vintage to be produced by these two wine-growers, and already they are in the *Guide*. They look to be worth keeping an eye on too for their evident skill in matching the Faugères *terroir* to the five grape varieties of the appellation. The bouquet is still pretty much closed up for now, opening only slightly to disclose some fruity notes, while the palate is still dominated by tannins that need time to soften. The delicacy of the wine's flavours demands patience. The similarly priced **rosé 2000** was commended by the Jury.

DOM. BERTRAND-BERGE
Cuvée Jean Sirven 1999★★★

2 ha | 2,000 | €23-30

This subtly oaky wine leads the field. A blend of Grenache, Carignan and Syrah, it is a superb, intense purple wine with mixed scents of spices, bay-leaves and ripe fruit. Its strikingly rounded, well-balanced character reveals an excellent marriage of fruit and oak on the palate. The sturdy, liquoricey tannins

Fitou

The Appellation

Fitou, the oldest AOC for a red wine in Languedoc-Roussillon (1948), is to be found in the Mediterranean part of the Corbières region. It covers nine communes, which are also authorised to produced Vin Doux Naturel Rivesaltes and Muscat Rivesaltes. In 2000 112,000 hl (2,956,800 gal) were produced. The wine is a beautiful deep ruby colour and has 12% of alcohol; maturation in casks takes a minimum of nine months.

● Feigel et Ribeton, 5, rue de L'Amour, 34480 Autignac, tel. 04.67.90.21.19, fax 04.67.90.21.19 ▼ by appt.

DOM. DU ROUGE GORGE 1999

n.c. | 50,000 | €3-5

Alain Borda has been working with vines since he was 15 years old. He established his own estate here in 1982, and offers this attractive Faugères with its notes of preserved fruits and its supple, elegant palate. The **rosé 2000** is commended for its fruitiness and well-balanced character.

● Alain Borda, Dom. Les Affanies, 34480 Magalas, tel. 04.67.36.22.86, fax 04.67.36.61.24, e-mail borda@terre.net.fr ▼ ev. day 8am-12 noon 2pm-6pm

DOM. DE SAUVEPLAINE Cuvée
Anne-Sophie Elevée en fût de chêne 1998★

35 ha | 200,000 | €5-8

This co-operative wine that uses 40% Carignan is highly successful. Its intense purple colour with black highlights encloses a universe of ripe red fruits and cocoa. The powerful, noble tannins are developing smoky notes. This is an emerging wine with a very fine future ahead of it.

● SCAV Les Coteaux de Laurens, chem. de Murelle, 34480 Laurens, tel. 04.67.94.48.73, fax 04.67.90.25.47 ▼ by appt.

DOMAINE BERTRAND BERGÉ

CUVÉE JEAN SIRVEN

FITOU

sustain the fruit content, and augment the wine's length.

❧ Dom. Bertrand-Bergé, av. du Roussillon, 11350 Paziols, tel. 04.68.45.41.73, fax 04.68.45.41.73 ☑ ☗ ev. day 8am–12 noon 1.30pm–7pm

DOM. DE LA ROCHELIERRE

Cuvée Privilège Elevé en fût de chêne 1999★★★

◼ n.c. 🍷 10,000 ◫◨ €8–11

Outside Pla, the Fitou vineyard claims its place among arid limestone hills, which shelter the vines inside rocky enclosures where one finds the odd *capitelle* (beehive-shaped stone shelter). Such is the origin of this ruby-coloured wine, a subtle marriage of ripe fruits and scents of the garrigue. The well-balanced palate is sustained by velvety tannins, and balanced by fleshy fruitiness and a very appealing toasty note. Drink with game.

❧ Jean-Marie Fabre, Dom. de La Rochelière, 17, rue du Vigné, 11510 Fitou, tel. 04.68.45.70.52, fax 04.68.45.70.52 ☑ ☗ by appt.

LE MARITIME

Elevé en fût de chêne 1999★

◼ 🍇 2 ha 🍷 8,000 ◫◨ €8–11

Leucate owes its name to the Greek sailors who called it so after the white cliffs (*leukos* in Greek) that are plainly visible from the sea. Le Maritime has a high proportion of Mourvèdre, a purple colour, and an intense bouquet of ripe fruits and venison. Its opening impression is forthright, soft and smoky, while the fruit content gives the wine its flesh, supported by some velvety tannins. The whole is very well integrated.

❧ Les vignerons du Cap Leucate, 2, av. F.-Vals, 11370 Leucate, tel. 04.68.40.01.31, fax 04.68.40.08.90 ☑ ☗ by appt.

DOM. LERYS

Elevé en fût de chêne 1999

◼ n.c. 🍷 10,000 ◫◨ €5–8

The maritime limestone-schist soils at Villeneuve take time to find. Follow the winding road through this wild and beautiful landscape. To pause, or even stay over, at the Lerys estate is well worth it. The oak maturation on this deeply coloured *cuvée* has been judged to perfection. Cherry scents mingle with leather and venison. The balance of tannin and fruit, on top of a light toasty note, bears witness that the wine has a fine future.

❧ Dom. Lerys, 11360 Villeneuve-les-Corbières, tel. 04.68.45.95.47, fax 04.68.45.86.11, e-mail domlerys@aol.com ☑ ☗ ev. day 10am–8pm

❧ Izard

DOM. LES MILLE VIGNES

Les Vendangeurs de la Violette 1999★

◼ 🍇 1 ha 🍷 4,000 ◫◨ €30–38

Jacques Guérin's idea of heaven is 5 ha (12 acres) of cherished vines and a harvest that is still a festivity. He has a weakness for long maceration and the Mourvèdre variety, underpinned by technical know-how. This is a seductive wine, with its deep, welcoming colour and still-wild bouquet evocative of blackberries and blackcurrants. It is surprisingly subtle on the palate, which centres on a sensation of cherry-like chewiness. Velvety tannin gives structure to a wine that is powerful, yet elegant, with a spicy finish. It will keep well.

❧ J. et G. Guérin, Dom. Les Mille Vignes, 24, av. Saint-Pancrace, 11480 La Palme, tel. 04.68.48.57.14, fax 04.68.48.57.14 ☑ ☗ by appt.

CH. DE NOUVELLES

Cuvée Vieilles vignes 1999

◼ 🍇 12 ha 🍷 20,000 ◫◨ €8–11

Daurat-Fort has a fine reputation for Fitou and this estate, lost beyond the Col d'Extrême, is one of the most historic in the region. The bouquet of this bright ruby-coloured 99 marries fruit and liquorice spice, notes that are echoed on the palate. The obvious tannic presence and generous finish call for a wild-boar stew.

❧ EARL R. Daurat-Fort, Ch. de Nouvelles, 11350 Tuchan, tel. 04.68.45.40.03, fax 04.68.45.49.21 ☑ ☗ by appt.

CH. DE SEGURE 1999★★

◼ 🍇 20 ha 🍷 60,000 ◫◨ €5–8

It is hard to choose among the remarkable range offered by the co-operative cellar at Tuchan. It draws on a production of fully 44,000 hl (1.16 m gallons) for its Fitou. The Jury liked both the **Baron La Tour 98** and the **Seigneur de Dom Neuve 99**, but best of all was this Château de Ségure. Along with its deep colour and honeyed scents of garrigue flowers and blackcurrants, it offers a full and ample palate full of fruit and liquorice flavours supported by well-balanced tannins. It all adds up to a fresh wine that may be enjoyed now.

❧ Les Producteurs du Mont Tauch, 11350 Tuchan, tel. 04.68.45.29.64, fax 04.68.45.45.29, e-mail contact@mont-tauch.com ☑ ☗ ev. day 9am–12 noon 2pm–6pm

CH. DU SEIGNEUR D'ARSE 1999★

◼ 🍇 30 ha 🍷 50,000 ◫◨ €5–8

After the terrible floods of November 1999, life has slowly returned to normal. The cellar here has been restored, thanks to widespread generosity. Seigneur d'Arse is a purple wine with aromas of very fresh, flavourful red fruits, sustained by tannins that are already quite gentle and liquorice-tinged. The finish is excellent. Although it may be drunk straight-away, this wine could also be kept a while.

➥ Les Maîtres Vignerons de Cascastel, Grand-Rue, 11360 Cascastel, tel. 04.68.45.91.74, fax 04.68.45.82.70 [V]
[Y] by appt.

DOM. DU TAUCH
Elevé en fût de chêne 1999★★

28 ha   150,000   €3-5

Domaine du Tauch is another *cuvée* from the Tuchan cellar. It is rather more classic in conception, but is eloquently expressive of the Haute-Corbière *terroir*. The wine is bright ruby in colour, with a note of the garrigue. Its small fruits with a note of the garrigue give full, rounded, silky yet firm tannins give structure to an attractively aromatic wine with a smoky finish. All it needs is a game dish to accompany. Not to be forgotten either is the **Cuvée Spéciale Sélection de Villeneuve 99**, which obtained a commendation from the Jury. It is very much a regional wine, being a fusion of the cellar at Villeneuve with that of Tuchan. Wait for two years, and then serve it decanted.

➥ Les Producteurs du Mont Tauch, 11350 Tuchan, tel. 04.68.45.29.64, fax 04.68.45.45.29,
e-mail contact@mont-tauch.com
[Y] ev. day 9am–12 noon 2pm–6pm

Minervois

Minervois is an AOC wine produced in 61 communes, 45 of which are in the Aude and 16 in the Hérault. This is a mainly limestone area of low hills with south-facing slopes, protected from the cold winds by the Montagne Noire. It produces white, rosé and red wines; the latter represent 95% of the production. In 2000 a total of 225,855 hl (5,962,572 gal) was produced in all three colours from an area of 4,560 ha (11,263 acres).

The Minervois vineyard is crossed by many enchanting tourist routes; the local Route des Vins is a signposted itinerary that offers numerous opportunities to visit tasting cellars along the way. The chief tourist attractions of the area include a famous historical site in the ancient city of Minerve, a host of Romanesque chapels and interesting churches in Rieux and Caune. The local wine Confrérie or brotherhood, the Compagnons du Minervois, has its headquarters at Olonzac. From now on, the commune of La Livinière is brought under the appellation Minervois la Livinière, comprising five communes. Production in 2000 was 8,930 hl (235,752 gal).

ABBAYE DE THOLOMIES 1999★

15 ha   30,000   €8-11

The cellar lies beneath the vaults of a thousand-year-old abbey, and its wine is a perfect blend of 40% Carignan with equal parts of Syrah, Grenache and Mourvèdre. It flatters the senses with a deep-purple appearance that is so enticing, one cannot wait to scent the heavenly aromas of rosses, rock-rosses and blackberries. The fleshy, full, rounded palate will please the most demanding taster.

➥ Lucien Rogé, Abbaye de Tholomiès, 34210 La Livinière, tel. 04.68.78.10.21, fax 04.68.78.36.04 [Y] by appt.

CH. DE BEAUFORT 1999★

10 ha   30,000   €11-15

Jérôme Portal has been in charge of this property since 1998, and has empowered the winery by harnessing the vineyard's potential. This superb 99, with its fine ruby colour and intense bouquet, is an immediate success for him. The tannins have presence, but are gracefully rounded, giving full expression to the red-fruit flavours. This is a Minervois of power and class. Its long vanilla finish is the sign of a great cask-aged wine, but it will need time to develop.

➥ SCEA Ch. de Beaufort, Dom. d'Artix, 34210 Beaufort, tel. 04.68.91.28.28, fax 04.68.91.38.38, e-mail contact@chateau-de-beaufort.com [V] [Y] by appt.
➥ Jérôme Portal

CH. BONHOMME Les Alaternes 1999

2.5 ha   6,000   €11-15

Made almost exclusively from Carignan grapes grown on 60-year-old vines, this distinguished *cuvée* has a surprising attack that bathes the palate in fruit and gentle vanilla. With its supple, elegant and warming finish, it would go well with *nouvelle cuisine*.

➥ SCE Ch. Bonhomme, Dom. de Bonhomme, 11800 Aigues-Vives, tel. 04.68.79.28.47, fax 04.68.79.28.48 [V]
[Y] by appt.

DOM. BORIE DE MAUREL
Cuvée Sylla 1999★★★

3.2 ha   11,000   €15-23

At Félines-Minervois, one can see some of the earliest examples of Neolithic flint arrows. This *terroir*, which lays claim to

Syrah, it unleashes enchanting aromas of spices, coffee, red fruits and vanilla. The perfectly balanced palate evolves on fine, full tannins. The seconds tick by as the finish goes on and on, giving the wine its lap of honour.
➤ Pierre Cros, 20, rue du Minervois, 11800 Badens, tel. 04.68.79.21.82, fax 04.68.79.24.03 [V] [Y] by appt.

CH. DU DONJON

Cuvée Prestige Elevé en fût de chêne 1999★★   10 ha   50,000   €5-8

Rich in vestiges of prehistory, the Minervois district is as interesting for its monuments and landscapes as for its vineyards. The traveller can thus satisfy the needs both of culture and idle pleasure. This fine estate of 50 ha (124 acres), part of which dates back to the 15th century, is part and parcel of the local life, as indeed is this wine, matured in oak casks for 12 months. Morello cherry in colour, with lively highlights, it has a rounded opening impression with notes of spices, raspberries and blackcurrants. The well-balanced, full-bodied palate leads on to a remarkable, vanilla-scented finish.
➤ Jean Panis, Ch. du Donjon, 11600 Bagnoles, tel. 04.68.77.18.33, fax 04.68.72.21.17, e-mail jean.panis@wanadoo.fr [Y] by appt.

YVES GASTOU 1998   2 ha   8,000   €5-8

The pretty village of Villalier contains the ruins of an episcopal palace. This is what one might call an 'haute-couture' wine bearing the wine-grower's own name on its label, its tannic strength derived from a 90% Syrah content, with the remainder Grenache. Silky aromas of leather and red fruits follow through to the finish. Drink it to accompany duck with olives.
➤ Yves Gastou, Dom. des Grandes-Marquises, 11600 Villalier, tel. 04.68.77.19.89, fax 04.68.77.58.94, e-mail yves.gastou@wanadoo.fr [Y] by appt.

CH. LA GRAVE Privilège 1999★   n.c.   12,000   €8-11

The château's banner unites parents, children and sons-in-law. This stronghold of the appellation was honoured with a Grappe de bronze from the Guide for its coup de cœur Expression 97 white. This year, it hoists its flag with this garnet-coloured 99, with its charming aromas of violet and vanilla. The sturdy tannins make for a vigorous opening statement, giving a solid, coherent structure to this strong, warming Minervois. The wine is a blend of the four red varieties of the appellation grown on gravel soils, with Syrah in the majority (60%).
➤ Jean-Pierre et Jean-François Orosquette, Ch. La Grave, 11800 Badens, tel. 04.68.79.16.00, e-mail chateaulagrave@wanadoo.fr [V] [Y] ev. day 9am–12 noon 2pm–7pm; Sat. & Sun. by appt.

thousands of years of expertise, has in the last 20 years undergone a quality revolution pioneered by the likes of Michel Escande, who now receives his sixth coup de cœur. This single-variety Syrah, grown on limestone-clay, no longer needs any introduction. It has the usual dark appearance, and the rich intoxicating intensity of truffle, violet, mocha and cocoa aromas rising up from the glass. On the palate, it is well integrated, mouth-filling, liquoricey and lush-textured, a wine to go with water-fowl.
➤ GAEC Michel Escande, rue de la Sallèle, 34210 Félines-Minervois, tel. 04.68.91.68.58, fax 04.68.91.63.92 [V] [Y] by appt.

DOM. CHABBERT-FAUZAN 2000★   2 ha   2,000   €5-8

The estate is located on the limestone heights of the hamlet of Fauzan. This year Clos La Coquille gains a commendation, but the star goes to the estate's intense rosé. It is both subtle and floral, and has a good balance of liveliness and fullness on a palate that develops slowly and elegantly. A characteristic blended rosé.
➤ Gérard Chabbert, Fauzan, 34210 Cesseras, tel. 04.68.91.23.64, fax 04.68.91.31.17 [V] [Y] by appt.

CH. COUPE ROSES 1999★★   6 ha   3,000   €5-8

As you leave La Caunette, a small troglodyte village where it is still possible to admire the 13th-century fortified gate, you may notice this distinguished cellar that makes a white from the only Roussanne grapes planted on schist soil. The bouquet is beautifully expressive, with a hint of menthol. A joy to the tastebuds, it happily juggles honeyed sweetness and mineral power on the palate. This is a fully mature 99 with a perfectly balanced finish.
➤ Frissant Le Calvez, Ch. Coupe Roses, 34210 La Caunette, tel. 04.68.91.11.73, fax 04.68.91.21.95, e-mail couperoses@wanadoo.fr [V] [Y] ev. day except Sat. & Sun. 8.30am–12.30pm 2 pm–6pm

DOM. CROS Les Aspres 1999★★★   1.5 ha   5,000   €15-23

The Grand Jury has delivered its verdict, and Pierre Cros only missed a coup de cœur by a mere whisker for this exceptional wine. A gorgeous, ruby-coloured, single-varietal

DOM. LA PRADE MARI

Chant de l'Olivier 1999★★

	n.c.	12,000	€8-11

On this garrigue *terroir*, where all is sound and light, the grower who has a sharp ear and much patience can achieve great things. This splendid ruby-red wine, wrested from vines growing on eroded slopes, has blackcurrant and cocoa aromas. Its structure is lively and powerful, with fleshy tannins that continue on to a finish where warmth combines with fullness.

Vignerons de La Méditerranée, ZI Plaisance,12, rue du Rec-de-Veyret, BP 414, 11104 Narbonne Cedex, tel. 04.68.42.75.00, fax 04.68.42.75.01, e-mail rhirtz@listel.fr
by appt.

DOM. LASSERRE

Clot de L'Oulo 1998★

	3 ha	20,000	€8-11

Clot de l'Oulo is a *lieu-dit* planted with Mourvèdre and Grenache. The two complementary varieties work snugly together here like the proverbial iron fist in the velvet glove. Developing gently on the palate, where there is an aromatic release of blackcurrants alongside pepper and vanilla, the wine has all the stuffing it needs to evolve well in the cellar. It was bottled by the Cave de Pouzols-Minervois, as the label mentions.

Vignerons de La Méditerranée, ZI Plaisance, 12, rue du Rec-de-Veyret, BP 414, 11104 Narbonne Cedex, tel. 04.68.42.75.00, e-mail rhirtz@listel.fr
by appt.

LAURAN CABARET 2000★

	6 ha	30,000	€3-5

This blend of Macabeu (80%), Grenache Blanc (10%) and Marsanne, macerated in their skins, will surprise some. It flashes with golden highlights as sweet acacia notes spill forth from the glass. The palate has a honeyed languor, and is concentrated and elegant with a warming finish. Drink now.

Cellier Lauran Cabaret, 11800 Laure-Minervois, tel. 04.68.78.12.12, fax 04.68.78.17.34 ev. day except Sun. 8am-12 noon 2pm-6pm; open Sun. in Jul.-Aug.

DOM. LE CAZAL

Le Pas de Zarat 1999★★★

	3 ha	15,000	€8-11

Zarat was an intrepid shepherd who led a risky life with his sheep on the steep, sharp inclines of La Caunette. Pierre and Claude Derroja have named this wine with its garnet tint after him. It is extremely aromatic, with subtle scents of the garrigue mixing with notes of jammy soft fruits. The palate is well balanced, sustained by tannins evocative of cocoa and cinnamon. The finish fades away slowly on notes of Virginia tobacco.

Vignerons de La Méditerranée, ZI Plaisance, 12, rue du Rec-de-Veyret, BP 414, 11104 Narbonne Cedex, tel. 04.68.42.75.00, fax 04.68.42.75.01, e-mail rhirtz@listel.fr
by appt.
P. et C. Derroja

CLOS L'ESQUIROL 1999★

	n.c.	10,000	€5-8

A regular in the *Guide*, this 'Squirrel' (*Esquirol* in the Oc dialect) emerges from its pine-forest with no less suppleness and subtlety than in previous years. A single-varietal Syrah, it is unequivocal in its aromas of cooked red fruits. The wine's acrobatics, supported by balance and gentleness, on the palate will amaze you. Tame it in your cellar or drink it now.

Coop. La Siranaise, 34210 Siran, tel. 04.68.91.42.17, fax 04.68.91.58.41

DOM. LIGNON

Les Vignes d'Antan 1998

	3 ha	15,000	€8-11

'Where are the vines of yesteryear (*les vignes d'antan*)?' asks the label. Here they are, on the steep, stony slopes that have yielded this densely coloured wine, redolent of ripe fruits mixed with unctuous roasted notes. This generous 98 offers a violet-toned finish. It should be kept.

Vignerons de La Méditerranée, ZI de Plaisance, 12, rue du Rec-de-Veyret, BP 414, 11104 Narbonne Cedex, tel. 04.68.42.75.00, fax 04.68.42.75.01, e-mail rhirtz@listel.fr
by appt.
Rémi Lignon

CH. MALVES-BOUSQUET

Cuvée Jordan le Noir 1998★

	n.c.	15,000	€8-11

Malves is a pretty village dominated by the four towers of the 16th-century château. A vast part of the former seigneurial lands now belongs to this estate. Its ruby-coloured wine is a blend of 70% Syrah with 30% Grenache planted on limestone-clay. The bouquet is very expressive, with notes of cooked fruits and vanilla, and the palate is rich and well balanced. It all leads up to a charming finish.

SCEA Christian et Jean-Louis Bousquet, Ch. de Malves, 11600 Malves-Minervois, tel. 04.68.72.25.32, fax 04.68.77.18.82
by appt.

CH. DE MERINVILLE 1999

	1 ha	5,500	€5-8

When stopping at Rieux, do not miss the splendid heptagonal church, nor indeed this wine, which is built on a triangular structure of spices, oak and fruit from 70% Syrah, 20% Grenache and 10% Carignan grapes. The palate is rounded, with well-structured tannins and a soft vanilla finish. Drink now or keep.

SCV les vignerons Mérinvillois, 41, av. Joseph-Garcia, BP 41, 11160 Rieux-Minervois, tel. 04.68.78.10.22, fax 04.68.78.13.03, e-mail cellier-de-merinville@wanadoo.fr by appt.

MOULIN DES NONNES 2000★

□ 10 ha 10,000 €5–8

Azille, a wine-growing village 4 km (2.5 miles) from Olonzac, has a 14th-century church. This estate of 100 ha (247 acres) has produced a very successful white wine with nine months of oak maturation. It has a bright golden colour with green highlights, and complex aromas of white flowers. This heady wine is no less lively on the palate, where flavours of lychees, vanilla and muscat grapes blend in sweet harmony, opening the door to paradise on the finish.

Frères Andrieu, Ch. La Rèze, 11700 Azille, tel. 04.68.78.10.19

DOM. PICCININI 2000★★

◪ 1 ha 6,000 €5–8

The steep little thoroughfares and the lovely church with its romanesque apse – a sanctuary and place of pilgrimage – make La Livinière special. Yet it also has a great *terroir* whose fine potential is demonstrated by this producer. While his **white 2000** gained many votes, the best rating went to this fuchsia-coloured rosé, a single-varietal Syrah with a bright, intense colour and rare aromatic complexity. The bouquet is enchantingly evocative of a basket of fruits and a bouquet of white flowers, while the palate is very powerful. Concentrated, warming flavours of citrus fruits tantalise on the finish. This remarkable wine would be ideal with grilled meats.

Jean-Christophe Piccinini, rte des Meulières, 34210 La Livinière, tel. 04.68.91.44.32 by appt.

CH. PIQUE-PERLOU

La Sellerie 1998★★

■ n.c. n.c. €23–30

This estate, bordering the Canal du Midi, puts its faith in old Carignan vines, which, together with 56% Syrah and two full years in oak, have produced this extraordinary wine. Purple in appearance and with a bouquet evocative of leather, it has a warming and powerful palate, well supported by sympathetic tannins and infused with rich aromas of mocha, black fruits and vanilla. The finish is long.

Serge Serris, 12, av. des Ecoles, 11200 Roubia, tel. 04.68.43.22.46, fax 04.68.43.22.46 by appt.

CH. PLO DU ROY

Le Balcon du Diable 1999★★★

■ 9.6 ha 32,000 €5–8

Not far from the wind-pumps at Sallèles blows the wind of success for this wine. It is seemingly an ill-named *cuvée*, for surely this 'devil's balcony' must be in paradise! Sixteen months in oak have left their mark on its purple colour and bouquet. Far from being a shady character, this is a wine that exudes spices, scents of the garrigue and preserved fruits. The velvety palate has excellent, perfectly balanced vanilla richness, which carries on to a magnificent, long finish. Spit-roasted game would be a fitting accompaniment, but

if you have no taste for the hunt, go for any strongly flavoured dish instead.

M. et Mme Franck Benazeth, 8, chem. de Bel-Mati, 11160 Villeneuve, tel. 04.68.26.13.64, fax 04.68.26.13.64

DOM. DU ROC Cuvée Tradition 1999★

■ 2.5 ha 12,000 €5–8

This dark red 99, a single-varietal Syrah, is as solid as the rock from which it takes its name, yet its heart is tender and aromatic. Notes of blackcurrants, cinnamon and fruits in brandy dance around a powerful, robust structure. This is a very successful and authentic example of its appellation. The producer may be a newcomer, but deserves his place among the famous names in your cellar. If you go to Pépieux, don't forget to view the Neolithic remains.

Alain Vies, 15, chem. de Rieux, 11700 Pépieux, tel. 04.68.91.52.14, fax 04.68.91.66.26, e-mail avies@club-internet.fr by appt.

DOM. SICARD

Cuvée la Cour de Jean 1998★

■ 3 ha 20,000 €8–11

Jean Sicard, whose estate is at Aigues-Vives, is an expert wine-grower and bee-keeper, with hives at the edges of his vineyard. This deep-purple 98 takes off majestically, thanks to its bouquet of spices and stewed fruits. Concentrated, fleshy and well balanced, it evokes violets and eucalyptus on the finish. Drink now.

Vignerons de La Méditerranée, ZI Plaisance,12, rue du Rec-de-Veyret, BP 414, 11104 Narbonne Cedex, tel. 04.68.42.75.00, fax 04.68.42.75.01, e-mail rhirtz@listel.fr by appt.

Jean Sicard

CH. VILLERAMBERT JULIEN 1999

■ 10 ha 42,000 €11–15

This estate has a *terroir* of mixed schist, marble and limestone-clay. Its claim to fame lies in this cherry-red wine that blends 40% Grenache with Syrah. This intensely flavoured 99 charts a course between soft vanilla and fruity freshness on the palate. An elegant, warming wine that is ready to drink.

Marcel Julien, Ch. Villerambert Julien, 11160 Caunes-Minervois, tel. 04.68.78.00.01, fax 04.68.78.05.34 ev. day 9am–11.30am 1pm–6.30pm; Sat. & Sun. by appt.

CH. DE VILLERAMBERT MOUREAU 1999

■ 5 ha   16,000   ■❚▲ €5-8

This huge estate of 120 ha (296 acres) is run by three brothers. They grow mainly Syrah vines with 10% Mourvèdre, planted on schist soils. The geology is reflected in this elegant and aromatically complex wine (notes of spices, minerals and violets) that is silky but well-structured. Although good to drink now, it will also keep.

➤ Marceau Moureau et Fils, Ch. de Villerambert, 11160 Caunes-Minervois, tel. 04.68.77.16.40, fax 04.68.77.08.14 [V]
Y ex. day except Sat. & Sun. 2pm–7pm

CH. DE VIOLET Cuvée Vieilles vignes

Elevé en fût de chêne 1999

■ n.c.   7,000   ■❚ €8-11

Venerable oak barrels sit cheek-by-jowl with the very latest equipment in this 11th-century château built over a Roman villa. This *cuvée* is well named, for it blends 20% Carignan from 60-year-old vines with 10% Grenache from 40-year-old vines and 70% Mourvèdre from 30-year-old vines. Ruby-red, with violet highlights, it offers excellent balance on a base of toasty vanilla. 'Let the tannins of this young wine throw off some of their friskiness first', commented one taster.

➤ Faussié, Ch. de Violet, 11160 Peyriac-Minervois, tel. 04.68.78.10.42, fax 04.68.78.30.01, e-mail chateau-de-violet@wanadoo.fr [V]
Y ex. day 9am–12.30pm 2.30pm–7pm

DOM. VORDY MAYRANNE

Cuvée de René 1999★

■ 2 ha   5,000   ■❚ €8-11

This famous estate 2 km (1.3 miles) from the Cathar town of Minerve hereby honours its ancestors, two grandfathers both named René, with a wine made of equal parts Mourvèdre and Grenache. Its purple colour and litany of cooked and ripe fresh fruits immediately catch the attention. This elegant, warming, vanilla-tinged 99 has fine balance. The tannins roll gracefully over the palate, and the finish shows a touch of acidity.

➤ Didier Vordy, Mayranne, 34210 Minerve, tel. 04.68.91.80.39, fax 04.68.91.80.39 [V]
Y by appt.

GRAND TERROIR

Elevé en fût de chêne 1999★★

■ 20 ha   20,000   ■❚ €5-8

Attention all wine-lovers! As the name indicates, this is a great *terroir* wine, fully true to its appellation. From the moment the wine

Minervois la Livinière

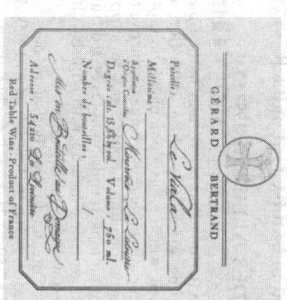

Le Viala is an exceptional limestone-clay *terroir* at an altitude of 120 m (392 ft) that yields a superbly intense and complex purple-red wine. Having hit the palate with stunning freshness, it goes on to play a harmonious score, in which notes of forest fruits, blackcurrants and vanilla resonate on a structure of obvious, yet well-rounded tannins. This full, powerful, robust wine is such a pleasure to the palate that a refill becomes a must.

hits the palate, the use of whole-grape maceration is detectable in the concentration of cooked fruits and vanilla richness. The palate is well integrated, powerful and balanced, with a tannic unity that guarantees good keeping, but also instant pleasure for the impatient.

➤ Cave coop. de La Livinière, rte de Notre-Dame, 34210 La Livinière, tel. 04.68.91.42.67, fax 04.68.91.51.77 [V]
Y by appt.

DOM. LA COMBE BLANCHE

La Galine 1999★

■ 6 ha   28,000   ■❚▲ €8-11

When Guy Vanlancker is asked which celebrities have visited his winery, he simply replies, 'Customers'. The surprising aspect of this wine is the playfulness of its blackcurrant and cherry aromas. On the palate, they are joined by vanilla in a contest between power and subtlety. Its tannins certainly need time to mature, but they guarantee good development.

➤ Guy Vanlancker, rue de La Taillanderie, 34210 La Livinière, tel. 04.68.91.44.82, fax 04.68.91.44.82 Y by appt.

CLOS DE L'ESCANDIL 1999★★

■ 5 ha   15,000   ■❚ €15-23

Matured for 20 months in the secrecy of the Clos, this wine really comes into its own once it is in the glass. Though vanilla excels in the bouquet, it has the discretion to give way to the delicately melting red fruits of the opulent, silky palate. Spices and prunes bring the whole to a warm and dazzling finish.

➤ Gilles Chabbert, Dom. des Aires Hautes, 34210 Siran, tel. 04.68.91.54.40, fax 04.68.91.54.40, e-mail gilles.chabbert@wanadoo.fr ■ Y by appt.

LE VIALA 1999★★★

■ 3 ha   11,000   ■❚ €30-38

• Dom. Gérard Bertrand, 34200 La Livinière, tel. 04.68.91.49.20 ☑ ▼ by appt.

CH. SAINTE-EULALIE
La Cantilène 1999★

■ 14 ha   30,000   €8-11

From Sainte-Eulalie, you can see the Pyrenees. The château offers a classy wine in which finely charred oak blends in with notes of undergrowth. A firm opening impression on the palate is sustained by tannins that are soft but well built. The finish is very elegant.
• Isabelle Coustal, Ch. Sainte-Eulalie, 34210 La Livinière, tel. 04.68.91.42.72, fax 04.68.91.66.09, e-mail icoustal@club-internet.fr ☑ ▼ by appt.

Saint-Chinian

Saint-Chinian has been a VDQS from 1945 and became an AOC in 1982. The appellation covers 20 communes spread over 2,977 ha (7,353 acres) and produces 143,636 hl (3,791,990 gal) of red and rosé wines. Located in the Hérault, north-west of Béziers, it lies on seaward-facing hills that rise to 100 and 200 m (328–656 ft). The soils are schists, which are mainly in the north, and limestone gravel in the south. The wine has a distinguished tradition, its name having been recorded as early as 1300. A Maison des Vins has been established in Saint-Chinian itself.

CH. DES ALBIERES 1998★★

■ 60 ha   15,000   €8-11

The Berloup cellar is a regular in the Guide, this time offering a white 2000 Berloup Schisteil, which gains a commendation, plus this very authentic terroir wine distinctive for its gentle opening impression and supple, elegant tannins. It ends on notes of red fruits and liquorice in a melting, warm finish – altogether a well-fashioned wine.
• Les Coteaux du Rieu Berlou, av. des Vignerons, 34360 Berlou, tel. 04.67.89.58.58, fax 04.67.89.59.21, e-mail cve.berloup@wanadoo.fr ☑ ▼ by appt.

CANET VALETTE
Le Vin Maghani 1998★★

■ 8 ha   18,000   €15-23

Respect for nature, a traditionally long vinification process with treading of the grapes, a good terroir, and excellent extraction have once again paid dividends for the Maghani cuvée. The complex bouquet of truffles, black olives, spices and violets is very attractive. On the palate, the wine has a good balance of roundness, tannins and alcohol. It finishes on a very sustained note of black fruits. A wine with a fine future.
• Marc Valette, Dom. Canet-Valette, rte de Causses-et-Veyran, 34460 Cessenon-sur-Orb, tel. 04.67.89.51.83, fax 04.67.89.37.50, e-mail earl-canet-valette@wanadoo.fr ☑ ▼ by appt.

DOM. CARRIERE-AUDIER
Cuvée Aurélie 1999★★

■ 3.4 ha   7,000   €3-5

Jérôme represents the fifth generation of growers on this estate. His Cuvée Aurélie has a high proportion of Mourvèdre and an array of pleasing mineral notes, dried figs, dried flowers and sweet spices. With its superb bouquet, this is exactly what a schist-soil wine should be, with the Grenache providing charm and suppleness. It is ready to drink.
• Dom. Carrière-Audier, Le Village, 34390 Vieussan, tel. 04.67.97.77.71, fax 04.67.97.34.14 ☑ ▼ by appt.
• Max Audier

CH. CAZAL VIEL
Cuvée L'Antenne 1999

■ 18 ha   45,000   €11-15

This estate was given over in 1202 to the monks of the abbey at Fontcaude, who managed it until the Revolution in 1789. Since then, it has continued to produce wine under the auspices of the Miquel family. Two wines caught the Jury's attention: first, the Vielle Vignes 99, and secondly, this Cuvée L'Antenne 1999. Both are good wines, but this one, which was oak-matured, has that little bit extra. The flavour of the well-balanced palate is of red fruits, sustained by tannins that are almost softened. Its subtlety and elegance mean that it can be drunk straight away.
• Ch. Cazal-Viel, Hameau Cazal-Viel, 34460 Cessenon-sur-Orb, tel. 04.67.89.63.15, fax 04.67.89.65.17 ☑ ▼ ev. day 9am–12.30pm 2pm–6pm; Sat. & Sun. by appt.
• Henri Miquel

CLOS BAGATELLE
La Gloire de mon Père 1999★

■ 3 ha   12,600   €15-23

The family settled here, cleared the scrub and first planted vines in 1643. Since then, the viticultural expertise has been passed on through the female line. The terroir is exceptional, and this reputable estate produces some great wines from it, as this intensely aromatic 99 shows. The bouquet is a mixture of white pepper and preserved raspberries, while the palate has structure and softness, a little too dominated by oak for the time being, but with convincing length. Wait two or three years before drinking this wine, whereupon it would go well with veal sautéed with olives. The Cuvée Mathieu et Marie de Val

Donnadieu 2000 was almost a two-star wine; it has youthful flavours of preserved black fruits, tapinade and musk, which will deserve a discerning palate in a year's time.
• Simon, Clos Bagatelle, 34360 Saint-Chinian, tel. 04.67.93.61.63, fax 04.67.93.68.84, e-mail closbagatelle@libertysurf.fr [V] by appt.

DOM. COMPS
Cuvée des Gleizettes 1999
4 ha   10,000   [€5-8]

The bouquet is discreet, with spicy nuances in which vanilla predominates. On the palate, the wine is attractively marked by red fruits, even if the structure is not huge.
• SCEA Martin-Comps, 23, rue Paul-Riquet, 34620 Puisserguier, tel. 04.67.93.73.15 [V] ev. day 9am–6pm
• Pierre Comps

CH. COUJAN Cuvée Bois Joli 1999
2 ha   6,450   [€8-11]

Long maceration has resulted in a dense, rich, tannic wine, which will need to be tasted again in a year or two. It is a fine Saint-Chinian, having a spicy, black-peppery character, together with full, yet still overfirm, body. Time will mature it and open it up.
• F. Guy et S. Peyre, Ch. Coujan, 34490 Murviel-les-Béziers, tel. 04.67.37.80.00, fax 04.67.37.86.23, e-mail coujan@mnet.fr [V] ev. day 9am–12 noon 2pm–7pm; Sun. by appt.

DOM. DESLINES Cuvée LC 1999★
3 ha   20,000   [€5-8]

Information technology could not compete for this grower with the poetry of becoming a *vigneron* at Babeau-Bouldoux. The 70-year-old vines of this schist *terroir* have yielded very fine results. There are complex aromas of fruits in brandy, of the garrigue, thyme, undergrowth and cloves in the wine. On the palate, it is rounded and supple, sustained by discreet tannins – an aromatically interesting and elegant Saint-Chinian.
• Line Cauquil, Dom. Deslines, 34360 Babeau-Bouldoux, tel. 04.67.38.19.95, fax 04.67.38.19.95, e-mail deslines@netcourrier.com [V] by appt.

DOM. DE GABELAS
Cuvée Juliette Elevé en fût de chêne 1999★
2.2 ha   5,000   [€8-11]

The talented Pierrette Cravero has owned this estate since 1972. Her oak-matured Cuvée Juliette, a predominantly Syrah wine (90%), is redolent of raspberry preserve and resin. It is beginning to reveal its potential. The attack cuts through immediately to the concentrated, very rounded body. A very true-to-type 99, this will go extremely well with Languedoc-style grilled lamb.
• Pierrette Cravero, Dom. de Gabelas, 34310 Cruzy, tel. 04.67.93.84.29, fax 04.67.93.84.29 [V] by appt.

DOM. DES JOUGLA Signature 1999★
3 ha   18,600   [€5-8]

The Signature *cuvée* is a great witness to the skills of the Jougla family, generations of whom have been tending vines here since the 16th century. Superbly deep purple in colour, the wine has a very complex bouquet of pepper, bay-leaves and preserved fruits. After a forthright opening impression, it immediately displays strong tannic presence on a fleshy palate. A very authentic Saint-Chinian.
• Alain Jougla, 34360 Prades-sur-Vernazobre, tel. 04.67.38.06.02, fax 04.67.38.17.74 [V]

CH. LA DOURNIE 2000★
3 ha   12,000   [€5-8]

Here is a rosé that is beautifully fresh, of a gentle pink hue with purple highlights. Its perfumes of flowers (roses) and red fruits are set off by a subtly balanced palate full of fresh, liquorice flavours – a true delight. The oak-matured Château Etienne La Dournie 98 red gains a commendation.
• EARL Ch. La Dournie, rte de Saint-Pons, 34360 Saint-Chinian, tel. 04.67.38.19.43, fax 04.67.38.00.37 [V]
• by appt.
• Etienne

DOM. LA MADURA 1999★★
8 ha   8,000   [€15-23]

Cyril Bourgne came here with his wife Nadia in 1998 after nine years of working in one of the finest crus of Bordeaux. Experience enabled him to recognise very quickly the exceptional quality of the Saint-Chinian *terroir*. Everything about this wine is magnificent and yet delicate: the brilliant colour, the elegance of the red-fruit aromas and smoky notes. The palate is dense with nuances of cherries and silky tannins. It needs to wait a bit, but this is a fine 99 from a very promising estate.
• Nadia et Cyril Bourgne, 61, av Raoul-Bayon, 34360 Saint-Chinian, tel. 04.67.38.17.85, fax 04.67.38.17.85, e-mail lamadura@wanadoo.fr [V] by appt.

DOM. DU LANDEYRAN
Cuvée Emilia 1999
n.c.   6,000   [€5-8]

Working a schist *terroir* set in a magnificent landscape, Michel Soulier (who discovered his passion for viticulture in 1993, after 20 years in banking) has produced this garrigue-scented wine. The bouquet also has aromas of red fruits, which make their mark as soon as the wine is swirled in the glass. Its rich, dense palate, with just a hint of tannin, guarantees a long life to this very promising *cuvée*.
• Dom. du Landeyran, rue de la Vernière, 34490 Saint-Nazaire-de-Ladarez, tel. 04.67.89.67.63, fax 04.67.89.67.63, e-mail domainedulandeyran@free.fr [V] by appt.

DOM. MARQUISE DES MURES
Cuvée Les Sagnes 1999★★

■ 10 ha 17,000 ▦ €8-11

This is a superb schist-soil wine from the village of Roquebrun. The Grand Jury was bowled over by its subtlety, elegance and authenticity. Grapes from century-old Carignan vines combine with Grenache and Syrah to balance one another in this *cuvée*. The bouquet is smoky, with pronounced charred notes, but then releases floral scents (violets and roses) that are not often encountered in a red wine. After a clean opening impression, the palate is full, well-balanced and harmonious. The same estate's **Cuvée Réserve des Marquises 99** gains one star. What marvellous wines!

➤ Jean-Jacques Mailhac, GAEC Dom. des Marquises, 34460 Roquebrun, tel. 04.67.89.55.63, fax 04.67.89.55.63
Y by appt.

MAS CHAMPART
Clos de La Simonette 1999★★

■ 1.3 ha n.c. ▦ €15-23

Isabelle and Mathieu Champart fell under the spell of this magnificent region in 1988, and planted terraces of vines in areas that had been abandoned. All their wines, red and white, have been well received. Clos de la Simonette has an intense purple colour and a delicious, rich bouquet of ripe fruits, the garrigue and rosemary on a bed of spices (liquorice particularly). The maturation has been very well judged, as is confirmed by the tannins on the palate, which remain quite soft. Though already excellent, this wine should age magnificently. Two other wines are commended: the **Causse du Bousquet red 99** and the **Coteaux du Languedoc white 99**. Don't forget that this estate won a *coup de cœur* last year.

➤ EARL Champart, Bramefan, rte de Villespassans, 34360 Saint-Chinian, tel. 04.67.38.20.09, fax 04.67.38.20.09, e-mail mas.champart@ibertysurf.fr
Y by appt.

CH. MAUREL FONSALADE
Cuvée La Fonsalade Vieilles vignes 1998★

■ 1.5 ha 6,800 ▦ ♦ €11-15

Strictly selected grapes from old vines on classic Saint-Chinian *terroirs* attest to the estate's striving for quality. This *cuvée* has a lovely carmine colour with deep-purple nuances. The expressive bouquet begins with fruits and herbs, after which the palate is full, rounded and powerfully structured – a galvanising combination of qualities. The **Felix Culpa 1997** has spent 30 months in oak, and receives a commendation.

➤ Philippe et Thérèse Maurel, Ch. Maurel Fonsalade, 34490 Causses-et-Veyran, tel. 04.67.89.57.90, fax 04.67.89.72.04
Y by appt.

CH. MILHAU-LACUGUE
Les Truffières 1998★

■ 1 ha 7,000 ▦ €11-15

This family-owned property is a former tenant estate of the Hospitallers of St John of Jerusalem, 3 km (2 miles) from Fontcaude Abbey. Les Truffières is a blend of Syrah (47%), Grenache (48%), Carignan (4%) and Cinsault (1%). Aromatically complex with notes of spices, red fruits and scents of the garrigue, this very fine wine is the product of excellent raw materials, and would be a joyous table-companion at a festive occasion. The estate's **Coteaux du Languedoc white 2000** also earns a star.

➤ Ch. Milhau-Lacugue, Dom. de Milhau, rte de Cazedarnes, 34620 Puisserguier, tel. 04.67.93.64.79, fax 04.67.93.51.93
Y ev. day 9.30pm–12 noon 1.30pm–5pm; Sat. & Sun. by appt.
➤ Lacugue

DOM. NAVARRE
Le Laouzil Terroir de schistes 2000★

■ 4 ha 10,000 ▦ €5-8

Although drinking it now would be too early to do it justice, this wine is nonetheless appreciably well made, especially on the palate, where it is very true to type. The Roquebrun *terroir* never fails. Here, its originality is evident in notes of thyme, the garrigue and a menthol finish, the product of careful wine-making. Serve in three to five years' time with *coq au vin* or a spit-roasted haunch of wild boar.

➤ Thierry Navarre, av. de Balaussan, 34460 Roquebrun, tel. 04.67.89.53.58, fax 04.67.89.70.88 Y by appt.

DOM. DES PRADELS
Elevé en foudre de chêne 1999★★

■ 3.3 ha 16,000 ▦ €5-8

Amidst the green oaks, this schist *terroir*, where members of the Quartironi family dedicate themselves to their vines, seems like the very edge of the world. This remarkable wine sports a fine garnet colour. Its bouquet has a range of floral (rose) and spicy notes. After a forthright opening impression, the palate is pleasingly and elegantly constructed on fine tannins. A well-balanced wine.

➤ Roger Quartironi, Dom. des Pradels, hameau le Priou, 34360 Pierrerue, tel. 04.67.38.01.53, fax 04.67.38.01.53
Y by appt.

CH. DU PRIEURE DES MOURGUES
Grande Réserve 1998★★

2 ha | 9,000 | €11-15

This 40-ha (99-acre) estate has managed to get the best out of its *terroir* in spite of the difficulties of the vintage. The subtly intense bouquet mixes aromas of liquorice, morello cherries and the garrigue. On the palate, the wine is full, long-lasting and well balanced. It should steadily improve in the months to come, and would then go very well with a joint of beef. The **Cuvée Principale red 99** gains a star for its elegant oakiness and aromatic complexity.

☛ SARL Vignobles Roger, Ch. du Prieuré des Mourgues, 34360 Pierrerue, tel. 04.67.38.18.19, fax 04.67.38.27.29, e-mail prieure.des.mourgues@wanadoo.fr ☑ by appt.

PRIEURE SAINT-ANDRE
Cuvée Andréus 1999

2 ha | 3,000 | €8-11

The tasting-cellar is in a 16th-century vaulted sheepfold. Cuvée Andréus is a dense red with aromas of blackberries, cherry jam and undergrowth. It is rich on the palate, with rounded tannins. This charming wine is ready for drinking.

☛ Michel Claparède, Prieuré Saint-André, 34460 Roquebrun, tel 04.67.89.70.82, fax 04.67.89.71.41 ☑ ev. day 10am–12.30pm 3pm–6.30pm

DOM. RIMBERT
Le Mas au Schiste 1999★

8.5 ha | 30,000 | €8-11

The old vines of Berlou, planted on schist, are what attracted Jean-Marie Rimbert here in 1996. All the secrets of the *terroir* are revealed in this *cuvée*. Carignan (40%), Syrah (25%), Grenache (20%) and Mourvèdre (15%) go to make up this fine, deep-red wine with its intensely smoky, toasty aromas of gun flint and morello cherries, accompanied by a floral note. The rounded, well-balanced palate leads up to a harmonious finish. This wine is ready to please.

☛ Jean-Marie Rimbert, 4, av. des Mimosas, 34360 Berlou, tel. 04.67.89.73.98, fax 04.67.89.73.98 ☑ by appt.

LES VINS DE ROQUEBRUN
Cuvée Roches noires 2000

25 ha | 130,000 | €8-11

The village of Roquebrun is part of the Haut-Languedoc national park and possesses a Mediterranean garden of great interest to botanists. The co-operative here oversees 480 ha (1,190 acres) of vines. The youthfulness of this wine prevented the members of the Jury from making many detailed comments, but they were able to get some idea of its originality and power. In two to three years' time, its promise will become fully evident, but it will need decanting.

☛ Cave Les Vins de Roquebrun, av. des Orangers, 34460 Roquebrun, tel. 04.67.89.64.35, fax 04.67.89.57.93, e-mail info@cave.roquebrun.fr ☑ by appt.

DOM. DU SACRE-COEUR
Cuvée Jean Madoré 1998★★

2 ha | 1,500 | €11-15

This wine has charisma, personality, warmth and generosity, like the father-in-law whom it honours. It illustrates the art of a grower able to make a wine speak from its roots and *terroir*. Strict selections of Carignan, Grenache and Syrah grapes, followed by 18 months' maturation in oak, have ensured that this fine 98 has cellaring potential. Serve it decanted, when ready, with game-birds.

☛ GAEC du Sacré-Cœur, 34360 Assignan, tel. 04.67.38.17.97, fax 04.67.38.24.52 ☑ ev. day 8.30am–12.30pm 2pm–6.30pm
☛ Marc et Luc Cabaret

DOM. SORTEILHO 2000★

30 ha | 160,000 | €5-8

To be young is no fault. Made on 15 September 2000, and then given six months' vatting, this wine was tasted on 10 April 2001. No matter: the strength of the *terroir* is clearly there. The floral, complex, spicy bouquet leads on to a fresh, densely textured palate with notes of cherry jam. The tannins are still a little obvious, but should have softened soon enough.

☛ Cave des Vignerons de Saint-Chinian, rte de Sorteilho, 34360 Saint-Chinian, tel. 04.67.38.28.41, fax 04.67.38.28.43 ☑ by appt.

DOM. DES SOULIE 2000★

10 ha | 50,000 | €3-5

Grown on limestone-clay soils that have been managed organically since 1968, this traditionally vinified 2000 is a delightful wine. Subtle and elegant, it displays fine maturity on the palate, and is very generous in style. Notes of eucalyptus and menthol supply freshness to a charming young wine that would go very well with leg of lamb.

☛ Aurore et Rémy Soulié, Dom. des Soulié, Carriera de la Teuliera, 34360 Assignan, tel. 04.67.38.11.78, fax 04.67.38.19.31 ☑ by appt.

DOM. DU TABATAU
Lo Tabataire 1999★★

2.5 ha | 6,500 | €8-11

Bruno Gracia quit everything in order to set up in business with his brother Jean-Paul, thus realising his dream of becoming a winegrower. His enthusiasm is evident in this dark *cuvée* with its intense, complex bouquet of cherries, spices (black pepper) and preserved fruits. It coats the palate with elegant flavours, and its balance and length take one pleasantly by surprise. A carefully made wine that would go very well with Languedoc cooking.

Cabardès

The wines of the Côtes de Cabardès and Obiel come from *terroirs* north of Carcassonne and west of the Minervois. The vineyard covers 514 ha (1,270 acres) in 18 communes. In 2000 production was 28,978 hl (765,019 gal) of both red and rosé wines, which mix vine varieties suited to both the Atlantic Mediterranean and the Atlantic areas of the appellation. The Atlantic influence in this, the most westerly appellation in the region, make its wines substantially different from other wines in Languedoc-Roussillon.

LES CELLIERS DU CABARDÈS 2000★★

▮ 2.07 ha 3,500 ▮ €5-8

This wine comes from vines situated around the superb village of Aragon in the heart of the appellation, where the rambler frequently comes across the most splendid *capitelles*, stone peasant-built huts dating from an era when agriculture dominated the whole region. This tender-looking rosé has a surprisingly strong and elegant bouquet evocative of rose-petals and crystallised fruits. Supple and generous, with a light, vivacious air, it is a very pleasing wine.

- SCV Les Celliers du Cabardès, rte de Fraisse, 11600 Aragon, tel. 04.68.24.90.64, fax 04.68.24.87.09 ▼ Y by appt.

DOM. DE CABROL

Cuvée Vent d'Est 1999★★★

▮ 6 ha 19,000 ▮ €5-8

Once again, Claude Carayol proves that talent and risk-taking in the form of harvesting at full maturity can result in very great wines. He expresses the strengths of the appellation perfectly and knows how to respect a great *terroir*. You will admire in this fine 99 its deep colour and very concentrated bouquet of overripe black fruits. This generous and complex *cuvée* is also endowed with a most attractive and long-lasting finish.

CH. VIRANEL

Elevé en fût de chêne 1999★★

▮ 2 ha 10,000 ▮ €8-11

This château has been in the same family since 1550! Is this a record in the *Guide?* It is said that 1999 was a difficult year, but you wouldn't guess it from the aromatic range of this Viranel, which mixes balsamic and clove aromas with an unusual hint of wax. The palate confirms these impressions inasmuch as the structure is extremely fine, with well-balanced yet evident tannins. This wine is already quite remarkable and would go best with classic dishes, such as game-birds.

- GFA de Viranel, 34460 Cessenon, tel. 04.90.55.85.82, fax 04.90.55.88.97 ▼
- Y by appt.
- Bergasse-Milhé

CH. VEYRAN

Cuvée Henri Elevé en fût de chêne 1999★★

▮ 4.75 ha 13,000 ▮ €15-23

The very least to be said of this wine is that it is powerful, round and pleasing. The authentic character of the limestone-clay Saint-Chinian *terroir* comes through in the tannins, warmth and balance of the palate. Preserved black fruits (bilberries) and garrigue aromas persist on the finish for no less than eight seconds. Another 12 months' keeping should make this wine more appealing still. It would go well with grilled kidneys or woodcock.

- Gérard Antoine, Ch. Veyran, 34490 Causses-et-Veyran, tel. 04.67.89.65.77, fax 04.67.89.65.77 ▼
- Y by appt.
- Vignerons de Saint-Chinian

DOM. DE TRIANON 1999★★

▮ 9 ha 40,000 ▮ €5-8

Not without good reason is Bruno Peyre's motto 'Wine-makers and Passions'. This oenologist offers a very attractive wine, whose aromatic range is characteristic of schist soils (charred, liquorice and jammy notes). The well-rounded tannins make their presence felt after a supple, rounded entry, and provide good structure.

- Vignerons et Passions, BP 1, 34725 Saint-Félix-de-Lodez, tel. 04.67.88.80.39, fax 04.67.88.86.39 ▼
- Y by appt.
- Vignerons de Saint-Chinian

CH. TENDON

Cuvée des Hirondelles 1999★★

▮ 3.5 ha 16,000 ▮ €5-8

In 1988, Jacques and Gisèle Belot cleared this limestone-clay part of the Saint-Chinian *terroir*. The torch now passes to Karine and Lionel. Cuvée des Hirondelles is an intense red colour, with a bouquet dominated by ripe red fruits, spices and notes of the garrigue. It displays a forthright opening impression and evident tannins, and both the balance and length on the palate are promising. Another star goes to their **L'Argilière du château Belot 98**.

- Gisèle et Jacques Belot, rte de Cazedarne, 34360 Saint-Chinian, tel. 04.67.38.28.48, fax 04.67.38.28.43

- Bruno et Jean-Paul Gracia, rue des Anciens-Combattants, 34360 Assignan, tel. 04.67.38.19.60, fax 04.67.38.19.54 ▼
- Y by appt.

♠ SARL Vignobles Alain Maurel, 1, pl. du Château, 11610 Ventenac-Cabardès, tel. 04.68.24.93.42, fax 04.68.24.81.16, e-mail alain-maurel@wanadoo.fr ☑ ⏱ ev. day except Sun. 8am–12 noon 2pm–6pm

Côtes de la Malepère AOVDQS

A total of 40,000 hl (1,056,000 gal) of wine is produced in this AOVDQS, which covers 31 communes in the Aude. The *terroir* receives Atlantic influences and is situated in the north-west of the Hauts-de-Corbières, which protect it from Mediterranean aridity. The red and rosé wines, full-bodied and fruity, come not only from Carignan grapes but also from Bordeaux varieties, mainly Cabernet Sauvignon, Cabernet Franc and Merlot, in addition to Grenache and Cot.

♠ Claude et Michel Carayol, Dom. de Cabrol, 11600 Aragon, tel. 04.68.77.54.90, fax 04.68.77.19.06, ☑ ⏱ ev. day 11am–12 noon 2pm–7pm

■ **CH. JOUCLARY**   n.c.   18,130   Elevé en fût 1999★

This vineyard was established in the 16th century. Robert Gianesini, who has owned it since 1969, has lately been joined by his son who, over the past four vintages, has revealed great wine-making talent. This *cuvée* has a pleasingly dark colour with deep-purple highlights and a bouquet of ripe fruits, enhanced by notes of vanilla and spices, followed on the palate by a straightforward opening impression and powerful tannic structure. This promising wine needs more time to harmonise.

♠ EARL Gianesini, Ch. Jouclary, 11600 Conques-sur-Orbiel, tel. 04.68.77.10.02, fax 04.68.77.00.21 ☑ ⏱ Sat. 11am–7pm

■ **CH. DE PENNAUTIER**   L'Esprit de Pennautier 1999★★   10 ha   26,000   €15-23

This 200-ha (494-acre) estate has seen all of Languedoc's history; among its famous guests in the past was one Molière. This 1999 is the product of particularly rigorously selected grapes and 18 months of oak maturation. Powerful and intense, full and generous on the palate, it has a fine oak element that contributes to its enjoyment. This very fine wine needs careful keeping. Note also the rosé **2000 de Pennautier** that was commended by the Jury.

♠ SCEA Ch. de Pennautier, 11610 Pennautier, tel. 04.68.72.65.29, fax 04.68.72.65.84, e-mail contact@Vignobles-Lorgeril.com ☑ ⏱ by appt.
♠ N. de Lorgeril

■ **CH. VENTENAC**   Traditionnel 1999★   40 ha   200,000   €5-8

Professionalism and high standards characterise the work of this grower, who is located in the foothills of the Massif Central on a soil of white limestone. His wine has a deep purple colour with youthful highlights. The bouquet is subtle and delicate, with scents of the garrigue and of red fruits. Supple at first on the palate, it displays a generous structure with good tannic support. A fine balance of the wine means that it can be enjoyed now.

Côtes de la Malepère AOVDQS

■ **DOM. DE FOUCAULD**   2000★★   n.c.   8,000   €3-5

The Arzens cellar distinguishes itself this year with its intense rosé, produced using state-of-the-art technology and possessed of fabulous aromatic power. Raspberries, blackberries, honey and spices dance together in a lively, merry quadrille. Its generosity on the palate develops with elegance and length. An ambassador of summer that will nonetheless be an excellent companion for your autumn salads and grills.

♠ Cave La Malepère, av. des Vignerons, 11290 Arzens, tel. 04.68.76.71.71, fax 04.68.76.71.72, e-mail oeno@cavelamalepere.com ☑ ⏱ ev. day except Sat. & Sun. 8am–12 noon 2pm–6pm

■ **DOM. DE LASSALLE**   1998★   1.5 ha   5,000   €5-8

Not long established and yet already in the *Guide*, this estate has produced a wine with a crystal-clear, intense colour of which the growers can be proud. Its complex bouquet plays on overripe fruits with hints of pepper and coriander. Full, well made, and with imposing structure, it is elegantly enhanced by a hint of vanilla. The well-balanced, warm finish will guarantee impeccable development both in the cellar and in the mouth.

Côtes de la Malepère AOVDQS

☛ Cave coop. de Rouffiac d'Aude,
5, av. des Carrassiers, 11250 Rouffiac
d'Aude, tel. 04.68.26.81.73,
fax 04.68.26.89.00 ▾

DOM. LE FORT
Elevé en fût de chêne 1998★★

■ 3 ha   20,000   ▦ €5-8

This young wine-grower strives for excellence on the slopes that produce this *cuvée*
with its engaging garnet-red colour. Oak maturation has produced a tough, fleshy wine
with a fine complexity of cooked fruits and
spices. The palate is full and well-balanced,
with a hint of vanilla. Some fairly evident
tannins guarantee the wine will keep well.
Time is on its side.

☛ Marc Pagès, Dom. Le Fort,
11290 Montréal-de-l'Aude,
tel. 04.68.76.20.11, fax 04.68.76.20.11 ▾
Ⓨ by appt.

DOM. DE MATIBAT
Elevé en fût de chêne 1999★

■ 5.4 ha 10,000   ▦ ◊ €5-8

Twelve months in oak and vat have produced a strong, characterful wine, and yet the
chocolate, vanilla and toasty overtones meld
together gently into a palate that is still quite
fresh. Balanced and subtle, with a smooth and
fruity finish, the wine is sustained by classy
tannins. It can wait.

☛ Jean-Claude Turetti, Dom. de Matibat,
11300 Saint-Martin-de-Villeréglan,
tel. 04.68.31.15.52, fax 04.68.31.04.29 ▾
Ⓨ by appt.

CH. MONTCLAR 1999★★★

■   20 ha 26,000   ▦ €5-8

Even though Château de Montclar has
gained top honours, **Domaine de Majou 2000**
and **Domaine de Fournery rosé 2000** are also
excellent wines. This three-star ruby-coloured
wine has aromas of undergrowth, raspberries
and quince. Unstinting praise was heaped
upon it for its power, and the warmth of its
concentrated, well-balanced palate. The
fruit-and-vanilla finish is a cause for celebration. Open it now or keep it.

☛ Cave du Razès, 11240 Routier,
tel. 04.68.69.02.71, fax 04.68.69.00.49,
e-mail cavedurazes@wanadoo.fr ▾
Ⓨ ev. day except Sat. & Sun. 8am–12 noon
2pm–6pm

Roussillon

Growing vines in Roussillon may date as far back as the
seventh century BC, perhaps instigated by Greek traders, drawn to the
Catalan coast by its rich mineral deposits. The trade was well developed by
medieval times, and the sweet wines of the region built a solid reputation
very early on. After their devastation by phylloxera in the early 20th
century, the vineyards were abundantly replanted to flourish once again on
the hills of France's southernmost vine-growing area.

Facing the Mediterranean, the Roussillon vineyards are
surrounded by three mountain ranges: the Corbières in the north, the
Canigou in the west and the Albères, which forms the border with Spain, in
the south. The Têt, Tech and Agly rivers have shaped a landscape of gravel
terraces where the washed, stony soils are ideally suited to produce wines
of quality, particularly Vin Doux Naturels (see page 1167). Also found are
soils from different origins made up of black or brown schists and sandy
granites as well as hills of Pliocene limestone.

The Roussillon vineyards enjoy a particularly sunny climate, with mild winters and high temperatures in summer. The rainfall – 350–650 mm (14–26 in) – is very uneven and often falls in torrential storms that are not beneficial for the vines. Fortunately, a dry, summer period follows, and the heat is intensified by the Tramontane wind, which helps the grapes to ripen.

Côtes du Roussillon and Côtes du Roussillon-Villages

The vines are trained in the traditional goblet shape and planted 4,000 to the hectare (1,620 to the acre). Tradition still plays a great part in cultivation, which is often only partly mechanised. However, the wine-making equipment in the cellars is being modernised in line with a diversification in vine varieties and vinification techniques. After being carefully checked for ripeness, the harvest is transported in trailers or small trucks without being crushed; some of the grapes are treated by carbonic maceration. Increasingly, temperature during vinification is controlled to protect the delicacy of the aromas: in Roussillon, tradition and modern technology work side by side.

These two appellations are produced from the best soils in the region. In 2000 the vineyards, about 8,800 ha (21,736 acres), produced 390,000 hl (10,296,000 gal) across the whole of the appellation. The Côtes du Roussillon-Villages are clustered in the northernmost part of the Pyrénées-Orientales department; four communes have an appellation with the village name: Caramany, Lesquerde, Tautavel and Latour-de-France. Gravel terraces, sandy granite and schist give the wines a richness and a qualitative difference that the wine-growers certainly know how to exploit.

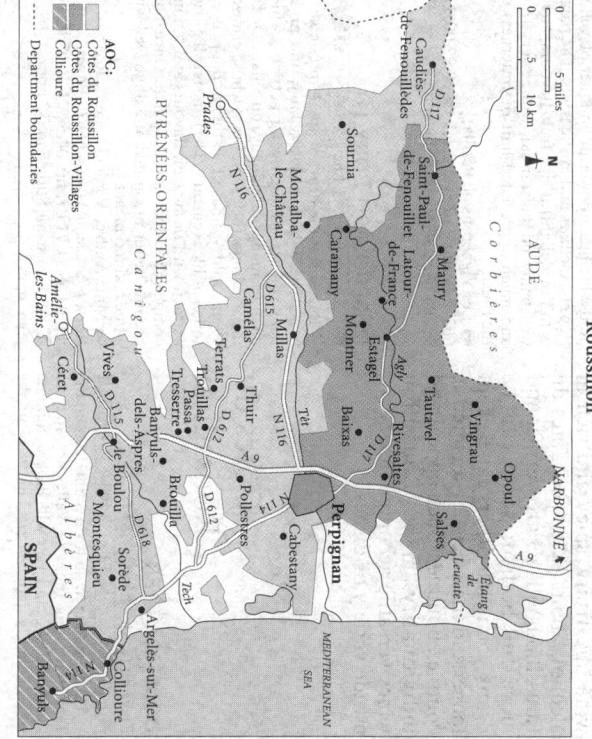

AOC:
- Côtes du Roussillon
- Côtes du Roussillon-Villages
- Collioure
- Department boundaries

0   5 miles
0   5   10 km

Roussillon

The vine varieties used to produce the white wines are mainly Macabeu, Malvoisie du Roussillon and Grenache Blanc, but Marsanne, Roussanne and Rolle are also used and are mainly vinified by direct pressing. The wines themselves are green in type, light and vigorous, with a fine, floral aroma and so go well with seafood, fish and shellfish.

The rosé and red wines are produced using several varieties: Carignan Noir (a maximum of 60%), Grenache Noir, Lladoner Pelut and Cinsault are the main varieties, with Syrah, Mouvèdre and Macabeu (10% maximum in the red wines) as additional varieties; two main varieties are required with another additional variety. All the varieties (except the Syrah) are pruned short down to two buds. Often, a proportion of the harvest is vinified by carbonic maceration: Carignan in particular produces excellent results with this method. The rosé wines are, of necessity, vinified by the *saignée*, or bleeding method.

The rosé wines are fruity, full-bodied and lively; the red wines are fruity, spicy and rich in alcohol, about 12%. The Côtes du Roussillon-Villages are warmer and more full-bodied; some can be drunk young but others can be kept longer and these develop an intense, complex bouquet. Such appeal and individuality make Roussillon wines versatile accompaniments to a wide variety of dishes.

Côtes du Roussillon

DOM. ALQUIER
Elevé en fût de chêne 1998★★

▪ 1.5 ha 2,500 ▥ €8-11

Take the time to go from Saint-Jean up the Tech and along the wild Vallespir valley to the Ares Pass, and you will have a sublime view of the Canigou *massif*. This 98 bears the stamp of the Albères *terroir* in its deep colour and dominant aromas of violets and wild mint. This is a substantial, rich, robust wine, which also has fleshy, velvety and marked by the earthy freshness of undergrowth. It finishes delightfully on a note of blackcurrant.
● Pierre Alquier, Dom. Alquier, 66490 Saint-Jean-Pla-de-Corts, tel. 04.68.83.20.66, fax 04.68.83.55.45 �byV
Y by appt.

ARNAUD DE VILLENEUVE
Vieilles vignes 2000

▪ n.c. 40,000 ▪ ◆

The new president of the region's oenological society has produced two very good wines here: an A. de Villeneuve red 2000, Vieilles Vignes, which earned a commendation, and this raspberry-hued rosé that, as soon as it is opened, releases strawberry and redcurrant aromas backed up by astonishing spicy notes. It is full and substantial on the palate, where its ripe fruit flavours give it a resolutely Mediterranean character. This is a rosé that will go well with food.
● Les Vignobles du Rivesaltais, 1, rue de la Roussillonnaise, 66602 Rivesaltes-Salses, tel. 04.68.64.06.63, fax 04.68.64.64.69, e-mail vignobles.rivesaltais@wanadoo.fr ▾
Y by appt.

CH. DE BLANES 1999★★

□ 4 ha 10,000 ▪ ◆ €3-5

This vineyard is in a sheltered southerly position, sloping gently down in little terraces from the La Dona Pass to the village, which stretches nonchalantly along the gravelly bank of the main branch of the Têt. This pale gold wine has a powerful bouquet of yellow flowers, medlars and exotic fruits. The palate is full of delightful ripe fruit flavours, and is well built and substantial, with a very fresh and much appreciated hint of bitterness on the finish.
● Les Vignerons de Pézilla, 66370 Pézilla-la-Rivière, tel. 04.68.92.00.09, fax 04.68.92.49.91 ▾ Y by appt.

DOM. JOSEPH BORY 1999

▪ 5.4 ha 2,500 ▥ €5-8

Bages is at the heart of the Aspres coastal area. The village is always busy, and prides itself on its wine-growing activity, which includes many individually run cellars. One of these belongs to Joseph Bory, whose crimson 99 has wild aromas of leather and a peppery touch of blackcurrant. The wine is full of rich extract, with fleshy fruit flavours and tannins competing to dominate the palate. Once it has become better integrated, it will go well with game and red meats.
● Mme Andrée Verdeille, Dom. Joseph Bory, 6, av. Jean-Jaurès, 66670 Bages, tel. 04.68.21.71.07, fax 04.68.21.71.07 ▾
Y ev. day except Sun. 9am–12 noon 3pm–6pm

DOM. BOUDAU Cuvée du Clos 2000★

■ 2 ha | 7,000 | €5-8

Pierre and Véronique Bouday are a very good brother-and-sister partnership, working together with skill and talent. This wine has a strong purplish-red colour, which shows that it is still young, and a very intense bouquet of crushed red berries with a more muted hint of fruit stones. The palate is rich, fruity, full and generous, with evident, sturdy tannins. Two to three years' time is needed for the wine to come into balance.

🍷 Dom. Véronique et Pierre Boudau, 6, rue Marceau, 66600 Rivesaltes, tel. 04.68.64.45.37, fax 04.68.64.46.26 ✓
🍽 from Jun. to Sep. ev. day except Sun. 10am–12 noon 3pm–7pm.

CH. DE CORNEILLA 1998★

■ 14 ha | 85,000 | €5-8

This château is full of history, the family having been here for centuries and achieving world renown by producing Olympic champions in fencing and horse-riding. The **Domaine Jonquières d'Oriola red 98** from here was much appreciated by the jury, and wins a commendation. This château wine has a brilliant garnet colour and a bouquet of ripe cherries, blackcurrants and fruits in brandy. On the palate, it is supple and surprisingly fresh and vigorous, with a note of sharp fruits and well-integrated tannins. Its spicy finish will make it a good accompaniment to Catalan charcuterie and *escalivade* (a baked vegetable dish of aubergine, peppers and tomatoes).

🍷 EARL Jonquères d'Oriola, Ch. de Corneilla, 66200 Corneilla-del-Vercol, tel. 04.68.22.73.22, fax 04.68.22.43.99, e-mail chateaudecorneilla@hotmail.com ✓

DOM BRIAL 1999★

■ n.c. | 20,000 | €3-5

Being in the world capital of the Muscat grape is not enough for the Cave des Vignerons de Baixas; this strong, reliable team has also shown great skill in creating an enviable position for itself among the élite. Its red Côtes du Roussillon has a colour somewhere between crimson and garnet, and a bouquet of red berries and undergrowth with accents of violet. The main impression on the palate is of cleanness: this is a supple, smooth, remarkably well-balanced wine with a spicy, silkily tannic finish.

🍷 Cave des Vignerons de Baixas, 14, av. Mal-Joffre, 66390 Baixas, tel. 04.68.64.22.37, fax 04.68.64.26.70, e-mail baixas@smi-telecom.fr ✓
🍽 by appt.

DOM. FERRER RIBIERE

Cana 1999★

■ 4 ha | 12,000 | €15-23

The partnership of Denis Ferrer and Bruno Ribière is more than ever concerned with the pursuit of high quality. Sustainable viticulture, careful selection of grapes by plot, hand-sorting, long maceration periods, a mastery of oak-maturation: all this has given us a brilliant garnet 99 Cana, characterised by preserved fruits, leather and undergrowth. It is full, substantial and powerful on the palate, where toast and fruit flavours are supported by very fine tannins. This is a very full, appealing wine with excellent ageing potential.

🍷 Dom. Denis et Bruno Ferrer Ribière, SCEA des Flo, 20, rue du Colombier, 66300 Terrats, tel. 04.68.53.24.45, fax 04.68.53.10.79 ✓ 🍽 by appt.

DOM. GARDIES Vieilles vignes 1999★

□ 2 ha | n.c. | €8-11

In autumn, the Vingrau vineyard, set in the limestone *cirque* of the high Corbières, offers a magnificent patchwork view from the top of the Escalette Pass. This wine has a pale yellow colour, and needs to breathe a while before it releases its aromas of overripe and exotic fruits. The rich, full palate has a fine hint of oak, which adds vanilla notes to the very fresh grapefruit flavour on the finish.

🍷 Dom. Gardies, 66600 Vingrau, tel. 04.68.64.61.16, fax 04.68.64.69.36 ✓
🍽 by appt.

JEAN D'ESTAVEL Prestige 1998

■ n.c. | 25,000 | €3-5

The whole art of the *négociant* lies in blending and maturation. This company's detailed knowledge of the regional *terroirs* is a considerable asset, as is shown by this wine, which comes from schist and limestone soils. It has a deep red colour, and a bouquet that, as it develops, is beginning to display aromas of venison and ripe fruits. Maturation has added charming softness to a well-balanced palate that is both fresh and spicy. The wine is ready to drink now with white meats or charcuterie.

🍷 SA Destavel, 7 bis, av. du Canigou, 66000 Perpignan, tel. 04.68.68.36.00, fax 04.68.54.03.54 ✓
🍷 M. G. Baissas

LE CELLIER DE LA BARNEDE 2000★

■ 3 ha | 4,500 | €5-8

The 'cave des artisans du vin' here shows a fine mastery of technique in this peony-coloured rosé with rose-petal aromas accompanied by pear-drop notes. A banana flavour gives way to a fruity finish on the palate, which is supple, fresh and well balanced.

🍷 SCV Les Producteurs de La Barnède, 5, av. du 8-Mai-1945, 66670 Bages, tel. 04.68.21.60.30, fax 04.68.37.50.13 ✓
🍽 by appt.

LA CASENOVE Cuvée Commandant François Jaubert 1998★

■ 20 ha | 18,000 | €15-23

They say that it was at Trouillas that Arnaud de Villeneuve discovered the principle of *mutage* for Vins Doux Naturels. The dry wines produced here are also expressive, however. This one, for example, is deeply coloured, with a strongly extracted character on the bouquet, where overripe fruit aromas mingle with peppery scents and more aggressive notes of undergrowth. This is a very ample wine that fills the palate with rich, fruity flavours.

- Ch. La Casenove, 6300 Trouillas, tel. 04.68.21.66.33, fax 04.68.21.77.81 ☑
- ev. day except Sun. 10am–12 noon 4pm–8pm
- Montes

DOM. LAFAGE 2000

■ 8 ha 42,000 ■ ◇ €5-8

The vineyard here is laid out along the contours of the last wine-growing foothills of the Aspres, where the fresh schist soils are well suited to the Syrah grape. This 2000 vintage has an intense garnet colour and aromas of roasting and gun flint which, although still muted, are beginning to break through. The full, substantial flavours of spices and toast combine well on a palate that leads to a well-structured finish. Still full of youthful fruit, the wine is suitable for long maturation.

- SCEA Dom. Lafage, mas Llaro, rte de Canet, 66100 Perpignan, tel. 04.68.67.12.47, fax 04.68.62.10.99, e-mail enofool@aol.com ☑
- ☑ by appt.

DOM. DE LA MADELEINE 2000★★

■ n.c. 3,000 ■ ◇ €5-8

The buildings and gardens of this property, located on the gravel terrace overlooking the Têt, seem to be watching jealously over the vineyard. This wine has a beautiful ruby colour with purplish highlights, and a surprising bouquet of preserved cherries and honeysuckle. More fruit flavours appear on the palate, giving it not just plenty of body, but also a very fresh touch of acidity. The tannins are still very much in evidence, ensuring that the wine has excellent prospects for the future. It will in time be a good accompaniment to game.

- Dom. de La Madeleine, chem. de Charlemagne, 66000 Perpignan, tel. 04.68.50.02.17, fax 04.68.50.02.17 ☑
- ☑ Wed. Sat. 9am–1pm
- Georges Assens

DOM. DE L'AURIS 1999★

■ 7 ha 32,200 ■ ◇ €5-8

Nobody happens upon Tarérach by chance, which is just as well, since it is essential to preserve, and deserve, the wild beauty of this high plateau, where patches of scrub cling to the ruin-like granite relief. One particular pleasure of the Canigou is this wine, which is made by the wine-growers of Tarérach and marketed in Perpignan. It has an intense, inviting red colour and a range of Syrah aromas, from violets to blackcurrants and cherry stalks, leading on to a fruity palate with a touch of liquorice. This elegant wine is ready to drink now.

- Méditerroirs, 264, chem. du Pas-de-la-Paille, BP 52114, 66012 Perpignan Cedex, tel. 04.68.55.88.40, fax 04.68.55.87.67, e-mail méditerroirs@ caramail.com ☑ ☑ by appt.

DOM. DU MAS BECHA 1999★

■ 3 ha 4,300 ■ ◇ €5-8

The hamlet of Nyls is trying to resist urbanisation, and thanks to Mas Bécha, it has been able since 1997 to boast a high-quality small producer, where previously there was only wine produced in bulk. The proof is in this cuvée, whose intense red colour evokes red cherries, while the aromas are more suggestive of toast, venison and spices. It is supple on the palate, with fine, velvety tannins and a toasty note on the finish. This attractive, aromatic 99 is ready to drink now. Also worthy of note here is the rosé 2000, a well-made wine that wins a commendation.

- Dom. Mas Bécha, 1, av. de Pollestres, 66300 Nyls-Ponteilla, tel. 04.68.54.52.80, fax 04.68.55.31.89 ☑ ☑ by appt.
- Perez

DOM. DU MAS CREMAT

Élevé en fût de chêne 1999★★★

■ 3 ha 12,000 ■ €11-15

It is hard to choose here between the unmaked 99 that, with its delightful aromas of ripe fruits and peppery cherries, its full, fine palate and its good ageing potential, also wins three stars and is excellent value for money, and this oak-aged 99, a heavier wine with a higher proportion of Mourvèdre. The fruit is masked on the bouquet by oak for now, although it comes to life on the palate. The balance between wine and oak is perfect, blending the power of the one with the finesse of the other to make for a substantial wine with magnificent, velvety tannins, giving great hope for the future.

- Jeannin-Mongeard, Dom. du Mas Cremat, 66600 Espira-de-l'Agly, tel. 04.68.38.92.06, fax 04.68.38.92.23 ☑
- ☑ by appt.

MAS D'EN BADIE 1998★

■ n.c. 8,000 €5-8

This vineyard has the advantage of being sheltered by the last wine-growing hills before the foothills of the Canigou and the Pyrenees. Safe from the wind, the area offers a festival of colour in the autumn. The colour of this wine is somewhere between crimson and garnet, showing that it is still young. Its aromas waver between undergrowth, game and overripe fruits. Silky tannins are accompanied by a note of roasting coffee beans on the palate, which is supple and velvety. The touch of gaminess will make this the perfect wine to drink with a whole range of game dishes in sauces.

- Vignerons de La Méditerranée, ZI Plaisance,12, rue du Rec-de-Veyret, BP 414, 11104 Narbonne Cedex, tel. 04.68.42.75.00, fax 04.68.42.75.01, e-mail rhirtz@iistel.fr ☑
- ☑ by appt.

DOM. DU MAS ROUS
Cuvée élevée en fût de chêne 1998★★★

| 9 ha | 53,000 | 📦 | €5-8 |

■

This splendid Albères *terroir* is set in a superb location between the Pyrenean foothills and the Mediterranean, where the vines have to be protected from property speculators, as well as the more usual pests. Once again, the vineyard has come up trumps with a wine whose deep colour is very much in keeping with its bouquet of small red berries, against a background of spices and toast. What is really exciting, however, is the full, velvety palate, which offers a combination of silky tannins and peppery cherries, pierced by the classic mineral note of the Albères soils – a truly superb wine. The **Cuvée Prestige 98** obtained one star.

↳ José Pujol, Dom. du Mas Rous,
66740 Montesquieu-des-Albères,
tel. 04.68.89.64.91, fax 04.68.89.80.88 Ⓥ
🍷 by appt.

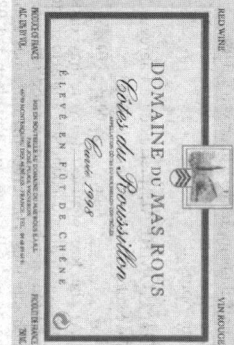

DOM. DE NIDOLÈRES
La Pierroune 1999

| 3 ha | 4,000 | ■ 📦 | €8-11 |

Looking out on the wild beauty of the Albères, this vineyard stretches over the terraces of the Tech at the entrance to the Vallespir valley, which is well known for its early cherries and mimosa. The wine has a crimson colour and an initially shy bouquet of red berries, spices and leather. There is a ripe cherry flavour at first, followed by powerful tannins and a note of oak on the palate, which will make this a good wine to drink with grilled meats and roast poultry.

↳ Pierre Escudié, Dom. de Nidolères,
66300 Tresserre, tel. 04.68.83.15.14,
fax 04.68.83.31.26 Ⓥ 🍷 by appt.

DOM. PAGES HURE 1999

| 11 ha | 33,600 | ■ ▮ | €5-8 |

With his great passion for wine, Jean-Louis Pagès changed tack to take over the family vineyard, which has a long history going back two centuries. In 1991, he launched himself into the direct sales side, and has succeeded, by a combination of modesty and enthusiasm, in making his dream a reality. This clear garnet 99 has intense aromas of cherries, blackberries and blackcurrant leaves in the bouquet, and corresponding flavours of slightly acid red berries on the palate, which is well knit, fresh and supple, yet substantial. Ready to drink.

↳ SCEA Pages Huré, 2, allée des Moines,
66740 Saint-Génis-des-Fontaines,
tel. 04.68.89.82.62, fax 04.68.89.82.62 Ⓥ
🍷 by appt.
↳ Jean-Louis Pagès

CH. MIRAFLORS
Cuvée Vilarnau 1998★

| 10 ha | 5,000 | ■ 🍷 | €5-8 |

Located between the town and the sea, the tower overlooking the old royal sheep pasture seems to watch over the vineyard and the archaeological excavations of the ancient city of Vilarnau. This three-way blend of Syrah, Carignan and Grenache has a garnet colour and aromas of undergrowth, preserved fruits and just a hint of game Its maturation period has given it a toasty, spicy note along with the ripe fruit flavour. This is an integrated, harmonious, well-balanced wine that is ready to be served now with red meats and cheeses.

↳ SA Cibaud-Ch. Miraflors et Belloch, rte de Canet, 66000 Perpignan,
tel. 04.68.34.03.05, fax 04.68.51.31.70,
e-mail vins.cibaud@wanadoo.fr Ⓥ
🍷 ev. day except Sun. 9am–1pm 3pm–7pm

DOM. PIQUEMAL
Elevé en fût de chêne 1999★★

| 4 ha | 27,000 | 📦 | €5-8 |

The problem encountered at the Piquemal estate is how to choose. The superb range here includes a delightfully fruity **unoaked 99** and a **2000 Les Terres Grillées white**, both of which win one star. This oak-matured 99 has a beautiful colour and an intense bouquet, in which cherries and blackberries are softened by vanilla. It won over the Jury with its fullness on the palate, and its combination of rich extract and high-quality oak. The wine finishes on notes of spices and peppery cherries, and would go well with game and red meats.

↳ Dom. Pierre et Franck Piquemal, 1, rue Pierre-Lefranc, 66600 Espira-de-l'Agly,
tel. 04.68.64.09.14, fax 04.68.38.52.94,
e-mail contact@domaine-piquemal.com Ⓥ
🍷 by appt.

CH. MOSSE
Coume d'Abeille 1999★★★

| 5.2 ha | 15,000 | | €5-8 |

■

Sainte-Colombe is not only the jewel of the Aspres; it also contains the cellars of the Mossé family, which is well known for its expertise in bringing out the qualities of its *terroirs*, and for its wonderful Vins Doux Naturels. The same know-how is also responsible for **Temporis 99**, which wins one star, and the deep red Coume d'Abeille with its wild, complex aromas of musk, boxwood and violets. This rich, generous wine is full of classic Syrah characteristics (violets, blackberries and blackcurrants), and the well-structured palate remains velvety and full-bodied to the finish. It is already full of flavour, but will also keep well.

↳ Jacques Mossé, Ch. Mossé, BP 8,
66300 Ste-Colombe-de-la-Commanderie,
tel. 04.68.53.08.89, fax 04.68.53.35.13,
e-mail chateau.mosse@worldonline.fr Ⓥ
🍷 by appt.

CH. PLANERES La Romanie 1999★★★

■   3.5 ha   10,000   III   €11-15

A new, intelligently designed cellar, an early grape harvest … No wonder the quality here is spot-on. The excellent **99 Château Planères red** wins two stars, yielding first place to the Romanie, which has a deep red colour and fruity aromas of cherries and red berries against a spicy background. The palate is ample, full of ripe fruit flavours, with fine, velvety tannins softened by the fleshiness of cherries, and a strong charred note on the finish.

➶• Vignobles Jaubert-Noury,
Ch. Planères, 66300 Saint-Jean-Lasseille,
tel. 04.68.21.74.50, fax 04.68.21.87.25,
e-mail contact@chateauplaneres.com ▼
Ⅰ by appt.

CH. PLANERES La Romanie 1999

☐   3 ha   8,000   €11-15

The Tourbat or Malvoisie of Roussillon is a rare grape variety. It used to be highly reputed, but then fell into neglect until a few vineyards such as this one re-established its pedigree. The wine has a pale gold colour, with honeyed notes of broom that combine well with the fruit scents. It is full and rich on the palate, where apricot and quince flavours are softened by vanilla, but nonetheless remains fresh through to its remarkably long finish.

➶• Vignobles Jaubert-Noury,
Ch. Planères, 66300 Saint-Jean-Lasseille,
tel. 04.68.21.74.50, fax 04.68.21.87.25,
e-mail contact@chateauplaneres.com ▼
Ⅰ by appt.

PUJOL La Montadella 1999★

■   1.8 ha   10,000   ▮   €8-11

Back full-time on the vineyard after spending some years championing Roussillon wines, Jean-Luc Pujol has given himself a new challenge by converting to organic growing methods. This darkly coloured wine is based on Carignan, and has appealing aromas of small purple berries (blackberries and blackcurrants). The tannins are clearly evident, still youthful and full of body, but well balanced with the richness of the ripe fruit flavours. This is a very fine, traditional wine that will be ready to drink with grilled meats in one to two years' time.

➶• Jean-Luc Pujol, EARL La Rourède,
Dom. La Rourède, 66300 Fourques,
tel. 04.68.38.84.44, fax 04.68.38.88.86,
e-mail vins-pujol@wanadoo.fr ▼
Ⅰ ev. day except Sun. 9am–12 noon
3pm–6.30pm

CH. DE REY 1998

■   10 ha   6,000   ▮   €5-8

Overlooking the lake at Canet, Dorf Potersen's château stands narrow and upright, proudly marking the end of the gravel terrace. Given the great heat on this *terroir*, it comes as no surprise to find a wine with dark colour, a bouquet of *eau-de-vie de noyau*, and a palate that is already well matured, full and integrated. Flavours of

prunes are supported by a charred tannic impression.

➶• Philippe and Cathy Sisqueille, EARL Ch. de Rey, 66140 Canet-en-Roussillon,
tel. 04.68.73.86.27, fax 04.68.73.15.03,
e-mail chateau-de-rey@libertysurf.fr ▼
Ⅰ ev. day except Sat. & Sun. 9am–12 noon
2pm–6pm

CH. ROMBEAU Pierre de La Fabrègue

Cuvée élevée en fût de chêne 1998★

■   n.c.   15,000   III   €5-8

At the Rombeau estate, you may taste wines, eat or attend a banquet, and also spend the night … which is often a good idea after such activities. The larger-than-life master of the house will serve you this deep red 98, which has heavy aromas of ripe grapes, undergrowth and leather. The seductive balance of this well-structured, finely oaky wine is sustained by full-bodied fruitiness that gives way on the finish to an attractive note of liquorice.

➶• P.-H. de La Fabrègue,
Dom. de Rombeau, 66600 Rivesaltes,
tel. 04.68.64.35.35, fax 04.68.64.64.66 ▼
Ⅰ ev. day 8am–7.30pm, groups by appt.

DOM. ROZES 1999★★

■   8.1 ha   19,000   ▮   ▮   €5-8

The turbulently flowing Agly runs its course before arriving at Espira, among the white of the limestone hills, the ochrous red of the clay and the ashy black of the marl-schist soils that have yielded this Côtes du Roussillon. It has a deep colour and is dominated by aromas of red berries, spices and grapey vinosity. The substantial, fruity palate has delightful finesse, thanks to the silkiness of the tannins. This serenely well-balanced wine is already a pleasure to drink.

➶• SCEA Tarquin – Dom. Rozès,
3, rue de Lorraine, 66600 Espira-de-l'Agly,
tel. 04.68.38.52.11, fax 04.68.38.51.38,
e-mail rozes.domaine@wanadoo.fr ▼
Ⅰ by appt.
➶• Antoine Rozès

DOM. SAINTE-BARBE

Elevé en fût de chêne 1998★

■   3 ha   6,000   ▮   ▮   €5-8

Robert Tricoire is a fascinating man with a great passion for his vines and his garden. It is a pleasure to talk to him about the 'Old Canine' and the 'Tassergal Tortoise' found at the fossil site at Serrat-d'en-Vaquer that overlooks the vineyard. The aromas of this deeply coloured 98 have barely begun to develop. It opens on the palate with a warming impression of ripe fruits – cherries in brandy, blackberries – enveloped in oak. The rich, powerful, liquoricey oak combines perfectly with a ripe fruit flavour that hovers between preserved cherries and prunes. Its tannins are well integrated, and the wine is ready to drink now.

➶• Vignerons et Passions,
BP 1, 34725 Saint-Félix-de-Lodez,
tel. 04.67.88.80.39, fax 04.67.88.86.39 ▼
Ⅰ by appt.

DOM. SALVAT Taichac 2000★★

☐ 11 ha · 20,000 · €5-8

Visitors to the Fenouillèdes district will discover a magnificent hinterland that was already valued in the Roman era, as also at Tautavu Acum, known these days as Taichac Salvat family. The freshness of this mountain *terroir* can be seen in the clear, brilliant colour of this 2000 vintage, and in the notes of flowers and citrus fruits in the bouquet. This is a fresh, lively, floral, well-integrated wine that has plenty of body, and finishes confidently on a slight touch of bitterness. Also worthy of note here is the lovely **99 Salvat red**, which receives a commendation.

🖙 Dom. J.-Ph. Salvat, 8, av. Jean-Moulin, 66220 Saint-Paul-de-Fenouillet, tel. 04.68.59.29.00, fax 04.68.59.20.44, e-mail salvat.jp@wanadoo.fr Ⓥ Ⓨ by appt.

DOM. SARDA-MALET
Terroir Mailloles 1998★★★

4 ha · 8,000 · €15-23

Suzy Malet, a woman with a passion for wine, allied to flair and charm, offers a **98 Réserved**, which wins one star, as well as the present *cuvée*, a youthful wine with a deep colour and a bouquet that is still more fruit than oak. Flavours of spices and toast emerge on the palate, along with richly constituted tannins. The wine is well set up for maturation in the bottle, and will go well with rib of beef or tournedos when ready.

🖙 Dom. Sarda-Malet, Mas Saint-Michel, chem. de Sainte-Barbe, 66000 Perpignan, tel. 04.68.56.72.38, fax 04.68.56.47.60 Ⓥ
Ⓨ by appt.
🖙 Suzy Malet

CH. DE SAU Cuvée réservée 1996

3 ha · 10,000 · €5-8

Hervé Passama took a bold risk in offering the tasters a 96. He has been here for 15 years, however, on a vineyard that has been in his family for over a century, and knows how to manage his *terroirs* and adapt his vinification methods to the requirements of the grape varieties. The colour of this wine is intense, but is beginning to turn brick red. Its bouquet opens with gamy notes, before releasing spicy aromas and a surprising cherry scent. As it continues to develop, the wine is becoming rounder on the palate. The tannins are still substantial, however, and there is a charred flavour on the finish that would make this a good wine to serve with grilled meats.

🖙 Hervé Passama, Ch. de Saü, 66300 Thuir, tel. 04.68.53.21.74, fax 04.68.53.29.07, e-mail chateaudesau@aol.com Ⓥ
Ⓨ by appt.

DOM. DU VIEUX CHENE
Lou Ginesta 2000★

6 ha · 8,000 · €5-8

This remarkably sited vineyard enjoys superb views. It also has the advantage of being only ten minutes from the town, at the point where the river Agly opens out onto the plain, and above all it has an enviable range of *terroirs*. This 2000 vintage has a fresh, intense garnet colour and a bouquet of red berries and blackcurrants, along with a wild note bordering on leather. The wine is well integrated and velvety on the palate, where the fruit flavours are accompanied by a mineral note that shows that it comes from schist soils. The palate is supported to the finish by very fine, slightly charred tannins. Another wine to note here is the **99 Haut Valoir white**, which receives a commendation.

🖙 Dom. du Vieux Chêne, Mas Kilo, 66000 Espira-de-l'Agly, tel. 04.68.38.92.01, fax 04.68.38.95.79 Ⓥ Ⓨ by appt.
🖙 Denis Sarda

Côtes du Roussillon-Villages

CH. AYMERICH Cuvée Augustin
Aymerich de Beaufort 1998★★

6 ha · 8,000 · €8-11

There can be no mistaking the 60% Syrah content and schist *terroir* that have produced this highly expressive wine, which has been perfectly matured in oak. Its aromas of wild red berries are combined with spicy notes, supported by tannins that are both liquoricey and full-bodied. Discreet, elegant notes of oak appear on the finish.

🖙 Ch. Aymerich, 52, av. Dr-Torreilles, 66310 Estagel, tel. 04.68.29.45.45, fax 04.68.29.10.35, e-mail aymerich-grau-vins@wanadoo.fr Ⓥ
Ⓨ by appt.
🖙 Grau-Aymerich

CH. DE BELESTA Schiste 1999

1.5 ha · 5,898 · €5-8

The wine-growers of Bélesta were among the first to practise selection of *terroirs*. This wine, which comes from vines planted on schist soils, is a perfect example. It is characterised by the roundness of its tannins, and by the fruity and spicy notes that continue on the palate right through to the finish.

🖙 SCV Les Vignerons de Cassagnes-Bélesta, 66720 Cassagnes, tel. 04.68.84.51.93, fax 04.68.84.53.82 Ⓥ
Ⓨ ev. day 10am-12 noon 3pm-6pm

DOM. REGIS BOUCABEILLE 1999★★

8 ha · 13,000 · €8-11

This indefatigable European business specialist successfully cultivates a small vineyard in Roussillon. His 1999 vintage is particularly notable for the softness of its fruit flavours and its very ripe tannins. The wine has just the right combination of finesse, complexity and length.

CH. DE CALADROY

Elevé en fût de chêne 1998★★★

◼ 🔾 2 ha 🍷 6,000 🍾 €8–11

Having won a *coup de coeur* last year for its 98 Les Schistes, the château now offers another *cuvée* from the same vintage, one that has been matured in oak. The oak flavour dominates at first, but then gradually gives way to notes of pink peppercorns, revealing very fine, meaty tannins cloaked by vanilla. A wine of excellent balance and length.

◦— SCEA ch. de Caladroy, 66720 Bélesta, tel. 04.68.57.10.25, fax 04.68.57.27.76, e-mail chateau.caladroy@wanadoo.fr ▼
Ⓨ ev. day except Sat. & Sun. 8am–12 noon 1.30pm–5.30pm

LES VIGNERONS DE CARAMANY

Caramany Elevé en fût de chêne 1998★

◼ 🔾 25 ha 🍷 72,000 🍾 €5–8

This oak-aged *cuvée* gives a new look to its appellation, offering evolved aromas of spices and toast. The oak is well balanced with the tannins on the palate, but dominates on the finish.

◦— SCV de Caramany, 66720 Caramany, tel. 04.68.84.51.80, fax 04.68.84.50.84 ▼
Ⓨ by appt.

DOM. DE CASTELL

Vieilli en fût de chêne 1998★

◼ 🔾 4.58 ha 🍷 3,000 🍾 €5–8

This vineyard lies on schist *terroirs* at the foot of the Força Réal hill. The wine has an appealing cherry colour with garnet highlights, and a bouquet of spicy and smoky aromas that give way to fruity notes on the palate. The tannic structure is still dominant, showing the strong concentration of a wine that has excellent prospects for the future.

◦— SCV Cellier Castell Réal, 152, rte Nationale, 66550 Corneilla-la-Rivière, tel. 04.68.57.38.93, fax 04.68.57.23.36 ▼
Ⓨ by appt.

VIGNERONS CATALANS

Haute Coutume Schistes de Trémoine 1998

◼ 🔾 5 ha 🍷 20,000 🍾 €8–11

Haute Coutume is the new name for the *cuvées de prestige* here at the Vignerons Catalans co-operative. This one comes from the schist vineyards of the famous Rasiguères *terroir*. It has been matured in new oak, which still dominates on the palate, but will develop if the wine is given time to mature.

◦— Vignerons Catalans, 1870, av. Julien-Panchot, 66011 Perpignan Cedex, tel. 04.68.85.69.03, fax 04.68.55.25.62, e-mail vignerons.catalans@wanadoo.fr
Ⓨ by appt.

LES VIGNERONS DES CÔTES D'AGLY

Mont d'Estagel Elevé en fût de chêne 1998★

◼ 🔾 3 ha 🍷 6,500 🍾 €11–15

This is a blend based mainly on Syrah and Mourvèdre with some Carignan. The garnet highlights in its colour anticipate a powerfully structured wine that is rounded out by oak. There are suggestions of very ripe red berries, the garrigue and spices on the palate, which is balanced and full-bodied, but this wine still needs to be kept.

◦— Les Vignerons des Côtes d'Agly, Cave coopérative, 66310 Estagel, tel. 04.68.29.00.45, fax 04.68.29.19.80, e-mail agly@little-france.com ▼
Ⓨ ev. day except Sat. & Sun. 8am–12 noon 2pm–6pm

CH. CUCHOUS

Caramany 1998★★

◼ 🔾 2 ha 🍷 6,600 🍾 €5–8

Château Cuchous is gradually building up its vineyard on the gneiss *terroirs* that tend to constitute the best expression of the Caramany appellation. Anyone tasting this wine will appreciate its fine, fruity aromas and spicy notes, and sense the delicate flesh of the grapes that are, without a doubt, what makes it such a delight to the tastebuds.

◦— SCV Les Vignerons de Cassagnes-Bélesta, 66720 Cassagnes, tel. 04.68.84.51.93, fax 04.68.84.53.82 ▼
Ⓨ ev. day 10am–12 noon 3pm–6pm

CH. DONA BAISSAS

Cuvée Vieille vigne Elevé en fût de chêne 1998★★

◼ 🔾 2 ha 🍷 45,000

This 98 is showing signs of development with its gorgeous aromas of preserved fruits and leather, combined with charred notes. Its ruby colour already shows nuances of vermilion, and it has very fine-grained tannins that give it delightful balance on the palate.

◦— Cellier de La Dona, 48, rue du Dr-Torreille, 66310 Estagel, tel. 04.68.29.10.50, fax 04.68.29.02.29 ▼
Ⓨ by appt.

DOM. FONTANEL

Tautavel Prieuré Vieilli en fût de chêne 1999★★★

◼ 🔾 n.c. 🍷 n.c. 🍾 €8–11

Just like the 98 that won a *coup de coeur* last year, this powerful 99 combines elegance with the mark of its *terroir*. Garnet in colour, with a bouquet of stone-fruits, it has a combination of blackberry and blackcurrant flavours on the palate. The fleshy tannins have accents of liquorice, giving an impression of richness and remarkable fullness. The **99 Cuvée Classique** is awarded two stars. It has not been matured in oak, and displays attractive notes of crushed red berries.

◦— Dom. Fontanel, 25, av. Jean-Jaurès, 66720 Tautavel, tel. 04.68.29.04.71, fax 04.68.29.19.44 ▼
Ⓨ ev. day 10am–1pm 2pm–7pm
◦— Fontaneil

LES HAUTS DE FORCA REAL

1999 ★★★   n.c.   15,000   €15-23

This vineyard is located on the arid, schist slopes of the Força Réal hill, and is made up of low-yielding Syrah and Mourvèdre vines. The wine has a bouquet of ripe fruits and garrigue blossom, and powerful, full-bodied, liquoricey tannins on the palate, against a background of toasty notes. A perfect combination of complexity, elegance and power.

🍷 J.-P. Henriquès, Dom. Força Réal, Mas de la Garrigue, 66170 Millas, tel. 04.68.85.06.07, fax 04.68.85.49.00, e-mail domaine@forca-real.com ☑
Ⴑ by appt.

DOM. GARDIES Tautavel 1999 ★★★

   n.c.   20,000   €8-11

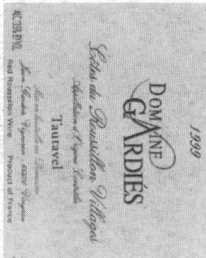

Could it be that every vintage at this estate produces an exceptional wine? This 99 certainly does nothing to counteract that impression. It has a beautiful crimson colour and a bouquet that releases pink peppercorn aromas with persistent notes of blackcurrant. After the powerful tannins have had their say on the palate, the delicacy of the oak and the richness of body create a magnificent symphony on the tastebuds.

🍷 Dom. Gardiès, 66600 Vingrau, tel. 04.68.64.61.16, fax 04.68.64.69.36 ☑
Ⴑ by appt.

DOM. GARDIES Les Millères 1999 ★★★

   10 ha   25,000   €5-8

Here a limestone *terroir* creates the structure, Syrah grapes provide the colour and aromas, and the know-how of a great wine-maker sets it all to music. The colour is an intense garnet, while the bouquet suggests the sunny garrigue as well as ripe red berries. Preserved fruits appear alongside full-bodied tannins on the palate, which goes to show that power and charm can go hand in hand.

🍷 Dom. Gardiès, 66600 Vingrau, tel. 04.68.64.61.16, fax 04.68.64.69.36 ☑
Ⴑ by appt.

CH. DE JAU Talon rouge 1998 ★

   4 ha   13,000   €15-23

A very modern label adorns this wine, the producer of which is also making wine in Chile. 'Talon Rouge' is noticeably fruity and lush on the palate, making it highly enjoyable right now with grilled cutlets. It has a lovely ruby colour veering towards garnet, and

notes of very ripe cherries both in the bouquet and on the palate.

🍷 Ch. de Jau, 66600 Cases-de-Pène, tel. 04.68.38.90.10, fax 04.68.38.91.33, e-mail daure@wanadoo.fr ☑ Ⴑ by appt.
🍷 Famille Dauré

JEAN D'ESTAVEL

Elevé en fût de chêne 1998 ★   n.c.   10,000   €5-8

This is a very well-developed 98, in which everything on the palate seems finely integrated: notes of cooked fruits, sweet spices, leather and roasting on the finish. The oak elements are in perfect balance with the finesse of the tannins.

🍷 SA Destavel, 7 bis, av. du Canigou, 66000 Perpignan, tel. 04.68.68.36.00, fax 04.68.54.03.54 ☑
🍷 M.G. Baïssas

DOM. JOLIETTE Cuvée Romain

Mercier Elevé en fût de chêne 1999 ★   4 ha   12,000   €8-11

The vineyard has managed to find itself a spot among the pine forests in the foothills of the Corbières, from where it overlooks Lake Leucate and the Mediterranean. Right from the start, the bouquet of this *cuvée* releases aromas of wild berries, the garrigue and rosemary. Substantially structured on the palate, it resonates with very ripe tannins and oaky notes that are softened by its elegant richness.

🍷 A. et Ph. Mercier, Dom. Joliette, rte de Vingrau, 66600 Espira-de-l'Agly, tel. 04.68.64.50.60, fax 04.68.64.18.82 ☑
Ⴑ by appt.

CH. LES PINS 1998 ★★

   n.c.   140,000   €8-11

Château Les Pins is both a viticultural Mecca, and the name of a range of wines developed by the Vignerons de Baixas. This *cuvée* has a deep ruby colour, fruity aromas enhanced by balsamic notes, and elegant, full-bodied tannins with the vanilla flavour of oak, which are well-integrated into the sheer power of the wine. All this goes very well with the famous Baixas *fraginat* (beef in a red pepper and tomato sauce).

🍷 Cave des Vignerons de Baixas, 14, av. Mal-Joffre, 66390 Baixas, tel. 04.68.64.22.37, fax 04.68.64.26.70, e-mail baixas@smi-telecom.fr ☑ Ⴑ by appt.

CAVE DE LESQUERDE

Lesquerde Les Arènes de Granit 1999 ★   3.3 ha   7,500   €5-8

A granitic sand *terroir* gives these wines delicate tannins and fine, well-rounded balance. Spicy aromas (mainly pepper on the palate) mingle with discreet smoky notes, resulting in a supple, full-bodied wine that will soon reach full maturity.

🍷 SCV Lesquerde, rue du Grand-Capitoul, 66220 Lesquerde, tel. 04.68.59.08.17 fax 04.68.59.08.17 Ⴑ ev. day except Sun. 8am-12 noon 2pm-6pm

829   ROUSSILLON

Côtes du Roussillon-Villages

CH. MONTNER 1999★

■ 85 ha 50,000 ■ ♦ €5-8

The vineyard here is mainly located on schist hillsides, giving the wine a sense of elegance on the tastebuds. The colour is brilliant red, and the bouquet a basket of red-fruit aromas. On the palate, its seductive flavours lead up to a finish of very good length.

→ Les Vignerons des Côtes d'Agly,
Cave cooperative, 66310 Estagel,
tel. 04.68.29.00.45, fax 04.68.29.19.80,
e-mail agly@little-france.com ☑ ▼ ev. day except Sat. & Sun. 8am–12 noon 2pm–6pm

LES VIGNERONS DE PEZILLA
1999

■ 35 ha 12,000 ■ ♦ €3-5

A brilliant, deep ruby colour, and aromas of lightly roasted red fruits distinguish this wine. Its tannic structure on the palate is gradually integrating with the richness of its flavours.

→ Les Vignerons de Pézilla,
66370 Pézilla-la-Rivière, tel. 04.68.92.00.09,
fax 04.68.92.49.91 ☑ ▼ by appt.

DOM. PIQUEMAL
Les Terres Grillées 1999★

■ 3 ha 18,000 ■ €8-11

Conditions in the Terres Grillées vineyard are perfectly suited to the Grenache grape, whose very ripe quality combines well with the burnt notes that maturation in oak gives the wine. This one has cherry highlights, followed by a harmony of wild red-berry flavours and tannic structure that will enable it to keep for a long time.

→ Dom. Pierre et Franck Piquemal,
1, rue Pierre-Lefranc, 66600 Espira-de-l'Agly,
tel. 04.68.64.09.14, fax 04.68.38.52.94,
e-mail contact@domaine-piquemal.com ☑
▼ by appt.

LES VIGNERONS DE
PLANEZES-RASIGUERES
Cuvée Moura Lympany Elevé en fût de chêne 1998★★★

■ 8 ha 25,000 ■ €5-8

A cuvée named after the renowned concert pianist offers a harmony between the effects of its schist terroir, a judiciously chosen grape blend, and oaky touches that accentuate the elegance of the flavours. Its red-berry fruit, vanilla notes, fine tannins, richness and good length play the entire concerto without striking a single false note.

→ Les Vignerons de Planèzes-Rasiguères,
5, rte de Caramany, 66720 Rasiguères,
tel. 04.68.29.11.82, fax 04.68.29.16.45 ☑
▼ by appt.

ROC DU GOUVERNEUR 1999

■ n.c. 30,000 ■ ♦

Red-fruit aromas develop around a structure that is as solid as the rock of the wine's name. With its appealing, fairly light ruby colour and clean, fresh bouquet, it would be a

good choice to drink with grilled meats, as a prelude to a visit to the Catalan region.

→ Les Vignobles du Rivesaltais, 1, rue de la Roussillonnaise, 66602 Rivesaltes-Salses,
tel. 04.68.64.06.63, fax 04.68.64.64.69,
e-mail vignobles.rivesaltais@wanadoo.fr ☑
▼ by appt.

DOM. DU ROUVRE
Les Feches 1998★★★

■ 1 ha 1,500 ■

Solid as an oak (rouvre in Catalan), this wine has powerful yet delicate tannins that are slightly vanilla-flavoured and softened by generous flesh. Ruby in colour with vermilion highlights indicating its maturity, it releases notes of spices, ripe fruits and undergrowth in turn. It would be an ideal accompaniment to venison.

→ GFA Domaines du Château Royal,
Los Parès, 66550 Corneilla-la-Rivière,
tel. 04.68.57.22.02, fax 04.68.57.11.63 ☑
▼ by appt.
→ Pouderoux

LES VIGNERONS DE SAINT-PAUL
Cuvée Monedariae Elevé en fût de chêne 1998★

■ 75.44 ha 6,000 ■ €5-8

Carignan, Grenache and Syrah in equal shares make up this oak-aged cuvée. It has a beautiful ruby-cherry colour with vermilion highlights, and aromas of toast, Oriental spices and vanilla-flavoured red fruits. The oaky structure with its elegant tannins cloaked in plump flesh makes for a full, rounded wine.

→ SCV Les Vignerons de Saint-Paul,
17, av. Jean-Moulin, 66220 Saint-Paul-de-Fenouillet, tel. 04.68.59.02.39,
fax 04.68.59.07.97 ☑ ▼ by appt.

DOM. DES SCHISTES
Tradition 1999★★

■ 10 ha 30,000 ■ ♦ €5-8

Jacques and Nadine Sire make two cuvées: one matured in oak (Les Terrasses), and this one, Tradition. The ruby-cherry colour still shows some violet highlights. Notes of cherries and pepper on the palate are in keeping with the wine's youthfulness. This full-bodied, velvety 99 can be enjoyed now, but also has real ageing potential.

● Jacques Sire, 1, av. Jean-Lurçat, 66310 Estagel, tel. 04.68.29.11.25, fax 04.68.29.47.17 [Y] by appt.

LES MAITRES VIGNERONS DE TAUTAVEL

Tautavel Vieilli en fût de chêne 1999★★ 58 ha 25,000 €5-8

This cellar located very close to the Prehistoric Museum regularly offers expressive wines. The oak-matured 99 from here has ruby and garnet highlights. Its flavours of very ripe red berries are enhanced by a touch of oak that combines well with its full-bodied tannic structure. Two stars were also awarded to the 99 Tautavel, which is not aged in oak and is characterised by red-fruit flavours and delicate tannins.

● Les Maîtres Vignerons de Tautavel, 24, av. Jean-Badia, 66720 Tautavel, tel. 04.68.29.12.03, fax 04.68.29.41.81, e-mail vignerons.tautavel@wanadoo.fr [V]
[Y] ev. day 8am–12 noon 2pm–6pm, groups by appt.

DOM. DU VIEUX CHENE

Terres Nègres Altes Elevé en fût de chêne 1999 5 ha 4,000 €8-11

In Catalan, Terres Nègres Altes means 'high black land', which is an allusion to the vineyard's hillside location on black schist soils. The wine's aromas of blackcurrants and the garrigue give way on the palate to balsamic notes supported by oak. It has a deep ruby colour and full, soft tannins.

● Dom. du Vieux Chêne, Mas Kiio, 66600 Espira-de-l'Agly, tel. 04.68.38.92.01, fax 04.68.38.95.79 [Y] by appt.
● Denis Sarda

Collioure

This very small appellation of 430 ha (1,062 acres) produces about 15,928 hl (420,499 gal). The soil is the same as that found in the Appellation Banyul. The four communes are Collioure, Port-Bendres, Banyuls-sur-Mer and Cerbère.

The vine varieties grown are principally Grenache Noir, Carignan and Mourvèdre, with Syrah and Cinsault as additional varieties. The exclusively red or rosé wines are made at the beginning of the harvest, before the grapes for Banyuls are picked. The small crop produces warm, full-bodied, highly coloured red wines, with aromas of well-ripened soft fruits. The roses are aromatic, rich but typically lively.

ABBAYE DE VALBONNE 1999★

43 ha 165,900 €11-15

Dominant notes of ripe fruits recall the end of harvest-time. They are combined on the palate with soft tannins and touches of cinnamon to accompany a harmony of flavours at once warm and gentle.

● Cellier des Templiers, rte du Mas-Reig, 66650 Banyuls-sur-Mer, tel. 04.68.98.36.70, fax 04.68.98.36.91 [V]
[Y] ev. day 10am–7.30pm

CH. DES ABELLES 1999★★★

24 ha 106,700 €11-15

With its sense of richness and persistent fruit flavours, this is an archetypal Collioure red. It has a cherry colour with vermilion highlights, and a bouquet of blackcurrants and blackberries, combined with lingering notes of sweet spice. Tannins are evident on a palate where finesse never yields to power. The refinement of the wine will best be shown by serving it with partridge cooked in the Catalan style.

● Cellier des Templiers, rte du Mas-Reig, 66650 Banyuls-sur-Mer, tel. 04.68.98.36.70, fax 04.68.98.36.91 [V]
[Y] ev. day 10am–7.30pm

DOM. DE BAILLAURY 1999★

n.c. n.c. €11-15

Baillaury means 'valley of gold' in Catalan, and this vineyard contributes to the sense of riches here. The still-youthful 99 can be enjoyed now for its notes of wild berries and spices (pepper). Its roundness on the palate gives free rein to this array of flavours.

● La Cave de L'Abbé Rous, 56, av. Charles-de-Gaulle, 66650 Banyuls-sur-Mer, tel. 04.68.88.72.72, fax 04.68.88.30.57

DOM. CAMPI 1999★

30 ha 33,400

A high percentage of Syrah gives this wine its purple highlights. There are blackcurrant and blackberry notes both in the bouquet and on the palate, along with a peppery edge. The finish is still dominated by powerful yet fine tannins, but these should become more supple with time.

● Cellier des Templiers, rte du Mas-Reig, 66650 Banyuls-sur-Mer, tel. 04.68.98.36.70, fax 04.68.98.36.91 [V] [Y] ev. day 10am–7.30pm

DOM. DE LA CASA BLANCA 1999

2 ha 7,000 €8-11

This 1999 was produced in an old, traditional cellar on the heights of the village of

Banyuls-sur-Mer. It has a ruby colour with garnet highlights, and notes of red berries and the garrigue in the bouquet. There are a few spicy touches on the palate, along with a tannic structure that is still quite muscular.

→ Dom. de La Casa Blanca, rte des Mas, 66650 Banyuls-sur-Mer, tel. 04.68.88.12.85, fax 04.68.88.04.08 [M] Y by appt.
→ Soufflet et Escapa

DOM. DE LA MARQUISE
Réserve 1999 ■ 1 ha 2,500 ■ ♦ €8-11

This wine has a beautiful, brilliant ruby colour and aromas of red berries, which develop especially on the palate, where there is a combination of richness, power and maturity. The stamp of overripe Grenache grapes shows in the notes of cooked fruits on the finish. The **2000 rosé de l'Arquete** wins a commendation. Its delicately salmon-pink highlights lead on to some spicy notes that blend in well with the very ripe fruit on the finish. This warming, powerful rosé will temper the hot flavours of certain Mediterranean dishes.

→ Jacques Py, Dom. de La Marquise, 17, rue Pasteur, 66190 Collioure, tel. 04.68.98.01.38, fax 04.68.82.51.77 [M] Y by appt.

DOM. LA TOUR VIEILLE
Puig Oriol 1999★★★ ■ 2 ha 9,660 ■ ♦ €11-15

DOMAINE LA TOUR VIEILLE
Collioure
APPELLATION COLLIOURE CONTRÔLÉE
RED COLLIOURE WINE
Puig Oriol
1999

Vincent and Christine Cantié offer another superb wine to follow on from their 97, which also won a *coup de cœur*. This cherry-red 99 with its still deep-purple highlights exudes aromas of blackcurrants and cloves. Lingering fruity notes are accompanied by deliciously soft tannins and a full-bodied impression on the finish. Two stars were awarded to the estate's **2000 Rosé des Roches**, which is peony-coloured with brilliant highlights and has a combination of wild red-berry and spice aromas. With its power, richness and elegant fruit, it would go well with a *suquet* (Catalan fish and potato soup).

→ Dom. La Tour Vieille, 3, av. du Mirador, 66190 Collioure, tel. 04.68.82.44.82, fax 04.68.82.38.42 [M] Y by appt.
→ Cantié et Campadieu

L'ETOILE Vieilli en montagne 1999★ ■ 10 ha 13,000 ■ ♦ €8-11

The aromas here are already fully mature, and range from spices to cut hay and liquorice. The ruby colour shows light brick-red highlights, and there are notes of grilled fruits on the palate around a structure still dominated by tannin.

→ Sté coopérative L'Etoile, 26, av. du Puig-del-Mas, 66650 Banyuls-sur-Mer, tel. 04.68.88.00.10, fax 04.68.88.15.10 [M] Y ev. day except Sat. & Sun. 8am-12 noon 2pm-6pm

DOM. DU MAS BLANC
Junquets 1998★ ■ 1 ha 4,000 ■ €15-23

Jean-Michel Parcé is assiduously following in the mythical footsteps of his father, the famous Doctor Parcé, especially with his Junquets *cuvée*, which has a beautiful crimson colour and a bouquet that releases its aromas little by little. The notes of blackcurrants and blackberries suggest very ripe Syrah. On the palate, its balanced structure is both substantial and rich, and bodes very well for the future.

→ SCA Parcé et Fils, 9, av. du Gal-de-Gaulle, 66650 Banyuls-sur-Mer, tel. 04.68.88.32.12, fax 04.68.88.72.24 [M] Y ev. day except Sat. & Sun. 9am-12 noon 2pm-6pm

MAS CORNET 1998★★ ■ n.c. 7,884 ■ ♦ €11-15

Wines produced at the Abbé Rous cellar are reserved for restaurants and wine-merchants. In this 98 vintage, notes of very ripe red fruits, toast and spices emerge gradually from within a strong tannic structure enveloped by richness and power. It will need to be kept further to achieve its full potential. The **2000 rosé** is lightly marked by oak and is a straightforward, perfectly integrated wine, both fruity and floral. It was awarded one star.

→ La Cave de L'Abbé Rous, 56, av. Charles-de-Gaulle, 66650 Banyuls-sur-Mer, tel. 04.68.72.72, fax 04.68.88.30.57

LES CLOS DE PAUILLES 2000★ ■ 18 ha 95,000 ■ ♦ €5-8

This rosé shows all the nobility of the Syrah grape in its almost ruby colour, intense notes of red fruits and touches of violet. Its richness and spicy flavours contribute to a delicious finish.

→ Les Clos de Pauilles, Baie de Pauilles, 66660 Port-Vendres, tel. 04.68.38.90.10, fax 04.68.38.91.33, e-mail daure@wanadoo.fr [M] Y ev. day 10am-11pm; cl. 1st Oct.-1st May
→ Famille Dauré

DOM. PIETRI-GERAUD 2000 ■ 1 ha 4,000 ■ ♦ €5-8

Laetitia Pietri-Géraud is successfully following in the footsteps of her mother Maguy, who gradually built up this vineyard. The wine has fuchsia highlights and a bouquet of red fruits in syrup, accompanied by a suggestion of *pain d'épice*. There is a strong sense of balance on the palate, where the flavours revolve around notes of pear drops.

♠ Maguy et Laetitia Piétri-Géraud, 22, rue Pasteur, 66190 Collioure, tel. 04.68.82.07.42, fax 04.68.98.02.58 ☒ ⍩ ev. day 10am–12.30pm 3.30pm–6.30pm; cl. Sun. & Mon. outside school holidays

DOM. DU ROUMANI 1999

| | 30 ha | 159,820 | ◼ | ◧ | €11-15 |

The wines at the Cellier des Templiers can be discovered all around the extraordinary 'circuit' that has been set up in the main cellar. This crimson 99 displays toasty notes, and has a slight aromatic hint of Banyuls. High-quality tannins give a good sense of balance on the palate.

♠ Cellier des Templiers, rte du Mas-Reig, 66650 Banyuls-sur-Mer, tel. 04.68.98.36.70, fax 04.68.98.36.91 ☒ ⍩ ev. day 10am–7.30pm

CELLIER DES TEMPLIERS
Cuvée Saint-Michel 1999★★

| | n.c. | 142,300 | ◼ | ◧ | €8-11 |

This wine is very much characterised by its schist *terroir*, which lends elegance and suppleness to the tannins of Grenache. It has an appealing colour with ruby highlights, and a bouquet of both fresh and preserved fruits. This is a powerful, lengthy wine whose richness and full-bodied flavours delight the tastebuds.

♠ Cellier des Templiers, rte du Mas-Reig, 66650 Banyuls-sur-Mer, tel. 04.68.98.36.70, fax 04.68.98.36.91 ☒ ⍩ ev. day 10am–7.30pm

DOM. DU TRAGINER
Cuvée Al Ribéral 1999★★

| | 2 ha | 4,000 | ◼ | ◫ | €15-23 |

The 'traginer' was the mule-drover who used to transport the grape harvest across the Banyuls terraces. This wine has been produced organically and offers a veritable basket of red fruit aromas, enhanced by touches of Oriental spice. It has a ruby colour, and fills the mouth with elegant tannins and toasty notes.

♠ Dom. du Traginer, 56, av. du Puig-del-Mas, 66650 Banyuls-sur-Mer, tel. 04.68.88.15.11, fax 04.68.88.31.48 ☒
⍩ by appt.
♠ J.-F. Deu

DOM. VIAL-MAGNÈRES
Les Espérades 1999

| | 1.25 ha | 7,000 | ◼ | ◫ | €11-15 |

As well as being a scientist, Bernard Sapéras is also a wine-maker, and a great advocate of the terraced landscape of the Banyuls vineyard with its multitudinous layers of schist. This wine has been matured in oak for eight months. Its dark purple highlights give evidence of its freshness, as do the flavours of red berries and spices on the palate, which shows a good balance of structure and richness.

♠ Dom. Vial-Magnères, Clos Saint-André, 14, rue Edouard-Herriot, 66650 Banyuls-sur-Mer, tel. 04.68.88.31.04, fax 04.68.55.01.06, e-mail al.tragou@wanadoo.fr ☒
⍩ by appt.
♠ M. et B. Sapéras

PROVENCE AND CORSICA

Provence

Provence means holidays, a place where 'the sun always shines', and where the people, with their melodious accents, take the time to live life as it should be lived … For the wine-growers it is also a place where the sun shines, for three thousand hours a year! Rain is rare, but violent storms and ferocious winds batter the terrain. When the Phocaean Greeks disembarked at Marseilles around 600 BC, they found vines already growing in the region, and began to cultivate them systematically. Vine-growing continued under the Romans, followed in medieval times by the abbeys and local aristocratic landowners up to and including the wine-grower king, René of Anjou, Count of Provence.

Eleanor of Provence, wife of Henry III of England, was the first to give the wines of Provence an international cachet, just as her mother-in-law, Eleanor of Aquitaine, had done for the wines of Gascony. In the centuries which followed, Provençal wines fell out of favour with the international shippers due to difficulties in transport compared with other wine areas. However, in recent decades the development of tourism has brought the wines back to prominence, particularly the rosés, which are fun to drink – perfect companions for summer holidays and delicious Provençal dishes.

The Provençal vineyard is a patchwork of numerous small areas, which helps explain why nearly half of the wine produced is organ-ised though co-operatives: there are no fewer than a hundred in the Var department alone. But the larger 'domaines' (which, for the most part, are also bottlers) have retained their influence, and their active presence in marketing and promoting the wines is considered invaluable throughout the region. The annual production reaches between 2 and 3 million hl (52,800,000–79,200,000 gal), of which between 700,000 and 800,000 (18,480,000–21,120,000 gal) come from the seven AOCs, and about one million from eight Appellations d'Origine. In the Var department, typical of the region, wine represents 45% of the total agricultural production and vineyards cover 51% of the area.

In common with other southern vineyards, quite a few vine varieties are grown: the Appellation Côtes de Provence allows a total of thirteen. And yet, sadly, the Muscats, the glory of the Provençal *terroirs* before the phylloxera devastation, have now vanished. The vines are for the most part pruned in the traditional low goblet shape; however, plants trained along cordons are becoming increasingly common. Rosé and white wines (the latter more rare but frequently surprisingly good), are generally drunk young. This might change if it were possible to find conditions for ageing in bottles that were less extreme than those offered by the local climate. The same thought applies to many of the lighter reds. However, the fuller-bodied reds from the Provençal appellations age very well.

The tiny Palette vineyard, at the gates of Aix, incorporates the old enclosure belonging to King René. Its whites, rosés and reds are worthy of attention.

Since Provençal is still spoken in some of the domaines, it is useful to know some of the local terminology: *avis* is the local word for *sarment* (wine shoot), a *tine* is a *cave* or vat, and a *crotte* is a *cave* or cellar. You may be told that one of the grape varieties is called *pecouitouar* or *queue tordue* (which means 'twisted tail'), while *ginou d'Agasso* means 'magpie knee', because of the peculiar shape of the stem of the bunch of grapes.

Côtes de Provence

This appellation has a substantial production 960,622 hl (25,361,476 gal) in 2000, and covers a good third of the department of the Var, with extensions into the Bouches-du-Rhône to the edge of Marseilles, and an enclave in the Alpes-Maritimes. The total area under production is more than 19,000 ha (46,930 acres). Three *terroirs* identify it: the crystalline rocks of the Maure mountains in the south-east, bordered to the north by a band of red sand from Toulon to Saint-Raphaël and, beyond, a sizeable massif of hills and limestone plateaux that prefigure the Alps. The charm of these wines lies in their sheer diversity: made from a number of different vine varieties in varying proportions, and grown on equally varied soils with as many different aspects, they share little but the influence of the fierce southern sun. Perhaps this was the charm that the Greek Protis, according to legend, tasted as early as 600 BC when Gyptis, the daughter of a local king, offered him a goblet of wine as a pledge of her love.

The whites from the coast are soft but lively, and are perfectly suited to very fresh seafood; those from a little further north are more 'focused' and will go very well with lobster à l'Américaine and tangy cheeses. The rosés can be either soft or lively and, depending on your mood or taste, are best combined with full flavours, such as soup with pesto, anchoïade, aïoli and bouillabaisse, as well as fish and seafood, particularly red mullet, sea urchins and shellfish. The soft reds (which should be drunk slightly chilled) go well with joints of meat, roasts and pot-au-feu and especially with cold pot-au-feu salad. Finally, some of the strong, full-bodied reds are suitable for daubes (rich, slowly cooked stews) and woodcock. And for those who are attracted by unexpected pairings, try cold rosé with mushrooms, red with stewed shellfish, or white with daube of lamb (made with white wine).

CH. DES ANGLADES 2000★

	2 ha	5,000		€5-8

This abandoned vineyard was renovated in 2000, which was an interesting year for its whites. Pale yellow in colour, it offers subtle citrus (grapefruit) aromas graduating to lime and may-blossom. The fruity sweetness persists on the delicate palate. The rosé 2000 also merits one star with its aromas of peach and pear drops and a warming roundness that derives from Grenache.

SCEA ch. des Anglades,
143, rue Marylou, 83130 La Garde,
tel. 04.94.21.34.66, fax 04.94.21.34.66
Gautier

Côtes de Provence

DOM. DES ASPRAS

Cuvée traditionnelle 2000★

▲ 3 ha 20,000 ▮ ♦ €5-8

Far from the major trunk roads, Correns is a village that takes care to preserve its environment; it claims to be the first ever 'organic' village in France. The Aspras estate subscribes to this philosophy. The initial floral and fruity tastes of its rosé, produced from old vines, reappear elegantly on the palate. The estate's **white Cuvée traditionnelle 2000** was also awarded a star.

● Lisa Latz, SCEA Dom. des Aspras, 83570 Correns, tel. 04.94.59.59.70, fax 04.94.59.53.92, e-mail mlatz@aspras.com ☑ ⊤ by appt.

CH. BARBANAU 2000★

▲ 6 ha 30,000 ▮ ♦ €5-8

Some kilometers from Cassis and planted under the shadow of Sainte-Baume, this unique *terroir* benefits from its closeness to the sea and the effects of its 300 m (984 ft) altitude. All this comes through in the wine, whose complexity is intensified by aromas that are both fruity and floral. The rounded palate is pleasantly balanced by true liveliness.

● GAEC Ch. Barbanau, Hameau de Roquefort, 13830 Roquefort-la-Bédoule, tel. 04.42.73.14.60, fax 04.42.73.17.85, e-mail barbanau@aol.com ☑ ⊤ ev. day except Sun. 10am–12 noon 3–6pm

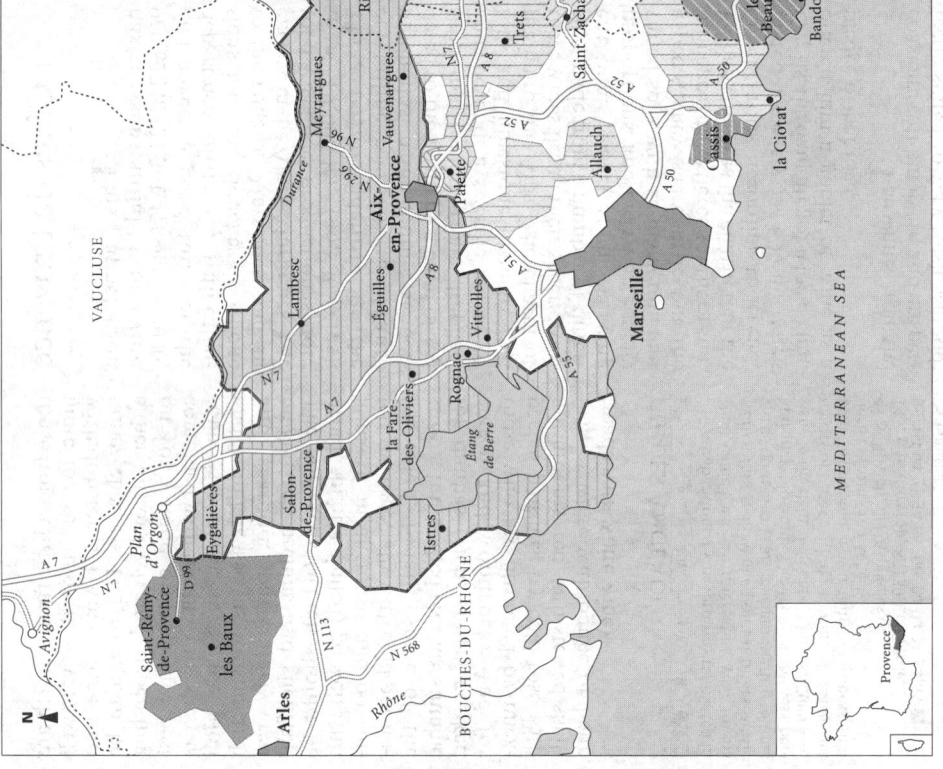

Provence

Côtes de Provence

CH. BARON GASSIER 2000★

25 ha · 133,333 · 43

The estate is set against a backdrop of Mont Sainte-Victoire, and the farmhouse lies at the heart of this scene. Its onion-skin tinted rosé with its attractive, fruity nose (red berries and yellow fruit) and full, pleasing palate, is balanced, lively and complex. This will go perfectly with bouillabaisse or similar fish soups.

Antony Gassier, Ch. Baron Georges, 13114 Puyloubier, tel. 04.42.66.31.38, fax 04.94.72.11.89 ☑ ⓨ by appt.

CH. BASTIDIERE 2000★★

3 ha · 15,000 · €5-8

Created in 1997, this 10-ha (25-acre) estate exports 50% of its production to Germany. The clear, salmon-coloured rosé offers a real balance of flavours, dominated by notes of crystallised orange and dried apricot. The palate has pleasant aromas of peach and orange before moving on to a fresher finish.

Dr Thomas Flensberg, Ch. Bastidière, 83390 Cuers, tel. 04.94.13.51.28, fax 04.94.13.51.29 ☑ ⓨ by appt.

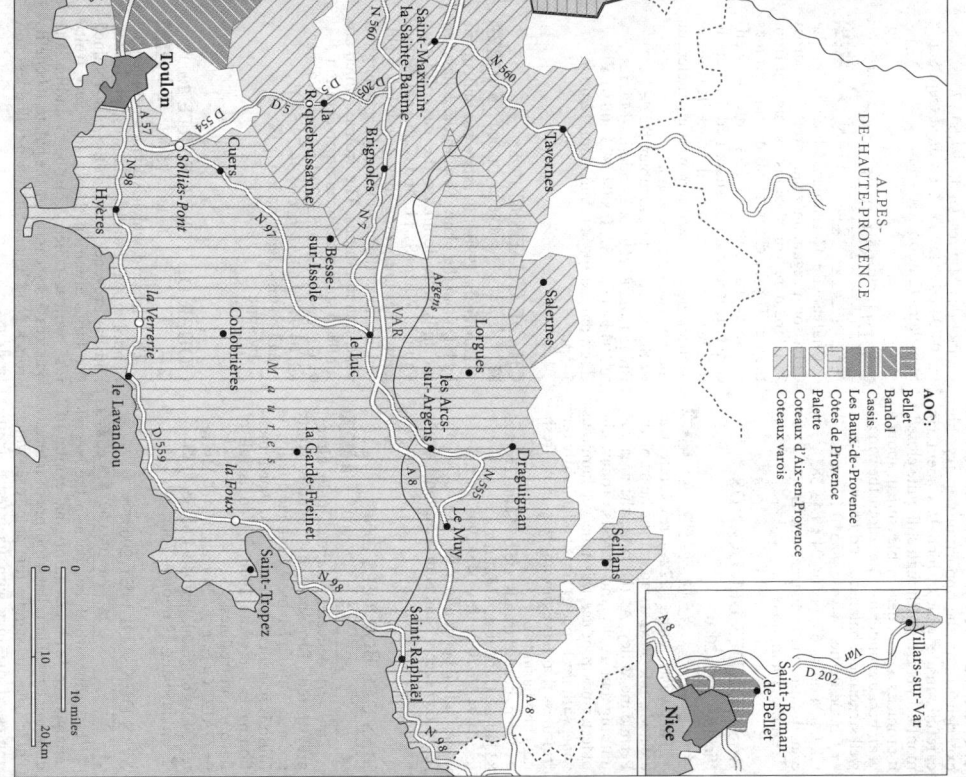

AOC:
Bellet
Bandol
Cassis
Les Baux-de-Provence
Palette
Côtes de Provence
Coteaux d'Aix-en-Provence
Coteaux varois

ALPES-DE-HAUTE-PROVENCE

Toulon

Saint-Maximin-la-Sainte-Baume

Brignoles

la Roquebrussanne

Cuers

Solliès-Pont

Hyères

la Verrerie

le Lavandou

Besse-sur-Issole

Collobrières

la Garde-Freinet

Saint-Tropez

Saint-Raphaël

le Luc

Les Arcs-sur-Argens

Draguignan

Le Muy

Lorgues

Salernes

Tavernes

Seillans

VAR

Maures

Argens

Nice

Saint-Roman-de-Bellet

Villars-sur-Var

la Faux

Côtes de Provence

DOM. DE BELOUVE 2000★★
■ ▪ €5-8
2.72 ha n.c.

Le Bélouvé means 'good grape' in Provençal, and the grapes have, indeed, been of good quality on the Bunan estates, producers well known for their Bandol. Lively aromas of soft red and black berries spring from this wine, which, though still young, lacks neither strength nor character. Its intensity is already pleasing, but its tannic backbone promises a good future.

➤ Domaines Bunan, Moulin des Costes, 83740 La Cadière-d'Azur,
tel. 04.94.98.58.98, fax 04.94.98.60.05,
e-mail bunan@bunan.com ☒ ⬝ by appt.

CH. DE BERNE Cuvée spéciale 2000★★★
□ ▥ €8-11
n.c. 30,000

Throughout the year Château de Berne organises cultural shows and wine tastings. You can therefore enjoy both the cultural experiences and the opportunity to try this carefully-made wine, which has spent six months in barrel. Although still quite closed, it promises a great deal of pleasure in about a year, because under its pale colour the wine is well structured, balanced and harmonious.

➤ Ch. de Berne, Flayosc, 83510 Lorgues,
tel. 04.94.60.43.60, fax 04.94.60.43.58,
e-mail vins@chateauberne.com ☒
⬝ ev. day 10am–6pm

BASTIDE DES BERTRANDS
Vieilles vignes 2000★
■ ▪ €5-8
9.4 ha 62,400

This vast, 90-ha (222-acre) estate was created some 30 years ago at the heart of the Permienne valley. At the time, the area was nothing but rocks and forests. Today, the oldest vines produce this pale yet luminous wine, with lively peony tints and a lightly tart fruitiness that leaves an impression of freshness and harmony.

➤ Dom. des Bertrands, rte de Saint-Tropez, 83340 Le Cannet-des-Maures,
tel. 04.94.99.79.00, fax 04.94.99.79.09,
e-mail info@bertrands.fr ☒
⬝ ev. day except Sun. 8am–12 noon 1–5pm
➤ Marotzki

MAS DES BORRELS 2000★
■ ▪ €5-8
n.c. 21,000

This very delicate, balanced, pale, almost grey-tinted, Provence rosé exudes fruity aromas. Although it has a feminine quality, its finish is nonetheless heady. Also worth mentioning is the **white 2000**, which is full of flavour and freshness.

➤ GAEC Garnier, 3° Borrels, 83400 Hyères,
tel. 04.94.65.68.20, fax 04.94.65.68.20 ☒
⬝ ev. day 9am–12 noon 3–7pm

MAS DE CADENET 2000★★
▥ 28.5 ha 100,000 ■ ▪ €5-8

This estate, which has been in the Négrel family since 1813, has an original exhibit of dinosaur eggs. The cellars, too, are of interest. There you can sample this pale rosé, which impressed the Jury with its intense, fruity aromas, developing on the sweet, refined palate. The **red Mas Négrel Cadanet 99**, matured in cask for 15 months, is seductive, with dense tannins, a generous leather character, red berries and smoke. It was awarded one star.

➤ Guy Négrel, Mas de Cadenet, 13530 Trets, tel. 04.42.29.21.59,
fax 04.42.61.32.09,
e-mail mas-de-cadenet@wanadoo.fr ☒
⬝ ev. day except Sun. 9am–12 noon 2–7pm

CH. CANNET 1998★
■ ▪ €5-8
7.3 ha 18,000

This estate, confiscated during the Revolution, has been re-assembled plot by plot by the descendants of Colbert. Today it boasts 41 ha (101 acres) and offers this deeply-coloured 98, altogether rich, full, harmonious and ready to drink from now onwards.

➤ Domaines de Colbert, RN 7, 83340 Le Cannet-des-Maures, tel. 04.94.60.77.66,
fax 04.94.60.95.59 ☒ ⬝ ev. day except Sat. Sun. 9am–12 noon 1.30–6pm

CH. DU CARRUBIER 2000★
■ ▪ €5-8
2 ha 10,600

Château du Carrubier, which is on the Cabasson-Brégançon road, stretches across 25 ha (62 acres) of siliceous soil, not far from the sea. This bright wine has opening aromas of soft fruit and violets and a well-concentrated palate, sustained by supple tannins which add to its elegance. It is ready to drink now but will retain its character for the next two or three years.

➤ SC du Dom. du Carrubier, rte de Brégançon, 83250 La Londe-les-Maures,
tel. 04.94.66.82.82, fax 04.94.35.00.01 ☒
⬝ ev. day except Sat. Sun. 8am–12 noon 1–5pm

CH. DE CHAUSSE 1998★
■ ▥ €8-11
6.96 ha 30,000

During the 1990s this estate was built up bit by bit, from the plantations to the cellars, on the hills that dominate the bay of Croix Valmer. When Syrah and Cabernet Sauvignon vines are young they give a low yield, which allows the production of a strong red wine, rich in tannins. The aromas, which are subtle to start with, open up on aeration.

➤ Ch. de Chausse, 83420 La Croix-Valmer,
tel. 04.94.79.60.57, fax 04.94.79.59.19,
e-mail chausse2@wanadoo.fr ☒
⬝ by appt.
➤ Y. Schelcher

COUER DE TERRE FORTE 2000★
▥ 13 ha 75,000 ■ ▪ €5-8

This vineyard, which is divided between the Bandol-growing area to the west of Toulon and the Provence coast to the east, retained the Jury's attention thanks to a very fruity rosé, with strawberry, raspberry and banana nuances. Very lengthy on the palate, it benefits from a good balance between roundness and freshness.

◆ SAS Gérard Dufforr, Le Rouve, BP 41, 83330 Le Beausset, tel. 04.94.98.71.31, fax 04.94.90.44.87 ☎ ev. day except Sat. Sun. 9am–12 noon 2–6pm; open Sat. summer

COMMANDERIE DE PEYRASSOL
Cuvée Eperon d'or 1998★   n.c.   n.c.

Having belonged to the Order of Malta, this property has been in the hands of the Rigord family since 1789. Françoise Rigord has run the vineyard for 25 years. Her ruby-tinted 98 benefits from decanting to open up its bouquet. The clean body is supported by a solid structure that will allow this wine to be kept for one or two years.
◆ Rigord, Ch. Commanderie-de-Peyrassol, 83340 Flassans, tel. 04.94.69.71.02, fax 04.94.59.69.23, e-mail peyrassol@caves-particulieres.com ☎ ev. day except Sat. Sun. 8am–12 noon 2–6pm

COSTE BRULADE
Réserve 3ème millénaire 2000★   50 ha   40,000   €5-8

This wine, pale in colour, but with purple-violet tints, is from a selection of Grenache (80%) and Syrah. The fruity (apricot, peach) aromas and notes of pear drops combine on the nose, while the fleshy palate leaves an impression of balance and length.
◆ Cellier Saint-Sidoine, rue de la Libération, 83390 Puget-Ville, tel. 04.98.01.80.50, fax 04.98.01.80.59, e-mail courrier@provence-sidoine.com ☎ ev. day except Sun. 9am–12 noon 2–6pm

CH. COUSSIN SAINTE VICTOIRE
1999★★   10 ha   60,000   €8-11

The base camp of the Roman battles against the Barbarians, led by General Marius in 102 BC, is the site of Château Coussin Sainte Victoire, which was created in the 17th century. The intensely purple 99 delivers a rich bouquet with notes of leather, toast, blackcurrant and pepper. Despite the austere palate, the solidly built, powerful body holds promise for future development. This wine should be kept for at least three years before opening. The rosé 2000, with a salmon tint, gained one star for its balance.
◆ Famille Elie Sumeire, Ch. Coussin Sainte-Victoire, 13590 Trets, tel. 04.42.61.20.00, fax 04.42.61.20.01, e-mail sumeire@chateaux-elie-sumeire.fr ☎ by appt.

DOM. DE CUREBEASSE 2000★
□   2.18 ha   5,000   €8-11

The Curebéasse estate, which is planted on volcanic soils, featured under the same name on 17th-century maps. This green-tinted Rolle opens with delicate aromas. The palate, supple at first, shows itself to be structured. It offers a lengthy and expressive finish. This wine will go well with seafood. Game, on the other hand, would complement the one star red 99 Roches noires, which has been matured in cask for six months. The nose evolves from red and black cherries towards charred notes; the palate is full bodied.
◆ Paquette, Dom. de Curebéasse, rte de Bagnols-en-Forêt, 83600 Fréjus, tel. 04.94.40.87.90, fax 04.94.40.75.18, e-mail curebeasse@infonie.fr ☎ by appt.

CH. D'ESCLANS
Cuvée spéciale 1998★★   3 ha   13,836   €8-11

The oak is still rather evident in this brilliant dark red Cuvée Spéciale, necessitating another year's maturation because of the rich, balanced, fruity body. The lengthy finish adds to this characterful wine's charm. It would be a good accompaniment to a sauced dish.
◆ Lars Torstensson, Ch. d'Esclans, rte de Callas, 83920 La Motte, tel. 04.94.60.40.40, fax 04.94.70.28.61, e-mail vin@rabiega.com ☎ ev. day 9am–12 noon 2–6pm; groups by appt.
◆ V. and S. Sprit

DOM. DES FERAUD 2000★
11.4 ha   53,000   €3-5

This ample, fruity, particularly lemony rosé derives from the finesse of a sandy terroir, nuances of original grape varieties, such as Tibouren, and well-controlled yields. Its silken palate has very good length.

CH. ESCARAVATIERS 1998★
1.8 ha   5,000   €5-8

The discovery of the remains of the veteran 9th Roman legion proves the antiquity of wine-making on this estate. This intense, ruby-coloured 98 is very fruity on the nose. Once the initial impression of firm tannins has passed, the palate gives way to a more convivial balance. The finely oaked white 2000, which was also awarded one star, reveals harmony that stems from careful wine-making and maturation.
◆ SCEA Domaines B.-M. Costamagna, Dom. des Escaravatiers, 83480 Puget-sur-Argens, tel. 04.94.19.88.22, fax 04.94.45.59.83, e-mail costam@wanadoo.fr ☎ by appt.

CH. DEFFENDS Cuvée première 2000★
2 ha   13,300   €5-8

This original terroir, located among the gravelly, sandy-clay alluvial and schist soils of the Maures, produces red wines that are always pleasing, even when young. This is true of the 2000, with its intense aromas of soft red fruit, rounded, it benefits from integrated tannins. Also awarded one star, the rosé Cuvée première 2000 is just as seductive.
◆ EARL Denise Verges, Ch. Deffends, 83660 Carnoules, tel. 04.94.28.33.12, fax 04.94.28.33.12 ☎ ev. day 8am–12 noon 1–7pm

● Dom. des Féraud, rte de La Garde-Freinet, 83550 Vidauban, tel. 04.94.73.03.12, fax 04.94.73.08.58 ✉
Ⴝ by appt.
● M. Fournier

CH. DES FERRAGES
Cuvée Roumery 2000★

4.5 ha 20,000 €5-8

Visible from Route Nationale 7, between Aix and Saint-Maximin, this 40-ha (99-acre) estate has been in the same family since 1912. José Garcia is responsible for the vinification and gets some good results, as is shown by the **white 2000 Tradition Prestige**, which was awarded only one star, as well as by this salmon-coloured rosé. Extremely fruity (peach, small red berries), it demonstrates, through its harmony in the tasting, perfectly mastered wine-making.

● José Garcia, Ch. des Ferrages, RN 7, 83470 Pourcieux, tel. 04.94.59.45.53, fax 04.94.59.72.49 ✉ Ⴝ by appt.

CH. FONT DU BROC 2000★★

4 ha 18,000 €8-11

In 1988 a fire destroyed the remains of Arcs-sur-Argens, and a vineyard was planted on the grounds that were left. This estate has already won over the Jury of preceding editions of the *Guide* with its red wines. The **white 99** definitely warrants a star, but the 2000 rosé also received a unanimous vote. Pale and glittering, the wine offers a basket of fruits. It develops elegantly, with length on the palate, in a plethora of fruit punctuated with mineral notes.

● Sylvain Massa, Ch. Font du Broc, 83460 Les Arcs-sur-Argens, tel. 04.94.47.48.20, fax 04.94.47.50.46 ✉ Ⴝ ev. day 10am–1pm 3–7pm

CH. DU GALOUPET 2000

Cru clas. 8 ha 35,000

It is difficult to remain indifferent to the somewhat baroque charm of this château, which is surrounded by palm trees and has a unique view over Porquerolles and the Giens peninsula. This vineyard has given birth to a lemon-tinted floral wine full of freshness.

● Ch. du Galoupet, Saint-Nicolas, 83250 La Londe-les-Maures, tel. 04.94.66.40.07, fax 04.94.66.42.40, e-mail galoupet@club-internet.fr ✉
Ⴝ by appt.
● S. Shivdasani

CH. DES GARCINIERES
Cuvée traditionnelle 2000★

8 ha 40,000 €5-8

This forested estate boasts a magnificent four-storey country house, an alley of age-old plane trees and a chapel dedicated to Saint Philomène. It has been producing wine for five centuries, only 6 km (almost 4 miles) from Saint-Tropez. The 20-ha (49-acre) vineyard offers a pale pink wine, round and fleshy, with lovely peach and citrus aromas.

● Famille Valentin, Ch. des Garcinières, 83310 Cogolin, tel. 04.94.02.85, fax 04.94.56.07.42, e-mail info@chateau-garcinières.com ✉
Ⴝ ev. day 9am–1pm 2–6 pm winter; 9am–1pm 4–8pm summer

DOM. GAVOTY
Cuvée Clarendon 2000★

3 ha 20,000 €5-8

This label honours Bernard Gavoty, a music critic who wrote under the pseudonym of Clarendon. The wine, made from Grenache and Cinsaut, has a fairly low volume of production. Very pale, it offers a fruity (citrus and peach) nose. The palate develops with length thanks to its good balance. The **white Cuvée Clarendon 2000** also gained a star for its aerated, fresh, expressive and generous character.

● Pierre et Roselyne Gavoty, Le Grand Campdumy, 83340 Cabasse, tel. 04.94.69.72.39, fax 04.94.59.64.04, e-mail domaine.gavoty@wanadoo.fr ✉
Ⴝ by appt.

CH. GRAND'BOISE 2000★

6.97 ha 26,000 €5-8

In 1879, three properties were joined to create Grand'Boise. The cultivation of vines quickly overtook that of lavender and silkworms and the forestry interests. Situated at approximately 300–600 m (985–1970 ft), this vineyard now covers over 42 ha (104 acres) on the north face of Sainte-Baume. Some of the vines are almost 100 years old. These contribute, in particular, to the expression of this fine, floral rosé. The palate is perfectly balanced between roundness and liveliness.

● SCEA La Grenobloise, Ch. Grand'Boisé, rte de Grisole, 13530 Trets, tel. 04.42.29.22.95, fax 04.42.61.38.71, e-mail contact@grandboise.com ✉
Ⴝ ev. day 8.30am–12 noon 2pm–6pm

HERMITAGE SAINT-MARTIN 2000★

4 ha 13,000 €8-11

In 1999, Guillaume Fayard, who works side by side with his father at the Château Sainte-Marguerite, acquired this 13-ha (32-acre) vineyard, whose medieval origins are linked with the monks of Saint-Victor. This wine has a very fruity palate and its violet tints indicate its youth; nevertheless, it demonstrates maturity in its tannic structure. Overall, it is dense, pleasing and is ready to drink now.

● Guillaume Fayard, Ch. Hermitage Saint-Martin, BP 1, 83250 La-Londe-les-Maures, tel. 04.94.00.44.44, fax 04.94.00.44.45 ✉
Ⴝ ev. day except Sun. 9am–12.30pm 2pm–5.30pm

DOM. DE JACOURETTE Cuvée
Genevière Elevé en fût de chêne 1998★★

0.5 ha 2,400 €8-11

Hélène Dragon was only 25 years old when she took over this 7-ha (17-acre) family estate in 1997. Wisely, she waited before submitting this 98 to the *Guide*, because today this wine shows all its attributes. Its complex palate opens on spicy notes of venison and black fruit; the palate has a harmonious balance between roundness and tannins. This is a good wine, which could still age another one or two years.

🍷 Dom. de Jacourette, rte de Trets, 83910 Pourrières, tel. 04.94.78.54.60, fax 04.94.78.42.07, e-mail hdragon@club-internet.fr Ⓥ
Ⓨ ev. day except Sun. Mon. 9.30am–12 noon 3pm–6.30pm in Jul. and Aug.
🍷 Hélène Dragon

CH. DE JASSON
Cuvée Eléonore 2000★★

| | 10.1 ha | 71,000 | | €8-11 |

In 1990, Benjamin de Fresne, a Parisian restaurateur, and his wife Marie-Andrée took over this estate of almost 16 ha (40 acres). Their rigour, passion and attention to detail won them two *coups de cœur* in 2000. This rosé collected votes for the intensity of its citrus and lilac aromas, as well as its complex, lengthy palate. The **white Cuvée Jeanne 2000**, aged in tank, received the same accolade. Demonstrating finesse with its grapefruit, exotic fruit and flower notes, it has a balanced structure. The fresh and lengthy finish enthused the Jury.

🍷 Benjamin de Fresne, Ch. de Jasson, RD 88, 83250 La Londe-les-Maures, tel. 04.94.66.81.52, fax 04.94.05.24.84, e-mail chateau.de.jasson@wanadoo.fr Ⓥ
Ⓨ ev. day 9.30am–12.30pm 2.30pm–7pm

LA BASTIDE DU CURE 2000★

| | 9.46 ha | 20,000 | | €3-5 |

Thanks to Giono and Pagnol, Provence is an open book. Rediscover the tastes of the vine in this aromatic, balanced, refreshing rosé: a pleasant, well-structured wine.

🍷 Coop. Vinicole La Vidaubanaise, 89, chem. Sainte-Anne, BP 24, 83550 Vidauban, tel. 04.94.73.00.12, fax 04.94.73.54.67 Ⓥ
Ⓨ by appt.

DOM. DE LA BASTIDE NEUVE 2000★★

| | 1.13 ha | 6,500 | | €8-11 |

A pale colour with tints of green ... A concentration of exotic fruits (peach, citrus, passion fruit) ... A full palate with pleasing harmony. ... This is Rolle with fine expression. The **rosé Perles de Rosé 2000**, also a great success, balances itself between roundness and liveliness to satisfy the gourmets.

🍷 SCEA Dom. de La Bastide Neuve, 83340 Le Cannet-des-Maures, tel. 04.94.50.09.80, fax 04.94.50.09.99, e-mail dmebastideneuve@compuserve.com
Ⓨ ev. day except Sat. Sun. 8am–12 noon 1pm–5.30pm
🍷 Hugo Wiestner

DOM. DE L'ABBAYE 2000★★

| | 2.5 ha | 12,500 | | €8-11 |

The Abbey of Thoronet is a masterpiece of Roman art from the 12th century. Stop there, meditate ... and, at the estate, taste this round full rosé, with aromas of dried fruits and flint stones. A Grand Jury finalist, this bottle would have pride of place on any table.

🍷 Franc Petit, Dom. de l'Abbaye, 83340 Le Thoronet, tel. 04.94.73.87.36, fax 04.94.60.11.62 Ⓨ ev. day 9am–7pm

DOM. DE LA BOUVERIE 2000★★

| | 34 ha | 60,000 | | €5-8 |

In the region of the ancient village of Roquebrune-sur-Argens, which dominates the Argens plain, this estate cultivates 32 ha (79 acres) of vines. A luminous salmon colour, this much-liked rosé has a rich, aromatic palate, where flowers (rose) and fruits (peach, apricot) intermingle. The elegant structure surrounds a rounded body and sustains the finish. The **white 2000**, matured in cask, also gains a star. Although the wood is still prominent, the wine is nevertheless fine and balanced.

🍷 Jean Laponche, 83520 Roquebrune-sur-Argens, tel. 04.94.44.00.81, fax 04.94.44.04.73 Ⓥ
Ⓨ ev. day except Sun. 9.30am–12 noon 2.30pm–7pm

DOM. DE LA COURTADE 1999★

| | 3.5 ha | 11,000 | | €15-23 |

Situated on the island of Porquerolles, this 30-ha (74-acre) vineyard contributes to the national park's fire protection: vines are an excellent barrier against flames. Richard Auther farms organically. The Rolle is very evident in this golden-yellow wine. The nose opens up to violets and narcissi, then moves on to fruit. Round, balanced by good liveliness, the wine carries on in the floral range. This wine will go well with poultry or fresh cheeses.

🍷 Dom. de La Courtade, 83400 Ile-de-Porquerolles, tel. 04.94.58.31.44, fax 04.94.58.34.12, e-mail la-courtade@terre-net.fr
Ⓨ by appt.
🍷 H. Vidal

CELLIER DE LA CRAU

Cuvée des Vieux Ceps 1999★

■ 14 ha 5,000 €3–5

The use of Syrah and a well-managed maturation stage allowed this Grand Toulon co-operative to successfully produce this pleasing, balanced, spicy red wine with woody aromas. It is ready to drink now.

Cellier de La Crau, 35, av. de Toulon, 83260 La Crau, tel. 04.94.66.73.03, fax 04.94.66.17.63 Y by appt.

DOM. DE LA CRESSONNIERE

Cuvée Mataro 1999★★

■ 1.25 ha 6,500 €8–11

Created in 1639, today the Maures estate, which until the nineteenth century was dedicated to the cultivation of silkworms, produces only wines. The oldest plantings are Syrah, a variety that dominates this blend, which has been judiciously produced and matured in wood. It demonstrates an elegant marriage between ripe fruit, vanilla aromas, volume, roundness and structure long into the finish. It still has a taste of youth though, which suggests it should be kept for three to five years.

GFA Dom. de La Cressonnière, RN 97, 83790 Pignans, tel. 04.94.48.81.22, fax 04.94.48.81.25, e-mail cressonniere@wanadoo.fr

Y ev. day except Sun. 10am–12 noon 3pm–6pm

Depeursinge

CH. DE LA DEIDIERE

Cuvée du Pigeonnier 1999★

■ 8.33 ha 50,000 €5–8

This old hunting lodge, of note due to its 18th-century pigeon-house, is surrounded by 80 ha (198 acres) of vines. The deep-red wine produced here has fruity aromas, including cherry, raspberry and blackcurrant. A touch of violet also appears in this mix. Tender and fresh, the palate maintains the real balance of flavours. It would accompany simple dishes, such as cold meats. The **white Château de l'Aumerade Cuvée Sully 2000** also gained a star.

SCEA des Dom. Fabre, Ch. de l'Aumerade, 83390 Pierrefeu, tel. 04.94.28.20.31, fax 04.94.48.23.09, e-mail hefabre@wanadoo.fr

Y ev. day except Sun. 8am–12 noon 1.30pm–5.30pm, groups by appt.

MAS DE LA GERADE 2000

◪ 3.5 ha 12,000 €5–8

A brilliant-coloured wine with marked aromas: pear drops, lime, peach and other fruits, all equally present on the palate. Fresh and balanced, the palate prolongs these sensations.

EARL de La Gérade, 1300, chem. des Tourraches, 83260 La Crau, tel. 04.94.66.13.88, fax 04.94.66.73.52, e-mail lagerade@aol.com

Y ev. day except Sun. 9am–12 noon

B. Henry

DOM. DE LA GISCLE

Moulin de l'Isle 2000★★

◪ 3 ha 15,000 €5–8

A flour mill then a silkworm farm were based here until the 16th century, when vines became all important to this *terroir*. The label recalls the prior activities of this estate. Appreciated by all, this rosé, with its lightly orange tints, is full of personality. It releases aromas of apricot and dried fruit. The unctuous, rounded palate develops into a long finish. One taster suggested that this wine could be served with a chocolate dessert.

EARL Dom. de La Giscle, hameau de l'Amirauté, rte de Collobrières, 83310 Cogolin, tel. 04.94.43.21.26, fax 04.94.43.37.53

Y ev. day 9am–12.30pm 2pm–7pm; Sun. 9am–12.30pm

Audemard

CH. LA GORDONNE 2000★

◪ 120 ha 800,000 €3–5

The Conseiller de Gourdon acquired this estate in 1650 and gave it its name. Since 1941, the 188-ha (465-acre) vineyard has been under the control of Domaines Listel. This clear rosé has generous red berry and pear drop aromas. The strong, full palate has a lengthy finish.

Domaines Listel, Ch. La Gordonne, 83390 Pierrefeu-du-Var, tel. 04.94.28.20.35, fax 04.94.28.20.35, e-mail njulian@listel.fr

Y ev. day 8am–12 noon 1pm–6pm; Sat. Sun. by appt.

DOM. DE LA GUINGUETTE 2000★

◪ 9.7 ha 50,000 €3–5

Scents of peach and pear drops give this fuchsia-tinted, very aromatic rosé a sense of lightness. The very fresh palate has a slightly sharp finish.

Les vignerons du Baou, rue Raoul-Blanc, 83470 Pourcieux, tel. 04.94.78.03.06, fax 04.94.78.05.50 Y by appt.

Tarabelli

DOM. DE LA JEANNETTE 2000★★

◪ 1.4 ha 15,500 €5–8

Situated at the entrance to the valley of Borrels, this charming Provençal estate is surrounded by 25 ha (62 acres) of vines. This pale, delicate wine releases very clean aromas reminiscent of yellow flowers, peach and green almond. Equally clear on the palate is its persistence and length. The **white 2000**, also awarded a star, is aromatic, fresh and ready to drink now.

🍷 SCIR Dom. de la Jeannette, 566, rte des Borrels, 83400 Hyères-les-Palmiers, tel. 04.94.65.68.30, fax 04.94.12.76.07

🍷 Limon

DOM. DE LA LAUZADE 2000★★
26 ha   140,000   €5-8

The communal archives of Luc mention that the Romans built the first Roman villa of this region here: Villa Lauza. The estate today owns 70 ha (173 acres) of vines. It is one of the few producers to have been awarded the Guide's *coup de cœur* on a number of occasions. The estate offers a bold, fuchsia-tinted rosé with aromas of fresh fruit, cherry and blood orange, with roundness and strength built around a well-structured palate. The unwooded **red 2000**, is an integrated, aromatic wine that is drinking well now. It was awarded one star.

🍷 SARL Dom. de La Lauzade, rte de Toulon, 83340 Le Luc, tel. 04.94.60.72.51, fax 04.94.60.96.26, e-mail lauzade.abouvier@wanadoo.fr

🍷 by appt.

CH. LA MARTINETTE
Cuvée Prestige 1999★★
2 ha   5,000   €8-11

This selection comes from the estate's oldest Syrah vines. The variety gives the wine spice and floral aromas, while it retains vanilla and roasted hints from its period in oak. The palate is rich, robust, balanced and full of promise.

🍷 Ch. La Martinette, 4005, chem. de la Martinette, 83510 Lorgues, tel. 04.94.73.84.93, fax 04.94.73.88.34

🍷 by appt.

🍷 Tarby-Liégeon

DOM. DE LA NAVARRE
Cuvée Les Roches 1999★
4.5 ha   25,000   €8-11

This estate owes its name to the Navarre family, who occupied it during the 18th century. Today, it is run by the religious order of Saint-Jean Bosco, founder of the congregation of Salesians. Nine months' barrel maturation has perfected the development of this lightly tinted wine with its delicate nose. The palate is agreeably supple and balanced with good aromatic length. This wine is drinking well now.

🍷 Fondation La Navarre, Cave du domaine, 3451, chem. de la Navarre, 83260 La Crau, tel. 04.94.66.04.08, fax 04.94.35.10.66

🍷 by appt.

CLOS LA NEUVE Prestige 2000★
1 ha   4,000

At the foot of the Aurélien mountains and exposed to the north, this estate's marl and sandstone soils are particularly suitable to Rolle, a variety with many similarities to the

Vermentino of Corsica or Italy. The resulting pale wine, intensely floral on the nose, has a palate that is seductively fine and balanced.

🍷 Fabienne Joly, Dom. de La Neuve, 83910 Pourrières, tel. 04.94.59.86.03, fax 04.94.59.86.42 🍷 ev. day 9am– 12 noon 2pm–7pm

DOM. DE L'ANGUEIROUN 2000★
n.c.   30,000   €5-8

This estate, previously a game reserve, owns a 35-ha (86-acre) vineyard surrounded by hills. Its complex rosé is floral, almost mineral on the nose. Round and warming, it also shows a degree of liveliness with slight bitterness on the finish. The **white 2000**, under the same label, is also a great success.

🍷 Eric Dumon, 1077, chem. de l'Angueiroun, 83220 Bormes-les-Mimosas, tel. 04.94.71.11.39, fax 04.94.71.75.51, e-mail angueiroun@libertysurf.fr

🍷 ev. day except Sun. 8am–12 noon 2pm–6pm

DOM. DE L'ANTICAILLE 2000★★★
2.3 ha   15,000   €5-8

This 35-ha (86-acre) estate lies in countryside that was dear to Cézanne, against the backdrop of Mount Sainte-Victoire. This pale, bright, expressive rosé has a nose which, though delicate, offers a fine array of exotic scents and red fruits. The full, balanced palate appears fleshy and lengthy. What generosity!

🍷 Martine Féraud-Paillet, Dom. de L'Anticaille, 13530 Trets, tel. 04.22.27.42.53, fax 04.42.29.22.64 🍷 by appt.

LES MAITRES VIGNERONS DE LA PRESQU'ILE DE SAINT-TROPEZ Carte noire 2000★★
7 ha   40,000   €5-8

The Jury's attention was held by this wine's finesse, complexity, balance and its touch of springtime fruits and flowers that would enliven any table. The **rosé Carte Noire, 2000** and the **red Carte Noire 2000** were equally seductive and achieved one star.

🍷 Les Maîtres vignerons de La Presqu'île de Saint-Tropez, 83580 Gassin, tel. 04.94.56.32.04, fax 04.94.43.42.57 🍷 ev. day except Sun. 9am–12 noon 3pm–7pm

Côtes de Provence

CH. L'ARNAUDE 2000★

10 ha   30,000   €5-8

Principally from Grenache and Cinsaut planted on chalky soil, this rosé inclines towards intense fruity aromas with mineral notes. Lively at first, this balanced wine, which has personality, opens to plenty of roundness and volume before finishing on a note of citrus fruit.

• Ch. L'Arnaude, rte de Vidauban, 83510 Lorgues, tel. 04.94.73.70.67, fax 04.94.67.61.69 ☑ ▼ ev. day 9.30am–12 noon 3pm–6pm; Sun. 10am–12 noon
• H.J. Knapp

DOM. DE LA ROUILLERE

Grande Réserve 2000★

3 ha   13,000   €5-8

Initially this pale pink wine appears delicate, but it evolves into deeper quality on the palate. Its initial suppleness rises strongly towards fruity notes. **The red Cuvée Grande Réserve 98**, twelve months in cask, is commended for its structure. It can be cellared for a year.

• Dom. de la Rouillère, rte de Ramatuelle, 83380 Gassin, tel. 04.94.55.72.60, fax 04.94.55.72.61, e-mail contact@domainedelarouillere.com ☑ ▼ ev. day except Sat. Sun. 8am–12 noon 2pm–5.30pm
• Letartre

DOM. DE LA SAUVEUSE 2000★

0.74 ha   5,200   €5-8

This 60-ha (148-acre) estate produces small quantities of this well-balanced wine. The pale colour, with green tints, invites you to discover a breadlike, toasty nose. The clean attack gives way to a full, soft structure right up to the finish. Everything comes together successfully in this elusive wine.

• SCEA Dom. de La Sauveuse, Grand-Chemin-Vieux, 83390 Puget-Ville, tel. 04.94.28.59.60, fax 04.94.28.52.48, e-mail sauveuse@wanadoo.fr ☑ ▼ ev. day except Sat. Sun. 8am–12 noon 1pm–5.30pm
• Salinas

DOM. LA TOUR DES VIDAUX

Cuvée Farnoux 1999★

3 ha   8,000   €8-11

The cellar is situated at the centre of an amphitheatre of vines that push the cork oaks back to the typical shale soil of the Maures. The estate has fixed daily menus and organises art exhibitions. The basis of this deep red wine, rich in spices and roasted aromas, is mainly Syrah, underlined by Grenache. The full, rich palate has integrated woody nuances, signifying a perfectly controlled maturation.

• V. P. Weindel, Dom. La Tour-des-Vidaux, quartier Les Vidaux, 83390 Pierrefeu-du-Var, tel. 04.94.48.24.01, fax 04.94.48.24.02, e-mail tourdesvidaux@wanadoo.fr ☑ ▼ ev. day except Sun. 8.30am–12 noon 2.30pm–6.30pm

DOM. LA TOURRAQUE 2000★★

3 ha   13,000   €5-8

This estate's 45 ha (111 acres) fall within the protected area of three headlands. As remarkable as its surrounding environment is this rosé, characteristic of both the vintage and the appellation, which displays a complex bouquet: floral yet citric with slight mineral hints. The round palate and lengthy finish add to its charm. Goat's cheese would complement it well.

• GAEC Brun-Craveris, Dom. La Tourraque, 83350 Ramatuelle, tel. 04.94.79.25.95, fax 04.94.79.16.08 ☑ ▼ ev. day except Sun. 9am–12 noon 2pm–6pm

CH. DES LAUNES

Cuvée spéciale 2000★★

2.5 ha   10,000   €5-8

This is a pretty 25-ha (62-acre) estate in the middle of the Maures forest. Château des Launes is a haven of serenity on the route to the Gulf of Saint-Tropez. It produces excellent wines, which regularly appear in the Guide. This very pale rosé with floral aromas has real presence on the palate. The balanced **white 2000**, produced from Rolle, is full of citrus fruit. It was awarded one star.

• Hans-Y. et Brigitte Handtmann, Ch. des Launes, RD 558 vers le Luc, 83680 La Garde-Freinet, tel. 04.94.60.01.95, fax 04.94.60.01.43 ☑ ▼ by appt.

LE GRAND CROS

L'Esprit de Provence 2000★★

5 ha   25,000   €5-8

This estate, whose main house dates back to the 17th century, reanimates the sprit of Provence in this rosé with its delicate, floral nose and total finesse. The Jury appreciated the intensity and balance on the palate, which plays on the essence of white flowers.

• EARL Dom. du Grand Cros, 83660 Carnoules, tel. 04.98.01.80.08, fax 04.98.01.80.09, e-mail info@grandcros.fr ☑ ▼ by appt.
• J.-H. Faulkner

CH. LE MAS 2000★

0.75 ha   4,000   €5-8

This estate celebrated its centenary in 2000. This wine is a fine testament to this anniversary. It owes its strength and richness to the clay-schist soil, while the Rolle and Clairette varieties give it elegant palate flavours. Well vinified and fresh on the palate, it won't disappoint.

• SCEA Ch. Le Mas, quartier La Tuilerie, 83390 Puget-Ville, tel. 04.94.48.30.21, fax 04.94.48.30.21, e-mail lemasaudibert@free.fr ☑ ▼ by appt.

CH. LES MESCLANCES

Cuvée Saint-Honorat 1999★

2 ha   3,000   €5-8

This wine comes from a 25-ha (62-acre) vineyard set on primary schist. It is a carefully designed mix of grape varieties; equal parts Cabernet Sauvignon, Syrah and Mourvèdre. Under a deep, violet-tinted colour lies a structured palate, balanced between the fruit and wood from the maturation. It is still characterised by tannins but will soften after cellaring for at least a couple of years.

➡ Xavier de Villeneuve-Bargemon, Les Mesclances, 83260 La Crau, tel. 04.94.66.75.07, fax 04.94.35.10.03, e-mail mesclances@yahoo.fr ▼ by appt.

DOM. DE L'ESPARRON

Cuvée Laurent Vieilli en barrique 1999

2 ha 9,000 € 3-5

This 40-ha (99-acre) estate is situated at the foot of the Maures a few miles from the village of Tortues. This red wine has spent eight months in the barrel, which is apparent from the intense vanilla aromas on the nose and palate. Well balanced but still somewhat austere, it would benefit from being kept for a while before opening.

➡ EARL Migliore, Dom. de l'Esparron, 83590 Gonfaron, tel. 04.94.78.32.23, fax 04.94.78.24.85 ▼ ev. day 8am–12 noon 1.30pm–7.30pm

CH. LES VALENTINES 1999★

3.5 ha 20,000 € 8-11

This wine, marked by its nine-month partial cask maturation, needs to be left in a good cellar for two or three years. It will then be the ideal accompaniment for a good Provençal stew. The dark, intense colour is superb. The subtle nose picks up on undergrowth, dried fruit and the charred taste of the barrels. The palate, underlined by everpresent and promising tannins, has similar characteristics.

➡ SCEA Pons-Massenot, 83250 La-Londe-les-Maures, tel. 04.94.15.95.50, fax 04.94.15.95.55, e-mail gilles.pons@wanadoo.fr ▼ ev. day except Sun. 9am–7pm

➡ Gilles Pons

CH. MAIME 2000★

6.12 ha 39,000 € 5-8

A chapel named Sainte-Maïme (Saint-Maxime in Provençal), dating back to 1640, gave its name to this 17-ha (42-acre) vineyard. Recent renovations have brought new life to the estate, an ancient hamlet where vines, olive trees and silk mulberry bushes were cultivated. This very pale, almost transparent rosé has delicate aromas of fresh fruit: peach, pear and strawberry. The palate picks up on these aromas with finesse.

➡ SCEA Ch. Maïme, quartier de La Maïme, 83460 Les Arcs-sur-Argens, tel. 04.94.47.41.66, fax 04.94.47.42.08, e-mail maime@terre-net.fr ▼ ev. day except Sun. 10am–12.30pm 3pm–7pm

➡ Sibran et Garcia

MANON 2000★★

n.c. 66,000 € 5-8

This Grenache (70%) and Syrah rosé has a sustained fuchsia-tinted colour. The well-structured palate, a happy aromatic marriage of fruit and flowers, makes for a wine that is both full and lively. It deserves fine food.

➡ Cellier Val de Durance, Le Grand Jardin, 84360 Lauris, tel. 04.90.08.26.36, fax 04.90.08.28.27

CH. MAROUINE 1999

3 ha 20,000 € 5-8

Dominating the valley, and planted in the remains of this old Provençal farmhouse, are vines surrounded by olive trees and springs. Carignan and Mourvèdre produce this violet-coloured wine which, thanks to a good extraction, has a promising future. Leave this wine for a minimum of two years to allow it to open.

➡ Marie-Odile Marty, Ch. Marouine, 83390 Puget-Ville, tel. 04.94.48.35.74, fax 04.94.48.37.61 ▼ ev. day except Sun. 9am–7pm

DOM. DE MAUVAN 2000★

3 ha 20,000 € 5-8

Yet again Gaëlle Maclou's rosé impressed the Jury. Called a 'singular wine' by one of the tasters, it is fine, elegant and full ... The sensations are open and balanced. The white 2000 is mentioned for its delicate floral character.

➡ Gaëlle Maclou, Dom. de Mauvan, RN 7, 13114 Puyloubier, tel. 04.42.29.38.33, fax 04.42.29.38.33 ▼ by appt.

CH. MINUTY

Cuvée de l'Oratoire 2000★ Cru clas.

7 ha 45,000 € 8-11

When Saint-Tropez was becoming more than a little fishing village, Minuty extended to 2,000 ha (5,000 acres). Today it occupies 65 ha (161 acres). This beautiful château is worth our attention for both its architecture and its wines. The wine based on Rolle remains good value. The 2000, very slightly tinted grey, offers elegant aromas of flowers and apricot and a strong, fine palate with durable length.

➡ Matton-Farnet, Ch. Minuty, 83580 Gassin, tel. 04.94.56.12.09, fax 04.94.56.18.38 ▼ ev. day except Sun. 9am–12 noon 2pm–6pm

DOM. DE MONT REDON

Cuvée Louis Joseph 2000★

1.5 ha 10,000 € 5-8

This intensely coloured, intensely aromatic wine is still youthful as seen in the freshness of its red berry, redcurrant and morello cherry aromas. It is full and silky on the palate due to its youthful, fine tannins. Seductive, it is equally a good wine for keeping. The rosé Cuvée Colombe 2000 is also very successful.

CH. MOURESSE
Grande Cuvée 1998★★

■ 2.5 ha 5,000 ▮▮ €8-11

The sandy soils of the Vidauban plain add great finesse to this red, which is made from Cabernet Sauvignon and Syrah. Clear with fruity, woody aromas, its body develops complexity around its solid structure. Despite being rich and mature, it could still benefit from a few years in the cellar. The **white 2000** was also awarded two stars for its ample, lengthy palate.

☛ Sophie et Patrick Horst, 3353, chem. de Pied-de-Banc, 83550 Vidauban.
tel. 04.94.73.12.38, fax 04.94.73.57.04, e-mail info@chateau-mouresse.com ☑
⏰ ev. day except Sun. 8am–12 noon 3pm–7pm
☛ Michel Horst

CH. DE PAMPELONNE 2000★★

■ 22 ha 100,000 ▮ €5-8

This pale pink wine, surrounded by intense aromas of exotic fruit, leaves a pleasing sensation on the palate due to its fleshiness. Finesse is the focus of its taste. Just as remarkable, the **white Prestige 2000**, with its intense floral aromas on the nose, has a palate which initially feels light but moves on to a warm finish.

☛ Ch. de Pampelonne, 83350 Ramatuelle.
tel. 04.94.56.32.04, fax 04.94.43.42.37
⏰ by appt.
☛ Pascaud

CH. PANSARD 2000★

■ 5 ha 30,000 ▮ €5-8

François de Canson, the son of the owners, is taking over the running of this estate with this fine pale pink, raspberry-tinted wine. The intense nose plays on woody strawberries, whilst the round and soft palate displays balance and length.

☛ Cave des vignerons Londais, quartier Pansard, 83250 La-Londe-les-Maures,
tel. 04.94.66.80.23, fax 04.94.05.20.10 ☑
⏰ by appt.
☛ de Canson

DOM. DE PARIS 2000★

■ 35 ha 100,000 ▮ €5-8

The Jury appreciated the fruit, freshness and roundness of this well-vinified, well-matured rosé.

☛ Les vins Jean-Jacques Bréban,
av. de La Burlière, BP 47, 83171 Brignoles,
tel. 04.94.69.37.55, fax 04.94.69.03.37,
e-mail vins_breban@hotmail.com ☑

DOM. PINCHINAT 2000★★

■ 3 ha 20,000 ▮▮ €5-8

This estate has been farming organically since 1990. This fine, expressive, salmon-tinted rosé stands out well. On the nose and the palate the fruit develops, giving a silken and lengthy structure. This balanced wine would go well with Mediterranean cuisine.

☛ Alain de Welle, Dom. Pinchinat,
83910 Pourrières, tel. 04.42.29.29.92,
fax 04.42.29.29.92 ☑ ⏰ by appt.

POMARIN Elevé en fût de chêne 1998★

■ 10 ha 28,000 ▮▮▮ €5-8

Situated at the foot of the Maures massif, 12 km (7 miles) from the coast, the village of Plan-de-la-Tour has an active co-operative incorporating almost all of its wine-makers. This original mix of Syrah and Mourvèdre creates an eloquent wine, with aromas of venison and jammy fruit. Well put together, it will drink comfortably over the course of the next two years.

☛ Les Fouleurs de Saint-Pons,
83120 Plan-de-la-Tour, tel. 04.94.43.70.60,
fax 04.94.43.00.55 ☑ ⏰ by appt.

CH. DE POURCIEUX 2000★

■ 8 ha 53,000 ▮ €5-8

Château de Pourcieux, along with its French gardens, has been classed as an historic monument. It has belonged to the Marquis d'Espagnet's family since 1760. The Jury has judged three wines very successful. This clear-cut, pink-tinted rosé, typical of its *terroir* with its fruity, peppery aromas and fresh structure, will match well with highly seasoned dishes. The more supple, delicately flavoured **white 2000** is ready to drink, as is the **red Grand Millésime 2000**.

☛ Michel d'Espagnet, Ch. de Pourcieux,
83470 Pourcieux, tel. 04.94.59.78.90,
fax 04.94.59.32.46, e-mail pourcieux@terre-net.fr ☑ ⏰ ev. day except Sat. Sun. 9am–12 noon 2pm–6pm

DOM. POUVEREL 2000★

■ 10 ha 60,000 ▮ €8-11

This lightly-tinted wine, with its very floral nose, can be found in the Cave des Vignerons in the gulf of Saint-Tropez. Roses and white flowers are pleasantly joined by nuances of peach. The balanced palate builds on these aromas: a wine to be enjoyed with exotic food.

☛ Dom. Pouverel, 83390 Cuers,
tel. 04.94.56.32.04, fax 04.94.43.42.57
☛ Massel

CH. DU PUGET
Cuvée de Chavette 1999★

■ 3 ha 3,600 ▮ €5-8

This 31-ha (77-acre) vineyard, planted on clay-chalk soil, surrounds a building dating back to 1640. This floral wine, predominantly Syrah and completed by Grenache, has a lively, light tint. It offers freshness, suppleness and balance. It is ready to drink now.

☛ Michel Torné, SCEA Dom. Mont Redon, 2496, rte de Pierrefeu, 83260 La Crau, tel. 04.94.66.73.86, fax 04.94.57.82.12, e-mail mont.redon@libertysurf.fr ☑ ⏰ by appt.

• SCEA Ch. du Puget, rue du Mas de Clappier, 83390 Puget-Ville, tel. 04.94.48.31.15, fax 04.94.33.58.55 ▼
Y ev. day except Sun. Mon. 9am–1pm 3.30pm–6.30pm
• Grimaud

CH. DE RASQUE 2000★
5 ha | 25,000 | €11-15

In the glass this wine is a bright, pale colour enlivened by green tints, with a delicate nose. It becomes more voluminous on the palate. Aromas of lime and grapefruit appear within a fresh, balanced body.

• Ch. Rasque, rte de Draguignan, 83460 Taradeau, tel. 04.94.99.52.20, fax 04.94.99.52.21 Y by appt.
• Biancone

CH. REAL D'OR 2000★★
2.5 ha | 12,000 | €5-8

Château Real d'Or cultivates vines at the foot of the Maures, between forests of chestnut and oak. This remarkable pale pink wine with violet tints gives hints of ripe apricot, red berries, pepper and mint that extend to the palate. Its structure and quality make it well able to stand up to a variety of cheeses. The more delicate but also **white 2000**, aged in tank, is more delicate but also warrants a mention.

• SCEA Ch. Real d'Or, rte des Mayons, 83590 Gonfaron, tel. 04.94.60.00.56, fax 04.94.60.01.05, e-mail realdor@free.fr Y ev. day 10am–1pm 3pm–7.30pm

CH. REILLANNE
Cuvée Prestige 2000★
5 ha | 30,000 | €5-8

Château Reillanne, a wine-growing estate at the heart of the Cannet-des-Maures plain, is surrounded by 100-year-old umbrella pines. This very pale, intensely floral rosé develops with finesse; peppery notes sustain the palate underlining its agreeable freshness.

• Comte G. de Chevron-Villette, Ch. Reillanne, rte de Saint-Tropez, 83340 Le Cannet-des-Maures, tel. 04.94.50.11.70, fax 04.94.47.92.06 Y ev. day except Sat. Sun. 8am–12 noon 2pm–5pm

CH. REQUIER Cuvée spéciale 1998★
11 ha | 14,472 | €8-11

Château Réquier benefits from a rich natural and cultural environment. Cabasse is famous for its megaliths, Gallo-Roman relics and the line of red rocks that run the length of the Issole. This 50-ha (124-acre) estate produces an elegant bright wine with fine tannins most appreciable after two years' maturation. This 98, fruity and lengthy on the palate, could still benefit from more time.

• Ch. Réquier, La Plaine, 83340 Cabasse, tel. 04.94.80.25.72, fax 04.94.80.22.01 Y ev. day 8.30am–5pm; Sat. Sun. by appt.

RESERVE DES VINTIMILLE 2000★
4 ha | 40,000 | €3-5

This co-operative cellar lies in the fertile valley surrounding Le Luc, an old town that

owed its past importance to its location on the ancient Aurélienne route from Fréjus to Aix-en-Provence. The success of this clear, luminous Réserve, with fine aromas in the floral register, comes from its round, balanced palate.

• Les Vignerons du Luc, rue de l'Ormeau, 83340 Le Luc-en-Provence, tel. 04.94.60.70.25, fax 04.94.60.81.03 ▼ Y by appt.

DOM. RICHEAUME
Cuvée Tradition 1999★★
8 ha | 20,000 | €11-15

It's been a long road for Henning Hoesch, who took over a tiny estate in 1970 and applied the 'return to nature' philosophy. Today, his wines are organically cultivated. This beautiful, alluring, deep-coloured 99, after a fine, intense nose, exhibits a well-structured but soft palate, which is evolving elegantly. This wine promises a good future.

• SCEA Henning Hoesch, Dom. Richeaume, 13114 Puyloubier, tel. 04.42.66.31.27, fax 04.42.66.30.59 ▼

RIMAURESQ 2000★★★
Cru clas. 4 ha | 23,000 | €8-11

This property, created at the dawn of the 20th century, was taken over in 1989 by a Scottish family. The estate covers 36 ha (89 acres) of schist *terroir*, with the mountain of Notre-Dame des Anges in the background. Careful cultivation and perfect technical mastery created this balanced wine with its elegant expression and intense citrus, exotic fruit aromas. Its fullness and length make it a popular choice. The **red 99** was awarded two stars. Its characteristics: rich and fine in equally proportions.

• SA Dom. de Rimauresq, rte de Notre-Dame-des-Anges, 83790 Pignans, tel. 04.94.48.80.45, fax 04.94.33.22.31, e-mail pierreduffort@wanadoo.fr ▼ Y ev. day except Sun. 8am–12 noon 1.30pm–5.30pm
• Wemyss

CAVE DE ROUSSET
Rouge Terres 1999★★
4.3 ha | 30,000 | €3-5

This lovely deep-coloured wine appears reserved at first, then red berries appear. The marked tannins in a fleshy body underline the lengthy finish. This mouth-filling 99 is strong enough to accompany red meats. It is drinking well now and will be for the next two or three years.

Cave de Rousset, quartier Saint-Joseph, 13790 Rousset, tel. 04.42.29.00.09, fax 04.42.29.08.63 ☑ Y by appt.

CH. DE ROUX 2000
4 ha 13,000 €5-8

This estate, planted on the site of the old village of Cannet-des-Majures, produces its wines under an original and simple label. This straightforward, consistent wine is perfectly balanced between roundness and liveliness.

Jean-Guy Cupillard-Ch. de Roux, rte de la Garde-Freinet, 83340 Le Cannet-des-Maures, tel. 04.94.60.73.10, fax 04.94.60.89.79 ☑ Y ev. day 10am–6pm
J.-G. Cupillard

DOM. SAINT-ANDRE DE FIGUIERE
Grande Cuvée Vieilles vignes 2000★★
2 ha 13,000 €8-11

Only the fruits of 35-year-old vines go into this wine, made from Cinsaut, Grenache and Mourvèdre grown on schist. Under a pale, salmon-tinted colour, this rosé expresses generous floral and fruit aromas. After a fresh, finely-perfumed attack, the palate displays roundness and complexity right up to the long, remarkable finish.

Dom. Saint-André de Figuière, BP 47, 83250 La Londe-les-Maures, tel. 04.94.00.44.70, fax 04.94.35.04.46 ☑ Y ev. day except Sun. 9am–12 noon 2pm–6pm
Alain Combard

CH. SAINTE-BEATRICE
Cuvée Vaussière 1998★★
8 ha n.c. €5-8

This estate, created twenty years ago, cultivates a fairly young vineyard on the chalky soil of a Triassic plateau. A judicious mix of Syrah, Grenache and Cabernet Sauvignon produces this complex wine. The fruity, charred aromas come together with a delicate, well-softened woodiness. This 98 wine has reached maturity: it is ready to drink now.

Ch. Sainte-Béatrice, 415, chem. des Peiroux, BP 112, 83510 Lorgues, tel. 04.94.67.62.36, fax 04.94.73.72.70 ☑ Y by appt.
J. Novaretti

DOM. SAINTE-CROIX
Clos Manuelle 1999★
8 ha 10,000 €5-8

Two brothers, Jacques and Christian Pélepol, manage this 70-ha (173-acre) estate. This barrel-matured wine shows very obvious fruitiness, which contributes to its harmony. The supple, balanced palate ends pleasantly.

SCEA Pélepol Père et Fils, Dom. Sainte-Croix, 83570 Carcès, tel. 04.94.04.56.51, fax 04.94.04.38.10 ☑ Y ev. day 9am–12 noon 3pm–7pm

CH. SAINTE-MARGUERITE
Cuvée Symphonie Or 1999★★
Cru clas. 1 ha 4,000 €15-23

Brigitte and Jean-Pierre Fayard bought this estate in 1977. The vineyard was created in 1929 by M. Chevillon, a concert pianist. The wine, Symphonie Or, is well named: golden yellow in colour, floral, seductive and honeyed in character with a complex palate. This well-balanced wine has personality. The red cuvée Symphonie Pourpre 99 was awarded one star. Matured for 12 months in the barrel, its rich structure has a well-softened woodiness that complements game, especially in the winter.

Jean-Pierre Fayard, Ch. Sainte-Marguerite, BP 1, 83250 La Londe-les-Maures, tel. 04.94.00.44.44, fax 04.94.00.44.45 ☑ Y ev. day except Sat. Sun. 9am–12.30pm 2pm–5.30pm

DOM. DE SAINTE MARIE
Cuvée de la Roche Blanche 2000★
2.4 ha 16,000 €8-11

While the name of this estate honours the apparition of the Virgin Mary in 1884, which reputedly stopped an epidemic of cholera, the name of this wine reflects the quartz rocks of the surrounding hillsides. This pale Grenache- and Syrah-based rosé offers fruity peach aromas which are rediscovered in the ample, lengthy palate. In the whites, the cuvée de la Roche Blanche 2000 was singled out for a special mention.

SA Dom. de Sainte-Marie, rte du Dom, RN 98, Vallée de La Mole, 83230 Bormes-les-Mimosas, tel. 04.94.49.57.15, fax 04.94.49.58.57 ☑ Y ev. day except Sun. 9am–1pm 2pm–7pm

CH. SAINTE-ROSELINE
Cuvée Prieuré 1999★★
Cru clas. 5 ha 24,500 €11-15

In its high and historic chapel that shelters the tomb of Sainte Roseline, this estate has received some of the best-known artists. Wine-making goes back a long way and from a selection of the oldest vines, planted on clay-limestone soil, comes this 99 wine displaying woody, smoky, grilled notes. The wine's concentrated body is structured around rich, ripe tannins: a wine to be kept.

SCEA Ch. Sainte-Roseline, 83460 Les Arcs, tel. 04.94.99.50.30, fax 04.94.47.53.06, e-mail chateau.sainte.roseline@wanadoo.fr ☑ Y ev. day 9am–12.30pm 2pm–6.30pm

DOM. DU SAINT-ESPRIT
Grande Cuvée 2000★
12 ha 5,000 €5-8

Rolle and Sémillon in equal parts, grown on clay-limestone soil, form the basis of this deep, golden-tinted wine. Its delicate aromas add to its elegant expression: there is no hint of aggressiveness in the way the fruit integrates with the wood. It is ready to drink now.

- Crocé Spinelli, rte des Nouradons, BP 31, 83460 Les Arcs-sur-Argens, tel. 04.94.47.45.05, fax 04.94.73.30.73
- by appt.

CH. DE SAINT-JULIEN D'AILLE
Cuvée des Rimbauds 1998★★

5 ha   n.c.   €8-11

This vast 170-ha (420-acre) estate, on the right bank of the Argens, submitted an intense ruby-coloured Côtes de Provence. Aromas of red berries give it an air of youth, surprising in a 98 wine. Woody, well-integrated notes complete its rich aromas. On the palate, roundness, as well as supple, well-softened tannins, display its maturity. This is a wine drinking well from now.
- Ch. de Saint-Julien d'Aille, 5480, rte de la Garde Freinet, 83350 Vidauban, tel. 04.94.73.02.89, fax 04.94.73.61.31
- by appt.
- B. Fleury

CH. DE SAINT-MARTIN

Cru clas. 5 ha   15,000   €5-8

The Saint-Martin site has been inhabited since the Gallo-Roman era. The monks of Lérins established a wine-growing priory here in the 13th century. The estate has belonged to the same family for 250 years, handed down from mother to daughter by each generation. This straw-coloured 2000, pleasing to the eye, with its expressive, dominant citrus fruit aromas (lemon and grapefruit) heralds a fresh, balanced palate, with good length.
- Adeline de Barry, Ch. de Saint-Martin, rte des Arcs, 83460 Taradeau, tel. 04.94.73.02.01, fax 04.94.73.12.36
- by appt.
- Mme de Gasquet

CH. SAINT-PIERRE
Cuvée du Prieuré 1999★

2 ha   10,000   €5-8

Restoration work on the cellar uncovered the remains of this priory, which dates back to the 11th century. This garnet-red wine,

DOM. DE SAINT-MARC
Cuvée Epicure 1999★★

1.2 ha   8,000   €8-11

Created in the 1970s by a Parisian and purchased in 1988 by a Japanese man, this 6-ha (15-acre) estate on mica-schist soil in the heart of the Maures massif has just changed its owner again. The dark-coloured **Cuvée Epicure** offers a strong, ripe body, underlined by dense but fine tannins. This is a generous, balanced wine that would be better kept for another two years. The **red Cuvée Grande Réserve Domini 99**, still affected by its year-long maturation in barrel, would benefit from a while longer. It is, nevertheless, very successful. Also requiring more time is the one star **rosé Grande Réserve Domini 2000**.
- SCEA dom. Ch. Saint-Marc, chem. de Saint-Marc et des Crottes, 83310 Cogolin, tel. 04.94.54.69.92, fax 04.94.54.01.41
- by appt.

DOM. DE SAINT-SER
Hauts de Sainte-Victoire 1999★★

2 ha   6,600   €11-15

This vineyard lies at the highest point on the southern flank of the Sainte-Victoire mountain. This wine, with its spicy and vanilla nose and seductive, well-balanced flavours, is initially round and supple on the palate. It becomes fuller as tasting progresses, thanks to velvety tannins, then ends on a fresh finish.
- Dom. de Saint-Ser, RD 17, 13114 Puyloubier, tel. 04.42.66.30.81, fax 04.42.66.37.51, e-mail saintser@europost.org ev. day 10am-12 noon 2pm-6pm; groups by appt.
- Pierlot

showing musky, woody notes, has a full palate that benefits from fine tannins, leaving a sensation of strength. This wine, which can be kept for two or three years, will complement game well. The **rosé Cuvée Marie 2000** also warrants a mention.
- Jean-Philippe Victor, Ch. Saint-Pierre, Les Quatre-Chemins, 83460 Les Arcs, tel. 04.94.47.41.47, fax 04.94.73.34.73
- by appt.

SAINT-ROCH-LES-VIGNES 2000★

60 ha   200,000   €5-8

Bottled by the winemakers of Saint-Tropez for the Cuers co-operative, this pale rosé, the colour of rose petals, opens with floral, fruity aromas. Its well-balanced palate rounds out as it develops.
- Cave de Saint-Roch-les-Vignes, rte de Nice, 83390 Cuers, tel. 04.94.28.60.60
- Mon. Tue. Thu. Fri. 9am-12 noon 2pm-6pm

CAVE DE SAINT-TROPEZ
Cuvée Paul Signac 2000

3 ha   13,000   €5-8

Paul Signac, considered the head of the neo-impressionist movement, lived in Saint-Tropez. He is doubly honoured this year: by a retrospective exhibition in Paris and by this wine. The floral nose on this bright, lemon-tinted wine opens up to ripe, dried fruit notes. It is pleasingly fresh on the palate. It can be served on its own, or is ideal with roast chicken.
- La Cave de Saint-Tropez, SCAV Est, av. Paul-Roussel, 83990 Saint-Tropez, tel. 04.97.01.60, fax 04.94.97.70.24, e-mail lacavesttropez@aol.com
- by appt.

DOM. SILVY Cuvée Mathilde 2000★

1 ha   6,666   €5-8

Pourrières can be found at the edges of Var and Bouches-du-Rhône. On the estate, pride of place goes to the Syrah variety that makes this straightforward rosé, which suggests pear drop aromas with nuances of red berries. The palate is harmonious due to the good balance between alcohol and acidity. The finish is fruity and long.

Côtes de Provence

Cathy et Alain Silvy, 5, rue de Galiniers, 83910 Pourrières, tel. 04.94.78.49.60, fax 04.94.78.51.16 ▼
Υ by appt.

DOM. SIOUVETTE
Cuvée Marcel Galfard 2000★★
■ 6.5 ha 45,000 ■ ♦ €5-8

The majority of the soil on this estate, located on the edges of the Maures massif, consists of clay and schist. This clear rosé, with raspberry tints, is perfumed with citrus fruit and woody strawberries. It refreshes the palate with flavours that are simultaneously soft and lively. It is a lovely wine, and is ready to drink now.

Sylvaine Sauron, Dom. Siouvette, 83310 La Mole, tel. 04.94.49.57.13, fax 04.94.49.59.12 ▼
Υ ev. day 9am–12.30pm 2pm–7pm

CH. TERREBONNE 2000★★
■ 25 ha 30,000 ■ ♦ €3-5

This estate belonged the musicologist Bernard Gavoty. It was taken over by Michel and Nathalie Mercier in 1997. This pale rosé makes a name for itself with its obvious, aromatic, harmony: citrus and exotic fruits. The palate is bold, balanced and lengthy. The very full flavoured **white 2000** is just as remarkable. It is expressive and full of vitality and will go well with fish dishes.

Dom. de Terrebonne, rte de Cabasse, 83340 Flassans, tel. 04.94.59.68.65, fax 04.94.69.74.35 ▼ Υ ev. day 9am–7pm
Mercier

DOM. DES THERMES 2000★
■ 3 ha 22,000 ■ ♦ €3-5

Remains of Roman baths have been discovered on the site of this estate. The first vintage of the estate (the **98**) received a *coup de cœur* and was the winner of the *Grappe de bronze* of the 2000 *Guide*. This elegant, pale-coloured rosé may not have the exuberance of the **98**, but offers a pleasing bouquet of citrus fruit, leaving an agreeable impression of lightness.

EARL Michel Robert, Dom. des Thermes, RN 7, 83340 Le Cannet-des-Maures, tel. 04.94.60.73.15, fax 04.94.60.73.15 ▼
Υ ev. day 8am–7.30pm

DOM. DU VAL DE GILLY
Cuvée Alexandre Castellan 2000★
■ 1 ha 6,000 ■ €5-8

Alexandre Castellan founded this estate in 1884. Vine cultivation has progressively taken over to the detriment of the olive plantations, most notably after the heavy frost during the exceptional winter of 1956. This traditionally-made, salmon-tinted rosé 2000 is a classic: though not exuberant, it successfully balances roundness and freshness right up to the fruity finish.

SARL Dom. du Val de Gilly, 83310 Grimaud, tel. 04.94.43.21.25, fax 04.94.43.26.27 ▼
Υ ev. day except Sun. 9am–12 noon 2pm–7.30pm; cl. am in Jan. Feb.
Castellan

CH. VANNIERES 1999★
■ 6 ha 18,000 ■■ €11-15

Essentially, this château produces Bandol, but its Côtes de Provence is a regular entry in the Guide. This deep-ruby 99 leaves lingering notes of musk and spice, which have a slight vanilla edge. Well-structured, it is developing its tannin structure, still young, which gives every indication of further good development over the next five years.

Ch. Vannières, 83740 La Cadière-d'Azur, tel. 04.94.90.08.08, fax 04.94.90.15.98, e-mail info@chateauvannieres.com ▼
Υ ev. day except Sun. 8am–12 noon 2pm–6pm
Eric Boisseaux

CH. DE VAUCOULEURS
Cuvée du Château 1999★★
■ 4 ha 50,000 ■■ €8-11

Situated on the edges of the Route Nationale 7, this 25-ha (62-acre) estate is surrounded by 100-year-old umbrella pines. Its pale 99 wine has expressive aromas of liquorice, with hints of musk. Balanced with silken tannins, the wine becomes fuller before finishing with long, spicy, flavours reminiscent of leather. The **rosé cuvée du Château 2000** merits one star.

P. Le Bigot, Ch. de Vaucouleurs, RN 7, 83480 Puget-sur-Argens, tel. 04.94.45.20.27, fax 04.94.45.20.27 ▼ Υ ev. day except Sun. Mon. 10am–12 noon 3pm–6pm; cl. 15 days Nov. 8 days Jan.

CH. VEREZ 2000★★
■ 21 ha 20,000 ■ ♦ €5-8

Nadine and Serge Rosinoer have headed up this property since 1994, exporting 50% of its produce to Germany and Japan. This candy pink wine will impress enthusiasts. Its delicious aromatic mixture reveals pear drops and fresh fruit in both the nose and the palate. Harmony, intensity and consistency – it lacks none of these. It is an authentic rosé.

Ch. Vérez, 5192, chem. de la Verrerie-Neuve-Le Grand Pré, 83550 Vidauban, tel. 04.94.73.69.90, fax 04.94.73.55.84, e-mail verez@wanadoo.fr ▼ Υ by appt.

Cassis

Accessible only over relatively high passes from Marseilles or Toulon, and tucked away at the foot of the highest cliffs in France, lies Cassis with its inlets, its anchovies and a particular fountain which, the inhabitants claim, makes their town more remarkable than Paris... However, there is also a vineyard over which powerful abbeys disputed ownership in the 11th century, finally calling upon the Pope to arbitrate. Nowadays, the vineyard covers about 177 ha (437 acres), of which 129 ha (319 acres) are planted with white varieties with an output of 7,515 hl (198,396 gal) in 2000. The wines are red and rosé but white above all. Mistral said of the whites that he smelled rosemary, heather and myrtle. Don't expect to find important vintages: as soon as they are made they are mostly consumed locally with bouillabaisse, grilled fish and shellfish.

DOM. LA FERME BLANCHE 2000

☐ 22 ha 120,000 €8-11

This estate became the property of the Garnier family during the 18th century. The wine's label carries their coat of arms: the king's sun, the county crown, three ears of wheat and an olive branch. Although this *cuvée* is short on length it possess roundness and complex aromas of a floral (acacia and broom flower) and fruity (quince and fruit sauce) nature.

🍷 Dom. de La Ferme Blanche, RD 559, 13260 Cassis, tel. 04.42.01.00.74, fax 04.42.01.73.94 Y ev. day 9am–7pm

🍷 F. Paret

DOM. DU PATERNEL 2000★

☐ 6.5 ha 38,000 €8-11

This 32-ha (79-acre) estate was created in 1951 by Pierre Cathinaud. Jean-Pierre Santini, who has been in control of the vineyard since 1962, directs his production to private clients and restaurants. The elegant, velvety palate of this 2000 wine, balanced between pear drop and buttery notes, seduces with its suppleness and length.

🍷 Jean-Pierre Santini, Dom. du Paternel, 11, rue Pierre-Imbert, 13260 Cassis, tel. 04.42.01.76.50, fax 04.42.01.09.54 ☑ Y ev. day except Sun. 10am–12 noon 2pm–6pm

CLOS VAL BRUYERE 1999★★

☐ 7.5 ha 30,000 €8-11

Château Barbanau has 7.5 ha (19 acres) of cassis vines. It also produces Côtes-de-Provence. This well-matured 99 has a really pleasant personality. Fresh and aromatic, the bold and lengthy palate is filled in a manner reminiscent of citrus (ripe lemon), white (peach) and dried fruits, with floral notes. It is one of the few wines that will go well with asparagus.

🍷 GAEC Ch. Barbanau, Hameau de Roquefort, 13830 Roquefort-la-Bédoule, tel. 04.42.73.14.60, fax 04.42.73.17.85, e-mail barbanau@aol.com ☑ Y ev. day except Sun. 10am–12 noon 3pm–6pm

🍷 Cerciello

DOM. DU BAGNOL

Marquis de Fesques 2000

☐ 4 ha n.c. €5-8

This estate cultivates its vineyard on the outskirts of the charming village of Cassis. Michelle Génovési has been running it since 1997. There is little extravagance in this pale white wine with hints of gold; the flavours are revealed with a simplicity that adds to its finesse, elegance and freshness.

🍷 Génovési, Dom. du Bagnol, 12, av. de Provence, 13260 Cassis, tel. 04.42.01.78.05, fax 04.42.01.11.22 ☑ Y ev. day except Sat. Sun. 9am–12 noon 2.30pm–6pm

CH. DE FONTCREUSE

Cuvée F 2000★★

☐ 14 ha 70,000 €5-8

Having received a *coup de cœur* for a number of consecutive years, this château – regarded since the 18th century as amongst the best of the wine-making châteaux of Provence – came very close to repeating the achievement with this wine. Its intense, rich, pleasant aroma combines with a full, well-constructed palate. This 2000 wine achieved centre of attention if served as an accompaniment to salmon. The perfumed, generous *rosé* 2000 was awarded one star.

🍷 SA J.-F. Brando, Ch. de Fontcreuse, 13, rue Pierre-Imbert, 13260 Cassis, tel. 04.42.01.71.09, fax 04.42.01.32.64, e-mail fontcreuse@wanadoo.fr ☑ Y ev. day except Sun. 8am–12 noon 2pm–6pm

851

Bellet

Only the privileged few know this minute vineyard, 39 ha (96 acres), on the heights above Nice, with a modest production (1,133 hl (29,911 gal) in 2000) of wines almost impossible to find anywhere other than in Nice itself. Its original, aromatic whites derive from the high-class Rolle vine variety and the Chardonnay (which is happy this far south when planted facing north and sufficiently high up). The rosés are supple and fresh, the reds sumptuous: two local varieties, the Fuella and the Braquet, give them their highly individual character. They form an entirely appropriate accompaniment to rich, very distinctive cuisine of Nice, with dishes such as chard pie, baked vegetables, estoficada (a local stew), tripe and pissaladière, and onion tart.

COLLET DE BOVIS 2000

2 ha　1,000　■ ♦ €8–11

The Fogolar estate received the artists Max Charvolen, Marcel Alocco and Manuela Cordenos during the festival 'Arts et Vin'. The year 2000 inspired this characteristic, salmon-tinted rosé, with aromas and flavours evoking apricot, strawberry or quince jam. This wine is straightforward, supple and well balanced.

➤ Jean Spizzo, Dom. du Fogolar, 370, chem. de Crémat, 06200 Nice, tel. 04.93.37.82.52, fax 04.93.37.82.52, e-mail fogolar@vin-de-bellet.com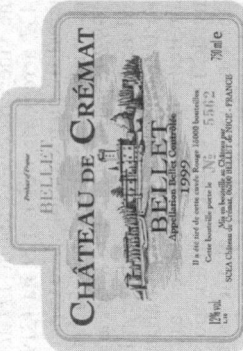
⟙ ev. day 8.30am–12 noon 2pm–7pm

CH. DE CRÉMAT 1999★★

4 ha　15,000　■■ €15–23

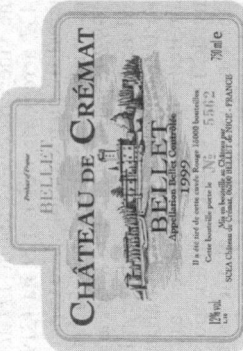

The Château de Crémat is closely associated with the history of the renaissance of the Bellet vineyard. This wine has great depth. Behind a dark colour, it opens up to reveal a rich, expressive nose; a varied selection of black berries, black smoked olives and grilled aromas. The palate, built on fine, elegant tannins, shows strength. The concentration in the body suggests that it should be allowed to develop further over the course of two to ten years.

➤ SCEA Ch. de Crémat, 442, chem. de Crémat, 06200 Nice, tel. 04.92.15.12.15, fax 04.92.15.12.13 ⟙ ev. day except Sun. 8am–12 noon 2pm–6pm
● Pisoni

CH. DE BELLET 2000★★

n.c.　n.c.　€11–15

During the 1960s, Rose de Bellet and her cavalry colonel husband reconstructed this estate, which had been badly affected by wartime restrictions. Their youngest son, Ghislain de Charnacé, took over in 1970. This year he submitted this characteristic pale rosé, with strong aromas of broom flower and very ripe strawberries. The palate, upfront in its attack, rounds out to recall these same flavours again. The white **Bellet 2000** was awarded a star for its youthful perfume and tight structure, at once both full and fresh.

➤ Ghislain de Charnacé, Ch. de Bellet, 440, chem. de Saquier, 06200 Nice, tel. 04.93.37.81.57, fax 04.93.37.93.83

CLOT DOU BAILE 1998★

2.8 ha　8,000　■ ■■ ♦ €11–15

The Clot Dou Baile has taken advantage of land that had previously lain fallow to put together its vineyard. From this pudding stone terroir comes this fairly pale-coloured wine with amber tints, characteristic of the vintage. This minerally, charred 98 achieves balance between its volume and freshness. It is drinking well now. The **white 2000**, awarded a mention, has a lively, rounded character, based on ripe fruit (pineapple and white peach).

➤ SCEA Clot Dou Baile, 277–305, chem. de Saquier, 06200 Nice, tel. 04.93.29.85.87, fax 04.93.29.85.87 ⟙ by appt.

LES COTEAUX DE BELLET 2000★

2.75 ha　10,000　■■ €11–15

In 2000 this association of four producers, whose **96** vintage received a coup de cœur, submitted a wine principally made from Rolle. Almost transparent, it opens with floral and light woody aromas. The frizante palate structure moves towards imprinted aromas of overripe fruit (pear and quince) returning to a lively finish. It is an elegant Bellet. Awarded a citation, the crystallised **rosé 2000** has a pleasant mineral, pear drop freshness.

➤ SCEA Les Coteaux de Bellet, 325, chem. de Saquier, 06200 Nice, tel. 04.93.29.92.99, fax 04.93.18.10.99 ⟙ by appt.
● Hélène Calviera

MASSA 2000★★

◻ 0.2 ha 1,000 🍷 €15-23

This very fine white wine is produced in very small quantities. Although the beeswax and fruit sauce aromas are still a little closed, the palate displays density and consistency. The palate develops roundness and length, moving to a soft finish. This Bellet should be enjoyed with blue cheese.

☛ GAEC Massa, 425, chem. de Crémat, 06200 Nice, tel. 04.93.37.80.02, fax 04.92.15.10.13 ☑ ⌶ by appt.

CLOS SAINT-VINCENT 1999★

◼ 2 ha 2,500 €15-23

The Folle Noire, a variety from the Nice area, owes its name (*fuella* in Nice patois) to the lengths of its tendrils. It makes up 90% of this lively, mauve-tinted red. This wine opens up giving a strong and complex nose: boxwood, red berries and grilled aromas. The expressive body is still characterised by tannins on the palate. If kept for at least three years it should soften entirely. Equally successful, the **rosé 2000** shows the supple, balanced, fruity character of another Nice variety – Braquet.

☛ Joseph Serge et Roland Sicardi, Collet des Fourniers, Saint-Romans-de-Bellet, 06200 Nice, tel. 04.92.15.12.69, fax 04.92.15.12.69, e-mail clos.st.vincent@wanadoo.fr ☑ ⌶ by appt.

Bandol

A fine wine produced, not in Bandol itself, but on the sun-scorched terraces of the surrounding villages, which cover an area of 1,419 ha (3,505 acres) and produced 54,652 hl (1,442,813 gal) in 2000. Bandol wines are white, rosé or red. The reds are very tannic and full-bodied, qualities contributed by the Mourvèdre variety, which makes up more than half the proportions of grapes used. This powerful wine, with its subtle aromas of pepper, cinnamon, vanilla and black cherry, is the perfect accompaniment to venison and red meats. It can be kept for a long time.

DOM. DES BAGUIERS
Cuvée Gaston Jourdan 1998★★

◼ 0.9 ha 3,300 🍷 €8-11

This wine honours the ancestry of the family who carried out the first bottling here in 1969. More than thirty years have passed since then and a *coup de cœur* celebrates the care taken with this deep, expressive 98. The complex nose combines the softest scents (blackcurrant, mulberry and spices) with the roughest (mineral, musk and leather). The palate reveals a concentrated structure, underlined with strong tannins that will soften if kept for at least five years.

☛ GAEC Jourdan, Dom. des Baguiers, 227, rue Micocouliers, 83330 Le Castellet, tel. 04.94.90.41.87, fax 04.94.90.41.87 ☑ ⌶ by appt.

DOM. BARTHES 2000

◻ 2.6 ha 13,000 🍷🍷 €8-11

This estate produced a white wine, balanced between pleasant liveliness and rounded structure. This fine, floral, fruity (pear) ensemble will go well with shellfish or fish grilled with olive oil.

☛ Monique Barthes, chem. du Val-d'Arenc, 83330 Le Beausset, tel. 04.94.98.60.06, fax 04.94.98.65.31 ☑ ⌶ by appt.

CH. DES BAUMELLES 1999★★

◼ 2.5 ha 10,000 🍷 €8-11

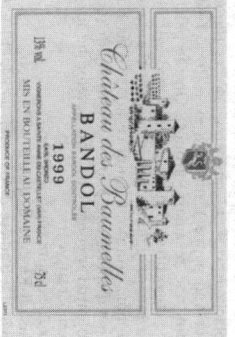

The 15th-century château, flanked by its towers, sits by a bend in the road on the route from Bandol to Saint-Cyr. Its 40-ha (99-acre) vineyard has produced this shimmering wine with its youthful colour. Opening with ripe fruit on the nose, this 98 develops pleasant peppery aromas on the mid-palate. Its round, ripe structure, built around fine tannins, make a well-balanced ensemble. It should be left for four or five years.

⚬➤ EARL Bronzo, 367, rte des Oratoires, 83330 Sainte-Anne-du-Castellet, tel. 04.94.32.63.20, fax 04.94.32.74.34, e-mail bastide.blanche@libertysurf.fr

Υ by appt.

⚬➤ GFA des Baumelles

DOM. DU CAGUELOUP
Vieilles vignes 1999★

■ 3.7ha 15,000 ‖‖ €11-15

Mentioned many times in the *Guide* for his white and rosé wines, Richard Prébost submitted a red Bandol, produced from old vines. This pleasant 99 releases a mix of aromas, from the fruity and spicy to the minty, displaying full flavour and length on the palate. Thanks to its tannic structure, this wine can be kept, which will allow it to soften. The pale salmon **rosé 2000** was also awarded one star for its richness and length.

⚬➤ SCEA Dom. de Cagueloup, quartier Cagueloup, 83270 Saint-Cyr-sur-Mer, tel. 04.94.26.15.70, fax 04.94.26.54.09 ◪

Υ by appt.

DOM. CASTELL-REYNOARD
1998★★★

■ 1 ha 4,500 ‖‖ €8-11

DOMAINE
Castell-Reynoard
BANDOL
APPELLATION BANDOL CONTRÔLÉE
1998

This estate, created at the end of the 19th century, is situated 2 km (1 mile) from La Cadière-d'Azur. It submitted this deep-tinted wine with a complex bouquet; hints of fruit (blackcurrant and mulberry), spices (liquorice and pepper), mineral, even floral (wild mint and rosemary) aromas. On the palate, the concentrated structure is tinged with the flavour of jammy cherries, whilst the dense tannins bring out liquorice notes. This rich wine displays exceptional length. With such potential it could carry on developing for a number of years.

⚬➤ Alexandre Castell, Dom. Castell-Reynoard, quartier Thouron, 83740La Cadière-d'Azur, tel. 04.94.90.10.16, fax 04.94.90.10.16 ◪ Υ by appt.

CH. DE CASTILLON 1999

■ 1.5 ha 5,000 ‖‖ €8-11

Matured in oak barrels for 18 months, this wine is still characterised by the wood. Nevertheless, it shows pleasant red berry and

brandied cherry aromas. With its robust, spicy character it will benefit from cellaring until it softens.

⚬➤ René de Saqui de Sannes, Dom. de Castillon, 408, rte des Oratoires, 83330 Sainte-Anne-du-Castellet, tel. 04.94.32.66.74, fax 04.94.32.67.36 ◪ Υ ev. day except Mon. Sun. 10am–12 noon 2pm–6pm

DUPERE-BARRERA India 1998

■ n.c. 3,000 ‖ ◆ €11-15

This wine comes from a recent business enterprise in the Provence region. Its ruby-tinted Bandol pleases with its kirsch, undergrowth, blackcurrant and strawberry aromas. The palate, slightly muted but supple, builds on the present tannin structure.

⚬➤ Emmanuelle Dupéré Barrera, 122, rue Dakar, 83100 Toulon, tel. 04.94.31.10.48, fax 04.94.31.10.48, e-mail vinsduperebarrera@hotmail.com ◪ Υ by appt.

DOM. DE FONT-VIVE 2000

□ 0.08 ha 400 ‖‖ €8-11

With a clean colour and clear green tints this wine opens freshly on the palate, thanks to the citrus fruit (lemon and grapefruit) aromas. This pleasing vigour should be enough to ensure good development.

⚬➤ Philippe Dray, Dom. de Font-Vive, 83330 Le Beausset, tel. 04.94.98.60.06, fax 04.94.98.65.31 ◪ Υ by appt.

DOM. DE FREGATE 1999★

■ 2.5 ha 6,000 ‖‖ €8-11

This estate's cellar, built into the rock, was constructed in 1971. It shelters this wine with its red berry and soft spice (vanilla and liquorice) aromas. The structure, which is good for this vintage, has fine tannins, so it is drinking well now, but in five to six years, further maturation will bring its aromatic fullness to light.

⚬➤ Dom. de Frégate, rte de Bandol, 83270 Saint-Cyr-sur-Mer, tel. 04.94.32.57.57, fax 04.94.32.24.22, e-mail domainedefregate@wanadoo.fr ◪ Υ ev. day except Sun. 9am–12 noon 2pm–5.30pm

CH. JEAN-PIERRE GAUSSEN 1999★

■ 4 ha 20,000 ‖‖ €11-15

This young, concentrated red Bandol possesses fruit, ripe tannins and real strength, all characteristics of the Mourvèdre variety. It will pay dividends if you have the patience to wait about five years. It should be particularly delicious if eaten with a spicy saddle of lamb.

⚬➤ Jean-Pierre Gaussen, La Noblesse, 1585, chem. de l'Argile, B.P. 23, 83740 La Cadière-d'Azur, tel. 04.94.98.75.54, fax 04.94.98.65.34 ◪ Υ by appt.

DOM. DU GROS'NORE 1999★

■ 9 ha 37,000 ‖‖ €11-15

This wine needs time to reveal its complex aromas. Already, red berries, toast and

LA BASTIDE BLANCHE 2000

18 ha 95,000 ◼ €8-11

This estate's red wines have regularly appeared in the Guide, but this year a rosé has distinguished itself. Pale and lightly coloured, releasing apricot aromas on the nose, it fills the palate with its balanced structure.

➤ EARL Bronzo, 367, rte des Oratoires, 83330 Sainte-Anne-du-Castellet, tel. 04.94.32.63.20, fax 04.94.32./4.34, e-mail bastide.blanche@libertysurf.fr ✓

Y by appt.

roasted aromas mingle on the mid-palate. The palate is promising, warming and elegant. A wine to leave for four of five years then serve with braised boar or venison.

➤ Pascal Alain, Dom. du Gros Noré, 675, chem. de l'Argile, 83740 La Cadière-d'Azur, tel. 04.94.90.08.50, fax 04.94.98.20.65 ✓

Y ev. day 10am–7.30pm

DOM. DE LA BÉGUDE 2000

4.5 ha 7,500 ◼ €8-11

Guillaume Tari, from the Bordelaise school, also has a property in AOC Côtes-de-Provence. His rosé Bandol comes from vines 400 m (1,310 ft) above sea level. It has the vintage's characteristic warmth, but enough body and aromas to absorb this.

➤ Guillaume Tari, SCEA du Dom. de La Bégude, 83330 Le Camp-du-Castellet, tel. 04.42.08.92.34, fax 04.42.08.27.02, e-mail domaines.tari@wanadoo.fr ✓

Y by appt.

LES VIGNERONS DE LA CADIERENNE 2000

245.45 ha 500,000 ◼ €5-8

La Cadière is a picturesque village at the centre of the appellation. Two co-operatives are active there. This one consists of almost 400 members, many based in the neighbouring village of Castellet. They have submitted this fairly full and balanced, well-coloured wine, which is a little timid in its aromatic expression.

➤ SCV La Cadièrenne, quartier Le Vallon, 83740 La Cadière-d'Azur, tel. 04.94.90.11.06, fax 04.94.90.18.73, e-mail cadierenne@wanadoo.fr ✓

DOM. LAFRAN-VEYROLLES 1999★

1.2 ha 5,600 ◼ €15-23

This 17th-century estate, named after the spreading oaks populating the *quartier* of La Cadière, has submitted this round 99, with fruity, leathery liquorice notes. On the palate it is velvety, due to its fine, dense tannins and length. Whilst drinking well now, it will be a pleasant rediscovery in a few years. The rosé 2000 is just as successful: very fruity, very fresh.

➤ Mme Jouve-Férec, Dom. Lafran-Veyrolles, 2115, rte de l'Argile, 83740 La Cadière-d'Azur, tel. 04.94.90.13.37, fax 04.94.90.11.18 ✓ Y by appt.

CH. LA ROUVIERE 2000★

3 ha 15,000 ◼ €8-11

The Bunan brothers' Château La Rouvière is situated in Castellet, but the wine-making is carried out at the Moulin des Costes in La Cadière. This tender-coloured rosé, rich in fruity aromas, comes from here. It stands out for its finesse and its balance between liveliness and roundness. The red Moulin des Costes 99 was awarded a mention. It is already developing a complex aromatic range (brush, heather, red berries and vanilla) but will benefit from further ageing to bring out its Mourvèdre expression.

➤ Domaines Bunan, Moulin des Costes, 83740 La Cadière-d'Azur, tel. 04.94.98.58.98, fax 04.94.98.60.05, e-mail bunan@bunan.com ✓ by appt.

DOM. DE LA RAGLE 1998★★

1 ha 5,000 ◼ €5-8

This red Bandol, produced by Les Vins Brébans, has complex aromas including jammy cherry and chocolate. Although this straightforward wine is still closed, it has a rough roundness and big, full, quality tannins. It would benefit from cellaring for a few years. The rosé Bandol Domaine de La Narrette 2000 awarded a mention by the Jury, is a characteristic delicate, elegant wine. It comes from a well-protected vineyard, owned by the coastal conservation society, situated above the port of Madrague, at Saint-Cyr-les-Lecques.

➤ Cave de La Roque, quartier Vallon, BP 26, 83740 La Cadière-d'Azur, tel. 04.94.90.10.39, fax 04.94.90.08.11

Y by appt.

DOM. DE LA LAIDIERE 2000★★

12 ha 55,000 ◼ €11-15

On this bottle's label is the Evenos coat of arms: a silver mountain with a golden cross on a blue background. Glittering with colour, this rosé sharpens the senses with its intensity and freshness. Its citrus fruit aromas appear from one end of the palate to the other. This expressive palate is also fine and lengthy. This is a real success for a *terroir* that has been badly battered by wind.

➤ SCEA Estienne, Dom. de La Laidière, 426, chem. de Font-Vive, 83330 Sainte-Anne-d'Evenos, tel. 04.94.90.35.29, fax 04.94.90.38.05, e-mail freddy-estienne@laidiere.com ✓ Y ev. day except Sun. 9.30am–12 noon 2pm–6pm; Sat. by appt.

855

DOM. LA SUFFRENE

Cuvée Les Lauves 1999★

■   2 ha   10,500   **IIII €11-15**

This 42-ha (104-acre) estate was created in 1996. The Cuvée des Lauves is as successful in the 99 vintage as the previous year. One can see fine grains of tannins within a balanced, open body. The aromas of spice and red fruits are openly expressive, giving immediate pleasure. The palate shows a good balance of straightforward fruit with fine-grained tannins. This stylish wine is, however, still young, as indicated by its violet tints. It would therefore benefit from being left for a while.

↬ Cédric Gravier, Dom. La Suffrene, 1066, chem. de Cuges, 83740 La Cadière-d'Azur, tel. 04.94.90.09.23, fax 04.94.90.02.21 ⛬
Y ev. day except Sun. 8.30am–12 noon 2pm–6.30pm

DOM. DE LA TOUR DU BON

1999★★

■   7 ha   26,000   **IIII €11-15**

This wine came close to a *coup de cœur*. Its characteristic Bandol expression is very generous and its closed tannins well integrated in a round, fleshy palate. Will its heady finish diminish its pleasure? Not at all, because this 99 wine keeps its balance from start to finish. It will not reach its peak for another five years, when the aromas will open fully. Just as remarkable is the floral and fruity **rosé 2000**, made from Cinsaut and Mourvèdre. It is fine and tasty.

↬ Dom. de La Tour du Bon, SCEA Saint-Vincent, 83330 Le Brûlat, tel. 04.98.03.66.22, fax 04.98.03.66.26, e-mail tourdubon@aol.com ⛬ Y by appt.
↬ Hocquard

DOM. DE LA VIVONNE 2000

▲   4.43 ha   29,000   **■ €8-11**

This estate cultivates 25 ha (62 acres) at the edge of the village of Castellet. This pale rosé with light orange tints is characteristic of Bandol with its mix of Mourvèdre (60%) and Grenache (40%). Round and balanced, it is fairly typical of the vintage. The **red Bandol 99**, cask matured, is also mentioned. It has good development potential.

↬ Walter Gilpin, Dom. de La Vivonne, 3345, montée du Château, 83330 Le Castellet, tel. 04.94.98.70.09, fax 04.94.90.59.98, e-mail infos@vivonne.com ⛬ Y by appt.

LE GALANTIN 2000

▲   12 ha   50,000   **■ €5-8**

This 25-ha (62-acre) estate exports 30% of its produce to the USA and Germany. A very pale orange colour, this wine opens up progressively to achieve a more intense expression. It then becomes smooth, lengthy and well balanced.

↬ EARL Pascal, Dom. Le Galantin, 690, chem. Le Galantin, 83330 Le Plan-du-Castellet, tel. 04.94.98.75.94, fax 04.94.90.29.55 ⛬ Y by appt.

DOM. LES LUQUETTES 2000★

▲   n.c.   32,600   **■ ♦ €5-8**

This 12-ha (30-acre) property has a flock of 40 ewes that contribute naturally to the fertilisation of its vineyard. The 2000 vintage is reflected in this attractive wine, which opens with fullness on to citrus fruit. The aromas persist for a long time on the palate. Awarded a mention, the still woody **red Bandol 98** had underlying fruitiness and a noticeable elegant structure.

↬ SCEA Le Lys, 20, chem. des Luquettes, 83740 La Cadière-d'Azur, tel. 04.94.90.02.59, fax 04.94.98.31.95, e-mail lesluquettes@libertysurf.fr
Y ev. day 8am–8pm

DOM. DE L'HERMITAGE 2000★

□   2 ha   8,000   **■**

Louis XV was fond of Rouve wines. Although the techniques and varieties have evolved since his day, the *terroir* remains unchanged. This Bandol is an illustration of the fact. With good balance, its aromas develop within a lively, light body. This wine would go well with a dry goat's cheese, fish dishes or can simply be sipped enjoyably on its own.

↬ SAS Gérard Duffort, Le Rouve, BP 41, 83330 Le Beausset, tel. 04.94.98.71.31, fax 04.94.90.44.87 ⛬ Y ev. day except Sat. Sun. 9am–12 noon 2pm–6pm; open Sat. summer

DOM. DE L'OLIVETTE 1999★

■   14 ha   60,000   **IIII €11-15**

When this estate was taken over in 1972, it had no more than 3 ha (7 acres) of vines. Today, it stretches over 55 ha (136 acres). 1 km (0.5 miles) to the north of the villages of La Cadière-d'Azur and Castellet. Its 99 wine has a complex seductive nose: fruitiness mixed with smoky, grilled aromas. On the palate, the supple, fleshy body covers the tannic structure; wood from the 18-month cask maturation appears on the finish, but the Bandol characteristic is left intact. It is a wine to be kept in the cellar. The **rosé 2000** was also awarded one star for its lively, aromatic character.

↬ SCEA Dumoutier, Dom. de L'Olivette, 83330 Le Castellet, tel. 04.94.98.58.85, fax 04.94.32.68.43, e-mail info@domaine-olivette.com ⛬

DOM. DU PEY-NEUF 2000★

▲   10 ha   53,333   **■ €8-11**

This family estate, created at the beginning of the 19th-century, today fills 36 ha (89 acres). It submitted a rosé, whose pale, salmon-tinted colour gives an impression of softness. The fruity, floral aromas form part of an elegant, fine character. Equally successful, the **white Bandol 2000** offers island scents (grapefruit, mango and lemon), followed on by liveliness and volume.

↬ Guy Arnaud, Dom. du Pey-Neuf, 367, rte de Sainte-Anne, 83740 La Cadière-d'Azur, tel. 04.94.90.14.55, fax 04.94.26.13.89 ⛬ Y by appt.

CH. DE PIBARNON 1999
■ 20 ha 100,000 ▦ ❚❚ €15-23

The individuality of the Pibarnon *terroir* lies in its Triassic soil, which is rich in limestone and trace elements. The vine gets all its resources and character from here. Intensely coloured, with violet tints, this wine releases a fruity aroma, delicately underlined by liquorice and a woody note. The supple, warming palate benefits from softened tannins. Do not keep this wine too long; for instant pleasure serve with stuffed pigeon.

↗ Eric de Saint-Victor, 410, chem. de la Croix-des-Signaux, 83740 La Cadière-d'Azur, tel. 04.94.90.12.73, fax 04.94.90.12.98, e-mail pibarnon@wanadoo.fr ✓ ⏰ by appt.

CH. SAINTE ANNE 1999★
■ 6 ha 20,000 ▦ ❚❚ €11-15

The family of the Marquis Dutheil de La Rochère moved to Sainte-Anne d'Evenos during the revolution. Even today, winemaking is conducted in the ancient 18th-century vaulted cellars. This red-coloured 99, underlined by violet tints, gives an impression of complexity, intensity and structure. The noticeable inherent woodiness, coming from maturation, will dissipate over time.

↗ Dutheil de La Rochère, Ch. Sainte-Anne, 83330 Sainte-Anne-d'Evenos, tel. 04.94.90.35.40, fax 04.94.90.34.20 ✓
⏰ ev. day except Sun. 9am–12 noon 2pm–7pm

DOM. DE SOUVIOU 1999★★
■ 21 ha 38,266 ❚❚ €11-15

This estate, which also produces olive oil, has recently changed owner. The 99 wine, made with the original equipment, is a standard-bearer. Garnet-red, with purple tints, still characterised by the initial woody aromas on the nose, it also reveals fruit. The tannins are somewhat austere – this is a characteristic of the vintage – but the palate impression of mulberry and raspberry notes is well put together. This balanced wine is evidence of well-managed maturation. It can be kept for between five and ten years.

↗ SCEA Dom. de Souviou, RN 8, 83330 Le Beausset, tel. 04.94.90.57.63, fax 04.94.96.62.74, e-mail contact@souviou.com ✓ ⏰ by appt.

CH. ROMASSAN-DOMAINES OTT
Cour de Grain 2000
■ 30 ha 140,000 ▦ ❚❚ ♦ €11-15

Château Romassan is one of the three flagships of the Ott family, who "emigrated" to Provence when France lost Alsace. From this *terroir* comes a very pale wine with a delicate, citrus fruit nose. Its balanced palate is advantageously fresh, suggesting it should be drunk within the year.

↗ SA Dom. Ott, Ch. Romassan, 601, rte des Mourvèdres, 83330 Le Castellet, tel. 04.94.98.71.91, fax 04.94.98.65.44, e-mail domaineott@wanadoo.fr ✓ ⏰ by appt.

Palette

A tiny vineyard just outside Aix, this includes the old enclosed vineyard that originally belonged to King René, Count of Provence.

Whites, rosés and reds are regularly produced from around 40 ha (99 acres), amounting to 1,848 hl (48,787 gal) of wine in 2000. The reds can be kept for a long time, during which they develop scents of violet and pine.

CH. CREMADE 1998★
■ 4.19 ha 12,900 ▦ ❚❚ €11-15

Like Cézanne, Emile Zola stayed at Château Crémade on a number of occasions. The writer is thought to have set the story *La Faute de l'Abbé Mouret* there. Today, as then, however, the main protagonist is the vine. Grown on limestone soil, this ruby-coloured wine has a complex, rich nose that evokes liquorice, vanilla and red berries. The ample palate rests on generous promising tannins. The **white Palette 2000**, also cask matured, was awarded a star for its prepossessing character and promising balance.

↗ SCEA Dom. de La Crémade, rte de Langesse, 13100 Le Tholonet, tel. 04.42.66.76.80, fax 04.42.66.76.81 ✓ ⏰ by appt.

DOM. DU GRAND COTE 1998★
■ 10.45 ha 55,000 ❚❚ €5-8

This wine, produced by the de Rousset co-operative, delivers very sweet aromas, evocative of spices and vanilla. Built on noticeable tannins, the palate develops roundness before it softens. It is stamped with red berry aromas. This pleasing 98 is drinking well now but has the structure for two to three years of ageing.

↗ Cave de Rousset, quartier Saint-Joseph, 13790 Rousset, tel. 04.42.29.00.09, fax 04.42.29.08.63 ✓ ⏰ by appt.

DOM. TEMPIER 2000
■ 10 ha 48,000 ■ ♦ €11-15

Mourvèdre is the Peyraud family's favourite variety. It dominates the mix of this pale-coloured rosé. The citrus fruit and *pêche de vigne* nose opens when exposed to the air, while the balanced palate continues harmoniously along crystallised, citrus fruit notes.

↗ SA Peyraud, Dom. Tempier, Le Plan-du-Castellet, 83330 Le Castellet, tel. 04.94.98.70.21, fax 04.94.90.21.65 ✓ ⏰ by appt.

CH. SIMONE 1998★

| | n.c. | 31,000 | €15-23 |

Chateau Simone is an ancient family property whose vineyard is based on north-facing hills. With 100 ha (247 acres), it sets aside about 20% of its grounds to various grape varieties. The wines are aged in ancient caves built in the 16th century by the Grands Carmelite monks. This 98 wine glitters with golden yellow tints and delivers a rich aroma of white truffle, honey and vanilla. On the palate are floral, grilled flavours within a fleshy, structured, lengthy body. It is a good wine for keeping. The rosé 99 was awarded a mention for its attractive colour and length on the palate. It is an Epicurean wine.

René Rougier, Ch. Simone, 13590 Meyreuil, tel. 04.42.66.92.58, fax 04.42.66.80.77

Coteaux d'Aix en Provence

The AOC Coteaux d'Aix en Provence belongs to the western part of the limestone area of Provence, situated between the Durance in the north and the Mediterranean in the south, the Rhodian plains to the west and a region of crystalline rocks from the Triassic period to the east. The relief is formed from a succession of secondary mountain chains running parallel to the sea coast and covered variously with scrub, aromatic moorland vegetation and pine woods: the Nerthe is near the Etang de Berre, and the chain of Costes in the north extends into the Alpilles.

Between these outcrops lie sedimentary basins of different sizes (the Bassin de l'Arc, the Bassin de la Touloubre, and that of the lower Durance) where vinegrowing is located. Here limestone and marly structures underlie a matrix of stony, alluvial clays, alternating with structures of molasses and sandstone underlying sandy soils or stony sand and alluvium. The total area of 3,910 ha (9,658 acres) produced 210,463 hl (5,555,223 gal) in 2000. The production of rosé wines has increased recently. Grenache and Cinsaut are still the mainstays, with Grenache predominant; Syrah and Cabernet Sauvignon are on the increase and are progressively replacing the Carignan.

The rosé wines are light, fruity and pleasant, and have benefited significantly from improved vinification techniques. They should be drunk young with local Provençal dishes: ratatouille, artichokes barigoules (braised with fat bacon), fish grilled with fennel, aïoli …

The reds are balanced, sometimes robust, giving of their best according to terroir and micro-climate. When young, these are fruity, supple wines, excellent with grilled meat and dishes topped with grilled cheese. They reach their peak after two or three years of keeping, when they should be served with meat dishes (particularly those with sauce) and game. These interesting reds are well worth looking out for.

The production of white wines is limited. They seem to do better in the northern part of the vineyard, where they combine the roundness of Grenache Blanc with the finesse of Clairette, Rolle and Bourboulenc.

CH. BARBEBELLE
Cuvée Madeleine 2000

| | 3 ha | 15,000 | €5-8 |

The Rognes village is known for its ochre-coloured crumbly stone, previously used to restore the historic centre of Aix. It also shelters this 17th-century château, whose wine – according to one taster – is dominated by Sauvignon. This variety actually makes up 50% of the blend. The result is a very fruity (rhubarb and citrus fruit) and fresh wine.

Brice Herbeau, Ch. Barbebelle, RD 543, 13840 Rognes, tel. 04.42.50.22.12, fax 04.42.50.10.20

ev. day 9am–12 noon 2pm–6pm

CH. BAS Pierres du Sud 2000★★

| | 5 ha | 16,000 | €5-8 |

Philippe Pouchin is the man for rosé: a man who knows how to respect the grape's expression and is a master technician. He has produced a clean, full 2000, with a fruity balance between raspberry and redcurrant. The rosé **Cuvée du Temple 2000** is just as remarkable, as much for the influence of its time in cask as its presence on the palate. Finally, the two-starred, unwooded **white Cuvée Pierres du Sud 2000** is a fleshy, round wine with pineapple flavours.

● EARL Georges de Blanquet, Ch. Bas, 13116 Vernègues, tel. 04.90.59.13.16, fax 04.90.59.44.35, e-mail chateaubas@ wanadoo.fr ▪ ⴷ by appt.

CH. BEAUFERAN

Etiquette noire Elevé en fût de chêne 1998*

15 ha   10,000   €8-11

Although the name Château Beauféran did not appear on labels until 1989, the family property goes back more than a century. The intensely-coloured 98 is a excellent testament to the long fermentation period and 12-month cask ageing. This wine will be appreciated by fans of vanilla-wood and lightly smoked notes. Firm tannins enriched with fleshy, crystallised fruit flavours support the palate. It is a wine to be kept in the cellar. The **Cuvée Tradition 98**, with its red label, was singled out for mention: unwooded, it already reveals a musky, peppery side. It should be kept for two years.

● Ch. Beauféran, 870, chem. de la Degaye, 13880 Velaux, tel. 04.42.74.73.94, fax 04.42.87.42.96,
e-mail chateaubeauferan@freesurf.fr ▪
ⴷ ev. day except Mon. 9am–12.30pm
● Sauvage-Veysset

CH. DE BEAUPRE

Collection du Château 1998**

3 ha   n.c.   €8-11

This country house and park are surrounded by 40 ha (99 acres). From its cellar comes a fine collection of wines, among which is the one star **white Collection du Château 2000**, which spent three months in cask, and this particular red 98. Though it is produced from 90% Cabernet Sauvignon, it is not at all monolithic. It is strong and supple, yet at the same time confirms mastery of the 12-month cask maturation stage. Memories of red berry, spice and mint aromas linger on. The unwooded **red Cuvée Classique 98**, is also a wine to be kept. The Jury awarded it a special mention.

● Christian Double, Ch. de Beaupré, 13760 Saint-Cannat, tel. 04.42.57.33.59, fax 04.42.57.27.90 ▪ ⴷ by appt.

CH. DE CALAVON 1999*

10 ha   10,600   €5-8

This ancient vineyard is planted on the terroir of the princes of Orange, at Lambesc, the second capital of Provence. This wine, composed of 70% Carignan and 30% Grenache, has a strong southern character. A good harvest and long maceration of the skins produce this dense red wine, which is balanced with suggestions of black fruit (blackcurrant), flowers and spice. This successful balance will allow it to be kept for two to three years. Serve it with rich braised meat.

● Michel Audibert, Ch. de Calavon, BP 4, 13410 Lambesc, tel. 04.42.21.56.84, fax 04.42.21.64.19, e-mail chateaudecalavon@club-internet.fr
▪ ⴷ ev. day except Sun. 9am–12 noon 3.30pm–6pm

CH. CALISSANNE

Cuvée Prestige 1999*

8 ha   30,000   €5-8

On arrival at Calissanne, one is seduced by both the mystery of the place and the harmony of the château, which dates from the 17th century. The property is sprinkled with Mediterranean influences and is a natural shelter for young partridges. Brush and vines sculpt the sumptuous grounds, brought to life by the sun. This dark, garnet-red wine evokes a panorama of aromas: blackcurrant, brown tobacco and cocoa. Well structured, it is drinking well now but can be kept for two or three years. The **red Cuvée du Château 2000** was awarded a mention, as was the **white Clos Victoire 2000** – a rarity at only 2,500 bottles – which comes from 75% Clairette variety and still needs a little time to balance out.

● Ch. Calissanne, RD 10, 13680 Lançon-de-Provence, tel. 04.90.42.63.03, fax 04.90.42.40.00, e-mail calissan@ club-internet.fr ▪
● Compass et AXA

DOM. CAMAISSETTE 2000

2.5 ha   13,300   €5-8

This 23-ha (57-acre) estate is situated on the edge of the Aurélienne road. Its centrepiece is a house in the typical style of 17th-century Provençal rural architecture. Its rosé, on the other hand, appears resolutely modern. The pear drop aromas are immediately apparent, while the palate is positively lively.

● Michelle Nasles, Dom. de Camaissette, 13510 Eguilles, tel. 04.42.92.57.55, fax 04.42.28.21.26, e-mail michelle.nasles@ wanadoo.fr ▪ ⴷ ev. day except Sun. 9.30am–12 noon 2.30pm–6.30pm

COMMANDERIE DE LA BARGEMONE

Cuvée Tournebride 1998*

2 ha   6,000   €5-8

The Commanderie, built during the 13th century, was a retreat for the Knights Templar on their return from the Holy Land. Named after M. Bargemon, who owned the land until 1968, the property was then taken over by Jean-Pierre Rozan. Thirty years later he submitted this wine, which evokes liquorice, brush and heather on the nose. The well-structured, concentrated palate has a predominance of violet aromas. This 98 wine, already pleasant, could be left for up to three years.

Jean-Pierre Rozan, SCMM DEP Agricole, La Bargemone, RN 7, 13760 Saint-Cannat, tel. 04.42.57.22.44, fax 04.42.57.26.39 ▸ by appt.

DOM. D'EOLE Cuvée Léa 1999★★ €11-15

5 ha   13,000

This vineyard is continuing its conversion to organic farming, a process which began in 1997. The yields, kept at the low level of 23 hl/ha, explain the richness of this wine, produced from Grenache and Syrah in equal parts. Deep purple, highlighted by violet tints, it reveals aromas of cocoa, tobacco, spice and prune. This is followed by a full structure, supported by silken tannins which demonstrate the integration between wood and wine. The lengthy finish echoes nuances of prune. The rosé 2000 du Domaine has at least six varieties in the blend. The Jury awarded it one star for its balance and full-flavoured notes of pear and pineapple.

EARL Dom. d'Eole, rte de Mouries, D 24, 13810 Eygalières, tel. 04.90.95.93.70, fax 04.90.95.99.85, e-mail domaine@domainedeole.com ▸ ev. day 8.30am–12.30pm 1.30pm–5.30pm; Sat. Sun. by appt.
▸ C. Raimont

CH. DES GAVELLES 2000 €5-8

11 ha   25,000

In Provençal, gavelles means vine shoots. This estate, close to 27 ha (67 acres), has been making wine since the 17th century, when its collection of beautiful vaulted cellars was built at the foot of Castelas, the old residence of the archbishops of Aix. The rosé 2000, with a sustained colour, has a fruity, long, aromatic range on the nose and the mid-palate. Its fullness leaves a smooth impression on the palate.

Ch. des Gavelles, 165, chem. de Maliverny, 13540 Puyricard, tel. 04.42.92.06.83, fax 04.42.92.24.12, e-mail mail@chateaudesgavelles.com ▸ ev. day 9.30am–12.30pm 3pm–7pm; Sun. 9.30am–12.30pm
▸ De Roany

DOM. DES GLAUGES 1999 €5-8

8 ha   40,000

This estate, between Crau and Alpilles, stretches its 42 ha (104 acres) into a beautiful valley. A new company was created in March 2000 and aims to restructure the vineyards. The ruby-red 99, though dominated by Syrah (60%), allows musky notes and red berry aromas to come through. The wine is balanced and ready to drink.

SAS Glauges des Alpilles, voie d'Aureille, BP 17, 13430 Eyguières, tel. 04.90.59.81.45, fax 04.90.57.83.19, e-mail glauges@wanadoo.fr ▸ by appt.

CH. GRAND SEUIL 1999★ €11-15

5 ha   17,000

By the sides of the river Trévaresse, the 12th- and 17th-century Château du Seuil and its estates testify to an age when Aix's parliamentary nobles found serenity in the countryside around their summer residences, with their cedar trees, fresh ponds, olive plantations, almond trees and vines. Today, the Jury appreciates wines from this estate. This red wine has an elegant spicy, floral, red berry nose. It is strong but not excessive and benefits from existing, pleasing, silken tannins. The white Château Grand Seuil 2000, matured in cask for eleven months, was also awarded a star. It leaves sweet memories of vanilla and almond aromas. Finally, the rosé Château du Seuil 2000 was awarded a mention.

Philippe et Janine Carreau-Gaschereau, Ch. du Seuil, 13540 Puyricard, tel. 04.42.92.15.00, fax 04.42.28.05.00 ▸ ev. day 9am–12 noon, 2pm–6pm.

CH. LA BOUGERELLE 1999★

2 ha   5,000

This vineyard was created in the 13th century, when Monseigneur de Vintimille built the property. There are long ties with the Granier family. Today the estate covers 25 ha (62 acres). This very intense wine, composed mainly of Cabernet Sauvignon with 25% Syrah, has an elegant, complex nose that evokes flowers, red berries and prunes, underlined by spicy, minty hints. The palate, with its musky note, is balanced between freshness and strength; the silken ever-present tannins suggest it will develop well in the future.

EARL Ch. La Bougerelle, 1360, rte de Berre, Les Granettes, 13090 Aix-en-Provence, tel. 04.42.20.18.95, fax 04.42.20.18.95 ▸ ev. day except Sun.10am–7pm (9am–7pm summer)
▸ Granier

DOM. LA CADENIERE 2000★ €3-5

3.45 ha   26,600

This estate, not far from the medieval village of Lançon-de-Provence and its château, increased its wine-growing area to 56 ha (138 acres) in 1985 after acquiring vines at the foot of the Alpilles. Its rosé caught the Jury's attention for its suppleness and freshness. It has light pear drop notes with complementary notes on fruity, faintly minty lines.

Tobias Freres, Dom. la Cadenière, 13680 Lançon-de-Provence, tel. 04.90.42.82.56, fax 04.90.42.82.56 ▸ ev. day except Sun. Mon. 8.30am–11.30am, 2.30pm–7pm.

CH. DE LA GAUDE 1999 €5-8

8 ha   10,000

Marcel Pagnol's Le Château de ma Mère was filmed in this 18th-century country house, whose buildings and gardens are classed as historic monuments. This blue-tinted, ruby 99 has a convivial temperament thanks to its supple body, marked by red berries; it asks to be drunk outdoors with a picnic.

Audibert-Beaufour, Ch. de La Gaude, rte des Pinchinats, 13100 Aix-en-Provence, tel. 04.42.21.64.19, fax 04.42.21.56.84 ▸ by appt.
▸ Beaufour

DOM. DE LA REALTIERE

Cuvée José 1999 ■ 3.05 ha 6,300 ▦ €8-11

Jean-Louis Michelland has owned this estate since 1994, after a long career as agricultural economist in the South Pacific. He is working towards converting his 8 ha (20 acres) of vines to organic farming. His 99 wine still needs to develop during the next three or four years, as at the moment the extracted tannins mask the aromatic strength of the fruit. It is, however, possible to see and appreciate the structure behind the cocoa, prune and stewed fruit aromas.

Y by appt.

☎ Jean-Louis Michelland, Dom. de La Réaltière, rte de Jouques, 83560 Rians, tel. 04.94.80.32.56, fax 04.94.80.55.70 ▼

LE MAGISTRAL DES VIGNERONS 1999

■ 50 ha 120,000 ▦ €5-8

The Berre cellar was created in 1998 when three co-operatives joined forces. This carefully-presented, modest wine, with its dark colour, is the result of well-executed cask maturation of 10 months.

☎ Les Vignerons de Mistral, av. de Sylvanes, 13130 Berre l'Etang, tel. 04.42.85.40.11, fax 04.42.74.12.55 ▼

Y ev. day except Sun. 9am–12 noon, 2pm–6pm.

DOM. LES TOULONS

Cuvée Sanlaurey 1998* ▲ 2 ha 5,333 ▦ €5-8

The main part of this estate, the farm, dates back to 1667 when the property was built on the ruins of a vast Roman winemaking villa. With 22 ha (54 acres), it has produced a firm, red 98 with roasted, dark berry aromas whose composition is atypical: 70% Cabernet Sauvignon, 30% Syrah. The concentrated palate rests on round tannins, making the wine drinkable both now and for up to two years. The rosé Domaine Les Toulons 2000, based on Syrah and Grenache, was awarded a mention.

☎ Denis Alibert, Dom. Les Toulons, 83360 Rians, tel. 04.94.80.37.88, fax 04.94.80.57.57

DOM. L'OPPIDUM DES CAUVINS 2000*

■ 12 ha 25,000 ▦ €3-5

This estate, situated in the Trévaresse massif, on the site of a Roman fort, covers 56 ha (138 acres). It has been awarded stars for two of its wines. This intensely-coloured red has inherited, from 12-month cask maturation, a complex nose dominated by coffee. The tannins, coming both from Syrah and wood, appear in the warming, balanced body along with aromas of ripe dark berries. The unwooded white 2000 was also awarded a star. Pale with green tints, it has a floral nose and a really fine palate with accents of exotic fruit. This wine would go well with Mediterranean fish.

CH. PIGOUDET

Cuvée La Chapelle 2000* □ 2 ha 6,000 ▦ €5-8

Château Pigoudet exports 60% of its produce to the UK and Germany. Although the red Grand 98, which spent 15 months in cask, was awarded a mention, this particular 50% Rolle, 50% Sauvignon wine was even more seductive with its terroir expression. It is fleshy, fresh with good length and elegant on the palate all at the same time.

☎ SCA Ch. Pigoudet, rte de Jouques, 83360 Rians, tel. 04.94.80.31.78, fax 04.94.80.54.25

▼ Y by appt.

☎ Schmidt-Rabe

DOM. DES OULLIERES

Réserve Louis Charles 1999** ▲ 15 ha 15,000 ▦ €8-11

The years roll by, but sometimes things don't change too much: this wine, remarkable in the 98 vintage, is just as much so in the 99. It is well constructed, and the integration between wood and fruit is successful. It has a complex structure supported by silken tannins, which give rise to aromas of cooked prune and stewed fruit. It has good keeping potential. One star was also awarded to the white 99 Dame des Oullières, which is 100% Vermentino and was cask matured.

☎ Les Treilles de Cézanne, RN 7, 13410 Lambesc, tel. 04.42.92.83.39, fax 04.42.92.70.83, e-mail contact@oullieres.com ▼ Y by appt.

☎ Rémy Ravaute, Dom. l'Oppidum des Cauvins, 13840 Rognes, tel. 04.42.50.13.85, fax 04.42.50.29.40 ▼ Y by appt.

DOM. DU MAS BLEU 2000

▲ 0.8 ha 4,000 ■ €5-8

Mas Bleu submitted a wine dominated by Sauvignon Blanc, whose fine floral aromas provide all its charm. Violet flavours add to a very rounded palate.

☎ EARL du Mas Bleu, 6, av. de la Côte Bleue, 13180 Gignac-la-Nerthe, tel. 04.42.30.41.40, fax 04.42.30.32.53 ▼

Y by appt.

☎ Marie-Claire Rougon

CH. MONTAURONE

Cuvée Réservée 2000 ◢ 40 ha 300,000 ■ €3-5

The 1907 earthquake completely destroyed this 18th-century château. It was rebuilt and the vineyard managed by the same dedicated proprietress for half a century. Today it is 82 ha (203 acres). It submitted a wine that is modern yet faithful to the terroir. It is made up of 40% Grenache and equal quantities of Syrah, Cabernet Sauvignon and Cinsault. While the aromas are based in red berries, without denigrating the complexity of the other varieties, the roundness from the Grenache is perceived straightaway.

☎ Pierre Decamps, Ch. Montaurone, 13760 Saint-Cannat, tel. 04.42.57.20.04, fax 04.42.57.32.80 ▼ Y by appt.

Coteaux d'Aix en Provence

CH. PONT-ROYAL Grande Cuvée 1998
n.c. 6,600 ◫ €5-8

Nuances of wild mulberry contribute to the strong, austere character of this wine. The palate's structure already shows quality, firmness and finish. It is wine to be revisited in two years.

➤ Sylvette Jauffret, Ch. Pont-Royal, 13370 Mallemort, tel. 04.90.57.40.15, fax 04.90.59.12.28,
e-mail chateau-pont-royal@mnet.fr ☑
Υ ev. day except Mon. Sun. 9am–12 noon 3pm–6.30pm

CH. REVELETTE 2000
4 ha 16,000 ◫ €5-8

This vineyard, situated in the north of the appellation, is farmed organically. Its wine shows the liveliness of Ugni Blanc, which is the mainstay of the blend. However, this says nothing against the influence of the Rolle, which is expressed in the floral, delicate character. It also benefits from Sauvignon Blanc's fleshiness.

➤ Ch. Revelette, 13490 Jouques, tel. 04.42.63.75.43, fax 04.42.67.02.04 ☑
Υ by appt.

LES VIGNERONS DU ROY RENE 2000
25 ha 50,000 ◫ €3

The Lambesc and Saint-Cannat co-operatives merged in 1998 to become one AOC. Three of their wines are mentioned in this selection: the **rosé d'un Roy Prestige 2000**, the **red Cuvée Jules Reynaud 99**, named after the founder of the co-operative, and this particular rosé, which comes from a blend of Grenache (70%) and Cinsaut. It is characteristic, expressive and well-balanced between liveliness and alcohol.

➤ Les Vignerons du Roy René, RN 7, 13410 Lambesc, tel. 04.42.57.00.20, fax 04.42.92.91.52 ☑ Υ by appt.

MAS SAINTE-BERTHE 2000★★
4 ha 25,000 ◫ €5-8

Geneviève Rolland and her children took over this 37-ha (91-acre) property during 2000. Christian Nief, the oenologist, is well-known, his work is regularly recognised in the *Guide*. His 2000 is expressive, releasing herbaceous, floral (white flowers) and fruity (grapefruit and lime) aromas all at the same time. The palate, which finishes softly, has surprising length.

➤ GFA Mas Sainte Berthe, 13520 Les Baux-de-Provence, tel. 04.90.54.39.01, fax 04.90.54.46.17 ☑ Υ by appt.

DOM. SAINT-HILAIRE 2000
3 ha 12,000 ◫ €5-8

This estate, previously dedicated to arboriculture and market gardening, changed direction to grow vines in 1973. It has progressively extended its land to reach its current size of 57 ha (140 acres). This finely herbaceous, slightly floral wine, though strongly

---

influenced by Clairette (70%), benefits considerably from Ugni Blanc's acidity. It would go well with bouillabaisse or a similar fish soup.

➤ Yves Lapierre, Dom. Saint-Hilaire, 13111 Coudoux, tel. 04.42.52.02.40, fax 04.42.52.05.45, e-mail st.hilaire@wanadoo.fr ☑ Υ ev. day except Sun. 9am–12 noon 3pm–6.30pm; groups by appt.

DOM. DE SAINT JULIEN LES VIGNES Cuvée du Château 2000★
12 ha 32,000 ◫ €5-8

This 150-ha (370-acre) estate lies 1 km (2 miles) from the ruins of Château des Grimaldi, an ambitious project that commenced in 1657 and had to be abandoned 50 years later. The estate submitted a round and warming rosé that should be served with food. It is a sunny wine, elegant due to its airy, fruity aromas which lie somewhere between strawberry and raspberry. The **white Cuvée du Château 2000** was awarded a mention.

➤ Famille Reggio, SCEA ch. Saint-Julien, rte du Seuil, 13540 Puyricard, tel. 04.42.92.10.02, fax 04.42.92.10.74, e-mail puyricard.st.julien@imageos.com ☑ Υ by appt.

CH. DE VAUCLAIRE
Vieilli en fût de chêne 2000★
n.c. n.c. ◫ €5-8

This property has been in the same family since 1774. This original pure Rolle was cask matured for seven months. Initial, very vanilla-scented aromas on the nose give way to almond, lychee and banana. The palate is fleshy and elegant though the wood does still dominate. This 2000 wine should be left until the body reappears and the wood becomes integrated.

➤ Uldaric Sallier, Ch. de Vauclaire, 13650 Meyrargues, tel. 04.42.57.50.14, fax 04.42.63.47.16 ☑ Υ ev. day except Sun. 9am–12 noon 2pm–6pm

CH. VIGNELAURE 1998★★
18 ha 90,000 ◫ €11-15

Vignelaure was created in the mid 1960s by Georges Brunet, who very soon made it a leading light. It was bought 30 years later by David O'Brien, who today exports 80% of its production within Europe as well as to the USA and Japan. This well-matured 98 suitably honours the estate. According to one taster, it is a 'noble and classy wine'. A touch of liquorice appears in the elegantly woody aromatic range. The palate develops a silky, warming expression. This wine could be left a little longer if it is to be appreciated at its best.

➤ Ch. Vignelaure, rte de Jouques, 83560 Rians, tel. 04.94.37.21.10, fax 04.94.80.53.39,
e-mail david.obrien@wanadoo.fr ☑ Υ ev. day 9.30am–12.30pm 2pm–6pm

CH. VIRANT Tradition 2000*

n.c. 50,000 🍷 €5-8

Originally a cellar and an oil mill, this estate now divides its production between 20 ha (49 acres) of Salonenque and Aglandau olives and 106 ha (262 acres) of vines. This well-balanced wine is produced using exactly equal amounts of Grenache, Syrah and Cabernet Sauvignon. The Grenache brings fleshiness, while the lengthy, aromatic bouquet is attributable to both Syrah and Cabernet Sauvignon.
- SCEA Ch. Virant,
13680 Lançon-de-Provence,
tel. 04.90.42.44.47, fax 04.90.42.54.81 ✅
- ev. day 7.30am–12 noon 2pm–6.30pm
- Robert Cheylan

Les Baux-de-Provence

The Alpilles, the most western secondary chain in the anticlinal mountains of Provence, is an eroded massif with a stunning landscape of crested oblique peaks made of limestone scree and Cretaceous marly limestone. This is paradise for the olive tree, and vines equally flourish on the stony deposits characteristic of the region. The terrace deposits are very thin and the fineness or otherwise of the composition is very important as the water retention ability of the soil depends on it. Here, around the fortified village of Baux-de-Provence, in the heart of the AOC Coteaux d'Aix-en-Provence, a distinctive microclimate makes for a highly productive area, 300 ha (741 acres), that is hot, sunny and rarely subject to frost or rain (650 mm (26 in)). Only reds (80%) and rosés are produced, but a detailed plan of action has been put in place to get the best out of this terroir.

More precise production regulations (lower yield, higher density of planting, harder pruning, development for a minimum of 12 months for the red wines, a minimum of 50% of 'bleeding' (saignée) for the rosés), more clearly defined vine varieties based on the pairing of Grenache and Syrah, sometimes augmented by Mourvèdre, are at the core of the renaissance of this sub-regional appellation nominated in 1995. Output in 2000 was 9,252 hl (244,253 gal), of which 258 hl (6,811 gal) was declared.

MAS DE GOURGONNIER
Réserve du Mas 1999*

🍷 5 ha 20,000 🍷 €6-11

This estate, with its farmhouse built at the beginning of the 18th century, has been farming organically since 1977, producing both olive oil and wine. The dark, almost black colour of the 99 announces its imposing structure. Although the nose is still closed, the palate opens boldly before continuing in a balanced fashion thanks to its tannins, which are noticeable but fine. This serious wine is worth leaving for four to five years.
- Mme Nicolas Cartier et ses Fils,
Mas de Gourgonnier, 13890 Mouriès,
tel. 04.90.47.50.45, fax 04.90.47.51.36 ✅
- ev. day 9am–12 noon 2pm–6pm; cl. Sun. in winter

LA STELE 1999

🍷 5.5 ha 29,300 🍷 €11-15

The vines at the Mas de La Dame are farmed organically. This deep-garnet-red wine is a blend of Syrah (60%) and Cabernet Sauvignon (40%). Its charm lies in its approachable palate. The tannins are just noticeable but softened enough to allow the fruit to appear on the finish. This wine will wait two to three years.
- Mas de La Dame, RD 5,
13520 Les Baux-de-Provence,
tel. 04.90.54.32.24, fax 04.90.54.40.67,
e-mail masdeladame@masdeladame.com ✅
- ev. day 8.30am–7.30pm
- A. Poniatowski, C. Missoffe

CH. ROMANIN 1999**

31 ha 48,000 🍷 €11-15

This 57-ha (141-acre) estate has been cultivated bio-dynamically since its creation in 1988, when Colette and Jean-Pierre Peyraud

joined Jean-André Charial, the owner of a gastronomic restaurant in Baux-de-Provence. The estate submitted, according to one taster, the best red from the 99 vintage. In fact this *cuvée*, which comes from very ripe grapes, expresses a strong profusion of liquorice and dark berry (blackcurrant and myrtle) aromas. The full palate benefits from its softened tannins and a fruity, elegant finish. The rosé 2000, awarded a mention for its fruity, floral aromas, is both round and fresh on the palate.

SCEA Ch. Romanin, 13210 Saint-Rémy-de-Provence, tel. 04.90.92.45.87, fax 04.90.92.24.36
by appt.

MAS SAINTE BERTHE

Cuvée Passe-Rose 2000★

9 ha   53,000   €8-11

This is a lovely rosé, rich in fine, fruity flavours such as nectarine and blackcurrant. The latter mixes together elegantly with raspberry on the round, lengthy palate. The red Cuvée Louis David 99 with its pleasant freshness, flavours of squashed grape and peppery finish, is equally successful. It is worth ageing it for a while for it to to gain complexity. Finally, the unwooded red Cuvée Tradition 99, awarded a mention, is simpler and can be drunk from now on.

GFA Mas Sainte-Berthe, 13520 Les Baux-de-Provence, tel. 04.90.54.39.01, fax 04.90.54.46.17   by appt.
Rolland

DOM. DES ALYSSES

Cuvée Angélique 1999★★

7 ha   20,000   €6-8

This entry in the *Guide* is a triumph for this estate, which has been farmed organically since its creation in 1977. This deeply-tinted wine is elegant. The nose shows a level of complexity in its expression of ripe red berries, pepper and minerals when released on aeration. The concentrated palate is fleshy enough to cover the noticeable but fine tannins. Its eloquence stretches into a long, flavourful finish. It is a wine to be drunk over the next two years. It will perfectly complement duck cooked with prunes.

Dom. des Alysses, Le Bas Deffens, 83670 Pontevès, tel. 04.94.77.10.36, fax 04.94.77.11.64   ev. day 8am–7pm

DOM. DES ANNIBALS 1998★

4.77 ha   4,400   €5-8

Bernard and Nathalie Coquelle have just acquired this estate, which is farmed organically. In their tasting cellar, which dates back to the 18th century, this 98 is typical of Alain Bellon. The wine expresses a varied, balanced palate: smoked, spicy, fruity and minty. Voluminous, it is built around youthful tannins that will drop out if the wine is kept for two years.

Nathalie Coquelle, SCEA Dom. des Annibals, rte de Bras, 83170 Brignoles, tel. 04.94.69.30.36, fax 04.94.69.50.70, e-mail bernard.coquelle@wanadoo.fr   ev. day 9am–7pm

Coteaux Varois

The Coteaux Varois wines are produced in the green, rolling countryside around Brignoles, in the heart of the Var. The wines, best drunk young, are fruity, fun and soft, very much in the image of this pretty little Provençal market town, once the summer residence of the counts of Provence. Coteaux Varois became an AOC on 26 March 1993, and the delimited area covers 1,740 ha (4,298 acres). In 2000 88,613 hl (2,339,383 gal) of rosé, red and white were produced.

CH. DE CANCERILLES

Cuvée Spéciale 1998

1.5 ha   8,000   €5-8

This château, situated in the wooded hills of Montrieux, used to be occupied by the monks of the Montrieux monastery, from which it inherited its cellars. They accommodate this strong red wine, characterised at the start of the tasting by truffle and spices. The supple palate is based on heightened tannins, which sustain the fruity finish. It is a wine to be kept for three to four years.

Chantal et Serge García, Ch. de Cancerilles, vallée du Gapeau, 83870 Signes, tel. 04.94.90.83.93, fax 04.94.90.83.93   ev. day 10am–7pm; cl. Mon. Oct. to Mar.

CH. DES CHABERTS

Cuvée Prestige 2000★★★

n.c.   13,000   €5-8

This Cuvée Prestige is prestigious! The balance between liveliness and fleshiness is brought out by the aromatic strength, baskets of citrus fruit equally evident on the nose as Cuvée Prestige 2000: a delicious rosé. The white Cuvée Prestige 2000 was awarded two stars. It has a luminous colour, supple, round structure and unreservedly, fruity aromas. The red **Cuvée Prestige 99**, characteristic of the appellation, was awarded one star. It can be left for another year or two.

• SCI Ch. des Chaberts, 83136 Garéoult, tel. 04.94.04.92.05, fax 04.94.04.00.97, e-mail chaberts@wanadoo.fr ▼ ev. day 9am–12 noon 2pm–7pm; Sun. by appt.

DOM. DE CLAPIERS 2000★

■ 1.03 ha █ 6,500 € 5-8

This estate, almost 59 ha (146 acres), was created on the site of an old co-operative cellar. It submitted a wine typical of this appellation, containing 75% Rolle in the blend. It is floral on the nose, becoming generously rounded on the palate while preserving aromatic finesse. Its finish, with its warmth, is bewitching. Just as well balanced and vivacious is the peach-pink **rosé 2000** (mainly Grenache). It was awarded one star for its balance and fresh aromas.

• Pierre Burel, Dom. de Clapiers, rte de Saint-Maximin, 83149 Bras, tel. 04.94.69.95.46, fax 04.94.69.99.36, e-mail clapiers@wanadoo.fr ▼ ev. day except Sun. 9am–12 noon 2pm–6pm

DOM. DU DEFFENDS
Clos de La Truffière 1999

■ 6 ha █ 25,000 ⫴♦ € 8-11

Planted on the edge of the Auréliens mountains, Clos de La Truffière produces a blend of Syrah and Cabernet Sauvignon, an intense garnet-red colour with violet tints which has youthful aromas of blackcurrant berries and leaves. The pleasantly supple palate benefits from its evident tannins. Lightly minty, spicy flavours make up the fresh finish. This wine should be left for a few years.

• J.-S. de Lanversin, Dom. du Deffends, 83470 Saint-Maximin, tel. 04.94.78.03.91, fax 04.94.59.42.69, e-mail deffends@terre-net.fr ▼ ev. day 9am–12 noon 3pm–6pm

CH. DUVIVIER Les Mûriers 1999★

■ 3.5 ha █ 17,000 ⫴♦ € 11-15

For almost ten years, this 30-ha (74-acre) estate has been run organically. The wine, exclusively matured in wood (half in vat, half in barrel) as evidenced by its attractive structure, still has quite intense tannins. The pear and vanilla bouquet remains youthful. This wine will become more refined if it is kept for about three years.

• SCEA Ch. Duvivier, La Geneviêre, rte de Draguignan, 83670 Pontevès, tel. 04.94.77.02.96, fax 04.94.77.26.66, e-mail antoine.kaufmann@delinat.com ▼ by appt.

DOM. FONTLADE
Cuvée Saint-Quinis 2000★

■ 4 ha █ 7,000 € 5-8

Frédéric Mistral mentions the name *Fuoant-Lado* ('large fountain') in his *Trésor du Félibrige*. From the beginning of the Middle Ages, Fontlade was a tollbooth on the

865

Aurélienne road. It later became the property of the Saint-Victor monks. Today, it distinguishes itself with well-balanced, flowery wines, such as this one, which is the ideal accompaniment to Provençal cooking.

• SCEA Baronne Philippe de Montrémy, Dom. de Fontlade, 83170 Brignoles, tel. 04.94.59.24.34, fax 04.94.72.02.88 ▼ by appt.

DOM. DE GARBELLE 2000★

■ 3 ha █ 10,000 € 3-5

Garéoult, a Roman farming colony set in the heart of vineyards in the Issole valley, produces this sensual, round, slightly pink rosé. A dash of flowers, a touch of fruit ... the aromatic expression is really good. The **red 99**, also awarded a mention, was cask matured so still needs to be cellared for a little while.

• Gambini, Dom. de Garbelle, Vieux chemin de Brignoles, 83136 Garéoult, tel. 04.94.04.86.30, fax 04.94.04.86.30 ▼ ev. day 8.30am–12 noon 2pm–6.30pm

DOM. LA BASTIDE DES OLIVIERS 2000

■ n.c. █ 15,000 € 5-8

Patrick Mourian, born into a family of winemakers, supervised his first vinification in 2000. His cherry-red wine with its violet tints may have the liveliness of youth but already aromas of fruits soaked in brandy and musk are beginning to appear. The evident tannins suggest the wine should be left for a couple of years.

• Patrick Mourian, 1011, chem. Louis-Blériot, 83136 Garéoult, tel. 04.94.04.03.11, fax 04.94.04.03.11 ▼ by appt.

CH. LA CALISSE 2000★★

■ 1 ha █ 5,000 € 8-11

This vineyard was previously a silkworm farm. Now Patricia Ortelli produces wine, lavender and olive oil. Her luminous 2000 is elegantly aromatic within a floral register of broom and pinks. The clean, open palate retains its aromatic freshness. The pleasant **red 2000** conjures up violet and liquorice notes and benefits from its balanced structure: it was awarded special mention.

• Patricia Ortelli, Ch. La Calisse, 83670 Pontevès, tel. 04.93.99.11.01, fax 04.93.99.06.10 ▼ ev. day 9am–7pm

CH. LAFOUX Cuvée Prestige 2000★

□ 1 ha █ 3,000 € 5-8

The year 2000 marks a new start for this estate, which is changing both ownership and name (it was previously the Domaine du Boulon). It is also a successful year as both wines, the fresh and fruity **rosé 2000** and this particular white, were awarded a star. This wine flatters the senses with its delicious body and long aromatic, fruity finish.

• SCEA Genevois, Ch. Lafoux, RN 7, 83170 Tourves, tel. 04.94.78.77.86 ▼

Coteaux Varois

DOM. DE LA GAYOLLE
Syagria 1999★ — ▮ ▮▮ 2.500 €5-8

This wine, produced in small quantities, has a label that depicts the sarcophagus of the La Gayolle chapel from the second century. This Coteaux Varois wine shows aromas of ripe red berries and nuances of vanilla and spice inherited from its 12-month cask maturation. The round, full-bodied palate has a fresh, fruity, woody finish. This well-matured wine is characteristic of its *terroir*. It needs two or three years' cellaring.

➼ Jacques Paul, RN 7, 83170 Brignoles,
tel. 04.94.59.10.88, fax 04.94.72.04.34,
e-mail gayolle@wanadoo.fr ☑ ✖ by appt.

DOM. LA ROSE DES VENTS 2000★★
◢ 8.5 ha 50,000 ▮ ⬥ €5-8

Jean-Louis Baude and his son, Gilles, have been working together since 1994. In 2000, a third associate, Thierry Josselin, joined them. Their delicate, pale Rosé des Vents is full and round. It is stamped with lengthy exotic aromas. This Coteaux Varois 2000 was submitted to the Grand Jury for the *coup de coeur*.

➼ EARL Baude, Dom. La Rose des Vents, rte de Toulon, 83136 La Roquebrussanne,
tel. 04.94.86.99.28, fax 04.94.86.91.75,
e-mail rose.des.vents@infonie.fr ☑
✖ ev. day except Sun. Mon. 9am–12 noon
2pm–6pm

LES ABEILLONS DE TOURTOUR 1999★★
◢ 2.6 ha 16,000 ▮ ▮▮ ⬥ €8-11

The village of Villecroze ('hollow town') probably owes its name to the tufa caves set in the impressive cliff. The influencing elements are the Romans, the monks of Saint-Victor from Marseille and the Knights Templar. This winemaking estate is well known to readers of the *Guide*, who will remember the 97 vintage *coup de coeur*. This dark 99, with its mixed bouquet of both rough (leather and musk) and delicate (red berries and spices) aromas, appears strong and characterful on the palate and full-bodied right up to the lengthy, spicy, stewed red berry finish. It is very pleasant to drink now and will continue to be so for the next three years.

➼ SCEA Les Abeillons, 83690 Villecroze,
tel. 04.94.70.63.02, fax 04.94.70.67.03 ☑
✖ by appt.
➼ Croquet

LES TERRES DE SAINT-LOUIS 2000★
◢ 74.6 ha 347,000 ▮ ⬥ –€3

This union of co-operatives has been awarded two distinctions. The **Domaine Le Gavelier 2000 rosé** was awarded a star for its irreproachable presentation, structure and warmth on the palate. This paler, particularly aromatic, cuvée rosé is generous, well-balanced and long on the palate. It offers excellent value for money.

➼ Le Cellier de Saint-Louis,
ZI Les Consacs, 83170 Brignoles,
tel. 04.94.37.21.00, fax 04.94.59.14.84,
e-mail cellier-saintlouis@wanadoo.fr

DOM. DU LOOU 1998
▮ 8 ha 26,000 ▮▮ €5-8

This pretty ruby-coloured wine liberates floral aromas, which are underlined by touches of bitter almond and mint. The palate, full on the attack, rests on a balanced structure. It also evokes cooked fruit. It is ready to drink from now on.

➼ SCEA Di Placido, dom. du Loou,
83136 La Roquebrussanne,
tel. 04.94.86.97, fax 04.94.86.80.11 ☑
✖ by appt.

CH. MIRAVAL 2000★★
▯ 4 ha n.c. ▮ €5-8

This estate is planted in the ancient village of Val, set in the Ribeirotte valley. The clear, slightly overripe Rolle is expressive, with a fresh, generous nose. The expressive round palate has lengthy fruity aromas. This is a pleasing wine that would be delightful as accompaniment to aperitif or dessert.

➼ SA Ch. Miraval, 83143 Le Val,
tel. 04.94.86.39.33, fax 04.94.86.46.79 ☑
✖ by appt.

DOM. DE RAMATUELLE 2000★
◢ 5 ha 35,000 ▮ ⬥ €3-5

The name Ramatuelle comes from the Arab *Ramat Allah*, which means 'God's gift'. The Moors named the estate thus when they settled here during the 12th and 13th century. This 2000 certainly has something to offer: an expressive, clear, pink wine, it has all the richness and fruitiness needed. It will go well with steak or baked cheese dishes. The rougher **red 99** would go well with braised meat and was commended.

➼ Bruno Latil, Dom. de Ramatuelle,
Les Gaëtans, 83170 Brignoles,
tel. 04.94.69.10.61, fax 04.94.69.51.41 ☑
✖ by appt.

CH. ROUTAS Pyramus 2000★
▯ 4 ha 20,000 ▮ ▮▮ ⬥ €5-8

Around 75% of this wine is exported, notably to the USA, UK and Germany. More expressive on the palate than on the nose, it develops with roundness and integrates harmoniously a delicate woodiness. The **red Cuvée Internet 99** is equally successful, thanks to controlled wood maturation. Its tannins will be refined in about two years.

➤ SARL Rouvière-Plane, 83149 Châteauvert, tel. 04.94.69.93.92, fax 04.94.69.93.61, e-mail rouviere.plane@wanadoo.fr ☑ ☒ by appt.

DOM. DE SAINT-JEAN LE VIEUX 1999★

■ 3 ha 15,000 ▮▮ €3-5

This estate is situated at the Bras end of Saint-Maximin, a town known for its inestimable basilica treasures, including its monumental organ, as well as its music festival. This 99 wine, supple on the attack, benefits from a well-balanced structure. Slightly musky, smoky, fruity flavours come from the pleasing body. It is ready to drink now. The very pale **rosé 2000**, awarded a mention, shows fresh fruit on a warm, round base.

➤ GAEC Dom. Saint-Jean-le-Vieux, rte de Bras, 83470 Saint-Maximin, tel. 04.94.59.77.59, fax 04.94.59.73.35 ☑ ☒ by appt.

CH. SAINT-JULIEN 2000

◤ 2 ha 13,000 ▮▮ €5-8

For the past two years, this producer has been completing the renovation of his cellar; it should be ready by next harvest. This pale rosé delivers generous pear drop aromas with musky nuances. Its roundness is pronounced.

➤ EARL Dom. Saint-Julien, rte de Tourves, 83170 La Celle, tel. 04.94.59.26.10, fax 04.94.59.26.10 ☑

☒ ev. day except Sun. 8am-12 noon 2pm-6pm

➤ M. Garassin

DOM. DE VALCOLOMBE 1999★

■ 2 ha 13,460 ▮▮ €5-8

An electric fence protects the vines just before harvest because, in the Haut Var, wild boars are very fond of grapes. Pierre and Marie Léonetti, both doctors, produce classic appellation wines. This one benefits from attractive tannins in a fairly supple structure perfumed with brush, mineral and fruity notes.

➤ Dom. de Valcolombe, chem. des Espèces, 83690 Villecroze, tel. 04.94.67.57.16, fax 04.94.67.57.16 ☒ ev. day except Tue. Fri. Sun. 10am-12 noon 3pm-6.30pm

➤ Léonetti

Corsica

'A mountain in the sea': the traditional definition of Corsica is as appropriate when applied to its tourist attractions. The topography of the whole island is folded and buckled to an extreme degree, and even the stretch called the west coast – and which, were it on the Continent would more properly be described as a coastal area – is far from lacking in elevation and relief. The vine is to be found virtually everywhere on this multiplicity of slopes and hills, normally sun-drenched, but kept relatively damp because of the influence of the sea. Only altitude limits its planting.

The production of wine, mostly Vin de Pays or table wine, is determined by the island's relief and the climatic variations it causes, in association with three main types of soil. The most common soil was originally granite; it covers nearly the whole of the south and west of the island; between this area and the schists of the north-east you find a small deposit of limestone soils.

In addition to the imported vine varieties are highly individual varieties native to Corsica, particularly the Niellucciu which has a dominant tannic characteristic and which excels on limestone. The Sciacarellu produces fruitier wines best appreciated when they are young. For the whites, the Malvasia (Vermentino or Malvoisie) is capable of producing the best wines grown on the shores of the Mediterranean.

Vins de Corse

As a general rule, the whites are better when young and this is even more the case for the rosés. Both go well with fish and seafood and with the excellent local goats' cheeses, as well as with brocciou, another local cheese made from goat's or ewe's milk. The reds, depending on bottle age and tannic strength, will complement a variety of different meat dishes and, naturally, all of Corsica's famous sheep's milk cheeses.

Vins de Corse

The vineyards of this appellation cover an area of 1,954 ha (4,826 acres). The proportions of grape varieties used, and the different nature of the *terroirs*, can produce variations in tone and colour from one region to another and between local vineyards. Mostly, these are accounted for by grouping them under the name of a sub-region associated with the appellation (Coteaux du Cap Corse, Calvi, Figari, Porto-Vecchio and Sartène). These wines may be produced virtually anywhere in Corsica except for the Patrimonio region. Most of the 87,050 hl (2,298,120 gal) vinified in 2000 came from the East Coast, where there are a large number of co-operatives.

successful. The **white Domaine Casabianca 2000** was awarded a mention.

Jean-Bernardin Casabianca, 20230 Bravone, tel. 04.95.38.81.91, fax 04.95.38.81.91 by appt.

CASONE 2000★★

40 ha   250,000   €3-5

This wine, a top-of-the-market selection from the Saint-Antoine cellar in Ghisonaccia, was in the running for a *coup de coeur* 2002. It has a clear, bright, pink colour with a seductive aromatic range of white flowers, brush and heather. The light, pleasurable palate is very lengthy. This wine will go well on its own, with *charcuterie* or some types of shellfish.

Coop. de Saint-Antoine, 20240 Ghisonaccia, tel. 04.95.56.61.00, fax 04.95.56.61.60 by appt.

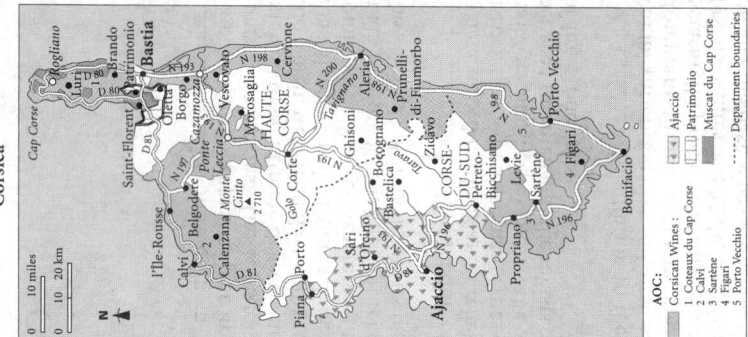

Corsica

DOM. D'ALZIPRATU

Calvi Cuvée Fiumeseccu 1999

5 ha   25,000   €5-8

The Alzipratu estate cultivates 31 ha (77 acres) of vine around Zilia, in Haute-Corse. Niellucciu and Sciacarellu are mixed to produce this garnet-red wine with herbaceous aromas on the nose and the palate. This wine is drinking well now.

Pierre Acquaviva, 20214 Zilia, tel. 04.95.62.75.47, fax 04.95.60.32.16 ev. day except Sun. 8am–12 noon 2pm–7pm

JEAN-BERNARDIN CASABIANCA

Centenaire du Fondateur 1999★

10 ha   65,000   €3-5

The Casabianca family heads of one of the biggest vineyards of the eastern coast (310 ha/766 acres); the blends are therefore very varied. This 'centenary' wine pays homage to the estate's founder. Its strength is obvious from the very first aromas of red berries and spices, and it lingers on the palate. With a little ageing this wine will be good. The red **Vin de Corse 99**, both characteristic of the estate, is equally

CORSICAN 2000★

50 ha | 100,000 | -43

This rosé, 90% Sciacarellu, was carefully vinified. Elegant fruity, spicy notes on the nose give rise to varietal characteristics on the palate, a fairly marked liveliness and good length. This rosé would go well with salmon dishes. The ruby-coloured red Corsican 99, with aromas of red berries and musky nuances, tinted by maturation, is equally successful. Rediscover it in 2003. Another selection from La Marana is the Terra Nosra 99, a very light red Nielluciu, which was also awarded a special mention.

SICA Uval, Rasignani, 20290 Borgo, tel. 04.95.58.44.00, fax 04.95.38.38.10, e-mail uval.sica@wanadoo.fr
ev. day 9am-12 noon 3pm-7pm

CLOS CULOMBU Calvi Cuvée Prestige 1999★

10 ha | 35,000 | €5-8

The ever-welcoming Etienne Suzzoni owns this vineyard on attractive granite-sand soil. His wine softens on long, grilled, vanilla aromas. The tasters noticed this wine's expressiveness. The qualities of the white and rosé Vins de Corse Calvi 2000, awarded a mention by the Jury, are also worth noting. The first, rather timid, is still awakening, while the latter is already showing floral aromas.

Etienne Suzzoni, Clos Culombu, chem. San-Pedru, 20260 Lumio, tel. 04.95.60.70.68, fax 04.95.60.63.46, e-mail culombu.suzzoni@wanadoo.fr
ev. day 9am-12 noon 3pm-8pm

DOM. FILIPPI 1999★

30 ha | 40,000 | €5-8

Toussaint Filippi, who received the coup de coeur for the preceding vintage of this wine, owns a vineyard in Linguizzetta, not far from the sea. Syrah and Mourvèdre support Nielluciu here to produce a strong, very aromatic wine: red berries, leather and coffee. The palate, echoing the aromatics with roasted notes, has a well-softened tannic structure. The rosé Vin de Corse 2000 was awarded a mention for its richness, which makes it an ideal wine to drink throughout a meal.

Toussaint Filippi, La Ruche Foncière, Arena, 20215 Venzolasca, tel. 04.95.58.40.80, fax 04.95.36.40.55, e-mail la-ruche-fonciere@wanadoo.fr
by appt.

DOM. DE LA FIGARELLA Calvi Cuvée Prestige 2000

4 ha | 7,500 | €5-8

This 34-ha (84-acre) estate is planted at Calenzana, an area rich in wine, honey and aromatic plants of which this wine is very characteristic. Intense citrus fruit (grapefruit) aromas and a lively palate make it an ideal accompaniment to grilled fish dishes.

Achille Acquaviva, dom. La Figarella, rte de l'Aéroport, 20214 Calenzana, tel. 04.95.65.07.24, fax 04.95.65.41.58
Wed. Sat. 3pm-6pm

CLOS LANDRY Calvi 1999

8 ha | 32,000 | €5-8

This estate, created in 1900, is situated near Calvi airport. For overseas visitors it may be the first step towards the discovery of Corsica! In addition to the white and rosé Vins de Corse Calvi 2000, the Jury awarded this light red, with its red berry aromas, a special mention. Crisp on the palate, it is a good wine to serve at barbecues.

Fabien et Cathy Paolini, Clos Landry, rte de l'Aéroport, 20260 Calvi, tel. 04.95.65.04.25, fax 04.95.65.37.56, e-mail closlandry@wanadoo.fr
ev. day except Sun. 9am-12 noon 2pm-7pm; cl. Dec.

DOM. MAESTRACCI Calvi E Prove 1998★★

6 ha | 32,000 | €8-11

This estate produced a successful trio with its E Prove range. This complex, strong red wine was cask matured. Its red berry aromas, underlined by musky notes, continue into the mid-palate, becoming velvety. It would go well with game. The Vin de Corse Calvi gris 2000 (light rosé), made up of Sciacarellu, has a surprisingly light spiciness on the nose and liveliness on the palate. It was awarded one star. The white 2000 was awarded a mention. It is a good example of Vermentino, with its citrus fruit notes. Michel Raoust also presented a lively rosé in the traditional Calvi vin gris style, under the label rosé Calivi Clos Reginu 2000. It was awarded one star and would be delicious served with North African spicy lamb dishes.

Michel Raoust, Clos Reginu, 20225 Feliceto, tel. 04.95.61.72.11, fax 04.95.61.80.16, e-mail clos.reginu@wanadoo.fr summer ev. day except Sun. 9am-12 noon 2pm-7.30pm

DOM. DU MONT SAINT-JEAN 2000★★

27 ha | 100,000 | €3-5

This estate is situated at Campo Quercio, in the village of Aléria. This year is its first time in the Guide, thanks to this bright, Sciacarellu rosé. Peppery notes on the nose and a minerally, lightly salty palate demonstrate its remarkable aromatic complexity. An original wine it is ideal to accompany oysters, fish dishes or just as an aperitif. Red Vin Corse 1999, awarded a mention by the Jury, appears promising.

SCA du Mont Saint-Jean, Campo Quercio, 20270 Aléria, tel. 04.95.38.59.96, fax 04.95.38.50.29, e-mail roger.pouyau@wanadoo.fr
R. Pouyau

Vins de Corse

CLOS D'ORLEA 2000★★
☐ 30 ha 150,000 🍷🍷 €5-8

François Orsucci would make anyone interested in Corsica, his Aléria region and the islands festivities. A fine gourmet, he introduces you to this rosé, with its fruity aromas and length on the palate, as an ideal wine with a fresh vegetable starter or as an accompaniment to simple grilled meat. The red **Clos d'Orlea 1999**, which develops spicy, peppery notes, has a velvety palate. The Jury awarded it one star. Finally, the **white 2000**, which was awarded a mention, goes well with cheese at the end of a meal.

➤ François Orsucci, SCEA Le Clos Léa, 20270 Aléria, tel. 04.95.57.13.60, fax 04.95.57.09.64 ☒ ▼ ev. day except Sat. Sun. 9am–12 noon 2pm–7pm

DOM. PERO-LONGO Sartène 2000
☐ 2 ha 9,000 🍷 €5-8

The Lion de Rocapina, situated quite close to this estate, has looked favourably on Pierre Richarme again this year. The producer submitted this attractive, clear white wine, faint on the nose but well balanced on the palate. The pronounced **rosé** generously reveals notes of red berries. Both wines were awarded a mention and go well with grilled fish or creamy Corsican sheep's cheese.

➤ Pierre Richarme, lieu-dit Navara, rte de Bonifacio, 20100 Sartène, tel. 04.95.77.10.74, fax 04.95.77.10.74 ☒ ▼ by appt.

DOM. DE PIANA 1999
☐ 15 ha n.c. 🍷 €5-8

Three special mentions have been awarded to this estate's wines: one each for red, white and rosé. This intense-ruby-coloured 99 has red berry flavours. It demonstrates liveliness and length on the palate. A light golden colour, the **white Vin de Corse 2000** shows delicate citrus aromas. Its balance and length make it a good wine with foods. The **rosé 2000** would be pleasing as an aperitif.

➤ Ange Poli, Linguizzetta, 20230 San Nicolao, tel. 04.95.38.86.38, fax 04.95.38.94.71 ☒ ▼ by appt.

DOM. PIERETTI Coteaux du Cap Corse Sélection Vieilles Vignes 1999★★★
☐ 2 ha 9,600 🍷 €5-8

Lina Pieretti is one of the first female winemakers in Corsica. Supported by her husband, she has run the estate since 1991, following in the footsteps of her father. This wine is from old Niellucciu and Elegante vines cultivated near the Macinaggio road. A deep ruby colour, it is generous with notes of spice and fruit. The palate flavours suggest fruit with a vanilla note, but one that is an expression of the variety and owes nothing to the wood. It is ready to drink now, or can be kept for a couple of years. From the same estate, the **white Vin de Corse Coteaux du Cap Corse 2000** is also a keeping wine. Its success is down to the lively, lengthy Vermentino aromas. It will go well with fish. The **rosé 2000**, matured in a modern way, was also awarded a star for the length of its fruit and flowers.

➤ Lina Pieretti Venturi, Santa-Severa, 20228 Luri, tel. 04.95.35.01.03, fax 04.95.35.01.03 ▼ by appt.

PRESTIGE DU PRESIDENT 2000
☐ 2.5 ha 8,000 🍷🍷🍷 €5-8

This pleasing white wine, with its citrus notes, has characteristics of Vermentino. Behind a pale colour is a lengthy palate. It goes well with grilled fish or grilled white meat. The open **red Vin de Corse Président Tradition 98** was also awarded a mention, because of its structure and intense aromas of spicy, smoked undergrowth.

➤ Union de Vignerons de L'Ile de Beauté, Cave coop. d'Aléria, 20270 Aléria, tel. 04.95.57.02.48, fax 04.95.57.09.59 ☒ ▼ by appt.

DOM. RENUCCI Calvi 2000★★★
☐ 2.3 ha 30,000 🍷 €5-8

This wine, partly made using the *saignée* method, is mainly Sciacarellu, supported by Niellucciu and Syrah. It impressed the tasters with its clear salmon colour, floral aromas of acacia and honeysuckle and perfect balance on the palate. It has a lively attack, structured softness and lengthy aromas of white fruit (peach and nectarine). It could be an aperitif or accompany lightly spiced dishes or soft cheeses. The **white Vin de Corse Calvi 2000** which has a floral, citrus nose, was awarded a mention.

➤ Bernard Renucci, 20225 Feliceto, tel. 04.95.61.71.08, fax 04.95.61.71.08 ☒ ▼ ev. day except Sun. 10am–12 noon 4pm–7pm; cl. Oct. to Apr.

DOM. SAN'ARMETTO Sartène 2000★
☐ 3 ha n.c. 🍷 €3-5

The Seroins, father and son, who had previously worked in a co-operative, went into private production in 1998. They submitted this white lively, expressive Vermentino. The nose has lengthy citrus fruit notes and it possesses a lengthy, pleasing palate. This could be a good aperitif wine. The restrained **rosé Vin de Corse Sartène 2000**, also awarded a star, will soon reveal its fruity, refreshing character and its lengthy, soft palate.

870

↪ EARL San Arnetto, Les Cannes, 20113 Olmeto, tel. 04.95.76.05.18, fax 04.95.76.24.47 ☑ ▼ by appt.

↪ Paul Gilles Serouin

DOM. DE SAN-MICHELE

Sartène 2000

| 6 ha | 35,000 | ▪ | €5-8 |

This rosé comes from the large property of San Michele, whose vines are spread across granite soil. It is fruity and floral with noticeable red berry flavours. Refreshing and lively, it could be a delicious aperitif.

↪ EARL Dom. San-Michele, 24, rue Jean-Jaurès, 20100 Sartène, tel. 04.95.77.00.60 ☑

TERRA NOSTRA

Cuvée Corsica 1999 ★★

| | n.c. | 40,000 | ▥ |

SANT'ANTONE 2000★

| 40 ha | 200,000 | ▪ | €3-5 |

This very aromatic rosé, suggesting raspberries, heather and flowers found in the brush, has a pleasing, round, supple palate. It would go well with aromatic grilled fish. The **red 2000**, from Niellucciu and Syrah, is equally successful. Its full body and red berry aromas will be ready to enjoy in a few more months.

↪ Coop. de Saint-Antoine, 20240 Ghisonaccia, tel. 04.95.56.61.00, fax 04.95.56.61.60 ☑ ▼ by appt.

DOM. DE TANELLA

Figari Cuvée Alexandra 1999★

| 8 ha | 35,000 | ▪▥▥ | €8-11 |

The Tanella estate is situated in the Figari area at the far south of Corsica, a region both bathed in sunshine and continually caressed (and sometimes battered) by the wind. Its owners created the Cuvée Alexandra when their daughter was born. This sombre, cerise-coloured wine is produced from Niellucciu and Sciacarellu. The mineral, iodine nose is fairly typical of this micro-region. A light oaky note enriches the aromas. This is an attractive wine, which will go well with game and whose tannins will complement a wine-based sauce.

↪ Jean-Baptiste de Peretti della Rocca, Dom. de Tanella, 20114 Figari, tel. 04.95.70.46.23, fax 04.95.70.54.49, e-mail tanella@wanadoo.fr ☑ ▼ by appt.

Alain Mazoyer, director of the Marana cellar, has personally invested in the production of this wine, only 40,000 bottles of which have been produced – a small amount for a co-operative cellar. Its deep ruby colour reveals aromas of red berries and liquorice. Extremely strong and structured, it delivers a softened woodiness and develops good balance. It is an ideal wine for celebrations but will also benefit from cellaring for two or three years.

↪ Cave coop. de La Marana, Rasignani, 20290 Borgo, tel. 04.95.38.44.00, fax 04.95.38.38.10, e-mail uval.sica@wanadoo.fr ☑ ▼ ev. day except Sun. 9am–12 noon 3pm–7pm

DOM. DE TORRACCIA

Porto-Vecchio 2000★

| 8 ha | 25,000 | ▪ | €5-8 |

This wine's colour is somewhere between clear pink and salmon. Its delicate fruity peach and cherry nose is seductive, and the same aromas appear on the pleasant, fresh palate. It is an attractive wine that will match well with salmon carpaccio in fennel and olive oil (the latter is also produced on this estate). The **white Vin de Corse Porto Vecchio 2000** was given special mention. Its lively good length makes it a good aperitif. The **red Orio 99**, notable for the spicy influence of Sciacarellu in the blend, was also awarded a mention.

↪ Christian Imbert, Dom. de Torraccia, Lecci, 20137 Porto-Vecchio, tel. 04.95.71.43.50, fax 04.95.71.50.03 ☑ ▼ ev. day 8am–12 noon 2pm–6pm

DOM. VICO 2000★★

| | 8.5 ha | 30,000 | ▪ | €5-8 |

The Vico estate is the only vineyard in the centre of the island of Corsica – in Ponte-Leccia. Jean-Marc Venturi, also the director of the Aléria cellar, joined with Yves Melleray, an oenologist from Casinca, to plant the vineyard in this difficult micro-region, with its intense cold spells in winter and huge heatwaves in summer. Judging by this limpid, expressive white wine with its aromas of flowers and summer fruit, the pair appear to have been successful. Slightly sharp notes balance the ample, sweet palate. It would perfectly complement fish or cheese pastry dishes. The estate's **rosé Vin de Corse 2000** is also very successful. Its full palate, with slightly vinous asides, match it with more highly seasoned food. The **red 99** was also awarded a star because, although still very much dominated by crisp fruit, its structure allows cellaring for quite a while.

Dom. Vico, 20218 Ponte-Leccia, tel. 04.95.47.61.35, fax 04.95.36.50.26
by appt.

Ajaccio

The vineyards of this appellation occupy 200 ha (494 acres) in a strip several dozen kilometres long running along the hills surrounding the chief town of southern Corsica and its famous gulf. The soils are mostly granitic, and Sciacarello is the main grape variety. The red wines are suitable for keeping and account for 60.5% of the 2000 production of around 6,558 hl (173,131 gal).

DOM. COMTE ABBATUCCI★

Cuvée Antoine Abbatucci 2000★

7 ha   15,000   €5-8

The Abbatucci estate, run organically since the end of 2000, is moving towards biodynamics. Jean-Charles Abbatucci, currently the president of the appellation, regularly proves how careful he is, as a producer, with both his white wines and his very successful **rosé 2000**, as well as his **red Ajaccio Cuvée Antoine Abbatucci 99**, which was awarded a mention by the Jury. The white Ajaccio shows Vermentino's citrusy fruit aromas and full palate. This wine is the ideal companion to slightly mature cheese. The very minerally rosé wine has seductive consistency and length.

Dom. Comte J.C. Abbatucci, Lieu-dit Chiesale, 20140 Casalabriva, tel. 04.95.74.04.55, fax 04.95.74.04.55, e-mail dom-abbatucci@infonie.fr
J.C. Abbatucci

CLOS D'ALZETO 1996★

10 ha   30,000   €5-8

This 43-ha (106-acre) estate is a must to visit; it stands at the edge of the appellation and has the unique position of being the highest vineyard in Corsica, at 500 m (1635 ft). Pascal Albertini, supported by his son, submitted this traditionally vinified, strong and elegant 96. This five-year-old wine demonstrates the potential of Ajaccio AOC wines. The **white Ajaccio 2000**, with delicate floral aromas, was awarded a mention.

Pascal Albertini, Clos d'Alzeto, 20151 Sari d'Orcino, tel. 04.95.52.24.67, fax 04.95.52.27.27   by appt.

CLOS CAPITORO 1999★

35 ha   160,000   €8-11

Jacques Bianchetti has been the mayor of Cauro since the end of March 2001. His estate covers a small part of this village and that of Porticcio. This 99 wine, Sciacarellu and Grenache, is rich in peppery aromas on a base of red berries. Its warming palate makes it a perfect accompaniment to quail cooked with grapes. The Clos Capitoro distinguishes itself equally with its successful spicy edged **rosé Ajaccio 2000**. The fresh, floral **white 2000** was awarded a mention.

Jacques Bianchetti, Clos Capitoro, Piscatella-Cauro, 20166 Porticcio, tel. 04.95.25.19.61, fax 04.95.25.19.33, e-mail info@clos-capitoro.com
by appt.

DOM. ALAIN COURREGES 1999★

4.4 ha   8,000   €5-8

This 28-ha (69-acre) vineyard is on the Porto Polo road. Alain Courrèges submitted this quite dark wine with a strong hint of undergrowth, leather and musk on the nose and palate. A structured Ajaccio, it will go well with game.

Alain Courrèges, 20123 Cognocoli, tel. 04.95.24.35.54, fax 04.95.24.38.07
by appt.

CLOS ORNASCA 2000★

n.c.   5,250   €5-8

Laetitia Tola is an energetic winemaker within her appellation: supported by her father, Vincent, she demonstrates her winemaking skills with this wine, based on the characteristics of Vermentino. This 2000 wine shows citrus fruit combined with aniseed fragrances on the nose, which continues for sometime on the palate. The **rosé Ajaccio 2000** is equally successful. Its generous expression of flowers is characteristic of Sciacarellu. It would go equally well alone as an aperitif or with roasted fish.

Laetitia Tola, Clos Ornasca, Eccica Suarella, 20117 Cauro, tel. 04.95.25.09.07, fax 04.95.25.96.05   ev. day except Sun. 8am-6pm; groups by appt.

DOM. COMTE PERALDI 2000★

n.c.   54,000   €5-8

The reputation of the Comte Péraldi estate is well established. Produced using equipment that is as dynamic as it is gentle, the **rosé 2000** and the **red 1999** are both very successful. The first has aromatic strength and great roundness on the palate, making it a very elegant wine. The **red Ajaccio** is intensely coloured with a well-presented structure showing musky, vanilla nuances. This pleasing wine should be cellared for one or two years and then drunk with marinated red meat or exotic more spicy dishes.

Guy Tyrel de Poix, Dom. Peraldi, chem. du Stiletto, 20167 Mezzavia, tel. 04.95.22.37.30, fax 04.95.20.92.91
by appt.

Patrimonio

This small enclave, occupying 389 ha (961 acres) in 2000, is made up of limestone *terroirs* extending east and mainly south from the Gulf of Saint-Florent. They are remarkably consistent from one to another and can with good management produce high-quality wines. The chief grape varieties are Nielluccio for reds and Malvasia for whites, and these look likely to become the only varieties used. They make very typical wines of excellent quality, especially the sumptuous reds which can be laid down for long maturing. Production was up to 17,435 hl (460,284 gal), of which 3,040 hl (80,256 gal) were whites.

DOM. DE PIETRELLA 1999 ■ 2 ha 9,000 €5-8

For this, its first appearance in the *Guide*, the Pietrella estate, situated in the Eccica Suarella area, was awarded a double mention: first for its clear **rosé Ajaccio 2000** with delicate red berry aromas, and then for this fine, elegant, aromatic red. Both wines would go well with full-flavoured summer dishes.

☙ Toussaint Tirroloni, Dom. de Pietrella, 2017 Cauro, tel. 04.95.25.19.19
Y by appt.

DOM. DE PRATAVONE 2000★★ ■ 4 ha 17,000 €3-5

Isabelle Courrèges, a winemaking oenologist, has received three *coups de cœur*. This clear, bold rosé, produced from Sciacarellu planted on sand-granite soil, opens to red berry (strawberry and raspberry) aromas. The palate, which is similarly fruity, continues for some time before leaving a very pleasant impression of freshness. The Jury awarded one star to the **red Ajaccio 98**, characteristic of the appellation. This wine lingers on the palate with spicy notes.

☙ Jean et Isabelle Courrèges, Dom. de Pratavone, Pila-Canale, 20123 Cognocoli-Monticchi, tel. 04.95.24.34.11, fax 04.95.24.34.74
Y ev. day except Sun. 8.30am-12 noon 3.30pm-7.30pm, out of season by appt.

CLOS DE BERNARDI
Crème de Tête 1999★ ■ n.c. 18,000 €5-8

Jean-Laurent de Bernardi neglects neither his vines nor his cellars, despite his current position as president of the appellation. He submitted a very open red wine with leathery flavours. The previous vintage received the *coup de cœur*. The lengthy palate is gamey, making it the perfect companion to boar, duck or venison. It will be just as pleasant next summer. The **white Patrimonio 2000** was awarded a mention: despite a delicate nose the palate echoes the nobility of its variety.

☙ Jean-Laurent de Bernardi, 20253 Patrimonio, tel. 04.95.37.01.09, fax 04.95.32.07.66
Y by appt.

DOM. DE CATARELLI 1999★★ ■ 2 ha 9,000 €8-11

Laurent Le Stunff's *savoir-faire*, knowledge of varietals and of soils have all contributed to his producing this lightly brick-red wine from small plots that plunge towards the Mediterranean. The nose, a pleasant mineral, iodine character, is quite rare for the Patrimonio appellation. On the palate, the finesse is carried on the strength, as the tannins appear softened. This wine, which would go well with a fillet of beef, can be left to age for two or three years.

☙ EARL Dom. de Catarelli, marine de Farinole, 20253 Patrimonio, tel. 04.95.37.02.84, fax 04.95.37.18.72
Y ev. day except Sun. 9am-12 noon 3pm-6pm
☙ Laurent Le Stunff

DOM. GENTILE
Sélection Noble 1998★★ ■ 2 ha 8,000 €11-15

A great wine offered in small quantities, this comes from a selection of small plots and has been vinified to age, thanks to well-controlled cask maturation. The nobility of Nielluccio appears in the lightly red-brick/

Patrimonio

DOM. LECCIA 2000★★ ☐ 3 ha 16,000 ▯ ♦ €8-11

PATRIMONIO

2000

DOMAINE LECCIA

APPELLATION D'ORIGINE PATRIMONIO CONTRÔLÉE
G.A.E.C. LECCIA A POGGIO D'OLETTA
PRODUCE OF FRANCE

garnet-red colour and the red berry aromas underlined by a touch of undergrowth. There is strength on the palate but the soft tannins are accompanied by incomparable aromatic length. Nobility calls to nobility, so this wine should be served with a baked capon stuffed with *foie gras*. Another wine for keeping is the **white Patrimonio 2000**, which was awarded a mention. With its aromas of pineapple and citrus fruit, supple and lengthy, it shows the characteristic of Vermentino.

☛ Dom. Gentile, Olzo, 20217 Saint-Florent, tel. 04.95.37.01.54, fax 04.95.37.16.69 ▣
Ⴤ ev. day except Sun. 9am–12 noon 2.30pm–6.30pm; by appt. out of season

DOM. GIACOMETTI
Cru des Agriates 2000★
☐ 5.43 ha 20,000 ▯ ♦ €5-8

The Giacometti estate, situated in the Agriates desert, presented its wines to the *Guide* for the first time this year. The success is evident: the **white Patrimonio 2000** and the **red 99** were both awarded a mention, while this intensely-coloured, fruity (strawberry and blackcurrant) rosé was awarded one star. It could be drunk throughout a meal, with grilled fish or couscous. It is ready to drink now but equally could be left for a few months.

☛ Christian Giacometti, Casta, 20217 Saint-Florent, tel. 04.95.37.00.72, fax 04.95.37.19.49 ▣ Ⴤ by appt.

DOM. GIUDICELLI 2000★★
☐ 0.8 ha 3,600 ▯ ♦ €8-11

This 12-ha (30-acre) vineyard is carefully maintained. A brand new cellar and vinification methods combine tradition with modernity, allowing Michel Giudicelli to produce this bold, bright rosé, which is on course for a *coup de coeur*. It suggests springtime with its floral and cherry aromas. Thanks to its strong, fresh palate it can be cellared for a while.

☛ Muriel Giudicelli, Paese Novu, 20213 Penta di Casinca, tel. 04.95.36.45.10, fax 04.95.36.45.10 ▣ Ⴤ by appt.

DOM. LAZZARINI 2000★★
☐ 4 ha 10,000 ▯ ♦ €3-5

The three Lazzarini brothers are welcoming and attentive winemakers. Thanks to experience and careful selection, they produced a complex, strong Vermentino with long aromas of exotic fruit. This 2000 wine would go well with scallops. The **rosé Patrimonio 2000** and the **red 99**, both from Niellucciu, were awarded a star each. The former is a clear pink with raspberry and mango aromas; the latter a refined ruby with highly evolved tannins.

☛ GAEC de la Cave Lazzarini, rte de la Cathédrale, 20217 Saint-Florent, tel. 04.95.37.13.17, fax 04.95.37.13.17 ▣ Ⴤ by appt.

A new year and new *coup de coeur* in the white category for this Leccia estate. This wine, an explosion of exotic fruit aromas accompanied by honey and mint notes, is gentle, supple and long on the palate. It would go well with roast duck.

☛ Dom. Leccia, 20232 Poggio-d'Oletta, tel. 04.95.37.11.35, fax 04.95.37.17.03 ▣
Ⴤ by appt.

DOM. LECCIA 1999★★
■ 10 ha 40,000 ▯ ♦ €8-11

Niellucciu, a difficult variety, expresses itself perfectly in this wine, with notes of red berries and spices. The structure, underlined by softened tannins, is accompanied by a lengthy aromatic development. This is a really full wine that would go well with game or sauced meats. The **rosé Domaine Leccia 2000**, produced from perfectly mature Niellucciu, evokes fruit and flowers on the nose and develops a rich palate, which continually remains light. It is a very successful food wine that would go well with slightly mature Corsican cheese.

☛ Dom. Leccia, 20232 Poggio-d'Oletta, tel. 04.95.37.11.35, fax 04.95.37.17.03 ▣
Ⴤ by appt.

CLOS MARFISI 2000★
☐ 2.56 ha n.c. ▯ ♦ €8-11

The 11-ha (27-acre) Clos Marfisi estate is carefully cultivated. A part of it is situated on the road from Nonza, towards the Cap Corse. This pale yellow wine with bright green tints comes from these vines. The nose offers a carnival of aromas including distinctive citrus fruit (lemon and grapefruit) notes, both characteristic of Vermentino. The **red Patrimonio 99** is equally successful. Niellucciu expresses itself as roasted and spicy aromas. It is a wine that goes well with grilled meat.

☛ Toussaint Marfisi, Clos Marfisi, av. Jules-Yentre, 20253 Patrimonio, tel. 04.95.37.01.16, fax 04.95.37.06.37 ▣
Ⴤ ev. day except Sun. 9am–7pm; cl. 1 Dec.–31 Mar.

CLOS MONTEMAGNI
Cuvée Prestige du Menhir 2000★★
1 ha ■ 5,000 €8-11

This clear-coloured, green-tinted 2000 evokes citrus fruit on the nose, with a touch of pear drops, quite rare in a white wine. The full, sweet palate characterises this crisp, long Patrimonio. It goes well with a seafood salad and salmon, or could be a lively aperitif. The **red Patrimonio Prestige du Menhir 99** was awarded one star. Its timid nose shows promise and its palate is supple, fruity, aromatic and musky. It would go well with quail roasted with chestnuts.

☙ SCEA Montemagni, 20253 Patrimonio, tel. 04.95.37.14.46, fax 04.95.37.17.15 ☑
🍷 ev. day 8am–12 noon 2pm–6pm
☙ L. Montemagni

DOM. LOUIS MONTEMAGNI
1999★★
20 ha ■ 30,000 €5-8

This strong, balanced, deep garnet-red wine was a *coup de cœur* finalist. Its expressive nose mixes spices with red berries. These intense aromas appear again on the palate underlined by a finely cut structure. This wine would go well with beef. Keep a few bottles back as it will age well in the cellar. The very successful **rosé Patrimonio 2000** is a *vin gris* (light rosé). It explodes with floral aromas of rose and apple blossom. The softness of the palate makes this a charming wine, which drinks well on its own, as an aperitif or with salads in creamy dressings.

☙ SCEA Montemagni, 20253 Patrimonio, tel. 04.95.37.14.46, fax 04.95.37.17.15 ☑
🍷 ev. day 8am–12 noon 2pm–6pm

ORENGA DE GAFFORY 2000
13 ha ■ 65,000 €8-11

The tasters appreciated this rosé's clear colour and the structure, which was at the same time sweet and fresh. It would go well with barbecued marinated meat. The **red Patrimonio Cuvée des Gouverneurs 99** was also awarded a mention. Still characterised by its 11-month wood maturation, it has aromas of vanilla and chocolate. Its structure will support cellaring for two to three years.

☙ GFA Orenga de Gaffory, Morta-Majo, 20253 Patrimonio, tel. 04.95.37.45.00, fax 04.95.37.14.25,
e-mail orenga.de.gaffory@wanadoo.fr ☑
🍷 by appt.

DOM. PASTRICCIOLA 2000
1.45 ha ■ 4,000

This estate, situated on the superb road from Patrimonio to Saint-Florent, was taken over in 1989 by men who are passionate about the restructuring of this vineyard. They submitted this bright white wine, with very fine, delicate aromas. The Vermentino shows itself in the characteristic citrus fruit notes. The **rosé Patrimonio 2000** was also awarded a mention. Very light with rose aromas, it would go well with a salad of fresh vegetables.

☙ GAEC Pastricciola, rte de Saint-Florent, 20253 Patrimonio, tel. 04.95.37.18.31, fax 04.95.37.08.83 ☑ 🍷 ev. day 9am–7pm

DOM. ALISO ROSSI
Fleurs d'Amandiers 2000
1 ha ■ n.c. €11-15

Fruity and lemony aromas, characteristic of Vermentino, come from this bright wine. The round palate indicates that this wine would go well with a sauced fish dish. The **red Patrimonio 99** was also awarded a mention. Its woody character will soften if it is kept for two or three years.

☙ Dominique Rossi, Dom. Aliso Rossi, 20246 Santo-Pietro-di-Tenda, tel. 04.95.37.15.96, fax 04.95.37.18.05 ☑
🍷 by appt.

DOM. SAN QUILICO 2000★
1.65 ha ■ 8,000 €5-8

The 35-ha (86-acre) San Quilico estate, run by a tenant, is situated in the village of Poggio d'Oletta. Its white Patrimonio gives out a basket of citrus and exotic fruit, aromas that appear again on the voluminous, supple and lengthy palate. The **rosé 2000** is equally successful. Unusually, its aromatic range is on similar lines to that of the white wine. It will go well with some desserts. Finally, the **red Patrimonio 2000** was awarded a mention for its pleasant structure and refreshing cherry flavours.

☙ EARL Dom. San Quilico, Morta-Majo, 20253 Patrimonio, tel. 04.95.37.45.00, fax 04.95.37.14.25 ☑ 🍷 by appt.

CLOS TEDDI 2000★
3 ha ■ 8,700 €5-8

The young winemaker Marie-Brigitte Poli-Juillard is making her first entry to the *Guide*. In 1996, she took over the reins of the family property situated in the Agriates desert, in the Casta village, helped by her husband. She has been well rewarded for her second vinification by the expressive **white 2000**, awarded a mention by the Jury, and this balanced rosé. It has a refreshing attack delivering a great range of floral, exotic fruit aromas.

☙ Marie-Brigitte Poli-Juillard, Hameau de Casta, sentier des Agriates, 20217 Saint-Florent, tel. 04.95.37.24.07, fax 04.95.37.24.07 🍷 by appt.

THE SOUTH-WEST

Grouping appellations as far apart as Irouléguy, on the border with Spain, Bergerac, on the Garonne, and Gaillac, on the Tarn, the wine-growing region of the south-west encompasses what the Bordelais call 'wines from the high country' and the Adour vineyard. Until the railway was laid, the vineyards of the Garonne and the Dordogne were subject to Bordeaux wine regulations. With the benefit of its strong geographical location and royal support, the port of Lune was in a position to establish laws controlling the wines of Duras, Buzet, Fronton, Cahors, Gaillac and Bergerac. These regions had to wait for the whole of the Bordeaux harvest to be sold, primarily to the English and Dutch, before their wines could be shipped, and they were routinely employed as 'dosing' wines to bolster certain clarets. The wines from the foothills of the Pyrenees were not subject to Bordeaux wine law but had to undergo a hazardous journey on the Ardour to reach Bayonne. Understandably, their reputation hardly extended beyond their immediate vicinity.

Yet these vineyards, among the oldest in France, represent a living history of the vines of ancient times. In no other area do you find such a range of varieties. The Gascon taste in wine, as in all else, has always been marked by a determined individualism and a preference for the particular. The Manseng, Tannat, Negrette, Duras, Len-de-l'el (Loin de l'œil), Mauzac, Fer Servadou, Arrufiac or Baroque (the Côt), as well as the charmingly named Raffiat de Moncade, are varieties that emerge from the mists of viticultural history and give the local wines their authentic identity, honesty and unmatchable style. Far from despising the term 'peasant' wine, these appellations embrace it with pride and give it due nobility. Wine-growing is far from the only agricultural activity in the region, and the wines have always been sold alongside other local produce that they accompany perfectly and naturally, making the south-west a region where one can still enjoy the privilege of a traditional gastronomy.

Today, all the vineyards of the region are burgeoning, driven along by the wine co-operative movement and by committed owners. The great efforts being made to raise quality standards, through improved methods of cultivation, by researching cloned varieties better suited to local soils and conditions and by modernising vinification techniques, mean that the wines are gradually becoming the best value for money in French wine.

Cahors

The Cahors vineyard, dating from Roman times, is one of the oldest in France. John XXII, the Pope of Avignon, recruited wine-makers from Quercy, in Cahors, to cultivate Châteauneuf-du-Pape. François I planted a vine variety from Cadurce in Fontainebleau that the Orthodox Church adopted as the wine for Mass, while the court of the Tsars chose it as a ceremonial wine. Yet the Cahors vineyard has had to come back from the brink. It was totally wiped out by frosts in 1956 and fell back to only 1% of its previous surface area. It was re-established in the meanders of the Lot valley and planted with traditional varieties, mainly Auxerrois, also known as Côt or Malbec, which represents 70% of the plantation along with Tannat (under 2%) and Merlot (about 20%). The terroir of Cahors has now regained the place it deserves among the areas producing wines of quality – 4,215 ha (10,411 acres) produced 254,900 hl (6,730,944 gal) in 2000. In addition, brave attempts are being made to re-establish vineyards on the limestone plateaux that were cultivated in the past.

Cahors wines are powerful and robust, with a deep colour that has given rise to the English term 'black wine'. These are undoubtedly wines to be kept, yet Cahors wine can also be drunk young: at that stage it is plump and aromatic with good fruit, to be drunk slightly chilled with grilled meat, for example. After two or three years' bottle age it becomes firm and austere, becoming harmonious again after about the same period of time, when it produces aromas of undergrowth and spices. At this stage, its round, mouthfilling qualities make it an ideal wine to accompany charcoal-grilled truffles, cep mushrooms and game of the region. Though the character of the terroir and the varieties planted tend to produce wines capable of being kept, there is also a current trend to produce lighter wines that can be drunk more quickly.

CH. ARMANDIERE 1999★

3 ha   20,000   €5-8

Bernard Bouyssou left the wine-growers' co-operative in 1998 to produce his own wine. The business is called Armandière, in honour of his grandfather Armand, founder of the Côtes d'Olt de Parnac co-operative. The first vintage was commended by the Guide; the next vintage is clearly of the same pedigree. Bluish-purple in colour, it has a beautiful appearance. The nose is still closed but has a degree of complexity, with game and fruit notes that intensify the attack. The full body gives an impression of strength because of the power of the tannins, but at the same time these are gentle and well-integrated. It is a warming wine.

☛ Bernard Bouyssou, Port de l'Angle, 46140 Parnac, tel. 05.65.30.72.47, fax 05.65.36.02.23, e-mail armandiere@aol.com ☑ � ev. day 8am–8pm

CH. DU BREL 1999★

11.73 ha   91,700   €5-8

This wine has a dark colour with hints of deep purple, and a nice nose, lively, fruity and well-seasoned. The palate seems balanced between coolness and warmth, and is both rich and meaty with a fruity body. It is pleasantly balanced.

☛ GAEC du Noble Cep, Le Brel, 46800 Fargues, tel. 05.65.36.91.08, fax 05.65.36.95.23 ☑ ☐ by appt.

CH. DE CAIX 1999

18 ha   56,000   €8-11

This is the vineyard of the Prince Consort of Denmark. The estate has been producing wine since 1993. This 99, although possibly somewhat overshadowed by the remarkable previous vintage, has all the character required to feature here. It is black with violet reflections. Initially, the nose is meaty; then oak, spice and toast aromas appear, with a subtle dark-berry tone. The palate is supple and unctuous on the attack, and then the tannins make their presence felt. The aromas on the nose are echoed on the palate, along with red berries.

☛ SCEA Prince Henrik, Ch. de Caïx, 46140 Luzech, tel. 05.65.20.80.80, fax 05.65.20.80.81, e-mail vigouroux@g-vigouroux.fr ☑ ☐ by appt.

DOM. DE CAUSE

Notre-Dame-des-Champs Elevé en fût de chêne 1999★★

1 ha   6,600   €8-11

The Costes took over the family business in 1994, and the estate first appeared in the Guide with the 1996 vintage. This wine, already remarkable last year, was born of pure Auxerrois. A deep, strong garnet colour, it has a direct and intense nose; the first impression is of meaty and spicy aromas, followed by liquorice sweets and fruit brandy, and finally a nuance of earth with Quercy truffles. The well-rounded palate reveals a fruity, well-integrated body. The tannins are very evident, but of high quality, and the oak character is elegant. It is a true Cahors.

☛ Serge et Martine Costes, Cavagnac, 46700 Soturac, tel. 05.65.36.41.96, fax 05.65.36.41.95, e-mail montalieu@infonie.fr ☑ ☐ ev. day 9.30am–12 noon 2pm–7pm; Sun. by appt.

CH. DU CEDRE Le Cèdre 1999★★★

8 ha   38,000   €23-30

In 12 years of inclusion in the Guide, this estate has seven coups de cœur to its credit. Three of these were for this Cuvée Le Cèdre, matured for 20 months in barrel, and which gained the same distinction for the 96 and 98 vintages. The 99 is a magnificent, shimmering violet colour with magenta reflections. Intense and pure, the nose is copiously garnished with dark berries and strong spice enveloped in a rich oak with a hint of smoke. The palate reveals a full-bodied, well-structured, rich, complex wine, with a tight,

Le Cèdre 1999
CAHORS
APPELLATION CAHORS CONTRÔLÉE
MIS EN BOUTEILLE AU CHÂTEAU

smooth, well-integrated tannin structure. High-quality oak finally brings just the right amount of mellowness to give length to the flavours. A 'highly crafted' wine. As for the **Cuvée Le Prestige 99**, also matured in oak, this is awarded two stars.
🔑 Verhaeghe, Bru, 46700 Vire-sur-Lot, tel. 05.65.36.53.87, fax 05.65.24.64.36 ☑
🍷 ev. day except Sun. 9am–12 noon 2pm–6pm

CH. DE CENAC Eulalie 1998★★

■ 1 ha 5,000 €11–15

This is the first vintage of this wine, made from 100% Côt grapes. The very intense red colour, almost black, shows pretty purple reflections. The nose has a good deal of depth; it develops through red- and dark-berry aromas with violet and spices to finish on a wave of gentle oak. The beautifully full, rich body is well-formed on a solid structure, and offers plenty of fruit and oak flavours lasting into a warming finish. It is an extremely well-balanced wine.
🔑 GAEC de Circofoul-Pelvillain, Circofoul, 46140 Albas, tel. 05.65.20.13.13, fax 05.65.30.75.67 ☑ 🍷 by appt.

CH. DE CHAMBERT Orphée 1999★

■ 4 ha n.c. €15–23

What was a 'hideout' in the 15th century became a château in the 19th century. The vineyard has undergone a renaissance since 1973. Its Cuvée Orphée is characterised by a fairly strong red colour, with hints of violet. Fine and elegant, the nose evokes a *coulis* (sauce) of red berries on buttered toast. The palate is pleasant, round, warming, smooth and balanced, with a good concentration of fruit despite a strong influence of oak at the finish. This is a wine for immediate pleasure.
🔑 Joël Delgoulet, Les Hauts Coteaux, 46700 Floressas, tel. 05.65.31.95.75, fax 05.65.31.93.56 ☑ 🍷 ev. day 8.30am–12.30pm 1.30pm–6.30pm

DOM. CHEVALIERS D'HOMS 1999★★

■ 2.35 ha 12,000 €8–11

The former stronghold of the Knights of Quercy is the birthplace of this pure Auxerrois wine, the fruit of 22 months'

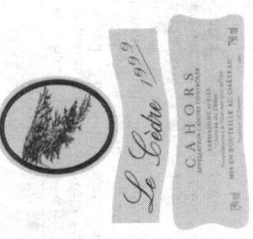

The South-West

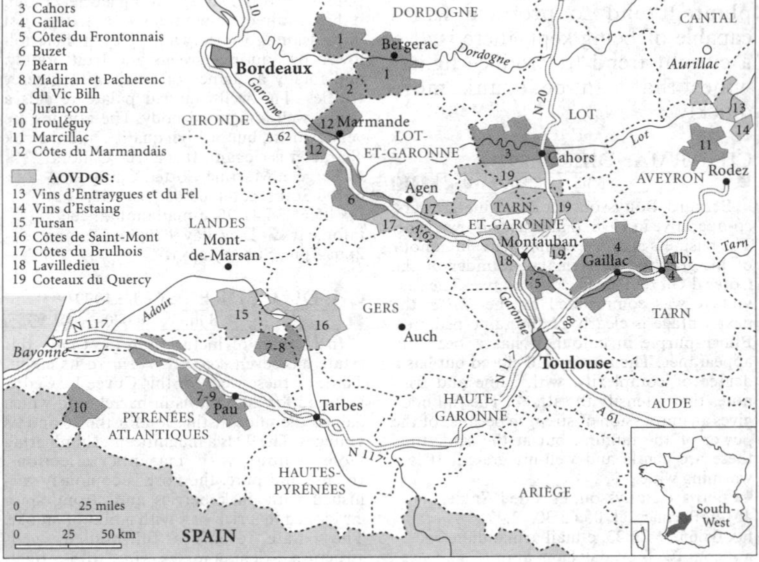
AOC:
1 Bergeracois
2 Côtes de Duras
3 Cahors
4 Gaillac
5 Côtes du Frontonnais
6 Buzet
7 Béarn
8 Madiran et Pacherenc du Vic Bilh
9 Jurançon
10 Irouléguy
11 Marcillac
12 Côtes du Marmandais
AOVDQS:
13 Vins d'Entraygues et du Fel
14 Vins d'Estaing
15 Tursan
16 Côtes de Saint-Mont
17 Côtes du Brulhois
18 Lavilledieu
19 Coteaux du Quercy
Périgueux
Brive-la-Gaillarde
CORRÈZE
CANTAL
Aurillac
DORDOGNE
Bergerac
Dordogne
Bordeaux
Garonne
GIRONDE
A 62
A 10
Marmande
LOT-ET-GARONNE
N 20
LOT
Lot
Cahors
AVEYRON
Rodez
Agen
TARN-ET-GARONNE
Montauban
Gaillac
Albi
Tarn
TARN
LANDES
Mont-de-Marsan
GERS
Auch
N 117
Adour
Bayonne
Pau
Tarbes
PYRÉNÉES ATLANTIQUES
HAUTES-PYRÉNÉES
HAUTE-GARONNE
Toulouse
N 88
A 61
AUDE
ARIÈGE
SPAIN
South-West
N
0 25 miles
0 25 50 km

vat-maturation, and a model of character, quality and authenticity. Its inky colour, with deep-purple reflections, is nothing short of superb. The bouquet rises in a crescendo, playing all the notes: floral, fruity, spicy, mineral and game, not to mention a touch of liquorice sweets. The attack is direct and the palate is concentrated. The body is consistent and rich and the structure robust, made up of sinewy tannins. The aromas are reiterated beautifully on the palate to give a finishing touch.

⤷ SCEA Dom. d'Homs, Les Homs, 46800 Saux, tel. 05.65.31.92.45, fax 05.65.31.96.21 ☑
🍷 ev. day 8.30am–7.30pm

CH. CROZE DE PYS 1999★

10.5 ha 80,000 €3-5

The Roche family acquired this château in 1966 and renovated the vineyard. They presented two wines, which obtained equal marks: the Cuvée Prestige 99, matured in barrel, and, in the lower price bracket, this classic and much more typical wine. The colour is a beautiful, deep red. The nose is immediate and delivers a profusion of red- and dark-berry scents against a background of spicy liquorice cachou Lajaunie. The fruit lasts in an extremely lively palate with a perfectly balanced structure and fine tannins.

⤷ SCEA des Dom. Roche, Ch. Croze de Pys, 46700 Vire-sur-Lot, tel. 05.65.21.30.13, fax 05.65.30.83.76, e-mail chateau-croze-de-pys@wanadoo.fr ☑
🍷 ev. day except Sat. Sun. 9am–12 noon 2pm–7pm
⤷ Jean Roche

CH. EUGENIE

Cuvée réservée de l'Aïeul 1999★★

8 ha 45,000 €8-11

In 1470, an *aïeul* (grandfather) was already cultivating this estate, as testified by the archives of Cahors. In the 18th century, the Russian czars used to buy wines from here. In 1985, the 82 vintage was described for the readers of the first *Guide*. So much for its noble origins. The 99 does credit to its past, with its deep colour, so dense it is opaque. Quite expressive on the nose, it delivers dark-berry fragrances in the form of crystallised fruit or brandy, carried by oak to a roasted coffee aroma. On the palate, it yields beautiful sensations, with rich concentration, powerful fruit and toasty aromas, with a good body and a nice structure, giving it a real presence.

⤷ Ch. Eugénie, 46140 Albas, tel. 05.65.30.73.51, fax 05.65.20.19.81 ☑
🍷 ev. day 8am–12 noon 1.30pm–7pm; Sun. and groups by appt.
⤷ Couture

DOM. DE FAGES

Cuvée VIe génération 1998★★

0.7 ha 3,200 €8-11

This wine, with its very dark-red colour with reflections of ink, is a pure Auxerrois. The nose, still a little closed and copiously oaky, allows complex aromas of very ripe red and dark berries, liquorice and spices to seep through. In the mouth the substance is beautiful, dense and rich, with an attractive fleshiness enveloping the tannins perfectly. The combination is already very integrated, pleasant and promising.

⤷ Jean Bel, Fages, 46140 Luzech, tel. 05.65.20.11.83, fax 05.65.20.12.99, e-mail belfages@aol.com ☑ 🍷 ev. day 9am–12.30pm 2pm–8pm; groups by appt.

DOM. DU GARINET

Elevé en fût de chêne 1998★★

1.6 ha 7,000 €8-11

Michael and Susan Spring settled at Le Boulvé in 1994. Their Cahors is made exclusively from Cot grapes. The domination of this local grape is shown in its sombre, dark-red colour. The intense, fairly complex nose mixes attractive, fruity notes with the butter and toasty aromas of the barrel. The palate is well-balanced, with flavoursome concentration and a pleasant freshness, good body and already-integrated tannins that accompany the aromas elegantly.

⤷ Michael et Susan Spring, Dom. du Garinet, 46800 Le Boulvé, tel. 05.65.31.96.43, fax 05.65.31.96.43, e-mail mike.spring@worldonline.fr ☑
🍷 ev. day 11am–6.30pm; Sun. 2pm–6.30pm

CH. DE GAUDOU Renaissance 1999★★

3.52 ha 21,000 €11-15

This vineyard dates from 1800. Even before the First World War, its wines used to win medals at the agricultural fair, and, ever since the first edition of the *Guide*, the estate has received two stars. Today, two of its wines are judged worthy of this grade: the Cuvée Château de Gaudou 99, matured in oak, and this Cuvée Renaissance. Both these wines are endowed with a dark, deep colour and an expressive, complex, elegant nose, a mixture of ripe fruits and spices. The difference between them is that more work goes into maturing this Cuvée Renaissance in barrel, giving it a fuller body, a more solid structure and a copious, long, oaky finish that will become more fully integrated.

⤷ Durou et Fils, Ch. de Gaudou, 46700 Vire-sur-Lot, tel. 05.65.36.52.93, fax 05.65.36.53.60 🍷 by appt.

Cahors

CH. DE HAUTE-SERRE
Cuvée Prestige Géron Dadine de Haute-Serre 1999★★

n.c. 19,000 ▥ €11-15

Georges Vigouroux produces wine from numerous châteaux within the appellation. The one at Haute-Serre offers this 99, remarkable for its potential, the result of careful maturation in oak. Its dark colour is a sign of good concentration. On the nose, the oak, which is very evident in vanilla, spice and toasted aromas, envelops a heart of stewed fruit. The direct attack precedes a robust body, standing out solidly against still-austere tannins. But the structure does not completely mask the fresh, aromatic richness. This wine needs to be kept so that it can mature. From the same château and worthy of note is the **Château de Mercuès Cuvée Prestige 99**, one star. Both are pure Auxerrois.

↳ GFA Georges Vigouroux,
Ch. de Haute-Serre, 46230 Cieurac,
tel. 05.65.20.80.80, fax 05.65.20.80.81,
e-mail vigouroux@g-vigouroux.fr ▼
Ⓨ by appt.

CH. LA CAMINADE
La Commandery 1999★★★

▪ 5.12 ha 28,000 ▥ ♦ €8-11

'First in its class,' this wine amazed the Jury. Not for the first time: it is one of the most frequent winners of stars and *coups de cœur* of the AOC (see the 87, 90 and 93). The colour is deep and black, so animated with reflections that it seems to be moving. It is captivating. You are gradually enveloped in the subtle fragrances of a bouquet overflowing with ripe fruit and elegant oak. The palate leaves a feeling of total fullness; the wine is powerful, full-bodied, round, well-balanced, full of floral, spicy vigour, lasting and very flavoursome.

↳ Resses et Fils, SCEA Ch. La Caminade,
46140 Parnac, tel. 05.65.30.73.05,
fax 05.65.20.17.04 ▼ Ⓨ by appt.

CH. LAGREZETTE
Le Pigeonnier 1998★★★

▪ 2.7 ha 6,600 ▥ €46-76

A real Renaissance château, complete with courtyard, is the setting for this wine. The producer is Michel Rolland, who provides long-macerated wines, long-matured in new barrels. This 99, a pure Auxerrois matured for 28 months in barrel, calls for a superlative

IMPERNAL *Vieilli en fût de chêne* 1999★

n.c. 90,000 ▥ €8-11

The Côtes d'Olt co-operative presents two very successful wines: the **Château Beauvillain-Monpezat 99**, matured in barrel like this Cuvée Impernal, which is an intense purple colour and a pure Auxerrois. The nose is intense too, with a milkiness containing suggestions of fruit and spice, then oak aromas with accents of cocoa beans. These aromas are reprised on the rather well-filled, dense palate, supported by a beautiful tannin structure. This is a well-made wine.

↳ Côtes d'Olt, 46140 Parnac,
tel. 05.65.30.71.86, fax 05.65.30.35.28 ▼
Ⓨ by appt.

Cahors

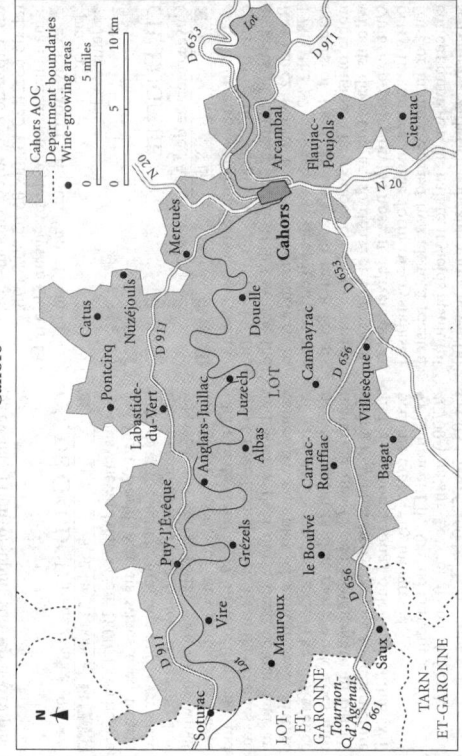

description. The colour is extremely dense and black, with purple reflections. The nose is rich, deep and concentrated, with a lot of oak, but well-balanced. The palate, very chewy, is impressive for its full-bodied structure, and is still dominated by oak but with well-balanced tannins; all the characteristics of a great wine, very ripe, of good extraction. This is an exceptional wine for laying down, and one which is worth waiting for. From the same producer, the **Cuvée Dame d'Honneur 98**, matured 18 months in barrel, is awarded two stars.

• Alain-Dominique Perrin,
SCEV Lagrezette, Dom. de Lagrezette,
46140 Caillac, tel. 05.65.20.07.42,
fax 05.65.20.06.95 Ⓥ Ⓣ ev. day 10am–7pm

CH. LAMARTINE
Cuvée particulière 1999★

10 ha 60,000 €8–11

Created in 1988, this Cuvée Particulière benefits from its producer's profound knowledge of the soil of the area. It was awarded a *coup de cœur* for the 96 vintage. The 99 has an opaque colour, impressive in its depth. The very expressive nose develops scents of flowers, spices and fresh fruits accompanied by a dash of menthol, all carefully oaked. The firm palate remains well-balanced and decidedly promising. Awarded the same marks, the **Cuvée Principale 99** has also been seen some oak.

• SCEA Ch. Lamartine, 46700 Soturac,
tel. 05.65.36.54.14, fax 05.65.24.65.31 Ⓥ
Ⓣ by appt.
• Alain Gayraud

DOM. DE L'ANTENET 1999★

4 ha 15,000 €5–8

This estate has converted to organic farming methods. The Cahors bursts with a deep, ruby-red colour. The nose is reserved, but with penetrating aromas of spice, tobacco and cocoa beans. The palate, more expressive with a more generous amount of fruit, is well-constructed and rests on fairly well-integrated tannins. It is a shy wine, but well-made.

• Bessières, Dom. de L'Antenet,
46700 Puy-l'Évêque, tel. 05.65.21.32.31 Ⓥ
Ⓣ ev. day 8am–9pm

CH. LA REYNE L'Excellence 1999★

0.5 ha 2,600

Johan Vidal, who took over in 1997, prides himself on having brought a fresh breath of modernisation to this traditional, family-run 20-ha (49.4-acre) estate, where five generations have devoted themselves to wine. Even before taking his place in the business, he talked of 'cutting grapes' (meaning green harvesting) to make a *Cuvée de Prestige*, much to the dismay of his grandfather. The result is an intense, dense red colour, almost black. It has an engaging nose evocative of dark berries, violets and spices on an oaky base, with a hint of vanilla. The palate is demonstrative, concentrated and very well-rounded, with body and pleasant. The tannins are well-rounded, good-quality tannins. This makes for a well-balanced combination.

• SCEA Ch. La Reyne, Teyssèdre-Vidal,
46700 Leygues, tel. 05.65.30.82.53,
fax 05.65.21.39.83 Ⓥ Ⓣ ev. day except Sun.
9am–12 noon 2pm–6pm
• Jean-Claude et Johan Vidal

CH. LES IFS 1999★★

8 ha 40,000 €5–8

This consistently good-quality estate offers two remarkable wines this year: the **Cuvée Prestige 99, Elevée en Fût** (barrel-matured), and this one, which comes close to being a *coup de cœur*. A deep colour with hints of violet, then a fine nose, fresh and intensely fruity, comprising red-berry, plum and dried apricot aromas, invites you to proceed with the tasting. The palate is delightfully balanced. It is full, very rich, warming, fruity, powerful and lasting resulting in a lovely harmony.

• Buri et Fils, EARL La Laurière,
46220 Pescadoires, tel. 05.65.22.44.53,
fax 05.65.30.68.52, e-mail chateau.les.ifs@
wanadoo.fr Ⓣ ev. day except Sun. 8am–
12 noon 2pm–7pm

CH. LATUC
Prestige Vieilli en fût de chêne 1998★

5 ha 20,000 €5–8

The colour of this wine is a beautiful cherry-red; the intense nose is enveloped in oak, vanilla and toasty aromas, still masking the fruit. The attack, which seems mellow, lasts on the palate without excessive extraction, and has a fullness which is modest but rather appealing. Oak characteristics are still in evidence. The finish lasts well, with a fine tannin structure.

• EARL Ch. Latuc, Laborie,
46700 Mauroux, tel. 05.65.36.58.63,
fax 05.65.24.61.57, e-mail duns@latuc.com
Ⓥ Ⓣ ev. day 11am–12.30pm 4.30pm–6.30pm
• Colin Duns

CH. LES GRAUZILS Héritage 1998★★

0.5 ha 2,500 €15–23

The 'estate', which has since become a 'château', has been included in the *Guide* ever since the first edition, when an 83 was judged remarkable. The 98 is no less worthy of note. Made purely from Cot grapes, it displays an intense, almost black colour, with purplish glints. The very open nose is a blend of generous oakiness, with a touch of vanilla and toast, and of violets, liquorice and dark berries. The very concentrated, rich, full palate is solid and robust, having dominant tannins, and the finish leaves an oaky taste. Powerful, solid and broad-shouldered, this wine will become more mellow.

• Philippe Pontié, Gamot, 46220 Prayssac,
tel. 05.65.30.62.44, fax 05.65.22.46.09 Ⓥ
Ⓣ ev. day except Sun. 9am–12 noon
2pm–7pm

CH. LES RIGALETS

La Quintessence 1999★

■ 2 ha 9,500 ▦ €15-23

Quintessence is the product of a meticulous Burgundian vinification method of punching down the cap of skins throughout the maceration period. The colour is so strong, it looks black. The powerful nose is first of all a profusion of aromas of oak and toast (or roasted coffee), then a touch of very ripe fruit, such as cherry and bilberry mixed with spices, comes into evidence. After a silky initial attack, a full palate follows, with flavours of fruits and spices in alcohol. This is supported by a robust structure made up of still-severe tannins. It is a serious wine, and one that needs to 'digest' the *barrique* (oak barrel). The **Cuvée Prestige 99**, also matured in oak for 15 months, was singled out by the Jury.

⦿ Bouloumié et Fils,
Les Cambous, 46220 Prayssac,
tel. 05.65.30.61.69, fax 05.65.30.60.46 ☑
☒ ev. day 8am–7pm; Sun. by appt.

METAIRIE GRANDE DU THERON 1999★

■ 12 ha 80,000 ▦ €5-8

This has a very attractive, intense garnet colour with black reflections. The characteristically fresh and fruity nose suggests a basket of fresh cherries, blackberries and bilberries. This impression lingers on the palate with a supple attack, an expressive and still-fruity body, loose structure, gentle texture and fine tannins. It has a clean, well-knit consistency, and is really pleasant.

⦿ Barat Sigaud, Métairie Grande du Théron, 46220 Prayssac, tel. 05.65.22.41.80, fax 05.65.30.67.32 ☑ ☒ by appt.

DOM. DU PEYRIE 1999★★

■ 3 ha 30,000 ▪ ▫ €5-8

This traditional Cahors has an attractive, cherry-red colour. The nose is vinous and well-matured, and has game aromas blended with scents of very ripe fruit, or jam. With a strong presence on the palate, this virile wine reveals the strength of its extraction, with a rich vigour reinforced by good vinosity and firm tannins.

⦿ EARL Dom. du Peyrie, 46700 Soturac, tel. 05.65.36.57.15, fax 05.65.36.57.15, e-mail domaine.peyrie@wanadoo.fr ☑
☒ ev. day except Sun. 8.30am–12 noon 1.30pm–6.30pm

CH. PINERAIE

Vieilli en fût de chêne 1998★

■ 30 ha 150,000 ▦ €5-8

The Burc family, established in Puy-l'Evêque since 1861, have been producing wine for five generations, and have been included in the *Guide* since its early days. Two of their Cahors are featured: **L'Authentique 98**, aged for 18 months in barrel, which is very oaky, and this one, matured in oak for a year, that the Jury preferred. It has a youthful appearance, cherry-coloured with deep-

purple reflections, but looking youthful does not mean it is delicate: the nose has a virile feel, gamey and spicy, with a toasty character. The round and powerful body is tannic and marked with vanilla oak on the finish. This wine is well-made, but still needs time to age.

⦿ Jean-Luc Burc, Ch. Pineraie, Leygues, 46700 Puy-l'Evêque, tel. 05.65.30.82.07, fax 05.65.21.39.65 ☑ ☒ by appt.

DOM. DU PRINCE

Elevé en fût de chêne 1998

■ 2 ha 12,000 ▦ €5-8

This estate derives its name from an early ancestor of Didier and Bruno Jouves, who supplied wine to the duke and was nicknamed the 'Prince' by the villagers when he came back. Their Cahors, made purely from Cot grapes, was likened by our tasters to 'strawberry *coulis* with deep purple reflections.' The well-expressed nose combines fruits and violet with a little touch of oak. The fresh, supple, fruity palate suggests youthfulness. Its modest extraction places this pleasant, well-balanced 98 in the category of easy-drinking wines.

⦿ J. Jouves et Fils, Cournou,
46140 Saint-Vincent-Rive-d'Olt,
tel. 05.65.20.14.09, fax 05.65.30.78.94 ☑
☒ ev. day except Sun. 8am–12 noon 2pm–7pm

CLOS RESSEGUIER 1999★

■ 13.54 ha 30,000 ▪ ▫ €3-5

The barrel store was built brick-by-brick by the great-grandfather when he founded the estate, using materials recovered from ruined buildings in the surrounding area. This Cahors does not match the image of virility associated with the wines of this appellation: it is more delicate. Is this a reason, as one taster suggested, for recommending it to the ladies? The aubergine colour is charming. The very distinctive nose combines red berries with a hint of more unusual fragrances of exotic fruits and ferns. The supple attack lingers onto a fruity palate, whose structure reveals a moderate extraction. It is a curious wine, but well-made.

⦿ EARL Clos Rességuier, 46140 Sauzet, tel. 05.65.36.90.03, fax 05.00.00.00.00 ☑
☒ ev. day except Sun. 9am–12 noon 3pm–7pm

CH. ROUQUETTE

Rêve d'Ange Vieilli en fût de chêne 1999★★

■ 1.89 ha 1,800 ▦ €11-15

This estate, founded in 1898, has only been bottling its wine since 1994, but has lost no time in presenting successful wines. Its **Cuvée d'Honneur 99**, matured in oak, was judged worthy of note; and this Rêve d'Ange was put forward as a *coup de coeur*. The colour is intense, dark garnet with reflections of deep purple. The subtle oak on the nose suggests scents of ripe fruit, violets and fresh pepper. The palate is supple, rich and fairly well-bodied, revealing an aromatic quality on a bed of fine tannins.

EARL Ch. Rouquette, Les Roques, 46140 Saint-Vincent-Rive-d'Olt, tel. 05.65.30.76.40, fax 05.65.30.52.99 ☑ ☷ by appt.

CH. SAINT-DIDIER-PARNAC
1999★★

■ | 37 ha | 260,000 | €5-8

The estate is run by Franck Rigal, now joined by his son David, an oenologist. This is a remarkable wine, christened in honour of Saint Didier, a bishop who once lived in these grounds. Its opaque colour indicates a powerful concentration. The nose, markedly oaky but of good extraction, moves into a second phase of dark berries and spices against a gamey background. Powerful, dense, muscular and demonstrative, the palate is reinforced by a rich oak flavour that will become more integrated in time. It has a style of its own. Another quite different wine from the same makers was awarded one star: the *Prieuré de Cénac 99*. Both were matured for 18 months in barrel.

SCEA Ch. Saint-Didier-Parnac, 46140 Parnac, tel. 05.65.30.70.10, fax 05.65.20.16.24 ☑ ☷ ev. day 9am–12 noon 2pm–6pm

DOM. DU THÉRON
Cuvée Prestige 1999★

■ | 5 ha | 25,000 | €11-15

This is an estate featured in the *Guide* since its first vintage, the 97, and a Cuvée Prestige is always included. The 99 is a deep-garnet colour. The nose, still a little closed, produces a few scents of fruit and spices with a touch of incense. The supple and pleasant attack lingers into a fresh, full palate with fine tannins. It is a wine of average structure, but very agreeable.

SCEA Dom. du Théron, Le Théron, 46220 Prayssac, tel. 05.65.30.64.51, fax 05.65.30.69.20, e-mail domaine.theron@libertysurf.fr ☑ ☷ by appt.
Vic Pauwels

CH. TREILLES 1998★

■ | 4 ha | 13,000 | €5-8

Established at the end of the 1970s, this vineyard offers a 98 made of the three Cahors grape varieties: Auxerrois (75%), Merlot (20%) and Tannat (5%). It is an enticing wine, beautifully radiant, with hints of violet. The rather fine nose is a blend of red berries and a delicate oaky scent with vanilla and butter. The straightforward palate reveals a good balance with sufficient structure and volume, and the finish is well-integrated.

SARL Dom. de Quattre, 46800 Bagat-en-Quercy, tel. 05.55.86.90.06, fax 05.00.00.00.00 ☷ by appt.

CLOS TRIGUEDINA
Balmont de Cahors 1999★

n.c. | n.c. | €5-8

After winning a *coup de coeur* last year, this time the Clos Triguedina offers a Cuvée Spéciale, matured 18 months in barrel. It has

a beautiful, cherry colour, with dark reflections. The nose is warming and concentrated, with fruit and liquorice notes. The powerful palate reveals a robust body, still young. The tannins, which really fill the palate, need to soften. The balance of oak and fruit will improve in two or three years, and will continue to improve for a long time.

Baldes et Fils, Clos Triguedina, 46700 Puy-l'Évêque, tel. 05.65.21.30.81, fax 05.65.21.39.28, e-mail triguedina@crdi.fr ☑ ☷ ev. day 9am–12 noon 2pm–6pm; groups by appt.
Jean-Luc Baldès

CH. VINCENS
Les Graves de Paul 1998★

■ | 0.6 ha | 3,000 | €11-15

This estate, established on the hillsides that dominate the Lot valley, presents a 98 of a matt appearance, with hints of blue. The rather intense nose delivers notes of overripe, or even stewed, fruits, enveloped in wreaths of smoke. A smooth attack is followed by a dense, supple, flavoursome palate, with a sweetness like jam. This all develops on a structure of quality tannins.

Michel Vincens, Ch. Vincens, 46140 Luzech, tel. 05.65.30.74.78, fax 05.65.30.15.83, e-mail chateau.vincens@aol.com ☑ ☷ ev. day except Sun. 9am–7.30pm

Coteaux du Quercy
AOVDQS

Located between Cahors and Gaillac, the Quercy wine region is of recent date although, as is common throughout the South-West region, vines were grown there in prehistoric times. In between, wine-making suffered several setbacks. In the first century AD, an edict by the Emperor Domitian banned the planting of new vines outside Italy: in the 15th century, the supremacy of Bordeaux spoiled the region's markets, and at the beginning of the 20th century the sheer volume of production in Languedoc-Roussillon had the same effect. Research aimed at improving quality was launched in 1965; hybrid stocks were replaced, and this raised the region to Vin de Pays status in 1976.

Coteaux du Quercy AOVDQS

Gradually, producers managed to sort out the best grape varieties and the best soils. These improvements in quality culminated in promotion to the AOVDQS category on 28 December 1999. The official territory extends across 33 communes in the departments of Lot and Tarn-et-Garonne.

Appellation wines are limited to reds and rosés. The red wines have a deep-purple colour and are full-bodied and hearty, with complex aromas deriving from their main variety which may account for up to 60% of a particular wine, the others being Tannat, Côt, Gamay Noir and Merlot, each up to a limit of 20%. The rosé wines are fruity and lively, and made from the same varieties.

Total production amounts to about 23,000 hl (607,200 gal) from vines covering nearly 500 ha (1,236 acres), and comes from about thirty producers, three of which are co-operatives.

DOM. D'ARIES

Cuvée du Marquis des Vignes 2000

| | 14.04 ha | 40,000 | ■ | ♦ | €3-5 |

Situated about 15 km (10 miles) from the Gorges de l'Aveyron, this estate covers 126 ha (311.22 acres) of vines. Intense and clear, the wine clearly expresses ripe dark berries on the nose, followed by body wrapped in tannins on the palate. The signs are that this wine is ready to drink now.

☛ GAEC Belon et Fils, Dom. d'Ariès, 82240 Puylaroque, tel. 05.63.64.92.52, fax 05.63.31.27.49 ✙ Ⓨ by appt.

DOM. DE CAUQUELLE 1999★

| | 10 ha | 20,000 | ■ | ♦ | €3-5 |

Grown in chalky clay soil, Cabernet Franc dominates the blend of this wine. Deep in colour, the wine produces fruit and spice aromas, characteristically accompanied by a little green pepper. It is harmonious and well-balanced on the palate, but needs to be kept a few years before it can express itself fully.

☛ GAEC de Cauquelle, Cauquelle, 46170 Flaugnac, tel. 05.65.21.95.29, fax 05.65.21.83.30 ✙ Ⓨ by appt.
☛ Sirejol

DOM. DE GUILLAU 2000

| | 2 ha | 6,600 | ■ | ♦ | €3-5 |

Prettily presented with its clear, light-red colour, with orange nuances, this wine has a clean, intense nose, suggesting notes of fruit, citrus, and pear drops. It lasts well on the palate and has body and balance. It is best drunk with paella, charcuterie or grilled meat dishes.

☛ Jean-Claude Lartigue, Saint-Julien, 82270 Montalzat, tel. 05.63.93.17.24, fax 05.63.93.28.06, e-mail jc.lartigue@worldonline.fr ✙ Ⓨ by appt.

JACQUES DE BRION 1999★★

| | 5.7 ha | 38,000 | ■ | ♦ | €3-5 |

This intense purplish-blue-coloured wine has pleasant aromas among which spices, green pepper, blackcurrant and fruit preserved in alcohol can be detected. The palate certainly reveals its tannic structure, but it still remains well-balanced and aromatic. Although already excellent now, this Coteaux du Quercy can be kept for several years.

☛ Cave de Lavilledieu-du-Temple, 82290 Lavilledieu-du-Temple, tel. 05.63.31.60.05, fax 05.63.31.69.11, e-mail cave.lavilledieu@wanadoo.fr ✙ Ⓨ by appt.

DOM. DE LAFAGE 1999★

| | 6 ha | 40,000 | ■ | ♦ | €5-8 |

This is a charming wine with an intense, radiant, purplish colour. Fruits and spices are blended in a range of aromas punctuated by subtly changing notes and a nuance of green pepper. On the palate, the same flavours revolve around still somewhat firm tannins that will soften with time. This 99 should go well with beef dishes.

☛ Bernard Bouyssou, 82270 Montpezat-de-Quercy, tel. 05.63.02.06.91, fax 05.63.02.04.55 ✙ by appt.

DOM. DE LA GARDE

Tradition 1999★★

| | 8 ha | 20,000 | ■ | ♦ | €5-8 |

This deep-purple 99 releases aromas of cooked fruit and spices, accompanied by vegetal, green pepper notes, attributable to the Cabernet Franc. The well-balanced palate has a long-lasting taste of red berries. The seductive power of this wine should remain intact for at least two years. The Jury also awarded one star to the **Cuvée 99 Elevée en Fût de Chêne** (matured in oak), a wine whose fruit dominates the oak.

☛ Jean-Jacques Bousquet, Le Mazut, 46090 Labastide-Marnhac, tel. 05.65.21.06.59, fax 05.65.21.06.59 ✙ Ⓨ by appt.

DOM. SAINT-JULIEN 1999★

| | 5 ha | 10,000 | ■ | ♦ | €3-5 |

Castelnau-Montratier is a charming village situated on a promontory. It offers the visitor the pleasure of discovering ancient houses with archways, a belfry, the remains of a château and, at its northern exit, three wind-mills. This is where the Saint-Julien estate produced this Coteaux du Quercy, an extremely radiant wine with a youthful, pur-plish colour. The nose, in which the Cabernet Franc grape is evident, has notes of fruit and vegetal notes that call to mind green pepper or freshly-mown grass, while the palate, full and fresh, is pleasantly evocative of cooked fruit.

♣ GAEC Saint-Julien.
Au Gros, 46170 Castelnau-Montratier,
tel. 05.65.21.95.86, fax 05.65.21.83.89 ▼
Y ev. day 9am-12 noon 2pm-7pm
♣ Vignals

Gaillac

Gaillac vineyard date back to the Roman occupation, as the Roman amphorae (terracotta wine vessels) made in Montels bear witness. In the 13th century, Raymond VII, Count of Toulouse, awarded his domains one of the first equivalents of an Appellation Contrôlée, while the Provençal poet, Auger Gaillard, sang the praises of sparkling Gaillac wine long before cham-pagne had been invented. The vine-yard (3,100 ha/7,657 acres) is divided into the Premières Côtes (or lower slopes), the Hauts Coteaux, the higher slopes on the right bank of the Tarn, and the plain, the area around Cunac and the district of Cordais. In total the appellation produces 138,700 hl (3,661,680 gal), of red wine and 45,850 hl (1,210,440 gal) of white wine.

The origins of the

The limestone slopes are ideal for the cultivation of traditional white vine varieties such as Mauzac, Len-de-l'En (Loin-de-l'œil), Ondenc, Sauvignon and Muscadelle. The gravel areas are reserved for red wine varieties such as Duras, Braucol or Fer Servadou, Syrah, Gamay, Bégrete, Cabernet and Merlot. The range of varieties gives rise to the wide palette of flavours to be found in Gaillac wines.

Among the whites are to be found fresh and aromatic

885

dry and sparkling wines, as well as the soft wines of the lower slopes, which are rich and supple. These wines draw their particular charac-ter from the Mauzac grape, histori-cally responsible for the reputation of Gaillac wines. Sparkling Gaillac can be made either by the tradi-tional local method of adding natural grape sugar, producing rather fruity wines, or by the Méthode Champenoise, which European legislation has decreed shall henceforth be known as Méthode Traditionelle. The easy-drinking rosés are produced by saignée method, which allows the colour of the red skins to bleed into the must, while the red wines, which are said to keep well, have striking character and bouquet.

MAS D'AUREL, Cuvée Alexandra 1999★

| 3 ha | 20,000 | ■ | ● | €5-8 |

While the **Gaillac Doux Cuvée Clara 2000** deserves to be singled out, the Jury considered this red wine even better. A brilliant cherry colour, it is evocative of blackcurrants, with a few notes of mint leaves and pepper. The slender, fruity palate demonstrates a good balance. The tannins make their presence felt in a very aromatic finish. This is a very charac-teristic Gaillac.

♣ Mas d'Aurel, 81170 Donnazac,
tel. 05.63.56.06.39, fax 05.63.56.09.21 ▼
Y ev. day except Sun. 8am-12 noon
2pm-7pm
♣ Albert Ribot

DOM. DE BALAGES 2000

| 1 ha | 5,000 | ■ | ● | €5-8 |

The Balagès estate is situated within the village of Lagrave, renowned for its château built on an outcrop over the Tarn. Syrah and Duras grapes are blended in this strawberry-coloured wine. The vinous nose is evocative of red berries, while on the palate, a fresh, mineral impression appears with the attack. A noticeable alcohol presence supports the fruit on the finish.

♣ Claude Candria, Dom. de Balagès,
81150 Lagrave, tel. 05.63.41.74.48,
fax 05.63.81.52.12 ▼
Y ev. day 9am-12 noon 2pm-7pm

DOM. BARREAU

□ Doux Caprice d'Automne 1999★★★

| 5 ha | 23,400 | ■ | €8-11 |

This wine is a good example of the new-generation Gaillacs, combining the tradi-tional character with the modern. A very brilliant gold colour, it leaves abundant tears on the surface of the glass before delivering its aromas of roasted raisins, honey and crystallised apricot. On the palate, the wine has good concentration, leaving an impression of richness and complexity. The finish is just as impressive for its length and freshness.

➤ Jean-Claude Barreau, Boissel, 81600 Gaillac, tel. 05.63.57.57.51, fax 05.63.57.66.37 ☑ 🍷 by appt.

BRUMES Doux 1999★★ €11-15

☐ 0.42 ha 800

The 25-ha (61.75-acre) Salesses estate offers 'an Occitan reverie in the thick autumn cloud.' Gold in colour, this wine shines brightly in the glass, inviting the discovery of a fine, complex nose, with scents of quince, crystallised pineapple, honey and soft spices. On the rich, full, generously aromatic palate, the flavours balance perfectly. The wine has good length, supported well by the alcohol. This already well-balanced Gaillac may be left to mature further.

➤ Dom. Les Salesses, Sainte-Cécile-d'Avès, 81600 Gaillac, tel. 05.63.57.26.89, fax 05.63.57.26.89 ☑
🍷 ev. day 8am–12 noon 2pm–7pm
➤ Litre

DOM. DES CAILLOUTIS 1999★ €3-5

■ 4 ha 21,000

Bernard Fabre, an oenologist, took over this vineyard in 1998. He presents this light, clear wine, with a clean nose well-marked by blackcurrant and blackberry fruits. The attack is subtle and the palate is well-balanced, fruity and very drinkable, ending

with a nice finish. This is a simple, fresh wine, ready to drink now.

➤ Dom. des Cailloutis, 81140 Andillac, tel. 05.63.33.97.63, fax 05.63.33.97.63, e-mail bf@rouge-blanc.com ☑ 🍷 by appt.
➤ Bernard Fabre

DOM. DE CAUSSE MARINES
Mysterre 1993★ €15-23

☐ 0.25 ha 654

At the Causse Marines estate, the names of the wines are chosen with talent. The Gaillac Doux Délires d'Automne 99 is every bit as much of a success as this white wine, but the latter is even more original, with its style similar to that of a Vin Jaune. Amber-coloured with hints of orange, it has a powerful 'oxidative' nose like fresh walnuts. Other aromas become evident, such as marc and plum brandy, and spices such as vanilla, cinnamon and saffron. The palate is surprising in that it develops, like a brandy, into an alcohol and acid taste with a hint of bitterness.

➤ Patrice Lescarret, Dom. de Causse Marines, 81140 Vieux, tel. 05.63.33.98.30, fax 05.63.33.96.23, e-mail causse-marines@infonie.fr ☑ 🍷 by appt.

DOM. D'ESCAUSSES
La Vigne Mythique 1999★★ €8-11

■ 1 ha 5,000

The Jury was unanimous in declaring this red Gaillac, made of pure Fer Servadou, a coup de cœur. With its deep red cherry colour, it reveals an intense, elegant nose with rich, spicy oak and red-berry aromas. The palate

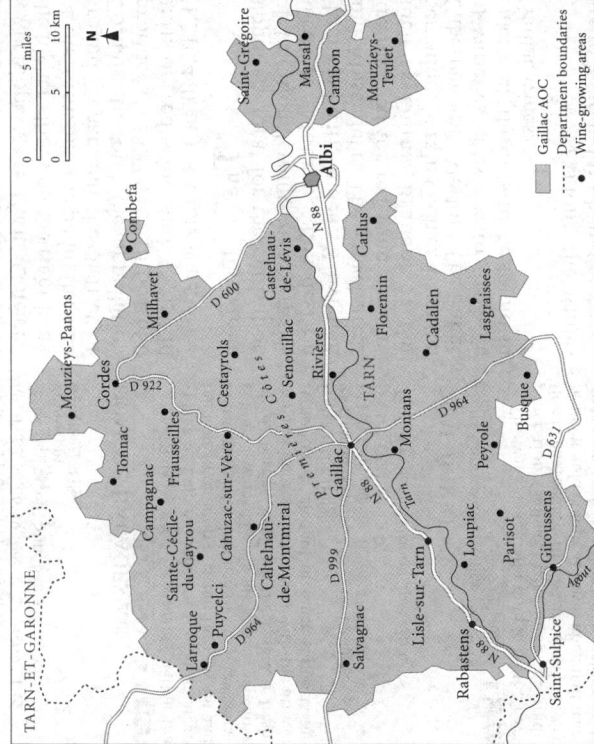

Gaillac

Gaillac AOC
···· Department boundaries
• Wine-growing areas

...gives an impression of concentration and a full body, with a well-integrated, solid structure. The oak permeates the whole blend and produces a long finish. The characteristic style is perfectly preserved. Awarded one star, the **Gaillac Doux Vendanges Dorées 99** is a characterful wine.

↳ EARL Denis Balaran, Dom. d'Escausses, 81150 Sainte-Croix,
tel. 05.63.56.80.52, fax 05.63.56.87.62,
e-mail jean-marc.balaran@wanadoo.fr ▼
☎ ev. day 9am–7pm; Sun. and groups by appt.

FASCINATION Sec 2000★

■ ■ 30,000 ■ €5-8

With its pale, crystalline colour, this wine has an aromatic nose, open and persistent. It produces nice aromas of boxwood, white flowers and lemon. The well-balanced, round, fruity palate is endowed with a pleasant freshness that blends in with the aromas perceived on the nose. This is a well-made white Gaillac.

↳ Cave de Técou, Técou, 81600 Gaillac,
tel. 05.63.33.00.80, fax 05.63.33.06.69,
e-mail passion@cavedetecou.fr ▼
☎ ev. day 9am–7pm; Sun. and groups by appt.

DOM. DE GINESTE

Grande Cuvée 1999★

n.c. ■ 1 ha ■ 4,000 ■ €11-15

This already famous estate is under the management of new owners. They have not only a **Gaillac Doux Cuvée Moine Albert 99**, which the Jury judged a great success, but also this wine, a dark red with purplish reflections. The intense nose, still closed, reveals oak with toast and menthol aromas and then develops into dark berries and spices. The tannins are very evident in the rich, concentrated palate, but they are well-balanced; although the oak is still noticeable, it contributes to the firm structure of the wine. This Gaillac will mellow if kept for a few years.

↳ EARL Dom. de Gineste, 81600 Técou,
tel. 05.63.33.03.18, fax 05.63.81.52.65,
e-mail domainedegineste@free.fr
☎ ev. day 10am–7pm
↳ Mangeais, Delmotte

MAS DE GROUZE

Cuvée des Graves 1999★

■ 5 ha ■ 25,000 ■ €3-5

A fairly deep, ruby colour, this wine is beginning to develop on the nose: it evokes lightly-cooked red berries and spices (pepper). After a supple initial attack, the palate is round and structured, supported by a strong, aromatic character. It is a typical Gaillac, which does not need to be aged.

↳ Mas de Grouze, 81800 Rabastens,
tel. 05.63.33.80.70, fax 05.63.33.79.48 ▼
☎ ev. day 8am–7pm; Sun. 10am–12.30pm
↳ Alquier

DOM. DE LABARTHE Doux Les Grains d'Or Elevé en fût de chêne 1999★★

■ 3 ha ■ 4,000 ■ €5-11

These 48 ha (118.56 acres) of vines have produced beautiful results. The **Gaillac Cuvée Guillaume red 99** and the dry white **Premières Côtes 2000** are each awarded one star. Honourable mention is given to this fresh, sweet white wine, made from 100% Len de l'el grapes. Golden-yellow, it leaves big tears on the surface of the glass. The intense nose begins with a strong oak aroma, with fragrances of balsamic essence. This is followed by fresh sensations of exotic fruits. With a powerful attack, the palate develops vivaciously into a wide range of flavours, still dominated by the oak. The finish gives an impression of warmth and sweetness. (50 cl bottles.)

↳ Jean-Paul Albert, Dom. de Labarthe, 81150 Castanet, tel. 05.63.56.80.14,
fax 05.63.56.84.81, e-mail jean.albert@wanadoo.fr ▼
☎ by appt.

CH. LABASTIDE 1999★

■ 65 ha ■ 250,000 ■ €5-8

This red Gaillac shows good potential, already perceptible in its deep colour with violet reflections. The rather intense nose evokes dark-berry preserves, with a touch of green pepper. With a straightforward attack, the palate is full, rich and chewy. The tannin structure becomes even more noticeable on the finish.

↳ Cave de Labastide de Lévis, 81150 Marssac-sur-Tarn, tel. 05.63.53.73.73,
fax 05.63.73.73.74 ☎ ev. day except Sun. 8am–12 noon 2pm–6pm

DOM. DE LA CHANADE

Elevé en fût de chêne 1999★

■ 1.5 ha ■ 8,000 ■ €5-8

This ancient estate is being revived by the efforts of an enthusiastic grandson, assisted by a young oenologist who is already very experienced. The vineyard covers 20 ha (49.4 acres). This bright, intensely-coloured wine initially reveals roasted aromas of toast and coffee, and then, when shaken, dark berries and spices. The generous, rich, fairly aromatic body is filled with velvety tannins, leading to a peppery finish.

↳ SCEA Dom. de La Chanade, La Chanade, 81170 Souel,
tel. 05.63.56.31.10, fax 05.63.56.31.10 ▼
☎ ev. day 9am–12 noon 2pm–7pm

DOM. LA CROIX DES MARCHANDS Fraîcheur perlée 2000★

■ 5 ha ■ 30,000 ■ €5-8

Pale yellow with nuances of more lively colours, this is a joyful *perlé* (slightly sparkling) wine, delicately floral and fruity, with a...

touch of pepper to give it a lift. The clean, pleasantly aromatic palate is well-balanced between roundness and freshness.

☛ J.-M. et M.-J. Bezios, av. des Potiers, 81600 Montans, tel. 05.63.57.19.71, fax 05.63.57.48.56, e-mail croixdesmarchands@wanadoo.fr Y ev. day except Sun. 9am–12 noon 1.30pm–7pm; groups by appt.

CH. LARROZE Sec 2000★★
☐ 5 ha 20,000 €5-8

The attractiveness of this Gaillac lies in its youth and vivacity. Clear, with hints of green, it releases delicate fragrances, blending a floral character with a little honey and a very clean lemon aroma. A fresh attack is followed by a good balance of flavours. The body and the nose remain in harmony right up to the fresh fruit finish.

☛ Ch. Larroze, La Colombarié, 81140 Cahuzac-sur-Vère, tel. 05.63.33.92.62, fax 05.63.33.92.49 V Y ev. day except Sun. 9am–12 noon 2pm–6pm

CH. LASTOURS
Cuvée spéciale Elevé en fût de chêne 1999★★ 4 ha 17,000 €8-11

Hubert and Pierric de Faramond work an estate of 40 ha (98.8 acres). While their **dry white Gaillac Les Graviers 2000** is a great success, this solid red wine, with its hints of purple, is attractive for its characterful nose, redolent of red-berry jam and spices. The full, round body possesses enough freshness to balance the spicy aromas and the final note of leather. The well-integrated tannins round off this charming, well-balanced blend.

☛ Hubert et Pierric de Faramond, Ch. Lastours, 81310 Lisle-sur-Tarn, tel. 05.63.57.07.09, fax 05.63.41.01.95 V Y ev. day except Sun. 8am–12 noon 1.30pm–6pm

LE PAYSSEL 2000
n.c. 5,000 €3-5

This is a pale rosé wine with hints of grey that pleases the senses with its floral, light menthol aromas. After a lively attack, the clean palate keeps fresh with its little hint of enlivening sparkle and aromas of minerals and fruit. This is a light and well-balanced wine.

☛ EARL Louis Brun et Fils, Vignoble Le Payssel, 81170 Frausseilles, tel. 05.63.56.00.47, fax 05.63.56.09.16, e-mail lepayssel@free.fr V Y ev. day 9am–12 noon 2pm–6pm; Sat. Sun. 4pm–6pm

DOM. DE LONG PECH 1999★★
1.5 ha 5,600 €5-8

Made from the Braucol, Cabernet Franc and Duras grapes, this wine is enticing because of its rich extraction and its potential. The intense colour, a deep, bright ruby, invites the discovery of a characterful nose: a basket of really ripe fruits and berries, cherry brandy and spices. The palate builds on this concentration with its rich, ripe texture. The

structure is full, composed of well-integrated tannins. The superb finish is the icing on the cake. Also worthy of note, the **Gaillac red Cuvée Jean-Gabriel 98**, matured in barrel, was judged very successful.

☛ GAEC Christian Bastide Père et Fils, Dom. de Long-Pech, Lapeyrière, 81310 Lisle-sur-Tarn, tel. 05.63.33.37.22, fax 05.63.40.42.06, e-mail dom.longpech@wanadoo.fr V Y ev. day except Sun. 9am–12.30pm 1.30pm–6.30pm

MANOIR DE L'EMMEILLE
Tradition 1999 3 ha 30,000 €5-8

Two wines from this estate deserve to be singled out, the **Gaillac Sec 2000** and this violet-red wine. The fruity nose is redolent of strawberry and raspberry, underlined by spices. After a supple attack, the palate becomes more lively, with a satisfactory balance. The finish is a little austere, but it is still a pleasant combination.

☛ EARL Manoir l'Emmeillé, 81140 Campagnac, tel. 05.63.33.12.80, fax 05.63.33.20.11 V Y ev. day except Sun. 9am–12 noon 2pm–7pm

☛ Charles Poussou

CH. MARESQUE
Cuvée Thomas 1999★★ 2 ha 11,000 €8-11

Béatrice Méhaye, a native of Pauillac, and Lucas Schutte, formerly a wine-grower in Burgundy, established this estate in March 1999, on an area of 12 ha (29.64 acres). Their deep, ruby Gaillac offers a concentrated nose with fragrances of dark berries, spices, liquorice and green pepper. The powerful, richly-structured palate evolves into elegant tannins, and the aromatic character develops into a lively finish. This wine has good potential.

☛ Béatrice Méhaye et Lucas Schutte, Maresque, 81600 Gaillac, tel. 05.63.57.53.32, fax 05.63.57.51.24, e-mail lucas.schutte@wanadoo.fr V Y by appt.

CH. MIRAMOND
Cuvée Antoine Elevé en fût de chêne 1999★★ 1.5 ha 3,600 €5-8

Château Miramond has put up a good performance, with its **Gaillac red 99**, matured in barrel, which is awarded one star; and this barrel-matured wine, made from 60% Syrah and 40% Fer Servadou grapes. An appreciation starts with the wine's garnet colour, with

its hints of darker hues. The fine nose releases elegant oak aromas, with fruit and spices, and a pleasant sensation of liquorice and menthol. Still aromatic, the fresh palate develops into a perfect balance.

♠ Pascal Trouche, Mas de Graves, Saint-Laurent, 81600 Gaillac, tel. 05.63.57.14.86, fax 05.63.57.63.44, e-mail ptrouche@online.fr ☑ Ⓨ ev. day except Sun. 10am–12 noon 4pm–7pm

CH. MONTELS Doux Les Trois Chênes
Elevé en fût de chêne 1999★★★

□ | 4 ha 4,200 €8-11

The Len de l'el (85%) and Muscadelle (15%) grapes that make up this wine are harvested into boxes after five or six passes through the vineyards. The result is a concentrated wine, like crafted gold and copper. The nose is full of character, reminiscent of baked apple topped with honey, sprinkled with a little star anise. The full, rich body confirms the range of aromas, adding further flavours of linden flowers and exotic fruits. It gives an impression of smoothness up to the finish. The **Gaillac red Cuvée des Trois Chênes 98** is awarded one star.

♠ Bruno Montels, Burgal, 81170 Souel, tel. 05.63.56.01.28, fax 05.63.56.15.46 ☑ Ⓨ ev. day 10am–12.30pm 2pm–7pm; Sun. by appt.

DOM. DU MOULIN
Vieilles vignes Elevé en fût 1999★

8 ha 32,000 €5-8

The deep, dark-red colour is indicative of this wine's quality. The nose is still only slightly open, vinous and spicy, but the round palate is full of richness and structure. There is a perception of fullness and fleshiness; more complex aromas will be revealed after the wine has been kept for a while. **The dry white Gaillac Vieilles Vignes Elevé en Fût** (matured in barrel) was also singled out.

♠ GAEC Hirissou, chem. de Bastié, 81600 Gaillac, tel. 05.63.57.20.52, fax 05.63.57.66.67, e-mail domainedumoulin@libertysurf.fr ☑ Ⓨ ev. day except Sun. 9.30am–12 noon 2pm–7pm

CH. PALVIE 1999★

1 ha 8,000 €8-11

Syrah and Braucol grapes have been blended to produce two very successful red Gaillacs: the **Château Palvié 99 Elevé en Fût** (matured in barrel) and this wine, matured in vat. Almost black, with a hint of violet, it reveals an intense nose, evocative of jam. The concentration and the overripe fruit aromas become stronger on the palate, giving a rich, powerful taste and strong tannins lasting up to the finish.

♠ Jérôme Bézios, 81140 Cahuzac-sur-Vère, tel. 05.63.57.19.71, fax 05.63.57.48.56 ☑

DOM. DES PARISES
Doux Loin de l'il 1999★

1.5 ha 3,500 €5-8

Jean Arnaud's estate has a new look: the 21-ha (51.87-acre) vineyard has been completely renovated, and the cellars are in the process of being refurbished. The results are promising, as seen in this radiant, amber-yellow Gaillac, with its generous legs. Its intense nose has aromas of dried or overripe fruit, gingerbread and quince jelly. The palate seems dense and rich, essentially carried by alcohol. The aromas detected on the nose are reiterated on the palate at the end, dominated by fruits steeped in brandy.

♠ SCEV Arnaud, rue de la Mairie, 81150 Lagrave, tel. 05.63.41.78.63, fax 05.63.41.78.63 Ⓨ by appt.
♠ Jean Arnaud

PERLE D'AMOUR 2000★

n.c. 60,000 €5-8

The Cave de Labastide de Lévis was the first co-operative established in the Tarn, in 1949. This wine is a clear, pale-yellow Gaillac, sprinkled with pearls. The intense nose produces not only fruit aromas (pear, apricot and lychee) but also flowers, with a little touch of butter. On the palate, the wine is light, supple and well-rounded: a fragrant bubble fading to a slight bitterness.

♠ Cave de Labastide de Lévis, 81150 Marssac-sur-Tarn, tel. 05.63.53.73.73, fax 05.63.53.73.74 ☑ Ⓨ ev. day except Sun. 8am–12 noon 2pm–6pm

DOM. DE PIALENTOU Les Gentilles
Pierres Elevé en fût de chêne 1999★

6.07 ha 6,000 €8-11

This 12-ha (29.64-acre) estate was taken over in 1998. This deep-violet wine gives an impression of freshness, with aromas of cherry and strawberry against a balsamic background. A smooth initial impression gives way to a light, well-rounded body developing with a structure of fine, flavoursome tannins. The finish is enveloped in sweet oak flavours.

♠ SCEA du Pialentou, Dom. de Pialentou, 81600 Brens, tel. 05.63.57.17.99, fax 05.63.57.20.51, e-mail domaine.pialentou@wanadoo.fr ☑ Ⓨ ev. day except Sun. 9am–12 noon 2pm–7pm
♠ J. et K. Gervais

MAS PIGNOU
Doux Les Hauts de Laborie 2000★

5 ha 27,000 €5-8

Rich in green hues, this wine offers a fairly intense, fresh nose with a hint of menthol. The aromas are both floral and fruity (passion-fruit). The palate pleases the senses with its balance and suppleness; the floral qualities of the wine are pleasantly persistent.

➤ Jacques et Bernard Auque, Dom. du Mas Pignou, 81600 Gaillac, tel. 05.63.33.18.52, fax 05.63.33.11.58, e-mail maspignou@free.fr ✉ ☱ ev. day 9am–12 noon 2pm–7pm; Sun. by appt.

VIN D'AUTAN DE ROBERT PLAGEOLES ET FILS Doux 1999★

☐ 3 ha 2,000 ■ ♦ €30-38

This wine of noble origin owes its character to the Ondenc grape, concentrated by *passerillage* (allowing the grapes to shrivel and dry on the vine) and controlled development of noble rot. The golden-yellow colour is followed by a powerful nose evoking gingerbread, quince jelly and dried fruits. Full and concentrated, the flavours on the palate develop generously and flow like honey.

➤ EARL Robert Plageoles et Fils, Dom. des Très-Cantous, 81140 Cahuzac-sur-Vère, tel. 05.63.33.90.40, fax 05.63.33.95.64 ☱ ev. day 8am–12 noon 2pm–7pm; Sun. by appt.

RAIMBAULT DES VIGNES 1999★

■ 30 ha 200,000 ■ ♦ €3-5

This cherry-red wine is an intense blend of red berries, spices, violet and mint in a fresh bouquet. The palate has a supple attack and is lightly structured, well-balanced and fresh. It is a delicious combination.

➤ Cave de Rabastens, 33, rte d'Albi, 81800 Rabastens, tel. 05.63.33.73.80, fax 05.63.33.85.82, e-mail rabastens@vins-du-sud-ouest.com ✉ ☱ ev. day 9am–12.30pm 2pm–7pm

DOM. RENE RIEUX Doux Concerto Elevé en fût de chêne 1999★★★

☐ 1.25 ha 2,000 ☷ €11-15

This 18.5-ha (45.7-acre) estate belongs to the Boissel Vocational Rehabilitation Centre. Three of its wines are featured, including the **Gaillac Mousseux Demi-Sec Symphonie 98**, which gets two stars, and the **Gaillac red Concerto 99 Elevé en Fût de Chêne** (matured in barrel), which was singled out. The Jury was impressed by this sweet, copper-gold wine. The nose explodes with white flowers, honey, baked apple and crystallised orange, while the concentrated palate is a balance between sweetness and great freshness, with a lasting concentration of flavours.

➤ Dom. René Rieux, 1495, rte de Cordes, 81600 Gaillac, tel. 05.63.57.29.29, fax 05.63.57.51.71, e-mail domaine.rene.rieux@wanadoo.fr ✉ ☱ ev. day except Sun. 9am–12 noon 1.30pm–7.30pm
➤ CAT Boissel

CH. RIVAT 1999★

■ 2 ha 5,000 ■ ♦ €5-8

This well-balanced, characteristic wine has a nice, clean, ruby colour. The nose has aromas of morello cherries with fruit brandy and pepper, and a floral touch. The well-filled, well-rounded body is balanced by alcohol and a soft tannic structure.

➤ Ch. Rivat, Rivat, 81600 Senouillac, tel. 06.09.88.08.15, fax 06.63.81.29.20 ✉
➤ F. Santandrea

DOM. ROTIER Doux Renaissance 1999★★★

☐ 3.6 ha 17,200 ☷ €11-15

This sweet Gaillac does real credit to the Len de l'el, a grape variety typically used in Gaillac wines. With its copper-gold colour, it produces a subtle bouquet with fragrances of orange and crystallised pineapple, *tarte Tatin* (an apple dessert), white flowers and honey. Intense on the attack, the palate reveals a wide range of flavours in a good balance between freshness, richness and alcohol. The finish is long. From the same producer, the **Gaillac red Renaissance 99** was singled out.

➤ Dom. Rotier, Petit Nareye, 81600 Cadalen, tel. 05.63.41.75.14, fax 05.63.41.54.56, e-mail rotier@terre-net.fr ✉ ☱ ev. day except Sun. 8am–12 noon 2pm–7pm
➤ Alain Rotier et Francis Marre

CH. DE SALETTES Doux 1999★★

☐ 2 ha 8,000 ☷ €5-8

Besides good wines, the Château de Salettes offers four-star accommodation and a gastronomical restaurant. Their sweet Gaillac is made from the Muscadelle grape. Gold-coloured and with noticeable legs, it immediately appears fine and complex with its floral characteristics of linden flowers and rose, with a little vanilla. The palate, lively at the start, retains its freshness while at the same time revealing a high degree of concentration and power. This wine stands out for its aromatic complexity and its happy marriage of fruit and oak.

➤ SCEV Ch. de Salettes, 81140 Cahuzac-sur-Vère, tel. 05.63.33.60.60, fax 05.63.33.60.61, e-mail chateau-de-salettes@wanadoo.fr ✉
➤ Roger Le Net

BARON THOMIERES Sec 2000★

☐ n.c. 8,000 ■ ♦ €3-5

Pale yellow with green tones, this intense wine at first seems fresh with its accents of lemon and menthol, then the aromas change to stewed fruit and honey. After a clean attack, its supple, smooth palate reveals a fruity character.

● Laurent Thomières, La Raffinie, 81150 Castelnau-de-Lévis, tel. 05.63.60.39.03, fax 05.63.53.11.99 ▼ ev. day except Fri. 3pm–6.30pm

■ DOM. DE VAYSSETTE 1999★

| 2 ha | 14,600 | €5-8 | V |

The Vayssette estate covers 23 ha (56.81 acres) of vines. Its red Gaillac is created from a blend of Syrah, Duras, Braucol and Cabernet Franc grapes. Peony-coloured, with hints of violet, it produces a subtle range of fragrances, evocative of black-currants, spices and liquorice. After a subtle attack, the palate develops a good balance between vivaciousness and alcohol. Its has a four-square structure, with integrated tannins. Also worthy of note is the **Gaillac Doux 99**, a very successful blend of Mauzac and Muscadelle grapes.

● Dom. de Vayssette, rte de Caussade, 81600 Gaillac, tel. 05.63.57.31.95, fax 05.63.81.56.84 ▼ by appt.

CH. VIGNE-LOURAC
Doux Vieilles vignes 1999★

| 6 ha | 30,000 | €5-8 |

Pale yellow with gold reflections, this rich, intense wine is a mixture of honey, jam and fruit jelly. Its full, round palate suggests richness, and good concentration. These characteristics develop powerfully on the mid-palate. It is a wine capable of long matura-tion, suitable for laying down.

● Vignobles Philippe Gayrel, BP 4, 81600 Gaillac, tel. 05.63.33.91.16, fax 05.63.33.95.76

Buzet

The Buzet vine-yard, sited between Agen and Marmande, has been recognised since the Middle Ages as an integral part of the Haut-Pays Bordelais area. It was originally a monastic domain, which was then developed by the burgers of Agen. Buzet faded into a memory after the devastation of the vineyards by phylloxera but, from 1956, it became a symbol of the renaissance of the vineyards in the Haut-Pays. Two individuals, Jean Mermillod and Jean Combabessouse, presided over the vineyard's revital-isation, which also owes a great deal to the Cave Coopérative des

Producteurs Réunis, where all the wines are brought on in hogsheads which are regularly renewed. The vineyard now stretches between Damazan and Sainte-Colombe on the lower slopes of the Garonne; it irrigates the tourist towns of Nérac and Barbaste.

The alternating terroirs of alluvial clay, pebbly soils and sandy limestones produce varied wines of striking character. The strong, deeply coloured, fleshy reds are velvety enough to rival some of their Girondin neighbours, and marvellous with local gastro-nomic dishes such as duck breast, confits (duck or goose preserved in fat), and rabbit cooked with prunes. Buzet wines are traditionally red, with 114,712 hl (3,028,397 gal) pro-duced from 1,916 ha (4,732.5 acres) in 2000, but white wines, of which 4,858 hl (128,251 gal) were pro-duced, add to a range that is never-theless dedicated above all to a palette of purples, garnets and vermilions.

□ BARON D'ARDEUIL
Elevé en fût de chêne 2000★

| 10 ha | 40,000 | €5-8 |

Pale, bright yellow with green reflections, this moderately-intense wine has exotic fruit aromas mixed with nuances of oak. Not very lively on the attack, the palate develops notes of exotic fruits and vanilla. This is a well-balanced Buzet, well-rounded, rich and ready to drink.

● Les Vignerons de Buzet, BP 17, 47160 Buzet-sur-Baïse, tel. 05.53.84.74.30, fax 05.53.84.74.24, e-mail buzet@vignerons-buzet.fr ▼ ev. day except Sun. 9am–12 noon 2pm–6pm

■ CH. DU BOUCHET 1999★★

| 18 ha | 84,075 | €5-8 |

The nose, both powerful and fine, reveals notes of green pepper and spices. The sweet, well-balanced attack leaves an initial taste of chocolate. The full, well-rounded, tannic structure supports the palate into a long finish. This characterful wine, pleasant when young, would complement a stew of veal with white sauce.

● Les Vignerons de Buzet, BP 17, 47160 Buzet-sur-Baïse, tel. 05.53.84.74.30, fax 05.53.84.74.24, e-mail buzet@vignerons-buzet.fr ▼ ev. day except Sun. 9am–12 noon 2pm–6pm

● Seava Padere

LES VIGNERONS DE BUZET

Grande Réserve 1998★★

■ 32 ha 96,320 ▮▮◧ ◆ €23-30

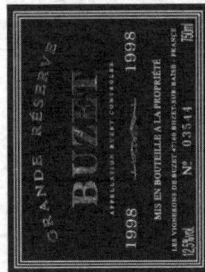

This Buzet is incontestably the most promising of the selection. The complex nose releases ripe-fruit aromas, underlined by a slightly burnt aroma. In the mouth, the tannins are particularly powerful and well-balanced; the oak taste, the result of nine months' maturation in the barrel, begins to melt, bringing a hint of leather. This wine looks to be very suitable for laying down. The **Cuvée Jean-Marie Hébrard red 98** is awarded one star. Still quite oaky, it is well-rounded with an expressive finish. It is a beautiful, dense, powerful wine that needs to wait.

➤ Les Vignerons de Buzet, BP 17, 47160 Buzet-sur-Baïse, tel. 05.53.84.74.30, fax 05.53.84.74.24, e-mail buzet@vignerons-buzet.fr ⊤ ev. day except Sun. 9am–12 noon 2pm–6pm

➤ J. de Royer

CH. DE GACHE 1999★★

■ 18 ha 68,568 ▮▮◧ ◆ €5-8

This 99 is deep ruby in colour. Its complex nose, both powerful and fine, emits notes of spice, pepper and ripe fruit. The palate has a good texture with lasting flavours. The wine and spice aromas are well-supported by a dense, concentrated structure. This well-balanced, flavoursome Buzet would go well with grilled red meats. The **Château de Bouigues 98**, not oak-aged, was awarded one star. The nose is dominated by blackcurrant aromas; the palate is full and well-supported by flavoursome tannins. It will be ready to drink in two or three years.

➤ Les Vignerons de Buzet, BP 17, 47160 Buzet-sur-Baïse, tel. 05.53.84.74.30, fax 05.53.84.74.24, e-mail buzet@vignerons-buzet.fr ⊤ ev. day except Sun. 9am–12 noon 2pm–6pm

CH. DE GUEYZE 1998★★

■ 78 ha 173,536 ▮▮◧ ◆ €8-11

The Château de Gueyze is one of the jewels in the crown of Buzet, with its uninterrupted 78-ha (192.66-acre) vineyard. The fine, powerful, oak aroma envelops the ripe fruit with its spicy and toasty notes. The range of flavours includes a hint of menthol and a touch

of fresh eucalyptus. This dense, well-balanced wine is supported by tight but supple tannins. It would go well with game, such as jugged wild boar.

➤ Les Vignerons de Buzet, BP 17, 47160 Buzet-sur-Baïse, tel. 05.53.84.74.30, fax 05.53.84.74.24, e-mail buzet@vignerons-buzet.fr ⊤ ev. day except Sun. 9am–12 noon 2pm–6pm

➤ Sté Gueyze

DOM. DE LA CROIX 1999★★

■ 55 ha 142,015 ▮▮◧ ◆ €5-8

Elegant and floral on the nose, this wine has a rich, full-bodied palate, structured by firm tannins. It also exhibits good acidity and a long finish. This classic, flavoursome Buzet is extremely well-balanced and can be drunk with every course of a meal. The **Cuvée Vieilles Vignes red 98** gets one star. It has ripe fruit aromas on the nose, typical of Cabernet, and a subtle oak character. The flavours on the palate give an impression of fresh fruit. This wine is ready to drink.

➤ Les Vignerons de Buzet, BP 17, 47160 Buzet-sur-Baïse, tel. 05.53.84.74.30, fax 05.53.84.74.24, e-mail buzet@vignerons-buzet.fr ⊤ ev. day except Sun. 9am–12 noon 2pm–6pm

CH. DE PADERE 1998★★

■ 45 ha 137,684 ▮▮◧ ◆ €5-8

The range of red-berry, blackcurrant and blackberry flavours are immediately appealing. After an initial impression of rich fruit, the palate reveals dense, tight, flavoursome tannins, leading to a fresh finish. This elegant, well-balanced wine can be kept for three or four years. It would go well with duck confit, or a *cassoulet* (stew).

➤ Les Vignerons de Buzet, BP 17, 47160 Buzet-sur-Baïse, tel. 05.53.84.74.30, fax 05.53.84.74.24, e-mail buzet@vignerons-buzet.fr ⊤ ev. day except Sun. 9am–12 noon 2pm–6pm

➤ Seava Padere

CH. SAUVAGNERES 1999★★

▮▮◧ ◆ €5-8 0.6 ha 4,000

This garnet-coloured wine develops resin and red-berry aromas, underlined by a little oak. After a supple attack, the palate releases a fresh spiciness. The body reveals oaky scents of vanilla, and is well-structured by firm tannins. It is best kept two or three years, and would go well with duck.

➤ Bernard Thérasse, Sauvagnères, 47310 Sainte-Colombe-en-Bru ilhois, tel. 05.53.67.20.23, fax 05.53.67.20.86, e-mail bernardtherasse@wanadoo.fr ☑ ⊤ by appt.

892

Côtes du Frontonnais

The Côtes du Frontonnais are Toulousain wines from a very old vineyard which was once the property of the Knights of the Order of Saint John of Jerusalem. During the siege of Montauban, Louis XIII and Richelieu were said to have succumbed to comparative tastings ... Rebuilt as a result of the establishment of the co-operative cellars of Fronton and Villaudric, the vineyard has stuck to its original varieties including the Negrette, a local variety found in Gaillac, as well as Côt, Cabernet Franc, Cabernet-Sauvignon, Syrah, Gamay and Mauzac.

The *terroir* of silts, clays and pebble layers covers about 2,000 ha (4,940 acres) of the terraces of the river Tarn. The red wines, with a high proportion of Cabernet, Gamay or Syrah, are light, fruity and aromatic. The wines with the greatest proportion of Negrette are stronger, tannic and have a distinctive flavour of the terroir. The rosés are clean, fresh and pleasantly fruity. Production was 119,804 hl (3,162,826 gal) in 2000.

CH. BELLEVUE LA FORÊT 1999★★
75 ha 580,000 ■ ■ €5-8

This vast 110-ha (271.7-acre) estate has enabled a great number of people to discover the wines of the Côte du Frontonnais, by virtue of the large volumes produced here. Quantity is not at the expense of quality: the **rosé 2000**, just like this red, came very close to being a *coup de coeur*. The former, pretty on the palate, is distinctive for its fullness and roundness. The latter, with its very intense, almost black, colour, has a deep nose releasing heady aromas of flowers, spices and dark berries. The palate asserts itself straightaway. Full, well-balanced and quite powerful, with even more aromatic qualities than the nose, the palate is supported by fine tannins. This is a beautifully-made wine.

➜ Ch. Bellevue la Forêt,
4500, av. de Grisolles, 31620 Fronton,
tel. 05.34.27.91.91, fax 05.61.82.43.21,
e-mail contact@chateaubellevuelaforet.com
☑ Ⴤ by appt.
➜ Patrick Germain

CH. BOUISSEL Cuvée Or 1999★
3 ha 21,000 ■ ■ €5-8

Established on an old river terrace of the Tarn, this estate got into the *Guide* through the front door, with its first bottled vintage, a superb 89 hailed as a *coup de coeur*. Made up of 50% Negrette grapes, 25% Syrah and the remaining 25% Cabernet Franc and Cot separately vinified, this 99 does not quite come up to the same standard: it could certainly have done with being more full-bodied, but it is a well-made, pleasant wine. It has its good points: an engaging, dark-garnet colour; a deep and quite complex nose with a blend of very ripe dark berries, spices and liquorice; and a fresh attack followed by a delicious, smooth, well-balanced, fruit-rich palate.

➜ EARL Pierre Selle, Ch. Bouissel,
82370 Campsas, tel. 05.63.30.10.49,
fax 05.63.64.01.22 ☑ Ⴤ ev. day except Sun.
9am–12.15pm 2pm–7.15pm; Wed. 2pm–7.15pm; groups by appt.

CH. CAHUZAC L'Authentique 1999★★
10 ha 80,000 ■ ■ €5-8

Bernard Ferran is known as a producer of quality wines. This year, **l'Authentique** was awarded one star for the **rosé 2000** and two for its red counterpart. Intense, clear and bright, this red wine presents a clean nose, perfectly characteristic, in which fruits and spices, with notes of violet, can be detected. The attack is fresh and velvety; the smooth, well-balanced mouth, with just enough body, is warming and full of flavour. It is noticeable for its ripe fruit. The 96 was a *coup de coeur*.

➜ EARL de Cahuzac, Les Peyronnets,
82170 Fabas, tel. 05.63.64.10.18,
fax 05.63.67.36.97 Ⴤ Ⴤ by appt.
➜ Ferran Père et Fils

CH. CLAMENS Cuvée Tradition 1999
5.2 ha 31,200 ■ ■ €3-5

This estate, with 15.5 ha (38.29 acres) of vines, has only been producing wine in its own cellars since 1998, and makes its début in the *Guide* with two wines that especially impressed the Jury: a **99 Vieilli en Fût de Chêne** (aged in oak barrels), with a high proportion of Cabernet grapes (90%), and this Cuvée Tradition, more typical (50% Negrette, some Cabernet Sauvignon and the tiniest amount of Syrah grapes). Purple in the glass, it has a moderately intense nose, gamey at first, then floral and spicy, with a few notes of ripe fruit. The soft initial impression is followed by a modest concentration, fluid and light but aromatic on the finish.

➜ Jean-Michel Bègue, 720, chem. du Tapas,
lieu-dit Caillol, 31620 Fronton,
tel. 05.61.82.45.32, fax 05.62.79.21.73 ☑
Ⴤ by appt.

Côtes du Frontonnais

CH. CLOS MIGNON
Villaudric Sélection 1999★★

■ 1.6 ha 13,000 ■ ◆ €3-5

In the year 2000 Olivier Muzart took over this estate, bought by his grandfather in 1952. This wine (from 20% Négrette, 40% Cabernet Sauvignon and 40% Syrah grapes) is an intense, purple colour, with hints of violet. The nose displays a good degree of maturity: deep and complex, it is a blend of gamey fragrances, jammy, stewed fruits and toasty aromas, all set off by a subtle touch of peony. After a supple attack, the palate appears extremely well-rounded and sweet. It becomes more powerful, accompanied by fruit and spicy liquorice flavours, supported by already-integrated tannins. It is a well-made wine.

➤ EARL du Ch. Clos Mignon,
31620 Villeneuve-les-Bouloc,
tel. 05.61.82.10.89, fax 05.61.82.99.14,
e-mail omuzart@aol.com ⊻ ⍓ by appt.
➤ Olivier Muzart

CH. DEVES 1999★

■ 11 ha 36,000 ■ ◆ €3-5

This long-macerated wine is made half from Négrette grapes, and a quarter each from the Cabernet and Syrah varieties. It is dark in colour, almost black, and it has an intense nose, with floral, fruity, mineral and spicy notes. Supported by a firm structure with smooth tannins, it has a full palate, with a profusion of ripe fruit. It concludes with a fairly long, warming finish.

➤ Sté André Abart et Fils, Ch. Devès,
31620 Castelnau-d'Estretefonds,
tel. 05.61.35.14.97, fax 05.61.35.14.97 ⊻
⍓ by appt.

DOM. FAOUQUET Villaudric 1999

■ 18 ha 20,000 ■ ◆ €3-5

This 30-ha (74.1-acre) estate, whose name was derived from a nickname given to the producer's great-grandfather, is established on pebbly, sandy soils. Ruby with a slight hint of brick-red, the 99 has a nose of medium intensity, which is characterised by a blend of red and dark berries with spices. After a supple attack, the palate is well-rounded, rather generous and warm, with a flavoursome finish. This wine is a little closed at first, but pleasant in the end.

➤ Robert Beringuier, 42, chem. des
Brugues, 31620 Bouloc, tel. 05.61.82.06.66,
fax 05.61.82.06.66 ⊻ ⍓ by appt.

COMTE DE NEGRET
Cuvée Excellence 1999★

■ n.c. 300,000 ⊪ ◆ €3-5

The Cave de Fronton is regularly featured in the *Guide*, especially for its Comte de Négret label, selected this year for two wines, both of which have been very successful: the **Cuvée Classique red 99**, matured in vat (500,000 bottles!), and the Cuvée Excellence. The latter is remarkable for its velvety, intense ruby colour. Every bit as intense, the nose, garnished with dark berries, gives an impression of sweetness. A clean attack is followed by a medium-bodied, youthful palate. The finish, on the other hand, has a tannic structure that is still quite tight. This wine still needs time to achieve balance.

➤ Cave de Fronton, av. des Vignerons,
31620 Fronton, tel. 05.62.79.97.79,
fax 05.62.79.97.70 ⊻ ⍓ ev. day except Sun.
8am–12.15pm 2pm–7pm

CH. COUTINEL 2000★

◀ 4.5 ha 35,000 ■ ◆ €3-5

This 44-ha (108.68-acre) estate is featured this year for its ready-to-drink **red 99** (singled out), and for this clear salmon-pink rosé. The nose is a generous blend of mixed fruits and pear drops, and its rather well-rounded palate is flavoursome and well-balanced between acidity and sweetness. This is a well-made wine.

➤ Jean-Claude Arbeau, BP 1,
82370 Labastide-Saint-Pierre,
tel. 05.63.64.01.80, fax 05.63.30.11.42,
e-mail coutinel@wanadoo.fr ⊻ ⍓ by appt.

CH. FERRAN 1999★

■ 25 ha 100,000 ⊪ ◆ €5-8

Nicolas Gélis is in charge of two estates, the production of both being controlled by the same oenologist: the Château Montauriol, singled out for its **Cuvée Mons Aureolus red 99**, which cannot hide the fact that it was aged in barrel, and the Château Ferran, offering this vat-matured wine preferred by the Jury. This wine is distinguished by its bright colour, an intense red, and by a nose that starts gamey and is then dominated by spices. The palate has a remarkable fullness and a firm structure. The tannins are spicy and are already well-integrated. It is a concentrated but well-balanced wine.

➤ Nicolas Gélis, Ch. Ferran,
31620 Fronton, tel. 05.61.35.30.58,
fax 05.61.35.30.59, e-mail chateau.ferran@
wanadoo.fr ⍓ by appt.

CH. FONVIEILLE
Excellence Elevé en fûts de chêne neufs 1999

■ 1 ha 10,000 ⊪ ◆ €5-8

This is a new label for Côtes du Frontonnais, and the wine is submitted by a négociant house at Montauban. This 99, made from Négrette (50%), Cabernet Sauvignon, Syrah and Côt grapes, is characterised by a dense garnet colour with black tones. The fairly intense nose has hints of floral aromas,

fruit and vegetal characteristics, accompanied by a slight note of oak. The supple attack is followed by a straightforward palate, with a good degree of freshness and fine tannins. The oak remains subtle. This is a well-balanced wine.
➤ SARL Aba, 149, av. Charles-de-Gaulle, 82000 Montauban, tel. 05.63.20.23.15, fax 05.63.03.06.64

■ **CH. JOLIET 1999★★**

5 ha | 30,000 | €5-8

This estate regularly produces wines that are judged 'successful,' 'remarkable,' or indeed, exceptional. The Négrette, Cabernet and Syrah grapes make this pretty wine what it is. It has a brilliant, ruby colour, and the nose is characterised by freshness and complex aromas of soft fruits, red and dark berries (such as blackcurrant), and pepper. After a smooth initial impression, the flavoursome palate is full, well-structured and sufficiently rich. This is a well-balanced wine.
➤ François Daubert, Dom. de Joliet, 31620 Fronton, tel. 05.61.82.46.02, fax 05.61.82.34.56, e-mail chateau.joliet@wanadoo.fr ✉ Y by appt.

■ **CH. LA COUTELIERE**
Vieilli en fût de chêne 1999

3.5 ha | 20,000 | €5-8

This wine is a beautiful, rather intense cherry colour, with hints of bronze. It has a warming nose, in which flower and fruit aromas are wrapped in a touch of vanilla. The palate is smooth on the attack, supple, fairly fresh and light; the epitome of an easy-drinking wine.
➤ Denis Bocquier, Entourettes, 31340 Villemur-sur-Tarn, tel. 05.61.82.14.97, fax 05.61.82.14.97

■ **CH. LA PALME Privilège 1999**

37 ha | 50,000 | €3-5

Since 1984, Martine Ethuin has been in charge of this estate, which her parents bought in 1963. This is her traditional wine, made using the appellation's five grape varieties: Négrette (50%), Cabernet, Syrah, Cot and Gamay. Ruby-coloured with a hint of orange, this 99 reveals a nose which is gamey and almost stewed-fruit aromas, with notes of spices and violets. The rather smooth, attractive palate becomes increasingly full of flavours, with a certain freshness.
➤ Ch. La Palme, 31340 Villemur-sur-Tarn, tel. 05.61.09.02.82, fax 05.61.09.27.01, e-mail chateau.la.palme@wanadoo.fr ✉ Y by appt.
➤ Ethuin

■ **LE ROC Cuvée Don Quichotte 1999★★**

3 ha | 15,000 | €5-8

Le Roc have been collecting stars for ten years; they have already been awarded the coup de cœur three times. Featured again this year, in the **99** vintage, are two of Frédéric Ribes's winning wines: the **Cuvée Réserve** and the Cuvée Don Quichotte. The latter is distinctive for the strong intensity of its purple colour. Its deep, dense, complex nose blends highly-ripened dark berries, cherries soaked in brandy and macerated spices with a touch of leather. The wine does still seem rather young, but it is already pleasant with its perfectly-structured palate, careful use of oak and evolving spicy liquorice flavours. This is a beautifully-made wine with a great future.
➤ Famille Ribes, Dom. Le Roc, 31620 Fronton, tel. 05.61.82.93.90, fax 05.61.82.72.38 ✉ Y by appt.

■ **CH. MARGUERITE 2000★**

13.1 ha | 104,500 | €3-5

This estate of some 75 ha (185.25 acres) has produced wine from its own cellars for about ten years. This is its rosé de saignée (a rosé wine made from black grapes subjected to a short maceration period) made from Négrette, Syrah and Cinsault grapes. It is a clear, salmon-pink colour. The pleasant, intense nose consists of lovely fermentation aromas; it is evocative of exotic fruits and pear drops. These characteristics are retained on the palate after a smooth attack. Rather full-bodied and rich, it is well-balanced and, although it is just the tiniest bit lacking in liveliness on the finish, it is a pleasing wine.
➤ SCEA Ch. Marguerite, 82370 Campsas, tel. 05.63.64.08.21, fax 05.63.64.08.21 ✉ Y by appt.

■ **CH. PLAISANCE** Thibaut de Plaisance
Vieilli en fût de chêne 1999★

2 ha | 10,500 | €5-8

This château, which has 24 ha (59.28 acres) of vines, has been mentioned in the Guide every year since it was established in 1990, and this wine was declared a coup de cœur in the last edition. The 99 is a beautiful, purple colour, deep and bright. The nose is rich in red berries and spices, enveloped in a smoky aroma with a hint of spicy liquorice. The attack is supple and the palate well-rounded and warming. A fairly noticeable oak character is still present on the finish, but this should soon blend in. In a lower price bracket, the **Château Plaisance Rosé 2000** especially impressed the Jury.
➤ EARL de Plaisance, pl. de la Mairie, 31340 Vacquiers, tel. 05.61.84.97.41, fax 05.61.84.11.26 ✉ Y by appt.
➤ Penavayre

■ **DOM. DE SAINT-GUILHEM**
Amadeus 1999★

2 ha | 5,000 | €5-8

This estate was established in the 19th century, then abandoned, and finally taken over by a young wine-grower about ten years ago. The Cuvée Amadeus is a deep, strong, cherry colour. The clean nose becomes more powerful, blending fruits and flowers with accents of menthol. The attack is supple; the well-rounded, robust palate, with its clean liquorice and light oak flavour, becomes more austere and warming on the finish. This,

Lavilledieu AOVDQS

however, does not make the wine any less satisfying.

☛ Philippe Laduguie,
Dom. de Saint-Guilhem,
31620 Castelnau-d'Estretefonds,
tel. 05.61.82.12.09, fax 05.61.82.65.59 ▼
☒ ev. day 8.30am–7.30pm; Sun. by appt.

CH. SAINT-LOUIS

L'Esprit Elevé en fût de chêne 1999★

■   0.4 ha   2,700   ▬ ▮▮▮ ♦   €5-8

It was ten years ago that Alain Mahmoudi bought this 25-ha (61.75-acre) estate. The renovation work on the cellars is paying off, with a very successful new wine, made from 60% Négrette and 40% Cabernet grapes. This 99 is a pretty, fairly intense garnet colour and has an open, powerful nose releasing aromas of overripe fruit in jam or brandy, set off by spices against an oaky background. The attack is clean and the palate well-balanced, with mature tannins and a charming oakiness. It is already well-developed.

☛ Alain Mahmoudi,
82370 Labastide-Saint-Pierre,
tel. 05.63.64.01.80, fax 05.63.30.11.42,
e-mail saintlouis@wanadoo.fr ▼
☒ by appt.

Lavilledieu AOVDQS

North of the Frontonnais, on the terraces of the Tarn and the Garonne, the little vineyard of Lavilledieu covers about 150 ha (370 acres) and produces red and rosé wines. The production, classified as AOVDQS, is still very little known. The Négrette (30%), Cabernet Franc, Gamay, Syrah and Tannat are the authorised varieties.

MAISTRE DES TEMPLIERS 1999

■   10 ha   40,000   ▬ ▮ ♦   €3-5

This wine is made from a combination of Négrette, Gamay, Syrah, Cabernet Franc and Tannat grapes, grown in a *boulbènes* soil (a type of alluvium-rich soil found in south-western France). Bright in colour, it is evocative of red berries, underlined by notes of undergrowth and spices. After a fresh attack, it develops a light richness with a structure of quality tannins. It should be drunk while still fruity. The Jury also singled out the Cuvée **Chevaliers du Temple du Christ 99**, a supple Lavilledieu, fruity and spicy.

☛ Cave de Lavilledieu-du-Temple,
82290 Lavilledieu-du-Temple,
tel. 05.63.31.60.05, fax 05.63.31.69.11,
e-mail cave.lavilledieu@wanadoo.fr
☒ by appt.

Côtes du Brulhois AOVDQS

Since November 1984, these former Vins de Pays have been AOVDQS, and are produced on both banks of the Garonne, in the departments of Lot-et-Garonne and Tarn-et-Garonne, near the small town of Layrac. The appellation covers an area of about 200 ha (494 acres). Production is mainly of reds from Bordelais varieties and the local Tannat and Côt. The majority of the wine-making is undertaken by two co-operative cellars.

CARRELOT DES AMANTS 2000

▮   30 ha   80,000   ▬ ♦   €3-5

The Vignerons du Brulhois cellars have a famous visitor, the singer Francis Cabrel, who grows grapes at Astaffort and brings them here. This raspberry-coloured wine sings of red fruits (cherries), before developing an agreeable suppleness with notes of fruit kernels. The red version, the **Parvis des Templiers 99**, characterised by its fruity aromas and a hint of game, also especially impressed the Jury.

☛ Vignerons du Brulhois, 82340 Dunes,
tel. 05.63.39.91.92, fax 05.63.39.82.83
☒ by appt.

CH. GRAND CHENE

Prestige Elevé en fût de chêne 1999★

■   20 ha   40,000   ▬ ▮▮▮   €5-8

This wine owes its name to the existence of a 600-year-old oak tree at the entrance to the estate. Intensely coloured, the aromas of cherry and cloves are also found on the palate, which is still marked by tannins. It needs to be laid down and left to mature for one or two years. The Cuvée **Couleur Fruits 2000**, which especially impressed the Jury, is a ready-to-drink **rosé**.

☛ Cave de Donzac, Chaline, 82340 Donzac,
tel. 05.63.39.91.92, fax 05.63.39.82.83 ▼
☒ ev. day except Sun. Mon. 9am–12 noon 2pm–6pm; groups by appt.

Côtes du Marmandais

Not far from the gravels of Entre-deux-Mers and the wines of Duras and Buzet, the Côtes du Marmandais wines are mainly produced by the co-operatives in Beaupuy and Cocumont on both banks of the Garonne. The white wines, generally made from Sémillon, Sauvignon, Muscadelle and Ugni Blanc, are dry, lively and fruity. The supple, pleasingly aromatic red wines are made mainly from Bordelais varieties, along with Abouriou, Syrah, Cot and Gamay. The vineyard covers about 1,500 ha (3,705 acres) and produced 55 hl (1,452 gal) of white wine and 89,525 hl (2,369,460 gal) of red in 2000.

BARON COPESTAING
Élevé en fût de chêne 1999★★
70 ha · 13,000 · €8-11

This is incontestably the best of the selection. Its fresh, fruity nose is underlined by toasty and vanilla aromas. Although oak dominates the attack, the palate evolves into red berries and spices; the supple, well-integrated tannins complete the general balance. Their rosé, the Cuvée Marescot 2000, is a great success, with its palette of red berries and fine balance.
↪ Cave de Cocumont, La Cure, 47250 Cocumont, tel. 05.53.94.50.21, fax 05.53.94.52.84, e-mail cave-cocumont@wanadoo.fr ☎ by appt.

CH. DE BEAULIEU
Cuvée de l'Oratoire 1998★
5 ha · 6,000 · €11-15

This wine is medium-deep in colour, with hints of light brick-red. On the nose, as on the palate, oak still dominates the fruit. Fruit and oak should balance out over the next two or three years.
↪ Robert et Agnès Schulte, Ch. de Beaulieu, 47180 Saint-Sauveur-de-Meilhan, tel. 05.53.94.30.40, fax 05.53.94.30.40, e-mail chateaudebeaulieu.com ☎ ev. day 9am–6pm; Sat. Sun. by appt.

PRESTIGE DE BEAUPUY 1999★
6 ha · 40,000 · €5-8

This wine was barrel-matured for 12 months, resulting in an oak character that does not dominate the wine and lets the red-berry aromas come through. These fruit characteristics are also present on the initial attack. Concentrated and powerful, this wine reflects good vinification and maturation techniques. The oak should integrate completely within three years.
↪ Les Vignerons de Beaupuy, Dupuy, 47200 Marmande, tel. 05.53.76.05.10, fax 05.53.64.63.90, e-mail contact@cavedebeaupuy.com ☎ ev. day except Sun. 8.30am–12 noon 2pm–6.30pm
↪ J.L. Bagot

DOM. DES GEAIS 1999★★
3 ha · 25,000 · €5-8

The rich, complex nose has red fruit and blackberry aromas. On the palate the wine is well-rounded, supple and well-balanced. The flavours explode and persist on the mid-palate. The tannins, still very present, should integrate with age. The Domaine Saint-Martin red 99 is awarded one star for its powerful structure and character. This wine is sold only through big retail stores.
↪ Vignobles Boissonneau, Cathelicq, 33190 Saint-Michel-de-Lapujade, tel. 05.56.61.72.14, fax 05.56.61.71.01 ☎ by appt.

LAFON FERRAN 2000★
40 ha · 60,000 · €3-5

This straightforward wine has aromas of passion-fruit mixed with pear and a touch of vanilla. Although the attack is still marked by oak, the fruit character re-asserts itself on the supple and rich mid-palate. Equally successful, the Prieur Saint-Christophe white 2000 is evocative of citrus and overripe fruits.
↪ Cave de Cocumont, La Cure, 47250 Cocumont, tel. 05.53.94.50.21, fax 05.53.94.52.84, e-mail cave-cocumont@wanadoo.fr ☎ by appt.

LA TOUR D'ASPE
Vieilli en fût de chêne 1999★
6 ha · 40,000 · €5-8

A promising wine on the nose, with its pronounced aromas of blackcurrant and a touch of oak. Initially supple on the palate, the body is firmly structured with well-balanced tannins and persistent nuances of fruit. It has good potential.
↪ Les Vignerons de Beaupuy, Dupuy, 47200 Marmande, tel. 05.53.76.05.10, fax 05.53.64.63.90, e-mail contact@cavedebeaupuy.com ☎ ev. day except Sun. 8.30am–12 noon 2pm–6.30pm
↪ J.L. Bagot

CH. LESCOUR 1999★
6 ha · 40,000 · €5-8

The tasters were immediately taken with this wine's nose of ripe fruits underlined by a little touch of spice. The fruit, underlined by of tasting, makes its mark on the structured palate, full, well-rounded and long; the tannins should come together with time. Also a great success, the Château de la Côte de France red 99 has a lot of fruitiness and a certain freshness. Two or three years' ageing should enable the sinewy tannins to integrate.

Vins d'Estaing AOVDQS

The vineyard of Aveyron is surrounded by the limestone plateaux of Aubrac, the Cantal mountains and the Lévezou plateau, so it should really be classified with the vineyards of the Massif Central. The little appellations here are very old: their original foundation by the monks of Conques goes back to the 11th century.

The Vins d'Estaing, 7 ha (17 acres), are divided between the fresh, perfumed reds (blackcurrant and raspberry) made from Fer Sevadou and Gamay and the very original whites from mixtures of Chenin, Mauzac and Rousselou. The latter are lively, flinty wines with strong *terroir* character.

Vins d'Estaing AOVDQS

➤ Les Vignerons de Beaupuy, Dupuy, 47200 Marmande, tel. 05.53.76.05.10, fax 05.53.64.63.90, e-mail contact@cavedebeaupuy.com ▼ 🍷 ev. day except Sun. 8.30am–12 noon 2pm–6.30pm
➤ J.L. Bagot

CH. SARRAZIERE 1999★
■ 75 ha 60,000 ■ 🍷 €8-11

The suppleness and fruitiness of this flattering wine is typical of the vintage. A light cherry colour, it reveals a nose that, though not very powerful, is elegantly composed of flowers and red berries. The palate is consistently fruity and well-balanced, with integrated tannins. The warm finish gives an impression of sweetness. The **Cuvée Mez Vinéa red 99** is also awarded one star. With its fruit flavour and pleasant tannins, it is well-balanced and ready to drink.

➤ Cave de Cocumont, La Cure, 47250 Cocumont, tel. 05.53.94.50.21, fax 05.53.94.52.84, e-mail cave-cocumont@wanadoo.fr ▼ 🍷 by appt.

TAP D'E PERBOS
Vieilli en fût de chêne 1999★★
■ 70 ha 25,000 ■ €5-8

The particularly complex bouquet includes powerful aromas of oak, roasted coffee and leather. The wine is well-balanced on the attack, and although the tannins are powerful and rich, leaving a hint of austerity on the finish, they are never aggressive on the palate. A very promising wine. Awarded one star, the **red Château Jacquet 99** evokes fresh and crystallised fruits with an earthy note. It is supple and characteristic of the *terroir*.

➤ Cave de Cocumont, La Cure, 47250 Cocumont, tel. 05.53.94.50.21, fax 05.53.94.52.84, e-mail cave-cocumont@wanadoo.fr ▼ 🍷 by appt.

TERSAC 1999★
■ 70 ha 40,000 ■ €5-8

This almost black Côtes du Marmandais pleases the nose with its oaky aromas of vanilla and toast, well-blended with notes of leather, blackcurrants and cooked fruit. The rich, supple body is supported by fine-grained tannins. Still dominated by oak, the wine will mature if cellared for five to ten years. The **Croix de Tucos red 99**, matured for 12 months in barrel, gets the same marks. After a distinct blackcurrant aroma on the nose, it fills the mouth with a round, rich sensation, without excessive tannins. This wine is characteristic of the *terroir*.

➤ Cave de Cocumont, La Cure, 47250 Cocumont, tel. 05.53.94.50.21, fax 05.53.94.52.84, e-mail cave-cocumont@wanadoo.fr ▼ 🍷 by appt.

LES VIGNERONS D'OLT 2000★
□ 0.8 ha 3,500 €3-5

This co-operative cellar uses Chenin and Mauzac grapes to produce a bright, limpid wine with a fruity, floral nose. The palate is delicious and fresh, punctuated by fine nuances of Muscat and minerals. It is best drunk with local charcuterie or goats' cheeses.

➤ Les Vignerons d'Olt, Z.A. La Fage, 12190 Estaing, tel. 05.65.44.04.42, fax 05.65.44.04.42 ▼ 🍷 by appt.

Vins d'Entraygues et du Fel AOVDQS

The white wines from Entraygues, 9 ha (22 acres), are cultivated on schist soils on narrow terracing cut into the steep hillsides. Made from Chenin and Mauzac, they are fresh and fruity: splendid with wild trout and the delicate Cantal cheese. The sturdy, earthy reds, made from Fel, are good paired with lamb from the Causses and *Potée Auvergnate* – a

substantial soup of vegetables and meat.

Marcillac

Cultivated in a natural hollow, the 'valley', with a propitious micro-climate, the Mansoi variety (also known as the Fer Servadou) gives the red Marcillac wines their great originality, marked by a tannic simplicity and aromas of raspberries. In 1990, this specialist approach was acknowledged with the award of an AOC, which now covers 146 ha (360.6 acres) and in 2000 produced 6,796 hl (179,414 gal) of a highly individual wine that is always instantly recognisable.

DOM. DU CROS
Lo Sang del País 1999★

14 ha   60,000

Lo Sang del País is quintessential Fer Servadou, grown on chalky rocky landscapes and *rougiers*. Deeply coloured, it has cherry and cocoa aromas, followed by a flavoursome, well-balanced palate, punctuated by notes of ripe fruit. After three months in barrel, the wine has a subtle oak character. The **Domaine du Cros Vieilles Vignes 99**, which especially impressed the Jury, was matured for 18 months in barrel, and is fruity and spicy.

✆ Philippe Teulier, Dom. du Cros, 12390 Goutrens, tel. 05.65.72.71.77, fax 05.65.72.68.80 ☑ ☎ by appt.

DOM. DES COSTES ROUGES 1999

n.c.   n.c.   €3-5

The Costes Rouges estate still features little in the *Guide*, but it has distinguished itself in this vintage by a characterful wine, expressive of red berries. On the palate it is very well-balanced with discreet notes of oak. Drink now to enjoy the fruitiness.

✆ Dom. des Costes Rouges, Combret, 1230 Nauviale, tel. 05.65.72.83.85 ☑

�‣ Vinas Costes

DOM. DU VIEUX NOYER 1999

3 ha   15,000   €3-5

Rather strongly coloured, this 99 has a distinctive bouquet consisting of tobacco and blackcurrant leaves, with a hint of blackberry. It has great finesse on the eye and lively on the palate. The **rosé 2000** is pleasant to the eye and lively on the nose and palate, with notes of rose and banana. Best drunk with charcuterie from Aveyron.

✆ Dom. du Vieux Noyer, Boyne, 12640 Rivière-sur-Tarn, tel. 05.65.62.64.57, fax 05.65.62.64.57 ☑ ☎ ev. day except Sun. 10am–12.30pm 2pm–7pm

➣ Carmen et Bernard Portalier

Côtes de Millau AOVDQS

The appellation AOVDQS Côtes de Millau was officially recognised on 12 April 1994. The wines are made from Syrah and Gamay Noir and, in a very small proportion, from Cabernet Sauvignon and Fer Servadou. Production reaches about 1,500 hl (39,600 gal).

JEAN-MARC VIGUIER
Cuvée spéciale 1999

0.8 ha   4,000   €5-8

With just over 5 ha (12.4 acres), Jean-Marc Viguier is regularly featured in the *Guide*. This is a wine made exclusively from the Chenin grape, with a floral and fruity nose. The palate echoes the aromas of the nose as it develops in a pleasant, well-balanced way.

✆ Jean-Marc Viguier, Les Buis, 12140 Entraygues, tel. 05.65.44.50.45, fax 05.65.48.62.72 ☑ ☎ ev. day except Sun. 8am–12 noon 2pm–7pm

JEAN-LUC MATHA
Cuvée spéciale 1999★

3 ha   12,000   €5-8

This deep wine has an oaky nose, with toasted and fruity aromas, such as red and black berries and prunes. Delicious and full in the mouth, it should be served with red meat dishes. The **99** in its **Classique** version deserves to be singled out: fruity, spicy and supple, it is vat-matured.

✆ Jean-Luc Matha, Bruéjouls, 12330 Clairvaux, tel. 05.65.72.63.29, fax 05.65.72.70.43 ☑ ☎ by appt.

LES VIGNERONS DU VALLON 1999★

n.c.   130,000

The co-operative vinifies the harvest of 90 ha (222 acres) within the appellation area. The intensely coloured 99 produces aromas of spice and red berries, such as cherry and raspberry. Its suppleness makes it a wine to drink while it is still fruity. The Vignerons du Vallon are also noted for their **Cuvée Réservée 99**, which especially impressed the Jury with its fruity aroma.

✆ Les Vignerons du Vallon, RN 140, 12330 Valady, tel. 05.65.72.70.21, fax 05.65.72.68.39 ☑ ☎ by appt.

Béarn

Béarn wines can be produced in three different areas. The first two are the same as for Jurançon and Madiran. The other, Béarn alone, encompasses the communes around Orthez and Salies-de-Béarn, including Bellocq. This AOC covers about 211 ha (521 acres) and produced 10,576 hl (279,206 gal) of wine in 2000, of which 67 hl (1,769 gal) was white.

The vineyard was reconstituted after the phylloxera epidemic and occupies the gravels and pre-Pyrenean hills of the Gave valley. The red varieties include Tannat, Cabernet Sauvignon and Cabernet Franc (Bouchy), as well as the old varieties of Manseng Noir, Courby Rouge and Fer Servadou. The wines are full-bodied and rich, and are good with 'garbure' (a local soup), and grilled squab. The rosés of Béarn, the best wines of the appellation, are lively but delicate with fine aromas from the Cabernet.

Irouléguy

Irouléguy wines are grown on the last remnants of a big Basque vineyard (known as Chacoli on the Spanish side), founded in the 11th century by the monks of Roncevaux abbey, and today's wine-makers are determined to maintain this ancient tradition. The vineyard is laid out on foothills in the communes of Saint-Etienne-de-Baïgorry, Irouléguy and Anhaux, covering some 205 ha (506 acres). In 2000 it produced 7,778 hl (205,339 gal) of wine, including 858 hl (22,651 gal) of white wine.

The older vine varieties have virtually disappeared in favour of Cabernet Sauvignon, Cabernet Franc and Tannat for red wines, and of Courbu and Gros and Petit Manseng for the whites. Practically the whole production is vinified by the co-operative in Irouléguy but new vineyards are now beginning to appear. The Irouléguy red is fragrant and somewhat tannic, worth trying with confits (duck or goose preserved in fat). The cherry-coloured rosé is lively, fragrant and light, and goes well with pipérade (eggs with peppers) and charcuterie.

BEAU VALLON 2000★

■ 20 ha 100,000 ▥ ◦ €3

The nose suggests fruit and spices, while the palate is already mouth-filling. Two years' ageing will be sufficient to perfect the balance. Also worthy of note in the **rosé** version and in the **2000** vintage are the **Domaine d'Oumprès** and the **Domaine Larribère**, which especially impressed the Jury.

☛ Cave des Producteurs de Jurançon, 53, av. Henri-IV, 64290 Gan, tel. 05.59.21.57.03, fax 05.59.21.72.06, e-mail cave.gan@ adour-bureau.fr ▨ ☎ ev. day except Sun. 8am–12.30pm 1.30pm–7pm

DOM. LAPEYRE 1999★

■ 3 ha 18,000 ▥ €8-11

The Lapeyre estate, regularly featured in the *Guide*, offers a deep purple-coloured Béarn, redolent of dark berries and spices. The well-structured, powerful body attests to the wine's potential, but it needs some time to mellow.

☛ EARL Pascal Lapeyre, 52, av. des Pyrénées, 64270 Salies-de-Béarn, tel. 05.59.38.10.02, fax 05.59.38.03.98 ▨ ☎ ev. day except Sun. 9am–12 noon 2.30pm–7.30pm; cl. in Jan.

DOM. ABOTIA 1999

■ 5.1 ha 24,000 ▥ €5-8

A deep red, this Irouléguy develops a nose of dark berries and spices. The fresh, spicy tone, which is echoed on the palate, makes this wine a good accompaniment to *ossau iraty*, the local ewe's cheese.

☛ Jean-Claude Errecart, Dom. Abotia, 64220 Ispoure, tel. 05.59.37.03.99, fax 05.59.37.23.57 ▨ ☎ by appt.

DOM. ARRETXEA

Cuvée Haitza 1999★

■ 1.2 ha 6,000 ▥ €11-15

The Arretxea estate vineyard is cultivated organically. A wine for laying down, the Cuvée Haitza reveals notes of oak, well-blended with aromas of black and red berries. Both fruity and spicy, the wine is full bodied but supported by still very noticeable tannins. Best kept for two or three years.

• Thérèse et Michel Riouspeyrous, Dom. Arretxea, 64220 Irouléguy, tel. 05.59.37.33.67, fax 05.59.37.33.67 ▽
Y by appt.

DOM. BRANA 1999

□ 11 ha 30,000 €8-11

The 22-ha (54-acre) Brana estate combines traditional growing methods with bio-dynamics. Its white wine has pleasant notes of flowers, fruit and honey. A menthol freshness gives it a bracing effect on the palate. It is ready to drink now, with fish, shellfish or ewe's cheese.

• Jean et Adrienne Brana, 3 bis, av. du Jai-Alai, 64220 Saint-Jean-Pied-de-Port, tel. 05.59.37.00.44, fax 05.59.37.14.28, e-mail brana.etienne@wanadoo.fr ▽
Y by appt.

DOM. ETXEGARAYA 1999★

4 ha 16,000 €5-8

Blackcurrant fruit and spices characterise this well-balanced, full-bodied wine. The tasters enjoyed its robustness and persistent finish. The Cuvée Lehengoa red 99 deserves to be singled out, as it is every bit as fruity and spicy.

• Joseph et Marianne Hillau, Dom. Etxegaraya, 64430 Saint-Etienne-de-Baïgorry, tel. 05.59.37.23.76, fax 05.59.37.23.76, e-mail etxegaraya@wanadoo.fr ▽
Y by appt.

DOM. LES TERRASSES DE L'ARRADOY 2000★

8.93 ha 23,000 €5-8

On the red sandstone that characterises this appellation area, the Tannat grape has been blended with two varieties of Cabernet to produce a fruity rosé. The pear drop aromas perceptible on the nose precede a lightly acidic and fresh palate. A wine to drink with fish, seafood or jambon de Bayonne.

• Les Vignerons du Pays Basque, CD 15, 64430 Saint-Etienne-de-Baïgorry, tel. 05.59.37.41.33, fax 05.59.37.47.76, e-mail irouleguy@hotmail.com ▽
Y by appt.

DOM. DE MIGNABERRY 1999★

23.05 ha n.c. €8-11

Twelve months of barrel maturation have gone into producing this dark wine, with its notes of morello cherries and spices. The well-structured palate has finely integrated oak characteristics. It is best cellared for two or three years. Also a great success, the Cuvée Omenaldia red 99, matured in oak barrels, is all spices and black berries; it is best kept a year or two.

• Les Vignerons du Pays Basque, CD 15, 64430 Saint-Etienne-de-Baïgorry, tel. 05.59.37.41.33, fax 05.59.37.47.76, e-mail irouleguy@hotmail.com ▽
Y by appt.

901

Jurançon and Jurançon Sec

'When I was a young woman, I made the acquaintance of a dazzling, imperious prince, as treacherous as any great seducer: Jurançon.' So wrote the novelist Colette. Jurançon has been famous since it was served at the baptism of Henri IV and thereafter became the wine of occasion at all royal ceremonies of the House of Navarre. This is the first historical appearance of the notion of Appellation Protégée – since it was forbidden to import foreign wines – as well as the first steps towards Cru and classification, since all the parcels of land were recorded, according to their value, by the Parliament of Navarre. Like the Béarn wines, those of the Jurançon, then both red and white, were shipped as far as Bayonne via the sometimes hazardous waters of the Gave. Much appreciated by the Dutch and the Americans, Jurançon acquired a star quality which was only extinguished by phylloxera. Under the dynamic leadership of the Cave de Gan and a few committed vineyard owners, the vineyard (1,013 ha/ 2,502 acres today) was completely replanted with traditional varieties grown and trained according to the old ways.

Here more than anywhere, year of vintage is extremely important, especially for the sweet Jurançons, for which the grapes must be ripened late on the vine by the passerillage method. In this traditional practice, the stalks of the grapes are pinched just above the clusters shortly before they are picked in late autumn, cutting off the passage of sap between the grapes and the vine. The grapes are then allowed to ripen thoroughly in the hot sun and, since no sap can get to them, they dry out, leaving the grapes extra-rich in natural sugar. This process allows the wine to

Jurançon

attain the legal minimum of 15% alcohol. The traditional varieties used for Jurançon are whites only, the Gros and Petit Manseng and the Courbu. In cultivation, the vines are trained high to avoid the frosts, and it is not unusual for the harvest to continue until the first snows.

The dry Jurançon, is a white wine made from white grapes (Blanc de Blancs), noted for its beautiful colour with glints of green, its aromas and its honeyed flavours. It is a good accompaniment to fresh trout and salmon from the river Gave. The sweet Jurançons have a lovely golden colour, and offer complex aromas of exotic fruits (pineapple and guava) and spices (such as nutmeg and cinnamon). Their balance between acidity and sweetness makes them a perfect foil for foie gras. Sweet Jurançons can be kept for a long time to provide big wines for a whole meal from aperitif to dessert, as well as to accompany fish with sauce and ewe's milk cheeses from the Ossau valley. The best vintages are: 1970, 1971, 1975, 1981, 1982, 1983, 1987, 1989, 1990 and 1995. In 2000 production reached 45,419 hl (1,199,062 gal).

DOM. BELLEGARDE
Cuvée Thibault 1999★★★

☐   5 ha   10,000   ▥ €11-15

The Jurançon produced at this estate of more than 15 ha (37.05 acres) was the best-liked of the selection. This wine really stands out, with its deep-golden colour with hints of orange. The remarkably dense, complex nose is evocative of a *tutti frutti* basket, a spray of flowers, a bouquet of spices, and a mouthful of honey. Pleasant and full, the palate reveals its wonderful lusciousness in a faultless balance. Its richly aromatic character, under-pinned by high-quality, well-balanced oak, continues into a sumptuous finish. The **Jurançon Sec 2000**, matured in vat, was awarded one star.

☛ Pascal Labasse, quartier Coos, 64360 Monein, tel. 05.59.21.33.17, fax 05.59.21.44.40, e-mail domaine.bellegarde@wanadoo.fr
𝕐 ev. day except Sun. 10am–12 noon 2pm–6.30pm

DOM. BORDENAVE
Cuvée des Dames 1999★

☐   10 ha   n.c.   ▮ ♦ €8-11

Though it may appear delicate with its pale, bright-gold colour, it reveals its intensity in a range of fresh exotic fruit and crystallised lemon aromas. This is a straightforward wine, with a smooth attack and a full body, which is lively and sweet at the same time, with aromas of citrus fruit that persist to the finish. The **Cuvée Savin 99** is also a great success with its nice balance and powerful aromas.

☛ Gisèle Bordenave, quartier Ucha, 64360 Monein, tel. 05.59.21.34.83, fax 05.59.21.37.32 ☑ 𝕐 ev. day 9am–6pm

BORDENAVE-COUSTARRET
Le Barou 1999★

☐   n.c.   1,500   ▥ €11-15

A beautifully-presented wine, with golden reflections. When shaken, it produces smoky, floral and soft fruit aromas. The lively attack precedes a well-balanced palate, fresh and delicately scented.

☛ Bordenave-Coustarret, quartier Baouch, 64290 Lasseube, tel. 05.59.21.72.66, fax 05.59.21.72.66 ☑
𝕐 ev. day 10am–6.30pm; Sun. by appt.

Jurançon

ETIENNE BRANA
Collection Royale Premières Neiges 2000★

☐   n.c.   n.c.   ▮ ♦ €8-11

The two Manseng grape varieties used in this light, bright-golden wine blend nicely. The intense nose suggests peach, apricot, pear and exotic fruits, underlined by a touch of rose. Straightforward and fairly full-bodied, the palate is enticing with its fine, intensely expressive flavours.

☛ Etienne Brana , 3 *bis*, av. du Jaï-Alaï, 64220 Saint-Jean-Pied-de-Port, tel. 05.59.37.00.44, fax 05.59.37.14.28, e-mail brana-etienne@wanadoo.fr ☑
𝕐 ev. day except Sat. Sun. 9am–12 noon 2pm–6pm

DOM. BRU-BACHE
La Quintessence 1999★★ n.c. n.c. ⊞ €11-15

This exceptional estate is among those that have collected the greatest number of stars and *coups de cœur* over the 18 editions of the *Guide*. *L'Éminence* was awarded two stars and a *coup de cœur* for the 98 vintage; the 99 is remarkable. However, La Quintessence is the star in this edition. Bursting with beautiful reflections of pure gold, it has an intense and elegant nose: honey and flowers, fruit jelly, a little touch of citrus zest, spices and hints of oak. Initially fresh, the mouth becomes progressively more full till the flavours dissipate into a slightly acidic finish. The wine is perfectly integrated.

🍷 Dom. Bru-Bache, rue Barada, 64360 Monein, tel. 05.59.21.36.34, fax 05.59.21.32.67 ☑ 🍷 by appt.

DOM. CAPDEVIELLE
Noblesse d'Automne 1999★★ 4.5 ha 12,000 ▪ €8-11

Ahead of its **Jurançon Sec Brise Océane 2000**, a great success, the Jury placed this intense, radiant, golden wine. The concentrated nose is redolent of crystallised fruits, mainly exotic (such as the nashi, an Asian fruit like a cross between an apple and a pear), and sweet spices. The supple attack precedes a mellow, warming palate with plenty of fullness and aroma. The finish is embellished with dried fruit and gingerbread undertones. This is an original, well-made wine.

🍷 Didier Capdevielle, quartier Coos, 64360 Monein, tel. 05.59.21.30.25, fax 05.59.21.30.25, e-mail domaine.capdevielle@wanadoo.fr ☑
🍷 ev. day 8.30am–12 noon 1pm–7pm; Sun. by appt.

CLOS CASTET Cuvée spéciale Vieilli en fût de chêne neuf 1999★★ 2 ha n.c. ⊞ €11-15

This wine has strong, floral aromas of honeysuckle and jasmine, with a fragrance of crystallised citrus fruits (orange, almost apricot) and currants, and a hint of barley-sugar sticks. It is concentrated, round and full-bodied on the palate.

🍷 Alain Labourdette, Clos Castet, 64360 Cardesse, tel. 05.59.21.33.09, fax 05.59.21.28.22 ☑
🍷 ev. day 9am–12 noon 2pm–7pm

DOM. CAUHAPE
Noblesse du temps 1999★★ 4 ha 12,000 ⊞ €23-30

Henri Ramonteu claimed to be a self-taught man when he established this estate in 1980. Since then, his wines have travelled the world, going from strength to strength. This intense wine is golden-straw coloured. After hints of oak and vanilla come aromas of citron blossom, acacia and crystallised apricot. The concentration is shown by the richness and warmth on the palate, but there is enough freshness to give the wine a good balance. The expressive flavours linger on the spicy finish. A characterful wine, for laying down. The estate's prize Jurançon, **Quintessence du Petit-Manseng 99**, is awarded one star; it can only improve as the years go by.

🍷 Henri Ramonteu, Dom. Cauhapé, quartier Castet, 64360 Monein, tel. 05.59.21.33.02, fax 05.59.21.41.82, e-mail domainecauhape@wanadoo.fr ☑
🍷 by appt.

CLOS GASSIOT Elégance 1999★ 3 ha 4,500 ⊞ ♦ €8-11

Vines have existed here since the 14th century, and the coat of arms depicted on the label testifies to the history of this family. This radiant, golden-yellow wine is infused with flowers, honey, crystallised fruit and sweet spices. A straightforward and agreeably lively wine, it stays well-balanced up to the long, fruity finish.

🍷 Antoine Tavernier, rte de Pau, 64360 Abos, tel. 05.59.60.10.22. fax 05.59.71.58.92 ☑ 🍷 by appt.

CLOS GUIROUILH
Petit Cuyalàa 1999★★ 1.3 ha 1,600 ⊞ €30-38

The **Jurançon Sec 2000** is a great success. This sweet, amber-coloured *moelleux* 99 is remarkable. It has overripe aromas of beeswax and fruity jam, underlined by a generous oakiness, the result of 22 months' maturation in barrel, as well as a full, rich body. Even though the oak has yet to integrate with the concentrated fruit, the wine is nonetheless superb now.

🍷 Jean Guirouilh, rte de Belair, 64290 Lasseube, tel. 05.59.04.21.45, fax 05.59.04.22.73 ☑

CH. JOLYS Epiphanie 1999★★ 1.8 ha 2,200 ⊞ €46-76

Château Jolys was in ruins when it was taken over in 1959. Since the first vines were planted in 1964, the vineyard has grown to a size of 36 ha (88.92 acres). Strong golden-yellow, its Cuvée Epiphanie already has a powerful and complex nose: ripe fruit (chestnut and medlar) and crystallised fruit (orange peel and exotic fruits) accompanied by a distinctly toasty note. The full, rich palate testifies to the technique of *passerillage* (drying on the vine). This well-balanced wine still bears the mark of its time spent in barrel, but it should mature well. Also noteworthy is the **Jurançon Vendanges Tardives 99** (late harvest), which is a great success.

🍷 Ste des Domaines Latrille, Ch. Jolys, 64290 Gan, tel. 05.59.21.72.79, fax 05.59.21.55.61 ☑ 🍷 ev. day except Sat. Sun. 8.30am–12 noon 1.30pm–5.30pm

Jurançon

CAVE DES PRODUCTEURS DE JURANÇON Prestige 1999★★

☐ 100 ha 100,000 ▮ ♦ €8-11

While the **Croix du Prince 99** was judged a great success, this Cuvée Prestige won the Jury's vote because the producer has managed to obtain a pure, sweet *moelleux* without employing artificial means. Golden-coloured with intense tones, this wine is subtly evocative of ripe, fresh fruit, with its range of juicy yellow-peach, mango, white-flower and mint aromas. The full-bodied palate is perfectly balanced, leading to a surprisingly full, rich finish. A delicacy.

☞ Cave des Producteurs de Jurançon, 53, av. Henri-IV, 64290 Gan, tel. 05.59.21.57.03, fax 05.59.21.72.06, e-mail cave.gan@ adour-bureau.fr ◪ ⍭ ev. day except Sun. 8am–12.30pm 1.30pm–7pm

DOM. LARREDYA
Sélection des terrasses 1999★★

☐ 2 ha 8,000 ▥ €11-15

Golden-yellow with very light glints of green, this wine opens generously when agitated, with fine, complex aromas of peach, mango and orange. The full-bodied palate has plenty of freshness and richness, and leads to a good finish. The wine is already agreeable and promising. The **Cuvée Simon Elevée en Fût** (matured in barrel) was also judged a great success.

☞ Jean-Marc Grussaute, La Chapelle-de-Rousse, 64110 Jurançon, tel. 05.59.21.74.42, fax 05.59.21.76.72 ◪ ⍭ by appt.

DOM. LARROUDE
Un Jour d'Automne 1999★★

☐ 1 ha 1,500 ▥ €15-23

The Larroudé estate really does itself credit with this 99 vintage. One autumn day was born this dense wine of old gold, which leaves pretty tears on the surface of the glass. Its rich nose evokes butter, honey, orange peel, toasted almonds and *crème catalane* sprinkled with cinnamon. After a smooth attack, the palate develops its full flavour and fragrances to enchant the senses with an impression of warmth and richness.

☞ Julien et Christiane Estoueigt, EARL du dom. Larroudé, s64360 Lucq-de-Béarn, tel. 05.59.34.35.92, fax 05.59.34.35.92 ◪ ⍭ by appt.

DOM. DE MALARRODE
Cuvée Prestige Vieilli en fût de chêne 1999★

☐ 2.5 ha 8,000 ▥ €8-11

A golden, clear Jurançon, with an intense nose of brioche, honey and butter, with hints of crystallised fruits, this wine is already delicious. After a fairly rich attack, it becomes full-bodied on the palate, still somewhat warming. A hint of honey unfolds, accompanied by well-integrated oak and a final note of spice.

☞ Gaston Mansanné, Dom. de Malarrode, 64360 Monein, tel. 05.59.21.44.27, fax 05.59.21.44.27 ◪ ⍭ by appt.

DOM. DE MONTESQUIOU
Grappe d'or 1999★★

☐ 2 ha 7,500 ▥ €8-11

Bright gold in colour, this wine reveals an assortment of white flower and dried fruit aromas, with notes of vanilla and resin and a hint of white truffle. After a sweet initial attack, the palate is well-structured, rich and soft. It retains its original floral and sweet fruit aromas.

☞ Gérard Bordenave-Montesquieu, Quartier Haut-Ucha, 64360 Monein, tel. 05.59.21.43.49, fax 05.59.21.43.49, e-mail info@domaine-de-montesquiou.com ◪ ⍭ by appt.

DOM. DE NAYS-LABASSERE 1999★★

☐ 4 ha 20,000 ▮ €8-11

For the past five years, the 7-ha (17.29-acre) Nays-Labassère estate has put forward a remarkable example of the appellation. Straw-coloured with tints of shimmering green, it reveals a basket of ripe, almost crystallised fruit, mingled with notes of aromatic plants. The full palate provides hints of jellied fruit and soft spices, all the time exhibiting a refreshing liveliness.

☞ Philippe de Nays, La Chapelle de Nays, 64110 Jurançon, tel. 05.59.21.70.57, fax 05.59.21.70.67 ◪ ⍭ by appt.

CH. DE ROUSSE 1999★

☐ 2 ha 6,500 ▥ €8-11

A former hunting lodge of Henri IV, the Château de Rousse today possesses 8 ha (19.76 acres) of vines. Its Jurançon, with its pronounced golden-yellow colour, shows its maturity by the complex aromas of flowers, exotic fruits and cinnamon on buttered toast. Dense and rich, the palate is evocative of fruit jelly, but it also has a good deal of freshness right up to its fruity and slightly acidic finish. It is an energetic combination.

☞ Marc Labat, Ch. de Rousse, La Chapelle-de-Rousse, 64110 Jurançon, tel. 05.59.21.75.08, fax 05.59.21.76.54, e-mail mlabat@nomade.fr ◪ ⍭ by appt.

CLOS THOU Cuvée Julie 1999★
n.c. n.c.

There are two very successful Jurançon wines presented by this estate: the **Suprême de Thou 99**, matured 18 months in barrel, and this intense, complex wine. The first impression on the nose is of white flowers and rose petals, which then continues to develop with accents of honey and a basket of exotic fruits. After a sweet attack, an increasingly lively acidity contributes to the balance of a rich and still-aromatic blend.

☛ Henri Lapouble-Laplace, chem. Larredya, 64110 Jurançon, tel. 05.59.06.08.60, fax 05.59.06.08.60 ▣
🍷 ev. day except Sun. 9am–12 noon 2pm–6pm

UROULAT 1999★
5 ha 20,000 €11-15

This magnificent clay-and-flint soil likes the Petit Manseng grape: here, it can express itself freely under the high authority of one of the AOC's great personalities. Behind its deep, yellow colour with hints of orange, a powerful range of aromas emerges; although oak and toasted aromas are still dominant, a little fruitiness breaks through. The full palate is a balance of freshness and sweetness. Being fruitier on the palate than on the nose is an indication that the traces of oak will break down with age.

☛ Charles Hours, quartier Trouilh, 64360 Monein, tel. 05.59.21.46.19, fax 05.59.21.46.90 🍷 by appt.

DOM. VIGNAU LA JUSCLE 1998
3 ha 3,000 €8-11

This wine-producing property from the 17th century remained abandoned for a long time, until Michel Valton took it over in 1987. His Jurançon is a golden-yellow colour, fairly intense in its fruity-floral aromas supported by a hint of honey and charred undertones. The lively attack indicates good supporting acidity, enhancing the delicious flavours on the palate. Although only medium-bodied, the range of aromatic qualities persists. All of these elements combine to produce a very agreeable wine.

☛ Michel Valton, Dom. Vignau-la-Juscle, 64290 Aubertin, tel. 05.59.83.03.66, fax 05.59.83.03.71 🍷 by appt.

CLOS BELLEVUE 2000
1 ha 6,000 €3-5

Two wines from this family-run estate deserve to be singled out: a **Jurançon Moelleux Cuvée Traditionnelle 99**, made from Gros Manseng, and this dry Jurançon, made from the same grape. The strong, yellow colour envelops intense aromas, rather fine,

Jurançon Sec

CLOS LAPEYRE Cuvée Vitage Vielh 1999★★★
n.c. 15,000 €8-11

Jean-Bernard Larrieu is currently in the process of converting his vineyard to organic production. The dry Jurançon wines from this producer have what it takes to appeal. The **Cuvée Lapeyre 2000** is already remarkable; matured in vat, it releases a complex nose of flowers and exotic fruits, then becomes well-rounded and well-balanced on the palate. As

DOM. DU CINQUAU 1999★
1 ha 3,500 €8-11

With an enticingly strong, yellow colour, this Jurançon has an intense nose with oaky fragrances at first (vanilla and toast), then fruit and honey. After a lively attack, the palate becomes richer and more powerful. It is very aromatic, but still dominated by a strong charred-oak taste. Also worthy of note is the **Jurançon Moelleux 99 Elevé en Fût de Chêne** (matured in oak barrels), which is a great success.

☛ Pierre Saubot, Dom. du Cinquau, Cidex 43, 64230 Artiguelouve, tel. 05.59.83.10.41, fax 05.59.83.12.93 ▣ 🍷 by appt.

DOM. CAUHAPE Noblesse 1999★★
2 ha 8,000 €15-23

Made purely from the Petit Manseng grape, this dry Jurançon has had the benefit of being matured in barrel on the lees for ten months. It is now a deep, gold colour with glimmers of orange. The powerful nose suggests crystallised orange peel with honey, spices and vanilla. On the palate, a surprisingly well-structured wine emerges. A complex balance is established between the alcohol and spicy aromas, with charred undertones. This is a beautiful creation.

☛ Henri Ramonteu, Dom. Cauhapé, quartier Castet, 64360 Monein, tel. 05.59.21.33.02, fax 05.59.21.41.82, e-mail domainecauhape@wanadoo.fr ▣ 🍷 by appt.

both floral and slightly fruity. The lively attack is followed by a fresh, but still fruity palate, with a hint of bitterness on the finish.

☛ Jean Muchada, Clos Bellevue, chem. des Vignes, 64360 Cuqueron, tel. 05.59.21.34.82, fax 05.59.21.34.82 🍷 by appt.

DOM. DE CABARROUY 2000★★
1 ha 7,000 €5-8

This intense, strong, yellow-coloured wine produces aromas of pear drops, pineapple and flowers. After a fresh attack, it becomes well-rounded and full on the palate, with a good deal of fruit, then continues with a balancing acidity. The **Jurançon Cuvée Sainte-Catherine 99**, a sweet and rich barrel-matured wine, is awarded one star.

☛ Dom. de Cabarrouy, 64290 Lasseube, tel. 05.59.04.23.08, fax 05.59.04.21.85 ▣ 🍷 ev. day 9am–12.30pm 2pm–7pm; Sun. by appt.

preference. Perfectly clear, with pretty green hints, it releases a range of intense aromas, rich in fruits (citrus fruits, pear and lychee) and underpinned by a floral note of broom. After a slightly sparkling attack, the balance on the palate is maintained throughout the mid-palate, and develops a fruitiness even more marked than on the nose.

Cave des Producteurs de Jurançon, 53, av. Henri-IV, 64290 Gan, tel. 05.59.21.57.03, fax 05.59.21.72.06, e-mail cave.gan@adour-bureau.fr ev. day except Sun. 8am–12.30pm 1.30pm–7pm

DOM. DE SOUCH
Cuvée de Marie-Kattalyn 2000★

1.8 ha   4,800   €8-11

Yvonne Hegoburu runs her 6.8-ha (16.8-acre) vineyard on biodynamic principles (a form of organic farming). Her dry Jurançon, a strong yellow in colour with green reflections, produces delicate aromas of white flowers, exotic fruits and spices. The straightforward attack precedes a beautiful structure on the palate. The finish, still reserved, reveals a hint of bitterness. The **Jurançon Moelleux Cuvée de Marie-Kattalyn 99**, matured in barrel, is also a great success.

Yvonne Hegoburu, Dom. de Souch, 64110 Laroin, tel. 05.59.06.27.22, fax 05.59.06.51.55 by appt.

for the Cuvée Vitage Vielh, this reveals itself under strong, yellow-coloured finery, leaving powerful aromas of dried and crystallised fruits, gingerbread and acacia honey in its trail. With a straightforward attack and just the right degree of liveliness, it fills the palate with its richness and structure. It strikes a perfect balance between well-proportioned acidity and rich, persistent concentration.

Jean-Bernard Larrieu, La Chapelle-de-Rousse, 64110 Jurançon, tel. 05.59.21.50.80, fax 05.59.21.51.83, e-mail jean-bernard.larrieu@wanadoo.fr ev. day except Sun. 9am–12 noon 2pm–6pm

DOM. NIGRI 2000★★

3 ha   18,000   €5-8

In charge of 10 ha (24.7 acres) of vines, Jean-Louis Lacoste presents this straw-coloured Jurançon, very intense and youthful in its expression: the nose combines floral and fruity aromas, accompanied by mineral notes. The straightforward attack, slightly sparkling, introduces a fresh and aromatic palate, with perfect balance and a long and pleasant finish. Also worthy of note is the **Jurançon Moelleux Réserve du Domaine Nigri 99**, which is awarded one star.

Jean-Louis Lacoste, Dom. Nigri, Candeloup, 64360 Monein, tel. 05.59.21.42.01, fax 05.59.21.42.59 ev. day 9am–12 noon 1.30pm–7pm; Sun. by appt.

PRIMO PALATUM Mythologia 1999

0.4 ha   1,200   €30-38

Primo Palatum is a firm of *négociants-éleveur* established in 1996 by oenologist Xavier Copel. This Jurançon, a strong, straw-yellow colour with hints of gold, has a warming, concentrated nose: charred notes precede aromas of crystallised fruits, mainly exotic. The same concentration is found on the rich, powerful, warming palate. The oak is still noticeable, but it will integrate with time.

Primo Palatum, 1, Cirette, 33190 Morizès, tel. 05.56.71.39.39, fax 05.56.71.39.40, e-mail primo-palatum@wanadoo.fr by appt.

CH. ROQUEHORT 2000★★

18 ha   24,000   €5-8

While the **Jurançon Sec Grain Sauvage 2000**, matured in vat, deserves to be singled out, the Château Roquehort was the Jury's

Madiran

Madiran has its origins in Roman times and, later, was the wine of pilgrims making the long journey to Santiago de Compostela in Spain. The gastronomy of the Gers region and its popularity in Paris have also helped to promote this Pyrenean wine. Much of the 1,290 ha (3,186 acres) of the appellation is planted with Tannat, which produces a wine that is tannic in youth, vividly coloured, with preliminary scents of raspberries; it develops after long ageing. Cabernet Sauvignon and Cabernet France (or Bouchy) and Fer Servadou (or Pinenc) are blended with it. The vines are trained to half-height. The production was 70,946 hl (1,872,974 gal) in 2000.

The Madiran is a supremely virile wine. Its vinification can be adapted so it can be drunk young when its fruitiness and suppleness can be best displayed. It goes well with goose confits (preserved in fat) and duck breasts served rare. The traditional Madiran, with its high proportion of Tannat, ages very well in wooden casks and can mature for a number of years. The mature Madirans are sensual, fleshy and full-bodied, with aromas of toasted bread, and go well with game and the ewe's milk cheeses from the high valleys.

CH. D'AYDIE Odé d'Aydie 1998★
■ 20 ha 100,000 €8-11

Elegant in its deep, bright blackness, the Odé d'Aydie leaves in its trail intensely smoky aromas, fragrances of vanilla and menthol, and notes of balsam too, which never overshadow the fruit. The same elegance can be perceived on the palate, in a successful blend of oak and wine. It is full-bodied, velvety and structured. With its **Pacherenc du Vic-Bilh Moelleux**, the **Château d'Aydie 99** is every bit as much of a success.

GAEC Vignobles Laplace, 64330 Aydie, tel. 05.59.04.08.00, fax 05.59.04.08.08, e-mail pierre.laplace@wanadoo.fr
Y ev. day 9am–12.30pm 2pm–8pm

CH. BARREJAT Tradition 1999★★
■ 12 ha 80,000 €3-5

A Cuvée Tradition in the purest Madiran style: 60% Tannat, 25% Cabernet Franc and 15% Cabernet Sauvignon grapes. Garnet with glints of scarlet, it has a fine nose, very expressive in its range of jammy blackberry and blackcurrant fruits, undergrowth and earth. Tannins are very evident on the well-balanced palate, which is supported by richness and concentration. It is full-flavoured with a persistent finish. Another Madiran, the **Cuvée des Vieux Ceps 99**, made from vines aged 80 to 100 years and matured in oak barrels, is awarded one star. Also worthy of note is the **Pacherenc du Vic-Bilh Moelleux, Cuvée de la Passion 99 Elevée en Fût de Chêne** (matured in oak barrels), which is a great success.

Denis Capmartin, Ch. Barréjat, 32400 Maumusson-Laguian, tel. 05.62.69.74.92, fax 05.62.69.77.54
Y ev. day except Sun. 8am–12 noon 2pm–7pm

DOM. BERNET Vieilli en fût de chêne 1999
■ n.c. 20,000

This wine is characterised by its intensity, in terms of both its dark-red colour and its warming nose, with dark-berry, liquorice and toasty aromas. After a smooth attack, the wine becomes increasingly powerful on the palate. Its unctuous body is supported by a good structure and a fairly high oak presence, before developing into a menthol-flavoured finish.

Yves Doussau, Dom. Bernet, 32400 Viella, tel. 05.62.69.71.99, fax 05.62.69.75.08
Y by appt.

CANTE PEYRAGUT Grande Réserve 1998★★
■ 100 ha 60,000 €5-8

Deep black with violet glints, this powerful wine combines fruits, spices and grilled

CH. BOUSCASSE Vieilles vignes 1999★
■ 10 ha 60,000 €15-22

Full credit goes to Alain Brumont for this 99 vintage. Ink-coloured, this Cuvée Vieilles Vignes combines the fragrances of high-quality oak with those of ripe, dark berries. Its concentrated, full, rich palate rests on a base of tannins, which are firm but already richly textured, giving length to the finish. This is a well-made wine, beautiful for laying down. Every bit as successful are the **Château Montus 99** and **Château Montus Cuvée Prestige 99**, made from 99% Tannat grapes, and the **Château Bouscassé 99**.

Alain Brumont, Ch. Bouscassé, 32400 Maumusson-Laguian, tel. 05.62.69.74.67, fax 05.62.69.70.46
Y ev. day except Sun. 9am–12 noon 2pm–7pm

DOM. BERTHOUMIEU Cuvée Charles de Batz 1998★★
■ 7.5 ha 45,000 €8-11

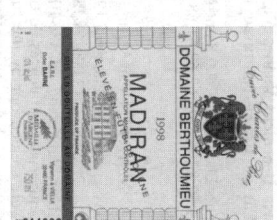

Well-accustomed to *coups de cœur*, Didier Barré has delighted the Jury again this year with a remarkable Madiran. Ink-black and extremely dense, the wine leaves long legs on the surface of the glass. The intense, elegant nose has ripe red- or dark-berry, soft fruit, cocoa, mint and liquorice aromas underpinned with light, grilled notes. The beautifully-ripe fruit is reinforced on the palate: though still firm and chewy, a richness and smoothness of texture can already be perceived. It is mouth-filling with a long finish. Distinguished last year in the 98 vintage, the **Cuvée Tradition 99** is awarded two stars. The **Pacherenc du Vic-Bilh Moelleux, Symphonie d'Automne 99** is also a great success.

Didier Barré, 32400 Viella, tel. 05.62.69.74.05, fax 05.62.69.80.64, e-mail barre.didier@wanadoo.fr
Y ev. day 8am–12 noon 2pm–7pm; Sun. by appt.

Madiran

aromas. The palate is initially rich and well-rounded, providing a solid structure. This rich, full wine is remarkably well-balanced, with well-integrated tannins. It can be kept between three and five years before drinking. The producers of Plaimont have also enjoyed success with two Madirans being awarded one star each: **La Mothe Peyran 98** and the **Arte Benedicte Vieilles Vignes 98 Elevé en Fût de Chêne** (matured in oak barrels).

☛ Producteurs Plaimont, 32400 Saint-Mont, tel. 05.62.69.62.87, fax 05.62.69.61.68 ✓
Ⴠ by appt.

DOM. CAPMARTIN Cuvée du

Couvent Elevé en fût de chêne neuf 1998★★
■   2 ha   12,000   ■ | | €8-11

Besides their **Pacherenc du Vic-Bilh Sec 2000** and **Liquoreux Confidences du Couvent 99**, which were singled out by the Jury, the Capmartin estate have submitted two Madirans. While the **Cuvée Tradition** is a deep success, this wine wins the vote with its opulent nose has aromas of violet and blue. The opulent nose has aromas of violet dark berries, cocoa, vanilla and liquorice over a background of toasted bread. The rich, smooth first impression is met by a beautiful, mouth-filling texture, supported by well-structured, high-quality tannins. The body is full of flavours that explode on the palate on the finish.

☛ Guy Capmartin, Le Couvent,
32400 Maumusson-Laguian,
tel. 05.62.69.87.88, fax 05.62.69.83.07 ✓
Ⴠ ev. day except Sun. 9am–12.30pm
2pm–7pm

CHAPELLE LENCLOS 1999★

■   6.5 ha 30,000   ■ | | ♦   €8-11

The two Madiran wines offered by Patrick Ducournau were a great success, the **Domaine Mouréou 99** and this one. An intense ink colour, the initially restrained nose soon opens out into ripe, dark-berry aromas over a background of soft oak and vanilla. From the initial rich attack, the wine becomes powerful, concentrated and firmly structured on the palate. Finely-grained tannins result in a fairly tight-knit framework that makes for a lasting finish.

☛ Patrick Ducournau,
32400 Maumusson-Laguian,
tel. 05.62.69.78.11, fax 05.62.69.75.87 ✓
Ⴠ by appt.

COURTET LAPERRE Grande Réserve

Vielles Vignes Elevé en fût de chêne 1998★★
■ 120 ha 80,000   ■ | | €5-8

Black and fringed with ruby and violet, this wine opens generously with gamey scents before developing into fragrances of fruits and spices, underpinned by toasty aromas. Straightaway, it conveys its great maturity and complexity. On the palate, it surprises by its almost unctuous attack, followed by a powerful, warming body, supported by

intense tannins. This wine should be kept at least eight years before drinking.
☛ Vignoble de Gascogne, 32400 Riscle,
tel. 05.62.69.62.87, fax 05.62.69.66.71 ✓
Ⴠ by appt.

CAVE DE CROUSEILLES

Carte d'Or 1999★★
■   250 ha 700,000   ■ | | ♦   €5-8

This is a beautifully-presented, garnet-coloured wine. A basket of red berries seasoned with spices are present on the intense, complex nose. The pleasantly smooth attack leads on to a flavour-filled palate, both rich and structured by integrated tannins. This is a well-balanced wine with a long finish.

☛ Cave de Crouseilles, 64350 Crouseilles,
tel. 05.59.68.10.93, fax 05.59.68.14.33 ✓
Ⴠ by appt.

DOM. DAMIENS

Cuvée vieillie en fût de chêne 1998★
■   2.5 ha 15,000   ■ | | ♦   €8-11

Nuances of cherry-red illuminate this wine's intense, bright colour. The initial impression on the nose is of kirsch, followed by spicy and toasty aromas. The palate has a degree of chewiness and firm tannins, while maintaining a balance between the flavours. This Madiran needs to be kept a while to integrate completely.

☛ André et Pierre-Michel Beheity, Dom. Damiens, 64330 Aydie, tel. 05.59.04.03.13, fax 05.59.04.02.74 ✓ Ⴠ ev. day 9am–12.30pm 2.30pm–7pm; Sat. Sun. by appt.

CH. DE DIUSSE Tradition 1999

■   10.5 ha 55,000   ■ | ♦   €5-8

A vocational rehabilitation centre, Diusse is very regular in its wine production. Crimson in colour with bright glints, this Madiran gives the impression of being already slightly matured with its cooked-fruit fragrances. The well-balanced palate, with its integrated tannins, has a good length.

☛ Ch. de Diusse, 64330 Diusse,
tel. 05.59.04.02.83, fax 05.59.04.05.77 ✓
Ⴠ by appt.

CLOS FARDET

Cuvée Moutoue Fardet 1998
■   1.2 ha   4,000 | | €8-11

With a bright, clear, ruby colour, this is a rustic Madiran. On the nose, the oak is made evident by intense toast and spice aromas; the fruits mix in with nuances of fruit jelly. On the palate, the supple attack develops into still-firm tannins, but the body is fresh and flavoursome.

☎ SCEA Moutoue Fardet, 3, chem. de Bellet, 65700 Madiran, tel. 05.62.31.91.37, fax 05.62.31.91.37 ▼ ▼ by appt.

☛ Savoret

CH. DE FITÈRE 1999

■ 5 ha   40,000   €5-8

A blend of 70% Tannat and 30% Cabernet Sauvignon grapes are used to make this sprightly Madiran. Dark with hints of garnet, the wine opens with a whole range of aromas, from vegetal notes to ripe fruit and spices. The attack is supple. The intense, spicy flavours on the palate do, however, end in a tannic finish supported by oak.

☎ René Casters, 32400 Cannet, tel. 05.62.69.82.36, fax 05.62.69.78.90 ▼

▼ ev. day except Sat. Sun. in winter 9am–12 noon 2pm–7pm

DOM. LABRANCHE LAFFONT

Vieilles vignes 1998★

■ 1.5 ha   9,000   €11-15

Dark, dense and strong, this Madiran is aubergine-coloured with glints of black. The nose is heavy with aromas of red berries mixed with liquorice, resin and cloves. The elegance on the palate stems from the beautiful flavours and good balance. It is as harmonious as a wine ever needs to be.

☎ Christine Dupuy, 32400 Maumusson-Laguian, tel. 05.62.69.74.90, fax 05.62.69.76.03 ▼

▼ by appt.

DOM. LAFFONT Hécate 1998★★

■ 0.4 ha   2,000   €11-15

Pierre Speyer offers three beautiful wines, one of which is a **Pacherenc du Vic-Bilh Sec 99 Elevé en Fûts de Chêne Neufs** (matured in oak barrels) while the other two are Madirans: the **Cuvée Erigone 98**, a great success, and this wine, with its decidedly dark, deep appearance, with hints of violet. The rich nose envelops fruit-brandy fragrances in a spicy, toasty oak. Powerful, rich and full on the palate, the wine is firmly structured but very well-integrated. The fine balance indicates near-perfect maturation.

☎ Pierre Speyer, Dom. Laffont, 32400 Maumusson-Laguian, tel. 05.62.69.75.23, fax 05.62.69.80.27 ▼

▼ by appt.

DOM. LAOUGUE 1999★

■ 2.4 ha   10,000   €11-15

Double honours for Pierre Dabadie for two highly-successful wines: one is a **Pacherenc du Vic-Bilh Moelleux 99** made purely from the Petit Manseng grape; the other is a Madiran.

The latter, a very dark wine, progressively reveals a range of oaky aromas (with vanilla, toasty and smoky characteristics) accompanied by some dark-berry notes. Rich and unctuous on the attack, the wine becomes more well-rounded and concentrated on the palate, while oak flavours remain at the heart. The finish is supported by integrated tannins, making for a well-balanced wine.

☎ Pierre Dabadie, rue de Madiran, 32400 Viella, tel. 05.62.69.90.05, fax 05.62.69.71.41 ▼

▼ ev. day 9am–12 noon 2pm–6pm

DOM. DU PEYROU 1998★

■ 0.3 ha   1,200   €5-8

Deep black with hints of violet, this intense wine reveals a range of aromas well-balanced between fruit and oak: a little spice and light, toasty aromas can be detected. A velvety attack, a blend of freshness and richness in the middle and a well-supported finish are what make this Madiran the success it is.

☎ Jacques Brumont, Dom. du Peyrou, 32400 Viella, tel. 05.62.69.90.12, fax 05.62.69.90.12.

▼ ev. day 8am–12 noon 2pm–8pm

☛ Georges Brumont

CH. SAINT-BENAZIT 1998★★

■ 24 ha   70,000   €5-8

The deep, red colour with violet reflections immediately shows a well-concentrated wine. The initial impression on the nose is of mocha and coffee followed by a release of red and dark berries in a basket of oak and spices. The tannins are still present on the palate, but the concentration is there: the finish, already long, indicates good ageing potential. This winery also distinguishes itself by its **Château Laroche Viella 98**, a great success.

☎ Vignoble de Gascogne, 32400 Riscle, tel. 05.62.69.62.87, fax 05.62.69.66.71 ▼

▼ by appt.

DOM. TAILLEURGUET

Elevé en fût de chêne 1998★

■ 1 ha   5,000   €5-8

The Tailleurguet estate has produced two successful **Madirans**, one of which, the **99** vintage, was matured in vat, and the other in barrel. The barrel-matured wine, cherry-coloured with violet tones, opens smoothly with notes of vanilla and butter. Then, notes of kirsch are released, accompanied by spices. The wine starts subtly, then quickly becomes fresh and fruity within a smooth but firm body, especially on the finish. Also noted, with one star, is the **Pacherenc du Vic-Bilh Sec 2000**.

☎ EARL Tailleurguet, 32400 Maumusson-Laguian, tel. 05.62.69.73.92, fax 05.62.69.83.69 ▼

▼ ev. day except Sun. 9am–1pm 2pm–7pm

☛ Bouby

Pacherenc du Vic-Bilh

Pacherenc du Vic-Bilh

From the same area as Madiran, this white wine is made from local varieties (Arrufiac, Manseng, Courbu) and others from the Bordelais (Sauvignon, Sémillon); this combination creates a notably rich aromatic palette. According to the climatic conditions of the year concerned, the wines can be dry and perfumed or medium and lively. Their finesse is quite remarkable; they are fleshy and strong with a nose melding almond, hazelnut and exotic fruits. Pacherenc du Vic-Bilh make excellent aperitif wines and, when medium, are perfect with a terrine of foie gras. In 1999 2,939 hl (77,590 gal) of dry wine and 5,949 hl (157,054 gal) of sweet wine were produced.

DOM. DU CRAMPILH
Moelleux 1999★★

☐   2 ha   n.c.   🍷 €8-11

The Jury awarded one star to the **Madiran Cuvée Baron 99**, made purely from the Tannat grape; this Pacherenc Moelleux was made entirely from the Petit Manseng variety. Golden-yellow with green tones, it has an intense, fresh nose. Fruit aromas dominate (pineapple and passion-fruit) and blend harmoniously with notes of vanilla. After a warming start, the full and always well-balanced palate develops a toasty taste. This is a well-made wine.

☛ Alain Oulié, 64350 Aurions-Idernes, tel. 05.59.04.00.63, fax 05.59.04.04.97, e-mail domaine-du-crampilh@epicuria.fr ☑
☉ ev. day except Sun. 9am–12 noon 2pm–7pm

FOLIE DE ROI Moelleux 1999★

☐   20 ha   30,000   🍷 €8-11

The Cave de Crouseilles offers three very successful **Pacherenc du Vic-Bilh Moelleux**: the **Automnal 99** and **Grain de Givre 99**, and this one, gold-coloured with light glimmers of green. The fairly intense nose seems fresh because of its predominantly fruity aromas, while the oak character remains subtle. The palate combines this fruity freshness with vanilla flavours to produce a charming blend.

☛ Cave de Crouseilles, 64350 Crouseilles, tel. 05.59.68.10.93, fax 05.59.68.14.33 ☑
☉ by appt.

CH. LAFFITTE-TESTON Sec Cuvée
Ericka Elevé en fût de chêne 2000★

☐   3 ha   20,000   🍷 €5-8

This is one of the most interesting wine cellars to visit, in terms of the set-up and wine-making methods. The Cuvée Ericka, a fresh, straw-coloured wine with brilliant tones, has an intense range of aromas consisting of exotic fruits, honey, butter and a gentle oak. The freshness can be detected on the attack, accompanied by a lingering flavour. The **Madiran Vieilles Vignes 99** was judged a great success.

☛ Jean-Marc Laffitte, 32400 Maumusson, tel. 05.62.69.74.58, fax 05.62.69.76.87 ☑
☉ by appt.

CH. DE LA MOTTE Moelleux 1999★★

☐   1 ha   3,000   🍷 ⚬ €8-11

Alongside a **Pacherenc du Vic-Bilh Sec 2000**, which is already a great success, this sweet wine is a little gem. The tasting starts with an intense, gold-coloured wine. The powerful, complex nose is like a cake made from overripe fruits: pear, quince, passion-fruit and citrus fruits, accompanied by attractive tertiary aromas. After a really rich attack, the palate is perfectly balanced between sugar, alcohol and acidity. The tasters were taken with the concentration and powerfulness of this wine, as well as its sweetness.

☛ Ghislaine Arrat, La Motte, 64350 Lasserre, tel. 05.59.68.16.98, fax 05.59.68.26.83 ☑ ☉ by appt.

CH. MONTUS Sec 2000★★

☐   3 ha   20,000   🍷 €11-15

Alain Brumont has a beautiful range of wines: ahead of his **Château Bouscassé Sec 2000**, singled out by the Jury, and his **Vendémiaire Doux 2000**, also a great success, this Château Montus is the winner. Rather an intense golden-yellow, it releases a fine nose, evocative of a bouquet of white flowers and a basket of ripe fruit (pear, pineapple and mango) on a bed of honey. The attack is fresh and the palate full and rich. Its well-balanced body is characterised by lasting fruit and brioche flavours.

☛ Alain Brumont, Ch. Bouscassé, 32400 Maumusson-Laguian, tel. 05.62.69.74.67, fax 05.62.69.70.46 ☑
☉ ev. day except Sun. 9am–12 noon 2pm–7pm

DOM. DU MOULIE
Moelleux Elevé en fût de chêne 1999★

☐   1 ha   3,000   🍷 €8-11

Clear yellow with green reflections, this wine has a good, intense nose, agreeably fresh because of the dominance of exotic and citrus fruits. Added to this, there is a hint of mint and a touch of oak. After a clean attack, the palate develops into a vanilla and coconut finish. Also worthy of note is the **Madiran Cuvée Chiffre 99**.

worthy of note and a great success is the **Madiran Vieill en Fût de Chêne 99** (matured in oak barrels).

➨ Alain Bortolussi, Ch. de Viella, rte de Maumusson, 32400 Viella, tel. 05.62.69.75.81, fax 05.62.69.79.18 ▣
Ⴤ ev. day except Sun. 8am–12.30pm 2pm–7pm

Tursan AOVDQS

This vineyard was once the property of Eleanor of Aquitaine. Nowadays the Tursan terroir covers some 460 ha (1,136 acres) and produces an average of 20,000 hl (528,000 gal) of red, rosé and white wines (35%). The most interesting are the whites made from the original vine variety, the Baroque. Dry, vigorous and inimitably perfumed, Tursan whites go very well with shad, elvers and grilled fish.

BARON DE BACHEN 1999

☐ | 17 ha | 19,000 | €11-15

This is the wine of a great chef, who in 1968 chose the charm of Eugénie-les-Bains for his fine gourmet restaurant. Rather pale and limpid, this 99 was matured in barrel for seven months, and this is reflected in the wine: toasty aromas are noticeable in a range of characteristics comprising honey and exotic fruits, also present on the palate, which still has noticeable oak. This wine needs to be kept a little longer.

➨ Michel Guérard, Cie hôtelière et fermière d'Eugénie-les-Bains, 40800 Duhort-Bachen, tel. 05.58.71.76.76, fax 05.58.71.77.77 ▣
Ⴤ by appt.
➨ SCA Ch. de Bachen

CH. DE PERCHADE 2000★

■ | 3.4 ha | 29,000 | €5-8

Tannat, Cabernet Franc and Cabernet Sauvignon grapes, planted in a clay-chalk soil, are the basis of this wine that is powerful and fine at the same time. Cherry and liquorice aromas are in evidence throughout. The **Château de Perchade white 2000** deserves to be singled out for its range of light fruit and gunflint aromas.

➨ EARL Dulucq, Château de Perchade, 40320 Payros-Cazautets, tel. 05.58.44.50.68, fax 05.58.44.57.75 ▣
Ⴤ ev. day except Sun. 8am–1pm 2.30pm–7pm

PRESTIGE DU VIEUX PAYS

Moelleux 1999★

☐ | 15 ha | 100,000 | €8-11

This producer presented three sweet wines, all of which were successful: the **Or du Vieux Pays 99**, the **Saint-Martin Vendanges de Novembre 99** and this Prestige du Vieux Pays, made from 50% Gros Manseng, 25% Petit Courbu, 5% Petit Manseng and 20% Arrufiac grapes. This 99, bright golden-yellow, is characterful and fine with its evocations of crystallised lemon, honey and spices. The palate, clean and well-balanced, reveals a pleasant sweetness and lasting crystallised fruit flavours.

➨ Vignoble de Gascogne, 32400 Riscle, tel. 05.62.69.62.87, fax 05.62.69.66.71 ▣
Ⴤ by appt.

DOM. SERGENT

Sec Elevé en fût de chêne 2000★

☐ | 0.3 ha | 2,400 | €5-8

These two highly-successful wines are beautiful examples of Pacherenc: a **Moelleux 99 Elevé en Fût de Chêne** (matured in oak barrels) and this wine, which was vinified dry and is a fresh-straw colour. This wine has an uncomplicated, intense nose with floral, soft-fruit and brioche aromas. The agreeably lively body provides a good balance between fruit and oak. Also worthy of note is the **Madiran 99** from this estate.

➨ EARL Dousseau, Dom. Sergent, 32400 Maumusson, tel. 05.62.69.74.93, fax 05.62.69.75.85 ▣ Ⴤ ev. day except Sun. 8am–12.30pm 2pm–7.30pm

CH. DE VIELLA Moelleux 1999★★★

☐ | 5 ha | 24,000 | €8-11

The *coup de coeur* was unanimously awarded to this Pacherenc du Vic-Bilh, made from 80% Petit Manseng and 20% Arrufiac grapes. It has a magnificent straw-gold colour and a powerful range of overripe aromas such as crystallised fruits, mainly exotic, which are balanced marvellously with the developed notes of undergrowth. After a warm attack, the palate delivers its full, rich concentration. The complex flavours last a long time. Also

➨ EARL Chiffre Charrier, Dom. du Moulié, 32400 Cannet, tel. 05.62.69.77.73, fax 05.62.69.83.66 ▣
Ⴤ ev. day except Sun. 8am–7pm
➨ Charrier

in no way old-fashioned. The golden colour is extremely bright; the nose expresses floral and citrus fruit aromas; and the fine, fruity palate gives an agreeable impression of freshness.

➤ Vignoble de Gascogne, 32400 Riscle, tel. 05.62.69.62.87, fax 05.62.69.66.71  Y by appt.

LES VIGNERONS DE TURSAN
Haute Carte 2000★

□ 40 ha   70,000   €3-5

The Tursan-Chalosse co-operative has distinguished itself with three selections from the 2000 vintage. While the **Cuvée Haute Carte rosé 2000** was singled out, its white counterpart is awarded one star. It is a pale, yellow colour with green reflections, and a nose that develops light fruit aromas, with mineral nuances of gunflint. Balanced by a very good acidity, this wine has a long finish, clearly expressing the Baroque grape that makes up one-third of the blend. Also worthy of note is the **Tursan Paysage red 2000**, a well-rounded wine, with morello-cherry aromas.

➤ Les Vignerons de Tursan, 40320 Geaune, tel. 05.58.44.51.25, fax 05.58.44.40.22, e-mail tursan.vin@wanadoo.fr   Y by appt.

DOM. DE MAOURIES 2000

1.5 ha   12,666   €3-5

This prettily-coloured rosé wine produces red- and dark-berry aromas: blackcurrant, raspberry and redcurrant. On the palate, it is supported by a good level of acidity, which makes it an ideal accompaniment to local charcuterie dishes.

➤ GAEC Dufau Père et Fils, Dom. de Maouries, 32400 Labarthète, tel. 05.62.69.63.84, fax 05.62.69.65.49, e-mail domaine.maouries@wanadoo.fr   Y by appt.

Côtes de Saint-Mont AOVDQS

This is a continuation of the Madiran vineyard. The Côtes de Saint-Mont is the most recent of the Pyrenean appellations (1981), producing wines of superior quality. The vineyard covers about 1,000 ha (2,470 acres), and annual production averages 60,000 hl (1,584,000 gal). The main red grape is the Tannat, the whites being made from Clairette, Arrufica, Courbu and the two Manseng varieties. Most of the production is managed by the dynamic Union des Caves Coopératives Plaimont. The red wines are vividly coloured and full-bodied, rapidly becoming round and pleasant. They are drunk with grilled meats and Garbure Gasconne, a local soup. The delicate rosés are appreciated for their fruity bouquet. The whites have a special flavour of the *terroir* and are dry and lively in character.

LE PASSE AUTHENTIQUE 2000★

□ 30 ha   200,000   €5-8

The Gros Manseng grape, the main ingredient here, was blended with the Petit Courbu and the Arrufiac to give birth to a wine that is

CH. DE SABAZAN 1999★★

■ 16 ha   35,000   €11-15

This intense red wine is a *coup de coeur*, with its nose of dark berries and spice. The oak is perfectly integrated in a powerful body structured and full, that lasts to a liquorice finish. This full-bodied wine can easily be kept for at least three years. Also worthy of note is the **Château de Sabazan red 98**, which is awarded one star, as is the **Cuvée Esprit des Vignes 99**, a red made from old vines and matured in barrel. In white, the **Cuvée Les Hauts de Bergelle 2000**, matured in barrel, especially impressed the Jury.

➤ Producteurs Plaimont, 32400 Saint-Mont, tel. 05.62.69.62.87, fax 05.62.69.61.68   Y by appt.

CH. SAINT-GO 1999★★

■ 38 ha   180,000   €8-11

This dark wine has beautiful dark-berry, leather, coffee and spice aromas. On the palate, the oak melts into a full-bodied wine, supported by silky tannins. A few years' keeping can only improve this wine, which will go well with red meat dishes, fillet of duck's breast or game. Also a great success, the **Cuvée Le Faître red 98** is a little oak-dominant, but this should soon integrate. The

Monastère de Saint-Mont red 98 was also singled out by the Jury.

● Vignoble de Gascogne, 32400 Riscle, tel. 05.62.69.62.87, fax 05.62.69.66.71 ▼

The wines of the Dordogne

The Dordogne vineyard is a natural extension of the Libournais wine-growing area, separated from it only by an administrative Gironde boundary. Planted with classic Gironde varieties, the Perigord vineyard is characterised by a very diverse production and a number of appellations. It stretches along slopes on both banks of the Dordogne.

The Appellation Régionale Bergerac comprises whites, rosés and reds. The Côtes de Bergerac offer fuller-bodied white wines with a delicate bouquet, along with reds that are well-structured and round, to be drunk with poultry and meat dishes with sauce. The Appellation Saussignac produces excellent fuller-bodied white wines with an ideal balance between freshness and sugar; they are drunk as aperitif wines, tasting somewhere between a Bergerac and a Monbazillac. Montravel, near Castillon, is the vineyard associated with Montaigne; production is divided into dry white Montravel, readily identifiable because of the Sauvignon, and the Côtes de Montravel and Haut-Montravel, fuller-bodied, elegant and stylish, which make excellent dessert wines. The Pécharmant is a red wine harvested on the slopes of the right bank where the soil, rich in iron, gives it a very distinctive taste of the *terroir*. A wine to keep, it has a fine, subtle bouquet and is a perfect accompaniment to the classic dishes of the Perigord. The Rosette is a semi-sweet wine, made from the

913

The wines of the Dordogne

Known as early as the 14th century, Monbazillac is one of the most famous 'sweet' wines. The vineyard is north-facing on limestone interbedded with molassic sands and marl. The localised micro-climate is particularly good for the development of a particular strain of botrytis, the 'noble rot'. Beautifully golden in colour, Monbazillac wines have scents of wild flowers and honey and a lingering flavour. They can be drunk as an aperitif, or enjoyed with foie gras, Roquefort cheese and chocolate desserts. They are fleshy and strong and, with age, become great sweet wines with a 'scorched' flavour.

same varieties as the Bordeaux wines, harvested in an enclave on the right bank of the Dordogne around Bergerac.

Bergerac

These wines are produced from the 90 communes of the district of Bergerac; the vineyard covers 6,447 ha (15,924 acres) devoted to red and rosé wines, and 3,375 ha (8,336 acres) to white. The rosé is fresh and fruity, and is frequently made from Cabernet; the red wine is aromatic and supple, a blend of traditional varieties. In 2000, production reached 195,056 hl (5,149,478 gal) of white wine and 383,047 hl (10,112,441 gal) of red or rosé wine.

CH. BEYLAT 1999 ■ n.c. 6,000 ■ €5-8

This 99 wine is ready to drink now, so as to enjoy its pretty nose of stewed fruits and its delicate, very drinkable palate, redolent of red berries. It is a classic of the appellation.

● EARL les Vignobles Beylat, Larroque, 24240 Thénac, tel. 05.53.58.43.71, fax 05.53.24.55.33 ▼ by appt.

CH. BRIAND 2000★ 0.75 ha 6,500 ■ ● €5-8

This 15-ha (37.05-acre) estate was formerly a dependency of the Château de Bridoire.

Half the vineyard is set aside for red grape varieties. This wine has quite a gamey nose, typical of a well-matured Merlot. The palate is concentrated and fruity, with well-ripened tannins and a touch of chocolate. The **Château Briand red 99 Vieilli en Fût de Chêne**, singled out, is still very oaky. It should achieve a better balance within two to three years. The **dry white Château Briand 2000** was also singled out for its citrus and exotic fruit aromas. It is a classic.

↝ Gilbert et Kathy Rondonnier, Les Nicots, 24240 Ribagnac, tel. 05.53.58.23.50, fax 05.53.24.94.63 ▣ ♈ by appt.

CH. BUISSON DE FLOGNY 2000★

■ 3 ha 15,000 ▦ €5-8

A 'black' wine, its colour is dark with violet reflections. Very fruity on the nose, it evokes ripe or cooked fruit. A somewhat fresh attack develops into ripe, well-integrated tannins. The finish is still austere, but should become more nicely balanced with time.

↝ Marc Bighetti de Flogny, Le Buisson, 24610 Saint-Méard-de-Gur çon, tel. 05.53.81.00.87, fax 05.53.80.61.39, e-mail flogny@aol.com ▣ ♈ by appt.
↝ SCEA Ch. Saint-Méard

CASANOVA 2000★

■ n.c. 20,000 ▦ ♦ €5-8

This wine was submitted by the de Conti family *négociants* (see Moulin des Dames), established in 1999. The Cuvée Casanova is truly seductive, with its pleasant, fruity nose, its well-rounded palate and its promising, ripe tannins. The **dry white Casanova 99**, singled out by the Jury, is just as charming, with its fruity, toasty nose. It is very oaky on the palate.

↝ SARL La Julienne, 24500 Saint-Julien-d'Eymet, tel. 05.53.57.12.43, fax 05.53.58.89.49 ▣ ♈ by appt.

CH. FAYOLLE-LUZAC

Cuvée Caroline Elevé en fût de chêne 1998

■ 11 ha 8,000 ▦ €5-8

Operating since 1998, this wine producer was featured in the *Guide* with his very first vintage. The nose reveals long barrel-maturation (12 months), dominated by oak and vanilla aromas. On the palate, the wine is powerful and dense. Vanilla tannins can be detected, integrated at the start but more austere on the finish.

↝ SCEA Ch. Fayolle, Fayolle, 33220 Fougueyrolles, tel. 05.53.73.51.68, fax 05.53.73.51.69, e-mail ch.fayolle.luzac@wanadoo.fr ▣ ♈ by appt.

CH. JONC-BLANC

Cuvée Symphonie 2000

■ 12 ha 24,000 ♦ €5-8

Jonc Blanc produces this red wine, with its pretty purple colour and its peppery, vanilla nose, very marked by ripe Cabernet. It has a well-rounded palate; fruity, concentrated, well-balanced and long. This is a well-made bottle, ready to drink, but it can also be kept for two to three years. This is the first vintage for these producers, who just started out in the year 2000.

↝ SCEA I. Carles et F. Pascal, Le Jonc Blanc, 24230 Vélines, tel. 05.53.74.18.97.

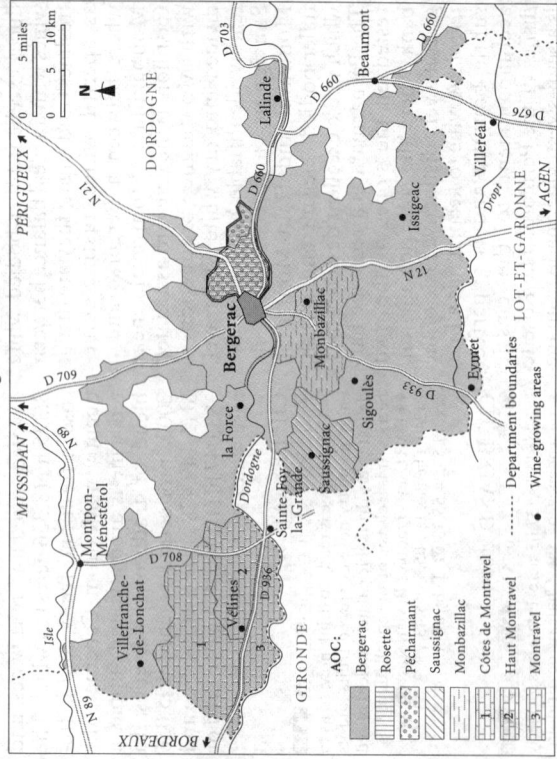

Bergerac

AOC:
Bergerac
Rosette
Pécharmant
Saussignac
Monbazillac
Côtes de Montravel
Haut Montravel
Montravel
······ Department boundaries
• Wine-growing areas

fax 05.53.74.18.97, e-mail jonçblanc@
hotmail.com ✉ ☎ by appt.

CH. LA GRANDE PLEYSSADE
Vieilli en fût de chêne 2000

| | 23 ha | 66,000 | ⊞ | €3-5 |

The major investments made in this estate over the past ten years have started to pay off with this wine. Clean and elegant, the nose delivers morello-cherry and vanilla fragrances. Full and concentrated, the palate has a long finish marked by somewhat austere tannins. This wine should be kept for two to three years before drinking.

➤ SCEA La Grande Pleyssade,
24240 Mescoules, tel. 05.53.73.21.79,
fax 05.53.24.27.61,
e-mail lagrandepleyssade@comp.serve.com
✉ ☎ by appt.

CH. LAMOTHE BELAIR 1999

| | 10 ha | 40,000 | ■ | €3-5 |

This is the epitome of a wine for pleasure: it has a powerful nose, blending blackcurrants, morello cherries and red berries, along with a mouthful of well-balanced tannins, sufficiently mellowed and with elegant fruity flavours. All this makes you want to open the bottle now, but it can be aged for two or three years.

➤ GAEC Jean Puyol et Fils,
Ch. Barberousse, 33330 Saint-Emilion,
tel. 05.57.24.74.24, fax 05.57.24.62.77 ✉
☎ by appt.

CH. L'ANCIENNE CITADELLE
1999

| | 5 ha | 4,000 | ■ | €5-8 |

The name of the estate refers to a castle tower, the relic of a fortress that was one of the most powerful in the Aquitaine region during the Hundred Years War. It also happens to be a few kilometres from the battlefield where in 1453 the decisive battle was fought that put a halt to that great medieval conflict. The vineyard straddles the south-facing hillside. It has yielded a likeable red Bergerac, dominated on the nose by red berries, with a hint of hazelnut and vanilla. Fresh, fruity and light on the palate, this wine offers soft tannins and good balance. It should be drunk soon, while it is still fruity.

➤ Jean-Luc Favretto, La Petite Rivière,
2430 Montcaret, tel. 05.53.57.59.29,
fax 05.53.57.59.29 ✉
☎ ev. day 9am–12 noon 2pm–5pm

DOM. DE L'ANCIENNE CURE
L'Extase 1999★

| | n.c. | 7,000 | ⊞ €15-23 |

To enjoy this wine at its best, it is advisable to wait four to five years. The intense, complex nose produces aromas of coffee, mocha and morello cherries. Both soft and powerful, the palate reveals noticeable tannins, accompanied by flavours of mocha, with nuances of vanilla and bilberry. This is a broad-shouldered wine, well-balanced and

CH. LA TILLERAIE 2000

| | 4.12 ha | 28,000 | ■ | €5-8 |

Situated in the Pécharmant area, the Château La Tilleraie also produces Bergeracs worthy of attention. This one has a rather delicate nose of green pepper and red berries. The palate is rich and well-balanced, with flavours of blackcurrant and raspberry on the mid-palate. The somewhat lively finish could make this wine suitable for accompanying soft cheeses such as Camembert. Readily singled out by the Jury, the rosé 2000 rather

CH. LA RAYRE 2000

| | 7 ha | 20,000 | ■ | €3-5 |

This 18.50-ha (45.7-acre) property was taken over in 1999 by the Vesselle family, who by the following year had already produced two wines that especially impressed the Jury. Their Bergerac red is made principally from Cabernet grapes (40% Cabernet Franc, 40% Cabernet Sauvignon), which dominate the nose with pepper and green-pepper aromas. The palate is supple, well-integrated and pleasant. This wine is not ambitious enough to last many years, but it will charm you now with its attractive balance. The Bergerac Sec 2000, with citrus (lemon) aromas, is enticingly fresh and lively.

➤ EARL Ch. La Rayre, La Rayre,
24560 Colombier, tel. 05.53.58.32.17,
fax 05.53.24.55.58, e-mail vincent.vesselle@
wanadoo.fr ✉ ☎ by appt.

CH. LA SALAGRE 2000★

| | 21.4 ha n.c. | | ■■▯ | €3-5 |

The colour of this wine is dark, almost violet. Its very pleasant, open nose has cherry, strawberry and blackcurrant aromas. After a supple attack, the palate is enticingly and exuberantly fruity up to the finish. A pleasant and very drinkable wine.

➤ SCEA Vignoble Rocher Cap de Rive, La
Salagre, 24240 Pomport, tel. 05.53.24.01.29,
fax 05.53.61.39.50 ☎ by appt.

CLOS LA SELMONIE 1999

| | n.c. | 5,000 | ■ | €5-8 |

A balance of Merlot (50%) and the two Cabernet grape varieties make up this Bergerac, which is a testament to skilled wine-making. The first of the two grape varieties dominates the nose, with somewhat musky aromas. The tannic body is powerful and elegant, and the finish lasts well. The Jury also singled out the lively, refreshing Côtes de Bergerac Moelleux 2000.

➤ Christian Beigner, Les Colombes,
24240 Mescoules, tel. 05.53.58.43.40,
fax 05.53.58.49.81 ✉ ☎ by appt.

very promising. The dry white Cuvée Abbaye 99 also deserves one star for its balance, harmony and floral fragrance evoking honeysuckle.

➤ Christian Roche, Ancienne Cure,
24560 Colombier, tel. 05.53.58.27.90,
wanadoo.fr ✉ ☎ by appt.

resembles a *clairet*, with its slightly bitter tannins. It is characterful enough to be drunk with charcuterie.
➤ SARL Ch. La Tilleraie, 24100 Pécharmant, tel. 05.53.57.86.42, fax 05.53.57.86.42 ☑ ▼ by appt.
• B. Faucomier

LA TOUR SAINT-VIVIEN 1999

■ 3 ha n.c. €3-5

Established in 1935, this co-operative has had three of its wines singled out, in the three colours. This bright ruby-red Bergerac is a blend of red berries, vanilla and liquorice on the nose. Dominated by fruit and tannins and with a lasting finish, the palate is pleasant. The Jury also liked the fruity, slightly sparkling rosé 2000, and in the **Côtes de Montravel 98**, a sweet, fruity **Chevalier de Saint-Avit**.
➤ Les Viticulteurs Réunis de Saint-Vivien-et-Bonneville, 24230 Saint-Vivien, tel. 05.53.27.52.22, fax 05.53.22.61.12 ☑
▼ by appt.

CH. LAULERIE

Vieilli en fût de chêne 1999★★ €5-8

n.c. 120,000

This Bergerac is a great classic. The 99 has a very toasty nose, with intense dark berries. The palate is enjoyable for its richness, its long finish and well-integrated oakiness. It is a particularly harmonious and well-balanced wine.
➤ Vignobles Dubard, Le Gouyat, 24610 Saint-Méard-de-Gurçon, tel. 05.53.82.48.31, fax 05.53.82.47.64, e-mail vignoblesdubard@wanadoo.fr ☑
▼ ev. day 8am–12.30pm 2pm–7pm

CH. LE CASTELLOT

Cuvée Prestige Elevé en fût de chêne 1999★ €8-11

12 ha 12,000

This 55-ha (135.85-acre) estate was originally controlled by the Knights Templar. Jean-René Ley inherited it from his parents in 1964 and expanded it. His red 99, with its open nose, releases ripe-fruit aromas accompanied by little nuances of oak. On the palate, the structure is dense, with well-integrated oak. This very promising wine will reach its potential in two to three years. Its white counterpart, the **Cuvée Prestige Bergerac white 99**, was singled out for its fruity aromas and delicate oak character. The elegant palate, soft, well-rounded and not too lively, makes this wine suitable for drinking with fish in sauce.
➤ GAF Ley, Dom. des Templiers, 24230 Saint-Michel-de-Montaigne, tel. 05.53.58.68.15, fax 05.53.58.79.99 ☑
▼ by appt.

CH. LE PAYRAL Cuvée Emilien 2000★

€8-11

1 ha 7,000

This wine cannot conceal the fact that it was matured in oak. The colour is dark and very rich. The oak dominates the nose, but when the glass is shaken, this gives way to aromas of red pepper and blackcurrant buds. The well-filled palate reveals a lot of fruit, but also a considerable amount of tannin. To be kept at least five years.
➤ Thierry Daulhiac, Le Bourg, 24240 Razac-de-Saussignac, tel. 05.53.22.38.07, fax 05.53.27.99.81 ☑
▼ by appt.

DOM. LES BRANDEAUX

Elevé en fût de chêne 1999 2.1 ha 6,200

This oak-matured Bergerac is attractive to the eye with its strong, garnet colour. The rather fine nose suggests aromas of oak and vanilla, as well as liquorice, coffee and red berries. After a clean, pleasant first impression, the rather full, well-rounded palate moves towards tannins somewhat dominated by oak, giving the finish an austere side. In the same vintage, the estate's **Cuvée Principale**, matured in vat, is pleasant and well-balanced, with a respectably simple range of aromas. This one gets the same rating.
➤ GAEC Piazzetta, Les Brandeaux, 24240 Puyguilhem, tel. 05.53.58.41.50, fax 05.53.58.41.50 ☑ ▼ by appt.

CH. LES MERLES 2000

€5-8

58 ha 100,000

This vast 72-ha (177.84-acre) estate produces large volumes of a well-made Bergerac: its attractive nose has a slightly toasty aroma with a pleasant fruitiness. The concentrated palate reveals velvety tannins, and has a long finish with spicy notes. This wine can be aged for three to four years.
➤ J. et A. Lajonie, GAEC Les Merles, 24520 Mouleydier, tel. 05.53.63.43.70, fax 05.53.58.06.46 ☑
▼ ev. day 9am–12 noon 2pm–6pm

CH. MAYNE GRAND PEY 2000

€3-5

15 ha 90,000

The rather deep, garnet-red colour immediately declares this to be a concentrated wine. The nose is of medium intensity and is dominated by red berries. The palate confirms the visual impression: it is beautifully full, fruity and dense, although the finish is still somewhat austere.
➤ Domaine de Sansac, Les Lèves, 33220 Sainte-Foy-la-Grande, tel. 05.57.56.02.02, fax 05.57.56.02.22, e-mail franckdelmas@wanadoo.fr
▼ by appt.

L'INSPIRATION DES MIAUDOUX

1999★ €8-11

2 ha 8,000

Gérard Cuisset has had a great career progression: he was an employee working on this estate, then he took over as tenant-manager in 1986, and subsequently purchased it in 1991. The wines that he produces, both Bergerac and Saussignac, are regularly complimented in the *Guide*. The 99 vintage is worth a star – three times. This Bergerac red *Cuvée Spéciale* has a nose that blends toasty aromas characteristic of oak maturation with cooked soft fruit. After a well-rounded first impression, the palate, with its high tannin level, has a long finish. The oak needs two to three more years to integrate. Also in **Bergerac** red, the **Château Miaudoux Elevé en Fût de Chêne** (matured in oak barrels) reveals a more supple structure and a little acidity on the finish. As for the **Saussignac Réserve**, this has a good potential for ageing, but the oak needs to integrate.

Gérard Cuisset, Les Miaudoux, 24240 Saussignac, tel. 05.53.27.92.31, fax 05.53.27.96.60, e-mail gerard.cuisset@terre-net.fr ☑ Y by appt.

MIRAGE DU JONCAL 1999★★

1.5 ha 2,860 €11-15

In spite of the difficulties of the 99 vintage, this bottle, presented with a very graphic triangular label, shows perfect continuity from the 1998 vintage, which was also awarded two stars. It has a very complex range of aromas revealing traces of charred, toasted oak, from the 18 months' barrel maturation; and also fruit, game and liquorice. Starting with the attack, the wine fills the palate nicely. The oak is perfectly integrated with the fruit. Keep for five years before drinking.

SCEA Le Joncal, Clos Le Joncal, 24500 Saint-Julien-d'Eymet, tel. 05.53.61.84.73, fax 05.53.61.84.73, e-mail roland.tatard@infonie.fr ☑
Y by appt.
J. Fonmarty

CH. MONDESIR 2000

10 ha 66,000 €5-5

This wine's dark, almost black, colour is fairly characteristic of the vintage. Its somewhat closed nose is dominated by ripe fruit. The palate is pleasant, with its clean attack and its tannins, which are of average concentration but well-integrated, leaving a chocolate flavour. The finish is a trifle austere, but that is the drawback of a young wine.

Closerie d'Estiac, Les Lèves, 33320 Sainte-Foy-la-Grande, tel. 05.57.56.02.02, fax 05.57.56.02.22
Y ev. day except Sun. Mon. 9.30am–12.30pm 3.30pm–6pm

CH. MONESTIER LA TOUR 2000

5.71 ha 48,000 €5-8

This château, originating from the 18th century, was visited by Henri IV. It has been magnificently restored. Matured 18 months in barrel, this red Bergerac has a nose that starts delicately, then opens up with fruit aromas. On the palate, while the tannins are still too forceful, the body is very concentrated. It needs to age for three to four years. The Jury also singled out the **Clos de Monestier 2000 Bergerac Sec**, a well-balanced wine, with distinct Sauvignon aromas.

SCEA Monestier La Tour, 24240 Monestier, tel. 05.53.61.87.87, fax 05.53.61.71.09 ☑ Y by appt.
Haseth Moller

CH. MOULIN CARESSE

Elevé en fût de chêne 1999★★

4.5 ha 28,000 €5-8

Sylvie and Jean-François Deffarge cultivate 23 ha (56.81 acres) of vines here. They have submitted some excellent wines, both Bergerac and Montravel. The Montravel can only serve to strengthen their reputation: its nose, a mixture of toasty and roasted aromas with red-berry fragrances, is one of the most elegant; the round, well-filled palate reveals a lot of concentration supported by well-integrated oak. This is a very concentrated, sweet wine that is a testament to careful maturation in barrel. It all adds up to a *coup de coeur*, the same as last year in the same AOC. It needs to be kept for three years before drinking. In the **Côtes de Bergerac 99**, the **Cuvée Prestige de Moulin Caresse** is awarded one star. Matured for 18 months in barrel, it is dominated by the oak despite the very pleasant touch of blackcurrant; it will need to be kept for four to five years before drinking. The **Montravel 99 Elevé en Fût de Chêne** (matured in oak barrels), with its very oaky finish, was also singled out.

EARL Sylvie et Jean-François Deffarge-Danger, Couin, 24230 Saint-Antoine-de-Breuilh, tel. 05.53.27.55.58, fax 05.53.27.07.39, e-mail moulin-caresse@libertysurf.fr ☑
Y ev. day 9am–12 noon 3pm–7pm; Sat. Sun. by appt.

MOULIN DES DAMES 2000★★

8 ha 35,000 €15-23

The de Conti family is already known, beyond the bounds of this area, for two wines often mentioned among the *Guide*'s top ratings: the Cuvée Moulin des Dames and the Château Tour des Gendres, both matured in oak. The first of these won the Jury's enthusiasm with its concentration, and was declared a *coup de cœur*. The oak dominates at present, but the future is promising. The **Cuvée La Gloire de Mon Père du Château Tour des Gendres** has produced a number of remarkable wines over the past ten years (including a *coup de cœur* with the 96). The **99** deserves two stars for the full, tight, firm structure of its tannins. A wine for laying down *par excellence*, it should be kept at least five years.

SCEA de Conti, Tour des Gendres, 24240 Ribagnac, tel. 05.53.57.12.43, fax 05.53.58.89.49 ▼ by appt.

CLOS DU PECH BESSOU 2000★   €3-5

2.74 ha n.c.

This estate has only been selling its wine in bottles since 1995. The Cabernet grape is the main constituent in their Bergerac, with its blackcurrant and cherry nose. The round, well-balanced palate is a pleasant surprise, reverting to a nice fruity blackcurrant and strawberry taste. It can be drunk now while fruity, or kept for two or three years and served with dishes like jugged rabbit.

GAEC Thomassin, La Ferrière, 24560 Plaisance, tel. 05.53.24.53.00 ▼ ev. day except Sun. 9am–12 noon 1.30pm–6pm

CH. RUINE DE BELAIR

Cuvée Merlot 2000★★   5 ha 15,000   €5-8

The 30-ha (74.1-acre) Rigal vineyards straddle the *départements* of the Dordogne and the Gironde; they produce Bordeaux and Bergerac. The 2000 vintage displays a deep, dark colour, testifying to a good degree of maturity. The powerful nose is dominated by the toasty, charred aromas of the oak. The palate becomes more powerful; the tannins assert themselves. Still a trifle marked by time spent in barrel, this wine will be well-integrated within three to four years. As for the **Domaine du Petit Négreaud 2000**, matured in vat, this wine is lighter and fruitier, and especially impressed the Jury.

EARL Vignobles Rigal, Dom. du Cantonnet, 24240 Razac-de-Saussignac, tel. 05.53.27.88.63, fax 05.53.23.77.11 ▼ by appt.

Jean-Paul Rigal

Cave Montravel Sigoulès, 24240 Sigoulès, tel. 05.53.61.55.00, fax 05.53.61.55.10 ▼ ev. day except Sun. 9am–12.30pm 2pm–6.30pm

CH. TOUR D'ARFON

Cuvée Prestige Vieilli en fût de chêne 1999   €5-8

0.75 ha 6,600

Established at this 15-ha (37.05-acre) property since 1998, this producer's 99 has a nose very marked by red berries, with toasty aromas. Very melting, almost fluid on the palate, this wine encourages you to drink the bottle quickly. The **Cuvée Classique 99**, which is not oak-matured, is also very supple and well-rounded, and gets the same rating.

H. et F. Ferté, La Tour d'Arfon, 24240 Monestier, tel. 05.53.73.36.49, fax 05.53.73.36.49 ▼ by appt.

CH. DU TUQUET DE BERGERAC   €3-5

1998   3 ha   4,600

Michel and Agnès Dameron took over this small 6.5-ha (16.06-acre) estate in 1998, and have now submitted their first vintage. The garnet colour attracts the eye. The fairly fruity nose is a mixture of red berries and prunes. The attack also has a pleasant touch of fruit; the finish is fairly warming.

Michel et Agnès Dameron, Le Tuquet, 24100 Bergerac, tel. 05.53.57.59.01, fax 05.53.57.59.01 ▼ ev. day 10am–6pm

CH. VEYRINES Cuvée Tradition 2000   €3-5

2 ha 10,000

Having started in 1996, Eric Lascombes was first featured in the previous edition of the *Guide*, with a Cuvée Boisée. This year, his Cuvée Classique is really all there. The nose is powerful, with a vinous, fruity character. The palate has strong tannins, but they are very supple and well-rounded. Pleasant to drink now, but it can also be kept for two to three years.

Eric Lascombes, Veyrines, 24240 Ribagnac, tel. 05.53.73.01.34, fax 05.53.73.01.34 ▼ by appt.

Bergerac rosé

DOM. DU BOIS DE POURQUIE   €5-8

2000★   1.5 ha 10,000

The quality of this estate goes from strength to strength. This rosé is almost *clairet*-coloured. Blackcurrant aromas, with a touch of Sauvignon, reveal the presence of the Cabernet grape. The palate has flavours of blackcurrant, violet and boxwood with a little touch of sugar and carbon dioxide sparkle. It is a modern, well-made rosé, with fruit and body. The new **Cuvée Révélation red 99** seems

LES VIGNERONS DE SIGOULES

Haute Tradition Vieilli en fût de chêne 2000★   65 ha 100,000   €5-8

This co-operative looks after the vinification of 250 ha (617.5 acres) of vines. It has produced this wine, which is sold through major retail outlets. Its very characterful nose is dominated by caramel aromas. The palate confirms this impression with a full-bodied attack, well-rounded, dense tannins and pleasant oak (although it is a trifle austere on the finish). From the same cellars, the Jury singled out the **Foncaussade red 2000**, a wine of average concentration but well-balanced.

...very promising, although it is still rather dominated by the oak. It especially impressed the Jury.

● Marlène et Alain Mayet, Le Bois de Pourquié, 24560 Conne-de-Labarde, tel. 05.53.58.25.58, fax 05.53.61.34.59 ☑
☐ by appt.

CH. FONTAINE DES GRIVES 2000

`1.3 ha  2,500  €3-5`

The colour of this wine is rather deep for a rosé. The Cabernet Sauvignon grape is expressed on the nose by somewhat vegetal aromas of blackcurrant and broom. The palate is very round because of the high sugar content, but there is still enough liveliness to balance the sweetness. It is an aperitif wine, or one for those who prefer the sweeter rosés.

● Mario Zorzetto, Ch. Fontaine des Grives, 24240 Thénac, tel. 05.53.58.46.73, fax 05.53.24.18.49 ☑ ☐ by appt.

DOM. LES GRAVES 2000

`0.5 ha  1,350  €3-5`

Lovers of slightly sweet rosé wines will enjoy this product. The colour is a pretty, pale pink. The nose is pleasant and floral. There is a lasting taste of violet in the mouth. Well-balanced between acidity and sugar, it is an aperitif wine.

● Bernard Barse, Dom. Les Graves, 24240 Gageac-Rouillac, tel. 05.53.24.01.11, fax 05.53.24.01.11 ☑ ☐ by appt.

LES JARDINS DE CYRANO

Larmandie 2000**★

`1 ha  6,000  €3-5`

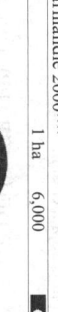

This wine, supplied by a *négociant*, won a unanimous *coup de cœur*. It is a very pale rosé. The nose is intense, with notes of boxwood and rose petal. The fruit is very elegant on the palate. Totally dry, with long-lasting aromatic qualities, it is very pleasant, but needs to be drunk soon. The Jury singled out the **dry white Cuvée Quatre Vents 2000** for its ripe-fruit and Muscat aromas.

● SARL Pascal Bonnac, 48, rue Joseph-Pères, 33110 Le Bouscat, tel. 05.57.22.87.87, fax 05.57.22.87.86

DOM. DU PETIT PARIS

Cuvée Tradition 2000

`3 ha  13,000  €3-5`

The colour is salmon-pink, almost brick-red. Dried flower and fruit aromas are combined on the nose. The palate is pleasant and rich, with crushed strawberry flavours. The small quantity of residual sugar gives it balance.

● EARL Dom. du Petit Paris, RN 21, 24240 Monbazillac, tel. 05.53.58.30.41, fax 05.53.58.30.27, e-mail petit-paris@wanadoo.fr ☑
☐ ev. day 8am-8pm; groups by appt.

Bergerac Sec

The mixed soils (limestone, gravel, clay, sand, alluvial deposits and stones) give rise to a range of aromas for these wines. When young, they are fruity and elegant, with a touch of vitality. If they are vinified in wood, it is necessary to wait for a year or two for the flavour of the terroir to become apparent.

CALISTA 2000

`0.68 ha  2,100  €15-23`

Among the Château de la Colline wines, there are two dry white Bergeracs that caught the attention of the tasters. The Cuvée Calista's range of aromas retains the memory of its 18 months' maturation in oak: a little oak mingles with the floral fragrance. On the palate, the oak is still noticeable, although the wine is fresh. This wine will improve if kept for two or three years. The **Cuvée Classique 2000** was also singled out: this wine has crystallised- and dried-fruit aromas.

● Charles Martin, Ch. de la Colline, 24240 Thénac, tel. 05.53.61.87.87, fax 05.53.61.71.09, e-mail la.colline.office@wanadoo.fr ☑ ☐ by appt.

CH. CAPULLE 2000

`1.16 ha  2,400  €3`

This greenish-white, dry Bergerac evokes the Sauvignon grape, with its characteristic, very floral aromas. On the palate, it is fresh on the attack, then develops a flavoursome fruit. It is a classic, and pleasant too.

CH. TOUR MONTBRUN 2000

`0.85 ha  6,000  €3-5`

The property is located on the site of the ancient citadel of Montravel. The intense, bold colour of this 2000 attracts the eye. The nose has fruit aromas, such as pear in particular. The very pleasant fruitiness, with notes of apple and pear, are reiterated again on the palate. This wine would be nice as an aperitif.

● Philippe Poivey, Montravel, 24230 Montcaret, tel. 05.53.58.66.93, fax 05.53.58.66.93, e-mail philippe-poivey@wanadoo.fr ☑ ☐ by appt.

DOM. DU CASTELLAT 2000 — 6 ha — 53,600 — €3-5

Jean-Paul Migot, Ch. Capulle, 24240 Thénac, tel. 05.53.58.42.67, fax 05.53.58.39.50 ▼ by appt.

This wine would be excellent served with seafood, escargots or the local cabécou (goat's cheese). It has a ripe fruit nose in keeping with a fairly rich, well-balanced palate, refreshed by a lively finish. It is a classic.

Jean-Luc Lescure, Le Castellat, 24240 Razac-de-Saussignac, tel. 05.53.27.08.83, fax 05.53.27.08.83 ▼ by appt. ▼ ev. day except Sun. 9am–7pm

DOM. DE COMBET 2000 — 2 ha — 8,000 — €3-5

The 30-ha (74.1-acre) Domaine de Combet estate has opted for maturation on the lees to produce this full-bodied wine. A clear yellow colour, it produces fairly delicate, but fine, crystallised fruit aromas. The palate is well-balanced and produces a fresh, fruity sensation.

EARL de Combet, 24240 Monbazillac, tel. 05.53.58.33.47, fax 05.53.58.33.47, e-mail combet@oreka.com ▼ ▼ by appt.

CH. DES GANFARDS 2000 — 5 ha — 18,000 — €5-8

From behind a pale, bright-yellow colour emerges an intense, complex nose, evocative of ripe fruit. Well-balanced on the attack, this dry Bergerac produces a sensation of freshness right up to the finish. It would go well with fish and seafood.

GAEC des Ganfards Haute-Fonrousse, 24240 Saussignac, tel. 05.53.58.30.28, fax 05.53.58.30.28, e-mail geraud.vins@wanadoo.fr ▼ ▼ ev. day except Sun. 8am–12 noon 2pm–7pm Serge et Jean-Claude Géraud

CH. HAUT-FONGRIVE 2000★ — 4.23 ha — 30,000 — €3-5

At the end of the 1980s, an English couple fell in love with this château and its views over the hillsides of the Thénac, and restored the buildings quite remarkably. Ten years later, in 1998, Sylvie and Werner Wichelhaus, in their turn, fell for its charms to the extent that they bought the 15-ha (37.05-acre) estate. They have produced a successful wine with a brillant, greenish-white appearance. The complex, delicate nose is dominated by floral notes. The palate has a round, fruity, well-balanced character. It will go well with fish and white meat dishes.

Sylvie et Werner Wichelhaus, Château Haut-Fongrive, 24240 Thénac, tel. 05.53.58.56.29, fax 05.53.24.17.75, e-mail hautfongrive@worldonline.fr ▼ by appt.

JULIEN DE SAVIGNAC 2000★ — 4 ha — 25,000 — €5-8

The Sauvignon grape, representing 60% of the blend, is clearly expressed on the nose, with its floral aromas and notes of citrus fruit. On the palate, this wine is rich, fine, long and pleasantly fresh. Ideal as an aperitif or with entrées. From the same producer, the rosé 2000 is a great success: fruity and full-bodied, it is the ideal accompaniment to the first courses of a meal. As for the Bergerac red 99, which was singled out, it is ready to drink now, with its well-rounded palate.

Julien de Savignac, av. de la Libération, 24260 Le Bugue, tel. 05.53.07.10.31, fax 05.53.07.16.41, e-mail julien.de.savignac@wanadoo.fr ▼ ▼ ev. day except Mon. 8.45am–12.15pm 2.45pm–7.15pm

CH. LA BRIE 2000★ — 10.5 ha — 80,000 — €3-5

Château La Brie was acquired by the Ministry of Agriculture in 1960. It covers 55 ha (135.85 acres), and since 1994 has had a viticultural training school, where this characteristic Bergerac is produced. This wine gives a lively first impression, punctuated by exotic fruit aromas (lychee and pineapple). This is a vivacious and delicate wine; its swift finish leaves a very pleasant sensation. From the same producer, the Monbazillac Cuvée Prestige 98, matured in oak barrels, deserves to be singled out.

Ch. La Brie, Lycée Viticole, Dom. de La Brie, 24240 Monbazillac, tel. 05.53.74.42.42, fax 05.53.58.24.08, e-mail expl.lpa.bergerac@educagri.fr ▼ ▼ ev. day except Sun. 10am–12 noon 1.30pm–5.30pm; cl. Jan.

PRESTIGE DE LA GRAPPE DE GURSON Hyacinthe 2000 — 12 ha — 60,000 — €3-5

It would be difficult to visit this co-operative without discovering, at a stone's throw, the Romanesque church of Carsac, built in the 12th century. La Grappe de Gurson awakened the interest of the tasters with this Bergerac, with its floral nose, so typically Sauvignon. These floral characteristics are reiterated on the palate, which is also vivacious, well-balanced and long-lasting.

La Grappe de Gurson, Le bourg, 24610 Carsac-de-Gurson, tel. 05.53.82.81.50, fax 05.53.82.81.60, e-mail grappe.gurson@wanadoo.fr ▼ by appt.

CH. DE LA JAUBERTIE 2000★ — 25 ha — 160,000 — €5-8

To harvest a fresher grape that will do better justice to its aromas, at La Jaubertie they have no compunction about picking at night-time. The result is worth the efforts they make. This Bergerac, characterised by the Sauvignon grape (60%), is rich, with a well-rounded palate and good length. Produced in accordance with the same strict requirements, the Bergerac rosé 2000 also deserves one star for its freshness, suppleness and blackcurrant aromas.

- SA Ryman, Ch. de La Jaubertie, 24560 Colombier, tel. 05.53.58.32.11, fax 05.53.57.46.22, e-mail jaubertie@ wanadoo.fr ▣ ▼ by appt.

DOM. LA TUILIERE 2000

1.5 ha	9,300	■	€3-5

The site occupied by La Tuilière (the Tile Makers) used to be a tile factory at the beginning of the 20th century, but the owners diversified into wine-making. The estate now covers 26 ha (64.22 acres). Made entirely from the Sauvignon grape, this dry Bergerac shimmers with yellow-green reflections. The citrus aromas on the nose express the characteristics of this grape. The fruit is every bit as noticeable on the palate, together with a well-balanced and long-lasting finish. This wine would be a good accompaniment to all kinds of fish.

- SCEA Moulin de Sanxet, Belingard-Bas, 24240 Pomport, tel. 05.53.58.30.79, fax 05.53.61.71.84 ▼ ev. day 9am-7pm; Sat. Sun. 2pm-7pm;
- M.-C. Larrue

CH. MALFOURAT 2000★★

3 ha	20,000	■	€3-5

A strict vinification process and very meticulous maturation on fine lees are the keys to the success of this dry Bergerac. Pale yellow with green reflections, this wine reveals traces of Sauvignon in its intense aromas of citrus and exotic fruits, accompanied by a slightly smoky touch. Fresh and pleasant on the attack, the palate develops a good concentration, with fresh fruit flavours. The effect is a well-balanced wine that can be enjoyed as an aperitif or with an entrée.

- EARL Vignobles Chabrol, Malfourat, 24240 Monbazillac, tel. 05.53.58.30.63, fax 05.53.73.86.89, e-mail patchabrol@ wanadoo.fr ▣ ▼ by appt.

MOULINS DE BOISSE

0.79 ha	3,000	■	€3-5

MOULINS DE BOISSE 2000

A few kilometres from the medieval village of Issigeac, the Moulins de Boisse estate is situated on a chalky hillock, where the Semillon grapes that make up this wine are grown. Pale yellow edged with green, with the tiniest hint of a mineral aroma. The palate is lightly sparkling and has a somewhat silky texture. It has 'xotic fruit flavours, then finishes with a slight bitterness.

- Bernard Molle, Cap del Bourg, 24560 Boisse, tel. 05.53.24.12.01, fax 05.53.24.12.01, e-mail moulins.de.boisse@wanadoo.fr ▣ ▼ by appt.

CH. REPENTY 2000★

4 ha	30,000	■	€3-5

Of the range of grape varieties used in making this dry Bergerac, the best part is played by the Muscadelle, a variety that is sadly rather overlooked. The nose is not misleading with its intense, delicate Muscat aromas, while the fruity palate produces a sensation of plumpness and balance. This is an original wine worth discovering.

- Jean-Pierre Roulet, Repenty, 24240 Monestier, tel. 05.53.58.41.96, fax 05.53.58.41.96 ▣ ▼ by appt.

SEIGNEURS DE BERGERAC 2000★

n.c.	n.c.	■	-€3

Seigneurs de Bergerac is a brand available in three colours. The best of the 2000 vintage is the white. This wine has an attractive yellow-green colour, and is showing complex, crystallised-fruit aromas. The silky, full flavoured palate is characterised by finesse and a good length.

- SA Yvon Mau, BP 1, 33193 Gironde-sur-Dropt Cedex, tel. 05.56.61.54.54, fax 05.56.71.10.45

DOM. DU SIORAC 2000

3.85 ha	10,000	■	€3-5

This pale-yellow wine with green reflections was created mainly from the Sauvignon grape, and also from some Sémillon. It has very fruity aromas of blackcurrant. The attack is rich as a result of maturation on the lees, and the palate maintains the fruity character. This is a well-balanced Bergerac that can be kept for a year or two.

- Dom. du Siorac, 24500 Saint-Aubin-de-Cadelech, tel. 05.53.74.52.90, fax 05.53.58.35.32 ▼ ev. day except Sun. 9am-12 noon 3pm-6pm
- Landat Fils

Côtes de Bergerac

This appellation conforms not to a *terroir* but rather to a set of more restrictive conditions for the harvest, intended to produce rich and well-structured wines. They are sought after for their concentration of flavour and their long-term keeping qualities.

CH. CAILLAVEL

Elevé en fût de chêne 1998★★

4 ha	5,000	▥	€5-8

This 98 wine has a dark, deep colour. The wine is characterised throughout by power, the power of the nose, with its well-balanced blend of nuances of toast, vanilla and fruit (blackcurrant and strawberry) and liquorice; the power of the palate, with its dominant oak; and the power of the attack, with its strong but fine tannins, which should become more refined within four to five years. Château Caillavel was also awarded one star for the **Monbazillac 98**, which is a blend of honey and the vanilla of the *barrique*.

☞ GAEC Ch. Caillavel, 24240 Pomport,
tel. 05.53.58.43.30, fax 05.53.58.20.31 ▼
♈ ev. day except Sun. 8am–7pm
☞ Lacoste et Fils

CH. COMBRILLAC 1999★

■ 3.41 ha 10,000 ▦ €11-15

This wine comes from a property of some 17 ha (41.99 acres), which changed hands in 1998. The 99 red, produced by maturing for 16 months in oak, starts off in a reserved manner before delivering a complex bouquet of dark fruit, spice and vanilla. The palate is all richness and power, but seems dominated by the oak. The finish, at present austere, should become supple within one to two years.

☞ GFA de Combrillac, Gravillac,
24130 Prigonrieux, tel. 05.53.57.63.61,
fax 05.53.58.08.12

DOM. DE GRIMARDY
Elevé en fût de chêne 1999

■ 0.65 ha 5,200

Marielle and Marcel Establet acquired this 12-ha (29.64-acre) property in 1998. On the nose, this 99 wine blends the red-berry aroma of the Cabernet Sauvignon grape (40% of the total make-up) with the farmyardy aromas of the Merlot (60%). The palate is a blend of freshness and roundness. It does not have an imposing structure, but it does have a flatteringly drinkable character, making it a bottle to drink soon. Uncork it with a pâté *en croûte*.

☞ Marcel et Marielle Establet,
Dom. de Grimardy, 24230 Montazeau,
tel. 05.53.57.96.78, fax 05.53.61.97.16,
e-mail m.establet@libertysurf.fr ▼
♈ by appt.

CH. LA BARDE-LES TENDOUX
Vieilli en fût de chêne 1999

■ 7.5 ha 9,000 ▦ €11-15

The 98 wine, included in the last edition, is a collector's wine that can be left to age. This less-structured 99 red will need to be drunk fairly young. The initial impression on the nose is of fruit, then a touch of oak surfaces. The attack is lively, but not very mouth-filling. On the palate, it is very mouth-filling, but the tannins are already well-integrated. The finish has enticing aromas of spices and cooked prunes.

☞ SARL de Labarde, Ch. La Barde,
24560 Saint-Cernin-de-Labarde,
tel. 05.53.57.63.61, fax 05.53.58.08.12
♈ by appt.

DOM. DE LA COMBE
Elevé en fût de chêne 1999★

■ 0.45 ha 3,200 ▦ €8-11

This 99 wine, matured for 13 months in oak after being somewhat reserved initially on the nose, has aromas of fruit married with attractive oak, subtle and well-integrated. The first impression is surprising powerful. Nuances

of mocha blend with blackcurrant and bilberry flavours, finishing up with a little vanilla. This is a very nice, well-balanced bottle of wine, to be enjoyed after two to three years. The **rosé 2000** from this estate gets the same rating for its freshness and dark-berry aromas.

☞ Sylvie et Claude Sergenton, Dom. de La Combe, 24240 Razac-de-Saussignac,
tel. 05.53.27.86.51, fax 05.53.27.99.87 ▼
♈ by appt.

CH. LA GRANDE BORIE
Cuvée CL 1998★

■ 1 ha 2,000 ▦ €11-15

Claude Lafaye has been in charge of this 30-ha (74.1-acre) vineyard for ten years. He has submitted an up-market wine, the result of a rigorous selection procedure and ageing in barrel. Starting with toasty and oaky aromas, the nose develops into dark berries (blackberry and blackcurrant), then a little spiciness surfaces. On the attack, the fruit dominates the oak. Full, well-rounded and fleshy, the palate has a lot of tannins on the finish: beautifully extracted, this is a wine that will mellow.

☞ Claude Lafaye,
La Grande Borie, 24520 Saint-Nexans,
tel. 05.53.24.33.21, fax 05.53.27.97.74,
e-mail cllafaye@wanadoo.fr ▼
♈ ev. day 9am–12 noon 2pm–7.30pm

CH. DE LA NOBLE
la Noblesse du Château 1999★★★

■ 3 ha 3,000 €11-15

Fabien Charron came into the family property in 1997, and has already demonstrated his know-how by being awarded one star for a Bergerac last year. This 99 red has a deep inky colour, which is indicative of its concentration. On the nose, very ripe fruit blends with fine toasty aromas, spices and nuances of chocolate to reinforce the complexity. The palate reveals an exceptional tannin structure, with oak that is very noticeable but subtle. A wine for laying down that will certainly last 20 years: this Noblesse lives up to its name. Far from this level of excellence, the **rosé 2000** from this estate especially impressed the Jury with its youthful fruitiness.

☞ Fabien Charron, La Noble,
24240 Puyguilhem, tel. 05.53.58.81.93,
fax 05.53.58.81.93 ▼ ♈ by appt.

CH. LA ROBERTIE La Robertie Haute

■ Elevé en fût de chêne 1999★ | 0.5 ha | 1,700 | €5-8

This estate, established in 1736 and remaining in the same family for more than three centuries, was taken over in 1998 by the Souliers, who have just renovated the cellar where the wine is produced. The vineyard covers an area of 20 ha (49.4 acres). This wine, made purely from Merlot, is initially dominated by the oak, but the nose soon gives hints of very ripe red-berry fragrances. The palate reveals good concentration and chewiness. The flavours are a blend of grilled cocoa beans, vanilla and raspberry. This wine is already well-balanced, but will improve if kept for five years. It will go well with beef. The estate is also singled out for the **Monbazillac Vendanges de Brumaire 99**, a wine whose sugar has not yet broken down. It needs a little time to acquire balance.

♠ SARL Ch. La Robertie, La Robertie, 24240 Rouffignac-de-Sigoulès, tel. 05.53.61.35.44, fax 05.53.58.53.07, e-mail chateau.larobertie@wanadoo.fr ☑
Ⴑ ev. day 9am-8pm
♠ J.-D. B. Soulier

CH. LES MARNIERES

Cuvée la Côte fleurie 1999★

■ | 1.1 ha | 1,700 | €15-23

Alain and Christophe Geneste have run this 23-ha (56.81-acre) estate since 1990. This up-market wine has won lots of stars (the 97 was a *coup de coeur*). The 99 vintage required very rigorous selection at harvest-time, hence the small volume of production this year. The complex nose reveals beautiful, fruity nuances of raspberry. There is a good structure on the palate, rich and full, with notes of chocolate, spices and cinnamon. This wine is already well-balanced and very promising. Another wine, the **Château Les Marnières 99 Elevé en Fût de Chêne** (matured in oak barrels) was singled out by the Jury. Its tannins are still a little firm.

♠ Alain et Christophe Geneste, GAEC des Brandines, 24520 Saint-Nexans, tel. 05.53.58.31.65, fax 05.53.73.20.34, e-mail christophe.geneste@wanadoo.fr ☑
Ⴑ by appt.

MALLEVIEILLE

Elevé en fût de chêne 1998

■ | 3 ha | 12,000 | €8-11

The colour of this wine is dense and deep. The nose is spicy at first, then has fruity aromas such as bilberry and raspberry. The palate has not reached its true balance because the oaky tannins need to integrate. A successful wine that needs to be kept for a while before drinking.

♠ Vignobles Biau, La Mallevieille, 24130 Monfaucon, tel. 05.53.24.64.66, fax 05.53.58.69.91, e-mail chateaudelamallevieille@wanadoo.fr
☑ Ⴑ ev. day 9am-12 noon 2pm-7pm

LADY MASBUREL 1999★★

■ | 8 ha | 13,500 | €8-11

The Château Masburel vineyard was established in 1740 by a First Consul of Sainte-Foy-la-Grande. It now covers 23 ha (56.81 acres) and was taken over in 1997 by Olivia and Neil Donnan, whose ambition is to restore it to its former lustre. They are going the right way about it, with two wines suitable for laying down, which win two stars each. This Lady Masburel has a complex nose, whose rich fruits hold the intensity of the vanilla in check. After a majestic start, a festival of flavours is discovered on the palate, as notes of toast and leather accompany a beautiful fruitiness to a spicy and perfectly-rounded finish. Also matured in oak (14 months), the **Château Masburel 99** seems rather more firm and wild. Just right for accompanying venison in *sauce Grand Veneur*.

♠ SARL Ch. Masburel, Fougueyrolles, 33220 Sainte-Foy-la-Grande, tel. 05.53.24.77.73, fax 05.53.24.27.30, e-mail chateau.masburel@accesinter.com ☑
Ⴑ ev. day except Sat. Sun. 9am-12 noon
♠ Olivia Donnan

L'EXCELLENCE DU CH. TOURS DES VERDOTS

Les Verdots selon David Fourtout 1999★

■ | 2.8 ha | 9,800 | €15-23

In charge of 30 ha (74.1 acres) of vines, the Fourtouts – father and son – have produced this wine, which seems delicate on the nose, although nice oak and forest-fruit aromas can be discerned. On the palate, the fruit flavours come out: fresh fruits give the attack a delicious quality and override the oak on the finish. The tannins are remarkably supple. This is a very well-balanced wine whose charms should be enjoyed without waiting. The **Clos des Verdots 2000** especially impressed the Jury. The composition is different from that of the other wine (80% Merlot and 20% Cabernet Franc grapes, while l'Excellence is made from 60% Cabernet Sauvignon and 40% Merlot), and it was matured in vat. It is a very pleasant bottle by virtue of its round, fleshy, supple palate.

♠ GAEC Fourtout et Fils, Les Verdots, 24560 Conne-de-Labarde, tel. 05.53.58.34.31, fax 05.53.57.82.00, e-mail fourtout@terre-net.fr ☑ Ⴑ ev. day except Sun. 9.30am-12.30pm 2pm-7pm

Côtes de bergerac moelleux

These are made from the same varieties as the dry white wines but are harvested when over-ripe to make popular and supple sweet wines with flavours of preserved fruits.

CH. BELLE FILLE
La Belle Inconnue 2000

☐ 0.5 ha | 10,000 | ▮ ◗ | € 5–8

In 1999, François de Conti took over a property dating from the 18th century, with a very ancient vineyard. This is the first wine he has produced. With toasty, hazelnut and almond aromas, the nose is very much influenced by oak. Round, lively and sweet all at the same time, the palate is similarly oak-dominated. This is a bottle to lay down for two years, to allow the oak to soften and the fruit to achieve a better expression.

● EARL François de Conti, Les Eymaries, 24240 Thénac, tel. 05.53.24.52.11, fax 05.53.24.56.29 ◪ ⌶ ev. day except Sun. 9am–12 noon 2pm–6pm; cl. 15 Jan.–15 Feb.

LES VIGNERONS DE SIGOULES
Haute Tradition 2000★

☐ 10 ha | 10,000 | ▮ ◗ | € 5–8

The grapes for this wine were picked and sorted in successive stages, as is usually done for sweet wines. The result is one of the most successful wines in a particularly light vintage. Honey and crystallised-fruit aromas are in evidence on the nose. After a fresh attack, a well-rounded, rich palate develops. The finish is persistent, but characterised by a little bitterness. This **Cuvée Haute Tradition** was singled out for the **Bergerac Sec 2000** (dry) for its harmonious balance between the fruit and the oak. In the same AOC, the abundant **Cuvée Perle de Diane 2000** (100,000 bottles), a great classic, also deserves a mention for its freshness and balance.

● Cave Montravel Sigoulès, 24240 Sigoulès, tel. 05.53.61.55.00, fax 05.53.61.55.10 ⌶ ev. day except Sun. 9am–12.30pm 2pm–6.30pm

---

soils bring intense aromas to the wines as well as a strong and complex structure. In 2000 45,597 hl (1,203,761 gal) were produced.

CH. BELINGARD
Blanche de Bosredon 1999★★

☐ 5 ha | 5,000 | ▥ | € 15–23

This château sums up all the charms of this rich and beautiful region. Its Monbazillac, vinified and matured in oak for 20 months, possesses an already-integrated oak. On the nose, tangerine and apricot aromas dominate the vanilla and toasty aromas. The rich palate consists mainly of crystallised fruits, honey and prune. The very sweet taste gives way to a fresh finish, so the wine does not feel heavy. This is a well-balanced wine, to be kept for two or three years before drinking. The Jury awarded one star to the **Bergerac Château Bélingard Grande Réserve red 2000**, with its particularly well-balanced structure, and to the château's **Cuvée Classique Bergerac red 2000**.

● SCEA Comte de Bosredon, Belingard, 24240 Pomport, tel. 05.53.58.28.03, fax 05.53.58.38.39, e-mail laurent.debosredon@wanadoo.fr ◪ ⌶ by appt.

CLOS DES CABANES
Chant d'Arômes 1998

☐ 0.8 ha | 2,700 | ▥ | € 8–11

Anne and Georges Lafont made a choice of lifestyle when they moved into wine-making on this estate of more than 10 ha (24.7 acres). Their first harvest has yielded a wine with a toasty, slightly fruity nose. After a well-rounded attack, the palate reveals its concentration, but its richness is still masked by the oak. This Monbazillac will need to be kept for a year or two to be fully appreciated. (50 cl bottles.)

● EARL des Vignobles Lafont, Clos des Cabanes, 24100 Saint-Laurent-des-Vignes, tel. 05.53.24.85.03, fax 05.53.24.85.03 ◪ ⌶ ev. day except Sun. 8am–12 noon 2pm–6pm; cl. Apr.
● Georges Lafont

CH. FONMOURGUES
Elevé en barrique 1998★

☐ 5 ha | 4,000 | ▥ | € 11–15

A little shy at first, this wine has leather and hazelnut aromas when allowed to breathe. On the palate, it has notes of citrus and dried fruits, delicate vanilla and liquorice in a good balance. Here, a liveliness persists that will enable the wine to age well for four or five years. The **Côtes de Bergerac red 98**, **Elevé en Barrique**, especially impressed the Jury. It is full of concentration, but the oak needs to integrate.

● Dominique Vidal, Ch. Fonmourgues, 24240 Monbazillac, tel. 05.53.63.02.79, fax 05.53.27.20.32 ◪ ⌶ by appt.

Monbazillac

Extending over 2,500 ha (6,175 acres), the Monbazillac vineyard produces rich wines made from grapes with 'noble rot'. The clay and limestone

GRANDE MAISON
Cuvée du Château 1999★

11 ha   3,500   €15-23

Thierry Desprès, who cultivates his 20 ha (49.4 acres) organically, declares 1999 an *Annus horribilis*. Following a poor crop and given the need for selective picking, it took 15 vines to produce one bottle, equivalent to one *barrique* per hectare. However, he can rest assured that the result is good. This fine, aromatic, fruity Monbazillac is a rich wine with a good, sweet taste. Toasty and crystal-lised-fruit flavours develop, with good length, into a finish with a great softness. This well-balanced wine ought to be drunk within the next four years.

↪ SARL Desprès et Fils, Grande Maison, 24240 Monbazillac, tel. 05.53.58.26.17, fax 05.53.24.97.36, e-mail grandemaison@aquinet.tm.fr V Y by appt.

RESERVE LAJONIE
Vieilli en fût de chêne 1999★

32 ha   25,000   €11-15

This is a well-balanced Monbazillac, with a fruity nose of apricot, quince and orange, with vanilla notes. Ripe fruit dominates the palate in a round, powerful body. The oak is well-integrated and the finish fresh, ending with a honey note. The **Bergerac Sec Château Pintouquet 2000** was singled out for its aromas of citrus and exotic fruits. It has a

DOM. DU HAUT-MONTLONG
Elevé en fût 1998

1 ha   3,000   €11-15

The moderately intense nose evokes peach and quince, and a fruity character that is echoed on the palate. The finish, however, is marked by the oak, and gives an impression of austerity which time will remedy. The **Bergerac Sec 2000** was also singled out by the Jury, who enjoyed its nose of flowers and citrus typical of the Sauvignon grape, as well as its long, well-balanced palate.

↪ Alain et Josy Sergenton et leurs Enfants, Dom. du Haut-Montlong, 24240 Pomport, tel. 05.53.58.81.60, fax 05.53.58.09.42, e-mail sergenton-haut-montlong@wanadoo.fr V Y ev. day 9am–12 noon 1.30pm–8pm; Sat. Sun. by appt.

CH. LADESVIGNES
Automne Elevé en fût de chêne 1999★

5 ha   5,000   €11-15

Crystallised fruits, beeswax, toasted bread and vanilla make up the main aromas of this wine's complex nose. After a supple attack, the palate is round and crisp, revealing a softness balanced by liveliness on the finish. This mature wine can be kept four or five years in the cellar. Also singled out from the same château were the **Côtes de Bergerac Le Petrocore red 98** and the **Bergerac Sec 99**.

↪ Ch. Ladesvignes, 24240 Pomport, tel. 05.53.58.30.67, fax 05.53.58.22.64, e-mail chateauladesvignes@wanadoo.fr V Y by appt. ↪ Monbouché

DOM. DE LA LANDE
Souvenir de Vendanges 1999

3 ha   4,000   €11-15

This young wine-maker took over the family property in 1999. He submitted this Monbazillac with crystallised-fruit aromas, still dominated by the oak in which it was matured. This fairly rich wine has a lot of freshness and elegance, and would be good as an aperitif. The **Bergerac red 2000** deserves to be singled out.

↪ Fabrice Camus, Dom. de La Lande, 24240 Monbazillac, tel. 06.08.56.92.36, fax 06.53.24.27.61 Y by appt.

CH. MONTDOYEN
Cuvée La Part des Anges 1999★★

2 ha   2,000   €11-15

Formerly known under the brand name Château du Puch, Château Montdoyen offers a pretty range of wines. This Monbazillac has all the characteristics of noble rot in its range of dried fruit, toasty and ripe-fruit aromas. The distinguished, well-rounded palate leaves a lingering taste of toast and apricot flavours. It is a rich, well-balanced wine. **La Part des Anges** is also available as a red or a dry white: the **Bergerac red 99** and the **Bergerac Sec 99** are two wines that especially impressed the Jury. The first of these is full-bodied, still dominated by the oak; the second, with its fruity aromas and delicate oakiness, is ready to drink now.

↪ SARL des Vignobles J.-P. Hembise, Ch. Le Puch, S24240 Monbazillac, tel. 05.53.58.85.85, fax 05.53.61.67.78, e-mail chateaumontdoyen@wanadoo.fr V Y ev. day 8am–12 noon 2pm–6pm; Sat. Sun. by appt.

DOM. DE PECOULA Cuvée Prestige
Vinifié en fût de chêne 1999★★

17 ha   6,900   €11-15

This has a highly powerful, complex nose. Although it is still a little marked by the oak, there are also pleasant aromas of honey, crystallised fruits and quince. The wine is mouth-filling, very soft and fruity. The oak is delicate on the palate. This wine should be kept two or

lively attack followed by a full palate. It will go well with oysters.

↪ SCEA Lajonie D.A.J., Saint-Christophe, 24100 Bergerac, tel. 05.53.57.17.96, fax 05.53.58.06.46 Y by appt.

three years before being opened, and it has the potential to keep a good deal longer.
➤ GAEC de Pécoula, 24240 Pomport.
tel. 05.53.58.46.48, fax 05.53.58.82.02 Ⓥ
Ⓨ by appt.
➤ GFA Labaye

DOM. DU PETIT MARSALET
Cuvée Tradition Elevé en fût de chêne 1999★
□ 2.5 ha 1,500 ▥ €11-15

This top-of-the-range wine from the estate has an intense nose, with suggestions of dried fruit, apricot and hazelnut. Although the attack is round, the palate becomes livelier as it develops, before concluding in a lasting finish of crystallised fruit. Nevertheless, it is a very rich wine, for laying down.
➤ Marie-Thérèse Cathal, Le Marsalet, 24100 Saint-Laurent-des-Vignes
tel. 05.53.57.53.36, fax 05.53.57.53.36 Ⓥ
Ⓨ by appt.

CH. POULVERE Cuvée Millénium 1999
□ 6 ha n.c. ▥ €8-11

Château Poulvère (86 ha/212.42 acres) has produced a warm wine with toasty aromas. Although delicate, the oak makes itself on the attack. The palate is characterized by crystallised fruit. The finish has a certain freshness. This Monbazillac needs to be kept long enough for the oak to integrate.
➤ GFA de Poulvère et Barses, Poulvère, 24240 Monbazillac, tel. 05.53.58.30.25, fax 05.53.58.35.87, e-mail poulvere@caves-particulieres.com Ⓥ Ⓨ ev. day except Sun. 9am–12 noon 2pm–7pm
➤ Borderie

CH. TIRECUL LA GRAVIERE
Cuvée Madame 1998★★★
□ 9.16 ha 10,000 ▥ ★76

Everything has been said about Bruno Bilancini's Cuvée Madame. The eye is attracted by the beautiful golden-yellow colour. The nose is met by intense aromas of white flowers, crystallised fruit and apricot. The palate is charmed by an abundance of richness and roundness, but the oak may not be completely integrated. This wine is remarkable for its power and finesse, and is already superb. This wine is remarkable for its power and finesse, and can be aged for ten to 20 years. (50 cl bottles).
➤ Claudie et Bruno Bilancini, Ch. Tirecul la Gravière, 24240 Monbazillac, tel. 05.53.57.44.75, fax 05.53.24.85.01, e-mail bruno.bilancini@free.fr Ⓨ by appt.

Montravel

The *terroir* of Montravel, extending over the hills from Port-Sainte-Foy and Ponchapt to Saint-Michel-de-Montaigne, produces dry and sweet wines noted for their elegance. In 2000, the output from 378 ha (934 acres) was 13,964 hl (368,650 gal) of Montravel, 2,239 hl (59,110 gal) of Haut-Montravel and 3,267 hl (86,249 gal) of Côtes-de-Montravel.

CH. DE SANXET
Millénium Elevé en fût de chêne 1999
□ 6.36 ha 9,000 ▥ €8-11

The Château de Sanxet is located on the site of a fortress built in the year 1000 and converted into a residence in the 15th century. This wine is typical of the appellation, light and round. The nose is a delicate blend of dried and crystallised fruits. After a supple attack, the palate develops fluidly to a rather fresh finish.
➤ Bertrand de Passemar, Ch. de Sanxet, 24240 Pomport, tel. 05.53.58.37.46, fax 05.53.58.37.46 Ⓥ Ⓨ by appt.

CH. THEULET
Antoine Alard Elevé en fût de chêne 1998★★
□ 2.5 ha 4,000 ▥ €15-23

This wine's fine nose has white-flower and crystallised-fruit aromas, with nuances of almond and toast. The rich, supple palate picks up the toasted almond flavours and then reverts to fruit and crystallised apricot. The lasting impression of this wine is one of extreme softness. It is ready to drink now. Another one to discover is the **Bergerac red 2000**, which especially impressed the Jury. Matured in barrel, it is fruity and light.
➤ SCEA Alard, Le Theulet, 24240 Monbazillac, tel. 05.53.57.30.43, fax 05.53.58.88.28 Ⓥ Ⓨ ev. day except Sun. 8am–12 noon 2pm–6pm

CH. BONIERES
La Dame de Bonières 2000★
□ 1.3 ha 4,500 ▥ €11-15

This Montravel is poles apart from a classic Sauvignon. The nose is finely toasted, with a lot of richness and fruit. The same sensations dominate the palate, with a strong oak presence. This wine should improve if kept for one to two years. Also judged worthy of being singled out, the **Cuvée Coeur de Vendanges red Bergerac 99** has ripe fruit aromas and fine, elegant tannins. This well-balanced wine has good laying-down potential.
➤ SCEA Vignobles André Bodin, Ch. Bonières, 33220 Fougueyrolles, tel. 05.53.24.15.16, fax 05.53.24.17.77, e-mail stevalentin@free.fr Ⓥ Ⓨ by appt.

CH. DAUZAN LA VERGNE

Sec Elevé en fût de chêne 1999★

| | 2 ha | 18,000 | 🍾 €8-11 |

This 200-ha (494-acre) estate was already known in the 13th century. This is a Montravel wine that has been long matured in oak. The nose is particularly toasty, very fine and elegant. The palate is enjoyable, with its good concentration and rich, fruity finish. This wine is still noticeably oaky and will improve with age. The **Haut-Montravel 99** was also matured in oak, but it has a beautiful, fresh lively attack and a nice, fruity palate.

☛ SNC Ch. Pique-Ségue,
Ponchapt, 33220 Port-Sainte-Foy,
tel. 05.53.58.52.52, fax 05.53.63.44.97,
e-mail chateau-pique-segue@wanadoo.fr ✔
🍷 by appt.
🚶 Philip et Marianne Mallard

CH. LE RAZ Sec 2000

| | 2.6 ha | 19,300 | 🍷 🍴 €3-5 |

Meticulous work in the vineyard, bunch-thinning and leaf-plucking, and a practical investment in a superb air-conditioned cellar are the factors that have contributed to the success of this production. The intense nose evokes citrus fruit. The attack is lively and sparkling, but it develops into the correct acid balance. The Jury also liked the **Bergerac rosé 2000** with its complex nose of red berries and blackcurrant. The palate is made even livelier by a little carbon dioxide sparkle. This is a nice wine for barbecues.

☛ Vignobles Barde, Le Raz,
24610 Saint-Méard-de-Gurçon,
tel. 05.53.82.48.41, fax 05.53.80.07.47 ✔
🍷 ev. day except Sun. 8.30am–12.30pm
2pm–7pm; Sat. by appt.

Côtes de Montravel

DOM. DE LA ROCHE MAROT

| | 0.16 ha | 1,200 | 🍾 €8-11 |

Crystallised fruits, very noticeable on the nose, indicate the presence of noble rot. The palate is mouth-filling and rich, with dried-fruit flavours and notes of apricot. The balance between liveliness and richness makes this 99 white a nice aperitif wine. As for the **Montravel 2000**, also singled out, the tasters noted its Sauvignon characteristics and its roundness.

☛ Yves et Daniel Boyer, GAEC de La
Roche Marot, 24230 Lamothe-Montravel,
tel. 05.53.58.52.05, fax 05.53.58.52.05 ✔
🍷 by appt.
🚶 Michel Boyer

Pécharmant

On a slope covered with 400 ha (988 acres) of vines, north-east of Bergerac, the 'Pech' produces very rich red wines with good keeping qualities. Often

---

DUC DE MEZIERE 1999

| | 3 ha | 7,000 | 🍾 €5-8 |

Hand-picking and meticulous selection, in addition to maturation in oak for seven months, have resulted in a simple, pleasant wine. The nose releases crystallised-fruit and apricot aromas, mingled with oak, while the palate, with its fresh attack punctuated by notes of vanilla, is rich, but not excessively so.

☛ Union de Viticulteurs de Port-Sainte-Foy,
78, rte de Bordeaux, 33220 Port-Sainte-Foy,
tel. 05.53.27.40.70, fax 05.53.27.40.71,
e-mail cavevitipsf@wanadoo.fr ✔ 🍷 ev. day
except Sun. 9am–12 noon 2pm–6pm

CH. LE BONDIEU

Cuvée Gabriel Elevé en fût de chêne 1999★

| | 1 ha | 1,500 | 🍾 €8-11 |

This Haut-Montravel is almost a *liquoreux* (sweet, syrupy wine). Its powerful nose suggests a basket of crystallised fruits underlined by delicate notes of oak. A clean, lively attack is counter-balanced by a fruity, rich, concentrated, almost unctuous, texture. This well-balanced wine can be kept for three to five years. (50 cl bottles).

☛ EARL d'Adrina, Le Bondieu,
24230 Saint-Antoine-de-Breuilh,
tel. 05.53.58.30.83, fax 05.53.24.38.21 ✔
🍷 by appt.
🚶 Didier Feytout

CH. PUY-SERVAIN Terrement 1999★

| | 1.5 ha | 3,600 | 🍾 €15-23 |

This wine received one star, in spite of a difficult vintage, and also won a *coup de cœur* last year. With this in mind, the reputation of the wines of Puy-Servain is already made. The nose is still somewhat closed, but already shows some concentration by its crystallised-fruit aromas. The round, rich palate is balanced by a little freshness, while the fruit flavours return beautifully on the finish. The **Montravel Cuvée Marjolaine 99**, matured in oak barrels, is also awarded one star because of its very ripe concentration underlined by a fine oakiness.

☛ SCEA Puy-Servain, Calabre,
33220 Port-Sainte-Foy, tel. 05.53.24.77.27,
fax 05.53.58.37.43 🍷 by appt.
🚶 Hecquet

brought on in hogsheads, these wines have considerable complexity and finesse. In 2000 production was 19,784 hl (522,298 gal).

CH. BEAUPORTAIL 1999 ■ 🍷 €8-11
4 ha   20,000

Beauportail is a wine-producing property dating from the 18th century. Now situated at the entrance to Bergerac, it has a vineyard area covering 10 ha (24.7 acres). Its 99 red has a powerful nose composed of vanilla, spices and fruits. On the palate, the fairly round tannins are accompanied by toasty notes. Although the tannins dominate the finish, they do not mask the fruit, and they give good structure to the whole blend.
➻ La Truffière Beauportail,
rte des Cabernets, 24100 Bergerac,
tel. 05.53.24.85.16, fax 05.53.61.28.63,
e-mail fabrice.feytout@wanadoo.fr ⓥ
⅄ by appt.
➻ F. Feytout

CH. CHAMPAREL 1999 ■ 🍷 €5-8
6.62 ha   45,000

At the top of the Pécharmant hillside, Château Champarel cultivates more than 8 ha (19.76 acres) of vines. The wine on offer here is deeply coloured. It is still shy on the nose, but it lets some spice and vanilla aromas peep through. The tannic concentration is rich and powerful. The palate has notes of overripe fruit and leather, fading to a still somewhat austere finish. This wine deserves to be left to age, to reach its potential.
➻ Françoise Bouché, Pécharmant,
24100 Bergerac, tel. 05.53.57.34.76,
fax 05.53.73.24.18 ⓥ ⅄ by appt.

CH. CORBIAC 1999★ ■ 🍷 👤 €11-15
13.5 ha   80,000

Grape cultivation had already been introduced to Corbiac in the Middle Ages. Furthermore, at Château Corbiac, wine-making activity can be dated from 1755 with certainty, by reference to the ledgers kept at the estate. This 99 is a wine with a fruity nose, underlined by nuances of chocolate. The palate is round but powerful, and exhibits solid tannins, still noticeable on the finish. It should be left for five or six years: it will certainly be good after this time.
➻ Bruno de Corbiac, Ch. de Corbiac,
24100 Bergerac, tel. 05.53.57.20.75,
fax 05.53.57.89.98, e-mail corbiac@
corbiac.com ⓥ ⅄ by appt.

DOM. DES COSTES 1999 ■ 🍷 €8-11
10 ha   30,000

Nicole Dournel works 12 ha (29.64 acres) of vines. In a vintage that was difficult because of the weather conditions, she has produced a rich wine that should be ready in

two or three years. A little charred-oak aroma is already perceptible on the nose, with ripe-fruit flavours on the palate. Right now, the oak certainly dominates the fruit, but the concentration is opulent.
➻ Nicole Dournel, Les Costes,
24100 Bergerac, tel. 05.53.57.64.49,
fax 05.53.61.69.08 ⓥ ⅄ by appt.
➻ Lacroix

DOM. DU HAUT PÉCHARMANT
Cuvée Nicolas Elevé en fût de chêne 1998★★ ■ 🍷 €11-15
1.5 ha   6,200

Michel Roches dedicates a *cuvée* to each of his grandchildren. Let's hope he has plenty of descendants, so that he can offer us more wines as remarkable as this one. On the first impression, red berries (blackcurrant and raspberry) are detected, which then give way to fine, oaky, vanilla aromas. On the palate, the balance is a harmony between powerful tannins and rich fruity flavours The tannins should mellow and integrate within the next eight to ten years. The **Cuvée Veuve Roches 99** especially impressed the Jury with its potential; it is a bottle to lay down for ten years.
➻ Michel et Didier Roches, Dom. du
Haut-Pécharmant, 24100 Bergerac,
tel. 05.53.57.29.50, fax 05.53.24.28.05 ⓥ
⅄ ev. day except Sun. 8am-12 noon
2pm-7pm

CH. HUGON 1998 ■ €5-8
1.18 ha   3,000

Château Hugon is a small vineyard covering just over 4 ha (9.88 acres). The yield is controlled by green harvesting (removing some of the grapes while still green to reduce the yield), and by hand-picking the entire crop. This Pécharmant presents an intense nose of red berries, based on a delicate vanilla oak. The initial attack on the palate is soft and then becomes more powerful, supported by solid tannins and a lot of oak. This pleasant wine needs to left to age for four or five years.
➻ Bernard Cousy, Haut-Pécharmant,
24100 Bergerac, tel. 05.53.63.28.44 ⓥ
⅄ ev. day 9am-12 noon 2pm-6pm

DOM. LA MÉTAIRIE 1998 ■ €8-11
6 ha   29,350

This Pécharmant reflects its 12 months' maturation in oak by its pronouncedly toasty aromas. When the wine is shaken, red-berry aromas are released. The silky attack introduces a supple and light palate. Also singled out, the **Côtes de Bergerac Château Fonfrède 98** is a very fruity wine, ready to drink now.
➻ SARL Dom. La Métairie en Pécharmant, Pommier, 24380 Creyssensac-et-Pissot, tel. 05.53.80.09.85, fax 05.53.80.14.72 ⓥ
⅄ by appt.

Fresh and not excessively sweet, it is a dessert wine.

CH. TERRE VIEILLE

Vieilli en fût de chêne 1999

7 ha 35,000 €8-11

At the heart of the vineyard, the owners of this château have discovered flints, scrapers and blade ends dating from prehistoric times. Some 3,000 stones are now on exhibition at the estate. From the same vineyard was born this Pécharmant, still largely dominated by oak and toasty aromas. It has a pleasant attack by virtue of the ripe fruits present on the palate. It also has good concentration, and it is worth keeping and rediscovering in a few years' time, when the oak has integrated.

➤ Gérôme et Dolores Morand-Monteil, Ch. Terre-Vieille, 24520 Saint-Sauveur-de-Berger ac, tel. 05.53.57.35.07, fax 05.53.61.91.77, e-mail gerome-morand-monteil@wanadoo.fr ✔ Y ev. day except Sun. 9am-7pm

CH. DE TIREGAND 1998

35 ha 97,000 €8-11

Established by Edward Tyrgan, illegitimate son of Henry III of England, this stately home possesses a park in the French style and a vineyard of 42 ha (103.74 acres). Its Pécharmant, with vanilla tones and a slight muskiness, also has red-berry (morello-cherry) aromas. The first impression is subtle, followed by ripe-fruit flavours developing on the palate, underlined by notes of vanilla, and concluding in a somewhat austere tone. The Millésime 99 du Château de Tiregand was also singled out.

➤ Comtesse F. de Saint-Exupéry, Ch. de Tiregand, 24100 Creysse, tel. 05.53.23.21.08, fax 05.53.22.58.49, e-mail chateautiregand@club-internet.fr ✔ Y by appt.

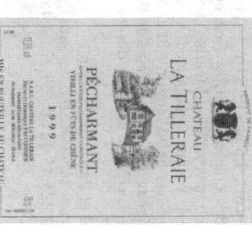

CH. LA TILLERAIE

Vieilli en fût de chêne 1999★★

6 ha 30,000 €5-8

➤ Gilles Gérault, Rosette, 24100 Bergerac, tel. 05.53.24.13.68, fax 05.53.73.87.65 ✔ Y by appt.

Château La Tilleraie comes back into the Guide decisively, with a masterly and unanimous coup de cœur. This Pécharmant has a particularly elegant nose, with roasted, toasty and spicy aromas reminiscent of pepper and cinnamon. Ripe fruit dominates a concentrated palate, supported by dense, fine-grained tannins. The balance is perfect between tannins, fruit and acidity. The 12 months' maturation was managed meticulously, so that the oak occupies just the right place. This wine is pleasant to drink now, but can be left to age for four or five years.

➤ SARL Ch. La Tilleraie, 4100 Pécharmant, tel. 05.53.57.86.42, fax 05.53.57.86.42 ✔ Y by appt.

➤ B. Fauconnier

CH. METAIRIE HAUTE 1999★

3 ha 20,000 €5-8

This négociant house has a wide range of wines, three of which are featured. Château Métairie Haute, with its very fine oaky nose and its palate of well-integrated tannins, is a well-made Pécharmant, ready to drink now. The Château Hautes-Fargues 99, singled out by the Jury, is full of fruit (cherries in brandy) and spices; the still-austere tannins should become more well-rounded within the next three years. Finally, the Monbazillac Château Les Marquises 98 was singled out by the Jury for its fine aromas.

➤ Producta SA, 21, cours Xavier-Arnozan, 33082 Bordeaux Cedex, tel. 05.57.81.18.18, fax 05.56.81.22.12, e-mail producta@producta.com Y by appt.

CH. DU ROOY 1999★

1.2 ha 6,600 €5-8

Château du Rooy commands a wide panoramic view over Bergerac and the Dordogne valley. It is one of the few estates to produce both Pécharmant and Rosette. In this 99 red, the complex range of aromas includes notes of prune, overripe fruit and a lightly-toasted oak. The taster detected nuances of chocolate and vanilla in the mouth, but the most impressive aspect is the tannic structure, making this a Pécharmant to keep in the cellar for at least three years. The Rosette 2000 was singled out for its floral and mineral aromas.

Rosette

Rosette is the least-known appellation and the best-kept secret of the region. It comes from the clay and gravel soils of hills overlooking the town of Bergerac from the north, and in 2000 production was 1,085 hl (28,644 gal).

CH. MONTPLAISIR 2000

□   0.6 ha   3,300   ▮ €3-5

This property, covering an area of just under 9 ha (22.23 acres), underwent major restructuring until the mid-1990s. Its floral Rosette, with its rose and white-flower aromas, surprises one with its liveliness on the palate, but its ethereal structure and aromatic length are really enticing.
➤ J.L. Blanc, Montplaisir,
24130 Prigonrieux, tel. 05.53.58.91.86,
fax 05.53.24.68.17, e-mail blanco@
wanadoo.fr ◪ Ƴ by appt.

Saussignac

Praised in the 16th century in François Rabelais's *Pantagruel* and located in a superb landscape of plateaux and hills, the terroir produces rich, sweet wines of great quality. In 2000 production was 2,154 hl (56,866 gal).

CH. GRINOU

Vinifié en fût de chêne 1998★★

□   2 ha   1,200   ▮▮ €15-23

It has a modest volume of production, but this wine is remarkable. The characterful nose is a subtle mixture of fruits, crystallised apple and caramel. After a touch of vanilla on the attack, the palate is supported by a solid structure, enveloped in a full-bodied wine, with good, long flavours. In **Bergerac red**, the **Grand Vin du Château Grinou 99** and the **Réserve 99**, two wines matured in the barrel for 12 months, especially impressed the Jury. They need to be kept two or three years.
➤ Catherine et Guy Cuisset, Ch. Grinou, 24240 Monestier, tel. 05.53.58.46.63, fax 05.53.61.05.66 ◪ Ƴ by appt.

CH. LA MAURIGNE

Cuvée La Maurigne 1998★

□   2.2 ha   4,000   ▮▮ €8-11

Owners of the estate since 1997, the Gérardins work 5.5 ha (13.59 acres) of vines. Their 1998 is characterised by fine, complex aromas, rich in crystallised fruits. The unctuous, smooth palate is balanced by a good acidity, and has good length. (50 cl bottles.) The **Saussignac 99** and the **Côtes de Bergerac red Cuvée La Maurigne 99** deserve to be singled out.
➤ Chantal et Patrick Gérardin,
La Maurigne, 24240 Razac-de-Saussignac,
tel. 05.53.27.25.45, fax 05.53.27.25.45 ◪
Ƴ ev. day 9am-7pm

CH. LE CHABRIER

Cuvée Eléna 1998★

□   2.38 ha   1,900   ▮▮ €15-23

Pierre Carle is in the process of converting his 20 ha (49.4 acres) of vines to organic viticulture. His Saussignac is distinguished by a complex nose of crystallised and overripe fruits and a rich, round palate. The oak is well-integrated. This wine is ready to drink now, but could be kept for a few years. The **Côtes de Bergerac red Cuvée Gros Caillou 99** and the **Bergerac Sec Cuvée Il était une fois … 99** are awarded one star. They need to be kept two or three years for the oak to integrate.
➤ Pierre Carle, Ch. Le Chabrier,
24240 Razac-de-Saussignac,
tel. 05.53.27.92.73, fax 05.53.23.39.03,
e-mail chateau.le.chabrier@wanadoo.fr ◪
Ƴ by appt.

CH. PETITE BORIE 2000★

□   4 ha   26,000   ▮ ♦ €5-8

This Saussignac of the *moelleux* (sweet) type is characteristic of the Sauvignon grape, with its boxwood aromas. On the palate, citrus fruits such as grapefruit come to the fore in a good balance between liveliness and fruity concentration. This is an ideal aperitif wine. Also highly successful, the **Château Court Les Mûts 99**, matured 18 months in barrel, is a very sweet, rich wine with aromas of apricot and crystallised fruits melted in oak. It needs to be kept two or three years.
➤ Vignobles Pierre Sadoux,
Ch. Court-Les-Mûts,
24240 Razac-de-Saussignac,
tel. 05.53.27.92.17, fax 05.53.23.77.21 ◪
Ƴ ev. day except Sun. 9am-11.30am
2pm-5.30pm; Sat. by appt.
➤ P.J. Sadoux

CH. TOURMENTINE 1999★

□   1 ha   2,500   ▮▮ €11-15

Jean-Marie Huré has been established in the Bergerac area since 1986. His Saussignac has a very fruity nose, dominated by quince and crystallised apricot. The same flavours return on the palate, within a round, full-bodied structure. The finish has good length, but is still a trifle austere. (50 cl bottles.) The **Bergerac red 99 Elevé en Fûts de Chêne** (matured in oak barrels) is also a great

Côtes de Duras

The Côtes de Duras vineyard, 2,000 ha (4,940 acres), is the natural extension of the plateau of Entre-Deux-Mers. There is a local story that, after the Revocation of the Edict of Nantes, exiled Gascon Huguenots used to have Duras wine shipped to them in their Dutch retreats. Tulips were planted at the ends of the rows of vines which they reserved for themselves.

Eroded over the ages by the River Dourdèze and its tributaries, the slopes are made up of sandy-clay and limestone soils naturally suited to the Bordeaux varieties. Sémillon, Sauvignon and Muscadelle are used for the white wines; Cabernet-Franc, Cabernet-Sauvignon, Merlot and Malbec for the reds. Also found are Chenin, Odenc and Ugni-Blanc. The glory of Duras is, above all, its dry white wine, made mainly from Sauvignon, with 46,136 hl (1,217,990 gal) produced in 2000. These are lively wines of pedigree with a specifically identifiable bouquet and are marvellous with seafood and saltwater fish. The red wines, of which 73,133 hl (19,307,191 gal) were produced in 2000; often vinified as varietal wines, are fleshy and round, with a good colour.

DOM. DES ALLEGRETS
Vinifié et élevé en fût de chêne 1999★★

	0.5 ha	1,700	€5-8

This wine's powerful, complex nose is a mixture of fruit and oak. The palate has a lot of concentration, and the noticeable oak character should soon become integrated. The Côtes de Duras Moelleux 99 Cuvée Breignes d'Or Vieilles Vignes, Vieilli en Fût de Chêne (aged in oak barrels), was judged a great success. It is a rich wine, expressing honey and dried fruit aromas, with a little touch of oak.

➤ SCEA Francis et Monique Blanchard, 47120 Villeneuve-de-Duras, tel. 05.53.94.74.56, fax 05.53.94.74.56
ev. day 10am-12 noon 2pm-7pm

DOM. AMBLARD Sauvignon 2000★

	10 ha	74,000	€3-5

The estate has grown progressively since it was purchased in 1936, and it now covers 130 ha (321.1 acres). The Sauvignon characteristics are expressed in notes of citrus and grapefruit, complemented by aromas of pear drops. The fruity, supple palate is well-balanced, and has a pleasant finish.

➤ Guy Pauvert, SCEA Dom. Amblard, 47120 Saint-Sernin-de-Duras, tel. 05.53.94.77.92, fax 05.53.94.27.12
ev. day except Sun. 8am-12.30pm 2pm-7pm

HAUTS DE BERTICOT
Elevé en fût de chêne 1999★

	9 ha	60,000	€5-8

Ripe fruit and notes of vanilla combine to create a pleasant nose; a clean, soft attack, supple, integrated tannins and a complex finish make for a flavoursome palate. The success, because it has a well-balanced blend of oak and fruit.

➤ Jean-Marie Huré, Tourmentine, 24240 Monestier, tel. 05.53.58.41.41, fax 05.53.63.40.52 ev. day except Sun. 9am-12 noon 2pm-6pm

CH. DES VIGIERS
Marguerite Vigier 1999

	2 ha	2,400	€11-15

This wine's nose is shy at first. When the glass is shaken, it produces notes of chocolate and menthol, then aromas of bitter orange and crystallised fruits. The palate is more expressive, with its suggestions of toasty roasted flavours and fruit. Endowed with a pleasant balance between richness and liveliness, it is a nice aperitif wine. (50 cl bottles).

➤ SCEA La Font du Roc, Ch. des Vigiers, 24240 Monestier, tel. 05.53.61.50.30, fax 05.53.61.50.31, e-mail vigiers@calvanet
by appt.
➤ Petersson

CLOS D'YVIGNE
Vendanges Tardives 1999★★

	3 ha	3,200	€23-30

This estate was awarded several coups de coeur in our previous editions. The 99 is remarkable, in spite of the difficult weather conditions. The highly-complex nose mingles crystallised fruits, toast, apricot, a touch of wax and a little oak. The palate is dominated by a sensation of richness, roundness and power; the notes of oak and vanilla melt nicely into a very lasting richness. (50 cl bottles.) The Jury singled out the Côtes de Bergerac Le Petit Prince red 99, matured in barrel.

➤ Patricia Atkinson, SCEA Clos d'Yvigne, Le Bourg, 24240 Gageac-Rouillac, tel. 05.53.22.94.40, fax 05.53.23.47.67, e-mail patricia.atkinson@wanadoo.fr
by appt.

Côtes de Duras

Cuvée Duc de Berticot red 99 and the **Cuvée Grande Réserve 99 Vieillie en Fût de Chêne** (aged in oak barrels) also receive one star each.

➤ SCA Vignerons Landerrouat-Duras, Berticot, 47120 Duras, tel. 05.53.83.75.47, fax 05.53.83.82.40 ▼ Ⓨ by appt.

BERTICOT Les Estivales 2000★

▢ 3 ha 20,000 ▥ ♦ €5-8

In the Berticot range, the Jury liked this dry white wine for its complex aromas of passion-fruit, white peach and apricot. This is a supple, rich Côtes de Duras, with a long finish, ready to drink now.

➤ SCA Vignerons Landerrouat-Duras, Berticot, 47120 Duras, tel. 05.53.83.75.47, fax 05.53.83.82.40 ▼ Ⓨ by appt.

CH. DES BRUYERES

Sauvignon 2000★

▢ 0.88 ha 5,800 ▥ ♦ €5-8

'Heide,' the owners' Dutch name, means 'bruyères' in French, or 'heather' in English: hence the name given to this château endowed with a vineyard of over 8 ha (20 acres). The 2000 vintage has produced this pleasant wine, with a powerful nose of Sauvignon and musky hints. The supple attack develops on the palate into somewhat wild fruit flavours.

➤ Piet et Annelies Heide, Ch. des Bruyères, 47120 Loubès-Bernac, tel. 05.53.94.22.61, fax 05.53.94.22.61, e-mail piet.heide@wanadoo.fr ▼
Ⓨ by appt.

DOM. DES COURS Sauvignon 2000★

▢ 5 ha 20,000 ▥ ♦ €3-5

The Côtes de Duras from the Domaine des Cours estate is renowned for its intense nose of boxwood and buds of blackcurrant and broom. This 2000 is no exception to the rule. It is characterised on the palate by a supple, unctuous body that takes up the wild flavours of the Sauvignon grape. The finish is complex and of good length.

➤ EARL Lusoli, Dom. des Cours, 47120 Sainte-Colombe-de-Duras, tel. 05.53.83.74.35, fax 05.53.83.63.18 ▼
Ⓨ by appt.

DOM. DE FERRANT

Elevé en fût de chêne 1998★

■ 1 ha 3,000 ▥ €5-8

This is an attractive, purple-coloured wine. The first aromas evoke lightly-crystallised fruits and morello cherries, then the well-integrated oak appears. After a supple attack, the palate is a balance between the fruit and the oak, although the finish is still austere. It is a pleasant wine that will mellow with age.

➤ SCEA Dom. de Ferrant, 47120 Esclottes, tel. 05.53.83.73.46, fax 05.53.83.82.80 ▼
Ⓨ ev. day except Sun. 8am–12.30pm 2pm–7pm

DOM. DU GRAND MAYNE

Sauvignon fût de chêne 2000★★

▢ 1.2 ha 10,000 ▥ €5-8

Andrew Gordon works 33.5 ha (82.75 acres) of vines. Each year, he invites his British customers to a grape-picking weekend. The Sauvignon grape thus harvested for the 2000 vintage produced a wine with powerful aromas of ripe fruits, pineapple and passion-fruit, underlined by a touch of fine oak. The lively attack allows aromas typical of the variety at perfect maturity to come through, mixed with a touch of vanilla. The mid-palate is complex, and the finish particularly long, with a little nuance of oak. This is the result of a real mastery of harvesting and maturing techniques. The **Cuvée Classique 2000**, not matured in oak, is awarded two stars for its fruity-floral aromas and its fresh balance.

➤ SARL Andrew Gordon, Le Grand Mayne, 47120 Villeneuve-de-Duras, tel. 05.53.94.74.17, fax 05.53.94.77.02, e-mail agordon@terre-net.fr ▼ Ⓨ by appt.

DOM. DU GRAND MAYNE

Elevé en fût de chêne 1999★★★

■ 3.22 ha 28,000 ▥ €5-8

This wine was nearly a *coup de cœur*. It was displaced only by the Côtes de Duras dry white. Its intense nose is predominantly of blackcurrant. The supple, round attack heralds a well-filled palate, supported by already-integrated tannins. The balance is harmonious and the flavour long. The **Cuvée Classique red 99** is notable for the way the fruity, round body is supported by the well-blended tannins.

➤ SARL Andrew Gordon, Le Grand Mayne, 47120 Villeneuve-de-Duras, tel. 05.53.94.74.17, fax 05.53.94.77.02, e-mail agordon@terre-net.fr ▼ Ⓨ by appt.

DOM. DE LA CHENERAIE

Prestige 1999

■ 1.5 ha 12,000 ▥ ♦ €3-5

This light-coloured wine has a pleasant range of red-berry aromas. It gives a supple impression on the palate, with the same fruity flavours. With its ethereal and well-balanced structure, it is ready to drink.

➤ Alain Mariotto, La Grand-Font, 47120 Esclottes, tel. 05.53.83.76.52, fax 05.53.89.03.06 ▼ Ⓨ by appt.

CH. LA MOULIERE
Sauvignon Grande Réserve 2000★★

☐ 10 ha 60,000 €3–5

This wine is intense and fine, with suggestions of well-ripened citrus fruits, which are dominant and persist to a long finish. It is a well-structured and well-balanced wine. The **Cuvée red Classique 99** from Château La Moulière is awarded one star. It is supple, fruity and already very drinkable.

Blancheton Frères, La Moulière, 47120 Duras, tel. 05.53.83.70.19, fax 05.53.83.07.30, e-mail blancheton@chateau-la-mouliere.com ☑ by appt.

CH. LA PETITE BERTRANDE
Grande Cuvée Vieilli en fût de chêne 1999★★

■ 3 ha 10,000 €8–11

This Côtes de Duras is original for its spicy, menthol nose, which comes from using 20% Malbec grapes in the blend. The nose develops into more classic, oaky aromas. After a powerful attack, the structured palate becomes round and fleshy, if a little oaky and austere on the finish. This wine possesses enough concentration for it to keep for three years, to allow it to mellow. The **Cuvée Classique 99** is awarded one star: it has a nose of ripe peaches and nectarines and a flavorsome, easy-to-drink quality.

Jean-François Thierry, Vignoble Les Guignards, 47120 Saint-Astier-de-Duras, tel. 05.53.94.74.03, fax 05.53.94.75.27, e-mail vguignards@aol.com ☑ ev. day except Sun. 10am–12.30pm 4pm–7pm

Alain Tingaud

DOM. DE LA SOLLE
Cuvée Fernand Elevé en fût de chêne 1999★

■ 0.4 ha 2,400 €8–11

Originally from the *Pays Nantais*, Jocelyne and Roger Visonneau moved to the South-West in 1994. Since then they have run a 9.5-ha (23.47-acre) vineyard. Their 99 wine, richly fruity and oaky on the nose, has a good structure. The tannins simply need to mellow and integrate for a few years in order to come together in a beautiful wine.

EARL Visonneau, Boussinet, 47120 Saint-Jean-de-Duras, tel. 05.53.83.07.09, fax 05.53.20.10.54 ☑ ev. day except Sun. 2pm–7pm

DOM. DE LAULAN Sauvignon 2000★★

☐ 12 ha 60,000 €3–5

A real personality in the history of his region, Gilbert Geoffroy plays a leading role in this appellation. His wines have been awarded numerous stars in past editions of the *Guide*. This wine gives off powerful scents of blackcurrant and broom, bearing the mark of the Sauvignon grape. After a clean and lively attack, it has a good weight on the palate, due to its complexity and balance, with a background of citrus flavours. The **Côtes de Duras Moelleux 99** was judged a great success by virtue of its well-balanced range of crystallised fruits, honey, prune and vanilla. The oaky character perceptible on the palate will integrate with time.

EARL Geoffroy, Dom. de Laulan, 47120 Duras, tel. 05.53.83.73.69, fax 05.53.83.81.54, e-mail domaine.laulan@wanadoo.fr ☑ ev. day except Sun. 8am–12 noon 2pm–6pm

CH. LES SAVIGNATTES
Sauvignon 2000

☐ 6.2 ha 30,000 €3–5

Boxwood and broom stand out on the nose of this classic wine, a very characteristic Sauvignon. The supple, rich palate has fruity flavours and a note of freshness. This is a bottle that may be put on the table as an aperitif and left there to accompany fish and shellfish.

Maurice Dreux, Les Savignattes, 47120 Esclottes, tel. 05.53.83.72.84, fax 05.53.83.82.97, e-mail bernadettedreux@wanadoo.fr ☑ ev. day except Sun. 9am–12 noon 3pm–7pm; 9am–12 noon Sat.

DOM. DU PETIT MALROME
Elevé en fût de chêne 1999★★

■ 1.5 ha 8,000 €5–8

Since the year 2000, Geneviève and Alain Lescaut have converted the whole of their 18.7-ha (46.19-acre) estate to organic farming. Their wines can be relied upon to give consistent value in Côtes de Duras, as testified by this fruity, concentrated wine. The raspberry aromas melt pleasantly into notes of oak. After a round attack, the palate preserves the fruity taste, and the overall balance is enticing, even if the oak does produce a certain austerity on the finish. It is an ideal accompaniment to red meats. The **Côtes de Duras Moelleux 99 Elevé en Fût de Chêne** (matured in oak barrels) was judged a great success. The nose of crystallised fruits, quince and vanilla is coupled by a concentrated palate, still somewhat characterised by oak.

EARL Geneviève et Alain Lescaut, 47120 Saint-Jean-de-Duras, tel. 05.53.89.01.44, fax 05.53.89.01.44 ☑ ev. day except Sun. 11am–7pm

DOM. DU VIEUX BOURG
Sauvignon 2000★

☐ 3 ha 22,000 €3–5

With 30 ha (74.1 acres) of vines, this producer is established in the ancient village of Pardaillan, which still houses the remains of a 12th-century fortified castle. He offers a quality dry white wine, that will go well with fish dishes. The nose releases powerful ripe-fruit aromas, which are reprised in a full, well-balanced palate.

Bernard Bireaud, Dom. du Vieux Bourg, 47120 Pardaillan, tel. 05.53.83.02.18, fax 05.53.83.02.37, e-mail vieux-bourg2@wanadoo.fr ☑ by appt.

THE LOIRE VALLEY AND THE CENTRE

This enormous area is dominated by a single great waterway, the 'royal' Loire. It would justify that epithet on its own merits, though it also became a favoured place of respite for kings and queens, and a cradle of Renaissance arts and culture. The changing countryside of the Loire valley is bathed in a unique light, arising from the subtle marriage of sky and water that enabled the 'Garden of France' to burgeon, and the vine to thrive. From the edge of the Massif Central to the estuary, vineyards stud the landscape along the river and a dozen of its tributaries, creating a vast wine-growing region which encompasses much more than the Loire valley itself, and is generally referred to as 'The Loire Valley and the Centre'. Tourism here is cultural, gastronomic and wine-based, and the roads that follow the river along the heights, or the back roads which run through the vineyards and forests, are unforgettable trails of discovery.

The Loire itself can be narrow and sinuous, or swift-flowing and turbulent, at times imposing and majestic in appearance, at times peaceful. Always the unifying factor in the landscape, it requires attention to its vagaries, particularly when it comes to the wines.

From Roanne or Saint-Pourçain as far as Nantes or Saint-Nazaire, vines grow on the slopes overlooking the banks, braving the nature of the soils and wide differences in climate and local traditions. For some 1,000 km (620 miles), a vineyard area of more than 50,000 ha (123,500 acres) produces greatly varying wines. In 1999, the volume of appellation wines was 2,743,582 hl (72,430,564 gal), that is to say 9.63% of the total production of France. The wines of this vast region share a freshness and delicacy of perfume that are essentially due to the northerly location of most of the producing areas.

All the same, to attempt to group all the different wines produced under the same heading is a little risky, since, even though they are classified as being northern, some vineyards are on a latitude which, in the Rhône valley, enjoys the influence of the Mediterranean climate ... Mâcon, for example, shares the same latitude as Saint-Pourçain and Roanne the same as Villefranche-sur-Saône. So it is the topography that works on the climate to limit the influence of the prevailing airflow: the Atlantic winds blow west to east along the corridor eroded by the Loire, weakening little by little as they encounter the hills around Saumur and the Touraine.

The wine areas that form identifiable entities are, thus, the Nantes region, plus Anjou and Touraine. However, we have also included the vineyards of Haut Poitou, the Berry, the Côtes d'Auvergne and the Côtes Roannaises; it is important to attach them to a big region, and this is the closest both geographically and as regards the wines that are produced. In general terms, it is appropriate to identify four big groupings, the first three mentioned plus the Centre.

In the lower Loire valley, the Muscadet area and part of the Anjou are on the Massif Armorican and made up variously of schists, gneiss and other sedimentary rocks, or of outcrops from the Primary era. The soils that have developed on these underlying structures are very well-suited to the vine and the wines produced are of excellent quality. The first entity, the most westerly area, still called the Nantais, has a gentle landscape in which the hard rocks of the Massif Armorican have been gouged away into almost vertical valley walls by little rivers. The steep valleys have no cultivable slopes and the vines are planted on hillocks on the plateau. The climate is maritime and fairly uniform throughout the year, and the maritime influence diminishes the seasonal variations. The winters are not particularly harsh and the warm summers are often humid; there is a good deal of sunshine, but Spring frosts sometimes disrupt growth.

Anjou is the transitional area between the Nantais region ('le pays Nantais') and the Touraine and, historically speaking, includes Saumur. This wine-growing region lies almost totally within the department of Maine-et-Loire but, geographically, Saumur should more appropriately be attached to western Touraine, with which it has more in common so far as *terroir* and climate are concerned. The sedimentary soils of the Paris Basin covered the Primary formations of the Massif Amoricain from Brissac-Quincé to Doué-la-Fontaine. Anjou falls into several sub-regions: the north-facing Coteaux de la Loire (an extension of the Nantais region) run gently down from the edge of the plateau; the Coteaux du Layon, very steep, on schist soils, together with the Coteaux de l'Aubance; finally, a transitional zone between Anjou and Touraine known chiefly for its rosés.

The Saumur *terroir* is essentially identified by creamy limestone, or tufa, on beds of chalk; underground, wine being aged in bottles competes with the cultivation of Paris mushrooms in the galleries and cellars dug out of the chalk. The hills provide shelter from the west winds, helping to create a semi-maritime/semi-continental climate. Across from Saumur, on the right bank of the Loire on the slopes outside Tours, you find the vineyards of Saint-Nicolas-de-Bourgueil. East of Tours, and on the same slopes (an extension of those of Saumur and Vienne), Vouvray and Chinon are the leading wines of the Touraine. Azay-le-Rideau, Montlouis, Amboise, Mesland and the Coteaux du Cher are other great names to remember from the 'Garden of France'. The little vineyards of the Coteaux du Loir, the Orléanais, Cheverny, Valençay and the Coteaux du Giennois should be considered with those of the Touraine. It is impossible to decide if you should visit the area for its wines, its châteaux or its goat's cheeses (Saint-Maure, Selles-sur-Cher, Valençay); in that case, why not all at once?

The Berry vineyards make up a fourth region, the Centre, which is quite different in *terroir* and climate from the other three. Here the soils are essentially Jurassic, as they are in Chablis, Sancerre's neighbour, and in Pouilly-sur-Loire, and the climate semi-continental, with cold winters and hot summers. For ease of presentation, Saint-Pourçain, the Côtes Roannaises and Forez are included in this fourth entity, despite further variations in the soils (primary rock from the Massif Central) and the climate (semi-continental to continental).

This guide follows the same geographic progression to examine the specific wine domains. Starting from the Atlantic coast, Muscadet owes its characteristics to a single grape variety (the Melon) producing a unique, dry, irreplaceable wine. In this area, the Folle Blanche variety is the base for another dry white wine, though of lesser quality, Gros-Plant. The region of Ancenis has been 'colonised' by Gamay.

In Anjou, Chenin (or Pineau de la Loire) is the main variety for white wines, although Chardonnay and Sauvignon have more recently been introduced. Chenin is the base for the great rich or, depending on how they develop, sweet wines of the area, as well as for excellent dry and sparkling wines. As for the red varieties the Grolleau Noir, once widely planted, traditionally produces semi-dry rosés, while Cabernet Franc (which used to be called 'Breton') and Cabernet Sauvignon produce fine, full-bodied red wines with good keeping qualities. The proverbial 'sweetness of the Anjou' arises from a combination of depth, due to its strong acidity, and a soft flavour from the presence of the remaining sugars, and this quality is to be found throughout the sometimes confusing multiplicity of wines produced.

Upstream from the Touraine region the main varieties are Chenin, planted in Saumur, Vouvray and Montlouis or on the slopes of the Loir, Cabernet Franc at Chinon, Bourgueil and Saumur, and Grolleau at Azay-le-Rideau. In the eastern region, Gamay for reds and Sauvignon for

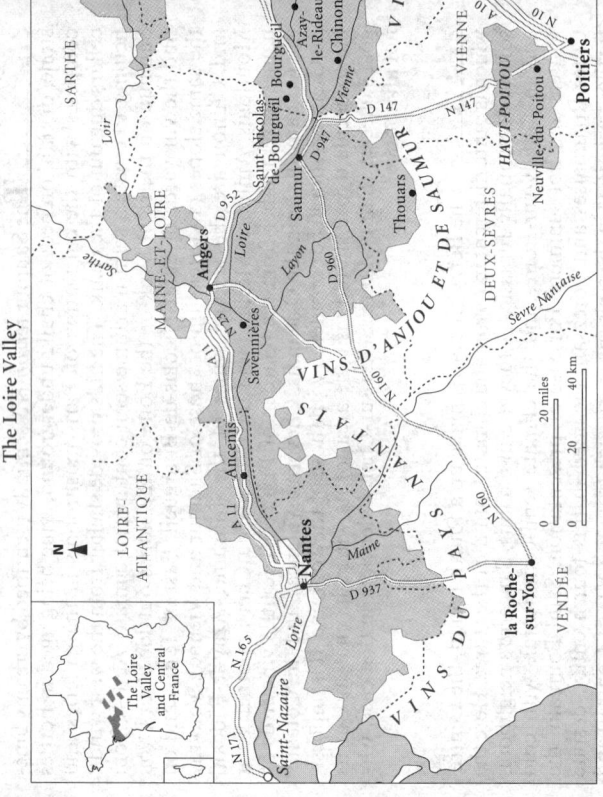

The Loire Valley

936

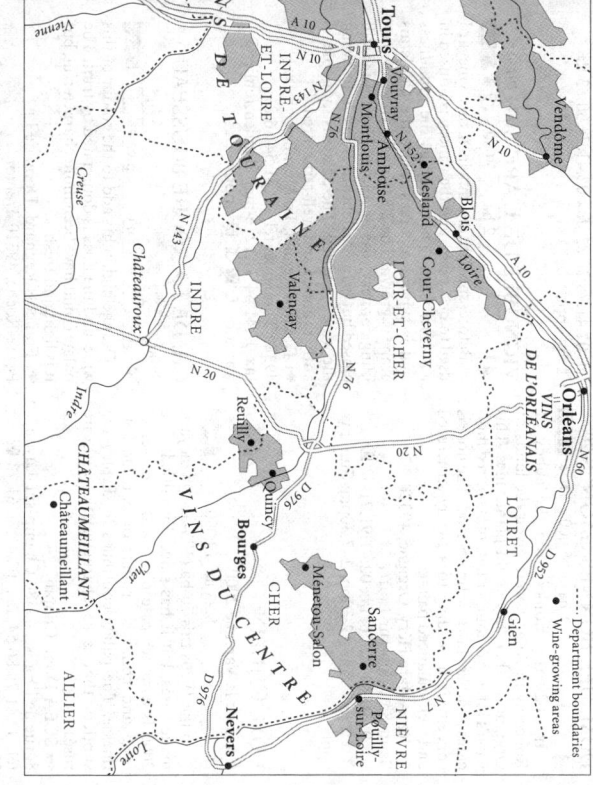

whites produce light, fruity and pleasant wines. Finally, for the sake of completeness, the Pineau d'Aunis from the Coteaux du Loir, which has peppery flavours, should be mentioned, along with the Gris Meunier in the Orléanais.

In the Centre, Sauvignon (making white wines) reigns supreme in Sancerre, Reuilly, Quincy and Menetou-Salon, as well as in Pouilly, where it is still called Blanc-Fumé. There it shares the slopes with the few remaining vineyards of Chasselas, which produce dry, lively wines. As for the reds, the influence of neighbouring Burgundy in the Pinot Noir wines of Sancerre and Menetou-Salon can already be discerned.

To complete this summary of Loire wines, a few words should be added about Haut Poitou, known for lively, fruity Sauvignons, well-structured Chardonnays, and light, robust reds from Gamay, Pinot Noir and Cabernet. Influenced by a semi-maritime climate, Haut Poitou is a zone of transition between the Loire Valley and Bordeaux. Between Anjou and Poitou lies the lesser-known Thouarsais vineyard (AOVDQS). In the Fiefs Vendéens region along the Atlantic coast, an AOVDQS *terroir* historically known as Vin des Fiefs du Cardinal, the best-known wines are the rosés from Mareuil, made with Gamay and Pinot Noir. The curiosity of the region is the Ragoûtant wine, made from the Négrette variety, but it is difficult to find.

LOIRE

The Loire Valley

The Val de Loire

Rosé de Loire

These wines from the Appellation Régionale, an AOC since 1974, can be produced within the boundaries of the regional AOCs of Anjou, Saumur and Touraine. Cabernet Franc, Cabernet Sauvignon, Gamay, Pineau d'Aunis and Grolleau are used for making dry rosé wines of which 65,000 hl (1,716,000 gal) were produced in 2000.

DOM. DES BONNES GAGNES 2000

1 ha   5,000   €3-5

In 1020 the monks from the abbey of Ronceray in Angers were given the lands of Orgigné so that they could plant vines. This wine's intense colour with its hints of red indicates a rather short vatting period. The nose is concentrated, leading to a firmly-structured and well-balanced palate.

☛ Jean-Marc Héry, Orgigné, 49320 Saint-Saturnin-sur-Loire,
tel. 02.41.91.22.76, fax 02.41.91.21.58
Y ev. day 9am–12.30pm 2–7.30pm; Sun. by appt.

DOM. CHUPIN

Croix de la Varenne 2000★

8.23 ha 70,000   €3

In the 1970s this 70-ha (173-acre) vineyard made rosés, but it has since diversified. The 2000 is a rather pale pink, with a powerful nose and complex aromas of considerable finesse. The palate continues to display the subtlety that is so characteristic of Loire rosés.

☛ SCEA Dom. Chupin,
8, rue de l'Eglise, 49380 Champ-sur-Layon,
tel. 02.41.78.86.54, fax 02.41.78.61.73
Y by appt.
☛ Guy Saget

DOM. DU FRESCHE 2000★

0.5 ha   2,900   €3-5

A pleasant pink colour with orange highlights, this wine has a very powerful nose with overtones of fruit. It is a lively but not aggressive wine, and the way it develops in the mouth is very pleasurable. The nose and the palate are extremely well balanced.

☛ EARL Boré, Dom. du Fresche, 49620 La Pommeraye, tel. 02.41.77.74.63,
fax 02.41.77.79.39 Y by appt.

LA GUIGNIERE 2000★

0.35 ha 2,000   €3

Everything about this wine suggests a lively character: the pure pink colour and the herbaceous and fruit characteristics which combine to give an extremely expressive nose. The palate has an interesting complexity and balance, producing a harmonious, silky feeling, which is most delightful. This successful wine makes one appreciate the appellation.

☛ Laurent Blouin, Les Hardières,
49750 Saint-Lambert-du-Lattay,
tel. 02.41.78.30.83, fax 02.41.78.30.83
Y by appt.

VIGNOBLE DE L'ARCISON 2000★

2 ha   5,000   €3-5

Before specialising in vines this vineyard used to be a farm, and the winery is housed in a former barn. The wine has the roundness that is typical of areas where the Choletais grape is grown. The 2000 is very vivid, a sparkling coppery rosé in colour. The nose is still closed but exhibits delicate, fruity notes when the wine is swirled. The palate is long, pleasantly rounded and well-structured.

☛ Damien Reulier, Le Mesnil,
49380 Thouarcé, tel. 02.41.54.16.81,
fax 02.41.54.31.12, e-mail damien.reulier@wanadoo.fr Y by appt.

CH. DE LA ROCHE BOUSSEAU 2000

n.c.   n.c.   €3-5

Orange highlights add to the colour of this wine, and the nose is dominated by fruit. The palate could have been more characterful, but it is light and fresh.

☛ François Regnard, Dom. de La Petite-Roche, 49310 Trémont,
tel. 02.41.59.43.03, fax 02.41.59.69.43
Y by appt.

CH. DE LA VIAUDIERE 1999 · 7 ha · 2,800 · €3

The Gélineau family has owned this vineyard for 400 years, handing it on from father to son. This rosé is fresh and delicate in colour with delightful golden highlights. The nose is interesting (lively at first then more fruity), while the palate is a perfectly balanced, soft and harmonious blend of fruit and flowers with a long finish.

EARL Vignoble Gélineau, Ch de La Viaudière, 49380 Champ-sur-Layon, tel. 02.41.78.86.27, fax 02.41.78.60.45, e-mail gelineau@wanadoo.fr · by appt.

LA VIGNE NOIRE 2000* · 2.49 ha · 2,000 · €3

Nathalie and Guillaume Cauty have been running the estate for only a few months, but they have been awarded a star for this rosé. The wine is dominated by the salmon pink colour of Cabernet. Cabernet characteristics are also apparent on the nose, where floral notes are prolonged with a very interesting and harmonious palate.

Nathalie et Guillaume Cauty, La Vigne Noire, 79290 Bouillé-Saint-Paul, tel. 05.49.96.83.19, fax 05.49.68.45.03 · ev. day except Sun. 8am–7.30pm.

LE CLOS DES MOTELES 2000 · 1.76 ha · 4,000 · €3-5

This vineyard is situated in Sainte-Verge, a small commune near Thouars, in the south of the Anjou wine-growing area, about 30 km (19 miles) from Saumur. The gravelly soil produces a rosé with a strong pink colour. When the wine is swirled the fruit opens out and lasts on the palate, giving a fresh, lively finish very typical of this appellation.

GAEC Le Clos des Motèles, Basset-Baron, 42, rue de la Garde, 79100 Sainte-Verge, tel. 05.49.66.05.37, fax 05.49.66.37.14 · by appt.

LE LOGIS DU PRIEURE 2000** · 4 ha · 5,000 · €3-5

The River Layon, canalised in the reign of Louis XVI, was once navigable and was used to transport coal and wine. The canal started from Concourson-sur-Layon, and today the riverbanks offer pleasant walks. This rosé is fresh and clean in appearance, and has a nose of fresh red berries with notes of blackcurrant and redcurrant. The palate is satisfyingly full, rounded and well balanced. This wine is a credit to the appellation.

SCEA Jousset et Fils, Le Logis du Prieuré, 49700 Concourson-sur-Layon, tel. 02.41.59.11.22, fax 02.41.59.38.18, e-mail logis.prieure@groupesirius.com · ev. day except Sun. 8am–12pm 2–7pm.

LES VIGNES DE L'ALMA 2000* · n.c. · 7,000 · €3-5

This small, 10-ha (24.7-acre) domaine is situated on a plateau with magnificent views of Saint-Florent-le-Vieil and the Loire valley. The rosé has an intense colour, bordering on a fiery red. The powerful nose generates floral aromas, while the rich, lively, palate is both opulent and insistent, with a long, agreeable finish. Try it as soon as possible!

Roland Chevalier, L'Alma, 49410 Saint-Florent-le-Vieil, tel. 02.41.72.71.09, fax 02.41.72.63.77 · ev. day except Sun. 8.30am–12.30pm 2–7pm.

DOM. DE L'ETE 2000 · 2.5 ha · 22,000 · €3-5

The name of this domaine dates from the 17th century, being mentioned in manuscripts in 1650. In the 21st century it has produced this light-coloured, salmon pink rosé, bright with reflected highlights. The nose is delicate, shows great finesse and is dominated by fermentation aromas when the wine is swirled. Lively on the palate, but still balanced, this is a very subtle rosé.

Dom. de l'Été, 49700 Concourson-sur-Layon, tel. 02.41.59.11.63, fax 02.41.59.95.16, e-mail domedelete@wanadoo.fr · by appt.
Catherine Nolot

DOM. DES MATINES 2000 · 3 ha · 5,000 · €3-5

This domaine, which has been run by the same family for four generations, offers a fuchsia-coloured wine. A hint of blue gives it an interesting appearance, and this is confirmed by the expressive aroma. This rosé has a distinct, well-balanced personality.

Dom. des Matines, 31, rue de la Mairie, 49700 Brossay, tel. 02.41.52.25.36, fax 02.41.52.25.50 · by appt.
Etchegaray

CH. MONTBENAULT 2000 · 1.8 ha · 10,000 · €3-5

The clarity of this rosé emphasises the hint of orange and lively colour. From the start the well-developed nose marries red berries and floral notes. Grolleau dominates, giving the wine a sound structure, and more complex aromas develop with aeration.

Yves et Marie-Paule Leduc, Ch. Montbenault, 49380 Faye-d'Anjou, tel. 02.41.78.31.14, fax 02.41.78.60.29 · ev. day except Sun. 9am–12 noon 2–7pm.

CH. DE MONTGUERET 2000
🔲 12.3 ha 70,000 €3-5

In 1987 André Lacheteau and his wife succumbed to the charms of Anjou and this Napoleon III château, a happy combination of chalky tuffeau, brick and schist. A delicate peony in colour, this wine has a powerful nose of fruit (raspberry) and flowers, with a fresh, lively feeling on the palate, which is supple and lasting.

📞 SCEA Ch. de Montguéret, Le Bourg, 49560 Nueil-sur-Layon, tel. 02.41.59.59.19, fax 02.41.59.59.02 ▼ ▼ by appt.
📞 Lacheteau

CH. DE PASSAVANT 2000★
🔲 6 ha 27,000 🍷 ♦ €3-5

Passavant-sur-Layon is a pleasant village on the shores of a lake formed by the Layon, which rises above it. The Château de Passavant is a large, 60-ha (148-acre) estate with a solid reputation. It produces a wine with a pronounced pink, almost red colour. Although initially somewhat muted, the fruity notes appear when the wine is swirled. Round, supple and well balanced on the palate, the fruity notes found initially on the nose linger on the finish, giving a lasting and well-balanced impression.

📞 SCEA David-Lecomte, Ch. de Passavant, rte de Tancoigne, 49560 Passavant-sur-Layon, tel. 02.41.59.53.96, fax 02.41.59.57.91, e-mail passavant@wanadoo.fr ▼ ▼ by appt.

DOM. DE SAINTE-ANNE 2000★
🔲 5 ha 10,000 🍷 ♦ €3-5

This domaine has been handed down from father to son for six generations. The special features of its *terroir* have produced a deep pink, salmon-tinted wine, which is a good representative of its appellation. Fermentation and varietal aromas mingle on the nose, while the palate is supple, agreeable and well balanced, with a fine-flavoured, persistent finish.

📞 EARL Brault, Dom. de Sainte-Anne, 49320 Brissac-Quincé, tel. 02.41.91.24.58, fax 02.41.91.25.87 ▼ ev. day except Sun. 9am–12 noon 2–7pm; Sat. 9am–12 noon 2–6pm.

DOM. DES TRAHAN
Le Logis de Preuil 2000
🔲 13 ha 8,000 🍷 ♦ €3-5

Just over 1 ha (2.47 acres) of Argenton gravel *terroir* is set aside for this wine on the 60-ha (148-acre) domaine in the south of the Anjou wine-growing area in the Deux-Sèvres *département*. It has a strong, natural colour with salmon pink tones. The nose is dominated by fruit and has overtones of fresh red berries. It is beautifully fresh on the palate, with body and a characterful finish that is typical of the appellation.

📞 EARL Les Magnolias des Trahan, 26, rue du Moulin, 79290 Cersay, tel. 05.49.96.80.38, fax 05.49.96.37.23 ▼

DOM. DES TROIS MONTS 2000★
🔲 10 ha 50,000 🍷 ♦ €3-5

The Guéneau family has been producing wine for four generations. The Trois Monts estate owes its name to the three hills that make up the commune of Trémont. The rosé is very pale, with glittering reflections. Subtle aromas of fresh red fruits appear unobtrusively, while the wine is light and agreeable on the palate, giving an impression of overall balance.

📞 SCEA Hubert Guéneau et Fils, 1, rue Saint-Fiacre, 49310 Trémont, tel. 02.41.59.45.21, fax 02.41.59.69.90 ▼ ▼ by appt.

DOM. DU VIEUX PRESSOIR 2000★
🔲 n.c. 4,500 🍷 ♦ €3-5

This estate, well known in the Saumur area, practises grassing down between the rows and produces one of the most seductive *rosés de saignée*. Tasters immediately appreciate its attractive colour, both cheerful and limpid, with a slight sparkle that brings the pink to life. The Cabernet Franc is well-expressed here, combining associations of fruit and flowers. The palate confirms the impressions on the nose.

📞 EARL B. et J. Albert, 205, rue du Château-d'Oiré, 49260 Vaudelnay, tel. 02.41.52.21.78, fax 02.41.38.85.83 ▼ ▼ by appt.

Crémant de Loire

Here again, the Appellation Régionale can be applied to sparkling wines produced within the boundaries of Anjou, Saumur, Touraine and Cheverny. The Méthode Traditionnelle or Champagne method works wonders here; production of these celebration wines is up to around 38,000 hl (1,003,200 gal). A number of grape varieties are grown: Chenin or Pineau de Loire, Cabernet Sauvignon and Cabernet Franc, Pinot Noir, Chardonnay, etc. Even though production is largely of white wines, some rosés are also made.

940

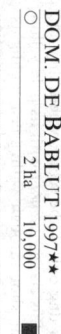

DOM. DE BABLUT 1997★★

2 ha   10,000   €5-8

The Daviau family have been wine-growers since 1546, which means that they know a good wine when they see one. The *terroir* in this area is unusual too: it is situated where the chalky soils of the Paris basin meet the schists of the Massif Armoricain. In an old mill that dates from the 12th century, visitors can taste one of the finest wines from this area. A lovely string of fine bubbles rises through a pale-yellow wine with green highlights. It is a complex wine, with peach aromas and grapefruit notes that develop on the palate in a remarkable way. Try this wine as soon as possible.

- SCEA Daviau, Dom. de Bablut, 49320 Brissac-Quincé, tel. 02.41.91.22.59, fax 02.41.91.24.77, e-mail daviau@refsa.fr
- ev. day except Sun. 8.30am-12 noon 2pm-6.30pm

BARONNIE D'AIGNAN 1997★

2 ha   16,000   €5-8

This *crémant* is a seductive golden-yellow colour with an even string of fine, persistent bubbles. Its rich freshness on the palate is surprising.

- Confrérie des Vignerons de Oisly-Thésée, 41700 Oisly, tel. 02.54.79.75.20, fax 02.54.79.75.29 ev. day except Sun. 9am-12 noon 2pm-5.30pm

DOM. DES BAUMARD

Cuvée Millésimée 1997

5 ha   n.c.   €8-11

The Baumard family have been making wine in Rochefort since 1634, and the domaine owes its success to Jean Baumard and his son, Florent. Fine bubbles accompany the light floral aromas, and these flavours recur in the richness and length of the palate.

- Florent Baumard, SCEA Dom. des Baumard, 8, rue de l'Abbaye, 49190 Rochefort-sur-Loire, tel. 02.41.78.70.03, fax 02.41.78.83.82 by appt.

BERGER FRERES

1.8 ha   7,000   €5-8

Montlouis is one of the birthplaces of fizzy and sparkling wines. The Berger *crémant* has a complex nose mingling toasty and creamy aromas. It is strongly effervescent at first, but settles down to a pleasant liveliness, making it good for celebrations.

- Berger Frères, 70, rue de Chenonceaux, 37270 Saint-Martin-le-Beau, tel. 02.47.50.67.36, fax 02.47.50.21.13 by appt.

DOM. DES BESSONS★

0.5 ha   3,000   €5-8

This is a lovely, delicate wine with a firm structure, plenty of mousse and a very elegant floral nose. Quite lively on the attack, the long finish evokes linden-flower flavours.

- François Péquin, Dom. des Bessons, 113, rue de Blois, 37530 Limeray, tel. 02.47.30.09.10, fax 02.47.30.02.25
- ev. day except Sun. 9am-7pm

DOM. DE BRIZE

3 ha   16,000   €5-8

This family estate has been handed down from father to son since the 18th century, and is now run by Marc and Luc Delhumeau, the fifth generation. Their *crémant* is a success: its golden, almost green colour is pleasing to the eye, and the complex range of aromas has fruit and lightly toasted nuances. The palate is full, fresh and long, finishing on a slightly acidic note.

- SCEA Marc et Luc Delhumeau, Dom. de Brizé, 49540 Martigné-Briand, tel. 02.41.59.43.35, fax 02.41.59.66.90, e-mail delhumeau.scea@free.fr
- Luc et Line Delhumeau

PAUL BUISSE

n.c.   10,000   €5-8

This Touraine *négociant* presents this *crémant* with its lasting bubbles and delicate spice aromas. It is a supple, well-balanced wine with a harmonious finish.

- SA Paul Buisse, 69, rte de Vierzon, 41402 Montrichard Cedex, tel. 02.54.32.00.01, fax 02.54.32.09.78, e-mail contact@paul-buisse.com
- ev. day except Sat. and Sun. 8am-12 noon 2pm-6pm; Fri. 8am-12 noon 2pm-5pm

FRANÇOIS CAZIN 1997

1 ha   5,000   €5-8

Still young, this *crémant* is an attractive pale-yellow with notes of linden flower and white peaches. It has a fine, long-lasting sparkle and should develop well.

- François Cazin, Le Petit Chambord, 41700 Cheverny, tel. 02.54.79.93.75, fax 02.54.79.27.89 by appt.

DE CHANCENY Blanc de Blancs 1995★

23 ha   100,000   €5-8

The Vignerons de La Noëlle, the main group of producers in the region, have presented a really vast range of wines. This one is pale-yellow with plenty of fine bubbles. The nose is delicate, but floral nuances dominate, while the fruity, well-balanced palate shows much finesse. This is an elegant wine which, it is suggested, would go well with mandarin sorbet.

Crémant de Loire

cellar dug out of the schist, where they can taste this classic *crémant* with its pale-yellow colour shot through with green highlights. The nose may be restrained, but the first impression is lively, with delightful notes of currants and honey making a striking introduction to a well-balanced wine.

➤ Daniel and Jean-Yves Moron, Dom. de Gagnebert, 2, chem. de la Naurivet, 49610 Juigné-sur-Loire, tel. 02.41.91.92.86, fax 02.41.91.95.50 ☑ ‖ ev. day except Sun. 9am–12 noon 3pm–7pm

FRANCIS ET PATRICK HUGUET　€5-8

○　1 ha　4,500

A sandy, pebbly soil has produced this well-balanced, golden-yellow *crémant*. The wine has a lively initial sparkle, which dissolves pleasantly on the palate into notes of brioche.

➤ GAEC Huguet, 12, rue de la Franchetière, 41350 Saint-Claude-de-Diray, tel. 02.54.20.57.36, fax 02.54.20.58.57 ☑

DOM. DE LA BESNERIE★　€5-8

○　0.6 ha　3,950

This *crémant* will enchant your guests with aromas of fresh brioche, lemon and white flowers and a well-balanced finish.

➤ François Pironneau, 41, rte de Mesland, 41150 Monteaux, tel. 02.54.70.23.75, fax 02.54.70.21.89 ☑ ‖ by appt.

DOM. DE LA DESOUCHERIE　€8-11

○　1 ha　9,000

This is a lovely, pale *crémant* with an astonishingly delicate, fruity and subtle nose. On the palate its finesse and length largely make up for its restraint.

➤ Christian Tessier, Dom. de La Désoucherie, 41700 Cour-Cheverny, tel. 02.54.79.90.08, fax 02.54.79.22.48, e-mail christian.tessier@waika9.com ☑ ‖ by appt.

MLLE LADUBAY　€5-8

○　n.c.　100,000　‖ ‖

This *négociant* is currently managed by the third generation of the Monmousseau family and situated in Saint-Hilaire-Saint-Florent, a village on the left bank of the Thouet, on a slope entirely riddled with cellars. They have produced a *crémant* with a delicate sparkle and a brilliant, pale-yellow colour with green highlights. The nose is a little restrained, with apple and pear aromas. The fresh, rounded, generous palate leaves a very well-balanced impression, resulting in a wine which should be discovered without delay.

➤ Bouvet-Ladubay, 1, rue de l'Abbaye, 49400 Saint-Hilaire-Saint-Florent, tel. 02.41.83.83.83, fax 02.41.50.24.32, e-mail bouvet-ladubay@saumur.net ‖ ev. day 8.30am–12 noon 2pm–6pm

---

➤ Les Vignerons de La Noëlle, bd des Alliés, BP 155, 44150 Ancenis, tel. 02.40.98.92.72, fax 02.40.98.96.70, e-mail vignerons-noelle@cana.fr ☑ ‖ by appt.

CHESNEAU ET FILS 1999　€5-8

○　0.75 ha　6,700

This wine is an example of finesse in all senses of the word. Delicate bubbles enhance its pale-yellow colour with subtle green highlights. It is an aperitif wine with delicate aromas and a pleasant palate.

➤ EARL Chesneau et Fils, 26, rue Sainte-Neomoise, 41120 Sambin, tel. 02.54.20.20.15, fax 02.54.33.21.91 ☑ ‖ by appt.

DELAUNAY PERE ET FILS 1999★　€5-8

○　3 ha　29,000

This domaine has been in the same family for four generations. The Jury was very impressed by their pale-yellow *crémant* with its fine, persistent sparkle. Light notes of brioche and honey are evident in a well-balanced, harmonious wine. One taster recommended that it be drunk throughout a meal.

➤ Dom. Delaunay Père et Fils, Daudet, 49570 Montjean-sur-Loire, tel. 02.41.39.08.39, fax 02.41.39.00.20, e-mail delaunay.anjou@wanadoo.fr ☑ ‖ by appt.

DOM. DUBOIS★　€5-8

◐　1 ha　5,000

The Saint-Cyr plateau is underlain by vast underground tuffeau quarries. In this village alone, there are about 180 km (111.8 miles) of tunnels, which are often used as cellars. This rosé *crémant* is a delight to the eye, with its fine, pleasing bubbles sparkling through a pale-pink colour. Cabernet dominates the nose and there are marked fruit aromas, introducing a balanced, harmonious palate which is both fresh and delicious.

➤ Dom. Michel and Jean-Claude Dubois, 8, rte de Chacé, 49260 Saint-Cyr-en-Bourg, tel. 02.41.51.61.32, fax 02.41.51.95.29 ☑ ‖ by appt.

XAVIER FRISSANT　€5-8

○　n.c.　5,000　‖ ‖

This wine was awarded the *coup de cœur* by the 2000 *Guide*. Xavier Frissant's *crémant* has a delightful floral intensity and a refreshing finish.

➤ Xavier Frissant, 1, chem. Neuf, 37530 Mosnes, tel. 02.47.57.23.18, fax 02.47.57.23.25, e-mail xavierfrissant@wanadoo.fr ☑ ‖ ev. day 8am–12.30pm 2pm–7pm; Sun. by appt.

DOM. DE GAGNEBERT 1997　€5-8

○　n.c.　12,000

The slaty schist subsoils of this domaine covering 60 ha (148.2 acres) in a single *commune* have been exploited since the 12th century. Visitors are made welcome in an old

CH. DE LA DURANDIERE 1999★

3.3 ha | 18,600 | €5-8

You will be delighted by the old town of Montreuil-Bellay, where the alleys and ancient houses have retained their old-world charm. This domaine, 600 m (654 yd) from the superb château, makes a pleasant destination for a stroll. It produces a *crémant* with a delicate sparkle and a delightful golden colour with hints of green. The bouquet is subtle, marrying fresh fruit with notes of crystallised fruit, which return most pleasurably on the palate. This is a well-made, well-balanced wine.

SCEA Bodet-Lhériau,
Ch. de La Durandière,
51, rue des Fusiliés, 49260 Montreuil-Bellay,
tel. 02.41.40.35.30, fax 02.41.40.35.31,
e-mail durandiere.chateau@libertysurf.fr V
ev. day 8am–7pm; Sat. Sun. by appt.

Hubert et Antoine Bodet

JOSE MARTEAU★

3.5 ha | 30,000 | €5-8

The Jury appreciated this pale-golden *crémant* with green highlights for its fruitiness, floral notes and a smoothness not normally found in Loire Valley wines. This wine has more of the Chardonnay character than the Chenin Blanc, although it contains both.

José Marteau, La Rouerie, 41400 Thenay,
tel. 02.54.32.50.51, fax 02.54.32.18.52 V
ev. day 8am–12.15pm 2pm–7pm; Sun.
8am–12.15pm

DOM. MICHAUD★★

1.6 ha | 12,000 | €5-8

This is a superb wine displaying all the wine-makers' blending skills. The delicate stream of bubbles, along with the green highlights in its pale-golden colour make this a truly royal *crémant*. Pinot, allied with Cabernet Franc, complements the Chardonnay and Chenin, giving a clean, lasting palate with a long finish. Its uncomplicated delightfulness proved irresistible to the Jury.

EARL Michaud, Les Martinières,
41140 Noyers-sur-Cher, tel. 02.54.32.47.23,
fax 02.54.75.39.19 V by appt.

DOM. MOREAU

0.5 ha | 2,000 | €5-8

Green highlights in a persistent stream of fine bubbles give this *crémant* a most convivial appearance, and the nose offers a touch of vanilla. It has a lively sparkle.

Catherine Moreau, Fleuray,
37530 Cangey, tel. 02.47.30.18.82,
fax 02.47.30.02.79 V by appt.

DOM. DE NERLEUX★

6 ha | 20,000 | €5-8

This family estate has been handed down from father to son for seven generations. The vines are grown on the chalky tuffeau, which is still quarried nearby. This is a pale-yellow *crémant*, enlivened with very fine bubbles, and the nose is both fruity and floral. The harmony, balance and length leave a feeling of freshness typical of this appellation.

SCEA Régis Neau, 4, rue de la Paleine,
49260 Saint-Cyr-en-Bourg,
tel. 02.41.51.61.04, fax 02.41.51.65.34,
e-mail rneau@terre-net.fr V
ev. day except Sun. 8am–12 noon 2pm–
6pm; Sat. 8am–12 noon

DOM. DU PETIT CLOCHER 1998★

12 ha | 12,000 | €5-8

This domaine has 54 ha (133.4 acres) under vines, and regularly produces fine wines such as this delightful *crémant* with its fine, lasting bubbles and light flower and spice aromas. This *brut* is fresh, aromatic and supple on the palate. It is pleasantly thirst-quenching and just the thing for an aperitif.

A. et J.-N. Denis, GAEC du Petit Clocher, 3, rue du Layon,
49560 Cléré-sur-Layon, tel. 02.41.59.54.51,
fax 02.41.59.59.70 V by appt.

CH. PIEGUE 1998★★

1 ha | 7,000 | €5-8

The Château de Piégué was built by M. Monon, a solicitor, in 1840. His son planted the first of the umbrella pines that give the domaine a Mediterranean air. Twenty-five hectares (61.8 acres) are currently under vine. This superb Crémant 98 was given unanimous approval. It has an astonishing freshness on the nose and a delightful stream of pear aromas are confirmed on the palate. Complex apple and pear aromas are confirmed on the palate.

Ch. Piégué, Piégué,
49190 Rochefort-sur-Loire,
tel. 02.41.78.71.26, fax 02.41.78.75.03,
e-mail chateaupiegue@groupesirius.com V
ev. day except Sun. 9am–12 noon 2pm–
6pm

Van der Hecht

Crémant de Loire

DOM. RICHOU 1998

○   2 ha   10,000   🔲 ♦ €8-11

Among the Richou family papers, there is a document dated 1550 which mentions one Maurice Joyau, wine-grower and supplier to the King of France. A beautiful string of fine bubbles attracts the eye in this golden-yellow *crémant*. This wine carries a strong scent of ripe, even stewed fruit, then reveals notes of crystallised fruit on the palate.

➤ GAEC Richou, Chauvigné, 49610 Mozé-sur-Louet, tel. 02.41.78.72.13, fax 02.41.78.76.05 ⊻ ♈ by appt.

DOM. DE RIS 1998

○   2 ha   8,000   🔲 ♦ €8-11

This domaine, once held by a lord, was not planted with vines until the end of the 19th century. Its *crémant* is supple, well-balanced and flavoursome, with a delicate sparkle. It will delight lovers of aperitifs with its smoothness and well-balanced style.

➤ Dom. de Ris, 37290 Bossay-sur-Claise, tel. 02.47.94.64.43, fax 02.47.94.68.46 ⊻ ♈ ev. day except Sun. 5.30pm–7pm; Sat. 10am–12 noon 2pm–7pm
➤ Gilbert Sabadie

DOM. DE SAINTE-ANNE 1999★

○   2 ha   10,000   🔲 ♦ €5-8

This vast domaine, passed from father to son for six generations, occupies one of the highest chalky clay hilltops in Saint-Saturnin-sur-Loire. This *terroir* has produced a delicate, pale-yellow *crémant* with long-lasting bubbles, which is typical of its appellation. The nose is still rather closed, but reveals toasted aromas. The palate is long, elegant and slightly sharp.

➤ Dom. de Sainte-Anne, EARL Brault, 49320 Brissac-Quincé, tel. 02.41.91.24.58, fax 02.41.91.25.87 ⊻ ♈ ev. day except Sun. 9am–12 noon 2pm–7pm; Sat. –6pm

CAVE DES VIGNERONS DE SAUMUR Cuvée de La Chevalerie 1998

○   n.c.   60,000   🔲 ♦ €5-8

As part of its modernisation programme, this co-operative built a new barrel store in 2000, the fifth stage after the new vinification tanks in 1957, 1968, 1978 and 1991. There are around 10 km (6.21 miles) of tunnels where wines are stored. This blend is delicate, pale-pink in colour, with long-lasting bubbles. Strong fruit aromas carry nuances of wild strawberry. The palate is fresh but not aggressive, carrying fruity overtones within a well-balanced structure.

➤ Cave des Vignerons de Saumur, rte de Saumoussay, 49260 Saint-Cyr-en-Bourg, tel. 02.41.53.06.06, fax 02.41.53.06.10, e-mail bernardjacob@ vignerondesaumur.com ♈ ev. day except Sun. 9am–12 noon 2pm–6pm

DANIEL TEVENOT 1998

○   0.72 ha   6,000   €5-8

This *crémant* is notable for its creamy mousse and very pale colour. The aromas are restrained, but brioche notes can be discerned. The wine is well-balanced, and the palate evokes flavours of apples and pears.

➤ Daniel Tévenot,
4, rue du Moulin-à-Vent, Madon,
41120 Candé-sur-Beuvron,
tel. 02.54.79.44.24, fax 02.54.79.44.24 ⊻
♈ by appt.

The Nantes Region

Some two thousand years ago the Roman legions introduced the vine to the Nantes area, at the crossroads of Brittany, the Vendée, the Loire and the Atlantic coast. After a terrible winter in 1709 when the sea froze solid along the shore and the vines were completely destroyed, the vineyards were replanted, mainly with the Melon variety from Burgundy.

The Pays Nantais vineyard area now covers 16,000 ha (39,520 acres) south and east of Nantes, extending slightly over the borders of the Loire-Atlantique into the Vendée and the Maine-et-Loire. The vines grow on sunny slopes exposed to maritime influences. The soils are rather light and stony, composed of both ancient and volcanic rocks. The region produces 968,000 hl (25,555,200 gal) of four AOC wines: Muscadet, Muscadet des Coteaux de Loire, Muscadet de Sèvre-et-Maine and Muscadet Côtes de Grand-Lieu, as well as the AOVDQS Gros-Plant du Pays Nantais, Coteaux d'Ancenis et Fiefs Vendéens.

The Muscadet AOCs and Gros-Plant from the Pays Nantais

These regulations are designed to maximise freshness, finesse and bouquet. Muscadet is a white wine, dry but not acid, with a generous bouquet, a wine for any occasion. It is the perfect accompaniment for fish, shellfish and seafood and also makes an excellent aperitif. It should be served chilled, but not ice-cold (8°–9°C). Gros-Plant is the ideal wine to drink with oysters.

Muscadet

Muscadet is a white wine that has been an AOC since 1936. It is made from a single grape variety: the Melon. The vineyard area covers 13,042 ha (32,244 acres). There are four Appellations d'Origine Contrôlée, identified according to their geographical location, which produced a total of 762,211 hl (20,122,370 gal) of wine in 2000: Muscadet de Sèvre-et-Maine, which alone represents 9,359 ha (23,116.7 acres) and 528,325 hl (13,947,780 gal); Muscadet Côtes de Grand-Lieu with 320 ha, 18,416 hl (790.4 acres, 486,182 gal), Muscadet des Coteaux de la Loire with 284 ha, 14,993 hl (701.5 acres, 395,815 gal) and Muscadet: 3,077 ha, 200,477 hl (7,600 acres, 5,292,592.8 gal).

Gros-Plant

Nantais, classified AOVDQS in 1954, is also a dry white wine, but made from a different grape variety, the Folle Blanche. In 2000 162,868 hl (4,299,715 gal) were produced from an area of 2,213 ha (5,466 acres).

Bottling on the lees

(sur lie) is a traditional technique in the region, subject to precise regulations which were made more stringent in 1994. In order to qualify for the sur lie suffix, the wines must spend no more than one winter in tanks or casks, having been matured on the lees and kept in the wine store where they were made until bottling. The wine bottling can take place only during precisely defined periods and in no circumstances before the 1st of March, and sales are permitted only after the third Thursday in March.

Muscadet des Coteaux de la Loire sur lie

DOM. DU CHAMP CHAPRON

2000★

| | 20 ha | 55,000 | | | €-3 |

This domaine is on rocky slopes above the Pont Truibert, the bridge between Brittany and Anjou where Marguerite la Boiteuse was taken prisoner by Duke Jean V in 1420. Its wine has a pleasant, vivid nose in which the initial floral aromas develop exotic-fruit notes. It is a typical, fresh-tasting wine, revealing plenty of power underneath its mineral character. It is the ideal accompaniment to Loire fish such as shad and pike-perch.

↳ EARL Suteau-Ollivier, Le Champ Chapron, 44450 Barbechat, tel. 02.40.03.65.27, fax 02.40.33.34.43, e-mail suteau.ollivier@wanadoo.fr ☑
⊤ by appt.

DOM. DES GALLOIRES

Cuvée de Sélection

| | 1.25 ha | 9,000 | | | €-5 |

Of the ancient manor of La Galloire, little is left but a small chapel and a few portions of wall which support the present-day cellar. The wine has an intense, sweet aroma of hawthorn. Its balanced, mineral character makes it very harmonious on the palate. The domaine also offers a **Coteau d'Ancenis Gamay 2000 red Cuvée de Sélection**, which was commended for its roundness and well-integrated tannins, together with red-berry flavours that are underpinned by a touch of liquorice and spices.

↳ GAEC des Galloires, Dom. des Galloires, 49530 Drain, tel. 02.40.98.20.10, fax 02.40.98.22.06 ☑ ⊤ by appt.

Muscadet de Sèvre-et-Maine

DOM. DU HAUT FRESNE 2000 · €3-5

☐　12 ha　15,000

This domaine, on very steep slopes on the left bank of the Loire, produces a wine with a rather mineral character that has a pleasing, slightly sparkling attack. It also offers two noteworthy wines under the label **Coteaux d'Ancenis Gamay 2000**: one is a strong **red** with a nose of black fruit, spicy, rich and long on the palate; the other is a fresh, rich **rosé**.

☛ Renou Frères, Dom. du Haut Fresne, 49530 Drain, tel. 02.40.98.26.79, fax 02.40.98.26.79 ♈ by appt.

CH. DE LA VARENNE 2000 · -€3

☐　4 ha　29,792

This château on an escarpment above the Loire offers a wine with exotic-fruit aromas, flowers and aniseed. It has a lively attack, evoking its local soil, and displays a satisfying roundness and length. This is a well-made wine.

☛ Pascal Pauvert, Le Marais, 49270 La Varenne, tel. 02.40.98.55.58

CH. MESLIERE 2000★★ · €5-8

☐　7.5 ha　20,000

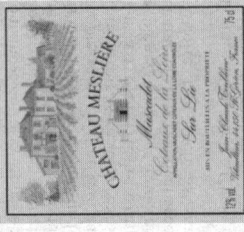

This château is magnificently situated overlooking the Loire, on the megalithic site of Pierres Meslières, and has already earned a *coup de cœur* from last year's *Guide*. This very pale Muscadet with hawthorn aromas has a fresh attack. It then reveals a well-balanced palate with plenty of mineral character so typical of Coteaux de Loire wines, giving it a definite *terroir* character. It is ready to drink now.

☛ Jean-Claude Toublanc, Les Pierres Meslières, 44150 Saint-Géréon, tel. 02.40.83.23.95, fax 02.40.83.23.95 ♈ by appt.

CLOS DES ALLEES Sur lie 2000 · €3-5

☐　5 ha　25,000

The landscape of the Landreau area is prettily dotted with windmills, the best-known of which are those of Pé Pucelle. Pierre Luneau-Papin, who exports 50% of his wine, has an interesting range of Muscadets, including those of the Coteaux de la Loire and Sèvre-et-Maine. This one lacks length, but is worth having for its pale-yellow colour with green highlights and its intense yet delicate mineral aromas.

☛ Pierre Luneau-Papin, Dom. Pierre de La Grange, 44430 Le Landreau, tel. 02.40.06.45.27, fax 02.40.06.46.62 ♈ by appt.

L'ORIGINAL DE BEDOUET · €5-8

Sur lie 1999★

☐　2 ha　8,000

Michel Bedouet, who has 18 ha (44.5 acres) of vines, set up the producers' association in the Nantes area. It now has 40 members. His wine, from the picturesque wine-making village of Pé-de-Sèvre, is pale with a delicate nose of floral and buttery notes. It is long and rich on the palate, with a nuance of iodine, a good example of the *sur lie* style with lots of elegance.

☛ Michel Bedouet, Le Pé-de-Sèvre, 44330 Le Pallet, tel. 02.40.80.97.30, fax 02.40.80.40.68, e-mail michel@ bedouet-vigneron.com ♈ by appt.

DOM. DE BEGROLLES Sur lie 2000★ · -€3

☐　1 ha　n.c.

The village of Bégrolles lies to the west of the town of La Haye-Fouassière, not far from the prehistoric site of Cavernes, on the banks of the Sèvre. Here Jean-Pierre Méchineau produces a clear, yet still closed, wine which is full of promise. Mineral on the nose, intense and rich on the palate, it shows a *terroir* character which is pronounced without being excessive.

☛ Jean-Pierre Méchineau, Bégrolles, 44690 La Haye-Fouassière, tel. 02.40.54.80.95, fax 02.40.54.80.95 ♈ by appt.

DOM. DU BOIS-JOLY★ · €3-5

Sur lie Harmonie 2000★

☐　4.5 ha　30,000

This pedigree wine, raised on the gabbro and mica-schist soils typical of the region, starts well then develops a full-bodied palate of citrus, apples and pears. It is worth keeping for another two or three years.

☛ Henri et Laurent Bouchaud, Le Bois-Joly, 44330 Le Pallet, tel. 02.40.80.40.83, fax 02.40.80.45.85 ♈ ev. day except Sun. 10am–12.30pm 1.30pm–7pm

Muscadet de Sèvre-et-Maine

DOM. DU BOIS MALINGE

Sur lie 2000★★ | 9 ha | 50,000 | €3-5

The northern part of the village of Saint-Julien-de-Concelles, along the Loire, is devoted to market gardening, whilst vines are grown on the slopes in the southern part. They have produced a good wine, as delicate and complex on the nose as on the palate. It has been remarkably well-made and its mineral, lively and slightly acidic character will develop its full potential in a few months' time. The **Gros-Plant du Pays Nantais sur lie 2000 Château de La Jousselinière** has also been awarded two stars. It has pleasant flower aromas and could be kept for a few more years.

➳ GAEC de La Jousselinière, La Jousselinière, 44450 Saint-Julien-de-Concelles, tel. 02.40.54.11.08, fax 02.40.54.19.90
➳ J-Gilbert Chon

DOM. GILBERT BOSSARD

Sur lie 1999★ | 5 ha | n.c. | €5-8

Gilbert Bossard, whose family has been growing vines at La Chapelle-Heulin for almost 500 years, owns 50 ha (123.5 acres) of vines. He has made a wine with well-developed dried-fruit aromas, supported by a note of broom. This 99 is full and rich, but still lively and ready to drink from now onwards.

➳ Gilbert Bossard, La Basse-Ville, 44330 La Chapelle-Heulin, tel. 02.40.06.74.33, fax 02.40.06.77.48
▼ ev. day except Sun. 8am–12.30pm 2pm–7pm

DOM. BONNETEAU-GUESSELIN

Sur lie 2000★ | 2 ha | n.c. | €5-8

This domaine has not been afraid to over-turn tradition by putting an egg-yellow label on its bottles of Muscadet. Its wine is traditional, though: hawthorn aromas and mineral notes are present on the nose and on the palate. It is lively and fresh and has plenty of length.

➳ Olivier Bonneteau-Guesselin, La Juiverie, 44690 La Haye-Fouassière, tel. 02.40.54.80.38, fax 02.40.36.91.17
▼ ev. day 9am–7pm

DOM. GILLES BOUFFARD

Sur lie 2000 | 1.7 ha | 13,300 | €3-5

This domaine in the Anjou area does not produce a large volume of wine, but it is of good quality. This wine is a light-golden colour with green highlights and, though admittedly young, as is perceptible in the delicate mineral and floral aromas, it is still rich, with elegant liveliness and acidic fruitiness. It is worth keeping for another year.

➳ Gilles Bouffard, La Brosse, 49230 Saint-Crespin-sur-Moine, tel. 02.41.70.43.42 ▼ by appt.

CLOS DES BOURGUIGNONS

Sur lie 1999★ | 3 ha | 15,000 | €5-8

After the terrible frosts of 1709, this *clos* (walled vineyard) was one of the first areas

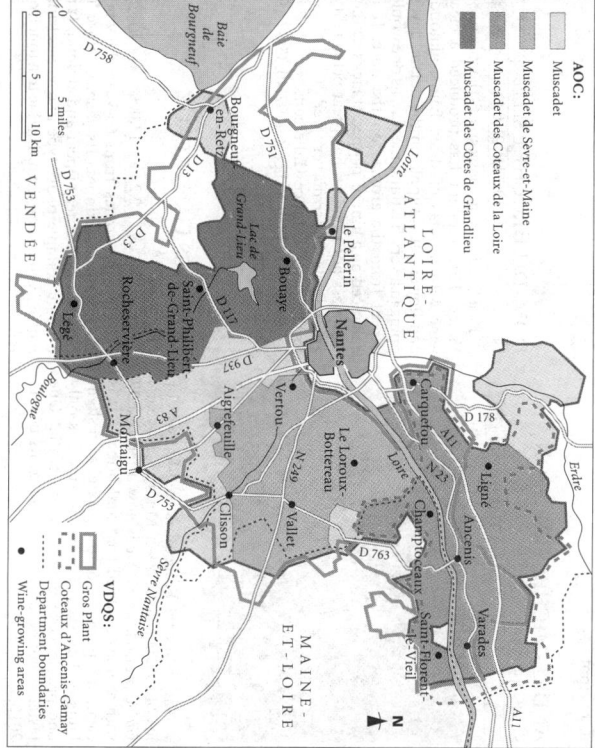

Pays Nantais

AOC:
- Muscadet
- Muscadet de Sèvre-et-Maine
- Muscadet des Coteaux de la Loire
- Muscadet des Côtes de Grandlieu

VDQS:
- Gros Plant
- Coteaux d'Ancenis-Gamay
- Department boundaries
- Wine-growing areas

Muscadet de Sèvre-et-Maine

of land that wine-growers from Burgundy replanted with Melon vines, and its name is a tribute to them. This golden wine has a nose of citrus fruits, ripe apples and pears, enriched with mineral and toast notes. It has a clean attack, both firm and balanced, leading to a long finish reminiscent of green apples.

► SCEA J.Y. Sécher et Associés, Dom. de La Loge, 44330 Vallet, tel. 02.40.33.97.08, fax 02.40.33.91.99, e-mail jysecher@multimania.com ☒ ⟙ ev. day 9am–12 noon 2.30pm–7pm; Sat. Sun. by appt.

BOURLINGUET Sur lie 2000★
☐ · 28 ha · 200,000 · ■ · ♦ · —€3

This Muscadet de Sèvre-et-Maine, with its fanciful name and amusing fisherman label, is produced by a major *négociant*. It is typical in its fruitiness (lemon, green apples) and has a lively attack, as well as being well-balanced.

► Donatien-Bahuaud, La Loge, BP 1, 44330 La Chapelle-Heulin, tel. 02.40.06.70.05, fax 02.40.06.77.11 ☒

CH. BRAIRON Sur lie 2000★★
☐ · 1.3 ha · 9,150 · ■ · ♦ · €3-5

Under the leadership of Serge Méchineau, the cellars of this estate in the western part of the AOC area have been active again for the last ten years. The vineyard has produced a high-class Muscadet which benefits from a slight stream of bubbles. It is very aromatic (fresh fruit), rich and rounded, typical of the appellation. It is an excellent accompaniment for delicate fish, such as pike-perch or John Dory.

► Serge Méchineau, Le Châtelier, 44690 Château-Thébaud, tel. 02.40.06.51.21, fax 02.40.06.57.76, e-mail serge.mechineau@free.fr ☒ ⟙ by appt.

ANDRE-MICHEL BREGEON
Sur lie 1997★★
☐ · 7.5 ha · 27,000 · ■ · ♦

André-Michel Brégeon is well-known for his Muscadets de Sèvre-et-Maine. Last year's *Guide* praised his 93. He is now offering a 97 with aromas of dried fruit and brioche. It is clean and powerful on the palate, with slight hints of liquorice. This great wine has only one problem: keeping it in the bottle! One taster announced that it will be at its best in 2010.

► André-Michel Brégeon, 5, Les Guisseaux, 44190 Gorges, tel. 02.40.06.93.19, fax 02.40.06.95.91 ☒ ⟙ ev. day except Sun. 10am–7pm

CH. DE BRIACE Sur lie 2000★
☐ · 10 ha · 60,000 · ■ · ♦ · €3-5

The private wine school of Briacé, east of Landreau, is housed in a mock-medieval château actually built in the 19th century, and is included in the *Guide* with noteworthy regularity. Its Muscadet de Sèvre-et-Maine 2000 is no exception to the rule. It is elegant and mineral, with an array of flowers and aromas that reflect the *terroir* on the nose. It is rich and rounded on the palate, revealing plenty of power. An amazing **Muscadet de Sèvre-et-Maine 99** is listed without a star: it has been macerated for a short time on the skins and has benefited from ageing in oak.

► Ch. de Briacé, Lycée agricole de Briacé, 44430 Le Landreau, tel. 02.40.06.43.33, fax 02.40.06.46.15 ☒ ⟙ by appt.

CLOS DES BRIORDS Sur lie 2000★★
☐ · 3 ha · 15,000 · ■ · ♦ · €3-5

This rich, powerful wine immediately evoked old vines to the tasters, and they were right. The 70-year-old vines give the wine a note of *terroir* which supports its nose of fresh lemon and grapefruit and its full palate marvellously. This is an ideal wine to drink with fish.

► Marc Ollivier, La Pépière, 44690 Maisdon-sur-Sèvre, tel. 02.40.03.81.19, fax 02.40.06.69.85 ☒ ⟙ by appt.

DOM. DU BROCHET Sur lie 2000★★
☐ · 10.8 ha · 20,000 · ■ · ♦ · €3-5

Brochet is an area west of the town of Vallet. This domaine has produced a clear wine with aromas of dried fruits, almonds and flowers. It is supple on the palate, developing in a very flavoursome way, as one would expect from the aromas on the nose. It is enhanced by a hint of pepper. It lacks neither freshness nor richness, has great personality, and reflects the *terroir* very well.

► Charles Fleurance-Hallereau, Le Brochet, 44330 Vallet, tel. 02.40.33.97.19 ☒ ⟙ by appt.

DOM. DES CANTREAUX
Sur lie 2000★
☐ · 2.2 ha · 13,000 · ■ · ♦

This wine comes from 60-year-old vines on mica-schist slopes. Its jasmine nose is enriched with notes of pear and almond. It is a good example of its type and is pleasant, with a freshness on the finish due to a touch of effervescence.

● Patrice Marchais, Les Cantreaux, 44430 Le Loroux-Bottereau, tel. 02.40.33.84.20, fax 02.51.71.90.36 ⚁ by appt.

CARDINAL RICHARD Sur lie 2000★
3 ha · 20,000 · €5-8

The name comes from a Parisian cardinal who was a former owner of the Château du Cleray. The wine is delicate, but its nose reveals dried-fruit, pear and broom aromas. The palate is supple and fresh, with a spicy note. This *vin de terroir* is already very enjoyable, but it will easily keep a few months more.

● SA Sauvion et Fils, Ch. du Cléray, 44330 Vallet, tel. 02.40.36.22.55, fax 02.40.36.34.62, e-mail sauvion44@aol.com ☑ ⚁ by appt.

DOM. DU CENSY Sur lie Vinifié en fût de chêne 1998★★
0.2 ha · 1,000 · €5-8

This wine comes from a plot of 50-year-old vines harvested by hand. It is then matured in oak barrels, making it something of a rarity. This is a pity, because its seductive flower and honey aromas, heralding a full palate, are a lovely balance of fruit and oak. Serve it with tuna steak with dill, for example.

● François Rivière, Le Gast, 44690 Maisdon-sur-Sèvre, tel. 02.40.03.86.28, fax 02.40.33.56.91 ☑ ⚁ by appt.

CH. DE CHASSELOIR Sur lie Comte Leloup de Chasseloir des Ceps Centenaires 2000★
3 ha · 20,000 · €5-8

At Chasseloir everything seems to be on a different scale, from the cellar with its Rabelaisian figures bringing in the fruit from their 20 ha (49.4 acres), to the very name of this wine. The vines are 100 years old, and they have created a wine of magisterial aromatic power, evoking flowers and dried fruit. The palate is rich and complex, finishing on a lemony note.

● Bernard Chéreau, 2, imp. Port de la Ramée, 44120 Vertou, tel. 02.40.54.81.15, fax 02.40.03.19.36, e-mail bernard.chereau@wanadoo.fr ☑ ⚁ ev. day except Sun. 9am-6pm

VIGNOBLE DU CHATEAU DES ROIS Sur lie 1996★★
6 ha · 30,000 · €3-5

Vignoble du Château des Rois — Muscadet-Sèvre et Maine sur lie — Gilbert GANICHAUD & FILS Viticulteurs - MOUZILLON (L.A.) FRANCE

In Mouzillon, 200 m (218 yd) from the Gallo-Roman bridge over the Sanguèze, Gilbert Ganichaud tends 27 ha (66.7 acres) of vines. Although the Château des Rois label shows only a baron's crown, this wine is truly royal, thanks to its impressive nose, which develops from currants, gentian and orange-flower into a more mineral aroma. This characterful Muscadet de Sèvre-et-Maine is clean, clear-cut and elegant on the palate and would go well with scallops.

● Gilbert Ganichaud et Fils, 9, rue d'Ancenis, 44330 Mouzillon, tel. 02.40.33.93.40, fax 02.40.36.38.79, e-mail oviti@aol.com ☑ ⚁ ev. day except Sat. Sun. 8am-12 noon 2pm-6pm

DOM. DES CHAUSSELIERES Sur lie Elevé en fût de chêne 1999
0.33 ha · 2,400 · €5-8

This characterful wine is produced in only small quantities, but does not reach perfection until a year or two later. Evidently oaked, the wine develops aromas of dried fruits, peach, apricot and even rum. It is powerful and heady on the palate but has not yet developed all of its complexity.

● Jean Bosseau, Dom. des Chausselières, 12, rue des Vignes, 44330 Le Pallet, tel. 02.40.80.40.12, fax 02.40.80.46.42 ☑

PHILIPPE CHENARD Cuvée des Buttays 2000★★
n.c. · 20,000 · €3-5

This pale-golden wine, as subtle on the nose as on the palate, is made by an estate on the slopes of Sanguèze, north-east of Pallet. This is a well-structured wine with plenty of length, and its delicate mineral notes and crystallised-fruit aromas make it a good wine to drink with fish in sauce.

● EARL Philippe Chénard, La Boissclière, 44330 Le Pallet, tel. 02.40.80.98.17, fax 02.40.80.44.38 ⚁ by appt.

DOM. DU COLOMBIER Sur lie Cuvée des Deux Colombes 2000★★
3 ha · 20,000 · €3-5

Tillières, on the borders of the Mauges and the Pays Nantais, is the first village where Muscadet is produced. Six hundred metres (654 yd) from the Guillou mill, Jean-Yves Brétadeau tends 27 ha (66.7 acres) of well-ordered vines. This Sèvre-et-Maine, which was awarded the *coup de coeur* in last year's *Guide*, confirms the talents of its producer. It is open and characterful, with flower and ripe-fruit aromas heralding a rich, concentrated palate. Body and richness are clearly perceptible, and this wine would go well with some desserts. A **Gros-Plant du Pays Nantais sur lie** from the same domaine, with intense flowery aromas spiced with a touch of lemon on the finish, received one star.

● Jean-Yves Brétaudeau, Le Colombier, 49230 Tillières, tel. 02.41.70.45.96, fax 02.41.70.36.17, e-mail bretodo@free.fr ☑ ⚁ by appt.

Muscadet de Sèvre-et-Maine

DOM. BRUNO CORMERAIS

Sur lie Cuvée Chambaudière 2000*

□   4 ha   17,000 ■● €3-5

From the footpath in the Maine valley, walkers can make out the barrel store of the Cormerais domaine. This wine, from the silts and granite of Clisson, is light-yellow in colour with dried-fruit aromas on the nose. It is well-structured and fairly flowery, with menthol notes on the palate.

➤ EARL Bruno et Marie-Françoise Cormerais, La Chambaudière, 44190 Saint-Lumine-de-Clisson, tel. 02.40.03.85.84, fax 02.40.06.68.74 ⊠ ⤶ by appt.

GILDAS CORMERAIS

Sur lie Prestige Vieilles vignes 2000*

□   2 ha   10,000 ■● €3-5

The 60-year-old vines on the flinty clays of the Maine slopes between Saint-Fiacre and Maisdon have produced a wine which is limpid, rich and powerful, as well as fruity on the nose and palate. This 2000 is supple and fresh, which makes it a good partner for fish in sauce.

➤ Dom. Gildas Cormerais, 17, La Bretonnière, 44690 Maisdon-sur-Sèvre, tel. 02.40.36.90.13, fax 02.40.36.99.95 ⊠ ⤶ ev. day except Sun. 9am–7pm

COLLECTION PRIVEE DES FRERES COUILLAUD 1997

□   n.c.   8,000 ■● €8-11

The Couillaud brothers tend 67 ha (165.5 acres) of vines around the Château de la Ragotière. The building, which was burnt down during the Revolution, was completely reconstructed at the beginning of the 19th century. Given the richness and concentration of their 97, these wine-growers have opted for 28 months of maturation *sur lie*. The result is a wine with a nose of ripe pears and liquorice flavours, whose ethereal structure invites you to start drinking it straight away. The flavoursome **Muscadet Sèvre-et-Maine sur lie Château de La Ragotière 2000**, which is evocative of ripe fruit, was also commended.

➤ Les Frères Couillaud, GAEC de La Grande Ragotière, La Regrippière, 44330 Vallet, tel. 02.40.33.60.56, fax 02.40.33.61.89, e-mail frères.couillaud@wanadoo.fr ⊠ ⤶ by appt.

MICHEL DELHOMMEAU

Sur lie Cuvée Harmonie 2000*

□   4 ha   20,000 ■● €3-5

This wine develops a balanced and characterful nose. It is lively and well-structured on the palate, with a definite *terroir* character.

➤ Michel Delhommeau, La Huperie, 44690 Monnières, tel. 02.40.54.60.37, fax 02.40.54.64.51 ⊠ ⤶ by appt.

DONATIEN-BAHUAUD

Cuvée des Aigles 2000*

□   28 ha   200,000 ■● –€3

This wine, half of which is destined for export, has a solemn Empire-green label. The intense yet delicate nose has notes of lemon and even cherries. It is supple and rounded, and both rich and lively on the palate.

➤ Donatien-Bahuaud, La Loge, BP 1, 44330 La Chapelle-Heulin, tel. 02.40.06.70.05, fax 02.40.06.77.11 ⊠

SELECTION CHRISTIAN GAUTHIER

Sur lie 2000**

□   4 ha   14,000 ■● €3-5

This wine, from the granite soils in the extreme south of the appellation area, makes an impression with a remarkably mineral nose. After a delightful attack it shows itself to be fresh, fruity and long. It can be drunk from now onwards, or can be cellared for another year at least.

➤ Christian Gauthier, 19, La Mainguionnière, 44190 Saint-Hilaire-de-Clisson, tel. 02.40.54.42.91, fax 02.40.54.25.83 ⊠ ⤶ by appt.

CH. DES GAUTRONNIERES

Sur lie 2000

□   8 ha   59,565 ■● –€3

This estate between La Chapelle-Heulin and Le Pallet has been in the same family for seven generations.This is a very dry wine in which the green-toned appearance is in keeping with a nose of hawthorn and lemon. The pronounced bitterness on the palate suggests leaving it for a few months more, but it is already suitable for drinking in kir.

➤ Claude Fleurance, Ch. des Gautronnières, 44330 La Chapelle-Heulin, tel. 02.40.06.74.06 ⊠ ⤶ by appt.

CH. DES GRANDES NOELLES

Sur lie 2000*

□   4 ha   20,000 ■❙❙● €5-8

The Poiron family have more than one string to their bow; in addition to their 36 ha (88.9 acres) of vines, they also own a vine nursery. This wine is golden-green, with a powerful nose of fresh fruit. It is perfumed and balanced, very pleasant on the palate and suitable for drinking with seafood or a dry goat's cheese.

➤ SA Henri Poiron et Fils, Les Quatre-Routes, 44690 Maisdon-sur-Sèvre, tel. 02.40.54.60.58, fax 02.40.54.62.05, e-mail poiron.henri@online.fr ⊠ ⤶ ev. day except Sun. 9am–12.30pm 2pm–6pm; Sat. 9am–12.30pm 2pm–5pm

DOM. DES GRANDES VIGNES

Sur lie 2000***

□   4 ha   n.c. ■● €5-8

With a vineyard of over 15 ha (37 acres) on sandy slopes, this is the right sort of *terroir* for wine-making. With its intense nose of gunflint, apples and pears and stimulating spicy and mineral notes, this wine is typical of its appellation. On the palate it progresses with a suppleness, supported by a delightful freshness, right up to the long finish. It could easily stay in the cellar for another two or three years.

🍷 Hermine, Daniel et Lionel Métaireau, Coursay, 44690 Monnières, tel. 02.40.54.60.08, fax 02.40.54.65.73, e-mail earl.metaireau@free.fr ☑
Ⓨ ev. day except Sun. 9am–12 noon 2pm–7pm; cl. 15–31 Aug.

GRAND FIEF DE LA CLAVELIERE
Sur lie 1999★

☐ 1 ha 6,000 ■ €3-5

This very clear wine comes from the sandy soils near the Maine. It has a characterful nose of ripe fruit, then a full, round palate with a rich finish. This wine is ready to drink now, but can also be kept another two or three years.

🍷 Louis Chatellier et Fils, La Clavelière, 44190 Saint-Lumine-de-Clisson, tel. 02.40.03.80.24, fax 02.40.06.69.02 ☑
Ⓨ ev. day 9.30am–7pm

GRAND FIEF DE LA CORMERAIE
2000★★
Sur lie Grande Réserve du Commandeur

☐ 2.5 ha 16,000 ■ €3-5

Grand Fief de la Cormeraie — MUSCADET SÈVRE & MAINE SUR LIE — par Véronique CHÂTEAU GÜNTHER Viticulteur à Monnières — MIS EN BOUTEILLE À LA PROPRIÉTÉ

stretching south-west of Vallet. Its pale wine with a delicate nose is pleasant, rich, fruity and well-balanced on the palate.

🍷 Jean Aubron, L'Audigère, 44330 Vallet, tel. 02.40.33.91.91, fax 02.40.33.91.31

ALAIN ET FRANCOISE GRIPON
Sur lie Vieilles vignes 2000★

☐ 3 ha 4,000 ■ €3-5

This domaine, where 18 ha (44.5 acres) of vines are cultivated, still has some traces of the ancient feudal castle mound to which it owes its name. This slightly sparkling wine has an intense, well-integrated nose of honey and rose. It starts freshly on the palate, revealing a well-rounded, balanced body with lemon, linden flowers and gunflint flavours. Altogether, this is a very elegant wine.

🍷 Françoise et Alain Gripon, Manoir de la Mottrie, La Levraudière, 44330 La Chapelle-Heulin, tel. 02.40.06.76.38, fax 02.40.06.76.38, e-mail agri.pont@wanadoo.fr ☑ Ⓨ by appt.

PHILIPPE GUERIN
Elevé en fût de chêne 1999

☐ 0.5 ha 2,600 ⊕ €5-8

The label bears the date 1795, when the Guérin family domaine was founded; the estate has been handed down from father to son ever since, and nowadays there are 22 ha (54.3 acres) of vines. The oak is very noticeable on this wine, along with notes of vanilla, beeswax and caramel, all of which do not obscure its *terroir* character. This 99 is a worthy accompaniment to white meats with cream sauces.

🍷 Philippe Guérin, Les Pellerins, 44330 Vallet, tel. 02.40.36.37.34, fax 02.40.36.40.73 Ⓨ by appt.

DOM. GUITONNIERE Sur lie 2000★

☐ 15 ha 15,000 ■ €3-5

From now onwards Thierry Beauquin will be in charge of this family domaine, which produces a slightly sparkling wine, still slightly closed on the nose, but with plenty of character on the palate. There is a touch of sparkle, giving freshness and liveliness to the fairly rounded palate.

🍷 EARL Beauquin et Fils, La Guitonnière, 44330 Vallet, tel. 02.40.36.33.03 ☑ Ⓨ by appt.

Véronique Günther-Chéreau's wines are the great classics of the Nantais vineyards. This one comes from an old *commanderie*, which was situated between Gorges, Monnières and Maisdon and was dismantled after the Revolution. There are 5 ha (12.4 acres) of vineyards. This Sèvre-et-Maine, with its delicate nose, both fruity and flowery, and its rich, long and well-structured palate, is very typical of its appellation. The **Château du Coing de Saint-Fiacre 2000** (one star), which is from vines planted at the confluence of the Sèvre and the Maine, is aromatic and fruity on both the nose and palate.

🍷 Véronique Günther-Chéreau, Ch. du Coing, 44690 Saint-Fiacre-sur-Maine, tel. 02.40.54.85.24, fax 02.40.54.80.21 ☑

GRAND FIEF DE L'AUDIGERE
Sur lie 2000★

☐ 46 ha 200,000 ■ €5-8

This former lord's domain is now a large 46-ha (113.6-acre) vineyard with lands

CH. DU HALLAY Sur lie 2000★

☐ 9 ha 65,000 ■ €5-8

On this 35-ha (86.5-acre) property, 9 ha (22.2 acres) are covered with vines. The Château du Hallay was destroyed towards the end of the Second World War, but it is pictured on this wine's original label. This straw-coloured wine develops complex aromas dominated by pineapple, white peach and dried fruit, accompanied by a few notes of bread and brioche. It is rich, soft and well-balanced on the palate and finishes with a hint of bitterness which ought to disappear in a few months' time.

Muscadet de Sèvre-et-Maine

HAUTE-COUR DE LA DEBAUDIERE Sur lie 2000★

☐ 12 ha 105,000 ▪ ● €3-5 🅥

Vines planted on the gabbro slopes of Sanguèze have produced a beautiful Muscadet with a subtle nose of citrus fruits. It is already well-balanced and very forward on the palate right from the start, although this impulsive wine needs longer to mature so that its structure can develop fully.

☛ Chantal et Yves Goislot, La Débaudière, 44330 Vallet, tel. 02.40.36.30.73, fax 02.40.36.20.23, e-mail yegoislot@aol.fr
🅥 🍸 by appt.

DOM. DE LA BAZILLIERE
Sur lie Prestige de la Bazillière 2000★

☐ 2 ha 17,000 ▪ ● €3-5

La Bazillière cultivates 16 ha (39.5 acres) of vines on the southern slopes of the Landreau, above the marshes of Goulaine. They produce a wine which has a *terroir* character, with a full, flavoursome palate. The 2000 is fresh, lively and supple with plenty of length.

☛ Jean-Michel Sauvêtre, La Bazillière, 44330 Le Landreau, tel. 02.40.06.40.14, fax 02.40.06.47.91 🅥 🍸 by appt.

DOM. DE LA BERNARDIERE
Sur lie 2000★

☐ 5 ha 12,000 ▪ ● €3

This vineyard nowadays covers almost 32 ha (79 acres). At the time of the Revolution, La Bernardière belonged to a Nantes shipowner who exported wine to Bruges and Hamburg. Northern Europe would benefit from rediscovering this flowery Muscadet de Sèvre-et-Maine with its marked apple and pear aromas. It is powerful on the palate, with plenty of structure and a note of acidity, and will happily keep a few more months.

☛ Dominique Coraleau, 14, rue des Châteaux, La Bernardière, 44330 La Chapelle-Heulin, tel. 02.40.06.76.21, fax 02.40.06.76.21 🅥 🍸 by appt.

CH. LA BERRIERE Sur lie 2000

☐ 28 ha 196,000 ▪ ● €3-5

This lovely little neoclassical château, which was rebuilt after the Vendée Wars, has been a major producer of Muscadet since 1737. Its 30-ha (74.1-acre) vineyard has produced a 2000 vintage which is pale in colour with a subtly fruity nose. The palate is well-made and has the same fruit qualities as the nose.

☛ SCEA La Berrière, Ch. de La Berrière, 44450 Barbechat, tel. 02.40.06.34.22, fax 02.40.03.61.96 🅥 🍸 by appt.
☛ de Bascher

DOM. DE LA BIGOTIERE
Sur lie 2000★

☐ 10 ha 60,000 ▪ ● €3-5

La Bigotière, halfway between the Sèvre and the Maine, covers 19 ha (46.9 acres), producing a Muscadet with a complex, mature nose. At first it has creamy notes, developing, after swirling, a new-mown hay aroma. It is full and powerful on the palate, very typical though still slightly austere, and needs to mature for a few more months, after which it will be the perfect wine to accompany fish dishes with sauce.

☛ EARL Pascal Batard, La Bigotière, 44690 Maisdon-sur-Sèvre, tel. 02.40.06.67.02, fax 02.40.33.56.79 🅥
🍸 by appt.

DOM. DE LA BLANCHETIERE
Sur lie 2000

☐ 21 ha 22,000 ▪ ● €3-5

A parchment dating from 1476 bears witness to the fact that there were already vines at La Blanchetière in the 15th century. Their descendants have produced a flowery wine that is delicate and slightly sparkling. Their **Gros-Plant du Pays Nantais sur lie 2000** is also recommended; it has an intense fruity nose and a fine palate, with a touch of acidity adding to its elegance.

☛ Christophe Luneau, Dom. de La Blanchetière, 44330 Le Loroux-Bottereau, tel. 02.40.06.43.18, fax 02.40.06.43.18 🅥
🍸 by appt.

CH. DE LA BOTINIERE Sur lie 2000

☐ 35 ha 260,000 ▪ ● €3

Although partially destroyed during the Revolution, La Botinière still retains some 16th- and 17th-century architectural features. It produces a wine with an original and flowery nose that evokes the clay soils of the vineyard. Although it does not have a great deal of length on the palate, it is pleasantly lively and fruity.

☛ SE Ch. de La Botinière, 44330 Vallet, tel. 02.40.06.73.83, fax 02.40.06.76.49 🅥
🍸 by appt.
☛ Jean Beauquin

CH. DE LA BOURDINIERE
Sur lie Tradition 2000★

☐ 15 ha 70,000 ▪ ● €5-8

This handsome château includes a tower and ramparts built by Pierre Landais, treasurer to Duke François II and defender of Breton independence in the 15th century. Its vineyard produces a well-structured wine with considerable overall harmony. The intense nose is a fruity and delicate introduction to a fresh, lively, flavoursome palate.

☛ Pierre et Chantal Lieubeau, La Croix de la Bourdinière, 44690 Château-Thébaud, tel. 02.40.06.54.81, fax 02.40.06.51.08, e-mail lieubeau.vigneron@wanadoo.fr 🅥
🍸 by appt.

☛ SCEA Dominique Richard, La Cognardière, 44330 Le Pallet, tel. 02.40.80.42.30, fax 02.40.80.44.37 🅥
🍸 by appt.
☛ Marie Richard

DOM. DE LA BRETONNIERE
Sur lie 2000★

| □ | 4.5 ha | 30,000 | ■ | €3-5 |

Y by appt.

This wine is a blend from the different forms of *terroir* in the domaine; this undoubtedly helps to make it typical of its appellation. It has a mineral character on the nose, with notes of lemon, flowers and coffee. It is supple and has a long but somewhat austere finish, indicating that it will benefit from being kept for a few more months.
➤ GAEC Charpentier-Fleurance, La Bretonnière, 44430 Le Landreau, tel. 02.40.06.43.39, fax 02.40.06.44.05

CH. DE LA CANTRIE Sur lie 2000★

| □ | 14.58 ha | 50,000 | ■ | €3-5 |

Y by appt.

All summer long, the ancient cellars of La Cantrie host art exhibitions; from there comes this wine. It has aromas of apples, pears and exotic fruit, underlined with a touch of broom. It is very rich and fleshy on the palate, even slightly heady, finishing on an attractive bitter note. The overall impression is that this is a wine that will develop well.
➤ Laurent Bossis, 11, rue Beauregard, 44690 Saint-Fiacre-sur-Maine, tel. 02.40.36.94.64, fax 02.40.54.87.60

DOM. DE LA CHAUVINIERE Sur lie 2000

| □ | 7 ha | 40,000 | ■ | €3-5 |

Yves Huchet tends 37 ha (91.4 acres) of vines on the granite soils that are a feature of Château-Thébaud. His wine is well-balanced, with developing aromas of citrus fruits, apples and pears. It also benefits from a fine initial attack, followed by a rich, fruity structure.
➤ Yves Huchet, La Chauvinière, 44690 Château-Thébaud, tel. 02.40.06.51.90, fax 02.40.06.57.13, e-mail domaine-de-la-chauviniere@wanadoo.fr Y by appt.

DOM. DE LA COGNARDIERE
Sur lie Bella Verte 2000

| □ | n.c. | 50,000 | ■ | €3-5 |

This wine from the domaine of La Cognardière has a label which is as original as its name. A typical Muscadet, it is pale in colour with plenty of intensity on the nose, while the fleshy palate leaves an impression of balance. It is ready to drink now.
➤ SARL Fabienne Richard de Tournay, La Cognardière, 44330 Le Pallet, tel. 02.40.80.42.30, fax 02.40.80.44.37 ev. day 8am-12 noon 2pm-6pm

CH. DE LA CORMERAIS Sur lie 2000

| □ | 4.5 ha | 30,000 | ◄3 |

This ancient estate once belonged to Richard de Bretagne, the brother of Duke Jean V. The château, surrounded by a 17-ha (41.9-acre) vineyard, is currently being renovated. Its wine is powerfully fruity on the nose, and the flavours prolong this impression with a full and fairly rich palate.
➤ Thierry Besnard, La Cormerais, 44690 Monnières, tel. 02.40.06.95.58, fax 02.40.06.50.76 Y by appt.

DOM. DE LA COUR DU CHATEAU DE LA POMMERAIE Sur lie 2000

| □ | 15 ha | 80,000 | ■ | €3-5 |

La Pommeraie, a famous Vallet *terroir*, is divided into many different parcels. This Muscadet de Sèvre-et-Maine is still slightly reserved, but seems representative of its year, thanks to an elegant sharpness on the palate.
➤ SARL Gilbert Chon, Le Bois Malinge, 44450 Saint-Julien-de-Concelles, tel. 02.40.54.11.08, fax 02.40.54.19.90
➤ Albert Poilane

CH. DE LA FERTE Sur lie 1998★

| □ | 2 ha | 12,000 | ■ | €3-5 |

This is a surprising wine. Although a mineral character dominates, its nose also reveals gamey and vegetal notes. It is rounded and well-balanced, and the finish is powerful, almost invasive. 'Keep it for people with experienced palates, said one of the tasters. The 2000 deserves to be singled out for its long citrus fruit flavours.
➤ Jérôme et Rémy Sécher, La Ferté, 44330 Vallet, tel. 02.40.33.95.54, fax 02.40.33.95.54 ev. day 9am-1pm 2pm-6.30pm

CLOS DE LA FEVRIE Sur lie 1999★

| □ | 1 ha | 6,000 | ■ | €3-5 |

Vincent Caillé is interested in using his 36 ha (88.9 acres) of vines to make wines suitable for ageing, but there is no point making this 99, with its nose of brioche and buttery aromas, wait any longer. It is firm on the palate and indicates successful vinification *sur lie*.
➤ Vincent Caillé, EARL Le Fay-d'Homme, 2, rue du Fief-Seigneur, 44690 Monnières, tel. 02.40.54.62.06, fax 02.40.54.64.20, e-mail lefaydhomme@wanadoo.fr Y by appt.

MANOIR DE LA FIRETIERE
Sur lie 2000★★★

| □ | 10 ha | 70,000 | ■ | €3-5 |

This country house between Le Loroux and La Chapelle-Heulin produces a pale-yellow wine with green highlights and a very clear, flowery nose. On the palate, this high-class Muscadet reflects the character of the *terroir* and reveals itself to be full, fleshy, rich and long, with dominant floral notes.
➤ Guillaume Charpentier, Les Noues, 44430 Le Loroux-Bottereau, tel. 02.40.06.43.76, fax 02.40.06.43.76 Y by appt.

DOM. DE LA FOLIETTE Sur lie
Tradition Vinifié en fût de chêne 1999★★

☐ 2 ha 9,000 ▭ €5-8

The Domaine de la Foliette covers 32 ha (79 acres). Its wine, which is fermented in oak casks, is pleasantly surprising in the complexity and richness of its combined aromas of apples and pears, citrus fruit, walnut, vanilla and toast. On the palate, it displays a good balance of oak and fruit before ending with a lively finish.

☛• Dom. de La Foliette, 35, rue de la Fontaine, 44690 La Haye-Fouassière, tel. 02.40.36.92.28, fax 02.40.36.98.16, e-mail domaine.de.la.foliette@wanadoo.fr ☑ ☎ by appt.

LE GRAND R DE LA GRANGE
Sur lie 2000★★

☐ 5 ha 30,000 ▭ €5-8

There are two Domaines de la Grange, each run by one of the Luneau brothers. The 'R' is the 30-ha (74.1-acre) estate belonging to Rémy. This Grand R is a blend of the year's best wines. It has a complex nose of flowers, apples and pears, heightened with a note of aniseed. Despite a lemony finish, it is well-balanced on the palate and would make a good partner for pike-perch in *beurre blanc*. The Jury awarded one star to a *Gros-Plant du Pays Nantais sur lie Vieilles vignes 2000*: the fresh fruit nose leads on to exotic nuances, while the delicate palate moves towards a long, lemony finish.

☛• Rémy Luneau, Dom. R de La Grange, 44430 Le Landreau, tel. 02.40.06.45.65, fax 02.40.06.48.17, e-mail domaine.r.delagrange@wanadoo.fr ☑ ☎ ev. day except Sun. 9am–12 noon 2pm–6pm

MANOIR DE LA GRELIERE
Sur lie Vieilles vignes Réserve 2000★★★

☐ 30 ha 200,000 ▭ €3-5

The oldest vines (aged between 50 and 100 years) on this property, which once belonged to the Dukes of Brittany, have produced an intense, complex wine reminiscent of honey and jasmine. It has a fullness on the palate, developing pear and quince flavours. This delightful Sèvre-et-Maine will benefit from being kept for a little longer. The domaine's *Cuvée Sélection 2000* is also worth mentioning, although it has no star. A well-rounded, slightly acid wine, it was not matured *sur lie*.

☛• Branger et Fils, Manoir de la Grelière, 44120 Vertou, tel. 02.40.05.71.55, fax 02.40.31.29.39, e-mail branger.vertou@wanadoo.fr ☑ ☎ by appt.

CH. DE LA GUIPIERE
Sur lie Tradition 2000★

☐ 10 ha 60,000 ▭ €3-5

This 30-ha (74.1-acre) domaine lies halfway between Vallet and La Chapelle-Heulin. It produces a wine that is a fine example of its type and representative of the appellation. This 2000 is fruity and mineral on the nose, with a fairly lively attack on the palate and an excellent structure.

☛• GAEC Charpentier Père et Fils, La Guipière, 44330 Vallet, tel. 02.40.36.23.30, fax 02.40.36.38.14 ☑ ☎ ev. day 9am–7pm; Sun. by appt.

LA FLEUR DU CLOS DE LA HAUTE CARIZIERE Sur lie 2000★

☐ 8 ha 50,000 €3-5

This wine, which is distributed by a Mouzillon wine-merchant, is actually produced west of La Haye-Fouassière. The explosive bouquet is astonishing; powerful apricot and hazelnut aromas are rather evocative of Sauvignon. It is rich and rounded on the palate, carrying notes of oak and vanilla from its six-month maturation in cask. This is not a typical Muscadet, but it is well-made and will suit fish dishes or white meat.

☛• Vinival, La Sablette, 44330 Mouzillon, tel. 02.40.36.66.00, fax 02.40.36.26.83

DOM. DE LA LANDELLE
Sur lie Vieilles vignes 2000★

☐ 2.5 ha 10,000 ▭ €3-5

No one will be surprised by the noticeable gunflint aromas in this wine. This 2000 comes from old vines planted on the friable, schisty soils of the Loroux. It is delicate and balanced, with a hint of toast. This wine has plenty of character and is very evocative of its *terroir*.

☛• Michel Libeau, La Landelle, 44330 Le Loroux-Bottereau, tel. 02.40.33.81.15, fax 02.40.33.85.37, e-mail domainelandelle@libertysurf.fr ☎ by appt.

DOM. DE LA LOUVETRIE
Sur lie Hermine d'Or 1999★★

☐ 7 ha 25,700 ▭ €5-8

The *Guide* has often mentioned this domaine situated on excellent soils along the banks of the Sèvre, just upstream of La Haye Fouassière. This wine is a good example of its type, with a delicate nose of dried and crystallised fruit. It is well-balanced and rich, with plenty of presence and fullness on the palate. It can easily spend another one or two years in the cellar. The **Domaine de La Louvetrie Eti-quette Noire 2000**, with a powerful nose of ripe fruit, was also awarded two stars. It is long and well-balanced on the palate, with a quality that reflects the *terroir* on the finish, making it a very lively wine. It could also keep a while longer.

☛• Joseph Landron, Les Brandières, 44690 La Haye-Fouassière, tel. 02.40.54.83.27, fax 02.40.54.89.82 ☑ ☎ by appt.

LA MAISON VIEILLE Sur lie 2000

☐ 1.5 ha 8,000 ▭ €3-5

Le Pé, which has all the charm one would expect of a wine-making village on the banks of the Sèvre, is a popular tourist destination and well worth a visit. This is the home of this 20-ha (49.4-acre) domaine where Christophe Maillard produces a straw-yellow wine with green highlights, as reliably and pleasantly fruity on the palate as on the nose. His **Gros-Plant du Pays Nantais 2000** (only 1,000 bottles) is also worth mentioning for its fresh-fruit character and refreshing slight sparkle.

☞ Christophe Maillard, Le Pé-de-Sèvre, 4330 Le Pallet, tel. 02.40.80.44.92 ▽
Ⴒ by appt.

DOM. LA MALONNIÈRE
Sur lie 2000★

□ 10 ha | 60,000 | ■ ▮ | €3-5

The Vignerons de la Noëlle export 40% of the wine they produce. The Domaine de la Malonnière, on the mica-schist soils of the Loroux Bottereau, produces a pale-golden wine with brilliant green highlights. The intense nose combines apples, pears and flowers, and these characteristics are also very evident on the palate. The fresh, full body is a sign of successful wine-making.

☞ Les Vignerons de La Noëlle, bd des Alliés, BP 155, 44150 Ancenis, tel. 02.40.98.92.72, fax 02.40.98.96.70, e-mail vignerons-noelle@cana.fr ▽
Ⴒ by appt.

LA MARQUISIÈRE Sur lie 2000★

□ 20 ha | 150,000 | ■ ▮ | €3

The La Marquisière name was created by the *negociant* at the beginning of 2001, and the wine enters the *Guide* with considerable success. Its almond and flower aromas and slight mineral notes make it fresh on the palate. It is lively and persistent, but not aggressive.

☞ Les Caves Saint-Florent, Le Buisson, BP 2, 49410 Chapelle-Saint-Florent, tel. 02.41.72.89.52, fax 02.41.72.77.13 ▽
Ⴒ by appt.

DOM. LANDES DES CHABOISSIÈRES Sur lie 2000★

□ 14.5 ha | 52,000 | ■ ▮ | €5-8

After centuries as pastureland, the heathlands of La Chaboissières have now been employed for a nobler purpose, with 22 ha (54.3 acres) of well-ordered vines. They have produced an intensely fruity 2000 which develops subtly; on the nose, citrus fruits dominate; on the finish, there are passion-fruit flavours.

☞ Georges et Guy Desfossés, 44330 Vallet, tel. 02.40.33.99.54, fax 02.40.33.99.54 ▽

DOM. DE LA PAPINIÈRE
Sur lie Sélection du Moulin 2000★

□ 15.5 ha | 9,000 | ■ ▮

On a slope cut by the stream of La Braudière, La Papinière is producing a wine with a clear, delicate nose with mineral and floral notes. It is well-rounded and full of freshness. The palate is supple, progressing towards a fruity finish.

☞ GAEC Cousseau Frères, Dom. de La Papinière, 49230 Tillières, tel. 02.41.70.46.31, fax 02.41.58.61.51 ▽
Ⴒ by appt.

'Neither vanity nor weakness,' proclaims the label. This Vallet wine has no weakness at all. It is very clear, developing a flattering nose of citrus fruits and ripe fruit; then it charms you with its straightforward attack and liquorice finish on the palate. This good *Vin de Terroir* can keep a few more months.

☞ Guilbaud-Moulin, 1, rue de la Planche, 44330 Mouzillon, tel. 02.40.36.30.55, fax 02.40.36.36.35 Ⴒ by appt.

DOM. DE LA ROCHE BLANCHE
Sur lie 2000★

□ 13.35 ha | 18,000 | ■ ▮ | €5-8

These 35 ha (86.5 acres) of clay-with-flint slopes have produced a wine which is typical in every respect. Its nose of apples and fresh pears is still slightly immature, but its rich, fruity, elegant palate lasts right through to an attractive point of bitterness on the finish. This 2000 can be kept for another two years.

☞ EARL Lechat et Fils, 12, av. des Roses, 44330 Vallet, tel. 02.40.33.94.77, fax 02.40.36.44.31 Ⴒ by appt.

DOM. LA ROCHE RENARD
Sur lie 2000★★

□ n.c. | 40,000 | ■ ▮ | €3-5

This domaine owes its name to alios, a ferruginous rock, formerly known as 'renard,' or fox. It produces a remarkable straw-yellow wine with green highlights. The floral nose is of average intensity, giving way to a very delicately fruity palate. The firm structure adds length to the finish and guarantees good potential development.

CH. LA PERRIÈRE Sur lie 2000

□ 10 ha | 25,000 | ■ ▮ | €3-5

This domaine in Pallet (where you should be sure to visit the interesting Vineyard Museum, *Musée du Vignoble*) offers a Muscadet with a good nose of crystallised fruit. It is lively and balanced on the palate and ready to drink now with seafood or fish.

☞ Vincent Loiret, Ch. La Perrière, 44330 Le Pallet, tel. 02.40.80.43.24, fax 02.40.80.46.99 ▽ Ⴒ by appt.

CH. DE LA PINGOSSIÈRE
Sur lie 2000★★★

□ 12 ha | 40,000 | ■ ▮ ▮ | €5-8

Muscadet de Sèvre-et-Maine

DOM. DE LA TOURMALINE 2000★

☐   4 ha   30,000 ■ €5-8

Michel and Christophe Gadais have recently moved, so their cellar is now on the western outskirts of the town of Saint-Fiacre. Their wine offers a complex nose of fruit and flowers. It has a straightforward attack, with suppleness and roundness on the palate, and finishes on a refreshing note of green apple.

➶ Gadais Père et Fils, La Grand'Maison, 44690 Saint-Fiacre, tel. 02.40.54.81.23, fax 02.40.36.70.25 ▼ ▼ by appt.

LA SANCIVE Sur lie 2000

☐   n.c.   172,000 ■ €3-5

This wine, widely known abroad, is made by one of the oldest *négociants* in the Nantes vine-growing area. It is fresh and lively on the palate, slightly sparkling, with unobtrusive mineral notes and plenty of fruitiness. Another wine, the **Domaine du Landreau-Village, Muscadet Sèvre-et-Maine sur lie 2000**, also made a favourable impression on the Jury.

➶ SA Les Vins Drouet Frères, 8, bd du Luxembourg, 44330 Vallet, tel. 02.40.36.65.20, fax 02.40.33.99.78, e-mail drouetsa@club-internet.fr ▼ ▼ by appt.

DOM. DE LA THEBAUDIERE

Sur lie 2000

☐   18.62 ha   10,500 ■ –€3

The vines of this domaine (almost 22 ha/54.3 acres) are planted on the well-known hillock of La Roche, pointed towards the heart of the Goulaine marshes. This pale Muscadet de Sèvre-et-Maine, born out of soil composed of sand and volcanic rock, releases delicate fruit aromas, and the richness of its palate is a good sign for the future.

➶ EARL Philippe Pétard, La Thébaudière, 44330 Le Loroux-Bottereau, tel. 02.40.33.81.81, fax 02.40.33.81.81 ▼ ▼ by appt.

CH. LA TOUCHE Sur lie 2000★

☐   10 ha   60,000 ■ €3-5

La Touche, a former nobleman's estate belonging to the Goulaine family, exports 40% of its wine to the United Kingdom and the United States. Their Sèvre-et-Maine has a *terroir* character, clearly mineral on both nose and palate. Its balance and finesse testify to the good work performed in the cellar.

➶ Boullault et Fils, La Touche, 44330 Vallet, tel. 02.40.33.95.30, fax 02.40.36.26.85, e-mail boullault-fils@wanadoo.fr ▼ ▼ by appt.

LA TOUR DU FERRE Sur lie 2000

☐   2 ha   15,000 ■ €3-5

Le Ferré is a famous *terroir* in the Vallet area, and has held the name for centuries. The tower belongs to Philippe Douillard's modern house. This straw-yellow wine with green highlights lies between tradition and modernity. The fruitiness is delicate on the nose at first, but is echoed more generously on the full palate.

➶ Philippe Douillard, La Champinière, 44330 Vallet, tel. 02.40.36.61.77, fax 02.40.36.38.30, e-mail fdouillard@terre-net.fr ▼ ▼ by appt.

CH. LES AVENEAUX Sur lie 2000★

☐   30 ha   180,000 ■ €3-5

This large 39-ha (93.3-acre) domaine lies between La Chapelle-Heulin and the Sèvre. It is undoubtedly one of the very few properties in the region to export a small proportion of its production to Russia. Its Sèvre-et-Maine develops flowery qualities on the nose, uplifted by a note of coffee. It has a generous attack with roundness and length, and is very refreshing.

➶ Charpentier Fils, Ch. Les Aveneaux, 44330 La Chapelle-Heulin, tel. 02.40.06.74.40, fax 02.40.06.77.72, e-mail chateau-les-aveneaux@wanadoo.fr ▼ ▼ by appt.

LES GRANDS PRESBYTERES

Sur lie 2000

☐   3 ha   20,000 ■ €5-8

In 2001 Nelly Marzelleau celebrated ten years of wine-making. She produced a Muscadet de Sèvre-et-Maine with a nose that reflects the *terroir* and that tastes full from the start. Although it has a rather herbaceous character, this 2000 also benefits from a good structure, which suggests a promising future.

➶ Nelly Marzelleau, Les Grands Presbytères, 44690 Saint-Fiacre-sur-Maine, tel. 02.40.54.80.73, fax 02.40.36.70.78, e-mail nelly.marzelleau@wanadoo.fr ▼ ▼ ev. day except Sun. 8am–9pm

DOM. LES JARDINS DE LA MENARDIERE Sur lie 2000

☐   2 ha   10,000 ■ €3-5

This estate, which lies at the heart of the triangle formed by Vallet, La Chapelle-Heulin and Le Pallet, produces a very gentle wine. The 2000 has a lively colour, intense flower and pink-grapefruit flavours, and a well-rounded structure.

➶ Benoît et Florence Grenetier, La Ménardière, 44330 Vallet, tel. 02.40.33.93.30 ▼ ▼ by appt.

LE SOLEIL NANTAIS Sur lie 2000★★

☐   25 ha   150,000 ■ €5-8

This wine is a selection by one of the region's top *négociants* and comes in a special bottle with a label shaped like the Breton stoat. It is a very characterful wine; the nose is open and generous with mineral notes. Thanks to a slight sparkle, good attack and a flavoursome finish on the palate, it is also a most seductive wine.

🕿 Guilbaud Frères, Les Lilas, 44330 Mouzillon, tel. 02.40.36.30.55, fax 02.40.36.36.35, e-mail guilbaud.muscadet@wanadoo.fr Ⓥ
Ⓨ by appt.

LES PRINTANIÈRES Sur lie 2000

18 ha	120,000			€5-8

Les Printanières is one of the brand-names of a major wine-merchant in the Nantes region. This wine has a complex nose that is rather mineral and subtle. On the palate, it starts with a good, fairly lively attack and plenty of fruit.

🕿 Barré Frères, Beau-Soleil, BP 10, 44190 Gorges, tel. 02.40.06.90.70, fax 02.40.06.96.52 Ⓥ Ⓨ ev. day except Sat. Sun. 8am–12.30pm 2pm–6pm.

🕿 Guilbaud

DOM. DE L'HYVERNIÈRE

Sur lie Collection Marine 2000★

17.5 ha	133,000			€3-5

The very modern winery at L'Hyvernière (with its capacity of 70,000 hl/1,848,000 gal, it could turn out 10% of all Muscadet!) has blended wines from different terroirs to make this wine. This is a typical Muscadet, with an elegant floral nose, a fruity palate and a flavoursome finish.

🕿 SA Marcel Sautejeau, Dom. de L'Hyvernière, 44330 Le Pallet, tel. 02.40.06.73.83, fax 02.40.06.76.49

DOM. MARTIN-LUNEAU 2000

2 ha	12,000			€3-5

The commune of Gorges extends over both banks of the Sèvre, as does that of Clisson. This 30-ha (74.1-acre) domaine lies north of the river. The supple, well-rounded wine produced here gives off interesting aromas of roasted coffee on the nose and dried fruit on the palate. The estate also has a gentle, fruity Cuvée Tradition 2000, an ideal aperitif wine, which also deserves a mention.

🕿 Martin-Luneau, Le Magasin, 44190 Gorges, tel. 02.40.54.38.44, fax 02.40.54.07.23 Ⓥ Ⓨ ev. day except Sun. 8am–12.30pm 2pm–6.30pm

LOUIS MÉTAIREAU Sur lie One 1995

6.5 ha	33,164			€11-15

It is difficult to produce a masterpiece every year to rival the Louis Métaireau 25 Août 1989, which won the Guide's coup de cœur last year. This 95 is no 89. Very mineral, delicate, and well-rounded, it has an attractive touch of bitterness. These characteristics bode well for the future. Another Louis Métaireau wine which deserves to be mentioned is the Muscadet Sèvre-et-Maine Grand Mouton Huissier 96, which is fruity and mineral, with a fine palate. Grand Mouton is the terroir and Huissier the ministerial official who certified the bottling sur lie.

🕿 Les Domaines Louis Métaireau G.I.E., La Fèvrie, 44690 Maisdon-sur-Sèvre, tel. 02.40.54.81.92, fax 02.40.54.87.83, e-mail manelucemetaireau@hotmail.com Ⓥ Ⓨ ev. day 9am–12.30pm 2pm–6pm; Sat. Sun. by appt.

DOM. DES MORTIERS GOBIN

Sur lie 1999

1.3 ha	3,000			€5-8

This golden-yellow wine develops a fresh, complex nose, with a combination of mineral and iodine notes together with honeysuckle and citrus fruits (lime and grapefruit). It is dry and lively on the palate and ideal for drinking with crab, lobster or prawns. It would be best kept for two to four years.

🕿 Robert Brosseau, 4, pl. de la Rairie, 44690 La Haye-Fouassière, tel. 02.40.54.80.66 Ⓨ by appt.

DOM. DE MOTTE CHARETTE

Sur lie 2000★★★

8 ha	59,597			€3

This estate on the left bank of the Sèvre, between Gorges and Monnières, has produced a wine with bluish highlights. It is very well-balanced, developing long mineral flavours which are particularly noticeable. This typical 2000 is characteristic of the terroir and is an example of good wine-making.

🕿 EARL Dom. de Motte Charette, La Simplerie, 44190 Gorges Ⓥ

🕿 Marie-Odile et Pierre Mabit

DOM. DU MOULIN Sur lie 2000★★

6 ha	40,000			€3-5

The mill of La Bourchinière, squeezed between the Sèvre and the Maine, which meet nearby, overlooks the vines of this domaine. They have produced a very straightforward wine with a nose that evokes healthy grapes. This 2000 is light, fresh and fruity and ready to drink now.

🕿 Bernard Déramé, 2, rue du Courtil-Bochet, La Bourchinière, 44690 Saint-Fiacre-sur-Maine, tel. 02.40.54.83.80, fax 02.40.54.80.87, e-mail derame@wanadoo.fr Ⓥ Ⓨ by appt.

DOM. DU MOULIN DAVID

Sur lie 2000

3 ha	10,000			€3-5

This domaine, situated above the Sanguèze, which forms the border here between Brittany and Anjou, has produced a well-rounded, fruity wine. This 2000 has a character that reflects the terroir and would go well with a warm goat's-cheese salad.

🕿 Didier Blanloeil, Les Corbeillères, 44330 Vallet, tel. 02.40.33.91.23, fax 02.40.51.79.01 Ⓨ by appt.

ALAIN OLIVIER Cuvée spéciale 1997★

1.8 ha	2,600			€5-8

'It's a little joy ... a poem,' was one taster's comment on this wine from the gabbro soils north-west of Vallet. This 97 is a delicate

Muscadet de Sèvre-et-Maine

wines. This wine is no exception; the nose has a nuance of liquorice and toasted almond, followed by a fruity, mineral palate with a lively sparkle on the attack.

�']️ GAEC Moreau, La Petite Jaunaie, 44690 Château-Thébaud, tel. 02.40.06.61.42, fax 02.40.06.69.45 ✔
⏲ ev. day except Sun. 8am–7pm

CLOS DES RATELLES Sur lie 1999 ■ €3-5
☐ 1.5 ha 5,000

This 30-ha (74.1-acre) property not far from the *Maison des Vins* in La Haye-Fouassière (an absolute must for travellers who love wine) has produced a well-rounded, fresh and slightly acidic wine. It shows potential and is an example of high-quality wine-making.

➥ Michel Ripoche, 8, rue de la Torrelle, 44690 La Haye-Fouassière,
tel. 02.40.36.91.95, fax 02.40.36.73.19 ✔
⏲ by appt.

DOM. DAMIEN RINEAU
Sur lie Fleur de Gabbro 2000★
☐ 3.3 ha 25,000 ■ €5-8

In the complicated geology of the Pays Nantais, gabbro, a very basic rock, is in a class of its own. This is a good example of the sort of wines it produces, with an interesting nose of apple, hawthorn and banana. It is rounded and well-balanced on the palate, finishing on a lively, lemony note.

➥ Damien Rineau, La Maison-Neuve, 44190 Gorges, tel. 06.71.98.48.21, fax 02.40.06.98.27 ✔ ⏲ by appt.

DOM. DES ROUAUDIERES
Sur lie 1997★★
☐ 2 ha 2,000 ■ €5-8

La Rouaudière, above the meandering Sanguèze, produces a very attractive wine with complex aromas of citrus fruit, hazelnut and toast. After a lively, flattering attack, this Muscadet develops a fresh, flavoursome palate recalling the notes of the bouquet. The complex, full-bodied, long-lasting palate has sufficient character to allow it to be kept for several years.

➥ Jacky Bordet, La Rouaudière, 44330 Mouzillon, tel. 02.40.36.22.46, fax 02.40.39.84 ✔ ⏲ by appt.

DOM. DE L'ABBAYE DE
SAINTE-RADEGONDE Sur lie 2000★ €3
☐ 18.5 ha 137,604

All that remains of this abbey, which was destroyed during the Revolution, are the cellars which house a Museum of Vines and Wine. This Sèvre-et-Maine stands out because of its intense nose, where an underlying mineral quality forms the backdrop to banana and lemon aromas. It is equally fruity on the palate and slightly salty, but this original wine is still representative of its appellation.

---

pale-gold with green highlights, and has aromas of hawthorn, almond and toast. It is clean on the palate and pleasant all the way to the finish.

➥ EARL Alain Olivier, La Moucletière, 44330 Vallet, tel. 02.40.36.24.69,
fax 02.40.36.24.69 ✔ ⏲ by appt.

DOM. DU PARADIS Sur lie 2000★ €3-5
☐ 13 ha 25,400 ■

This 'Paradise' near Monnières has its own elegant 'Lourdes grotto' above the river Sèvre. The wine produced has complex aromas of crystallised fruit and honey on the nose, with hazelnut on the palate. This 2000 is developing some suppleness, but still has a touch of austerity on the finish. It will benefit from being kept for a few more months.

➥ Alain Caillé, 6, rue du Fief Seigneur, 44690 Monnières, tel. 02.40.54.63.57, fax 02.40.54.63.57 ✔ ⏲ by appt.

STEPHANE ET VINCENT PERRAUD
Sur lie Sélection des Cognettes 2000★★ €3-5
☐ 2.8 ha 12,000

Stéphanie and Vincent Perraud farm over 32 ha (79 acres). They have just launched a vine-leasing scheme. This enables their customers, who obtain their wine after Easter, to follow its development during the year before they receive it. There ought to be some enthusiasts for this level of traceability, if the quality of the wine is anything to go by; the wine has an intense nose of apricot, pear and almonds. This 2000 is well-balanced and long but still a little firm on the finish, suggesting that it will benefit from further maturation.

➥ Stéphane et Vincent Perraud, Bournigal, 44190 Clisson, tel. 02.40.54.45.62, fax 02.40.54.45.62 ✔ ⏲ ev. day except Sun. 8.30am–1pm 2pm–7pm

CH. DU POYET
Sur lie Elevé en fût de chêne 1999★ €5-8
☐ 0.7 ha 1,800

This very special wine, for the connoisseur, comes from a single parcel of vines planted in 1948. Nine months of barrel-ageing have given it delicate vanilla notes, and these flavours support the character of the wine, giving it a certain smoothness on the finish. Nevertheless, this Sèvre-et-Maine is still wholly typical in its lively attack and its suppleness. It is enjoyable on its own, or equally with grilled fish or a veal chop in cream sauce.

➥ EARL Famille Bonneau, Le Poyet, 44330 La Chapelle-Heulin,
tel. 02.40.06.74.52, fax 02.40.06.77.57.
e-mail chateau.dupoyet@wanadoo.fr ✔
⏲ ev. day except Sun. 9am–12.30pm 2pm–7pm

PRESTIGE DE L'HERMITAGE
Sur lie 2000★ €3-5
☐ 5 ha 33,000 ■

L'Hermitage, on slopes with gneiss and mica-schist subsoils above the river Maine, has a good reputation for the quality of its

CH. DU SAUT DU LOUP
Sur lie 2000★

2 ha | 7,000 | €3

This château was destroyed by a fire in 1900, and all that remains are the outbuildings and the entrance. The vineyard produces a wine with a complex nose of flowers and citrus fruit. The 2000 is well-made, with the palate revealing a good balance of richness and fruit, and a character that reflects the *terroir*.

Dominique Bouchaud, Le Patis Vinet, 44120 Vertou, tel. 02.40.06.15.37, fax 02.40.06.15.37 by appt.

DOM. YVES SAUVETRE
Sur lie 2000★

7 ha | 15,000 | €3-5

This wine from the schist soils of Loroux has a complex, fruity nose. After a straightforward attack, it shows itself to be rich and full, with long Williams pear flavours.

Yves Sauvêtre et Fils, La Landelle, 90, rue de la Durandière, 44430 Le Loroux-Bottereau, tel. 02.40.33.81.48, fax 02.40.33.87.67 by appt.

ANTOINE SUBILEAU
Sur lie Marie-Louise 2000

167 ha | 1,160,000 | €3

For a very widely sold wine, this is more than honourable. It has everything it ought to have and all in the right places: a clear appearance, a lemony nose and slight acidity on the palate with a pleasant attack.

SA Antoine Subileau, 6, rue Saint-Vincent, 44330 Vallet, tel. 02.40.36.69.70, fax 02.40.36.63.99, e-mail antoine-subileau@wanadoo.fr

SCEA Abbaye de Sainte-Radegonde, 44430 Le Loroux-Bottereau, tel. 02.40.03.74.78, fax 02.40.03.79.91 ev. day 9am-12 noon 2pm-6pm; Sun. by appt.

DOM. DU VAL-FLEURI
Sur lie 2000★

15 ha | 60,000 | €3-5

Yves and Jacqueline Delaunay took over a 27-ha (66.7-acre) vineyard in 1992. This wine, from a gneiss-amphibolite soil, has golden highlights and makes a powerful impression on the palate with its richness, fullness and balance.

Yves et Jacqueline Delaunay, Le Val-Fleuri, 44430 Le Loroux-Bottereau, tel. 02.40.33.86.84, fax 02.40.33.88.99, e-mail y.delaunay@infonie.fr by appt.

DANIEL ET GERARD VINET
Sur lie 1997★★

n.c. | n.c.

Some parcels of land in the Domaine de La Quilla belonged to Charles Héron, one of the eight wine-growers who founded the Muscadet appellation. This wine is still very lively and will appeal to experienced palates, with its balance, fine expression of flavours (citrus fruit and dried fruit plus a touch of liquorice) and its length.

Daniel et Gérard Vinet, La Quilla, 44690 La Haye-Fouassière, tel. 02.40.54.88.96, fax 02.40.54.89.84 ev. day except Sun. 8am-12.30pm 1.30pm-5pm

Muscadet Côtes de Grand Lieu

DOM. DU FIEF GUERIN
Sur lie 2000★★

17 ha | 115,000 | €3-5

This 2000, with its green highlights, has an intense nose of white peaches. It is fresh, delicate and aromatic, with a slightly salty touch that is typical of the appellation. The **Clos de La Sénaigerie 2000** is also worth mentioning, and comes from vines right on the banks of the Lac de Grand-Lieu.

Luc et Jérôme Choblet, 44830 Bouaye, tel. 02.40.65.44.92, fax 02.40.65.58.02 by appt.

L'ACHENEAU
Sur lie 2000★

20 ha | 120,000 | €3-5

The Acheneau runs from the Lac de Grand-Lieu to the Loire or the other way, depending on the tides and seasons. It has given its name to this supple, full-bodied Muscadet with its long finish, charming balance and finesse. In the wide range offered by the Vignerons de La Noëlle, the memorable **Coteaux d'Ancenis Gamay La Pierre Couvretière 2000 red**, with its ripe-fruit and spice aromas, was also commended.

Les Vignerons de La Noëlle, bd des Alliés, BP 155, 44150 Ancenis, tel. 02.40.98.92.72, fax 02.40.98.96.70, e-mail vignerons-noelle@cana.fr by appt.

DOM. DE LA GUILLAUDIERE
Sur lie Vieilles vignes 2000★

3.6 ha | 25,000 | €3

Although it is located right in the Sèvre-et-Maine area, the Château des Gillières has extended its activities as far as the Côtes de Grand Lieu, and not without success. After a very fruity nose with notes of honey and white peach, this wine has a soft, gentle attack on the palate before a long finish.

SAS des Gillières, Ch. des Gillières, 44690 La Haye-Fouassière, tel. 02.40.54.80.05, fax 02.40.54.89.56

DOM. DE LA PIERRE BLANCHE

Sur lie 2000 · €3

□ · 7.5 ha · 10,600 · ■ · ● · ■

This wine is undoubtedly original; the only Muscadet from the Vendée in the 2002 *Guide*. Apart from this detail, its slight sparkle, fresh nose, the fine, soft attack on the palate and lively finish, make it a very typical Muscadet of the Côtes de Grand Lieu.

➽ Gérard Épiard, La Pierre Blanche,
85660 Saint-Philbert-de-Bouaine,
tel. 02.51.41.93.42, fax 02.51.41.91.71 Ⓥ
Ⴅ by appt.

Gros-Plant AOVDQS

Gros-Plant is a dry, white wine, Nantais is a dry, white wine, AOVDQS since 1954, made from a single grape variety, Folle Blanche, originally from the Charente, and here called Gros-Plant. The vineyard area is 2,213 ha (5,466 acres), producing around 162,868 hl (4,299,715 gal) in the year 2000. Like Muscadet, Gros-Plant can be bottled on the lees and is perfect for seafood in general and shellfish in particular. It should also be served chilled, but not ice-cold at 8°–9° C (46.4–48.2° F)

DOM. DES BEGAUDIERES

Sur lie 2000★★

□ · 3.05 ha · 5,000 · ■ · ● · €3-5

'A wine made in the old-fashioned way,' said one of the tasters, which is hardly surprising when you know that vines have been grown on this domaine since at least the 17th century. This wine, with its floral nose and finesse on the palate, is very typical and will please traditionalists.

➽ GAEC Jauffrineau-Boulanger,
Bonne-Fontaine, 44330 Vallet,
tel. 02.40.36.22.79, fax 02.40.36.34.90 Ⓥ
Ⴅ by appt.

DOM. DE BEL-AIR Sur lie 2000★

□ · 2 ha · 4,000 · ■ · ● · €3

Right next to Nantes-Atlantique international airport, this domaine produces a pale Gros-Plant with a pleasant nose from 35-year-old vines on a sand and pebble subsoil. It is well-balanced and supple on the palate.

➽ EARL Bouin-Jacquet, Dom. de Bel-Air,
44860 Saint-Aignan-de-Grand-Lieu,
tel. 02.51.70.80.80, fax 02.51.70.80.79 Ⓥ
Ⴅ ev. day except Sun. 2pm–7pm; Sat. 9am–12 noon

DOM. DE BELLEVUE 2000★★

□ · 2 ha · 5,000 · ■ · ● · €3

On the Nantes-Montaignu road, just before Aigrefeuille, Jean-Yves Templier offers a typical Gros-Plant. The nose is very classical, with nuances of hawthorn and citrus fruit. The structure on the palate is good, with a slightly acidic finish, which gives it length.

➽ Jean-Yves Templier, Dom. de Bellevue,
44140 Aigrefeuille-sur-Maine,
tel. 02.40.03.86.90, fax 02.40.03.86.90 Ⓥ
Ⴅ ev. day 8.30am–7pm

DOM. GUY BOSSARD Sur lie 2000★

□ · 2.3 ha · 9,000 · ■ · ● · €3-5

In 1972 Guy Bossard started growing grapes organically, and between 1972 and 1996 he employed biodynamic methods. Nowadays he is a standard-bearer for the anti-GM revolution. He produces a Gros-Plant with a warm, intense nose of ripe fruit. It is fruity on the palate and very dry. This pleasant wine has a long finish with notes of lemon.

➽ Guy Bossard, La Bretonnière,
44430 Le Landreau, tel. 02.40.06.40.91,
fax 02.40.06.46.79 Ⓥ Ⴅ by appt.

DOM. DE CHANTEGROLLE

Prestige Sur lie 2000★

□ · 0.75 ha · 7,000 · ■ · ● · €3-5

This Gros-Plant, from the friable, granite soil that is a feature of Château-Thébaud, has a very intense perfumed-floral nose. It is supple and rounded on the palate, with a touch of mineral and excellent long flavours on the finish.

➽ Jean-Michel Poiron, Chantegrolle,
44690 Château-Thébaud,
tel. 02.40.06.56.42, fax 02.40.06.58.02 Ⓥ
Ⴅ by appt.

CLOS DES ROSIERS Sur lie 2000★

□ · 1.5 ha · 2,000 · ■ · ● · €3

The *Guide* has often been enchanted by the Les Rosiers Gros-Plant. The 2000 is slightly sparkling, supple, rounded and rich, though still very typical. It is a shame that so little of it is produced.

➽ Philippe Laure, Les Rosiers, 44330 Vallet,
tel. 02.40.33.91.83, fax 02.40.36.39.28 Ⓥ
Ⴅ by appt.

DOM. DU HAUT BOURG

Sur lie 2000★

□ · 5 ha · 8,000 · ■ · ● · €3

Michel Choblet and his son, Henri, are well-known for their Gros-Plant. The 2000 is very typical of the appellation, with its slight sparkle and golden highlights. It has a floral nose with mineral nuances and a slightly acidic palate finishing on a lemony note.

☎ Michel et Hervé Choblet, Dom. du Haut-Bourg, 44830 Bouaye, tel. 02.40.65.47.69, fax 02.40.32.64.01 ▽
🍷 by appt.

CH. DE LA BOITAUDIERE 2000★

4 ha | 41,318 | →3

This large domaine north of Landeau has produced a clear Gros-Plant with very typical green highlights. Although its nose is a little immature, its palate of green apple reveals a good balance before finishing on a mineral, slightly acidic note.
☎ EARL Ch. de La Boitaudière, La Boitaudière, 44430 Le Landreau, tel. 02.40.06.42.69
🍷 Serge Sauvètre

LA CHATELIERE Sur lie 2000★★

40 ha | 400,000

Although the village of Tillières is situated in Maine-et-Loire, it is part of the Nantes region from the viticultural point of view. The wines it makes are good, as we can see for this typical Gros-Plant, likeable and long on the palate. Further confirmation comes from the two stars awarded to the **Muscadet Sèvre-et-Maine sur lie Cave de Val et Mont 2000** from the same winemakers; it is powerful, well-balanced and fresh. One star was awarded to the **Gros-Plant 2000 Cave de La Perrière**, which is also a good example of its type: dry and straightforward with a lemony finish.
☎ Rolandeau SA, La Frémondière, BP 2, 49230 Tillières, tel. 02.41.70.45.93, fax 02.41.70.43.74, e-mail rolandeau@free.fr

DOM. DE LA COGNARDIERE 2000

1.55 ha | 6,000 | €3-5

This domaine between the Sèvre and Goulaine produces a Gros-Plant with green highlights and a typical nose. The palate has the classic aromas of green apple, lifted by a note of acidity.
☎ Jean-Claude et Pierre-Yves Nouet, 1, imp. des Pressoirs, La Cognardière, 44330 Le Pallet, tel. 02.40.80.41.72, fax 02.40.80.41.72 🍷 by appt.

CH. LA FORCHETIERE Sur lie 2000★

20 ha | 40,000

This wine from this vast estate in the extreme south of the Loire-Atlantique is a good ambassador for Gros-Plant. The nose is developed, with intense floral notes, and complements the supple and delightful palate with just the amount of liveliness it needs.
☎ SCEA Champteloup La Forchetière, 44650 Corcoué-sur-Logne, tel. 02.40.36.66.00, fax 02.40.36.26.83

DOM. DE LA MOMENIERE Sur lie 2000★★

5 ha | 10,000 | €3-5

Above the Gueubert, which separates the commune of Landreau from that of Vallet, La Momenière produces a well-balanced Gros-Plant that is a good example of the appellation, with just the right amount of acidity. It would be interesting to keep a few bottles in the cellar for a while, because the jury think that it will benefit from a little ageing.
☎ EARL Joseph Audouin, Dom. de La Momenière, 44430 Le Landreau, tel. 02.40.06.43.04, fax 02.40.06.47.89 ▽
🍷 ev. day 9am–7pm

DOM. DE LA ROCHERIE

Sur lie 2000★ 1.5 ha | 5,000 | →3

Even if La Rocherie only uses 6% of its area for Gros-Plant, this one deserves a round of applause; last year it was awarded a *coup de cœur*. It is very typical in appearance, slightly sparkling, with a floral nose and a rather mineral palate. The overall effect is one of finesse.
☎ Daniel Gratas, La Rocherie, 44430 Le Landreau, tel. 02.40.06.41.55, fax 02.40.06.48.92 ▽
🍷 ev. day except Sun. 8am–8pm

DOM. DE LA TOURLAUDIERE

Sur lie 2000 1.6 ha | 9,000 | €5-8 | →3

This domaine is almost always included in the *Guide*, either for its Muscadet or its Gros-Plant (they were even awarded a *coup de cœur* two years ago). Though this wine lacks an intense nose, it is interesting because of its palate, which has a very typical character that reflects the local *terroir*.
☎ EARL Petiteau-Gaubert, La Tourlaudière, 44330 Vallet, tel. 02.40.36.24.86, fax 02.40.36.29.72, e-mail contact@jtourlaudiere.com ▽
🍷 ev. day 9.30am–12.30pm 2pm–7.30pm

DOM. DE L'AUBINERIE 2000★

1.5 ha | 11,000 | €3-5

Viticulture in the Pays Nantais owes a great deal to the meanderings of the Sanguèze, which has carved out many favourable slopes. This domaine, above one of these meanders, has produced a long, very lively, white Gros-Plant with a flowery nose and fruity palate.
☎ Jean-Marc Guérin, 26, La Barillère, 44330 Mouzillon, tel. 02.40.36.37.06, fax 02.40.36.37.06 🍷 by appt.

LE DEMI-BOEUF Sur lie 2000

4 ha | 11,000

Under this mysterious name (it recalls a meal which the Vendéen rebels of 1793 did not have time to finish), there is a very typical Gros-Plant with an aromatic bouquet and well-balanced palate.
☎ EARL Michel Malidain, Le Demi-Boeuf, 44310 La Limouzinière, tel. 02.40.05.82.29, fax 02.40.05.95.97 🍷 by appt.

DOM. LES COINS Sur lie 2000★

n.c. | 10,000

Right down in the south of the Loire-Atlantique, the soils of Corcoué-sur-Logne are reputed to be well-suited to the Gros-

Fiefs Vendéens AOVDQS

Historically these domains were the property of Cardinal Richelieu. The name of this appellation is evocative of the history of these wines, replanted in the Middle Ages, as so often at the instigation of the monks, and later enjoyed by the Cardinal. The denomination AOVDQS was awarded in 1984 in recognition of the efforts made to improve quality and these continue on the 449 ha (1,109 acres) planted with vines.

The Mareuil region produces rosés and fine reds with good bouquet and fruit from Gamay, Cabernet and Pinot Noir; the whites are little known. The Brem vineyard, not far from the sea, produces dry whites from Chenin and Grolleau Gris, but also some rosés and red wines. In the area round Fontenay-le-Comte, dry whites are made (from Chenin, Colombard, Melon and Sauvignon), while rosés and reds (Gamay and Cabernet) come from the regions of Pissotte and Vix. These wines should be drunk young, partnering the appropriate dishes.

CH. DE L'OISELINIERE
Sur lie 1999★★

☐   1.7 ha   2,000   ▯ ♦ €3-5

In 1635, L'Oiselinière was the first estate in the region to be planted with Melon de Bourgogne. Its Italianate architecture, which is typical of the town of Clisson, has earned it historic-monument status. It is especially well-known for its Muscadet, but also produces a small quantity of Gros-Plant, which has a mineral nose with notes of brioche. It is full and rich on the palate, revealing an acidic structure that gives it freshness as well as plenty of persistent flavour.

☛ SC Aulanier, Ch. de L'Oiselinière, 44190 Gorges, tel. 02.40.06.91.59, fax 02.40.06.98.48, e-mail oiseliniere@chateau-oiseliniere.com ✉ 🍷 by appt.

DOM. DU PARC Sur lie 2000★

☐   15 ha   90,000   ▯ ♦ €3

The green-rock, amphibolite subsoils are said to be favourable for the Gros-Plant, and the vines from this domaine give a very typical wine with delicate, flowery aromas and richness on the palate. The same year produced a **Muscadet Côtes de Grand Lieu Domaine du Parc** (one star) which is worth investigating. It is a typical wine, rich, rounded and well-balanced, with mineral notes dominating the nose and green-fruit aromas uppermost on the palate.

☛ Pierre Dahéron, Le Parc, 44650 Corcoué-sur-Logne, tel. 02.40.05.86.11, fax 02.40.05.94.98 ✉ 🍷 by appt.

DOM. DES PETITES COSSARDIERES Sur lie 2000★★

☐   1.8 ha   8,000   ▯ ♦ €3

This Gros-Plant offers quality, not quantity. It is well-balanced and a good example of its type, with plenty of freshness. This perfectly made wine would go well with mussels or oysters, or on its own, just for the pleasure of it.

☛ Jean-Claude Couillaud, 17, rue de la Loire, 44430 Le Landreau, tel. 02.40.06.42.81, fax 02.40.06.49.14 ✉ 🍷 by appt.

CH. DU ROCHER Sur lie 2000★

☐   4 ha   41,290   ▯ ♦ €3

This lovely 18th-century property would have been the region's first wine-growing estate. However, the cultivation of the vine around here doubtless dates back to the Romans. This Gros-Plant develops a complex

nose, floral at first then veering towards citrus fruits. It is long and supple, and the palate shows a style that is very characteristic of the area.

☛ Hervouet et Bes de Berc, Ch. du Rocher, 44310 Saint-Philbert-de-Grand-Lieu, tel. 02.40.78.83.03 ✉

Plant. Jean-Claude Malidain's wine develops a nose of toast and is slightly evocative of Sauvignon, but is nevertheless perfectly typical on the palate, with a mineral, slightly acidic finish.

☛ Jean-Claude Malidain, Le Petit Coin, 44650 Corcoué-sur-Logne, tel. 02.40.05.95.95, fax 02.40.05.80.99, e-mail jeanclaude.malidain@free.fr ✉ 🍷 by appt.

XAVIER COIRIER
Pissotte Sélection 2000★

▮   10 ha   60,000   ▯ ♦ €5-8

Pinot Noir, Gamay and Cabernet have come together to produce this candy-pink wine with an intense nose. The palate is full of the flavour of red berries (cherry, blackcurrant and raspberry) and is animated by a slight vivacity. It would go well with charcuterie (pork products).

☛ Xavier Coirier, 15, rue des Gélinières, 85200 Pissotte, tel. 02.51.69.40.98, fax 02.51.69.74.15 ✉ 🍷 by appt.

DOM. DES DAMES

Mareuil Les Agates 2000★★

4 ha | 14,000 | €3-5

This domaine, run by women, has brought together Gamay Noir, Cabernet Franc and a little Négrette to produce this wine with ruby highlights and earthy, red-berry aromas. It is quite tannic on tasting and will benefit from keeping for several months. The **Mareuil Les Pierres Blanches 2000 white** was awarded two stars for its balance and persistence. A well-balanced **Mareuil rosé** and the **Les Aigues Marines 2000** also deserve a mention.

GAEC Vignoble Daniel Gentreau, Follet, 85320 Rosnay, tel. 02.51.30.55.39, fax 02.51.28.22.36
ev. day except Sun. 9am–12.30pm, 2.30pm–7.30pm; 15 Sept–15 June by appt.

DOM. DE LA CHAIGNÉE Vix 2000★

5 ha | 30,000 | €5-8

At the edge of the amazing Marais Poitevin, this domaine (one of the world leaders in vine grafting) has produced a ruby-coloured wine with a fruity nose. After a lively attack, the palate reveals a gamey note and a definite tannic character, which suggests it would benefit from keeping for several more months.

Vignobles Mercier Frères, La Chaignée, 85770 Vix, tel. 02.51.00.65.14, fax 02.51.00.67.60, e-mail info@mercier-groupe.com by appt.

DOM. DE LA VIEILLE RIBOULERIE

Mareuil Cuvée des Moulins brûlés 2000★

4 ha | 8,000 | €5-8

This *cuvée*, one would think, owes its name to 'collateral damage' during the wars in the Vendée. It has a raspberry colour and an intense, earthy fruit nose with a peppery note. On the palate it is well-balanced and sufficiently long. The domaine also produces a very successful **Mareuil 2000 white** (one star) with a fresh attack and aromas of very ripe apple.

Hubert Macquigneau, Le Plessis, 85320 Rosnay, tel. 02.51.30.59.54, fax 02.51.28.21.80 by appt.

DOM. DU LUX EN ROC

Brem 2000

2.5 ha | 5,000 | €3-5

Négrette and Gamay Noir, supported by a little Cabernet Sauvignon, come together to produce this deep-red wine with a purple rim. It is well-balanced on the palate, revealing a rustic, tannic character.

Jean-Pierre Richard, 5, imp. Richelieu, 85470 Brem-sur-Mer, tel. 02.51.90.56.84 by appt.

CH. MARIE DU FOU Mareuil 2000★

3.73 ha | 30,000 | €5-8

White Mareuil is a little-known wine, which is a shame, if this one is anything to go by. This wine has been barrel-aged in the cellars of a medieval fortress. Although the nose is still very dominated by oak, on the palate it is rich, sufficiently long and enlivened by a light acidity.

Jean et Jérémie Mourat, 5, rue de la Trémolle, 85320 Mareuil-sur-Lay, tel. 02.51.97.20.10, fax 02.51.97.21.58, e-mail chateau.marie.du.fou@wanadoo.fr
ev. day except Sun. 8am–12 noon 2pm–6pm

Coteaux d'Ancenis AOVDQS

CH. DE ROSNAY

Mareuil Vieilles vignes 2000★★

16 ha | 50,000 | €3-5

This little 19th-century château between the Yon and the Lay has married Pinot Noir and Gamay Noir to produce a light-pink wine. It is very aromatic on the nose (boiled sweets), and on the palate it starts with a lively attack and develops a pleasant note of red berries. The **Mareuil Prestige 2000 white** and the **Mareuil Elegance 2000 red** from the same domaine are both noteworthy, having being awarded a star each, the first for its grapefruit aromas and fresh attack and the second for its intense red-berry nose and promising tannins.

Jard, 5, rue du Perrot, 85320 Rosnay, tel. 02.51.30.59.06, fax 02.51.28.21.01 by appt.

DOM. SAINT-NICOLAS

Brem Cuvée Prestige 2000★★

5 ha | 18,000 | €5-8

This large domaine is situated on the edge of the former salt marshes of the Pays des Olonnes. It produces a candy-pink wine, its fruity nose combining with a hint of broom. It is well-balanced and rich, developing attractive raspberry and strawberry flavours on the palate. The **Cuvée Prestige 99 red** is also singled out (one star). It is very intense and tannic, and should be aged for one or two more years.

M.-J. Michon et Fils, 11, rue des Vallées, 85470 Brem-sur-Mer, tel. 02.51.33.13.04, fax 02.51.33.18.42, e-mail caves.michon@cer85cernet.fr by appt.

Coteaux d'Ancenis AOVDQS

The Coteaux d'Ancenis wine region has been classified AOVDQS since 1954. Four single-variety wines are produced: from Gamay (80% of production), Cabernet, Chenin and Malvoisie. The area under vines is 253.6 ha (626.39 acres) and in 2000 production was 16,556 hl (437,078 gal), of which about 200 hl (5,280 gal) was white wine.

Anjou

The geographical area of this regional appellation, made up of a group of nearly 200 communes, incorporates all the Anjou AOCs. White wines are produced (57,989 hl/1,530,910 gal) in 2000 and so are reds (255,358 hl/6,741,451 gal). For many, Anjou covers about 14,500 ha (35,815 acres) and produces from 800,000 to 1 million hl (21,120,000–26,400,000 gal), depending on the weather.

As always, the combination of *terroir* and climate determines the character of the local wines. However, it is important to identify the clear difference between those grown on 'Anjou Black' soils, of schists and other primary rocks from the Massif Armorican, and those produced on 'Anjou White', or Saumurois, the sedimentary soils of the Paris Basin, where white, chalky limestone is most in evidence. The rivers and streams of the region have also played an important role in the wine trade: one can still find ruins of the little loading ports on the Layon. Planting density is between 4,500 and 5,000 plants per hectare; pruning, which used mainly to be in goblet or fan shapes, is now more usually in cordons.

Anjou has always been best known for its sweet white wines, those from the Coteaux du Layon being the most highly rated. However, wine styles are changing, moving more towards semi-dry or dry white wines and to red wines. In Saumur, the reds are the most highly regarded, alongside the sparkling wines which have seen a significant increase, particularly the AOC Saumur-Mousseux and Crémant de Loire.

Anjou-Saumur

The Anjou and Saumur vineyards occupy Maine-et-Loire, extending a little into the north of the Vienne and the Deux-Sèvres. This undulating landscape, criss-crossed with numerous watercourses, lies at the northern limits of vine cultivation, under the influence of an Atlantic climate.

Vines have always been grown on the slopes of the Loire, the Layon, the Aubance, the Loir and the Thouet. At the end of the 19th century, the vineyard was at its most extensive. Dr Guyot, in a survey for the Minister of Agriculture, reported 31,000 ha (76,570 acres) under vines in Maine-et-Loire. Phylloxera was to decimate the vineyard, as everywhere else in France. Replanting took place at the beginning of the 20th century, with further efforts in the 1950s and 1960s, though it fell back thereafter. Today, the vineyard

---

DOM. DU BUISSON Gamay 2000

5 ha · 49,600 · –€3

On the eastern border of the Coteaux d'Ancenis, in the Anjou fringes of the Nantais vineyard area, this domaine produces a Gamay rosé with a pleasant nose of mango and fresh butter, slightly tart on the palate and with a very persistent finish. The **Gros-Plant sur lie 2000**, supple and very typical, also impressed the Jury.

☛ EARL Dom. du Buisson, Le Buisson, 49410 La Chapelle-Saint-Florent, tel. 02.41.72.89.52, fax 02.41.72.77.13 ▼
▼ by appt.

DOM. DES GENAUDIERES

Malvoisie 2000★★

□ 1 ha · 5,000 · €5-8

In the broad range of Genaudières wines, this Malvoisie certainly occupies a marginal position, but it is interesting because of its nose (tropical and citrus fruit) and its well-rounded, rich, integrated palate with very immediate flavours. This is a very fine bottle of wine for aperitifs or dessert.

☛ EARL Athimon et ses Enfants, Dom. des Génaudiéres, 44850 Le Cellier, tel. 02.40.25.40.27, fax 02.40.25.35.61 ▼
▼ ev. day except Sun. 8.30am–12.30pm 2pm–6.30pm

wine is synonymous with sweet or medium white wines made with Chenin or Pineau de la Loire. However, in line with the trend towards drier wines, local producers have opted for mixing in Chardonnay or Sauvignon, to a maximum limit of 20%. Production of red wines, from Cabernet Franc and Cabernet Sauvignon, is in the process of altering the image of the region.

■ **CH. DE BELLEVUE 2000** 3 ha 10,000 ⧉ €3-5

The 19th-century château was acquired by the grandfather in 1894. Every year in July, the Fête des Vins Liquoreux d'Anjou, a celebration of the local sweet wines, is held in its grounds. The 28-ha (69.2-acre) vineyard is run by M. Tijou and his son. Their Anjou, which is red with a touch of black and purple highlights, releases aromas of fruit macerated in brandy. The fruity palate is pleasant, though a little austere on the finish. It is a well-made wine which is worth keeping for a year or two.

EARL Tijou et Fils, Ch. de Bellevue, 49190 Saint-Aubin-de-Luigné, tel. 02.41.78.33.11, fax 02.41.78.67.84 ▼ by appt.

■ **DOM. DE BRIZE 2000★★★** 3 ha 13,000 ⧉ €3-5

This domaine of 40 ha (98.8 acres) or so is managed by Luc Delhumeau, an oenologist who is married to another oenologist. His sister is an oenologist too. It is hardly surprising that their entry is covered with stars in every edition of the *Guide*. This wine is a model for the appellation. Everything about it is seductive: its lively ruby colour; its subtle palette of aromas, mingling red berries, flowers and amylic notes; and its luscious palate, which leaves a sensation of ripe fruit

Domaine de Brizé
2000
ANJOU
APPELLATION ANJOU CONTRÔLÉE
ROUGE
Mis en bouteille au domaine par
Marc et Luc DELHUMEAU S.C.A.
Domaine de Brizé · 49540 Martigné-Briand · France
750 ml

Anjou and Saumur

Legend:
- Anjou
- Coteaux de l'Aubance
- Anjou-Coteaux de la Loire
- Savennières
- Coteaux du Layon
- Saumur
- Saumur-Champigny
- 1 Bonnezeaux
- 2 Quarts de Chaume
- ⸺⸺ Department boundaries
- ● Wine-growing areas

0 5 miles
0 5 10 km

N

DEUX-SÈVRES
MAINE-ET-LOIRE
VIENNE
ET-INDRE
LOIRE

Cholet, Chemillé, Vihiers, Thouarcé, Doué-la-Fontaine, Thouars, Montreuil-Bellay, Allones, Montsoreau, Saumur, Saint-Georges-sur-Loire, Chalonnes-sur-Loire, Saint-Clément-de-la-Place, Savennières, Beaulieu-sur-Layon, Brissac, Angers, Chefres, Seiches-sur-le-Loir, Cornillé-les-Caves, Durtal

965 THE LOIRE VALLEY

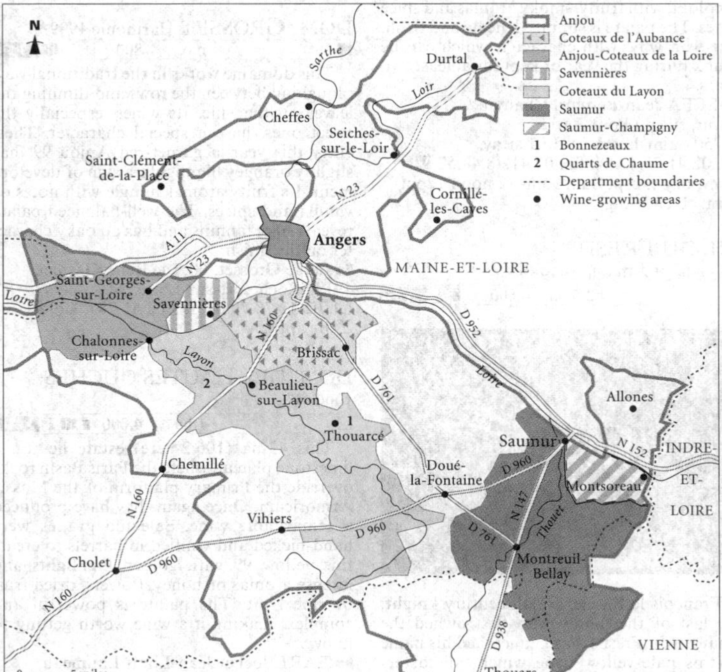

and freshness. This wine has a remarkable balance, combining lightness and richness, delicacy and intensity.

➤ SCEA Marc et Luc Delhumeau, Dom. de Brizé, 49540 Martigné-Briand, tel. 02.41.59.43.35, fax 02.41.59.66.90, e-mail delhumeau.scea@free.fr ☑
☐ by appt.
➤ Luc et Line Delhumeau

DOM. DES CHESNAIES 2000★
■ n.c. 10,000 €3-5

As soon as he was settled in this domaine (acquired in 1998). Olivier de Cenival gained a place in the *Guide* with this intense black Anjou, with intense red-berry and spice aromas and a full, supple palate, slightly austere on the finish. This is a powerful, richly structured wine, which needs to age further. Wait at least a year before drinking it.

➤ Olivier de Cenival, La Noue, 49190 Denée, tel. 02.41.78.79.80, fax 02.41.68.05.61, e-mail odcenival@aol.com ☑ ☐ by appt.

DOM. DE CLAYOU 2000★
■ 2 ha 14,000 €3-5

J.-B.Chauvin has taken up the baton in defence of the wine-growers of Saint-Lambert-du-Lattay, the Anjou village with the highest proportion of vines. His red Anjou, light and well-balanced, is well-representative of the appellation. It is bright ruby in colour, with fruity, smoky aromas and spice notes. The palate is supple, delicate and fresh. This is a wine with character, which can be drunk during the year or kept for at least two years.

➤ SCEA Jean-Bernard Chauvin, 18 bis, rue du Pont-Barré, 49750 Saint-Lambert-du-Lattay, tel. 02.41.78.42.84, fax 02.41.78.48.52 ☑ ☐ ev. day except Sun. 9am–12 noon 12pm–7pm; cl. end Aug.

CH. DU FRESNE
Chevalier Le Bascle 1999★★★
☐ 2.5 ha 6,600 ■ ♦ €5-8

François le Bascle, a 17th-century knight, the last of the family who first owned the Château du Fresne, has bequeathed his name to this pale-yellow wine which, all tasters agreed, is a model Anjou white. Its aromas of apples and pears, ripe fruit and flowers are enhanced by the fact that the harvest was

hand-picked, while the unctuous palate, both rich and delicate, gives the impression of chewing golden, overripe grapes. This wine would be a good complement to fish in sauce.

➤ Vignobles Robin-Bretault, Ch. du Fresne, 49380 Faye-d'Anjou, tel. 02.41.54.30.88, fax 02.41.54.17.52, e-mail fresne@voila.fr ☑ ☐ by appt.

DOM. GAUDARD 2000★★
☐ 3.32 ha 10,000 €5-8

Pierre Aguilas has been President of the Fédération Viticole des Vins d'Anjou-Saumur (Anjou-Saumur Wines Viticultural Federation) for many years. Judging by his wines, which have been regularly selected by the *Guide* since the very first edition (often being highly placed), his responsibilities do not prevent him from taking good care of his domaine. This clear-ruby Anjou is remarkable for its balance, freshness and fruitiness, which is the key to the tasting. Its delicate nose mingles red and black fruit. The same delicious sensation of fruitiness comes across again on an attractive palate. It is clear that behind all these attractive features lies a very ripe vintage.

➤ Pierre Aguilas, Dom. Gaudard, rte de Saint-Aubin, 49290 Chaudefonds-sur-Layon, tel. 02.41.78.10.68, fax 02.41.78.67.72 ☑ ☐ ev. day except Sun. 9am–12 noon 2pm–7pm

DOM. GROSSET Harmonie 1999★
■ n.c. 800 ■▯ €5-8

This domaine works in the traditional way, ploughing between the rows and thinning the leaves on the vine. Its wines, especially the sweet ones, have a special character. Their entry this year, a garnet-red Anjou 99, has slightly orangey highlights, a sign of development. Its fruity aromas mingle with notes of vanilla and spices. The well-balanced palate reveals silky tannins and has an oaky character on the finish.

➤ Serge Grosset, 60, rue René-Gasnier, 49190 Rochefort-sur-Loire, tel. 02.41.78.67, fax 02.41.78.79.79 ☑ ☐ by appt.

DOM. DES HAUTES OUCHES 1999★★
☐ 1 ha 4,000 ■▯ ♦ €5-8

This 43-ha (106.2-acre) estate lies on a limestone plateau where the Paris Basin rocks override the Primary platform of the Massif Armoricain. Once again they have produced a remarkable wine. Selected grapes were hand-picked and vinified in barrels to create this yellow 99 with golden highlights and intense aromas of honey, flowers, dried fruit or ripe fruit. The palate is powerful and complex, making it a wine worth getting to know.

➤ EARL Joël et Jean-Louis Lhumeau, 9, rue Saint-Vincent, Linières, 49700 Brigné-sur-Layon, tel. 02.41.59.30.51, fax 02.41.59.31.75 ☑ ☐ by appt.

DOM. DES IRIS 2000★

12 ha　93,330　€3-5

This elegantly labelled wine is an intense red colour and releases light, delicate aromas of fruit macerated in brandy, red berries and roasted coffee beans. In spite of being supported by firm, well-structured tannins, the palate is not lacking in charm. This is a wine which is ready to drink, but also suitable for keeping another four years.

Jack Petit, La Roche Coutant, 49540 Tigné, tel. 02.41.40.22.50, fax 02.41.40.22.60, e-mail j.verdier@wanadoo.fr

DOM. DE LA BELLE ANGEVINE

Vieilles vignes Cuvée Or 1999★

0.25 ha　1,000　€5-8

The Belle Angevine is the heroine of an old local legend. The domaine on the Coteaux du Layon was established in 1993 and is run by Florence Dufour, whose wines are regularly mentioned in the *Guide*. This Cuvée Or is a pale, clear yellow and has an interesting balance. Its citrus fruit aromas (lemon and grapefruit) and liveliness on the palate combine to give a feeling of freshness that suggests it should be drunk with grilled fish or seafood.

Florence Dufour, Dom. de La Belle Angevine, La Motte, 49750 Beaulieu-sur-Layon, tel. 02.41.78.34.86, fax 02.41.72.81.58, e-mail fldufour@club-internet.fr by appt.

DOM. DE LA CROIX DES LOGES 2000★

10 ha　10,000　€3-5

This 40-ha (98.8-acre) domaine, which is regularly mentioned in the *Guide*, has particularly distinguished itself with two consecutive *coups de coeur* for its Cabernet d'Anjou. Their talents are not limited to rosé: this 2000 shows that they also know how to make powerful reds with a lot of potential (even better than one would expect from this AOC). This Anjou is an intense red, with red-berry and spice aromas. It is well-balanced, with a rich palate and a fairly imposing but well-integrated tannic structure. It should be kept for at least one year.

SCEA Bonnin et Fils, Dom. de La Croix des Loges, 49540 Martigné-Briand, tel. 02.41.59.43.58, fax 02.41.59.41.11, e-mail bonninlesloges@aol.com

DOM. LA GABETTERIE 2000

2 ha　7,000　€3-5

This 40-ha (98.8-acre) estate, a few kilometres from the hamlet of Bonnezeaux, produces an intense ruby-coloured Anjou with a good balance, which was appreciated by the Jury. The aromas are of red berries and fruit.

macerated in brandy. The palate is pleasant, though slightly astringent on the finish. This wine is ready to be drunk, but it can be kept for a year or two.

Vincent Reuiller, La Gabetterie, 49380 Faveraye-Machelets, tel. 02.41.54.14.99, fax 02.41.54.33.12 by appt.

DOM. DE LA GRETONNELLE 2000★

1 ha　1,000　€3-5

This is one of the most successful Anjou whites, from a domaine in the north of the *département* of Deux-Sèvres. Its nose is dominated by notes of pear drops and citrus fruit, linked to careful fermentation and vinification at a temperature to preserve aromas. These aromas are complemented by fragrances such as flowers and ripe fruit, which testify to a ripe vintage. The wine as a whole is very well-balanced, leaving a sensation of freshness that is typical of Loire white wines.

EARL Charruault-Schmale, Les Landes, 79290 Bouillé-Loretz, tel. 05.49.67.04.49 by appt.

LES VIGNES DE L'ALMA 2000★★

3.5 ha　10,000　€3-5

This is a small 10-ha (24.7-acre) property on a plateau in the west of the *département* of Maine-et-Loire. From the domaine there is a view over the Loire Valley and Saint-Florent-le-Vieil, an ancient city where some of the decisive events of the Vendée War (1793–1795) took place. These vines have produced a garnet-red wine that has been highly complimented. The nose is reminiscent of ripe-fruit, grenadine and smoky aromas. The palate is unctuous and delicious, leaving an intense sensation of red berries, with a few vegetal, green-pepper notes on the mid-palate. This is a very fine representative of the appellation.

Roland Chevalier, L'Alma, 49410 Saint-Florent-le-Vieil, tel. 02.41.72.71.09, fax 02.41.72.63.77 ev. day except Sun. 8.30am–12.30pm 2pm–7pm

LES CAVES DE LA LOIRE

Prestige 2000★

13 ha　100,000　€5-8

This wine has a strong red colour, intense red- and black-berry aromas, with a few green-pepper flavours on the mid-palate, and an attractive tannic structure on the finish. This all makes for a very successful wine that is ready to drink now, but could be kept for a year or two.

Les Caves de La Loire, rte de Vauchrétien, 49320 Brissac-Quincé, tel. 02.41.91.22.71, fax 02.41.54.20.36, e-mail loire-wines@vapl.fr by appt.

DOM. DU LANDREAU 1999★

■ 20 ha 100,000 ■ ↓ €5-8

In summer, there is an interesting Museum of Anjou Vines and Wines in Saint-Lambert-du-Lattay, a village famous for Coteaux-du-Layon. The Landreau estate has 50 ha (123.5 acres) of vines, 20 ha (49.4 acres) of which are dedicated to making Anjou red. This wine's bouquet suggests musky notes of meat and leather. The palate is very well-structured. Give it time to breathe before serving with game.

➤ Raymond Morin, Dom. du Landreau, 49750 Saint-Lambert-du-Lattay, tel. 02.41.78.30.41, fax 02.41.78.45.11, e-mail rmorin@domaine-du-landreau.com ☑ Ⲩ ev. day except Sun. 8am–12.30pm 2pm–7pm; Sat. 8am–12.30pm

VIGNOBLE DE L'ARCISON 2000

■ 3 ha 8,000 ■ ↓ €5-8

This 26-ha (64.2-acre) domaine in the village of Thouarcé produces a simple, pleasant, well-made wine. It has a strong red colour, with aromas of green pepper, spices and red berries. The palate is supple, light and fresh. This Anjou is ready to drink, but could be kept for a little while (one to two years).

➤ Damien Reulier, Le Mesnil, 49380 Thouarcé, tel. 02.41.54.31.12, e-mail damien.reulier@wanadoo.fr ☑ Ⲩ by appt.

CH. DE LA ROULERIE

Les Maronis 2000★

■ 4 ha 24,000 ■ ↓ €5-8

Though it is situated at the foot of the Coteau de Chaume, the centre for production of the great sweet wines of Anjou, the Château de La Roulerie has not forgotten how to make red wines. This Anjou has an intense red colour and a powerful nose of red berries. The full palate has a lovely tannic structure with a richness that should become more refined with time. This wine, which is similar to an Anjou-Villages, needs to be kept for at least another year.

➤ Vignobles Germain et Associés Loire, 49380 Thouarcé, tel. 02.41.68.94.00, fax 02.41.68.94.01, e-mail loire@vgas.com ☑ Ⲩ by appt.

DOM. DE LA VILLAINE

Cuvée spéciale 1999★

□ 0.5 ha 1,500 ⬛ €5-8

This domaine, which was created by amalgamating a lot of smaller vineyards in the 1970s, now extends over 23 ha (56.8 acres). Its clear, pale-yellow Cuvée Spéciale, which is has fruity and floral aromas, along with oaky notes. It is full, intense and unctuous on the palate, which for the moment is dominated by oak on the finish. It is certainly a little atypical, but it is an extremely successful wine.

➤ GAEC des Villains, La Villaine, 49540 Martigné-Briand, tel. 02.41.59.75.21, fax 02.41.59.75.21 ☑ Ⲩ by appt.

LEDUC-FROUIN Cuvée Alexine 2000★

□ 1 ha 3,000 ■ ↓ €5-8

This domaine, well-known to readers of the *Guide*, is now run by the younger generation, represented by Antoine Leduc and his sister Nathalie. Their Cuvée Alexine had not yet reached its full potential on the day it was tasted. However, its complex range of aromas (a mixture of overripe grapes, citrus fruit and ripe fruit) and its palate (both rich and light) are unmistakable signs that this is a promising wine which will amaze the drinker by the beginning of 2002. The **Anjou red 2000 Domaine Leduc-Frouin La Seigneurie** was also well-received by the Jury. It can be drunk now or kept for several years.

➤ SCEA Dom. Leduc-Frouin, Sousigné, 49540 Martigné-Briand, tel. 02.41.59.42.83, fax 02.41.59.47.90, e-mail domaine-leduc-frouin@wanadoo.fr ☑ Ⲩ by appt.

➤ Nathalie et Antoine Leduc

LE LOGIS DU PRIEURE

Le Gâte-Acier 2000★

□ 0.5 ha 2,500 ■ ↓

The Layon was canalized by Louis XVI and used as a navigable waterway for transporting coal and wine until the Revolution. The Jousset estate is on the slopes overlooking this river. Its Cuvée Gâte-Acier can be drunk from now onwards or kept for two to three years. It is a golden-toned yellow with intense flower and dried-fruit aromas. The palate is both soft and fresh, finishing on fruity notes with a touch of hazelnut, making a very successful marriage of power and delicacy. The domaine's **Anjou red 2000** got the same mark for its complex aromas of ripe fruit, green pepper and gamey notes and its well-rounded, well-balanced palate. It should be drunk this year.

➤ SCEA Jousset et Fils, Le Logis du Prieuré, 49700 Concourson-sur-Layon, tel. 02.41.59.11.22, fax 02.41.59.38.18, e-mail logis.prieure@groupesirius.com ☑ Ⲩ ev. day except Sun. 8am–12 noon 2pm–7pm

DOM. LES GRANDES VIGNES

Varenne de Combre 2000★★

□ 1.65 ha 4,800 ⬛ €8-11

This domaine, managed by three brothers and sisters who have built a solid reputation in only a few years, made a remarkable Bonnezeaux last year; now they have a dry white Anjou, from carefully selected grapes. Pale-yellow in colour, with green-gold highlights, its nose recalls sweet, rich aromas (crystallised or concentrated fruit, walnut, quince and cooked apple). The palate is both richly textured and fresh. It will be at its best at the start of 2002.

➤ GAEC Vaillant, Dom. Les Grandes Vignes, La Roche Aubry, 49380 Thouarcé, tel. 02.41.54.05.06, fax 02.41.54.08.21, e-mail gaecvaillant@wordonline.fr ☑ Ⲩ by appt.

LES TERRIADES 2000★★

□   20 ha   150,000 ■ ▲   -€3

This co-operative near the Château de Brissac was set up in 1951, bringing together producers with around 1,800 ha (4,446 acres). The Les Terriades wines correspond to different *terroirs* vinified separately. This white Anjou is a clear pale-yellow, enchanting with its finesse, elegance and balance. It has a delicate nose, and the palate leaves a very pleasant impression of lightness. It is a classic wine of this appellation and will be at its best at the start of 2002.

✦ Les Caves de La Loire, rte de Vauchrétien, 49320 Brissac-Quincé, tel. 02.41.91.22.71, fax 02.41.54.20.36, e-mail loire-wines@vapl.fr ☑ ☖ by appt.

■

DOM. DES MAURIÈRES 2000★

□   0.75 ha   4,000 ■ ▲   €5-8

This traditional domaine, well-known for its *vins liquoreux* or sweet wines (even cultivating several parcels in the Quarts de Chaumes), has made a fine red Anjou with an intense ruby colour, a sloe-berry nose with liquorice and spices and a pleasing palate with a touch of austerity on the finish. This is a slightly tannic, traditional-style wine, which is ready to drink now but should become more refined if kept.

✦ EARL Moron, Dom. des Maurières, 8, rue de Perinelle, 49750 Saint-Lambert-du-Lattay, tel. 02.41.78.30.21, fax 02.41.78.40.26 ☑ ☖ by appt.

■

DOM. DE MIHOUDY 2000★★

□   2 ha   5,000 ◧ ▲   €5-8

This family estate of 50 ha (123.5 acres) or so, in the heart of the Coteaux du Layon vineyards, is one which has contributed to the renaissance of viticulture in Anjou. It regularly receives stars (often two at a time) in the *Guide*, and was awarded the *Grappe de bronze* in the 1997 edition. Its Anjou white is made from grapes selected by hand and vinified in barrel. Pale-yellow with green highlights, it has a nose of tropical fruit, citrus fruit and bergamot. The palate reveals a rich, fresh structure, finishing on a note of dried fruit. It is a well-balanced and delicate wine. The **red 2000, La Cuvée Les Tréjeots** was awarded one star and is a straightforward, fresh, fruity wine to serve with grilled red meat or small game.

✦ Cochard et Fils, Dom. de Mihoudy, 49540 Aubigné-sur-Layon, tel. 02.41.59.46.52, fax 02.41.59.68.77 ☑ ☖ by appt.

■

CH. MONTBENAULT 2000★

□   3 ha   10,000 ■ ▲   €5-8

This traditional Anjou estate has made a wine with an old-style tannic character. It is a brilliant red colour in the glass, mingling ripe fruit with vegetal (green pepper) notes on the nose. After a pleasant attack dominated by ripe fruit, the palate leaves an impression of austerity on the finish. This wine should be ready to drink by the start of 2002.

✦ Yves et Marie-Paule Leduc, Ch. Montbenault, 49380 Faye-d'Anjou, tel. 02.41.78.31.14, fax 02.41.78.60.29 ☑ ☖ ev. day except Sun. 9am–12 noon 2pm–7pm

---

■

GILLES MUSSET ET SERGE ROULLIER 2000★★

□   1 ha   6,000 ■ ▲   €5-8

With regard to vine-training, choice of harvest dates and careful vinification, this domaine sets the standard for the region's vineyards. This Anjou white is yet another proof of their abilities. It is intense and powerful, with complex, delicate aromas, mingling apples and pears, citrus fruit, lemon and ripe fruit. It has remarkable balance. Their red, the **Cuvée d'Automne 2000** also gained two stars, with its brilliant stewed-fruit and spice character.

✦ Vignoble Musset-Roullier, Le Pélican, 49620 La Pommeraye, tel. 02.41.39.05.71, fax 02.41.77.75.76, e-mail musset.roullier@wanadoo.fr ☖ ☖ by appt.

■

DOM. PERCHER 2000★

□   3 ha   6,000 ■ ◧ ▲   €3-5

This domaine at the foot of the slopes of Verchers-sur-Layon, in the little hamlet of Savonnières, produces a very pleasant Anjou. It has a lively red colour, light, delicate aromas of small red berries and spices, and a pleasant and fresh palate with notes of ripe raspberries. This wine can be drunk from now onwards or kept for one to two years.

✦ SCEA Dom. Percher, Savonnières, 49700 Les Verchers-sur-Layon, tel. 02.41.59.76.29, fax 02.41.59.90.44 ☑ ☖ ev. day except Sun. 8am–12 noon 2pm–6pm

---

■

DOM. DU PETIT CLOCHER

Élevé en fût de chêne 2000★

□   1 ha   4,000 ■ ◧ ▲   €5-8

The Layon rises at Cléré, on the edge of the *département* of Deux-Sèvres, to the south of the Anjou vineyards. It is here that the Denises farm 54 ha (133.4 acres) of vines. Their barrel-aged Anjou white is a good example of Chenin harvested at full ripeness, and shows evidence of its maturation in oak. Its nose mingles fresh fruit, citrus fruit and flowers with vanilla and smokey notes. It is a distinctive wine that will attract a following. The **Anjou red 2000** (60,000 bottles) is just as successful: it is a typical Anjou, with redberry and blackcurrant aromas and a palate that leaves a light, fresh impression.

✦ A. et J.-N. Denis, GAEC du Petit Clocher, 3, rue du Layon, 49560 Cléré-sur-Layon, tel. 02.41.59.54.51, fax 02.41.59.70 ☖ by appt.

■

DOM. DES PETITES GROUAS 2000★

□   2 ha   10,000 ■ ▲

At Martigné-Briand in the high Layon, there are still the remains of the renaissance château that was burned down during the

---

Vendée War. The Domaine des Petit Grouas is situated on a limestone plateau where the rocks of the Paris Basin straddle the schists of the Massif Armoricain. Its Anjou red is well-made, with a fine structure and black-currant aromas. On the whole this is a very pleasant wine, and one that will find no lack of enthusiasts.

EARL Philippe Léger, Cornu, 49540 Martigné-Briand, tel. 02.41.59.67.22, fax 02.41.59.69.32 ▼ by appt.

DOM. DES PETITS QUARTS
2000★★★ 1 ha 4,000 €3-5

The 'Champion of Bonnezeaux' (we have not forgotten its three *coups de coeur* in 95, 96 and 97) now proves that its talents are not limited to *vins liquoreux*. This Anjou red is a real classic. An intense garnet-red in colour, it also has an interesting, impressively complex nose, mingling red and black berries, liquorice and notes of smoke. As for the palate, it is delicate, unctuous and fresh, all at the same time. 'A perfect wine,' said one taster.

Godineau Père et Fils, Dom. des Petits Quarts, 49380 Faye-d'Anjou, tel. 02.41.54.03.00, fax 02.41.54.25.36 ▼ ev. day except Sun. 8am–12 noon 2pm–6pm

CH. DE PIMPEAN
Cuvée du Festival 2000★ 13 ha 40,000 €5-8

The Château de Pimpéan was built in 1450. Its chapel vaults are decorated with splendid 15th-century paintings. In late summer of this wine. The 2000 is an intense ruby colour, with a nose of ripe fruit, fruit in brandy and prune. The palate is rich, concentrated and fresh. This is a characterful wine, but it gives an impression of lightness, being both well-structured and easy to drink.

SCA Dom. de Pimpéan, 49320 Grézillé, tel. 02.41.68.95.96, fax 02.41.45.51.93, e-mail maryset@pimpean.com ▼ ev. day 8am–12 noon 1.30pm–5.30pm

Gilles Tugendhat

CH. DE PUTILLE 2000
2.5 ha 10,000 €3-5

The Château de Putille and its owner, Pascal Delaunay, have been associated with the revival of Anjou reds, but their whites are just as highly regarded. This one surprised the Jury, who found it well-developed for its year, due to the late harvest. It is an intense yellow, with a flower and citrus-fruit nose and an unctuous palate with very little acidity. This is an original wine that will be ideal as an aperitif or with white meats.

Pascal Delaunay, EARL Ch. de Putille, 49620 La Pommeraye, tel. 02.41.39.02.91, fax 02.41.39.03.45 ▼ ev. day except Sun. 8.30am–12.30pm 2pm–7.30pm

DOM. RICHOU Les Rogeries 1999★★★
4 ha 10,000 €8-11

In the history of the Richou family there is a reference to Maurice Joyau, supplier of wines to the king in 1550. The family has always been important in Anjou wine-making and was involved in reviving the region's wines. This wine is from vines grown on a line of rhyolite rock (an acid rock made of solidified volcanic ash), the original *terroir* of the Coteaux de l'Aubance. It is a brilliant yellow, with aromas of quince, ripe fruit and flowers suggesting *vendange triée* (harvesting selecting only the ripest fruit). Its unctuous palate leaves an impression of finesse; it is a superb wine which is both powerful and delicate.

GAEC D. et D. Richou, Chauvigné, 49610 Mozé-sur-Louet, tel. 02.41.78.72.13, fax 02.41.78.76.05 ▼ by appt.

MICHEL ROBINEAU 2000★★
1 ha 4,000 €3-5

Michel Robineau created this estate in 1990. He knows how to do everything, judging from the *coups de coeur* to his credit. This Anjou 2000 delivers complete satisfaction, with its intense garnet-red colour, powerful ripe-fruit aromas (blackcurrant and blackberry) and rich, concentrated palate. It has more potential than is normal for this appellation. It needs another year or two in the cellar.

Michel Robineau, 3, chem. du Moulin, Les Grandes Tailles, 49750 Saint-Lambert-du-Lattay, tel. 02.41.78.34.67 ▼ by appt.

CH. DES ROCHETTES 2000★★
10 ha 20,000 €5-8

The Fief des Rochettes was already covered in vines in the 15th century, when it was owned by Louis XV. In the middle of the vineyard, on the side of the hill, there was once a windmill, the site of violent combat during the Vendée War. The domaine is famous for its Coteaux du Layon, honoured time and time again by *coups de coeur*, but its other wines are also worth lingering over. This Anjou red, for example, earned two stars for its fruitiness and balance. It is a lively garnet-red colour, with delicate, small red-berry aromas, and a well-integrated, pleasing

DOM. DU PRIEURE 2000★
0.56 ha 4,000 €3-5

Franck Brossaud took over the domaine in 2000, after completing a doctoral thesis on the effect of *terroir* on viticulture, and dealing in particular with the phenolic compounds in red wines. Now it's time for some hands-on work! This well-balanced Anjou, both fruity and supple, is already an encouraging result. Garnet-red, it shows classic red-berry aromas, accompanied by a few herbaceous notes. The palate is pleasant and fresh, leaving an impression of ripe fruit.

Franck Brossaud, 1 bis, pl. du Prieuré, 49610 Mozé-sur-Louet, tel. 02.41.45.30.74, fax 02.41.45.30.74 ▼ by appt.

palate, leaving an impression of freshness and ripe fruit.

♠ Jean Douet, Ch. des Rochettes, 49700 Concourson-sur-Layon, tel. 02.41.59.11.51, fax 02.41.59.37.73 ☑
Y by appt.

DOM. ROMPILLON 2000
■ 0.6 ha 4,500

This domaine on the Coteaux du Layon was recently enlarged and now covers 15 ha (37 acres). Its Anjou red mingles confected notes with red-berry aromas. It is well-made and so light that it can be drunk chilled like a Rosé de Loire. This bottle is an initiation into the red wines of the Loire Valley.

♠ Jean-Pierre Rompillon, L'Olluliere, 49750 Saint-Lambert-du-Lattay, tel. 02.41.78.48.84, fax 02.41.78.48.84 ☑
Y by appt.

DOM. DES SABLONNIERES
Cuvée des Vignes rouges 2000
■ 2 ha 4,000

Doué-la-Fontaine is a town that specialises in rose cultivation, but here vines hold their own. The Domaine des Sablonnières, on 16.5 ha (40.8 acres), was probably named after the particular *terroir* where it is situated, a bank of *faluns* (calcareous sands, rich in marine fossils). Its Anjou red has a brilliant colour, with interesting red-berry and smoke aromas. It has very pronounced austere tannins on the finish, perhaps due to the high level of extraction. There are those who will appreciate its honest rusticity.

♠ EARL Pierre et Eliane Bébin, 387, rue Jean-Gaschet, 49700 Doué-la-Fontaine, tel. 02.41.59.00.41, fax 02.41.59.99.27, e-mail lessablonnieres@wanadoo.fr ☑
Y by appt.

DOM. SAINT-ARNOUL 2000★★
■ 4.17 ha 8,000 €3-5

George Poupard, who founded this domaine in 1963, retired in the year 2000. His eldest son, Alain, who joined him on the estate in 1986, has teamed up with Xavier Maury, an oenologist, who was formerly in charge of one of the Anjou viticultural laboratories. This fruitful partnership lies behind a very well-made Anjou from a very ripe harvest. The 2000 leaves an impression of lightness, fruitiness and balance, which make this wine a pleasure to drink. In other words, it is a perfect example of its appellation.

♠ GAEC Poupard et Maury, Dom. Saint-Arnoul, Sousigné, 49540 Martigné-Briand, tel. 02.41.59.43.62, fax 02.41.59.69.23, e-mail saint-arnoul@wanadoo.fr ☑ Y by appt.

DOM. DES VARENNES 2000★★
■ 4 ha 5,000 €6-8

This 16-ha (39.5-acre) estate in the Coteaux du Layon area was created in 1930 and is run by the Richards, father and son. Their Anjou red is as remarkable as it was the year before. It is cherry-red in colour, obtained by short maceration and traditional pumping-over, and manages to be light while showing character. From the nose, which releases notes of fresh fruit after aeration, to the finish of very ripe cherries, one appreciates its delightful aromatic continuity. It is altogether a balanced wine.

♠ GAEC A. Richard, 11, rue des Varennes, 49750 Saint-Lambert-du-Lattay, tel. 02.41.78.32.97, fax 02.41.74.00.30 ☑
Y by appt.

DOM. VERDIER 2000★
■ 1 ha 7,000 €3-5

This 22-ha (54.3-acre) family domaine in the Coteaux du Layon area has produced a powerful, richly structured wine with a rather austere finish. This signifies very ripe grapes and a firm extraction, making it slightly atypical of the appellation. In colour, it is an intense purple with hints of black, and herbaceous notes (blackcurrant buds) and spices combine on the nose.

♠ EARL Verdier Père et Fils, 7, rue des Varennes, 49750 Saint-Lambert-du-Lattay, tel. 02.41.78.35.67, fax 02.41.78.35.67 ☑
Y ev. day 8.30am–12.30pm 2pm–6.30pm; Sun. by appt.; cl. 25 Aug–3 Sept.

MANOIR DE VERSILLE 2000★
■ 5 ha 20,000 €3-5

Versillé is a village in the Coteaux de l'Aubance region, on the north side of this river, facing the town of Saint-Melaine. The manor house is austerely beautiful, with two main buildings at right angles, connected by a square 16th-century tower. The Anjou red shows the same austerity, with a fairly astringent finish, doubtless due to the effect of a firm extraction on a very ripe harvest. However, the deep-red colour, stewed-fruit aromas and intensely fruity palate make a good impression. This bottle should be cellared for at least a year.

♠ Francine Desmet, EARL du Manoir de Versillé, Versillé, 49320 Saint-Jean-des-Mauvrets, tel. 02.41.45.22.00, fax 02.41.45.22.00, e-mail manoir.versille@wanadoo.fr ☑
Y by appt.

Anjou-Gamay

A red wine made from the Gamay Noir grape. On the area's more schisty soils, when well-vinified, it can produce an excellent carafe wine. Several growers have specialised in this type of wine, which has no ambition other than seeking to please in its year of harvest. In 2000, production was 16,642 hl (439,349 gal)

DOM. DES BONNES GAGNES 2000 ■ 2 ha 6,000 ■ ♦ €3-5

The soils of Bonnes Gagnes were planted with vines by monks in the 11th century. Ten centuries or so later, they have produced a very attractive ruby-coloured wine with pink highlights and simple aromas of ripe grapes and spices, along with a fresh, fruity palate. It is a typical Gamay, which could be drunk throughout a meal.

➤ Jean-Marc Héry, Orgigné, 49920 Saint-Saturnin-sur-Loire, tel. 02.41.91.22.76, fax 02.41.91.21.58 ▼ ev. day 9am–12.30pm 2pm–7.30pm; Sun. by appt.

DOM. CHUPIN 2000★★ ■ 3.8 ha 30,000 ■ ♦ €3-5

This enormous Anjou domaine of about 80 ha (197 acres) has made a Gamay which is a good example of the grape variety. It is a purplish, garnet-red colour, and has simple, vivid, fresh-fruit aromas (strawberry) along with confected notes, such as banana, on the nose. On the palate, it is fresh, delicate, and fruity. The concentration is remarkable for this year.

➤ SCEA Dom. Chupin, 8, rue de l'Eglise, 49380 Champ-sur-Layon, tel. 02.41.78.86.54, fax 02.41.78.61.73 ▼ by appt.

DOM. PIED FLOND 2000 ■ 0.4 ha 3,500 ■ ♦ €3-5

The estate is overlooked by an old 15th-century country house, which was later occupied by monks and, since 1864, by the Gourdon family. This wine is simple, light and pleasant, leaving a sensation of small red berries and freshness. Drink it within the year.

➤ EARL Franck Gourdon, Dom. de Pied Flond, 49540 Martigné-Briand, tel. 02.41.59.92.36, fax 02.41.59.92.36 ▼ by appt.

by the steep hillsides of Layon. The soils are deep, and the special nature of the *terroir* is also influenced by the proximity of the Loire, which guards against extreme variations in temperature. In 2000 the harvest produced 13,800 hl (364,320 gal).

DOM. PATRICK BAUDOUIN 1999★ ■ n.c. 5,000 ■ €8-11

Patrick Baudouin left his bookshop in Belleville to become a wine-grower. He started in 1990, after training with Pierre Aguilas, and his domaine has grown from 2 ha (4.94 acres) to 8 ha (19.76 acres) in only a few years. Although he is passionate about the Coteaux du Layon, he has not neglected his Cabernet vines either. His Anjou-Villages 99 is a sparkling, intense purple. Its berry aromas charm the nose and a rich, generous attack precedes a well-balanced, persistent palate. This wine will reach its peak in three years.

➤ Patrick Baudouin, Prince, 49290 Chaudefonds-sur-Layon, tel. 02.41.78.66.04, fax 02.41.78.66.04, e-mail contact@patrick-baudouin-layon.com ▼ by appt.

DOM. DES BLEUCES

Vignes rouges Vieilli en fût de chêne 1999★ ■ 0.3 ha 2,000 ■ €5-8

Benoît Proffit, who took over this domaine back in 1994, started by improving the vineyard. These 'red vines' whose grapes have spent only a short time in oak (nine months), have produced a most attractive, brilliant-ruby 99. The nose is fairly intense, and combines fruity, toasty, and black-berry aromas. There is a slight hint of oak on the palate, subtly balanced, and the finish is underpinned by silky tannins.

➤ EARL Proffit-Longuet, Dom. des Bleuces, 49700 Concourson-sur-Layon, tel. 02.41.59.11.74, fax 02.41.59.97.64, e-mail domainedesbleuces@coteaux-layon.com ▼ ▼ ev. day except Sun. 8am–12pm 2pm–5.45pm
➤ Benoît Proffit

Anjou-Villages

The *terroir* of this AOC is drawn from a selection of regions within the Anjou appellation. To qualify, soils must be healthy, early-flowering and well-exposed. They mainly lie on schists, whether altered or not. The ten communes making up the geographical area of the AOC Anjou-Village-Brissac, recognised in 1998, occupy a plateau sloping gently down to the Loire, bordered to the north by the river and to the south

DOM. CHUPIN 1999 ■ 4.31 ha 30,000 ■ ♦ €3-5

This is a large domaine of over 78 ha (192.7 acres). It belongs to Guy Saget, who is well-known for his vineyards in the Pouilly region. His 99 has a moderate concentration, but this does not stop it from being pleasant. It is not deep-ruby in colour, but it looks attractive. Sloe, wild strawberry and liquorice notes mean that there is much to appreciate aromatically. On the palate it is supple and well-made.

➤ SCEA Dom. Chupin, 8, rue de l'Eglise, 49380 Champ-sur-Layon, tel. 02.41.78.86.54, fax 02.41.78.61.73 ▼ ▼ by appt.
➤ SA Guy Saget

DOM. DE GATINES 1999★★

2.5 ha 12,000 | €5-8

The Domaine des Gatines covers 35 ha (86.5 acres) in the upper Layon. In 1996 the third generation of the family took it over. France's champion vine-pruner can also mount the podium for Anjou-Villages on occasion: the 95 won the *Guide's coup de cœur*. This 99 is from the same stock. It is an intense garnet-red in the glass, leaving rich tears on the sides when swirled. Ripe black fruit dominates the extremely concentrated nose. The palate is generous, full and rich, with powerful but silky tannins, features which show that the grapes were gathered at the peak of ripeness and that the extraction was perfect. This remarkable wine will become even better in a few years' time.

↪ EARL Vignoble Dessèvre, Dom. de Gatines, 12, rue de la Boulaie, 49540 Tigné, tel. 02.41.59.41.48, fax 02.41.59.94.44 Y ev. day except Sun. 8am-12.30 2pm-7pm

DOM. DE LA CROIX DES LOGES
Les Grenues 1999★★

1 ha 5,000 | €5-8

The estate of Bonnin (40 ha/98.8 acres) is situated near the village on the Gennes road. The son of the family took it over in 1998, and the compliments paid to this wine will encourage him. It is ruby-coloured with bluish highlights, and though it is initially restrained on the nose, when swirled it opens up a whole range of complex aromas where red berries mingle with floral notes, evoking iris and peony. The palate is smooth, has a good tannic structure and a long, elegant finish.

↪ SCEA Bonnin et Fils, Dom. de La Croix des Loges, 49540 Martigné-Briand, tel. 02.41.59.43.58, fax 02.41.59.41.11, e-mail bonninlesloges@aol.com Y by appt.

DOM. DE LA MOTTE
Cuvée fût de chêne 1999★★★

0.5 ha 1,000 | €8-11

This 18-ha (44.5-acre) family estate, established in 1935, was restarted by Gilles Sorin in 1995. His 99 was judged to be so fine that it was placed on the list of possible *coups de cœur*. This is the ultimate wine for laying down. In colour it is a strong, dark garnet-red with violet highlights. The nose is pronounced: fruity, with notes of spices and roasted coffee beans. It is very well-structured on the palate and rich, even opulent. The fact that the grapes were harvested at the ideal level of ripeness, and the wine has had the ideal type of vinification are undoubtedly the keys to this superb bottle, which will give a great deal of pleasure in two or three years' time.

↪ Gilles Sorin, 35, av d'Angers, 49190 Rochefort-sur-Loire, tel. 02.41.78.72.96, fax 02.41.78.75.49 Y ev. day except Sun. 8.30am-6.30pm

CH. DE LA MULONNIERE 1998

3 ha 8,000 | €5-8

The Château de La Mulonnière, on the river Layon which crosses the domaine, was built by Charles Messe, a former artillery officer under Napoléon III, in 1876. The present owners acquired it in 1991. Their 98 is a ruby-red, with garnet highlights. The nose reveals herbaceous nuances with a touch of oak and for the moment the palate is austere. It needs to be kept for a year or two.

↪ SCEA B. Marchal-Grossat, Ch. de La Mulonnière, 49750 Beaulieu-sur-Layon, tel. 02.41.78.47.52, fax 02.41.78.65.63, e-mail chateau@domaine-mulonniere.com Y by appt.

DOM. DU LANDREAU 1999★★

8 ha 15,000 | €5-8

This domaine was founded in 1961 and developed well after opting for private sale. It now covers 50 ha (123.5 acres). Its Anjou-Villages 99 immediately inspired one of the tasters, who said its ruby colour was 'singing'. The nose, just as pleasant, plays elegantly on the theme of red berries. The palate reveals a good, sound structure and has a flattering finish. This wine is still a little young, but those who are impatient could uncork it when the *Guide* comes out.

↪ Raymond Morin, Dom. du Landreau, 49750 Saint-Lambert-du-Lattay, tel. 02.41.78.30.41, fax 02.41.78.45.11, e-mail rmorin@domaine-du-landreau.com Y ev. day except Sun. 8am-12.30pm 2pm-7pm, Sat. 8am-12.30pm

DOM. DE LA VILLAINE Les Rôtis
Cuvée spéciale Elevé en fût de chêne 1999★

0.5 ha 2,500 | €5-8

This 23-ha (56.8-acre) domaine was set up in the 1970s and taken over by Jean-Paul Carré and Pascal Batail in 1997. Their Cuvée Les Rôtis, which has been barrel-aged for 12 months, is ruby-red with brilliant highlights. At first the nose suggests delicate, attractive fruit aromas, which are then complemented with well-integrated toast and vanilla notes. The attack is straightforward and full, and the tannins on the finish are rather pronounced, but will certainly be better-integrated after the wine has been kept for a little while.

↪ GAEC des Villains, La Villaine, 49540 Martigné-Briand, tel. 02.41.59.75.21, fax 02.41.59.75.21 Y by appt.

DOM. LES GRANDES VIGNES 1999

10 ha 62,000 | €5-8

This 50-ha (123.5-acre) domaine is in Thouarcé, in the Coteaux du Layon. Its wines are often mentioned in the *Guide*. This one is dark-ruby with crimson highlights, with a nose of overripe fruit. The finish is not one of the longest, and at the moment the tannins overpower the fullness of the fruit, but it has enough balance and harmony to develop after it has been kept for a while.

GAEC Vaillant, Dom. Les Grandes Vignes, La Roche Aubry, 49380 Thouarcé, tel. 02.41.54.05.06, fax 02.41.54.08.21, e-mail gaecvaillant@worldonline.fr
Y by appt.

LUC ET FABRICE MARTIN 1999★

1 ha 2,500 €5-8

Luc and Fabrice Martin, who represent the fourth generation of this domaine, became a GAEC (farmers' economic interest grouping) in 1997. Their 99 is a dense purple with very delicate aromas. The attack gives way to a well-structured, powerful, full-bodied palate which has persistent, fine tannins.
GAEC Luc et Fabrice Martin, 2 bis, rue du Stade, 49290 Chaudefonds-sur-Layon, tel. 02.41.78.19.91, fax 02.41.78.98.25
Y ev. day 8am–12 noon 2pm–8pm

CH. DES NOYERS 1999★

8 ha 4,000 €3-5

The 18.5-ha (45.7-acre) vineyard is overlooked by a fine 16th-century château defended by three dry moats and large angular towers. It has produced a 99 that is very attractive both for its intense colour and its delicate meniscus. The nose is soft and fairly complex, reminiscent of stewed red berries. The palate is supple and well-balanced, with plenty of persistence, and gives a great deal of pleasure.
SCA Ch. des Noyers, Les Noyers, 49540 Martigné-Briand, tel. 02.41.54.03.71, fax 02.41.54.27.63, e-mail webmaster@chateaudesnoyers.fr Y by appt.
Besnard

DOM. OGEREAU 1999★★

8 ha 15,000 €5-8

The results from this domaine are often awaited with impatience, because in recent years the wine-maker, Vincent Ogereau, has produced brilliant wines, both *vins liquoreux* and reds. In this AOC he obtained two consecutive *coups de cœur* in the 2000 and 2001 editions of the *Guide*. The 99, after a very long maceration (one month), is purple with hints of violet. The nose is very open, with red berries and a touch of oak. The palate is very pleasant, as it gives an impression of suppleness and lightness while still being well-structured and remarkably long.
Vincent Ogereau, 44, rue de la Belle-Angevine, 49750 Saint-Lambert-du-Lattay, tel. 02.41.78.30.53, fax 02.41.78.43.55 Y by appt.

DOM. DU PETIT METRIS 1997★★

Clos de Midion 1.1 ha 5,000 €5-8

Every year we expect white wine: Quarts de Chaume, Coteaux du Layon, Savennières and so on. With this 97, Le Petit Métris has shown that it can also make something good from Cabernet. With the first sniff this attractive garnet-red wine shows off its richness and generosity, delivering plenty of black fruit. This impression is confirmed on the palate, where a full, voluminous body, and a well-integrated structure is evident. The secret is that the grapes are picked at optimum ripeness and the extraction of the grape's noble constituents is skilfully managed. This bottle is worth a try right now, but it could also wait another three to five years.
GAEC Joseph Renou et Fils, Le Grand Beauvais, 49190 Saint-Aubin-de-Luigné, tel. 02.41.78.33.33, fax 02.41.78.67.77, e-mail domaine.petit.metris@wanadoo.fr
Y by appt.

DOM. DE PUTILLE 1999★★

0.85 ha 3,000 €5-8

The 13-ha (32.1-acre) Domaine de Putille is situated in the heart of the Loire Valley, 30 km (18.6 miles) from Angers. *Guide* readers know it well because, with Chenin, Gamay and Cabernet, it offers a rich variety of Anjou wines, which are regularly praised by our Juries. This 99, which has been macerated for a long time, is without doubt the finest red tasted here. On swirling, the intense colour creates a brilliant garnet-red meniscus. The elegant and complex nose has fine, stewed red-berry aromas. After a superb attack comes a fine body, a full, rounded, silky structure and a very good balance. The finish goes on forever!
Isabelle Sécher, Dom. de Putille, 49620 La Pommeraye, tel. 02.41.39.80.43, fax 02.41.39.81.91 Y by appt.

DOM. JEAN-LOUIS ROBIN-DIOT 1999★★

Le Haut du Cochet 2 ha 5,300 €6-11

This domaine has just added an underground cellar and barrel store, and this remarkable Anjou-Villages was, of course, aged in oak. The intense garnet colour of this 99 shows highlights which indicate that it is just starting to develop. The nose is a potpourri of flowers (violet), dried fruit (fig) and charred notes. The palate is well-integrated and finishes on silky tannins. This is a really well-balanced wine.
Dom. Jean-Louis Robin-Diot, Les Hauts-Perrays, 49290 Chaudefonds-sur-Layon, tel. 02.41.78.68.29, fax 02.41.78.67.62 Y by appt.

MICHEL ROBINEAU 1999★

■ 0.8 ha 3,000 ⬛⬛ €5-8

Ten years ago Michel Robineau set up this estate, and he knows how to get the best out of it. His 99 is a very pure purple, with an attractive rim. The nose is restrained at first, but opens out when the wine is swirled, emitting game and spice notes. It is very finely balanced on the palate. A slight astringency diminishes during tasting, giving way to a silky harmony.

↝ Michel Robineau,
3, chem. du Moulin, Les Grandes Tailles,
49750 Saint-Lambert-du-Lattay,
tel. 02.41.78.34.67 ☙ Ⅴ by appt.

DOM. ROBINEAU CHRISLOU 1999★

■ 0.7 ha 4,500 ⬛⬛ €5-8

Louis Robineau took over the family domaine in 1991. His 99 is a ruby-red with sparkling violet highlights. The nose is pronounced, developing very soft, spicy notes. The supple attack is followed by a well-structured palate. In summary, this is a balanced and harmonious wine.

↝ Louis Robineau, 14, rue Rabelais,
49750 Saint-Lambert-du-Lattay,
tel. 02.41.78.42.65, fax 02.41.78.42.65 ☑
☙ Ⅴ by appt.

SAUVEROY Cuvée Antique 1999★

■ 5.5 ha 36,000 ⬛⬛ €5-8

The Sauveroy domaine has developed rapidly over the last 15 years. The wine-maker is interested in vinification in small tanks, which means that grape maturity has to be carefully ascertained. This painstaking work allows him to produce fine wines like this Cuvée Antique: the 96 was awarded a coup de cœur. After long maceration, this 99 is a confidence-inspiring, intense deep, gleaming ruby-red colour, the sign of masterful extraction. The nose confirms the impression that the grapes were picked very ripe, being very fruity, intense and subtle. There is great persistence on the palate.

↝ Pascal Cailleau, Dom. du Sauveroy,
49750 Saint-Lambert-du-Lattay,
tel. 02.41.78.30.59, fax 02.41.78.46.43,
e-mail domainesauveroy@terre-net.fr ☑
☙ Ⅴ by appt.

DOM. DES TROTTIERES 1999★

■ 4.57 ha 28,000 ⬛

This vast domaine, with 80 ha (197.6 acres) under vines which cover the slopes of the Layon valley, was created in 1905. In 1985 it was taken over and modernised by the Lamottes. This 99 looks elegant, halfway between ruby and purple in colour. The nose suggests very ripe or overripe grapes, with a note of stewed fruit. On the palate the wine develops very noticeable but ripe, rich tannins.

↝ Dom. des Trottières, Les Trottières,
49380 Thouarcé, tel. 02.41.54.14.10,
fax 02.41.54.09.00, e-mail lestrottieres@
worldonline.fr ☙ Ⅴ by appt.

DOM. DE BABLUT 1999

■ n.c. 30,000 ⬛⬛ €5-8

The 80-ha (197.6-acre) Domaine de Bablut has been in the same family since 1546. The wine-grower, who also tends the vines at the Château de Brissac, has converted to organic methods. The property, which produces all types of Anjou wines, has been mentioned regularly since the first edition of the Guide and is listed every year for this AOC. The 99 is an attractive red with violet highlights, and has very flattering fruit and floral aromas on the nose which are most pleasantly echoed on the palate. Though not particularly long, its freshness makes it attractive, and it is very well-balanced.

↝ SCEA Daviau, Dom. de Bablut,
49320 Brissac-Quincé, tel. 02.41.91.22.59,
fax 02.41.24.77, e-mail daviau@refsa.fr
☑ Ⅴ ev. day except Sun. 8.30am–12 noon
2pm–6.30pm

CH. DE BRISSAC 1999★

■ n.c. 40,000 ⬛⬛ €5-8

The building – two round, pointed 15th-century towers framing a 17th-century façade – has been described as a 'half-built new château in a half-ruined old château'. It is still the property of the Dukes of Brissac, as is the entire vineyard, which was planted in a year which our French readers will remember with no difficulty – 1515. Its 80 ha (197.6 acres) are now farmed according to biodynamic principles. As the domaine is symbolic of the appellation, it would be a shame if it disappointed. This 99 lives up to expectations. It is garnet-red with violet highlights. On the nose, black-fruit and earthy notes mingle, and it is well-balanced, full, rounded and long on the palate. The 96 was awarded a coup de cœur.

↝ SCEA Daviau, Dom. de Bablut,
49320 Brissac-Quincé, tel. 02.41.91.22.59,
fax 02.41.24.77, e-mail daviau@refsa.fr
☑ Ⅴ ev. day except Sun. 8.30am–12 noon
2pm–6.30pm
↝ Duc de Brissac

DOM. DES CHARBOTTIERES

Les Richoux 1999★

■ 1.1 ha n.c. ⬛⬛ €8-11

Using biodynamic principles, Paul-Hervé Vintrou farms 5 ha (12.35 acres) of Chenin for Coteaux de l'Aubance and 5 ha (12.35 acres) of Cabernet for Anjou-Villages-Brissac. The vines grow on clay and schist soils. Although not from the Anjou area, he knows his subject, as he comes from a family of négociants and has trained as a sommelier. The nose is dense and concentrated with black fruit accompanied by roasted-coffee notes. The palate reveals a sumptuous and very tannic structure, a guarantee of ageing potential. This intense 99 would suitably accompany red meat or even game. It should be very balanced once the tannins have become more integrated.

↘ Paul-Hervé Vintrou, Clabeau, 49320 Saint-Jean-des-Mauvrets, tel. 02.41.91.22.87, fax 02.41.66.23.09, e-mail contact@ domainedescharbotieres.com ✉ Y by appt.

DOM. DITTIERE 1999
■ 1.5 ha 9,000 €5-8

The Domaine Dittière has been in existence for a century, and is currently run by two brothers, Joël and Bruno. The vines grow on sandy/gravelly soil which is characteristic of the village of Vauchrétien and makes for characterful wines. Those wines from this estate, especially the reds, figure regularly in the *Guide*, and an 89 was even awarded a *coup de cœur*. This 99 has aromas of ripe, slightly stewed fruit or of prunes. These fruity notes persist on a light, lively palate. This is a well-balanced, well-made wine.

↘ Dom. Dittière, 1, chem. de la Grouas, Vauchrétien, 49320 Brissac, tel. 02.41.91.23.78, fax 02.41.54.28.00, e-mail domaine.dittiere@wanadoo.fr ✉ Y by appt.

DOM. DE GAGNEBERT
Clos de Grésillon 1999★
■ 5 ha 20,000 €5-8

Schist has been quarried for slates at Juigné since the 12th century, and the old open quarries are still visible. In a cellar dug out of the schist you can taste this very pleasant 99, which was grown on schist, as one might expect. An intense ruby in colour, with violet highlights, it has a delicate, fairly intense nose mingling red berries with notes of vanilla and roast coffee, conferred by a year's ageing in oak. On the palate, the flavours become more powerful, culminating in a finish supported by silky tannins. It has good structure and harmony.

↘ Daniel et Jean-Yves Moron, Dom. de Gagnebert, 2, chem. de la Naurivet, 49610 Juigné-sur-Loire, tel. 02.41.91.92.86, fax 02.41.91.95.50 ✉ Y ev. day except Sun. 9am–12 noon 3pm–7pm

DOM. DE MONTGILET 1999★★
■ 5.92 ha 33,000 €5-8

This 36-ha (88.92-acre) domaine is right in the heart of the Coteaux de l'Aubance and, like its labels, it is all grey and blue; this is a schist roofing-slate area. It has often introduced us to superb *vins liquoreux*, but it also excels in reds (an Anjou-Villages 87 was the *coup de cœur* in the 1990 *Guide*). This garnet-red 99 with brown highlights represents the appellation well, showing concentrated aromas, combining black fruit with a herbaceous touch. It has a full-bodied, opulent palate with persistent, fruity notes. Enjoy it now and in the future.

↘ Victor et Vincent Lebreton, Dom. de Montgilet, 49610 Juigné-sur-Loire, tel. 02.41.91.90.48, fax 02.41.54.64.25, e-mail montgilet@terre-net.fr ✉ Y ev. day except Sun. 9am–12 noon 2pm–7pm

DOM. RICHOU
Les Vieilles vignes 1999★
■ 4 ha 22,000 €5-8

Members of this family have been working with wine since the 16th century, and are proud of having discovered a document dated 1550 which mentions a certain Maurice Joyau, who was a wine-maker and supplier to the king. With this wine-making background it is not surprising that they show a level of expertise which has made this domaine one of Anjou's safe bets. They have been well-known since the first edition of the *Guide*. Their Cuvée Vieilles Vignes is intense in colour, but has a subtle nose, opening with toast and black-fruit notes. The palate reveals an opulent structure, which only needs to mature. It's one to wait for.

↘ GAEC D. et D. Richou, Chauvigné, 49610 Mozé-sur-Louet, tel. 02.41.78.72.13, fax 02.41.78.76.05 ✉ Y by appt.

DOM. DE ROCHAMBEAU 1999★★
■ 2 ha 8,000 €5-8

This 17-ha (42-acre) vineyard on the slopes of the Coteau dominates the Aubance and is organically farmed. Its 99 gives a feeling of richness and concentration throughout the tasting. The garnet-red colour is intense, and the nose has aromas of black fruit, such as blackcurrant. As for the palate, it is supple, yet well-structured and balanced. There is a seductive, long-lasting fruitiness on the finish.

↘ EARL Forest, Dom. de Rochambeau, 49610 Soulaines-sur-Aubance, tel. 02.41.57.82.26, fax 02.41.57.82.26, e-mail rochambeau@wanadoo.fr ✉ Y by appt.

DOM. DES ROCHELLES 1999★★
La Croix de Mission 1999★★
■ 5 ha 20,000 €8-11

La Croix de Mission
DOMAINE DES ROCHELLES
1999
ANJOU VILLAGES BRISSAC
J.Y.A. LEBRETON
49320 SAINT-JEAN-MAUVRETS FRANCE
MIS EN BOUTEILLE AU DOMAINE

Jean-Yves Lebreton makes high-quality red wines, as this one showed when it won over the Jury. In colour it is intense, deep and vibrant. The nose is warm and powerful, while still elegant. On the nose the complex range of aromas combine very ripe red berries with stewed black fruit. On the palate it is full and well-structured, prolonging and

Rosé d'Anjou

Although very successful in export markets, nowadays this medium-dry wine is hard to sell. The principal variety is Grolleau, which used to be trained in the goblet shape, when it produced light rosé wines called 'rougets'. It is increasingly being vinified as light red table wine or Vin de Pays.

DOM. DE SAINTE-ANNE 1999★
3 ha   10,000   € 5-8

This domaine, situated on one of the highest chalky-clay hilltops in Saint-Saturnin-sur-Loire, proves its quality with great regularity; it has been mentioned in the *Guide* since the first edition. Its Anjou-Villages-Brissac 99 has a lively garnet-red colour. It needs aeration to bring out the fruity notes, which suggest it has the potential to develop some aromatic complexity. The attack is full, rich and delicious and the finish leaves nuances of black fruit and jam in its wake. It is a very attractive wine.
➤ Dom. de Sainte-Anne, EARL Brault, 49320 Brissac-Quincé, tel. 02.41.91.24.58, fax 02.41.91.25.87 ☎ ev. day except Sun. 9am–12 noon 2pm–7pm; Sat. 6pm

DOM. DES HAUTES OUCHES 2000★
3 ha   7,000   € 3-5

This family-owned domaine in full expansion has 43 ha (106.2 acres) of vines. Each edition of the *Guide* shows their ability with rosé (they obtained the *coup de coeur* for the 96 in this AOC). This 2000 is extremely pleasant. Limpid but intense in colour, it has strong, elegant red-berry aromas and is smooth, well-balanced and fruity on the palate.
➤ EARL Joël et Jean-Louis Lhumeau, 9, rue Saint-Vincent, Limières, 49700 Brigné-sur-Layon, tel. 02.41.59.30.51, fax 02.41.59.31.75 ☎ by appt.

DOM. LEDUC-FROUIN
La Seigneurie 2000★★
7 ha   5,000   € 3-5

The brilliant salmon-pink colour is attractive. Intense, elegant citrus-fruit aromas assail the nose. The palate is well-rounded, lively

La Seigneurie
DOMAINE LEDUC-FROUIN
Rosé d'Anjou
Appellation Rosé d'Anjou Contrôlée
2000
MIS EN BOUTEILLE AU DOMAINE
Mme Georges LEDUC - Propriétaire à VAUCHRÉTIEN - 49320 MARITIME-GRAND - France
11,5%vol   75cl

developing these first impressions. The aromas on the nose are there again as flavours on the palate, only more intense. This is a bottle which will not let itself be forgotten!
➤ J.-Y.A. Lebreton, Dom. des Rochelles, 49320 Saint-Jean-des-Mauvrets, tel. 02.41.91.92.07, fax 02.41.54.62.63, e-mail jy.a.lebreton@wanadoo.fr ☎ by appt.

Rosé d'Anjou

the characteristic Anjou aromatic richness. Drink it from now onwards.
➤ SCEA Dom. de Champteloup, 49700 Brigné-sur-Layon, tel. 02.41.59.65.10, fax 02.41.59.63.60

CHANTAL FARDEAU
Rosé lumineux Demi-sec 2000★
0.62 ha   5,700   € 5-8

This domaine is situated in the lower Layon, near its confluence with the Loire, at the foot of the Anjou corniche. This 'luminous rosé' is a delightful salmon-pink. It has a subtle nose, but a delicate palate which is both balanced and refreshing.
➤ Dom. Chantal Fardeau, Les Hauts Perrays, 49290 Chaudefonds-sur-Layon, tel. 02.41.78.67.57, fax 02.41.78.68.78 ☎ by appt.

FLANERIE DE LOIRE 2000
n.c.   300,000   € 3-5

This *négociant* house distinguished itself in this appellation with a very fine 99. The following year is more modest, but it has everything one would expect of a rosé: pale salmon-pink colour, elegant fruity and floral perfumes and a fine, rounded palate with persistent flavours.
➤ SA Lacheteau, ZI de La Saulaie, 49700 Doué-la-Fontaine, tel. 02.41.59.26.26, fax 02.41.59.01.94

DOM. DES BLEUCES 2000★
6.1 ha   50,000   € 3

Benoît Proffit took over the 29-ha (71.63-acre) domaine in 1994. His rosé is a lovely orangey-pink, with elegant aromas of small red berries and a fresh, harmonious, well-balanced palate.
➤ EARL Proffit-Longuet, Dom. des Bleues, 49700 Concourson-sur-Layon, tel. 02.41.59.11.74, fax 02.41.59.97.64, e-mail domainedesbleues@ coteaux-layon.com ☎ ev. day except Sun. 8am–12 noon 2pm–5.45pm

CH. DE CHAMPTELOUP
10 ha   60,000   € 3

A third of this property's vineyard area is used for producing rosés. This one is a beautiful, pale salmon-pink, with intense but delicate red-fruit perfumes on the nose. It is smooth and elegant on the palate, developing

Cabernet d'Anjou

The best examples come from the fossiliferous sands of the Tigné region and the Layon.

DOM. MICHEL BLOUIN 2000★ ■ ♦ €3-5
1.61 ha 8,000

The sixth generation of the Blouin family is beginning to take over the reins. For the time being, Michel Blouin runs this estate of some 21 ha (51.9 acres), which he took over in 1970. His Cabernet d'Anjou is fairly pale-coloured, but has a surprisingly intense bouquet with slightly tart aromas. This tartness recurs on the palate, which is rounded, fine and full of flavour. This is an excellent wine for casual drinking.

Dom. Michel Blouin, 53, rue du Canal-de-Monsieur, 49190 Saint-Aubin-de-Luigné, tel. 02.41.78.33.53, fax 02.41.78.67.61 ☑ ♈ by appt.

DOM. BODINEAU 2000★ ■ ♦ €3-5
3 ha 3,000

The Boudineau family have been growing vines since 1850. This year's Cabernet d'Anjou is just as it should be: a clear, brilliant pale-pink in colour, with a straightforward but vivid range of light red-berry aromas on the nose. The palate is rounded and balanced. This is a well-made wine.

Dom. Bodineau, Savonnières, 49700 Les Verchers-sur-Layon, tel. 02.41.59.22.86, fax 02.41.59.86.21 ☑ ♈ by appt.

DOM. DE CLAYOU 2000★★ ■ ♦ €3-5
6 ha 50,000

Continuing a long-established wine-making tradition, J.-B. Chauvin has produced a balanced and very delicate Cabernet d'Anjou from clay-schist soils. The Jury were charmed by the orangey-pink colour with coppery glints, the bouquet's intense aromas of red berries and the smooth palate, which is very fruity and has good length.

SCEA Jean-Bernard Chauvin, 18 bis, rue du Pont-Barré, 49750 Saint-Lambert-du-Lattay, tel. 02.41.78.42.84, fax 02.41.78.48.52 ☑ ♈ ev. day except Sun. 9am–12 noon 2pm–7pm; cl. end Aug.

COTEAU SAINT-VINCENT 2000★ ■ ♦ €3-5
4 ha 10,000

This 19-ha (46.9-acre) family estate was taken over in 1992 by Michel Voisine, who in 1999 was joined by his son Oliver, an oenologist. Their Cabernet d'Anjou is very pleasant. Pale-pink in the glass, its bouquet is certainly still restrained, but it releases elegant and very fruity flavours on the palate, and has plenty of liveliness and length.

Michel et Olivier Voisine, Le Coteau Saint-Vincent, 49290 Chalonnes-sur-Loire, tel. 02.41.78.18.26, fax 02.41.78.18.26, e-mail licheur@infonie.fr ☑ ♈ by appt.

---

and long, leaving a very attractive, slightly acidic note. The Jury was won over, and La Seigneurie elevated to the ranks of royalty!

SCEA Dom. Leduc-Frouin, Sousigné, 49540 Martigné-Briand, tel. 02.41.59.42.83, fax 02.41.59.47.90, e-mail domaine-leduc-frouin@wanadoo.fr ☑ ♈ by appt.

DOM. LE POINT DU JOUR 2000★ ■ ♦ €3
5 ha 30,000

This rosé comes across very well. It is an attractive pink with salmon tints, and the fruity, floral aromas of violet develop elegantly on the palate, with plenty of persistent flavours. What more could anyone ask?

Réthoré, 51 bis, rue d'Anjou, 49540 Tigné, tel. 02.41.59.65.10

DOM. DES MAURIERES 2000 ■ ♦ €5-8
1.57 ha 5,000

This domaine is often mentioned for its Coteaux de Layon, but also knows how to make rosés. This one is typical – orange-pink, with an intense nose of flowers and fruit. This fruitiness recurs on the well-balanced, velvety palate.

EARL Moron, Dom. des Maurières, 8, rue de Perinelle, 49750 Saint-Lambert-du-Lattay, tel. 02.41.78.30.21, fax 02.41.78.40.26 ☑ ♈ by appt.

CH. DE MONTGUERET 2000★ ■ ♦ €3-5
10 ha 80,000

André and Dominique Lacheteau bought this enormous domaine in 1987. They offer a delightful rosé. It is a limpid salmon-pink in colour, with an intense range of aromas on the nose that develop pleasantly on the palate. The wine finishes on a slightly acidic note, which gives the whole thing a dynamic quality.

SCEA Ch. de Montguéret, Le bourg, 49560 Nueil-sur-Layon, tel. 02.41.59.59.19, fax 02.41.59.59.02 ☑ ♈ by appt.

A. et D. Lacheteau

Cabernet d'Anjou

There are some excellent medium-dry rosés made from the Cabernet Franc and Cabernet Sauvignon varieties in this appellation. Served chilled, they go well with melon as a starter or with desserts that are not too sweet. As they age, the wines take on a tile-red colour and can be drunk as an apéritif. Production was 167,654 hl (4,426,066 gal) in 2000.

Cabernet d'Anjou

DOM. DITTIERE 2000
6 ha 3,000 €3-5

This 34-ha (84-acre) estate stands in the middle of the Anjou wine region. It is run by Joël Dittière, who was joined by Bruno in 1993, and the two have made steady progress. Their Cabernet d'Anjou is worth noting for its classic appearance and its bouquet, which, although still closed, hints at interesting aromas to come. The palate is pleasant and balanced.

♦ Dom. Dittière, 1, chem. de la Grouas, Vauchrétien, 49320 Brissac, tel. 02.41.91.23.78, fax 02.41.54.28.00, e-mail domaine.dittiere@wanadoo.fr ☑

DOM. FARDEAU 2000★
1.29 ha 10,000 €5-8

Stéphanie Fardeau joined her father in 1994 at this small family estate whose cellars are located on the hills of Chaudefonds. This Cabernet d'Anjou is typical of its appellation, with its orangey-pink colour, prevailing aromas of red berries, and delicate, slightly sharp palate. It is ready to drink now.

♦ Dom. Chantal Fardeau, Les Hauts Perrays, 49290 Chaudefonds-sur-Layon, tel. 02.41.78.67.57, fax 02.41.78.68.78 ☑
Ⓣ by appt.

DOM. DE GATINES 2000
3 ha 20,000 €3-5

The property register of 1765 listed this site as the manor house and lands of Gatines. It became a presbytery before it was acquired by the grandfather of the present owners. The Dessèvre family have always taken care over the quality of their Cabernet d'Anjou, which has appeared in the last three editions of the Guide. The 2000 version has a smart orangey-pink colour, and the fruity aromas of the bouquet and flavours on the palate were again thought to be true examples of the appellation. It has a fine balance.

♦ EARL Vignoble Dessèvre, Dom. de Gatines, 12, rue de la Boulaie, 49540 Tigné, tel. 02.41.59.41.48, fax 02.41.59.94.44 ☑
Ⓣ ev. day except Sun. 8am–12.30pm 2pm–7pm

DOM. LA CROIX DES LOGES
2000★★
8 ha 8,000 €3-5

The Martigné-Briand estate is ever-present in the Guide, and this year, by an overwhelming majority, wins a third coup de cœur for its Cabernet d'Anjou. The 2000 vintage follows the style of the 97 and 98 versions. It has a very characteristic bouquet with delicate, light aromas together with fruity, slightly sharp notes, and excellent balance. This is a very fine, balanced wine.

♦ SCEA Bonnin et Fils, Dom. de La Croix des Loges, 49540 Martigné-Briand, tel. 02.41.59.43.58, fax 02.41.59.41.11, e-mail bonninlesloges@aol.com ☑
Ⓣ by appt.

DOM. DE L'ANGELIERE 2000★
3.5 ha 6,000 €3-5

The Angelière estate is now run by the family's fifth generation, and produces about ten AOC wines on some 40 ha (98.8 acres). This Cabernet d'Anjou is salmon-pink in colour with beautiful highlights, and has very pleasant aromas of red berries on the nose, followed by a soft, well-balanced palate and remarkable length.

♦ GAEC Boret, Dom. de L'Angelière, 49380 Champ-sur-Layon, tel. 02.41.78.85.09, fax 02.41.78.67.10 ☑
Ⓣ ev. day except Sun. 9am–7pm

DOM. DE LA PETITE CROIX 2000★
7 ha 10,000 €3-5

Although this estate produces one of the most highly-rated crus in Anjou, the Bonnezeaux, all its wines are worth trying. This Cabernet d'Anjou has a delightful orangey-pink colour and aromas of small red berries. The palate is already well-balanced but has not yet reached its full potential. However, it has all the qualities it needs to improve in time. It should be kept for a while.

♦ A. Denechère et F. Geffard, Dom. de la Petite Croix, 49380 Thouarcé, tel. 02.41.54.06.99, fax 02.41.54.30.05 ☑

DOM. DE L'ARBOUTE 2000
2 ha 8,500 €3-5

In 1955, Jules Massicot took over this 19-ha (46.9-acre) estate, which dates from the 18th century. Since 1980, it has been run by Yves and his wife, who are now joined by their son Sébastien. This pale-pink Cabernet releases notes of very ripe fruit, both on the nose and on the palate, and has a light, balanced finish. Its all-round qualities make it a 'good little rosé' to be enjoyed without fuss.

♦ Yves Massicot, L'Arboute, 49380 Faye-d'Anjou, tel. 02.41.54.03.38, fax 02.41.54.40.57 Ⓣ by appt.

CH. DE LA ROCHE BOUSSEAU
2000
30 ha 100,000 €3-5

This Cabernet d'Anjou is a fine example of its year. It is pink with orangey glints, and floral and fruity qualities combine on the palate with a refreshing note of acidity, making it a wine to enjoy.

Cabernet d'Anjou

François Regnard, Dom. de La Petite-Roche, 49310 Trémont, tel. 02.41.59.43.03, fax 02.41.59.69.43
 by appt.

LE CLOS DES MOTELES 2000★★ €3-5
1.23 ha 4,000

This family estate of some 18 ha (44.5 acres) is located in a small commune in the southern part of the Anjou wine region, near Thouars. This Cabernet, grown on gravelly soils, was universally praised for its intense orangey-pink colour and delicate aromas of red fruits and flowers. The palate is remarkably well-structured with peach and nectarine flavours prominent all the way to the finish. This is a superb rosé.
 GAEC Le Clos des Motèles Basset-Baron, 42, rue de la Garde, 79100 Sainte-Verge, tel. 05.49.66.05.37, fax 05.49.66.37.14 by appt.

LE LOGIS DE PREUIL 2000 €3-5
1.8 ha 8,000

Jean-Marc Trahan has been renting the Logis du Preuil for just one year, and has produced a wine with a pretty, pale and slightly orange colour. The bouquet's aromas are still somewhat herbaceous, with notes of ivy mixed with white flowers and citrus fruits. The palate is very fruity and well-balanced.
 EARL Les Magnolias des Trahan, 26, rue du Moulin, 79290 Cersay, tel. 05.49.96.80.38, fax 05.49.96.37.23 by appt.

LE LOGIS DU PRIEURE 2000★ €3-5
5 ha 5,000

This 30-ha (74.1-acre) estate was founded in 1850, and was already well-known for its Anjou wines when Vincent Jousset took it over in 1982. Since then, he has developed it in his own way, for example with this very fine, fresh Cabernet d'Anjou. It has a fruity aroma of strawberries and a hint of vanilla. This enjoyable wine is ready to drink now.
 SCEA Jousset et Fils, Le Logis du Prieuré, 49700 Concourson-sur-Layon, tel. 02.41.59.11.22, fax 02.41.59.38.18, e-mail logis.prieure@groupesirius.com ev. day except Sun. 8am–12 noon 2pm–7pm

LES GRANDS CAVEAUX DE FRANCE Demi-sec Cuvée Chopin 1998 €3-5
n.c. 2,400

This business was set up in 1991 and sells bottled wines from various estates. This Cabernet d'Anjou is very pleasant, combining a lovely pale-pink colour with fruity notes and leaving an impression of freshness and lightness. It is a delicious wine.
 Les Grands Caveaux de France, 5, La Grossinière, 79150 Saint-Maurice-la-Fougereuse, tel. 05.49.65.94.77, fax 05.49.80.31.87 by appt.
 Paul Froger

DENIS MARCHAIS L'Âme du Terroir 2000★ -€3
7 ha 40,000

This Cabernet d'Anjou is produced by an estate in the Loire-Atlantique *département*, on the right bank of the Sèvre, near the historic site of La Guérivière. It has a most attractive pink colour, and powerful aromas combining fruity notes with others of brioche and pear drops. The palate is lively, and a slightly acidic finish completes the tasting pleasantly.
 Vinival, La Sablette, 44330 Mouzillon, tel. 02.40.36.66.00, fax 02.40.36.26.83

DOM. MATIGNON 2000★ €3-5
3 ha 10,000

The property now consists of 37 ha (91.4 acres) and was inherited from a grandfather who was a cooper. From it you can see the chimneys of the Château de Martigné-Briand. This Cabernet has a delightful appearance, fine and delicate aromas and a balanced and refreshing palate. It has a long finish that makes you want to try it again immediately.
 EARL Yves Matignon, 21, av. du Château, 49540 Martigné-Briand, tel. 02.41.59.43.71, fax 02.41.59.92.34, e-mail domaine.matignon@wanadoo.fr by appt.

DOM. DES PETITES GROUAS 2000★★ €3-5
1 ha 5,000

In all, this property consists of 12.5 ha (30.9 acres), made up of many small plots. It was taken over by Philippe Léger in 1989. His Cabernet d'Anjou has everything going for it: an intense pink colour, fascinating fruity aromas and a balanced, light, soft palate which makes an excellent overall impression. It's a pity there is so little of it.
 EARL Philippe Léger, Cornu, 49540 Martigné-Briand, tel. 02.41.59.67.22, fax 02.41.59.69.32 by appt.

DOM. SAINT-ARNOUL 2000★ -€3
3.85 ha 15,000

Georges Poupard, who founded this estate, retired in 2000, and its 29 ha (71.6 acres) are now cultivated by Alain Poupard and Xavier Maury, an oenologist. This Cabernet has a lovely pink colour and elegant aromas of red berries, which emerge as flavours on the full and pleasantly long palate.
 GAEC Poupard et Maury, Dom. Saint-Arnoul, Sousigné, 49540 Martigné-Briand, tel. 02.41.59.43.62, fax 02.41.59.69.23, e-mail saint-arnoul@wanadoo.fr by appt.

DOM. DES TROIS MONTS 2000★ €3-5
10 ha 50,000

The Guéneau family, wine-growers for over four generations, specialise in Coteau du Layon and Anjou Villages. They have done well with this Cabernet d'Anjou. It has an intense pink colour and aromas of fruit and flowers, along with a lively, rounded and very well-balanced palate. The long finish with hints of strawberries and exotic fruits combine to make this an extremely pleasant bottle of wine.

➻ SCEA Hubert Gueneau et Fils, 1, rue Saint-Fiacre, 49310 Trémont, tel. 02.41.59.45.21, fax 02.41.59.69.90 ▼
▼ by appt.

DOM. DES TROTTIERES 2000
25.59 ha   150,000   €3-5

This estate was laid out in 1905 over an unbroken 110 ha (271.7 acres). Today it works 80 ha (197.6 acres) of vines on the hillside overlooking the Layon valley. It was bought in 1985 by the Lamottes, who have modernised it. Their clear, pale-pink Cabernet d'Anjou has an intense bouquet of red and black berries. The palate is long, fresh and balanced, but finishes on an acidic note.

➻ Dom. des Trottières, Les Trottières, 49380 Thouarcé, tel. 02.41.54.14.10, fax 02.41.54.09.00, e-mail lestrottieres@worldonline.fr ▼ ▼ by appt.
➻ Lamotte

DOM. DU VIGNEAU 2000
2 ha   3,000   €3-5

This well-made Cabernet d'Anjou has a typical, pale-pink colour, fruity aromas both on the nose and on the palate, and a generous character. The lightness of the palate is refreshing.

➻ Patrick Robichon, pl. de l'Eglise, 49560 Passavant-sur-Layon, tel. 02.41.59.51.04, fax 02.41.59.51.04 ▼

DOM. DE BABLUT Noble 1999 ▢
n.c.   7,500   €15-23 ★★★

The Daviau family use biodynamic methods on their estate, and have certainly got the best out of the 99 vintage. The eye is drawn immediately to the amber colour. The bouquet releases a magnificent range of aromas of citrus fruits and crystallised fruits

Coteaux de l'Aubance

The banks of the little Aubance river are schist slopes planted with old Chenin vines, giving a sweet white wine which improves with age. Production was 4,710 hl (124,344 gal) in 2000. This appellation imposes strict limits on production.

Domaine des Deux Moulins 1999 — Coteaux de l'Aubance

DOM. DES DEUX MOULINS ▢
Cuvée Exception 1999 ★★
3 ha   3,500   €8-11

With this superb Cuvée Exception, D. Macault goes to the top of the list for this appellation. Its intense golden colour shows straight away that this isan exceptional creation. An impression of richness and

with lightly oaky notes. The palate is impressively concentrated and full. This is a truly noble wine.

➻ SCEA Daviau, Dom. de Bablut, 49320 Brissac-Quincé, tel. 02.41.91.22.59, fax 02.41.91.24.77, e-mail daviau@refsa.fr
▼ ▼ ev. day except Sun. 8.30am-12 noon 2pm-6.30pm

DOM. DE BABLUT
Grandpierre 1999 ★★
n.c.   4,000   €11-15

This wine has tremendous structure. It has an amber-yellow colour and a concentrated bouquet of dried and crystallised fruits. Opulent, perfectly balanced flavours explode on the palate. It will go well with sweet dishes but, like the Cuvée Noble, is best enjoyed on its own. It is ready to drink now, but has the potential for long cellaring. The Cuvée Sélection 99 was awarded a star for its authenticity and potential.

➻ SCEA Daviau, Dom. de Bablut, 49320 Brissac-Quincé, tel. 02.41.91.22.59, fax 02.41.91.24.77, e-mail daviau@refsa.fr
▼ ▼ ev. day except Sun. 8.30am-12 noon 2pm-6.30pm

DOM. DES CHARBOTIERES
Clos des Huttières 1999 ★
0.8 ha   1,000   €23-30

Paul-Hervé Vintrou, a former *sommelier*, has gone from the table to the cellar, and from the South-West of France to Anjou, where he uses biodynamic methods on his land. The colour of this Huttières is like liquid gold. The nose is still somewhat closed, but when swirled in the glass releases notes of crystallised and dried fruit. The palate is concentrated, fresh and dried fruit. This is a wine with lots of potential.

➻ Paul-Hervé Vintrou, Clabeau, 49320 Saint-Jean-des-Mauvrets, tel. 02.41.91.22.87, fax 02.41.66.23.09, e-mail contact@domainedescharbotieres.com
▼ ▼ by appt.

concentration dominates the wine. A combination of honey and crystallised fruits is most in evidence in the elegant range of aromas. Meanwhile, the palate retains an extraordinary freshness.

➤ Dom. des Deux Moulins, 20, rte de Martigneau, 49610 Juigné-sur-Loire, tel. 02.41.54.36.05, fax 02.41.54.67.94, e-mail les.deux.moulins@wanadoo.fr ☒ ☎ by appt.

➤ GAEC Dom. Richou, Chauvigné, 49610 Mozé-sur-Louet, tel. 02.41.78.72.13, fax 02.41.78.76.05 ☒ ☎ by appt.

Anjou-Coteaux de la Loire

This appellation is limited to white wines made from Chenin, known here as Pineau de la Loire. Production, which was 608 hl (16,051 gal) in 2000, is limited by the size of the area, a dozen communes situated exclusively on schists and limestone at Montjean. Careful picking encourages the grapes to reach over-ripeness, giving the generally medium-dry wines a greener colour than those of Coteaux de Layon. In this region, as elsewhere in Anjou, there is an increasing shift towards the production of red wines.

DOM. DE HAUTE PERCHE

Les Fontenelles 1999★
▢ 4,000 ▊❙❘ ♦ €8-11

Christian Papin has taken over and considerably increased the Haute Perche estate, which today has 34 ha (84 acres). Mainly he has planted Chenin and Cabernet. This 99 vintage notes of very ripe fruit and dried fruit on the nose. The powerful, rich and full-bodied palate, both lively and well-structured, has hints of crystallised fruit and a marvellous finish.

➤ EARL Agnès et Christian Papin, 9, chem. de la Godelière, 49610 Saint-Melaine-sur-Aubance, tel. 02.41.57.75.65, fax 02.41.57.75.42 ☒ ☎ by appt.

DOM. DE MONTGILET

Les Trois Schistes 1999★★★
12.02 ha 8,726 ▊❙❘ €11-15

The estate's attractive labels recall its blue-slate clay terroirs. Its wines have already won four coups de cœur. This one is another in the same mould. Made from very ripe grapes, it has a golden-yellow colour and a bouquet of concentrated aromas combining exotic fruits, crystallised fruits and floral notes. The palate is full, complex, fresh and very long. One of the Jury suggested trying it with a fig tart. Another wine, Le Clos Prieur 99, was awarded two stars. Although rich, and already great to drink now, it will really improve with ageing (half-litre bottles).

➤ Victor et Vincent Lebreton, Dom. de Montgilet, 49610 Juigné-sur-Loire, tel. 02.41.91.90.48, fax 02.41.54.64.25, e-mail montgilet@ierre-net.fr ☒ ☎ ev. day except Sun. 9am–12 noon 2pm–7pm

DOM. RICHOU

Les Trois Demoiselles 1999★★
4 ha 5,000 ▊❙❘ €15-23

Henri Richou, and now his sons, have brought distinction to this estate and to the Anjou wine region. Their vintages of 97, 96 and 94 have won three coups de cœur for the Richou estate's Les Trois Demoiselles since the Guide began (see the 1996, 1999 and 2000 editions). In considering the 99 vintage, the Jury liked its straw-yellow colour and its concentrated aromas of dried, exotic and very ripe fruits. The palate is impressively full with a hint of fleshiness: this is a great vin liquoreux which just needs time to open up.

GILLES MUSSET ET SERGE ROULLIER 2000
▢ 2 ha 4,000 ▊ ♦ €8-11

From the estate there is a splendid view of the church of Montjean-sur-Loire, which seems to hang over the vineyard. This Coteaux de la Loire is pale-yellow in colour and is developing delicate, light aromas along with notes of very ripe fruit (stewed apple) and a slight, attractive bitterness on the finish. Overall this is very fine and well-balanced.

➤ Vignoble Musset-Roullier, Le Pélican, 49620 La Pommeraye, tel. 02.41.39.05.71, fax 02.41.77.75.76, e-mail musset.roullier@wanadoo.fr ☒ ☎ by appt.

CH. DE PUTILLE

Cuvée Pierre Carrée 1999★★
▢ n.c. 4,000 ▊ ♦ €8-11

On the road leading to the Château de Putille, you pass some old ruined limekilns. Pascal Delaunay, a wine-grower who appears regularly in the Guide, charmed the Jury with this wine, remarkable both for its fine, intense gold colour and its concentrated aromas of dried and exotic fruits. The palate gives an impression of richness and its very fine range of flavours are a great pleasure to experience. This is almost a very great wine. The second wine offered by this estate is a Clos du Pirouet 2000, which delighted the tasters with its lightness and finesse: a straw-yellow colour with golden glints, delicate aromas of quince,

Savennières

These are dry white wines made from Chenin, mainly produced in the commune of Savennières. The schists and purple sandstone of the area give the wines a particular character which has led them in the past to be defined as part of the Coteaux de la Loire, but they deserve a place in their own right. The wines are a little firm, but full of aromatic flavour, excellent with cooked fish. The production of Savennières and the growths Coulée-de-Serrant and Roche-aux-Moines was 4,769 hl (125,902 gal) in 2000.

DOM. EMILE BENON
Clos du Grand Hamé Réserve 1999

5.5 ha   6,000   €8-11 ★★

This 13-ha (32.1-acre) estate was formed ten years ago. For the last three years it has been highly praised in the *Guide*, particularly for last year's Savennières, which won a *coup de cœur*. Its range of aromas is surprisingly complex, with notable hints of flowers, reminiscent of a *vin liquoreux*. The palate is full, rounded, very fruity and long, and has the right note of bitterness found in these wines. The mineral qualities of this wine are well-balanced by its full, richly concentrated character. It is a magnificent wine that will develop more complexity in the course of time.

Dom. Emile Benon, rte de la Lande, Epiré, 49170 Savennières, tel. 02.41.77.10.76, fax 02.41.77.10.07, e-mail earl.benon@wanadoo.fr ev. day except Sun. 8am–12 noon 2.30pm–7pm; cl. 15–31 Aug.

DOM. DU CLOSEL Les Vaults 2000 ★

6 ha   20,000   €8-11

The Les Vaults 2000 takes its name from the feudal domain to which this estate belonged. These lands were recorded as having been under vine in 1495. Its holders included the Walshes, Comtes de Serrant (a shipowning family), then a Marquis de Las Cases, grandson of Napoleon's chamberlain, from whom the present owners are descended. The château took on its present appearance during the Second Empire. The vineyard consists of several plots fanning out across the hills overlooking Savennières and the Loire Valley. The Les Vaults has an attractive pale-yellow colour, while the nose is initially restrained, but elegant. On the palate it is mouth-filling, yet delicate, complex and very well-balanced. A second wine, **Les Caillardières 2000**, also wins one star. Yellow in colour with green glints, it is still somewhat closed on the nose, but the palate is pleasantly lively, fresh and rich.

Mesdames de Jessey, Dom. du Closel, Ch. des Vaults, 49170 Savennières, tel. 02.41.72.81.00, fax 02.41.72.86.00, e-mail closel@savennieres-closel.com ev. day 9am–12.30pm 2pm–7pm

CLOS DE COULAINE 1999

4 ha   26,000   €8-11

The wine-grower at Clos de Coulaine is none other than Claude Papin, the leading producer of Coteaux du Layon and Anjou red and an expert on the geology of the Anjou terroirs. He operates from the château Pierre-Bise, which has wonderful views over the Layon hills. His 99 wine is pale-yellow with green highlights and charmed the Jury with its elegant fruity and floral aromas, which re-emerge on a clean palate. This wine's long finish is a guarantee that it will improve with age.

Claude Papin, Ch. Pierre-Bise, 49750 Beaulieu-sur-Layon, tel. 02.41.78.31.44, fax 02.41.78.41.24
by appt.
F. Roussier

CH. D'EPIRE 2000 ★

6.5 ha   30,000

People have been growing vines here since the early Middle Ages, and the estate has been in the same family since the 17th century. The château dates from 1850, and the cellar has occupied a Romanesque building since 1906, the village's former church. The present 11-ha (27.2-acre) vineyard (including 9 ha/22.2 acres used for this appellation) is located on the upper slopes of the appellation. It has

mandarin and exotic fruit such as mango. The sweet, richly textured palate finishes with an impression of fresh acidity, which accentuates the notes of crystallised fruits. Overall, this is a very well-balanced wine which deserves a star.

EARL Ch. de Putille, 49620 La Pommeraye, tel. 02.41.39.02.91, fax 02.41.39.03.43 ev. day except Sun. 8.30am–12.30pm 2pm–7pm.
Pascal Delaunay

produced a Savennières with typical fresh and bitter characteristics. It is a lovely pale-yellow colour, and has an intense nose with aromas of very ripe fruits. The palate is clean and straightforward, with a mineral note, and the structure suggests good ageing potential. The **Cuvée Spéciale 2000** is also awarded one star. This wine is yellow with bronze highlights and the nose is delicate and appealing. The palate is full-bodied and richly textured, with a delicate mineral note on the finish. This is a classic, very approachable wine. Drink now or keep for several years.

➤ SCEA Bizard-Litzow, Chais du château d'Epiré, 49170 Savennières,
tel. 02.41.77.15.01, fax 02.41.77.16.23,
e-mail luc.bizard@wanadoo.fr ▢ ❢ ev. day except Sun. 9am–12 noon 2pm–6.30pm

NICOLAS JOLY 1999★

▢ n.c. 12,000 €11-15

The name of Nicolas Joly has long been linked with biodynamic methods. He was one of its first practitioners in France (converting to it at the beginning of the 1980s) and remains a staunch supporter. His Savennières have captured all the scents of autumn with its aromas of ripe, stewed plums and slightly overripe fruits (pears, sorb apples and medlars). The palate is light, fresh and well-balanced.

➤ Nicolas Joly, Ch. de La Roche-aux-Moines, 49170 Savennières,
tel. 02.41.72.22.32, fax 02.41.72.28.68,
e-mail couleedeserrant@wanadoo.fr
❢ ev. day except Sun. 8.30am–12 noon 2pm–6pm

CH. LA FRANCHAIE 1999★★

▢ 2 ha 10,000 ▯ ▮ ⚘ €8-11

This dry, thoroughbred wine has an astonishingly rich range of aromas: flowers (hawthorn, broom, acacia and linden flower) mingle with ripe fruits, dried fruits and mineral notes typical of the appellation. The palate is warm, full of character and well-balanced. It recalls Chenin grapes and slate-schist soil, and mirrors the soft light of the Anjou region.

➤ SCEA Ch. La Franchaie, Dom. de La Franchaie, 49170 La Possonnière,
tel. 02.41.39.18.16, fax 02.41.39.18.17 ▢
❢ by appt.
➤ Chaillou

DOM. DE LA MONNAIE
L'Enclos 1998★★

▢ 2 ha 2,500 ▯ €11-15

Eric Morgat has been running this 5-ha (12.4-acre) estate since 1995. The house was formerly a tollhouse on the banks of the Loire, hence the estate's name. This 98 wine is very typical of the appellation. It has an attractive, strong yellow colour and an intense and complex bouquet that releases aromas of overripe fruit reminiscent of sweet wines. The palate is unctuous and very concentrated, with a hint of bitterness on the finish. This wine has excellent potential for the future,

when it should become even more richly flavoured.

➤ Eric Morgat, Dom. de la Monnaie, 49170 Savennières, tel. 02.41.72.22.51,
fax 02.41.78.30.03 ▢ ❢ by appt.

CLOS LA ROYAUTE 1999★

▢ 6 ha 18,000 ▯ €11-15

The Laffourcade family owns the estate of l'Echauderie Jaune d'Or. This 99 wine has intense and complex aromas of violets, honeysuckle and honey. These characteristics are repeated on the rounded, rich and balanced palate, added to toast and crystallised-fruit notes. It will improve with age.

➤ Vignobles Laffourcade, Ch. de l'Echarderie, 49170 Rochefort-sur-Loire,
tel. 02.41.54.16.54, fax 02.41.54.00.10,
e-mail laffourcade@wanadoo.fr ❢

CLOS DU PAPILLON
Moelleux Cuvée d'Avant 1999

▢ 1.2 ha 5,000 ▯ €15-23

The 15th-century Château de Chamboureau was redesigned in the 17th century, and is worth a visit as much for its architecture as for its wines, which have appeared in the *Guide* since its first edition. The Clos du Papillon (butterfly) is a plot of land which owes its name to its shape. The 99 vintage displays a strong yellow colour. The bouquet is attractively powerful, with scents of crystallised and exotic fruits, characteristic of a very ripe vintage. The palate is intense and fairly sweet, but leaves an impression of freshness.

➤ EARL Pierre Soulez, Ch. de Chamboureau, 49170 Savennières,
tel. 02.41.77.20.04, fax 02.41.77.27.78 ▢
❢ by appt.

CH. DE PLAISANCE Le Clos 1999★

▢ 1.5 ha 3,000 ▯ ▮ ⚘ €11-15

Located in the middle of the Chaume wine region, Guy Rochais has produced many notable sweet wines, which have featured regularly in the *Guide*. His Savennières are no less successful. This 99 vintage is a classic of the appellation, with its intense golden colour, its delicate, elegant aromas of honey and caramel and its fresh, balanced palate, which leaves an impression of great finesse. It is a wine to be savoured.

➤ Guy Rochais, Ch. de Plaisance, 49190 Rochefort-sur-Loire,
tel. 02.41.78.33.01, fax 02.41.78.67.52 ▢
❢ by appt.

DOM. TAILLANDIER
Demi-sec 1999★

▢ 7 ha 7,000 ▮ €8-11

Two brothers, Eric and Marc Taillandier, have created a brand-new vineyard on a south-facing hillside on the outskirts of Savennières. Their 99 vintage has a slightly golden-yellow colour with a delicate, fruity bouquet releasing aromas of crystallised fruits and honey. The same pattern re-emerges on the palate, which is also balanced,

Savennières Roche-aux-Moines

harmonious and long, with ripe fruits very much in evidence.

☛ Dom. Eric Taillandier,
Varennes, 49170 Savennières,
tel. 02.41.72.23.70, fax 02.41.72.23.70,
e-mail mtaill4788@aol.com ✔ ⍩ by appt.

CH. DE VARENNES 1999★

7 ha   45,000   €11-15

This 7-ha (17.3-acre) vineyard is one of the Anjou estates acquired by Bernard Germain, who also owns vineyards in the Bordeaux region. His well-made 99 has a clear, brilliant golden-yellow colour and a bouquet combining floral and dried-fruit notes, with nuances of toast and finely integrated oak. The palate is full-bodied and elegant with good length. This is a pedigree wine with good ageing potential.

☛ Vignobles Germain et Associés Loire,
49380 Thouarcé, tel. 02.41.68.94.00,
fax 02.41.68.94.01, e-mail loire@vgas.com ✔
⍩ by appt.

CH. DE CHAMBOUREAU

Cuvée d'Avant 1999★

5.36 ha 25,000   €15-23

The hillside at La Roche-aux-Moines is a rocky spur overhanging the Loire Valley. The Château de Chamboureau reflects the age and prestige of its vineyard. Its Cuvée d'Avant is a lovely pale-gold. Its aromas of floral, honeyed notes are typical of a very ripe harvest. The palate is full, powerful and warm, and also very long. This is a classic of the appellation.

☛ EARL Pierre Soulez,
Ch. de Chamboureau, 49170 Savennières,
tel. 02.41.77.20.04, fax 02.41.77.27.78 ✔
⍩ by appt.

CH. DE CHAMBOUREAU Chevalier

Buhard Cuvée d'Avant Doux 1999★★★

0.35 ha 1,500   €15-23

This Chevalier Buhard 99 was fermented and left for ten months on the lees in a *barrique* that had been mellowed by being used for more than two wines. It was then set boldly before the Jury in its golden-yellow livery and proved delicious throughout the tasting. The nose has some aromas of development, reminiscent of nuts and dried grapes. The palate, with its excellent structure, is lively and rich at the same time, revealing all the finesse of the *terroir*. This is a rare and magnificent wine (half-litre bottles).

☛ EARL Pierre Soulez,
Ch. de Chamboureau, 49170 Savennières,
tel. 02.41.77.20.04, fax 02.41.77.27.78 ✔

Savennières Roche-aux-Moines Savennières Coulée-de-Serrant

It is difficult to distinguish between two growths so similar to each other in character and quality. The Coulée de Serrant is grown on a smaller area (6.85 ha (16.9 acres)), sited on both sides of the valley of the little Serrant river, but mainly on a steep slope with a south-westerly exposure. Totally owned by the Joly family, this appellation has attained the highest reputation at national level for its quality and value for money. It takes five or ten years for the wines to reach their peak. La-Roche-aux-Moines is owned by several growers and covers a declared area of 19 ha (47 acres) (though not all planted), producing an average of 600 hl (15,840 gal). Even though quality is not as consistent, you can find certain vintages of which its namesake would not be ashamed.

NICOLAS JOLY

Clos de la Bergerie 1999★★

n.c.   7,000   €15-23

According to Nicolas Joly, the biodynamic method allows soils to breathe and is the best way to ensure that wines retain the true taste of their *terroir*, or place of origin. 'I don't want a good wine, I want a true wine,' he once explained. Fortunately, the two aims are not at all incompatible, and his Savennières feature regularly in the *Guide*. This Clos de la Bergerie has something exuberant about it, with its heady aromas of fruits macerated in alcohol, ripe fruits and dried fruits. The palate imparts simultaneously both richness and freshness. This is a very individual wine.

☛ Nicolas Joly, Ch. de La Roche-aux-Moines, 49170 Savennières, tel. 02.41.72.22.32, fax 02.41.72.28.68, e-mail couleedeserrant@wanadoo.fr ✔
⍩ ev. day except Sun. 8.30am–12 noon 2pm–6pm

Savennières Coulée-de-Serrant

NICOLAS JOLY 1999★★

n.c. 26,000 €38-46

This historic estate was first developed in the 12th century by the Cistercians, who have contributed so much to the history of winemaking in Europe. It owes its present worldwide fame to Nicolas Joly. His Coulée-de-Serrant wines feature regularly in the *Guide*, beginning with his '76 vintage in the first edition. His wines are vinified in oak but very little of it is new, so as not to overpower the wine. The '91 and '94 wines both won a *coup de coeur*. The '99 vintage is more restrained, and is not a wine for people in a hurry. Its mysterious aromas recall wood used for cabinet-making, nuts and earthy, woodland notes. The palate is fresh, and the general impression is of autumn days: gentle, full of light and inner contemplation.

Nicolas Joly, Ch. de La Roche-aux-Moines, 49170 Savennières, tel. 02.41.72.22.32, fax 02.41.72.28.68, e-mail couleedeserrant@wanadoo.fr
ev. day except Sun. 8.30am–12 noon 2pm–6pm

DOM. DES BARRES Chaume 2000★★

1.5 ha 2,300 €8-11

Patrice Achard has been in charge of this family estate of 25 ha (61.8 acres) for ten years. He has often been mentioned in the *Guide*, thanks to excellent wines like this 2000 vintage, the product of four *tries successives* (several pickings to harvest only the ripest fruit). His quest for a crop of overripe grapes has produced a wine with a golden-yellow colour, a range of aromas consistent with noble rot, including notes of honey, white flowers and concentrated fruit. The palate combines power and delicacy with very good balance.

Patrice Achard, Dom. des Barres, 49190 Saint-Aubin-de-Luigné, tel. 02.41.78.98.24, fax 02.41.78.68.37
by appt.

DOM. PATRICK BAUDOUIN

Grains nobles 1999★★

5 ha 9,000 €30-38

Patrick Baudouin has been at his 10-ha (24.7-acre) vineyard at Chaudefonds-sur-Layon since 1990, and has made a name for himself both in the region and abroad, exporting 80% of his production. He makes true *vins liquoreux*; this one, from a harvest with a natural potential alcohol of more than 17.5%, has been aged in barrel for 16 months. It has an orangey-yellow colour and a bouquet combining coffee, toast, dried banana and old rum. The palate is also splendidly complex, being both powerful and concentrated. It is a fine example of noble rot.

Patrick Baudouin, Prince, 49290 Chaudefonds-sur-Layon, tel. 02.41.78.66.04, fax 02.41.78.66.04, e-mail contact@patrick-baudouin-layon.com
by appt.

CHARLES BEDUNEAU

Vieilles vignes 2000★

10 ha 3,500 €5-8

This small family estate has been in business since 1958, cultivating 20 ha (49.4 acres), of which 10 ha (24.7 acres) are set aside for sweet wines. This vintage made a very good impression with its blend of richness and freshness. It is pale straw-yellow and has restrained aromas of ripe fruits and white flowers. The palate is delicate and fairly sweet with a long, balanced finish. This is a wine full of promise.

Dom. Charles Béduneau, 18, rue Rabelais, 49750 Saint-Lambert-du-Lattay, tel. 02.41.78.30.86, fax 02.41.74.01.46
by appt.

DOM. MICHEL BLOUIN

Saint-Aubin 2000

3.22 ha 8,000 €5-8

The village of Saint-Aubin-de-Luigné, the 'pearl of Layon,' has many old houses and several lanes for visitors to explore. Michel Blouin's vineyard of just over 21 ha (51.9 acres) is beside the river. His 2000 vintage is memorable for its firm structure. The aromas

Coteaux du Layon

These are medium-dry, medium-sweet and sweet white wines, of which 50,249hl (1,326,574 gal) were produced in 2000, from the slopes of 25 communes on the banks of the Layon, from Nueil to Chalonnes. Chenin is the only variety grown. Several villages have a reputation for quality: the best known is Chaume, producing from 78 ha (193 acres). Six other names can also be added to the appellation: Rochefort-sur-Loire, Saint-Aubin-de-Luigné, Saint-Lambert-du-Lattay, Beaulieu-sur-Layon, Rablay-sur-Layon and Faye-d'Anjou. They are subtle wines, golden green at Concourson, yellower and stronger downstream, with aromas of honey and acacia from the over-ripe grapes. Their ability to keep is exceptional.

combine very ripe fruits with a hint of iodine. The finish has an attractive note of bitterness.

🞄 Dom. Michel Blouin,
53, rue du Canal-de-Monsieur, 49190 Saint-Aubin-de-Luigné, tel. 02.41.78.33.53, fax 02.41.78.67.61 ☑
🍷 by appt.

DOM. DES BOHUES
Cuvée des Martyrs 2000★★
□ 0.8 ha 1,800

Denis Roussillon won a *coup de coeur* last year for his 99 vintage, and narrowly missed winning another with this Cuvée des Martyrs. It has an intense yellow colour, an exuberant bouquet of apricots and a full, rich and smooth palate with an impression of unctuousness that lasts throughout the wine. This is a wine to lay down for several years in the cellar.

🞄 Denis Retailleau, Les Bohues, 49750 Saint-Lambert-du-Lattay, tel. 02.41.78.33.92, fax 02.41.78.34.11 ☑
🍷 by appt.

CH. DU BREUIL
Beaulieu Vieilles vignes 1999★
□ 8 ha 2,500 €11-15

This Cuvée Vieilles Vignes was vinified in barrel and truly deserves its name, being made from 100-year-old vines. It appears in the *Guide* for the third year running. The bouquet of this golden-yellow 99 is initially restrained, but when swirled in the glass it releases subtle scents of crystallised fruits or fruits steeped in brandy. The rich, powerful palate has a complex range of flavours combining lemon, grapefruit, honey, linden flower and vanilla. Given time to breathe, this is a surprisingly delicate wine.

🞄 Ch. du Breuil, 49750 Beaulieu-sur-Layon, tel. 02.41.78.32.54, fax 02.41.78.30.03, e-mail ch.breuil@wanadoo.fr ☑ 🍷 by appt.
🞄 Morgat

CH. DE BROSSAY
Sélection de grains nobles 1999★★
□ 3 ha 1,600 €11-15

The Château de Brossay has a 36-ha (88.9-acre) vineyard in the Upper Layon, not far from the source of the river. Like the Sélection de Grains Nobles in last year's remarkable vintage, this one was made with grapes containing naturally more than 17.5% potential alcohol. It is straw-yellow, and after being swirled in the glass the nose releases aromas of ripe or concentrated fruit mixed with spices. The powerful palate is currently dominated by the oak and the long finish gives an impression of great richness. This wine will be even better at the start of 2002 and should improve over the next year or two.

🞄 Raymond et Hubert Defrois, Ch. de Brossay, 49560 Cléré-sur-Layon, tel. 02.41.59.59.95, fax 02.41.59.58.81, e-mail chateau.brossay@wanadoo.fr ☑
🍷 ev. day except Sun. 8am–12.30pm 2pm–7pm

DOM. CADY Saint-Aubin Grains nobles
Cuvée Volupté 1999★★
□ 3 ha 2,600 €11-15

Having won stars galore and with more than one *coup de coeur* to its credit, the 20-ha (49.4-acre) Cady estate is a safe bet when it comes to sweet wines. This Cuvée Volupté is an intense orange-yellow and justifies its name through the extremely sweet impression it makes on the palate. The bouquet of spices and crystallised fruits is characteristic of noble rot. The flavours on the palate are a sumptuous blend of peach, apricot jam, and crystallised fruits. This wine will become even more complex in years to come. A **Coteaux du Layon Les Varennes** comes from a south-facing hill where layers of green schist from the Primary era break through to the surface. It is yellow with green tones, and after swirling in the glass releases an array of complex aromas such as ripe peaches, apricots, crystallised quince, honey and spices. It is fresh and balanced on the palate with an appealing hint of bitterness on the finish (half-litre bottles).

🞄 Dom. Cady, Valette, 49190 Saint-Aubin-de-Luigné, tel. 02.41.78.33.69, fax 02.41.78.67.79, e-mail cadypb@wanadoo.fr ☑ 🍷 by appt.

DOM. PIERRE CHAUVIN
Rablay Vieilles vignes 1999★
□ n.c. 2,500 €8-11

The village of Rablay-sur-Layon has an unusual *terroir* consisting of layers of sand and gravel several metres thick in places and lying on the schistose platform of the Massif Armorican. These are the soils that produced this intensely yellow 99 with its light but delicate bouquet mingling ripe fruits, apple and pear jam, spices and vanilla. This harmonious, well-balanced wine finishes on a note of crystallised fruits and impresses more with its elegance than its power.

🞄 Dom. Pierre Chauvin, 45, Grande-Rue, 49750 Rablay-sur-Layon, tel. 02.41.78.32.76, fax 02.41.78.22.55, e-mail domaine.pierrechauvin@wanadoo.fr ☑ 🍷 by appt.

DOM. DE CLAYOU 2000★
□ 7 ha 5,000 €5-8

Saint-Lambert-du-Lattay is the most intensive wine-growing village in Anjou. It also contains a Museum of Vines and Wine. Jean-Bernard Chauvin cultivates 21 ha (51.9 acres), and two of his wines are well worth noting. Firstly, his **Coteau du Layon Saint-Lambert 99**, is a light wine typical of the vintage but with a fairly good potential to age (for five years). It is a pleasant wine with a bouquet of dried fruits and green apples and is fresh and balanced on the palate. Then there is this pale-yellow 2000 with its delicate bouquet of ripe fruits and honey, and its pleasant palate combining liveliness and sweetness. The hint of bitterness on the finish is typical of the year and should disappear. Allow it time to breathe before serving.

◗ SCEA Jean-Bernard Chauvin, 18 bis, rue du Pont-Barré, 49750 Saint-Lambert-du-Lattay, tel. 02.41.78.42.84, fax 02.41.78.48.52 ⋈ ev. day except Sun. 9am–12 noon 2pm–7pm; cl. end Aug.

DOM. DU CLOS DES GOHARDS
Cuvée spéciale 2000★
n.c.   6,000   €5-8

This family estate was founded in 1924 and now has 34 ha (84 acres). Its Coteau du Layon 2000 is pale-yellow and the tasters reported that it was very well-balanced for the year. They liked its fine bouquet of white flowers and ripe fruits, and the latter recur on the full-flavoured but delicate palate.

◗ EARL Michel et Mickaël Joselon, Les Oisonnières, 49380 Chavagnes-les-Eaux, tel. 02.41.54.13.98, fax 02.41.54.13.98 ⋈ by appt.

DOM. DES CLOSSERONS
Faye Elevé en fûts de chêne 1999★★★
2.6 ha   4,000   €15-23

Jean-Claude Leblanc founded this vineyard in 1956 and was joined by his sons Yannick and Dominique in the 1980s. The estate has close to 51 ha (126 acres), and is one of those which set out to replant the steep slopes where Chenin does so well. They have succeeded in their aim, and in recent years have had several wines mentioned in the *Guide*. This lovely, amber 99 was the result of four *tries* (harvesting at different times to pick the ripest fruit). The nose is intense but delicate, combining concentrated fruit, quince, honey and spices. The full palate is both rich and fresh, finishing with a dazzling display of flavours.

◗ EARL Jean-Claude Leblanc et Fils, Dom. des Closserons, 49380 Faye-d'Anjou, tel. 02.41.54.30.78, fax 02.41.54.12.02 ⋈ by appt.

DOM. PHILIPPE DELESVAUX
Sélection de grains nobles 1999★★
10 ha   6,000   €23-30

Philippe Delesvaux has been running this estate of some 15 ha (37 acres) since 1978. He uses *les vendanges par tries* (a selective-picking method), and is one of those winegrowers who have campaigned for recognition of the distinction 'Sélection de Grain Nobles'

for the sweet wines of Anjou. This wine was vinified and matured in barrel for 18 months. It has an intense straw-yellow colour and a complex bouquet of ripe and concentrated fruit. It is full on the palate, with a chewy, curranty flavour. This is a powerful wine which nevertheless leaves an impression of lightness and delicacy typical of the great sweet wines of the Loire.

◗ Philippe Delesvaux, Les Essards, La Haie-Longue, 49190 Saint-Aubin-de-Luigné, tel. 02.41.78.18.71, fax 02.41.78.68.06 ⋈ by appt.

DOM. DHOMME 1999★★★
4 ha   1,700   €11-15

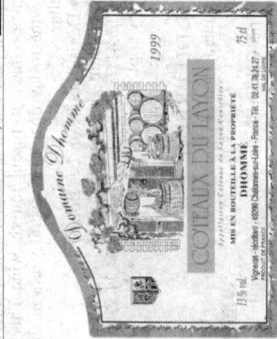

Chalonnes-sur-Loire was an active inland port during the Ancien Régime. The best wines of Anjou were shipped from this market town at the confluence of the Layon and the Loire to Holland and its colonies. The Dhommé family, who run a 18-ha (44.5-acre) estate founded in 1960, featured in the first edition of the *Guide*. They now make a triumphant return with this superb straw-yellow 99 so typical of the Loire valley, made with grapes having a natural potential alcohol of more than 17.5%. Everything about it is pleasing, from the complex, delicate bouquet blending mineral and floral notes, shades of dried fruits (currants and apricots) and spices, to the palate, which is both concentrated and fresh. This is a great wine which will become even greater.

◗ Dhommé, Le Petit Port-Girault, 49290 Chalonnes-sur-Loire, tel. 02.41.78.24.27, fax 02.41.74.94.91 ⋈ by appt.

DOM. DULOQUET
Cuvée prestige 2000★
3 ha   2,320   €8-11

This estate was founded by the grandfather, modernised by the father and taken over in 1991 by the grandson, Hervé Duloquet, who has established its fame. Although this year's wine may seem a little short of certain previous vintages, it will not disappoint winelovers. Its yellow colour is true to type; the nose has a good intensity with very elegant notes of ripe and concentrated fruit that recur as flavours on the unexpectedly rich and full palate.

DOM. DES EPINAUDIERES

Saint-Lambert 2000★

□ 1 ha ■ 4,000 €5-8

Roger Faideau has made excellent progress since he first took over the vineyard as a tenant (in 1966) and was joined by his son ten years ago. Today this estate has 21 ha (51.9 acres) and features regularly in the *Guide*. This 2000 wine starts with an orange-yellow colour and a bouquet comprising dried fruits and linden flowers. The palate is rounded, rich and well-balanced, and finishes on notes of apricot. This very successful wine will be ready for drinking at the start of 2002.

➤ SCEA Fardeau, Sainte-Foy,
4750 Saint-Lambert-du-Lattay,
tel. 02.41.78.35.68, fax 02.41.78.35.50,
e-mail fardeau.paul@club-internet.fr ▼
Y by appt.

DOM. DES FORGES

Saint-Aubin Cuvée des Forges 2000★★

□ 10 ha ■ 3,000 €8-11

The first plot here was acquired in 1890. Today the estate comprises 38 ha (94 acres) and in 1996 welcomed Stéphane Branchereau, representing the fifth generation. It has already won three *coups de coeur* for this appellation. This Cuvée des Forges is yellow with green glints and has attractive aromas of apricots, honey and spices. The palate is balanced, fresh and long. This wine is true to type, leaving a dual impression of delicate elegance and character.

➤ Vignoble Branchereau, Dom. des Forges,
rte de la Haie-Longue,
49190 Saint-Aubin-de-Luigné,
tel. 02.41.78.33.56, fax 02.41.78.67.51 ▼
Y by appt.

CH. DU FRESNE Clos des Cocus 1999★

□ 1.15 ha ■ 2,000 €15-23

This plot is just a tiny part of a large estate of 76 ha (187.7 acres), but its name is nonetheless famous. It has produced a wine which should be enjoyed for its intrinsic qualities and not because its name stirs thoughts of a certain Bacchic tradition. This straw-yellow 99 has delicate aromas of ripe and dried fruits together with some herbaceous notes. The palate is balanced and pleasant, with the flavours of dried fruits (quince and apricot) recurring on the finish.

➤ Vignobles Robin-Bretault, Ch. du Fresne,
49380 Faye-d'Anjou, tel. 02.41.54.30.88,
fax 02.41.54.17.52, e-mail fresne@voila.fr ▼

DOM. DE GATINES

Cuvée Juliette 1999★

□ 3 ha ■ 1,500

This 35-ha (86.5-acre) estate is proud of being voted the best at pruning in the whole of France. Its Cuvée Juliette was made after

DOM. GROSSET

La Motte à Bory Rochefort 2000★

□ 1.6 ha ■ 3,500 €11-15

At this traditional estate they stick to the old ways of cultivating their vines and vinifying the grapes in barrel. This La Motte à Bory is a delicate wine. Its restrained bouquet nevertheless has a complex range of aromas including peaches, quince, honey, apricots and linden flower. The quince and honey flavours return on the fresh, balanced, light palate. This elegant wine is a good advertisement for the sweet wines of the Loire.

➤ Serge Grosset, 60, rue René-Gasnier,
49190 Rochefort-sur-Loire,
tel. 02.41.78.67, fax 02.41.78.79.79 ▼
Y by appt.

DOM. DE LA BERGERIE

Cuvée Fragrance 1999★★

□ 2.5 ha ■ 2,000 €23-30

This 34-ha (84-acre) estate features regularly in the *Guide*, especially for its Cuvée Fragrance. Its sweet wines are highly regarded. They work very thoroughly on their vines (short pruning, thinning and controlling vigour), and vinification is carried out in barrel. This 99 wine was in barrel for 15 months and makes an extremely powerful impression. Its range of aromas is surprisingly rich, a mixture of exotic fruits,

a fourth *trie* (selective harvest) was carried out. The must had a natural potential alcohol content of 20.6%. It has an intense yellow colour and an equally intense, very delicate, nose that blends mineral notes with those of noble rot. The palate is a combination of power, elegance and balance.

➤ EARL Vignoble Desserre, Dom. de Gatines, 12, rue de la Boulaie, 49540 Tigné, tel. 02.41.59.41.48, fax 02.41.59.44.44 ▼
Y ev. day except Sun. 8am-12.30pm
2pm-7pm

DOM. GAUDARD Saint-Aubin 2000★

□ 2 ha ■ 3,500 €8-11

Pierre Aguilas has been campaigning for almost ten years to promote the Anjou wine region. This year, two of his Coteaux du Layon, though very different from each other, have been awarded one star. The Saint-Aubin revealed the ripeness of the vintage at every stage of the tasting. Starting with a straw-yellow colour, it has a bouquet mingling white flowers, apricots, honey and orange peel. The balanced palate leaves an impression of ripe fruits and finishes with a pleasant hint of bitterness. His other wine, **Les Varennes 2000**, has a bright-yellow colour with straw highlights, and although it is not very concentrated, is delicate with subtle aromas of white flowers and pears. The palate is fresh and well-balanced.

➤ Pierre Aguilas, Dom. Gaudard,
rte de Saint-Aubin,
49290 Chaudefonds-sur-Layon,
tel. 02.41.78.10.68, fax 02.41.78.67.72 ▼
Y ev. day except Sun. 9am-12 noon
2pm-7pm

➤ Hervé Duloquet, Les Mousseaux, 4, rte du Coteau, 49700 Les Verchers-sur-Layon, tel. 02.41.59.17.62, fax 02.41.59.37.53 ▼
Y by appt.

crystallised fruits, honey and spices. It still needs time to reach its full potential. It should acquire more finesse and will be really wonderful in a few years (half-litre bottles).
➤ Yves Guégniard, Dom. de La Bergerie, 49380 Champ-sur-Layon, tel. 02.41.78.85.43, fax 02.41.78.60.13, e-mail domaine.de.la.bergerie@wanadoo.fr
ⓥ ♈ ev. day except Sun. 9am–12 noon 2pm–6.30pm

DOM. DE LA COUCHETIERE 2000 €5-8
1.8 ha   3,500

This family property took up wine-growing in 1969. Its 2000 vintage has an intense yellow colour and its bouquet offers a blend of white flowers and ripe fruits. The palate is balanced and fresh. This is a simple Coteau du Layon, pleasant and well-made, and will be ready at the start of 2002.
➤ GAEC Brault Père et Fils, Dom. de La Couchetière, 49380 Notre-Dame-d'Allençon, tel. 02.41.54.30.26, fax 02.41.54.40.98 ⓥ
♈ ev. day except Sun. 8.30am–12.30pm 2pm–7.30pm

LA DUCQUERIE
Saint-Lambert Prestige 1999★★
5 ha   4,000   €8-11

This estate won a coup de coeur last year for its white Anjou. This wine was made after a meticulous selection in the vineyard and vinification in barrel. It has an intense yellow colour with amber glints. After swirling in the glass, the bouquet releases aromas of white flowers (acacia), citrus fruits (grapefruit) and ripe fruits. The palate is concentrated and intense and finishes on a note of dried fruit. It is a remarkable wine (half-litre bottles).
➤ EARL La Ducquerie, 2, chem. du Grand-Clos, 49750 Saint-Lambert du Lattay, tel. 02.41.78.42.00, fax 02.41.78.48.17 ⓥ ♈ by appt.

DOM. DE L'ANGELIERE
Faye d'Anjou 1999★
3 ha   8,000   €8-11

This estate has been in the same family for six generations and now has 40 ha (99 acres) of vines. The plot producing this 1999 wine is on a high south-facing slope from which you can see the towers of nine churches. The wine leaves an impression of elegance and finesse. Its aromas of citrus fruit such as mandarin and white flowers are typical of a harvest affected by noble rot. The light palate is very pleasant. This delicate wine is ready to be enjoyed straight away.
➤ GAEC Boret, Dom. de L'Angelière, 49380 Champ-sur-Layon, tel. 02.41.78.85.09, fax 02.41.78.67.10 ⓥ ♈ ev. day except Sun. 9am–7pm

DOM. DE LA PETITE CROIX 2000★★
n.c.   4,000   €8-11

The Jury were full of praise for this Coteaux du Layon made from selected grapes.

It has an intense golden-yellow colour and its range of aromas is typically concentrated with notes of acacia, stewed fruits and crystallised fruits. The palate is silky, even voluptuous, and finishes with a hint of bitterness which will disappear as the wine matures.
➤ A. Denechère et F. Geffard, Dom. de la Petite Croix, 49380 Thouarcé, tel. 02.41.54.06.99, fax 02.41.54.30.05 ⓥ ♈ by appt.

DOM. DE LA ROCHE AIRAULT
Rochefort Vieilles vignes 1999★
1.5 ha   4,000   €5-8

This 14-ha (34.6-acre) estate is located at the foot of the Anjou Ledge, which overhangs the Loire and Layon Valleys. The 97 vintage of its Rochefort Vieilles Vignes was remarkable. The 99 version is yellow with grey-green glints and is a very successful, fairly light wine. The nose is a combination of peaches, blackberries and menthol; the palate is fruity, fresh and balanced, revealing a hint of bitterness on the finish. Keep it for a year.
➤ Pascal Audio, La Roche Airault, 49190 Saint-Aubin-de-Luigné, tel. 02.41.78.74.30, fax 02.41.78.89.03 ⓥ ♈ by appt.

DOM. DE LA ROCHE MOREAU
Chaume Sélection de Grains Nobles Cuvée Alexis 1999★
n.c.   n.c.   €11-15

Before the Industrial Revolution, they used to mine coal in this region. Some of the old mining galleries are still around, one of them being used to store the older vintages of this 21-ha (51.9-acre) estate, which stands on the Anjou Ledge. Its tasting room is a chalet with a panoramic view over the Loire Valley and the Layon hills, and its wines are well worth coming to try. This Cuvée Alexis is made from fruit with a natural alcohol potential of more than 17.5%. The colour is golden-yellow and the aromas are those associated with noble rot. The rich, powerful and fairly sweet palate contains notes of honey. Drink it as an aperitif.
➤ André Davy, Dom. de La Roche Moreau, La Haie-Longue, 49190 Saint-Aubin-de-Luigné, tel. 02.41.78.34.55, fax 02.41.78.17.70, e-mail davy.larochemoreau@wanadoo.fr ♈ by appt.

DOM. LEDUC-FROUIN
Le Grand Clos La Seigneurie 2000★★
3 ha   2,000   €8-11

This 28-ha (69.2-acre) estate was once a stately home. It was acquired in 1933 by the Leduc-Frouin family, who had been cultivating it since 1873. The management of the estate was recently handed over to a new generation. Their wine has plenty of character, being made from grapes of remarkable quality for the year, and leaves an impression of surprising concentration. The intense aromas on the nose recall dried fruits such as grapes and apricots. The palate is powerful, rich and sweet. This is a remarkable wine which it would be advisable to keep for a while.

• SCEA Dom. Leduc-Frouin, Sousigné, 49540 Martigné-Briand, tel. 02.41.59.42.83, fax 02.41.59.47.90, e-mail domaine-leduc-frouin@wanadoo.fr
☑ Y by appt.

DOM. LEROY Cuvée Divinité 2000

2 ha   3,000   €8-11

The 11th-century church of Aubigné-sur-Layon has interesting *trompe-l'œil* frescos dating from the 18th century. Facing it is this very old estate, founded in 1612: the vineyard was started in 1840. There you can try a **Coteaux du Layon Vieilles Vignes 2000**, which the Jury singled out, finding it pleasant, simple and well-made. It is pale-yellow and has notes of toast and dried fruits such as apricots on the nose, together with a light, fresh palate.

• Jean-Michel Leroy, rue d'Anjou, 49540 Aubigné-sur-Layon, tel. 02.41.59.61.00, fax 02.41.59.96.47 ☑ Y by appt.

DOM. LES GRANDES VIGNES 2000★★

5.72 ha   9,600   €5-8

Three brothers and sisters run this 50-ha (123.5-acre) estate. In recent years their remarkable Bonnezeaux and Coteaux du Layon have been featured in the *Guide*. This wine was matured in barrel for one year and drew two kinds of comment. Everyone was agreed that it should be kept for a while. They also agreed that behind certain imperfections of youth they could sense a complex range of aromas including dried fruits (apricots and almonds) and spices. Everyone also liked its impression of balance and surprising finesse. This outstanding wine should already have improved by the time you read this.

• GAEC Vaillant, Dom. Les Grandes Vignes, La Roche Aubry, 49380 Thouarcé, tel. 02.41.54.05.06, fax 02.41.54.08.21, e-mail gaecvaillant@wordonline.fr ☑ Y by appt.

DOM. OGEREAU Saint-Lambert Clos des Bonnes Blanches 1999★★★

2 ha   5,000   €15-23

This wine has a golden-yellow colour. The intense and complex nose has notes of dried, ripe, and concentrated fruit, spices and honey,

DOM. DE PAIMPARE Saint-Lambert 2000

4 ha   2,000   €5-8

Michel Tessier has been at Saint-Lambert-du-Lattay since 1990. This is one of the strongholds of Coteaux du Layon, and it has appeared regularly in the *Guide*. This vintage certainly lacks the richness of the two 97 wines he produced two years ago, but allowances must be made for the wetness of the latter part of the season in 2000. This has given the wine a bright-yellow colour, a bouquet with notes of citrus-fruit flowers and ripe fruits, and a palate which is pleasant, light and fresh. This simple, well-made wine will be ready to drink at the start of 2002.

• SCEA Michel Tessier, 32, rue Rabelais, 49750 Saint-Lambert-du-Lattay, tel. 02.41.78.43.18, fax 02.41.78.41.73 ☑ Y by appt.

DOM. DES PETITS-QUARTS Faye 2000★★

2.3 ha   3,300   €8-11

The vineyard was founded in 1887. The Goudineau family use organic methods, producing sweet wines of a consistently high quality, both Coteaux du Layon and Bonnezeaux, which have won several *coups de cœur* in the *Guide*. This 2000 wine has an intense golden colour, aromas of honey, quince and exotic fruits, and a sweet, long

all of which are typical of overripe harvests. The opulent palate imparts a feeling, appropriate to great sweet wines, of chewing currants. This vintage has just sailed around the world in the boat of Michel Desjoyaux, winner of the Vendée-Globe. One hopes it will travel more and make itself known in other continents because, while the two previous vintages were very distinguished, this one has been voted champion of the AOC. It confirms the talents of a wine-grower who, both in Anjou and Coteaux du Layon, has been gathering up *coups de cœur* for his wines from the region.

• Vincent Ogereau, 44, rue de la Belle-Angevine, 49750 Saint-Lambert-du-Lattay, tel. 02.41.78.30.53, fax 02.41.78.43.55 Y by appt.

DOM. OGEREAU Saint-Lambert Cuvée Prestige 1999★★★

6 ha   7,500   €11-15

Here is a different style of Coteau du Layon that is just as good as the previous wine. Partly aged in barrel and partly in tank, it is less powerful but has excellent finesse and delicacy. Straw-yellow with amber reflections, it has aromas of overripeness, dried fruits (apricots), hazelnuts and ripe fruits. The palate is very well-balanced and leaves an impression of lightness despite its overall richness.

• Vincent Ogereau, 44, rue de la Belle-Angevine, 49750 Saint-Lambert-du-Lattay, tel. 02.41.78.43.55 ☑ by appt.

palate flavoured by very ripe pears. It is a splendidly rich and fine wine.

➤ Godineau Père et Fils, Dom. des Petits Quarts, 49380 Faye-d'Anjou,
tel. 02.41.54.03.00, fax 02.41.54.25.36 ▼
Ⓨ ev. day except Sun. 8am–12 noon 2pm–6pm

DOM. DU PETIT-VAL 2000

☐　2 ha　7,000　▪ ♦　€5–8

Vincent Goizil and the Petit-Val estate were mentioned in the first edition of the *Guide*. Since then, the business has been taken over by his son Denis (in 1988). It still keeps up its appearances in the *Guide*, especially for its sweet wines (19 ha/46.9 acres out of the estate's 34 ha/84 acres are allocated to Chenin grapes). The 2000 wine is typical both of the appellation and the year. It has a lovely yellow colour, aromas of the desired intensity and a rich and concentrated palate. Although it was not entirely balanced at the time of tasting, it should have improved by the end of 2001.

➤ EARL Denis Goizil, Dom. du Petit-Val, 49380 Chavagnes, tel. 02.41.54.31.14, fax 02.41.54.03.48 ▼ Ⓨ by appt.

CH. PIERRE-BISE

Rochefort Les Rayelles 2000★★

☐　3.57 ha 4,000　▪ €11–15

This vineyard was founded in 1910 and has 53 ha (131 acres). It has been in the *Guide* since the first edition, producing outstanding sweet wines which have already won five *coups de coeur* (in Coteaux du Layon and Quarts-de-Chaume). Its Les Rayelles wine was a winner for its 99 and 97 vintages. The 2000 version had still not reached its full potential on the day of the tasting, but the Jury could see it had all the signs of a remarkable future ahead of it: an intense colour with straw-gold highlights, a complex range of aromas mingling dried apricots, crystallised fruits, honey, wax and honeysuckle, and a powerful palate with notes of overripe grapes. It will be ready from the beginning of 2002. A second wine, the **Coteaux du Layon Chaume 2000**, was full of concentrated fruit and should be kept for a year. It was awarded one star (half-litre bottles).

➤ Claude Papin, Ch. Pierre-Bise, 49750 Beaulieu-sur-Layon,
tel. 02.41.78.31.44, fax 02.41.78.41.24 ▼ Ⓨ by appt.

CH. DE PLAISANCE

Chaume Les Charmelles 1999★★

☐　4 ha 5,000　▪ ♦ €11–15

The first *coup de coeur* for this AOC was a 1970 Château de Plaisance. This 30-ha (74-acre) estate is located in the middle of the vines on the Chaume hillside, a very good site for the appellation. Its Les Charmelles is very typical of sweet wines from theregion, combining delicacy with richness and power. Its complex aromas suggest white flowers (acacia), citrus fruits and ripe grapes. The attractions of the palate lie in its apparent lightness, great freshness and the finish, which lasts a surprisingly long time. Another wine

from the same appellation, **Les Zerzilles 99**, was also singled out and should be put in the cellar to mature for a year or two.

➤ Guy Rochais, Ch. de Plaisance, 49190 Rochefort-sur-Loire,
tel. 02.41.78.33.01, fax 02.41.78.67.52 ▼ Ⓨ by appt.

DOM. JEAN-LOUIS ROBIN-DIOT

Rochefort Cuvée Intégrale 1999★★

☐　3 ha　n.c.　Ⅲ €15–23

Jean-Louis Robin has been here for more than 30 years and is president of the Union of Coteaux du Layon. He was one of the wine-growers who started this appellation's revival. His Cuvée Intégrale was vinified and aged for one year in barrel and comes from 60-year-old vines. It is still dominated by aromas stemming from its maturation in oak (vanilla, smoky and toasty notes) along with others typical of overripe grapes (dried fruits, crystallised fruits, quince, wax and linden flower). The palate is rich, delicate and harmonious. The balance is excellent (half-litre bottles).

➤ Dom. Jean-Louis Robin-Diot, Les Hauts-Perrays,
49290 Chaudefonds-sur-Layon, tel. 02.41.78.68.29, fax 02.41.78.67.62 ▼ Ⓨ by appt.

DOM. JEAN-LOUIS ROBIN-DIOT

La Pierre d'Ardenay 2000★

☐　n.c.　3,000　▪ €8–11

This selection, made from old vines, has a pale-yellow colour and a charming delicacy. Its subtle, light bouquet is reminiscent of roses. The palate is light, smooth and refined with a finish marked by pleasant notes of ripe fruits (greengages, pears and plums). Jean-Louis Robin's **Clos du Cochet Rochefort 99**, matured in barrel, was also made from old vines and wins one star. Yellow with golden glints, its bouquet combines fresh fruits (apricots and quince), honey and linden flower with oaky notes. The palate is fruity, rich and fresh, leaving an impression of delicacy and balance. Drink now if you can't wait, but it will be better kept for a few years.

➤ Dom. Jean-Louis Robin-Diot, Les Hauts-Perrays,
49290 Chaudefonds-sur-Layon, tel. 02.41.78.68.29, fax 02.41.78.67.62 ▼ Ⓨ by appt.

MICHEL ROBINEAU Saint-Lambert

Sélection de grains nobles 1999★★

☐　2 ha　3,000　Ⅲ €11–15

Michel Robineau has been running this vineyard since 1990, and loves tending his vines (he uses methods of short pruning, controlling the yield and hand-picking). For this reason, people wait eagerly for his latest wines, especially this Sélection de Grains Nobles de Saint-Lambert, which most years wins at least one star (the 93 was awarded a *coup de coeur*). The 99 vintage was made from grapes with a natural potential alcohol of more than 17.5%. This initial richness accounts for the intense aromas and flavours released during the tasting. The colour is a deep-gold with orangey tones. The aromas are typical of noble rot and the powerful palate is strongly marked by fruity notes. This Coteaux du Layon could be kept for more than 20 years.

● Michel Robineau, 3, chem. du Moulin, Les Grandes Tailles, 49750 Saint-Lambert-du-Lattay, tel. 02.41.78.34.67 ▼ ▼ by appt.

CH. DES ROCHETTES
Sélection de Vieilles vignes 2000★★
□ 4 ha   10,000   €8-11   ▼ ▼ by appt.

Three wines were submitted (see also the next entry), and won seven stars between them. The Château des Rochettes is exemplary. Both the 2000 wines on offer were thought to be remarkable. This Sélection de Vieilles Vignes leaves an impression of ripe fruits and won over the tasters with its powerful and complex range of aromas mingling floral notes, concentrated fruits and spices. The Moelleux 2000 is lighter and very well-balanced. It has a charmingly delicate bouquet combining aromas of honey, white fruits and spices.

● Jean Douet, Ch. des Rochettes, 49700 Concourson-sur-Layon, tel. 02.41.59.11.51, fax 02.41.59.37.73 ▼ by appt.

CH. DES ROCHETTES
Sélection de Grains Nobles Cuvée Folie 1999★★★
□ 2 ha   2,000   €15-23

During the Revolution, this vineyard was the scene of violent fighting between the Blues and the Vendéens. Two centuries later, it is leading another campaign, this time a peaceful one, to promote the excellence of grapes affected by noble rot. This Cuvée Folie, which has three coups de coeur to its credit, will further boost the fame of this type of wine. It is made from grapes with a natural potential alcohol of more than 20%, and was fermented and aged in barrel for 18 months. The result is a surprisingly powerful wine. Its straw-yellow colour is enlivened by marvellous golden glints. The bouquet is heavenly, releasing aromas of stewed fruits, bergamot orange and caramel. The palate is opulent, the finish dazzling. This is not so much a dessert wine as 'a dessert all by itself', as one taster put it, a wine to be savoured calmly and at length.

● Jean Douet, Ch. des Rochettes, 49700 Concourson-sur-Layon, tel. 02.41.59.11.51, fax 02.41.59.37.73 ▼

DOM. ROMPILLON
Saint-Aubin Le Défay 1999★
□ 2 ha   2,500

Jean-Pierre Rompillon's estate stands on the Wine Route which, between Saint-Lambert-du-Lattay and Saint-Aubin-de-Luigné, winds amongst the vines and passes beneath the famous Quarts-de-Chaume cru. This 99 wine comes from Saint-Aubin and is a classic of the appellation. It has a clear straw-yellow colour and delicate aromas of ripe fruits (pears) and concentrated fruit along with oaky notes. The palate is balanced, fresh and concentrated, and marked on the finish by oaky flavours. Keep it for at least a year. The estate also offered a Clos des Forières Saint-Lambert 99 which wins a mention. This wine needs swirling in the glass to release its scents of white flowers and ripe fruits. The palate is fairly light, fresh and well-balanced.

● Jean-Pierre Rompillon, L'Olluière, 49750 Saint-Lambert-du-Lattay, tel. 02.41.78.48.84, fax 02.41.78.48.84 ▼

SAUVEROY
Saint-Lambert Cuvée Nectar 1999★★
□ 1.04 ha   4,100   €11-15

This family estate was founded in 1947 and now has 27 ha (66.7 acres). Its 99 vintage has all the characteristics of a wine made with overripe grapes: a strong yellow colour with orangey highlights; delicate aromas of dried fruits, concentrated fruit and spices; a powerful and elegant palate; and a long and intense finish.

● Pascal Cailleau, Dom. du Sauveroy, 49750 Saint-Lambert-du-Lattay, tel. 02.41.78.30.59, fax 02.41.78.46.43, e-mail domainesauveroy@terre-net.fr ▼ by appt.

CH. SOUCHERIE
Beaulieu Cuvée de La Tour 1998★
□ 4 ha   2,500   €11-15

This 30-ha (74.1-acre) estate has a lovely view over the Layon and Chaume hillsides. Its Cuvée de La Tour is yellow with golden glints, and was matured in barrel for 12 months. On the nose, ripe fruits and dried fruits are combined with smoky, toasty notes. The pleasant palate blends fruity and oaky characteristics, such as vanilla and coconut, and the finish is delicately marked by flavours of honey and crystallised fruits (half-litre bottles).

● P.-Y. Tijou et Fils, Ch. Soucherie, 49750 Beaulieu-sur-Layon, tel. 02.41.78.31.18, fax 02.41.78.48.29 ▼ by appt.

DOM. DES VARENNES
Saint-Lambert Cuvée des Varennes 1999★
□ 1 ha   3,000   €11-15

Founded in 1930, this vineyard adopted the name 'Varennes' in 1983. Locally, the term refers to the surface stones which appear on the schistose platform of the Massif Armorican. This Cuvée des Varennes has a strong colour with orangey glints. After swirling in the glass, it releases aromas reminiscent of citrus fruits (grapefruit) and other ripe fruits. The palate is fairly light, balanced and pleasant. This wine could be kept for five years.

● GAEC A. Richard, 11, rue des Varennes, 49750 Saint-Lambert-du-Lattay, tel. 02.41.78.32.97, fax 02.41.74.00.30 ▼ by appt.

Bonnezeaux

Dr Maisonneuve said in 1925 that this wine was 'inimitable' as an accompaniment for desserts. At the time it was the custom to consume great sweet wines either with dessert, or in the afternoon, socially amongst friends. Nowadays, this very perfumed and vigorous Grand Cru is more generally appreciated as an aperitif. It owes its qualities to an exceptional *terroir*: the three steep little slopes of schists (La Montagne, Beauregard and Fesles) above the village of Thouarcé.

In 2000, the volume of production reached 1,964 hl (51,850 gal). The area of production includes 130 ha (321 acres) of plantable land. This is a good value, consistently reliable wine that will keep a long time.

DOM. DES COQUERIES 1999

☐   2 ha   5,000   ▦ Ⅲ▯ ◈   €11-15

This traditional estate of 8.5 ha (21 acres) was taken over in 1998 by Philippe Gilardeau, who has made its name with this appellation (see the 2000 edition). This Bonnezeaux has an attractive greeny-gold colour. The bouquet is still restrained, with notes of apples and pears, and the attack is light and fresh. It is generally a well-balanced wine.

•᛫ EARL Philippe Gilardeau, Les Noues, 49380 Thouarcé, tel. 02.41.54.39.11, fax 02.41.54.38.84 ☒ ☿ by appt.

CH. DE FESLES 1999★

☐   15 ha   18,000   ▦ Ⅲ▯   €30-38

The vineyard won the first *coup de coeur* for this appellation (an 83 wine in the 86 edition) and was awarded another last year for its 98 wine. The château has changed hands several times in the last ten years. Originally belonging to the Boivin family, it was handed over to Gaston Lenôtre in 1991 and sold to Bernard Germain in spring 1996. This 99 vintage has a strong colour and a delicate bouquet veering towards mirabelle plums. These subtle flavours re-emerge on a full but balanced and fresh palate, which has good length.

•᛫ Vignobles Germain et Associés Loire, 49380 Thouarcé, tel. 02.41.68.94.00, fax 02.41.68.94.01, e-mail loire@vgas.com ☒ ☿ by appt.

Bonnezeaux

DOM. DES GAGNERIES

Les Hauts fleuris 1999★★

☐   4 ha   8,000   ▦ Ⅲ▯ ◈   €8-11

This estate, located in the middle of the appellation, was acquired by the Rousseau family in 1890. It has already produced some remarkable vintages (96, 95, 90 and 89) but this is the first time it has won a *coup de coeur*. This wonderful 99 seems both concentrated and fresh, and has an impressive range of aromas. Keep it for as long as you can.

•᛫ EARL Christian et Anne Rousseau, Dom. des Gagneries, 49380 Thouarcé, tel. 02.41.54.00.71, fax 02.41.54.02.62 ☒ ☿ by appt.

DOM. LA CROIX DES LOGES

1999★

☐   1.5 ha   5,000   Ⅲ▯   €11-15

This 40-ha (98.8-acre) estate stands on the road to Gennes, near Martigné, and appears regularly in the *Guide*. Its 99 wine is a very attractive straw-yellow colour, and has strikingly intense aromas marked by earthy notes, which recur on the attack. The flavours on the finish suggest a careful selection of very ripe grapes. This is a wine to lay down for a long time.

•᛫ SCEA Bonnin et Fils, Dom. de La Croix des Loges, 49540 Martigné-Briand, tel. 02.41.59.43.58, fax 02.41.59.41.11, e-mail bonninleslogs@aol.com ☒ ☿ by appt.

DOM. DE LA PETITE CROIX

Cuvée Prestige 2000★

☐   3.5 ha   3,000   ▦ Ⅲ▯ ◈   €11-15

This wine has a very fine ageing potential. The bouquet initially releases linden flower aromas, followed by notes of overripeness reminiscent of dried apricots. The palate is rounded, powerful and fresh. This wine will come into its own in a few years.

•᛫ A. Denechère et F. Geffard, Dom. de la Petite Croix, 49380 Thouarcé, tel. 02.41.54.06.99, fax 02.41.54.30.05 ☒ ☿ by appt.

CH. LA VARIERE

Les Melleresses 1999★

☐   2.3 ha   6,000   Ⅲ▯ ◈   €15-23

Jacques Beaujeau is the latest in a line of wine-growers going back to 1850. This 95-ha

(234.7-acre) estate has 2.3 ha (5.68 acres) set aside for Bonnezeaux; its buildings date from the 13th and 15th centuries. Its Les Melleresses is straw-yellow with lovely green highlights. The nose combines wax and apricots, and is beginning to open out. The attack seems rounded and rich without being mouth-filling. The flavours of baked apples which rush in on the finish lend it a luxurious quality.

♠ Ch. La Varière, 49320 Brissac, tel. 02.41.91.22.64, fax 02.41.91.23.44, e-mail chateau.la.variere@wanadoo.fr ✉
⊤ by appt.

DOM. LES GRANDES VIGNES
1999★
□ 2.1 ha 4,800 €11–15

This 99 wine has a delightfully complex range of aromas including notes of flowers, fruits and vanilla. The palate has a strong, rich structure which leaves an impression of elegance and delicacy. This wine can be kept for 20 years or more.

♠ GAEC Vaillant, Dom. Les Grandes Vignes, La Roche Aubry, 49380 Thouarcé, tel. 02.41.54.05.06, fax 02.41.54.08.21, e-mail gaecvaillant@wordonline.fr ✉
⊤ by appt.

DOM. DES PETITS QUARTS
Le Malabé 2000★★
□ 3 ha 3,300 €11–15

Although they have left the Bonnezeaux appellation area, the Godineau family are not neglecting their 'Malabé.' Admittedly, their new home at Faye-d'Anjou is only half a mile from the old one. This wine is a *coup de coeur* champion in the AOC, having won four (the 90, 95, 96 and 97 vintages). The colour of the 2000 wine is a strong yellow, and its aromas recall exotic and crystallised fruits. The palate has all the qualities expected of a sweet wine (rounded, full-bodied, sweet, balanced and long). This is a wine of remarkable richness.

♠ Godineau Père et Fils, Dom. des Petits Quarts, 49380 Faye-d'Anjou, tel. 02.41.54.03.00, fax 02.41.54.25.36 ✉
⊤ ev. day except Sun. 8am–12 noon 2pm–6pm

DOM. RENE RENOU
Cuvée Zénith 1999★★
□ 8.36 ha n.c. €38–46

This is the Bonnezeaux of the president of INAO. This year he organised the appellation's 50th birthday celebrations. René Renou is a betting man, and this estate of some 8 ha (19.8 acres), which he took over in 1995, marks a new stage in the journey of the man who presides over the AOC's Union. The wine has a slightly amber, straw-yellow colour, and releases strong aromas of white flowers and white peaches. The attack is smooth, fine and distinguished, and the long finish is reminiscent of the overripe, perfectly selected grapes used to make it.

♠ René Renou, 1, pl. du Champ-de-Foire, 49380 Thouarcé, tel. 02.41.54.11.33, fax 02.41.54.11.34, e-mail domaine.rene.renou@wanadoo.fr ✉
⊤ by appt.

Quarts de chaume

The original noble-man owner kept a quarter ('quart') of the production for himself; naturally, he kept the best, meaning the wine produced on the best soil. The appellation, which covers 40 ha (99 acres), is located on a hump of a hill, facing due south, at Rochefort-sur-Loire. A total of 576 hl (15,206 gal) was produced in 2000.

The combination of old plants, the southerly exposure and the capabilities of the Chenin variety means that only a limited amount of wine is produced, although of very high quality. Selective picking during harvest encourages over-ripening of the grapes, giving a sweet white wine that is firm and full of flavour, and ages well.

DOM. DES FORGES 1999★
□ 1 ha 2,000 €23–30

This fresh and complex wine has a lovely golden-yellow colour, a fairly light structure with aromas of dried fruits and honey and a very well-balanced, intense and delicate palate.

DOM. DE TERREBRUNE
Séduction 1999★
□ 2.3 ha 6,000 €11–15

This 45-ha (111.2-acre) estate produces a good deal of rosé wine, but we also remember that it offered the *Guide* a Bonnezeaux 92 which won three stars and a *coup de coeur*. The 1999 vintage has a restrained bouquet and needs to be swirled in the glass. It appears to be more forthcoming on the palate. It is powerful, full and classy, and will reach its full potential in a few years (half-litre bottles).

♠ Dom. de Terrebrune, La Motte, 49380 Notre-Dame-d'Allençon, tel. 02.41.54.01.99, fax 02.41.54.09.06, e-mail domaine-de-terrebrune@wanadoo.fr
✉ ⊤ by appt.

CHATEAU DE L'ECHARDERIE

1999

Clos Paradis

☛ Vignoble Branchereau, Dom. des Forges, rte de la Hale-Longue, 49190 Saint-Aubin-de-Luigné, tel. 02.41.78.33.56, fax 02.41.78.67.51 ☑
Ⴣ by appt.

DOM. DE LA BERGERIE 1999★

☐　　1.25 ha　2.500　　▦ €23-30

Yves Guégniard's grandmother bought the La Bergerie estate in 1961 in order to expand the family's vineyard holdings. Since 1979 it has been run by Yves. This 99 wine has an attractive, strong yellow, slightly golden colour. The palate exudes richness and gives the impression of chewing very ripe fruit. Drink it now or keep it in the cellar for decades.

☛ Yves Guégniard, Dom. de La Bergerie, 49380 Champ-sur-Layon, tel. 02.41.78.85.43, fax 02.41.78.60.13, e-mail domainede.la.bergerie@wanadoo.fr ☑ Ⴣ ev. day except Sun. 9am–12 noon 2pm–6.30pm

DOM. DE LA POTERIE 1999

☐　　0.88 ha　800　　▦ €30-38

This wine is pale-yellow with greenish glints. The bouquet is still restrained and the palate has a good, fruity balance, at present dominated by fairly prominent oak notes. Lay it down for a while.

☛ Guillaume Mordacq, La Chevalerie, 16, av. des Trois-Ponts, 49380 Thouarcé, tel. 02.41.54.12.29, fax 02.41.52.26.41 ☑ Ⴣ by appt.

CH. LA VARIERE

Les Guerches 1998★★

☐　　1.3 ha　3,000　　▦ €30-38

Located very near the Château de Brissac, this estate contains buildings dating from the 13th and 15th centuries and has been in the same family since 1850. It produces a golden-yellow wine with a very rich bouquet and a similar palate, combining floral and fruity notes with just the right amount of oak. This 98 wine has an excellent future and can be left to slumber in the cellar for 20 years or more (half-litre bottles).

☛ Ch. La Varière, 49320 Brissac, tel. 02.41.91.22.64, fax 02.41.91.23.44, e-mail chateau.la.variere@wanadoo.fr ☑ Ⴣ by appt.

CH. DE L'ECHARDERIE

Clos Paradis 1999★★

☐　　7 ha　16,000　　▦ €23-30

L'Echarderie is located in the middle of the Quarts-de-Chaume AOC. The estate's buildings are outbuildings of a noble domain destroyed during the Vendée Wars. Vines have been growing on this *terroir* since the Middle Ages. This 99 wine has a magnificent colour and an exceptional structure with aromas of honey and dried fruits. It is powerful and sweet on the palate with a finish marked by ripe fruits, making it a great *vin liquoreux*.

☛ Vignobles Laffourcade, Ch. de l'Echarderie, 49190 Rochefort-sur-Loire, tel. 02.41.54.16.54, fax 02.41.54.00.10, e-mail laffourcade@wanadoo.fr ☑ Ⴣ by appt.

CH. PIERRE-BISE 2000★★

☐　　2.75 ha　3,000

Claude Papin is nicknamed 'Monsieur *Terroir*' of Anjou, and when you meet him, if only for a few moments, you understand why. This Quarts-de-Chaume has an impressive structure and a very strong golden colour. The bouquet is muted, but opens up wonderfully after swirling in the glass, while the rich palate is balanced and delicious – the true sign of a great *vin liquoreux*.

☛ Claude Papin, Ch. Pierre-Bise, 49750 Beaulieu-sur-Layon, tel. 02.41.78.31.44, fax 02.41.78.41.24 ☑ Ⴣ by appt.

CH. DE PLAISANCE 1999★

☐　　1.5 ha　3,000　　▦ €23-30

The Château de Plaisance is the only estate building to stand in the middle of its vines, and seems to be the guardian of this exceptional site, a tongue of land in the Chaume. The colour of this 99 wine is already a pleasure to behold; on the nose, the aromas are at first still restrained, but flavours emerge on the palate mingling notes of dried and crystallised fruits. The finish leaves an impression of finesse and balance.

☛ Guy Rochais, Ch. de Plaisance, 49190 Rochefort-sur-Loire, tel. 02.41.78.33.01, fax 02.41.78.67.52 ☑ Ⴣ by appt.

The area of production, 2,735 ha (6,755 acres) covers 36 communes. In 2000, a total of 193,391 hl (5,105,522 gal) of red and white (both dry and lively) wine was produced. This included 98,664 hl (2,604,730) of sparkling wines, from the same grape varieties as the AOC Anjou wines. All keep well.

The vineyards stretch along the slopes overlooking the Loire and the Thouet. The white Turquant and Brézé wines were well thought of in the past; the red wines of Puy-Notre-Dame, Montreuil-Bellay and Tourtenay, among others, have acquired a good reputation. However, the appellation is best known for its sparkling wines, and it is worth stressing how much makers, all of whom are based in Saumur, own cellars hollowed out of the tufa that are well worth a visit.

DOM. DU BOIS MIGNON 2000★

■ 14 ha 20,000 ■ ♦ €3-5

This estate is located in the Vienne *département*, in the south of the Saumur wine region, where more than two-thirds of its area is planted with Cabernet. It should therefore not be a surprise to see its Saumur red winning one star. Although it has a strong red colour with violet glints, the nose is initially restrained, but after swirling in the glass suggests notes of very ripe cherries and cloves. The finish is a little tannic, but the palate retains its balance. Altogether, it is a harmonious wine.

☛ SCEA Charier Barillot, Dom. du Bois Mignon, 86120 Saix, tel. 05.49.22.94.59, fax 05.49.22.94.51 ☑ ▼ by appt.

BOUVET LADUBAY Trésor 1999★★

○ n.c. 60,000 ⬛ €11-15

Bouvet-Ladubay was founded around 1850, like many other estates in Saint-Hilaire-Saint-Florent. The company has a reputable name and runs a wine-tasting academy. This Cuvée Trésor now wins its third *coup de cœur* (the others appeared in the 1990 and 1992 editions of the *Guide*). Its fine sparkle and strong golden colour are very pleasing to the eye. Although it is too oaky at the moment, this will help to improve the elegance of its flavours. The palate is full, silky and well-balanced and reveals a perfect marriage of oak and wine at the finish.

☛ Bouvet-Ladubay, 1, rue de l'Abbaye, 49400 Saint-Hilaire-Saint-Florent, tel. 02.41.83.83.83, fax 02.41.50.24.32, e-mail bouvet-ladubay@saumur.net ☑ ▼ ev. day 8.30am–12 noon 2pm–6pm

ACKERMAN Cuvée 1811 2000

○ n.c. 390,700 ♦ €3-5

Saint-Hilaire-Saint-Florent stretches out over a hillside which has been liberally pitted with caves since the Middle Ages, and was once known as Saint-Hilaire-des-Grottes. It was Jean Ackerman, the son of an Anvers banker, who in 1811 had the idea of using them to process wines by the Dom Pérignon method. The Ackerman company is now the largest producer of sparkling Saumur wines. This one has an attractive sparkle which enlivens its colour (pale-yellow with green glints). The intense bouquet is typical of the Cabernet grape variety. The palate is distinctively rounded and elegant.

☛ Laurance Ackerman, BP 47, 49400 Saumur, tel. 02.41.53.03.10, fax 02.41.53.03.19 ▼ ev. day except Sun. Mon. 9am–12 noon 2pm–6pm

CH. DE BEAUREGARD

Blanc de blancs★

○ 4.52 ha 35,000 ■ ♦ €8-11

The château was rebuilt in the 19th century, but retains some elements from the 17th century and even traces dating from the 13th century, when the vast collegiate church which dominates Le Puy-Notre-Dame (a famous place of pilgrimage in the Middle Ages) was built. This sparkling Saumur is made of 80% Chardonnay and 20% Chenin, and has plenty of fine bubbles to add to its attractions. On the nose, exotic fruits and floral notes are mingled. The palate is smooth with good length and is very pleasant.

☛ SCEA Alain Gourdon, Ch. de Beauregard, 4, rue Saint-Julien, 49260 Le Puy-Notre-Dame, tel. 02.41.52.25.33, fax 02.41.52.29.62 ☑ ▼ by appt.

DOM. DES CHAMPS FLEURIS

1999★★

□ 4 ha 7,000 ⬛ €8-11

A few miles from the estate is the abbey of Fontevraud, where Henri II, Eleanor of Aquitaine and Richard the Lionheart are buried. The vineyard is in the Saumur-Champigny area, but the region, and particularly the hillside where the estate is located, was a centre for making white wines before it was colonised by Cabernet. This pale-yellow 99 with golden glints was made from selected grapes and matured for one year in barrel. Its bouquet releases light and delicate scents of ripe fruits, flowers and spices. The palate is rounded and sweet and finishes on a oaky note. This is a rich and complex wine that reflects the efforts made by the wine-growers of Saumur to produce interesting white wines.

Saumur

DOM. ARMAND DAVID

Vieilles vignes 2000★★

■   4 ha   20,000   ■ ●   €5-8

This 15-ha (37-acre) estate was founded in 1932 and is now run by the third generation. It is located on the Jurassic formations of Vaudelnay, and the owners plant grass around the vines and vinify their grapes in natural caves. They made a brilliant début in the *Guide* with their sparkling wines (see the *coups de cœur* in the 1995 and 1996 editions). In recent years they have also been producing red wines, and this 2000 vintage is proof of their skill. It has a strong purple colour with black glints and a bouquet mingling morello cherries, blackcurrants, violets and earthy notes. The full, fleshy palate is just as complex. Already a remarkable wine, this is a Saumur of great promise.

☛ Dom. Armand David. Messemé, 49260 Vaudelnay, tel. 02.41.52.20.84, fax 02.41.38.28.51 ⊠ ▼ ev. day. 9am–7pm

CH. D'ETERNES 1998★★

■   12 ha   8,500   ▥ €11-15

This vineyard, which today has 18 ha (44.5 acres), belonged in the Middle Ages to the abbey of Fontevraud, 4 km (2 miles) away. It produced, we are told, the abbesses' favourite wine. What we can be sure of is that this intense ruby 98 with brown highlights really delighted the Jury. It was aged for 18 months in barrel and is slightly removed from the normal run of the appellation, but won support for its remarkable range of aromas and flavours throughout the tasting: strawberries, blackcurrants, spices and smoky notes captivated the nose and the tastebuds. The palate is smooth, rounded and rich and reveals an astonishingly good structure for this difficult year. It calls for game or an entrecôte steak with shallots.

☛ EARL Ch. d'Eternes, 86120 Saix, tel. 05.49.22.34.77, fax 05.49.22.34.77, e-mail lea.sherina@libertysurf.fr ⊠
▼ By appt.
☛ Marteling

LOUIS FOULON Tête de Cuvée 1997★

○   n.c.   110,000   ■ ●   €5-8

The place-name 'Doué' comes from a Gallic word meaning 'source.' The word Fontaine was then added to it, rather needlessly, to recall a spring which was harnessed

---

☛ EARL Rétiveau-Rétif, 50–54, rue des Martyrs, 49730 Turquant, tel. 02.41.38.10.92, fax 02.41.51.75.33 ⊠
▼ by appt.

CH. DE CHAMPTELOUP

Cuvée Prestige

○   3 ha   4,000   €3-5

This Saumur *brut* is distributed by a company in Mouzillon, in the Nantes region, but it was certainly made in Anjou. The eye is drawn to its fine, elegant and long-lasting sparkle. The bouquet is lively with floral aromas. These characteristics recur on the balanced palate and are evidence of the wine's good length.

☛ Vinival, La Sablette, 44330 Mouzillon, tel. 02.40.36.66.00, fax 02.40.36.26.83

DOM. DES CLOS MAURICE 2000★

■   4 ha   20,000   ■ ●   €3-5

Although Varrans, a large wine-growing village typical of the Saumur region, is a leader in the production of Saumur-Champigny, it also makes good-quality white wines, and this estate produces impressive vintages in either colour. This Saumur red is a brilliant-ruby colour and tastes delicious. It is definitely light, but is delightfully smooth and fruity. The bouquet releases attractive scents of strawberries, spices and menthol, while the palate is no less pleasing with its flavours of fresh fruits. This wine is good for drinking throughout a meal with friends. The Jury also singled out the **white 2000**, which has similar qualities: lightness, fruit and white-flower aromas and a lively freshness.

☛ Maurice et Mickael Hardouin, 10, rue du Ruau, 49400 Varrains, tel. 02.41.52.93.76, fax 02.41.52.44.32 ⊠ ▼ ev. day except Sun. 8am–12 noon 2pm–6pm

COMTE DE COLBERT

Cuvée spéciale★

○   1.97 ha   16,000   ■ ●   €8-11

Here you will find a real château, open to visitors, with foundations dating back to the 11th century and surrounded by impressive moats dug out of the tuffeau. It is connected with great figures from French history such as Diane de Poitiers (the wife of Louis de Brézé) and the Grand Condé (who in 1682 handed over this château to the ancestors of the present owners, the Dreux-Brézé). Its vineyard now comprises about 30 ha (74.1 acres) and is rooted in the regional wine-making tradition. Its sparkling Saumur, made from 60% Chenin and equal proportions of Chardonnay and Cabernet, has an attractive sparkle and a brilliant-yellow colour with green glints. The delicate bouquet is elegantly fruity, and these flavours continue on the palate along with floral hints. This is a delicious wine: fresh, rounded and full-bodied.

☛ Comte Bernard de Colbert, Ch. de Brézé, 49260 Brézé, tel. 02.41.51.62.06, fax 02.41.51.63.92 ⊠ ▼ ev. day 10am–5pm

in the 18th century. This village seems devoted to water, but is also a small centre of wine-production. This Saumur has an attractive, long-lasting sparkle. The bouquet is somewhat restrained but pleasantly light. The palate is elegant, well-balanced, long and very satisfying.

↳ SA Lacheteau, ZI de La Saulaie, 49700 Doué-la-Fontaine, tel. 02.41.59.26.26, fax 02.41.59.01.94

DOM. GUIBERTEAU
Cuvée de Printemps 2000 ★★

■ | 1 ha | 7,300 | €5-8 | ⛛ by appt.

Here is a grower who was brought up in the city but wanted to follow in the footsteps of his grandfather. He moved to the family property in 1996 and cultivates about 12 ha (29.6 acres) near Montreuil-Bellay. He produces a Cuvée de Printemps and a Cuvée d'Automne – two different styles, but both of these 2000 wines are most interesting. All in all, the former is preferred for its fruity friendliness. The grapes were macerated for eight days, producing an intense garnet colour and varied aromas with orange peel and spices mingling with red berries. The palate is rounded and fruity. The second wine (one star) was macerated for 32 days and aged for longer in oak, and is a little harsh with some herbaceous notes. Keep this for a year or two.

↳ EARL Guiberteau, 3, imp. du Cabernet, 49260 Saint-Just-sur-Dive, tel. 02.41.38.78.94, fax 02.41.38.78.94, e-mail domaine.guiberteau@wanadoo.fr ⛛

DOM. DES GUYONS
Cuvée Vent du Nord 2000 ★★

□ | 0.66 ha | 5,400 | €3-5

This estate of some 10 ha (24.7 acres) has been taken over by Franck Bimont, who has made a remarkable pale-yellow Saumur 2000 with green glints. The Jury liked its subtle aromas of flowers and fruits and its fresh, light and very well-balanced palate. This is a most attractive wine which has that delicate harmony that is so pleasing to find in wines from the Loire Valley.

↳ Franck et Ingrid Bimont, 6, rue du Moulin, 49260 Le Puy-Notre-Dame, tel. 02.41.52.21.15, fax 02.41.52.21.15 ⛛ by appt.

DOM. DES HAUTES VIGNES
Cuvée du Fief aux Moines 2000

■ | 3 ha | 20,000 | €5-8

This estate began in 1961 with 0.5 ha (1.24 acres) and now has 45 ha (111.2 acres). It is frequently mentioned in the *Guide*. The name of its Fief aux Moines wine may refer to an old priory at Distré, where there is still a church with a Romanesque nave. Be that as it may, the vines here have produced a typical Saumur red with an intense ruby colour and a nose mingling black fruits (bilberries), red fruits and liquorice. The delicate, smooth palate is very pleasant. This wholesome wine

---

will be ready at the start of 2002 and can be kept for a year or two.

↳ SCA Fourrier et Fils, 22, rue de la Chapelle, 49400 Distré, tel. 02.41.50.21.96, fax 02.41.50.12.83, e-mail a.fourrier@free.fr ⛛ by appt.

CH. DU HUREAU 1999 ★★★

□ | 2.5 ha | 10,000 | €8-11

The grapes here are scrupulously selected in the course of up to five separate pickings. They are then aged for a year in barrel. This gives them a brilliant golden-yellow colour and exuberant scents reminiscent of overripe fruits and jam, which continue on a superbly rich palate with accents of stewed ripe fruits and quince jelly. This complex and delicate Saumur white has excellent balance.

↳ Philippe et Georges Vatan, Ch. du Hureau, 49400 Dampierre-sur-Loire, tel. 02.41.67.60.40, fax 02.41.50.43.35, e-mail philippe.vatan@wanadoo.fr ⛛ ev. day except Sat. Sun. 9am-12 noon 2pm-5pm

DOM. JOULIN 2000 ★

□ | 1 ha | 1,000 | €6-8

Philippe Joulin set up here in 1994 and cultivates 13 ha (32.1 acres). Chacé is in the Saumur-Champigny area, but it is the estate's Saumur whites that have featured in the *Guide*. This brilliant pale-yellow 2000 loses its restraint after being swirled in the glass, releasing notes of white flowers and stewed fruits (apples and pears). The palate is rich and sweet. Keep it for at least a year to allow it to reach its full potential.

↳ Philippe Joulin, 58, rue Emile-Landais, 49400 Chacé, tel. 02.41.52.41.84, fax 02.41.52.41.84 ⛛ by appt.

CLOS DE L'ABBAYE 1999

○ | 1.3 ha | 10,000 | €5-8

In 1964, Henri Aupy, who comes from Algeria, acquired this reputable vineyard, which takes its name from the abbey of Asnières. He has been joined by his son, Jean-François. The estate is situated on a hillside, and its cellars are formed from enormous galleries dug out of the tuffeau in the Middle Ages. They were once used to grow Paris mushrooms before being converted so that this vineyard could benefit from their constantly cool temperature. Our Juries have already praised this vineyard for its sparkling wines. This one has a fine sparkle and a restrained but fine and fairly complex bouquet, dominated by a fruitiness that continues on the palate. The dosage has been carefully handled.

↳ EARL Henri Aupy et Fils, Clos de l'Abbaye, 49260 Le Puy-Notre-Dame, tel. 02.41.52.26.71, fax 02.41.52.26.71, e-mail j.verdier@wanadoo.fr

DOM. DE LA BESSIÈRE 2000 ★

Thierry Dézé is in charge at Souzay-Champigny, a typical Saumur village with its tuffeau hillside peppered with galleries and cave dwellings. His 2000 white wine is pleasant and light, and leaves an impression of delicate, fruity freshness. It is a classic of the appellation.

Thierry Dézé, Dom. de La Bessière, rte de Champigny, 49400 Souzay-Champigny, tel. 02.41.52.42.69, fax 02.41.38.75.41 ▼
Y by appt.

CH. DE LA DURANDIERE
Vieilles vignes 2000★

■   3.5 ha   20,000   ■ ♦   €5-8

Montreuil-Bellay is well worth a visit for its medieval wall, fortified gates and superb château, rebuilt in the 15th century. La Durandière and its park were built on the banks of the Thouet. The 38-ha (93.9-acre) vineyard has produced a garnet-coloured Saumur with restrained fruity aromas of strawberries and blackcurrants and a smooth, well-balanced palate. This 2000 vintage will open out more fully in a few months and can be kept for five years. While visiting the vineyard, you will notice an interesting curiosity – a chapel hollowed out beneath the vines.

SCEA Bodet-Lhériau, Ch. de La Durandière, 51, rue des Fusillés, 49260 Montreuil-Bellay, tel. 02.41.40.35.30, fax 02.41.40.35.31, e-mail durandiere.chateau@ibertysurf.fr ▼
Y ev. day 8am–7pm; Sat. Sun. by appt.
Hubert et Antoine Bodet

DOM. DE LA FUYE 2000★

■   4 ha   24,000   ■   €2-5

The word 'Fuye' means a dovecote mounted on pillars, a typical feature of Anjou. Another curiosity is that the estate's cellars – 3,000 m (3,270 yd) of vaulted galleries hollowed out in the tufeau – were used as a prison by the town of Thouars in the 15th and 16th centuries. Today they house a garnet-coloured Saumur with violet glints. It has aromas of fruits macerated in brandy and of liquorice, with a full, warm palate finishing beautifully on long notes of stewed fruits. This 23-ha (56.8-acre) estate uses organic growing methods.

Philippe Elliau, 225, rue du Château, Sanziers, 49260 Vaudelnay, tel. 02.41.52.29.75, fax 02.41.38.87.31 ▼
Y by appt.

DOM. DE LA GUILLOTERIE 2000★★

■   15 ha   35,000   ■   €2-3

This large 50-ha (123.5-acre) family estate has emerged brilliantly from a blind tasting with this intensely coloured red wine. The complex range of aromas combines spices, liquorice and earthy notes with the classic aromas of red berries, which are echoed on the finish. The palate is full and balanced. This is an excellent ambassador for the appellation. The white from the same year is not at all bad (one star) with its brilliant pale-yellow colour, aromas of fresh fruits and flowers and its lively palate. It will go well with seafood but can be enjoyed by itself.

SCEA Duveau Frères, 63, rue Foucault, 49260 Saint-Cyr-en-Bourg, tel. 02.41.51.62.78, fax 02.41.51.63.14, e-mail dom.guilloterie@wanadoo.fr ▼
Y by appt.

DOM. LANGLOIS-CHATEAU
Vieilles vignes 2000★★★

□   3.5 ha   21,000   ⫿⫿   €8-11

This family estate was dedicated to making sparkling wines before it enlarged its range with still wines. Today it has a much wider scope, with vines not only in Anjou but also in the Nantes and Sancerre regions. This Cuvée Vieilles Vignes was made from several selections of grapes. Fermentation was carried out in barrel, and the wine was matured in oak for one year with stirring of the lees. This is a fairly new procedure for the region. Following the 94 vintage, which won a *coup de cœur* in the *Guide*, this wine has a superb structure with all the delicacy of great Loire Valley wines. Drink it with poultry or fish in sauce. From the same estate, the **2000 red** was matured in barrel and wins one star for its aromas of stewed black fruits and spices and its soft, warm palate.

Langlois-Chateau, 3, rue Léopold-Palustre, 49400 Saint-Hilaire-Saint-Florent, tel. 02.41.40.21.40, fax 02.41.40.21.49, e-mail langlois.chateau@wanadoo.fr ▼
Y ev. day 10am–12.30pm 2.30pm–6.30pm; cl. Jan.

DOM. DE LA PALEINE 2000★★

■   4 ha   16,000   ■ ♦   €5-8

The community of Puy-Notre-Dame stands on a vine-covered hill overlooked by the three spires of its collegiate church. In geological terms it is a Turonian hill. Joël Lévi has been there since 1991. This wine has a velvety quality in common with many others grown on limestone soils. Its fine structure is the product of pleasantly silky tannins. Its rich range of aromas combines fresh fruits, spices, and smoky notes and the wine leaves an impression of balance and harmony. The **Méthode Traditionelle** from this grower was also praised by the Jury. It has a long-lasting sparkle, aromas of ripe and dried fruits with a toasty note, and a fairly lively but balanced palate.

Joël Lévi, Dom. de La Paleine, 9, rue de la Paleine, 49260 Le Puy-Notre-Dame, tel. 02.41.52.21.24, fax 02.41.52.21.66 ▼
Y by appt.

DOM. LES MERIBELLES 2000★★

□   2 ha   5,000   ■   €3-5

This 11-ha (27.2-acre) family estate is on the Saumur hillside, a plateau overlooking the Loire. Its white Saumur is well-made, pleasant and delicate, with aromas recalling fresh fruits, especially citrus fruits, and white flowers. The palate makes a fresh impression both on the attack and at the finish. It is a delicious wine, best drunk this year.

• Jean-Yves Dézé, 14, rue de la Bienboire, 49400 Souzay-Champigny, tel. 02.41.67.46.64, fax 02.41.67.73.77 [V] [Y] by appt.

DOM. DES MATINES
■ Cuvée Vieilles vignes 2000★★

□ 20 ha 20,000 [€5-8]

This family estate owes much to its 'patriarch', who dug the cellar into the rock. This 2000 vintage shows Saumur reds at their best. It has an intense ruby colour and a bouquet with rich aromas of red berries; the palate is rounded, very tasty and fresh and leaves an impression of chewing fresh fruits. This delicious wine is ideal for grilled meats and poultry, though it could well be drunk with strawberries. The estate's **Saumur white 2000** was awarded one star. It has aromas of citrus fruits (mandarins) mixed with exotic fruits like pineapples, and a light, delicate and balanced palate that finishes on a lemony note and leaves a pleasant impression of freshness.
• Dom. des Matines, 31, rue de la Mairie, 49700 Brossay, tel. 02.41.52.25.36, fax 02.41.52.25.50 [V] [Y] by appt.

MANOIR DE LA TETE ROUGE
■ Bagatelle 2000★

□ 0.5 ha 4,000 [€3-5]

[Y] by appt.

This 15-ha (37.1-acre) manor house and estate with its picturesque name was taken over in 1996 by Guillaume Reynouard, and has been cultivated by organic methods since 1999. This golden-yellow Bagatelle has an intense nose with aromas of cooked fruits. The palate is medium-sweet and rich. The wine should be surprisingly pleasant by the start of 2002.
• Guillaume Reynouard, 3, pl. J.-Raimbault, 49260 Le Puy-Notre-Dame, tel. 02.41.38.76.43, fax 02.41.38.29.54, e-mail guillaume-reynouard@free.fr [V]

DOMINIQUE MARTIN
■ Vieilles vignes 2000★★

□ 2 ha 5,000 [€5-8]

Located near the Château de Brézé, this family estate comprises 20 ha (49.4 acres). Its cellar, dug from the tuffeau, houses a wine which is rich, delicate, structured and silky, and is a true reflection of its limestone *terroir*. The lovely finish leaves an impression of fresh fruits. It is nearly ready to drink but could be kept for five years.
• Dominique Martin, 20, rue du Puits-Aubert, 49260 Brézé, tel. 02.41.51.60.28, fax 02.41.51.60.28, e-mail martin-chantreau@wanadoo.fr [V] [Y] by appt.

CH. DU MARCONNAY La Favorite
■ Vieilles vignes Elevé en fût de chêne 1999★★

□ 0.3 ha 1,350 [€8-11]

Hervé Goumain took over this family estate in 1997. His Favorite, a white wine, was much enjoyed by the Jury. It was fermented in barrel and matured for 13 months in oak, and is still overly oaky. However, the tasting revealed a remarkably good structure for the year, and the wine should open out once the oakiness has softened. It is a wine to keep.
• Hervé Goumain, Ch. du Marconnay, 49730 Parnay, tel. 02.41.50.08.21, fax 02.41.50.23.04, e-mail marconnay@wanadoo.fr [V] [Y] ev. day 10am–12 noon 2pm–6pm; 1 Oct.–31 Mar. by appt.

DOM. DU MOULIN DE L'HORIZON 1999★★

There is no longer a windmill on the horizon. It used to stand on this estate's vineyard, which is laid out on the Puy Notre-Dame hill and is the highest in the Loire valley at 118 m (386 ft). It is hardly surprising that the storm of December 1999 should have got the better of it. The vineyard survived, however, and has been especially successful this year. The fine, long-lasting sparkle enlivens this wine's pale-yellow colour. Toasty, even smoky notes add to the delicacy of the bouquet, while the Chenin (90% of the blend) brings a straightforward character to the palate. A long finish brings the tasting to a pleasant end. The same estate's **Sympathic red 2000** wins one star for its delicious notes of ripe cherries. This is a light wine to be drunk while young. One final point: the estate uses organic methods and plants grass around the vines.

LYCEE VITICOLE DE MONTREUIL-BELLAY
■ Cuvée des Hauts de Caterne 2000★

2.75 ha 22,000 ■ [€5-8]

In addition to providing wonderful evidence of Anjou in medieval times, Montreuil-Bellay educates the wine-growers of tomorrow in its wine-growing academy, a public foundation started in 1967. This 2000 vintage is made from 40% Cabernet Sauvignon and 60% Cabernet Franc, and releases notes of blackcurrant leaves and peppers, which is a little surprising for this appellation. The Jury liked its intense ruby colour and presence on the palate. It is still a little tannic, but this will soften in time.
• Lycée Prof. Agricole de Montreuil-Bellay, rte de Méron, 49260 Montreuil-Bellay, tel. 02.41.40.19.20, fax 02.41.40.19.27 [V] [Y] by appt.

CH. DE MONTGUERET 2000★

□ 10 ha 70,000 [€3-5]

This is a very well-made wine that is typical of its appellation. It has a pale-yellow colour and is very fruity both on the nose and on the balanced palate. It finishes on a note of freshness and is ready to drink now.
• SCEA Ch. de Montguéret, Le bourg, 49560 Nueil-sur-Layon, tel. 02.41.59.59.19, fax 02.41.59.59.02 [V] [Y] by appt.
• A. et D. Lacheteau

Saumur

vinifies the production of 1,400 ha (3,458 acres) of wines (about 30% of the volume of each AOC). The wines are housed in 10 km (6 miles) of galleries dug in the tuffeau. The co-operative makes its wines according to their place of origin; this Cuvée de La Croix Verte is thus a selection made from limonitic-clay soils. It has a purple colour and a bouquet which opens out after the glass is swirled to reveal scents of red berries and stewed fruits; the palate is balanced, rounded and smooth. This is a fairly rich wine which can be drunk straight away or kept for up to five years. A second wine selected by the Jury, the **Les Pouches white 2000** comes from magnesic-limestone soils. It was vinified from ripe grapes, is well-made and releases aromas of fresh fruits and citrus fruits. The palate has the freshness typical of white wines of this appellation.

↬ Cave des Vignerons de Saumur, rte de Saumoussay, 49260 Saint-Cyr-en-Bourg,
tel. 02.41.53.06.06, fax 02.41.53.06.10,
e-mail bernardjacob@vignerondesaumur.com
Ⓨ ev. day except Sun. 9am–12 noon 2pm–6pm

VEUVE AMIOT
Cuvée Elisabeth Amiot 1995★
○   n.c.   8,000   €8-11

Founded in 1884, Veuve Amiot specialises in traditional methods. Its Cuvée Elisabeth Amiot (after the deserving widow who founded the business) has a fine, long-lasting sparkle which is immediately attractive. On the nose, floral notes are combined with toasty notes and *pain d'épice* (a spiced bread). These favourable impressions are confirmed on the palate, which has a good structure and balance, with notes of honey adding to its complexity. The other wine offered by this wine-merchant is **L'Esprit de Veuve Amiot**, singled out for its lovely colour and fine sparkle, its intense, fruity and floral bouquet and its complex palate, which is long and retains the fruitiness.

↬ Veuve Amiot, BP 67,
49426 Saint-Hilaire-Saint-Florent,
tel. 02.41.83.14.14, fax 02.41.50.17.66 Ⓥ
Ⓨ ev. day 9am–6pm; cl. Nov.-Apr.

DOM. DU VIEUX PRESSOIR
2000★★
■   10 ha   55,000   ■ Ⓢ   €3-5

The 2000 vintage is a blend of Cabernet Franc (70%) and Cabernet Sauvignon, and has plenty of character. Its remarkable structure has been brought out well by the grower. It has a brilliant purple colour and a delicate nose with red- and black-berry aromas. The palate is smooth and fresh and leaves an impression of fresh fruits.

↬ EARL B. et J. Albert, 205, rue du Château-d'Oiré, 49260 Vaudelnay,
tel. 02.41.52.21.78, fax 02.41.38.85.83 Ⓥ
Ⓨ by appt.
↬ Bruno Albert

↬ Jacky Clée, 1, rue du Lys, Sanziers, 49260 Le Puy-Notre-Dame,
tel. 02.41.52.24.96, fax 02.41.52.48.39 Ⓥ
Ⓨ by appt.

NEMROD
○   2 ha   5,000   ■ Ⓢ   €5-8

The Les Rochettes property was already planted with vines when it was acquired by the Douet family in the 18th century, and had previously belonged to Louis XI in the 15th century. This sparkling wine has lovely, fine bubbles and a pale-yellow colour. The bouquet releases well-formed fruity notes which are even more evident on the palate. It is a well-balanced wine.

↬ Jean Douet, Ch. des Rochettes,
49700 Concourson-sur-Layon,
tel. 02.41.59.11.51, fax 02.41.59.37.73 Ⓥ
Ⓨ by appt.

DOM. SAINT-JEAN 2000★★
□   2 ha   8,000   ■ Ⓢ   €3-5

A new trend is appearing in white Saumur wines: manual selection of very ripe grapes. Here, this has produced a richly structured wine whose power and delicacy will have increased by the end of 2001. It has a pale-yellow colour and releases intense scents of overripe fruits. The palate seems rounded and sweet while remaining fresh, making this a lovely wine from the Loire Valley.

↬ Jean-Claude Anger, 16, rue des Martyrs,
49730 Turquant, tel. 02.41.38.11.78,
fax 02.41.51.79.23 Ⓥ Ⓨ by appt.

DOM. DE SAINT-JUST 2000★★
■   7 ha   42,000   ■ Ⓢ   €5-8

Yves Lambert took over this 38-ha (93.9-acre) estate in 1997. He has been quick to make his name in the world of wine. This year, he demonstrated his skills with this garnet-coloured red wine with black glints. On the nose, it does not reveal its secrets immediately, but releases a complex bouquet of ripe fruits and leather with hints of smoki-ness. The palate is rich, warm and balanced and the finish is intense and long. It is a wine to keep for several years. Just as remarkable is the **La Coulée de Saint-Cyr white 2000**, made from carefully selected grapes and vinified in barrel, which releases attractive scents of white flowers, exotic fruits and vanilla. The palate is beautifully balanced and imparts a feeling of freshness. This wine will be ready to drink by the time this *Guide* is published.

↬ Yves Lambert, Dom. de Saint-Just,
12, rue Prée, 49260 Saint-Just-sur-Dive,
tel. 02.41.51.62.01, fax 02.41.67.94.51,
e-mail domainedesaint-just@wanadoo.fr Ⓥ
Ⓨ ev. day except Sat. Mon. 9am–12 noon 2pm–6pm

CAVE DES VIGNERONS DE SAUMUR La Croix Verte 2000★
■   6 ha   50,000   ■ Ⓢ   €3-5

The Saumur Wine-growers' Co-operative was founded in 1957 and has an important position in the region, with 300 members. It

Cabernet de Saumur

CH. DE VILLENEUVE
Les Cormiers 1999★★★

☐　2 ha　9,000　€11-15

Go to the Saumur-Champigny section of this 2002 edition and you will find a very fine red wine. The château has achieved a very similar feat with this white wine. The grapes were selected in three pickings and have a natural alcohol content of 14%. Vinification was done wholly in barrel. The range of aromas is complex and delicate, reminiscent of citrus fruits, stewed fruits, ripe fruits and white flowers. The tasting revealed an exceptionally good structure, which retains that freshness so characteristic of Loire wines.

🕿 SCA Chevallier, Ch. de Villeneuve, 3, rue Jean Brevet, 49400 Souzay-Champigny, tel. 02.41.51.14.04, fax 02.41.50.58.24, e-mail jpchevallier@chateau-de-villeneuve.com ☑
🍷 ev. day except Sun, 9am–12 noon 2pm–6pm

BOURDIN 2000★

1 ha　3,000　€3-5

Even though produced only in small quantities, with 3,176 hl (83,846 gal) in 2000, the Appellation Cabernet de Saumur rosé holds its own due to Cabernet finesse and the limestone *terroir*.

The management of this 12-ha (29-acre) estate has recently been taken over by the younger members of the family, and they produced this immediately appealing rosé. Clear, pale pink in colour, it has intense aromas of apples, pears and lemon drops, which linger on the palate.

🕿 EARL Bourdin, 27, rue des Martyrs, 49730 Turquant, tel. 02.41.38.11.83, fax 02.41.51.47.71 ☑
🍷 ev. day except Sun, 9am–12 noon 2–7pm

DOM. DES SANZAY 2000

0.54 ha　4,000　€3-5

Didier Sanzay has been head of the family estate since 1991, and he has developed an attractive, pale pink Cabernet. Intense, tangy notes on the nose carry through to the attractive palate. It has a good overall balance.

🕿 Didier Sanzay, Dom. des Sanzay, 93, Grand-Rue, 49400 Varrains, tel. 02.41.52.91.30, fax 02.41.52.45.93, e-mail didier-sanzay@domaine-sanzay.com ☑
🍷 by appt.

Coteaux de Saumur

They received their patents of nobility long ago: Coteaux de Saumur, the Saumurois equivalent of Anjou's Coteaux du Layon, is made exclusively from Chenin grapes grown on the chalky tuffeau. In 2000, only 110 hl (2,904 gal) were produced.

L'ORMEOLE 1999★

2 ha　2,000　€11-15

This small estate, which lies on the side of a hill, was bought up in 1998. The attractive, strong yellow-coloured 99 has a concentrated scent of overripe fruit and a well-balanced palate of ripe fruit. Well worth seeking out. The 97 was awarded a *coup de cœur*.

🕿 EARL Yves Drouineau, 3, rue Morains, 49400 Dampierre-sur-Loire, tel. 02.41.51.14.02, fax 02.41.50.32.00, e-mail yves.drouineau@club-internet.fr ☑
🍷 by appt.

Saumur-Champigny

Touring the narrow streets of Saumurois villages, you will find yourself in heaven among the tuffeau cellars, which shelter many aged bottles. Even though this vineyard, which covers 1,300 ha (3,211 acres), has only recently expanded, the red wines from Champigny have been renowned for many centuries. Production comes from nine villages, using Cabernet Franc (or Breton) grapes, and the wines are light, fruity, agreeable. In 2000, output was 85,818 hl (2,265,595 gal). The Winemakers' Cellar in Saint-Cyr-en-Bourg has been influential in the development of the vineyard.

DOM. DU BOIS MIGNON
Le Saut aux Loups 2000

3.5 ha　6,000　€5-8

Located in the Vienne, the southern part of the appellation, this small estate has just celebrated its 100th year of business, producing what one taster described as a 'vin de copains' (a wine to be drunk among friends); a pleasant, light, lively wine, which can be enjoyed on its own.

🕿 SCEA Charier Barillot, Dom. du Bois Mignon, 86120 Saix, tel. 05.49.22.94.59, fax 05.49.22.94.51 ☑ by appt.

Saumur-Champigny

DOM. DU BOIS MOZE PASQUIER
Vieilles vignes 2000★   €5-8
0.5 ha   4,000

In 1994 Patrick Pasquier took over this 6-ha (15-acre) estate, founded by his parents in 1955. His deep ruby Vieilles Vignes 2000 is clean on the nose and strong yet tannic on the palate. A potentially interesting wine, it needs time to mature. If you are looking for a wine to drink within the year, you need look no further than the estate's main vintage, the Clos du Bois Mozé 2000. It is a lighter wine, leaving a suggestion of fresh fruit (strawberries, cherries and blackcurrants) and was especially singled out by the Jury.
☞ Patrick Pasquier, 9, rue du Bois-Mozé, 49400 Chacé, tel. 02.41.52.42.50, fax 02.41.52.59.73 [V] [Y] by appt.

CH. DE CHAINTRES 2000★   €5-8
17 ha   120,000

Lying in the centre of the appellation, the village of Chaintres is typical of the area, with its tuffeau buildings and cloisters. The château dates from the mid-17th century. The vineyards go back even further, to the 16th century. The 2000 vintage is an interesting blend of strength and delicacy. It has an intense ruby colour, and a nose that reveals a well-structured, subtle palate, indicating that the wine should have a fine future. It may be drunk from the end of 2001 onwards, with red meat or game.
☞ SA Dom. Vinicole de Chaintres, 49400 Dampierre-sur-Loire, tel. 02.41.52.90.54, fax 02.41.52.99.92, e-mail chaintres@wanadoo.fr [V]
[Y] weekdays 9am–12 noon 2–6pm; Sat., Sun. by appt.
☞ G. de Tigny

DOM. DES CHAMPS FLEURIS 1999★   €8-11
3 ha   12,000

On a hillside within the Saumur-Champigny appellation, this is one of the young enterprises which have, by their industry and their knowledge brought distinction to the appellation. Its supple, balanced 99 has a dark ruby colour revealing hints of brown, which convey the beginning of its development. Its delicate nose is accompanied by scents of iris, violet and red berries. The palate is not that long, but the well-integrated flavours are rather seductive nevertheless, and on the finish there are interesting flavours of liquorice and dark chocolate.
☞ EARL Rétiveau-Rétif, 50–54, rue des Martyrs, 49730 Turquant, tel. 02.41.38.10.92, fax 02.41.51.75.33 [V]
[Y] by appt.

DOM. DES CLOSIERS 2000   €5-8
12 ha   10,000

Parnay is well known among ornithologists for its islet in the middle of the Loire, home to sizeable colonies of sea birds. Wine-lovers, on the other hand, will head off in the opposite direction, towards the cellars of the Domaine des Closiers, which is built into the tuffeau and situated along the narrow road leading from the Château de Tardé to the top of the vineyard slope. The estate produces a pleasant, well-made wine, with a flavour of red berries that lasts right through tasting. This simple wine should be drunk informally.
☞ EARL Elie Moirin, 8, rue Valbrun, 49730 Parnay, tel. 02.41.38.12.32, fax 02.41.38.11.14 [V] [Y] by appt.

DOM. DES COUTURES 2000   €5-8
11 ha   10,000

This domaine, 4 km (2.5 miles) from Fontevraud Abbey, a Plantagenet necropolis, renovated its wine-making cellar in 1999. Its latest vintage, light ruby in colour, offers simple aromas of red berries and capsicum. It has a fresh palate and is lively on the finish. A light wine to be served chilled.
☞ SCA Nicolas et Fils, rue des Martyrs, 49730 Turquant, tel. 05.49.91.63.76, fax 05.49.91.68.21, e-mail marc-rene.nicolas@wanadoo.fr [V]
[Y] ev. day except Sun. 8am–1pm 2–6pm

YVES DROUINEAU
Les Beaumiers 2000★   €5-8
16 ha   80,000

Yves Drouineau has managed this 21-ha (52-acre) estate for 10 years, and its wines have been regularly featured in the Guide. Its Beaumiers, produced from 50-year-old vines, represents three-quarters of the estate's total output. The dark red colour and full palate give it a rich appearance and suggest considerable potential. Its slightly tannic finish suggests that it needs to mature further.
☞ EARL Yves Drouineau, 3, rue Moraine, 49400 Dampierre-sur-Loire, tel. 02.41.51.14.02, fax 02.41.50.32.00, e-mail yves.drouineau@club-internet.fr [V]
[Y] by appt.

DOM. DUBOIS
Cuvée d'automne 2000★★   €8-11
2 ha   12,000

This estate, which has a solid reputation in the local area, has produced more than just the occasional exceptional bottle of wine. This Cuvée d'Automne has a rare structure and complexity. It is an intense, dark-red colour, and on the nose it reveals scents of blackberries, blackcurrants and damp woodland; it has a well-balanced, delicate palate of some length. The Cuvée de Printemps 2000 (one star) is a more lively wine, with hints of violets, iris and fresh fruit. It leaves a fresh, light feeling on the palate, well representative of the appellation.
☞ Dom. Michel et Jean-Claude Dubois, 8, rte de Chacé, 49260 Saint-Cyr-en-Bourg, tel. 02.41.51.61.32, fax 02.41.51.95.29 [V]
[Y] by appt.

DOM. FOUET La Rouge et Noire
Cuvée Vieilles vignes 1999★★★   €8-11
1 ha   5,000

Patrice Fouet runs the vineyard, while his son Julien works in the winery. The former has managed the family estate for more than 20 years, while Julien joined him in 1995. They make a sound partnership, judging from the *Guide's* selection: all the wines submitted have been accepted by the Jury. The Rouge et Noire, matured in barrel for a year, was unanimously acclaimed. Its dark garnet colour, the complex scents, combining blackberries and currants, liquorice and herbs, and its powerful, warm flavours won it recognition. Matured in vat, both 2000 vintages, **Cuvée Domaine** and **Cuvée de Printemps**, were awarded a star for their balance and for the sensation of fresh fruit left on the palate.

➤ Fouet, 3, rue de la Judée, 49260 Saint-Cyr-en-Bourg, tel. 02.41.51.60.52, fax 02.41.67.01.79, e-mail j-fouet@domaine-fouet.com [V]
♈ ev. day except Sun. 8am–12 noon 2–6pm

DOM. DES FROGERES
Cuvée Prestige 2000 ■ 9 ha 30,400 ■ €5–8

This domaine, covering 13 ha (32 acres), converted to organic farming in 1988, and it also employs biodynamic techniques. Its Cuvée Prestige has a garnet colour with slightly brownish highlights. On the nose it mixes ripe fruit with gamey aromas. This flavoursome mixture comes together in a supple palate. It is a pleasant wine to be drunk young.

➤ Michel Joseph, 11 bis, rue de Champigny, 49400 Chacé, tel. 02.41.52.95.25, fax 02.41.52.95.25 ■ ♈ by appt.

CH. DU HUREAU
Cuvée des Fevettes 2000★★★ ■ 2 ha 10,000 ■ €11–15

Cuvée des Fevettes — CHATEAU DU HUREAU — SAUMUR-CHAMPIGNY — 2000 — Philippe et Georges VATAN — 750 ml — 12.8% vol.

Philippe Vatan has managed this 20-ha (49-acre) estate since 1987, and his first vintage gained two stars. Moreover, he has achieved no fewer than seven *coups de cœur* over the past 15 years: for his 89, 94, 95, 96, 97, 99 vintages and for this Cuvée des Fevettes 2000, awarded its third *coup de cœur* this time round (following those for the 96 and the 99 vintages), is characterised by a dark ruby colour with hints of black and a complex palate suggestive of stewed fruit, berries, spices and tobacco. Powerful yet delicate, the wine leaves an impression of richness and balance. The **Cuvée Lisagathe 2000**, more structured and less expressive, should reveal much more.

➤ Philippe et Georges Vatan, Ch. du Hureau, 49400 Dampierre-sur-Loire,

tel. 02.41.67.60.40, fax 02.41.50.43.35, e-mail philippe.vatan@wanadoo.fr [V]
♈ ev. day except Sat. and Sun. 9am–12 noon 2–5pm

DOM. DE LA BESSIERE
Vieilles vignes 2000 ■ 2 ha 5,000 ■ €5–8

With its tufeau plateau concealing a labyrinth of galleries and cave dwellings, Souzay-Champigny is a characteristic village within the wine-producing Anjou region. Thierry Dézé has run a 15-ha (37-acre) estate here since 1987. His light, fruity wine is typical of the appellation. Ruby in colour, it exudes a scent of red berries on the nose, together with a vegetal note. Supple and well balanced on the palate, it remains lively on the finish. The wine should be drunk within the year.

➤ Thierry Dézé, Dom. de La Bessière, rte de Champigny, 49400 Souzay-Champigny, tel. 02.41.52.42.69, fax 02.41.38.75.41 [V]
♈ by appt.

DOM. LA BONNELIERE
Les Poyeux Prestige 2000 ■ 2 ha 15,000 ■ €5–8

Renamed in 1995, the estate got its name from its founders, André Bonneau and his wife, who set it up in 1972 with just a few hectares of old vines. Their two sons have joined them on the estate, which now covers a total of 20 ha (49 acres). They have produced a traditional Saumur-Champigny with an intense ruby colour, aromas of soft fruit and a rounded, well-balanced palate.

➤ EARL Bonneau et Fils, 45, rue du Bourg-Neuf, 49400 Varrains, tel. 02.41.52.92.38, fax 02.41.52.92.38 [V]

DOM. DE LA CUNE
Chai'Anne 2000★★ ■ 2.5 ha 15,000 ■ €5–8

A 16-ha (39-acre) estate at the very heart of the appellation, this domaine has presented the Jury with Chai'Anne, a product of the clay-limestone soil and 28 days' maceration on the skins. The 2000 vintage is excellent: an intense garnet colour, it starts off rather timidly on the nose, then gradually lets through hints of undergrowth, fruit purée and crystallised fruit, and displaying strength and structure on the palate. The wine is at its best now.

➤ Jean-Luc et Jean-Albert Mary, Chaintres, 49400 Dampierre-sur-Loire, tel. 02.41.52.91.37, fax 02.41.52.44.13 [V]
♈ by appt.

DOM. DE LA GUILLOTERIE 2000★
■ 25 ha 50,000 ■ €5–8

Several generations have run this family estate, where the winery and reception area have recently been renovated. The latest vintage, with its intense garnet red colour, is fresh, fruity and complex. Its delicate aromas evoke fruit purée, flowers and liquorice. Supple, rounded and well balanced on the palate, it finishes on a delicious and lasting note of red berries.

☛ SCEA Duveau Frères, 63, rue Foucault, 49260 Saint-Cyr-en-Bourg, tel. 02.41.51.62.78, fax 02.41.51.63.14, e-mail dom.guilloterie@wanadoo.fr ☑ ⟁ by appt.

DOM. DE LA PERRUCHE
Clos de Chaumont 2000★

■ 4 ha　20,000　⚭ ⚬ €8-11

This traditional estate has been run by five generations of wine-producers, who carefully control and manage the vines. The harvest takes place quite late in the year (around 23 October in the case of the 2000 vintage). The garnet colour of the wine, together with its scents of undergrowth and leather, give an initial impression of strength. However, on the palate it reveals a surprising structure, which requires refinement for a further year or two. On visiting the estate, visitors will discover one of the most attractive villages in the Anjou region, with its château still haunted by the memory of Alexandre Dumas' character, the Dame de Montsoreau.

☛ EARL Rouiller, 29, rue de La Maumenière, 49730 Montsoreau, tel. 02.41.51.73.36, fax 02.41.38.18.70 ☑ ⟁ ev. day except Sun. 9.30am–12.30pm 2.30–6.30pm

DOM. DE LA PETITE CHAPELLE 2000★

■ 7 ha　40,000　⚭ ⚬ €5-8

Laurent Dézé has been producing wine from his 30 ha (74 acres) of vines for some 10 years now. His traditional Saumur cellar, carved out of the tuffeau, is home to this intense garnet-coloured wine, with its complex aromas of ripe fruit and spices, mixed with a discernible hint of leather. The pleasant, rounded palate offers a slightly lively finish. This is a well-produced, enjoyable wine, highly representative of the limestone soil of its appellation.

☛ Laurent Dézé, 4, rue des Vignerons, 49400 Souzay-Champigny, tel. 02.41.52.41.11, fax 02.41.52.93.48 ☑ ⟁ by appt.

LA SEIGNERE
Clos de la Seignère 2000★★

■ 5.4 ha　22,000　⚭ ⚬ €5-8

Clos de la Seignère keeps on going: the hillside vineyard, acquired by Yves Drouineau in 1998, has produced a remarkable wine from small yields and 30 days of maceration. Its rich palate lends it a certain opulence, while its tannic structure is impressive. A wine to lay down, it will be at its best after five years.

☛ EARL Yves Drouineau, La Seignère, 3, rue Morains, 49400 Dampierre-sur-Loire, tel. 02.41.51.14.02, fax 02.41.50.32.00, e-mail yves.drouineau@club-internet.fr ☑ ⟁ by appt.

DOM. LAVIGNE Les Aïeules 2000★★

■ 8 ha　49,000　⚭ ⚬ €5-8

Produced from clay-limestone soil, Les Aïeules is powerful but, at the same time, harmonious and complex. Fresh and fruity, it gives you the impression that you are chewing red berries; everything you would expect from a Saumur-Champigny, in fact. The main **2000 Cuvée** is almost at the same level (one star) and also leaves a very pleasant fruity sensation.

☛ Dom. Lavigne, 15, rue des Rogelins, 49400 Varrains, tel. 02.41.52.92.57, fax 02.41.52.40.87. e-mail sca.lavigne-veron@wanadoo.fr ☑ ⟁ ev. day except Sun. 9am–12 noon 2–6pm

RENE-NOEL LEGRAND
Les Terrages 2000★

■ 2 ha　12,000　⚭ ⚬ €5-8

This 15-ha (37-acre) estate in the wine-producing village of Varrains is run by a geology enthusiast. The 2000 vintage is lighter than the previous year's, but it is well balanced, harmonious and very pleasant. Its dark ruby colour, delicate aromas of red and black berries and generous, elegant, fruity palate give it a young, fresh feel. Drink it within a year.

☛ René-Noël Legrand, 13, rue des Rogelins, 49400 Varrains, tel. 02.41.52.94.11, fax 02.41.52.49.78 ☑ ⟁ by appt.

DOM. DES MATINES 2000

■ n.c.　n.c.　⚭ ⚬ €5-8

Lying in the heart of the Saumur region, between the villages of Saumur, Montreuil-Bellay and Doué-la-Fontaine, this 50-ha (123-acre) domaine has produced a dark ruby-coloured wine deemed *gourmand* by the Jury. With its perfumes of red berries and violets and its fruity, balanced palate, it is a delight to the senses.

☛ Dom. des Matines, 31, rue de la Mairie, 49700 Brossay, tel. 02.41.52.25.36, fax 02.41.52.25.50 ☑ ⟁ by appt.

DOM. DE NERLEUX
Clos des Chatains 2000★★

■ 5 ha　20,000　⚭ ⚬ €8-11

Records of this estate go back to 1578, when it belonged to a lord. Today, the estate covers some 45 ha (111 acres). Its Clos des Chatains is surprisingly rich, as is immediately clear from its almost black colour. Its complex scents are a mixture of ripe fruit, toast and vanilla. The wine is just as complex on the palate, at the same time both powerful and harmonious. The finish is one of silky tannins, and it has an uncommon length. **Les Nerleux 2000** is also an interesting wine with aromas of fresh fruit; it was awarded one star by the Jury.

☛ SCEA Régis Neau, 4, rue de la Paleine, 49260 Saint-Cyr-en-Bourg, tel. 02.41.51.61.04, fax 02.41.51.65.34, e-mail rneau@terre-net.fr ☑ ⟁ Mon.-Fri. 8am–12 noon 2–6pm; Sat. 8am–12 noon

DOM. DES ROCHES NEUVES

Terres Chaudes 2000★★

■ 6 ha 15,000 €8-11

Comprising 22 ha (54 acres) taken over by Thierry Germain in 1992, this domaine has adopted organic farming methods. Its Terres Chaudes 2000, matured for 12 months in barrel, is characterised by its superb structure. It has hints of stewed fruit, spices and black berries. The wine will be at its peak in a year or two. The **Cuvée Principale 2000**, matured in tank, offers a series of highly seductive, complex aromas, among which you can discern black berries and undergrowth. It was awarded one star by the Jury.

↳ Thierry Germain, 56, bd Saint-Vincent, 49400 Varrains, tel. 02.41.52.49.30, e-mail thierry-germain@wanadoo.fr by appt.

DOM. DES SABLES VERTS

Cuvée des Sables Verts 2000★

■ 1 ha 8,000 €8-11

Alain and Dominique Duveau took over this 15-ha (37-acre) estate in 1985, and they farm it using their own particular methods, such as grassing down between the rows of vines. The name 'Sables Verts' ('green sands') derives from a limestone and detrital formation. The 2000 vintage, produced from 40-year-old vines, is surprisingly powerful, the result of very thorough vineyard management. Its colour, together with its aromas of undergrowth, spices and puréed fruit, immediately give it a rich feeling. The wine will fulfil its true potential within two or three years. The simpler and lighter **Cuvée Ligérienne 2000**, on the other hand, should be drunk within a year: it was especially singled out by the Jury.

↳ GAEC Dominique et Alain Duveau, 66, Grand-Rue, 49400 Varrains, tel. 02.41.52.91.52, fax 02.41.38.75.32 by appt.

DOM. SAINT-JEAN

Les Vignolles 2000★

■ 2 ha 16,000 €5-8

Run for the past ten years by Jean-Claude Anger, this estate has seen five generations of wine-producers. At the beginning of the 20th century it consisted of 5 ha (12 acres), whereas it now covers some 23 ha (57 acres). Les Vignolles 2000 is representative of the appellation: it reveals aromas of fresh fruit which last right through tasting. Ready to drink, it may nevertheless be kept for a few years. Similar but lighter, the **Cuvée Classique 2000** was especially singled out by the Jury.

↳ Jean-Claude Anger, 16, rue des Martyrs, 49730 Turquant, tel. 02.41.38.11.78, fax 02.41.51.79.23 by appt.

DOM. SAINT-VINCENT

Les Adrialys 2000★★

■ 4 ha 10,000 €5-8

The estate has grown over recent years, thanks to improvements made to both its vineyards and its winery. Les Adrialys, which was awarded a coup de cœur for the 1991 vintage, is of remarkable quality once again this year: a combination of intensity, richness and strength, together with balance and delicacy, and aromas of red and black berries, as well as violets and tobacco. The lighter **Les Trézellières 2000** (60,000 bottles), with its hints of fresh fruit, was awarded one star.

↳ EARL Patrick Vadé, Dom. Saint-Vincent, 49400 Saumur, tel. 02.41.67.43.19, fax 02.41.50.23.28, e-mail pvade@st-vincent.com ev. day 9am–12 noon 2pm–6pm

DOM. DES SANZAY

Vieilles vignes 2000★★

■ 2 ha 10,000 €5-8

Didier Sanzay, who took over the management of his 27-ha (67-acre) family estate ten years ago, has worked hard on improving the quality of his vineyards, managing to bring production up to a good level. His Vieilles Vignes 2000 seduces with its garnet colour laced with hints of black, its aromas of puréed fruit and its velvety palate. 'Excellent soil' and 'perfect harvest' are the descriptions given in the tasting notes. **Cuvée Principale 2000** is a lighter, fruity wine, also worthy of note: in fact, it was awarded one star, and sells four times the quantity of Vieilles Vignes 2000.

↳ Didier Sanzay, Dom. des Sanzay, 93, Grand-Rue, 49400 Varrains, tel. 02.41.52.91.30, fax 02.41.52.45.93, e-mail didier-sanzay@domaine-sanzay.com by appt.

CH. DE TARGÉ 2000★

■ 20 ha 120,000 €5-8

Although the manor of Targé came into the family through one of Louis XIV's secretaries, the château itself became a republican stronghold, home to two of the founders of the Third Republic, Gambetta and Jules Ferry. Mention should also be made of the role played by Fresnette Ferry and her husband, Edgar Pisani, in reorganising the vineyard. Pisani, while Minister of Agriculture under General de Gaulle, was an important figure in European agricultural policy during the 1960s. The estate has been run since 1978 by Edouard Pisani-Ferry, an agronomist. The 2000 vintage is a well-structured wine that will improve with age. Of an intense ruby colour, it offers a subtle nose of soft fruit, black berries and a hint of toast, together with a generous, supple, persistent palate. A delicate wine with plenty of depth.

↳ SCEA Edouard Pisani-Ferry, Ch. de Targé, 49730 Parnay, tel. 02.41.38.11.50, fax 02.41.38.16.19, e-mail edouard@chateaudetarge.fr Mon.–Fri. 8am–12.30pm 1.30pm–6pm, Sat. am by appt.

DOM. DU VAL BRUN

Vieilles vignes Les Folies 2000★★★

■ 3 ha 10,000 €5-8

On a sloping site, this vineyard is well worth a visit. It has been awarded several coups de cœur (for its 85 and 89 vintages),

Saumur-Champigny

and Les Folies, with its intense, almost black colour and its aromatic, majestic palate, is exceptional. It is ready to drink now. **Cuvée Principale 2000** (one star), while almost as dark in colour, is a much lighter wine, leaving hints of fresh fruit and cocoa on the palate.
➤ Charruau et Fils, 74, rue Val Brun, 49730 Parnay, tel. 02.41.38.11.85, fax 02.41.38.16.22 ☑ ▼ by appt.

DOM. DES VARINELLES
Vieilles vignes 2000★
■ 3.5 ha 20,000

Established in 1850, the 40-ha (99-acre) Domaine des Varinelles successfully combines tradition – with its cellar carved out of the tuffeau – and modernity – a gleaming series of stainless-steel tanks and a perfect command of the latest vinification methods. Matured in barrel, like the majority of the estate's red wines, the 2000 vintage displays considerable body. Currently an austere wine, barricaded behind its tannins, it promises a pleasant surprise when those tannins begin to soften.
➤ SCA Daheuiller et Fils, 28, rue du Ruau, 49400 Varrains, tel. 02.41.52.90.94, fax 02.41.52.94.63 ☑ ▼ Mon.-Fri: 8am–12 noon 2pm–7pm; Sat. by appt.

CH. DE VARRAINS 2000★★★
■ 5 ha 30,000 ▮▯ ♦ €11-15

Langlois-Château runs several estates in the Loire Valley using the same high-quality methods. The 2000 vintage, the product of a strict harvest selection process and perfectly controlled production, was matured for a third of the total time in new 500-l (26,500-pt) casks. It has a dark-garnet colour, and hints of ripe fruit, spices and strong scents of pungency. It has a rounded palate that proves particularly seductive due to its finely textured tannins. A superb wine!
➤ Langlois-Château,
3, rue Léopold-Palustre,
49400 Saint-Hilaire-
Saint-Florent, tel. 02.41.40.21.40,
fax 02.41.40.21.49, e-mail langlois.chateau@wanadoo.fr ☑ ▼ e. day 10am–12.30pm 2.30pm–6.30pm; cl. Jan.

DOM. DU VIEUX BOURG
Vieilles vignes 2000★
■ n.c. 12,000 ▮▯ ♦ €8-11

This traditional estate is characterised by its strictly controlled vines and its cellar. Its 2000 vintage appears of a one-dimensional quality on first tasting, but invariably possesses greater potential given the intensity of its dark-garnet colour, the fine texture of its tannins and its softness on the palate. This is a wine that will have significantly improved in a few months.
➤ Dom. du Vieux Bourg, 30, Grand-Rue, 49400 Varrains, tel. 02.41.52.91.89, fax 02.41.52.42.43 ☑ ▼ by appt.

CH. DE VILLENEUVE 2000★★★
18 ha 80,000 ▮▯ ♦ €8-11

Château de Villeneuve, dominating the Loire Valley, is a haven of peace and quiet, a true mecca for wine-lovers in the Saumur. The vineyard dates from the 15th century, while the elegant tuffeau-stone château was built in the 18th. In 1985 Jean-Pierre Chevallier, an oenologist by profession, took over the 25-ha (62-acre) estate previously acquired by his family in 1969. He restored the ancient cellars where the Saumur-Champigny ages in 500-l (26,500-pt) casks (locally known as 'tonnes'). The main 2000 vintage is simply stunning: an intense dark-garnet colour, it delivers extremely promising aromas (of puréed fruit, spices, undergrowth and liquorice). Extremely rounded on the palate, it has an exceptional finish. The **Vieilles Vignes 99** (one star), completely cask-matured, should be cellared for a few years.
➤ SCA Chevallier, Ch. de Villeneuve, 3, rue Jean Brevet, 49400 Souzay-Champigny, tel. 02.41.51.14.04, fax 02.41.50.58.24, e-mail jpchevallier@chateau-de-villeneuve.com ☑ ▼ ev. day except Sun. 9am–12 noon 2pm–6pm

Touraine

The interesting collections housed in the Musée des Vins de Touraine (Touraine Wine Museum) in Tours exhibit the history of advances made in vine-growing and wine in the region. It relates semi-mythical accounts of the life of Saint Martin, the bishop of Tours in 380, and illuminates the 'Golden Legend' with images relating to vine cultivation and wines. By the year 1000, the Abbey at Bourgueil was already cultivating the Breton (Cabernet Franc) variety in its famous enclosed vineyard and, years later, Rabelais, the great French writer, was eloquently singing its praises during the 16th century. History is still much in evidence today along the tourist routes from Mesland to Bourgueil on the right bank (through Vouvray, Tours, Luynes, Langeais), and from Chaumont to Chinon on the left bank (through Amboise and Chenonceaux, the Cher valley, Saché, Azay-le-Rideau and the forest of Chinon).

The Touraine vineyard has been famous for a considerable time, but underwent its most significant expansion at the end of the 19th century. Its present-day area, which is about 13,000 ha (32,110 acres), is actually less than it was before the phylloxera disaster; it lies mainly within the departments of Indre-et-Loire and Loir-et-Cher but, in the north, encroaches into the Sarthe. Tasting very old wines from 1921, 1893, 1874 or even 1858, for example at Vouvray, Bourgueil or Chinon, reveals characteristics fairly close to the wines of today. Thus, despite developments in cultivation techniques and the science of winemaking, the 'style' of Touraine wines remains relatively unchanged, probably because each of the appellations is founded upon a single grape variety. The climate also plays its part: maritime and continental influences find expression in the wines, the slopes forming a screen from the north winds. In addition, the east-west valleys of the Loir, the Loire, the Cher, the Indre and the Vienne create a multitude of tuffeau slopes propitious for vine-growing, enjoying a local climate that shows little variation and maintains a healthy level of humidity. The tuffeau, a soft, creamy-yellow limestone, is hollowed out into innumerable subterranean caves. In the valleys, clay is mixed with limestone or sand and sometimes silica, while down on the banks of the Loire and the Vienne gravelly soils predominate.

These local variations are reflected in the wines. Each valley corresponds to an appellation, and each year the wines

have different individual characteristics depending on the weather. The association of the year of bottling with the description of the cru is thus essential.

In 1989, a hot dry year, the wines were rich and full, with the promise of long life. In 1984, a year when the vines flowered late and the weather was dull, the white wines were drier and the reds lighter, and are only now reaching their full development. Due to these factors, the best vintages from recent decades are as follows: 1959, 1961, 1964, 1969, 1970, 1976, 1981, 1982, 1983, 1985, 1986, 1988, 1989, 1990, 1995 and 1996. Nevertheless, self-evidently, this classification varies between the tannic reds of Chinon or Bourgueil (softer when they are grown on gravelly soils, better structured when they come from the slopes), and the lighter growths from the Appellation Touraine, sometimes sold en primeur. There are also variations in the rosés, which are drier or not so dry depending on the amount of sunshine; the same is true of the whites of Azay-le-Rideau or Amboise, and of those from Vouvray and Montlouis, where the styles range from dry to sweet and include sparkling wines. Specific local vinification techniques also play their part. The tuffeau caves provide an excellent storage environment at a constant temperature of around 12°C (53.6°F), ideal for ageing; in addition, the vinification of the white wines is carried out at a controlled temperature, fermentation sometimes lasting several weeks, or even several months for the sweet wines. The light Touraine reds are produced from short periods of fermentation; with Bourgueil and Chinon, however, fermentation is longer: two to four weeks. While the reds undergo malolactic fermentation, the whites and rosés owe their freshness, conversely, to the presence of malic acid. Generally speaking, 55% of the production, which in good years

Touraine

approaches some 700,000 hl (18,480,000 gal), is sold by shippers. Direct sales represent 30% and the co-operatives sell 15%.

Touraine

T HE Appellation Régionale Touraine covers 5,250 ha (12,967 acres), stretching from the outskirts of Montsoreau in the west as far as Blois and Selles-sur-Cher in the east. It is located principally in the valleys of the Loire, the Indre and the Cher. Tuffeau emerges rarely; the soils most often overlie clay with silica. The main variety for red wines is Gamay, alongside more tannic varieties such as Cabernet Franc and Côt, depending on the terrain. The majority of red wines, including the light and fruity *vins* *primeurs*, are made exclusively with Gamay. Reds made from a mixture of two or three of the main varieties keep well in bottle. The dry white wines are made with the Sauvignon, which in the last forty years has replaced all other varieties. A proportion of the white wines is made as sparkling wines by the Méthode Traditionelle, or Champagne method. Finally, the rosés are always dry, fresh and fruity, made with the red wine grape varieties of the region.

I T is worth mentioning the historic vineyard to the south of Tours which produces dry rosé Appellation Touraine wines formerly known as Noble Joué, a denomination now revived. The varieties in use here are the three Pinots: Pinot Gris (the majority), Pinot Meunier and Pinot Noir.

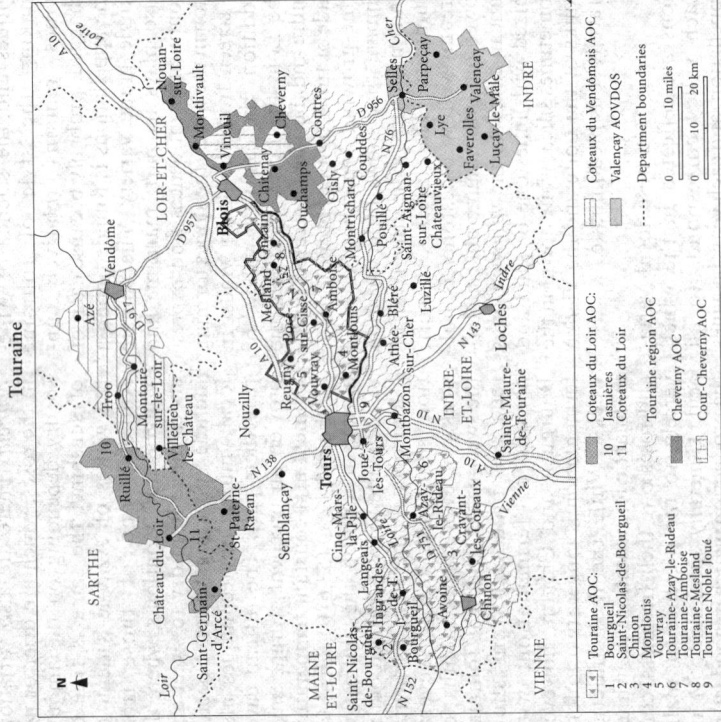

Touraine

Touraine AOC:
1 Bourgueil
2 Saint-Nicolas-de-Bourgueil
3 Chinon
4 Montlouis
5 Vouvray
6 Touraine-Azay-le-Rideau
7 Touraine-Amboise
8 Touraine-Mesland
9 Touraine Noble Joué
10 Jasnières
11 Coteaux du Loir

Coteaux du Loir AOC:
Touraine region AOC
Cheverny AOC
Cour-Cheverny AOC
Coteaux du Vendômois AOC
Valençay AOVDQS
Department boundaries

0   10 miles
0   10   20 km

JACKY ET PHILIPPE AUGIS

Méthode traditionnelle ★★ ○ 2.5 ha 20,000 ▦▦ €5–8

The term 'traditional method' used in wine-making circles is the right name for this floral, brightly coloured wine. The exotic fruitiness given off at the finish is beyond criticism.

➤ GAEC Jacky et Philippe Augis, Le Musa, rue des Vignes, 41130 Meusnes, tel. 02.54.71.01.89, fax 02.54.71.74.15, e-mail paugis@net-up.com ⓥ

☐ ev. day except Sun. 8am–12 noon 2pm–7.30pm; cl.15–31 Aug.

CELLIER DU BEAUJARDIN

Gamay 2000 ★ ▪ 30 ha 40,000 ▦ €3

This Gamay is full, firm and supple; a good example of its variety, with its characteristic colour, slightly musty nose and fruity palate. An attractive Touraine wine worth discovering.

➤ Cellier du Beaujardin, 32, av. du 11-Novembre, 37150 Bléré, tel. 02.47.30.33.44, fax 02.47.30.33.44, e-mail cellier.beaujardin@wanadoo.fr ⓥ

☐ ev. day except Sun. 8am–12 noon 2pm–6.30pm

DOM. BEAUSEJOUR

Cuvée Vincent 2000 ★★ ▪ 5 ha 30,000 ▦▦ €3–5

A fine example of a Touraine wine that the Jury judged worthy of a *coup de cœur*. The Cuvée Vincent 2000 is made from Gamay grapes alone, grown on sand and clay overlaying silica. Its fine ruby colour is accompanied by a surprisingly intense floral note of soft fruit: it is a pleasure to find the same intensity on the palate in a style that is highly characteristic of this appellation. It will delight wine-lovers.

➤ GAEC Trotignon et Fils, Dom. Beauséjour, 10, rue des Bruyères, 41140 Noyers-sur-Cher, tel. 02.54.75.06.73, fax 02.54.75.06.73 ⓥ ☐ ev. day 8am–12 noon 2pm–7pm

DOM. BEAUSEJOUR

L'Authentique Elevé en fût 1999 ★★ ▪ 5 ha 5,000 ▥ €5–8

This is another excellent blended vintage, produced from vines grown in the *perruche* (sandy clay soil with underlying clay subsoil) on the lower slopes of the Cher. It is a fine Touraine characterised by its dark colour, and aromas of liquorice and woodland. Powerful and well-balanced, it will invariably appeal to lovers of more mature wines.

➤ GAEC Trotignon et Fils, Dom. Beauséjour, 10, rue des Bruyères, 41140 Noyers-sur-Cher, tel. 02.54.75.06.73, fax 02.54.75.06.73 ⓥ

☐ ev. day 8am–12 noon 2pm–7pm

DOM. DES CAILLOTS

Tradition 1999 ★ ▪ 3 ha 20,000 ▦▦ €3–5

This Touraine echoes the past, as people have been cultivating the Cabernet Franc and Côt grape varieties on this same soil for generations – traditional varieties from this beautiful Cher Valley. A full-ruby colour with brick-red reflections, it blossoms out into peony aromas on a note of soft fruit and peppers. A well-balanced, full palate with a subtle, rounded quantity of tannin characterise this excellent Touraine. The estate also submitted its **Touraine Sauvignon 2000**, an interesting wine with an exotic note and a pleasant structure, which especially impressed the Jury.

➤ EARL Dominique Girault, Le Grand Mont, 41140 Noyers-sur-Cher, tel. 02.54.32.27.07, fax 02.54.75.27.87 ⓥ ☐ ev. day 8.30am–12 noon 2pm–7pm; Sun. by appt.

DOM. CHARBONNIER

Sauvignon 2000 ★ ☐ 5 ha 6,000 ▦▦ €3

Daniel, Michel and, as of 2001, Stéphane open their estate's doors to visitors on the first Sunday of December. This is an excellent opportunity to taste and buy this fine wine, which offers not only aromas of boxwood and citrus fruit but also a supple, well-balanced opening on the palate with just a hint of bitterness. It is an agreeable, well-produced Touraine.

➤ GAEC Charbonnier, 4, chem. de la Cossaie, 41110 Châteauvieux, tel. 02.54.75.49.29, fax 02.54.75.40.74 ⓥ ☐ by appt.

CH. DE CHENONCEAU

Sauvignon 1999 ★ ▪ 5 ha 26,000 ▦▦ €5–8

Built in 1513, 'on the water, in the air', as Flaubert once described it, Château de Chenonceau is between the two banks of the Cher. However, it is not only a fine example of Renaissance architecture, but is also a wine-producing château. This vintage is produced on the slopes of Touraine, where the Chenin grape variety, a difficult one to manage, performs miraculous feats: it possesses a honeyed nose and a lithe body that will satisfy the most demanding of purists. It should be laid down immediately.

→ SA Chenonceau-Expansion,
Ch. de Chenonceau, 37150 Chenonceaux,
tel. 02.47.23.44.07, fax 02.47.23.89.91,
e-mail chateau.de.chenonceau@wanadoo.fr
☑ ▼ ev. day 11am–6pm; cl. Nov.–Mar.

DOM. DES CHEZELLES★

Sauvignon 2000★

☐   10 ha   80,000   ■ ●   €5-8

Alain Marcadet has produced this expressive wine, in which hints of blackcurrant leaves, boxwood and grapefruit bubble up to the top of the glass, followed by a generous, rich palate. The vegetal notes in its finish do not alter the positive overall impression. If you are looking for a youthful Gamay type, then you will not be disappointed by this estate's 2000 vintage, now ready for drinking, which was also awarded a star.

→ EARL Alain Marcadet, Le Grand Mont, 41140 Noyers-sur-Cher, tel. 02.54.75.13.62, fax 02.54.75.44.09 ☑ ▼ ev. day except Sun. 8.30am–12 noon 2pm–7pm

LES VIGNERONS DES COTEAUX ROMANAIS

Sauvignon Cuvée Saint-Vincent 2000★

☐   50 ha   400,000   ■ ●   €3-5

Engaged in a qualitative move, together with its suppliers, this co-operative based in Saint-Romain has presented the Jury with an elegant wine with aromas of boxwood and tobacco. A good balance on the palate is followed by a finish that was still a little harsh at the time of tasting, but which should have improved by now. The perfect wine to drink with local pike or perch cooked in butter.

→ Les Vignerons des Coteaux Romanais, 50, rue Principale,
41140 Saint-Romain-sur-Cher,
tel. 02.54.71.70.74, fax 02.54.71.41.75 ☑ ▼ ev. day except Sun. Mon. 8am–12 noon 2pm–6pm

DOM. DE CRAY Sauvignon 2000★

☐   3.5 ha   31,000   ■ ●   €3-5

The attractive label on this Sauvignon is the result of the partnership between a British wine-merchant and a Montlouis wine-producer. The wine is an extremely elegant, pale-gold colour with a hint of green. On the nose it reveals hints of exotic fruit and brioche. Warm and smooth on the palate, the wine seduces right through to the balanced finish.

→ Boutinot, SARL La Chapelle de Cray, rte de l'Aquarium, 37400 Lussault-sur-Loire, tel. 02.47.57.17.74, fax 02.47.57.11.97, e-mail chapelledecray@wanadoo.fr
▼ by appt.

DOM. JOEL DELAUNAY

Sauvignon 2000★

☐   7.5 ha   50,000   ■ ●   €5-8

Thierry, Joël Delaunay's son, rejoined the estate in 1998. Together they have produced a highly enjoyable wine. A strong aroma of broom, together with a refreshing taste, fail to conceal the unique character of this wine.

→ EARL Thierry et Joël Delaunay,
48, rue de la Tesnière, 41110 Pouillé,
tel. 02.54.71.45.69, fax 02.54.71.55.97,
e-mail joeldelaunay@terre-net.fr ▼
▼ ev. day except Sun. 9am–12 noon 2pm–6pm

VIGNOBLE DUBREUIL

Sauvignon 2000

☐   9.5 ha   3,000

This family-owned vineyard was renovated between about 1965 and 1970, and 30 years on the Sauvignon vines have produced a highly aromatic wine characterised by hints of boxwood and a round, elegant palate. A thirst-quenching wine. Do not forget to visit the church at the centre of the village; it dates from the 11th and 12th centuries.

→ Rémi Dubreuil, La Touche,
41700 Couddes, tel. 02.54.71.34.46,
fax 02.54.71.09.64 ▼ ▼ by appt.

DOM. DE FLEURAY

Sauvignon 2000★★   →€3

A small dish of fried fish from the Loire would be the perfect match for this wine produced from 20-year-old Sauvignon vines. The Jury was impressed by the elegance of the 2000 vintage, with its highly expressive nose of citrus fruit and its remarkable aromatic length.

→ Dom. Cocteaux, Fleuray, 37530 Cangey, tel. 02.47.30.01.44, fax 02.47.30.05.09 ▼ ▼ ev. day except Sun. 8am–6.30pm; Sat. 8am–1pm

CHANTAL ET PATRICK GIBAULT 2000★★

☐   2 ha   10,000   ■ ●   €3-5

Meusnes is proud of its Romanesque church dating from the 11th century, as well as its museum. This rosé is an attractive, lively colour and abounds in subtle nuances of fruit. It reveals a surprising complexity that is uncommon in a rosé, and boasts a long, fresh, balanced finish. The estate's **Sauvignon 2000** was awarded one star: a subtle wine with scents of exotic fruit and grapefruit, together with a ripe palate, it is characterised by fruity sweetness.

→ EARL Chantal et Patrick Gibault,
183, rue Gambetta, 41130 Meusnes,
tel. 02.54.71.02.63, fax 02.54.71.58.92,
e-mail gibault.earl@wanadoo.fr ▼
▼ ev. day 8am–7pm; Sun. 10am–12 noon

DOM. DU HAUT CHESNEAU

Sauvignon 2000

☐   6 ha   10,000   ■ ●   €3-5

On the right bank of the Cher, this 17-ha (42-acre) estate was built in 1789, its attractive cellars carved out of the rock. A brilliant pale-yellow colour, the Sauvignon 2000 offers a vegetal note characteristic of its youth. It attains a good balance between the fleshy and the acidic, and also has an appealing liveliness, which makes it a good wine to drink with shellfish.

● Jean-Marc Villemaine, La Ramée, 41140 Thésée, tel. 02.54.71.52.69, fax 02.54.71.52.69, Y by appt.

DOM. DE LA BERGEONNIERE
Gamay 2000 ★★ — 2.3 ha | 10,000 | ■

Old Gamay vines planted on silica soil have produced an extremely pleasant wine, which reflects both the importance given to the harvest and the producers' passion for their work. A brilliant, attractive colour, the wine releases floral notes against a mineral background, and then reveals flavours of red berries on a refreshing finish.

● Jean-Claude Bodin, La Bergeonnière, 41140 Saint-Romain-sur-Cher, tel. 02.54.71.70.43, fax 02.54.71.72.92 [V] Y by appt.

DOM. DE LA BERGEONNIERE
Pinot noir 2000 ★ — 0.5 ha | 4,000 | ■ | €3-5

It is a limited vintage produced on Jean-Claude Bodin's 15-ha (37-acre) estate, but an interesting one nevertheless: this *vin gris* is somewhat rare in an area dominated by the Gamay grape, as it is produced using the Pinot Noir grape, which gives it such an expressive nose. As a result, it is lacking in that freshness that usually characterises rosés, but this means that it will be a good wine to drink with more substantial dishes.

● Jean-Claude Bodin, La Bergeonnière, 41140 Saint-Romain-sur-Cher, tel. 02.54.71.70.43, fax 02.54.71.72.92 [V] Y by appt.

DOM. DE LA BERGERIE
Cabernet 1999 ★ — 4 ha | 15,000 | ■ | €3-5

A product of the *perruche* (sandy clay soil with underlying clay subsoil) found in the Cher Valley, this is a classic, extremely balanced, fuchsia-red wine. This Touraine, highly characteristic of its grape variety, reveals scents of redcurrant on the nose, which are prolonged in the mouth: it is destined to charm. The pale-coloured **Touraine Sauvignon 2000** gives off aromas of blackcurrant leaf and grapefruit. It is a supple wine that may be served with all kinds of foods.

● François Cartier, La Tesnière, 41110 Pouillé, tel. 02.54.71.51.54, fax 02.54.71.74.09 [V] Y ev. day except Sun. 8am–12 noon 2pm–6pm

DOM. DE LA CROIX BOUQUIE
Gamay 2000 ★★ — 4 ha | 15,000 | ■ | €5-8

A siliceous soil overlaying clay clearly shows its affinity with the Gamay variety here. This wine's attractive cherry colour is a sign of its success: it offers subtle hints of soft fruit, is full and well-structured, and will be the perfect partner to roast leg of lamb.

● Christian Girard, 1, chem. de la Chaussée, 41400 Thenay, tel. 02.54.32.50.67, fax 02.54.71.52.69, Y by appt.

DOM. DE LA CROIX BOUQUIE
Cuvée Prestige 1999 ★★ — 1.5 ha | 5,000 | ■ | €5-8

Produced from 75% Côt (Malbec) and Cabernet grape varieties, this attractive garnet-coloured Cuvée Prestige 99 is a good example of what a Touraine red wine should be like. Its complex aromatic qualities are immediately evident. Well-structured and powerful, it is a wine for cellaring for a few years, although it may nevertheless be drunk straight away.

● Christian Girard, 1, chem. de la Chaussée, 41400 Thenay, tel. 02.54.32.74.17 [V] Y by appt.

DOM. DE LA GIRARDIERE
Sauvignon 2000 ★★ — 5 ha | 10,000 | ■ | €3-5

Patrick Léger has run the family estate, founded by his grandfather, since 1988. A product of clay on silica, the Sauvignon 2000 has crystalline greenish-gold reflections and complex scents of citrus fruit and blackcurrant. It opens on the palate with a slightly sparkling feeling, but then develops in a more balanced fashion, leaving the palate fresh. It is a truly enjoyable wine.

● Patrick Léger, La Girardière, 41110 Saint-Aignan, tel. 02.54.75.42.44, fax 02.54.75.21.14 [V] Y by appt.

DOM. DE LA GIRARDIERE
Méthode traditionnelle 1999 ★★ — 0.45 ha | 4,000 | ○ | €5-8

A dry blanc de blancs made from 15% Chardonnay and 85% Chenin grapes, this subtle wine is a brilliant, pale-yellow colour and is nicely fruity on the nose: a well-balanced, harmonious, enjoyable Touraine, full of freshness and charm.

● Patrick Léger, La Giraudière, tel. 02.54.75.42.44, 41110 Saint-Aignan, tel. 02.54.75.21.14 Y by appt.

LA HERPINIERE
Cabernet 1999 ★★★ — 1.5 ha | 8,500 | ■ | €5-8

The wines of La Herpinière are matured in a cellar that was cut into the rock during the 15th century: ideal conditions for the wine-producer. Matured in barrel for six months, this blend of Cabernet Franc (70%) and Cabernet Sauvignon grapes is the product of the *perruche* (sandy clay soil with underlying clay subsoil). It possesses a strikingly brilliant ruby colour, together with a nose of intense cherry nuances. It opens on the palate with powerful flavours of red berries, and then reveals a strong tannic structure, promising a positive future for this particular Cabernet.

● Christophe Veronneau, 16, La Vallée, 37190 Varennes, tel. 02.47.45.92.39, fax 02.47.45.92.38, e-mail laherpiniere@aol.com [V] Y ev. day 10am–7pm; cl. Jan.

DOM. DE LA RENNE Côt 1999★★ €3-5

n.c. 6,800

The Côt grape variety, which covered a third of the Cher Valley 40 years ago, contributed significantly towards making the region known. The scent of morello cherries and leather precede its rounded, still slightly tannic palate, followed by flavours that indicate the wine's potential for ageing. The wine is ready to drink now, but it could equally be kept to see in the New Year in 2005.

• Guy Lévêque, 1, chem. de la Forêt, 41140 Saint-Romain-sur-Cher, tel. 02.54.71.72.79, fax 02.54.71.35.07 ☑ ☘ by appt.

CH. DE LA ROCHE Sauvignon 2000★ €5-8

8 ha 60,000

Château de la Roche, 3 km (1.8 miles) from Clos Lucé – a must-see for the visitor as it is home to the wonderful 'machines' invented by Leonardo da Vinci – is an estate of 75 ha (185 acres). It presented a **Touraine Gamay 2000**, which the Jury singled out for its rounded, fruity character, and this pretty bottle with its powerful nose of lychees and fresh mangoes. It opens in a lively manner, and then develops unctuously, making it a worthy representative of Touraine wines.

• SCA Dom. Chainier, Ch. de La Roche, 37530 Chargé, tel. 02.47.30.73.07, fax 02.47.30.73.09 ☘ by appt.

DOM. DE LA ROCHETTE Sauvignon 2000★★ €3-5

15 ha 75,000

In the centre of the Loire châteaux, François Leclair's vineyard is on the lower slopes of the Cher Valley. The *perruche* (sandy clay soil with underlying clay subsoil), with a high silica content, is the key to the 2000 vintage: light-coloured and tinged with green, this is one for true wine-lovers. Its intense scents of oranges on the nose and its fullness on the palate would suggest that the wine needs to age for a year or two before drinking, when it will make an ideal match for shellfish or white meat.

• François Leclair, 79, rte de Montrichard, 41110 Pouillé, tel. 02.54.71.44.02, fax 02.54.71.10.94, e-mail info@ vin-rochette-leclair.com ☑ ☘ ev. day 8am– 11.30am 2pm–5.30pm; Sat. Sun. by appt.

CAVES DE LA TOURANGELLE Sauvignon 2000★

n.c. n.c.

This white Touraine is a pleasant success, with its restrained scents and simple flavours: a wine to be drunk with friends.

• Les Caves de La Tourangelle, 26, rue de la Liberté, 41400 Saint-Georges-sur-Cher, tel. 02.54.32.65.75, fax 02.54.71.09.61

DOM. DE L'AUMONIER Gamay 2000★

12.5 ha 40,000 €3-5

Thierry Chardon has been running his 32-ha (79-acre) estate since 1996. The dark-coloured Gamay 2000 reveals scents of fruit hinting of pepper on the nose. On the palate, the first impression is one of roundness, but this gives way to flavours of blackcurrant and strawberry. It is an agreeable wine. The **Touraine Sauvignon 2000** (100,000 bottles) is equally worthy; it offers a delightful bouquet of white flowers mixed with blackcurrant leaves. Tender, balanced but also refreshing, this wine is a good example of its type.

• Thierry Chardon, Villequemoy, 41110 Couffy, tel. 02.54.75.21.83, fax 02.54.75.21.56, e-mail domaine-aumoniertchardon@ wanadoo.fr ☘ by appt.

PRESTIGE DE LA VALLEE DES ROIS Gamay 2000★ €5-8

6 ha 50,000

Seven wine-producers got together in 1961 to set up this co-operative: today there are 52 of them. The Gamay 2000 will benefit from a little ageing, to allow its tannins to soften; but with its dominant flavours of red berries, it is nevertheless a success now.

• Confrérie des Vignerons d'Oisly et Thésée, Le Bourg, 41700 Oisly, tel. 02.54.79.75.20, fax 02.54.79.75.29 ☑ ☘ by appt.

DOM. LEVEQUE Cabernet 1999★ €3-5

4 ha 5,000

Noyers-sur-Cher boasts a 13th-century Angevin church; this vineyard is found along the RN76. An attractive, intense colour, its Cabernet is fruity and fresh, with hints of blackcurrants.

• Dom. Luc Lévêque, Le Grand Mont, 41140 Noyers-sur-Cher, tel. 02.54.71.52.06, fax 02.54.75.47.65 ☑ ☘ ev. day except Sun. 8.30am–12 noon 2pm–6.30pm

CAVE PIERRE LOUET
Cuvée Prestige 1999★

1.5 ha | 9,000 | €3-5

South of Blois, between the Loire and the Cher, is a wine-producer whose passion for her work is contagious. Her 99 Cuvée Prestige, made from Cabernet grapes, brings to mind ripe blackcurrants with its dark-garnet colour. Round, balanced, tannic – but not exceedingly so – and well balanced, the wine will please the average wine-lover with its fruitiness.

♠ Mme Jacqueline Louet,
Cave Pierre Louet, Le Marchais,
41120 Monthou-sur-Bièvre,
tel. 02.54.44.01.56, fax 02.54.44.01.18
Y ev. day 8am-12 noon 2pm-6pm; Sat. Sun. by appt.

JEAN-CHRISTOPHE MANDARD
Sauvignon 2000★★

3.5 ha | 25,000 | €5-8

Jean-Christophe Mandard represents the fourth generation of his family to produce wine on the slopes along the left bank of the Cher, and he has managed to fully exploit the fine silica soil in his Sauvignon 2000. An enjoyable, balanced wine, it has intense scents of citrus mixed with boxwood, together with a lively, fresh taste that lingers on the finish. The Touraine Tradition 99, a mix of Cabernet Franc and Côt varieties, impressed the Jury. Its tannins need to mature somewhat.

♠ Jean-Christophe Mandard,
Le Haut-Bagneux, 41110 Mareuil-sur-Cher,
tel. 02.54.75.19.73, fax 02.54.75.16.70,
e-mail mandard.jc@wanadoo.fr
Y by appt.

DOM. LOUET-ARCOURT 1999★

5 ha | 7,000 | €3-5

Among fresh, light wines, this is a Touraine with an intense ruby colour, one that offers highly attractive notes of red berries; sufficiently round and slightly acidic, it is an excellent wine for all-round drinking. Cuvée de Réserve Côt 99 is equally successful: it is a rich, well-structured wine to be laid down in the cellar for some time.

♠ EARL Dom. Louet-Arcourt,
1, rue de la Paix, Labertaudière,
41120 Monthou-sur-Bièvre,
tel. 02.54.44.04.54, fax 02.54.44.15.06
Y by appt.

LOUET GAUDEFROY
Cabernet 1999★★

3 ha | 9,500 | €3-5

This Touraine, with its deep-garnet colour, got an enthusiastic reception from the Jury for its ageing potential. The wine opens on the nose rather timidly, with hints of undergrowth, but then a cocktail of soft fruit explodes on the palate. Well-balanced with silky tannins, it offers a lengthy finish. It is a highly pleasurable wine. The estate also produces a Touraine Sauvignon 2000, which was singled out by the Jury.

♠ GAEC Louet Gaudefroy, Les Sablons,
41140 Saint-Romain-sur-Cher,
tel. 02.54.71.72.83, fax 02.54.71.46.53
Y ev. day 8am-7pm

DOM. MESLAND
La Pindorgerie 2000★★

0.8 ha | 6,000 | €5-8

On the right bank of the Loire, north-east of Amboise, Limeray is an interesting village, full of caves, with hiking trails enabling visitors to explore the surrounding countryside. This excellent wine is not to be missed: hints of honey and a note of toast on the nose are followed by extremely pleasant full, round flavours in the mouth and a lengthy finish. The wine should be drunk as an aperitif, or with cheeses.

♠ Dom. Mesland, 15 bis, rue d'Enfer,
37530 Limeray, tel. 02.47.30.11.15,
fax 02.47.30.02.89 Y ev. day 8am-9pm; groups by appt.

DOM. MAX MEUNIER Brut★★★

n.c. | 5,000 | €5-8

On the lower slopes of the left bank of the Cher, this 15-ha (37-acre) domaine was set up in 1911. It presented the Jury with a magnificent party wine, a sparkling Touraine that persistently teased the taste buds. It opens freshly, and is perfectly balanced by the multitude of fruity flavours that return on the finish.

DOM. JACKY MARTEAU
Sauvignon 2000

8.5 ha | 55,000 | €5-8

At Pouillé, excavations have revealed the existence of a Gallo-Roman village of potters. Jacky Marteau runs a 24-ha (59-acre) estate here, producing this fine, brilliant golden-yellow wine. Its colour is the preface to delicate nuances of grapefruit mixed with acacia. Unambiguous, enhanced by a slightly sparkling lightness on the palate, it lingers on the finish.

♠ Jacky Marteau, 36, rue de La Tesnière,
41110 Pouillé, tel. 02.54.71.50.00,
fax 02.54.71.75.83 Y by appt.

GUY MARDON L'Elégante 2000★

n.c. | 8,000 | €5-8

Guy Mardon set up the estate in 1961, and Jean-Luc Mardon came in to help in 1995. That is what is known as 'continuity.' Here is a beautifully mature wine where hawthorn blends with acacia over notes of blood orange. Velvety on the tongue, its hint of sparkle refreshes the lengthy finish. It is a successful, characteristic wine.

♠ Guy et Jean-Luc Mardon, Dom. du Pré
Baron, 41700 Oisly, tel. 02.54.79.52.87,
fax 02.54.79.00.45 Y ev. day except Sun. 9am-7pm

Touraine

DOM. DE MONTIGNY Côt 1999★
■ 1 ha 5,500 ■ ♦ €3-5

Management of this family-run estate changed hands in 1998, and this year's was the second harvest for Annabelle, the present manager. This dark-coloured Touraine is a rounded wine that releases subtle scents of morello cherry mixed with leather. Well-structured and powerful, it will delight lovers of this old Touraine grape variety.

● Annabelle Michaud, Dom. de Montigny, 41700 Sassay, tel. 02.54.79.60.82, fax 02.54.79.07.51 ▼ by appt.

DOM. OCTAVIE Sauvignon 2000 ■ ♦ €5-8
□ 10.37 ha 50,000

Octavie was the name of the first owner of this estate, back in 1885; her descendants, Isabelle and her husband Noë, today manage nearly 23 ha (57 acres). The modern set-up that characterises the present estate has not really changed the nature of the family's wines. The pale-coloured 2000 vintage reveals a complex aromatic intensity, a mixture of citrus fruit and boxwood: a supple, rounded wine with a warm finish.

● Noë Rouballay, Dom. Octavie, Marcé, 41700 Oisly, tel. 02.54.79.54.57, fax 02.54.79.65.20, e-mail octavie@netcourrier.com ▼ ev. day 9am–12.30pm 2pm–6.30pm; Sun. by appt.

DOM. MICHAUD Gamay 2000★★
■ 4 ha 22,000 ■ ♦ €3-5

The Michaud estate is a benchmark for wine-lovers in the attractive Cher Valley, and this Gamay 2000 has a remarkable structure and a slightly peppery nose, with soft fruit clearly present on the palate. The estate's **Ad Vitam 99** goes back to the Touraine tradition of blending Côt and Cabernet Franc grapes. It boasts a dark-garnet colour, with soft fruit (cherries) discernible throughout. It is well-balanced with tannins that are yet subtle. The wine was awarded one star.

● EARL Michaud, Les Martinières, 41140 Noyers-sur-Cher, tel. 02.54.32.47.23, fax 02.54.75.39.19 ▼ by appt.

MONMOUSSEAU
Cuvée J. M. Brut Blanc de Blancs 1997★★
○ 42 ha 404,535 ■ ♦ €5-8

The Monmousseau caves have been owned by a group from Luxembourg since 1986: this group has proven its ability to safeguard local know-how in the production of sparkling wines. The light bubbles in this blanc de blancs rise up to the rim of the glass; its fruity nuances immediately come to the fore as whole baskets of exotic fruits, and it offers a balanced, harmonious finish. A true party wine.

● SA Monmousseau, BP 25, 71, rte de Vierzon, 41401 Montrichard Cedex 01, tel. 02.54.71.66.66, fax 02.54.32.56.09, e-mail monmousseau@monmousseau.com ▼ ev. day 10am–6pm; groups by appt.; cl. Sat. Sun. 1 Nov.–31 Mar.

● Bernard Massard

JAMES PAGET Cuvée Tradition 1999★
■ 1.5 ha 8,000 ■ Ⅲ ♦ €3-5

James Paget produces excellent Touraine-Azay-le-Rideau rosé wines, and his Cuvée Tradition is a well-balanced wine featuring silky tannins. Restrained on the nose, its pleasant lightness on the palate makes it an ideal wine to accompany white meats.

● EARL James Paget, 13, rue d'Armentières, 37190 Rivarennes, tel. 02.47.95.54.02, fax 02.47.95.45.90 ▼ by appt.

CH. DE MONTFORT 1999★
□ 5.58 ha 10,000

This 99 white wine is a charming, pale-yellow vintage made from the Chenin grape. A highly expressive nose of honey, followed by honeyed notes on the palate which remain on the finish, are signs of balance. Although the label does not say so, the wine may be defined as 'off-dry', with 5g/l of residual sugar.

● SC Ch. de Montfort, Les Quarts, 37210 Chançay, tel. 02.47.52.14.57, fax 02.47.52.06.09 ▼ by appt.

● SA Blanc Foussy

CAVES DU PERE AUGUSTE
Côt 1999★★
■ 8 ha 20,500 ■ ♦ €3-5

Founded by Robert Godeau's ancestors in 1850, and 1 km (0.6 miles) from Château de Chenonceau, this estate is famous for the warm welcome it offers visiting wine-lovers. The reader will be equally attracted by this wine, with its strong colour and its flavours of morello cherry with a dash of peppery freshness. An elegant vintage, full of softened tannins, the Côt 99 is an excellent representative of Touraine wines. The estate's **Gamay 2000** was also awarded a star: it is a well-structured wine that can be enjoyed until the 2002 harvest comes round.

● Robert Godeau, Caves du Père Auguste, 14, rue des Caves, 37150 Civray-de-Touraine, tel. 02.47.23.93.04, fax 02.47.23.99.58 ▼ ev. day except Sun. 9am–12 noon 2pm–7pm

DOM. DES QUATRE VENTS
Vieilles vignes 1999★　n.c.　15,000

This is a truly attractive wine, made using the original grape varieties in the valley, Côt and Cabernet. Well-balanced, it offers a powerful, slightly vinous nose followed by flavours of soft fruit on a full-bodied, lengthy palate.

José Marteau, La Rouerie, 41400 Thenay, tel. 02.54.32.50.51, fax 02.54.32.18.52. ev. day 8am–12.15pm 2pm–7pm; Sun. 8am–12.15pm

CH. DE QUINCAY 1999　5 ha　8,000　€5-8

The château, built in 1830, produces this clean Touraine. Garnet tinged with brick-red in colour, the 99 has peony and gamey hints accompanied by a fine structure. The extremely young tannins present on the finish need another year or two to mature. The **Touraine Sauvignon 2000** was singled out by the Jury for its pleasant balance and floral scents. It is ready to drink.

Cadart Père et Fils, Ch. de Quinçay, 41130 Meusnes, tel. 02.54.71.77.72. by appt.

SEIGNEUR CLEMENT DU DOM. DE RIS 1999★　2 ha　8,000　€5-8

The Claise is a small river bordered by attractive, vine-covered hillsides. Along its banks are not only a series of pretty little villages and Romanesque churches, but also a number of vineyards like this one. The 99 Touraine, now ready for drinking, has a well-developed colour, with a mixture of strawberry and gamey notes on the nose that give it a smooth character, typical of the fresh Loire Valley wines.

Dom. de Ris, 37290 Bossay-sur-Claise, tel. 02.47.94.64.43, fax 02.47.94.68.46. ev. day except Sun. 5.30pm–7pm; Sat. 10am–12 noon 2pm–7pm
Gilbert Sabadié

JEAN-FRANCOIS ROY　Côt 1999★　1.5 ha　n.c.　€5-8

Jean-François Roy, a wine producer within the Valençay appellation, also cultivates the Côt variety on AC Touraine soil and matures the wine in wooden barrels for a year. The 99 vintage is a pleasant, bright colour, and reveals subtle hints of vanilla against an excellent, balanced structure. The woody flavour dominates at present, making it a rather unusual wine for its appellation, but of considerable interest to informed wine-lovers. It has sufficient body for it to be laid down for three or four years.

Jean-François Roy, 3, rue des Acacias, 36600 Lye, tel. 02.54.41.00.39, fax 02.54.41.06.89. by appl.

DOM. SAUVETE Privilège 1999★　3 ha　10,000　€5-8

Do not miss the chance to buy this fine wine, with its garnet colour and its clear flavours of soft fruit, made from 70% Côt and 30% Cabernet. At present, the wine's structure is dominated by its tannins, but four or five years of maturing will bring out the very best of its potential.

Dom. Sauvète, chem. de La Bocagerie, 41400 Monthou-sur-Cher, tel. 02.54.71.48.68, fax 02.54.71.75.31. ev. day except Sun. 9am–12 noon 2pm–7pm

DOM. DES SEIGNEURS
Pineau d'Aunis 2000★　2 ha　14,500　€3

Laurent Avignon took over the family estate in 1994, and he has produced a very elegant rosé with a light colour and a freshness on the nose. It opens in the mouth rather subtly, but has excellent structure and a lengthy finish.

Dom. des Seigneurs, Les Tassins, 41110 Couffy, tel. 02.54.75.01.01, fax 02.54.75.39.31. by appt.

DOM. MICHEL VAUVY
Sauvignon 2000　4 ha　10,000　€5-8

A golden colour and interestingly complex flavours will be appreciated by both the uninitiated and aficionados of Touraine white wine. This would go well with moules marinières.

Michel Vauvy, 81, rue Nationale, 41140 Noyers-sur-Cher, tel. 02.54.75.26.57, fax 02.54.75.26.57. by appt.

Touraine Noble-Joué

Known at the court of Louis XI, this wine's reputation was at its peak during the 19th century. The vineyard nearly disappeared, nibbled away by the urbanisation of Tours, but has been reborn due to the efforts of winegrowers who reconstituted it. This *vin gris*, made from a blend of Meunier, Pinot Gris and Pinot Noir, now regains its historic place thanks to its recognition as a new AOC.

REMI COSSON 2000　1.7 ha　5,000　€3-5

On the nose, this rosé is redolent of surprisingly intense cooked fruit, while cherries dominate on the palate. On the finish, the wine is typical of the freshness of this new appellation.

➤ Rémi Cosson, La Hardellière, 37320 Esvres-sur-Indre, tel. 02.47.65.70.63 ▼ ▲ by appt.

ANTOINE DUPUY 2000 ▲ ■ €3-5
4 ha 15,000

A light-pink colour, this 2000 has a fine, restrained nose as well as a freshness on the palate that make it an ideal wine for afternoon drinking. The finish is sharp, although not excessively so.

➤ EARL Antoine Dupuy, Le Vau, 37320 Esvres-sur-Indre, tel. 02.47.26.44.46, fax 02.47.65.78.86 ▼ ▲ by appt.

JEAN-JACQUES SARD 2000 ▲ ■ €3-5
3.8 ha 13,000

A pale-pink colour and clear, burnt vegetal scents, followed by a rounded, lively palate, combine well to give the impression of a naturally elegant wine. This is a vintage worth discovering.

➤ Jean-Jacques Sard, La Chambrière, 37320 Esvres-sur-Indre, tel. 02.47.26.42.89, fax 02.47.26.57.59 ▼ ▲ by appt.

three grape varieties. The *terroir* is clearly present in the wine, a bottle to be drunk with Sunday lunch.

➤ François Péquin, Dom. des Bessons, 113, rue de Blois, 37530 Limeray, tel. 02.47.30.09.10, fax 02.47.30.02.25 ▼ ▲ ev. day except Sun. 9am–7pm

GUY DURAND ■ €8-11
Cuvée HM Moelleux 1999★★
1 ha 1,200

The Chenin grape is definitely one of the best white wine varieties when handled by an expert like Guy Durand. A yield worthy of a Grand Cru together with a patient wait for the wine to mature to its optimal level contribute to this excellent wine, which is named after the founder of the estate. Pears blend into over-ripe rhubarb, making this a superb Saumur wine with a surprising, honeyed length of flavour on the finish.

➤ Guy Durand, 11, chem. Neuf, 37530 Mosnes, tel. 02.47.30.43.14, fax 02.47.30.43.14 ▼ ▲ ev. day 8am–8pm

Touraine-Amboise

Sited on both banks of the Loire and dominated by the 15th- and 16th-century Château d'Amboise, the vineyard of the Appellation Touraine-Amboise, which is between 150 and 200 ha (370–494 acres) is not far from the Manoir Clos-Lucé, where Leonardo de Vinci spent his last days. Production is mainly of red wines (10,815 hl / 285,516 gal) from Gamay, Côt and Cabernet Franc. These are full wines with only a little tannin; when the Côt and Cabernet are dominant, the wines have some keeping potential. The same varieties also produce dry, charming rosés that are fruity and well defined. The whites, 1,799 hl (47,494 gal) in 2000, are dry or medium-dry, depending on the year, and they, too, may be kept.

DOM. DES BESSONS ▲ ■ €3-5
Cuvée François Ier 1999★
1 ha 8,000

Limeray church, with its beautiful stone St Madeleine dating from the 16th century, is well worth a visit, after which, travelling down the Rue de Blois, you have the chance to discover this well-made Touraine-Amboise, with its spicy notes and perfectly balanced blend of

DOM. DUTERTRE ▲ ■ €5-8
Clos du Pavillon 1999
4 ha 7,000

Domaine Dutertre has always given priority to the quality of its products, as shown by the decidedly mineral intensity of this dry white. Although immature at the time of tasting, the 99 releases honeyed nuances on the finish, which would suggest it will be at its best by early 2002.

➤ Dom. Dutertre, 20–21, rue d'Enfer, 37530 Limeray, tel. 02.47.30.10.69, fax 02.47.30.06.92 ▼ ▲ ev. day 8am–12.30pm 2pm–6pm; Sun. by appt.

DOM. DE LA PERDRIELLE 2000 ▲ ■ €3-5
1 ha 5,500

An attractive salmon-pink dotted with tiny bubbles created by the carbon dioxide still present at the time of tasting, this rosé will enthuse wine-lovers with its fermenting nuances of banana and its refreshing, lingering finish.

➤ EARL Gandon, Dom. de La Perdrielle, 24, Vallon de Vauriflé, 37530 Nazelles-Négron, tel. 02.47.57.31.19, fax 02.47.57.77.28, e-mail vgandon@club-internet.fr ▼ ▲ ev. day 9am–12.30pm 2pm–7pm; Sun. by appt.

DOM. DE LA PRÉVÔTÉ 2000 ★★

10 ha · 15,000 · €3-5

The house of Bonnigal boasts considerable knowledge of blending those red grape varieties cultivated within the appellation. This wine's attractive salmon-pink colour and nose full of soft fruit (blackcurrants and strawberries) blend perfectly with its elegant, fresh flavours.

↳ Dom. de La Prévôté, GAEC Bonnigal, 17, rue d'Enfer, 37530 Limeray, tel. 02.47.30.11.02; fax 02.47.30.11.09
Y by appt.

DOM. DE LA RIVAUDIÈRE 2000 ★

1 ha · 7,000 · €5-8

Winner of a coup de coeur last year for its 98 red, this estate has produced an extremely enjoyable, salmon-pink rosé full of soft fruit flavours. Very round and balanced, slightly warm, the wine finishes on a very pleasant note of freshness.

↳ EARL Perdriaux,
3, Les Glandiers, 37210 Vernou-sur-Brenne, tel. 02.47.52.02.26, fax 02.47.52.04.81

DOM. DE LA TONNELLERIE 1999 ★

1 ha · 1,000 · €3-5

An ancient cooper's workshop gave its name to this estate back in 1850. Since 1996 it has had its own symbol, that of the cooper and his staves. Vincent Péquin, a young wine-producer who loves his trade, has produced a very attractive, golden-coloured white with a lovely smell of honey. A straightforward wine, it was a great success in 1999.

↳ Vincent Péquin,
71, rue de Blois, 37530 Limeray,
tel. 02.47.30.13.52, fax 02.47.30.06.23
Y ev. day except Sun. 8am-8pm

L'ORÉE DES FRESNES 1999

1 ha · 6,000 · €5-8

Xavier Frissant, who has managed this estate since 1990, blends equal quantities of Côt and Cabernet Franc grapes harvested from 30-year-old vines to produce a wine that is a perfect match for game; it is ready for drinking. Its strong colour and concentrated flavours over silky tannins make it the perfect wine for the dinner table.

↳ Xavier Frissant, 1, chem. Neuf,
37530 Mosnes, tel. 02.47.57.23.18,
fax 02.47.57.23.25, e-mail xavierfrissant@wanadoo.fr Y ev. day 8am-12.30pm
2pm-7pm; Sun. by appt.

DOM. MESLAND

La Besaudière Cuvée François Ier 1999 ★

0.54 ha · 4,000 · €5-8

This wine, matured six months in oak, is a great success. Complex flavours of soft fruit mixed with liquorice, together with integrated tannins, give the wine a rich, velvety feel. This successful production is due in large part to the correct management of the vineyard and the grape harvest.

↳ Dom. Mesland, 15 bis, rue d'Enfer,
37530 Limeray, tel. 02.47.30.11.15,
fax 02.47.30.02.89
Y ev. day 8am–9pm; groups by appt.

ROLAND PLOU ET SES FILS 1999 ★

3 ha · 10,000 · €3-5

This family-run estate is 4 km (2.5 miles) from the Château d'Amboise. Its 99 white is intensely aromatic, and the perfect wine to drink with cold meats or fish. Its balanced finish was popular with the tasters.

↳ EARL Plou et Fils, 26, rue du
Gal-de-Gaulle, 37530 Chargé,
tel. 02.47.30.55.17, fax 02.47.23.17.02,
e-mail rplou@terre-net.fr
Y ev. day 9am–1pm 3pm–7.30pm
by appt.

VIGNOBLE DES QUATRE ROUES 1999

1 ha · 5,000 · €3-5

During the 19th century, Pocé-sur-Cisse, 3 km (2 miles) from Amboise on the right bank of the Loire, had a foundry, some of the products of which can still be viewed in the village church. This is a pleasant wine: scents of undergrowth and spices rise on the palate, and the tannins discernible in the mouth should soften fairly quickly.

↳ Vignoble des Quatre Roues,
27, Fourchette, 37530 Pocé-sur-Cisse,
tel. 02.47.57.26.96, fax 02.47.57.26.96
Y by appt.

THIERRY BESARD 2000

0.47 ha · 1,500 · €3-5

The Grolleau grape variety, grown on the banks of the Loire and the Indre, distinguishes this characterful fruity rosé, an easy-drinking wine.

↳ Thierry Besard, 10, Les Priviers,
37130 Lignières-de-Touraine,
tel. 02.47.96.85.37, fax 02.47.96.41.98

Touraine-Azay-le-Rideau

Grown on 150 ha (370 acres) along both banks of the Indre, the wines here are as elegant as the riverside château of Azay-le-Rideau after which they are named. Half are particularly fine whites – 955 hl (25,212 gal) in 2000 – from Chenin Blanc (Pineau de la Loire), which range from dry to soft, and age well. Grolleau (60% minimum of a mixed wine), Gamay and Côt (with a maximum 10% of Cabernets) make very fresh dry, fruity rosés – 1,689 hl (44,590 gal) in 2000.

CH. DE LA ROCHE 1999★

`1.74 ha` `9,800` `€5-8`

Looking out over the Loire and Indre Valleys, this magnificent château, at the heart of the vineyards, benefits from a microclimate that is particularly suited to the cultivation of the Pineau de la Loire and Chenin grape varieties. This 99, full of nuances, is the perfect match for white meats.

• Ch. de La Roche,
La Roche, 37190 Cheillé,
tel. 02.47.45.46.05, fax 02.47.45.29.60,
e-mail gentil.la-roche@wanadoo.fr ⚊
Ⓨ ev. day 9am–12.30pm 2pm–7pm

JAMES PAGET 2000★

`2 ha` `10,000` `€5-8`

James Paget is an expert wine-producer who harvests late and skilfully blends Grolleau, Gamay and Côt to produce this delicate rosé with its well-developed floral aromas, length of flavour and freshness.

• EARL James Paget,
13, rue d'Armentières, 37190 Rivarennes,
tel. 02.47.95.54.02, fax 02.47.95.45.90 ⚊
Ⓨ by appt.

PASCAL PIBALEAU 2000★

`3 ha` `10,000` `€5-8`

Pascal Pibaleau is the fourth generation of wine-makers to work these vineyards on the banks of the Indre. He arrived in 1996 and quickly proved his ability to produce a fruity, fresh, bright-pink rosé from 40-year-old Grolleau vines. This charming wine is a delight to drink with delicately flavoured cooked meats. The highly aromatic **white 99** was also singled out.

• EARL Pascal Pibaleau,
68, rte de Langeais, 37190 Azay-le-Rideau,
tel. 02.47.45.27.58, fax 02.47.45.26.18,
e-mail pascal.pibaleau@wanadoo.fr ⚊
Ⓨ ev. day except Sun. 8am–12.30pm
1.30pm–7pm

FRANCOIS ROLLAND 1999★

`1.07 ha` `1,000` `€5-8`

The 12th-century church of Lignières-de-Touraine contains frescoes from the 13th century. After having admired these interesting works of art, you must try this wine. It will take another few months for the hints of oak to merge into extremely pleasant flavours of citrus fruit and the full palate that this vintage promises. A fine example of the influence of the *terroir* on the Chenin.

• Francis Rolland, 30, rue de Villandry,
37130 Lignières-de-Touraine,
tel. 02.47.96.83.55, fax 02.47.96.69.08 ⚊
Ⓨ by appt.

ERIC TOULME 2000★

`1.86 ha` `1,164` `€3-5`

Beyond Azay-le-Rideau, take the D57 to reach Lignières-de-Touraine. It is here that Eric Toulmé runs the family's 5.5-ha (13.5-acre) vineyard. A bright prawn colour, this rosé, with its clear scents of raspberry on the nose, gives pleasant hints of biscuit and toast on the palate. An ideal wine to drink with pork.

• EARL Eric Toulmé, 2, Les Carrés,
37130 Lignières-de-Touraine,
tel. 02.47.96.72.36, fax 02.47.96.69.69 ⚊
Ⓨ by appt.

Touraine-Mesland

The vineyard of this appellation covers 200 ha (494 acres) on the right bank of the Loire, north of Chaumont and downstream from Blois. In 2000, 6,199 hl (163,654 gal) of wine were produced, including 851 hl (22,466 gal) of white. The soils are a mixture of flinty clays covered here and there with Eocene sands and gravel. Production is mostly of red wines, from Gamay mixed with Cabernet or Côt, with good structure and character. Dry whites (mainly from Chenin) and rosés are also produced.

DOM. D'ARTOIS 2000

`10 ha` `70,000` `€3-5`

Its strong garnet colour reveals a wine rich in aromas of spiced fruit, a wine that will improve with ageing in the bottle. Tannins are present, but not overtly so, and the finish is smooth.

• SCEA Dom. d'Artois, La Morandière,
41150 Mesland, tel. 02.54.70.24.72,
fax 02.54.70.24.72 ⚊ Ⓨ by appt.
• J.L. Saget

CH. GAILLARD 2000★★

`5 ha` `30,000` `€5-8`

Vincent Girault is a great believer in the local soil and vines, and as such has managed here to create a successful 2000 white full of quince and humus: a wine full of character and lively on the palate.

• Ch. Gaillard, 41150 Mesland,
tel. 02.54.70.25.47, fax 02.54.70.28.70 ⚊
Ⓨ by appt.
• Vincent Girault

CLOS DE LA BRIDERIE

Vieilles vignes 2000★★

`n.c.` `48,000` `€5-8`

A Touraine-Mesland served in the best restaurants in the region, the 2000 vintage seduced the Jury with its balance, its strong colour and its powerful, complex nose that blends ripe fruits, spices and grilled flavours, together with a finish of great length. A superb product that the Jury rightly awarded a *grand coup de coeur*. The enjoyable **rosé**

Bourgueil

The Appellation Contrôlée Bourgueil area, which covers 1,250 ha (30,875 acres), lies on the right bank of the Loire, west of the Touraine and on the borders of Anjou. In 2000 75,598 hl (1,995,787 gal) of the distinctive Bourgueil red wines were produced from the Cabernet Franc variety, also known as Breton. These are thoroughbred wines, graced with elegant tannins, which have undergone a long period of fermentation; those from the yellow tuffeau slopes have great keeping qualities. The best vintages (1976, 1989 or 1990, for example) continue to develop for decades. Those from the terraces of gravelly and sandy soil are smoother and fruitier in character. A few hundred hectolitres (several thousand gallons) are vinified as dry rosés. It is worth pointing out that the members of the Coopérative de Restigné (a quarter of the Bourgueil growers) often age their wines in their own cellars.

DOM. DE LUSQUENEAU 2000★

n.c.   13,600   €3-5

A rosé with an attractive, clear appearance, full, firm and fresh wine that reveals hints of ripe fruit; an enjoyable bottle that is ready for drinking.

☛ SCEA Dom. de Lusqueneau, rue du Foyer, 41150 Mesland, tel. 02.54.70.25.51, fax 02.54.70.27.49 ▼

DOM. DE RABELAIS 2000

n.c.   n.c.   €3-5

This is a powerful rosé, with an attractive, light colour, which, although slightly lacking the fruitiness you would expect from this type of wine, is pleasant on the finish.

☛ Chollet, 23, chem. de Rabelais, 41150 Onzain, tel. 02.54.20.79.50, fax 02.54.20.79.50 ▼ ▼ by appt.

DOM. DES TERRES NOIRES 2000

0.4 ha   2,000   €3-5

The three Rédiguère brothers set up their GAEC in 1993 on the right bank of the Loire. Their rosé is an attractive, strong pink colour; an intensity on the nose of red berries blossoms into a suitably weighted, spring-like morning freshness on the finish, making this a wine to be drunk among friends wishing to discover the delights of the appellation.

☛ GAEC des Terres Noires, 81, rue de Meuves, 41150 Onzain, tel. 02.54.20.72.87, fax 02.54.20.85.12 ▼ ev. day 9am–7pm

JACQUES VEUX 2000

1 ha   2,400   €3-5

A Gamay rosé of an elegantly lightish hue, with a full and firm body. An attractive bottle.

☛ Jacques Veux, 3 bis, Château-Gaillard, 41150 Mesland, tel. 02.54.70.26.27 ▼ ev. day 10am–7pm

YANNICK AMIRAULT
Le Grand Clos 1999★★

1.5 ha   n.c.   €8-11

This producer has two wines equally deserving praise: the Grand Clos and La Coudraye. Both fine cuvées will delight lovers of Bourgueil wines with their concentration, richness, volume and silky tannins. The Grand Clos, well-balanced, has a nose of blackberry with a hint of vanilla, and a finish that goes on forever. La Coudraye is the product of young vines that nevertheless fail to compromise its merits: the only evidence is a certain freshness, proof of its origins. These two remarkable wines were submitted for a coup de cœur, awarded third and fourth place by the Grand Jury.

☛ Yannick Amirault, 5, Pavillon du Grand Clos, 37140 Bourgueil, tel. 02.47.97.78.07, fax 02.47.97.94.78 ▼ ▼ by appt.

JEAN-MARIE AMIRAULT
Cuvée Prestige 1999★

2 ha   5,000   €5-8

This is an ideal wine for a family meal: it is uncomplicated and full of fruit, with blackcurrant dominating. Its supple, round tannic structure gives it sufficient body, without any pretence of its being a wine for laying down; it finishes on an elegant note.

Bourgueil

DOM. DU CHENE ARRAULT

Cuvée Vieilles vignes 1999★★

■ 1.33 ha 8,000 ■ €5-8

The merger of paternal and maternal grandparents' properties in 1990 led to the foundation of this attractive 13-ha (32-acre) estate. Cuvée Vieilles Vignes is very fruity on the nose, with hints of undergrowth; its tannins are of average intensity, devoid of any rawness, while the wine leaves a cooked sensation on the finish. This enjoyable wine can be aged, although the Jury loved it just as it was. The **Cuvée du Chêne Arrault**, a smooth, light wine ready for drinking, was also singled out.

↘ Christophe Deschamps,
4, Le Chêne-Arrault, 37140 Benais,
tel. 02.47.97.46.71, fax 02.47.97.82.90,
e-mail domaine.du.chene.arrault@
wanadoo.fr ☑ ⟙ by appt.

HUBERT AUDEBERT

Vieilles vignes 1999★

■ 2 ha 12,000 ■ €5-8

A traditional, family-run 10-ha (25-acre) estate located on the sandy soil of Restigné. The Audeberts' wines are usually fresh and delicate, and this is definitely the case with their Vieilles Vignes 99, a well-structured, smooth, mouth-filling wine giving off scents of undergrowth, leading to a pleasant finish. The vintage may be aged for a further year or two. The estate's **Jolinet 99** bears a clearer sandy influence: it especially impressed the Jury, and is ready for drinking.

↘ Hubert Audebert,
5, rue Croix-des-Pierres, 37140 Restigné,
tel. 02.47.97.42.10, fax 02.47.97.77.53 ☑
⟙ by appt.

VIGNOBLE AUGER 1999★

■ 20 ha 15,000 ▥ €5-8

Christian Auger's 20-ha (50-acre) vineyard consists of a variety of terrains, but the harvest is blended into just one *cuvée* designed to be representative of the appellation: this it very much is, with a nose redolent of the Cabernet Franc, a well-structured palate at the same time both lively and well-balanced. It is a fine wine that will age well.

↘ Vignoble Auger, 58, rte de Bourgueil,
37140 Restigné, tel. 02.47.97.41.37,
fax 02.47.97.49.78 ☑ ⟙ by appt.

CATHERINE ET PIERRE BRETON

Les Galichets 1999★

■ 3 ha 10,000 ▥ €8-11

Les Galichets is produced from organically grown grapes on a 3-ha (7-acre) vineyard. The wine is matured in oak barrels, which give it clear vanilla hints both on the nose and on the palate. However, through careful management its tannins have softened and ripened around a significant degree of fruitiness.

↘ Pierre et Catherine Breton, 8, rue du
Peu-Muleau, Les-Galichets, 37140 Restigné,
tel. 02.47.97.30.41, fax 02.47.97.46.49,
e-mail catherinetpierre.breton@libertysurf.fr
☑ ⟙ by appt.

BRUNO ET ROSELYNE BRETON

Elevé en fût de bois 1999★

■ 3 ha 16,000 ☑ €5-8

This cuvée, produced from three of the 20 ha (7.5 of the 50 acres) cultivated by Bruno and Roselyne Breton, possesses surprisingly smooth tannins, which give a supple, extremely fruity sensation on the palate. A wine to be enjoyed now, perhaps with charcuterie that will not be overshadowed by its power.

↘ Roselyne et Bruno Breton, EARL du
Carroi, 45, rue Basse, 37140 Restigné,
tel. 02.47.97.31.35, fax 02.47.97.49.00 ☑
⟙ by appt.

SERGE DUBOIS Cuvée Prestige 1999★

■ 2.5 ha 15,000 ▥ €5-8

Serge Dubois has ably managed this estate since he arrived in 1973. Starting with 2 ha (5 acres), he now cultivates an attractive 14-ha (35-acre) vineyard. Recently he has built a modern winery where he can work more easily. This Cuvée Prestige is well-developed on the nose, evoking lilac, followed by smoke and then oak. The tannins are perceptible, but already well-smoothed and subdued by the wine's body. It is already a balanced wine, although a further two or three years ageing are conceivable, as they will invariably further the complexity of the wine.

↘ Serge Dubois, 49, rue de Lossay,
37140 Restigné, tel. 02.47.97.31.60,
fax 02.47.97.43.33, e-mail serge.dubois9@
wanadoo.fr ☑ ⟙ by appt.

LAURENT FAUVY 1999★

■ 3 ha 4,000 ■ €3-5

The wine-producers of Benais are a lucky breed: the excellent management of vinification means that the wines are characterised by their fine constitution. This is the case with this 99, which offers a round, fleshy palate leading to a lengthy finish. Laurent Fauvy also presents the Jury with his **Cuvée Vieilles Vignes**, of a similar style and just as highly appreciated. They are two attractive wines destined for success.

↘ Laurent Fauvy, 14, rte de Saint-Gilles,
37140 Benais, tel. 02.47.97.46.67,
fax 02.47.97.95.45 ☑ ⟙ by appt.

DOM. DES FORGES

Cuvée Vieilles vignes 1999★

■ 4 ha 15,000 ■ €5-8

Les Forges, where a blacksmith once plied his trade, has become this wine-producer's home, situated amid 18 ha (44 acres) of vineyard. One of Jean-Yves Billet's ancestors kept a diary, in which he noted in 1846 that he produced 'a first-class wine in considerable quantity.' Cuvée Vieilles Vignes 99 is definitely a first-class wine. As for the quantity, let us have faith in this producer's ability to modify his yields. The wine gives off plenty of fruit on

1022

the nose and the palate, with a slight hint of coffee and smoke. The tannins are of the right kind, giving it roundness and balance as well as an elegant finish. **Cuvée des Bezards 99** was marked very similarly: in fact, the two wines seem almost like twins.

♦ Jean-Yves Billet, Dom. des Forges,
pl. des Tilleuls, 37140 Restigné,
tel. 02.47.97.32.87, fax 02.47.97.46.47,
e-mail J.Y.Billet@wanadoo.fr [V] [Y] by appt.

DOM. HUBERT Vieilles vignes 1999

■ 3 ha 15,000 [€5-8]

Vieilles Vignes 99 is produced from grapes grown on 50-year-old vines, resulting in a wine with rather harsh tannins at present. Further ageing will give it considerable potential.

♦ EARL Franck Caslot, La Hurolaie,
37140 Benais, tel. 02.47.97.30.59,
fax 02.47.97.45.46 [V] [Y] ev. day 9am–
12 noon 2.30pm–7pm; Sun. by appt.

DOM. DE LA CHANTELEUSERIE

Cuvée Vieilles vignes 1999★

■ 4 ha 10,000 [€5-8]

Domaine de la Chanteleuserie is a family-run vineyard, covering some 20 ha (49 acres), dating back to 1822; it gets its name from the song of the lark. Thierry Boucard takes care with his harvest, using a grading table that enables any plant debris and bad or unripe grapes to be eliminated. The result is excellent: the wine is highly expressive on the nose, full of red berries and toast; strong tannins that nevertheless reveal the right degree of smoothness and elegance; and a lengthy finish. These ingredients add up to a very pleasant wine that may be enjoyed now but will improve after some time in the cellar. A second cuvée, **Beauvais 99**, is similar, and needs to be laid down for two or three years before drinking.

♦ Thierry Boucard, La Chanteleuserie,
37140 Benais, tel. 02.47.97.30.20,
fax 02.47.97.46.73, e-mail tboucard@
terre-net.fr [V] [Y] ev. day except Sun.
8.30am–12 noon 2pm–7pm

DOM. DES GALLUCHES

Cuvée Tradition 1999★

■ 3 ha 12,000 [€5-8]

In 1997 James Petit took over this estate from his uncle, Jean Gambier, who retired but continues to be well-known within the Bourgueil area. The vineyard covers more than 16 ha (39 acres) on the top terrace of the appellation. This fine, ripe cherry-coloured 99 has straightforward, subtle scents evoking green peppers, which is so characteristic of Cabernet Franc, and flavours rich in liquorice, walnuts and tobacco. The tannins should mellow during the course of ageing for a year or two.

♦ James Petit, La Petite Mairie,
37140 Restigné, tel. 02.47.97.30.13 [V]
[Y] by appt.

♦ Jean Gambier

DOM. DES GELERIES

Cuvée Prestige 1999

■ 1.5 ha 6,000 [€5-8]

Jeannine Rouzier-Meslet, who took over her husband's vineyard when he retired, is nowadays helped by her son. Her Cuvée Prestige, matured for three months in oak barrels, has a surprisingly robust structure: fruity in taste, its strong tannins are still evident. They will require some time to mature.

♦ Jeannine Rouzier-Meslet,
2, rue des Gélètes, 37140 Bourgueil,
tel. 02.47.97.72.83, fax 02.47.97.48.73 [V]
[Y] by appt.

DOM. DES GESLETS

Cuvée de Garde 1999★★

■ 2.1 ha 9,400 [€8-11]

In 1988 Vincent Grégoire took over where his father had left off, and continues to give a certain momentum to this estate's wine production. He works a lot with large wooden casks and barrels, careful of the constitution of his wines. This wine, following longer maturing, is remarkable for its considerable richness and the dimension of its tannins which, clearly present, merge well with the body of the wine. However, the wine will benefit from ageing for another year or two.

♦ EARL Vincent Grégoire,
Dom. des Geslets, 37140 Bourgueil,
tel. 02.47.97.06, fax 02.47.97.73.95,
e-mail domainedesgeslets@oreka.com [V]
[Y] ev. day 9.30am–6.30pm

DOM. DE LA CHEVALERIE

Cuvée des Busardières 1999★★★

■ n.c. 13,000 [€5-8]

12.5% Vol.
MIS EN BOUTEILLE À LA PROPRIÉTÉ
DOMAINE DE LA CHEVALERIE
APPELLATION *Bourgueil* CONTROLÉE
Cuvée des Busardières
750 ml · PRODUCT OF FRANCE

While the house is in the lower part of the appellation, the vineyards, covering nearly 32 ha (79 acres), mostly cultivated by a tenant, are on the hillside where great wines are made. The cellars, carved out of the same hillside, provide an ideal environment for maturing these wines. Pierre Caslot has pulled off a masterstroke: sniffing immediately shows that this is a wine of considerable character. It gives off aromas of very ripe – almost overripe – fruit, accompanied by a hint of vanilla. The well-rounded tannins have not completely matured yet, but the wine is full.

rich and fleshy, with a long finish. A superb wine.

Pierre Caslot, Dom. de La Chevalerie, 37140 Restigné, tel. 02.47.97.37.18, fax 02.47.97.45.87 ev. day 9am–12 noon 2pm–6pm; Sun. by appt.

DOM. DE LA CROIX MORTE 1999

0.5 ha · 3,000 · €5-8

Fabrice Samson, a young wine-producer, continues to work the 3 ha (7.5 acres) his father and grandfather cultivated before him using traditional methods. This smooth 99 is well-balanced, of average length, and could be defined as a spring wine due to its freshness and fruity character.

Fabrice Samson, La Croix-Morte, 37140 Restigné, tel. 02.47.97.49.48, fax 02.47.97.49.48 by appt.

DOM. DE LA LANDE

Cuvée Prestige 1999★

2.5 ha · 12,000 · €5-8

This 14-ha (34-acre) family-owned vineyard is run very much according to tradition: ploughing the rows of vines, hand-picking the grapes and maturing the wines in large wooden casks – no new wood here. This Cuvée Prestige is the result of well-managed maturation. The tannins are already rounded, and the aromas are of preserved fruit. Furthermore, balance has been skilfully achieved. It is ready to drink now, but could equally be left to mature further. **Graviers 99**, produced by the same wine-makers, especially impressed the Jury.

Delaunay Père et Fils, Dom. de La Lande, 20, rte du Vignoble, 37140 Bourgueil, tel. 02.47.97.80.73, fax 02.47.97.95.65 ev. day except Sun. 8.30am–12 noon 2pm–6pm

DOM. DE LA VERNELLERIE 1999★

1 ha · 3,000 · €5-8

Founded during the 15th century, the estate today consists of a country house and a series of imposing buildings set in 15 ha (37 acres) of vineyards. The 99 offers consistent aromas of soft fruit; a fine opening on the palate followed by a sensation of light tannins; and a sufficiently long finish. It is a totally classical wine.

Camille Petit, EARL Dom. de La Vernellerie, 37140 Benais, tel. 02.47.97.31.18, fax 02.47.97.31.18 by appt.

LE COUDRAY LA LANDE

Vieilles vignes 1999

4 ha · 18,000 · €5-8

This estate was demolished in 1905 and completely rebuilt in 1980, the year in which Jean-Paul Morin arrived on the scene. A well-made Vieilles Vignes, the 99 has a well-developed nose of the utmost finesse. Intense on the palate due to rounded tannins, the finish gives an overall impression of balance and of a wine that is already perfectly mature.

Jean-Paul Morin, Le Coudray-la-Lande, 37140 Bourgueil, tel. 02.47.97.76.92, fax 02.47.97.98.20 by appt.

DOM. LES PINS Vieilles vignes 1999★

2 ha · 10,000 · €5-8

Five generations of the same family have owned this 18-ha (44-acre) estate, and a 16th-century building in the centre of the vineyard is proof of its historical importance. The Vieilles Vignes 99 boasts fine, silky tannins. A round, full wine with musky hints, it could be matured further. The **rosé 2000** has traditional Bourgueil character, both fruity and fresh, and was singled out by the Jury.

Pitault-Landry et Fils, Dom. Les Pins, 1 et 8, rte du Vignoble, 37140 Bourgueil, tel. 02.47.97.91, fax 02.47.97.98.69 by appt.

MICHEL ET JOELLE LORIEUX

Chevrette 1999

2 ha · 5,000 · €5-8

Michel and Joëlle Lorieux inherited their grandfather's love and knowledge of the vine and wine-making. Today, on their 10-ha (25-acre) vineyard at the foot of a hillside, they recall his advice as they go about the business of producing quality wines like this rounded, supple 99, ready to be served at the dining table.

Michel et Joëlle Lorieux, Chevrette, 26, rte du Vignoble, 37140 Bourgueil, tel. 02.47.97.85.86, fax 02.47.97.85.86 by appt.

DOM. LAURENT MABILEAU 1999

3.5 ha · 25,000 · €5-8

This is a wine that can only benefit from being matured a little longer. It has real potential, and is worth looking after carefully. The clearly evident tannins will soften in time, and on the nose and palate the wine will show its true potential after two or three years.

Dom. Laurent Mabileau, La Croix du Moulin-Neuf, 37140 Saint-Nicolas-de-Bourgueil, tel. 02.47.97.74.75, fax 02.47.97.99.81, e-mail domaine@mabileau.fr ev. day except Sun. 8am–12 noon 2pm–7pm

DOM. DES MAILLOCHES

Cuvée Samuel 1999

0.5 ha · 3,000 · €5-8

Samuel Demont, who has been working alongside his father since January 2000, has his part to play in the production of this cuvée that bears his name. One should wait a while before drinking this well-balanced wine, with its elegant woody character: its harmony will improve with time, while the woody nuances will persist.

J.-F. Demont, Les Mailloches, 37140 Restigné, tel. 02.47.97.33.10, fax 02.47.97.43.43, e-mail infos@domaine-mailloches.fr by appt.

HERVE MENARD
Vieilles vignes 1999★

■   0.5 ha   n.c.   ■ €5-8

Hervé Ménard took over his grandfather's estate in 1994, and in the meantime has increased its productive area to some 7 ha (17 acres). His Vieilles Vignes is intensely redolent of red berries on the nose, and its excellent presence on the palate gives an impression of a very ripe – almost overripe – harvest. The silky, long tannins are beyond reproach, and overall this is a wine that is characteristic of the 99 vintage: a wine to be enjoyed as it is.

↬ Hervé Ménard, 5, L'Echelle, 37140 Bourgueil, tel. 02.47.97.72.65, fax 02.47.97.72.65 ⟁ by appt.

CH. DE MINIERE Cuvée Rubis 1999

■   7 ha   10,000   ■ €5-8

Château de Minière, built of tuffeau during the 17th century in the centre of the vineyard, is run by Jean-Yves Billet. Together with the owner, Evelyne de Mascarel, he successfully combines modern and traditional methods, helped by the fine local terroir. This soil produces an attractive wine dominated by an aroma of blackcurrants. Its tannins are clearly present, although they do not compromise the roundness of the vintage. An elegant finish ends on a note of liquorice. This is a pleasant wine ready for drinking.

↬ Ch. de Minière, 37140 Ingrandes-de-Touraine, tel. 02.47.97.32.87, fax 02.47.97.46.47 ⟁ by appt.

DOM. REGIS MUREAU 1999★★

■   4 ha   15,000   ■ ● €5-8

With its impressive, well-equipped buildings, Régis Mureau's estate does not go unnoticed when you come into the Bourgueil from Tours. He has managed to produce a balanced, full, round, fruity wine characterised by integrated tannins. At the start the wine gives off gamey scents, but then soft fruit emerges in the mouth, followed by spices on the finish. Well-produced, the 99 holds considerable promise. Domaine de La Gaucherie 99 received a star for its intensity on the palate.

DOMINIQUE MOREAU 1999

■   1 ha   5,000   ▦ €5-8

Restigné marks the beginning of the upper Loire terrace. It is a long way from the hillside, and the soils are sandy and gravelly. Fruity, fresh wines are produced in this part of the Loire. This vintage has still to attain the right balance, as the wine struggles a little to open out on the nose, and the tannins are still very evident. All this will be redressed after a year's further ageing.

↬ Dominique Moreau, L'Ouche Saint-André, 37140 Restigné, tel. 02.47.97.31.93, fax 02.47.96.83.30 ▣

DOM. DES OUCHES
Clos Princé 1999★★

■   3.5 ha   12,000   ▦ €5-8

The recently built winery adjoins the beautiful wine cellars, where the wines are guaranteed to mature well. As in 1998, this producer's outstanding wine is the Clos Princé. It has a superb constitution, offering nuances of berries on the nose, and it splendidly fills the mouth with a tight, intensely tannic structure. Its substantial character makes it a wine for laying down. The woody Vieilles Vignes 99 also impressed the Jury.

BERNARD OMASSON 1999★

■   2 ha   3,000   ▦ ●

Dark, almost purple in colour, this 99 has distinct scents of the Cabernet Franc on the nose, and a solid, structured palate which merges into a finish of red berries and hazelnuts. It only needs a few months in the cellar and it will be ready to drink.

↬ Bernard Omasson, La Perrée, 54, rue de Touraine, 37140 Ingrandes-de-Touraine, tel. 02.47.96.98.20 ⟁ by appt.

ALAIN OMASSON 1999★

■   1 ha   1,500   ▦ ● €5-8

Saint-Patrice is the first village you come to in the Bourgueil appellation. This is where the Loire upper terrace rises up, an area dominated by gravelly, sandy soils. Alain Omasson's 4.5-ha (11-acre) vineyard produces some very attractive wines, such as the present one, a wine destined for further maturing. The tannins are young and clearly evident, although not at all raw. It merely requires a little more time for it to develop to the full, as this is a wine with body.

↬ Alain Omasson, 21, rue du Port-Véron, 37130 Saint-Patrice, tel. 02.47.96.90.26, fax 02.47.96.90.26 ⟁ by appt.

NAU FRERES Vieilles vignes 1999★

■   6 ha   4,000   ▦ ● €5-8

The Nau brothers' estate was once a farm that adopted the polyculture approach, producing cereals, fruit, vegetables and milk. Around the 1970s it converted to monoculture farming, concentrating on the cultivation of vines. Nobody could complain about this radical change, having tasted this colourful 99 with its fruity character, full but needing more time for the tannins to fully mature – perhaps a further year or two.

↬ GAEC Nau Frères, 52, rue de Touraine, 37140 Ingrandes-de-Touraine, tel. 02.47.96.98.57, fax 02.47.96.90.34 ▣ ⟁ ev. day except Sun. 8am–7pm

↬ Régis Mureau, 16, rue d'Anjou, 37140 Ingrandes-de-Touraine, tel. 02.47.96.97.60, fax 02.47.96.93.43 ▣ ⟁ ev. day except Sun. 8am–12 noon 2pm–7pm

LOIRE

the vigour of his vine stocks: a tried and tested natural technique which has greatly contributed towards the success of his Cuvée des Couplets 99, recipient of a *coup de coeur*. It is a dark-purple – amost black – colour, close to that of blackcurrants, with intense ripe fruit on the nose. It is round and generous on the palate, with evident tannins within a fine body of some length. This is a remarkable wine which has still to mature completely. **Brunetières 99** is another excellent wine, with pronounced aromas of oak, which received special mention from the Jury. This estate has clearly been blessed this year.

☛ EARL Jean-Marc Pichet, Le Petit Bondieu, 30, rte de Tours, 37140 Restigné, tel. 02.47.97.33.18, fax 02.47.97.46.57, e-mail jean-marcpichet@wanadoo.fr
Ⓨ ev. day except Sun. 9am–12 noon 2pm–7pm

DOM. PONTONNIER

Cuvée Vieilles vignes 1999★

■ 1.3 ha 9,000 ■ ⅠⅠⅠ €5-8

Domaine Pontonnier consists of 14 ha (35 acres) of vineyards planted on clay-chalk soil in a favourably sunny position. Vieilles Vignes 99 is clearly a quality wine. Very floral on the nose initially, its scents evolve into more intense hints of leather and marc. Its elegant, lengthy tannins blend in well. The nuances of marc reappear on a lengthy finish. The wine will only improve from being laid down for some time.

☛ Dom. Pontonnier, 4, chem. de L'Epaisse, 37140 Saint-Nicolas-de-Bourgueil, tel. 02.47.97.84.69, fax 02.47.97.48.55
Ⓨ by appt.

DOM. DES RAGUENIERES

Cuvée Clos de la Cure 1999

■ 1.1 ha 6,000 ■ ⅠⅠⅠ ♦ €5-8

Two wine-producers run this estate, which is almost 19 ha (47 acres) on clay-chalk soil and in a sunny position. The tuffeau cellars are well worth visiting, and a warm welcome awaits visitors to the tasting room. The 99 vintage is a wine for shorter maturing. The scents on the nose are reminiscent of blackcurrant, and its first impression on the palate is one of fruit followed by a marked tannic quality. This is a wine that requires a little further ageing.

☛ R. Viemont-D. Maître-Gadaix, Dom. des Raguenières, 11, rue du Machet-Benais, 37140 Bourgueil, tel. 02.47.97.30.16, fax 02.47.97.46.78  Ⓨ by appt.

VIGNOBLE DES ROBINIERES 1999

■ 3 ha 7,000 ■ ♦ €5-8

The two Marchesseau brothers work together at the Robinières vineyard located on the upper terrace of the Bourgueil appellation, characterised by its clay-chalk soil. This is a wine with potential. Still firm on the nose and tannic on the palate, it needs maturing further for its tannins to round out; it should be left for a further three years at least.

☛ Paul Gambier et Fils, 3, rue des Ouches, 37140 Ingrandes-de-Touraine, tel. 02.47.96.98.77, fax 02.47.96.93.08, e-mail domaine.ouches@wanadoo.fr
Ⓨ by appt.

ANNICK PENET 1999

■ 0.8 ha 2,500 ■ ⅠⅠⅠ €5-8

Annick Penet has been cultivating her small vineyard for donkey's years. This small vineyard has been handed down from generation to generation ever since the Bourgueil existed, so they say. The estate boasts a patch of 100-year-old vines that are still very productive. The working of the soil, the vine stocks and the wine production are still performed following traditional methods. The 99 is of a bright-ruby colour, while on the nose it is still young, with hints of red berries and undergrowth. Following a fine first impression in the mouth, roundness emerges on the palate, although it remains somewhat astringent. It is a wine ready for drinking which, however, will have improved in a year's time.

☛ Annick Penet, 29, rue Basse, 37140 Restigné, tel. 02.47.97.33.68, fax 02.47.97.88.47  Ⓨ by appt.

DOM. DES PERRIERES

La Cuvée de Vénus 1999★★

■ 3 ha 5,000 €5-8

Guy Delanoue represents the sixth generation of family wine-producers to cultivate this 7-ha (17-acre) estate near the small town of Bourgueil. His Cuvée de Vénus, rich in thyme, laurel and red berries on the palate, with mature, well-rounded tannins, is a well-balanced wine which should be drunk immediately so as not to miss its remarkable bouquet. The estate's **Cuvée Principale** was awarded one star.

☛ Guy Delanoue, 10, rte du Vignoble, Les Perrières, 37140 Bourgueil, tel. 02.47.97.82.29, fax 02.47.97.48.20
Ⓨ ev. day 8.30am–1pm 2pm–7.30pm; cl. Jan.

DOM. DU PETIT BONDIEU

Cuvée des Couplets 1999★★

■ n.c. 6,500 ■ ♦ €5-8

The main concern of this estate is to keep yields within acceptable limits in order to produce quality wines. Jean-Marc Pichet adopts the grassing-down method to temper

Saint-Nicolas-de-Bourgueil

The commune of Saint-Nicolas-de-Bourgueil (a single parish that was detached from Bourgueil in the 18th century) has its own appellation, even though the *terroir* is similar to the neighbouring area of Bourgueil.

At least two-thirds of the slopes are made up of the sandy, gravel terraces of the Loire. At the top, the hill is protected from the north wind by forest and a covering of sand overlies the tuffeau outcrops. Saint-Nicolas-de-Bourgueil wines are made from a mixture of varieties, and are generally regarded as being lighter than the Bourgueils (not always the case with wine grown on the heights). In 2000, they produced 56,409 hl (1,489,198 gal).

YANNICK AMIRAULT

La Source 1999★ ■ ♨ ♦ €5-8 | 2 ha | 15,000

Yannick Amirault's estate, on the border between two appellations – Bourgueil and Saint-Nicolas – surprised everyone this year with his Saint-Nicolas produced from young vines. You would expect the wine to be light and fruity, but you would be wrong: this 99 vintage may well be a little fruity, but it is also a full, round wine that could certainly be aged for a while. The result is proof yet again of the producer's ability to excel through the proper management of yields and vinification, keys to the production of a great wine.

✆ Yannick Amirault, 5, Pavillon du Grand Clos, 37140 Bourgueil, tel. 02.47.97.94.78 ☑ ☎ by appt.

DOM. AUDEBERT ET FILS 1999

■ ♨ ♦ €5-8 | 8 ha | 40,000

This is a 21-ha (52-acre) family-run estate whose top vines lie on the hillside. The son took over the wine-production in 1996, and this is therefore one of his first vintages, an encouraging sign indeed. Rather underdeveloped on the nose, with musky hints still perceptible, the wine is smooth, round and balanced on the palate – easy to drink, and ideal for mealtimes.

✆ Dom. Audebert et Fils, av. Jean-Causeret, 37140 Bourgueil, tel. 02.47.97.70.06, fax 02.47.97.72.07, e-mail audebert@micro-vidéo.fr ☑ ☎ ev. day 8.30am–12 noon 2pm–6pm; Sat. Sun. by appt.

DOM. DES BERGEONNIERES

Cuvée Rondeau 1999★★ ■ ♨ €5-8 | 1.5 ha | 8,000

The vines here are rooted in the warm, well-drained, gravelly soil of the south-facing slopes, protected from the cold northern winds. As a result, the estate has produced this Cuvée Rondeau, which won a *coup de cœur*. On the nose, the wine opens with aromas of dried fruit and morello cherries. The ripe, powerful body fills the palate for some considerable time, while the tannins are unobtrusive and blend in well. A remarkable

DOM. DU ROCHOUARD 1999

■ ♨ €5-8 | 2 ha | 4,000

On the border between two appellations – Bourgueil and Saint-Nicolas – this 7-ha (17-acre) estate lies within the Bourgueil. It has been planted on gravel, particularly suited to producing fresh, fruity wines such as this particular vintage: a round, smooth wine that is ready for drinking.

✆ GAEC Duveau-Coulon et Fils, 1, rue des Gelières, 37140 Bourgueil, tel. 02.47.97.85.91, fax 02.47.97.99.13 ☑ ☎ ev. day 8.30am–12.30pm 2pm–7pm

JEAN-MARIE ROUZIER

Cuvée Tradition 1999 ■ ♨ ♦ €5-8 | 2 ha | 9,000

Jean-Marie Rouzier has a father from the Chinon and a mother from the Bourgueil, but it matters little to him, as Cabernet Franc always constitutes the basis of his wines. He has produced a Cuvée Tradition with a smooth, fruity character, suitably intense and slightly woody on the nose: a wine to drink straightaway.

✆ Jean-Marie Rouzier, Les Gelières, 37140 Bourgueil, tel. 02.47.97.74.83, fax 02.47.97.48.73 ☑ ☎ ev. day except Sun. 9am–12.30pm 2pm–7pm

DOM. THOUET-BOSSEAU

Cuvée Vieilles vignes 1999 ■ ♨ €5-8 | 1.8 ha | 7,000

Jean-Baptiste Thouet-Bosseau manages his small 7-ha (17-acre) vineyard, which he inherited from his father, and also runs the Abbey's vineyard with the help of another wine-producer. He thus has plenty to do, but still manages to produce pleasant wines such as this Vieilles Vignes, a smooth, balanced wine with an interesting structure and farmyard scents and flavours. The wine needs a further year's ageing.

✆ Jean-Baptiste Thouet-Bosseau, l'Humelaye, 13, rue de Santenay, 37140 Bourgueil, tel. 02.47.97.73.51, fax 02.47.97.44.65 ☑ ☎ by appt.

✆ EARL Marchesseau Fils, 16, rue de l'Humelaye, 37140 Bourgueil, tel. 02.47.97.47.72, fax 02.47.97.46.36 ☑ ☎ ev. day except Sun. 9am–7pm

Saint-Nicolas-de-Bourgueil

wine, it also has clear potential for ageing. The **Cuvée Principale du Domaine 99**, on the other hand, was awarded one star, and is a highly characteristic, well-produced wine, which is ready for drinking but will certainly improve with another year or two in the bottle.

☛ André Delagoutière, Les Bergeonnières, 37140 Saint-Nicolas-de-Bourgueil, tel. 02.47.97.75.87, fax 02.47.97.48.47 ☒
Ⓨ by appt.

DOM. DU BOURG
Cuvée Prestige 1999★
■   2 ha   10,000   ⬛⬛   €5-8

This highly efficient winery, in the centre of the village of Saint-Nicolas, is a perfect blend of traditional and modern methods. Its stainless-steel vats and thermoregulation system work side by side with a series of casks and barrels used to age the wine. A well-designed tasting room welcomes visitors, where they can taste some fine wines such as this fruity, highly drinkable Cuvée Prestige 99, which is ready for drinking. **Les Graviers 99**, which is produced in greater quantities (70,000 bottles), was especially singled out by the Jury.

☛ EARL Jean-Paul Mabileau, 6, rue du Pressoir, 37140 Saint-Nicolas-de-Bourgueil, tel. 02.47.97.82.02, fax 02.47.97.70.92.
e-mail jean.paul.mabileau@wanadoo.fr
Ⓨ by appt.

CAVE BRUNEAU DUPUY
Vieilles vignes 1999★
■   5 ha   30,000   ⬛⬛   €5-8

Bruneau Dupuy is now associated with his son, Sylvain, in the management of these 15 ha (37 acres) of vineyards, two-thirds of which are of a respectable age. Sited on these clay-limestone slopes, they are in the ideal situation for the production of fine wines. This smooth, fruity Vieilles Vignes, characterised by good balance, is ready for drinking.

☛ EARL Bruneau-Dupuy, La Martellière, 37140 Saint-Nicolas-de-Bourgueil, tel. 02.47.97.75.81, fax 02.47.97.43.25, e-mail cave-bruneau.dupuy@netcourrier.com ☒ Ⓨ by appt.

DOM. DU CLOS DE L'EPAISSE
Cuvée des Clos Vieilles vignes 1999★★
■   2.3 ha   15,000   ⬛   €5-8

This remarkable Saint-Nicolas, a wine for laying down, owes a large part of its success to the clay-limestone soil of the slopes on which the vines grow. Its almost purple colour reveals an interesting blend of ripe red berries with a slightly musky nuance. Just-ripe grapes gathered at harvest-time are discernible, which means the wine is rich and exceptionally intense on the palate, as are tannins, which are never excessive nevertheless. With its fine, perfectly balanced structure, this wine should be matured further.

☛ Yvan Bruneau, 50, av. Saint-Vincent, 37140 Saint-Nicolas-de-Bourgueil, tel. 02.47.97.90.67, fax 02.47.97.49.45 ☒
Ⓨ by appt.

BERNARD DAVID
Vieilles vignes 1999★
■   3 ha   11,000   ⬛⬛   €5-8

This 16-ha (39-acre) estate presented the Jury with a wine made by means of carbonic maceration. With ripe fruit on the nose and a first impression of balance, it is smooth and charming on the palate, and on the finish it seems to go on forever. A quality wine destined to improve with age, it is also a fine wine to be drunk straight away.

☛ Bernard David, La Gardière, 37140 Saint-Nicolas-de-Bourgueil, tel. 02.47.97.81.51, fax 02.47.97.95.05
Ⓨ by appt.

PATRICE DELARUE
Cuvée Vieilles vignes 1999★
■   0.5 ha   3,000   ⬛   €5-8

This is a wine to be drunk in the late spring, at the same time as the strawberries and raspberries that flavour this vintage are ripening. It boasts a supple, fresh, round palate of some length. The tannins merge perfectly, resulting in a well-balanced wine – very pleasant.

☛ Patrice Delarue, La Perrée, 37140 Saint-Nicolas-de-Bourg ueil, tel. 02.47.97.94.74 ☒ Ⓨ by appt.

DOM. DES GRAVIERS 1999★
■   2 ha   15,000   ⬛   €5-8

'Wine-making is an art that requires the producer's constant attention,' were Hubert David's thoughts on the matter. Today his wife carries on from where her husband left off, and runs the estate's wine-production with considerable success. Ample proof lies in this Saint-Nicolas, perfect for shorter maturation, with its scents of toasted almonds and its evident tannins, which need to ripen only for a further couple of years to give a surprisingly good wine.

☛ EARL Hubert David, La Forcine, 37140 Saint-Nicolas-de-Bourgueil, tel. 02.47.97.86.93, fax 02.47.97.48.50 ☒
Ⓨ ev. day except Sun. 8.30am–12.30pm 2pm–7pm

DOM. DU GROLLAY 1999★★
■   1.5 ha   10,000   ⬛⬛   €3-5

This wine-producer ought to be proud of his success. Starting from a small area of vines back in 1977, he today manages a 12-ha (29-acre) estate that boasts two cellars and a tasting room. This particular wine has a clearly identifiable character, with its power, its full body and its excellent tannins. It has enormous potential, and will fully mature in about ten years.

☛ Jean Brecq, 1, Le Grollay, 37140 Saint-Nicolas-de-Bourgueil, tel. 02.47.97.78.54, fax 02.47.97.78.54 ☒
Ⓨ ev. day 9am–2.30pm 1.30pm–8pm

DOM. GUY HERSARD
Vieilles vignes 1999★
■ 5 ha | 20,000 | ■ ♣ | €5-8 ▼

This 9.5-ha (23-acre) estate has produced this wine on gravelly soil in the southern part of the appellation, an area that traditionally yields light, fruity wines. This is exactly what this vintage is; fruity and slightly peppery on the nose, it is highly aromatic and balanced on the palate, evolving into smoothness. It is a pleasant wine to be drunk now.
➽ Guy Hersard, 5–7 Le Fondis, 37140 Saint-Nicolas-de-Bourgueil, tel. 02.47.97.76.13, fax 02.47.97.92.06 ▼
Y by appt.

DOM. DE LA COTELLERAIE-VALLEE 1999★
■ 18 ha | 80,000 | ■ ♣ | €5-8

Claude Vallée, who received the *coup de coeur* for his Maugerets 98, was awarded one star this year for his **Les Maugerets 99** cuvées, rich in tannins and clearly suitable for laying down, and for this Vallée 99, a very dark wine evoking peppers and a hint of spice on the nose, roundness and richness on the palate, and a slight woodiness on the lengthy finish. It needs more time to fully mature.
➽ Gérald Vallée, La Cotelleraie, 37140 Saint-Nicolas-de-Bourgueil, tel. 02.47.97.75.53, fax 02.47.97.85.90, e-mail gerald.vallee@fnac.net ▼
Y ev. day except Sun. 9am–6.30pm

VIGNOBLE DE LA JARNOTERIE
Cuvée M R 1999★
■ n.c. | 90,000 | ■◗♣ | €5-8 ▼

A purple colour and a fragrance of soft fruits are two of the main characteristics of Saint-Nicolas-de-Bourgueil wines. This is not exactly the case with this particular vintage, a rather immature wine concealing its real potential, which needs more time to mature. On the palate it is round and powerful, with a persistence on the finish that nevertheless leaves the taster a little thirsty. **Concerto 99**, produced from 50-year-old vines, is a dark-red colour and shows a good balance based on clearly present tannins that are, however, concealed behind an elegant structure, making this a wine to be drunk over the next five years.
➽ EARL Jean-Claude Mabileau et Didier Rezé, La Jarnoterie, 37140 Saint-Nicolas-de-Bourgueil, tel. 02.47.97.75.49, fax 02.47.97.79.98 ▼
Y by appt.

LES QUARTERONS 1999★
■ 1.36 ha | 10,000 | ■◗♣ | €5-8

Thierry Amirault has never ceased to make improvements to this estate, which is over 100 years old, after taking over from his father Claude, a well-known figure in the Saint-Nicolas wine-making community. The Jury were divided in their views on Les Quarterons: some members saw it as a powerful, woody-flavoured wine, while others believed that its body and fruity character were signs of great future potential. All agreed that it was a successful vintage that would blossom in time. **Vieilles Vignes 99**, matured for 12 months in cask, is woody in character; it was especially singled out by the Jury.
➽ Thierry Amirault, Clos des Quarterons, 37140 Saint-Nicolas-de-Bourgueil, tel. 02.47.97.75.25, fax 02.47.97.97.97 ▼
Y by appt.

MICHEL ET JOELLE LORIEUX
1999
■ n.c. | n.c. | ■◗♣ | €5-8

As often happens, it was their grandfather who encouraged Michel and Joëlle Lorieux to learn the art of wine-making and helped them set up their business. Firmly settled in Bourgueil, they cultivate a vineyard at Saint-Nicolas. Their 99 has a powerful, fleshy opening, followed by a rich yet structured character with subtle tannins. Gamey nuances dominate both on the nose and on the palate. This is a wine that needs to be left to mature.
➽ Michel et Joëlle Lorieux, Chevrette, 26, rte du Vignoble, 37140 Bourgueil, tel. 02.47.97.85.86, fax 02.47.97.85.86 ▼
Y by appt.

PASCAL LORIEUX
Les Maugerets La Contrie 1999★
■ 3 ha | 15,000 | ■◗♣ | €5-8 ▼

Pascal and Alain Lorieux are each responsible for the management of a separate vineyard – one in Saint-Nicolas and the other at Chinon – but pool their equipment and marketing facilities. Pascal, who manages the vineyard in Saint-Nicolas, is extremely careful about respecting the natural environment. His Les Maugerets La Contrie, produced from 12-year-old vines growing on the gravel plateau, is a well-balanced wine, generous, rich and round on the palate and extremely elegant on the finish. It gives the impression of a very ripe harvest, a success story for this dynamic, likeable producer. The **Cuvée Principale 99** is also a successful vintage, the product of 30-year-old vines, and will improve with age; it receives a star as well.
➽ EARL Pascal et Alain Lorieux, Le Bourg, 37140 Saint-Nicolas-de-Bourgueil, tel. 02.47.97.92.93, fax 02.47.97.47.88, e-mail earl.lorieux@worldonline.fr ▼
Y by appt.

FREDERIC MABILEAU
Eclipse 1999★★
■ 1 ha | 6,000 | ■◗ | €8-11

L'Eclipse appears from time to time in the *Guide*, always with very positive tasting notes. Now it makes an appearance once again, rich and round, with well-matured grape tannins, while its wood tannins emerge briefly only to quickly merge with the others, giving an elegant character. Overall, this excellent wine will achieve perfect harmony in a few years, a superb product thanks largely to the ability of the producer. Frédéric Mabileau also produces a cask-conditioned **Rouillères 99**.

Saint-Nicolas-de-Bourgueil

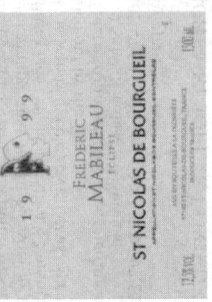

Especially singled out by the Jury, this light, smooth wine reveals pleasant flavours of soft fruit.

☛ Frédéric Mabileau, 17, rue de la Treille, 37140 Saint-Nicolas-de-Bourgueil, tel. 02.47.97.79.58, fax 02.47.97.45.19, e-mail mabileau-frederic@wanadoo.fr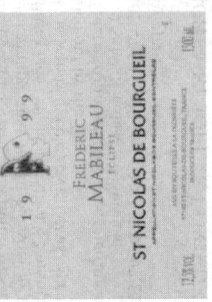
Ⓨ by appt.

JACQUES ET VINCENT
MABILEAU Cuvée Vieilles vignes 1999

■ 4 ha 18,000 ☷ ♦ ᐃ €5-8

It seems likely that La Gardière has a future producing wine for longer maturing, based on tasting this Vieilles Vignes produced from 50-year-old vines. Its clearly discernible tannins give it considerable potential. It is a wine to be drunk in two or three years' time.

☛ EARL Jacques et Vincent Mabileau, La Gardière, 37140 Saint-Nicolas-de-Bourgueil, tel. 02.47.97.75.85, fax 02.47.97.98.03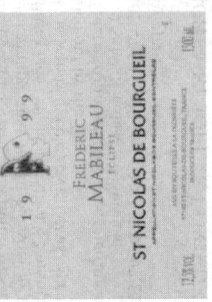
Ⓨ by appt.

LYSIANE ET GUY MABILEAU
1999★

■ 1.5 ha 10,000 ☷ ♦ ᐃ €5-8

Lysiane and Guy Mabileau present the Jury with their number one product, a wine that is guaranteed to be a success. Pleasant fruit aromas on the nose, and roundness and fullness on the palate, with well-balanced, mild tannins, make this wine a pleasure to drink now. **Vieilles Vignes 99** was especially singled out, and seems to be particularly suited to longer maturing.

☛ GAEC Lysiane et Guy Mabileau, 17, rue du Vieux-Chêne, 37140 Saint-Nicolas-de-Bourgueil, tel. 02.47.97.70.43, fax 02.47.97.70.43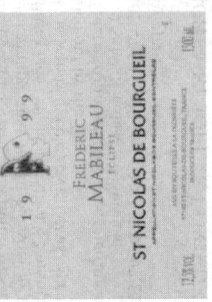
Ⓨ ev. day 9am–7pm

DOM. OLIVIER
Cuvée du Mont des Olivier 1999★

■ 3 ha 19,000 ☷ ♦ ᐃ €5-8

Juice from the grapes gathered on Mont des Olivier goes into this wine. A bright ruby colour, this full-bodied vintage boasts roundness on the palate, with well-matured tannins, and a strong flavour of soft fruit; a slight nuance of vanilla embellishes the finish. The Jury felt that it should be laid down for a further two or three years before drinking. Special mention was also given to the **Cuvée Principale du Domaine Olivier 99** (160,000 bottles).

☛ EARL Dom. Olivier, La Forcine, 37140 Saint-Nicolas-de-Bourgueil, tel. 02.47.97.75.32, fax 02.47.97.48.18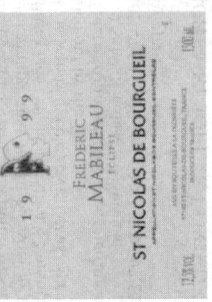
Ⓨ by appt.

THIERRY PANTALEON
Haut de la Gardière 1999

■ 2 ha 12,000 ☷ ♦ ᐃ €5-8

In La Gardière, the clay-limestone soil and sunny position guarantee the production of a truly expressive wine. This characteristically light, delightfully aromatic vintage reveals strong aromas of soft fruit. Well-rounded on the palate, it is still a little rough on the finish, so, as it is not fully matured, it needs another year's ageing.

☛ Thierry Pantaléon, La Gardière, 37140 Saint-Nicolas-de-Bourgueil, tel. 02.47.97.87.26, fax 02.47.97.47.71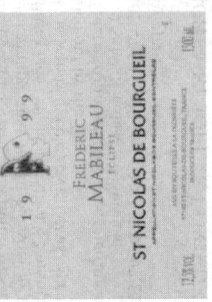
Ⓨ by appt.

LES CAVES DU PLESSIS
Sélection Vieilles vignes 1999★

■ 3.3 ha 26,000 ☷ ♦ ᐃ €5-8

The Renou family's estate is on a sunny hillside overlooking the Saint-Nicolas plain. This favourable position, together with the 60-year-old vines and the skills of Claude and his son Stéphane, have together produced a powerful wine with depth on the nose. It should be laid down for two years. **Réserve Stéphane 99**, which also received a star, is matured for ten months in oak casks, and reveals a more woody character on the nose than on the palate, where it also displays great promise.

☛ Claude Renou, 17, La Martellière, 37140 Saint-Nicolas-de-Bourgueil, tel. 02.47.97.85.67, fax 02.47.97.45.55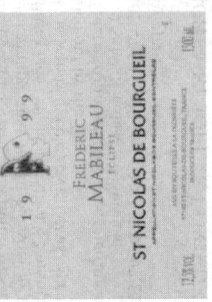
Ⓨ by appt.

DOM. PONTONNIER
Cuvée des Générations 1999★

■ 0.5 ha 4,500 ☷ ⅢⅠ ♦ ᐃ €8-11

The wine-producers of the Bourgueillois have the greatest respect for their elders, who planted the vineyards and gave them their name. Guy Pontonnier has named his latest vintage Cuvée des Générations after these elders. A fine blend of the traditional and the modern, the wine was carefully monitored while maturing for six months in oak. It offers powerful, balanced flavours on the palate, and, although already well-rounded, promises to blossom further with time.

☛ Dom. Pontonnier, 4, chem. de L'Epaisse, 37140 Saint-Nicolas-de-Bourgueil, tel. 02.47.97.84.69, fax 02.47.97.48.55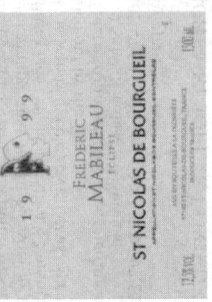
Ⓨ by appt.

DOM. CHRISTIAN PROVIN
Coteau 1999★★

■ 7 ha 30,000 ☷ ♦ ᐃ €5-8

L'Epaisse, one of the last houses on the hillside, looks down over the beautiful Saint-Nicolas plateau. The soil is rich in clay overlaying tuffeau, and as such tends to produce well-structured wines. This vintage is the characteristic Saint-Nicolas wine for

The AOC Chinon, which covers 2,000 ha (4,940 acres), surrounding the old medieval fort from which it takes its name, lies amid countryside made famous by Rabelais in his epics *Gargantua* and *Pantagruel* (1534). The various *terroirs* include the ancient gravel terraces of the Vienne (a triangle formed by the confluence of the Vienne and the Loire), the low, sandy terraces of the Vienne (Cravant) valley, the higher slopes on both sides of the valley (Sazilly) and chalk (Chinon). Cabernet Franc, known as Breton, made 113,536 hl (2,997,350 gal) of delicious red wines in 2000, plus a few thousand hectolitres (hundred thousand gallons) of dry rosé which equal Bourgueil in quality: they have pedigree, elegant tannins and keep well, for several decades in the case of some exceptional vintages! Less known outside the area, but very original, is white Chinon, of which 1,892 hl (49,949 gal) were produced in 2000, a rather dry wine that softens with bottle age.

G. ET M. ANGELLIAUME
Cuvée Vieilles vignes 1999★

6 ha 35,000 €5-8

This old family from the Chinon area produce their wines much as their ancestors did, in the incredible Coteau de Cravant cellars. This Vieilles Vignes is extremely promising on the nose, it evokes morello cherry and blackcurrant, while the first impression on the palate is more towards coffee and spices. Its body is almost immediately perceptible, partially concealed by vigorous tannins. A typical wine of the area, it should be laid down: it promises some pleasant surprises in the future.

DOM. DU ROCHOUARD 1999★

2 ha 8,500 €5-8

Christian Provin, L'Epaisse, 37140 Saint-Nicolas-de-Bourgueil, tel. 02.47.97.85.14, fax 02.47.97.47.75
by appt.

The harvested grapes are carefully sorted, and any leaves, shoots, green or damaged grapes thrown out before the grapes are put into casks. This is an indispensable prerequisite for quality wine, and the Rochouard estate is a great believer in this practice. This bright ruby-coloured wine evokes hints of fresh red berries on the nose, with clearly evident strawberry aromas. Supple on the palate, a hint of spice leaves an impression of considerable length. It achieves good overall balance, and is a considerably enjoyable wine that may be drunk immediately.

GAEC Duveau-Coulon et Fils, 1, rue des Galeries, 37140 Bourgueil, tel. 02.47.97.85.91, fax 02.47.97.99.13
ev. day 8.30am–12.30pm 2pm–7pm

JOEL TALUAU Le Vau Jaumier 1999★★

3.5 ha 19,000 €5-8

Joël Taluau, the founder of a fine 20-ha (49-acre) estate, is gradually letting one of his sons-in-law, well-versed in the art of wine-production, take over the management of the vineyards. Le Vau Jaumier, one of his latest acquisitions, covers 5 ha (12 acres) of sunny, chalky-clay soil. This 99 is surprisingly smooth and fruity, a good representative of the Saint-Nicolas appellation, which so enthused the Jury that it was very close to being awarded a *coup de cœur*. **Vieilles Vignes 99**, which also received a good mark, constitutes another success for a wine-producer who has never compromised on quality, and great satisfaction for wine-lovers, who will appreciate its fruitiness.

EARL Taluau-Foltzenlogel, Chevrette, 37140 Saint-Nicolas-de-Bourgueil, tel. 02.47.97.78.79, fax 02.47.97.95.60, e-mail joel.taluau@wanadoo.fr
Joël Taluau

DOM. DES VALLETTES 1999★

14 ha 80,000 €5-8

This property, which has always been owned by the same family, has appeared in the *Guide* every year since 1985. It covers some 18 ha (44 acres) of mainly gravelly soil situated in the very heart of the appellation. A highly colourful appearance and well-rounded flavours are signs of grapes that have been harvested when very ripe. Its length of flavour makes it an ideal wine for longer maturation. It should be left for about a year, and may be drunk for some years after; it can only improve with age.

longer maturing: fleshy, powerful, with solid, well-rounded, balanced tannins. **Vieilles Vignes 99**, which received one star, needs more time to mature fully. As for the **Prestige 99**, which was singled out by the Jury, it has good balance and may be drunk straight away.

Francis Jamet, Dom. des Vallettes, 37140 Saint-Nicolas-de-Bourgueil, tel. 02.41.52.05.99, fax 02.41.52.87.52, e-mail francis.jamet@les-vallettes.com
by appt.

EARL Angelliaume, La Croix de Bois, 37500 Cravant-les-Coteaux, tel. 02.47.93.06.35, fax 02.47.98.35.19
by appt.

DOM. CLAUDE AUBERT
Cuvée Prestige 1999

2.5 ha 14,000 €3-5

This wine emerged from the vat full of well-rounded tannins, indicating a rich body, and with a supple, enjoyable palate that lingers well on the finish. It may be served straight away or aged for a number of years.

EARL Dom. Claude Aubert, 4, rue Malvault, 37500 Cravant-les-Coteaux, tel. 02.47.93.33.73, fax 02.47.98.34.70, e-mail domaine.c.aubert@libertysurf.fr
ev. day 9am–12.30pm 2pm–7.30pm; cl. 15 July.

DOM. DE BEAUSÉJOUR 1999★★

27 ha 100,000 €5-8

Domaine de Beauséjour (30 ha/74 acres run by a sole tenant) was set up in the 1970s by Gérard Chauveau, who before becoming a wine-producer had worked as an architect and town-planner. He has produced a well-made wine, smooth on the palate, where fruit flavours suddenly come to the fore, leaving very little space for the strong tannins. The finesse on the finish contrasts with the intensely aromatic nose. This is a superb wine that should mature well, but which also may be enjoyed now. The same producer also presented the Jury with his Angelot 99, which was rightly awarded one star.

Gérard et David Chauveau, Dom. de Beauséjour, 37220 Panzoult, tel. 02.47.58.64.64, fax 02.47.95.27.13, e-mail dom.beausejour@wanadoo.fr
by appt.

DOM. DES BEGUINERIES
Vieilles vignes 1999★

4 ha 20,000 €5-8

Jean-Christophe Pelletier took over this small estate on the banks of the Vienne in 1995. However, he had already gained invaluable experience from 1987 onwards at Château de Saint-Louand (see name). Today he continues to run the cellar there while cultivating his own 11-ha (27-acre) vineyard. His Vieilles Vignes 99 is a well-made wine, beautifully balanced on the palate, with a fine body and mild tannins. The woody taste will mellow with time, and this is a wine definitely worth waiting for.

Jean-Christophe Pelletier, Clos de la Rue Braie, Saint-Louand, 37500 Chinon, tel. 06.08.92.88.17, fax 06.47.93.37.16
by appt.

DOM. DE BEL AIR
La Croix Bossée 1999★

1 ha 4,000 €11-15

Jean-Louis Loup, who took over in 1997, manages his 13-ha (32-acre) vineyard well-aware of the diversity of the various soil types. In fact, the grapes from each plot of land are vinified separately. La Croix Bossée is a 1-ha (2.5-acre) south-facing vineyard on the hillside. The Cabernet Franc shows all its strength here: very strong aromas of soft fruit and vanilla on the nose, supple and aromatic on the palate, with vanilla coming to the fore. The strong yet classy tannins give this Chinon a slightly uncharacteristic quality, showing that it needs ageing. The same producer has also made his rosé 2000, Cuvée Pauline, a fresh, fruity, balanced wine which especially impressed the Jury.

Jean-Louis Loup, Dom. de Bel Air, 37500 Cravant-les-Coteaux, tel. 02.47.98.42.75, fax 02.47.93.98.30
by appt.

VINCENT BELLIVIER 1999★

1 ha 5,800 €5-8

A small estate (3.5 ha/8.6 acres), this is sheltered from the northerly winds by the Chinon forest. Vincent Bellivier uses production methods similar to those of bygone days. He neither adds yeasts nor filters his wines: they are produced in the most natural way possible. The results are excellent, as shown by this wine, with its highly characteristic aromas and tannic structure. On the nose, the Breton is surprisingly evident; on the palate, it still possesses the flavour of ripe grapes, and the finish is smooth and lengthy. A pleasant wine, it should be laid down for a while. Nnoune de Noune 99 was singled out by the Jury for its fruity qualities.

Vincent Bellivier, La Tourette 12, rue de la Tourette, 37420 Huismes, tel. 02.47.95.54.26, fax 02.47.95.54.26
by appt.

CHRISTIAN CHARBONNIER 1999★★

2 ha 10,000 €3-5

This was one of the cereal farms that converted to wine-production during the 1960s when an agreement to grant farmers authorisation to do so was signed. Today, the estate has more than 12 ha (29 acres) of vineyards planted on clay-silicate soil. It would have been a shame had the vineyard never come into being: this superb 99, with soft fruit aromas on the nose, a fine lengthy structure and an elegant finish, leaves no doubts about that. The vintage may be drunk now or left to mature a little longer.

EARL Christian Charbonnier, 2, rue Balzac, 37220 Crouzilles, tel. 02.47.97.02.37, fax 02.47.97.02.37 ev. day except Sun. 9am–12 noon 2pm–7pm

DOM. DANIEL CHAUVEAU
Cuvée Domaine 1999★

4 ha 20,000 €5-8

Covering nearly 12 ha (29 acres), this estate is divided into hillside vineyards and those planted on gravelly soil. Cuvée Domaine is produced from old vines (more than 30 years old) growing on the hillside. Boasting highly seductive aromas and balanced tannins, the wine is smooth and easy to drink, which is fairly typical of the Cabernet wines of this particular appellation. It can be served immediately.

↝ Dom. Daniel Chauveau, Pallus, 37500 Cravant-les-Coteaux. tel. 02.47.93.06.12, fax 02.47.93.93.06, e-mail domaine.daniel.chauveau@ wanadoo.fr � ▼ by appt.

DOM. DES CLOS GODEAUX 2000★

■　4 ha　20,000　◨◨ €3-5

Philippe Brocourt owns a fine 17-ha (42-acre) vineyard covering the Rivière hill-sides that slope gently down towards the Vienne. Often praised for its reds, this year it has produced a rosé which opens on a fresh, lively note with a silky, fruity body. On the finish it is light, with ever-present flavours of fresh tobacco and peaches.

↝ Philippe Brocourt, 3, chem. des Caves, 37500 Rivière, tel. 02.47.93.34.49, fax 02.47.93.97.40 ▼ ▼ by appt.

DOM. DU COLOMBIER

Cuvée Vieilles vignes 1999★

■　1.5 ha　7,000　■ ● €5-8

The use of a grading table during the harvest helps to improve the quality of the finished product. Yves Loiseau has been using this device for a long while now, as it enables him to eliminate any plant debris before putting the grapes into casks. This serious approach to wine-making is clearly reflected in the quality of this Vieilles Vignes, which, although highly characterised by the Cabernet, remains a round, enjoyable wine, with soft fruit dominating on the nose. The estate's Cuvée Principale 99 likewise reveals the strong influence of the vine stock, and was also singled out by the Jury. Finally, Yves Loiseau received a star for his Clos du Centenaire 2000 white, a highly aromatic wine, fleshy and elegant on the palate.

↝ EARL Loiseau-Jouvault, Dom. du Colombier, 37420 Beaumont-en-Véron, tel. 02.47.58.43.07, fax 02.47.58.93.99, e-mail chinon.colombier@club-internet.fr ▼ ▼ ev. day except Sun. 8am-12 noon 2pm-7pm

DOM. COTON

■　13 ha　18,000　◨◨ €3-5

From the 1960s onwards, Guy Coton began to specialise his farm's production, up until then based on polyculture and livestock breeding, and for the past 12 years he has concentrated his efforts exclusively on wine-making. Judging by this wine, the choice was the right one. It is full-bodied, with well-rounded tannins, and has already attained the right balance. On the finish, it features ripe fruit. A wine to be enjoyed immediately, it is not at all suited to further ageing.

↝ EARL Dom. Coton, La Perrière, 37220 Crouzilles, tel. 02.47.58.55.10, fax 02.47.58.55.69 ▼ ▼ by appt.

RENAUD DESBOURDES

Les Ribottées Cuvée de Printemps 1999★

■　4 ha　4,500　■ ■ €5-8

Four oaks more than a century old growing at the entrance bear witness to the history of this 12-ha (29-acre) family estate, taken over by Renaud Desbourdes in 1999 after he had worked 15 years on another wine-making

CH. DE COULAINE

Clos de Turpenay 1999★

■　1.1 ha　4,500　◨◨ €8-11

Rabelais wrote about this very old family estate, which boasts a 15th-century castle and a 12-ha (29-acre) vineyard dating from the 13th century. For a dozen years or so, the estate has been up and running again, after the terrible phylloxera crisis that devastated wine-making. It has certainly been a trium-phant renaissance, with this Clos de Turpenay, awarded a coup de cœur last year and revealing a good balance this year. Its bouquet of red and black berries, and its generous opening on the palate, supported by mature tannins and finishing on a note of blackcurrants, constitute a Chinon that can be aged safely for several years.

↝ Étienne et Pascale de Bonnaventure, EARL Ch. de Coulaine, 37420 Beaumont-en-Véron, tel. 02.47.98.44.51, fax 02.47.93.49.15 ▼ ▼ by appt.

COULY-DUTHEIL

Clos de l'Echo 1999★

■　22 ha　80,000　◨◨ €11-15

The Couly estate celebrated its 80th anni-versary in 2001. Run by Pierre and Jacques Couly, it has of late taken on a younger air, with the growing involvement of their sons Bertrand and Arnaud in the technical and commercial sides of the business. The estate's Clos de l'Echo, inherited from Rabelais' family, once again offers a well-made red with a fruity character, and clearly evident body and tannins (currently concealed behind an omnipresent woody flavour). If it is left to age for a few years, everything should blend perfectly to give a fine, balanced wine.

↝ SCA Couly-Dutheil Père et Fils, 12, rue Diderot, 37500 Chinon, tel. 02.47.97.20.20, fax 02.47.97.20.25, e-mail webmaster@ coulydutheil-chinon.com ▼ ▼ by appt.

JEAN-PIERRE CRESPIN

L'Arlequin 1999★

■　1.4 ha　7,000　◨◨ €5-8

The product of small hillside vines, this wine, matured for 15 months in oak barrels, is a wine to be laid down for a considerable time, given its body, its balance and, above all, its clearly woody character, to mature into a truly harmonious wine.

↝ Jean-Pierre Crespin, 12, rue Grande, 37220 Tavant, tel. 02.47.97.01.48, fax 02.47.97.01.48, e-mail jean-pierre.crespin@mageos.com ▼ ▼ by appt.

↝ GFA Champ Martin

estate. His Cuvée de Printemps is a fruity wine which opens cleanly and develops in a well-balanced fashion, displaying a light tannic structure. It should be served slightly chilled. The **Réserve de la Marinière 99 Vieillie en Fût**, a more solid wine needing further ageing, was especially singled out.

➤ Renaud Desbourdes, La Marinière, 37220 Panzoult, tel. 02.47.95.24.75, fax 02.47.95.24.75 ⊻ by appt.

DOM. DOZON 2000★★

€5-8 · 0.6 ha · 4,000

A 23-ha (57-acre) estate planted on chalky clay soil, this domaine produces substantial red wines, generally well-suited to laying down. However, this year it is a white wine that wins the honours. Highly aromatic in the nose, it blends hints of honeysuckle, mint and lychee. Mint re-emerges on a fresh, lemony palate that lingers on the finish. It is a wine to savour with grilled fish.

➤ Dom. Dozon, Le Rouilly, 37500 Ligré, tel. 02.47.93.17.67, fax 02.47.93.95.93, e-mail dozon@terre-net.fr ⊻ ev. day except Sun. 9am–12 noon 2pm–6pm

DOM. DES GELERIES

Cuvée Prestige 1999★

€5-8 · 2 ha · 6,000

On the small estate she inherited from her husband, Jeannine Rouzier-Meslet produces mainly Bourgueil wines. Cuvée Prestige is extremely promising and very aromatic on both the nose and the palate. A gamey first impression is followed by clearly evident tannins that still need to mature fully, making this a wine that should be left for some time in the cellar so that its beautiful structure can be allowed to develop to its full potential.

➤ Jeannine Rouzier-Meslet, 2, rue des Geléries, 37140 Bourgueil, tel. 02.47.97.72.83, fax 02.47.97.48.73 ⊻ by appt.

GOURON ET FILS 2000

€3-5 · 1 ha · 5,000

Coming away from the Gourons' hillside winery, you should take time to admire the Cravant vineyard below spreading across the gravelly terraces of the Vienne. This family, which for three generations has produced wine here, this year has produced a really fruity rosé with a fresh yet mild opening in the mouth followed by a lengthy presence on the palate.

➤ GAEC Gouron, La Croix de Bois, 37500 Cravant-les-Coteaux, tel. 02.47.93.15.33, fax 02.47.93.96.73, e-mail info@domaine-gouron.com ⊻ by appt.

VIGNOBLE GROSBOIS

Cuvée Printemps 1999

€3-5 · 2 ha · 18,000

Jacques Grosbois cultivates 8 ha (19 acres) of vines on the sunny, chalky clay hillside of Panzoult, where he has successfully produced two wines, one of which is this Cuvée Printemps, a wine that opens smoothly and avoids any excessive richness of body or tannins: this makes it an enjoyable wine that is pleasant and easy to drink, with a fine aromatic bouquet. The **Vieilles Vignes 99**, which also impressed the Jury, is a warming wine suitable for longer maturing.

➤ Jacques Grosbois, Le Pressoir, 37220 Panzoult, tel. 02.47.58.66.87, fax 02.47.95.26.52, e-mail vignoble.grosbois@wanadoo.fr ⊻ by appt.

DOM. HERAULT

Cuvée Vieilles vignes 1999★

2.63 ha · 19,000 · €5-8

The cellar alone is a good reason to stop off at Eric and Elodie Hérault's domaine. Established in 1975, this small property dates from the 13th century, and covers almost half a hectare (1.2 acres). A palm tree greets visitors at the entrance, a sign of the mild climate. The wines they produce are also of interest, such as this Vieilles Vignes, a seductively elegant wine, round, fresh and well-balanced on the palate: altogether an appealing, easily drinkable wine.

➤ EARL Hérault, Le Château, 37220 Panzoult, tel. 02.47.58.56.11, fax 02.47.58.69.47 ⊻ by appt.

DOM. CHARLES JOGUET

Clos du Chêne Vert 1999★★★

2 ha · 10,000 · €11-15

Charles Joguet retired in 1997, but his philosophy of giving great importance to the terroir lives on. Clos du Chêne Vert, which was considered exceptional last year, once again received three stars from the Jury and came within a hair's breadth of the coup de coeur. Its intensity first fills the nose with ripe fruit or jam, and then develops hints of vanilla out of a slightly woody essence. A smooth, fleshy opening is followed by an elegant display of fine tannins. This is a highly promising Chinon that requires ageing for its woody character to mellow sufficiently.

➤ SCEA Charles Joguet, La Dioterie, 37220 Sazilly, tel. 02.47.58.55.53, fax 02.47.58.52.22, e-mail joguet@charlesjoguet.com ⊻ by appt.

DOM. DE L'ABBAYE 1999★

20 ha · 100,000 · €5-8

This sizeable, 50-ha (123-acre) estate, spread over eight villages, has its roots in the Parilly estate, which was already famous for its vineyards back in the 11th century. Guillaume de Sainte-Maure, a local lord, gave it as a gift to Noyers Abbey. The Abbey has not survived, but the name has remained with the estate. It produces wines of quality, as can be seen by the one star awarded to three separate Chinons. The main wine is rather closed on the nose, which nevertheless reveals a hint of blackcurrant. After a smooth, powerful first impression, fruit explodes on to the palate, while the tannins are well-blended. This wine will express its true potential after a further two years in the bottle. **Vieilles Vignes**

99 red, matured in barrel, is equally promising, while the well-made **rosé 2000** is fresh and fruity.

↝ Michel Fontaine,
Le Repos Saint-Martin, 37500 Chinon,
tel. 02.47.93.35.96, fax 02.47.98.36.76 ▣
Ⴤ ev. day 9am–12 noon 2pm–6.30pm;
cl. Sun. 15 Nov.–15 Mar.

MANOIR DE LA BELLONNIÈRE
Vieilles vignes 1999★★

■ 5 ha 15,000 ▣ €5-8

This magnificent 15th-century building possesses some 25 ha (61 acres) of vines, some of which grow on the banks of the Vienne river, while the others (20%) are on the hillside. This Vieilles Vignes is seductively open on the nose, where soft fruits blend with dried fruit and liquorice. On the palate, which is well-endowed with fine tannins, it opens cleanly to then reveal an elegantly constituted body. A serious wine, it needs to be aged for some time.

↝ Béatrice et Patrice Moreau,
La Bellonnière, 37500 Cravant-les-Coteaux,
tel. 02.47.93.45.14, fax 02.47.93.93.65 ▣
Ⴤ by appt.

CLOS DE LA GRILLE 1999

■ 2.5 ha n.c. ▣ €5-8

This 12-ha (29-acre) estate on a chalky hillside has produced a wine that was appreciated by the Jury for its fruity, rounded character. Its harmonious tannins give it an overall balance that is immediately evident.

↝ Marie-Pierre Raffault,
Les Loges, 37500 Chinon,
tel. 02.47.93.17.89, fax 02.47.93.92.60,
e-mail marie-pierre.raffault@wanadoo.fr ▣

CH. DE LA GRILLE 1999★★

■ 27 ha 180,000 ▣ €11-15

The 16th-century château was restored during the 19th century by Gustave de Coigny, chairman of the French Archaeological Association at that time. Today it belongs to the Gosset family, who have been making wine for 14 generations. Using a combination of traditional and modern methods, they have produced a superb wine in an elegant bottle, a copy of an 18th-century champagne bottle. The wine is matured for 15 months in wooden barrels, and the result is expressive on the nose, with clear scents of cedar. A supple, full opening proves well-balanced and lengthy. Nothing is missing here. A bottle of considerable class (both container and contents), it is destined to go a long way.

↝ Laurent et Sylvie Gosset, Ch. de La Grille, BP 205, 37502 Chinon Cedex,
tel. 02.47.93.01.95, fax 02.47.93.45.91 ▣
Ⴤ by appt.

DOM. DE LA HAUTE OLIVE
Cuvée Vieilles vignes 1999

■ 4 ha 20,000 ▣ €5-8

A dark ruby colour together with hints of strawberry and blackcurrant on both nose and palate, solid tannins that have had their rough edges smoothed, and a body that is perceptible for some considerable time, make this an interesting wine that needs to be kept for two years in the cellar before serving.

↝ EARL Dom. de La Haute Olive,
38, rue de la Haute-Olive, 37500 Chinon,
tel. 02.47.93.04.08, fax 02.47.93.99.28 ▣
Ⴤ by appt.
↝ Yves Jaillais

BEATRICE ET PASCAL LAMBERT
Cuvée Marie 1999★★★

■ 2 ha 8,500 ▣ €11-15

Béatrice and Pascal Lambert run a well-equipped vineyard, covering more than 10 ha (25 acres) at the foot of the Cravant hillside. They place a great deal of importance on ageing in wood, and their cellar features rows of oak barrels, 30% of them new. They took the utmost care over the production of this particular wine, and they have reaped the rewards in all departments. Of a dark, almost violet colour, it is very pleasant on the nose, with red and black berries enhanced by a mere hint of vanilla. Full, rich and deep on the palate, supported by mature tannins, a hint of wood is apparent on the finish. Its considerable intensity, fine body and perfectly conducted maturation all contributed towards the decision to award it a *coup de cœur*. This Chinon deserves to be matured further: the question is, will the wine-lover be able to wait?

↝ Pascal Lambert, Les Chesnaies,
37500 Cravant-les-Coteaux,
tel. 02.47.93.13.79, fax 02.47.93.40.97,
e-mail lambertchesnaies@aol.com ▣
Ⴤ by appt.

DOM. DE LA NOBLAIE 1999★★

■ 11.3 ha 35,000 ▣ €5-8

Domaine de la Noblaie, at Le Vau Breton, lies at the heart of the Chinon area: this is the valley where the 'Breton' grows, the name Rabelais gave the Cabernet Franc grape variety. Set up by Pierre Manzagol in 1952, the estate has since been taken over by his son-in-law, Pierre Billard. The 99 is a fine expression of the local *terroir*: it boasts smooth, elegant tannins that give an impression of strength. On the nose it reveals scents of soft fruit, a characteristic of this grape. It may be aged a little, although this is not compulsory. The estate's **white 2000** also received a good mark.

DOM. DE LA PERRIERE

Vieilles vignes 1999★★

■   7.5 ha   40,000   ▥ €5-8   ▥

☛ SCEA Manzagol-Billard, Dom. de La Noblaie, Le Vau Breton, 37500 Ligré, tel. 02.47.93.10.96, fax 02.47.93.26.13 ▥ ⅋ by appt.

In the same family for six centuries, this domaine, on the gravelly terraces of the Vienne, produces very fragrant, often finely structured wines. The 99 vintage, the product of 40-year-old vines, just failed to win the *coup de coeur*. A typical Breton nose is followed by hints of coffee and liquorice on the palate, revealing a rich body and balanced tannins. It has considerable potential for further ageing. The **Grande Cuvée 99**, which can hardly conceal its 15 months in cask, received special mention from the Jury, while the very oaky **white 2000**, otherwise known as **Confidentiel**, was awarded one star.

☛ Christophe Baudry, Dom. de La Perrière, 37500 Cravant-les-Coteaux, tel. 02.47.93.15.99, fax 02.47.98.34.57 ▥ ⅋ by appt.

VIGNOBLE DE LA POELERIE

2000★

▨   n.c.   3,000   ■   €3-5

François Caillé has run his 19-ha (47-acre) estate, sited on the flood plain of the Vienne, since 1990. His rosé immediately reveals considerable balance: pleasant on the nose, winding its way among fruit and flowers, its unambiguous, fruity opening on the palate is followed by a lengthy finish. It is a charming, highly drinkable wine. The estate's **Vieilles Vignes** was also especially singled out by the Jury. With its supple, fruity palate, it is characteristic of those Chinon wines produced on gravelly soils.

☛ François Caillé, Le Grand Marais, 37220 Panzoult, tel. 02.47.95.26.37, fax 02.47.58.56.67 ⅋ by appt.

DOM. DE LA POTERNE 2000★

▨   0.35 ha 2,000   ■ ▪ €5-8

A well-balanced, attractive wine, this is rather fleshy for a rosé. Fruity scents and a sweet, lengthy finish make it a pleasant wine, with a fresh, spontaneous verve. Deep gravelly soils clearly favour the production of such readily enjoyable wines, although the skill of the wine-maker is also of considerable importance.

☛ EARL Christian et Robert Delalande, Montet, 37220 L'Ile-Bouchard, tel. 02.47.58.67.99, fax 02.47.58.67.99 ▥ ⅋ by appt.

DOM. DE LA ROCHE HONNEUR

Diamant Prestige 1999★★

▨   3 ha   10,000   ▥ €5-8

A 15-ha (37-acre) estate between the Loire and the Vienne, Domaine de La Roche Honneur produces diverse wines from vines grown on a variety of different soils. This one, matured for 15 months in cask, is the brainchild of Stéphane Mureau. On the nose, it is a complex combination of woody notes and ripe soft fruit. A first impression of richness quickly merges into a fleshy, generous body where woody hints reappear again. Its silky tannins contribute towards the remarkable balance of a wine that deserves to be aged further. The estate also produces a **rosé 2000**, a rich, full, fresh vintage awarded one star by the Jury.

☛ Dom. de La Roche Honneur, 1, rue de la Berthelonnière, 37420 Savigny-en-Véron, tel. 02.47.58.42.10, fax 02.47.58.45.36, e-mail domaine.de.roche.honneur@libertysurf.fr ▥ ⅋ by appt.

☛ Stéphane Mureau

CAVES DE LA SALLE

Vieilles vignes 1999

■   n.c.   10,000   ■ €5-8

The house and its outbuildings date from the 18th century, but the vineyard buildings and winery were built in 1988. As well as managing the estate's production, Rémi Desbourdes also runs a farm campsite and breeds donkeys. However, his main interest is wine-making. Last year he was awarded the *coup de coeur*, and this year he gained acknowledgement for three fine wines: this well-balanced Vieilles Vignes, with its smooth tannins and clear aromas of Cabernet, is ready for drinking; the **Fief de la Rougellerie 99**, characterised by its harmonious tannins and good balance, was awarded one star; and finally, the **white 2000**, revealing an aromatic palate of grapefruit and mineral nuances, was singled out by the Jury.

☛ Rémi Desbourdes, La Salle, 37220 Avon-les-Roches, tel. 02.47.95.24.30, fax 02.47.95.24.83 ▥ ⅋ ev. day except Sun. 8am–12 noon 2pm–6pm

DOM. DE LA SEMELLERIE

Cuvée Déborah Vieilles vignes Elevé en fût de chêne 1999★

■   1 ha   5,000   ▥ €5-8

'Semellerie' was the name once given to a vineyard's very best crus. The estate has undoubtedly kept the name as a result of its superb position, sited as it is at the highest point of the village, facing south, with a clay-silicate soil rich in stones. This wine is produced from 50-year-old vines. An intense bouquet is dominated by blackcurrant, with several more developed nuances and a hint of grilled food. On the palate the wine is supple,

➤ Fabrice Delalande, La Semellerie, 37500 Cravant-les-Coteaux, tel. 02.47.93.18.70, fax 02.47.93.94.00 ☑
☗ by appt.

DOM. DE LA TOUR
Cuvée Vieilles vignes 1999

6 ha	n.c.	€8-11

Guy Jamet's vineyard covers some 14 ha (34 acres) of land in a sunny spot at the highest point in the village. This well-matured 99 is rounded on the palate, with silky tannins and flavours of soft-fruit jam on the finish. An extremely pleasant wine, it is ready for drinking.

➤ Guy Jamet, Dom. de La Tour, 37420 Beaumont-en-Véron, tel. 02.47.58.47.61, fax 02.47.58.47.61 ☑
☗ by appt.

DOM. DE LA TRANCHEE 1999

2 ha	5,000	€5-8

The vineyards within the village of Beaumont are mainly planted on chalky-clay soil directly overlaying tuffeau – warm, well-drained terrain that suits the vines. This product of these vineyards is a simple, pleasant, balanced wine of good length.

➤ Pascal Gasné, 33, rue de la Tranchée, 37420 Beaumont-en-Véron, tel. 02.47.58.91.78, fax 02.47.58.85.25, e-mail pascal.gasne@club-internet.fr ☑

➤ Pierre Ferrand, Ch. de Ligré, 37500 Ligré, tel. 02.47.93.16.70, fax 02.47.93.43.29, e-mail pierre.ferrand4@wanadoo.fr ☑ ☗ ev. day 8.30am–12 noon 2pm–6pm; Sat. Sun. by appt.

DOM. DES MILLARGES
Elevé en fût 1999★

3 ha	12,600	€5-8

The wine-production centre in Chinon is closely associated with agricultural training and education, and as such provides local wine-producers with information about the selection of vines and a variety of other wine-related advice. The product of a well-equipped winery, this vintage is dominated by wood, although it is not without fruit or body. The tannins are still rather strong, and it clearly needs time to mature into a more balanced wine. The Centre was also singled out for its **white 2000**, a wine that opens elegantly and develops a smooth body and fine overall balance. This is an enjoyable wine ready for drinking.

➤ Centre viti-vinicole de Chinon, Les Fontenils, 37500 Chinon, tel. 02.47.93.96.20, fax 02.47.93.96.20 ☑
➤ Lycée agricole

DOM. DU MORILLY 2000

0.6 ha	4,500	€3-5

Chinon rosés have an interesting structure, as well as an often generous fruity character, which puts them among those refreshing summer wines which go so well with starters and cold meats. This particular vintage is an aromatic, fresh, light, balanced wine that would go well with a spicy, exotic dish.

➤ EARL André-Gabriel Dumont, Malvault, 37500 Cravant-les-Coteaux, tel. 02.47.93.24.93, fax 02.47.93.45.05 ☑
☗ by appt.

round and of appreciable length. The tannins suggest that the wine needs ageing further if it is to attain the correct balance.

➤ Pierre Ferrand, Ch. de Ligré, [...]

CH. DE LIGRE
La Roche Saint-Paul 1999★

5 ha	25,000	€5-8

Consisting of more than 30 ha (74 acres) on the left bank of the Vienne, this estate has been in the same family for three generations. La Roche Saint-Paul opens on a clean, fresh note before revealing a pleasant roundness followed by rather evident tannins. The structure of the wine is not easily forgotten, and it will certainly improve with a little age. Pierre and Fabienne Ferrand also impressed the Jury with their aromatic, elegant **white 2000**.

LE LOGIS DE LA BOUCHARDIERE
Les Clos 1999★★

6.3 ha	42,000	€5-8

This is an estate of 45 ha (111 acres), three-quarters of which is on the hillside, the remaining quarter on the gravelly terraces along the Vienne. Les Clos is a product of vines grown on the clay-silicate soil of the slopes, terrain that usually yields fleshy, tannic wines, as proven by the 99 vintage. However, it should be pointed out that its tannins show that it can either be served now or laid down to mature further.

➤ Serge et Bruno Sourdais, Le Logis de la Bouchardière, 37500 Cravant-les-Coteaux, tel. 02.47.93.04.27, fax 02.47.93.38.52 ☑

CLOS DE NEUILLY 1999★

n.c.	15,000	€5-8

This wine fills the mouth with fine tannins before notes of soft fruit appear on a lengthy finish; it is a good wine, although the Jury differed on whether it should be drunk now or left to age. Both options seem feasible, according to one's individual preference. The **Domaine du Carroi Portier 2000 rosé** is a wine for a fine summer's day; it is ready for drinking.

➤ Dom. Spelty, Le Carroi Portier, 37500 Cravant-les-Coteaux, tel. 02.47.93.08.38, fax 02.47.93.93.50, e-mail spelty@free.fr ☑ ☗ by appt.

J.-L. PAGE
Cuvée Vieilles vignes 1999★

1.4 ha	5,000	€5-8

After leaving agricultural college, in 1977 Jean-Louis Page took over the running of this small estate left to him by his grandfather. This, then, is one of his first vintages, and it has proven quite a success. Its characteristic Breton bouquet reveals rounded tannins, and its full, powerful body makes it an ideal wine for longer maturing.

Jean-Louis Page, 12, rte de Candes, La Halbardière, 37420 Savigny-en-Véron, tel. 02.47.58.96.92, fax 02.47.58.86.65 by appt.

JAMES PAGET Vieilles vignes 1999★

1.5 ha   7,000   €5-8

Although Azay-le-Rideau is the centre of James Paget's business and professional activities, in fact, it is here that he cultivates a small vineyard located on gravelly soil that produces 'spring' wines. This fine Vieilles Vignes, a supple wine with discernible tannins and aromas of soft fruit, falls neatly into this category: a wine to drink immediately.
EARL James Paget, 13, rue d'Armentières, 37190 Rivarennes, tel. 02.47.95.54.02, fax 02.47.95.45.90 by appt.

DOM. CHARLES PAIN★★
Cuvée Prestige 1999★

10 ha   30,000   €5-8

Domaine Charles Pain covers some 25 ha (61 acres) in three different *communes* to the far east of the appellation area. Its Cuvée Prestige has a number of excellent qualities: a clean bouquet of ripe blackcurrants and strawberries, a fleshy opening on the palate and dense, fine tannins. A balanced wine that fills the mouth, this Chinon should be left to mature further. **Cuvée du Domaine 99** is made from vines grown on sandy, gravelly terraces along the Vienne. A seductive wine full of soft fruit and smooth tannins, it was awarded one star by the Jury. The winey **Rosé de Saignée 2000** received special mention.
EARL Dom. Charles Pain, Chezelet, 37220 Panzoult, tel. 02.47.93.06.14, fax 02.47.93.04.43, e-mail charles.pain@wanadoo.fr by appt.

DOM. DU PUY Vieilles vignes 1999

6 ha   13,000   €3-5

Alexis Delalande set up Domaine du Puy in 1820, and since then five generations of producers have tended the estate's vines. The estate now covers 24 ha (59 acres) and is run by Patrick Delalande, a wine-maker who remains faithful to his ancestors' traditional methods. His 99 is a clean, round, well-balanced vintage with pleasant tannins, a harmonious yet light wine that ought to be served immediately.
Patrick Delalande, EARL Dom. du Puy, RN 11, Le Puy, 37500 Cravant-les-Coteaux, tel. 02.47.98.42.31, fax 02.47.93.39.79 by appt.

JEAN-MAURICE RAFFAULT 2000★

2 ha   13,000   €3-5

Jean-Maurice Raffault's ancestor, Mathurin Bottreau, a labourer, bought the first vineyard back in 1693. Today the estate covers 45 ha (111 acres) of diverse soil types. If you are looking for a wine to be enjoyed immediately, then you need look no further than this aromatic, fresh rosé. His **La Cuvée du Puy 99 red**, on the other hand, is a wine that needs more time to mature, even though it is already balanced in character. The product of the estate's chalky-clay slopes and low yields (the grapes are thinned out during August), it is matured in new barrels for nearly two years before bottling. Thus, the wine hides very few surprises on the palate, with nuances of wood and roasting coming to the fore. It especially impressed the Jury, as did the **Clos d'Isoré 99 red**, matured for one year in wood: a wine that may be drunk a little earlier than the former.
EARL Jean-Maurice Raffault, La Croix, 37420 Savigny-en-Véron, tel. 02.47.58.42.50, fax 02.47.58.83.73, e-mail rodolphe.raffault@wanadoo.fr by appt.

DOM. DU RAIFAULT 1999★

5 ha   30,000   €5-8

Since 1997, Julien Raffault has been following in the footsteps of his father, a man who died prematurely, leaving his son this well-established 28-ha (69-acre) estate along the banks of the Vienne. The domaine's main wine, dark ruby in colour, is immediately appealing. The pleasant scent of new oak is clear on the nose, but on the palate it tends to conceal the flavours of Cabernet. Perfect tannins are an ideal match for the lively finish. This is a very successful vintage that true admirers of Chinon will leave to mature into a more balanced wine.
Julien Raffault, 23–25, rte de Candes, 37420 Savigny-en-Véron, tel. 02.47.58.44.01, fax 02.47.58.92.02 ev. day 8am–7pm; Sun. 9am–12 noon.

PHILIPPE RICHARD 1999★

2 ha   5,000   €5-8

The cellars on this small (6-ha/15-acre) estate were carved out of the tuffeau by the present owner's father and grandfather. The Chinon 99 has a rather musky bouquet, which evolves into strawberry when the wine is swirled in the glass. On the palate, it opens smoothly to reveal a good structure with fine tannins, although it remains a little harsh on the finish. The wine is the result of a well-managed process of maturation, and it would be a shame to drink it too early.
Philippe Richard, Le Sanguier, 37420 Huismes, tel. 02.47.95.52.50, fax 02.47.95.45.82 ev. day 9am–7pm

DOM. DU RONCEE 1999★★

20 ha   100,000   €5-8

Domaine du Roncée is an ancient fiefdom that during the 12th century fell within the manor of Ile-Bouchard. In the 15th century the vineyards were walled in, and today the estate's wines bear the names of those ancient vineyards. The main wine itself, a careful blend of grapes from various plots, greatly impressed the Jury: a truly balanced, smooth, elegant wine, with a strong body and tannins, and no one element upstaging the others. This is a wine with considerable potential, well-suited to laying down for some time. The same domaine also makes **Coteau des Chenanceau 99 red**, which was awarded one

...star and is of a completely different character: at present it is too severe and needs to be left to mellow.

● Dom. du Roncée, La Morandière, 37220 Panzoult, tel. 02.47.58.53.01, fax 02.47.58.64.06, e-mail info@roncee.com [V] [Y] by appt.

DOM. DES ROUET
Cuvée des Battereaux Vieilles vignes 1999

2.3 ha 10,000 €5-8

Cuvée des Battereaux has often been mentioned in the *Guide*, and this vintage deserves its place due to its almost garnet colour, its flavours on the palate – a blend of blackcurrant, cherry and violets – and its ample structure, the result of well-managed maturing in wood. It may be drunk immediately, although ageing will see it become more rounded.

● Dom. des Rouet, Chezelet, 37500 Cravant-les-Coteaux, tel. 02.47.93.19.41, fax 02.47.93.96.58 [V] [Y] ev. day 9am–6pm; Sun. by appt.

CH. DE SAINT-LOUAND
Réserve de Trompegueux 1999★

5.75 ha 25,000 €5-8

Covering 6.5 ha (16 acres), this vineyard was bought in 1898 by Charles Walther, surgeon and chairman of the Medical Academy, who probably never failed to recommend Chinon wine to his patients. The vines grow on chalky-clay soil overlooking the Vienne. Réserve de Trompegueux, a dark-red colour, opens on the nose with hints of cherries. On the palate, it reveals a smoky flavour before the tannins take over, making this promising wine one that needs time to fully mature.

● Bonnet-Walther, Saint-Louand, 37500 Chinon, tel. 02.47.93.48.60, fax 02.47.98.48.54 [V] [Y] by appt.

PIERRE SOURDAIS
Réserve Stanislas 1999★

3.5 ha 20,000 €5-8

A visit to this estate's Cravant vineyard reveals a variety of soils – flinty, clay and gravelly – on which a range of grapes are produced to be blended into this Réserve Stanislas. It opens on a fruity, smooth note with a certain degree of elegance, although the tannins also make their presence felt, and are an indication of good maturation.

● Pierre Sourdais, Le Moulin à Tan, 37500 Cravant-les-Coteaux, tel. 02.47.93.31.13, fax 02.47.98.30.48 [V] [Y] by appt.

CH. DE VAUGAUDRY
Clos du Plessis-Gerbault 1999★

1 ha n.c.

Although the present château dates only from the 19th century, the site was mentioned by Rabelais in his writings. Situated on a terrace cut into the hillside running along the left bank of the Vienne, the estate faces the ancient fort of Chinon. The 12-ha (29-acre) vineyard is completely walled in, and as a result benefits from its own microclimate. The 99 vintage has strong aromas of soft fruit on the nose and on opening on the palate, and then develops a strongly tannic, woody character, a sign that it will have to be laid down for some time if it is to mellow to the right degree.

● SCEA Ch. de Vaugaudry, Vaugaudry, 37500 Chinon, tel. 02.47.93.23.08 [V] [Y] by appt.
● Belloy

Coteaux du Loir

This AOC and its cru, Jasnières, the only two vineyards in the Sarthe, occupy the slopes of the Loir valley. About twenty-five years ago, Coteaux du Loir was on the verge of extinction, but is now fully revived. The vines are planted on silicious clays over tuffeau. The wines have great appeal, and include nearly 2,068 hl (54,595 gal) of light, fruity reds (Pineau d'Aunis, Gamay or Côt) and rosés, together with 1,175 hl (31,020 gal) of dry white (Chenin, known here as Pineau Blanc de la Loire).

DOM. DE CEZIN
2000★★

4 ha 10,000 €5-8

The Jury were quick to award this fine, brightly coloured white a *coup de coeur*. Its aromatic intensity first surprises then amazes, with its complex mixture of mango and orange followed by peach over a background of blackcurrant leaf. It opens cleanly, then reveals the flavours found on the nose on a lengthy palate. A remarkable wine, typical of the appellation, it lends itself to longer maturing.

Jasnières

'Three times in a century, Jasnières is the best white wine in the world.' Experts recommend it as an elegant accompaniment for *marmite Sarthoise*, a local speciality, as well as for other delicacies of the region, such as chicken and rabbit dishes with steamed vegetables. A rare wine in every sense – a discovery waiting to be made.

BERNARD CROISARD 2000★
☐ 1.5 ha 7,000 ▮▯▯ €5–8

This 200-year-old estate has been in the Croisard family all that time. Bernard Croisard has made a pale golden-coloured wine with an intense bouquet of ripe citrus fruit, while on the palate its flavours, though well-developed, give it a certain youthful character. It needs to mature in the cellar before it can be fully appreciated.

● Bernard Croisard, La Pommeraie, 72340 Chahaignes, tel. 02.43.44.47.12 ▼
Ⲩ by appt.

DOM. DE LA GAUDINIERE 1999★
▮ 1.3 ha 6,000 ▮▮▯ €3–5

An attractive light-ruby colour and peppery aromas blended with a hint of leather give this wine stature. The spices on the palate – a hint of originality – through a supple structure are what characterise this 99 vintage.

● EARL C. et D. Cartereau, La Gaudinière, 72340 Lhomme, tel. 02.43.44.55.38, fax 02.43.44.55.38 ▼
Ⲩ by appt.

LES MAISONS ROUGES
Pineau d'Aunis Vieilles vignes 1999★
▮ 0.35 ha 1,000 ▮▮▯ ♦ €3–5

Set up in 1994 with half a hectare (1.2 acres) of vines, this estate has since bought a number of old vines, such as these 60-year-old Pineau d'Aunis, which are well-suited to the soil in this Loire Valley. A light ruby colour, this 99 reveals a fresh, characteristic hint of pepper, followed by smooth tannins that line the palate. It is a good wine.

● Elisabeth et Benoît Jardin, Les Maisons Rouges, Les Chaudières, 72340 Ruillé-sur-Loir, tel. 02.43.79.50.09, fax 02.43.44.46.80, e-mail benoit-jardin@libertysurf.fr ▼ Ⲩ by appt.

GASTON CARTEREAU 2000★
☐ 0.75 ha 4,000 ▮▯▯ €5–8

With its highly developed balsamic and mineral bouquet and bright colour with straw-yellow reflections, this remarkably balanced wine is highly characteristic of the Jasnières cru. Its harmony is just waiting to be discovered.

● Gaston Cartereau, Bordebeurre, 72340 Lhomme, tel. 02.43.44.48.66 ▼
Ⲩ by appt.

DOM. DE CEZIN 2000★★
☐ 2 ha 10,000 ▮▮▯

François Fresneau, a yearly presence in the *Guide*, has produced a great wine that could only have come from superb soil. A beautiful straw colour, this is a charming vintage, with its nuances of apricot and peach that then develop along a more virile note, with grapefruit and grilled tones. It ought to be laid down a while, although it is already a delightful wine. The Jury awarded it a *coup de cœur*.

● François Fresneau, rue de Cézin, 72340 Marçon, tel. 02.43.44.13.70, fax 02.43.44.13.70, e-mail earl.francois.fresneau@wanadoo.fr
▼ Ⲩ by appt.

DE RYCKE Cuvée Prestige 2000★
☐ 1.5 ha 6,000 ▮▯▯ ♦ €5–8

These two young wine-producers, who have been working their Jasnières vineyards for about ten years, have succeeded in getting the best from their old vines. Their Cuvée Prestige is a generous, seductive wine offering delicate aromas and a very charming finish: a vintage that may well surprise Jasnières purists.

● François Fresneau, rue de Cézin, 72340 Marçon, tel. 02.43.44.13.70, fax 02.43.44.13.70, e-mail earl.francois.fresneau@wanadoo.fr
▼ Ⲩ by appt.

Jasnières

T his cru within Coteaux du Loir is precisely delimited on a single south-facing slope, 4 km (2.5 miles) long and only a few hundred metres (yards) wide. In 2000 it produced 2,627 hl (69,353 gal) of single-variety white Chenin which can be quite sublime in great years. As one authority wrote:

Montlouis

This appellation of 1,000 ha (2,470 acres) of vines including 400 (988 acres) in the AOC Montlouis, is bounded by the Loire to the north, the forest of Amboise to the east and the Cher to the south. The flinty clay soils, with sandy overlays in places, are planted with Chenin (Pineau de la Loire) and produce lively white wines of considerable finesse; they can be dry or sweet, still or sparkling. In 2000, 16,480 hl (435,072 gal), were produced. The dry wines are aged in bottle in tuffeau cellars, and can be kept for a good ten years.

DOM. DE LA GAUDINIERE 2000★

☐ 2 ha 8,000 ■ €5-8

A worthy representative of this small estate, this wine delighted the tasters with its presence and serenity. A nervy yet perfectly balanced vintage; it ought to reach perfection in four or five years.

☛ EARL C. et D. Cartereau, La Gaudinière, 72340 Lhomme, tel. 02.43.44.55.38, fax 02.43.44.55.38
☑ ☥ by appt.

JEAN-JACQUES MAILLET 2000★

☐ 3 ha 10,000 ■ ⑪ €5-8

Twenty-five-year-old vines planted on 6 ha (15 acres) of silicate-clay soil have produced a fine wine well worth discovering: the intensity of its grapefruit flavours contends with white flowers against a mineral backdrop. To appreciate its balance in full, leave it to age for a further few months.

☛ Jean-Jacques Maillet, La Paquerie, 7340 Ruillé-sur-Loir, tel. 02.43.44.47.45, fax 02.43.44.35.30 ☑ ☥ by appt.

DOM. J. MARTELLIERE 2000★

☐ 1 ha 5,000 ⑪ €5-8

A well-made Jasnières 2000 from an estate that is often mentioned in the *Guide*, this wine is full on both the nose and the palate, its initial vegetal flavours gradually fading to give way to a pleasant finish characteristic of its *terroir*.

☛ SCEA du Dom. J. Martellière, 46, rue de Fosse, 41800 Montoire-sur-le-Loir, tel. 02.54.85.16.91, fax 02.54.85.16.91 ☑ ☥ by appt.

DOM. DES MOLIERES 2000

☐ 7.4 ha 50,000 ■ €5-8

René Renou has learned his trade in vineyards where the Chenin Blanc, a multifaceted grape from the Loire Valley, has earned a reputation as being sweet and rich. In this particular case, it has produced a fine dry white wine, still rather harsh, but which will mature in time.

☛ René Renou, 1, pl. du Champ-de-Foire, 49380 Thouarcé, tel. 02.41.54.11.33, fax 02.41.54.11.34, e-mail domaine.rene.renou@wanadoo.fr
☥ by appt.

CLAUDE BOUREAU

Les Maisonnettes Sec 1999

☐ 1 ha 2,600 ⑪ €5-8

Claude Boureau, who has run this small 7-ha (17-acre) estate since 1969, defines himself as an 'artisan wine-maker'. He looks after his vines, works the land, meticulously sorts the grapes, and will not let anyone touch his wines while they age in the cellar. This wine is smooth and dry, with characteristic notes of aniseed on the nose. It is a versatile wine to enjoy during meals, or as an aperitif.

☛ Claude Boureau, 1, rue de la Résistance, 37270 Saint-Martin-le-Beau, tel. 02.47.50.61.39 ☑ ☥ by appt.

DOM. DES CHARDONNERETS

Demi-Sec 1998★

◯ 1 ha n.c. ■ ◖ €5-8

This estate, situated 2 km (1.2 miles) from the Touraine Aquarium, covers nearly 14 ha (35 acres) of gravelly slopes descending gently down towards the Cher river. It often features in the *Guide*, and this year offers a sparkling, medium-dry white whose nose is still somewhat closed, but already reveals a certain elegance. Its sweet palate of honey merges into a very crisp finish, which clearly reflects the local *terroir* and the Chenin Blanc varietal. A wine well worth having in your cellar, and the perfect match for fruit desserts that are not too sweet. The **Brut 99** (with an oval label) was singled out by the Jury.

☛ GAEC Daniel et Thierry Mosny, 6, rue des Vignes, 37270 Saint-Martin-le-Beau, tel. 02.47.50.61.84, fax 02.47.50.61.84 ☑
☥ ev. day 8am–7pm

☛ De Rycke, Le Coteau de la Pointe, 72340 Marçon, tel. 02.43.44.46.43, fax 02.43.79.63.54 ☑ ☥ by appt.

FRANCOIS CHIDAINE
Les Choisilles Sec 1999★

◻   4 ha   12,000   ▥   €8-11

The colour of this dry wine, rich yellow with green highlights, is immediately seductive. Strong notes of crystallised fruit on the nose are followed by an elegant palate. The finish is firm and structured. It is a wine that successfully blends fruit and oak, which although immediately enjoyable, could also be laid down for a while. François Chidaine runs this 15-ha (37-acre) estate, situated on the slopes of the Loire, along biodynamic lines. He makes another dry wine, the **Clos du Breuil 99**, which has good body, and especially impressed the Jury. The producer has opened a tasting room on the banks of the Loire, which is open to visitors practically every day from Easter through to the grape harvest, and by appointment during the rest of the year.

☛ EARL François Chidaine,
5, Grande-Rue, 37270 Montlouis-sur-Loire,
tel. 02.47.45.19.14, fax 02.47.45.19.08 ▥
Ⴤ by appt.

YVES CHIDAINE
Méthode Traditionnelle Brut★

○   1 ha   8,000   ■   €5-8

Yves Chidaine has chaired the Montlouis Grower's Association for many years now, while at the same time cultivating a fine estate situated on the prime slopes of the Loire: he has thus dedicated his entire career to promoting the wines of the Montlouis Appellation. He is now completely retired, although he continues to sell his wines. This traditional-method *brut* is the product of rich, well-selected base wines. The palate is supple, and very dry. This wine almost certainly spent some time *sur lattes* (stored in bottle while lying on wooden slats), and while somewhat atypical, it is most definitely attractive. A simple, yet appealing **Pétillant Demi-Sec** was singled out by the Jury.

☛ Yves Chidaine, 2, Grande-Rue, Husseau,
37270 Montlouis-sur-Loire,
tel. 02.47.50.83.72, fax 02.47.45.02.16 ▥
Ⴤ ev. day except Sun. 8am–12 noon
2pm–7pm

FREDERIC COURTEMANCHE
Sec 1999★

◻   1 ha   3,000   ■   €5-8

Frédéric Courtemanche meticulously cultivates this small 5-ha (12-acre) vineyard, working among the vines, grading the grapes at harvest time and using the method of maturing on the lees. The results are excellent, as proven by this dry Montlouis with its perfect balance, mineral flavours, and very long finish. A hint of pear on the nose is a clue to the hidden delights of this appealing wine.

☛ Frédéric Courtemanche, 12, rue
d'Amboise, 37270 Saint-Martin-le-Beau,
tel. 02.47.50.60.89 ▥ Ⴤ by appt.

DELETANG
Méthode Traditionnelle Brut★

○   5.6 ha   50,000   €5-8

Having obtained a *coup de cœur* last year for a traditional-method wine, this estate shines once again for its sparkling production. The 22 ha (54 acres) of vines planted on the sunny slopes of the Cher Valley undoubtedly contribute towards this success, but they so do the skills of the wine-maker. This is a wine characterised by its fine mousse, and a nose that is very expressive of the Chenin grapes. A lively, balanced wine, where the mark of the grape variety reappears as lemony crispness on the palate. The finish is smooth and elegant.

☛ EARL Deletang, 19, rue d'Amboise,
37270 Saint-Martin-le-Beau,
tel. 02.47.50.67.25, fax 02.47.50.26.46,
e-mail deletang.olivier@wanadoo.fr ▥
Ⴤ by appt.

DANIEL FISSELLE 1999★

◻   1 ha   2,000   €5-8

Daniel Fisselle set up this estate in 1972, and proceeded to expand it over the years. Today he cultivates some 8 ha (20 acres) on the slopes of Montlouis, where the siliceous topsoil overlays limestone. This soil is warm, well-drained and good for the ripening of the grapes: greatly contributing towards the success of the wines. This is a medium-dry wine with a powerful, elegant palate, and a fruity, lengthy, very lightly-sweet finish. This wine will benefit from ageing. A **dry white 99** also received the same marks, and can be enjoyed immediately.

☛ Daniel Fisselle, Les Caves du Verger,
74, rte de Saint-Aignan,
37270 Montlouis-sur-Loire,
tel. 02.47.50.93.59 ▥ Ⴤ by appt.

LA CHAPELLE DE CRAY
Méthode Traditionnelle Brut

○   16 ha   n.c.   ■ ●   €5-8

This company is the result of a partnership between a grower from Montlouis and an English *négociant*, and has attained a certain importance within the local economy. It has already set aside 15 ha (37 acres) of its vineyards for the production of this traditional-method *brut*. Its fresh, floral nose is very appealing, and the mousse is persistent and contributes to the well-balanced palate. A straightforward wine for every occasion.

☛ Boutinot, SARL La Chapelle de Cray, rte de l'Aquarium, 37400 Lussault-sur-Loire,
tel. 02.47.57.17.74, fax 02.47.57.11.97,
e-mail chapelledecray@wanadoo.fr
Ⴤ by appt.

DOM. DE LA MILLETIERE
Méthode Traditionnelle Demi-Sec 1996

○   2 ha   13,000   ▥   €5-8

Wine-producers since 1545, the Dardeau family know what they are talking about when it comes to Montlouis traditions: they harvest by hand, very carefully grade and select their grapes, and ferment exclusively in

DOM. DE L'ENTRE-COEURS
Méthode Traditionnelle Brut★★

○ 2 ha 15,000 €5-8

Alain Lelarge runs this 15-ha (37-acre) estate, situated on sandy clay soil with underlying clay subsoil. His most remarkable wine is undoubtedly this traditional-method brut. A rather dainty nose with floral notes opens up into a well-balanced, rounded palate. The finish is excitingly floral. It is an excellent wine, which anyone would be proud to serve as an aperitif. The **Demi-Sec 99** is a well-balanced, stylish, medium-dry wine that especially impressed the Jury.

☛ Alain Lelarge, 10, rue d'Amboise, 37270 Saint-Martin-le-Beau, tel. 02.47.50.61.70, fax 02.47.50.68.92 ▼

CLAUDE LEVASSEUR Sec 1999★

□ 1.8 ha 8,200 €5-8

This estate's splendid wine-making cellars, and its 13 ha (32 acres) of vines on the best silicious slopes of Montlouis, near to the Loire, are a true godsend. However, Claude Levasseur's *savoir-faire* also makes the difference here. He presents this dry 99, fermented

DOM. DE LA TAILLE AUX LOUPS
Cuvée des Loups 1999★

□ 1 ha 1,000 €23-30

Jacky Blot founded this estate in 1989 from three small vineyards, and since then has expanded operations, with almost 14 ha (35 acres) of vines currently being cultivated, together with the Clos de Venise on the Vouvray *terroir*. All his wines are fermented and matured in barrels. This wine is rich and sweet (with 80 g/l of residual sugar), and the full body and oak flavours are in happy balance. A well-made wine which, thanks both to the selection and grading of grapes, and to the vinification process, produces a perfect blend of sweetness and acidity. It has awarded a star by the Jury. It is only lightly oaked, and will repay cellaring. The **Cuvée Principale**, on the other hand, is matured eight months in barrel, and was singled out by the Jury.

☛ Dom. de La Taille aux Loups, 8, rue des Aîtres, 37270 Montlouis-sur-Loire, tel. 02.47.45.11.11, fax 02.47.45.11.14, e-mail La-Taille-Aux-Loups@wanadoo.fr ☛ ev. day 9am-7pm; cl. Sun. Nov.-Feb.
☛ Jacky Blot

wooden barrels. This wine shows the benefits of such care. Its colour is pale yellow, with a fine bead. The nose is dainty and floral, leading to a supple palate and lingering finish. A medium-dry wine to enjoy with desserts, especially fruit-based desserts that are not too sweet.

☛ Jean-Christophe Dardeau, 14, rue de la Milière, 37270 Montlouis-sur-Loire, tel. 06.85.20.30.98, fax 06.47.50.82.60, e-mail dardeau@club-internet.fr ▼ ev. day 9am-12 noon 2pm-7pm; Sun. by appt.

DOM. DE L'OUCHE GAILLARD
Sec 1999

□ 1 ha 4,100 €5-8

This is a well-made dry white from a difficult year. However, at l'Ouche Gaillard, Régis Dansault expertly manages his wine-making processes to give a bright, pale wine. The nose has aromas of peach and pear. The palate is full and has considerable length, and is characterised by a crisp liveliness. It goes extremely well with goat's cheese. Two traditional-method wines, one **Brut** and the other **Demi-Sec**, were singled out by the Jury.

☛ SCEA Dansault-Baudeau, 94, av. George-Sand, 37700 La Ville-aux-Dames, tel. 02.47.44.36.23, fax 02.47.44.95.30 ▼
☛ by appt.

CAVE DE MONTLOUIS-SUR-LOIRE Cuvée Réservée Méthode Traditionnelle Brut★

○ n.c. n.c. €5-8

This fine co-operative plays an important role in the local economy. It is run with the help of an expert oenologist, and produces wines of excellent quality; in particular, sparkling wines. The cellar, set into the rock, is an impressive one, well worth visiting, and you are guaranteed a warm welcome on your arrival. This wine has spent 24 months *sur lattes*, and is a fine expression of the *terroir*. Honey and almonds mingle on the nose, followed by a rich, lengthy palate, which together indicate a well-matured, well-made wine.

and matured in barrels, and using *bâtonnage*, the yeast-stirring technique. The wine is fresh and fleshy, with an impression of volume. Overall, it is a well-structured wine, a 'true Montlouis,' as one member of the Jury defined it. It can be drunk immediately.

☛ Claude Levasseur, 38, rue des Bouvineries, 37270 Montlouis-sur-Loire, tel. 02.47.50.84.53, fax 02.47.45.14.85 ▼

DOM. DES LIARDS
Vieilles Vignes Moelleux 1999★

□ 2 ha 8,000 €5-8

This 19-ha (47-acre) estate, covering some of the best slopes of the Cher Valley, was first set up in 1959 by two brothers, who subsequently handed it down to the younger members of the family. Despite the very difficult vintage, this *moelleux* boasts a nose which opens on aromas of ripe grapes and figs. The palate is full and round, and kept in balance by the wine's acidity. The finish leaves a flavour of peach and pear. It is a promising wine, which will benefit from time in the cellar.

☛ Berger Frères, 70, rue de Chenonceaux, 37270 Saint-Martin-le-Beau, tel. 02.47.50.67.36, fax 02.47.50.21.13 ▼
☛ by appt.

• Cave Coop. des Producteurs de Montlouis-sur-Loire, 2, rte de Saint-Aignan, 37270 Montlouis-sur-Loire,
tel. 02.47.50.80.98, fax 02.47.50.81.34, e-mail cave-montlouis@france-vin.com ▼
⊤ ev. day 8am–12 noon 2pm–6pm

DOMINIQUE MOYER
Méthode Traditionnelle Brut 1998

◯ 3 ha 10,000 ▥ €5–8

The Moyer family offer visitors an excellent welcome to their 17th-century home, an ancient hunting lodge belonging to the Duke of Choiseul. Their elegantly-produced wines include this golden-coloured, traditional-method *brut*, with hints of ripe fruit on the nose. The palate is refined, with apple flavours. It is a pleasant aperitif wine, or one to accompany white meats.
• Dominique Moyer,
2, rue de la Croix-des-Granges, 37270 Montlouis-sur-Loire,
tel. 02.47.50.94.83, fax 02.47.45.10.48 ▼
⊤ ev. day 9am–12 noon 2pm–6pm

CH. DE PINTRAY
Cuvée Tradition 1999

☐ 2ha 3,500 ▤ ◑ €5–8

The Château de Pintray is a beautiful home that provides rooms for guests (*chambres d'hôte*). The visitor may enjoy not only the gardens, but also the surrounding vineyard of nearly 7 ha (17 acres), planted on clay and flint soils on the slopes of Lussault-sur-Loire. The river's warming influence aids maturation. This particular wine, defined as "lightly sweet" by the Jury, is rich in aromas of ripe fruit and honey, and is highly representative of the appellation. It is already well-rounded, and may be enjoyed immediately.
• Marius Rault, Ch. de Pintray,
37400 Lussault-sur-Loire,
tel. 02.47.23.22.84, fax 02.47.57.64.27 ▼
⊤ by appt.

DOM. DE SAINT-JEROME
Moelleux 1999★

☐ 4 ha 2,000 ▥ €5–8

An attractive 10-ha (25-acre) vineyard sited on the higher slopes of Montlouis, not far from the Loire, where the clay-silicate soils are suited to the production of powerful wines. This *moelleux* has a rich body, and shows the care taken in the vineyard to select only the ripest grapes. Its balance of sugar and acidity is quite remarkable. It was matured in oak barrels, which have left a subtle oaky flavour with hints of exotic spices. It may be served with a goat's cheese such as Sainte Maure de Touraine.
• EARL Jacky Supligeau, Dom. de Saint-Jérôme, 7, quai Albert-Baillet, 37270 Montlouis-sur-Loire,
tel. 02.47.45.07.75, fax 02.47.45.07.75 ▼
⊤ ev. day 9am–7.30pm; Sun. 9am–12.30pm; groups by appt.

J.-C. THIELLIN Sec 1999

☐ 0.75 ha 2,500

The Thiellins are one of the old Montlouis families of growers who helped to make a name for this appellation. Well-made, this off-dry, straightforward wine (7 g/l of residual sugar) fills the palate. It is supple, delicate and highly characteristic of Montlouis dry wines, and is ready to drink immediately.
• Jean-Claude Thiellin, 46, rue des Bouvineries, 37270 Montlouis-sur-Loire, tel. 02.47.45.12.21, fax 02.47.45.08.69 ▼
⊤ ev. day except Sun. 9am–7pm

Vouvray's full qualities become apparent only after a long time in cellar and in bottle. These whites come from an appellation of 2,000 ha (4,940 acres) in the north of the Loire, stretching across the wide valley of the river Brenne, with the A10 motorway cutting through its northern tip (though the TGV express train goes through a tunnel). Here Chenin (Pineau de la Loire) and Sauvignon are used in the production of still wines, dry or sweet depending on the year, of very high quality. Fizzy or sparkling wines with a high alcohol content, are also produced. The sparkling wines should be drunk young, while the still wines can be kept for a long time, giving them time to develop aromatic complexity. Fish and goat's cheese go well with some, delicate dishes or light desserts with others, and the wines also make excellent aperitifs. In 2000, 115,909 hl (3,059,998 gal) were produced.

AIGLE BLANC
Cuvée Abbé Baudoin 1999★

☐ 9 ha 6,500 €8–11

This is an off-dry wine that would have made the Abbot of Beaudoin, an 18th-century clergyman, proud. The Abbot greatly contributed towards the selection of Chenin Blanc at Vouvray, and left his name to a vineyard of some fame belonging to the Poniatowski family. An attractive, bright-yellow colour, this wine has aromas of citrus fruit and hazelnuts. Well-balanced, rounded

1044

and immensely fresh on the palate, it is a wine to savour with a dish of Touraine cold meats.
♦ Philippe Edmond Poniatowski, clos Baudoin, Vallée de Nouy, 37210 Vouvray, tel. 02.47.52.71.02, fax 02.47.52.60.94, e-mail pep@magic.fr ▼ by appt.

JEAN-CLAUDE ET DIDIER AUBERT

Moelleux 1999★ □ 3 ha 10,000 ■ ▮ ◈ €5-8

A father-and-son partnership successfully manages this 21-ha (52-acre) estate situated on the best slopes of the Coquette Valley. The vineyards overlook the Loire, and receive the beneficial effects of the river below. The result is this elegant *moelleux* (20 g/l of residual sugar), characterised by its fine overall structure, roundness, and cooked-fruit aromas. This is a wine that asks for no more than time to mature to perfection. The estate also produces a fine **Vouvray Sec 99** (one star), with its powerful aromas of quince, acacia and apple. A surprisingly lively, clean attack merges into a balanced palate of some length.
♦ Jean-Claude et Didier Aubert, 10, rue de la Vallée-Coquette, 37210 Vouvray, tel. 02.47.52.71.03, fax 02.47.52.68.38 ▼
▼ ev. day 8.30am–12.30pm 2pm–7pm

DOM. DES AUBUISIERES

Brut 8 ha 60,000 ○ ■ €5-8

Bernard Fouquet presents a characteristic traditional-method *brut*, which must have been kept longer than the regulation nine months *sur lattes*, such is its mature character. This lends it a certain grilled and toasted nose, and a touch of coffee on the finish. It is a very classic aperitif wine.
♦ Bernard Fouquet, Dom. des Aubuisières, 37210 Vouvray, tel. 02.47.52.67.82, fax 02.47.52.67.81, e-mail info@vouvrayfouquet.com ▼ by appt.

PASCAL BERTEAU ET VINCENT MABILLE

Brut★ 17 ha n.c. ○ ■ €5-8

Pascal Berteau and Vincent Mabille's wine-making expertise is clearly evident in this sparkling *brut*, a blend of seven *cuvées* that is highly characteristic of the estate's production. It has astonishing floral aromas, with hazelnut and crystallised fruit bursting through. A balanced palate gives it a certain elegance, making it a thoroughly enjoyable aperitif.
♦ GAEC BM, Vaugondy, 37210 Vernou-sur-Brenne, tel. 02.47.52.03.43, fax 02.47.52.03.43 ▼
▼ by appt.

JEAN-PIERRE BOISTARD

Pétillant Demi-Sec Cuvée Prestige 1996 0.5 ha 3,500 ○ ■

A beautiful, well-run 10-ha (25-acre) estate situated on the slopes overlooking the banks of the Loire enables Jean-Pierre Boistard to produce this classic medium-dry Vouvray. The palate bursts with dried fruits and almonds, and together with the well-balanced, lively body, makes this a joyful, lightly-sparkling wine. It would be the perfect match for a plum or apricot tart.
♦ Jean-Pierre Boistard, 216, rue Neuve, 37210 Vouvray, tel. 02.47.52.18.73, fax 02.47.52.19.95 ▼
▼ by appt.

DOM. BOURILLON-DORLEANS

Brut Cuvée Hélène Doriéans 1997★ n.c. 15,000 ○ ■ €5-8

Hélène Doriéans, already acknowledged last year for her traditional-method wine, is a young producer who has come to the attention of the tasters once again, this time with this *brut*. Its fresh nose, with hints of fruit and a smoky/toasty note, paves the way for a lengthy, rich, harmonious palate. Its slightly rounded character makes it an ideal aperitif. The same producer has also succeeded with her **Vouvray Sec Argilo 99**, singled out for its good texture and suppleness.
♦ Dom. Bourillon-Dorléans, 30 *bis*, rue de Vauloynard, 37210 Rochecorbon, tel. 02.47.52.83.07, fax 02.47.52.83.07 ▼
▼ by appt.

MARC BREDIF

Brut n.c. 60,000 ○ ■ €8-11

This is a refreshing wine, with good balance and aromas of apples and pears, which would be ideal as an aperitif. The Brédif estate owns magnificent cellars on the banks of the Loire, and has years of experience in the production of sparkling wines. In fact, it was one of the pioneers in this area, where it has been making wines since 1893.
♦ Marc Brédif, 87, quai de la Loire, 37210 Rochecorbon, tel. 02.47.52.50.07, fax 02.47.52.53.41, e-mail bredif.loire@wanadoo.fr ▼ ▼ ev. day except Sun. 9am–12.30pm 2pm–6.30pm
♦ de Ladoucette

YVES BREUSSIN

Brut★ 3 ha 15,000 ○ ■ €5-8

If you have the chance to visit Yves Breussin's estate when you come to Vaugondy, you will learn a lot about Vouvray and the lives of its inhabitants. Yves is always ready to recount the history of the place to visitors, while offering them a taste of his traditional-method sparkling wine. This wine has a fine, light nose, together with a smooth, very fruity palate where apples and peaches jostle for attention. It is a joyful young wine, ready for drinking now. The estate's slightly sparkling medium-dry **Pétillant Demi-Sec** possesses a good balance of sweetness and acidity, as well as a lengthy finish, and especially impressed the Jury.
♦ GAEC Yves et Denis Breussin, Vaugondy, 37210 Vernou-sur-Brenne, tel. 02.47.52.18.75, fax 02.47.52.13.66 ▼
▼ by appt.

Vouvray

VIGNOBLES BRISEBARRE Brut
○ 10 ha 20,000 ▥ ▪ ♦ €5-8

Philippe Brisebarre sells the majority of his wine abroad (about 80%). His success is the result of the guaranteed quality of his wines. This one is a traditional-method sparkler with a fruity nose and a slightly floral note (linden flowers). The palate opens in a lively fashion, but it quickly acquires balance. It has a smooth finish on a peach and citrus-fruit note.

↣ Philippe Brisebarre, la Vallée-Chartier, 37210 Vouvray, tel. 02.47.52.63.07, fax 02.47.52.65.59 ▣ ⅄ ev. day 9am–7pm; Sun. by appt.

DOM. GEORGES BRUNET Brut 1997
○ 9 ha 10,000 €5-8

This small estate once belonged to the Château de Sens, a fine building overlooking the Loire, which is now owned by a computer company. Georges Brunet presents a traditional-method wine with aromas of fruit and grilled bread. A smooth, fleshy, fairly round palate and excellent body make this *brut* a fine aperitif.

↣ Dom. Georges Brunet, 12, rue de la Croix-Mariotte, 37210 Vouvray, tel. 02.47.52.60.36, fax 02.47.52.75.38 ▣ ⅄ by appt.

CLOS DE CHAILLEMONT
Moelleux 1999★★★
□ 1.5 ha 5,000 ▥ €8-11

This superb Vouvray *moelleux* is from 1999, commonly considered to have been a difficult year for this style of wine. A very floral, honeyed nose is followed by a well-balanced, rounded palate of crystallised fruit, with honey once more on the finish. Although this 99 may be matured further, it can already be drunk as an aperitif wine. As for the slightly sparkling **Brut de Jean-François Delaleu**, it is a young, lively wine with pleasant fruit, which was singled out by the Jury.

↣ Jean-François Delaleu, la Vallée-Chartier, 37210 Vouvray, tel. 02.47.52.63.23, fax 02.47.52.69.27 ▣ ⅄ by appt.

DOM. CHAMPION Brut 1998
○ 3 ha 4,900 €5-8

The Cousse Valley is one of the most picturesque valleys in Vouvray, with its series of houses built onto a hillside into which cellars have been cut, and where several of the appellation's best wines are now made. This traditional-method sparkler saw the light of day in cellars owned by this father-and-son partnership, who together manage a 13-ha (32-acre) estate. Rich aromas of vanilla and pear are followed by a surprisingly lively palate: a sign of the wine's youth. The finish is an elegant one, and this wine is certainly worth maturing a little longer.

↣ GAEC Champion, 57, Vallée-de-Cousse, 37210 Vernou-sur-Brenne, tel. 02.47.52.02.38, fax 02.47.52.05.69 ▣ ⅄ ev. day except Sun. 8am–12.30pm 2pm–7pm

DOM. DU CLOS DES AUMONES
Demi-Sec 1999
□ 1.5 ha 8,000 €5-8

'To Vouvray the fame, to Rochecorbon the good', is often the toast among locals over a glass of mature wine in the cellars of this rural village close to Tours. The prime slopes of the appellation are to be found there, and Philippe Gaultier knows it. He has produced a medium-dry wine with a full nose, a fruity palate and excellent overall balance. Although it may be matured further, it is already a highly drinkable wine.

↣ Philippe Gaultier, 10, rue Vaufoynard, 37210 Rochecorbon, tel. 02.47.54.69.82, fax 02.47.42.62.01 ▣ ⅄ by appt.

CLOS DU PORTAIL Demi-Sec 1999
□ 0.4 ha 2,600 ▥ €8-11

Didier and Catherine Champalou are in the *Guide* again, this time with a well-made 99 medium-dry wine from their 19-ha (47-acre) estate in the hills of Vouvray. A hint of vanilla from new wood gives way to the wine's fruity character, which lasts well on the palate. Their **Vouvray Brut**, a fresh young wine, was also singled out.

↣ Didier et Catherine Champalou, 7, rue du Grand-Ormeau, 37210 Vouvray, tel. 02.47.52.64.49, fax 02.47.52.67.99 ▣

MICHEL DUBRAY Brut 1999
○ 1.2 ha 6,000 ▥ €5-8

For over ten years, Michel Dubray has been running this 8-ha (20-acre) estate situated on the Vernou plateau. The vineyards are bathed in sunshine, and soils are stoney, with cooler clay soil below. Using traditional methods, he has produced a very attractive *brut*, with fine bubbles and a lively, fresh palate.

↣ Michel Dubray, 18, La Rauderie, 37210 Vernou-sur-Brenne, tel. 02.47.52.04.22, fax 02.47.52.04.22 ▣ ⅄ by appt.

FRANÇOIS VILLON Brut
○ n.c. 70,000 ▥ €5-8

Christian Dumange, amongst a variety of activities, runs the 17-ha (42-acre) Clos des Pentes de Rochecorbon, a vineyard with some fine buildings where he specialises in the production of sparkling wines. This very bubbly *brut* is a golden-yellow colour, and offers a pleasant, supple palate. It is a refreshing wine.

↣ Christian Dumange, Dom. François Villon, Les Maisons, 37210 Rochecorbon, tel. 02.47.52.54.85, fax 02.47.52.82.05

JEAN-PIERRE FRESLIER
Brut Réserve★
○ 2.5 ha 15,000 ▥ €5-8

Winner of a *coup de cœur* last year for a sparkling wine the Jury classified among the *Vins de Terroir* (typical regional wines), this year Jean-Pierre Freslier presents a very attractive Vouvray *brut*. Its colour is bright gold, with tiny, light bubbles. Its lengthy finish denotes a full body. It is a wine with

CLOS DU GAIMONT Sec 1999

□   4 ha   9,000   ▯▮◗   €5-8

The Clos du Gaimont is, like the Clos de Nouys, one of the most illustrious vineyards in the region. This dry, lively wine boasts a solid structure and aromas of tobacco and spice. While not offering any real surprises now, this wine will undoubtedly develop considerable character on maturing.

🔹 F. Chainier, Clos de Nouys, 46, rue de la Vallée de Nouys, 37210 Vouvray, tel. 02.47.30.73.07, fax 02.47.30.73.09

DOM. GANGNEUX Sec 1999

□   1 ha   5,700   ▯▮◗   €5-8

Gérard Gangneux is a great believer in tradition. 'Nature should not be forced, but given support and direction,' he loves to repeat. His dry Vouvray is a classic, with vanilla aromas and a firm palate with floral notes. An elegant wine to be drunk right now.

🔹 Gérard Gangneux, 1, rue de Monnaie, 37210 Vouvray, tel. 02.47.52.60.93, fax 02.47.52.67.66 ▼ ev. day except Sun. 8am–12 noon 2pm–7pm

CH. GAUDRELLE Sec 1999★★

□   8 ha   23,000   ▯▮◗   €5-8

An ancient manor house dating back to the 16th century, according to local records, and a well-sited 14-ha (35-acre) vineyard make up this exceptional estate run by Alexandre Monmousseau. His dry Vouvray was highly praised by the entire Jury. Its lightly-oaked character with hazelnut to the fore, a round attack that fills the palate and a finish that is strongly influenced by the *terroir* are the ingredients of a superb wine, the perfect accompaniment for scallops.

🔹 Ch. Gaudrelle, 87, rte de Monnaie, 37210 Vouvray, tel. 02.47.52.67.50, fax 02.47.52.67.98, e-mail gaudrelle@libertysurf.fr ▼ ▼ ev. day except Sat. Sun. 9am–12 noon 2pm–5.30pm

DOM. SYLVAIN GAUDRON Demi-Sec 1999★

□   n.c.   5,000   ▯▮◗   €5-8

In 1975 Sylvain Gaudron purchased these enormous 13th-century cellars carved out of the rock to make his traditional-method Vouvray, and to mature his still wines. His son Gilles now presents three well-made wines: this medium-dry 99 is a fruity wine with great length, good overall balance and a lively opening, which makes it ideal to drink with numerous different dishes. The **Vouvray Brut Symphonie du Nouveau Monde 96** is also

deemed a success, while the **Vouvray Sec 99** was singled out by the Jury for its balance. The oak-aged, slightly sparkling **Vouvray Pétillant Brut** especially impressed the Jury.

🔹 Jean-Pierre Fresler, 92, rue de la Vallée-Coquette, 37210 Vouvray, tel. 02.47.52.76.61, fax 02.47.52.78.65 ▼ 1.30pm–7.30pm

DOM. GENDRON
Brut Cuvée Extra Réserve 1997

□   4 ha   7,200   ▯▮◗   €5-8

Philippe Gendron started wine-making by cultivating a tiny vineyard in 1982, using equipment he had been left by his father. He gradually expanded operations, and currently heads a fine 22-ha (54-acre) estate. This bright-golden wine leaves small, discreet bubbles in the glass, while offering a pleasant, slightly shy, nose of exotic fruit. It is a supple wine, to be drunk as an aperitif.

🔹 Philippe Gendron, 5, rue de la Fuye, 37210 Vouvray, fax 02.47.52.74.71 ▼ ev. day except Sun. 8am–12 noon 2pm–8pm

CHRISTIANE GREFFE
Brut Tête de Cuvée★

○   n.c.   18,000   ▯▮◗   €5-8

Christiane Greffe has recently taken over the family estate, and aims to maintain the high quality that has always been a mark of this small winery. She presents a traditional-method *brut* that represents the top of their product range. The nose reveals flowers followed by apples and pears. After a rather racy start, the palate comes through in a very powerful and rounded fashion, a sign of elegance. It is a well-balanced wine.

🔹 Christiane Greffe, 35, rue Neuve, 37210 Vernou-sur-Brenne, tel. 02.47.52.12.24, fax 02.47.52.09.56, e-mail jac-savard@club-internet.fr ▼ ev. day except Sat. Sun. 8am–12 noon 1.30pm–5.30pm

🔹 Jacques Savard

DOM. GUERTIN BRUNET
Moelleux Vieilles Vignes 1999★★

□   1.5 ha   8,000   ▮   €5-8

Gérard Guertin took over the management of this estate from his father-in-law in 1978. Since then, he has not stopped making improvements to his vineyard and his winery, and today he manages some 12 ha (30 acres). The tasting room, situated in the La Verrine cellar along the main road leading to Vouvray, gives visitors the chance to try his range of wines. This particular wine offers a surprisingly powerful nose of honey and acacia, merging into vanilla, hazelnuts and apricot. The full, supple palate develops nuances of overripe grapes, together with honey and a hint of coffee. Volume and length are perfectly matched. You can, of course, age this wine in the cellar, although it is already very pleasant to drink.

•↘ Gérard Guertin, 24, rue de la
Croix-Mariotte, 37210 Vouvray,
tel. 02.47.52.77.71; fax 02.47.52.65.13 ▼
Υ ev. day 10am–8pm

DOM. DE LA BLOTIERE Brut 1998★
☐ 3 ha 13,000 **€5-8**

Jean-Michel Fortineau lives in one of those
traditional Touraine houses of white tuffeau
stone that brighten up the landscape around
Vouvray. Perched on the hillside, and encircled by more than 10 ha (25 acres) of vines,
his home looks out over slopes gently
descending to the Loire. He presents a fine,
floral, traditional-method sparkler with tiny,
persistent bubbles and a lively palate. Overall,
a well-balanced aperitif wine for family
reunions.
•↘ EARL Jean-Michel Fortineau,
La Blotière, 37210 Vouvray,
tel. 02.47.52.74.24, fax 02.47.52.65.11 ▼
Υ by appt.

DOM. DE LA CHATAIGNERAIE
Sec 1999★
☐ 5 ha 9,000 **€5-8**

Recently, Benoît Gautier celebrated 20
years of business by opening a special reception and tasting room: a good reason to go
and taste the wines he produces on the prime
slopes of Rochecorbon, overlooking the
Loire. The first wine to try should be this
Vouvray. It is a bright-coloured, fleshy, dry
wine with a pleasant overall suppleness. The
nose reveals hints of linden flowers and
acacia. The palate is both lively and full,
creating a fine wine that can be drunk straight
away. The Jury also singled out the estate's
Vouvray de Gautier Brut 98.
•↘ Benoît Gautier, Dom. de La
Châtaignerae, 37210 Rochecorbon,
tel. 02.47.52.84.63, fax 02.47.52.84.65,
e-mail info@vouvraygautier.com ▼
Υ by appt.

JEAN-PIERRE LAISEMENT
Blanc 1999★
☐ 1 ha 4,000 **€5-8**

Jean-Pierre Laisement is now reaping the
fruit of three generations' hard work on this
beautiful 13-ha (32-acre) estate. He made his
own contribution to the property by having a
vast tasting room built, and chose the decor
and furnishings himself. Thus he has created
the right environment in which to appreciate
this medium-dry wine (20 g/l of residual
sugar). The taster is surprised by the balance,
whereby no one feature dominates the others.
This elegant wine flows smoothly, with clean
aromas of quince on the nose. It is a classic
wine, ready to be served.
•↘ Jean-Pierre Laisement,
15 et 22, Vallée-Coquette, 37210 Vouvray,
tel. 02.47.52.74.47, fax 02.47.52.65.03 ▼
Υ ev. day 8am–12.30pm 1.30pm–7pm;
groups by appt.

DOM. DE LA MABILLIERE
Moelleux Les Hautbois 1999★★
☐ n.c. 2,000 **€11-15**

The organic winery has produced a
moelleux of great class and richness (50 g/l of
residual sugar). This is a refined, elegant
Vouvray wine, dominated by quince. Its balanced structure promises well for the future.
•↘ Pierre Mabille, 16, rue Anatole-France,
37210 Vernou-sur-Brenne,
tel. 02.47.52.10.03, fax 02.47.52.14.98 ▼
Υ by appt.

DOM. DE LA POULTIERE
Demi-Sec 1999★
☐ 5 ha 3,200 **€5-8**

Damien Pinon has just joined together with
his father, Michel, to set up a company and
run this 17-ha (42-acre) estate. Michel Pinon
is an excellent wine-maker who undoubtedly
has left his mark on this medium-dry wine
(30 g/l of residual sugar). It is a really good
wine, with a supple, delicate, fruity palate
where sugar and acidity are perfectly balanced. Its simplicity makes it the perfect
match for poultry, veal or cheese. Michel and
Damien Pinon also make an attractive,
oak-aged **Vouvray Moelleux 99.**
•↘ GAEC Michel et Damien Pinon,
29, rte de Châteaurenault,
37210 Vernou-sur-Brenne,
tel. 02.47.52.15.16, fax 02.47.52.07.07 ▼
Υ ev. day 9am–7pm; Sun. by appt.

DOM. DE LA ROCHE FLEURIE
Brut★
☐ 3.5 ha 25,000 **€3-5**

Michel Brunet started off business on a
small scale, renting a patch of vines and a
cellar at first. He worked hard, planting,
renting and then buying vines, and now owns
a fine 13-ha (32-acre) estate. His latest creation is a reception room where he welcomes
his customers, who can sample his very successful wines such as this traditional-method
brut. It has a very floral nose, and a fleshy,
harmonious palate of some length.
•↘ Michel Brunet, 6, rue Roche-Fleurie,
37210 Chançay, tel. 02.47.52.90.72 ▼
Υ ev. day except Sun. 8am–12 noon 2pm–
7pm; cl. 15–31 Aug.

DOM. DE LA ROULETIERE
Brut 1998
○ 7 ha 60,000 **€5-8**

This 14-ha (35-acre) family-run vineyard is
situated on the same site where the Abbot of
Marmoutier planted his first vines during
the sixth century. Another trump card is the
estate's cellar, carved out of the rock on two
floors, where this traditional-method *brut*
with its supple attack and balanced palate was
produced. It is not short of aromas either,
making it a pleasant aperitif wine.
•↘ SCEA Gilet, 20, rue de la Mairie,
37210 Parçay-Meslay, tel. 02.47.29.14.88,
fax 02.47.29.08.50, e-mail scea.gilet@
wanadoo.fr ▼ **Υ** by appt.

DOM. DE LA TAILLE AUX LOUPS

Sec Clos de Venise 1999★ □ | 1 ha | 5,000 | €8-11

Jacky Blot's skill at producing Montlouis wines are well-known, but seeing him in Vouvray is a true surprise. All wine-lovers should be thoroughly pleased, hoping that he manages to be just as successful as he has been in the past. This dry white has been deemed a success all around: its white-peach and citronella aromas together with its rounded, long, well-made character leave a favourable impression on the palate. It should be drunk now when celebrating both small and great occasions.

↳ Dom. de La Taille aux Loups, 8, rue des Aîtres, 37210 Montlouis-sur-Loire, tel. 02.47.45.11.11, fax 02.47.45.11.14, e-mail LA-TAILLE-AUX-LOUPS@wanadoo.fr ev. day 9am–7pm; cl. Sun. Nov.–Feb.
↳ Jacky Blot

DOM. DES LAURIERS

Moelleux Grande Réserve 1999★★ □ | 1 ha | 2,000 | €11-15

A whole line of wine-makers from the same family preceded Laurent Kraft at this 13-ha (32-acre) estate. Proof of this is in the ability to produce a great *moelleux* in a difficult year, by choosing individual plots of vines, and harvesting the grapes in a careful fashion. The nose reveals intense aromas of crystallised fruit, while the palate points to a harvest characterised by botrytis, with crystallised fruit once more to the fore. It is a great Vouvray, without doubt, and a wine guaranteed to age well.

↳ Laurent Kraft, 29, rue du Petit-Coteau, 37210 Vouvray, tel. 02.47.52.61.82, fax 02.47.52.61.82, e-mail lkraft@wanadoo.fr ev. day 8am–7pm

DOM. LE CAPITAINE 1999

□ | 5 ha | 5,000 | €5-8

The two Le Capitaine brothers, a constant presence in the *Guide*, have produced a dry wine which, despite the summer of 1999, is a success. Its nose seduces with its mineral qualities and aromas of acacia flower, while the balanced palate reveals a roundness that takes over from a slight liveliness. A good all-round wine, ideal for every occasion.

↳ Dom. Le Capitaine, 23, rue du Cd-Mathieu, 37210 Rochecorbon, tel. 02.47.52.53.86, fax 02.47.52.85.23
by appt.

DOM. DES LOCQUETS Brut 1999★

○ | 8 ha | 20,000 | €5-8

Stéphane Deniau now works alongside his father Michel, and together they run this 12-ha (30-acre) estate at Parçay, where the Abbot of Marmoutier had planted the very first vineyards in Vouvray. Their Brut will be popular for its overall balance. A floral nose, with a slight hint of smoke, is followed by a lengthy palate releasing nuances of peach and citrus fruits on the finish.

↳ Michel Deniau, 27, rue des Locquets, 37210 Parçay-Meslay, tel. 02.47.29.15.29, fax 02.47.29.15.29 ev. day except Sun. 2pm–8pm

FRANCIS MABILLE Brut 1999★

○ | 1.5 ha | 13,650 | €5-8

Francis Mabille represents the fourth generation of his family running this small 12-ha (30-acre) estate. The rather bare slopes of the Vaugondy Valley have a sound reputation as being ideal for growing vines. This traditional-method *brut* is a tribute to such origins. Well-made, rather straightforward: it is a supple, fresh wine that is a pleasure to drink.

↳ Francis Mabille, 17, Vallée-de-Vaugondy, 37210 Vernou-sur-Brenne, tel. 02.47.52.01.87, fax 02.47.52.19.41
by appt.

MARC ET LAURENT MAILLET

Moelleux Coulée d'Or Réserve 1999★★ □ | 1.75 ha | 1,800 | €8-11

The Maillet brothers run La Caillerie, nearly 19 ha (47 acres) of vines situated on the rocky slopes of the sunny Vallée Coquette. Balzac described this valley in his *Illustre Gaudissart* as being the ideal terrain for producing sweet wines, provided the grapes are carefully harvested. This *moelleux* has remarkable aromatic qualities (a blend of honey and crystallised fruit), with all ingredients combining to produce the perfect balance. It would be an excellent wine to lay down, if one has the patience to wait!

↳ EARL Marc et Laurent Maillet, 101, rue de la Vallée-Coquette, 37210 Vouvray, tel. 02.47.52.76.46, fax 02.47.52.63.06
ev. day 9am–7pm; groups by appt.

MARECHAL Brut 1997★

○ | 1 ha | 5,519 | €5-8

A traditional Vouvray house in the Vallée Coquette, at the very heart of the wine-producing *terroir*. It boasts sizeable, well-equipped cellars, and the managers are also experienced tasters. They have all it takes to produce successful blends and *cuvées*. This Vouvray seduces with its suppleness and fruity character. Its golden colour and fine bubbles give it an undeniable advantage. It is a wine that stimulates the appetite.

↳ SARL Maréchal, 36, Vallée Coquette, BP 1, 37210 Vouvray, tel. 02.47.52.71.21, fax 02.47.52.61.05

DOM. DU MARGALLEAU

Brut 1998★ ○ | 3 ha | 20,000 | €5-8

The grandfather set up the business in 1938; his two children took over in 1955, followed by his two grandchildren in 1995. Today these two grandsons, Bruno and Jean-Michel, continue to run this 25-ha (62-acre) estate situated on the slopes of the Vallée de Vaux. Here they produce this traditional-method wine which favourably impressed the Jury with its aromatic qualities and elegance. Well-balanced and persistent, it

also possesses a pleasant, youthful character. The medium-dry, still, **Vouvray Tranquille Demi-Sec 99** was singled out by the Jury.
➤ GAEC Bruno et Jean-Michel Pieaux, Vallée de Vaux, rue du Clos-Baglin, 37210 Chançay, tel. 06.08.62.54.92, fax 02.47.52.25.51 [V] [Y] by appt.

MÉTIVIER ET FILS
Brut Cuvée Vincent 1996★

○ 3,000 ■ €5-8

This nearly 14-ha (35-acre) estate situated on the slopes overlooking the main bank of the Loire is run by a mother-and-son partnership. This year, they present a very supple, elegant, rich traditional-method *brut* with aromas of quince and hazelnut. Its fine bubbles slowly rise up against a bright, straw-coloured background. It is difficult not to be tempted by such an attractive wine.
➤ GAEC Métivier, 51, rue Neuve, 37210 Vernou-sur-Brenne, tel. 02.47.52.01.95, fax 02.47.52.06.01 [V] [Y] by appt.

MAISON MIRAULT Brut

n.c. 20,000 ■■♦ €5-8

This traditional firm places great importance on the selection of the must and the wines, as well as in their blending, in its well-equipped cellars. It specialises in the production of sparkling wines, such as this lively, refreshing Vouvray. It is a wine characterised by its aromas of apple and dried fruit, with hints of citrus fruit even, which together give it a very pleasant taste. The firm's **Vouvray Effervescent Demi-Sec**, a sparkling, medium-dry wine with perfumes of ripe fruit, also especially impressed the Jury.
➤ Maison Mirault, 15, av. Brûlé, 37210 Vouvray, tel. 02.47.52.71.62, fax 02.47.52.60.90, e-mail maison.mirault@wanadoo.fr [V] [Y] ev. day 8am–12 noon 2pm–6.30pm; Sun. by appt.

CH. DE MONTFORT Demi-Sec 1999★

□ 8.2 ha 62,000 ■ ♦ €3-5

The Château de Montfort winery covers some 23 ha (57 acres) situated on the beautiful Quarts plateau within the local borough of Chançay. The soil, covered with stones on the surface but clay underneath, enables the vines to build up reserves. This balanced, fleshy, medium-dry wine stretches out and fills the palate with honeyed aromas. It should be cellared for several years.
➤ SC Ch. de Montfort, Les Quarts, 37210 Chançay, tel. 02.47.52.14.57, fax 02.47.52.06.09 [Y] by appt.
➤ SA Blanc Foussy

CH. MONCONTOUR Demi-Sec 1999

□ 40,000 ■ ♦ €5-8

The Château Moncontour produces this extremely refined, medium-dry wine. Aromas of honey and wax appear on the nose, and pleasantly persist for some time on the palate. The slightly lively opening is a sign of delicacy. It is a successful wine, in what was a difficult year.
➤ Ch. Moncontour, 37210 Vouvray, tel. 02.47.52.60.77, fax 02.47.52.65.50, e-mail info@moncontour.com [Y] ev. day 10am–6pm
➤ M. et Mme Feray

MONMOUSSEAU Brut 1997★

○ 24.5 ha 173,701 ■ €5-8

The Monmousseau firm, founded in 1886 and owned by the same family for many years, now belongs to the Bernard Massard Group based in Luxembourg. The company's production is characterised by its local expertise, as shown by this excellent traditional-method *brut*. The bubbles rise steadily, against a bright-coloured background. The nose is floral, with apple and pear, and finally a hint of vanilla. The same flavours are also found on the palate, together with a supple, balanced body. This is a well-made wine that is bound to please.
➤ SA Monmousseau, BP 25, 71, rte de Vierzon, 41401 Montrichard Cedex 01, tel. 02.54.71.66.66, fax 02.54.32.56.09, e-mail monmousseau@monmousseau.com [V] [Y] ev. day 10am–6pm; groups by appt.; cl. Sat. Sun. 1 Nov.–31 Mar.
➤ Bernard Massard

DOM. D'ORFEUILLES Brut 1997★★

○ 3 ha 20,000 ■ ♦ €5-8

The estate's office is situated in an outbuilding of a former medieval château, which the estate is named after, although the castle no longer exists. The fine vineyard spreads out all around, currently covering 17 ha (42 acres), and is skilfully run by Bernard Hérivault. The village of Reugny, with its flinty soil, seems to be entirely dedicated to the production of quality base wines to be used in the blending of sparkling wines. This *brut*, with its intense nose of flowers and fruit, is proof of this, as it achieves a completely natural balance between freshness and fruitiness on its full, rich palate. This 97 will cheer you up when drunk as an aperitif. The medium-dry **Vouvray Demi-Sec Les Coudraies 99** also impressed the Jury.
➤ EARL Bernard Hérivault, La Croix-Blanche, 37380 Reugny, tel. 02.47.52.91.85, fax 02.47.52.25.01, e-mail earl.herivault@france-vin.com [V] [Y] by appt.

VINCENT PELTIER Brut 1997★

○ 1 ha 6,500 ■ €5-8

Vincent Peltier has established a fine business, with a modern winery situated on the hillside, and maturation cellars carved out of the rock. This set-up has undoubtedly played its part in the success of this particular dry Vouvray sparkling wine. Its brioche-scented nose reveals hints of honeysuckle. The round, fruity palate finishes quickly, but leaves a delicate impression of suppleness. The estate's medium-dry, lightly-sparkling **Vouvray Pétillant Demi-Sec 97** was also awarded one star.

➳ Vincent Peltier, 41 bis, rue de la Mairie, 37210 Chançay, tel. 02.47.52.93.34, fax 02.47.52.96.96 V Y ev. day except Sun. 8am–12.30pm 2pm–7.30pm

CLOS DU PETIT MONT
Moelleux 1999★★
□ 2 ha   5,000   €5-8

Daniel Allias, head magistrate in the town for two terms of office, decided not to run for a third term, but to dedicate his time to his first love: his vineyard. He wanted to help his son Dominique run the family's beautiful 12-ha (30-acre) estate situated along the upper reaches of the Vallée Coquette. His return will be celebrated with this sparkling wine, with its ever-present aromas of botrytis and crystallised fruit. It is a remarkably full-bodied, balanced wine, given the rather difficult harvest, and one that is destined to mature further.

➳ GAEC Allias Père et Fils, 106, rue de la Vallée-Coquette, 37210 Vouvray, tel. 02.47.52.74.95, fax 02.47.52.66.38 V Y ev. day except Sun. 8am–12 noon 2pm–7pm

DOM. PIERRE DE RONSARD Brut
□ n.c.   40,000   €5-8

Raoul Diard, the previous owner of this 18-ha (45-acre) vineyard, was an important figure in Vouvray. His famous vineyard is now run by the Dumange family, specialists in the production of traditional-method sparkling wines. This Vouvray is a brilliant pale-yellow colour, and has an extremely floral nose and well-balanced palate. A lively attack gives it a pleasing freshness.

➳ Ève Dumange, Dom. Pierre de Ronsard, Les Maisons, 37210 Rochecorbon, tel. 02.47.52.54.85, fax 02.47.52.82.05

VINCENT RAIMBAULT Doux 1999
□ 1 ha   2,000   €8-11

Vincent Raimbault has been cultivating his 16 ha (40 acres) of vines on the hillsides bordering the Brenne (a tributary of the Loire) for over 20 years now. His vineyard benefits from the warming influence of the river, which encourages the grapes to ripen. This sparkling Vouvray (containing 48 g/l of residual sugar) falls within the category of sweet wines. It opens in a lively fashion, and offers mineral notes on the finish. It needs to be allowed to mature further in order to develop fully.

➳ Vincent Raimbault, 9, rue des Violettes, 37210 Chançay, tel. 02.47.52.92.13, fax 02.47.52.24.90 V Y ev. day except Sun. 9.30am–12.30pm 2pm–7pm

DOM. DU VIEUX VAUVERT
Brut Tête de Cuvée 1999★
○ n.c.   40,000   €5-8

This company set up in Vouvray in 1966, currently cultivates 25 ha (62 acres), and specialises in the production of traditional-method sparkling wines. It owns huge cellars highly-suited to this kind of wine production. This dry 99 is a golden-straw colour, with firm, tiny bubbles, together with a dainty nose and a palate of exotic fruit. A vinous wine with considerable length, it faithfully reflects the local terroir.

➳ SCA du Vieux Vauvert, 8, rue Vauvert, 37210 Rochecorbon, tel. 02.47.52.54.85, fax 02.47.52.82.05

DOM. DE VAUGONDY Sec 1999★
○ 4 ha   18,000   €5-8

The Vaugondy Valley runs into that of the Brenne River, which in turn flows into the Loire. In fact, the wine-producing Touraine is made up of a whole series of rocky-sided valleys, often sunny and exposed to the beneficial influence of the river. In this particular case, the sun has definitely left its mark on this dry Vouvray. The wine is lively and strongly mineral, light, and yet not lacking in aromatic presence, with green apples, cut hay and thyme coming to the fore. This wine will become more rounded after ageing for a further two years.

➳ EARL Perdriaux, 3, Les Glandiers, 37210 Vernou-sur-Brenne, tel. 02.47.52.02.26, fax 02.47.52.04.81 V by appt.

CHRISTIAN THIERRY
Brut Réserve 1997
○ 1 ha   2,500   €5-8

Christian Thierry has been running this 10-ha (25-acre) estate on the slopes of the Vallée de Cousse since 1982. He has worked towards improving the vineyard's equipment, while continuing to employ traditional methods in all else. This dry Vouvray presents an elegant nose of grilled bread. The palate opens with some verve, and then fills out with fruit and reveals considerable length, leaving an overall impression of youthfulness. This wine will continue to improve if left to mature in the cellar.

➳ Christian Thierry, 37, rue Jean-Jaurès, la Vallée-de-Cousse, 37210 Vernou-sur-Brenne, tel. 02.47.52.18.95, fax 02.47.52.13.23, e-mail christianthierry-vins@wanadoo.fr V Y ev. day 10am–12 noon 2pm–7pm; Sun. and groups by appt.; cl. end Aug.

CHRISTOPHE THORIGNY★
○ 2 ha   12,000   €5-8

The estate, set up in 1989 on a small plot of land, today consists of some 8 ha (20 acres) of relatively young vines, capable of producing excellent base wines. This Vouvray releases fine, steady bubbles, and develops a nose of quince and peach. The rather floral palate has notes of grilled bread on the finish. A well-produced wine to be drunk as an aperitif.

➳ Christophe Thorigny, 30, rue des Auvannes, 37210 Parçay-Meslay, tel. 02.47.29.13.33, fax 02.47.29.13.33 V Y ev. day except Sun. 9am–12 noon 2pm–7pm

DOM. VIGNEAU-CHEVREAU
Moelleux 1999★★ · 10 ha 20,000 €5-8

Five generations have contributed towards the creation and expansion of this beautiful 26-ha (64-acre) vineyard. The latest operation, overseen by Michel Vigneau, involved the replanting of the plot situated within the walls of Marmoutier Abbey. Legend has it that St. Martin planted the first vineyard of the Vouvray on this very spot back in the year 372. This *moelleux* has a palate that explodes with flavours of quince, linden flowers and honey that compete with a pleasant hint of *terroir*. Its length is proof of the wine's rich body. This is a wine that will mature happily in the cellar for many years. The same producer also presents two other wines which the Jury judged favourably: a sparkling **Vouvray Moelleux 99**, quite sweet given its 45 g/l of residual sugar, and matured in wooden casks; and a dry **Vouvray Sec Clos de Rougemont 99**, matured in barrel.

➽ EARL Vigneau-Chevreau, 4, rue du Clos-Baglin, 37210 Chançay, tel. 02.47.52.93.22, fax 02.47.52.23.04
➽ J.-M. Vigneau
➻ by appt.

Cheverny

Classified as VDQS in 1973, Cheverny proceeded to AOC in 1993. The appellation area extends a considerable way along the left bank of the Loire, from Sologne, in the Blésois, to the outskirts of Orléans. Numerous grape varieties are planted in this appellation of 400 ha (988 acres) of vineyards in an area of more than 2,000 ha (4,940 acres), where the *terroir* is predominantly sandy (sand on Sologne clay and the terraces of the Loire). The producers have managed to establish a Cheverny 'style' from a mixture of varieties in proportions that vary slightly depending on the *terroir*. In 2000 12,563 hl (331,663 gal) of red wine were produced, mainly from Gamay and Pinot Noir. They are fruity in youth, later developing an animal muskiness in harmony with the hunting traditions of the region. The Gamay rosés are dry and perfumed. The whites, of which 8,887 hl (234,617 gal) were produced in 1999, and for which a little Chardonnay is added to Sauvignon, are floral and finely made.

PASCAL BELLIER
Cuvée Prestige 2000★★ · 6 ha 27,000 €5-8

When producing this wine from a blend of Gamay, Pinot and Cabernet, the producer matured 40% of the Pinot Noir and 10% of the Cabernet in new casks for four months. This is the secret behind this excellent, very dark-red wine with its charming, elegant nose. Its fleshy character fills the palate, and ends on a note of spicy oak and flavours of very ripe soft fruit.

➽ Dom. Pascal Bellier, 3, rue Reculée, 41350 Vineuil, tel. 02.54.20.64.31, fax 02.54.20.58.19 ➽ ev. day except Tue. Thur. Sun. 2pm–7pm; Sat. 9am–12 noon 2pm–7pm

ERIC CHAPUZET
Cuvée Les Souchettes 2000★ · 5 ha n.c. €3-5

Eric Chapuzet's estate was once an old farm belonging to Fougères-sur-Bièvre castle. The Jury deemed this Cheverny white wine to have considerable potential. Intense aromas of citrus fruit and pear drops and a light, fresh palate characterise this wine. The cherry-coloured **Mont-Crochet 2000 red** has a pleasant, supple palate, and may be drunk now. It was singled out by the Jury.

➽ Eric Chapuzet, La Gardette, 41120 Fougères-sur-Bièv re, tel. 02.54.20.27.21, fax 02.54.20.28.34, e-mail e.chapuzet@wanadoo.fr
➻ by appt.

CHESNEAU ET FILS 2000★★
0.52 ha 4,000 €3-5

This very attractive wine, highly characteristic of the appellation, is a success for the Chesneau estate. A beautiful orangey colour, this rosé develops aromas of flowers and toasted almonds. A balanced wine with good length on the palate, this superb Cheverny goes perfectly with grilled and cold meats. The **red 2000** was especially singled out by the Jury for its cherry colour, its surprising spicy nose and its well-balanced palate.

➽ EARL Chesneau et Fils, 26, rue Sainte-Neomoise, 41120 Sambin, tel. 02.54.20.20.15, fax 02.54.33.21.91
➻ by appt.

MICHEL CONTOUR 2000
0.28 ha 1,800 €3-5

In 1984, Michel Contour replanted his vineyard with quality vines. This blend of equal parts of Pinot Noir and Gamay is characterised by a very attractive structure. This wine is ready to drink with grilled meats.

DOM. DU CROC DU MERLE 2000

■   4 ha   10,000   ■ ♦   €3-5

This evocatively-named estate received a *coup de cœur* for a 98 red. This white wine is a pale-yellow colour with green highlights; a very attractive, natural, lively wine that deserves to be singled out.

➤ Patrice et Anne-Marie Hahusseau, Dom. du Croc du Merle, 38, rue de La Chaumette, 41500 Muides-sur-Loire, tel. 02.54.87.58.65, fax 02.54.87.02.85 ◪ ev. day 9am–7.30pm; Sun. 9am–12 noon

MICHEL DRONNE 2000

■   3.11 ha   9,300   ■ ♦   €5-8

The Gamay (60%) dominates the Pinot Noir in this light Cheverny red, with its fruity palate and pleasant finish. It should be drunk lightly chilled, among friends.

➤ Michel Dronne, 1, voie des Perraudières, Cave l'Ebat, 41700 Cheverny, tel. 02.54.79.92.15, fax 02.54.79.92.15 ◪ by appt.

MICHEL GENDRIER

Le Pressoir 2000

■   n.c.   20,000   ■ ♦   €5-8

Michel Gendrier's estate is currently being converted to biodynamic methods. He presents a red made from 20% Gamay and 80% Pinot Noir. The latter clearly dominates both nose and palate. It is ready to drink immediately.

➤ Jocelyne et Michel Gendrier, Les Huards, 41700 Cour-Cheverny, tel. 02.54.79.97.90, fax 02.54.79.26.82 ◪ ev. day 9am–12 noon 2pm–7pm; Sun. by appt.

HUGUET 2000★★

■   5 ha   16,000   ■ ♦   €3-5

While the Cheverny **white 2000** is singled out for its powerful nose dominated by boxwood, it was this red that almost bowled the Jury over. Its nose opens on complex, delicate aromas of soft fruit. The palate is clean and round, while the velvety tannins hold their charm right through to the finish. It was but a hair's breadth away from a *coup de cœur*.

➤ GAEC Huguet, 12, rue de la Franchetière, 41350 Saint-Claude-de-Diray, tel. 02.54.20.57.36, fax 02.54.20.58.57 ◪

DOM. DE LA DESOUCHERIE

2000★★

■   9 ha   35,000   ■ ♦   €5-8

This estate carried off a fine crop of stars with three Cheverny wines. Its strongly-coloured **rosé 2000** is intense and delicate on the nose, has good length and a well-balanced palate, for which it received one star. The **Christian Tessier 2000 white** 'caresses the palate', according to one member of the Jury.

The product of perfectly ripe grapes, it is round on the palate with a fresh, clean flavour. However, it was this red wine which really stole the show, with its beautiful ruby colour with violet highlights, an intense nose dominated by very ripe blackberries, and an unctuous palate of suppleness and elegance.

➤ Christian Tessier, Dom. de La Désoucherie, 41700 Cour-Cheverny, tel. 02.54.79.90.08, fax 02.54.79.22.48, e-mail christian.tessier@waika9.com ◪ by appt.

DOM. DE LA GAUDRONNIERE

Cuvée Laëtitia 2000★★

■   5.14 ha   19,000   ■ ♦   €5-8

At the end of your visit to the Château de Beauregard, with its magnificent collection of Dutch earthenware tiles, stop off at Christian Dorléans' to taste his delightful Cuvée Laëtitia. A complex nose of white blossom and fruit, heightened by a note of brioche, precedes a supple and perfectly-balanced palate.

➤ Christian Dorléans, Dom. de La Gaudronnière, 41120 Cellettes, tel. 02.54.70.40.41, fax 02.54.70.38.83 ◪ by appt.

DOM. DE L'AUMONIERE 2000★

■   3.94 ha   10,000   ■ ♦   €5-8

This 17-ha (42-acre) estate has been in Gérard Givierge's family since 1836. His attractive wine is a pale-yellow colour with golden reflections. Nose and palate are powerful and stylish, and the wine has good length and a fine balance. It should be drunk now as an accompaniment to fish.

➤ Gérard Givierge, Dom. de l'Aumonière, 41700 Cour-Cheverny, tel. 02.54.79.25.49, fax 02.54.79.27.06 ◪ ev. day except Sun. 8am–12 noon 2pm–7.30pm

LE PETIT CHAMBORD 2000

■   5 ha   30,000   ■ ♦   €3-5

François Cazin manages the 18-ha (45-acre) family estate situated 2 km (1.2 miles) from the Château de Cheverny, 'one of the finest examples of Louis XIII architecture.' This attractive, pale-coloured wine is all floral aromas on the nose, and surprisingly round and pleasant on the palate.

➤ François Cazin, Le Petit Chambord, 41700 Cheverny, tel. 02.54.79.93.75, fax 02.54.79.27.89 ◪ by appt.

DOM. LE PORTAIL 2000

■   8 ha   40,000   ■ ♦   €3-5

This is a pleasant, typical Cheverny white blended from 85% Sauvignon and 15% Chardonnay: a classical mix. It offers interesting herbal notes of boxwood and a nicely rounded palate.

➤ Michel Cadoux, Le Portail, 41700 Cheverny, tel. 02.54.79.91.25, fax 02.54.79.28.03 ◪ by appt.

Cheverny

DOM. MAISON PERE ET FILS 2000★

☐   20 ha   25,000   🍷   €5-8

The first vines were planted here in 1906. Chardonnay grapes account for 40% of the blend in this bright, pale-coloured white. The nose is a mixture of white blossoms and blackcurrants. Fresh on the palate, it is a good wine to drink with a fish dinner. The Jury singled out the **rosé 2000**, a rather timid, albeit supple, wine which will open up in a year or two.

• Dom. Maison Pere et Fils, 22, rue de la Roche, 41120 Sambin, tel. 02.54.20.22.87, fax 02.54.20.22.91 ⊠ ⅄ ev. day 8am–7pm
• Jean-François Maison

JEROME MARCADET

Cuvée de l'Orme 2000★

■   2 ha   10,000   🍷   €3-5

The three wines offered by this producer all charmed the Jury. This straw-yellow wine exhales spring flowers on the nose, and its slight prickle highlights its youth and freshness. The **rosé 2000** is equally as successful, with its subtle nose, round palate and fresh finish. The **red Cuvée des Gourmets 2000**, a young wine that releases hints of red berries (strawberries), also impressed the Jury.

• Jérôme Marcadet, L'Orme Favras, 41120 Feings, tel. 02.54.20.28.42, fax 02.54.20.28.42 ⊠ ⅄ ev. day 8am–12 noon 2pm–7pm; Sun. by appt.

DOM. DE MONTCY

Cuvée Louis de La Saussaye 2000★

■   3.2 ha   19,000   🍷   €5-8

This estate produces three Cheverny wines, each of which was awarded a star by the Jury. This fine Cuvée Louis de La Saussaye is a ruby-red colour, and is distinguished by its elegant, complex nose, supple structure on the palate, and a tannic finish. The **Cuvée des Cendres** of the same year has a lot of class, is well-balanced and promises well for the future.

• R. et S. Simon, La Porte dorée, 32, rte de Fougères, 41700 Cheverny, tel. 02.54.44.20.00, fax 02.54.44.20.50, e-mail domaine-de-montcy@wanadoo.com ⊠ ⅄ ev. day except Sun. 10am–12 noon 2pm–6pm; Sat. by appt.; cl. 26 Aug.–6 Sept.

LES VIGNERONS DE MONT-PRES-CHAMBORD 2000★★

■   25 ha   180,000   🍷   €5-8

This winery has just celebrated its 70th anniversary, and continues to offer some truly splendid wines. The Jury all agreed on awarding a *coup de cœur* to this superb red, for its dark colour, somewhere in between purple and ruby, and for its complex nose that blends aromas of red berries with mineral notes. The rich body fills the palate. A true gem of a Cheverny. The same co-operative also presents a **rosé 2000**, singled out for its flavoursome complexity and its extremely fresh finish.

• Les Vignerons de Mont-près-Chambord, 816, la Petite-Rue, 41250 Mont-Prés-Chambord, tel. 02.54.70.71.15, fax 02.54.70.70.65, e-mail cavemont@club-internet.fr ⊠ ⅄ ev. day except Mon. am 9am–12 noon 2pm–6pm

DOM. DU MOULIN 2000★

■   4 ha   20,000   🍷   €5-8

Beyond the Château de Beauregard and the partly Roman church, the village of Cellettes offers industrial-history enthusiasts the chance to see a well-preserved water-mill on the Beuvron river. There is also the Moulin estate, producer of wines characterised by their soft fruit aromas (blackberries and cherries mainly), and their supple tannins. This 2000 is a well-balanced wine with a palate that is plump and rounded.

• Hervé Villemade, Dom. du Moulin, 41120 Cellettes, tel. 02.54.70.41.76, fax 02.54.70.37.41 ⊠ ⅄ by appt.

LES VIGNERONS DE OISLY ET THESEE 2000★

☐   6 ha   45,000   🍷   €5-8

This co-operative has been going since 1961, and presents here a fine, clear, bright white wine with a floral nose. The intensity of the aromas and the balanced palate give this Cheverny considerable charm.

• Confrérie des Vignerons de Oisly et Thésée, Le Bourg, 41700 Oisly, tel. 02.54.79.75.20, fax 02.54.79.75.29 ⊠ ⅄ by appt.

DOM. DU SALVARD 2000★★

☐   12 ha   50,000   🍷   €5-8

The two Cheverny whites presented by this estate both seduced the Jury: perhaps more so this blend of Chardonnay and Sauvignon (clearly dominated by the latter). It is a wine that reveals both strength and balance. As for the **Cuvée L'Héritière**, this is again a powerful and flavourful wine with good balance, which has already earned itself a star.

• EARL Delaille, Le Salvard, 41120 Fougères-sur-Bièvre, tel. 02.54.20.28.21, fax 02.54.20.22.54 ⊠ ⅄ ev. day except Sat. Sun. 8am–12 noon 2pm–6.30pm

DOM. SAUGER ET FILS 2000★

☐   4 ha   10,000   🍷   €3-5

The Sauger family have been wine-producers since 1870. The three wines they

have presented this year all attracted the interest of the Jury, although this Cheverny white was judged of particular interest, with its intense nose of white blossoms. The palate is silky, well-balanced and of good length. As for the two **Cheverny reds**, each impressed the Jury: the first, produced from 25-year-old vines, is slightly oaky with a good structure on the palate; the second is a young, yet elegant, wine with a promising future ahead.

♠ Dom. Sauger et Fils, Les Touches, 41700 Fresnes, tel. 02.54.79.58.45, fax 02.54.79.03.35 ☑ ☒ ev. day except Sun. 9am–12 noon 2pm–6pm; by appt. 15 Sept.–15 Mar.

DANIEL TEVENOT 2000

☐ n.c. 7,500 €3-5 ☒ by appt.

Daniel Tévenot is not only interested in wine, but also in the history and culture of this region north of the Sologne. He has written a book about Candé and Madon, a small hamlet inhabited since Merovingian times. The historical importance of the Vallée du Beuvron should not distract from the important feature of this estate: a wine whose aromas of blackcurrant and well-balanced palate will certainly not disgrace your dining table.

♠ Daniel Tévenot, 4, rue du Moulin-à-Vent, Madon, 41120 Candé-sur-Beuvron, tel. 02.54.79.44.24, fax 02.54.79.44.24 ☑

DOM. PHILIPPE TESSIER

Le Point du Jour 2000★

☐ n.c. 11,000 €5-8

Awarded a *coup de cœur* last year for his 99 vintage, Philippe Tessier proposes two 2000 wines, both produced using organic methods and judged positively by the Jury. This dark Cheverny red offers a surprising blend of floral aromas and red berries. A supple palate reveals clearly the character of the Pinot Noir in the finish. The **La Charbonnerie 2000**, a fine, golden-coloured white wine, gives off aromas of the *terroir*, which together with its refined palate make it an extremely pleasant bottle.

♠ EARL Philippe Tessier, 3, voie de la rue Colin, 41700 Cheverny, tel. 02.54.44.23.82, fax 02.54.44.21.71 ☑ ☒ by appt.

DOM. DU VIVIER 2000★

3.15 ha 13,000 €5-8

Jean-François Deniau has navigated the waters of diplomacy and French and European politics, as well as those of the world's oceans. A lover of the sea and of literature, the author of several novels and essays, he is also clearly fond of the land, having purchased this vineyard near to Cheverny. It is a return to his roots, since on his father's side his ancestors were either wine-producers or foresters in the Sologne region. The wine-maker is none other than Michel Gendrier, and the wine he produces is all you would expect from a Cheverny: aromas of soft fruit, freshness and elegance.

♠ Jocelyne et Michel Gendrier, Les Huards, 41700 Cour-Cheverny, tel. 02.54.79.97.90, fax 02.54.79.26.82 ☑ ☒ ev. day 9am–12 noon 2pm–7pm; Sun. by appt.

Cour-Cheverny

A decree dated 24 March 1993 recognised Cour-Cheverny as a separate AOC, limited to white wines made using only the Romorantin variety. The area of production comprises the former AOS Cour-Cheverny Mont-Près-Chambord and a few surrounding communes where the variety was maintained. The *terroir* is typical of the Sologne (sand on clay). Production in 2000 totalled 2,262 hl (59,717 gal).

DOM. DES HUARDS 1999

☐ n.c. 30,000 €5-8

This estate has been in the Gendrier family since 1846, and has recently converted to using biodynamic methods of cultivation. It produces a floral, elegant Cour-Cheverny which is a pleasure to drink now.

♠ Jocelyne et Michel Gendrier, Les Huards, 41700 Cour-Cheverny, tel. 02.54.79.26.82 ☑ ☒ ev. day 9am–12 noon 2pm–7pm; Sun. by appt.

DOM. DE LA DESOUCHERIE 1999

3.4 ha 25,000 €5-8

Cour-Cheverny organises walking itineraries for visitors which may be of interest to wine-enthusiasts; in which case, they should include a visit to this estate en route. This golden-coloured wine boasts real body and richness, as well as a very balanced palate. The true connoisseur cannot go wrong here.

PASCAL BELLIER 1999

0.5 ha 4,100 €5-8

At the Pascal Bellier estate, the harvest starts in November, as it is a known fact that the Romorantin is a late variety. This wine is a fine example of its type. It has a refined nose that abounds in citrus fruit and white blossoms, with a hint of brioche, and a pleasant palate with a lively structure. Drink now or cellar for a year.

♠ Dom. Pascal Bellier, 3, rue Reculée, 41350 Vineuil, tel. 02.54.20.64.31, fax 02.54.20.58.19 ☑ ☒ ev. day except Tue, Thur, Sun. 2pm–7pm; Sat. 9am–12 noon 2pm–7pm

Coteaux du Vendômois

Coteaux du Vendômois was recognized as an AOC in 2001. This unique appellation, between Vendôme and Montoire, produces the highly distinctive *vin gris* de Pineau d'Aunis, noted for its very pale colour and

the nose just now, although well-balanced on the palate. It needs to be laid down for a few months before it can be fully appreciated.

☛ Les Vignerons de Mont-près-Chambord, 816, la Petite-Rue,
41250 Mont-Près-Chambord,
tel. 02.54.70.71.15, fax 02.54.70.70.65,
e-mail cavemont@club-internet.fr ⱱ
Ⓨ ev. day 9am–12 noon 2pm–6pm

PIERRE PARENT 1999 €5-8

☐ 1.13 ha 4,400

This wine is forthcoming on the nose, and offers those nuances of acacia and linden flowers so characteristic of Romorantin wines. On the palate, the fresh impression suggests that it would be the ideal wine to drink now with freshwater fish (pike or perch).

☛ Pierre Parent, 201, rue de Chancelée,
41250 Mont-Près-Chambord,
tel. 02.54.70.73.57, fax 02.54.70.89.72 ⱱ
Ⓨ by appt.

DOM. PHILIPPE TESSIER 1999★★ €5-8

☐ 2 ha 10,000

Last year, the estate's Le Point du Jour 99 was awarded the *coup de cœur* for the AOC Cheverny. This year sees the reappearance of Philippe Tessier, who took over the estate in 1988, for this organically-produced Cour-Cheverny: a seductive wine of a golden-amber colour, due to the perfectly ripe grapes. It reveals charming, intense aromas of honey and acacia blossom. The palate develops in a very well-balanced fashion, to give a wine with considerable potential.

☛ EARL Philippe Tessier, 3, voie de la rue Colin, 41700 Cheverny, tel. 02.54.44.23.82, fax 02.54.44.21.71 ⱱ Ⓨ by appt.

☛ Christian Tessier, Dom. de La Désoucherie, 41700 Cour-Cheverny, tel. 02.54.79.90.08, fax 02.54.79.22.48, e-mail christian.tessier@waika9.com ⱱ
Ⓨ by appt.

DOM. DE LA GAUDRONNIERE €5-8
Mûr Mûr de la Gaudronnière 1999★

☐ 1.45 ha 2,200

The grapes for this attractive, straw-coloured wine are picked towards the end of October. The resulting wine is strongly flavoured, with hints of honey, acacia and toast blending perfectly. A well-balanced palate bodes well for the future of this wine.

☛ Christian Dorléans, Dom. de La Gaudronnière, 41120 Cellettes, tel. 02.54.70.40.41, fax 02.54.70.38.83 ⱱ
Ⓨ by appt.

LE PETIT CHAMBORD 1999★ €5-8

☐ 4.3 ha 25,000

The Romorantin is the oldest vine-stock planted on the estate, and is the one that François Cazin uses to make this fine 99, with its golden-yellow colour reflecting the ripeness of the grapes. A full palate leads into a honeyed, mineral finish. With 9 g/l residual sugar, this medium-dry wine may be aged in the cellar.

☛ François Cazin, Le Petit Chambord, 41700 Cheverny, tel. 02.54.79.93.75, fax 02.54.79.27.89 ⱱ Ⓨ by appt.

PHILIPPE LOQUINEAU
Fleurs de Lis 1999

☐ 1.5 ha 6,000

The product of a vineyard currently being converted to organic methods, this wine develops aromas of linden flowers on the nose. This Fleurs de Lis is a balanced wine with an agreeable presence on the palate.

☛ Philippe Loquineau, Dom. de La Plante d'Or, La Demalerie, 41700 Cheverny, tel. 02.54.44.23.09, fax 02.54.44.22.16 ⱱ
Ⓨ by appt.

DOM. DE MONTCY 2000★ €5-8

☐ 1.7 ha 5,200

Forty-year-old vines produce the grapes that went into this golden-coloured, classic appellation wine. Its exotic (mango) and floral aromas, together with its good overall harmony, are going to delight the wine-enthusiast. This estate was awarded the *coup de cœur* for its 98 vintage.

☛ R. et S. Simon, La Porte dorée,
32, rte de Fougères, 41700 Cheverny,
tel. 02.54.44.20.00, fax 02.54.44.20.50,
e-mail domaine-de-montcy@wanadoo.fr
ⱱ Ⓨ ev. day except Sun. 10am–12 noon 2pm–6pm; Sat. by appt.; cl. 26 Aug.–6 Sept.

LES VIGNERONS DE MONT-PRES-CHAMBORD 1999 €5-8

☐ 9 ha 30,000

Forty-year-old vines have produced a beautifully golden-coloured wine, a little closed on

peppery aromas. The whites, made from Chenin, resemble those from the neighbouring AOC Coteaux de Loire and Jasnières, which are grown on similar soils.

The range of red wines is a newer development, in response to consumer demand. The delicately spicy liveliness of the Pineau d'Aunis is combined with Gamay for smoothness, and either improved in finesse by including Pinot Noir or in tannin by using Cabernet.

On average, production is 10,000 hl (264,000 gal). Visitors can enjoy walking by the Loir and exploring the surrounding hillsides with their 'troglodyte' cave dwellings and cellars carved out of the tuffeau.

DOM. DU CARROIR Tradition 2000★

6 ha   10,000   €3-5

Ronsard, in one of his Epicurean songs, said that you need to know 'where good wine is sold.' There can be no doubt that this estate has come up with one such wine: this fine blend with its aromas of red berries. It opens firmly, with silky tannins clearly evident, an encouraging sign for the future. The **white 2000** is a rich wine, singled out by the Jury for its suppleness and unctuousness on the palate. It is a thoroughbred Vendômois.

✦ GAEC Jean et Benoît Brazilier, 17, rue des Ecoles, 41100 Thoré-la-Rochette, tel. 02.54.72.81.72, fax 02.54.72.77.13
Y by appt.

DOM. CHEVAIS 2000★

0.34 ha   2,500   €5-8

This estate is situated a few kilometres (about a mile and a half) from one of the prettiest villages in the Vendômois, Lavardin: the village church owns an exceptional collection of murals, the oldest of which date back to the 12th century. This pale-yellow wine offers hints of white peach and apple. It is an elegant, rich wine that opens well and persists on the palate. The Jury were also impressed by the **Vin Gris**, which was singled out for its characteristic pale-pink colour, its elegance and freshness.

✦ GAEC Chevais Frères, Les Portes, 41800 Houssay, tel. 02.54.85.30.34
Y by appt.

PATRICE COLIN Gris 2000★

6 ha   9,000

The initial attraction is provided by the colour of this *vin gris*: pink with orange highlights. Then you notice the excellent aromatic intensity so characteristic of the Pineau d'Aunis, and the fine balance, both of which confirm the potential inherent in the wine's colour. The **Cuvée Pierre-François 2000 red** impressed the Jury with the complexity of its aromas and its roundness on the palate; it is a pleasant wine ready for drinking. Then there is the **Pentes des Coutis 2000 white**, a pale-yellow Chenin which is still rather reserved on the nose, but which has a seductive personality all the same.

✦ Patrice Colin, Dom. Gaudetterie, 41100 Thoré-la-Rochette, tel. 02.54.72.80.73; fax 02.54.72.75.54
Y by appt.

DOM. DU FOUR A CHAUX 2000

2 ha   9,000   €3-5

The lime kiln which gives its name to this estate is characteristic of the Thoré-la-Rochette region, and can be found on the premises; it has since been restored, and can be visited. The estate is also of interest for its wines, of course, including this brilliant pale-yellow-coloured white wine: an elegant one that is worth ageing a while in order to behold its true potential. The Jury also singled out the **Coteaux du Vendômois 2000 red**, with its violet highlights and great charm. It is also young, and will repay cellaring.

✦ GAEC Dominique Norguet, Berger, 41100 Thoré-la-Rochette, tel. 02.54.77.12.52, fax 02.54.77.86.18
Y by appt.

CHARLES JUMERT 2000★

1.3 ha   4,000   €3-5

Of the three wines Charles Jumert presented, it was this *vin gris* that got the Jury's vote. A very characteristic pale colour with salmon-pink reflections, it possesses surprising balance and freshness on the palate. The **white 2000**, a fresh, well-balanced wine, was singled out, as was the **red 2000**, which is an exciting wine with aromas of cherry and blueberry and a youthful palate. Both are ready to drink immediately.

✦ Charles Jumert, 4, rue de la Berthelotière, 41100 Villiers-sur-Loir, tel. 02.54.72.94.09, fax 02.54.72.94.09
Y by appt.

DOM. DE LA CHARLOTTERIE Gris 2000★

0.75 ha   4,000   €5-8

With a perfect pink colour, and a subtle nose with floral notes, this *vin gris* also displays balance and freshness on the finish. It's a fine example of a Coteaux du Vendômois. Equally successful was the **red Tradition**, which was awarded the *coup de cœur* in the 1998 edition of the *Guide*. The 2000 has all the makings of an excellent wine: a beautiful colour (a sign of the ripeness of its young tannins. It was also awarded one star by the Jury. The **white 2000** was singled out for its elegant, rich nose, and is ready to drink now.

✦ Dominique Houdebert,
2, rue du Bas-Bourg, 41100 Villiersfaux, tel. 02.54.80.29.79, fax 02.54.73.10.01
Y by appt.

Valençay AOVDQS

DOM. J. MARTELLIÈRE
Réserve Jean Vivien 2000★

■　　　　2 ha　　6,000　■ ⅢⅡ €3-5

This estate presents two interesting wines, both red. This first wine offers aromas of red berries which flatter both nose and palate. It has a round palate, but where the rather angular tannins need time to mature; this means it is a wine to wait for. The **Cuvée Balzac** is ready for drinking straight away: a bright cherry colour, it is also balanced on the palate, and impressed the Jury, as did the **Cuvée Jasmine 2000**. This is a *vin gris* made from Pineau d'Aunis. Its very pale colour and peppery aromas are characteristic of this grape variety.

●➤ SCEA du Dom. J. Martellière, 46, rue de Fosse, 41800 Montoire-sur-le-Loir, tel. 02.54.85.16.91, fax 02.54.85.16.91 ☑
❦ by appt.

CLAUDE MINIER 2000

■　　n.c.　　n.c.　■ ⅢⅡ ◇ €3-5

Two of this estate's wines especially impressed the Jury: a pleasant **rosé 2000**, supple initially and well-balanced overall; and this red, which is very powerful on the palate with aromas of soft red fruits. It is a wine that needs to be matured for a further few months.

●➤ GAEC Claude Minier, Les Monts, 41360 Lunay, tel. 02.54.72.02.36, fax 02.54.72.18.52 ☑ ❦ by appt.

DOM. JACQUES NOURY
Rouge Tradition 2000★

■　　1.1 ha　6,000　■ ⅢⅡ €3-5

Near to the very attractive village there are a number of cellars inside cave dwellings cut into the hillside. The Jury loved this wine, with its colourful appearance and its aromas of morello cherry and blackcurrant. Its well-balanced palate and still-evident tannins are signs that this wine will improve with age. The **white 2000**, singled out by the Jury, is a typical, crisp appellation wine, and should be served with a dish of seafood.

●➤ Dom. Jacques Noury, Montpot, 41800 Houssay, tel. 02.54.85.36.04, fax 02.54.85.19.30 ☑ ❦ by appt.

LES VIGNERONS DU VENDÔMOIS Gris 2000★

◢　　9 ha　60,000　■ ⌖ €3-5

The wall paintings in the church of Villiers-sur-Loir are well worth seeing. They depict scenes from the life of Saint Éloi, together with a strange version of the 16th-century 'three dead' and 'three alive.' Then, pleased with the fact that you belong to the latter category, you should pay a visit to the cellar of the Vignerons du Vendômois. They present a characteristic *vin gris*, with good balance on the palate, and a pleasing freshness on the finish. It is a very attractive wine overall. On the other hand, you may prefer their **white 2000**, an appealing wine with slightly lemony aromas and a lengthy palate, that was singled out by the Jury.

●➤ Cave des Vignerons du Vendômois, 60, av. du Petit-Thouars, 41100 Villiers-sur-Loir, tel. 02.54.72.90.69, fax 02.54.72.75.09 ☑
❦ ev. day except Sun. Mon. 9am–12 noon 2pm–6pm

Valençay AOVDQS

Bordering Berry, Sologne and the Touraine is an area of mixed agriculture, forestry and husbandry (particularly goat-rearing) in which the vine plays its part. The soils are mainly clay and silica or alluvial clay. There are more than 300 ha (741 acres) under vines, half of which is declared as Valençay, offering wines for early drinking from the classic varieties of this part of the Loire. Sauvignon produces aromatic wines with notes of blackcurrant or broom, and an added fullness when mixed with Chardonnay. The red wines are assembled from Gamay, Cabernet, Côt and Pinot Noir in various proportions. Production in 2000 was 1,386 hl (36,590) of white wine and 3,330 hl (87,912 gal) of red.

The great French statesman Talleyrand (1754–1838) had strong associations with the Valençay region, which is also famous for its goat's cheese, awarded an AOC in 1998. Depending on how mature they are, the little pyramids of goat's cheese will accompany any of Valençay's red and white wines.

JACKY ET PHILIPPE AUGIS 2000★

▢　　1.2 ha　8,000　■ ⌖ €3-5

Pale-yellow with green highlights, this Valençay reveals complex aromas of apples, pears, honey and acacia. It opens well on the palate, before finishing on a very refreshing note. The same producer also presents a richly-coloured **Valençay 2000 red**, a wine enhanced by a clean nose and a well-rounded palate, which especially impressed the Jury.

●➤ GAEC Jacky et Philippe Augis, Le Musa, rue des Vignes, 41130 Meusnes, tel. 02.54.71.01.89, fax 02.54.71.74.15, e-mail paugis@net-up.com ☑
❦ ev. day except Sun. 8am–12 noon 2pm–7.30pm; cl. 15–31 Aug.

DOM. BARDON 2000★

3 ha — 15,000 — €5-8

Two Valençay wines were presented by this producer: one red and one white, each of which was awarded a star. The attractively-coloured red, with violet highlights further enhancing its appearance, offers a whole basketful of soft fruit on the nose, which together with its rounded palate makes it a very attractive wine. The **white 2000** is characterised by its golden-yellow hue, the sign of a well-made wine which does the appellation proud.

● Dom. Denis Bardon,
22, rue Paul-Couton, 41130 Meusnes,
tel. 02.54.71.01.10, fax 02.54.71.75.20
Y by appt.

CLOS DU CHATEAU DE VALENCAY 2000★

1.5 ha — 12,000 — €3-5

The red and white, both from the same vintage, were awarded a star each. The red reveals a rather shy, albeit promising, nose, while the palate expresses the true harmony of the local *terroir*. It is an easy wine to drink throughout the meal. The fruity **white** has aromas of pear drops, and boasts a refreshing finish.

● SCEV Clos du Château de Valençay,
Chez Hubert Sinson, 41130 Meusnes,
tel. 02.54.71.00.26, fax 02.54.71.50.93
Y by appt.

DOM. FRANCK CHUET 2000

0.5 ha — 4,000 — €3-5

This brightly-coloured Valençay offers interesting aromas of red berries with just a hint of caramel. It should be drunk immediately.

● Dom. Franck Chuet, rue Debussy,
41130 Meusnes, tel. 02.54.71.01.06 Y ev. day except Sun. 8am-12 noon 1.30pm-7pm

CHANTAL ET PATRICK GIBAULT 2000★

2 ha — 12,000 — €3-5

Still a rather young wine, this producer's **white 2000** was awarded one star for its promising character. As for this red 2000, it evokes soft fruits throughout. A wine with the taste of its *terroir*, and with a surprisingly balanced nature.

● EARL Chantal et Patrick Gibault,
183, rue Gambetta, 41130 Meusnes,
tel. 02.54.71.02.63, fax 02.54.71.58.92,
e-mail gibault.earl@wanadoo.fr
Y ev. day 8am-7pm; Sun. 10am-12 noon

FRANCIS JOURDAIN

Cuvée des Griottes 2000★

1.5 ha — 8,000 — €3-5

Francis Jourdain, who won a *coup de cœur* in the 2000 *Guide* for the estate's 98 *cuvée*, this year presents three wines, each of which was awarded one star. The **white Cuvée Chevrefeuille** has a nose that mirrors the complexity of the *terroir*, and a well-balanced palate which leads into a smoky finish. The

red **Cuvée Terroir** is a blend of Gamay, Pinot Noir and Côt/Malbec. An attractive ruby-coloured wine, it reveals a supple, silky palate, and is ready for drinking straight away. As for this wine, the deep colour supports a generous nose of soft red fruit, and the wine goes on to fill the palate. It has considerable ageing potential.

● Francis Jourdain, Les Moreaux,
36600 Lye, tel. 02.54.41.01.45,
fax 02.54.41.07.56 Y by appt.

MONTBAIL 2000★

2 ha — 13,000 — €3-5

Sauvignon and Chardonnay are blended to produce this fine, pale-coloured Valençay. While the nose may appear a little closed, the palate is full and powerful. It is ready to drink, perhaps with fresh river fish or *feuilleté d'escargots*.

● Dom. Garnier, 81, rue Eugène-Delacroix,
Chamberlin, 41130 Meusnes,
tel. 02.54.00.10.06, fax 02.54.05.13.36
Y by appt.

DOM. JACKY PREYS ET FILS

Cuvée Princière 2000

n.c. — n.c. — €3-5

Two of the estate's 2000 reds were singled out by the Jury: the **Cuvée Prestige**, a blend of Gamay, Pinot Noir and Côt/Malbec, which promises great things in years to come; and this wine, which releases a rose fragrance on the nose. Although it is still rather young, it will last years, thanks to its tannins.

● Dom. Jacky Preys et Fils, Bois Pontois,
41130 Meusnes, tel. 02.54.71.00.34
Y by appt.

JEAN-FRANCOIS ROY 1999★

6 ha — 48,000 — €3-5

This beautiful, ruby-red Valençay with orange highlights is the product of a flinty clay soil, and is a blend of 50% Gamay, 35% Pinot Noir and 15% Côt/Malbec. The nose reflects the subtle aromas of the Pinot Noir, while its balanced palate and fruity flavours make it a well-made wine. One star was also awarded to the **Valençay 2000 white**: an intensely aromatic wine that opens cleanly and develops an all-embracing palate redolent with citrus fruit.

● Jean-François Roy, 3, rue des Acacias,
36600 Lye, tel. 02.54.41.00.39,
fax 02.54.41.06.89 Y by appt.

HUBERT SINSON ET FILS

Prestige 2000★

6 ha — 15,000 — €3-5

This estate has seen four generations of wine-makers, and continues to produce some much-loved wines. First of all, there is this red wine (a blend of 40% Gamay, 40% Pinot Noir and 20% Côt/Malbec), with its powerful, elegant nose that merges into a balanced, classy palate. The firm tannins in the finish are a signature of Côt/Malbec, and guarantee this wine a long life. Next is the **Valençay 2000 white**, an elegant young wine which also received one star. Finally, there is the **Cuvée Michel Denisot 2000 red**, singled out for its aromas of fruit (particularly blackberries), its balanced palate and its tannic finish.

➤ GAEC Hubert Sinson et Fils, 1397, rue des Vignes, 41130 Meusnes, tel. 02.54.71.00.26, fax 02.54.71.50.93 ☑ ⊻ ev. day 8am–12 noon 2pm–6pm; Sun. by appt.; cl. 15–31 Aug.

CAVE DES VIGNERONS REUNIS DE VALENCAY Terroir 2000
☐   3.7 ha   29,000   ▮ ◆   €3-5

This co-operative, set up in 1964, presents two wines, both of which were singled out. Firstly, this pleasant white Valençay, made from very ripe grapes, impressed the Jury with its clean, fresh character. Next is the **Terroir 2000 red**, a smooth red in its ruby finery. It should be drunk slightly chilled.

➤ Cave des Vignerons Réunis de Valençay, 36600 Fontguenand, tel. 02.54.00.16.11, fax 02.54.00.05.55, e-mail vigneronvalencay@aol.com ☑ ⊻ ev. day except Sun. 8am–12 noon 2pm–6pm; groups by appt.

Poitou

Haut-Poitou AOVDQS

In 1865 Dr Guyot reported that the Vienne vineyard covered 33,560 ha (82,893 acres). Nowadays, apart from the vineyard attached to the Saumur area in the north of the department, wine-growing is reduced to the area around the cantons of Neuville and Mirebeau. Marigny-Brizay is the commune with the largest number of individual growers. The others grouped together to set up the Cave de Neuville-de-Poitou. The wines of Haut-Poitou produced 28,324 hl (747,754 gal) in 2000, 14,320 (378,048 gal) of which were whites.

The soils of the Neuville plateau, a mixture of limestone and Marigny clay as well as marl, are well suited to the different varieties of this appellation; the best known of them is Sauvignon (for white wines).

CAVE DU HAUT-POITOU 2000
▮   10 ha   95,000   ▮ ◆   €3-5

The Cave du Haut-Poitou was set up in 1948, and it produces 90% of the appellation's wines. This red is made from a blend of three grape varieties: Gamay, Pinot Noir and Cabernet Franc. It possesses the lightness and the aromatic character found in the red wines of the Loire (notes of red berries such as strawberry and raspberry) with a hint of liveliness on the palate. It is ready to enjoy now.

➤ SA Cave du Haut-Poitou, 32, rue Alphonse-Plault, 86170 Neuville-de-Poitou, tel. 05.49.51.21.65, fax 05.49.51.16.07, e-mail c-h.p@wanadoo.fr ☑ ⊻ by appt.

DOM. DE LA GRANDE MAISON 2000★
▮   1 ha   7,200   ▮ ◆   €3-5

Marigny-Brizay is situated on a limestone hillock that is well-known within the appellation. The estate, which lies 3 km (1.9 miles) from the Futuroscope Park, has made a full-bodied Cabernet that is pleasant and easy to drink. A dark-garnet colour defines the wine, together with floral and vegetal aromas, and a hint of red berries. The palate is well-balanced and rounded, while the finish is just slightly tannic.

➤ GAEC Grassien Lassale, Saint-Léger-la-Palu, 86380 Marigny-Brizay, tel. 05.49.52.08.73, fax 05.49.62.33.73 ☑ ⊻ ev. day except Sat. Sun. 9am–7pm

DOM. DE LA ROTISSERIE Cabernet 2000★
▮   3.5 ha   10,000   ▮   €3-5

Before the Haut-Poitou vineyard was granted VDQS status, this estate was called the *Domaine des Coteaux de Marigny*. The cellar is cut out of the local tuffeau. Two 2000 reds were each awarded a star. This Cabernet, with its bright-red colour, offers intense aromas of fresh fruit, an agreeable, fresh palate and a rather austere finish. Secondly, a **Gamay** offers soft fruit perfumes with just a hint of animal leather, together with a powerful palate indicating considerable body.

➤ Jacques Baudon, 35, rue de l'Habit-d'Or, 86380 Marigny-Brizay, tel. 05.49.52.09.02, fax 05.49.37.11.44 ☑ ⊻ ev. day except Sat. Sun. 8am–12 noon 1.30pm–7pm

DOM. DE LA TOUR SIGNY Cuvée Poitevine 2000★★
▮   6 ha   15,000   ▮   €3-5

This 15-ha (37-acre) estate has produced a remarkably fine, balanced wine from a mixture of Cabernet (40%) and Gamay (60%). It is a garnet colour, with complex aromas of red berries, spices and vanilla, followed by a rich, lively, well-structured palate. A stylish and characteristic wine from this vineyard.

➤ Christophe Croux, Dom. de La Tour Signy, 2 rue de Tue-Loup, 86380 Marigny-Brizay, tel. 05.49.55.31.21, fax 05.49.62.36.82 ☑ ⊻ by appt.

this wine has intense aromas of fruit and spices and a firm, fruity palate. The wine and the estate are both well worth getting to know.

🛒 Pascale Bonneau,
pl. du Champ-de-Foire, 86110 Mirebeau,
tel. 05.49.50.53.66, fax 05.49.50.90.50,
e-mail pascale.bonneau@libertysurf.fr ✅
🕐 ev. day except Sun. 8am–7.30pm; Sat.
9.30am–7pm

Wines from Central France

From the hills of Forez to the Orléans area, the main wine-growing sectors of the Centre are located on the best exposed sites of hills and plateaux eroded through successive geological eras by the Loire and its tributaries, the Allier and the Cher. These areas, on the hillsides of the Côtes d'Auvergne, in parts of Saint-Pourçain and Châteaumeillant, are located on the eastern and northern flanks of the Massif Central, and yet still open onto the Loire basin.

The vine-growing soils are either silica or limestone, always well situated and exposed, sustaining a limited number of varieties of which the most common are Gamay for red and rosé wines and Sauvignon for white wines. A few special local varieties are grown here and there: the Tressallier at Saint-Pourçain and the Chasselas at Pouilly-sur-Loire for whites; Pinot Noir at Sancerre, Menetou-Salon and Reuilly for reds and rosés, plus the delicate Pinot Gris, again in the latter vineyard; finally, the Meunier which, near Orléans, makes the original Gris Meunier. When all is said and done, it is a notably rich selection.

Whatever the *terroir*, all the wines made from these varieties share a light, fresh and fruity character which makes them particularly appealing, pleasant and drinkable, especially when matched with the gastronomic specialities of the region. The green, peaceful countryside of the Auvergne, the Bourbonnais, the Nivernais, the Berry or the Orléanais encompasses a region of wide horizons and varied landscapes. The wines are grown in vineyards that are often family-owned and run in traditional ways, and, secure in their roots and traditions, the wine-makers are expert in showing off their worthy wines to best advantage.

DOM. DES LISES 1.2 ha 4,000 €3-5 Cabernet 2000

Pascale Bonneau, an oenologist by profession, took over the family estate in 1995, and the following year built a vinification cellar situated at the entrance to the medieval town of Mirebeau, in the château quarter. His wine has a full body, with that necessary touch of young tannins on the finish. A rich red colour,

Châteaumeillant AOVDQS

Châteaumeillant AOVDQS

Here, the Gamay is raised on *terroirs* of volcanic soils, in an old established wine region. In 2000 this covered 84 ha (208 acres) with an output of 4,770 hl (125,928 gal).

The reputation of Châteaumeillant was founded on its famous *gris*, a wine made from the first pressing of Gamay grapes, and notable for its remarkable texture, freshness and fruitiness. The reds (which should be drunk young and chilled), combine bouquet, smoothness and sheer drinkability.

DOM. DU CHAILLOT 2000★
■ 3.5 ha ■ 30,000 ■ ♦ €5–8

Produced from vines grown on a *terroir* of mica schists and Tertiary sediment, this wine smells of blackcurrants and fresh-grape brandy. On the palate, tannins are light and well-integrated. A rather reserved wine, but one with clear definition and character.
➤ Dom. du Chaillot, pl. de la Tournoise, 18130 Dun-sur-Auron, tel. 02.48.59.57.69, fax 02.48.59.58.78, e-mail pierre.picot@ wanadoo.fr ☑ Ⴒ by appt.
➤ Pierre Picot

VALERIE ET FREDERIC DALLOT
Tradition 1999
■ 3 ha ■ 7,000 ■ ♦ €3–5

This wine is a light-ruby colour, with notes of amber at the rim showing maturity. The nose is elegantly fruity and ripe (cherry jam), and the palate is smooth, with light, supple tannins.
➤ Frédéric et Valérie Dallot, 42, rue Saint-Genest, 18370 Châteaumeillant, tel. 02.48.56.31.84 ☑ Ⴒ by appt.

DOM. GEOFFRENET MORVAL
Cuvée Jeanne Vieilles Vignes 2000★
■ 0.5 ha ■ 3,000 ■ ♦ €5–8

Laure and Fabien Geoffrenet are new producers who took over this old vineyard in 2000. Their first wine is the product of vines that are more than 50 years old. Both aroma and palate show flavours of cherry and woody herbs. Tannins are firm and silky, and the finish has hints of leather and black tea. This wine will benefit from one to two years in the cellar, and will be a good match for poultry.
➤ EARL Geoffrenet Morval,
2, rue de La Fontaine, 18190 Venesmes, tel. 02.48.60.50.15, fax 02.48.24.62.91 ☑ Ⴒ by appt.

Châteaumeillant AOVDQS

DOM. LANOIX 2000
■ 3 ha ■ 18,000 ■ ♦ €3–5

This wine is full of surprises. Its colour is onion-skin pale, but the nose is rich with aromas of cooked plums and fruit pits. The palate is supple, round and warming. This wine is ready to drink now.
➤ EARL Dom. Patrick Lanoix, Beaumerle, 18370 Châteaumeillant, tel. 02.48.61.39.59, fax 02.48.61.42.19 ☑ Ⴒ by appt.

LEGIER DE LA CHASSAIGNE 2000★
■ 6.2 ha ■ 43,000 ■ ♦ €3–5

Produced by the co-operative, this wine bears the name of the person who, in 1753, introduced vines from Lyon. The wine's colour is dark, ruby-garnet, with hints of black. Aromas of strawberry and raspberry are enveloped in a light smoky veil, and titillate both nose and taste buds. The tannins are still young and angular, but will mature with time. A fine wine to serve with red meat in sauce.
➤ Cave du Tivoli, rte de Culan,
18370 Châteaumeillant, tel. 02.48.61.33.55, fax 02.48.61.44.92, e-mail chateaumeillant@ wanadoo.fr ☑ Ⴒ ev day 8am–12 noon 1.30pm–5.30pm; cl. Sun. July–April

DOM. DES TANNERIES 2000★
■ 5 ha ■ 25,000 ■ ♦ €5–8

Nohant, home of the writer George Sand, lies only 18 km (11 miles) from this Châteaumeillant vineyard. This wine has a noticeably spicy character, with notes of pepper and smoke on the nose. A meaty palate leads into young, somewhat rebellious tannins. Time in the cellar will bring maturity, and show a well-made wine.
➤ Raffinat et Fils, Dom. des Tanneries, 18370 Châteaumeillant, tel. 02.48.61.35.16, fax 02.48.61.44.27 ☑ Ⴒ by appt.

Côtes d'Auvergne AOVDQS

Whether grown on the volcanic hills called *puys*, in Limagne, or on the hills (*dômes*) on the eastern edge of the Massif Central, Auvergne wines are made with the Gamay variety, which has been cultivated in the region for centuries, as well as Pinot Noir for red and rosé wines and Chardonnay for the whites. Produced from about 374 ha (924 acres) of vines, these wines have had the right to the denomination AOVDQS since

1977. The unusual rosés and easy-drinking reds (two-thirds of the production) are particularly recommended as companions for the famous local charcuterie and regional dishes. The best growths can acquire surprising character, fullness and personality. In 2000, 17,360 hl (458,304 gal) were produced, including 496 hl (13,094 gal) of white wine.

JACQUES ABONNAT Boudes 2000
2.5 ha   9,000

This estate is situated at Chalus, a strategic point of old, overlooking the Lembron. This wine is a lively, bright-red colour. In taste it is both youthful and generous, and as such should be kept for a while before drinking.

Jacques Abonnat, 63340 Chalus, tel. 04.73.96.45.95, fax 04.73.96.45.95   by appt.

MICHEL BLOT
Boudes Cuvée d'Antan 2000★
0.3 ha   1,700

The beautiful, dark-red colour of this wine is a sign of its perfect health. A spicy nose and a generous, fleshy palate, with a hint of warmth on the finish, complete the picture. Tannins are firm but silky, making this an altogether enjoyable wine.

Michel Blot, 63340 Boudes, tel. 04.73.96.41.42, fax 04.73.96.58.34, e-mail sauvat@terre-net.fr   ev. day except Sun. 9am–12 noon 2pm–7pm

HENRI BOURCHEIX-OLLIER
Chanturgue 2000
1.3 ha   6,600

A wine that smacks of cherry right the way through, from its colour to its nose. A crisp finish makes this Côtes d'Auvergne a refreshing wine.

Henri Bourcheix, 4, rue Saint-Marc, 63170 Aubière, tel. 04.73.26.04.52, fax 04.73.27.96.46   by appt.

NOEL BRESSOULALY 2000★★
2 ha   10,000

Noël Bressoulaly has set up a living museum to preserve old Auvergne wine stocks. He uses Gamay and Pinot Noir to make this Côtes d'Auvergne red, with its purple and violet hues and a remarkable nose. The spicy scents blend closely with aromas of morello cherry, on both nose and palate. An extremely well-balanced palate and a stimulating character make this a very intriguing wine.

Noël Bressoulaly, chem. des Pales, 63114 Authezat, tel. 04.73.24.18.01, fax 04.73.24.18.01   by appt.

CHARMENSAT Boudes Cuvée Grandes Vignes Elevé en Fût de Chêne 2000
0.2 ha   1,000

Boudes has preserved the vestiges of its ancient fort, together with a Romanesque church whose steeple features on this wine's label. On the nose, it releases scents of tobacco, while the palate is fresh and mouth-watering. A wine that would go well with a selection of local cheeses.

GAEC Charmensat, rue du Coufin, 63340 Boudes, tel. 04.73.96.44.75, fax 04.73.96.58.04, e-mail charmensat@lokace-online.com   by appt.

PIERRE GOIGOUX
Châteaugay 2000★★
1.7 ha   11,000

This estate is situated about 500 m (545 yd) from the 14th-century Château de Châteaugay, with its crenellated tower. It has produced a clear, salmon-pink wine with aromas of very ripe red fruits. A rounded palate, well-balanced and elegant, makes this one of the best wines in the region. The Jury also singled out the estate's Côtes d'Auvergne 2000 red: cherry-coloured, with a red-fruit nose and pleasant palate.

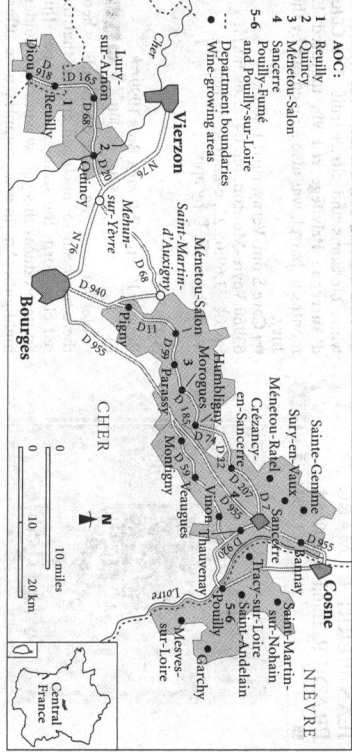

AOC:
1   Reuilly
2   Quincy
3   Menetou-Salon
4   Sancerre
5–6   Pouilly-Fumé and Pouilly-sur-Loire
···   Wine-growing areas
Department boundaries

Wines from Central France

Côtes d'Auvergne AOVDQS

This cherry-red wine with violet highlights received unanimous approval from the Jury. A distinctive nose of very ripe red fruits with a hint of pear-drops precedes a soft, rather delicate palate. Silky tannins accompany a long, fragrant finish. The Jury gave one star to this producer's **white 2000**, and singled out the **rosé 2000 du Cru Corent**, with its lovely 'partridge-eye' colour.

☞ Jean-Pierre et Marc Pradier,
9, rue Saint-Jean-Baptiste, 63730 Les Martres-de-Veyre, tel. 04.73.39.86.41, fax 04.73.39.88.17  Y by appt.

CHRISTOPHE ROMEUF 2000★ €3-5

3.5 ha   n.c.

A beautiful garnet-red colour with hints of orange, this 2000 boasts a full, rich nose followed by a well-balanced palate. Tannins are firm yet silky on the finish.

☞ Christophe Romeuf, 1 *bis*, rue du Couvent, 63670 Orcet, tel. 06.08.85.01.69, fax 06.73.84.07.83  Y by appt.

DOM. ROUGEYRON

Châteaugay Cuvée Bousset d'Or 2000★ ▣ ▪ ♦ €5-8

1.7 ha   13,300

In the Limagne, each village church has a statue of Saint Verny, patron saint of wine-growers. He is usually represented complete with his possessions: a vine, a beggar's pouch, a little hoe and a cask. This wine is a bright, straw colour; proof of wine-making expertise. On the nose are hints of almond, and the palate is warming, unctuous and powerful.

☞ Michel et Roland Rougeyron, 27, rue de La Crouzette, 63119 Châteaugay, tel. 04.73.87.24.45, fax 04.73.87.23.55, e-mail domainerougeyron@terre-net.fr  Y by appt.

CAVE SAINT-VERNY

Première Cuvée 2000★ ▣ ▪ ♦ €3-5

35 ha   60,000

This winery, placed under the protection of Saint Verny, patron-saint of wine-makers, presents three excellent wines. This, the first, is a deep cherry-red colour, and reveals fresh and youthful aromas. On the palate, the silky tannins blend perfectly with the roundness of the finish. The Jury also awarded one star to the **rosé 2000 du Cru Corent**, with aromas of white blossoms and citrus fruit. The **Côtes d'Auvergne Privilège red 99**, matured 12 months in barrel, was also singled out by the Jury.

☞ Cave Saint-Verny, rte d'Issoire, 63960 Veyre-Monton, tel. 04.73.69.60.11, fax 04.73.69.65.22, e-mail saint.verny@ wanadoo.fr  Y by appt.

SAUVAT

Boudes Prestige Elevage Bois 1999★★ ▣ ▣ €8-11

1.5 ha   4,000

Not far from the Vallée des Saints, where there has been so much soil erosion that the red clays form the strangest of shapes, this estate produces this yellow wine with golden highlights. An intense, complex nose offers

---

☞ GAEC Pierre Goigoux,
22, rue des Caves, 63119 Châteaugay, tel. 04.73.87.67.51, fax 04.73.78.02.70  Y ev. day 10am–11.30am 3pm–6.30pm; by appt. 15 Sept.–15 April

ODETTE ET GILLES MIOLANNE

Volcane 2000★★ ▣ ▪ ♦ €5-8

1.15 ha   5,000

A fine salmon colour, the result of a particularly successful blend of Gamay and Pinot Noir. Fragrant, and with a well-balanced palate, this wine does its appellation proud.

☞ EARL de La Sardissère, 17, rte de Coudes, 63320 Neschers, tel. 04.73.96.72.45, fax 04.73.96.25.79, e-mail gilles.miolanne@ wanadoo.fr  Y by appt.
☞ Odette et Gilles Miolanne

GILLES PERSILIER Gergovia 2000★★ €5-8

1 ha   4,000

As the name of this remarkable wine suggests, the estate has taken Vercingétorix (ancient leader of the Gauls, who fought an important battle at the ancient city of Gergovia) as its symbol, and it has certainly won a clear victory with this lemon-yellow wine. The intensity of aromas on the nose, a combination of citrus fruit and hazelnuts, comes as something of a surprise. With its supple palate, this is a truly elegant, classy wine.

☞ Gilles Persilier, 27, rue Jean-Jaurès, 63670 Gergovie, tel. 04.73.79.44.42, fax 04.73.87.56.95  Y by appt.

YOHANNA ET BENOIT
PORTEILLA Cuvée de la Louve 2000 ▣ ▪ ♦ €3-5

1 ha   4,500

This wine is produced from vines growing on basalt soil near to the small village of Dallet. A strong red-garnet colour, it has good balance on the palate, but needs further time in the cellar before its potential can be fully appreciated.

☞ Porteilla, Caveau de Loup, 4, imp. de la Halle, 63111 Dallet, tel. 04.73.83.05.21, fax 04.73.23.05.21, e-mail caveaudeloup@ wanadoo.fr  Y ev. day 10am–6pm; Sun. 10am–1pm; groups by appt.; cl. 1–15 Sept.

JEAN-PIERRE ET MARC
PRADIER Tradition 2000★★ ▣ ▪ ♦ €3-5

3 ha   12,000

---

vanilla and citrus-fruit aromas, followed by a supple, delicate, rather unctuous palate. A woody note adds to a beautifully complex finish. The **Prestige Boudes Elevé Sous Bois 1999 red** received one star, as did the **Demoiselles Oubliées du Donazat Boudes 2000 red**.

• Claude et Annie Sauvat, 63240 Boudes, tel. 04.73.96.41.42, fax 04.73.96.58.34, e-mail sauvat@terre-net.fr ☒ Y ev. day 9am–12 noon 2pm–7pm; Sun. 3pm–7pm

Côtes du Forez

Great efforts have gone into maintaining this smart and spectacular vineyard, covering 181 ha (447 acres) in 21 communes around Boën-sur-Lignon (Loire).

Nearly all the excellent dry, robust rosé and red wines, made exclusively from Gamay, are grown on Tertiary terrains in the north and Primary soils in the south. Production comes mainly from a splendid Cave Coopérative. These wines which received an AOC in the year 2000, when production amounted to 6,863 hl (181,183 gal), are best drunk young.

GILLES BONNEFOY
La Madone 2000★★

0.4 ha	2,000	€3-5

At Champdieu, stop and visit the Auvergne-style Romanesque Benedictine church, before proceeding to Gilles Bonnefoy's winery, set up between 1997 and 1999. Some of his vines are cultivated on the slopes of the Pic de Purchon, on top of which there is a statue of the Madonna. This rosé was made from those grapes: a pretty, lively-pink colour, with scents of citrus fruit and passion-fruit, linden flowers and hawthorn. Its generous, powerful palate remains supple and crisp. It is a stylish wine, whose balance and elegance will be enjoyed in the next few years. It would be a fine match with grilled meats.

• Gilles Bonnefoy, Le Pizet, 42600 Champdieu, tel. 04.77.97.07.33, fax 04.77.97.17.76 Y by appt.

LES VIGNERONS FORÉZIENS
Cuvée Dellenbach 2000

3.5 ha	10,000	€5-8

The *Vignerons Foréziens* played a fundamental role in the granting of AOC status to the Côtes du Forez wines in 2000, and they love recounting how this vineyard originally dates back to the year 980. This clear, bright, purple-coloured wine has clean, grapey aromas, with nuances of raspberry and cloves and hints of liquorice. An elegant mineral note points to the volcanic origins of this vineyard. Lively, persistent, fruity flavours mean that this classy wine is ready to drink immediately. The **Cuvée Tradition 2000** was also singled out by the Jury.

• Les Vignerons Foréziens, Le Pont-Rompu, 42130 Trélins, tel. 04.77.24.00.12, fax 04.77.24.01.76 ☒ Y by appt.

DOM. DE LA PIERRE NOIRE
2000★

1.5 ha	9,000	€3-5

Young, eight-year-old vines produce the wine for the **Cuvée Jeunes Vignes 2000**, singled out by the Jury, while the oldest vines (60 years old) are reserved for the **Cuvée Spéciale 99**, which was judged a great success. Those vines considered to be in their prime (20 years old), planted on migmatites, provided the raw material for this deep, purple-coloured wine, with its rich aromas of raspberry and redcurrant. Fresh fruitiness fills the palate, supported by firm, elegant tannins. This is a well-balanced wine, which should be enjoyed over the next few years, accompanied by *poitrine roulée*, perhaps.

• Christian Gachet, Dom. de l'Abreuvoir, Noire, chem. de l'Abreuvoir, 42610 Saint-Georges-Hauteville, tel. 04.77.76.08.54 ☒ Y ev. day except Sun. 9am–12 noon

DOM. DU POYET 2000

4 ha	30,000	€3-5

Marcilly-le-Châtel is famous for its *Volerie du Forez*, where falcons are trained. After a visit to the Château Sainte-Anne, you might like to travel the 1 km (0.6 miles) to this estate, set up in 1995, where this ruby-coloured wine was produced. It has a rich scent of raspberry, together with hints of blackcurrant and strawberry. It is a supple, lip-smacking wine full of red-fruit flavours. Medium-to-full in body, it is ready to drink now.

• Jean-François Arnaud, Dom. du Poyet, au Bourg, 42130 Marcilly-le-Châtel, tel. 04.77.97.48.54, fax 04.77.97.48.71 ☒ Y ev. day 8am–8pm; groups by appt.

O. VERDIER ET J. LOGEL
La Volcanique 2000★★

3 ha	10,000	€3-5

Just a few kilometres (about a mile and a half) from the Château de la Bastie d'Urfé, a masterpiece of Renaissance architecture that served as the setting for Honoré d'Urfé's pastoral novel *L'Astrée* in the 17th century, you come to Odile Verdier and Jacky Logel's family estate, which the two took over in 1992. The vines, planted on basalt soil, have produced this wine, which for the first time comes within the Appellation Contrôlée category. The Jury unanimously awarded it a *coup de coeur.* A deep-red colour, the wine is fragrant with aromas of raspberry and very ripe cherry. The palate is rounded and flavourful, with firm, young tannins. This is a concentrated, balanced wine to be enjoyed now with red-meat dishes.

Odile Verdier et Jacky Logel, La Côte, 42130 Marcilly-le-Châtel, tel. 04.77.97.41.95, fax 04.77.97.48.80, e-mail cave.verdierlogel@wanadoo.fr ev. day 9am–12 noon 2pm–7pm; Sun. by appt.

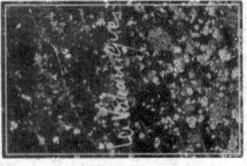

Coteaux du Giennois

This appellation, classified as AOC in 1998, covers silicious or limestone soils stretching along the hills of the upper Loire into the Nièvre and the Loiret. In 2000, three traditional varieties, Gamay, Pinot Noir and Sauvignon, produced 6,947 hl (183,401 gal), including 2,923 hl (77,167 gal) of light, fruity white wines with little tannin, expressing the highly distinctive *terroir*. They can be kept for up to five years and can be drunk with all meat dishes.

Planting is progressing appreciably in the Nièvre and also increasing somewhat in the Loiret, promising continuing good health for this vineyard, which covers 148 ha (366 acres).

JOSEPH BALLAND-CHAPUIS 2000 — 7.5 ha — 60,000 — €5-8

This wine comes from a fine 20-ha (49-acre) estate, owned by Jean-Louis Saget since 1998. This wine is open and fresh, and the nose is initially herbaceous, then fruity. Lightness, suppleness and roundness are the main features of the palate. This is a wine to be matched with salads or cold meats.

SCEA Dom. Balland-Chapuis, 6, allée des Soupirs, 45420 Bonny-sur-Loire, tel. 02.38.31.55.12, fax 02.48.54.07.97
by appt.
Jean-Louis Saget

DOM. DES BEAUROIS 2000 — 2.2 ha — 15,000 — €5-8

The Domaine des Beaurois, situated 10 km (6 miles) from the medieval site of Guédelon, is the result of a reconversion project carried out in 1998. The estate's silicious soil produces a very crisp white wine, with floral notes blended with aromas of moss and undergrowth. It is the perfect accompaniment for a mixed salad.

Anne-Marie Marty, Dom. des Beaurois, 89170 Lavau, tel. 03.86.74.16.09, fax 03.86.74.16.09 ev. day 11am–12.30pm 4pm–7pm

LYCEE AGRICOLE DE COSNE-SUR-LOIRE 2000 — 1.59 ha — 3,400 — €3-5

The Agricultural College at Cosne-sur-Loire is a training ground for prospective wine-makers, and it produces wines such as this 2000. The nose opens slowly, releasing a range of fruity and floral aromas. The palate is both supple and balanced. This is a fresh, aromatic wine that may be served with asparagus.

Lycée Agricole de Cosne-sur-Loire, 66, rue Jean-Monnet, BP 132, 58206 Cosne-sur-Loire, tel. 03.86.26.99.84, fax 03.86.26.99.84 ev. day except Sat. Sun. 8am–12.30pm 1.30pm–5.30pm

CH. DE LA CHAISE 2000★ — 4 ha — 20,000 — €3-5

The nose on this wine is young and shy, but promises complexity with notes of cooked fruit, herbs, spices, and orange zest. The tannins are well-integrated. This wine is already drinking well, but will benefit from some time in the cellar. The white **2000**, a supple and pleasant wine, was singled out by the jury.

Philippe Auchère, 36, rue de Venoire, 18300 Bué, tel. 02.48.78.05.15, fax 02.48.78.05.15, e-mail philippe.auchere@vinsdesancerre.com by appt.

MICHEL LANGLOIS 1999 — 1.2 ha — 8,000 — €5-8

Catherine and Michel Langlois are among those young, enthusiastic wine-makers in the Coteaux du Giennois area. They have produced a beautiful, light-coloured rosé with orange highlights. The nose offers nuances of redcurrant and white blossoms. The palate is rounded, juicy and delicious. It would be a fine match with cold meats or Asian dishes.

ALAIN PAULAT
Les Têtes de Chats 1999★★

■ 1.2 ha n.c. ■ €5-8

Alain Paulat's motto, 'Passion-Respect-Tradition,' sums up this fine wine. The initial fragrances are of leather with a hint of vanilla, and are followed after aeration by attractive spicy notes. The tannins are firm and concentrated. A promising Coteaux du Giennois that will become rounder and more open with some time in the cellar. The **Les Belles Forrasses 99 red** also especially impressed the Jury.

⌒ Alain Paulat, Villemoison, 58200 Saint-Père, tel. 03.86.26.75.57, fax 03.86.28.06.78 ☑ by appt.

POUPAT ET FILS Rivotte 2000

■ 2.03 ha 17,000 ■ €5-8

A regular presence in the *Guide*, Philippe Poupat appears here again with two of his wines. This white wine has an initial light, fresh structure, then takes on weight, becoming fleshier and offering good length in the finish. Its rich aromas of peach and citrus fruit are gay and colourful. The Jury also liked the **Cuvée Trocadéro 2000 rosé** (one star).

⌒ Poupat et Fils, Rivotte, 45250 Briare, tel. 02.38.31.39.76, fax 02.38.31.39.76 ☑ by appt.

DOM. DES RATAS Les Ratas 2000★

■ 0.3 ha 1,700 ■ €5-8

Emile Balland, a descendant of a famous family of wine-producers, is the cellarmaster at the Domaine des Ratas. His white wines are a true success. This wine, matured in wood, has intense fruit, a fleshy, long palate, and would be the perfect match for a dish of poultry in cream sauce. Warming and well-structured, it has everything it needs to please. The **Cuvée Domaine** was singled out by the Jury.

⌒ SCEA Dom. des Ratas, Les Ratas, RN 7, 45420 Bonny-sur-Loire, tel. 02.38.85.31.52, fax 02.38.98.16.61 ☑ by appt.

SEBASTIEN TREUILLET 2000

■ n.c. 2,500 ■ €3-5

A bright, pale-salmon colour, with a slight brick-red hue, this 2000 requires some aeration to reveal its distinctly floral aromas (peony). The palate is pleasantly firm, round, and clean. The **red 2000** was especially singled out by the Jury, who enjoyed its supple tannins.

⌒ Sébastien Treuillet, Fontenille, 58150 Tracy-sur-Loire, tel. 03.86.26.17.06, fax 03.86.26.17.06 ☑ ev. day 8am-12 noon 1pm-7pm

⌒ Michel Langlois, 58200 Pougny, tel. 03.86.28.06.52, fax 03.86.28.59.29 ☑ ev. day except Sun. 9am-1pm 3pm-7pm

Saint-Pourçain AOVDQS

DOM. DE VILLARGEAU 2000★★

□ 4.1 ha 32,000 ■ €5-8

The Thibault family successfully produces wine in their new cellar, which is better-suited to the estate's current production than the old one was. After their 99, this 2000 also received plaudits from the Jury. The nose is powerful, very Sauvignon in all its grassy herbaceousness with fruity notes. The well-balanced palate is supple and fresh. Such elegance and breed enthused the Jury, who consequently awarded this wine a *coup de cœur*. The **Les Licotes 2000 red** also impressed the Jury.

⌒ GAEC Thibault, Villargeau, 58200 Pougny, tel. 03.86.26.23.24, fax 03.86.28.47.00, e-mail fthibault@wanadoo.fr ☑ by appt.

DOM. DE VILLEGEAI 2000★

□ 0.72 ha 6,000 ■ €5-8

This wine has an attractive golden colour with clear, youthful reflections, pleasant floral aromas on the nose, and a structure and overall balance that satisfy the palate. The fine **Terre des Violettes 99 red** was also singled out by the Jury.

⌒ SCEA Quintin Frères, Villegeai, 58200 Cosne-Cours-sur-Loire, tel. 03.86.28.31.77, fax 03.86.28.20.27 ☑ by appt.

Saint-Pourçain AOVDQS

Gentle, fertile Bourbonnais boasts a lovely vineyard, in nineteen communes, stretching over 512 ha (1,265 acres) south-west of Moulins. In 2000, production amounted to 32,680 hl (862,752 gal) of wine.

Limestone or gravelly slopes and plateaux, skirting the banks of the charming Sioule river, grow Gamay and Pinot Noir which combine to give the red and rosé wines their fruity appeal.

In the past, the native Tressallier variety made remarkable white wines that established Saint-Pourçain's reputation. Today, the original Tressallier is assembled with Chardonnay and Sauvignon to make distinctively aromatic wine worthy of more than a passing comment.

ATLANTIS 2000★

n.c.   40,000   ■ ⬥ €3-5

This fine wine, with its evocative name, is straw-coloured with pale-silver highlights and has a very floral nose. The palate is rich and supple, with elegant citrus-fruit flavours on a long finish. This Saint-Pourçain could be the perfect match with freshwater fish.

↦ Union des vignerons de Saint-Pourçain, rue de la Ronde,
03500 Saint-Pourçain-sur-Sioule,
tel. 04.70.45.42.82, fax 04.70.45.99.34,
e-mail udv.stpourcain@wanadoo.fr ☑
Ⓨ ev. day 8.30am–12.30pm 1.30pm–6.30pm; groups by appt.

DOM. DE BELLEVUE

Grande Réserve 2000★

4.9 ha   30,000   ■ ⬥ €3-5

Jean-Louis Pétillat is following in the steps of his grandfather, Marc, and is making an excellent job of it. This is an attractive, pale-yellow Grande Réserve. Flowers and citrus fruit fill the nose, and the palate is fresh and lively. It is a wine for friends, company and conversation. The **Grande Réserve 2000 red** was also singled out by the Jury.

↦ Philippe Pétillat, Bellevue,
03500 Saint-Pourçain-sur-Sioule,
tel. 04.70.42.09.75 ☑ Ⓨ by appt.

DOM. DE CHINIERE 2000★

5.3 ha   30,000   ■ ⬥ €3-5

The village of Saulcet boasts a Roman-esque church with an interesting series of wall paintings, which is worth visiting before going on to the Domaine de Chinière. This estate has produced a pale-yellow wine with green highlights. The wine has aromas of white fruit (especially peaches), and the palate is well-balanced, with a tasty finish.

↦ Jean-Louis Pétillat, Chinière,
03500 Saulcet, tel. 04.70.45.45.66,
fax 04.70.45.43.16

excellent 99, obtained a star. A blend of 90% Chardonnay and 10% Tresallier, it is a pretty straw colour, and has a complex nose of fruit and herbs. Its good balance and suppleness are very attractive.

↦ Cave Courtinat, Venteuil, 03500 Saulcet,
tel. 04.70.45.44.84, fax 04.70.45.80.13 ☑
Ⓨ ev. day 8am–12.30pm 2pm–8pm

BERNARD GARDIEN ET FILS

Nectar des Fées 2000★

5 ha   30,000   ■ ⬥ €3-5

Bernard Gardien and his sons hit the jackpot last year, with a double *coup de coeur*. Their Nectar des Fées 2000 is also a fine wine. Bright-yellow with silvery highlights, it offers fruity aromas on the nose. The palate is supple and fleshy, with flavours of white peach. A lemony zing on the finish adds to the balance and freshness.

↦ Dom. Gardien, Chassignolles,
03210 Besson, tel. 04.70.42.80.11,
fax 04.70.42.80.99, e-mail c.gardien@
03.sideral.fr ☑ Ⓨ ev. day except Sun. 8am–
12 noon 2pm–7pm

DOM. GROSBOT-BARBARA

Le Vin d'Alon 2000★

1.2 ha   9,600   ■ ⬥ €3-5

Once again, the estate has come up with some very good wines. The expertise of these two producers, Elie Grosbot and Denis Barbara, who have worked together for five years now, is clear from these two white wines. This wine is pale with green highlights, and offers a generous nose of fresh citrus fruit. The palate is extremely supple, and the crisp finish emphasises its freshness. The **La Vreladière 2000** is well-balanced with a lengthy finish: a very promising wine.

↦ Dom. Grosbot-Barbara, Montjournal, rte de Montluçon, 03500 Cesset,
tel. 04.70.45.26.66, fax 04.70.45.54.95 ☑
Ⓨ ev. day 10am–12 noon 2pm–7pm

DOM. HAUT DE BRIAILLES 2000★

2 ha   13,000   ■ ⬥ €5-8

A chapel appears almost set into the estate's vineyard. As well as the **Réserve de la Chapelle 2000 white**, singled out for its rich palate, the Jury also liked this dark, red-coloured wine with violet highlights. The nose releases scents of soft red fruit, while the palate is balanced and slightly tannic on the finish. It is a wine to be enjoyed now.

↦ Jean Meunier, Dom. Haut de Briailles,
03500 Saint-Pourçain-sur-Sioule,
tel. 04.70.45.38.88, fax 04.70.45.60.07,
e-mail jeanmeunier@freesbee.fr ☑
Ⓨ by appt.

DOM. DE LA CROIX D'OR 2000★

3.5 ha   20,000   ■ ⬥ €3-5

Chemilly lies at the entrance to the Saint-Pourçain vineyards, and marks the beginning of a wine trail, signposted using a special logo. Furthermore, there are no less than five châteaux in the parish, four of which are listed buildings. This estate has produced a

CAVE COURTINAT 2000★

1.5 ha   8,000   ■ ⬥

An ancient 14th-century convent, flanked by a tower, and a traditional Bourbonnais dovecote make up this estate, which has spe-cialised in the production of wines for many years. It has proven highly successful, as can be seen, since this white, following an

Volcanic soils on valley slopes in the east, south and south-west create a *terroir* in which the Gamay is very much at home.

Fourteen communes, covering 183 ha (452 acres) situated on the left bank of the river produce excellent red wines and rather unusual, fresh rosés. Vinification, which totalled 11,344 hl (299,482 gal) in 2000, takes place on the growers' own properties; they create original wines of character appealing to the most prestigious chefs in the region. The area's wine-growing traditions are on show at the Musée Forézien in Ambierle.

Slowly but surely the vineyard is expanding. More important, however, is the attention the shippers and distributors now pay to Côte Roannaise wines, which helps to reinforce the originality and quality of the growth.

Chardonnay is gradually being introduced and makes wines that are bottled as Vin de Pays d'Urfé.

ALAIN BAILLON Montplaisir 2000★★   1.7 ha   9,000   ■   €5-8

Ambierle is a historical town with a Benedictine abbey dedicated to Saint Martin. It is popular with tourists and is a thriving wine-making centre. This dark-garnet vintage made from old vines was awarded a *coup de cœur*. Its powerful bouquet releases lovely scents based on very ripe fruits, black-currants, violets, white pepper and cinnamon. Its rich and balanced structure reveals young and promising tannins and long-lasting aromas, which confirm the quality of the

wine with a beautiful straw-yellow colour and a complex nose of white flowers and apricot. The firm, well-balanced palate has a finish that is crisp and fresh.

☛ Jean-François Colas, La Croix d'Or, 03210 Chemilly, tel. 04.70.45.99.34, fax 04.70.45.99.34 [V]

LAURENT Cuvée Prestige 1999★   3 ha   12,000   ■   €5-8

This family estate has been at Saulcet for several centuries. This Saint-Pourçain vineyard is one of the oldest in France, and its wines were served at royal feasts. This 99 seduced the Jury with its complex nose of raspberries and caramel, and its fine balance on the palate.

☛ Famille Laurent, Montifaud, 03500 Saulcet, tel. 04.70.45.45.13, fax 04.70.45.60.18, e-mail cave.laurent@wanadoo.fr [V], ev. day except Sun. 8am–12 noon 2pm–6.30pm

NEBOUT Cuvée de la Malgarnie 1999★★   3 ha   15,000   ■   €5-8

On the nose, scents of white flowers blend delightfully with aromas of ripe fruit. The palate is silky, with a long, lingering finish. While it may be drunk immediately, it will benefit from a year or two in the cellar. The Saint-Pourçain 2000 red is an attractive wine, worthy of the star it received. It is a blend dominated by Gamay, with the balance in Pinot Noir, which contributes to the orange notes in the colour. Aromas of red fruits and toast add depth to the fresh and well-balanced palate.

☛ EARL Nebout, rte de Montluçon, 03500 Saint-Pourçain-sur-Sioule, tel. 04.70.45.31.70, fax 04.70.45.55.85 [V], ev. day except Sun. 8am–7pm

FRANCOIS RAY Cuvée des Gaumes 2000   2.53 ha   16,000   ■   €5-8

This is an enjoyable, cherry-coloured wine that proves fresh and fruity, supple and balanced. Drink it with a selection of local Auvergne cheeses.

☛ Cave François Ray, Venteuil, 03500 Saulcet, tel. 04.70.45.35.46, fax 04.70.45.64.96 [V], ev. day except Sun. 9am–12 noon 2pm–7pm; groups by appt.

LES VIGNERONS DE SAINT-POURCAIN Vin Gris 2000★   n.c.   40,000   ■   €3-5

A fine 'partridge-eye' colour, this rosé displays a very floral nose, together with all the characteristics of a summer wine: suppleness, freshness and balance. The easy-to-drink **Réserve Spéciale 2000 red**, pleasant and rounded on the palate, was also singled out.

☛ Union des Vignerons de Saint-Pourçain, rue de la Ronde, 03500 Saint-Pourçain-sur-Sioule, tel. 04.70.45.42.82, fax 04.70.45.99.34, e-mail udv.stpourcain@wanadoo.fr [V], ev. day 8.30am–12.30pm 1.30pm–6.30pm; groups by appt.

wine-making. It is ready to drink now, or could be kept for another two or three years.

☛ Alain Baillon, Montplaisir,
42820 Ambierle, tel. 04.77.65.65.51,
fax 04.77.65.65.65 ▨ 🍷 by appt.

JEAN-PIERRE BENETIERE

Cuvée Vieilles vignes 2000

■ 1.4 ha 9,000 ■ ◆ €5-8

This wine-growing estate also has an interesting workshop making wickerwork baskets. No less interesting is this wine made from old vines: it has a strong ruby colour and well-formed, complex aromas of peonies and undergrowth. Smooth on the palate, with flavours of pepper and liquorice, this agreeable, elegant 2000 is ready for drinking, and makes an ideal companion for charcuterie.

☛ Jean-Pierre et Paul Bénétière,
pl. de la Mairie, 42155 Villemontais,
tel. 04.77.63.18.29, fax 04.77.63.18.29 ▨
🍷 by appt.

CH. DE CHAMPAGNY

Grande Réserve 2000★★

■ 1.5 ha 8,000 ■ ◆ €3-5

Saint-Haon-le-Vieux is very close to the medieval town of Saint-Haon-le-Châtel. Explore the latter's lanes and alleyways and go 2 km or so (around a mile) further on to this estate. The Jury awarded it one star for the **Château de Champagny 2000**, made from younger vines, and two stars for this dark-red Grande Réserve, with its impressive bouquet of very ripe red berries and blackcurrants combined with hints of spices and oak. This rich, warm wine with characteristic mineral notes is full, fleshy and powerful, and should be drunk in the next two or three years.

☛ André et Frédéric Villeneuve,
Champagny, 42370 Saint-Haon-le-Vieux,
tel. 04.77.64.42.88, fax 04.77.62.12.55 ▨
🍷 by appt.

DOM. DE LA PAROISSE 2000

■ 4 ha 15,000 ■ ◆ €3-5

After visiting Saint-Haon-le-Châtel, a fine medieval village with ramparts of pink porphyry, you can visit this estate, which dates from 1610 and is regularly featured in the *Guide*. This year, it has been singled out for a **Cuvée à l'Ancienne 2000**, and for this wine with a strong ruby colour and fairly powerful, pleasant aromas of red berries, blackcurrants and spices. The smooth, fruity first impression blends with slightly harsh tannins rounded off with notes of wild berries. Imbued with hints of its *terroir*, the wine should be drunk within the next two years.

☛ Jean-Claude Chaucesse, La Paroisse,
42370 Renaison, tel. 04.77.64.26.10,
fax 04.77.62.13.84 ▨ 🍷 by appt.

MICHEL ET LIONEL MONTROUSSIER

Cuvée La Baude 2000★

■ 4 ha 20,000 ■ ◆ €3-5

The commune of Saint-André-d'Apchon has two main tourist attractions: a château

dating from the 15th century and a Flamboyant church with 16th-century windows. It has been a wine-growing village since the Middle Ages. The history of this estate began in 1680, and in 1999 father and son joined forces. That year, they produced a **Cuvée de Bouthéran**, which impressed the Jury, and this garnet-coloured La Baude, which is developing fairly powerful and complex aromas of red berries and blackcurrants enlivened by notes of cinnamon and peonies. Lively on the palate – full and well-structured, with good tannins – this rich, substantial wine could be kept for two to three years.

☛ GAEC Michel et Lionel Montroussier,
La Baude, 42370 Saint-André-d'Apchon,
tel. 04.77.65.92.76, fax 04.77.65.92.76 ▨
🍷 by appt.

DOM. DU PAVILLON 2000★★

■ 7 ha 40,000

Not far from the abbey of Ambierle, where you can see a triptych by Van der Weyden and a crafts museum, this domaine has produced a strongly garnet-coloured wine with expressive aromas of fruits and flowers combined with spices and a mineral hint. The wine is a rich, balanced and well-made version of the appellation, with a velvety, mouth-filling palate and long-lasting flavours of spices and flowers. Drink it in the next two or three years.

☛ Maurice Lutz, GAEC Dom. du Pavillon,
42820 Ambierle, tel. 04.77.65.64.35,
fax 04.77.65.69.69 ▨ 🍷 by appt.

JACQUES PLASSE Bouthéran 2000

■ 2.1 ha 19,000 ■ ◆ €3-5

Jacques de Saint-André, Marshal of France and adviser to Henri II (16th century), designed this château. Its tower and main building are well worth visiting, as is this estate, which has been run by Jacques Plasse since 1999. He has produced a wine with a strong ruby colour and a fairly intense bouquet suggesting red berries and spices. This fruity Bouthéran has good length and is charming and smooth. Drink it within a year.

☛ Jacques Plasse, Bel-Air,
42370 Saint-André-d'Apchon,
tel. 04.77.65.84.31 ▨ 🍷 by appt.

ROBERT SEROL ET FILS

Les Vieilles vignes 2000

■ 5 ha 30,000 ■ ◆ €3-5

The estate has done a good job in updating its labels for its 2000 wine. Made from 45-year-old vines, this Vieilles Vignes has a strong ruby colour and intense aromas recalling raspberries and strawberries and a decided hint of blackcurrants. Its fine, well-balanced structure, supported by fairly rounded, fresh tannins, is allied to a pleasant liveliness that will make it enjoyable to drink in the next two years. A second wine from the estate, **Les Originelles**, also impressed the Jury; its 99 version was awarded a *coup de cœur*.

L'Orléanais AOVDQS

Orléans had their moment of glory in medieval times, but the vine still prospers on about 107 ha (264 acres) among the gardens, nurseries and famous orchards of the Orléanais. The tradition was kept going mainly on the sandy, gravelly terraces of the south bank of the Loire between Olivet and Cléry, where the church houses the tomb of Louis XI, who died in 1483.

Pinot Meunier, otherwise mainly used in Champagne, here produces original red and rosé wines. The supple rosés are sometimes described as *vin gris*.

Since the 10th century, the wine-makers have adapted the following varieties, which it is claimed were imported from the Auvergne, but which are identical to the ones in Burgundy: Auvernat Rouge (Pinot Noir), Auvernat Blanc (Chardonnay) and Gris Meunier, to which was added Cabernet (or Breton) with its aromas of red- and blackcurrants. The wines should be drunk with partridge and roast pheasant, game pâtés from neighbouring Sologne and ash cheeses from the Gâtinais. In 200, the production of red reached 4,628 hl (122,179 gal); white wine production is more limited at 1,050 hl (27,720 gal).

VIGNOBLE DU CHANT D'OISEAUX Gris meunier 2000★★

◻ 0.5 ha 3,000 €3-5

The year 2000 seems to have inspired Jacky Legroux, who offered a lovely, salmon-coloured rosé which gives a lively first impression in the mouth and is pleasantly fruity on the palate, revealing its youthfulness. It surprised the Jury with its richness and freshness. The ruby- coloured red 2000 is balanced on the palate and is slightly tannic at the finish; it wins one star.

Jacky Legroux, 315, rue des Muids, 45370 Mareau-aux-Prés, tel. 02.38.45.60.31, fax 02.38.45.62.35 by appt.

SAINT AVIT 2000★

◻ 0.58 ha 4,000 €3-5

This wine has a lovely light-pink colour. Its bouquet is still restrained, but it is rounded and very pleasant on the palate. Two **reds** especially impressed the Jury, one made from Cabernet for its characteristic peppery flavours on the palate; the other, made from Pinot Meunier and Pinot Noir, is pleasant and very drinkable, with a refreshing finish.

Javoy Père et Fils, 450, rue du Buisson, 45370 Mézières-lez-Cléry, tel. 02.38.45.66.95, fax 02.38.45.69.77 ev. day except Sun. 8am-12 noon

CLOS SAINT-FIACRE 2000★★

◻ 6.02 ha 45,000 €5-8

Bénédicte and her husband Hubert Piel have taken over this estate. While they settle down, this lovely wine may be enjoyed, with its refined bouquet giving off scents of red berries combined with cocoa beans and spices. Very well-balanced on the palate, with rounded tannins, the wine is ready for drinking. Another **red 2000** from the same estate, made from Cabernet, wins one star; its bouquet releases aromas of blackcurrants. After a good first impression on the palate, showing a well-balanced wine, this vintage could do with further ageing. Another star was won by the **rosé 2000**, which has an elegant, thoroughbred palate.

GAEC Clos Saint-Fiacre, 560, rue Saint-Fiacre, 45370 Mareau-aux-Prés, tel. 02.38.45.61.55, fax 02.38.45.66.58 by appt.

Montigny-Piel

Robert Sérol et Fils, Les Estinaudes, 42370 Renaison, tel. 04.77.64.44.04, fax 04.77.62.10.87 ev. day 8.30am-12.30pm 1.30pm-7pm; Sun. by appt.

PHILIPPE ET JEAN-MARIE VIAL 2000

◻ 1 ha 6,000 €5-8

This clear, bright-pink wine comes from vines planted on granite sands. It opens on the nose with notes of dried flowers and cherry brandy, while on the palate it is pleasantly fruity, lively and balanced. Over the next year or so, this slightly sharp wine, which is delightfully refreshing, will be good with a barbecue.

GAEC Vial, Bel-Air, 42370 Saint-André-d'Apchon, tel. 04.77.65.81.04, fax 04.77.65.91.99 by appt.

Menetou-Salon

Menetou-Salon

Menetou-Salon owes its vinous beginnings to the proximity of the medieval metropolis of Bourges. Unlike many other once-famous wine regions this one has remained a wine-growing area; the present vineyard is of high quality and covers 374 ha (924 acres).

Menetou-Salon's favoured slopes share the same soils as its prestigious neighbour, Sancerre, and grow the same varieties, Sauvignon Blanc and Pinot Noir. From these, the appellation produces fresh, spicy white wines, delicate, fruity rosés, and harmonious, scented reds, all of which should be drunk young. They are the pride of viticulture in Berry and splendidly accompany full-flavoured classic dishes (as an aperitif or with hot starters for the whites; with fish, rabbit or charcuterie for the reds, which should be served slightly chilled). Production reached 24,511 hl (647,090 gal) in 2000, of which 15,447 hl (907,801 gal) were white wines.

The white has a restrained bouquet, but is already revealing its complexity with notes of liquorice and apricots. On the palate, it is just as rounded as it is fresh. The **rosé** also wins one star; well-balanced and fruity, it was judged the best wine for this appellation. The **red** is also recommended.

➤ G. Chavet et Fils, GAEC des Brangers, 18510 Menetou-Salon, tel. 02.48.64.80.87, fax 02.48.64.84.78, e-mail contact@chavet-vins.fr ☑ ▼ ev. day except Sun. 8am–12 noon 2pm–6pm

DOM. DE COQUIN 2000 ∎ €5-8

∎ 3 ha 25,000

Francis Audiot took over his 10-ha (25-acre) family estate in 1993 and has developed its direct sales business. It has been in the *Guide* for the last four years, and last year won a *coup de cœur* for its white wine. The red 2000 has a pretty, strong ruby colour, and swirling the glass brings out the true worth of its intense bouquet. This is a well-balanced wine with appreciable length – a typical Menetou-Salon.

➤ Francis Audiot, Dom. de Coquin, 18510 Menetou-Salon, tel. 02.48.64.80.46, fax 02.48.64.84.51 ☑ ▼ by appt.

DOM. GILBERT 2000★★★ ∎ €8-11

∎ 13.4 ha 108,000

Although their property is only 100 years old, the family has been in wine-making since 1768. The latest generation took over in 1998. This wine was flawless throughout the tasting and was certainly well-blessed by nature, but it also reveals perfect wine-making techniques. The fruity bouquet is intense, recalling blackberries, blackcurrants and cherries. The tannins are very smooth and well-blended. In addition to these excellent impressions, it is well-balanced and has good length. The Jury praised it unanimously. The same growers also received recommendations for their **white 2000** and their **Les Renardières 99 red**, matured in barrel.

➤ Dom. Gilbert, Les Faucards, 18510 Menetou-Salon, tel. 02.48.66.65.90, fax 02.48.66.65.99 ▼ by appt.

DOM. DE CHATENOY 2000 ∎ €8-11

∎ 8 ha 70,000

This property dates from 1709 – one of the worst years in the 'little Ice Age,' with a bitterly cold winter when, apparently, wines froze in the glass. It has featured in the *Guide* since the first edition, winning one *coup de cœur* (for a white 91). This wine has an attractive dark-red ruby colour with violet glints. The bouquet has already developed aromas of red berries (blackcurrants, raspberries and blackberries) but needs time to open out. On the palate, with its still somewhat lively tannins, the wine also needs softening. This is a well-made wine, but one for keeping.

➤ SCEA B. Clément et Fils, Dom. de Chatenoy, BP 12, 18510 Menetou-Salon, tel. 02.48.66.68.70, fax 02.48.66.68.71 ☑ ▼ by appt.

G. CHAVET ET FILS 2000★ □ €5-8

□ 9.34 ha 75,000

A family-run estate of some 20 ha (49 acres), this has been in every edition of the *Guide* and has won more than one *coup de cœur*. Once again it has done well, its **2000 vintage** being singled out in all three colours.

LA TOUR SAINT-MARTIN □ €5-8

Morogues 2000★★ □ 6.3 ha 55,000

Bertrand Minchin took over in 1987, and in the 1990s showed himself to be one of the mainstays of the appellation. His

La Tour Saint Martin

MENETOU-SALON
MOROGUES
Appellation Menetou-Salon Contrôlée
2000
Mis en bouteille à la propriété

• Dom. Henry Pellé, rte d'Aubinges, 18220 Morogues, tel. 02.48.64.36.88, fax 02.48.64.42.48, ☰ ev. day except Sat. Sun. 8am–12 noon 1.30pm–5.30pm; cl. 15 Aug.–1 Sep.

DOM. DU PRIEURE 2000★

■ 8.86 ha 50,000 €5-8

This estate of some 19 ha (47 acres) offers a wine full of verve, with spices and pepper contending with strawberries and morello cherries. On the palate, the wine is so smooth that the tannins are hardly noticeable. The estate's **white 2000** is recommended.

• SCEA du Prieuré, 14, rte de la Gare, 18510 Menetou-Salon, tel. 02.48.64.88.39, fax 02.48.64.85.95, e-mail gogue-prieure@terre-net.fr ☑ by appt.

DOM. JEAN TEILLER 2000★

□ 7 ha 48,000 €5-8

An 85 red was awarded a *coup de cœur* in one of the early editions of the *Guide*, and since then the wines of Jean-Jacques Teiller and his wife Monique have been regularly singled out. This one has both character and originality; it is well structured, with a touch of vanilla, and is also marked by boxwood and blackcurrant leaves. The **rosé 2000** also receives one star.

• Dom. Jean Teiller, 13, rte de la Gare, 18510 Menetou-Salon, tel. 02.48.64.80.71, fax 02.48.64.86.92, e-mail domaine-teiller@wanadoo.fr ☑ ☰ ev. day except Sun. 8.30am–12 noon 2pm–6pm

CHRISTOPHE ET GUY TURPIN

Morogues 1999

■ 5 ha 3,000 €5-8

This lovely rosé, with salmony and golden glints, was fermented for a long time after direct pressing of the grapes, then matured on the lees. Its soft, smooth aromas are mainly fruity, and there is a successful balance between fleshiness and the necessary acidity, making this a pleasant wine. The **red Morogues**, light and very drinkable, is also recommended.

• GAEC Turpin Père et Fils, 11, pl. de l'Eglise, 18220 Morogues, tel. 02.48.64.32.24, fax 02.48.64.32.24 ☑ by appt.

grandfather, a wine-grower in the 1930s, would certainly be proud of him for winning a *coup de cœur* for the third time. This white wine releases aromas of ripe grapes in lovely golden bunches. Mouth-filling and fleshy on the palate, teasing out fine, long-lasting flavours of flowers and fruits, this full, rounded, complex wine is magnificent.

• Albane et Bertrand Minchin, EARL La Tour Saint-Martin, 18340 Crosses, tel. 02.48.25.02.95, fax 02.48.25.05.03, e-mail tour.saint.martin@wanadoo.fr ☑ by appt.

LE PRIEURE DE SAINT-CEOLS

Cuvée des Bénédictins 1999

□ 1 ha 8,000 €5-8

Pierre Jacolin operates from a very beautiful building, an old Benedictine priory which belonged to the abbey of La-Charité-sur-Loire, itself a dependency of Cluny. The vineyard is recent, having been planted by Pierre Jacolin in 1986. This wine-grower has been steady and careful in his work, and is often mentioned in the *Guide*, especially for this Cuvée des Bénédictins made from his finest plots. His 99 vintage is subtle on the nose, with mineral notes and hints of dried fruits, and in the mouth it has a fleshy quality enlivened by an appropriate touch of freshness, and a good length. The **red 2000** from the estate is also recommended.

• Pierre Jacolin, Le Prieuré de Saint-Céols, 18220 Saint-Céols, tel. 02.48.64.40.75, fax 02.48.64.41.15, e-mail sarl-jacolin@libertysurf.fr ☑ ☰ ev. day 8am–7pm; Sun. by appt.

DOM. HENRY PELLE

Les Cris 2000★★

□ 3 ha 22,000 €11-15

The Pelles have supported the Menetou-Salon appellation since the 1950s and have been in every edition of the *Guide*. Anne Pellé and her oenologist, Julien Zernott, have been looking after the estate since 1995. Three of its **2000 vintage** wines have been selected, but the red stands apart from the other two. It is blended from equal parts of wines matured in barrel and in tank, and is a harmonious combination of intense fruitiness and oak: an alliance of power and finesse. The **Morogues white** wins one star, and the **Clos des Blanchais** (whose 98 vintage won a *coup de cœur*) is recommended.

Pouilly-Fumé and Pouilly-sur-Loire

The delightful vineyard of Pouilly-sur-Loire was first established by Benedictine monks. The Loire pounds against a limestone promontory as it turns

1073

THE LOIRE VALLEY

LOIRE

north-east, and the soil, less chalky than at Sancerre, provides excellent growing conditions for the south-south-east facing slopes. The main variety is Sauvignon Blanc Fumé, which will shortly have entirely supplanted the traditional Chasselas, previously the source of appealing white wines when cultivated on silica soils. Pouilly-sur-Loire covers 38 ha (94 acres) while Pouilly-Fumé represents 1,078 ha (2,663 acres). Total production was 72,603 hl (1,916,719 gal) of a wine that has all the qualities associated with a limestone *terroir*, marked by a freshness which does not lack a certain structure, and a full array of varietal aromas. It is matured within the area where it is grown according to certain conditions under which the must is fermented.

Pouilly-Fumé

MICHEL BAILLY ET FILS
Les Bines 1999★

| | 1 ha | 7,000 | ■ | ● | €5-8 |

Bines is the local name for the cicadas heard chirping at Les Loges. Herbaceous scents of boxwood and broom are the main elements of the 99 vintage, its balance achieved by a blend of liveliness and roundness. The vines are fairly old, and long maturation on lees has given the wine a fleshy quality that is very pleasant.

➤ Dom. Michel Bailly et Fils,
Les Loges, 58150 Pouilly-sur-Loire,
tel. 03.86.39.04.78, fax 03.86.39.05.25,
e-mail domaine.michel.bailly@wanadoo.fr
▨ ▼ by appt.

CEDRICK BARDIN
Cuvée des Bernadats 2000★★

| | 1 ha | 6,000 | ■ | ● | €8-11 |

Cédrick Bardin has been running this family business for ten years. It has vines in the Sancerre region as well as around Pouilly. The year 2000 was a good one for him, with both his Pouilly-Fumés being highly praised, especially this Cuvée des Bernadats, the product of vines grown on marl soil. A wine of remarkable power, its main features are intense fruitiness and fleshiness, excellent qualities on the palate. Also recommended is the **Cuvée Principale**, which received one star for its mineral content.

➤ Cédrick Bardin, 12, rue Waldeck-Rousseau,
58150 Pouilly-sur-Loire, tel. 03.86.39.11.24,
fax 03.86.39.16.50 ▨
▼ by appt.

DOM. BARILLOT 2000

| | 4 ha | 28,000 | ■ | ● | €5-8 |

This Pouilly-Fumé has an intensity and an aromatic richness that are immediately attractive, the principal aroma being characteristic gunflint. The clear-cut first impression continues with a certain liveliness, probably caused by the wine's youthfulness. Drink this with seafood.

➤ Barillot Père et Fils, Le Bouchot,
58150 Pouilly-sur-Loire, tel. 03.86.39.15.29,
fax 03.86.39.09.52 ▨ ▼ ev. day except Sun.
9am–12.30pm 1.30pm–7pm; groups by appt.

FRANCIS BLANCHET 2000

| | 4.7 ha | 17,000 | ■ | ● | €5-8 |

The eye takes in the pronounced green shining amid the golden colour of this wine, then the nose enjoys the intense scents combining fruits and chopped acacia. The wine has a balanced opening on the palate and also reveals a subtle hint of bitterness at the finish. It can easily be kept for two to three years.

➤ EARL Francis Blanchet, Le Bouchot,
58150 Pouilly-sur-Loire, tel. 03.86.39.05.90,
fax 03.86.39.13.19 ▼ by appt.

GILLES BLANCHET 2000★

| | 4.6 ha | 25,000 | ■ | ● | €5-8 |

Gilles Blanchet has appeared regularly in the *Guide* (with a *coup de cœur* for his 96 wine), and now presents his tenth vintage. Its bouquet is restrained at first, opening with a fruity aroma close to crystallised fruit, then releases lemony nuances. On the palate, its roundness is tempered by a slightly acid quality, and it has a good length of flavour on the finish.

➤ Gilles Blanchet, Le Bourg,
58150 Saint-Andelain, tel. 03.86.39.14.03,
fax 03.86.39.14.03 ▼ by appt.

BRUNO BLONDELET 2000★

| | 10.3 ha | 60,000 | | | €5-8 |

This wine flirts with paradox, as though to imprint itself on the memory, opening in the mouth with both fullness and acidity. Aromas of gooseberries and apricots open out, captivating from start to finish. It is a promising wine.

➤ Bruno Blondelet, Cave des Criots,
Le Bouchot, 58150 Pouilly-sur-Loire,
tel. 03.86.39.18.75, fax 03.86.39.06.65 ▨
▼ by appt.

BOUCHIE-CHATELLIER
Premier millésimé 2000★★

| | 1.3 ha | 10,000 | ■ | ● | €11-15 |

Around 1939, Bernard Bouchié's grandfather cleared the woods, chased the foxes out and planted vines on siliceous-clay soils. Some 60 years later, Bernard has an estate of 13 ha (32 acres) overlooking the Loire Valley, and he knows how to get the best out of the

HENRI BOURGEOIS
La Demoiselle de Bourgeois 2000★★
3.8 ha　26,000　€11-15

Henri Bourgeois cultivates 65 ha (160 acres) of vines around Pouilly and in the Sancerre region. His Demoiselle de Bourgeois appears regularly in the *Guide*, and this one is both elegant and classy. The complex bouquet combines flowers and ripe fruits with mineral shades. The first impression in the mouth is warm and balanced by a tasty freshness, and the wine is full on the palate with a lengthy finish. A remarkable wine, it needs two or three years to achieve its full potential.

• Dom. Henri Bourgeois, Chavignol, 1300 Sancerre, tel. 02.48.78.53.20, fax 02.48.54.14.24, e-mail domaine@bourgeois-sancerre.com [V] [Y] by appt.

DOM. DU BOUCHOT 2000★★
8.5 ha　55,000　€5-8

This property, taken over by the Kerbiquet family in 1968, consists of 9 ha (22 acres) of vines planted on south-west-facing clay-limestone soils. The 2000 vintage is a great success. The bouquet develops in various directions, from ripe lemons to crystallised notes, and from white berries to boxwood. Fine and full on the palate, supported by a touch of bitterness, its flavours are marked by notes of exotic and dried fruits. A remarkable Pouilly-Fumé that is ready to drink now but could be kept for a few years. In a higher price bracket, the **Prestige 2000** is also recommended.

• Dom. du Bouchot, BP 31, 58150 Saint-Andelain, tel. 03.86.39.13.95, fax 03.86.39.05.92 [V] [Y] by appt.

• Kerbiquet

HENRY BROCHARD
Sélection 2000★★
n.c.　25,000　€8-11

wonderful Sauvignon grape variety. Take this wine, made from 45-year-old vines, which this year narrowly missed winning the *coup de cœur*. It has a charming bouquet, with floral notes and very fresh nuances (green apples), and on the palate the wine is firm, complex and rich, continuing on notes of narcissus. This is a great wine to keep. In a lower price bracket, his **La Châtellière** and **La Renardière** are recommended (no stars).

• EARL Bouché-Chatellier, Dom. La Renardière, 58150 Saint-Andelain, tel. 03.86.39.14.01, fax 03.86.39.05.18, e-mail pouilly.fume.bouchie.chatellier@wanadoo [V] [Y] by appt.

People will love this wine, if they are prepared to wait for it. Although its bouquet is still closed, it is already showing remarkable finesse. Its rounded, rich, fleshy qualities fill the palate with its rich, fruity base. It has a very promising future.

• Dom. Henry Brochard, Chavignol, 18300 Sancerre, tel. 02.48.78.20.10, fax 02.48.78.20.19, e-mail lesvinshenrybrochard@wanadoo.fr [V]

DOM. A. CAILBOURDIN
Les Cornets 2000
2.5 ha　16,000　€8-11

This 15-ha (37-acre) estate is regularly mentioned in the *Guide*. Les Cornets comes from clay-limestone soils (kimmeridge marls), which have produced a lovely golden-coloured wine with metallic glints, and a subtle bouquet reminiscent of quince. On the palate it reveals a harmonious flow of sensations, with just the right amount of bitterness to show it will come into its own in a year's time. Another wine from the same producer was also singled out by the Jury: **Les Cris 2000** – a product of the limestone slopes.

• EARL Alain Cailbourdin, Maltaverne, 58150 Tracy-sur-Loire, tel. 03.86.26.17.73, fax 03.86.26.14.73 [Y] by appt.

DOM. CHAMPEAU 2000
14.4 ha　80,000　€5-8

The aromas are released slowly, suggesting yellow flowers and bitter almonds, and on the palate this wine is very rounded and smooth. Ready for drinking, the wine should go well with white meats.

• SCEA Dom. Guy et Franck Champeau, Le Bourg, 58150 Saint-Andelain, tel. 03.86.39.15.61, fax 03.86.39.19.44, e-mail domaine.champeau@wanadoo.fr [V] [Y] by appt.

JEAN-CLAUDE CHATELAIN 2000★
19 ha　150,000　€8-11

Jean-Claude Chatelain represents the 11th generation of wine-growers on this estate, founded in 1630. Now that his son Vincent has arrived on the scene, the succession is assured. With their 2000 vintage, they chose to make a wine that is not at all restrained. Its scents are strongly marked by broom and boxwood, with floral notes, and on the palate it is well-balanced with a lengthy finish.

• SA Dom. Chatelain, Les Berthiers, 58150 Saint-Andelain, tel. 03.86.39.17.46, fax 03.86.39.01.13, e-mail jean-claude.chatelain@wanadoo.fr [V] [Y] by appt.

DOM. CHAUVEAU La Charnette 2000
7 ha　30,000　€8-11

Benoît Chauveau, who has been in charge of his family business for three years, receives his third mention in the *Guide*. This wine is classic in style, its intense bouquet initially herbaceous, then marked by citrus fruits; on the palate it is lively, but still rather subdued on the finish.

EARL Dom. Chauveau, Les Cassiers, 58150 Saint-Andelain, tel. 03.86.39.15.42, fax 03.86.39.19.46, e-mail pouillychauveau@aol.com
ev. day 9am–12 noon 2pm–8pm

GILLES CHOLLET 2000★

3 ha 25,000 €5-8

The pronounced golden colour of this vintage augurs well for its later development. The bouquet mingles white flowers and citrus fruits, and it is very fleshy on the palate as well as mischievously lively with notes of liquorice and aniseed. It is a most charming wine.

Gilles Chollet, 6 bis, rue Joseph-Renaud, Le Bouchot, 58150 Pouilly-sur-Loire, tel. 03.86.39.02.19, fax 03.86.39.06.13
ev. day 9.30am–7pm; Sun. 9.30am–1pm

PATRICK COULBOIS

Les Cocques 2000 8 ha 35,000 €5-8

Comprising 8.7 ha (21 acres), this estate is planted mainly on the siliceous-clay slopes of Saint-Andelain. Their Les Cocques has often been mentioned in the *Guide* and is again singled out this year. It releases very pronounced scents of blood orange, rounded off with a touch of linden flowers. The palate is rounded and smooth and marked by a very ripe fruitiness with accents of exotic fruits and stewed plums. It is a very accessible wine.

Patrick Coulbois, Les Berthiers, 58150 Saint-Andelain, tel. 03.86.39.15.69, fax 03.86.39.12.14 by appt.

DIDIER DAGUENEAU

En Chailloux 1999★ 5 ha n.c. €15-23

This wine's fermentation was carried out in new oak barrels, and it was matured in tank to show off its fine *terroir* in mineral aromas with accents of gunflint, a lively first impression and a rounded and long palate with a fruity base. This is just the sort of good wine you can drink now or keep in the cellar for several years.

Didier Dagueneau, Le Bourg, 58150 Saint-Andelain, tel. 03.86.39.15.62, e-mail Silex@wanadoo.fr by appt.

JEAN-CLAUDE DAGUENEAU

Cuvée d'Eve Vieilles vignes 1999 2.5 ha 15,000 €8-11

Cuvée d'Eve is made from selected grapes from the estate's best plots. It was partly matured in oak, so you should not be surprised to find toasty notes as the bouquet opens. Powerful fruity qualities emerge later. This light but typical Pouilly-Fumé will be enjoyable to drink immediately.

SCEA Dom. des Berthiers, Les Berthiers, BP 30, 58150 Saint-Andelain, tel. 03.86.39.12.85, fax 03.86.39.12.94, e-mail sauldre@fournier-père-fils.fr
ev. day 9am–5pm; Sat. Sun. by appt.

MARC DESCHAMPS

Vieilles vignes 2000 1.6 ha 10,000 €8-11

When he took over this property in 1992, Marc Deschamps was already an experienced wine-grower. His wine, made from 50-year-old vines, is well-structured, with aromas of pineapples and citrus fruits. Although its liveliness is still very evident at the finish, all should be well if it is kept for a while.

Marc Deschamps, Les Loges, 58150 Pouilly-sur-Loire, tel. 03.86.69.16.43, fax 03.86.39.06.90 by appt.
Colette Figeat

JEAN DUMONT

Les Coques Vieilles 2000★ 12 ha 100,000 €8-11

The whole attraction of this wine stems from its rich aromas. The clay-limestone soil has produced a bouquet of white flowers and a procession of herbaceous scents (broom and gorse), with notes of lemon and pineapple developing on the palate. The wine is a true example of the appellation. Another wine, Le Grand Plateau, also won one star.

Jean Dumont, RN 7, La Castille, 58150 Pouilly-sur-Loire, tel. 03.86.39.56.60, fax 03.86.39.08.30 by appt.

CH. FAVRAY 2000★

14 ha 95,000 €8-11

Château Favray's vineyards were destroyed by phylloxera and were restored by Quentin David from 1981. The limestone soil has produced an unusual wine with a floral bouquet briefly touched by a herbaceous note. Its youthful liveliness will mature, introducing more freshness. This is an interesting and original wine.

Ch. Favray, 58150 Saint-Martin-sur-Nohain, tel. 03.86.26.19.05, fax 03.86.26.11.59 by appt.

ANDRE ET EDMOND FIGEAT

Côte du Nozet 2000★ 2 ha 10,000 €8-11

André and Edmond Figeat have taken their place in a line of five generations of winemakers. A photograph of their ancestors, Louis and Ferdinand, at the winepress figures prominently, and explains their fondness for tradition. Their forefathers would certainly have approved of their 2000 vintage, with its intense nuances of exotic fruits. Although still closed on the palate and difficult to enjoy, this is a wine of substance and temperament which needs time to improve.

André et Edmond Figeat, Côte du Nozet, 58150 Pouilly-sur-Loire, tel. 03.86.39.19.39, fax 03.86.39.19.00 by appt.

DOM. DES FINES CAILLOTTES

2000*

☐ 15 ha 132,000 €8-11

Consisting of more than 20 parcels of land, this domaine takes its name from the white limestone pebbles that are locally known as *caillottes* and are often found in clay-limestone soils. Alain Pabiot knows how to harvest extremely ripe grapes, as this wine clearly shows, with its intense fruity and floral aromas already joined by shades of honey and liquorice. On the palate, it is very rounded and smooth, without a trace of harshness, revealing a very fleshy, almost sweet character. This sort of wine should go well with fish or poultry.

➜ Jean Pabiot et Fils, 9, rue de la Treille, Les Loges, 58150 Pouilly-sur-Loire, tel. 03.86.39.10.25, fax 03.86.39.10.12 ☑
Ⓨ ev. day 8am–12 noon 2pm–6pm; Sat. Sun. by appt.

FOUCHER-LEBRUN

Les Deux Collines 2000

☐ n.c. 4,600 €8-11

This wine-merchant's firm was founded in 1921 by a cooper, Paulin Lebrun, and today is run by Jacky Foucher. His Pouilly-Fumé is well-made, with a bouquet of boxwood and ivy hinting of minerals. Its lack of liveliness makes it very drinkable, and it is ready for drinking now.

➜ Foucher-Lebrun, 29, rte de Bouhy, 58200 Alligny, tel. 03.86.26.87.27, fax 03.86.26.87.20

DOM. DE LA MARNIERE 2000

☐ 5 ha 40,000 €8-11

Pale-gold with characteristic green glints, this Pouilly-Fumé offers a fairly intense bouquet dominated by the herbaceous notes that are typical of Sauvignon. Clear-cut and lively on the palate, it will go well with seafood or asparagus.

➜ Loiret Frères, 4430 Le Pallet, tel. 02.40.80.40.27, fax 02.40.80.41.32
➜ Maurice Parizot

LA MOYNERIE 1999

☐ 26 ha 250,000 €8-11

Aromas of citrus fruits are evidence of careful vinification, and herbaceous notes are a reflection of this wine's *terroir*. Open and lively on the palate, the wine is not ostentatious, but true to the appellation.

➜ SA Michel Redde et Fils, La Moynerie, 58150 Pouilly-sur-Loire, tel. 03.86.39.14.72, fax 03.86.39.04.36, e-mail michel-redde@ michel-redde.fr ☑ Ⓨ by appt.
➜ Thierry Redde

LES VIEILLOTTES 2000***

☐ 6 ha 40,000 €8-11

Caves de Pouilly-sur-Loire, founded in 1948 and one of the region's largest producers, have just taken on a new wine-maker, Frédéric Jacquet. The siliceous-clay soils that produced Les Vieillottes come through in the mineral notes and the delicate fruity aromas

JOSEPH MELLOT Le Troncsec 2000

☐ n.c. 84,000 €8-11

Boxwood and white flowers are the main aromas of this wine, which is typical of Sauvignon. On the palate, it reveals a slight sparkle, with a hint of bitterness on the finish (which is not a defect).

➜ Vignobles Joseph Mellot Père et Fils, rte de Ménétréol, BP 13, 18300 Sancerre, tel. 02.48.78.54.54, fax 02.48.78.54.55, e-mail alexandre@joseph-mellot.fr ☑
Ⓨ ev. day 8am–12 noon 1.30pm–5.30pm; Sat. Sun. by appt.

JEAN-PAUL MOLLET 2000*

☐ n.c. 9,733 €8-11

Jean-Paul Mollet has recently taken over this old family estate, and this is his first year of production. Already he has proved himself successful. The very subtle aromas of this 2000 wine combine flowers with apples and pears. This mouth-filling wine is an accomplished Pouilly-Fumé.

of peaches and quince, their power evidence of the wine's maturity. This is a great wine that can only become more refined. Another mainstay of the co-operative is **Les Moulins à Vent 2000**, which wins one star.

➜ Caves de Pouilly-sur-Loire, Les Moulins à Vent, BP 9, 58150 Pouilly-sur-Loire, tel. 03.86.39.10.99, fax 03.86.39.02.28, e-mail caves.pouilly.loire@wanadoo.fr ☑
Ⓨ by appt.

JACQUES MARCHAND 2000

☐ n.c. n.c. €8-11

This wine's fruitiness runs right through the tasting, from bouquet to finish. It is a ripe fruitiness particularly reminiscent of citrus fruits (oranges and grapefruits) and also, in the background, pears. A fairly rounded opening in the mouth is followed by a sensation of a well-structured and tasty wine on the palate.

➜ SARL Jacques Marchand, Les Loges, rue Francs-Bourgeois, 58150 Pouilly-sur-Loire, tel. 02.48.78.54.55, fax 02.48.78.54.55 ☑
Ⓨ by appt.

PIERRE MARCHAND ET FILS

2000

☐ 2.4 ha 20,000 €5-8

Pierre Marchand belongs to a line of wine-makers dating from 1650, and he has managed to transmit his passion to his two sons, who work with him on this 14-ha (34-acre) property. Their Pouilly-Fumé is pleasant, the bouquet opening with scents of fermentation (bananas and blackcurrants), then suggesting floral nuances. It is smooth and easy to drink, and finishes on a note of grapefruit.

➜ EARL Pierre Marchand et Fils, Les Loges, 9, rue des Pressoirs, 58150 Pouilly-sur-Loire, tel. 03.86.39.14.61, fax 03.86.39.17.21 ☑
Ⓨ ev. day 9am–12.30pm 2pm–7.30pm

SCEV des Renardières, 11, rue des Écoles, Boisgibault, 58150 Tracy-sur-Loire, tel. 02.48.54.02.26, fax 02.48.54.02.26

DOM. DIDIER PABIOT 2000

☐ 12 ha 100,000 ◼◾ €8-11

From the door of Didier Pabiot's cellar you have an unbeatable view over the Loire Valley. Inside, he will offer you a Pouilly-Fumé with a restrained bouquet of wax, bread and oranges, and a smooth palate finishing on notes of grapefruit peel. It would be an ideal companion for goats' cheese.

Didier Pabiot, Les Loges, BP 5, 58150 Pouilly-sur-Loire, tel. 03.86.39.01.32, fax 03.86.39.03.27 ⚑ by appt.

DOM. ROGER PABIOT ET SES FILS

Silex de Tracy 1999★★

☐ 1.75 ha 15,000 ◼◾ €8-11

Matured for 18 months, this charming wine comes from Tracy's siliceous soils. The intensity of its bouquet lacks nothing in finesse, and on the palate its rounded, fleshy qualities are enlivened by a slight sparkle; fruity flavours of peaches and prunes are apparent on the lengthy finish. It is an excellent wine. Another wine from this estate, Pouilly-Fumé **Coteau des Girarmes 2000**, is recommended and wins one star.

Dom. Roger Pabiot et ses Fils, 13, rte de Pouilly, Boisgibault, 58150 Tracy-sur-Loire, tel. 03.86.26.18.41, fax 03.86.26.19.89, e-mail domainerogerpabiot@wanadoo.fr ⚑ by appt.

DOM. RAIMBAULT-PINEAU

La Montée des Lumeaux 2000★

☐ 1.64 ha 13,000 ◼◾ €8-11

Ten generations have run this vineyeard, from Pierre-Alexandre, born in 1701, to Lucien, born in 1990. Their mastery of their trade comes through in this very well-balanced wine, with its charming bouquet of citrus fruits. Smooth and full on the palate, its scents on the nose re-emerge on the lengthy finish.

Dom. Raimbault-Pineau, rte de Sancerre, 18300 Sury-en-Vaux, tel. 02.48.79.33.04, fax 02.48.79.33.04 ⚑ ev. day 9am–12 noon 2pm–6pm; Sun. by appt.; cl. 1–15 Aug.

DOM. DE RIAUX 2000

☐ 9 ha 55,000 ◼◾ €5-8

This wine comes from vines grown on siliceous-clay soils, and clearly bears their mark. It is restrained, timid at first, with a mineral bouquet and accents of gunflint, and a firm, slightly charred note on the palate. Give it time to mature, and it will not disappoint you.

GAEC Jeannot Père et Fils, Dom. de Riaux, 58150 Saint-Andelain, tel. 03.86.39.11.37, fax 03.86.39.06.21 ⚑ by appt.

GUY SAGET Les Chantalouettes 2000★

☐ 4 ha 30,000 ◼◾ €8-11

Herbaceous notes of fennel and menthol elegantly combine with the fruitness of pears in this wine's bouquet, while on the palate it is no less interesting: well-structured and enlivened by vigorous accents of green apples and white peaches. All in all, this is a wine with plenty of depth. Another wine, **Les Logères 2000**, often mentioned in the *Guide*, is recommended again this year.

Guy Saget, La Castille, 58150 Pouilly-sur-Loire, tel. 03.86.39.57.75, fax 03.86.39.08.30, e-mail saget@guy-saget.com ⚑ by appt.

J.-L. Saget

DOM. TABORDET 2000★

☐ 5.9 ha 50,000 ◼◾ €8-11

The open, charming bouquet, with its scents of crystallised lemon and very ripe fruits, is a pleasant introduction to the body of this wine. The bouquet's aromas recur on the palate, when a touch of liveliness adds depth to the fairly smooth whole. It has the elegance and restraint of a classic wine.

Yvon et Pascal Tabordet, Chaudoux, 18300 Verdigny, tel. 02.48.79.34.01, fax 02.48.79.32.69 ⚑ by appt.

DOM. THIBAULT 2000★

☐ 12.51 ha 87,000 ◼◾ €8-11

This wine has succulent scents of honeyed white flowers (acacia and elder) and fruit (blackcurrants and plums), as well as fresh, smooth, tasty sensations on the palate. It is a very well-flavoured Pouilly-Fumé that relies more on finesse than power.

SCEV André Dezat et Fils, Chaudoux, 18300 Verdigny, tel. 02.48.79.38.82, fax 02.48.79.38.24 ⚑ by appt.

F. TINEL-BLONDELET

L'Arret Buffatte 2000★

☐ 3.5 ha 28,000 ◼◾ €8-11

Annick Tinel-Blondelet offers one of those wines that are mainstays of the appellation because they are open, natural and true to type. The intense bouquet, suggestive of gunflint and boxwood, and its light but no less excellent flavours (flowers and white berries) make this a very elegant wine.

Dom. Tinel-Blondelet, La Croix-Canat, 58150 Pouilly-sur-Loire, tel. 03.86.39.13.83, fax 03.86.39.02.94 ⚑ by appt.

SEBASTIEN TREUILLET 2000★

☐ 1 ha 8,000 ◼◾ €5-8

This wine comes from a clay-silt soil, and reveals a youthful character. After swirling the wine in the glass, the bouquet opens with smoky notes and mandarins. It still has a slight sparkle, which adds a lemony acidity on the finish. Although ready for drinking now, it could be kept for two years.

Sébastien Treuillet, Fontenille, 58150 Tracy-sur-Loire, tel. 03.86.26.17.06, fax 03.86.26.17.06 ⚑ ev. day 8am–12 noon 1pm–7pm

DOM. DE BEL AIR 2000★

0.6 ha 2.500 €3-5

Domaine de Bel Air has 13 ha (32 acres). Its Pouilly-sur-Loire 2000 is particularly successful. The maturity of the Chasselas grapes provides fine fruity scents (apples) and, above all, typical almond notes. The flavours are harmoniously balanced, and its freshness and fullness combine perfectly.

➥ EARL Mauroy-Gaultez, Dom. de Bel Air, Le Bouchot, 58150 Pouilly-sur-Loire, tel. 03.86.39.15.85, fax 03.86.39.19.52, e-mail mauroygaultez@aol.com ☑
☗ ev. day 8.30am–12.30pm 1.30pm–6.30pm

DOM. CHAMPEAU 2000

1.8 ha 10.000 €5-8

The estate that produces this successful wine is opposite the church of Saint-Andelain. The aromas are light, but have a complexity rare in a Pouilly-sur-Loire: exotic fruits, spices and vanilla. This 2000 wine – from very old vines, as is often the case with Chasselas plantations – is fresh and fine, and ready for drinking.

➥ SCEA Dom. Guy et Franck Champeau, Le Bourg, 58150 Saint-Andelain, tel. 03.86.39.15.61, fax 03.86.39.19.44, e-mail domaine.champeau@wanadoo.fr ☑
☗ by appt.

LA MOYNERIE 1999★

1 ha 6.500 €8-11

With grey-brown highlights in its golden colour, and an intense bouquet of linden flowers and fresh nuts, this Pouilly-sur-Loire is rounded and full, and its full-bodied structure and elegance come as a pleasant surprise. This dashing wine deserves special attention.

➥ SA Michel Redde et Fils, La Moynerie, 58150 Pouilly-sur-Loire, tel. 03.86.39.14.72, fax 03.86.39.04.36, e-mail thierry.redde@michel-redde.fr ☑ ☗ by appt.
● Thierry Redde

DOM. ROGER PABIOT ET SES FILS 2000★

0.4 ha 3.000 €5-8

Roger Pabiot and his sons have got the best out of Tracy's *terroir* to produce good wines made with Chasselas grapes. This one's aromas are particularly expressive and elegant, reminiscent of quince and very ripe apples. Its freshness and balance make it a classic wine, very true to type, which will be pleasant with a light meal.

➥ Dom. Roger Pabiot et ses Fils, 13, rte de Pouilly, Boisgibault, 58150 Tracy-sur-Loire, tel. 03.86.26.18.41, fax 03.86.26.19.89, e-mail domainerogerpabiot@wanadoo.fr ☑

DOM. DE RIAUX 2000★

0.4 ha 1.500 €5-8

This lovely Pouilly-sur-Loire was made from grapes grown on vines planted almost 50 years ago. The finesse of its aromas, recalling white flowers and undergrowth in spring, was enjoyed by the tasters. On the palate, the wine is rounded, with a fleshy finish. It is a charming wine.

➥ GAEC Jeannot Père et Fils, Dom. de Riaux, 58150 Saint-Andelain, tel. 03.86.39.11.37, fax 03.86.39.06.21 ☑
☗ by appt.

The vineyards of Quincy and Brinay cover 171 ha (442 acres) on plateaux covered with sand and ancient gravels along the banks of the Cher, not far from Bourges and Mehun-sur-Yèvre, in an area rich in the history of the 16th century.

Quincy wines, of which 10,288 hl (271,603 gal) were produced in 2000, are made only from Sauvignon, and are fresh, fruity and extremely drinkable, with real finesse and personality.

If, as the French wine authority Doctor Guyot wrote, Quincy determines character, Quincy also provides evidence that the same variety can provide different wines in the same region depending on the structure of the soils. The wine-lover will find this one of the most elegant of the Loire wines, to be drunk with fish and seafood, as well as with the goat's cheeses of the region.

SYLVAIN BAILLY
Les Grands Coeurs 2000★

4 ha 30.000 €5-8

Les Grands Coeurs is suitably open-hearted, offering rich and intense fruity aromas. It is rounded and rather firm, with a lemony note on the finish, and has the balance to make it enjoyable.

➥ Sylvain Bailly, 71, rue de Venoize, 18300 Bué, tel. 02.48.54.02.75, fax 02.48.54.28.41 ☗ ev. day 8am–12 noon 2pm–6pm; Sun. by appt.

HENRI BOURGEOIS 2000★   7 ha   55,000   €5-8

The Henri Bourgeois estate, which started life in the Sancerre region, offers a very successful Quincy made from a good selection of grapes and careful vinification. This wine is smooth and fleshy, and completely fills the mouth with fruity flavours, peaches to the fore – very elegant.

Dom. Henri Bourgeois, Chavignol, 18300 Sancerre, tel. 02.48.78.53.20, fax 02.48.54.14.24, e-mail domaine@bourgeois-sancerre.com by appt.

DOM. DES BRUNIERS 2000   10 ha   50,000   €5-8

A very light-golden colour, with particularly noticeable green glints, this wine is consistently good on the palate, with its flavours of fruits and flowers. It is a classic Quincy.

Jérôme de La Chaise, Les Bruniers, 18120 Quincy, tel. 02.48.51.34.10, fax 02.48.51.34.10 by appt.

DOM. DES CAVES 2000   4.3 ha   35,000   €5-8

Bruno Lecomte is one of the many growers who opted for an integrated wine-making policy. His Quincy has a strong bouquet with charred notes. However, on the palate the wine, though pleasant, still reveals a hint of bitterness. It needs time to mature to reach its best.

Bruno Lecomte, 105, rue Saint-Exupéry, 18520 Avord, tel. 02.48.69.27.14, fax 02.48.69.16.42, e-mail bruno.lecomte@wanadoo.fr by appt.

DOM. DE CHAMP MARTIN 2000   4 ha   30,000   €5-8

Didier Rassat offers a Quincy 2000 whose unusually strong gold colour immediately draws the eye. This is certainly a singular wine of some character, with its intense aromas and balanced structure combining smoothness and liveliness.

Didier Rassat, Champ Martin, 18120 Cerbois, tel. 02.48.51.70.19, fax 02.48.51.79.27 ev. day 9am–12 noon 3pm–7pm

DOM. DES COUDEREAUX 2000   8 ha   60,000   €5-8

From a vineyard about ten years old, this Quincy is true to the clay-silt soils it comes from. The bouquet clearly emphasises the mineral aspect of the Sauvignon grape. Although the sensations on the palate are somewhat light in their make-up, they are none the less full of quality and very pleasant.

SCEA Les Coudereaux, 34, rte de Bourges, 18510 Menetou-Salon, tel. 02.48.64.88.88, fax 02.48.64.87.97 by appt.

DOM. DES CROIX 2000   1.25 ha   8,000   €5-8

Sylvie Rouzé-Lavault has made a successful 2000 vintage marked by broom and boxwood, with a youthful vigour recalling grapefruit. It is a very pleasant wine.

Rouzé-Lavault, rte de Lury, 18120 Quincy, tel. 02.48.51.08.51, fax 02.48.51.05.00 by appt.

LES VIGNERONS DU DUC DE BERRY 2000★   8 ha   60,000   €5-8

The maturity of this wine is clearly evident in its fruity, long-lasting notes. Even so, it has a lively, even sharp temperament with a touch of bite. This kind of wine is good with seafood and shellfish.

SICA Vignerons du Duc de Berry, 34, rte de Bourges, 18510 Menetou-Salon, tel. 02.48.64.88.88, fax 02.48.64.87.97 by appt.

PIERRE DURET 2000★★   n.c.   n.c.   €5-8

Although bearing the name of its former proprietor, this vineyard is owned by the Joseph Mellot company. Its 2000 vintage is full of good things: not only the fine, fruity aromas, but also the sensations of roundness and fleshiness on the palate, which brilliantly cloak its liveliness and charm the taste buds. In short, this is a rich wine.

SARL Pierre Duret, rte de Lury, 18120 Quincy, tel. 02.48.78.05.01, fax 02.48.78.54.55 by appt.

Alexandre Mellot

DOM. DU GRAND ROSIERES 2000   3.8 ha   15,000   €5-8

Since he took over in 1994, Jacques Siret has prudently increased the size of his vineyard. His wine remains balanced, from the smooth first impression to the lively finish. It could be served as an aperitif.

Jacques Siret, Dom. du Grand Rosières, 18400 Lunery, tel. 02.48.68.90.34, fax 02.48.68.03.71 by appt.

DOM. DE LA COMMANDERIE 2000   2.95 ha   25,000   €5-8

Made from selected grapes, this wine combines notes of broom and citrus fruits, and is characterised by a clear-cut opening in the mouth and by a lightness and smoothness on the palate, which give it a youthful brightness.

EARL Jean-Charles Borgnat, 27, rue de Jacques-au-Bois, 18120 Preuilly, tel. 02.48.51.30.16, fax 02.48.51.32.94, e-mail jcborgnat@aol.com by appt.

DOM. MARDON 2000   11 ha   n.c.   €5-8

The bouquet is still closed, but it gives off hints of flowers (violets) and fruits (lychees and peaches). The first impression is clear-cut, and on the palate the wine reveals real smoothness. Although the wine has good quality, it should be aged to allow its many qualities to emerge.

intensely evident, and tasting ends on a lengthy finish of ripe lemon. Drink this with shellfish.

↝ SARL Jean-Michel Sorbe, La Quervée, 18120 Preuilly, tel. 02.48.51.99.43, fax 02.48.51.35.47 ☑ ♈ by appt.

DOM. DU TONKIN 2000

3.25 ha 25,000 🗓️ €5-8

Jacques Masson's property is gradually getting larger (now 3.25 ha/8 acres). His Quincy is dominated by intense herbaceous nuances and completed by fruity and mineral notes. On the finish, the wine has a hint of dryness, which does no harm to the general impression.

↝ Dom. du Tonkin, Le Tonkin, 18120 Brinay, tel. 02.48.51.11.67 ☑ ♈ by appt.

↝ Jacques Masson

DOM. DU TREMBLAY

Cuvée Nouzats-Coudereaux 2000★

3.5 ha 25,000 🗓️ €5-8

Jean Tatin has been running the 7.5-ha (18.5-acre) Domaine du Tremblay since 1993, and can tell you a thing or two about the appellation's soils. His Nouzats-Coudereaux happily combines the harvests of two parcels of land located in the communes of Quincy and Brinay. Its roundness and balance provide good support for the flavours, which have yet to give their best.

↝ Jean Tatin, Le Tremblay, 18120 Brinay, tel. 02.48.75.20.09, fax 02.48.75.70.50, e-mail jeantatinviticulteur@hotmail.com ☑ ♈ by appt.

DOM. TROTEREAU 2000★★

n.c. 45,000 🗓️

Once again, Pierre Ragon has delighted the jury with the very personal style he brings to his wines, which are in the top bracket. This vintage has a charming and smooth fruitiness (mango) enhanced by herbaceous and floral touches. It has good body, with roundness and fullness bordering on the fleshy. A real *vin de terroir*, which all of the tasters enjoyed.

↝ Pierre Ragon, rte de Lury, 18120 Quincy, tel. 02.48.51.37.37, fax 02.48.26.82.58 ☑ ♈ by appt.

↝ Dom. Mardon, 40, rte de Reuilly, 18120 Quincy, tel. 02.48.51.31.60, fax 02.48.51.35.55 ☑ ♈ by appt.

JOSEPH MELLOT Le Rimonet 1999★

10 ha 80,000 🗓️ €5-8

This pale, green-gold 99 has retained much of its youthfulness. The fresh bouquet recalls passion-fruit, and on the palate the wine reveals a good touch of acidity before the flavours of crystallised fruit appear, the result of ageing. Balanced and full, this 99 will be ready to drink in the course of 2002.

↝ SA Joseph Mellot, rte de Ménétréol, BP 13, 18300 Sancerre, tel. 02.48.78.54.54, fax 02.48.78.54.55, e-mail alexandre@joseph-mellot.fr ☑ ♈ ev. day except Sat.-Sun. 8am–12 noon 1.30pm–5.30pm

---

DOM. ANDRÉ PIGEAT 2000★

2.45 ha 5,000 🗓️ €3-5

Domaine André Pigeat was established in 1999. It has a functional cellar and modern equipment, which has proved ideal for this vintage. It has a delightful freshness recalling grapefruit and lemon, and is well-structured on the palate. It would go well with fish.

↝ Dom. André Pigeat, 18, rte de Cerbois, 18120 Quincy, tel. 02.48.51.31.90, fax 02.48.51.31.90 ☑ ♈ by appt.

PHILIPPE PORTIER 2000★

9 ha 70,000 🗓️ €5-8

The vineyard has been planted on gravel soils with a clay subsoil (both good for Sauvignon), a careful and creative wine-maker and good-quality production methods. The 98 vintage won a *coup de cœur*. The 2000 combines scents of ivy and passion-fruit spiced with toasty notes, making it an original Quincy with a good general structure.

↝ EARL Philippe Portier, Bois-Gy-Moreau, 18120 Brinay, tel. 02.48.51.09.02, fax 02.48.51.00.96 ☑ ♈ by appt.

JACQUES SALLE Silice 1998★

4 ha 15,000 ⫿ €11-15

In 1996, after writing a lot about wine, Jacques Sallé decided to try producing wine himself. He bought about ten parcels of old vines and opted for organic cultivation. His Silice bears the mark of being aged in barrel for nine months, with weekly stirring: toasty, vanilla and buttery notes are to the fore. These flavours are balanced on the palate by a nice freshness. This is one for enlightened wine-lovers.

↝ Jacques Sallé, Chem. des Vignes, 18120 Quincy, tel. 02.54.04.04.48, e-mail jacquessalle@aol.com ♈ by appt.

JEAN-MICHEL SORBE 2000★

2.5 ha 20,000 🗓️ €5-8

Immediately apparent in this wine are its aromas of fermentation along with hints of bread. Swirling in the glass results in the scents of the Sauvignon grape becoming

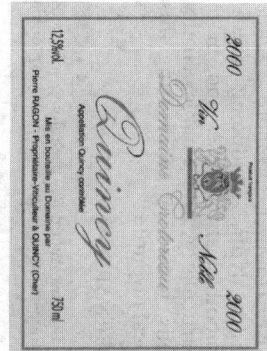

Reuilly

Steep, sunny hills and remarkable soils make Reuilly a natural environment for the vine.

The appellation covers 138 ha (341 acres) ranging over seven communes in the Indre and the Cher, a charming region crossed by the green valleys of the rivers Cher, Arnon and Théols. It produced 8,296 hl (219,014 gal) of wine in 2000.

Reuilly white wines are dry, fruity Sauvignons, which can achieve notable fullness; production was 4,606 hl (121,598 gal) in 2000. Pinot Gris provides a rosé from direct pressing that is as delicate and distinguished as one might wish. However, the more versatile Pinot Noir, producing fresh, smooth, lustrous rosés and, more particularly, full, complex, fruity reds, is rapidly supplanting this local favourite.

BERNARD AUJARD 2000★★   1.7 ha   12,000   €5-8

Bernard Aujard has been doing very well. After winning a *coup de coeur* last year for his rosé, he collects another one this year for a red. It exhales lovely scents of spices, cinnamon and pepper, and also pears. The tannins are still a little harsh, and the wine needs to be kept for two or three years before drinking. The **white 2000** is recommended for its mineral note followed by a touch of citrus fruit.

Bernard Aujard, 2, rue du Bas-Bourg, 18120 Lazenay, tel. 02.48.51.73.69, fax 02.48.51.73.69 ☑ ☑ by appt.

LES BERRYCURIENS

Les Chatillons 2000   0.5 ha   3,000   €8-11

The passion for good wine leads people far afield, even as far as producing their own. That has been the story of the BerryCuriens, a group of enthusiasts, since 1995. The colour of this wine, made from Pinot Gris planted on sloping alluvial soils, is bright peony. Its other attractions are linked to its fruitiness: stewed fruits in the bouquet, fresh fruits on the palate, and fruits in brandy to round it off. It is a balanced and pleasant wine.

SCEV des BerryCuriens, 9, rte de Boisgissons, 18120 Preuilly, tel. 02.48.51.30.17, fax 02.48.51.35.47 ☑ by appt.

DOM. HENRI BEURDIN ET FILS   €5-8

2000   7.25 ha   50,000

This estate, 5 km (3 miles) from the abbey of Manzay-Limeux, won a *coup de coeur* last year for its 99 white. This vintage is also not short of energy, revealing its liveliness in a bitter note that the wine's richness extends. The bouquet of flowers and citrus fruit is delicate. It is an original wine that has a charm of its own.

SCEV Henri Beurdin et Fils, 14, Le Carroir, 18120 Preuilly, tel. 02.48.51.30.78, fax 02.48.51.34.81 ☑ ☑ by appt.

DOM. DU BOURDONNAT 2000   €5-8

1.5 ha   8,000

Slightly silvery and pale-pink in colour, this pleasant Pinot Gris rosé has a fresh bouquet of white peaches and citrus fruit. An impression of sweetness prevails on the palate, with flavours of fruits followed by a faintly spicy freshness, and these are still there on the finish.

François Charpentier, Dom. du Bourdonnat, 36260 Reuilly, tel. 02.54.49.20.18, fax 02.54.49.29.91 ☑ ☑ by appt.

CHANTAL ET MICHEL CORDAILLAT 2000   €5-8

1.7 ha   12,000

Starting with a plot he acquired in 1995, Michel Cordaillat has gradually built up a property, and a name for himself. His 2000 white opens straightforwardly with a pale golden-yellow colour and delicate floral and herbaceous aromas. It then asserts its

Reuilly

DOM. DE VILLAIN 2000★   €5-8

3 ha   16,000

In its second year of production, Domaine de Villain has made a successful wine that gets it into the *Guide*. On the palate, the wine has impressive presence and length, and touches of acidity and bitterness made the Jury optimistic about its future quality after it has been aged for a while.

Dom. de Villain, Le Grand Villain, 18120 Quincy, tel. 02.48.51.34.98, fax 02.48.51.34.98 ☑ ☑ by appt.

Marchand

openness and firmness and finishes on lemony nuances.

☛ Chantal et Michel Cordaillat, Le Montet, 18120 Méreau, tel. 02.48.52.83.48, fax 02.48.52.83.09 **V**
Y ev. day except Sun. 4pm–7pm

DOM. DES COUDEREAUX 2000★

| 0.72 ha | 6,000 | | €5-8 |

'This is an unfinished sculpture,' wrote an oenologist at the tasting. The aromas are still of citrus fruit, but floral qualities are beginning to show through, and the Jury was confident that very soon both balance and a fine richness would appear. This is a typical 2000 Reuilly, one that can be trusted.

☛ SCEA Les Coudereaux, 34, rte de Bourges, 18510 Menetou-Salon, tel. 02.48.64.88.88, fax 02.48.64.87.97 **V**
Y by appt.
☛ Jean-Paul Godinat

PASCAL DESROCHES
Clos des Varennes 2000★

| 3.8 ha | 30,000 | | €5-8 |

Very successfully, this Clos des Varennes was matured on fine lees. The intense bouquet of flowers mingled with spices produces a warm, rich impression. The wine creates silky, fleshy and 'comfortable' (as one Jury member put it) sensations on the palate, and there is some acidity, but not too much. This Reuilly white is a full-bodied wine. Also try the rosé **Clos des Lignis 2000**, which was awarded one star.

☛ Pascal Desroches, 13, rte de Charost, 18120 Lazenay, tel. 02.48.51.71.60, fax 02.48.51.71.60 **V** **Y** by appt.

JEAN-SYLVAIN GUILLEMAIN
2000

| 0.8 ha | 7,000 | | €5-8 |

This Reuilly white comes from eight-year-old vines grown on a newish estate which started in 1992. Its aromas of citrus fruit are distinctly of the fermented kind, but behind them are notes of wild flowers. This well-structured wine already has finesse and promises to mature well, sharpening and developing both body and roundness.

☛ Jean-Sylvain Guillemain, Palleau, 18120 Lury-sur-Arnon, tel. 02.48.52.99.01, fax 02.48.52.99.09 **V** **Y** by appt.

CLAUDE LAFOND La Raie 2000★★

| 7 ha | 59,500 | | €5-8 |

Claude Lafond does credit to the Reuilly appellation with his high-quality 2000 wines. The La Raie white's aromas gush forth like a volcanic outburst (ripe peaches, brioche and butter, with a herbaceous touch). It is simultaneously rounded, fleshy and tender, with a slightly acid structure, and wins the *coup de cœur*. From the same year, **Les Grandes Vignes** red is recommended (one star).

☛ SARL Claude Lafond, Le Bois-Saint-Denis, 36260 Reuilly, tel. 02.54.49.22.17, fax 02.54.49.26.64, e-mail claude.lafond@wanadoo.fr **V**
Y by appt.

ALAIN MABILLOT 2000★★

| 1 ha | 6,000 | | €5-8 |

Alain Mabillot has been running his estate since 1990, and won a *coup de cœur* for his 99 wine. His tenth-anniversary vintage confirms the quality of his wines. Deep-ruby in colour, this wine gives off a musky scent at first, followed by an intensely fruity one of blackcurrants. On the palate, the wine is still closed, and the tannins are powerful but smooth, and it has enough body and consistency to cope with a long period in the cellar.

☛ Alain Mabillot, Villiers-les-Roses, 36260 Sainte-Lizaigne, tel. 02.54.04.02.09, fax 02.54.04.01.33 **Y** by appt.

GUY MALBÊTE 2000

| 3 ha | 20,000 | | €5-8 |

On Guy Malbête's estate, the black grapes are picked by hand and de-stemmed. His 2000 wine reveals the rather herbaceous aromas of Pinot Noir, along with spices. On the palate, the still fairly young tannins emphasise the flavours of cherries and undergrowth, but these will have softened very soon to give a very drinkable Reuilly.

☛ EARL Guy Malbête, 16, chem. du Boulanger, Bois-Saint-Denis, 36260 Reuilly, tel. 02.54.49.25.09, fax 02.54.49.27.49 **V** **Y** by appt.

JOSEPH MELLOT Les Milets 1999

| n.c. | n.c. | | €5-8 |

Alexandre Mellot's wine labels remind people that his company was founded in 1513. The scents of this 99 wine have already come through (crystallised fruits, plums and wax). Rounded and with a pleasant sweetness on the palate, a degree of liveliness brings freshness and demonstrates the wine's good structure. It can be drunk immediately.

☛ SA Joseph Mellot, rte de Ménétréol, BP 13, 18300 Sancerre, tel. 02.48.78.54.54, fax 02.48.78.54.55, e-mail alexandre@joseph-mellot.fr **V** **Y** ev. day except Sat. Sun. 8am–12 noon 1.30pm–5.30pm

DOM. VALERY RENAUDAT 2000★

| 0.7 ha | 3,500 | | €5-8 |

Valéry Renaudat is a young wine-maker who just started out in 1999. This wine has a lovely spray of aromas – white flowers, broom and citrus fruits. The flavours on the palate are accompanied by good smoothness and body. This charming wine has great potential.

Sancerre

The hilltop village of Sancerre, overlooking the Loire, commands a magnificent panorama of well-exposed, sheltered slopes, perfect for winegrowing, stretching over 11 communes. The *terroir* is composed variously of limestone and chalky marl, which suit the vine and contribute to the quality of the wines. About 2,541 ha (6,276 acres) are planted, and produced 162,632 hl (4,293,485 gal) in 2000, of which 129,774 hl (3,426,034 gal) were white wine.

Two varieties reign supreme in Sancerre: Sauvignon and Pinot Noir, both uniquely capable of expressing the spirit of the *terroir* to the full. This is amply demonstrated in the wines: fresh, young, fruity whites (the most numerous wines); supple, subtle rosés, and light, perfumed, complex reds.

In addition to this, Sancerre represents, in a unique way, the contribution of wine-growers and wine-makers. It requires great skill and dedication to produce a great wine from Sauvignon, which is a late-ripening variety, so near to the northern limit of vine-growing, and at heights of 200 and 300 metres (656–984 ft). Add to these human challenges the vagaries of the local climate, slopes that are among the steepest in the country, and the fact that fermentation takes place at a critical moment at the end of a late season!

White Sancerre is particularly to be appreciated with dry goat's cheeses, such as the famous Crottin de Chavignol, from a village which itself produces wines. It also goes well with hot starters or fish that are not too strongly seasoned. The reds go well with poultry and the meat dishes of the region.

JACQUES RENAUDAT 2000★★   ■ 3.12 ha 18,000 ■ ♦ €5–8

An old, restored residence is the venue for tasting this superb, intensely coloured mauvish-purple Reuilly flecked with black-cherry highlights. After swirling the wine in the glass, the bouquet opens up with rich and very fruity aromas (blackberries and blackcurrants). The integrated tannins add fullness and fleshiness. This very harmonious wine should be cellared for several years.

☛ Jacques Renaudat, Seresnes, 36260 Diou, tel. 02.54.49.21.44, fax 02.54.49.30.42 ▼
▼ ev. day 8am–12 noon 2pm–7pm; Sun. by appt.

DOM. DE REUILLY 2000★   ■ 3.7 ha 30,000 ■ ♦ €5–8

Ruby red in colour, this wine has aromas of red berries and a restrained note of violets. The tannins are still vigorous, which means that this well-made Reuilly will become more refined as it matures. You may like the **2000 whites**: the **Domaine** and **Les Pierres Plates** are both recommended.

☛ SCE Dom. de Reuilly, chem. des Petites-Fontaines, 36260 Reuilly, tel. 02.38.66.16.74, fax 02.38.66.74.69, e-mail denis.jamain@wanadoo.fr ▼
▼ ev. day 8am–6pm
☛ Jamain

JEAN-MICHEL SORBE 2000★★   ■ 3 ha 20,000 ■ ♦ €5–8

A delightfully brilliant, strong salmon-pink colour, this wine has enchanting aromas of roses and yellow peaches. Full on the palate, with chewy fruit flavours and a lengthy finish, it is the sort of wine to be enjoyed with an iced dessert. The **Reuilly white 2000** is successful and recommended (no star).

☛ SARL Jean-Michel Sorbe, La Quervée, 18120 Preuilly, tel. 02.48.51.99.43, fax 02.48.51.35.47 ▼ ▼ by appt.

JACQUES VINCENT 2000★   □ 2.5 ha 18,000 ■ ♦ €5–8

Although the **rosé** manages regularly to please the tasters, and is again recommended for the long aromas of the **2000**, it is the white that this year won over the Jury. Its golden colour is barely marked, but the scents of blackcurrant leaves are strong. They will no doubt soften in the maturing process to leave more room for floral and spicy flavours. Taken as a whole, the wine is smooth, balanced and very enjoyable.

☛ Jacques Vincent, 11, chem. des Caves, 18120 Lazenay, tel. 02.48.51.73.55, fax 02.48.51.14.96 ▼ ▼ ev. day 9am–12 noon 2pm–7pm; Sun. by appt.

DOM. AUCHERE 2000★

■ 2 ha 15,000 ■ ‖ €8–11

The family estate nestles in the middle of a natural hollow where vines grow well. This wine, made from old vines, releases aromas of citrus fruit and acacia. Its liveliness and length will enhance a dish of seafood.

🍷 Jean-Jacques Auchère, 18, rue de l'Abbaye, 18300 Bué, tel. 02.48.54.15.77, fax 02.48.78.03.46 ☑ by appt.

B. BAILLY-REVERDY 1999★

■ 5 ha 27,000 ■ €5–8

This lovely ruby-coloured 99, with brick-red glints and a fruity (plums) and peppery bouquet, was matured for 12 months in barrel. On the palate, it is powerful yet rounded and smooth, enlivened by flavours of fruits (cherries) and violets. Ready for drinking, it makes an ideal partner for white meats.

🍷 SA Bailly-Reverdy 43, rue de Venoize, 18300 Bué, tel. 02.48.54.18.38, fax 02.48.78.04.70 ☑ ☑ by appt.

DOM. JEAN-PAUL BALLAND
1999★

■ 4.5 ha 30,000 ■ ‖‖ €8–11

Created by a mainstay of the Sancerre region, this red wine, made from hand-picked grapes, was partly vinified in barrel. Its maturation has equipped it with notes of vanilla and roasting which merge with red berries, and as it matures it is becoming musky on the palate. This will go well with game. The **Grande Cuvée 99 white** is recommended: its very old vines come through in its fruitiness and balance.

🍷 Dom. Jean-Paul Balland, chem. de Marloup, 18300 Bué, tel. 02.48.54.07.29, fax 02.48.54.20.94, e-mail balland.jean.paul@wanadoo.fr ☑ by appt.

PASCAL BALLAND 1999★

■ 7.5 ha 50,000 ■ ■ €5–8

Pascal Balland has been running his very old family business since 1984. He has had a great success with this 99, with its powerful, fine bouquet releasing simultaneously fruity, floral (honeysuckle), charred and slightly mineral notes. On the palate, it is lively and, above all, very full, with flavours of citrus fruit and pepper.

🍷 EARL Pascal Balland, 18300 Bué, tel. 02.48.54.22.19, fax 02.48.78.08.59 ☑ ev. day 8am–7pm; Sun. 2pm–7pm

JOSEPH BALLAND-CHAPUIS
Le Chatillet 2000★★

■ 4 ha 32,000 ■ ‖ €5–8

The Joseph Balland-Chapuis estate has again done well, with two fine 2000 wines. Le Chatillet, with its aromas of butter and coffee, has surprising richness and complexity. On the palate, notes of roasting follow the fresh flavour of citrus fruit. This is an atypical wine, but no less remarkable for that: try it. The **Vallon white** wins one star; it releases

delightful mineral and fruity notes, and its liveliness and roundness make it a character-istic wine for the year.

🍷 SARL Joseph Balland-Chapuis, La Croix-Saint-Laurent, 18300 Bué, tel. 02.48.54.06.67, fax 02.48.54.07.97 ☑ by appt.

CEDRICK BARDIN 2000★

■ 3.2 ha 25,000 ■ ‖ €8–11

The family vineyard stretches over both banks of the Loire: to the north, in the Pouilly-sur-Loire appellation, and to the south, on the slopes of the Sancerre region. This 2000 vintage is particularly floral, with some herbaceous notes. Its lively first impression is quickly replaced by roundness. A very attractive wine, it is ready for drinking.

🍷 Cédrick Bardin, 12, rue Waldeck-Rousseau, 58150 Pouilly-sur-Loire, tel. 03.86.39.11.24, fax 03.86.39.16.50 ☑ by appt.

ROGER BONTEMPS ET FILLES
Cuvée Josyane Bontemps 2000

■ 0.3 ha 1,600 ■ ‖ €8–11

The vineyard has been in the hands of the Bontemps family since 1852. This wine bears typical traces of the Sauvignon grape: broom and citrus fruit. It is powerful and well-structured, and the scents of the bouquet recur on the palate along with flavours of damp hay.

🍷 Roger Bontemps et Filles, rte de Sancerre, 18300 Ménétréol-sous-Sa ncerre, tel. 02.48.54.25.41, fax 02.48.54.07.63 ☑ ev. day 8am–12 noon 2pm–6pm

HENRI BOURGEOIS
La Côte des Monts Damnés 2000★★

■ 3.1 ha 18,000 ■ ‖ €11–15

The huge Henri Bourgeois estate – it runs to 65 ha (160 acres) – is a pillar of the Sancerre region. In 2000 it installed a gravity-led winery with a panoramic view. It presented the Jury with two very fine Sancerre whites, both from the clay-limestone slopes of the Monts Damnés. La Côte des Monts Damnés opens with a fine bouquet mingling peaches and grapefruit, then reveals freshness and vivacity enhanced by fruitiness and menthol. The **Grande Réserve** is also a great success: its mineral notes show it has a greater affinity to its *terroir*. It will go well with white meats.

🍷 Dom. Henri Bourgeois, Chavignol, 18300 Sancerre, tel. 02.48.78.53.20, fax 02.48.54.14.24, e-mail domaine@ bourgeois-sancerre.com ☑ ☑ by appt.

DOM. HUBERT BROCHARD
2000★★

■ 25 ha 200,000 ■ ‖ €8–11

This vineyard's estate occupies the best *terroirs* in Sancerre. Its main wine is typical of the appellation, and has a lovely harmony. Its dry, fruity character is reinforced by good balance and mineral notes. It definitely has a good future. **Cuvée Silex** is also recom-mended. Made from grapes from old vines planted on silty soil, it releases aromas of exotic fruit and gunflint up to a lengthy finish.

➤ Dom. Henry Brochard, Chavignol, 18300 Sancerre, tel. 02.48.78.20.10, fax 02.48.78.20.19, e-mail domaine-hubertbrochard@ wanadoo.fr ☑

DOM. DES BUISSONNES 2000

☑ 1.85 ha 8,000 ▮ ♦ €8-11

To the west of the Bois de Charmes, Sury-en-Vaux is a centre for ramblers. This co-operative has produced a wine for laying down: it has a lovely dark-ruby colour, an intense bouquet of red and black fruits (morello cherries, blackberries and strawberries) and, although rich and well-structured on the palate, it has rather harsh tannins, a result of its youthfulness.

➤ Cave Roger Naudet, SCEA des Buissonnes, Maison Sallé, 18300 Sury-en-Vaux, tel. 02.48.79.34.68, fax 02.48.79.34.68 ☑ ⵏ ev. day 8.30am–12 noon 2pm–6pm

ROGER CHAMPAULT
Les Pierris 2000

☑ 7 ha 55,000 ▮ ▮ ♦ €8-11

To taste this wine, you enter a lovely 16th-century dovecote. Les Pierris comes from clay-limestone soils and has a fruity, musky bouquet and a full (but not aggressive) body. Serve it with white meats.

➤ Roger Champault et Fils, Champtin, 18300 Crézancy-en-Sancerre, tel. 02.48.79.00.03, fax 02.48.79.09.17 ☑ ⵏ by appt.

DANIEL CHOTARD 2000★★

☑ 0.64 ha 5,000 ▮ ♦ €8-11

Daniel Chotard's ancestors were winemakers well before 1789. He is a music enthusiast who plays the accordion and guitar and organises musical get-togethers in the cellar in which he presents his wines. This well-balanced rosé combines expressiveness, finesse, freshness and good body. Its strawberry notes will go well with exotic salads. The **red 99** is very successful, a delicious showcase for Pinot Noir. Made from very ripe grapes, it is full of red fruits with a hint of vanilla.

➤ Daniel Chotard, Hameau de Reigny, 18300 Crézancy-en-Sancerre, tel. 02.48.79.08.12, fax 02.48.79.09.21, e-mail daniel.chotard@wanadoo.fr ☑ ⵏ by appt.

COMTE DE LA PERRIERE 2000★

☑ 5 ha 35,000 ▮ ♦ €8-11

One-third of the vineyards of this property (10 ha/25 acres out of 30 ha/75 acres) are on silty soils, and this wine reflects its *terroir* through its mineral notes. Its lively, rounded character will make it an excellent accompaniment for fish and mature cheese. Also worth trying is the **Mégalithe 99**, with its complex bouquet and interesting blend of oakiness and fruit.

➤ SA Pierre Archambault, Caves de la Perrière, 18300 Verdigny, tel. 02.48.54.16.93, fax 02.48.54.11.54 ☑ ⵏ by appt.

➤ J.-L. Saget

DOM. ROBERT ET MARIE-SOLANGE CROCHET 2000★

☑ 0.6 ha 4,800 ▮ ♦ €5-8

This captivating rosé has a beautiful orangey-pink colour and aromas of red berries, including strawberries. The white **Le Chêne Marchand** and **Cuvée Principale du Domaine** are recommended, the former for its bouquet of pepper and pears, the latter for its mineral qualities; both reflect the serious aims of the estate.

➤ Robert et Marie-Solange Crochet, Marcigoué, 18300 Bué-en-Sancerre, tel. 02.48.54.21.77, fax 02.48.54.25.10 ☑ ⵏ ev. day 9am–7pm; Sun. by appt.

DANIEL CROCHET 2000

☐ 2.5 ha 20,000 ▮ ♦ €5-8

Here is a wine made from grapes grown on *caillottes*, or white stones. It has a brilliant pale-gold colour, a pleasant bouquet with hints of white flowers and rhubarb, and on the palate it is smooth, rich and floral. Try it as an aperitif.

➤ Daniel Crochet, 61, rue de Venoize, 18300 Bué, tel. 02.48.54.07.83, fax 02.48.54.27.36 ☑ ⵏ ev. day 9am–12 noon 2pm–7pm

DOM. DOMINIQUE ET JANINE CROCHET 2000

☐ 2.5 ha 15,000 ▮ ▮ €8-11

This red wine's lovely ruby colour suggests that it has good potential, and, indeed, it needs some time before it will be at its best. Already it is releasing scents of cherries and raspberries. On the palate, it is balanced and well-structured, but slow to open up. Keep it until spring 2002.

➤ Dom. Dominique et Janine Crochet, 64, rue de Venoize, 18300 Bué-en-Sancerre, tel. 02.48.54.19.56, fax 02.48.54.12.61 ☑ ⵏ ev. day 8am–12 noon 2pm–7pm

DOM. DAULNY
Le Clos de Chaudenay 1999★

☐ 1 ha 7,500 ▮ ▮ ♦ €8-11

Cuvée Principale 2000, with its pale-golden glints, comes from vines planted on clay-limestone soils; it wins one star. Lovers of Sancerre will be delighted with its intense fruity bouquet, which continues on the well-balanced palate. Le Clos de Chaudenay 99 is a great success: it comes from old vines planted on marl soils. This lovely wine has a superb golden colour, a complex bouquet combining white flowers and peaches, and a finish which is full and very pleasant on the palate.

➤ Etienne Daulny, Chaudenay, 18300 Verdigny, tel. 02.48.79.33.96, fax 02.48.79.33.39 ☑ ⵏ by appt.

• Langlois-Chateau, 3, rue Léopold-Palustre,
49400 Saint-Hilaire-Saint-Florent,
tel. 02.41.40.21.40, fax 02.41.40.21.49,
e-mail langlois.chateau@wanadoo.fr

DOM. VINCENT DELAPORTE ET FILS Vieilles vignes Fût de chêne Cuvée Maxime 2000★

1 ha   5,000   [icons] £8-11

The village of Chavignol is full of charm; it is just as famous for its *crottin*, a goat's cheese of rare finesse, as it is for the vineyard planted on the lovely hills that surround it. Matured in barrel, this wine has an intense bouquet of mainly charred scents accompanied by vanilla notes and subtle hints of exotic fruit, while on the palate it is well-balanced. It needs ageing for two years. The **Domaine** wine was not matured in barrel, and has distinctive, long-lasting floral and grapey notes. Ready for drinking immediately, it wins one star.

• SCEV Vincent Delaporte et Fils,
Chavignol, 18300 Sancerre,
tel. 02.48.78.03.32, fax 02.48.78.02.62
Y by appt.

DOM. DOUDEAU-LEGER 2000★★

0.09 ha   700   [icons] €5-8

The market town of Sury is well worth a visit, both for its church and the countryside that surrounds it. This rosé has an intense bouquet of strawberries, while on the palate it is full, flavoursome and balanced. Drink it with grills. The **white 2000** is also a great success, with its very fine aromas of white flowers and pears. A first impression of liveliness gives way to elegant roundness.

• Dom. Doudeau-Léger, Les Giraults,
18300 Sury-en-Vaux, tel. 02.48.79.32.26,
fax 02.48.79.29.80 Y by appt.
• Pascal Doudeau

GERARD FIOU
La Cabarette Cuvée Silex 1999

0.3 ha   1,500   [icons] £11-15

The label features a tall woman in a tailcoat waving from a stage, obviously suggesting La Cabarette be drunk during an evening with friends. It is blended from a wine matured in stainless-steel vats and one matured in oak barrels for ten months. It could be left to mature longer to allow the oak to soften, but herbaceous and mineral notes are already in evidence on the nose, and on the palate it is well-structured and round.

• Gérard Fiou, 13–15, rue Hilaire-Amagat,
18300 Saint-Satur, tel. 02.48.54.16.17,
fax 02.48.54.36.89 Y by appt.

CH. DE FONTAINE-AUDON 2000★

8.36 ha   70,000   [icons] £8-11

The vineyard, which completely surrounds the château, is on a south-facing incline at Sainte-Gemme, in the north of the Sancerre region. The Sauvignon grapes are planted on clay-silt soils, which come through in the wine's mineral notes. It has the pale-yellow colour, glinting of green, of a young wine, and a complex bouquet combining white flowers, minerals and vegetation. Lively and clear-cut on the palate, its acidity means that it will go well with shellfish.

FOURNIER 2000★

15.57 ha   120,000   [icons] €5-8

The hamlet of Chaudoux is on the D 134 to the north of Verdigny. The Fournier family have produced a very well-balanced wine with a lovely pale-gold colour. On the nose, it gives off complex scents redolent of white flowers, fruit (pineapples) and, above all, a lemony element: flavours which are apparent on the palate, which means the wine will go well with seafood and fish.

• Fournier Père et Fils,
Chaudoux, BP 7, 18300 Verdigny,
tel. 02.48.79.35.24, fax 02.48.79.30.41,
e-mail claude@fournier-père-fils.fr
Y ev. day 8am–6.30pm; Sat. Sun. by appt.
• GFA Chanvrières

DOM. MICHEL GIRARD ET FILS 2000★

0.65 ha   5,000   [icons] £8-11

This 13-ha (32-acre) property has belonged to the Girards for seven generations. Their rosé, made from Pinot Noir, is characteristic of the appellation, with its orangey-pink colour, fine, fruity aromas (strawberries and raspberries) and rich, equally fruity (strawberries and citrus fruit) flavours that linger on the palate. The estate's **Sancerre 2000 red** is recommended. A lovely ruby colour, it releases scents of vegetation and cherries, while, on the palate, its lightness and fruity flavours make it a very drinkable wine, ready to open now.

• Dom. Michel Girard et Fils, Chaudoux,
18300 Verdigny, tel. 02.48.79.33.36,
fax 02.48.79.33.66 Y by appt.

DOM. DES GRANDES PERRIERES Vieilles vignes 2000

1 ha   7,000   [icons] €5-8

Made from vines more than 25 years old, this wine has a bouquet of white flowers and citrus fruit, and lively, rich flavours in the mouth that replicate the scents on the nose. This is a balanced wine to serve with white meats.

• Jérôme Gueneau, Dom. des
Grandes-Perrières, 18300 Sury-en-Vaux,
tel. 02.48.79.39.31, fax 02.48.79.40.27 Y
by appt.

PASCAL JOLIVET
La Grande Cuvée 1998

1.7 ha   9,000   [icons] £15-23

Founded in 1986, this wine-merchant acquired its own winery in 1999. Its 98 vintage won a *coup de cœur* last year, and the **Le Chêne Marchand 99 white** is recommended, as is this golden Grande Cuvée, with its fairly well-developed bouquet (despite the presence of floral aromas). It is well-balanced, with clear acidity bringing a lovely freshness to the palate, and is ready for drinking.

Sancerre

➤ Pascal Jolivet, rte de Chavignol,
18300 Sancerre, tel. 02.48.27.28.29,
fax 02.48.27.28.20, e-mail info@
pascal-jolivet.com ▼ Ⴤ ev. day except Sat.
Sun. 9am–12 noon 2pm–5pm

DOM. DE LA GARENNE 2000★
☐　6.5 ha　52,000　■ ♦　€8-11

When it was founded in 1978, Domaine de
la Garenne intended its wine to be solely for
export. Now you can find it in France too. It
has an intense, fine bouquet marked by exotic
fruit and citrus fruit. After a lively opening in
the mouth, it reveals richness, balance and
length.

➤ Bernard-Noël Reverdy, Dom. de la
Garenne, 18300 Verdigny-en-Sancerre,
tel. 02.48.79.35.79, fax 02.48.79.32.82 ▼
Ⴤ by appt.

SERGE LALOUE
Silex Cuvée réservée 2000★
☐　2 ha　13,000　■ ♦　€8-11

Serge and Franck Laloue run 18 ha
(44 acres) of vines planted on a mainly
clay-silt soil. This gives their Silex Cuvée its
particular characteristics. A pale-gold colour,
it releases a restrained bouquet of fine aromas
of oranges and herbaceous notes. Fresh and
lively on the palate, it should be given time to
open out. Also recommended is the **red 99**,
which is not filtered and has a very charming
bouquet with notes of charring, undergrowth
and liquorice.

➤ Serge Laloue, Thauvenay,
18300 Sancerre, tel. 02.48.79.94.10,
fax 02.48.79.92.48, e-mail laloue@
terre-net.fr ▼ Ⴤ by appt.

DOM. LA MOUSSIERE 2000★
☐　25 ha　150,000　■ ♦　€8-11

Alphonse Mellot runs a huge vineyard of
48 ha (118 acres). This is a lovely pale-gold
wine with golden glints, which releases
aromas of citrus fruit, aniseed and liquorice.
Full-bodied and balanced on the palate, it
has the same citrus flavours. The Jury also
re-tasted the 99 vintage, **La Génération XIX**,
with its mineral, charred and vanilla notes;
the tannins from the oak are softening well on
a palate which is lively on opening in the
mouth and rounded on the finish.

➤ Alphonse Mellot, Dom. La Moussière,
18300 Sancerre, tel. 02.48.54.07.41,
fax 02.48.54.07.62, e-mail mellot@
sfiedi.com ▼ Ⴤ by appt.

DOM. DE LA PERRIERE 2000★
☐　7 ha　55,000　■ ♦　€8-11

This wine is faithful to the Sauvignon it is
made from, releasing aromas of citrus fruit,
asparagus, boxwood, white flowers and exotic
fruit. It is elegant, fruity and complex, has
good balance and can be served on all sorts of
occasions: as an aperitif, with freshwater fish
or with a spicy zabaglione.

➤ Dom. de La Perrière, Cave de la Perrière,
18300 Verdigny, tel. 02.48.54.16.93,
fax 02.48.54.11.54 ▼ Ⴤ by appt.
➤ SA Pierre Archambault

DOM. SERGE LAPORTE 1999
☐　2.5 ha　16,000　■　€8-11

The cellar is in the middle of the village of
Chavignol. This wine, which comes from
vines grown in soil of clay limestone and
caillottes (white stones), has an elegant,
complex bouquet of herbaceous notes, citrus
fruit, ginger and sweet almonds, and it has
retained all its freshness. The lemony and
mineral flavours linger to a lengthy finish.

➤ Dom. Serge Laporte, Chavignol,
18300 Sancerre, tel. 02.48.54.30.10,
fax 02.48.54.28.91 ▼ Ⴤ by appt.

DOM. LES GRANDS GROUX 2000
☐　8.03 ha　35,000　■ ♦　€8-11

In 2000, Benoît Fouassier joined his
parents at the vineyard. Their wine attracted
the tasters with its intense bouquet of white
fruit combined with a hint of spices and,
overall, citrus fruit (lemon and grapefruit).
On the palate, it is smooth and fairly lively,
and lemony on the finish. Also recommended
is **Le Clos de Bannon white 2000**, notable for
its bracing aromas and structure.

➤ SA Fouassier Père et Fils,
180, av. de Verdun, 18300 Sancerre,
tel. 02.48.54.02.34, fax 02.48.54.35.61,
e-mail fouassier@terre-net.fr ▼
Ⴤ ev. day 9am–12 noon 2pm–6pm

DOM. RENE MALLERON 2000★
☐　0.86 ha　7,400　■　€11-15

Champtin, a hamlet next to Crézancy, is
very pleasant. Goats and mixed farming flank
the vineyard, which has produced this high-
quality rosé. Only 1 ha (2.5 acres) out of
13 ha (32 acres) is devoted to the wine, made
from hand-picked grapes. It has the colour of
onion skin, and a power and body that do not
impair its fruitiness and finesse.

➤ Dom. René Malleron,
Champtin, 18300 Crézancy-en-Sancerre,
tel. 02.48.79.06.90, fax 02.48.79.42.18 ▼
Ⴤ by appt.

THIERRY MERLIN-CHERRIER
Le Chêne Marchand 1999
☐　0.8 ha　2,000　■　€8-11

The village of Bué is at the end of a valley
5 km (3 miles) south-west of Sancerre. Here
you will find a cellar offering two wines that
are typical of the 99 vintage. First, this white
wine, which comes from limestone soil. It is
pale-gold in colour, and releases fairly strong
aromas of peaches and fruit. It opens on the
palate with a lively first impression and then
becomes more more rounded. The estate's **red 99**
has all the classic characteristics of a Pinot
grown on a clay-limestone soil: the slightly
brick-red ruby colour reveals its age, and,
light in style, it gives out flavours of very ripe
red berries on the palate; it is ready for
drinking.

1088

● Thierry Merlin-Cherrier, 43, rue Saint-Vincent, 18300 Bué, tel. 02.48.54.06.31, fax 02.48.54.01.78 ▼ ev. day except Sun. 9am–12 noon 2pm–6pm; cl. 15–31 Aug.

DOM. PAUL MILLERIOUX 2000
☐ 13.5 ha 90,000 ■ ⚬ €8-11

Paul Millerioux is passionate about wine-making, and will gladly tell you the history of the appellation. He will offer you this straightforward wine, with its typical Sancerre bouquet and a lively first impression, which releases flavours of boxwood and broom, finishing on hints of aniseed.
● Paul Millerioux, Champtin, 18300 Crézancy-en-Sancerre, tel. 02.48.79.07.12, fax 02.48.79.07.63, e-mail millerio@terre-net.fr ☑ ▼ ev. day 8am–12 noon 2pm–8pm; Sun. by appt.

DOM. FRANCK MILLET 2000 ★
■ 2 ha 15,000 ■ ▥ ⚬ €8-11

Franck Millet's wine has a brilliant dark-ruby colour, which reveals the maturity of the grapes used. Red berries gush forth on the nose and recur on the palate. This is a well-balanced wine, both rounded and fine, with well-integrated tannins. Drink it with meat or charcuterie.
● Franck Millet, rue Saint-Vincent, 18300 Bué, tel. 02.48.54.25.26, fax 02.48.54.39.85, e-mail franck.millet@wanadoo.fr ☑ ▼ by appt.

DOM. GERARD MILLET 2000 ★
☐ 12.5 ha 109,000 ■ ⚬ €8-11

Gérard Millet, who has won a coup de coeur in the 2000 Guide, has now produced this very fine wine. Although restrained, it has an attractive pale-yellow colour with glints of green, and delightfully delicate scents of wild flowers in spring. Long and lively on the palate, this is a wine to savour.
● Gérard Millet, rte de Bourges, 18300 Bué, tel. 02.48.54.38.62, fax 02.48.54.13.50, e-mail gmillet@terre-net.fr ▼ by appt.

FLORIAN MOLLET 2000 ★★
☐ n.c. 16,000 ■ ⚬ €8-11

Florian Mollet has got into the Guide with his first harvest, a Sancerre with a distinctive intensity. The fruity, slightly grapey bouquet is beautifully echoed on the palate, which opens with liveliness and then becomes pleasantly rounded and long. Another wine to try is the Cuvée Le Roc de l'Abbaye white, with mineral notes reflecting its silty-clay terroir and others suggesting grapefruit.
● EARL Clos du Roc, 84, av de Fontenay, 18300 Saint-Satur, tel. 02.48.54.02.26, fax 02.48.54.02.26 ▼ ev. day 9am–12 noon 2pm–6pm; Sun. by appt.

ROGER MOREUX
Les Monts Damnés 1999 ★
☐ 1 ha 6,000 ■ ⚬ €8-11

Roger Moreux has succeeded in making a lovely wine that reflects the soul of its terroir, the famous Monts Damnés. This 99 is very intense, with a very complex bouquet, a real mixture of flowers, white fruit (peaches), exotic fruit (lychees and mangoes), minerals and vanilla. On the palate it also offers an absolute cocktail, with a lively first impression followed by flavours that are gaining in power.
● Roger Moreux, Chavignol, 18300 Sancerre, tel. 02.48.54.05.79, fax 02.48.54.09.55, e-mail moreux912@aol.com ☑ ▼ ev. day 8am–12 noon 2pm–7pm; Sun. 8am–12 noon

MOULIN DES VRILLERES
Perle blanche 1999 ★
☐ n.c. 6,000 ■ ⚬ €5-8

Although pale-looking in the glass, this has surprisingly fine aromas of mineral notes and acacia flowers shaded by ferns and boxwood. On the palate, its very mineral aspect is faithful to its origins. It is a lively and well-balanced wine.
● Christian Lauvergeat, SCEA Moulin des Vrillères, 18300 Sury-en-Vaux, tel. 02.48.79.38.28, fax 02.48.79.39.49, e-mail lauvergeatchristian@wanadoo.fr ☑ ▼ by appt.

DOM. DU NOZAY 2000 ★★
☐ 6 ha 45,000 €5-8

Philippe de Benoist's vineyard is planted all in one piece in a huge natural hollow. He belongs to a family with a long military tradition, but 30 years ago he chose to be a wine-maker and moved into an 18th-century château. Both his wines have been singled out by the Jury. One, the Château de Nozay 2000 white, is distributed by the wine-merchant Pascal Jolivet, who selected the blend himself. It is superb, and more expensive; a real dry Sancerre. The other, listed above, is perhaps more suited to Anglo-Saxon tastes, with its residual sugar of 2.8 g/l. Rounded and full, it clearly reflects both its terroir and its grape variety. Its aromas mingle mirabelle plums, quince and white flowers (acacia). This is a wine of character.
● Philippe de Benoist, Dom. du Nozay, Ch. du Nozay, 18340 Sainte-Gemme-en-Sancerrois, tel. 02.48.79.36.64, e-mail nozay@aol.com ☑ ▼ by appt.

PAUL PRIEUR ET FILS 2000 ★★★
☐ 9.28 ha 80,000 ■ ⚬ €8-11

This family has its roots in Verdigny, which has a museum of wine-making. Paul, Didier and Philippe Prieur submitted three wines, all of which were singled out. The Jury preferred this remarkable white wine, with its flashes of green, its complex and elegant bouquet (lilies, peaches, lychees, broom and grapefruit) – which on the palate reveals a lovely balance –

and its liveliness, reinforced by a citrus aspect. It narrowly missed a *coup de cœur*. The **red 99** is a highly successful wine (one star), being both very fruity and well balanced. Finally, the Jury also commended a fine and fruity **rosé 2000**.

• Dom. Paul Prieur et Fils,
rte des Monts-Damnés, 18300 Verdigny,
tel. 02.48.79.35.86, fax 02.48.79.38.85
Y ev. day 9am–12 noon 2pm–6pm;
Sun. by appt.

DOM. DU P'TIT ROY 2000★★

| | 2 ha | 10,000 | | | €8-11 |

Made from Pinot Noir planted on the famous *caillottes* (white stones) of Sancerre, this wine has a lovely, intense cherry colour with mauvish glints, indicating morello cherry maturity, which is confirmed by scents of morello cherries and blackcurrants on the nose. On the palate, the wine is delightfully rounded and balanced, and its tannins well-integrated. It is a very elegant wine.

• Pierre et Alain Dezat, Maimbray,
18300 Sury-en-Vaux, tel. 02.48.79.34.16,
fax 02.48.79.35.81  **Y** by appt.

NOEL ET JEAN-LUC RAIMBAULT
Les Chailloux 2000★

| | 1.5 ha | 13,300 | | | €5-8 |

The Raimbaults have had an excellent year 2000, thanks primarily to this wine, which has an intense bouquet of herbaceous notes (boxwood and broom), citrus fruit and minerals that recurs on the palate. It opens smoothly, followed by a liveliness that is typical of the year. The age of the grapes used means that the **Les Cotelins 2000 red** should keep well. It is recommended for its attractive, restrained flavours of crystallised fruit and spices.

• Noël et Jean-Luc Raimbault,
Lieu-dit Chambre, 18300 Sury-en-Vaux,
tel. 02.48.79.36.56, fax 02.48.79.36.56
Y by appt.

DOM. HIPPOLYTE REVERDY
2000★

| | 10 ha | 65,000 | | | €8-11 |

Elegance and complexity are the two main assets of this wine. On the nose, it releases sweet scents of peaches, orange peel, lemons, lilies and aniseed. The first impression is clear-cut and lively, and the wine is robustly smooth and fruity, with a long finish. Try it with a casserole of assorted shellfish. Also worth tasting is the very successful **red 2000**, with its dark-cherry colour. The maturity of the grapes at harvest time gives this wine its character: notes of soft fruits, with discernible but refined tannins, and a long finish.

• Dom. Hippolyte Reverdy,
Chaudoux, 18300 Verdigny-en-Sancerre,
tel. 02.48.79.36.16, fax 02.48.79.36.65
Y by appt.

PASCAL ET NICOLAS REVERDY
2000★★

| | 7 ha | 55,000 | | | €5-8 |

The Reverdys won a *coup de cœur* for their red Sancerre 95, and this time repeat the feat with a white wine. The 2000 vintage has a pale-yellow colour, and pleasantly surprised the Jury with its very intense bouquet of, predominantly, ripe fruit along with citrus fruit (grapefruit), broom and boxwood. After a clean first impression, on the palate it is very balanced, and quite as appetising as its bouquet. It is very long and fruity on the finish. 'Try drinking this wine with sole in orange sauce,' suggested one of the tasters. The **red 2000**, aged for six months in barrel, was also awarded two stars. Very dark in colour, flavours of very ripe fruit (raspberries, blackcurrants and prunes) and violets appear both on the nose and on the palate. The fine tannins are typical, but sufficiently evident to warrant ageing the wine for a year.

• Pascal et Nicolas Reverdy,
Maimbray, 18300 Sury-en-Vaux,
tel. 02.48.79.37.31, fax 02.48.79.41.48
Y ev. day except Sun. 2.30pm–7pm

DOM. BERNARD REVERDY ET FILS 2000★★

| | 0.83 ha | 6,000 | | | €8-11 |

This wine was presented to the Jury as one of the few candidates for the *coup de cœur*. A rosé made from direct pressing, it demonstrates all the skills of the Reverdys. It is lovely to look at, with its bright, almost candy-pink colour, and releases very fruity notes verging on jam. Dry, fleshy, straightforward and still very fruity on the palate, it will go well with food. The **white Sancerre 2000**, rounded and pleasant, has aromas of citrus fruit and bananas; it was awarded one star, and will be a good match for white meat.

• Dom. Bernard Reverdy et Fils,
rte des Petites-Perrières, Chaudoux,
18300 Verdigny, tel. 02.48.79.33.08,
fax 02.48.79.37.93  **Y** by appt.

JEAN REVERDY ET FILS
La Reine Blanche 2000★

| | 9 ha | 60,000 | | | €8-11 |

La Reine Blanche won the *coup de cœur* last year for its 99 vintage. Coming from a limestone and silt soil, the 2000 has a lovely pale-yellow colour glinting with gold. The intense bouquet recalls citrus fruit on a honey

base, and the wine's lively first impression gives way to extreme roundness on the palate.
- Jean Reverdy et Fils, 18300 Verdigny, tel. 02.48.79.31.48, fax 02.48.79.32.44 Ⓥ
Y by appt.

CLAUDE RIFFAULT La Noue 2000

2.3 ha | 18,000 | €5-8

An intense and brilliant ruby colour, La Noue's bouquet releases herbaceous notes and goes on to soft fruit, including strawberries. A clear-cut opening on the palate is followed by fruity flavours, and the tannins are well-integrated. The wine is still young, but has good prospects. Serve it, perhaps, with chicken.
- SCEV Claude Riffault, Maison-Sallé, 18300 Sury-en-Vaux, tel. 02.48.79.38.22, fax 02.48.79.36.22 Ⓥ Y ev. day 8am–12 noon 2pm–7pm; Sun. by appt.

DOM. DU ROCHOY 2000★★

8.2 ha | 60,000 | €8-11

With its lovely golden colour, a bouquet predominantly of orange peel, and lively, round and long-lasting flavours on the palate echoing the aromas of the bouquet, this very well-balanced wine is typical of the appellation, and will enhance grilled fish. Another successful wine is the **La Cresle de Laporte 2000 white**, made from vines planted on *caillottes* (the local term for limestone), which has delightful notes of white flowers.
- Laporte, Cave la Cresle, rte de Sury-en-Vaux, 18300 Sury-en-Vaux, tel. 02.48.78.54.20, fax 02.48.54.34.33 Ⓥ Y by appt.

DOM. DE SAINT-PIERRE

Cuvée Maréchal Prieur 1999★★★

n.c. | 4,400 | €11-15

Pierre Prieur and his sons grow grapes on vineyards in the best soils of Sancerre. This 99, matured for a year in barrel, charmed the Jury, who chose it by an overwhelming majority. It has an intense and very youthful-looking ruby colour, as well as a bouquet that combines floral, musky, vanilla and fruity aromas typical of Sancerre. On the palate, it is complex, concentrated and balanced. The wine demonstrates a perfect alliance between the Pinot Noir, the *terroir*, the oak of the barrels and the skills of the winemakers.

DOM. DE SAINT-ROMBLE 2000★

7.5 ha | 30,000 | €5-8

Pale in colour, this wine is too young for its scents to have developed. On the palate, however, it indicates that it has an excellent future; it is very fleshy, with a good length on the finish. Be patient. Also recommended is the estate's **red 99**, which is fruity, light and smooth. These wines are distributed by Fournier at Verdigny, which has been running the estate since 1996.
- SARL Paul Vattan, Dom. de Saint-Romble, Maimbray, BP 45, 18300 Sury-en-Vaux, tel. 02.48.79.30.36, fax 02.48.79.30.41, e-mail claude@fournier-pere-fils.fr Ⓥ Y ev. day 9am–12 noon 2pm–6pm; Sat. Sun. by appt.

DOM. CHRISTIAN SALMON 1999★★

3.33 ha | 26,666 | €8-11

Christian Salmon's vineyard straddles the clay-limestone slopes of the village of Bué. Its best wine this year is this Sancerre, matured for 18 months in barrel, which is at its best in terms of fullness. It releases aromas of very ripe fruit, roasting and vanilla; well-balanced on the palate, with hints of fruitiness and cocoa beans, its well-integrated tannins reveal an excellent blend of grapes and oak. Two other wines are recommended: the lively and fruity **rosé 2000** and the elegant **white 2000**, with its scents of flowers and citrus fruit.
- SA Christian Salmon, Le Carroir, 18300 Bué, tel. 02.48.54.20.54, fax 02.48.54.30.36

CAVE DES VINS DE SANCERRE

Cuvée réservée 2000

n.c. | 13,300 | €5-8

Formed in 1963, this co-operative changed premises in 2001. It has produced a wine typical of the appellation, with an intense bouquet dominated by vegetal, mineral and fruity scents. After a lively, fresh opening on the palate, the wine has body and roundness, with a hint of spices on the finish.
- Cave des Vins de Sancerre, av. de Verdun, 18300 Sancerre, tel. 02.48.54.19.24, fax 02.48.54.16.44, e-mail infos@vins-sancerre.com Ⓥ Y by appt.

GERARD ET HUBERT THIROT

Elevé en fût de chêne Cuvée Pierre 1999★

0.5 ha | 3,000 | €8-11

The Thirots have been growing wine here for three centuries. Maturing this wine in oak has given it notes of vanilla, coffee and cocoa beans along with natural fruit. On the palate, it opens smoothly, but the tannins are still very evident: wait for them to soften.

- SA Pierre Prieur et Fils, Dom. de Saint-Pierre, 18300 Verdigny-en-Sancerre, tel. 02.48.79.31.70, fax 02.48.79.38.87 Ⓥ Y ev. day except Sun. 8.30am–12 noon 2pm–6pm

☎ Gérard et Hubert Thirot, allée du Chatilier, 18300 Bué, tel. 02.48.54.16.14, fax 02.48.54.00.42 ☑ 🍷 by appt.

DOM. THOMAS Le Pierrier 2000★

☐   11.5 ha   70,000   ■ 🍸 ♦   €8-11

This estate was founded in the 17th century, and introduced Paris to Sancerre at the beginning of the 20th century. This wine has a bouquet that opens on mineral notes, then develops a delicate scent of pears. On the palate, it is full, rounded, powerful and balanced; its slight bitterness will fade with time. The **Terres Blanches 99 red** is recommended too: maturing in oak has preserved the fruitiness of the grapes.

☎ Dom. Thomas et Fils, Verdigny, 18300 Sancerre, tel. 02.48.79.38.71, fax 02.48.79.38.14 ☑ 🍷 ev. day 9am–12 noon 2pm–7pm; Sun. by appt.

CLAUDE ET FLORENCE THOMAS-LABAILLE
Les Aristides Vieilles vignes 2000★

☐   1.5 ha   7,500   ■ 🍶   €8-11

With its original label, this wine is restrained and pleasant on the nose, with fruity and mineral notes. Rounded, with good intensity and real finesse on the palate, it will go well with *crottin de Chavignol*, the famous local goats' cheese. Also worth trying is **L'Authentique 2000**, which is more mineral and lively and was not matured in oak.

☎ Claude et Florence Thomas-Labaille, Chavignol, 18300 Sancerre, tel. 02.48.54.06.95, fax 02.48.54.07.80 ☑ 🍷 by appt.

DOM. DES TROIS NOYERS 2000★

☐   7 ha   30,000   ■ 🍶   €8-11

A lovely pale-golden colour, this wine has a fine, elegant bouquet dominated by lemons and grapefruit, scents in perfect keeping with its well-balanced liveliness on the palate. It will go well with marinated mussels. The same estate produces the **Domaine des Trois Noyers 2000 red**, which wins one star. On the palate, it gives fruity flavours (cherries and raspberries), though the tannins are still a little firm: keep it for a while.

☎ Reverdy-Cadet et Fils, rte de la Perrière, Chaudoux, 18300 Verdigny, tel. 02.48.79.38.54, fax 02.48.79.35.25 ☑ 🍷 by appt.

DOM. VACHERON 1999★★

■   11 ha   50,000   ▥   €8-11

Domaine Vacheron, which appears regularly in the *Guide*, stands on the famous Sancerre peak. This wine was matured for a year in barrel, which has given it notes of vanilla, coffee and roasting. Its fullness increases on the palate, with its bursting flavours of stewed fruit and soft fruit. Fleshy and well-structured, it lingers on the finish.

☎ Dom. Vacheron, rue du Puits-Poulton, 18300 Sancerre, tel. 02.48.54.09.93, fax 02.48.54.01.74 ☑ 🍷 by appt.

DOM. ANDRÉ VATAN
Maulin Bele 2000

☐   0.45 ha   3,900   ■ 🍶 ♦   €8-11

This is a Sancerre to drink with a pastry. It has a lovely, onion-skin colour and releases powerful aromas of exotic fruit. Also recommended is the **Les Charmes 2000 white**. Yellow with green glints, it releases typically Sauvignon scents of boxwood, broom and citrus fruit. The flavours of white flowers dominate on the palate: a fine, lively wine.

☎ André Vatan, Chaudoux, 18300 Verdigny, tel. 02.48.79.33.07, fax 02.48.79.36.30 ☑ 🍷 by appt.

DOM. DU VIEUX PRÊCHE 2000★★

■   0.5 ha   4,700   ■   €8-11

A very small vintage but a great wine, this *coup de coeur* delighted the tasters straight away with its clean red colour tinged with purple. Flavours of very ripe red fruit (raspberries, blackcurrants and cherries) and cocoa beans linger on the palate, which is smooth, firm and well-balanced, indicating a great future.

☎ SCEV Robert Planchon et Fils, Dom. du Vieux Prêche, 3, rue Porte-Serrure, 18300 Sancerre, tel. 02.48.54.22.22, fax 02.48.54.09.31 ☑ 🍷 by appt.

As the mighty Rhône races south towards the Midi and the sun, it unites rather than divides the great tracts of country either side of it. Along both its banks stretch vineyards that are among the oldest in France, prestigious in some places, yet unknown in others. In terms of producing fine wines, the Rhône valley is the second largest viticultural area in France, after Bordeaux. In terms of quality it can compete at the highest level with some of the Bordeaux crus and can excite the interest of connoisseurs just as much as some of the most highly prized Bordeaux and Burgundies.

For a long time, however, Côte du Rhône wine was under-estimated: it was considered to be a nice, popular little bar wine and, as such, appeared only rarely on dinner tables. It was known as a *vin d'une nuit* (a one-night wine), because its fleeting stay in the vat made it light, fruity and a little tannic, quite at home alongside Beaujolais in the Lyonnais *bouchons* (bars). Nonetheless, true wine-lovers had always appreciated the Grands Crus, tasting a Hermitage with the respect reserved for great bottles. Nowadays, thanks to the efforts of the 12,000 Rhône winegrowers and their professional organisations, along with a constant improvement in quality, the image of the Côte du Rhône wines has improved. While they still flow joyously in bars and bistros, they are also taking their place at the best tables and, while their true richness remains in their diversity, they have reclaimed the success they enjoyed in times past.

Few wine regions are able to lay claim to so glorious a past, and from Vienne to Avignon there is no single village that is not recorded in some of the most memorable pages of French history. The oldest vineyard in the country is said to be on the banks of the Vienne, originally created by Phocaean Greeks who journeyed up from Marseille, and further developed by the Romans. By the 4th century BC, vineyards are recorded in the areas now famous as Hermitage and Côte Rôtie, while those in the region of Die appeared at the very beginning of the Christian era. The Templars, in the 12th century, planted the first vines at Châteauneuf-du-Pape, and the work was continued by Pope John XXII two centuries later. As for the Côte du Rhône wines in the Gard, they used to be very fashionable in the 17th and 18th centuries.

Today, in the southern sector, on the left bank of the river, the medieval château of Suze-la-Rousse has been reconverted to serve the wine industry: the Université du Vin has its headquarters there and organises courses, professional training and various events.

Looking at the valley as a whole, some commentators make a distinction between the wines of the left bank as being heavier and more heady, and the wines on the right bank which are lighter. More generally they distinguish between two main sectors which are clearly differentiated: the sector of the northern Côtes du Rhône, north of Valence, and that of the southern Côtes du Rhône, south of Montélimar, divided from each other by an area about 50 km (31 miles) deep where no vines are grown.

The neighbouring appellations of the Rhône valley should not be left out. Even though they are less well known to the general

Côtes du Rhône

public, they nonetheless produce original wines of quality. These are the Coteaux du Tricastin in the north, the Côtes du Ventoux and the Côtes du Luberon in the east, and the Côtes du Vivarais in the north-west. There are three further appellations which are geographically more distant still from the valley proper: the Clairette de Die and the Châtillon-en-Dios in the Drôme valley, on the edge of the Vercors, and the Coteaux de Pierrevert, produced in the department of the Alpes-de-Haute-Provence. Finally, it is worth noting the two appellations of Vins Doux Naturels (naturally sweet wines) of the Vaucluse: Muscat de Beaumes-de-Venise and Rasteau (see the chapter on Vins Doux Naturels).

Looking at the variations of soils and climate, it is still possible to identify three sub-groupings within the vast region of the Rhône valley. North of Valence, the climate is temperate with a continental influence, the soils are mostly granites or schists, deposited on hills with very steep slopes; the red wines come from a single variety, Syrah, and the whites from Marsanne and Roussanne, while the Viognier variety is used to make Château-Grillet and Condrieu. In the Dios, the climate is influenced by the mountain relief and the limestone soils are made up of screes at the foot of the slopes, good conditions for the Clairette and Muscat varieties. South of Montélimar the climate becomes Mediterranean and the very varied soils are spread out on a limestone stratum (terraces of rolled pebbles, red clay and sand soils, molasses and sands). Grenache is the main variety here, but the extremes of climate force the wine-growers to use a number of varieties to obtain perfectly balanced wines: these include Syrah, Mourvèdre, Cinsault, Clairette, Bourboulenc and Roussanne.

After a considerable reduction in the planted area in the 19th century, the vineyard of the Rhône valley was extended again, and today it is still expanding. In general terms it covers 59,000 ha (145,730 acres) producing on average 2.9 million hl (76,560,000 gal) a year; nearly 50% of the wine produced in the northern area is sold by shippers, and 70% is sold by cooperatives in the southern area.

Côtes du Rhône

The Appellation Régionale Côtes du Rhône was defined by decree in 1937. In 1996, a new decree set conditions regarding the vine types planted, to be implemented from 2004: for red wines, Grenache should form a minimum proportion of 40%, Syrah and Mourvèdre should also be included. Naturally enough, this arrangement only applies to vineyards south of Montélimar. White wine varieties will, in future, only be allowed where vines for rosés are grown. The AOC extends into six departments: the Gard, the Ardèche, Drôme, Vaucluse, Loire and Rhône. Produced on 41,000 ha (101,270 acres), nearly all in the southern sector, these wines make 2,200,000 hl (58,080,000 gal), the red wines having the lion's share with 96% of the production, rosés and whites each producing 2%. The 10,000 wine-makers are divided up into 1,610 individual cellars (35% of the volume) and 70 Caves Coopératives (65% of the volume). Out of three hundred million bottles sold each year, 40% are consumed in people's homes, 30% in restaurants and 30% are exported.

Because of the variations in microclimate, the differences in the soil and the vine varieties, these vineyards produce wines that can satisfy every palate. Long-keeping red wines that are rich, tannic and strong, ideal with red meat, are produced in

Côtes du Rhône

The Rhône Valley (Northern)

the hotter areas and on the diluvial alpine soils (Domazan, Estezargues, Courthézon, Orange, etc). Fruity, firmer reds are grown on soils that are lighter (Puyméras, Nyons, Sabran, Bourt-Saint-Andéol, etc). Finally, nouveau wines (about 15 million bottles), fruity and smooth and designed to be drunk very young, are released from the third Thursday in November, and are enjoying an ever-growing success.

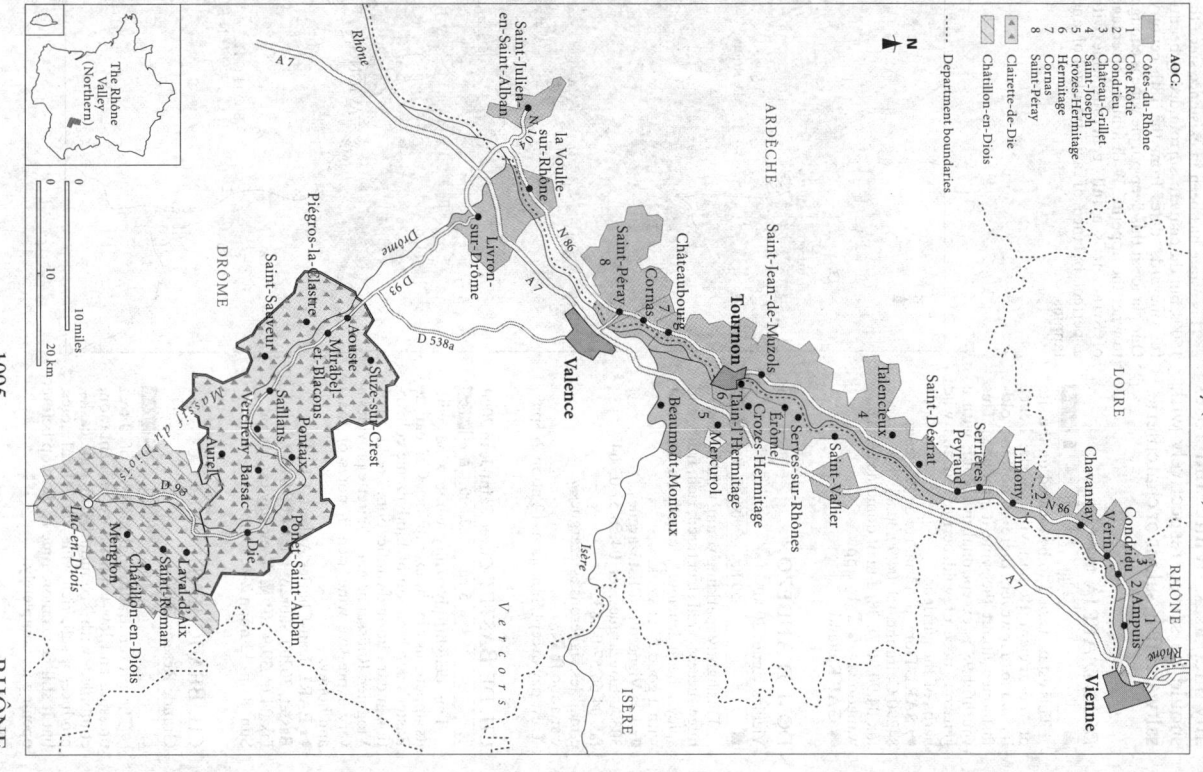

AOC:

1 Côtes-du-Rhône
2 Côte Rôtie
3 Condrieu
4 Château-Grillet
5 Saint-Joseph
6 Crozes-Hermitage
7 Hermitage
6 Cornas
8 Saint-Péray

Clairette-de-Die

Châtillon-en-Diois

----- Department boundaries

The Rhône Valley (Northern)

Côtes du Rhône

    In the case of the whites and rosés, the summer heat promotes a characteristic balance and roundness. Careful cultivation and modern oenological techniques mean that the aromas can be maximised to produce fresh, delicate wines for which demand continually increases. White and rosés should be served respectively with saltwater fish, salads or charcuterie.

DOM. D'AERIA 1998★

◼   2 ha   4,000   ◼ €5-8

This estate is said to be located on the site of the ancient Roman villa Aéria, hence its name. However, there is nothing old-fashioned about the wine it produces. This youthful 98 is exceptional in colour, with a generous nose of wild berry fruit and wild herbs of the garrigue.

☛ SARL Dom. d'Aéria, rte de Rasteau, 84290 Cairanne, tel. 04.90.30.88.78, fax 04.90.30.78.38, e-mail domaine.aeria@wanadoo.fr ✉ ❢ by appt.
☛ GAP Rolland

DOM. D'ANDEZON
Vieilles vignes 2000★

◼   50 ha   200,000   ◼ ●   €5-8

This lightly sparkling young wine is again a huge success. Well structured, rich, fruity and spicy, it has a deliciously long finish. Excellent with a good fillet steak.

☛ Les Vignerons d'Estézargues, 30390 Estézargues, tel. 04.66.57.03.64, fax 04.66.57.04.83, e-mail les.vignerons.estezargues@wanadoo.fr
❢ ev. day except Sun. 8am–12 noon 2–6pm

CH. DE BASTET Cuvée Saint-Jean 2000

☐   5 ha   16,000   ◼ €5-8

This delightfully fruity white wine, with its appetising finish, exemplifies Château de Bastet's combination of biodynamic cultivation and traditional vinification. The blend of Viognier, Roussanne and Clairette provides a very expressive wine, rich in notes of toast and honey.

☛ EARL Jean-Charles Aubert, Ch. de Bastet, 30200 Sabran, tel. 04.66.89.69.14, fax 04.66.39.92.01 ✉ ❢ ev. day except Sat. Sun. 8am–12 noon 2–6.30pm

CH. BEAUCHENE
Grande Réserve 2000

☐   3 ha   20,000   ◉◻ €5-8

The proven traditional method of direct pressing and low-temperature fermentation, combined with six months in oak casks, produces a full, rich wine with floral notes, but it still needs more time to develop before opening out completely.

☛ Michel Bernard, ch. Beauchêne, rte de Beauchêne, 84420 Piolenc, tel. 04.90.51.75.87, fax 04.90.51.73.36, e-mail chateaubeauchene@worldonline.fr ✉ ❢ ev. day except Sat. Sun. 8am–12 noon 1.30–5.30pm

CH. DE BEAULIEU
Cuvée Prestige 1998★★

◼   2 ha   10,000   ◼ €5-8

This estate has been in existence since the 1500s, but the château, surrounded by beautiful vineyards, dates from the 18th century. One glance at this deep purple wine is enough to whet the appetite. With a high percentage of Syrah, it is a full, generous wine with a perfect balance of acidity, alcohol and tannins.

⌐ SCEA Merle et Fils, Ch. de Beaulieu, rte de Sérignan, 84100 Orange, tel. 04.90.34.07.11, fax 04.90.34.07.11 ☑
Υ by appt.
⌐ François Merle

⌐ Jean-Paul Benoit, 584, plateau de Campbeau, 84470 Chateauneuf-de-Gadagne, tel. 04.90.22.29.76 ☑ Υ by appt.

DOM. DU BOIS DE SAINT-JEAN

2000★

□   1.5 ha   6,000   €5-8

Viognier, the grape variety used in Condrieu, is grown here in the sandy soil of the south near Avignon and is producing some interesting results. Here is a rich, fleshy wine with a powerful, mouth-watering flavour. The **Côtes du Rhône-Villages Cuvée du Comte d'Hust et du Saint-Empire 99** was commended by the Jury. Muscular and well structured, this is a wine worth watching.

DOM. JEAN-PAUL BENOIT

Plateau de Campbeau Cuvée spéciale 1999★

■   n.c.   1,000   €5-8

This is a rich, fleshy wine for laying down. The complex bouquet ranges widely through damp undergrowth, spices and red fruit, with a final hint of leather. The fine tannins offset the overripe berries to give a long finish topped with a dash of liquorice.

The Rhône Valley (Southern)

AOC communes

Côtes du Rhône-Villages

1 Beaumes-de-Venise
2 Cairanne
3 Chusclan
4 Laudun
5 Rasteau
6 Roaix
7 Rochegude
8 Rousset-les-Vignes
9 Sablet
10 Séguret
11 Saint-Gervais
12 Saint-Maurice-sur-Eygues
13 Saint-Pantaléon-les-Vignes
14 Valréas
15 Vinsobres
16 Visan

Other AOCs:

A Coteaux du Tricastin
B Côtes du Ventoux
C Côtes du Luberon
D Côtes du Vivarais
E Coteaux de Pierrevert

Côtes du Rhône

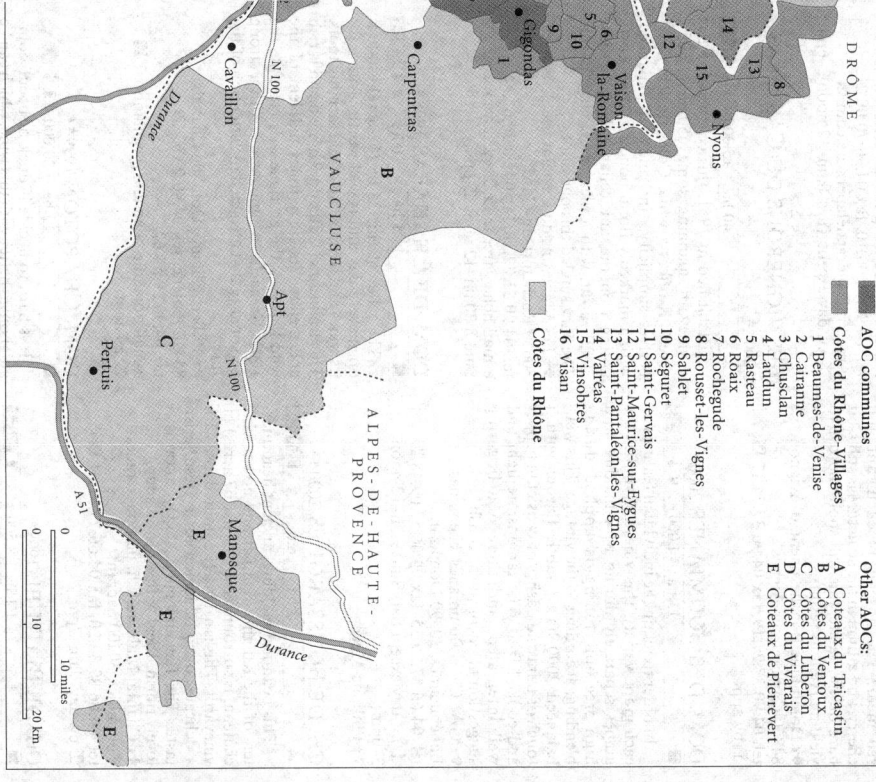

DRÔME
VAUCLUSE
ALPES-DE-HAUTE-PROVENCE

Cavaillon
Carpentras
Gigondas
Vaison-la-Romaine
Nyons
Apt
Pertuis
Manosque

N 100
A 51
Durance
Durance

0   10   20 km
0   10 miles

Côtes du Rhône

HENRY BOUACHON

Rhône Prestige 2000★★

☐   40 ha   50,000   ▪ ♦   €5-8   Ⓥ

Prestigious indeed! Noblesse oblige for this wine with its golden highlights. An explosion of honey and crystallised fruit. Although rich and full, this wine is beautifully fresh, achieving remarkable balance.

● Henry Bouachon, BP 5,
84230 Châteauneuf-du-Pape,
tel. 04.90.83.58.35, fax 04.90.83.77.23 Ⓥ
Ⓨ by appt.

DOM. BOUCHE La Truffière 1999★★★

☐   5 ha   26,000   ▪ ♦   €8-11   Ⓥ

A wine made with uncrushed grapes (Grenache and Syrah) to drink with all types of red meat. The nose is blackcurrant and cherry, and although the structure is still a bit hard on the palate, this will soon improve to yield marvellous results.

● Dominique Bouche, chem. d'Avignon,
84850 Camaret-sur-Aigues,
tel. 04.90.37.27.19, fax 04.90.37.74.17 Ⓥ
Ⓨ by appt.

DOM. DES BOUMIANES 2000★

☐   13 ha   4,000   ▪ ♦   €3-5   Ⓥ

In order to retain the individual features of each grape variety, this vineyard vinifies the grapes separately during wine-making, and high-precision tuning is applied during blending, according to the vintage. This well-balanced 2000 has a subtle flavour with a touch of mint and dashes of capsicum pepper and cooked fruit. The tannins are light and well integrated, and there is a lingering suggestion of cocoa at the finish.

● GAEC des Boumianes, chem. des Bohémiennes, 30390 Domazan,
tel. 04.66.57.29.35, fax 04.66.57.09.48 Ⓥ
Ⓨ ev. day except Sat. Sun. 9am–12 noon 2–6pm
● Philippe Meger

CH. DE BOUSSARGUES 2000★

☐   2 ha   n.c.   ▪ ♦   €3-5

This beautiful building, ancient headquarters of the Knights Templar and now a wine château, is surrounded by 27 ha (67 acres) of vineyards. This is a densely coloured rosé with a delicate touch of lemon for a fresh, crisp taste. The flavours build slowly towards a lovely finish. Ideal with a pistou soup.

● Chantal Malabre, Ch. de Boussargues Colombier, 30200 Sabran,
tel. 04.66.89.32.20, fax 04.66.79.81.64 Ⓥ
Ⓨ ev. day. 9am–7pm

CH. DE BRUTHEL 1999★

☐   1.1 ha   8,500   ▪ ♦   €5-8

The château was built in the late 17th century, its 99 was matured for six months in large wooden casks. Automatically classified for laying down because of the tannin levels, it is already a full, well-balanced wine, with berries macerated in brandy and faint hints of vanilla. It needs to be left in the cellar for two or three years to reach its peak.

● Christian Reynold de Seresin, Ch. de Bruthel, 30200 Sabran, tel. 04.66.79.96.24, fax 04.66.39.80.88 Ⓥ Ⓨ ev. day except Sun. 9am–12 noon 2–5pm.

CH. CARBONEL 2000★

☐   15 ha   90,000   ▪ ♦   €3-5

Red or **rosé**? This very young vintage is value for money, whichever the choice. The red is strong in fruit, with good spicy overtones; the rosé is more delicate, with a soft rose-petal fragrance. 'Expertly made wine,' was the Jury's verdict. In this same AOC the **Château Joanny cuvée Prestige white 2000** and the **rosé 2000** were both singled out for mention.

● Famille Dupond, Ch. Carbonel, rte de Piolenc, 84830 Serignan-du-Comtat,
tel. 04.90.70.00.10, fax 04.90.70.09.21,
e-mail info@bracdelaperriere.com Ⓥ
Ⓨ ev. day except Tues. 8am–12 noon 2–6pm

LES VIGNERONS DU CASTELAS 2000★★

☐   40 ha   15,000   ▪ ♦   €3-5

Established in 1951, this co-operative has a vineyard spanning some 650 ha (1,605.5 acres). It offers a white Côtes du Rhône of perfect simplicity, fine and well balanced, with a markedly floral bouquet. Also worth noting, from the same cellar, is the **2000 white vielli en fût**, with a pleasantly oaky flavour. The Jury singled this one out.

● Les Vignerons du Castelas, rte de Nîmes, 30650 Rochefort-du-Gard,
tel. 04.90.31.72.10, fax 04.90.26.62.64,
e-mail ncha@free.fr Ⓥ Ⓨ ev. day except Sun. 8.30am–12 noon 2–6pm

DOM. DE CHANABAS 1998★

☐   1 ha   6,000   ▪ ♦   €3-5

The cellar of this 25-ha (62-acre) estate is open every day and is well worth visiting for its wines and its museum of old farming tools. This traditional Côtes du Rhône blend is rich and mellow, its spicy tones redolent of the wild herbs of the garrigue. Also sample the **100% Grenache**, a supple wine with a strong personality that attracted the attention of the Jury.

● Robert Champ, Dom. de Chanabas, 84420 Piolenc, tel. 04.90.29.63.59, fax 04.90.29.55.67,
e-mail domaine-chanabas@wanadoo.fr Ⓥ
Ⓨ by appt.

DOM. CHAPOTON 1999★★

☐   15 ha   20,000   ▪ ♦   €5-8

It is hard to decide if duck or boeuf bourguignon go better with this wine, which can be drunk from now on, even on its own. The aroma of black fruit and game supplements

● EARL Vincent et Xavier Anglès, 126, av. de la République, 84450 Jonquerettes,
tel. 04.90.22.53.22, fax 04.90.22.53.22 Ⓥ
Ⓨ ev. day. 8am–12 noon 2–8pm

on the lovely colour. Superbly balanced and long on the palate, this is a beautiful quality wine.
☛ Serge Remusan, rte du Moulin, 26790 Rochegude, tel. 04.75.98.22.46, fax 04.75.98.22.46 ☑ ▼ ev. day except Sun. 10am–12.30pm 3–6pm; cl. Jan. Feb.

CELLIER DES CHARTREUX 2000★

☐ | n.c. | 21,000 | €5–8

This white wine glimmers with gold and green in the glass, with a strong character of citrus fruit on the nose, but it proves astonishingly harmonious and well balanced. The exemplary quality control practised by the winery (established in 1929) suggests that the new cellars built for the 2001 vintage will produce very promising results.
☛ SCA Cellier des Chartreux, 216, chem. des Vignerons, 30150 Sauveterre, tel. 04.66.82.53.53, fax 04.66.82.89.07 ☑
▼ by appt.

DOM. CHARVIN 1999

13 ha | 34,000 | €5–8

What better than a tender leg of lamb studded with garlic to set off this wine to its best? Powerful and rustic, the wine, which is 85% Grenache, has opened up a little to produce dense, spicy aromas. It is very pleasant to drink right now, but could be drunk over the next two years.
☛ EARL Gérard Charvin et Fils, Dom. Charvin, chem. de Maucoil, 84100 Orange, tel. 04.90.34.41.10, fax 04.90.51.65.59, e-mail domaine.charvin@free.com ☑
▼ by appt.

CH. CHEVALIER BRIGAND 1999

6 ha | 15,000 | €5–8

The members of Jean-Marie Saut's family have been wine-makers since 1609. Every single vine plant is scrupulously vetted to ensure the wine's quality. This particular vintage is strongly influenced by the 60% Syrah grape that gives it an intense, musky aroma, while Grenache adds the warmth of the southern sun.
☛ Jean-Marie Saut, Le Pont de Codolet, 30200 Codolet, tel. 04.66.90.18.64, fax 04.66.90.11.57 ☑ ▼ ev. day except Sat. Sun. 9am–12 noon 2–6.30pm

DOM. CLAVEL 2000

1.93 ha | 13,000 | €3–5

Maximum skill and care have always been the hallmarks of the wines from this estate. This year the outstanding wine is the *rosé de saignée*, which is lovely on the eye, the nose and the palate.
☛ Denis Clavel, rue du Pigeonnier, 30200 Saint-Gervais, tel. 04.66.82.78.90, fax 04.66.82.74.30 ☑ ▼ ev. day except Sun 9am–12 noon 2–6pm

CAVE COSTES ROUSSES

Cuvée réservée 2000★

30 ha | 7,848 | €3–5

Bernard Roustand, the well-known oenologist, took over this winery in 1998. He has created a rosé that is lively, yet remains fruity and elegant. It is ideal with cold cuts of every description.
☛ SCA Cave Costes Rousses, 2, av. des Alpes, 26790 Tulette, tel. 04.75.97.23.18, fax 04.75.98.38.61 ☑ ▼ by appt.

DOM. COULANGE

Cuvée Rochelette 1999★★

5 ha | 1,660 | €5–8

A splendid advertisement for the beautiful *département* of Ardèche! Two stars for the **Cuvée Mistral 99** affirm the quality of this vintage from an estate awarded the *coup de coeur* for its **Cuvée Rochelette**. Fruity flavours explode on the palate and in the throat. This dark wine is a real pleasure to drink and has attracted compliments galore: immediate, supple, persistent, powerful, well-balanced, liquorice-flavoured, spicy … to quote just a few.
☛ Maurice et Christelle Coulange, quartier Saint-Ferréol, 07700 Bourg-Saint-Andéol, tel. 04.75.54.56.26, fax 04.75.54.56.26, e-mail domaine.coulange@free.fr ☑
▼ by appt.

DOM. NICOLAS CROZE

Cuvée Notre Dame de Mélinas 1999★★★

n.c. | 10,000 | €3–5

This wine only just missed out on the *coup de coeur* for its splendid quality. An elegantly coloured wine, with superbly luscious fruits and spices, subtly balanced, dense and complex, it will provide delight for another three or four years. The **Cuvée vieille en fût red** was awarded a star for its rich velvet texture with oak undertones. The **Cuvée fleurie white 99**, 100% Viognier, is beginning to show all the qualities of this most important variety of the Rhône valley. Powerful in aroma and excellently balanced, this is a wine well worth discovering.
☛ Maurice et Nicolas Croze, 1, rue Max-Ernst, 07700 Saint-Martin-d'Ardèche, tel. 04.75.04.67.11, fax 04.75.04.62.28 ☑
▼ by appt.

CELLIER DES DAUPHINS

Cuvée Grand Millésime 1998

140 ha | 500,000 | €3–5

This enormous complex of Rhône co-operatives offers a fruity, chewy wine on a framework of finely structured tannins, for immediate drinking.

Côtes du Rhône

GALLIFFET 2000★   4 ha   5,300   €15-23

☐

The 'estate of the President's wife', from which this wine originates, does not signify, as some believe, the private residence of the wife of the President of France. The name, in fact, is a tribute to the wife of the President of Provence. This Viognier white has strong character, and is richly textured, with ripe fruit and a touch of almond. It is worth noting that the principal **Domaine de La Présidente rosé 2000** selection bears the same mark. Fresh and delicate, it is a splendidly elegant wine.

☛ SCEA Max Aubert, Dom. de La Présidente, 84290 Sainte-Cécile-les-Vignes, tel. 04.90.30.79.73, fax 04.90.30.72.93, e-mail aubert@presidente.fr ⊻ ⊤ by appt.

CH. GIGOGNAN
Vigne du Prieuré 2000★   0.5 ha   3,300   €5-8

This is the 'classic' Rhône Valley rosé: a blend of Grenache and Cinsault, one for warmth, the other for fragrance, and produced in *saignée*, resulting in a beautifully balanced wine. Its aroma, body and elegance cannot be faulted. It is delicious with poultry.

☛ Ch. Gigognan, chem. du Castillon, 84700 Sorgues, tel. 04.90.39.57.46, fax 04.90.39.15.28. e-mail info@chateau-gigognan.fr ⊻ ⊤ ev. day 10am–12 noon 2pm–6pm; Sun. by appt.

☛ Callet

DOM. DES GIRASOLS
Cuvée Bienveillante 1998★   1.5 ha   10,200   €8-11

The Domaine des Girasols has created a charming 98 wine from the illustrious soil of Rasteau. The **Vieilles vignes** attracted the Jury's commendation. It combines 10% Cinsault with Grenache: jammy red fruit flavours dominate, but there are also hints of chocolate. The more traditional *Cuvée* has a spicy floral bouquet and is nicely rounded and well-structured on the palate, though still very young. A star, too, for the **Côtes du Rhône-Villages Rasteau 98** whose exuberant tannins bode well for its future.

☛ Famille Paul Joyet, Dom. des Girasols, 84110 Rasteau, tel. 04.90.46.11.70, fax 04.90.46.16.82. e-mail domaine@girasols.com ⊻ ⊤ ev. day. 8am–12 noon 2pm–7pm

DOM. DES GRANDS DEVERS
1999★   2.81 ha   15,000   €5-8

In this vineyard, in the very heart of the 'Enclave des Papes', Grenache grows alongside truffles! This southern 100% Syrah wine, with its fruity nose laced with violets, delighted the Jury. Nicely coloured, its impact is supple and smooth, enhanced by the delicate tannins which ensure a wonderful finish.

☛ Cellier des Dauphins, BP 16, 26790 Tulette, tel. 04.75.96.20.47, fax 04.75.96.20.22, e-mail cellier.des.dauphins@wanadoo.fr

DOM. JEAN DAVID 1999★   10 ha   14,000   €5-8

This well-structured wine comes from organically cultivated grapes, with Grenache dominating the other five southern grape varieties. With its powerful berry bouquet, the wine is already smooth on the palate, and there is no need to lay it down.

☛ Dom. Jean David, quartier Le Jas, 84110 Séguret, tel. 04.90.46.95.02, fax 04.90.46.86.21 ⊻ ⊤ ev. day except Sun. 9am–7pm; cl. Nov.

DOM. DES FILLES DURMA 1999★★   n.c.   12,000   €5-8

This is a traditional 99 of a deep violet colour. Its strong fruity aroma instantly fills the palate, matching the fleshy, rich texture built on sturdy tannins, which is likely to take up to three years to blend completely.

☛ EARL Durma Soeurs, quartier Hautes-Rives, 26110 Vinsobres, tel. 04.75.27.64.71, fax 04.75.27.64.50 ⊤ by appt.

DOM. DES ESCARAVAILLES 1999★   n.c.   10,000   €3-5

The name of the estate derives from the Provençal for 'scarab', the term applied to the penitents from Avignon who once owned this land. Today these vines produce a pleasantly well-rounded, wine, full of flavour that releases surprising hints of honey. The **Côtes du Rhône-Villages Rasteau, 99** won compliments from the Jury as a worthy representative of its AOC.

☛ GAEC Ferran et Fils, Dom. des Escaravailles, 84110 Rasteau, tel. 04.90.46.14.20, fax 04.90.46.11.45 ⊻ ⊤ by appt.

DOM. DE FONTAVIN 2000★   1 ha   6,000   €5-8

This 42-ha (103.74-acre) family estate lies close to the village of Courthézon, famous for its many springs. If proof were still needed that women have won their fair place among wine-makers, La Fontavin can do just that. Hélène Chouvet, oenologist, has created this quite delightful wine. 'I love this wine for the fragrance alone,' said one member of the Jury. The long, well-rounded finish is equally notable. The vintage **white Vin du Domaine** was singled out for special mention. It is racy and fresh, a rare combination in southern Côtes du Rhône whites. A good choice with shellfish.

☛ EARL Hélène et Michel Chouvet, Dom. de Fontavin, 1468, rte de la Plaine, 84350 Courthézon, tel. 04.90.70.72.14, fax 04.90.70.79.39, e-mail helene-chouvet@fontavin.com ⊻ ⊤ ev. day except Sun. 9am–12.30pm 2pm–6.30pm; Summer 9am–7pm

● Paul-Henri Bouchard et ses Frères, Dom. des Grands-Devers, 84600 Valréas, tel. 04.90.35.15.98, fax 04.90.34.49.56, e-mail phbouchard@grandsdevers.com ▼ by appt.

DOM. DU GROS PATA
Cuvée Sabine Vieilli en fût de chêne 1999★

| 1.53 ha | 10.666 | €5-8 |

Whether or not inspiration comes from Romulus' rape of the Sabines, as the label suggests, this estate has an intriguing history. The name of the vineyard stems from the taxes levied on produce by nearby Vaison-la-Romain. A classical blend has produced a round, full-bodied wine with a fragrance of stone fruit and a touch of toast. This nicely balanced 99 could be put away for a few months without the loss of any attributes.
● Gérald Garagnon, Dom. du Gros-Pata, 84110 Vaison-la-Romaine, tel. 04.90.36.23.75, fax 04.90.28.77.05 ▼

DOM. JAUME 1999★

| 23 ha | 150,000 | €3-5 |

All three Côtes du Rhône wines are celebrated here. The **rosé 2000**, commended by the Jury, is a ripe and pleasant accompaniment to cold cuts; the **white 2000**, with its overwhelmingly powerful floral bouquet, was awarded a star; and the **red 99** has a good solid structure, with an aroma of fresh fruits and mellow hints of liquorice. The finish is simply superb.
● Dom. Jaume, 24, rue Reynarde, 26110 Vinsobres, tel. 04.75.27.61.01, fax 04.75.27.68.40 ▼ ev. day except Sun. 8am-12 noon 1.30pm-7pm

LA BASTIDE SAINT DOMINIQUE 1999

| 4 ha | 21,000 | €5-8 |

Given faultless grapes, the punching-down technique that has been widely adopted for Côtes du Rhône wines often yields striking results, as is the case here, where well-rounded tannins are complemented by entrancing touches of jammy fruit.
● Gérard Bonnet, La Bastide-Saint-Dominique, 84350 Courthézon, tel. 04.90.70.85.32, fax 04.90.70.76.64, e-mail contact@bastide-st-dominique.com ▼ ev. day: 9am-12 noon 1.30pm-6.30pm; Sun. by appt.

LA CABOTTE 1999★

| 27 ha | 50,000 | €5-8 |

A single 45-ha (111-acre) vineyard plot in the heart of the Massif d'Uchaux meant love at first sight for Marie-Pierre Plumet back in 1981. She bought it on the spot. This wine is recommended to be served with rabbit cooked with prunes. Deceptively simple and discreet on the nose, the fruit expands on the palate to reveal a rich, lingering, well-balanced texture.

● Marie-Pierre Plumet, La Cabotte, 84430 Mondragon, tel. 04.90.40.60.29, fax 04.90.40.60.62 ▼ by appt.

DOM. LA CHARADE
Vieilli en fût 1999★

| 22 ha | n.c. | €5-8 |

Lots of special skill and care goes to making this wine, aged in oak barrels. It has maintained its complex vanilla and toasted aroma, and the powerful structure has earned it a star. From the same estate, the **Cuvée non Boisée** also has won recognition from the Jury. A good, honest wine.
● M. et L. Jullien, Dom. La Charade de Peyrolas, 30760 Saint-Julien-de-Peyrolas, tel. 04.66.82.18.21, fax 04.66.82.33.03 ▼ ev. day except Sun, 9am-12 noon 2pm-7pm

DOM. DE LA CHARITÉ 1999★★★

| 16 ha | 100,000 | €3-5 |

The Grand Jury gave this wine three stars for its high quality blend of Grenache (60%), Syrah (30%) and Carignan. The wine-maker and its oenologist, Noël Rabot, have produced an exceptional Côtes du Rhône from the clay-limestone soil. The deep rich colour is rivalled by the aroma, in which jammy black and red currants blend with liquorice. Full-bodied and fleshy, its flavour is built upon lovely rich tannins. This wine is already superb, but will gain even more after a time in the cellar. The **white Domaine de La Charité 2000**, singled out for mention by the Jury, has all the characteristics of southern whites including strongly dominant Grenache (70%) over the Viognier.
● EARL Valentin et Coste, 5, chem. des Issarts, 30650 Saze, tel. 04.90.31.73.55, fax 04.90.26.92.50, e-mail earlvc@club-internet.fr ▼ ev. day except Sun. 2pm-7pm

DOM. DE LA CHARTREUSE DE VALBONNE
Cuvée de La Font des Dames 1999★★

| 1.6 ha | 12,000 | €5-8 |

Nestled in the bottom of a valley, this architectural treasure, a monastery until the French Revolution, is now an agricultural advisory centre. The monastery is used for wine-making and cultural activities. Because of its unusual *terroir*, the wine produced here is often out of the ordinary; the flavour is very intense, with violet and spices blending happily with wild fruit to delight the palate; ideal with tender roast lamb. Harmony, structure, complexity and a long finish spell perfection for the next three years.

➼ ASVMT, Dom. de La Chartreuse de Valbonne, 30130 Saint-Paulet-de-Caisson, tel. 04.66.90.41.24, fax 04.66.90.41.23, e-mail chartreuse.de.valbonne@wanadoo.fr ⓥ ⓣ by appt.

DOM. DE LA CROIX-BLANCHE 1999★

◼ 0.3 ha 2,000 ⓦ €5-8

In the cool shade of its stone walls at the heart of this magnificent village in Ardèche, the vineyard offers a wide range of really good-quality wines, and this one in particular. Deep red, it has a strong aroma of smoked wood. A well-structured wine to accompany a tasty dish of wild game.

➼ Daniel Archambault,
Dom. de La Croix-Blanche,
07700 Saint-Martin-d'Ardèche,
tel. 04.75.04.65.07, fax 04.75.98.77.25, e-mail daniel.archambault@free.fr ⓥ ⓣ by appt.

CH. LA CROIX CHABRIERES 2000★

☐ n.c. 9,000 ◼ €5-8

Bollène offers much for the visitor, and the most interesting building is the *Collégiale Saint-Martin* founded in the 11th century. Nearby is this 34-ha (84-acre) estate with its **La Festivalière 98** and **Terre Nette 99**, both red, and both awarded a star, as was this château white, blended from equal parts of Grenache, Roussanne and Marsanne. Supple but well structured, with a delightful citrus fruit fragrance, the wine is worth sampling with a tasty fillet of sea bream.

➼ Ch. La Croix Chabrière,
rte de Saint-Restitut, 84500 Bollène,
tel. 04.90.40.00.89, fax 04.90.40.19.93 ⓥ ⓣ ev. day 9am–12 noon 2pm–6pm; Sun. 9am–12 noon; groups by appt.
➼ Patrick Daniel

CH. LA DECELLE 1999★

◼ 3 ha 5,000 ◼ €5-8

Very close to Barry, the village famous for its ancient cave-dwellings, Château La Decelle produces white table wine. Even stronger on the palate than on the nose, the subtle blending of Marsanne and Viognier yields powerful results. Terrific with monkfish, especially when cooked Breton-style.

➼ Ch. La Décelle, rte de Pierrelatte, D 59, 26130 Saint-Paul-Trois-Châteaux,
tel. 04.75.04.71.33, fax 04.75.04.56.98, e-mail anne-marie.seroin@wanadoo.fr ⓥ ⓣ ev. day 9am–12 noon 2.30pm–6.30pm; groups by appt.
➼ Seroin

LA DEVEZE 1999

◼ 6.5 ha 8,928 ◼ €3-5

This wine is ready to drink right now with grilled meats. Its spicy, fresh bouquet makes a

powerful impression, but the silky tannins recommend it for drinking within the year.

➼ EARL Dionysos, 28 bis, av. F.-Mistral, BP 18, 84101 Orange, tel. 04.90.34.06.07, fax 04.90.34.79.85 ⓥ ⓣ by appt.
➼ Farjon

DOM. LA FAVETTE 2000★

◼ 6 ha 23,000 ◼ €3-5

Philippe Faure has only recently taken over the family vineyards, but already has ambitious plans. His deep, richly-coloured 2000 has an aroma of red fruit steeped in alcohol. Long and balanced well by fine tannins, it is one of the more interesting new wines. The intriguing potential of the barrel-aged **Roche-Sauve 99** selection was recognised by the Jury.

➼ Philippe Faure, Dom. La Favette, rte des Gorges, 07700 Saint-Just-d'Ardèche, tel. 04.75.04.61.14, fax 04.75.98.74.56 ⓥ ⓣ by appt.

DOM. DE LA FAVIERE 1999★

☐ 0.2 ha 1,300 €11-15

Cultivated in soil consisting largely of granite, this Viognier has turned out to be a wine with huge potential for laying down. Open on the nose, well-balanced and aromatic on the palate, with a lingering finish, it would be great even now with goat's cheese from Condrieu.

➼ Pierre Boucher, Dom. de La Favière, 42520 Malleval, tel. 04.74.87.15.25, fax 04.74.87.15.25,
e-mail domainedelafaviere@.com ⓥ ⓣ by appt.

DOM. LAFOND ROC EPINE 1999★

◼ 17 ha 125,000 €5-8

Even in the *terroir* of the great rosé wines, fine reds like this can turn up. The colour is beautiful, the attack well balanced, the flavour fresh and pleasantly harmonious. Take note of this delightful Côtes du Rhône.

➼ Dom. Lafond, rte des Vignobles, 30126 Tavel, tel. 04.66.50.24.59, fax 04.66.50.12.42, e-mail lafondrocepine@wanadoo.fr ⓥ ⓣ by appt

DOM. LA FOURMENTE 2000★

◼ 6 ha 12,000 ◼ €5-8

A straightforward wine with a deep violet glow, fresh red fruit on the nose, nicely structured on the palate, yet delicate, fruity and elegant. One member of the Jury, a *sommelier*, recommends this wine with a red meat dessert, or, in a year's time for maturing, to accompany meat cooked with fruit. The **rosé** was given the same mark for its strength and complex aroma. A beautifully smooth wine.

➼ Jean-Louis Pouizin, Grange-Neuve, 84820 Visan, tel. 04.90.41.91.87, fax 04.90.41.91.87,
e-mail domainelafourmente@wanadoo.fr ⓥ ⓣ ev. day except Sun. 10am–12 noon 2pm–7pm

LA GAILLARDE
Cuvée Pied Vaurias 2000
▲ | 10 ha | 12,600 | ■ ■ | €3-5

The Valréas co-operative produces wines from 1,660 ha (4,100 acres) of vines. This year it offers a pale-coloured rosé de saignée, with a fine floral bouquet and a vibrant fresh flavour. A suitable wine for an entrée.

↣ Coop. vinicole La Gaillarde, av. de l'Enclave-des-Papes, BP 95, 84602 Valréas Cedex, tel. 04.90.35.00.66, fax 04.90.35.11.38 ☑ by appt.

DOM. DE LA GRAND'RIBE
Les Garrigues d'Éric Beaumard et Christophe Lambert 1999★★
■ | 11 ha | 70,000 | ■ ▮▮ ▯ ▮

Two stars for this very fine wine, cask-matured for a year. The subtle hints of oak give a fine flavour with toasted overtones. This wine has a good strong structure, but is cleverly balanced all the same, and can be happily served for two or three years with dishes such as veal cutlet and wild mushrooms.

↣ Jérôme Muratori, Dom. de La Grand'Ribe, rte de Bollène, 84290 Sainte-Cécile-les-Vignes, tel. 04.90.30.83.75, fax 04.90.30.76.12 ☑
☒ ev. day except Sat. Sun. 9am-12 noon 2pm-6pm
↣ Abel Sahuc

DOM. DE LA GUICHARDE
Cuvée Ninon Vieilli en fût de chêne 1999★
n.c. | 3,000 | ▮▮ | €8-11

A very fine 99 for two of its wines, commended by the Jury for two of its wines. The Ninon, with aromas of undergrowth and spices allied to an intriguing, toasty, smoked flavour, will soon be ready for drinking with jugged rabbit and wild mushrooms. The red **Vin d'Isabelle**, composed of 100% Grenache grape, has a fruity flavour with suggestions of gunflint. The initial impression is clean and rich, giving way to ripe fruit that lingers on the palate. This wine can be drunk before the Ninon.

↣ Arnaud et Isabelle Guichard, Dom. de La Guicharde, 84430 Mondragon, tel. 04.90.30.17.84, fax 04.90.40.05.69 ☑
☒ ev. day except Sun. 10am-6pm

DOM. DE LA JANASSE 2000★
□ | 1.5 ha | 6,000 | ■ ■ | €8-11

This vineyard hand-picks its grapes, and exercises the most scrupulous control in cultivation methods to extract the best from white Grenache, a notoriously capricious grape, but with what class! Supplemented by Clairette and Bourboulenc, this is a classical Côtes du Rhône white.

↣ EARL Aimé Sabon, 27, chem. du Moulin, 84350 Courthézon, tel. 04.90.70.86.29, fax 04.90.70.75.93 ☑
☒ ev. day. 8am-12 noon 2pm-7pm; Sat. Sun. by appt.

DOM. DE L'AMANDINE 2000★
□ | 1 ha | n.c. | ■ ■ | €5-8

This 50-ha (124-acre) estate was created in 1973 in Séguret, a beautiful hillside village classified for its historic trust, and famed for attracting artists. Special mention was made of the 250,000 bottles of **L'Amandine red 2000**. Unanimous praise, too, from the Jury for this white wine, made from equal parts of Roussanne and Viognier. A delightful fragrance of citrus fruits and citronella lingers on the palate. Perfect with shellfish.

↣ Jean-Pierre Verdeau, rte de Roaix, 84110 Séguret, tel. 04.90.46.11.64, fax 04.90.46.16.64, e-mail domaine.amandine@wanadoo.fr ☑
☒ ev. day except Sun. 9am-12 noon 2pm-6pm

DOM. DE LA MORDOREE 2000★
La Dame Rousse 2000★
n.c. | n.c. | ■ ■ | €5-8

This red wine, from an excellent estate, comes from the Garde region, originally the home of Tavel. The deep red Dame Rousse, shot with violet highlights, has an intense aroma of ripe fruit blended with cherry jam. This is a warm wine with velvety tannins. Combining power and elegance, it boasts real quality.

↣ Dom. de La Mordorée, chem. des Oliviers, 30126 Tavel, tel. 04.66.50.00.75, fax 04.66.50.47.39 ☑
☒ ev. day 8am-12 noon 2pm-5.30pm
↣ Delorme

DOM. LA REMEJEANNE
Les Arbousiers 2000★
5.5 ha | 40,000 | ■ ■ | €5-8

Here are two wines that are always included among the great Côtes du Rhône. Each has individual personality and true breeding. These Arbousiers, from Grenache (60%) and Syrah, need no extra frills. The intense flavour of ripe fruit and quince jam is mouth-filling. The **Les Chèvrefeuilles** is more delicate, yet strongly perfumed with red fruit.

↣ EARL Ouahi et Rémy Klein, Dom. La Rémèjeanne, Cadignac, 30200 Sabran, tel. 04.66.89.44.51, fax 04.66.89.64.22, e-mail remejeanne@wanadoo.fr ☑
☒ by appt.

LE CLOS DE LASCAMP 2000★★
15 ha | 20,000 | ■ ■ | €5-8

This estate's **white 2000** was singled out by the Jury. Tasters enthusiastically described it as having a delicious fruity flavour, and being well structured, nicely balanced, long on the palate, with a hint of pear drops - and with reason: the combination of Viognier and Grenache grape varieties is perfectly crafted to extract the best of each. It is a rich, powerful wine with a full floral and white peach flavour.

↣ EARL Clos de Lascamp, Cadignac, 30200 Sabran, tel. 04.66.89.69.28, fax 04.66.89.62.44 ☑ by appt.
↣ Imbert

Côtes du Rhône

DOM. DES LAUSES
Vieilles vignes 1999★
■ 3 ha 14,000 ⅢⅢ €5-8

The Vieilles vignes from this estate comes from grapes cultivated in sandstone soil. The nose is intense and varied, with hints of oak that provide a perfect blend. The pepper and vanilla spices surprise and delight the palate at the first taste.

❧ Dom. des Lauses, quartier des Pessades, 84830 Sérignan-du-Comtat,
tel. 04.90.70.09.13, fax 04.90.70.09.13 ⅤⅤ
Ⅰ by appt.
❧ Gilbert Raoux

DOM. DE LA VERDE 1999★
■ 10 ha 60,000 ● €3-5

In a blindfold tasting of this wine, unaware that the vineyard was windswept by the Mistral, the Jury immediately recognised the resolve of this wine-grower to extract as much body as possible and liked its 'healthy texture'. Fruit and spices blend happily on the palate. A good choice with poultry.

❧ Dom. de La Verde,
La Grand-Comtadine, 84190 Vacqueyras,
tel. 04.90.65.85.91, fax 04.90.65.89.23 ⅤⅤ
Ⅰ by appt.
❧ Annie Camalonga

LA VIGNERONNE
Cuvée des Templiers 2000
◨ n.c. ■ €3-5

The Cuvée des Templiers does honour to the cellar that produces this wine, blended equally from Grenache and Syrah, which explains the deeper-than-usual colour and the pleasant, mellow texture.

❧ Cave La Vigneronne, 84110 Villedieu,
tel. 04.90.28.92.37, fax 04.90.28.93.00 ⅤⅤ
Ⅰ by appt.

LE CLOS DU CAILLOU
Bouquet des garrigues 2000★★
◻ 2 ha 10,000 ■ ● €5-8

Cultivated on sand and smooth pebbles, this refreshing, sparkling golden wine has a sweet fruity flavour that lingers enticingly on the palate. A relaxing wine, the composition is of rare complexity, and the long finish is an unexpected surprise.

❧ Jean-Denis Vacheron, Clos du Caillou,
84350 Courthézon, tel. 04.90.70.73.05,
fax 04.90.70.76.47 ⅤⅤ Ⅰ ev. day except Sun.
8.30am–12 noon 1.30pm–5.30pm

DOM. LE COUROULU 1999
■ 3 ha 21,000 ⅢⅢ ● €5-8

The 20-ha (50-acre) vineyard was established in 1920. This Côtes du Rhône from Vacqueyras is kept in barrels for six months, and although the grapes are de-stemmed during harvesting, the tannins are still rather fierce, although doubtless a year in the cellar will complete integration nicely. Strong red fruit on nose and palate.

❧ Guy Ricard, Dom. Le Couroulu, La Pousterle, 84190 Vacqueyras,
tel. 04.90.65.84.83, fax 04.90.65.81.25 ⅤⅤ
Ⅰ by appt.

DOM. LE PUY DU MAUPAS
Cuvée Isabelle Elevé en fût de chêne 1999★
◻ 1 ha 3,200 ⅢⅢ €8-11

Puyméras, near Vaison-la-Romaine, is the site of a ruined castle destroyed in 1789 during the French Revolution. The Puy du Maupas vineyards were restored about 20 years ago, and produce delightful wines such as this example aged in oak casks. The oaky taste is well integrated, the flavour is delicate and beautifully balanced, and the initial aroma lingers until the finish. A wine to be watched, but for a limited clientèle, it will be perfect in two years or so as an accompaniment to white fish dishes garnished with a cream sauce.

❧ Christian Sauvayre, Dom. Le Puy du Maupas, 84110 Puyméras,
tel. 04.90.46.47.43, fax 04.90.46.48.51 ⅤⅤ
Ⅰ ev. day 9am–12 noon 2pm–7pm

CH. LES AMOUREUSES
La Barbare 2000★
■ 1 ha 4,000 ⅢⅢ €8-11

This estate won the *coup de coeur* last year. This year it offers a blend of Syrah (70%) and Grenache grown in clay-limestone soil exposed to full sun. The vines are assiduously cultivated and hand-harvested to ensure the choicest ingredients for this characteristic wine, rich and long, with a complex flavour that includes chocolate and stone fruits. Worth keeping for a couple of years.

❧ Alain Grangaud, chem. de Vinsas,
07700 Bourg-Saint-Andéol,
tel. 04.75.54.51.85, fax 04.75.54.66.38,
e-mail alain.grangaud@wanadoo.fr ⅤⅤ
Ⅰ by appt.

LES BROTTIERS Prestige 1998★
■ 12 ha 60,000 ⅢⅢ €5-8

This very young 98 is a deep ruby colour shot with violet. The nose is ripe, delicately oaky with additional touches of liquorice, vanilla and toast. Round and full, the flavour is every bit as complex and well balanced. Nice to drink for the next three years with game.

❧ Laurent-Charles Brotte, Le Clos, BP 1,
84231 Châteauneuf-du-Pape,
tel. 04.90.83.70.07, fax 04.90.83.74.34,
e-mail brotte@wanadoo.fr ⅤⅤ
Ⅰ ev. day 9.30am–12 noon 2pm–6pm

DOM. DE L'OLIVIER 2000★
◻ 1.9 ha 12,000 ⅢⅢ ● €3-5

Well-maintained vineyards and a perfectly-equipped cellar have helped to create this prize-winning wine. Delicate yet complex aromas, a strong attack and a well-crafted structure, plus an exceptional finish, characterise this excellent specimen of its appellation. Moreover, the **L'Olivier red 99** was awarded a star by a Jury captivated by the lightly spiced nose and somewhat gamey flavour; it needs a few years to show off its full potential.

● Eric Bastide, EARL Dom. de L'Olivier, 1, rue de la Clastre, 30210 Saint-Hilaire-d'Ozilhan, tel. 04.66.37.08.04, fax 04.66.37.00.46 ▼
Ⓨ by appt.

DOM. DE LUMIAN 1998
■ 5 ha ■ 35,000 ■ €5-8

Enhancing the sunny, slightly orange tints of this wine is a warm, pungent perfume with a trace of pepper worthy of the Spice Islands, and there is genuine chocolate among the flavour elements. Ready for drinking now.

● Gilles Phétisson, Dom. de Lumian, 84600 Valréas, tel. 04.90.35.09.70, fax 04.90.35.18.38, e-mail domaine delumian@terre-net.fr ▼
Ⓨ ev. day 8am–8pm

CH. MALIJAY
Les Genévriers Réserve du château 1999★
■ 100 ha ■ 200,000 ■ €3-5

This château, an authentic historical monument in the region since the 11th century, was bought by the Compagnie des Salins du Midi (Southern France Saltmarsh Company) in 1989. The wine produced here has proved very successful. Lightly structured, with a very white fruit fragrance, it is smooth and aromatic – very pleasant to drink.

● Ch. Malijay, 84150 Jonquières, tel. 04.90.70.33.44, fax 04.90.70.36.07 ▼
Ⓨ by appt.

DOM. MARIE-BLANCHE 1999★
■ 10 ha ■ 30,000 ■ €3-5

Naming the estate after his wife virtually obliges Jean-Jacques Delorme to produce quality wines on a regular basis. No problems for this delicious 99, which is fresh and fruity, full-bodied and ready to drink straight away.

● Jean-Jacques Delorme, Dom. Marie-Blanche, 30650 Saze, tel. 04.90.31.77.26, fax 04.90.26.94.48 ▼

CH. DE MARJOLET 2000★
□ 3 ha ■ 17,000 ■ €3-5

This wine-maker's wide experience in his special field (aromas) has stood him in good stead for this vintage. The fleshy texture is manifest in the strong, mouth-filling flavour. This wine is marvellous value, considering its quality.

● Bernard Pontaud, Vignobles de Marjolet, 30030 Gaujac, tel. 04.66.82.00.93, fax 04.66.82.92.58, e-mail marjolet@ fr.pachardbell.org ▼ by appt.

CLOS DES MIRAN 1999★★
■ 15.15 ha ■ 9,000 ■ €3-5

Romain Flésia discovered the remains of an ancient Roman farm on part of the property he bought in 1998 on the outskirts of Ardèche. Not content with winning a star for his **red Cuvée des Proxumes 99**, for its intense

DOM. DU MOULIN 2000★★
□ 2 ha ■ 5,000 ■ €5-8

Continuous investment has enabled this estate to maintain a high position among the Côtes du Rhône quality wines. Grape-skin maceration and gentle pressing precede temperature-controlled fermentation to create this superb wine. It has a particularly pleasant impact, with elegant balance, very good structure and a lingering finish. To do it justice, serve with shellfish or maybe smoked trout or salmon.

● Denis Vinson, Dom. du Moulin, 26110 Vinsobres, tel. 04.75.27.65.59, fax 04.75.27.63.92 ▼ ev. day except Sun. 8am–12 noon 1.30pm–7pm

DOM. MOULIN DU POURPRE 1998
■ 4.5 ha ■ 32,666 ■ €3-5

Equal parts Syrah and Grenache: this is a traditional but highly reliable blend. Françoise Simon is an accomplished wine-maker. If the nose is still a little reticent at the moment, the flavour is already savoury. This is a round, nicely textured wine ideal with a Sunday roast.

● Françoise Simon, Colombier, 30200 Sabran, tel. 04.66.89.73.98, fax 04.66.89.73.98 ▼ ev. day 8am–8pm

flavour and fine oaky touch, his traditional wine won two stars for its outstanding structure and delicious bouquet of overripe black fruit, spices and nuts. It is well worth waiting a couple of years to taste this one.

● Romain Flésia, clos des Miran, plaine de mas Conil, 30130 Pont-Saint-Esprit, tel. 04.66.82.76.94, fax 04.20.78.77.21 ▼
Ⓨ by appt.

CH. MONGIN 1999★
■ 4 ha ■ 20,000 ■ €3-5

A great introduction for this agricultural college. Very sound wine-making, thanks to a well-designed, functional cellar. With its flavour of undergrowth and leather, this nicely-balanced wine will be superb in a few years.

● Lycée viticole d'Orange, Ch. Mongin, 2260, rte du Grès, 84100 Orange, tel. 04.90.51.48.04, fax 04.90.51.11.92 ▼
Ⓨ by appt.

CH. DE MONTFAUCON 1999★★
□ 5 ha ■ 30,000 ■ €5-8

Although still a very young appellation, the château is notable for its neo-medieval architecture (reconstruction dates to the 19th century) and is renowned for its wines. This one is remarkable, with an intense aroma of musk layered above overripe red fruit, delighting both nose and palate. Its wonderful, richly-textured, long structure ranks it once again among the great Côtes du Rhône.

● Rodolphe de Pins, Ch. de Montfaucon, 30150 Montfaucon, tel. 04.66.50.37.19, fax 04.66.50.62.19 ▼ ev. day except Sat. Sun 2pm–6pm; groups by appt.

CH. DE PANERY 2000

■ 1 ha 5,000 ▮ ♦ €3-5

This vineyard is one of the former farms that belonged to the Château de Pouzilhac (one of the largest properties in the Gard region, with 528 ha/1,426 acres). Here is a very well-structured rosé loaded to the hilt with red fruit plus some hints of pear drops.

➥ SCEA Ch. de Panery, rte d'Uzès, 30210 Pouzilhac, tel. 04.66.37.04.44, fax 04.66.37.62.38,
e-mail chateaudepanery@wanadoo.fr ▾
Ⴤ ev. day 10am–6pm
➥ Roger Gryseels

DOM. DU PARC SAINT CHARLES

Cuvée Saint-Charles 1998★

■ 3 ha 3,850 ▮ ♦ €5-8

In the very south of the Côtes du Rhône, this vineyard is set on a magnificent stony plateau on the right bank. It is definitely worth sparing time for a visit to taste this subtly balanced wine. The red **Côtes du Rhône Elevé en Fût 98** was specially mentioned by the Jury, and is ready now.

➥ SCEA du Parc Saint-Charles, Dom. du Parc Saint-Charles, 30490 Montfrin, tel. 04.66.57.22.82, fax 04.66.57.54.41, e-mail florent.combe@wanadoo.fr ▾
Ⴤ by appt.
➥ Combe Frères

DOM. PELAQUIE 2000

□ 5 ha 15,000 ▮ ♦ €5-8

Absolutely not to be missed by lovers of southern white wines, this year the estate has produced a blend from Roussanne, white Grenache and Clairette which is smooth on the palate but with very pronounced floral nuances. No big surprises perhaps, but with all the typical characteristics of its *terroir*. The **red 99** was singled out too for its intense tannins and gentle spices. Lovely with a side of lamb or cutlets.

➥ Dom. Pélaquié, 7, rue du Vernet, 30290 Saint-Victor-la-Coste, tel. 04.66.50.06.04, fax 04.66.50.33.32, e-mail domaine@pelaquie.com ▾
Ⴤ ev. day except Sun. 9am–12 noon 2pm–6pm
➥ GFA du Grand Canet

DOM. ROGER PERRIN

Prestige blanc 2000★

□ 1 ha 4,000 ▮ ♦ €5-8

This white wine is cultivated on fine lees. The nose is intense and complex, the palate well-balanced and harmonious. Nicely rounded, it will go well with white meats.

➥ Dom. Roger Perrin, rte de Châteauneuf-du-Pape, 84100 Orange, tel. 04.90.34.25.64, fax 04.90.34.88.37 ▾
Ⴤ ev. day except Sun. 8.30am–12 noon 2pm–7pm
➥ Luc Perrin

CLOS PETITE BELLANE 2000★

■ 3.5 ha 24,260 ▮ ♦ €5-8

This high-tech cellar vats the wine for six days to obtain its fine, fruity texture. Black and white currants and wild fruit add to its complex flavour. Worth noting is the **white**, commended by the Jury, composed of 50% Roussanne and 50% Viognier planted in a hot, sunny, clay-limestone soil. It has a decent volume and, with the intense fruity nose, affords a lovely warm sensation.

➥ SARL sté nouvelle Petite Bellane, rte de Vinsobres, chem. de Sainte-Croix, 84600 Valréas, tel. 04.90.35.22.64, fax 04.90.35.19.27 ▾ Ⴤ by appt.
➥ Olivier Peuchot

DOM. PHILIPPE PLANTEVIN

1998★★

■ 0.8 ha 4,000 ▮▮▮ ♦ €5-8

This 98 red, blended from Grenache (65%), Syrah (30%) and Carignan, is remarkably developed. The noble grape varieties from the Rhône Valley create a deeply-textured, beautifully-balanced wine. Aged for 12 months in barrels, this wine is made by traditional methods, and today has reached its peak. It would be ideal with wildfowl, but could be served with the entire meal.

➥ EARL Plantevin Père et Fils, La Daurelle, 84290 Cairanne, tel. 04.90.30.71.05, fax 04.90.30.77.75 ▾
Ⴤ by appt.

DOM. RIGOT

Jean-Baptiste Rigot 2000★★

■ 8 ha 10,000 ▮ ♦ €5-8

This 99 selection celebrates the centenary of the estate. Dedicated as usual to the founder of the vineyard, the 2000 red is outstanding. Equal parts of Grenache and Syrah have been perfectly blended and extracted to produce a deep purple wine glowing with violet reflections. Dense and velvety, its mellowness warms the palate and there is always the reminder of the glorious initial scent of ripe fruit. Delicious with mulberry or blueberry tart.

➥ Camille Rigot, Les Hauts Débats, 84150 Jonquières, tel. 04.90.37.25.19, fax 04.90.37.29.19 ▾ Ⴤ by appt.

CH. ROCHECOLOMBE 1999★★

■ 8 ha 40,000 ▮ ♦ €3-5

These vines, planted on the sunny slopes of Bourg-Saint-Andéol in Ardèche by a Belgian author and composer, and managed today by his daughter and grandson, have produced three delightful wines. The **white Rochecolombe 2000**, 100% Clairette (rare for a Côtes du Rhône), attracted the attention of the Jury for its concentrated aroma and potential. The rich, full-bodied, **rosé Rochecolombe 2000**, was awarded one star, and now here is another for this full-blown, beautifully-structured wine, dark cherry in colour and shot with mauve: the sign of excellent vinification. The rest follows, from crushed red fruit to spices, to finish on a sublime high note.

➥ EARL G. Herberigs, Ch. Rochecolombe, 07700 Bourg-Saint-Andéol, tel. 04.75.54.50.47, fax 04.75.54.80.03 ▾
Ⴤ ev. day 9am–12 noon 2pm–7pm

CAVE DE ROCHEGUDE 2000★

2 ha | 8,000 | €3-5

The high proportion of Viognier grapes (85%) gives this wine its full-bodied volume. The fruity flavour can be enjoyed from start to finish. Nicely balanced, and at the same time powerful and elegant, this wine is proof indeed that these are not mutually exclusive attributes.

Cave des Vignerons de Rochegude, 26790 Rochegude, tel. 04.75.04.81.84, fax 04.75.04.84.80, ev. day 9am–12 noon 2pm–6pm

DOM. DE ROCHEMOND
Fût de chêne 1999★★

2 ha | 10,000 | €5-8

Two very high-quality wines are on offer from this 85-ha (210-acre) rosé vineyard. The principal choice, **Rochemond red 2000**, awarded a star, is very young, blood-red ruby, and boasts a fruity bouquet with delightful herbal touches and soft tannins. This cask-matured 99 with its intense nose of white figs and dried prunes is strong and rich, the oaky tones are perfectly integrated and the lengthy finish is superb. This is a wine to go with game or (for those who disapprove of hunting) with guinea fowl cooked with grapes.

EARL Philip-Ladet, Éric Philip, Dom. Rochemond, 1, chem. des Cyprès, 30200 Sabran, tel. 04.66.79.04.42, fax 04.66.79.04.42, by appt.

DOM. DES ROCHES FORTES 1999★

2 ha | 12,000 | €5-8

This estate won the *coup de coeur* in the 2000 *Guide* for its 100% Syrah wine. **La Cuvée Prestige 99** was commended by the Jury: this is the white label wine, strong in character, with well-integrated hints of liquorice wood (plus an attractive touch of liquorice). The gold label wine presented here is light and dazzling in colour. Smoothly flower-flavoured, the overall effect is first-class.

EARL Brunel et Fils, Dom. des Roches Fortes, quartier Le Château, 84110 Vaison-la-Romaine, tel. 04.90.36.03.03, fax 04.90.28.77.14, ev. day except Sun. 10.30am–12 noon 1.30pm–6.30pm

CH. SAINT-ESTEVE D'UCHAUX
Jeunes vignes 1999★

2 ha | 8,000 | €5-8

The D11 highway that winds from Orange to Uchaux follows the ancient Roman road that crossed the limestone mountain range. Young Viognier vines thrive well under sustained farming methods in this arid, shallow soil. The initial bouquet of this wine has power and the taste is rich, fine and full-bodied. Another wine, the **Vionysos 99**, 100% Viognier grape, also won a star. With a floral, fruity nose, mingled with lime blossom and honey, this wine is fresh and succulent. The long finish is amazing.

Ch. Saint-Estève d'Uchaux, 84100 Uchaux, tel. 04.90.40.62.38, fax 04.90.40.63.49, ev. day except Sun. 9am–12 noon 2pm–6pm
Gérard et Marc Français

CH. SAINT NABOR 2000

2 ha | 25,000 | €3-5

Roussane (90%), well ripened on the hills above the magnificent village of Cornillon, combined with a pinch of white Grenache and Clairette, has created a wine with a bouquet chock-full of citrus and exotic fruits. Exceptionally refreshing.

Gérard Castor, EARL Vignobles Saint-Nabor, 30630 Cornillon, tel. 04.66.82.24.26, fax 04.66.82.31.40, ev. day 8am–12 noon 2pm–6pm

DOM. DE SERVANS 2000★★★

0.53 ha | 1,200 | €8-11

This wine, from a single Viognier, made and aged in oak casks, is reserved for an exclusive clientèle. It is a vintage to rank among the great northern prize-winning names. The Grand Jury unanimously applauded the sheer perfection of the crafting. An unbelievably complex nose, layer upon layer of honey, nuts, flowers and fruit, and above all, those beautiful traces of apricot. This is a wine to accompany fine pastries. Blessed are those few who get to taste it.

Pierre et Philippe Granier, av. de Provence, 26790 Tulette, tel. 04.75.98.31.47, fax 04.75.98.31.47, e-mail domainedeservans@wanadoo.fr, by appt.

CH. SIMIAN
Saint Martin de Jocundaz 2000★★

0.8 ha | 2,000 | €11-15

On this exceptional *terroir* down the southern slopes of the Uchaux, well sheltered from the Mistral, the Serguier family have wrought miracles: a shower of stars for three wines, each of a different colour! Two for this 100% Viognier white, cultivated in a village *terroir*, floral and lingering. The **rosé 2000** *saignée*, rich and fruity, gets one star; and two stars for the **red 99**, strong and full-bodied, but still very young. It should be put away for two to five years before drinking.

Jean-Pierre Serguier, Ch. Simian, 84420 Piolenc, tel. 04.90.29.50.67, fax 04.90.29.62.33, e-mail chateau-simian@wanadoo.fr, ev. day 9am–7.30pm

year he showed his talent again with this poetically named wine ('hedge of thrushes'), suggesting its suitability with wildfowl. It is the result of carefully selected blends, very rich and full-bodied, as is immediately evident from its deep, concentrated colour. It has great ageing potential (three to five years), the 86 vintage being the Jury's choice for the *coup de coeur*.

⚬ Jean-Claude et Béatrice Bouché, rte de Vaison-la-Romaine, rue Buisseron, 84850 Camaret-sur-Aigues, tel. 04.90.37.25.07, fax 04.90.37.76.84, e-mail contact@bouche-duvieuxchene.com
▾ ev. day except Sun. 9am–12 noon 2pm–6pm

DOM. DU SOLEIL ROMAIN

Dame Laurence 2000

□   1 ha   2,000   ■   €5-8

A bottleful of tropical fruit and hot sun. The strong pineapple bouquet is the prelude to a pleasantly balanced wine. The Jury suggested it be served with grilled fish or perhaps with lemon cake. Also commended was the **rosé 2000**, full-bodied and fleshy on the palate, and expertly structured.

⚬ GAEC Giély et Fils, quartier Saint-Martin, 84110 Vaison-la-Romaine, tel. 04.90.36.12.69, fax 04.90.28.71.89 ▾
Y by appt.

DOM. SOLEYRADE

Cuvée Champaneó 1999★

■   4 ha   5,500   ■   €5-8

The grandfather, nicknamed Champaneó in the village, gave his name to this estate wine, which was described by all tasters as very subtle. Its forthright, fresh attack is followed by an explosion of red fruit on the palate, especially at the finish. This elegant, well-balanced wine would be perfect with roasts or with a Provençale-style stew.

⚬ Denis Raymond, quartier La Combe, 84830 Sérignan-du-Comtat, tel. 04.90.70.07.79, fax 04.90.70.07.79 ▾
Y ev. day 9am–1pm 3pm–8pm; Sun. by appt.

DOM. DES TAMARIS 1998

■   20 ha   10,000   ■   €5-8

This year's *Guide* features quite a few Côtes du Rhône wines from Ardèche – a reflection of the quality consciousness of the vineyards concerned. Here is a wine blended from Grenache and Syrah. Nicely mature, the deliciously fruity flavours are enhanced by touches of chocolate. It is ready to drink now, but could really wait another couple of years.

⚬ EARL Faure-Paulat, Dom. des Tamaris, rte des Gorges, 07700 Saint-Just-d'Ardèche, tel. 04.75.98.79.16, fax 04.75.98.74.68 ▾
Y by appt.
⚬ Bernadette Faure

DOM. DE VAL FRAIS 1998★

■   n.c.   7,000   ■   €5-8

'This is Grenache as we like it.' The proportion is 80% Grenache in this wine with its moderately developed nose which expands to include ripe fruit and dried prunes. Fleshy and full, with hints of peanut, it has a spicy finish. One taster called it 'a very sensual wine'. Judge for yourselves.

⚬ SCEA André Vaque, Dom. de Val-Frais, 84350 Courthézon, tel. 04.90.70.84.33, fax 04.90.73.61 ▾ ev. day except Sun. 9am–12 noon 2pm–6pm

DOM. DU VIEUX CHENE

Cuvée de la Haie aux Grives 1999★

■   10 ha   40,000   ■   €5-8

Oenologist Jean-Claude Bouche took over this lovely estate in 1978, to apply biological farming methods. His wines have regularly attracted praise. Although 99 was a difficult

DOM. DU VIEUX COLOMBIER

1999★★

■   6 ha   30,000   ■   ♦   €5-8

The label on the **Cuvée du XX's**, shows some of the technical innovations that have left their mark over the last century. An interesting point about that wine is that although it was awarded a star, it was outranked by this selection which received higher marks during tasting for its richness, aromatic complexity, fine tannins and violet colour. The flavour leaves a final impression of pure pleasure. The wine-maker and his oenologist, Bruno Sabatier, have done a fantastic job.

⚬ Jacques Barrière et Fils, Dom. du Vieux Colombier, 30200 Sabran, tel. 04.66.89.98.94, fax 04.66.89.98.94 ▾
Y by appt.

Côtes du Rhône-Villages

Within the Côtes du Rhône area, some communes have *terroirs* that produce wines with characteristics and qualities that are unanimously acknowledged and appreciated. The conditions of production for these wines, which is about 184,000 hl (4,875,600 gal) are more restrictive than for the Côtes du Rhône, especially with regard to boundaries, yield and alcohol content.

There are two categories of *Côtes du Rhône-Villages* wines. On the one hand, there are those entitled to included the name of a commune; the 16 names that have been recognised historically are: Chusclan, Laudun and Saint-

1108

Gervais in the Gard; Beaumes-de-Venise, Cairanne, Sablet-Séguret, Rasteau, Roaix, Valréas and Visan in the Vaucluse; Rochegude, Rousset-les-Vignes, Saint-Maurice, Saint-Pantaléon-les-Vignes and Vinsobres in the Drôme. These wines comprise 25 communes in all and cover an declared area of 4,787 ha (11,824 acres) with an output of 192,773 hl 5,089,207 gal) in 2000.

On the other hand, there are the Côtes du Rhône-Villages where no commune name is specified, their territory covering the remainder of all the communes in the Gard, the Vaucluse and the Drôme within the area of the Côtes du Rhône.

Seventy communes have been included. The purpose of defining the territory had the primary objective of making it possible to produce wines that would keep. In 2000, an output of 143,376 hl (3,785,126 gal) was declared from 3,239 ha (8,000 acres).

■ **DOM. AMIDO** 1999   5.25 ha 30,000 €5-8

This vineyard produces both Tavel and Côtes du Rhône-Villages, and this year it presented a characterful 99. The fruit, spices, fine tannins and lasting aroma combine to make a delightful wine.
↳ Christian Amido, rue des Carrières, 30126 Tavel, tel. 04.66.50.04.41, fax 04.66.50.04.41 ❦ by appt.

■ **DOM. DE BEAUMALRIC**
Beaumes de Venise 1999★   5 ha 25,000 €5-8

This well-made wine, with its traditional flavour yet strong personality, has a gamey aroma and touches of undergrowth. Nicely balanced on the palate, it expands with a rich, red fruity flavour. It still retains its young, deep ruby colour.
↳ EARL Begouaussel, Dom. de Beaumalric, BP 15, 84190 Beaumes-de-Venise, tel. 04.90.65.01.77, fax 04.90.62.97.28 ❦

■ **DOM. BEAU MISTRAL**
Rasteau Sélection du Terroir 2000★   3 ha 6,000 ❦

Here is one instance of the Mistral exercising a beneficial effect on the grapes: doubtless this explains the name of the vineyard, whose

rosé de saignée has won popular acclaim for its brilliant rose-petal colour, and finely tuned nose of aniseed, mint and red fruit - a bouquet that accounts for the wine's refreshing flavour.
↳ Jean-Marc Brun, Le Village, rte d'Orange, 84110 Rasteau, tel. 04.90.46.16.90, fax 04.90.46.17.30 ❦ by appt.

■ **DOM. DE BEAURENARD**
Rasteau 1999   4 ha 50,000 €5-8

From Châteauneuf-du-Pape, this *village* wine, a lovely rich garnet-red, opens with an oak aroma overlaid with red fruit. More crushed berries on the palate, and tannins that should blend well with time. The results of long vatting time and months in cask are immediately recognisable.
↳ SCEA Paul Coulon et Fils, Dom. de Beaurenard, av. Pierre-de-Luxembourg, 84231 Châteauneuf-du-Pape, tel. 04.90.83.71.79, fax 04.90.83.78.06, e-mail paul.coulon@beaurenard.fr ❦ ev. day except Sun. 9am-12 noon 1.30pm-5.30pm; groups by appt.

■ **DOM. DE BELLE-FEUILLE** 1999★   3 ha 18,000 €5-8

This estate has made large-scale investments in vinification and maturation, and it has reaped rewards with this wine – one for laying down to be fully appreciated. The colour is a deep garnet-red, and the complex aroma ranges from spices to hints of musk. After a straightforward attack, this wine is beautifully balanced on the palate, demonstrating great ageing potential. Gilbert Louche was awarded a star for his **white Côtes du Rhône 99**: fresh, complex, and carrying on beautifully to a good finish, it should be served with white fish.
↳ Gilbert Louche, Dom. de Belle-Feuille, 30200 Vénéjan, tel. 04.66.79.27.33, fax 04.66.79.22.82 ❦ ev. day except Sun. 8am-12 noon 1pm-6.30pm

■ **LOUIS BERNARD** 2000★   n.c. 300,000 €5-8

After an initial impression of wild strawberry, there is a lengthy, well-balanced flavour with tannins that linger. The **Domaine Sarrelon 2000** was also commended by the Jury.
↳ Les Domaines Bernard, rte de Sérignan, 84100 Orange, tel. 04.90.11.86.86, fax 04.90.34.87.30, e-mail sagon@domaines-bernard.fr

■ **DOM. BOISSON** Cairanne 1999   8 ha 35,000 €5-8

This vineyard started out in 1945 with 8 ha (20 acres) and cultivates over 40 ha (148 acres) today. Two .99 selections are worth remembering: the **Clos de la Brussière**, with its pleasing liquorice flavour, impressed the Jury; while the **Cairanne**, stronger in character with its dashes of pepper, spices and leather, is a well-balanced wine with a lasting fragrance.

Côtes du Rhône-Villages

☛ Cave de Cairanne, 84290 Cairanne, tel. 04.90.30.82.05, fax 04.90.30.74.03 ▼ Ⅱ by appt.

CASTEL MIREIO Cairanne Prestige
Elevé en fût de chêne neuf 1999★

5 ha 15,000 ▥ ▤ ◗ €8-11

This wine, with its charming Provençal name, comes from a 24-ha (60-acre) vineyard. The initial attack is compelling: game and red fruit, and a hint of oaky spices at the finish. Particularly notable are the good structure and the overripe fruit aromas and mellow liquorice-flavoured tannins complete the picture.

☛ Dom. Michel et André Berthet-Rayne, rte d'Orange, 84290 Cairanne, tel. 04.90.30.88.15, fax 04.90.30.83.17 ▼ Ⅱ by appt.

DOM. DIDIER CHARAVIN
Rasteau Les Parpaïouns 1999★

2 ha 7,000 ▤ €8-11

'The very incarnation of the AOC' was the Jury's comment. Beautifully structured and lengthy on the palate, this wine is rich in fine, spicy tannins with a dash of pepper and red fruits continue to dominate the flavour. It should be given two years in the cellar. The main selection, the **red 99**, singled out by the Jury for particular mention, conjures up Grenache and Syrah vines, lush and ripe on the hillsides of Cairanne, with its spicy, musky nose and flavour, and its smoothly integrated tannins.

☛ Didier Charavin, rte de Vaison, 84110 Rasteau, tel. 04.90.46.15.63, fax 04.90.46.16.22 ▼ Ⅱ ev. day 9am–12 noon 2pm–6pm

DOM. CHAUME-ARNAUD
Vinsobres Cuvée La Cadène 1999★

2 ha 8,800 ▥ €11-15

This wine immediately releases the essential aromas of the three main AOC grape varieties. Mulberry and blueberry in the bouquet, combined with soft tannins on the palate: red fruit is predominant, the balance outstanding. The estate's **white 2000** has a strong floral nose, and tastes rich and fruity. The pure gold colour is evidence of expert vinification. In fact, the Jury singled it out, together with the **rosé 2000**, which is every bit as enjoyable.

☛ EARL Chaume-Arnaud, Les Paluds, 26110 Vinsobres, tel. 04.75.27.66.85, fax 04.75.27.69.66 ▼ Ⅱ by appt.

DOM. DU CORIANÇON
Vinsobres Le Haut des Côtes 1999

3 ha 5,000 ▥ ▤ €11-15

The vast Coriançon family estate has been run by François Vallot since 1976. Coriançon produces a special wine, this year blended from 80% Grenache with 15% Syrah and 5% Mourvèdre. Thirty days' maceration produce this deep colour and lovely tannins. The bouquet is strong and forthright, of ripe spicy fruit. It is worth waiting two years to let the oakiness integrate to perfection.

☛ Régis Boisson, Les Sablières, 84290 Cairanne, tel. 04.90.30.70.01, fax 04.90.30.89.03 ▼ Ⅱ ev. day except Sun. 9.30am–12 noon 2pm–7.30pm; groups by appt.

DOM. BRESSY-MASSON
Cuvée la Souco d'or Rasteau 1999★★

2 ha 6,000 ▥ €8-11

This vineyard boasts two *coups de cœur* for two different wines. The Grand Jury expressed a slight preference for the 'Souco d'Or', with its nose of iris, cocoa and spices over a base of black fruit (blackcurrant, mulberry and blueberry) that reappear at the finish. Good strong tannins, well integrated with oak, fill the palate. The finish is full-blown and ripe, very spicy with a dash of strong pepper. The **Cuvée Paul-Emile 99** is every bit as good.

☛ Marie-France Masson, Dom. Bressy-Masson, rte d'Orange, 84110 Rasteau, tel. 04.90.46.10.45, fax 04.90.46.17.78 ▼ Ⅱ ev. day 9am–12 noon 2pm–7pm; groups by appt.

DOM. BRUSSET
Cairanne Coteaux des Travers 2000

□ 2 ha 4,000 ▥ ▤ ◗ €5-8

The huge 87-ha (215-acre) estate was awarded a *coup de cœur* in 2000 for another wine produced under the name of Laurent Brusset. This rich, blooming 2000 is dominated by a very ripe grape fragrance. The bouquet opens on a floral note, and continues on the palate with cloves and white fruit. The acidity level is well measured to give a very pleasant finish.

☛ Dom. Brusset, 84290 Cairanne, tel. 04.90.30.82.16, fax 04.90.30.73.31 ▼ Ⅱ by appt.

CAVE DE CAIRANNE
Cuvée antique 1998★

80 ha 65,000 ▥ €8-11

Loaded with power and promise: this is a real prize-winner, intense and fruity, with hints of leather and game. Smooth mouth-filling tannins supplement the wine's complex character, to finish in perfect balance. To do justice to this excellent 98, serve it with Tournedos Rossini.

✆ François Vallot, Dom. du Coriançon, 26110 Vinsobres, tel. 04.75.26.03.24, fax 04.75.26.44.67, e-mail françois.vallot@wanadoo.fr ☑ ✗ ev. day except Sun. 9am-12 noon 2pm-7pm

DOM. DES COTEAUX DES TRAVERS
Rasteau Cuvée Prestige 1999★★

n.c.	14,000	€8-11

A very fine wine with a deep, rich red glow. The strong, concentrated aroma impresses on the palate, and gives way to very pronounced flavours of red fruit and undergrowth. Beautifully balanced tannins mellow it entirely. This is a wine that will do you proud at a celebration dinner. The **Cairanne** by the same wine-maker won two stars.

✆ Robert Charavin, Dom. des Coteaux des Travers, BP 5, 84110 Rasteau, tel. 04.90.46.13.69, fax 04.90.46.15.81, e-mail robert.charavin@wanadoo.fr ☑ ✗ by appt.

CH. COURAC Laudun 1999★★

9.64 ha	53,000	€5-8

This château is set on the hilltop over Tresques and surrounded by its vineyards. The young proprietors have opened up a cellar where visitors can taste this dark, deeply-coloured *village* wine. The aroma is concentrated, gamey and robust, rich in fresh fruit and bay leaf, full and ripe on the palate. The beautifully crafted, silky tannins blend well with the consistent flavour of overripe black plum.

✆ SCEA Frédéric Arnaud, Ch. Courac, 30330 Tresques, tel. 04.66.82.90.51, fax 04.66.82.94.27 ☑ ✗ by appt.

DU PELOUX 1998★

n.c.	n.c.	€5-8

A very satisfying, deep garnet-red wine. A little tight at the start, the aroma expands with a flavour of red berries, the structure on the palate is delicious, and an aftertaste of musky undergrowth lingers at the finish.

✆ Vignobles Du Peloux, quartier Barrade, RN 7, 84350 Courthézon, tel. 04.90.70.42.00, fax 04.90.70.42.15 ☑ ✗ by appt.

DOM. DE DURBAN
Beaumes-de-Venise 1999★

17.74 ha	67,000	€5-8

The walk to this estate, with its fabulous view, is marvellous and the range of wines to be discovered and sampled on arrival is equally rewarding. This *village*, ripened on the sunny slopes, is crammed with red fruit and spices. Full-bodied, well-balanced, with smooth tannins, the wine finishes on a long fruity note.

✆ SCEA Leydier et Fils, Dom. de Durban, 84190 Beaumes-de-Venise, tel. 04.90.62.94.26, fax 04.90.65.01.85 ☑ ✗ ev. day except Sun. 9am-12 noon 2pm-5.30pm

DOM. REMY ESTOURNEL
Laudun 2000★

1 ha	3,000	€5-8

Located about 150 m (163.5 yd) from the old village, this estate is familiar to readers of the *Guide*. Here is a delightful white Gard wine, pale yellow with flashes of gold. The strong floral nose has suggestions of white fruits and apricot. The taste is at once rich and refreshing. The **white Côtes du Rhône 2000** is a worthy representative of southern white wines, and was awarded a star.

✆ Rémy Estournel, 13, rue de Plaineautier, 30290 Saint-Victor-la-Coste, tel. 04.66.50.01.73, fax 04.66.50.21.85 ☑

DOM. DE FENOUILLET
Beaumes-de-Venise Cuvée des Générations 1999★★

1.5 ha	4,000	€8-11

A really magnificent wine with a superb blend of fruit and oak. At the moment, the oak predominates, though not overwhelmingly, with notes of spice and vanilla and an underlying hint of red fruit. This is a wine to put away in the cellar. On the other hand, drink the star-winning **Cuvée Yvon Soard 99** straight away.

✆ GAEC Patrick et Vincent Soard, Dom. de Fenouillet, allée Saint-Roch, 84190 Beaumes-de-Venise, tel. 04.90.62.95.61, fax 04.90.62.99.67, e-mail pv.soard@freebee.fr ☑ ✗ by appt.

FERDINAND DELAYE
Visan 1999★

17 ha	90,000	€5-8

This wine, presented by the hillside co-operative of Visan, holds a lot of interest. The Jury termed it rustic and well constructed, and the ripe fruit fragrance expands nicely on a sound tannin base. This is a good, well-balanced wine that has matured very well.

✆ Cave Les Coteaux, B.P. 22, 84820 Visan, tel. 04.90.28.50.80, fax 04.90.28.50.81, e-mail cave@coteaux-de-visan.fr ☑ ✗ by appt.

DOM. FOND CROZE 1998★★
■ 3 ha 8,600 ▪ ■ €5-8

Two brothers run this very young estate, established in a vineyard that had previously supplied a co-operative. Fond Croze has produced a brilliantly-coloured wine with a delightful nose of sun-ripened black fruit. The flavour is full, rich, rounded and balanced – a promise, one hopes, of continuing success.

↦ Dom. Fond Croze, Le Village, 84290 Saint-Roman-de-Malegarde, tel. 04.90.28.94.30, fax 04.90.28.97.07, e-mail fondcroze@hotmail.com ▼
↦ Bruno et Daniel Long

DOM. DU GOURGET
Rochegude 2000★
□ 1 ha 3,200 ■ €8-11

This is a really refreshing white wine. The attack is discreet and refined, and the balance of alcohol and acidity on the palate is admirable. The honeyed flavour, blended with white fruit, would make this Rochegude ideal for serving with white meats in sauce, or with fish.

↦ Mme Tourtin-Sansone, Dom. du Gourget, 26790 Rochegude, tel. 04.75.04.80.35, fax 04.75.98.21.21 ▼
Y by appt

CH. DU GRAND MOULAS
Cuvée de l'Ecu Grande Réserve 1999★
■ 5 ha n.c. €8-11

Syrah grapes (95%) and a clay-limestone soil are the prerequisites for this deep red wine. Blackcurrant leaves and red fruit on the nose follow through to the palate. This is a cleverly-balanced wine that finishes with a hint of pepper.

↦ Marc Ryckwaert, Ch. du Grand Moulas, 84550 Mornas, tel. 04.90.37.00.13, fax 04.90.37.05.89, e-mail ryckwaert@grand.moulas.com ▼ Y by appt.

DOM. GRAND NICOLET
Rasteau 1999★★★
■ 5 ha 15,000 ▪ ■ €5-8

Here is a classical example of a great Rasteau. Mainly Grenache, with the addition of 20% Syrah, the result is exceptional. It is a deep, glowing garnet-coloured wine with an intense initial aroma of cocoa and spices. The flavour is superb, balanced by delightfully silky tannins. The cocoa returns at the finish, mingled with black fruit to linger on and on.

↦ Jean-Pierre Bertrand, quartier Petit-Paris, 84110 Rasteau, tel. 04.90.46.12.40, fax 04.90.46.11.37, e-mail cave-nicolet-leyraud@wanadoo.fr ▼
Y by appt.

DOM. JAUME Vinsobres 1999★★
■ 4 ha 25,000 ▪ ■ €5-8

The present owner's great-grandfather helped to get Vinsobres recognised as a *dénomination villages* in 1937. Today, his descendants present this deeply-coloured red wine. A strong direct impact on the nose overflows with floral notes and gingerbread. Full and mellow on the palate, the wine blends the vanilla-toned tannins and the red fruit flavour with great skill. Oak and grape are bonded with elegance. A marvellously well-balanced wine that can safely wait four or five years.

↦ Dom. Jaume, 24, rue Reynarde, 26110 Vinsobres, tel. 04.75.27.61.01, fax 04.75.27.68.40 ▼ Y ev. day except Sun. 8am–12 noon 1.30pm-7pm

CH. JOANNY 1999★
■ 7 ha 35,000 ▪ ■ €5-8

The expertise of this estate can be measured by the vinification of this elegant red wine. Glowing purple colour, scent of wild fruit that gradually expands on the palate, exquisite balance: here is a combination to guarantee a first-class product. The **Château La Renjardière 99** is the merchant wine sold by the Pierre Dupont wineries of Villefranche. It was awarded the same marks.

↦ Famille Dupont, Ch. Carbonel, rte de Piolenc, 84830 Sérignan-du-Comtat, tel. 04.90.70.00.10, fax 04.90.70.09.21, e-mail info@bracdelaperriere.com
Y ev. day except Tues. 8am–12 noon 2pm-6pm

DOM. DE LA CHARTREUSE DE VALBONNE
Cuvée Terrasses de Montalivet 2000
□ 1.3 ha 5,000 ▪

Like a multicoloured jewel set in green velvet, La Chartreuse, with its painted roof tiles, is reminiscent of Burgundy and its perennially close links with the Rhône valley. This 2000 white, created exclusively from Viognier, is transparent, shimmering with yellow-green reflections. The aroma, full of flowers and white fruit, unfurls on the palate in a ripe, full, perfectly-balanced flavour. A lovely wine.

↦ ASVMT. Dom. de La Chartreuse de Valbonne, 30130 Saint-Paulet-de-Caisson, tel. 04.66.90.41.24, fax 04.66.90.41.23, e-mail chartreuse.de.valbonne@wanadoo.fr ▼ by appt.

DOM. LA COMBE JULLIERE
Rasteau 2000
■ 3.5 ha 16,000 ▪ ■ €5-8

This is still a very young wine, with ruby highlights in its garnet colour, and a fine spicy aroma with a touch of pepper. The tannins are firm and the red fruit flavour lasts well. A year in the cellar will give the wine the maturity it needs.

↦ EARL Le Bouquet, 84110 Rasteau, tel. 04.90.12.32.42, fax 04.90.12.32.49
↦ M. Laurent

LA FONT D'ESTEVENAS
Cairanne 1999★
■ 2 ha 8,000 ▪ ■ €8-11

The Alary family trace their roots to 1692, when their ancestors already farmed this soil. This very pleasant ruby/garnet-red wine is composed of Grenache and Syrah. The strongly concentrated nose of overripe red fruit follows through to the palate in liaison with matured tannins. Definitely a wine for laying down.

DOM. DE LA MONTAGNE D'OR
Séguret 1999   3 ha   10,000   [€5-8]

Cherry-red tinged with violet, with an aroma of red berry fruits sprinkled with pepper, this wine offers an attractive balance of light tannins and spices. It can be served now.

● Alain Mahinc, La Combe, 84110 Vaison-la-Romaine, tel. 04.90.36.22.42, fax 04.90.36.22.42 Y ev. day 8am–12 noon 2pm–7pm

DOM. LA REMEJEANNE
Les Eglantiers 2000★   n.c.   4,800   [€11-15]

This Eglantiers won the *coup de coeur* for its 98 Côtes-du-Rhône, in the 2000 *Guide*. This time their winning wine is a very young, but extremely promising *village*, primarily because of its complexity. The aroma is not yet fully developed but is already concentrated and strong in black fruits. The tannins are well structured and blend well with the oak flavour, promising a wine of great maturity. The fruit and the spices are there: all you need is the patience to wait a while.

● EARL Ouahi et Rémy Klein, Dom. La Reméjeanne, Cadignac, 30200 Sabran, tel. 04.66.89.44.51, fax 04.66.89.64.22, e-mail remejeanne@wanadoo.fr V

DOM. DE LA RENJARDE
Réserve de Cassagne 1999★★   10 ha   20,000   [€8-11]

● Dom. Daniel et Denis Alary, La Font d'Estévenas, rte de Rasteau, 84290 Cairanne, tel. 04.90.30.82.32, fax 04.90.30.74.71 Y ev. day except Sun. 8am–12 noon 2pm–7pm

This vineyard is situated on an ancient Roman *oppidum*. The terraced vines with full southern exposure, plus the nature of the soil, are conducive to very full-bodied wines of great quality. Simply try these two fine **99 Réserve de Cassagne**, composed exclusively of Grenache and Mourvèdre. Deep garnet, with a complex aroma of toasted grain, vanilla, resin, spices and liquorice, the initial impact is strong, followed by a densely textured flavour

of stewed fruit, tobacco and a hint of coffee. The **Domaine de la Renjarde**, from the same *cuvée*, was also judged very successful.

● Dom. de La Renjarde, rte d'Uchaux, 84830 Sérignan-du-Comtat, tel. 04.90.83.70.11, fax 04.90.83.79.69, e-mail alaindugas@chateau-la-nerthe.com V Y by appt.

DOM. LA SOUMADE
Rasteau Prestige 1999   8 ha   30,000   [€11-15]

The first impression is of a rich, full wine, with all the characteristics of well-ripened Grenache, the noble grape of the southern region. The nose begins with strawberry, followed by undertones of bay leaf. The flavour is complex, with a nicely balanced structure of warm tannins and a touch of undergrowth.

● André Romero et Fils, 84110 Rasteau, tel. 04.90.46.11.26, fax 04.90.46.11.69 Y ev. day except Sun. 9am–11.30am 2pm–6pm

LAURUS Cairanne 1999★★   2 ha   3,000   [€8-11]

This is the prestige wine range from Laurus, who offers a remarkably expressive Cairanne, where the utmost attention has been devoted to fermentation and maturation. The subtle bouquet of oak is supplemented by vanilla and grilled and toasted elements, all enhanced by superbly crafted tannins. The estate wine **Château La Différence 2000 Séguret**, awarded two stars, is packed with wild fruits and spices.

● Gabriel Meffre, Le Village, 84190 Gigondas, tel. 04.90.12.30.22, fax 04.90.12.30.29, e-mail gabriel-meffre@meffre.com V Y by appt.

DOM. DE LA VALERIANE 1999★   2 ha   3,500   [€5-8]

The Grenache and Syrah vines, cultivated a few kilometres from Avignon on smooth pebbled terraces with full southern exposure, go to make this deep purple wine for laying down, its strong spicy nose overlaid with a touch of toasty liquorice. The tannins are still too hard, but will be perfect in a year or two. The spicy liquorice finish is sheer delight. The **white Côtes du Rhône 2000** was singled out as well. It is a good choice with shellfish.

● Mesmin Castan, rte d'Estézargues, 30390 Domazan, tel. 04.66.57.04.84, fax 04.66.57.04.84 Y by appt.

LA VINSOBRAISE Vinsobres 1999   4 ha   13,000   [€5-8]

This year the Vinsobres winery offers a brilliant ruby-coloured 99. The strong spicy attack is followed by a very pleasant, slightly spicy flavour on the palate. The wine is ready to drink now.

● Cave La Vinsobraise, 26110 Vinsobres, tel. 04.75.27.64.22, fax 04.75.27.66.59 V Y ev. day 8am–12 noon 2pm–6pm

DOMAINE DE LA RENJARDE — CÔTES DU RHÔNE VILLAGES — RED TABLE WINE

DOM. LE CLOS DU BAILLY 2000★

▲ €3-5 ■ 2 ha 7,000

After a visit to the Pont du Gard, stop at this vineyard to taste its delightful salmon-coloured rosé. The nose is smoky with notes of jasmine and dried roses, and the delicately refreshing red fruit flavour lingers on the palate. This wine offers great pleasure at a bargain price.

➤┬ Richard Soulier, 17, rue d'Avignon, 30210 Remoulins, tel. 04.66.37.12.23, fax 04.66.37.38.44 ▼ ▼ by appt.

DOM. LES HAUTES CANCES

Cairanne Cuvée Col du Débat 1998★

■ €8-11 ■ 2.85 ha 7,600

A sound achievement for this wine-maker, who goes in for organic farming. This deep garnet-coloured wine has an immediate, fine, oaky nose mingled with dried fruits. The liquorice, sweet almonds and vanilla fill out with the smooth tannins to create a lovely blend.

➤┬ SCEA Achiary-Astart, quartier Les Travers, 84290 Cairanne, tel. 04.90.30.76.14, fax 04.90.38.65.02, e-mail contact@hautescances.com ▼ ▼ by appt.

LES QUATRE CHEMINS

Laudun 2000★

□ €3-5 ■ 5 ha 20,000

Since he set up his winery, Pierre Pappalardo, manager of this estate, has specialised in blending delicious white wines to delight the taste buds of his fans. The nose of this one is full of grapefruit and white flowers, opening up into a flavour of ripe citrus fruit. Elegant with a beautiful balance, it has all the right qualities.

➤┬ Cave des Quatre-Chemins, 30290 Laudun, tel. 04.66.82.00.22, fax 04.66.82.44.26 ▼ ▼ ev. day except Sun. 8am–12 noon 2pm–6pm

CH. LES QUATRE FILLES

Cairanne Elevé en fût de chêne 1999★

■ €8-11 ■ 5 ha 4,200

A special wine this time, from a vineyard changing over to organic farming. A long vatting period followed by nine months in barrel have produced a good vintage for laying down. Deep carmine red, giving out an expansive aroma of very ripe fruit and charred oak that continues on the palate with delicious hints of truffle, the tannins still require some blending time.

➤┬ Roger Flesia, Ch. Les Quatre-Filles, rte de Lagarde-Paréol, 84290 Sainte-Cécile-les-Vignes, tel. 04.90.30.84.12, fax 04.90.30.86.15, e-mail 4filles@worldonline.fr ▼ ▼ ev. day 8am–8pm

DOM. DE L'ORATOIRE SAINT-MARTIN

Cairanne Réserve des Seigneurs 1999★★

■ €8-11 ■ 10 ha 40,000

Winner of a *coup de coeur* last year, this 25-ha (62-acre) vineyard is named after the old stone and terracotta oratory built in 1948. The three classic varieties used here, Grenache, Morvèdre and Syrah, grown in the magnificent Cairanne *terroir*, guarantee an outstanding wine. The soft flavour of red fruit mingles with elegant floral notes on the palate. The tannins, though prominent, are nicely blended. Although ready now, this excellent wine is bound to improve after another three to four years.

➤┬ Frédéric et François Alary, Dom. l'Oratoire St-Martin, rte de Saint-Roman, 84290 Cairanne, tel. 04.90.30.82.07, fax 04.90.30.74.27 ▼ ▼ ev. day except Wed. Sun 8am–12 noon 2pm–7pm

MARQUIS DE LA CHARCE

Saint Maurice Cuvée Prestige 1998★★

■ €5-8 ■ 4 ha 8,000

An excellent wine this, with its attractive dark colour and powerful aroma of overripe black fruit. The sturdy structure, built on beautifully balanced tannins, does not overpower the fruity flavour.

➤┬ Cave des Coteaux de Saint-Maurice, 26110 Saint-Maurice-sur-Eygues, tel. 04.75.27.63.44, fax 04.75.27.67.32 ▼ ▼ by appt.

MAS DE LIBIAN 1999★

■ €8-11 ■ 3 ha 15,000

This attractive garnet-coloured wine comes from the sunny slopes of Saint-Marcel-d'Ardèche. Elegantly refined, loaded with red fruit on the nose and palate with a touch of liquorice at the finish, this is a full-bodied, nicely-structured wine with a superbly rich texture.

➤┬ Thibon, Mas de Libian, 07700 Saint-Marcel-d'Ardèche, tel. 04.75.04.66.22, fax 04.75.98.66.38 ▼ ▼ by appt.

DOM. DU MOULIN

Vinsobres Cuvée Charles Joseph 1998★

■ €8-11 ■ 1.5 ha 5,500

This estate has completed its second cellar, built underground for laying down. The deep ruby 98 is ready for tasting, and the Jury was unanimous in praising its distinction. The nose is at first peppery and musky with hints of violet creeping though. The marvellous tannins announce superb ageing potential. The **Domaine du Moulin 99** won a star for its long aroma of liquorice over stone fruit. The **white 2000**, which should also be ready by now, was commended by the Jury for its fragrance of citrus fruits and Muscat, and for the beautifully balanced fresh fruit palate.

➤┬ Denis Vinson, Dom. du Moulin, 26110 Vinsobres, tel. 04.75.27.65.59, fax 04.75.27.63.92 ▼ ▼ ev. day except Sun. 8am–12 noon 1.30pm–7pm

DOM. DE MOURCHON
Séguret Grande Réserve 1999★
▪ 3 ha · 18,000 · €8-11

Take two parts of Grenache to one of Syrah, ripen well on the hills above the charming village of Séguret and you get a very promising wine, strong in spices and jammy black fruit. The palate is young and full; more spices and blackcurrant blend beautifully and release a concentrated aroma. This wine has a splendid future.

• Dom. de Mourchon, 84110 Séguret, tel. 04.90.46.70.30, fax 04.90.46.70.31, e-mail mourchon@free.fr — by appt.

DOM. DU PETIT BARBARAS
Sélection 1999
▪ 7 ha · 6,000 · €5-8

This 99 is a lovely deep purple, with a nose that develops gradually to burst powerfully on the palate in an oaky finish. A really pleasant wine to accompany red and grilled meats.

• SCEA Feschet Père et Fils, Dom. du Petit-Barbaras, 26790 Bouchet, tel. 04.75.04.80.02, fax 04.75.04.84.70 — ev. day except Sun. 9am–12 noon 2pm–6pm; groups by appt.

CLOS PETITE BELLANE
Valréas Les Echalas 2000★
▪ 1.5 ha · 6,300 · €8-11

It is worth visiting Valréas, a town in the heart of the *Enclave des Papes*, for its charming buildings and the excellent vineyards. The 100% Syrah *Cuvée* from this recently established estate drew much praise from the tasters. Deep red with flashes of violet, the nose of red fruit makes a pleasant impact and continues on the palate with the support of silky tannins.

• SARL sté nouvelle Petite Bellane, rte de Vinsobres, chem. de Sainte-Croix, 84600 Valréas, tel. 04.90.35.22.64, fax 04.90.35.19.27 — by appt.
• Olivier Peuchot

DOM. DE PIAUGIER
Sablet Montmartel 1999★
▪ 2 ha · n.c. · €11-15

Give this wine two or three years in the cellar before opening. At present the wood dominates, but already there is enticing anticipation of stewed fruit (plums) and liquorice. The palate is very well structured on good solid tannins that are just beginning to mix in, closing on a note of liquorice and spices that leaves a woody finish.

• Jean-Marc Autran, Dom. de Piaugier, 3, rte de Gigondas, 84110 Sablet, tel. 04.90.46.96.49, fax 04.90.46.99.48, e-mail piaugier@wanadoo.fr — by appt.

DOM. DU POURRA
Séguret La Combe 1999★
▪ 7.5 ha · 34,700 · €5-8

J.-C.Mayordome took over the family estate in 1977. Cultivated in Séguret *terroir* and matured in Sablet, this cherry-coloured wine has a delightful red cherry bouquet. The structure is fleshy and full-textured on the palate over a touch of cocoa. This can be served readily until 2003.

• J.-C. Mayordome, SCEA Dom. du Pourra, rte de Vaison, 84110 Séguret, tel. 04.90.46.93.59, fax 04.90.46.98.71 — ev. day except Sat. Sun. 8am–5.30pm

DOM. ROC FOLASSIERE
Elevé en fût de chêne 1999
▪ 4.5 ha · 25,200 · €5-8

This is a prestige wine from a co-operative which produces wines from 700 ha (1,729 acres) of vineyard. Grenache and Syrah in equal measure create a deep-coloured wine, with refined woody tones blended with very ripe fruit in a nicely balanced palate.

• Les Vignerons producteurs de Saint-Hilaire-d'Ozilhan, av. Paul-Blisson, 30210 Saint-Hilaire-d'Ozilhan, tel. 04.66.37.16.47, fax 04.66.37.35.12, e-mail contact@cotesdurhone-wine.com — ev. day except Sun. 9am–12.30pm 2pm–4.30pm

CAVE DE RASTEAU
Rasteau Tradition 2000★
▪ 250 ha · 300,000 · €5-8

Some 65% of the Rasteau appellation will be cellar matured from now on. The deep garnet colour prefaces a strong attack with a jammy aroma full of spices and fig. The rich, warm palate is still influenced by powerful tannins whose length will be appreciated later.

• Cave de Rasteau, rte des Princes-d'Orange, 84110 Rasteau, tel. 04.90.10.90.10, fax 04.90.46.16.65, e-mail rasteau@rasteau.com — by appt.

DOM. ROCHE-AUDRAN
Visan 1998★★
▪ 4 ha · 12,000 · €5-8

This is a wonderful 98, remarkable for its smooth refinement. The garnet colour is still brilliant and the complex aroma of red fruit and blackcurrant fills the nose. A truly delicious, full-bodied wine, with beautifully-balanced tannins and a lingering fragrance that ends on a note of truffles and ripe fruit.

• Vincent Rochette, Dom. Roche-Audran, 84110 Buisson, tel. 04.90.28.90.96, fax 04.90.28.96.96, e-mail vincent.rochette@mnet.fr — by appt.

DOMINIQUE ROCHER
Cairanne 1999★★
▪ 4.7 ha · 25,150 · €8-11

This estate was established in 1996, and a vast amount of work has obviously gone into producing such a fine wine. A powerful attack, strong in blackcurrant, develops with a long, concentrated flavour on the palate, excellently balanced between fruit and integrated tannins. This is a superb *village* that should be laid down for several years. The cask-matured **Monsieur Paul** was awarded a star. The tannins are still rather too

Côtes du Rhône-Villages

prominent, but will no doubt gradually harmonise with the fruit.

➤ Dominique Rocher, rte de Saint-Roman, 84290 Cairanne, tel. 04.90.30.87.44, fax 04.90.30.80.62, e-mail contact@rochervin.com  ▼ ev. day except Sun. 8am–12 noon 2pm–7pm.

DOM. DES ROMARINS 1998★

Les Romarins | 5 ha | 12,000 | ■ | €5-8

Grenache and Syrah, sun-ripened on smooth pebbled soil in Domazan, have produced this 98, which retains its wild gamey aroma. However, this wine shows great promise and is well worth putting away at the back of the cellar.

➤ SARL Dom. des Romarins, rte d'Estézargues, 30390 Domazan, tel. 04.66.57.05.84, fax 04.66.57.14.87, e-mail domromarin@aol.com ▼ ▼ Wed. Fri. Sat. 3pm–7pm
➤ Francis Fabre

DOM. ROUGE GARANCE

Rouge Garance 1999 | 5 ha | 20,000 | ■ | €5-8

On your way back from Pont du Gard, stop to visit this estate, which is associated with French film actor Jean-Louis Trintignant. The bottle bears a label designed by Bilal. This deep, dark wine, with its aroma of charred wood, roasted coffee and cocoa, is fleshy and full-bodied. The tannins have all the hallmarks of a good wine to be laid down.

➤ SCEA Dom. Rouge Garance, chem. de Massacan, 30210 Saint-Hilaire-d'Ozilhan, tel. 06.14.41.52.88, fax 04.66.37.06.92, e-mail rougegarance@waika9.com ▼ ▼ by appt.

DOM. SAINTE-ANNE

Saint-Gervais 1999★★★ | 2 ha | 10,000 | ■

The estate is one of the élite circle to have won a large number of *coup de cœur* awards over the last 17 years. Not only did the Jury give the **Cuvée Notre Dame des Cellettes 1999** a star (Grenache and Syrah), it also acclaimed this Saint-Gervais. The nose wafts from leather to liquorice, herbs from the garrigue, spices and stewed fruit, and continues on the palate, cushioned by velvety tannins. Morvèdre and Grenache blend yet again for a wine that promises to be simply superb after a good time in the cellar.

➤ EARL Dom. Sainte-Anne, Les Cellettes, 30200 Saint-Gervais, tel. 04.66.82.77.41, fax 04.66.82.74.57 ▼ ▼ ev. day except Sat. Sun. 2pm–6pm; 9am–11am by appt.
➤ Steinmaier

DOM. SAINT-ETIENNE

Les Galets 2000★★ | n.c. | n.c. | ■ | €5-8

This Galets is remarkable for its elegant cherry and blackcurrant blend. The full, well-balanced palate is surprisingly refreshing. This wine should be almost ready now. The red **Côtes du Rhône Les Albizzias 2000** also won a star. Delicately floral notes on the nose mark this nicely balanced wine with its delicious fruity finish of cherry and raspberry.

➤ Michel Coullomb, Dom. Saint-Etienne, fg du Pont, 30490 Montfrin.
tel. 04.66.57.50.20, fax 04.66.57.22.78 ▼ ▼ by appt.

DOM. DE SAINT-GEORGES

Chusclan 1998★ | 7.5 ha | 40,000 | ■ | €8-11

The estate has produced a prize-winner with this wine, ideal for drinking with game. Well-matured with a slightly orange colour, the nose is intense and musky with ripe fruit and a touch of leather. It is gamey on the palate with good strong touches of stewed fruit, and a lovely long finish.

➤ André Vignal, Dom. de Saint-Georges, 30200 Vénéjan, tel. 04.66.79.23.14, fax 04.66.79.20.26 ▼ ▼ by appt.

CAVE DES VIGNERONS DE SAINT-GERVAIS

Saint-Gervais Cuvée spéciale SG 1999★ | 15 ha | 10,000 | ■ | €5-8

Our tasters spent a long time over this Special Cuvée with its superb nose of truffles, spices and undergrowth. On the palate these are replaced by red fruits and tannins that develop in well-structured accord. The **Prestige 99** (no star) is recommended.

➤ Cave des Vignerons de Saint-Gervais, Le Village, 30200 Saint-Gervais, tel. 04.66.82.77.05, fax 04.66.82.78.85, e-mail cave@saint-gervais.com.fr ▼ ▼ ev. day except Sat. Sun. 8.30am–12 noon 2.30pm–6pm

DOM. SAINT-LUC 1999★

| 15 ha | 36,000 | ■ | €5-8

Take a young guinea-fowl with garlic sauce and a drop of olive oil, and serve it as accompaniment to this well-built wine with its silky tannins and long red fruit flavour. Delightfully fresh and radiant.

➤ Ludovic Cornillon, Dom. Saint-Luc, 26790 La Baume-de-Transit, tel. 04.75.98.11.51, fax 04.75.98.19.22 ▼ ▼ by appt

CH. SAINT-MAURICE L'ARDOISE
Laudun Vieilles vignes Elevé en fût de chêne 1999★

■ 5 ha 21,000 €8-11

Christophe Valat cultivates about 100 ha (247 acres). This wine comes from 50-year-old vines and is compelling for its red fruit aroma and is balanced by the slightly oaky tannins. The attack on the palate is direct, and the flavour is nicely balanced by the slightly oaky tannins.
♠ Christophe Valat, Ch. Saint-Maurice, L'Ardoise, 30290 Laudun, tel. 04.66.50.29.31, fax 04.66.50.40.91 [V]

CH. SAINT-NABOR
Clos de Roman 1998

■ 2 ha 10,000

This red fruit- and violet-flavoured 98 is still young. On the palate the tannins are silky, and the subtle structure is a blend of oak, black cherry and vanilla. It is a wine to taste in the château cellar, where visitors are accorded a warm family welcome.
♠ Gérard Castor, EARL Vignobles Saint-Nabor, 30630 Cornillon, tel. 04.66.82.24.26, fax 04.66.82.31.40 [V]
Ⴘ ev. day 8am-12 noon 2pm-6pm

DOM. DU SEIGNEUR
Laudun 1999★★

■ 16 ha 80,000 €5-8

You will come across this beautiful sunny estate, surrounded by vines, along the road to Saint-Victor-la-Coste. Here they produce this excellent deep red 99, with an intense black-currant and spicy aroma that flows from nose to palate with a good lengthy finish. A perfect balance, which the Jury called 'a great quality wine'.
♠ Frédéric Duseigneur, rte de Saint-Victor, 30126 Saint-Laurent-des-Arbres, tel. 04.66.50.02.57, fax 04.66.50.02.57, e-mail freduseigneur@infonie.fr [V]
Ⴘ by appt.

DOM. DU SERRE-BIAU
Laudun 2000

■ 2 ha 2,600 €5-8

The vineyard lies near a Gallo-Roman aqueduct. Grenache and Clairette are grown in a sandy *terroir* to produce this beautifully smooth white wine. The nose is all white fruit and delicate spices, and the palate mouth-filling but well balanced, further enhanced by delicious citrus fruit. Try it with monkfish à la provençale.
♠ Faraud et Fils, 4, chem. des Cadinières, 30290 Saint-Victor-la-Coste, tel. 04.66.50.04.20, fax 04.66.50.04.20 [V]
Ⴘ ev day. 9am-12 noon 2pm-7pm; Sun. by appt.

DOM. DU TERME
Sablet 2000★

■ 1 ha 4,000

This wine is best tasted in the cellar situated on the little square of Gigondas. It is 50% Roussanne, 50% Viognier, fully ripened on a well-exposed hillside. Pale, almost transparent, yellow, with greenish highlights, and with a nose heavy with white fruit, the flavour is of strong peach with a subtle added touch of bitterness for a refreshing finish.
♠ Rolland Gaudin, Dom. du Terme, 84190 Gigondas, tel. 04.90.65.86.75, fax 04.90.65.80.29 [V] Ⴘ by appt.

CH. DU VIEUX TINEL 1999

■ 27 ha 120,000 €3-5

One of the tasters commented, 'It's amazing: this 99 is the spitting image of the old wines we used to drink years ago.' Solid black, with muscle and strength, this is great stuff for those who like wines you can chew on.
♠ La Compagnie Rhodanienne, Chemin-Neuf, 30210 Castillon-du-Gard, tel. 04.66.37.49.50, fax 04.66.37.49.51

DOM. VIRET
Saint-Maurice Maréotis 1999★★

■ 3 ha 8,500 €11-15

This wine-maker is an expert in *cosmo-culture* (a type of biodynamic vine-growing), with a cellar built from 3-6 tonne (6,600-13,200 lb) stone blocks from the Gard quarries. This Maréotis is a deeply concentrated garnet, and the nose, intense but marvellously refined, is full of ripe fruit and spices, dominated by violets. There is more fruit in the lovely texture on the palate where the tannins are already very well blended. This is a wine with a great future.

TERROIR DU TRIAS
Beaumes de Venise 1999★

■ 73 ha 80,000 €8-11

The wine-makers' cellar in Beaumes-de-Venise is mainly renowned for its famous Muscat, but its other wines are well worth a detour as well. The range includes this dark garnet 99 with a powerful stewed wild fruit aroma. This is a round, full wine in which the tannins, while well integrated, play the star role.
♠ Cave des Vignerons de Beaumes-de-Venise, quartier Ravel, 84190 Beaumes-de-Venise, tel. 04.90.12.41.00, fax 04.90.65.02.05, e-mail vignerons@beaumes-de-venise.com
[V] Ⴘ by appt.

DOM. DE VERQUIERE
Sablet 1997★

■ 5 ha 16,000 €8-11

The 'great house' on this estate dates back to the 17th century. The *village* is already four years old, but remains beautifully drinkable because of its excellent balance. The nose is still fresh and vibrant, full of red fruit, followed by a stronger, riper fruit flavour that lingers on the palate.
♠ Bernard Chamfort, 84110 Sablet, tel. 04.90.46.90.11, fax 04.90.46.99.69 [V]
Ⴘ by appt.

yet complete, but it seems to have all the right qualities. It needs a while for the oak to integrate completely.

● E. Guigal, Ch. d'Ampuis, 69420 Ampuis, tel. 04.74.56.10.22, fax 04.74.56.18.76, e-mail contac@guigal.com ✕ ✕ by appt.

DE BOISSEYT-CHOL
Côte blonde 1999
■　0.6 ha　3,000　|||　€ 23-30

This wine attracts attention for its very fine cherry bouquet. Although not strongly concentrated in flavour, the full texture is wholly dominant. Ready for drinking immediately.

● De Boisseyt-Chol, RN 86, 42410 Chavanay, tel. 04.74.87.23.45, fax 04.74.87.07.36, e-mail deboisseyt.chol@net-up.com ✕ ✕ ev day except Sun. 9am–12 noon 2pm–6pm; cl. 15 Aug.–15 Sep.
● Didier Chol

DOM. DE BONSERINE 1999★★★
■　7 ha　23,000　|||　€ 15-23

This vineyard is producing some magnificent wines, and this, the principal vintage, can compete with any prize-winning name in the region. The royal purple colour alone indicates its fabulous potential. The nose is still very young and opens with black fruits and hints of vanilla. The palate is filled with a dense texture, strong tannins, a good length and an oak flavour that will vanish with time. Lock it up in your cellar for ten years and hide the key.

● Dom. de Bonserine, 2, chem. de la Viallière, 69420 Ampuis, tel. 04.74.56.14.27, fax 04.74.56.18.13 ✕ ✕ ev. day 9am–6pm; Sat. Sun. by appt.

DOM. DE BONSERINE
Les Moutonnes 1999★★★
■　n.c.　n.c.　|||　€ 38-46

Given that this *Cuvée principale* contains only 3% Viognier, this is practically pure Syrah, cultivated in an exceptional *terroir*. The cask has left the nose somewhat austere for now, but the palate is exceptional, with a perfect balance between body and alcohol. This is worth queuing for when they open the cellar door in five to ten years' time. The **La Garde 99** is also remarkable.

● Dom. Philippe Viret, EARL Clos du Paradis, quart. les Escoulenches, 26110 Saint-Maurice, tel. 04.75.27.62.77, fax 04.75.27.62.31 ✕ ✕ by appt.

Côte Rôtie

Situated at Vienne, on the right bank of the river, this is the oldest vineyard of the Rhône Valley. In 2000, its output was 8,591 hl (226,802 gal) from a production area of 200 ha (494 acres), spread through the communes of Ampuis, Saint-Cyr-sur-Rhône and Tupins-Sémons. The vines are cultivated on hills that are so steep as to be almost vertiginous. If the Côte Blonde has a separate identity from the Côte Brune it could, according to one story, be in memory of a Maugiron noble who, in his will, divided his lands between his two daughters, a blond and a brunette. It is perhaps worth observing that the wines of the Côte Brune are more full-bodied while the Côte Blonde wines are more delicate.

The soils are the richest in schist in the region. Only red wines are produced, made from the Syrah variety and a proportion of Viognier, which may be added to a maximum of 20%. The Côte Rôtie wine is deep red in colour, its delicate, fine bouquet dominated by aromas of raspberry and spices, with a touch of violet. Well-structured, tannic and richly flavoured, it holds an unchallenged position at the top of the range of Rhône wines, a perfect accompaniment to all dishes that deserve great red wines.

CH. D'AMPUIS 1997
■　6 ha　25,000　|||　€ 30-38

The copperplate engraving on the label of this wine shows the Château d'Ampuis, a superb property that is the headquarters of Marcel Guigal's estates and business. This very problematic year, the third in which he produced, gives us this red wine glowing with amber, strongly influenced by the cask in which it was kept for 38 months. Ageing is not

☛ Dom. de Bonserine, 2, chem. de la Viallière, 69420 Ampuis, tel. 04.74.56.14.27, fax 04.74.56.18.13 ☑ Ⓨ ev. day. 9am–6pm; Sat. Sun. by appt.

BERNARD BURGAUD 1999★

■ 4 ha 20,000 ▥ €15-23

What a wine! Dark and deep with garnet highlights; an aroma of violet, blackcurrant, stewed fruit and spices, this youthful 99 promises a brilliant future. The palate is well-balanced but young, lively and full of flavour.

☛ Bernard Burgaud, Le Champin, 69420 Ampuis, tel. 04.74.56.11.86, fax 04.74.56.13.03 ☑ Ⓨ by appt.

CAVES DES PAPES La Serine 1999

■ n.c. 6,000 ▥ €15-23

This large group was created from the fusion of the trademarks of several *négociants* (wine-merchants). Twelve months in cask has made this a nicely-balanced wine, suave, with a pleasant flavour of leather and spices. Very characteristic of the 99 vintage, it can be put away for three or four years.

☛ Ogier-Caves des Papes, 10, bd Pasteur, 84230 Châteauneuf-du-Pape, tel. 04.90.39.32.32, fax 04.90.83.72.51, e-mail ogier.caves.des.papes@ogier.fr ☑ Ⓨ ev. day except Sat. Sun. 8am–5pm

M. CHAPOUTIER La Mordorée 1999★★

■ 3 ha 7,000 ▥ +76

This is one of the stars of the Côte Rôtie, a once-in-a-lifetime experience. If the price is too much of a shock, try the **Les Bécasses 98**, which won a star and will have much the same effect. This wine, however, has all the attributes to last at least another ten years, boasting an excellent structure and skilful oak integration that renders the tannins beautifully silky. Both these wines are ideal accompaniments to duck or other water-fowl.

☛ M. Chapoutier, 18, av. du Dr-Paul-Durand, 26600 Tain-l'Hermitage, tel. 04.75.08.28.65, fax 04.75.08.81.70, e-mail chapoutier@chapoutier.com ☑ Ⓨ by appt.

EDMOND ET DAVID DUCLAUX 1999★★★

■ 4.5 ha 20,000 ▥ €23-30

This estate is situated in the Pilat regional park, and this year's 99 justifies the *coup de cœur* awarded last year. It is among the aristocrats of the AOC, although it will need some time before the oak is perfectly integrated. The wine has all the right attributes (full body and good balance) with the extra touch of red fruit and spices.

☛ Edmond et David Duclaux, RN 86, 69420 Tupin-Semons, tel. 04.74.59.56.30, fax 04.74.56.64.09 ☑ Ⓨ by appt.

DOM. ANDRE FRANCOIS 1999★

■ 3 ha 10,000 ▥ €15-23

This is a wine that requires you to wait with patience. Despite a slight hint of bitterness in the finish, the tannins are still young and it holds lots of promise. 'It is all there,' said the Jury. An elegant, oaky flavour with a complex blend of coffee, liquorice and red fruit. Wonderful sensations throughout.

☛ André François, Mornas, 69420 Ampuis, tel. 04.74.56.13.80, fax 04.74.56.19.69 ☑ Ⓨ by appt.

PIERRE GAILLARD 1999★★

■ 2.5 ha 10,000 ▥ €15-23

Pierre Gaillard already exports 50% of his production, so hurry if you want a few bottles of this excellent wine. It is long, full-bodied and round, thanks to its good oak assimilation which lets the fruit just creep through. The **Rose Pourpre 99** (an allusion perhaps to Woody Allen's *Purple Rose of Cairo*?) was awarded a star for its aroma of brandied plums, its full body, nicely integrated oak and long finish.

☛ Pierre Gaillard, lieu-dit Chez Favier, 42520 Malleval, tel. 04.74.87.13.10, fax 04.74.87.17.66, e-mail vinsp.gaillard@wanadoo.fr ☑ Ⓨ by appt

JEAN-MICHEL GERIN Champin le Seigneur 1999★★★

■ 5 ha 25,000 ▥ €23-30

This blend by Jean-Michel Gerin won showers of stars for previous vintages. This wine has similarly been inundated with compliments: 'magnificent, a truly great wine, excellent ...'. The nose, with its jammy black fruit seeping with sugar, signals a truly excellent structure. On the palate, the well-integrated oak matches the full body. Lay it down for ten years and keep the cellar key in the bank.

☛ Jean-Michel Gerin, 19, rue de Montmain, Vérenay, 69420 Ampuis, tel. 04.74.56.16.56, fax 04.74.56.11.37, e-mail gerin.jm@wanadoo.fr ☑ Ⓨ by appt.

LAURUS 1999★

■ 1 ha 3,600 ▥ €23-30

A long maturation: 18 months in the barrel for this Laurus 99, deep red with flashes of violet. The nose is complex: undergrowth with hints of vanilla. The palate is loaded with very ripe fruit, truffles and good strong coffee built on tannins to make you sigh with pleasure.

➤ Gabriel Meffre, Le Village, 84190 Gigondas, tel. 04.90.12.30.22, fax 04.90.12.30.29, e-mail gabriel-meffre@meffre.com ▼ by appt.

B. LEVET 1998★
■ 3.5 ha 15,000 ▥ €15-23

Bernard Levet took over this vineyard from his in-laws in 1983. His Côte Rôtie was matured in *demi-muid* (450-l oak casks) and the resultant colour is such a dark purple as to be almost black. Toast competes with violet in the remarkable bouquet but, although the structure is massive, the palate has not yet reached complete balance. The tannins need a good three to five years to blend.

➤ Bernard Levet, 26, bd des Allées, 69420 Ampuis, tel. 04.74.56.15.39, fax 04.74.56.19.75 ▼ ▼ by appt.

MARQUIS DES TOURNELLES 1999
■ n.c. 12,000 ▥ €15-23

A wine from a southern *négociant* (Châteauneuf-du-Pape) in this northern AOC. The colour is not very strong, and the floral nose is equally delicate; but supple, silky tannins are suave to just the right point, making this a wine to be savoured long before others.

➤ Caves Saint-Pierre, BP 5, 84230 Châteauneuf-du-Pape, tel. 04.90.83.58.35, fax 04.90.83.77.23 ▼ ▼ ev. day except Sun. 9am–12 noon 2pm–5pm

MONTEILLET 1999
■ 0.4 ha 1,800 ▥ €38-46

First, one week's maceration at a cool temperature, followed by three weeks' at a warm temperature: 100% de-stemming, then 100% ageing in new barrels. This wine's maturation is still progressing. The nose is still closed but the wine has the right structure to be worth waiting four or five years for.

➤ Vignobles Antoine et Stéphane Montez, Le Monteillet, 42410 Chavanay, tel. 04.74.87.24.57, fax 04.74.87.06.89, e-mail stephane.montez@worldonline.fr ▼ ▼ by appt.

ANDRÉ ET JEAN-CLAUDE MOUTON 1999★
■ 0.5 ha 2,100 ▥ €15-23

Father and son have worked together to present this very well-made 99. The lovely young bright colour is eye-catching. The bouquet starts with a liquorice note followed by concentrated red fruit, in elegant balance. The gamey finishing touch provides a strongly concentrated flavour and a lot of potential. This needs at least five years to calm down.

➤ André et Jean-Claude Mouton, Le Rozay, 69420 Condrieu, tel. 04.74.87.82.36, fax 04.74.87.84.55 ▼ ▼ ev. day 9am–12 noon 12 noon–6pm; groups by appt.

DOM. DE ROSIERS 1999★
■ 7 ha 35,000 ▥ €15-23

This wine-maker is good value for money. He won a *coup de cœur* for his 97 wine. This one is still somewhat closed. One taster called it 'solid and elegant', while another said 'a touch too rigid'. It is a good honest wine with a strong, deep colour and a very promising structure. The long floral flavour makes it suitable for three or more years in the cellar.

➤ Louis Drevon, 3, rue des Moutonnes, 69420 Ampuis, tel. 04.74.56.11.38, fax 04.74.56.13.00, e-mail idrevon@terre-net.fr ▼ ▼ by appt.

SAINT COSME 1999
■ n.c. 6,000 ▥ €15-23

Louis and Cherry Barruol set up their small *négociant* winery in 1997. This wine, with its deep ruby colour glowing with garnet highlights, has a dominant touch of oak that needs to settle down. It is nice and fresh, worth waiting two to three years.

➤ EARL Louis Barruol, Ch. de Saint-Cosme, 84190 Gigondas, tel. 04.90.65.80.80, fax 04.90.65.81.05 ▼ ▼ by appt.

DANIEL ET ROLAND VERNAY 1998
■ 4.47 ha 10,000 ▥ €15-23

This wine gave the Jury a few headaches: technically very good, it does not have all the qualities for its appellation. Supple and fruity in flavour right to the finish, the fruit, in fact, tastes somewhat exotic and unusual. Open this in a year's time.

➤ GAEC Daniel et Roland Vernay, Le Plany, 69560 Saint-Cyr-sur-Rhône, tel. 04.74.53.18.26, fax 04.74.53.63.95 ▼ ▼ by appt.

DOM. GEORGES VERNAY
Maison rouge 1998
■ 0.5 ha 4,000 ▥ €23-30

The renowned Condrieu wine-maker Georges Vernay offers a well-made Côte Rôtie, with elegance and delicacy of structure built on a solid foundation. The fruit is nicely dominant in this wine, where the preponderance of Syrah is completed by 10% Viognier. Good for drinking in two years' time, and subsequently for five years; ideal with wild game and fowl.

➤ Dom. Georges Vernay, 1, rte Nationale, 69420 Condrieu, tel. 04.74.56.81.81, fax 04.74.56.60.98 ▼ ▼ by appt.

DOM. J. VIDAL-FLEURY
La Chatillonne Côte Blonde 1998★★
■ 0.8 ha 3,500 ▥ €30-38

The Jury's plaudits leave little doubt as to the quality of this Côte Blonde: 'Near to perfection', 'A "must have" for the wine-lover'... The remarkable aroma combination of Muscat and very ripe red fruits is equalled by the balance of the flavour elements and the tannins. Wait five years for this wine, and drink it for ten. The estate's main wine, the **Vidal-Fleury Côtes Brune et Blonde 98**, won a star. This is a wine to savour immediately, but may be put away for five to eight years.

J. Vidal-Fleury, 19, rte de la Roche, 69420 Ampuis, tel. 04.74.56.10.18, fax 04.74.56.19.19 ☑ Ⴤ by appt.

GILLES BARGE 1999★

1 ha	4,000	€15-23

A distinguished name among the northern Rhône appellations, Gilles Barge is more of a Côte Rôtie man since establishing his estate in Ampuis. However, he has been making Condrieu wines for 20 years. It is no surprise

---

Condrieu

The vineyard is on granite soils, 11 km (7 miles) south of Vienne, on the right bank of the Rhône. Only wines made exclusively from the Viognier variety are entitled to the appellation which, in seven communes and three departments, covers a mere 102 ha (252 acres). All its characteristics contribute to Condrieu's image as a white wine of very rare quality. Rich in alcohol, fleshy and supple but at the same time fresh, it is highly perfumed, releasing floral aromas – the scent of apricot. This is a unique wine, exceptional and unforgettable, and while it can be drunk young (with all fish dishes) it can also develop with bottle age. In recent years wines from late harvesting have appeared which are made from successive pickings (sometimes as many as eight times in a harvest).

DOM. FARION
Les Graines dorées 1999★★★

0.35 ha	600	€23-30

Here, though reserved for only a few, is an example of the art of wine-making in all its glory. Nothing is missing in this rich wine, made from grapes overripened to perfection. Only superlatives can describe this superb offering, in which the powerful blend of sweet spices and jammy fruit erupts in a creation of total balance.

Thierry Farjon, Morzelas, 42520 Malleval, tel. 04.74.87.16.84, fax 04.74.87.16.84 Ⴤ by appt.

PHILIPPE FAURY La Berne 2000

0.5 ha	3,000	€23-30

This wine was tasted too soon. Matured on yeast lees, as yet it reveals few of its secrets. Nevertheless, the well-built structure was appreciated by the Jury, as well as its dark gold colour with flashes of green, holding out plenty of promise. Leave it for four to five years in the cellar.

EARL Philippe Faury, La Ribaudy, 42410 Chavanay, tel. 04.74.87.26.00, fax 04.74.87.05.01 ☑ Ⴤ by appt.

PIERRE GAILLARD 2000★★

2 ha	8,000	€15-23

Two Condrieu wines: one dry and the other sweet, both superb and worthy of interest. The latter, **Fleurs d'automne 2000**, is long and silky, smooth, and ripely exotic: powerful yet not overwhelming. Already lovely to drink, it may be kept another ten years. As for the dark gold 2000, which has spent only six months in the barrel, the nose is concentrated with a nice dialogue between the slight hint of toast and the ripe peach and apricot. The flavour is just

---

to see him chosen for this supple round wine, with its light fruity flavour and no excessive frills. Everything is well attuned, and the cask aroma is perfectly measured for the last word in style.

Gilles Barge, 8, bd des Allées, 69420 Ampuis, tel. 04.74.56.13.90, fax 04.74.56.10.98 Ⴤ ev. day except Sun. 9am–12 noon 2pm–6pm

CAVE DE CHANTE-PERDRIX 1999★

1 ha	4,500	€15-23

Chante-Perdrix won a *coup de cœur* for its Condrieu in 97. This 99 is a subtle blend of vat and cask (30%) to give a very well-rounded wine with a prominent but well-integrated oak flavour. The delicate nose has a few notes of liquorice. Fleshy and well-balanced, this wine will develop fully in a couple of years. A good choice to accompany white meats served with vegetables *au gratin*.

Philippe Verzier, Izeras, La Madone, 42410 Chavanay, tel. 04.74.87.06.36, fax 04.74.87.07.77, e-mail chanteperdrix.verzi@free.fr ☑ Ⴤ by appt.

Condrieu

as good, perfectly balanced. The 99, incidentally, won a *coup de cœur* last year.

☛ Pierre Gaillard, lieu-dit Chez Favier, 42520 Malleval, tel. 04.74.87.13.10, fax 04.74.87.17.66, e-mail vinsp.gaillard@ wanadoo.fr ▼ ⵏ by appt.

LA GALOPINE 1999★
　　□　　　　n.c.　　13,000　　€15-23

The Jury really enjoyed tasting this wine, with its lovely sparkling colour and a strong bouquet of grapefruit, mandarin and honey. The same fruity flavour has an added note of overripe apricot. Fleshy and rich, very long-tasting, this is a 99 in all its glory.

☛ Delas Frères, ZA de l'Olivet, 07302 Tournon-sur-Rhône, tel. 04.75.08.60.30, fax 04.75.08.53.67, e-mail jacques-grange@delas.com ▼ ⵏ by appt.

DOM. DU MONTEILLET 1999★★
　　□　　1.6 ha　5,000　📖 🍷 €15-23

Centuries of cultivation on arid terraces, experimental plantings in the United States and Australia, and here we have a Viognier the way it should taste. Even when matured by means of grape-skin maceration, and kept for two weeks at 0°C (32°F), it retains all the features of a Condrieu with its touches of liquorice and apricot. A lovely round, full and fleshy palate, this wine is worthy of its name.

☛ Vignobles Antoine et Stéphane Montez, Le Monteillet, 42410 Chavanay, tel. 04.74.87.24.57, fax 04.74.87.06.89, e-mail stephane.montez@worldonline.fr ▼ ⵏ by appt.

ANDRE ET JEAN-CLAUDE MOUTON Côte Châtillon 2000★
　　□　　0.7 ha　1,900　📖 🍷 €15-23

Côte Châtillon normally blends wines matured 40% in vat and 60% in barrel; the **Côte Bonnette 2000** exactly reverses the procedure. Both wines have been awarded a star. The former seems a little fuller, with a delicate touch of oak sustaining the very open floral bouquet. The flavour is rich and well-balanced, with an underlying but tasty mineral note.

☛ André et Jean-Claude Mouton, Le Rozay, 69420 Condrieu, tel. 04.74.87.82.36, fax 04.74.87.84.55 ▼ ⵏ ev. day 9am–12 noon 2pm–6pm; groups by appt.

ANDRE PERRET Chery 1999★★
　　□　　3 ha　8,000　📖 🍷 €23-30

André Perret is a biologist who, during the 1980s, developed the wine-making sector of the family estate. He cultivates 10 ha (25 acres), and this is one of several good wines, blends of 66% aged in the cask and 33% in the vat, following a malolactic fermentation. An attractive pale straw yellow, this 99 has a complex aroma in which dried apricot and spices predominate. The lovely harmony and incredible length make it a good accompaniment to fresh shrimp.

☛ André Perret, Verlieu, 42410 Chavanay, tel. 04.74.87.24.74, fax 04.74.87.05.26 ▼ ⵏ by appt.

CHRISTOPHE PICHON 2000★
　　□　　4 ha　17,000　📖 🍷 €15-23

An ivory-coloured label for the dry Condrieu, and dark green for the **Moelleux 2000**. The latter is still too young for the overripe aroma to be trusted, but has been singled out for its considerable promise. The dry wine was preferred, even though it, too, is still rather closed, but its light supple structure shows good balance. A fine and pleasantly refreshing wine.

☛ Christophe Pichon, Le Grand Val, Verlieu, 42410 Chavanay, tel. 04.74.87.06.78, fax 04.74.87.07.27, e-mail christophe.pichon@terre-net.fr ▼ ⵏ by appt.

DOM. DE PIERRE BLANCHE 1999
　　□　　0.7 ha　3,000　📖 🍷 €15-23

Michel and Xavier Mourier created the vineyard on these steep hillsides in 1990. Completely matured and yeast-stirred in oak casks, this Condrieu bears a label that summarises its features very well: a naïve painting in a framework of greenery. The floral aroma is very refreshing and the oak is so well blended as to be imperceptible. This is an interesting wine to put down for a year or two, then sample with freshwater fish.

☛ Xavier Mourier, RN 86, Verlieu, 42410 Chavanay, tel. 04.74.87.04.07, fax 04.74.87.04.07 ▼ ⵏ by appt.

CAVE DE SAINT-DESIRAT 2000★
　　□　　2 ha　8,000　📖 🍷 €15-23

Established in 1961, this co-operative invested in a barrel store for *barrique* ageing. It is well worth a visit, both for the equipment and for the wine which, with its full flavour and good solid structure, bodes well for the future. Worth trying with the celebrated goat's cheese *rigotte de Condrieu*.

☛ Cave de Saint-Désirat, 07340 Saint-Désirat, tel. 04.75.34.22.05, fax 04.75.34.30.10 ▼ ⵏ by appt.

DOM. GEORGES VERNAY Les Chaillées de l'Enfer 1999★★
　　□　　1 ha　4,000　📖 🍷 €23-30

The estate has turned out some top-quality wines this year. The **Coteau de Vernon 99** was awarded a star (perfect blend and balance), as was the **Les Terrasses de l'Empire 99**, both without a trace of oak. There is a strong preference for Les Chailles de l'Enfer that has led us not into hell (*l'enfer*), but straight to paradise, without passing through purgatory? Just plain rich fullness and nothing else. The smooth sweetness is supplemented by apricot, liquorice and juniper berries. Doubtless, too, the length contributed to its awards.

• Dom. Georges Vernay, 1, rte Nationale, 69420 Condrieu, tel. 04.74.56.81.81, fax 04.74.56.60.98 ▼ Y by appt.

FRANCOIS VILLARD
Quintessence 1999★

☐ 1 ha 3,500 €30-38

Condrieu is producing an increasing number of sweet wines. This Quintessence is the product of grapes selected from 10 October onward. Typically, the wine is vinified and matured in the barrel, and has 110 g/l of residual sugar. The aroma is enticingly intense, the coppery gold colour is already eye-catching, and the strong flavour does not prejudice the refined structure. This is a marvellously fresh wine with hints of ripe exotic fruit.

• François Villard, Montjoux, 42410 Saint-Michel-sur-Rhône, tel. 04.74.56.83.60, fax 04.74.56.87.78 ▼
Y by appt.

Saint-Joseph

The appellation stretches over about 900 ha (2,223 acres) along the right bank of the Rhône, in the Ardèche and Loire departments, on steep gravel slopes with beautiful views of the Alps. Mount Pilat and the Doux gorges. Saint-Joseph reds are made from Syrah grapes, and are elegant, relatively light and soft, with subtle aromas of raspberry, pepper and blackcurrant, which open when accompanying grilled chicken and certain cheeses. In 2000, 34,972 hl (923,261 gal) were produced. The

white wines, made from the Roussanne and Marsanne varieties, are reminiscent of the Hermitage whites. They are fleshy with a delicate perfume of flowers, fruit and honey, and are best drunk fairly young. In 2000, 3,432 hl (90,605 gal) were produced.

GABRIEL ALIGNE 1999★

■ 1 ha 4,000 €8-11

There has been a real 'invasion' of Beaujolais *négociants* in Rhône Valley appellations, and it has paid dividends with this still very young Saint-Joseph. Strongly flavoured, with ripe red fruit on nose and palate, this wine is powerful and beautifully rounded.

• Les Vins Gabriel Aligne, La Chevalière, 69430 Beaujeu, tel. 04.74.04.84.36, fax 04.74.69.29.87 ▼ ev. day except Sat. Sun. 8am–12 noon 2pm–6pm

DOM. DES AMPHORES
Les Mésanges 1999★

■ 0.5 ha 2,500 €8-11

When visiting Chavanay, along the Pélussinois circuit in the Pilat regional park, do not miss the medieval ruins and the 16th- and 17th-century houses. Close by is this estate which offers an excellent wine, typical of the region. Full-bodied and well-structured on fine tannins, which release the blackcurrant, it filters through to a lingering finish that includes cloves and other spices.

• Véronique et Philippe Grenier, Dom. des Amphores, Richagnieux, 42410 Chavanay, tel. 04.74.87.65.32, fax 04.74.87.65.32 ▼
Y by appt.

DE BOISSEYT-CHOL 1999

■ 5 ha 25,000 €11-15

Share-croppers under the French monarchy, the Chol family purchased the Boissie vineyard in 1797, originating the estate that descendant Didier Chol has been running since 1988. Here is a 35-year-old Syrah, the wild, youthful character of which stood out when it was tasted. Strongly concentrated, with a good solid structure and tannins, the wine has a gamey liquoricy nose and will not be tamed for some while yet.

• De Boisseyt-Chol, RN 86, 42410 Chavanay, tel. 04.74.87.23.45, fax 04.74.87.07.36, e-mail deboisseyt.chol@net-up.com ▼ ev. day except Sun. 9am–12 noon 2pm–6pm; cl. 15 Aug–15 Sep.
• Didier Chol

BOUCHER Cuvée panoramique 1999

■ 0.6 ha 2,500 €8-11

Here is a Saint-Joseph to drink with the Sunday roast. It has a lovely intense colour, with a very agreeable flavour of red fruit and well-integrated tannins.

• GAEC Michel et Gérard Boucher, Vintabrin, 42410 Chavanay, tel. 04.74.87.23.38, fax 04.74.87.08.36 ▼
Y by appt.

CALVET
Cuvée JM Calvet Elevé en fût de chêne 1999★
■ n.c.　20,000　€8-11

This Rhône wine from the famous Bordeaux firm is simple yet elegant, dark, almost black, in colour, with a red fruit bouquet and a touch of cocoa. There is chocolate, too, on the palate, together with prominent but well-blended long tannins. Good in two or three years' time.
• Calvet, 75, cours du Médoc, BP 11, 33028 Bordeaux Cedex, tel. 05.56.43.59.00, fax 05.56.43.17.78, e-mail calvet@calvet.com

M. CHAPOUTIER Les Granits 1999
■ 2 ha　5,000　€38-46

The white Les Granits 2000 and the red 99 from this vineyard won the same mark. Still very youthful, both wines have strong potential, unexploited at the time of tasting: impressive texture combined with full body and young tannins. This red needs time for the tannins to assimilate and allow the fruit to prevail over the woody spices that are too strong at present.
• M. Chapoutier, 18, av. du Dr-Paul-Durand, 26600 Tain-l'Hermitage, tel. 04.75.08.28.65, fax 04.75.08.81.70, e-mail chapoutier@chapoutier.com
Y by appt.

DOM. DU CHENE 1999★
□ 1.5 ha　4,000　♦ €8-11

This estate is known on three continents, and here it offers two good wines. The red Anaïs 98 was matured 18 months in barrel, and needs to be left until 2003. The main 99 vintage has a delicious nose of peach and apricot, perhaps a little overripe. This is an interesting feature even though the wine is still rather closed; but the lovely length and elegance are immediately obvious.
• Marc et Dominique Rouvière, Le Pêcher, 42410 Chavanay, tel. 04.74.87.27.34, fax 04.74.87.02.70　Y by appt.

CLOS DE CUMINAILLE 1999★★
■ 4 ha　13,000　€11-15

This delightful Clos only just missed the coup de cœur. Good strong oak tones give it a wonderfully complex flavour. Red fruit and spices blend to create the intense young texture. The flavour is very open, direct, tannic and toasty, but the fruit is also there. A wine with good laying-down potential. The slightly oaky white Cuvée Principale 2000 won a star, as did the very spicy red Les Pierres 99, which needs another three years in the cellar.
• Pierre Gaillard, lieu-dit Chez Favier, 42520 Malleval, tel. 04.74.87.13.10, fax 04.74.87.17.66, e-mail vinsp.gaillard@wanadoo.fr　Y by appt.

DOM. DU CORNILHAC 1999★
■ 2 ha　8,000　€11-15

The younger generation of the Salette family converted to biodynamic farming in 1997. After the great freeze of 1998, they are back with their 99, well ripened on the vine, and perhaps even a little overripe judging by the notes of stewed fruit and cinnamon on a very concentrated texture, sustained by the incipient tannins.
• SCEA Salette, Dom. du Cornilhac, Le Cornilhac, 07300 Tournon, tel. 04.75.08.02.80, fax 04.75.82.95.08　Y by appt.

DOM. COURBIS Les Royes 1999★★
■ 5 ha　19,000　€15-23

Meet the genuine Saint-Joseph! Beautifully textured, this wine reveals a skilful blend of aroma and structure, and an equally excellent balance of silky tannins and full-bodied mellowness. It attracts for its complexity rather than its strength. The nose is wonderful, with very ripe black fruit and touches of cloves, pepper and vanilla. The estate's main offering, the red Domaine de Courbis 99 was awarded a star. In short, a superb wine.
• Dom. Courbis, rte de Saint-Romain, 07130 Châteaubourg, tel. 04.75.81.81.60, fax 04.75.40.25.39, e-mail domaine-courbis@wanadoo.fr
Y by appt

PIERRE COURSODON
Le Paradis Saint-Pierre 1999★★
□ 0.8 ha　2,400　€15-23

Pierre Coursodon and his son Jérôme have registered the trademark for this unusual wine. It is made from a small quantity of 100% Marsanne, hand-picked and carried manually from the vine because the hillsides are too steep for machine-cultivation. The grapes must be superb, judging by the tasters' chorus of praise. It is indeed an excellent wine with good ageing potential. Very pure and elegant, it fills the nose and palate refreshingly. Three red wines won a star each: Le Paradis Saint-Pierre, L'Olivaie and La Sensonne, with long silky tannins and a bouquet tinged with spices, oak and game.
• EARL Pierre Coursodon, pl. du Marché, 07300 Mauves, tel. 04.75.08.18.29, fax 04.75.08.75.72　Y ev. day 8am–12 noon 2pm–6pm

DIASKOT Cuvée Prestige 1999★
■ n.c.　5,000　€8-11

This négociant certainly knew his ingredients for blending this powerfully fruity, persistent wine. The nose is perfect, with an intense attack of red and black fruit. The full-bodied texture has a complex flavour that needs two or three years before ideally serving with roast pheasant.

ERIC ET JOEL DURAND

Les Coteaux 1999

4 ha   16,000   €11-15

Even though this wine was only partially matured in barrel (70%) the oak is very prominent. The structure is already supple, light, open and harmonious. Make the most of this wine over the next two years.

☞ Eric et Joël Durand, imp. de la Fontaine, 07130 Châteaubourg, tel. 04.75.40.46.78, fax 04.75.40.29.77 ✓ by appt.

DOM. FARJON 1999★

0.26 ha   1,300   €11-15

This is Thierry Farjon's tenth wine, matured and yeast-stirred in barrel for six months. It is of superb quality, the oak sufficiently subtle to leave room for the white peach, violet, white flowers and spices. Round and well-balanced, the palate is pleasantly smooth and suave.

☞ Thierry Farjon, Morzelas, 42520 Malleval, tel. 04.74.87.16.84, fax 04.74.87.16.84 ✓ by appt.

PHILIPPE FAURY

La Gloriette Vieilles vignes 1999★

1 ha   4,500   €11-15

This is the third time Philippe Faury has offered a *cuvée spéciale* from his 11-ha (27-acre) vineyard, which has produced several prize-winners since 1979. This Gloriette is already lovely to drink and will get even better over the next two or three years. The colour is very young and bright, with a tempting oaky flavour and refreshing aroma. Very fine tannins, red fruits and good maturation combine to perfection. Serve this with white meats.

☞ EARL Philippe Faury, La Ribaudy, 42410 Chavanay, tel. 04.74.87.26.00, fax 04.74.87.05.01 ✓ by appt.

PIERRE FINON Les Rocailles 1999★★

2 ha   5,000   €11-15

The estate's principal offering, the **red** Pierre Finon 99, was awarded a star and may be served for a good five years. Blended from much older vines, this wine is distinctive for its complex flavour of red fruits, spices and flowers, together with solid, well-assimilated tannins. It is a wholly characteristic and very elegant wine.

☞ Pierre Finon, Picardel, 07340 Charnas, tel. 04.75.34.08.75, fax 04.75.34.06.78 ✓ by appt.

GILLES FLACHER

Cuvée Prestige 1999

1.5 ha   5,000   €11-15

When tasted on 30 March 2001, this wine was still closed and hard to judge because of the overstrong woody flavour. However, it has a lot of body despite spending only 14 months in barrel. Well structured, it has a superb colour. The jury took a chance, giving it four to five years to mature. The **white Cuvée Principale 99** was awarded the same marks. It is round and supple, blending sweet spices and white fruit.

☞ Gilles Flacher, 07340 Charnas, tel. 04.75.34.09.97, fax 04.75.34.09.96 ✓ by appt.

DOM. FLORENTIN

Clos de l'Arbalestrier 1998

4 ha   16,000   €11-15

Completely surrounded by walls, here is an authentic *clos* (walled vineyard) that dates back to the 16th century. The estate offers a **white Cuvée 99** blended from 50-year-old vines, which is ready to drink now. This wine shows all the signs of a well-developed structure with a good gamey flavour plus odd notes of plum. The tannins are fine but could do with being put away for a few more years.

☞ Dom. Florentin, 32, av. Saint-Joseph, 07300 Tournon, tel. 04.75.08.60.96, fax 04.75.08.60.97 ✓ by appt.

PIERRE GONON 1999★★

5.5 ha   27,000   €11-15

'A natural wine which fully reflects the quality of the grape,' wrote one of the tasters; and the other members of the jury were equally enthusiastic. Here is an excellent producer who has made a wine of great promise, still somewhat closed, but with the deep colour that reflects the full-bodied richness at first glance. The **white Saint-Joseph Les Oliviers 99** won a star for its delightful bouquet. This is ready to drink over the next two years.

☞ Pierre Gonon, 11, rue des Launays, 07300 Mauves, tel. 04.75.08.07.95, fax 04.75.08.65.21 ✓ by appt.

BERNARD GRIPA 1999★

6 ha   28,000   €11-15

Bernard Gripa has 30 years' experience behind him, and is considered one of the pillars of the AOC. This wine still has a taste of the cask, needing four to five years for the oak to blend in. At the moment, the flavour is more complex than the nose: full of spices, red fruit, and long, really powerful tannins.

☞ Bernard Gripa, 5, av. Ozier, 07300 Mauves, tel. 04.75.08.14.96, fax 04.75.07.06.81 ✓ by appt.

PASCAL JANET Côte Sud 1999

0.5 ha   1,600   €8-11

Pascal Janet studied at the Beaune agricultural college of wine-making, then set up his vineyard in 1992. This, his first wine, made from very young five-year-old vines cultivated

Saint-Joseph

on mica-schists and gneiss, has a delicate nose with some toasted notes. A light wine, serve it this winter alongside a stew with potatoes.

➤ Pascal Janet, RN 86, 07370 Arras-sur-Rhône, tel. 04.75.07.09.61, fax 04.75.07.09.61 ⛉ by appt.

DOM. DE LA FAVIERE 1999★   €8-11

Malleval, a medieval village, is situated in the Pilat regional park. Pierre Boucher has been working his estate here since 1970. While the red 99 was selected by the Jury and needs a few more months in the cellar, this young white wine has proved very successful. A classical blend of Marsanne (85%) and Roussanne, it has no touch of wood. Pale and glistening, this is a straightforward, fresh, mellow wine with a lingering, mouth-filling flavour. It should be even better in two or three years' time.

➤ Pierre Boucher, Dom. de La Favière, 42520 Malleval, tel. 04.74.87.15.25, fax 04.74.87.15.25, e-mail domainedelafaviere@.com ⛉ by appt.

LES COMBAUD 1999★   1.5 ha   8,000   €11-15

Twenty years a wine-maker, Sylvian Bernard uses organic farming methods. Beautifully complete, with a strong aroma of violet and wild fruit, well-balanced and structured, and very persistent, this 99 will keep well. The red Domaine de Fauterie 99 was commended for its classic attributes.

➤ Sylvain Bernard, Dom. de Fauterie, 07130 Saint-Péray, tel. 04.75.40.46.17, fax 04.75.81.06.60 ⛉ by appt.

J. MARSANNE ET FILS 1999   0.4 ha   1,800   €8-11

This estate converted to direct sale more than 30 years ago. This wine was cultivated on clay and granite. The clear, brilliant colour has a nose of honey, nuts and spices. Forthright, supple and quite full-bodied, it will be good for two years.

➤ Jean Marsanne et Fils, 25, av. Ozier, 07300 Mauves, tel. 04.75.08.86.26, fax 04.75.08.49.37 ⛉ by appt.

MAS DU PARADIS 1999   4 ha   10,000   €8-11

It will be five years before this Paradis with its young tannins is ready to drink. Deep in colour, the bouquet abounds with game and spices. This wine is bottled by the négociant Gabriel Meffre.

➤ André Morion, Epitaillon, 42410 Chavanay, tel. 04.90.12.32.42, fax 04.90.12.32.49

DOM. DU MONTEILLET
Cuvée du Papy 1999★★   2.5 ha   9,000   €11-15

The renowned Cuvée du Papy always receives excellent marks from Juries. This is a genuine Saint-Joseph that missed winning a coup de coeur by a single vote. Strong, but harmonious and complex, it typifies the great wines of this appellation which are built on supple, well-blended and balanced tannins that ensure excellent keeping. One of the tasters commented: 'It needs further maturation to let the body develop.' The white Domaine de Monteillet 99 was awarded a star. It is good with fish in cream sauce. The red La Cabriole 99, which also won a star, needs to wait a little as well.

➤ Vignobles Antoine et Stéphane Montez, Le Monteillet, 42410 Chavanay, tel. 04.74.87.24.57, fax 04.74.87.06.89, e-mail stephane.montez@worldonline.fr ⛉ by appt.

DIDIER MORION Les Echets 1999★   0.4 ha   3,500   €8-11

Schist is the favourite terroir for Syrah vines which, as in this case, reach their peak after 30 years. Deep red with violet flashes so dark that they seem almost black, this wine is still young and bears the signs of its maturation. Notes of liquorice and vanilla form a delightful, complex nose that carries on to the palate. Clean and fresh, long and mellow, the wine still needs some time (three years at least) in a good cellar to draw out the fruit.

➤ Didier Morion, Epitaillon, 42410 Chavanay, tel. 04.74.87.26.33, fax 04.74.87.26.33 ⛉ by appt.

ALAIN PARET 420 Nuits 1999★   2 ha   13,000   €15-23

This estate won the coup de coeur last year for its 98. The 99 demonstrates the skill and hard work put in by Alain Paret to create wine along the lines followed by his grandfather. Dark red, shot with violet, this wine is very well balanced. Spicy with notes of oak, the bouquet does not overpower the fruity flavour that warms the palate. Notes of pepper and cinnamon continue through to the long finish of blended tannins that still retain their harvest scent.

➤ Alain Paret, pl. de l'Eglise, 42520 Saint-Pierre-de-Bœuf, tel. 04.74.87.12.09, fax 04.74.87.17.34 ⛉ by appt.

CUVEE PARSIFAL 1999   9 ha   50,000   €8-11

Although the name is suggestive of a Wagnerian wine, it more nearly resembles a Debussy: delicate and gentle, expanding supple and smooth on the palate. Nicely balanced, this is a good wine to drink for the next five years with wild-fowl.

➤ Les Vignerons de Rasteau et de Tain-l'Hermitage, rte des Princes-d'Orange, 84110 Rasteau, tel. 04.90.10.90.10, fax 04.90.10.90.36, e-mail vrt@rasteau.com

ANDRE PERRET Les Grisières 1999★   1 ha   4,000   €11-15

After studying biology, André Perret trained in vinification and oenology before joining the family estate. His Grisières are made with 50-year-old Syrah grapes.

Matured for 18 months in barrel (20% of the barrels were new), this wine has a prominent yet classy flavour of oak. Other fine points are the gloriously young colour of ripe cherry with violet tints, and the nose of liquorice blending with musk and black fruit. The long elegant tannins are full of promise.
- André Perret, Verlieu, 42410 Chavanay, tel. 04.74.87.24.74, fax 04.74.87.05.26 ☑ by appt.

CAVE DES VIGNERONS RHODANIENS Cuvée réservée 1999

■ n.c. n.c. €8-11

This co-operative was established in 1929 and reconverted to AOC in 1970. In this wine, the attack is very clean, revealing a touch of richness that is soon dispersed by the very strong tannins. The powerful, complex bouquet of blackcurrant, truffles and spices is mouthwatering. However, it will take three to five years to develop.
- Cave des Vignerons Rhodaniens, 35, rue du Port-Vieux, 38550 Le Péage-de-Roussillon, tel. 04.74.86.20.69, fax 04.74.86.57.95, e-mail vignerons.rhodaniens@wanadoo.fr ☑

DOM. RICHARD
Vieilles vignes 1999★★

■ 1 ha 6,000 €11-15 ☑

Hervé Richard took over his grandfather's estate in 1989. This small selection, made from 35-year-old Syrah grapes, delighted the Jury with its beautiful balance of fruit and well-measured oak. The colour is brilliant deep red, almost black, with a violet glow. The nose is superbly complex, blending red fruit and blackcurrant, leather, spices and a few delicate touches of musk. The attack on the palate is very direct, cushioned by mellow, oaky tannins. The **red Tradition 99** was singled out for mention by the Jury.
- Hervé et Marie-Thérèse Richard, Verlieu, 42410 Chavanay, tel. 04.74.87.07.75, fax 04.74.87.05.09 ☑ by appt.

CAVE DE SAINT-DÉSIRAT 2000★

□ 15 ha 50,000

This co-operative has set up a 'teaching vineyard': a sort of small conservatory for regional grapes. This Saint-Joseph is nicely refreshing with touches of hazelnut and floral honey. The texture is mouth-filling, rich and fresh in a lovely balance.
- Cave de Saint-Désirat, 07340 Saint-Désirat, tel. 04.75.34.22.05, fax 04.75.34.30.10 ☑ by appt.

CAVE DE SARRAS Cuvée
Champtenaud Élevé en fût de chêne 1998★

■ 7 ha n.c. €8-11

The cellar, on the right bank of the Rhône, in the Haut-Vivarais region near Saint-Vallier, produced three very successful 98 red wines in the same price range: **La Mandragore, Domaine de Bonarieux** and this **Champtenaud**, typical of its year with fine, well-balanced tannins on a rich complex aroma of spices and ripe fruit. Wait until 2004 before opening these three wines.
- Cave de Sarras, Le Village, 07370 Sarras, tel. 04.75.23.14.81, fax 04.75.23.38.36 ☑ by appt.

CAVE DE TAIN L'HERMITAGE
Nobles Rives 1999

■ n.c. n.c. €8-11

The well-known Cave de Tain estate has cask-matured this deep-coloured wine, with its aroma of wild herbs from the garrigue and some charred notes. The first impression is fresh and clean, and the palate is well balanced with nicely blended tannins that guarantee good keeping for three to five years.
- Cave de Tain-l'Hermitage, 22, rte de Larnage, BP 3, 26601 Tain-l'Hermitage Cedex, tel. 04.75.08.20.87, fax 04.75.07.15.16, e-mail commercial.france@cave-tain-hermitage.com ☒ by appt

DOM. DE VALLOUIT 1999★

□ 0.6 ha 2,300 €11-15 ☒ by appt

An earlier vintage of this wine was one of those served at the dinner given by the President of France at the Élysée during the bicentennial celebrations of the French Revolution. This one, produced ten years after the anniversary wine, is a blend of 70% Marsanne and 30% Roussanne, blended and matured in oak casks, with an excellent texture. The oak flavour combines well with white peach to give a well-rounded effect augmented by a note of beeswax. Just as successful is the **red Domaine de Vallouit 99** which received a star. The strong tannins in this young wine need two to five years to blend fully.
- Dom. de Vallouit, 24, av. Désiré-Valette, BP 61, 26240 Saint-Vallier, tel. 04.75.23.10.11, fax 04.75.23.05.58 ☒ by appt.

DOM. GEORGES VERNAY 1999

■ 1.5 ha 6,000 €11-15

A full 12 months in barrel (20% of the barrels were new) has given this very pleasant wine a full flavour of ripe, jammy fruit. The attack is strong and refreshing. The palate is full and tastes of fruit preserved in alcohol. Open in a year or two.
- Dom. Georges Vernay, 1, rte Nationale, 69420 Condrieu, tel. 04.74.56.81.81, fax 04.74.56.60.98 ☑ by appt

Crozes-Hermitage

This appellation, which is on land that is easier to cultivate than Hermitage, extends over 11 communes around Tain-l'Hermitage. It is the largest vineyard of the northern appellations: the area of production is 1,238 ha (3,058 acres), and produces 57,628 hl (1,521,378 gal). The soils, which are richer than those of the Hermitage appellation, produce less powerful, fruity wines that are better drunk young. The red wines are fairly supple and aromatic; the whites are dry and fresh, light in colour, with a floral aroma. Like the Hermitage whites, they go splendidly with freshwater fish.

M. CHAPOUTIER

Les Varonniers 1999★★

2.5 ha   5,300   €38–46

'Seven years in the planning'... But then, what a treat! This is a great wine which was presented to the Grand Jury and only narrowly missed a *coup de coeur*. From the intense colour through to the finish where cinnamon and vanilla blend with black fruits, strong on the palate, and built on tightly structured tannins, it is thoroughly delicious.

M. Chapoutier, 18, av. du Dr-Paul-Durand, 26600 Tain-l'Hermitage, tel. 04.75.08.28.65, fax 04.75.08.81.70, e-mail chapoutier@chapoutier.com   by appt.

DOM. BERNARD CHAVE

Tête de Cuvée 1999★★★

3.6 ha   16,670   €11–15

Blind-tasting never fails to demonstrate that the Tête de Cuvée is streets ahead of other wines, including those from estates with excellent reputations. The **red Cuvée Traditionnelle 99** and **white Domaine Bernard Chave 99** were both awarded a star. A laurel wreath, too, for this Tête de Cuvée with its brilliant, almost black colour, and aroma loaded with black fruit, oak and chocolate. The palate is equally fine, strongly concentrated, pleasantly full, and with the exceptional length that is the sign of a wine that will be superb after its time in the cellar.

Yann Chave, La Burge, 26600 Mercurol, tel. 04.75.07.42.11, fax 04.75.07.47.34   by appt.

Bernard Chave

DOM. BERNARD ANGE

Rêve d'Ange 1998★

0.8 ha   3,000   €11–15

Bernard Ange, with an estate in what was once a riverside mansion, won a *coup de coeur* last year for his 97 wine. This, the following vintage, is deep in colour, strong in fruit and with excellent tannic balance. The **Cuvée Principale 99** is somewhat more austere and was singled out by the Jury for mention.

Bernard Ange, Pont-de-l'Herbasse, 26260 Clérieux, tel. 04.75.71.62.42, fax 04.75.71.62.42   ev. day except Sun. 9am–7pm.

JEAN BARONNAT 1999★

n.c.   n.c.   €5–8

This Beaujolais family estate is run by the founder's grandson. His Crozes-Hermitage is fine and well-balanced, with a fruity opening and a flavour of black cherries blended with soft tannins.

Maison Jean Baronnat, Les Bruyeres, 491, rte de Lacenas, 69400 Gleizé, tel. 04.74.68.59.20, fax 04.74.62.19.21, e-mail info@baronnat.com   by appt

BOIS FARDEAU 1999

4 ha   20,000   €5–8

Two wines here, neck and neck: the **red Les Murières 99** and this Bois Fardeau, both of which rely less on strength than on immediately perceptible harmony and spicy flavour.

Gabriel Meffre, Le Village, 84190 Gigondas, tel. 04.90.12.30.22, fax 04.90.12.30.29, e-mail gabriel-meffre@meffre.com   by appt.

CAVE DES CLAIRMONTS 1999★

18 ha   113,500   €8–11

Renovated in 1997, this estate offers two Crozes, awarded the same marks. The **red Cuvée des Pionniers 99**, matured in cask, has better ageing potential (five years): supple and rich, full of red and black fruit with touches of spice. For immediate drinking, try this Cave des Clairmonts, very typical of its appellation.

SCA Cave des Clairmonts, Vignes-Vieilles, 26600 Beaumont-Monteux, tel. 04.75.84.61.91, fax 04.75.84.56.98   ev. day except Sun. 9am–12 noon 2pm–6pm; groups by appt.

DOM. COLLONGE 1999

| | 30 ha | 30,000 | ■ | €5-8 |

This wine, from a 44-ha (109-acre) estate and bearing a classically smart label, is still, quite naturally, feeling its way but shows a lot of promise. Delicately fruity, it should be ready in a year or two.

➥ GAEC Collonge, La Négociale, 26600 Mercurol, tel. 04.75.07.44.06, fax 04.75.07.44.06 ☑ ❢ ev. day. 8.30am–12 noon 1.30pm–6.30pm; Sun. 9.30am–12 noon; groups by appt.

DOM. DU COLOMBIER

Cuvée Gaby 1999★★

| | n.c. | 15,000 | ▥ | €11-15 |

A prestige wine from this 14-ha (35-acre) estate, and matured a year in cask. Charming the Jury, who passed it on to the Grand Jury, it is one of the best wines of its year. Touches of cinnamon and clove, strongly textured, with excellent tannins; all it needs is time to develop. The **red Domaine du Colombier, Cuvée principale 99 and white 2000** were each awarded a star.

➥ Dom. du Colombier, SCEA Viale, Mercurol, 26600 Tain-l'Hermitage, tel. 04.75.07.44.07, fax 04.75.07.41.43 ☑
❢ by appt.
❢ Viale

CH. CURSON 1999★★

| | 7 ha | 23,000 | ▥ | €11-15 |

This 18-ha (44-acre) estate offers a very successful **white Crozes-Hermitage 2000** that still retains the savour of the cask, but with a delicious fresh flavour (awarded one star), and this 99, similarly cask-matured. The rich texture, concentration and well-blended tannins substantiate its fabulous potential.

➥ Dom. Pochon, Ch. de Curson, 26600 Chanos-Curson, tel. 04.75.07.34.60, fax 04.75.07.30.27 ☑ ❢ by appt

DELAS Les Launes 1999★

| | n.c. | 180,000 | ▥ ▮ | €8-11 |

A new vat room and reorganised barrel stores for this very old estate, energetically administered by Frédéric Rosset, who ensures it remains one of the finest in the region. This very dark, violet-tinted wine is very enticing both on nose and palate, where the well-blended tannins are set off by an elegant hint of truffle.

DOM. COMBIER 1999★

| | n.c. | 30,000 | ▥ | €8-11 |

This vineyard, whose vines are organically cultivated, offers its principal wine, matured ten months in cask. It is very well balanced and characteristic of its AOC, based on prominent but silky tannins that do not overpower the fruit.

➥ EARL Dom. Combier, RN 7, 26600 Pont-de-l'Isère, tel. 04.75.84.61.56, fax 04.75.84.53.43 ☑ ❢ by appt

LE GRAND COURTIL 1999★

| | 1.5 ha | 6,000 | ▥ | €15-23 |

These grapes are cultivated organically, matured in open oak casks without destemming, and pumped over twice a day. This produces very good wines to put away (five years or more), with strong but balanced tannins. Aromas of black cherry and spice, a clean attack, followed by a liquorice flavour on a long finish.

➥ Ferraton Père et Fils, 13, rue de la Sizeranne, 26600 Tain-l'Hermitage, tel. 04.75.08.59.51, fax 04.75.08.81.59, e-mail ferraton.pereetfils@wanadoo.fr ☑ ❢ by appt.

DOM. DU MURINAIS

Cuvée Vieilles vignes 1999★

| | 2.5 ha | 12,000 | ▥ | €8-11 |

Luc Tardy adventurously took over the family estate in 1998 and established a cellar for wine that had previously gone to the co-operative. This, from his second vintage, is a modest blend, aged in barrel, deep in colour

LA MAURELLE 1999★

| | 50 ha | 40,000 | ▥ ▮ ♦ | €8-11 |

The Jury thought that this wine, with its ripe flavour of jammy fruit, needed a couple of years to express itself completely, although it is already mouth-filling, with well-blended tannins.

➥ Henry Bouachon, BP 5, 84230 Châteauneuf-du-Pape, tel. 04.90.83.58.35, fax 04.90.83.77.23 ☑

LA CHASSELIERE 1998

| | n.c. | 12,000 | ▥ | €5-8 |

This 45-ha (111-acre) family estate has been run by Robert Michelas for 40 years. Serve this 98 wine with a *terrine* of wild boar this winter. A nice honest classic with well-integrated tannins.

➥ Dom. Michelas Saint Jemms, Bellevue-les-Chassis, 26600 Mercurol, tel. 04.75.07.86.70, fax 04.75.08.69.80, e-mail michelas.st.jemms@wanadoo.fr ☑ ❢ by appt

GUYOT Le Millepertuis 1999

| | 50 ha | 55,000 | ▥ | €8-11 |

Strength and solidity in this wine that is as yet a bit rough on the palate with very prominent tannins that should soften up after a few months in the cellar. The 33% proportion of new barrels probably explains the taste.

➥ SA Guyot, montée de l'Eglise, 69440 Taluyers, tel. 04.78.48.70.54, fax 04.78.48.77.31, e-mail guyotvin@vins-guyot.com ☑ ❢ Thurs. Fri. Sat. 8.30am–12 noon 1.30pm–6pm

➥ Delas Frères, ZA de l'Olivet, 07302 Tournon-sur-Rhône, tel. 04.75.08.60.30, fax 04.75.08.53.67, e-mail jacques-grange@delas.com ☑ ❢ by appt

with violet reflections, with a delicious nose of black fruit and spices and a well-rounded palate supported by softening tannins. It needs a couple of years to express itself successfully.
➤ Luc Tardy, Champ-Bernard, 26600 Beaumont-Monteux, tel. 04.75.07.34.76, fax 04.75.07.35.91
Y by appt.

ERIC ROCHER Chaubayou 2000★ 1.4 ha 4,800 €8-11

Violet glimmers through the deep red colour of this wine, well-balanced and pleasantly refreshing thanks to the fruity flavour that lasts until the finish.
➤ Eric Rocher, Dom. de Champal, quartier Champal, 07370 Sarras, tel. 04.78.34.21.21, fax 04.78.34.30.60,
e-mail vignobles-rocher@wanadoo.fr
Y by appt.

LES ALLEGORIES D'ANTOINE OGIER 1999★ n.c. 6,000 €8-11

This large southern firm of *négociants* markets its northern wines as 'allegories'. Although one can only guess at the significance of the label (a cup held by two cherubs) the wine, with its smooth silky tannins that accord prominence to the fruity flavour, is wholly recommendable. The **Oratorio 99** is very similar.
➤ Ogier-Caves des Papes, 10, bd Pasteur, 84230 Châteauneuf-du-Pape, tel. 04.90.39.32.32, fax 04.90.83.72.51, e-mail ogier.caves.des.papes@ogier.fr
Y ev. day except Sat. Sun. 8am–5pm

DOM. PRADELLE 2000 18 ha 100,000 €8-11

Lovely flashes of purple in this dark wine, full of promise. An intense bouquet of musk, followed by blackcurrant and violet, which lasts to the very finish. The tannins are ready, so that the wine can be served this winter.
➤ GAEC Pradelle, 26600 Chanos-Curson, tel. 04.75.07.31.00, fax 04.75.07.35.34
Y ev. day except Sun. 8am–12 noon 2pm–6pm

DOM. DES REMIZIERES Cuvée Christophe 1999★ n.c. 12,000 €11-15

Although St Christopher, patron saint of travellers, is unlikely to have personally influenced the name of this wine, it provides an excuse for the salutary reminder not to drink and drive! Anyway, this 99 should be sampled with moderation, for it will afford even greater pleasure in three or four years. The deep colour is eye-catching, but the aroma is not yet developed. The palate is somewhat closed, but dense, so decant the wine to let its red fruit and spice fragrance expand freely. Its tannins and fruit harmonise beautifully.
➤ Cave Desmeure, rte de Romans, 26600 Mercurol, tel. 04.75.07.44.28, fax 04.75.07.45.87 Y by appt.

MESSIRE LOUIS REVOL 1999 2 ha 10,000 €5-8

This is a refreshing wine, judging by the number of times the word 'fresh' was written on the tasting cards. Red fruit (cherry) follows a straightforward but delicate attack.
➤ Léon Revol, 6, rue Yves-Farges, 69700 Givors, tel. 04.72.49.50.29, fax 04.78.73.16.87

CAVE DE TAIN L'HERMITAGE Nobles Rives 1999★★ n.c. n.c. €8-11

Deserved applause for this cellar, which pulled off a rare exploit: two *coups de coeur* from the Grand Jury! First the **red Les Hauts du Fief 98**, with its silky tannins, ready to win the heart right away, and then this **Noble Rives**, great for putting away and full of promise. For the time being, both wines breathe concentrated power, kept in check by the tightly knit tannins, but the texture is dense, concentrated and beautifully full: superb with a long, long finish.
➤ Cave de Tain-l'Hermitage, 22, rte de Larnage, BP 3, 26601 Tain-l'Hermitage Cedex, tel. 04.75.08.20.87, fax 04.75.07.15.16, e-mail commercial.france@cave-tain-hermitage.co Y by appt.

CHARLES ET FRANCOIS TARDY Les Pends 1999★ 1 ha 5,000 €11-15

The Pends hillsides are clay-limestone. Its grape varieties are 80% Marsanne, the rest Roussanne. The Jury was very appreciative of this selection, produced by oak and yeast lees maturation with over a month's fermentation, resulting in a fresh, well-integrated oaky flavour. Toasted notes with apricot make this an excellent choice with white meat or grilled lobster. The **red 99, Les Machonnières** was commended.
➤ Dom. des Entrefaux, quartier de la Beaume, 26600 Chanos-Curson, tel. 04.75.07.33.38, fax 04.75.07.35.27 Y by appt.

Hermitage

The Hermitage slope is located north-east of Tain-l'Hermitage, with an excellent southerly aspect. Vine cultivation there goes back to the 4th century BC, but the origin of the appellation's name is attributed to the knight Gaspard of Sterimberg who, on his return from the Albigensian crusade in 1224, decided to withdraw from the world. He built a hermitage, cleared the land and planted vines.

The appellation covers about 131 ha (324 acres). To the west, the granite soils of the Tain mountain provide an ideal terrain for producing red wines (Les Bessards). In the south-east, the soils of broken stones and loess (deposits of fine-grained, wind-blown silt and sand) are suited to producing white wines (Les Rocoules, Les Muerts).

The Hermitage red is a very big, tannic wine that is extremely aromatic and needs to be aged from five to ten years, and even up to twenty years, before it develops its bouquet, which is of rare richness and quality. After so long in the bottle, it should be opened well in advance and served at between 16°-18°C (60.8-64.4°F) with game and tasty red meat. Production in 2000 was 4,570 hl (120,648 gal). The Hermitage white (made from the Roussanne and particularly the Marsanne varieties) is a very fine wine that lacks acidity, but is supple, fleshy and very perfumed. It can be enjoyed from the first year but reaches its full expression after between five and ten years' bottle age. In 2000, 1,012 hl (26,717 gal) were produced. However, for both white and red wines, the great years can be kept for as long as thirty or forty years.

DOM. DE THALABERT 1999★★ 40 ha n.c. €15-23

Michel, Philippe and Jacques Jaboulet sell their prestige wines all over the world, and have won awards from our juries since the *Guide* was first published in 1983. This 99 is no exception. The colour is breathtakingly black and intense, promising a marvellously full wine. With its concentrated flavour, rich and round, this is loaded with spices, oak tones and black fruit that all last and last. Keep this wine for a long time.
☞ Paul Jaboulet Aîné, Les Jalets, BP 46, 26600 La Roche-de-Glun, tel. 04.75.84.68.93, fax 04.75.84.56.14, e-mail info@jaboulet.com ▼ by appt.

THOMAS FRÈRES 1999★ n.c. 50,000 €5-8

The deep red colour of this wine gives notice of a very concentrated aroma full of mulberry, blackcurrant and stewed fruit. The fruity flavour lingers on the palate with a tang of overripe richness.
☞ Thomas Frères, BP 6, 2071 Nuits-Saint-Georges Cedex, tel. 03.80.62.42.00, e-mail thomasfrères@wanadoo.fr ▼ ev. day 10am-6pm

DOM. JEAN-LOUIS CHAVE 1998★★★ 5 ha n.c. €46-76

This beautifully delicate Hermitage has enormous refinement and class. Hints of freesia appear at first impact, followed quickly by a full floral bouquet that brings to mind innumerable blossoms scattered in the air. But make no mistake: like all the great whites of this appellation, this is a wine to put away for a long time, for with all its delicacy it is marvellously full and rich. The perfect balance is a true delight.

DOM. BERNARD CHAVE 1999★★ 1.12 ha 5,970 €30-38

Bernard Chave's son Yann has been working on this estate since 1996. Matured in *demi-muid* (450-l wooden casks) this very young wine is like an exuberant puppy, but when it calms down it will show fantastic potential. Some of the most experienced tasters say it will be exceptional. Nothing ordinary about this 99, just tremendous power: leather, very ripe red fruit (black cherry), elegant high-class tannins. Put it away in the cellar for at least four years. Then drink it slowly, so that, as they say, 'the last glass is the best'.
☞ Yann Chave, La Burge, 26600 Mercurol, tel. 04.75.07.42.11, fax 04.75.07.47.34
▼ by appt.
☞ Bernard Chave

Hermitage

but will need two to three years for complete balance.

☛ Ferraton Père et Fils, 13, rue de la Sizeranne, 26600 Tain-l'Hermitage, tel. 04.75.08.59.51, fax 04.75.08.81.59, e-mail ferraton.pereetfils@wanadoo.fr
Ⓨ by appt.

LES ALLEGORIES D'ANTOINE OGIER 1999★

◼ n.c. 1,000 ▥ €23-30

Castelpapale offers this delightful 99 Hermitage, typifying its AOC. Nicely structured, with a good texture, it is still a little strong in cask flavour and should wait another four to five years.

☛ Ogier-Caves des Papes, 10, bd Pasteur, 84230 Châteauneuf-du-Pape, tel. 04.90.39.32.32, fax 04.90.83.72.51, e-mail ogier.caves.des.papes@ogier.fr
Ⓨ ev. day except Sat. Sun. 8am–5pm

DOM. DES REMIZIERES
Cuvée Emilie 1999★★★

◼ n.c. 11,000 ▥ €23-30

A month in the vat has enabled the wine-maker to extract all the harvest essentials for a great wine. The colour is bright and almost black, the powerful bouquet redolent of toast and very ripe red fruit. Wine and wood tannins are smooth but somewhat dominant. This wine needs four years in the cellar. Typical of its AOC, it will be great to put away. The same white **Cuvée 99** received one star.

☛ Cave Desmeure, rte de Romans, 26600 Mercurol, tel. 04.75.07.44.28, fax 04.75.07.45.87  Ⓨ by appt.

LES VIGNERONS REUNIS A TAIN L'HERMITAGE 1996

☐ 1.5 ha 6,000 ◼ ♦ €11-15

This 96 wine is ready to drink straight away. It has delightful colour with green highlights, a heady floral nose (acacia) followed by hints of honey. Fresh and supple, it will not disappoint.

☛ Les Vignerons de Rasteau et de Tain-l'Hermitage, rte des Princes-d'Orange, 84110 Rasteau, tel. 04.90.10.90.10, fax 04.90.10.90.36, e-mail vrt@rasteau.com

1132

DOMAINE JEAN-LOUIS CHAVE

☛ Jean-Louis Chave, 37, av. du Saint-Joseph, 07300 Mauves, tel. 04.75.08.24.63, fax 04.75.07.14.21

DOM. JEAN-LOUIS CHAVE
1998★★★

◼ 10 ha n.c. ▥ €46-76

One very experienced taster concluded: 'Too much of a good thing does no harm!' The other members of the Jury apparently agreed as they all noted the rich strength of this wine, deeply concentrated with loads of personality. Perfectly matured, this Hermitage has an intense bouquet, developing on silky tannins that linger on the palate. Those who get to drink this wine are truly fortunate.

☛ Jean-Louis Chave, 37, av. du Saint-Joseph, 07300 Mauves, tel. 04.75.08.24.63, fax 04.75.07.14.21

DOM. DU COLOMBIER 1998

◼ 1.5 ha 7,000 ▥ €30-38

It is surprising how much the blackcurrant dominates the taste of this supple and tantalising Hermitage. It is ready for drinking immediately with red meat.

☛ SCEA Viale, Dom. du Colombier, Mercurol, 26600 Tain-l'Hermitage, tel. 04.75.07.44.07, fax 04.75.07.41.43
Ⓨ by appt.

PAUL JABOULET AINE
Le Chevalier de Sterimberg 1999★

☐ 5 ha n.c. ▥ €38-46

This is one of the great names of France, famous for its label, the emblem of the AOC. This Chevalier is a highly presentable wine, pale yellow flashed with green highlights, strongly floral (hawthorn) with delicate hints of oak, full, balanced, mellow and harmonious. Leave it for four years in a good cellar and then serve with prime fish.

☛ Paul Jaboulet Aîné, Les Jalets, BP 46, 26600 La Roche-de-Glun, tel. 04.75.84.68.93, fax 04.75.84.56.14, e-mail info@jaboulet.com  Ⓨ by appt.

LES DIONNIERES 1999

◼ n.c. 8,000 ▥ €46-76

This estate goes in for organic farming and also operates as a *negociant*. Bright red, shot with violet, this is a wine with a jammy flavour of stewed and brandied fruit. The oaky aroma is pleasantly rounded and almost integrated,

CAVE DE TAIN-L'HERMITAGE
□
Nobles Rives 1999 ★★

130 ha　n.c.　€15-23

Unanimous praise from the Jury for this 99 Nobles Rives, described as 'a very fine wine'. It is very generous, both in aroma and structure, strongly individual, with a tang of apricot, hazelnut and vanilla pastry, full and rich on the palate.

Cave de Tain-l'Hermitage, 22, rue de Larnage, BP 3, 26601 Tain-l'Hermitage Cedex, tel. 04.75.08.20.87, fax 04.75.07.15.16, e-mail commercial.france@ cave-tain-hermitage.com ✓ ▼ by appt.

Cornas

Lying across the river from Valence, the appellation covers only the commune of Cornas, about 93 ha (230 acres). The granite soils, on fairly steep ground, are held in place by low walls. Cornas is a virile, well-structured wine that must be aged for at least three years (but can often wait a good deal longer) to allow it to express its fruity, spicy aromas. Serve it with red meats and game. In 2000, 4,233 hl (111,751 gal) were produced.

CHANTE-PERDRIX 1997 ★
■

n.c.　10,000　€15-23

This estate, founded in 1835, belongs to Deutz Champagne, which is part of the Roederer group. This wine, from a good harvest, is already mature. Even though the colour is still a little young with its violet notes, the wood tannins are integrated. Vanilla and undergrowth do not overpower the fruit flavour. Serve this wine with game and wild mushrooms.

Delas Frères, ZA de l'Olivet, 07302 Tournon-sur-Rhône, tel. 04.75.08.60.30, fax 04.75.08.53.67, e-mail jacques-grange@delas.com ✓ ▼ by appt

DOM. CLAPE 1999 ★★★
■

4 ha　18,000　€23-30

Deep and intense, the colour of this wine is extraordinary. Notes of fresh marc (grape skins) seeping with grape juice appear on the nose straight away, followed by long floral aromas (iris and violet). This is a very young wine, but is strong on the palate without being aggressive. The lovely balance and roundness

demand a very long time in the cellar. It is a great vintage to put away for ten years. You will need to spend some time at the best wineries to find it, but it will be well worth the effort.

SCEA Dom. Clape, 146, rte Nationale, 07130 Cornas, tel. 04.75.81.01.98, fax 04.75.40.33.64, ▼ by appt.
A. et P. Clape

CHARLES DESPESSE Les Côtes 1999
■

0.3 ha　1,500　€11-15

Jérôme Despesse is a new arrival in the *Guide*, and offers a wine that has already attracted the Jury's attention. Fifty-year-old vines have produced this very good traditional-style Cornas, matured for 14 months in oak barrels. This wine shows its granite *terroir* origins; it is rustic and a bit closed when young and needs some time to open up. The colour is intense, and the palate has good strong tannins full of promise. In five years' time it will be ready to drink.

Jérôme Despesse, 10, Basses-Rues, 07130 Cornas, tel. 04.75.80.03.54, fax 04.75.80.03.26 ✓ ▼ by appt
Charles Despesse

DUMIEN-SERRETTE
■
Vieilles vignes 1999

1.8 ha　5,000　€11-15

This estate is now run by the third generation of the owning family. The vines are 50 years old and this wine is characteristic, worthy of its appellation. The strong colour announces a good aroma, well balanced between fruit and flower. It has all the fullness to be able to open up nicely in two or three years.

Dumien-Serrette, 18, rue du Ruisseau, 07130 Cornas, tel. 04.75.40.41.91, fax 04.75.40.41.91 ▼ by appt.

ERIC ET JOEL DURAND 1999 ★★
■

2.5 ha　13,200　€15-23

'Aristocratic,' commented one taster as he admired the refinement of this wine. Or it could be described as a fine athlete with a good strong body. The structure is full and rounded, the superb colour is deep and intense, and the luscious flavour of mulberry and blackcurrant follows through to its finish. This wine is wholly characteristic of its AOC.

pure 'Cornas' but it will be appreciated abroad when matured.

● Eric et Joël Durand, imp. de la Fontaine, 07130 Châteaubourg, tel. 04.75.40.46.78, fax 04.75.40.29.77 by appt.

LES EYGATS 1999★

€23-30 · 1.5 ha · 7,000

The 24-ha (59-acre) Courbis estate has this year offered three Cornas wines, all of which were retained by a very exacting Jury who had to examine 26 wines from this AOC. The **Sabarotte 99** was kept 16 months in barrel. One taster exclaimed, 'Now here is a real Cornas', because the fruit is allowed to show through and the palate is well-structured and complex. It won a star for its elegance. The **Champelrose 99**, slightly more toasty despite spending less time in the barrel, was singled out by the Jury. As for this Les Eygats, it has a marked taste of oak but is very promising: mingling red fruit and spices (liquorice) it is a complex and elegant blend which makes a very successful ensemble.

● Dom. Courbis, rte de Saint-Romain, 07130 Châteaubourg, tel. 04.75.81.81.60, fax 04.75.40.25.39. e-mail domaine-courbis@wanadoo.fr by appt.

JOHANN MICHEL 1999★

€15-23 · 2.5 ha · 7,300

François Michel was the man responsible for the recognition of the AOC. His great-grandson, Johann, has carried on the family tradition since 1997, introducing modern techniques with 12-month maturation in oak casks. This additional feature, far from corrupting the spirit of the appellation, supplements and enhances the quality, proclaiming that this AOC is not synonymous with conservatism or stagnation. An intense deep purple colour indicates the long, well-balanced texture that will be lovely in two to three years with red meat or game.

● Johann Michel, 52, Grand-Rue, 07130 Cornas, tel. 04.75.40.43.16, fax 04.75.40.43.16. ev. day 8am–12 noon 2pm–6pm

DOM. DE ROCHEPERTUIS 1999

€11-15 · 9 ha · 20,000

From 45-year-old vines and 12 months in the cask: at the moment the woody flavour of this wine dominates, with touches of toast and mocha. All the same, this is a well-balanced 99 full of promise. It may not be a pure 'Cornas' but it will be appreciated abroad when matured.

● Jean Lionnet, 48, rue de Pied-la-Vigne, 07130 Cornas, tel. 04.75.40.36.01, fax 04.75.81.00.62 by appt.

DOM. DU TUNNEL 1999★

€11-15 · 1 ha · 3,693

Although steam trains no longer run through this old tunnel in Saint-Péray, it is still surrounded by the ancient vines taken over by Stéphane Robert in 1994. Readers of the *Guide* will appreciate this wine as a solid, honest Cornas. Ruby-red shot with violet, the nose is of red fruit with strong spicy touches (pepper and liquorice). The same flavour is supplemented by rich tannins. It should be laid down for three years. The **Cuvée Prestige 1999**, produced from vines that are almost 100 years old, is still rather closed, but has a fine oak aroma with underlying blackcurrant. Wait three to four years for this wine.

● Stéphane Robert, Dom. du Tunnel, 20, rue de la République, 07130 Saint-Péray, tel. 04.75.80.04.66, fax 04.75.80.06.50 ev. day 2pm–8pm

Saint-Péray

Situated on the opposite bank of the river from Valence, the vineyard of Saint-Péray, 62 ha (153 acres), is dominated by the ruined château of Crussol. Saint-Péray has a relatively cooler micro-climate and richer soils than elsewhere in the region, producing white wines (2,600 hl/ 68,640 gal in 2000) that are more acid, drier, and lower in alcohol, but ideal for making sparkling Blanc de Blancs by the Méthode Traditionelle, or champagne method. This, the main type of wine made under this appellation, is one of the best sparkling wines in France.

DOM. DARONA 1996★

€5-8 · 2.5 ha · 1,500

Here is a sparkling wine dominated by 93% Marsanne. The fine bubbles release an aroma of aniseed and liquorice. This wine has the natural maturation of a 96 but this has not affected the tidy balance and length.

● Dom. Darona, Les Faures, 07130 Saint-Péray, tél. 04.75.40.34.11, fax 04.75.81.05.70 ev. day except Sun. 8.30am–12.30pm 2pm–7.30pm

DOM. DE FAUTERIE 1999

1 ha | 5,000 | €5-8

This is a good aperitif wine. The aroma exudes camomile and verbena with a hint of toast and delicate peach.

♠ Sylvain Bernard, Dom. de Fauterie, 07130 Saint-Péray, tel. 04.75.81.06.60 ☑ ▼ by appt.

BERNARD GRIPA 1999★★

2 ha | 8,000 | €8-11

Had the bouquet been a little more expressive, this wine would certainly have won a *coup de cœur*. It is certainly packed with promise, but is still somewhat closed. The attack is delicate with acacia flowers and a touch of citrus (grapefruit), followed by a finish of lemon). This would be perfect with a fillet of red mullet.

♠ Bernard Gripa, 5, av. Ozier, 07300 Mauves, tel. 04.75.08.14.96, fax 04.75.07.06.81 ☑ ▼ by appt.

CAVE DE TAIN-L'HERMITAGE
Nobles Rives 1999★★

65 ha | n.c. | €5-8

This Noble Rives has a lovely clear transparent colour. With all the attributes of a true Saint-Péray, it would be tempting to drink it on the riverbank (*Rive*). Vigorous and fresh, but very well balanced, the delightful fragrance of acacia and citrus fruit continues from nose to palate. One taster recommends this wine with a *terrine* of wild rabbit.

♠ Cave de Tain-l'Hermitage, 22, rte de Larnage, BP 3, 26601 Tain-l'Hermitage Cedex, tel. 04.75.08.20.87, fax 04.75.07.15.16, e-mail commercial.france@ cave-tain-hermitage.co ☑ ▼ by appt.

JEAN-LOUIS ET FRANCOISE THIERS Brut★

4 ha | 21,000 | €5-8

The estate presents two wines this year, one sparkling, the other still, and both received a star. The first is a party wine, young and vital with notes of lemon. The nose opens with white flowers, conveying a flavour of spring-time to the palate. The second, the **white 99**, was produced from 50-year-old vines and made exclusively with Marsanne. The nose contains strong mineral notes combined with white peach, spices and citrus fruit. Try serving with warm oysters *au gratin* and white butter sauce.

♠ Jean-Louis Thiers, EARL du Biguet, 07130 Toulaud, tel. 04.75.40.49.44, fax 04.75.40.33.03 ☑ ▼ by appt.

DOM. DU TUNNEL 2000

0.8 ha | 3,962 | €5-8

The vines of this estate were planted around a tunnel of stone blocks, hence the name. Although the **Cuvée Prestige**, 30% matured in new casks, and this more traditional wine from the same year both won the same award, the latter seems more typical of its appellation. Very fresh and well-balanced, it is full of white peach and citrus fruit.

♠ Stéphane Robert, Dom. du Tunnel, 20, rue de la République, 07130 Saint-Péray, tel. 04.75.80.04.66, fax 04.75.80.06.50 ☑ ▼ ev. day 2pm–8pm

Gigondas

The famous Gigondas vineyard, at the foot of the breath-taking Dentelles de Montmirail mountains, covers a series of slopes and valleys within the commune of Gigondas itself. Wine-making here is a very ancient tradition, but its real development dates from the 14th century (the vineyards of le Colombier and les Bosquets), greatly assisted by Eugène Raspail. Gigondas was originally classed as a Côtes du Rhône, then in 1966 a Côtes du Rhône-Villages, until it finally obtained its 'letters patent' in 1971, when it became a specific appellation. It covers nearly 1,250 ha (3,088 acres).

Soil and climate combine to make Gigondas red wines, 44,316 hl (1,169,942 gal) in 2000, very rich in alcohol, powerful, well-structured and well-balanced, with fine aromas of liquorice, spices and stone fruits. The wines develop slowly in the bottle and can retain their qualities for many years, making a very suitable accompaniment to game dishes. Gigondas rosés are powerful and heady in character.

PIERRE AMADIEU
Romane-Machotte 1999

60 ha | 100,000 | €8-11

Even though this wine is blended from Mourvèdre, Syrah and a little Cinsault, it is dominated by Grenache. The aroma is a mixture of fruit and vegetable (fennel) and the flavour, initially full and supple, is nicely balanced. Good with small game.

♠ Pierre Amadieu, 84190 Gigondas, tel. 04.90.65.84.08, fax 04.90.65.82.14, e-mail pierre.amadieu@pierre-amadieu.com ☑ ▼ by appt. ♠ Jean-Pierre Amadieu

HENRI BOUACHON

Grande Tradition Gourmet 1998★

■ 45 ha 30,000 ⦀ 🍶 €8-11

The region has left its mark in this deep, slightly amber-coloured wine. The wild herbs of the garrigue are strong but subtle on the nose. A jammy black fruit flavour in a full-bodied, well-balanced palate finishes with the same herbal taste. The **red Cuvée Duc de Montfort 98** is every bit as successful, as the delicate oak bouquet lets through a hint of red fruit. The finish is superb.

👉 Caves Saint-Pierre, BP 5,
84230 Châteauneuf-du-Pape,
tel. 04.90.83.58.55, fax 04.90.83.77.23 Ⓥ
Ⓨ ev. day except Sun. 9am–12 noon 2pm–5pm

DOM. DE CASSAN 1999

■ 7.5 ha n.c. ⦀ 🍶 €8-11

This wine has a very unusual, faintly minty aroma, with touches of smoke and tobacco. Tightly-knit tannins provide an excellent structure. The wine is strong yet not austere; in fact it exudes a sense of power and individuality which requires a little time to express itself to the full.

👉 Dom. de Cassan,
SCIA Saint-Christophe, Lafare,
84190 Beaumes-de-Venise,
tel. 04.90.62.96.12, fax 04.90.65.05.47,
e-mail domainedecassan@wanadoo.fr Ⓥ
Ⓨ ev. day except Sun. 10am–12 noon 2pm–6pm
👉 Famille Croset

DOM. DU CAYRON 1999★

■ 16 ha 60,000 ⦀ €8-11

An aroma of cherry with a touch of musk is allied to a delicate hint of oak. Already nicely full, the flavour proves even more delicious, for it is supported by good-quality, tightly-knit and silky tannins. This is an attractive, elegant wine for laying down.

👉 EARL Michel Faraud, Dom. du Cayron,
84190 Gigondas, tel. 04.90.65.87.46,
fax 04.90.65.88.81 Ⓨ by appt.

CLOS DU JONCUAS 1999★

■ n.c. n.c. ⦀ €11-15

All the richness that derives from established vines marks the flavour of this warm, rounded wine. The ripe fruit aroma finishes on a note of kirsch. Here is a full, generous Gigondas that has not yet said its final word. Give it one or two years, but no more, as the alcohol may take over.

👉 Fernand Chastan, Clos du Joncuas,
84190 Gigondas, tel. 04.90.65.86.86,
fax 04.90.65.83.68 Ⓥ Ⓨ ev. day except Sat.
Sun. 8am–12 noon 2pm–5.30pm

DOM. DES ESPIERS

Cuvée Tradition 1999

■ 2.5 ha 11,000 ⦀ 🍶 €11-15

A bouquet of spices, liquorice and nutmeg ... and yet this wine still seems a little closed. Typical of its appellation, with a strong attack

and integrated tannins, it should move up the scale once it has matured some more.

👉 Philippe Cartoux, rte de Jaison,
84190 Vacqueyras, tel. 04.90.65.81.16,
fax 04.90.65.81.16 Ⓥ Ⓨ by appt.

DOM. DE FONTAVIN

Cuvée Les Terrasses 1999★

■ 2.5 ha 9,300 ⦀ 🍶 €8-11

This is the first outing for this estate with its blend of Grenache and Mourvèdre. The nose is rich in stone fruit, very ripe blackcurrant and leather, and the impression on the palate is full-bodied and powerful.

👉 EARL Hélène et Michel Chouvet,
Dom. de Fontavin, 1468, rte de la Plaine,
84350 Courthézon, tel. 04.90.70.72.14,
fax 04.90.70.79.39, e-mail helene-chouvet@fontavin.com Ⓨ ev. day except Sun. 9am–12.30pm 2pm–6.30pm; summer 9am–7pm

DOM. GIROUSSE 1999★

■ 1.36 ha 4,500 ⦀ €8-11

This very small estate, where the vines are planted on the slopes of the Trignon valley, shows once again that limited quantity may be synonymous with quality. Although the nose is still slightly dominated by the cask, it has attractive hints of smoke and liquorice. The flavour is round and full, built on elegant, nicely integrated tannins. This wine will very soon be exquisite.

👉 Girousse, Le Cours, 84410 Bédoin,
tel. 04.90.12.81.47, e-mail benoit.girousse@free.fr Ⓥ Ⓨ by appt.

DOM. DU GRAND BOURJASSOT

Cuvée Cécile 1998★

■ 2 ha 4,000 ⦀ €11-15

This wine delighted the tasters with its strong aroma of beautifully blended liquorice and ripe black fruit. Nicely balanced, it benefits from a good *terroir* and quality vinification. The **red Cuvée Goutte Noire 99** and the **rosé 2000** are also worth a star.

👉 Pierre Varenne, quartier Les Parties,
84190 Gigondas, tel. 04.90.65.88.80,
fax 04.90.65.89.38 Ⓥ Ⓨ ev. day except Sun.
10am–12 noon 2.30pm–6.30pm

DOM. DU GRAND MONTMIRAIL

Cuvée Vieilles vignes Vieilli en fût de chêne 1999★

■ 5 ha 20,000 ⦀ €8-11

With its dark colour and beautiful blend of overripe fruit and spices, this wine strikes a nice balance between body and tannins thanks to its time in cask. It needs another two or three years.

👉 Dom. du Grand-Montmirail, ferme du Grand-Montmirail, 84190 Gigondas,
tel. 04.90.65.00.22 Ⓥ Ⓨ by appt.

DOM. DU GRAPILLON D'OR 1999

■ 14 ha 55,000 ⦀ 🍶 €11-15

The almost black hue of this wine, with its deep aroma of ripe fruit, leather and tobacco, shows the maturity of the grape. The attack

LABASTIDE 1999★

■ 0.9 ha | ■ 6,000 | € 15-23

The initial impact of blackcurrant, liquorice and clove follows through on the palate with an unusual flavour of red fruit, bringing a fresh touch to this well-balanced, skilfully worked wine. It should reach its peak in five to eight years.

☛ Gabriel Liogier, 21420 Aloxe-Corton, tel. 03.80.26.44.25, fax 03.80.26.43.57

LA BASTIDE SAINT VINCENT
Costevieille 1999★★

■ 1 ha | ■ 4,000 | € 11-15

This wine is a fine example of good maturation. Although the nose retains its initial suggestion of oak, a lingering range of flavours follows: spices and, above all, black fruit (blackcurrant, mulberry and blueberry). The tasters found this wine silky, smooth, and remarkably rich and harmonious.

☛ Guy Daniel, La Bastide Saint-Vincent, 84190 Violès, tel. 04.90.70.94.13, fax 04.90.70.96.13, e-mail bastide.vincent@free.fr ᵞ ev. day 8.30am-12 noon 2.30pm-7pm; cl.1-15 Jan.

DOM. LA BOUISSIERE 1999★★

■ 5.1 ha | ■ 20,000 | € 8-11

DOMAINE LA BOUISSIÈRE
Gigondas
1999

The deep colour of this wine is equalled by the concentrated flavour. The nose is intense and complex with a blend of liquorice, blackcurrant and vanilla. The dense taste, too, impressed the Jury. It is obvious that considerable skill and care went into the manufacture of this Gigondas, which rivals the quality of the great wines of yesteryear. The **red Cuvée La Font de Tonin 99**, matured in barrel, is very successful and worth waiting for. The Jury made special mention of the **rosé 2000**.

☛ EARL Faravel, rue du Portail, 84190 Gigondas, tel. 04.90.65.87.91, fax 04.90.65.82.16 ᵞ by appt.

DOM. DE LA MAVETTE 1999

■ 6 ha | ■ 22,000 | € 8-11

Classical aromas of red fruit are accompanied by notes of rock-rose, thyme and bay leaf, finishing on a muskier note (especially leather). A full, joyous flavour too, silky and long-lasting. This wine is already good to drink with red meat.

☛ EARL Lambert et Fils, Dom. de La Mavette, 84190 Gigondas, tel. 04.90.65.85.29, fax 04.90.65.87.41, e-mail mavette@club-internet.fr ᵞ by appt.

DOM. DE LA TOURADE
Cuvée Morgan Fût de Chêne 1999★

■ 1.45 ha | ■ 6,800 | € 15-23

The nose of this wine bursts with overripe fruit, liquorice, honey and touches of toast and vanilla. The tannins are still rather prominent, but the full-bodied mellowness can already be tasted. A little patience …

☛ EARL André Richard, Dom. de La Tourade, 84190 Gigondas, tel. 04.90.70.91.09, fax 04.90.70.96.31 ᵞ ev. day 9am-7pm

LAURUS 1999★

■ 6.5 ha | ■ 25,000 | € 11-15

The Laurus range exemplifies the prestige wines of Gabriel Meffre. This Gigondas is rich, full, and well structured on velvety tannins. The flavour is long in red fruits (cherry) with truffle and undergrowth. The **red Domaine de La Daysse 99**, owned by Jack Meffre, is also well worth tasting.

☛ Gabriel Meffre, Le Village, 84190 Gigondas, tel. 04.90.12.30.22, fax 04.90.12.30.29, e-mail gabriel-meffre@meffre.com ᵞ by appt.

LES REINAGES 1999★★

■ n.c. | ■ 20,000 | € 11-15

This wine is a classic example of this appellation. An aroma of well-ripened morello and black cherries, oak and spice blend on the palate to create a well-structured, full-bodied wine balanced by excellent tannins.

☛ Delas Frères, ZA de l'Olivet, 07302 Tournon-sur-Rhône, tel. 04.75.08.60.30, fax 04.75.08.53.67, e-mail jacques-grange@delas.com ᵞ by appt.

L'OUSTAU FAUQUET
Cuvée Cigaloun 1999★★

■ 4 ha | ■ 15,000 | € 11-15

The subtle and elegant bouquet starts with a floral aroma, and follows through to a more intense and complex flavour with black fruit, hawthorn, spices and juniper. Quality does not always depend on age, and here the tannins are completely integrated in a rich, full-bodied palate. However, those with the patience to wait a few years will be well rewarded. Meantime, enjoy the **Cuvée Traditionnelle du Petit Montmirail 99** that was commended by the Jury.

Gigondas

DOM. NOTRE DAME DES PALLIERES Fût neuf 1999

■ 1 ha 2,700 ▥ €11-15

This wine was matured in barrel under controlled procedures for a year. The vanilla aroma of the cask is still prominent on nose and palate, although already the harmony can be appreciated. This is a wine that can be safely kept for a few years. On the other hand, the **rosé 2000** should be served now. It has a slightly sharp but subtle taste that comes from the Cinsault that was dominant in this blend.

🟐➤ Jean-Pierre et Claude Roux,
Dom.Notre-Dame des Pallières,
chem. Tuileries, 84190 Gigondas,
tel. 04.90.65.83.03, fax 04.90.65.83.03,
e-mail nd_pallieres@hotmail.com ▼
🍷 by appt.

🟐➤ Roger Combe et Filles,
Dom. La Fourmone, rte de Bollène,
84190 Vacqueyras, tel. 04.90.65.86.05,
fax 04.90.65.87.84 ▼ 🍷 ev. day 9.30am–
12 noon 2pm–6pm; cl. Feb.

MONTIRIUS 1999

■ 16 ha 30,000 ▥ €11-15

After a forthright but subtle attack, the flavour combines red fruit with a toasty, spicy note that carries through to the finish. Well-matured and robust, this wine has all the body and attributes of a ready-to-drink Gigondas.

🟐➤ Christine et Eric Saurel, SARL Montirius, Le Deves, 84260 Sarrians, tel. 04.90.65.38.28, fax 04.90.65.38.28, e-mail montirius@wanadoo.fr ▼
🍷 by appt.

CH. DE MONTMIRAIL Cuvée de Beauchamp 1999

■ 24 ha 100,000 ▥ €8-11

Take time to breathe in this aroma several times to appreciate the development: fruit, followed by kirsch, and then roasted notes. The tannins blend well with the supple texture and a finish that goes on and on ...

🟐➤ Archimbaud-Bouteiller, Ch. de Montmirail, cours Stassart, BP 12, 84190 Vacqueyras, tel. 04.90.65.86.72, fax 04.90.65.81.31,
e-mail chateau-montmirail@interlog.fr ▼
🍷 ev. day except Sun. 9am–12 noon 2pm–6.30pm

MOULIN DE LA GARDETTE Cuvée Ventabren 1998★

■ 2 ha 10,000 ▥ €15-23

Grapes ripened under a white-hot sun have left their mark on this Gigondas. The nose is full of prune and brandied fruit, then truffle and a musky scent of undergrowth. Subtle touches of vanilla, redolent of the cask, complement the full, strong-bodied flavour for a thoroughly well-balanced wine. The **red Cuvée Tradition 99** was given a mention. Sturdy and well-built, it will stand the test of time.

🟐➤ Jean-Baptiste Meunier, moulin de la Gardette, pl. de la Mairie, 84190 Gigondas, tel. 04.90.65.81.51, fax 04.90.65.86.80 ▼
🍷 by appt.

DOM. DE PIAUGIER 1999★

■ 3.4 ha n.c. ▥ €11-15

Although the nose is somewhat reticent, the fruit and spices are there in this wine. The texture is already warm and firm but needs two to five years for the touch of Mourvèdre to expand and make this wine a worthy example of its appellation.

🟐➤ Jean-Marc Autran, Dom. de Piaugier, 3, rte de Gigondas, 84110 Sablet, tel. 04.90.46.96.49, fax 04.90.46.99.48, e-mail piaugier@wanadoo.fr ▼ 🍷 by appt.

PRÉFÉRENCE BOSQUETS 1999★★

■ 2 ha 6,800 ▥ €23-30

The initial impact of ripe red fruit soon gives way to a fine mix of toast, undergrowth and mushroom to form a complex bouquet. The structure is well-balanced, full and skilfully built on tannins that are subtle yet potentially strong enough to ensure good development. The **red Domaine des Bosquets 99** was singled out for its blend of red fruit, violet and liquorice, and for its full-bodied texture.

🟐➤ Dom. des Bosquets, 84190 Gigondas, tel. 04.90.65.80.45, fax 04.90.65.80.45 ▼
🍷 by appt.

CH. RASPAIL 1999★★

■ 42 ha 20,000 ▥ €8-11

The nose is complex yet delicate, with intriguing charred, fruity and floral notes. The solid tannin structure is already integrated to provide a long, pure, harmonious flavour. However, this very characteristic wine is far from unveiling all its qualities. In five to eight years it will be superb.

🟐➤ Christian Meffre, Ch. Raspail, 84190 Gigondas, tel. 04.90.65.88.93, fax 04.90.65.88.96, e-mail château.raspail@wanadoo.fr ▼ 🍷 ev. day except Sat. Sun. 8am–12.30pm 1.30pm–5.30pm; cl. 15-31 Aug.

DOM. RASPAIL-AY 1998

■ 18 ha 50,000 ▥ €8-11

This wine is a classical blend of Grenache (80%), Syrah and Mourvèdre, exuding a strong, elegant aroma. The palate is already nicely rounded and the wine can be served straight away.

🍇 Dominique Ay, Dom. Raspail-Ay, 84190 Gigondas, tel. 04.90.65.83.01, fax 04.90.65.89.55 ▼ by appt.

■ CH. REDORTIER 1999
5 ha · 22,000 · €8-11

Full body and elegance need not be incompatible; the proof is this deep purple wine shot with violet and its heady aroma of the garrigue: wild herbs, juniper and thyme. There are enticing suggestions on the palate of chanterelle mushrooms, blood oranges and berries.

🍇 EARL Ch. Redortier, 84190 Suzette, tel. 04.90.62.96.43, fax 04.90.65.03.38 ▼
Υ by appt.
🍇 Etienne de Menthon

■ DOM. DU ROUCAS DE SAINT PIERRE Le coteau de mon père 1999★
1.3 ha · 6,000 · €8-11

A dark, intense garnet-red, the nose is a lovely blend of cocoa and overripe red fruits, toast, smoke and liquorice. The flavour is equally evocative, gaining strength without shedding its balance, and with a lingering chocolatey finish. Definitely a wine to put away.

🍇 Dom. du Roucas de Saint-Pierre, 84190 Gigondas, tel. 06.10.44.02.98 ▼
Υ by appt.
🍇 Yves Chéron

■ CH. DE SAINT COSME 1999★
15 ha · 60,000 · €8-11

This estate offered two wines and both were acclaimed. This Gigondas was singled out for its refined structure and pleasant flavour based on silky tannins. The **Cuvée Valbelle 98**, just as successful, needs to wait a while to show its full potential.

🍇 EARL Louis Barruol, Ch. de Saint-Cosme, 84190 Gigondas, tel. 04.90.65.80.80, fax 04.90.65.81.05 ▼ by appt.

■ DOM. SAINT-DAMIEN 1999
4 ha · 4,000 · €8-11

This blend of Grenache and Mourvèdre is characterised by its strong texture. Stewed fruit and leather fill the nose and the full-bodied palate is richly structured. The tannins need about five years to tone down.

🍇 SCEA Joël Saurel, Dom. Saint-Damien, 84190 Gigondas, tel. 04.90.70.96.42, fax 04.90.70.96.42 ▼ by appt.

■ DOM. SAINT-GAYAN Fontmaria 1999★★
1 ha · 2,000

This wine is spellbinding. An aroma such as this of overripe prune and fig is rare and unusually powerful, and the mellow flavour lingers wonderfully on the palate. Clearly the wine has been very skilfully matured. The **red Domaine Saint Gayan 99** is likewise

outstanding. Rich and well-balanced, it fills the mouth with liquorice and vanilla.

🍇 EARL Jean-Pierre et Martine Meffre, Dom. Gigondas, 84190 Gigondas, tel. 04.90.65.86.33, fax 04.90.65.85.10 ▼ Υ by appt.

■ ANDEOL SALAVERT Elevé en fût de chêne 1999
n.c. · 30,000 · €8-11

Unexpected notes of toasted almond and vanilla give this dark garnet wine a very fine aroma. Good maturation yields a delicate oak flavour, well-blended and long on the palate.

🍇 Caves Salavert, Les Mures, rte de Saint-Montan, 07700 Bourg-Saint-Andéol, tel. 04.75.54.77.22, fax 04.75.54.47.91, e-mail caves.salavert@wanadoo.fr
Υ by appt.

■ DOM. DU TERME 2000
0.5 ha · 3,000 · €8-11

The colour of this wine is bright red with dark reflections. The nose is pleasantly delicate and the impression on the palate is warm and long. This Gigondas can be served straight away.

🍇 Rolland Gaudin, Dom. du Terme, 84190 Gigondas, tel. 04.90.65.86.75, fax 04.90.65.80.29 ▼ Υ by appt.

■ DOM. DES TOURELLES 1999★
9 ha · 30,800 · €8-11

The nose, even now, has richness and power, but it will surely open up more with time. This wine, from 45-year-old vines, (mainly Grenache, with a little Syrah and a very small proportion of Mourvèdre and Cinsault) is some way from its peak, but the structure is already very impressive with a rich fleshy body wrapped around fine tannins.

🍇 Roger Cuilleral, SCEA Les Tourelles, le Village, 84190 Gigondas, tel. 04.90.65.86.98, fax 04.90.65.89.47, e-mail domaine-des-tourelles@wanadoo.fr
▼ by appt.

■ DOM. DES TROIS EVEQUES 1999★★
1 ha · 3,500 · €11-15

The aroma range of this wine is dominated by almonds and spices, but it will increase in complexity and eventually build up into a superb bouquet. The tannins are still prominent, but the texture is fleshy enough to create a beautifully integrated wine within three to five years.

🍇 Jérôme Evesque, Quartier Cabassole, 84190 Vacqueyras, tel. 04.90.65.80.58, fax 04.90.65.87.10 ▼ by appt.

■ DOM. VARENNE Vieux fût 1999★★
1 ha · 6,000 · €11-15

Does the best wine come from old casks? This 99 would seem to confirm the rule. A fabulous aroma of the southern French countryside, composed of morello cherries, cep mushrooms, undergrowth and vanilla. There is body and harmony right to the finish, loaded with cherry, raspberry and wild fruit.

Vacqueyras

The Appellation d'Origine Contrôlée Vacqueyras, made according to conditions of production defined in the decree of 9 August 1990, is the 13th and most recent of the local AOCs of the Côtes du Rhône.

It competes with Gigondas and Châteauneuf-du-Pape in the hierarchy of the Vaucluse department. Lying between Gigondas to the north and Beaumes-de-Venise to the south-east, the territory it covers stretches over the two communes of Vacqueyras and Sarrians. The 1,236 ha (3,053 acres) of vines produced 48,084 hl (1,269,418 gal) of wine in 2000, including 628 hl (16,579 gal) of white wine.

Twenty-three bottlers, a Cave Coopérative and three merchant growers sell 1.5 million bottles of Vacqueyras annually.

The red wines (95% of production), made mainly from Grenache, Syrah, Mourvèdre and Cinsault, are capable of ageing (three to ten years). The rosés (4% of production) are from the same varieties. The whites remain less well known (varieties: Clairette, Grenache Blanc, Bourboulenc, Rousanne).

LOUIS BERNARD 1999★★

n.c.　20,000　🍶　€5-8

The dark strong nose of stewed fruit, prune, morello cherry and jam makes an immediate impact. The cask flavour is still there but to excellent effect. The structure, although slightly astringent, is on a par with the rest. The tannins are integrated, and the flavour is fresh and beautifully rounded. It is sufficiently pleasurable to be drunk right now, but will be incomparably better after two or three years.

☞ Les Domaines Bernard, rte de Sérignan, 84100 Orange, tel. 04.90.11.86.86, fax 04.90.34.87.30, e-mail sagon@domaines-bernard.fr

DOM. CHAMFORT 1999★★

10 ha　40,000　🍶▮◖　€5-8

Smooth pebbles on clay-limestone soil, 30-year-old vines and skilful ageing have produced a very pleasant and palatable wine. The strong nose blends garrigue herbs, red fruit and spices. The wine is very characteristic and highly seductive. Velvety smooth tannins complete the excellent harmony.

☞ Denis Chamfort, La Pause, 84110 Sablet, tel. 04.90.46.94.75, fax 04.90.46.99.84, e-mail denis.chamfort@wanadoo.fr ☒
👁 by appt.

LA BASTIDE SAINT-VINCENT 1999★

▮　5 ha　24,000　▮◖　€5-8

Guy Daniel's family has owned this estate since the 18th century, and today this 21-ha (52-acre) vineyard belongs among those not to be missed by wine-lovers. This wine has a nose of morello and wild (kirsch) cherries, and a palate of fresh and dried fruits, predominantly red, which continue to the long finish.

1140

DOM. DES AMELERAIES

Fût de chêne 1999★

▮　5.2 ha　24,000　🍶▮◖　€5-8

This wine has a medal-winning aroma of ripe strawberry, liquorice and gingerbread, with touches of toast. Ageing in cask has left its mark. On the palate, subtle flavours of caramel and leather follow a fleshy attack that develops with a full, almost sensual impression. A few more years, and this wine will be at its peak.

☞ La Compagnie rhodanienne, chemin Neuf, 30210 Castillon-du-Gard, tel. 04.66.37.49.50, fax 04.66.37.49.51
👁 by appt.

Another wine well worth tasting is the remarkable **rosé 2000**: intense and beautifully balanced on the palate. The **red Cuvée Principale du Domaine 99** was singled out by the Jury.

☞ Dom. Varenne, Le village, 84190 Gigondas, tel. 04.90.65.86.55, fax 04.90.12.39.28 ☒ 👁 ev. day. 10am–12 noon 2pm–6pm; cl. Jan.

wine its characteristic flavour.
- Guy Daniel, La Bastide Saint-Vincent, 84150 Violès, tel. 04.90.70.94.13, fax 04.90.70.96.13, e-mail bastide.vincent@ free.fr ☑ Y ev. day 8.30am–12 noon 2.30pm–7pm; cl. 1–15 Jan.

DOM. DE LA CHARBONNIERE
1999★   4.33 ha 20,000   €11–15

Fantaisise a little and liken the experience of tasting this wine to a trip on a quiet river: upstream, a lovely intense impression of brandied fruit with hints of pepper, mellow and mouth-filling; downstream, the sense of confident, warm strength. No rapids to shoot, no bends to negotiate, nothing but blissful relaxation.
- Michel Maret, Dom. de la Charbonnière, 26, rte Courthézon, 84230 Châteauneuf-du-Pape, tel. 04.90.83.74.59, fax 04.90.83.53.46 ☑ Y by appt.

LA FONT DE PAPIER
1999★   n.c. n.c.   €8–11

These vines, cultivated by organic farming methods, have produced a delightful fresh, fruity wine, with a lovely intense flavour and pleasantly smooth tannins. It may not be one to last for decades, so drink it right now just for the sheer pleasure.
- Fernand Chastan, Clos du Joncuas, 84190 Gigondas, tel. 04.90.65.86.86, fax 04.90.65.83.68 ☑ Y ev. day except Sat. Sun. 8am–12 noon 2pm–5.30pm

DOM. LA FOURMONE
Trésor du Poète 1999★★   11 ha 20,000   €8–11

This is a very complete and fairly complex wine, like most produced by this estate, which is also a *coup de cœur* winner (see the Gigondas section). Subtle hints of nuts, spices and garrigue wild herbs, plus a tiny touch of mint, give an attractively original taste. The volume and strength of this wine are impressive. Full and rich, this poetical treasure inspires lyrics and will be remembered. Delightfully refreshing, it should be sampled right now. The **Cuvée des Ceps d'Or** 99, accomplished and beautifully refined, will satisfy even the most discerning palate.
- Roger Combe et Filles, Dom. La Fourmone, rte de Bollène, 84190 Vacqueyras, tel. 04.90.65.86.05, fax 04.90.65.87.84 ☑ Y ev. day 9.30am–12 noon 2pm–6pm; cl. Feb.

DOM. LA GARRIGUE
Cuvée de l'Hostellerie 1999★★   30.58 ha 12,000   €5–8

This typically Provençal 65-ha (160.5-acre) estate has been in the same family since 1850. Impressions of undergrowth, musk and leather are somehow evocative of the garrigue, from which the vineyard derives its name. The strong, rich flavour is finely structured, the tannins are well blended ... all the qualities are there to make this Vacqueyras a very fine wine that will improve considerably to reach its crowning glory in five to ten years.
- EARL A. Bernard et Fils, Dom. La Garrigue, 84190 Vacqueyras, tel. 04.90.65.84.60, fax 04.90.65.80.79 ☑ Y ev. day 8am–12 noon 2pm–7.30pm; Sun. by appt.

DOM. LE CLOS DE CAVEAU
Cuvée Prestige 1998★   2 ha 5,000   €8–11

This estate has applied organic techniques since 1989, and also accepts guests in its *gîte rural*. The wine presented here is strong and complex on the nose but also very traditional with its notes of blackcurrant and spices (liquorice). It is a harmonious Vacqueyras with a deep, dark colour, a solid structure and tightly knit tannins to give a lovely balance and long flavour on the palate. Its motto could be 'length and strength'.
- SCA Dom. Le Clos de Caveau, rte de Montmirail, chem. de Caveau, 84190 Vacqueyras, tel. 04.90.65.85.33, fax 04.90.65.83.17 ☑ Y by appt.

DOM. LE CLOS DES CAZAUX
Cuvée de Saint Roch 1999★   7 ha 30,000   €5–8

This wine won the *coup de cœur* in our first *Guide* in 1986, and the estate has built up its vineyards with painstaking patience over the years. It has often been a prize-winner, and this year again only missed by a hair. This 99 is a still a bit reticent, but undergrowth, mushrooms and liquorice are all there. The taste is pleasantly full and the tannin-alcohol balance is good. This is a high-quality wine worthy of its excellent *terroir*.

DOM. LA MONARDIERE
Cuvée Vieilles Vignes 1999★★   2.5 ha 9,500   €11–15

The name of this wine specifies its origins: 60-year-old vines for a *Vieilles Vignes*. The nose is delicate but fragrant, and the oak has left its mark with a beautiful balance and elegant texture. This is a wine made to last. The Mourvèdre (20%) has not yet unveiled all its treasures. In the meantime, therefore, sample the **Réserve des Deux Monardes** 99, whose balsamic aroma with hints of resin intrigued the tasters. The palate is agreeably supple.
- Dom. La Monardière, Les Grès, 84190 Vacqueyras, tel. 04.90.65.87.20, fax 04.90.65.82.01, e-mail monardiere@ wanadoo.fr ☑ Y ev. day except Sun. 10am–12 noon 2pm–7pm
- Christian Vache

DOM. DE L'OISELET 1999★

■ ❙ €8-11 ■ n.c. n.c.

This wine releases a beautifully mature bouquet of leather, ripe fruit, sweet spices and almonds. The attack is direct and the overall harmony compensates the slightly closed flavour on the palate. The tasters were convinced that within two to four years this wine will give excellent results.

➤ Vignobles du Peloux, quartier Barrade, RN 7, 84350 Courthézon,
tel. 04.90.70.42.00, fax 04.90.70.42.15 ☑
Ⴤ by appt.

DOM. L'OUSTAU DES LECQUES 1999★

Cuvée Bernardin
■ 2 ha 6,000 ■ ⬛ ♦ €5-8

Bernard Chabran took over the reins of the family estate in 1996. This Cuvée Bernardin is well crafted, with a straightforward impact and a good strong structure. Some tasters found it austere, others called it 'virile', but all were unanimous in describing it as highly promising. Wait another year or two.

➤ Dom. L'Oustau des Lecques, Les Lecques, 84190 Vacqueyras,
tel. 04.90.65.84.51, fax 04.90.65.81.19,
e-mail oustau.des.lecques@wanadoo.fr ☑
Ⴤ by appt.
➤ Bernard Chabran

CLOS MONTIRIUS 1999

■ 8.5 ha 30,000 ■ ⬛ ♦ €8-11

A total of 54 ha (133 acres) of organic farming for this estate, which was left fallow 11 years ago. Today it offers this wine with an intense aroma where red fruit and spices blend with touches of undergrowth. Although the palate is not yet wholly realised, the balance is improving, and the tannins, body and length will soon combine for an attractive wine to drink with grilled meat.

➤ Christine et Eric Saurel, SARL Montirius, Les Deves, 84260 Sarrians,
tel. 04.90.65.38.28, fax 04.90.65.38.28,
e-mail montirius@wanadoo.fr Ⴤ by appt

CH. DE MONTMIRAIL

Cuvée des deux Frères 1999★

■ 10 ha 40,000 ■ ♦ €8-11

Here is the perfect example of a successful marriage between *terroir* and grape variety. This wine is still very young and fruity with notes of herbs from the garrigue. Fresh, round and nicely balanced, it was judged a good specimen of its appellation. The Cuvée de l'Ermite 99, ready to drink now, was awarded a star.

➤ Archimbaud-Bouteiller,
Ch. de Montmirail, cours Stassart, BP 12, 84190 Vacqueyras, tel. 04.90.65.86.72,
fax 04.90.65.81.31,
e-mail chateau-montmirail@interlog.fr ☑
Ⴤ ev. day except Sun. 9am–12 noon 2pm–6.30pm

DOM. LE SANG DES CAILLOUX

Cuvée Doucinello 1999★★

■ 4 ha 12,000 ■ ⬛ ♦ €11-15

In the first *Guide* of 1986, this estate was awarded the initial *coup de cœur*, its entry benefiting from the wonderful *terroir* of smooth pebbles on clay-limestone. This year's wine continues the tradition of the great wines. The Jury enthused over the black fruit aroma blended with other appetising background scents. The tannins bring a high note to the palate in a wine that is all supple harmony, and there is cooked fruit in the finish. With its solid structure, this will be a splendid wine when mature.

➤ Dom. Le Sang des Cailloux, rte de Vacqueyras, 84260 Sarrians,
tel. 04.90.65.88.64, fax 04.90.65.88.75,
e-mail le-sang-des-cailloux@wanadoo.fr ☑
Ⴤ by appt.
➤ S. Férigoule

LES GRANDS CYPRES 1998

■ 25 ha 40,000 ■ ⬛ ♦ €5-8

The vines located at the foot of the Dentelles de Montmirail are surrounded by cypresses that have given their name to this subtle but characteristic Vacqueyras, which will soon open up. The flavour is fairly intense and quite harmonious. This is a round warm wine to grace a family dinner.

➤ Gabriel Meffre, Le Village, 84190 Gigondas, tel. 04.90.12.32.42,
fax 04.90.12.32.49

DOM. DE L'ESPIGOUETTE 1999★

■ 3.5 ha 7,000 ■ ⬛ ♦ €5-8

Cherry jam with cinnamon, vanilla-flavoured stewed fruit, and maybe a touch of liquorice: this is the initial impact. The palate, full and mellow, packed with ripe fruit, is delicious. This well-built Vacqueyras is refined but powerful, perfect with partridge or similar fowl.

➤ Bernard Latour, EARL Dom. de L'Espigouette, 84150 Violes,
tel. 04.90.70.95.48, fax 04.90.70.96.06 ☑
Ⴤ by appt.

GABRIEL LIOGIER Montpezat 1999★

■ 0.5 ha 2,000 ■ ♦ €15-23

Although this wine is a blend of four varieties, Grenache is undoubtedly predominant, with the traditional flavour of the Vacqueyras of former years. Quite strong in fruit, pleasantly supple on the palate, it still needs a little time to loosen up. Good served alongside duck with olives.

➤ Gabriel Liogier, 21420 Aloxe-Corton,
tel. 03.80.26.44.25, fax 03.80.26.43.57

DOM. LE CAILLOUX

➤ EARL Archimbaud-Vache, Dom. Le Clos des Cazaux, 84190 Vacqueyras,
tel. 04.90.65.85.83, fax 04.90.65.83.94 ☑
Ⴤ ev. day except Sat. Sun. 9am–11am 2pm–6pm
➤ Maurice Vache

Châteauneuf-du-Pape

This appellation, which was the first legally to define its conditions of production in 1931, covers nearly the whole commune from which it derives its name, together with similar *terroirs* in the neighbouring communes of Orange, Courthézon, Bédarrides and Sorgues, 3,084 ha (7,617 acres). The vineyard is located on the left bank of the Rhône, 15 km (9 miles) north of Avignon. The unique character of its wines comes from a *terroir* largely composed of vast terraces at different heights, covered with layers of pebbly red clay. The vine varieties are very varied with a predominance of Grenache, Syrah, Mourvèdre and Cinsault. The yield is not greater than 35 hl/ha (378 gal per acre).

The Châteauneuf-du-Pape wines are noted for their intense colour and good keeping qualities, although the time they can be kept varies with the vintage. They are expansive, well-structured, full-bodied wines with a strong, complex bouquet, excellent companions to red meat, game and fermented cheeses. The whites, produced in small quantities (7,266 hl/191,822 gal in 2000), counterbalance their strength with flavour and the finesse of their aromas. The appellation's total annual production was 110,380 hl (2,914,032 gal) in 2000.

ANCIEN DOMAINE DES PONTIFES Cuvée Elise 1999★
□ n.c. n.c. €11-15

This wine is notable for its exceptional finesse. Regular yeast stirring has given it a smooth texture, and hints of almonds and hazelnut are already showing through. Drink this in about three years' time with fish in a cream sauce.

Françoise Granier, 13, rue de l'Escatillon, 30150 Roquemaure, tel. 04.66.82.56.73, fax 04.66.90.23.90 Y by appt.

DOM. PAUL AUTARD Cuvée La Côte ronde 1999★
12 ha n.c. n.c. €20-38

Equal proportions of Grenache and Syrah have produced this powerful wine loaded with spicy red fruit. A lengthy 18 months in barrel has conferred a satisfactory length with a vanilla finish. If you are in the vicinity, make sure to visit the cellar of this estate, tucked away in the hillside.

Dom. Paul Autard, rte de Châteauneuf-du-Pape, 84350 Courthézon, tel. 04.90.70.73.15, fax 04.90.70.29.59, e-mail jean-paul.autard@wanadoo.fr ev. day except Sun. 9am-12.30pm 3pm-6.30pm

DOM. DE MONTVAC 1999
■ 10 ha n.c. n.c. €5-8

The nose is dominated by red fruit and undergrowth, and the surprise is the flavour, fresh and full, yet long and well balanced. Time should improve the harmony.

Cécile Dusserre, Dom. de Montvac, 84190 Vacqueyras, tel. 04.90.65.85.51, fax 04.90.65.82.38 Y ev. day except Sat. Sun. 9am–12 noon 2pm–6pm

OGIER-CAVES DES PAPES Les Truffiers 1999
■ n.c. 60,000 €5-8

The lovely flavour of this wine is for tasting right now. The nose culminates in a complex aroma of fruit, spices and musk. The fullness and length on the palate are likewise appealing. From grape to vinification, this wine is tradition to a T, and is it good!

Ogier-Caves des Papes, 10, bd Pasteur, 84230 Châteauneuf-du-Pape, tel. 04.90.39.32.32, fax 04.90.83.72.51, e-mail ogier.caves.des.papes@ogier.fr Y ev. day except Sat. Sun. 8am–5pm

DOM. DES TROIS EVEQUES 1999
■ 8 ha 10,000 €5-8

Surrounded by wooded hillsides, Vacqueyras is the essence of Provence. This 12-ha (30-acre) estate offers a wine unusual for its resinous nose and mineral finish. It is somewhat austere, and will benefit from a couple of years in the cellar.

Jérôme Evesque, Quartier Cabassole, 84190 Vacqueyras, tel. 04.90.65.80.58, fax 04.90.65.87.10 Y by appt.

DOM. DE VERQUIERE 2000
■ 2.5 ha 13,000 €5-8

A high proportion of Grenache (75%), the remainder Syrah and Cinsault, plus traditional vinification, have gone to produce this full, mouth-filling yet elegant wine: qualities associated with its youth. The red fruit flavour is still prominent, and the silky tannins promise a happy development.

Bernard Chamfort, 84110 Sablet, tel. 04.90.46.90.11, fax 04.90.46.99.69 V

Châteauneuf-du-Pape

CH. BEAUCHENE

Vignobles de La Serrière 1999★★

■ 4 ha ◆ 4,000 ▥ €11-15

Michel Bernard bought the estate in 1971, and this château now presents two excellent wines: a **red Domaine de La Serrière 99**, and this one with a slightly different name. The Jury liked them both equally. Nicely matured with just the right touch of cask, the colour is deep with a flavour of light vanilla on black fruit. Beautifully balanced and very characteristic, these wines are to be put away for five or six years, then served with jugged hare.

☞ Michel Bernard, ch. Beauchène, rte de Beauchène, 84420 Piolenc,
tel. 04.90.51.75.87, fax 04.90.51.73.36,
e-mail chateaubeauchene@worldonline.fr ▣
☖ ev. day except Sat. Sun. 8am–12 noon 1.30pm–5.30pm

DOM. DE BEAURENARD 1999★★★

■ 23.73 ha ◆ 80,000 ▥ €11-15

Even though this wine failed by one Jury vote to gain a *coup de cœur*, it is of exceptional quality. The rich bouquet, strong structure and harmonious palate are quite admirable. This is a wine to keep for a long time—five to ten years). The **Cuvée Boisrenard 99**, left in cask much longer, received a star. It is still tannic and strong, but will integrate well.

☞ SCEA Paul Coulon et Fils, Dom. de Beaurenard, av. Pierre-de-Luxembourg, 84231 Châteauneuf-du-Pape,
tel. 04.90.83.71.79, fax 04.90.83.78.06,
e-mail paul.coulon@beaurenard.fr ▣
☖ ev. day except Sun. 9am–12 noon 1.30pm–5.30pm; groups by appt.

DOM. BERTHET-RAYNE 1999★

□ n.c. ◆ 2,600 ▯ €8-11

Courthézon offers a view of wonderful 12th-century ramparts. After visiting the town, take the D 72 highway west of the A 7 motorway to find this estate, which offers its delightfully rich and complex wine, with an elegant floral aroma laced with mint. Long and nicely balanced, with a flavour of nuts and honey, this is a wine that you can confidently put away in the cellar without fear of disappointment. The **red Vieillie en Fût de Chêne 99** is an equally good choice. It was given a star for its lovely bouquet of ripe fruit blended with oak. Put it away for three to four years.

☞ Christian Berthet-Rayne, 2334, rte de Caderousse, 84350 Courthézon, tel. 04.90.70.74.14, fax 04.90.70.77.85 ▣
☖ ev. day 8am–7pm; Sat. Sun. by appt.

☞ Monique et Daniel Chaussy, quartier Boislauzon, 84100 Orange,
tl. 04.90.34.46.49, fax 04.90.34.46.61 ▣
☖ ev. day except Sun. 10am–12 noon 1pm–6pm; groups by appt.: cl. 15–30 Sept.

BOSQUET DES PAPES 1999

■ 2 ha ◆ 6,000 ▯▯ €15-23

The description 'Cuvée Grenache' on the neck label identifies this wine produced by an estate 300 m (327 yd) from the castle of Châteauneuf-du-Pape. It is a lovely clear red with a nose of red fruit. Nicely matured tannins and a full round palate guarantee rich potential within three or four years.

☞ Maurice Boiron, Dom. Bosquet des Papes, 18, rte d'Orange,
84230 Châteauneuf-du-Pape,
tel. 04.90.83.72.33, fax 04.90.83.50.52 ▣
☖ by appt.

LAURENT-CHARLES BROTTE

1998 ▯▯ 9 ha ◆ 40,000

This is a well-made wine, with a fresh and fruity bouquet. The attack is immediate and palate is delightfully elegant. The tannins need another five years to assimilate. The **red Clos Bimard 98** from the same *négociant* was singled out by the Jury, and it will be ready to drink in another two years. Also commended is the **red Gigondas 98**: jammy black fruit and hints of toasted pepper, against a background of wild herbs from the garrigue, give strong individuality to this wine, sturdily structured on solid tannins.

☞ Laurent-Charles Brotte, Le Clos, BP 1, 84231 Châteauneuf-du-Pape,
tel. 04.90.83.70.07, fax 04.90.83.74.34,
e-mail brotte@wanadoo.fr ▣ ☖ ev. day.
9.30am–12 noon 2pm–6pm

DOM. DU CAILLOU 1999

□ 6 ha ◆ n.c. ▯▯ €11-15

Among the attractions to visit in Courthézon is a 17th-century bell-tower. Both the wines from this estate were successful: the **red Cuvée Réserve 99**, matured in barrel for 16 months, and the *Cuvée Principale* with only a year in cask. The latter already reveals a well-matured structure, amber reflections in the colour, and a preponderance of brandied fruit. This wine shows all the hallmarks of traditional vinification. It can be put away for several years.

☞ Jean-Denis Vacheron, Clos du Caillou, 84350 Courthézon, tel. 04.90.70.73.05, fax 04.90.70.76.47 ▣ ☖ ev. day except Sun. 8.30am–12 noon 1.30pm–5.30pm

DOM. CHANTE CIGALE 2000★

□ 4.5 ha ◆ 21,000 ▯ €8-11

This estate was founded in 1930 by M. Favier's grandfather. The delightful name evokes the atmosphere of Provence as does the wine, which still has time, but is rich in honey, very ripe fruit and hawthorn.

1144

Full-bodied and long, this will be delightful to drink for five years.
♠ Dom. Chante-Cigale, av. Louis-Pasteur, BP 46, 84230 Châteauneuf-du-Pape,
tel. 04.90.83.70.57, fax 04.90.83.58.70 [V]
Y ev. day except Sun. 8am–6pm
♣ Favier

■ **DOM. CHANTE PERDRIX** 1999★   19 ha   60,000   €8-11

The estate, created in 1896, and just to the west of Châteauneuf on the D 17 highway, is run by father and son. The 6,500 bottles of this **2000 white** were awarded a star. It is a generous, vibrant wine that needs another two or three years to round off. This red wine has a summer freshness with its notes of cherry and strawberry. The Grenache features strongly on the spicy palate. Matured in the huge 1,000-l vat, this wine will please those allergic to the wooden cask and will sit patiently in a good cellar for two years.
♠ Guy et Frédéric Nicolet, Dom. Chante-Perdrix, BP 6, 84230 Châteauneuf-du-Pape,
tel. 04.90.83.71.86, fax 04.90.83.53.14,
e-mail chante-perdrix@wanadoo.fr [V]
Y ev. day except Sun. 9am–11.30am 3pm–7pm; cl. Sept.

■ **CLOS SAINT-MICHEL** Cuvée réservée 1998★★   4 ha   15,000   €15-23

Three nice wines were presented this year by this 30-ha (84-acre) estate. This, the first, is seductively dark, almost black; the nose deep, with ripe fruit, chocolate and touches of vanilla; the palate full, based on good solid tannins, and the oak flavour harmonious. This is a superb, characteristic wine that can be put away happily for five years. The estate's principal offering, the **red Clos Saint-Michel 99** is not as strong, but is very pleasant. It was awarded a star, as was the **white Clos Saint-Michel 99**, as floral as could be wished, ready for an aperitif.
♠ EARL Vignobles Guy Mousset et Fils, Le Clos Saint-Michel, rte de Châteauneuf, 84700 Sorgues, tel. 04.90.83.56.05, fax 04.90.83.56.06 [V]
Y ev. day 9am–6pm

■ **DOM. DE CRISTIA** 1999★   10 ha   20,000   €8-11

Here is a well-made wine, perfectly matured. It is great now – so why wait? Make the most of the red fruit bouquet and its well-balanced structure. Try it with wood-smoked breast of duck.
♠ Alain Grangeon, 33, fbg Saint-Georges, 84350 Courthézon, tel. 04.90.70.89.15, fax 04.90.70.77.43,
e-mail grangeonbaptiste@hotmail.com [V]
Y by appt.

■ **DIFFONTY** Cuvée du Vatican 1999   20 ha   57,000   €11-15

This wine was left 18 months in a huge oak vat using traditional methods that have given it a taste of brandied fruit. Here is the wine for lovers of old-style Châteauneuf. Keep it at least five years in the cellar before serving it with well-marinated game.
♠ SCEA Félicien Diffonty et Fils, 10, rte de Courthézon, BP 33, 84231 Châteauneuf-du-Pape Cedex,
tel. 04.90.83.70.51, fax 04.90.83.50.36,
e-mail cuvée-du-vatican@mnet.fr [V]
Y by appt.

■ **DOM. DURIEU** 1999   20 ha   n.c.   €11-15

This is a 99 for those who appreciate a strong oak flavour, and who have a decent cellar to put it away. It will take at least three to five years for these tannins to make their mark. The musky flavour and fleshy texture make it a delicious wine to drink with jugged hare.
♠ Paul Durieu, 10, av. Baron-le-Roy, 84231 Châteauneuf-du-Pape,
tel. 04.90.37.28.14, fax 04.90.37.76.05 [V]
Y by appt.

□ **CH. DES FINES ROCHES** 2000   4.5 ha   21,000   €11-15

The present owner's grandfather bought the marvellous medieval-style château depicted on the label. Here is a pleasantly successful wine, ideal for an aperitif, or with goat's cheese. The bouquet is floral, but not too strong, and the nicely balanced flavour contains kiwi and citrus fruits. This is a good wine to drink immediately without thinking twice.
♠ SCEA des Ch. des Fines Roches et du Bois de La Garde, 1, av. du Baron-Leroy, 84230 Châteauneuf-du-Pape,
tel. 04.90.83.51.73, fax 04.90.83.52.77,
e-mail scea.chateau.des.fines.roches@libertysur [V]
Y ev. day except Sun. 9am–7pm; cl. Jan. Feb.
♣ Robert Barrot

■ **CH. FORTIA** 1998   22 ha   80,000   €11-15

Before the Second World War, Baron le Roy was one of the great architects of the *appellation d'origine*, and in 1935 created what is now the *Institut National des Appellations d'Origine*. Today this estate offers a delightfully fresh, juicy wine full of red fruits, predominantly cherry, on the palate. Taste it while still young, but keep it if need be in a good cellar. It goes well with grilled meat (especially rib of beef).
♠ Bruno Le Roy, SARL Ch. Fortia, BP 13, 84231 Châteauneuf-du-Pape Cedex,
tel. 04.90.83.72.25, fax 04.90.83.51.03 [V]
Y by appt.

■ **DOM. DU GALET DES PAPES** Tradition 1999★   9 ha   20,000   €11-15

This estate was founded in the reign of Napoleon III, and is broken up into a variety of *terroirs*. This blend has produced a *Cuvée Tradition* with an attractive terracotta colour and a bouquet of prune and spices. The

Châteauneuf-du-Pape

tannins are silky on the palate. It can be tasted now and drunk for three to five years.

➤ Jean-Luc Mayard, Dom. Galet des Papes, 15, rte de Bédarrides,
84230 Châteauneuf-du-Pape,
tel. 04.90.83.73.67, fax 04.90.83.50.22,
e-mail galet.des.papes@terre-net.fr ☑
🍷 ev. day except Sun. 9am–12 noon 2.30pm–6.30pm

DOM. DU GRAND TINEL 1999★★

☐　　2 ha　9,000　　▥ 🍷 €11–15

Careful fermentation has given this wine remarkable quality. The nose is rich in flowers and nuts and the flavour is exceptionally long with a subtle balance between acidity and mellowness. The wine will be ready in about four to five years.

➤ Les Vignobles Elie Jeune, rte de Bédarrides, 84230 Châteauneuf-du-Pape, tel. 04.90.83.70.28, fax 04.90.83.78.07, e-mail eliejeun@terre-net.fr 🍷 ev. day 9am–12 noon 2pm–6pm; Sat. Sun. by appt.; cl. Aug.

DOM. GRAND VENEUR

La Fontaine 2000★

40 ha　n.c.　　▥ 🍷 €15–23

Orange, with its ancient theatre for music and opera, celebrated the centenary of the death of Verdi in 2001. The town is only about 10 km (6.2 miles) from Châteauneuf-du-Pape. Music and wine often go hand in hand, and this selection has all it takes to satisfy a discerning palate. The Roussanne is strongly dominant, with a bouquet of white flowers and honey. The balance between fruit and vanilla-flavoured oak is very successful. A wine to serve for four or five years.

➤ Alain Jaume, Dom. Grand Veneur, rte de Châteauneuf-du-Pape, 84100 Orange, tel. 04.90.34.68.70, fax 04.90.34.43.71, e-mail jaume@domaine-grand-veneur.com ☑ 🍷 by appt.

LA BASTIDE-SAINT-DOMINIQUE 2000★

☐　　1.8 ha　5,000　　▥ 🍷 €11–15

A beautifully balanced trio of white Grenache, Clairet and Roussanne has produced this pleasant, supple wine. The nose is rich in citrus fruits and white flowers. Drink it with a warm goats' cheese salad.

➤ Gérard Bonnet, La Bastide-Saint-Dominique, 84350 Courthézon, tel. 04.90.70.85.32, fax 04.90.70.76.64, e-mail contact@bastide-st-dominique.com ☑ 🍷 ev. day. 9am–12 noon 1.30pm–6.30pm; Sun. by appt.

LA BELLE DU ROY 1999★

☐　　n.c.　15,000　　▥ €8–11

This is a good *négociant* wine universally applauded for its quality and price. The nose is floral with acacia and wisteria, and touches of honey and beeswax. Lovely ripe fruit appears on the palate. This cherishable wine can be kept for four years.

➤ Caves Salavert, Les Mures, rte de Saint-Montan, 07700 Bourg-Saint-Andéol, tel. 04.75.54.77.22, fax 04.75.54.47.91, e-mail caves.salavert@wanadoo.fr

DOM. LA BOUTINIERE 1999★

■　　n.c.　10,000　　▥ €11–15

This 9.5-ha (23.5-acre) estate has been in the family since 1920. Its wine is light and elegant. Don't shake it, treat it gently and discover its fresh musky flavour with touches of spice and mint. Take care to serve it with a dish that will not submerge its delicate flavour.

➤ Gilbert Boutin, Dom. La Boutinière, 17, rte de Bédarrides, 84230 Châteauneuf-du-Pape, tel. 04.90.83.75.78, fax 04.90.83.76.29 ☑ 🍷 by appt.

DOM. DE LA CHARBONNIERE

Cuvée Vieilles vignes 1999★★

■　　1.3 ha　6,000　　€15–23

The vines of this estate are ideally situated on a plain of smooth pebbles. The **white 2000** (given one star) is a lovely luminous colour with an interesting aroma of citrus fruit, honey and vanilla, and is full and nicely balanced on the palate. Better still is this dark, rich red wine, with its powerful bouquet loaded with ripe fruit. Full-bodied and complex, it has a solid, promising tannic structure: one to put away for five to eight years, and to serve with game.

➤ Michel Maret, Dom. de La Charbonnière, 26, rte Courthézon, 84230 Châteauneuf-du-Pape, tel. 04.90.83.74.59, fax 04.90.83.53.46 ☑ 🍷 by appt.

DOM. DE LA COTE DE L'ANGE

Cuvée Vieilles vignes 1999★★

■　　0.6 ha　2,000　　▥ €15–23

The label of this excellent Vieilles Vignes shows a chapel encircled by vines and an angel holding a chalice … or perhaps a wine glass? This wine was matured for a year in oak casks. Musky, its tannins are still a little on the wild side, but five to eight years should tame them nicely. It would be perfect with game.

➤ Jean-Claude Mestre et Yannick Gasparri, La-Font-du-Pape, BP 79, 84230 Châteauneuf-du-Pape, tel. 04.90.83.72.24, fax 04.90.83.54.88 ☑ 🍷 ev. day 9am–12 noon 2pm–7pm

LA CRAU DE MA MERE 1999

■　　8 ha　35,000　　▥ ▥ 🍷 €11–15

This wine has a good, solid, almost rustic structure of tannins. The nose is full of blackcurrant and brandied cherry. It can be put away for a good three to four years, and that is not long for a plot that is 100 years old.

➤ Dom. du Père Pape, 24, av. Baron-le-Roy, 84230 Châteauneuf-du-Pape, tel. 04.90.83.70.16, fax 04.90.83.50.47 ☑ 🍷 by appt.

➤ Mayard

DOM. LA DESTINEE 1998

1 ha ▮ 3,000 ⫴ €11-15

This estate, bought in 1997, boasts 50-year-old vines. The second vinification produced a complex, classy wine with a vibrant appeal, packed with the scent of wild garrigue herbs, red fruit and touches of mint. This is already delightful to drink, but if necessary can be kept two or three years.

☛ Pierre Folliet, Ch. de La Gironde, 84100 Orange, tel. 04.90.11.06.85, fax 04.90.11.06.85 ▼ by appt.

DOM. DE LA FONT DU ROI 1999★

16 ha ▮ 65,000 ⫴ €11-15

Here is a wine with 60% Grenache, 15% each of Syrah and Cinsault, and 10% of Muscardin – a variety found only in Châteauneuf, and included in Pierre Galet's *Dictionnaire encyclopédique des cépages*. This wine for laying down can be put away for a long time. The tannins can already be tasted, but are so good that they require four to five years to integrate, when the flavour of black fruit, spice and undergrowth will be at its best.

☛ EARL Cyril et Jacques Mousset, Ch. des Fines-Roches, 84230 Châteauneuf-du-Pape, tel. 04.90.83.73.10, fax 04.90.83.50.78, e-mail domaines-mousset@enprovence.com ▼ ev. day 10am–7pm; cl. Jan. Feb

CH. DE LA GARDINE 1999★★

48 ha ▮ 200,000 ⫴ €15-23

The origin of this marvellously rich, full wine for laying down is a stony plain typical of the AOC *terroir*. For now it keeps its light under a bushel, but the tannin potential is simply magnificent. In four years' time and then for another ten, this wine will be superb with game. Ask the owner of the estate for one of his recipes. If you are as good a chef as he is, you will not be disappointed.

☛ Brunel, Ch. de La Gardine, rte de Roquemaure, BP 35, 84230 Châteauneuf-du-Pape, tel. 04.90.83.73.20, fax 04.90.83.77.24, e-mail chateau@gardine.com ▼ ev. day except Sat. Sun. 8.30am–12 noon 1pm–6pm

CH. DE LA GARDINE 2000★

□ 5 ha ▮ 17,000 ⫴

This wine takes us through an authentic initiation course from the sweet flavours (syrupy honey) right through to beeswax: everything, indeed, apart from the actual buzzing of the bees – one can even detect the wooden hive. No need to squirrel this one away, drink it now with fish in sauce.

☛ Brunel, Ch. de La Gardine, rte de Roquemaure, BP 35, 84230 Châteauneuf-du-Pape, tel. 04.90.83.73.20, fax 04.90.83.77.24, e-mail chateau@gardine.com ▼ ev. day except Sat. Sun. 8.30am–12 noon 1pm–6pm

CUVÉE DE LA REINE DES BOIS
Domaine de la Mordorée
1999
CHÂTEAUNEUF-DU-PAPE
RED RHONE WINE

DOM. DE LA MORDOREE

Cuvée de la Reine des Bois 1999★★★

■ 3.5 ha ▮ 14,000 ⫴ €23-30

One of the most famous AOC estates wins yet another *coup de coeur*. This time it is their Reine des Bois which receives the crown. A glorious violet, purple colour, a bouquet of morello cherry and ripe fruit, this wine is superb. A wonderful attack on the nose is followed by a full, round flavour with a powerful finish. The oak is delicate and well-integrated. The length of the aroma is exceptional. This is a wine that will need to wait another five to eight years before serving with wild boar or a similarly strong meat.

DOM. DE LA JANASSE 1999★

5 ha ▮ 12,000 ⫴ €15-23

Christophe Sabon joined his father on this lovely estate in 1991. For 45 years grapes have been grown here on smooth, pebbled soil. Matured in cask (20%) and large barrels (80%), this wine is well-built with nice fleshy tannins, combined with red berries and spices. The length is incredible (seven *caudalies*). This is a wine to drink immediately with fruit, but it can wait another five years to develop a much more complex flavour. Also note the **Chaupin** and the **red Vieilles Vignes 99** from the same estate.

☛ EARL Aimé Sabon, 27, chem. du Moulin, 84350 Courthézon, tel. 04.90.70.86.29, fax 04.90.70.75.93 ▼ ev. day. 8am–12 noon 2pm–7pm; Sun. by appt.

DOM. DE LA JANASSE

Prestige 1999★★

□ 0.5 ha ▮ 1,000 ⫴ €30-38

Fourteen months in barrel gave this wine its delicate structure. The aroma is intense and floral, followed by hints of toasted wood. The overall harmony is heavenly. Unfortunately the estate produced only 1,000 bottles of this nectar. It can be put away for five or six years. Serve with *poularde de Bresse*.

☛ EARL Aimé Sabon, 27, chem. du Moulin, 84350 Courthézon, tel. 04.90.70.86.29, fax 04.90.70.75.93 ▼ ev. day 8am–12 noon 2pm–7pm; Sat. Sun. by appt.

Châteauneuf-du-Pape

● Dom. de La Mordorée, chem. des Oliviers, 30126 Tavel, tel. 04.66.50.00.75, fax 04.66.50.47.39 ☑ ☒ ev. day.8am–12 noon 2pm–5.30pm
● Delorme

CH. LA NERTHE 2000★★

☐ 6 ha 28,000 €15-23

Château La Nerthe
Châteauneuf-du-Pape

Many tourists will know of this handsome château, and there is additional pleasure in the discovery of this remarkable wine blended with such exceptional care. The blend is partly fermented in cask, and 30% is matured in oak as well. Alain Dugas and Philippe Capelier have produced very finely-integrated oak tannins capable of maintaining this wine for years, as it was bottled seven months after harvesting. Here is a prestige vintage to be served with the most delicate fish dishes.
● SCA Ch. La Nerthe, rte de Sorgues, 84230 Châteauneuf-du-Pape,
tel. 04.90.83.70.11, fax 04.90.83.79.69,
e-mail la.nerthe@wanadoo.fr ☑
☒ ev. day. 9am–12 noon 2pm–6pm
● Pierre Richard

CH. LA NERTHE
Cuvée des Cadettes 1998★★

■ 3 ha 11,000 €30-38

This Cadettes constitutes La Nerthe's prime offering for 98. Its originality lies in the very high proportion of Mourvèdre (37%) that sustains the structure. A direct but sweet attack, a splendid flavour and incredible length. Although the new oak is well blended, this is still a great wine to keep for at least five years.
● SCA Ch. La Nerthe, rte de Sorgues, 84230 Châteauneuf-du-Pape,
tel. 04.90.83.70.11, fax 04.90.83.79.69,
e-mail la.nerthe@wanadoo.fr ☑
☒ ev. day. 9am–12 noon 2pm–6pm

DOM. DE LA SOLITUDE 1999★

■ 30 ha 100,000 €15-15

This very deep red wine has an intense nose of fruit with hints of violet. The flavour is mouth-filling with prominent tannins, and the nice long finish is fruity, topped with a touch of vanilla. The wine can wait two or three years, and will be good with red meat served in sauce.

● SCEA Dom. Pierre Lançon, Dom. de La Solitude, BP 21,
84230 Châteauneuf-du-Pape,
tel. 04.90.83.71.45, fax 04.90.83.51.34 ☑
☒ ev. day 8am–6pm

LA TIARE DU PAPE 1998★

■ 20 ha 30,000 ▥ ♦ €15-23

Here is a good *négociant* wine that should be earmarked for putting away in a good cellar: it has very strong potential but is unlikely to reach its peak for another four or five years. The deep colour is shot with violet highlights, and the bouquet has touches of musk and spice. The structure is solid, with promise for the future. Put it aside for serving with a tasty dish of red meat or game.
● Henry Bouachon, BP 5,
84230 Châteauneuf-du-Pape,
tel. 04.90.83.58.35, fax 04.90.83.77.23 ☑
☒ by appt.

DOM. DE LA VIEILLE JULIENNE
Réservé 1999★

■ 2.1 ha 6,600 ▥ €23-30

This 32-ha (79-acre) estate has produced a wine for those prepared to wait four or five years until the tannins soften. This 99 has a very good alcohol–acidity balance, the oak is not too prominent, and the liquorice on the finish is promising. It would be a good accompaniment to woodcock with a side dish of *julienne* vegetables.
● EARL Daumen Père et Fils, 84100 Orange, Vieille Julienne, Le Grès, 84100 Orange,
tel. 04.90.34.20.10, fax 04.90.34.10.20,
e-mail jpdaumen@club-internet.fr ☑
☒ by appt.

DOM. LOU FREJAU 1999★

☐ 1 ha 1,600 €11-15

The name of this estate in *patois* means 'smooth pebbles', and the reason is easy to understand. This is more than simply a good, honest wine. The nose is delicate, with notes of nut, and the palate is full and nicely balanced. The wine can be kept three to five years.
● SCEA Dom. Lou Fréjau, chem. de la Gironde, 84100 Orange, tel. 04.90.34.83.00,
fax 04.90.34.48.78
● Serge Chastan

MARQUIS ANSELME MATHIEU
Vignes centenaires 1998

■ 2.5 ha 11,500 ▥ €15-23

This wine has had the advantage of 18 months in cask. Strongly influenced by the Grenache, the flavour is strong in musk and other spices, following through to brandied fruit. The tannins are assimilated but still perceptible. Keep the wine two to three years.
● Dom. Mathieu, rte de Courthézon, 84230 Châteauneuf-du-Pape,
tel. 04.90.83.72.09, fax 04.90.83.50.55,
e-mail dnemathieu@aol.com ☑ ☒ ev. day. 9am–12 noon 2pm–6pm; Sat. Sun. by appt.; cl. 1–10 Dec.

GABRIEL MEFFRE

Cuvée du Concordat 1999★

▪   4.5 ha   20,000   ▪ ▯ €11-15

The Cuvée du Concordat from the Meffre winery has a straightforward attack and well-measured tannins. Nose and palate breathe fruit (prunes) and spices (pepper and coriander). A nicely balanced wine, this can wait another five years at least, and be served with roast meats.

☛ Gabriel Meffre, Le Village, 84190 Gigondas, tel. 04.90.12.32.42, fax 04.90.12.32.49

MOILLARD 1999★

▪   n.c.   10,000   ▪ ▯ €15-23

Visit this *négociant* and you will not be in Châteauneuf, but in Nuits-Saint-Georges. In fact, since the 19th century, the Burgundy wineries who controlled the bottling industry bought the wine and sold bottles of Châteauneuf. This is full, fruity, with touches of liquorice and spices, and is built on elegant tannins with excellent potential. Lovely, for example, with a side of lamb.

☛ Moillard, 2, rue François-Mignotte, 21700 Nuits-Saint-Georges, tel. 03.80.62.42.22, fax 03.80.61.28.13, e-mail nuicave@wanadoo.fr ▼
🍷 ev. day 10am–6pm; cl. Jan.

CH. MONGIN 1999

▪   2 ha   9,000   ▪ ▯ €11-15

All agricultural colleges that specialise in wine-making must have a good vineyard in order to put theory into practice. The college in Orange boasts vineyards of a very respectable age. This deep-coloured wine shadowed with violet has an intense gamey nose. The attack is fruity, and carries on to the finish. Drink it, for example, with red meat served in sauce.

☛ Lycée viticole d'Orange, Ch. Mongin, 2260, rte du Gres, 84100 Orange, tel. 04.90.51.48.04, fax 04.90.51.11.92 ▼
🍷 by appt

CH. MONT-REDON 1999

▪   84 ha   360,000   ▪ ▯ €15-23

Anselme Mathieu, the Provençal poet, was among the many owners of this very old wine estate, whose history can be traced back six centuries. This 99 has well-crafted oak to support the solid structure. Its gamey scent requires some time to breathe. The palate of red fruit is very pleasant. It should be drunk within two or three years, after decanting.

☛ Famille Abeille-Fabre, Ch. Mont-Redon, BP 10, 84230 Châteauneuf-du-Pape, tel. 04.90.83.72.75, fax 04.90.83.77.20, email chateaumontredon@wanadoo.fr ▼
🍷 by appt.

DOM. MOULIN-TACUSSEL 1999★★

▪   8.5 ha   15,000   ▪ ▯ ▮ €11-15

One of the founder's granddaughters has run this estate since 1976. Here she offers a well-made wine built on imposing tannins. The oak resulting from cask maturation is

well-integrated. This wine will develop and open up its spicy mint flavour in time. It will keep well, and should be left in the cellar for three or four years.

☛ Dom. Moulin-Tacussel, 10, av. des Bosquets, 84230 Châteauneuf-du-Pape, tel. 04.90.83.70.09, fax 04.90.83.50.92 ▼
🍷 by appt.

DOM. DE NALYS 2000★★

▫   10 ha   40,000   ▪ ▯ €11-15

Created in the 18th century, the Nalys estate covers 51 ha (126 acres), and has belonged to Groupama since 1976. It is noted for its constant remarkable quality over the years, and for its prices, which have remained reasonable. The white flower bouquet of this 2000 is designed to stimulate the tastebuds, and the palate is full and rounded by virtue of the dominant Grenache. The wine can be appreciated straight away with shellfish or fish, such as grilled bream. The **red Nalys 99** was commended by the Jury. Well-balanced, it combines black fruit, spices and charred elements.

☛ Dom. de Nalys, rte de Courthézon, 84230 Châteauneuf-du-Pape, tel. 04.90.83.72.52, fax 04.90.83.51.15 ▼
🍷 ev. day except Sun. 8am–12 noon 1.30pm–6pm; Sat by appt.
🍷 Groupama

DOM. DE PANISSE 1999★

▪   6 ha   8,000   ▪ ▯ €11-15

Maître d'hôtel to Louis XII in 1498, Dominique de Panisse probably did not come here often. Jean-Marie Olivier has run this 18-ha (44.5-acre) estate since 1992. His wine is deep and dark, with plenty of tears, but in no way associated with tragedy. The nose is full of black fruit and mulberry syrup. The sound balance between tannins and alcohol in this harmonious 99 promises excellent potential for keeping three to five years.

☛ Jean-Marie Olivier, Dom. de Panisse, 161, chem. de Panisse, 84350 Courthézon, tel. 04.90.70.78.93, fax 04.90.70.81.83, e-mail panisse@viticulture.net ▼ 🍷 ev. day except Sun. 9am–12 noon 1.15pm–6pm

---

DOM. DES RELAGNES

La Cuvée vigneronne 1999★

▪   2 ha   6,400   ▪ ▯ €15-23

Here is a fine Cuvée Vigneronne. The harvested grapes are not de-stemmed and are kept in casks on yeast lees. The dominant effect is of red fruit with liquorice, and the tannins are prominent but well-harmonised. Drink this over the next five years.

☛ SCEA Dom. des Relagnes, rte de Bédarrides, 84230 Châteauneuf-du-Pape, tel. 04.90.83.73.37, fax 04.90.83.52.16 ▼
🍷 by appt.
🍷 Henri Boiron

Châteauneuf-du-Pape

DOM. SAINT-BENOIT
Soleil et Festins 1999★

■　　　4 ha　　19,000　　€15-23

Here is an estate that, thanks to its export turnover, operates a *négociant* business as well. Two Châteauneuf wines, the one on offer here, and the **Truffière 98**, received the same marks from the Jury. With little to choose between them, buy both and keep for at least five years.

☛ Marc Cellier, EARL Saint-Benoît, rte de Sorgues, BP 72, 84232 Châteauneuf-du-Pape Cedex, tel. 04.90.83.51.36,
fax 04.90.83.51.37 ▽ ▼ by appt

DOM. SAINT-LAURENT 1999★

　　　3 ha　　n.c.　　■ ▥ ♦ €11-15

François Sinard established this estate at the end of the 19th century and supplied the archbishop with wine for Mass. This year's 99 red is delicate in colour, and the aroma of black fruit is matched in the light, airy palate with its long finish. It can be served immediately with small game.

☛ Robert-Henri Sinard,
1375, chem. Saint-Laurent, 84350 Courthézon, tel. 04.90.70.87.92, fax 04.90.70.78.49,
e-mail sinard@domaine.saint-laurent.com
▽ ▼ by appt.

DOM. DES SENECHAUX 2000★★

□　　　3 ha　14,000　■ ▥ ♦ €11-15

Here is an elegant wine with a delicately refined nose that evokes white flowers. The palate is rich and full, with a flavour of very ripe grape. This Châteauneuf would be perfect with scallops at the start of a celebration dinner, served now or in four years' time.

☛ Pascal Roux, Dom. des Sénéchaux,
3, rue la Nouvelle-Poste,
84231 Châteauneuf-du-Pape,
tel. 04.90.83.73.52, fax 04.90.83.52.88 ▽
▼ ev. day except Sun. 8.30am–12.30pm
1.30pm–7pm; groups by appt.

CH. SIMIAN 1999★★

■　　　3.35 ha 15,000 ■ ▥ ♦ €11-15

Château Simian still matures its production in huge oak casks for eight months. This gives an intense bouquet of brandied fruit that lingers on the palate. Solidly structured, full-bodied and rich, it can be served with jugged hare or wild boar. It can also be put away for four or five years.

☛ Jean-Pierre Serguier, Ch. Simian,
84420 Piolenc, tel. 04.90.29.50.67,
fax 04.90.29.62.33, e-mail chateau-simian@wanadoo.fr ▽ ▼ ev. day 9am–7.30pm

DOM. PIERRE USSEGLIO ET FILS 1999★★

■　　15 ha　50,000　■ ▥ €11-15

This estate is renowned for the skilful blending of remarkable wines for putting away. The initial impact on the nose of this wine is fruity, tending towards a jammy aroma. The palate is rich and fleshy, with tannins at the finish, but these will smooth with time. It is a good solid wine, with a

beautifully balanced flavour, that can be kept for at least four to five years: a delightful *coup de coeur*.

☛ Dom. Pierre Usseglio et Fils, rte d'Orange, 84230 Châteauneuf-du-Pape, tel. 04.90.83.72.98, fax 04.90.83.72.98 ▽
▼ by appt.

DOM. RAYMOND USSEGLIO ET FILS 1999★★

■　　10 ha　10,000　■ ▥ ♦ €11-15

Stéphane Usseglio took over the family estate in 1998, and his superb 99 wine is along the same lines as those made by his father. It is for long keeping, well-balanced, with great personality and silky tannins. The flavour of red fruit and spices delighted the Jury.

☛ Raymond Usseglio et Fils,
16, rte de Courthézon, BP 29,
84230 Châteauneuf-du-Pape,
tel. 04.90.83.71.85, fax 04.90.83.50.42 ▽
▼ ev. day except Sun. 9am–12 noon
1.30pm–7pm

DOM. DE VAL FRAIS
Cuvée Prestige 1998

　　　3 ha　　3,600　　■ ▥ €15-23

There is some contrast in this *Cuvée Prestige*: warm and full, yet beautifully tender. Its lengthy time – eighteen months – in barrel has left a fine oak flavour. Put it away for another four or five years.

☛ SCEA André Vaque, Dom. de Val-Frais, 84350 Courthézon, tel. 04.90.70.84.33,
fax 04.90.70.73.61 ▽ ▼ ev. day except Sun 9am–12 noon 12 noon–6pm

CH. DE VAUDIEU 2000★

□　　10 ha　10,500　■ ♦ €15-23

The Italian sports car enthusiasts' Club des Belles Italiennes meets annually at this 18th-century castle, so maybe it's possible to see their technical excellence in this prestige white, beautifully crafted and without equal. The nose is rich and complex, following on the palate with subtle harmony. It is already good to drink, but will improve even more in two to three years.

☛ Ch. de Vaudieu,
84230 Châteauneuf-du-Pape,
tel. 04.90.83.70.31, fax 04.90.83.51.97 ▽
▼ by appt.
☛ Brechet

Lirac

Lirac has produced quality wines since the 16th century, when the magistrates of Roquemaure authenticated them by burning the letters 'C d R' into the barrels with a red-hot iron. The climate and *terroir* are nearly the same here, in an area between Lirac, Saint-Laurent-des-Arbres, Saint-Geniès-de-Comolas and Roquemaure, as at Tavel, further north. Since Vacqueyras became an AOC, Lirac is no longer the only southern cru to make three colours of wine. Lirac roses and whites are full of grace and perfume; they go pleasantly with fish from the Mediterranean nearby and should be drunk young and cool. The reds are strong, with a pronounced *terroir* character, and offer an ideal accompaniment to red meat. In 2000, Lirac produced 29,750 hl (785,400 gal) from nearly 700 ha (1,729 acres).

DOM. VERDA 1999★   2 ha   3,000   €11-15

This fruity, spicy wine is rich and full. Thanks to a long time in cask, the tannins are prominent and well blended with strongish alcohol. Drink it straight away with a T-bone steak.

☛ Dom. André Verda, 2749, chem. de la Barote, 30150 Roquemaure, tel. 04.66.82.87.28, fax 04.66.82.87.28 ▼

☎ ev. day except Sun. 8am–12 noon 2pm–6pm

DOM. AMIDO 1999★★   6 ha   30,000   €5-8

Grenache, Syrah and Mourvèdre: the classic trio provides the last word in aroma and flavour. Truffles, pepper, apricot, prune and caramel – this is definitely a superb wine for laying down, beautifully balanced with integrated tannins and a deep red colour with dark brown highlights.

☛ Christian Amido, rue des Carrières, 30126Y, tel. 04.66.50.04.41, fax 04.66.50.04.41 ▼ ☎ by appt.

DOM. LAFOND ROC-EPINE 1999   12 ha   50,000   €8-11

It requires 20 days in the vat followed by four months in cask to extract these strong aromas of apricot, coconut, and very ripe fruit. The palate is equally rich with hints of toast and cocoa.

☛ Dom. Lafond Roc-Epine, rte des Vignobles, 30126 Tavel, tel. 04.66.50.24.59, fax 04.66.50.12.42, e-mail lafond.roc-epine@wanadoo.fr ▼ ☎ by appt.

DOM. DU JONCIER 1999   13 ha   55,000   €5-8

'Joncier' means 'broom' in Provençal. This area was covered in broom before it was converted to vineyards in 1970. Here is a good wine for keeping, with a strong musky aroma, nice prominent tannins, and a flavour of tree bark and crystallised orange. Even so, it needs a good five years to settle down.

☛ Marine Roussel, rue de la Combe, 30126 Tavel, tel. 04.66.50.27.70, fax 04.66.50.34.07 ▼ ☎ ev. day except Sun. 8am–12 noon 2pm–6pm; Sat. by appt.

DOM. DUSEIGNEUR 1999   12.5 ha   70,000   €8-11

The wine cellars of this estate are situated in the heart of the vines, which are planted on old garrigues. You are sure of a warm welcome to taste this dark wine shot with blue. A fragrance full of overripe fruit and spices is followed by a delightfully pleasant pleasant flavour loaded with strawberry jam and hints of smoke, ending with a spicy finish.

☛ Frédéric Duseigneur, rte de Saint-Victor, 30126 Saint-Laurent-des-Arbres, tel. 04.66.50.02.57, fax 04.66.50.02.57, e-mail fredseigneur@infonie.fr ▼ ☎ by appt.

DOM. DE CASTEL OUALOU 2000   10 ha   60,000   €8-11

Overripe fruit fills the nose: a blend of marc and fig jam. This 2000 cushions the palate beautifully. Better served with a meal than as an aperitif, this rosé would go well with Asian food.

☛ Assémat, 30150 Roquemaure, tel. 04.66.82.65.65, fax 04.66.82.86.76 ▼ ☎ by appt.

CH. D'AQUERIA 1999   n.c.   66,000   €8-11

This 99 from the Château d'Aquéria has been well matured. Its colour is deep red with flashes of terracotta, and the nose exudes leather and spice. The leather carries on in the full-bodied flavour with a hint of tobacco. Drink now.

☛ Ch. d'Aquéria, 30126 Tavel, tel. 04.66.50.04.56, fax 04.66.50.18.46, e-mail contact@aqueria.com ▼ ☎ ev. day except Sun. 8am–12 noon 2pm–6pm; Sat. by appt.

☛ V. de Bez

DOM. LA GENESTIERE

Cuvée Raphaël 1999

◼ 20 ha 40,000 ◼▯◆ €5-8

The tasters said this wine will be ready to drink by the time the *Guide* is published. So by the time you read this, the red fruit and kernels will be even stronger on the nose. The flavour is already rich and full but well-balanced and delightfully harmonised.

• Jean-Claude Garcin, Dom. La Genestière, 30126 Tavel, tel. 04.66.50.07.03, fax 04.66.50.27.03, e-mail genestiere@paewan.fr ▼ ✕ ev. day. 8am–6pm; Sat. Sun. by appt.

DOM. DE LA MORDOREE

Cuvée de la Reine des Bois 2000★

▢ n.c. n.c. €8-11

The colour is brilliant, transparent and slightly golden, with an intense, complex aroma dominated by pineapple. This fruit figures strongly in the flavour as well, nicely balanced with a delicious fleshy texture and length. Also a star winner, the red **Cuvée de la Reine des Bois 99** is a truly young wine. The bouquet is fresh and fruity, while the flavour is blended with very good tannins. This wine finishes on a note of delicate brandied fruit.

• Dom. de La Mordorée, chem. des Oliviers, 30126 Tavel, tel. 04.66.50.00.75, fax 04.66.50.47.39 ▼

• Delorme

DOM. LA ROCALIERE 1999★★

◼ 3.7 ha 18,600 ◼▯◆ €5-8

Grenache, Mourvèdre and Syrah, cultivated on a sunny *terroir* of smooth pebbles, produce this magnificent deep red wine with blue reflections. An intense nose of liquorice, undergrowth and ripe fruit on the nose, with a glorious flavour on the palate, well blended with its tannins. Great maturity in this wine, to be put away.

• Dom. La Rocalière, Le Palai-Nord, BP 21, 30126 Tavel, tel. 04.66.50.12.60, fax 04.66.50.23.45, e-mail rocaliere@wanadoo.fr ▼ ✕ ev. day 8am–12 noon 12pm–6pm; Sat. Sun. by appt.

• Borrelly-Maby

LAURUS 1999★

◼ 3 ha 8,000 ◼▯◆ €8-11

This *négociant* has blended its wine wisely and well. Deep red, slightly orange in colour, this Lirac has a a musky leather aroma with hints of toast and nuts. On the palate are full-ness, fleshy richness and integrated tannins, with a finish of very ripe cherry and spices.

• Gabriel Meffre, Le Village, 84190 Gigondas, tel. 04.90.12.30.22, fax 04.90.12.30.29, e-mail gabriel-meffre@meffre.com ▼ by appt.

CH. LE DEVOY MARTINE 2000

◼ 30 ha 100,000 ◼▯◆ €5-8

This wine is still very young and needs some time to release all the aromas that are trapped inside. However, the red fruit appears through the violet on the nose and the tannins hold out promise of an excellent balance. Put this away for two years.

• SCEA Lombardo, Ch. Le Devoy Martine, 30126 Saint-Laurent-des-Arbres, tel. 04.66.50.01.23, fax 04.66.50.43.58 ▼ ✕ ev. day 9am–12 noon 2pm–5pm

LES LAUZERAIES

Elevé en fût de chêne 1999

◼ 10 ha 30,000 ◼▯◆ €5-8

A good successful wine for Les Lauzeraies, matured in barrel, and with a ruby colour shot with orange. Stewed fruit blends with a light oak fragrance on nose and palate, and well-integrated tannins with a finish of vanilla and cinnamon bark. A truly well-made wine.

• Les Vignerons de Tavel, 30126 Tavel, tel. 04.66.50.03.57, fax 04.66.50.46.57, e-mail tavel.cave@wanadoo.fr ✕ ev. day 9am–12 noon 2pm–6pm

DOM. MABY La Fermade 1999

◼ 20 ha 60,000 ◼▯◆ €8-11

This estate was rebuilt in 1995. The wine-maker has produced a delightful wine with a deep intense colour, a lovely aroma of stewed fruit and spices, and a strong flavour of underground from the Mourvèdre grape. This is a wine to keep and will cause general delight when opened.

• Dom. Roger Maby, rue Saint-Vincent, 30126 Tavel, tel. 04.66.50.03.40, fax 04.66.50.43.12 ▼ ✕ ev. day except Sat. Sun. 8am–12 noon 1.30pm–5.30pm

CH. MONT-REDON 2000★

▢ 5.300 ◼▯◆ €8-11

The wine-maker only has to cross the Rhône to work on his AOC Lirac vineyards, then the wine is bottled at the château. This rosé, clear and brilliant, has a strong aroma and taste of red fruit (currants and strawberry). Fresh, fleshy, well-balanced, it is a lovely wine that should be served really cold. The 99 was awarded the *coup de coeur* last year.

• Famille Abeille-Fabre, Ch. Mont-Redon, BP 10, 84230 Châteauneuf-du-Pape, tel. 04.90.83.72.75, fax 04.90.83.77.20, email chateaumontredon@wanadoo.fr ▼ by appt.

DOM. DES MURETINS 1999

◼ n.c. 8,000 ◼▯◆ €8-11

Despite eight months in cask, this dark violet 99 has retained all its fresh, powerful aroma of garrigue herbs, boxwood and rockrose. Full and with strong individuality, this is well-balanced and long on the palate.

• Les Domaines Bernard, rte de Sérignan, 84100 Orange, tel. 04.90.11.86.86, fax 04.90.34.87.30, e-mail sagon@domaines-bernard.fr

• J.-L. Roudil

Considered by many to be the finest rosé in France, this great wine from the Côtes du Rhône comes from a vineyard situated in the department of the Gard, on the right bank of the river. The vines are grown on land around Tavel, together with a few parcels in the commune of Roquemaure, on 938 ha (2,317 acres) of sand, alluvial clay or smoothed pebbles. Tavel is the only Rhône appellation to produce rosé wines; production is 42,992 hl (1,134,989 gal). A wine of great character, with a floral, then fruity bouquet, Tavel should be served as an accompaniment for fish dishes with sauce, charcuterie and white meats.

DOM. PELAQUIE
Vitis Flora Le Prestige 1999★

■ 4 ha 6,000 ▮ €8-11

This 99 releases a very fine delicate aroma of stewed ripe fruit with hints of spice. After measured maturation in barrel, the flavour is harmonious and the tannins silky; balance and elegance that tempt the drinker to open this wine immediately.

🍷 Dom. Pélaquié, 7, rue du Vernet, 30290 Saint-Victor-la-Coste, tel. 04.66.50.06.04, fax 04.66.50.33.32, e-mail domaine@pelaquie.com ☑
🍽 ev. day except Sun. 9am–12 noon 2pm–6pm

CH. SAINT-ROCH
Cuvée confidentielle □

0.5 ha 2,500 ▮ €11-15

Long wine-making experience is immediately evident in this magnificent blend of Grenache and Clairette, with an intense nose of fruit, white flowers and vanilla. Fermentation in cask has not disturbed the balance, and the delicate oak flavour combines well with the floral bouquet; a truly great wine. The **red Cuvée Confidentielle 99** was mentioned by the Jury, and is ready for drinking now. The liquorice aroma, round, solid structure, and lingering flavour of jammy fruit, will make this a splendid choice with a long-simmered meat dish.

🍷 Maxime et Patrick Brunel, Ch. Saint-Roch, chem. de Lirac, 30150 Roquemaure, tel. 04.66.82.82.59, fax 04.66.82.83.00, e-mail brunel@chateau-saint-roch.com ☑
🍽 ev. day except Sat. Sun. 8am–12 noon 2pm–5pm

CELLIER SAINT-VALENTIN 2000

■ 7.14 ha 40,000 ▮ €5-8

This pale-coloured rosé has a pleasantly fruity nose, very nicely balanced with the full, vibrant flavour. There is a follow-through of wild fruit on the finish.

🍷 SCA Cellier Saint-Valentin, 1, rue des Vignerons, 30150 Roquemaure, tel. 04.66.82.82.01, fax 04.66.82.67.28 ☑
🍽 by appt.

DOM. VERDA Cuvée de la Barotte 1999

■ 3.5 ha 2,000

The extreme ripeness of the harvested grapes used in this wine is responsible for the powerful nose of macerated fruit, with a touch of mint. The overripe fruit flavour returns strong on the palate, supported by silky tannins.

🍷 Dom. André Verda, 2749, chem. de la Barotte, 30150 Roquemaure, tel. 04.66.82.87.28, fax 04.66.82.87.28 ☑
🍽 ev. day except Sun. 8am–12 noon 2pm–6pm

BALAZU DES VAUSSIERES 2000★★

▲ 3 ha 5,000 ▮ €5-8

Christian Charmasson inherited this small vineyard from his grandfather, nicknamed Balazu, and went on to plant 3 ha (7.4 acres) of Tavel vines. This 2000 is a good table wine. With a nice harmonious colour, the nose is fine, spicy with a hint of pepper and mint. The long flavour of overripe fruit is strong in texture.

🍷 Dom. Christian et Nadia Charmasson, chem. de la Vaussière, 30126 Tavel, tel. 04.66.50.44.22, fax 04.66.50.44.22 ☑
🍽 ev. day 8am–9pm

LOUIS BERNARD 2000★★

▲ n.c. 75,000 ▮ €5-8

Brilliant baby pink in colour, this Tavel has a bouquet of strawberry and caramel and a full, mouth-filling flavour of very ripe fruit. The well-balanced structure of the wine makes it suitable to serve with fish in sauce, or white meats.

🍷 Les Domaines Bernard, rte de Sérignan, 84100 Orange, tel. 04.90.11.86.86, fax 04.90.34.87.30, e-mail sagon@domaines-bernard.fr

DOM. LAFOND ROC-EPINE 2000★★

▲ 38 ha 200,000 ▮ €8-11

This wine is the personification of its appellation. Blended from five grape varieties – Grenache, Clairette, Cinsault, Syrah and Bourboulenc – it is elegant with a very refined floral aroma over wild fruit (berries). The pleasantly fresh fruit flavour lingers on the palate with notes of cinnamon and liquorice. A balanced structure completes the overall harmony.

☛ Dom. Lafond Roc-Epine, rte des Vignobles, 30126 Tavel, tel. 04.66.50.24.59, fax 04.66.50.12.42, e-mail lafond.roc-epine@wanadoo.fr ☒
� Y by appt.

LA FORCADIERE 2000★★

☐ 18.51 ha 100,000 ☐ ◦ €5-8

The very old family estate is well-known for its fine-quality Tavels. This 2000 has a brilliant, slightly violet colour. The delicate aroma releases currants and raspberry, while the palate, strong and vibrant, is elegantly balanced. The notes of berries and almonds last nicely on the finish.
☛ Dom. Roger Maby, rue Saint-Vincent, 30126 Tavel, tel. 04.66.50.03.40, fax 04.66.50.43.12 ☒ Y ev. day except Sat. Sun. 8am–12 noon 1.30pm–5.30pm
☛ Roger Maby

DOM. LA ROCALIERE 2000★

☐ 23 ha 138,000 ☐ ◦ €5-8

This wine has a coral colour and an aroma that opens on a mineral note. Jammy fruit flavours appear in the strong concentrated palate. The balance is good.
☛ Dom. La Rocalière, Le Palai-Nord. BP 21, 30126 Tavel, tel. 04.66.50.12.60, fax 04.66.50.23.45, e-mail rocaliere@wanadoo.fr ☒ Y ev. day. 8am–12 noon 2pm–6pm; Sat. Sun. by appt.
☛ Borrelly-Maby

LA ROUVIERE 2000★

☐ 28 ha 100,000 ☐ ◦ €8-11

A delightful rosé with a brilliant cherry colour, and a nose of red fruit and hazelnut in harmony with the long finish. The flavours on the mid-palate carry a suggestion of spice, ending on a slightly tart note.
☛ Henry Bouachon, BP 5, 84230 Châteauneuf-du-Pape, tel. 04.90.83.58.35, fax 04.90.83.77.23 ☒ Y by appt.

LES ESPERELLES 2000★

☐ 20 ha 100,000 ☐ ◦ €5-8

Coral tones with violet reflections: this Tavel releases an aroma of jammy red fruit. The palate is refreshing and long with a cherry aftertaste.
☛ Les Vignerons de Rasteau et de Tain-l'Hermitage, rte des Princes-d'Orange, 84110 Rasteau, tel. 04.90.10.90.10, fax 04.90.10.90.36, e-mail vrt@rasteau.com

PRIEURE DE MONTEZARGUES

2000 ☐ 34 ha 100,000 ☐ ◦ €8-11

This priory is surrounded by 55 ha (136 acres) of vineyard. The Tavel from the estate is deep and brilliant in colour. The aroma is elegant, hinting at morello cherry and raspberry. Mineral notes provide the fresh flavour.

☛ Allauzen Lucenet Gaff, Prieuré de Montézargues, 30126 Tavel, tel. 04.66.50.04.48, fax 04.66.50.30.41 ☒ Y by appt.

DOM. ROC DE L'OLIVET 2000★★

☐ 2 ha 8,660 ☐ ◦ €5-8

Just 2 ha (5 acres) of 30-year-old vines have produced 8,600 bottles of this fine salmon-coloured rosé. The nose is fresh and fruity, revealing a spicy note that returns discreetly on the palate.
☛ Thierry Valente, chem. de la Vaussière, 30126 Tavel, tel. 04.66.50.37.87, fax 04.66.50.37.87 ☒ Y by appt.

LES VIGNERONS DE TAVEL

Cuvée royale 2000★

☐ 12 ha 70,000 ☐ ◦ €5-8

This salmon-coloured Tavel is a blend of six varieties (Grenache, Cinsault, Syrah, Clairette, Bourboulenc and Carignan). The fruity aroma is followed by hints of almond and spice. After the direct attack, the palate is rich with a slightly sharp touch on the finish. The Cuvée Tableau 2000 was awarded a star.
☛ Les Vignerons de Tavel, 30126 Tavel, tel. 04.66.50.03.57, fax 04.66.50.46.57, e-mail tavel.cave@wanadoo.fr ☒ Y ev. day. 9am–12 noon 2pm–6pm

CH. DE TRINQUEVEDEL 2000★★

☐ 30 ha 120,000 ☐ ◦ €5-8

Gérard Demoulin runs this 30-ha (74-acre) estate, producing AOC Tavel. Here is a brilliant rosé with violet flashes, and a flavour that evokes delicate hints of currant and stewed morello cherry. The palate is fresh and full in a pleasant balance, culminating in the long red berry flavour on the finish.
☛ Ch. de Trinquevedel, 30126 Tavel, tel. 04.66.50.04.04, fax 04.66.50.31.66, e-mail f30trinque@aol.com ☒ Y by appt.
☛ Demoulin

DOM. VERDA 2000★

☐ 2.2 ha 4,000 ☐ ◦ €5-8

André Verda is a new arrival in the AOC Tavel category, and his début is certainly a success. This brilliant wine, flashed with violet highlights, is full of raspberry and blackcurrant, and the result is well-balanced and elegant.
☛ Dom. André Verda, 2749, chem. de la Barotte, 30150 Roquemaure, tel. 04.66.82.87.28, fax 04.66.82.87.28 ☒ Y ev. day except Sun. 8am–12 noon 2pm–6pm

Clairette de Die

Clairette de Die is one of the oldest known wines in the world. The vineyard occupies the hillsides of the middle valley of the Drôme, between Luc-en-Diois and Aouste-sur-Sye. A sparkling wine is produced mainly from the Muscat variety (75% minimum). The fermentation stops naturally in the bottle, according to ancient Die practice. No 'liqueur de tirage' (a mixture of yeasts, old wine and sugar) is added. Production was 75,045 hl (1,981,188 gal) in 2000.

CAROD Tradition 1999★
35 ha · 250,000 · €5-8

The Carod family aims to produce very characteristic, high-quality wines, and has also opened a museum in order to publicise this appellation and the local wine-making traditions of the early 20th century. This wine, matured after careful *dosage* – three-quarters Muscat with one-quarter Clairette – has improved with time. The mousse is very delicate and the touch of muscat does not overpower. Peach and apricot flavours appear on the palate.
☞ Carod Frères, RD 93, 26340 Vercheny, tel. 04.75.21.73.77, fax 04.75.21.75.22, e-mail info@caves-carod.com [V]
Y ev. day 8am–12 noon 2pm–6pm

DIDIER CORNILLON Tradition 1999★
10 ha · 60,000 · €5-8

Fine, frothy mousse explodes when you open this wine. It is a marvellous, beautifully balanced blend of white flowers and fruit, with light, airy touches of muscat.
☞ Didier Cornillon, 26410 Saint-Roman, tel. 04.75.21.81.79, fax 04.75.21.84.44 [V]
Y ev. day. 10.30am–12.30pm 2pm–7pm; Oct–Mar. by appt.

JAILLANCE Tradition★
70 ha · 540,000 · €5-8

This co-operative offers a great trio of Clairette de Die: the **Cuvée Impériale**, this **Cuvée Issue de l'Agriculture Biologique**, the **Cuvée Tradition**. All three are outstanding and were each awarded a star for rosé wines. They are beautifully delicate and underlined by a lovely finish.
☞ Cave coop. de Die Jaillance, 26150 Die, tel. 04.75.22.30.00, fax 04.75.22.21.06
Y by appt.

ALAIN POULET Tradition 1999
12 ha · 76,000 · €5-8

Here is a Clairette de Die to drink as an aperitif. Gently frothy with fine bubbles, it is lovely light wine full of springtime freshness.
☞ Alain Poulet, la Chapelle, 26150 Pontaix, tel. 04.75.21.22.59, fax 04.75.21.20.95 [V]
Y by appt.

RASPAIL Tradition 1999
3.5 ha · 23,000 · €5-8

This estate always extends a warm welcome, whether you stay at the *gîte rural* or in the camping park. Visitors appreciate the direct contact with the wine-maker, and the patient way in which he explains his craft. This Clairette stands out for its impact of lychees and very delicate hint of roses. Jammy white fruits and berries fill the palate, with an excellent balance of aroma and freshness.
☞ EARL Georges Raspail, rte du Camping municipal, La Roche, 26340 Aurel, tel. 04.75.21.71.89, fax 04.75.21.71.89 [V]
Y by appt.

JEAN-CLAUDE RASPAIL Tradition 1999★★
n.c. · 29,659 · €5-8

With his organic farming methods, Jean-Claude Raspail produces a remarkable Clairette. The fine frothy mousse is perfumed with white flowers and peach. The elegant touch of muscat and the delicious long finish make this a wine not to be missed.
☞ Jean-Claude Raspail, Dom. de la Mûre, 26340 Saillans, tel. 04.75.21.55.99, fax 04.75.21.57.57 [V] Y ev. day. 9am–12 noon 2pm–6pm; cl. 5–31 Jan.

SALABELLE Tradition Cuvée Adline 1999★
n.c. · n.c. · €5-8

The estate, dating back to 1845, has opted for organic farming, with very successful results. This Clairette, pale yellow shot with flashes of green, is very straightforward. The peach and grapefruit nose is supplemented by hints of mango to produce a real fruit cocktail.
☞ GAEC Salabelle, 26150 Barsac, tel. 04.75.21.70.78, fax 04.75.21.70.78 [V]
Y by appt.

Crémant de Die

The AOC Crémant de Die was recognised by decree on 26 March 1993. It is made solely from the Clairette variety by the 'Champagne' method involving secondary fermentation in the bottle.

CAROD 1998★
3.5 ha · 26,000 · €5-8

Notes of undergrowth and hazelnut appear in this sparkling wine that maintains its strength throughout. Pale and transparent

Châtillon-en-Diois

with green highlights, and a long frothy mousse, this wine will go well with white meat.

⚬━ Carod Frères, RD 93, 26340 Vercheny, tel. 04.75.21.73.77, fax 04.75.21.75.22, e-mail info@caves-carod.com
Ⓨ ev. day. 8am–12 noon 2pm–6pm

CHAMBERAN 1997 €5-8

○ 2.8 ha 15,000

Seven wine-makers pooled their vineyards to create a single estate of 61 ha (150.6 acres) that they run jointly, from vine to market, under the Chamberan trademark. Set at the foot of the natural park of Vercours, the vines are planted on stony hillsides that are well exposed but difficult to harvest. The Crémant 97 is strong and sparkling on the palate, with a delicate fragrance of white flowers. Altogether well-balanced and pleasant.

⚬━ Union des Jeunes Viticulteurs récoltants, rte de Die, 26340 Vercheny, tel. 04.75.21.70.88, fax 04.75.21.73.73, e-mail ujvr@terre-net.fr
Ⓨ ev. day. 8.30am–12 noon 2pm–6.30pm

DIDIER CORNILLON
Brut absolu 1998★★★ €5-8

○ 1 ha 5,000

This wine won second place in the Grand Jury's selection of *coups de cœur* for this appellation. Round and fleshy with a buttery pastry flavour that lingers, it is perfectly balanced and is beautiful to drink throughout the meal.

⚬━ Didier Cornillon, 26410 Saint-Roman, tel. 04.75.21.81.79, fax 04.75.21.84.44
Ⓨ ev. day. 10.30am–12.30pm 2pm–7pm; Oct.–Mar. by appt.

JAILLANCE★★ €5-8

○ 4 ha 26,000

This wine, 100% Clairette, is organically cultivated. With its fine mousse and long flavour, pale yellow with transparent highlights, this is a very fruity wine (ripe pear, white fruit and pineapple), long on the palate. Also worth tasting is the **Cuvée Traditionnelle**, awarded a star for its excellent balance.

⚬━ Cave coop. de Die Jaillance, 26150 Die, tel. 04.75.22.30.00, fax 04.75.22.21.06
Ⓨ r.-v.

MARCEL MAILLEFAUD ET FILS
1997★★★ €5-8

○ 0.75 ha 5,000

'This *Crémant* can be served throughout an entire meal', according to one member of the Jury. The wine is sufficiently rich and full-bodied to last a long time. With strong notes of butter and toast, it has an exceptionally long finish.

⚬━ Marcel Maillefaud et Fils, GAEC des Adrets, 26150 Barsac, tel. 04.75.21.71.77, fax 04.75.21.75.24
Ⓨ ev. day. 8am–12 noon 2pm–6pm

Châtillon-en-Diois

The vineyard of Châtillon-en-Diois covers 50 ha (123 acres) on the slopes of the high valley of the Drôme, between Luc-en-Diois, at 550 m (1,804 ft) altitude, and Pont-de-Quart, 465 m (1,525 ft). The appellation produces light and fruity reds (from the Gamay variety), to be drunk young, and whites (from the Aligoté and Chardonnay varieties) that are pleasant and firm. Total production was 3,288 hl (86,803 gal) in 2000.

CLOS DE BEYLIERE 1999★★

□ 0.5 ha 2,500

This year has seen very successful white wines from the domaine, including this one which was complimented by the Jury. It is fine and complex: pineapple, peach and apricot, a veritable basketful of fruit. The **Aligoté 2000** was also judged remarkable for its intense fruity flavour (grapefruit).

⚬━ Didier Cornillon, 26410 Saint-Roman, tel. 04.75.21.81.79, fax 04.75.21.84.44
Ⓨ ev. day. 10.30am–12.30pm 2pm–7pm; Oct.–Mar. by appt.

DOM. DE LA GOUYARDE 2000 €3-5

□ 1.57 ha 10,000

This co-operative offers an *Aligoté* which the Jury considered to have interesting potential even though the nose is still somewhat closed. Rich and supple, it is also very thirst-quenching: a good wine for an aperitif.

Coteaux du Tricastin

This appellation covers 2,000 ha (4,940 acres), in 22 communes on the right bank of the Rhône, from La Baume-de-Transit in the south, through Saint-Paul-Trois-Châteaux, to Granges-Gontardes in the north. The very pebbly ancient alluvial soils and the sandy slopes situated at the limit of the Mediterranean climate produced about 121,634 hl (3,211,138 gal) of wine in 2000. The boundaries of this appellation have recently been redrawn.

DOMAINES ANDRE AUBERT
Le Devoy Vieilli en fût de chêne 1998★

n.c. | 4,500 | €5-8

A fairly limited production of a wine whose originality is in its floral bouquet, blended with herbal fragrance and harvested hay. The flavour opens in nice balance with soft tannins on the palate, and the oak taste has all but gone. Good to drink with small game.

- GAEC Aubert Frères, Le Devoy, 26290 Donzère, tel. 04.75.51.63.01, fax 04.75.51.63.01 [V] [Y] by appt.

DOM. DE MAUPAS 2000★★

1.4 ha | 8,400 | €5-8

For certain tasks in the vineyard, the wine-maker still uses heavy, strong cart-horses, definitely not terms to apply to this wine, which is direct and vibrant, with a delicious aroma of pear that makes it ideal for a *tarte Tatin*.

- Jérôme Cayol, Dom. de Maupas, 26410 Châtillon-en-Diois, tl. 04.75.21.18.81, fax 04.75.21.14.54, e-mail domaine-de-maupas@wanadoo.fr [V] [Y] by appt.

- Cave coop. de Die Jaillance, 26150 Die, tel. 04.75.22.30.00, fax 04.75.22.21.06 [V] [Y] by appt.

DOM. DE GRANGENEUVE
Cuvée Vieilles vignes 1999★

20 ha | 100,000 | €5-8

Between 1964 and 1970, Odette and Henri Bour planted their vines on the stony terraces invaded by the garrigue and truffle oaks. The vineyard presently covers 65 ha (160.5 acres), and their wines have kept pace with progress. This selection from old vines is so well structured that it could be served today. The **red** Cuvée Tradition 99 has a very successful, classic bouquet of red fruit and hints of pepper. Lovers of cask-matured wines may prefer the **red** La Truffière 99, but will need to wait a couple of years before opening.

- Domaines Bour, Dom. de Grangeneuve, 26230 Roussas, tel. 04.75.98.50.22, fax 04.75.98.51.09, e-mail domainesbour@wanadoo.fr [V] [Y] by appt.

CH. LA CROIX CHABRIERE 2000★

2 ha | 14,000 | €3-5

A striking contrast between this wine's rich bouquet (spices, kernel and fruit) and its plain but very pleasant impact on the palate. Perhaps the relatively strong proportion of Cinsault explains the flavour. This is a wine to drink among friends with the first truffles of the season. For an aperitif, choose the **white** 2000, long and balanced, with a nose of coconut and mango.

- Ch. La Croix Chabrière, rte de Saint-Restitut, 84500 Bollène, tel. 04.90.40.00.89, fax 04.90.40.19.93 [V] [Y] ev. day 9am-12 noon 2pm-6pm; Sun.
- Patrick Daniel

CH. LA DECELLE 1999

6 ha | 20,000 | €5-8

Crushed strawberry in combination with other scents have supplemented this wine's enchanting bouquet which derives in the main from the grapes of which it is constituted. The aroma of the **red** Cuvée S 99, from *vieilles vignes*, is even stronger, although very different (musk and game), yet it is the fruit that lingers on the palate. Keep it in the cellar for a while.

- Ch. La Décelle, rte de Pierrelatte, D 59, 26130 Saint-Paul-Trois-Châteaux, tel. 04.75.04.71.33, fax 04.75.04.56.98, e-mail anne-marie.seroin@wanadoo.fr [V] [Y] ev. day. 9am-12 noon 2.30pm-6.30pm; groups by appt.
- Seroin

LE DOME D'ELYSSAS
Cuvée des Echirouses 1999

55 ha | 11,000 | €3-5

The garrigue and its perfumes galore ... the **Cuvée du Gros Chêne 99** is already well rounded and strong on the palate. It was singled out by the Jury, although preference was given to the Cuvée des Echirouses, much stronger in style and structure. The subtle bouquet is a blend of violet and a touch of spice. This is ready to drink, but can wait a little longer.

- SARL d'Elyssas, 26290 Les Granges-Gontardes, tel. 04.75.98.61.55, fax 04.75.98.63.12 [V] [Y] ev. day except Sun. 9am-12 noon 3pm-7pm; groups by appt.

Côtes du Ventoux

This vineyard is at the foot of the limestone Massif du Ventoux, the 'giant of the Vaucluse' (1,912 m/6,271 ft), on soil composed of tertiary sediments, and stretches over 51 communes (6,888 ha/17,013 acres) between Vaison-la-Romaine in the north and Apt in the south. The wines produced are essentially reds and rosés. The climate, cooler than that of the Côtes du Rhône, causes the grapes to ripen later. The red wines have a lesser alcoholic content, but are fresh and elegant when young; they are better structured in the more westerly communes (Caromb, Bédoin, Mormoiron). The rosé wines are pleasant and need to be drunk young. Total production reached 307,850 hl (8,127,240 gal) in 2000.

DOM. DE MONTINE ★★
Élevé en fût de chêne 1999

■ 10 ha ■ 20,000 ■ ▥ €5-8

The colour is dark ruby, with a complex nose of spices blended with musky notes and intense touches of vanilla. The attack is straightforward, the development smooth, and the flavour long and mouth-filling. Nothing is missing, and the velvety structure will soon be apparent. The very successful **red 98** is striking for the violet fragrance and the unusually long flavour on the palate: a wine with loads of personality.

•➤ Jean-Luc et Claude Monteillet, Dom. de Montine, GAEC de la Grande Tuilière, 26230 Grignan, tel. 04.75.46.54.21, fax 04.75.46.93.26, e-mail domainedemontine@wanadoo.fr ▥
Ⴘ by appt.

RABASSIERE 1999
■ n.c. ■ ▥ €3-5

This traditional blending had the added advantage of careful maturation in barrel. Vanilla and kernels mingle smoothly with brandied fruit on the palate. The **rosé Cuvée Le Lutin 2000** has a very pleasant sharp taste on the finish. It, too, was commended.

•➤ SCV La Suzienne, 26790 Suze-la-Rousse, tel. 04.75.04.80.04, fax 04.75.98.23.77 ▥
Ⴘ by appt.

DOM. RASPAIL
Réserve du Domaine 2000★

■ n.c. ■ ▥ €3-5

'Powerful' was the key word in tasting. The bouquet conjures up concentrated fruit flavours and hints of musk. The flavour harmonises with the rest: strong texture and velvety tannins. Here is an example of successful collaboration between wine-grower and wine-maker. The **red Cuvée Louis Bernard 2000** is just as good.

•➤ Les Domaines Bernard, rte de Sérignan, 84100 Orange, tel. 04.90.11.86.86, fax 04.90.34.87.30, e-mail sagon@domaines-bernard.fr

DOM. DU VIEUX MICOCOULIER 1999★

■ 100 ha ■ 250,000 ■ ▥ €5-8

This is a perfectly matured wine: darkest colour in harmony with ripe fruit and intense spices. The heat from the smooth pebbles of the vineyard seems to have permeated the solidly-built, powerful, lingering flavour on the palate. The tannins, too, are very acceptable. The combination of *terroir* and the grower's expertise has paid rich dividends.

•➤ SCGEA Cave Vergobbi, Le Logis de Berre, 26290 Les Granges-Gontardes, tel. 04.75.04.02.72, fax 04.75.04.41.81 ▥
Ⴘ ev. day. 9.30am–12 noon 2.30pm–6.30pm; Sun. by appt.

DOM. AYMARD Prestige 1999★
■ 1 ha ■ 4,000 ■ ▥ €5-8

The Aymard family is very concerned with environmental protection, and this philosophy underpins the methods applicable to its vineyard. The *Cuvée Prestige* has a complex bouquet with well-integrated oak and the fragrance of overripe red fruit. Charm and elegance are the main features of this 99 that should be kept another two years.

•➤ Dom. Aymard, Les Galères, Serres, 84200 Carpentras, tel. 04.90.63.35.32, fax 04.90.67.02.79 ▥ Ⴘ by appt.

CAVE DE BEAUMONT DU VENTOUX Vieilli en fût de chêne 1999
■ 4 ha ■ 20,000 ■ ▥ €5-8

Here is a delightful brilliant-red wine with garnet highlights, and an aroma loaded with red fruit and blackcurrant, with a few musky notes. The flavour on the palate is balanced fruit blended with well-balanced oak. This wine will be complete in two or three years.

•➤ Coopérative vinicole de Beaumont-du-Ventoux, rte de Carpentras, 84340 Malaucène, tel. 04.90.65.11.78, fax 04.90.12.69.88 ▥
Ⴘ by appt.

CH. BLANC 1999★★
■ 10.18 ha ■ 60,000 ■ ▥ €3-5

This estate is in Roussillon, one of the most beautiful villages in France, against its background of ochre cliffs. The colour of this 99 wine, however, is dark garnet-red, with a well-developed bouquet of ripe fruit (dried apricot) and spicy notes over the oaky finish.

The solid structure has a subtle elegance. It is ready now.
✆ SCEA Ch. Blanc, quartier Grimaud, 84220 Roussillon, tel. 04.90.05.64.56, fax 04.90.05.72.79 [V]
☎ ev. day 8am–7pm; groups by appt.
✆ Chasson

CAVE DE BONNIEUX
Élevé en fût de chêne 1999★

■ 5 ha   5,021   €5-8

The oldest co-operative winery in Vaucluse offers a dark purple 99 with an aroma that is still a little closed. However, the character is there, with its full, well-balanced flavour. Beautifully expressive, the tannins are rather too prominent and must be allowed time to soften down.
✆ Cave vinicole de Bonnieux, quartier de la Gare, 84480 Bonnieux, tel. 04.90.75.80.03, fax 04.90.75.92.73, e-mail vignerons-bonnieux@wanadoo.fr [V]
☎ ev. day except Sun. 9am–12 noon 2pm–6pm

DOM. DU BON REMEDE 2000
■ 0.5 ha   2,400   €3-5

This rosé wine has a delightful, brilliant colour of pink flecked with violet. The nose is loaded with fruit: grapefruit, pineapple, strawberry ... The strong, lively and persistent flavour makes it a wine that will keep well, but it can certainly be drunk right away with meat and cold cuts.
✆ Frédéric Delay, 1248, rte de Malemort, 84380 Mazan, tel. 04.90.69.69.76, fax 04.90.69.69.76 [V] ☎ by appt.

DOM. DE FENOUILLET 2000
■ 0.6 ha   4,000   €5-8

After 50 years of cultivating their vines, the Soard family decided to make their own wine in 1989. Their summer rosé is easy on the palate without any sharpness. It is round and well-blended, with touches of red and even exotic fruits.
✆ GAEC Patrick et Vincent Soard, Dom. de Fenouillet, allée Saint-Roch, 84190 Beaumes-de-Venise, tel. 04.90.62.95.61, fax 04.90.62.90.67, e-mail pv.soard@freesbee.fr [V] ☎ by appt.

DOM. DE FONDRECHE
Cuvée Persia 1999★★

■ 3 ha   6,000   €8-11

Tying up the vines, snipping the buds, green harvesting – the hard work put in by this estate to achieve quality has reaped dividends. The intense garnet-red of this *Cuvée Persia* wine is eye-catching, and the complex nose of flower and fruit, a touch overripe and musky, is rich and powerful. Appreciative Jury members piled on the superlatives – very elegant, magnificent, superb, exceptional – and unanimously awarded it a *coup de cœur*. The **white Cuvée Persia 2000** is an excellent marriage of wine and oak, and the touch of toast does not overpower the fruit. Its two stars would grace a chicken pot-au-feu with truffles. The same marks went to the **red Cuvée Nadal 99**: mulberries, blueberries, morello cherries, and a good solid structure. It will be lovely with jugged hare or boar in two or three years' time.
✆ Dom. de Fondrèche, quartier Fondrèche, 84380 Mazan, tel. 04.90.69.61.42, fax 04.90.69.61.18 [V] ☎ by appt.
✆ Vincent et Barthélemy

DOMAINE DE FONDRÈCHE — Côtes du Ventoux — Appellation Côtes de Ventoux Contrôlée — Cuvée PERSIA 1999 — Mis en bouteille à la propriété — 84380 MAZAN – FRANCE — 75cl

DOM. DES HAUTES ROCHES
Cuvée Les Pourrats 1999

■ 11 ha   60,000   €5-8

A new arrival in the *Guide*, and for good reason: this vineyard was only established in April 1999. The delightfully drinkable **rosé Pourrats 2000**, singled out by the Jury, is exemplary: the nose is still slightly closed, but full of sloe and heady flower fragrance, whereas the flavour is plainer and more traditional.
✆ SCEA Bourgue-Hardoin, Dom. des Hautes-Roches, Roquefure, 84400 Apt, tel. 04.90.74.19.65, fax 04.90.74.19.65, e-mail sceabourguehardoin@free.fr [V]
☎ ev. day. 9am–12.30pm 3pm–7pm
✆ Lionel Bourgue

DOM. DE LA BASTIDONNE
Élevé en fût de chêne 1999★★

■ n.c.   10,000   €5-8

This family estate is on the tourist route between Fontaine-de-Vaucluse and Gordes. Long fermentation and then a year in barrel has given superb colour to this deep violet 99 with almost black reflections. Brandied fruit on the nose is followed by oak and touches of vanilla. This is a slightly unusual wine, but really delicious, worth drinking with a tasty main dish. Equally well made is the **rosé 2000**, with strong individuality, which can be served throughout the meal.
✆ SCEA Dom. de La Bastidonne, 84220 Cabrières-d'Avignon, tel. 04.90.76.70.00, fax 04.90.76.74.34 [V]
☎ ev. day except Sun. 9am–12 noon 2pm–6pm
✆ Gérard Marreau

CH. DE LA BOISSIERE 1999★
■ n.c.   20,000   €3-5

M. Rambaud, manager of this winery, has produced this wine with its pleasant flavour of very ripe fruit. A good example of its appellation, it would be perfect immediately with Provençal dishes or red meat.

• Cave La Montagne Rouge,
84570 Villes-sur-Auzon, tel. 04.90.61.82.08,
fax 04.90.61.89.94 ▼ ev. day except Sun.
8am–12 noon 2pm–6pm

DOM. DE LA COQUILLADE 2000★
□ ▦ €3-5
1ha 4,000

La Coquillade is a little village that dates back to the 13th century, near Pont Julien, the oldest Roman bridge in France, and Roussillon, famous for its ochre cliffs. The lovely golden highlights in this white wine and the very fine nose of white flowers, followed by citrus fruits with notes of oak and vanilla, harmonise well and promise good development. Another star was awarded for the **99 red**, aged in oak casks, which one member of the Jury described as 'well structured at every stage of development'.
• Dom. de La Coquillade, Hameau de La Coquillade, 84400 Gargas,
tel. 04.90.74.54.67, fax 04.90.74.71.86 ▼
ev. day except Sun. 10am–12 noon 3pm–7pm; cl. Dec. Feb.
• M. et W. Pluck

LA COURTOISE
Cuvée le Courtois 2000★
▦ €1-3
n.c. 50,000

The lovely deep purple colour envelops the intense aroma of blackcurrant and mulberry, with its supple palate and silky tannins. Interesting and very pleasant, this wine can wait another two or three years.
• SCA La Courtoise, 84210 Saint-Didier,
tel. 04.90.66.01.15, fax 04.90.66.13.19 ▼
by appt.

DOM. DE LA FERME SAINT-MARTIN
Clos des Estaillades 1999
▦ ♂ €5-8

A successful presentation for this 99 with its aroma of liquorice and blackcurrant, spicy and peppery flavour, and prominent tannins. It needs another two years to open up completely.
• Guy Jullien, Dom. de la Ferme Saint-Martin, 84190 Suzette,
tel. 04.90.62.96.40, fax 04.90.62.90.84 ▼
by appt.

DOM. DE LA VERRIERE Le Haut de la Jacotte Elevé en fût de chêne 1999★
▦ €5-8
1.2 ha 6,930

This domaine is where King René of Provence set up his glass-makers from Italy in the 15th century. Today it is a vineyard, and offers a delightful **rosé 2000** that was awarded a star, and this wine, which is just as successful. It still has some of the oak flavour but is strong enough in jammy red fruits. The wine has a fine texture that guarantees promising development.
• Jacques Maubert, Dom. de La Verrière, 84220 Goult, tel. 04.90.72.20.88,
fax 04.90.72.40.33, e-mail laverriere2@wanadoo.fr ▼ ev. day except Sun. 9am–12 noon 2pm–6pm

DOM. LES HERBES BLANCHES 2000★★
▦ €3-5
n.c. 58,000

Here is a wine with a very good value for money. This 2000 is redolent of Provence, breathing thyme, savory, pepper and juniper. A good wine for putting away, it will do justice to game or meat in three or even four years.
• Les Domaines Bernard, rte de Sérignan, 84100 Orange,
tel. 04.90.11.86.86, fax 04.90.34.87.30,
e-mail sagon@domaines-bernard.fr

LES ROCHES BLANCHES Vieilles vignes 2000★★
▦ €3-5
n.c. n.c.

This wine is a dark, intense garnet-red, and the nose, though still slightly closed, soon opens on notes of mineral and red fruit. It is mouth-filling, well textured, nicely full and supple.
• Cave Les Roches blanches, 84570 Mormoiron. tel. 04.90.61.80.07,
fax 04.90.61.97.23 ▼ ev. day except Sun. 8am–12 noon 2pm–6pm

DOM. LES TERRASSES D'EOLE 2000★★
□ €5-8
2.5 ha 16,000

In the Mazan area, a recently discovered Gallo-Roman wine jar dating from 40BC would have been worthy of this perfectly made white wine, with its subtle bouquet of green almonds, citrus fruit and hazelnut. Good for drinking on its own or with a fruit dessert, you can enjoy this treat immediately. The **red Cuvée Lou Mistrau 99** received the same marks for its complex, fragrant bouquet of undergrowth, musk, roasted coffee and red fruit.
• Claude et Stéphane Saurel, chem. des Rossignols, 84380 Mazan.
tel. 04.90.69.84.82, fax 04.90.69.84.90,
e-mail terrasses.eole@online.fr ▼
by appt.

DOM. LE VAN 1999★
▦ ♂ €5-8
5.5 ha 18,100

This estate was established at the foot of Mount Ventoux in 1993. Under the old monarchy, the farm was a chapel called 'Our Lady of the Wind'. This ruby red 99 has a good strong aroma dominated by red fruit (mulberry, morello cherry) and, as one Jury member put it, 'the lovely scent of the sunny garrigue'. On the palate it is round and full, finishing on well-rounded tannins. This is a good wine to serve with dishes in sauce for three to five years.
• Mertens-Sax, SCEA Le Van, rte de Carpentras, 84410 Bédoin,
tel. 04.90.12.82.56, fax 04.90.12.82.57,
e-mail domaine.levan@wanadoo.fr ▼
ev. day 8.30am–7.30pm; 1 Oct.–31 Mar. by appt.

CAVE DE LUMIERES
Les Quatre Vents 2000★

■ 10 ha ▪ 1,800 ▪ €3-5

This *rosé de saignée* is a lovely clear pink with strong highlights. The bouquet breathes red fruit and flowers, the palate is full and round, with the addition of red fruit. Lovely as an aperitif, with a plate of mixed cold cuts.
- Cave de Lumières, 84220 Goult, tel. 04.90.72.20.04, fax 04.90.72.42.52, e-mail info@cavedelumieres.com ☑
- Y by appt.

MARQUIS DE SADE 1998★

■ 8 ha ▪ 50,000 ▪ €5-8

This 98 with its strong bouquet of red fruit dominated by ripe blackcurrant is ready to drink right now, as indicated by the silky tannins and lovely finish. The **white Cuvée Canteperdrix 2000** won the same marks with its luminous colour flecked with green, a strong bouquet of ripe fruit and a flavour ranging from flowers to ripe bananas. It is great to drink with grilled white fish or shellfish. Finally, there is the **red Cuvée Prestige 98** which also won a star for its fleshy texture. In two or three years it will be perfect with red meat or game.
- Les Vignerons de Canteperdrix, rte de Caromb, BP 15, 84380 Mazan, tel. 04.90.69.70.31, fax 04.90.69.87.41 ☑
- Y ev. day except Sun. 8am–12 noon 2pm–6pm

DOM. PELISSON 2000

■ n.c. ▪ n.c. ▪ €5-8

This winery at the foot of the Gordes is tucked away in the middle of its vineyards. All the wines produced here are cultivated organically 'from vine to table' and are marked by strong individuality which will afford a pleasant surprise in two years' time.
- Patrick Pelisson, 84220 Gordes, tel. 04.90.72.28.49, fax 04.90.72.23.91
- Y by appt.

CH. PESQUIE Perle de rosée 2000★

■ 0.6 ha ▪ 3,700 ▪ €5-8

Even though the current architecture dates from the 18th century, Pesquié goes back to the 13th century, and organic farming has characterised the area long before modern fashion decreed it. This beautiful estate's magnificent rosé is dressed to kill: a frosted bottle, prestige label and rose-petal colour. The nose is fresh and strongly floral, and the palate is loaded with red fruit (blackcurrant and redcurrant) 'A rosé by any other name ...?'
- GAEC Ch. Pesquié, rte de Flassan, BP 6, 84570 Mormoiron, tel. 04.90.61.94.08, fax 04.90.61.94.13, e-mail pesquier@infonie.fr Y by appt.
- Chaudière

CAVE SAINT-MARC 2000★

■ 5.2 ha ▪ 35,000 ▪ €3-5

Visitors get a warm welcome in this brightly lit cellar, used for art exhibitions and a display of ancient farming tools. Taste this splendidly refined wine, developed with love and care by Olivier Andrieu, the cellar master, and strikingly original for its flavour of minerals and citrus fruits. It is ready to drink now. The **red Cuvée du Sénéchal 99** was also awarded a star for its complex nose of musk, hummus and gamey truffles.
- Cave Saint-Marc, 84330 Caromb, e-mail cave@st-marc.com ☑
- Y ev. day 8am–12.30pm 2pm–7pm

CH. SAINT-SAUVEUR 1998

■ 1.1 ha ▪ 6,600 ▪ €5-8

As you leave Aubignan, you cannot miss this Romanesque chapel which dates from the 12th century and is used today for wine tasting. It is cool in summer but the welcome is warm; and the heady aroma of the pleasant wine on offer here is enough to make you giddy.
- EARL les Héritiers de Marcel Rey, Ch. Saint-Sauveur, rte de Caromb, 84810 Aubignan, tel. 04.90.62.60.39, fax 04.90.62.60.46 ☑ Y by appt.
- Guy Rey

DOM. DE TARA Hautes Pierres 1999★

▥ 1 ha ▪ 3,700 ▪ €8-11

A blend of 90% Syrah and 10% Grenache, fermented by traditional methods, has produced this 99 with its intense bouquet of vanilla and spices, minerals, ripe blackcurrant and blueberry. The full body and elegant young tannins combine in a well-balanced wine with a lovely spicy finish. It can be drunk for two or three years, say with roast game stuffed with wild mushrooms. A special mention was made by the Jury of the **white Hautes Pierres 99**, for its full body and long flavour.
- Dom. de Tara, Les Rossignols, 84220 Roussillon, tél. 04.90.05.74.87, fax 04.90.05.71.35 ☑
- Y ev. day except Sun. 2pm–6pm
- Droux

TERRE DU LEVANT 2000★★

■ n.c. ▪ n.c. ▪ €3-5

This intense deep purple 2000 impressed the Jury with its powerful bouquet dominated by ripe red fruit that will become even stronger with time. Beautifully round and full, with a Syrah that expands to perfection, this wine can be served for three to four years to accompany to a rack of lamb with Provençal herbs.
- Cellier de Marrenon, BP 13, 84240 La Tour d'Aygues, tél. 04.90.07.40.65, Tour d'Aygues, tél. 04.90.07.30.77, e-mail marrenon@marrenon.com ☑ Y ev. day 8am–12 noon 2pm–6pm (Summer 3pm–7pm); Sun. 8am–12 noon

DOM. TROUSSEL 1999

■ 2.5 ha 1,300 ⬛ €8-11

This wine is a blend of equal parts Grenache and Syrah, with nice tannins that still need to be put away with the wood. Good in two years with white meats or cheese.

➤ Dom. Troussel, 2059, av. Saint-Roch, 84200 Carpentras, tel. 04.90.67.28.35, fax 04.90.60.68.99 ▼ ⚹ by appt.

DOM. DES YVES 2000★★

▮ 15 ha n.c. ■ ⚹ €3-5

Plenty of Grenache (70%) and a lesser amount of Syrah form this wine with its complex aroma and rather original musky flavour. This is a wine to be put away, and to be appreciated in three or four years with meat or jugged hare. Two tasters recommended decanting.

➤ Cellier Val de Durance, Le Grand Jardin, 84360 Lauris, tel. 04.90.08.26.36, fax 04.90.08.28.27

Côtes du Luberon

The Appellation Côtes du Luberon was created on 26 February 1988.

The 36 communes included in this appellation extend over the northern and southern slopes of the limestone mountains of the Luberon, and the vineyard covers nearly 3,000 ha (7,410 acres) and in 2000 169,132 hl (4,465,085 gal) were produced. Côtes du Luberon produce good red wines with a marked character from the quality of the varieties used (Grenache, Syrah) and the distinctive *terroir* on which they grow. The climate is cooler than in the Rhône valley and the late harvests explain the large proportion of white wines (25%) and the acknowledged quality for which they are sought.

CAVE COOPÉRATIVE DE BONNIEUX Cuvée Prestige 2000★

▮ 5 ha 19,020 ■ €3-5

Equal parts Grenache and Syrah, with *saignée* fermentation for this Cuvée Prestige. It is a brilliant pale rose colour with a prominent bouquet of exotic fruit (mango) and blackcurrant, and would be good with grilled meat. The **white Cuvée Tradition en 2000**, also

---

mentioned by the Jury, is very refreshing and nicely balanced, with a long finish. It is recommended to be served with grilled fish.

➤ Cave vinicole de Bonnieux, quartier de la Gare, 84480 Bonnieux, tel. 04.90.75.80.03, fax 04.90.75.92.73,

e-mail vignerons-bonnieux@wanadoo.fr ▼ ⚹ ev. day except Sun. 9am–12 noon 2pm–6pm

DOM. CHASSON Vitis Flora 1999

■ 2 ha 3,000 ⬛ €8-11

This 99 was made from half Grenache and half Syrah, but that does not explain why the wood is so dominant at the moment. It will need to wait a year or two for the oak to integrate.

➤ SCEA Ch. Blanc, quartier Grimaud, 84220 Roussillon, tel. 04.90.05.64.56, fax 04.90.05.72.79 ▼ ⚹ ev. day. 8am–7pm; groups by appt.

DOM. CHATEAU D'AIGUES 2000★

■ 8 ha 40,000 ⬛ ⚹ €3-5

This wine has a glorious cherry-red colour and a strongly intense bouquet of truffle, spices, bayleaf and thyme, plus red fruits. This is a harmonious wine that can safely wait a year before serving with red meat. This winery was also cited for its **red Domaine de Messery 2000** and **red Domaine de La Devention 2000**, two very fruity wines for drinking now.

➤ Cellier Val de Durance, Le Grand Jardin, 84360 Lauris, tel. 04.90.08.26.36, fax 04.90.08.28.27

CH. DE CLAPIER Cuvée réservée 2000★

☐ 1 ha 5,000 ⬛ €5-8

This estate was the former property of the Marquis de Mirabeau, and the Clapier vineyards have belonged to the Montagne family since 1880. Thomas Montagne took over the estate in 1995 and has gradually modernised it. He can be justly proud of his *Cuvée Réservée*, with its slightly closed nose but very pleasant vanilla flavour. The very fine structure and the lovely finish combine to make a very well-crafted wine.

➤ Thomas Montagne, Ch. de Clapier, RN 96, 84120 Mirabeau, tel. 04.90.77.01.03, fax 04.90.77.03.26,

e-mail thomas.montagne@wanadoo.fr ▼ ⚹ ev. day except Sun. Tues. 9am–12 noon 1.30pm–5.30pm

CH. CONSTANTIN-CHEVALIER Cuvée des Fondateurs 2000★★

☐ 6 ha 4,500 ⬛⬛ ⚹ €5-8

The Constantin estate lies within the bounds of the Aygues Brun river which, as it hollowed out the valley of Lourmarin, left a layer of smooth pebbles along its banks. Apart from this geological feature, the vineyard has the benefit of a favourable microclimate. Fermentation is completed in barrel, followed by four months' ageing, giving this wine a wonderfully refreshing flavour of fresh fruit. Well-balanced with a particularly long savoury finish, it is a remarkable wine to be served with grilled fish or shellfish.

• EARL Constantin-Chevalier et Filles, Ch. de Constantin, 84160 Lourmarin, tel. 04.90.68.38.99, fax 04.90.68.37.37 ⊻
⅄ by appt.

■ DOM. FAVEROT 1999 — 3 ha — 13,000 — ■ — €5-8

Established in an 18th-century Provençal *mas* (farmhouse), and converted to wine-growing in 1920, this estate is a newcomer to the *Guide*, presenting its first wine, which has proved quite successful, although some may be taken aback by the high proportion of Carignan. The nose is complex and solid, giving out scents of the garrigue, black olive and stick liquorice. The tannins are well integrated, with a hint of ripe morello cherry.

• Dom. Faveror, L'Allée, BP 9, 84660 Maubec, tel. 04.90.76.65.16, fax 04.90.76.65.16 ⊻ ⅄ by appt.

▽ DOM. FONDACCI Cuvée spéciale 2000 — 10 ha — 18,500 — €5-8

This wine is produced by an even combination of *saignée* and pressing. It is a smooth rosé with a caressing blend of wild strawberry and raspberry and a touch of lemon. 'A nice wine for drinking cool under the linden trees,' remarked one of the Jury members.

• Guy Fondacci, quartier La Sablière, 84580 Oppède, tel. 04.90.71.40.38, fax 04.90.71.40.38 ⊻ ⅄ by appt.

■ DOM. DE GERBAUD 1999★ — 2 ha — 8,000 — ■ — €5-8

Equal proportions of Grenache and Syrah for this dark violet 99, the nose loaded with very ripe black fruit, and a flavour of cocoa, vanilla and overripe fruit. Strong and well-built, this wine can wait happily two or three years.

• SCA Cave de Lourmarin-Cadenet, montée du Galinier, 84160 Lourmarin, tel. 04.90.68.06.21, fax 04.90.68.25.84 ⊻ ⅄ ev. day except Sun. 8am–12 noon 2pm–6pm

□ GRANDE TOQUE 2000★ — n.c. — n.c. — ■ — €3-5

The Marrenon winery, established in 1966, is a union of 13 co-operative ventures. It offers two wines from the same *cuvée*, both awarded a star. The first, pale yellow, slightly golden and brilliant in colour, is blended from 60% white Grenache and 40% Vermentino and gives out a strong scent of yellow fruit, including banana. It goes well with white fish or goat's cheese. The **rosé 2000** has a superb cherry colour with a strong bouquet of red fruit (raspberry, cherry and mulberry). Acidity, richness and alcohol blend delightfully in an elegant harmonious wine.

• Cellier de Marrenon, BP 13, 84240 La Tour d'Aygues, tel. 04.90.07.40.65, fax 04.90.07.30.77, e-mail marrenon@marrenon.com ⊻ ⅄ ev. day 8am–12 noon 2pm–6pm (Summer 3pm–7pm); Sun. 8am–12 noon

□ CH. LA CANORGUE 2000★ — 10 ha — n.c. — ■ — €5-8

The magnificent château dates back to the 17th century, Jean-Pierre Margan, who runs this estate, opted for organic farming methods 15 years ago. He has produced two wines that were very much appreciated by the Jury. This 2000 white, pale yellow with brilliant green reflections, complex and very refined, stands out for the long flavour of white flowers and fruit. Nicely balanced, it will go excellently with red mullet. The **red Château La Canorgue 99** is deep violet tinged with red, its nose of morello cherries and sweet spices still rather closed but with excellent potential for ageing. Leather and pepper feature prominently on the palate in an extraordinarily complex range of flavours. This wine can wait two or three years before serving with leg of lamb.

• EARL Jean-Pierre et Martine Margan, Ch. La Canorgue, 84480 Bonnieux, tel. 04.90.75.81.01, fax 04.90.75.82.98, e-mail chateaucanorgue.margan@wanadoo.fr ⊻ ⅄ by appt.

■ DOM. DE LA CITADELLE Cuvée Le Châtaignier 2000★ — 1.2 ha — 8,000 — ■ — €5-8

Ménerbes is an ancient château fortress of the 16th century, the citadel itself shaped like a ship's prow. In 2002 a wine and truffle centre will be opened here. The estate presents its Châtaignier, with a very fine nose of flowers, beeswax and honey. Fresh and well-balanced, it will go very well with fish in white sauce. The same estate was singled out for its smooth, very well-balanced **rosé 2000**, recommended with rich foods.

• Yves Rousset-Rouard, Dom. de La Citadelle, 84560 Ménerbes, tel. 04.90.72.41.58, fax 04.90.72.41.59, e-mail citadelle@pacwan.fr ⊻ ⅄ ev. day, 9am–12 noon 2pm–6pm; cl. Sun. in winter.

▽ CH. LA DORGONNE L'Expression du terroir 2000★ — 0.75 ha — 2,500 — €5-8

This estate is very close to La Tour-d'Aygues, a large market town in the centre of which are the ruins of a 16th-century château. It offers a particularly successful Cuvée Expression du Terroir, unanimously acclaimed by the Jury. It is fruity and floral with a lovely fragrance of apple, ripe pear and white flowers, good for serving with Mediterranean fish. The same domaine also won a mention from the Jury with its very pale **rosé 2000**.

• SCEA Dom. de La Dorgonne, rte de Mirabeau, 84240 La Tour d'Aygues, tel. 04.90.07.50.18, fax 04.90.07.56.55 ⊻ ⅄ ev. day 8am–8pm

■ DOM. DE LA ROYERE Cuvée spéciale 1999 — 3 ha — 9,300 — ■ — €5-8

Anne Hugues runs her estate with great efficiency. Her attractively dark red wine has

an intense bouquet of ripe fruit, pepper, leather and herbs from the garrigue. It is beautifully blended with good ageing potential. It can wait two years to accompany a meat dish with sauce. The **white Cuvée Spéciale 2000** received the same mark.
• Anne Hugues, Dom. de La Royère, 84580 Oppède, tel. 04.90.76.87.76, fax 04.90.20.85.37, e-mail info@royere.com ▼ ￥ ev. day except Sun. 9am–12 noon 2.30pm–6.30pm; cl. Dec–Mar.

LES BUGADELLES 2000 n.c. n.c. €3–5

The *négociant* offers here a brilliant pale yellow wine with a complex nose of jasmine, peach and citrus fruits. The flavour, too, is floral (elder blossom) with touches of honey and lemon: delightfully balanced and with a good long finish.
• Vignobles du Peloux, quartier Barrade, RN 7, 84350 Courthézon, tel. 04.90.70.42.00, fax 04.90.70.42.15 ▼
￥ by appt.

DOM. LES VADONS 2000★★ 1 ha 7,000 €3–5

This family estate was taken over in 1998 by Louis-Michel Brémond, who immediately set up a winery: and to good effect, for his *Cuvée 2000* is remarkable, red-violet, with a nose of red fruit and blackcurrant jam, and a very pleasant supple palate. A wine, perhaps, to go with small game. The **red Cuvée Aquarelle 2000** from the same domaine was singled out for mention by the Jury. Deep garnet-red colour, a fine nose full of red fruit and a full, silky flavour make this a wine to drink with a raspberry trifle.
• EARL Dom. Les Vadons, La Resparine, 84160 Cucuron, tel. 06.03.00.10.29, fax 06.90.77.13.40, e-mail vadonbreba@terre-net.fr ▼ ￥ by appt.
• Louis-Michel Brémond

CH. DE L'ISOLETTE Cuvée Prestige Vieilles vignes 1999 15 ha 60,000 €8–11

The Château de l'Isolette is built in an area that is still wild and untouched, with some traces of Stone Age relics. This estate is often quoted in the *Guide*, and this time has produced a wine that has spent a long time in cask and does nothing to conceal the fact – which is part and parcel of the wine-maker's craft. Richly smooth on the palate, with a bouquet of mint, pepper and other spices, it is a wine recommended by the tasters for drinking now.
• Ch. de l'Isolette, rte de Bonnieux, 84400 Apt, tel. 04.90.74.16.70, fax 04.90.04.70.73 ▼ ￥ ev. day except Sun. 8am–12 noon 2pm–5.30pm
• EARL Luc Pinatel

DOM. DE MAYOL Cuvée l'Antique 1998★★ 1.2 ha 3,000 €11–15

The domaine, which goes in for organic farming, only just missed out on the *coup de coeur*. The Jury complimented this 98, with its dark, almost black, colour, its predominantly blackcurrant bouquet and its well-balanced palate with a hint of liquorice in the finish. The wine can be put away another two or three years, and will be perfect with poultry or white meat. The **99 red Vieilli en Fût de Chêne**, from the same estate, won a star for its complex bouquet of stewed black fruit, spices and leather.
• Bernard Viguier, Dom. de Mayol, rte de Bonnieux, 84400 Apt, tel. 04.90.74.12.80, fax 04.90.04.85.64, e-mail mayol@worldonline.fr ▼ ￥ ev. day except Sun. 9am–12 noon 2.30pm–7pm

CH. SAINT ESTEVE DE NERI Cuvée de garde 1999 1 ha 6,000 €5–8

This estate is a mile from the village of Ansouis perched on the hillside and dominated by the terraced vineyards of the château. It presented two wines of the same selection, and both were given a special mention, but this one was a neck ahead of the **red Cuvée Grande Réserve Fût de Chêne**. This wine is very well-crafted, with touches of toast, morello cherry and raspberry, but needs a little time to mature.
• SA Ch. Saint Estève de Néri, 84240 Ansouis, tel. 04.90.09.90.16, fax 04.90.09.89.65, e-mail saintestevedeneri@free.fr ▼
￥ by appt.
• Rousselliers

CH. SAINT-PIERRE DE MEJANS 2000 3.5 ha 5,300 €5–8

The estate is a former Benedictine priory with a very lovely inner courtyard. It has produced a strongly coloured rosé, dominated by the 60% Cinsault which aims neither for richness or power. The flavour of raspberry and wild strawberry is light and refreshing.
• Laurence Doan de Champassak, 84160 Puyvert, tel. 04.90.08.40.51, fax 04.90.08.41.96, e-mail bricedoan@yahoo.fr ▼ ￥ by appt.

CH. VAL JOANIS 2000 10 ha 60,000 €5–8

The Chancel family has owned this vast 165-ha (408-acre) estate since 1977. A blend of white Grenache and Roussanne in equal proportions has produced this pale yellow wine shot with green, and an intense bouquet of white flowers and camomile. Fleshy and long, it would be just as good for an aperitif to accompany fish or white-sauce dishes.
• SC du Ch. Val Joanis, 84120 Pertuis, tel. 04.90.79.20.77, fax 04.90.09.69.52, e-mail info.visites@val-joanis.com ▼
￥ by appt.

DOM. DES VAUDOIS 2000★ 10 ha 10,000 €3–5

This estate, a very old Vaudois freehold, has belonged to the family since the 17th century. The vaulted cellar, formerly a cave-dwelling, dates back to 1604. This very elegant 2000, with its subtle floral bouquet, is refreshing and nicely balanced, with good acidity and length on the palate. The estate was also commended for its *rosé 2000*. Fruity and refined, it will go well with southern French recipes.

☞ François Aurouze, rue du Temple, 84240 Cabrières-d'Aigues, tel. 04.90.77.60.87, fax 04.90.77.69.44 ▼

⚲ by appt.

Côtes du Vivarais

CH. DE ROUSSET 2000

6.5 ha	n.c.	€5-8

This lovely 17th-century château offers a 2000 rosé with a deep colour, *saignée* from half Grenache and half Syrah, and an early bouquet strong in confected fruit. This wine is smooth, pleasant, well-balanced, and should be served as soon as possible.

☞ H. et R. Emery, Ch. de Rousset, 04800 Gréoux-les-Bains, tel. 04.92.72.62.49, fax 04.92.72.66.50 ▼ ⚲ ev. day except Sun 2pm–6.30pm; Sat. by appt.

Coteaux de Pierrevert

Located in the Alpes-de-Haute-Provence department, the appellation lies mostly on the slopes of the right bank of the Durance (Corbières, Saint-Tulle, Perrevert, Manosque, etc), on about 210 ha (519 acres). Climatic conditions restrict cultivation to about ten communes of the 42 legally included in the area of the AOC. The red, rosé and white wines, at 17,896 hl (472,454 gal), are fairly low in alcohol, but lively enough, and are enjoyed by the many who travel through this tourist region. The Coteaux de Pierrevert were recognised as an Appellation d'Origine Contrôlée by the INAO National Committee of the INAO in 1998.

DOM. LA BLAQUE Réserve 1998★

5 ha	25,000	€8-11

Three wines were presented, and all three prize-winners. The **white Cuvée 2000** and the **red Cuvée Principale 2000** were both singled out for special mention. This 98 had a long fermentation, followed by a year in the barrel. It is deep red, with a complex bouquet of black fruit, liquorice, and toast, and a delicious flavour that includes caramel and vanilla. Well-balanced, with supple, prominent tannins, the wine can wait a couple of years.

☞ Gilles Delsuc, Dom. de Châteauneuf, 04860 Pierrevert, tel. 04.92.72.39.71, fax 04.92.72.81.26, e-mail domaine.lablaque@wanadoo.fr ▼

⚲ by appt.

Côtes du Vivarais

At the north-western limit of the southern Côtes du Rhône, the Côtes du Vivarais straddle the departments of the Ardèche and the Gard, covering 577 ha (1,425 acres). The communes of Orgnac (famous for its potholes), Saint-Ramèze and Saint-Montan are authorised to add their name to that of the appellation. These wines, produced on limestone soils, are mainly reds made from Grenache (30% minimum) and Syrah (30% minimum), with some typically fresh rosés, which should be drunk young. This former VDQS, which was recognised as an AOC in May 1999, produced 26,980 hl (712,272 gal) of wine in 2000.

BEAUMONT DES GRAS 1999★

n.c.	100,000	€3

This co-operative, which exports half its production, offers a delightful wine with a blended bouquet of fruit and spice. The palate is equally harmonious because of the velvety tannins. Although rich, it is lovely to drink right now.

☞ Les Vignerons Ardéchois, quartier Chaussy, 07120 Ruoms, tel. 04.75.39.98.00, fax 04.75.39.69.48, e-mail vpc@uvica.fr ⚲ ev. day except Sun. 8am–12 noon 3pm–7pm

DOM. DU BELVEZET 1999★

8 ha	8,000	€3-5

The wines from this estate are popular in France, Germany and the Netherlands. Although this 99 may be a little closed, it has a well-balanced flavour built on solid tannins that promise nice development. Good to serve with autumn or winter dishes.

Côtes du Vivarais

☛ René Brunel, rte de Vallon-Pont-d'Arc, 07700 Saint-Remèze, tel. 04.75.04.05.87, fax 04.75.04.05.87, e-mail belvezet.brunel@wanadoo.fr ▼ ❢ by appt.

DOM. DE COMBELONGE 2000 ■ ◊ ▬ €3

□   n.c.   13,000   ▬ ▬ €3

White wine is not a speciality of the region with its stony limestone soil, but this one, a blend of white Grenache and Marsanne, attracted the attention of the jury for its strong, lively flavour. It is ready to drink immediately.

☛ Denis Manent, Dom. de Combelonge, 07110 Vinezac, tel. 04.75.36.92.54, fax 04.75.36.99.59 ▼ ❢ by appt.

DOM. DE LA BOISSERELLE 1999 ▬ €3-5

■   4 ha   20,000   ▬ €3-5

Syrah dominates the Grenache by 70% in this deep red wine, which seems to have retained the flavour of its *terroir*, a dry plain with strong climatic contrasts. Delightfully fruity on nose and palate.

☛ Richard Vigne, Dom. de La Boisserelle, 07700 Saint-Remèze, tel. 04.75.04.24.37, fax 04.75.04.24.37, e-mail domainedelaboisserelle@wanadoo.fr ▼ ❢ by appt.

UNION DES PRODUCTEURS

Réserve 1999   ■   60 ha   80,000   ▬ €3-5

This dark wine opens with strongly concentrated fruit which dominates the palate as well without a false note. The **rosé 2000** with its fresh, lively flavour, is recommended with meat and cold cuts.

☛ Union des Producteurs, 07150 Orgnac l'Aven, tel. 04.75.38.60.08, fax 04.75.38.65.90 ❢ ev. day except Sat. Sun. 8am–12 noon 2pm–6pm

LES VIGNERONS DE LA CAVE DE SAINT-MONTAN 2000   ▬ €3

▬   10 ha   13,000   ▬ €3

This rosé, predominantly Grenache, was cultivated on a plain in Ardèche, and is a nice fleshy wine. Fruity and light floral notes blend well. The **red Côtes du Vivarais 99** is also worth noting: rich in flavour, it will go well with grilled meat.

☛ SCA les Vignerons la Cave de Saint-Montan, Bas Viressac, 07220 Saint-Montan, tel. 04.75.52.61.75, fax 04.75.52.56.51, e-mail cavesaintmontan@free.fr ▼ ❢ by appt.

DOM. DE VIGIER Cuvée Prestige 1999 ▬ €3-5

■   2 ha   13,000   ▬ €3-5

This estate, close to the Ardèche gorges, has produced a red wine with a strong musky aroma. Round and full, it seems perfect to serve with cold cuts. From the same estate comes **white Côtes du Vivarais 2000**, a blend of Clairette, Grenache and Marsanne that is worth a mention for its fresh citrus fruit aroma. This would be perfect as an aperitif after a walk in the Ibie valley.

☛ Dupré et Fils, Dom. de Vigier, 07150 Lagorce, tel. 04.75.88.01.18, fax 04.75.37.18.79 ▼ ❢ by appt

BERNARD VIGNE 2000★★

■   2 ha   13,000   ▬ ◊   €3-5

Equal parts of Grenache and Syrah for this blended red wine with its strong nose and palate of violet and blackcurrant. Nicely balanced, it can be served right now, but is likely to improve with time.

☛ Bernard Vigne, Vallée de l'Ibie, 07150 Lagorce, tel. 04.75.37.19.00 ▼ ❢ by appt.

The wine-makers of Roussillon have made highly regarded the principle of 'mutage'. This involves adding brandy to the must of red or white wines at the moment of full fermentation, a process that prevents further fermentation but preserves a certain quantity of sugar.

The AOC of these sweet wines stretches discontinuously through various parts of southern France: Pyrénées-Orientales, Aude, Hérault, Vaucluse and Corsica — but never too far from the Mediterranean. The principal grape varieties used are the Grenaches (Blanc, Gris and Noir), Macabeu, Malvoisie du Roussillon, also called Tourbat, Muscat à Petit Grains and Muscat d'Alexandrie. Compulsory regulations govern the way the vines are grown and pruned.

The yields are low and, at harvest, the must is required to have a minimum 252 g of sugar per litre. The sugar released at harvest varies depending on the region. Individual wines are accepted only after meeting rather stringent criteria: they must have reached between 15% and 18% alcohol by volume, have a minimum 45 g of sugar per litre (up to more than 100 g per litre for the Muscats), and have a total alcohol level (alcohol content plus strength of alcohol) of at least 21.5%. Some are sold only after three years' ageing in wooden barrels, the traditional method. The level is maintained by topping up with younger wines. Wines aged in this way acquire the particular flavour described as 'rancio', which is a legal definition in wine law. In 2000 total production of these wines was 447,538 hl (11,815,003 gal).

Banyuls and
Banyuls Grand Cru

This exceptional *terroir* is on the extreme east of the Pyrenees, with steeply sloping hills overlooking the Mediterranean. Only the four communes of Collioure, Port-Vendres, Banyuls-sur-Mer and Cerbère are entitled to the appellation. The terraced vineyards (roughly 1,400 ha (3,458 acres) are on schistous soils with a rocky substratum which, when not immediately visible, is often covered with a thin layer of topsoil. Thus the *terroir* is poor, often acid, and supports only very ordinary vine varieties, such as Grenache, producing a very low yield, often less than about 20 hl per ha (216 gal per acre).

In 2000 production of Banyuls was 29,289 hl (773,230 gal).

On the other hand, the amount of sunshine is maximised by the terraced cultivation (the wine-growers have to maintain the terraces by hand to protect the soil, which can be washed away by the slightest storm). With the additional benefit of proximity to the Mediterranean, the grapes become gorged with sugar and aromatic qualities.

Old Grenache vines predominate. Vinification involves macerating the bunches of grapes; 'mutage' (the addition of brandy) may be carried out at this stage, allowing substantial maceration lasting more than ten days, a method known as maceration in alcohol.

Banyuls

have a characteristic bouquet of dried grapes, cooked fruit, grilled almonds, coffee and prune brandy. The *rimages* retain their aromas of soft fruit, cherry and cherry brandy. Banyuls wines should be served at temperatures from 12–17°C (53.6–62.2°F), according to their age. They may be drunk as an apéritif, with dessert (some consider Banyuls the only wine to drink with a chocolate dessert, for example), with coffee and a cigar, but equally with foie gras, duck with cherries or figs and also with certain cheeses.

The way in which the wine is brought on plays an essential part. In general, it tends to favour the oxidative development of the wine, either in wood (large barrels of 200–300 hectolitres or wooden casks of 600 litres) or in *bonbonnes* (squat, bulbous containers) exposed to the warmth of the sun under the roofs of the cellars. The different vintages brought on in this way are blended with the greatest care by the cellar-master to create the numerous types of wine that we know. In some contrary cases, the wine is brought on in a way specifically designed to maintain its youthful fruitiness and prevent oxidisation: thus, different wines are obtained with highly specific characteristics; these are called the *rimages* or 'varieties'. To earn the Appellation Grand Cru, wines must brought on in wooden casks for 30 months.

The wines range in colour from ruby to mahogany, and

Banyuls

BERTA-MAILLOL Rimage 1999

■ ▬ 4 ha ● 9,000 ■ ♦ €8–11

The sculptor Aristide Maillol was born at Banyuls in 1861, and he often returned to the village where he had spent his childhood. He owned this 15-ha (37-acre) estate, which was

Vins Doux Naturels

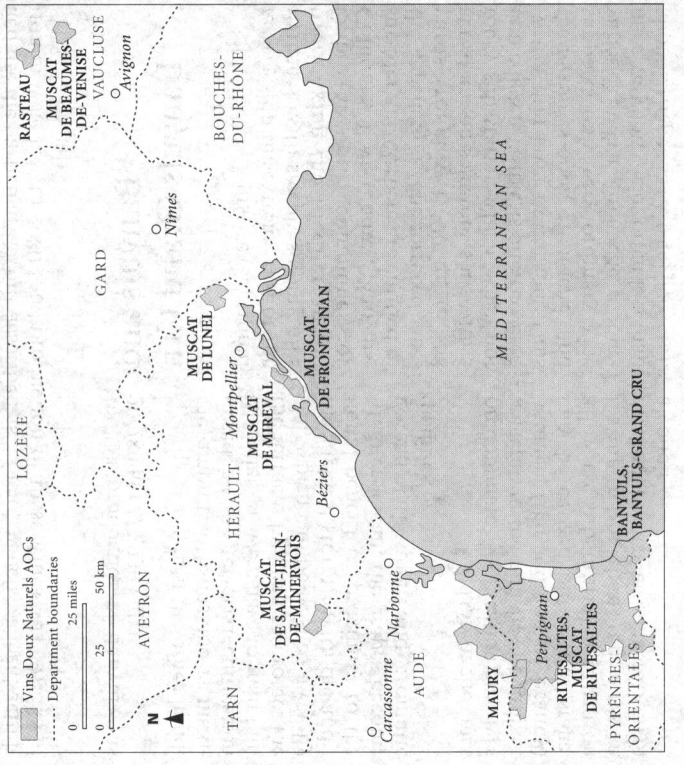

established in 1873, and although it was certainly not the straight lines of the terraces that inspired him, it is possible to find in his female nudes an echo of the roundness, flesh and fruit of the Banyuls *rimages*. This deep red wine conjures up ripe fruit, fresh harvest and undergrowth. Crisp cherry and pronounced tannins feature on the palate, which is very sweet.

➤ Yvon et Jean-Louis Berta-Maillol, mas Paroutet, 66650 Banyuls-sur-Mer, tel. 04.68.88.00.54, fax 04.68.88.36.96 ▼

Ⓨ by appt.

CORNET Rimage 1998★★★

■   n.c.   5,304   ■ €11-15

Cornet is a brand of La Cave de l'Abbé Rous, which perpetuates the memory of François Rous, one of the pioneers of direct selling in the 1880s. This magnificent 98 *rimage*, sold only to the trade (cellarmen and restaurateurs), displays its youth as much by its very sustained colour as by its intense aroma of morello cherries overlying leather and damp undergrowth. Fruits and spices combine in a rich, full palate, which is well structured yet velvety. What would go with it? Fruit salad or duck with cherries. La Cave was also awarded a star for a **1999 Régis Cuvée Boucabeille Rimage**.

➤ La Cave de l'Abbé Rous, 56, av. Charles-de-Gaulle, 66650 Banyuls-sur-Mer, tel. 04.68.88.72.72, fax 04.68.88.30.57

CROIX-MILHAS★★

■   n.c.   13,000   ⬥ €5-8

At the end of the 19th century, the Violet family made the medieval city of Thuir into the capital of the aromatised wine-based aperitif. Relics of this era are the barrel stores and the 95-m (104-yd) -long station hall, which was built by the Eiffel workshop of gigantism, where the 'largest oak vat in the world' (1,000,200 l/264,053 gals) is a tourist attraction, 13,000 bottles are just a drop in the ocean. The brick red colour of this Banyuls and the aromas of prunes, crystallised fruit and a spicy touch of old oak indicate a light maturation. The palate is rich, full and well balanced with toasty notes accompanying a

fruity body, and it opens out into a remarkable finish with notes of tobacco and spices.

➤ Cusenier, 6, bd Violet, BP 1, 66300 Thuir, tel. 04.68.53.05.42, fax 04.68.53.31.00 ▼

Ⓨ ev. day 9am-11.45am 2.30pm-5.45pm; cl. 1-15 Jan.

DOMINICAIN

Vieilli en fût de chêne 1991★★

■   n.c.   20,000   ⬥ €8-11

Collioure, a bright little port on the Vermilion Coast, has retained a rich architectural heritage. During the Revolution the Dominican monastery, founded in 1290, met with the same fate as a number of other monastic establishments: it was nationalised and then taken over by the army. In 1926 the commune's wine-producers bought the various buildings, largely consisting of a Gothic church. This wine cellar, which is open throughout the year, is situated to the south of the town, on the road to Port-Vendres. Discover this excellent brick red Banyuls with hints of mahogany, which releases aromas of coffee and warm minerals. This perfectly balanced 91 wine is rich, harmonious and sweet on the palate. It is marked by aromas of prunes and crystallised fruit, giving way to roasted notes in the finish.

➤ Cave Le Dominicain,
pl. Orfila, 66190 Collioure,
tel. 04.68.82.05.63, fax 04.68.82.43.06,
e-mail ledominicain@wanadoo.fr ▼

Ⓨ ev. day 9am-12 noon 2pm-6pm

DOM. DE LA CASA BLANCA 1999★

□   1 ha   2,000   ■ ⬥ €8-11

The estate, which was awarded a *coup de coeur* in the last edition of the *Guide* (a *coup de coeur* in the last edition of the *Guide* for a 97 wine), is featured this year for its rare white Banyuls produced from 80-year-old vines. It is a 50/50 blend of Grenache Blanc and Gris, with the silvery glints being typical of this latter grape variety. There are aromas of broom and honeyed heathland flowers on the nose, then a supple attack unveils fruit, quickly followed by bitter almonds, on the palate leading to a very fresh finish. Slightly dry, this wine is a good example of the local *terroir*.

➤ Dom. de La Casa Blanca, rte des Mas, 66650 Banyuls-sur-Mer, tel. 04.68.88.12.85, fax 04.68.88.04.08 ▼ Ⓨ by appt.

➤ Soufflet et Escapa

DOM. LA TOUR VIEILLE

Vintage 1999★

■   1 ha   n.c.   ■ ⬥ €11-15

It is no surprise to find this estate appearing again. Managed with passion by Vincent Cantié and Christine Campadieu, its wines, whether dry or sweet, are regularly singled out in the *Guide*. The enterprise also exports a large proportion (40%) of its production. A deep red, this young vintage has a very marked ripe cherry aroma, a flavour that continues on the palate, where it mingles with strawberries. Sweet and supple in the attack, it reveals strong tannins, indicating a wine capable of long ageing.

VDN

well structured, rich and full, and blends a toasted note with aromas of *pain d'épice*.

☛ Maguy et Laetitia Piétri-Géraud, 22, rue Pasteur, 66190 Collioure, tel. 04.68.82.07.42, fax 04.68.98.02.58 **Ⓜ** **Ⓨ** ev. day 10am–12.30pm 3.30pm–6.30pm cl. Sun. Mon. out of school holidays

CELLIER DES TEMPLIERS

Rimatge 1999   n.c.   106,900 **●** **€11-15**

With several *coups de coeur* to its credit (including one for an 85 *rimatge*), the Cellier des Templiers is a definite asset to this region. Produced from Grenache Noir, the *rimatge* ('harvest' in Catalan) Banyuls are prepared without oxidative maturation to preserve the fruit. This one is dark ruby in colour, with vivacious cherry and blackcurrant aromas, accompanied by brandied fruit and very spicy tannins, all of which give an excellent idea of the wine's youth. Altogether an excellent wine.

☛ Cellier des Templiers, rte du Mas-Reig, 66650 Banyuls-sur-Mer, tel. 04.68.98.36.70, fax 04.68.98.36.91 **Ⓜ**
Ⓨ ev. day 10am–7.30pm

L'ETOILE

Cuvée spéciale 75ème anniversaire ★★★

■   3 ha   6,000   **■** **Ⓜ** **€23-30**

This co-operative produces wine from 140 ha (346 acres) of vines. It has numerous *coups de coeur* to its credit for its Banyuls and Banyuls Grand Cru, stretching back to the very first edition of the *Guide*. This year's production is also memorable: the **Extra-Vieux 88** is still as good as it was last year, and the **Macéré Tuilé 89** is in the same class, as is this wine, which celebrates the 75th anniversary of the cellar. A surprising aged and copper-coloured wine, it has grilled hazelnut aromas mingling with fruit kernel brandy. The palate is superb and full, with dominant aromas of dried hazelnut, roasted hazelnut and coffee, and it has a very lengthy finish with notes of nuts and *rancio*.

☛ Sté coopérative L'Etoile, 26, av. du Puig-del-Mas, 66650 Banyuls-sur-Mer, tel. 04.68.88.00.10, fax 04.68.88.15.10 **Ⓜ** **Ⓨ** ev. day except Sat. Sun. 8am–12 noon 2pm–6pm

LES CLOS DE PAULILLES

Rimage mise tardive 1998   **Ⓜ** **€11-15**

■   2 ha   6,000

Planted on the vertiginous slopes that plunge into one of the prettiest coves of the Vermilion Coast, south of Cape Béar, this vineyard is one of the wine-growing jewels of the Dauré family, who are well known abroad (Les Clos exports 60% of its production). This wine-maker has produced a Banyuls that, in contrast to a classic *rimage*, has undergone a short maturation in wood before being bottled. The process aims to achieve good fruit and long ageing potential. Here it has given rise to an intense red colour and aromas of mulberries mixed with cherry brandy and spices. Warming and peppery, with notes of cherry and zesty acidity, the palate has a tannic character that guarantees a good future.

☛ Les Clos de Paulilles, baie de Paulilles, 66660 Port-Vendres, tel. 04.68.38.90.10, fax 04.68.38.91.33, e-mail daure@wanadoo.fr **Ⓜ** **Ⓨ** ev. day 10am–11pm; cl. 1 Oct.–1 Jun.
☛ Famille Dauré

DOM. DU TRAGINER 1996★

■   3 ha   6,000

For many years men and mules toiled together on the narrow vineyard terraces of Banyuls. Jean-François Deu has farmed this estate since 1975 and, although it is modest in area (slightly less than 9 ha or 22 acres), it is nevertheless well-known abroad, exporting half of its wines. He remains faithful in his labours to the rustic and ancestral beast of burden; indeed, *traginer* means 'muleteer' in Catalan. The result of this alliance of strength and intelligence, this Banyuls reflects the 'kick' of the wine-producer and the contribution of the Grenache Gris, which constitutes 30% of the blend. The colour contains hints of fawn, and old casks contribute notes of leather, venison and cocoa. On the palate mellow tannins mingle with crystallised fruit and drier notes of cocoa and dark tobacco to excellent effect.

☛ Dom. du Traginer, 56, av. du Puig-del-Mas, 66650 Banyuls-sur-Mer, tel. 04.68.88.15.11, fax 04.68.88.31.48 **Ⓜ**
Ⓨ by appt.

DOM. PIETRI-GERAUD 1999★

□   1 ha   3,000   **Ⓜ** **€11-15**

White Banyuls represent scarcely 10% of the production in this appellation, yet this is the second, and again very successful, example mentioned in the *Guide*. It bears the name of Maguy Piétri-Géraud and her daughter, Laetitia, who run the 32-ha (79-acre) family estate, established in 1890 and situated at the heart of Collioure. Produced from 60-year-old white Grenache vines, this gold-coloured 99 wine has a perfume of honeyed flowers. The palate is

LES VIGNERONS CATALANS

1995★   **Ⓜ** **€6-11**

□   4 ha   12,000

For their entry in the Banyuls section of the *Guide* the Vignerons Catalans have backed Grand Cru and wood maturation. This Banyuls is a beautiful brick-red in colour, and the nose mingles aromas of undergrowth, prunes, spices and tobacco. The palate is supple and velvety, with grilled notes accented with cocoa. A mature wine, it is ready to drink. Serve it with a chocolate dessert. (50 cl bottles)

☛ Vignerons Catalans, 1870, av. Julien-Panchot, 66011 Perpignan Cedex, tel. 04.68.85.04.51, fax 04.68.55.25.62, e-mail vignerons.catalans@wanadoo.fr

Y by appt.

CLOS CHATART 1990 ★★★

■ 0.5 ha   750   € 23-30

Together with a distinguished **Banyuls 98**, Jacques Laverrière submitted this limited-edition, beautifully matured *cuvée*. It is a warm brick-red in colour and has a complex aromatic palate of leather, peat, cocoa and dried fruit. Full, mellow and harmonious, it finishes with roasted notes. Drink it with chocolate, coffee or a Havana cigar.

☛ Clos Chatart, 66650 Banyuls-sur-Mer, tel. 04.68.88.12.58, fax 04.68.88.51.51

Y by appt.

☛ J. Laverrière

JEAN D'ESTAVEL Prestige ★

■ n.c.   n.c.   € 8-11

While numerous Banyuls producers will be going it alone in future, the local *négociant* continues to invest in production. The house of Destavel offers a most successful Grand Cru. Still rich in colour, it releases aromas of prune, cocoa and roasting, which underline its 30-month maturation in barrels. The full, rich palate develops inviting notes of tobacco, peat, chocolate and brandied fruit.

☛ SA Destavel, 7 bis av. du Canigou, 66000 Perpignan, tel. 04.68.68.36.00, fax 04.68.54.03.54

LA CAVE DE L'ABBE ROUS
Cuvée Christian Reynal 1993 ★★

■ n.c.   5,387   € 30-38

This subsidiary of GICB sells only to restaurateurs and cellarmen. The **Cornet 95** was much enjoyed (one generous star), and as for this Christian Reynal, it offered more than simply a remarkable wine, providing complete satisfaction for the wine-lover. Having spent six years in the barrel, this wine is a brick-red colour, close to *rancio*. Red fruit gives way to hazelnut, raisin and walnut aromas, the initial impression is confirmed on the palate with figs, quince and spices, opening out to walnut again and a very long, spicy finish.

☛ La Cave de L'Abbé Rous, 56, av. Charles-de-Gaulle, 66650 Banyuls-sur-Mer, tel. 04.68.88.72.72, fax 04.68.88.30.57

L'ETOILE Doux paillé Hors d'âge ★★★

■ 3 ha   6,700   € 23-30

This co-operative is well known to readers of the *Guide*, and this new bottling of its straw-coloured sweet wine is a delight. It has undergone maturation in wooden casks, spent time in demijohns, where it was exposed to the sun, then had a rest period in vats, all under the patient care of Jean-Paul Ramio and his oenologist, Patrick Terrier. During the ageing process, the initial red colour has turned a lovely, brilliant russet-amber. The nose is expressively powerful and elegant, developing walnut, mild tobacco, hay, honey and dried apricot aromas. An outstanding, full and generous palate has apricots mingling with crystallised fruit and toast flavours leading to a long lingering *rancio* finish.

☛ Sté cooperative L'Etoile, 26, av. du Puig-del-Mas, 66650 Banyuls-sur-Mer, tel. 04.68.88.00.10, fax 04.68.88.15.10

Y ev. day except Sat, Sun. 8am-12 noon 2pm-6pm

CELLIER DES TEMPLIERS
Cuvée Président Henry Vidal 1988 ★★

■ n.c.   57,500   € 23-30

If you have visited the Cellier des Templiers at Banyuls-sur-Mer, you will have seen the wooden casks of various shapes and sizes ageing in the sun. You will certainly have come across those in which the superb one-star **Mas de la Serra 93** is maturing, together with this President Henry Vidal wine, whose vintages, described in successive editions of the *Guide*, range from remarkable to exceptional. The initial impression is faultless. The nose is rich in promise but the palate is a delight, with its suppleness, elegance and great finesse, and flavours of grilled hazelnut, tobacco and cocoa blended with crystallised fruit. It is a well-balanced wine, ready to serve with a chocolate dessert, coffee or a Havana cigar.

☛ Cellier des Templiers, rte du Mas-Reig, 66650 Banyuls-sur-Mer, tel. 04.68.98.36.70, fax 04.68.98.36.91

Y ev. day 10am–7.30pm

VIAL-MAGNERES
Cuvée André Magnères 1991 ★★

■ 1.25 ha   4,000   € 15-23

Monique and Bernard Sapéras feature most often in the *Guide* for their white Vintage type and their old Banyuls, but they have also been included in the past with a Grand Cru of this same wine, awarded a *coup de coeur* for the 88 vintage. With a faded colour, this 91 wine has hints of *rancio* and aromas of kernelled fruit, brandy and toast. Dominated by walnut and the oily *rancio* note, the palate is surprisingly pleasant in its richness, fullness and velvety texture. It is a remarkable wine.

or blackberry. They may be drunk as an aperitif or with dessert, and should be served at a temperature from 11–15°C (51.8–59°F), depending on their age.

➤ Dom. Vial-Magnères, Clos Saint-André, 14, rue Edouard-Herriot, 66650 Banyuls-sur-Mer, tel. 04.68.88.31.04, fax 04.68.55.01.06, e-mail al.tragou@wanadoo.fr ▣ ▼ by appt.
➤ M. and B. Saperas

Rivesaltes

In terms of area this is the biggest appellation of Vins Doux Naturels, with 14,000 ha (34,580 acres) producing 264,000 hl (6,969,600 gal) in 1995. In 1996 nearly 4,000 ha (9,880 acres) fell victim to frost; production slumped below 200,000 hl (5,280,000 gal), and the Rivesaltes Plan was introduced to re-organise the vineyard, now in economic difficulties, but in 2000 production was 131,000 hl (3,458,400 gal). The *terroir* of Rivesaltes lies in Roussillon and in a very small part of Corbières, on poor, dry, hot soils that produce well-ripened grapes. Four varieties are permitted: Grenache, Maccabeu, Malvoisie and Muscat, although only small proportions of Malvoisie and Muscat are included. White wines are generally vinified normally, but maceration is also used, especially for the Grenache Noir, to achieve a maximum in colour and tannin.

How the Rivesaltes wines are brought on is crucial in determining quality. Whether brought on in the vat or in wooden casks, they develop very different bouquets. (In difficult years, there is also an option for the wines to be downgraded as Appellation Grand Roussillon.)

The wines range in colour from amber to tile-red, with a bouquet, at its most expressive, recalling roasting coffee, dry fruit or the nutty flavour of *rancio*. When young, red Rivesaltes have aromas of soft fruit: cherry, blackcurrant

ARNAUD DE VILLENEUVE
Ambré Hors d'âge 1982★★
▣ n.c. 8,980 €15-23

The hardest thing about wine-making is having to wait almost 20 years until the perfect blend of the old Ambrés (Muscat and Grenache) finally comes together. Here, the amber colour has softened with ageing in old barrels and is tinged with russet. Crystallised orange peel dominates the exotic notes of kumquat and the smoky, woody *rancio*. Mellow and sweet, yet still fresh, the whole is pleasant, full of citrus fruit leading to a finish with roasted notes, softened by hazelnut.

➤ Les Vignobles du Rivesaltais, 1, rue de la Roussillonnaise, 66602 Rivesaltes-Salses, tel. 04.68.64.06.63, fax 04.68.64.64.69, e-mail vignobles.rivesaltais@wanadoo.fr ▼
▼ by appt.

CH. BELLOCH Vieux Hors d'âge★★
▣ 7 ha 5,000 €8-11

Between Perpignan and the Mediterranean the last terraces of the Têt carry vines right up to the lake, forming a beautiful vista of blues and greens. Amber and russet in colour, the result of cask ageing, this wine has aromas of raisins, fruits in syrup, citrus fruit and quince jelly, indicating very ripe grapes. The fruit flavours continue on the mature and full palate, with crystallised fruit pleasantly offset by touches of roasting and toasted almond.

➤ Cibaud SA ch. Miraflors et Belloch, rte de Canet, 66000 Perpignan, tel. 04.68.34.03.05, fax 04.68.51.31.70, e-mail vins.cibaud@wanadoo.fr ▼
▼ ev. day except Sun. 9am–1pm 3pm–7pm
➤ Cibaud

DOM. JOSEPH BORY 1999★★★
▣ 10 ha 1,500 €5-8

All wine-lovers should visit this estate at Bages for its architecture, delightful atmosphere and the quality of its range of wines. This 99 offering is very deep and rich in colour, with a lovely blend of aromas of ripe fruit, cherries and strawberries with spicy undertones. Very pleasant on the palate, it is full, well structured, very fruity and already showing a remarkable mellowness. It is a perfectly balanced wine.

➤ Mme Andrée Verdeille, Dom. Joseph Bory, 6, av. Jean-Jaurès, 66670 Bages, tel. 04.68.21.71.07, fax 04.68.21.71.07 ▼
▼ ev. day except Sun. 9am–12 noon 3pm–6pm

DOM. BOUDAU Sur grains 1999 €8-11

■ 5 ha 10,000

Véronique Boudau is cellar-master of this 80-ha (198-acre) estate and it is worth meeting her to hear her talk enthusiastically about the old Grenache vines, the rounded pebbled soil, alcohol being added directly to the grape berries and the long maceration periods practised. Go for this remarkably well-balanced 99, which is dark red in colour, with an initial impression of cherries and mulberries followed by fruit and silky tannins.

Dom. Véronique et Pierre Boudau, 6, rue Marceau, 66600 Rivesaltes, tel. 04.68.64.45.37, fax 04.68.64.46.26 ⊻ ev. day except Sun.10am-12 noon 3pm-7pm Jun.-Sept.

CH. DE CALADROY Tuilé Cuvée Bacchus

■ 5 ha 15,000

The history of this château, built on the ancient border between Roussillon and the kingdom of France, is lost in the mists of time. Having changed hands in 1999, it is now beginning a new millennium. This Bacchus wine has developed a lovely brick-red colour and a characteristic nose of prunes and sweetness from the time it has spent in large, old wooden casks. Notes of crystallised fruit and prunes in alcohol vie on the palate, leading to an astonishing citrus fruit finish.

SCEA ch. de Caladroy, 66720 Bélesta, tel. 04.68.57.10.25, fax 04.68.57.27.76, e-mail chateau.caladroy@wanadoo.fr ⊻ ev. day except Sat. Sun. 8am-12 noon 1.30pm-5.30pm

CAVE DE CASES DE PENE Vieux Hors d'âge Tuilé Vieilli en fût de chêne ★

■ 7 ha 4,000 €5-8

Having spent five years maturing, Rivesaltes can lay claim to being hors d'âge. Brick red-orange with an amber patina, its maturation in old oak casks brings out intense scents of prune, quince and hay. There is a wonderful balance between the fruit's richness and the mellowness of the tannins and between honeyed tobacco and bitter cocoa. This wine is ready to drink, particularly with dessert.

Ch. de Pena, 2, bd Mal-Joffre, 66600 Cases-de-Pène, tel. 04.68.38.91.91, fax 04.68.38.92.42, e-mail chateau-de-pena@wanadoo.fr ⊻ ev. day except Sun. 8am-12 noon 2pm-6pm

DOM. CAZES Cuvée Aimé Cazes 1976 ★★★

□ 6.7 ha 10,000 €46-76

At Cazes, the difficulty lies in choosing. The Jury selected a lovely **Vintage 95** (one star), the superb **Ambré 91** (two stars), which has great finesse and is excellent value for money, as well as this unmissable Cuvée Aimé Cazes '76, a tribute to the family's exceptional father, who died recently. After 22 years in oak barrels, the gold colour has coppery glints with aromas of bitter orange and dry apricot mingling with the milky sweetness of coconut. The perfectly balanced palate is a delight, and the wine is smooth, mellow and full, with honeyed tobacco and cut hay flavours leading to a magnificent finish enhanced by hints of lemon.

André et Bernard Cazes, 4, rue Francisco-Ferrer, BP 61, 66602 Rivesaltes, tel. 04.68.64.08.26, fax 04.68.64.69.79, e-mail info@cazes-rivesaltes.com ⊻ by appt.

COLLECTION Ambré 1995 ★★

□ 4 ha 12,000 €5-8

The Vignerons Catalans, the main producer of Côtes du Roussillon, can also produce stunning Rivesaltes as shown in this Collection. Copper-amber in colour, with aromas of kumquat and dried apricot, this is a wine of delicacy and finesse. Orange and apricot accompany a woody note and a silky texture. Drink it with biscotti. (50 cl bottles)

Vignerons Catalans, 1870, av. Julien-Panchot, 66011 Perpignan Cedex, tel. 04.68.85.04.51, fax 04.68.55.25.62, e-mail vignerons.catalans@wanadoo.fr ⊻ by appt.

CH. DE CORNEILLA Rubis 1989 ★★★

■ 2.5 ha 6,000 €11-15

This 12th-century château was built by the Templars, and has been a family estate for more than 500 years. The family has borne the colours of France in international fencing and riding competitions and its history continues in the field of viticulture, with this wine, whose colour lies between brick red and mahogany. The milky sweetness of chocolate, silky tannins, honeyed notes of mild tobacco, roast cocoa and finally a hint of malt, all combine to provide a perfectly-balanced, exceptional wine.

EARL Jonquères d'Oriola, Ch. de Corneilla, 66200 Corneilla-del-Vercol, tel. 04.68.22.73.22, fax 04.68.22.43.99, e-mail chateaudecorneilla@hotmail.com ⊻ by appt. Philippe Jonquères d'Oriola

LES VIGNERONS DES COTES D'AGLY Tuilé Cuvée François Arago Vieilli en fût de chêne 1994★

■ 10 ha n.c. ■ ⅢD ♦ €8–11

Estagel lies in the heart of the Agly Valley, and has named this wine in honour of the 19th-century scientist and politician, François Arago. An intense, deep mahogany-red colour, this wine exudes aromas of brandied plums and Havana cigars. Robust, with good fruit structure, the palate has smoky and cut-hay notes. Enjoy it with coffee or a cigar.

☛ Les Vignerons des Côtes d'Agly, Cave coopérative, 66310 Estagel,
tel. 04.68.29.00.45, fax 04.68.29.19.80,
e-mail agly@little-france.com ☒ ⅄ ev. day except Sat. Sun. 8am–12 noon 2pm–6pm

CROIX-MILHAS Ambré★

☐ n.c. 50,000 ■ €5–8

The Cusenier house, at Thuir, is a piece of history in a unique setting where 800 large wooden casks sit alongside Eiffel's architecture. It is a 'must see'. You can also taste this wine: a clear, brilliant, ambered old gold, with honeyed notes of wood patina, dried apricot and a hint of citrus fruit that continues on the round, supple palate and finishes with hints of brandied fruits.

☛ Cusenier, 6, bd Violet, BP 1, 66300 Thuir,
tel. 04.68.53.05.42, fax 04.68.53.31.00 ☒
⅄ ev. day 9am–11.45am 2.30pm–5.45pm; cl. 1–15 Jan.

DOM BRIAL Ambré 1996★★★

☐ n.c. 15,000 ⅢD €5–8

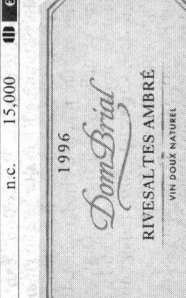

1996

Dom Brial

RIVESALTES AMBRÉ

VIN DOUX NATUREL

This bawdy monk established his mark in the *Guide* a long time ago, working on the amber-coloured *Vins Doux Naturels* rather than the gold of the remarkable altar-piece at Baixas. This 1996 wine is clear, russet-amber in colour, and on the nose, it is a riot of honey, wax, mild tobacco and cut hay. Full, rich, fine and fresh on the palate, a balance of ripe fruit and toast, this harmonious wine has hazelnut notes on the finish.

☛ Cave des Vignerons de Baixas,
14, av. Mal-Joffre, 66390 Baixas,
tel. 04.68.64.22.37, fax 04.68.64.26.70,
e-mail baixas@smi-telecom.fr ☒ ⅄ by appt.

DOM. ELS BARBATS Garance 1998★★★

☐ 2 ha 1,866 ■ ♦ €8–11

Situated next to the experimental station for Roussillon wines, which is of invaluable use to the wine-producers, this 18-ha (45-acre) estate offers a superb Garance wine. It is an attractive brick-red colour with

well-developed scents of prune, leather and dried fruit. The rich and mellow palate is dominated by ripe fruit offset by toasty notes. The roasted finish calls for coffee and chocolate.

☛ Paul Milhe Poutingon, Mas Els Barbats,
66300 Tresserre, tel. 04.68.83.28.51,
fax 04.68.83.28.51 ☒ ⅄ by appt.

DOM. JOLIETTE Vintage 1998

■ 2 ha 6,000 ■ ♦ €8–11

A superb estate with a view of the sea and lakes where red clay soil gently gives way to black marls. The name 'Joliette' does not do justice to the wine! Deep red in colour, with pronounced undergrowth and ripe-cherry aromas, robust and powerful, this is a wine for ageing. Drink with chocolate.

☛ A. et Ph. Mercier, Dom. Joliette,
rte de Vingrau, 66600 Espira-de-l'Agly,
tel. 04.68.64.50.60, fax 04.68.64.18.82 ☒
⅄ by appt.

CH. LA CASENOVE Tuilé 1998

■ 20 ha 6,000 ■ €11–15

A dedicated and talented wine-maker now occupies the historic property built by the Templars bordering the capricious Réart. This wine has an intense red colour and dominant aromas of morello cherry and mulberry, grippy tannins but with good fruit balance. It could accompany a fruit salad.

☛ Ch. La Casenove, 66300 Trouillas,
tel. 04.68.21.66.33, fax 04.68.21.77.81
⅄ ev. day except Sun. 10am–12 noon 4pm–8pm
☛ Montes

DOM. DE LA MADELEINE Tuilé 1997★

■ 3 ha n.c. ■ €8–11

This estate, situated between the town and the sea on the ancient route of the Via Domitia, was taken over in 1996 by Georges Assens, who successfully presents his first vintage with this wine. Brick-red in colour, the wine is at an early stage of development, but is still very fruity and full-bodied. With prunes and silky tannins, the wine is well-balanced and ready to drink.

☛ Dom. de La Madeleine,
chem. de Charlemagne, 66000 Perpignan,
tel. 04.68.50.02.17, fax 04.68.50.02.17
⅄ Wed. Sat. 9am–1pm

DOM. LA ROUREDE Hors d'âge★★★

☐ 1 ha 1,500 ⅢD €15–23

Jean-Luc Pujol was a passionate, charismatic leader in the wine industry who decided to spend more time with his vines and cellar. Ten years of maturation in wood have produced this luminous, russet-amber coloured wine, rich in honeyed scents of tobacco, spices, fig and orange zest. The palate is seductively full, rich and mellow, with hints of ripe apricots; and on the finish, dried fruit and roasted notes.

CH. DE NOUVELLES Tuilé 1994★

■ 4 ha 4,000 ⊪ €8-11

Recommended for its AOC Fitou, this old family estate merits a detour. It is a veritable oasis of Corbières, where it is a pleasure to wander amongst the casks. Cask ageing produces a mahogany-coloured wine with pronounced hay, damp undergrowth and cocoa aromas. Supple and velvety, the palate opens up to kirsch-fruit notes, toasted tannins, and tobacco and chocolate, which add a touch of bitterness, giving length.

↣ EARL R. Daurat-Fort, Ch. de Nouvelles, 11350 Tuchan, tel. 04.68.45.40.03, fax 04.68.45.49.21 ☑ ⵏ by appt.

DOM. PAGES HURE Grenat 1998

■ 3 ha 8,000 ▣ €8-11
Hors d'âge

Two centuries of wine-growing on this family estate have provided Jean-Louis Pagès with a rich viticultural heritage, and he still retains all the passion with which he took over the estate ten years ago. Intense in colour, with leather, liquorice and spice on the nose, this is a supple, fine and very velvety wine with a peppery and robust finish.

↣ SCEA Pages Huré, 2, allée des Moines, 66740 Saint-Génis-des-Fontaines, tel. 04.68.89.82.62, fax 04.68.89.82.62 ☑ ⵏ by appt.

LES VIGNERONS DE PEZILLA

□ 250 ha 10,000 ⊪ €8-11
Hors d'âge★★★

Taking the Col de la Donne road from the village allows you to discover both the vineyard and the diversity of the Roussillon *terroirs*. This wine is amber-gold in colour, and has prevalent crystallised oranges with hints of fruit-kernel brandy. The Jury appreciated its balance and fullness as well as the blend of citrus and roasted, dried fruits with walnuts appearing on the finish.

↣ Les Vignerons de Pezilla, 66370 Pézilla-la-Rivière, tel. 04.68.92.00.09, fax 04.68.92.49.91 ☑ ⵏ by appt.

DOM. DE RANCY

□ n.c. n.c. ⊪ €8-11
Ambré 4 Ans d'âge Elevé en fût de chêne★★

Going against the fashion and remaining faithful to *Vins Doux Naturels*, J.-H. Verdaguer continues to prove that one's passion can be a driving force. Here is another wine for cognoscenti. Its colour is between amber and mahogany, jam-packed with leather and tobacco, then walnut brandy aromas. This is definitely *rancio* country, where crystallised fruit, dark tobacco, malt and prunes give way to walnut flavours.

↣ Jean-Hubert Verdaguer, Dom. de Rancy, 11, rue Jean-Jaurès, 66720 Latour-de-France, tel. 04.68.29.03.47, fax 04.68.29.06.13 ☑ ⵏ by appt.

CH. LES PINS Ambré 1995★★

□ n.c. 5,000 ⊪ €11-15

Sun, pebbly terraces, old vines and a touch of Malvoisie, a legendary grape variety also known as Tourbat, creates a perfect recipe. Two years in new *barriques* results in an old gold-amber colour; intense crystallised oranges and mild tobacco aromas; harmonious balance on the palate; a touch of the exotic; toasted wood and a fine, minty finish.

↣ Cave des Vignerons de Baixas, 14, av. Mal-Joffre, 66390 Baixas, tel. 04.68.64.22.37, fax 04.68.64.26.70, e-mail baixas@smi-telecom.fr ☑ ⵏ by appt.

MAS CRISTINE 1997

□ 4 ha 13,000 ⊪ €11-15

Here, at the start of the the superb, rocky coast at the Mas Cristine, cork-oak trees give way to vines, and the mountains give way to the sea. Clear amber in colour, this wine has hints of honey, gingerbread and roasted almonds on the nose, with citrus-fruit notes on the palate. A fresh wine with good length.

↣ Mas Cristine, Château de Jau, 66600 Cases-de-Pène, tel. 04.68.38.90.10, fax 04.68.38.91.33, e-mail dauré@wanadoo.fr

↣ Famille Dauré

CH. MOSSE Hors d'âge 1967★★★

□ 3 ha 4,000 ⊪ €46-76

The village is a jewel set against the backdrop of the Mediterranean and the Canigou range. This sublime wine is the colour of a walnut husk, with *rancio* glints. Walnut brandy, old wooden casks, peat, dark tobacco and musk comprise its cornucopia of aromas. The palate is tremendous: the typical, oily mellowness of *rancio* accompanies crystallised figs and prunes, then liquorice, tobacco and never-ending peat.

↣ Jacques Mossé, Ch. Mossé, 66300 Sainte-Colombe-de-la-Commanderie, tel. 04.68.53.08.89, fax 04.68.53.35.13 ☑

↣ by appt.

↣ Jean-Luc Pujol, EARL La Rourède, Dom. La Rourède, 66300 Fourques, tel. 04.68.38.84.44, fax 04.68.38.88.86, e-mail vins-pujol@wanadoo.fr ☑ ⵏ ev. day except Sun. 9am–12 noon 3pm–6.30pm

VDN

Rivaltes

DOM. ROSSIGNOL Tuilé 1997★

■ 1 ha 2,000 ⊞ €11-15

After two generations of co-operative membership, grandson Pascal Rossignol dreamed of independence, and from 1995 has been making his own wine. First he produced an **Ambré 96**, now a Tuilé 97 that is still young-looking and has surprising elegance. On the palate, the wine is supple and mellow, with lots of crystallised fruits. The finish has roasted and sweet hazelnut notes.

☛ Pascal Rossignol, rte de Villemolaque, 66300 Passa, tel. 04.68.38.83.17,
fax 04.68.38.83.17 ⊠ ⅄ ev. day except Sun. 10.30am-12.30pm 4.30pm-7.30pm

DOM. ROZES Muté sur grain 1992★

■ n.c. 12,000 €8-11

Famous for its Muscat, the estate has distinguished itself this year with this 92 Muté sur Grain. The initial impression is of an aggressive wine, but on the palate, the wine is supple, rich and very reminiscent of kirsch. Fruit dominates on the finish, taking over from the tannins.

☛ SCEA Tarquin – Dom. Rozès, 3, rue de Lorraine, 66600 Espira-de-l'Agly, tel. 04.68.38.52.11, fax 04.68.38.51.38, e-mail rozes.domaine@wanadoo.fr ⊠
⅄ by appt.

SIGNATURE RENE SAHONET
Ambré Elevage en fût 1997★

□ 5 ha 4,000 ⊞ ◊ €8-11

René Sahonet is descended from a very long line of wine-makers, and it was only recently that he made a huge investment in a wine cellar for tasting and maturation. His Ambré 97, russet-amber in colour, has good fruit and honeyed-tobacco aromas. It opens up to surprising citrus notes on the palate followed by apricots, which give the wine substance. This is an intense wine with light tannins.

☛ René Sahonet, 13, rue Saint-Exupéry, Clos de Bacchus, 66450 Pollestres, tel. 06.60.87.60.12 ⊠ ⅄ by appt.

DOM. SARDA MALET
La Carbasse 1999

■ 2 ha 3,000 ■ ◊ €11-15

Nestling in the foothills just outside the town of Perpignan, this 48-ha (119-acre) estate is far removed from the city's chaos. Susy Malet says that the spirit of Bacchus blows over the land. This beautiful garnet wine, with its classic cherry notes, is initially very supple and well-structured, with youthful tannins. It should be laid down for four to five years.

☛ Dom. Sarda-Malet, Mas Saint-Michel, chem. de Sainte-Barbe, 66000 Perpignan, tel. 04.68.56.72.38, fax 04.68.56.47.60 ⊠
⅄ by appt.
☛ Suzy Malet

CH. DE SAU Ambré Hors d'âge★★

□ 2 ha 4,500 ⊞ €11-15

Hervé Passama produces wine in the region between Perpignan and Thuir. This is a remarkable, amber-coloured wine with hints of *rancio* perceptible to the eye and confirmed on the nose. On the palate, it has citrus-fruit and honeyed-peach aromas, which set off toasted notes, peat and a hint of cinnamon. Walnuts stamp the finish.

☛ Hervé Passama, Ch. de Saü, 66300 Thuir, tel. 04.68.53.21.74, fax 04.68.53.29.07, e-mail chateaudesau@aol.com ⊠
⅄ by appt.

CAVE DE TAUTAVEL Tuilé 1983★

■ 75 ha 12,000 ⊞ €8-11

Tautavel was an important centre in prehistoric times, and now has great potential for producing superb wines, borne out by those from the local co-operative. This brick-red wine was matured in wood, taking on the aromas of old casks mingled with notes of wax and old Armagnac. Full, rich and round, the palate opens out from crystallised to dried fruits with hints of spices, and finishes on a note of dark chocolate.

☛ Les Maîtres Vignerons de Tautavel, 24, av. Jean-Badia, 66720 Tautavel, tel. 04.68.29.12.03, fax 04.68.29.41.81, e-mail vignerons.tautavel@wanadoo.fr ⊠
⅄ ev. day 8am 12 noon 2pm-6pm; groups by appt.

TERRASSOUS
Ambré Vinifié en fût de chêne 1995

□ 5 ha 5,000 ⊞ €8-11

Although a distance from the main road between the Canigou range and the Mediterranean, Terrats is at the heart of Aspres, and exists only for wine-production. Its Ambré 95 is light and supple. Mutage in barrel produces Cointreau overtones mingled with floral notes. Fine and delicate, with honeyed flowers, this wine is ready to drink as an aperitif accompanied by dried fruit.

☛ SCV Les Vignerons de Terrats, BP 32, 66302 Terrats, tel. 04.68.53.02.50, fax 04.68.53.23.06, e-mail scv-terrats@wanadoo.fr ⊠ ⅄ ev. day except Sun. 8am-12 noon 2pm-6pm

TERRE ARDENTE★★

■ n.c. 10,000 €5-8

Fitou's red, chalky-clay soils and hot sunshine are ideal for the production of lovely Rivesaltes. This is an attractive wine; its russet-brown colour complements roasted aromas of spices, prune and leather. Velvety and well-balanced, the toasty tannins and hint of cocoa would go well with a dessert.

☛ Vignerons de La Méditerranée, ZI Plaisance, 12, rue du Rec-de-Veyret, BP 414, 11104 Narbonne Cedex, tel. 04.68.42.75.00, fax 04.68.42.75.01, e-mail rhirtz@listel.fr ⊠
⅄ by appt.

VAQUER Post scriptum 1995★

n.c. 3,000 €11-15

A touch of humour in the name of this wine, 'forgotten' for five years in vats and now writing a new page in the wine-making annals of the Vaquer family. It is an attractive brick-red, exuding scents of undergrowth and leather mingled with cooked fruit. On the palate, there are figs and ripe fruits, followed by tobacco and enhanced by a delicate bitterness on the finish. (50 cl bottles).
⬥ Dom. Bernard Vaquer, 1, rue des Écoles, 66300 Tresserre, tel. 04.68.38.89.53, fax 04.68.38.84.42 ☒ Ⓨ by appt.

DOM. DU VIEUX CHENE

Vieux 1989★

☐ 10 ha 16,000 €15-23

Le Vieux Chêne, producing top-quality wines, is uniquely situated, with beautiful countryside and splendid views over the Roussillon. This wine is russet-amber in colour with tinges of apricot. The aromatic palate is well-balanced, with a blend of crystallised fruit, dried hay, spices and tobacco. The palate is full, rich and generous with bitter oranges on the finish.
⬥ Dom du Vieux Chêne, Mas Kilo, 66600 Espira-de-l'Agly, tel. 04.68.38.92.01, fax 04.68.38.95.79 ☒ Ⓨ by appt.
⬥ Denis Sarda

Maury

The *terroir* covers the commune of Maury, north of Agly, together with some of the bordering communes. The vines (Grenache Noir) grow on steep schistous slopes, producing about 32,094 hl (847,282 gal) of wine in 2000.

Vinification is often achieved through long maceration, and the way in which the wine is brought on encourages the production of some remarkable vintages.

When young, the wines are garnet in colour, later turning mahogany. The bouquet is initially of soft fruit, developing aromas of cocoa, cooked fruit and coffee with age. Maury wines can be enjoyed as an aperitif or with desserts and sweet foods, but also with spicy dishes.

CHABERT DE BARBERA 1983★★

1.85 ha 5,000 €30-38

It is impossible to tire of the Chabert made by the wine-makers of Maury. Russet-amber in colour, it has scents of hazelnut, honeyed tobacco and crystallised figs. This 1983 wine is unforgettable, with its impressive palate of crystallised fruit, spices and toast backed by walnut kernels. It is very versatile; try it with a Havana cigar, Black Forest gâteau or walnut cake.
⬥ SCAV Les Vignerons de Maury, 128, av. Jean-Jaurès, 66460 Maury, tel. 04.68.59.00.95, fax 04.68.59.02.88 ☒ Ⓨ by appt.

DOM. DE LA COUME DU ROY

Cuvée Agnès 1998★

19.3 ha 20,000 €11-15

This old estate has been in the same family for five generations and has some very old vintages within its cellars. It is a feminine wine: Paule de Volontat originally owned the estate now managed by Agnès de Volontat-Bachelet, whilst Hélène Grau takes care of the wine-making. A dark red, this Cuvée Agnès exudes intense scents of cherry and spices that lengthen in the mouth; the fruit is crisp with good tannins. Serve this wine with a *soupe de fruits*.
⬥ Agnès Bachelet, Dom. de la Coume du Roy, 5, rue Emile-Zola, 66460 Maury, tel. 04.68.59.67.58, fax 04.68.59.67.58, e-mail de.volontal.bachelet@wanadoo.fr ☒ Ⓨ by appt.

CAVE JEAN-LOUIS LAFAGE

Prestige Vieilli en fût de chêne 1988★★

0.42 ha 1,250 €11-15

A 92 **rancio** matured for six years in wood was highly appreciated by the Jury (one star), but Jean-Louis Lafage has achieved the highest distinction with this 88 wine, matured in large wooden casks. The colour is still a sustained brick-red, with cooked fruit and toasted wood on a background of Mediterranean summer vegetation on the nose. Full and generous in the mouth, the fruit gives way to roasted cocoa. A *coup de coeur* was also awarded to the 86 vintage.
⬥ Jean-Louis Lafage, 13, rue Dr-Pougault, 66460 Maury, tel. 04.68.59.12.66, fax 04.68.59.13.14 ☒ Ⓨ by appt.

Muscat de Rivesaltes

of this vineyard covers more than 4,000 ha (9,880 acres) and produced 149,215 hl (3,939,276 gal) in 2000. The two varieties permitted are Muscat à Petits Grains and Muscat d'Alexandrie. The first, frequently called Muscat Blanc or Muscat de Rivesaltes, ripens early and is happy in relatively cool soils, preferably limestone. The second, also known as Muscat Romain, is a later-ripening variety which is very resistant to dry conditions.

Vinification is either by direct pressing, or by maceration for a shorter or longer time, according to the wine-maker's judgement. The must is kept in a closed container, to prevent the first aromas released from being oxidised.

The wines are required to have a minimum of 100 g of sugar per litre. They should be drunk young, served at 9–10°C (48.2–50°F), with desserts such as lemon, apple or strawberry tarts, sorbets, ice creams, fruit, touron and marzipan. They are also good with Roquefort cheese.

MAS AMIEL 1980★★

▦ | 10 ha | ▥ 40,000 | ▦ 30–38

In the past, the Mas Amiel has been a true exponent of the appellation, but it changed hands in 1999, so it will be interesting to follow its future progress. Included in the *Guide* since the very first edition, it has produced no less than five *coups de coeur* and eight exceptional wines during the last decade. This year, wines produced by the previous owner include: a very noteworthy **ten-year-old** (one star) and this superb 20-year-old. With a good colour, it has aromas of leather, cocoa and dark tobacco. The palate is intense, full, rich, generous and velvety, with tobacco and cocoa accompanied by a fruity sweetness, and a remarkable *rancio* finish.

●▸ Dom. du Mas Amiel, 66460 Maury, tel. 04.68.29.01.02, fax 04.68.29.17.82 ▼
▸ ev. day 10am–12 noon 2pm–5.30pm
●▸ O. Decelle

DOM. POUDEROUX Hors d'âge★★

▦ | 2 ha | ▥ 2,000 | ▦ | ● 11–15

R. Pouderoux produces a range of wines from Grenache Noir, from a young, powerful **99** (one star), to this truly mellow *hors d'âge* wine. It is the colour of aged mahogany, with initial aromas of undergrowth followed by prunes and dark tobacco. Supple, fine and well-balanced, the palate has silky tannins with a long finish and hints of cocoa.

●▸ Dom. Pouderoux, 2, rue Emile-Zola, 66460 Maury, tel. 04.68.57.22.02, fax 04.68.57.11.63 ▼ ▸ by appt.

DOM. DES SCHISTES

La Cerisaie 1999

▦ | 3 ha | ▥ 4,000 | ▦ | ● 11–15

This estate produces delightful Rivesaltes and Côtes du Roussillon-Villages, and the schist soils are also ideal for Maury Vin Doux Naturel. This is a dark-red 99 produced from very old vines (50 years old), with a long alcohol maceration and a short time in wood. Prunes and wood notes dominate on the nose, and fruit and spices on the mellow palate. It finishes on cocoa notes.

●▸ Jacques Sire, 1, av. Jean-Lurçat, 66310 Estagel, tel. 04.68.29.11.25, fax 04.68.29.47.17 ▼ ▸ by appt.

DOM. AMOUROUX 1999★★

€ 5–8

▦ | 10 ha | ▥ 5,000 | ▦ | ●

Situated right in the heart of Aspres, the 70-ha (172-acre) Amouroux estate has particularly distinguished itself this year with this old-gold 99. The palate is full and persistent, with complex aromas evoking exotic fruit, overripe grapes and crystallised oranges. This very attractive wine with good length can be found in the estate's shop in Argelès-sur-Mer.

●▸ Dom. Jean Amouroux, 15, rue du Pla-del-Rey, 66300 Tresserre, tel. 04.68.38.87.54, fax 04.68.38.89.90 ▼
▸ by appt.

DOM. D'AUBERMESNIL

Cuvée Apinae 1999★

€ 5–8

▦ | 15 ha | ▥ 28,000 | ▦ |

A staging post for ancient Greek navigators, the village of Leucate draws its name from the whiteness (from the Greek *leucos*; white) of its cliff, which descends into the sea. Its chalky soil is particularly suited to Muscat à Petits Grains. Characteristic of its type, particularly when aged, this 99 has a brilliant, old-gold colour and offers aromas of overripe grapes with nuances of citrus fruit and honey. It is a lovely dessert Muscat, rich, full and powerful with a long finish.

Muscat de Rivesaltes

This sweet 100% Muscat can be made anywhere in Rivesaltes, Maury and Banyuls provided the blend is composed exclusively of Muscat varieties. The area

DOM. DE BESOMBES SINGLA
Vieilles vignes 2000

0.7 ha · 4,000 · ■ €8-11

Situated close to Salses, this very old estate has been in the same family since 1760 and has now produced a powerful wine, sustained gold in colour. Its aromas evoke ripe grapes and citrus fruit, and on the palate, notes of orange marmalade combine with crystallised lemon. A beautiful, traditional Muscat.

● Dom. de Besombes-Singla, 4, rue de Rivoli, 66250 Saint-Laurent-de-la-Salanque, tel. 04.68.28.30.68, fax 04.68.28.30.68, e-mail ddbs@libertysurf.fr ▼ by appt.

DOM. BONZOMS 2000

5 ha · 2,500 · ■ €5-8

Situated in Les Fenouillèdes, surrounded by arid mountains, the village of Tautavel is known throughout the world for its important prehistoric deposits. The *terroir* produces a Côtes du Roussillon-Villages *appellation communale*. The Muscats, too, are excellent here. A lovely straw-gold colour, this wine mingles flowers and green tea on the nose, with the palate developing nuances of citrus fruit and fresh grapes, in an elegant balance of freshness and richness.

● EARL Dom. Bonzoms, 2, pl. de la République, 66720 Tautavel, tel. 04.68.29.40.15, e-mail domaine.bonzoms@clubinternet.fr ▼ ev. day 10am–12.30pm 3pm–7pm; cl. 1 Oct–31 Mar.

DOM. BOUDAU 2000★

6 ha · 20,000 · ■ €8-11

For several years now, Pierre and Véronique Boudau have been equipping their wine cellar to do better justice to the different *terroirs* on their vast 80-ha (198-acre) estate. Featured in the *Guide* in 1995, 1997 and 1998, they have now produced a delightful, well-balanced, fresh, rich Muscat with a wonderful blend of fresh apricots, yellow peaches and exotic fruit.

● Dom. Véronique et Pierre Boudau, 6, rue Marceau, 66000 Rivesaltes, tel. 04.68.64.45.37, fax 04.68.64.46.26 ▼ ev. day except Sun. 10am–12 noon 3pm–7pm Jun.–Sept.

DOM. CAZES 2000★

35 ha · 140,000 · ■ €11-15

This 160-ha (395-acre) estate is one of the largest and most famous in the region because it offers a good range of consistently high-quality wines. Its 2000 Muscat, clear, limpid and brilliant gold, is distinguished by the finesse and elegance of its aromas of mangoes, pineapples and ripe grapes, accompanied by hints of aniseed and fresh violets. The palate is full, floral and lemony.

● André et Bernard Cazes, 4, rue Francisco-Ferrer, BP 61, 66602 Rivesaltes, tel. 04.68.64.08.26, fax 04.68.64.69.79, e-mail info@cazes-rivesaltes.com ▼

● Vignerons de La Méditerranée, ZI Plaisance, 12, rue du Rec-de-Veyret, BP 414, 11104 Narbonne Cedex, tel. 04.68.42.75.00, fax 04.68.42.75.01, e-mail rhitrz@listel.fr ▼ by appt.

CH. AYMERICH 2000

2.15 ha · 6,000 · ■ €6-11

This family estate is situated at Estagel, a large wine-growing commune in Les Fenouillèdes. Its 2000 Muscat is a brilliant, pale-gold colour with silvery glints. On the nose there are light floral notes with touches of lemons, grapefruit and peaches: and on the well-balanced, long palate, notes of peaches in syrup.

● Jean-Pierre et Catherine Grau-Aymerich, Ch. Aymerich, 52, av. Dr-Torrelles, 66310 Estagel, tel. 04.68.29.45.45, fax 04.68.29.10.35, e-mail aymerich-grau-vins@wanadoo.fr ▼ by appt.

CH. BELLOCH 2000

9.5 ha · 3,000 · ■ €5-8

This 25-ha (61.75-acre) estate is devoted to the production of Vins Doux Naturels. Its 2000 Muscat is clear and fresh, with sweet, lemony aromas of exotic passion-fruit, pineapple and bananas. The well-balanced palate has a lively finish.

● SA Cibaud-Ch. Miraflors et Belloch, rte de Canet, 66000 Perpignan, tel. 04.68.34.03.05, fax 04.68.51.31.70, e-mail vins.cibaud@wanadoo.fr ▼ ev. day except Sun. 9am–1pm 3pm–7pm

DOM. BERTRAND-BERGE 2000★★

2 ha · 5,300 · ■ €8-11

The Bertrand-Bergé estate is in superb countryside, close to the Cathare fortresses of Quéribus and Peyrepertuse. The power and lightness of its Muscat 2000 particularly impressed the Jury. It fully deserves a *coup de cœur*. Its colour is very pale gold: its nose fine, lemony and floral, evoking broom and acacia. The lovely, full palate opens to an extraordinary aromatic palate of roses, honey, verbena, citrus blossom and exotic fruit.

● Dom. Bertrand-Bergé, av. du Roussillon, 11350 Paziols, tel. 04.68.45.41.73 ▼ ev. day 8am–12 noon 1.30pm–7pm

VDN

Muscat de Rivesaltes

LES VIGNERONS DES COTES D'AGLY 2000★

80 ha   30,000   ■ ♦   €5-8

This co-operative produces wine from 1,250 ha (3,088 acres) of vines. Its Muscat is a lovely pale yellow with green glints, and mingles exotic fruit, lemon and rose. The palate is fresh in the attack then round, sweet and rich with very good balance and delicate apricot notes on the finish.

➤ Les Vignerons des Côtes d'Agly, Cave coopérative, 66310 Estagel, tel. 04.68.29.00.45, fax 04.68.29.19.80, e-mail agly@little-france.com ⊠ ▼ ev. day except Sat. Sun. 8am–12 noon 2pm–6pm

HENRI DESBŒUFS

Le Vieux Bailli 2000★

2 ha   2,000   ■ ♦   €8-11

Close to Rivesaltes, Espira-de-l'Agly developed around a priory founded in the 12th century, and there still remains a lovely fortified Roman church. Here, too, Henri Desboeufs farms a 25-ha (62-acre) vineyard. His Muscat offers a remarkable quality in quality. The 2000 vintage is a beautiful, straw-coloured gold with intense aromas of crystallised orange peel, raisin and honey. The palate is rich, full and has good length.

➤ Henri Desboeufs, 39, rue du 4-Septembre, 66600 Espira-de-l'Agly, tel. 04.68.64.11.73, fax 04.68.38.56.34 ⊠ ▼ by appt.

DOM BRIAL 2000★★

n.c.   70,000   ■ ♦   €5-8

Not far from Perpignan, the village of Baixas still retains a good proportion of its surrounding walls and fortified gates. The Baixas wine cellar is one of the main producers of Muscat in Roussillon, processing grapes from 2,100 ha (5,188 acres) of vines. Quantity and quality go hand in hand in this magnificent village, borne out by this wonderful 2000 Muscat. Brilliant golden-yellow with green highlights, the wine has an aromatic palate of finesse, complexity and elegance: a bouquet of roses and mimosas, as well as passion-fruit, pineapples, mangoes and lemons. It also has a remarkable balance between richness and freshness. The Jury had no hesitation in awarding it a *coup de cœur*.

➤ Cave des Vignerons de Baixas, 14, av. Mal-Joffre, 66390 Baixas, tel. 04.68.64.22.37, fax 04.68.64.26.70, e-mail baixas@smi-telecom.fr ⊠ ▼ by appt.

LES VIGNERONS D'ELNE

Passion de Pyrène 2000

4 ha   5,000   ■ ♦   €8-11

Elne is the ancient *Illibéris* of the Iberians. Visitors can see its Roman cathedral, which has a magnificent cloister, and on the way through can taste this attractive Muscat from the co-operative. It has a light, brilliant, clear-gold colour, shot with green. The nose is fine and complex, with aromas of white peaches and pears, crystallised lemons and touches of verbena. The balance on the palate is pleasant, rich and warming.

➤ Les Vignerons d' Elne, 67, av. Paul-Reig, 66200 Elne, tel. 04.68.22.06.51, fax 04.68.22.83.31 ⊠ ▼ ev. day except Sun. 8am–12 noon 2pm–6pm; Sat. 8am–12 noon

LES VIGNERONS DE FOURQUES

2000

20 ha   n.c.   ■ ♦   €8-11

Situated in the Aspres, the village of Fourques still has vestiges of its surrounding wall. The co-operative produces wine from grapes grown on 420 ha (1,037 acres) of vines. Its 2000 Muscat is a brilliant yellow-gold with green glints, and clean and intense aromas of flowers (nasturtium, rose, pink and acacia) and fresh fruit (lychees, kumquats and pears). Its acidity, fullness and ripeness achieve a good balance on the palate.

➤ SCV les Vignerons de Fourques, 1, rue des Taste-Vin, 66300 Fourques, tel. 04.68.38.80.51, fax 04.68.38.89.65 ⊠ ▼ by appt.

CH. DE JAU 2000

10 ha   40,000   ■ ♦   €8-11

Situated at Cases-de-Pène, in Les Fenouillèdes (between Corbières and Roussillon), this vast estate of 134 ha (331 acres) is a regular in the *Guide*. Newly presented in a 50-cl bottle, the 2000 Muscat remains a good classic wine of this appellation. A brilliant golden-yellow with green nuances, it offers clean, fine and complex aromas of ripe grapes, white fruit, citronella, ginger and greengages. A lovely dessert wine to serve with lemon tart or prunes.

➤ Ch. de Jau, 66600 Cases-de-Pène, tel. 04.68.38.90.10, fax 04.68.38.91.33, e-mail daure@wanadoo.fr ⊠ ▼ by appt.

➤ Famille Dauré

CELLIER DE LA BARNEDE

Cuvée du 3e Millénaire 2000

23 ha   10,000   ■ ♦   €8-11

This large wine cellar in the Aspres region is the birthplace of the Roussillon's *vins verts*, antecedents of the Côtes du Roussillon Blanc AOC. The co-operative processes grapes from 500 ha (1,235 acres) of vines, and produces some 25,000 hl (660,000 gal) of wine per year. Its Cuvée du Troisième Millénaire has dominant aromas of pears and peaches. Full-bodied on the palate, it has good balance and length.

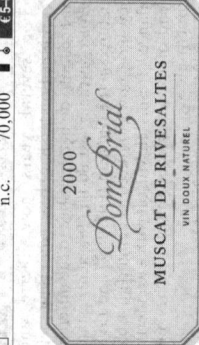

2000
Dom Brial
VIN DOUX NATUREL
MUSCAT DE RIVESALTES

SCV Les Producteurs de La Barnède, 66670 Bages, tel. 04.68.21.60.30, fax 04.68.37.50.13 Y by appt.

DOM. LAFAGE 2000★
15 ha 40,800 €8–11

Jean-Marc and Eliane Lafage, young oenologists, took over this 72-ha (178-acre) estate in 1995 and are in the process of establishing its reputation. The Jury chose their 2000 Muscat for the quality of its aromas (pears, crystallised oranges, bananas and fresh grapes), and for its structure, which is full, sweet and rich without being heavy. It is a powerful wine.

SCEA Dom. Lafage, mas Llaro, rte de Canet, 66100 Perpignan, tel. 04.68.67.12.47, fax 04.68.62.10.99, e-mail enofool@aol.com Y by appt.

CAVE DE LESQUERDE 2000★
7.5 ha 30,000 €5–8

The wine cellar of Lesquerde is famous above all for its production of Côtes du Roussillon-Villages Lesquerde, but also makes Muscats with lovely finesse. A brilliant, clear gold, the wine is dominated by aromas of lemons, limes and orange peel, and is very well-balanced on the palate with exotic nuances of pineapples and ginger.

SCV Lesquerde, rue du Grand-Capitoul, 66220 Lesquerde, tel. 04.68.59.02.62, fax 04.68.59.08.17 Y ev. day except Sun. 8am–12 noon 2pm–6pm

CH. LES FENALS 2000
5.26 ha 7,000 €8–11

Voltaire's nephew, the steward of the château, used to supply the court of Louis XV with its 'Liqueur du Cap de Salses.' Nowadays the estate comprises 17.5 ha (42 acres) and was taken over by a midwife-turned-wine-grower, who brought this wonderful Muscat into the world in 2000. The wine is golden, lively and robust. While it has fragrant aromas of fresh mint and lemon, it is also round and nicely balanced.

Roustan Fontanel, Les Fenals, 11510 Fitou, tel. 04.68.45.71.94, fax 04.68.45.60.57 Y ev. day except Sun. 9am–12 noon 2.30pm–6.30pm; cl. pm out of season

DOM. LES MILLE VIGNES 2000★
0.5 ha 3,000 €11–15

This small estate, situated on the north bank of the lake of Leucate, was founded in 1979 with 1,000 vines, hence the name Mille Vignes. Nestling between the lake and sun-drenched hills, it possesses a very special charm. In a 50-cl bottle, the 2000 Muscat has a lovely, brilliant appearance, with nuances of yellow-gold. On the nose, there are notes of fresh fruit (pears, white peaches and bananas) and berlingot (boiled sweets), whilst the rich and full palate opens up to reveal hints of roses and grapefruit. A well-balanced whole.

J. et G. Guérin, Dom. Les Mille Vignes, 24, av. Saint-Pancrace, 11480 La Palme, tel. 04.68.48.57.14, fax 04.68.48.57.14 Y by appt.

CH. MOSSE 1998★★
n.c. 23,000 €8–11

This wine has a youthful, pale-golden colour with developing aromas of lime blossom. Muscat brandy and dried apricots. Intense on the palate, the wine is fresh, sweet and rich, and has a very good length.

SA Destavel, 7 bis, av. du Canigou, 66000 Perpignan, tel. 04.68.68.36.00, fax 04.68.54.03.54

DOM. PARCE 2000
4.6 ha 6,300 €5–8

This family estate opted for quality in 1982 when it decided to replace its high-yield varieties with distinctive grape varieties, and to bottle on the estate. Its 2000 Muscat, pale-gold in colour with green glints, has delicate menthol aromas mingled with peaches, lemon and lime blossom. Full, fresh and well-balanced on the palate, it has a pleasant finish.

EARL A. Parcé, 21 ter, rue du 14-Juillet, 66670 Bages, tel. 04.68.21.80.45, fax 04.68.21.69.40 Y ev. day except Sun. 9.30am–12.15pm 4pm–7.30pm

LES VIGNERONS DE PEZILLA, Cuvée Prestige n.c.
n.c. 5,000 €5–8

Founded in 1935, the wine cellar of Pézilla processes grapes from 800 ha (1,976 acres) in the region. Its Cuvée Prestige, with its beautiful, brilliant pale-gold colour and its fine

CH. L'HOSPITALET 1999★★
1.5 ha 9,900 €8–11

The estate – nowadays 1,000 ha (2,470 acres), of which 60 ha (148 acres) are vines – was established on the Clape Massif by the Hospitalier monks in 1561. It makes a lovely spot for a cultural and gastronomic break. This remarkable 99, clear gold in colour, has enticing aromas of overripe grapes, gunflint, blackcurrant leaf and orange blossom. An original wine, slightly atypical, but highly complex.

Dom. de L'Hospitalet, 11100 Narbonne, tel. 04.68.45.27.10, fax 04.68.45.27.17, e-mail info@domaine.hospitalet.com Y by appt.

DOM. DU MAS CREMAT 2000★
4 ha 9,000 €8–11

The mas takes its name from the charred-looking black schist soils, an exceptional terroir from which Jean-Marc Jeannin continues to produce beautifully expressive wines. This 2000 Muscat, brilliant gold in colour with green highlights, epitomises elegance and finesse. Its aromas evoke lime blossom, white flowers and citrus fruit, with a hint of eucalyptus. On the palate the wine is well-balanced with a long finish.

Jeannin-Mongeard, Dom. du Mas Cremat, 66600 Espira-de-l'Agly, tel. 04.68.38.92.06, fax 04.68.38.92.23

Muscat de Rivesaltes

herbaceous (verbena and lime blossom) and floral aromas with exotic notes on the palate, is recommended. A well-balanced, rich wine with a good length.

☛ Les Vignerons de Pézilla,
66370 Pézilla-la-Rivière, tel. 04.68.92.00.09, fax 04.68.92.49.91 ▨ ▾ by appt.

DOM. PIETRI-GERAUD 2000
▢   3.2 ha   4,000   €8-11

The 32-ha (79-acre) vineyard was established in the 1890s, and is currently run by Maguy Piétri-Geraud and her daughter, Laetitia. You will find their wine cellar in a shady street in the dazzling city of Collioure. A very pale gold with green tints, their 2000 Muscat has the fresh aromas of orange blossom and chopped mint opening out on the palate to reveal great sweetness. It is well-balanced, with nuances of lemons on the finish.

☛ Maguy et Laetitia Piétri-Geraud,
22, rue Pasteur, 66190 Collioure,
tel. 04.68.82.07.42, fax 04.68.98.02.58 ▨
▾ ev. day 10am–12.30pm 3.30pm–6.30pm;
cl. Sun. Mon. out of school holidays

DOM. PIQUEMAL
Coup de Foudre 1997★★
▢   1 ha   4,000   ▥ €15-23

Pierre and Franck Piquemal, regulars in the *Guide*, farm 60 ha (148 acres), and this year offer a rare vintage of old wine matured for two years in large oak casks. Straw in colour, it has an aromatic palate of lovely complexity, with crystallised fruits, cinnamon, vanilla, caramel and cardamom. The balance is sweet, rich and very mellow. The **Cuvée Principale 2000** (one star), is also seductively complex, with its exotic fruits, pears and white peaches mingled with honey, mace and crystallised ginger. It is a powerful wine with a long finish, which would be ideal with recipes containing blue cheese (such as a Roquefort pastry).

☛ Dom. Pierre et Franck Piquemal, 1, rue Pierre-Lefranc, 66600 Espira-de-l'Agly, tel. 04.68.64.09.14, fax 04.68.38.52.94, e-mail contact@domaine-piquemal.com ▨ ▾ by appt.

CH. PRADAL 2000
▢   8 ha   30,000   ▥ €5-8

Established in 1810, this is a tenacious vineyard, which is resisting the spread of the town of Perpignan (today it is only a short distance from the station). The 2000 vintage is a clear, gold wine with intense aromas of ripe bananas and brandied fruit. The palate is full, sweet and rich, with nuances of crystallised lemon and mimosa.

☛ André Coll-Escluse, Ch. Pradal,
58, rue Pépinière-Robin, 66000 Perpignan, tel. 04.68.85.04.73, fax 04.68.56.80.49 ▨
▾ ev. day except Sun. 10am–12.30pm 5pm–7.30pm

RIERE CADENE 2000★★
▢   5 ha   5,000   ▥ ♠ €5-8

This 40-ha (99-acre) estate, worked by the fourth generation of the family, has particularly distinguished itself this year with this brilliant Muscat, gold with green glints. On the nose, there are complex aromas of exotic fruit, overripe grapes and apricots, lemon peel and acacia. There are touches of resin on the beautifully balanced, fresh, rich palate.

☛ Laurence et Jean-François Rière, Mas Bel-Air, chem. Saint-Genis-de-Tanyères, 66000 Perpignan, tel. 04.68.63.87.29, fax 04.68.63.87.29, e-mail riere@club-internet.fr ▨ ▾ ev. day except Sat. Sun. 9am–12 noon 2pm–6pm

ROC DU GOUVERNEUR 2000
▢   n.c.   15,000   ▥ €8-11

This co-operative processes grapes from 3,000 ha (7,410 acres). The 2000 vintage from Roc du Gouverneur, one of its two brands, is a brilliant, pale yellow with green glints. The delicate Muscat nose mingles flowers, pears, lychees and light herbaceous notes. Well-balanced, with a supple attack, the wine is wonderfully rich and full with a fresh finish.

☛ Les Vignobles du Rivesaltais, 1, rue de la Roussillonnaise, 66602 Rivesaltes-Salses, tel. 04.68.64.06.63, fax 04.68.64.64.69, e-mail vignobles.rivesaltais@wanadoo.fr ▨ ▾ by appt.

RENE SAHONET 2000
▢   4 ha   9,000   ▥ ♠ €5-8

The Sahonet family have been producing wines since before 1662 on their 12-ha (30-acre) estate, at Pollestres, on the Aspre wine route. In 1999 they built a vast storage hall and a *barrique* store for the maturation of Vins Doux Naturels. Their 2000 Muscat, a lovely, clear, brilliant gold, has fine, lightly floral aromas, with hints of ripe pears, apples, pineapples and citrus fruit and a very attractive balance, reflecting the care and skills of their wine-making.

☛ René Sahonet, 13, rue Saint-Exupéry, Clos de Bacchus, 66450 Pollestres, tel. 06.60.87.60.12 ▨ ▾ by appt.

DOM. SALVAT 2000★
▢   10 ha   10,000   ▥ ♠ €8-11

Saint-Paul-de-Fenouillet marked the boundary of the Kingdom of France from 1258–1659. The city of Les Fenouillèdes is situated close to the Galamus Gorges, bisected by the turbulent River Agly. The Salvats farm 70 ha (173 acres) of vines in this area and produce a very attractive Muscat with a clear, brilliant colour shot with green. The intense nose is marked by floral, lemon and menthol notes. A lovely, lively, fresh wine, it has very good length.

☛ Dom. J.-Ph. Salvat, 8, av. Jean-Moulin, 66220 Saint-Paul-de-Fenouillet, tel. 04.68.59.29.00, fax 04.68.59.20.44, e-mail salvat.jp@wanadoo.fr ▨ ▾ by appt.

DOM. SAN MARTI
Muscat de Noël 2000★

| 1.5 ha | 4,600 | €8-11 |

This 31-ha (77-acre) estate, established in 1914, is now farmed organically. Its Muscat de Noël, golden-yellow with silvery tinges, has intense lemon-zest, grapefruit, pineapple and ripe-banana aromas. After a clean, fresh opening, the palate is well-balanced with aromas of peppered geranium and ginger, and is wonderfully rich and sweet on the finish.

• Clos Saint-Martin,
20, av. Lamartine, 66430 Bompas,
tel. 04.68.63.26.09, fax 04.68.63.14.04,
e-mail domaine-san-marti@free.fr
♈ by appt.
• Coronat

CH. VALFON 2000

| 1.17 ha | 4,000 | €5-8 |

The 28-ha (69-acre)Valfon estate was created in 2000 from the amalgamation of two vineyards. Its 2000 wine is a brilliant, clear gold with green glints, clean and lively on the nose with aromas of honeysuckle, jasmin, grapes, peaches and pears. The palate is well-balanced and wonderfully fresh.

• Anne-Marie Jeanjean, Dom. du Mas Rouge, 34110 Vic-la-Gardiole,
tel. 04.67.88.80.01, fax 04.67.96.65.67

CH. DE LA PEYRADE Solstice 2000

| 26 ha | 4,000 | €8-11 |

Here, regulations permit Vins de Liqueur to be made with mutage of the must before fermentation, making for wines that are much richer in sugar (about 125 g per litre). In some cases, bringing on the Muscats in old, large barrels causes a slight oxidisation which gives the wines a distinctive flavour of dried grapes.

This wine, of a particularly clear colour shot with green, shows great originality and freshness. The aromas are pleasing, with notes of gunflint and redcurrant. The discreet palate is slightly acidic. Drink as an aperitif.

• Yves Pastourel et Fils,
Ch. de La Peyrade, 34110 Frontignan,
tel. 04.67.48.61.19, fax 04.67.43.03.31
♈ by appt.

Muscat de Frontignan

CH. DE LA PEYRADE
Cuvée Prestige 2000★★

| 26 ha | 30,000 | €8-11 |

The château of La Peyrade has done it again this year as far as coups de coeur are concerned; this is the fifth time it has received this distinction, after exceptionally lovely wines in 1991, 1993 and 1995 (not to mention those judged exceptional in 1987, 1988, 1990, 1994 and 1996). So as usual, the Pastourel family appears in the catalogue of elegance. The Cuvée Prestige 2000, a very pale-gold colour with green lights, offers very fresh aromas: pear, exotic fruit (pineapple) and Viburnum-tinus flower mix happily. The palate, fleshy and lively, reveals nuances of aniseed and grapefruit.

• Yves Pastourel et Fils,
Ch. de La Peyrade, 34110 Frontignan,
tel. 04.67.48.61.19, fax 04.67.43.03.31
♈ by appt.

DOM. DU MAS ROUGE 1999★

| 4.5 ha | 16,000 | €5-8 |

This wine is a brilliant straw colour. The nose, very fresh, mingles herbaceous nuances, grapefruit and citronella, while crystallised orange-peel notes appear on the palate. Very rich and full, the palate is pleasantly enhanced by a slightly sparkling point.

• Anne-Marie Jeanjean, Dom. du Mas Rouge, 34110 Vic-la-Gardiole,
tel. 04.67.88.80.01, fax 04.67.96.65.67

CH. DE SIX TERRES 2000★

| n.c. | 37,000 | €8-11 |

Dominating the lake of Thau and facing the town of Sète, the estate's wine is made by the co-operative winery. The 2000 vintage, a good yellow colour, has aromas of crystallised fruits, as well as hints of fruit jelly, syrup pears and verbena. On the palate are notes of ripe wine, lively with balanced rich sweetness, and is typical of the appellation.

• SCA Coop. de Frontignan,
14, av. du Muscat, 34110 Frontignan,
tel. 04.67.48.12.26, fax 04.67.43.07.17
♈ ev. day 9am-12 noon 2pm-6.30pm;
groups by appt.

Muscat de Beaumes-de-Venise

Located north of Carpentras, beneath the impressive mountains of the Dentelles de Montmirail, the landscape is one of grey limestones and red marls. The *terroir* is partly composed of sands, marls and sandstone together with weathered, faulted terrain dating from the Triassic and Jurassic eras. Here again, the only grape variety used is the Muscat à Petits Grains, although, on some parcels of land, a mutation has led to pink or red grapes. Muscat de Beaumes-de-Venise wines, of which 13,929 hl (367,726 gal) were produced in 2000, are required to contain a minimum of 110 g of sugar per litre of must; aromatic, fruity and elegant, they are perfect as an aperitif or with cheese.

Henry Bouachon, BP 5,
84230 Châteauneuf-du-Pape,
tel. 04.90.83.58.35, fax 04.90.83.77.23
Y by appt.

DOM. BOULETIN 2000★

☐   6 ha   24,000   ■ ◊ €8-11

A clear straw colour, this fresh Muscat has pear, apricot, green peach and lime blossom aromas, and a full and rich palate with nuances of tangerine, enhanced on the finish by a slight petulance.

EARL Bouletin et Fils, quartier Les Plantades, 84190 Beaumes-de-Venise,
tel. 04.90.62.95.10, fax 04.90.62.98.23 ☑
Y by appt.

DOM. DE FONTAVIN 2000★★

☐   3.59 ha   7,500   ■ ◊ €8-11

This Muscat is produced in an area called Costebelle, and lives up to the name. The previous vintage obtained a *coup de coeur*, and this brilliant yellow-gold wine is in the same class. Very fresh lemon-peel aromas abound on the palate with touches of citron jam. The Jury recommends serving it with fromage frais.

EARL Hélène et Michel Chouvet, Dom. de Fontavin, 1468, rte de la Plaine,
84350 Courthézon, tel. 04.90.70.72.14, fax 04.90.70.79.39, e-mail helene-chouvet@fontavin.com ☑ **Y** ev. day except Sun. 9am–12.30pm 2pm–6.30pm; summer 9am–7pm

DOM. DE LA PIGEADE 2000★★

☐   23 ha   92,000   ■ ◊ €8-11

A *coup de coeur* was unanimously awarded to this estate's fifth vintage. The *terroir* and the young wine-maker's art have combined to produce a clear, golden wine with an exceptionally intense and complex nose dominated by rosewater, pears and exotic fruits. Drink with oriental pastries.

Thierry Vaute, Dom. de La Pigeade,
84190 Beaumes-de-Venise,
tel. 04.90.62.90.00, fax 04.90.62.90.90,
e-mail th.vaute@lapigeade.fr ☑ **Y** by appt.

LES MUSCADIERES 1998★

☐   2 ha   8,000   ■ ◊ €8-11

Great care has been taken during the harvest: grape sorting, skin maceration and cooling to 18 °C (64 °F) before the beginning of fermentation. This has resulted in a pale-

DOM. DE BEAUMALRIC 2000★

☐   7.83 ha   31,000   ■ ◊ €8-11

This estate is frequently mentioned in the *Guide*. Its 2000 Muscat is clear gold with green lights, a wine with a great deal of finesse on the nose with herbaceous, exotic and green pear nuances. Initially full on the palate, with hints of citronella, there is a good rich, fresh balance.

EARL Begouaussel,
Dom. de Beaumalric, BP 15,
84190 Beaumes-de-Venise,
tel. 04.90.65.01.77, fax 04.90.62.97.28 ☑
Y by appt.

BOIS DORE 1998★★

☐   50 ha   20,000   ▥ €11-15

A good colour, this wine has incredibly intense aromas of crystallised fruits, lime blossom and verbena liqueur. These mingle with pronounced nuances of vanilla with roasted coffee flavours on a very long finish.

Cave des Vignerons de Beaumes-de-Venise, quartier Ravel,
84190 Beaumes-de-Venise,
tel. 04.90.12.41.00, fax 04.90.65.02.05,
e-mail vignerons@beaumes-de-venise.com
☑ **Y** by appt.

HENRY BOUACHON 1998★

☐   50 ha   10,000   ■ ◊ €11-15

This is 'balm to the soul.' Weighty, but also very rich and velvety, this wine is slightly subdued with some depth.

yellow wine with explosive but delicate violet aromas and resinated notes. A mellow wine with good Muscat character; it has wonderful elegance.

☛ Pascal, rte de Gigondas, 84190 Vacqueyras, tel. 04.90.65.85.91, fax 04.90.65.89.23 ☒ ☖ by appt.

DOM. DES RICHARDS 1999

n.c. ▮ 30,000 ▮ €11-15

This wine is in a lovely old-gold with brilliant glints and mingling lemon, tangerine and quince jelly aromas. On the palate, it is sweet and rich with a touch of acidity, beautifully balanced, with orange peel nuances.

☛ Gabriel Meffre, Le Village, 84190 Gigondas, tel. 04.90.12.32.42, fax 04.90.12.32.49 ☖ by appt.

RESERVE J. VIDAL-FLEURY 2000★

3 ha ▮ 12,000 ▮ €11-15

This *négociant*, founded in 1781, claims to be the oldest in the Rhône Valley and to have entertained Thomas Jefferson during his long journey through Europe. Its latest wine has a good golden colour and well-developed aromas opening out to crystallised apricots and ripe pineapples. On the palate, there are nuances of faded roses underpinning a particularly aromatic finish.

☛ J. Vidal-Fleury, 19, rte de la Roche, 69420 Ampuis, tel. 04.74.56.10.18, fax 04.74.56.19.19 ☒ ☖ by appt.

Muscat de Lunel

A sweet (minimum 125 g of sugar per litre) wine made only from Muscat à Petits Grains. Located around Lunel, the hilltop vineyards sit amid a typical landscape of rolled stones on red clay earth over alluvial folds. A total of 10,191 hl (269,042 gal) was declared in 2000.

CLOS BELLEVUE

Cuvée Vieilles vignes 2000★

5 ha ▮ 13,000 ▮ €11-15

With ten years in the *Guide*, two *coups de coeur* and a profusion of stars, Francis Lacoste is a past master of the art of producing very fine Muscats. This 2000 wine continues the tradition, with its clear gold colour with silver glints, and its light aromas of redcurrants and acid drops. The balance on the palate is attractive: lively, fleshy and elegant.

CH. TOUR DE FARGES 1999★★

n.c. ▮ 2,400 ▮ €5-8

This vineyard, the oldest in the appellation, now has its grapes processed by the co-operative cellar. The jury was unanimous about its 1999 wine, with its beautiful, brilliant and sustained gold colour. The aromas are remarkable for their intensity and complexity: ripe Muscat grapes, apricots and crystallised orange mingle with the bouquet of mint and verbena. The palate is lively, sweet and rich, and has very good length.

☛ Les Vignerons du Muscat de Lunel, rte de Lunel-Viel, 34400 Vérargues, tel. 04.67.86.00.09, fax 04.67.86.07.52 ☒

☛ Francis Lacoste, Dom. de Bellevue, rte de Sommières, 34400 Lunel, tel. 04.67.83.24.83, fax 04.67.71.48.23, e-mail muscatlacoste@wanadoo.fr ☒ ☖ ev. day except Sun. 9am–7pm; groups by appt.

CH. GRES SAINT-PAUL

Sévilane 1999★

8.15 ha ▮ 15,000 ▮ €8-11

This is a wine of character, with a sumptuous old-gold colour and evolving nuances of dried roses, crystallised apricots, grapefruit zest and orange peel, with a round yet vivacious palate. Lovers of mature wine will appreciate it.

☛ Ch. Grès Saint-Paul, rte de Restinclières, 34400 Lunel, tel. 04.67.71.27.90, fax 04.67.71.73.76, e-mail contact@gres-saint-paul.com ☒ ☖ ev. day except Sun. 10am–12 noon 3pm–7pm

DOM. DE SAINT-PIERRE DE PARADIS Vendanges d'Automne 1999★★

n.c. ▮ 5,200 ▮ €8-11

This is an original, mature wine, amber in colour with camphor touches, and mushroom and vanilla aromas on the nose. There are finely toasted flavours on the palate, finishing on notes of coffee and gentian. Full, with well-integrated wood, it is beautifully balanced.

☛ Les Vignerons du Muscat de Lunel, rte de Lunel-Viel, 34400 Vérargues, tel. 04.67.86.00.09, fax 04.67.86.07.52 ☒

Muscat de Mireval

This vineyard is bordered by the Etang de Vic, and stretches between Sète and Montpellier on the south-facing slope of the Massif de la Gardiole. The soils are of ancient Jurassic alluvium, smoothed stones and the predominant limestone. The single grape variety is Muscat à Petits Grains.

Mutage is carried out fairly early, because the wines must reach a minimum of 125 g of sugar per litre; they are sweet, fruity and rich. In 2000 7,343 hl (193,855 gal) were produced.

DOM. DU MAS NEUF 2000★★ ■ ◆ €5–8

☐ 68.4 ha 77,000

Blue, like the nearby Mediterranean, the bottle is reminiscent of flasks of orange-flower water. B.-P. Jeanjean's wine is remarkable for its youth and elegance. The colour is brilliant, clear gold shot with green. It has green notes, too, on the nose, with a hint of blackcurrant leaf. Wonderfully complex on the palate, it has mixed exotic fruit, floral, resin and grapefruit peel aromas. This crescendo of flavours calls for a *coup de coeur*. The 1994 vintage was awarded the same distinction.

☛ Bernard-Pierre Jeanjean, Mas neuf des Aresquiers, 34110 Vic-la-Gardiole, tel. 04.67.78.37.44, fax 04.67.78.37.46

DOM. DU MOULINAS 1999 ■ ◆ €5–8

☐ 16 ha n.c.

This wine has a brilliant, clear straw colour with intense aromas revealing crystallised fruits, apricots and verbena liqueur. The latter dominates on the palate. The colour is enhanced by touches of lime. Full, lively and well balanced, this is a classic.

☛ SCA Les Fils Aymes, Dom. du Moulinas, 24, av. du Poilu, BP1, 34114 Mireval, tel. 04.67.78.13.97, fax 04.67.78.57.78 ▼

Muscat de Saint-Jean de Minervois

This Muscat is produced on parcels of land amid the garrigue, the classic high (average 200 m/656 ft) stony moorland of south-west France. It follows that the harvest is late, about three weeks after the other Muscat appellations. Some vines are on primary schist terrain but most grow on limestone interspersed with red clays. Muscat à Petits Grains is the single variety planted; the wines must have a minimum sugar content of 125 g per litre. They are very aromatic with great finesse and characteristic floral notes. This is the smallest Muscat AOC, producing 4,808 hl (126,931 gal) in 2000.

DOM. DE BARROUBIO 1999★ ■ €5–8

☐ 1 ha 5,000

A family estate, which has already been awarded three *coups de coeur* in previous editions of the *Guide*, has produced this 1999 wine. It is a clear golden-yellow colour, and has an attractive nose of ripe grapes and lime blossom, with crystallised apricots, orange zest and verbena leaves on the palate. A lovely classic wine. (50 cl bottles).

☛ Raymond Miquel, Dom. de Barroubio, 34360 Saint-Jean-de-Minervois, tel. 04.67.38.14.06, fax 04.67.38.14.06 ▼

☖ ev. day 9.30am–12 noon 3pm–7pm

DOM. DE BARROUBIO
Vieilles vignes Cuvée Nicolas 1999★ ■ €15–23

☐ n.c. 5,000

This special wine is sold in 50-cl bottles. A lovely russet gold, slightly amber, it has wonderfully original aromas with touches of fruit steeped in alcohol. The palate, with plums in brandy flavours, has warmth and balance, and ends on a pleasantly bitter finish.

☛ Raymond Miquel, Dom. de Barroubio, 34360 Saint-Jean-de-Minervois, tel. 04.67.38.14.06, fax 04.67.38.14.06 ▼

☖ ev. day 9.30am–12 noon 3pm–7pm

LES VIGNERONS DE SEPTIMANIE Petit Grain ■ ◆ €8–11

☐ 30 ha 60,000

The old-gold colour denotes maturity, as does the aromatic palate with its nuances of quince, crystallised tangerine and cooked peaches. There are herbaceous notes and dried flowers on the palate, with an attractive bitterness on the finish.

bring out the best in Grenache Noir, in both dry and sweet wines. A brilliant, dark red, this 1995 wine has cherry aromas on the nose, with pervasive fruit on the supple and velvety (but powerful) palate. It needs time to fully develop.

• Cave de Rasteau, rte des Princes-d'Orange, 84110 Rasteau, tel. 04.90.10.90.10, fax 04.90.46.16.65, e-mail rasteau@rasteau.com ☒ ▼ by appt.

• Vignerons de La Méditerranée, ZI Plaisance, 12, rue du Rec-de-Veyret, BP 414, 11104 Narbonne Cedex, tel. 04.68.42.75.00, fax 04.68.42.75.01, e-mail rhirtz@listel.fr ▼ by appt.

Rasteau

Located in the very north of the Vaucluse department, this vineyard is spread over two distinct geological formations: sand, marl and pebbles in the north, and ancient alluvial terraces left by the Rhône (from the Quaternary era) with smoothed pebbles in the south. The Grenache varieties (Noir, Blanc, Gris) are responsible for all the wines here. In 2000, production amounted to 189 hl (4,990 gal) of white wine and 876.53 hl (23,140 gal) of red.

DOM. BEAU MISTRAL
Vieilli en fût de chêne 1999★

□ 2 ha 4,000 €5-8

This Rasteau, produced from 50-year-old Grenache vines particularly suited to this soil, has been matured for a year in barrel. Mahogany to russet-amber in colour, it has permeating aromas of dried fruits overlying toasted notes, with almonds and grapes in brandy opening out to unexpected *rancio* notes.

• Jean-Marc Brun, Le Village, rte d'Orange, 84110 Rasteau, tel. 04.90.46.16.90, fax 04.90.46.17.30 ☒
▼ ev. day 9am–12 noon 2pm–6pm

DOM. BRESSY MASSON 1999★

■ n.c. 4,000 €8-11

This estate, known usually for its *rancio*, has distinguished itself this year with a macerated red wine which is sustained, intense and generous. The palate, with pronounced red fruit, particularly cherries, overlying spices, is full, with firm tannins. It is a powerful wine that is ready for drinking now, but will also keep.

• Marie-France Masson, Dom. Bressy-Masson, 84110 Rasteau, tel. 04.90.46.10.45, fax 04.90.46.17.78 ☒
▼ ev. day 9am–12 noon 2pm–7pm

CAVE DE RASTEAU Signature 1995

■ 3 ha 10,500 €8-11

Amalgamated into a co-operative since 1925, the Rasteau's wine-makers know how to

Muscat du Cap Corse

The Appellation Muscat du Cap Corse was officially recognised in 1993, the culmination of lengthy efforts made by a handful of wine-makers working on the limestone soils of Patrimonio and the schist soils of the AOC Vin de Corse-Coteaux du Cap Corse. The AOC is located in 17 communes in the extreme north of the islands, and covered 84 ha (207 acres), producing 2,095 hl (55,308 gal) in 1998.

Since 1993, AOC wines have been limited to Muscat Blanc à Petits Grains and have had to fulfil the stipulated production conditions of Vin Doux Naturels, which require at least 95 grams of residual sugar per litre.

CLOS DE BERNARDI 2000

□ 5 ha 2,000 €8-11

The Clos de Bernardi has been in existence since 1884. Jean-Laurent de Bernardi's father was a great advocate of the Corse appellations, in particular the Patrimonio. The estate's 2000 wine is a lovely, golden colour with pronounced Muscat aromas on the nose and a well-balanced palate. It is definitely worthwhile.

• Jean-Laurent de Bernardi, 20253 Patrimonio, tel. 04.95.37.01.09, fax 04.95.32.07.66 ▼ by appt.

DOM. DE CATARELLI 2000★

□ 2 ha 6,000 €11-15

The Catarelli estate is a beautiful 11-ha (27-acre) property, situated in the village of Farinole, on the west coast of the Cap Corse. This seductive, well-balanced 2000 Muscat

VDN

has wonderfully aromatic exotic-fruit aromas. The Jury recommends serving it with *foie gras* with morels. It should be kept for a special occasion.

● EARL, Dom. de Catarelli, Marine de Farinole, 20253 Patrimonio,
tel. 04.95.37.02.84, fax 04.95.37.18.72 ☑
Ⴤ ev. day except Sun. 9am–12 noon 3pm–6pm
● Le Stunff

DOM. GENTILE 2000★
☐ 3.5 ha 16,000 ▪ ♦ €11-15

Dominique Gentile's Muscat has again distinguished itself with its intensity and character. A pretty straw-yellow colour, it has citrus notes on the nose and on the powerful palate. It is traditional in style.

● Dom. Gentile, Olzo, 20217 Saint-Florent, tel. 04.95.37.01.54, fax 04.95.37.16.69 ☑
Ⴤ ev. day except Sun. 9am–12 noon 2.30pm–6.30pm; by appt. out of season

DOM. GIUDICELLI 2000★
☐ 5.17 ha 16,000 ▪ ♦ €8-11

Muriel Guidicelli, a young Patrimonio wine-maker who set up in 1997, makes consistently good wines, producing, this year, a very aromatic Muscat derived from a wine-making process that links tradition and modernity. Golden-straw coloured, the wine has original notes of rose, Turkish Delight and coconuts, and is very elegant on the palate. This wine can be drunk as an aperitif and also with an exotic-fruit-based dessert.

● Muriel Giudicelli, Paese Novu, 20213 Penta di Casinca, tel. 04.95.36.45.10, fax 04.95.36.45.10 ☑ Ⴤ by appt.

DOM. LECCIA 2000★
☐ 3 ha 10,000 ▪ ♦ €11-15

The Leccia estate, included in the *Guide* since the beginnings of the appellation, already has a reputation for both dry and sweet wines. It has often entered remarkable Muscats, and this wine, golden-coloured with straw glints, is no exception. The nose is complex, with Muscat notes and touches of dried fruits and almonds. The palate is very sweet, with great length.

● Dom. Leccia, 20232 Poggio-d'Oletta, tel. 04.95.37.11.35, fax 04.95.37.17.03 ☑
Ⴤ by appt.

CLOS MARFISI 2000★
☐ 3.5 ha 10,000 ▪ ♦ €11-15

Toussaint Marfisi, a very conscientious wine-maker at Patrimonio since 1956, has produced a clear, brilliant Muscat, wonderfully sweet and elegant with Muscat aromas and menthol notes on the palate. It is ready to drink now, and would go well with figs poached in wine – Muscat, obviously!

● Toussaint Marfisi, Clos Marfisi, av. Jules-Ventre, 20253 Patrimonio, tel. 04.95.37.01.16, fax 04.95.37.06.37 ☑
Ⴤ ev. day except Sun. 9am–7pm; cl. 1 Dec.–31 Mar.

CLOS MONTEMAGNI
Cuvée Prestige du Menhir 2000★★
☐ 7 ha 10,000 ▪ ♦ €8-11

Corsica is famous for its prehistoric menhirs, one of which has been discovered near Patrimonio. It is an ancient name, then, for this modern, very pale wine, with its floral aromas mingled with honey and apricots. With its perfect balance on the palate between residual sugar and alcohol, this wine narrowly missed the *coup de coeur*.

● SCEA Montemagni, 20253 Patrimonio, tel. 04.95.37.14.46, fax 04.95.37.17.15 ☑
Ⴤ ev. day 8am–12 noon 2pm–6pm

ORENGA DE GAFFORY 2000★★
☐ 7.56 ha n.c. ▪ ♦ €11-15

Orenga de Gaffory's estate has achieved its fourth *coup de coeur* in this appellation, with this Muscat produced from chalky-clay soil vineyards, a wine very much in the modern style. On the nose, there are rich and varied aromas of white flowers and asphodel honey. The balance between sugar and alcohol, sweetness and power is perfect. This is a wine to serve with grilled white meat or a simple fresh-fruit salad. It could also keep for several months before drinking chilled, without ice.

● GFA Orenga de Gaffory, Morta-Majo, 20253 Patrimonio, tel. 04.95.37.45.00, fax 04.95.37.14.25, e-mail orenga.de.gaffory@wanadoo.fr ☑
Ⴤ by appt.
● H. Orenga et P. de Gaffory

DOM. PIERETTI 2000★
☐ 0.75 ha 3,200 ▪ ♦ €11-15

The old wine cellar dates from the 17th century, and up until 1992 the grapes were pressed, as in the good old days, by foot. Lina Pieretti Venturi, taking over in 1991, introduced a new approach. She planted some of her Muscat vines at Pietracorbara, on land fanned by the west winds, where the grapes ripen very early. This is now her third vintage. It is a clear wine, with a discreet but fine nose. On the palate, nuances of dried fruit mingle with the characteristic aromas of the grape variety. Try it with blue cheese.

● Lina Pieretti Venturi, Santa-Severa, 20228 Luri, tel. 04.95.35.01.03, fax 04.95.35.01.03 ☑ Ⴤ by appt.

Muscat du Cap Corse

DOM. SAN QUILICO 2000★

n.c.   n.c.   ■ ♦ 6-11

The San Quilico estate, a very attractive, large, undivided property, is managed by Henri Orenga de Gaffory. In past years he has produced superb Muscats (one of which, a 98, was awarded a *coup de cœur*). This is a modern-style wine, crystal-clear with lemon glints. With toasty and vanilla fragrances on the nose that continue through on the palate, it would be a delightful accompaniment to a plate of fresh fruit or for drinking in the early evening.

↣ EARL Dom. San Quilico, Morta Majo, 20253 Patrimonio, tel. 04.95.37.45.00, fax 04.95.37.14.25 ⅄ by appt.

VINS DE LIQUEUR

This type of wine is the result of blending must with grape brandy during fermentation. In all cases, wines described as Vins de Liqueur must have between 16% and 22% of alcohol by volume. The addition of brandy to the musts is called mutage; both brandy and must should originate from the same vineyard. The AOC (the equivalent of the EU designation VLQPRD) used to apply only to Pineau des Charentes (apart, in rare instances, from a few Frontignans). However, Floc de Gascogne (classified 27 November 1990) and Macvin du Jura (classified 14 November 1991) have now also joined the Appellation Contrôlée Vin de Liqueur.

Pineau des Charentes

Pineau des Charentes is produced in the Cognac region on an extensive plain sloping gently westwards from a maximum altitude of 180 m (590 ft) towards the Atlantic Ocean. The climate, maritime in character, is typified by a remarkable amount of sunshine and very even temperatures, factors which promote the slow ripening of the grapes.

More than 83,000 ha (205,010 acres) of vines are planted on limestone slopes in a hinterland watered by the Charente river. The grapes are intended mainly for the production of Cognac. Pineau des Charentes is produced by mixing Cognac with partially fermented grape must.

According to legend, a somewhat distracted wine-maker once made the mistake of filling a hogshead that still contained some Cognac with grape must. Noticing that the barrel did not ferment, he left it in the back of the cellar. A few years later, when he was preparing to empty the hogshead, he discovered a clear, delicate liquid with a sweet, fruity flavour: this is said to be the origin of Pineau des Charentes. The legend dates from the 16th century, but the blend is still current today, as is the traditional method of production,

because Pineau des Charentes may only be made by wine-growers. Its reputation remained localised for a long time before gradually achieving first national, then international recognition.

The grape musts for white Pineau des Charentes come mainly from Ugni-Blanc, Colombard, Montils and Sémillon, while Cabernet-Franc, Cabernet-Sauvignon and Merlot are used for the rosé. The vines are trained low and cultivated without nitrogenous fertilisers. The grapes have to produce a must of over 10% alcohol by volume. After the blending process, Pineau des Charentes is aged in oak casks for a minimum of one year before bottling.

As is the case with Cognac, it is not the practice to show the vintage. On the other hand, the age of the wine is frequently indicated. The term Vieux Pineau is reserved for Pineau that is more than five years old and Très Vieux Pineau for Pineau that is more than ten years old. In both cases, it must be aged exclusively in the hogshead, and the quality of this ageing process has to be checked by the Commission de Dégustation (the tasting panel). Alcoholic strength must be between 17% and 18% by volume and the content of non-fermented sugar from 125–150 g/l; the rosé is typically sweeter and fruitier than the white, which is firmer and drier. The annual production exceeds 100,000 hl (2,640,000 gal): 55% of it is white, 45% rosé. Five hundred producer-growers and about seven co-operatives make and sell Pineau des Charentes. A hundred shippers are responsible for more than 40% of retail sales.

This is a nectar of honey and fire, its marvellous sweetness camouflaging real power. Pineau des Charentes can be drunk young (after two years) when all its fruit aromas (even fuller in the rosé) are on show. With age, these aromas take on a nutty *rancio* character. Traditionally, Pineau des Charentes is drunk as an aperitif or with desserts; however, its roundness also perfectly accompanies foie gras and Roquefort. Its sweetness intensifies the natural flavour and sweetness of some kinds of fruit, particularly melon (Charentais melon), strawberries and raspberries. Pineau des Charentes is also used as an ingredient in traditional regional dishes such as mussel stew.

CLAUDE AUDEBERT Vieux★

□ 6 ha · 5,000 · €15-23

Romanesque churches and a Gallo-Roman theatre are within easy reach of this traditional Charentais enterprise, which has buildings constructed from local stone and an 18th-century porch. An attractive amber colour with bright gold glints, the wine has aromas of dried fruit and hazelnuts, pleasantly dominated by oak. Round and perfumed, the dried fruit flavours linger on the palate, accompanied by a mellow *rancio* note, and finish with a delicate hint of oak.

● Claude Audebert, Les Villairs, 16170 Rouillac, tel. 05.45.21.76.86, fax 05.45.96.81.36, e-mail erclaude@wanadoo.fr ☑
☖ ev. day. 7.30am-1pm, 2-8pm

ANDRE ARDOUIN★

□ 4 ha · n.c. · €8-11

This property, in the north of Charente-Maritime, has been cultivating vines for six generations. It is situated in an exceptionally attractive tourist region, and the Romanesque church of Aulnay is about 4 km (2.5 miles) away. The wine has a lovely gleaming gold colour. However, the nose, though both elegant and subtle, lacks intensity. It is fruity on the palate with a well-balanced touch of acidity.

● André Ardouin, 6, rue des Anges, 17470 Villemorin, tel. 05.46.33.12.52, fax 05.46.33.14.47 ☑ ☖ by appt.

BARBEAU ET FILS Sélection

▲ 0.95 ha · 10,000 · €8-11

For over a century the Barbeau family has handed down to each generation their tried and tested expertise. This wine has a deep rose colour with orange glints and aromas of blackcurrant, redcurrant and raspberry. A full, rich Pineau with a lovely fresh finish.

● Maison Barbeau et Fils, Les Vignes, 17160 Sonnac, tel. 05.46.58.55.85, fax 05.46.58.53.62 ☑ ☖ by appt.

MICHEL BARON Vieux 1990★★

▲ 2 ha · 4,000 · €11-15

The Logis du Coudred, 5 km (5 miles) from Cognac, is situated within the vineyard of Les Borderies. The Baron family has owned this property since 1851. This vintage white Pineau is a clear, brilliant straw-yellow colour and has a delicate nose with traces of *rancio* aromas and hints of lemon and exotic fruit. The round, rich and complex palate has lemony, spicy notes sweetened with hints of honey. It has excellent length and a mellow, delicate *rancio* flavour. This producer was awarded yet another *coup de coeur* this year.

● Michel Baron, Logis du Coudret, 16370 Cherves-Richemont, tel. 05.45.83.16.27, fax 05.45.83.18.67, e-mail veuvebaron@wanadoo.fr ☑
☖ ev. day. excl. Sun. 2-6.30pm

RAYMOND BOSSIS 1998★

▲ 4 ha · 6,000 · €8-11

Raymond Bossis has featured regularly in the *Guide* and won a *coup de coeur* last year. He handed over to his son in 1993. Once again the rosé is one of those that came through the Jury's harsh assessment with flying colours. It is an intense, clear, brilliant ruby colour and has cherry and violet aromas. The attack is supple and round, followed by a long, full mouth finishing with crystallised fruit flavours.

● SCEA Les Groies, 1750 Saint-Bonnet-sur-Gironde, tel. 05.46.86.02.19, fax 05.46.70.66.85 ☑
☖ ev. day. 9am-12 noon 2-7pm
● Raymond Bossis

Pineau des Charentes

BRARD BLANCHARD 1997★★

☐ 1.31 ha 24,000 🍶 €8-11

The vineyard is situated on clay and limestone slopes that sweep down to the Charente river and the gateway to Cognac. The unusual blend of grape varieties (Ugni Blanc, Colombard and Montils) and the organic cultivation produce a very typical yet original Pineau. It is a beautiful, delicate, clear, pale yellow with glimmers of gold. The complex nose is a combination of white-fleshed fruit, very ripe *pêche de vigne*, a particularly aromatic variety of peach, exotic fruit and dried fruit. Both full and rich, it opens out on the palate with citrus tones (mandarin and kumquat). The attractive palate has great length and a wonderful finish with dried fruits (figs), banana and apricot. A well-made Pineau Blanc.

➥ GAEC Brard-Blanchard, 1, chem. de Routreau, Boutiers, 16,000 Cognac, tel. 05.45.32.19.58, fax 05.45.36.53.21 ☑ 🍷 ev. day ex Sun. 9am–12 noon and 2–6pm; closed 15 Aug–1 Sept.

FREDDY BRUN★

☐ 2 ha 4,000 🍶 €5-8

The original blend of grape varieties (50% Colombard, 30% Sémillon and 20% Ugni Blanc, from 30-year-old vines planted on clay and limestone soil) produces this Pineau. Bright with glints of yellow gold, the rich, complex nose shows well-balanced oak and some development. Mouth filling with good fruit and delicious honey flavours.

➥ Freddy Brun, Chez Babouf, 16300 Barret, tel. 05.45.78.00.73, fax 05.45.78.98.81 ☑ 🍷 by appt.

CALISINAC Extra vieux★

☐ 50 ha 2,500 🍶 €8-11

Coopérative du Liboureau was established in 1953 and vinifies the harvests from some 230 ha (568 acres) belonging to around 100 wine-growers. It produces Cognac, Pineau and Vins de Pays. This Pineau is a lovely old-gold colour and exceptionally bright and clear. It has a very fine nose with hints of orange flower, honey, walnut and a well-balanced *rancio* flavour. The palate is full, rich and long, with a roundness that adds to the overall harmony.

➥ SCA Cave du Liboureau, 18, rue de l'Océan, 17490 Siecq, tel. 05.46.26.61.86, fax 05.46.26.68.01, e-mail cave.du.liboureau@wanadoo.fr ☑ 🍷 by appt.

JEAN-NOEL COLLIN 1997

▲ 3 ha 3,000 🍶 €8-11

The vineyard, established in 1850, is on the clay and limestone soils of Grande Champagne. The Pineau is pinkish in colour and flecked with orange, clear and very bright. A subtle, intense nose is packed with strawberry and redcurrant. The palate is rich and round, with flavours of red fruits and a refreshing liveliness. Enjoy it with a chocolatey dessert.

➥ Jean-Noël Collin, La Font-Bourreau, 16130 Salles-d'Angles, tel. 05.45.83.70.77,

fax 05.45.83.66.89, e-mail jean-noel.collin@wanadoo.fr ☑ 🍷 ev. day. 8am–8pm.

RICHARD DELISLE★

☐ n.c. 15,000 🍶 €8-11

The headquarters of this wine-shipper are in Grande Champagne, near the Château de Bourg-Charente and the church of Saint Jean-Baptiste. This golden colour glints with coppery-orange hues and is slightly tile-red. The intense flowery nose has subtle hints of figs with well-balanced oak. The sweetness on the palate opens and reveals flavours of dried fruits, figs and a well-structured *rancio* flavour.

➥ SARL Hawkins Distribution, Moulineuf, 16200 Bourg-Charente, tel. 05.45.81.11.30, fax 05.45.81.11.31, e-mail contact@hawkinsdistribution.com ☑

DROUET ET FILS Vieux X'Cep★

☐ 1 ha 2,000 🍶 €15-23

A blend of Colombard (25%) and Ugni Blanc (75%), which proves to be very successful. This Vin de Liqueur is produced using traditional cultivation methods with limited manuring and sustainable agricultural methods. This Pineau is neither fined or filtered. Its amber colour is bright with fiery sparks. The nose presents delicate aromas of dried fruit with well-balanced oak and a light *rancio* character. It has great length yet remains fresh because of a pleasant acidity, which harmonises perfectly with the wood and *rancio*. A well-crafted Pineau with typical exotic fruit aromas.

➥ Patrick et Stéphanie Drouet, 1, rte du Maine-Neuf, 16130 Salles-d'Angles, tel. 05.45.83.63.13, fax 05.45.83.65.48 ☑ 🍷 ev. day. 9am–7pm; Sun. by appt.

DUPUY Très Vieux★

☐ n.c. n.c. 🍶 €8-11

The family enterprise, founded in 1852, is situated in the centre of the town of Cognac. It produces Cognacs and Pineaux by traditional methods. This Pineau Très Vieux is old-gold in colour with slightly orange glints. The nose has beautiful aromas of orange peel, apricot and honey. Well balanced on the palate, with mature flavours of crystallised fruits.

➥ A. Edmond Dupuy, 32, rue de Boston, BP 62, 16102 Cognac Cedex, tel. 05.45.32.07.45, fax 05.45.32.52.47, e-mail c-b-g@cognac-dupuy.com ☑

HENRI GEFFARD 1996★★

☐ 1 ha 9,000 🍶 €8-11

A family-run vineyard, this is not far from the Vallée du Né (where the Gérard Klein film *Va Savoir* was shot). Without doubt this is a Pineau to get to know. Clear with an intense vermilion-yellow colour. It has a fine floral nose with citrus fruits, lemon, honey and lime flower. The attack is supple and, although not powerful, the palate opens to reveal lingering flavours of peach and grapefruit finishing with a touch of pleasant and refreshing acidity.

GUILLON-PAINTURAUD

Extra Vieux★   0.61 ha   1,000   €15-23

This family-run vineyard was established in 1610 and is situated in the heart of Grande Champagne, the premier cru of Cognac. A great many events take place here over the summer months. The rosé colour of the wine has tile-red hues that indicate its long ageing. The nose explodes with aromas of crystallised orange peel, oak and *rancio*. The Jury enjoyed its prominent fruitiness on the palate and its well-balanced character.

▸ Guillon-Painturaud, Biard, 16130 Segonzac, tel. 05.45.83.41.95, fax 05.45.83.34.42. e-mail guillon-painturaudepicuria@wanadoo.fr ☑ Ⓣ by appt.

DOM. DE LA PETITE FONT VIEILLE★   0.5 ha   3,000   €5-8

This was a dairy farm as well as a vineyard until the end of the 1970s, when the owners decided to buy a still and concentrate exclusively on wine-growing. The Ugni Blanc produces this clear, glittering, buttercup-yellow wine with an appealing nose showing some maturity. Fruity and well balanced, it is a good, classic, harmonious Pineau.

▸ Eric et Carole Aiguillon, 10, rue Grimard, 17520 Jarnac Champagne, tel. 05.46.49.55.54, fax 05.46.49.55.54 ☑ Ⓣ by appt.

DOM. DE LA VILLE★★   n.c.   1,000   €5-8

This vineyard, established in 1934, is situated on the clay and limestone soils of the hills overlooking the Gironde estuary. This is a deep ruby-coloured Pineau rosé with dazzling carmine glints and aromas of perfectly ripened grapes. The Jury appreciated strawberries and raspberries on the nose and enjoyed the soft mellow palate, which is pleasant and very rich. The fruit flavours expand and finish in perfect harmony.

▸ SA Dom. de La Ville, 1710 Saint-Thomas-de-Conac, tel. 05.46.86.03.33, fax 05.46.70.67.00, e-mail domainedelaville@voila.fr ☑ Ⓣ by appt.

CH. DE L'OISELLERIE

Gerfaut rubis 1998   5 ha   2,000   €8-11

The hunting falcons of the French court used to be trained here. When François I was freed by Charles V, he came to live with his sister, Marguerite of Angoulême, and often hunted with falcons. Now it is an agricultural college. L'Oisellerie makes a beautiful, clear, bright rose-coloured Pineau with hints of orange and with subtle strawberry and redcurrant. Well balanced, with red fruit flavours and a lively finish.

▸ Lycée agricole Oisellerie, 16400 La Couronne, tel. 05.45.67.36.89, fax 05.45.67.16.51, e-mail expl.legta-angouleme@educagri.fr ☑ Ⓣ by appt.

LISCA MONT★   0.5 ha   750   €8-11

These young wine-growers settled in Petite Champagne in 1994 near Pons where the Château des Enigmes and the Donjon de Pons are open to the public. Their very pale gold Pineau is limpid with saffron glints. It has a powerful, flowery nose with aromatic

MARQUIS DE DIDONNE★   50   80,000   €8-11

The Marquis de Didonne has distinguished himself again. This wine is a blend of Ugni Blanc and Colombard grown on siliceous clay soil by the members of this co-operative near Royan. It is straw-yellow in colour, with flecks of copper. The nose is packed with quince, fig and a touch of strawberry and shows some maturity. It has good length with evident oak.

▸ Vignerons des Côtes de Saintonge, B.P. 5, Fontbedeau, 17200 Saint-Sulpice-de-Royan, tel. 05.46.06.01.01, fax 05.46.06.92.72, e-mail info@didonne.com ☑ Ⓣ by appt.

MENARD★   n.c.   20,000   €8-11

Since 1946 the Menard family has enjoyed a legendary reputation in the Charentais region, endorsed by entries in successive editions of the *Guide*. This year the Pineau is a very clear rosé with salmon-pink glints and aromas of blackcurrant, blackberry and cherry brandy. After a firm attack it becomes full and pleasant, and the fruity tones become more prominent. Good length where the oak is evident. The white **Très Vieux Pineau** with its honey and dried fruit aromas is also awarded a star.

▸ J.-P. Ménard et Fils, 2, rue de la Cure, BP 16, 16720 Saint-Même-les-Carrières, tel. 05.45.81.90.26, fax 05.45.81.98.22, e-mail menard@cognac-menard.com ☑ Ⓣ ev. day ex Sat. Sun. 8am–12 noon 2–6pm

J.Y. ET F. MOINE   **Très Vieux★**   2 ha   4,000   €15-23

These two brothers took over the family vineyard in 1970. In 1990 they dreamed up the 'Circuit de Chêne' (the oak circuit), a visit for tourists that takes in the distillery, a cooperage and the workshop where the wood is cut for barrel-making. Their golden-yellow Pineau has flecks of brilliant orange and aromas of vanillary wood and crystallised fruits. The powerful, rich palate is supple and round, which adds to the overall harmony of aromas.

▸ Jean-Yves et François Moine, Villeneuve, 16200 Chassors, tel. 05.45.80.98.91, fax 05.45.80.96.01, e-mail lesfreres.moine@wanadoo.fr ☑ Ⓣ by appt.

notes of honey and tea. The palate is fruity combining walnut, honey and a noticeable *rancio*, or nutty, flavour.

Lisca Mont, 8, rue de la Mare, 17800 Biron, tel. 05.46.91.36.49, fax 05.46.91.36.49, e-mail cognac.mont@cognac.fr ev. day. 9am–8pm

DOM. DE MONTLAMBERT ★★

0.31 ha 2,676 €11–15

The Tourny family has owned this vineyard since 1850. After the death of her grandfather, Rémy Tourny, Marie-Laure Saint-Martin created the Montlambert brand. Her old-gold, crystal-clear Pineau is remarkable. The nose is precise and fairly powerful, rich in aromas of white-fleshed fruit. The palate is supple and well balanced, with just the right amount of liveliness, and shows some development.

SARL de Montlambert, Dom. de Montlambert, 16100 Louzac-Saint-André, tel. 05.45.82.27.86, fax 05.45.82.91.32, e-mail remytourny@wanadoo.fr by appt.

GERARD PAUTIER ★

1.32 ha 2,000 €8–11

A magnificent domaine on the banks of the Charente, where there are pleasant walks along the tow path. The vineyard has produced a pretty Pineau rosé, which is deep pink with glints of garnet with an attractive clarity. There are notes of blackcurrant, redcurrant and raspberry on the nose and palate, which is rich and has good length.

Gérard Pautier, SCA de la Roméde, Veillard, 16200 Bourg-Charente, tel. 05.45.81.24.89, fax 05.45.81.04.44 ev. day. 9am–6pm

ROBERT POUILLOUX ET SES FILS Rubis 1998

4 ha n.c. €8–11

These limestone soils have been cultivated by the same family since 1764, and they produce an intensely pink Pineau with carmine-red glints. The aromas of blackcurrant, myrtle and red fruit jam are pleasantly surprising. The rich, supple and mouth-filling palate has great character, and the finish is impressive.

EARL Robert Pouilloux et ses Fils, Peugrignoux, 17800 Pérignac, tel. 05.46.96.41.41, fax 05.46.96.35.04 ev. day. 8am–8pm

DAVID RAMNOUX ★

1 ha 3,600 €8–11

The Ramnoux domaine was established in 1946 and since 1993 has been practising organic production methods. This Pineau, the first to be officially certified organic, is a blend of the 1997 and 1998 harvests. Brilliant yellow-gold in colour, it has a well-developed nose dominated by perfumes of flowers and honey. The palate is well balanced and has a lovely freshness on the finish, which is in perfect harmony with the fruit and honey.

David Ramnoux, Le bourg, 16170 Mareuil, tel. 05.45.35.43.88, fax 05.45.96.94, e-mail david-ramnoux@hotmail.com by appt.

REMY-MARTIN ★

50 ha 80,000 €8–11

The great shipper, founded in 1724, not only markets Grande and Petite Champagne cognacs to the five continents but also sells Pineau. This one is an intense, ripe-straw colour with copper hints. Its nose is already well developed with the beginnings of a walnutty, *rancio* character and flowery, woody notes. A powerful palate, where the strong *rancio* flavours compliment the fruitiness. This good, well-made wine is the perfect accompaniment to Roquefort cheese.

Remy-Martin, 20, rue de la Société-Vinicole, B.P. 37, 16100 Cognac, tel. 05.45.35.76.00, fax 05.45.35.02.85 by appt.

ROUSSILLE Rosé spécial 1997 ★

3.35 ha 7,000 €8–11

This vineyard is 6 km (nearly 4 miles) outside Angoulême and has been run by the same family for nearly a hundred years. The Pineau rosé is deep pink bordering on ruby and has orangey glints. The nose shows fine crystallised red fruit aromas. The palate, which is surprisingly round, is very rich and has great length.

SCA Pineau Roussille, 16730 Linars, tel. 05.45.91.05.18, fax 05.45.91.13.83 ev. day. 9am–12 noon 1–7pm
Pascal Roussille

ANDRE THORIN Extra vieux ★

2 ha 6,000 €11–15

The family-run vineyard in Grande Champagne on clay-limestone soils. This Pineau Extra Vieux, made from Ugni Blanc grapes, is a bright pale straw colour and has a lightly oaked nose with lots of cherry and ripe fruit. It is mellow and supple on the palate, with a hint of *rancio* among the cherry and spicy notes.

Claude Thorin, Chez Boujut, 16200 Mainxe, tel. 05.45.83.33.46, fax 05.45.83.38.93 ev. day ex. Sun. 9.30am–7pm

Floc de Gascogne

Floc de Gascogne is produced in the same geographical area as the Appellation Bas Armagnac, Ténarèze and Haut Armagnac, as well as in all the communes within the Appellation Armagnac. The wine-growing region is part of the Pyrenean foot-hills and extends into three departments: the Gers, the Landes and the Lot-et-Garonne. To give themselves extra power, the wine-makers of Floc de Gascogne established a new principle. Instead of describing and defining specific growing areas, as is the case for wines, or a simple geographical area, as for brandies, they propose an annual list of growing areas for approval by the INAO.

The whites are produced from Colombard, Gros Manseng and Ugni Blanc, and, together, these must make up at least 70% of the range of varieties planted. Since 1996, no individual variety can exceed 50%; other varieties included are Baroque, Folle Blanche, Petit Manseng, Mauzac, Sauvignon and Semillon. Rosés are produced from Cabernet Franc and Cabernet-Sauvignon, as well as from Cot, Fer Servadou, Merlot and Tannat, which last may not exceed 50% of the varieties planted.

The regulations laid down by the producers are highly restrictive: a maximum of 3,300 plants per hectare (1,336 per acre), trained en guyot or in cordons, the number of buds to the hectare to be fewer than 60,000 (24,291 per acre). Artificial irrigation of the vines is strictly forbidden in any season, and the basic yield from the parcels of land must be less than or equal to 60 hl/ha (648 gal per acre).

Every year, each wine-grower must submit a declaration of intent to make the wines and send it to the INAO, so that the organisation may actually inspect the conditions of production on the ground. The musts harvested may not have less than 170 g/l of must sugar. Once the grapes have been stripped from the stalks and separated from the sediment, they are placed in a receptacle where the must undergoes the beginnings of fermentation. No addition of external products is permitted. The mutage of the must takes place with Eau de Vie

d'Armagnac at a minimum of 52% alcohol by volume. The result is left to rest for at least nine months. It may be brought out of the vat room only after 1 September of the year following the harvest. All the lots of wine are tasted and analysed. Given the variations that arise in this type of product, the best of the wine emerges only after ageing in the bottle.

BAUT BARON★   1.33 ha 8,450   €6-11

Only a few turns of the wheel from Notre-Dame-des-Cyclistes at Labastide-d'Armagnac, this co-operative has two Flocs among the winners. The very successful rosé is a deep bright red with aromas of overripe fruit and contrasting sweetness and acidity that adds balance. The white is impressive, with attractive aromas of dried fruits and a roundness that makes it smooth and easy to drink.

☛ Cave coop. de vinification de Cazaubon, rte de Mont-de-Marsan, 32150 Cazaubon, tel. 05.62.08.34.00, fax 05.62.69.50.98 ▼
Ⴑ by appt.

DOM. DE BILE   1.84 ha 3,249   €5-8

The Domaine de Bilé is one of the few remaining wine-growing properties in the Haut-Armagnac region. The Della-Vedove family deserves even more praise for submitting this white Floc. Straw-yellow in colour with an almondy nose, it is expansive on the palate. An appealing wine.

☛ EARL Della-Vedove, Dom. de Bilé, 32320 Bassoues-d'Armagnac, tel. 05.62.70.93.59, fax 05.62.70.93.59 ▼
Ⴑ ev. day, 8am-8pm

BORDENEUVE-ENTRAS★★   1.04 ha 13,500   €6-11

This property in the heart of the Ténarèze is respected by its peers. It presented two well-made wines. The remarkable rosé has a bright, intense colour, and the nose is packed with aromas of crystallised fruits. Lightly oaked, the palate is very attractive, its roundness, balance and length delicately flavoured by the armagnac. The white is commended for its deep straw-yellow appearance and well-structured nose and palate.

☛ GAEC Bordeneuve-Entras, 32410 Ayguetinte, tel. 05.62.68.11.41, fax 05.62.68.15.32 ▼ ev. day, 9am-6pm; summer (9am-8pm); groups by appt.
☛ Maestrojuan

Floc de Gascogne

DOM. DES CASSAGNOLES★★★

☐ €5-8

▲ 5 ha 6,200

It is hardly surprising that this Floc rosé has been awarded a *coup de coeur*, since the Baumann family constantly produce wines of quality. This one has a deep, intense red colour and a delicate, complex nose with intense blackcurrant aromas. Fleshy and round on the palate, it is packed with red fruit flavours, perfectly balanced and with great length. Another achievement is the **white Floc**. This is crystal-clear yellow with a delicate flowery nose and an elegant well-balanced palate. Worthy recognition for well-handled maturation and high quality armagnac.

☞ J. et G. Baumann, Dom. des Cassagnoles, EARL de la Ténarèze, 32330 Gondrin, tel. 05.62.28.40.57, fax 05.62.28.42.42 ☑
Ⓣ ev. day. 8.30am–5.30pm; Sun. by appt.

DOM. DE CHIROULET

▐▌ €8-11

▲ 5 ha 16,000

Chiroulet means 'whistle' in Gascon — and the one belonging to the Fezas family makes itself heard loud and clear. Highly recommended again, the Floc Rosé has a lively, intense colour. A powerful nose, fine and complex with red fruit aromas (blackberries, strawberries and raspberries). Supple with a lovely richness; very pleasant.

☞ EARL Famille Fezas, Dom. de Chiroulet, 32100 Larroque-sur-l'Osse, tel. 05.62.28.02.21, fax 05.62.28.41.56 ☑
Ⓣ by appt.

CAVE DES COTEAUX DU MEZINAIS★★

☐ ▬ ♦ €5-8

0.1 ha 910

Situated in the north of Ténarèze, this co-operative is run on family lines, and the members are actively involved in the wine-making. It presented two Flocs for consideration; this white has greenish glints and an elegant nose with an intense flowery palate. The very successful **rosé** is awarded one star. It is a brilliant pale pink with ripe fruit aromas and a very sweet palate. Both wines are very well balanced and typically representative of the AOC. Don't miss a visit to the Musée du Bouchon et du Liège (cork museum), only 500 m (545 yds) from the co-operative.

☞ Cave des Coteaux du Mézinais, 1, bd Colome, 47170 Mézin, tel. 05.53.65.53.55, fax 05.53.97.16.73, e-mail ccm3@libertysurf.fr ☑
Ⓣ ev. day. ex Mon. 9am–12.30pm 3–6pm

CH. DE CASSAIGNE★

☐ €8-11

15 ha 11,000

The 13th-century château, with its 16th-century kitchens and old armoury (now the barrel store), is one of the most popular places to visit in the Gers. This Floc is straw yellow with more intense glints. On the nose, as on the palate, the aromas are slightly heavy, which denotes some development, although it loses none of its elegance. To be enjoyed with *foie gras* – from the Gers, of course.

☞ Ch. de Cassaigne, 32100 Cassaigne, tel. 05.62.28.04.02, fax 05.62.28.41.43, e-mail chateaudecassaigne@teleparc.net ☑
Ⓣ ev. day. 10am–12 noon 2–7pm; groups by appt; closed Feb.

DOM. DE CAZEAUX

☐ €11-15

10 ha 4,000

The story goes that this is where the first bottle of Floc de Gascogne was made. This one is pale yellow, with a fruity nose and quince on the palate. The **rosé** has a ruby hints and a crystallised red fruit nose. It is round yet not heavy on the palate. These two Flocs are in the Kauffer family tradition.

☞ Eric Kauffer, Dom. de Cazeaux, 47170 Lannes, tel. 05.53.65.73.03, fax 05.53.65.88.95, e-mail domaine.de.cazeaux@wanadoo.fr ☑
Ⓣ ev. day. 9am–6pm; groups by appt.

CH. GARREAU★

▐▌ €8-11

☐ 12 ha 40,000

Dr Garreau is renowned in Cognac. He battles constantly against systems run by various administrations, yet he is still a serious wine-maker. This flowery, golden-yellow Floc is a little heady on the palate because of the armagnac. Nevertheless, it still has appealing hints of honey and ripe fruit. The star is well deserved.

☞ Ch. Garreau, Côtes de la Jeunesse, Ecomusée de L'Armagnac, 40240 Labastide-d'Armagnac, tel. 05.58.44.84.35, fax 05.58.44.87.07, e-mail chateau.garreau@wanadoo.fr ☑ Ⓣ by appt.

CH. DE JULIAC★★

☐ €8-11

35 ha n.c.

The château is built on the ruins of an old fortress in Bas-Armagnac, on soils described as 'sables fauves' (tawny sands). The Jury was pleasantly surprised by this brilliant, pale yellow Floc, with its aromatic nose of dried fruit. The same flavours follow through on the palate, where they are coupled with sweetness (honey). Good balance and harmony.

☞ Pierre Cassagne, Dom. de Juliac, 40240 Betbezer-d'Armagnac, tel. 05.58.44.88.64, fax 05.58.44.81.16 Ⓣ ev. day. 8am–6pm

CH. DE LAUBADE

6 ha   18,000   €5-8

The Château de Laubade, well known for producing Bas-Armagnacs of fine quality, submitted two examples of white Floc, which is fine and delicate and endowed with a good armagnac-style finish.

↪ SCA Ch. de Laubade, 32110 Sorbets, tel. 05.62.09.06.02 ☑ ☒ by appt.
↪ Lesgourgues

DOM. DE LAUROUX★

1.2 ha   5,000   €8-11

Rémy Fraisse is a regular in the *Guide* and has been acknowledged yet again. Bright straw-yellow in colour, this Floc is flowery, lively and fresh on the nose. On the palate, the flavours are light and well balanced. It is very characteristic. The rosé is singled out for its appearance and fine, subtle nose and palate.

↪ Rémy Fraisse, EARL de Lauroux, 32370 Manciet, tel. 05.62.08.56.76, fax 05.62.08.57.44 ☑ ☒ by appt.

CH. DE MONS★★★

1 ha   6,500   €8-11

The Mons estate is owned by the Chambre d'Agriculture du Gers and also houses the headquarters of the Centre technique de la Vigne et du Vin. The two Flocs presented were selected. The white is pale yellow and has a fresh, complex nose with hints of peaches. Well balanced on the palate, with strong flowery flavours and a long, lingering finish, it has class. The rosé, awarded one star, has mature red fruit flavours and pronounced sugariness, yet it is well balanced and seductive.

↪ Dom. de Mons, Chambre d'agriculture du Gers, 32100 Caussens, tel. 05.62.68.30.30, fax 05.62.68.30.35, e-mail chateau.mons.cda.32@wanadoo.fr ☑ ☒ by appt.

CH. DE PELLEHAUT★

1 ha   n.c.   €8-11

The Béraut family has been in the region for more than 300 years. At the 18th-century château in Ténarèze on the old Roman road, they plant the clay and limestone soil with two grape varieties, Ugni Blanc and Colombard. This results in a golden straw-yellow Floc with a complex nose of flowers, honey and hazelnuts. There is a little oak (vanilla) on the palate with good sugariness and a hint of armagnac on the finish. A well-made Floc, which is particularly appreciated by connoisseurs.

↪ SCV Béraut, Ch. de Pellehaut, 32250 Montréal-du-Gers, tel. 05.62.29.48.79, fax 05.62.29.49.90, e-mail chateau@pellehaut.com ☑ ☒ by appt.

DOM. DE POLIGNAC★

5 ha   12,000   €5-8

The Domaine de Polignac lies on stony clay and limestone soil. Two Flocs were submitted. Both delighted the tasters and each won a star. This rosé is a beautiful pure colour and

has fine, yet powerful, blackcurrant and raspberry aromas. It has a clean attack and is aromatic on the palate. The white is a brilliant, limpid golden-yellow with floral aromas and a touch of armagnac. Two wines to be drunk simply for pleasure.

↪ EARL Gratian, Dom. de Polignac, 32330 Gondrin, tel. 05.62.28.54.74, fax 05.62.28.54.86 ☑
☒ ev. day. 10am-1pm 3-8pm

DOM. SAN DE GUILHEM

3 ha   20,000   €8-11

The president of the appellation was highly praised this year. His pale yellow white, scented with peach aromas, is light and airy on the palate. The rosé glitters with brown flecks, and both the nose and palate show crystallised fruits with good length. Two Flocs for drinking without a second thought.

↪ Alain Lalanne, Dom. San de Guilhem, 32800 Ramouzens, tel. 05.62.06.57.02, fax 05.62.06.44.99, e-mail domaine@sandeguilhem.com ☑
☒ ev. day. ex Sun. 8am-12 noon 2-6pm

CH. DU TARIQUET★★★

n.c.   n.c.   €8-11

The Grassas, who own the 12th-century château, need no introduction as their products are known worldwide, and Tariquet is synonymous with quality. This exceptional Floc was a close call for a *coup de coeur*. A golden-yellow colour, with an aromatic nose with flowery hints, it is particularly distinguishable by its rich, lightly honeyed palate that has great fullness and length. The quality of the armagnac goes a long way to explain its success.

↪ SCV Ch. du Tariquet, 32800 Eauze, tel. 05.62.09.87.82, fax 05.62.09.89.49, e-mail contact@tariquet.com ☑
↪ Famille Grassa

TERRES DE GASCOGNE★

n.c.   40,000   €5-8

Condom, the capital of the Ténarèze, has a rich, distinguished history. In order to profit from the tourist windfall, the producers of this Cave concentrated on quality. They have been successful and, as a result, make regular appearances in the Guide. This year the white Floc is awarded one star. It is pale yellow with green flecks and a fine fruity nose. A clean and lively first impression is followed by a freshness that lasts through to the finish.

↪ Cave coop. de Condom-en-Armagnac, 59, av. des Mousquetaires, 32100 Condom, tel. 05.62.28.12.16, fax 05.62.28.23.94

DOM. DE TOUADE★

n.c.   n.c.   €5-8

One star for this white Floc, submitted by a new producer. In this rugby-crazed part of France it could be described as a try that needs to be converted – next year! It is pale yellow with golden glints and complex on the nose and palate. After a floral attack, spiced aromas emerge. It leaves a long, sweet, warming sensation.

GAEC de Touade, 32190 Mourède, tel. 05.62.06.40.82, fax 05.62.06.40.82
by appt.

ISABELLE ZAGO★

1.5 ha   1.520   €5-8

The Zagos respect tradition. Even the harvest is hand picked to ensure better quality control. This white proves the point. It is an intense straw-yellow and mingles white blossom and dried fruit (hazelnut) aromas. On the palate it opens out and becomes vivacious and long. Drink it with a *croustade* (savoury tart) for a real indulgence.

EARL de Cassagnaous, Au Cassagnaous, 32250 Montreal-du-Gers, tel. 05.62.29.44.81, fax 05.62.29.44.81, e-mail isabelle.zago@freesbee.fr
by appt.
Isabelle Zago

Macvin du Jura

This highly distinctive wine could equally well have been called Galant, the name by which it was known in the 14th century, when Marguerite of France, Duchess of Burgundy and wife of Philip the Bold, declared it her favourite wine.

The Macvin – historically Maquevin or Marc-vin – was probably first made in the medieval abbey of Château-Chalon. It was recognised as an AOC under the name of Macvin du Jura by decree on 14 November 1991. The Société de Viticulture began the procedures for AOC recognition in 1976. The inquiry took a long time because agreement had to be reached on a definitive approach to making the wine. Macvin began as a 'cooked' wine, with herbs and spices added to it; it then became Mistelle, a fortified wine made from musts that were concentrated by heating (cooking them), then a Vin de Liqueur muted with eau-de-vie from the Franche-Comté. The last method was the one ultimately agreed upon; for the AOC, this means using a Vin de Liqueur with must that has undergone a very slight initial fermentation, muted with Marc Eau-de-Vie made from wines from the AOC Franche-Comté, which have to come from the same property as the musts. The must should come from vine varieties and a production area with the right to the AOC. The Eau-de-Vie should be *rassise*, that is, aged in an oak cask for a minimum of 18 months.

After this final mixing, the Macvin should rest for a year, without being filtered, in oak casks, since it cannot be sold before 1 October of the year following its harvest.

Production, which is growing, is about 1,700 hl (44,880 gal) from 36 ha (89 acres). Macvin du Jura is enjoying an appreciable development since it is greatly enjoyed, particularly locally, as the aperitif of choice for connoisseurs of Jura wines. It completes the range of appellations in the Comté area and is perfect served with local specialities.

CH. D'ARLAY★

11-15   0.25 ha   2,400

There are few red Macvins, and the Count de Laguiche, therefore, presents an original product, which is nevertheless made according to the rules of the appellation. The Pinot Noir grape gives it a deep cherry-red colour heightened by violet glints. Its nose is certainly unusual, but the aroma of small, red-berry fruits is pleasant. The attack is round, then the flavours open out on the palate with the same nuances as the nose. An astonishing experience.

Alain de Laguiche, Ch. d'Arlay, rte de Saint-Germain, 39140 Arlay, tel. 03.84.85.04.22, fax 03.84.48.17.96, e-mail chateau@arlay.com
ev. day ex Sun. 8am–12 noon 2–6pm

BERNARD BADOZ★

11-15   0.06 ha   800

The Poulsard grape is a typical Jura variety, and Bernard Badoz selected it for his Macvin, which is a deep rose colour enlivened by hints of violet. Must and *eau-de-vie* are both evident on the nose, with a subtle mix of red fruit and marc. The palate is harmonious and well balanced with an underlying fruitiness. This is an unusual Macvin because of its colour, but it is very well made.

1198

● Bernard Badoz, 15, rue du Collège, 39800 Poligny, tel. 03.84.37.11.85, fax 03.84.37.11.18 ☒ ☗ ev. day: 8am–7pm

DOM. BAUD PÈRE ET FILS 1998★★

0.5 ha	4,000	€11-15

The Baud family has already won two *coups de cœur* with this appellation. In 2000 the tasting room was totally refurbished to provide an ideal environment for appreciating their wines. This Macvin has an almost perfect nose, somewhere between honey, fruit in brandy and currants. Although its aromatic complexity is less evident on the palate, it is consistent through to the finish. Ready for drinking.

● Dom. Baud Père et Fils, rte de Voiteur, 39210 Le Vernois, tel. 03.84.25.31.41, fax 03.84.25.30.09 ☒ ☗ by appt.

BERNARD FRÈRES 1994★

n.c.	1,200	€11-15

The intense, complex nose is a mixture of fruit in brandy, spiced bread, raisins and marc. The same aromatic components are evident on the palate. The alcohol has softened well and leaves an attractive finish. There is a touch of vintage marc to this Macvin which is rather misleading. It is not the fruity aspect that characterises it, but it leaves a good impression. The six-year maturation period in wood is probably responsible for its character.

● Bernard Frères, 15, rue Principale, 39570 Gevingey, tel. 03.84.47.33.99 ☒ ☗ by appt.

CAVEAU DES BYARDS 1998★

0.5 ha	2,300	€11-15

Chardonnay must is used in this blend. The first impressions on the nose are somewhat overpowered by the marc, but then aromas of raisins, dried fig and caramel emerge. The palate has a pleasing roundness even though the finish is somewhat unbalanced by sweetness. A fine Macvin, it is ready to drink though it may improve if left to age. Try it with melon.

● Caveau des Byards, 39210 Le Vernois, tel. 03.84.25.33.52, fax 03.84.25.38.02 ☒

JEAN-MARIE COURBET 1998★

0.5 ha	2,500	€11-15

President of the Société de Viticulture du Jura, Jean-Marie Courbet knows only too well how long it took for what he describes as 'the great ancestral liqueur' to be recognised as an AOC. This is Macvin from the top of the range, made using marc and Savagnin must. It is round and balanced on the palate and will continue to improve as it ages.

● Jean-Marie Courbet, rue du Moulin, 39210 Nevy-sur-Seille, tel. 03.84.85.28.70, fax 03.84.84.68.88 ☒ ☗ by appt.

D. ET P. CHALANDARD 1999

■ 0.5 ha	1,500	€11-15

Red Macvins do exist even though they are not numerous. Daniel and Pascal Chalandard have made it their speciality. This one, which blends with violet flecks. A fine nose with hints of sour-cherry jam. Round on the palate, even a little fiery, with nuances of kirsch.

● GAEC du Vieux Pressoir, rte de Voiteur, BP 30, 39210 Le Vernois, tel. 03.84.25.31.15, fax 03.84.25.37.62 ☒ ☗ by appt.

CH. GRÉA 1998★★

0.2 ha	500	€11-15

Almost copper-coloured, or at least intensely amber, this Macvin draws the eye but is reticent about revealing itself on the nose. It is still closed, giving off a few scrawny notes of spice and caramel. The palate is round, almost silky, with an attractive aromatic display of spices, caramel and vanilla. The alcohol is well integrated with no aggressive tones. It is sweetness itself but has character all the same. The must in this Macvin comes from Savagnin only; the grape variety used for Vin Jaune.

DOM. GRAND FRÈRES★

n.c.	7,000	€11-15

This Macvin was made with grapes from 50-year-old Chardonnay vines. Pale yellow but bright, there is a concentrated nose of citrus fruits, almond and dried fruits. On the palate there is just the right amount of sugar and alcohol to give sweetness and balance. In spite of a stab of alcohol at the finish, there an overall impression of elegance.

● Dom. Grand Frères, rue du Savagnin, 39220 Passenans, tel. 03.84.85.28.88, fax 03.84.44.67.47 ☒ ☗ ev. day: 9-12 noon 2–6pm: closed Sat., Sun. in Jan. and Feb.

DOM. GENELETTI★

0.3 ha	1,800	€11-15

The term used could appear unappetising to the uninitiated, but the *eau-de-vie* used to make the Macvin du Jura should be *rassise* (stale), which means it must have aged for at least 18 months. Indeed, this *eau-de-vie* strikes strongly on the nose of Michel Geneletti's Macvin as well as on the palate. However, there is also a deal of finesse to uncover. The must comes from Chardonnay grapes.

● Dom. Michel et David Geneletti, 373, rue de l'Eglise, 39570 L'Etoile, tel. 03.84.47.46.25, fax 03.84.47.38.18 ☒ ☗ by appt.

DOM. VICTOR CREDOZ★

0.5 ha	2,500	€11-15

Here the must is from Savagnin grapes. The wine is not very clear, but the straw-yellow is attractive. The nose starts on herbaceous aromas that open out to reveal aromas of crystallised fruit. The round palate is well balanced between the marc and the grape juice. This harmonious Macvin would be a particularly good aperitif.

● Dom. Victor Credoz, 39210 Menétru-le-Vignoble, tel. 06.80.43.17.44, fax 06.84.44.62.41 ☒ ☗ ev. day: 8am–12 noon 1–7pm

structured and with an attractive finish, this Macvin will appeal to some as an aperitif or to others as a dessert wine. The must used comes from Chardonnay grapes.

Nicolas Caire, Ch. Gréa, 39190 Rotalier, tel. 06.81.83.67.80, fax 06.84.25.05.47 by appt.

CAVEAU DES JACOBINS★   €11-15

0.45 ha   5,200

On the nose the alcohol is evident but not aggressive. In the same vein, the palate is round, almost alcoholic. The general harmony is there all the same. Why not try it with ice cream?

Caveau des Jacobins, rue Nicolas-Appert, 39800 Poligny, tel. 03.84.37.01.37, fax 03.84.37.30.47, e-mail caveaudesjacobins@free.fr ev. day. 9.30-12 noon 2-6.30pm

CLAUDE JOLY 1999★★   €11-15

0.5 ha   2,000

In the Jura and particularly south of Revermont, where Claude and Cédric Joly set up, nearly all the proprieters make Macvin. This one is immediately attractive to look at, with its intense straw-yellow colour and silvery glints. The intensity on the nose is evidence of good blending. There are aromas of crystalised fruits, apricot and grape. Well balanced and complex, the palate has lovely harmony.

EARL Claude et Cédric Joly, chem. des Patarattes, 39190 Rotalier, tel. 03.84.25.04.14, fax 03.84.25.14.48 by appt.

DOM. DE LA PINTE★   €11-15

2 ha   3,000

In a vinous kingdom where Savagnin is king, it was inevitable that the variety used to make Vin Jaune should play a part in the making of Macvin. The Savagnin grape provides 80% of the must used. The nose is clean, concentrated and slightly vanillary. The homogeneous palate also reflects vanilla along with interesting fig flavours. One of our tasters summed it up as 'good right down the line'.

Dom. de La Pinte, rte de Lyon, 39600 Arbois, tel. 03.84.66.06.47, fax 03.84.66.24.58 ev. day. 9am-12 noon 1.30-6pm; Sun. by appt.

DOM. DE LA TOURNELLE★   €11-15

0.2 ha   2,500

Pascal Clairet chose to blend Chardonnay must with marc. The resulting Macvin is pale yellow with silver glints. It has a powerful nose that complements the round, well-balanced palate.

Pascal Clairet, 5, Petite-Place, 39600 Arbois, tel. 03.84.66.25.76, fax 03.84.66.27.15 ev. day except Sun. 10am-12 noon 2.30-7pm

CH. DE L'ETOILE★★   €11-15

0.5 ha   5,000

An extravagant coppery colour with a refined nose. Flavours of spiced bread, dried fruits, fig, caramel and crystallised orange create a mature, aromatic palate. Well

Vandelle et Fils, Ch. de L'Etoile, 994, rue Bouillod, 39570 L'Etoile, tel. 03.84.47.33.07, fax 03.84.24.93.52 by appt.

LIGIER PERE ET FILS★★   €11-15

0.5 ha   2,500

Nearly a quarter of Macvin exports go to Belgium and Switzerland, and by all accounts they approve of the gastronomic pairing of Macvin with chocolate mousse. The marc is much in evidence here, but well integrated with the must (Savagnin). Both the nose and palate show finesse, balance, length and complexity (dried fruits and toasty flavours). A wine for romantics.

Dom. Ligier Père et Fils, 7, rue de Poligny, 39380 Mont-sous-Vaudrey, tel. 03.84.71.74.75, fax 03.84.81.59.82, e-mail ligier@netcourrier.com by appt.

DOM. DE MONTMOURGEAU   €11-15

0.5 ha   n.c.

The must is from Chardonnay grapes. Typical Macvin aromas emerge from the glass: caramel, dried fruits as well as eau-de-vie. The structure is a little unsteady on the palate, but the raw materials are good quality and the result is agreeable. Recommended as an aperitif.

Jean Gros, Dom. de Montbourgeau, 39570 L'Etoile, tel. 03.84.47.32.96, fax 03.84.24.41.44 by appt.

DESIRE PETIT ET FILS   €11-15

0.6 ha   5,800

Gérard and Marcel Petit's cellar closes only on Christmas Day and New Year's Day, so there are 363 days to taste their beautifully coloured Macvin. The amber colour is as pleasing as the intense macerated fruit aromas. It has already developed well and is ready to drink.

Dom. Désiré Petit, rue du Ploussard, 39600 Pupillin, tel. 03.84.66.01.20, fax 03.84.66.26.59 by appt.

Gérard et Marcel Petit

FRUITIERE VINICOLE DE PUPILLIN★   €5-8

2 ha   10,000

This little co-operative right in the heart of the vineyards uses only Chardonnay grapes for its Macvin is a golden-yellow with amber tones. It has a complex nose with hints of apricot, spiced bread and crystallised fruit. The flavours of marc are powerful on the palate, but the blending has been well handled. It gives a good general impression particularly because of its length.

Fruitière vinicole de Pupillin, 39600 Pupillin, tel. 03.84.66.12.88, fax 03.84.37.47.16 by appt.

XAVIER REVERCHON ★

0.2 ha   1,500   €11-15

This house recommends the gastronomic coupling of chocolate and Macvin. They are not wrong. There is intensity in both the straw-yellow colour and the nose, where the alcohol is evident. The attack is round, with a marked aroma of *eau-de-vie*. The palate reveals a few citrus notes (lemon and grapefruit). This good quality wine will certainly improve with time.
☛ Xavier Reverchon, EARL de Chantemerle, 2, rue de Clos, 39800 Poligny, tel. 03.84.37.02.58, fax 03.84.37.00.58 ☑ Y by appt.

PIERRE RICHARD ★★

0.5 ha   2,000   €11-15

This Macvin starts with a brilliant, limpid straw-yellow colour and an expressive, elegant and fresh nose with welcoming aromas of raisins, honey and spices. The lively attack stimulates the senses and is followed by a rewarding roundness. The alcohol is detectable but is well integrated without harshness. A high quality product with balance and finesse.
☛ Dom. Pierre Richard, 39210 Le Vernois, tel. 03.84.25.33.27, fax 03.84.25.36.13 ☑ Y by appt.

ANDRE ET MIREILLE TISSOT ★

1 ha   4,000   €11-15

This domaine adopted organic methods in 1999. The must comes in equal quantities from Poulsard and Savagnin grapes. It is a slightly coppery ochre-yellow and has a lovely nose, with fig, caramel, apricot and cinnamon combined with the marc. The alcohol is evident but of good quality and therefore results in overall harmony.
☛ André et Mireille Tissot, 39600 Montigny-lès-Arsures, tel. 03.84.66.08.27, fax 03.84.66.25.08 ☑ Y by appt.
☛ André et Stéphane Tissot

JACQUES TISSOT 1998 ★

2 ha   8,000   €11-15

Savagnin is used in this Macvin: its golden-yellow colour gives it away. Marc, crystallised fruit and apricot flavours combine on this interesting aromatic palate. The marc does not over-dominate. Good length with a hint of raisins on the finish. A harsh style, but it will give pleasure.
☛ Jacques Tissot, 39, rue de Courcelles, 39600 Arbois, tel. 03.84.66.14.27, fax 03.84.66.24.88 ☑ Y by appt.

JEAN TRESY ET FILS 1999 ★

0.3 ha   2,500   €11-15

Chardonnay must is used in this blend. It is light in colour but has a powerful, complex nose. Although this elegant Macvin is a little fiery, the fruit is evident. Time will sort this out, then it will be perfect as an aperitif.
☛ Jean Tresy et Fils, rte des Longevernes, 39230 Passenans, tel. 03.84.85.22.40, fax 03.84.44.99.73, e-mail tresy.vin@wanadoo.fr ☑ Y by appt.

FRUITIERE VINICOLE DE VOITEUR 1999 ★★★

2 ha   12,000   €11-15

Château-Chalon is the high temple of Vin Jaune but the Cooperative de Voiteur, at the foot of the château, shows that it too can make fine Macvin. The nose has great aromatic richness (honey, spices, dried grass, beeswax), which is due to the well-handled blending. It is a winner: after an initial refreshing touch of citrus flavours, raisins, apricots and peaches flood the palate. The sugar and alcohol are extremely well balanced and add to the great overall length. This is a knockout combination, which also has a delicious sweetness.
☛ Fruitière vinicole de Voiteur, 60, rue de Nevy-sur-Seille, 39210 Voiteur, tel. 03.84.85.21.29, fax 03.84.85.27.67, e-mail voiteur@fruitiere-vinicole-voiteur.fr ☑ Y by appt.

VIN DE PAYS

Although the phrase *vin de pays* has been used since 1930, it has only recently been officially defined as a 'table wine that is representative of the district, *département* or region from which it originates'. A law of 4 September 1979 established basic guidelines for the production of Vin de Pays, recommending preferred grape varieties and setting maximum yields. It also stipulated analytical standards, such as the volume of alcohol, the degree of acidity and the quantity of permitted additives. Because of this stringent regulation, Vins de Pays are some of the best table wines produced in France. As with AOC wines, a tasting panel must approve Vins de Pays. However, while AOC wines are regulated by the INAO, Vins de Pays are overseen by the *Office national interprofessionnel des vins*, ONIVINS. Made up of wine professionals and trade associations responsible for maintaining the regional character of each Vin de Pays, ONIVINS also supervises the marketing of Vins de Pays at home and abroad. Its efforts have made Vin de Pays an important contributor to France's wine exports.

There are three categories of Vin de Pays. First, there are the wines named for the *département* in which they are produced. The exceptions are the *départements* of Jura, Savoie and Corsica, which are also the names of an AOC. A second category consists of wines from designated VDP zones. The third category is of 'regional' Vin de Pays. There are four large regions, each of which contains several *départements*. Vins de Pays within a region may be blended to produce wines of a consistent style. The regions are Jardin de la France (Val de Loire), Comté Tolosan, Pays d'Oc and Comtés Rhodaniens. The 1979 law regulates the conditions of production for all three categories of Vin de Pays. In addition, each zone and region of Vin de Pays has a directive setting out more specific, and restrictive, regulations for wine production.

Most of the 7.8 million hectolitres (206 million gal) of Vin de Pays produced annually are made by co-operatives. Between 1980 and 1992 production of Vin de Pays almost doubled (from 4 to 7.8 million hl). Of this, 200,000 to 250,000 hl (5–6.6 million gal) are classed as *primeur* or 'nouveau'. Varietal wines, the majority (85%) of which come from vineyards in the Midi, make up another significant proportion of Vins de Pays. Good, ordinary wines with character, Vins de Pays are table wines for casual occasions. Sampling local Vin de Pays when you are travelling around France can provide an insight into regional differences in wine-making styles. The wines will also often complement local food specialities. Listed below are the zones of production for Vins de Pays, with regional boundaries as defined by the legislation. These do not correspond to the AOC and AOVDQS wine regions. Note that the 4 May 1995 directive excluded the Rhône, Bas-Rhin, Haut-Rhin, Gironde, Côte d'Or and Marne *départements* from Vin de Pays production.

Calvados

ARPENTS DU SOLEIL 2000★

☐   0.15 ha   1,200   ■ €5–8

In 1995 Gérard Samson restored this little Calvados vineyard, which dates from the 17th century. This year it was his Pinot Gris 2000 that won the Jury's favour. In particular, this wine was praised for its aromas of exotic fruits, its clear-cut freshness and good length of finish.

❀ Gérard Samson, 3, rue d'Harmonville, 14170 Saint-Pierre-sur-Dives, tel. 02.31.20.80.41, fax 02.31.20.29.70 ▶

Vallée de la Loire

The wines of the Loire Valley.

This vast region is the agglomeration of 13 *départements*: Maine-et-Loire, Indre-et-Loire, Loiret, Loire-Atlantique, Loir-et-Cher, Indre, Allier, Deux-Sèvres, Sarthe, Vendée, Vienne, Cher and Nièvre. In addition, it includes Vins de Pays of Retz (south of the Loire estuary), Marches de Bretagne (south-east of Nantes) and the Coteaux Charitois (around Charité-sur-Loire).

At present, the region produces a total of 600,000 hl (15.8 million gal), mostly vinified from traditional Loire grape varieties. The whites, 45% of the wine produced, are dry, fresh and fruity. They are made from Chardonnay, Sauvignon Blanc and Grolleau Gris grapes. Gamay, Cabernet Sauvignon and Grolleau Noir grapes are used to make reds and rosés.

For the most part, these Vins de Pays should be drunk young. Occasionally, a varietal Cabernet Sauvignon from a good vintage will benefit from cellaring.

Jardin de la France

Jardin de la France, a regional classification, make up 95% of Vin de Pays production in the Loire Valley.

DOM. DES BONNES GAGNES

Sauvignon 2000★

☐ 1.7 ha 5,000 ■ ♦ €5-8 ☑

This pale yellow wine has the intense grassy aroma that is typical of Sauvignon wines. It is a refreshing wine with a supple, well-structured palate and a lively finish.

♠ Jean-Marc Héry, Orgné,
49320 Saint-Saturnin-sur-Loire,
tel. 02.41.91.22.76, fax 02.41.91.21.58 ☑
𝖸 ev. day 9am-12.30pm 2-7pm; Sun. by appt.

Jardin de la France

DE PREVILLE Chardonnay 2000★

☐ 6.5 ha n.c. ■ ♦ €3

This white wine, with silvery-green highlights, has a subtle but very fine, toasty aroma. A light hazelnut flavour is perceptible on the lively, fresh and well-balanced palate. The **Sauvignon Blanc De Préville 2000** was also awarded a star by the Jury.

♠ SA Lacheteau, ZI La Saulaie, 282, rue Lavoisier, 49700 Doué-la-Fontaine,
tel. 02.41.59.26.26, fax 02.41.59.01.94

DAME DE LA VALLEE

Sauvignon 2000★

☐ n.c. 400,000 €3

This fine, clean-tasting Sauvignon has aromas of flowers and fruits (bananas). The wine's power intensifies on the palate showing strong citrus fruit flavours, with the aromas shown on the nose coming through on the finish. It is an attractive, thirst-quenching wine. The **Chardonnay 2000** were also singled out by the Jury.

♠ Rémy-Pannier, rue Léopold-Palustre,
BP 47, 49400 Saint-Hilaire-Saint-Florent,
tel. 02.41.53.03.10, fax 02.41.53.03.19
𝖸 ev. day except Mon. Sun. 9am-12 noon 2-6pm

CADET ROUSSELLE Gamay 2000★★

■ n.c. 160,000 ■ ♦ €3

Made entirely from the Gamay grape, this is a rich ruby-coloured wine with violet highlights. A complex, subtle aroma of ripe fruit, prunes and golden tobacco is followed by a rounded, full-bodied, supple palate and a fruity finish. The Jury also singled out the **Chardonnay 2000** and the **Sauvignon 2000**.

♠ SA Bougrier, 1, rue des Vignes,
41400 Saint-Georges-sur-Cher,
tel. 02.54.32.31.36, fax 02.54.71.09.61
𝖸 by appt.

DOM. BRUNO CORMERAIS

Elevé en fût de chêne 1999★

■ 0.75 ha 4,000 ▥ ♦ €5-8

A carefully balanced blend of three grape varieties, Cabernet Franc, Cabernet Sauvignon and Abouriou, has produced a very appealing wine. It is a rich red colour with an intense, fruity nose of great elegance. Equally full of flavour, the palate is nicely balanced with noticeable but silky tannins. This 99 would be a perfect companion for any red meat dish.

♠ EARL Bruno et Marie-Françoise Cormerais, La Chambaudière,
44190 Saint-Lumine-de-Clisson,
tel. 02.40.03.85.84, fax 02.40.06.68.74 ☑
𝖸 by appt.

Vins de pays

1 Vin de Pays des Coteaux de Coiffy
2 Vin de Pays de Franche-Comté
3 Vin de Pays des Coteaux de l'Auxois
4 Vin de Pays de Sainte-Marie-la-Blanche
5 Vin de Pays des Coteaux du Cher et de l'Arnon
6 Vin de Pays des Coteaux charitois
7 Vin de Pays du Bourbonnais
8 Vin de Pays d'Allobrogie
9 Vin de Pays d'Urfé
10 Vin de Pays des Balmes dauphinoises
11 Vin de Pays des Coteaux du Grésivaudan
12 Vin de Pays des Coteaux de l'Ardèche
13 Vin de Pays des Collines rhodaniennes
14 Vin de Pays des Coteaux des Baronnies
15 Vin de Pays du Comté de Grignan
16 Vin de Pays des Coteaux du Verdon
17 Vin de Pays du Mont-Caume
18 Vin de Pays des Maures
19 Vin de Pays d'Argens
20 Vin de Pays de la Petite Crau
21 Vin de Pays d'Aigues
22 Vin de Pays de la Principauté d'Orange

23 Vin de Pays des Sables du Golfe du Lion
24 Vin de Pays du Duché d'Uzès
25 Vin de Pays des Cévennes
26 Vin de Pays de la Vistrenque
27 Vin de Pays des Côtes du Vidourle
28 Vin de Pays de la Vaunage
29 Vin de Pays des Coteaux de Cèze
30 Vin de Pays des Coteaux du Pont du Gard
31 Vin de Pays des Coteaux Flaviens
32 Vin de Pays du Val de Montferrand
33 Vin de Pays du Mont Baudile
34 Vin de Pays des Côtes du Ceressou
35 Vin de Pays des Monts de la Grage
36 Vin de Pays des Coteaux d'Enserune
37 Vin de Pays des Coteaux du Libron
38 Vin de Pays de Pézenas
39 Vin de Pays des Coteaux de Murviel
40 Vin de Pays des Coteaux de Laurens
41 Vin de Pays des Côtes de Thongue
42 Vin de Pays de la Bénovie
43 Vin de Pays de Cassan
44 Vin de Pays de la Haute Vallée de l'Hérault
45 Vin de Pays des Gorges de l'Hérault
46 Vin de Pays des Coteaux de Bessilles
47 Vin de Pays de l'Ardailhou
48 Vin de Pays des Côtes du Brian
49 Vin de Pays de Cessenon
50 Vin de Pays des Coteaux du Salagou
51 Vin de Pays de la Vicomté d'Aumélas
52 Vin de Pays des Collines de la Moure
53 Vin de Pays de Caux
54 Vin de Pays des Coteaux de Fontcaude

55 Vin de Pays de Bessan
56 Vin de Pays de Bérange
57 Vin de Pays des Côtes de Thau
58 Vin de Pays des Côtes de Peyriac
59 Vin de Pays de la Haute Vallée de l'Aude
60 Vin de Pays des Coteaux de Narbonne
61 Vin de Pays des Côtes de Prouilhe
62 Vin de Pays de la Cité de Carcassonne
63 Vin de Pays de Cucugnan
64 Vin de Pays du Val de Dagne
65 Vin de Pays des Coteaux du Littoral audois
66 Vin de Pays des Côtes de Pérignan
67 Vin de Pays des Coteaux de la Cabrerisse
68 Vin de Pays des Hauts de Badens
69 Vin de Pays du Torgan
70 Vin de Pays des Côtes de Lastours
71 Vin de Pays du Val de Cesse
72 Vin de Pays de la Vallée du Paradis
73 Vin de Pays des Coteaux de Miramont
74 Vin de Pays d'Hauterive
75 Vin de Pays des Vals d'Agly
76 Vin de Pays des Coteaux des Fenouillèdes

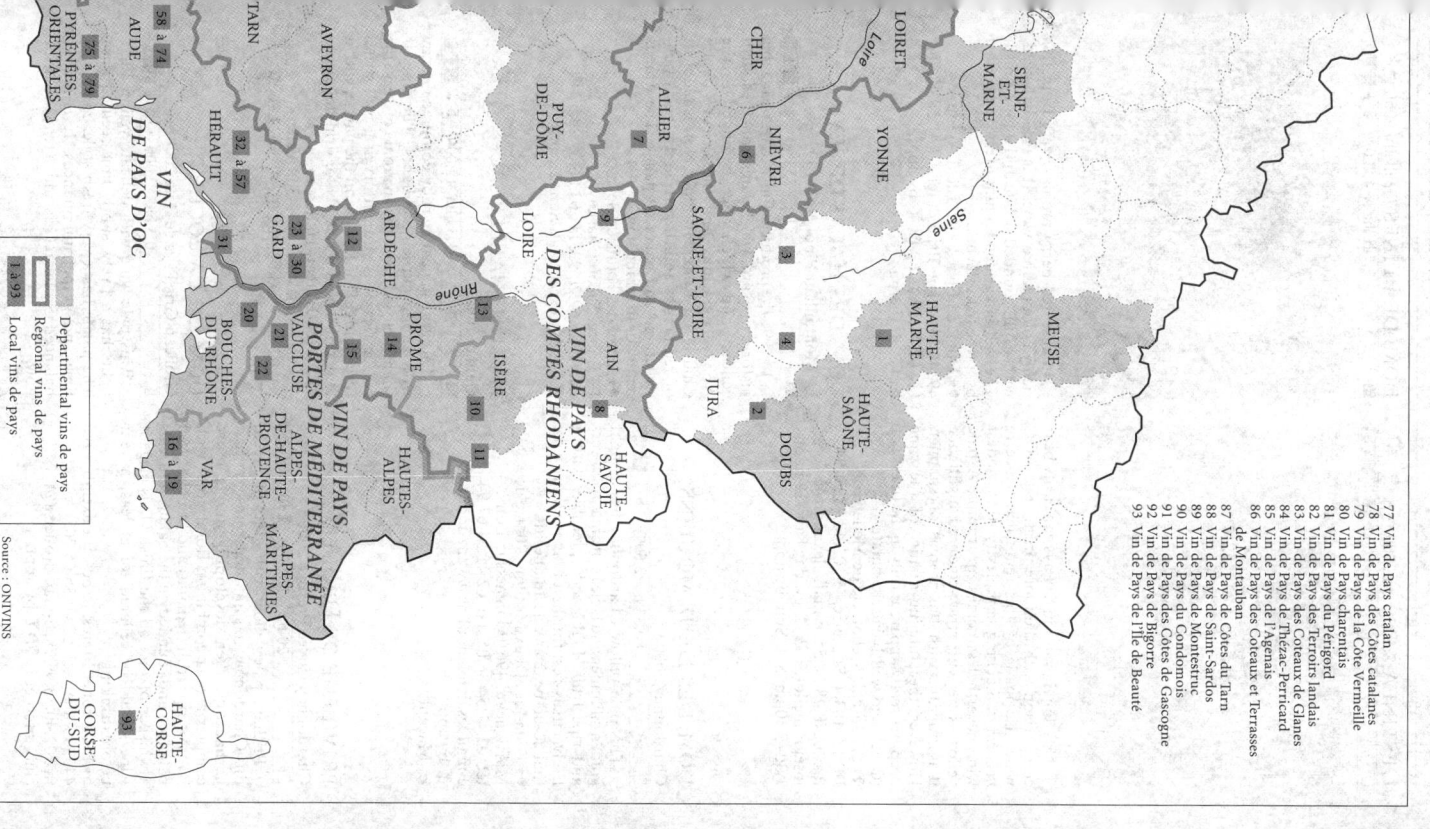

PYRÉNÉES-ORIENTALES

75 à 79

AUDE

58 à 74

VIN DE PAYS D'OC

TARN

HÉRAULT

32 à 57

GARD

31

23 à 30

AVEYRON

PUY-DE-DÔME

ALLIER

7

CHER

LOIRET

SEINE-ET-MARNE

ARDÈCHE

12

9

LOIRE

Loire

NIÈVRE

6

YONNE

Seine

Seine

ANEUS-ET-ROL

VIN DE PAYS DES CÔMTÉS RHODANIENS

SAÔNE-ET-LOIRE

3

HAUTE-MARNE

1

MEUSE

Rhône

Rhône

DRÔME

14

13

ISÈRE

AIN

JURA

4

HAUTE-SAÔNE

2

DOUBS

Departmental vins de pays

1 à 93

Regional vins de pays

1 à 93

Local vins de pays

VIN DE PAYS PORTES DE MÉDITERRANÉE

BOUCHES-DU-RHÔNE

VAUCLUSE

20

21

22

ALPES-DE-HAUTE-PROVENCE

15

10

11

HAUTES-ALPES

HAUTE-SAVOIE

8

VAR

16 à 19

ALPES-MARITIMES

CORSE-DU-SUD

HAUTE-CORSE

93

77 Vin de Pays catalan
78 Vin de Pays des Côtes catalanes
79 Vin de Pays de la Côte Vermeille
80 Vin de Pays charentais
81 Vin de Pays du Périgord
82 Vin de Pays des Terroirs landais
83 Vin de Pays des Coteaux de Glanes
84 Vin de Pays de Thézac-Perricard
85 Vin de Pays de l'Agenais
86 Vin de Pays des Coteaux et Terrasses de Montauban
87 Vin de Pays des Côtes du Tarn
88 Vin de Pays de Saint-Sardos
89 Vin de Pays de Montestruc
90 Vin de Pays du Condomois
91 Vin de Pays des Côtes de Gascogne
92 Vin de Pays de Bigorre
93 Vin de Pays de l'Île de Beauté

Source : ONIVINS

Jardin de la France

DESTINÉA Sauvignon 2000★★★

□ ▪ n.c. ▪ 80,000 ▪ ◈ ▪ €5-8

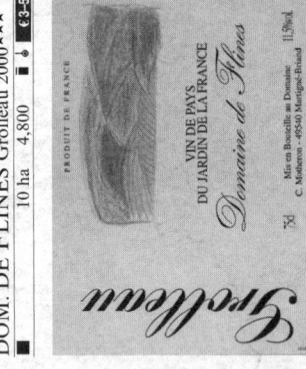

This Sauvignon Vin de Pays can easily bear comparison with the more prestigious AOC wine also made by this renowned Sancerre *négociant*. Lacking complexity, this modest wine nevertheless comes up trumps. A pale yellow wine with straw-coloured highlights, it is fragrant with the aromas of summer. However, the stunning quality of the wine becomes really apparent only in the finesse of its rich and well-balanced palate.

• SA Joseph Mellot, rte de Ménétréol, BP 13, 18300 Sancerre, tel. 02.48.78.54.54, fax 02.48.78.54.55, e-mail alexandre@joseph-mellot.fr ☑ Ⓨ ev. day 8am–12 noon 1.30–5.30pm; Sat. Sun. by appt.

DOM. DES DEUX MOULINS
Chardonnay 2000★

□ ▪ 0.33 ha ▪ 2,500 ▪ ◈ ▪ €3-5

This pale yellow Chardonnay has a slight golden shimmer and a clean aroma of flowers and ripe fruit. Light and agreeable, with a lively, citrus-zest finish, it is a refreshing wine that could be drunk as an aperitif.

• Dom. des Deux Moulins, 20, rte de Martigneau, 49610 Juigné-sur-Loire, tel. 02.41.54.36.05, fax 02.41.54.67.94, e-mail les.deux.moulins@wanadoo.fr ☑ Ⓨ by appt.
• Macault

PRIVILEGE DE DROUET
Chardonnay Cuvée Prestige 2000★★

□ ▪ 20 ha ▪ 35,000 ▪ ▪◍ ◈ ▪ €3-5

Brilliant pale yellow with hints of green, this Chardonnay has an intense nose: at first herbaceous, then developing into a more complex aroma combining floral notes with hints of ripe fruit (banana) and brioche. Well balanced and rounded on the palate, it reveals a whisper of oak on the finish. This elegant wine should be cellared for at least a year before drinking.

• SA Drouet Frères, 8, bd du Luxembourg, 44330 Vallet, tel. 02.40.36.65.20, fax 02.40.33.99.78, e-mail drouetsa@club-internet.fr ☑ Ⓨ by appt.

DOM. DE FLINES Grolleau 2000★★★

▪ 10 ha ▪ 4,800 ▪ ▪ ◈ ▪ €3-5

Intense red-berry aromas waft from this richly coloured red wine. It is well balanced, with a full, rounded palate and a long finish. The well-integrated tannins are accompanied by a ripe fruit flavour.

• Dom. de Flines, 102, rue d'Anjou, 49540 Martigné-Briand, tel. 02.41.59.42.78, fax 02.41.59.45.60 ☑ Ⓨ by appt.
• C. Motheron

DOM. DES HAUTS DE SEYR
Le Montaillant Pinot Noir 1999★

□ ▪ 2.5 ha ▪ 25,000 ▪ ▪ ◈ ▪ €5-8

In 1991 the producer finished restoring this historic vineyard, which dates from the fourth century and which once belonged to the Abbaye de Cluny and the Prieuré de La Charité-sur-Loire. His Pinot Noir is redolent of red berries and flowers, and it has a well-structured and balanced palate. The wine is ready for drinking now.

• Dom. des Hauts de Seyr, Le Bourg, 58350 Chasnay, tel. 03.86.69.20.93, fax 03.86.69.28.57 ☑ Ⓨ ev. day except Sat. Sun. 2–6pm

HUTEAU-HALLEREAU
Gamay 2000★

▪ ▪ 1.33 ha ▪ 12,000 ▪ ▪ ◈ ▪ €3-5

This is an appealing ruby-coloured Gamay with subtle garnet highlights. The fine, if slightly closed, nose has an aroma of very ripe red berries. It is straightforward, well structured and full of flavour on the palate, with a long finish, and it is ready for drinking now.

• EARL Huteau-Hallereau, 41, rue Saint-Vincent, 44330 Vallet, tel. 02.40.33.93.05, fax 02.40.36.29.26 ☑ Ⓨ by appt.

DOM. DE LA COCHE
Grolleau Gris Pays de Retz 2000★

□ ▪ 0.5 ha ▪ 2,000 ▪ ▪ ◈ ▪ €3

This pale wine with delicate yellow highlights has a lively, subtly lime-scented nose. The palate has a very fresh style, combining lime and grapefruit nuances. It is a well-balanced Grolleau Gris and is ready to drink now.

• Emmanuel Guitteny, La Coche, 44680 Sainte-Pazanne, tel. 02.40.02.44.43, fax 02.40.02.44.43, e-mail eguitteny@aol.com ☑ ♈ by appt.

DOM. DE LA COUCHETIERE

Grolleau 2000★

■ 2 ha | 18,000 | €3

A deep red wine with violet highlights, this Grolleau has a very fruity nose, dominated by ripe cherries. Its full, well-balanced palate echoes the aromas of the nose, which persist through a long finish. This is an appealing wine, which is ready to drink now, ideally with a plate of pork charcuterie.

• GAEC Brault Père et Fils, Dom. de La Couchetière, 49380 Notre-Dame-d'Allençon, tel. 02.41.54.30.26, fax 02.41.54.40.98 ☑ ♈ ev. day except Sun. 8.30am–12.30pm 2–7pm

DOM. DE LA COUPERIE

Cabernet 2000★

■ 2.5 ha | 10,000 | €3-5

Made from a blend of 85% Cabernet Sauvignon and 15% Cabernet Franc grapes, this wine has an intense, complex nose. Its supple and well-structured palate lives up to the promise of the aromas. Already drinking well, this wine will continue to improve over the coming months.

• EARL Claude Cogné, La Couperie, 49270 Saint-Christophe-la-Couperie, tel. 02.40.83.73.16, fax 02.40.83.76.71 ♈ by appt.

LA DIVA

Sauvignon 2000★★

□ n.c. | 100,000 | €5-8

This Sauvignon with pale yellow highlights has clean, fairly intense aromas of citrus fruit and nut (almond, hazelnut). A supple and well-structured palate leads into a long, delicate finish. The Jury was also impressed by the **Chardonnay La Diva 2000**.

• Donatien-Bahuaud, La Loge, BP 1, 44330 La Chapelle-Heulin, tel. 02.40.06.70.05, fax 02.40.06.77.11 ☑

DOM. DE LA GRETONNELLE

Sauvignon 2000★

□ 0.8 ha | 2,000 | €3-5

La Gretonnelle estate occupies 25 ha (62 acres) around the village of Deux Sèvres in Bouillé-Loretz, the most southerly part of the Anjou vineyards. It offers a pale yellow Sauvignon with green highlights and a powerful floral nose. This well-balanced wine has a long finish and is ready to drink now.

• EARL Charruault-Schmalz, Les Landes, 79290 Bouillé-Loretz, tel. 05.49.67.12.52 ☑ ♈ by appt. fax 05.49.67.04.49,

DOM. DE LA GUENIPIERE

Cabernet vieilli en fût de chêne 2000★

■ 0.88 ha | 5,300 | €3

The Suteau family has been in Landreau since 1921 and currently cultivates 17 ha (42 acres) of vines. Their garnet red Cabernet Sauvignon has a complex, spicy, red-fruit aroma of great finesse, and well-integrated tannins contribute to the suppleness of the palate. This well-balanced wine is for immediate consumption.

• Patrick Suteau, Dom. de La Guenipière, 44690 Le Landreau, tel. 02.40.06.42.08, fax 02.40.06.47.63 ☑ ♈ by appt.

DOM. LA PRAIRIE DE LA MOINE

Gamay 2000★

▲ 1.5 ha | 2,000 | €3

This congenial, appealing rosé made from Gamay grapes is an archetypal Vin de Pays. The Jury enjoyed the fruitiness (cherries) apparent on both the nose and the palate and welcomed its light, drinkable style. It is a perfect wine to share with friends at a barbecue.

• Hubert Chapeleau, La Garnière, 49230 Saint-Crespin-sur-Moine, tel. 02.41.70.41.55, fax 02.41.70.49.44 ☑

DOM. DE LA ROCHERIE

Cabernet vieilli en fût de chêne 1999★★

■ 1 ha | 6,000 | €3

Jammy red fruits and a hint of oak are apparent on the subtle nose of this pure Cabernet wine, which has been matured in barrels for a year. On the palate, it is structured and well balanced, with well-integrated tannins and an echo of vanilla on the mid-palate.

• Daniel Gratas, La Rocherie, 44430 Le Landreau, tel. 02.40.06.41.55, fax 02.40.06.48.92 ☑ ♈ ev. day except Sun. 8am–8pm

DOM. DE LA ROULIERE

Chardonnay 2000★

□ 7 ha | 80,000 | €3

This bright, yellow-green Chardonnay has a spring-like aroma with hints of exotic fruit. The fresh and fruity palate has a favourable balance and length. This wine could be drunk now or cellared for one year.

• René Erraud, Ch. de La Roulière, 44310 Saint-Colomban, tel. 02.40.05.80.24, fax 02.40.05.53.89 ☑ ♈ by appt.

HUBERT LEGRAND

Gamay 2000★

■ n.c. | 150,000 | €3-5

This is a classic Gamay wine. It is dark red with purple highlights and has a red-berry aroma tinged with the scent of forest undergrowth. The palate is crisply fruity, with evident but well-integrated tannins. It is a wine for immediate consumption.

• Hubert Legrand, 58150 Pouilly-sur-Loire, tel. 03.86.39.57.75, fax 03.86.39.08.30

LE MOULIN DE LA TOUCHE ★★★
Pays de Retz Chardonnay 2000★★★

☐   n.c.   12,000   ■ ◨   €3-5

In the last edition of the *Guide* Joël Hérisse's Chardonnay was recognised as being very good value for money. The 2000 vintage is not only reasonably priced but also received the highest accolades from the Jury. A remarkable, intense honeysuckle and grapefruit nose introduces a beautifully fresh, well-balanced palate. Delightful citrus fruit flavours appear on the finish. The **Sauvignon 2000 Pays de Retz** was awarded one star.

➤ Joël Hérissé, Le Moulin de la Touche, 44580 Bourgneuf-en-Retz,
tel. 02.40.21.47.89, fax 02.40.21.47.89 ▼
⟁ by appt.

DOM. DE L'EPINAY
Cabernet élevé en fût de chêne 1999★

■   1.1 ha   6,000   ▥   €5-8

This estate cultivates 28 ha (69 acres) near the medieval village of Clisson. Its dark ruby Cabernet has an expressive aroma and a well-structured palate.

➤ EARL Albert Paquereau, Dom. de L'Epinay, 44190 Clisson, tel. 02.40.36.13.57, fax 02.40.36.13.57 ▼ ⟁ by appt.

DOM. DE L'ERRIERE ★★
Cabernet 2000★★

■   1.98 ha   6,000   ■ ◨   −€3

A rich red colour with violet highlights, this Cabernet Sauvignon has a concentrated berry (blackcurrant, strawberry) nose. Berry flavours are also evident on its well-balanced palate, which is nicely structured by silky tannins. This well-crafted Vin de Pays is ready for drinking now but will also keep for another two years.

➤ GAEC Madeleineau Père et Fils, Dom. de L'Errière, 44430 Le Landreau, tel. 02.40.06.43.94, fax 02.40.06.48.82 ▼ ⟁ by appt.

MARQUIS DE GOULAINE ★★
Chardonnay 2000★★

☐   20 ha   50,000   ■ ◨   −€3

Pale-yellow with green highlights, this well-balanced wine has a fine lime-blossom and grapefruit nose. The palate is extremely aromatic, and quite delicate in structure.

➤ Vinival, La Sablette, 44330 Mouzillon, tel. 02.40.36.66.00, fax 02.40.33.95.81

DOM. DE MONTGILET ★
Grolleau 2000★

■   6 ha   15,000   ■ ◨   €3-5

The wine's intense red-fruit nose (blackberry, cherry, blueberry) has vegetal and leather overtones. The fruity aromas are reprised on a full-bodied, fleshy palate which is balanced by firm tannic structure and a long finish.

➤ Victor et Vincent Lebreton, SCEA Dom. de Montgilet, 49610 Juigné-sur-Loire, tel. 02.41.91.90.48, fax 02.41.54.64.25, e-mail montgilet@terre-net.fr ▼ ⟁ ev. day except Sun. 9am–12 noon 2pm–7pm

DOM. DU PETIT VAL ★★
Grolleau 2000★★

■   0.5 ha   6,000   ■ ◨   −€3

A mastery of vinification techniques, and the judicious acquisition of new wine-making equipment has allowed Denis Groizil to produce a remarkable Grolleau wine. It is very intense and fruity, and has firm tannins that will enable it to age well.

➤ EARL Denis Goizil, Dom. du Petit-Val, 49380 Chavagnes, tel. 02.41.54.31.14, fax 02.41.54.03.48 ▼ ⟁ by appt.

DOM. DES PRIES
Pays de Retz Grolleau 2000★

■   2.25 ha   10,000   ■ ◨   €3-5

Wine experts describe the colour of this wine as very pale pink, and typical of Grolleau rosés from the Pays de Retz. The wine has a complex aroma of fruits of the forest, redcurrants and citrus fruits (grapefruit). A freshness lingers on the palate through the long and well-balanced finish.

➤ Gérard Padiou, Les Priés, 44580 Bourgneuf-en-Retz, tel. 02.40.21.45.16, fax 02.40.21.47.48 ▼ ⟁ by appt.

DOM. DU PRIEURE ★
Rouge du Prieuré 2000★

■   1.14 ha   2,000   ■ ◨   −€3

Made from a blend of Grolleau (80%) and Gamay grapes, this richly-coloured wine has a generous yet delicate aroma. On the palate, it displays a clean style and a strong morello-cherry flavour that lingers through a medium-to-long finish.

➤ Franck Brossaud, 1 *bis*, pl. du Prieuré, 49610 Mozé-sur-Louet, tel. 02.41.45.30.74, fax 02.41.45.30.74 ⟁ by appt.

DOM. DES QUATRE ROUTES
Gamay 2000★

■   0.69 ha   n.c.   ■ ◨   €3-5

Henri Poiron and his sons own two estates that cover a total of 36 ha (89 acres): Le Manoir and Les Quatre Routes. The second vineyard has produced a wine with a restrained, delicate nose and a supple, fruity

DOM. DE L'IMBARDIERE ★
Chardonnay 2000★

■   1.7 ha   4,000   ■ ◨   −€3

This well-balanced Chardonnay has a white-flower aroma. Initial freshness continues through into a lively, delicately-herbaceous palate.

➤ Joseph Abline, L'Imbardière, 49270 Saint-Christophe-la- Couperie, tel. 02.40.83.90.62, fax 02.40.83.74.02 ▼ ⟁ by appt.

and rounded palate. It is a cheerful rosé that can accompany a meal from start to finish.

☛ SA Henri Poiron et Fils, Les Quatre-Routes, 44690 Maisdon-sur-Sèvre, tel. 02.40.54.60.58, fax 02.40.54.62.05, e-mail poiron.henri@online.fr ☑ ♈ by appt.

CLOS SAINT-FIACRE Gamay 2000★★ ▇ ● 2.67 ha 30,000 ▮▮▮ €3-5

This is a richly-coloured wine with musky, leathery aromas and a nicely-structured palate. Ripe tannins fill the mouth and give the wine a rounded character.

☛ GAEC Clos Saint-Fiacre, 560, rue Saint-Fiacre, 45370 Mareau-aux-Prés, tel. 02.38.45.61.55, fax 02.38.45.66.58 ☑
♈ by appt.
♈ Montigny-Piel

YVONNICK ET THIERRY SAUVETRE

Marches de Bretagne Gamay 2000★★ ▇ ● 1.5 ha 6,000 ▮▮▮ €3

The Jury was impressed by the distinctive style of this elegant Gamay. Blackberry, blackcurrant and prune aromas can be found on the nose, while the full palate is under-pinned by soft, supple tannins.

☛ Yves Sauvètre et Fils, La Landelle, 90, rue de la Durandière, 44430 Le Loroux-Bottereau, tel. 02.40.33.81.48, fax 02.40.33.87.67 ☑ ♈ by appt.

AMPELIDAE Le K 1999★★ ▇ ● 2 ha 10,000 ▮▮▮ €11-15

La Vienne

Since 1995, the Brochet family has been cultivating the vineyards of the Manoir de Lavauguyot, which lie at the top of the Marigny-Brizat hills in the wine village of Vienne. Le Rouge K Ampelidae 1999 has a fine aroma, a rounded and well-balanced palate and voluptuous tannins, all of which testifies to a perfectly-vinified, very ripe harvest. This wine should be cellared for one to two years before being served with beef or game.

Aquitaine and Charentes

This region, made up of the Charente, Charente-Maritime, Gironde, Landes, Dordogne and Lot-et-Garonne départements, almost completely surrounds the vineyards of Bordeaux. It produces 60,000 hl (1.6 million gal) of wine annually. The majority of the wines are supple, aromatic reds made in the Aquitaine district, using Bordeaux grape varieties blended with some more rustic local varieties (Tannat, Abouriou, Bouchalès, Fer). Charentes and Dordogne mostly produce white Vins de Pays that can be fine and light (Ugni Blanc, Colombard), rounded (Sémillon blends) or robust (Baroque). Charentais, Agenais, Terroirs Landais and Thézac-Perricard are sub-regional designations; Dordogne, Gironde and Landes are based on the départements.

☛ Brochet, Manoir de Lavauguyot, 86380 Marigny-Brizay, tel. 05.49.88.18.18, fax 05.49.88.18.85, e-mail ampelidae@ampelidae.com ☑
♈ ev. day 9am–12.30pm 2pm–6pm

JEAN TREUILLET Sauvignon 1999 ☐ ▇ 2 ha 10,000 ▮▮▮ €3-5

This Sauvignon has a buttery aroma with a hint of fruit. Initially, the palate seems slightly sweet, with citrus and dried-fruit flavours. This is balanced by a burst of liveliness on the finish.

☛ Madeleine Treuillet, 58150 Tracy-sur-Loire, tel. 03.86.26.17.06, fax 03.86.26.17.06 ☑
♈ ev. day 8am–12 noon 1pm–7pm

Charentais

HENRI DE BLAINVILLE 2000★
■ 10 ha 15,000 🍷 ■ -€3

This estate, which dates from the 1950s, originally produced Cognac. Later, it began to make Pineau des Charentes. In the 1980s it focused its attention on Vins de Pays production. Its rosé is both rounded and fresh, making it a quaffable, thirst-quenching wine. This bottle would be an ideal accompaniment to a light luncheon dish.
➤ SCA Cave du Liboreau,
18, rue de l'Océan, 17490 Siecq,
tel. 05.46.26.61.86, fax 05.46.26.68.01,
e-mail cave.du.liboreau@wanadoo.fr ▼
Ⓣ by appt.

BRARD BLANCHARD 2000★
□ 1.56 ha 16,000 🍷 ■ €3-5

This bright-white wine has a pear-drop aroma. Light and delicate on the palate with a fresh finish of medium length, it would perfectly complement seafood or any selection of cold dishes.
➤ GAEC Brard Blanchard, 1, chem. de Routreau, Boutiers, 16100 Cognac,
tel. 05.45.32.19.58, fax 05.45.36.53.21 ▼
Ⓣ ev. day except Sun. 9am–12 noon 2pm–6pm; cl. 15 Aug.–1 Sep.

DOM. DU BREUIL Sauvignon 2000★
□ 0.6 ha 4,800 🍷 ■ -€3

A golden-yellow Sauvignon, which has been left to lie for two months on its lees during wine-making to maximise extraction. It is full and fleshy on the palate, and quite long on the finish. It could be served with fish or shellfish.
➤ Guy et Jean-Pierre Morandière,
Le Breuil, 17150 Saint-Georges-des-Agoûts,
tel. 05.46.86.02.76, fax 05.46.70.63.11 ▼
Ⓣ ev. day 9am–7pm

DOM. BRUNEAU Merlot 2000★
■ 6 ha 10,000 🍷 ■ €3-5

Twenty years ago, this estate gave up mixed farming to concentrate on viticulture. Judging from the quality of this clean red wine, the conversion was a good decision. This is a smooth, easy-to-drink Merlot that is fruity both on the nose and on the palate.
➤ Alain Pillet, Chez Bruneau,
17130 Rouffignac, tel. 05.46.49.04.82,
fax 05.00.00.00.00 ▼ Ⓣ by appt.

COULON ET FILS
Ile d'Oléron Sauvignon 2000

This wine-maker cultivates 30 ha (74 acres) on the Ile d'Oléron. His Sauvignon vines, which are only six years old, have produced an attractive, pale-yellow wine. A delicate aroma is followed by a supple and fruity palate, and a memorable finish.
➤ EARL Coulon et Fils, Saint-Gilles,
17310 Saint-Pierre-d'Oléron,
tel. 05.46.47.02.71, fax 05.46.75.09.74 ▼
Ⓣ by appt.

DOM. GARDRAT Colombard 2000★
■ 2 ha 20,000 🍷 ■ €3-5

This wine-maker exports 20% of his wine to Germany. He has made a pale-yellow Colombard with the full, expressive nose characteristic of that variety. A supple and rounded palate is given a lift by the lively finish.
➤ Jean-Pierre Gardrat, La Touche,
17120 Cozes, tel. 05.46.90.86.94,
fax 05.46.90.95.22, e-mail lionel.gardrat@wanadoo.fr ▼ Ⓣ by appt.

THIERRY JULLION 2000★
■ 4 ha 40,000 🍷 ■ €3-5

The estate, which covers more than 31 ha (76 acres), has been in Thierry Jullion's family for five generations. His Merlot (75%) and Cabernet Sauvignon blend is fruity, warming and supple. It is ready for drinking now.
➤ Thierry Jullion, Montizeau,
17520 Saint-Maigrin, tel. 05.46.70.00.73,
fax 05.46.70.02.60 ▼ Ⓣ ev. day except Sat. Sun. 2pm–7pm

DOM. DE LA CHAUVILLIERE
Chardonnay 2000★
□ 9.5 ha 45,000 🍷 ■ €3-5

This producer specialises in wines for immediate consumption, and this Chardonnay certainly fits the bill. Starting with an agreeable freshness, aromas explode on the palate and linger through the long, lively finish.
➤ EARL Hauselmann et Fils, Dom. de La Chauvillière, 17600 Sablonceaux,
tel. 05.46.94.44.40, fax 05.46.94.44.63 ▼
Ⓣ by appt.

DOM. LE PETIT COUSINAUD
Chardonnay 2000★
□ 2 ha 6,000 🍷 ■ €5-8

This straw-yellow Chardonnay has a pleasant floral aroma. On the palate, it is lively and long, with a delicate cut-grass flavour. This wine is an ideal partner for seafood.
➤ Maurice Denis, Le petit Cousinaud,
16480 Guizengeard, tel. 05.45.98.72.68,
fax 05.45.98.45.20 ▼ Ⓣ by appt.

MOULIN DE MERIENNE
Merlot 1999
■ 6 ha 20,000 🍷 ■ €3-5

The estate is named after a 13th-century mill. Its 20-year-old Merlot vines have produced a fruity (cherry, overripe fruit) and full-bodied wine. A vegetal note is just perceptible on the palate but it is not enough to unbalance the wine. This 99 is ready to drink now, but could also be cellared for another few months.

SCA du Clos de Mérienne, 1, chemin du Clos de Mérienne, BP 87, 16200 Gondeville, tel. 05.45.81.13.27, fax 05.45.81.74.30, e-mail cognac-charpentron@hotmail.com
Y by appt.
Charpentron

DOM. PIERRIERE GONTHIER 2000*

2.5 ha | 16 000 | €3-5

This 21-ha (52-acre) estate planted its first red wine vines in 1993, and vinified its first red vintage 1996. The 2000, a Merlot-Cabernet Sauvignon blend, has a powerful leather and coffee aroma. A well-structured palate suggests that this wine will age very well.
Pascal Gonthier, Nigronde, 16170 Saint-Amant-de-Nouère, tel. 05.45.96.42.79, fax 05.45.96.42.79
Y by appt.

ROSE DES DUNES Ile de Ré 2000*

75 ha | 300,000 | €3

This wine is named after the pine tree and tamarisk-covered sand dunes of the Ile de Ré. An elegantly-coloured and firm, refreshing, cut-grass aroma and an agreeably lengthy finish.
Coop des Vignerons de L'île de Ré, 17580 Le Bois-Plage-en-Ré, tel. 05.46.09.23.09, fax 05.46.09.09.26
Y by appt.

SORNIN Cabernet 2000*

15 ha | 40,000 | €3

Although this Cabernet Sauvignon needs a little longer to develop fully, it already displays all the hallmarks of the variety. Nicely-structured and firm, it would complement Charentais recipes. The red Privilège 99 from the same producer was also awarded a star by the Jury.
SCA Cave de Saint-Sornin, Les Combes, 16220 Saint-Sornin, tel. 05.45.23.92.22, fax 05.45.23.11.61, e-mail contact@cavesaintsornin.com
Y by appt.

Agenais

DOM. DE CAMPET Moelleux Vin de Novembre 2000*

2.4 ha | 2,400 | €5-8

This wine, made from Gros Manseng grapes harvested on 10 November 2000, could be served with foie gras. It is a bright, clear, straw colour with golden highlights, and has a delicate aroma of honey mixed with pears and quince syrup. Pear is also evident on the full and rounded palate, which displays just the right balance of acidity and sweetness.

SCA du dom. de Campet, 47170 Sos, tel. 05.53.65.63.60, fax 05.53.65.36.79, e-mail domainecampet@club-internet.fr
Y by appt.

COTES DES OLIVIERS 2000*

2 ha | 7,300 | €3-5

The estate also produces walnuts and the famous Agen prunes. Its dark-purple wine has a red berry and green pepper aroma, suggesting a ripe harvest. After a supple opening, this is a rich and concentrated wine with a long, slightly tannic finish.
Jean-Pierre Richarte, Les Oliviers, 47140 Auradou, tel. 05.53.41.28.59, fax 05.53.49.38.89
Y ev. day 9am-12 noon 2pm-7pm

LOU GAILLOT Prestige 2000*

4 ha | 8,000 | €3-5

This estate, which has been run by Gilles Pons since 1999, possesses 100-year-old oak barrels. Its Prestige cuvée is a bright ruby-coloured Merlot with spicy, vanilla and ripe-fruit (jammy or brandied) aromas. The wine's alcohol, acidity and tannins are well balanced. With its supple, rounded and full-bodied palate and long, unctuous finish, this is a perfect wine to serve alongside a roast joint. If duck breasts are going to be the centrepiece of your meal, the Reserve 99, which has been matured in barrels for nine months, may be more appropriate; it was also awarded a star by the Jury.
Gilles Pons, Les Gaillots, 47440 Casseneuil, tel. 05.53.41.04.66, fax 05.53.01.13.89 Y ev. day 9am-12.30pm 2pm-7.30pm; groups by appt.

CAVE DES SEPT MONTS Sauvignon Instant Choisi 2000*

5 ha | 32,000 | €3-5

This co-operative, which was formed in the 1960s, currently vinifies 10,000 hl (264,000 gal) of wine each year. Its brilliantly clear, pale-gold wine has a delicate, lemony nose with floral and exotic-fruit overtones. The Sauvignon's varietal character is evident in the subtle herbaceous flavour of the supple, fleshy and rounded palate, leading to quite a long finish.
Cave des Sept Monts, ZAC de Mondésir, 47150 Monflanquin, tel. 05.53.36.33.40, fax 05.53.36.44.11
Y ev. day 9am-12.30pm 3pm-6.30pm

DOM. DU SERBAT Cuvée Orival 2000*

0.4 ha | 2,933 | €3-5

This estate is a Centre d'Aide par le Travail, part of a government initiative by which the disabled can learn a profession under supportive conditions. It has selected a very attractive label for this pure Merlot wine. The wine's colour is dark, purple-garnet. The floral nose has brandied fruit, red berry and blackcurrant overtones. Ripe, rounded tannins indicate that this wine is ready for

Thézac-Perricard

flavour reflects the fact that it was made from a ripe harvest. This wine is ready to drink now. The Jury was also impressed by the co-operative's delicately fruity **red Fleur des Landes 2000**, made from a blend of Cabernet Sauvignon and Tannat grapes.

• CAT Lamothe-Poulin, Dom. du Serbat, 47340 Laroque-Timbaut, tel. 05.53.95.71.07, fax 05.53.95.79.61, e-mail domaine-serbat@wanadoo.fr ▼ ev. day except Sun. 8.30am–5.30pm; Sat. 8.30am–12 noon

Thézac-Perricard

VIN DU TSAR Le Bouquet 1999★
■   4 ha   34,000 ■ ◆   €3-5

It is rumoured that France's President Armand Fallières introduced Tsar Nicholas II to Agenais wines. The garnet-coloured 99 has subtle brick-red highlights, and a spicy, exotic-fruit aroma. Its powerfully fruity palate is rounded and well balanced. The spiciness of the nose reappears on the finish along with slightly chewy tannins that need time to mature.

• Les Vignerons de Thézac-Perricard, Plaisance, 47370 Thézac, tel. 05.53.40.72.76, fax 05.53.40.78.76, e-mail info@vin-du-tsar.tm.fr ▼ ▼ ev. day 8.15am–12.15pm 2pm–6pm; Sun. 2pm–6pm

Périgord

LE RELAIS DE KREUSIGNAC 1998★
□   0.5 ha   3,400   ▥ €11-15

This bright, rich, ruby-coloured 98 is made from a blend of 60% Merlot, 30% Cabernet Sauvignon and 10% Cabernet Franc grapes. The oaky nose has vanilla and ripe-fruit aromas. The palate is supple at first, but then develops a firmer, more powerful character with a subtle oak flavour that does not overpower its well-balanced style. This wine will repay several years of ageing.

• SCEA Dom. de Kreusignac, Pommier, 24380 Creyssensac-et-Pissot, tel. 05.53.80.09.85, fax 05.53.80.14.72 ▼

Thézac-Perricard

immediate consumption, perhaps with a roast.

MICHEL GUÉRARD 2000★
■   n.c.   n.c.   €5-8

Michel Guérard, the famous chef whose restaurant is in Eugénie-les-Bains, has been restoring the Bachen wine estate since 1983. He has made a pure Merlot wine whose delicately toasty aroma and fruity palate are proof of a ripe harvest. Supple, rounded and with a lingering finish, this wine is ready for drinking now.

• Michel Guérard, Cie hôtelière et fermière d'Eugénie-les-Bains, 40800 Duhort-Bachen, tel. 05.58.71.76.76, fax 05.58.71.77.77 ▼ by appt.

DOM. DE HAUBET 2000
□   14 ha   n.c.   €3

This estate in the centre of the Armagnac region is part of a village with seven churches. Its 92 vintage was selected as a *coup de cœur* by the 1994 edition of the *Guide*. While the pale-coloured 2000 may not live up to that standard, it is a fresh and lively wine that will happily accompany seafood.

• Philippe Gudolle, EARL de Haubet, 40310 Parleboscq, tel. 05.58.44.95.99, fax 05.58.44.95.99 ▼ by appt.

DOM. DE LABAIGT 2000★
□   2 ha   14,000   ■ ◆   €3-5

This is a bright white wine with a fine aroma of exotic fruits, especially pineapples. The wine is supple, gentle and well balanced on the palate. Ready for drinking now.

• Dominique Lanot, Dom. de Labaigt, 40290 Mouscardès, tel. 05.58.98.02.42, fax 05.58.98.80.75 ▼ ▼ ev. day except Sun. 8.30am–12 noon 2pm–6.30pm

DOM. DE LABALLE Sables Fauves 2000★
□   17 ha   110,000   €3

This estate has been in the family since 1820 when the founder, Jean-Dominique Laudet, settled here after a career as a trader in the Antilles. This year, the estate has produced an appealing, bright, pale-coloured white wine with lemon-yellow highlights. A restrained but balanced palate, which ends with a persistent ripe-fruit (nectarine pulp) flavour.

• Noël Laudet, Le Moulin de Laballe, 40310 Parleboscq, tel. 05.58.44.33.39, fax 05.58.44.92.61, e-mail n.laudet@wanadoo.fr ▼ ev. day 9am–12 noon 2pm–5pm

Terroirs Landais

GAILANDE 2000★
□   10 ha   40,000   €3

Like the Landes pine forests depicted on the label, this rich yellow wine is powerfully aromatic (white flowers). Its good length of

Pays de la Garonne

The city of Toulouse is at the centre of this wine region. The 'Vin de Pays du Comté Tolosan' designation includes the following *départements*: Ariège, Aveyron, Haute-Garonne, Gers, Lot, Lot-et-Garonne, Pyrénées-Atlantiques, Hautes-Pyrénées, Tarn and Tarn-et-Garonne. The sub-regional or local designations are: Côtes du Tarn; Coteaux de Glanes (Haut-Quercy, to the north of Lot – reds worth ageing); Coteaux du Quercy (south of Cahors – structured reds); Saint-Sardos (the left bank of the Garonne River); Coteaux et Terrasses de Montauban (light reds); Côtes de Gascogne, Côtes du Condomois and Côtes de Montestruc (the Armagnac growing area of Gers – mostly white wines); and Bigorre. Haute-Garonne, Tarn-et-Garonne, Pyrénées-Atlantiques, Lot, Aveyron and Gers are designations which correspond with *départements*.

In total, this extremely varied region produces about 200,000 hl (5.3 million gal) of red and rosé wine; with Gers and Tarn producing 400,000 hl (10.6 million gal) of white wine. The diverse soils and *climats* of the region, and the additional variation caused by the influence of the Atlantic Ocean on the area south of the Massif Central, are combined with an especially wide range of grape varieties. Such diversity has prompted efforts to produce blended wines, with a recognisable and consistent style. Since 1982, these have been labelled Vin de Pays du Comté Tolosan. At the moment this accounts for only 40,000 hl (1.1 million gal) per year, about one-fifteenth of the area's total wine production.

LA FLEUR D'ESPERANCE

Tradition 2000★

15 ha   13,000   €3

The estate, which dates from the 17th century, has long been a producer of Armagnac. These days, it also offers cooking courses run by famous chefs. Its clear, bright, pale-white wine is made from an equal blend of Ugni Blanc, Colombard, Sauvignon Blanc and Gros Manseng. An elegant floral nose is followed by a well-balanced palate, and a fine, lingering finish.

• Claire de Montesquieu, Dom. d'Espérance, 40240 Mauvezin-d'Armagnac, tel. 05.58.44.89.93, fax 05.58.44.85.93, e-mail info@esperance.com.fr

DOM. PERCHADE 2000★

0.9 ha   9,800   €3-5

This is a richly-coloured red wine made from 40% Cabernet Sauvignon, 40% Cabernet Franc, and 20% Tannat. It has a youthful fruity aroma, and a long and powerful palate. This rounded, supple wine is ready for drinking now.

• EARL Dulucq, Château de Perchade, 40320 Payros-Cazautets, tel. 05.58.44.50.68, fax 05.58.44.57.75   ev. day except Sun. 8am–1pm 2.30pm–7pm

SABLOCEAN Sables de l'Océan 2000★

n.c.   n.c.   €3-5

This famous vineyard, planted on the sandy soil between the forests and the Atlantic Ocean, dates from 1691, but has only recently been restored. Its brightly-coloured rosé 2000 has a delicate and elegant red-berry aroma. After a full yet supple first impression, the palate finishes on a soft and refreshing note.

• Les vignes du Chemin de Camentron, Camentron, 40660 Messanges, tel. 05.58.48.99.08
• M. Dutirou

DOM. DU TASTET Coteaux de Chalosse Elevé en Fût de Chêne 2000★

0.5 ha   4,000   €3-5

This latest vintage from an estate that dates back to 1684 is a deep ruby-coloured wine. It is powerfully aromatic on both nose and palate. The Tannat grape is the dominant constituent (80%) in this wine, and its role is evident in the well-developed tannins which will allow the wine to age well.

• EARL J.-C. Romain et Fils, Dom. du Tastet, 2350, chem. d'Aymont, 40350 Pouillon, tel. 05.58.98.28.27, fax 05.58.98.27.63, e-mail domaine-tastet@voila.fr   ev. day 8am–7pm; Sun. 8am–12.30pm

Comté tolosan

Comté tolosan

TOUR DES CASTELLANES 2000★★

■ 12 ha 100,000 ■ ♦ €3

Those who appreciate young, lively, rather fruity red Vins de Pays will not be disappointed with this wine. It has a fragrant aroma, and a supple yet lively palate, with a delicate flavour of red berries. Subtle, mature tannins ensure a long finish without disrupting the rounded style of the wine.

➽ Ets Nicolas, 4, imp. Abbé-Arnoult, 31620 Fronton, tel. 05.62.22.97.40, fax 05.62.22.97.49

LIBRA 2000★

□ 250 ha 200,000 ■ ♦ €3-5

Two Gascon varieties, Colombard and Gros Manseng, have been blended to make this Vin de Pays de Comté Tolosan. The result is a faultless white wine with a good balance of richness and vigour. It is a perfect introduction to Gascony.

➽ Producteurs Plaimont, 32400 Saint-Mont, tel. 05.62.69.62.87, fax 05.62.69.61.68 ▼ ▼ by appt.

LES PASTELIERS 2000★★

▮ 25 ha 250,000 ■ ♦ —€3

The Cave de Rabastens makes a wide variety of colourful red and rosé wines. Its pretty salmon-pink rosé is supple, rounded and well balanced. The powerful aromas of both the nose and the palate have a strong boiled-sweets tone. The cellar's Gamay also impressed the Jury.

➽ Cave de Rabastens, 33, rte d'Albi, 81800 Rabastens, tel. 05.63.33.73.80, fax 05.63.33.85.82, e-mail rabastens@vins-du-sud-ouest.com ▼ ▼ ev. day 9am–12.30pm 2.30pm–7pm

LES RIALS 2000★

□ 4.1 ha 36,000 ■ ♦ €3-5

This wine certainly has plenty to recommend it. An inviting pale-yellow colour, it has a delicate, complex, floral and fruity nose. Pear and peach dominate the equally flavourful palate.

➽ SCEA Dom. de La Chanade, 81170 Souel, tel. 05.63.56.31.10, fax 05.63.56.31.10 ▼

▼ ev. day 9am–12 noon 2pm–7pm
➽ Hollevoet

Côtes du Tarn

COSTE BLANCHE 2000★★

■ 8.24 ha 90,000 —€3

The powerful, spicy aromas of this wine make a strong impression. Spicy notes are also present on the palate, where they merge seamlessly with the flavour of very ripe red berries. The wine's tannins are well developed and refined.

➽ David, Les Fortis, 81310 Lisle-sur-Tarn, tel. 05.63.40.47.80, fax 05.63.40.45.08, e-mail clement-termes@wanadoo.fr ▼

▼ by appt.

DOM. DE LA BELLE

Muscadelle 2000★

□ 2 ha 15,000 ■ ♦ €3-5

The Muscadelle grape variety is quite difficult to vinify successfully, since its characteristics are all about subtlety and finesse. With this wine, Pascale Roc-Fonvieille has succeeded in drawing out the best from this noble variety. It has an orange-blossom and sweetbrier aroma, and a truly silky palate. A beautifully-made wine.

➽ Pascale Roc-Fonvieille, Saint-Salvy, 81310 Lisle-sur-Tarn, tel. 05.63.40.47.46, fax 05.63.40.31.93, e-mail borie-vieille.pascale@wanadoo.fr ▼

▼ ev. day 9am–12 noon 2pm–6pm; Sat. Sun. by appt.

Saint-Sardos

CAVE DES VIGNERONS DE SAINT-SARDOS

Cuvée Pech de Boisgrand 1996★★

■ 3.5 ha 7,800 ▥ €5-8

Saint-Sardos has always produced distinctive wines, and the 96 vintage is no exception. Although it is five years old, it is in prime condition. Fine, yet powerful, tannins are perceptible on the nose and on the palate. The wine's rich, supple, full-bodied character, and well-developed, long-lasting flavours will delight the taster. Don't miss the chance to sample this wine.

➽ Cave des vignerons de Saint-Sardos, Le Bourg, 82600 Saint-Sardos, tel. 05.63.02.52.44, fax 05.63.02.62.19 ▼

▼ by appt.

Côtes de Gascogne

DOM. DE BRACHIES Tannat 1998★

■ n.c. 20,000 ■ ♦ €3-5

When vinifying Tannat into Vin de Pays it is hard to make a distinctive varietal that is not too harsh. Jean-Claude Fontenay has succeeded with this spicy, blackcurrant-scented wine. Fine, ripe tannins make the palate, full-bodied and fleshy, with a long finish.

☛ Jean-Claude Fontan, Dom. de Maubet, allée du Colombard, 32800 Noulens, tel. 05.62.08.55.28, fax 05.62.08.58.94, e-mail alinefontan@wanadoo.fr ▣
Ⳡ by appt.

LA GASCOGNE PAR ALAIN BRUMONT
◻ Gros Manseng-Sauvignon 2000★

| | | 25 ha | 266,666 | ▪ | ♦ | €3–5 |

Alain Brumont knows how to successfully vinify a wide range of grape varieties. All of his wines, whether single varietal or blended, aged in barrels or vats, attest to the quality of this vineyard on the border between Gascony and the western Pyrenees. The Jury selected his Gros Manseng–Sauvignon Blanc blend, a particularly fine example of the estate's wines. It has a citrus-fruit aroma and a long palate, where exotic-fruit flavours merge with a hint of smoke.

☛ SA Dom. et Ch. d'Alain Brumont, Ch. Bouscassé, 32400 Maumusson, tel. 05.62.69.74.67, fax 05.62.69.70.46 ▣
Ⳡ ev. day 9am–12 noon 2pm–7pm

DOM. DES CASSAGNOLES 2000★
▪

| | | 3 ha | 22,000 | | | €3 |

This estate makes a number of distinctive Vins de Pays. This richly-coloured wine has a pure, powerful aroma. Strong green-pepper flavours burst forth on the smooth, rounded and supple palate. Full of character!

☛ J. et G. Baumann, EARL de la Ténarèze, 32330 Gondrin, tel. 05.62.28.40.57, fax 05.62.28.42.42, e-mail tenareze@club-internet.fr ▣ Ⳡ ev. day 8.30am–5.30pm; Sun. by appt.

CAPRICE DE COLOMBELLE 2000★
◻

| | | 400 ha | 450,000 | | | €3–5 |

Plaimont's Caprice de Colombelle follows in the footsteps of its famous Colombelle *primeur*. The Caprice is even more distinctive, with generous citrus-fruit aromas on the nose and on the palate.

☛ Producteurs Plaimont, 32400 Saint-Mont, tel. 05.62.69.62.87, fax 05.62.69.61.68 ▣ Ⳡ by appt.

DOM. DE LA HIGUERE
Cuvée Boisée 1999★
▪

| | | 15 ha | 18,000 | ▥ | €5–8 |

La Higuère has long been recognised as an estate that produces well-made red Vins de Pays. Its rich, garnet-red Cabernet Sauvignon–Merlot blend has a complex aroma on the nose, and a smoky, red-berry flavour on the palate. The full-bodied wine has a fleshy yet structured style which has benefited from ageing in barrels. This oak ageing has been carefully managed so as not to overwhelm the character of the grapes used.

☛ Paul et David Esquiro, Dom. de la Higuère, 32390 Mirepoix, tel. 05.62.65.18.05, fax 05.62.65.13.80, e-mail esquiro@free.fr ▣ Ⳡ by appt.

DOM. DE MONLUC
◻ Moelleux 1999★★★

| | | 15 ha | 55,000 | ▥ | €3–5 |

An absolute marvel! To produce a sweet wine of this quality while retaining the character of the Gascon grape varieties from which it is made, is a rare achievement. The Monluc estate has succeeded with this exceptional Gros Manseng.

☛ Dom. de Monluc, Ch. de Monluc, 32310 Saint-Puy, tel. 05.62.28.94.00, fax 05.62.28.55.70, e-mail monluc-sa-office@wanadoo.fr ▣ Ⳡ ev. day 10am–12 noon 3pm–7pm; cl. Jan. and Sun. am

DOMAINE DE MONLUC
1999
12% vol. VIN DE PAYS DES CÔTES DE GASCOGNE
MIS EN BOUTEILLE AU DOMAINE 75 cl

DOM. DE SAINT-LANNES 2000★★
◻

| | | 31.75 ha | 200,000 | | | €3–5 |

This estate is noted in Gascony for its well-crafted wine. It knows how to produce the best possible wines from local grape varieties. The full-bodied, complex and fruity 2000 is yet another in a long line of well-made wines from the Côtes de Gascogne. Pays that have forged the fine reputation of the Côtes de Gascogne wines.

☛ Michel Duffour, Dom. de Saint-Lannes, 32330 Lagraulet-du-Gers, tel. 05.62.29.11.93, fax 05.62.29.12.71, e-mail duffour.michel@wanadoo.fr ▣ Ⳡ by appt.

DOM. DU TARIQUET
◻ Sauvignon 2000★★

| | | 38 ha | 445,000 | | | €5–8 |

This is a truly powerful, generous and distinctive Sauvignon, with a subtle, lemony, leafy aroma. It is a fine example of the wide range of varietals that the Domaine du Tariquet has been producing for many years.

☛ SCV Ch. du Tariquet, Saint Amand, 32800 Eauze, tel. 05.62.09.87.82, fax 05.62.09.89.49, e-mail contact@tariquet.com ▣ ☛ Famille Grassa

Lot

LE GRAVIS 2000★

◻ 4 ha ▣ 12,000 ◧ ◡ €3-5

The wine has a pretty pink colour with violet highlights, and a fresh, expressive nose. It is fleshy, full-bodied and lively on the palate, with a predominantly floral aroma that reveals a hint of banana.

☛ Maradenne-Guitard, EARL de Nozières, 46700 Vire-sur-Lot, tel. 05.65.36.52.73 ▣ ☖ ev. day 8am–12 noon 2pm–6pm; Sun. by appt.

☛ Cave viticole de Branceilles, Le Bourg, 19500 Branceilles, tel. 05.55.84.09.01, fax 05.55.25.33.01 ▣ ☖ ev. day except Sun. 10am–12 noon 3pm–6pm.

Côtes du Condomois

COROLLE 2000★

◻ 30 ha ▣ 100,000 ◧ €3-5

The Côtes Condomois is a small red-wine producing area surrounded by the white-wine vineyards of Gers. This is a young and fruity Vin de Pays with an aroma of blackcurrants. Restrained, discreet tannins mark its agreeable finish. This is an easy-to-drink wine for all occasions.

☛ Les producteurs de la Cave de Condom, 59, av. des Mousquetaires, 32100 Condom, tel. 05.62.28.12.16, fax 05.62.28.23.94 ☖ by appt.

Coteaux de Glanes

LES VIGNERONS DU HAUT-QUERCY
Cuvée des Fondateurs 2000★★

◻ 3 ha ▣ 21,000 ◧ €5-8

This co-operative, set in the beautiful countryside to the north of Lot, has made a beguiling Vin de Pays. The wine opens with a powerful, spicy aroma. On the palate, supple fruit is followed by the emergence of tannins that help to sustain a good length of flavour. This remarkable wine provides the perfect excuse for visiting the charming vineyards of Haut-Quercy.

☛ Les Vignerons du Haut-Quercy, 46130 Glanes, tel. 05.65.39.75.42, fax 05.65.38.68.68 ▣ ☖ by appt.

Coteaux et terrasses de Montauban

DOM. DU BIARNES 2000★★

◻ 1.6 ha ▣ ◡ 3,000 ◧ €3-5

The wine is a beautiful, bright, pale-pink colour. Although it has a powerful and complex nose, the full richness, intensity and complexity of its composition only become apparent on the palate. This is a rounded, supple and full-bodied wine with the hint of vitality that marks a good rosé. A remarkable wine. The winery's equally appealing **red 2000** is also very promising.

☛ Léo Béteille, Dom. du Biarnés, 82230 La Salvetat-Belmontet, tel. 05.63.30.42.43, fax 05.63.30.42.43 ▣ ☖ by appt.

Corrèze

MILLE ET UNE PIERRES
Elevé en Fût de Chêne 1999★★

◻ 11.5 ha ▣ 80,000 ▦ €5-8

Made from a blend of 80% Cabernet Franc and 20% Merlot grapes, this is a bright, clear, garnet-coloured 99 with purple highlights. Oaky vanilla, red berries, and the aromas of a ripe harvest combine with a hint of musk (game, leather) to create a complex nose. Supple at first, the well-balanced palate develops a rounded, fleshy and full-bodied character with a gentle note of oak. This wine is worthy of being served with a truffle omelette.

DOM. DE MONTELS 2000★

◻ 2 ha ▣ 6,000 ◧ €3-5

The levels of sugar and acidity in this delicate, honeyed, sweet wine are nicely balanced, giving it a memorable style and elegance.

☛ Philippe et Thierry Romain, Dom. de Montels, 82350 Albias, tel. 05.63.31.02.82, fax 05.63.31.07.94 ▣ ☖ ev. day except Sun. 8am–12 noon 2pm–7pm

Pyrénées-Atlantiques

CABIDOS Petit Manseng 2000

□   3 ha   13,000   🍷 €5-8

The Pyrénées-Atlantiques region makes some unusual, but distinctive, Vins de Pays. Minty aromas are perceptible on both the nose and the palate of this golden Cabidos. It is an interesting wine worth seeking out.

☞ Vivien de Nazelle, Ch. de Cabidos, 64410 Cabidos, tel. 05.59.04.43.41, fax 05.59.04.43.41 ☑ ⊤ ev. day except Sat. Sun. 8am–12 noon 2pm–5.30pm

ARNAUD DE VILLENEUVE

Chardonnay Elevé en Barrique de Chêne 2000★

□   n.c.   20,000   🍷 €5-8

This golden wine is named after the medieval Catalonian alchemist who first made Vin Doux Naturel. The agreeably oaky nose shows finesse, and the rich yet lively palate is very well structured and long.

☞ Les Vignobles du Rivesaltais, 1, rue de la Roussillonnaise, 66602 Rivesaltes, tel. 04.68.64.06.63, fax 04.68.64.64.69, e-mail vignobles.rivesaltais@wanadoo.fr ☑ ⊤ by appt.

Languedoc and Roussillon

Shaped like a vast amphitheatre overlooking the Mediterranean, the Languedoc-Roussillion region has vineyards that roll from the Rhône down to the eastern Pyrénees. It is the largest wine-growing area in France, producing almost 80% of all Vins de Pays. Aude, Gard, Hérault and Pyrénées-Orientales (eastern Pyrenees) are the four designations which correspond to *departments*. Inland, there are numerous smaller designations. Together, these two categories of Vin de Pays produce almost 5.5 million hl (145 million gal) of wine each year. Finally, there is the 'Vin de Pays d'Oc' regional designation which produced 2.6 million hl (69 million gal) of wine in 1996/1997 (60% red, 16% rosé, 24% white).

Languedoc-Roussillon Vins de Pays are made by individually vinifying the selected harvests. Traditional grape varieties such as Carignan, Cinsault, Grenache and Syrah are grown for red wines, with Clairette, Grenache Blanc, and Macabeu varieties grown for whites. In addition, wine-makers grow some varieties not generally associated with the South of France – Cabernet Sauvignon, Merlot or Pinot Noir for reds; Chardonnay, Sauvignon Blanc and Viognier for whites.

DOM. DE BACHELLERY

Merlot 2000★

■   10 ha   15,000   ⬛ €3

This estate lies off the route of the Voie Domitia, a Roman road that crosses Languedoc-Roussillon on the way to Spain. Its barrel-aged, bright, deep-garnet Merlot has a delicate, lightly spicy, fruity nose. The same aromas are echoed on the well-balanced, full-bodied palate, and long finish. This wine would benefit from a few months in cellar.

☞ Bernard Julien, Dom. de Bachellery, rte de Bessan, 34500 Béziers, tel. 04.67.62.36.15, fax 04.67.35.19.38, e-mail vinbj@club-internet.fr ☑

DOM. DE BAUBIAC

Viognier Roussanne 1999★

■   0.97 ha   2,100   🍷 €5-8

This Vin de Pays has been made from the harvest of four-year-old Viognier and Roussanne vines, blended in equal parts. An attractive golden colour, it has subtle smoke and wood aromas, and a silky, full, well-balanced palate.

☞ SCEA Philip Frères, Dom. de Baubiac, 30260 Brouzet-lès-Quissac, tel. 04.66.77.33.45, fax 04.66.77.33.45, e-mail philip@dstu.univ-montp2.fr ☑ ⊤ by appt.

DOM. BELOT Viognier 2000★★

□   1 ha   3,700   ■ €5-8

This estate, which lies on lands that were royal hunting grounds in the 12th century, is now managed by Karine and Lionel Belot, the founder's children. They have made a rich, aromatic, pale-white wine with golden highlights. It has an intensely floral nose and a long, balanced, full-bodied palate. This is a powerful, yet elegant wine.

☞ Karine et Lionel Belot, rte de Cazedarnes, 34360 Pierrerue, tel. 04.67.38.08.96, fax 04.67.38.14.14 ☑ ev. day 9am–12.30pm 1.30pm–7pm; cl. Jan.

VIGNERONS DU BERANGE

Merlot 2000★

◾ n.c. 11,000 ▪ ♦ -€3

The Berange co-operative has made a pretty, dark-purple Merlot with violet highlights. A smooth and well-balanced wine, it has an elegant fruity aroma, and a very supple palate.

•➤ Groupement de producteurs Gres, 19, rue de la Coopérative, 34740 Vendargues, tel. 04.67.87.68.68, fax 04.67.87.68.69 ☑ ☥ ev. day except Sun. 9am–12 noon 2pm–6pm

DOM. BOIS BORIES Chardonnay Les

Peyrades Elevé en Fût de Chêne 2000★★

▫ 2.18 ha 6,500 ⅢⅡ €8-8

The Raymond family has been cultivating these vineyards since 1919. They have made a remarkable, brilliant-gold wine. It has an expressive, refreshing aroma of citrus fruits and elegant, delicately-oaked palate. Spicy, floral flavours emerge on the long finish.

•➤ SCEA Paul Raymond et Fils, Les Bories, 34800 Clermont-L'Hérault, tel. 04.67.96.98.03, fax 04.67.96.98.03 ☑ ☥ by appt.

DOM. DU BOSQUET

Cabernet Sauvignon 2000★

◾ 13.57 ha 148,000 ▪ ♦ €3-5

Apparently, this estate harvests its grapes at night in order to avoid the harmful effects of the high summer temperatures in Languedoc. The resulting wine, which is very good, is bottled by the Virginie group in Béziers. A bright, clear-red colour, it has a subtle, light aroma and a pleasant, well-balanced palate.

•➤ SCI Dom. du Bosquet, Dom. La Grangette, 34440 Nissan-lez-Enserune, tel. 04.67.11.88.00, fax 04.67.49.38.39

CALVET DE CALVET

Chardonnay 2000★

▫ n.c. 65,000 ▪ ♦ €3-5

The clear and bright white wine has a delicate, honeyed, white-flower aroma. Fresh and well-balanced on the palate, it also has a good length of flavour.

•➤ Calvet, 75, cours du Médoc, BP 11, 33028 Bordeaux Cedex, tel. 05.56.43.59.00, fax 05.56.43.17.78, e-mail calvet@ calvet.com

DOM. CAMPRADEL 2000★

◾ n.c. 100,000 ▪ €3-5

The dark-garnet wine has a rather restrained aroma, with smoky overtones. Ripe red-berry flavours are found on the rounded and well-structured palate. This wine could be drunk now, but it would also benefit from some time in the cellar.

•➤ Les Domaines Bernard, rte de Sérignan, 84100 Orange, tel. 04.90.11.86.86, fax 04.90.34.87.30, e-mail sagon@ domaines-bernard.fr

DOM. CAZAL-VIEL

Cuvée Finesse 2000★

▫ 8 ha 20,000 ▪ ♦ €5-8

The Cuvée Finesse certainly lives up to its name. It is a bright, pale-white wine with a floral Muscat aroma (Muscat grapes make up a quarter of the blend, which also includes 25% Sauvignon Blanc, 25% Viognier and 25% Chardonnay grapes). The well-balanced palate is flavoursome and fresh. The Jury also awarded one star to Henri Miquel's Viognier **2000**.

•➤ Ch. Cazal-Viel, Hameau Cazal-Viel, 34460 Cessenon-sur-Orb, tel. 04.67.89.63.15, fax 04.67.89.65.17 ☑ ☥ ev. day 9am–12.30pm 2pm–6pm; Sat. Sun. by appt.

•➤ Henri Miquel

CIGALUS 2000★★

ⅢⅡ €23-30

The Cigalus 2000, made from a blend of 70% Chardonnay, 25% Viognier and 5% Sauvignon Blanc, has been barrel-aged for eight months. The resulting wine is bright gold, with well-integrated oak aromas, and notes of vanilla and stewed fruit. On the palate, it is velvety, voluptuous and very well balanced, with a good length of flavour.

•➤ Gérard Bertrand, Dom. Cigalus, 11100 Bizanet, tel. 04.68.42.68.68 ☑ ☥ by appt.

DOM. COSTEPLANE

Cuvée Terroir 2000★

◾ 3.3 ha 13,300 ▪ ♦ €5-8

This estate, which is even older than the 500-year-old oak tree that sits on its border, practises organic viticulture. From an equal blend of Syrah and Grenache, it has made an attractive, dark, garnet-coloured wine with an expressive garrigue aroma. The full-bodied and well-structured palate has a warming finish. Excellent tannins balance this powerful wine, and ensure that it will age well if one can keep from drinking it right away.

•➤ Françoise et Vincent Coste, Mas Costeplane, 30260 Cannes-et-Clairan, tel. 04.66.77.85.02, fax 04.66.77.85.47, e-mail vetf.coste@free.fr ☑ ☥ by appt.

DOM. DE COUDOULET

Muscat Sec de Petits Grains 2000★★

▫ 1 ha 6,600 ▪ ♦ €5-8

Pierre-André and Jean-Yves Ournac jointly manage this beautiful 43-ha (106-acre) estate in Minervois. They have made a light-coloured wine with golden highlights, whose pure Muscat origin is evident in its expressive, very floral, aroma. Lively, fresh, well-balanced and long on the palate, this wine is for drinking now.

•➤ GAEC Dom. de Coudoulet, chem. de Minerve, 34210 Cesseras, tel. 04.68.91.15.70, fax 04.68.91.15.78 ☥ by appt.

DOM. COUSTELLIER
Rosé de Syrah 2000★

■   1.6 ha   9,000   ■ ● ♦   €3

Roland Coustellier realised his dream of returning to his native village when he bought his first vineyard in Florensac in 1967. The estate is now in the hands of the second generation. They have made a bright reddish-orange rosé, with an intensely fresh and fruity aroma of red berries. Firm and full-bodied on the palate, this is a well-balanced and elegant wine.

☛ GAEC Coustellier, 16, rue Gal-Montbrun, 34510 Florensac, tel. 04.67.77.01.42, fax 04.67.77.94.39, e-mail gaec.coustellier@wanadoo.fr

🍷 by appt.

DOM. DES CROZES-SENACQ
Merlot Elevé en Fût de Chêne 1999★

■   5 ha   40,000   ■ ● ♦   €5-8

The Euzet vineyards, near the city of Alès, are set in the beautiful Cévennes countryside. This clear, bright, garnet-coloured wine made by the local co-operative has a delicate fruity aroma. The rounded and full-bodied palate is marked by a well-integrated oak flavour that will complement white meat dishes.

☛ Cave d'Euzet-les-Bains, rte d'Alès, 30360 Euzet, tel. 04.66.83.51.16, fax 04.66.83.68.33

🍷 ev. day 9am–12 noon 2pm–7pm

DOM. ELLUL-FERRIERES
Vieilles Vignes 1998★

■   3 ha   12,000   ■ ● ♦   €5-8

This estate's first-ever vintage, the 97, was awarded one star in the 2000 edition of the *Guide*. Its second star goes to a rich, ruby-coloured 100% Grenache with an aroma of over-ripe, as well as dried, fruits. On the palate, it is full, fresh, silky and well structured. This is a beautifully-balanced wine.

☛ Dom. Ellul-Ferrières, 151, rue Jacques Bounin, 34070 Montpellier, mob. 06.15.38.45.01, fax 04.67.16.04.49, e-mail ellulferrieres@aol.com

🍷 ev. day 5pm–7pm

LOUIS FABRE Sauvignon 2000★★

□   3 ha   26,000   ■ ● ♦   €3-5

One member of the tasting panel enthused that the colour of this Sauvignon resembled 'Venetian gold'. The wine's concentrated and complex bouquet of citrus, exotic and crystallised fruits, and lively yet full palate are also impressive. This is a fleshy and structured wine, with a good length of flavour.

☛ Louis Fabre, rue du Château, 11200 Luc-sur-Orbieu, tel. 04.68.27.10.80, fax 04.68.27.38.19, e-mail chateau.luc@aol.com

🍷 by appt.

DOM. DE FLORIAN
Les Chênes Blancs 1998★★

■   n.c.   3,000   ■ ● ♦   €5-8

At one time, this estate belonged to the writer Jean-Pierre Claris de Florian, a member of the Académie Française and Voltaire's great-nephew. The Jury was impressed by this attractive, dark-ruby wine with purple highlights. It has a delicate but richly evocative aroma of spices, fruits and garrigue. The full-bodied and heady palate fulfills the promise of the nose with its good structure, and exceptional balance.

☛ SCEA Dom. de Florian, rte d'Anduze, 30610 Logrian, tel. 04.66.77.48.22, fax 04.66.77.48.22. 🍷 ev. day except Sun. 9am–12 noon 1.30pm–6.30pm

☛ Louis Rico

DOM. GALETIS
Cabernet Sauvignon 2000★★

■   10 ha   120,000   ■ ● ♦   €3

This estate has been owned by the same family since 1855. Its handsome, bright-purple 2000 has a well-developed spicy aroma, and a lively, long and well-balanced palate. This wine is bottled by the Virginie group.

☛ SCI du Dom. Galetis, 11170 Moussoulens, tel. 04.67.11.88.00, fax 04.67.49.38.39

DOM. DU GRAND CRES 1999★★

□   2 ha   8,000   ■ ● ♦   €8-11

The Jury was very impressed by this wine from Le Grand Crès, a beautiful vineyard in the Corbières region. The 35% Viognier, 60% Roussane and 5% Muscat blend was left in contact with the skins for only a short time during maceration. The resulting wine has a remarkable golden colour with green highlights, and a delicate, complex, floral and fruity aroma. After a fine first impression, the well-balanced palate gives further proof of this wine's elegant style.

☛ Hervé et Pascaline Leferrer, Dom. du Grand Crès, 40, av. de la Mer, 11200 Ferrals-les-Corbières, tel. 04.68.43.69.08, fax 04.68.43.58.99

🍷 by appt.

GRANGE DES ROUQUETTE
Agrippa 2000★★

■   2 ha   8,000   ■ ● ♦   €5-8

The Roquettes are a branch of the Boudinaud family and the *grange* once harboured the estate's wine-cellars, olive oil press and sheep-fold — hence Grange des Rouquette. The wine is very dark, almost black, with purple highlights. It has a powerful, ripe-fruit nose and a rich suppleness to the well-balanced palate, with a long finish. Altogether, a very elegant wine.

☛ Vignobles Boudinaud, 30210 Fournes, tel. 04.66.37.27.23, fax 04.66.37.27.23, e-mail boudinaud@infonie.fr 🍷 by appt.

DOM. DE LA BAUME 1998★

■ 8.1 ha 22,680 ⅢⅠ €8-11

Made from a 50–50 blend of Merlot and Cabernet Sauvignon grapes, this ruby-coloured wine has a generous and complex aroma that is both oaky and fruity. Its robust style is confirmed by a well-balanced palate with warm, chewy, tannins and maturing aromas. The Jury was equally impressed by the estate's **white 98**.

•⚲ Dom. de La Baume, rte de Pezenas, 34290 Servian, tel. 04.67.39.29.49, fax 04.67.39.29.40, e-mail charlotte-habit@labaume.com ☒ ⅄ by appt.

LA CHAPELLE DES PENITENTS
Chardonnay 1999★★

▢ n.c. 13,600 ■ ♦ €15-23

The straw-yellow wine with golden highlights from the négociant, Daniel Bessière, has a concentrated, complex, butter-and-honey aroma. Its equally elegant palate is full-bodied, fleshy and round, and balanced by good acidity. This is a very fine wine that is ready for drinking now, but could also be cellared for several months.

•⚲ SA Bessière, 40, rue du Port, 34140 Mèze, tel. 04.67.18.40.40, fax 04.67.43.77.03

DOM. LA CONDAMINE
BERTRAND Cabernet Sauvignon
Cuvée Promesse 1999★★

▢ 0.5 ha 2,000 ⅢⅠ €23-30

An appealing dark-purple colour with amber highlights, this wine has a rich and complex aroma of ripe fruits, spices, and forest undergrowth. Its palate is aromatic and well-balanced, with mature tannins and good length. The firm structure of this 99 means it will keep for some time yet.

•⚲ Bertrand Jany et Fils, Ch. Condamine Bertrand, 34230 Paulhan, tel. 04.67.25.27.96, fax 04.67.25.07.55, e-mail chateau.condamineber@free.fr ☒ ⅄ by appt.

DOM. DE LA DEVEZE Viognier
Elevé en Barrique de Chêne 2000★★

▢ 0.7 ha n.c. ⅢⅠ €8-11

The enormous, 30-ha (74-acre), La Devèze estate is right on the Cévennes Fault in historic territory. A pretty, golden wine, it has a fine, rich, floral aroma. The oaky palate is elegant and well structured with a remarkably good length of flavour.

•⚲ Marcel Damais, GAEC du Dom. de la Devèze, 34190 Montoulieu, tel. 04.67.73.70.21, fax 04.67.73.32.40, e-mail domaine@deveze.com ☒ ⅄ by appt.

DOM. DE LA FERRANDIERE
Grenache Gris 2000★

◢ 6 ha 60,000 ■ ♦ €3-5

The estate, established in the early 20th century, cultivates 70 ha (173 acres) of vineyards and 25 ha (62 acres) of apple orchards. Its blush-pink Grenache Gris reveals aromas of great finesse and elegance, and is lively,

fresh and well balanced on the palate. This wine would make a good accompaniment to charcuterie.

•⚲ SARL Les Ferrandières, 11800 Aigues-Vives, tel. 04.68.79.29.30, fax 04.68.79.29.39, e-mail fergau@terre-net.fr ☒ ⅄ ev. day except Sat. Sun. 8am–12 noon 2pm–6pm

DOM. LALANDE
Cabernet Sauvignon 2000★★

■ 10.03 ha 60,000 ■ ♦ €3

The Canal du Midi flows past the lower slopes of this estate, which is located 3 km (1.9 miles) from Carcassonne. The Lalande is a beautiful, bright, cherry-red 2000 with a delicately spicy aroma. Full, well balanced and structured, it has a good length of flavour on the palate. This wine will show at its very best with a little time in the cellar.

•⚲ SCEA Ch. Lalande, Dom. Lalande, 11610 Pennautier, tel. 04.67.37.22.36 ☒ ⅄ by appt.
•⚲ B. Montariol

DOM. LALAURIE Merlot 1999★

■ 12 ha 15,000 ⅢⅠ ♦ ❚ €5-8

The estate has been in the same family for nine generations! Seventy per cent of this deep-garnet wine was matured in barrels, resulting in an oaky, complex, leather-and-moss-scented nose. The palate is structured with firm tannins. This well-balanced wine should be served with small game or a roast joint.

•⚲ Jean-Charles Lalaurie, 2, rue Le-Pelletier-de-Saint-Fargeau, 11590 Ouveillan, tel. 04.68.46.84.96, fax 04.68.46.93.92, e-mail jean-charles.lalaurie@libertysurf.fr ☒ ⅄ by appt.

DOM. LAMARGUE Merlot 2000★

■ 2.33 ha 10,000 ⅢⅠ €8-11

The Jury was equally impressed by both the estate's **Syrah 2000** and this rich, garnet-coloured Merlot. Its delicately-oaked, fruity aroma preceeds a powerful, full-bodied palate that is structured by solid tannins. This wine is ready for drinking now, but could also age for a time.

•⚲ SCI du Dom. de Lamargue, rte de Vauvert, 30800 Saint-Gilles, tel. 04.66.87.31.89, fax 04.66.87.41.87, e-mail domaine.de.lamargue@wanadoo.fr ☒ ⅄ by appt.
•⚲ C. Bonomi

DOM. DE LA VALMALE
Cuvée Alphonse 2000★

◢ 5 ha 25,000 ■ ♦ €3

The founders' grandchildren have been managing this 79-ha (195-acre) estate since 1994. The bright-purple Grenache (60%), Syrah (25%) and Merlot (15%) blend has violet highlights. Ripe fruit aromas dominate the generous nose while the structured, inviting palate has a good length of flavour.

• Alain Clarou, Dom. de la Valmale, 34550 Bessan, tel. 01.43.54.42.49, fax 01.40.46.89.01 Y by appt.

DOM. LE CLAUD Cuvée Sélectionnée Comtesse Louis de Boisgelin 1999★

■ n.c. 5,600 ▦ €5-8

The estate is located in a village 4 km (2.5 miles) outside Montpellier, where there is evidence of the presence of prehistoric man. The vineyards are much more recent, having been completely replanted in 1976. The dark-purple 98, with its amber highlights, has a subtle oaky aroma. On the palate, it is pleasant and well balanced, with a very good length of flavour.

• SCEA de Boisgelin, Dom. Le Claud, 34430 Saint-Jean-de-Védas, tel. 04.67.27.63.37, fax 04.67.47.28.72 Y by appt.

LE CORDON DE ROYAT Syrah 2000★

■ n.c. n.c. ■ €3-5

Thierry Boudinaud oversees the management of this huge wine estate whose headquarters are in Gigondas. This brand-name wine is a rich, dark-purple colour with an aromatic red-berry and violet nose. The palate is rounded and supple, making this a very balanced and elegant wine.

• Domaines du Soleil, Ch. Canet, 11800 Rustiques, tel. 04.90.12.32.42, fax 04.90.12.32.49

LES COLLINES DU BOURDIC Muscat 2000★★

□ 5 ha 27,000 ■ €3-5

The marl soils of the Bourdic vineyards in Gard have produced a clear and bright Muscat, that displays its varietal character from its intensely aromatic nose, to its fresh and well-balanced palate. The Jury also awarded one star each to the co-operative's **Chardonnay 2000** and **Cabernet Sauvignon 2000**.

• SCA Les Collines du Bourdic, chem. de la Gare, 30190 Bourdic, tel. 04.66.81.20.82, fax 04.66.81.23.20 Y by appt.

LES JAMELLES Sauvignon 2000★

□ 10.5 ha 70,000 ▦ €5-8

This Sauvignon is vinified by a couple of Burgundians from the Côte-d'Or, and bottled in Saône-et-Loire. It is pale yellow with green highlights, and has an intensely floral aroma. The fresh and lively palate is well balanced and long-lasting.

• Badet Clément et Cie, 39, rte de Beaune, 21220 L'Etang-Vergy, tel. 03.80.61.46.31, fax 03.80.61.42.19, e-mail contact@badetclement.com Y ev day except Sat. Sun. 9am–12 noon 2pm–5pm

LES QUATRE CLOCHERS Cabernet Sauvignon Vieilles Vignes Elevé en Fût de Chêne 1999★

■ n.c. n.c. ▦ €8-11

This co-operative, located just outside Limoux, is one of the biggest players in the French wine industry. Although it generally specialises in whites, it does make some reds. Here is a dark-purple 99, with an open, spicy, oaky nose, and a balanced and well-structured palate with evident tannins. This wine may be enjoyed right away, or cellared for several months.

• Aimery-Sieur d'Arques, av. de Carcassonne, BP 30, 11303 Limoux Cedex, tel. 04.68.74.63.00, fax 04.68.74.63.12, e-mail service@sieurdarques.com Y by appt.

DOM. LES YEUSES Chardonnay 2000★

□ n.c. 10,000 ▦ €5-8

The estate was converted from a green-oak yeuse, plantation into a vineyard in the 18th century. Its limpid, golden Chardonnay has a rich, intensely floral nose, and a full-bodied and fleshy palate. This is a beautifully-balanced wine.

• Jean-Paul et Michel Dardé, Dom. Les Yeuses, rte de Marseillan, 34140 Mèze, tel. 04.67.43.80.20, fax 04.67.43.59.32, e-mail jp.darde@worldonline.fr Y ev. day except Sun. 9am–12 noon 3pm–7pm

DOM. DE MAIRAN Chasan 2000★

□ 5 ha 30,000 ■ €3-5

The estate is on the site of an ancient Roman villa. It cultivates a vineyard of 'Chasan' grapes, a Listan-Chardonnay cross that generally tends to produce wine that is quite low in alcohol. This Chasan wine is unusually alcoholic at 13%. It is a brilliant, pale-yellow colour with green highlights, and has a strong citrus-fruit aroma. The developed, well-structured palate shows that the wine is ready for drinking now. The Jury was equally impressed by the estate's **Cabernet Sauvignon 98**.

• Jean Peitavy, Dom. de Mairan, 34620 Puissergier, tel. 04.67.93.74.20, fax 04.67.93.83.05 Y ev. day 9am–12 noon 2pm–7pm

DOM. DE MALAVIEILLE Merlot 2000★

■ 2 ha 6,000 ▦ €3-5

In the 18th century, a Malavieille nobleman abandoned this estate when he fled to the French colony of Louisiana. Centuries later, the current owner, one of his descendants, purchased the estate. Her dark, ruby-red Merlot has a lightly-oaked, toasty and floral nose. Spicy aromas mark the smooth and rounded palate, which has a good length of flavour.

• Mireille Bertrand, Malavieille, 34800 Mérifons, tel. 04.67.96.34.67, fax 04.67.96.32.21 Y by appt.

DOM. PAUL MAS
Cabernet Sauvignon Merlot 2000★★ 18.2 ha 27,000 €5-8

The chapel of the Château de Cornas, restored in 1985, is worth a visit, as are the château's cellars, which have been used to age wine since 1995. The dark-purple wine with amber highlights has a rich and complex (spicy) bouquet. The well-balanced palate is also quite rich, as well as being long and aromatic.

• Dom. Paul Mas, Ch. de Conas, 34210 Pezenas, tel. 04.67.90.16.10, fax 04.67.98.00.60, e-mail info@paulmas.com ▼ Ⓣ by appt.

DOM. DU MAS DE PIQUET
Chardonnay 2000★★ 3.34 ha n.c. €3-5

The agricultural college has made a clear, bright Chardonnay, with a hint of effervescence. It is beguilingly floral, fruity and spicy on the nose, with a lively and elegant palate that is both silky and well balanced.

• Lycée Agropolis, Dom. du Mas de Piquet, rte de Ganges, 34790 Grabels, tel. 04.67.52.26.59, fax 04.67.52.26.59, e-mail piquet-dom@educagri.fr ▼ Ⓣ ev. day except Sun. 9am–12 noon 3pm–7pm; Sat. 9am–1pm

MAS MEYRAC 1999★ 16.5 ha 20,000 €8-11

After acquiring the estate in July 2000, the new owners invested six million francs to modernise the wine-making equipment. The dark-garnet 99 with its amber highlights has a generous fruity aroma (cherries, plums, crystallised fruit), and a fleshy, rounded palate. Very pleasant.

• Ch. Capendu, pl. de la Mairie, 11700 Capendu, tel. 04.68.79.00.61, fax 04.68.79.08.61 ▼ Ⓣ by appt.

MAS MONTEL Cuvée Jéricho 1999★ 3 ha 15,000 €5-8

The brilliant, dark-ruby wine has a rich bouquet of spices, garrigue and eucalyptus. The complexity of the nose continues on the full-bodied, well-balanced palate, with a long finish.

• EARL Granier, Mas Montel, 30250 Aspères, tel. 04.66.80.01.21, fax 04.66.80.01.87, e-mail montel@wanadoo.fr ▼ Ⓣ ev. day except Sun. 9am–12 noon 2pm–7pm

DOM. DE MOLINES
Sauvignon Réserve 2000★ 2 ha 15,000 €5-8

Michel Gassier would have preferred that the Molines *terroir* be classed as an AOC, but that does not prevent him from continuing to aspire to the production of great wines. To this end, he has chosen to grow Sauvignon vines even though they are more commonly associated with cooler climates. His straw-gold wine has a scintillating aroma of flowers and dill. The aromas of the nose are echoed on the rich and fleshy palate.

• Vignobles Michel Gassier, Ch. de Nages, chem. des Canaux, 30132 Caissargues, tel. 04.66.38.44.30, fax 04.66.38.44.21, e-mail m.gassier@chateaudenages.com ▼ Ⓣ by appt.

OPUS TERRA Merlot et Syrah 2000★ 12 ha 100,000 €3-5

Hervé Durand is renowned for having established the Orpailleur vineyard in Quebec. This wine is the product of his Languedoc vineyards. The wine's elegant and fruity bouquet suits its bright-purple colour. The fine aromas reappear on the well-balanced palate. 'This wine is very beguiling,' remarked one of the tasters. While it is ready to drink now, it will also age well.

• Hervé et Guilhem Durand, 30300 Beaucaire, tel. 04.66.59.19.72, fax 04.66.59.50.80 ▼ Ⓣ by appt.

LE BLANC D'ORMESSON 2000★ 4 ha 10,000 €5-8

This wine is a surprising blend of Sauvignon Blanc (30%), Roussanne (30%), Viognier (20%) and Petit Manseng (20%) grapes. The bright, pale colour of the wine complements its delicate white-flower aroma. On the palate, it is crisp, fresh and very aromatic. The estate's **Sauvignon 2000** and **Cabernet Sauvignon 99** also impressed the Jury.

• Jérôme d'Ormesson, Le Château, 34120 Lézignan-la-Cèbe, tel. 04.67.98.29.33, fax 04.67.98.29.32 ▼ Ⓣ ev. day 9am–12 noon 2pm–6pm

DOM. DE PANERY 2000★ 2 ha 7,000 €3-5

This blend of 70% Merlot and 30% Syrah comes from one of the vast estates of the Gard region. The dark-purple wine slowly releases a spicy aroma of black pepper mixed with vanilla. Its well-balanced palate is rounded, full and very pleasant.

• SCEA Ch. de Panery, rte d'Uzès, 30210 Pouzilhac, tel. 04.66.37.04.44, fax 04.66.37.62.38, e-mail chateaudepanery@wanadoo.fr ▼ Ⓣ ev. day 10am–6pm
• Roger Gryseels

PAVILLON DU BOSC
Cabernet Franc 2000★ 2 ha 4,000 €5-8

The Jury awarded one star each to two of this producer's wines: the **red Moulin du Bosc 2000** and this salmon-pink rosé. An expressive, herbaceous nose with liquorice notes is followed by a warm and rounded palate. This is a very elegant wine.

• SICA Delta Domaines, Dom. du Bosc, 34450 Vias, tel. 04.67.21.73.54, fax 04.67.21.68.38 ▼ Ⓣ by appt.

LES VIGNERONS DU PIC
Sauvignon 2000★★

	n.c.	10,000	🍾	€3-5

This bright, pale-white wine with green highlights is beautiful to look at. It has a delicate nose; festive and floral, with acacia and white peach. Similar flavours appear on the expressive palate, which balances fullness and vigour, and has a lingering finish.

Les Vignerons du Pic, 285, av. de Sainte-Croix, 34820 Assas, tel. 04.67.59.62.55, fax 04.67.59.56.39 ☑ ev. day except Mon. 9am–12 noon 2pm–6pm; groups by appt.

DOM. DE POUSSAN LE HAUT
Chardonnay 2000★

	n.c.	26,000	€5-8

A bright, pale-yellow colour with green highlights, this wine has a rich, floral, fruity aroma. Its lively and rounded palate is well balanced and long. This is a finely-made wine. The Jury also selected the Syrah du Domaine des Rosiers and the Domaine de la Barrière, and awarded a star each to the Domaine des Guillards Chardonnay and the Cuvée Mythique, all of which were produced by this association of co-operatives.

Vignerons de La Méditerranée, ZI Plaisance, 12, rue du Rec-de-Veyret, BP 414, 11104 Narbonne Cedex, tel. 04.68.42.75.00, fax 04.68.42.75.01, e-mail rhirtz@listel.fr
by appt.

DOM. REYNAUD
Chardonnay 2000★

2.75 ha	4,000	€3-5

This wine has a bright, scintillating appearance and a delicate, subtle aroma. Its fresh, rounded palate is fruity and well balanced. The estate's Merlot 2000 also impressed the Jury.

EARL Reynaud, Dom. Reynaud, 30700 Saint-Siffret, tel. 04.66.03.18.20, fax 04.66.03.12.95 ☑ ev. day except Sun. 10am–12 noon 4pm–6pm

DOM. SAINT JEAN DE CONQUES
2000★

▲	1 ha	8,000	€3-5

This pretty pink rosé with purple highlights has a spicy aroma of dried fruits and red berries. A fresh finish makes a nice counter-point to the rounded palate.

François-Régis Boussagol, Dom. Saint-Jean de Conques, 34310 Quarante, tel. 04.67.89.34.18, fax 04.67.89.35.46 ☑ by appt.

DOM. SAINT MARTIN DE LA GARRIGUE Chardonnay 1999★★

2.08 ha	13,000

This estate is in a beautiful setting, with both a chapel that dates back to the ninth century and a fascinating château nearby. This remarkable straw-yellow wine has golden highlights, and an intense aroma of flowers and crystallised fruits. The well-

structured, balanced palate develops the flavours of the nose, and has a lengthy finish.

SCEA Saint-Martin de la Garrigue, 34530 Montagnac, tel. 04.67.24.00.40, fax 04.67.24.16.15, e-mail jczabalia@stmartingarrigue.com ☑ ev. day 8am–12 noon 1pm–5pm; Sat. Sun. by appt.

DOM. DE TERRE MEGERE
Merlot 1999★★

■	3 ha	30,000	🍾	€3-5

The bright-purple Merlot with amber highlights has a rich and complex nose, and a supple palate with fully-integrated tannins.

Michel Moreau, Dom. de Terre Mégère, Cour de Village, 34660 Cournonsec, tel. 04.67.85.42.85, fax 04.67.85.25.12, e-mail terremegere@wanadoo.fr ☑ ev. day except Sun. 3pm–7pm; Sat. 9am–12.30pm

TERRE D'AMANDIERS 1998★★

	n.c.	50,000	€11-15

Phillipe Maurel and Stéphane Vadeau jointly run a wine company that exports 90% of its production. This Chardonnay is perfectly elegant from start to finish. The colour is straw-yellow with golden highlights. Aromas are delicate yet richly fruity and floral. Finally, the fresh and rounded palate with its good length of flavour contributes to making this a remarkable wine.

Maurel Vedeau, ZI La Baume, 34290 Servian, tel. 04.67.39.21.20, fax 04.67.39.22.13

SYRCAB Comte Cathare 1999★

■	n.c.	10,000	€11-15

The slightly odd name of this wine is simply a contraction of the grape varieties, Cabernet Sauvignon (80%) and Syrah (20%), which were blended to produce it. A deep garnet colour, the wine develops a rich, complex bouquet that is both oaky and fresh. The balanced and lengthy palate is quite substantial, which will enable this wine to age. Drink now, or cellar.

Grands Vignobles en Méditerranée, La Tuilerie, 34210 La Livinière, tel. 04.68.91.42.63, fax 04.68.91.62.15, e-mail franboissier@compuserve.com ☑ by appt.

F. DE SKALLI Merlot 1998★

■	n.c.	28,000	€15-23

The author Paul Valéry was born in the town where this company, one of the most important enterprises in Vins de Pays production, is headquartered. The wine, which has been barrel-aged for 18 months, has a bright garnet colour and an intensely oaky nose. It is very well structured, warm and balanced on the palate.

Les vins Skalli, 278, av. du Mal-Juin, BP 376, 34204 Sète Cedex, tel. 04.67.46.70.00, fax 04.67.46.71.99, e-mail info@vinskalli.com ☑ ☒ by appt. except Jul. Aug. 10am–1pm 2pm–6pm

Sables du Golfe du Lion

TERRES BLANCHES
Muscat Sec 2000★

☐ 22.5 ha 100,000 ■ €5-8

The Frontignan co-operative vinifies 630 ha (1,556 acres). It makes a Vin Doux Naturel as well as this unusual dry Muscat. The golden 2000 has the delicate flowery aromas generally associated with Muscat grapes, and a fresh and elegant palate with a good length of flavour.

☛ SCA Coop. de Frontignan,
14, av. du Muscat, 34110 Frontignan,
tel. 04.67.48.12.26, fax 04.67.43.07.17 ⊠
🍷 ev. day 9am–12 noon 2pm–6.30pm; groups by appt.

VERMEIL DU CRES
Chardonnay 2000★

☐ 3 ha 20,000 ■ ♦

This pale Chardonnay glitters with green, rather than golden, highlights. It has a delicate fruity nose, and a lively, full and well-balanced palate.

☛ SCAV les Vignerons de Sérignan,
av. Roger-Audoux, 34410 Sérignan,
tel. 04.67.32.23.26, fax 04.67.32.59.66 ⊠
🍷 ev. day except Sun. 9am–12 noon 3pm–6pm

EXCELLENCE DE VIRGINIE
n° 10 2000★

n.c. 100,000 ■ ⅢⅠ ♦ -€3

This estate numbers its wines the way Chanel numbers its perfumes. The dark-red 'Number 10' is a blend of 50% Syrah, 20% Cabernet Sauvignon, 20% Merlot and 10% Grenache. It has a delicately-oaked, spicy and toasted palate, and a full and flavoursome palate that is elegantly structured. This wine is ready now, but will also keep well in the cellar.

☛ Les domaines Virginie, av. Jean-Foucault,
ZI du Capiscol, 34500 Béziers,
tel. 04.67.11.88.00, fax 04.67.49.38.39

Sables du Golfe du Lion

DOM. DU PETIT CHAUMONT
2000★

■ 5 ha 35,000 ■ ♦ €3-5

This vineyard has been in the same family for five generations. In 1973 it was completely re-planted with 'noble' grape varieties. The dark-purple 2000 has a spicy, red-berry nose and an elegant, well-balanced palate with good length of flavour. It is ready for drinking now.

☛ GAEC Bruel, Dom. du petit Chaumont,
30220 Aigues-Mortes, tel. 04.66.53.60.63,
fax 04.66.53.64.41, e-mail chaumont@
caves-particulieres.com ⊠ 🍷 ev. day except
Sun. 9am–12 noon 3pm–6.30pm; groups by appt.

Gard

DOM. DE TAVERNEL 2000★★

☐ 10.58 ha 30,000 ■ €3-5

At one time, the *mas* belonged to the family of the Occitane poet, Frédéric Mistral. The estate's inspired Vermentino and Muscat blend has a very pale, bright colour, and a flowery bouquet of great finesse and complexity. On the palate, it is crisp, delicate and well balanced, with lingering and seductive flavours.

☛ GFA Dom. de Tavernel, rte de Fourques,
30300 Beaucaire, tel. 04.66.58.57.01,
fax 04.66.59.38.30,
e-mail tavernel.domaine@ilibertysurf.fr ⊠
🍷 ev. day except Sun. 10am–6pm; Sat. by appt.
☛ M. Amphoux

Côtes de Thongue

DOM. BOURDIC Grenache 1999★★

■ 0.85 ha 3,800 ⅢⅠ €5-8

This organic vineyard has used a combination of traditional and modern vinification methods to produce a well-balanced and harmonious wine. The purple 99, with amber-coloured highlights, has a distinctive, subtly-oaked nose, and a very silky and flavourful palate. This wine is ready for drinking now.

☛ Christa Vogel et Hans Hürlimann, Dom. Bourdic, 34290 Alignan-du-Vent,
tel. 04.67.24.98.08, fax 04.67.24.98.96,
e-mail bourdic2@wanadoo.fr ⊠ 🍷 by appt.

DOM. LA CROIX BELLE
N° 7 1998★★

■ 3.5 ha 13,000 ⅢⅠ €11-15

Although the primary component of this wine is Syrah, five other varieties have been included in the blend. A dark, glowing wine, it has a delicate, lightly-oaked nose. The remarkably well-structured palate has an excellent length of flavour. One taster declared it to be a 'very high quality wine'.

☛ Jacques et Françoise Boyer,
Dom. La Croix-Belle, 34480 Puissalicon,
tel. 04.67.36.27.23, fax 04.67.36.60.45 ⊠
🍷 by appt.

DOM. DE L'ARJOLLE

Paradoxe 1999★

4 ha	15,000	€15-23

This rich garnet-coloured 99 has a light, vanilla-scented nose. A blend of Syrah, Cabernet Franc and Merlot grapes has given a well-structured wine that remains austere, though well balanced, after 16 months of barrel ageing. It will be a very good wine in a few months' time when the tannins have softened.

☛ Dom. de L'Arjolle, 6, rue de la Côte, 34480 Pouzolles, tel. 04.67.24.81.18, fax 04.67.24.81.90, ✔ ▼ ev. day except Sun. 9am–12.30pm 2pm–6pm

LES VIGNERONS DE MONTBLANC Chardonnay 2000★★

□

29 ha	30,000	€3-5

This is an expressive and elegant wine. Limpid and bright, it has a very complex, attractive aroma of flowers with citrus and exotic fruits. On the palate, it is fresh and well balanced, with a long, lingering finish.

☛ Les Vignerons de Montblanc, av. d'Agde, 34290 Montblanc, tel. 04.67.98.50.26, fax 04.67.98.61.00 ✔

DOM. DE MONT D'HORTES

Cabernet Sauvignon 2000★

■

5.5 ha	40,000	€3-5

This bright and deeply-coloured red wine has a delicate aroma redolent of overripe, jammy fruit. The palate is powerful, well balanced and long, with a slight liquorice flavour. This attractive 2000 is ready for drinking now.

☛ Dom. de Mont d'Hortes, 34630 Saint-Thibéry, tel. 04.67.77.88.08, fax 04.67.30.17.57 ✔ ▼ by appt.

☛ J. Anglade

DOM. MONTROSE

Les Lézards 2000★★

■

3 ha	17,000	€5-8

A dark, almost black wine with purple highlights, which is remarkable for its complex, powerful aroma of ripe fruits. Enticing, exuberant flavours are found on a heady and full-bodied palate. The Jury also liked the estate's rosé 2000.

☛ Dom. Montrose, RN 9, 34120 Tourbes, tel. 04.67.98.63.33, fax 04.67.98.65.27 ✔ ▼ by appt.

DOM. SAINT-GEORGES D'IBRY

Chardonnay 1999★★★

□

3.62 ha	3,000	€8-11

Henceforth, this estate, established in 1860, will be practising sustainable agriculture. The Jury was unanimous in its decision to select this superb, straw-yellow Chardonnay with golden highlights as a coup de cœur. It has a delicate, elegant, intensely floral aroma with a subtle hint of oak. The palate is full and well balanced, with a lingering finish. A beautiful wine to drink now.

☛ Michel Cros, Dom. Saint-Georges-d'Ibry, rte d'Espondeilhan, 34290 Abeilhan, tel. 04.67.39.19.18, fax 04.67.39.07.44, e-mail st-georges-ibry@worldonline.fr ▼ by appt.

DOM. DE RAVANES Les Gravières du Taurou Grande Réserve 1998★★★

■

1.18 ha	5,500	€15-23

There is evidence that the original Roman villa, whose ruins are on the estate, was involved in wine-making. Centuries later, the vineyards have produced a deep-red 98 with a powerful, complex, fruity and oaky (vanilla) nose. Its well-structured palate has softened tannins, and a good length of flavour. This wine is ready to drink.

☛ Guy et Marc Benin, tel. 04.67.36.00.02, fax 04.67.36.35.64, e-mail ravanes@wanadoo.fr ✔ ▼ by appt.

RESSAC

Le Muscat des Garrigues 2000★★

□

20 ha	10,000	€5-8

This straw-yellow Muscat has golden highlights and an expressive floral nose. An impressive length of flavour marks its fresh and supple palate. The Cabernet Sauvignon 2000, made by the same co-operative, also impressed the Jury.

☛ Cave coopérative de Florensac, BP 9, 34510 Florensac, tel. 04.67.77.00.20, fax 04.67.77.79.66 ✔ ▼ by appt.

Hérault

LE ROUGE DE L'ABBAYE DU FENOUILLET Cuvée Barroque 1999★

■ 5.5 ha 20,000 ◖◗ €11–15

There has been a building on the site of this historic abbey since 1293. Twenty per cent of the barrels that have been used to age the estate's 'Cuvée Barroque' are made of American oak. The resulting dark-coloured wine has purple highlights, and a powerful toasty, roasted, black-fruit aroma. The palate is structured, full-bodied and flavourful. This is a well-balanced wine.

🔑 Toni Schuler, SARL Abbaye du Fenouillet, 34270 Vacquières, tel. 04.67.59.03.15, fax 04.67.59.03.15, e-mail toni.schuler@schuler.ch ☑
Y by appt.

DOM. LA FADEZE Sauvignon 2000★

☐ 4.8 ha 30,000 ▮ ♁ €5–8

During wine-making, this Sauvignon was allowed a short period of contact with the skins. The resulting clear, bright wine has fruity and flinty aromas, and a crisp, well-balanced palate. An excellent wine to serve with seafood.

🔑 GAEC Dom. La Fadèze, 34340 Marseillan, tel. 04.67.77.26.42, fax 04.67.77.20.92 ☑ Y ev. day except Sun. 9am–12 noon 2pm–7pm

DOM. DE MOULINES Merlot 2000★

■ 10.8 ha 110,000 ▮ ♁ €3–5

This estate has been owned by the same family since 1914; the third generation is now managing the vineyards. Its dark-purple Merlot has an enticing aroma of ripe fruits. The palate is firm, fruity and well structured, and has a good length of flavour.

🔑 Michel Saumade, GFA Mas de Moulines, 34130 Mudaison, tel. 04.67.70.20.48, fax 04.67.87.50.05 ☑ Y ev. day except Sun. 9am–12 noon 2pm–7pm

DOM. DE PETIT ROUBIE L'Arbre Blanc 1999★

■ 1.5 ha 10,000 ◖◗ €8–11

Olivier Azan, who has owned this estate for 20 years, cultivates his vineyards organically. His pure Syrah wine is an attractive dark-garnet colour, and has a rich, complex nose of spice (vanilla, caramel), and damp woodlands. Silky tannins balance the palate.

🔑 Olivier Azan, EARL Les dom. de Petit Roubié, BP 4, 34850 Pinet, tel. 04.67.77.09.28, fax 04.67.77.76.26, e-mail roubie@club-internet.fr ☑
Y by appt.

DOM. DU POUJOL La Bête Noire 1998★

■ 2 ha 9,000 ◖◗ €8–11

The Bête Noire 98 is a 50–50 blend of Carignan and Cabernet Sauvignon that has been barrel-aged for 16 months. A bright, rich, ruby-red colour, it has a complex aroma of ripe fruits and forest undergrowth. The long and structured palate is beautifully well balanced. This wine is ready to drink now, but will also repay cellaring.

🔑 Dom. du Poujol, rte de Grabels, 34570 Vailhauquès, tel. 04.67.84.47.57, fax 04.67.84.43.50, e-mail cripps.poujol@wanadoo.fr ☑ Y by appt.

Hauterive

DOM. DE CRUSCADES 1999★

■ 3 ha 20,000 ▮ ◖◗ ♁ €5–8

This estate has recently been bought by an agronomist returning from an extended stay in China. Judging from this wine, his first vintage, his decision to become a wine-maker was a good one. The dark-ruby 99 with purple highlights has an aroma of flowers and red berries. A substantial and structured palate helps to make this a well-balanced wine.

🔑 Régis Loevenbruck, 2, rue de la République, 11200 Cruscades, tel. 04.68.27.68.88, fax 04.68.27.16.56, e-mail loevenbruck@terre-net.fr ☑
Y by appt.

Coteaux des Fenouillèdes

DOM. SALVAT Fenouill 2000★★

■ 15 ha 48,000 ▮ ♁ €3–5

This is a blend of Merlot (50%), Syrah (40%) and Grenache from the Pays Cathare. A bright ruby colour, it has a rich, complex garrigue and caramel nose, and an equally expressive, very flavourful palate. The Fenouill 2000 is ready to drink now.

🔑 Dom. J.-Ph. Salvat, 8, av. Jean-Moulin, 66220 Saint-Paul-de-Fenouillet, tel. 04.68.59.29.00, fax 04.68.59.20.44, e-mail salvat.jp@wanadoo.fr ☑ Y ev. day except Sat. Sun. 10am–12 noon 2pm–6pm

Catalan

DOM. DU MAS ROUS Cabernet Sauvignon Elevé en Fût de Chêne 1998★

■ 2.5 ha 14,000 €5-8

The current owner's great-grandfather was blond, or *'ros'* in Catalan. Hence *el Mas del ros* or *le Mas du Rous*, the blond man's house, later shortened to *le Mas Rous*. The purple Cabernet Sauvignon 98, with its aroma of ripened red berries and heady palate, is a very appealing, well-balanced wine.

☎ José Pujol, Dom. du Mas Rous, 66740 Montesquieu-des-Albères, tel. 04.68.89.64.91, fax 04.68.89.80.88 ⍁ by appt.

DOM. MOSSE Carignan 1998★

■ 3.25 ha 5,000 €8-11

This garnet-coloured Carignan with purple highlights, has a lightly spicy, overripe red-berry aroma, and a well-balanced palate. Its silky tannins are very appealing.

☎ Jacques Mossé, Ch. Mossé, BP 8, 66301 Ste-Colombe-de-la-Commanderie, tel. 04.68.53.08.89 fax 04.68.53.35.13, e-mail chateau.mosse@worldonline.fr ☑

Côtes Catalanes

DOM. BOUDAU Le Petit Closi 2000★★

■ 4 ha 15,000 €3-5

Siblings Véronique and Pierre Boudau are the third generation of this family to run the estate. Their bright, blush-pink rosé has a fruity aroma and a fresh yet full, well-balanced palate. This is a very elegant wine.

☎ Dom. Véronique et Pierre Boudau, 6, rue Marceau, BP 60, 66602 Rivesaltes, tel. 04.68.64.45.37, fax 04.68.64.46.26 ☑ ⍁ ev. day except Sun. 10am–12 noon 3pm–7pm from Jun. to mid-Sep.

DOM. DE MARTINOLLES Pinot Noir Grande Réserve 1999★

■ 1.3 ha 4,300

An aroma of ripened red berries wafts from this ruby-red Pinot Noir. It is a heady wine with a well-balanced palate, and mature, integrated tannins.

☎ Vignobles Vergnes, Dom. de Martinolles, 11250 Saint-Hilaire, tel. 04.68.69.41.93, fax 04.68.69.45.97, e-mail martinolles@wanadoo.fr ☑ ⍁ ev. day except Sat. Sun. 8am–12 noon 1.30pm–6.30pm; groups by appt.

Cévennes

DOM. DE BARUEL Cuvée Fontanilles 1998★★

■ 1.5 ha 4,000 €15-23

This estate, renowned for its truffles, dates back to the wars of the Camisards (Huguenot rebels) in the early 18th century. The dark, gleaming 98 is thus the product of a centuries-long wine-making tradition. The wine's complex, rich, leathery, fruity nose is still a little closed. The palate is full, very concentrated and beautifully structured. This wine should be cellared for a few more years.

☎ SCEA Baruel, Dom. de Baruel, 30140 Tornac, tel. 04.66.77.58.52 ☑ ⍁ by appt.

☞ Coudène

DOM. DE GOURNIER Chardonnay 2000★

□ 5 ha 35,000 €3-5

This bright Chardonnay, with green highlights, has an expressive aroma of honey and white flowers. The well-balanced palate is lightly oaked, and has a good length of flavour. The Jury also awarded one star to the estate's **Sauvignon 99**.

☎ SCEA Barrouin, Dom. de Gournier, 30190 Sainte-Anastasie, tel. 04.66.81.20.28, fax 04.66.81.22.43 ☑ ⍁ by appt.

Coteaux d'Ensérune

PUECH AURIOL 2000★

■ 0.5 ha 1,600 €3-5

A blend dominated by Grenache (30%) and Carignan (20%) grapes, whose vines grow around Béziers in chalky soils derived from fossilised oyster shells. Grape and *terroir* together have produced a bright, fruity rosé with a fresh, very well-balanced palate.

☎ Stéphane Yerle, La Courtade, rte de Capestang, 34500 Béziers, mob. 06.14.03.21.83, fax 04.67.28.30.68, e-mail la-cepa@wanadoo.fr ☑ ⍁ by appt.

Aude

Cassan

Depending on soil and climate conditions, they are blended either with unusual, old-fashioned local varieties such as the Counoise and Roussanne of Var, or with varieties associated with other wine-growing regions, such as the Cabernet Sauvignon and Merlot of Bordeaux, and the Syrah grape of the Rhône Valley. The following designations are based on *départements*: Vaucluse, Bouches-du-Rhône, Var, Alpes-de-Haute-Provence, Alpes-Maritimes and Hautes-Alpes. Principauté d'Orange, Petite Crau (south-east of Avignon), Mont Caumes (west of Toulon), Argens (between Brignoles and Draguignan, in Var), Maures, Coteaux du Verdon (Var), Ile de Beauté (Corsica) and the recently-recognised Aigues (Vaucluse), are sub-regional or local designations.

DOM. SAINTE MARTHE
Syrah Elevé en Fût 2000★

n.c.   n.c.   €3-5

The dark garnet-coloured wine makes an immediate impression with its powerful, oaky, toasted aromas. Full-bodied and long on the palate, it is as solidly-structured as a Roman church. This wine will repay cellaring; ideally, six months to a year.
➤ Olivier Bonfils, Dom. de Sainte-Marthe, rte Pouzolles, 34320 Roujan, tel. 04.67.93.10.10, fax 04.67.93.10.05

Coteaux du Libron

DOM. LA COLOMBETTE
Lledoner Pelut 1998★

3 ha   10,000   €11-15

The Lledoner Pelut is a Spanish grape variety (*Garnacha Peluda*) that is rarely grown in France. It has been made into an extremely well-balanced, dark-red 98 with warm highlights. Elegant, oaky, toasty vanilla notes are perceptible on the subtle nose. On the palate, it is both structured and complex, with a good length of flavour. While this wine is ready for drinking now, it will benefit from up to a year in the cellar.
➤ François Pugibet, Dom. de La Colombette, anc. rte de Bédarieux, 34500 Béziers, tel. 04.67.31.05.53, fax 04.67.30.46.65 ✉ ☎ ev. day 8am–12 noon 2pm–7pm

Ile de Beauté

DOM. AGJHE VECCHIE
Vecchio Chardonnay 2000★★★

0.83 ha   2,000   €5-8

Provence, Basse Vallée du Rhône, Corsica

The bulk of the wines produced by this vast zone are red; they constitute 70% of the 700,000 hl (18.5 million gal) yield of the Provence-Alpes-Côte d'Azur administrative region. The rosés (25%) are mostly made in Var, and the whites are the product of Vaucluse and the area north of the Bouches-du-Rhône. Although a wide range of the southern grape varieties are grown here, they are rarely made into varietal wines.

This wine has been oak-aged for nine months. Although it will reach full maturity after another year or two in the cellar, it is already an extremely attractive wine. In the glass, it shines with golden highlights, and has an intense aroma of butter and hazelnuts. On the palate, it is powerful and long. The distinctive morello-cherry aromas of the **Vecchio Pinot Noir 2000** earned one star from the Jury.
➤ Jacques Giudicelli, 20230 Canale di Verde, tel. 04.09.50.73.36, fax 04.95.38.03.37, e-mail jerome.girard@attglobal.net ✉ ☎ by appt.

DOM. DU MONT SAINT-JEAN

Aleatico 2000★

| 7 ha | 30,000 | €3-5 |

The Aleatico is a dark-berried Italian grape variety occasionally grown in Corsica. The slightly musky-tasting grapes, which are also quite nice to eat, have been made into a clear, fruity and floral, light-red wine. Modest tannins add definition to the clean-tasting palate.

➤ SCA du Mont Saint-Jean, Campo Quercio, 20270 Aleria, tel. 04.95.38.59.96, fax 04.95.38.50.29, e-mail roger-pouyau@wanadoo.fr ☎ ▾ by appt.
➤ Roger Pouyau

A TORRA 2000★★

| 50 ha | 30,000 | €3 |

A pale, clear, salmon-pink colour, this rosé has an elegant spicy-fruit aroma. The aromas of the nose are echoed on the fresh, long, well-balanced palate.

➤ Cavec coop. d'Aghione, Samuleto, 2070 Aghione, tel. 04.95.56.60.20, fax 04.95.56.61.27 ▾ ☎ ev. day except Sat. Sun. 8am–12 noon 2pm–6pm

---

GASPA MORA 2000★

| 20 ha | 200,000 | €3 |

The Saint-Antoine co-operative's Gaspa Mora rosé 2000 impressed the Jury, but this red is even better. A rich garnet colour with a delicate fruity aroma, it is well balanced and firm, with a good length of flavour.

➤ Coop. Saint-Antoine, 20240 Ghisonaccia, tel. 04.95.56.61.00, fax 04.95.56.61.60 ▾ ☎ by appt.

DOM. DE LISCHETTO

Chardonnay 2000★★★

| 60 ha | 140,000 | €5-8 |

The vineyards of the La Marana co-operative's 60-ha (148-acre) Lischetto estate are planted on clay-schist soil. The Chardonnay 2000, although it is not a *coup de cœur* like the previous vintage, is still an exceptional wine. The clear, straw-yellow wine has the buttery, creamy aromas typical of a Chardonnay. It is well balanced and fresh on the palate.

➤ Cave coop. de La Marana, Rasignani, 20290 Borgo, tel. 04.95.38.40.01, fax 04.95.38.81.10, e-mail uval.sica@wanadoo.fr ☎ ▾ ev. day except Sun. 9am–12 noon 3pm–7pm

---

MODERATO 2000

| 33 ha | 104,000 | €8-11 |

Made from the partially-fermented must of small-berried Muscat grapes, this unusual wine has 100 g/l of residual sugar. It has the characteristic honeyed and grapey aromas of Muscat, and a clean, rich palate.

➤ Jean-Bernardin Casablanca, 20230 Bravone, tel. 04.95.38.81.91, fax 04.95.38.81.91 ☎ by appt.

MONTE E MARE 2000★★

| 20 ha | 210,000 | €3 |

This ruby-coloured wine has been made from Niellucciu grapes, blended with a small quantity (20%) of Merlot. An expressive, fruity aroma is echoed by the flavours on the palate. The wine is fresh and supple, with moderate tannins.

➤ Coop. Saint-Antoine, 20240 Ghisonaccia, tel. 04.95.56.61.00, fax 04.95.56.61.60 ▾ ☎ by appt.

DOM. TERRA VECCHIA 2000★★★

| n.c. | n.c. | €8-11 |

The Terra Vecchia estate has made a wine of distinction in each colour. The **Terra Vecchia Merlot 2000** and **rosé 2000** were awarded one star each, but this Chardonnay and Vermentino blend earned the highest marks. It has a powerful, yet delicate, floral aroma and a very expressive, well-balanced fleshy palate. Delicious with seafood.

➤ SICA Coteaux de Diana, Les vins Skalli, Dom. Terra Vecchia, 20270 Tallone, tel. 04.95.57.20.30, fax 04.95.57.08.98

PRATICCIOLI 2000★

| 6 ha | n.c. | €3 |

The 14-ha (35-acre) estate has granitic soils. Its pale, garnet-coloured wine is still rather youthful, but is pleasant and promising.

➤ GFA de Praticcioli, Linguizzetta, 20230 San Nicolao, tel. 04.95.38.86.38, fax 04.95.38.94.71 ☎ by appt.

VIGNERONS DES PIEVE Cabernet

Sauvignon Cuvée San Michelone 1999★★

| 50 ha | 50,000 | €5-8 |

The concentrated style of this wine, which has been aged in barrel for eight months, is immediately apparent from its dark-ruby colour, and powerful aroma of spicy, black fruits. The palate is supple, despite its concentrated substance, and has a good length of flavour.

➤ Uval, Rasignani, 20290 Borgo, tel. 04.95.58.44.00, fax 04.95.38.10, e-mail uval.sica@wanadoo.fr ☎ by appt.

VIGNERONS DES PIEVE

Cabernet Sauvignon Terra Mariana 2000★★

| 100 ha | 150,000 | €3 |

The Jury selected two reds from the Terra Mariana range of wines. The **Terra Mariana Merlot 2000** earned one star. It is an appealing, well-balanced wine whose aromas are still a little restrained. This garnet-coloured Cabernet Sauvignon is rich and aromatic, with a supple and fruity, well-balanced palate.

➤ Uval, Rasignani, 20290 Borgo, tel. 04.95.58.44.00, fax 04.95.38.10, e-mail uval.sica@wanadoo.fr ☎ by appt.

Principauté d'Orange

TERRA VECCHIA

Vermentino 2000★★★

☐   n.c.   ■ ◆ n.c.   **€3-5**

This exceptional wine has the distinctive character of the Vermentino grape, native to Corsica and Sardinia. The nose is perfumed with white flowers, and it has a fleshy and well-balanced palate.

•➥ SICA Coteaux de Diana, Les vins Skalli, Dom. Terra Vecchia, 20270 Tallone, tel. 04.95.57.20.30, fax 04.95.57.08.98

DOM. DANIEL ET DENIS ALARY★

La Grange 2000★

☐   5 ha   30,000   ■ ◆ **€5-8**

This is a balanced and elegant wine made from grapes grown in pebbly soils. It has a rich garnet colour with mauve highlights, and a jammy red-berry aroma. The full-bodied palate has well-integrated tannins, and reveals fruity and spicy flavours on a long finish.

•➥ Dom. Daniel et Denis Alary, La Font d'Estévenas, rte de Rasteau, 84290 Cairanne, tel. 04.90.30.82.32, fax 04.90.30.74.71 ✔ ▼ ev. day except Sun. 8am–12 noon 2pm–7pm

Petite Crau

CAPRICE DE LAURE 2000★★

■   n.c.   66,000   **€3**

This is a dark-red Merlot–Cabernet Sauvignon blend. It has jammy, toasted aromas, and a full-bodied palate, which is well-structured and attractive. In a year's time it will have matured fully, and become even more enjoyable. Two other **red** wines from the producer received equally high marks: the **Cuvée Prestige 99**, oak-aged for eight months, and the **Cuvée d'Amour 2000**.

•➥ SCA Cellier de Laure, 1, av. agricol-Viala, 13550 Noves, tel. 04.90.94.01.30, fax 04.90.92.94.85 ▼ ▼ ev. day except Sun. 8am–12 noon 2pm–6pm

Portes de Méditerranée

DOM. LA BLAQUE Viognier 2000★★

☐   6 ha   28,000   ■ ◆ **€5-8**

This Viognier has violet-scented aromas, both on the nose and on the palate. An elegant drink from start to finish, it would make a delightful aperitif. It could also partner sweet-and-sour oriental food.

•➥ Gilles Delsuc, Dom. de Châteauneuf, 04860 Pierrevert, tel. 04.92.72.39.71, fax 04.92.72.81.26, e-mail domaine.lablaque@wanadoo.fr ▼ ▼ by appt.

Mont-Caume

DOM. DU PEY-NEUF 2000★

☐   2 ha   12,000   ■ ◆ **€3-5**

This appealing wine is made up of 30% Rolle (also known as Vermentino) grapes, blended with Clairette and Ugni Blanc. Pale-yellow with green highlights, it has fruity aromas of quince, pear and apricot on both nose and palate. It is a charming and slightly sweet wine. The Jury also singled out this producer's **red Domaine du Pey-Neuf 2000**, which is aged both in vats and in barrels.

•➥ Guy Arnaud, Dom. du Pey-Neuf, 367, rte de Sainte-Anne, 83740 La Cadière-d'Azur, tel. 04.94.90.14.55, fax 04.94.26.13.89 ▼ ▼ by appt.

LE VIOGNIER DU PESQUIE 2000

☐   3.5 ha   14,000   ■ ◆ **€5-8**

This year the Château Pesquié has expanded its range of wines to include a pure Viognier in this newly-created (1999) regional denomination. The result appealed to the Jury. The pale-yellow 2000 with green highlights has an intense apricot aroma. Its equally fruity palate is luscious, yet lively, and ends on a spicy note.

•➥ GAEC Ch. Pesquié, rte de Flassan, BP 6, 84570 Mormoiron, tel. 04.90.61.94.08, fax 04.90.61.94.13, e-mail pesquier@infonie.fr ▼ ▼ by appt.

•➥ Chaudière Bastide

Vaucluse

CANORGUE Chardonnay 2000
□ 1 ha · 2.600 · €8-11

The requirement for anonymity during the judging meant that the tasters were unable to appreciate this wine's elegant label. Instead, they selected the refreshing Chardonnay because of its floral nose, and its plump palate, with apple and pear flavours, and a lingering finish.

DOM. DE LA CITADELLE
Chardonnay 2000★
□ 1.3 ha · 8.000 · €5-8

This Chardonnay has a seductive floral nose, with hints of pear-drops. Its silky palate has dainty floral flavours accented with banana. The Viognier 2000 from the Domaine de La Citadelle also earned one star for its floral aroma, and unctuous, apricot-flavoured palate.
● Yves Rousset-Rouard, Dom. de La Citadelle, 84560 Paris, tel. 04.90.72.41.58, fax 04.90.72.41.59, e-mail citadelle@paewan.fr ☑ ▼ ev. day 9am–12 noon 2pm–6pm; cl. Sun. in winter

DOM. DE LA BASTIDONNE
Viognier 2000★
□ 1.5 ha · 3.000 · €5-8

This wine has an attractive straw-gold colour, and a delicious floral scent, but it is the opulent apricot and nectarine-flavoured palate that really makes it special. This is a distinctive, well-made wine.
● SCEA Dom. de La Bastidonne, 84220 Cabrières-d'Avignon, tel. 04.90.76.70.00, fax 04.90.76.74.34 ☑
▼ ev. day except Sun. 9am–12 noon 2pm–6pm
● Gérard Marreau

Maures

DOM. DE L'ANGLADE 2000
□ 4 ha · 12.500 · €5-8

This is a pale rosé wine made from a blend of Cinsaut and Grenache grapes. It has pronounced red-berry aromas, with discreet notes of boiled sweets. The flavours are fruity, with a warm finish. The Jury also singled out the estate's vat-aged Merlot 2000.
● Bernard Van Doren, Dom. de l'Anglade, av. Vincent-Auriol, 83980 Le Lavandou, tel. 04.94.71.10.89, fax 04.94.15.15.88 ☑
▼ by appt.

DOM. DE L'ESPARRON Syrah 2000
■ 2 ha · 10.000 · €3

There were few Syrah wines in the Vins de Pays tastings, since the variety is mostly used to make blended wines in the Var region. This one caught the Jury's attention because it has all of the hallmarks of this Rhône grape variety: liquorice aromas, good structure and integrated tannins. The Cabernet Sauvignon 2000 from the same estate was also singled out.
● EARL Migliore, Dom. de l'Esparron, 83590 Gonfaron, tel. 04.94.78.32.23, fax 04.94.78.24.85 ☑
▼ ev. day 8am–12 noon 1.30pm–7.30pm

DOM. DE REILLANNE
Plan Genet 2000★
■ 7 ha · 60.000 · €3

This wine is made from a blend of Cinsault and Tibouren grapes. Legend has it that Tibouren vines were first brought to the Golfe de Saint-Tropez in the 18th century, by a naval captain called Antiboul. The variety continues to be appreciated for the delicacy it imparts to rosé wines. It is floral on both nose and palate, and has an elegant finish.
● Comte G. de Chevron Villette, Ch. Reillanne, rte de Saint-Tropez, 83340 Le Cannet-des-Maures, tel. 04.94.50.11.70, fax 04.94.47.92.06 ☑ ▼ ev. day except Sat. Sun. 8am–12 noon 2pm–5pm

Vaucluse

● EARL Jean-Pierre et Martine Margan, Ch. La Canorgue, 84480 Bonnieux, tel. 04.90.75.81.01, fax 04.90.75.82.98, e-mail chateaucanorgue.margan@wanadoo.fr ☑ ▼ by appt.

DOM. DE COMBEBELLE 2000
□ 4 ha · 2.500 · €3-5

A portion of this estate in the Vaucluse region, giving the owner the right to use the denomination for this pale-pink rosé wine. Red-berry aromas and a hint of dill are found on the nose. The wine is so rounded that it slips across the tongue. Serve this wine with grilled meats (beef or lamb).
● Eric Sauvan, EARL Dom. de Combebelle, 26110 Piegon, tel. 04.75.27.18.96, fax 04.75.27.15.62 ☑
▼ ev. day except Sun. 9am–12.15pm

DORE DE FENOUILLET
Muscat à Petits Grains 2000
□ 0.5 ha · 5.600 · €5-8

Only small-berried Muscat grapes could have produced this golden wine. Modern vinification techniques have helped to create a wine with an enticing grapey aroma, a rich palate and a soft, sweet finish. This is a dessert wine, par excellence.
● GAEC Patrick et Vincent Soard, Dom. de Fenouillet, allée Saint-Roch, 84190 Beaumes-de-Venise, tel. 04.90.62.95.61, fax 04.90.62.90.67, e-mail pv.soard@freesbee.fr ☑ ▼ by appt.

DOM. DE LA VERRIERE
Viognier Elevé en Fût de Chêne 2000 ▦ €5-8

Six months in the barrel have added a subtle vanilla scent to the citrus-fruit aromas of this wine. It is unctuous on the palate, and marked by the liquorice and crystallised apricot flavours that distinguish a Viognier. Serve this wine with a salmon steak, that has been grilled and then caramelised using a teaspoon of sugar.

Jacques Maubert, Dom. de La Verrière, 84220 Goult, tel. 04.90.72.20.88; fax 04.90.72.40.33, e-mail laverriere2@wanadoo.fr ☒ ▼ ev. day except Sun. 9am–12 noon 2pm–6pm

DOM. LES CONQUES-SOULIERE
Chardonnay 2000★ ▮ €3-5

This is a very beguiling Chardonnay. A ripe banana nose is followed by a rich, almost voluptuous palate, tasting of cooked fruit (apples, bananas). A delightful freshness appears at the finish. It would complement any grilled fish.

GAEC Lanchier-Degioanni, bd du nord, 84160 Cucuron, tel. 04.90.77.20.87, fax 04.90.77.15.29 ☒

DOM. DE MAROTTE 2000 €5-8
■ 5.8 ha 24,000 ▮ ◆

Three Rhône Valley grape varieties (Grenache Blanc, Viognier, Roussanne) have been blended to create a pale-yellow wine. While the aromas on the nose are floral (hyacinth), the palate tastes of apples and pears. This is a fleshy wine, making it a perfect accompaniment for chicken breasts or fish.

EARL La Reynarde, Dom. de Marotte, ptit chem. de Serres, 84200 Carpentras, tel. 04.90.63.43.27, fax 04.90.67.15.28, e-mail marotte@wanadoo.fr ☒ ▼ by appt.
Van Dykman

DOM. MEILLAN-PAGES
Viognier 2000★ ▮ €5-8
■ 0.34 ha 3,000 ▮ ◆

In the last edition of the Guide, Jean-Pierre Pagès's Sauvignon was selected as a coup de coeur. This year, he has made a well-developed, straw-yellow Viognier with golden highlights. It has an intense, floral and dried-apricot nose. Similar flavours appear on the fleshy palate, confirming the wine's elegant style. There is a subtle note of crystallised ginger on the finish. This wine is for drinking now.

Jean-Pierre Pagès, Quartier La Garrigue, 84580 Oppède, tel. 04.90.76.94.78; fax 04.90.76.94.78 ▼ ev. day 10am–8pm

DOM. DU VIEUX CHENE
Cuvée de la Dame Vieille 2000 ▮ €5-8
■ 2 ha 13,000

The old Grenache vines that have produced this wine have strongly influenced the taste of the wine. It has a spicy leather and prune nose, and a chewy palate whose tannins should mature over the next twelve months. This would be a good wine to serve with a standing rib roast.

Jean-Claude et Béatrice Bouché, rte de Vaison-la-Romaine, rue Buisseron, 84850 Camaret-sur-Aigues, tel. 04.90.37.25.07, fax 04.90.37.76.84, e-mail contact@bouche-duvieuxchene.com ☒ ▼ ev. day except Sun. 9am–12 noon 2pm–6pm

DOM. DE BEAULIEU Syrah 2000★ ▮ €3
■ 10 ha 80,000 ▮ ◆

The powerful old-rose aromas of this rosé are even more arresting than its deep pink colour. On the palate, it is rich, warming and well balanced with a good length of flavour. Serve this wine with a vegetable *tian* or as an aperitif, with toast spread with *tapenade* or *caviar d'aubergine*.

Ch. de Beaulieu, 13840 Rognes, tel. 04.42.50.13.72, fax 04.42.50.19.53 ▼ ev. day except Sun. Mon. 9am–12 noon 2pm–5pm

DOM. HOUCHART
Syrah-Cabernet 2000★ ▮ €3
■ 3 ha 15,000 ▮ ◆

At present, this attractive dark-red wine with violet highlights has a slightly restrained nose, but it should develop fully within the year. Initially supple, then firm and tightly-knit, the elegant palate has a particularly good length of flavour. A fine Cabernet Sauvignon–Syrah blend, which will accompany vegetable *gratins* or grilled meats.

Vignobles Jérôme Quiot, av. Baron-Le-Roy, 84231 Châteauneuf-du-Pape, tel. 04.90.83.73.55, fax 04.90.83.78.48, e-mail vignobles@jeromequiot.com ▼ by appt.

DOM. LA MICHELLE 2000 ▮ €5-8
■ 1.5 ha 8,000 ▮ ◆

The rosé 2000 is the first vintage produced by this estate. A pure Grenache, it is a rather dainty wine with a pale pink colour, fruity nose and soft palate. It is ready now for drinking with light meals.

Les Vignerons du Garlaban, 8, chem. Saint-Pierre, 13390 Auriol, tel. 04.42.04.70.70, fax 04.42.72.89.49 ▼ by appt.

DOM. DE L'ILE SAINT PIERRE

2000

30 ha — 30,000 — €3

Pale gold with green highlights, this wine has an elegant floral and exotic-fruit nose, with a subtle Muscat overtone (Muscat grapes account for 15% of this blend, which is dominated by Chardonnay and Sauvignon Blanc). On the palate, it is complex and full-bodied, but not heavy, and has the warming finish often found in southern wines. An excellent match with grilled fish.

Marie-Cécile et Patrick Henry, Dom. de l'Isle-Saint-Pierre, 13104 Mas Thibert, tel. 04.90.98.70.30, fax 04.90.98.74.93

by appt.

DOM. L'OPPIDUM DES CAUVINS

Cassus 2000★

n.c. — 25,000 — €3

A blend of Grenache, Syrah and Cabernet Sauvignon grapes has produced a well-balanced wine that gleams with purple highlights. The red-berry aromas of the nose harmonize with the flavours on the palate, which is structured by supple tannins. The Sauvignon 2000 was also awarded one star.

Rémy Ravaute, Dom. l'Oppidum des Cauvins, 13840 Rognes, tel. 04.42.50.13.85, fax 04.42.50.29.40

by appt.

DOM. DE LUNARD

Cabernet Sauvignon 1999★

3.5 ha — 15,000 — €5-8

This Cabernet Sauvignon, with brick-red highlights, has been barrel-aged for 12 months. It has an aroma of leather and forest undergrowth, and a subtly-oaked, jammy palate with a warm finish. The Sélection 2000 rosé, a blend of Grenache and Caladoc grapes, was also awarded one star by the Jury.

EARL Dom. de Lunard, 13140 Miramas, tel. 04.90.50.93.44, fax 04.90.50.73.27

ev. day 9am–12 noon 3pm–7pm

MAS DE LONGCHAMP 2000★

22 ha — 40,000 — €3

The richly-coloured rosé wine is extremely rounded on the palate. The nose may still be a little closed, but the potential is already evident. This would be the perfect wine to serve with a Provençal dish.

SCIEV, Quartier de la Gare, BP 17, 13940 Mollèges, tel. 04.90.95.19.06, fax 04.90.95.42.00

ev. day except Sun. 9am–12 noon 2pm–6pm

MAS DE REY Caladoc 2000★

10 ha — 20,000 — €5-8

The Caladoc grape variety, a crossing of Grenache Noir and Malbec/Côt, gets its name from the fusion of Galabert (a lake in the Bouches-de-Rhône) and Languedoc. It is used to make elegant rosé wines like this bright-pink 2000. A long and supple palate follows the nose with a hint of confected fruit. The Jury also awarded one star to the complex white Chasan 2000, with its unusual, exotic aromas.

M. Mazzoleni, SCA Mas de Rey, Trinquetaille, 13200 Arles, tel. 04.90.96.11.84, fax 04.90.96.59.44, e-mail mas.de.rey@provnet.fr

ev. day 9am–12 noon 2pm–7pm; cl. Sun. from Nov. until Mar.

LES VIGNERONS DE MISTRAL

Cuvée Notre Dame 2000★

50 ha — n.c. — €3-5

This is a well-balanced wine. Caladoc (70%) and Syrah (30%) grapes have been vinified apart before being blended to make a red-berry-scented 2000 with a supple palate. Enjoy this wine with a *gardiane*, a stew made with the meat of a Gard bull from the Camargue. (Other rich, meaty dishes would be equally appropriate.)

Les Vignerons de Mistral, av. de Sylvanes, 13130 Berre l'Etang, tel. 04.42.85.40.11, fax 04.42.74.12.55

ev. day except Sun. 9am–12 noon 2pm–6pm

LES VIGNERONS DU ROY RENE

Cabernet Sauvignon 2000

5 ha — 20,000 — €3

The enticing cherry-red wine with violet highlights has a very expressive, gamey nose. Notes of blackcurrant appear as the wine is swirled in the glass, and the palate is supple and firm. This would be the perfect wine for a barbecue.

Les Vignerons du Roy René, RN 7, 13410 Lambesc, tel. 04.42.57.00.20, fax 04.42.92.91.52

by appt.

DOM. DE VALDITION

Tête de Cuvée 2000★

4 ha — 7,000 — €3-5

This pale-gold Macabeu and Chasan blend has a subtle bouquet of soft, mossy aromas. Firm acidity introduces the delicate palate, which is complex, rich and well balanced. The mineral flavours that emerge on the finish make this wine a particularly appetizing match with seafood.

GFA Valdition, Dom. de Valdition, rte d'Eygalières, 13660 Orgon, tel. 04.90.73.08.12, fax 04.90.73.05.95, e-mail valdition@wanadoo.fr

ev. day except Sun. 9am–5.30pm

spices and garrigue. The co-operative's **Cabernet Sauvignon 2000** also earned two stars, while the **Vin de Pays des Maures Cellier de la Crau 2000** made from a Merlot-Carignan blend was judged worthy of one star.

➤ Cellier de La Crau, 35, av. de Toulon, 83260 La Crau, tel. 04.94.66.73.03, fax 04.94.66.17.63 ▼ Ⓨ by appt.

DOM. DE LA GAYOLLE

Chardonnay 2000★ ■ ♦ €5-8

□ 3 ha 12,000

The La Gayolle Chardonnay has a very expressive citrus-fruit (grapefruit and lemon) aroma on both the nose and the palate, and a fine balance of freshness and acidity. Enjoy this wine with prawns or a sole meunière.

➤ Jacques Paul, Dom. de La Gayolle, RN 7, 83170 Brignoles, tel. 04.94.59.10.88, fax 04.94.72.04.34, e-mail gayolle@wanadoo.fr ▼ Ⓨ ev. day 9.30am–12.30pm 2.30pm–7pm in summer

DOM. DE LA LIEUE

Chardonnay 2000 ■ ♦ €5-8

□ 4 ha 20,000

The estate, which covers almost 80 ha (198 acres), cultivates its vineyards organically. Its Chardonnay has a fruity and floral nose. The palate is clean and fresh, fruity and nicely rounded.

➤ Jean-Louis Vial, Ch. La Lieue, rte de Cabasse, 83170 Brignoles, tel. 04.94.69.00.12, fax 04.94.69.47.68, e-mail chateau.la.lieue@wanadoo.fr ▼ Ⓨ ev. day 9am–12.30pm 2pm–7pm

LES VIGNERONS DE LA SAINTE-BAUME

Chardonnay 2000★ ■ ♦ €3-5

□ 5 ha 15,000

Both of the two wines submitted to the Jury by this co-operative were judged worthy of one star. This Chardonnay is bright gold, and smells of citrus fruits and orange flowers. The palate is fresh and firm, with great finesse. The **Syrah 2000** is a rounded, delicious rosé with pear-drop flavours.

➤ Les Vignerons de La Sainte-Baume, rte de Brignoles, 83170 Rougiers, tel. 04.94.80.42.47, fax 04.94.80.40.85 ▼ Ⓨ by appt.

DOM. DE L'ESCARELLE

Cuvée Frédéric Mistral Chardonnay 2000★ ■ ♦ €5-8

□ n.c. 10,000

This pale-yellow Chardonnay has elegant, toasty, citrus-fruit aromas. On the palate, it is well balanced and firm, with attractive toasty, spicy flavours of good length. This wine would be perfect as an aperitif, or to go with a fish terrine.

➤ Dom. de L'Escarelle, 83170 La Celle, tel. 04.94.69.09.98, fax 04.94.69.55.06, e-mail l'escarelle@free.fr ▼ Ⓨ by appt.

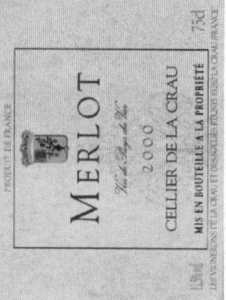

PRODUIT DE FRANCE

MERLOT

2000

CELLIER DE LA CRAU

MIS EN BOUTEILLE A LA PROPRIÉTÉ

75cl

Var

LES CAVES DU COMMANDEUR

Cabernet 2000★★ ■ ♦ €5-8

■ 30 ha 26,000

The Jury awarded the **Merlot 2000** one star, but was even more impressed by this Cabernet Sauvignon. An inky-purple colour, it has subtle aromas of cocoa, herbs and liquorice, and a well-structured palate. This wine will mature nicely for three to five years, but could also be enjoyed now, with beef dishes.

➤ Les caves du Commandeur, 19, Grand-Rue, 83570 Montfort-sur-Argens, tel. 04.94.59.59.02, fax 04.94.59.53.71 ▼ Ⓨ by appt.

LE MAS DES ESCARAVATIERS

2000★ ■ ♦ €3

■ 4.41 ha 30,000

This is an elegant Vin de Pays made from a blend of 70% Cabernet Sauvignon and 30% Carignan grapes. Both varieties give the wine structure and substance. As a result, the well-balanced 2000 has fine, tightly-knit tannins that give the palate a good length of flavour. The wine also has a complex aroma of ripe black fruits and spices.

➤ SCEA Domaines B.-M. Costamagna, Dom. des Escaravatiers, 83480 Puget-sur-Argens, tel. 04.94.19.88.22, fax 04.94.45.59.83, e-mail costam@wanadoo.fr ▼ Ⓨ by appt.

DOM. DE GARBELLE 2000 ■ ♦ €5-8

□ 0.75 ha 2,600

There are not many wines made only from Vermentino grapes. Here is one with a pale-yellow colour and a floral nose of heather and hawthorne. It is well balanced on the palate, and finishes on a fresh, citrus-fruit note. This wine should be served as an aperitif, or alongside grilled fish.

➤ Mathieu Gambini, Dom. de Garbelle, Vieux chemin de Brignoles, 83136 Garéoult, tel. 04.94.04.86.30, fax 04.94.04.86.30 Ⓨ ev. day 8.30am–12 noon 2pm–6.30pm; 7pm in summer

CELLIER DE LA CRAU

Merlot 2000★★ ■ ♦ €3

■ 10 ha 10,000

This rich and concentrated, darkly-coloured Merlot is redolent of cloves, black pepper,

THUERRY

L'Exception Cabernet Sauvignon 2000★

2.5 ha | 11,000 | €8-11

This is a well-crafted Cabernet Sauvignon. The wine has been barrel-aged for ten months, resulting in a spicy, ripe-fruit (black-berry) aroma with a subtle hint of vanilla. Full-bodied and powerful on the palate, it is structured by well-integrated, ripe tannins. This would be a fine match with game.

• SCEA Les Abeillons, Ch. Thuerry, 83690 Villecroze, tel. 04.94.70.63.02, fax 04.94.70.67.03 ☑ Ⓨ by appt.
• Croquet

DOM. DE TRIENNES

Sainte Fleur 2000★★

5.11 ha | n.c. | €8-11

This is a powerful and well-balanced Viognier. Apricots and dried fruits are already showing on the nose, which will develop more fully in a few months' time. Exuberant apple and pear flavours fill the palate, and persist through the long finish. This bottle will make a lovely accompaniment to chicken, veal and pork dishes. The **Domaine de Triennes** *vin gris* 2000, a Cinsault rosé that was deemed worthy of one star, is also worth sampling.

• Dom. de Triennes, RN 560, 83860 Nans-les-Pins, tel. 04.94.78.91.46, fax 04.94.78.65.04, e-mail triennes@triennes.com ☑ Ⓨ by appt.
• J. Seysses

VAL D'IRIS Cabernet Sauvignon 2000★★

3.35 ha | 6,500 | €5-8

The Jury was unanimous in its appreciation of this rich and complex wine. Its enticing dark purple-red colour leads on to a spicy, green-pepper and black fruit nose. The palate is firm and generous, with velvety tannins. This Cabernet Sauvignon is ready to drink

Alpes-de-Haute-Provence

now, but may also be cellared for two to three years.

• Anne Dor, Val d'Iris, chem. de la Combe, 83340 Seillans, tel. 04.94.76.97.66, fax 04.94.76.89.83, e-mail valdiris@wanadoo.fr ☑ Ⓨ by appt.

Hautes-Alpes

DOM. ALLEMAND 2000

2 ha | 12,000 | €3-5

Although it does not say so on the label, this wine has been made from small-berried Muscat grapes. Delicate spicey-grape aromas are present on the nose, while the palate has a more flowery character. This rounded wine would make a pleasant aperitif.

• EARL Allemand et Fils, La Plaine de Théus, 05190 Théus, tel. 04.92.54.04.20, fax 04.92.54.41.50 ☑ ev. day except Sun. 9am–12 noon 2pm–6pm

LA VALSERROISE 2000

10 ha | 14,000 | €3

The Mollard is a common red-wine grape in the Hautes-Alpes, but it makes up only 10% of this blend, which is dominated by Cabernet Sauvignon and Merlot. Red with purple highlights, it has a distinctive, clean and powerful aroma. The lively palate is very youthful. Try serving this wine as an accompaniment to cured Alpine sausages.

• Cave La Valserroise, 05130 Valserres, tel. 04.92.54.33.02, fax 04.92.54.31.34 ☑ Ⓨ by appt.

Alpes-de-Haute-Provence

LA MADELEINE

Cabernet Sauvignon 2000★★

1.5 ha | 10,000 | €3-5

Judging from the success of this wine, Cabernet Sauvignon vines thrive in the clay-limestone soils of this vineyard, far from their native Bordeaux. The wine has a beautiful, bright, rich-red colour, and a beguiling red-berry aroma. On the palate, it is powerful yet delicate, with a persistent, ripe flavour. The vat-aged **Merlot 2000** from the same producer is also a very remarkable wine that is worth trying.

Alpes-de-Haute-Provence

Alps and Pays Rhodaniens

Stretching from the Auvergne to the Alps, this region includes the eight *départements* of the Rhône-Alpes and the Puy-de-Dôme. Thus the *terroirs* are particularly varied, resulting in a diverse range of regional wines. Burgundy grape varieties (Pinot, Gamay, Chardonnay) and southern varieties (Grenache, Cinsault, Clairette) are all present. They march alongside the regional grapes – Syrah, Roussanne, Marsanne in the Rhône Valley; the Mondeuse, Jacquère and the Chasselas from Savoie; along with Etraire de la Dui and Verdesse, oddities from the Val d'Isère. Bordeaux varieties (Merlot, Cabernet Sauvignon, Sauvignon Blanc) have also been planted, further extending the range of the wines.

Production levels are increasing, approaching 450,000 hl (11.9 million gal), with Ardèche and Drôme making the majority of the red wines. On the whole, each wine is made from just one variety. Ain, Ardèche, Drôme, Isère and Puy-de-Dôme are *département* designations. The eight regional designations are: Allobrogie (Savoie and Ain, 7,000 hl/ 185,000 gal of mostly white wines), Coteaux du Grésivaudan (central Isère Valley, 2,000 hl/53,000 gal), Balmes Dauphinoises (Isère, 1,000 hl/ 26,400 gal), Urfé (Loire Valley between Forez and Roannais, 2,000 hl/53,000 gal), Collines Rhodaniennes (10,000 hl/ 264,000 gal, mostly reds), Comté de Grignan (south-west of Drôme, 25,000 hl/660,000 gal, primarily reds), Coteaux des Baronnies (south-east of Drôme, 35,000 hl/ 924,000 gal of reds) and Coteaux de l'Ardèche (320,000 hl/8.5 million gal, reds, whites and rosés).

In addition, there are two large zonal Vins de Pays designations. The first, Vin de Pays des Comtés Rhodaniens (approximately 25,000 hl/660,000 gal),

● Pierre Bousquet, Cave de la Madeleine, 04130 Volx, tel. 04.92.72.13.91 ▼ ev. day except Sun. 9am–12 noon 2pm–6.30pm

DOM. DE REGUSSE ★★★

Muscat Blanc Moelleux 2000 ★★★

☐ | 15 ha | 30,000 | ■ | ♦ | €5–8

This *vin moelleux* is filled with delicate Muscat aromas: orange-flowers and spice. Elegant and balanced, this is a superb wine that would be perfect with a piece of Roquefort cheese. The Domaine de Régusse also impressed the Jury with its **Chardonnay Vieilli en Fût de Chêne 2000.**

● M. Dieudonné, Dom. de Régusse, rte de Bastide-des-Jourdans, 04860 Pierrevert, tel. 04.92.72.30.44, fax 04.92.72.69.08 ▼
▼ ev. day 8am–12 noon 2pm–7pm

DOM. DE ROUSSET Viognier 2000 ★★

☐ | 1 ha | 5,000 | ■ | ♦ | €5–8

The bright and limpid Viognier has the classic varietal aroma of violets and apricots. These aromas are echoed on the fleshy, long and very well-balanced palate. This is a wine for drinking as an aperitif, or with fish in a cream sauce.

● Ch. de Rousset, 04800 Gréoux-les-Bains, tel. 04.92.72.62.49, fax 04.92.72.66.50 ▼
▼ ev. day except Sun. 2pm–6.30pm; Sat. by appt.
● H. et R. Emery

was established in 1989. It is made up of the eight Rhône-Alpes *départements* (Ain, Ardèche, Drôme, Isère, Loire, Rhône, Savoie, Haute-Savoie). The second, Vin de Pays des Portes de Méditerranée, established in 1999, includes seven *départements* (Alpes-de-Haute-Provence, Hautes-Alpes, Alpes-Maritimes, Ardèche, Drôme, Var and Vaucluse).

DOM. ROCHE BUISSIERE 2000★

4 ha   5.000   ■   €5-8

This wine was made from a blend of organically-grown Grenache and Syrah grapes. It has an expressive red-berry and green-pepper nose, and an agreeable, but slightly tannic, palate. Try this wine as an accompaniment to *tapenade*.

● Antoine Joly, rte de Vaison, 84110 Faucon, tel. 04.90.46.49.14, fax 04.90.46.49.11 ☑ Y ev. day 10am-12 noon 3.30pm-7.30pm; cl. Nov.-Apr.

Comté de Grignan

DOM. ROCHE BUISSIERE 2000★

1 ha   6.000   ■   €5-8

This wine-maker, who vinifies his harvest with great care, has farmed his vineyards organically for over 20 years. A selectively-harvested, *trié*, blend of 90% Cabernet Sauvignon and 10% Grenache grapes was siphoned off into open vats, so that the cap of skins could be punched down during fermentation, maximising extraction. The resulting richly-coloured wine has a complex, expressive aroma of leather, mushrooms and game, that is echoed on the warm, fleshy and well-structured palate. Try this wine with aged Gouda, or smoked wild-boar ham. This wine will repay several years of cellaring.

● Antoine Joly, rte de Vaison, 84110 Faucon, tel. 04.90.46.49.14, fax 04.90.46.49.11 ☑ Y ev. day 10am-12 noon 3.30pm-7.30pm; cl. Nov.-Apr.

Allobrogie

LE CELLIER DE JOUDIN

Jacquère 2000★

4 ha   40.000   ■   €3

This family estate succeeds in maintaining the quality of its wines year after year. Lovers of the Jacquère grape will adore the brilliant pale-yellow 2000. It has aromas of mineral, vine-blossoms and rhubarb. Lively, and very slightly sparkling, it could inspire shad cooked with sorrel, or a simple *raclette*.

● Pierre Demeure, Le Cellier de Joudin, 73240 Saint-Genix-sur-Guiers, tel. 04.76.31.61.74, fax 04.76.31.61.74 ☑ Y ev. day except Sun. pm. 9am-12 noon 2pm-6pm

Coteaux des Baronnies

Collines Rhodaniennes

DOM. LA ROSIERE Viognier 1999

3.5 ha   10,000   ■   €5-8

Serge Liotaud and his oenologist son Valéry regularly make wines with great character. Their Viognier, barrel-aged for four months, is an attractive golden-yellow colour. Its intense aroma is redolent of dried apricots and toasted almonds, with a hint of blackcurrant leaves. This supple 99 could either be enjoyed as an aperitif, or as an accompaniment to fresh goat's cheese.

● EARL Serge Liotaud et Fils, Dom. La Rosière, 26110 Sainte-Jalle, tel. 04.75.27.30.36, fax 04.75.27.33.69, e-mail vliotaud@yahoo.fr ☑ Y ev. day 9am-7pm

EMMANUEL BAROU

Syrah Cuvée des Vernes 2000★

1 ha   4.000   ■   €5-8

Emmanuel Barou makes wines with character from organically-grown grapes. He has used traditional vinification methods to produce a dark-purple wine, with a leathery, red-berry nose, and a supple palate. Serve this wine as an aperitif.

● Emmanuel Barou, Picardel, 07340 Charnas, tel. 04.75.34.02.13, fax 04.75.34.02.13, e-mail e-barou@club-internet.fr ☑ Y by appt.

Coteaux de l'Ardèche

DOM. POCHON 2000★★

■   4 ha   28,000   ■ ♦   €3-5

This is a beautifully-made Syrah and Merlot blend. The Jury was seduced by its rich-purple colour, and its aroma of cooked red berries, cocoa and tobacco. Its fleshy, full palate is equally pleasing, and has a good length of flavour. Enjoy this well-balanced wine with a chicken liver pâté or grilled peppers.

●┐ Dom. Pochon, Ch. de Curson, 26600 Chanos-Curson, tel. 04.75.07.34.60, fax 04.75.07.30.27 ✓ ▼ by appt.

99, and awarded it a *coup de coeur*. It has crystallised fruit, cocoa and vanilla aromas, and a fleshy and well-structured palate. Two other wines caught the attention of the tasting panel: the **Merlot Cuvée de la Paysage 99** with its jammy red-berry, prune and truffle aromas (two stars), and the reasonably tannic **Prestige 99**, a Merlot, Syrah and Cabernet Sauvignon blend. Either of these wine would be perfect for drinking with a Provençal *daube*.

●┐ Les Vignerons Ardéchois, quartier Chaussy, 07120 Ruoms, tel. 04.75.39.98.00, fax 04.75.39.69.48, e-mail vpc@uvica.fr ✓ ▼ ev. day except Sun. 8am–12 noon 3pm–7pm

Coteaux de l'Ardèche

CAVE COOP. D'ALBA
Pinot Noir 2000★

■   33 ha   75,000   ■■ ♦   €5-8

This co-operative is one of the 27 wine-producers that make up the renowned *Vignerons Ardéchois* group. This wine is made from de-stemmed, manually-harvested grapes, and 35% of this Pinot Noir has then been oak-aged. The colour is garnet-red, with amber notes. It has an intense aroma of morello cherries and vanilla, which is echoed on a smooth and supple palate that is structured by well-integrated tannins. Try this wine with a plate of cured Ardèche sausages.

●┐ Cave coop. d'Alba, La Planchette, 07400 Alba-la-Romaine, tel. 04.75.52.40.23, fax 04.75.52.48.76, e-mail cave.alb@free.fr ✓ ▼ ev. day except Sun. 9am–12 noon 1.30pm–6pm

LES VIGNERONS ARDECHOIS
Syrah Cuvée Prestige 1999★★

■   n.c.   40,000   ▥   €3-5

DOM. DE CHAZALIS Merlot 2000★

■   1.5 ha   5,000   ■ ♦   €3-5

Gérard Champetier has followed family tradition in making this elegant, garnet-coloured Merlot with its delicate red-berry and rose aroma, and rounded, well-balanced palate. Enjoy this with a pigeon *salmis*.

●┐ Champetier, Dom. de Chazalis, 07460 Beaulieu, tel. 04.75.39.32.09, fax 04.75.39.38.81, e-mail chazalis@terre-net.fr ✓ ▼ by appt.

DOM. DE COMBELONGE
Cuvée des Pérèdes 2000★★

■   n.c.   9,500   ▥   €3-5

This vineyard on the Vinezac hillsides consistently produces elegant wines, and this garnet-coloured, pure Cabernet Sauvignon, made from hand-harvested grapes, is no exception. Its has a powerful, cooked-red-berry, cinnamon and vanilla nose. The same flavours are found on the full-bodied, stylish palate. This is a wine for drinking over the next two years with boar sausage, or a stew.

●┐ Denis Manent, Dom. de Combelonge, 07110 Vinezac, tel. 04.75.36.92.54, fax 04.75.36.99.59 ✓ ▼ by appt.

GEORGES DUBOEUF
Viognier Or Blanc 2000★

□   n.c.   40,000   ■   €5-8

Georges Duboeuf's Hameau en Beaujolais, a wine centre and museum in Romanèche-Thorins, has become a required stop for wine-lovers. Besides its AOC wines, the *négociant* also offers this fresh Viognier. Citrus fruit, peach and apricot aromas are all present in a lovely wine that can be served with a cold first course, or with *pélardon*, a local goat's cheese.

●┐ SA Les Vins Georges Dubouf, quartier de la Gare, BP 12, 71570 Romanèche-Thorins, tel. 03.85.35.34.20, fax 03.85.35.34.25, e-mail mcvgd@csi.com ✓ ev. day 9am–6pm at the Hameau en Beaujolais; cl. 1–15 Jan.

CUVEE PRESTIGE
1999

CEPAGE SYRAH
VIN DE PAYS DES
COTEAUX DE L'ARDECHE

Here is further proof, if it were needed, of the huge improvements in wine quality made over the past three decades by this group of 27 co-operatives from the southern Ardèche. The Jury was extremely taken with this Syrah

CAVE LA CEVENOLE
Chatus Cuvée Monnaie d'Or 1999★

10 ha | 8,000 | €5-8

Since 1989, the Rosières co-operative has been striving to rehabilitate the reputation of the Chatus grape, a traditional Ardèche red-wine variety first described by Olivier de Serres in 1599. The 99 perfectly expresses the varietal characteristics of this grape. It is a dark-garnet colour, and has a powerful aroma of macerated red berries, gingerbread and toast. The spicy, well-structured and robust palate has a subtle vanilla flavour, the mark of 16 months in oak barrels. Chewy tannins suggest that this Chatus will continue to mature over the next three to four years. It would complement a *civet of boar*.

➤ Cave coop, La Cévenole, Le Grillou, 07260 Rosières, tel. 04.75.39.52.09, fax 04.75.39.92.30 ☑ ⊤ by appt.

LOUIS LATOUR
Chardonnay Grand Ardèche 1999★★★

50 ha | 250,000 | €8-11

The famous Burgundy *négociant*, Louis Latour, has owned vineyards in Ardèche since 1979. It has made a thoroughly engaging Chardonnay – *a coup de cœur*. Oak-aged for ten months, the wine has a clear, golden-yellow colour and a powerful, elegant bouquet of vanilla, exotic fruits, honey and subtle spices. Wonderfully rounded and fleshy on the palate, it displays honey and ginger-bread flavours that persist in a long and stylish finish. This classy wine epitomises the perfectly-oaked Chardonnay. It should be cellared for two years before being served with turbot in puff pastry or, more casually, roast chicken.

➤ Maison Louis Latour, La Téoule, 07400 Alba-la-Romaine, tel. 04.75.52.45.66, fax 04.75.52.87.99 ☑ ⊤ by appt.

MAS DE BAGNOLS
Cuvée Marjorie 2000★

2 ha | 14,000 | €3-5

This family-owned estate began using its new winery in 1999. The dark-red 2000 has been made from a Merlot-dominated blend. Ripe fruit, cocoa and even strawberry-jam aromas can be found on the nose. It is power-ful and fleshy on the palate, with well-integrated tannins. The Cuvée Marjorie is a well-made wine that would complement a slowly-roasted leg of lamb, or grilled duck breast.

➤ Pierre Mollier, Mas de Bagnols, 07110 Vinezac, tel. 04.75.36.83.10, fax 04.75.36.98.04 ☑ ⊤ ev. day except Sun. 8am–12 noon 2pm–6pm

LES CHAIS DU PONT D'ARC
Chardonnay 2000★

3 ha | 4,000 | €5-8

This co-operative is only 12 km (7.5 miles) down the road from the Grotte Chauvet, a cave famous for its paintings by Paleolithic Man. By allowing the Chardonnay juice to have prolonged skin contact during macera-tion, the co-operative has made a bright, straw-yellow wine that is full of aromas of grapefruits, peaches and mangos. The fresh, rounded and supple 2000 is for enjoying with freshwater fish, or local goat's cheese.

➤ SCA Les Chais du Pont d'Arc, rte de Ruoms, 07150 Vallon-Pont-d'Arc, tel. 04.75.88.02.16, fax 04.75.88.11.50 ☑ ⊤ by appt.

CAVE DE VALVIGNERES
Viognier 2000★

60 ha | 25,000 | €5-8

This is a very fresh and fruity Viognier, made from grapes grown in a spectacular valley. Citrus fruit, peach and apricot aromas combine to make it an agreeable wine that could accompany a cold first course, or fresh goat's cheese.

➤ Cave coop. de Valvignères, quartier Auvergne, 07400 Valvignères, tel. 04.75.52.60.60, fax 04.75.52.60.33, e-mail cavevalvigneres@free.fr ☑ ⊤ ev. day except Sun. 9am–12 noon 1.30pm–6pm

DOM. DE VIGIER **Syrah 2000★**

4 ha | 32,000 | €5-8

This Syrah wine, which has been oak-aged for eight months, is a worthy ambassador for an estate that dates back to 1789. Dark-red with bluish highlights, it has an intense black fruit and rosewood aroma, and a soft and supple blackcurrant, liquorice and vanilla-flavoured palate. The estate's **Cuvée Thomas 2000** is an oak-aged Cabernet Sauvignon-Merlot blend with youthful tannins.

➤ Dupré et Fils, Dom. de Vigier, 07150 Lagorce, tel. 04.75.88.01.18, fax 04.75.37.18.79 ☑ ⊤ by appt.

Drôme

CAVE DE LA VALDAINE
Syrah 2000★★

n.c. | 6,900 | €3

The La Valdaine wine cellar, near Montélimar, has spent years restoring its vineyards and perfecting its vinification tech-niques. With *a coup de cœur* for its Syrah, the co-operative has finally fulfilled its potential.

Saône-et-Loire

SYRAH
Vin de Pays de la Drôme

The shining, dark-garnet Syrah has a red-berry, violet and peony nose that is still a little closed. It is, however, very expressive on the palate, with a firm structure and rich, floral flavours. This 2000 has chewy tannins, and would be a perfect partner for an entrecôte grilled over vine shoots, or a mutton stew. The cellar's stylish Cabernet Sauvignon **rosé 2000** was also singled out by the Jury.

↘ Cave de La Valdaine, rue Marx-Dormoy, 26160 Saint-Gervais-sur-Roubion, tel. 04.75.53.80.08, fax 04.75.53.93.90 ☑
Ⴤ by appt.

VIN DES FOSSILES
Chardonnay 1999★

    □   n.c.   n.c. ▉ ♠   €3–5

This wine is a captivating rich-yellow colour with golden highlights, and has an intense, forward yet elegant, ripe-fruit aroma. Complex flavours emerge on the fresh and opulent palate. The well-made, expressive **Gamay 99 Vieilles Vignes** also impressed the Jury.

↘ Jean-Claude Berthillot, Les Chavannes, 71340 Mailly, tel. 03.85.84.01.23 ☑

HAUT-BRIONNAIS 2000★
 ▉   2.37 ha   16,800   €3–5

Fifty-year-old vines have produced a ruby-coloured wine with a subtle yet fine, red-berry (raspberry, redcurrant) nose. Fruity flavours are also found on the clean and lively palate. A distinctive, enjoyable Gamay, and ready for drinking now.

↘ Les Coteaux du Brionnais, 71340 Mailly, tel. 03.85.84.19.21, fax 03.85.84.19.21 ☑
Ⴤ Sat. 9am–12 noon

Franche-Comté

The East

The vineyards of this region, having been decimated by the phylloxera epidemic of the 1860s, now produce only small quantities of unusual wines. Before phylloxera, these vineyards basked in the reflected glory of their prestigious neighbours in Burgundy and Champagne. Grape varieties associated with those regions are still cultivated here, complemented by some varieties from Alsace and Jura. In general, wines are made from single varieties, and thus express the character of their grapes: Chardonnay, Pinot Noir, Gamay or Pinot Gris (for rosés). The occasional blend may include Auxerrois, a white variety similar to Pinot Blanc.

Vins de Pays de Franche-Comté, de la Meuse or de l'Yonne are all agreeable, light, fresh, and aromatic wines. Although production is increasing, especially in white wines, at present only 3,000 hl (79,200 gal) are produced each year.

VIGNOBLE GUILLAUME
Pinot Noir Vieilles Vignes 1999★★★

 ▉   3 ha   18,000   ▮▮   €5–8

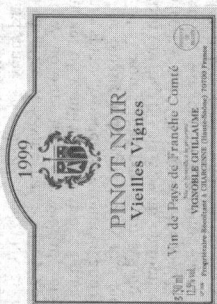

PINOT NOIR
Vieilles Vignes
Vin de Pays de Franche-Comté
VIGNOBLE GUILLAUME

The Vignoble Guillaume consistently produces excellent wines. There were no dissenting votes when its Pinot Noir Vieilles Vignes was selected as a *coup de cœur*. A very bright, attractive, dark-red colour; it has an extremely expressive red-berry Pinot Noir aroma, with a hint of muskiness. The palate is rounded and firm, silky and fruity, and it is balanced by supple tannins on the finish. This wine is ready for drinking now, but will also keep. The **Pinot Noir 99**, the product of younger vines, was awarded one star for its balance and its fine, well-integrated tannins. The powerful, fleshy, well-oaked Chardonnay Vieilles Vignes 99 earned two stars.

↘ Vignoble Guillaume, 70700 Charcenne, tel. 03.84.32.80.55, fax 03.84.32.84.06 ☑
Ⴤ by appt.

E. ET PH. ANTOINE Gris 2000★

2 ha 20,000 €3-5

All three of the wines that this producer presented to the Jury were selected. The best one was this fresh and lively Gamay (75%) and Auxerrois (25%) blend. The **white 2000** was also awarded one star. It's a 50-50 Chardonnay and Auxerrois blend, with an intense, exotic citrus-fruit aroma, and a supple and balanced palate. Finally, the jury selected the **red 99**, a silky Pinot Noir that is ready to drink now.

Philippe Antoine, 6, rue de l'Eglise, 55210 Saint-Maurice, tel. 03.29.89.38.31, fax 03.29.90.01.80 by appt.

DOM. DE COUSTILLE
Chardonnay 2000

1.5 ha 4,500 €3-5

A yellow colour with green highlights, this Chardonnay has a flowery fragrance underscored by hazelnut aromas. Agreeably supple and fresh on the palate, it should be drunk while still young.

SCEA de Coustille, 23, Grand-Rue, 55300 Buxerulles, tel. 03.29.89.33.81, fax 03.29.90.01.88 by appt.
Philippe

LAURENT DEGENEVE Gris 2000

1.25 ha 10,000 €3

Laurent Degenève also grows the famous Alsatian plum, the mirabelle, on this small 3-ha (7.4-acre) estate. His salmon-pink *vin gris* has a fruity bouquet. Fruity red-berry flavours are also found on its light and delicate palate.

Laurent Degenève, 7, rue des Lavoirs, 55210 Creuë, tel. 03.29.89.30.67, fax 03.29.89.30.67 ev. day 8am-12 noon 1.30pm-7pm

L'AUMONIERE Chardonnay 2000

2.3 ha 7,000 €3

This Chardonnay has a rich colour and aroma, and a firm palate, which is balanced and quite well developed. This wine is ready to drink now.

GAEC de L'Aumonière, Vieville-sous-les-Côtes, 55210 Vigneulles-les-Hattonchâtel, tel. 03.29.89.31.64, fax 03.29.90.00.92 ev. day 8am-8pm

DOM. DE MONTGRIGNON 2000

1 ha 5,800 €3

The Pierson brothers farm 6 ha (15 acres) on the clay-limestone hillsides of the Meuse river. Their pale-yellow Pinot Gris has a fairly expressive, fruity and floral nose. On the palate, it is fresh from start to finish.

GAEC de Montgrignon Pierson Frères, 9, rue des Vignes, 55210 Billy-sous-les-Côtes, tel. 03.29.89.58.02, fax 03.29.90.01.04 by appt.

DOM. DE MUZY Pinot Noir 1999★★

n.c. 8,000 €5-8

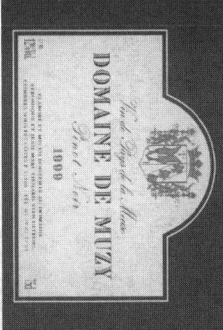

The Domaine de Muzy has made two wines, both of which were selected as a *coup de coeur*. The deep cherry-red Pinot Noir amazed the Jury with its intense aromas, and its balance and structure. While it is ready for drinking now, it will also keep well for another two years. The **vin gris 2000**, made from a blend of 70% Gamay, 20% Auxerrois and 10% Pinot Noir, is equally remarkable. It has a raspberry-scented nose, and a long and supple palate.

Véronique et Jean-Marc Liénard, Dom. de Muzy, 3, rue de Muzy, 55160 Combres-sous-les-Côtes, tel. 03.29.87.37.81, fax 03.29.87.35.00 by appt.

Coteaux de Coiffy

FLORENCE PELLETIER
Pinot Noir Vieilli en Fût de Chêne 1999

1 ha 4,290 €5-8

This vineyard has finally produced its first vintage after having been completely replanted five years ago. The wine has a fruity nose, but the supple and rounded palate is rather shy, and finishes on a slightly tannic note.

Florence Pelletier, Caves de Coiffy, 52400 Coiffy-le-Haut, tel. 03.25.90.21.12, fax 03.25.84.48.69, e-mail caves-de-coiffy@wanadoo.fr by appt.

Haute-Marne

LE MUID MONTSAUGEONNAIS 1999★

Pinot Noir Elevé en Fût de Chêne 1999★   🍾 €5-8

1.3 ha   10,200

This vineyard, devastated by the phylloxera epidemics of the 19th century, was finally re-planted a few years ago. It has now produced a dark, richly-coloured wine with a nose that begins on a toasty note, and then develops a more fruity (cherry) aroma, with hints of leather. Oak and cherry flavours are also found on the well-structured, long and rounded palate. The tannins are still very firm on the finish, which suggests that this wine should be cellared for a year or two.

☛ SA Le Muid Montsaugeonnais, 2, av. de Bourgogne, 52190 Vaux-sous-Aubigny, tel. 03.25.90.04.65, fax 03.25.90.04.65
Y by appt.

thirds was matured in vats. Red-fruit (cherry) aromas are found on the nose and on the light, supple palate. Serve this wine lightly chilled, with grilled meats.

☛ SA des Coteaux Villaines-les-Prévôtes Viserny, 21500 Villaines-les-Prévôtes, tel. 03.80.96.71.95, fax 03.80.96.71.95
Y ev. day except Sun. 2pm–6pm; Sat. 9am–1pm

VIGNOBLE DE FLAVIGNY 1999★

Pinot Noir Fût de Chêne 1999★   🍾 €5-8

2.34 ha   6,000

The vineyard is located 2 km (1.24 miles) from the ruins of the ancient Gallic city of Alésia. Its purple-red wine with violet highlights has an expressive aroma of cherries, blackberries, cooked fruits and leather. It is fleshy, luscious and chewy on the palate with powerful but well-integrated tannins, and a lengthy finish. Rarely does one find such a combination of finesse and vigour in one wine; these qualities would be highlighted by serving it with a richly-sauced meat dish.

☛ SCEA Vignoble de Flavigny, Dom. du Pont Laizan, 21150 Flavigny-sur-Ozerain, tel. 03.80.96.25.63, fax 03.80.96.25.63
Y by appt.
☛ Vermeere

Yonne

DOM. LA FONTAINE AUX MUSES

Pinot Noir 2000★   €3-5

0.5 ha   2,000

La Fontaine aux Muses is a famous hotel-restaurant, housed in a 17th-century building that was restored in the 1960s. It also has its own vineyards. The dark-coloured Pinot Noir has a powerful, spicy nose, and a full-bodied, concentrated and savoury palate with a slightly tannic finish. Two years' cellaring will give the wine a chance to develop and soften.

☛ Vincent Pointeau-Langevin, La Fontaine aux Muses, 89116 La Celle-Saint-Cyr, tel. 03.86.73.40.22, fax 03.86.73.48.66
Y ev. day except Mon. 10am–10pm

Coteaux de l'Auxois

DEVILLAINES LES PREVOTES ET VISERNY 2000★

Pinot Noir 2000★   €5-8

1 ha   6,000

One-third of this purple Pinot Noir was matured in barrels for ten months, and two-

Sainte-Marie-la-Blanche

LES CAVES DE LA VERVELLE

Melon 2000   0.33 ha   3,400

Melon grapes have given this bright, pale-yellow wine a fresh, citrus-fruit aroma of great finesse. The palate is both rounded and fresh. This is a well-balanced wine, with a very good length of flavour. The co-operative's **Pinot Noir 2000**, also selected by the Jury, has tannins that need to mature for another year or two.

☛ Caves de La Vervelle, rte de Verdun, 21200 Sainte-Marie-la-Blanche, tel. 03.80.26.60.60, fax 03.80.26.54.47
Y ev. day except Sun. 8am–12 noon 2pm–6pm

The Grand Duchy of Luxembourg is a small, prosperous state in the very heart of the European Union, located at a pivotal point where the Germanic and Latin worlds meet. Since Roman times Vines have been cultivated here on slopes that follow the sinuous course of the Moselle. Today, Luxembourg produces dry, lively and aromatic white wines, and wine consumption in the Grand Duchy approaches the levels recorded in France and in Italy.

The production of wine in Luxembourg is limited to 160,000 hl (4,224,000 gal), in keeping with its modest area of 1,350 ha (3,334 acres). However, wine is taken very seriously, and Luxembourg has its own minister of agriculture and viticulture.

The Moselle vineyard first rose to fame in the 4th century, when Trèves (which is very near to the present border of the Grand Duchy) became an Imperial seat as one of the four capitals of the Roman Empire. Today, from Schengen to Wasserbillig, the slopes on the left bank of the Moselle form a continuous belt of vineyards through the cantons of Remich and Grevenmacher. Facing south and south-east, they benefit from the advantageous influences of the river waters, which moderate the cold airflow from the north and east in spring and the strength of the sun in summer. Because of their northerly latitude (49° north), the Luxembourg vineyards produce almost exclusively white wines. Nearly 35% of the wines come from the Rivaner (or Müller-Thurgau) variety. The Elbling, which is a typical Luxembourg variety (12% of the wine-growing area), makes a light, refreshing wine. Other varieties include Auxerrois, Riesling, Pinot Blanc, Chardonnay, Pinot Gris, Pinot Noir and Gewurztraminer. Co-operatives account for more than two-thirds of the viticultural area. Remich is the headquarters of a research centre and the official viticultural organisation.

The Marque Nationale des Vins de la Moselle Luxembourgeoise, which has official backing, was set up in 1935 with the aims of encouraging improvements in quality and to give the consumer a choice. In 1985 the Appellation Contrôlée Moselle Luxembourgeoise was established. There is also a scale in the classification of the wines (Marque Nationale: Appellation Contrôlée, Vin Classé, Premier Cru and Grand Premier Cru). The originality of the classification system should be emphasised. The wines are marked for quality each year: wines gaining between 18 and 20 points qualify as Grand Premier Cru, those with between 16 and 17.9 points as Premier Cru, those with between 14 and 15.9 points as Vin Classé, those with between 12 and 13.9 points as Vin de Qualité but with no specific description, and those gaining fewer than 12 points as simple table wines. The Appellation Cremant du Luxembourg was created in 1991.

Moselle Luxembourgeoise

CEP D'OR

Stadtbredimus Primerberg Pinot gris 1999 ★★

☐ Gd 1er cru 0.8 ha 4,000 ▪ ♦ €8-11

Distinguished last year by a *coup de coeur* for its *crémant*, the estate run by the Vesque family continues to attract praise. Its Pinot Gris is greenish yellow in colour and features a pronounced nose that is both fine and very powerful, with fruity and floral aromas. This power persists on the palate, together with an elegance reflected in touches of citronella. This is a well-balanced, harmonious wine with very good length. The estate's **Crémant de Luxembourg** is recommended: a fine and persistent mousse accompanies a discreet nose of astonishing elegance. On the palate, a clean opening and definite mousse confirm that this is indeed a *crémant* of quality.

➤ SA Cep d'Or, 15, rte du Vin,
5429 Hëttermillen, tel. 76.83.83,
fax 76.91.91, e-mail cepdor@pt.lu ✅
☕ by appt.
➤ Famille Vesque

DOM. CLOS DES ROCHERS

Domaine et Tradition Riesling 1999

☐ 0.75 ha 4,831 ▪ ♦ €5-8

The surface of this wine is clear and brilliant, its colour a pale gold with greenish tinges. The nose combines nuances of flowers and citrus fruit. The palate is smooth and light after a vigorous opening. Crisp citrus notes appear in the palate aroma. This is a well-balanced wine of decided freshness.

➤ Dom. Clos des Rochers, 8, rue du Pont, 6773 Grevenmacher, tel. 75.05.45, fax 75.06.06, e-mail bermas@pt.lu ✅
☕ ev. day except Sun. 9.30am–6pm; cl. 1 Nov.–1Apr.

DOM. CHARLES DECKER

Remerschen Kreitzberg Riesling Aiswäin 1999 ★★

☐ n.c. n.c. ♦ €23-30

Charles Decker's *Vin de Glace* (ice wine) is really special. Topaz highlights gleam within the yellow, and it has a brilliant, crystal clear surface. The nose reveals sumptuous aromas of strongly perfumed honey, dried fruit and currants. The palate completes the picture: it is full, elegant, round and fleshy, and finishes on a touch of crystallised apricot.

➤ Dom. Charles Decker, 7, rte de Mondorf, 5441 Remerschen, tel. 60.95.10, fax 60.95.20, e-mail deckerch@pt.lu ✅
☕ by appt.

DOM. MME ALY DUHR

Ahn Hohfels Pinot gris 1999

☐ 2 ha 6,000 ▪ €8-11

This yellow-green Pinot Gris is animated by brilliant glints. Elegant and intense at the same time, the nose is made up of very complex floral tones. The wine is full bodied, with a voluminous palate, which is shot through with the mineral aromas so typical of this grape variety. Also recommended, the **Riesling 99 Wormeldange Nussbaum**, which is intense and complex, with aromas of crystallised fruit opening out on the nose. A lovely opening leads into a long and concentrated palate.

↦ Dom. Mme Aly Duhr, 9, rue Aly-Duhr, 5401 Ahn, tel. 76.00.43, fax 76.05.47 ▼

DOM. GALES
□ Domaines et tradition Auxerrois 1999★★

| 0.33 ha | 2,000 | €5-8 |

Nowadays the estate, which is planted mainly with Riesling and Pinot Gris, is managed by Marc Gales, grandson of the founder. Thomas Hein, an oenologist, has helped him produce this pale yellow Auxerrois, which enchanted the Jury with the complexity of its aromas of honey, lemon and raisins, obtained by using partially overripe grapes. This opulent, wonderfully balanced wine has retained a certain freshness. The finish has a touch of caramel, and the impression of elegance and harmony takes a long time to fade. It can age for a long while yet.

↦ Caves Gales, BP 49, 5501 Remich, tel. 69.90.93, fax 69.94.34 ▼ ▼ by appt.

A. GLODEN ET FILS Schengen
□ Gd 1er cru
Markusberg Gewurztraminer 1999★

| 0.14 ha | 1,900 | €5-8 |

A double success for this estate, which is to be congratulated first on this golden yellow Gewurztraminer. The attraction of its nose lies in the pleasing intensity of its aromatic range of spices (cumin) and flowers (yellow rose). Its palate is powerful and full bodied, well balanced and persistent. It should be laid down for another two years in order to achieve its full potential. A **Riesling 99 Schengen Markusberg** also receives the same accolade (one star). Its generous nose mingles notes of citrus fruit and pineapple with nuances of overripe grapes. Full on the palate, this is a rich and complex wine and promises a delightful future.

↦ A. Gloden et Fils, 2. Albaach, 5471 Wellenstein, tel. 69.83.24, fax 69.81.32, e-mail a.gloden-fils@village.uunet.lu ▼
▼ by appt.
↦ Jules Gloden

CAVES DE GREIVELDANGE
Greiveldange Herrenberg Auxerrois 2000★
□ Gd 1er cru

| 5.39 ha | 20,000 | €5-8 |

Reflecting the uniqueness of the Auxerrois grape variety, this wine is an attractive golden yellow. On the nose, it unfurls an astonishing aromatic richness, revealing nuances of apple and pear. The initial good impression is confirmed by a mellow, very rich palate. The **Pinot Blanc 99 du Grand Premier Cru Greiveldange Primerberg** is recommended.

↦ Les domaines de Vinsmoselle, Cave de Greiveldange, 1, Hamersgaasse, 5427 Stadtbredimus, tel. 69.83.14 ▼

CAVES DE GREVENMACHER
Grevenmacher Riesling Vin de glace 1999★★
□ Gd 1er cru

| 1.1 ha | 900 | €15-23 |

With a surface as clear as crystal, this *Vin de Glace* (ice wine) sparkles with lovely, intense golden glints. The grapes were harvested by hand beginning on 21 December 1999, and the quality is evident in the exceptionally complex aromas of dried fruit, crystallised grape, honey, apricot and peach. The full, rich, fruity palate also makes its elegant mark, then a fleshy, round mid-palate develops into a lively, crisp finish. This harmonious wine is well balanced between sweetness and acidity and would make a good accompaniment to an apricot dessert and, of course, *foie gras*. But you've still got plenty of time: from two to four years.

↦ Les domaines de Vinsmoselle, Caves de Grevenmacher, 6718 Grevenmacher, tel. 75.01.75, fax 75.95.13, e-mail info@vinsmoselle.lu ▼ ▼ ev. day except Sun. 10am–5pm; 1 Sept.–30Apr. by appt.

DOM. ALICE HARTMANN
Wormeldange Koeppchen Riesling 1999★★★
□

| 0.6 ha | 3,500 | €8-11 |

DOMAINE ALICE HARTMANN
WORMELDANGE KOEPPCHEN
RIESLING · 1999

The 3-ha (7-acre) estate is planted mainly with old Riesling vines in original terraced vineyards. The Jury was very enthusiastic about this wine, which has a lovely brilliance, and an intense nose that unfurls citrus (lemon and grapefruit) scents. The attack is fresh, lively and light, and is followed by a palate that is all finesse. A delightfully fresh and elegant wine.

↦ SA Dom. Alice Hartmann, rue Principale 72–74, 5480 Wormeldange, tel. 76.00.02, fax 76.04.60 ▼

DOM. R. KOHLL-LEUCK
Rousemen Pinot gris 2000★★★
□ Gd 1er cru

| n.c. | 2,000 | €5-8 |

This family estate has been in existence since the end of the 19th century. Raymond and Marie-Cécile have been running it for 29 years and are thinking of handing over soon to their son. In the meantime, they have produced an exceptional wine. Its outstanding qualities are legion, and include an appealing colour, the freshness and finesse of its floral

Moselle Luxembourgeoise

aromas, its supple, very lacy opening and its overall balance. This Pinot Gris will be at its best in two to three years' time. The same estate receives a mention in **Crémant de Luxembourg** for its **Cuvée Gust Kohll** which has aromas of dried fruit and caramel accompanied by a persistent mousse. A good attack is followed by a well-balanced, very fruity palate.

↝ Dom. viticole Raymond Kohll-Leuck, 4, an der Borreg, Ehnen, 5419 Wormeldange, tel. 76.02.42, fax 76.90.40

DOM. MICHEL KOHLL-REULAND

Crémant de luxembourg La cuvée du domaine 1999★★★

◯　　　n.c.　　n.c.　　€5-8

Michel Kohll-Reuland has been head of the estate since 1973. His 5 ha (12 acres) of vines extend over the chalk slopes of Ehnen and Wormeldange and his wine *crémant* is very typical of the appellation and does him proud. It is yellow with green glints, and aromas of very ripe fruit unfold on the nose. The palate is well balanced and has an impressive structure. This is a wine that would please the forebears of the master of the house.

↝ Michel Kohll-Reuland, 5, am Stach, 5418 Ehnen, tel. 76.00.18, fax 76.06.40, e-mail mkohll@pt.lu
Ⴤ by appt.

KRIER FRERES

Remich–Primerberg Riesling Givré 1999★★★

☐　　0.2 ha　800　　　　€38-46

Golden yellow with a lovely brilliance, this *Vin de Glace* (ice wine) is a winner. Its nose exudes delicious fruity aromas of white peach, mango and lychee. After a luscious, elegant attack, the palate unfurls with great finesse. The roundness of the mid-palate leads melodiously towards a sweet finish, which is punctuated by a pleasing spark of freshness. Two other wines presented by this cellar are recommended: the **Crémant du Luxembourg Saint-Cunibert**, which surprised the Jury with its strong personality, the finesse and richness of its palate and the dominant fruitiness of its nose, and the **Pinot Noir Rubis 99, Bech-Kleinmacher Enschberg** with its powerful aromatic expression, tending strongly towards red-berry fruit (redcurrant and strawberry). Very typical of the appellation, this wine features freshness, balance and good fruit.

↝ Caves Krier Frères, 1, montée Saint-Urbain, 5501 Remich GDL, tel. 69.82.82, fax 69.80.98, e-mail cave@krierfreres.lu
Ⴤ by appt.

DOM. KRIER-WELBES

Bech-Kleinmacher Jongeberg Gewurztraminer 1999★

☐　　0.2 ha　n.c.　　　€5-8

This pale Gewurztraminer gleams with green and yellow, and delicate aromas of rose and fine spices arise on its nose. It is a full-bodied, well-structured wine that opens out with finesse in the tasting, onto a charming balance of alcohol, sweetness and acidity. It would go best with a characterful cheese or a well-seasoned exotic dish. The Jury also recommended the **Grand Premier Cru Wellenstein Foulschette en Pinot Gris 2000** from the same estate, which stands out because of its intense ripe grape aromas. A well-structured wine, it has fine, elegant acidity, lovely length and a good balance. Lay it down for a year.

↝ Dom. viticole Krier-Welbes, 3, rue de la Gare, 5690 Ellange-Gare, tel. 67.71.84, fax 66.19.31, e-mail guykrier@pt.lu
Ⴤ by appt.
↝ Guy Krier

LAURENT BENOIT

Crémant de Luxembourg★

◯　　0.5 ha　7,000　　　€5-8

This estate is recommended for its **Grand Premier Cru Riesling 2000 Koltschberg** with its aromas of citrus and white fruit, so typical of this grape variety. A lively, well-balanced wine, long and harmonious; the Jury predicts a fine future for it. As for this *crémant*, its intense and persistent mousse and fine bubbles make it a most successful wine. On the palate, subtle scents are enveloped in a lively structure.

↝ Laurent and Benoît Kox, 6A, rue des Prés, 5561 Remich, tel. 69.84.94, fax 69.81.01, e-mail kox@pt.lu
Ⴤ by appt.

CAVES LEGILL

Schengen Markusberg Pinot blanc 1999

☐　Gd 1er cru　0.28 ha　2,700　　€5-8

The Legills have been growing wine for six generations, and their estate has submitted two lovely wines from the 99 vintage, one white and the other red. This Premier Grand Cru is derived from Pinot Blanc, a well-balanced wine with aromas typical of the grape variety; the palate has a light but elegant structure and leaves an impression of freshness. The second wine, a **Pinot Noir Coteaux de Schengen**, is recommended for its lovely, intense, deep ruby colour with violet highlights, which envelops an aroma of cherries. The palate is both pleasant and complex. Serve in three or four years' time with red meat.

↝ Caves Legill et Fils, 27, rte du Vin, 5445 Schengen, tel. 66.40.38, fax 60.90.97

CAVES HENRI RUPPERT

Schengen Markusberg Pinot blanc 1999★★

☐ | 0.2 ha | 1,350 | ▮▮ | €5-8

This estate is less than 5 ha (12 acres) in area and has been in existence since 1920. The expertise acquired here over the years is evident in this Pinot Blanc, and the Jury was impressed by the very fruity nose with its aromas of citrus fruit and fruit of the forest. After a soft attack the palate opens up, picking out nicely-balanced fruity notes. The finish is lovely, characterised by an elegant acidity. From the same estate and the same vintage, an **Auxerrois** is recommended for its floral (lilac) and fruity (apple and pineapple) touches. Warm, nicely persistent, unfolding with finesse and balance, it is already drinkable but will be at its best in three to five years.

↳ Henri Ruppert, rte du Vin, 100, 5445 Schengen, tel. 66.42.30, fax 66.44.83 ☑
Ⴤ by appt.

CAVES SAINT-REMY-DESOM

Remich Primerberg Pinot gris 2000★

☐ | 0.85 ha | 8,000 | ▮▮ | €5-8

This *négociant* has been in business since 1922 and occupies 18th century buildings, whose wine cellars have been enlarged over the years. Its Pinot Gris was much appreciated: this lovely clear wine with green glints has a fresh nose of crystallised fruit and peach, with a touch of smokiness. A lovely alcohol-sweetness-acidity balance endows the wine with great charm. Well-structured, round and long, the opulent palate has a characteristic flavour that would go well with a *magret de canard*. A **Grand Premier Cru Pinot Blanc 2000 Remich Primerberg** is singled out for the perfect maturity of its grapes, its lively and generous palate and its finish that mingles lemony notes and floral nuances.

↳ Caves Saint-Rémy-Desom, 9, rue Dicks, 5521 Remich, tel. 69.93.47, fax 69.93.47 ☑
Ⴤ by appt.

DOM. JEAN LINDEN-HEINISCH

Ehnen Wousselt Riesling 1999

☐ | Gd 1er cru | 0.4 ha | 4,500 | ▮▮ | €5-3

This most appealing wine has a clear, brilliant colour. The grape variety is expressed in the aromas of citrus fruit and honey, accompanied by a mineral spark. The tasting unfolds with the greatest of balance; the palate reveals itself to be full, rich, lively and elegant in the attack, then rounds out before ending in a very mellow finish.

↳ Jean Linden-Heinisch, 8, rue Isidore-Cones, 5417 Wormeldange, tel. 76.06.61, fax 76.91.29 ☑ Ⴤ by appt.

MATHES ET CIE

Crémant de luxembourg Sélection 2000

○ | 2.64 ha | 21,500 | ▮▮ | €11-15

A fine, abundant mousse, and golden yellow in colour. A generous *crémant*, full-bodied with a lovely harmony: a wine to be recommended.

↳ Dom. Mathes, BP 3, 5507 Wormeldange, tel. 76.93.93, fax 76.93.90, e-mail mathes@pt.lu ☑ Ⴤ by appt.

POLL-FABAIRE

Crémant de Luxembourg★★

○ | 5 ha | 50,000 | ▮▮ | €5-8

The Vinsmoselle estates belong to a group of six cooperative wine cellars spread throughout Luxembourg's Moselle region, and they trade under the Poll-Fabaire brand name. The Wormeldange cellar's *crémant* is brilliant and clear with straw-coloured glints. Its aromas come through subtly in nuances of white flowers and peach, and its palate demonstrates all the finesse and balance of a quality wine. The **Cave de Grevenmacher** has produced a very successful **Crémant de Luxembourg Poll-Fabaire**. The aroma of caramel accompanies white flowers on the nose, before developing into a fresh harmony. The **Crémants Poll-Fabaire** from the **Stadbredimus** and **Wellenstein cellars** deserve a mention.

↳ Les Domaines de Vinsmoselle, 115, rte du Vin, 5481 Wormeldange, tel. 76.82.11, fax 76.82.15, e-mail info@vinsmoselle.lu Ⴤ by appt.

CAVES DU SUD REMERSCHEN

Schengen Markusberg Pinot gris 1999

☐ | Gd 1er cru | 17.11 ha | 27,593 | ▮▮ | €5-8

Of the 210 ha (518 acres) processed by this co-operative, 17 ha (42 acres) are devoted to this wine, which is produced entirely from Pinot Gris. Yellow, gleaming green, it has very pleasantly pronounced floral and fruity aromas. The palate has a powerful body, balanced with rich honeyed notes. This wine makes a harmonious impression and cries out to be shared with friends.

↳ Les Domaines de Vinsmoselle, Caves du sud Remerschen, 32, rte du Vin, 5440 Remerschen, tel. 66.41.65, fax 66.41.66, e-mail info@vinsmoselle.lu ☑ Ⴤ by appt.

CAVES JEAN SCHLINK-HOFFELD

Cuvée personnelle Wormeldange Heiligenhäuschen Pinot gris 2000

☐ | Gd 1er cru | 0.15 ha | 1,200 | ▮▮ | €5-8

This estate, managed by René and Jean-Paul Schlink since 1993, produced a brilliant, clear Pinot Gris, with a lovely golden yellow colour and an expressive nose of citrus fruit and white peach mingled with a touch of smokiness. A heady wine, opulent and full-bodied, it is supported by a good structure. The finish is long, fine and subtle. This Pinot Gris would go well with pork fillet and vegetables.

↳ Caves Jean Schlink-Hoffeld, 1, rue de l'Eglise, 6841 Machtum, tel. 75.84.68, fax 75.92.62, e-mail cschlink@pt.lu ☑ Ⴤ ev. day except Sun. 8am–6pm; groups by appt.

Moselle Luxembourgeoise

SCHMIT-FOHL

Ahn Goellebour Gewürztraminer 2000★ ■ ♦ €5–8

☐ 0.5 ha 2,000

A pale yellow Gewurztraminer with light hints of green. The nose is closed initially, then opens out into fresh notes of flowers (rose) and spices. The palate is characteristically well balanced in its aromatic expression and structure. Wait for two or three years because this wine is one that will live up to its promise.

☛ Maison viticole Schmit-Fohl, 8, rue de Niederdonven, 5401 Ahn, tel. 76.02.31, fax 76.91.46, e-mail hsf@pt.lu
☥ by appt.
☛ Armand Schmit

DOM. PIERRE SCHUMACHER-LETHAL ET FILS

Wormeldange Heiligenhäuschen Pinot blanc 2000 €5–8

☐ Gd 1er cru n.c. 3,500

This Pinot Blanc 2000 is bedecked in pale green glints that match the tonality of its exquisitely delicate and elegant aromas. Fine floral threads embroider the palate. Full and rich in body, this wine is seductively well balanced, and would be a welcome addition to any wine cellar.

☛ Dom. Schumacher-Lethal et Fils, 114, rue Principale, 5450 Wormeldange, tel. 76.01.34, fax 76.85.04 ☥ ☥ by appt

CAVES DE STADTBREDIMUS

Stadtbredimus Dieffert Pinot blanc 1999★ €5–8

☐ Gd 1er cru 3.33 ha 6,600

The nose releases very fine aromas accented with melon and honey. An unobtrusive acidity gives this wine a pleasant freshness. Like an echo of the nose, the palate seems full of honey and fruit.

☛ Les domaines de Vinsmoselle, Caves de Stadtbredimus, Kellereiswe, 5450 Stadtbredimus, tel. 69.83.14, fax 69.91.89 ☥ by appt.

DOM. THILL FRERES

Crémant de luxembourg Cuvée Victor Hugo 1998★★★ €5–8

○ 1 ha n.c.

This estate was awarded a *coup de coeur* last year for a Pinot Blanc, and this year the *crémant*, named after Victor Hugo, whose picture figures on the label, was pronounced exceptional. Accompanied by a beautiful, persistent mousse, the nose expresses itself with great aromatic richness, followed by a vigorous palate with good vinosity. An elegant and well-balanced wine, honouring the name it bears.

☛ Dom. Thill Frères, 39, rte du Vin, 5445 Schengen, tel. 75.05.45, fax 75.06.06, e-mail bermas@pt.lu ☥ ☥ by appt.

CAVES DE WELLENSTEIN

Bech-Kleinmacher Naumberg Sélection des vignerons Pinot gris 1999★ ■ ♦ €8–11

☐ Gd 1er cru 30.87 ha 1,000

Just over 30 ha (74 acres) are devoted to this Premier Grand Cru. The Jury liked its pale yellow colour with green highlights, which introduces a nose of pronounced floral aromas. Complex ripe fruit notes appear in the well-balanced, mellow palate. A wonderfully harmonious wine. (50 cl bottles.)

☛ Les domaines de Vinsmoselle, Caves de Wellenstein, 13, rue des Caves, 5471 Wellenstein, tel. 66.93.21, fax 69.76.54, e-mail info@vinsmoselle.lu ☥ ☥ by appt.

CAVES DE WORMELDANGE

Wormeldange Mohrberg Pinot blanc 2000★★ €5–8

☐ Gd 1er cru 3 ha 25,000 ■ ♦

Robed in a beautiful sustained colour with yellow glints, this Pinot Blanc offers the nose a plethora of exotic fruit. The palate is all power and concentration. A wine that won the hearts of the Jury, who see it as a good accompaniment to fish in a sauce.

☛ Les Domaines de Vinsmoselle, 115, rte du Vin, 5481 Wormeldange, tel. 76.82.11, fax 76.82.15, e-mail info@vinsmoselle.lu ☥ ☥ by appt.

SWITZERLAND

Compared to its other European neighbours, Swiss vineyards cover the comparatively small area of 14,900 ha (36,803 acres). They extend over the area of three great river basins drained by the Rhône to the west of the Alps, by the Rhine to the north and by the Po to the south of the mountain chain. As a result, they encompass a great variety of soils and microclimates, creating an array of different *terroirs* in spite of their relative proximity. Cultivated by traditional methods on sunny slopes, some steep, some terraced, the vineyards determine the character of the landscape. Three main wine-growing regions can be identified, based on the linguistic divisions of the country. However, they are far from uniform, and the contrasts they display are significant. In the west the vineyards of the Suisse Romande account for more than three-quarters of the whole of Switzerland's wine-growing area. From Geneva they extend into the heart of the Alps in the canton (a Swiss administrative region) of Valais and hug the shoreline of Lake Geneva in the canton of Vaud. Further north they rise above the shores of lakes Neuchâtel, Morat and Bienne (in the canton of Berne) in the foothills of the Jura. The Swiss–German vineyards are much less continuous and account for a total of 17% of the wine-growing area. Starting from Basle, they are dotted along the Rhine valley, following the course of the river into the east of the country and extend equally far into the interior, where they are to be found on the best sites on hills overlooking numerous lakes and valleys. In Italian-speaking Switzerland vine-growing is centred in the southern valley of the Ticino, where natural conditions on the south-facing slopes of the Alps are significantly different from those in other Swiss wine-growing regions. Apart from a whole range of 'specialities', the wine-makers of Swiss Romande traditionally favour the Chasselas variety for whites. The most commonly cultivated red variety is Pinot Noir, followed by Gamay. In the Swiss–German region, Pinot Noir dominates, but is grown side by side with white Müller-Thurgau and various other local varieties, which are much sought after by wine-lovers. In Italian-speaking Switzerland, where white grape varieties are very poorly represented, the best wines – red, white and rosé – are made from Merlot. Finally, a major event in the viticultural life of Switzerland should be mentioned: the Fête des Vignerons de Vevey (Festival of the Wine-growers of Vevey). With its roots in the Middle Ages, this splendid festival brings together the wine-growers and the local population to celebrate their work in the vineyards. The most recent was held in August 1999 and the next is due to be held in 2021 to 2023.

Vaud

In the Middle Ages, Cistercian monks cleared a substantial area of Vaud and planted out the vineyard. By the middle of the 19th century Vaud was Switzerland's primary wine-growing canton (ahead of the Zürich vineyard), but the ravages of phylloxera made complete replanting essential. Today the vineyard covers 3,850 ha (9,510 acres), and ranks second after the Valais.

For more than 450 years, the Vaud has cherished an authentic wine-growing tradition, relying on its châteaux – there are about 50 of them – as much as it does on the experience of the great wine-making and shipping families.

The climatic conditions mark out four large wine-

Vaud

growing zones. The Vaud side of Lake Neuchâtel and the shores of the Orbe produce fruity wines with delicate perfumes. Between Geneva and Lausanne the shores of Lake Geneva produce wines of great finesse. Here the vines are sheltered by the Jura mountains to the north, and benefit from a temperate microclimate influenced by the lake. The vineyards of Lavaux, between Lausanne and Château-de-Chillon, with the terraced vineyards of Dézalay at their heart, benefit from radiated heat from their low-walled enclosures and reflected light from the lake. They produce structured, complex wines often characterised by notes of honey and toasted flavours. Finally, the vineyards of the Chablais are located north-east of Lake Geneva and climb up the right bank of the Rhône. The *terroirs* are typically made up of stony soils, and the climate is much influenced by the Foehn (a hot, dry wind that blows in the Swiss Alps); the wines are strong with flavours of gunflint.

The Vaud vineyard has very good soil for Chasselas (70% of the vines planted), which reaches full ripeness here.

The red varieties represent 27% of the whole (15% of Pinot Noir and 12% of Gamay). These two varieties are frequently blended together, and the wines are known under the name Appellation d'Origine Contrôlée Salvagnin.

A few 'specialities' represent 3% of the wine produced: Pinot Blanc, Pinot Gris, Gewurztraminer, Muscat Blanc, Sylvaner, Auxerrois, Charmont, Mondeuse, Plant-Robert, Syrah, Merlot, Gamaret, Garanoir, and so on.

ANTAGNES
Ollon Vieilli en fût de chêne 1997★★
■   0.3 ha   1,170 | **€8-11**

A blend of Pinot Noir and Gamay, this wine exhibits a moderately deep colour with some dark highlights. The intense nose is redolent of soft fruit (raspberry, strawberry and cherry) with a suggestion of over-ripeness. A

subtle hint of burnt vanilla comes from 12 months' barrel maturation. Despite its age, the wine has retained an attractive freshness. The palate shows obvious fruit with a structure underpinned by fine, rich tannins and an elegant, long finish.

➤ Hugues Baud, av. du Chamossaire 14, 1860 Aigle, tel. 024.466.47.27, fax 024.466.47.27 ✉ ☎ by appt.

ANCIENNE PROPRIETE AUBERJONOIS
Tartegnin Chasselas 2000★
□   1 ha   8,000 | ▮ ♦   **€5-8**

The attractive label featuring a painting of a couple of grape-pickers is the work of René Auberjonois (1872–1957), son of the former owner of this estate. The fine balance of this Chasselas emerges in the glass. Nicely open, the wine displays a range of flower (lime blossom) and fruit (peach, apricot) flavours. The palate is slightly sweet, balanced by a subtle acidity. Fruity and mineral flavours emerge, followed by a touch of attractive bitterness on the finish.

VAUD Wine-growing areas

DOM. DE BEAU-SOLEIL

Mont-sur-Rolle Chasselas 2000★★

☐ 5 ha □□□ 55,000 ■ €5-8

This 6-ha (15-acre) estate offers superb views over Lake Geneva and the Alps beyond. The Chasselas has exotic overtones, with lemon and pineapple slightly overshadowing the floral notes. The wine is deliciously smooth on the palate, with a touch of saltiness leading to a fresh finish.

☛ Thierry Durand, rte de la Noyère 5, 1185 Mont-sur-Rolle, tel. 021.825.49.21, fax 021.825.49.21, e-mail t.durand@ bluewin.ch ✉ ☎ by appt.

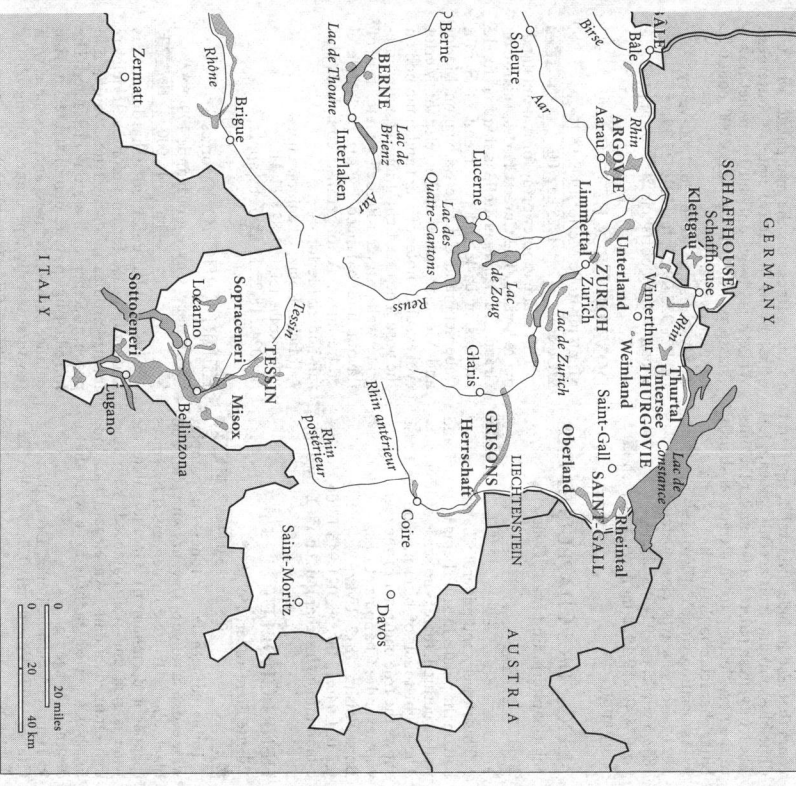

DOM. DES BIOLLES

Founex Chasselas 2000★★

☐ 3 ha ☐ 25,000 €5-8

This pleasantly fresh Chasselas would be ideal as an aperitif. The citrus flavours, notably lemon and grapefruit, linger on the palate, combining a lively character with a velvety mid-palate. The finish is still a little austere but should mellow in a year or so to allow the wine's delicious fruit character to emerge.

☛ Jean-Pierre Deblüe, rue du Vieux-Pressoir 2, Chataigneriaz, 1297 Founex, tel. 079.632.58.58, fax 072.776.05.43 ✉ ☎ by appt.

DOM. BOVY

Saint-Saphorin Chasselas 2000★★

☐ 3 ha ■ 18,000 ■ €8-11

Massive ornately decorated oak vats dominate the cellars of this 7-ha (17-acre) estate. This Chasselas, which has never been in contact with oak, is a good example of a wine produced from a clay-limestone soil. Lime

Switzerland

SWITZERLAND

blossom and peach flavours combine on a soft, velvety mid-palate. The finish is powerful and long, with a characteristic touch of bitterness. The **Saint-Saphorin Chasselas Vieilles Vignes 2000** is equally noteworthy.

↝ Dom. Bovy, rue du Bourg-de-Plait 15, 1071 Chexbres, tel. 021.946.51.25, fax 021.946.51.26,
e-mail info@domainebovy.ch [V]
Ⓨ ev. day except Sun. 9am–6pm; Sat. 9am–12 noon

DOM. DES CAILLATTES

Tartegnin Chasselas 2000★★
□ Gd cru   1.5 ha   13,000   ■   €5-8

Aromas of lime blossom combine with a hint of lemon to yield a clean, fresh bouquet. On the palate the softness of the structure is perfectly balanced by a hint of freshness, leading to a very fruity finish. This is a most elegant wine.

↝ SA Hammel, Les Cruz, 1180 Rolle, tel. 021.825.11.41, fax 021.825.47.47, e-mail hammel@span.ch [V] Ⓨ by appt.

CHANT DES RESSES

Yvorne Chasselas 2000★
□   6.6 ha   90,000   €5-8

Pepper and spice complete a range of flavours that also includes mineral notes, floral (lime blossom) and fruit accents (pineapple). The fruity, fresh palate shows similar flavours to the nose, leading to an attractive, slightly bitter character on the finish.

↝ Association viticole d'Yvorne, Les Maisons Neuves, case postale 95, 1853 Yvorne, tel. 024.466.23.44, fax 024.466.59.19, e-mail avy@span.ch [V] Ⓨ by appt.

HENRI CHOLLET

Villette Plant-robert 1999★★★
■ 0.5 ha   5,000   €8-11

Ruby red with deeper tones, this complex wine evokes a range of flavours with plum and black cherry fruits complemented by spices (pepper and cinnamon). On the palate the wine is rich and well balanced, with fine, tight-grained tannins. An elegant and long finish is a perfect endnote for a wine that is destined for ageing.

↝ Henri et Vincent Chollet, Dom. du Graboz, 1091 Villette, tel. 021.799.24.85 [V] Ⓨ by appt.

CLOS DE LA GEORGE

Yvorne Chasselas 2000★★
□ Gd cru   4 ha   25,000   €11-15

Perched on a steep hillside at an altitude of between 380 and 500 m (1,420–1,635 ft), this venerable vineyard now occupies more than 6 ha (15 acres). On a soil of gravel scree and clay-limestone, the vines are encircled by walls and protected from winds by the valley below. From this special *terroir* emerges a rich and complex Chasselas. Pale in colour, the nose has a mineral, almost stony, character along with notes of citrus fruits. Rich and full-bodied, with a lively, fresh structure leading to a classic mineral finish.

↝ Clos de la George, 1852 Versvey-Roche, tel. 021.825.11.41, fax 021.825.47.47 [V] Ⓨ
↝ Famille Rolaz-Thorens

CLOS DU ROCHER

Yvorne Chasselas 2000★★
□ Gd cru   10 ha   80,000   ■ ♦ €11-15

The estate, which covers 10 ha (25 acres) of well-protected terraced vineyards, is represented here by a Chasselas wine. A stony character comes through among a range of rich flavours, notably pineapple and lime blossom. The wine's distinct personality is attributable to the softness on the mid-palate, which is offset by an attractive note of bitterness. While it is always difficult to predict how a Chasselas will develop, this 2000 could be kept for five years.

↝ SA Obrist, av. Reller 26, 1800 Vevey, tel. 021.925.99.25, fax 021.925.99.15, e-mail obrist@obrist.ch [V] Ⓨ by appt.

ALEXANDRE CHAPPUIS ET FILS

Saint-Saphorin En Lavaux Chasselas 2000★★
□   2 ha   15,000   ■ €8-11

This flowery and mineral Chasselas is very soft on the palate. Despite being both rich and well structured, there is no sense of heaviness. The slight touch of bitterness on the finish shows the true character of the region.

↝ Alexandre Chappuis et Fils, Bons-Voisins, 1812 Rivaz, tel. 021.946.13.06, fax 021.946.13.06, e-mail info@vins-chappuis.ch [V] Ⓨ by appt.

DOM. DE CROCHET

Mont-sur-Rolle Merlot 1999★★
□ Gd cru   0.25 ha   700   €15-23

This estate is noteworthy for two outstanding red wines. The **Cuvée Charles Auguste du Grand Cru Mont-sur-Rolle** is matured for 12 months in cask and is a blend of Syrah, Cabernet Franc, Cabernet Sauvignon, Merlot and Viognier varieties. The elegant Merlot evokes subtle notes of plum and cinnamon on the nose. The fine, tight-grained tannins integrate well into a rounded palate, full of flavour and balanced by the perfect level of freshness. A long finish completes this full-bodied Merlot.

↝ Michel Rolaz, Chem. porchat 4, 1180 Rolle, tel. 021.825.11.41, fax 024.818.25.11 [V] Ⓨ by appt.

HENRI CRUCHON Morges

Chardonnay Cuvée gourmande 1999★★★
□   4 ha   16,000   €11-15

This golden-coloured Chardonnay is matured in cask for nine months. It delivers intense aromas of citrus fruits, vanilla and peach, together with a stony character. The long-lasting palate demonstrates a fine balance between richness and freshness, with flavours of fully ripe grapes joining all the nuances expressed on the nose.

DOM. DU DALEY Villette Chasselas

Réserve du domaine 2000★★

□ Gd cru   4.7 ha   10,000   ■   € 8–11

The estate belonged to the monks of the Order of Saint Nicolas of Fribourg for more than 500 years until 1937, when it passed into the care of the Bujard family. This Chasselas is true to type, revealing lime blossom overlaid by peach aromas. The wine shows some sweetness on the palate but has the benefit of a restrained acidity, which brings out even more of the fresh fruit. The finish has a characteristic slightly bitter note. The **red Reserve du Domaine Barrique Assemblage**, a blend of Gamaret, Garanoir and Pinot Noir varieties, also merits two stars.

☏ Dom. du Daley, chem. des Moines, 1095 Lutry, tel. 021.791.15.94, fax 021.791.58.61 ☑ ▼ by appt.

CHRISTIAN DUGON

Côtes de l'Orbe Gamaret 1999★★

  0.4 ha   3,000   ■   € 5–8

Gamaret, a Swiss grape variety created by crossing Gamay and Reichensteiner, is renowned for producing wines that are rich in colour and tannins. The wine is characterised by a deep colour and roundness, supported by fine and rich tannins. The lingering flavours are redolent of blackberries and cinnamon, with a suggestion of violets behind. Christian Dugon also produces an excellent **red Côte de l'Orbe Cuvée Arpège 99**.

☏ Christian Dugon, La Grande-Ouche, 1353 Bofflens, tel. 024.441.35.01, fax 024.441.35.36 ☑ ▼ by appt.

ES EMBLEYRES

Dézaley Chasselas 2000★★

  1.2 ha   12,000   ■   € 11–15

Ninety per cent of the 3.7 ha (9 acres) of vines in this estate are Chasselas. The wine perfectly illustrates the union between the soil of Dézelay and the Chasselas variety: it is clear in colour, has a flowery and mineral nose and is round yet fresh on the palate, imbued with a range of flavours. It may be a little closed at present but should improve over the next five years.

☏ Jean-François Chevalley, Dom. de la Chenalettaz, 1096 Le Treytorrens-en-Dézaley, tel. 021.799.13.00, fax 021.799.39.21, e-mail jf.chevalley@lavaux.ch ☑ ▼ by appt.

DENIS FAUQUEX

Epesses Chasselas 2000★★

□   0.41 ha   4,200   ■   € 8–11

As a rule, the wines of Epesses lend themselves to ageing. Even if this Chasselas would benefit from keeping, it is already revealing its true personality. Flowery and slightly

☏ Henri Cruchon, Cave du Village SA, 1112 Echichens, tél. 021.801.17.92, fax 021.803.33.18 ☑ ▼ ev. day except Sun.10am–12 noon 2–6pm; Sat. 8am–12 noon

---

mineral, it shows richness on the palate and the hint of bitterness that is so typical of the region.

☏ Denis Fauquex, rte de la Corniche 17, 1097 Riex, tel. 021.799.11.49, fax 021.799.11.49, e-mail denis-fauquex@bluewin.ch ☑ ▼ by appt.

GROGNUZ FRERES ET FILS

Saint-Saphorin Syrah 1999★★★

■   0.12 ha   1,000   ▮▮   € 15–23

SAINT-SAPHORIN

Syrah 1999

This dark, almost black Syrah seduced the Jury. Extremely expressive and very characteristic of the variety, it shows aromas of pepper, violets and cinnamon. The same complexity is obvious on the velvety palate, which reveals a rich tannic structure. The finish is especially long and, together with the good concentration, indicates that the wine can be kept for 10 years. Also recommended is the **Chasselas Chez les Rois 2000**, which was awarded one star.

☏ Grognuz Frères et Fils, chem. des Bulesses 91, 1814 La tour-de-Peilz, tel. 021.944.41.28, fax 021.944.41.28 ☑ ▼ by appt.

DOM. DE LA CAPITE

Luins Chasselas 2000★★★

□   4 ha   20,000   ■   € 5–8

A hint of saltiness complements a range of subtle mineral, flowery and fruit aromas of lime blossom, peach and lemon. These reappear on the palate in an attractive balance between richness and freshness. The structure is sturdy, yet not too heavy, and this wine can be kept for between five and seven years.

☏ Claude Berthet, La Capite-Luins, 1268 Begnins, tel. 022.366.11.16, fax 022.366.11.16 ☑ ▼ by appt.

LA CELESTE Vinzel Chasselas 2000★★

□   1.5 ha   10,000   ■   € 5–8

The name Céleste is applied to a range of wines created in 1998 in which Sauvignon and Chasselas varieties play the dominant roles. The attractive orange and gold label featuring a vine stock encourages one to try this lemony and flowery Chasselas, which is still somewhat closed. The well-structured palate shows a good balance between fullness and freshness. The sweet mid-palate reveals a subtle blend of lemon and pineapple flavours, which eventually give way to a most attractive touch of bitterness.

➤ Gustave et Yann Menthonnex, Dom. Delaharpe, La Tourelle, 1183 Bursins, tel. 021.824.22.30, fax 021.824.22.30, e-mail menthonnex@hotmail.com ✉ ♈ by appt.

DOM. LA COLOMBE
Mont-sur-Rolle Petit Clos Chasselas 2000★★
☐　　1.5 ha　10,000　🍷 ♦ €8-11

The estate takes its name from the dove (*colombe*) that features on the coat of arms of the Paccot family. This slightly salty Chasselas comes from the Petit Clos, a plot of vines at an altitude of 500 m (1,635 ft). The aromas conjure up flowers, peaches and a subtle hint of lemon, which also combine in perfect harmony on the fresh, fruity palate. The wine may be enjoyed as an aperitif or with food.

➤ Raymond Paccot, Dom. La Colombe, 1173 Féchy, tel. 021.808.66.48, fax 021.808.52.84, e-mail raypaccot@freesurf.ch ✉ ♈ by appt.

LA MAISON DU LEZARD
Yvorne Pinot noir Vinifié et élevé en barrique de chêne 1999★★
■　　1 ha　9,510　🍷🍷 €15-23

This estate designates specific areas for Pinot Noir on the limestone soils of Aigle, Ollon and Yvorne. This last-named *terroir* provides a dark red wine, focused on fruit (strawberry, raspberry and cherry), with the oak flavours derived from the cask remaining in the background. The palate is that of a classic Pinot Noir with a structure of rounded tannins and an emerging fresh, fruity character. The long finish shows a subtle hint of vanilla.

➤ Henri Badoux, av. du Chamossaire 18, 1860 Aigle, tel. 024.468.68.88, fax 024.468.68.89, e-mail badoux.vins@bluewin.ch ✉ ♈ by appt.

LA TRINQUETTE
Epesses Chasselas 2000★★
☐　　1.05 ha　7,500　🍷 ♦ €8-11

Flecks of gold enliven the colour of this Chasselas, which is still quite closed. The nose begins to reveal the mineral character typical of this variety, together with some floral notes. The palate is marked by softness, with a stony character and some lime blossom flavours behind. The wine could be drunk right away or over the next three years.

➤ Pascal Fonjallaz-Spicher, La Place, 1098 Epesses, tel. 021.799.37.56, fax 021.799.37.56, e-mail pascal.fonjallaz@urbanet.ch ✉ ♈ by appt.

LE CAVISTE Ollon Chasselas 2000★★
☐　　15 ha　100,000　🍷 ♦ €8-11

Lime blossom is dominant on the palate of this Chasselas, which is also characterised by a stony minerality, typical of the *terroir*. A judicious balance between roundness and freshness gives a harmonious wine, an excellent aperitif.

➤ Association viticole d'Ollon, rue Demesse, 1867 Ollon, tel. 024.499.11.77, fax 024.499.24.48, e-mail info@avollon.ch ✉ ♈ by appt.

LES BLASSINGES
Saint-Saphorin Chasselas 2000★★
☐　　1.2 ha　12,000　🍷 ♦ €8-11

Grown on dry-stone terraces, this is Chasselas at its best. Golden in colour, it yields fruit aromas and predictable hints of lime blossom, underlined by a slight mineral note. Rounded and fine on the palate, there are suggestions of pineapple and a slightly peppery note of *pêche de vigne*. The finish holds up well.

➤ Pierre-Luc Leyvraz, chem. de Baulet 4, 1071 Chexbres, tel. 021.946.19.40, fax 021.946.19.45, e-mail pl.leyvraz@freesurf.ch ✉ ♈ by appt.

LE SENDEY
Blonay Montreux Chasselas 2000★★
■　　0.6 ha　6,500　🍷 ♦ €8-11

This sophisticated Chasselas with flavours of blackcurrant jelly and lime blossom will whet the appetite. Soft with a slight, attractive bitterness on the palate, the wine is characteristic of the region. It can be drunk over the next two or three years.

➤ Henri et François Montet, Chaucey 14, 1807 Blonay, tel. 021.943.53.35, fax 021.943.53.35 ♈ by appt.

LES FOSSES
Saint-Saphorin Chasselas 2000★★★
☐　　n.c.　30,000　🍷 ♦ €8-11

Although this Chasselas is ready for drinking now, it demonstrates good ageing potential. With a light colour, there are wafts of intense floral scents, enhanced by an elegant mineral note. This flavour profile together with a slightly spicy note provides a smooth and fresh fruity palate. The overall balance is sustained through to a long finish that exhibits that attractive note of bitterness so typical of the region.

➤ Le Fils Rogivue, rue Cotterd 6, 1071 Chexbres, tel. 021.946.17.39, fax 021.946.32.83, e-mail info@rogivue.ch ✉ ♈ by appt.

CH. DE LUINS Luins Chasselas

Réserve du propriétaire 1998★★★

☐ | 10.08 ha | 🍷 | n.c.

Golden-coloured, this Chasselas owes a period of cask maturation for its spicy aromas of pepper and cinnamon mixed with a plethora of flowers and fruits, notably peach and apricot. The rich and deliciously fresh taste exhibits a subtle liveliness that retains these flavours right through the finish. Here is a successful example of a wine that has managed to enhance its range of flavours through a period of ageing.

☞ Rémi Baechtold, Ch. de Luins, 1184 Luins, tel. 021.824.13.84, e-mail lbaechto@worldcom.ch ☑
☦ by appt.

CH. MAISON BLANCHE

Yvorne Chasselas 2000★★★

☐ | Gd cru | 6.44 ha | 70,000 | €8-11

The Yvorne vineyards are on a gravel soil with a deep limestone base. A landslide in 1584 effectively destroyed the village, covering the ground with a scree known as *ovaille* or *orvale* which meant 'disaster' in Old French. Some most attractive Chasselas are produced on this terrain, as evidenced by this soft and rich 2000. With a range of mineral, flower and fruit flavours, it exhibits attractive peachy notes on the middle of the palate. The mineral character and touch of bitterness on the finish bear witness to its origins.

☞ SA ch. Maison Blanche, CP 76, 1180 Rolle, tel. 021.822.02.02, fax 021.822.03.99 ☑ ☦ by appt.

DOM. DE MARCELIN

Morges Chasselas 2000★★

☐ | 2.42 ha | 12,500 | €5-8

The 7.5-ha (18.5-acre) Marcelin estate belongs to the College of Agriculture and Viticulture in Morges. The estate has produced a very pure Chasselas 2000, redolent of lime blossom. With a good balance between weight and acidity, the freshness on the palate reflects this floral character. The wine would be an excellent accompaniment to hard cheeses.

☞ Dom. de Marcelin, av. Marcelin, 1110 Morges, tel. 021.803.08.33, fax 021.803.08.36 ☑ ☦ by appt.

DOM. DU MARTHERAY

Féchy Chasselas 2000★★

☐ | Gd cru | 13.85 ha | 100,000 | €5-8

Clear and bright, this Chasselas shows a moderately powerful nose, a stony character along with peach, pineapple and lime-blossom aromas. Quite rounded on the palate, it has good freshness balanced by flavours of fruits and mineral notes, which extend into a pleasantly bitter finish. This wine demonstrates both good length and regional character and would go well with a soft cheese such as vacherin.

PIERRE MONACHON

Saint-Saphorin Merlot 1999★★★

■ | 0.1 ha | 6.00 | €15-23

This red-black Merlot matured in 18th-century vaulted cellars for a full year, boasts a fine and complex range of flavours recalling tobacco, cinnamon, smoke, plum and black cherries. The velvety taste is supported by tight-grained tannins and richness. Ripe and beautifully made as indicated by the very fruity finish, this wine can be enjoyed for the next five to eight years.

☞ Pierre Monachon, Cave de Dereyeu, 1812 Rivaz, tel. 021.946.15.97, fax 021.946.37.91 ☑ ☦ by appt.

LE CELLIER DU MAS

Tartegnin Pinot-gamay 2000★

■ | 1 ha | 🍷 | 6,000 | €8-11

A blend of 60% Pinot Noir and 40% Gamay has resulted in a fresh, deep ruby-red wine. The nose combines black-cherry and violet notes, whereas on the palate, fruit is to the fore with a solid tannic background. The wine's body is well integrated with a light acidity. There are still some noticeable tannins on the finish but these should soften by the end of 2002.

☞ Blanchard Frères, Le Cellier-du-Mas, 1185 Mont-sur-Rolle, tel. 021.825.19.22, fax 021.825.49.03, e-mail fblanchard@ blue-win.ch ☑ ☦ by appt.

☞ Fernand Blanchar

P.A. MEYLAN

Ollon Gamaret Elevé en barrique 2000★★

■ | 0.65 ha | 3,000 | €23-30

At the centre of this 4.2-ha (10.4-acre) vineyard stands a Savoyard-style house dating from the 18th century. Here, Gamaret grapes blended with 15% of the Garanoir variety yield a well-rounded wine, redolent of blackberries, black cherries and pepper, with a perceptible but unobtrusive hint of vanilla. The taste is rich and tannic leading to a moderately long finish.

☞ Meylan et Cavé, Le Raisin, 1867 Ollon, tel. 024.499.37.07, fax 024.499.37.08, e-mail chapellelaroche@bluewin.ch ☑
☦ by appt.

☞ SA dom. du Martheray, CP 76, 1180 Rolle, tel. 021.822.02.02, fax 021.822.03.99 ☑ ☦ by appt.

Vaud

PARFUM DE VIGNE
Coteau de Vincy Grain noir 2000★★
■ ▥ €11-15 · 0.4 ha · 3,500

This wine is an amalgam of all the typical red grape varieties of the Vaud: Gamaret, Garanoir, Diolinoir and Pinot Noir. They are blended together to give a wine of intense colour with a violet rim, a typical indication of youth. The expressive aroma is one of red and black fruit such as raspberry, blackberry and cherry, with a light suggestion of pepper and violets. The full-bodied palate shows tannins at first, but these evolve into a softer, velvet character with plenty of fruit at the finish. To allow better integration, this wine should be kept for a year.

➤ Jean-Jacques Steiner, Sous-Les-Vignes, 1195 Dully, tel. 021.824.11.22, fax 021.824.23.38, e-mail jjcsteiner@smartfree.ch ▣ Ⴟ by appt.

PONNAZ ET FILS
Calamin Chasselas 2000★★
□ Gd cru €8-11 · 0.5 ha · 5,000

The golden colour of this Chasselas presages its opulent aromas of peaches, apricots, mangoes and lime blossom. On the palate, it tastes simply exotic. The wine is well balanced, allying a delightfully fresh fruit taste with a slight sweetness. In the wake of the flowery and fruity flavours comes the touch of bitterness on the finish, typifying the wines of the region.

➤ Ponnaz et Fils, rte de Vevey 7, 1096 Cully, tel. 021.799.13.18, fax 021.799.13.26, e-mail ponnaz-et-fils@bluewin.ch ▣ Ⴟ by appt.

RESERVE DU PATRON Vully Pinot noir Elevé en barrique de chêne 2000★
□ ▥ €11-15 · 0.25 ha · 1,700

Some darker hints are evident in this pale-intensity red. Pronounced aromas of raspberry and black cherry with obvious oak flavours carry through to the palate. The mid-palate shows a structure of moderately powerful, rounded tannins.

➤ Daniel Matthey, pl. du Village, 1586 Vallamand-Dessus, tel. 026.677.13.30, fax 026.677.31.64, e-mail info@mattheydaniel.ch ▣ Ⴟ by appt.

ROBIN DES VIGNES
Villette Chasselas 2000★
□ €8-11 · 2.5 ha · 25,000

The scent of *pêche de vigne* can be detected alongside the more typical aroma of lime blossom. In which colour attests to a ripe wine, in which a touch of sweetness is balanced by attractive acidity. The finish betrays the attractive bitterness typical of the region.

➤ Association viticole de Lutry, Chem. Culturaz 21, 1095 Lutry, tel. 021.791.24.66, fax 021.791.67.24, e-mail avl@i-net.ch ▣ Ⴟ ev. day except Sun. 8.30am–12am 1.30pm–6pm; Sat. 8am–12am; groups by appt.

LOUIS-PHILIPPE ROUGE ET FILS
Epesses Chasselas La Réserve du Vigneron 2000★★★
■ ▥ ♦ €15-23 · 1 ha · 6,000

Floral notes, a mineral note and fruit too: in short, here are all the makings of a rich, full-bodied wine. Lime-blossom, peach, spice and gun-flint flavours fill the long-lasting palate. The wine, while excellent as an aperitif, also goes well with fish, white meat and cheese.

➤ Louis-Philippe et Philippe Rouge, cave de la Cornalle, 1098 Epesses, tel. 021.799.41.22, fax 021.799.26.64 ▣ Ⴟ by appt.

DOM. SERREAUX-DESSUS
Luins Chasselas 2000★★★
□ Gd cru €8-11 · 6.5 ha · 20,000

This pale-coloured Chasselas is an extremely fine and harmonious wine, obviously from a great *terroir*. With aromas of lime blossom, salty and mineral overtones, the acidity and rounded body provide an elegant structure that lasts through to the finish. The wine has excellent ageing potential.

➤ Hoirie Matringe, Serreaux-Dessus, 1268 Begnins, tel. 022.366.29.47, fax 022.366.28.57, e-mail serreauxdessus@bluemail.ch ▣ Ⴟ by appt.

SYMPHONIE DORÉE Epesses 2000★★
□ ▥ €15-23 · 0.2 ha · 700

A veritable golden symphony of Chasselas is joined by 10% of Sylvaner grapes to give a nose that hints at overripeness in its aromas of peach, apricot and mandarin orange. On the palate, the wine is as sweet as one could wish, yet with just the right amount of acidity to offset its richness, right through to a long finish.

➤ Michel Blanche, Dom. d'Aucrêt, 1091 Bahyse-sur-Cully, tel. 021.799.36.75, fax 021.799.38.14, e-mail cave.aucret@worldcom.ch ▣ Ⴟ ev. day 8am–12am 1.30pm–6pm

Valais

The valley of the Haute-Rhône is a land of contrasts, fashioned through the millennia by the advance and retreat of the glacier. Many of the vineyards on the steep hills are laid out in terraces.

Valais is like a part of Provence in the heart of the Alps. Close to the eternal alpine snows, vines grow alongside apricot trees and asparagus. On the pathways of the *bisses* (a local name for irrigation channels), a walker will come across almond trees, pheasant's eye, sweet chestnut trees, cactus, praying mantises and scorpions, and find absinthe, wormwood, hyssop and thyme growing along the walls.

More than 40 grape varieties are grown in the Valais, some not to be found elsewhere, including Arvine, Humagne, Amigne and Cornalin. Here, Chasselas is called Fendant and a local cross between Pinot Noir and Gamay creates the Dôle. Both are AOC Crus and, according to the *terroir*, range from fruitiness to a greater elegance in character.

ARDEVINE Chamoson 1999★

1 ha   6,000   €11-15

This blend of Cabernet Sauvignon, Syrah, Humagne and Merlot is matured in cask for a year. The nose gives intense but fine flavours of spices and the palate is full and silky. There is a touch of tannin still noticeable on the finish, but the wine should develop an attractive harmony within about two years from now.

• Michel Boven, Latigny 4, 1955 Chamoson, tel. 027.306.28.36, fax 027.306.74.00, e-mail michel.boven@revaz.com ☑ ☗ by appt.

ANTOINE ET CHRISTOPHE BETRISEY Saint-Léonard Pinot noir

Elevé en fût de chêne 1999★

0.3 ha   3,000   €11-15

From a light gravel-limestone soil with a substantial slate content, this intense ruby-red Pinot Noir gives aromas from its ten months in cask: roasted coffee beans, toast, and vanilla. Excellent tannins frame this full and well-structured wine, which still has noticeable oak flavours. It should be ready for

TRIADE

Réserve Elevé en barrique 1999★★

0.2 ha   2,100   €11-15

Pinot Noir, Gamaret, and Garanoir form an elegant triad in this deep-red wine, whose colour is almost tinged with black. Aromas of pepper, cinnamon and berry fruits accentuate a light touch of oak. The wine fills the palate with its richness, sustained by tight-grained tannins. A suggestion of vanilla features in the long finish. Here is a wine that can be laid down for at least five years.

• Association vinicole de Corseaux, rue du Village 20, 1802 Corseaux, tel. 021.921.31.85, fax 021.821.31.10, e-mail info@avc-vins.ch ☑ ☗ by appt.

VALLON DE L'AUBANNE

Lavigny Chasselas Elevé sur lie 2000★★

0.5 ha   4,100   €8-11

This Chasselas demands food and would be an excellent accompaniment for fish in white sauce. The golden colour delivers a range of aromas redolent of flowers offset by a touch of saltiness. Deliciously fresh and fruity, it leaves an impression of roundness on the palate and should develop well over the next five years.

• Jacques et Stéphane Schmidt, cave du Vallon, 1175 Lavigny, tel. 021.808.61.92, fax 021.808.61.92, e-mail info@caveduvallon.ch ☗ by appt.

DOM. DE VILLAROSE

Vully Chardonnay Fleur de vigne 2000★

0.3 ha   n.c.   €8-11

This attractively golden Chardonnay opens on fresh aromas of citrus fruits and peaches which are sustained on the palate and underscored by an admirable freshness. The finish shows a certain amount of richness as well as good length, though the wine will be at its best whilst still young.

• Alain Besse, Dom. de Villarose, 1787 Mur, tel. 026.673.12.40, fax 026.673.14.95, e-mail p.a.besse@bluewin.ch ☑ ☗ by appt.

CH. DE VINZEL

Vinzel Chasselas 2000★★

Gd cru   8.34 ha   70,000   €5-8

Until the 18th century, the vineyards of the Château de Vinzel and those of the neighbouring Château La Bâtie formed part of a single estate. Today, Vinzel has 8.3 ha (20 acres). Their Chasselas has a mineral and slightly salty character allied to aromas of lime blossom and *pêche de vigne*. The wine is soft but full, with that undeniable hint of bitterness that is the hallmark of wines from the Vaud.

• SA Ch. de Vinzel, CP 76, 1180 Rolle, tel. 021.822.02.02, fax 021.822.03.99 ☑ by appt.

ALBERT BIOLLAZ

Belle Provinciale Petite arvine 2000★★

| | 0.2 ha | 3,000 | | | €11–15 |

This Belle Provinciale is yellow with tinges of gold with a floral perfume, including notes of wisteria. The palate is well structured, showing a straightforward, lively and fresh fruit character. The **red Renaissance Humagne 2000** is awarded one star.

☞ Les Hoirs Albert Biollaz, rue du Prieuré 5, 1956 Saint-Pierre-de-Clages,
tel. 027.306.28.86, fax 027.306.62.50,
e-mail info@biollaz-vins.ch ☑ ⟂ by appt.

CHARLES BONVIN FILS

Humagne blanche 1999★★

| | n.c. | 2,000 | | | €15–23 |

The Charles Bonvin company was founded at the end of the 18th century. In 1992, it joined forces with the merchant Varone based at Champsec, and today they share wine-making facilities while each retains its autonomy. This dry white is a pale yellow with tinges of grey and gives a delicately floral nose and a fresh fruity palate. Flavours of peach and apricot give way to an elegant suggestion of bitterness on the finish. The Jury awarded a star to two wines: the **Heida 2000**, a dry white which combines strength and freshness, and the **Dôle du Château Cuvée Réservée 2000.**

☞ Charles Bonvin Fils, Grand Champsec 30, 1950 Sion 4, tel. 027.203.41.31,
fax 027.203.47.07, e-mail info@
charlesbonvin.ch ☑ ⟂ ev. day except Sun.
10am–12am 2pm–6.30pm

CAPRICE DU TEMPS

Coteaux de Sierre Chardonnay 2000★

| | 0.23 ha | 2,000 | | | €8–11 |

Good weather for the 2000 vintage conspired with the limestone soil and southern exposure here to produce an enjoyable Chardonnay, ready to drink now. Pale yellow with some intensity, it shows floral notes on the nose and citrus fruits on the palate. Long and concentrated there is good, balancing acidity.

☞ Hugues Clavien et Fils, Cave Caprice du Temps, rte la Coin-du-Carro, 3972 Miège,
tel. 027.455.76.40, fax 027.455.76.40,
e-mail clavien@capricedutemps.com ☑
⟂ by appt.

CHAMPORTAY Martigny Dôle 2000★★

| ■ | n.c. | n.c. | | | €8–11 |

Dry-stone walls support this 14-ha (35-acre) terraced vineyard on the slopes above the town of Martigny. This deep-red Dôle has tinges of violet and offers aromas of ripe fruit (strawberry, raspberry and blackcurrant), before filling the palate to give a rounded body structured by noticeable, but

---

fleshy tannins. This is a wine that has already achieved good balance but will continue to be appreciated for at least three more years. The **Gamay de Champortay 2000** is equally remarkable.

☞ Gérald et Patricia Besse, Les Rappes, 1921 Martigny-Combe, tel. 027.722.78.81, fax 027.723.21.94 ☑ ⟂ by appt.

CAVE CHANTEVIGNE

Petite arvine 2000★

| | 0.1 ha | 700 | | | €6–11 |

Raphaël Vergère, who set up this family producer in 1984, is also a nurseryman by profession and is therefore a specialist in grape varieties. His golden-coloured Petite Arvine comes from a soil of clay with black schist and gives off fragrances of citrus and exotic fruits. Tasting straightforward and fresh at the start, it gives a suggestion of sweetness and is well structured on the middle palate. On the finish the flavours of grapefruit and lemon give way to a characteristic hint of saltiness.

☞ Raphaël Vergère, Cave de Chantevigne, rue de Conthey 25, 1963 Vétroz,
tel. 027.346.34.48, e-mail r.vergere@
netplus.ch ☑ ⟂ by appt.

THIERRY CONSTANTIN

Johannisberg Larme de décembre 1999★★★

| ◨▯ | 0.28 ha | 900 | | | €15–23 |

Thierry Constantin opened a small tasting cellar on this 5.5-ha (14-acre) estate in April 2001. His sweet Johannisberg (alias the Sylvaner grape), a gold-coloured wine with hints of straw yellow, boasts strong flavours of damp undergrowth, crystallised pears and chestnuts. Rich and unctuous, the palate shows some good botrytis notes and presents excellent balance that will delight the senses for years to come. Sold in 50-cl bottles, it will be best left to age for three years. The Jury awarded two stars to another sweet wine, the **Larme d'Or Petite Arvine 99 (37.5-cl bottles).**

☞ Thierry Constantin, rte de Savoie, 1962 Pont-de-la-Morge, tel. 079.433.16.81, fax 077.346.60.20, e-mail tyconstantin@
tvsznet.ch ☑ ⟂ by appt.

CAVE CORBASSIERE

Saillon Malvoisie 2000★★

| | 0.3 ha | 3,000 | | ♦ | €11–15 |

Flecks of gold herald the imposing presence of this sweet wine with its aromas of raisins and quince. The taste achieves a fine balance between sweetness and fresh acidity sustained by flavours of walnut. This fine

---

drinking in between one and three years from now.

☞ Antoine et Christophe Bétrisey, rue du Château, 12, 1958 Saint-Léonard,
tel. 027.203.11.26, fax 027.203.40.26,
e-mail betrisey@bluewin.ch ☑ ⟂ by appt.

wine deserves to be laid down for two years, a time enough in which to appreciate the highly successful **Johannisberg de Saillon 2000**, a fully rounded dry white redolent of grilled almonds and orange blossom.

- Cave Corbassière, rte de Traux, 1913 Saillon, tel. 027.744.14.03, fax 027.744.39.20, e-mail info@ cave-corbassiere.ch Ⓥ

CORNULUS Cornalin Antica 1999★★★

| ■ | 0.6 ha | 2,500 | ■ | € 15-23 |

The Cornalin, also known as the *vieux rouge* of the Valais, is a typical Swiss grape variety from the Alpine regions that was chronicled in the register of Anniviers in 1313. Today very rare, Cornalin finds its true expression in this marvellous 99. With a deep-ruby, violet-tinged colour and aromas of morello cherry, red berries, spices and hints of minerals, the beautifully rich and powerful palate of spiced fruit is perfectly balanced by distinctive tannins. The finish is long and sustained. The Cornulus estate also offers a remarkable **Octoglaive Hermitage Grain Noble 99** and a most successful **Clos des Corbassières Chasselas Vieilles Vignes 2000**.

- Dom. Cornulus, Stéphane Reynard et Dany Varone, 1965 Savièse, tel. 027.395.25.45, fax 027.395.25.45, e-mail cornulus@bluewin.ch Ⓥ by appt.

PIERRE-ANTOINE CRETTENAND

Gamaret 2000★

| ■ | 0.3 ha | 1,000 | ■ | € 8-11 |

The Gamaret variety harvested on the schist soil of this estate has given rise to a dark red, spicy wine. The palate is lively at the start and the middle of the palate reveals a full body sustained by fine tannins. The finish is long.

- Pierre-Antoine Crettenand, rte de Tobrouk, 1913 Saillon, tel. 027.744.29.60, fax 027.744.29.60 Ⓥ by appt.

JEAN-YVES CRETTENAND

Saillon Humagne rouge 2000★

| ■ | n.c. | 1,000 | ■ | € 8-11 |

A violet edge attests to the wine's youth although the nose is already strongly evocative of ivy flowers. The palate opens fresh and lively but it has sound structure and length with underlying flavours of damp forest undergrowth and violets. This wine should be laid down for between two and five years to allow full integration of the tannins.

- Jean-Yves Crettenand, 1913 Saillon, tel. 027.744.12.73, fax 027.744.21.08 Ⓥ by appt.

PHILIPPE DARIOLY

Ermitage Grains nobles 1999★

| □ | 0.13 ha | 900 | ■ | € 25-30 |

The Ermitage grape is none other than the Marsanne of the Rhône Valley. Its *grains nobles* or botrytis-affected berries are at the heart of this amber-gold-coloured wine with its hints of white truffle, raspberry liqueur, forest undergrowth and crystallised oranges.

Sweetness is the first impression, presaging a taste that is powerful and overripe yet balanced with a distinct acidity. The finish is agreeably long.

- Philippe Darioly, Fusion 160, 1920 Martigny, tel. 027.723.27.66 Ⓥ by appt.

DESFAYES-CRETTENAND

Leytron Syrah 2000★★

| ■ | 1 ha | 6,000 | ■ | € 11-15 |

This delightful young Syrah from the schistose soils of Leytron has an intense violet colour and a bouquet of spices, notably pepper. It seems already perfectly balanced on the palate, with obvious tannins that should allow the wine to age well over the next four years.

- Desfayes-Crettenand, 1912 Leytron, tel. 027.306.28.07, fax 027.306.28.84 Ⓥ by appt.

GILBERT DEVAYES

Leytron Petite arvine 2000★

| □ | 0.5 ha | 2,700 | ■ | € 11-15 |

The wines from this estate are nurtured in old, vaulted 18th-century cellars. This yellow-coloured wine from the Petite Arvine variety shows green tinges and intense aromas of citrus and exotic fruits. Immediate freshness is evident on the palate and the flavours echo the fruity notes of peach and blackberries, culminating in a touch of saltiness. The **Fendant de Leytron 2000** is also awarded a star.

- Gilbert Devayes, Cave La Dôle Blanche, ruelle de la Cotze, 1912 Leytron, tel. 027.306.25.96, fax 027.306.63.46 Ⓥ by appt.

BLAISE DUBUIS

Lentine Fendant 2000★

| □ | 0.25 ha | n.c. | ■ | € 8-11 |

The aroma of lime blossom imbues this pale yellow wine with a pleasing freshness. On the palate, fruit and mineral notes combine to produce a most successful and well-balanced wine.

- Blaise Dubuis, rte de Drône, 1965 Savièse, tel. 079.606.52.46 Ⓥ by appt.

HENRI DUMOULIN

Savièse Fendant 2000★

| □ | 0.5 ha | 5,000 | ■ | € 5-8 |

The pronounced fruitiness of this characteristic Chasselas makes it an excellent accompaniment to cheese and fish dishes. Pale yellow, with strong aromas of lime blossom, this wine is simple, but lively and very easy-drinking.

- Henri Dumoulin, rte de Zambotte, 1965 Savièse, tel. 027.395.10.69, fax 027.395.10.69, e-mail eddydumoulin@ bluewin.ch Ⓥ by appt.

SIMON FAVRE-BERCLAZ

Humagne rouge 1999★★

■ 0.045 ha 2,900 ■ ▲ €8-11

This dark red wine with tinges of violet shows notes of leather and game. These flavours persist on the powerful palate, which is structured by noticeable tannins. A rather rustic, albeit characteristic wine that would be best kept for four or five years. By the same token, the cask-matured, powerful and remarkably flavoursome **Chardonnay Grain Noble 98** from grapes harvested at the end of January 1999, deserves to be kept a good ten years.

➤ Simon Favre-Berclaz, Cave d'Anchettes, 3973 Venthône, tel. 027.455.14.57, fax 027.455.14.57 ☑ ⅄ by appt.

HERVÉ FONTANNAZ

Amigne de Vétroz 2000★

□ Gd cru 0.5 ha 2,800 ■ ▲ €11-15

With aromas of mandarin orange peel and crystallised mandarins on the nose, and very ripe pineapple showing through on the powerful palate, this wine has a slight sweetness due to 4 g per litre residual sugar. The strong finish betrays subtle tannins. This Amigne would be ideal as an accompaniment to breast of duck in a honey sauce.

➤ Hervé Fontannaz, chem. du Repos 8, 1963 Vétroz, tel. 027.346.47.47, fax 027.346.47.47, e-mail info@cavelatine.ch ☑ ⅄ ev. day except Sun. 8am–12am 1.30pm–6pm; Sat. 8am–12am; Mon. 1.30pm–6pm

JO GAUDARD

Leytron Humagne blanc 2000★

□ 0.1 ha 800 ■ ▲ €8-11

The Humagne Blanc variety dates back to the 12th century but is rare today, planted on perhaps no more than a dozen hectares (around 30 acres) in the canton of Valais. This pale yellow 2000 with its gold highlights is a very representative example of the variety. On the nose it shows distinct lime blossom aromas, and on the palate a subtle taste of resin is followed by an enjoyable fresh fruit character that carries through to the finish.

➤ Jo Gaudard, rte de Chamoson, 1912 Leytron, tel. 027.306.60.69, fax 027.306.72.18, e-mail jogaudard@bluewin.ch ☑ ⅄ by appt.

MAURICE GAY

Dôle les Mazots 2000★★

□ 3 ha 25,000 ■ ▲ €8-11

Three wines of the Les Mazots range caught the attention of the Jury. One star was awarded to the **Petite Arvine Les Mazots 99**, an oak-aged dry white that retains its full fruit flavour against a background of toast and vanilla. A star was also awarded to the **Fendant de Sion Les Mazots 2000**. The Dôle was rated higher on account of its distinctive character and balance. It offers a deliciously fresh nose with concentrated aromas of red berries, followed by a fresh and

straightforward palate indicating that it is ready for drinking.

➤ SA Maurice Gay, Vignoble de Ravanay, 1955 Chamoson, tel. 027.306.53.53, fax 027.306.53.88, e-mail mauricegay@mauricegay.ch ☑ ⅄ ev. day except Sat. & Sun. 8am–5pm; cl. 23 Jul.–10 Aug.

ROBERT GILLIARD Syrah 1999★★

■ 2 ha 15,000 ▥ €15-23

Robert Gilliard has a vineyard area of 40 ha (99 acres) on a schist and sandstone soil, including one parcel, Domaine de la Cotzette, that is supported by a 20-m-high (65-ft) dry-stone wall. This Syrah shows floral aromas accompanied by spices and woodland berries. Floral notes also show through on the complex and well-structured palate, whose intense, classic fruity flavours are pleasantly long. The **Vendémiaire Pinot Noir 99** and the red **Antares 98**, both also matured in oak, were each awarded a single star.

➤ SA Robert Gilliard, rue de Loèche 70, 1950 Sion, tel. 027.329.89.29, fax 027.329.89.27, e-mail vins@gilliard.ch ☑ ⅄ by appt.

MAURICE ET XAVIER GIROUD-POMMAR

Chamoson Fendant 2000★

□ 0.5 ha 4,500 ■ ▲ €5-8

This Chasselas exhibits the obligatory lime blossom and mineral notes but asserts its individuality in the pineapple and lemon flavours found on the long palate. There is a good balance between the wine's weight and acidity.

➤ Maurice et Xavier Giroud-Pommar, Pommey 21, cave la Sisezarche, 1955 Chamoson, tel. 027.306.44.52, fax 027.306.90.19 ☑ ⅄ by appt.

DOM. DU GRAND-BRULE

Petite arvine 2000★

□

For their viticultural research, the Valais cantonal authorities have chosen a site on gravel limestone with scattered bushes and thickets of Scots pine. The Petite Arvine is one of twenty-four grape varieties grown here. This 2000 is a complex wine with aromas of flowers and grapefruit, whose lively and forthright taste is one of sustained fruit underscored by a hint of saltiness.

➤ Vignoble de l'Etat du Valais, 1912 Leytron, tel. 027.306.21.05, fax 027.306.36.05 ☑ ⅄ by appt.

GRANDGOUSIER Fendant 2000★★

□ 6 ha 35,000 ■ ▲ €5-8

A brilliant colour with touches of gold is a feature of this floral and fruity Fendant with discreet hints of lime blossom. Elegant and deliciously fresh and fruity on the palate, there is a happy liaison between this grape variety and the estate's limestone-schistose soil.

● SA Les Fils Maye, Rte des Caves, 1908 Riddes, tel. 027.305.15.00, fax 027.305.15.01 ▼ Y by appt.

O. HUGENTOBLER

Le Préféré Pinot noir 2000★

■ 1 ha | 25,000 | €8-11

This Pinot Noir could be served right away as an accompaniment to red meat or a cheese-board. Behind the deep ruby-red colour, the flavours run the gamut of red berries, while the tannins have already softened, imparting a most agreeable balance.

● Vins O. Hugentobler, Varenstr. 50, 3970 Salgesch, tel. 027.455.18.62, fax 027.455.18.56 ▼ Y by appt.

IMESCH VINS SIERRE

Petite arvine 2000★★

■ 2 ha | n.c. | €15-23

The Imesch family have been vine-growers in the Valais since the late 19th century and currently manage some 50 ha (124 acres) of vineyards, with ten in the area around the town of Sierre. This bright, yellow-green Petite Arvine shows a range of exotic fruit (pineapple) punctuated by a hint of minerals and iodine. The palate is refreshing and powerful and preserves its fruity character through to the typical salty note on the finish. Equally noteworthy is the **Marsanne Noble Cépage 99**, which is rich and powerful. The **Pinot Noir Les Communes Soleil de Sierre 2000**, is also a great success.

● SA Imesch Vins Sierre, place Beaulieu 8, 3960 Sierre, tel. 027.452.36.80, fax 027.452.36.89, e-mail imesch.vins@ swissonline.ch ▼ Y by appt.

CAVE LABACHOLLE

Chamoson Humagne rouge 2000

■ 0.3 ha | 2,000 | €8-11

The dark-red colour still shows some violet tinges. Gamey notes combine with red fruit in a strongly concentrated nose. On the palate, the flavours of fruit dominate. Though the tannins are still marked, they are already beginning to integrate with the richness of the wine. It should be kept for one or two years.

● Jacques Remondeulaz et Fils, chem. neuf 11, 1955 Chamoson, tel. 079.332.12.44, fax 077.306.51.44 ▼ Y by appt.

CAVE DE LA COMBE

Chamoson Johannisberg 2000★

■ 0.2 ha | 2,000 | €5-8

Bertrand Gaillard took over the reins of this family estate in 2000 and his first year of production is acknowledged here with this harmonious Johannisberg. With a yellow colour showing flashes of gold and green, it has a nose of pronounced fruit and bitter almond. Similar flavours continue on the palate before it finishes on a characteristic touch of bitterness. The wine can be enjoyed now.

● Bertrand Gaillard, Cave de La Combe, 1957 Ardon, tel. 027.306.13.33, fax 027.306.59.87 ▼ Y by appt.

LA TORNALE

Chamoson Chasselas 2000★★

■ n.c. | 15,000 | €5-8

Glints of green sparkle amid the pale yellow of this fruity and mineral-flavoured wine. The palate is fresh at the start and this is emphasised on the middle of the palate by a touch of sparkle that agreeably brings out the fruit.

CAVE DE L'ANGELUS

Lacrima Grain noble Confidentiel 1996★

■ n.c. | 2,700 | €23-30

A blend of Pinot Gris, Ermitage (Marsanne) and Johannisberg (Sylvaner) has resulted in this Grain Noble (a designation of at least 15 years of age, a minimum natural sugar content at harvest, and maturation in cask for at least 12 months). Glints of ochre-orange punctuate the colour, presaging a concentrated range of flavours of honey, walnuts and apricots. On the palate, there are suggestions of dark chocolate, raisins and caramel. Rich and long, this wine is balanced by a welcome hint of acidity.

● G. Liand et Fils, cave de L'Angélus, rte de Bonse, 1965 Saviese, tel. 027.395.12.33, fax 027.395.12.06, e-mail guyliand@ bluewin.ch ▼ Y by appt.

CAVE LA MADELEINE

Amigne de Vétroz 2000★★

■ Gd cru | 0.4 ha | 2,000 | €11-15

This 2000 Amigne grown on the schistose terraces of Vétroz has pronounced mineral notes coupled with mandarin-orange aromas. The straightforward, rounded palate is well structured and sustained, and the wine is ready for drinking now. The **Fendant de Vétroz 2000** is also awarded two stars.

● André Fontannaz, Cave La Madeleine, 1963 Vétroz, tel. 027.346.45.54, fax 027.346.45.54 ▼ Y by appt.

CAVE DE LA CRETTAZ

Venthône Humagne blanche 2000★

■ 0.1 ha | 830 | €11-15

The locality known as La Crettaz lies less than 1 km (½ mile) from the Château de Venthône and is known for its plantings of the Humagne Blanche variety. This pale yellow 2000 exudes a fragrance of honey and mineral notes. The wine is very fresh on the palate showing touches of gun-flint flavour. This is a wine to be enjoyed right away, perhaps together with a carpaccio of tuna on a bed of bean sprouts in sesame oil.

● Guy Berclaz, chem. de Fontanay, 3973 Venthône, tel. 027.456.16.32, fax 027.456.16.32, e-mail guyberclaz@ bluewin.ch ▼ Y by appt.

LA TOURMENTE

Chamoson Humagne rouge 1998★★★

■   n.c.   1,800   ■   €11-15

On a schistose-clay soil that emerged from the alluvial cone of Chamoson more than 5,000 years ago this fully south-facing vineyard has produced an exemplary 98 wine. With a shimmering red-black colour, the nose shows the characteristic fruit of the Humagne grape variety, underscored by hints of violet and tobacco. Full-bodied and rich, this is an elegant wine that boasts a pleasant freshness on the palate, with well-integrated tannins. It needs another two to five years of ageing. The Jury also awarded two stars to the **Syrah de Chamoson 98**.

☛ Bernard Coudray et Fils, Cave La Tourmente, Tsavez 6, 1955 Chamoson, tel. 027.306.18.32, fax 027.306.34.56, e-mail tourmente.cave@bluewin.ch ⓥ Ⓨ by appt.

LE BOSSET Humagne rouge 2000★

■   0.6 ha   4,000   ■ €11-15

In 1999, Romaine Blaser-Michellod assumed sole charge of this estate which she had managed jointly with her father over the previous decade. Her Humagne Rouge 2000 is a powerful red on a silky tannin base, where the aroma of black cherry extends on the palate into flavours of wild berries, chocolate and spices.

☛ Michellod et Romaine Blaser, Cave Le Bosset, chem. des Ecoliers, 1912 Leytron, tél. 027.306.18.80, fax 027.306.18.80 ⓥ Ⓨ by appt.

LES FUMEROLLES Fendant 2000★

□   1 ha   10,000   ■   € €8-11

The estate lies on the hill of Montorge that enjoys the effects of the waters of a small lake. This Chasselas amply reflects the harmony of the surrounding countryside. Pale yellow-green, it exudes notes of lime blossom and lemon on the nose, which give way to a more mineral flavour on the palate. The fresh taste is structured and long.

☛ SA Cave de Montorge, La Muraz, 1950 Sion, tel. 027.327.50.60, fax 027.395.13.60 ⓥ Ⓨ ev. day except Sat. & Sun. 8am–12am 1.30pm–5.45pm

LEUKERSONNE

Pinot gris Strohwein 2000★

□   0.15 ha 415   ■ € €15-23

The intensely gold colour of this 'straw wine' is attributable to drying the grapes on a bed of straw. Swirling the glass releases strong aromas of honey and quince. The palate strikes a happy balance between sweetness and acidity. This wine will be fully appreciated three years from now and for a decade to come.

☛ Weinkellerei Leukersonne – R. Seewer und Söhne, Sportplatzstte 5, 3952 Susten, tel. 027.473.20.35, fax 027.473.40.15, e-mail info@leukersonne.ch ⓥ Ⓨ by appt.
☛ René Seewer

L'ORMY Chasselas 2000★★★

■   0.3 ha   3,000   ■ € €8-11

True-to-type this Chasselas is a pale yellow with green tinges and presents strong aromas of banana and lemon. There is immediately obvious fruit on the palate and a very good balance between liveliness and roundness. Ready for drinking now, the finish is of good length and pleasantly fresh.

☛ Nicolas Zufferey, rte des Bernunes, 3960 Sierre, tel. 027.656.51.41, fax 027.456.51.10 ⓥ Ⓨ by appt.

L'ORPAILLEUR Petite arvine 2000★

□   0.1 ha   750   ■   € €8-11

For the past three years, Frédéric Dumoulin has worked as a wine-producer in his own right, alongside his daytime job as oenologist in a wine company. He currently has close on 3 ha (7.5 acres) of vineyards, partly on lease. His Petite Arvine with its yellow-green colour is a classic example from the region. Aromas of exotic fruits (pineapple) and citrus fruits explode from the glass. The palate is full and rich with soft overtones of wisteria and grapefruit. The finish is fresh and elegant.

☛ Frédéric Dumoulin, rue du Chemin de Fer 140, 1958 Uvrier, tel. 079.640.90.21, fax 077.203.37.10, e-mail orpailleur@ bluewin.ch ⓥ Ⓨ by appt.

MABILLARD-FUCHS

Venthône Gamay 2000★

■   0.22 ha 1,800   ■ € €5-8

The 2000 is a classic Gamay: purply-red, strongly redolent of black fruits, fresh and fruity on the palate, and with distinct, yet soft tannins, it achieves the ideal balance to accompany either charcuterie or a barbecue. The **Chasselas de Venthône**, an equally

☛ Vincent Favre – La Tornale, rue des Plantys 22, 1955 Chamoson, tel. 027.306.22.65, fax 027.306.64.43, e-mail jd.favre@bluewin.ch ⓥ Ⓨ by appt.

successful balance between freshness and full-ness, is characterised by elegant aromas of lime blossom.

MAJOR ROUGE
Salquenen Pinot noir 1998★

0.4 ha 2,500 €8-11 by appt.

This small family concern was founded by Arthur Schmid in 1959 and is managed today by brothers Reinhard and Christian Schmid. The Pinot Noir 98 is a wine of character, with strong fruit flavours showing through on both the nose and the palate. It is structured by good tannins and has attractive roundness and suppleness.

Famille Arthur Schmid, Weinschmiede, Tschuetrigstrasse 27, 3970 Salgesch, tel. 079.329.21.65, fax 077.322.80.61, e-mail chris.family3@bluewin.ch

ADRIAN MATHIER Cornalin 1999★★
n.c. 2,500 €15-23

This ruby-red wine with tinges of mauve comes from Cornalin vines planted on a lime-stone scree soil. Aromas of spices and cloves are followed by a lively fruitiness on the mid-palate with well-integrated, supple tannins and an elegant finish. Mention should also be made of the most accomplished **Johannisberg Weidmannstrunk 2000** and the **Pinot Noir Oeil-de-perdrix La Matze 2000**, respectively a dry white and a rosé.

Adrian Mathier, Nouveau Salquenen S.A., Bahnofstrasse 50, 3970 Salgesch, tel. 027.455.75.75, fax 027.456.24.13, e-mail info@mathier.com by appt.
Yvo Mathier

SIMON MAYE ET FILS
Chamoson Syrah 2000★★★

1.5 ha 7,000

The pretty village of Saint-Pierre-de-Clages is justifiably proud both of its 11th-century Roman church and its vineyards growing on the gravel-limestone soil. This Syrah also deserves to be a source of pride for its grower: rich in colour, it exudes sustained aromas hinting at cherries, blackcurrant and

clove. Richly structured, evident tannins are well integrated with ripe fruit. Overall, the palate is smooth and balanced and the wine can be enjoyed in around three years from now. The Jury also found the **Humagne Rouge de Chamoson 2000** to be excellent.

Simon Maye et Fils, Collombey 3, 1956 Saint-Pierre-de-Clages, tel. 027.306.85.82, fax 027.306.80.02, e-mail simon.maye@swissonline.ch
by appt.

BERNARD MERMOUD
Petite arvine 2000★★

0.1 ha 800 €5-8

Flashes of gold glisten in this sweet-tasting 2000. Aromas of citrus and exotic fruits are evident on the nose, whereas the palate shows a distinct taste of grapefruit. The balance is sustained through to a touch of saltiness on the finish, typical for the Petite Arvine variety. This 2000 may be enjoyed immediately and over the next six years. (50-cl bottles)

Bernard Mermoud, Cave l'Or du Vent, chem. des Vendanges, 3968 Veyras, tel. 027.455.88.20, fax 027.455.88.20, e-mail bernardmermoud@swissonline.ch
by appt.

MITIS Amigne de Vétroz
Grains nobles confidentiel 1998★★★

n.c. n.c. €15-23

The Amigne grape variety dates back to Roman times but today is extremely rare: of the 24 ha (59 acres) under cultivation world-wide, some 18 ha (45 acres) are grown here in the vineyards of Vétroz. This sweet 1998 flies the Amigne flag with pride. A deep yellow with glints of green-gold, it has a slightly charred aroma that complements the intense nose of pear, apricot jam and saffron. The palate is rich and offers an attractive balance between sweetness and acidity leading to a very long finish. This producer has also dis-tinguished itself with two other noteworthy wines: the **red Gally 99**, a blend of Gamay with the Diolinoir variety, and the **red Humagne 99**. The **Fendant de Vétroz** is awarded a single star.

S.A. Germanier Bon Père Balavaud, 1963 Vétroz, tel. 027.346.12.16, fax 027.346.51.32, e-mail wine@bonpere.com by appt.
Jean-René Germanier

DOM. DU MONT D'OR

Saint-Martin Johannisberg 1999★★★

☐   2 ha   3,500   ▥ €15-23

The Johannisberg grape has been grown on this limestone-schist and sandstone *terroir* since 1870. Living up to the past, on the eve of the new millennium, Mont d'Or produced a Johannisberg of rich-gold colour with a powerful nose redolent of sultanas and crystallised fruit. Rounded and voluptuous, its taste of overripe grapes lingers long on the palate, retaining finesse throughout. By way of confirmation of the excellence of this grape variety, two stars are also awarded to the *cuvée* **Premier Décembre 99**, while the **Dôle Perle Noire 2000** achieves an honourable mention and is awarded one star.

➤ Dom. du Mont d'Or SA-Sion, Pont-de-la-Morge, case postale 240, 1964 Conthey 1, tel. 027.346.20.32, fax 027.346.51.78, e-mail montdor@ montdor-wine.ch ▨ ▼ by appt.

OPALINE Petite arvine 2000★

☐   6 ha   6,000   ▤ ♦ €11-15

Louis-Bernard Emery boasts a *carnotzet* (a converted underground gallery or tunnel) directly below his vineyard at Saint-Léonard. Here, in this attractive tasting cellar, one can enjoy his golden Petite Arvine with its aromas of honey and green walnut. The palate shows good acidity and delivers a generous, refreshing and fully rounded taste, finishing on a salty note, typical of this grape variety.

➤ Cave Emery, Argnou, 1966 Ayent, tel. 079.221.10.86, fax 077.398.14.68, e-mail louis.bernard.emery@span.ch ▨ ▼ by appt.

➤ Louis Emery

PERLES DU SOLEIL

Coteaux de Sierre Fût de chêne 1999★

☐   0.5 ha   1,600   ▥ €15-23

Vines grown in this 4.5-ha (11-acre) vineyard on the limestone slopes of Sierre enjoy a great deal of sunshine. Full advantage of this has been taken by the Chardonnay and Petite Arvine that make up this harmonious wine. Golden-yellow, it exhibits distinctive aromas of citrus and tropical fruits followed by that unmistakable touch of saltiness, revealing the presence of the typical Valais grape variety, Petite Arvine. Well balanced, the wine can age for a full ten years. The **Fendant des Coteaux de Sierre** is also awarded a star.

➤ Claudy Clavien, Les Champs, 3972 Miège, tel. 027.455.24.23, fax 027.455.24.23 ▨ ▼ by appt.

LES FRERES PHILIPPOZ

Leytron Marsanne 1999★★★

☐   0.4 ha   2,000   ▤ ♦ €11-15

The Philippoz brothers have produced a memorable Marsanne in 99, a glittering golden-yellow wine that emits strong aromas of white truffles and raspberry liqueur. The full, fleshy palate has an elegant balance. An extremely fine wine, it reveals all the complexity of the grape variety. Equally remarkable is the **Malvoisie Flétrie de Leytron 99** which, in line with the *grains nobles* quality charter requirements, prescribing eighteen months in the barrel, has mellowed into a full and complex wine with a subtle oak flavours. Meanwhile, the **Petite Arvine Flétrie de Leytron Grains Nobles** is no less worthy of its two stars.

➤ Philippoz Frères, rte de Riddes 13, 1912 Leytron, tel. 027.306.30.16, fax 027.306.71.33 ▨ ▼ by appt.

PLANCHE-BILLON

Petite arvine 2000★

☐   0.36 ha   2,100   ▤ ♦ €11-15

Oswald Vallotton began his estate in 1928 by buying up vineyards in Combe d'Enfer, Claives and Planche-Billon. From the last-named vine parcel on a gneiss soil comes this 2000 Petite Arvine. A clear yellow with green highlights, it conjures up aromas of wisteria and a mixture of citrus fruits: This is a successful balance between slight sweetness and fresh acidity, together with attractive hints of grapefruit underpinned by some salty notes.

➤ Henri Vallotton, rue Morin, 1926 Fully, tel. 027.746.28.89, fax 027.746.28.38, e-mail vallottonhenri@bluewin.ch ▨ ▼ by appt.

LA CAVE A POLYTE

Chamoson Pinot blanc 2000★

☐   0.1 ha   700   ▤ ♦ €11-15

This pale-greenish wine exudes aromas of walnuts and some tropical fruit character. Very soft to begin with, the palate reveals a sense of richness before finishing on a fresh note.

➤ Jacques Disner, La Cave à Polyte SA, 5, rue de la Place, 1955 Chamoson, tel. 079.220.35.11, fax 077.306.26.66, e-mail info@polyte.ch ▨ ▼ by appt.

CAVE DU PARADOU Gamay 2000★

▉   0.2 ha   1,500   ▤ €5-8

The Paradou vineyard planted at an altitude of 1,200 m (3,925 ft) in the Val d'Hérens plays host to some fifteen different grape varieties, amongst them Gamay. The wine reveals a pronounced morello-cherry aroma mixed with some spices and peony. On the well-structured palate silky tannins underpin the sustained flavours.

➤ Cave du Paradou, La Villettaz, 1973 Nax, tel. 027.203.23.59, fax 027.203.60.13 ▨ ▼ by appt.

PRIMUS CLASSICUS

Cornalin 2000★★★

▉   2 ha   10,000   ▤ ♦ €15-23

The Cornalin from Caves Orsat was noteworthy in 1999 and has progressed in 2000 to be described as exceptional. With deep red brightened by touches of mauve, it reveals a wonderful bouquet that wine-lovers will acknowledge, commingling spices, morello cherry, black cherries and raspberries. It is full and nicely structured on the palate, benefiting from soft tannins that ensure an overall impression of finesse. This is a wine to be enjoyed now but which will improve with age. The **Primus Classicus Petite Arvine** is awarded two stars in recognition of its fresh and attractive flavours.

🍷 SA Caves Orsat, rte du Levant 99, 1920 Martigny, tel. 027.721.01.01, fax 027.721.01.03, e-mail info@ cavesorsat.ch ☑ ⊤ by appt.

PROVINS-VALAIS

□ Corbassières Fendant 2000★

| 1 ha | 5,000 | €5-8 |

The schist soil of this small, 2-ha (5-acre) vineyard has yielded a Chasselas which is both round and fresh with excellent length. Lime-blossom aromas and mineral notes contribute to its overall balanced flavour.

🍷 Provins Valais, rue de l'Industrie 22, 1950 Sion, tel. 027.328.66.66, fax 027.328.66.60, e-mail madeleine.cay@ provins.ch ☑ ⊤ by appt.

PIERRE-LUC REMONDEULAZ

□ Chardonnay 2000★

| 0.12 ha | 950 | €8-11 |

Golden yellow, both floral and fruity, this Chardonnay shows an attractive freshness. The bouquet of citrus fruit adds to the pleasure. Enjoy this well-balanced wine with fillet of sole or with reblochon cheese.

🍷 Pierre-Luc Remondeulaz, rue de Latigny 27, cellier de la Dzaquette, 1955 Chamoson, tel. 027.306.55.68, fax 027.307.14.08 ☑ ⊤ by appt.

CAVE DES REMPARTS

■ Muscat 2000★

| 0.2 ha | 1,500 | €8-11 |

This attractive pale-coloured Muscat shows hints of gold and an intense, yet fine aroma of rose petals. The palate is initially straightforward and powerful, but continues in a more delicate vein. Rich fruit shows well on the sustained finish.

🍷 Yvon Cheseaux, Cave des Remparts, 1913 Saillon, tel. 027.744.33.76, fax 027.744.33.76, e-mail cavedesremparts@ bluewin.ch ☑ ⊤ by appt.

JEAN-MARIE REYNARD

■ Dôle 2000★

| 0.3 ha | 2,100 | €8-11 |

The Dôle is a deep-red blend of Pinot Noir, Diolinoir and Gamay varieties. Aromas of red fruits and blackcurrants are evident on the nose and these persist on the well-structured palate. Distinct but soft tannins indicate that the wine is ready for drinking.

🍷 Jean-Marie Reynard, 1965 Romaz-Savièse, tel. 027.395.24.23 ☑ ⊤ by appt.

RIVES DU BISSE

■ Cornalin Fût de chêne 2000★★★

| 1 ha | 8,500 | €15-23 |

This Cornalin, grown on a limestone soil derived from the alluvial cones along the banks of the Bisse (irrigation channel), has produced an intensely coloured wine. The

Rouge d'Enfer
Appellation d'origine contrôlée Valais
CUVÉE DU MAÎTRE DE CHAIS
PROVINS VALAIS

The *Guide* has regularly singled out wines produced by this co-operative set up in 1930. The Rouge d'Enfer 99 is a blend of Cornalin, Syrah and Pinot Noir varieties and boasts a dark-ruby colour with intense red-fruit aromas. The palate is immediately powerful, in which the richness lasts well to the sustained finish. The wine needs to be left for five to eight years. Also worthy of mention is the

nose combines red fruits with aromas derived from eight months in the barrel. Elegance on the palate is shown by a strand of fruity and spicy, long-lasting flavours. This significant wine is rich with well-structured tannins. The **Petite Arvine 2000** and **Humagne Rouge 2000**, both aged in the vat, were also found to be excellent.

🍷 SA Gaby Delaloye et Fils, Vins Rives du Bisse, rue de la Fonderie 5, 1957 Ardon, tel. 027.306.13.15, fax 027.306.64.20 ☑ ⊤ by appt.

ELOI ET GERARD RODUIT

□ Fully Humagne blanche 2000★

| 0.3 ha | 1,500 | €11-15 |

This family estate at Fully is made up of very scattered vineyards with a total of 7 ha (17 acres) at altitudes up to 800 m (2615 ft). The white Humagne has mostly floral notes on the nose, with a lemon character on the refreshing palate. The wine is ready for drinking now and ideal with fish.

🍷 Eloi et Gérard Roduit, chem. de Liaudise 31, 1926 Fully, tel. 027.746.28.10, fax 027.746.28.10 ☑ ⊤ by appt.

SERGE ROH

■ Cornalin 2000★★

| 0.15 ha | 1,800 | €11-15 |

Morello or even black cherry describes the shade of colour, as well as the flavour of this robust and well-structured Cornalin. Already balanced, this 2000 will improve even more over the next four years. The oak-aged **Syrah Elevée en Barrique 99** is equally noteworthy and suitable for ageing.

🍷 Serge Roh, Cave Les Ruinettes, rue de Conthey 43, 1963 Vétroz, tel. 027.346.13.63, fax 027.346.50.53, e-mail serge.roh@ bluewin.ch ☑ ⊤ by appt.

ROUGE D'ENFER

■ Cuvée du Maître de chais 1999★★★

| 10 ha | 10,000 | €15-23 |

remarkable dry white **Amigne de Vétroz 99**, and three further well-made wines: the sweet white **Marsanne Cuvée Tourbillon Vin de l'Evêché 99**, the **Petite Arvine de Fully 2000**, and the **Johannisberg de Chamoson 2000**.

➤ Provins Valais, rue de l'Industrie 22, 1950 Sion, tel. 027.328.66.66, fax 027.328.66.60, e-mail madeleine.cay@provins.ch ⊠ Ⴤ by appt.

ROUVINEZ Johannisberg 2000★★★
□   0.7 ha   7,600   €8–11

Jean-Bernard Rouvinez owns around 40 ha (99 acres) of vineyards on the right bank of the Rhône, some on the hills and others on the plain. His Johannisberg is grown on a light-granite soil and exhibits a pale-yellow colour, revealing aromas of pineapple underpinned by almonds. Softened by a touch of richness, the wine has sustained flavours of ripe fruit. The red **Château Lichten 2000** and the **Château Lichten Petite Arvine 2000** are awarded two stars; the **Dôle rosé 2000** was judged to be a success.

➤ Vins Rouvinez, Colline de Géronde, 3960 Sierre, tel. 027.452.22.52, fax 027.452.22.44, e-mail info@rouvinez.com ⊠ Ⴤ by appt.

SAINTE-ANNE Humagne rouge 2000★
■   0.3 ha   4,000   €8–11

The three estates that comprise this company are located at Molignon, Crétalonza and Chamoson. The chapel of Saint-Anne de Molignon gives its name to this excellent range of wines. Alongside the **Johannisberg Sainte-Anne 2000** and the **Pinot Noir Sainte-Anne 2000** the Humagne Rouge was enjoyed for its dark-red, bright colour, and for its aromas of cinnamon and black cherry underpinned by the suggestion of ground ivy, characteristic of this grape variety. The soft tannic structure imbues the palate with a silky feel.

➤ SA Cave Héritier et Favre, av. Saint-François 2, case postale, 1950 Sion 2 Nord, tel. 027.322.24.35, fax 027.322.92.21, e-mail heritierfavre@swissonline.ch ⊠ Ⴤ by appt.

SOLEIL NOIR 2000★
■   0.5 ha   3,000   €8–11

The Soleil Noir is a blend of Pinot Noir, Diolinoir and Syrah varieties grown on the hillside of Gérande. Spicy and with a strong tannic structure, the wine is long on the palate. It can be enjoyed right away together with food.

➤ Frédéric Zufferey, rue de Fond-Villa 16, 3965 Chippis, tel. 029.213.26.80, fax 027.455.19.31, e-mail zuffereyfredericvins@netplus.ch ⊠ Ⴤ by appt.

FREDERIC VARONE
Petite arvine 2000★★★
□   1.5 ha   10,000   ■ ⚬ €11–15

Petite Arvine vines grown on slate and schistose soil have resulted in a brilliant-gold wine with a nose that is powerfully redolent of rhubarb and grapefruit. A slight mineral taste emerges on a balanced palate, together with suggestions of saltiness that last through to the finish. The wine proves itself to be an accomplished and characteristic example of this grape variety. The **Cornalin 2000** and the **Valroc Pinot Noir 2000** both earn two stars.

➤ Vins Frédéric Varone, av. Grand Champsec 30, 1950 Sion 4, tel. 027.203.56.83, fax 027.203.47.07, e-mail info@varone.ch ⊠ Ⴤ ev. day except Sun. 10am–12 noon 2pm–6.30pm

VERTIGES Fendant 2000★
■   1 ha   10,000   ■ ⚬ €5–8

Jean-Louis Mathieu's vineyards are situated on three clay-limestone ridges covering a total area of 11 ha (27 acres). The Chasselas variety is very expressive here. A pale green colour lies behind a classic range of aromas on the nose including lime blossom and lemon. The taste is of tropical fruit with a fresh, mineral overtone.

➤ Jean-Louis Mathieu, rte du Téléphérique, 3966 Chalais-Sierre, tel. 027.458.27.63, fax 027.458.42.44, e-mail je.matieu@bluewin.ch ⊠ Ⴤ by appt.

CAVE DE VIDOMNE
Chamoson Fendant 2000★
□   1 ha   10,000   ■ ⚬ €5–8

This floral and fruity Chasselas commends itself as an accompaniment to a convivial raclette or a cheese fondue. The nose betrays a touch of gun-flint flavour and the palate is well structured. Balanced with some attractive freshness, the flavours persist through to a good finish.

➤ Albert Gaillard et Fils, Cave du Vidômne, rue du Prieuré 8, 1956 Saint-Pierre-de-Clages, tel. 027.306.27.80, fax 027.306.27.02 ⊠ Ⴤ by appt.

CAVE VILLA SOLARIS
Chamoson Pinot gris 2000★★
■   0.09 ha   600   ⏗ €15–23

This family estate on the edge of Saint-Pierre-de-Clages offers a medium-sweet wine with delicate aromas and lively sparkle. With a judicious balance of fruity flavours on the palate, the lemony character persists well.

➤ Sylvio-Gérald Magliocco, Villa Solaris, rte de Bessoni, 1956 Saint-Pierre-de-Clages, tel. 027.306.64.45, fax 027.306.64.29, e-mail s-g.magliocco@chamoson.ch ⊠ Ⴤ Thu., Fri. 5pm–9pm; Sat., Sun. 11am–9pm

Geneva

Vine-growing in the canton of Geneva dates from before the Christian era, and it survived the vicissitudes of history to flourish to the full after the close of the 1960s.

The Geneva vineyard is divided into 32 appellations, all of which enjoy a temperate climate (due to the proximity of the lake), very good sunshine and favourable soils. Efforts made to improve the potential of the wines include environmentally friendly methods of cultivation and the choice of lower cropping grape varieties suited to a soil that generally has a high limestone content. The results guarantees a wine of high quality. The regulations imposed reflect the determination of both the authorities and the professionals to put on the market wines that will meet the requirements of the AOCs.

The diversity of the grape varieties has widened with the addition of speciality wines to the range. In addition to the main growths from Chasselas for white wines, from Gamay and Pinot Noir for the reds, specialities such as Chardonnay, Pinot Blanc, Aligoté, Gamaret and Cabernet are enjoying great success among knowledgeable wine-lovers.

DOM. DES ABEILLES D'OR
Choully Chasselas 2000★
11 ha 6,000 €5-8

The estate takes its name from the coat of arms of the Desbaillets, one of Geneva's oldest families. Twenty-one-year old Laurent Desbaillet has been in charge of wine-making since 1999. This subtly fruity wine proves that he has already mastered both the art and the methodology. With its deliciously fresh and fruity palate this Chasselas would be ideal with a cheese fondue or raclette.

🍷 Dom. des Abeilles d'Or, 3, rte du Moulin-Fabry, 1242 Satigny, tel. 022.753.16.37, fax 022.753.80.20, e-mail abeillesdor@geneva.link.ch

Ⓨ by appt.

🍷 René Desbaillets

Bourdigny is a wine-growing hamlet attached to Satigny, Switzerland's largest wine-growing village. It is part of a vast region known as Le Mandement, which inherited some of the Episcopal estates of the Middle Ages. The Alouettes estate has 17 ha (42 acres) of vines from which it has produced a well-balanced, rounded Chasselas full of fine fruit.

🍷 Jean-Daniel Ramu, 36, chem. de la Vieille-Servette, 1242 Satigny, tel. 022.753.13.70, fax 022.753.13.70

Ⓨ by appt.

DOM. DES ALOUETTES
Satigny Chasselas 2000
6.64 ha 9,000 €5-8

J. ET C. BOCQUET-THONNEY
Sézenove Chardonnay Elevé en barrique 1999
0.45 ha 3,000 €8-11

This oak-matured Chardonnay is distinguished by an elegant range of flavours. The grape variety is fully expressed on the full-bodied palate, which shows a good balance between weight and acidity. Although ready now, it could be kept for a year or two.

🍷 Jacques et Claude Bocquet-Thonney, 9, chem. des Grands-Buissons, 1233 Bernex, tel. 022.757.45.63, fax 022.757.45.63

Ⓨ by appt.

DOM. DE CHAMPVIGNY
Chardonnay Elevé en fût de chêne 1999★
0.3 ha 1,500 €5-8

Satigny, the starting point for a tour around the historic region of Mandement, abounds with architectural interest, including a temple built on the site of a medieval church and a fort dating back to the 16th century. This estate offers a barrel-aged Chardonnay where the oak flavours do not overwhelm the characteristics of the grape variety. Toasty notes on the nose lead on to a lightweight and mellow palate.

🍷 Raymond Meister, 29, rte de Champvigny, 1242 Satigny, tel. 022.753.01.35, fax 022.753.01.78, e-mail champvigny@capp.ch

Ⓨ by appt.

DOM. DES CHARMES
Peissy Les Crecelles Chasselas 2000★★
0.88 ha 8,000 €5-8

This estate lies above Satigny and extends over 10 ha (25 acres) of vines on the slopes of Peissy. The cellars are housed in an old, 17th-century farm building. One of eight varieties grown here, the Chasselas is grown in a vineyard plot called La Moraine. The well-balanced 2000 demonstrates its development in its floral character and its full, rounded taste. With a welcome freshness, the finish is long.

🍷 Anne et Bernard Conne, Dom. des Charmes, 11, rte de Credery, Peissy, 1242 Satigny, tel. 022.753.22.16, fax 022.753.18.45 Ⓨ Wed.-Fri. 11am–12 noon 5pm–6pm; Sat. 9am–1pm

SWITZERLAND

Geneva

CLOS DES PINS

Dardagny Chasselas 2000★★

☐ 2 ha 10,000 ■ ◆ €5-8

Dardagny boasts a listed 17th-century château featuring splendid *trompe l'œil* wall decorations dating from the 18th century. The Clos des Pins owns 9 ha (22 acres) of vineyards close to the village. Its Chasselas reveals the distinct mineral character and pleasant fruitiness so typical of the region. In addition, there is the freshness on the palate that one expects from this variety.

☛ Marc Ramu, Clos des Pins, rte du Mandement 458, 1282 Dardagny, tel. 022.754.14.57, fax 022.754.17.23
♈ by appt.

DOM. DU CREST

Jussy Chasselas 2000★★★

☐ 3 ha 30,000 ■ ◆ €8-11

This estate has been in the Micheli family since 1637 and has been extended from one generation to the next to reach 12 ha (30 acres) of vines today. The wines are matured in vaulted cellars dating back to 1823, which were restored seven years ago. This characteristic Chasselas is nicely developed with aromas of pineapple on the nose. The palate is well balanced between weight and acidity, with a long finish.

☛ G. Bené et J. Meyer, Ch. du Crest, 1254 Jussy, tel. 022.759.06.11, fax 022.759.11.22  ♈ by appt.

RESERVE DES FAUNES

Dardagny Chardonnay 2000

☐ 3 ha 15,000 ■ ◆ €8-11

The 10-ha (25-acre) Faunes estate is set in verdant hill-walking country above Dardagny. It has produced a fine Chardonnay with citrus fruit aromas. Full-bodied with an agreeable roundness on the palate it would be excellent with cheeses such as vacherin.

☛ Gilbert et Danielle Mistral-Monnier, Dom. Les Faunes, 1282 Dardagny, tel. 022.754.14.46, fax 022.754.19.46, e-mail info@les-faunes.ch  ♈ ev. day except Sun. 4pm–6pm; Sat. 8am–12 noon

LA CAVE DE GENEVE

Côtes de Russin 2000

■ 1.25 ha 10,600 ■ ◆ €5-8

Russin lies on the edge of the Mandement region between Dardagny and Peney. The

Cave de Genève offers a blackcurrant and morello-cherry-flavoured Gamay grown on clay-limestone slopes. Distinct, yet soft tannins provide structure on the palate and give a spicy edge to the finish.

☛ SA La cave de Genève, 140, rte du Mandement, 1242 Satigny, tel. 022.753.11.33, fax 022.753.21.10
♈ by appt.

GRAND'COUR

Peissy Kerner Sauvignon 2000★

☐ 0.52 ha 3,400 ★ €11-15

Perched on the hilltop of Peissy, this vineyard dates back to between the 15th and 17th centuries. The estate takes its name from a vaulted archway and various outbuildings. This blend of Kerner and Sauvignon grapes exudes an intense nose with aromas of blackcurrant leaves. The palate is full and rich, filled with flavours of tropical fruit. It could well prove the ideal accompaniment to Oriental food.

☛ Jean-Pierre Pellegrin, 1242 Satigny, tel. 022.753.15.00, fax 022.753.15.00
♈ by appt.

LE CLOS DE CELIGNY

La Côte-Céligny Chasselas 2000★

☐ 2.55 ha 30,000

The Clos de Céligny is set in countryside between fields and woodlands with a view towards Lake Geneva and the Alps beyond. Here is a Chasselas showing characteristic flavours of the local *molasse* (a soft sandstone) soil, which complement the local Geneva cuisine well. The wine is rounded and well balanced on the palate with a pleasantly long finish.

☛ H. Schütz et R. Moser, Le Clos de Céligny, rte de Céligny 38, 1298 Céligny, tel. 022.776.32.05, fax 022.776.07.85, e-mail moser@clos-de-celigny.ch
♈ by appt.

LE CRET 2000★★

■ 1 ha 2,500 ▥ €11-15

Pinot Noir is blended with equal parts of the Gamaret and Garanoir varieties to make up this *cuvée*. Gamaret, a cross between the Gamay Noir and Reichensteiner varieties, brings colour and tannic richness to the blend, while Garanoir, from the same antecedents, adds the fruit. The resultant wine is richly fruity, with a full and rounded, developed taste underpinned by noticeable tannins. Although enjoyable now, the wine could be aged for a further year or two.

☛ SA Marcel Berthaudin, 11, rue Ferrier, 1202 Genève, tel. 022.732.06.26, fax 022.732.84.60, e-mail info@ berthaudin.ch ♈ by appt.

LES PERRIERES Peissy Chardonnay

Elevé en fût de chêne 1999

■ n.c. n.c. ▥ €8-11

This Chardonnay from the silty-clay and *molasse* (local sandstone) soil of Peissy shows

1268

DOM. DES PENDUS

Coteaux de Peney Cuvée Victoria Syrah
Elevé en fût de chêne 1999★★

■ 1er cru 0.45 ha 3,600 ■ ⦿ €11-15

The estate takes its name from the tragic events of 1534 at the Catholic stronghold of the Château de Peney, when Reformists from Geneva laid siege to the castle and were subsequently hanged (*pendus*) from the trees around it. Today, the estate comprises 7 ha planted with a very wide range of vine varieties covers barely 6% of the area. However, the apparently limited...

(17 acres) of vineyards along the banks of the Rhône. This Syrah offers a typically spicy aroma on the nose and has a well-structured palate, full and long with pronounced tannins that will allow it to age well.

↗ Christian Sossauer, 1, rte de Peney-Dessus, 1242 Satigny, tel. 022.753.19.61, fax 022.753.19.61, e-mail csossauer@domaine-des-pendus.ch ▼ by appt.

DOM. DU PARADIS

Satigny Pinot blanc 2000★★

□ 4 ha 9,000 ■ €8-11

The Paradis label portrays a little devil hidden behind an angel's wing, an appropriate image for an estate that claims to produce *vins d'enfer* ('wines from hell'). The appeal of this 2000 lies in its distinctively delicate nose of white peaches, juxtaposed with a light smoky aroma. The taste is full and rich, extending smoothly to a long finish.

↗ Roger Burgdorfer, 275, rte du Mandement, 1242 Satigny, tel. 022.753.18.55, fax 022.753.18.55, e-mail info@domaine-du-paradis.ch ☑ ▼ Sat. 9am–12 noon 1pm–5pm; cl. Oct.

LE VIEUX CLOCHER

Peissy Pinot noir 2000★★

■ 5 ha 30,000 ■ ♦ €8-11

The estate was taken over in 1971 by two cousins, one trained in banking, who administers the estate, the other a qualified agronomist. The Vieux Clocher name refers to the 11th-century bell tower of Peissy. The 47-ha (117-acre) vineyard, run essentially by a single tenant, is farmed along organic lines and the wine comes from the 'Oberlin' Pinot Noir variety developed at the Changins research station. The nose is a typical amalgam of morello cherry and raspberry, while the taste is full and deep with a fine tannic structure.

↗ Leyvraz et Stevens, 27, rte de Maison Rouge, 1242 Peissy, tel. 022.753.11.60, e-mail bossons@infonie.ch ☑ ▼ by appt.

good development on the nose with vanilla aromas, evidence of its period in oak. The taste is balanced and rich.

↗ Bernard et Brigitte Rochaix, 54, rte de Peissy, 1242 Satigny, tel. 022.753.90.00, fax 022.753.90.00 ▼ by appt.

Le Vieux Clocher
Pinot noir de Peissy 2000
appellation d'origine contrôlée
LEYVRAZ & STEVENS

DOM. DES TROIS ETOILES Peissy

Chardonnay Elevé en fût de chêne 1999★★

□ 1 ha 6,233 ■ €8-11

Not a three-star wine perhaps but nevertheless an excellent example from this estate: a superbly made wine, showing successful integration between oak and fruit. Toasted vanilla aromas on the nose are followed by a full and fleshy palate, typical of Chardonnay. The wine has fine structure and is ready for drinking.

↗ Jean-Charles Crousaz, 41, rte de Peissy, Dom. des Trois Etoiles, 1242 Satigny, tel. 022.753.16.14, fax 022.753.41.55, e-mail info@trois-etoiles.ch ☑ ▼ by appt.

Neuchâtel

The vineyards of the Neuchâtel canton have a highly privileged position, receiving reflected sun from the lake and shelter from the lower foothills of the Jura. The vines stretch for 40 km (25 miles) along a narrow band between Le Lauderon and Vaumarcus. The dry, sunny climate of the region and the Jurassic limestone soils that predominate have always combined to create excellent conditions for vine cultivation. The first vineyard was officially planted there in 998, a fact that makes wine-making in Neuchâtel over one thousand years old.

In this little wine-growing area, which covers 610 ha (1,507 acres), Chasselas and Pinot rule; there are indeed a few 'special-ities' (Pinot Gris, Chardonnay, Gewurztraminer and a Riesling-Sylvaner cross), but cultivation of these varieties covers barely 6% of the area. However, the apparently limited range of vine varieties planted hides a very wide palette of different wines and flavours, thanks to the expertise of the wine-makers and the diverse nature of the *terroirs*.

The reds, from Pinot Noir, are elegant and fruity, often with good keeping qualities. The very typical Oeil-de-Perdrix is a superb rosé, originating from the Neuchâtel vineyards, along with Perdrix Blanche, which is made by being pressed with no maceration. Some growers even make a sparkling wine.

The variety of soils in the canton, from east to west, as well as the personal styles of the wine-makers, result in many different flavours and aromas in the white wines made from Chasselas. These promise an interesting voyage of discovery for the curious, and it is worth highlighting two local speciality wines made from the same variety: the 'non-filtré' Vin Primeur, which cannot be put on sale before the third Wednesday in January, and the 'sur lie' wines, which have been kept on the lees.

Each of the 18 wine-producing communes makes its own appellation, yet the Appellation Neuchâtel can apply to all primary category wines from the canton.

DOM. DU CHATEAU
Vaumarcus 2000★★
4 ha 26,000 €8-11

APPELLATION D'ORIGINE CONTROLÉE

VAUMARCUS
DOMAINE DU CHÂTEAU

11% vol   CAVES CHATENAY-BOUVIER SA • BOUDRY • SUISSE   75 cl

The 200-year old Château Vaumarcus estate, owned by the Caves Châtenay-Bouvier at Boudry, nestles between rocky outcrops warmed by the sun and the waters of the Lac de Neuchâtel. The rich, complex and well-structured Chasselas found favour with the Jury, who awarded it a *coup de coeur*. This is a well-made wine, powerful, yet elegant with a ripe and sustained palate. An attractive richness and good complexity of flavours make it ideal to enjoy both as an aperitif and with fine food.

SA Caves Châtenay-Bouvier,
rte du Vignoble 27, 2017 Boudry,
tel. 032.842.23.33, fax 032.842.54.71,
e-mail chatenay@worldcom.ch
by appt.

ALAIN GERBER Oeil-de-perdrix 2000★
1.2ha 9,000 €8-11

Alain Garnier has been at the helm of this 7-ha (17-acre) family-owned estate for the past three years. His Oeil-de-Perdrix 2000 is seductively elegant, and characterised by flavours of quince. A lively wine, its ethereal quality will delight lovers of classic Neuchâtel rosés.

Alain Gerber, imp. Alphonse-Albert 8, 2068 Hauterive, tel. 032.753.27.53, fax 032.753.02.41 by appt.

GRILLETTE Chasselas 2000★★
2 ha 15,000 €8-11

The family-owned enterprise of La Grillette was founded in 1884 in the heart of the village of Cressier and has since firmly established itself as part of Neuchâtel's wine-growing heritage. Director Thierry Lüthi and oenologist Jean-Claude Martin have brought a fresh impetus to La Grillette, which features in the *Guide* for the second year running. This wine is remarkably delicate and floral, with the distinct aromas of hawthorn and lime blossom that are a familiar feature of the Chasselas variety grown on the limestone rocky soils of Cressier. The palate is lively but with a richness of fruit that ensures perfect balance. Here is a wine that can be enjoyed as an aperitif or, ideally, with the regional fish dishes.

CH. D'AUVERNIER
Pinot noir Elevé en barrique 1999★
1 ha 4,000 €15-23

Auvernier, a typical wine-growing village is well worth a visit to see its vintners' houses dating back to the 16th and 17th centuries. Estate manager Thierry Grosjean, who welcomes visitors to the château in the shade of the trees in the old parkland, has opted to mature this Pinot Noir in the barrel, a bold choice for the 99 vintage. His reward is an excellent wine with delicate hints of vanilla that accentuate rather than detract from the balance. Characteristic of the region, the wine is already ready for drinking.

Ch. d'Auvernier, 2012 Auvernier, tel. 032.731.21.15, fax 032.730.30.03, e-mail wine@chateau-auvernier.ch
by appt.

Berne

The wine-growing area in the Berne canton stretches along the shore of Lake Bienne, clinging to the slopes at the foot of the Jura range and surrounding the picturesque villages of the region. Some 55 per cent of the vineyard area is planted with Chasselas, 35% with Pinot Noir and 10% with speciality vine varieties such as Pinot Gris, a Riesling-Sylvaner cross, Chardonnay, Gewurztraminer and so on. The temperate lakeside climate and the shallow limestone soil give the wines finesse and character. The local Chasselas is a light, slightly sparkling white, ideal as an aperitif or to accompany a dish of lake salmon. The Pinot Noir is a light, elegant, fruity red. The wine-growing domains are family concerns of 2–7 ha (5–17 acres), where traditional and modern methods are combined to good effect.

In the other Swiss wine-growing cantons, vines grow in northerly locations. Despite the rigour of the climate, these regions produce a majority of red wines (frequently from Pinot Noir), representing 70% of total production. White wines come mostly from a Riesling-Sylvaner cross.

A. PORRET

Cortaillod Pinot noir 1999★★

3.5 ha · n.c. · €8-11

While enjoying a walk at Cortaillod, you will probably come across the Domaine des Cèdres overlooking the Lac de Neuchâtel. The château is worth a visit as is the wine museum close by at Boudry. The Porret family have been wine-growers here since 1858. The Jury awarded a coup de cœur to this seductive and complete Pinot Noir. With soft, silky tannins and aromas of forest undergrowth it also has that characteristic hint of smokiness prevalent in the great Pinot wines.

● A. Porret et Fils, Dom. des Cèdres, Goutte d'Or 20, 2016 Cortaillod, tel. 032.842.10.52, fax 032.842.18.41 ✉ Ⴤ Sat. 8am–12 noon; weekdays by appt.

A. PORRET CORTAILLOD NEUCHATEL 1999 · 70cl · 12,5% vol.

DOM. E. DE MONTMOLLIN FILS

Auvernier Goutte d'or 2000★★

2 ha · 10,000 · €5-8 · Ⴤ by appt.

The Montmollin family have been vine-growers since the 16th century. Their estate has gradually expanded over the centuries to become the largest vineyard in the canton of Neuchâtel. Today it has a vineyard area of 47 ha (116 acres) and cellars in the heart of the village of Auvernier. The 'Golden Drop' 2000 boasts a complex tropical-fruit nose with citrus fruits and citronella helping to bring out the freshness. A very light sparkle seduces the taste buds.

● Dom. E. de Montmollin Fils, Grand-Rue 3, 2012 Auvernier, tel. 032.731.21.59, fax 032.731.88.06, e-mail info@montmollinwine.ch ✉ Ⴤ by appt.

DOM. DE L'ETAT DE NEUCHATEL

Auvernier 1999★

2.2 ha · 16,000 · €11-15 · Ⴤ by appt.

This viticultural test station, set up a little over a century ago at the time of the phylloxera crisis, doubles as a research facility and as the cantonal wine-growing administration. Director Eric Beuret is in charge of the canton's wine cellars. This well-structured wine has yet to reveal all its secrets but it already boasts a complex plethora of flavours together with most elegant tannins. It needs a few years of ageing.

● Encavage de l'Etat de Neuchâtel, Fontenettes 37, 2012 Auvernier, tel. 032.846.29.17, fax 032.730.24.39, e-mail eric.beuret@ne.ch ✉ Ⴤ by appt.

J.C. KUNTZER ET FILS Saint-Sébaste

Pinot noir Oeil-de-perdrix 2000★★

4 ha · 25,000 · €8-11 · Ⴤ by appt.

Year in, year out, this family-owned concern produces excellent wines. This classic and elegant Pinot Noir rosé has a really lovely balance between liveliness and alcoholic strength. The Kuntzers also have on offer a first-rate red Pinot Noir Saint-Sébaste 99. Ready for drinking, it will delight those who enjoy smooth wines.

● Jean-Pierre Kuntzer, Daniel-Dardel 11, 2072 Saint-Blaise, tel. 032.753.14.23, fax 032.753.14.57, e-mail info@kuntzer.ch ✉ Ⴤ by appt.

● Grillette Dom. de Cressier, rue Molondin 2, 2088 Cressier, tel. 032.758.85.29, fax 032.758.85.21, e-mail info@grillette.ch ✉ Ⴤ by appt.

AUBERSON ET FILS

Neuveville Pinot blanc 2000★

☐　　🏺 0.9 ha　2,500　◼ ◈　€11-15

This family-owned estate overlooking the rooftops of the old town of La Neuveville offers a Pinot Blanc of astonishing elegance and finesse with delicate hints of lime blossom. The wine opens out fully on the palate and is a delicious accompaniment to soft cheeses.

● Auberson et Fils, Tirage 25,
2520 La Neuveville, tel. 032.751.18.30,
fax 032.751.53.83 ⓥ Ⓨ by appt.

DOM. DE LA VILLE DE BERNE

Schafiser Chasselas 2000★★

☐　　　12 ha　80,000　◼ ◈　€8-11

This 21-ha (52-acre) estate, belonging to the city of Berne and managed by the Louis family, is the largest vineyard on the Lac de Bienne. The original cellars have been transformed into a reception area. The Jury was captivated by this extremely flowery Chasselas with its touch of sparkle in the glass. The palate is fresh and lively with a lovely balance of rich fruit. It might be best appreciated while looking out towards Jean-Jacques Rousseau's beloved Ile Saint-Pierre and eating a fillet of perch from the lake or a portion of the local tête de moine cheese.

● Dom. de la ville de Berne,
2520 La Neuveville, tel. 032.751.21.75,
fax 032.751.58.03 ⓥ Ⓨ by appt.
● H. Louis

DOM. DE L'HOPITAL DE SOLEURE Schafiser Chasselas 2000★★

☐　　　2 ha　6,000　◼ ◈　€8-11

The Hôpital de Soleure wine estate boasts one of the oldest vineyards in all of Switzerland. The city fathers of Berne acquired the first vines in around the year 1350 and the estate was established in 1466 under the provisions of a legacy. For the past four years, the cellars have been looked after by a young wine-maker who has produced this soft, slightly sparkling Chasselas that reflects its origins perfectly. It could be enjoyed either as an aperitif or with a fish dish.

● Dom. de l'Hôpital de Soleure, Russie, 8,
2525 Le Landeron, tel. 032.751.46.01,
fax 032.751.46.01 Ⓨ by appt.

HEINZ TEUTSCH

Schafiser Schlössliwy Pinot noir 2000★

◼　　🏺 2 ha　15,000　◼ ◈　€8-11

Owned by the Teutsch family since 1830, the origins of this estate can be traced back to 1570. The cellars were lovingly restored some 15 years ago and now house the oak barrels. This ruby-red Pinot Noir with its floral and cherry aromas reflects the regional character well. On the palate, the 2000 shows good acidity which will allow it to improve over the next year or two, when it should be an ideal accompaniment to a leg of lamb.

● Heinz Teutsch, Im Schlössli,
2514 Schafis, tel. 032.315.21.70,
fax 032.315.22.79, e-mail teutsch@
rebgut-schloessli.ch ⓥ Ⓨ by appt.

BAUMGARTNER Tegerfelden

Pinot noir Edelblut barrique 1998★

◼　　🏺 0.6 ha　2,000　◼ ◈　€11-15

Run by a father and son, this family business has been devoted to the art of wine-production on a full-time basis since 1975. Certainly the work involved is obvious in their 98 Pinot Noir. The nose shows an attractive interplay between fruit and oak, and the palate is absolutely as it should be, with well-integrated oak and an enjoyable sweetness of fruit, all boding well for the future.

● Baumgartner Weinbau,
Dorfstrasse 37, 5306 Tegerfelden,
tel. 056.245.28.01, fax 056.245.17.00,
e-mail baumgartner.weinbau@pop.agri.ch
ⓥ Ⓨ Sat. 9am–12 noon 1pm–4pm

CHALMBERGER Kerner 2000★★

☐　　　0.17 ha　700　　　　€6-11

Konrad and Sonja Zimmermann have run this estate of almost 7 ha (17 acres) since 1990. This yellow-coloured wine exudes intense aromas of fresh Muscat grapes and of mint. The palate is rounded and full-bodied, achieving a good balance between sweetness and acidity.

● Chalmberger Weinbau, Rebbergstrasse 24, 5108 Oberflachs, tel. 052.443.26.39,
fax 056.443.06.81, e-mail zimmermann@
chalmberger.ch ⓥ Ⓨ by appt.
● K. et S. Zimmermann

E. ET D. FURST

Hornusser Federweiss Fürstlicher 2000★★

◼　　🏺 0.5 ha　3,000　◼ ◈　€8-11

This estate grows a little more than 3 ha (7.5 acres) of vines, with Pinot Noir, Pinot Gris, Müller-Thurgau and Dornfelder varieties giving a wide range of wines. This attractive pale-pink rosé shows a classic nose of some distinction, and the palate follows with plenty of soft, fleshy fruit. 'Exactly how it

IM LEE
Döttingen Pinot noir Malbec 1999★★

■ n.c. 1,200 €11-15

Established since 1828, this family estate of 7 ha (17 acres) boasts an impressive mix of indigenous, international and innovative grape varieties. In addition they act as a vine nursery and own a gastronomic restaurant. An attractive deep colour, this distinguished 99 has a rich nose, full of aromas and a fleshy, flavoursome palate. The jury awarded a star to the white 2000, an opulent, rather than lively, Sauvignon Blanc with an attractive elderberry flavour.
☛ Andreas Meier & Co, Weingut zum Sternen, Rebschulweg 2, 5303 Würenlingen, tel. 056.297.10.02, fax 056.297.10.01, e-mail office@weingut-sternen.ch ▾
▾ by appt.

HARTMANN
Sommerhalder Blauburgunder Spätlese
Elevé en fût de chêne 1999

■ 1.2 ha 7,000 €11-15

The Hartmann family have been wine-growers since 1985 and are committed to an ecological approach. For them quality is more important than yield. Their Pinot Noir 99 is from grapes that were late-harvested at a very high sugar content. This has resulted in a wine that still reveals a youthful nose but neverthe-less shows plenty of weight on the palate.
☛ Bruno Hartmann, Rinikerstrasse 17, 5236 Remigen, tel. 056.284.27.43, fax 056.284.27.28. e-mail weinbau.hartmann@pop.agri.ch ▾
▾ by appt.

should be summed up one Jury member. The white Cuvée Création Désirée, from the Müller-Thurgau variety, is awarded one star. Its nose reveals attractive fruit and floral notes and the palate shows a good balance between sweetness and acidity. Also first-rate is the Blauburgunder Spätlese 99 Pinot Noir de Vendanges Tardives, which boasts classic aromas of cherries and wild berries.
☛ Daniel et Erika Fürst, Fürstliche Weinkultur, 5075 Hornussen, tel. 062.871.55.61, fax 062.871.85.66 ▾
▾ by appt.

SIEBE-DUPF-KELLEREI
Prattler Blauburgunder 2000★★

■ 1.4 ha 13,000 €8-11

Johannes Schwob purchased this property and installed the cellars in 1875. Still in the family, today it is managed by Paul Schwob. Two wines were offered to our Juries this year. This youthful, purple-coloured Pinot Noir has a fine and classic aroma tinged with violet. Its overall balance won over the Jury who unhesitatingly awarded it a *coup de coeur*. The glitteringly pale-yellow Sissacher Kerner 2000 was also singled out. Fruity and floral, the palate is initially quite delicate but shows good balance.
☛ Siebe-Dupf-Kellerei, Kasernenstrasse 25, 4410 Liestal, tel. 061.921.13.33, fax 061.921.13.32 ▾ ▾ by appt.

Bâle

NAUER Tegerfelder Räuschling 2000★

□ 0.5 ha 600 €8-11

This pale yellow-green wine shows attractive overall harmony with a nose suggesting lemon and honey. The palate reveals both class and weight, and the zippy acidity gives it freshness.
☛ Gebrüder Nauer Ag, Postfach, 5620 Bremgarten 2, tel. 056.648.27.27, fax 056.648.27.17 ▾ ▾ ev. day except Sun. & Mon. 9am–12 noon 2pm–6pm

Grisons

COTTINELLI Malanser 1999★

■ n.c. n.c. €11-15

The Malanser 99 has a pale, pretty colour and a fruity nose with a suggestion of vanilla. On the palate, the wine is full and rounded with good structure.

Schaffhouse

GRENDELMEIER-BANNWART

Zirzerser Blauburgunder Auslese 1999★

■ 0.5 ha 3,00 ▥ **€8-11**

The 98 vintage from this family-owned estate that started marketing their wine in 1992 received a *coup de coeur* last year. This Pinot Noir is from grapes harvested on 29 October 1999 and was matured in oak barrels for nine months. The nose is elegant with delicate coffee beans and a light fruit character. Well-balanced, it is full and rich and will age well.

☛ Weinbau Grendelmeier-Bannwart, 7205 Zizers, tel. 081.322.62.58, fax 081.322.92.66 ▥ Ⲩ by appt.

LEVANTI Pinot noir 1998★

■ 1.5 ha 5,500 ▥ **€11-15**

The deep-red colour of this Pinot Noir remains youthful with really pretty glints of purple. The intense nose shows both aromas of red fruits in brandy and some oak notes from the cask. The palate is rich and characteristic, revealing a truly authentic wine.

☛ Elli Süsstrunk, Hindergasse 62 B, 7603 Fläsch, tel. 081.302.78.28, fax 081.302.28.78 ▥ Ⲩ by appt.

LIESCH Malans Malanser

Blauburgunder Barrique 1999★★★

■ 0.7 ha 3,500 ▥ **€11-15**

Blackberries appear initially on both the colour and the nose of this complex 99, which gradually reveals a wide range of flavours including elderberry, tea and mint. The palate is powerful, balanced and youthful, and should be able to age gracefully thanks to its good tannins. The **Blauburgunder Auslese 99** is a well-balanced wine too. From late-harvested Pinot Noir, the nose is less classical than the same wine from the previous vintage, awarded a *coup de coeur* last year, but nevertheless this remains a wine most worthy of mention.

☛ Ueli et Jürg Liesch, Treib, 7208 Malans, tel. 081.322.12.25, fax 081.330.05.85 ▥ Ⲩ by appt.

WEGELIN ET BARGAHR

Blauburgunder Elevé en fût 1999★★

■ 1 ha 3,000 ▥ **€15-23**

This Pinot Noir has been aged for 14 months in the barrel and shows pronounced oak aromas although these do not dominate the aroma of red-fruit jam. Full-bodied and long, the wine is still young enough to lay down. Equally notable is the **white Silvestri 98**, a sweet, rich and well-balanced white harvested on 1 November.

☛ Peter Wegelin et Silvia Bargähr, Scadenagut, 7208 Malans, tel. 081.322.11.64, fax 081.322.11.64 ▥ Ⲩ by appt.

Schaffhouse

GRAF VON SPIEGELBERG

Hallauer Blanc de pinot noir 2000★

□ 3 ha n.c. ■ ♦ **€6-11**

It is probably the legendary Count Spiegelberg himself, resplendent in his armour, who graces this label. Whether he was as loquacious as the very expressive wine that bears his name is open to question. However, the Jury were captivated by its classic nose of fruits and sweets, and its soft, rounded palate evoking flavours of bergamot and mirabelle plums.

☛ Rimuss-Kellerei Rahm, 8215 Hallau, tel. 052.681.31.44, fax 052.681.40.14 ▥ Ⲩ by appt.

STAMM Cuvée Stoffler

Elevé en barrique de chêne 1999

■ 1 ha n.c. ▥ **€15-23**

Here, 50% Merlot is blended with equal parts of Pinot Noir and a Gamay-Reichensteiner cross. The result is a very young, dark-ruby wine still showing hints of purple. The nose reveals black fruits macerated in brandy as well as oak notes from its period in the cask. Showing good acidity, the palate is packed full of fruit.

☛ Thomas et Mariann Stamm, Aeckerlistrasse 20, 8240 Thayngen, tel. 052.649.24.15, fax 052.649.25.16, e-mail stammson@datacomm.ch ▥ Ⲩ by appt.

Thurgovie

ESCHENZ Müller Thurgau 2000★

□ 0.3 ha 2,754 ■ **€8-11**

Though not the product of a late harvest, this wine demonstrates that character as it was made from very ripe grapes. With a high alcoholic content, it is full-bodied and will age well.

☛ Johannes Hanhart, Hauptstrasse 10, 8265 Mammern, tel. 052.741.24.74, fax 052.741.23.87 ▥ Ⲩ by appt.

A. ET A. SAXER

Nussbaumen Pinot gris 2000★★

■ 0.25 ha 1,120 ■ **€8-11**

This wine company based at Nussbaumen owns around 8 ha (20 acres) of vines, the majority of which are of the Pinot Noir and Müller-Thurgau (also known as Riesling-Sylvaner) varieties. This, however is a mellow Pinot Gris and was singled out for its fine balance and its sweet taste. The first-rate **red Assemblage No. 13 2000** has aromas of blackcurrant liqueur, strawberry, cherry, liquorice

Weinhaus Cottinelli, Karlihof, 7208 Malans, tel. 081.300.00.30, fax 081.300.00.40 Ⲩ by appt.

1274

and black tea which sustain on the palate through a long finish. The youthful and classy white **Assemblage No. 11 2000** merits attention on account of its pear-drop aroma overland by hints of fruit and elderberries.
◆ A. & A. Saxer, St-Anna-Kellerei, Stammheimerstrasse 9, 8537 Nussbaumen, tel. 052.745.23.51, fax 052.745.27.34 Ⓥ
Ⓨ by appt.

JURG SAXER'S
Neftenbach Nobler weisser 2000★
□ 1.8 ha 5,000 ■ ⑅11-15

The brand-new vinification cellars of the Bruppach estate are ready to receive the 2001 harvest. In the meantime, this 'noble white' 2000 is truly classy, redolent of fresh citrus fruits with a palate that exhibits commendable honesty and vivacity.
◆ Jürg Saxer, Weingut Bruppach, 8413 Neftenbach, tel. 052.315.32.00, fax 052.315.32.30 Ⓥ
Ⓨ Fri. 4pm–7pm, Sat. 11am–4pm

DER ANDERE Nº 3
Schlossgut Pinot noir 1999★★
■ 0.7 ha 3,000 ⑅15-23

Château Bachtobel has been in the hands of Hans Ulrich Kesselring's family since 1784. He is a consistently innovative wine-producer, as this Pinot Noir 99 illustrates: a complex nose of blackberries and a touch of oak leads into a young but well-structured palate. In all, this is very well-balanced wine that promises to age well.
◆ Hans Ulrich Kesselring, Bachtobel, 8561 Ottoberg, tel. 071.622.54.07, fax 071.622.76.07 Ⓥ Ⓨ by appt.

PANKRAZ Pinot noir Prestige 1998★★
■ 2 ha 12,000 ⑅11-15

Originally part of a Catholic monastery dating from medieval times, this estate was taken over by the City of Zurich in 1862. An elegant label adorns the Pinot Noir, which reveals a complex, fruity nose. The palate is rich with good structure and is characterised by notes of stewed fruit.
◆ Caves Mövenpick SA, Staatskellerei Zürich, Klosterplatz, 8462 Rheinau, tel. 052.319.29.10, fax 052.319.31.82 Ⓥ
Ⓨ by appt.

AUGUST PÜNTER
Sternenhalde Stäfa Rubin 1999★★
■ 0.2 ha 1,500 ■ ⑅8-11

Three grape varieties, all ideal for making wines to age, join together in this wine: 80% Pinot Noir, blended with Malbec and Diolinoir (the latter is a cross, created in Switzerland in 1970 at the Pully research station in the canton of Vaud). The Rubin 1999 is so-called on account of its ruby colour. Extremely fruity, the nose reveals a whole range of wild berries. The palate has it all too, with fine, subtle tannins and a good structure with overall, perfect balance.
◆ August Pünter, Glärnischstrasse 53, 8712 Stäfa, tel. 1.926.12.24, fax 1.796.36.24
Ⓥ Ⓨ by appt.

Ticino

The Ticino vineyard stretches from Giornico in the north to Chiasso in the south, covering an area of 900 ha (2,223 acres). Many of the 3,800 wine-growers of the canton own small plots of land, which they cultivate in their leisure time. In the last few years, about 30 of them have specialised in wine-growing, vinifying and selling. About a hundred wine-growers work full time on their vines and sell their grapes to co-operatives. The key variety in the canton is Merlot, originating from Bordeaux, which was introduced into the canton at the beginning of the 20th century. Nowadays, Merlot covers 85% of the wine-growing area of the Ticino and gives white, rosé and red wines. The red Merlot, by far the majority production, can be a light or full-bodied wine, which can be kept, depending on the time it spends in the vat. Some are brought on in hogsheads. The average amount of Merlot produced in Ticino over the last decade has climbed to 55,000 quintals (a local measure equivalent to 100 kg, 220 lb).

AMPELIO Merlot del Sopraceneri 1998★
n.c. n.c. ⑅15-23

From a producer who is also renowned for both whites and rosés comes this fresh and attractive, intense-ruby Ampelio. With scents of dry wood, fruit and musk emerging on the nose, it is just a shame that the wine still remains a little closed. However, the palate does reveal a good structure.

CAMORINO

Merlot Affinato in barrique 1997★

■ n.c. 5,200 | €15-23

☛ SA Vinicola Carlevaro, via San Gottardo 123, 6500 Bellinzona, tel. 091.829.10.44, fax 091.829.14.56, e-mail carlevaro@unitbox.ch ☑ ☒ by appt.

This 1997 Merlot retains a youthful and lively appearance. The palate is full-bodied with a good level of acidity guaranteeing that the wine will age well. The fine and elegant nose is beginning to show some development, with evident complexity.

☛ SA Cagi-Cantina Giubiasco, via Linoleum 11, 6512 Giubiasco, tel. 091.857.25.31, fax 091.857.79.12, e-mail cagi@ticino.com ☑ ☒ by appt.

FATTORIA MONCUCCHETTO

Merlot Lugano Riserva 1999★

■ n.c. 2,500 | €15-23

This dark ruby-red Merlot 99 comes from 35-year old vines and is a relatively fiery wine with a nose that betrays its maturation in the cask. The palate is assertive and shows an attractive balance without particularly great length. This successful wine would go well with red meat, game or cheese.

☛ Niccolò and Lisetta Lucchini, via Crivelli 30, 6900 Lugano, tel. 091.966.73.63, fax 091.922.71.77, e-mail niluc@bluewin.ch ☒ by appt.

PURPURATUM Riserva 1998★★★

■ n.c. n.c. | €15-23

The tasting panel almost ran out of adjectives to describe this attractively deep-coloured wine which fully lives up to the promise of the flamboyant coat of arms displayed on the label. Complex aromas of spices and tar on the nose are followed by a rich, supple, full-bodied and well-balanced palate which reveals good ageing potential.

☛ SA La Cappellaccia, Strada Regina 1, 6928 Manno, tel. 091.605.44.76, fax 091.604.64.71

ROMPIDEE Affinato in barrique 1997★★

■ n.c. 13,000 | €23-30

From 100 % Merlot and made in a traditional way by wine-maker Fabio Arnaboldi, this wine boasts a deep-ruby colour. The nose is spicy with a slightly vegetal character and some floral notes. Evident tannins on the palate add to the balance and give the wine great individuality.

☛ SA Cantina Chiodi, via Delta 24, 6612 Ascona, tel. 091.791.16.82, fax 091.791.03.93 ☑ ☒ by appt.

SASSI GROSSI Merlot 1998★★

■ 0.3 ha 20,000 | ▮ ♦ | €23-30

Elegance is the distinguishing characteristic of the taste of this excellent red wine. Some development is evident in the intense-red colour and this leads onto spicy oak aromas on the nose, and a palate that is both well-structured and long.

☛ SA Casa Vinicola Gialdi, via Vignoo 3, 6850 Mendrisio, tel. 091.646.40.21, fax 091.646.67.06 ☑ ☒ by appt.

SINFONIA

Merlot del Ticino Barrique 1998★

■ 4 ha 12,000 | €15-23

Produced from a sandy soil, here is a red with an intense colour showing some signs of development. Fruity on the nose, one taster detected an aroma of cherries in brandy. The palate is marked by its richness and complexity, with judicious tannins and good length.

☛ SA Chiericati vini, Via Convento 10, casella postale 1214, 6501 Bellinzona, tel. 091.825.13.07, fax 091.826.40.07, e-mail chiericati@freesurf.ch ☑ ☒ by appt.

☛ Angelo Cavalli

SOTTOBOSCO – TENIMENTO DELL'OR Rosso del Ticino 1997★★★

■ 3 ha 10,000 | €15-23

Historical records confirm that this vineyard dates back to the 17th century. So many years of experience should bear fruit, and fruit there is in this excellent 97. The tasters loved the intensely dark-ruby colour as well as the complex aromas and oak flavours on the nose. Still young on the palate, it already shows good length and extremely good ageing potential.

☛ SA Agriloro, Tenimento Dell'Or, 6864 Arzo, tel. 091.646.74.03, fax 091.640.54.55, e-mail clinicasantalucia@bluewin.ch ☒ by appt.

☛ M.C. Perler

TENUTA MONTALBANO

Merlot Riserva

■ 1.35 ha 5,760 | €15-23

Ultramodern wine-making equipment coupled with a traditional vinification and

some time in oak has yielded a most attractive
98. Made from old vines, it exhibits a light-
ruby colour with slight development and
aromas of liquorice and game on the nose.
The palate is both soft and balanced making
this ideal for drinking in 2003 with a tournedos Rossini.

● Cantina sociale Mendrisio,
Via Bernasconi 22, 6850 Mendrisio,
tel. 091.646.46.21, fax 091.646.43.64 ▼
Y by appt.

TERA CREDA Merlot Riserva 1999★   0.2 ha   2,000   €23-30
■

This lively and attractively coloured
Merlot 99 was vinified in the style of a Bordeaux. The Jury enjoyed the minty freshness
on the nose and the fullness on the palate,
although the high alcohol content was felt to
be slightly obtrusive.

● Tenuta Vitivinicola Trapletti, via Mola
34, 6877 Coldrerio, tel. 091.646.45.08,
e-mail 105486@ticino.com ▼
Y by appt.

VIGNA D'ANTAN
Rosso Ticinese 1999★★   1.5 ha   15,000   €15-23
■

The cellars here were carved out of the rock
back in 1900. The Jury applauded not only
the violet-tinged colour but also the enjoyable
spicy aroma of this intense 99. It seems that
the 30% Cabernet Franc grapes were a
welcome contribution to the blend. The
palate is attractive from the start and demonstrates balanced tannins and good length.

● SA I Vini di Guido Brivio, Via Vignoo 8,
6850 Mendrisio, tel. 091.646.07.57,
fax 091.646.08.05, e-mail brivio@brivio.ch
▼ Y by appt.

GLOSSARY

1er Cru. See 'Premier Cru'.

Acerbic. Describes a wine made tart and sour from having far too much tannin and acidity. A very serious defect.

Acidity. In moderation, acidity helps the balance of a wine, giving it freshness and vigour. But if there is too much, it is a defect, making the wine biting and sour. Too little, however, and the wine will be flabby and lacking in grip.

Aggressive. A wine that is too strong (usually in tannins) and attacks the palate in an unpleasant way.

Agreeable. A pleasant, nicely balanced wine in every respect.

Alcohol. The next largest component of wine after water, ethyl alcohol gives wine its warming character. But if there is too much, the wine is said to be hot.

Alcoholic strength. This is generally expressed in degrees or per cent corresponding to the alcoholic content of the wine by volume.

Aligoté. White grape variety used for making Bourgogne Aligoté, an everyday wine to be drunk young.

Altesse. White grape variety used to make very fine Roussette-de-Savoie.

Amber. If white wines are aged for a long time or are oxidised prematurely, they sometimes take on an amber colour.

Amigne. Traditional white grape variety grown in tiny quantities in the Valais, Switzerland, making dry and sweet wines of high quality.

Ampelography. The study of vine varieties, especially grape vines.

Ample. Term for a harmonious wine which appears to fill the mouth well.

Amylic. Smell of amyl acetate, similar to pear-drops, banana or bubble-gum. Usually detected on young white or rosé wines that are made using cool fermentation, or on reds made with carbonic maceration.

Animal. Smells evoking the animal kingdom: musk, venison, leather. Mostly found in old red wines.

AOC. Appellation d'Origine Contrôlée. A regulatory system which guarantees the authenticity of a wine made in a particular area. Almost all the great wines come from AOC regions.

Aroma. In the technical language of wine-tasting, this term is used for olfactory sensations perceived in the nose and, sometimes, on the palate. It is particularly used for the simple fruit smells of young wines to differentiate from 'bouquet', which is used for smells of more mature wines. The adjective 'aromatic' may describe a generally pleasant smell. See also 'Bouquet'.

Arvine. See 'Petite Arvine'.

Assemblage. A blending of several lots of wine from the same area to obtain the desired final blend. Term used in particular in Champagne for the blending of the base wine *cuvées*, and in

Bordeaux for the final blending for the Grand Vin or main Château wine.

Astringency. A rather rough, rasping taste or, technically, a tactile sensation around the gums and on the roof of the mouth. It is often found in young red wines having more tannin than fruit.

Auxerrois. White grape variety used to make Alsace Klevner; the name is also a synonym for the red Malbec variety in Cahors.

Balanced. Describes a wine with a good balance of acidity and sweetness in whites, or tannin and fruit in red wines.

Balsamic. Used to describe smells evoking the world of perfume, including, among others, vanilla, incense, resin and benzine.

Balthasar. Very large bottle containing the equivalent of 16 ordinary bottles (12 litres).

Barrique. Barrel or cask, usually made of oak; it generally refers to a barrel of around 225l as traditionally used in Bordeaux, and now increasingly elsewhere.

Bâtonnage. Stirring the yeast in a barrel with a pole or baton. Particularly used for fine barrel-fermented whites.

Bitartrate deposit. Technical term for the deposit of tartaric acid crystals, often known simply as tartrates and sometimes found in bottled wines.

Bitterness. Caused by tannins overwhelming the fruit. Bitterness can be an advance warning of astringency, which can soften out, while bitterness is an abiding fault.

Blanc Fumé. Name given to Sauvignon at Pouilly-sur-Loire, where the Pouilly-Fumé appellation comes from (not to be confused with Pouilly-Fuissé from Burgundy, which is made from the Chardonnay grape).

Blend. May refer to a wine made from more than one grape variety, or a wine from grapes sourced in different vineyards, or in Champagne, for example, wine produced from different vintages. It may also be used simply to refer to a selected wine from a producer or estate that may make more than one wine. See also 'cuvée'.

Blending. The mixing together of different lots of wines; see also 'Assemblage' and 'Blend'.

Body. Characteristic of a well-structured, warming and fleshy wine.

Botrytis cinerea. A fungus which attacks the skins of grapes. Although detrimental to red grape varieties, it can be beneficial for certain whites given certain climatic conditions. In such cases it concentrates the sugars and flavours of the grape enabling the great sweet wines to be made. See also 'Noble rot'.

Botrytised. Grapes that have been affected by *botrytis cinerea* or noble rot.

Bouquet. Smells sensed by the nose while sniffing wine in the glass. Technically used to refer to the smells in more mature wines that emerge as the wine ages. This differentiates it from 'aroma', which is used for smells in younger wines. See also 'Aroma'.

Bourboulenc. Medium-quality white grape variety from the Rhône Valley and Southern France.

Breton. Name given to Cabernet Franc in the Loire Valley.

Brilliant. Said of wine having a very bright or brilliant colour which glints strongly in the light.

Burning. Describes a wine containing too much or an excessive balance of alcohol, leaving a burning sensation in the mouth.

Burnt. Sometimes ambiguous term for smells ranging from caramel to burnt wood, usually associated with ageing in oak.

Brut. Term for dry sparkling wines and champagnes containing very little sweetness (just enough to temper the wine's acidity); 'Extra Brut' or, in French, *brut zéro* means there is virtually no added sugar, giving a very dry sparkling wine.

Cabernet Franc. Red grape variety blended with Cabernet Sauvignon and/or Merlot in Bordeaux, also the main quality red grape in the Loire Valley. It is capable of producing a very fine wine for long-term keeping.

Cabernet Sauvignon. Noble red grape variety predominant in the Médoc and Graves regions of Bordeaux, also used elsewhere in South-West and Southern France and producing wines for long-term keeping.

Carignan. Red grape variety from Southern France producing very well-structured, robust wines.

Casse. Fault in wine caused by oxidation or chemical reduction which makes wine lose its clarity.

Carbonic maceration. Method of vinifying red wine by macerating whole grapes in vats saturated with carbon dioxide. It is used mainly to produce wines to be drunk very young (Vins de Primeur) and is widely used in Beaujolais.

Chaptalisation. The addition of sugar to fermenting must to obtain a more robust wine by increasing its richness in alcohol when this is too weak; this process is subject to legal controls.

Chardonnay. Noble white grape variety from Burgundy, also grown in other regions such as Jura. It produces fine wines likely to age well. It is also a key grape variety for champagne and other sparkling wines.

Chasselas. White grape variety grown chiefly as a table grape but also used for making dry wine (in Switzerland, Alsace and Savoie).

Château. Term often used to describe a wine estate even though – sometimes – it does not contain a real château.

Chenin or Chenin Blanc. White grape variety very common in the Loire Valley, producing fine, balanced wines likely to keep well.

Cinsaut or Cinsault. Red grape variety from the Rhône Valley and South of France which makes very fruity wines.

Clairet. Light, fruity red wine, or dark rosé wine produced in Bordeaux.

Clairette. White grape variety from the Rhône

Valley and South of France producing fairly fine dry and sparkling wines.

Claret. English term for red wine from Bordeaux.

Clarification. Separating the sediment from grape juice or wine; see also 'Filtration' and 'Fining'.

Clavelin. Unusually shaped bottle holding 62 cl and used for the Vins Jaunes or yellow wines of the Jura.

Climat. In Burgundy, refers to an area characterised by soil type and micro-climate.

Clonal selection (of vines). A contemporary method of selection and propagating vines from the strongest or most disease-resistant plants in a vineyard. New plantings are increasingly with clonally selected vines.

Clone. Group of vinestocks grown from cuttings that have been multiplied from a single parent stock.

Clos. Term used in some regions, especially Burgundy, to describe an enclosed vineyard usually surrounded by walls (e.g. Clos de Vougeot).

Colombard. White grape variety from the South-West of France, producing fairly ordinary, everyday wines.

Cornalin. Obscure red grape variety grown in the Valais, Switzerland.

Cot or Côt. Name given to the Malbec grape variety in the Loire Valley.

Coulure. Poor fruit set following wet or windy weather resulting in the fruit (as small, unformed berries) falling off after flowering.

Corked. A wine suffering from a tainted smell and taste from a faulty cork. The typical smell is musty, mousy or corky.

Crémant. Sparkling AOC wine.

Cru. French term for a vineyard, often translated as 'growth'. The meaning of this term varies from region to region and may be linked to a quality system. See also 'Premier Cru' and 'Grand Cru'. It may be used to denote certain superior areas of vineyards, e.g., the Beaujolais crus such as Juliénas or Fleurie. May also be used loosely to mean a particular wine.

Cru Bourgeois. Classification for châteaux in the Médoc region of Bordeaux which is below that of the 1855 classification.

Crushing. The process of breaking up the grape skins to extract the juice.

Cuve. Vat, tun or tank used for the fermentation and storage of wine.

Cuvée. Literally, the produce from one vat but is generally a very loose French term to imply a selected wine from a producer or estate that may make more than one wine.

Decant. To transfer a wine from its bottle into a carafe or decanter to separate the wine from its sediment and allow the wine to breathe.

Dégorgement. See disgorgement.

Demi-sec. Medium dry, for still wines. For a sparkling wine, the term means medium-sweet.

De-stemming. Removing the stems or stalks from the grapes. If grapes are not de-stemmed, they can give wine a certain astringency.

Deposit. Solid particles in a wine, particularly in old wines, which are removed by decanting before the wine is served.

Diolinoir. Red grape crossing giving deep-coloured wines and grown in Switzerland, mainly in the canton of Vaud. Sometimes used in a blend.

Disgorgement. The act of expelling the sediment caused by the secondary fermentation in the bottle of sparkling wine. This is followed immediately by topping up and insertion of the final cork.

Dosage. French term for the sweetened wine added to a sparkling wine or champagne after the yeast deposit has been removed. The level of dosage determines the final style, e.g., Doux, Demi-sec or Brut.

Doux. Term applied to sweet wines rich in sugar and to highly dosed wines in Champagne.

Dry. In still wines, describes a wine with virtually no residual sweetness (less than 4g/l); on the sweetness scale of sparkling wines, it means having little sugar (between 17 and 35g/l), which gives a medium-dry taste.

Duras. Red grape variety mainly produced in Gaillac in South-West France. (Not to be confused with the appellation of the same name.)

Eau-de-vie. Brandy i.e. distilled product from grapes or other fruit.

Echelle des crus. Term used in Champagne for the classification or grading of Premier and Grand Cru vineyards.

Empyreumatic. Term for smells recalling things burnt, cooked or smoked.

Espalier. Rare method of training vines.

Fat. Synonym for mellow or unctuous.

Feminine. Said of wines suggesting tenderness and lightness.

Fer or **Fer Servadou.** Red grape variety used to make wines for long-term keeping in South-West France.

Fermentation. Process by which grape juice becomes wine through the action of yeasts which turn the grape sugar into alcohol.

Fillette. Small bottle holding 35 cl, used in the Loire Valley.

Filtration. The process of filtering out deposits from must or wine to clarify it.

Finesse. Term for a wine that is delicate and elegant.

Fining. Process for clarifying wine by adding a coagulant (e.g. egg white, isinglass) which draws off particles still in suspension. These are subsequently filtered out.

Flavour. Overall sensation in the mouth imparted by a wine's taste and its aromas.

Flesh, fleshy. Said of a wine that gives an impression of fullness and density in the mouth, without any roughness.

Folle Blanche. White grape variety producing very fresh, lively wine (Gros Plant).

Foudre. Large oak barrel or cask of indeterminate size.

Foxy. Term for a smell given off by wine made from certain hybrid grape varieties.

Free-run juice. The juice of fermenting wine that runs freely from the vat, as opposed to the juice obtained by pressing the skins. (Only applies to red wines.)

Fresh. Said of a wine that is lightly but not

excessively acid, and imparts a feeling of freshness or liveliness.

Full. Said of a wine which has the requisite qualities of a good wine and leaves a feeling of fullness in the mouth.

Fût. Small barrel, usually of new oak.

Gamaret. Red grape crossing grown in Switzerland, mainly in the cantons of Geneva and Vaud. Similar parentage to Garanoir. Potentially of high quality.

Gamay. Red grape variety, the only one permitted in Beaujolais, also grown widely in the Loire Valley. Makes a very fruity, lively wine.

Gamey. Tasting term used in a positive way for the smell of red wines that is reminiscent of the smell of various game birds or animals.

Garanoir. Red grape crossing grown in Switzerland, mainly in the cantons of Geneva and Vaud. Similar parentage to Gamaret.

Garrigue. Scrub or scrubland in southern France that is usually full of wild herbs such as thyme, mint and rosemary. When used as a tasting term, describes a particular flavour reminiscent of the smell of the garrigue and often found in red wines from the Rhône Valley or southern France.

Generic. Term having several applications but often describing a brand-name wine rather than a Cru or Château wine, sometimes directed in a derogatory way at regional appellations such as Bordeaux, Burgundy, etc.

Generous. Said of a wine that is ripe and strong in alcohol but not tiresomely so, as in a heady wine.

Gewürztraminer. Very aromatic white grape variety from Alsace.

Glycerol. A higher alcohol and by-product of fermentation. Present in most wines, it is found in greater concentration in botrytised wines. It adds to the sweetness and oiliness of a wine.

Goût de terroir. Literally the taste from (not of) the soil. The notion of *terroir* includes soil, climate and exposure. In modern terms, a *goût de terroir* refers to a wine that tastes of where it comes from. See also 'Terroir'.

Grafting. Method used since the phylloxera disaster whereby a vine is grafted onto a rootstock (usually American) resistant to the phylloxera plant louse.

Grains nobles. Grapes that have been affected by noble rot or *botrytis cinerea* and usually used to make a sweet wine. See also *Selection de Grains Nobles*.

Grand Cru. Literally 'Great Growth', usually left untranslated. Generally refers to the best category in the AOC classification systems that exist in Alsace and in Burgundy. Vineyards may be classified as Grand Cru (also in Champagne) and the wine made from grapes harvested in those vineyards may subsequently be called Grand Cru. The term is also used in various individual classification systems that exist in Bordeaux, and is incorporated into the AOC St-Emilion Grand Cru.

Grand Vin. Term used by the Crus Classés châteaux of Bordeaux to describe the first wine of the château, e.g. in Margaux, Château Margaux is the Grand Vin of that château and Le Pavillon Rouge de Château Margaux is the second wine.

Gravel. Soil consisting of rounded pebbles and gravel, giving very good drainage. Very suitable for making high-quality red wines and found particularly in the Médoc and Graves areas of Bordeaux.

Green. Said of a wine that is too acidic.

Grenache. Red grape variety grown principally in the Rhône Valley and in some regions of South such as Banyuls and Languedoc-Roussillon, giving a fruity and very alcoholic wine.

Grolleau. Red grape variety from the Loire Valley used mainly in the production of rosé wines.

Gris, Vin. Pale rosé wine usually made by direct pressing of red grapes which results in a slightly coloured white wine.

Gros Plant. Name given to the Folle Blanche grape variety in the Nantes area of the Loire Valley.

Hard. Said of wine that is too astringent and acid, with too much tannin.

Harmonious. Describes a wine, usually a mature wine, in which the different characteristics are balanced and make a well-rounded whole.

Harshness. A rough, rather biting feeling, caused by far too much tannin.

Heady. Term for a wine that is very high in alcohol and possibly unbalanced.

Heavy. Said of an excessively rich wine.

Heida. White aromatic grape variety grown in some of the highest vineyards of the Valais, Switzerland and thought to be related to the Savagnin of Jura.

Herbaceous. Term (often used pejoratively) for aromas recalling grass or vegetation.

Hogshead. Barrel.

Humagne. Traditional red grape variety giving rustic wines in the Valais, Switzerland. There is also a white Humagne Blanche.

Hybrid. Term for grape varieties created from two different species of vine, as distinct from a grape crossing. Hybrids are rarely grown in France today and may only be used for table wines.

INAO. Institut National des Appellations d'Origine. Public body established to administer AOC and AOVDQS wines and regulate their production conditions.

Jacquère. White grape variety found in Savoie which makes a wine to be drunk fairly young.

Jeroboam. Large bottle holding the equivalent of four bottles (three litres) in Champagne and six bottles (4.5 litres) in Bordeaux.

Johannisberg. Wines made from the Sylvaner grape are named Johannisberg in the Valais canton of Switzerland.

Jurançon. Little-used white grape variety still found in Charente; also a red variety from the South-East used to make fairly ordinary wine. It is also the name for a dry or sweet white AOC wine made from the Gros et Petit Manseng and Courbu varieties in South-West France around the Jurançon commune.

Lactic acid. Acid obtained during malolactic fermentation (q.v.).

Lees. The natural precipitation of yeast cells and colouring matter that forms as a wine matures in a vat or barrel. When this happens in the bottle, it is called sediment.

Len de l'el. An obscure grape variety grown in the appellation of Gaillac in South-west France.

Lie, sur. A white wine may be referred to as having matured *sur lie* when it has been left in vat or barrel in contact with the lees or dead yeast cells and other deposits. This may impart more flavour to the wine and is particularly used in Muscadet in the Loire Valley where the term *sur lie* when used on labels means the wine is subject to certain stringent production rules.

Lieu-dit. Literally means a named place. Usually refers to a small part of a hamlet or village and is widely used in Burgundy to refer to wines coming from a particular small area.

Light. Said of a light-coloured wine with little body, but well-balanced and pleasant. In general, a wine to be drunk fairly young.

Limpid. Said of a clear, brightly coloured wine having no sediment.

Liquoreux. Particularly sweet and rich in sugar. The Vins Liquoreux are made from grapes allowed to develop noble rot and have a generally honeyed bouquet.

Lively. Said of a fresh, light wine, a little bit acid but still pleasant.

Long. Tasting term used when the flavours of a wine make a pleasing and persistent impression in the mouth after tasting; wine is also said to have 'length' or 'good length'.

Macabeo. White grape variety from the Roussillon that makes a pleasant wine to be drunk young.

Maceration. When the must and the grapes' solid matter (skins, pips, etc) are still in contact during fermentation.

Maderised. Said of a white wine which is slightly oxidised, taking on an amber colour while ageing and a taste like madeira.

Magnum. Bottle holding the equivalent of two bottles (1.5 litres).

Malbec. Name given in Bordeaux to the Cot grape variety.

Malic acid. Acid naturally present in all wines and which may be turned into lactic acid by malolactic fermentation.

Malolactic fermentation. The transformation, through the action of lactic bacteria, of malic acid into lactic acid and carbon dioxide. It is considered essential for stability in red wines and is sometimes used for whites. Its effect is partly to make the wine less acid, and for whites to develop a generally softer or creamier character.

Malvoisie. Synonym used in the Valais, Switzerland for the Pinot Gris grape.

Manseng. Gros Manseng and Petit Manseng are two of the white grape varieties used to make Jurançon.

Marc. Solid material left over after pressing; also the popular name of the marc brandy made from it.

Marsanne. White grape variety grown in Hermitage and elsewhere in the Rhône Valley and the South.

The traditional alternative to clonal selection.

Maturation. The period of time the wine spends between the end of the vinification or wine-making process and it being drunk. Maturation may take place in vats or oak barrels, or later in the bottle. The French word *maturation* refers to the ripening process of the grapes, which in English is simply called ripening.

Mauzac. White grape variety cultivated in South-ern and South-West France, making a fine wine for early drinking; it is also used as the base for sparkling wines.

Melon de Bourgogne. Originally from Burgundy, Melon is a synonym for the white Muscadet grape grown in the Nantes area of the Loire Valley.

Merlot. Main red grape variety in the Pomerol and St-Emilion districts of Bordeaux and blended with the Cabernets.

Methuselah. Name used in Champagne for a large bottle equivalent to eight ordinary bottles (six litres). In Bordeaux, this is also called the imperial bottle.

Mildew. Vine disease caused by a parasitic fungus which attacks the stems and leaves.

Millerandage. A condition that causes bunches of grapes to have uneven sizes of berries following poor setting of the fruit. It often follows *coulure*. Not always viewed badly as the condition leads to a reduction in yield that may even improve quality.

Mistelle. Sweet mixture of grape must and alcohol. The fermentation of the must of fresh grapes is stopped by the addition of alcohol. See also 'VDN' and 'VDL'.

Moelleux. Term generally used for very sweet white wines.

Mondeuse. Red grape variety from Savoie which makes a high-quality wine for long-term keeping.

Mourvèdre. Red grape variety from Provence and the Rhône Valley producing fine wines which keep very well.

Mousse. Sparkle or fizziness as seen and tasted in champagne and other sparkling wines.

Mousseux. French word for sparkling which can be applied to sparkling wines made using all methods.

Muscadelle. White grape variety from Bordeaux which is blended with Sémillon and Sauvignon.

Muscadet. White grape variety grown in the Loire Valley which makes a very fresh wine generally made to be drunk young.

Muscat. A family of grape varieties which all have a similar grapey or floral aroma. The word is also used for wines made from Muscat grapes.

Musky. Said of a smell that recalls musk.

Must. The sugary juice extracted from grapes.

Musty. Describes a wine that has lost some or all of its bouquet through partial oxidation or other faults.

Mutage. Process of stopping the must's alcoholic fermentation by adding wine-based spirit. Mistelle, Vins de Liqueurs and Vins Doux Naturels are made this way.

Nebuchadnezzar. Giant bottle in Champagne, equivalent to 20 ordinary bottles (15 litres).

Négociant, négociant-éleveur. See 'Wine-merchants'.

Négrette. Red grape variety in South-West France giving a rich, strongly coloured wine with little acidity.

Nervy. Said of a lively wine which leaves pronounced flavours and some acidity on the palate, but not too much.

Niellucciu. Red grape variety planted in Corsica, giving high-quality wines for long-term keeping (particularly Patrimonio).

Noble rot. Name given to the action of the *Botrytis cinerea* on white grapes to make the finest sweet white wines.

Nouveau. Wine from the latest harvest to be drunk young. See also 'Primeur'.

Oenologist. Trained, professional wine-taster or wine-maker.

Oenology. The scientific study of wine.

Oidium. Powdery mildew, a fungal disease of the vine which can attack stalks, leaves or grape bunches and leaves a powdery grey residue which severely affects yields; can be treated with sulphur.

OIV. Office International de la Vigne et du Vin. Based in France, this is the inter-governmental body which supervises technical, scientific and economic matters related to growing vines and making wine.

Old. Term with several applications, usually describing a wine which is several years old and has aged in the bottle after its period in the barrel; but may also be said of a wine that is simply past its best.

Onivins. The French Interprofessional Office for Wines. This body succeeded Onivit in its mission to direct and regulate the wine market.

Organoleptic. Describes the qualities and properties noted by the senses during wine-tasting, e.g. colour, smell or taste.

Ouvrée. Measurement of land area. 23 ouvrées = 1 hectare.

Oxidation. The action of oxygen (air) on wine. If there is too much, the colour fades and both the smell and taste of the wine are affected.

Pasteurisation. Heat-sterilising process perfected by Louis Pasteur.

Pêche de vigne. Small, fairly sour peach used mainly in cooking and traditionally found in vineyards. The aroma of certain white wines are likened to that of *pêche de vigne*.

Persistence. Length of time that the flavours of a wine remain in the mouth after swallowing. Good persistence, or length, is a positive sign.

Pétillant. A Vin Pétillant is a lightly sparkling wine, less fizzy than Vin Mousseux.

Petite Arvine. Traditional white grape variety grown in the Valais, Switzerland and producing wines of high quality.

Petit Verdot. In the Médoc district of Bordeaux, a minor red grape variety which may be blended in small quantities with the Cabernets and Merlot.

Phylloxera. Plant louse which between 1860 and 1890 ravaged French vineyards by eating vine roots and thus killing the vines. It is controlled today by grafting vines onto phylloxera-resistant rootstocks. See also 'Grafting'.

Pineau d'Aunis. Minor red grape variety grown

in some regions of the Loire Valley and producing a pale-coloured wine.

Pinot Blanc. White grape variety grown mainly in Alsace.

Pinot Gris. High-quality white grape variety grown mainly in Alsace, where it used to be known as Tokay.

Pinot Meunier. Red grape variety which is mainly used in Champagne as part of the blend. It is a hardier and earlier-ripening grape than Pinot Noir, to which it is related.

Pinot Noir. The main red grape variety in Burgundy, where it gives wines with immediate fruitiness which nevertheless keep well. It is also an important part of the blend for champagne, where it is pressed quickly so as not to extract colour. It is the only permitted red grape in Alsace, and small quantities are grown in the South.

Piquant. Said of a wine with a sharp, acid taste.

Poulsard. Red grape variety grown mainly in the Jura and producing pale-coloured wines sold as rosé or red.

Powerful. Said of a wine which combines a full body with generosity and a rich bouquet.

Premier Cru. Literally First Growth, usually left untranslated. In Burgundy it refers to the second best category in the AOC classification systems. Vineyards may be classified as Premier Cru (also in Champagne) and the wine made from grapes harvested in those vineyards may subsequently be called Premier Cru. In Bordeaux the term may be used for certain châteaux that are classified as Premier Cru Classés.

Pressing. Process of pressing the grapes to extract juice or wine, leaving the skins and other solid matter behind.

Pricked. Property of a wine suffering from acescency, which gives it a sour, vinegary smell.

Primeur. A Vin de Primeur is from the latest harvest and is made to be drunk very young. See also 'Nouveau'.

Racking. Process of transferring a wine from one barrel or vat to another to separate it from the lees or sediment.

Rancio. Originally Spanish, this tasting term is applied to some wines, especially VDN, which, when they age, may take on a vaguely nutty, almost maderised character.

Rasping. Said of a rough, astringent wine.

Ratafia. Vin de Liqueur made in Champagne by mixing grape spirit and fermenting must.

Remuage. Riddling. During the secondary fermentation in the bottle in the traditional (Champagne) method, this is the shaking and turning process by which the remaining sediment is brought down to rest on the cork so that it can be disgorged. Formerly done by hand, it can now be done mechanically with rotating pallets.

Rich. Said of a well-balanced, generous, powerful wine with good colour.

Riesling. White grape variety grown in Alsace and making wines of great distinction.

Rimage. Term used in some areas, especially Banyuls and Beaujolais to denote a higher quality selection of wine.

Roasted. Characteristic taste and aromas of crystallised fruits in sweet wines made from grapes affected by noble rot. Also refers to red wines made from grapes that have been literally 'roasted' by the sun.

Robust. Said of a wine having body.

Rolle. White grape variety from Provence which makes very fine wines.

Romorantin. Rare white grape variety grown in some parts of the Loire Valley.

Rootstock. The part of the vine that is not visible, i.e. which is below ground. Most European grape varieties are grafted onto American rootstocks, since these are resistant to phylloxera.

Rough. Describes a very astringent, rasping wine.

Round, rounded. Said of a supple, ripe and fleshy wine which leaves a pleasant, harmonious feeling in the mouth.

Roussanne. White grape variety grown mainly in the northern Rhône Valley, a little in the southern Rhône and in small quantities in Savoie, giving a very fine wine for long-term keeping.

Saignée. Rosé de. Rosé wine run off the skins of red grapes after a very short maceration period.

Salmanazar. Very large bottle in Champagne containing the equivalent of 12 ordinary bottles (nine litres).

Sauvignon. White grape variety grown in many regions, but especially in the Loire Valley and Bordeaux, and making a fine wine which keeps well and has a characteristic smoky aroma.

Savagnin. Grape variety from the Jura giving the famous Vin Jaune or yellow wine and making up part of the blend for other Jura white wines. It may be related to the Klevner and Gewurztraminer from Alsace.

Scent. Another word for smell, indicating something scented or perfumed, or delicately aromatic.

Sciacarello. Red grape variety grown in Corsica and giving a fleshy, fruity wine.

Sediment. Solid particles held in suspension in must or wine.

Sélection de Grains Nobles. Term used traditionally in Alsace, but increasingly adopted elsewhere for a wine made from grapes affected by noble rot or botrytis cinerea.

Sémillon. Noble white grape variety grown mainly in Bordeaux and making sweet wines such as Sauternes as well as fine dry wines.

Sensory analysis. Technical term for wine-tasting.

Short. Said of a wine having little length in the mouth after tasting; 'short in the mouth' is also used.

Silky. Said of a supple, mellow, velvety, pleasantly harmonious and elegant wine.

Smoky. Term for a smell like that of smoked foods, characteristic of, among others, the Sauvignon grape variety (hence the name Blanc Fumé or 'smoky white').

Smooth. A smooth or supple, pleasant wine, easy to drink and which 'slips down well'.

Solid. Said of a well-constituted, well-structured wine.

Sour. Having a highly acid character, accompanied by a smell very like that of vinegar.

Sparkling. Term for wines that have dissolved carbon dioxide, usually the result of a second fermentation.

Stabilisation. All the processes, such as filtration and fining, used before bottling to ensure a wine is kept in good condition. Especially refers to the process of removing tartaric acid crystals before bottling.

Stale. A wine that has lost some or all of its bouquet, usually through oxidation.

Stemming. Alternative term sometimes used for de-stemming (q.v.).

Still wine. Non-sparkling wine.

Straightforward. Said of a frank wine with a well-defined character.

Structure. Describes the general form and constitution of a wine, especially its acidity and tannin.

Substantial. Said of a wine that has a strong colour and in the mouth feels rather heavy and thick.

Sulphur. A sulphur solution may be added to must or wine to protect it from faults such as oxidation, or, at the point of fermentation, to kill off certain unwanted yeast strains. Sulphuring refers to the treatment of the vine by spraying with copper sulphate, to prevent fungal diseases.

Supple. A smooth wine, its mellowness prevailing over its astringency.

Sylvaner. White grape variety from Alsace which generally makes straightforward wine for early drinking.

Syrah. High-quality red grape variety mainly planted in the Rhône Valley and Languedoc-Roussillon.

Tannat. Red grape variety grown in the South-West and producing very well-structured fine wines which keep well.

Tannic. A rough, astringent sensation in a wine caused by tannin.

Tannin. Substance found in grape skins, pips and stems which helps wine to keep for a long time and forms part of its structure. Particularly noticeable in young reds.

Tartrates. Tartaric crystals that form in the cask, vat or bottle if the wine has been subjected to intense cold.

Tastevinage. Seal awarded by the Confrérie des Chevaliers du Tastevin to certain Burgundy wines.

Tears. Term for the traces of wine on the glass, sometimes also called 'legs'.

Temperature regulation. Technique for checking and adjusting the temperature in the vat during fermentation and storage.

Terroir. A place where wine is grown. Each terroir has its own physical characteristics (soil, subsoil, exposure, etc) which influence the kind and quality of the wine produced there. See also 'Goût de terroir'.

Thermovinification. A method of fermentation employing heat, used mainly for red wines. It may result in soft, fruity, early-drinking red wines.

Tired. Term for a wine that has lost some of its quality. This may be temporary (for example after being transported) and it may just need time to recover.

Tokay. Name given in Alsace to Pinot Gris, a quality white grape variety. No relation to the Hungarian wine of the same name.

Topping up. Process of adding wine to the barrel to keep it full and prevent the wine from coming into contact with air.

Traditional method. Method of making sparkling wines which includes a secondary fermentation in the bottle, as is done for champagne. Identical to the 'Champagne method'.

Trousseau. Red grape variety from the Jura, producing wine with a darker colour than the Poulsard or Pinot Noir.

Ugni Blanc. White grape variety grown in the South (and in Charente to make Cognac under the name of St-Emilion) and giving a fairly acid wine which does not keep well.

Ullage. Space left at the top of a closed bottle. If there is too much ullage, the wine will oxidise. Also refers to the space left in the top of a barrel. See also 'Topping up'.

Unctuous. Said of a wine that is pleasantly mellow, fleshy and full-bodied in the mouth.

VDL. Vin de Liqueur. A sweet wine made by mixing must and alcohol (e.g. Pineau des Charentes). These sweet wines do not conform to the legal norms for the VDNs.

VDN. Vin Doux Naturel. A sweet wine made from Muscat, Grenache, Macabeu or Malvoisie grapes. The wine is obtained by stopping the fermentation of the must with the addition of grape spirit, in line with strict conditions about the wine's sweetness and how it is made.

VDP. Vin de Pays. A wine legally belonging to the table wines group, ie below that of AOC and AOVDQS wines, but which carries a mention on the label of the geographical region it comes from. Some VDP may be of high quality.

VDQS. Now AOVDQS: Appellation d'Origine Vin Délimité de Qualité Supérieure. The regional wines in this group are made according to strict regulations.

Vegetal. Said of the bouquet or aromas of a wine (generally a young one) which recall grasses or vegetation.

Vermentino. White grape variety grown particularly in Corsica where it is known sometimes as Malvoisie. It may be the same as Rolle in Provence.

Village. As well as the normal usage of the word, this term may be used in Burgundy to denote a wine that has the simple village appellation rather than the grander Premier or Grand Cru appellation e.g. Volnay as opposed to Volnay Premier Cru.

Villages. Term used in some regions to single out a superior area within a larger appellation (Beaujolais, Côtes du Rhône, Mâcon).

Vin de glace. Term used in Luxembourg for very sweet 'ice wine' produced from frozen grapes harvested in early winter after the first heavy frost.

Vin de Paille. Term used mainly in Jura for sweet wine made from grapes that have been harvested and then left for several months to dry and for the natural sugars and flavours to concentrate. Traditionally the grapes were laid out on straw (paille), but today they are often simply left in wooden crates or suspended from the rafters in a well-ventilated room.

Vin Gris. See 'Gris, Vin'.

Vinification. The various methods and techniques of processing grapes into wine. It is followed by a period of maturation before bottling the wine.

Vin Jaune. Unusual 'yellow wine' produced in Jura from the Savagnin variety. The wine is stored for over six years in old oak casks that are not topped up. A '*voile*' or film of yeast forms on the surface protecting the wine from extreme oxidation and imparting a special flavour.

Vinous. Said of a wine fairly rich in alcohol which seems to sum up neatly the differences between wine and other alcoholic drinks.

Vintage. The year in which the wine was harvested.

Viognier. White grape variety grown in the Rhône Valley and the South and producing a fine, high-quality wine.

Virile. Said of a well-structured, full-bodied and powerful wine.

Voile, sous. Literally 'beneath a veil'. Refers to the ageing of Vin Jaune in the Jura.

VQPRD. Vin de Qualité Produit dans une Région Déterminée. This category includes the French AOC and VDQS wines and sets them apart from the table wines category in the European Union.

Warming. Said of a wine conveying an impression of warmth, usually because of its alcoholic strength.

Well structured. Said of a well-constituted wine with plenty of acidity and tannin that will probably age well.

Wine-merchants. In the French wine business, there are straightforward wine-merchants and shippers (*négociants*), but also others (*négociants-éleveurs*) who, especially in the big appellation regions, not only buy and sell wine but take over the maturation of young wine and see it through every stage up to bottling. In Champagne, the *négociant-manipulateur* buys grapes to make his own champagne wine.

Yeasts. Microscopic single-celled organisms which convert sugar to alcohol during fermentation.

Young. Very relative term, used for a wine in its first year as well as for the taste of an older wine that has not yet developed to its full potential.

INDEX OF APPELLATIONS

INDEX OF COMMUNES

COMMUNES

INDEX OF PRODUCERS

PRODUCERS

Jacquinet-Dumez, 707
Maison Louis Jadot, 513, 533, 616, 623
Jaeger-Ligneul, 707
Jaffelin, 559, 591, 597, 619
André Jaffre, 161
Yves Jalliet, 779
EARL Pierre Jamain, 707
E. Jamart et Cie, 708
Bruno Jambon, 160
Laurent Jambon, 164
Gabriel Jambon, 169
Dominique Jambon, 189
Francis Jamet, 1031
Guy Jamet, 1037
EARL Jane et Sylvain, 513
Pascal Janet, 1126
Michel Janin, 178
SCEV Janisson-Baradon, 378
Sté Pierre Janny, 480, 490, 640, 663
François Janouëix, 266
Bertrand Jany et Fils, 1220
Bertrand Jany, 793
Jard, 963
Elisabeth et Benoît Jardin, 1040
SCEV Champagne René Jardin, 708
Ch. de Jau, 829, 1180
Vignobles Jaubert-Noury, 826
Sylvette Jauffret, 862
GAEC Jauffrineau-Boulanger, 960
Dom. Jaume, 1101, 1112
Alain Jaume, 1146
Javoy Père et Fils, 1071
Dom. Guy-Pierre Jean et Fils, 453
SCEA du Ch. Jean Voisin, 300
Michel Jean, 313
Jean-Gabriel Devay, 154
Anne-Marie Jeanjean, 1183
Bernard-Pierre Jeanjean, 1186
Gérard Jeanjean, 794
Philippe et Frédéric Jeanjean, 799
Jeanjean, 806
Champagne Jeanmaire, 708
Christophe Jeanmet, 175
Jeanmin-Mongeard, 824, 1181
Dom. Rémi Jobard, 464, 468
Dom. Emile Jobard, 603
SCEA Charles Joguet, 1034
Jean-Luc Joillot, 464, 585
SCEV Joinaud-Borde, 293
EARL Joliet Père et Fils, 508
Pascal Jolivet, 1088
Jean-Marc Jolivet, 214
Hervé Jolly, 708
Antoine Joly, 1237
Joly, 736
EARL Claude et Cédric Joly, 755, 1200
Fabienne Joly, 843
Nicolas Joly, 984-986
Pierre et Jean-Michel Jomard, 193
Jean-Hervé Jonquères d'Oriola, 823, 1173
SCA Les Vignerons de Jonquières, 785
Frédéric Jordy, 796
EARL Bertrand Jorez, 708
EARL Michel et Mickaël Joselon, 988

Michel Joseph, 1005
EARL M.-C. et D. Joseph, 173
SA Josmeyer et Fils, 121
Jean-Pierre Josselin, 708
EARL Dom. Gabriel Jouard Père et Fils, 614, 623
Dom. Vincent et François Jouard, 614
Cave Françoise et Philippe Jouby, 453
Alain Jougla, 815
Philippe Joulin, 999
Francis Jourdain, 1059
Gilles Jourdan, 464, 549
GAEC Jourdan, 853
SCEA Jousset et Fils, 939, 968, 980
Mme Jouve-Férec, 855
J. Jouves et Fils, 882
Famille Paul Joyet, 1100
EARL Joyet, 153
SC Vignobles Jugla, 410
Anne-Marie Juillard, 167
Dom. Michel et Laurent Juillot, 562, 565, 639
Diane Julinet, 171
Julien de Savignac, 920
Bernard Julien, 1217
Eric Julien, 256
Xavier Julien, 457
Marcel Julien, 812
M. et L. Julien, 1101
Guy Jullien, 1160
Jean-Pierre Jullien, 791
Thierry Jullien, 1210
Charles Jumert, 1057
SARL Roger Jung et Fils, 91, 133
Daniel Junot, 453
Cave des Producteurs de Jurançon, 900, 904, 906
Eric Kauffer, 1196
Hans Ulrich Kesserling, 1274
SCEA Vignoble famille Khayat, 255
Jean-Charles Kieffer, 101
René Kientz Fils, 116
Cave de Kientzheim-Kaysersberg, 101
André Kientzler, 85, 124
Philippe Kirmann, 113
Pierre Kirschner, 123
Peter Kjellberg, 304
EARL Henri Klée et Fils, 91, 137
EARL Jean Klack et Fils, 134
Françoise et Jean-Marie Klein – Aux Vieux Remparts, 101
EARL Ouahi et Rémy Klein, 1103, 1113
Joseph et Jacky Klein, 95, 142
Klein-Brand, 111
André Kleinknecht, 116
GAEC René et Michel Koch, 128
Pierre et François Koch, 85
Koeberlé Kreyer, 124
Jean-Marie Koehly, 91
Dom. viticole Raymond Kohll-Leuck, 1246
Michel Kohll-Reuland, 1246
Jan de Kok, 435
Laurent et Benoît Kox, 1246
Laurent Kraft, 1049
Domaines Kressmann, 355, 366-368
Kressmann, 390
SCEA Dom. de Kreusignac, 1212
Elke Kreuzfeld, 806
Dom. Marc Kreydenweiss, 111, 126
EARL Hubert Krick, 116, 141
Caves Krier Frères, 1246
Dom. viticole Krier-Welbes, 1246
Krug Vins fins de Champagne, 709
EARL Paul Kubler, 101, 138

Kuehn SA, 102
R. Kuentz et Fils, 136
Jean-Pierre Kuntzer, 1271
Coop. des Vignerons de l'Ile de Ré, 1211
La Cave de l'Abbé Rous, 831-832, 1169, 1171
SCA Ch. de L'Amarine, 788
Michel L'Amoullier, 244
Dom. de L'Arjolle, 1225
Dom. de L'Ariot, 546
Ch. L'Arnaude, 844
GAEC de L'Aumonière, 1241
SCI de L'Ecluse, 170
Dom. de L'Ecole, 116
SCEA du Ch. L'Enclos, 270, 275
SCEA Ch. L'Enclos, 342
SCEA du Ch. de L'Engarran, 798
Arnaud L'Epine, 801
Dom. de L'Escarelle, 1234
SCEA Ch. L'Escart, 233
Dom. de l'Eté, 939
Ch. L'Etampe, 305
Encavage de l'Etat de Neuchâtel, 1271
Sté coopérative L'Etoile, 832, 1170-1171
Dom. de L'Hospitalet, 799, 1181
Union de Vignerons de L'Ile de Beauté, 870
Ch. de l'Isolette, 1164
Cave de L'Ormarine, 799
Dom. de L'Orme, 485
Dom. L'Oustau des Lecques, 1142
Cooperative vinicole L'Union, 711
Dominique Léandre-Chevalier, 245
Dom. France Léchenault, 631
Patrick Léger, 1013
EARL Philippe Léger, 970, 980
B. Léger-Plumet, 664
Bernard Legrand, 455, 485
Eric Léglise, 403
Famille Patrick Léon, 260
Lésineau, 807
Dom. Luc Lévèque, 1014
Guy Lévèque, 1014
GFA Françoise et Henri Lévèque, 353
Yves et Catherine Léveillé, 451
Joël Lévi, 1000
Sté viticole du Dom. de Lézin, 330
Henri Liddecke, 226, 349
Mas de la Barben, 796
SCV Les Producteurs de La Barnède, 823, 1181
SCEA La Bassonnerie, 267
SCEA Dom. de La Bastide Neuve, 841
Cellier de La Bastide, 203, 209, 235, 338
Ch. La Bastide, 781
SCEA Dom. de La Bastidonne, 1159, 1231
Dom. de La Barrière, 1220
SCEA La Berrière, 952
SA Ch. La Bienfaisance, 311
Dom. de La Boitinière, 961
SE Ch. de La Bôtinière, 952
EARL Ch. de La Bougerelle, 860
SCEA La Braulterie-Morisset, 244
Ch. La Brie, 920
Cave coop. La Cévenole, 1239
SCV La Capdérenne, 855
SA La Cappellaccia, 1169
Cave cooperative La Carignano, 793
Dom. de la Casa Blanca, 832, 1169
Ch. La Casenove, 824, 1174

SCEA Ch. La Chèze, 346
La Chablisienne, 487, 495, 500
Jérôme de La Chaise, 1080
SCEA Dom. de La Chanade, 887, 1214
Dom. de La Chapelle de Vâtre, 162
Ch. La Chapelle Maillard, 342
SCEA du Ch. La Chapelle, 320
Cave coop. La Clairette d'Adissan, 778
SARL Direct Wines Ch. La Clarière Laithwaite, 220, 329
EARL Ch. La Commanderie, 417
La Compagnie rhodanienne, 788, 1140
Dom. de La Coquillade, 1160
Dom. de La Courtade, 841
SCA La Courtoise, 1160
SCEA Dom. de La Crémade, 857
Cellier de La Crau, 842, 1234
GFA Dom. de La Cressonnière, 842
Ch. La Croix Chabrière, 1102, 1157
SCEA Ch. La Croix de Mouchet, 325
Dom. La Croix de Pez, 415
SCEA Ch. La Croix Jacquelet, 636, 640
SA La Croix Merlin, 212
GAEC Dom. de La Croix Saunier, 162
SC Ch. La Décelle, 267, 270
Ch. La Décelle, 1102, 1157
Mas de La Dame, 863
SARL de La Diligence, 278
Cellier de La Dona, 828
SCEA Dom. de La Dorgonne, 1163
EARL Ch. La Dournie, 815
EARL La Ducquerie, 990
P.-H. de La Fabrègue, 826
GAEC Dom. La Fadèze, 1226
SCE Ch. la Fagnouse, 301
Dom. de La Ferme Blanche, 851
Dom. de La Feuillata, 155
de La Filolie, 302
SCE Ch. La Fleur Milon, 413
SC du Ch. La Fleur-Pétrus, 268
Dom. de La Folie, 636
Dom. de La Foliette, 954
SCEA La Font du Roc, 931
Cave coop. La Fontesole, 800
SCEA Ch. La Forêt, 346
SC de La Frérie, 331
SCEA Ch. La Fruitaie, 984
EARL de La Gérade, 842
Coop. vinicole La Gaillarde, 1103
SC du Ch. La Garde (Dourthe), 366
SC de La Gironville, 389
SCEA Dom. de La Giscle, 842
SCEA La Grande Pleyssade, 915
SCE du Ch. La Grande-Barde, 321, 326
La Grappe de Gurson, 920
SCEA Dom. La Grave, 355
SCEA La Gravette, 805
EARL Dom. de La Haute Olive, 1035
SCIR Dom. de La Jeannette, 843
GAEC de La Jousselinière, 947
SARL La Julienne, 914
Ch. La Lagune, 391

PRODUCERS

INDEX OF PRODUCERS

PRODUCERS

SCEA du Val du Lel, 741
SC du Val Joanis, 1164
EARL P.L. Valade, 330
Vignoble de l'Etat du Valais, 1260
Christophe Valat, 1117
Dom. de Valcolombe, 867
GFA Valdition, 1233
Cave des Vignerons Réunis de Valency, 1060
Thierry Valente, 1154
EARL Valentin et Coste, 1101
Famille Valentin, 840
Christine Valette, 313
EARL Thierry Valette, 331
Marc Valette, 814
Gérald Vallée, 1029
Jean-François Vallat, 804
Jean-Claude Vallois, 735
Les Vignerons du Vallon, 899
François Vallot, 1111
Henri Valloton, 1264
Dom. de Vallouit, 905
Michel Valton, 905
Cave coop. de Valvignères, 1239
Bernard Van Doren, 1231
Vandelle et Fils, 759, 1200
Guy Vanlancker, 813
Ch. Vannières, 850
Jean-Yves Vantey, 629
Jean-Yves Vapillon, 758
SCEA André Vaque, 1108, 1150
Dom. Bernard Vaquer, 1177
Pierre Varenne, 1136
Dom. Varenne, 1140
SCI Ch. de Varennes, 164
Champagne Varnier-Fannière, 735
SCI Dom. des Varoilles, 515
Vins Frédéric Varoure, 1266
André Vatan, 1092
Philippe et Georges Vatan, 999, 1005
SARL Paul Vattan, 1091
Vaucher Père et Fils, 477, 588, 609
De Vaudieu, 1150
Christophe Vaudoisey, 593
Vaudoisey-Creusefond, 588
SCEA Ch. de Vaugaudry, 1039
SCEA Dom. de Vauroux, 492, 498
Thierry Vaute, 1184
Famille Vauthier, 286, 307
Frédéric Vauthier, 317
Champagne Vauversin, 735
Michel Vaury, 1017
Xavier Vayron, 263
Dom. de Vayssette, 891
Champagne Vazart-Coquart, 735
SA Maurice Velge, 416
Cave des Vignerons du Vendômois, 1058
Champagne de Venoge, 735
GAEC Venot, 466, 631
Venture, 798
Dom. André Verda, 1151, 1153-1154
Jean-Hubert Verdaguer, 1175
Jean-Pierre Verdeau, 1103
Mme Andrée Verdeille, 822, 1175
Alain Verdet, 472
Odile Verdier et Jacky Logel, 1066
EARL Verdier Père et Fils, 971

Denise et Cécile Verdier, 344
SC Ch. Verdignan, 395
Raphaël Vergère, 1258
EARL Denise Vergès, 839
GAEC Verger Fils, 280, 327
Robert Verger, 172
François-Joseph Vergez, 389
Vignobles Jacques Vergez, 1227
SCEV J.-L. Vergnon, 736
SCGEA Cave Vergobbi, 1158
Verhaeghe, 878
Jacques et Yannick de Vermont, 165
GAEC Daniel et Roland Vernay, 1120
Dom. Georges Vernay, 1120, 1123, 1127
SCA du Ch. Vernous, 384
Armand Vernus, 168
Laurent Verot, 455, 642
Dom. Verret, 466, 469, 492
Christophe Verronneau, 1013
Philippe Verzier, 1121
Georges Vesselle, 736, 740
Maurice Vesselle, 736, 740
Dom. Vessigaud Père et Fils, 661
Denis Vessot, 631
SA Veuve Ambal, 482
Veuve Amiot, 1002
Veuve Clicquot-Ponsardin, 736
Veuve Henri Moroni, 466, 611
Veuve Maître-Geoffroy, 737
Jacques Veux, 1021
Chantal Veyry, 283
Eric Vezain, 243
Charles Viénot, 550, 600
GAEC Vial, 1071
Jean-Louis Vial, 1234
Vialard, 386, 388
SCEA Viale, 1132
GAEC Dom. Viallet, 765
Dom. Vial-Magnères, 833, 1172
Champagne Viard Rogué, 737
Champagne Florent Viard, 737
Dom. de Viaud, 251
SAS Ch. de Viaud, 278
Dom. Vico, 872
Jean-Philippe Victor, 849
Dominique Vidal, 924
J. Vidal-Fleury, 1121, 1185
Françoise Vidal-Leguénédal, 243
Cave vinicole du Vieil-Armand, 86, 129
Vieilles Caves de Bourgogne & de Bordeaux, 472
R. Viemont-D. Maître-Gadais, 1026
Alain Vies, 812
Dom. du Vieux Bourg, 1008
SC du Vieux Château Certan, 273
Dom. du Vieux Chêne, 827, 831,1177
SC du Ch. Vieux Lartigue, 286
Dom. du Vieux Noyer, 899
GAEC du Vieux Pressoir, 753-754, 757, 1199
SCE Ch. Vieux Robin, 384
SCA du Vieux Vauvert, 1051
Alain Vigier, 277
André Vignal, 1116
Bernard Vigne, 1166
Richard Vigne, 1166

EARL Vigneau-Chevreau, 1052
Ch. Vigneleure, 862
Vignerons et Passions, 818, 826
Cave de Vignerons réunis, 193
GAEC des Vignerons, 467, 635
GAEC du Dom. des Vignes sous Les Ouches, 641
SA Champagne Vignier-Lebrun, 712
Alain Vignol, 459
Dom. Fabrice Vigot, 537
GFA Georges Vigouroux, 880
Bernard Viguier, 1164
Jean-Marc Viguier, 899
A. et P. de Villaine, 631-632
GAEC des Villains, 968, 973
Dom. de Villalin, 1082
Ch. de Villambis, 396
SA Henri de Villamont, 530, 572, 605
François Villard, 1123
Claire Villars, 401-402, 412
Céline Villars-Fouhet, 392, 407
Hervé Villemade, 1054
Jean-Marc Villemaine, 1013
GAEC Villeneuve et Fils, 212
André et Frédéric Villeneuve, 1070
Xavier de Villeneuve, 845
SC villeneuvoise, 228
Ch. de Villers-la-Faye, 472
Elise Villiers, 459
Champagne Vilmart et Cie, 737
Michel Vincens, 883
Jacques Vincent, 1084
Jean-Marc Vincent, 627
Daniel et Gérard Vinet, 959
Vinival, 954, 980, 998, 1208
Cie des Vins d'Autrefois, 587, 605
Vins et Vignobles, 167
Les domaines de Vinsmeselle, 1245, 1248
Les Domaines de Vinsmoselle, 1247-1248
Denis Vinson, 1105, 1114
Paul-Hervé Vintrou, 976, 981
SA Ch. de Vinzel, 1257
Georges Viornery, 169
Dom. Philippe Viret, 1118
Les domaines Virginie, 1224
Alain Vironneau, 234
SCEA des Vignobles Visage, 282, 326
EARL Visonneau, 933
Gérard Vitteaut-Alberti, 482
Christian Vivier-Merle, 157
Emile Voarick, 469, 580, 644
SCEA Michel Voarick, 564
Dom. Vocoret et Fils, 492, 498, 501
Dom. Yvon Vocoret, 486
Christa Vogel et Hans Hürlimann, 1224
EARL Laurent Vogt, 142
Dom. Joseph Voillot, 588, 593
SCEV Voirin-Desmoulins, 738
Michel et Olivier Voisine, 978

Fruitière vinicole de Voiteur, 751, 756, 1201
Laurent Vonderheyden, 404
Jean-Pierre Vorburger et Fils, 95, 112
Didier Vordy, 813
Vranken, 738
Dom. Vrignaud, 498
EARL Jean Vullien et Fils, 766-767
Guy Wach, 127
Pascal Walczak, 742
Bernard Walter, 113
Charles Wantz, 87, 106
Waris-Larmandier, 738
GAEC Jean-Paul Wassler, 107
Bernard Weber, 122
GAEC Odile et Danielle Weber, 142
Peter Wegelin et Silvia Bargähr, 1274
Maurice Wehrlé, 118, 122
Dom. Weinbach-Colette Faller et ses Filles, 107, 124
V. P. Weindel, 844
Jean Weingand, 113
Gérard Weinzorn et Fils, 118, 134
Alain de Welle, 846
Bernadette Welty et Fils, 113
EARL Dom. Jean-Michel Welty, 107
Nadine Wendling, 374
Besthcim – Cave de Westhalten, 99
Sylvie et Werner Wichelhaus, 920
SCEA Wiehle, 84, 136
Alsace Willm, 95
Ronald Wilmot, 259
Albert Winter, 107, 131
EARL André Wittmann et Fils, 139
Cave vinicole Wolfberger, 131
Wunsch et Mann, 107
Willy Wurtz et Fils, 128
Bernard Wurtz, 135
Vignobles Florence et Alain Xans, 285, 301
SCEA Vignobles Daniel Ybert, 313
Stéphane Yerle, 1227
Consorts Yerles, 329
SCEA Pierre Yung et Fils, 346
SCEA Charles Yung et Fils, 347
Yvan Bruneau, 1028
Association viticole d'Yvorne, 1252
Yannick Zausa, 354
E. et N. Zecchi, 206
G. Zeyssolff, 87
EARL Fernand Ziegler et Fils, 95
Albert Ziegler, 130
Jean Ziegler, 95
Jean-Jacques Ziegler-Mauler Fils, 107, 133
EARL A. Zimmermann Fils, 95
SARL Paul Zinck, 123
Pierre-Paul Zink, 96
EARL Maison Zoeller, 120
Mario Zorzetto, 919
Nicolas Zufferey, 1262
Frédéric Zufferey, 1266
Zumbaum-Tomasi, 805

DOM. RENE MALLERON, 1088
MALLEVIEILLE, 923
CH. MALMAISON, 408
CH. MALROME, 216
L'ESPRIT DE MALROME, 234
MALTOFF, 455
CH. MALVES-BOUSQUET, 811
CAVE DES VIGNERONS DE MANCEY, 455
DOM. MANCIAT-PONCET, 653, 659
JEAN-CHRISTOPHE MANDARD, 1015
HENRI MANDOIS, 716
CH. MANGOT, 305
CH. MANIEU, 260
ALBERT MANN, 116, 123-124
JEAN-LOUIS ET FABIENNE MANN, 130
MANOIR DE L'EMMEILLE, 888
MANOIR DE LA TETE ROUGE, 1001
DOM. MANOIR DU CARRA, 157
CH. DE MANON, 246
MANON, 845
MANSARD, 717
DOM. DE MAOURIES, 912
DOM. MARATRAY-DUBREUIL, 565
CH. MARBUZET, 418
DIDIER MARC, 717
PATRICE MARC, 717
JEROME MARCADET, 1054
CH. MARCEAU, 338
DOM. DE MARCELIN, 1255
DENIS MARCHAIS, 980
PIERRE MARCHAND ET FILS, 1077
DOM. MARCHAND FRERES, 513, 520
JACQUES MARCHAND, 1077
RENE MARCHAND, 157
JEAN-PHILIPPE MARCHAND, 471
CH. DU MARCONNAY, 1001
GUY MARDON, 1015
DOM. MARDON, 1080
MARECHAL, 1049
CATHERINE ET CLAUDE MARECHAL, 455, 553, 586, 597
GHISLAINE ET BERNARD MARECHAL-CAILLOT, 468, 553, 570
CH. MAREIL, 381
CH. MARESQUE, 888
DOM. DE MARIGNAN, 191
PIERRE MAREY ET FILS, 559, 566
DOM. MAREY, 465
CLOS MARFISI, 874, 1188
A. MARGAINE, 717
DOM. DU MARGALLEAU, 1049
CH. MARGAUX, 403
DOM. JEAN-PIERRE MARGERAND, 180
GERARD ET NATHALIE MARGERAND, 191
DOM. DES MARGOTIERES, 599
CH. MARGOTON, 348
CH. MARGUERITE, 895
MARGUET-BONNERAVE, 717
DOM. DU MARGUILLIER, 184
CH. MARIE DU FOU, 963
MARIE STUART, 717
DOM. MARIE-BLANCHE, 1105
MARINOT-VERDUN, 628
CH. DE MARJOLET, 1105

CH. MARJOSSE, 338
CH. DE MARMORIERES, 799
DOM. MAROSLAVAC-LEGER, 604, 620
ROLAND MAROSLAVAC-LEGER, 607
DOM. DE MAROTTE, 1232
CH. MAROUINE, 845
MARQUIS D'ABEYLIE, 234
MARQUIS DE DIDONNE, 1193
MARQUIS DE GOULAINE, 1208
MARQUIS DE LA CHARCE, 1114
MARQUIS DE SADE, 1161
MARQUIS DE SAINT-ESTEPHE, 418
CH. MARQUIS DE TERME, 403
MARQUIS DES TOURNELLES, 1120
DOM. MARQUISE DES MURES, 816
DOM. DU MARQUISON, 157
DOM. DES MARRANS, 180
DOM. DU MARRONNIER ROSE, 163
DOM. DES MARRONNIERS, 455, 485
CH. MARSAC SEGUINEAU, 403
CLOS MARSALETTE, 369
CH. DE MARSANNAY, 216
J. MARSANNE ET FILS, 506, 515, 521, 534
CH. MARSAU, 333
DOM. DE MARSOIF, 455
DOM. JACKY MARTEAU, 1015
JOSE MARTEAU, 943
MARTEAUX-GUYARD, 717
G. H. MARTEL & Co, 718
DOM. J. MARTELLIERE, 1041, 1058
DOM. F. MARTENOT, 537
MAISON FRANCOIS MARTENOT, 640
CH. MARTET, 343
DOM. DU MARTHERAY, 1255
DOM. MARTIN FAUDOT, 748
DOMINIQUE MARTIN, 1001
CEDRIC MARTIN, 163
PATRICE MARTIN, 163
JEAN-JACQUES ET SYLVAINE MARTIN, 191
DOM. JEAN-CLAUDE MARTIN, 496
P. LOUIS MARTIN, 718
LUC ET FABRICE MARTIN, 974
CH. MARTINAT, 251
DOM. MARTIN-DUFOUR, 553
CH. MARTINENS, 403
DOM. MARTIN-LUNEAU, 957
DOM. MARTINOLLES, 1227
LAURENT MARTRAY, 168
MARX-BARBIER ET FILS, 718
MARZOLF, 102
MAS AMIEL, 1178
DOM. DU MAS BECHA, 824
DOM. DU MAS BLANC, 832
DOM. DU MAS BLEU, 861
MAS CHAMPART, 816

MAS CORNET, 832
DOM. DU MAS CREMAT, 824, 1181
MAS CRISTINE, 1175
DOM. D'EN BADIE, 824
MAS DE BAGNOLS, 1239
MAS DE LIBIAN, 1114
MAS DE LONGCHAMP, 1233
DOM. DU MAS DE PIQUET, 1222
MAS DE REY, 1233
MAS DU PARADIS, 1126
MAS MEYRAC, 1222
MAS MONTEL, 1222
DOM. DU MAS NEUF, 1186
DOM. DU MAS ROUGE, 1183
DOM. DU MAS ROUS, 825, 1227
LE CELLIER DU MAS, 1255
LADY MASBUREL, 923
MASSA, 853
DOM. MASSE PERE ET FILS, 631, 644
REMY MASSIN ET FILS, 718
D. MASSIN, 718
THIERRY MASSON, 718
JEROME MASSON, 624
CH. DES MATARDS, 246
JEAN-LUC MATHA, 899
MATHIES ET CIE, 1247
DOM. MATHIAS, 456, 648, 662
ADRIAN MATHIER, 1263
MARQUIS ANSELME MATHIEU, 1148
SERGE MATHIEU, 718
DOM. DE MATIBAT, 820
DOM. MATIGNON, 980
DOM. DU MATINAL, 186
DOM. DES MATINES, 939, 1001, 1006
CH. MATRAS, 306
DOM. MATRAY, 180
DENIS ET VALERIE MATRAY, 189
CH. MAUCAILLOU, 408
CH. MAUCAMPS, 392
PROSPER MAUFOUX, 607, 659
JEAN-PAUL MAULER, 127
ANDRE MAULER, 91
DOM. DE MAUPAS, 1157
DOM. DU MAUPAS, 173
LOUIS MAX, 534
SIMON MAYE ET FILS, 1263
CH. MAYLANDIE, 783
CH. MAYNE BLANC, 318
CH. MAYNE D'IMBERT, 357
MAYNE D'OLIVET, 222
CH. MAYNE DU CROS, 357
CH. MAYNE GRAND PEY, 916
CH. MAYNE LALANDE, 398
MAYNE SANSAC, 222
CH. MAYNE-CABANOT, 338
CH. MAYNE-GUYON, 246
CH. MAYNE-VIEIL, 260
DOM. DE MAYOL, 1164
CH. MAZERIS, 256
CH. MAZERIS-

BELLEVUE, 256
CH. MAZERS, 800
PASCAL MAZET, 719
ANNE MAZILLE, 193
DOM. MAZOYER, 631
GUY MEA, 719
GABRIEL MEFFRE, 1149
DOM. MEILLAN-PAGES, 1232
MEISTERMANN, 111
DOM. DU MEIX-FOULOT, 641
PASCAL MELLENOTTE, 465
JOSEPH MELLOT, 1077, 1081, 1083
CH. MEMOIRES, 348, 425, 427
DOM. L. MENAND PERE ET FILS, 641
HERVE MENARD, 1025
MENARD, 1193
MERCIER, 719
DE MERIC, 719
DE MERINVILLE, 811
DOM. DU MERLE, 468, 481
DOM. DE MERLET, 369
CH. MERLIN FRONTENAC, 212
THIERRY MERLIN-CHERRIER, 1088
BERNARD MERMOUD, 1263
CH. MERVILLE, 783
DOM. MESLIAND, 1015, 1019
CH. MESLIERE, 946
ROBERT MESLIN, 502
MESTRE PERE ET FILS, 624
LOUIS METAIREAU, 957
METAIRIE GRANDE DU THERON, 882
CH. METAIRIE HAUTE, 929
METIVIER ET FILS, 1050
DOM. METRAT ET FILS, 177
GERARD METZ, 102
HUBERT METZ, 137
METZ-GEIGER, 92
D. MEUNEVEAUX, 563
CH. MEUNIER SAINT-LOUIS, 783
DOM. MAX MEUNIER, 1015
DOM. VINCENT MEUNIER, 641
CH. DE MEURSAULT, 604
DOM. RENE MEYER, 102
GILBERT MEYER, 111
RENE MEYER, 123
DENIS MEYER, 92
JEAN-LUC MEYER, 96
MEYER-FONNE, 92
P.A. MEYLAN, 1255
CH. MEYRE, 393
MEZIAT-BELOUZE, 157
L'INSPIRATION DES MIAUDOUX, 916
CH. MICALET, 393
DOM. MICHAUD, 943, 1016
CH. DES MICHAUDS, 187
DOM. RENE MICHEL ET FILS, 656
GUY MICHEL ET FILS, 720
JOHANN MICHEL, 1134
DOM. MICHEL, 653
J.B. MICHEL, 719
PAUL MICHEL, 719
DOM. MICHELOT MERE ET FILLE, 604
DOM. DE MIGNABERRY, 901
MIGNON ET PIERREL, 720
CHARLES MIGNON, 720
PIERRE MIGNON, 720
DOM. DE MIHOUDY, 969
MILADY, 240
JEAN MILAN, 720

WINES

WINES

WINES

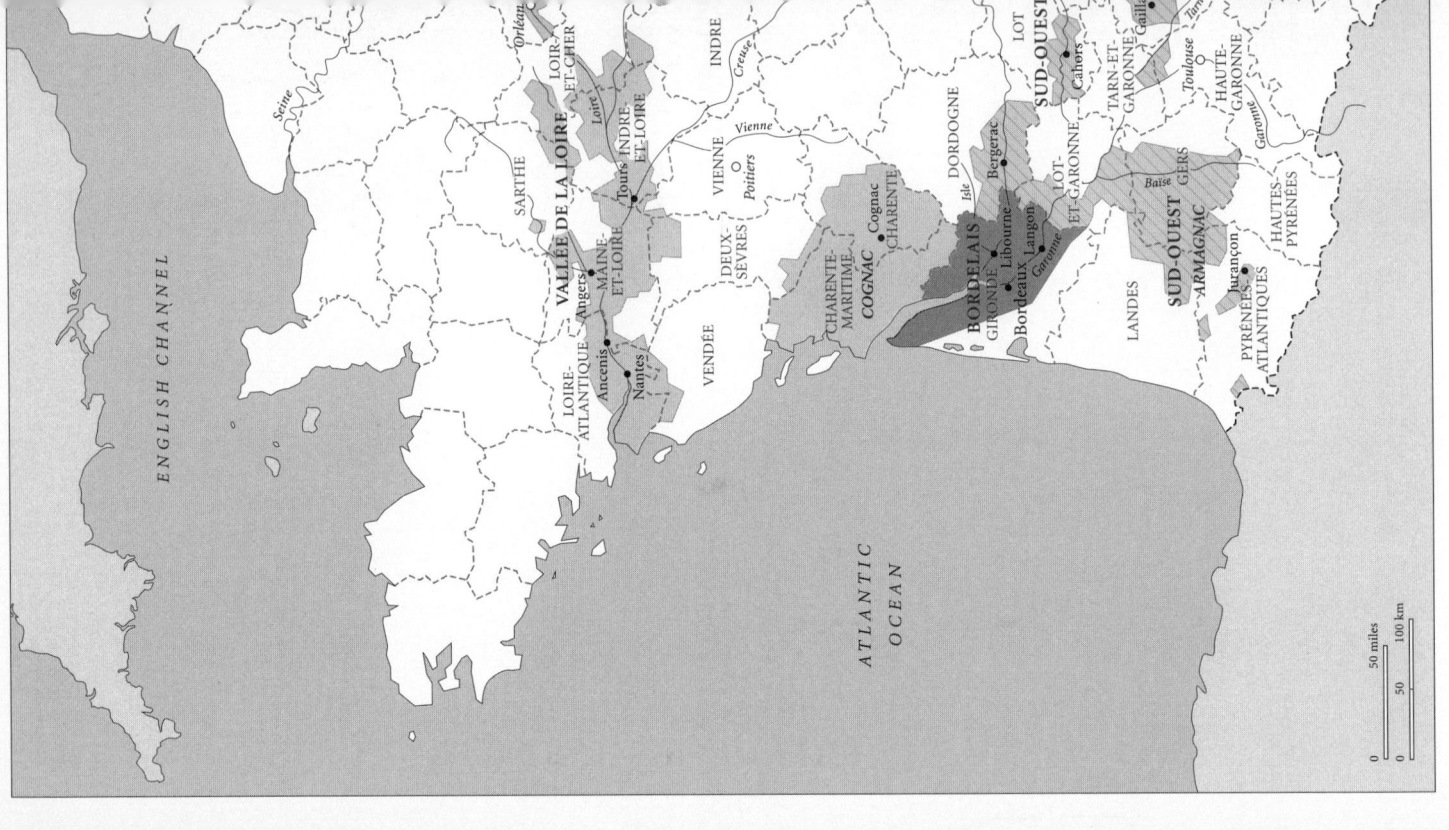